HIST

OF

WESTERN MARYLAND.

BEING A HISTORY OF

FREDERICK, MONTGOMERY, CARROLL, WASHINGTON, ALLEGANY, AND GARRETT

COUNTIES

FROM THE EARLIEST PERIOD TO THE PRESENT DAY;

INCLUDING

BIOGRAPHICAL SKETCHES

OF THEIR

REPRESENTATIVE MEN.

BY

J. THOMAS SCHARF, A.M.,

AUTHOR OF "CHRONICLES OF BALTIMORE," "HISTORY OF BALTIMORE CITY AND COUNTY," "HISTORY OF MARYLAND;" MEMBER OF THE MARYLAND HISTORICAL SOCIETY AND ACADEMY OF SCIENCES; MEMBER OF THE HISTORICAL SOCIETY OF PENNSYLVANIA; HONORARY MEMBER OF THE GEORGIA HISTORICAL SOCIETY; CORRESPONDING MEMBER OF THE HISTORICAL SOCIETIES OF NEW YORK, WISCONSIN, MINNESOTA, SOUTH CAROLINA, AND VIRGINIA; OF THE HISTORICAL AND PHILOSOPHICAL SOCIETY OF OHIO; OF THE NEW ENGLAND HISTORIC-GENEALOGICAL SOCIETY, ETC., ETC.

IN TWO VOLUMES, ILLUSTRATED.

VOL. II.

CLEARFIELD COMPANY & WILLOW BEND BOOKS

1995

Originally Published
Philadelphia, 1882

Reprinted
Regional Publishing Company
Baltimore, 1968

Reprinted 1995, 2003
for Clearfield Company, Inc. by
Genealogical Publishing Co., Inc.
Baltimore, Maryland
in conjunction with
Willow Bend Books
Westminster, Maryland

Library of Congress Catalogue Card Number 68-26127
International Standard Book Number: 0-8063-5205-1
Set Number 0-8063-4565-9

Made in the United States of America

CONTENTS OF VOLUME II.

ILLUSTRATIONS IN VOLUME II.

HISTORY

OF

WESTERN MARYLAND.

CARROLL COUNTY.

CHAPTER XXXVIII.

INTRODUCTORY.

First Settlers—Land Grants—Erection of Carroll County—Elections—Bench and Bar—Distinguished Men—County Officers—School Statistics.

THE territory embraced within the limits of Carroll County was settled at an early period in the history of Maryland. The first settlers were Scotch-Irish, Germans, and the descendants of the English from Southern Maryland. The Indians, before the advent of the whites, had retired across the South Mountain into the Cumberland Valley. A remnant of the "Susquehannocks," numbering between sixty and seventy, lived within less than a mile of Manchester (then a part of Baltimore County) until 1750 or 1751, and were probably the last aborigines residing in the county. About that period, without any stir or apparent preparation, with the exception of two, they all disappeared in a single night. The exceptions were a chief named Macanappy and his wife, both old and infirm, and they survived the departure of their race but a few days. The similarity of names has given rise to the impression that this tribe found its way to Florida, and that Miconopy, the celebrated chief, who afterwards gave the United States so much trouble, was one of the descendants of the old Indian left to die near Manchester. In the Land Office at Annapolis patents are recorded for land grants in this portion of the State as early as 1727. In that year "Park Hall," a tract of land containing two thousand six hundred and eighty acres, was surveyed for James Carroll. This land was then situated in Prince George's County, between New Windsor and Sam's Creek. In 1729 "Kilfadda" was granted to John Tredane, and subsequently sold to Allan Farquhar. It now embraces a part of the town of Union Bridge and the farm of E. J. Penrose. "Brierwood" was surveyed for Dr. Charles Carroll in 1731. "White's Level," on which the original town of Westminster was built, was granted to John White in 1733. "Fanny's Meadow," embracing the "West End" of the present town of Westminster, was granted to James Walls in 1741. "Fell's Retirement," lying on Pipe Creek, and containing 475 acres, was granted to Edward Fell in 1742. "Arnold's Chance," 600 acres, was granted to Arnold Levers in 1743. "Brown's Delight," 350 acres, situated on Cobb's Branch, near Westminster, was granted to George Brown in 1743. "Neighborly Kindness," 100 acres, to Charles Carroll in 1743. "Cornwell," 666 acres, on Little Pipe Creek was patented in 1749, and afterwards purchased by Joseph Haines and his brother. "Terra Rubra" was patented to Philip Key in 1752, for 1865 acres; "Ross' Range" to John Ross in 1752, for 3400 acres; "Spring Garden," on part of which Hempstead is built, to Dunstan Dane in 1748; "Brothers' Agreement," near Taneytown, to Edward Diggs and Raphael Taney in 1754, for 7900 acres; "Foster's Hunting Ground" to John Foster, 1439 acres; "German Church" to Jacob Schilling and others in 1758, for a German Reformed and Lutheran church at Manchester; "Five Daughters" to Carroll's daughter, 1759, for 1500 acres; "New Market," on which Manchester is built, to Richard Richards in 1754; "Rattlesnake Ridge" to Edward Richards in 1738; "Caledonia" to William Lux and others in 1764, for 11,638 acres; "Bond's Meadow" to John Ridgely in 1753, for 1915 acres (Westminster is partly situated on this tract); "Brother's Inheritance" to Michael Swope in 1761, for 3124 acres; "Ohio," north of Union Mills, to Samuel Owings in 1763, for 9250 acres; "New Bedford," near Middlebury, to Daniel McKenzie and John Logsden in

1762, for 5301 acres; "Gilboa" to Thomas Rutland, 1762, for 2772 acres; "Runnymeade," between Uniontown and Taneytown, to Francis Key and Upton Scott in 1767, for 3677 acres; "Hale's Venture" to Nicholas Hale in 1770, for 2886 acres; "Windsor Forest" to John Dorsey in 1772, for 2886 acres; "Rochester" to Charles Carroll of Carrollton in 1773, for 4706 acres; and "Lookabout," near Roop's mill, to Leigh Master in 1774, for 1443 acres.

Among the earliest settlers in this section of Maryland was William Farquhar, whose energy, thrift, and wisdom aided materially in the development of the country. His ancestors emigrated from Scotland to Ireland, where he was born July 29, 1705. When sixteen years of age he left Ireland with his father, Allen Farquhar, and settled in Pennsylvania. Allen Farquhar, as was mentioned above, acquired from John Tredane a large tract of land on Little Pipe Creek; but there is no evidence that he actually resided there. In 1735 he conveyed this tract, known as "Kilfadda," to his son William, one of the conditions of the gift being that he should remove from Pennsylvania to "ye" province of Maryland. In compliance with the terms of the deed, William Farquhar, with his wife Ann, came to Maryland and entered into possession of his estate. The country was then a wilderness and destitute of roads, except such paths as were made by wild beasts and Indians, and no little intrepidity was required for such a journey, clogged with a helpless family. Farquhar had learned the trade of a tailor, and by his skill and industry in making buckskin breeches, the garments then most in vogue, he prospered. He invested his savings in land, and in 1768 he was the possessor of two thousand acres, in which was included all the ground upon which the present town of Union Bridge is built. He was a counselor and peace-maker, and it is related of him that upon one occasion he rode home in the evening and found his house surrounded with emigrant-wagons belonging to settlers who had been driven from their homes by the Indians and had fled to him for protection. They had their stock and movable property with them, and were afraid to go back to their lands. Farquhar visited the Indians and soon pacified them, and the settlers returned to their homes and were never afterwards molested. Between the years 1730 and 1740 great advances were made in the settlement of what is now known as Carroll County. "The Marsh Creek settlement," in the western section of York County, Pa., including the region around Gettysburg, composed almost exclusively of Scotch-Irish, furnished a number of industrious and enterprising immigrants, and Hanover and Conewago, in the same county, settled entirely by Germans, provided a large contingent. The latter located principally in the Manchester and Myers Districts, where many of their descendants now live.

Many were attracted thither also from St. Mary's, Prince George's, Anne Arundel, and Baltimore Counties, on the Western Shore of Maryland. The dispute concerning the boundary line between the provinces of Pennsylvania and Maryland was a fruitful source of trouble to those who possessed interests in the debatable ground. A strip of land six or eight miles wide was claimed both by the province of Pennsylvania and the proprietary of Maryland. John Digges obtained a Maryland grant of six thousand eight hundred acres in the vicinity of Hanover, and Charles Carroll procured a similar grant in the neighborhood of Fairfield or Millerstown, and the latter now goes by the name of the Carroll Tract. Hanover, at that time known as McAllisterstown, or Kallisterstown, was within the disputed territory, and became a refuge for disorderly characters, and hence was called "Rogues' Harbor."

This vexatious boundary question, which had agitated the two colonies since the arrival of William Penn in America in 1682, was decided, as we have shown elsewhere, in favor of the province of Pennsylvania in 1769 by Mason and Dixon, two surveyors sent out from London for that purpose, and Mason and Dixon's line has ever since remained the unquestioned boundary between the two commonwealths. The dispute having reached a definite conclusion, an impetus was given to development. Settlers multiplied, the country was cleared up, and convenient farm-buildings were erected. The inhabitants soon learned to appreciate the fine water-powers so abundant in this portion of Maryland, and in 1760 David Shriver, the grandfather of the older members of the family of that name now living in Western Maryland, purchased a tract of land on Little Pipe Creek and erected a mill and tannery. Mr. Shriver was a prominent and useful citizen. He represented Frederick County in the convention called in 1776 to frame a constitution for the State of Maryland, and for a number of years he was the representative of that county in the Senate and House of Delegates. In May, 1765, a bateau loaded with iron was successfully navigated from the Hampton furnace on Pipe Creek to the mouth of the Monocacy River, in Frederick County. There is no record of the establishment of this furnace, but that it must have been in operation for some time prior to the date given above is evident from the advertisement which appeared May 28, 1767, in which Benedict Calvert, Edward Digges, Normand Bruce, William Digges, Jr., and James Canady offer for sale the "Hampton Furnace, in Frederick County, together with upwards of three thousand acres of land. The furnace (with casting-bellows) and bridge-houses were built of stone, also grist-mill and two stores, the whole situated on a branch of Monocacy River."

The entire stock of negroes, servants, horses, wagons, and implements belonging to the works were offered for sale. There was on hand at the time coal for six months, fourteen hundred cords of wood, five hundred tons of ore at the side of the furnace and four hundred tons raised at the banks. The advertisement concludes with the announcement that Normand Bruce lived near the works.

Solomon Shepherd, grandfather of Thomas, Solomon, and James F. Shepherd, married Susanna Farquhar, the youngest child of William Farquhar, Oct. 27, 1779, and settled on a portion of the Farquhar estate, about three-quarters of a mile east of Union Bridge. Mr. Shepherd was a wool-comber and fuller, and established a fulling-mill where the factory now stands. For some time after the construction of his mill he was without a house of his own, and boarded with his father-in-law, at some distance down Pipe's Creek; and it is related of him that in walking back and forth along the banks of the stream from the mill to the house at night he was wont to burn the ends of a bunch of hickory sticks before he would set out on his hazardous journey, and when the wolves (which were savage and ravenous) approached too near he would whirl his firebrand about him to drive them away. He afterwards moved into a log house, which is still standing, and in 1790 built the brick house in which Shepherd Wood now resides. The latter was at that time considered a palatial extravagance, and the neighbors dubbed it "Solomon's Folly." In 1810 he built the present factory, and put in carding and spinning-machines and looms for the manufacture of cloths, blankets, and other fabrics. In 1815 he purchased land of Peter Benedune, and removed to the place now owned and occupied by E. G. Penrose, where he lived until his death in 1834.

In 1783, David Rhinehart and Martin Wolfe walked from Lancaster County, Pa., to Sam's Creek, where they purchased a tract of land and soon afterwards settled on it. Wolfe was the grandfather of Joseph, Samuel, and Daniel Wolfe. He was somewhat eccentric after a very unusual fashion, and is said to have been unwilling to dispose of property for a price which he believed to exceed its real value. David Rhinehart was the grandfather of David, Daniel, William H., E. Thomas, J. C., and E. F. Rhinehart. William H. Rhinehart, the great American sculptor, received his first lessons on the farm now owned and occupied by Daniel Rhinehart, twelve miles southeast of Union Bridge.

Joel Wright, of Pennsylvania, married Elizabeth Farquhar, daughter of William Farquhar, and settled on a part of the land acquired by his father-in-law. He was a surveyor and school-teacher, and superintended a school under the care of Pipe Creek Monthly Meeting, at that time one of the best educational institutions in the State. His pupils came from all parts of the surrounding country, and many were sent to him from Frederick City and its vicinity. It was common in those days for ladies to make long journeys on horseback to attend religious meetings or to visit friends. Mrs. Wright traveled in this way to Brownsville, then called "Red Stone," in Pennsylvania, to attend meeting and to visit her relatives. She brought back with her, on her return, two small sugar-trees and planted them, and from these have sprung the many beautiful shade-trees of that species which adorn the vicinity of Union Bridge.

Francis Scott Key, whose name the "Star-Spangled Banner" has made immortal, was born at Terra Rubra, near the Monocacy, in what is now the Middleburg District of Carroll County, Aug. 9, 1780. In his day he was well known as an able lawyer and Christian gentleman, but with the lapse of time his reputation as a poet has overshadowed his many other excellent qualities.

Col. Joshua Gist was an early settler in the section of Maryland now embraced within the limits of Carroll County. He was an active partisan in the Revolutionary war, and during the administration of President John Adams, near the close of the last century, was marked in his disapproval of the riotous and insurrectionary proceedings of those opposed to the excise duty laid upon stills. The disturbance, known in history as the "Whisky Insurrection," became so formidable, especially in Western Pennsylvania, that Mr. Adams appointed Gen. Washington commander of the forces raised to suppress it. The excitement extended to this region, and the Whisky Boys in a band marched into Westminster and set up a liberty-pole. The inhabitants of the town becoming alarmed sent out for Col. Gist, who then commanded a militia regiment. The colonel, a very courageous man, mounted his horse, rode into town, drew his sword, and ordered the pole to be cut down, which was at once done, and placing his foot on it, he thus remained until it was hewn in pieces. The Boys, concluding discretion to be the better part of valor, stole out of town, and the incipient revolution was stayed by the coolness and judgment of a single individual. In 1748, Frederick County was created by the Colonial Legislature, and that portion of the present county of Carroll which had previously belonged to Prince George's was embraced within its limits, as was almost the whole of Western Maryland. Col. Gist and Henry Warfield were elected to the House of Delegates of Maryland towards the close of the eighteenth century, for the express purpose of securing a division of the county into election districts for the convenience of the inhabitants, who were at that time compelled to cross the Monocacy and go all the way to Frederick City to vote.

Joseph Elgar, in the latter part of the last century, established a factory at Union Bridge for the manufacture of wrought nails,—that is, the nails were so designated, but in reality they were cut from the bar of iron, lengthwise with the fibre of the bar, which gave them ductility and clinching qualities equivalent to wrought nails. Elgar subsequently removed to Washington and entered the service of the United States, where his genius was duly appreciated. About the year 1809, Jacob R. Thomas, a neighbor of Elgar, conceived the idea that the very hard labor of cutting grain in the harvest-field could be done by machinery driven by horse-power. Prior to this time, and for some years afterwards, the old system of cradling grain was the only process generally known for harvesting, and the reaping-machine may be truthfully said to have been invented by him. Thomas worked at his machine with great assiduity, and added to it an automatic attachment to gather the cut grain into sheaves, it being substantially the self-raker of the present day. During the harvest in the summer of 1811 his machine was so far perfected as to admit of a trial. It had not been furnished with a tongue and other appurtenances for attaching horses, and was therefore pushed into the harvest-field and over the grain by a sufficient number of men. Thomas Shepherd, recently deceased, and William Shepherd, his brother, and father of Thomas F. Shepherd and Solomon Shepherd, and Rudolph Stern, father of Reuben W. Stern, of Westminster, were three of the men who aided in the trial, and their testimony is unanimous that it cut the grain well and perfectly, but that its delivery was defective and did not make a good sheaf. There is no evidence on record as to the manner in which the gathering attachment was constructed, whether it was like or unlike any of the automatic rakes of the present day, but the cutting apparatus was the same in principle as those now in use on the best reapers, mowing in the same shears-like manner, which has been universally approved and adopted as the best method of cutting grain, and differing only in the manner of attaching the knives to the sickle-bar. In modern machines the knives are short and broad and riveted fast to the sickle-bar, while in Thomas' machine the knives were longer and pivoted in the middle, and attached to the sickle-bar by a pivot at the rear end. Thomas was extremely sensitive, and unable to bear up against and overcome the incredulity and ridicule consequent upon the partial failure of the machine, and it was never finished by him. He afterwards built a factory for the manufacture of flax into linen, but it did not prove remunerative. He subsequently removed to Baltimore, where he kept the Globe Inn, on Market Street, and then to Frederick City, where he kept the City Hotel, and afterwards to Point of Rocks, on the Potomac River, where at the time of his death he was engaged in the construction of a steam canal-boat invented by himself. Obed Hussey, the pioneer in the manufacture of practical reaping-machines, was a cousin of Jacob R. Thomas. They were intimately acquainted, and Hussey afterwards perfected Thomas' invention, and from that McCormick's, and all others cutting on the same principle, were framed. The pathetic story of Jacob R. Thomas is the same so often repeated in the lives of inventors and discoverers. The spark of genius went out amid the vapors of poverty, while his quick-witted imitators reaped the golden showers which should have been poured into his own lap. The region of country afterwards known as Carroll County now grew apace. The lands were cleared of their dense forests, the magnificent water-courses were utilized for mills and manufactures, towns sprang into existence, and the inhabitants, following the motto of the commonwealth, increased and multiplied. Taneytown, Westminster, Manchester, Hampstead, Union Bridge, Middleburg, and New Windsor became prosperous villages. At the close of the last war between Great Britain and the United States agricultural products commanded excellent prices. Wheat-flour was sold in the Baltimore markets for fourteen dollars per barrel, and other commodities realized proportionate prices. The value of land had greatly appreciated. In April, 1814, Peter Benedune sold out all his land in the vicinity of Union Bridge at prices ranging from one hundred to one hundred and twenty dollars per acre, and removed to the Valley of Virginia. About this time also the spirit of progress was abroad. The Westminster Fire-Engine and Church Lottery was drawn in Frederick City, July 10, 1813. A bank was established in Westminster, and it is learned from the newspapers of the day that the old martial spirit, fanned into a flame during the Revolution, and rekindled in 1812 by the invasion of the British, was still active and vigorous. Under date of Oct. 13, 1821, the Frederick *Herald* says, "At a meeting of the Columbian Independent Company, commanded by Capt. Nicholas Snider, of Taneytown, and the Independent Pipe Creek Company, commanded by Capt. Thomas Hook, at Middleburg, in Frederick County, . . . information of the death of Gen. John Ross Key was received."

The people were virtuous and God-fearing. The corner-stone of the German Reformed and English Presbyterian church was laid in Taneytown, Sept. 5, 1821. It was about this date also that the inhabitants awakened to a sense of the value of regular postal communication, and a postal service on horseback was established from Frederick City to Westminster *via* Union Bridge and back once a week. The people were gradually becoming sensible of the overgrown bulk and unmanageable interests of the immense counties of Frederick and Baltimore, and the leading men residing in either county in the vicinity of Westminster began to take an active interest in politics. Joshua Cockey became a prominent politician in this end of Frederick County, and represented his constituents in the Senate and House of Delegates. Isaac Shriver also represented the county several times. William P. Farquhar and John Fisher were also members of the House of Delegates. Peter Little and Elias Brown, of Freedom District, represented the Baltimore District in Congress between the years 1818 and 1828. In 1832 the feeling, which had been gaining strength for years, that a new county was absolutely needed for the convenience and prosperity of those dwelling in the eastern portion of Frederick and the western portion of Baltimore Counties culminated in a memorial to the Legislature of Maryland petitioning for a division of these counties and the establishment of a new one to be called "Westminster."

When the area and population of Frederick and Baltimore Counties are considered it seems extraordinary that this movement should have been so long delayed or that it should have met with such decided opposition when inaugurated. The two counties contained nearly one-fifth of the territorial area of the State, and, exclusive of the city of Baltimore, they possessed a population of upwards of eighty-five thousand inhabitants, or very nearly one-fifth of the whole number of inhabitants in the State. The bounds of the new county, as proposed by the memorialists, were as follows: "Beginning at Parr's Spring, at the head of the western branch of the Patapsco River, and running with said branch, binding on Anne Arundel County, to the north branch of said river; thence running up said north branch, excluding the same, to the old mill on Dr. Moore Falls' land, including said mill; thence north seventeen degrees east to the Pennsylvania line; thence, binding on said line, westwardly to Rock Creek, one of the head-waters of the Monocacy River; thence with said creek and river, excluding the same, to Double Pipe Creek; thence with said creek, and with Little Pipe Creek and Sam's Creek, including their waters, to Maurois' mill, excluding said mill, and thence with a straight line to Parr's Spring, the beginning."

It was estimated that the new county would contain about twenty-five thousand inhabitants. The town of Westminster, beautifully situated in the valley between the head-waters of Little Pipe Creek and those of the north branch of the Patapsco, on the road leading from Baltimore to Pittsburgh, generally known as the Reisterstown turnpike road, and containing a population of seven hundred souls, was to be the county-seat. The people in some of the districts were now thoroughly aroused. Complaints were frequent and vehement of the distance to be traversed to reach the seats of justice in Baltimore and Frederick Counties respectively, and the difficulties and delays encountered because of the overcrowded dockets of the courts. The *Star of Federalism*, a newspaper, was established at Uniontown, and at different periods three papers were published at Westminster by George Keating, Mr. Burke, and George W. Sharpe, all strenuously advocating a division. The latter afterwards removed to Frederick and established the Frederick *Citizen*. The support of these papers was small, and they were soon discontinued. Although the sentiment in favor of a division was general, the people were very much divided in opinion as to how it should be done. Some favored a division of Frederick County alone, some were in favor of separating Baltimore County from the city and locating the seat of justice at a central point, while the inhabitants of Westminster and its vicinity, which was on the dividing line between the two counties, were anxious to take a portion of each of those counties and form a new one with Westminster as the county-seat. The memorial mentioned above was presented to the Legislature of Maryland in 1833, and referred to a committee of which William Cost Johnson, of Frederick, was chairman. Mr. Johnson was a man of great ability and popularity. He introduced a bill into the Legislature which created a county with the metes and bounds prayed for by the memorialists, and it was mainly through his efforts that it passed both houses. It had been the original intention of the petitioners to give the name of Westminster to the new county, but the bill as passed named it "Carroll," in honor of Charles Carroll of Carrollton, then recently deceased, a man who in character, ability, patriotism, and usefulness has never been surpassed in Maryland.

The act of Assembly was clogged with a provision requiring its submission to the vote of the people who lived in the sections of the two counties proposed to be cut off, and further exacting a majority of the voters in its favor in each segment. The vote was to be taken *viva voce*, at the October election in 1833. The people were now fully alive to the importance of the question, and the issue was fairly joined. Col. John K. Longwell established the *Carrolltonian* at Westminster, June 28, 1833, a journal whose aim was to advocate the division and educate the people up to a full knowledge of the advantages likely to accrue from the creation of the new county. The paper was conducted with marked ability and zeal, and the division, which occurred four years later, was measurably due to its unflagging energy and fidelity. As the fall election approached public meetings were held in the districts interested and the merits of the proposed division very thoroughly discussed. A very large meeting was held at Westminster and an able address issued, which was published in pamphlet form in the English and German languages and very freely circulated in the counties. A committee composed of the following-named gentlemen was appointed to further the object of the meeting: C. Birnie, Sr., William Murray, Edward Dorsey, Joshua C. Gist, Thomas Hook, John McKaleb, Archibald Dorsey, William Sheppard, Mordecai G. Cockey, John McKellip, Joseph Steele, John Baumgartner, Nicholas Algire, William Shaw, of H., George Richards, William Roberts, Frederick Ritter, Samuel Galt, Nicholas Kelley, James C. Atlee, Washington Van Bibber, Evan L. Crawford, Peter Hull, Philip G. Jones, Peter Erb, Jacob Shriver, William Brown, Evan McKinstry, Basil D. Stevenson, Philip Englar, Abraham Bixler, Jacob Landes, William Caples, David Kephart, Sr., Joshua Sellman, William B. Hebbard, John Malehorn, J. Henry Hoppe, Michael Miller, John Swope, George Warfield, William Jordan, George Crabbs, Sebastian Sultzer, John C. Kelley, David Foutz, Jesse Slingluff, Nathan Gorsuch, Joseph Keifer, Abraham Null, Jesse L. Warfield, George Cassell.

It would seem that with such an array of citizens of worth and excellence in its favor there should have been no difficulty in securing the passage of the bill, but a strong opposition was developed in the districts which belonged to Baltimore County. Their attachment to the county clouded their judgments, and they refused to listen to reason or to consult their own interests. The campaign in behalf of the new county was one of the most memorable and exciting that had ever taken place in Western Maryland, and after a canvass which embraced every nook and corner of the districts in Frederick and Baltimore Counties to be segregated the election took place, and the new county failed to receive a majority of the votes in the Baltimore County segment, and the division was consequently defeated, as the following vote by districts will show:

FREDERICK COUNTY.

Districts.	For.	Against.
Westminster	610	139
Taneytown	398	187
Liberty	4	101
New Market	0	22
	1012	449

BALTIMORE COUNTY.

Districts.	For.	Against.
Dug Hill	150	304
Freedom	141	208
Woolery's	250	53
Wise's	0	11
Reisterstown	13	17
	554	593

The election was a severe blow to the friends of the new county. They had not anticipated defeat: indeed, they thought that the measure would be approved by a large majority of the voters. They did not make sufficient allowance for county attachments and the influence of tradition, nor did they properly estimate the jealousy of other villages and the prejudice and fear of increased taxation, but they were not dismayed by the disaster. They now knew both their weakness and strength, and they went manfully to work to retrieve their mistakes. More meetings were called, the people were reasoned with, and a public sentiment created in favor of the measure in places where the stoutest opposition had been developed. In 1835 the Whigs nominated Dr. William Willis as a member of the House of Delegates from Frederick County, and the Democrats nominated Isaac Shriver. They were both elected, many of the friends of the new county voting for them. Willis and Shriver, with their colleagues, Robert Annan and Daniel Duvall, originated and boldly pressed another bill on the attention of the Legislature. By this act a large portion of the Liberty District in Frederick County and all of the New Market District were excluded from the limits of the new county by making the Buffalo road the line from Sam's Creek to Parr's Spring, and thus were removed the objections of the people residing in those districts, who were almost unanimously opposed to separation from the old county. The delegates were supported in their action by a petition containing 1800 names, and after laboring diligently during the whole session they had the satisfaction of procuring the passage of the bill by both branches of the Legislature.

A confirmatory act by the next Legislature was necessary before the bill could become a law, and it was expected that the measure would have to encounter determined opposition, especially from the representatives of Baltimore County, as the project was strongly opposed there, and her representatives considered themselves under obligations, if possible, to defeat it.

The political campaign of 1836 was one of the most exciting and closely-contested struggles that has ever taken place in the State, and resulted in important changes of the organic law. Senatorial electors were to be chosen, two from each county, who were to meet in Annapolis and select the Senate, then consisting of fifteen members. The Whigs of Frederick County nominated Evan McKinstry and Gideon Bantz, and the Democrats, John Fisher and Casper Quynn. A strong party in favor of reform in the State Constitution caused the election of Fisher and Quynn. Of the whole number of electors the Whigs elected twenty-one and the Democrats nineteen. The constitution prescribed that twenty-four electors should constitute a quorum. The electors met in Annapolis, but the nineteen Democrats claimed a majority of the senators as Reformers, inasmuch as they represented a large majority of the popular vote of the State, and declined to enter the electoral college until their proposition was granted. The Whigs indignantly refused to accede to their demand, and the Democrats left for their homes in a body, receiving from their friends the appellation of the "Glorious Nineteen."

The withdrawal of the Democrats from Annapolis produced a profound sensation in Maryland. By the Whigs it was considered revolutionary, and many persons became alarmed. The Whig friends of the new county were afraid that it would cause the rejection of their favorite scheme.

When the Whig and Democratic senatorial electors were nominated in Frederick County, a ticket was named by each party for the House of Delegates. The Whig ticket was composed of Jacob Matthias, Francis Brengle, Joshua Doub, and George Bowlus. Isaac Shriver was again placed on the Democratic ticket. Francis Thomas, afterwards Governor of Maryland, was at that time the leader of the Democracy in the western portion of the State. The action of the Democratic electors, and the feeling in the party consequent thereupon, led him to believe that the time was ripe for a change in the constitution. He therefore advised the withdrawal of the Democratic legislative ticket, and proposed instead the selection of delegates to a Constitutional Convention at the regular election. This was done, and the Whig delegates in Frederick County were elected without opposition. In other portions of the State the secession of the "Glorious Nineteen" was not regarded with favor, and the reaction in public sentiment gave the Whigs a large majority in the House of Delegates, a number of counties in which they had been defeated at the September elections sending solid Whig delegations to Annapolis.

Five of the Democratic senatorial electors considered themselves instructed by this decisive manifestation of the will of the people, and agreed to unite with the twenty-one Whigs and elect a Senate. William Schley, of Frederick, and Elias Brown, of Baltimore County, were chosen as two of the fifteen senators. The proposition to hold a Constitutional Convention was abandoned. It was conceded, however, that some reform was needed, and accordingly, upon the assembling of the Legislature, Governor Veazy, in his annual message, recommended that the election of Governor and senators should be given to the people, and that Carroll County be created, so as to diminish the size of the largest two counties and give an addition of four members to the popular branch of the Legislature. These measures received the sanction of public approval, the constitution was amended to meet the views of the Governor, and the confirmatory act creating Carroll County passed the House of Delegates by a majority of twenty-eight, and every senator, with the exception of Elias Brown, cast his vote in favor of it. It was signed by the Governor, and became a law Jan. 19, 1837, so that in all probability the course pursued by the "Glorious Nineteen," instead of proving adverse to the creation of the new county, had the tendency to bring to its support, as a conciliatory measure, many of the representatives from the smaller counties of the State. This long-deferred victory was hailed with demonstrations of delight by the citizens of Westminster and the surrounding country. It was celebrated by a procession, with arches, banners, and an illumination, and an address was delivered in the Old Union church by James Raymond.

The following is the act of Assembly, passed March 25, 1836, for the creation of Carroll County:

"WHEREAS, a considerable body of the inhabitants of Baltimore and Frederick Counties, by their petition to this General Assembly, have prayed that an act may be passed for a division of said counties, and for erecting a new one out of parts thereof; and whereas, it appears to this General Assembly that the erecting of a new county out of such parts of Baltimore and Frederick Counties will greatly conduce to the ease and convenience of the people thereof; therefore

SEC. 1. *Be it enacted by the General Assembly of Maryland*, That after the confirmation of this act such parts of the aforesaid counties of Baltimore and Frederick as are contained within the bounds and limits following, to wit: beginning at the Pennsylvania line where Rock Creek crosses said line, thence with the course of said creek until it merges in the Monocacy river, thence with the Monocacy to the point where Double Pipe Creek empties into Monocacy, thence with the course of Pipe Creek to the point of junction of Little Pipe Creek and Big Pipe Creek, thence with the course of Little Pipe Creek to the point where Sam's Creek empties into Little Pipe Creek, thence with Sam's Creek to Warfield's mill, thence with the road called the Buffalo road, and to a point called Parr's Spring, thence with the western branch of the Patapsco Falls to the point of its junction with the northern branch of the Patapsco Falls, thence with the northern branch of said falls to the bridge erected over said falls on the turnpike road leading from Reisterstown to Westminster, thence with a straight course to the Pennsylvania line, running north seventeen degrees east, thence with the Pennsylvania line to the place of beginning, shall be erected into a new county by the name of Carroll County, and that the seat of justice thereof be established at Westminster.

"SEC. 2. *And be it enacted*, That the inhabitants of Carroll County shall have, hold, and enjoy all the immunities, rights, and privileges enjoyed by the inhabitants of any other county in this State.

"SEC. 3. *And be it enacted*, That the taxes which shall be levied by the commissioners of Baltimore County, prior to the confirmation of this act, on such parts of Baltimore County as are to constitute a part of Carroll County shall be collected and paid to the treasurer of Baltimore County, and the same be applied precisely as if this act had not passed; and that the taxes which shall be levied by the justices of the Levy Court of Frederick County, prior to the confirmation of this act, on the parts of Frederick County as are to constitute Carroll County shall be applied precisely as if this act had not passed.

"SEC. 4. *And be it enacted*, That all causes, processes, and pleadings which shall be depending in Frederick County Court and Baltimore County Court when this act shall be confirmed shall and may be prosecuted as effectually in the courts where the same be depending as if this act had not been made.

"SEC. 5. *And be it enacted*, That the county of Carroll shall be a part of the Third Judicial District of this State, and the justices of the said district for the time being shall be the judges of the County Court of Carroll County, and the said County Court shall be held as may be directed by law, and shall have and exercise the same powers and jurisdiction, both at law and in equity, as other County Courts of this State.

"SEC. 6. *And be it enacted*, That the election districts in Carroll County shall be nine in number, and their limits, as well as the limits of the election districts in Baltimore and Frederick Counties, shall be established after the confirmation of this act as shall be directed by law.

"SEC. 7. *And be it enacted*, That after the confirmation of this act by the next General Assembly, a writ of election shall issue for holding an election in said county for four delegates to represent said county in the General Assembly which shall then be in session.

"SEC. 8. *And be it enacted*, That if this act shall be confirmed by the General Assembly, after the next election of delegates at the first session after such new election, according to the constitution and form of government, that in such case this alteration and amendment of the constitution and form of government shall constitute and be valid as part thereof, and everything therein contained repugnant to or inconsistent with this act be repealed and abolished."

The county was created, but much remained to be done. Carroll was in an embryotic condition. She was as helpless as a newly-born babe. Public buildings were to be erected, courts of justice established, officers chosen, and the county must be districted. Mr. Matthias, who had labored zealously for the creation of the new county, now applied himself to bringing order out of chaos. Bills were introduced into the Legislature for the working machinery and to set it in motion. At that time the register of wills was chosen by the Legislature. After a sharp contest between a number of candidates, John Baumgartner, of Taneytown District, was elected. Acts of Assembly were introduced and passed providing for the appointment of county commissioners, for the assessment of real and personal property, for the meeting of the County Court, for the establishment of the Orphans' Court, for the opening of public roads, for the purchase of sites and the erection of public buildings thereon, for the election of a sheriff and the appointment of subordinate officers, and for the election of four delegates to the General Assembly, and at the end of the session of 1837 Carroll County was fairly on its legs and provided with the necessary legislation for the career of prosperity and progress upon which it was about to enter.

The following-named gentlemen were appointed to lay off the election districts: Samuel Galt, James C. Atlee, Thomas Hook, Samuel W. Myers, Joshua Smith, Abraham Wampler, Daniel Stull, Mordecai G. Cockey, Stephen Gorsuch, Joseph Steele, George W. Warfield, Frederick Ritter, and William McIlvain. They divided the county into nine districts as follows: Taneytown, Uniontown, Myers', Woolery's, Freedom, Manchester, Westminster, and Franklin. Since then the districts of Middleburg, New Windsor, and Union Bridge have been added. The districts were marked out Feb. 15, 1837, and the report of the commission was filed with the county clerk June 20, 1837, but not recorded until May 18, 1846. In March, 1837, an election was held for sheriff, the first that had taken place in Carroll County, and as a matter of interest the judges and clerks of election are given:

District No. 1, John Clabaugh, Jacob Correll, John Thomson, Jacob Wickert, James McKellip.

District No. 2, Moses Shaw, Sr., Israel Norris, David Foutz, John Hyder, Wm. C. Wright.

District No. 3, Wm. Coghlan, Peter Bankard, David B. Earhart, John Erb, Jacob H. Kemp.

District No. 4, Wm. Jameson, Edward E. Hall, George Jacobs, Wm. Jordan, Wm. Stansberry.
District No. 5, Robert Hudson, Nicholas Dorsey, Benjamin Bennett, Wm. Whalen, Otho Shipley.
District No. 6, Henry N. Brinkman, Frederick Ritter, Jarrett Garner, John Kerlinger, Joseph M. Parke.
District No. 7, Joshua Smith, David Uhler, Lewis Wampler, Jonathan Norris, Charles W. Webster.
District No. 8, Wm. McIlvaine, George Richards, John Lamotte, John Fowble, George Richards, Jr.
District No. 9, James Douty, Thomas Barnes, Robert Bennett, Joshua C. Gist, Thomas E. D. Poole.

A number of candidates sought the suffrages of the citizens, and the contest between Nicholas Kelley, Isaac Dern, and Basil Root, the leading aspirants, was very close, resulting in the election of Nicholas Kelley as the first sheriff of the county. The inauguration of the county government took place the first Monday in April, 1837. On that day the Circuit Court, the Orphans' Court, and the county commissioners all met in Westminster.

The Circuit Court met in the dwelling of Dr. Willis, now owned by Mr. Boyle, Judges Dorsey and Kilgour on the bench. After an appropriate introductory address, Judge Dorsey announced the appoint- of Dr. William Willis as county clerk, which was received with unqualified approval by those present. The court then appointed James Keiffer court crier, and accepted the bonds of the clerk and sheriff. William P. Maulsby, James Raymond, James M. Shellman, A. F. Shriver, and T. Parkin Scott were admitted as attorneys of the Carroll County bar. Mr. Maulsby was appointed and qualified as State's attorney for the county. The court then adjourned to meet in the old Union church, where its sessions were afterwards held until a court-house was built.

The Orphans' Court of Carroll County convened for the first time April 10, 1837, in the Wampler mansion, on the corner of Church Street, which building it occupied until the erection of a court-house. The commissions of Judges Abraham Wampler, William Jameson, and Robert Hudson were received from Theodoric Bland, chancellor of the State of Maryland, and read and recorded, after which the judges qualified and proceeded to business. John Baumgartner was qualified as register of wills, and appointed George B. Shriver assistant register. The first business of a general nature transacted by the court was the appointment of Peter Gettier and Peter Utz to view and estimate the annual value of the real estate of Julia, Mary, George, Joseph, Peter, and Amos Sauble, minors, in the hands of Dr. Jacob Shower, their guardian. A notice was filed from Elizabeth, widow of Peter Sauble, refusing to administer on decedent's estate; also a similar notice from John and Michael, brothers of the deceased.

April 17th. The court directed Nelly Demmitt to dispose of the personal property of William Demmitt as administratrix.

May 1st. James Raymond was admitted as an attorney in this court, the first mentioned in the proceedings, and William P. Maulsby was admitted at the same time.

May 8th. Nancy Koutz was appointed guardian to Joshua Koutz.

June 5th. In the case of Jacob Sellers, administrator of Philip Sellers, deceased, *vs.* George Wareham, a citation was issued, the first citation going out of this court.

June 12th. On application of Jesse Lee, John Barney, a colored boy, aged six years, was bound to said Lee until the said boy arrived at twenty-one years of age.

The first administrators mentioned at the April term were Dr. Jacob Shower, of Peter Sauble's estate; Nelly Demmitt, of her husband, William Demmitt; Adam Feeser, of Elizabeth Feeser.

The first executors were Joseph Cookson, of the estate of Samuel Cookson, deceased; Karahappuck Towson, of James Towson; and Peter Nace, of Peter Nace, Sr.

The first petition filed in any suit was that of George Wareham *vs.* Jacob Sellers, administrator of Philip Sellers, deceased. The first suit was indorsed "No. 1."

The following is a list of the wills admitted to probate during the first two years subsequent to the organization of the county:

1. Elizabeth Tawney, April 10, 1837. Witnesses, David Roop, John Schweigart, John Roop, Jr. Before John Baumgartner, register, and the judges of the Orphans' Court.
2. Samuel Cookson, April 17th. Witnesses, Joseph, Samuel, and John Weaver.
3. James Towson, April 17th. Witnesses, John Philip and Jacob Frine.
4. Peter Nace, the elder (dated 1827), and admitted to probate in Baltimore County, Dec. 27, 1831. Certified copy recorded in Carroll County, April 17, 1837.
5. Lauranty Freed, of Baltimore County. Certified copy of its probate there. Recorded April 17, 1837.
6. Lydia Hatton, April 17th.
7. Jacob Hoffman, May 1, 1837.
8. Solomon McHanney, June 5th.
9. Elizabeth Ann Howard, July 25th. Witnesses, Samuel Greenhalt, Asbury O. Warfield, D. W. Naill.
10. Henry Wareham, July 22d. Witnesses, J. Henry Hoppe, Jacob Matthias, of George, Daniel Stowsifer, John Baumgartner.
11. David Geirman, August 9th. Witnesses, David Lister, of Jacob, George Croul, David Myerly.

12. Ann Brown, August 30th. Witnesses, N. Dorsey, Abel Scrivenar, Geo. W. Warfield.
13. Eliza C. Dorsey, August 30th. Witnesses, Edward Frizzell, Joseph Black, Thomas Beasman.
14. Aquila Garrettson, September 5th. Witnesses, George Bramwell, Mordecai G. Cockey, John Malehorn.
15. Jonathan Parrish, September 11th.
16. John Menche, October 17th. Witnesses, Peter Sawble, Michael Gettier, Jacob Kerlinger.
17. John Foltze, November 6th. Witnesses, Jacob Gitt, George Weaver, of H., James Marshall.
18. John Krumine, November 27th. Witnesses, Jacob Baumgartner, Philip Wentz, Jonathan Sterner.
19. Adam Frankforter, Jan. 1, 1838. Witnesses, Henry N. Brinckman, Jacob Gitt, Jacob W. Boesing.
20. Mary Ann Engel, January 2d. Witnesses, John Baumgartner, George Hawk.
21. John Gilliss, January 13th. Witnesses, Augustus Riggs, Wm. Curlien, James L. Riggs.
22. Archibald Barnes, January 22d. Witnesses, Joshua C. Gist, Joshua Franklin, Benjamin Bennett.
23. Joseph Arnold, February 12th. Witnesses, David Leister, George Croul, John Baumgartner.
24. Richard Manning, Sr., February 19th. Witnesses, Wm. Jameson, David Tawney, Peter Flater.
25. Catharine Manro, February 26th. Witnesses, Joshua C. Gist, Joseph Harden, Jacob Hiltabeidel.
26. John Lambert, March 26th. Witnesses, John Smelser, David Smelser, David Gorsuch.
27. James Steele, April 2d. Witnesses, N. Browne, Beale Buckingham, Vachel Buckingham.
28. Ezekiel Baring, May 7th.
29. Rachel Wentz, May 14th.
30. Mary Hooker, June 25th.
31. Baltzer Hesson, July 9th. Witnesses, Sterling Galt, Josiah Baumgartner, F. J. Baumgartner.
32. Nicholas H. Brown, July 13th.
33. George Tener, July 30th.
34. Jacob Brown, September 3d. Witnesses, Michael Sholl, Jr., John Streavig, George Koons.
35. Peter Shriner, September 4th. Witnesses, Evan McKinstry, David Engler, John P. Shriner.
36. Patrick Hinds, October 8th.
37. Margaret Reid, October 8th. Witnesses, A. B. R. McLine, Samuel Naill, James Maloney.
38. Veronica Peters, October 8th.
39. Margaret Durbin, October 8th.
40. Hannah Wampler, October 15th. Witnesses, Jacob Yingling, Wm. Yingling, Wm. Zeppe.
41. Peter Arbaugh, October 29th. Witnesses, Solomon Wooley, William Lockard, Stephen Ourslers.
42. Jacob Reid, October 29th.
43. Elizabeth Keys, October 29th.
44. Mary Lampert, November 19th. Witnesses, James H. Gorsuch, Henry Long, Jacob Frine.
45. Susannah Loveall, Jan. 14, 1839. Witnesses, Henry Ebaugh, of George, George Ebaugh, John Rinehart.
46. Peter Shoemaker, Dec. 31, 1838. Witnesses, John Nusbaum, Abraham Hesson, Jacob Sell, Peter Dehoff.
47. Solomon Foutz, Feb. 11, 1839. Witnesses, Abraham Myers, John Flegle, Philip Boyle.
48. Michael Wagner, March 4th. Witnesses, John Hyder, John Smith, John Nusbaum.

The first death was recorded April 4, 1837. It was that of Basil D. Stevenson, surviving executor of Samuel Stevenson, deceased, to Hannah Shipley for four hundred and sixty-nine acres, adjoining "Fell's Dale;" consideration, $2665. Dated April 1, 1837.

The first mortgage was recorded April 5th, and was from John Knox to James Knox *et al*, and dated March 2, 1837.

The second deed was from J. Mason Campbell, trustee, to the president and directors of the Union Bank of Maryland, and was recorded April 8th. Dated April 1, 1837; consideration, one dollar. The land conveyed was Lot No. 6, of ninety acres, and was called "Legh Castle," being part of the late Legh Master's estate. It adjoined tracts called "Bond's Meadow Enlarged," "Long Valley," and "Brown's Delight." It was a part of the tract issued to the late William Winchester and his heirs by James Clark and Joseph G. J. Bend, surviving trustees of Rev. Legh H. Master, by an indenture of March 14, 1812.

The third deed was recorded April 8th, and was from Basil D. Stevenson, surviving executor of Samuel Stevenson, deceased. Its date of execution and record were the same. It conveyed one hundred and forty-seven acres, three roods, and twelve perches, and was parts of tracts called "The Resurvey on Father's Gift," "Rich Meadows," and "Pigeon's Hill." Consideration, $1034.76.

The second mortgage was recorded April 11th, and was from William Jordan to Richard Johns. It was on one hundred and thirty-nine and a half acres called "Curgafergus," and two hundred and fifty acres called "Mount Pisgah."

The fourth deed was recorded April 11th, from Jacob Reese and wife to Jacob Roop, dated March 25, 1837. It was for one-half acre of "Bond's Meadow." Consideration, $600.

The following are the first marriage licenses issued by the clerk of the court for a period of two years after the creation of the county of Carroll:

1837.

April 8. John Kroh and Julia Weaver.
May 1. Thomas Bosley and Elizabeth Wheeler.
" 9. Samuel Dayhoffe and Nancy Wheeler.
" 14. Silas M. Horner and Elizabeth McAlister.
" 17. Samuel L. Linah and Maria Six.
June 5. Shadrach Bosley and Serepta Sater.
" 6. Joseph Bowers and Elizabeth Cullison.
" 6. Wm. F. Smyth and Elizabeth Bixler.
" 8. Jeremiah Robinson and Ann Smith.
" 16. Geo. B. Shipley and Ann Shipley.
" 20. Wm. Naill, Jr., and Mary A. Rudisel.
July 8. Abraham Reaver and Catharine Jones.
" 15. Jacob Michael and Eve Grogg.
" 26. Wm. W. Warfield and Jemima Formwalt.
" 26. Daniel Lampart and Julian Loveall. (Rev. E. Keller.)

Sept. 1. Conrad Koons and Mary E. Zunbunn.
" 15. Porcius Gilleys and Rachel Evans. (Rev. Lloyd Selby.)
" 23. David Haines and Sarah W. Durbin.
" 25. Thos. C. Thomson and Mary Shunk. (Rev. E. Keller.)
Oct. 2. James Shaeffer and Margaret Cottrider.
" 7. George Bixler and Mary Grittier.
" 9. Andrew C. Fowble and Elizabeth Murray.
" 16. Nicholas Dorsey and Rachel Clemson. (Rev. Dr. Reese.)
" 16. Peter Rinamon and Margaret Strickling. (Rev. J. Geiger.)
" 25. George W. Manro and Elizabeth Kelly. (Rev. Samuel Gore.)
Nov. 11. John Sweeden and Charlotte Weaver.
" 28. Josiah Roop and Elizabeth Shafer. (Rev. William Prettyman.)
Dec. 6. Elisha Shreeve and Minerva Bennett.
" 20. D. W. Houck and Rachel F. Allgire.
" 22. Aaron Goswell and Ann Leatherwood.
" 26. Elisha Wheeler and Sarah Shambarger.
" 27. Beall Sellman and Mary B. Weaver.
" 29. Thomas Rudisell and Ann M. Snyder. (Rev. E. Keller.)

1838.

Jan. 15. John Weist and Elizabeth Mouse. (Rev. Jacob Geiger.)
Feb. 1. Jacob Lynn and Louisa Crabbs. (Rev. D. Zollickoffer.)
" 3. George W. Grimes and Eliza Buffington. (Rev. E. Keller.)
" 8. George W. Litzenger and Martha A. Keefer.
" 10. Samuel Myers and Eliza C. Dagen. (Rev. Daniel Zollickoffer.)
" 12. Jacob Gieman and Julian Haines. (Rev. Jacob Geiger.)
" 28. Joseph Kelly and Naomi Ross. (Rev. N. Harden.)
March 3. William E. Shipley and Mary A. Dorsey. (Rev. Hood.)
" 6. Samuel Price and Catharine Ripple.
" 7. James Smith and Catharine Diffenbaugh. (Rev. Israel Haines.)
" 8. Jacob Flatter and Elizabeth Bush.
" 12. Jacob Smith and Angeline Christ. (Rev. Miller.)
" 18. Thomas Loveall and Jane A. Cushing. (Rev. Jonathan Forrest.)
" 19. John Myerly and Emmaline Little. (Rev. Israel Haines.)
" 22. George Richards, Jr., and Lucinda Allgire.
" 26. Henry S. Black and Rachel Maring. (Rev. E. Keller.)
" 30. N. B. Stocksdale and Elizabeth Cover. (Rev. Lloyd Selby.)
April 3. Noah Brown and Bartholow Richards. (Rev. Aaron Richards.)
" 3. Christopher Weisman and Mary A. Guthing. (Rev. Jacob Geiger.)
" 5. Peter Nace and Susanna Meyselman.
" 14. Lewis J. Grove and Carrilla Barnes. (Rev. Hunt.)
May 9. Alexander H. Senceny and Lavinia Englar. (Rev. David Englar.)
" 14. John Roberts and Catharine A. Boyle. (Rev. N. Zocchi.)
" 21. Joseph Wilson and Sarah E. Vanzant. (Rev. Samuel Grove.)
May 21. Elisha Bennett and Rachel Prugh. (Rev. Jonathan Forrest.)
" 25. John Warner and Susanna Fisher.
" 30. Ephraim Lindsey and Eliza Fringer. (Rev. Samuel Gore.)
" 31. Benjamin W. Bennett and Margaret Clemson. (Rev. Daniel Zollickoffer.)
June 11. John Loveall and Elizabeth Houck.
" 23. Aaron Wheeler and Matilda Barnes.
" 26. Washington Wilson and Margaret Smith. (Rev. Daniel Zollickoffer.)
" 30. Robert Collins and Honor Elder. (Rev. William Hunt.)
July 25. David Shipley and Mary A. Wheeler.
Aug. 13. Jacob Ocker and Barbara Fleegle.
" 13. John W. Ogborn and Eliza Pole. (Rev. Daniel Zollickoffer.)
" 21. Larkin Shipley and Rebecca Shipley. (Rev. S. Gore.)
" 31. Giles Cole and Mary Merryman. (Rev. William Hunt.)
Sept. 12. John Baile and Sarah L. Eby. (Rev. Boyle.)
" 15. Obadiah Buckingham and Mary A. Barlow.
" 17. Dones Groff and Mary S. Biggs. (Rev. William Prettyman.)
" 20. Ephraim Shultz and Jane Crawford.
" 22. John M. Blizzard and Ann Welsh.
" 25. John Slyder and Catharine Wentz.
Oct. 6. Thomas Wright and Caroline Frizzell.
" 11. Dr. David Diller and Ann E. Matthias. (Rev. N. Zocchi.)
" 15. Washington Senceney and Mary A. Grimes. (Rev. Daniel Zollickoffer.)
" 18. Henry Nicodemus and Margaret McCreery. (Rev. William Prettyman.)
" 18. William S. Brown and Carrilla Manning.
" 27. Samuel B. Shipley and Leah Shipley.
" 27. William Otter and Elizabeth Lathem.
" 30. John Reigle and Catharine Reaver. (Rev. E. Keller.)
Nov. 6. John Omergoast and Barbara Leister.
" 20. John Elder and Rebecca Selby. (Rev. Samuel Gore.)
" 20. Jacob Ecker and Sarah Dudderar. (Rev. Webster.)
" 22. Dennis Grimes and Sarah A. Pool. (Rev. Nicholas Harden.)
" 27. Levin Williams and Susan Haines. (Rev. N. Harden.)
" 28. John Walker and Mary A. Tucker. (Rev. Lloyd Selby.)
Dec. 5. Michael Smith and Maria Haines.
" 14. W. W. Garner and Harriet Murray.
" 19. Joseph Marriott and Sarah Shipley.
" 22. Benjamin Davis and Mary Ward.
" 24. Wm. Warner and Rebecca Warner. (Rev. Daniel Zollickoffer.)
" 28. Abraham Wilson and Delilah Hervey.

1839.

Jan. 17. Jesse Baker and Eliza E. Bailey. (Rev. S. Gore.)
" 23. John T. Fisher and Sophia Stansbury. (Rev. Harple.)
Feb. 8. Jonas Engler and Hannah Stoner.
" 14. Geo. Croft and Anne Ruby. (Rev. Richards.)
" 18. Levi Hiner and Mary Medcalf. (Rev. Daniel Zollickoffer.)

Feb. 26. James Thompson and Mary A. Hitterbridle. (Rev. Robert S. Grier.)
" 28. Conrad Moul and Lydia A. Kesselring. (Rev. Josiah Varden.)
March 2. Michael Bartholow, Jr., and Elizabeth A. Plaiten.
" 9. Hanson Carmack and Harriet Clabaugh.
" 11. Josiah Baugher and Mary Babylon. (Rev. Daniel Zollickoffer.)
" 13. Levi Davis and Julian Shriver. (Rev. Josiah Varden.)
" 13. James Parrish and Ruth Creswell.
" 15. Samuel Shriner and Mary A. Merring.
April 1. Isaac Magee and Margaret Dayhoffe.
" 1. Henry E. Beltz and Julian A. Motter.
May 4. Michael Hubbard and Rachel Durbin. (Rev. D. Zollickoffer.)
" 15. John Roop, Jr., and Lydia Engle.

On Oct. 5, 1840, at Annapolis, Hon. James G. Berrett, of Carroll County, was married by Rev. Mr. McIlheney to Miss Julia W., only daughter of the late John W. Bordley, of the former place.

The following is the first marriage license issued in the new county:

"*Whereas*, application has been made to me by John Kroh, of Carroll County, and Julia Weaver, of Carroll County, for License to be joined in Holy Matrimony.

"These are therefore to authorize and license you to solemnize the Rites of Matrimony between said persons according to law, there appearing to you no lawful cause or just impediment by reason of any Consanguinity or Affinity to hinder the same.

"Given under my hand and the seal of my office this 8th of April, in the year 1837.

[SEAL] "GEORGE MACKUBIN,
"*Treasurer Western Shore.*

"To the REV. JACOB GEIGER or any other person authorized by law to celebrate the marriage in the State of Maryland.

"WILLIAM WILLIS,
"*Clerk C. C., Md.*"

Sheriff Kelley converted a portion of the brick mansion in Westminster now owned by William Reese into a jail, and used it as such until the present prison was built. There was but one prisoner confined in it, and he is said to have made his escape by sliding down the spouting. The county commissioners met in a room of the Wampler tavern, and organized with Otho Shipley as clerk, and Thomas Hook county collector. A number of places were suggested as sites for the public buildings, including the land on which they now stand, the lot at present occupied by the Dallas mansion, and the ground on which the Reformed church is built. The advantages of all were fairly considered by the commissioners, and on May 25, 1837, they accepted for the site of the court-house an acre of ground from Isaac Shriver, immediately in rear of his tavern-stand, and about three hundred yards from Main Street, with ground for streets on three sides of it. For the jail they accepted an acre of land a short distance northeast of the court-house site, and about four hundred yards from Main Street. This was donated by the heirs of David Fisher.

The jail was built in 1837, by B. F. Forester and Johnzee Selby, at a cost of four thousand dollars, and since that time the jail-yard and other improvements have been added.

The second term of the Circuit Court was held Sept. 4, 1837. Chief Justice Thomas B. Dorsey presided, with Thomas H. Wilkinson as associate judge. The grand jury, the first in the new county, appeared, and was sworn as follows: William Brown (foreman), Jonathan Dorsey, Charles Devilbiss, Daniel Stull, John T. Mathias, William McIlvain, David Z. Buchen, Jacob Kerlinger, Daniel Horner, Nathaniel Sykes, Frederick Ritter, William Caples, William Fisher, John Jones, Jacob Grove, Michael Sullivan, Andrew C. Fowble, Thomas Sater, Samuel L. Swarmstead, Edward Dorsey, Joseph Shaffer, Isaac Dern, and John Henry Hopper.

Nicholas Kelley was sheriff, William Willis, clerk, and Emmanuel Gern and Henry Geatty, bailiffs. The grand jury returned true bills against George Ramsbery for resisting an officer; Jacob Boring, breach of the peace; Whitfield Garner, the same; Charlotte White, colored, larceny; Michael Wagner, assault; B. Eck, maltreatment to his slave "Poll;" William Coghlan and Peter Bankert, misdemeanor in office; William Grimes, Benjamin Davis, Resin Franklin, Jacob Gilavier, Nimrod Booby, Jacob Sanders, selling liquor without a license. The presentments against the last four were withdrawn by the grand jury and not returned. It will be observed from the perusal of the above that the offenses committed in 1837 did not differ materially from those of which the county courts take cognizance nowadays, though there was a commendable absence of the higher crimes, such as murder, arson, burglary, and robbery, which too frequently deface the present records of judicial tribunals. James Keifer was appointed court crier. James Mybrea filed a declaration of his intention to become a citizen of the United States and renounce his allegiance to the King of Great Britain. Henry Short, a native of Holland, also appeared and gave notice of his intention to become a naturalized citizen of this country. The following was the petit jury, the first in the county: John Cover, Jacob Gitt, John Kuhn, Sr., Basil Root, Evan L. Crawford, William Shaw, Joshua F. Copp, Robert Crawford, Isaiah Pearce, Nicholas H. Brown, Elijah Bond, Henry H. Harbaugh, Benjamin Bennett, Daniel Yeiser, Evan Garner, Thomas Smith, Thomas Bartholow, Nimrod Frizzell, Benjamin Yingling, Mordecai G. Cockey,

Hezekiah Crout. The first case tried was that of an appeal of William Naill *vs.* Jesse Reifsnider. The witnesses for appellant were Elias Grimes and Elias Naill, and for appellee, Samuel Reindollar and Israel Hiteshue. The jury found for the appellant without leaving the box. The next cause was that of James Smith *vs.* Samuel Gatt, William Shaw, Silas Hauer, Washington Hauer, and Jacob Shoemaker, trustees of the church, an appeal. The witnesses were John W. McAlister for appellant, and James Bar, David Kephart, John Thompson for appellee. Judgment was affirmed with costs. Godfried Guyser, a native of Würtemberg, Germany, John Reisly, of the same place, and Jacob Lewis and Philip Yoost, natives of Darmstadt, Germany, all filed their intentions to become American citizens. Fifty-six witnesses testified before the grand jury, among whom were the following constables: John Shockney, Jacob Frankfortder, Thomas Brummel, Andrew P. Barnes, George Ogg, Emanuel Gernand, Warren P. Little, Evan Black, John Krantz, William Grunbine, Abraham England, William Stansbury, Samuel Lammott, John Clabaugh, David Kephart, George Willott, Frederick Yingling, Joseph Smith. On the petition of John S. Murray to inquire whether George Ecklar was an insane person and a pauper the jury refused an inquisition. The first criminal case tried was that of the State of Maryland *vs.* Charlotte White (colored), indicted for larceny, and the jury found a verdict of not guilty. The second State case was that of George Ramsbery for resisting a constable, in which a verdict of guilty was returned. The defendant was ordered to pay a fine of five dollars and be imprisoned sixty days. The third session of the County Court met Sept. 3, 1838, when the following grand jury was sworn: Jacob Landes (foreman), John A. Byers, John Adlisperger, Josiah Shilling, Peter Lippy, George W. Manro, Eli Hewitt, George Miller, Thomas Shepherd, Nimrod Woolery, Robert J. Jameson, Richard Smith, Samuel W. Myers, Robert B. Shipley, Joseph Poole, William Lockert, Solomon Myerly, Lewis Shuey, Benjamin B. Forrester, Henry Cover, Martin Krole, Adam Beiser. The petit jury were John McCollum, David Weaver, Julius Bennett, Nelson Norris, David Buffington, Isaac Powder, John Fowble, Francis Haines, David P. Deal, Henry W. Ports, Daniel Hoover, Micajah Rogers, Richard Owings, Denter Shipley, Horatio Price, Beal Buckingham, David Fowble, John Krouse, John Gornell, Michael Sullivan, John H. Hoppe, Francis Shriver, George Bramwell, Jacob Null.

The corner-stone of the present court-house of Carroll County was laid in June, 1838, with appropriate military and civic ceremonies. It was an occasion of general rejoicing, and a large concourse of people assembled to mark the event. Four military companies marched in the procession, commanded by Capts. Skinner, of Hanover, Swope, of Taneytown, Bramwell, of Finksburg, and Longwell, of Westminster. The stone was laid by Andrew Shriver, assisted by Col. Joshua Gist, then in his ninety-fourth year, a brother of Gen. Mordecai Gist, of Maryland, who won an imperishable name during the Revolution as a soldier and patriot, he having especially distinguished himself in the battles of Long Island and Camden. An address was delivered by Samuel D. Lecompte, and a number of impromptu speeches were made by prominent citizens. Conrad Moul was the contractor for the building, and the masonry of both the court-house and jail was done by Ephraim Swope and Thomas W. Durbin. The court-house was built at a cost of eighteen thousand dollars, and notwithstanding it was erected more than forty years ago it is now a substantial and durable edifice, and a credit to the commissioners under whose administration it was constructed.

In 1838 the county government was perfected, all necessary subordinate officers had been elected or appointed, those who had opposed the creation of a new county had become reconciled to the situation, and thenceforward Carroll took its proper place among the older organizations as one of the most vigorous, progressive, and influential counties of Maryland.

Carroll County is bounded on the north by Pennsylvania, on the south by the Patapsco River, which separates it from Howard County, on the east by Baltimore County, and on the west by Frederick County. Its natural advantages are great. The surface is undulating, the gently sloping hills, like the billows of the ocean, swelling gradually in the direction of the Catoctin range, a spur of the Blue Ridge. The tributaries of the Patapsco and Monocacy Rivers permeate the soil in every direction, not only supplying abundant water for farming purposes, but affording to the miller and manufacturer unlimited power for their handicrafts. The soils comprise all the varieties of the Blue Ridge division of the State, as white and red isinglass, slate, mica, limestone, and the "Red Lands." They are for the most part exceedingly fertile, the county possessing probably a smaller proportion of poor land than almost any other in Maryland, and where impoverished they are readily susceptible of improvement by careful cultivation and the use of lime, which exists in such abundance beneath the surface. The county is well wooded, and the scenery picturesque and beautiful, abounding in charming valleys, hemmed in by hills, on which the growth of the heaviest forest-trees gives the necessary shading to the landscape, and where a view of the distant Blue Ridge can be obtained, which is the case in many portions of the county, very happy effects are produced. The inhabitants have always been thrifty and energetic, and agriculture has received here its most perfect development. Fine farms abound. Wheat, rye, oats, and corn, the various grasses, fruits, and vegetables are grown, and magnificent herds of cattle and improved breeds of horses, sheep, and hogs are the principal productions of the farmers, while much attention is paid to the dairy business, the proximity to the city of Baltimore by means of the railroads and turnpikes insuring profitable returns to those engaged in it. Tobacco has been grown to some extent, and small crops are still raised in parts of the county, but the expense and uncertainty attending its production have been so great as to render it unpopular with the majority of farmers. Well-tilled farms and fine residences are confined to no particular district, but are freely distributed through the county. There are numerous mills and manufacturing establishments, and a large number of tanneries in the county, the last induced, doubtless, by the heavy growth of oak timber, which forms the body of the woods in that section of country. Large supplies of granite, marble, limestone, and brick clay are to be had for building purposes.

There are also large quarries of the best variety of soapstone near Marriottsville, adjacent to the Baltimore and Ohio Railroad. The stone is of the purest quality, and at the factory is sawed into every imaginable shape, and used for many varied purposes, its uses having multiplied greatly of late years. Even the refuse stone and dust are valuable in various ways.

Some of the finest hematitic iron ore in the United States, and also some excellent specimens of oxide of manganese, have been found in Carroll. The climate is salubrious, and the lay of the land and purity of the water favorable to health, so much so as to make many portions of the county favorite places of resort for the citizens of Baltimore during the summer months. The county is rapidly increasing in population, wealth, and enterprise, and the public-spirited citizens who have managed its affairs have adopted all judicious means for social and material advancement. The Baltimore and Ohio Railroad on its southern border, the Western Maryland Railroad which passes almost directly through the centre of the county, the Frederick and Pennsylvania Line Railroad which runs across the northwestern portion, and numerous fine turnpikes, as well as an admirable system of public roads, constitute the means of transportation, and few sections of the country possess greater conveniences in this regard. Through these channels it is placed in direct communication with the city of Baltimore, where a ready market is found for its productions, and the rapid transportation furnished by the railroads has enabled its citizens to build up a trade in the products of the dairy unsurpassed probably elsewhere in Maryland. The prices of land vary of course with the quality of the soil and its proximity or remoteness to the highways of travel, but one hundred and fifty dollars per acre is not unusual, and many who have purchased land at that rate have had no cause to regret it. As far back as April, 1814, Peter Benedune, who was a restless speculator, sold out all his land in the vicinity of Union Bridge at from one hundred to one hundred and twenty dollars per acre, and removed to the Valley of Virginia. The accessibility of the lands in Carroll County, their healthfulness, and the social advantages in many of the neighborhoods, render them desirable either as residences or safe investments. The brown sandstone, so highly valued for building purposes, is found in the western part of Carroll, and will compare very favorably with the Connecticut sandstone, so generally in use in the construction of the finer class of edifices in large cities. In Emmittsburg, among the upper layers of brown sandstone are found strata of flagging. Some of it separates into flags from two to four inches thick, with smooth surfaces ready dressed for paving. The boundaries of Carroll County were made for political convenience and not as divisions between distinct varieties of soil or different geological formations. The "Red Lands," beginning in the northwestern part of the county and extending through the Taneytown and Middleburg Districts into portions of the Union Town District, are similar in geological formation to those found in Frederick County, differing only in their agricultural value, the former being more decomposed, thereby insuring a deeper soil. These lands are underlaid by compact shales, among which red sandstone is frequently found sufficiently durable for building purposes. The value of these lands is materially influenced by the proximity of these shales or sandstones to the surface. When they are immediately beneath it the soil is unproductive, being easily affected by droughts, as there is not sufficient depth to retain the necessary supply of water for the crops. When this is the case the remedy is always at hand. The land should be subsoiled and heavily manured with lime.

Slate soils are a continuation of those found in Frederick County, and differ materially from the red land described above. The slates from which the soils overlying them are formed are mica slate, talc slate, chlorite slate, and blue, or roofing slate, the composition of all of which is, in an agricultural point of view, so nearly allied as to render any separate description of them unnecessary, and they are so intimately mixed that it would require almost an innumerable number of analyses to determine the special composition of each.

The lands drained by the waters of the Little Pipe Creek and its tributary branches are composed mainly from the disintegrated particles of these rocks or slates. They have by various influences become thoroughly decomposed, have been well manured and well cultivated, and are equal in productive value to the average of the best in the State. These lands are formed from the same rocks, and have the same composition in every particular, as all the lands in this section of the State are underlaid by the slates above spoken of; and the question naturally arises, why should some of them be so barren and some so productive? Why should the soils of the same formation on Parr's Ridge, running through the county to Manchester and the Pennsylvania line, be generally unproductive? Their mechanical texture must be examined for an explanation of their different degrees of fertility. Most of the soil in this part of the county, as it has been formed, has been washed off, and there has not been enough of it left to meet the wants of plants, by retaining a sufficiency of moisture for their support, or a proper quantity of nutrient materials to develop their growth and structure. To obviate these difficulties the soil must be deepened, decomposed, and the mineral set free which it has in a crude state.

There are also the light red sandy loams of this county, at the foot of Parr's Ridge, represented by the lands which extend over the whole county in a line more or less directly parallel with Parr's Ridge. They are famous for producing a variety of tobacco known as the Bay Tobacco, which sells at a very high price.

The red clay loam begins at the eastern border of the above-described lands, and extends eastward to where they meet the granite or isinglass soil. The next varieties met after going eastward from these are the white isinglass, soils formed from the disintegration of granite rocks. These are easily recognized, the bright shining spangles of mica, or isinglass, glistening everywhere. They are exceedingly light and dry, and are occasionally very barren. These comprise the chief soils of Carroll; they follow each other in regular succession, from west to east, in the order in which they are named, and can be readily recognized by their location as well as by their description.

The limestones of Carroll are fully equal to those found in any other portion of Western Maryland. Many of them are used only in the neighborhood where they are located, but there are many excellent limestone-quarries both for agricultural and building purposes. The principal limestones in the upper part of the county are as follows:

No. 2, a white limestone of fine crystalline texture, Uniontown, Maryland.

No. 2, a dark gray variety, slatish, with crystals of calc spar imbedded.

No. 3, a dark gray and homogeneous mass of fine crystalline texture, and small white veins of calc spar traversing. They were found to be composed as follows:

	No. 1.	No. 2.	No. 3.
Carbonate of lime	99.5	68.3	98.8
Carbonate of magnesia		11.5	0.5
Sand slate, etc.	0.5	20.2	0.7
	100	100	100

and will, therefore, produce, when burnt, of

Caustic lime	56.0	38.3	55
Caustic magnesia		5.5	0.2

and when water-slacked, of

Water-slacked lime	73.7	50.6	73.10
Water-slacked magnesia		8.0	0.3

The second series are those of the western flank of Parr's Ridge. They usually have a fine grain resembling that of Carrara marble, and they vary in color from white to grayish blue. They contain little silicious matter, and in general but small proportions of magnesia or other impurities. They have sometimes a slaty structure. Near the southern limits of the formation the proportion of magnesia is somewhat larger.

Iron ores occur in immense quantities in connection with the limestones before mentioned. They range from the Pennsylvania line (north of Westminster) southwesterly for ten or twelve miles. Westminster lies on the eastern edge of the range. There are the ruins of an iron-furnace about two and a half miles southwest of Westminster, on the property of Mr. Vanbibber, where these ores were smelted many years ago. The Western Maryland Railroad reaches this range of ore at Westminster, and passes through it for several miles. This affords every facility for transporting the ore or the iron that may be made therefrom.

The magnetic oxide of iron is the richest of iron ores, and when pure (as is sometimes the case in Sweden) contains seventy-two per cent. of metal. It is usually, however, more or less mixed up with earthy matters, and sometimes contains the oxides of titanium and manganese.

It has a metallic lustre and a dark gray or almost black color, the latter being also the color of its powder. It strongly attracts the magnetic needle, and when in small grains it is attracted by the magnet. Some of its varieties are sufficiently magnetic to attract iron filings and needles, hence the name of loadstone, which was formerly applied to it. These characters distinguish it from all other ores of iron.

It occurs in small quantities about seven miles west-northwest from Baltimore, near the Bare Hill's Copper-Mine, and again near Scott's mills, about eighteen miles north-northwest of Baltimore. It is found in massive as well as in octahedral crystals and grains. An iron-furnace at Sykesville is in part supplied by ore which is mined in that vicinity.

When the northwestern edge of the mica slates is reached, there is found what may be termed a metalliferous range, extending from the northern part of Cecil County through Harford, Baltimore, Carroll, Howard, and Montgomery Counties.

In addition to the magnetic iron ores of this range already referred to, there are ores of copper, chrome, and gold. Indications of copper may be seen at various points, and several mines have been opened in this county, one of which, at Springfield, near Sykesville, continues to be profitably worked. Near Finksburg a copper-mine was successfully worked during several years, and, if proper skill and sufficient capital are applied, it will probably prove productive. The ore consists of yellow or pyritous copper and still richer quartz, called purple copper ore.

Sulphuret of cobalt was discovered among the products of this mine, but this rare and valuable material occurred in very small quantity, and has not been found elsewhere in this State. Other mines have been opened in this range, between Finksburg and Sykesville, and at one of them native gold was discovered.

Northeastward from Finksburg there are indications of copper at many points, especially near the forks of the Gunpowder River, about twenty-two miles north of Baltimore. Some explorations and diggings have been made without discovering the ore in quantity. It appears to be associated with the magnetic oxide of iron of this formation.

There are also abundant traces of copper in the northwest part of the county, in the red shales. They give so little promise of profitable mines, however, that it is almost useless to expend money in digging for the ore.

Copper ore accompanies (in very small proportion) the magnetic oxide of iron, which is associated with steatite in veins in mica slate rock. Some years ago certain parties caused a shaft to be sunk on one of these veins with the hope that copper might be obtained in available quantities beneath, but they were disappointed. The Springfield mine was a success, and a similar result might happen at the Gunpowder veins, but the cost of sinking deep shafts is too great for the chances of a favorable result. In following this metalliferous range southwestward no indications of either chrome or copper are encountered until the vicinity of Finksburg is reached. From this point for about seven miles, to Springfield (one mile and a half north of Sykesville, on the Baltimore and Ohio Railroad), there are numerous indications of copper ores. A mine was opened near Finksburg about thirty years ago, and for some time was worked with success. The ore was found in a true vein, and consisted at first principally of carbonate of copper, which, as usual, was succeeded by a sulphuret of copper ore, containing sixty per cent. of metal when free from gangue, or about thirty per cent. after bring prepared for sale. At depths of from fifty to one hundred feet the ore was abundant, and it was usual for them to mine thirty tons a week.

Subsequently the vein became thinner, or pinched off, to use a mining term, but there is every reason to believe that with more knowledge of such matters on the part of the owners the vein might have been reached at a lower depth as rich as it was above. Veins of this kind are irregular in thickness, but mining to depths of two to three thousand feet has never yet reached the bottom of one of them. Another vein was slightly explored a short distance from this opening, but the owners became discouraged and suspended operations.

Another mine was opened at Mineral Hill, about seven miles southwest of Finksburg, in the same range. It was penetrated to a considerable depth. Cobalt ore has been found at Mineral Hill in small quantity, and native gold in the outcrop in inappreciable amount. The veins were opened and some work done about two miles southwest of this point. In the Springfield mine the main shaft has been carried down on the large vein to a distance of seven hundred feet, with much better indications at the greatest depth penetrated than near the surface, where there was little copper, but a considerable thickness of magnetic oxide of iron. In fact, this mine was originally worked for iron, but as it progressed in depth the proportion of copper continued to increase, so that for several years it was worked as a copper-mine, and turned out better than any other in the State.

The ore consisted of pyritous copper, which, when pure, contains usually about thirty-three per cent. of the metal, but owing to the mixture of vein-stone, or gangue, the proportion of metal was about thirteen per cent. The ore sold for about fifty dollars per ton to the copper-smelting works of Baltimore. Chrome ores occur at many points in a serpentine formation which stretches from New Lisbon four miles west to Rockville, Montgomery Co., and nearly to the Potomac River. The ore has been worked at several points, and is found to vary considerably in quality.

The range of limestone, useful as marble, is on the western flank of Parr's Ridge, extending southwestward from a little northwest of Manchester, passing near and west of Westminster, and extending into Frederick County. They are usually stratified, and consist of very small crystalline grains, and ore generally white or some light shade of blue. It is found, however, towards the southern limits of this range more variegated, with shades of red less pure, and the stratification more disturbed. The different layers of this vary considerably, and even in the same quarry there are strata of pure white and light blue, and sometimes variegated with light and dark shades of red. They take a fine polish, and are free from the grains or masses of quartz and other minerals which sometimes exist in the older limestones. The quarries, with cheap transportation, will increase their depths. The effect of this will be to bring to light the marble, less acted upon by the weather, at less cost than when large quantities of stone have to be quarried and thrown aside in order to get unaltered blocks of marble of large size.

Carroll County is well supplied with railroad facilities. The Western Maryland Railroad was chartered in January, 1852, and work was commenced on it in July, 1857. It was completed to Union Bridge in 1861, and to Williamsport, on the Potomac River, in 1873. In its inception it was a Carroll County enterprise, the inhabitants of that section subscribing for nearly all of the original stock of the company. William Roberts, the president, and William W. Dallas, John Smith, Samuel McKinstry, J. Henry Hoppe, and John K. Longwell, directors, contracted with Messrs. Irwin, Taylor & Norris to build the road to Union Bridge, the contractors to receive the stock subscription, amounting to one hundred and sixty thousand dollars, and six hundred thousand dollars in first mortgage bonds. It was subsequently completed to its present terminus on the Potomac River by Baltimore capitalists, who were very materially aided by Baltimore City. The presidents of the company have been Robert Magraw, Nathan Haines, William Roberts, Augustus Shriver, Robert Irwin, John Smith, John Lee Chapman, Wendell Bollman, George M. Bokee, Robert T. Banks, James L. McLane, Alexander Reiman, and the present very able and efficient executive, J. M. Hood. The value of this road to Carroll County can scarcely be overestimated. It passes directly through the centre of the county, entering Woolery District on its eastern border, and passing up through the northern corner, it skirts the southern extremity of Hampstead; thence through the centre of Westminster District, and taking in the county-seat, it crosses the New Windsor District, passing through the town of New Windsor; thence across the Union Bridge District, embracing the town of that name, and then along the southwestern portion of Middleburg District into Frederick County. At Bruceville, in Middleburg District, it intersects the Frederick and Pennsylvania Line Railroad, through which Frederick City, Taneytown, and points in Pennsylvania are reached. The scenery along the line of the road in Carroll County is exquisitely beautiful, and affords to the tourist in the summer months abundant opportunities for the study of nature in her loveliest and most varied forms. The land through which it passes is fertile, productive, highly cultivated, and teeming with the fruits of the earth. The road is intersected at many points by rapid, sparkling, and limpid streams, which promise in the near future to furnish power for innumerable mills and factories. Already the spirit of progress has manifested itself. Many mills have been erected along the course of the road, and the tanneries and ore-mines show that the confidence of the projectors of the enterprise was not misplaced. Property of every description in the vicinity of the railroad has greatly appreciated in value, and an unmistakable impetus has been given to all industries which the county is capable of sustaining. The stations in Carroll County are Carrollton, Gorsuch Road, Westminster, Avondale, Wayside, New Windsor, Linwood, Union Bridge, Middleburg, Frederick Junction, York Road (Bruceville), and Double Pipe Creek.

The Bachman's Valley Railroad begins at the Chestnut Hill iron ore mines, about the centre of the Manchester District, and runs almost due north across the line into Pennsylvania until it intersects the Hanover Branch Railroad. Immense quantities of iron ore are transported over this road to furnaces in Pennsylvania. The officers for 1881 were: President, Capt. A. W. Eichelberger; Directors, Stephen Keifer, H. C. Shriver, Joseph Dellone, Joseph Althoff, C. L. Johnson, J. W. Gitt, Levi Dubbs, Perry Wine, Edwin Thomas, Samuel Thomas, E. W. Henidele, and Adam Newcomer. The Hanover Railroad was built from Reisterstown, on the Western Maryland Railroad, to Hanover in 1879. It passes through Hampstead and Manchester Districts. Its officers are: President, Capt. A. W. Eichelberger; Directors, Stephen Keifer, Mr. Meltheimer, W. H. Hoffman, William Slagle, Calvin C. Wooden, and J. W. Gitt.

The Frederick and Pennsylvania Line Railroad runs from Frederick City, Md., through Middleburg and Taneytown Districts, in Carroll County, taking in the extreme western corner of Myers District, to Hanover, in Pennsylvania. It intersects the Western Maryland Railroad at Bruceville, in Middleburg District, and furnishes several outlets for the produce of the remarkably fertile grain-growing and grazing country through which it passes.

Prior to the building of railroads turnpikes were the readiest means of commercial intercourse between the great centres of trade and the outlying districts. So important were they considered that the policy of a great party in this country was to some extent based upon the advisability of their construction by the national government, and many severe contests were waged over this question in Congress.

At an early period in the history of the section now known as Carroll County the increase in population and trade made it necessary to secure greater facilities for transportation, and in 1805 the Baltimore and Reisterstown Turnpike Company was chartered. The capital needed for its construction, six hundred thousand dollars, was subscribed for by the merchants and capitalists of Baltimore, and in 1807 the road was constructed through this county. It entered Woolery District near Finksburg, and passing through Westminster, connected with the Hanover Branch. It is sixty miles in length, including the latter. The goods and produce carried over this road in early days was immense. The large Conestoga wagons, so familiar to denizens of the West as "schooners of the desert," passed each other, hundreds in a day, on their way to and from Pittsburgh and Baltimore, and the jingling of bells, the cracking of whips, the horses gayly caparisoned, and the drivers in picturesque costumes constituted an animating and enlivening spectacle, the recollection of which occasionally excites regret in the bosoms of the old-timers, and arouses a fleeting wish for the populous roads and the good old country inns which have been so effectually superseded by the trailing smoke and lightning dash of the steam-engine.

The Westminster and Hagerstown turnpike was begun about 1824, but before much progress had been made railroads had become a question of absorbing interest to enlightened people all over the world, and doubtless occasioned a lukewarmness with reference to pikes which materially interfered with the completion of the enterprise. At many points on the line sections of road were made, but the only portion finished was between Westminster and Uniontown.

The Liberty turnpike passes through the southern portion of the county, and there are short turnpikes at Union Bridge, New Windsor, and Finksburg. In 1851, about the time that the mania for plank-roads was at its height in the United States, it was determined to build one from Westminster to Emmittsburg, but, fortunately perhaps, it was never completed.

The following is a correct list of the judges, county clerks, sheriffs, State's attorneys, registers, and subordinate officers of Carroll County since its creation in 1837 to this present writing:

Judges of the Circuit Court.

1837–52, Thomas B. Dorsey, Thomas H. Wilkinson, Nicholas Brewer;[1] 1851–64, Madison Nelson; 1864–67, John E. Smith; 1867–81, Oliver Miller, Edward Hammond, Wm. N. Hayden.

County Clerks.

1837–41, Dr. William Willis; 1841–49, Dr. Jacob Shower; 1849–57, John B. Boyle; 1857–62, George E. Wampler; 1862–67, William A. McKellip; 1867–73, John B. Boyle; 1873–81, Dr. Frank T. Shaw.

Sheriffs.

1837–39, Nicholas Kelly; 1839–42, Jacob Grove; 1842–45, J. Henry Hoppe; 1845–48, Lewis Trumbo; 1848–51, Hanson T. Webb; 1851–53, William S. Brown; 1853–55, John M. Yingling; 1855–57, Joseph Shaeffer; 1857–59, William Wilson; 1859–61, William Segafoose; 1861–63, Jeremiah Babylon; 1863–65, Joseph Ebaugh; 1865–67, Jacob D. Hoppe; 1867–69, Thomas B. Gist; 1869–71, John Tracey; 1871–73, George N. Fringer; 1873–75, Edward Devilbiss; 1875–77, James W. White; 1877–79, Peter Wood; 1879–81, George N. Fringer.

Court Criers.

1837–57, James Kieffer; 1857–68, Benjamin Yingling; 1868–81, William S. Brown.

State's Attorneys.

1837–46, William P. Maulsby; 1846, James Raymond; 1847–49, William N. Hayden; 1849–51, Charles W. Webster; 1851, A. N. Hobbs; 1852–56, Daniel L. Hoover; 1856–67, Charles W. Webster; 1867–71, Charles T. Reifsnider; 1871–75, Richard B. Norment; 1875–81, David N. Henning.

Registers of Wills.

1837–53, John Baumgartner; 1853–65, Joseph M. Parke; 1865–67, Henry H. Herbaugh; 1867–73, Joseph M. Parke; 1873–79, Henry E. Beltz; 1879–81, J. Oliver Wadlow.

Judges of the Orphans' Court.

1837–39, Abraham Wampler, William Jameson, Robert Hudson; 1839–42, Nimrod Frizell, Michael Sullivan, Michael Barnitz; 1842–45, Michael Sullivan, Jesse Manning, John

[1] Judge Charles J. Kilgour attended the first court, but was killed by an accident in August, and was succeeded by Judge Brewer.

B. Boyle; 1845–48, Jacob Matthias, William Shepherd, Mordecai G. Cockey; 1848–51, Basil Hayden, William Fisher, George W. Manro; 1851–55, George W. Manro, Levi Buffington, Michael Sullivan; 1855–59, Michael Sullivan, Horatio Price, Thomas S. Brown; 1859–63, Horatio Price, John Thomson, Joshua C. Gist; 1863–67, John Thomson, Joseph Schaeffer, Thomas S. Brown, Michael Baughman (part of 1863); 1867–70, Jacob Powder; 1867–71, Levi Buffington, Hanson T. Webb; 1870–71, Ira E. Crouse; 1871–79, Adam Shower, Isaac C. Baile; 1871–72, Upton Roop; 1872–79, L. P. Slingluff, Granville T. Hering (chief justice), William Frizell, Milchour F. Allgire.

Auditors to the Circuit Court as a Court of Equity.

September term, 1837, James M. Shellman; April term, 1851, Abner Neal; April term, 1862, Charles T. Reifsnider; Jan. 1, 1867, Augustus D. Shaeffer; Nov. 29, 1867, John J. Baumgartner.

County Surveyors.

Charles W. Hood, Jacob Kerlinger, James Kelly, J. Henry Hoppe, J. William Everhart, Francis Warner, J. Henry Hoppe (deceased in 1881).

County School Commissioners.

Aug. 7, 1865, to April 27, 1868, Jacob H. Christ, Washington Senseney, Zachariah Ebaugh, Andrew K. Shriver, Joshua Yingling, Andrew J. Wilhelm, James V. Cresswell, Peter Engel; Secretary, William A. Wampler. April 27, 1868, to Jan. 3, 1870 (appointed by county commissioners), Sterling Galt, Reuben Saylor, Isaac Winchester, L. A. J. Lamotte, Dr. J. W. Steele, George A. Shower, John K. Longwell, Lewis Green, W. P. Anderson, Jacob Sharrets, Peter Shriner; Joseph Davis, counsel; Joseph M. Newson, secretary, treasurer, and examiner. Jan. 3, 1870, to Jan. 3, 1872 (elected by the people), Daniel H. Rudolph, Robert C. McKinney, Charles H. Gilbert, Jacob H. Cranmer, W. N. Matthews, Dr. J. W. Steele, David T. Schaeffer, Isaac Winchester, Joseph B. Dehoff, W. P. Anderson, Solomon Shepherd, Job Hibberd; Counsel, R. B. Norment; Secretary, Treasurer, and Examiner, J. M. Newson. Jan. 3, 1872, to 1881 (appointed by the court), Dr. William Reindollar *vice* R. C. McKinney, Alfred Zollickoffer, Francis H. Hering, David Prugh, William Reese; Counsel, John E. Smith; Secretary, Treasurer, and Examiner, Joseph M. Newson.

County Commissioners.

1837–39, William Shepherd, Sterling Galt, John Erb, Joshua C. Gist, Joseph Steele, Jacob Reese, John Lamotte, Nimrod Gardner, Henry N. Brinkman; 1839 to 1843, William Shaw, John Roop, of Joseph, Daniel Stull, Peter Hull, Eli Hewitt, Frederick Ritter, Jacob Shaeffer, William Houck, Joshua Barber; 1843–45, William Shaw, John Adelsperger, John Roop, Lewis Shue, Peter Hull, George Bramwell, Eli Hewitt, James Morgan, Frederick Ritter, Jacob Shaffer, William Houck, Larkin Buckingham; 1845–48, Henry Carter, Samuel Evans, Peter Geiger, Richard Richards, David B. Earhart, David Cassell, Frederick Bauchman, Elias Grimes, G. W. Gorsuch; 1848–51, James Crouse, Cornelius Baust, David Feevér, Daniel Bush, John H. Lindsey, George Crouse, Joseph Orendorff, George Richards, Jr., Bennett Spurrier; 1851–54, James Crouse, Thomas Smith, George L. Little, Jacob Wickert, Julius B. Berrett, George Crouse, Jacob Grove, George Richards, Jr., Bennett Spurrier; 1854–56 (now elected by the people), John Cover, Jonathan Dorsey, Michael Baughman; 1856–58, Benjamin Shunk, Jacob H. Christ, John Malehorn; 1858–60, Andrew K. Shriver, Jacob Morelock, G. W. Gorsuch; 1860–62, A. K. Shriver, H. W. Dell, Zachariah Ebaugh; 1862–64, Benjamin Shunk, Thomas F. Shepherd, John H. Chew; 1864–66, same board; 1866–68, Thomas Paynter, John H. Chew, Thomas F. Shepherd; 1868–70, Josiah Adelsperger, Upton Roop, Jabez A. Bush; 1870–72, Jacob Sharretts, Josiah Adelsperger, Upton Roop; 1872–74, Josephus H. Hoppe, G. K. Frank, Joseph Spurrier; 1874–76, M. C. McKinstry, John W. Murray, John O. Devries; 1876–78, same board; 1878–80, Jonas S. Harner, John J. Abbott, David Fowble; 1880–82, J. K. Longwell, W. C. Polk, Francis Warner.

Clerks to Commissioners.

1837–39, Otho Shipley; 1839–45, Basil Root *vice* Andrew Grammer, resigned; 1845–48, Otho Shipley; 1848–56, Jacob Myerly; 1856–64, James Blizzard; 1864–68, Levi Valentine; 1868–72, James Blizzard; 1872–78, James A. Bush; 1878–80, L. C. Trumbo; 1880–82, Joseph A. Waesche.

Collectors of Taxes.

1837–39, Thomas Hook; 1839–45, Tobias Cover; 1845–48, Josiah Baumgartner; 1848–51, Richard Manning; 1851–54, Tobias Cover; 1856–58, S. R. Gore; 1858–60, John T. Diffenbaugh; 1860–62, James Campbell;[1] 1874–78, Jabez Bush; 1878–80, L. C. Trumbo; 1880–82, Joseph A. Waesche.

Attorneys to Commissioners.

1837–39, James Raymond; 1843–45, William P. Maulsby; 1845–48, C. Birnie, Jr.; 1848–51, Joseph M. Parke; 1851–56, E. F. Crout; 1856–60, C. W. Webster; 1868–76, Charles B. Roberts; 1876–81, Richard B. Norment.

Members of Congress.

Peter Little, Elias Brown, Dr. Jacob Shower, Charles B. Roberts.

Members of Constitutional Conventions.

1851, Elias Brown, Dr. Jacob Shower, Joseph M. Parke, A. G. Ege, Mordecai G. Cockey; 1864, Dr. John Swope, John E. Smith, Jonas Ecker, William S. Wooden; 1867, William N. Hayden, George W. Manro, Thomas F. Cover, Sterling Galt, Benjamin W. Bennett, John K. Longwell.

State Senators.

1838–44, William P. Maulsby; 1844–50, William Roberts; 1850–55, John K. Longwell; 1855–57, Dr. Francis T. Davis; 1857–62, John E. Smith; 1862–64, Jacob Campbell; 1864–67, Dr. James L. Billingslea; 1867–70, Dr. Nathan Brown; 1870–74, John K. Longwell; 1874–78, James Fenner Lee; 1878–82, Henry Vanderford.

Members of the House of Delegates.

1837–38, Dr. Jacob Shower, James G. Berrett, John B. Boyle, Jacob Powder; 1839, Joseph M. Parker, George Bramwell, George Crabbs, Thomas Hook; 1840, John B. Boyle, Dr. Jacob Shower, Samuel D. Lecompte, Daniel Stull; 1841, John B. Boyle, Jacob Powder, Dr. Francis T. Davis, Daniel Stull; 1842, Elias Brown, Samuel D. Lecompte, Jacob Powder, William Shaw; 1843, Samuel Ecker, Jacob Powder, William Shaw, Daniel Stull; 1844, James Raymond, John Thomson, Micajah Rogers, Joseph Ebaugh; 1845, Thomas Hook, James M. Shellman, Abraham Wampler; 1846, A. G. Ege, James M. Shellman, Upton Scott, Charles Devilbiss; 1847, John B. Boyle, Nicholas Kelly,

[1] A collector for each district was then appointed, which system remained in force until 1874.

Tobias Cover, Jacob Powder; 1849, Elias Brown, Samuel A. Lauver, George Motter, Lewis Trumbo; 1851, Elijah F. Crout, Dr. J. E. H. Ligget, Daniel Stull; 1854, Thomas Smith, Robert T. Dade, Josiah Baugher; 1856, Stephen T. C. Brown, David Buffington, John E. Smith; 1858, Samuel McKinstry, Milton Day, Samuel Reindollar; 1860, Dr. B. Mills, John W. Gorsuch, David Roop; 1861, Somerset R. Waters, George Everhart, Warren L. Little (December session); 1862, Jonas Ecker, John N. Starr, Somerset R. Waters; 1864, Moses Shaw, George Everhart, John W. Angel, William S. Wooden, N. D. Norris; 1865, William A. Wampler, Benjamin Poole, James V. Criswell, E. F. Benton, S. R. Gore; 1868, Henry S. Davis, John H. Jordon, John W. Hardin, Benjamin Worthington; 1870, William H. Crouse, Airhart Winters, George A. Shower, John H. Jordon; 1872, James H. Steele, Lewis A. J. Lamotte, Trusten Polk, H. H. Lamotte; 1874, Henry Vanderford, Henry Galt, Dr. S. R. Waters, Thomas C. Brown; 1876, Frank Brown, H. H. Lamotte, Dr. Jacob Rinehart, Dr. S. R. Waters; 1878, Frank T. Newbelle, T. Herbert Shriver, Robert Sellman, Sr., Frank Brown; 1880, William T. Smith, T. Herbert Shriver, Robert Sellman, Sr., Benjamin F. Crouse; 1882, Henry Galt, Edward W. Leeds, David A. C. Webster, Joseph W. Berret.

Miscellaneous Officials in 1881.

Assistant School Examiner, Orlando Reese; Deputy County Clerks, George A. Miller, N. Bruce Boyle, James A. Diffenbaugh; Deputy Register of Wills, George M. Parke.

Justices of the Peace in Carroll County since its Organization as a County—When Appointed or Elected.

1839, John Manning, Basil Root, James Keefer, John C. Kethy, Adam Fieser, Michael Smith, Josiah Shilling, Henry Drach, Jonathan Dorsey, Jacob Wickert, Thomas B. Owings, Wilton Burdett, John Jones, of John, Michael Lynch, John Kerlinger, John F. Reese, Charles Denning, Jacob Farver, Thomas Ingels, George W. Manro; 1840, J. Henry Hoppe; 1841, Jabez Gore, Jesse Brain, John Lockard; 1842, Benjamin Williams, Samuel Moffett, Jabez Gore, Thomas J. Carter, J. Henry Hoppe, John Potherer, Jacob Grove, Abraham Lamott, Josiah Shilling, George Williams; 1843, Thomas Grisley, John Malehorn, Jacob Kerlinger, John Rinehart, Samuel Lamott, James Heind, David Roop, Basil Hayden; 1844, Jacob Myerly, Julius B. Berret, Elijah Woolery, Michael Smith; 1845, Otho Shipley, James Smith, Benjamin Shunk, John Lochitz, Washington Van Bibber, Isaac Dern, Jeremiah Bartholow, Daniel Stonesifer, William Ecker, James Kelly, David C. Frankforter, George D. Klinefelter, Abraham Bixler, Henry H. Herbaugh, Stephen Oursler, Nimrod Stevenson, Charles Devilbiss, Abraham England, James McKellip, John K. Longwell, Henry V. Buchen, Richard A. Kirkwood, Jacob Stone, Archibald Dorsey, Frank Yingling, Joshua H. Shipley, Zachariah Ebaugh, James Douty, John Hood. Jr., Solomon Stocksdale, Geo. E. Wampler, Richard Owings, Charles Stevenson, William Shaw, Washington Barnes, Samuel Swarmstedt, Warren L. Little, Alexander Gilliss, Nicholas Dorsey, Thomas Hook, Horatio F. Bardwell, David B. Earhart, Moses Myers, Joshua Smith, G. Ogg, Henry Stamf; 1846, John Leatherwood, James Rodgers, Jonathan Morris, David Kephart, Wm. Jordan, John Delaplane, Peter E. Myers, Thomas W. Durbin, Daniel Banker, Joshua Stansbury, Jacob Zumbrun, Franklin J. Smith; 1847, Geo. W. Wilson, Stephen Gorsuch; 1848, Jabez Gore, Jacob Grove, Jacob Myerly, Joseph Gernand, George Everhart, James Baker, J. Henry Hoppe, Geo. W. Manro, Jonathan Dorsey, Eli Hewitt, George Foster, William Fisher, Thomas Hook, George Miller, Daniel L. Hoover, Samuel A. Lauver, Daniel J. Geiman, D. F. Lamott, Thos. S. Brown, John Mauss, Geo. L. Little, Michael Sullivan, David Bussard, Samuel Messinger, Michael Smith, Kelpher Crawmer, Julius B. Berrett, Francis J. Crawford, D. W. Houck, John C. Price, Charles Denning, Jacob Kerlinger, Joseph Spurrier, George Bramwell, William Lockard, George P. Albaugh, Joseph Creager, John Rinehard, Thos. B. Buckingham, George Williams, Jesse Manning, David Bussard, James Rodgers, William Tagg, Samuel Messinger, Geo. W. Daniel, Peter B. Mikesell, David Hope, Richard Harris, Larkin Buckingham; 1849, Michael Sullivan, Joseph Stonesifer; 1850, David Wolf, Geo. L. Little, Jacob Wickert, Michael Smith, D. F. Lamott, John Rinehart, Charles Dunning, David Bussard, Elijah Woolery, D. W. Houck, George Foster; 1851, John W. McAllister; 1852, Jacob Myers, Jesse Manning, J. Henry Hoppe, David Wolf, Wm. Jordan, David Feeser, James Rodgers, John Mauss, Eli Hewitt, George Miller, William Tagg, James Baker, Jacob Kerlinger, Larkin Buckingham, George Foster, Basil Hayden, William Fisher, George Everhart, Thos. B. Owings, George Ogg, Joseph Spurrier, John W. McAlister, George Bramwell, D. F. Lamott, Thos. S. Brown, Kelpher Crawmer, Joshua Lamott, Peter B. Mikesell, Henry W. Deel, Henry H. Herbaugh, E. L. Crawford, David Hape, Richard Harris, John C. Price; 1853, Jesse Hollingsworth, D. W. Houck, Richard Deel, Mordecai G. Cockey, Benj. Shunk, J. Henry Hoppe, David B. Earhart, Wm. Gensfribe, Jesse Manning, Wm. A. Wampler, Charles Denning, James McKellip, Wm. Haugh, Wm. R. Currey, Wm. Walter, Jacob Kerlinger, Richard Harris, John C. Price, F. O. Franklin, H. H. Herbaugh, John Koontz, Isaac Dern, David Otto, Joshua Switzer, John Hood, Thomas B. Owings, Alex. Gilliss, Abraham Lamott; 1854, Bennett Spurrier; 1855, Wm. Walter, Henry Fleagle, George Miller, Jacob Kerlinger, Henry Motter, John Fowble, of Jacob, Edwin A. Atlee, W. A. Wampler, Jacob Shurve, Abraham Albaugh, H. H. Herbaugh, Reuben Conaway, Mordecai G. Cockey, Aquila Pickett, J. Henry Hoppe, A. H. Jenkins, Geo. Richards, John T. Lowe, Joseph Matthias, David Otto, Nathan Gorsuch, Nicholas D. Norris, M. B. L. Bassard, John Delaplane, Wm. Crouse, Elijah Woolery, Daniel Stonesifer, Geo. L. Little; 1856, Daniel L. Hoover, John C. Price; 1857, J. Henry Hoppe, F. O. Franklin, Wm. Crouse, David B. Flegal, M. G. Cockey, Hanson M. Drach, Joseph Matthias, Reuben Conaway, Aquila Pickett, Benjamin W. Bennett, N. D. Norris, W. G. Shipley, Peter B. Mikesell, Daniel Stonesifer, Henry Glaze, Jesse B. Christ, F. A. Switzer, Elijah Woolery, Benj. Shunk, Geo. Miller, Frederick H. Crabbs, John C. Price, Wm. Haugh, Geo. Richards, Jr., Wm. Walter, Abraham Albaugh, John Delaplane, Nathan Gorsuch, D. Otto, H. H. Herbaugh, H. Geatty; 1859, E. A. Atlee, Joseph Mathias, A. S. Yentz, W. A. Wampler, James Lockard, J. Henry Hoppe, Wm. Walter, H. M. Drach, D. B. Flegal, John T. Young, Henry Motter, John Mauss, P. B. Mikesell, Jacob Zumbrun, Jacob Shriver, Benjamin Shunk, John Delaplane, Samuel A. Lauver, Aquila Pickett, W. G. Shipley, John C. Price, William Crouse, Joshua Switzer, F. A. Switzer, M. G. Cockey, H. H. Herbaugh, Jesse Braun, Israel Norris, Evan Thompson; 1861, J. Washington Cochran, Joseph Mathias, W. A. Wampler, John Hesson, Emanuel Gernand, John Mauss, Jacob D. Hopple, John Delaplane, William Lockard, H.

H. Herbaugh, John G. Ways, M. G. Cockey, William Lensfield, J. William Everhart, Nathan Gorsuch, E. A. Atlee, George P. Albaugh, George Miller, John Fultz, Jacob Zumbrun, Joshua Switzer, John T. Young, William Haugh, Henry Motter, A. Pickett, Eli Hewitt, John C. Price, Jetson L. Gill, D. B. Flegal, Thomas Tipton, Solomon S. Ecker, William Fisher; 1863, William Tensfield, W. J. Mitten, Joseph Mathias, William E. Shriner, Richard Harris, George Miller, William Haugh, Amon Brice, Aquila Pickett, John Hesson, Joseph Brummel, Joseph H. Gilliss, J. C. Price, Henry Frack, H. H. Herbaugh, J. W. Cochran, Nathan Gorsuch, S. B. Stocksdale, Thomas Tipton, Levi D. Frock, Eli Hewitt, George E. Buckingham, John Delaplane, William Fisher, Henry Motter, Francis Warner, Joshua Switzer, Solomon S. Ecker, John Mauss; 1864, William Lockard, George E. Buckingham; 1865, John S. Wampler, William Lockard, Benjamin Shunk, James Kelly, William Haugh, George Miller, John T. Ways, J. Williams, D. E. Earhart, David Otto, J. William Everhart, Thomas Tipton, Henry Glaze, Aquila Pickett, George E. Wampler, Joshua Switzer, Joshua Oain, J. L. Gill, Peter A. Shipley, John Hesson, Solomon S. Ecker, John Fultz, John W. Cochran, Nicholas S. F. Harden, Eli Hewitt, Michael Babylon; 1866, George E. Wampler, J. L. Gill, Thomas Demoss, Michael Babylon, Joshua Cain, Peter Ritter; 1867, John W. McAlister, John Lamott, Cornelius Jenkins, William Fisher, Henry Galt, W. H. Stocksdale, Levi Yingling, Joshua Cain, Francis Warner, John Maus, Nathan Gorsuch, Azariah Oursler, A. Neal, Stephen Gorsuch, W. J. Mitten, J. Henry Hoppe, Eli Hewitt, John W. Jones, D. H. Hoffacker, J. B. Summers, William T. Smith, J. Oliver Wadlow, Henry Bussard, Henry Motter, David Otto, Michael Babylon; 1868, Peter B Mikesell, William Fisher, W. L. Tracy, Henry Galt, Simon Bange, Charles Denning, Joshua Switzer, Joshua Cain, W. H. Stocksdale, W. T. Smith, Levi Yingling, C. W. Hood, Henry Bussard, J. W. McAlister, Charles Sykes, David Otto, John Lamott, J. Henry Hoppe, J. B. Summers, W. J. Mitten, John Maus, J. Oliver Wadlow, C. Jenkins, Henry Motter, J. W. Jones, A. Neal, Nathan Gorsuch, Thomas B. Buckingham, G. W. Gilbert; 1870, W. L. Tracy, G. A. Flicking, G. W. Gilbert, C. W. Hood, A. Oursler, N. Gorsuch, Henry Bussard, William Fisher, T. C. Jenkins, W. G. Byers, J. Henry Hoppe, J. Oliver Wadlow, Stephen Gorsuch, William T. Smith, W. H. Stocksdale, Henry Motter, John W. Jones, Henry Galt, Thomas B. Buckingham, George L. Stocksdale, J. B. Dehoff, John W. McAlister, A. J. Houck, P. B. Mikesell, Charles Denning, E. Legore, W. J. Mitten, A. Neal, Joshua Switzer, Andrew Grammer; 1872, Ezra Legore, Stephen Gorsuch, Henry Galt, William Fisher, J. William Everhart, C. Jenkins, William J. Mitten, Abner Neal, Joshua Switzer, J. Oliver Wadlow, William T. Smith, William L. Tracy, Azariah Oursler, George A. Flickinger, Henry Motter, A. J. Houck, Henry Bussard, Charles W. Hood, James Morgan, William Stocksdale, Nathan Gorsuch, Peter B. Mikesell, Thomas B. Buckingham, George L. Stocksdale, George W. Gilbert, Samuel Shunck; 1873, John W. Abbott; 1874, Charles W. Hood, James Morgan, S. B. Stocksdale, Henry Galt, Joel Brown, J. Henry Hoppe, J. F. Malehorn, J. Oliver Wadlow, Charles Denning, Lewis Dielman, William T. Smith, Henry Motter, Joshua Switzer, Ezra Legore, William J. Mitten, William L. Tracy, G. A. Flickinger, A. Oursler, Jacob P. Baltover, J. W. Abbott, Eli Erb, Vincent Brown, G. W. Gilbert, C. W. Hood, J. B. Summers, Thomas B. Buckingham, Abner Neal, Stephen Gorsuch, Peter B. Mikesell, William H. Crouse, Samuel Shunk, Henry A. McAtee; 1875, Francis Warner; 1876, J. P. Baltozer, Francis Warner, Louis Dielman, G. A. Flickinger, Joab Brown, John B. Summers, W. T. Smith, Joshua Switzer, W. H. Fogle, G. W. Matthews, Jesse A. Legore, Samuel Messinger, J. K. Kearney, Thomas Tipton, W. J. Mitten, J. Henry Hoppe, G. W. Crapster, J. E. Ward, A. Oursler, James Morgan, J. W. Abbott, J. Oliver Wadlow. Charles Denning, Henry Galt, Stephen Gorsuch, Henry Motter, William Fisher, Dr. H. M. Drach, J. E. Christ, John Elgen, Howard McGill, Isaiah Hann, C. W. Hood, G. F. Yingling, Thomas Jones, Charles R. Favour; 1877, Richard Dell; 1878, Jacob P. Baltozer, Samuel S. Spalding, Dr. H. M. Drach, Peter B. Mikesell, Azariah Oursler, J. Henry Hoppe, J. U. Legore, J. H. Knipple, G. A. Flickinger, Henry Galt, Louis Dielman, W. J. Mitten, Joab Brown, John W. Abbott, P. Bennett, William Fisher, Gustavus W. Crapster, H. McGill, Thomas Jones, Thomas B. Buckingham, J. B. Summers, Francis Warner, John Elgen, James Morgan, J. K. Kearney, J. Bowman, Isaiah Hann, Daniel E. Christ, William T. Smith, J. Oliver Wadlow, W. H. Stocksdale, Richard Dell, Henry Motter, Thomas Tipton, Nathan Gorsuch, John P. Fowler, Charles R. Favour, D. Calvin Warner, J. Frank Shipley; 1880, Joab Brown, Henry Galt, Azariah Oursler, J. P. Baltozer, William Fisher, James C. Davis, S. S. Spalding, Richard Dell, Thomas Tipton, John W. Abbott, Dr. Hanson, M. Drach, Louis Dielman, Thomas Jones, William J. Mitten, S. H. Hoffacker, G. W. Crapster, John Burgoon, E. E. Lovell, John Elgen, Ira E. Crouse, John P. Fowler, Thomas B. Buckingham, Peter B. Mikesell, Henry Motter, John Bowman, D. Calvin Warner, W. H. Stocksdale, J. Henry Knipple, Charles R. Favour, Nathan Gorsuch, J. F. Shipley, J. K. Kearney, John B. Summers, David H. Reindollar, Jesse F. Billmyer, Henry Crook; 1881, Joseph Arnold, Andrew J. Dougherty.

Registers of Voters.

1866-67.—1st District, W. A. Hiteshue, Washington Galt; 2d, J. H. Jordan; 3d, Peter E. Myers, Abraham Long; 4th, Thomas Gorsuch; 5th, Jesse Hollingsworth; 6th, Jacob Linaweaver; 7th, Benjamin Williams, George W. Shriver; 8th, Richard Harris; 9th, Abraham Albaugh; 10th, David Otts; 11th, Jesse Lambert.

1868.—R. B. Warden, W. H. Lamott, John M. Yingling, Abraham Albaugh, George Shower, S. G. Harden, W. A. Hiteshue, Peter E. Myers, Jeremiah Malshorn, Jesse Lambert, William Valentine, G. W. Crapster.

1869.—Uriah B. Mikesell.

1870.—Jesse Lambert, G. W. Crapster, W. H. Lamott, Abraham Albaugh, George Shower, William H. Hull, Uriah B. Mikesell, John R. Haines, William Valentine, Samuel G. Harden, Jeremiah Malshorn.

1871.—8th District, Jacob Coltrider.

1872.—1st District, G. W. Crapster; 2d, John R. Haines; 3d, Eli Erb; 4th, William H. Lamott; 5th, S. D. Warfield; 6th, George Shower; 7th, Uriah B. Mikesell; 8th, Jacob Coltrider; 9th, Abraham Albaugh; 10th, William Valentine; 11th, Jesse Lambert; 12th, John Hartsock.

1873.—7th District, Lee McElroy.

1874.—1st District, William Fisher; 2d, John R. Haines; 3d, Jonas Frock; 4th, Daniel Ebaugh; 5th, Surratt D. Warfield; 6th, George Shower; 7th, Lee McElroy; 8th, Jacob Coltrider; 9th, Abraham Albaugh; 10th, Levi Buffington; 11th, Jesse Lambert; 12th, John Hartsock.

1876.—1st District, William L. Rudisel; 2d, John R. Haines; 3d, Jonas Frock: 4th, Daniel Ebaugh; 5th, Samuel S. Spalding: 6th, George Shower; 7th, Lee McElroy; 8th,

Francis L. Hann; 9th, Abraham Albaugh; 10th, John Shunk; 11th, Jesse Lambert; 12th, John Hartsock.

1877.—4th District, Noah Stocksdale.

1878.—1st District, W. L. Rudisel; 2d, John R. Haines; 3d, Jonas Frock; 4th, Noah Stocksdale; 5th, Dr. Joseph W. Steele; 6th, George Shower; 7th, Lee McElroy, G. W. Matthews; 8th, Francis L. Hann; 9th, Abraham Albaugh; 10th, John Shunk; 11th, Jesse Lambert; 12th, John Hartsock.

1880.—1st District, Charles A. Waesche; 2d, John R. Haines; 3d, William G. Byers; 4th, John Frick; 5th, Dr. J. W. Steele; 6th, George Shower; 7th, George W. Matthews; 8th, James W. Hann; 9th, Lewis C. Franklin; 10th, John Shunk; 11th, Jesse Lambert; 12th, John Hartsock.

Tax Collectors.

1866.—1st District, Samuel T. Clingan; 2d, T. H. Routson; 3d, Benjamin Hesson; 4th, Stephen Oursler; 5th, William D. Frizzell; 7th, Henry Shreev; 8th, David Grogg; 9th, John Hood; 10th, John Root; 11th, Mordecai Engler.

1867.—1st District, S. T. Clingan; 2d, T. H. Routson; 3d, Benjamin Hesson; 4th, Stephen Oursler; 5th, W. T. Frizzell; 6th, Jesse Schultz; 7th, Henry Shreev; 8th, David Grogg; 10th, Jacob Shriner; 11th, Mordecai Engler.

1868.—7th District, Jacob Holmes; 8th, Benjamin Jackson; 9th, Joseph Spurrier; Edward Spalding, Henry T. Eck, Nathan Hanna, G. K. Frank, Samuel A. Lauver, James Gilbert, James White, Freeborn Gardner, Edward Spalding.

1869.—Henry T. Eck, James Gilbert, Freeborn Gardner, Nathan Hanna, Samuel A. Lauver, Benjamin Jackson, James W. White, George K. Frank, Jacob Holmes, Edward Spalding, Joseph Spurrier.

1870.—1st District, A. F. Arndorff; 2d, James Gilbert; 3d, W. T. Feeser; 4th, Samuel A. Lauver; 5th, Freeborn Gardner; 6th, George K. Frank; 7th, Jacob Holmes; 8th, Benjamin Jackson; 9th, Joseph Spurrier; 10th, William A. Grimes; 11th, D. W. Snader.

1871.—Same, excepting Isaiah Hann in 10th and John N. Selby in 9th, *vice* Grimes and Spurrier.

1872.—1st District, Edward Spalding; 2d, Dennis Cookson; 4th, Jesse Long; 6th, John J. Abbott; 7th, George P. Albaugh; 8th, Benjamin Jackson; 9th, John N. Selby; 10th, Isaiah Hann.

1873.—1st District, Edward Spalding; 2d, Dennis Cookson; 3d, Daniel Myers; 4th, Jesse Long; 5th, Freeborn Gardner; 6th, John J. Abbott; 8th, Benjamin Jackson; 9th, Henry S. Davis; 10th, Isaiah Hann; 11th, D. W. Snader.

1874.—1st District, Edward Spalding; 2d, J. Hamilton Singer; 3d, Daniel Myers; 4th, Jesse Long; 5th, Freeborn Gardner; 6th, Joseph Weimer; 7th, George P. Albaugh; 8th, W. H. Armacost; 10th, Jacob Sharretts; 11th, D. W. Snader.

1875.—1st District, Edward Spalding; 2d, J. H. Singer; 3d, Daniel Myers; 4th, Jesse Long; 6th, Joseph Weimer; 7th, G. P. Albaugh; 8th, J. Thomas Green; 9th, Byron S. Dorsey; 10th, Jacob Sharretts; 11th, D. W. Snader.

1876.—1st District, Edward Spalding; 2d, J. H. Singer; 3d, Daniel Myers; 5th, Freeborn Gardner; 6th, Joseph Weimer; 7th, G. P. Albaugh; 8th, J. Thomas Green; 9th, Byron S. Dorsey; 11th, Joseph A. Waesche.

1877.—1st District, Washington Reaver; 2d, J. H. Singer; 3d, Daniel Myers; 4th, Jesse Long; 5th, R. H. Wadlow; 6th, Joseph Weimer; 7th, G. P. Albaugh; 8th, Isaac T. Green; 9th, B. S. Dorsey; 10th, Jacob Sharretts; 11th, J. A. Waesche.

1878.—1st District, W. Reaver; 2d, Benjamin Reaver; 5th, G. W. Manro; 6th, G. K. Frank; 7th, W. G. Rinehart; 8th, Isaac T. Green; 9th, B. S. Dorsey; 10th, J. H. Diffendal; 11th, J. A. Waesche; 12th, George P. Buckley.

1879.—1st District, W. Reaver; 2d, Benjamin Reaver; 3d, Daniel Myers; 4th, Jesse Long; 5th, G. W. Manro; 6th, G. K. Frank; 7th, W. G. Rinehart; 8th, J. T. Green; 9th, B. S. Dorsey; 10th, J. H. Diffendal; 11th, J. A. Waesche; 12th, G. P. Buckley.

1880–81.—Same, save D. P. Smelzer in 11th.

It is sometimes interesting to glance over the results of successive elections held during a given period and to note the gradual changes effected in public sentiment by the lapse of time, the march of enlightenment, or the happening of exciting events which exert an influence on the minds of electors. A philosophic study of such statistics will enable a careful student to evolve the outline of the history of a people, the bent of their minds, and even their character and habits.

The names of the principal candidates for office at every prominent election held in Carroll County since 1847 to the present time (1881) is given below, together with the number of votes cast for each candidate:

Gubernatorial Vote, 1847.

Districts.	Francis Thomas. (Democrat.)	Goldsborough. (Whig.)
Taneytown	203	296
Uniontown	261	358
Myers'	205	79
Woolery's	195	94
Freedom	106	208
Manchester	352	72
Westminster	262	203
Hampstead	159	64
Franklin	109	150
Total	1854	1524

Vote for Delegates, 1847.

Boyle	1831	Kelly	1785
Ege	1493	Hood	1465
Powder	1791	Cover	1512
Ecker	1538	Wampler	1513

Third Congressional District.

	Ligon.	Philpot.
Baltimore County	2401	1902
Five Wards of Baltimore	2509	1612
Howard District	726	661
Carroll County	1801	1531
Total	7447	5706

Vote for Sheriff, 1848.

Districts.	Sullivan. (Democrat.)	Gore. (Dem.)	Webb. (Whig)	Earhart. (Whig)	Bishop (Ind.)
Taneytown	132	173	261	186	5
Uniontown	148	166	324	114	14
Myers'	117	109	79	124	5
Finksburg	122	163	131	28	19
Freedom	37	95	249	103	7
Manchester	286	246	60	28	5
Westminster	222	237	200	70	10
Hampstead	119	115	73	10	29
Franklin	95	78	131	59	2
Total	1278	1382	1508	722	96

Vote for President, 1848.

Districts.	Lewis Cass.	Zachary Taylor.
Taneytown	195	318
Uniontown	208	373
Myers'	181	100
Woolery's	142	134
Freedom	88	258
Manchester	362	75
Westminster	245	262
Hampstead	154	73
Franklin	97	170
Total	1672	1763

Gubernatorial and Senatorial Vote, 1850.

Districts.	Governor.		Senator.	
	Clark. (Whig.)	Lowe. (Democrat.)	Langwell. (Whig.)	Liggett. (Democrat.)
Taneytown	321	162	293	189
Uniontown	358	218	357	217
Myers'	80	157	82	155
Woolery's	116	155	120	149
Freedom	215	88	221	80
Manchester	79	361	80	359
Westminster	261	250	288	226
Hampstead	77	146	81	140
Franklin	157	74	160	71
Total	1664	1611	1682	1586

Vote for Delegates to Constitutional Convention, 1850.

Democratic Ticket.

Districts.	Cockey.	Brown.	Edge.	Parke.	Shower.
Taneytown	273	268	328	288	283
Uniontown	171	135	190	185	180
Myers'	114	100	116	115	113
Woolery's	153	126	135	133	134
Freedom	74	61	65	66	70
Manchester.	273	271	273	280	282
Westminster	225	197	220	232	217
Hampstead	117	112	115	116	119
Franklin	51	41	31	64	68
Total	1431	1309	1473	1479	1466

Whig Ticket.

Districts.	Wampler.	Ecker.	Swope.	Frankforter.	Grimes.
Taneytown	96	98	134	79	91
Uniontown	230	287	236	239	232
Myers'	48	54	45	50	48
Woolery's	97	93	90	85	90
Freedom	154	161	161	156	166
Manchester.	61	59	60	81	56
Westminster	236	222	221	218	225
Hampstead	50	48	45	46	45
Franklin	114	142	128	127	157
Total	1086	1164	1117	1081	1110

Vote on the Adoption of the New Constitution, June 4, 1851.

Districts.	For.	Against.
Taneytown	227	124
Uniontown	145	274
Myers'	90	97
Woolery's	205	39
Freedom	73	201
Manchester	287	37
Westminster	227	162
Hampstead	151	40
Franklin	66	121
Total	1071	1095

Vote for Congressman, Oct. 1, 1851.

Districts.	Hammond. (Democrat.)	Lynch. (Whig.)
Taneytown	185	100
Uniontown	112	80
Myers'	158	27
Woolery's	94	6
Freedom	59	89
Manchester	253	33
Westminster	191	131
Hampstead	211	
Franklin	115	86
Total	1378	552

Vote for State Comptroller, November, 1851.

Districts.	P. F. Thomas. (Democrat.)	G. C. Morgan. (Whig.)
Taneytown	246	277
Uniontown	250	376
Myers'	204	89
Woolery's	170	128
Freedom	82	206
Manchester	317	90
Westminster	269	269
Hampstead	170	73
Franklin	87	146
Total	1795	1654

For Court of Appeals, John T. Mason 1604, Fred'k A. Schley 1672.

For Circuit Judge, Madison Nelson 1732, R. H. Marshall 865, W. M. Merrick 153, J. M. Palmer 724.

For Clerk of Court, John B. Boyle 1882, John McCollum 1596.

For Sheriff, W. S. Brown 2199, S. J. Jordan 1491, Otho Shipley 973.

For Register of Wills, Joseph M. Parke 1607, J. J. Baumgardner 1902.

For State's Attorney, D. L. Hoover 1807, C. W. Webster 1543.

For Orphans' Court, M. Sullivan 1707, G. W. Manro 1800, Levi Buffington 1784, J. C. Gist 1398, H. Price 1493, John Thomson 1362, D. B. Earhart 214, B. Hayden 378.

For Assembly, E. F. Crout 1730, D. Stull 1702, J. E. H. Ligget 1793, Thos. Hook 1505, E. G. Cox 1346, G. E. Wampler 1668, R. R. Booth 234, A. Lamott 300.

For Surveyor, J. Henry Hoppe 1582, James Kelly 1828.

Vote for President, 1852.

Districts.	Pierce.	Scott.
Taneytown	153	236
Uniontown	244	341
Myers'	201	79
Woolery's	182	103
Freedom	94	236
Manchester	423	89
Westminster	279	252
Hampstead	166	83
Franklin	108	163
Middleburg	69	120
Total	1919	1702

Vote for School Commissioners, Nov. 3, 1852.

Districts.	Shriver.	Holmes.	Cookson.	Hiteshue.	Herbaugh.	Earhart.	Nat. Mon.
Taneytown	62	59	63	101	59	60	$8.62
Uniontown	54	17	51	37	73	31	5.00
Myers'	85	40	52	9	8	72	.20
Woolery's	56	59	54	2	3	1	4.75
Freedom	25	30	25	28	28	27	1.78
Manchester	102	104	104	14	13	14	5.00
Westminster	96	99	100	73	79	74	13.34
Hampstead	25	24	24	20	8	7	6.00
Franklin	28	29	29	17	19	19	1.32
Middleburg	19	14	21	30	27	18	2.05
Total	552	475	523	331	317	323	$48.07

Average Democratic majority 193.

Gubernatorial Vote, 1853.

Districts.	T. W. Ligon. (Democrat.)	R. J. Bowie. (Whig.)
Taneytown	136	221
Uniontown	289	329
Myers'	216	91
Woolery's	202	121
Freedom	100	202
Manchester	410	88
Westminster	300	282
Hampstead	180	81
Franklin	134	184
Middleburg	79	103
Total	2046	1702

For Congress, Dr. Jacob Shower 2053, John Wethered 1654.

For Delegates, Josiah L. Baugher 1882, Thomas Smith 1909, Robert Dade 1918, George E. Wampler 1859, Joseph Ebaugh 1744, Stephen Oursler 1648.

For Register of Wills, J. J. Baumgardner 1782, J. M. Parke 1903.

For Sheriff, J. M. Yingling 2077, S. J. Jordan 1751.

For School Commissioners, Samuel Ecker 1669, J. H. Shipley 1498, J. W. Earhart 1730, J. C. Cookson 2009, A. K. Shriver 2061, Jacob Holmes 2011.

For County Commissioners, J. B. Chenowith 1731, J. C. Gist 1780, John Cover 1853, Michael Baughman 2038, Jonathan Dorsey 1927, Isaac Appler 1726.

Vote for State Comptroller, 1855.

Districts.	W. H. Purnell. (American.)	W. W. W. Bowie. (Democrat.)
Taneytown	249	134
Uniontown	487	180
Myers'	110	183
Woolery's	216	119
Freedom	306	85
Manchester	103	444
Westminster	303	313
Hampstead	123	146
Franklin	221	134
Middleburg	134	73
Total	2252	1811

Presidential Vote, 1856.

Districts.	Buchanan.	Fillmore.
Taneytown	147	270
Uniontown	154	343
Myers'	227	113
Woolery's	175	207
Freedom	105	314
Manchester	494	122
Westminster	334	274
Hampstead	171	133
Franklin	99	195
Middleburg	71	156
New Windsor	122	221
Total	2099	2348

Gubernatorial Vote, 1857.

Districts.	J. C. Groome. (Democrat.)	T. H. Hicks. (American.)
Taneytown	161	260
Uniontown	165	343
Myers'	230	108
Finksburg	186	207
Freedom	118	294
Manchester	502	135
Westminster	336	270
Hampstead	186	126
Franklin	107	204
Middleburg	74	145
New Windsor	114	224
Total	2179	2316

Vote for State Comptroller, 1859.

Districts.	A. L. Jarrett. (Democrat.)	W. H. Purnell. (American.)
Taneytown	157	279
Uniontown	176	351
Myers'	252	106
Finksburg	220	208
Freedom	139	290
Manchester	501	139
Westminster	373	324
Hampstead	184	132
Franklin	122	186
Middleburg	73	165
New Windsor	128	228
Total	2325	2408

For County Officers.

Sheriff, William Legafoose 2417, M. F. Shilling 2319.

State's Attorney, Edmund O'Brien 2322, C. W. Webster 2333.

Register of Wills, J. M. Parke 2435, Jacob Campbell 2293.

Judges of Orphans' Court, D. S. Herring 2301, G. W. Manro 2314, Jonas Ecker 2361, John Thompson 2393, J. C. Gist 2376, Horatio Price 2401.

Presidential Vote, 1860.

Districts.	Breckenridge.	Bell.	Douglas.	Lincoln.
Taneytown	126	289	18	7
Uniontown	155	292	6	36
Myers'	209	100	7	1
Woolery's	110	189	59	...
Freedom	95	323	26	1
Manchester	431	137	49	...
Westminster	247	295	85	9
Hampstead	133	133	47	...
Franklin	109	171	18	...
Middleburg	60	152	11	4
New Windsor	122	214	8	1
Total	1797	2295	334	59

Gubernatorial Vote, 1861.

Districts.	A. W. Bradford. (Republican Union.)	B. C. Howard. (Democrat.)
Taneytown	375	94
Uniontown	452	86
Myers'	195	172
Woolery's	268	184
Freedom	398	98
Manchester	319	323
Westminster	478	245
Hampstead	215	113
Franklin	259	68
Middleburg	188	45
New Windsor	260	94
Total	3405	1522

Vote for County Commissioners.

Benjamin Shunk 3371, Thomas F. Shepherd 3348, John H. Chew 3376, H. S. Davis 1531, Samuel A. Lauver 1568, George K. Frank 1522.

Vote for Comptroller of State, 1863.

Districts.	H. H. Goldsborough. (Independent.)	S. S. Maffit. (Unionist.)
Taneytown	268	147
Uniontown	294	86
Myers'	10	275
Finksburg	61	299
Freedom	232	13
Manchester	97	257
Westminster	108	501
Hampstead	135	134
Franklin	106	83
Middleburg	133	37
New Windsor	177	80
Total	1617	1912

Vote for Sheriff.

Joseph Ebaugh 2054, J. M. Yingling 1406, R. W. Stern 1138, H. P. Albaugh 161.

Presidential Vote, 1864.

Districts.	Lincoln.	McClellan.
Taneytown	303	119
Uniontown	287	173
Myers'	90	243
Finksburg	124	180
Freedom	211	121
Manchester	156	375
Westminster	325	315
Hampstead	107	169
Franklin	136	67
Middleburg	149	62
New Windsor	169	61
Total	2057	1885

Vote for Sheriff, 1865.

Districts.	Jacob D. Hoppe. (Republican.)	J. A. Bush. (Independent.)
Taneytown	237	14
Uniontown	252	17
Myers'	86	19
Finksburg	90	47
Freedom	151	13
Manchester	97	30
Westminster	289	51
Hampstead	77	22
Franklin	75	16
Middleburg	69	9
New Windsor	106	8
Total	1529	250

For Commissioners.

T. F. Shepherd 1421, Thomas Paynter 1471, John H. Chew 1728, Israel Norris 372, John H. Jordan 268.

Surveyor.

James Kelley 1749.

Register.

H. H. Harbaugh 1800.

Vote for State Comptroller, 1866.

Districts.	Robt. Bruce. (Republican.)	W. J. Leonard. (Democrat.)
Taneytown	322	55
Uniontown	339	145
Myers'	123	127
Finksburg	166	204
Freedom	223	135
Manchester	153	78
Westminster	371	309
Hampstead	129	138
Franklin	131	88
Middleburg	159	66
New Windsor	143	149
Total	2259	1494

Vote on the Adoption of the Constitution, Sept. 18, 1867.

Districts.	For.	Against.
Taneytown	103	293
Uniontown	145	269
Myers'	251	91
Finksburg	217	157
Freedom	156	195
Manchester	441	124
Westminster	383	334
Hampstead	166	102
Franklin	111	115
Middleburg	66	105
New Windsor	148	135
Total	2187	1920

Vote for Calling Constitutional Convention, April 10, 1867.

Districts.	For.	Against.
Taneytown	80	275
Uniontown	96	238
Myers'	245	85
Finksburg	166	137
Freedom	116	164
Manchester	373	142
Westminster	307	308
Hampstead	123	99
Franklin	69	96
Middleburg	39	94
New Windsor	107	117
Total	1721	1755

Vote for Delegates.

Districts.	Longwell.	Manro.	Galt.	Bennett.	Cover.	Hayden.
Taneytown	79	79	79	79	79	79
Uniontown	96	96	96	96	96	96
Myers'	245	245	243	245	244	245
Finksburg	166	166	166	166	166	166
Freedom	115	116	115	115	115	114
Manchester	378	372	372	372	372	373
Westminster	310	309	309	309	309	309
Hampstead	123	123	123	123	123	123
Franklin	69	68	69	70	69	69
Middleburg	39	39	39	39	39	39
New Windsor	108	104	109	109	109	108
Total	1723	1717	1720	1723	1721	1721

The Republicans voted against calling a convention, and placed no candidates for delegates in the field.

Gubernatorial Vote, 1867.

Districts.	Oden Bowie. (Democrat.)	Hugh L. Bond. (Republican.)
Taneytown	143	336
Uniontown	245	316
Myers'	283	106
Finksburg	290	173
Freedom	243	222
Manchester	483	167
Westminster	475	366
Hampstead	204	144
Franklin	160	145
Middleburg	95	150
New Windsor	195	166
Total	2815	2291

For Senator, Nathan Browne 2789, D. H. Swope 2352.

For Delegates, H. S. Davis 2806, J. H. Jordan 2786, Benjamin Worthington 2799, John W. Harden 2777, Robert Russell 2334, W. W. Naill 2324, Jesse Andrews 2352, Jacob C. Turner 2327.

For Clerk, John B. Boyle 2716, William A. McKellip 2406.

For Register of Wills, Joseph M. Parke 2710, H. W. Herbaugh 2358.

For State's Attorney, C. T. Reifsnyder 2780, A. D. Schaeffer 2350.

For Sheriff, Thomas B. Gist 2804, Washington Galt 2327.

For Surveyor, Francis Warner 2707, James Kelley 2340.

For Orphans' Court, H. T. Webb 2786, Jacob Powder 2719, Levi Buffington 2770, Joseph Shaeffer, 2370, Jacob Campbell 2378, David Pugh 2350.

Presidential Vote, 1868.

Districts.	Seymour.	Grant.
Taneytown	122	328
Uniontown	216	306
Myers'	272	108
Finksburg	241	174
Freedom	215	216
Manchester	463	173
Westminster	469	375
Hampstead	201	136
Franklin	140	158
Middleburg	81	149
New Windsor	187	177
Total	2607	2300

Vote for State Comptroller, 1869.

	Levin Walford.	Wm. A. McKillip.
Taneytown	119	302
Uniontown	235	278
Myers'	248	105
Finksburg	221	169
Freedom	160	180
Manchester	459	144
Westminster	419	394
Hampstead	208	138
Franklin	150	132
Middleburg	77	134
New Windsor	162	174
Total	2458	2150

Vote for Sheriff, 1869.

John Tracey (Democrat) 2522, Michael Baughman (Republican) 2073, John M. Yingling (Independent) 42.

Congressional Vote, 1870.

Districts.	John Richie.	John E. Smith.
Taneytown	138	309
Uniontown	266	349
Myers'	280	104
Finksburg	307	159
Freedom	251	268
Manchester	473	164
Westminster: Precinct No. 1	288	285
" " No. 2	262	228
Hampstead	218	119
Franklin	192	193
Middleburg	86	160
New Windsor	205	220
Total	2966	2558

Gubernatorial Vote, 1871.

Districts.	W. P. Whyte. (Democrat.)	Jacob Tome. (Republican.)
Taneytown	144	322
Uniontown	236	354
Myers'	256	92
Finksburg	284	169
Freedom	256	266
Manchester	486	172
Westminster: Precinct No. 1	278	285
" " No. 2	255	229
Hampstead	211	123
Franklin	180	185
Middleburg	71	157
New Windsor	195	234
Total	2858	2583

Presidential Vote, 1872.

Districts.	Greeley.	Grant.
Taneytown	127	325
Uniontown	177	295
Myers'	249	105
Woolery's	235	154
Freedom	162	276
Manchester	474	156
Westminster: Precinct No. 1	260	269
" " No. 2	247	231
Hampstead	192	128
Franklin	117	193
Middleburg	43	141
New Windsor	162	195
Union Bridge	60	139
Total	2505	2587

Vote for State Comptroller, 1873.

Districts.	Levin Wolford. (Democrat.)	H. H. Goldsborough. (Republican.)
Taneytown	155	315
Uniontown	213	289
Myers'	278	108
Finksburg	296	178
Freedom	249	272
Manchester	493	180
Westminster: Precinct No. 1	302	295
" " No. 2	257	241
Hampstead	200	131
Franklin	181	177
Middleburg	62	132
New Windsor	207	214
Union Bridge	71	134
Total	2964	2666

Congressional Vote, 1874.

Districts.	Charles B. Roberts. (Democrat.)	John T. Ensor. (Republican.)
Taneytown	123	299
Uniontown	188	230
Myers'	239	81
Woolery's	252	138
Freedom	183	210
Manchester	490	141
Westminster: Precinct No. 1	289	181
" " No. 2	264	256
Hampstead	167	117
Franklin	141	137
Middleburg	61	93
New Windsor	185	170
Union Bridge	82	102
Total	2664	2155

Gubernatorial Vote, 1875.

Districts.	John Lee Carroll. (Democrat.)	J. Morrison Harris. (Republican.)
Taneytown	124	355
Uniontown	197	292
Myers'	267	135
Finksburg	291	182
Freedom	222	295
Manchester	464	191
Westminster: Precinct No. 1	267	237
" " No. 2	260	325
Hampstead	195	162
Franklin	153	222
Middleburg	66	138
New Windsor	171	250
Union Bridge	76	130
Total	2753	2914

Presidential Vote, 1876.

Districts.	Tilden.	Hayes.
Taneytown	148	370
Uniontown	213	309
Myers'	294	133
Woolery's	346	218
Freedom	304	270
Manchester	544	175
Westminster: Precinct No. 1	307	245
" " No. 2	303	331
Hampstead	247	145
Franklin	215	196
Middleburg	86	146
New Windsor	204	228
Union Bridge	94	136
Total	3305	2902

Vote for State Comptroller, 1877.

Districts.	T. J. Keating.	Dr. G. Ellis Porter.
Taneytown	148	338
Uniontown	184	275
Myers'	265	108
Finksburg	280	172
Freedom	272	215
Manchester	477	168
Westminster: Precinct No. 1	280	237
" " No. 2	257	293
Hampstead	216	135
Franklin	179	164
Middleburg	62	114
New Windsor	178	209
Union Bridge	75	121
Total	2873	2549

Vote for Sheriff, 1877.

Peter Woods 2725, Edmund A. Ganter 2563, Abraham Greider 104.

Congressional Vote, 1878.

Districts.	J. Fred. C. Talbott. (Democrat.)	G. B. Milligan. (Independent.)
Taneytown	104	94
Uniontown	120	49
Myers'	221	27
Finksburg	178	45
Freedom	163	112
Manchester	393	92
Westminster: Precinct No. 1	213	170
" " No. 2	205	197
Hampstead	147	54
Franklin	160	4
Middleburg	56	36
New Windsor	147	104
Union Bridge	68	66
Total	2175	1050

The vote was 2000 short. McCombs also received 89 votes, Morling 27, and Miller 11.

Gubernatorial Vote, 1879.

Districts.	W. T. Hamilton. (Democrat.)	J. A. Gary. (Republican.)
Taneytown	179	399
Uniontown	241	348
Myers'	295	124
Finksburg	327	253
Freedom	322	290
Manchester	545	186
Westminster: Precinct No. 1	329	276
" " No. 2	304	348
Hampstead	253	147
Franklin	229	227
Middleburg	98	144
New Windsor	188	230
Union Bridge	107	149
Total	3417	3121

Presidential Vote, 1880.

Districts.	Hancock.	Garfield.
Taneytown	190	375
Uniontown	234	348
Myers'	297	127
Finksburg	335	229
Freedom	307	326
Manchester	570	194
Westminster: Precinct No. 1	339	249
" " No. 2	298	348
Hampstead	281	160
Franklin	228	238
Middleburg	91	147
New Windsor	206	248
Union Bridge	116	149
Total	3492	3138

Weaver (Greenback candidate) received 42 votes.

Vote For or Against Liquor License, 1880.

Districts.	For.	Against.
Taneytown	182	336
Uniontown	224	310
Myers'	321	77
Finksburg	286	242
Freedom	286	288
Manchester	591	138
Westminster: Precinct No. 1	301	238
" " No. 2	335	269
Hampstead	262	148
Franklin	239	188
Middleburg	103	123
New Windsor	133	185
Union Bridge	102	146
Total	3375	2688

Bench and Bar.—The bar of Maryland since the days of Luther Martin has enjoyed a national reputation for the ability, eloquence, and sound opinions of its members. It has been mainly recruited from the counties of the State, and some of its most eloquent advocates have been reared amid rural surroundings and their pure influences. The local bars at the smaller county-seats are seldom heard of beyond the circumscribed area of their practice, and yet men frequently pass their lives at these provincial points whose energies and abilities, exerted in wider fields, would have commanded fame and wealth. They are useful in their day and generation, and perhaps, after all, the approval of their own consciences, and the esteem of those who know them best, is a more enduring reward than the fleeting praises of the multitude, or the honors which leave canker and corrosion behind.

At the first meeting of the Circuit Court of Carroll County in 1837, William P. Maulsby, James Raymond, James M. Shellman, Arthur F. Shriver, and T. Parkin Scott were admitted to practice. Of these but one now remains.

Col. William P. Maulsby, in the fullness of years, but with unabated vigor, still represents the interests of his clients in the leading courts of the State, and many a more youthful attorney envies the elasticity of mind and knowledge of law which he displays. Col. Maulsby was born in Harford County, Md., and after careful training selected law as a profession. He removed to Frederick, where he practiced until the creation of the county of Carroll, when he removed to Westminster, and was appointed by the court the first State's attorney of the new county. He filled this position with great credit until 1846. He was also the first State senator from Carroll, and was an active and influential member of the higher branch of the State Legislature for eight years. At the breaking out of the civil war Col. Maulsby's convictions were decidedly in favor of the Union, and he gave practical direction to his opinions by taking command of a

Maryland regiment in the Army of the Potomac, where he saw much active service. Upon his retirement from the army he resumed the practice of his profession in Frederick City, and he was appointed by the Governor, Jan. 20, 1870, chief judge of the Sixth Judicial District of Maryland, composed of the counties of Frederick and Montgomery, to fill the vacancy occasioned by the death of Judge Madison Nelson. He filled this position acceptably until his successor was chosen at the November election. He is now the senior member of the bar in Carroll County, has an extensive practice, and stands deservedly high in the legal profession.

Thomas Parkin Scott, one of the pioneers of the Carroll County bar, was born in Baltimore in 1804, and educated at St. Mary's College. He studied law with an elder brother, and was admitted to the bar in Baltimore, where he soon acquired a large practice. He was the auditor of the Equity Court for many years. He was at one time a member of the City Council of Baltimore, and served several terms in the Maryland Legislature, of which body he was a member at the breaking out of the war in 1861. He was arrested by the military because of his sympathies with the South, and confined successively in Forts McHenry, Lafayette, and Warren during a period of fourteen months. It is related of him that while confined in Fort Warren a Northern preacher requested to be allowed to preach to the Southern prisoners, which was acceded to provided the latter were permitted to select the text. Judge Scott selected Acts xxv. 27 : "It seemeth to me unreasonable to send a prisoner and not withal to signify the crimes laid against him." The prisoners did not receive the benefit of the clergyman's ministrations on that occasion. Judge Scott was elected judge of the Circuit Court of Baltimore City in 1867, and was made chief judge of the Supreme Bench in the following year, both of which positions he held until his death, Oct. 13, 1873. In politics he was a stern, uncompromising Democrat, and in religion a sincere convert to the Catholic faith. As a judge, he was upright, impartial, and wise, and as a man, he was beloved and lamented by the community in which he had lived.

Col. James M. Shellman was born in Louisville, Ga., Sept. 8, 1801. His wife was a daughter of Philip Jones, of the "Gallipot" farm, in Baltimore County, who was a soldier in the war of 1812. The grandfather of Mrs. Shellman was the first register of wills for Baltimore County, and her great-grandfather was Philip Jones, the surveyor who laid out the town of Baltimore in 1730. Col. Shellman was the auditor of the court of Carroll County from its organization in 1837 until his death, which occurred Jan. 14, 1851. His long service is sufficient evidence of the faithful performance of the duties appertaining to the position. He was an active and influential member of the House of Delegates of Maryland in 1845 and 1846.

James Raymond was State's attorney from 1846 to 1847, and a member of the House of Delegates of Maryland in 1844.

Samuel D. Lecompte was a member of the House of Delegates in 1842.

Charles W. Webster was a son of Rev. Isaac Webster, a pioneer preacher, and served several years as deputy attorney-general.

John E. Smith was judge of the Circuit Court from 1864 to 1867, and his law-partner, Col. William A. McKellip, was clerk of the court from 1862 to 1867.

Hon. John E. Smith was born at Westminster, on the 19th of January, 1830, and received his education at Pennsylvania College, Gettysburg, where he graduated in 1849. Returning home he determined to study law, and entered the office of the distinguished lawyer, J. M. Palmer, at Frederick City. After a thorough course of study he was admitted to the bar at Westminster, on the 2d of September, 1851, and at once secured the respect and esteem of the profession and the confidence of his fellow-citizens. His success at the bar was rapid and pronounced, and he soon acquired an extensive popularity and influence in politics. In 1856 he was elected to the State Legislature, and took a very active and prominent part, with Hon. Anthony Kennedy, William M. Travers, William T. Merrick, and others, in securing the repeal of the stamp tax and in effecting other reforms.

In 1857 he was elected to the Senate of Maryland, and in 1859 re-elected to the same body. In 1864 he was elected a member of the Constitutional Convention which abolished slavery in this State. Upon the adoption of the constitution of 1864, Judge Smith was elected judge of the Fourth Judicial Circuit, comprising the counties of Carroll and Howard. During the three years he occupied a position on the bench he discharged his duties in so careful and impartial a manner that when the State was redistricted under the constitution of 1867, he retired with the confidence and respect of the people of the two counties without reference to party. In 1870 he was the Republican candidate for Congress in the Fourth, now the Sixth, Congressional District, but was defeated. During the session of the Legislature of that year, upon the election of Governor Whyte to the United States Senate, Judge Smith was unanimously selected

Charles B. Roberts.

by the Republican members and voted for as Governor of the State, but was defeated by Governor Groome. Judge Smith has repeatedly served as elector at large upon the Republican Presidential ticket, and as delegate to various district, State, and National Conventions. On the death of Judge Giles he was prominently mentioned for United States District Judge of Maryland, and again in 1879 as Republican candidate for Governor of Maryland. On the latter occasion he publicly announced that he was not an aspirant for any office, and that he intended thenceforth to devote himself exclusively to the pursuit of his profession. This declaration was received with regret by the general public, as well as by his many friends of all shades of political opinion throughout the State, as Judge Smith had always borne, and still bears, the highest reputation as a lawyer and a man. He is now in the prime of life, and in the active practice of his profession, which is very large and lucrative. Judge Smith is regarded as being one of the soundest and ablest lawyers in the State, and enjoys a personal influence in his community which is the legitimate fruit of a life of the strictest rectitude in all his relations, and of scrupulous fidelity in discharging every trust that has been confided to him. He has never sought office, and all the nominations bestowed upon him were entirely without any solicitation on his part. In fact, it was only after repeated and urgent requests that he ever consented to serve the people. He has never been a bitter partisan, but at the same time has always been a zealous and consistent member of the Republican party; and to his uniformly conservative and temperate course is to be ascribed much of the well-earned popularity which he enjoys.

Hon. Charles Boyle Roberts, ex-congressman and one of Carroll County's leading lawyers, was born in Uniontown, Carroll Co., April 19, 1842. His father (John Roberts) and his mother (Catharine A. Boyle) were natives of Uniontown, and his ancestors were among the earliest settlers of the vicinity. Charles B. Roberts was educated at Calvert College, New Windsor, where he graduated in 1861. Directly thereafter he began the study of the law with Hon. William N. Hayden (now one of the associate judges of the Circuit Court for the Fifth Judicial Circuit), and in 1864, being admitted to the bar, made his residence in Westminster, where he has lived and practiced his profession ever since. In 1868 he was chosen on the Democratic ticket as one of the Presidential electors from Maryland, and six years later (in 1874) was elected to Congress from the Second District of Maryland, composed of the counties of Cecil, Harford, and Carroll, and all of Baltimore County save the First and Thirteenth Election Districts. His majority over John T. Ensor, the Republican candidate, was 2444 in a total vote of 18,920. During his term he served on the Committee of the Levees of the Mississippi River and on the Committee of Accounts, of which latter he became the chairman upon the transfer of the former chairman (James D. Williams) to the Governorship of Indiana. Mr. Roberts introduced a bill providing for the equalization of the tax on State and national banks, and supported his measure in a speech that attracted marked attention. His record in the Forty-fourth Congress was so creditable that he was nominated by acclamation for a seat in the Forty-fifth, and out of a total vote of 27,017, gained over J. Morrison Harris, the Republican candidate, a majority of 3149. His earlier experience and the generous development of his capacity as a statesman rendered his service in the Forty-fifth Congress singularly useful not only to his own district but to the State of Maryland. He served as chairman of the Committee on Accounts, and discharged his duties with rare discrimination and judgment. He was likewise a member of the Committee on Commerce, and in that capacity accomplished much beneficial work for the State. He secured liberal appropriations for the improvement of Baltimore Harbor, and was chiefly instrumental in the passage of the bill granting a portion of the Fort McHenry reservation as the site of the new dry-dock. He bent his best energies to effect a revision of the tariff law, under which Baltimore has suffered the loss of her sugar and coffee trade, and opposed with earnestness and vigor the proposed subsidy to John Roach's line of Brazilian steamers. In a strong speech against that measure he concluded as follows:

"In conclusion, Mr. Speaker, permit me to say that while the pending amendment may possess attractions for some because of the supposed advantages which are expected to accrue to the localities named in it, and while the prosperity of a thrifty and enterprising city may be destroyed by the exercise of an unjust, arbitrary, and doubtful power of the Federal government in seeking to build up and foster a trade which private enterprise has failed to develop, I yet sincerely question whether the victory thus gained will commend itself to the plain, sober second thought of those who are its advocates to-day. The wrong thus accomplished will not fail to seek a compensation. Time will furnish the opportunity, and circumstances will shape the occasion. We are not here to legislate for any particular locality, but we come here under the provisions of the Constitution, which in plain terms declares that 'no preference shall be given by any regulation of commerce or revenue to the ports of one State over those of another.' It is but a few weeks since we passed the inter-State commerce bill, in obedience to a public sentiment which demanded that unjust discriminations should not be imposed upon the citizens of one State or locality in favor of those of another; and if this amendment is to become a law it will very manifestly appear that we do not object to the general government's crushing the prosperity of a great and flourishing city, but we will not permit the corporations of the country to exercise any such right, that being a special reservation of Congress. How different was Mr. Webster's view of this subject, as presented in his speech in the Senate, March 7, 1850, when he said,—

"'If there be any matter pending in this body, while I am a member of it, in which Massachusetts has an interest of her own not averse to the general interests of the country, I shall pursue her instructions with gladness of heart and with all the efficiency which I can bring to the occasion. But if the question be one which affects her interest, and at the same time equally affects the interests of all the other States, I shall no more regard her particular wishes or instructions than I should regard the wishes of a man who might appoint me an arbitrator or referee to decide some question of important private right between him and his neighbor and then instruct me to decide in his favor. If ever there was a government upon earth it is this government; if ever there was a body upon earth it is this body, which should consider itself as composed by agreement of all, each member appointed by some, but organized by the general consent of all sitting here, under the solemn obligations of oath and conscience, to do that which they think to be best for the good of the whole.'

"Sir, when we shall have reached the conclusion that the highest obligations we owe to the government is to make it subserve the wants of one State, utterly disregarding the rights of the others; when we shall resort to combinations of doubtful propriety to purchase successful legislative action; when we can afford to ignore past friendly relations, and upon mercenary motives seek new alliances, personal and political, it will not be long ere we shall realize—

'How nations sink, by darling schemes oppressed,
When Vengeance listens to the fool's request.'"

As chairman of the Committee on Commerce, Mr. Roberts perfected a measure for a thorough reorganization of the United States Life-Saving Service, and enjoyed the gratification not only of securing the passage of the act, but of receiving the warmest approval of his work abroad as well as at home. At the close of his term in the Forty-fifth Congress he decided to resume the practice of the law and to retire from public life. In recognition of his valuable services in Congress he was tendered, in the spring of 1879, by leading citizens of Baltimore, a complimentary banquet at the Mount Vernon Hotel. The following is the letter of invitation:

"BALTIMORE, March 7, 1879.

"HON. CHARLES B. ROBERTS, Westminster, Md.:

"DEAR SIR,—A number of your friends here among our business men have been desiring for some time to make you some acknowledgment of the earnestness and ability with which you have dedicated yourself in the House of Representatives to the furtherance of the business interests of this community. There has been no measure of importance to the prosperity of Baltimore in the promotion of which you have not taken an active and useful part, or in which we have not had occasion to be grateful to you for your accessibility and courtesy, as well as for the intelligence and great efficiency of your labors. The adjournment of Congress affords us the desired opportunity, and we beg that you will do us the favor to meet us at dinner on Thursday, the 13th of March, at 7 P.M., or at such other time as may better suit your convenience.

"It will be agreeable to you, we are sure, to know that while the gentlemen whom you will oblige by accepting this invitation represent all shades of political opinion, they are of hearty accord in their estimate of your impartial fidelity as a public servant, and in their high personal respect and esteem for you.

"We are, dear sir, with great regard,

"Truly yours,

"S. T. Wallis.	William H. Perot.
John W. Garrett.	Henry C. Smith.
Decatur H. Miller.	Christian Ax.
Enoch Pratt.	Daniel J. Foley.
James Hodges.	J. D. Kremelberg.
Washington Booth.	S. P. Thompson.
Robert A. Fisher.	James A. Gary.
John I. Middleton.	John S. Gilman.
Israel M. Parr.	Robert Garrett.
Stephen Bonsal.	Walter B. Brooks.
C. W. Humrickhouse.	Charles D. Fisher.
Richard D. Fisher.	Charles A. Councilman.
James Carey Coale.	James E. Tate.
Robert T. Baldwin.	William Keyser.
John E. Hurst.	Louis Muller.
William H. Graham.	F. C. Latrobe.
R. W. Cator.	H. M. Warfield.
George B. Coale.	Basil Wagner.
John L. Thomas, Jr.	P. H. MacGill.
George P. Frick.	S. E. Hoogewerff."
James Sloan, Jr.	

Although he has not been a candidate for public office since the close of his last congressional term, Mr. Roberts has nevertheless been frequently called to occupy positions of prominence in connection with public and private enterprises. In June, 1880, he was sent as a delegate to the National Convention at Cincinnati that nominated Gen. Hancock to the Presidency, and as a member of the Democratic State Convention of 1881, was appointed one of the committee selected to draft a new registration bill for the State. He is one of the managers of the Maryland House of Correction, and in his own town and county occupies a prominent place in connection with projects devoted to the public welfare. He is a director of the Union National Bank of Westminster, as well as of the Westminster Gaslight Company, and of the Mutual Fire Insurance Company, and president of the recently-organized Westminster Water-Works Company. In 1875 Mount St. Mary's College, of Emmittsburg, Md., conferred upon him the degree of Doctor of Laws. His chosen profession has ever found in him an ardent devotee, and to its pursuit he gives his warmest efforts and most zealous ambition, encouraged by the knowledge that his labors find ample reward and bear abundant fruit. He was married Nov. 10, 1863, to Annie E., daughter of Col. John T. Mathias, of Maryland. At his home in Westminster he dispenses a genial hospitality that is widely known and warmly esteemed among the many who have from time to time been privileged to share it.

Politically, Mr. Roberts has always been a zealous but conservative Democrat, and while he has steadily adhered to the regular organization of that party, he has exhibited on all occasions an independence and conscientiousness in the discharge of his duties, both as a member of the Democratic party and as a public official, which have secured him the highest confidence and respect of the best elements in both parties. He has frequently been mentioned in various quarters as the Democratic candidate for Governor. With exceptional abilities as a lawyer Mr. Roberts combines the qualities of a sound and practical judgment and remarkable business energy and tact, qualities which, together with his attractive personal characteristics, have secured him an enviable popularity throughout the State as well as in his own immediate community, where he is best known and most thoroughly appreciated. In fact, he is one of the most enterprising, progressive, and influential gentlemen in the State, not only as a public man of the best and most honorable type, but also as a sound and well-read lawyer and a highly-successful and prosperous business man.

The three attorneys who have been longest at the bar of Carroll County are Judge Maulsby, C. W. Webster, Joseph M. Parke, the last having been register of wills from 1869 to 1873.

The list given below includes all the attorneys who have been regular practitioners at the Carroll County bar, together with the names of eminent lawyers from other parts of the State who have been specially admitted for the trial of particular causes:

1837.
April 3. William P. Maulsby.
" 3. James M. Shellman.
" 3. James Raymond.
" 3. Arthur F. Shriver.
" 3. T. Parkin Scott.
Sept. 7. Samuel D. Lecompte.
" 7. Isaac Van Bibber.
1838.
Madison Nelson.
Edward Shriver.
George Schley.
Joseph Breck.
R. J. Bowie.
1839.
Sept. 6. Charles W. Webster.
" 6. James M. Coale.
" 6. B. S. Forrest.
" 6. Wm. Cost Johnson.
1840.
Sept. 7. Joseph M. Parke.
1843.
Sept. W. H. G. Dorsey,
John T. B. Dorsey.
1844.
Sept. 2. William N. Hayden.
" 4. John H. Ing.
" 4. Nathaniel Williams.
" 4. G. Eichelberger.
1845.
April 7. W. T. Palmer.
" 7. John J. McCullough.
" 9. Elijah F. Crout.
July 1. Clothworthy Birnie.
1846.
April 7. Elbridge G. Kilbourn.
" 7. R. Willson, Jr.
" 7. Wm. McSherry.
" 7. James McSherry.
" 8. Covington D. Barnitz.
" 15. Wm. G. Matthias.
Sept. 9. J. J. Baumgardner.
" 9. Michael G. Webster.
1847.
April 6. Geo. K. Shellman.
Sept. 7. Joseph C. Boyd.
" 7. Will Motter.
1848.
April 4. H. F. Bardwell.
Sept. 5. James Cooper.
1849.
April 7. Daniel L. Hoover.
Sept. 4. Edmund L. Rogers.
" 4. Wm. C. Sappington.
" 5. Thomas Whelan, Jr.
" 5. G. W. Nabb.
Dec. 3. R. G. McCreary.
1850.
April 1. E. Holloway.
" 1. E. G. Day.
1851.
April 7. A. H. Hobbs.
Sept. 1. Robert Lyon Rogers.
" 2. Wm. M. Merrick.
" 2. John E. Smith.
1852.
April 5. M. B. Luckett.
" 6. James Hungerford.
" 7. Ephraim Carmack.
" 15. Dennis H. Poole.
" 15. John S. Tyson.
Sept. 7. Worthington Ross.
" 7. Bradley T. Johnson.
" 7. Frederick Nelson.
1854.
April 8. Isaac E. Pearson.
Sept. 6. Thomas Donaldson.
" 8. J. T. M. Wharton.
1855.
April 2. Oscar Baugher.
" 3. W. H. Dallam.
" 5. M. P. Galligher.
" 10. John Ritchie.
1856.
Sept. 1. Wm. G. Read.
1858.
April 6. Wm. A. Fisher.
" 8. John A. Lynch.
Sept. 8. E. O'Brien.
" 8. W. Scott Roberts.
" 9. James T. Smith.
1859.
April 4. John T. Ensor.
" 6. E. Louis Lowe.
Sept. 5. T. S. Alexander.
" 8. S. Morris Cochran.
1860.
Sept. 4. Samuel E. Kuch.
" 4. J. S. Yellott.
1861.
April 1. C. C. Raymond.
" 4. Wm. Schley.
Sept. 4. R. R. Boarman.
" 4. W. P. Preston.
" 9. C. H. Busby.
1862.
July 15. David Wills.
" 16. D. McConnaughy.
1863.
S. J. Frank.
1864.
April 5. Charles B. Roberts.
Sept. 1. Milton G. Urner.
1865.
May 10. W. C. Griffith.
" 10. C. T. Reifsnider.
" 10. Milton Whitney.
" 10. Abner Neal.
" 31. H. Winter Davis.
" 31. A. Stirling, Jr.
" 31. W. E. McLaughlin.
Nov. 14. Peter W. Crain.
" 14. Joseph Davis.
1866.
Nov. 12. Isaac E. Pearson, Jr.
" 28. W. Fernandis, Jr.
1867.
May 13. S. D. Webster.
" 13. James A. C. Bond.
" 14. Wm. Price.
Aug. 1. James W. McElroy.
Oct. 28. R. B. Norment.
Nov. 13. B. F. M. Hurley.
" 13. Wm. A. McKellip.
1868.
June 11. Wm. Reynolds, Jr.
" 11. W. W. Sullivan.
Sept. Wm. Waterman.
" D. W. Zepp.
Dec. 1. F. C. Latrobe.
" 4. D. H. Roberts.
" 4. J. A. C. Bond.
" 4. A. D. Schaeffer.
1869.
Nov. 8. D. G. Wright.
" 29. R. G. Keene.
Dec. 11. John W. Breaver.
1870.
Feb. 14. W. W. Dallas.
May 17. Orville Horwitz.
" 17. R. J. Gittings.
" 31. Thos. R. Clendinen.
Nov. 14. Wm. Rowland.
1871.
May 13. A. K. Syester.
" 16. A. H. Norris.
Nov. 7. A. S. Diller.
" 28. T. Sturgis Davis.
" 28. W. H. Cowan.
1872.
May 13. D. N. Henning.
Aug. 12. Harris J. Chilton.
Nov. 23. W. J. Jones.
1873.
May 12. Z. S. Claggett.
" 24. Henry A. McAtee.
Nov. 10. E. J. D. Cross.
" 17. George Freaner.
1874.
May 14. James Fenner Lee.
" 14. J. Q. A. Jones.
" 18. T. H. Edwards.
" 18. T. Q. Kennedy.
" 18. Wm. T. Hamilton.
" 18. H. K. Douglas.
Aug. 13. J. E. K. Wood.
1875.
May 11. A. H. Robertson.
" 25. Edward Stake.

May 25. R. Chemfours.
July 15. L. L. Cunard.
" 20. J. J. Alexander.
Aug. 9. M. B. Settle.
Nov. 17. B. Frank Crouse.
1876.
May 31. Trueman Smith.
June 1. James W. Pearre.
Aug. 15. Thos. W. Brundige.
Nov. 15. S. L. Stockbridge.
Dec. 11. W. M. Busey.
" 14. W. A. Hammond.
1877.
May 25. William Grason.
" 25. D. G. McIntosh.
" 30. O. F. Mack.
June 2. John S. Shillson.
Nov. 27. O. P. Macgill.
Dec. 12. J. T. Mason.
1878.
May 13. S. F. Miller.
" 14. John R. Buchanan.
" 17. T. W. Hall.
" 20. W. C. N. Carr.
June 17. Frank X. Ward.
Aug. 13. Jas. A. Diffenbaugh.
Nov. 12. George E. Cramer.
" 30. W. H. Washington.
1879.
May 12. John Berry.
May 12. Charles E. Fink.
" 19. Benj. I. Cohen.
June 6. Wm. L. Seabrook.
" 10. L. L. Billingslea.
" 17. G. W. Pearce.
Nov. 10. Charles L. Wilson.
" 19. Frank L. Webb.
" 28. —— Shull.
Dec. 8. John Sterrat.
" 15. John McClean.
" 23. William Walsh.
" 23. D. D. Blackeilton.
" 23. James E. Ellegood.
1880.
May 10. W. J. Keech.
" 10. John F. Courep.
" 10. N. W. Watkins.
June 3. Douglas B. Smith.
Aug. 9. H. W. Crowl.
Nov. 8. C. P. Meredith.
" 9. H. M. Clabaugh.
" 10. George Whitelock.
" 16. A. Hinton Boyd.
1881.
May 20. John S. Donaldson.
" 20. Thos. K. Bradford.
" 20. Joseph C. Boyd.
" 20. John H. Handy.
" 30. Frederick E. Cook.

Literature and art are essentially the products of life in the country. The freedom of the woods and fields, the rippling streams, the hills and valleys, and the health-giving atmosphere uncontaminated by the thousand impurities of large cities, seem necessary for the nurture and development of genius. Nature in her simplest and grandest forms there excites the imagination and fosters the creative faculty in man. However great may be the influence of culture and accumulated experience and example, only to be obtained in great cities, the narrow ruts of life in a metropolis and the concentration of all the powers of body and mind in one direction are unfavorable to the production or early development of genius, and hence it is found that a very large proportion of the really great poets, painters, and sculptors of the world have been born in the country, and very many have passed their early years there. Carroll County in this regard has been no exception to the rule. Artists and poets have been born within her borders whom the world will not willingly let die, some whose works have received the approval of distant lands and whose names are spoken with homage in all cultivated households. The aggregations of books and master-pieces in large cities and the splendid advantages which wealth has extended through the instrumentality of schools of design, conservatories, and colleges makes it of the first importance that the devotees of art and literature should seek the great centres of civilization and avail themselves of the resources so lavishly supplied. True genius is never appalled by obstacles, and so it generally happens that those who recognize its promptings sooner or later work their way to the attainment of their wishes, and the city rather than the country is a gainer by their reputation. Few countries can present nature to the inspired student of art in more beautiful or more varied aspects than are to be found in Carroll County. Almost every phase of natural scenery is illustrated within her borders, from the landscapes of simple pastoral beauty to the rugged and sublime outlines of the lofty peaks of the Blue Ridge, and some of these scenes have been faithfully reflected in the works of her sons, who have sought the distinction elsewhere that they could not expect at home.

In 1850 there was to be seen at the Chesapeake Bank a sculptured bust of Andrew Jackson, which had been presented to Col. J. S. Gittings by the Messrs. F. M. & H. F. Baughman. It was the work of an apprentice to the Messrs. Baughman, named Reinhart. It was executed chiefly at night, after the hours of labor, and was the first effort of his chisel. "The excellence of the work gives promise of high attainment in this beautiful art, and leads us to hope that Maryland may yet be able to give to the world some enduring memento of the age in one of the most admirable departments of human genius." Such was the greetings of encouragement which the first work of young Reinhart received, and the contemporaneous description of the first work of his chisel.

William H. Reinhart was born in Carroll County, Md., about the year 1826; his father was a well-to-do farmer of German descent, living near Westminster, in that county, and characterized by thrift, perseverance, and economy. All the children were actively employed about the farm, and received the rudiments of an English education at a school in Westminster. When a mere boy young Reinhart evinced very great interest in the working of the marble quarries that abounded in the neighborhood, and in this particular he found opportunity for the bent of his genius in the quarry and stone-cutting yard on his father's farm. At the age of sixteen, with his father's consent, he came to Baltimore, and presented himself at the store of Andrew Gregg, on Franklin Street, to whom his father was in the habit of consigning produce of his farm. He told Mr. Gregg that he desired to apprentice himself to some useful trade, and preferred that of marble-working, with which he already had some familiarity. He was immediately taken to the marble-yard and stone-cutting establishment of Baughman & Bevan, and engaged as an apprentice by that firm. He proved himself to be a steady and industrious youth, with a taste for reading and study which he gratified at night by regular attendance at the Maryland Institute and School of Design, where his favorite studies were mythology, ancient history, anatomy, architecture, and books on art and artists. He continued the improving studies for several years, and before his majority his chisel and proficiency obtained for him the execution of all the fine work on mantles of the establishment of the Messrs. Baughman. When twenty-three years of age he was made foreman of the establishment and gave full satisfaction to his employers. In 1855 he left Baltimore for Italy to prosecute the higher studies of his art with a full knowledge of practical marble-working. He prosecuted his studies with great diligence at Florence, where he went to reside, working with other young artists on trial for wages. He returned to Baltimore in 1857, bringing with him two beautiful *basso-relievos* in panel of "Night and Morning," which were purchased by Augustus J. Albert. He returned to Italy in 1858, and made his residence at Rome, where he remained, with the exception of short trips to Baltimore, until his death in 1874.

Probably the greatest event in the life of the young artist was the unveiling of the Taney statue at Annapolis, Dec. 10, 1872. This heroic statue of Chief Justice Roger B. Taney in bronze had been ordered by the Legislature of Maryland, and was erected in front of the State-House. On that occasion there were assembled in the Senate chamber the leading representatives of the State in politics, at the bar, in literature and art, to hear the addresses of S. Teackle Wallis and Governor William Pinkney Whyte. Mr. Wallis alluded to the fact that the appropriation by the State had not been sufficient compensation to the artist for such a work, and recognized the liberality and public spirit of the artist in accepting and executing the work notwithstanding. "The figure," Mr. Wallis said, "had been treated in the spirit of that noble and absolute simplicity which is the type of the highest order of greatness, and is therefore its grandest, though its most difficult, expression in art." In 1872 the statue of Clytie, which is Reinhart's masterpiece in marble, was exhibited in Baltimore, attracting the admiration of thousands of her people. It was purchased by John W. McCoy, and placed in the Peabody Gallery of Art as a gift to the citizens of Baltimore. Among the other works of this artist are the bronze doors of the Capitol at Washington, begun by Crawford, and completed after four years of labor by Reinhart; the statuettes on the clock of the House of Representatives, as well as the statue on the fountain in the General Post-office at Washington; Endymion, now owned by J. W. Garrett; Antigone, owned by Mr. Hall, of New York; Hero, for A. J. Albert, of Baltimore; Leander, owned by Mr. Riggs, of Washington; the Woman of Samaria, for W. T. Walters, of Baltimore; the bronze monumental figure at the tomb of Mrs. W. T. Walters, in Greenmount Cemetery; and the "Sleeping Children," in marble, in the lot of Hugh Sisson, as well as many other works in Mount Auburn Cemetery, Boston, Loudon Park Cemetery, Baltimore, and many busts of citizens of Baltimore.

William H. Reinhart died in Rome on Wednesday, Oct. 28, 1874, in the forty-eighth year of his age, having fully enabled his native State, Maryland, "to give to the world" not only "some," but many "enduring mementoes of the age in one of the most admirable departments of human genius." By his will he attested further his great love for art; after amply providing for relatives he directed that his executors, W. T. Walters and B. F. Newcomer, of Baltimore, should apply the residue of his estate, according to their best judgment, to the promotion of interest in and cultivation of taste for art, by the following clause of his will:

"Third, Being desirous of aiding in the promotion of a more highly cultivated taste for art among the people of my native State, and of assisting young men in the study of the art of sculpture who may desire to make it a profession, but having at the present time no definite plan in view for the accomplishment of these objects, I give, devise, and bequeath all the rest and residue of my estate, real, personal, and mixed, and wheresoever situated, unto my two personal friends, William T. Walters and Benjamin F. Newcomer, of the city of Baltimore, or the survivor of them, or the heirs, executor, or administrator of such survivor, in trust and confidence, with the injunction that the whole of said residue of my estate or the proceeds thereof shall be devoted and appropriated by them, according to their best judgment and discretion, to the promotion of the objects and purposes named above; and if in the opinion of my said trustees this can be best accomplished by any concert of action with the trustees of the Peabody Institute, or by the establishment of a professorship in connection with the Gallery of Art, which at some future time is to be provided for by that corporation, or by the investment of any portion of the funds so held by them in trust, and aiding from the income derived from such investments deserving young men who are desirous of pursuing their studies abroad, but are without the means of doing so, they, my said trustees, are at liberty to adopt any or all or none of these methods, or to transfer the trust or the estate so held by them in trust to any corporation which in their judgment would best serve the purpose indicated."

Willie T. Hoppe was the second son of Hannah and the late Jacob D. Hoppe, of Carroll County. His life in some important features resembled that of Chatterton, the boy-poet of England. At an age when most children realize their highest pleasure in a game of marbles or hide-and-seek, his mind was at

work like the piston rod of a steam-engine, grinding out tales, editorials, and local histories in a ceaseless flow. His mental faculties and energy far outstripped his weak and sickly body, and absolutely wore it out before he arrived at man's estate. His first essay in literature was as the editor and publisher of an amateur journal entitled *The Boys' Rights*, which astounded the neighbors and friends of his family by the extraordinary precocity exhibited in its contents. He subsequently conducted the *Amphion Journal* and *Cupid's Messenger*, and, as president of the Amateur Press Association, still surprised his friends and the public not only by the marvelous maturity of his intellect, but by a display of executive ability which his years and experience did not appear to justify. In 1878 he entered the office of Charles Poe, of Baltimore, as a law-student, but it soon became painfully evident that while his mind was ripening and brightening with study and training, his body was gradually wasting away before the inroads of some insidious malady, and he died July 24, 1880, in the twentieth year of his age. In his literary efforts and on his papers he was frequently assisted by Miss Mary Shellman, a lady of rare literary attainments, whose historical contributions to the press have earned for her a merited reputation as a writer.

Dr. Washington Chew Van Bibber was born in Frederick, now Carroll, Co., Md., July 24, 1824. His family settled in that section very early in the history of the State, and soon acquired influence and prominence. After a thorough course of study at a number of colleges, Dr. Van Bibber entered the office of Prof. Nathan R. Smith, of Baltimore, and matriculated at the University of Maryland, from whence he graduated in 1845. After some years spent in the South, where he had an opportunity to familiarize himself with the yellow fever in all its phases,—that dread pest of Southern cities,—he returned to Baltimore and began the practice of his profession. His practice rapidly increased, and with it his reputation as a skillful and excellent physician, and to-day he is fully the equal of any of the galaxy of physicians who have made Baltimore famous as a centre of instruction in the healing art. As a writer, Dr. Van Bibber deserves especial mention. Few have recently added more to the literature of medicine. From 1856 to 1859 he was associate editor of the *Virginia Medical Journal*, and from 1859 to 1861 he was associate editor of the *Maryland and Virginia Medical Journal*, and he has contributed a large number of papers to the various medical periodicals of the day, replete with interest and valuable scientific information.

Thomas E. Van Bibber, a relative of Dr. Van Bibber, is a native of Carroll County, but is now a resident of California. He early developed a taste for literature, and many of his youthful efforts will compare favorably with those of more pretentious poets and authors. He is best known by his poem, "The Flight into Egypt," a work exhibiting considerable power, a beautiful fancy, and a true conception of the poet's vocation. It was very favorably received by American critics, and has stood the test of time remarkably well. His many miscellaneous prose efforts have added to his reputation as a cultured and popular writer.

For many years the meetings of the "Addison Reunion Association" constituted a delightful feature of society in Westminster. The organization was literary in character, and a number of the most cultivated and influential citizens were members and contributors. The intention was to combine social with literary recreation, and for a longer time than usually occurs to such associations the effort was successful. The papers read before it took a wide range, embracing poetry, history, art, science, and the various branches of polite literature. In 1871, Dr. Charles Billingslea compiled "The Addison Reunion Papers," a neat volume of three hundred pages, containing the choicest of the papers delivered before the society during its existence, and embracing selections from the writings of Emma Alice Browne, the poetess, and authoress of "Ariadne," Rev. Josiah Varden, Rev. James T. Ward, D.D., Mrs. Albert Billingslea, Rev. David Wilson, D.D., Dr. Charles Billingslea, Isaac E. Pearson, Mrs. Carrie Brockett Anderson, Miss Ada Billingslea, and Thomas E. Van Bibber. The "Addison Reunion Association" gave its closing entertainment June 9, 1871, at the "Montour House," a noted hostelry, which derived its name from the famous Indian chief of that name who flourished in colonial times.

The religious denominations of Carroll County recognizing the paramount value of religious instruction through the instrumentality of Sabbath-schools, and anxious to extend their influence and usefulness, consulted together as to the best method of accomplishing this desirable result. Their deliberations culminated in 1867 in a county Sabbath-school association, to be composed of delegates from all the Protestant denominations in the county. The second annual convention of the society was held in the Lutheran church at Westminster, Sept. 8, 1868. Rev. J. T. Ward, of the Methodist Protestant Church, was called to the chair, and H. B. Grammer appointed secretary. The districts were called, and the following delegates enrolled: Finksburg, John H. Chew, D. Ebaugh, A. Geisley, R. A. Smith, Wm. Cruise, Rev. W. T. Dunn; Hampstead, S. Ruby, Joseph Lippy; New Windsor, Clinton Hanna, Wm. A. Norris, Isaac C. Baile, Rev. Mr. Scarborough; Manchester, Rev. R. Weiser, Jacob Campbell, Edmund Gonder, D. Frankforter, Jos. Shearer, H. B. Lippy, D. W. Danner, J. T. Myers, Misses F. Crumrine, S. Trump, Ellen Trump, V. C. Weizer, Lizzie Earle; Myers, Jacob Wolfe, T. T. Tagg, J. Bankard; Middleburg, Thos. Newman, Wm. H. Boust, John W. Angell, Jacob Koons, A. E. Null, Albert Koons, John Feezer, Eli Hahn; Taneytown, Peter Mark, G. Stover, J. T. Clay; Uniontown, Revs. P. A. Strobel, J. T. Ward, J. T. Hedges, Van Meter, E. H. Smith, J. Monroe, W. C. Creamer, H. B. Grammer, Wm. H. Cunningham, G. W. Cecil, F. Herr, M. Baughman, H. L. Norris, E. Koons, R. Gorsuch, Josh Sellman, N. Pennington, J. N. Williams, Mrs. M. A. Wagner, Mrs. M. Cunningham, Misses Sanford, Sue Cassell, Annie Ocker. The committee appointed to select permanent officers reported the following nominations, which were unanimously confirmed:

President, Hon. John E. Smith; Vice-Presidents, J. W. Angell, David H. Webster, —— Debough, Jacob Campbell, Alfred Zollicoffer, A. McKinney, C. D. Frieze, Joseph Ebaugh; Secretaries, H. B. Grammer and Wm. A. Baker.

The convention continued their interesting exercises until Thursday, June 10th, when they adjourned until their annual meeting in 1869.

The German Baptists sought the region embraced in Carroll County very soon after its settlement by white people, conceiving it to be a favorable field for their ministrations. Congregations have been established at Pipe Creek, Meadow Branch, Sam's Creek, New Windsor, Union Bridge, and Westminster. They are all under the charge of an ordained elder, who has five or six assistants. Philip Englar was the first elder in charge of whom there is any record, and served in this position from 1780 to 1810, when he was succeeded by David Englar, who had been his assistant for some years. The latter served from 1810 to 1833, and was followed by Philip Boyle, who occupied the position for thirty-five years, having been assisted by Michael Petry, Jesse Royer, Jesse Roop, David Miller, Howard Hillery, Hanson Senseny, and Solomon Stoner. Rev. Mr. Boyle was succeeded by Hanson Senseny as ordained elder. He served in that capacity until 1880, and was assisted by Solomon Stoner, E. W. Stoner, William Franklin, Amos Caylor, Joel Roop, and Uriah Bixley. The denomination in the county numbers between four and five hundred members.

Pipe Creek congregation, the mother of all the other German Baptist organizations in the county, and one of the oldest in Western Maryland, was established prior to the year 1780, and worshiped in a log building which stood at Pipe Creek. In 1806 their present church edifice was erected, since when it has been used constantly by the congregation. The church was repaired in 1866, having been enlarged and remodeled. It is now a plain brick structure, thirty-five by seventy-one feet, with a seating capacity for six hundred persons. The congregation numbers about one hundred members, who are very active in the interests of their church.

Meadow Branch church is situated about two miles from Westminster, on the plank road, and was erected in 1850. It is a stone structure, and was originally built thirty-five by fifty-five feet in dimensions, but was recently enlarged to the size of thirty-five by eighty feet. The congregation numbers about ninety members.

Sam's Creek German Baptist church was erected in 1860. It is situated on the old Liberty road, about two miles from Naill's Mill, up Sam's Creek, in New Windsor District. It is a frame building, very neat in appearance, about thirty by forty feet in size, and capable of holding one hundred and fifty people. About fifty members worship here.

New Windsor church was built and the congregation formed about the year 1873. It is a fine brick building, erected at a cost of sixteen hundred dollars, and is conveniently located on Church Street, in the town of New Windsor. The building in size is thirty by forty feet. About fifty members constitute the congregation at the present time, which is steadily increasing.

Union Bridge church, a beautiful little edifice, was erected in the town of Union Bridge in 1877. It is a brick building, situated on Broadway Street, thirty by forty-five feet in size, and cost eighteen hundred dollars. The seats are so arranged as to comfortably seat about four hundred persons. Fifty members comprise the congregation.

Westminster church was purchased by the German Baptist denomination from the Baptist Church in 1879, at a cost of two thousand two hundred dollars.

It has been several times attempted to divide the church in this county into three congregations or charges, viz.: Pipe Creek, to be composed of Pipe Creek and Union Bridge; Meadow Branch, to embrace Meadow Branch Church and Westminster; and Sam's Creek, composed of Sam's Creek and New

Windsor. Although the efforts have thus far proved unsuccessful, doubtless this division will occur sooner or later.

A short distance from the German Baptist church at Pipe Creek, and one and a quarter miles from Uniontown, is the large German Baptist Cemetery, the first grave in which was dug in the year 1825. Among the names of those buried are the following:

Catharine Garber, died Dec. 30, 1847, aged 73 years, 10 months, 5 days.

Lydia A. Garber, died May 4, 1861, aged 38 years, 10 months, 10 days.

Johannes Garber, born April 4, 1769, died Oct. 4, 1839.

Christian Roop, Jr., died Aug. 14, 1825, aged 20 years, 9 months, 13 days.

Esther Roop, born Feb. 11, 1776, died July 2, 1850.

Christian Roop, born Nov. 4, 1764, in Lancaster County, Pa. He removed in 1784 to the precinct in which he died, March 18, 1855.

Abraham Roop, died Sept. 11, 1871, aged 74 years, 7 months, 12 days; Lydia, his wife, died Oct. 6, 1858, aged 56 years, 6 months, 10 days.

Isaac Slingluff, born Aug. 5, 1807, died April 30, 1852.

Elizabeth Foutz, died July 1, 1860, aged 67 years, 11 months, 12 days.

John Stoner, born Feb. 21, 1796, died March 14, 1874.

Mary Stoner, died May 19, 1853, aged 57 years, 11 months, 1 day.

Sarah, wife of John Stoner, died June 6, 1835, aged 38.

Betsey, wife of William Warner, died Nov. 15, 1830, aged 58.

Ann, wife of Otho Warner, died Oct. 1, 1836, aged 42 years, 6 months, 22 days.

Joseph Roop, Sr., died May 3, 1829, aged 69 years, 9 months, 6 days; Mary Roop, his wife, born Feb. 15, 1767, died July 25, 1853.

Margaret Snader, born Aug. 7, 1794, died Aug. 27, 1877.

Mary Snader, died Feb. 4, 1835, aged 65.

Jacob Snader, died Dec. 2, 1847, aged 85 years, 3 months, 13 days.

Michael Garber, died Jan. 4, 1847, aged 53 years, 7 days.

Hetty Garber, born Feb. 5, 1778, died March 2, 1857.

Samuel Bare, born March 29, 1793, died Jan. 22, 1845.

Jacob Rhodes, died July 26, 1846, aged 77 years, 7 months, 9 days.

Sarah Rhodes, born Oct. 15, 1763, died Jan. 8, 1854.

Lydia Bare, died Aug. 16, 1858, aged 59 years, 11 months, 13 days.

Daniel Harman, born Jan. 1, 1821, died Aug. 20, 1862.

William Plaine, died May 4, 1847, aged 65 years, 8 months, 7 days; and Margaret, his wife, Jan. 15, 1849, aged 65 years, 4 months, 20 days.

Daniel Plaine, born June 19, 1783, died July 2, 1872; and Penelope, his wife, Aug. 24, 1853, aged 76 years, 4 months, 17 days.

Catharine Wantz, died Aug. 14, 1866, aged 51 years, 6 months, 20 days.

Philip Boyle, died Aug. 15, 1872, aged 65 years, 6 months, 4 days; Rachel, his wife, and daughter of Jacob and C. Zimmerman, died Sept. 15, 1859, aged 74 years 10 days.

William H. Shriner, died Feb. 14, 1856, aged 32 years, 3 months, 16 days.

John P. Shriner, died April 18, 1849, aged 32 years, 7 months, 3 days.

Eliza, wife of Joseph Stouffer, died June 20, 1855, aged 48.

Jacob Roop, born Sept. 4, 1785, died Jan. 19, 1860; Sarah, his wife, died June 20, 1866, aged 79 years, 2 months, 22 days.

Jacob Shriner, died Dec. 28, 1866, aged 76 years, 16 days; Elizabeth, his wife, died Feb. 1, 1881, aged 85 years, 4 months, 11 days.

Isaac W. Shriner, born Dec. 13, 1818, died Dec. 3, 1872; Rachel Ann, his wife, died Aug. 2, 1875, aged 55 years, 11 months, 23 days.

Benjamin Bond, died Sept. 12, 1863, aged 72.

Matilda Bond, died Dec. 17, 1860, aged 58 years, 11 months.

Joseph Englar, died July 4, 1872, aged 72 years, 4 months; Susannah, his wife, died May 20, 1861, aged 59 years, 3 months, 10 days.

Elizabeth, consort of John Englar, died Feb. 2, 1879, aged 54 years, 2 months, 6 days.

Tobias Cover, died March 26, 1865, aged 65; Elizabeth, his wife, died Feb. 14, 1869, aged 69.

David Gilbert, born Nov. 22, 1798, died Sept. 5, 1865.

William Ecker, born Aug. 10, 1809, died Oct. 7, 1865; Mary A., his wife, born Sept. 6, 1813, died Oct. 2, 1869.

Mary A., wife of William Bloxsten, born Nov. 11, 1804, died Sept. 5, 1879.

William Bloxsten, born Sept. 2, 1802, died March 11, 1876.

Henry Riael, died Dec. 4, 1867, aged 85; Mary, his wife, died July 10, 1869, aged 75.

Eliza A., wife of Thomas A. Franklin, born April 15, 1812, died April 3, 1876.

Ezra Stoner, born July 19, 1830, died June 4, 1867.

Elizabeth, wife of William Gilbert, died March 22, 1870, aged 49 years, 7 months, 1 day.

Josiah Englar, died Oct. 25, 1878, aged 69 years, 7 months, 1 day.

Elizabeth, wife of Daniel S. Diehl, died Aug. 6, 1879, aged 40 years, 4 months, 6 days.

Lucretia, wife of Levi N. Snader, died June 13, 1876, aged 49 years, 1 month, 16 days.

Nathan Crumbacker, born Aug. 27, 1811, died Aug. 31, 1880.

David Crumbacker, born Aug. 12, 1808, died Feb. 5, 1881.

Ezra O. Englar, born Aug. 10, 1845, died Oct. 31, 1879.

Robert M. Jenkins, born May 12, 1811, died April 19, 1879.

William Segafoose, died Aug. 29, 1876, aged 69 years, 9 months, 22 days.

David Engel, of D., born Jan. 13, 1784, March 31, 1854.

David Engel, born Oct. 23, 1754, died July, 1802; Elizabeth Engel, his wife, died Oct. 2, 1841, aged 90 years, 10 months, 2 days.

Elizabeth, wife of Jacob Stem, died Sept. 19, 1836, aged 32 years, 2 days.

Hannah Ecker, died May 13, 1862, aged 71 years, 1 month, 4 days.

Elizabeth, daughter of P. and H. Myers, died Dec. 16, 1845, aged 20 years, 11 months, 23 days.

Daniel Engel, died Jan. 16, 1874, aged 76 years; Thiriza A., his wife, died July 14, 1878, aged 64 years, 8 months, 22 days.

Eleanor M., wife of George Ebb, born Oct. 28, 1820, died Jan. 6, 1873.

Anna M., consort of Daniel Engel, died March 12, 1859, aged 53 years, 4 months, 27 days.

William Hoffman, died March 7, 1838, aged 60 years.

Peter Engel, died April 5, 1833, aged 53 years, 5 months, 17 days; Hannah, his wife, died Feb. 8, 1867, aged 84 years, 10 months, 25 days.

John Engel, born Sept. 13, 1785, died June 21, 1870; Nancy, his wife, died May 11, 1871, aged 71 years, 8 months, 18 days.

Jacob Smith, died Feb. 24, 1869, aged 87 years, 5 months, 2 days.

Jacob Highmiller, of Company F, Seventh Regiment Maryland Volunteer Infantry, born Jan. 11, 1839, "died in the service of his country," Jan. 30, 1864.

Daves Lightner, died Sept. 14, 1867, aged 67 years, 10 months, 2 days.

Joseph Roop, born July 24, 1810, died Oct. 3, 1877.

Mary, wife of Daniel Petry, died June 16, 1865, aged 63 years, 1 month.

Jacob Erb, died April 1, 1862, aged 65 years, 3 months, 13 days.

Nathan W. Stem, died Dec. 29, 1862, aged 46 years, 4 months, 6 days; Eliza, his wife, died Dec. 18, 1854, aged 38.

John Roop, died March 14, 1872, aged 76 years, 5 months, 8 days.

Upton Stoner, born March 24, 1796, died May 30, 1876.

Joseph Myers, born July 7, 1801, died April 8, 1880; Elizabeth, his wife, born Feb. 14, 1801, died Nov. 1, 1864.

Mary Roop, died Nov. 10, 1847, aged 49 years, 6 months, 27 days.

Conrad Englar, born Oct. 13, 1804, died Sept. 3, 1842.

Margaret Brown, born Sept. 1, 1800, died May 2, 1862.

Mary Englar, died Jan. 1, 1854, aged 81 years, 8 months, 22 days.

Abraham Englar, died March 13, 1879, aged 67 years, 7 months, 12 days.

Jacob Diehl, died Dec. 28, 1848, aged 49 years, 6 months, 5 days.

Rachel Warner, died Dec. 11, 1853, aged 47 years, 8 months, 10 days.

Samuel Leaming, died May 25, 1837, aged 48 years, 9 months, 14 days.

Alfred F. Mering, born Dec. 6, 1835, died Feb. 21, 1879.

Lewis G. Lindsay, died Nov. 9, 1879, aged 65 years, 7 months, 25 days.

Deborah Weaver, died Dec. 25, 1871, aged 76 years, 9 months, 22 days.

John K. Weaver, died Dec. 13, 1878, aged 88 years, 26 days.

Joseph Weaver, born Sept. 16, 1779, died Oct. 14, 1866.

John Weaver, born 1753, died 1823.

Susannah Weaver, born 1753, died 1833.

Samuel Weaver, born May 25, 1786, died May 21, 1863.

Elizabeth Weaver, born Oct. 14, 1803, died June 15, 1856.

Philip Weaver, died Jan. 10, 1873, aged 74.

Ann Weaver, born June 24, 1827, died Aug. 23, 1837.

Susie Weaver, born Oct. 10, 1844, died July 19, 1866.

McKendrie Weaver, died May 29, 1870, aged 22 years, 10 months.

Jesse Weaver, died July 24, 1878, aged 48 years, 11 months, 7 days.

Frederick Englar, born May 10, 1811, died Nov. 17, 1878.

Ann, consort of M. Smith, died Feb. 21, 1849, aged 37 years, 7 months, 10 days.

Catharine, wife of Jacob Zimmerman, died May 30, 1827, aged 63 years, 5 months, 19 days.

Jacob Zimmerman, died Sept. 30, 1834, aged 28 years, 4 months, 5 days.

David Johnson, born Oct. 19, 1800, died April 20, 1879; Susanna, his wife, died Jan. 21, 1861, aged 64 years, 9 months, 22 days.

Anna, wife of William Zimmerman, and only daughter of William and Anna Shirk, born Nov. 17, 1834, died Nov. 17, 1869.

Catharine Martin, died Nov. 5, 1864, aged 91.

John Hess, died Oct. 5, 1861, aged 76; Mary, his wife, died April 24, 1865, aged 67 years, 8 months, 25 days.

Jacob Bower, born Nov. 19, 1761, died April 11, 1825.

Margaret Bower, died March 25, 1835, aged 59 years, 4 months, 14 days.

Catharine, wife of J. P. Haines, and daughter of Christopher and S. Johnson, died Jan. 30, 1871, aged 77 years, 4 months, 26 days.

Jacob Switzer, died June 20, 1854, aged 84 years, 3 months, 13 days; Susanna, his first wife, died Nov. 25, 1827, aged 52 years, 6 months, 19 days; Elizabeth, his second wife, died Jan. 1, 1865, aged 76 years, 4 months, 19 days.

Samuel Switzer, died March 1, 1829, aged 27 years, 7 months, 24 days.

Esther, wife of Jos. Bower, died Oct. 31, 1834, aged 40 years, 3 months, 28 days.

Barbara, wife of John Hess, died Feb. 11, 1829, aged 46 years, 1 month, 26 days.

George Urner, died Oct. 7, 1830, aged 25 years, 8 months, 19 days.

Margaret Walter, born Dec. 29, 1780, died Oct. 4, 1876, aged 95 years, 5 months, 9 days.

Elizabeth Urner, died Oct. 8, 1828, aged 28 years, 9 months, 15 days.

Jonathan Plaine, died April 27, 1835, aged 48 years, 6 months, 26 days; Lydia, his wife, died Oct. 3, 1866, aged 85 years, 1 month, 14 days.

George Harris, Sr., died April 14, 1838, aged 40 years, 5 months, 17 days.

Margaret Harris, died July 24, 1870, aged 78.

Samuel Plaine, born Dec. 10, 1778, died Oct. 5, 1865.

Catharine, wife of David Plaine, died 26th of 9th mo., 1826, aged 76.

Elizabeth Nusbaum, died April 17, 1851, aged 85 years, 8 months.

John Nusbaum, died Aug. 8, 1825, aged 70.

Isaac Hiltabidle, died Sept. 4, 1827, aged 27 years, 3 months, 12 days; Mary Ann, his wife, died Sept. 19, 1845, aged 44 years, 10 days.

Joseph Englar, died Feb. 23, 1845, aged 64 years, 8 months, 25 days; Esther, his wife, died June 27, 1867, aged 82 years, 9 months, 9 days.

David Englar, died Aug. 9, 1839, aged 66 years, 6 months; Elizabeth, his wife, died Nov. 12, 1849, aged 72 years, 4 months, 22 days.

Deborah, wife of Henry Cover, died Feb. 2, 1858, aged 74 years, 9 months, 25 days.

Henry Cover, died Nov. 20, 1857, aged 76 years, 4 months, 20 days.

Deborah, wife of Joseph McKinstry, died Dec. 14, 1845, aged 32 years, 18 days.

Elizabeth Stoner, died Oct. 24, 1851, aged 85 years, 11 days.

Margaret Stoner, died April 19, 1849, aged 17 years, 2 months, 17 days.

Margaret Crumback, died Aug. 14, 1844, aged 67.

Hannah Nicodemus, died Aug. 10, 1852, aged 48 years, 3 months, 26 days.

Philip Englar, born May 13, 1778, died Dec. 19, 1852.

Hannah Englar, born Nov. 22, 1799, died Jan. 20, 1873.

John Stoner, died Sept. 2, 1852, aged 64 years, 1 month, 10 days.

Samuel Boightel, died Dec. 13, 1846, aged 43 years, 11 months, 8 days.

Ephraim Englar, born June 4, 1806, died Nov. 8, 1857; Agnes, his relict, and wife of Jos. Stouffer, died Jan. 19, 1863, aged 52 years, 9 months, 14 days.

Samuel Johnson, born June 15, 1804, died March 13, 1869.

Jacob Plowman, born Feb. 4, 1816, died Feb. 7, 1870.

Rufus K. Bowers, born Feb. 1, 1830, died April 30, 1875.

Samuel Hoffman, died June 19, 1874, aged 53 years, 9 months, 13 days.

Daniel Ogle, born Aug. 16, 1805, died Dec. 8, 1865.

Philip Snader, born Jan. 2, 1802, died Feb. 4, 1864, aged 62 years, 1 month, 2 days.

David W. Snader, died April 4, 1877, aged 47 years, 4 months, 10 days; Sophia, his wife, died April 7, 1875, aged 42 years, 3 months, 14 days.

Abraham Wolfe, born Dec. 21, 1782, died Oct. 22, 1863; Sarah, his wife, born Oct. 24, 1786, died July 11, 1880.

Israel Rinehart, born June 25, 1792, died Nov. 21, 1871; Mary, his wife, died Dec. 15, 1865, aged 68 years, 1 month, 26 days.

John M. Wolfe, died March 15, 1876, aged 54.

Mary A., wife of Hiram Davis, died Oct. 9, 1878, aged 58 years, 7 months, 5 days.

Joseph Foutz, born Oct. 5, 1793, died Jan. 13, 1878; Margaret, his wife, born July 10, 1801, died May 26, 1869.

Mary A., wife of Richard B. Foutz, died Sept. 8, 1857, aged 55.

Maria Naill, wife of Jacob Snader, born Sept. 26, 1806, died Dec. 21, 1875.

Martha A., wife of J. T. Devilbiss, died Jan. 26, 1875, aged 34 years, 9 months, 19 days.

Eve E., wife of Jacob Souble, died Aug. 4, 1877, aged 70 years, 25 days.

Louisa, wife of Asa Zent, died Aug. 21, 1877, aged 77 years, 2 months, 21 days.

Hannah Little, born May 20, 1804, died Oct. 10, 1877.

Jacob Harman, died Aug. 13, 1871, aged 76 years, 2 months, 18 days; Mary, his wife, died June 28, 1875, aged 80 years, 11 months, 19 days.

Hannah, wife of John Warehime, born April 11, 1801, died March 2, 1873.

Peter Utz, born Sept. 4, 1796, died July 27, 1878.

Jacob Rider, died May 31, 1871, aged 58 years, 6 months, 5 days.

George Hess, died Dec. 20, 1863, aged 80 years, 5 days.

Susanna Hess, died Feb. 24, 1870, aged 88 years, 5 days.

George Kelly, born Dec. 21, 1834, died Sept. 24, 1874; Sarah, his wife, died April 24, 1868, aged 37 years, 1 month, 1 day.

John Banker, born Feb. 4, 1790, died Aug. 23, 1870.

Catharine Banker, born Dec. 8, 1793, died Feb. 20, 1873.

Mary, wife of S. Hamilton Shouser, born Jan. 30, 1828, died Dec. 4, 1869.

David S. Golly, died Dec. 27, 1863, aged 50 years, 7 months, 4 days.

Eliza Golly, died Aug. 6, 1878, aged 67 years, 6 months, 28 days.

Samuel Bower, died January, 1867, aged 60 years, 5 months, 13 days; Nancy Ann, his wife, died April 22, 1866, aged 54 years, 6 months, 8 days.

Ephraim Powell, died March 2, 1872, aged 52.

Peter M. Calwith, died June 10, 1866, aged 74 years, 5 months.

Rachel Calwith, died Feb. 26, 1860, aged 35 years, 5 months, 6 days.

Washington Wilson, born Jan. 12, 1815, died Jan. 17, 1856.

John M. Romspert, born May 7, 1838, and "was instantly killed while on duty by the explosion of No. 4 engine on W. M. R. R.," Oct. 24, 1876.

Ulrick Messler, born June 30, 1811, died March 9, 1870.

Martha Messler, died Dec. 27, 1858, aged 40.

Julia Ann Shriver, died Oct. 29, 1861, aged 48 years, 5 months, 18 days.

Martin Billmeyer, born March 23, 1779, died Sept. 3, 1856.

Salome, relict of Jacob Yon, born Dec. 10, 1769, died Nov. 22, 1855.

Hannah Yon, born April 3, 1793, died Oct. 11, 1868.

Samuel Meyers, died Sept. 11, 1856, aged 35 years, 5 months, 7 days; Eliza C., his wife, died Dec. 30, 1875, aged 68 years, 6 months, 3 days.

Stephen Bower, died March 12, 1856, aged 76 years, 7 months.

Mary Bower, died Feb. 5, 1855, aged 71 years, 10 months.

John Rheam, died June 25, 1853, aged 67 years, 6 months, 18 days.

Elizabeth Rheam, died Jan. 12, 1871, aged 81 years, 8 months.

Eliza, consort of Abraham Myers, born Dec. 12, 1801, died Nov. 21, 1855.

Anna Myers, died March 6, 1847, aged 78 years, 6 months, 6 days.

Jacob Myers, died April 25, 1876, aged 69 years, 8 months, 15 days; Lydia, his wife, died Sept. 5, 1866, aged 49 years, 1 month, 13 days.

John Englar, born March 11, 1812, died July 29, 1860.

Daniel Englar, died June 12, 1840, aged 63.

Mary A. Englar, died Oct. 6, 1867, aged 50 years, 4 months, 27 days.

David Englar, died Jan. 21, 1841, aged 64 years, 6 months.

Ann Singer, born July 31, 1811, died Oct. 28, 1876; Jacob, her husband, born April 9, 1813, died Feb. 27, 1877.

Magdalena Sherbig, died July 23, 1825, aged 87 years, 10 days.

Jacob Cowell, died March 23, 1841, aged 84 years, 5 months, 27 days.

Elizabeth Cowell, died Oct. 17, 1849, aged 74 years, 2 months, 18 days.

G. M. Jordan, died Aug. 20, 1841, aged 84 years, 5 months, 27 days.

Anna M. Jordan, born March 19, 1758, died July 17, 1825.

Abraham Caylor, died May 25, 1857, aged 64 years, 5 months; Anna, his wife, died March 24, 1841, aged 46 years, 9 months, 5 days.

Dorothy Wildermute, born Jan. 10, 1780, died Sept. 9, 1823.

"M. R.," died 1827.

Henry Fulkerth, died July 2, 1848, aged 84.

Margaret Fulkerth, died Dec. 21, 1837, aged 69 years, 6 months.

Ebenezer Carlyle, died July 27, 1840, aged 66 years, 1 month; Margaret, his wife, died April 26, 1839, aged 53 years, 9 months, 18 days.

Anna Carlyle, died Aug. 1, 1880, aged 68 years, 3 months, 23 days.

Rachel O'Brien, died Dec. 25, 1870, aged 70.

Sarah Boman, died July 7, 1857, aged 71.

Jacob Zimmerman, born Dec. 30, 1787, died Feb. 5, 1859.

Peter Little, died Dec. 11, 1839, aged 37 years, 3 months, 15 days.

Sophia Little, died March 11, 1852, aged 50.

John Moore, died Aug. 1, 1860, aged 86 years, 5 months, 19 days.

Rachel Smith, died July 28, 1840, aged 52 years, 1 month, 24 days.

Barbara Keim, born Sept. 15, 1786, died Aug. 30, 1852.

Jacob Keime, died March 16, 1849, aged 80.

Priscilla, wife of William Stoner, died March 25, 1864, aged 38 years, 4 months, 10 days.

Henry Row, born Dec. 10, 1812, died Dec. 10, 1871.

George Row, died May 5, 1857, aged 84 years, 7 months, 10 days; Margaret, his wife, born Aug. 1, 1793, died Feb. 11, 1870.

Carroll County was not altogether free from the vicissitudes which characterized the war between the

North and the South. At the beginning of the unfortunate struggle there was the same diversity of sentiment which existed in the other counties of Maryland, but those who favored the South were far inferior in numbers to the supporters of the Union. The young men volunteered freely in defense of their opinions, and it is estimated that the Federal army was supplied with eight hundred recruits from this section, while two hundred enthusiastic young men of Southern sympathies made their way through the Union lines into the camps of the Southern army. The contingents of Carroll in both armies fully maintained the character of her people for gallantry and true manhood. In June, 1863, the soil of Carroll echoed the tread of large bodies of armed men from both armies. A portion of the cavalry force belonging to the army of Northern Virginia passed through Westminster on its way to Gettysburg, and encountered a battalion of cavalry, which it dispersed or captured after a slight skirmish. The troops rested in the city during the night and proceeded on their way with the dawn. They had scarcely emerged from the city when the Sixth Corps of the Army of the Potomac entered from the opposite side. Much excitement prevailed among the citizens, who had seen but little of either army, but their fears were groundless, as both detachments behaved with exemplary courtesy and evidenced thorough discipline. For some days the transportation wagons of the Union army were parked around the town and the streets presented an animated appearance, but they were moved to the front prior to the battle of Gettysburg. The booming of the cannon on that fatal field was heard with conflicting emotions by the friends of the combatants, and as the echoes died away the town relapsed into its wonted quiet. It was roused again in the succeeding year for a brief period by a raid of the Confederate forces under Gen. Bradley T. Johnson and Maj. Harry Gilmor, but as they had learned by experience that the presence of troops was not such a serious infliction as their fears had painted, the short visit of the Confederates was made rather an occasion of rejoicing than sorrow.

The ex-Federal soldiers from Carroll County met in Westminster, March 13, 1880, and formed a post of the Grand Army of the Republic, to be known as Burns' Post, after W. H. Burns, of the Sixth Maryland Regiment. Col. William A. McKellip was elected Commander, Capt. A. Billingslea, Senior Vice-Commander; Capt. Charles Kuhns, Junior Vice-Commander; Dr. William H. Rippard, Surgeon; Lee McElroy, Quartermaster; Sylvester Mathias, Adjutant; and John Matthews, Chaplain. The officers were installed March 27th by department commander Gen. William Ross and staff, of Baltimore.

The Carroll County Agricultural Society was incorporated March 8, 1869, by John E. Smith, Jeremiah Rinehart, William A. McKellip, Richard Manning, David Fowble, Hashabiah Haines, George W. Matthews, and John L. Reifsnider. The object of the association was "to improve agriculture by attracting the attention, eliciting the views, and combining the efforts of the individuals composing the agricultural community of Carroll County, and aiming at the development of the resources of the soil so as to promote the prosperity of all concerned in its culture." Grounds containing thirty acres of land were purchased on the Baltimore turnpike at the east end of Westminster, just outside of the corporation limits. They were inclosed with a substantial fence, and stabling was erected for the accommodation of five hundred head of stock. A race-track, half a mile in length, was made from a diagram furnished by George W. Wilkes, of the *Spirit of the Times*, and all the necessary preparations completed for the annual exhibitions of the association. The constitution of the society requires the members to meet three times a year, and Article III. of that instrument defines the aims of the association to be, in addition to others, "to procure and improve the implements of husbandry; to improve the breed of domestic animals . . . ." The first officers of the society were John E. Smith, president; Jeremiah Rinehart, vice-president; William A. McKellip, secretary; Richard Manning, treasurer; David Fowble, George W. Matthews, Edward Lynch, Hashabiah Haines, and John F. Reifsnider, directors. At a meeting of the board of directors in 1869, the following committees were appointed to solicit subscriptions to the capital stock of the society:

District No. 1, Samuel Swope, Jno. McKellip, Samuel Smith; No. 2, Reuben Saylor, Thomas F. Shepherd, Jeremiah Rinehart; No. 3, H. Wirt Shriver, Geo. W. Shull, Samuel Cover; No. 4, James Lee, Jeremiah Babylon, P. A. Gorsuch; No. 5, S. T. C. Brown, David Prugh, J. Oliver Wadlow; No. 6, George A. Shower, Edwin J. Crumrine, P. H. L. Meyers; No. 7, Wm. A. McKellip, Richard Manning, Hashabiah Haines, Augustus Shriver; No. 8, David W. Houck, Wm. Houck, John W. Murray; No. 9, Dr. F. J. Crawford, Col. J. C. Gist, Robert D. Gorsuch; No. 10, Geo. Harris, Joseph Davis, John Winemiller; No. 11, L. P. Slingluff, Wm. A. Norris, Sol. S. Ecker, Jos. A Stouffer.

Preparations having all been completed, and the society having fully realized their anticipations of support from the people of the county, on the 3d of July, 1869, the grounds of the association were opened with much ceremony and with a fine exhibition, which embraced the varied productions of the county and admirable specimens of improved stock and horses. A grand tournament attracted a large concourse of people, after which some interesting trotting races took place. Among the cattle exhibited were beautiful selections from Durham, Devon, Ayrshire, and Alderney breeds. The exhibition of horses was worthy of careful inspection, the large majority of the animals having been raised by the enterprising farmers of Carroll County.

The following is a list of the officers of the society during each year, including 1881:

1870.—President, John E. Smith; Vice-President, Jeremiah Rinehart; Secretary, Wm. A. McKellip; Treasurer, Richard Manning; Directors, David Fowble, Edward Lynch, H. Haines, W. G. Rinehart, Joseph H. Hoppe.

1871.—President, Augustus Shriver; Vice-President, Jeremiah Rinehart; Secretary, Wm. A. McKellip; Treasurer, Richard Manning; Directors, Edward Lynch, David H. Byers, Geo. W. Matthews, David Fowble, Josephus H. Hoppe.

1872.—President, Augustus Shriver; Vice-President, Jeremiah Rinehart; Secretary, Wm. A. McKellip; Treasurer, Richard Manning; Directors, David Fowble, Edward Lynch, H. E. Morelock, Joseph Shaeffer, Louis P. Slingluff.

1873.—President, Granville S. Haines; Vice-President, Jeremiah Rinehart; Secretary, Wm. A. McKellip; Treasurer, Richard Manning; Directors, Edward Lynch, David Fowble, Joseph Shaeffer, Dr. C. Billingslea, Noah Shaeffer, E. O. Grimes, Louis P. Slingluff, Lewis H. Cole.

1874.—President, Granville S. Haines; Vice-President, George W. Matthews; Secretary, C. V. Wantz; Treasurer, Richard Manning; Directors, F. H. Orendorff, H. E. Morelock, Joseph Hibberd, Thomas F. Shepherd, E. J. Crumrine.

1875.—President, Granville S. Haines; Vice-President, Joseph Shaeffer; Secretary, C. V. Wantz; Treasurer, Richard Manning; Directors, H. E. Morelock, F. H. Orendorff, David Fowble, Thos. F. Shepherd, Samuel Roop.

1876.—President, Jeremiah Rinehart; Vice-President, Noah Shaeffer; Secretary, George W. Matthews; Treasurer, Richard Manning; Directors, David H. Byers, Samuel Lawyer, Henry B. Albaugh, John Sellman, David Stoner.

1877.—President, Col. William A. McKellip; Vice-President, David Fowble; Secretary, G. W. Matthews; Treasurer, Richard Manning; Directors, Dr. Jacob Rinehart, Granville S. Haines, L. P. Slingluff, Edward Lynch, Orlando Reese.

1878.—(Same board.)

1879.—Same board, save Francis H. Orendorff, secretary, *vice* G. W. Matthews.

1880.—Same board; Assistant Secretary, Frank W. Shriver; Chief Marshal, Joseph W. Berret; Assistant Marshals, Robert M. Hewitt, Wesley A. Steele, G. Edwin Hoppe, William N. Sellman; Committee on Grounds and Side Shows, David Fowble, Granville S. Haines, Edward Lynch; Superintendents of Departments, Henry E. Morelock, Wm. J. Morelock, D. H. Byers, Thomas B. Gist, Elias Yingling, Charles N. Kuhn, Francis Sharrer, Lee McElroy, W. G. Rinehart; Vice-Presidents, Dr. Samuel Swope, Frank Brown, J. C. Brubaker, A. G. Houck, Emanuel Myers, Geo. W. Manro, P. H. L. Myers, John W. Murray, Solomon Shepherd, Lewis Dielman, Benj. Poole, David Rinehart; Committee of Reception, Hon. Charles B. Roberts, Hon. John E. Smith, Henry Galt, Thomas F. Shepherd, Samuel Cover, John H. Chew, E. J. Crumrine, R. D. Gorsuch, L. A. J. Lamotte, A. Augustus Roop, J. H. Steele, E. H. Clabaugh. The fair this year was held September 28th to October 1st, and in the trials for speed there were six trots, in which $775 were given as awards.

1881.—President, Col. William A. McKellip; Vice-President, David Fowble; Secretary, Francis H. Orendorff; Treasurer, Richard Manning; Directors, Edward Lynch, Dr. Jacob Rinehart, Jeremiah Rinehart, John B. Boyle, William J. Morelock.

The Agricultural Hall, for the productions requiring shelter, is eighty-five by forty feet, and two stories high. The pavilion seats over two thousand persons, and a music-stand, octagonal in form, is erected in the centre of the track. This society has a capital of nearly thirty thousand dollars invested in its properties. The quality of horses, cattle, hogs, sheep, and mules in the county, as annually exhibited, is superb, and makes a good return in profits to the growers and owners. It is universally admitted that the generous rivalry in their exhibitions has stimulated the farmers to more active exertions, and the machinists have been aroused to the necessity of producing implements of superior quality.

As has been before observed in these pages, the inhabitants of Carroll County have always been a peaceful and law-abiding people. The records of the court have seldom been defaced by the more heinous offenses which sometimes mar the moral symmetry of other communities. There have been but two executions in the county since its creation in 1837. Rebecca McCormick, a colored woman, was tried at the April term of the Circuit Court for 1859 for the murder of a colored boy, fourteen years of age. She was convicted of murder in the first degree, and executed in the month of June following.

On the 5th of April, 1872, Abraham L. Lynn, a miller near Lynwood Station, was found dead in his grain-bin with his skull fractured in several places. It was at first supposed that he had accidentally fallen into the bin, but the suspicious movements of a young man named Joseph W. Davis, employed in the mill, attracted attention, and he was arrested and charged with the murder. Hamilton Shue, a shoemaker in the village, was also arrested as an accomplice. The trial of Davis before the Circuit Court of Carroll County, in June, 1872, resulted in a disagreement of the jury. His case was then removed to Washington County, where he was tried in September, 1872, and convicted of murder in the first degree. There succeeded a series of delays almost unexampled in the history of jurisprudence. The evidence was entirely circumstantial, and his counsel, Col. Maulsby and J. A. C. Bond, believed implicitly in his innocence.

The case was taken on a bill of exceptions to the Court of Appeals, and the decision of the lower court affirmed. Subsequently, in deference to the appeals of counsel, the case was reopened by the highest court in the State and reargued, with the same result as before. An appeal was now made to the Governor for pardon, and the case elaborately argued before him, but he declined to interfere. Again, on the supposed discovery of new evidence, it was argued before the Governor with a like result. Some mistakes were then discovered in the court papers, and a writ of error was sued out by the counsel of Davis, which was heard by the Court of Appeals, and decided adversely to Davis. As a last resort an application for interference was made to the Legislature, which was then in session, but while the proceedings were pending before this body Davis made a full confession, acknowledging his guilt and exonerating Shue, who had already been acquitted. Davis was executed in the jail-yard at Westminster, Feb. 6, 1874. A fearful storm of wind and snow prevailed during the day, but the case had become so generally known through the extraordinary efforts of counsel in his behalf, that thousands of people were drawn thither to witness the last act in the tragedy. He broke down utterly at the last, and had to be borne up the steps of the gallows. His confession was sold to the spectators while he was delivering his farewell to the populace, and appeared the next day in the morning papers.

The financial exhibit of Carroll County for the year ending June 30, 1881, was very gratifying to the taxpayers. There was a reduction of $10,641.61 in the public debt over the previous year, and an increase of $5172.41 in assets, making a general improvement of $15,787.02. The liabilities over assets were $12,532.82, which was about the actual debt of the county. The tax levied was fifty cents on a hundred dollars, the lowest in the State. The expenses of the Circuit Court for August and November, 1880, and for February and May, 1881, were $8303.46; for sundry attorneys, $121.33; for the Orphans' Court, $1573.81; for county commissioners, $1868.50; for county jail, $2390.59; for public schools, $21,000; for registers of voters, $825; for collection of taxes, $2635; for justices of the peace, $457.68; for constables, $464.79; for public printing, $722.83; for taxes refunded, $14 10; for State witnesses, $41 58; for laying out and opening public roads, $109; for inquests, $166.94; for sundry minor expenses, $970.55; for county roads, small bridges, and culverts, $9369.90; for bridges, $3732.-88; for county indebtedness, $14,230.31; for judges and clerks of election, $286; for out-door pensioners, $2803; for special pensions by order, $619.60; for miscellaneous accounts, $2364.36; for the almshouse, $3822.70. The liabilities of the county on June 30, 1881, were given by Joseph A. Waesche, the treasurer, as follows: County certificates outstanding, $47,495; note due Union National Bank, $5000; Daniel Bush estate, $1200; George W. Armacort, $400; total, $54,095. The amount of liabilities June 30, 1880, $64,709.61. The assets were stated as follows: Outstanding taxes in hands of collectors for former years, $38,230.71; cash in bank, $2396.97; due from Baltimore City and Allegany County, $935.50; total, $41,563,18. Amount of assets July 30, 1880, $36,390.77. The commissioners were John K. Longwell, president; Francis Warner, William C. Polk.

The following statistics in regard to Carroll County are furnished from the census bureau: Total value of real estate assessed for the year ended June 30, 1880, $11,215,334; personal property, $5,030,142; aggregate value of real and personal property assessed, $16,245,476. Receipts from taxes for all purposes except schools, $90,687.65; for school purposes, $37,245.47; total receipts from State taxes for all purposes except schools, $14,214.79; total receipts from State taxes (or apportionment) for schools, $16,245.47. Expenditures for schools, $37,245.47; State roads or bridges, $11,996.71; poor, $7590; all other purposes, $24,337.95. Total, $81,170.13. The bonded indebtedness is based on the issue of bonds bearing 6 per cent. interest in 1864 and 1865, as bounties for volunteer soldiers, which matured in 1866 and 1867. The amount paid is $16,675; outstanding, $48,325. Assets, par value outstanding taxes in the hands of collectors, $36,390.17; almshouse property, containing 175 acres of land, $15,000. Total, $51,390.17; estimated value, $51,390.17.

The total population of the county in 1880 was 30,992, of which the males numbered 15,495, and the females 15,497.

The population of Carroll County, according to previous census returns, has been as follows:

	1870.	1860.	1850.	1840.
White	26,444	22,525	18,667	15,221
Colored	2,175	1,225	974	898
Slave	....	783	975	1,122
Total	28,619	24,533	20,616	17,241

The cereal production of Carroll County, as returned by the census of 1880, was as follows:

	Acres.	Bushels.
Barley	133	3,724
Buckwheat	972	12,543
Indian corn	31,983	1,003,986
Oats	11,972	262,458
Rye	5,269	54,879
Wheat	40,077	579,333
Tobacco	162	137,171

Summary of School Statistics for 1880.

Number of school-houses (frame 32, brick 63, log 18, stone 12)	125
Number male teachers (principals)	82
" female " "	49
" " " assistants	1
" fenced lots	9
" schools having outbuildings	105
" " " good blackboards	110
" " " " furniture	112
Different pupils for the year (white)	6152
" " " " (colored)	307

Receipts.

Balance on hand Sept. 30, 1880	$180.30
State school tax	12,662.30
" free school fund	1,942.02
County school tax at 16 cents on the $100	20,000.00
Book fees	7,811.60
State appropriation to colored schools	2,171.88
License	201.33
Rent	25.00
Total	$44,994.43

The total disbursements were $44,994.43, of which $36,991.40 were teachers' salaries, $1579.96 for fuel, $4902.89 for stationery; $4033.12 for colored schools (included in the above disbursements), and the balance (save $3146.07 cash on hand) for various incidental and contingent expenses.

According to the United States census of 1880, the total number of persons in Carroll County who cannot read is 1419, and of those who cannot write 2125. Of the latter, 1209 are native white, 66 foreign white, and 850 colored. Of the white population who cannot write, 95 males and 61 females, total, 156, are between 10 and 14 years of age; 43 males and 49 females, total, 92, are from 15 to 20 years of age; and 383 males and 644 females, total, 1027, are 21 years and over. Of the colored population who cannot write, 43 males and 51 females, total, 94, are from 10 to 14 years old; 42 males and 58 females, total, 100, are from 15 to 20 years; and 320 males and 336 females, total, 656, are 21 years and over.

CARROLL COUNTY DISTRICTS.

CHAPTER XXXIX.

TANEYTOWN DISTRICT, No. 1.

THE metes and bounds of this district are as follows:

"Beginning at the Pennsylvania line where Rock Creek crosses said line; thence with the course of said creek until it empties into the Monocacy River; thence with the Monocacy to the point where Double Pipe Creek enters the river; thence with the course of Pipe to the point of junction with Little Pipe Creek and by Pipe Creek; thence with the course of Little Pipe Creek to Eckart's Ford; thence with a straight line to Sick's Ford on Big Pipe Creek; thence up Big Pipe Creek to Grove's Mill; thence with the stone road to Littlestown turnpike; thence with the turnpike to the Pennsylvania line; thence to the place of beginning."

The district is bounded on the north by Pennsylvania, on the east by the Myers' and Uniontown Districts, on the south by the Uniontown and Middleburg Districts, and on the west by Frederick County. Its western boundary line is the Monocacy River, and Big Pipe Creek separates it from the Uniontown District. Alloway's Creek, which rises in Pennsylvania, passes through the northwest corner of the district and empties into the Monocacy River, and Piney Creek, which takes its rise in the same State, passes diagonally through the district, dividing it into two nearly equal parts, and finds its outlet in the Monocacy. Upon the tributaries of these streams many mills have been erected, some of them prior to the Revolutionary war. Taneytown District was first settled by the Scotch-Irish Presbyterian Covenanter stock, who were either natives of the north of Ireland or the descendants of those who came to Pennsylvania very early in the history of the colonies. Among them were the Gwynns, McKalebs, McKellips, Galts, Birnies, Knoxes, and Rudesils. The Goods, Crouses, Swopes, Hesses, Nalls, Hecks, Reindollars, Thompsons, and Shunks are names intimately associated also with the first settlement of the district. Frederick Taney was the earliest settler of whom any record is preserved. He took up a tract of land in the vicinity of Taneytown, at present the business centre of the district, in 1740, and in 1754 "Brother's Agreement," a tract of seven thousand nine hundred acres, was patented to Edward Digges and Raphael Taney. About 1750 a heavy tide of immigration set in from Pennsylvania. John McKellip, Sr., a sea-captain, was born in the County Antrim, Ireland, where his parents had removed from the neighborhood of Castle Stirling, England. He married, Nov. 9, 1780, Mary Drips, his first wife, and after her death, Ann Adams, of Maryland. He settled in the Taneytown District in 1780, whither he had come from Ireland in company with Rogers Birnie. He died March 10, 1834, aged eighty years. His first wife died Feb. 15, 1799, and his second, Dec. 14, 1827, she being sixty-four years of age. Three of his brothers, William, Hugh, and David, settled in America. John McKellip's son James by his second wife was born Nov. 5, 1805, and died May 4, 1859. He was the father of Col. William A. McKellip, a prominent lawyer of Westminster. The early settlers were all stanch Whigs during the Revolution, and contributed largely in troops and treasure to its success. "Brother's Inheritance," a grant of three thousand one hundred and twenty-four acres, was patented to Michael Swope in 1761.

If longevity be an indication of the salubriousness of a climate, Taneytown District has reason to be proud of its record in this regard. John Welty was born in Eppingen, Germany, Sept. 4, 1722. He came to this country and settled in the Taneytown District, and died near Emmittsburg, Jan. 16, 1817, aged ninety-four years, four months, and two days. His son, Frederick Welty, was born on Piney Creek, near Taneytown, March 12, 1779, and afterwards removed to Deilsburg, York Co., Pa., where he died April 28, 1877, aged ninety-eight years, one month, and sixteen days; Elizabeth Knitz, a daughter of John Welty, lived to be one hundred and three years of age; Susanna Hornaker died in March, 1855, aged eighty-four years, four months, and two days; Casper Welty, a son of John, died Feb. 27, 1856, aged eighty-eight years, nine months, and twenty-one days; Bernard Welty, another son, died April 1, 1856, aged eighty-two years, eight months, and eleven days; Mary Hoovs, another daughter, died Sept. 17, 1866, aged ninety-one years; Abraham Welty, died May 2, 1874, aged ninety-seven years, eleven months, and twenty-two days. Their aggregate ages amounted to six hundred and fifty-seven years, giving an average of ninety-four years to each member of the family, probably the most remarkable instance of longevity since the days of the patriarchs.

Piney Creek Presbyterian Church.—"April 13, 1763, Tom's Creek and Pipe Creek Churches ask leave to apply to the Presbytery of New Brunswick for a young man to supply them." The answer to this request is not recorded, but the Rev. Samuel Thompson was appointed to preach at Tom's Creek, and the Rev. Robert McMardil was at the same time appointed to preach at Pine Creek, on the fourth Sabbath of April. At this point in the history the name of Pipe Creek disappears from the record, and that of Pine, then Piney Creek, is substituted, showing that the congregation now adopted a new name, if it did not also change its place of worship. The church was supplied during the next autumn and winter by William Edmeston and John Slemons, licentiates of the Donegal Presbytery, by William Magau, a licentiate of the Presbytery of Philadelphia, and by the Rev. Robert Smith. For the summer of 1764, Mr. Slemons had three appointments at Piney Creek. During the next five years Tom's Creek and Piney Creek had occasional supplies, appointed chiefly at the stated meetings of the Presbytery in April and October. Andrew Bay, John Slemons, John Craighead, Hezekiah James Balch, Samuel Thompson, and Robert Cooper were among their preachers. Rev. John Slemons was born in Chester County, Pa. His parents were emigrants from Ireland. He was a graduate of Princeton College, and was licensed by the Presbytery of Donegal in 1762 or 1763. He was unanimously called to Lower Marsh Creek on the third Saturday of November, 1764. He also received calls from Tom's Creek and Piney Creek about the same time. At Philadelphia, May 8, 1765, the Presbytery desired his answer respecting the calls under consideration, when "he gave up that from Piney Creek and Tom's Creek." Not being "clear" with respect to the call from Lower Marsh Creek, the Presbytery "recommend him to come to a determination as soon as he can in that matter."

On the 23d of May he declared his acceptance of the call to Lower Marsh Creek, and was ordained and installed by the Presbytery of Carlisle. Oct. 30, 1765, Mr. Slemons frequently supplied Tom's Creek and Piney Creek, both before and after his settlement at Marsh Creek. His relation to this church had dissolved in 1774. He was pastor of Slate Ridge and Chanceford from their organization until his death, June, 1814, in the eightieth year of his age. His remains, and those of his wife Sarah, who died June 2, 1823, are interred in the Piney Creek burying-ground. Mrs. Slemons was the daughter of the Rev. Joseph Dean, a co-laborer of the Tennents, who was buried in the Neshaminy Church graveyard. Two brothers and a sister of Mr. Slemons, and the children of one of the brothers, are buried in the Lower Marsh Creek burying-ground. Piney Creek had meanwhile asked for the appointment of the Rev. Joseph Rhea "in particular" as supply, and had also requested that some member of the Presbytery be deputized to assist in the preparation of a call to Mr. Rhea. He had already been before the congregation, having become a member of the Presbytery, October, 1770. That Mr. Rhea's ministrations were highly acceptable is evinced by the fact that not only Piney Creek, but also Upper Marsh Creek (now Gettysburg) and the united churches of Tuscarora and Cedar Springs, all presented calls to him in April, 1771. Hanover, in Dauphin County, likewise asked for him as supply at the same time. The call from Tuscarora and Cedar Spring was withheld for correction. That from Upper Marsh was presented to Mr. Rhea, and taken into consideration by him.

The commissioners from Piney Creek were Patrick Watson and Matthew Galt. They stated that subscriptions amounting to £110 or £112 had been secured for Mr. Rhea's support; that if he became pastor they proposed to maintain his family for the first year in addition to the salary, and that this agreement had been entered of record in their "Book of Congregational Affairs."

The Presbytery found the call to be regular and the people unanimous, but an existing difficulty between Tom's Creek and Piney Creek was an impediment in the way of placing it in Mr. Rhea's hands. Another committee was now raised to hear and determine the matters now in dispute. This committee consisted of the Rev. Messrs. Thompson, Roon, Duffield, and Cooper, and was directed to put the call in Mr. Rhea's hands, if no sufficient objections arose out of the questions submitted for their decision.

The committee was directed to meet on the Monday following their appointment, but in this they failed, and so reported to the Presbytery in June, when the reasons assigned for the failure were sustained. During the delay occasioned by these efforts of conciliation Mr. Rhea declared his acceptance of the call to Upper Marsh Creek, but afterwards declined it under circumstances which led the Presbytery to disapprove of his conduct "as having too great an appearance of inadvertency and instability," and recommending him to be "more cautious in the future with respect to such matters."

Piney Creek now urged the Presbytery to put their call into Mr. Rhea's hands, and in case of his acceptance to have him installed as soon as convenient. The same obstacle being still in the way as at the April meeting, action upon this request was again deferred.

But, in order to expedite the business, a new committee, consisting of the Rev. Messrs. Cooper, Craighead, and Duffield, with Robert Dill and Robert McPherson as elders, was appointed to determine the matter in debate, and if the way should be clear, put the call into Mr. Rhea's hands and receive his answer.

The committee met at Tom's Creek on the fourth Tuesday of June, 1771, all the members being present except Mr. Craighead and Elder Dill. Mr. Cooper was chosen moderator, and Mr. Duffield clerk. The commissioners from Piney Creek were Patrick Watson, Abraham Heyter, Benjamin McKinley, James Galt, and James Hunter; from Tom's Creek a committee of four.

When the committee and the parties came together, there were two subjects of dispute to be considered. The first was that Piney Creek desired a separation from Tom's Creek and the settlement of a pastor of their own; whereas Tom's Creek favored the continuance of the former union and a joint settlement of a pastor. After a full and patient hearing of the arguments on both sides, the committee decided this first question in favor of Piney Creek, and dissolved the union.

The second subject of controversy was that of the boundary line between the two congregations. It will be remembered that in April, 1765, this question was considered and apparently settled. The following is the concluding part of the committee's decision:

> "The committee therefore determine that although Monocacy does appear to be a just and natural boundary to Tom's Creek, yet for the present such persons as live between the above-mentioned Stony Ridge and Marsh Creek, or Monocacy, and choose to join with Piney Creek, shall be at liberty so to do. But that in case of Tom's Creek obtaining a minister, it shall be deemed more regular in them to join with Tom's Creek (within whose reasonable bounds they are to be esteemed residing), as being more conducive to the general good of the church, even though they should still continue a connection with Piney Creek as being nearer to them as that house is now seated."

In the judgment and determination of the committee the commissioners of both congregations acquiesced, and thus disposed of questions which had been sources of controversy and distraction. The way was now clear for presenting the call to Mr. Rhea. It was accordingly placed in his hands by the committee. After due deliberation he accepted it. The record omits the arrangements for his installation, but this doubtless soon followed, as from this time he discharged the duties of the pastorate. Thus after depending upon the Presbytery for supplies for nearly ten years, Piney Creek had, for the first time, a settled minister. At what precise time the first house of worship was erected at Piney Creek is unknown. It was, however, prior to the settlement of Mr. Rhea, as is shown by the deed conveying the lot of ground, and the house built upon it, to the trustees. The original Piney Creek church, as stated above, erected prior to Mr. Rhea's settlement in 1771, was a very plain log structure. Its pews were

> "—— Straight-backed and tall,
> Its pulpit, goblet formed,
> Half-way up the wall,
> The sounding-board above."

It was removed about the year 1818, when the present brick church was built upon the same site, and much after the same fashion. It was remodeled and modernized in 1869, during the pastorate of Mr. Patterson. The number of pews in the second church before the last improvements were made were fifty-eight.

The deed of the old church is dated Feb. 15, 1771, and was given for a consideration of five shillings, by

Abraham Heyter, of Frederick County, province of Maryland, to Patrick Watson, James Galt, and John McCorkle, of the same county and province, and James Barr and James Hunter, of York County, province of Pennsylvania, in trust for a church and burying-ground. The grant contained two acres of land, and the use of a spring of water contiguous thereto, on the southeast side of the land, and was situated in Piney Creek Hundred, Frederick Co. In shape it was a parallelogram, with lines running north and south twenty perches, and east and west sixteen perches. The grantor restricted the use and privilege of the land to "a congregation of people called Presbyterians, who shall hold or continue to hold that system of doctrine contained in the Westminster confession of faith, catechisms, and directory, as the same principles are now professed and embraced by the Synod of New York and Philadelphia, to which they are now united."

While Piney Creek was enjoying the regular ministrations of a settled pastor, Tom's Creek was dependent upon the Presbytery for supplies. In 1772 subscriptions to the amount of fourteen pounds were taken up in Piney Creek for the benefit of Nassau Hall College, New Jersey. In June, 1775, Mr. Rhea informed the Presbytery that he desired to visit some parts of Virginia, and that his people had given consent to his absence. The Presbytery permitted him to carry out his purpose, and furnished him with the usual traveling credentials.

Mr. Rhea tendered his resignation as pastor of the Piney Creek Church in April, 1776. His reasons for doing so are not upon record, but subsequent proceedings show that his salary was in arrears. The commissioners of the congregation were Robert Bigham and Adam Hoop. Upon their acceding to Mr. Rhea's request, the Presbytery, after due deliberation, dissolved the pastoral relation. An agreement was, however, previously entered into whereby Mr. Rhea engaged to receipt in full for his salary upon the payment of one hundred and fifty pounds. He also agreed that if upon examination of accounts it should appear that any moneys had been received for which due credit had not been given, the proper deductions should be made. The date of these transactions was April 11, 1776.

Mr. Rhea obtained leave to spend the following summer in Virginia, and was furnished with the usual Presbyterial certificate.

Being unable to effect a settlement with Mr. Rhea, the congregation applied to the Presbytery in October of the same year for a committee to adjudicate the matter. The Rev. Messrs. Balch and Black, with Elders William Blair and David McConaughy, were appointed said committee, and directed to meet at Piney Creek, when Mr. Rhea could be present. But as he had gone to Virginia, the meeting was necessarily delayed, and before it could be arranged for his convenience he died. This event occurred Sept. 20, 1777. Mr. Rhea was a native of Ireland. Piney Creek was his only pastorate in this country. His remains lie in the burying-ground attached to this church. His tombstone bears the following inscription:

"Sacred to the memory of the Rev. Joseph Rhea, who died in 1777, aged about sixty-two years. Erected at the request and the expense of a grandson of the deceased, in 1839, by the elders of the Piney Creek Church, where he preached seven years."

In October, 1778, a paper signed by Patrick Watson, Robert Bigham, Samuel McCune, James Watson, and William Linn showed that the arrears due to the heirs of Mr. Rhea had been collected, and all the obligations of the congregation to him honorably discharged. Supplies were appointed for Piney Creek at this meeting, and from time to time for the next two years.

On the 22d of May, 1777, the Rev. James Martin, a member of the Associate Presbytery of Pennsylvania, was received by the Synod and assigned to the Presbytery of Donegal. He was enrolled as a member of this latter body June 18th. In 1780 he accepted a call to Piney Creek Church. The support promised was "four hundred bushels of wheat per year, or the current price thereof in money, and as much more as the circumstances of the congregation would admit." He was installed Nov. 9, 1780, by a committee consisting of the Rev. Messrs. James Hunt, John Slemons, and John Black. The pastorate of Mr. Martin was continued eight and a half years. In October, 1788, he applied to the Presbytery of Carlisle for a relief from his charge. The commissioners of the congregation had not been instructed to acquiesce in this application, but they presented a memorial showing that their financial affairs were not in a healthy condition. The church was cited to appear at the next meeting and show cause why Mr. Martin's request should not be granted, and a committee consisting of Rev. Messrs. Black, McKnight, and Henderson, with Elders John Linn, Robert McPherson, and James McKnight, was directed to meet at Piney Creek on the first Tuesday of December and inquire into the condition of affairs.

The committee reported, April 15, 1789, that the whole amount paid Mr. Martin in nine years was £612 12*s.* 8*d.*, that £297 7*s.* 4*d.* were still due, that for his future support they can only raise seventy pounds per annum, and will only be responsible for forty pounds of the said sum. The pastoral relation was therefore unanimously dissolved, and the congregation was directed to use every honorable effort to liquidate their indebtedness to Mr. Martin. At the same meeting Mr. Martin accepted a call to East and West Penn's Valley, Warrior Mark, and Half-Moon, in Pennsylvania, within the present bounds of the Presbytery of Huntingdon. Here he labored until his death, June 20, 1795. He was a native of the County Down of Ireland. He came to this country before its independence was declared, and labored for a season in South Carolina. Piney Creek was his first settlement here, though he had preached for some years in his native land. He was one of the original members of the Presbytery of Huntingdon, which was constituted April 14, 1795. He died at the age of sixty-seven, and was buried in Penn's Valley, where he resided after he moved to Maryland. Tradition speaks of him as an able and popular preacher. He is said to have been a very earnest and animated speaker. Like all the preachers of that day, and those especially of the denomination from which he originally came, his sermons were long, perhaps seldom less than an hour and a half, and sometimes considerably longer. On a warm summer day it was not unusual for him to take off his coat and preach in his shirt-sleeves. In the pulpit he was very forgetful of himself and his personal appearance, so intensely was he taken up in his subject. He would first take off his coat, then begin to loosen his cravat, and conclude by taking off his wig, holding it in his hand and shaking it in the face of the congregation, and sometimes during the course of his sermon his wig would become awry, the back part turned to the front, and he utterly unconscious of the metamorphosis. Surely a man of such earnestness was above and beyond the ridicule of the profane. Mr. Martin was twice married. His first wife was Annie McCullough; his second, Ellen Davidson, of York County. After his death she returned to her home. She had no children. Mr. Martin had four sons,—James, Samuel, John, and Robert.

The pulpit remained vacant for several years after Mr. Martin's resignation, and depended upon the Presbytery for preaching and the administration of the sacraments. The process of liquidating their indebtedness went on slowly.

In October, 1792, a statement of accounts between the congregation and their late pastor showed a remaining indebtedness of £96 17*s.* 11*d.* The only other reference to the subject is in April, 1793, when the people are again directed to take all proper measures to secure a speedy discharge of their obligations to Mr. Martin.

In August, 1793, the advice of the Presbytery was sought in the following case: "A certain widow of Piney Creek, with her husband in his lifetime, applied to a certain man who passed under the name of a gospel minister and had the ordinance of baptism in appearance administered to her two children; but it was afterwards discovered that the said administrator had never been authorized by any regular church of Christ to act as a gospel minister." The Presbytery decided the act of the impostor to be invalid, and advised that the children be baptized by a regularly ordained minister.

In October, 1801, the Piney Creek Church, which had been vacant since the resignation of Mr. Martin, April 15, 1789, extended a call to Mr. Davidson, offering him £87 10*s.* for one-half of his ministerial and pastoral services. A commissioner informed the Presbytery that Tom's Creek had been consulted, and had agreed that Mr. Davidson's services should be divided between the two congregations. The call was accordingly presented to Mr. Davidson, and upon his acceptance of it the arrangement was consummated.

Tom's Creek and Piney Creek were now for the first time in a period of forty years united under the same pastor. The union then established has, however, been continued with entire harmony through successive pastorates for three-quarters of a century. Mr. Davidson's labors were continued in the two congregations until the autumn of 1809.

At the Presbytery meeting at Carlisle, Sept. 26, 1810, charges of a serious nature were made against Mr. Davidson by Mr. Emmit. "Only six were deemed relevant: 1. A charge of fraud and falsehood in a business transaction with said Emmit. 2. Of fraud towards the purchasers of certain lots of ground in the above transaction. 3. Of falsehood in renting to Anthony Troxel a brick house only, and afterwards giving him possession of orchard, clover, and garden, though said property was claimed by said Emmit according to contract. 4. Of fraud and falsehood (1) in settling an account with Robert Holmes, and (2) in his dealings with Lewis Weaver, wherein he promised to settle with said Weaver before he (Davidson) removed to Frederick, but violated said promise. 5. Of cruel and unchristian conduct in ejecting George Hockensmith, wife, and children, with beds and furniture, during a heavy rain, despite all said Hockensmith's entreaties to give him two or three days, for which he would pay him two dollars, and in refusing to give him time for his children to eat a mouthful of breakfast, though it was provided for them and already on the table. 6. Of a breach of the Sabbath, in June, 1805, in dealing with Solomon Kephart for harvest liquors."

A committee consisting of the Rev. John McKnight, D.D., chairman, and the Rev. Messrs. William Paxton and David McConaughy, with Elders Alexander Russel, Walter Smith, and John Eadie, appointed to hear and take testimony in the case, met at the house of Patrick Reed, in Emmittsburg, on the first Tuesday of November, 1810, and entered upon an examination of the charges. Mr. Davidson declined to make any defense. The committee reported to the Presbytery April 11, 1811. The charges were taken up seriatim, and after mature consideration it was decided that none of them had been sustained. It was thereupon

"*Resolved*, That the Presbytery declare their high disapprobation of the conduct of William Emmit, in instituting and prosecuting charges evidently unjust, slanderous, and vexatious."

It was also ordered that an attested copy of this resolution be read from the pulpit of the churches.

Of the internal and spiritual condition of Piney Creek during Mr. Davidson's pastorate little is known. In 1806 the total membership was 124; in 1807, 113; in 1808, 108. In 1805 the additions to the church were 10; in 1807, 8; in 1808, 7; in 1809, 9. The baptisms in 1806 were 14; in 1807, 8; in 1808, 24; in 1809, 10; in 1810, 14.

The next pastor of the united congregations was the Rev. Robert Smith Grier. A complete roll of the membership of Piney Creek was prepared in January, 1824, from which it appears that there were then one hundred and forty-four communicants; of these eighty-nine were females. Piney Creek had at that date thirty-seven members more than Tom's Creek, and was most probably as strong as at any period of its history. Emigration westward, by which it has been greatly depleted of late, had not then fairly set in. The elders were Alexander Horner, John McAlister, Samuel Thompson, and John Barr. Many names then on the list of members have since disappeared. The Adairs, the Baldwins, the Blacks, the Darbys, the Fergusons, the Heagys, the McCrearys, the Reids, the Wilsons, and others familiar doubtless to many now living are no longer upon the register.

In May, 1825, Catharine Harris, Susan Jamison, Sarah and William Thompson, Rebecca Wilson, Henry Dinwiddie, Amelia Rhinedoller, and Sophia Deukart were received, and in September Robert Flemming and Miss Eliza Graham. In 1830 the Session received Jacob Shoemaker, who became a useful member of the church, and was ordained to the eldership in 1838. He died Feb. 4, 1869. Mrs. Margaret Shoemaker, wife of Jacob, was received at the same time; she was a diffident though a sincere and humble Christian woman. At her death, which occurred Oct. 26, 1875, it was discovered that she had bequeathed two thousand dollars to the board of the church.

John Adair was treasurer of Piney Creek Church from 1814 to 1822; James Barr, from 1822 to 1836. The position of doorkeeper was held by Abraham Shoemaker from 1815 to 1819; James Ross, from 1819 to 1822; Elijah Currens, from 1823 to 1837. The number of persons subscribing to the pastor's salary in 1806 were 95; in 1810, 75; in 1816 and 1817, 100, which appears to be the maximum number so far as can be ascertained. The subscriptions ranged from one to ten dollars, the average being about three, and were paid semi-annually.

The pastorate of Mr. Grier, though covering more than half a century, was quiet and uneventful. He lived during a large part of his ministry upon his farm, three miles north of Emmittsburg, and over the line separating Maryland and Pennsylvania. After the decease of Mr. Grier both churches were supplied for a few months by Rev. Daniel B. Jackson, then a licentiate, but now pastor of the Black River Falls Church, Wis. Early in the summer of 1866 they were visited by the Rev. Isaac M. Patterson, pastor of the Annapolis Church, and a member of the Presbytery of Baltimore. This visit resulted in a call to the pastorate of both churches. Mr. Patterson commenced his labors early in August, and was installed at Piney Creek November 13th, and on the next day at Emmittsburg. Mr. Patterson's ministry lasted seven years. In the summer of 1873 he resigned his pastoral charge with a view to accept a call to Milford, N. J., which is his present field of labor. The relations of the present pastor to the united churches of Emmittsburg, Piney Creek, and Taneytown were constituted in December, 1873, by a committee of the Presbytery of Baltimore.

In January, 1824, there were in the church at Piney Creek four elders,—Alexander Horner, John McAllister, Samuel Thompson, and James Barr,—and the following are the names of the communicants:

Alexander Horner, Sarah Horner, Eli Horner, Ann Walker, John Horner, Ann Thompson, Robert McCreery, Robert Thompson, Eleanor Thompson, Ann McCreery, Mary Thompson, Andrew Walker, Maria McCreery, Sarah Horner, James Horner, James Black, Jane Black, Philip Heagy, Esther Heagy, Jesse Quinn, Margaret Linor, William Walker, William Stevenson, Peggy Stevenson, John McCallister, J. W. McCalister, Betsy McCalister, Mary McCalister, Elizabeth Henry, Frances Weemes, Jane Cornell, Margaret Paxton, William Paxton, Caroline Harris, Jane McCrea, Elijah Baldwin, Matthew Galt, Mary Galt, Elizabeth Galt, Susan Galt, Rebecca Galt, Abraham Linor, Sterling Galt, Margaret Galt, Samuel Galt, Mary Galt, Mary Jones, Elizabeth McCrea, Thompson McCrea, Samuel Thompson, Archibald Clingan, Ann Clingan, William Clingan, Elizabeth Clingan, Hugh Thompson, Margaret Snyder, Elijah Baldwin, Elizabeth Baldwin, Mary Baldwin, Kizeah Baldwin, Rachel Miller, Sarah Drummond, James Smith, Sarah Smith, —— Alison, Martha Alison, Mary Ann Alison, Isabella Barr, James Barr, Margaret Barr, Sally Barr, Mary Cornell, Esther Cornell, Sarah Galt, Martha Breckenridge, Margaret Birnie, Hester Birnie, Charles Birnie, Hester Birnie, Jr., Rose Birnie, John McKaleb, Mary Jane Annan, John McKillip, Ann McKillip, Mary Gillelan, Sarah Claubach, Catherine Musgrove, John Ferguson, Sr., John Ferguson, Rebecca Ferguson, John Adair, Esther Adair, Sarah Adair, Samuel Adair, Hannah Adair, Frances Alison, Margaret Reid, Margaret Reid, Jr., Mary Reid, Weemes Black, Elizabeth Larrimore, Lucinda McCalister, Thomas McCune, Thomas McCune, Jr., Mary McCune, John Thompson, Andrew Guin, Margaret Hunter, Susanna Hunter, Jane Hunter, Elizabeth Hunter, John Hunter, Andrew Horner, Margaret Horner, William Horner, Elizabeth Horner, Nancy Bentley, John Darby, Catharine Darby, Elizabeth Smith, Mary Wilson, Jane Wilson, John Wilson, Betsy Larimore, George Guin, Elizabeth Baldwin, John McClanahan, Ann McClanahan, James McCalester, James McCalister, Jr., Mary McCalister, Alexander McCalister, James McIlhenny, Maria McIlhenny, Sally McIlhenny, Robert McKinney, Susanna McKinney, Esther McKinney, James Smith, Jane Longwell, Sally Jamison, Miss Jamison, Kitty (colored), Jack (colored).

The following is a list of the persons subscribing to the pastor's salary in the year 1817:

Adair, John.
Adair, Samuel.
Alison, Francis.
Alexander, William.
Armstrong, Isaac.
Barr, James.
Breckinridge, William.
Black, James.
Birnie, Clotworthy.
Baldwin, Daniel.
Beard, William.
Breckinridge, Widow.
Brannon, Margaret.
Cornall, Thomas.
Cornall, William.
Crabbs, John.
Currens, Elijah.
Currens, William.
Cornall, Jesse.
Cornall, Smith.
Clingan, Archibald.
Clingan, William.
Crabster, John.
Crabster, John, Jr.
Darby, John.
Dorborrow, Isaac.
Drummond, James.
Ferguson, John.
Ferguson, William.
Galt, John.
Galt, Matthew.
Guin, George.
Galt, Moses.
Gilliland, John.
Guin, Andrew.
Gordin, Mary.
Horner, Alexander.
Hill, Hannah.
Hunter, Joseph.
Horner, William.
Horner, Andrew.
Horner, John.
Hunter, John.
Heagy, Philip.
Hays, Joseph.
Hunter, Susanna.
Heagy, George.
Jamison, Widow.
Jamison, John.
Jones, John.
Linn, James.
Linn, Samuel.
Love, Robert.
Leech, Robert.
Linah, Abraham.
Larimore, Thomas.
Linn, Samuel, Jr.
Little, Susanna.
McCreary, Robert.
McAlister, John.
McAlister, James.
McKaleb, John.
McKalip, John.
McCune, Thomas.
McIlvane, Moses.
Major, Robert.
McKinney, John.
McCune, Thomas.
McIlhenny, John.
McCrea, Elizabeth.
McCrea, Thomson.
Musgrove, Samuel.
McIlhenny, James.
Paxton, William.
Paxton, Thomas.
Paxton, Margaret.
Ross, James.
Robinson, Robert.
Reed, Francis.
Smith, Samuel.
Smith, James.
Stevenson, William.
Shoemaker, William.
Snyder, Nicholas.
Shaw, Hugh.
Six, George.
Sink, George.
Smith, Obadiah.
Shoemaker, Abraham.
Stevenson, James.
Thomson, John.
Thomson, Samuel.
Thomson, Robert.
Thomson, Hugh.
Wilson, William.
Walker, Mary.
Walker, William.
Wilson, Charles, Jr.
Wharton, James.
Weems, Fanny.
Walker, Andrew.

Rev. Sterling M. Galt was born in Taneytown District, Carroll Co., Md., Feb. 28, 1837. He was the son of Sterling Galt, a wealthy and influential citizen of the county and a descendant of one of the oldest settlers. He entered Princeton College, and pursued a thorough course of study both in the academic and theological departments. He was licensed to preach by the Presbytery of New Brunswick in 1861. He began his ministrations at Newark and Red Clay Creek, Del., within the bounds of the Presbytery of New Castle, where he was ordained in 1862 and installed pastor of these churches. After three years of incessant labor in this his only charge, he fell a victim to typhoid fever, Oct. 24, 1865.

Piney Creek has done her share to replenish the ministerial ranks. John W. Smith was the only son of Stephen and Frances Smith. He entered himself as a student of Pennsylvania College, at Gettysburg, and studied at the same time for the Presbyterian ministry. He was a young man of talent, and gave promise of eminent usefulness, but was taken off by disease, May 26, 1872, in the twentieth year of his year. The inscription upon his tombstone in Piney Creek graveyard tells that "he was a candidate for the ministry."

Rev. James Grier Breckinridge, son of Robert and Mary Grier Breckinridge, and brother of Mrs. Matilda Allison, of Emmittsburg, was born in Carroll County, Md., May 30, 1808. His parents were members of the Piney Creek Church. His mother was a daughter of Rev. James Grier, a convert of Whitefield, and pastor of the Deep Run Church, Bucks County, Pa., from 1776 to 1791. Mr. Breckinridge received his collegiate education at Dickinson College, studied theology at Princeton, and was licensed by the Presbytery of Carlisle. In the autumn of 1831 he assisted in protracted services held at Bedford, Pa., after which he supplied the Bedford Church for some months. In May, 1833, a colony of thirty members from this congregation formed a new church at Schellsburg, of which Mr. Breckinridge became the first pastor. Accompanied by his wife he attended the sessions of the Carlisle Presbytery, at Chambersburg, in October, 1833. After the adjournment they visited their relatives in Carroll County, Md., and while there were prostrated by an attack of typhoid fever, from which neither of them recovered. Mr. Breckinridge died Nov. 1, 1833, when but twenty-six years of age, and Mrs. Breckinridge on the 19th of the same month, aged thirty years. They were both buried in the graveyard of Piney Creek Church.

John Motter Annan, the son of Dr. Andrew and Elizabeth Motter Annan, was born in Emmittsburg, Md., March 17, 1841. Early in life he exhibited a decided predilection for the church, and with a view to prepare for the ministry entered Lafayette College Sept. 7, 1859. At the breaking out of the civil war he left school and joined the Union army, enlisting in Company C, First Regiment of the Potomac Home Brigade, Maryland Cavalry, Capt. John Horner, of which company he was chosen first lieutenant. While at Camp Thomas, Frederick, Md., before the company had been in active service, he was accidentally killed by the discharge of a carbine in the hands of a soldier with whom he was conversing, Nov. 13, 1861. He was a young man of some talent, and possessed of moral qualities which would have made themselves felt in the community had he lived and carried out his original intentions.

The pastors of the Piney Creek Church have been:

1763–70, vacant, with occasional supplies; 1771–76, Rev. Joseph Rhea; 1776–80, vacant, with occasional supplies; 1780–89, Rev. James Martin; 1789–1800, vacant, with occasional supplies; 1801–10, Rev. Patrick Davidson; 1811–13, vacant, with occasional supplies; 1814–66, Rev. Robert S. Grier; 1866–73, Rev. Isaac M. Patterson; 1873, Rev. William Simonton.

Taneytown is the oldest village in Carroll County. It was laid out about the year 1750 by Frederick Taney, who came from Calvert County, Md. It is situated on the main road from Frederick to York, Pa., and prior to the Revolutionary war, and for many years afterwards, was the principal thoroughfare between the North and South. Frederick Taney, the founder of the town, was a member of the family of Roger B. Taney, the late eminent chief justice of the Supreme Court of the United States, whose remains now repose in a cemetery in Frederick after a grand but stormy career, in which heroic devotion to duty and extraordinary judicial acumen were so faithfully illustrated that his bitterest enemies have united to do justice to his memory. The ancestors of Frederick Taney were among the earliest settlers in the province of Maryland, and were large landed proprietors in Calvert County for many generations before his birth. Raphael Taney, in conjunction with Edward Digges, patented a tract of seven thousand nine hundred acres of land in this vicinity in 1754, but the Taney estate passed into other hands many years ago. The Good family succeeded by purchase to Taneytown. The land eventually fell into the hands of an old bachelor named Taney, who was a hard drinker. When not in his cups he was crusty and disagreeable, and could not be brought to entertain a proposition for the disposal of his property. Certain parties familiar with his habits, and anxious to secure the land, probably for speculative purposes, plied him with liquor, and when reduced to the convenient state of intoxication induced him to sign the papers which conveyed away his property. From the Good family the property descended by inheritance to the Gwinns, and from them, by sale and otherwise, to John McCaleb, the most extensive owner, Crouse, McKellip, Swope, Knox, Birnie, Rudisel, Hess, Null, Galt, and other families, until to-day there are but few acres within a radius of several miles around the town owned by parties bearing the names of those who were the proprietors sixscore years ago. Exception must be noted in the case of Sterling Galt. His estate has been the homestead of the family for one hundred and thirty-five years. In the original plan of Taneytown it was intended that a public square should be placed at the intersection of York Street and the Emmittsburg pike, now known as Bunker Hill, but the idea, an excellent one, was never carried out.

On a lot at the southeast angle of the intersection above mentioned, and directly opposite the residence of John Reindollar, stood the oldest house in the village, supposed to have been built one hundred and forty-five years ago. When Peter Heck was a boy, in 1799, it was a very old house. It was owned by Mrs. Margaret Angel, and in 1876 it was taken down.

In the latter part of the eighteenth century there stood on or near what is now the lime-kiln in Taneytown a long, low frame building, in which were manufactured, by a Mr. Sroyer, such implements as fire-shovels, tongs, hoes, nails, and guns. The venerable Mrs. Elizabeth Thompson has in her possession a heavy pair of tongs made at this primitive factory, on which is inscribed the date of manufacture, 1796. The establishment was under the supervision of the government, or at least that portion which embraced the manufacture of firearms, and was annually visited and inspected by government officials. The machinery was very crude and simple. Instead of the belts, pulleys, emery-wheels, and ordinary appurtenances of a modern factory, regulated by steam, and by means of which a gun-barrel or other iron implements can be polished in a few moments, the only contrivance then known and used was a huge grindstone turned by an old horse. With these limited facilities, however, many guns were made for the government. The factory burned down early in the present century, and was never rebuilt, the government factory having been subsequently transferred to Harper's Ferry, Va.

Taneytown, situated on the great highway of travel between the North and South, doubtless witnessed more of the conflict between Tory and Federal partisans than has been recorded or remembered. On more than one occasion the British and their allies rendezvoused at the head-waters of the Elk, in Cecil County, and sent out marauding parties, who ravaged the country and committed many outrages which time has suffered to lapse into oblivion. It would be strange, indeed, if in some of their raids they had not directed their energies against the rich country now forming Carroll County, and the road passing through Taneytown offered inducements of no ordinary nature to the baser class of army followers. The most annoying feature of these raids must have been the idiotic search made for prominent patriots. Houses were entered, the inmates insulted, and the furniture ransacked and broken to pieces. The late Mrs. Elizabeth Galt, whose death occurred some thirty-five years ago, was wont to exhibit with pride to interested visitors several bed-quilts which in "the days that tried men's souls" had been perforated by the swords or bayonets of the soldiers in search of some victim. The fires of patriotism burned very brightly in the vicinity of Taneytown, and Tories were seldom rash enough to brave the anger of the people by an open expression of their sentiments. The martial spirit pervaded the neighborhood. A company of light horse was organized here, of which the father of Mrs. Elizabeth Thompson, an old and highly esteemed resident, was a member. They were accustomed to assemble for drill at stated times in full regimentals in what is now known as "the race-ground field," a short distance east of the village. As the country had need of every soldier that could be spared from the ordinary avocations of life, it is probable that this company took the field early in the struggle and combated gallantly for the rights of the people. On one occasion during the Revolution Gen. Washington, accompanied by his wife, halted in Taneytown on his way North to join the army, and remained there overnight. The log house, since then covered in with a casement of brick, still stands where the general and his wife passed the night. It is the building on Frederick Street now owned and occupied by Ephraim Hackensmith, but at that time kept as a tavern by Adam Good. Many old citizens remember the quaint sign which hung above the door, and whose creaking of a chill winter's night, accompanied by the shrill blasts of wind, filled the souls of the small fry with awe and dread, suggesting ghosts and hobgobblins to their impressionable minds. It is related of Washington that when asked what he would have for supper he replied "mush and milk," and Mrs. Washington having some leisure moments during the evening, drew from her reticule an unfinished stocking and began to knit. After the death of Adam Good, the proprietor of the inn where the distinguished guests were entertained, his furniture was sold at auction, and Matthew Galt, the father of Sterling Galt, purchased the table upon which the very modest supper was served to Gen. Washington and his wife. It has since then passed through a number of hands in the same family, and is now the property of John McKellip.

As far as is known there are no other existing relics or vestiges of colonial times, save the almost undistinguishable remains of an old burial-ground about a mile and a half southwest of the village, in the woods, on the farm of William Brubaker. The only stone remaining upon which characters can be traced is one bearing the date 1764. Mr. Brubaker has a stone taken from there on which is inscribed the date 1701. Inasmuch as the oldest inhabitants have no knowledge of those buried there, and that there has been no mention made of the spot for several successive generations, it is inferred that the pioneers of this section, persons who penetrated the wilderness before the advent of Taney or the building of Taneytown, were laid to rest in this spot of ground, and that many friendly Indians are peacefully sleeping their last sleep in company with their white brethren. The tribes of Indians scattered through this region in early days were on the most friendly terms with the whites, and tradition tells of a friendly contest in marksmanship which took place many years before the Revolution between the whites and Indians in the vicinity of Taneytown. There were excellent marksmen on both sides, and the struggle was prolonged until all the lead was used up. An Indian offered to bring them within an hour an abundance of lead if they would provide a conveyance. He was furnished with a fleet horse, and the hour had scarcely expired when he returned, bringing with him a huge lump of crude lead. Where he got it has always been a mystery. At the time efforts were made to induce the Indians to reveal the whereabouts of this lead-mine, but the red men were too wary for the whites, and no expedient could draw from them a disclosure of their secret. This vein of lead is popularly supposed to lie somewhere near Monocacy Creek, but repeated attempts have been made to discover it without success.

During the war of 1812 a company of volunteers was organized in Taneytown, and commanded by Capt. Knox and Lieut. Galt, and forty men responded to the call of the United States government during the war between the North and South, some of whom laid down their lives in defense of the Union.

In 1836 an act was passed by the General Assembly of Maryland incorporating the inhabitants of Taneytown, and prescribing the following metes and bounds for the municipality: Beginning at the southwest corner of lot number one, at the public square of the town; thence in a straight line to a stone planted at the fork of the road leading from Taneytown to Westminster and Uniontown; thence a straight line to a branch where it crosses the main road leading from Taneytown to Fredericktown, at Ludwick Rudisel's tan-yard, and down the bed of said branch to its intersection with Spark's Run; thence in a straight line to Piney Run, where said run crosses the main road leading from Taneytown to Gettysburg; thence by a straight line to a spring run, where said run crosses the main road leading from Taneytown to Littlestown, where said run passes into John McKaleb's meadow; thence in a straight line to a stone planted at the fork of the roads leading from Taneytown to Westminster and Uniontown; thence in a straight line to the place of beginning. And that the taxable limits of the said town shall be as follows: including all that part of the town now improved, or which the citizens may at any time hereafter improve.

In 1838 another act of Assembly was passed supplementary to the above, and changing somewhat the boundaries of the town, but as both of the acts were allowed to expire by limitation it is not necessary to give the latter here. The village is accredited by the census of 1880 with a population of five hundred and nineteen.

The Reformed Church was among the first places of worship established in Taneytown. There are no records preserved of a date prior to 1770. In that year Rev. W. Faber accepted the pastorate, and remained in charge of the church until 1785. The next pastor was old Mr. Nicodemus, who was deaf as a post. He ministered to the spiritual wants of the congregation between 1790 and 1800. His successor was Rev. W. Rabauser, a young man who remained but a short time. He was followed by Rev. W. Runkle, who came from Germantown, Pa., and is reputed to have been an excellent preacher. He did not stay longer than one year. The congregation at that time numbered about six hundred members. Father Greeves succeeded Mr. Runkle. He remained several years, and was then called to Woodstock, Va. Jacob Helfenstein succeeded him, and was noted for his zeal and anxious-bench system. Rev. W. Aurand followed, and created some difficulty about his salary, which is still remembered in the neighborhood. Father Greeves was recalled, and remained in charge of the congregation until his death, leaving a good name behind him. The church was now vacant for some time. Rev. N. Habbert, of the Presbyterian denomination, was subsequently called, and promised to council himself with the German Reformed Church, but never did. At this time Rev. W. Leidy officiated, and preached in the German language. He is said to have been very eccentric. During this period the congregation thinned out considerably. After the departure of Mr. Leidy the charge was vacant until Rev. W. Heiner settled in Emmittsburg and took the church under his pastoral charge. In 1838, Rev. Daniel Felte took charge of the congregation, and served until June, 1841. He was followed by Rev. J. G. Wolf, who retired from the charge June 1, 1850, and was succeeded by Rev. Charles M. Jameson in February, 1851. Mr. Jameson remained only a year, when Rev. John G. Fritchey was called. He entered upon his duties April 1, 1852, and was installed pastor of the charge June 7, 1852, by a committee consisting of the following divines: William F. Colliflower, M. Shuford, and George Hughenbaugh. Rev. W. F. Colliflower preached the installation sermon. At a meeting in June, 1854, the number of elders was increased to four.

At a joint consistorial meeting, held at Mount Union church on Nov. 28, 1864, Rev. John G. Fritchey tendered his resignation, which after some consideration was accepted with a great deal of reluctance. A call was then extended to the Rev. N. E. Gibbs, of St. Clairsville, Bedford Co., Pa., who accepted the same, and entered upon the pastoral work in May, 1865. After two years he resigned the charge to accept a call to Mechanicstown. In September, 1873, Rev. P. D. Long, of Navarre, Ohio, was called to the charge by a unanimous vote of the congregation. He took charge of the church Nov. 14, 1873, and was installed March 25, 1874.

This congregation worshiped in the "Old Yellow" Union church until 1822. On Sept. 6, 1821, the corner-stone of their present edifice was laid, the sermon and services being delivered by Rev. J. B. Winebrenner. The estimated cost of their church was about three thousand five hundred dollars, the members numbering about two hundred at that time. The church has since been remodeled and repaired, and now presents a handsome appearance. Their parsonage, which is occupied by the present pastor, was built in 1848. The congregation numbers about two hundred members, and the officers are David Buffington, Wm. Hough, Joshua Houtz, Abraham Shriner, elders; Thomas Shriner, Jonas Harner, James Shriner, Michael N. Fringer, deacons; Abraham Hess, Wm. Fisher, Americus Shoemaker, and Toba Fringer, trustees.

Among the persons buried in the German Reformed Cemetery are the following:

Elizabeth Blair, died Nov. 30, 1831, aged 14 years.

John Shriner, born March 18, 1796, died July 24, 1874; and Susanna, his wife, March 12, 1848, aged 40 years.

Rachel Newcomer, wife of Samuel, died Jan. 29, 1849, aged 38 years, 10 months, 2 days.

Lydia, daughter of J. Shriner, born Dec. 26, 1837, died July 6, 1865.

Sarah Clabaugh, aged 64.

Jacob Clabaugh, aged 48.

John T., son of J. Hann, died Nov. 6, 1830, aged 2.

Henry Hann, died Sept. 12, 1812, aged 71.

Elizabeth Hann, died June 10, 1821, aged 71.

John Hann, died June 10, 1830, aged 34.

William Hann, son of J. Hann, died Oct. 3, 1835, aged 20.

Namary A. Lindin, died Sept. 11, 1787, aged 27.

A. Bigal Lind, died June 23, 1819, aged 29.

Nicholas Lind, died Feb. 21, 1823, aged 73 years, 3 months, 4 days.

Harmon Hersh, died November, 1818, aged 75.

Susan E. Baemer, born January, 1731, died September, 1804.

Philip Baemer, born 1729, died 1806.

Elizabeth Baemer, born Sept. 2, 1779, died Nov. 1, 1805.

Elizabeth Baemer, born Oct. 26, 1806, died Dec. 20, 1806.

Catharine, wife of Jacob Hape, died Sept. 29, 1838.

George Koons, born Jan. 21, 1790, died March 12, 1815.

Matthias Hann, died Feb. 17, 1831, aged 92 years, 9 months.

Mary Hann, died March 29, 1829, aged 72 years.

Elizabeth Koons, died April 19, 1830, aged 35.

John Fuss, died Feb. 4, 1826, aged 29 years, 2 months, 22 days.

Daniel Fuss, died July 29, 1834, aged 47 years, 2 months, 9 days.

John Fuss, born May 20, 1754, died Jan. 25, 1836.

John Crabb, died Feb. 11, 1829, aged 62.

Mary A. Fuss, died June 14, 1831, aged 38 years, 9 months, 12 days.

Catharine Fuss, died Sept. 20, 1849, aged 62 years, 5 months, 12 days.

Mary, wife of John Fuss, died May 27, 1840, aged 80 years.

Elizabeth, consort of J. H. Hays, died Jan. 4, 1846, aged 30.

James Slick, died Dec. 22, 1844, aged 33 years, 16 days.

Nicholas Fringer, born Aug. 27, 1751, died July 12, 1840.

Margaret Fringer, died Aug. 12, 1850, aged 86.

George Fringer, died Oct. 20, 1846, aged 43 years, 10 months, 20 days.

Wilhelm Slick, died March 20, 1804, aged 40 years.

Rebecca Homer, died 1806.

W. Hiner, died April 8, 1801, aged 32.

Mary Hiner, died Dec. 15, 1808, aged 64.

Herbert Hiner, died Oct. 16, 1806, aged 65.

Henry Koontz, of John, died July 30, 1825, aged 50 years, 6 months, 8 days; and Margaret, his wife, Jan. 27, 1835, aged 52 years, 7 months.

Peter Shriner, born Oct. 25, 1767, died Aug. 5, 1861.

Mary Shriner, born Aug. 6, 1773, died March 17, 1814.

Cot Munshower, born March, 1737, died in 1792.

Nicholas Munshower, born 1743, died Oct. 1, 1814.

Conrad Orndorff, born Sept. 16, 1722, died Nov. 26, 1795.

Mary B. Shriner, born Aug. 9, 1770, died Sept. 1, 1825.

Henry Shriner, born Feb. 15, 1763, died April 11, 1835.

William Otto, died Dec. 26, 1806, aged 64 years, 2 months.

E. Burke, 1866.

John Kehn, died March 9, 1868, aged 80 years, 6 months, 27 days.

Louis Reindollar, died Jan. 10, 1848, aged 67 years, 8 months.

Henry Reindollar, died July 7, 1830, aged 51 years.

Rebecca Starr, died May 8, 1831, aged 21 years, 3 months, 1 day.

Elizabeth McKellip, wife of James, and daughter of H. Reindollar, Sept. 2, 1851, aged 24.

James Reindollar, died April 8, 1825, aged 22.

John Kraus, born 1737, died 1777.

Joseph Crouse, died May 1, 1850, aged 52 years, 11 months; Elizabeth, his wife, died Oct. 26, 1850, aged 52 years, 2 months.

George Krabbs, died March 27, 1810, aged 66.

John Six, died May 15, 1869, aged 79 years, 9 days; and Sarah A., his wife, born March 11, 1809, died March 26, 1874.

Catharine Heagy, died March 8, 1852, aged 42 years, 6 months, 7 days.

Samuel Heagy, died Oct. 15, 1837, aged 36 years, 9 months, 6 days.

George Keefer, died Jan. 25, 1831, aged 55 years, 4 months, 26 days.

Joseph Shaner, died Aug. 24, 1880, aged 79.

David Fleagle, died Jan. 4, 1865, aged 79 years, 7 months, 18 days.

Margaret, his wife, died Sept. 12, 1844, aged 48 years, 5 months, 22 days.

Benjamin Koons, died May 14, 1851, aged 44 years, 1 month, 10 days.

Polly Frock, born Oct. 9, 1817, died March 15, 1835.

Philip Frock, born June 14, 1813, died April 10, 1863.

Daniel Frock, born June 30, 1777, died May 30, 1857.

Elizabeth, his wife, born Feb. 9, 1779, died May 22, 1857.

John Frock, born Dec. 18, 1801, died May 14, 1858; and Mary, his wife, Aug. 5, 1875, aged 68 years.

Ann, wife of J. Shaner, born Oct. 25, 1805, died March 20, 1874.

Abraham Haugh, died Oct. 17, 1835, aged 18 years, 5 months, 18 days.

Paul Haugh, Jr., died June 15, 1819, aged 1 year.

Josiah Haugh, died March 13, 1829, aged 18.

Susannah, consort of John Crapster, born July 1, 1766, died June 23, 1855.

Walter O'Nea, died June 27, 1827, aged 39 years, 6 months.

Margaret Wilt, died Nov. 23, 1869, aged 58 years, 6 months, 25 days.

John Weant, died Sept. 11, 1858, aged 81 years.

Catharine, his wife, died Aug. 26, 1853, aged 71 years.

Jacob Weant, died July 25, 1850, aged 44 years.

Peter Orndorff, died Jan. 16, 1847, aged 58 years, 5 months, 14 days; and Elizabeth, his wife, died Nov. 20, 1851, aged 69 years, 8 months, 20 days.

Henry Kiser, died June 30, 1850, aged 47 years, 19 days.

Phœbe, his wife, died Oct. 27, 1870, aged 65 years, 8 months, 11 days.

Mary Heiner, born May 28, 1793, died May 17, 1837.

John Cover, born 1798, died 1864; and Susan, his wife, Oct. 3, 1876, aged 78.

Peter Ridinger, born Oct. 28, 1793, died May 11, 1842.

Henry Keefer, died Aug. 30, 1848, aged 35 years, 8 months, 28 days.

Christiana Koons, died June 23, 1844, aged 33 years, 4 months, 23 days.

Jacob Koons, died May 22, 1879, aged 68 years, 5 months, 21 days; and Elizabeth, his wife, March 28, 1861, aged 47 years, 4 months.

Catharine, wife of Jacob Koons, Sr., died Feb. 15, 1846, aged 69 years, 11 months, 19 days.

Jacob Koons, Sr., died Dec. 31, 1845, aged 68 years, 1 month, 28 days.

Margaret, wife of Jacob Koons, Jr., died June 8, 1848, aged 39.

Thomas Keefer, born Jan. 8, 1797, died aged 53 years, 4 months, 29 days.

Ephraiam Koons, died Oct. 14, 1856, aged 42 years.

Rev. John Lantz, pastor of the German Reformed Church, died Jan. 26, 1873, aged 62.

Daniel Sell, died Nov. 19, 1874, aged 90 years, 10 months, 10 days.

Mary, his wife, died Feb. 28, 1874, aged 85 years, 20 days.

Samuel Longwell, Sr., died Aug. 24, 1854, aged 86 years, 6 months, 15 days; and Margaret, his wife, Jan. 4, 1845, aged 68 years, 3 months.

Joseph Bargar, Sr., died June 17, 1842, aged 65.

Robert Arthur, died Feb. 23, 1869, aged 88.

Agnes Arthur, died March 11, 1846, aged 64.

Paul Haugh, Sr., died March 5, 1847, aged 67 years, 1 month, 16 days.

Elizabeth Rech, died Dec. 25, 1845, aged 55 years, 6 months, 17 days.

Abraham Hiteshew, born March 28, 1789, died Aug. 1, 1873.

Catharine, his wife, died April 3, 1858, aged 69.

Henry Koons, born Jan. 18, 1789, died Dec. 25, 1853.

Emily Koons, died April 2, 1867, aged 39 years, 11 months, 18 days.

Jacob Keefer, born March 28, 1780, died Sept. 28, 1855.

Catharine Keefer, died March 29, 1859, aged 68 years, 6 months, 15 days.

Isaac Newcomer, died April 10, 1870, aged 55 years, 5 months, 23 days.

Jacob Newcomer, died Jan. 5, 1869, aged 64 years, 8 months, 5 days.

George Crabbs, Sr., died Jan. 6, 1859, aged 65 years, 10 months, 16 days.

Hugh Thomson, died Dec. 18, 1852, aged 68.

Nicholas Snider, born May 9, 1786, died June 11, 1856.

Margaret, his wife, died July 20, 1865, aged 86 years.

Ann, wife of George Shriner, died July 16, 1853, aged 72 years.

Elizabeth, wife of John Slogenhaupt, died March 18, 1865, aged 48 years, 2 months, 23 days.

Elijah Fleagle, died March 19, 1871, aged 50 years, 4 months, 20 days.

Mary A., his second wife, died Oct. 17, 1854, aged 27 years, 1 month, 11 days.

Francis Slick, died Feb. 8, 1857, aged 63.

Magdalena Slick, born Nov. 26, 1790, died April 6, 1853.

John Fleagle, died Dec. 24, 1873, aged 93 years, 2 months, 15 days.

Susanna Fleagle, died April 23, 1851, aged 76 years, 2 months, 11 days.

Samuel Newcomer, died July 4, 1848, aged 75 years, 7 months, 1 day.

Barbara Newcomer, died March 6, 1853, aged 75 years.

John Henry, son of J. and B. Ocker, born Feb. 10, 1843, died April 30, 1862, "of typhoid fever, whilst a volunteer in the defense of his country's honor."

Jacob, son of J. and B. Ocker, "killed on Maryland Heights by an explosion, June 30, 1863," aged 21 years, 10 months, 28 days. "He was beloved by his officers and companions, and was a faithful and obedient son to a widowed mother."

Mary Wilson, died May 16, 1864, aged 78.

Michael Ott, born Oct. 16, 1793, died May 20, 1872.

Mary, his wife, born Dec. 12, 1796, died Oct. 10, 1871.

Isabella G. Reaver, died March 11, 1880, aged 45 years, 7 months.

Lewis Maus, born Nov. 8, 1777, died Sept. 26, 1826.

"D. M.," died 1817.

Daniel Hawn, born Sept. 9, 1802, died Jan. 30, 1877; Magdalena, his wife, born Oct. 9, 1801, died March 25, 1877.

Wm. Shaner, born Feb. 2, 1798, died June 16, 1850; Rosanna Shaner, died Feb. 12, 1868, aged 67 years, 10 months, 18 days.

Henry Hiner, born Jan. 28, 1836, died Oct. 23, 1873.

Eleanor Fluegal, died March 31, 1839, aged 43 years, 2 months, 13 days. Sarah, wife of John Stockslayer, born July 22, 1795, died June 13, 1865.

Mary Hawn, died Dec. 19, 1872, at an old age.

Henry Hawn, born Dec. 10, 1781, died Jan. 25, 1867; Anna M., his wife, died Aug. 9, 1859, aged 64 years, 7 months, 6 days.

Matthias Hawn, born Feb. 20, 1794, died April 1, 1858.

Jacob Hawn, born Nov. 6, 1785, died May 25, 1878.

Elizabeth, wife of Samuel Hough, died March 26, 1877, aged 50 years, 9 months, 27 days.

Reuben Stonesifer, died Dec. 1, 1876, aged 52 years, 8 months, 16 days.

Elizabeth Tracy, died Aug. 7, 1878, aged 90.

John Angel, died April 16, 1872, aged 72 years, 5 months, 9 days.

Magdalena Angel, died Feb. 18, 1880, aged 42 years, 3 months, 21 days.

Elizabeth Angel, wife of John A., Sr., died Jan. 18, 1864, aged 64 years, 7 months, 22 days.

Elizabeth, wife of Samuel Hough, died March 26, 1877, aged 50 years, 9 months, 27 days.

Harvey T., son of S. and M. Null, who fell at Loudon Heights, Jan. 10, 1864, aged 21 years, 4 months, 25 days.

"Sweet be the slumbers of him who fell for his country fighting for liberty and law."

Jacob Shriner, born Jan. 5, 1800, died April 13, 1874; Catharine, his wife, died Feb. 6, 1868, aged 63 years, 9 mos., 23 days.

Mary Ann Stultz, died Aug. 4, 1879, aged 55 years, 4 months, 19 days.

Ann Stultz, born Jan. 31, 1804, died Jan. 28, 1875.

Samuel F. Stultz, born Sept. 20, 1835, died Aug. 10, 1870.

Maria Smith, died Feb. 13, 1871, aged 37 years.

Eli Sowers, born Jan. 6, 1805, died Nov. 3, 1878; Elizabeth, his wife, and daughter of Peter Shriner, died Sept. 16, 1838, aged 64 years, 8 months, 22 days.

Wm. Newcomer, died Jan. 10, 1872, aged 40.

Henry Peters, died Dec. 4, 1872, aged 63 years, 1 month, 28 days.

Samuel Newcomer, born Oct. 30, 1807, died April 19, 1877; Frances, his wife, born July 16, 1807, died Feb. 14, 1878.

Philip Hann, born Oct. 22, 1777, died Dec. 31, 1863; Elizabeth, his wife, died March 10, 1860, aged 78 years, 10 days.

Philip W. Hann, died April 8, 1867, aged 67 years; Susannah, his wife, died March 29, 1864, aged 78 years.

Frederick Dotterea, died Aug. 25, 1854, aged 66 years, 1 month, 5 days.

Lydia, wife of John Shoemaker, born Aug. 14, 1798, died Feb. 15, 1867.

Esther Shoemaker, died Nov. 20, 1861, aged 86 years, 1 month, 15 days.

Joseph Shoemaker, died March 28, 1863, aged 57 years, 2 months, 1 day.

John Davidson, born May 12, 1795, died Dec. 23, 1873; Margaret, his wife, born July 11, 1793, died March 30, 1872.

Maria E., wife of George Baird, died Nov. 3, 1867, aged 72 years, 12 days.

Frederick Crabbs, died Oct. 3, 1861, aged 62 years, 4 months, 23 days; Matilda, his wife, died Jan. 13, 1878, aged 79 years, 7 months, 8 days.

George W. McConkey, born Sept. 20, 1799, died June 30, 1880; Eliza, his wife, died Dec. 27, 1876, aged 71.

Jesse Heck, born March 3, 1807, died Sept. 4, 1866.

James Crouse, died March 27, 1868, aged 68.

Elizabeth Crouse, died Feb. 14, 1877, aged 68.

Barbara, wife of George Crise, died Nov. 5, 1873, aged 82 years, 4 months, 12 days.

Sarah, wife of James Heck, died March 28, 1872, aged 63 years, 3 months, 3 days.

Susanna, wife of Philip Shriner, died Aug. 10, 1863, aged 83 years, 10 months, 27 days.

John Koons, died March 6, 1869, aged 51 years, 11 months, 15 days.

John Kuhns, died May 12, 1875, aged 58 years, 7 months, 2 days; Lovey, his wife, died Feb. 8, 1868, aged 39 years, 11 months, 22 days.

Michael Fringer, died July 12, 1879, aged 72 years, 6 months, 16 days.

Nicholas Fringer, born Dec. 20, 1798, died Sept. 2, 1869.

Israel Hiteshue, born Dec. 1, 1803, died Sept. 13, 1856.

Gideon Hiteshue, died April 9, 1865, aged 71 years; Mary Ann, his wife, died June 26, 1879, aged 76 years, 8 months, 19 days.

Margaret Arthur, died July 22, 1870, aged 50 years, 4 months, 10 days.

Adam Tobias Hokensmith, died Oct. 27, 1865, aged 35 years, 7 months, 11 days.

George Crabbs, died Jan. 6, 1859, aged 65 years, 10 months, 16 days.

John Shoemaker, born March 11, 1822, died Feb. 2, 1878.

Catharine Buffington, aged 44 years, 5 months, 11 days.

John M. Cover, died Jan. 9, 1877, aged 46 years, 3 months, 14 days.

J. B. Harmish, died Feb. 23, 1879, aged 49 years, 6 months, 26 days.

Lutheran Church.—This congregation was organized about the year 1780. They worshiped in the "Old Yellow" church, a structure weather-boarded and painted yellow, which was situated on the graveyard lot. No regular pastor was employed, but Dr. Melsheimer and Dr. Runkel, from Gettysburg, delivered sermons to the congregation occasionally in German. About the year 1800 the congregation removed to the church they now occupy. Rev. John Grubb was the regular pastor in 1815 and for some time before, and it was he that first introduced English preaching. About the year 1817 he nearly made a failure, owing to his not being familiar with the language. He would open his sermon in English, and in his efforts to convey an idea in that language would become confused and finish his expression in German. Rev. John N. Hoffman succeeded Mr. Grubb, and was the first regular English pastor. He continued in this charge for some years, and was followed by Rev. Ezra Keller, who upon resigning his position after some years' services was appointed a professor of the Wurtemburg College, Springfield, Ohio. Rev. Solomon Sentmen was their next pastor, and continued for seventeen years and a half to attend to the duties of the church. He was succeeded by Rev. Levi T. Williams, who occupied the pulpit about seven years. Rev. Bertgresser followed him, and was succeeded by Rev. Williams, whose failing health compelled his resignation, and Rev. W. H. Luckenbach was his successor. In 1878 their present pastor, Samuel G. Finckel, was called to the church. The salary of the pastors was always paid by voluntary subscriptions up to the new organization of the congregation and the remodeling of the church, since when the salary has been raised by assessment, each member paying according to his wealth or worth. The present officers are Samuel Shriner, Jacob Sherratts, elders; Charles Hess, Daniel Null, Jacob Mehring, William Clutz, deacons; Dr. George T. Motter, John Reindollar, David Mehring, John Renner, Elijah Currans, Dr. Samuel Swope, trustees. The congregation numbers between four and five hundred members, and possesses a fine and substantial parsonage.

The following names of persons buried in the Lutheran Cemetery are given:

Jacob Snider, born Oct. 15, 1796, died Aug. 29, 1868; Hester, his wife, died Nov. 9, 1871, aged 60 years, 6 months, 22 days.

George Snider, died Aug. 29, 1871, aged 74 years, 7 months, 14 days.

Levi Snider, died May 24, 1874, aged 39 years, 6 months, 19 days.

Sarah, wife of J. Angell, died Feb. 23, 1871, aged 62 years, 1 month, 25 days.

Elizabeth Norris, born Aug. 20, 1820, died July 1, 1870.

Jacob Clutts, died Sept. 4, 1870, aged 66 years, 7 months, 12 days; Rosanna, his wife, died Dec. 21, 1870, aged 65 years, 8 months, 13 days.

Wm. Reaver, died March 31, 1871, aged 58 years, 11 months, 12 days.

Mary A., wife of Daniel Null, died Feb. 1, 1877, aged 43 years, 4 months, 25 days.

David Kephart, died Jan. 22, 1874, aged 77 years, 9 months, 27 days.

Susan, his wife, died April 15, 1872, aged 70 years, 8 months.

Samuel Crouse, died May 31, 1871, aged 61 years, 3 months, 12 days.

George Reifsnider, born April 22, 1803, died May 14, 1869; Catharine, his wife, born Sept. 21, 1807, died Dec. 1, 1876.

Daniel H. Rudolph, born Oct. 5, 1821, died Jan. 9, 1871.

Amelia Jean, wife of Elijah Currens, died April 20, 1880, aged 71 years, 9 months, 7 days.

Samuel R. Hess, born March 17, 1823, died Sept. 12, 1871.

John Hess, born Dec. 21, 1802, died March 22, 1875; Barbara, consort of John Hess, born Aug. 30, 1803, died April 3, 1877.

John Baumgardner, born Dec. 6, 1797, died Feb. 15, 1874.

Dr. John Swope, died Sept. 3, 1871, aged 74 years, 1 month.

Daniel H. Swope, died April 19, 1873, aged 64 years, 7 months.

Catharine, wife of John Renner, died Jan. 14, 1879, aged 59 years, 10 months, 21 days.

Andrew Harner, born Jan. 2, 1788, died March 12, 1873; Sarah, his wife, born May, 1801, died Oct. 1, 1872.

Jacob Sheets, died Jan. 27, 1826, aged 65 years, 5 months, 26 days. "A soldier of the war of 1776. Enlisted under Washington as he passed through Taneytown."

Hannah Sheets, died May 5, 1852, aged 85 years, 4 months, 11 days.

Jacob Sheets, died Nov. 11, 1866, aged 76 years, 4 months, 6 days.

Elizabeth, wife of Wm. Koons, died June 5, 1867, aged 74 years, 3 months, 15 days.

Mary Null, died Jan. 7, 1812, aged 71.

Regina Noel, born 1745, died Dec. 5, 1812.

Valentine Null, died Nov. 21, 1815, aged 79.

Michael Null, died Feb. 15, 1817, aged 70; Anna Maria, his wife, died May 25, 1818, aged 80.

Michael Null, born Nov. 5, 1770, died Dec. 11, 1850.

Elizabeth Null, born May 7, 1778, died Oct. 19, 1856.

Abraham Null, born Jan. 12, 1799, died April 26, 1851; Mary, his wife, died April 6, 1849, aged 49.

Ulrich Rieber, aged 79.

Margaret Wolf, born Aug. 4, 1799, died Dec. 5, 1821.

Elizabeth Kephart, died June 20, 1814, aged 80 years, 4 months, 12 days.

David Kephart, born Nov. 17, 1729, died June 5, 1792.

Margaret Kephart, died Oct. 15, 1852, aged 73.

David Kephart, died Nov. 24, 1836, aged 74.

Joseph Davidson, died Aug. 15, 1801, aged 30 years, 6 months.

Phinehas Davidson, died March 16, 1798, aged 72 years, 11 months, 20 days.

Susan Davidson, died June 12, 1845, aged 64 years, 3 months.

James Matthews, died Jan. 4, 1872, aged 74.

Adam Black, died Dec. 18, 1818, aged 74 years, 6 months.

Margaret Black, born in 1752, died in 1773.

John, son of Lawrence and Hannah Bowers, died Oct. 29, 1816, aged 11 days.

Frederick Black, died Nov. 3, 1826, aged 85.

Rebecca Black, daughter of Frederick Black, "who came into this world in the year of our Lord 1785, the 29th day of January, at 9 o'clock in the morning," and wife of George Houk, died Aug. 12, 1834, aged 49 years, 6 months, 12 days.

Elizabeth Bernhart, 1791.

Philip Rever, died Nov. 22, 1843, aged 78.

Gritzena Rever, died August, 1841, aged 81.

Elizabeth, wife of John B. Grobp, died April 15, 1835, aged 69.

Jacob Buffington, born Aug. 10, 1756, died Aug. 7, 1831; Mary Magdalena, his wife, died Dec. 15, 1840, aged 81 years, 16 days.

Peter Schener, died Dec. 13, 1790, aged 52.

Joshua Delaplane, died Oct. 14, 1830, aged 42.

Hannah Delaplane, died Aug. 4, 1879, aged 93 years, 6 months, 12 days.

Wm. Cover, born July 1, 1814, died Oct. 4, 1824.

Wm. Jones, born Aug. 20, 1796, died Jan. 12, 1818.

Wm. Jones, died Sept. 25, 1824, aged 76.

James Ickes, died March 4, 1852, aged 57 years, 2 months, 24 days.

M. M. Hess, died April 26, 1841.

H. A. Hess, died April, 1833.

Mary Hess, born May 1, 1797, died March 5, 1850.

Samuel Hess, born Nov. 11, 1796, died Dec. 24, 1873.

George Ott, died July 23, 1834, aged 77.

John Baumgardner, born Nov. 10, 1781, died Sept. 6, 1828.

Margaret Ott, consort of George, born Sept. 8, 1764, died Sept. 5, 1828. Her maiden name was Margaret Sluthur.

Nicholas Ott, died Dec. 16, 1833, aged 25 years, 4 months, 21 days.

Abraham Herner, born 1803, died 1825.

Susan Neher, born 1802, died ——.

Amanda E. Ott, died April 7, 1854, aged 18.

Mary E., wife of Wm. L. Crapster, died April 17, 1848, aged 45 years, 11 months, 7 days; and five of her children, from one to ten years of age.

Catharine Swope, daughter of H. and E., died Nov. 16, 1805, aged 1 year, 5 days.

Jesse Swope, son of the same, died Sept. 21, 1805, aged 4 years, 6 months, 21 days.

Henry Swope, born April 5, 1767, died Feb. 13, 1842; Elizabeth, his consort, died June 13, 1843, aged 68 years, 8 months, 18 days.

Jacob Sheetz, died Oct. 27, 1806, aged 81.

Catharine Sheetz, died May 5, 1803, aged 75 years, 4 months, 11 days.

Henry Clutz, died Sept. 10, 1831, aged 67 years, 14 days.

Elizabeth Clutz, born March 12, 1762, died Oct. 6, 1821.

John D. Miller, son of George and Eliza Miller, "who fell in the defense of his country near Petersburg, Va., June 22, 1864," aged 24 years, 2 months, 16 days.

Susanna Cover, born Nov. 26, 1775, died Feb. 7, 1824.

Jacob Cover, died Sept. 29, 1873, aged 64 years, 9 months.

Philip Rudisel, born March 20, 1785, died Nov. 21, 1810.

Elizabeth Koberger, born 1763, July 23d, died Aug. 21, 1801.

Lewis Rudisil, born Feb. 27, 1783, died Aug. 11, 1805.

G. Rudisil, born March 15, 1770, died March 13, 1795.

Maria Rudisil, born Feb. 15, 1765, died April 23, 1784.

Tobias Rudisil, born April 4, 1736, died March 26, 1816.

T. Louis Rudisil, born April 7, 1743, died December, 1821.

Magdalena Weiwell, died Aug. 25, 1796, aged 25 years, 5 months, and 26 days.

Michael Sawyer, died Nov. 25, 1825, aged 63.

Ann Mary, his wife, died Aug. 8, 1829, aged 65 years, 1 month, and 16 days.

John Foire, died Dec. 13, 1827, aged 42 years, 11 months, and 13 days.

Anna B., his wife, died May 25, 1867, aged 75 years, 7 months, and 27 days.

Peter Slyder, born July 25, 1759, died May 25, 1840. On his left are his two wives, Mary, born Sept. 8, 1763, and died Jan. 11, 1796; Elizabeth, born April 3, 1780, died Sept. 22, 1830.

Jacob Cornell, died July 9, 1863, aged 66 years, 11 months, and 10 days.

Mary Cornell, died Nov. 27, 1815, aged 59 years, 8 months, and 6 days.

Conrad Shorb, died Oct. 16, 1863, aged 77.

John Harman, born Sept. 8, 1792, died Aug. 7, 1870.

Hezekiah Harman, born Feb. 1, 1831, died Aug. 15, 1866.

Elizabeth, wife of John Good, died Sept. 29, 1865, aged 56 years, 1 month, and 6 days.

John Good, born Feb. 28, 1802, died May 11, 1879.

Samuel Naill, died Oct. 19, 1869, aged 83.

Elizabeth Naill, died Jan. 27, 1878, aged 76.

Elizabeth Naill, wife of Samuel, died Aug. 28, 1826, aged 34 years, 9 months, and 28 days.

Anna Naill, wife of Jacob Mering, born Feb. 8, 1805, died February, 1824.

Mary Naill, born Feb. 28, 1778, died Nov. 17, 1815.

Dr. Wm. B. Hibberd, died March 14, 1839, aged 61; Ann, his first wife, died Feb. 18, 1835, aged 44.

Christian Naill, born Jan. 5, 1747, died June 15, 1815.

William Naill, died April 6, 1846, aged 67 years, 9 months, and 25 days. Elizabeth, his wife, died Feb. 26, 1853, aged 73.

William Naill, died June 28, 1868, aged 54 years, 9 months, and 16 days. Mary Ann, his wife, died July 11, 1869, aged 54 years, 3 months, and 20 days.

John Raitt, died Feb. 14, 1833, aged 31.

Basil Raitt, died July 10, 1839, aged 32 years and 7 months.

John Rudisel, born Aug. 25, 1772, died March 25, 1840.

Barbary Shunk, born 1757, died 1826.

Peter Shunk, died June 19, 1834, aged 87 years, 10 months, and 14 days.

Joseph Shunk, died May 28, 1840, aged 60 years, 3 months, and 5 days; Aberrilla Shunk, his wife, died June 6, 1852, aged 67.

Elizabeth S. Sawyer, died Sept. 29, 1834, aged 45 years, 7 months, and 29 days.

Abram Buffington, died Aug. 5, 1872, aged 85 years, 7 months, and 28 days; Anna, his wife, died April 19, 1854, aged 61 years, 6 months, and 21 days.

Hammond Raitt, died Feb. 1, 1858, aged 82.

Harriet Raitt, died Jan. 22, 1852, aged 52.

Eleanor, consort of Hammond Raitt, died June 9, 1847, aged 69.

Jacob Zumbrum, died Sept. 13, 1868, aged 74 years and 2 months; Margaret, his wife, died Jan. 16, 1852, aged 57 years and 8 months.

David Harper, died Feb. 28, 1844, aged 43 years, 5 months, and 15 days.

Rachel, wife of Tobias Haines, died Feb. 1, 1852, aged 40 years, 1 month, and 17 days.

John K. Hilterbrick, born Sept. 27, 1796, died Nov. 18, 1869.

Anna M. Slyder, born Dec. 21, 1800, died April 29, 1877.

Sarah Reaver, died March 29, 1867, aged 66 years, 11 months, and 29 days.

Maria Apolonia Hoeffner, born May 8, 1776, died May 2, 1841.

Magdalena Mock, died Feb. 24, 1852, aged 66 years, 2 months, and 8 days.

Daniel Harman, Sr., died Aug. 10, 1864, aged 64 years, 5 months, and 15 days.

Thomas Mathias Greaves, born Aug. 22, 1823, died Feb. 7, 1853.

Sophia Kregelo, died Aug. 30, 1872, aged 81 years, 11 months, and 15 days.

Jacob Kregelo, born Oct. 28, 1865, aged 80 years, 6 months, and 26 days.

Rev. J. M. Kregelo, died Nov. 11, 1854, aged 27.

Isaac McGee, born Dec. 24, 1795, died Jan. 9, 1881.

Dorothy McGee, died Jan. 2, 1836, aged 34 years, 2 months, and 6 days.

John Kregelo, Sr., died Nov. 30, 1871, aged 87 years, 7 months, and 27 days.

John Kregelo, died May 29, 1837, aged 55 years, 8 months, and 5 days.

John Kregelo, died Sept. 13, 1880, aged 70 years, 9 months, and 1 day.

Margaret, wife of Isaac McGee, died Aug. 20, 1860, aged 52 years, 3 months, and 13 days.

Dorothy Harner, died May 27, 1851, aged 93.

Christian Harner, died June 24, 1840, aged 91.

Catharine, wife of Frederick Harner, died June 7, 1859, aged 73 years, 6 months, and 9 days.

Frederick Harner, died Sept. 18, 1862, aged 79 years, 9 months, and 12 days.

Samuel Harner, died May 13, 1867, aged 60 years, 2 months, and 8 days.

Susannah Null, born March 11, 1797, died Feb. 11, 1868.

Samuel Null, born Feb. 15, 1793, died Feb. 4, 1853.

Abraham Null, died Feb. 27, 1850, aged 78 years, 11 months, and 19 days.

Catharine Null, died April 3, 1860, aged 88 years, 4 months, and 19 days.

Tobias Rudisel, died Dec. 24, 1863, aged 50 years, 3 months, and 11 days. Mary J., his wife, died Jan. 21, 1873, aged 54 years, 4 months, and 17 days.

Nancy Rudisel, born Sept. 7, 1787, died Sept. 9, 1861.

Ludwick Rudisel, born Feb. 25, 1778, died June 28, 1842.

Susanna, wife of Samuel Babylon, died Dec. 6, 1861, aged 52 years, 9 months, and 21 days.

Elizabeth, consort of David Reifsnider, born July 25, 1783, died Oct. 19, 1844.

David Reifsnider, Sr., died Feb. 26, 1841, aged 66.

Joseph Reever, died Aug. 11, 1853, aged 65 years, 11 months, and 11 days; Margaret, his second wife, died January, 1852, aged 48; Mary, his first wife, died April 25, 1845, aged 49 years, 2 months, and 13 days.

Hanna Reven, died Feb. 14, 1848, aged 41 years, 2 months, and 25 days.

Amelia, wife of Henry Picking, died Oct. 23, 1865, aged 51 years, 1 month, and 3 days.

Eliza L., consort of Rev. Solomon Sentman, born Sept. 28, 1811, died Dec. 4, 1855.

George Lambert, died Oct. 25, 1875, aged 89; Elizabeth, his wife, died Oct. 4, 1859, aged 64 years, 4 months, and 16 days.

Anna M., wife of Jacob Lambert, died March 27, 1852, aged 49 years, 2 months, and 4 days.

Elizabeth N. Clabaugh, died May 25, 1852, aged 75 years, 10 months, and 25 days.

Margaret, wife of Henry Black, born May 24, 1799, died Dec. 14, 1868.

Elizabeth, wife of Henry Hess, died Oct. 13, 1860, aged 67 years, 1 month, and 19 days.

Henry Hess, born Feb. 20, 1794, died Aug. 20, 1874.

Thomas Ohler, died Dec. 8, 1843, aged 63 years.

Margaret Fair, wife of George H., died April 8, 1866, aged 52 years, 11 months, and 5 days.

Eliza, wife of John Cownover, born Jan. 26, 1812, died Dec. 16, 1871.

John Cownover, died March 24, 1851, aged 42.

Christian Naill, died July 13, 1869, aged 63 years, 8 months, and 3 days; Lydia Naill, his wife, died Aug. 14, 1868, aged 56 years, 8 months, and 3 days.

Margaret Hawk, born Oct. 12, 1802, died May 6, 1879.

George Hawk, born Oct. 17, 1776, died Dec. 29, 1855.

Sophia, wife of Nicholas Heck, born April 27, 1818, died May 7, 1868.

Mary A. Bower, died Dec. 14, 1880, aged 70 years, 7 months, 10 days.

John Shoemaker, born Aug. 19, 1803, died June 18, 1864.

Lawrence Bower, died Nov. 30, 1842, aged 69 years, 9 months, 16 days.

Hannah Bower, died April 11, 1855, aged 76 years, 5 months, 8 days.

Susanna Stoner, died March 24, 1843, aged 57 years, 7 months, 24 days.

Wm. Mering, died March 16, 1856, aged 50.

Rebecca, wife of Jacob Snider, born Feb. 4, 1812, died Jan. 20, 1860.

Jacob Snider, died Jan. 30, 1850, aged 81 years, 6 months, 5 days.

Thomas Rudisel, died Jan. 18, 1880, aged 68 years, 3 months, 4 days.

Anna Rudisel, died March 22, 1874, aged 50 years, 9 days.

Anna M., wife of Thomas Rudisel, died June 7, 1857, aged 44.

William Rudisel, died Oct. 16, 1866, aged 56 years, 8 months, 10 days.

John Moring, born Dec. 4, 1795, died March 24, 1857.

Henry Baumgardner, born Dec. 11, 1810, died Nov. 16, 1880.

Jacob Null, died March 20, 1873, aged 68 years, 6 months, 16 days.

Wm. Shoemaker, born Dec. 24, 1817, died Jan. 11, 1864.

Mary A., wife of James McKellip, born Oct. 11, 1811, died Jan. 25, 1854.

Mary A., consort of Samuel Shriner, died Nov. 13, 1866, aged 49 years, 6 months, 10 days.

Michael Mentzer, born Sept. 11, 1775, died Dec. 23, 1848; Magdalena, his wife, and daughter of John and Ann Diller, born Sept. 28, 1787, died Oct. 29, 1846.

Elizabeth, wife of John D. Woods, born Nov. 1, 1781, died Dec. 18, 1860.

John D. Woods, born Dec. 23, 1786, died Jan. 29, 1869.

Daniel Shunk, born Jan. 15, 1788, died April 5, 1860.

Euphemia Shunk, died Nov. 31, 1861, aged 76 years, 6 months, 21 days.

Benjamin Shunk, died Oct. 30, 1876, aged 70 years, 8 months, 15 days; Rebecca, his wife, died Dec. 20, 1863, aged 61 years, 7 days.

John White, born Aug. 18, 1796, died March 31, 1863; Mary White, his wife, died Aug. 4, 1850, aged 57 years, 6 months, 26 days.

John Ott, died Dec. 14, 1857, aged 52 years, 2 months, 21 days; Mary, his wife, died May 10, 1856, aged 47 years, 9 months, 28 days.

Catharine Ott, died July 26, 1851, aged 64 years, 6 months, 11 days.

Elizabeth Baumgardner, died June 10, 1851, aged 66 years, 1 month, 10 days.

George Reed, born July 12, 1782, died Nov. 3, 1857. Mary, his wife, died Sept. 29, 1856, aged 73 years, 3 months, 12 days.

James Aring, born Dec. 29, 1866, aged 67 years, 9 months, 23 days.

Jacob Valentine, born May 18, 1790, died Aug. 15, 1863.

David Reifsnider, died July 20, 1858, aged 50 years, 6 months, 3 days.

Anna M. Mering, died April 29, 1867, aged 85 years, 5 months, 18 days.

Jacob Heltibridle, died March 21, 1866, aged 79 years, 6 days; Barbara, his wife, died July 21, 1863, aged 74 years.

Jacob Slagenhaupt, died 1863, aged 73.

Elizabeth Slagenhaupt, died 1844, aged 52.

Philip M. Smith, died Dec. 4, 1860, aged 43 years, 6 months, 9 days; Rebecca Smith, died Dec. 14, 1865, aged 46 years, 7 months.

Jacob Bushey, died Aug. 31, 1861, aged 75 years, 8 months, 12 days.

Mary Bushey, died Feb. 8, 1862, aged 72 years, 21 days.

Susanna, consort of David Buffington, born in 1802, died in 1859, aged 57 years, married in 1822.

Magdalena Wolf, died March 10, 1869, aged 58 years, 3 months, 10 days.

The founder of Taneytown was a Catholic, and it is reasonable to suppose there were others of the same faith living in the vicinity of the town at an early period. As far back as 1790 there are records of mass having been said at private dwellings by Fathers Frambaugh, Pellentz, Brosuis, and Cefremont. In 1804, Prince Geliven visited the village, and built St. Joseph's church. Father Zocchi, an Italian priest of great learning and remarkable executive ability, was the first pastor of St. Joseph's, and remained in charge of the parish during the extraordinary period of forty-one years. He died in 1845, regretted by all who knew him, and there was no priest regularly assigned to the charge until 1851. From the latter date until 1862 the parish was under the control of Father Thomas O'Neill, who was succeeded by Father J. Gloyd, who remained in charge until Jan. 1, 1879. Father Gloyd's first assistant was Rev. Richard Haseman, from May, 1871, to January, 1873; his second, Rev. Casper Schmidt, from 1873 to 1874; and his third, Rev. John T. Dulaney, from 1874 to Jan. 1, 1879. At this date the mission was divided, Father Dulaney retaining charge of St. Joseph's, and St. Thomas', at New Windsor, while Father Gloyd took charge of St. John's, Westminster, and St. Bartholomew's, Manchester. Father Dulaney is a native of Baltimore, and was educated in that city. Though comparatively a young man he is a thorough classical scholar, and while scrupulously discharging the onerous duties of his pastorate is also a laborious student. His many engaging qualities and his unflagging zeal in the cause of religion and charity have not only endeared him to the people of his parish, but have won for him the confidence and respect of the entire community without reference to denominational lines. Taneytown was the headquarters of the mission until 1869, when the residence of Father Gloyd was changed to Westminster by Archbishop Spalding.

The following persons are buried in the Catholic cemetery:

Rev. Nicholas Zocchi, late pastor of Taneytown Catholic Church, died Dec. 17, 1845, aged 72 years.

Mary J., daughter of Dr. John Swope, died July 30, 1846, aged 43 years, 10 months.

Robert McGinnis, born Jan. 17, 1817, died Oct. 12, 1871; Catharine, his wife, born Jan. 8, 1815, died June 24, 1874.

Samuel P. Chase, born March 30, 1831, died Nov. 10, 1872.

Susan McAllister, daughter of Lewis Eliot, born Nov. 23, 1853, died Feb. 4, 1879.

Lucinda, daughter of J. and M. Orndoff, died April 22, 1877, aged 23 years, 8 months.

Anna, wife of Anthony Wivell, died June 12, 1876, aged 68 years, 10 months, 14 days.

Margaret, wife of Samuel J. Wivell, born Aug. 26, 1819, died May 22, 1872.

Joseph Hawk, born Jan. 31, 1811, died May 28, 1871.

Margaret Hawk, born Oct. 20, 1809, died September, 1875.

Honora Donnelly, died Oct. 29, 1874, aged 79.

Wilhemina, wife of Joseph Ries, born May 14, 1814, died Feb. 25, 1878.

Catherine Sebald, born in Berks County, Pa., July 11, 1786, died Dec. 27, 1827.

Joseph Wivel, born Dec. 12, 1790, died Jan. 10, 1853.

Christena Wivel, his wife, died March 23, 1848, aged 55.

George Spalding, born Oct. 4, 1792, died Aug. 9, 1854; Mary, his wife, born Aug. 10, 1797, died Feb. 22, 1875; Edward F., their son, died Feb. 16, 1878, aged 53 years, 4 months, 8 days.

Mary Diffendall, born Sept. 11, 1808, died Sept. 26, 1878.

John Diffendall, born Aug. 14, 1788, died May 4, 1876.

Andrew Kuhns, died July 8, 1874, aged 81; Rachel, his wife, died July 18, 1864, aged 64 years.

Paul Kuhns, died March 15, 1815, aged 55 years, 18 days.

Mary A. Kuhns, born March 24, 1758, died June 23, 1844.

Elizabeth Baumgardner, died June 23, 1819, aged 27 years, 11 months, 29 days.

Peter Diffendal, died March 19, 1849, aged 54 years, 19 days; Mary, his wife, died April 20, 1863, aged 67 years, 6 months, 9 days.

Samuel Diffendall, born March 14, 1781, died July 11, 1855.

Christiana Diffendall, died June 12, 1859, aged 88.

John Eline, died Jan. 30, 1846, aged 83; Catharine, his wife, died Sept. 14, 1844, aged 56 years, 5 months, 4 days.

Juliana, daughter of John Adlesperger, died Oct. 8, 1854, aged 40 years, 10 months, 13 days.

John Adlesperger, born Jan. 17, 1785, died June 22, 1859; Margaret Adlesperger, born April 30, 1784, died Aug. 16, 1867; Mary, their daughter, born March 15, 1812, died Aug. 12, 1867.

Magdalena, wife of Jacob Yingling, died September, 1855, aged 42.

John Althoff, died Jan. 13, 1873, aged 85 years, 6 months, 28 days; Mary C., his wife, died July 26, 1867, aged 86.

Daniel Rose, died Nov. 9, 1815, aged 13 years.

Peter Hamburg, died Jan. 24, 1869, aged 73 years, 2 months, 29 days; Mary, his wife, died July 26, 1870, aged 71 years, 11 months, 21 days.

Mary Hamburg, died Oct. 6, 1863, aged 31 years, 11 months, 15 days.

James Taney, died Oct. 2, 1817, aged 19.

Dorothy Taney, wife of Joseph, died April 17, 1817, aged 61.

Catherine Boyle, died April 12, 1814, aged 97 years.

Ann Boyle, died Sept. 16, 1811, aged 22 months.

Roger Joseph Boyle, died Jan. 14, 1841, aged 25.

Henry Boyle, died Feb. 14, 1855, aged 37 years.

Mary H. Boyle, died May 2, 1821, aged 41 years.

Daniel Boyle, died Dec. 5, 1830, aged 66 years.

Jane, wife of Raphael Brooke, died Nov. 19, 1818, aged 67 years.

Raphael Brooke, died July 7, 1816, aged 69 years.

Ann, wife of Francis Jamison, died Dec. 11, 1792, aged 35.

Catherine Wilson, died Dec. 20, 1815, infant.

Joseph C. Clements, died March, 1807.

Francis Elder, died Oct. 1, 1809, aged 54; Catherine, his wife, died April 12, 1834, aged 67.

Mary Mourie, born 1743, died Jan. 30, 1810.

James Clabaugh, died March 16, 1867, aged 80 years, 4 months, 16 days; Monica, his wife, born July 22, 1787, died Nov. 30, 1851.

Ann M., wife of John Classon, born Dec. 3, 1802, died Sept. 4, 1864.

Rebecca, wife of Levi Murren, died July 22, 1844, aged 23 years, 5 months, 8 days.

Caroline, wife of David S. Smith, died Jan. 3, 1857, aged 30 years, 7 months.

Barbara, wife of Joseph Gartner, died June 5, 1852, aged 27.

Mary Gardner, died March 23, 1846, aged 25 years, 15 days.

Joseph Gardner, died March 4, 1879, aged 69 years, 9 months, 24 days.

Jacob Eckenrode, died July 22, 1865, aged 81 years, 9 months; Mary, his wife, died Feb. 10, 1859, aged 71 years.

Mary Ann, consort of Christopher Storm, died Jan. 3, 1863, aged 88 years, 11 months, 13 days.

John Burk, died Dec. 6, 1839, aged 46 years; Catharine, his wife, died Sept. 7, 1819, aged 22 years.

Joseph Welty, born Aug. 8, 1810, died Jan. 24, 1864.

Peter A. S. Noveel, died Jan. 23, 1837, aged 21.

Elizabeth, wife of Basil Brooke, died Aug. 27, 1827, aged 34 years.

John Spalding, died Dec. 23, 1807, aged 28 years.

Henry Spalding, died Feb. 19, 1816, aged 69 years; Ann, his wife, died Jan. 17, 1800, aged 54 years.

Cecila, daughter of Geo. and Mary Spalding, born Sept. 30, 1836, died Feb. 25, 1856.

Margaret Adams, died Sept. 8, 1805.

Henry O'Hara, died June 14, 1815, aged 85 years.

Elizabeth Stigers, died Feb. 17, 1828, aged 31 years, 11 months, 14 days.

Thomas Adams, died Jan. 18, 1826, aged 64 years.

Magdalena Adams, wife of Thomas, who died at the age of 104, "loaded with years and virtuous deeds," Jan. 21, 1826.

Margaret, wife of John Dougherty, died Oct. 17, 1860, aged 79 years.

Margaret A., daughter of James and Rebecca Adlesperger, born Aug. 16, 1862, died May 12, 1880.

"This stone laid by Capt. John Gwinn, U.S.N., and Dr. Wm. Gwinn," for their mother, Mary, who died April 8, 1837, aged 60.

P. Hinds, died Sept. 23, 1828, aged 79 years.

Easter Hinds, died May 28, 1835, aged 65 years.

John Eckenrode, born April 2, 1780, died Nov. 25, 1849; Elizabeth, his wife, born July 6, 1788, died Sept. 20, 1850.

Lydia E., their daughter, and wife of Samuel B. Horner, died May 13, 1871, aged 58 years, 10 months, 11 days.

Ann Louisa, wife of Jos. A. Orendorff, died Aug. 15, 1872, aged 38 years, 2 months, 27 days.

Elizabeth Eline, died July 14, 1873, aged 68 years, 10 months, 25 days; Wm. Eline, her husband, died Dec. 11, 1879, aged 79 years, 4 months, 29 days.

Louisa C., wife of John M. McCarty, born Oct. 9, 1843, died April 3, 1880.

John Gonker, died Dec. 4, 1814, aged 71 years.

Barbara Gonker, died Dec. 27, 1827, aged 77 years.

Eliza Gonker, died Oct. 16, 1858, aged 75 years.

Hannah Gonker, died April 21, 1878, aged 81 years.

Mary Gonker, died Oct. 26, 1861, aged 86 years.

J. Burk, died 1814, at an old age.

Jacob Welty, died March 7, 1816, aged 26 years.

John, son of John and Eliza Welty, died March 25, 1816, aged 12 years.

John Welty, died Sept. 15, 1816, aged 54 years.

Mary Welty, died Dec. 20, 1816, aged 24 years.

Elizabeth, consort of John Welty, died Nov. 22, 1843, aged 72 years, 3 months, 18 days.

Alexander Frazier, died Oct. 9, 1872, aged 59 years, 5 months, 26 days; Polly, his wife, died June 30, 1854, aged 39 years.

Ann C., wife of Henry Althoff, died Oct. 11, 1845, aged 92 years.

Frederick Shoemaker, died March 31, 1864, aged 48 years, 11 months, 28 days.

Wm. Clabaugh, died Nov. 7, 1855, aged 34.

Sylvester N. Orndorff, died August, 1854, aged 19 years, 5 months, 20 days.

Joseph Eck, died Jan. 15, 1856, aged 62.

Margaret Eck, born July 7, 1816, died July 15, 1853.

Paul Eck, died Sept. 12, 1860, aged 63 years.

Wm. Staubb, died Oct. 23, 1842, aged 43 years, 22 days.

Peter Mathias, died Feb. 4, 1827, aged 37 years.

Klara, wife of Francis J. Albrocht, born Dec. 2, 1819, died May 4, 1858.

Catherine Snovell, died Oct. 17, 1761, aged 79.

Elizabeth, wife of Daniel Snovell, died Feb. 11, 1852, aged 37 years, 5 months. Elizabeth, his second wife, died Sept. 21, 1853, aged 27 years, 2 months.

Isaac T. Stonesifer, died Aug. 21, 1867, aged 26 years, 3 months, 17 days.

Elizabeth F. Watson, died Aug. 19, 1854, aged 24 years, 1 month, 24 days.

Wm. Watson, born November, 1798, died Feb. 16, 1861.

Mary A. Sewell, died March 16, 1871, aged 39 years.

John Hopkins, died June 20, 1833, aged 58.

Wm. Cash, born Dec. 24, 1800, died April 3, 1872.

Ann E. Cash, died Feb. 12, 1858, aged 22 years.

Anthony Arnold, died April 3, 1854, aged 78 years, 7 months, 11 days.

Ann, wife of Augustine Arnold, died Dec. 30, 1863, aged 62 years.

Taneytown Presbyterian Church.—Prior to 1820 German preaching was the rule in Taneytown, English the exception. Indeed, a strong prejudice existed against preaching in the English language. It is related that when the corner-stone of what is the original part of the present Lutheran church was laid, in 1812, the Rev. John Grope, pastor at that time, remarked to the bystanders, "This corner-stone is laid on a German foundation, and there is to be no English preaching here only when there must be."

But the world moves, and men must move with it. Some of the persons who heard the remark to which reference has been made lived to hear the same minister preach in the English language. About the year 1820 the younger portion of the German-speaking part of the community began to manifest a desire to have preaching in the English language. This desire was strenuously opposed by the older persons.

The house in which the German Reformed congregation worshiped at this time, known as the "Yellow Church," was in a very dilapidated condition. This, together with the desire of many members of the German Reformed congregation to have service in the English language, opened the way for the formation of certain "articles of association" between the members of the latter church at Taneytown and the members of the Presbyterian Church of the same place, to unite for the purpose of building a Union church.

In virtue of the seventh of these "articles of association," the parties concerned, in March, 1821, elected five persons as a building committee, and vested in them full power to purchase a lot or lots in such locality as they might think would best suit the different congregations, and to build thereon said church.

This committee, the members of which were Nicholas Snider, William B. Hilberd, George Shriner, Abraham Linn, and Samuel S. Forney, bought of Elizabeth Hughs, the widow of John Hughs, lots Nos. 78 and 80, situated in Taneytown, for the sum of eighty-nine dollars sixty-eight and a half cents ($89.68½). These lots were conveyed to the persons composing said committee, to be held by them in trust for the German Reformed and Presbyterian congregations until such time when said congregations may become corporate bodies, and thus by law be authorized to have and to hold the same by their trustees.

The corner-stone was laid on the 5th or 6th of September, 1821. Rev. John Winebrenner preached on the occasion from Zachariah iv. 7. Rev. Mr. Reilly also preached at the same time from Isaiah lxvi. 1.

The erection of the building progressed slowly. In the autumn of 1822 the church was dedicated. The Presbyterian element, during the interval between 1822 and 1828, worshiped with the German Reformed congregation, which was during that time served by the following-named pastors: Rev. Jacob Helfenstein, Rev. Mr. Aurand, a short time, and Rev. Deatrick Graves.

In the year 1828 the "Presbyterian Church of Taneytown" was organized.

The Presbytery of Baltimore met in Taneytown on the 24th of February, 1828, and ordained Rev. Austin O. Hubbard, who had been licensed in 1826. On the 30th of March, 1828, Rev. Mr. Hubbard ordained Philip Hann and William Cormack ruling elders, and administered the communion. On Sabbath, June 22, 1828, the church was regularly organized by the admission of the following-named persons as members: Mrs. Elizabeth Hann, Mrs. Alah Clabaugh (probably Alice), Miss Mary Ann McCollough, Miss Mary Musgrove on confession of their faith, and Miss Margaret Birnie, Miss Hester Birnie, Miss Margaret Ried, Miss Mary Ried by certificate.

Mr. Hubbard's pastorate extended from his ordination, Feb. 24, 1828, until the 18th of November, 1829, during which three persons were received into the church, two on confession of their faith and one by certificate. From the close of Mr. Hubbard's pastorate to Jan. 13, 1838, a period of eight years, the church was ministered to by Rev. George W. Kennedy, Rev. Nathan Harnad, Rev. Mr. Ammerman, and Rev. Jaleel Woolbridge.

Rev. George W. Kennedy was licensed, received, and ordained by the Presbytery of Baltimore in 1831, and dismissed in 1833. From Sessional records he appears to have been in Taneytown Church during the year 1831, and may have been pastor. Of the others, they served here a short time as supplies. During these eight years twelve persons were received as members of the church. On Sunday, May 13, 1838, Rev. John P. Carter, appointed by the "General Assembly's Board of Missions," commenced preaching in Taneytown church. Mr. Carter was installed pastor Oct. 29, 1838. His pastorate extended five years, to Dec. 17, 1843. After his resignation the church was vacant until the 1st of September, 1844, when Rev. Jacob Belville, a licentiate, was unanimously elected pastor, and soon afterwards ordained and installed a pastor of the church by the Presbytery of Baltimore. He was pastor four years. His pastorate closed about the 1st of September, 1848. The pulpit was then supplied between September, 1848, and June 2, 1849, by Rev. Mr. Connell.

In a Sessional record Rev. James Williamson, pastor elect, is spoken of as being present. He was soon after installed as pastor, and served the church as such until some time during the year 1854. He was dismissed from the Presbytery of Baltimore in 1854. It appears that the church was vacant from the close of Mr. Williams' pastorate to April 13, 1857, during which time the pulpit was supplied for a few months by Rev. Mr. Dodder, a licentiate. April, 1857, Rev. William B. Scarborough was ordained and installed pastor. Mr. Scarborough was pastor until the latter part of December, 1868, making a pastorate of eleven years and seven months. He handed his resignation to the Session 22d of November, 1868, to take effect in December. The Presbytery having granted the congregation the privilege of supplying their own pulpit, Rev. Isaac M. Patterson was unanimously elected stated supply, and entered upon his duties on the first Sabbath of January, 1869. In October, 1871, Mr. Patterson was installed pastor by a committee of the Presbytery of Baltimore. He resigned July, 1873, and preached his last sermon on the 27th of the same month.

After the union between the Old and the New School branches of the church, changes in the bounds of Synods and Presbyteries threw Emmittsburg and Piney Creek into the Presbytery of Baltimore, thus opening the way for Mr. Patterson to become pastor of Taneytown, in connection with Emmittsburg and Piney Creek. Since Mr. Patterson's installation, October, 1871, Emmittsburg, Piney Creek, and Taneytown have constituted, and at this time constitute, a pastoral charge. When the church became vacant by Mr. Patterson's resignation it united with the other churches of the charge in unanimously calling Rev. William Simonton, of Williamsport, Pa. Mr. Simonton accepted and soon entered upon his duties. His pastorate dates from Oct. 1, 1873, and still continues.

Philip Hann and William Cormack were ordained ruling elders at the organization of the church. Mr. Hann died Dec. 31, 1863, having served as an elder for a period of thirty-five years. Of Mr. Cormack it is recorded, "Did not apply for a certificate—joined the Methodists." Clotworthy Birnie, Sr., united with the church by certificate Sept. 8, 1832, and was ordained a ruling elder Aug. 8, 1838. He died June 2, 1845. He was a member of this church almost thirteen years, and a ruling elder seven years, four of which he was clerk of the Session. The members of the Session at present are Rogers Birnie, ordained Aug. 4, 1844; Andrew McKinney and Clotworthy Birnie, M.D., ordained Nov. 27, 1864; John W. Davidson and Andrew Arthur, ordained May 5, 1872. Rogers Birnie, the senior member, was clerk twenty-three years. Andrew McKinney has been clerk since 22d of November, 1868. Clotworthy Birnie, M.D., is a grandson of Clotworthy Birnie, Sr., who was a member of the Session during the earlier history of the church.

Taneytown Church was organized with ten members. In 1840 it had increased to twenty-six; in 1850 to thirty-five; and at present has a membership in full communion of forty-two. The whole number of persons who have been members of the church is about two hundred; and while the number in communion at any given time has always been small, the fact may be noted that it was never less at any period than it had been at an earlier date in the church's history. Two of the original members still survive.

In 1853, during Mr. Williamson's pastorate, the congregation bought a house and lot in Taneytown for the sum of nine hundred dollars; this was conveyed by deed, executed by John K. Longwell and Sarah Longwell to Rogers Birnie and Philip Hann, elders, and their successors, in trust, to be held for the benefit of their congregation. The property was used most of the time as a parsonage, except the latter part of Mr. Scarborough's pastorate, during which he resided in New Windsor. After the congregation became part of the pastoral charge of Emmittsburg and Piney Creek it was deemed best to dispose of the parsonage, which was accordingly done on the 29th of October, 1870, and on the 1st of April, 1871, it was conveyed to Thomas Rudisel by Rogers Birnie, Clotworthy Birnie, and Andrew McKinney, elders, for the sum of $3126. The congregation was incorporated by the laws of the State of Maryland, January, 1871; previous to that time the members of the Session attended to the secular interests of the church, and since then it has been governed by a board of trustees.

The pastors and stated supplies have been:

1828-29, Rev. Austin O. Hubbard; 1829-38, vacant, with supplies; 1838-43, Rev. John P. Carter; 1843-44, vacant, with occasional appointments; 1844-48, Rev. Jacob Bellville, D.D.; 1848-49, vacant, with supplies; 1849-54, Rev. James Williamson; 1854-57, vacant, with occasional supplies; 1857-68, Rev. William B. Scarborough; 1868-73, Rev. Isaac M. Patterson, S. S. and P.; 1873, Rev. William Simonton.

Taneytown Academy.—This institution was incorporated Jan. 25, 1844, with the following trustees: Solomon Sentman, Israel Hiteshue, Thomas Rudisel, John B. Boyle, John Thompson.

The Church of the United Brethren in Christ was incorporated March 10, 1858, with the following trustees: Henry Shriner, Daniel Frock, Joseph Witherow, John Ridinger, and Peter Mark.

A lodge of Knights of Pythias was organized in Taneytown Sept. 17, 1877. Their charter and paraphernalia were purchased from the Frederick City Lodge, and were issued to them in 1871. The first officers of the lodge were as follows:

C. C., C. C. Steiner; Master at Arms, G. T. Crouse; Dr. C. Birnie, Prelate; David Fogle, V. C.; L. D. Reed, K. of R. and S.; J. E. Davidson, M. of E.; Ezekiah Hawk, O. G.; Elwood Burns, I. G.; E. K. Weaver, M. of F. The present officers are S. E. Reindollar, V. C.; D. R. Fogle, C. C.; J. E. Davidson, M. of E.; E. K. Weaver, M. of F.; C. C. Stuller, K. of R. and S.; W. T. Hawk, P.; L. D. Reed, O. G.; J. Hahn, I. G.; B. B. Miller, P. C.

They have twenty-one members in good standing, and hold their meetings in Reindollar's Hall. The lodge is in a very prosperous condition, and is steadily increasing in numbers.

The Regulator and Taneytown Herald was published by Samuel P. Davidson, who was also the editor, "in Church Street, adjoining Mr. Sebastian Sultzer's tavern, Taneytown, Md." The eighteenth issue, dated Sept. 7, 1830, contains among its news the names of Isaac Shriner, John Kinzer, Madison Nelson, and Daniel Kemp, of Henry, who are published as candidates on the Jackson Republican ticket for members of the Assembly from Frederick County, and the candidates on the National Republican ticket were David Kemp, Jno. H. Melford, Evan McKinstry, and David Richardson.

From the market reports, copied from the Baltimore *American*, we learn that wheat was worth 98 cents to $1.00 per bushel; rye, 47 and 50 cents; corn, 45 and 47 cents; whisky, 22 and 24 cents per gallon; plaster, $3.80 per ton.

But two marriages are published, one of which is that of Mr. Adam Bowers and Miss Mary Ann Currans.

A. Reck, secretary, gives notice that the Evangelical Lutheran Synod of Maryland and Virginia will assemble at Taneytown on the third Sunday of October (1830).

Michael Wagner advertises a stray heifer. Nathan Hendricks announces a barbecue at Bruceville on the 23d of September. Samuel Thompson, Sterling Galt, and David Martin, trustees, advertised for "a man of good moral character, who is well qualified to teach reading, writing, arithmetic, and mathematics in a school-house lately erected within one mile of Taneytown." The teacher secured was J. M. Newson, the present superintendent of public schools. Mathias E. Bartgis, Wm. H. Cannon, Abner Campbell, and Peter Brengle published cards announcing themselves as candidates for sheriff of Frederick County. John N. Hoffman, agent, gives notice to the subscribers to the theological seminary at Gettysburg that three installments are due. David H. Fries, seven miles from Taneytown, near Smith's tavern, advertises public sale of personal property. James Raymond, trustee, advertises sale of land of Abraham Derr, near Taneytown. Nathan Hendricks, "desirous of leaving Frederick County," advertises Bruceville Mills at public sale. Louisa Rinedollar and Abraham Lichtenwalter, executors, give notice to the creditors of Peter Micksell. James Heird advertises the Fairview races to come off on the 6th, 7th, and 8th of September, and offers three purses,—$25, $15, $20. John Hughes nominates himself for the Assembly as the Workingmen's independent candidate, "who is a friend to railroads, canals, and turnpikes," etc. "A valuable family of negroes" is offered for sale, "but not to traders," and another negro is also advertised for sale; those desiring to buy are requested to inquire at the office of the *Regulator*. C. Birnie offers Merino rams for sale. Israel Hiteshew and James Kridler announce a dissolution of partnership "in tavern and tailoring."

The *American Sentinel*, published in Westminster, is a combination of *The Regulator*. The paper was bought from Mr. Davidson by Col. John K. Longwell, who moved the office to Westminster in May, 1833, and changed its name to *The Carrolltonian*. The paper was moved there solely to advocate the formation of Carroll County. In 1838 a Democratic journal called *The Democrat* was established here by Wm. Shipley, Jr., when *The Carrolltonian* was announced as a Whig journal. Col. Longwell continued the publication of the paper until 1844, when Francis T. Kerr, a brother-in-law to the late John J. Baumgartner, Esq., succeeded to its proprietorship. Upon the death of Mr. Kerr in 1846 or 1847, George D. Miller, of Frederick, took charge of the paper, and was shortly after succeeded by W. H. Grammer, in 1850. In 1854, upon the rise of Know-Nothingism, the name of the paper was changed to the *American Sentinel*, its present title.

Among the early physicians were Dr. Joseph Sim Smith, a patriot in the Revolution and a brave soldier. He died Sept. 6, 1822. William Hubbert and Dr. Boyle were also among the first physicians in Taneytown. The latter and Henry Swope were among the earliest merchants. John White and Joseph Lanubert were the blacksmiths of the village in the olden time. A tavern was kept by Mary Crouse in the house now occupied by Mr. Stonesifer as a hotel, and the Crabsters kept the inn just opposite and across the street. The following advertisement appeared in a newspaper of Dec. 16, 1801:

"For sale, the tavern 'American Coat of Arms,' in Taneytown. Apply to James McSherry, Littlestown, Pennsylvania, or Richard Coale, Libertytown, Maryland."

Harney is a small hamlet about four and a half miles from Taneytown and near the Monocacy River, which is at this point a small stream. It was named in honor of the late Gen. Harney, of the United States army. The United Brethren, a religious denomination, have built a church in the village recently, of which Rev. J. Whitlock is pastor. D. L. Shoemaker is the village postmaster. A number of mills are located here, under the charge of William Starner, John Unger, and Peter Selt. There is a hotel in the village, kept by W. F. Eckenrode, and John Eckenrode keeps an assortment of general merchandise. There are also two excellent physicians, John C. Bush and E. B. Simpson. The population of the Taneytown District, according to the census of 1880, is 2596.

For many years the old free-school system, which obtained so extensively in the rural districts of Maryland, was in vogue in Carroll County. At the public schools the children were taught the three R's,—"reading, 'riting, and 'rithmetic,"—and if they desired further education, they either had to teach themselves or attend one of the many excellent private schools within reach. During the civil war there was an awakening of the public mind to the advantages of general education, and a cumbersome system, expensive in character, resulted from inexperienced legislation. This was superseded by the present system, now general throughout all the counties of the State, which gives all necessary advantages, and has the additional recommendation of simplicity. The following is a list of public school trustees for 1881 and 1882 in the Taneytown District:

1. Pine Hill.—William Clutz, Michael Humbert, Charles M. Hess.
2. Piney Creek.—Franklin Keppert, Daniel Hesson, Richard Hill.
3. Walnut Grove.—Samuel Brown, Upton Harney, David W. Bowers.
4. Washington.—No appointments.
5. Oak Grove.—Samuel P. Baumgartner, Henry Eck, Hezekiah Hahn.

6, 7, and 8. Taneytown, Nos. 1, 2, and 3.—William S. Rudisell, Jesse Haugh, Ezra K. Reaver.

9. Oregon.—Gabriel Stover, William W. Koontz, Ezra Stuller.
10. Martin's.—Valentine Harman, Jacob Shriner, Martin L. Buffington.
11. Shaw's.—Daniel Harman, Edward Shorb, William Smith.

The teachers for the term ending April 15, 1881, were:

1, H. C. Wilt, 53 pupils; 2, S. F. Hess, 48 pupils; 3, J. H. Lambert, 51 pupils; 4, J. Ross Galt, 44 pupils; 5, Calvin T. Fringer, 51 pupils; 6, Levi D. Reid, 55 pupils; 7, Mrs. Emma L. Forrest, 54 pupils; 8, James F. Fringer, 47 pupils; 9, John T. Reck, 68 pupils; 10, George W. Hess, 51 pupils; 11, C. A. Waesche, 29 pupils; 1 (colored school), C. H. Stuller, 20 pupils.

The following is the vote for local officers from 1851 to 1861, inclusive:

1851.—Vote for Primary School Commissioners: Israel Hiteshue 190, Benjamin Shunk 155, Israel Hiteshue 159, John H. Clabaugh 85, Benjamin Zumbrum 41.

1853.—For Justices: William Haugh 227, George Miller 172, Benjamin Shunk 246, James McKellip 232; Constables: Thomas Jones, Jr., 250, James Burke 64, John Reindollar 238, David Kephart 87; Road Supervisor: Patrick Burke 103, James Thompson 243.

1855.—For Justices: George Miller 246, William Haugh 248, Jacob Shriner 249, George Crabbs 132, James Crouse 132, L. Buffington 137; Constables: Thomas Jones, Jr., 256, Henry Rinaman 242, Michael Fogle 127, James Rodgers 135; Road Supervisor: James Thompson 220, J. Newcomer 131.

1857.—For Justices: B. Shunk 216, William Haugh 250, George Miller 245; Constables: H. Rinaman 138, A. Shoemaker 238, W. Slates 240; Road Supervisor: William Henier 262.

1859.—For Justices: William Fisher 157, Jacob Zumbrum 253, Benjamin Shunk 267, Jacob Shriner 266; Constables:

James Burke 152, Wendell Slates 270, J. E. Delaplane 259; Road Supervisor: William Hess 272.

1861.—For Justices: William Haugh 377, William Fisher 191, J. Zumbrum 207, George Miller 356; Constables: W. Slates 247, Joel Bowers 284, David Kephart 206; Road Supervisor: Gabriel Stover 266, John Reindollar 105, W. Shoemaker 82, William Hess 2.

UNIONTOWN DISTRICT, No. 2.

The metes and bounds of Uniontown District are as follows:

"Beginning at Grove's Ford, on Big Pipe Creek; thence down Big Pipe Creek to Sick's Ford; thence with a straight line to Eckart's Ford on Little Pipe Creek; thence up Little Pipe Creek to Sam's Creek to Landis' mill; thence with a road leading between the farms of Jacob Sneader and the late Henry Nicodemus to a stone on the Buffalo road; thence near Levi Devilbiss' house, now occupied by Jacob Nusbaum, leaving said house in District No. 9 (thence near John Myers' house, leaving the same in District No. 9); thence to Philip Nicodemus' mill; thence down Turkeyfoot Branch to where it intersects Little Pipe Creek; thence up said creek to Haines' mill, running through Widow Haines' farm, leaving her house in District No. 2; thence through Joseph Haines' farm, leaving his house in No. 7; thence through Michael Morelock, Sr.'s farm, leaving his house in No. 2; thence to Morelock's tavern, on the Uniontown turnpike, leaving his house in No. 7; thence through Shaffer's farm, leaving his house and factory in District No. 7; thence with a straight line to Smith's old tavern on the Taneytown turnpike, leaving said house in District No. 7; thence to Husson's house, leaving his house in No. 2; thence to Messing's mill, leaving his dwelling in No. 7; thence to the stone road near Stoneseifer's house; thence with the stone road to place of beginning."

This district is bounded on the north by Myers', northwest and west by Taneytown, east by Westminster, south by New Windsor, and west by Union Bridge and Middleburg. Big Pipe Creek divides it from Taneytown District, and Little Pipe Creek skirts its southwestern corner, forming for a short distance the boundary line with New Windsor. Bear and Meadow Branches flow westerly through its centre and empty into Big Pipe Creek. Wolf-Pit Branch flows southwest, and Log Cabin Branch northwest, emptying respectively into Little and Big Pipe Creeks. The population of the district, according to the census of 1880, is two thousand six hundred and three.

The district was settled before 1745, and about 1760 the population increased rapidly. Among the pioneers were the Herbaughs, Norrises, Eckerds, Nicodemuses, Harrises, Babylons, Roops, Shepherds, Zollickoffers, Senseneys, Hibberds, Farmwalts, Brubakers, Hiteshews, Roberts, McFaddens, Stoneseifers, Erbs, Markers, Zepps, and Myerlys. The early settlers were largely Germans, with a sprinkling of English and Scotch-Irish. The Barnharts were the original owners of the land on which A. Zollicoffer now lives, and the land now owned by Capt. Brubaker was formerly in the possession of the Cover family. Mrs. Mehring owns the land upon which the Grammers lived. The Stouffers also took up a large tract south of Uniontown.

Uniontown is situated in an undulating and healthy country, two and a half miles from Linwood, seven from Westminster, and forty-three from Baltimore. Before there was any town here, more than a hundred years ago, Peter Moser kept a tavern, which is marked on the old Maryland maps, on the road from Baltimore through Westminster and Moravian Town (Graceham) to Hagerstown.

The first house built in the village was situated at the forks of the Hagerstown and Taneytown road, a log building one and a half stories high, containing three rooms. It was used as a hotel and store, and was kept first by Peter Moser, before the Revolution, and afterwards by Mr. McKenzie, and then by Mr. Hiteshew, who conducted it until 1809. It was built on the lot now occupied by Nathan Heck, and was torn down in 1831. The second house, a low structure, was built by Stephen Ford, and is now occupied by Mr. Segafoose. Mrs. Green's hotel was built in 1802 by Conrad Stem, and was first kept by John Myers. The next house was built in 1804, and is now occupied by Charles Devilbiss. It was first occupied by a family named Myers. That in which Reuben Matthias lives was erected in 1805. Its first occupant was John Kurtz, who kept a store. The town was then called "The Forks," and its name was changed in 1813 to Uniontown, when the people were trying to secure a new county, which it was proposed to call "Union County," with this town as the county-seat. The project failed, but the village retained the name of Uniontown. The first physician was Dr. Hobbs, and he was succeeded by Dr. Boyer, who lived outside of the town. His successor was Dr. Hibberd. The first blacksmith was Nicholas Hiteshew, whose shop was at the foot of the hill leading to the Stouffer residence. His shop was there in 1800. Wm. Richinacker and George Attick were the pioneer carpenters of the hamlet. The first schoolmaster was Thomas Harris, who taught in 1807 in the house now occupied by Mr. Segafoose. Moses Shaw came here in 1816 and kept a tavern on the property now owned by Charles Devilbiss. In 1817, Jacob Appler was a wealthy citizen living near town. Charles Devilbiss, David Stouffer, Isaac Hiteshew, Upton Norris, Capt. Henry Anders, Mr. Harris, Samuel Shriner, Thomas Metcalf, and many others from Uniontown and its vicinity volunteered for the defense of Baltimore during the war of 1812. The first school-house was erected in 1810, in the lower part of the town. It has been removed several times and is still standing. Cardinal McCloskey, of New York City, was born in Uniontown, in a log house opposite the cemetery. In 1818 St. Lucas' church was built, under the pastorate of Rev. Winebrenner. Subsequent pastors were Revs. Helfenstein and Graves. It is now occupied by the Church of God. In those days it was customary to raise funds for the erection of churches and other public enterprises by means of lotteries. Below is given the scheme by which the money was obtained to build St. Lucas' church:

UNIONTOWN DISTRICT.

Stationary Prizes.

1	prize of $1200 is	$1200
1	" 500 is	500
1	" 200 is	200
4	" 100 is	400
10	" 50 is	500
60	" 10 is	600
250	" 8 is	2000
800	" 7 is	5600
1127	prizes	
1073	blanks.	
2200	tickets at $5 is	$11,000

"1st drawn 300 tickets, each $7.
"1st drawn ticket after 1000, $500
"1st drawn ticket after 2000, $1200.

"Part of the above prizes will be paid in part as follows: prize of $1200 by 100 tickets in 2d class, Nos. 1 and 100 inclusive; prize of $500 by 50 tickets in 2d class, Nos. 101 and 150 inclusive; prize of $200 by 15 tickets in 2d class, Nos. 151 and 166 inclusive; prizes of $10, $8, and $7 by 1 ticket in 2d class, commencing with first drawn of ten dollar prizes with No. 167, and so upwards in regular succession with said prizes of $10, $8, and $7. Ticket in 2d class valued at $5 each.

"SECOND CLASS.

1	prize of $1000 is	$1000
1	" 400 is	400
1	" 200 is	200
2	" 100 is	200
6	" 50 is	300
20	" 20 is	400
122	" 10 is	1220
155	" 8 is	1240
720	" 7 is	5040
1028	prizes.	
972	blanks.	
2000	tickets at $5 is	$10,000

"*Stationary Prizes.*

"1st drawn 200 tickets, each $7.
"1st drawn ticket after 1500, $1000.

"Part of the above prizes will be paid in part as follows: prize of $1000 by 80 tickets in 3d class, Nos. 1 and 80 inclusive; prize of $400 by 40 tickets, Nos. 81 and 121 inclusive; prize of $200 by 15 tickets, No. 122 and 137 inclusive; prizes of $10, $8, and $7 by 1 ticket each, commencing with No. 138 to the first drawn ten dollar prize, and continuing regularly up with said prizes. Tickets valued in 3d class at $5 each.

"THIRD CLASS.

1	prize of $1500 is	$1500
1	" 600 is	600
1	" 300 is	300
2	" 100 is	200
20	" 50 is	1000
26	" 15 is	390
261	" 10 is	2610
400	" 8 is	3200
600	" 7 is	4200
1312	prizes.	
1488	blanks.	
2800	tickets at $5 each is	$14,000

"*Stationary Prizes.*

"1st drawn 250 tickets, each $7.
"1st drawn ticket after 1000, $300.
"1st drawn ticket after 2300, $1500.

"Prizes subject to a deduction of 20 per cent. in each class, and payable ninety days after the completion thereof. The managers in offering the above scheme to the public, for the purpose of appropriating the proceeds to a church, feel confident that they will meet with a general support. Perhaps no scheme has been offered heretofore that affords so great a chance to adventurers, there being more prizes than blanks, and only few tickets in each class.

"Those persons who purchased tickets in the original scheme will please to exchange them for tickets in the first class as soon as possible, as the managers are very reluctantly obliged to abandon it, as a duty they owe to the church and the public, in consequence of the magnitude of the original scheme. As a number of tickets are already held in the first class, the managers pledge themselves to commence the drawing as soon as possible.

"MANAGERS.

"Jacob Appler, Sr.[1]	Thomas Boyer.
Nicholas Snider.	John Dager..
Moses Shaw.	Jacob Shriver.
John Crabb.	John Shates.
William B. Hubbard.	

"UNIONTOWN, MD., April, 1817."

In 1807, Mr. Cover established a tan-yard. The tan-yard now operated by Mr. Hoffman was opened in 1842 by Charles Devilbiss. The Methodist church was built in 1822. In 1813 the Masonic Temple was erected where the house of the Misses Yingling now stands. It was torn down between 1825 and 1830, and its brick used in building a house on Mr. Zollikoffer's farm. The town has been several times incorporated, but its charters expired for want of elections or failure to conform to them. In 1807 the house now used as a dry-house in the tannery was removed from Westminster by Frederick Stem. It had been a Catholic church, and its brick was brought from England. The post-office was established here about 1813, and the first postmaster was John Hyder, who laid out the town after a few houses had been

[1] On Thursday, Aug. 28, 1817, Jacob Christ was married to Miss Elizabeth Appler, daughter of Jacob Appler, by Rev. Curtis Williams.

built. In 1817, Jonas Crumbacker advertised the "Boorhaveau Lotion" for sale at his store as a grand anti-rheumatic tincture. In 1817 the Frederick County Court, at its October term, ordered a public road to be laid out from Liberty Town through Union Town to Andrew Shriver's mill. Dr. Clement Hubbs in 1817 lived on his farm called "Valley Farm."

Moses Shaw and John Gibbony advertised that races would be run over a handsome course near Uniontown, Wednesday, Sept. 10, 1817, and a purse of ninety dollars was free for any horse, mare, or gelding running four miles and repeat, carrying weight agreeable to the rules of racing. And on the Thursday following a purse of forty dollars was offered, free as the above, the winning horse of the preceding day excepted, two miles and repeat, carrying a feather; and on Friday a purse of seventy dollars, free as above, the winning horses the preceding days excepted, running three miles and repeat, carrying a feather. Four horses to be entered each day or no race, to be entered the day previous to running or pay double entrance, entrance to pay one shilling in the pound. No jostling or foul riding to be countenanced.

Uniontown is one of the most enterprising villages in Carroll County. According to the last census it contained three hundred and eighteen inhabitants. It is the commercial centre of the district, the polling-place for the voters, and a popular resort for the energetic and intelligent population by which it is surrounded. A number of charitable, social, and business organizations have been formed in the town, or have moved thither from other portions of the county, and are all in a flourishing condition.

Door to Virtue Lodge, No. 46, of Ancient Free and Accepted Masons, moved Nov. 7, 1813, to Uniontown from Pipe Creek, where the members met uninterruptedly until 1824.

At the communication of November 21st, "Brothers William P. Farquhar, J. Cloud, and Jacob R. Thomas were appointed a committee to prepare a petition to the Legislature for a lottery to defray the expense of building the Uniontown Masonic Lodge Hall," but the committee never reported, the lottery was never granted, and the hall was never built.

The officers from December, 1813, to June, 1814, were William P. Farquhar, W. M.; J. R. Thomas, S. W.; C. Ogborn, J. W.; and Jesse Cloud, Sec.; J. Wright, Treas. From June to December, 1814, William P. Farquhar, W. M.; J. R. Thomas, S. W.; Joseph Wright, J. W.; Henry Gassaway, Sec.; and Enoch Taylor, Treas. From December, 1814, to June, 1815, Jesse Cloud, W. M.; J. R. Thomas, S. W.; J. Wright, J. W.; William Bontz, Sec.; and John Richnicker, Treas. From June to December, 1815, Jacob R. Thomas, W. M.; William P. Farquhar, S. W.; Henry Gassaway, J. W.; William Bontz, Sec.; and Isaac Lyon, Treas. From December, 1815, to June, 1816, Joseph Wright, W. M.; Isaac P. Thomas, S. W.; John C. Cockey, J. W.; William P. Farquhar, Sec.; and Charles Devilbiss, Treas.

During this term, at a meeting held Feb. 25, 1816, the lodge manifested its appreciation of the importance of "proficiency" by passing the following resolution: "That every member shall make himself well acquainted with such degrees of Masonry as have been conferred upon him before he can be permitted to advance further into Masonry," thus anticipating by forty-four years the standing resolution of the Grand Lodge of May, 1860. The officers from June to December, 1816, were Wm. P. Farquhar, W. M.; J. R. Thomas, S. W.; Isaac Lyon, J. W.; John C. Cockey, Sec. From June, 1817, to June, 1818, Wm. P. Farquhar, W. M.; Isaac Lyon, S. W.; Joseph Wright, J. W.; J. C. Cockey, Sec.; and John Richnecker, Treas.

The lodge, from the beginning, had always held its stated meetings on Sunday, but on the 28th of December, 1817, it was resolved, "That the meetings shall for the winter season be on the Saturday evening preceding the fourth Sunday, at 6 o'clock P.M." In the following spring we find the brethren again assembling as usual on the first day of the week. The officers from June to December, 1818, were Wm. P. Farquhar, W. M.; Joseph Wright, S. W.; Israel Lyon, J. W.; J. C. Cockey, Sec.; and George W. Gist, Treas. On the 18th June, this same year, the lodge had its first funeral procession. It was at Libertytown, and in honor of Enoch Taylor, who was one of the original or charter members, the first senior deacon, and afterwards junior warden, senior warden, and treasurer.

The first junior warden, William Slaymaker, it appears, also died during this term, as the lodge, on the 13th of September, appointed a committee "to take in subscriptions to be applied to the erection of a tombstone over his remains, and to wait on the widow and trustees of the church on this subject to obtain their consent," etc.

The officers from December, 1818, to June, 1819, were Wm. P. Farquhar, W. M.; Alexander McIlhenny, S. W.; Charles Devilbiss, J. W.; J. C. Cockey, Sec.; and George W. Gist, Treas. At the meeting of Feb. 22, 1819, "a memorial was presented from Wm. H. McCannon, Thomas Gist, and others, Master Masons, eight in number, for a recommendation to the

Grand Lodge for a charter for new lodge, to be established in Westminster. On motion, the further consideration thereof was postponed until the fourth Sunday in March," and the postponement seems to have been indefinite, as nothing more is heard of the memorial. " The craft then moved in procession down to the lodge-hall, where an oration was delivered in honor of the day by Upton Scott Reid, in the presence of the lodge and the public, after which the craft returned to the lodge-room, and the honors of the lodge were conferred on Bro. Reid for his oration." On the 25th of April it was

" *Resolved*, That hereafter the stated meetings of this lodge shall be on the evening of the day of every full moon at two o'clock P.M., except from the first of November until the first day of April, during which time the lodge shall meet at ten o'clock A.M., unless the moon shall be full on Sunday, in which case the meeting shall be held at the same hour on the Friday preceding."

The officers from June to December, 1819, were Alexander McIlhenny, W. M.; George W. Gist, S. W.; Benjamin Yingling, J. W.; Upton S. Reid, Sec.; and Dr. William B. Hebbard, Treas. The festival of St. John the Baptist (June 24th) was kept this year in true Masonic style. The number of brethren present, including visitors, was over one hundred, and after conferring the third degree " a procession was formed and the craft proceeded to St. Lucas' church, where divine service was performed and a discourse delivered by the Rev. Bro. John Armstrong." By a resolution passed July 7th the fee for each of the three degrees was fixed at ten dollars, and it was also " *Resolved*, That if a candidate for initiation be elected, and does not attend at the first or second meetings after such an election, having been duly notified thereof, his petition shall be returned, and his deposit retained for the benefit of the institution." The officers from December, 1819, to June, 1820, were Alexander McIlhenny, W. M.; Upton S. Reid, S. W.; Benjamin Yingling, J. W.; John Hyder, Sec.; and Dr. William B. Hebbard, Treas.; from June to December, 1820, Upton S. Reid, W. M.; Benjamin Yingling, S. W.; John W. Dorsey, J. W.; John Hyder, Sec.; and W. B. Hebbard, Treas. On St. John's day (June 24th) " a discourse was delivered by the W. M., highly gratifying to all the brethren present." Soon after, on the 25th of July, the lodge, for the first time, was compelled to visit upon an unworthy member the severest penalty known to their laws. The offender was an unaffiliated Master Mason, formerly a member of Mechanics' Lodge, No. 153, New York, whose application for membership in this lodge had been twice rejected. He was tried on the charge of " unmasonic conduct. Specification 1st. Using profane language at Uniontown, or or about the 1st of May, 1820." To which the accused pleaded " guilty." " Specification 2d. Being intoxicated on the evening of the said day at Uniontown." Pleaded " guilty." " Specification 3d. Giving the G—— and S——, etc., to persons, or in the presence of persons, who were not Masons, at New Windsor, some time in the spring of 1819." Pleaded " not guilty." " The testimony being closed," says the record, " the accused made his defense and then retired." The lodge then proceeded to consider the case, and after mature consideration did find the accused guilty of the charge, and sentenced him to be expelled from all the rights and benefits of Masonry." The officers from December, 1820, to June, 1821, were U. S. Reid, W. M.; W. H. McCannon, S. W.; Joshua W. Owings, J. W.; John Hyder, Sec.; and W. B. Hebbard, Treas.; from June to December, 1821, Alexander McIlhenny, W. M.; Benjamin Yingling, S. W.; James Blanchford, J. W.; William Curry, Sec.; and W. B. Hebbard, Treas.

On the 24th of June, " it was unanimously resolved, in conformity with the recommendation of the Grand Lodge at its last Grand Annual Communication, that this lodge in future abandon and desist from the practice of using spirituous liquors at their refreshments in and about the lodge."

On the 11th of October there was a solemn procession and commemorative services in honor of the Grand Master of the State, Charles Wirgman, who had recently died. The sermon was preached in St. Lucas' Reformed Church, by the Rev. R. Elliott, P. M. of Columbia Lodge, No. 58, Frederick, who generously returned the fee of ten dollars offered him " into the charity fund, with his hearty and most sincere thanks and prayers for their welfare in this world and eternal happiness hereafter." The officers from December, 1821, to June, 1822, were A. McIlhenny, W. M.; B. Yingling, S. W.; James Blanchford, J. W.; William Curry, Sec.; and W. B. Hebbard, Treas.

On the 7th of January, 1822, it was unanimously resolved, " that hereafter our stated meetings shall be held on the fourth Sunday in the month, as originally printed in the by-laws of 1813." Soon after, on the 28th of the same month, at Taneytown, the lodge buried with Masonic honors its late Past Master, Upton Scott Reid. The chaplain on this mournful occasion was the Rev. Daniel Zollikoffer.

The officers from June to December, 1822, were William P. Farquhar, W. M.; William H. McCannon, S. W.; Nicholas Snider, J. W.; Alexander McIlhenny, Sec.; and W. B. Hebbard, Treas. From December, 1822, to June, 1823, Benjamin Yingling, W. M.; John Giboney, S. W.; James Blanchford, S. W.; William Curry, J. W.; A. McIlhenny, Sec.; and W. B. Hebbard, Treas. From June, 1823, to December, 1823, W. P. Farquhar, W. M.; N. Snider, S. W.; William Curry, J. W.; A. McIlhenny, Sec.; and W. B. Hebbard, Treas. On the 24th of February, 1823, the fee for the three degrees was reduced to twenty dollars, viz., seven for the first, five for the second, and eight for the third. From December, 1823, to June, 1824, W. P. Farquhar, W. M.; N. Snider, S. W.; Jacob Glazer, J. W.; A. McIlhenny, Sec.; and Israel Bentley, Treas.

From June 4, 1815, there had been connected with this lodge a "Mark Lodge," for the purpose of conferring the degree of Mark Master, which is now given only in Royal Arch Chapters, but at the meeting held Feb. 22, 1824, "Door to Virtue Mark Lodge" was declared to be defunct and its books closed.

On the 13th of April, 1824, there was a special meeting at "Shriver's Inn," Westminster, the object of which was to pay proper Masonic respect to the memory of a deceased brother, John Holmes, of No. 1, Ohio.

On the 13th of June the lodge went into mourning for sixty days for the death of the Grand Master, Gen. W. H. Winder. The officers from June to December, 1824, were W. P. Farquhar, W. M.; John C. Cockey, S. W.; Joshua W. Owings, J. W.; W. H. McCannon, Sec.; and Michael Bornetz, Treas.

Wyoming Tribe, No. 37, I. O. R. M., was instituted March 18, 1860, and the charter was granted April 23, 1860, to the following members, who then composed the lodge: Frank E. Roberts, John S. Devilbiss, Jr., George H. Routson, B. Mills, C. S. Devilbiss, and C. A. Gosnell, all residing within Uniontown. The first officers of the lodge were, viz.: Prophet, F. E. Roberts; Sachem, Dr. B. Mills; Senior Sagamore, John S. Devilbiss; Junior Sagamore, George H. Routson; Chief of Records, Charles Gosnell; Keeper of Wampum, C. S. Devilbiss.

The tribe numbers sixty-eight members in good standing, and the present officers are as follows: Prophet, John A. Brown; Sachem, B. L. Waltz; Senior Sagamore, J. Hamilton Singer; Junior Sagamore, William Strimme; Chief of Records, H. P. Englar; Keeper of Wampum, Jesse T. H. Davis; Guard of Wigwam, G. A. Davis; Guard of the Forest, William H. Baker.

Brothers' Relief Division, No. 136, Sons of Temperance, was incorporated by the General Assembly, Feb. 24, 1860. The incorporators were Alfred Zollickoffer, S. Hope, E. Bankerd, J. Bankerd, E. Adams, Samuel Anders, D. Stultz, J. H. Christ, T. H. Adams, M. Jenkins, J. Bean, J. H. Gordon, J. Zepp, J. McHenry, T. Welling, A. Bitesell, R. Sharpley, A. Hurley, W. S. Lantz, J. E. Starr, William Eckard, D. Seller, Charles Myers, Lewis Byers, N. N. Meredith, T. H. Routson, F. A. Devilbiss, J. A. Eckard, J. N. Galwith, G. H. Brown, William H. Bankerd, G. Kugle, G. Winter, T. A. Eckard, John W. Kinney, J. Little, P. Smith, T. Eckard, G. Hamburg, G. W. Gilbert, A. Eckard, A. Little, P. Little.

The Uniontown Academy was incorporated by the General Assembly by an act passed March 26, 1839, making Samuel Cox, Dr. James L. Billingslea, John Smith, Henry Harbaugh, and William Roberts trustees, and making them and their successors a body politic.

The Carroll County Savings Institution was organized in Uniontown Feb. 27, 1871, by an act of the General Assembly, with the following gentlemen as incorporators: Robert B. Varden, William H. Starr, Levi Caylor, David Foutz, Dennis Cookson, John Gore, Daniel S. Deight, Emanuel Formwalt, J. Hamilton Singer, and Levi Engler, all citizens of Carroll County. The amount of capital of the corporation was twenty thousand dollars, and the above gentlemen were appointed a board of directors.

The present officers of the institution are D. Stoner, president; W. H. Starr, treasurer; Levi Caylor, secretary; and T. H. Davis, assistant secretary. Board of trustees, D. N. Stoner, D. Foutz, Levi Caylor, Edwin J. Gilbert, Daniel S. Diehl, T. H. Davis, W. H. Stoner, Dr. J. J. Weaver.

The institution is in a very prosperous condition, and has been successful since its formation.

The Maryland Mutual Benefit Association of Carroll County for Unmarried Persons was incorporated under the laws of Maryland with its home-office in Uniontown. The officers are: President, Thomas H. Routson; Vice-President, Philip H. Babylon; Secretary, Jesse T. H. Davis; Treasurer, Edwin G. Gilbert; Agent, John A. Brown; Attorney, Charles T. Reifsnider. The board of trustees are Thomas H. Routson, Edwin G. Gilbert, Jacob J. Weaver, Jr., M.D., P. H. Babylon, John A. Brown, Thomas F. Shepherd, Jesse T. H. Davis.

A copy of the *Engine of Liberty and Uniontown Advertiser*, No. 22 of Volume I., dated Feb. 3, 1814, a newspaper published by Charles Shower, at two dollars per annum, contains among other matters the proceedings of the Legislature of Maryland, Louis Gassaway, clerk, and a short extract of the proceedings of the Massachusetts Legislature.

The editor advertises for subscriptions to a novel entitled "The Storm," in two volumes, price seventy-five cents; also that the office of the *Engine of Liberty* is removed "to the new brick building of Mr. Henry Meyers, nearly opposite to where it was formerly kept." Some news is given from New York, January 29th, and Richmond, January 27th, with an account of the camp at New Point Comfort, and describing the enemy's fleet. An account of an earthquake at Showanoetown, Illinois Territory, Dec. 13, 1813, is published; also a resolution passed by the New York Legislature, January 29th, appropriating fifty thousand dollars for the relief of the sufferers of the Niagara frontier.

Among the advertisements Morris Meredith advertises for sale a lot of twenty-five acres of valuable land adjoining Uniontown, on the road leading from Baltimore to Hagerstown.

Joshua Gist offers for sale his dwelling-house and plantation, containing six hundred acres, within two miles of Westminster. The said Westminster is expected to be the county town of a new county that is to be made out of Baltimore and Frederick Counties. Also two hundred and eighty acres about three or four miles from Westminster.

Israel Rinehart and Ulrich Switzer, executors of David Rinehart, deceased, and Hannah Urner and John Rinehart, administrators of Jonas Urner, give notice to creditors.

On the fourth page is given a column of foreign news, embracing England, France, and Germany. Jacob Appler, Sr., advertises three lots of land in Libertytown, also seven and a half acres of woodland adjoining the lands of Abraham Albaugh.

Ann Willis offers her farm of two hundred and eighty-two and a half acres, on Sam's Creek, on the road leading from Libertytown to Baltimore, for sale.

Beal Dorsey, near Freedom Town, advertises one hundred and fifteen acres of land, near McMurray's tavern.

John Shriver offers for sale a dwelling-house, wheelwright-shop, and two lots in Uniontown.

Samuel Lookingpeale, at Capt. John Williams', desires to sell sixty-five acres of land within half a mile of Philip Cromer's tavern.

Edward Stevenson, within four or five miles of the Sulphur Springs, Frederick County, advertises his farm of two hundred and ten acres.

Henry C. Dorsey offers his mill-seat and farm, on the waters of Sam's Creek, three-quarters of a mile below Mr. Londes' mill, also two hundred and twenty-three acres in Hampshire County, Va., for sale.

John Williams, desiring to move to the Western country, wishes to sell his farm of two hundred and thirty-eight acres, situate on the waters of Sam's Creek.

This copy was about one-fourth the size of the *Democratic Advocate*, is well printed, and seems to have been well sustained, judging from its advertising patronage.

A copy of the *Engine of Liberty*, bearing date Nov. 25, 1813, which was published at Uniontown, contains nine columns and a half of Judge Luther Martin's charge to the grand jury of Baltimore County and the grand jury's reply.

The marriages of Philip Bishop, of Adams County, Pa., and Miss Mary Senseney, of Frederick County, on the 23d of November, 1813, and Daniel Stoner and Miss Ann Roop, both of Frederick County, on the 25th of the same month, are published; also the death, on the 12th of November, of Philoman Barnes, aged about ninety years.

A meeting of the citizens of Uniontown and vicinity is called to meet on December 7th, at the house of George Herbach, to petition Congress for a post-route from Westminster to Fredericktown; also to petition the next Legislature to grant them a lottery to raise money to purchase a fire-engine.

Some war news is reported, including an account of his victory over the Creek Indians on November 4th by Gen. Jackson. One or two articles published showed that the editor, like most Federalists, was opposed to the war of 1812–14.

Among the advertisements are the sale of farming utensils and household goods by Francis Hollingsworth, Little Pipe Creek; auction sale of dry goods, etc., by John Kurtz, at Uniontown; the sale of one hundred and twenty acres of land on Meadow Branch, one mile from Uniontown, by Christian Stouffler; also notices of two petitions to the General Assembly of Maryland, one of which, signed by citizens of Baltimore and Frederick Counties, is a prayer for a new county. The metes and bounds asked for are substantially the same as those granted twenty-four years later, when the bill was passed creating the county of Carroll.

The other petition was for a law "to open a road from New Windsor to intersect the old Liberty road, on the line between Eli Dorsey and James Pearre, about a quarter of a mile below Conrad Dudderar's tavern."

The *Star of Federalism*, a small newspaper of four pages, each with five columns, was established March,

1816, by Charles Sower, with the motto, "Nothing extenuate, nor aught set down in malice." Its terms were two dollars per annum, and it was printed in the building now occupied by R. J. Matthias. Its agents were:

LibertyTown, Nathan England; Sam's Creek, Jacob Landis; New Windsor, William Brawner, Chr. Ecker; Baltimore County, Thomas Pole; Westminster, Thomas Gist, Nicholas Lemon; New Market, William Hodgkiss; Taneytown, Nicholas Snider; Middleburg, J. C. and G. W. Gist; Pipe Creek, W. P. Farquhar; Union Bridge, Moses B. Farquhar; Emmittsburg, P. Reid, of Alexander; Baltimore, Edward J. Coale; Cumberland, Francis Reid; Mount Pleasant, David Stem; Norristown, Christopher Sower, Nathan Potts; Triadelphia, Andrew Graff; Darnes Town, Robert Groomes, John Candler; Hyatt's Town, William Hyatt; Pickneyville, D. Holliday.

It was in size thirteen by twenty inches, and after its publication in Uniontown for a year was removed to Frederick Town, and there published by Mr. Sower as late as December, 1819.

The Enterprise was established in 1856 by William Sedwick and Dr. Mills. It was a small sheet, and was published until the close of the year, when it was merged into a larger paper called *The Weekly Press*. The latter was first issued in January, 1857, with J. H. Christ as editor, its publishers being those of its predecessor, Dr. Mills and William Sedwick. It was published as late as July 26, 1861.

Church of God.—Religion appears to have taken firm hold of the people of Uniontown and its vicinity at an early date. Allusion has already been made to the building of St. Lucas' church by a lottery, under the auspices of the Presbyterian denomination. The congregation of the Church of God was organized in 1833, numbering at that time about fifty members, and the Presbyterian faith not having proved as popular in the community as was expected, St. Lucas' was transferred to the new organization. Abraham Appler was the elder of the church, and Isaac Appler, deacon. Edward West was the first regular pastor, and was succeeded by Rev. Maxwell, Rev. Jacob Linninger, Rev. Joseph Adams, Rev. William McFadden, Joseph Bombarger, R. C. Price, Rev. I. L. Richmond, Rev. Saletymer, and several others. The congregation now numbers about fifty members, and is under the care of Rev. Mr. Lugenbeel. This church is the mother of the churches at Middletown, Mayberry, Frizzelburg, and Greenwoods, which are all now in this charge. The Warfield, Winfield, and Carlton Churches at one time belonged to the same charge, and were under the supervision of this church. Their annual camp-meeting is held a few miles from Uniontown.

The Church of God Cemetery is situated immediately in rear of the church. The remains of the following persons are buried within its limits:

M. M. Currey, died July 5, 1830, aged 35.
Martha Currey, died May 16, 1852, aged 56.
Eleanor Banks, died Dec. 31, 1859, aged 81.
John M. Ferguson, born Sept. 8, 1786, died Oct. 20, 1861.
Rebecca, his wife, died Sept. 16, 1843, aged 60.
James Currie, died Aug. 26, 1827, aged 64.
Rebecca Eckard, died Feb. 6, 1842, aged 39 years, 3 months, 9 days.
John W. Davis, born March 22, 1813, died Aug. 9, 1877.
Mary Davis, born March 5, 1792, died Jan. 8, 1865.
Jonathan G. Davis, born March 28, 1779, died Jan. 4, 1842.
Edward Davis, died Aug. 2, 1825, aged 8.
John S. Shriver, born Aug. 26, 1794, died Dec. 6, 1814.
Elizabeth Ann Mary Martha Grammar, died April 26, 1833.
Andrew Werble, died April 29, 1849, aged 65 years, 6 months, 4 days.
Rachael Metcalf, died April 12, 1826, aged 54 years.
Solomon Beam, born July 11, 1798, died June 20, 1819.
Isaac Hiteshew, died March 19, 1829, aged 34 years, 2 months, 15 months.
Sivilla Reck, died March 15, 1826, aged 27 years, 1 month, 13 days.
Ezra Metcalfe, died Jan. 4, 1841, aged 29 years, 2 months, 25 days.
Conrad Stuller, born June 8, 1823, died July 3, 1876.
Henry Hiner, born March 9, 1770, died Sept. 12, 1847.
Hannah Hiner, died Dec. 11, 1847, aged 62 years, 3 months.
Samuel Hiner, born April 5, 1817, died Nov. 8, 1876.
Esther Hiteshew, died Oct. 31, 1844, aged 72 years, 14 days.
David Yingling, born Oct. 20, 1804, died April 23, 1874.
William H. Christ, born April 25, 1831, died Nov. 9, 1862.
Morgan A. Christ, died Jan. 2, 1870, aged 34 years, 3 months, 25 days.
Jacob Appler, died April 23, 1823, aged 34 years, 4 months, 1 day.
Abraham Appler, born Dec. 10, 1790, died Feb. 1, 1878.
Rebecca, his wife, and daughter of Jacob Hoffman, of Bainbridge, Lancaster Co., Pa., died Aug. 28, 1866, aged 70, and who was a member of the church for 50 years.
Mary J., wife of D. R. Carlyle, died Feb. 19, 1875, aged 50 years, 5 months.
Jacob Christ, born Sept. 22, 1789, died Nov. 30, 1872.
Elizabeth, his wife, died May 16, 1867, aged 68 years, 10 months, 12 days.
Abraham Garner, died Aug. 2, 1789, aged 63 years, 10 months, 25 days.
Mary Cover, born Dec. 20, 1754, died March 17, 1828.
Sarah, wife of Dan. Smith, died July 4, 1844, aged 66 years, 3 months, 14 days.
Barbara, relict of Barton Bean, died May 12, 1858, aged 74 years, 1 month, 5 days.
Sophia Yingling, aged 70.
William Wilson, died Nov. 12, 1849, aged 73 years, 9 months, 28 days.
Elizabeth, his wife, died Dec. 28, 1869, aged 84 years, 4 months, 7 days.
Margaret, wife of Ephraim Garner, died Aug. 12, 1855, aged 34 years, 2 months, 6 days.
Oliver, son of William and Elizabeth Hiteshew. Enlisted in Co. E, 203d Regiment P. V., Aug. 31, 1864, and was killed Jan. 15, 1865, whilst in the act of planting the flag on Fort Fisher, aged 18 years, 3 months, 17 days.

James Hiteshew, died Nov. 21, 1874, aged 24 years.

Anna, wife of John Gore, died March 10, 1874, aged 63 years, 6 months, 16 days.

Rebecca Grammar, born Sept. 10, 1793, died June 8, 1864.

Sarah C. Grammar, born June 22, 1824, died April, 1864.

Mary D. C., wife of John Grammar, died Aug. 23, 1856, aged 57 years, 8 months.

Elizabeth, wife of A. Koons, died Aug. 2, 1874, aged 82.

Angeline, wife of John T. Wilson, died Feb. 5, 1878, aged 62 years, 3 months, 26 days.

Annie Clay, died Feb. 19, 1877, aged 69 years, 10 months.

Mary Ann Hollenberger, died Jan. 4, 1855, aged 37 years, 5 months, 10 days.

Peter Hollenberger, died March 22, 1860, aged 70 years, 4 months, 22 days.

Magdalena, his wife, died Feb. 23, 1862, aged 76.

Rachel Yingling, born Jan. 28, 1801, died July 30, 1865.

Jacob Bloom, born July 20, 1794, died Sept. 19, 1862.

Mary, his wife, born Jan. 20, 1800, died March 24, 1877.

Samuel Anders, died April 26, 1865, aged 61 years, 10 months, 5 days.

Lydia, his wife, died Dec. 12, 1876, aged 74 years, 8 months, 28 days.

John Garner, died Sept. 13, 1860, aged 57 years.

Hannah Hetshue, died March 1, 1876, aged 74.

Ary, wife of James Few, died April 30, 1861, aged 69 years, 3 months, 19 days.

Thomas Metcalf, born Dec. 5, 1783, died March 17, 1862.

George Warner, died June 18, 1862, aged 79.

Elender A. Warner, born Dec. 22, 1786, died Feb. 26, 1867.

Catharine Hollenberger, born July 4, 1825, died April 7, 1874.

John P. Glass, a member of Co. G, 6th Md. Potomac Home Brigade, who died at Frederick Hospital, Sept. 12, 1863, aged 29 years, 4 months, 3 days.

Lieut. Peter Wolfe, Co. G, Md. P. H. B., died Aug. 1, 1862, aged 34 years, 4 months, 3 days.

Mary Smith, died Jan. 11, 1863, aged 54.

Sarah Burgoon, died Nov. 20, 1878, aged 71 years, 11 months, 20 days.

John Eckard, born Jan. 24, 1795, died Sept. 8, 1872.

Elizabeth Eckard, born Jan. 12, 1799, died Dec. 30, 1865.

John A. Eckard, born Aug. 29, 1831, died Aug. 21, 1870.

Anna Fuss, died Dec. 1, 1863, aged 88.

Elizabeth Bare, born Oct. 15, 1777, died Feb. 12, 1865.

Lydia Senseney, died Oct. 20, 1869, aged 64 years, 6 months, 19 days.

Washington Senseney, born May 28, 1815, died Dec. 18, 1868.

Mary A., his wife, born July 27, 1815, died June 20, 1875.

Joanna Gilbert, died March 8, 1873, aged 37 years, 5 months, 6 days.

Sarah Herbach, born Oct. 16, 1801, died April 12, 1872.

Mary Bentley, died Sept. 27, 1821, aged 24 years, 6 months, 18 days.

Rebecca Steele, died April 6, 1879, aged 65 years, 6 months, 16 days.

William Hollenberry, born Nov. 13, 1817, died Feb. 23, 1870.

Peter Christ, born July 19, 1786, died March 2, 1876.

Elizabeth, his wife, died Oct. 17, 1868, aged 81.

James Gilbert, died July 15, 1877, aged 73 years, 5 months, 6 days.

Alamanda Eckard, died July 13, 1879, aged 43 years, 8 months, 12 days.

Henry Eckard, died April 21, 1876, aged 45.

Edward Arntz, died Oct. 16, 1867, aged 26 years, 1 month, 3 days.

St. Paul's Evangelical Lutheran congregation was formed Dec. 29, 1869. It was then under the charge of Rev. J. F. Deiner, and numbered eight members. The elders were Dr. J. J. Weaver and Jacob Ecker; the deacons, O. M. Hitshew, W. H. Hoffman, and J. Routson. Mr. Deiner held the position as pastor of the charge until 1872, when he was succeeded by Rev. G. W. Anderson; the membership at this time was steadily increasing. They held their services in a hall until the erection of their present edifice. The church, which was built by a general contribution, cost about two thousand dollars. The corner-stone was laid Oct. 24, 1874, and the building was dedicated in December of the same year, under the supervision of Rev. D. Morris, of Baltimore. After three years of untiring services Mr. Anderson resigned his charge, in May, 1876, when the Rev. David B. Floyd was called to occupy the pulpit. The estimated cost of their handsome parsonage, which is now under erection, is two thousand dollars. The present officers of the church are: Elders, Dr. Weaver and Jacob Ecker; Deacons, O. M. Hitshew and J. Routser, who have occupied those respective positions since the organization of the church. The congregation now numbers forty members, and the amount of contributions for 1881 was about four hundred dollars. This church has in its charge three other congregations, viz., "Winter's Church," "Baust Church," and "Mount Union;" it has also a Sunday-school attached to it which is in a very flourishing condition. Rev. Mr. Floyd has been the pastor for five years and gives entire satisfaction, and is untiring in his efforts to promote the interests of his church.

The Pipe Creek Circuit of the Methodist Protestant Church was organized in 1829, and has steadily increased in power and influence. Below is given the names of the pastors who have successively ministered to the various congregations under their charge in Uniontown and its vicinity:

1829, D. E. Reese; 1830, F. Stier, J. Hanson; 1831, F. Stier, I. Ibbertson; 1832, Isaac Webster, C. W. Jacobs; 1833, Isaac Webster, W. Sexsmith; 1834, Josiah Varden, H. Doyle; 1835, H. Doyle, J. W. Everest, A. A. Lipscomb; 1836–37, J. S. Reese, J. W. Porter; 1838, Eli Henkle, J. W. Porter; 1839, G. D. Hamilton, E. Henkle; 1840, G. D. Hamilton, B. Appleby; 1841, J. S. Reese, J. T. Ward; 1842, L. R. Reese, P. L. Wilson, J. Elderdice; 1843, J. S. Reese, S. L. Rawleigh, W. T. Eva; 1844, W. Collier, T. L. McLean, J. D. Brooks; 1845, W. Collier, P. L. Wilson, J. K. Nichols; 1846, W. Collier, J. K. Nicholas; 1847, J. Morgan, T. D. Valiant; 1848, J. Morgan, W. Roby; 1849, D. E. Reese, T. L. McLean; 1851, H. P. Jordan, J. Roberts; 1852, H. P. Jordan, H. J. Day; 1853, T. M. Wilson, H. J. Day; 1854, J. A. McFadden; 1855, J. A. McFadden, F. Swentzell; 1856, N. S. Greenaway, F. Swentzell; 1857–60, J. T. Ward, J. T. Murray; 1860, D. E. Reese, J.

B. Jones; 1861, D. E. Reese; 1862–65, P. L. Wilson; 1865–68, R. S. Norris; 1868-71, D. Wilson; 1871, J. R. Nichols; 1872–74, H. C. Cushing; 1874–77, J. W. Charter; 1877–80, C. H. Littleton.

The following are the names of some of the persons buried in Uniontown cemetery:

Washington, son of Moses and S. B. Brown, died March 15, 1874, aged 39 years, 3 months, 2 days. He was a member of Co. I, 4th Regiment Md. Vols.

Anna Carlyle, died Aug. 1, 1880, aged 80 years, 3 months, 23 days.

Rachel O'Brien, died Dec. 25, 1870, aged 70.

Sarah Boham, died July 7, 1857, aged 71.

Jacob Zimmerman, born Dec. 30, 1787, died Feb. 5, 1859.

Mary, wife of John Babylon, died March 2, 1859, aged 45 years, 9 months, 14 days.

William Roberts, died March 29, 1860, aged 61; and his wife, Eleanor R., May 13, 1875, aged 70.

Philip Babylon, born Oct. 6, 1776, died Jan. 10, 1842.

Elizabeth Babylon, born Oct. 12, 1782, died July 19, 1857.

Rachel Hammond, died July 23, 1846, aged 82 years, 5 months, 6 days.

Eleanor Roberts, died Feb. 28, 1846, aged 77.

Rachel Brooks, born Dec. 18, 1818, died Jan. 31, 1851.

Caroline Zollickoffer, died Dec. 20, 1850, aged 84.

John M. A. Zollickoffer, died May 20, 1836, aged 51 years, 3 months, 10 days.

William Wright, died Jan. 25, 1838, aged 36.

Rev. Daniel Zollickoffer, died Nov. 1, 1862, aged 72; and Elizabeth, his wife, died July 5, 1851, aged 57.

Rev. Dr. William Zollickoffer, died April 6, 1853, 59 years, 5 months; and Sarah, his wife, died May 24, 1843, aged 44 years, 10 months, 20 days.

Richard Brown, born Dec. 23, 1793, died March 14, 1850; and Susan, his wife, born June 10, 1787, died Sept. 24, 1872.

Samuel Roberts, died June 15, 1838, aged 32 years, 5 months, 8 days.

Charles Stephenson, died Sept. 10, 1832, aged 91 years, 8 months, 26 days.

John D. Norris, died Feb. 4, 1829, aged 23.

Elizabeth Norris, died April 11, 1841, aged 57.

Nicholas Stevenson, born May 18, 1780, died Aug. 8, 1838.

Nancy Stevenson, died May 21, 1848, aged 70.

Sarah Stevenson, died April 10, 1844, aged 60.

William Devilbiss, born April 30, 1790, died Sept. 1, 1834.

Jemima Stevenson, died May 7, 1852, aged 70.

Peter Senseney, born Feb. 3, 1789, died March 21, 1855.

Keturah Senseney, died June 11, 1858, aged 70.

Richard Parrish, born May 10, 1822, died Dec. 2, 1851.

Rachel Rebecca Senseney, died March 19, 1862, aged 36.

Michael Spousler, died Oct. 25, 1832.

George Herbach, died April 28, 1836, aged 69 years, 4 months; and Elizabeth, his wife, born Dec. 24, 1774, died July 28, 1858.

Zachariah Weeling, died Sept. 16, 1870, aged 65.

Abraham Shriver, died Aug. 24, 1855, aged 80 years, 5 months, 29 days.

John Shriver, died April 25, 1869, aged 51.

Robert Dungan, born March 28, 1818, died April 18, 1858.

Emily Dungan, born Jan. 16, 1811, died April 28, 1863.

Elizabeth Wright, died July 14, 1867, aged 85 years, 7 months, 6 days.

Rev. Francis G. Wright (of M. P. Church), died Feb. 23, 1859, aged 35 years, 7 months.

Norris Meredith, died Sept. 12, 1860, aged 90 years, 10 months, 15 days.

Lydia Meredith, died Jan. 23, 1867, aged 70 years, 11 months, 10 days.

Catharine Meredith, died Feb. 24, 1867, a6ed 75 years, 9 months, 5 days.

William N. Meredith, died Jan. 14, 1868, aged 53 years, 9 months, 20 days.

Mary G. Meredith, died Jan. aged 16, 1868, aged 61 years, 2 months, 29 days.

Elizabeth B. Meredith, born Feb. 22, 1802, died Nov. 20, 1875.

Nathaniel N. Meredith, born April 5, 1798, died Dec. 25, 1874.

Nathan Roop, born May 3, 1835, died April 10, 1874.

Michael Nusbaum, died March 8, 1877, aged 66 years, 2 months, 8 days; and Catharine, his wife, Jan. 19, 1873, aged 77 years, 7 months, 3 days.

William Shaw, died April 18, 1869, aged 68 years, 3 months.

Anna Maria, wife of Rev. David Wilson, died May 29, 1870, aged 41 years, 4 months, 11 days.

Dennis Cookson, died July 22, 1879, aged 44 years, 4 months, 10 days.

Joseph Cookson, born Aug. 24, 1793, died June 1, 1846.

Rachel Cookson, born Feb. 1, 1800, died Jan. 24, 1875.

Samuel Cookson, born Sept. 17, 1762, died Dec. 22, 1836; and Rachel, his wife, born 1779, died 1853, aged 74.

John W. Babylon, died Nov. 19, 1866, aged 21 years, 8 months, 18 days.

John N. Starr, born March 24, 1808, died May 26, 1880; and Mary, his wife, born March 10, 1810, died Aug. 27, 1878.

Hannah M., wife of Milton S. Starr, died Jan. 13, 1874, aged 29 years, 5 months, 27 days.

Mordecai Haines, died Jan. 19, 1861, aged 40.

Louisa Babylon, died Dec. 6, 1854, aged 38 years, 9 months, 17 days.

Deborah, wife of David Foutz, died Sept. 25, 1842, aged 41.

Charles Devilbiss, born Aug. 13, 1786, died Sept. 29, 1862; and Elizabeth, his wife, died Feb. 27, 1864, aged 76 years, 1 month, 21 days.

Ann Eliza, consort of John S. Devilbiss, died April 4, 1869, aged 34 years, 6 days.

Martha Devilbiss, died Jan. 19, 1868, aged 37 years, 15 days.

Mary E. Devilbiss, died Oct. 17, 1870, aged 46 years, 1 month, 4 days.

Wm. H. Devilbiss, born Jan. 13, 1821, died April 3, 1880.

Edward Devilbiss, born Oct. 5, 1822, died Jan. 1, 1880; and Louisa C., his wife, born Sept. 11, 1825, died Feb. 2, 1879.

John B. Williams, died July 23, 1861, aged 66; and Temperance, his wife, died Nov. 19, 1872, aged 69 years, 7 days.

John Smith, died Aug. 7, 1868, aged 70 years, 4 months, 9 days; and Mary, his wife, died Nov. 6, 1878, aged 77 years, 7 months, 16 days.

William Goswell, died July 20, 1839, aged 56.

Matilda Morelock, died April 15, 1851, aged 53 years, 6 months.

Nancy Wilson, wife of George Harris, died March 1, 1858, aged 65.

Mary Brisco, died Aug. 17, 1869, aged 75.

John Hyder, born Aug. 22, 1787, died March 20, 1878; and Catharine, his wife, born April 16, 1788, died March 13, 1863; Englid Hyder, their son, born Aug. 31, 1814, died Feb. 12, 1853.

"Sydney Hyder Johnson, aged 23."

Below are given the votes polled for district officers since June 4, 1851:

1851.—Vote for Primary School Commissioners: Isaac Slingluff 253, Wm. Hughes 117, Henry H. Herbaugh 157, William Ecker 44.

1853.—For Justices: Richard Dell 280, Helpher Crawmer 55, John Smelzer 33, H. W. Dell 17, H. H. Herbaugh 354, Samuel Shunk 259, W. R. Currey 292, Joshua Switzer 321; Constables: Wm. Segafoose 384, Wm. Brown 225, Wm. Wilson 311, Wm. Delphy 197; Road Supervisor: Frederick Tawney 240, Thos. F. Shepherd, 302.

1855.—For Justices: Henry Fleagle 476, H. H. Herbaugh 486, E. A. Adee 481, John T. Lowe 480, John Smelzer 147; Constables: Wm. Delphy 463, Wm. Wilson 466, W. Segafoose, 232; Road Supervisor: Hiram Englar, 488.

1857.—For Justices: H. H. Herbaugh 378, D. B. Fleagle 353, J. B. Christ 304, S. Anders 340; Constables: Wm. Brown 166, J. T. Myers 328, Isaac B. Wright 338; Road Supervisor: J. B. Williams 342.

1859.—For Justices: W. H. Haines 153, Caleb Baring 138, W. H. Herbaugh 341, D. B. Fleagle 334, Joshua Switzer 345, John Hesson 355; Constables: Frederick Tawney 137, J. R. Haines 361, Levi Haifley 351; Road Supervisor: Samuel Beck 330.

1861.—For Justices: H. H. Herbaugh 454, John Hesson 447, Levi Fleagle 445, Joshua Switzer 449; Constables: A. S. Warner 346, Wm. Singer 412, J. W. Segafoose 202; Road Supervisor: Wm. Beck 364, W. S. Lantz 91, Noah Plowman 74.

The public school trustees for 1881 and 1882 have been:

1 and 2. Uniontown.—J. C. Brubaker, Jesse J. H. Davis, Wm. H. McCollum.
3. Tunker Meeting-house.—George H. Brown, Levi Caylor, John H. Jordan.
4. Moredock's.—David Roop, John Royer, Henry Brunner.
5 and 6. Frizellsburg.—Dr. Jacob Rinehart, Alfred Warner, Leonard Zile.
7. Pleasant Valley.—Wm. Bowers, Noah Powell, Uriah Feaser.
8. Baust Church.—Jesse Unger, Wm. Neusbaum, Wm. Farmwalt.
9. Fairview.—Davis Myers, Daniel Diehl, David Stoner.
10. Bear Mount.—Samuel Wantz, David E. Morelock, George W. Hull.
1. Middletown African School.—John Thompson, Summerfield Roberts, Lloyd Coats (colored).

The teachers and number of pupils for the term ending April 15, 1881, were:

1, H. P. Engler, 49; 2, Ella Beam, 42; 3, T. H. Adams, 30; 4, S. P. Weaver, 54; 5, Thomas Tipton, 41; 6, J. J. Reindollar, 48; 7, J. P. Earnest, 42; 8, Francis L. Delaplane, 51; 9, A. H. Diffenbaugh, 47; 10, Sue L. Langly, 34; 1 (colored school), T. F. McCann, 20.

Frizzellburg.—The village of Frizzellburg is five miles from Westminster, and pleasantly situated near Meadow Branch. It was named in honor of the Frizzell family, early identified with the settlement.

Among the first families located in the immediate vicinity of the town were the Smiths, Haifleys, Harmans, Blacks, Roops, and Warners.

The house now owned by Jeremiah Rinehart was the first erected in the village, and was occupied by Daniel Smith, one of the first residents of the town, in 1814, and was built probably prior to the year 1800. In the year 1814, Nimrod Frizzell, accompanied by his family, settled in the neighborhood and worked at his trade, that of a blacksmith. At that time there were but few houses within the village limits. The Haifleys lived in the house now occupied by Larry Freeman. George Harman built and resided in the present residence of Edward Six. Jacob Black lived in the house which is now the home of Mrs. Vance. In 1818, Nimrod Frizzell built the house which is now owned and occupied by Judge Frizzell. He lived there and kept a hotel, together with a small store, which was conducted in his name after his death until 1860. Frank Lytle was the first school-teacher in the village, and was followed by Samuel Moffat and Francis Matthias. Dr. Cook was the first regular physician, and located here about the year 1847. He remained but a short time, and was followed by Dr. Baker, Dr. Shipley, Dr. Roberts, Dr. Kennedy, and Dr. Price respectively. In 1864, Dr. J. E. Rinehart located here. He was a native of Carroll County, and was born in Hampstead District. He came to the vicinity of Frizzellburg in 1836, attended the public schools at this point, and in 1849 entered the Gettysburg Academy, Pa., where he graduated in 1855. He attended lectures in Philadelphia, and graduated at the Medical College in 1858. After locating and remaining in Pennsylvania during the war, he permanently located in Frizzellburg. He was married to Maggie, a daughter of Peter Greeble, of Emmittsburg, Frederick Co., Md. Mr. Rinehart represented his county in the Maryland Legislature in 1876. Richard Brown was the earliest merchant, and was succeeded by Darius Brown, who opened his place of business in the front room of the house now occupied by Ephraim Cover. In 1849 he built himself a store-room and removed his goods to that building. Campbell & Everheart succeeded to his business in 1851. Mr. Brown having died the previous year, they built themselves a larger storehouse to accommodate the rapidly-increasing trade of the village. A gentleman by the name of Richard Dell, and also a Mr. Holliberry, were the successors of Messrs. Campbell & Everheart, and were themselves succeeded, in 1881, by Mr. Kerster.

In 1842, Isaac Appler built the dwelling and storehouse now owned and occupied by Mr. Warner. Mr. Appler sold it to Mr. Gilbert, who kept a grocery-store, and who subsequently sold it to Valentine Vance. A dry-goods and grocery-store has since been established here, Mr. Warner having purchased the property from Mrs. Vance in 1860.

Mr. Frizzell, the son of Nimrod Frizzell, from whom the village received its title, was born in the year 1818, and has always been a resident of the place. For three years he held the position of leather inspector of the city of Baltimore. He married, in 1844, Miss Barbara N., daughter of John and Mary Swigart. Mr. Frizzell is at present one of the judges of the Orphans' Court.

Church of God.—This congregation was formed under the auspices of Rev. William McFadden. The church was erected and dedicated in the year 1842, at a cost of seven hundred and fifty dollars. Rev. Joseph Bombarger delivered the dedicatory sermon. The following gentlemen composed the building committee, and were authorized to collect all the subscriptions: Benjamin Fleagle, Levi Fleagle, James Gilbert, Caleb Boring, and Henry Fleagle. The congregation at that time numbered forty members.

Rev. Mr. Lugenbeel is the present pastor, and Levi Fleagle the elder. The latter has held that position since the organization of the church. The trustees for the year 1881 are Levi Fleagle, Wm. L. Fleagle, Benjamin Fleagle, and John T. Baust, and the number of members fifteen. In the rear of the church is the Church of God cemetery, in which are buried several children, and there are also many unmarked graves. Among the names recorded are Eliza Jabes, died Jan. 22, 1862, aged sixty-five years, four months, four days, and Thomas Jones, died Aug. 11, 1873, aged fifty-two years.

The building in which are held the sessions of the Frizzellburg Academy is commodious and amply provided with all the necessary paraphernalia for proper training and education. The school is graded to suit the ages and development of scholars, and is supplied with an excellent corps of teachers.

Within four miles of the village, on the banks of the Big Pipe Creek, there stood until recently an old stone mill and dwelling, erected in 1776 by two Tories named Graffs. They were driven from Philadelphia because of the intemperate expression of their unpopular opinions and sympathies, and fled to Carroll County (at that time Frederick) for refuge. They settled upon this stream and prospered, their calamities having taught them the wisdom of moderation and taciturnity.

Tyrone.—The village of Tyrone is situated thirty-two miles west of Baltimore and six miles west of Westminster, on what is generally known as "the plank road" leading from Westminster to Taneytown. It contains a handsome church, a mill, a store for general merchandise, and a number of dwelling-houses. The Farmwalt family, early settlers in the neighborhood, founded the town. William L. Fleagle is the postmaster and principal merchant, and W. H. Rider superintends the mill.

Emmanuel Church, or Baust's church, in which the Lutheran and Reformed congregations jointly worship, was built many years ago, but was thoroughly repaired and almost completely remodeled, Oct. 18, 1868. The congregations were originally organized prior to the year 1794, and worshiped in an old log school-house which stood upon the site of the present church, the land having been deeded Jan. 10, 1794, by Valentine and Maria Baust, to build a church and school-house, and it was from the donors that the church derived its former name.

The two congregations were incorporated by an act of the General Assembly of Maryland passed Jan. 12, 1835. The incorporators were John Fleagle, Sr., John Derr, Michael Morelock, and Peter Haifley. At a meeting of the two congregations in 1838 there were present John Derr, Peter Dayhoff, Peter Golle, George Maxwell, John Fleagle, Jr., Valentine Wentz, and Jacob Valentine.

The officers of the church at this time were as follows:

German Reformed Congregation: Elders, John Fleagle, Peter Golle; Deacons, Peter Dayhoff, John Fleagle; Trustees, George Maxwell, John Derr. Lutheran Congregation: Elders, M. Morelock, Andrew Babylon; Deacons, Henry Hahn, Jacob Valentine; Trustees, Valentine Wentz, Peter Halfleigh.

The ministers who have served the Lutheran congregation, as far as can be ascertained, are as follows: John Grupp was the first, and was at the time also the pastor of Taneytown, Krider's, Winter's, and Silver Run Lutheran Churches. He was followed in 1819 by Henry Graver; Rev. John N. Hoffman, 1833; Samuel Finckle, 1834; Ezra Keller, 1835; Solomon Sentman, 1840; Rev. Philip Willard, 1845; Cornelius Reimensnider, John Winters, 1850; Samuel Henry, 1855 to 1868; Mr. Deiner, 1872; Rev. G. W. Anderson, and the present pastor, Rev. David B. Floyd.

This church was in the Emmittsburg and Taneytown charge until 1840, when it was transferred to the Westminster Circuit. Again, about the year 1870, it was transferred to the Uniontown Circuit, to which it now belongs. The present officers of the two congregations are:

Lutheran: Elders, William Nusbaum and Jacob Myers; Deacons, Dr. J. E. Rinehart, Lewis Myers; Trustees, Jeremiah Rinehart, Ephraim Winter. This congregation numbers ninety members. German Reformed: Elders, Jesse Unger, Joshua Crawford; Deacon, Josiah Erb; Trustees, Jacob Sell, Wm. Farmwalt. Joint Board: President, William Nusbaum; Secretary, Dr. J. E. Rinehart. Jacob Myers, joint treasurer; Jacob Myers, treasurer Lutheran Congregation; Jesse Unger, treasurer Reformed Congregation.

As was said above, in 1868 the church was thoroughly remodeled and rededicated, the services being interesting and impressive. The preparatory exercises were conducted by Rev. Griffith Owen, of Baltimore, and the sermon was preached by Rev. P. A. Strobel, of Westminster. The dedicatory services were performed by Rev. J. Steiner. The debt of the church was liquidated by subscriptions raised during the services. The name of the church was also changed at that time, and it has since been known as Emmanuel. The following persons are buried in Baust Church Cemetery:

Abraham Hann, died Oct. 5, 1862, aged 80 years, 11 months, 25 days.

Josiah Hafley, died Nov. 29, 1855, aged 36 years, 5 months, 13 days.

Margaret Fluegal, born Jan. 3, 1770, died Dec. 4, 1842.

John Fluegal, born Nov. 17, 1762, died Sept. 3, 1845.

Uriah Baust, born Nov. 23, 1822, died Nov. 16, 1849.

Abraham Hann, born May 4, 1817, died March 16, 1841.

Jacob Keefer, died July 13, 1837, aged 34 years, 6 months, 21 days.

Lydia Hesson, wife of John Hesson, and daughter of John Taney, died Aug. 27, 1842, aged 17.

Peter Haiffle, born April 11, 1786, died Jan. 11, 1869.

Levi Haifley, died July 3, 1830, aged 17.

Margaret, wife of Peter Hafley, died Dec. 23, 183–, aged 43 years, 1 month, 23 days.

Sophia Wagner, died Aug. 13, 1836, aged 62 years, 7 months.

Mary Wantz, died March 25, 1842, aged 24 years, 9 months, 28 days.

Catharine Shoemaker, died 1834.

Peter Shoemaker, died Dec. 24, 1838, aged 81 years, 8 months, 24 days.

Mary E. Wentz, died 1833, aged 40.

George Warner, died April 30, 1836, aged 77 years, 10 months, 10 days.

Johannes Bischoff, born 1740, died July 9, 1813, aged 73 years, 4 months.

Maria Bischoff, died Dec. 21, 1824, aged 80.

Jacob Bishop, died Aug. 31, 1832, aged 59 years, 9 months, 7 days; and Elizabeth, his wife, died Dec. 4, 1824, aged 35 years, 9 months, 18 days.

Margaret Mock, died Jan. 2, 1815, aged 64.

Peter Mock, died April 3, 1812, aged 85.

Jacob Honer, died 1798.

Frederick Wentz, Jr., died Sept. 27, 1824, aged 63.

Geo. Frederick Wentz, died Feb. 3, 1833, aged 78 years, 1 month, 15 days.

Frederick Keefer, born Dec. 2, 1795, died Aug. 4, 1855.

Elizabeth Shreiner, born in 1771, died in 1773.

Sarah Swigart, died March 28, 1813, aged 25 years, 10 months, 2 days.

"Wagner, born 1755, died 1801."

Michael Wagner, born Nov. 6, 1752, died Feb. 21, 1839.

Barbara Yar, born Deo. 4, 1784, died Dec. 2, 1806.

Ulrich Stollern, born April 15, 1737, died September, 1816.

John Marker, died Aug. 16, 1824, aged 65; and Susannah, his wife, born Feb. 12, 1774, died March 3, 1839.

Elizabeth Moler, born Nov. 14, 1776, died Feb. 18, 1813.

Magdalena Derr, died July 19, 1822, aged 25.

Abraham Derr, died May 11, 1829, aged 62.

Elizabeth Derr, died Nov. 13, 1822, aged 55.

Jacob Derr, born Nov. 12, 1788, died Dec. 23, 1819.

Valentine Wentz, died Feb. 19, 1843, aged 56 years, 11 months, 20 days.

Catherine Bishop, born Oct. 13, 1783, died June 13, 1845.

John F. Haifley, died Sept. 14, 1845, aged 55 years, 5 months, 13 days.

George Eckard, died Nov. 9, 1822, aged 65 years, 11 months, 20 days.

Aaron P. Erviesse, died Aug. 24, 1829, aged 6.

Mary Seel, died Aug. 27, 1813, aged 80.

Sarah Worley, born March 6, 1799, died Sept. 13, 1857.

Lydia Worley, born June 18, 1803, died Feb. 17, 1858.

Lydia, wife of Daniel Myers, died July 16, 1856, aged 40 years, 11 months.

Elizabeth Hann, died March 20, 1855, aged 69 years, 2 months, 1 day.

Peter Hesson, born July 21, 1783, died Dec. 16, 1865; and Susannah, his wife, born Dec. 15, 1797, died Jan. 25, 1857.

Catherine, wife of John Fleet, died Dec. 11, 1856, aged 72.

Peter Zepp, died Aug. 21, 1879, aged 71 years, 1 month, 14 days; and Catherine, his wife, born April 28, 1810, died Jan. 23, 1855.

Abraham Hesson, died Feb. 19, 1855, aged 81 years, 11 months, 21 days.

Louisa Hesson, died Jan. 14, 1859, aged 70 years, 11 months, 27 days.

Eli Hesson, died Sept. 9, 1859, aged 47 years, 6 months, 12 days.

John L. Powell, born June 23, 1779, died April 15, 1855; and Elizabeth, his wife, born April 12, 1782, died May, 1864.

Peter Gatle, died July 7, 1865, aged 76 years, 10 months, 16 days; and Catherine, his wife, Feb. 25, 1862, aged 68 years, 8 months, 3 days.

Josiah Bankard, born Oct. 25, 1836, died July 17, 1873.

Abraham Bankard, died Oct. 30, 1879, aged 80 years, 22 days.

Ezra Haifley, "Co. A, 6th Md. Regt. Vols.," born Sept. 27, 1840, died Oct. 14, 1864.

Wm. Gregg, born April, 1818, died April, 1866.

Lydia, wife of Josiah Babylon, died Aug. 10, 1867, aged 47 years, 10 months, 9 days.

Joseph Cox, born Aug. 10, 1801, died Oct. 29, 1879; and Rachel, his wife, born Nov. 8, 1811, died May 24, 1872.

"John Mathew, honest and faithful servant to Abraham Hesson, died Sept. 9, 1855, aged 61."

Valentine Wantz, died June 25, 1876, aged 65 years, 6 months, 23 days; and Susannah, his wife, born July 8, 1800, died March 5, 1870.

Mathias Copenhover, died Jan. 8, 1877, aged 68 years, 8 months, 22 days; and Mary, his wife, died May 4, 1875, aged 72 years, 8 months, 8 days.

Sarah, their daughter, born Dec. 5, 1830, died March 18, 1864; and Elizabeth, another daughter, born Dec. 3, 1835, died August, 1863.

John Fleagle, a soldier of 1812, born June 25, 1793, died March 15, 1879; and Rachel, his wife, born Jan. 22, 1795, died May 8, 1865.

Uriah Fleagle, of "Co. G, 1st Regt. Md. Vols." (P. H. B.), born Feb. 21, 1843, fell at the battle of Gettysburg, July 3, 1863, aged 20 years, 4 months, 9 days.

Amos Fleagle was killed at the battle of Murfreesboro', December, 1862.

George Fleagle, died Feb. 27, 1880, aged 81 years, 7 months, 4 days.

Anna Louisa, wife of Amos Hull, died Dec. 22, 1876, aged 38.

Margaret Rinehart, died June 5, 1863, aged 49.

Samuel Fitze, died Nov. 30, 1871, aged 49 years, 2 months, 27 days.

Valentine Wantz, born Jan. 27, 1820, died March 11, 1860.

Anna Maria Meyers, born Dec. 21, 1777, died Oct. 3, 1863.

Susan, wife of Jacob Eckard, died Jan. 9, 1861, aged 51.

John Lampert, died June 20, 1874, aged 76; and Louisa, his wife, Feb. 17, 1877, aged 78 years, 11 days.

Hezekiah Lambert, born Oct. 24, 1825, died April 7, 1860.

George Warner, born July 15, 1814, died Feb. 6, 1872.

Sarah Warner, born May 24, 1795, died May 16, 1872.

Elizabeth Warner, born May 26, 1776, died Oct. 1, 1857.

William Warner, died Dec. 30, 1853, aged 36 years, 7 months, 15 days.

Michael Dotzour, died March 19, 1858, aged 35 years, 5 months, 10 days.

Margaret Dotzour, died May 6, 1872, aged 68.

John Babylon, born May 10, 1803, died March 1, 1862.

John Dell, born Dec. 17, 1773, died Oct. 23, 1871.

Mary Dell, born July 26, 1777, died Sept. 28, 1851.

Michael Babylon, died Dec. 12, 1870, aged 70 years, 8 months, 23 days.

Andrew Babylon, born Aug. 20, 1779, died Oct. 21, 1851.

Susanna Babylon, died Feb. 8, 1870, aged 91 years, 9 months, 17 days.

David Babylon, born Dec. 21, 1820, died July 15, 1857; and Mary, his wife, born Feb. 13, 1821, died Feb. 4, 1857.

George Rodkey, born Dec. 8, 1790, died Nov. 25, 1851.

Mary Eckard, born Dec. 13, 1765, died Jan. 31, 1856.

Solomon Farmwalt, born Sept. 4, 1793, died Feb. 22, 1881; and Elizabeth, his wife, born April 28, 1800, died March 22, 1852.

Ellenoore Fromfelter, died Feb. 15, 1870, aged 76 years, 3 months, 4 days.

John Nusbaum, born March 25, 1793, died June 1, 1866; and Elizabeth, his wife, born July 28, 1799, died Dec. 6, 1864.

Henry Beard, died Aug. 4, 1861, aged 41 years, 6 months, 5 days.

Cornelius Baust, born Feb. 10, 1785, died April 26, 1868; and Elizabeth, his wife, born Sept. 6, 1791, died March 1, 1865.

Charles Crawford, died Dec. 11, 1871, born May 23, 1805.

Fred. Wantz, born March 3, 1778, died Jan. 24, 1857; and Mary, his wife, died Feb. 8, 1852, aged 64 years, 2 months, 8 days.

George Wantz, died May 6, 1866, aged 36 years, 1 month, 11 days.

Eliza Hunger, died May 2, 1877, aged 63 years, 25 days.

Catharine, wife of Jesse Babylon, died April 5, 1878, aged 62.

Elizabeth, wife of Joshua Stansbury, born Aug. 13, 1813, died Feb. 1, 1874.

Wm. Lampert, born Sept. 1, 1826, died April 7, 1878.

Dr. David B. Fleagle, died Feb. 26, 1878, aged 35 years, 9 months, 6 days.

Jacob Foglesong, born Jan. 12, 1807, died Nov. 27, 1880.

Nusbaum's Cemetery.

Peter Babylon, born Nov. 14, 1781, died Jan. 28, 1850.

Hannah Foutz, born Nov. 26, 1770, died Aug. 28, 1815.

Elizabeth Foutz, died Sept. 27, 1830, aged 43.

Solomon Foutz, died Feb. 14, 1839, aged 78 years, 10 months, 25 days.

Jacob Youn, died January, 1830, aged 60.

Mary Youn, died March 15, 1824, aged 37 years, 2 months, 13 days.

Mary, infant daughter of Wm. Youn, died May 4, 1825.

John Yon, born April 1, 1829, died Jan. 1, 1831.

Catherine Yon, born 1785, died 1797.

Elizabeth Babylon, born Dec. 22, 1790, died April 26, 1813.

Samuel Farnhord, born Oct. 9, 1817, died June, 1818.

Leonard Kitzmiller, born April 27, 1732, died March 1, 1820.

David Stouffer, died Dec. 15, 1867, aged 76 years, 11 months, 14 days; and Mary, his wife, died March 26, 1841, aged 48 years, 4 months, and 12 days.

Emma Kate, daughter of N. and C. Heck, died Aug. 30, 1869, aged 7 months, 21 days.

Susannah Holloway, daughter of Samuel and Elizabeth Holloway, died 1809.

"P. W., died 1785."

Alexander McIlheny, died Jan. 25, 1835, aged 56 years, 10 months, 20 days; and Elizabeth, his wife, born Aug. 1, 1779, died May 2, 1853.

Mayberry is a small village five miles from Taneytown, near Bear Branch. N. H. Fleagle is the postmaster and merchant of the place, and William Stonesifer and Henry Eck are the millers.

Pleasant Valley, another small village, is five miles from Westminster. Samuel Lawyer is the postmaster; H. B. Albaugh, merchant; and F. L. Yingling & Son, mill-owners. St. Matthew's Reformed church was built at a cost of $2400, and dedicated Nov. 30, 1879.

MYERS DISTRICT, No. 3.

Myers District, or the Third District of Carroll County, is bounded on the north by Pennsylvania, on the east by Manchester District, on the south by the districts of Uniontown and Westminster, and on the west by Taneytown District. Big Pipe Creek, Silver Run, and their tributaries flow through the district in many directions, and Piney Creek forms the boundary line on the northwestern border; these fine streams furnishing excellent power for mills, which has been utilized to a considerable extent by the inhabitants. Union Mills, Myersville, Silver Run, and Piney Creek Station, on the Frederick and Pennsylvania Line Railroad, are flourishing villages. The metes and bounds of the district, as laid out by commission appointed in 1837, are as follows:

"Beginning at the end of Royer's and Guyman's lane, on Baughman's county road; thence with said road to Lawyer's Branch; thence down said branch to Big Pipe Creek; thence with a straight line through Peter Bixler's farm, leaving said Bixler in District No. 6; thence with a straight line to a branch known by the name of Ohio, where said branch crosses Trump's county road; thence up said branch through to Wine's farm, up said branch to its head; thence with a straight line to the nearest point on Rinehart's county road; thence on said road to the Pennsylvania line; thence with Pennsylvania line to Littlestown and Westminster turnpike; thence down said turnpike to the stone road; thence with said stone road to Grove's Ford on Big Pipe Creek; thence with said road to the aforesaid turnpike at the 33d mile stone; thence with said turnpike to Rinehart's county road; thence with said road to Rinehart's mill; thence up the road by Rinehart's dam; thence with said road, between Frederick Baughman's farm and Jacob Snyder's, to Andrew Angel's, leaving said Angel in District No. 7; thence to Bixler's tan-yard, leaving said Bixler in District No. 7; thence with a straight line to the beginning."

By an act of the General Assembly of Maryland, passed April 2, 1841, the division line between the Third (Myers) and Seventh (Westminster) Districts was altered and made as follows: "Beginning at the natural boundary at the intersection of Big Pipe Creek, in Peter Bixler's meadow, and running thence by a direct line to Jacob Frock's dwelling-house, leaving the same in the Seventh Election District; thence by a direct line to Adam and William Bishe's dwelling-house, leaving the same in the Seventh Election District, and thence to the Westminster and Littlestown turnpike road, at the intersection of the stone road, which was then the boundary line between the Third and Seventh Election Districts." The district in 1880 had a population of 1959.

Union Mills was made the place for holding the polls. The district was named in honor of the Myers family, one of the first to settle in this portion of Carroll County, one of whose descendants, Samuel W. Myers, assisted in laying out the nine districts into which Carroll was originally divided in 1837.

A tract of land known as "Ohio," containing nine thousand seven hundred and fifty acres, was patented to Samuel Owings in 1763.

The early settlers were almost entirely Germans from York and Lancaster Counties, in Pennsylvania, or directly from the Palatinate, and to this day there are in its limits but few families not of German extraction.

For the first half-century of its history and settlement the German was the only tongue spoken, and after that, for a generation, the German and English languages were spoken indiscriminately, but since 1835 the English only has been used. These settlers were a hardy and thrifty race, of strong religious sentiments, and rapidly increased in numbers and wealth. Among the pioneers were Joseph Leaman, Nicholas Deal, George Michael Derr, Charles Angel, the Erbs, Myerses, Bankerds, Naills, Krouses, Yinglings, Farmwalts, Hessons, Flicklingers, Koontz', Frocks, Bixlers, Bachmans, Groffs, Hahns, Wivels, Kesselrings, Leppoes, and afterwards there came the Burgoons, Joneses, Morelocks, Gearharts, Fishers, and others.

Over a century ago "Bankerd's mill" was in operation on the site of the present Union Mills, and "Groff's mill" was located where now James E. Dodrer has a saw and grist-mill, both on Big Pipe Creek.

The Shriver Family and Union Mills.—Andrew Shriver, son of David and Rebecca (Ferree) Shriver, was born on Little Pipe Creek (Westminster District), Nov. 7, 1762, and was the eldest of nine children. His parents were among the first settlers in this section of country. He was married Dec. 31, 1786, to Miss Elizabeth Shultz, daughter of John Shultz, at his house in Baltimore, by Rev. William Otterbein, a distinguished clergyman of that day. His wife was born Aug. 15, 1767, and died Sept. 27, 1839. Their children were John Shultz, born March 1, 1788; Thomas, born Sept. 2, 1789; Rebecca, born Dec. 29, 1790; Matilda, born Oct. 3, 1792; James, born at Littlestown, Pa., April 4, 1794; William, born at same place, Dec. 23, 1796, and died June 11, 1879; Elizabeth, born at Union Mills, March 14, 1799; and Andrew Keyser, born at the same place, March 25, 1802; Ann Maria, born March 13, 1804; Joseph, born Jan. 11, 1806; and Catharine, born May 27, 1808.

All of these children grew up and married respectably, and left surviving children to perpetuate their name and lineage.

After the death of his wife, Elizabeth, in 1839, Andrew Shriver continued to live at the old homestead at Union Mills until his death, Sept. 20, 1847, aged nearly eighty-five years. In the fall of 1784, when twenty years of age, with a capital of four hundred and sixty pounds, having been assisted to this extent, perhaps, by his father, who had accumulated considerable means, Andrew Shriver engaged in the mercantile business on Little Pipe Creek, and subsequently in Baltimore. After his marriage in 1786 he continued to make his home with his wife on Little Pipe Creek until 1791, when he removed to Littlestown, Pa., where he kept a store and tavern until 1797. On June 26th of that year he removed with his family, then comprising six children, to the Union Mills property, which he bought, in partnership with his brother David, of the heirs of Jacob Bankerd, deceased. This property is located on the northern branch of Pipe Creek, in what was then Frederick, now Carroll, County, five miles southeast of the Pennsylvania State line. Andrew and David Shriver experienced great difficulty in gaining possession of their property. David Shriver, Sr., was then, and for some thirty years afterwards, employed by them to get a chancery decree for the sale of the land of the Bankerd estate. He was at length successful, and was appointed trustee for the sale of the property. Andrew Shriver became the purchaser of a large part of the land, together with the mill, then almost on the same site as that occupied by the present structure. They got possession of the property with difficulty, even after its sale, some of the heirs not being willing to yield. By arrangement of the above partners with John Mung, a millwright, work on the mill was completed satisfactorily for the sum of four hundred and thirty dollars. This agreement was witnessed by James McSherry, Dr. S. Duncan, and Susannah Showers (sister of Andrew and David Shriver), and dated Jan. 26, 1797. An agreement of the same parties, of the same date, with Henry Kohlstock, carpenter,—

"Witnesseth that for and in consideration of one hundred pounds to be paid by the said Andrew and David Shriver to the said Henry Kohlstock, he, the said Kohlstock, agrees to finish two small houses, fourteen by seventeen feet each, to be connected by a porch and passage about ten feet wide,—that is to say, he is to do all the joiner work so as to complete said houses, passage, porch, and stairways, agreeably to a plan thereof now produced; also to do all the carpenter work of a mill house forty by fifty feet, and to complete the whole thereof in a sufficient and neat, workmanlike manner, as expeditiously as possible; and further, finally to complete the whole, he is to paint the work, both dwelling and mill house, in a proper and sufficient manner; they, Andrew and David Shriver, to find all the materials, paint, oil, etc.

"R. McIlhenny, John Mong, *Witnesses*."

This house was completed according to the agreement and occupied, and one of the rooms on the ground-floor was used for a store. The partnership between the brothers suggested the name of the "Union Mills" to their homes, which was subsequently extended to embrace the whole village. The date of the dissolution of the firm is not exactly known. David was afterwards employed in locating and constructing the National road from Baltimore through Fredericktown, Hagerstown, and Cumberland to Wheeling, on the Ohio River. He displayed great skill in working iron, having made some of the most difficult parts of the mill-machinery (the appliances at hand being embraced in an ordinary blacksmith-shop at this place), some of which are still about the premises, and will compare favorably with the productions of the best workmen of the present day. A couple of pair of steelyards, with his name stamped upon them, are now in use, and are perfectly reliable, the State inspector of weights and measures having certified to their accuracy some twenty years since. The Shriver family developed great skill in working iron. At a very early date they had a shop at Little Pipe Creek, in which they all worked at times for different purposes, and Isaac Shriver took a contract from the government to furnish a large quantity of gun-barrels, to be delivered at a stated time. Although the designated time was short for that day, he finished the contract according to the terms and to the satisfaction of the authorities. Andrew Shriver, after the removal of his brother David from the mills, continued to keep a store for the sale of general merchandise, and secured for the village a post-office, of which he took charge. He also held the office of magistrate for a long time, and it was chiefly owing to his influence that the public road was opened from Union Mills to Hanover, Pa. He was afterwards instrumental in getting the turnpike from Baltimore to Chambersburg through the village. With a growing family and continued prosperity in business, Mr. Shriver required more house-room, and wings were added at different periods to the original building. Architectural beauty was not much studied, but the mansion is quaint and picturesque. It still stands with but little alteration, and is now occupied by Andrew K. Shriver, one of the sons, born under its ancient roof. Andrew Shriver, although an active politician, as was also his father, never held any public office other than magistrate, which position he filled during the greater part of his life, having been retained through all the political changes which occurred in the State. His magisterial services were highly appreciated, and were characterized by moderation and dignity. Very few appeals from his decisions to the higher court were made, thus saving expense to the county, as well as to individuals. In his judicial business, which extended over a wide region, he exerted a large personal influence, often acted as peacemaker between litigants, and brought about amicable settlements where a continued appeal to law tended only to make matters worse. Elizabeth Shriver, wife of Andrew Shriver, as mistress of a large household and mother in the family, was an admirable Christian woman, and her influence had much to do in moulding the character and shaping the future of her children. The children of Andrew and Elizabeth Shriver were married thus: John Shultz to Henrietta Myers, of Baltimore; Thomas, three times,—first, to Ann Sharp, of York, Pa., and the third time to Miss Sherrard; Rebecca Ferree to James Renshaw, of York, Pa.; Matilda to Michael H. Spangler, of York, Pa.; James to Elizabeth B. Miller, of Uniontown, Pa.; William to Mary Owings, of Littlestown, Pa.; Elizabeth (Eliza) to Lawrence J. Brengle, of Frederick (after the decease of Catharine Shriver, his first wife); Andrew Keyser, on Feb. 16, 1837, to Catharine Wirt, of Hanover, Pa. (who died Aug. 24, 1873); Ann Maria to William Tell Steiger, of Washington, D. C.; Joseph to Henrietta Coston, of Washington, D. C.; Catharine to Lawrence J. Brengle, of Frederick. The children of these several family unions form a large connection, and are scattered over a wide extent of country, though the majority of them are living in the vicinity of the old homestead. Andrew K. and William, two of the sons, with parts of their families, retain the mill property in their possession at this date, 1881. This place is on the Baltimore and Reisterstown turnpike,—the old road to Pittsburgh,—over which noted thoroughfare in the days of stage-coaches there was an immense deal of travel. Among the many eminent men who tarried overnight or stopped for meals at the old Shriver mansion was Washington Irving, who spent the Sabbath there, and a chapter of the recollections of his stay is found in his writings, but the scene is laid in England. The first postmaster was Andrew Shriver, the present efficient officer Andrew K. Shriver, and William Shriver once held the office. For nearly fourscore years, save a brief space of time, this office has always been in the Shriver family. B. F. Shriver & Co. now operate the flouring-mill, and run a large canning-factory, while the tannery is run by A. K. Shriver & Sons on the same site where the first enterprise of that character was located in 1795.

William Shriver was born at Littlestown, Pa., Dec. 23, 1796, and at the time of his death, which occurred in 1879, was one of the proprietors of the flour-mills, and of the old estate there, which had been in the family many years. He was a brother to the late John S. Shriver, so well known as the president of the Ericsson line of steamboats between Baltimore and Philadelphia. He had several brothers, one of them, Thomas Shriver, living in New York City, ninety years old. Mr. Shriver's father was a very old man when he died, and the family is generally long-lived. He left an aged wife and a large number of children and great-grandchildren. He celebrated the fiftieth anniversary of his wedding several years ago. Few persons had a larger personal acquaintance or more friends than the deceased.

The following is a list of persons living within a radius of four or five miles of Union Mills, and all, with a few exceptions, in Myers District, who were seventy years old and upwards in 1879:

	Years.		Years.
Christina Yingling	80	Samuel Lookingbill	77
William Shriver	83	Isaac Beal	76
Mrs. Mary Shriver	72	George Stegner	88
Andrew K. Shriver	77	Mrs. Rebecca Leppo	80
Peter Yingling	82	Mrs. Catharine Meyers	84
Mrs. Yingling	74	Mrs. Mary Yeiser	91
Mrs. Willet	73	Mrs. Sarah Little	75
Jacob Slyder	84	John Stonesifer	84
John Koontz	76	Mrs. Rachel Warner	85
Philip Arter	75	Mrs. Margaret Duce	71
John Frock, of J.	72	Henry Duttaror	73
Isaac Bankert	77	Mrs. Mary Kelly	79
John Flickinger	73	John Study	74
Jacob Leister	77	Jacob Mikesell	90
Mrs. Elizabeth Kump	94	Daniel Leppo	73
Jacob Hahn	76	John Snyder	76
Samuel Hahn	75	Mrs. Elizabeth Myers	77
Mrs. Sarah Shull	79	George Fleagle, Sr.	82
George Bowman	77	Mrs. Lydia Fleagle	76
Andrew Stonesifer	77	Mrs. Judith Crumrine	81
Mrs. Mary Stonesifer	74		

Directly across Big Pipe Creek is a village laid out by Peter E. Myers and called Myersville; but as the post-office is called Union Mills, the latter is the name by which the mills and the village are generally known. The Methodist Episcopal church was erected in 1880, and has a flourishing Sunday-school attached to it, of which William Yingling is superintendent.

Carroll Academy was organized in 1838, and a stone building was erected by stock subscriptions. The first trustees were William Shriver, William N. Burgoon, John Erb, Peter E. Myers, and Isaac Bankerd; secretary of the board, A. K. Shriver. The first principal was James Burns, an Irishman, the second, James Small, and among their successors were Bushrod Poole, Christian Erb, Samuel S. Shriver, John G. Wolf, John A. Renshaw, Bernard McManus, and Mr. Bardwell. Upon the creation of the public school system, the academy passed under the control of the school authorities. Mr. Burns, the first teacher of the academy, organized the first Sunday-school in the district,—a union school and not denominational. Dr. William R. Cushing is the physician of the town. F. M. Hall is a prominent merchant in Union Mills. William Bankerd, Joseph Erb, Samuel Stonesifer are coopers; John Beemiller, Jesse Koontz, shoemakers; W. G. Byers, undertaker; J. William Everhart, surveyor; Jesse Legare is a justice of the peace; Jeremiah Myers carries on a saw-mill; Jesse Myers and P. Wolf are millers; John Myers is a manufacturer of brick. The blacksmiths are Samuel Stansbury, Samuel Orem, William Tagg & Sons; William Rennaker is a carpenter; Ephraim and Ezra J. Yingling are tinners; and Martin Yingling, a cabinet-maker.

Silver Run is on the turnpike from Westminster to Littlestown, Pa., nine miles from the former and five from the latter. Its postmaster is John N. Mark, and assistant, Augusta J. Mark. The village is near the stream, Silver Run, from which it takes its name. The village store is kept by Albaugh & Haines, and the hotel by Andrew Wisner. J. Henry Knipple is justice of the peace, and Dr. James M. Marshall, the physician. The various industries are represented by Elias Bankerd, wheelwright; Joseph Beemiller, J. W. Little, shoemakers; Mrs. T. Kesselring, millinery and confectionery; Henry and Jacob Koontz, blacksmiths; George L. Little, cabinet-maker; and Rufus Strouse, constable.

St. Mary's Church is on "Silver Run," and is the

joint place of worship of the German Reformed and Lutheran congregations. The present church edifice is of stone, and was erected in 1822. It is on a tract of land called "Dyer's Mill Forest," adjoining a survey called "Lewis' Luck." It occupies the site of the first church, a rude log structure, built in 1768. The deed for the fifteen acres on which it is located was made by Joseph Dyer in 1768 to John Leaman, Nicholas Deal, George Michael Derr, Charles Angel, of the "Dutch Congregation of Silver Run," a committee of the Lutheran and Reformed Calvinists. The consideration named in the conveyance is £4 3*s.* 9*d.* The witnesses to its execution were William Blair and Abraham Hayton. It was duly acknowledged March 21, 1769, before "His Lordship's Justices of the Peace," William Blair and Thomas Price. On the back of this instrument is a receipt from Christopher Edelin acknowledging to have received "7 pence half-penny stirling," as alienation fee on the said fifteen acres, from Daniel, of St. Thomas Jenifer, his lordship's agent. This was ground-rent money due the Lord Proprietor, and payable semi-annually at the two annual feasts at St. Mary's, but which had to be paid before a good conveyance could be obtained. This deed was recorded March 27, 1769. Rev. J. G. Noss is the present Reformed pastor, and Rev. J. M. Alleman the Lutheran, and H. W. Shriver the superintendent of the Reformed Sunday-school.

Immediately above the junction of Silver Run with Big Pipe Creek, on the latter, John Wiest has large flouring-mills, and David B. Earhart has a fulling-mill.

West of Union Mills, on Big Pipe Creek, James E. Dodrer has flouring-mills, once called "Old Graves' mills," but put down on the old maps, made a century ago, as "Groff's mill."

Piney Creek Station is on the Frederick and Pennsylvania Line Railroad, in the northwestern part of the district. C. Shere is the postmaster and merchant, and P. M. Wiest has charge of a mill on the Westminster turnpike. At the boundary line dividing Myers from Westminster District is "Mount Pleasant Academy," built in 1854, and a store kept by John Crouse. There is a saw- and grist-mill on the estate of the late Dr. Study, on Big Pipe Creek. Near the Hanover road, in the north of the district, are large beds of iron ore. In the eastern part, on Big Pipe Creek, A. Fusir has a store and flour-mill.

The first physicians who practiced in the district were Dr. Wampler, of Hanover, Dr. Shorb, of Littlestown, and the Taneytown doctors. There were no resident physicians for many years after the first settlement. Dr. Study, long ago deceased, was the pioneer in his profession, and he was succeeded by his son, Dr. John Study, who still practices in the neighborhood.

The following is a list of public school trustees and teachers for Myers District for 1881 and 1882:

1. Mount Pleasant.—J. Crouse, Frank Burgoon, John C. Bankert.

2 and 3. Carroll Academy.—Jacob Humbert, H. W. Shriver, John Bemiller.

4. Wisner's.—Jacob Feever, Larkin Belt, John H. Baum.

5. Bishe's.—Emanuel Yeizer, Samuel Getting, Josiah Steiner.

6. Humbert's.—Ezra M. Lawyer, Lewis Morelock, George Humbert.

7. Mauss'.—John Maus, Cyrus Feever, Absalom Koontz.

8. Green Mount.—Jacob P. Hull, John Starr, John Boose.

9. Erb's.—Jesse Lemon, S. Keefer, Jacob Marker.

10. Good Hope.—George Bowers, William Yingling, John Leister.

11. Cover's.—Samuel Cover, Solomon Boose, Joseph Mathias.

12. Cherry Grove.—Peter Kump, David Shull, William A. Lippo.

The teachers for the term ending April 13, 1881, were:

1, C. H. Bixler, 43 pupils; 2, John Burgoon, 20 pupils; 3, Isaac Wright, 44 pupils; 4, G. W. Yeizer, 50 pupils; 5, J. H. Stonesifer, 40 pupils; 6, G. F. Morelock, 30 pupils; 7, John N. Mark, 49 pupils; 8, A. F. Galt, 43 pupils; 9, George Fleagle, 63 pupils; 10, N. H. Kester, 45 pupils; 11, Richard Dell, 41 pupils; 12, A. S. Morelock, 35 pupils.

Below are given the votes cast for local officers in Myers District from 1851 to 1861 inclusive:

1851.—Vote for Primary School Commissioners: William Earhart 89, A. K. Shriver 59, Samuel Bowers 37, J. William Earhart 134, P. B. Mikesell 49.

1853.—For Justices: William Tagg 135, John Koontz 196, D. B. Earhart 157, Daniel Stonesifer 153; Constables: Perry Rumler 125, Peter Wolf 204, Samuel Bowers 92, Peter Lingenfelter 88, John Hornberger 56; Road Supervisor: David Circle 77, James E. Dodrer 146, Peter E. Myers 17.

1855.—For Justices: Samuel Bowers 42, J. W. Earhart 99, D. B. Earhart 72, Eli Erb 28, Henry Shuler 122, Peter Kump 117, D. Stonesifer 68; Constables: D. E. Leister 79, W. H. Lippy 56; Peter Rumler 102; Daniel Shull 167, J. H. Wimert 122; Road Supervisor: Peter E. Myers 98, Abraham Koontz 190.

1857.—For Justices: D. Stonesifer 177, P. B. Mikesell 223, William Tagg 108, D. B. Earhart 71; Constables: J. H. Knipple 203, J. L. Farmwalt 185, P. Rumler 130, B. J. Matthias 51; Road Supervisor: Daniel Lippo 232.

1859.—For Justices: John Maus 257, P. B. Mikesell 262; Constable: J. H. Knipple 219, Gershom Huff 235, W. N. Burgoon 134; Road Supervisor: Daniel Lippo 183, Emanuel Yeiser 132.

1861.—For Justices: J. W. Earhart 183, D. H. Rudolph 150, D. B. Earhart 55, John Maus 194, Eli Erb 129; Constables: D. L. Feeser 170, Levi Bish 127, Joshua Wisner 53, G. Huff 193, B. J. Matthias 154; Road Supervisor: Moses Troxell 182, Michael Shull 185.

WOOLERY DISTRICT, No. 4.

Woolery District, or District No. 4, of Carroll County, is bounded on the north by Hampstead, on the west by Baltimore County, on the south by Freedom District, and on the west by the district of Westminster.

Deep Run, Middle Run, Beaver Run, and the Patapsco River, with their tributaries, furnish abundant water-power for manufacturing and milling purposes. In addition to the numerous excellent public roads and the Chambersburg turnpike, the Western Maryland Railroad passes through the northeastern portion of the district, and furnishes admirable facilities for travel and transportation. The metes and bounds of the district, as originally laid down by the commission of 1837, were as follows:

"Beginning at the twenty-sixth milestone on the Reisterstown turnpike road; thence with a straight line to the late Richard Gorsuch's house, leaving said house in No. 4; thence to the Patapsco Falls; thence down said Falls to Stansbury's house, leaving said house in District No. 4; thence with the county road to Brown's meeting-house; thence to Brown's mill; thence to Williams' school-house, binding on the road leading past John Kelly's; thence to Edward Bond's; thence with the county line to the bridge over the Patapsco Falls, near John Ely's mill; thence with the Patapsco Falls to Beasman's bridge; thence with the Deer Park road to the road leading from Philip Nicodemus's mill to the Calico House; thence with said road to Pool's school-house; thence to Morgan's Run, near Thomas Beasman's barn; thence up Morgan's Run to Hawkins' Branch; thence up Hawkins' Branch to the county road leading past Benjamin Gorsuch's; thence with said road until it intersects a county road leading from the 'Stone Chapel' to the Washington road; thence with said road to the Washington road; thence with a straight line to the place of beginning."

Daniel Weaver's was made the place for holding the polls.

By an act of the General Assembly of Maryland, passed May 23, 1853, it was provided that "so much of the Fourth Election District lying north and west of the Washington road should thereafter be deemed and taken as part of the Seventh Election District; and that the division line between Election Districts Five and Nine should be so far altered and changed as to commence at a point where the then division line crossed the new Liberty road, and running thence with a straight line to the dwelling-house then occupied by James McQuay, leaving said McQuay's in district number nine; thence with a straight line to the dwelling-house then occupied by John Hess, leaving said Hess in district number nine; thence to the Washington road; thence with said road to Morgan's Run, and up said run to the original division line." Woolery District had 2743 inhabitants in 1880.

The German element predominated to a large extent in the first settlement of this district, which was part of Baltimore County until the creation of Carroll in 1836. Among the early settlers were the Woolerys (from whom the district received its name), Stockdales, Garners, Jacobs, Gorsuches, Shipleys, Barneses, Cockeys, Finks, Leisters, Zepps, Armacosts, Prughs, Conaways, and Flaters.

Finksburg, the most prominent town in the district, is twenty miles from Baltimore and about one mile from the Western Maryland Railroad. It was laid out in 1813 by a Mr. Quigly, a contractor on the Chambersburg turnpike, then being built through it. It is situated on a survey called "Hooker's Meadow," and was named Finksburg in honor of Adam Fink, who built the first house. Mr. Fink lived and kept tavern on the land now owned by Daniel Frazier, and was succeeded by William Horner, Sr., who kept the inn for twenty years. Mr. Fink had fifteen acres of land, eleven of which Daniel Frazier now owns, but the house (tavern) built by the former was long ago taken down. Mr. Quigly laid out the town for Mr. Fink on the latter's land. The oldest house is that of Thomas Demoss. Thomas Ward kept the first store, Samuel Hughes was the first blacksmith, and his shop was that now occupied and carried on by Thomas Demoss. The first physician was Dr. Forrest, and the first teacher Charles W. Webster, an attorney-at-law of Westminster, son of Rev. Isaac Webster, who taught the school in Finksburg in 1831, in a log school-house on the site of the present school building. The oldest man in the village is John Nelson Whittle, aged seventy-three years, who married, June 11, 1830, Miss Cynthia Ann, daughter of Thomas Ward, an old settler and the first merchant of the place. The merchants are George W. Horner and H. S. Thompson,—the latter being the postmaster. Dr. S. L. Morris is the resident physician, and the venerable Samuel Stansbury keeps the toll-gate at the east end of the village.

Zion Methodist Protestant church was erected in 1856, under the auspices of Rev. Scott Norris. Frank Hering is superintendent of the Sunday-school.

The pastors of Zion Methodist Protestant Church have been:

1856, R. S. Norris, A. Anderson; 1857, R. S. Norris, C. H. Littleton; 1858, J. A. McFadden, N. S. Greenaway; 1859, J. A. McFadden, C. M. Whiteside; 1860, J. Elderdice, C. H. Littleton; 1861, C. H. Littleton, G. W. Weills; 1862, J. F. Whiteside, G. W. Weills; 1863, J. F. Whiteside, J. W. Gray; 1864, T. M. Bryan, G. D. Edmondston; 1865, T. M. Bryan, C. T. Cochel; 1866, C. T. Cochel, F. M. Hawkins; 1867, C. T. Cochel; 1868–70, W. T. Dunn; 1870–72, J. H. Ellegood; 1872, A. D. Dick, J. G. Sullivan; 1873, A. D. Dick; 1874, A. D. Dick, S. B. Tredway; 1875, G. D. Edmondston; 1876, S. S. T. Ferguson, J. B. Butler; 1877, S. S.

T. Ferguson, G. F. Farring; 1878, S. S. T. Ferguson, J. M. Brown; 1879–81, J. W. Charlton; 1881, W. D. Litsinger.

The church building of the Methodist Episcopal Church South was erected in 1856 by the Methodist Episcopal Church, but shortly after the late war the church organization became so feeble and so reduced in numbers that the building was sold to the Methodist Episcopal Church South. Its first pastor under the Church South was Rev. William Etchison, and the present incumbent is Rev. Mr. Brown, of Reisterstown.

In the rear of the church is a graveyard, with only a few interments, among which are William L. Crawford, born December, 1834, died January, 1879.

The two most prominent burials are those of Judge Mordecai G. Cockey, who died July 29, 1872, aged 70; and his wife Eurith, who died Dec. 27, 1843, aged 42.

In a field adjoining are the graves of the following-named persons: Ann E. Corbin, wife of William Corbin, born Sept. 12, 1800, died April 30, 1829; and Keturah Wheeler, died June 15, 1829, aged 2 years and 20 days.

The Independent Order of Mechanics was instituted in 1872, in which year it built its hall, which was sold recently to George W. Horner. He has enlarged and beautified it, and the order continues to hold its meetings there. Its officers are:

W. M., Frank Stocksdale; S. M., John Simmons; J. M., Conrad Mann; Sec., Alfred Williams; F. S., John W. Barrett; Treas., L. A. J. Lamott.

The Excelsior Literary Society, an association for entertainment and instruction, is in a flourishing condition. Its officers for 1881 were:

Pres., B. L. Fair; Sec., Dixon Leister; Treas., Miss Alverdie Lamott; Vice-Pres., F. L. Hering.

Samuel Shoemaker, the wealthy and distinguished Baltimore railroad and express man, was raised in this village, and Lewis H. Cole lives near the town, on his elegant farm known as "Clover Hill." Abraham Leister owns part of the old Leister estate, among the first located in the district. That portion of this farm near the railroad is owned by William Zepp. Thomas Gorsuch came to this section of country at an early day from Baltimore County, and settled where Elias Gorsuch now lives, before whose time George W., son of Thomas Gorsuch, owned it.

The Garner Graveyard is on the road from Finksburg to the railroad station, and is a private burial-lot, in which only three of the tombstones have inscriptions, as follows:

"In memory of Flinn Garner, who departed this life Feb. 20, 1859, aged 93 years. He was a member of the Methodist Church 69 years."

"In memory of Cary Garner, wife of Flinn Garner, the mother of 13 children."

"Sarah Fresh, died Sept. 19, 1822, aged 28."

Carrollton is a romantic and pretty village on the Western Maryland Railroad, seven miles from Westminster and twenty-six from Baltimore. The North Branch of the Patapsco River passes by the hamlet, and furnishes an abundance of water for manufacturing and other purposes. Thomas Chapel, Pleasant Grove, and Bethel churches are near. Edward H. Bash is a merchant, railroad agent, and postmaster. J. A. Bush, a surveyor, lives here, as does also W. J. Houck, the undertaker.

Patapsco.—This village lies on the Western Maryland Railroad, twenty-seven miles from Baltimore and six from Westminster. Ezra Chew is postmaster. J. H. Chew & Co., J. W. Sanders, and John S. Martin are merchants in the village. P. Lingenfelter keeps the hotel, and E. E. Koons, a miller and lumberman, resides there.

Bird Hill is on the "Nicodemus road," six miles from Westminster, and near Morgan's Run. John W. Nelson is the postmaster of the village and keeps a store.

Louisville is also on the "Nicodemus road," six miles from Finksburg, ten from Westminster, and twenty from Baltimore. There are copper-mines situated on Morgan's Run, within a half-mile of the town, containing large deposits of copper, and operated by John Vial. S. H. Patterson is postmaster, and John Reed and Nicholas Benson, merchants. The village has two churches,—Mount Pleasant Methodist Episcopal and Providence Methodist Protestant. The millers are G. W. McComas and George F. Branning. The town is partly in Woolery's and partly in Freedom District,—the "Mineral Hill Copper-Mine" being in the latter.

Mechanicsville.—This pleasant village, rapidly growing in business and population, lies on the Nicodemus road, midway between Bird Hill and Louisville. It has a Methodist church and cemetery, two stores, several shops, and is the home of an industrious people.

Shamberger's Station, on the Western Maryland Railroad, is an important shipping-point, and has large and excellent flouring-mills.

The following is a list of persons seventy years old and over living in the district in 1879:

Mrs. Margaret Wickert, aged 95 years; her son, Jacob Wickert, 77; her daughter, Mrs. Margaret Crapster, 75; Mrs. Rachel Roache, 79; her sister, Mrs. Mary Criswell, 74; Samuel Stansbury, 75; his wife, Rachel, 75; John Whittle, 71; Mrs. Lavina Grumbine, 73; her sister, Mrs. Eliza Stocksdale, 71; Mrs. Catharine Stocksdale, 71; her brother,

Supervisor: John D. Powder 176, Elijah Wooden 113, A. Taylor 12.

1855.—For Justices: M. G. Cockey 228, N. Gorsuch 199, E. Woolery 184, J. D. Powder 121, S. Wilderson 38; Constables: S. Flater 165, Jesse Magee 146, D. D. Byers 198; Road Supervisor: Lewis Taylor 200, Amon Allgire 123.

1857.—For Justices: S. A. Lauver 188, Daniel Stull 184, L. Lamott 186, M. G. Cockey 208, Nathan Gorsuch 206, Elijah Woolery 191; Constables: J. Shilling 178, J. H. Uhler 172, Samuel Flater 204, D. D. Byers 204; Road Supervisor: G. Mummaugh 193, H. T. Bartholow 198.

1859.—For Justices: Joseph Poole 187, James Lockard 208, S. A. Lauver 198, M. G. Cockey 203, Azariah Oursler 188, Nathan Gorsuch 186; Constables: William Crusey 192, Lewis Taylor 170, Jesse Magee 203, William Gorsuch 212; Road Supervisors: Henry Taylor 203, Joseph Bromwell 214.

1861.—For Justices: William Lockard 240, M. G. Cockey 232, N. Gorsuch 213, N. Burgett 48, Azariah Oursler 166, J. W. Steele 182, L. A. J. Lamott 187; Constables: P. Gorsuch 271, Jesse Magee 272, Jer. Taylor 161, D. D. Byers 163; Road Supervisor: Peter Flater 268, John Uhler 180.

One of the best-known farmers in this district is Col. James Fenner Lee, who was born in Providence, R. I., July 9, 1843. He is the eldest living son of Stephen S. and Sarah F. (Mallett) Lee, who removed to Baltimore the year of his birth. In that city he was placed under the instruction of the best masters, and in 1855 sent to Europe, where he was for several years in one of the first schools of Switzerland. He completed his collegiate studies in Paris, at the Lycée St. Louis, and after having traveled over the continent returned to Baltimore. There he entered as a law student the office of Brown & Brune, and before applying for admission to the bar spent a term at the Law School of Harvard University. In 1866 he married Mrs. Albert Carroll, daughter of Hon. William George Read, and granddaughter of Col. John Eager Howard. On this occasion his parents presented him with a farm in this district, and he decided to devote himself to agricultural pursuits as soon as he could dispose of his law business and complete the third volume of the "Maryland Digest," which he had, in conjunction with his friend, Jacob I. Cohen, undertaken to publish. Having in time accomplished this and settled upon his farm, he soon became identified with, and earnest in the promotion of, every material interest of the county. In a short time, such was his popularity, he was constantly chosen to represent the interests of his district in the Democratic County Conventions, and frequently in the State councils of that party. In 1874 he was appointed by Governor Groome one of his aide-de-camps, with the rank of colonel. He was nominated in 1875 for State senator by the Democratic party, and elected after a most active and exciting campaign. In the Senate he was chairman of the joint Committee on Printing, and did good service to the State by reducing the expenditures of the same twenty thousand dollars. This position he retained in the second session of the Legislature, in which he was equally successful in his efforts to secure economy in that department. At the assembling of the Senate he was unanimously chosen president of the temporary organization, and was very often called to the chair during the absence of Col. Lloyd, the permanent president. It was mainly through the efforts of Col. Lee that the endowment of twenty-six free scholarships was obtained from the State for the Western Maryland College at Westminster. His children are Arthur F., Sarah J. Fenner, and Stephen Howard Lee.

FREEDOM DISTRICT, No. 5.

Freedom District, or District No. 5, of Carroll County, is bounded on the north by Woolery District, on the east by Baltimore County, on the south by Howard County, and on the west by Franklin District. It is intersected by Piney Run, Big and Little Morgan's Runs, Owings' Run, and their tributaries, and the North and West Branches of the Patapsco form the eastern and southern boundary lines of the district respectively. In addition to a number of turnpikes and excellent public roads, the Baltimore and Ohio Railroad skirts the southern portion of the district, affording the most ample facilities for traffic with points of commercial importance. Freedom District in 1880 had a population of 3154. The following are the metes and bounds of the district as originally laid out by the commission appointed in 1837:

"Beginning at the mouth of Gillis' Falls where it enters in the Western Falls; thence running with said falls to its junction with the Northern Branch; thence with the Northern Branch to Beasman's bridge; thence with the Deer Park road to the road leading from Philip Nicodemus's mill to the Calico House; thence with said road at Pool's school-house; thence to Morgan's Run, near Thomas Beasman's barn; thence up Morgan's Run to District No. 9; thence with District No. 9 to the place of beginning."

Freedom was made the place for holding the polls. The above lines were somewhat changed by an act passed May 3, 1853, readjusting the bounds of the Fifth, Ninth, and Fourth Districts. This is the largest district in the county in area, and was the first settled. Its pioneers were mostly of English descent, with some of Welsh and Scotch-Irish extraction. Among the first to make their homes in the district were John Welch, Abel Brown, Robert Twis, Edward Dorsey, John Elder, Joshua Glover, Samuel Sewell, Grove Shipley, the Littles, Mr. O'Donald, the Steeles, Dorseys, Wadlows, Scriveners, Gores, Lees, Binghams, Ritters, Parishes, Bennetts, Gardners, Buckinghams, Enoch Baker, Joseph Willis, John Beard, Lindsays, and Hoods. The Shipley family, embracing several branches, was the most numerous, and is to the present day.

The founder of the Ritter family in Maryland was Elias Ritter, who settled on the Western Shore of the province in 1650

He was a native of Bedingen, Hesse-Darmstadt, Germany, where, it is said, he possessed an estate covering twenty-four square miles of land, embracing three towns within its bounds. Bedingen, the main town, was fortified, and contained the "Ritter Castle," the walls of which were still standing in 1848. The family furnished men and munitions to the Protestant cause during the "Thirty Years' War," and at the close of that struggle was sent into exile and their property confiscated. Elias Ritter went to England during the protectorate of Oliver Cromwell, there joined one of the expeditions sent by Lord Baltimore to Maryland, and settled in the western part of Anne Arundel County.

At the time of the formation of Frederick County the family was located on the banks of the Monocacy River. The names of the principal members of the family at that time were Elias, John, William, Tobias, Michael, and Ludwig, or Lewis.

John, a son of the founder of the family, assisted William Penn in surveying the province of Pennsylvania in 1682, for which service he received five thousand acres of land in Berks County, Pa. A descendant of this Ritter occupied a seat in the Twenty-eighth and Twenty-ninth Congresses. William and Elias Ritter were members of Capt. William Keeport's company, Stricker's battalion, Maryland line of 1776.

Tobias Ritter, another brother, was a member of the third company of Col. Armand's Pennsylvania Legion.

Lewis Ritter, born Oct. 20, 1778, in Frederick County, Md., married Margaret Stall in 1803. This lady was the daughter of John Stall, of Franklin County, Pa., whose wife had been made a prisoner of war by the French and Indians after Braddock's defeat, and taken to France, where she remained until 1770, when she was restored to her family. The husband had been with Braddock's army.

Jacob Ritter, born Nov. 20, 1804, near Fayetteville, Franklin Co., Pa., married, December, 1829, Elizabeth, eldest daughter of Philip J. Neff, a soldier in the war of 1812, and eldest son of Col. Michael Neff, a drill-officer under Washington during the American Revolution. Col. Neff served under Frederick the Great during his "Seven Years' War" as one of the "Light Horse" and the king's body-guard. At the commencement of the Revolutionary war Col. Neff resided in Tyrone township, Adams Co., Pa., where Philip J. Neff, his eldest son, was born. At the time of the marriage of Jacob Ritter and Elizabeth Neff, Philip J. Neff resided near Fayetteville, Franklin Co., Pa.

In 1836, Jacob Ritter was commissioned as first lieutenant of Company A, One Hundred and Fifty-fifth Regiment of State Militia, by Governor Joseph Ritner, of Pennsylvania, and served in that capacity six years.

In August, 1847, he removed to Finksburg, Carroll Co., Md., and in 1850 to Eldersburg, Freedom District, same county, where he died in 1870.

William L. Ritter, the son of Jacob Ritter, was born near Fayetteville, Franklin Co., Pa., on the 11th of August, 1835. He began his career with only a common-school education, which by diligence and perseverance he supplemented in after-years with all that was needed for the part he was called upon to play in life.

At the age of twenty-two he was appointed mail-agent under the Buchanan administration, and held this position until the breaking out of the war. When hostilities began his convictions led him to embrace the cause of the South, and without a moment's delay he resolved to cast his lot with the Confederate army. Accordingly, on the 24th of October, 1861, in connection with Capt. Henry B. Latrobe and Lieuts. F. O. Claiborne, John B. Rowan, and William T. Patton, he recruited and organized the Third Battery Maryland Artillery. When the company was mustered into service he was appointed orderly sergeant.

Soon afterwards the battery was ordered to East Tennessee, where it remained until Gen. E. Kirby Smith marched into Kentucky, in August, 1862, when it accompanied his army to Covington, opposite Cincinnati, Ohio. After the army returned to Tennessee the battery was ordered to Vicksburg, Miss. Capt. Latrobe there retired from service, and Lieut. Claiborne was placed in command. On the 17th of March, 1863, Sergt. Ritter was elected second lieutenant to fill the vacancy caused by the promotion of his superior officer. Not long after his promotion he was sent to Gen. Ferguson's command, on Deer Creek, Miss., above Vicksburg, to take charge of a section of light artillery of the Third Maryland Battery, then operating on the river in connection with a section of Capt. Bledsoe's Missouri Artillery. Lieut. Ritter distinguished himself during this service for bravery and skill, and when during the long siege of Vicksburg Capt. Claiborne was killed, he was promoted to the rank of first lieutenant. In the seven days' fight around Jackson, Miss., Lieut. Moore was wounded, and Ritter took command. In the October following he rejoined his old battery at Decatur, Ga. At the battle of Resaca, in May, 1864, he was wounded, but refused to retire from the field. He dressed his own wound, and although urged by the battalion surgeon to go to the hospital, kept his post, and in the absence of Capt. Rowan, withdrew the guns from one of the most exposed positions on the line. At the siege of Atlanta, Lieut. Ritter took command of the battery, Capt. Rowan having been called to the command of the battalion. At the death of Capt. Rowan, who was killed at the battle of Nashville, in December, 1864, he assumed command of the battery, and worked the guns until the enemy drove his men from the pieces at the point of the bayonet. At Columbus, Miss., Lieut. Ritter was promoted to captain to fill the vacancy caused by the death of Capt. Rowan, his commission dating from the 16th of December, 1864.

He remained in active service until the troops were surrendered and paroled at Meridian, Miss., never having taken a furlough nor spent a day in the hospital during the entire term of his service.

In February, 1866, he returned to Maryland, and on the 26th of November, 1867, married Mrs. Sarah Howard Rowan, widow of Capt. John B. Rowan, his late companion in arms, and daughter of Col. Thomas Howard, of Elkton, Md.

The Springfield Estate.—George Patterson was the youngest son of William Patterson, well known in Baltimore, who was possessed of a large amount of real estate in that city. He was also the brother of Mrs. Elizabeth Patterson, the first wife of the late Jerome Bonaparte. He took possession of his estate in Carroll County, containing about three thousand acres of land, in 1824, and made it his home until the time of his death, which occurred Nov. 19, 1869, in his seventy-fourth year. He was possessed of considerable wealth, and was largely engaged in importing and raising improved stock. He was an extensive exhibitor at the agricultural fairs held in the State before the beginning of the late war, but never competed for premiums, taking pride only in adding to the interest of the show by the presence of his fine animals. His immense farm was called "Springfield," and was situated near Sykesville. He was an esteemed citizen, and his death was lamented by a large circle of friends and acquaintances.

Springfield is one of the most admirable and complete farming establishments in Maryland. It is situated a short distance from the Sykesville Station, on the Baltimore and Ohio Railroad, and contains about two thousand acres of land, fifteen hundred of which in 1870 were under cultivation. It is furnished with a flour-mill, saw-mill, and a comfortable country-house, with room enough for the uses of home and the claims of a generous hospitality, with lawns, orchards, and outhouses of every description and variety. It is high, healthy, rich, well watered and wooded.

More than forty years of Mr. Patterson's life were spent in changing this excellent homestead from "a naked surface, incapable almost of cultivation," to a rich, highly-cultivated farm. "Time and grass were at the bottom of all" his achievements in this respect. Every field has had two hundred bushels of lime to the acre, and each "passed six years of nine in grass." The great pasture, in full view from the front door of the dwelling, has not been broken for many years, and being constantly pastured by the beautiful Devons, has grown richer and richer, and grasses native and exotic strive there for the mastery.

His system of farming was first corn, manured on sod broken deeply, and yielding an average of twelve barrels to the acre. This was followed by a crop of oats, and then two years of clover. Next a crop of wheat, on which ammoniated phosphate was used for the purpose of ripening the crop. At the time the wheat was sown the field was set to grass for hay, and for three years after the wheat crop was taken off mown, and the next year grazed. Manure was applied during the last year and the sod again broken for corn, beginning the regular nine years' course.

Mr. Patterson raised Berkshire hogs instead of Chester, Southdown, and Shropshire sheep, and game chickens instead of fancy fowls. His stock of horses was unsurpassed. Many Marylanders will long remember Mr. Patterson's stout, well-proportioned, powerful, and active horses at the State fairs.

Under the cultivation of Mr. Patterson, Springfield became the most celebrated, and was truly what he designed it should be, the *model* farm of Maryland. He erected his mansion on an eminence overlooking the farm and surrounding country. It is one hundred and seventy-five feet front by fifty feet deep. The front has a two-story porch supported by pillars. The house, which is somewhat classical in style, is unique in its arrangements and a perfect country home. The iron and copper-mines upon this property, discovered in 1850, were profitably worked until 1861, and more recently leased to Graff, Bennett & Co., of Pittsburg, and Read, Stickney & Co., of Baltimore, who have begun operations with indications of valuable results. "Springfield Farm" is distinctively noted for its *Devon* cattle, Mr. Patterson having made, in 1817, the first importation of thoroughbred Devons into the United States, through his brother Robert, and as a present from Mr. Coke, afterwards Earl of Leicester.[1] The following were his importations in order, as recorded in the "Devon Herd-Book": Bulls, Anchises, No. 140; Eclipse, No. 191; Herod, No. 214; Norfolk, No. 266; Chatsworth, No. 182; Dick Taylor, No. 486; the President, Nos. 639 and 904. From these most of the Devon herds of this country are descended.

George Patterson married Prudence A. Brown, the daughter of Thomas C. and sister of Stephen T. C. Brown, who survives him and lives in Baltimore. Their only child, Florence, married James Carroll, of Charles. She died in 1878, much lamented. After Mrs. Carroll's death, Mrs. Patterson and Mr. Carroll decided to sell "Springfield" to Frank Brown, which was done in 1880. Mr. Brown inherited the estate known as "Brown's Inheritance" from his father, Stephen T. C. Brown. The land had been brought to the highest state of cultivation by Mr. Brown's father and his grandfather, Thomas C. Brown, and is one of the best farms in the State. He combined the two farms, and has since been actively engaged in cultivating and improving the whole estate. As consolidated, his farm now contains two thousand five hundred acres, and is not surpassed in point of cultivation by any in the State. Mr. Brown has not only maintained the reputation of Devon cattle, but has even improved it.

It will be seen that these two farms have been blended together from their origin in the close alliance of the families of their respective owners.

Frank Brown, proprietor of the one farm by inheritance and of the other by purchase, is the only son and heir of the late Stephen T. C. and Susan Bennett Brown. He was born Aug. 8, 1846, on "Brown's Inheritance." The ancestor of the family in this country was Abel Brown, who emigrated from Dumfries, Scotland, to near Annapolis, Md., in 1730; he removed later to this part of Carroll (then Baltimore County), and purchased a large tract of land adjoining Springfield. This he brought to a high state of cultivation; it came into the possession of Elias Brown, Sr., who erected a stone saw and flour-mill, the corner-stone of which bears the date of 1798. He was a prominent citizen, and actively participated in civil affairs. He had four sons,—Thomas Cockey, Elias, Jr., William, and Stephen,—all of whom served in the war of 1812. Elias Brown, Jr., became prominent in the State, was a member of the United States Congress, and a Democratic Presidential elector a number of times. Thomas C. Brown inherited the estate, a division of which having been made, William Patterson, of Baltimore (the distinguished merchant and citizen, one of the organizers of the Baltimore and Ohio Railroad, the father of Robert, George, Joseph, Edward, Henry, and Elizabeth Patterson,—Madame Bonaparte), purchased a portion which contributed largely to make up his "Springfield" estate. Thomas C. Brown married Susan Snowden, a descendant of Baptiste Snowden, of St. Mary's County, Md., who had removed to the vicinity on a farm which he called Branton, on which he built a house of cut straw and clay, still standing in a good state of preservation. Col. Francis Snowden, the son of Baptiste, married Miss Miles, of St. Mary's, and these are the maternal great-grandparents of the subject of this sketch. The children of Thomas C. Brown were Lewis, Prudence A., the widow of George Patterson, and Stephen T. C., the father of Frank Brown.

Stephen T. C. was born in 1820, reared on the "Inheritance," and in 1842 married Susan Bennett; was a member of the State Legislature, one of the original subscribers to the Maryland Agricultural College, a most useful citizen, a representative man and agriculturist of the country. He was an official and leading member of the Springfield Presbyterian Church, which was established and supported by him and George Patterson, and whose edifice and parsonage were erected by their combined efforts. Mr. Brown was a man of decided character, strong convictions, benevolent spirit and works, Christian consistency and activity, and universally esteemed. He died in December, 1876.

Frank Brown is the only son of the last mentioned. At the age of eighteen his father gave him a farm, well stocked and furnished, adjoining the homestead, which he successfully managed for several years. He entered the agricultural implement and seed-house of R. Sinclair & Co., of Baltimore, where he received valuable training, of practical use in his after-years. He was later placed in charge of the Patterson estates in Baltimore, which he managed to the satisfaction of the heirs. He was subsequently appointed by Governor Bowie to a responsible place in one of the State tobacco warehouses, which position he held for six years. In 1875 he was elected to the House of Delegates, Maryland Assembly, and in 1878 re-elected. His success was a gratifying proof of the public confidence in him. At the close of his second term he withdrew from political affairs, the care of "Springfield" and the Patterson interests having devolved upon him after his father's death, who for six

---

1 "American Devon Herd-Book," vol. iii, and old *American Farmer*, vol. iv. p. 29.

Frank Brown

years subsequent to George Patterson's demise had the management of them. This was a task requiring the exercise of financial wisdom and good executive ability, but Mr. Frank Brown has been equal to these great responsibilities. Naturally endowed with business capacity, his early experience fitted him for the management of his trusts. Like his father, he, too, takes a lively interest in the affairs of the county and his vicinity, and in many respects supplies his place. He was elected a trustee of Springfield Presbyterian Church, to fill the vacancy caused by his father's death. He was also made trustee under Mrs. James Carroll's (*née* Florence Patterson) will, for her legacy to the church of five thousand dollars. He is one of the executive committee of the Maryland State Agricultural Association, and a director of the Maryland Live-Stock Breeders' Association. At the late tenth annual meeting of the Maryland Agricultural and Mechanical Association, held Oct. 27, 1881, he was elected its president.

Mr. F. Brown married (December, 1879) Mary R. Preston, *née* Miss Ridgely, daughter of David Ridgely, of Baltimore. They reside on the farm during summer and in Baltimore during the winter.

Below is given a list of persons in Freedom District in 1879 who had reached the age of eighty years. The names of twenty-two persons are given, whose ages amount to 1881 years, or an average of eighty-five and a half years:

Mrs. Jane C. Smith, 83; Joshua Hipsley, 81; Mrs. Rebecca Hiltabidle, 84; Daniel Gassaway (colored), 85; Mrs. P. Wilson, 84; Samuel Jordan, 84; Mrs. E. Ware, 83; Nathaniel Richardson, 86; Jacob Beem, 86; Rev. Dr. Piggot, 84; J. Linton, 83; Mrs. Matilda Phillips, 84; George Haywrath, 82; Nathan Porter, 85; Mrs. Susanna Warfield, 83; Sebastian Bowers, Sr., 86; Ruth Shipley, 99; James Morgan, 85; Ruth Frizzle, 94; P. Diens (colored), 90; Kate Philips, 85; Susan Dixon (colored), 85.

Defiance, a small village, is situated on the western edge of the district. Horace L. Shipley here has a store, formerly kept by his father, Larkin Shipley, a son of John Shipley, one of the oldest settlers.

St. Stephen's Lodge, No. 95, I. O. O. F., located at Defiance, was instituted in May, 1857. Its charter members were Jesse Leatherwood, Larkin Shipley, Dr. Francis J. Crawford, Abraham Greenwood, Hanson Leatherwood. Its first officers were:

N. G., Jesse Leatherwood; V. G., Larkin Shipley; Sec., Dr. F. J. Crawford; Treas., Hanson Leatherwood.

Its present officers (second term, 1881) are:

N. G., John W. Pickett; V. G., F. L. Criswell; Sec., Augustus Brown; Per. Sec., Thomas L. Shipley; Treas., C. R. Pickett; Con., T. N. Shipley; Chapl., Dr. D. F. Shipley; Marshal, A. Brown; Warden, David H. Haines; Dist. Dep., Horace L. Shipley.

Its neat frame hall, forty-four by twenty-two feet, was built in 1880. The trustees are John H. Conoway, William H. Pickett, F. L. Criswell. Number of members, seventy.

Bethesda Methodist Episcopal church is situated north of the hamlet of "Pleasant Gap." It is a substantial brick structure, erected in 1880. Immediately in its rear is the old log church, in which services were held from 1810, the date of its erection, until the completion of the new church in 1880. The graveyard adjoining contains the following interments:

Ruth, wife of James Parish, died July 24, 1875, aged 60.

Vachel Buckingham, died Sept. 4, 1866, aged 76; and his wife, Eleanor, Feb. 8, 1871, aged 71.

Prudence A. Lindsay, died Jan. 3, 1879, aged 63; John A. Lindsay, died Jan. 10, 1877, aged 64.

Eliza J., wife of Andrew Wheeler, died Jan. 5, 1878, aged 19.

Henry S. Buckingham, died March 26, 1872, aged 43.

Ellen Nora Elizabeth, wife of Richard M. Chenoweth, died Nov. 13, 1863, aged 22.

Ann, wife of Joseph Willis, died Sept. 7, 1865, aged 88.

Elizabeth, wife of Grove Shipley, born Sept. 11, 1776, and died July 8, 1854; and her husband, born April 4, 1776, died Oct. 20, 1849.

Louisa, wife of Grove Shipley, Jr., died June 21, 1846, aged 42.

James Parish, born April 15, 1773, died March 29, 1853.

Kiturah Parish, died June 1, 1848, aged 76.

Thomas Barnes, died Feb. 29, 1860, aged 43.

Array Parish, wife of Moses Parish, and daughter of Richard and Array Condon, died Nov. 29, 1861, aged 62. Moses Parish, born Sept. 6, 1795, died April 27, 1862; and his wife, Micha, daughter of Grove and Elizabeth Shipley, died Sept. 21, 1839, aged 43.

Nicholas Shipley, born Jan. 28, 1805, died Jan. 15, 1837.

Sarah Shipley, born Nov. 20, 1797, died Jan. 22, 1873.

Sarah, wife of William A. Gibson, died March 12, 1873, aged 39.

William Baker, born April 27, 1806, died July 20, 1876.

Enoch Baker, died June 27, 1864, aged 97; and Mary, his wife, July 8, 1863, aged 87.

Elizabeth, wife of Samuel Hughes, died May 1, 1854, aged 31.

Hannah, wife of Reese Brown, born Sept. 19, 1789, died Sept. 29, 1864.

John Beard, born Aug. 24, 1789, died Aug. 28, 1859.

James W. Parish, died June 13, 1871, aged 50.

Elizabeth, wife of John W. Parish, born March 25, 1830, died April 24, 1878.

The Methodist Protestant church, built about 1840, is just south of "Pleasant Gap." It is a frame structure, originally built of logs, and then weather-boarded. It has one gallery, and is two stories high. In the graveyard adjoining are only a few graves, among which is that of Abraham, son of Nicholas and Mary J. Wilson, born April 12, 1867, died Jan. 2, 1872. Most of them have no tombstones.

Nathan Manro was born in the State of Rhode Island, Sept. 29, 1730, and was married, Nov. 21,

1750, to Miss Hannah Allen, of that State. She was born April 14, 1733. Their children were Hannah, Sarah, Elizabeth, Squire, Lydia, Nathan, Mary, Jonathan, David, Allen, and Thomas. Of these, Jonathan, the eighth child, was born Nov. 28, 1766, and came to Maryland from near Providence, R. I., with his brother Nathan, who died in 1827. Jonathan settled in Baltimore, and became a rich and prosperous merchant. He owned several ships that were engaged in the London and West India trade. He was married, Jan. 15, 1795, to Sarah Conner, daughter of James Conner, and died Jan. 22, 1848. They had thirteen children, of whom two survive, Mrs. Dr. Turnbull, of Baltimore, and Judge George W. Manro. The latter was born in Baltimore, March 22, 1810, and was liberally educated in the schools of that city. He followed the high seas for ten years on merchant vessels owned by his father, and served as second mate under Capt. James Beard. Before he quit the seas he had command of the ship "Ocean," owned by the Osgoods. In 1837 he removed to the farm on which he now resides, and which was a part of the lands purchased at an early date by his mother's father, James Conner. Mr. Conner owned six hundred and three acres, made up of tracts surveyed and patented to Samuel Sewell and Joshua Glover. One of these, "Buck's Park," was surveyed for Samuel Sewell, April 16, 1759, for fifty acres. Another, "Sewell's Park," of twenty acres, was surveyed March 17, 1745, and another, of one hundred and twenty-one acres, "Buck's Park," at another date. "William's Neglect," of thirteen and three-fourths acres, was surveyed for Joshua Glover, Dec. 9, 1795. Judge Manro was married, Oct. 26, 1837, to Elizabeth Kelly, daughter of William and Martha (Loveall) Kelly, by Rev. Samuel Gore. Her brother, Nicholas Kelly, was the first sheriff of Carroll County. Judge Manro was one of the first magistrates appointed in the new county of Carroll, and held this office for a long term of years. He was appointed one of the judges of the Orphans' Court in 1848, and served three years, and was elected in 1851 for the term of four years, according to the provisions of the new constitution adopted that year. He was elected in 1867 one of the six members from this county to the Constitutional Convention, and aided in framing the organic law under which Maryland is now governed. In 1868 he was appointed by Governor Oden Bowie inspector of tobacco, which position he held several years. At present he is collector of taxes. Both on the bench and in all other public positions held by Judge Manro, his administration of affairs has been characterized by the ability, purity, and suavity of manner that has ever distinguished his life, and has made him a popular and valued public servant. He is a zealous member of the Masonic order, in which, over thirty years ago, he received its first three degrees. He has been a lifelong Democrat, devoted to the interests of his party, to which, under all vicissitudes, he has strongly adhered, and to whose counsels he ever gave his voice, and for the success of which his vote was always freely given. He is connected with the Methodist Episcopal Church South at Freedom, in the erection of whose church edifice in 1868 he liberally contributed, and was chairman of its building committee. The judge resides on his splendid farm of three hundred and one acres, located a mile north of Eldersburg, where he and his accomplished lady dispense old-fashioned Maryland hospitality. The name of his estate is "Buck's Park," called after two of the original surveys made of the grant.

Geo W. Manro

Freedom.—The village of Freedom is four miles from Sykesville, and adjacent to Morgan's Run and Piney Falls. It is situated on land belonging to Mr.

O'Donald, a very large landed proprietor in this district at an early date. O'Donald, in laying out the village, gave the alternate lots to those who purchased lots, and his liberality and *freedom* in his transactions gave the name to the village, and when the district was organized, in 1837, it took its name from the village, which was founded shortly after the Revolution. The residence of Dr. Joseph W. Steele, a log structure weather-boarded, was built about 1769, and during the Revolution and until a few years ago was occupied as a tavern. John Little kept it for many years. The village is on the old Liberty road, built in olden times by convicts, but before its construction there was an older road, which ran back of Dr. Steele's residence (the old tavern). The Berret family is an old one in this region, and its first head here was a Hayti refugee, who married a daughter of O'Donald, the great land-owner. Mary E. Wadlow is postmistress, and J. Wadlow & Sons, merchants. J. Oliver Wadlow, the popular and efficient register of wills of Carroll County, resides here.

The physician of the town is Dr. Joseph W. Steele, who has been engaged in the practice of his profession at this point since 1856. He was born near the village, March 6, 1831 (also the day of the birth of J. Oliver Wadlow), and is, on his father's side, of Irish extraction. His grandfather was John Steele, who taught school and kept store at an early date a few miles distant (now in Franklin District). John Steele met for the first time his future wife, Mary Hays, during the Revolution, at the tavern in Freedom at a social party. The doctor's grandmother on his maternal side was a Gore, one of the oldest settlers, and his wife was Margaret J. Smith, a descendant of the earliest settlers of Baltimore Town. Where the village stands the only house for many years was the old tavern, whose high mantels and unique hand-carving betoken its great age. Dr. Nathan Browne, who lived near here and died in 1873, was a celebrated physician. He was born on the Eastern Shore of Maryland, and was distinguished for his philanthropy. He never married, and lived with his beloved nieces. He was a State senator from 1867 to 1871, and held other positions of great trust. He practiced here forty-five years.

Dr. W. M. Hines resides just west of the village. Dr. Hines has steadily practiced medicine in Carroll County since 1846, save for a period of three years, and it may therefore be easily understood that he is pretty well known all over the county as well as in adjacent sections. He was born July 23, 1825, in the town of Liberty, Frederick County. There also his father, David, was born. David Hines was educated at Georgetown, D. C., and passed a busy life as farmer and merchant. He ow..ed and farmed in early life the valuable tract known as "Glade Garden." As a merchant he was prominent in Liberty, Frederick, and Baltimore, in which latter city he ended his days. His wife was Jane C.,

Wm. M. Hines

daughter of Samuel Marshall. His father, Philip Hines, served with considerable distinction in the war of the Revolution. The living sons and daughters of David Hines are Mrs. Augustus Webster and Mrs. Ignatius Gore, of Baltimore, and Dr. Hines, of Carroll County. Dr. Hines passed his early youth at Glade Garden farm, and at the age of fifteen was sent to Dickinson College, at Carlisle. At the end of four years of study he occupied a place in the junior class, from which he was forced to retire by reason of ill health. A brief rest recuperated his energies, and in 1844 he began the study of medicine under Dr. Nathan R. Smith, one of Baltimore's most distinguished surgeons. Young Hines attended lectures at the University of Maryland, and graduated at that institution in March, 1846. Very soon thereafter he located in Carroll County, near his present home, and gave himself with such energy and vigorous determination to the practice of his profession that he found himself in due time in active demand in all the country roundabout. His field was a large one, and his calls so numerous that for a time in his early experience he almost literally lived in the saddle. For a period of three years he was connected with the United States custom-house at Baltimore, and for three months during the war of 1861–65 was a surgeon in the Federal army, with his station at Convent Hospital, Baltimore. Excepting these absences Dr. Hines has been regularly, in season and out of season, one of Carroll County's leading physicians, and now, after a practice of thirty-six years, is hale, hearty, and vigorous, and still rides a large circuit and attends upon his numerous patients with wellnigh as much briskness and ambitious spirit as marked the younger portions of his career. Like his father before him, he was an Old-Line Whig. Later he became and remains a Republican. Although alive to the progress of political events and deeply interested therein, he has steadily from the outset of his manhood's experience held consistently aloof from the business of office-seeking or office-holding. In 1855 he married Frances H., daughter of Rev. Augustus Webster, of Baltimore. Mrs. Hines died Oct. 3, 1877. There are three living children, two of them being sons, Augustus W. and William M.

Freedom Lodge, A. F. and A. M., No. 112, was chartered in 1862, with the following charter members:

W. M., Warren N. Little; S. W., Dr. Joseph W. Steele; J. W., Nicholas L. Rogers; Sec., J. Oliver Wadlow; Treas., John Deckabaugh.

The lodge built its hall before obtaining its charter. It is a two-story frame building, twenty-four by forty-five feet, the lower part being used for a public school. Of the fourteen charter members the following are living: John Deckabaugh, Thomas Paynter, Lewis Ohler, J. Oliver Wadlow, Dr. J. W. Steele, John L. Nicholas, and Robert Clark. Its Worshipful Masters have been John Deckabaugh, J. Oliver Wadlow, Dr. J. W. Steele, Lewis Ohler, and Warren N. Little.

Officers for 1881:

W. M., John Deckabaugh; S. W., Thomas Paynter; J. W., Samuel W. Barnet; Sec., Dr. J. W. Steele; Treas., J. Oliver Wadlow.

It numbers forty-seven Master Masons, two Fellow Crafts, and one Entered Apprentice. Dr. J. W. Steele has served as Grand Standard Bearer in the Grand Lodge. At a single festival this lodge took in fourteen hundred dollars, which cleared it of all debts, and left a surplus for charitable purposes.

The Methodist Episcopal church, built in 1822, is between Freedom and Eldersburg. It is a handsome edifice, displaying considerable architectural taste.

In its cemetery are the graves of the following persons:

Nicholas Dorsey, died Sept. 9, 1876, aged 60.

Elizabeth Dorsey, died March 2, 1881, aged 76.

Samuel Bingham, died Aug. 17, 1876, aged 66.

Ruth Bingham, died Aug. 27, 1880, aged 72.

Caroline Brown, born April 15, 1815, died July 17, 1878.

Jesse W. Brandenburg, born Dec. 19, 1838, died Jan. 9, 1879.

Caroline, wife of William Cooley, died March 3, 1877, aged 49.

Sarah, wife of David Slack, died Feb. 20, 1878, aged 91.

Rebecca, wife of William D. Frizzell, born March 17, 1829, died Feb. 25, 1866; and her husband, born March 7, 1829, died March 24, 1875.

John Frizzell, died March 31, 1870, aged 69.

John Wadlow, died Sept. 10, 1854, aged 50; and Jemima, his wife, April 8, 1872, aged 67.

Anna Maria Shipley, born Feb. 27, 1775, died Jan. 15, 1857.

Frances Hollis, wife of Dr. William M. Hines, died Oct. 3, 1877.

Achsa, wife of William Scrivenor, died April 8, 1872, aged 82.

Israel Frizzell, born March 23, 1807, died Aug. 6, 1876.

Stephen R. Gore, born April 1, 1818, died Feb. 25, 1872.

Jabez Gore, died Jan. 7, 1851, aged 39.

Rev. Samuel Gore, died Sept. 4, 1858, aged 75 (a local preacher of Methodist Episcopal Church for 50 years); and Theresa, his wife, born Nov. 20, 1789, died Feb. 29, 1864.

Nathan Clark, died Sept. 22, 1852, aged 68.

Joseph Steele, died Aug. 25, 1855, aged 61; and his wife Charlotte, April 22, 1857, aged 58.

John T. Steele (a Freemason), died Aug. 9, 1863, aged 42.

Cecilia, wife of William Beam, and third daughter of Matthew and Catharine Chambers, born Jan. 24, 1806, died Dec. 18, 1870.

Matthew Chambers, died Aug. 15, 1825, aged 52.

Col. Peter Little, died Feb. 5, 1830, aged 54; and his wife, Catharine, July 18, 1867, aged 79.

Sophia Levely, died Sept. 17, 1845, aged 53.

Warren Little (a Freemason), born Feb. 29, 1811, died Feb. 21, 1863.

John Little, died Sept. 5, 1853, aged 80.

Mrs. Catharine Steele, eldest daughter of John and Anna Little, died April 11, 1865, aged 55.

David Little, died Aug. 23, 1857, aged 62.

George Clift, died Feb. 9, 1852, aged 75.

Elizabeth Clift, died Dec. 30, 1858, aged 94.

Elizabeth Hines, died May 3, 1867, aged 68.

Hannah Lindsey, died Aug. 31, 1862, aged 74.

Joshua Lee, died March 4, 1871, aged 88; and his wife, Susannah, Nov. 21, 1869, aged 83.

Jesse Lee, died March 23, 1866, aged 68.

Thomas Lucy, died July 16, 1853, aged 92.

Margaret, wife of John Elder, born Jan. 10, 1774, died May 8, 1849.

Thomas Bingham, died May 5, 1854, aged 80.

Mary, wife of John Twemmy, born Aug. 9, 1812, died Jan. 21, 1855.

Julia, wife of William C. Lindsay, died Aug. 6, 1874, aged 49.

Honor Lee, wife of Thomas Lee, died June 30, 1853, aged 64; and her husband, Nov. 5, 1851, aged 75.

Larkin Fisher, died Feb. 21, 1876, aged 71.

The corner-stone of the Methodist Episcopal Church South, a handsome brick structure, lying between Freedom and Eldersburg, was laid April 13, 1868, when Rev. Wm. Etchison was pastor. Judge George W.

Mauro was chairman of the building committee. Its present pastors are Revs. Watters and Martin.

In the churchyard are buried the following persons:

John W. Brown, born Oct. 9, 1811, and died March 7, 1877.

Jemima E., wife of John G. Pearce, born Sept. 14, 1827, died Jan. 12, 1875.

Their son, Elias J., born Feb. 2, 1856, died Aug. 23, 1876.

Jacob Ritter, born Nov. 20, 1804, died Dec. 26, 1870,—descendant of the earliest Ritter of 1650,—and Elizabeth, his wife, born Feb. 17, 1806, died March 23, 1879.

Juliet Welsh, wife of Luther Welsh, died June 1, 1869, aged 63.

Ruth, wife of Freeborn Gardner, died March 29, 1870, aged 62.

Elizabeth, wife of Samuel W. Barnett, died July 7, 1871, aged 44.

Cornelius Shipley, died Feb. 3, 1862, aged 61.

Eldersburg.—The town of Eldersburg, three and a half miles from Sykesville and thirty-two from Baltimore, was named in honor of John Elder, who laid it out before 1800, and who was an early settler, owning large tracts of land in the vicinity. It has a lodge of I. O. Good Templars, and Grange No. 139 of Patrons of Husbandry, of which N. D. Norris is Master, and George M. Prugh, secretary. Among the business men of the town are T. A. Barnes, postmaster and merchant; Dr. H. C. Shipley, physician; L. H. W. Selby, undertaker; J. & L. H. Selby, millers; and J. Collins, shoemaker.

Holy Trinity Parish, Protestant Episcopal Church, originated on March 8, 1771, when John Welch entered into a bond in the penal sum of two hundred pounds, English sterling, to convey to Abel Brown, Robert Twis, Edward Dorsey, and John Elder two acres of land, provided the said persons would build a "Chappell of Ease" for the benefit of "Delaware Hundred," the name of their election district. The church was built (a stone structure), and became a part of St. Thomas' Parish, Baltimore County. In the lapse of time the congregation thinned out, Episcopal services were no longer held, and the Baptists for some years occupied the edifice. After a time the Baptists were unable to maintain their congregation, and the building was not used for religious services, but became the abode of cattle and horses.

On June 1, 1843, Holy Trinity Parish was formed out of St. Thomas', and this ancient building repaired, rebuilt, and refurnished, and on Oct. 31, 1843, consecrated anew. The vestrymen then chosen were George F. Warfield, Wm. H. Warfield, James Sykes, Jesse Hollingsworth, George W. Mauro, John Colhoon, Nicholas Dorsey, and Warner W. Warfield, and the Register, Washington L. Bromley. Its pastors and rectors have been:

1843–47, Rev. D. Hillhouse Buell; 1847, Rev. Wm. E. Snowden; 1848–51, Rev. S. Chalmers Davis; 1851–69, Rev. Thomas J. Wyatt; 1869, Rev. J. Worrall Larmour; Dec. 6, 1869, Rev. Robert Pigott, D.D., present rector.

The officers for 1881 were: Vestrymen, L. W. W. Selby, Dr. C. C. Moorehead, Thomas B. Jones, Capt. J. W. Bennett, John Grimes, W. B. Shipley, A. Voorhees, John Barnes, Sr., Wm. P. Grimes, and George W. Holmes; Wardens, George W. Holmes, John Grimes; Register, Charles R. Favour, Esq.

In the churchyard the following persons are buried:

Kate, wife of Z. Hollingsworth, died Sept. 21, 1858.

Their son, Zebulon, died April 3, 1861, aged 34.

Elizabeth, wife of Edward Ireland, Jr., died Jan. 19, 1862, aged 32.

Emma E. Lucy, died Nov. 14, 1861, aged 41.

Barbara, daughter of Andrew and Martha Fite, born July 16, 1831, died April 7, 1865.

Jesse Hollingsworth, born March 19, 1800, died April 8, 1872.

Anna Baker, daughter of Jesse and Sophia Hollingsworth, born April 21, 1829, died April 10, 1870.

George Fraser Warfield, born March 20, 1769, died Dec. 11, 1849; and his wife Rebecca (daughter of Abel Brown), born Dec. 24, 1774, died March 4, 1852.

William Warfield, born Aug. 3, 1807, died March 26, 1857.

Augustus Edward Dorsey, died Dec. 9, 1869, aged 60.

James Soper, died Oct. 10, 1811, aged 45.

Springfield Presbyterian church, a fine three-story structure, was erected in 1836 by George Patterson and Stephen T. C. Brown. A few years later the parsonage, adjoining, was built. The building has been used both as a church and school. The school was incorporated as "Springfield Academy" by an act of the Legislature passed Jan. 6, 1838. The first trustees designated in this act were Dr. Hawes Goldsborough, Dr. R. D. Hewitt, Dr. Nathan Browne, Eli Hewitt, Nathan Gorsuch, Joseph Steele, and Cornelius Shipley. The last pastor of the church was Rev. Charles Beach, who had charge of the academy now conducted by his daughters. The present trustees of the academy are Frank Brown, Wm. C. Polk, Lewis Shultz, Richard J. Baker, Joliner Wadlow, J. O. Devries, Joshua D. Warfield, P. W. Webb, and Robert C. McKinney. Miss Florence Patterson, who died in 1878, left to the church and academy a bequest of five thousand dollars, which is held by Frank Brown in trust for the interests of the church.

In the graveyard in the rear of the church and academy the following persons are buried:

George Devries, over whom there is erected an elegant Scotch granite monument with simply his name.

Sarah L., his wife, died Aug. 26, 1877.

Stephen T. C. Brown, born Nov. 12, 1820, died Dec. 6, 1876.

Mary, daughter of Stephen T. C. and Susan A. Brown, born Aug. 29, 1843, died May 30, 1863.

Susan, wife of Thomas C. Brown, born Feb. 1, 1791, died Sept. 19, 1861.

Florence, wife of James Carroll, and daughter of George and

Prudence A. Patterson, born June 13, 1847, died Oct. 15, 1878 (resting on her breast was the body of her infant son).

George Patterson, born Aug. 26, 1796, died Nov. 26, 1869.

George, son of George and Prudence A. Patterson, born Sept. 9, 1844, died Dec. 21, 1849.

Eli Hewitt, died April 10, 1868, aged 62; and Ann B., his wife, Jan. 18, 1859, aged 52.

Susanna, wife of John L. Nicholas, died July 14, 1862, aged 38.

Nicholas Harry, born in parish Tywardreath, County Cornwall, England, May, 1809, died Feb. 5, 1862.

Catharine Buckingham, died Nov. 1, 1875, aged 71.

Augustus Smith, died June 15, 1862, aged 42.

Jane, wife of Henry Nicholas, died Aug. 25, 1858, aged 37.

Sykesville is on the Baltimore and Ohio Railroad, thirty-two miles from Baltimore, and by turnpike twenty-two, and seventeen from Westminster. It is pleasantly located on the West Branch of the Patapsco River, which supplies abundance of water for milling and other purposes. It is a flourishing town, and a large business is done here in lumber, lime, coal, fertilizers, and general merchandise. It has become a favorite resort for the families of Baltimoreans, many of whom board at the farm-houses in the neighborhood during the summer. The town was named after James Sykes, son of John Sykes, a famous Baltimore merchant. He came here in 1825, and bought a thousand acres of land in different tracts, including the site of the town, on which at that time the only building was a saw- and grist-mill. He replaced the old mill by a new and substantial structure in 1830–31, and erected a five-story stone hotel to meet the requirements of the railroad then built to this place, and for a summer resort. It was fifty by seventy-four feet in dimensions, and the finest hotel in Maryland outside of Baltimore at that date. In 1837, when John Grimes (the present hotel-keeper) came here, there were but four or five houses, and John Garrett kept the big hotel. In 1845, Mr. Sykes enlarged his stone mill and converted it into the "Howard Cotton-Factory," and also built large houses for his operatives. He carried it on until 1857, employing over two hundred hands, when the monetary crisis caused his suspension. This factory has not been in operation since, except for a short time, when run by L. A. Purennet and Miller for a year or so, and for a brief period during the war by James A. Gary on certain lines of manufactured goods. Mr. Sykes died in the spring of 1881, universally esteemed and respected. The oldest house standing is a log hut occupied by George Collins. The first house built on the site of the town was carried off by the flood of 1868, which did immense damage, sweeping away many buildings, including the large hotel then kept by John Grimes, and the store of Zimmerman & Shultz. This firm lost all their goods, and also their iron safe with its contents of money, books, etc. The safe was never found. The first physician to settle here was Dr. Array Owings in 1846. J. M. Zimmerman is postmaster, railroad and express agent, and Dr. C. C. Moorhead, the physician of the neighborhood. Messrs. Zimmerman & Shultz, merchants, came here from Frederick in 1858, and have built up an immense trade, having been very successful in business. After being washed out by the great freshet in 1868 they built another fine stone house across the street and opposite their old place of business. John McDonald & Co. erected their elegant stone store in 1865, and have an extensive trade. Samuel R. Duvall has just completed a large building, where he carries on a big business in agricultural implements, hardware, etc. Messrs. Zimmerman & Shultz own the mill property and factory formerly belonging to Mr. Sykes. All these houses, together with the Methodist Episcopal and Episcopal churches, are on the Howard County side of the river. E. M. Mellor is also engaged in the merchandise business. When Mr. Sykes came to this spot in 1825 there were only three houses or buildings, including the mill, but to-day the population is over four hundred.

The Methodist Episcopal church, a handsome stone edifice, was erected in 1878 on a very high eminence overlooking the town. It has stained windows and a well-toned bell. It was built under the pastorate of Rev. C. W. Baldwin, who was in charge from 1878 to 1879. His successor, Rev. T. M. West, remained from 1879 to 1881, when the present incumbent, Rev. A. J. Gill, entered upon the discharge of his duties as pastor. The Sunday-school superintendent is J. E. Gaither.

Previous to the erection of the church building in 1878 the congregation held its services in a large frame building opposite the cotton-factory.

St. Joseph's Catholic church, a handsome structure, is near the depot, and on a beautiful site. It was begun before the war, and completed in 1867. Its pastor is Father Loague, of Woodstock College, and the congregation is large and zealous.

The Protestant Episcopal church in Holy Trinity Parish was built in 1850, on June 11th of which year the corner-stone was laid. Its rector then was Rev. S. Chalmers Davis, who, in 1851, was succeeded by Rev. Thomas J. Wyatt, who continued to 1869, during which year Rev. J. Worrall Larmour officiated a few months. The present rector, the learned and venerable Robert Pigot, D.D., came to the parish Dec. 6, 1869. The church edifice is a substantial stone structure of imposing architecture, and located on the Howard County side, with a fine view of the whole town. The list of its officers is given above, being the same as those in charge of the Eldersburg Church, which with this forms Holy Trinity Parish, made out of St. Thomas' in 1843. Its rector, Rev. Dr. Pigot, was born May 20, 1795, in New York City. His father was a native of Chester, England, came to America a soldier in the king's army, and was present, Sept. 13, 1759, at the battle of Quebec, under Gen. Wolfe, where he witnessed that famous commander's victory and death. He located after the close of the French and Indian war in New York City, where before and after the Revolution he was a successful school-teacher. During the French and Indian war he was one of the secretaries of Lord Amherst, the commander of all the king's forces in America.

The doctor's family was founded in England by Pigot, Baron of Boorne, in Normandy, one of the forty knights who accompanied William the Conqueror. An elder branch settled at Chetwynd Park and Edgemont, in Shropshire, where it yet continues, another possessed Doddeshall Park, in Bucks, and the third removed to Ireland. Its arms were—sanguine—three pickaxes—argent crest—a greyhound, *passant*, sable; mottoes, *labore et virtute*, and *conanti debitum;* seats, Archer Lodge, Sherfield upon Lodden Hants, and Banbury, Oxfordshire. On the maternal line, Dr. Pigot is descended from Cerdic, a Saxon prince, who invaded England 495 and 519 B.C. He was brought up in the church, and ordained Nov. 23, 1823, by Bishop White. He came to Maryland from Pennsylvania in 1837, and was made rector of North Sassafras, Cecil Co. In 1840 he became rector of Grace Church, Elkridge Landing, and Ellicott Chapel, Anne Arundel County. In 1842 he was chosen principal of Darlington Academy, and in 1844, missionary and rector of Redemption Church, in Baltimore, to which, in 1845, was added Cranmer Chapel. In 1847 he was made professor in Newton University of Baltimore, in 1850 was city missionary. In 1855 he was an assistant in the University of Maryland, and chancellor of the Protestant University. His first rectorship was St. Mark's, Lewistown, Pa., from 1825 to 1828. In 1869 he came to Holy Trinity Parish, and on March 30, 1870, his house burned down, and he lost by the fire the church register, all his literary labors for fifty-three years, and all his sermons for forty-seven. This venerable divine is one of the oldest Freemasons in America, having received the three first degrees in Masonry in 1824. Since then he has taken all the degrees to and including the thirty-second. He belongs to the Maryland Commandery, No. 1, of Baltimore, from which he was the recipient of a splendid sword, presented to him as a Sir Knight. A handsome Masonic medal, bearing date of his initiation into the order (1824), was also presented to him, with the Latin inscription, "*Tolle crucem et coronam.*" He has repeatedly, and for many years, served as chaplain in various Masonic organizations and bodies, both in Pennsylvania and Maryland.

Another noted family connected with Holy Trinity Parish since its establishment in 1843 is that of the Warfields. Richard Warfield, a native of Wales, came to this country in 1638, and pitched his tent nine miles from Annapolis, Md., at a place now known as the " Black Horse Tavern." His second son was Alexander, whose third son was Hazel Warfield. The latter was twice married. By his first wife were born Henry Warfield, a member of Congress, Dr. Charles Alexander Warfield, Dr. Peregrine Warfield, Dr. Gustavus Warfield; and by his second wife, George Frazer Warfield and Sally Waters, of Tennessee, whose daughter married Dr. Robinson, who was the father of the wife of Judge Henning, of New Orleans, whose daughter married Gen. Hood, of the Confederate army. Dr. Charles A. Warfield was a stanch patriot (as were all the Warfields) in the Revolution, and was a lieutenant in the Continental army. He was with the party which boarded the British vessel " Peggy Stewart" and burned her with her cargo of tea at Annapolis. George Frazer Warfield was born March 20, 1769, in Baltimore, and became a noted merchant of that city. In 1834 he removed to his country-seat, " Groveland," in the vicinity of Sykesville, where he died Dec. 11, 1869. His wife was Rebecca Brown, daughter of Abel Brown, and a sister of ex-Congressman Elias Brown. She was born near Sykesville, Dec. 24, 1774, and died March 4, 1852. The Warfield family was largely instrumental in creating the parish of Holy Trinity, rebuilding the church edifice at Eldersburg, and building the one at Sykesville, and three of its members, William H., George F., and Warner W., were members of the first vestry in 1843. George Frazer Warfield's children were Lewis, George F., Warner W., William H. (of United States army), Susanna, Rebecca, married to Richard Holmes, and Elizabeth, married to Mr. Wade, a lawyer of Massachusetts. Miss Susanna Warfield lives at " Groveland" with her nephew, George W. Holmes. She was born in 1794, and is a well-preserved lady of the old school,—dignified and courtly, paying great attention to current events, and specially interested in the church. George Frazer Warfield was one of the defenders of Baltimore, and named his country-seat "Groveland" at the suggestion of Miss Bentley, a sister of his son George's wife. "Aunt Harvey," a sister of Abel Brown, and aunt to Mrs. George Frazer Warfield, was murdered by the Indians near Harper's Ferry, while on her way to the West, about 1775, and one of Abel Brown's brothers was killed under Braddock at this unfortunate general's defeat.

In the Protestant Episcopal graveyard there are a few interments, among which are the following:

James Berry, died Sept. 13, 1865, aged 78.

Mamie E., daughter of John K. and Rachel A. Mellor, born Oct. 17, 1869, died Feb. 26, 1872.

Ida Helena, daughter of William L. and Ann E. Long, born Oct. 20, 1867, died Jan. 31, 1869.

Margaret, wife of William Dean, died Feb. 14, 1858, aged 68.

Catharine H., wife of William H. Hooper, died Feb. 3, 1854, aged 31.

Mary Gill, died March 26, 1863, aged 57.

Fanny Isabel, born July 27, 1814, died Oct. 24, 1876.

Marcellus Warfield, died June 3, 1855, aged 35.

Warner W. Warfield, born March 20, 1788, died July 28, 1867.

Elba furnace lies just below Sykesville, but has not been worked since the flood of 1868. It was opened and operated years ago by the Tysons.

Elias Brown, a son of Abel Brown, one of the first settlers and largest landed proprietors of the district, died July 3, 1857. He was a Presidential elector for Monroe in 1820, and for Gen. Jackson in 1828, and in 1824 his brother, William Brown, was also a Presidential elector for Jackson in the great quadruple contest. Elias Brown was for several years a member of Congress. He was a delegate to the State Constitutional Convention of 1851, and a member of the House of Delegates from Carroll County in 1849. He had frequently represented Baltimore County in the Legislature before the creation of Carroll County in 1837.

Col. Peter Little was born in 1776, and died Feb. 5, 1830. He was of a family that settled in the district before 1765. He was at one time a member of Congress from the Baltimore district, and an active and zealous officer in the militia. He served with honor in the war of 1812.

Porter's is a small village on the Liberty road, six miles from Sykesville, and near Piney Run, and derives its name from an old family which settled in the vicinity many years ago. Branchburg's Methodist Protestant church is near the hamlet. Mrs. M. E. Trenwith is postmistress, and keeps the only store in the place.

Hood's Mills is on the Baltimore and Ohio Railroad, thirty-four miles from Baltimore, and fifteen from Westminster. It was named after the Hood family, as one of them, James Hood, and John Grimes erected the famous mills in 1845. Winfield S. Robb is postmaster, railroad and express agent, and keeps the only store. Watson Methodist Episcopal chapel is near here. Gen. J. M. Hood, the estimable president of the Western Maryland Railroad, was born and raised here, and Charles W. Hood, a successful land surveyor in his early life, died in the vicinity, Jan. 19, 1877, aged sixty years.

Morgan is on the Baltimore and Ohio Railroad, thirty-four miles from Baltimore, and near the Patapsco River. John A. Dushane, of Baltimore, has an extensive paper-mill here, giving employment to a number of persons, and manufacturing all grades of paper. George F. Jones is the superintendent of the paper-mill, postmaster, and railroad agent.

Woodbine.—This station is on the Baltimore and Ohio Railroad, thirty-seven miles from Baltimore, and near the Patapsco River. Morgan chapel (Methodist Episcopal) is near the village. A. Owings is postmaster and railroad agent. E. A. Owings and Mrs. H. A. Ways are the store-keepers. J. A. Albaugh keeps the hotel, and J. M. Baker has charge of the mill. The Warfield family in America is of Welsh descent. The first representative was Richard Warfield, an emigrant from Wales, who came to this country in 1637 and settled nine miles from Annapolis, at a place now called "Black Horse Tavern." A descendant of this emigrant was Charles A. Warfield, of Howard County, whose son, Charles A., married Julianna Owings and resided near Lisbon, in that county. Of their six children,—five sons and one daughter,—the next to the youngest was Charles A., born Oct. 16, 1836, in Howard County, near Sykesville. He was raised on his father's farm, a mile and a half from the Carroll County line, and was early inured to labor by tilling the soil and taking care of the stock on the farm. He received a good education in the English branches at the public schools of the neighborhood. In December, 1862, he removed to Freedom District, and purchased one hundred and sixty-two acres of land of George Wethered. This is the splendid farm he now owns, and to which the previous owner, Mr. Wethered, a soldier in the Mexican war, gave the romantic name of "Chihuahua," a name it still retains. Mr. Warfield was married, Nov. 16, 1864, to Caroline A. Devries, daughter of Christian and Jemima Devries, near Marriottsville. Their son, Wade Hampton Devries Warfield, was born Oct. 7, 1865. Mr. Warfield's farm is three-fourths of a mile north of Sykesville, in a fertile country, surrounded by picturesque scenery. His mansion is an elegant three-story frame building, delightfully located on an eminence, with pleasant surroundings of lofty trees and beautiful shrubbery. In the heated term during the summer months he entertains summer boarders from the cities, who find his place a delightful resort. He is specially engaged in dairying, and sends a daily average of forty-five gallons of milk to "Olive Dairy," Pennsylvania Avenue, Baltimore. He was one of the first in this section to embark in this business, and his dairy is the largest in this region, save that on the Frank Brown estate. His family and himself are attendants on the Springfield Presbyterian Church. He is a Democrat in politics, but has never held or sought office. His farm is in an excellent state of cultivation, and its buildings, fences, and general improvements indicate the best qualities of a thorough and successful farmer, while the tidiness and order of the house betoken rare domestic graces in his estimable wife.

Below is given the vote for local officers in the district from 1851 to 1861, inclusive:

1851.—Vote for Primary School Commissioner: John Warden 182, L. Gardner 91, John W. Wadlow 110.

1853.—For Justices: Jesse Hollingsworth 201, Alex. Gillis 200, William Tensfield 215; Constables: L. H. Boring 200, Aaron Gosnell 199; Road Supervisor, Reuben Conoway 221.

1855.—For Justices: R. Conoway 310, N. D. Norris 312, N. H. Jenkins 312; Constables: W. C. Lindsay 310, J. H. Conoway 310; Road Supervisor, J. Hollingsworth 310.

1857.—For Justices: J. Morgan 73, J. Dorsey 13, R. Conoway 289, W. G. Shipley 293, N. D. Norris 303; Constables: P. Welsh 12, A. Gosnell 303, W. C. Lindsay 294; Road Supervisor: A. Evans 12, Joshua Lee 297.

1859.—For Justices: C. W. Hood 75, James Morgan 61, N. D. Norris 285, Larkin Shipley 262, W. G. Shipley 251; Constables: J. H. Hood 121, W. C. Lindsay 255, Aaron Gosnell 243; Road Supervisor: W. H. Harden 160, Brice Shipley 249.

1861.—For Justices: Eli Hewitt, Sr., 397, John T. Ways 396, William Tensfield 378, E. Thompson 97, James Morgan 98, Abel Scrivnor 97; Constables: Aaron Gosnell 397, W. C. Lindsay 389; Road Supervisor: Wesley Day 373, O. Buckingham 112.

The public school trustees for 1881 and 1882 were:

1. Oakland.—Joseph Gist, John Melvin, William Baesman.
2. Stony Ridge.—John O. Devries, John Pearce, Austin Arrington.
3. Mechanicsville.—No trustees.
4. Sykesville.—Lewis H. Shultz, S. P. Duvall, Charles R. Favar.
5. Hood's Mills.—Solomon Shoemaker, Zachariah Wolfe, R. C. McKinney.
6. Brandenburg's.—J. M. Dorsey, Henry Cook, Joseph Barnes.
7. Pleasant Gap.—James H. Shipley, Brice Shipley, Cornelius Shipley.
8. Farver's.—Thomas L. W. Conden, Joseph Wilson, David McQuay.
9. Jenkins.—No appointments.
10. Woodbine.—George E. Buckingham, Elisha Young, R. H. Harrison.
11. Freedom.—Joseph W. Berret, J. Deckabaugh, Thomas Painter.
1. White Rock (African).—Isaac Dorsey, Wesley Costly, Aaron Austin (all colored).

The teachers for the term ending April 15, 1881, were:

1, Celie E. Gorsuch, 41 pupils; 2, Lizzie A. Bennett, 35 pupils; 3, C. L. Hughes, 22 pupils: 4, Isabel N. Hale, 51 pupils; 5, S. Spalding, 26 pupils; 6, Sue M. Matthews, 41 pupils; 7, Libbie Shipley, 27 pupils; 8, L. A. Koontz, 50 pupils; 10, M. L. Hoffman, 46 pupils; 11, Minta Shipley, 33 pupils; 1 (colored school), Emma V. Randolph, 70 pupils.

MANCHESTER DISTRICT, No. 6.

Manchester District, the Sixth District of Carroll County, is bounded on the north by Pennsylvania, on the east by Baltimore County and Hampstead District, on the south by the districts of Hampstead and Westminster, and on the west by Westminster and Myers Districts. The principal stream in the district is the Gunpowder Falls Creek, which passes through the northeastern portion and flows into Baltimore County, and which has several small tributaries. Big Grave Run has its source in the centre, and flows southeast into Baltimore County, and the head-waters of Big Pipe Creek and the North Branch of the Patapsco take their rise in the district. The population of Manchester District was in 1880 three thousand five hundred and one. The metes and bounds of Manchester District, as laid out by the commission of 1837, are as follows:

"Beginning at the forks of the county road leading from Westminster to the town of Hampstead and George Richards' mill; thence to the falls of Aspin Run and Long Glade Branch; thence up said branch to the spring near the house of Joseph Bowser, deceased; thence to the spring near the house of John Orendorff; thence to the forks of the most northern branch of Patapsco Falls and Bosley's Spring Branch, where they unite in Wm. Albaugh's meadow; thence through the farms of John Reed and Joshua Bosley, Sr., leaving said Reed and Bosley in District No. 6; thence to Michael Baker's tavern on the Hanover and Baltimore turnpike road, leaving said Baker in District No. 6; thence across said turnpike east of Shriver's tan-yard; thence through the lands of Daniel Caltuder, leaving said Caltuder in District No. 6; thence through the lands of (Gist's; thence through the land of) George Caltuder, deceased, and John Wareham, leaving said Caltuder and Wareham in District No. 8; thence to Michael Miller's well on the middle road; thence to Joshua Stansbury's spring, near the house on the Falls road; thence through the lands of Hair, leaving said Hair in District No. 8; thence to Henry Zimmerman's county road, where said road crosses Carroll and Baltimore county line, at a blazed hickory-tree; thence on said county line to the Pennsylvania line; thence with said line to Rinehart's county road; thence with said road to a point nearest to the head spring of

Ohio Branch; thence down said branch to where it crosses Trump's county road; thence through Peter Bixler's farm to Big Pipe Creek, where Lawer's Branch unites with Big Pipe Creek, leaving said Bixler in District No. 6; thence up said branch to Baughman's county road; thence with said road to the mouth of a lane between Royer and German; thence through the farm of Abraham Shaffer, leaving said Shaffer in District No. 7; thence to the forks of Manchester and Hampstead road; thence to the place of beginning."

Manchester was made the place of holding the polls.

Among the earliest surveys were "Rattlesnake Ridge," of 50 acres, surveyed July 18, 1738, for Edward Richards, and patented in 1739; "Three Brothers," of 300 acres, surveyed Aug. 2, 1746; "Easenburg," Aug. 26, 1761; "Shilling's Lot," of 40 acres, Oct. 3, 1751; "Heidelburgh," Aug. 10, 1752, and resurveyed Feb. 22, 1762, for Elias Harange; "Frankford," surveyed Jan. 27, 1761, for Conrad Barst; "Motter's Choice," resurveyed December, 1751, for 162 acres; "Potter's Lot," of 40 acres, for John Prlack, Oct. 30, 1760; "Richard's Chance," of 50 acres, Jan. 1, 1749, for Richard Richards; "Pomerania," near Whistler's Mill, now Bixler's, for 50 acres, to William Winchester, Jan. 8, 1755; "Johnsburg," of 130 acres, resurveyed for John Shrempling, May 20, 1761; "Mount Hendrick," of 48 acres, to James Hendrick, March 3, 1768; "McGill's Choice," of 50 acres, to Andrew McGill, June 12, 1744; "Winchester's Lot," Oct. 23, 1751; "Everything Needful," to Richard Richards, May 16, 1763, and for 1646 acres; same afterwards resurveyed, Nov. 14, 1786, as "Everything Needful Corrected," to Samuel Owings, in three parts, one of 1573 acres and one of 58½, Ulrich Freeland getting the latter; "Warms;" "Bridgeland," Feb. 28, 1754; "California," of 490 acres, March 26, 1765; and "Dey's Chance," June 10, 1755.

The earliest actual settlers were Germans, mostly from Pennsylvania, and some from the Fatherland. Among these may be mentioned the Showers, Ritters, Jacob Shilling, Philip Edleman, Jacob Utz, Michael Burn, Kerlingers, Faess, Gethiers, Motters, Werheims, Weavers, Steffers, Everharts, Bowers, Warners, Bachmans, Ebaughs. Paul Everhart, an emigrant from Germany, settled first at Germantown, Pa., and in 1761 removed to this district. His son George, then seven years old, died in 1851. Paul settled where are now the iron-ore works. His great-grandson, George Everhart, born in 1800, is still living.

Manchester, the commercial centre of the district, is the second town in size and importance in Carroll County, containing in 1880 six hundred and forty inhabitants. It is situated on the Hanover turnpike, and contains a population of about nine hundred inhabitants, with a number of churches, a Masonic Hall, an Odd-Fellows' Hall, an academy, and a number of stores and manufactories. The people, as a rule, are educated and enterprising. A number of railroads have been projected, which if completed will make the town a centre for business second to none in Maryland outside of Baltimore. Of late years an æsthetic taste has been manifested by the inhabitants, which has given rise to associations for the culture of literature and music, and the town now possesses all the elements for enlightened existence in the country remote from the temptations and embarrassments of a large city.

From 1760 to 1790 a few houses stood where the site of the present thriving village is situated. In 1790, Capt. Richard Richards, an Englishman, living in the Hampstead settlement, laid out the town and called it "Manchester," after that city in England, from which he had emigrated many years before. It was part of a survey of fifty acres, called "New Market," patented to him in 1754, but which was surveyed for him March 5, 1765, and thirty-three of which he laid out in lots. These lots were sold subject to an annual ground-rent, and to this day on one and one-fourth acres of land George Everhart pays a yearly rent of five dollars to Judge John E. Smith, of Westminster, the representative of or successor to the Richard rights. The ground-rents on all the other lots have expired. "The German Church Lands," of twenty-five acres, adjoining the above and a part of the town, were surveyed Dec. 20, 1758, to Jacob Shilling, Philip Edleman, Jacob Utz, and Michael Burns, as trustees. The church at the present time receives from its ground-rents on these lands or lots an annual sum of more than one hundred and fifty dollars. The town is designated on the old maps as "on the original road leading to Baltimore and near Dug Hill." The oldest man in the town is George Everhart, aged eighty-two, who came here from the country in 1826, and was nearly half a century in the mercantile business. The oldest house in the village is an old log building now owned by Edward Oursler. It was formerly kept as a tavern by Christian Heibly. On the lot now owned by Mr. Brinkman, the jeweler, a tavern once stood before any other house had been built in the town. The first physician was Dr. Urnbaugh, who was followed by Dr. Turner and Dr. Jacob Shower. The last began practice in 1825. Among the first schoolmasters was a Mr. Keller, who taught part of his pupils in the German, and the others in the English language. About the first storekeeper was George Motter, and in 1826, George

Everhart bought out Mark Spencer (an Eastern man from the State of New York), and continued in business until 1877. George Linaweaver was the earliest blacksmith. George Gettier, born here in 1791, was a soldier in the war of 1812, and died in Cincinnati, Ohio.

The town was incorporated in 1833, and a supplementary act of 1836 revived the incorporation, confining the limits of the town to the lots on the several tracts of land known as "New Market" and "German Town." The corporation was reorganized by an act of 1870, before which the records are mislaid or lost. Since that time the officers have been:

1871.[1]—Mayor, E. A. Ganter; Councilmen, George Everhart, Adam Shower, John Weaver, James Kelly, Henry Reagle; Secretary, L. C. Myerly; Treasurer, John Weaver; Bailiff, James Greenhultz.

1872.—Mayor, John C. Danner; Councilmen, Wm. Walter, Geo. Everhart, John Weaver, James Kelly, Henry Reagle.

1873.—Mayor, John Carl; Councilmen, James Kelly, Henry Reagle, Simon J. Grammer, Henry E. Masenheimer, D. Hoffacker.

1874.—Mayor, John Carl; Councilmen, John Fultz, W. L. Tracy, S. J. Grammer, H. Masenheimer, D. Hoffacker.

1875.—Mayor, John Carl; Councilmen, Henry Reagle, H. E. Masenheimer, D. Shultz, Edward Oursler, S. J. Grammer.

1876.—Mayor, Jacob Campbell; Councilmen, Emanuel Shaffer, Henry Reagle, Edward Oursler, Luther Tramp, Oliver Lippy; Secretary, Ferdinand A. Dieffenbach.

1877.—Mayor, Jacob Campbell; Councilmen, John J. Lynerd, Henry Reagle, Luther Tramp, John Bentz, Edward Oursler; Secretary, G. W. J. Everhart.

1878.—Mayor, H. W. Thomas, who resigned, and George M. Stien took his place; Councilmen, Cornelius Miller, E. A. Ganter, E. Shaffer, Geo. M. Stein, Dr. J. F. B. Weaver; Secretary, G. W. J. Everhart.

1879.—Mayor, John H. Lamott; Councilmen, E. A. Ganter, N. W. Sellers, P. Gober, Emanuel Shaffer, Cornelius Miller; Secretary, G. W. J. Everhart.

1880.—Mayor, John H. Lamott; Councilmen, Edward A. Ganter, N. W. Sellers, P. G. Ober, Emanuel Shaffer, Cornelius Miller.

1881.—Mayor, Henry H. Keller; Councilmen, E. A. Ganter, E. Shaffer, Oliver Lippy, John J. Lynerd, Edward J. Sellers; Secretary, G. W. J. Everhart; Treasurer, E. A. Ganter; Bailiff, Wm. J. Eisenbrown.

In 1878 the first crossings were laid to the streets; in 1879 the town was supplied with street-lamps, and in 1881 the streets were all graded.

Zion Church, with two exceptions, was the oldest congregation in Baltimore County (in which Manchester was located until 1836). It was organized Feb. 12, 1760, by a union of the Lutheran and German Reformed congregations. During that year was erected the first meeting-house, a log structure, which stood until 1798, when a brick edifice was built. It was repaired in 1836, and a steeple built from the ground up in November of that year. During these repairs Rev. Jacob Albert was chief manager, and Philip Grove and Charles Miller, assistants. Jacob Houck was the contractor for making the repairs, John Matthias was the contractor for building the steeple, Michael Gettier did the masonry, John M. Miller was the gilder and painter, and Jarret Garner furnished the materials; Jacob Weyant, Peter Shultz, Joshua F. Copp, Jesse Shultz, H. and W. Brinkman, Jacob Garrett, and Philip Crumrine were the under-workmen; Rev. Jacob Albert (Lutheran) and Rev. Jacob Geiger (German Reformed) were the pastors. In June, 1862, this church was taken down, and each of the two congregations erected a separate church building, that of the Lutherans being on part of the old church tract. The first church (log) of 1760 and the second (brick) of 1790 stood in the graveyard lot. This church was popularly known as the "Union Church," from the fact that two congregations worshiped peacefully therein. The Lutheran pastors who preached in it were:

1760–83, Rev. Newburg; 1783–90, Johan Daniel Schroeder; 1791–96, Rev. Meltzheimer (the elder); 1797–1825, John Herbst; 1826 (six months), Emanuel Keller; 1827–37, Jacob Albert; 1837–38, Jeremiah Harpel; 1838–42, Philip Williard; 1843–44, Frank Ruthrauff; 1844–48, Elias Swartz; 1848–53, Jacob Kaempfer; 1853–62, Daniel J. Hauer, D.D.

The German Reformed pastors to 1862 were: from 1823 to 1848, Rev. Jacob Geiger, C. F. Colliflower, and Henry Wissler. The names of subsequent pastors are not accessible.

Emanuel Lutheran Church, after the old "Zion Church" was torn down in 1862, erected in that and the following year its present edifice. Its pastors have been:

1862–65, Peter River; 1866–69, R. Weiser; 1870–81, G. Sill; 1881 (April 1), E. Manges.

The superintendent of Sunday-school is D. H. Hoffacker.

After the taking down of the "Zion church" in 1862, the Trinity Reformed Church congregation erected its present building, which was completed in 1863. The German Reformed pastors of Zion and Trinity Churches from 1760 to 1881, as far as ascertainable, were: 1823 to 1848, Jacob Geiger, C. F. Colliflower, Henry Wisler, J. W. Hoffmeirer, D. W. Kelley, and William Rupp, the latter the present pastor, who came July 2, 1877. The superintendent of the Sunday-school is J. P. Baltozer; elders, J. P. Baltozer, George Bixler; deacons, Emanuel Shaffer, Charles Brillhart.

[1] The total valuation this year of the real estate was $232,-930.

The corner-stone of the Methodist Episcopal church edifice was laid in 1839, before which there was a mission here with occasional preaching. At the erection of the building Rev. E. G. Ege was the pastor, and the present incumbent is D. Benton Winstead.

The erection of the Manchester Bethel church (United Brethren in Christ) was begun in 1870, and was completed in the same year. The building is a handsome brick structure. It was dedicated on Sunday, Jan. 1, 1871. At its dedication Bishop J. Weaver, of Baltimore, was present, and preached morning and night to a large congregation. Rev. John Shaeffer, of Baltimore, preached in the afternoon in the German language. The spire is forty feet above the roof, and presents a fine appearance. The first pastor, under whose auspices the building was erected, was Rev. Mr. Hutchinson ; the next one, Rev. J. B. Jones; and the present incumbent, Rev. Mr. Quigly, who took charge in 1881. In the rear of the church is a neat graveyard, in which are buried

Mary M. Baring, born July 25, 1752, died Jan. 29, 1830; and her husband, Ezekiel, who died March 30, 1838, aged 87.

Rev. Ezekiel Baring, born Jan. 16, 1780, died Feb. 14, 1861.

John Baring, died Dec. 17, 1869, aged 85.

Villet Baring, wife of Jacob Swartzbaugh, born Jan. 17, 1796, died March 2, 1857.

Margaret A. Stultz, born April 1, 1780, died April 23, 1861.

Elizabeth, wife of John Young, died Nov. 18, 1873, aged 76.

Catherine Lynerd, died Nov. 5, 1873, aged 73.

Martha Burkett, died July 17, 1866, aged 83.

Levi Beecher, died Oct. 11, 1866, aged 52; and his wife, Eve, Nov. 22, 1865, aged 53.

This church organization had a log church prior to 1870, on the same lot where the brick building now stands. Its trustees in 1857 were Samuel Dehoff, Joseph H. Little, Jacob W. Baring, Amos Williams, and Henry W. Steffy.

St. Bartholomew's Catholic church was built by the Redemptorist Fathers of Baltimore, who had charge of it until 1876, when it was placed under the pastorate of Father John Gloyd, pastor of St. John's Church, Westminster. It was erected under the supervision of Mr. Frederick, an eminent architect and builder of Baltimore.

The Manchester United Academy was incorporated March 3, 1829. The first trustees were Rev. Joseph Geiger, Rev. Jacob Albert, Dr. Jacob Shower, Solomon Myerly, George Motter, John Weaver, George Everhart, Peter Sable, Martin Kroh, George Shower, and Frederick Ritter. The building was erected in 1831, and its first teacher was Hon. Joseph M. Parke.

Irving College was incorporated by the Legislature Feb. 1, 1858, with the following trustees: Ferdinand Dieffenbach, John H. Falconer, John W. Horn, and Henry B. Roemer. Mr. Dieffenbach was a refugee of the Revolution of 1848, and a fine scholar and educator. This institution opened with two pupils, and soon became flourishing and noted. Its able head died in March, 1861, when it was for some time carried on under the auspices of his widow. Subsequently Lewis C. Myerly was at its head, and in 1880 Prof. D. Denlinger took charge, under whose management it yet remains. He changed its name to Irving Institute, and has made it a boarding-school for students of both sexes. Its aims are to prepare students for business, for teaching advanced classes in college, or the study of a profession. The course of study embraces Latin, Greek, French, German, mathematics, the sciences, music, painting, and drawing. Since the abandonment of the old "academy" this institution receives all the advanced scholars of the town and neighborhood.

The Thespian Society was incorporated in 1835, and the Manchester Band in 1836. The latter was reorganized in 1855. Its first leader for a few months was Dr. Charles Geiger, and since then it has been under the direction of Edward A. Ganter. The following are its present members: Edward A. Ganter (leader), C. J. H. Ganter, C. Frankforter, D. Frankforter, Jesse Leese, Nelson Warheim, Jeremiah Yingling, John Stump, Ephraim Freyman, Aaron Hoffman, J. D. Lotz, N. W. Sellers, Jacob Hoffman, William Hoffman, R. L. Simpers, S. F. Frankforter.

The first Sunday-school was organized in 1828.

The first newspaper was issued Nov. 14, 1870, by W. R. Watson as editor, and J. A. Bartley, assistant. It was called the *Manchester Gazette*, an independent journal, and was published up to March, 1872, when it was sold to Messrs. Smith & Sites, who removed the paper and presses to Glen Rock, Pa , where they established a new journal. The next paper was the *Manchester Enterprise*, established in November, 1880. It is a sprightly four-page sheet of twenty-eight columns, devoted to general and local news, "independent in all things, neutral in nothing." Joseph S. Cartman, late of Carlisle, Pa., is its editor, a journalist of ability and experience.

The Lutheran and Reformed cemetery was set apart for burial purposes in 1760, and interments began to be made in that year. Among the persons buried there are the following:

Frederick Ritter, died Feb. 9, 1864, aged 76.

George Motter, born Nov. 27, 1751, died Oct. 1, 1800.

Erwar Conrad Kerlinger, born 1731, died October, 1798.

Henry N. Brinkman, died Oct. 22, 1867, aged 76.

John Kerlinger, died Nov. 27, 1823, aged 51.

Elizabeth Kopp, died March 18, 1861, aged 75.

John Manche, born March 19, 1771, died Sept. 11, 1837.
Catharine Faess, died March, 1850, aged 86.
Carl Faess, born 1752, died 1815.
Catharine Gettier, born Oct. 27, 1822, died 1826.
Anthony Hines, died Nov. 29, 1825.
Hannes Motter, born April 10, 1771, died March 28, 1819.
Jacob Motter, died 1798.
John Peter Gettier, died Dec. 2, 1837, aged 80; and Elizabeth, his first wife, Aug. 22, 1791; and his second, Mary E., Oct. 14, 1856.
George Kerlinger, born Nov. 18, 1795, died Oct. 6, 1797.
Catharine Motter, born 1782, died 1790.
Daniel Bowman, born Feb. 27, 1783, died May 24, 1854.
Johannes Swartzbaugh, died Feb. 7, 1825, aged 86.
Heinrich Werheim, born 1758, died 1828.
Elizabeth Kantz, died Oct. 28, 1854, aged 86.
Joseph Kopp, died Jan. 26, 1852, aged 75; was in all the Napoleonic wars.
John Ritter, died March 17, 1831, aged 73.
John Ports, Sr., died July 19, 1854, aged 82.
Henry Glase, died Feb. 24, 1879.
George Warner, born Jan. 17, 1791, died Aug. 24, 1874.
George Yingling, died May 14, 1879, aged 85.
Michael Ritter, died Oct. 1, 1878, aged 81.
Henry Beltz, born June 27, 1783, died March 19, 1858.
Johannes Schaurer (now Shower), born 1730, died 1810; married in 1764, Anna Maria Eine, who was born in 1740, and died Aug. 10, 1833.
John Adam Shower, died Aug. 27, 1833, aged 59; and his wife, Anna E., Feb. 13, 1854, aged 81.
George Weaver, born Jan. 27, 1776, died Jan. 15, 1852; and his wife, Mary Magdalene, March 23, 1850, aged 69.
Elizabeth Utz, born 1742, married 1766, to Peter Utz, and died 1797.
Margaret, second wife of Peter Utz, died Jan. 3, 1826, aged 75.
Peter Utz, born 1740, died 1820.
Martin Kroh, died May 23, 1866, aged 83.
Elizabeth, wife of John Sellers, born Feb. 5, 1768, died Sept. 26, 1860.
George Utz, born Oct. 7, 1774, died 1842.
Henry Lamott, died Feb. 15, 1845, aged 75.
Daniel Hoover, born Sept. 9, 1792, died Aug. 16, 1864.
Louisa, wife of Jacob Bear, born Aug. 30, 1761, died March 9, 1856.
Jacob Sherman, born Jan. 19, 1779, died April 8, 1861.
Michael Miller, died Jan. 10, 1845, aged 80.
George Lineweaver, died April 12, 1844, aged 75.
Michael Steffee, born Dec. 16, 1769, died May 18, 1850; and his wife, Christina, born April 8, 1760, died June 16, 1854.
George Everhart, died July 4, 1857, aged 86; and his wife, Elizabeth, March 7, 1868, aged 90.
Rev. Jacob Geiger (31 years and 6 months pastor), died Oct. 19, 1848, aged 55 years and 2 days; and his first wife, daughter of Jacob and Mary Seltzer, born June 1, 1801, died March 12, 1835.

The Union Fire Company was incorporated by act of the General Assembly, March 26, 1839. The incorporators were Solomon Myerly, Jacob Sellers, Lewis Riggle, George Messamore, David Lippy, Elias Buckingham, Jacob Houck, George E. Weaver, George Everhart, George Trump, William Crumrine, Jacob Lineweaver, Henry Krantz, Henry Brinkman, John Shultz, Jesse Shultz, Andrew Pleifer, Ezekiel Baring, James Davis, Jacob Frankforter, David Frankforter, Joseph Gouter, George Baker, Joseph Gardner, Jacob Wentz, Frederick Hamburg, Jacob Kerlinger, Jacob Miller, Charles Miller, S. B. Fuhrman, George Matter, David Houck, Amos Gauman, Jacob Campbell, Adam Shower, J. F. Kopp, John Kuhn, Michael Gettier, George Lineweaver, Levi Maxfield, Michael Matter, Garret Garner, Richard Jones, James Stansbury, Henry E. Beltz, Joseph M. Parke, Philip Crumrine, Frederick Smith, John N. Steffy, Levi Mansfield, Henry Lippy, John Krantz, John Everhart, David Whiteleather.

The Carroll Literary Society was organized Feb. 12, 1881, with J. P. Baltover, president; Dr. J. W. Bechtel, vice-president; Joseph S. Carnman, secretary; P. G. Ober, treasurer. The object of the association is general improvement and the development of a taste for belles-lettres.

The school-house for the pupils of the public schools is a fine brick building, seventy-five by forty-five feet, erected in 1878.

The dispensation of the Knights of Pythias, Manchester Lodge, No. 78, was dated Sept. 14, 1872, and the lodge was instituted on the 17th of that month. The first officers were:

C. C., J. W. Dehoff; Prel., Aaron Miller; V. C., J. S. Kerlinger; M. of E., Cornelius Miller; M. of F., E. A. Ganter.

The charter was dated January, 1878, and the charter members were John W. Dehoff, Aaron Miller, J. S. Kerlinger, E. A. Ganter, H. Falkenstine, Jr., C. J. H. Ganter, James Cross, M.D., G. W. J. Everhart, Daniel Dubbs, C. Miller, George Pfeiffer, Luther Trump. The officers for the second term, 1881, were:

P. C., Emanuel Sherrick; C. C., John W. Burns; Vice C., Charles F. Bergman; Prel., D. M. Brillhart; M. of E., Jacob Wink; M. of F., Cornelius Miller; K. of R. and S., J. P. Baltover; M. at A., Aaron Hoffman; I. G., D. F. Boose; O. G., J. C. Hoffman; Rep. to Grand Lodge, J. E. Mensenheimer; Dist. Dep., R. Lee Simpers; Trustees, Christian Buchanan, A. Appold, Charles Brillhart.

Number of members, 40.

Lebanon Lodge, A. F. and A. M., No. 175, was instituted Oct. 9, 1856, as No. 104, and its first officers were:

W. M., William L. Nace; S. W., Ferdinand Dieffenbach; J. W., John H. Lamott; Sec., Dr. Jacob Shower; Treas., George Shower; S. J., Amos L. Wolfang; Tyler, John Bentz.

It lost its charter, but on May 14, 1879, it was rechartered as No. 175. Its officers then were Dr. Theodore A. Shower, W. M.; E. G. Sellers, S. W.; John M. Bush, J. W. Its officers for 1881 were:

W. M., Lewis C. Myerly; S. W., Wm. C. Murray; J. W., E. T. Sellers; Sec., Adam Shower; Treas., Samuel Miller; S. D., John Fultz; J. D., Jacob Fink; Tyler, John H. Lamott.

Number of members, 25.

The present secretary, Adam Shower, was initiated in 1859, and became secretary in 1861.

Daniel and Jacob Lodge, I. O. O. F., No. 23. A petition was sent to the Maryland Grand Lodge of I. O. O. F. in 1834 for a lodge to be located here, the two first petitioners on the list being Daniel Hoover and Jacob Shower. The petitioners designating no name for the proposed lodge, the Grand Lodge named Daniel and Jacob, in honor of Daniel Hoover and Jacob Shower. The charter was dated Oct. 17, 1834, and signed by James L. Ridgely, G. M., and Robert Neilson, G. S. Its first officers were: N. G., Dr. Jacob Shower; V. G., Daniel Hoover; Sec. and Treas., Jacob Kerlinger.

At the first meeting the following were the initiates: Samuel Lamott, Wm. Crumrine, Henry Brinkman, John Lamott. The second set of officers were: N. G., Daniel Hoover; V. G., William Crumrine; Sec. and Treas., Jacob Kerlinger. The officers for 1881 were:

S. P. G., John Fultz; N. G., Henry Boose; V. G., Nimrod Armstrong; Rec. Sec., G. W. J. Everhart; Per. Sec., E. A. Ganter; Treas., Edward Oursler; Marshal, Wm. A. Wolf; R. S. N. G., N. W. Sellers; L. S. N. G., Henry Reagle; R. S. V. G., John Wink; L. S. V. G., George L. Beltzer; I. G., John Emmel; O. G., A. Pfeiffer.

The lodge owns a fine hall, and has 74 members. Its accumulated funds are $1500. The district deputy is William A. Wolf.

The charter of Carroll Encampment, No. 17, I. O. O. F., dated Oct. 26, 1866, was granted by J. L. Baugher, G. P., and John M. Jones, G. S. The charter members were Wm. Crumrine, Henry Falkenstine, Henry Zimmerman, Samuel Wilhelm, C. Frankforter, Adam Barns. The first officers were: W. C. P., Conrad Frankforter; H. P., Henry E. Beltz; J. W., Samuel Wilhelm; Scribe, Henry Falkenstine.

The following were the initiates at the first meeting, Oct. 26, 1866: Theo. J. Kopp, J. Alfred Kopp, E. A. Ganter, G. W. J. Everhart, E. H. Croutch. The officers for 1881 were:

W. C. P., John C. Denner; H. P., Wm. J. Eisenbrown; S. W., D. H. Hoffacker; J. W., Samuel Miller; Rec. Sec., G. W. J. Everhart; Per. Sec., A. N. Ganter; Treas., N. W. Sellers; Dist. Dep., Samuel Miller.

Number of members, 39.

Bachman's Mills is a small village on the road leading to Hanover turnpike, seven miles from Westminster, five from Manchester, and at the head of Big Pipe Creek. This was formerly Bower's mills, erected about 1780. William and A. C. Bachman own the mills, and the latter is postmaster. The village lies in a beautiful and productive valley, which was settled early in the eighteenth century.

Jerusalem Church was organized in 1799 by the Lutheran and Reformed congregations, who have jointly used the same building in their worship. The first edifice was a log structure, but the present is a substantial brick building, and was erected but a few years ago. Since 1825 its pastors have been the Lutheran and Reformed preachers living in Manchester.

Lazarus Church is also a union church of the Lutheran and Reformed congregations. It was erected in 1853. The building committee were V. B. Wentz, John Kroh, and George Weaver. The Lutheran congregation organized Sept. 5, 1853, and held its first communion June 4, 1854. Since 1863 the Lutheran and Reformed pastors have been the Manchester preachers. Its flourishing Sunday-school is under the charge of Francis Warner as superintendent.

On Feb. 27, 1770, Jonathan Plowman conveyed to John Davis (pastor), John Whitaker, and Samuel Lane fifteen acres of land "for the sole use of a meeting-house for the worship of God forever." In 1828, the Particular Baptist Gunpowder Church was incorporated by the General Assembly, and Thomas Layman, John Perigoy, and Benjamin Buckingham were designated in the act as its trustees. Of these, two died, and one removed from the neighborhood. The meeting-house fell into decay, and the congregation was broken up. The Particular Baptist Church of Black Rock, Baltimore County, being the nearest church of the same faith and order, appointed John B. Ensar, Joshua Plowman, and James Blizzard as trustees, who began erecting thereon a suitable house of worship. To cure all existing and supposed legal disabilities of the trustees, and to ratify their proceedings, the Legislature incorporated this church again, March 4, 1858, retaining the trustees above named.

St. John's church is used jointly by the Reformed and Lutheran congregations, and was built in 1846. It is a log structure weather-boarded. It is five miles from Westminster, which supplies it with pastors.

The Baltimore and Hanover Railroad Company was organized under the general railroad act passed by the General Assembly of Maryland in 1876. Its southern terminus is at Emory Grove, nineteen miles from Baltimore City, on the Western Maryland Railroad. Thence it passes north through Baltimore and

Carroll Counties to Black Rock Station, where it connects with the Bachman Valley Road, the latter forming a connecting link with the Hanover Junction, Hanover and Gettysburg Railroad. The Baltimore and Hanover road forms a most valuable and important connection of the Western Maryland company, by which it is enabled to drain the rich and fertile territory of Southern Pennsylvania. The officers of the company are A. W. Eichelberger, president; William H. Vickery, vice-president; L. T. Melsheimer, secretary; R. M. Wirt, treasurer; Directors, Stephen Keefer, Hanover, Pa.; William H. Hoffman, Baltimore County, Md.; Charles W. Slagle, William H. Vickery, Baltimore; C. C. Wooden, Carroll County, Md.; L. F. Melsheimer, Hanover, Pa.

Bachman's Valley Railroad runs from the iron-ore banks and intersects the Hanover Railroad. Its present officers are: President, Capt. A. W. Eichelberger; Directors, Stephen Kiefer, H. C. Shriver, Joseph Dellone, Joseph Althoff, C. L. Johnson, J. W. Gitt, Levi Dubbs, Perry Wine, Edwin Thomas, Samuel Thomas, E. W. Heindel, and Adam Newcomer.

Parr Ridge Gold and Silver Mining Company.—Many years ago gold was discovered in various places on a ridge extending through Manchester town from Cranberry Valley. In 1879, Messrs. Keeport and Lafeber, of Littlestown, made a thorough examination of the gold region, and found by assays that it was in sufficient quantities to pay for digging. In the summer of 1881 this company was organized with Daniel Beckley as president, and C. J. H. Ganter as secretary. On Aug. 13, 1881, the stockholders at a called meeting voted to purchase the necessary machinery to proceed to work, and the work is being pushed to an apparently successful conclusion. The largest quantities of gold have been found right in the town, or on farms close to the corporation limits. The company has leased several farms, and is actively engaged now in searching for the treasure.

The Dug Hill Mutual Fire Insurance Company has been in operation several years, insuring buildings and general farm property against loss by fire. Its president is P. H. L. Myers, and secretary, John Strevig. Its main and home office is in Manchester. Its former secretary was Francis Warner.

The Shower Foundry, a large manufactory, was established in 1851 by Jacob Shower, who used to employ some thirty hands in the manufacture of different kinds of machinery, of which the larger part was agricultural implements. It is now operated by his son, William H. Shower, and employs some fifteen persons in its various departments. This foundry cast a cannon which was successfully used on the Fourth of July, 1881.

The following are the district officers serving at this date (1881): Justices of the Peace, Henry Motter, J. P. Boltoser, Samuel Hoffacker; Constables, George P. Burns, Geo. Reagle.

Ebbvale is a village on the Bachman's Valley Railroad, nine miles from Westminster, and near to Big Pipe Creek. C. Wentz is postmaster. Of the iron-ore mines located here C. L. Johnson is superintendent, Martin Hugenborn and F. Schenck, engineers, and F. Tragesser, mine boss.

Melrose is on the same railroad, and thirty miles from Baltimore. C. B. Wentz is postmaster. Dr. J. S. Ziegler, physician, C. R. Wentz & Sons, merchants, and Levi Hoff, hotel-keeper.

Springfield Grange, No. 158, is located near Bahn's Mill, and has seventy members. Officers for 1881:

Master, Francis Warner; Sec., J. D. Sharer; Treas., Joseph Miller; Lecturer, John Hinkle; Door-keeper, D. Resh; Steward, J. H. Hoffman; Pomona, Mrs. J. A. Bahn; Flora, Mrs. Francis Warner; Ceres, Mrs. E. Sharer; Lady Assistant Steward, Mrs. Lydia Sharer.

This is the best-conducted grange in the county, and is well officered.

The names of the following persons, residents of the district, aged seventy years and upwards in 1879, are given as a matter of local interest:

Josiah Dehoff, 78; Mrs. Nancy Dehoff, 88; George Yingling, 85; Mrs. Yingling, 82; Mrs. Catherine Ganter, 78; Mrs. Mary Frankforter, 76; Henry Steffy, 84; George Leese, 79; Mrs. Susannah Leese, 80; John Sellers, 84; Mrs. Sellers, 74; Mrs. Elizabeth Martin, 83; Mrs. Sarah Bixler, 83; Mrs. Mary Gettier, 89; Henry Glaze, 79; David Lippy, 73; Geo. Everheart, 79; Dr. Jacob Shower, 76; Mrs. Mary Shower, 74; George Shower, 74; Mrs. Rachel Shower, 76; Mrs. Barbara Warner, 78; Mrs. Elizabeth Shaffer, 85; Mrs. Lydia Black, 75; Mrs. Catherine Zepp, 75; Henry Lucabaugh, 85; Mrs. Mary Yingling, 85; Mrs. Anna M. Wolfgang, 77; Ephraim Tracy, 76; John Redding, 76; John Everheart, 76; George Trump, 71; George Warehime, 89; Stephen Reys, 78; Christian Kexel, 78; Adam Merkel, 83; Mrs. Martha Stansbury, 76; John Bentz, 72; Mrs. Maria Bentz, 75; Mrs. Mary Stansbury, 79; Sarah Butler (colored), 81; Nicholas Warner, 81; John H. Bordleman, 76; Benjamin Lippy, 71; Elizabeth Gettier, 73. Females, 22; aggregate ages, 1741; average, 79. Males, 23; aggregate ages, 1803; average, 78.

Mr. John Sellers, one of the soldiers of the war of 1812, and a member of Capt. Adam Shower's company, died at his residence, in Manchester District, on Feb. 27, 1879, aged 84 years, 4 months, and 11 days.

Dr. Jacob Shower, a prominent citizen of this county, and well known in former years throughout the State as a Democratic leader, died at his residence in Manchester on Sunday, May 25, 1879, aged seventy-seven years. He was the son of Col. Adam Shower, who represented Baltimore County in the

House of Delegates for many years during the early part of this century. Dr. Shower entered politics when quite young, and served in the House of Delegates from Baltimore County several years prior to the organization of Carroll County in 1837, and was in the Legislature when the bill for its formation was passed. He was upon the first ticket nominated in this county for the House of Delegates, and was elected. He was elected for a second, and declined a nomination for the third term. In 1841 he was appointed to the position of clerk of the court, made vacant by the death of Dr. Willis, and served about seven years. In 1851 he was elected a member of the Constitutional Convention, but declined the position. Since his term in Congress, from 1854 to 1856, he had not been in public life, but had ever evinced a great interest in State and national politics. He was a member of the first Andrew Jackson Club in this State, which was formed at the Washington Hotel, on Gay Street, Baltimore, in the year 1824, and which adopted the die for the figure-head, "Jackson and Liberty." Dr. Shower was possessed of a strong mind. His genial disposition and general fund of information endeared him to all who knew him, and his society was much sought by the politicians of the State. As a politician he was a link between the past and the present. He saw the rise of the Democratic party, was a participator in all its contests, saw its overthrow, and again witnessed its triumph. He left a large circle of relatives and friends to mourn his death. His was one of the most familiar faces in all the State Democratic conventions from the time of his first connection with politics until his death. He was arrested by the United States provost-marshal in 1863 upon some trivial charges, and imprisoned for some months.

The following is a list of school trustees and teachers for this district for 1881 and 1882, with number of pupils:

1 and 2. Grammar School and Primary No. 1.—J. H. La Motte, D. H. Hoffacker, John M. Gettier.

3 and 4. Primary Nos. 2 and 3.—G. W. Everhart, Jacob Wink, H. K. Grove.

5. Miller's.—George K. Frank, George P. Miller, John P. Frank.

6. Zimmerman's.—Benjamin Bowser, J. David Shearer, John Hilker.

7. Kroh's or Lippy's.—Joseph Price, Francis Warner, C. R. Wentz.

8. Tracey's.—Jonas Warner, Wm. Zepp, A. J. P. Rhoads.

9. Wentz's.—Peter Gettier, Phaniel Wentz, G. Bixler.

10. Krideler's.—Edward Krideler, Philip Yoatz, Samuel Shaeffer.

11. Bachman's Mill.—D. S. Palmer, Jacob Shaeffer, Samuel Wine.

12. Royer's.—Daniel Reese, Christian Royer, Jeremiah Mathias.

13. Union.—J. J. Abbott, H. B. Houck, Nathaniel Leister.

14. Old Fort (Nace's).—Charles Grove, Jacob Boring, L. Kreitzer.

15. Bosley's.—H. M. Menshey, D. Burns, D. Garrett.

16. Ebbvale.—Oliver Hoover, C. Wentz, Edward Garrett.

The teachers for the term ending April 15, 1881, were:

1, Nellie R. Lilley, 40 pupils; 2, J. P. Baltzer, 41 pupils; 3, Willie Cox, 45 pupils; 4, Lizzie Trump, 39 pupils; 5, E. S. Miller, 55 pupils; 6, Emma Lorrenger, 38 pupils; 7, V. B. Wentz, 58 pupils; 8, Noah Peterman, 42 pupils; 9, J. R. Strevig, 58 pupils; 10, J. F. Peterman, 47 pupils; 11, G. T. Palmer, 42 pupils; 12, Mary C. Bixler, 47 pupils; 13, J. A. Abbott, 65 pupils; 14, G. W. J. Everhart, 34 pupils; 15, Laura M. Burnee, 27 pupils; 16, T. R. Strevig, 33 pupils.

The following were the votes cast from 1851 to 1861, inclusive, for local officers:

1851.—Vote for Primary School Commissioner: George Crouse 229, Philip H. L. Myers 76, David Bachman 56, John C. Price 30.

1853.—For Justices: George Everhart 234, Jacob Kerlinger 386, John C. Price 324, Wm. Walter 358; Constables: John Shultz 455, Anthony Hines 358; Road Supervisor: Frederick Ritter 488.

1855.—For Justices: J. Kerlinger 445, W. Walter 445, Henry Motter 423, Geo. Bixler 104; Constables: J. A. Hines 435, Henry Krantz 425, Emanuel Trine 63, John Shultz 113; Road Supervisor: Frederick Ritter 437, Samuel Witter 102.

1857.—For Justices: John C. Price 479, Wm. Walter 474, Henry Motter 134, Henry Glaze 401; Constables: J. A. Hines 501, Henry Krantz 501; Road Supervisor, Michael Ritter 497.

1859.—For Justices: Henry Motter 476, John C. Price 480, Wm. Walter 490, Michael Sullivan 134; Constables: Henry Krantz 491, Eli Myers 474, John Shultz 151; Road Supervisor: Michael Ritter 491.

1861.—For Justices: Henry Motter 326, John C. Price 318, D. T. Shaeffer 311, Henry Glaze 299, Geo. Hartley 309, John Fultz 318; Constables: Henry Krantz 330, John Lockard 281, Henry Reagle 308, Henry Cramer 264; Road Supervisor: D. H. Hoffacker 329, Henry Fair 307.

Among the thrifty and industrious German emigrants to Pennsylvania in 1720 was Jacob Warner, a young man from the kingdom of Bavaria, who settled in York County of that State. His son, Melchior Warner, removed, about 1780, to that part of Baltimore County now forming a part of Manchester District, in Carroll County. His son, Jacob H. Warner, was the father of Francis Warner, who was born July 28, 1826, three miles east of Manchester. He lived on a farm until the twenty-first year of his age. He was liberally educated at the noted "White Hall Academy," near Harrisburg, Pa. He was elected magistrate by the voters of his district during the late civil war (1863), and was subsequently repeatedly appointed to this office, which he held with complete satisfaction to the public for eight successive years. He was twice elected surveyor of Carroll County, and in 1879 was chosen county commissioner, which position he now most acceptably fills, having for his colleagues Col. John K. Longwell, of Westminster, and William C. Polk, of Freedom District. He was for nine consecutive years a director of the "Farmers' Mutual Insurance Company of Dug Hill," and its secretary and treasurer for five years. He resides on "Dug Hill," an historical part of the district, situated on the Pennsylvania State line, and settled about the middle of the past century. He takes great interest in educational matters, having been engaged in teaching fourteen years, and is one of the trustees of School No. 7. He is superintendent of the Sunday-school of Lazarus Church, jointly erected and occupied by the Reform and Lutheran congregations. A practical farmer, and thoroughly conversant with agriculture in all its minutiæ, he has ever zealously labored for the material interests of the tillers of the soil. He is Master of Springfield Grange, No. 158, located near Bahn's Mill,—the most flourishing organization of the kind in the county,—formed and chiefly built up under his management. He was married, Nov. 8, 1859, to Adaline C. Wolfgang, daughter of Jacob Wolfgang, by whom he has three children,—two daughters and a son. Besides having served two terms as county surveyor, he has for many years been engaged in private surveying, in which profession he stands deservedly high because of his proficiency and skill. He has filled all public positions intrusted to him with credit, and the board of county commissioners has rarely had a member who paid closer attention to the wants and interests of the public than Mr. Warner.

HAMPSTEAD DISTRICT, OR DISTRICT No. 8,

of Carroll County, is bounded on the north by Manchester District, on the east by Baltimore County, on the south by Woolery's, and on the west by the districts of Westminster and Manchester. The east branch of the Patapsco Falls flows south through the centre of the district, and Aspen and White Oak Runs intersect the western portion, and empty into the Patapsco. In addition to the turnpikes and private roads the Hanover Railroad furnishes an outlet for the products of the district in a northern direction, and the Western Maryland Railroad passes along its southwestern edge. In 1880 it had a population of 1983. The metes and bounds of the district as determined by the commission of 1837 are as follows:

"Beginning at the forks of the county roads leading from Westminster to Hampstead and George Richards' mill; thence to the forks of Aspen Run and Long Glade Branch; thence up said branch to the spring near the house of Joseph Bowser, deceased; thence to the spring near the house of John Orendorff; thence to the forks of the most northern branch of Patapsco Falls and Bosley's spring branch, where they unite in William Albaugh's meadow; thence through the farms of John Reed and Joshua Bosley, Sr., leaving said Reed and Bosley in District No. 6; thence to Michael Becker's tavern, on the Hanover and Baltimore turnpike road, leaving said Becker in District No. 6; thence across said turnpike east of Shriver's tan-yard; thence through the lands of Daniel Caltuder, leaving said Caltuder in District No. 6; thence through the lands of ——— Gist; thence through the lands of George Caltuder, deceased, and John Wareham, leaving said Wareham and Caltuder in District No. 8; thence to Michael Miller's mill, on the middle road; thence to Joshua Stansbury's spring, near the house on the Falls road; thence through the lands of Hair, leaving said Hair in District No. 8; thence to Henry Zimmerman's county road where said road crosses the Carroll and Baltimore County line at a blazed hickory-tree; thence on Baltimore County line to Edward Bond's; thence with the lines of District No. 4 to Richard Gorsuch's farm on Patapsco Falls; thence with a straight line to the place of beginning."

Hampstead was made the place for holding the polls. The tract of land known as "Transylvania" was originally surveyed for Thomas White, Aug. 8, 1746, but resurveyed and patented to Capt. Richard Richards, June 10, 1751.

The district took its name from Hampstead in England, a town from which Capt. Richard Richards emigrated about 1735. The early settlers were Capt. Richard Richards and his brother-in-law, Christopher Vaughn, the Coxes, Stansburys, Henry Lamott, the Fowbles, Houcks, Snyders, Ebaughs, Murrays, Browns, Leisters, Rubys, Lovealls, Cullisons, Gardners, Hammonds, and Armacosts. The first settlers were generally English, but afterwards the Germans came into the district in large numbers.

Hampstead, a village containing upwards of three hundred inhabitants, is located on surveys called "Spring Garden," patented to Dustane Dane in 1748, and "Landorff." It was called "Coxville" for over fifty years in honor of John Cox, its first settler, but finally took the name of Hampstead from the district. About a century ago, Col. Johns, of Baltimore County (in which this district was then situated), built a warehouse of logs to receive and store wheat for his mills, near Dover. That house was afterwards weatherboarded and sold by Col. Johns to John Cox, the first actual settler, who kept a tavern in it. Cox subsequently sold it to Henry Lamott. It is the oldest house in the town, and is now owned by Micajah Stansbury. The town was laid out about 1786 by Christopher Vaughan, a brother-in-law of Capt. Richard Richards. They were both Englishmen, and during the Revolution Richards sympathized with the British, but Vaughan was an active Whig. Henry

Lamott came to the village in 1798 from Havre de Grace, when there were only a few houses in it. He was the son of John Lamott, a French nobleman, who settled in Maryland about 1760, and was the first of this family in America. The first physician of the town was Dr. Urnbaugh, who had been a Hessian soldier, and lived a short time in nearly all the villages of the county. The first schoolmaster was a Mr. Parks. After Dr. Urnbaugh, Dr. Hall, who lived several miles distant, attended patients here, and the next resident physician was Dr. Richard C. Wells, with whom Drs. Roberts Barthulow and Hanson M. Drach studied in 1850–51 and '52. The last two married daughters of John Lamott. John Fowble kept the first store. Peter Frank kept the first tavern, and was succeeded by John Cox. Capt. Richard Richards owned fifteen hundred acres of land near the town.

The village is on the Hanover pike, and is one of the best stations on the Hanover Railroad. Its oldest citizens are Col. John Lamott and William Tall Hammond, who both served in the war of 1812, the latter being now (1881) eighty-seven years old. Col. Lamott was born in 1795, and was three years old when his father, Henry Lamott, moved to Hampstead. In the war of 1812 he was in Capt. Adam Shower's company of Col. Shultz' regiment, of which Conrad Kerlinger was major. He was in the battle of North Point, and draws a pension for his services. His father, Henry Lamott, kept a tavern here forty-five years, and died in 1851. Since the completion of the railroad in 1879 the town has rapidly increased in population, and the value of real estate has doubled. The physicians are Drs. Richard C. Wells and his sons, Edward and Constant Wells, Hanson M. Drach, John W. Stansbury, and W. W. Wareheim. C. M. Murray is postmaster, and Lewis C. Myerly, attorney-at-law. The latter was admitted to the bar during his residence in Indiana. He was born Jan. 24, 1829, in Westminster District, and was a son of Jacob, and grandson of George, Myerly. The latter was one of two brothers who came from Germany before 1775. The Myerly family is of German and French extraction. Jacob Myerly married Eve Bishop, by whom he had the following children: Rachel, Benjamin, Reuben C. (wounded in the Mexican war, and died in Lima, La.), Jacob, Mary J., Lewis Cass, and Susanna. It was owing largely to the efforts of Lewis C. Myerly that the Hanover Railroad was located and built on its present road-bed. John Armacost, aged ninety-two years, lives near town with his wife, to whom he has been married seventy years, and during all of that time he has been a member of the M. E. Church. Shane Cullison, living near, died in 1877, aged ninety-six years.

The first edifice of the Methodist Episcopal Church was a log structure, built about 1800, which is now occupied by Charles Roat. It was used also as a school-house. The present stone church was erected in 1845 by Richard Richards as contractor. The parsonage was built in 1878. Rev. D. Benton Winstead is the pastor. The graveyard ground in its rear was a donation from John Lamott. Interred there are

Maria, wife of Jackson Belt, who died June 7, 1880, aged 62.
Elizabeth, wife of John Cox, died Aug. 20, 1872, aged 77.
Nicholas Gardner, died Nov. 3, 1874, aged 65.
Jeremiah Malehorn, died Feb. 28, 1871, aged 47.
Anna, wife of Christian Wisner, died March 28, 1869.
Leonard Belt, died Nov. 7, 1871, aged 59.
Mary, wife of Caleb Blizzard, died July 7, 1866, aged 56.
Susan, wife of Elisha Gorsuch, died July 1, 1863, aged 62.
Keziah Caltrider, died Oct. 3, 1876, aged 71; and her husband, John Caltrider, born March 5, 1795, died Feb. 28, 1863.
Elizabeth, wife of Richard D. Armacost, died July 16, 1859, aged 68.
Moses Myers, died Nov. 18, 1851, aged 58; and his wife, Jane, March 18, 1868, aged 67.
Elender, wife of Dr. Henson L. Drach (U. S. Army), died Oct. 3, 1864, aged 32; and Susan, wife of Dr. Roberts Bartholow (U. S. Army), died July 6, 1862, aged 28, both daughters of John and Rachel Lamott. The latter (Rachel) died Jan. 11, 1850, aged 46.
George Ports, died April 18, 1872, aged 70.
Joshua Tipton, born Aug. 14, 1800, died Sept. 20, 1853.
Dr. J. Ebaugh, died Oct. 13, 1848, aged 24.
Absalom Null, died Feb. 24, 1862, aged 40.

Rev. Amon Richards was the first preacher of this church, and died but a few years ago nearly one hundred years old.

The United Brethren church is situated one mile from town, at Greenmount, on the Hanover pike. Its pastor is Rev. J. R. Snake.

The Lutheran congregation has no church edifice, but holds its services in the hall of the Independent Order of Red Men. Rev. H. Burk is pastor.

Dehoff's church, not now standing, was near Greenmount, and was built over seventy years ago by John Dehoff, who preached himself, although a plain farmer with limited education.

Red Jacket Tribe, No. 24, of the Independent Order of Red Men, was instituted about 1845. It owns a fine hall and is in a flourishing condition. William A. Murray is its Chief of Records and Keeper of Seal.

Snydersburg is on the east branch of the Patapsco, three and a half miles from Manchester, seven and a half miles from Westminster, and twenty-nine miles from Baltimore. The merchants are E. Snyder and J. H. Lippy, the latter being the postmaster.

St. Mark's church was erected in 1878 by the Lutheran and Reformed congregations, who jointly use it in worship. The building committee were Michael Brillhart (Reformed), Jacob Yingling, and Mr. Ruby (Lutheran). The house was consecrated Sept. 29, 1878. The Lutheran organization was perfected March 9, 1879, when Jacob Yingling and Elisha Snyder were elected elders, Edmund Reed and Daniel S. Hann, deacons.

Houcksville is three miles from Patapsco, near the Patapsco River, thirty-four miles from Baltimore, and fifteen from Westminster. The merchants are S. A. Lauver & Son, G. W. Keller, and A. J. Houck. The latter is postmaster, and it is from his family that the place takes its name. Geo. W. Keller has an extensive paper manufactory here. Dr. C. S. Davis is the physician of the town, and Dr. George Rupp the dentist. Mr. Keller's paper-factory gives employment to many mechanics and laborers. The water-power of the Patapsco at this point is magnificent, and numerous mills and factories are successfully operated.

The Bartholow family is one of the oldest in this district, and has given to the country a man distinguished at home and in Europe for his great medical learning and attainments. Dr. Roberts Bartholow was born and raised near Hampstead, and educated at Calvert College, after which he graduated at the University of Maryland. During the war of 1861–65 he was brigade surgeon on the staff of Gen. McClellan. After his resignation he took a professorship in the University of Maryland, and from there he removed to Cincinnati, Ohio, at which place he was chosen Professor of Materia Medica of the Ohio Medical College. He is the author of several meritorious medical works. In March, 1879, this most skillful and scientific physician was appointed Professor of Materia Medica and Therapeutics in the Jefferson Medical College of Philadelphia. Dr. Bartholow, within the past ten years, has attracted the attention of his profession, both in Europe and America, by the freshness and vigor of his writings and the variety of his contributions to science. In the literature of his profession he is now an acknowledged authority, and the fact that Jefferson Medical College chose him for the responsible position named is an evidence that this standard institution is determined to keep abreast of the age. He studied medicine with Dr. Thomas W. Wells, graduated on March 9, 1852, and practiced his profession at New Windsor until his removal to Cincinnati, Ohio. He married Susan, daughter of John and Rachel Lamott.

The following is a list of public school trustees in this district for 1881 and 1882, together with the names of teachers and number of pupils in each school:

1. Jesse Brown's.—Leven Wright, John E. Houck, Adam Shaffer.
2 and 3. Snydersburg (Nos. 1 and 2).—J. Switzer, Wm. H. Ruby, John T. Reed.
4. Eberg.—John Strickland, George Gross, George Shaffer.
5 and 6.—Hampstead (Nos. 1 and 2).—James Sugars, William Houck, Jacob Caltrider.
7. Houcksville.—Michael Buchman, Joseph Brummel, A. J. Houck.
8. Emory Chapel.—Appointments deferred.
9. Lowe's.—Miles Long, D. Leister, Lewis Green.
10. Salem.—J. M. Bush, John P. Murray, John A. Armacost.
11. Mount Union Mills.—Thomas J. Gorsuch, Casper Millander, William Kagle.

The teachers for the term ending April 15, 1881, were:

1, E. S. Martin, 39 pupils; 2, A. Eugenia Foltz, 36 pupils; 3, J. H. L. Boyer, 39 pupils; 4, G. A. Leister, 46 pupils; 5, Mettie Miller, 44 pupils; 6, W. A. Abbott, 42 pupils; 7, Joel Sykes, 58 pupils; 8, Anna M Buckingham, 27 pupils; 9, J. Thomas Green, 27 pupils; 10, Sadie E. Myers, 34 pupils; 11, John W. Rilb, 48 pupils.

The justices are Dr. Hanson T. Drach, John W. Abbott; Constable, Benjamin Croft.

Below are given the votes cast for local officers in this district from 1851 to 1861, inclusive:

1851.—Vote for Primary School Commissioner: F. J. Smith 101, Daniel Hoover 89, F. J. Smith 126, Daniel Hoover 88.
1853.—For Justices: D. W. Houck 184, Richard Harris 160, H. Jordan 68; Constables: John Marsh 67, Jetson L. Gill 179; Road Supervisor: Joseph Armacost 174, Jacob Lippo 72.
1855.—For Justices: Richard Harris 122, Jesse Brown 103, John Fowble 141, George Richards 150; Constables: J. L. Gill 137, J. Campbell 121; Road Supervisor: E. Ebaugh 110, Leonard Belt 154.
1857.—For Justices: Dr. H. M. Drach 183, George Richards 189, J. L. Gill 120, Daniel Richards 116; Constables: H. W. Ports 177, Jerome Ebaugh 121; Road Supervisor: L. Belt 172, C. P. Frick 121, William Corbin 8.
1859.—For Justices: H. M. Drach 162, Jesse Brown 149, John Lamotte 62, R. Harris 137; Constables: J. G. Gittinger 175, Jerome Ebaugh 134; Road Supervisor: Leonard Belt 179, Henry Stansbury 130.
1861.—For Justices: W. S. Wooden 209, Jacob Miller 194, Jesse Brown 116, Richard Harris 131; Constables: Elisha Bromwell 216, Alfred Ruby 108; Road Supervisor: William Houck 199, Leonard Belt 132.

The reputation of Hampstead District for good order has been uniformly excellent, and there has seldom happened anything of an exciting character to arouse the feelings of the inhabitants. On the night of Feb. 12, 1870, however, at a place known as Houck & Hoffman's fulling-mill, and about one mile from the store of D. W. Houck, Edward Woolman, a German, stabbed Samuel P. Linkinhofer to the heart with a shoemaker's knife, killing him instantly. At the subsequent investigation Woolman was discharged from custody, it having been shown that the homicide was committed in self-defense.

FRANKLIN DISTRICT, No. 9.

The Ninth District of Carroll County, known as Franklin, is bounded on the north by the districts of New Windsor and Westminster, on the west by Freedom, on the south by Howard County, and on the west by Frederick County. Morgan's Run waters the northern portion of the district, Gillis' Falls the centre and south, and a number of small streams pass through the western part of Franklin. The southern extremity of Franklin District is traversed by the Baltimore and Ohio Railroad, which offers unlimited facilities for the disposal of produce, and the Western Maryland passes through New Windsor, not very far from the northern boundary. The following are the metes and bounds prescribed by the commission of 1837, which were afterwards slightly altered by an act of Assembly passed May 23, 1853, and already given:

"Beginning at Parr's Spring; thence with the Western Branch of Patapsco Falls to the junction of Gillis's Falls; thence with Gillis's Falls to James Steel's, leaving him in District No. 5; thence with a straight line to a branch crossing the new Liberty road near Conway's; thence with a straight line to Crawford's road at the old Liberty; thence up the old Liberty road to Farfer's old fields; thence with the road running near Gideon Mitchel's, leaving him in District No. 9; thence with said road to Morgan's Run; thence up Morgan's Run to Hawkins' Branch, to a road leading from Benjamin Gorsuch to George Warfield's store; thence with the road leading to the 'Stone Chapel;' thence with Howard's road to Turkey Foot Branch; thence down said branch to Philip Nicodemuses mill; thence with the lines of District No. 2 to Sandis' Mill; thence with the county line to the place of beginning."

Franklinville was made the place for holding the polls. The district contained 2225 inhabitants in 1880.

This district was settled by the English and emigrants from the southern counties of the province of Maryland. Among the first settlers were the Franklins, from whom the district took its name, Charles and Alexander Warfield, John and David Evans, Rawlingses, Beaches, Samuel Kitzmiller, the Waterses, Brashearses, Spurriers, Gosnells, Barneses, Ingelses, Buckinghams, Lindsays, Dorseys, Bennetts (Samuel, Benjamin, and Lloyd), Selbys, Hoods, and Elgins.

Ebenezer church (M. E.), a frame building, is situated in the eastern part of the district, on the road from Winfield to Defiance, and was built in 1854. For the past six years it has been a part of the New Windsor Circuit, and before that was connected with Westminster. Its pastors for 1881 were Revs. James Cadden and Howard Downs. In the graveyard adjoining the church are buried

Perry C. Harp, died April 26, 1879, aged 80.

Eliza Ann, wife of R. L. Farver, died Oct. 17, 1872, aged 40.

Nicholas H. Jenkins, died Jan. 31, 1877, aged 61.

Arrey, wife of Warner Pickett, born June 29, 1821, died Jan. 28, 1871.

Marcilia, wife of J. T. Jenkins, born Oct. 16, 1848, died Aug. 2, 1872.

Joseph Atkins, of First Massachusetts Cavalry, died July 8, 1863, aged 34.

Catharine Harp, died Nov. 16, 1874, aged 73.

John Day, died March 5, 1871, aged 60; and his wife, Emily, born Jan. 29, 1818, died April 30, 1876.

Joshua Grimes, died April 12, 1867, aged 61.

David A. Hiltabidel, born Aug. 23, 1818, died Nov. 21, 1862; and Temperance, his wife, died Dec. 31, 1866, aged 51.

Samuel Choate, born Jan. 28, 1822, died Nov. 1, 1862.

Hamilton P. Skidmore, died March 17, 1878, aged 51.

Ruth Ann, wife of Basil Shipley, died Feb. 24, 1859, aged 27.

Cordelia, wife of Perry G. Burdett, died April 28, 1857, aged 28.

Catharine, wife of Joseph Frizzell, died Jan. 16, 1871, aged 63.

John W. Criswell, died Nov. 18, 1858, aged 42; and Ruth, his wife, Dec. 28, 1879, aged 66.

Sarah A. Rawlings, born Nov. 3, 1809, died May 29, 1878.

Catharine, wife of Dr. J. Rinehart, died Dec. 19, 1879, aged 25.

Corrilla, wife of John A. Snider, died Jan. 23, 1872, aged 39.

Taylorsville was named in honor of Gen. Zachary Taylor, and the first house was built in it in May, 1846, by Henry D. Franklin. Mr. Franklin still resides therein, and has adjoining a wagon-making shop, which he carries on. The second settler in the place was David Buckingham, who keeps a store and is the postmaster.

The Methodist Episcopal church is a neat frame edifice erected in 1878, before which services were held in a building constructed in 1850, and now used as a band hall. The present pastor is Rev. Mr. Shriner, and the Sunday-school superintendent is Thomas Shipley. In the cemetery attached to the church are buried James Beach, born Aug. 19, 1846, died Oct. 29, 1880; Charles G. Franklin, died Dec. 24, 1878, aged seventy; N. Harvey Shipley, died Feb. 4, 1881, aged eighteen; Louisa, wife of David Buckingham, died July 22, 1849, aged forty-two.

Franklinville is seven and a half miles from Mount Airy, and near Parr's Falls, a small stream which drains the neighborhood. It was settled in the beginning of the century, and named for the Franklin family, one of the first to settle in the district, about 1745. R. Dorsey is merchant and postmaster, and Dr. R. O. D. Warfield, the physician of the village. William Long, John Elgin, and John T. Derr have shoe-shops, and George Pickett and Jesse Wilson are the millers. It is the voting-place of the district, and is pleasantly situated on the old Liberty road.

The Methodist Episcopal Church South (Bethany)

was organized in 1871, under the auspices of Rev. A. Q. Flaherty, and its neat frame edifice was built in the same year. Its pastors have been:

1871–73, Rev. A. Q. Flaherty; 1873–76, Rev. David Bush; 1876–79, Rev. W. R. Stringer; 1879–82, Rev. M. G. Balthis.

In the graveyard in its rear are, among others, the following interments:

Levin Gosnell, died Dec. 21, 1879, aged 86.

Bennett Spurrier, died Nov. 9, 1879, aged 75; and his wife, Rachel, died Dec. 25, 1879, aged 77.

Lizzie M., wife of Samuel Elgin, died March 1, 1875, aged 68.

Lewis Lindsay, died Nov. 21, 1878, aged 57.

Casadora Lindsay, died June 18, 1876, aged 28.

Charles W. Franklin, died March 1, 1874, aged 53.

Samuel Kitzmiller, died Sept. 15, 1854, and born May 10, 1790; and his wife, Catharine, born June 8, 1799, died June 22, 1865.

Thomas B. Franklin, died Oct. 30, 1878, aged 65.

Winfield is six miles from the Baltimore and Ohio Railroad at Woodbine, and was named in honor of Gen. Winfield Scott. The Bethel Church of God, Rev. Mr. Palmer, is located here. The village was established about 1851 and 1852. Franklin Grange, No. 117, of Patrons of Husbandry, of which Dr. F. J. Crawford was for a long time Master, holds its meetings in Winfield. H. M. Zile is a merchant in the village, and James Easton postmaster. Dr. F. J. Crawford is the physician. Its schools, Pine Orchard and Jenkins', are among the best in the county.

Mount Airy, so named from its elevated and healthy location, is on the Baltimore and Ohio Railroad. J. C. Duvall is postmaster and track foreman. The store-keepers are J. B. Runkles, S. E. Grove, A. Anderson, and Cochran & Harrington. The hotels are kept by R. A. Nelson and C. A. Smith. Drs. B. H. Todd and J. E. Bromwell are the physicians, and T. P. Mullinix, railroad and express agent. The Mount Airy Coal and Iron Company was incorporated March 9, 1854, with F. A. Schley, J. M. Schley, Thomas Hammond, George Schley, and John G. Lynn as incorporators.

Newport, a small hamlet, lies near the Frederick County line.

Parrsville and **Ridgeville,** small villages, lie south of the Baltimore and Ohio Railroad. In the former is a Methodist Episcopal church, and between it and Mount Airy is the Presbyterian church.

Hooper's Delight, a neat brick school-house, a mile from Sam's Creek, was built in 1875.

Bethel Methodist Episcopal church, a brick building of two stories and a basement, was erected in 1860 on the site where the old log structure stood in 1815. It belongs to the New Windsor Circuit, and its pastors for 1881 were Rev. Howard Downs and J. A. Fadden. The beautiful cemetery adjoining the church contains the graves of the following persons:

Thomas Devilbiss, died July 12, 1878, aged 77.

Benjamin Bennett, born Aug. 21, 1809, died Dec. 23, 1863.

Robert Bennett, died March 26, 1856, aged 78; and Elizabeth Bennett, died Jan. 4, 1846, aged 78.

Nathan B. Stocksdale, born Feb. 2, 1806, died Jan. 20, 1865.

Jesse M. Zile, born July 26, 1831, died June 11, 1875.

Lewis Keefer, born July 31, 1803, died Sept. 7, 1880; and Rachel, his wife, died July 26, 1873, aged 63.

Mahlon, son of Casper and A. E. Devilbiss, died Nov. 8, 1878, aged 44.

Casper Devilbiss, died March 4, 1868, aged 73.

Mary Hiteshew, died Dec. 10, 1871, aged 88.

Sarah T. Sebier, died Nov. 21, 1871, aged 55.

Mary Nusbaum, died Jan. 1, 1864, aged 44.

David Nusbaum, died Sept. 24, 1861, aged 60.

Benjamin Sharrets, born Feb. 19, 1808, died Aug. 24, 1873.

Mary M. Sharrets, born April 3, 1812, died March 26, 1874.

John L. Reigler, born July 5, 1805, died April 12, 1879; and Annie, his wife, died March 24, 1862, aged 58.

Ursala Barbara Reigler, born Dec. 14, 1814, died March 5, 1874.

John Greenwood, born Feb. 25, 1817, died Feb. 12, 1878.

Ellen Chase, died June 19, 1874, aged 62.

Mary E., wife of R. Dorsey, born Oct. 20, 1829, died April 17, 1873.

Urland Greenwood, died Dec. 3, 1875, aged 57.

Stephen Gorsuch, died June 5, 1880, aged 80.

Jane Gorsuch, born June 19, 1786, died Sept. 3, 1856.

Nathan, son of Stephen and Jane Gorsuch, born Jan. 26, 1826, died April 6, 1849.

Thomas Poole, died Aug. 31, 1821, aged 37.

Dr. Lewis Kelly, died April 13, 1872, aged 30.

Alexander Warfield, died Jan. 6, 1835, aged 70; and his wife, Jemima, died Nov. 20, 1847, aged 72.

Elizabeth Worthington, born Oct. 22, 1826, died July 6, 1851.

Rev. Joshua Jones, died Sept. 19, 1836, aged 70; and his wife, Annie, March 12, 1811, aged 33.

Horatio J. Warfield, died Aug. 5, 1877, aged 53.

Rev. Geo. W. Johnson, born Oct. 10, 1841, died May 28, 1874.

Francis A. Davis, died Dec. 7, 1850, aged 50; and his wife, Cecilia, died Aug. 28, 1849, aged 40.

Rev. John Davis, died April 28, 1847, aged 85.

Joshua Warfield, died April 1, 1880, aged 79.

Evelina C. Warfield, died May 24, 1877, aged 47.

David Warfield, died March 4, 1871, aged 43.

Virginia S., wife of J. P. Naill, died July 22, 1874, aged 28.

Near this church—but a few yards away—is the old Alexander Warfield homestead. It is now occupied by Rev. Charles A. Reid, a native of Virginia, who began preaching in the Methodist Episcopal Church in 1842. He married Elizabeth, daughter of Joshua Warfield, and granddaughter of Alexander Warfield. The latter's father was one of the earliest settlers in the district, and owned all the land around the Bethel church. Alexander Warfield was first married to Elizabeth Woodward, Dec. 30, 1788, by whom he had four children. He was again married March 11, 1797, to Jemima Dorsey. His house, built over a hundred years ago and now occupied by Rev. Dr. Reid, was the early stopping-place of Bishop Asbury and all the circuit riders and preachers. Bishop Asbury visited it last in 1816. Mr. Warfield was church steward in 1801, and active in the church services until his death, Jan. 6, 1835. At John Evan's old house, now owned by Jesse Stern, was likewise a home for preachers, and preaching held there as late as 1809, when services were transferred to the house of Benjamin Bennett. The Evan's house was a log structure one and a half stories high. Samuel and Lloyd Bennett were early converted to Methodism, and became noted in the church.

Creameries.—Pinkney J. Bennett owns two creameries, both of which are in successful operation, one of which is located in the Franklin District and the other in New Windsor. He is the largest butter producer in Maryland. His establishments are fitted up with the best of machinery, and together have a capacity of ten thousand pounds of butter daily. His varied appliances include five horse engines. At present he is making about five thousand pounds daily, while the average daily yield throughout the year is six thousand pounds. The lands in the vicinity are finely adapted to the business, producing the best of blue grass and clover, and are free from noxious weeds. Mr. Bennett gets his milk from thirty-five farmers, and the amount used is the product of a herd of four hundred cows, all healthy and vigorous animals. The butter is made by machinery, and is never touched by the employés during its manufacture. He also makes ice-cream and ships milk, but makes no cheese. He does not think that the increased value of the product is equivalent to the extra labor, and believes his butter will keep longer. The yield per hundred pounds of milk he also thinks to be greater than cheese-makers realize, and by returning the sour milk to the farmers for their pigs, he can buy for less than if it were retained for cheese-making.

The price the farmers get for the milk is equivalent, if they made it into butter, to about twenty-five cents per pound of butter.

The creameries are two stories high, thirty-five by forty feet, with engine-houses ten by twelve feet, and are erected over streams of running water.

The farmers of the county are awakening to the importance of creameries, and at their solicitation Mr. Bennett is considering the establishment of two more.

He has been in the business since 1876, and since the first difficulties were overcome, of the educating of the farmers of his vicinity to keeping pastures and the necessity of cleanliness, he has been quite successful in his enterprises. He is a progressive and energetic gentleman, and has ample means to back him.

Harrisville, a small hamlet, is in the western part of Franklin District and on the Frederick County line.

Hood & Clary have a store here, and the place has a mill and several shops.

Watersville is a village situated in the Franklin District, on the Baltimore and Ohio Railroad, about forty miles from Baltimore. The Methodist Episcopal and Baptist congregations have a place of worship. England & Kenly are the merchants of the town, and the former is postmaster. Dr. S. R. Waters is the practicing physician for the village and the surrounding country, and it is from his family, one of the oldest in the district, that the town derives its name. Joshua Hall is the railroad foreman stationed at this point, and D. L. Kenly is the railroad and express agent. The country in the vicinity of the village is noted as a tobacco-growing region.

David Crawford, one of the first settlers in New Windsor District, where in early days he was a leading man in public affairs, was a native of Pennsylvania. He married Miss Lloyd, from which union were born seven sons and two daughters. Of these, Evan Lloyd Crawford married Isabella Smith, a daughter of Duncan Smith. She was born at Inverness, Scotland, near the city of Edinburgh, and came to America with her parents when a little girl. Evan Lloyd Crawford was the father of one son and four girls, who grew up to maturity, and of the latter three yet survive. The son, Francis Jesse Crawford, was born on the farm on which he now resides, then in Baltimore County, Nov. 1, 1819. Until twenty-one years of age he worked on the farm, and attended the neighborhood schools during the winter months. He then attended for three years the academy at Johnsville, Frederick Co., of which that eminent instructor, Prof. John S. Sandbatch, was principal. Among his classmates was Judge William N. Hayden, of Westminster. He taught school for several winters near home, in both Baltimore and Frederick Counties, to acquire funds sufficient to enable him to prosecute his studies for the medical profession. He then read medicine with Dr. James H. Claggett, of Washington County, one of the most distinguished physicians of his day, after which he attended the lectures of Washington University, in Baltimore, where he graduated in the class of 1843 and '44. In that institution he was under the tutelage of such eminent and learned men as Drs. Baxley, Vaughan, Jennings, Moncur, and Webster, great lights in the medical world. After his graduation he returned to his

Francis J. Crawford, M.D.

home in Franklin District and began the practice of his profession, in which he has been successfully engaged for thirty-eight years. In that period of time he has not been excelled as a practitioner, and before the war his practice extended over a field now filled by some eight physicians. In one year he paid two thousand two hundred medical visits, of which sixty-five were in obstetrical cases. The doctor is a strong Democrat in politics and active in the counsels of his party, and, although often solicited by his friends, has ever firmly refused to be an aspirant for office. Some thirty years ago he became a member of Salem Lodge, No. 60, I. O. O. F., at Westminster, and subsequently of Columbia Encampment, No. 14, of the same place. On the institution of St. Stephen's Lodge, No. 95, I. O. O. F., at Defiance, in May, 1857, he was one of its charter members, and since then has passed all the chairs, and has been a representative to the Grand Lodge. He is Master of Franklin Grange, Patrons of Husbandry, No. 117, and was largely instrumental in its organization. Although connected with no denomination, he is a liberal giver to all the churches in his neighborhood. He was married in May, 1853, to Ruth Elizabeth Bennett, daughter of Benjamin Bennett, of Franklin District, by which union he has five children: Fannie Belle, married to Dr. R. O. D. Warfield; Kate Emma, married to Henry S. Davis; Francis Albert, William Lloyd, and Charles Clement, besides two daughters who died young. Dr. Crawford's fine farm of three hundred and seventy acres, known as Waterloo, is within some sixty yards of the Frederick County line. He is a self-made man, who, with no resources with which to begin life but a firm will and energy, has by his ability and industry reached an eminent place in his profession, and has been otherwise very successful in life. He is the most noted fox-hunter in the county, and has a pack of eighteen hounds unsurpassed in this part of Maryland. He is also a fine horseman, and in breeding horses has made the Morgan stock a specialty, having years ago purchased from Col. Carroll a pure-blooded Morgan mare. His horses are among the first in Carroll County. In cattle he prefers Alderneys or Jerseys, and his herds take rank with the best and purest in the State.

Below are given the votes cast for local officers in this district from 1851 to 1861, inclusive:

1851.—Vote for Primary School Commissioner: Charles Dunning 87, Stephen Gorsuch 86, Charles Denning 156, Evan L. Crawford 44.

1853.—For Justices: Thos. B. Owings 145, Charles Denning 164, E. L. Crawford 52, John Hood 171, David Buckingham 117, Aquila Pickett 139; Constables: Joshua Shuster 175, Lewis Lindsey 116, H. B. Skidmore 53, Nimrod Buckingham 118; Road Supervisor: F. J. Crawford 148, A. P. Barnes 160.

1855.—For Justices: Milton Bussard 209, Aquila Picket 203, A. Albaugh 215, T. B. Owings 135, C. Denning 127, G. W. Chase 87; Constables: John Hood 222, J. Criswell 233, Henry Lida 117; Road Supervisor: Wm. Gosnell 223, J. Nausbaum 127.

1857.—For Justices: T. B. Owings 105, A. Pickett 166, Abraham Albaugh 172, F. A. Switzer 183, John Hood 83; Constables: Vachel Hammond 199, J. V. Criswell 212; Road Supervisor: G. H. Davis 124, W. Gosnell 177.

1859.—For Justices: T. B. Owings 116, John Hood 174, F. A. Switzer 163, Aquila Pickett 164, J. Thomas Young 185; Constables: W. W. Pickett 184, J. B. Runkles 173; Road Supervisor: Jesse Jarrett 98, Kanan Sprinkle 67.

1861.—For Justices: J. W. Cochran 256, John T. Young 255, Aquila Pickett 247; Constables: W. W. Pickett 248, W. P. Davis 264; Road Supervisor: W. H. Barnes 261.

The following is a list of public school trustees for 1881 and 1882, together with the names of teachers and number of scholars:

1. Parr's Ridge.—No appointments.
2. Chestnut Grove.—James H. Steele, Wesley P. Gosnel, Dr. S. R. Waters.
3. Cabbage Spring.—J. N. Selby, S. Hood, N. Davis.
4. Franklinville.—Ambrose G. Franklin, W. H. Barnes, G. W. Baker.
5. Pine Orchard.—Augustus Brown, David Zile, David Cover.
6. Salem.—Wm. Y. Frizzell, John B. T. Sellman, Vincent Cresswell.
7. Hooper's Delight.—No appointments.
8. Ridge.—Richard J. Brashears, Wesley Harrison, James Hood.
1. Fairview (African).—No appointments.

The teachers for the term ending April 15, 1881, were:

1, Ettie Shipley, 41 pupils; 2, Sallie N. Waters, 25 pupils; 3, Clara Selby, 40 pupils; 4, Jacob Farver, 44 pupils; 5, A. W. Buckingham, 44 pupils; 6, Louisa A. Hoffman, 41 pupils; 7, C. W. Reagan, 32 pupils; 8, Geo. A. Davis, 41 pupils; 1 (colored school), John H. Henderson, 38 pupils.

MIDDLEBURG DISTRICT, No. 10.

The Tenth District of Carroll County, generally known as Middleburg, is bounded on the north by the Taneytown District, on the west by the districts of Uniontown and Union Bridge and by Frederick County, on the south by Frederick County. The Monocacy River, Double Pipe Creek, and Little Pipe Creek separate the district from Frederick County, while Big Pipe Creek flows through the centre of the district. These streams and their tributaries supply an abundance of water for all purposes. The Western Maryland Railroad passes through the southern portion of the district, and the Frederick and Pennsylvania Line Railroad divides it very nearly into equal portions, these roads furnishing ample facilities for outside communication, trade, and traffic. The district in 1880 had a population of 1221.

Middleburg District was created by an act of the General Assembly of Maryland, passed March 24, 1852, in which William Shepperd, William Shaw, and John Clabaugh were named as commissioners to ascertain and fix the boundaries. The town of Middleburg was chosen as the place for holding the polls. The first settlers in the district were Scotch-Irish. They entered upon and cleared up a large amount of land between 1750 and 1770.

Among the pioneers in this portion of the State were Normand Bruce, Philip and Francis Key, Upton Scott, the Delaplanes, Dernses, and Landises. "Terra Rubra," a tract of eighteen hundred and sixty-five acres, was patented in 1752 to Philip Key, and "Runnymeade," of three thousand six hundred and seventy-seven acres, to Francis Key and Upton Scott in 1767.

Normand Bruce was sheriff of Frederick County before the Revolution under the proprietary government, and the most important personage in this part of the county. "New Bedford," of five thousand three hundred and one acres, was patented in 1762 to Daniel McKenzie and John Logsden.

John Ross Key, son of Philip Key, the owner of "Terra Rubra," was born in 1754. He was a lieutenant in the First Artillery, which went from Maryland at the outbreak of the Revolutionary war, and owned a large estate in Middleburg District, then a part of Taneytown, in Frederick County. His wife, Anne Phebe Key, was born in 1775. Their mansion was of brick, with centre and wings and long porches. It was situated in the centre of a large lawn, shaded by trees, and had attached to it an extensive terraced garden adorned with shrubbery and flowers. Near by flowed Pipe Creek through a dense woods. A copious spring of the purest water was at the foot of the hill. A meadow of waving grass spread out towards the Catoctin Mountain, which could often be seen at sunset curtained in clouds of crimson and gold. When the labors of the farm were over, in the evening, the negroes were summoned to prayers with the family, which were usually conducted by Francis Scott Key when he was there, and by his mother when he was away. After prayers, almost every night, as was common on plantations in Maryland, music and dancing might be heard at the quarters of the negroes until a late hour. It was at this happy home that Roger Brooke Taney, then a young attorney, and subsequently chief justice of the United States, married, Jan. 7, 1806, Anne Phebe Charlton Key, daughter of the proprietor of the estate. John Ross Key died Oct. 9, 1821, and his wife, Anne Phebe, July 8, 1850. Both are buried in Frederick City, in Mount Olivet Cemetery. Their daughter, the wife of Judge Taney, died of yellow fever at Point Comfort, Va., Sept. 29, 1855, and is buried near her parents in the same lot, by the side of her daughters, Ellen M. and Alice Carroll.

No man in Frederick County took a more active part in the Revolutionary struggle than John Ross Key, who fought on the field, and was of great service to the patriot cause in committees and as a counselor. As early as 1770, when a mere boy, he attended the preliminary meetings of the pioneers held at Taneytown to consult as to the odious stamp measures then oppressing the colonies. He was the father of the wife of Chief Justice Taney and of the author of "The Star-Spangled Banner,"—one a woman of rare virtues and graces, and the other the favorite national poet.

Francis Scott Key, the author of the "Star-Spangled Banner," was a native of Middleburg District, where he was born Aug. 1, 1779. A graduate of St. John's College, Annapolis, he adopted the law as his profession, began his practice at Frederick, and thence removed to Georgetown, D. C. He was for many years district attorney for the District of Columbia. His only sister was the wife of Roger B. Taney, chief justice of the United States. Hon. George H. Pendleton, of Ohio, is one of his sons-in-law.[1]

In personal appearance Mr. Key was tall and thin, cleanly shaven, with a head of heavy brown hair, disposed to curl slightly. He had a face of marked beauty, of peculiar oval form, and a notable sweetness of expression. He had large, dreamy, poetic eyes, and a genuinely sympathetic and mobile countenance. A portrait in possession of his daughter, Mrs. Turner, who with some of her descendants lives in California, has been copied for the statue to adorn the monument which is to be erected to him in accordance with the $150,000 bequest for that purpose of James Lick, the millionaire.

Mr. Key died in Baltimore, Jan. 11, 1843, while on a visit to his son-in-law, Charles Howard, and was buried in the Monumental City. At the death of his wife, in 1857, his remains were removed and placed by the side of her remains in Mount Olivet Cemetery, Frederick City, under the direction of his son-in-law, Hon. George Hunt Pendleton, United States senator from Ohio, who married his daughter Alice, the favorite niece of Chief Justice Roger Brooke Taney.

Daniel Turner, who graduated at the head of the

[1] A full sketch of him will be found in the history of Frederick County.

first class which went out from West Point Military Academy, was a nephew of Jacob Turner, one of three commissioned officers who, with six soldiers, were killed in the battle of Germantown.

After the war of 1812, Turner retired from the army and became a member of Congress from North Carolina. John Randolph, then in Congress, an intimate friend of John Ross Key, and a frequent visitor at his hospitable home, took Mr. Turner there and introduced him into the Key family, one of whose daughters he married.

The Scott family was an old one in the district, and one of its most noted members, Hon. Upton Scott, was born in Annapolis in 1810, when his mother was on a visit to her relatives. He was a delegate to the General Assembly in 1846, and in 1866 removed to Baltimore County, and later to Baltimore City. Governor Whyte appointed him a justice of the peace for the city, and he was reappointed by Governor Carroll. Mr. Scott died in Baltimore, Aug. 3, 1881. He was the father of Mrs. Judge William N. Hayden, and brother-in-law of Hon. John B. Boyle, both of Westminster. His father, John Scott, married a daughter of Normand Bruce.

Middleburg, the largest village in the district, is situated on the Frederick road. The land on the south side of that road was originally owned by the Brooks family, and it was a dense woods in 1800. The town in 1817 comprised the following houses: The old stone house now occupied by William Dukart was then kept as a tavern by William Neal. An old stone house also stood upon the site of J. H. Winebrenner's dwelling, a part of which was, in 1817, used by Mr. Clapsaddle as a blacksmith-shop. Mr. Fulwiler, a tailor, lived in the house now occupied by Dr. Thompson, which was built about the year 1800 by John Dust, and is the oldest house in the village. The stone house now owned by Arnold was built in 1815, or thereabouts, and was then owned by Dickey Brooks. The tavern now owned by Lewis Lynn was also built about the year 1815. The building now occupied by Mr. Williams, and which belongs to Mary Koontz, was built in 1816, and was intended to be used as a bank, as at that time there was talk of organizing a county, and Middleburg was to be the county-seat. Dr. William Zollicoffer was the physician, and moved here in 1817, and lived in a shed-house which was attached to the Williams property. Mr. Steiner kept a store in the house where Mr. Thompson now lives, there being then an additional building attached to it, which has since been removed. Mr. Zultzer kept a store in the Williams property. The old well which is situated on the pike south of Mr. Arnold's residence was dug by an Irishman, named Elick Fulton, in 1803. It is supposed that the town received its name from the fact that it is situated about middle way between Westminster and Frederick. It did not improve much until after the war of 1812–14, when, under the lead of Mr. Winemiller, several fine houses were erected. The house now occupied by Susanna Dehoff was standing in 1817, and was owned by her mother.

At a meeting of the "Columbian Independent Company," commanded by Capt. Nicholas Snider, of Taneytown, and the "Independent Pipe Creek Company," under the command of Capt. Thomas Hook, held at Middleburg, Oct. 13, 1821, information of the death of Gen. John Ross Key was first received. Middleburg is on the Western Maryland Railroad, forty-eight miles from Baltimore and fifteen from Westminster, in a fertile and thriving section of country. The merchants are Ferdinand Warner and H. D. Fuss; the physician, Dr. Charles Thompson; and the hotel-keeper, Lewis F. Lynn. A large pottery establishment is conducted by U. T. Winemiller.

The congregation of the Methodist Episcopal Church, which is quite old, held its services in the old log school-house until 1850, when the church was built. Rev. William Keith was the pastor in 1866, and was succeeded by Rev. Mr. Haslet, who was followed by Rev. J. D. Moore, Rev. William Ferguson, Rev. George Madewell, Rev. Charles West, Rev. Mr. Smith, and others. E. O. Elridge is the present pastor. The officers of the church are C. Brooks, Mr. Buffington, J. A. Miller, E. C. Utter. Attached to this church is a neat cemetery, and the following persons are buried there:

Isaac Dern, died March 9, 1864, aged 75.

Mary, wife of Joshua Delaplane, died Aug. 11, 1862, aged 87 years, 4 months, 20 days.

John Delaplane, born Aug. 10, 1793, died Feb. 10, 1868.

Abraham L. Lynn, born Aug. 13, 1844, died April 5, 1872.

Anna E., wife of D. H. Lynn, died Aug. 17, 1873, aged 20 years, 7 months, 7 days.

Anna R., wife of C. W. Winemiller, died April 7, 1876, aged 32 years, 5 months, 19 days.

Michael Magkley, born April 16, 1799, died Dec. 19, 1878.

Joshua Parrish, died March 27, 1862, aged 59 years, 7 months, 24 days.

John Wesley Wilson, born April 7, 1818, died Oct. 11, 1856.

Mary Dayhoof, died Jan. 1, 1858, aged 47 years, 1 month, 13 days.

Joseph Dayhoof, died Feb. 16, 1862, aged 57 years, 18 days.

William Koons, born July 2, 1794, died Dec. 18, 1852.

John Nipple, born Jan. 27, 1815, died Dec. 31, 1877.

Margaret Souder, wife of Joshua S., died June 18, 1850, aged 50 years, 7 months, 14 days.

Henrietta, wife of Evan C. Otts, died March 24, 1856, aged 35 years, 9 days.

Catharine, wife of George Hope, died Jan. 22, 1853, aged 86.

Frederick Dern, Jr., died May 20, 1863, aged 35 years, 11 months, 23 days.

Mary J., his wife, died May 31, 1861, aged 36 years, 4 months, 18 days.

Frederick, Sophia, John W., their three children.

Ann P., daughter of J. and M. Winemiller, died Dec. 11, 1859, aged 16 years, 2 months, 25 days.

John H. Winemiller, died March 14, 1879, aged 59 years, 8 months, 12 days.

Susan Alice, their daughter, died Dec. 2, 1859, aged 11 years, 10 months, 7 days.

John N. F. Winemiller, died Dec. 8, 1859, aged 8 years, 1 day.

Thomas Hook, died May 12, 1869, aged 77 years, 23 days.

Sarah Hook, died May 17, 1868, aged 83 years, 4 months, 23 days.

Elizabeth C. Hook, died June 13, 1858, aged 33 years, 14 days.

Regina E., daughter of J. M. and Agnes McAllister, died Jan. 4, 1863, aged 16 years, 10 months, 1 day.

Lavina Margaret, wife of Abendago Flick, died Nov. 8, 1855, aged 27 years, 23 days.

John W. McAllister, died Nov. 10, 1880, aged 82 years, 8 months, 12 days.

Agnes McAllister, died Oct. 23, 1880, aged 75 years, 9 months, 13 days.

David Hope, died Nov. 1, 1859, aged 57 years, 4 months, 22 days.

Keysville, a small village, received its title from the fact that the land upon which the old school-house and church were built was presented to the inhabitants by Francis Scott Key.

Though the house in which Mr. Key was born has disappeared, a large barn and spring-house, which he built not long before he died, are still standing on the farm now owned by John Winemiller, and occupied by Jacob Wentz.

Double Pipe Creek is on the Western Maryland Railroad, fifty-one miles from Baltimore. Double Pipe Creek, from which it takes its name, is near, and furnishes water sufficient for milling and other purposes. The improvements recently made indicate the zeal and energy of the people. Of the Dunker Church, here located, Revs. D. Panel and Daniel R. Sayler are the preachers. The merchants are John T. Ott, J. W. Weant, and J. H. Angell; the latter is also postmaster. The physician is Dr. Charles H. Diller. William T. Miller has a cooper's factory, and C. B. Anders runs the flouring-mill. There are several shops and local industries that give considerable business to the place.

The old stone mill at Double Pipe Creek, now owned and operated by C. B. Anders, has stood since 1794, in which year it was founded by Joshua Delaplaine, although it was not completed until 1800, as an inscription upon a stone in the "fire arch" bears witness. Joshua Delaplaine was a manufacturer of some note in his day, and carried on not only the grist-mill, but a woolen-mill on the opposite side of the creek. The last-named structure still stands, but no looms have made music within its walls for these many years. In 1836, Henry Waspe built an addition to the grist-mill, making it what it now is. In 1878, C. B. Anders bought the mill and other property of Thomas Cover. Mr. Anders was born at Double Pipe Creek in 1850, and in the old Delaplaine mill his father, Aaron, was a miller many years ago. Aaron Anders removed to Linganore, and in the mill at that place followed his calling upwards of twenty-five years. C. B. Anders was placed in the Linganore mill when sixteen years of age, and has ever since followed the occupation of a miller. His mill, three stories in height, is furnished with four pairs of burrs, has a capacity of one hundred barrels of flour daily, and is devoted almost exclusively to merchant-work. The motive power is supplied by two turbine-wheels measuring, respectively, fifty-four and thirty-six inches in diameter, with a head of nine feet. The manufacturing apparatus includes all the latest devised mill improvements. All the barrels used are manufactured in the mill. The total number of employés is seven. Choice Red Longberry wheat is chiefly used in the production of flour for shipment, and in Baltimore the "Double Pipe Creek" brand ranks high. Mr. Anders owns also the old Delaplaine woolen-mill property, a brick residence on the Frederick County side of the creek, and two residences on the Carroll County side, besides the railroad warehouse. His home, near the railway depot, is a handsome two-story structure of imposing appearance. He built it in 1878, and spared no expense to make it a model of its kind. It is a striking object in the architecture of the village, and is conceded to be one of the most completely appointed homes in Carroll County.

Bruceville is a small village about the centre of the district. Long before the Revolutionary war, Normand Bruce, a Scotchman, emigrated to this country and settled in the Middleburg District, in the locality now known as Keysville. At that time the land in and about Bruceville was owned by John Ross Key. Bruce desiring the Key property for the purpose of building a mill on Big Pipe Creek, entered into negotiations with Key, which resulted in an exchange of their estates. Bruce erected a large stone mill, which stood until February, 1881, when it was partially destroyed by fire. He also built a dwelling-house, the same which is now occupied by Frederick Mehring. The town was laid out by Bruce and named about the close of the eighteenth century. Bruce had three children,—Betsey, who married John Scott, the parents of the late Upton Scott, Mrs. Daniel Swope, and Mrs. John Brook Boyle. Charles Bruce,

RESIDENCE MILL AND WAREHOUSE OF C. B. ANDERS

DOUBLE PIPE CREEK, CARROLL CO. MD.

one of his sons, was born in Middleburg District, but in early life left this country and resided in the West Indies. While on a visit to his birthplace he first saw his sister, she then being a wife with a large family. Bruce was the third son. The Landis family came from Scotland in 1812, and located on a part of the Key estate. John Landis, one of the sons, who is still living, was in Washington in the year 1814, learning his trade, and was among the first who saw the British fleet sailing up the Potomac.

Nicholas Kuhen was the earliest blacksmith in the town, and Jesse Cloud kept the hotel. Dr. Leggett was the physician, and Mr. Trego the merchant. Hudson and Brooks were prominent farmers who resided near the mill at the time of its erection.

What was at one time quite an extensive cemetery is at present a thick growth of underbrush, and contains only five graves the inscriptions upon which can be deciphered:

Basil Brooks, eldest son of Raphael and Jane, died Jan. 24, 1829, aged 56.

Robert T. Dodds, died April 17, 1806, aged 74, "a native of East Lothian County, Scotland, of Haddington, of Aberlada;" Selkirk Dodds, his wife, "a native of Edinburgh, Scotland," died April 24, 1825, aged 73.

John Dodds, their son, died Oct. 17, 1816, aged 42.

John Scott, died Feb. 28, 1814, aged 71.

It is stated that the body of Normand Bruce lies in this yard, but should the same be true, it is unmarked by even a grave.

Double Pipe Creek Division, No. 36, of Sons of Temperance, was incorporated by an act of the Legislature, passed March 3, 1847. The incorporators were John E. H. Ligget, George H. Warsche, Isaac Dern, Eli Otto, Noah Pennington, Benjamin Poole, Martin Grimes, Nicholas Stansbury, Hiram Fogle, George Landers, James Thomas, William Carmack, Abednego Slick, Francis Carmack, Joseph Fogle, Jesse Anders, William Miller, Edward Carmack, Samuel Birely.

York Road is the station and post-office for Bruceville. It is a small village, at the junction of the Western Maryland Railroad with the Frederick Division of the Pennsylvania Line Railroad, and is sixteen miles from Westminster by rail. David Hiltabidle is the railroad and express agent and postmaster. Dr. M. A. Lauver is the physician.

The following is the vote for local officers in this district from 1853 to 1861, inclusive:

1853.—Vote for Justices: Isaac Dern 113, David Otto 73, David Hope 67, J. W. McAllister 57; Constable: John Six 105; Road Supervisor: J. W. Wilson 43, Thomas Hook 90, Philip W. Hann 47.

1855.—For Justices: J. Delaplane 123, David Otto 128, Thomas Hook 71, J. W. McAllister 74; Constables: John Six 115, A. Slick 91; Road Supervisor: John Angell 109, H. Clabaugh 98.

1857.—For Justices: David Otto 174, John Delaplane 144; Constables: John Six 160, J. S. Shriner 149; Road Supervisor: Jacob Sayler 177.

1859.—For Justices: Thomas Hook 93, John Delaplane 130, A. S. Zentz 146; Constables: John Six 158, John A. Mackley 148; Road Supervisor: Ephraim Hiteshue 163.

1861.—For Justices: Samuel Angell 182, John Delaplane 181; Constables: John Six 188, Samuel T. Linn 178; Road Supervisor: Nicholas Koons 149, A. S. Zentz 81

The following are the public school trustees for 1881 and 1882, together with the names of teachers and number of pupils:

1. Mount Union.—John Shunk, J. Thaddeus Starr, Henry Williams.
2. Middleburg.—Dr. C. Thomson, Lewis Lynn, Moses Seabrook.
3. Bruceville.—Jacob Buffington, John Biehl, M. Fringer.
4. Franklin.—Samuel Waybright, Joshua Dutterer, Sylvester Valentine.
5. Keysville.—Aaron Weant, Peter Writter, Benjamin Poole.
6. Double Pipe Creek.—J. W. Weant, A. N. Forney, Lewis Cash.

The teachers for the term ending April 15, 1881, were:

1, W. J. Crabbs, 50 pupils; 2, S. Jannetta Dutterer, 39 pupils; 3, C. F. Reindollar, 46 pupils; 4, S. Lina Norris, 41 pupils; 5, James B. Galt, 46 pupils; 6, Luther Kemp, 27 pupils.

The justices of the peace are Calvin Warner, Joseph Arnold; Constable, Moses Seabrook.

NEW WINDSOR DISTRICT, No. 11.

The Eleventh District of Carroll County, generally known as New Windsor, is bounded on the north by Uniontown District, on the east by Westminster, on the south by Franklin, and on the west by Frederick County and Union Bridge. Sam's Creek separates the district from Frederick County, and Little Pipe Creek flows east from Westminster through the northern portion. The Western Maryland Railroad passes directly through the district, and furnishes excellent facilities for trade and travel. In 1880 it contained 2199 inhabitants.

This district was created by an act of the General Assembly of Maryland, passed March 10, 1856, out of parts of the Second, Seventh, and Ninth Districts. Its boundaries were defined as follows:

"Beginning at the intersection of the county line with the Buffalo road at Sam's Creek, and running up a branch of said creek to a spring near the dwelling of Abraham Albaugh, Esq.; thence by a straight line to a point on the road leading from Mount Airy to Westminster, directly opposite the dwelling of Maj. Benjamin Gorsuch; thence with said road to the Nicodemus road; thence with said Nicodemus road westwardly to the house of A. Brown (colored); thence by a straight line to Cassell's mill, on Little Pipe Creek; thence down said creek to the Melville mills; thence by a straight line to Upton Roop's saw-mill, and down the branch; thence to said Pipe Creek, and with it to the bridge on the road leading from McKinstry's mills to Uniontown; thence by a straight line to the bridge over Sam's Creek, near Rinehart's marble-quarries; thence up said creek, the county line, to the place of beginning."

The same act established the following primary school districts: Priestland, No. 1; Greenwood, No. 2; Snader's, No. 3; Bailes', No. 4; Carroll, No. 5; Wakefield, No. 6; Springdale, No. 7; and New Windsor, No. 8.

Early Settlers.—"Park Hall," a tract of 2680 acres, was surveyed for James Carroll in 1727. It lies between New Windsor and Sam's Creek, and was the first survey recorded in this portion of Maryland. Among the early settlers were Rev. Robert Strawbridge, John Maynard, Henry Willis, David Evans, Hezekiah Bonham, John and Paul Hagarty, the Poulsons, Baxters, Durbins, Wakefields, Joshua Smith, Richard Stevenson, the Devilbisses, Naills, Nausbaums, Pearres, Nicodemuses, Buckinghams, Englars, Lamberts, Roops, Michael Bartholow. The tract of land known as "Cornwall," for 666 acres, patented in 1749, lies on Little Pipe Creek, and was purchased by Joseph Haines and his brother. "Windsor Forrest," of 2886 acres, was patented to John Dorsey in 1772.

Rev. David Englar, a preacher in the Society of Dunkers, died August, 1839, aged sixty-seven years.

The Strawbridge Pipe Creek, or Sam's Creek, Methodist Episcopal Church was established in 1760, in Frederick County (now Carroll), the birthplace of American Methodism. At that time Frederick embraced the counties of Montgomery, Washington, Allegany, Carroll, and Garrett, and in 1774 appeared the first record of the Frederick Circuit, which was in less than a hundred years to expand until it encircled with its Briarean arms every State and Territory within the limits of the United States. For years it was a frontier circuit, extending as far as Fairfax County, Va., and the pioneer preachers who traveled it came prepared to endure hardships and encounter dangers from which the advance of civilization has happily freed them. Its first appointments were Pipe Creek, Frederick-Town, Westminster, Durbin's, Saxon's, Seneca, Sugar-Loaf, Rocky Creek, Georgetown (District of Columbia), and Adams.

Rev. Robert Strawbridge, the *first* Methodist preacher in America, was a native of Drummer's Nave, near Carrick-on-Shannon, County Leitrim, Ireland. Upon his arrival in this country with his wife and children he settled on Sam's Creek. As soon as he had arranged his house he began to preach in it, as early as 1760, and besides his appointment in his own house he had another, in 1762, at the house of John Maynard, who was a Methodist, where he baptized his brother, Henry Maynard, aged six years, at a spring in the same year,—the *first* Methodist baptism in America. Henry Maynard died in 1837, aged eighty-one years. The society formed by Mr. Strawbridge consisted of about fifteen persons, among whom were David Evans, his wife and sister, and Mrs. Bennett. The latter, who was living in 1856, aged eighty-nine years, described Mr. Strawbridge as of medium size, dark complexion, black hair, and possessing a very sweet voice. When Mr. Asbury first visited the society, in 1772, he found there such names as Hagarty, Bonham, Walker, and Warfield. Hezekiah Bonham had been a Baptist until influenced by Mr. Strawbridge's preaching, when he became a Methodist, and was much persecuted by his former sect. At this time Mr. Asbury heard him speak in public, and seeing that he had gifts as a speaker he gave him license to exhort. He afterwards became a preacher, and in 1785 his name is in the minutes of the Conference among the itinerants. His son, Robert Bonham, was also a traveling preacher. Paul Hagarty was a member of the Pipe Creek Society, as was also his brother, John Hagarty, who became a traveling preacher, and could hold service in both German and English. Robert Walker had been converted by Mr. Whitefield at Fagg's Manor, Chester Co., Pa. He afterwards removed to this county and joined the Pipe Creek Society. He subsequently removed to Sandy River, S. C., where he entertained Bishops Asbury and Whatcoat in 1800. Dr. Alexander Warfield was a kind and useful friend to the organization. Mr. Asbury dined with him on his first visit to Pipe Creek, and Dr. Warfield's wife was a member of Mr. Strawbridge's first society. Rev. Lott Warfield, formerly of the Philadelphia Conference, was of this family.

Not far from Pipe Creek lived William Durbin, who with his wife joined the Methodists in 1768. Their house was an early stand for preaching, and their son, John Durbin, was a traveling preacher in the beginning of this century. In the same region lived George Saxton, whose house was a preaching place at that early date. Mr. Strawbridge also extended his labors to Baltimore and Harford Counties. Samuel Merryman visited Pipe Creek, and was converted by the remarkable preacher who could pray without a book and preach without a manuscript sermon, which was regarded by many in that age and place as an impossibility. From that day the old and noted Merryman family of Baltimore County were Methodists. Methodist preaching was first introduced into Frederick Town by Mr. Strawbridge, on an invitation from Edward Drumgole, who, when he came from Ireland in 1770, bore a letter to Mr. Strawbridge, and heard him preach at Pipe Creek. Mr. Strawbridge was the first of Mr. Wesley's followers to preach on the Eastern Shore, in 1769, at the house of John Randle, in Weston, Kent Co. He built up the *first society* of Methodists, and built the first Methodist chapel in America, which was on Pipe Creek. In 1764 a log meeting-house was erected, about a mile from Mr. Strawbridge's house. It was twenty-two feet square; on one side the logs were sawed out for a door, on the other three sides there were holes for windows, but it does not appear that it ever was finished. It stood without windows, door, or floor until 1844, when it was demolished, and hundreds of canes manufactured out of its logs. William Fort sent one to each of the bishops, then in New York, and one to Dr. Bond.

STRAWBRIDGE'S LOG MEETING-HOUSE.

Mr. Strawbridge continued to reside at Sam's Creek about sixteen years, and then removed to the upper part of Long Green, Baltimore Co., to a farm given him for life by the wealthy Capt. Charles Ridgely, by whom he was greatly esteemed, and who often attended his preaching. It was while living here, under the shadow of "Hampton" (Capt. Ridgely's beautiful seat), that in one of his visiting rounds he was taken sick at the house of Joseph Wheeler and died, in the summer of 1781. His funeral sermon was preached by Rev. Richard Owings, to a vast concourse of people, under a large walnut-tree. His grave and that of Mrs. Strawbridge (who died in Baltimore) were in the small burying-ground, about eight miles from Baltimore, in the orchard south of the house, and a large poplar-tree has grown up between them as a living monument.

Mr. Strawbridge had six children,—Robert, George, Theophilus, Jesse, Betsey, and Jane. Two of his sons, George and Jesse, grew up and became carpenters. Bishop Asbury, on Sunday, Nov. 22, 1772, preached in the log meeting-house on Pipe Creek; and in 1801, at the residence of Henry Willis, held his Conference. During the session of that Conference he made the significant entry in his journal, "Here Mr. Strawbridge founded the first society in Maryland or *America*," underscoring the latter word. The home of Mr. Strawbridge was on the farm now owned by Charles Devilbiss, and the log chapel was on that now owned by Peter Cover, but when torn down was owned by Peter Engle. The site of this first American chapel is a few yards from Mr. Cover's barn, and is now a part of a corn-field, and is unmarked. David Engle is the only living man who has a personal knowledge of the exact site, and he assisted in removing the logs of the rude fabric to another place. During 1866, the centennial year of American Methodism, denominational relic-hunters removed these logs, and thus every vestige of the building disappeared. The last log was presented by the Rev. Charles A. Reid to the Rev. Frank S. De-Hass, D.D., to be placed in the Metropolitan Methodist Episcopal church at Washington, D. C., where it was converted into an ornament. Before they were taken away they were measured, and from their length it was inferred that this primitive structure was about twenty-four feet in length and breadth. A part of one of the logs was sawed out by Charles Devilbiss, who presented it to Rev. S. V. Leech, D.D., of Frederick Methodist Episcopal Church. He had the remnant made into canes and mallets, which were presented to various parties as mementos.

About twelve years ago the remains of Mr. Strawbridge were removed to the "Preachers' Lot" in Mount Olivet Cemetery, Baltimore, and the beautiful monument that marks his grave was presented to the National Local Preachers' Association, through its president, Rev. Isaac P. Cook, by the late Rev. Geo. C. M. Roberts, M.D.

Mr. Strawbridge did not own any land until March 8, 1773, when, according to the county records, he purchased the fifty acres on which he had resided for thirteen years from John England. The property was known as "Brothers' Inheritance" and "England's Chance," nor did he ever sell it. Nearly six years after his decease his only heir, Robert Strawbridge, conveyed it to Richard Stevenson. This deed is dated Jan. 23, 1787. The log church of Strawbridge, on Sam's, or Pipe Creek, was built two years before the chapel erected by Philip Embury in New York City in 1766, and was the first church building erected by the Methodists on the American continent. When Rev. Thomas S. Rankin, Mr. Wesley's envoy, met the preachers in Philadelphia in 1773, that first Conference in America ordered that no local preacher should administer baptism or the Lord's Supper, Robert Strawbridge only excepted and by name, and permission was given him to administer these rites under direction of the regular Wesleyan missionaries. Mr. Strawbridge was a brave, self-denying, and successful evangelist, and the site of his rude log chapel is the Mecca to which annually hundreds of Methodists repair to view the cradle of their faith in this country. Four miles north of the site of the old Pipe, or Sam's Creek church of Robert Strawbridge stands the building known as "Stone Chapel." When Mr. Strawbridge's log structure was abandoned a small log chapel known as "Poulson's" was erected, which was torn down in 1783, and "Stone Chapel" built on the site. It was the Pharos of Western Maryland Methodism during several decades. Memorable revivals have marked its history, and distinguished men of early Methodism have preached from its pulpit.

Stone Chapel antedates the organization of the Methodist Episcopal Church in America. It is a two-story edifice, with small windows and galleries on three sides. There is on the front, high up, next to the apex, a tablet, on which are first three stars, then the initials "J. D." (Jesse Durbin); below there is an eagle with the initials "B. B." (Benjamin Bennett) to its left, and beneath the inscription:

"Bt. 1783
Rebt. 1800."

Jesse Durbin and Benjamin Bennett were very active in their efforts for its erection.

This church is only a few feet from the Westminster District line. Right opposite to it, on the other side of the road, is a small graveyard, in which are interred

Abraham Koontz, died Jan. 18, 1873, aged 83.

John N. Koontz, died Nov. 21, 1873, aged 32.

Eliza, wife of James Robertson, and daughter of Thomas and Mary Stevenson, died Feb. 11, 1879, aged 39.

Joseph Cushing, died Jan. 20, 1873, aged 83; and his wife, Susan, died Feb. 14, 1871, aged 78.

Mary, wife of Mahlon Bowers, died April 13, 1874, aged 42.

Jeremiah H. Smith, born Oct. 23, 1835, died Dec. 8, 1874.

Ann Poulson, died Dec. 21, 1875, aged 78.

Elizabeth Nicodemus, died July 10, 1870, aged 71.

Maranda, wife of Joshua Sellman, died July 7, 1871, aged 68.

William Wagner, born Aug. 9, 1833, died April 18, 1875.

Sarah Hooper, born Jan. 10, 1793, died Feb. 8, 1875 (daughter of Michael and Ann Bartholow).

Washington Barnes, son of Elisha and Amelia Barnes, born July 10, 1804, died Oct. 25, 1873.

The neighborhood of the old Strawbridge farm is dotted with venerable houses rich in early associations. Near it is the old mansion of Alexander Warfield, Asbury's friend and host. The room where the great bishop slept is there, as is the table upon which he wrote his journals. For twenty years that mansion was a circuit-preaching appointment, and Bishop Asbury visited it for the last time in 1816, two years before his death. It is now occupied by Rev. C. A. Reid, whose wife is Alexander Warfield's granddaughter.

Near to it is the Willis house, where the Rev. Henry Willis died. Here Bishop Asbury held a Conference in 1801, attended by forty preachers. Willis preached as far north as New York and as far south as Charleston, S. C. Within a circuit of six miles are the residences of William, Jesse, and John Durbin, Joshua Smith, Adam Poulson, William Poulson, the Wakefields, Baxters, Joseph, Jacob, and Leonard Cassell. Mrs. Henry Willis was the daughter of Jesse Hollingsworth, and was born Feb. 9, 1769. Her six children were William, Jesse, Mary Yellott, Jeremiah, and Francis Asbury. Henry Maynard was born Aug. 17, 1759, and died in 1839. Henry Willis died in 1800.

Among the old settlers in this district is Judge Louis Philip Slingluff. Judge Slingluff was born in Uniontown District (now New Windsor), Frederick County (now Carroll), March 15, 1831; the eldest child of Isaac and Julianna (Englar) Slingluff. The family is of German origin. His grandfather, Jesse Slingluff, was born in Springfield township, Philadelphia Co., Pa., Jan. 1, 1775. When a boy he removed to Baltimore, and eventually, under the firm-name of Bohn & Slingluff, carried on an extensive grocery trade for many years in that city. He married Elizabeth Deardoff, of Adams County, Pa., by whom he had ten children, viz.: Charles D., Sarah Ann, Isaac, George W., Joseph, Esther Ann, Catharine, Elizabeth, Jesse, and Upton. Except Catharine and Elizabeth, who died when young, all were married and raised families. Charles D. was a prominent merchant in Baltimore, and left a large family. George W. was a merchant and farmer in Canal Dover, Ohio. He left one son, now living there. Joseph was a prominent physician in Canal Dover. Two sons survive him and are still living there. Esther Ann was wife of Joseph Poole; eight children survive her. Upton was a merchant in Baltimore. He left five children. Sarah Ann is the widow of Thomas E. Hambleton, residing in Baltimore. She has seven children. Jesse is president of the Commercial and Farmers' Bank, of Baltimore, and has eight children. Isaac, father of Judge L. P., was born in Baltimore, Aug. 5, 1807. At the time Baltimore was threatened by the British in the war of 1812–14, Jesse Slingluff moved his family from the city and settled on what was known as the "Avalon" farm, in New Windsor. Having secured the safety of his family, he returned to give his services in the defense of the city. He became the owner of a large tract of land in New Windsor, and the latter years of his life were spent upon his estate. He died June 30, 1836. Both himself and wife are buried in Greenmount Cemetery, Baltimore. Upon the death of his father Isaac came into possession of the "Avalon" farm. He married Julianna, daughter of Philip Englar, of New Windsor. Their children were Louis

Philip, subject of this sketch; Mary Elizabeth, born Jan. 27, 1833, widow of Jesse Weaver; four children; Jesse, born April 14, 1835, died Oct. 9, 1836; Frances Hannah, born April 7, 1838, widow of Ezra Stouffer, living in New Windsor; six children. Isaac Slingluff died April 30, 1852; his wife, Dec. 14, 1848.

Upon the death of his father Louis Philip became the possessor of the "Avalon" farm, by purchase from the heirs. He was educated in Calvert College, New Windsor, under President A. H. Baker. Though thoroughly devoted to his occupation as a farmer, Judge Slingluff has always taken a lively interest in the political questions of the day. He has been identified actively with the Democratic party since he became a voter. In 1872 he was appointed by Governor William P. Whyte to fill the unexpired term of Judge Upton Roop as judge of the Orphans' Court, and upon the expiration of that term was elected for another term of four years. For the last six or seven years he has been one of the board of directors and the board of trustees of "New Windsor," formerly "Calvert," College.

Though not a member of any church, the judge is a liberal contributor to the support of all churches and benevolent institutions of his neighborhood. He married, Oct. 18, 1855, Ellen, daughter of George W. Slingluff, of Canal Dover, Ohio. Mrs. Slingluff died Sept. 8, 1856. He married for his second wife Margaret Alverda, daughter of Thomas and Catharine (Stouffer) Cromwell, March 19, 1861. The latter was born Aug. 24, 1839, in Walkersville, Frederick Co., Md. Her grandfather, Philemon Cromwell, who was a descendant of Oliver Cromwell, came from Baltimore County, and settled in Frederick County, Md. Her father, after the death of his first wife, married again, moved to Tiffin, Ohio, and died there.

Judge and Mrs. Slingluff have five children, viz.: Isaac Jackson, born Dec. 17, 1861; Thomas Cromwell, born Dec. 21, 1862; Nellie, born June 24, 1866; Catharine Cromwell, born Dec. 22, 1867; Robert Lee, born Jan. 14, 1877; all living at home.

Many Germans from the old country and Pennsylvania settled in this part of New Windsor District as early as the year 1750. They worshiped at their homes until the increase in their numbers necessitated the building of a church. George F. Winter, one of the prominent men at that time, generously donated an acre of ground, upon which, in the year 1766, under the direction of the building committee,—Jacob Haines, Adam Swigart, John Engleman, and Mr. Prugh,—the church was erected. It is one and a half miles from New Windsor, on the road to Uniontown. It was built by the Lutheran congregation, assisted slightly by the German Reformed congregation, who were allowed to use the church for their worship.

The first pastor of whom there is any record was the Rev. Mr. Grubb, who occupied this position in 1800. He was followed by the Reverends Mr. Wachter, Reuben Weiser, and Mr. Kiler. After Mr. Kiler the congregation had no regular minister for some years, but was supplied with occasional preaching by ministers from Baltimore. Rev. Solomon Sentman, fearing the congregation would lose many of its members by this mode of ministering, organized a church council, and Rev. Philip Willard was appointed to the charge. The church at this time was in the Taneytown charge, but was subsequently joined to the Westminster charge. Rev. Mr. Reinsnider was the next pastor, and was followed by Rev. John Winter, who began his duties about the year 1848. He was succeeded in the year 1853 by Rev. Samuel Henry. Rev. Dr. Martin, Rev. H. C. Holloway, Rev. J. F. Deiner, Rev. A. Strobel, Rev. G. W. Anderson, and Rev. David B. Floyd, respectively.

About the year 1870 the church was again changed, and put in the Uniontown Circuit, where it now stands. About eighty members worship at this church, and it is in a very prosperous condition. The present trustees are Elmer Hyde, Ephraim Haines, Levi Winter, Wm. Winter, Samuel Gilbert, Jonas Effert; Elders, Elmer Hyde, Levi Bankart; Deacons, Robert Davidson, John Wilhelm.

In the Winters Cemetery, which is attached to the church, the following persons are buried:

John Lambert, died March 1, 1838, aged 80 years, 1 month, 23 days; Ellen, his wife, died April 4, 1829, aged 68 years, 17 days.

Jacob Haynes, died July 2, 1820, aged 73 years, 4 months, 10 days.

Ester Hens, born March 6, 1756, died March 9, 1804.

Mary M. Greenwood, died Dec. 2, 1812, aged 63.

Jacob Morman, born 1786, died 1804.

Rosanna Shuey, died April 10, 1839, aged 83.

Anna M. Greenholtz, died June 19, 1815, aged 53.

Jacob Greenholtz, died aged 85.

Catharine Greenholtz, died aged 45.

Rachel Greenholtz, died aged 75.

John Greenholtz, died Dec. 29, 1870, aged 84.

Isaac B. Norris, died March 19, 1849, aged 64.

Jacob Smelser, died May 19, 1819, aged 31 years, 9 months, 27 days.

Henry Haines, died Feb. 25, 1873, aged 83 years, 12 days; Magdalena, his wife, died Sept. 2, 1868, aged 75 years, 9 months, 25 days.

Sarah, relict of John Lantz, died Dec. 2, 1874, aged 77 years, 10 months, 22 days.

Andrew Myers, died July 12, 1823, aged 30 years, 5 months.

Mary Myers, died Aug. 27, 1817, aged 21 years, 7 months, 3 days.

Peter Myers, died Feb. 22, 1814, aged 54 years, 21 days.

Magdalena Myers, died Jan. 14, 1829, aged 68 years, 5 months, 16 days.

Noah Worman, died Oct. 9, 1868, aged 83 years, 5 months, 4 days; Catharine, his wife, born July 26, 1787, died Aug. 2, 1853.

Rebecca Myers, died Jan. 11, 1867, aged 66 years, 11 months, 11 days.

John Engleman, died April 18, 1841, aged 52 years, 7 months, 4 days.

Julia A. Sellman, died July 19, 1880, aged 82.

Mary Engleman, died Dec. 15, 1822, aged 57 years, 6 months.

John Engleman, Sr., died Dec. 25, 1835, aged 75 years, 9 months.

Henry Shriner, died Sept. 25, 1823, aged 7 months.

Mary Myers, born April 16, 1826, died Oct. 9, 1858.

Jacob Myers, born July 29, 1787, died May 13, 1833; Mary, his wife, died Jan. 4, 1822, aged 34 years, 4 months, 18 days.

Martin Winter, died July 7, 1876, aged 72 years, 6 months, 6 days.

Catharine Winter, died Aug. 20, 1851, aged 77 years, 10 days.

Jacob Winter, died Dec. 1, 1845, aged 58 years, 1 month, 18 days.

Elizabeth, wife of Geo. Winter, died Jan. 16, 1866, aged 73 years, 1 month, 20 days.

Geo. Winter, Sr., died Aug. 6, 1831, aged 45 years, 11 months, 7 days.

Catharine Garner, died Aug. 22, 1831, aged 47 years, 8 months, 19 days.

George Garner, died Aug. 5, 1840, aged 68 years, 8 months, 15 days.

James Crawford, died Feb. 2, 1839, aged 77 years, 3 months, 14 days.

Catharine, his wife, died May 7, 1828, aged 60 years, 3 months, 13 days.

Charlotte Boblets, daughter of Geo. Lambert, died March 13, 1830, aged 33 years, 5 days.

Wm. Brawner, died Aug. 1, 1828, aged 76; Catharine, his wife, died Oct. 25, 1824, aged 69.

Elizabeth Crawford, died Dec. 24, 1872, aged 86 years, 9 months, 5 days.

Elizabeth Randel, died Oct. 6, 1849, aged 67 years, 8 months, 27 days.

Mary Lamberd, born Sept. 21, 1822, died March 30, 1872.

Abraham Lambert, died Sept. 3, 1862, aged 56 years, 10 months.

Joshua Metcalf, born June 30, 1787, died April 16, 1860; Eleanor, his wife, born Feb. 21, 1799, died June 8, 1864.

David Shuey, died June 5, 1845, aged 45.

Catharine Shuey, born Aug. 2, 1778, died May 10, 1855.

Margaret Kiler, died April 23, 1853, aged 51 years, 7 months, 12 days.

Rachel Blizzard, born Sept. 12, 1807, died May 31, 1874.

Mary Traxell, died April 10, 1870, aged 95.

Jacob Kiler, died Nov. 15, 1844, aged 82 years, 9 months, 5 days.

Simon Kiler, died Oct. 1, 1839, aged 73 years, 9 months.

Elizabeth, wife of Jacob Kiler, died April 2, 1836, aged 72.

Fred. Buser, died June 21, 1821, aged 16.

Josiah Prugh, died Aug. 7, 1813, aged 16.

Lucia M. Prugh, died July 19, 1816, aged 67 years, 5 months, 3 days.

Geo. Dagen, died Dec. 17, 1810, aged 72.

Elizabeth Dagen, died March 19, 1821, aged 32 years, 8 months, 9 days.

Henry Cook, died Jan. 14, 1820, aged 74.

Mary Swigart, died March 5, 1835, aged 84.

Michael Smelser, died Nov. 10, 1831, aged 74 years, 4 months.

Adam Swigart, born 1724, died 1796.

Adam Swigart, born Oct. 25, 1784, died March 17, 1825.

Adam Swigart, died Jan. 9, 1832, aged 82 years, 8 months, 22 days.

Elizabeth Swigard, died Jan. 15, 1812, aged 59 years, 4 days.

Elizabeth Hanes, died March 10, 1822, aged 37 years, 11 months, 9 days.

Geo. Smelser, born Nov. 1, 1811, died April 29, 1872.

Mary, wife of Michael Smelser, died July 25, 1836, aged 77 years, 7 months, 11 days.

David Smelser, died Feb. 22, 1864, aged 63 years, 7 months, 11 days.

Mary Magdalena Hanna, died Jan. 25, 1841.

Barbara Long, died April 18, 1841, aged 34 years, 6 months, 25 days.

Michael S. Norris, died April 3, 1866, aged 75.

Isaac N. Smelser, born May, 1821, died May, 1850.

Elizabeth Lambert, born Oct. 6, 1785, died Feb. 3, 1862.

John Lambert, died March 30, 1855, aged 58 years, 6 months, 1 day.

Esther, his wife, died Oct. 16, 1876, aged 74 years, 11 months, 9 days.

Joshua Yingling, born Oct. 5, 1801, died Dec. 9, 1856.

Mary M. Yingling, born June 13, 1802, died Aug. 19, 1875.

Mary A., wife of Samuel Lamberd, died Jan. 24, 1856, aged 25.

Peter Geiger, born May 19, 1784, died Aug. 7, 1858; Charlotte, his wife, born April 26, 1793, died Sept. 6, 1863.

Magdalen Cook, died June 4, 1849, aged 96 years, 4 days.

Catharine Bayar, died Oct. 1, 1811, aged 48 years, 4 months.

J. Fasler, born 1781.

Tobias Gearner, born 1754, died 1793.

Margaret Gearner, born 1750, died 1807.

Israel Cook and Ephraim, infants, died 1820.

David Brower, died Jan. 7, 1823, aged 19.

Rebecca Eckman, died 1820, aged 11 months.

Michael, wife of John Brower, died June 22, 1849, aged 80 years, 7 months, 15 days.

Richard Adams, died April 2, 1867, aged 68.

Hannah Adams, died Jan. 29, 1852, aged 52.

Lewis Boublets, born 1802, died April 20, 1867.

Elizabeth Frownfelter, died Nov. 26, 1879, aged 39 years, 6 months, 7 days.

Jacob Z. Buchan, died May 24, 1813, died July 15, 1877.

Michael Bagner, born 1723, died 1795.

M. Bagner, born 1725, died 1789.

J. Winter, died Oct. 13, 1731, aged 61.

John Winter, died June 3, 1827, aged 43 years, 5 months, 26 days.

Christian Winter, died March 9, 1810, aged 25 years, 3 months.

Fred. Milins, born in Etzdorf, kingdom of Saxony, Germany, Sept. 15, 1767, died Oct. 28, 1852; Mary E., his wife, born Dec. 10, 1785, died Nov. 21, 1874.

John Shannon, died March 28, 1853, aged 65; Sarah, his wife, died April 21, 1859, aged 75.

Samuel Townsend, died June 11, 1825, aged 21 years, 10 months.

David Townsend, died May 16, 1835, aged 30 years, 3 months, 4 days.

Thomas Townsend, died Nov. 10, 1851, aged 73 years, 3 months; Elizabeth, his wife, born Aug. 28, 1776, died April 27, 1850.

Joseph Winter, born Feb. 9, 1797, died Dec. 2, 1863.

Elizabeth Engleman, died Dec. 16, 1879, aged 89 years, 8 months, 14 days.

Mary Engleman, died April 20, 1879, aged 85 years, 6 months, 18 days.

Lewis Engleman, died Nov. 19, 1870, aged 78 years, 11 months, 8 days.

Josiah Pearce, died Dec. 5, 1830, aged 53 years, 3 months, 28 days.

Elizabeth Pearce, died Oct. 10, 1852, aged 72 years, 10 months, 22 days.

Sarah A., wife of Elmer Hyde, born March 6, 1829, died April 1, 1875.

Isaac Hyde, born Jan. 9, 1798, died March 3, 1872; Mary, his wife, died May 14, 1876, aged 74 years, 1 month, 29 days.

Jonathan Hyde, died July 31, 1802, aged 75.

Ann Hyde, born June 16, 1728, died July 8, 1812.

Elizabeth Hyde, born June 3, 1765, died Dec. 14, 1814.

Ann Hyde, died March 22, 1858, aged 87 years, 3 months, 23 days.

Columbus Engleman, died March 27, 1877, aged 39 years, 5 months, 11 days.

George Mering, died Oct. 24, 1868, aged 67 years, 2 months, 9 days.

Catharine Frownfelter, born Aug. 22, 1824, died Sept. 15, 1865.

Magdalene Herman, born Dec. 27, 1799, died March 14, 1861.

Thomas King, died July 26, 1879, aged 65.

George Gisleman, died June 19, 1878, aged 84 years, 1 month, 18 days; Regina, his wife, died Dec. 5, 1876, aged 80 years, 7 months, 28 days.

Francis Wagner, died Oct. 7, 1869, aged 34 years, 4 months, 4 days.

Peter Nace, died June 15, 1866, aged 53.

George Wilhelm, died Feb. 17, 1872, aged 34 years, 10 months, 16 days.

Sophia L. Wilhelm, born April 27, 1805, died Feb. 7, 1875.

Helper Grammer, born April 14, 1790, died April 17, 1869; Margaret Grammer, his wife, died Oct. 5, 1868, aged 83 years, 5 months.

Adam Fuss, died Aug. 28, 1879, aged 60 years, 2 months, 17 days.

Louisa Muller, died Jan. 21, 1880, aged 61 years, 9 months, 26 days.

New Windsor.—This town is twenty-eight miles from Baltimore, and is the commercial centre of the district. It is in an exceedingly fertile section of the county, and a branch of Little Pipe Creek passes along its outer edge. It is one of the important stations on the Western Maryland Railroad, has a bank, two institutions of learning, a number of churches, a warehouse, some well-stocked stores, and contains a population of more than 400 inhabitants. In the immediate vicinity there are a number of lime and stone-quarries, and some valuable mills. The town was incorporated by an act of the General Assembly of Maryland, passed Jan. 25, 1844.

On March 15, 1817, Joshua Metcalfe took charge of the Merino factory, a valuable property, formerly carried on by Silas Hibberd, near New Windsor. Mr. Metcalfe had been foreman in the factory for many years. Aug. 22, 1817, Charles W. Pearre, who had been in business for a number of years, notified all those in debt to him to call and settle at Lemuel Pearre's store their accounts by September 20th.

The following advertisement appeared in the *Star of Federalism* of Nov. 19, 1819:

"German Redemptioners.—About one hundred and sixty German Redemptioners, who are principally young people, and among whom are farmers and tradesmen of every kind, have just arrived in the Dutch ship 'Batavia,' Capt. B. Ehlers. Apply to the captain on board at the Cove, Spring Garden, or to Chas. W. Karthaus & Co., 50 South Gay Street, Baltimore."

Of these redemptioners, several who were bought came to this region and settled in the rear of the town of New Windsor.

The first physician in New Windsor was Dr. Robert Dodds, a native of Scotland, who died July 27, 1833.

New Windsor was formerly called "Sulphur Springs," in consequence of an excellent mineral spring on the farm of Isaac Atlee, now owned by Dennis H. Maynard. The first officers of the town, who were elected to serve from 1844 to 1845, were:

Henry W. Dell, burgess; Samuel Ecker, Jesse Lambert, Isaac Blizzard, commissioners; Samuel Hoffman, collector.

1845-46.—H. W. Dell, burgess; Samuel Hoffman, Jesse Lambert, Samuel Ecker, commissioners.

1846-47.—Samuel Ecker, burgess; H. W. Dell, Jesse Lambert, Jonas Ecker, commissioners.

1847-48.—Jonas Ecker, burgess; Jesse Lambert, Andrew Baker, Samuel Ecker, commissioners.

1848-49.—Jonas Ecker, burgess; Thomas Bartlow, Andrew Baker, Lewis Fowler, commissioners.

1849-50.—H. W. Dell, burgess; Jesse Lambert, Jonas Ecker, Lewis Fowler, commissioners. Dell resigned, and Samuel Hoffman was appointed in his place.

1850-51.—Jonas Ecker, burgess; H. W. Dell, Nathan Hanna, Jesse Lambert, commissioners.

1851-52.—Jonas Ecker, burgess; Henry Geaty, N. Hanna, Jesse Lambert, commissioners.

1852-53.—Jonas Ecker, burgess; Jesse Lambert, William R. Curry, William Delphey, commissioners.

1853-54.—The same re-elected.

1854-55.—Jonas Ecker, burgess; Jesse Lambert, Elijah Ensor, Henry W. Dell, commissioners.[1]

1861-62.—Henry Geaty, burgess; Ezra Stouffer, Levi N. Snader, Jesse Lambert, commissioners.

1862-63.—Jacob Roop, burgess; Levi N. Snader, Ezra Stouffer, N. Hanna, commissioners.

1863-64.—James Earhart, burgess; Dr. Buffington, Joseph A. Stouffer, Jesse Lambert, commissioners.

1864-65.—Levi N. Snader, burgess; Jesse Lambert, Lewis Shully, Daniel Stouffer, commissioners.

By an act of the March session of the General Assembly of Maryland, the charter of the corporation was revived, and the limits extended as follows:

"Beginning at a sycamore-tree on Dickinson's branch, opposite the foot of Main Street, southeast of said branch to the mouth of Ray's branch; thence with the northeast side of the mill dam to Chew's bridge, leaving the dam and bridge outside of the corporation; thence northeast on the west side of the road to the division line between Jesse Lambert and E. W. Englar, leaving said road outside of said corporation; thence with said line to a point directly opposite the line between Andrew H. Baker and Josiah Hibbert, on the east side of Calvert College; thence from this point northerly through the lands of A. H. Baker, and the division line between the said Baker and Hibbert, to the northeast corner of the lands of said Baker, to a ten-pin alley, and westwardly with the lines between said Baker and Hibbert, Frownfelter, and others to the lands of D. H. Maynard; then with a straight line parallel with said Maynard's garden fence, and with it to said Maynard's outer gate; thence with a straight line to a sycamore-tree, the place of beginning."

1867.—Joseph A. Stouffer, burgess; A. H. Baker, Dr. J. F. Buffington, E. S. Stouffer, commissioners.

1868-69.—A. H. Baker, burgess; Dr. J. F. Buffington, E. S Stouffer, Joseph Stouffer, commissioners.

1869.—Jesse Lambert, burgess; Jacob Frownfelter, Jesse Haines, Charles P. Baile, commissioners.

1870-71.—Jesse Lambert, burgess; Charles P. Baile, Jacob Frownfelter, Jesse Haines, commissioners.

[1] During the year 1855 the corporation died out, but in 1860 Jacob Roop was elected mayor or burgess; Dr. John Buffington, Daniel Stouffer, and Winson Brown, commissioners.

1871-72.—Peter Baile, burgess; Lewis Dielman, William Vansant, James Devilbiss.

1872-73.—The same re-elected.

1873-74.—The same re-elected.

1874-75.—Peter Baile, burgess; Lewis Dielman, Jacob Frownfelter, James Devilbiss, commissioners.

1875-76.—P. Baile, burgess; Lewis Dielman, C. P. Baile, Jacob Frownfelter, commissioners.

1876-77.—P. Baile, burgess; William Vansant, W. A. Norris, Dr. J. F. Buffington, commissioners.

1877-78.—Charles P. Baile, burgess; W. A. Norris, William Vansant, Jeremiah Bailey, commissioners.

1878-79.—Peter Baile, burgess; Lewis Dielman, Samuel Hoffman, Jacob Frownfelter, commissioners.

1879.—Peter Baile, burgess; Jacob Frownfelter, George S. Gitt, C. P. Baile, commissioners.

1880-81.—Peter Baile, burgess; George A. Gitt, F. J. Devilbiss, James Lambert, commissioners.

1881.—Peter Baile, burgess; Jacob Frownfelter, Charles E. Norris, C. C. Engel, commissioners.

Prior to 1871 one of the commissioners served as a clerk to that body, but since that date Lewis Dielman has occupied that position.

A correct list is given of thirty-one persons, living within a radius of five miles of New Windsor in 1879, who had lived to the age of seventy years and upwards:

Males.—William Engleman, 82; Jacob Sauble, 88; Israel Switzer, 74; Abner Baile, 71; Israel Norris, 80; Samuel McKinstry, 71; Samuel Winter, 79; Jacob Snader, 74; Joseph Stouffer, 73; Daniel Lambert, 72; Esau Randall, 90; D. Woodegard (colored), 88; David Crumbacker, 77; David W. Naill, 84; Joshua Warfield, 82; Josiah Hibberd, 70; Thomas King, 70; David Engel, 77. *Females.*—Mrs. Sallie Wolfe, 92; Elizabeth Eckman, 88; Elizabeth Shriner, 83; Elizabeth Crumbacker, 84; Elizabeth Engleman, 89; Mary Diehl, 90; Julia Earhard, 76; Polly Engleman, 86; Nelly Engleman, 71; Honor Williams, 82; Nancy Sanders[2] (colored), 110; Rebecca Crowl, 86; Sally Baile, 76.

The First National Bank of New Windsor was chartered in 1860. Its officers have been: President, Thomas F. Shepperd; Cashiers, Joseph A. Stouffer, Nathan H. Baile; Directors, Job Hibberd, Solomon

[2] Nancy Sanders, a colored woman residing at Landis' Mill, in an interview, states: "I belonged to Mr. George Robeson, way down in 'Gomery County, and about the time the first wa' with the English closed I came to Carroll County, on Sam's Creek. Then I was sixteen years old. In a few years there was another war with the English, and just as Mr. Peter Naill, Lud. Greenwood, and Massa Clemson Skyles were about to start to jine the army, the English captain was killed down near Baltimore, and then the war stopped." Judging from her account, she was born in 1767, was sixteen years of age when the Revolutionary war ended (in 1783), and is consequently one hundred and fourteen years old now. She says if she was not in such a bad state of health she could do more work than any woman in the county. She claims that her age does not hurt her, for she can thread a needle, and laughs at her youngest son, George, who is sixty, because he wears spectacles. Her mind seems clear on all subjects, except she thinks some one has put a "spell" on her.

S. Ecker, Samuel Hoffman, Upton Root, Peter Engle, and Joseph H. Hibberd.

New Windsor was thrown into a state of intense excitement Saturday morning, Jan. 23, 1868, by the discovery that the bank had been robbed. For some days previous two strangers had been in the neighborhood, who represented themselves as drummers for Baltimore houses. About two o'clock on Saturday morning a physician who was called up to see a patient saw a man standing near the bank building, and although it was unusual to see any person on the street at that hour, he suspected nothing wrong. Saturday morning the officers of the bank went as usual to their place of business, but discovered that the safe could not be opened. One of them immediately started for the city of Baltimore, and called on the independent police firm of Smith, Pierson & West. The detectives went immediately to New Windsor, and found that the lock had been successfully picked, and that important portions of it had been removed. Upon opening the safe it was apparent that the whole contents had been removed.

Ninety-nine thousand dollars in all had been taken. Of this amount ninety thousand dollars were in the following securities, which were the property of private parties, and had been deposited with the bank for safe-keeping:

United States five-twenties of 1862, Nos. 3260, 7650, of five hundred dollars each; United States five-twenties of 1864, Nos. 39,663, 20,152, 20,153, 20,154, one thousand dollars each; United States five-twenty bonds of 1865, January and July, Nos. B, 64,031; A, 2881; E, 177,342; B, 70,191; B, 57,982, of five hundred dollars each; United States ten-forties, No. 19,747, of five hundred dollars; Central Pacific Railroad bonds, first mortgage, Nos. F, 7648; F, 4561; F, 4562; G, 8978; G, 8981; G, 8982; G, 8971; G, 8972; F, 4571; F, 4572; F, 4569; F, 7648; Union Pacific Railroad, Nos. 2982, 9417, 9419, 9416, 8487, 8491, 7258, 7259, 8486, amounting to $13,931.56; Western Maryland Railroad first mortgage bonds, Nos. 93, 125, 107, of one thousand dollars each; Nos. 447, 444, 449, 555, 448, 564, 525, 559, 526, 566, 441, of five hundred dollars each; Western Maryland Railroad second mortgage bonds, indorsed by Washington County, Nos. 11, 13, 78, 81, 7, 47, 43, 44, of one thousand dollars each; 7, 67, 68, 670, of five hundred dollars each; 761, 690, of one hundred dollars each; Washington County bonds, Nos. 65, 66, 91, 39, 7, 55, of one thousand dollars each; 33, 30, 64, 65, 66, 67, 31, 21, 36, 37, 53, of five hundred dollars each; 53, 51, 26, of one hundred dollars each; New Orleans and Opelousas Railroad first mortgage, Nos. 962, 963, 967, 968, 1803, 999, 428, 216, 427, 998, 1806, 1592, 1610, 1593, 1599, 1479, 188, 1807, 966, 1804, 972, 1805, 474, 209, 997, 906, 475, of one thousand dollars each; and others.

The remaining nine thousand dollars were in greenbacks, of the denominations of one thousand dollars and five hundred dollars, and were the property of the bank.

An examination of the premises disclosed that the burglars had but little difficulty in gaining access to the bank. The upper part of the house was not occupied, and the entrance was effected through a second-story window, after which, with the aid of burglar's tools, the doors were easily opened. One of the tools, a jimmy, made with a screw-thread on one end, by which it could be converted into a brace, was found on the premises, where it had been left. The robbery was done by expert burglars, and it is supposed the arrangements for its consummation had been perfected for some time, so easily and thoroughly was it accomplished. Messrs. Smith, Pierson & West took charge of the matter at once.

A new and elegant light jagger-wagon, badly mashed, was found beyond the limekiln, close to Lawrence Zepp's entrance, near Westminster. William S. Brown found tied to his garden fence a very fine horse with a set of silver-mounted harness on him. The harness and blankets were new and of costly make. The impression was at the time that the robbers had intended to meet an accomplice here. The burglars left New Windsor in a hand-car, and ran down to within a mile of Westminster, at Hollow Rock limestone-quarries. Here they threw the car off the track, and walked to Westminster, where they took the early train for Baltimore. A reward of ten thousand dollars was offered for the apprehension of the robbers. The detective learned that several persons, whose description he had with him, had registered at the hotels in Baltimore at different times previous to the robbery, and no doubt remained on his mind that these were the robbers. The police in prosecuting the search visited Philadelphia, and gave the detective force there a description of a man whose identity could be established more readily than that of the others, and asked the co-operation of the Philadelphia officers. The latter recognized in him Mark Schinbourn, a notorious New York burglar, who was then in New York, and for whose apprehension the New Hampshire authorities were offering a reward of one thousand dollars, he being an escaped convict from that State. An additional reward was also offered for his arrest by the Lehigh Coal and Navigation

Company, from whose office at White Plains he had stolen fifty-six thousand dollars' worth of bonds. The Baltimore detective officers, in continuation of their investigation, went to New York, and applied for assistance to the chief of police, relating the circumstances and their suspicion of Schinbourn. Nothing further was heard of the robbers or their booty for about two weeks, at which time a man appeared at the New Windsor Bank with ninety thousand dollars of the missing securities, which he paid over, with a deduction of twenty per cent. (nineteen thousand dollars) for his trouble and expense. It then leaked out that Schinbourn and an associate named McQuade had been arrested, and were confined in the New York Police Central Office for about a week, and it is said when they turned over the securities they were allowed to depart in peace.

New Windsor College, situated in the heart of one of the healthiest and most picturesque sections of Maryland, was chartered in 1843 by the Presbyterians. In 1852 it was reorganized by Andrew J. Baker and others, and though still under the auspices of the Presbyterian Church is not a sectarian institution, the pupils being allowed to worship in accordance with their religious convictions. The buildings are commodious, and fitted with all the modern appliances for health and comfort. The institution has preparatory and collegiate departments, to which both sexes are admitted, with such restrictions only as the nature of the case demands. Rev. J. P. Carter was the first president. He was succeeded in 1852 by Andrew J. Baker, who presided until 1877, when Rev. A. M. Jelly, D.D., the present excellent principal, took charge.

The college suffered greatly during the war, and for some years afterwards from financial embarrassments, but through the able management of Dr. Jelly it weathered the storm and entered upon a career of prosperity and usefulness. The college is essentially two separate institutions with two boards of instructors, located on the same ground and under the same general management, and thus parents are enabled to educate both their sons and daughters without separating them. The students enjoy the advantages of a large and well-selected library and the "William Andrews" cabinet of geology, containing twenty thousand specimens.

There are three literary societies,—the Alexandrian, in the academical department; the Minnehaha, in the Ladies' Seminary; and the Union Society, composed of the other two, which meets once a week for mental culture. The faculty is composed of graduates from Yale, Princeton, Wooster University, University of Maryland, and Washington and Jefferson College, as well as from the best female schools.

During the college year Joseph T. Smith, M.D., of the University of Maryland, delivers twice a week lectures upon anatomy, physiology, and hygiene, and there is a course of lectures during the session on general topics. The institution has also a printing department, under the management of W. R. A. Kohl, of Baltimore, where the college printing is done.

The curators are

Rev. John C. Backus, D.D., LL.D., Baltimore; Rev. Joseph T. Smith, D.D., Baltimore; Rev. John Leyburn, D.D., Baltimore; Rev. J. A. Lefevre, D.D., Baltimore; Rev. H. Fulton; Rev. J. P. Carter, Baltimore; Rev. J. T. Leftwitch, Rev. J. S. Jones, D.D., Rev. W. T. Brantly, D.D., Rev. D. J. Beale, Rev. W. H. Gill, Rev. George E. Jones, Rev. Joseph F. Jennison, W. W. Spence, Esq., W. S. Carroll, Esq., W. B. Canfield, Esq., E. M. Cole, Esq., C. Dodd McFarland, Esq., John L. Reed, Esq., E. H. Perkins, M.D., all of Baltimore; Rev. Byron Sunderland, D.D., Washington, D. C.; Rev. John R. Paxton, D.D., Washington, D. C.; Rev. Wm. Simonton, Emmittsburg, Md.; Robert L. Annon, M.D., Emmittsburg, Md.: E. Hall Richardson, M.D., Belair, Md.; Rev. R. H. Williams, Arlington, Md.; Hon. Alexander H. Stephens, Georgia; Rev. J. A. Rondthaler, Hagerstown, Md.; Rev. George Morrison, Aberdeen, Md.; Rev. Joseph Nesbitt, Lock Haven, Pa.; Rev. John Ewing, Clinton, N. J.; S. D. Bull, Esq., Lock Haven, Pa.; J. D. Skilling, M.D., Lonaconing, Md.; T. W. Simpson, M D, Liberty, Md.; Hon. Thos. C. Action, New York City; Rev. Wm. H. Cooke, Havre de Grace, Md.; Rev. Thos. Nelson, Madonna, Md.; Rev. Wm. T. L. Kieffer, Churchville, Md.; Rev. W. H. Hortzell, Glenville, Md.

Trustees.—Hon. L. P. Slingluff, president; Rev. A. M. Jelly, D.D., vice-president, New Windsor; D. P. Smelser, James Erhard, Joseph A. Stouffer, Job Hibberd, Jeremiah Baile, Levi N. Snader, Solomon S. Ecker, C. H. Chapman, A.M., secretary, all of New Windsor.

Faculty and Instructors.—Rev. A. M. Jelly, D.D., president, Professor of Mental and Moral Philosophy; C. H. Chapman, A.M., Professor of Physical Science and Greek; James B. Green, A.B., Professor of Latin and Mathematics; Joseph T. Smith, M.D., Professor of Anatomy, Physiology, Hygiene, and Chemistry; A. H. Chapman, A.M., in Book-keeping, Banking, Commercial Forms, Type-writing; Charles Gola, Professor of Music; J. B. Greene, Instructor in German Language. The president and vice-president, Instructors in Rhetoric and Elocution. The vice-president, Custodian of the Library. J. A. C. Bond, Attorney-at-Law, Resident Counselor; J. F. Buffington, M.D., Resident Physician.

Board of Instructors.—Ladies' Seminary.—Rev. A. M. Jelly, D.D., president; Mrs. A. M. Jelly, principal of the seminary; James B. Greene, A.B., Professor of Mathematics and German; Miss Nannie W. McVeigh, Teacher of English Branches, French, and Music; Joseph T. Smith, M.D., Professor of Anatomy, Physiology, Hygiene, and Chemistry; A. H. Chapman, A.M., Instructor in

NEW WINDSOR COLLEGE,

NEW WINDSOR, CARROLL CO., MD.

Physical Development. Calisthenics, and Gymnastics; Charles Gola, Professor of Music. Special instructors in normal and Kindergarten training, type-writing, telegraphy, phonography, book-keeping, and penmanship. Special artists in drawing, painting, wax flowers, and fancy work. Miss Kate L. Miller, matron; J. F. Buffington, resident physician.

Calvert College, in the town of New Windsor, for many years one of the finest classical schools in the State, was under the auspices of the Catholic Church, and was noted for the thoroughness of its academic departments. Many of the leading men of the State and county were here educated, among whom were Hon. Charles B. Roberts, of Westminster, Dr. Roberts Bartholow, of Jefferson Medical College, Philadelphia, and Dr. Hanson M. Drach.

Sulphur Spring Lodge, No. 130, I. O. O. F., was instituted in August, 1878, by the following charter members: Gustavus Barnes, Chas. F. Myers, John W. Myers, P. J. Bennett, Samuel Harris, Lewis H. Greenwood, David Nusbaum. The first officers were: N. G., Gustavus Barnes; V. G., C. F. Myers; Sec., J. W. Myers. The lodge then numbered nine members. The officers from January to July, 1879, were:

Chas. F. Myers, N. G.; J. Myers, V. G.; C. C. Ingle, Sec.; Lewis H. Greenwood, Treas. July, 1879, to January, 1880, N. G., J. H. Myers; V. G., L. H. Greenwood; Sec., C. C. Ingle; Treas., L. Greenwood. January to July, 1880, N. G., Lewis H. Greenwood; V. G., C. C. Ingle; Sec., D. C. Ingle; Treas., Jesse Crawner. July, 1880, to January, 1881, N. G., C. C. Ingle; V. G., W. B. Bowersox; Sec., C. C. Repp; Treas., Eph Haines. January to July, 1881, N. G., W. C. Bowersox; V. G., Jesse Crawner; Sec., J. W. Myers; Treas., H. Geatty.

The lodge now numbers thirty members in good standing, which is a showing of an increase of twenty-one members in three years. They hold their meetings in the Town Hall, on Bath Street. The present officers are: N. G., Jesse Crawner; V. G., Chas. T. Repp; Sec., C. C. Ingle; Treas., D. O. Bankard.

The Methodist Episcopal Church was incorporated Feb. 17, 1844, by the General Assembly of Maryland. The first trustees were Andrew Nicodemus, David Cassell, Jeremiah Bartholomew, Dr. J. L. Warfield, H. W. Dell, Thomas Devilbiss, Cooper Devilbiss, Daniel Danner, and H. A. Davis. The pastors for 1881 were Revs. J. A. Fadden, Howard Downs.

St. Thomas' Catholic church was built by Rev. Thomas O'Neill about 1861. He was the priest then in charge of the Carroll County mission. From November, 1862, to 1879, Father John Gloyd had charge of this church, and since then Father John T. Delaney, of Taneytown, under whose ministrations the two churches have formed one mission since 1879.

The Presbyterian cemetery surrounds the Presbyterian church, and the following, among others, are buried there:

Joshua C. Gist, born Sept. 15, 1792, died March 27, 1878.

Samuel J. Atlee, died Aug. 10, 1861, aged 69 years, 1 month, 15 days.

Augusta A. Atlee, born March 22, 1840, died Dec. 11, 1862.

Isaac Richardson Atlee, son of Col. Samuel John Atlee, of the Revolutionary war of 1775, born 1767, died 1842, aged 82.

Mary Clemson, wife of Isaac R. Atlee, born 1769, died 1834, aged 64.

Wm. Richardson Atlee, attorney-at-law, brother of Isaac R. Atlee, and son-in-law of Maj.-Gen. Anthony Wayne, of the Revolutionary war, born 1764, died 1844, aged 80.

James C. Atlee, born Aug. 14, 1798, died May 3, 1855; Sarah S., his wife, born May 8, 1809, died Nov. 1, 1876.

Elhanan Stouffer, died Dec. 27, 1877, aged 34.

John Lambert, born Sept. 19, 1836, died June 4, 1869.

Jacob Hull, born June 12, 1782, died May 1, 1853.

Anna M., wife of Jacob Wikert, died March 29, 1871, aged 83 years, 10 months, 7 days.

William Hull, born Dec. 13, 1824, died Sept. 20, 1853.

Mary A. H., wife of Wm. Mitten, died Dec. 14, 1874, aged 64.

B. F. Bartholow, died at Henderson, N. C., May 18, 1873, aged 39.

Jeremiah Bartholow, died in Baltimore, July 19, 1854, aged 67; Pleasant, his wife, died Jan. 28, 1876, aged 80.

Wesley Bartholow, M.D., died in New Windsor, July 31, 1848, aged 29.

Wm. H. Clay, died April 4, 1870, aged 33.

Sarah E. Smith, died May 4, 1879, aged 48 years, 4 months, 12 days.

Thomas Bond, born April 26, 1768, died Sept. 27, 1827.

James B. Bond, born Oct. 8, 1782, died Oct. 20, 1827.

Elijah Bond, died Sept. 15, 1853, aged 64 years, 3 months.

Mary A., born Jan. 21, 1801, died Feb. 25, 1843.

George Erhard, died July 28, 1868, aged 85; Julia A., his wife, died April 16, 1880, aged 83 years, 5 days.

Robert Dods, M.D., "born at Prova, county of Haddington, Scotland," died at New Windsor, July 27, 1833, aged 48.

Margaret Dods, died June 11, 1862, aged 82.

Sarah Dods, died June 1, 1849, aged 62.

Anna, wife of H. W. Geatty, born Sept. 28, 1828, died Sept. 15, 1879.

Jonas Ecker, died Aug. 22, 1870, aged 57.

Francis Ecker, died May 19, 1880, aged 64.

Jeremiah Currey, born April 1, 1801, died June 11, 1835; Sarah S., his wife, born June 18, 1805, died Oct. 18, 1874.

Jacob Repp, died Feb. 21, 1871, aged 84 years, 6 months, 13 days.

Ann Mumford, born Dec. 13, 1798, died Dec. 25, 1867.

Jacob Wilt, died Oct. 27, 1872, aged 82; Elizabeth, his wife, died Oct. 2, 1856, aged 61 years, 1 month, 2 days.

Ferdinand Matthes, a native of Germany, died Jan. 16, 1876, aged 70 years, 4 months, 8 days.

Jacob Nusbaum, died Dec. 11, 1876, aged 69 years, 11 months, 10 days; Mary, his wife, died April 2, 1865, aged 54 years, 7 months, 25 days.

Jacob Stem, born April 30, 1793, died Nov. 23, 1855; Mary A., his wife, died Jan. 29, 1864, aged 42 years, 3 months, 25 days.

John W. Durbin, born Nov. 5, 1821, died Nov. 30, 1859.

Nancy Durbin, born 1789, died Feb. 20, 1865.

Abraham Albaugh, born Aug. 29, 1780, died Feb. 27, 1854; Mary C., his wife, died Oct. 17, 1851, aged 57 years, 1 month, 19 days.

John Haines, died July 6, 1859, aged 76; Susannah, his wife, died May 2, 1857, aged 63.

Jos. Bigham, born Feb. 22, 1818, died April 5, 1860, aged 42 years, 1 month, 14 days.

John Haines, born Sept. 4, 1806, died March 23, 1870; Mary, his wife, born Dec. 23, 1800, died July 23, 1858.

Honor Williams, born Nov. 29, 1803, died Oct. 2, 1879.

Francis Smith, died April 4, 1861, aged 32.

Henry Townsend, of Co. C, First U. S. Sharpshooters, killed in battle at Kelly's Ford, Va., Nov. 7, 1863, aged 23.

Levi Picking, died Jan. 14, 1862, aged 50.

Anna M. Condon, died Aug. 14, 1870, aged 38 years, 6 months, 8 days.

Elizabeth Barnes, died Nov. 10, 1858, aged 39.

Thos. Wm. Barnes, died May 5, 1858, aged 19 years, 7 days.

Richard Smith, born Dec. 13, 1768, died Dec. 22, 1783.

Mary Leppo, died May 21, 1880, aged 80 years, 4 months, 11 days.

Ludwick Baille, born Sept. 28, 1853, aged 69.

Catharine, wife of Peter Baile, born May 5, 1820, died June 27, 1859.

Christiana A. Diehl, died Jan. 5, 1866, aged 40 years, 3 months, 4 days.

Nimrod T. Bennett, died Sept. 17, 1870, aged 27 years, 8 months, 19 days.

Levi T. Bennett, died Dec. 9, 1865, aged 56 years, 1 month, 14 days.

Edwin G. Shipley, died Nov. 5, 1865, aged 40 years, 8 months, 10 days.

Ann Shipley, died Sept. 3, 1867, aged 85 years, 9 months, 5 days.

Dr. Joseph Shuey, an alumnus of Calvert College, and a graduate of the University of Maryland, died Jan. 10, 1865, aged 25 years, 10 months, 16 days.

Mary E., wife of J. L. Shuey, died Jan. 22, 1863, aged 32 years, 4 months, 18 days.

Hester Brawner, died April 8, 1844, aged 55.

Wm. Thoburn, born Oct. 11, 1803, died Dec. 28, 1870; Eliza McRea, his wife, died Jan. 11, 1870, aged 60 years, 7 months.

Joseph Poole, born Oct. 4, 1802, died Jan. 23, 1850; Esther, his wife, died April 2, 1864, aged 61.

Washington M. Naill, born Feb. 20, 1826, died Feb. 24, 1876.

The *New Windsor Herald* was established in 1881, and is issued semi-monthly. F. J. Devilbiss is associated with Mr. Koehl in its publication.

My Maryland was established in August, 1881, and is the fifth newspaper now published in the county.

The New Windsor Library Company was incorporated by the Legislature Jan. 13, 1841. The incorporators were Rev. John P. Carter, Dr. J. L. Warfield, Isaac Slingluff, Samuel Eiker, Michael Smith, J. H. Hibberd, William A. Norris, William Pole, Jr., Ephraim Bowersox, Jesse Lambert, Jonas Eiker, William Kelley, Theodore Hibberd, James C. Atlee, G. W. Willson, Nathan Haines, of Joseph, William Eiker, Josiah Hibberd, Isaac Blizzard, Silas Hibberd, Jacob Nasbaum, Catherine M. Brawner, Lewis Shull.

Mount Vernon is a pretty little village situated a mile northeast of Sam's Creek, and is on the road to Stone Chapel. It has a store and several small shops.

Denning's is four and a half miles from New Windsor, near Sam's Creek. It has a Dunker Church. Joseph T. Stern is the merchant and postmaster, and Dr. L. A. Aldridge is the physician of the village and the surrounding country.

St. James' Chapel (M. E. Church South), a substantial and commodious structure, was erected in 1879, under the auspices of Rev. W. R. Stringer, who was its pastor that year. Since then it has been under the pastorate of Rev. M. G. Balthis.

Wakefield is on the Western Maryland Railroad, forty miles from Baltimore, and near Little Pipe Creek. It is in the midst of a fertile portion of the county known as "Wakefield Valley." "The Wakefield Valley Creamery," a stock company composed of farmers of that vicinity, is an important business enterprise, consuming six hundred gallons of milk daily in the manufacture of butter and cheese. Joseph Hoover is postmaster, H. S. Roberts, merchant, and Joseph A. Waesche, florist.

McKinstry's Mills is two miles from Linwood, twelve from Westminster, and is situated near Sam's Creek. The postmaster, Samuel McKinstry, from whom the post-office derives its name, is the oldest officer in official servitude in the State. He received his appointment from Amos Kendall, postmaster-general under Andrew Jackson, and has held it continuously from that time to the present. M. C. McKinstry and Jacob Zumbrum & Sons operate the mills. John McKinstry keeps the store, and Benjamin Jones the blacksmith shop.

Sam's Creek Post-Office is three and a half miles from New Windsor, near Sam's Creek, a small but historical stream, from which it derives its name. Rev. Charles A. Reid is pastor or local preacher of the M. E. Church. D. E. Stern is merchant and postmaster; John W. and William Yingling and Jesse T. Wilson are blacksmiths.

Linwood is on the Western Maryland Railroad, ten miles from Westminster, and forty-three from Baltimore. John Q. Senseney was the original proprietor of the land, and Reuben Haines laid off the town. The merchants are Josiah Englar and sons. Joseph Englar is railroad and express agent and postmaster; J. & J. Englar operates the mills, and Dr. L. Royer is the resident physician.

Pipe Creek Beneficial Society was incorporated by the Legislature on Feb. 28, 1844. The trustees were Abraham Jones, Francis Jones, Dr. Thomas Sim, Jesse Wright, Israel Norris, Robert Nelson, and R. S. Reese.

"Door to Virtue" Lodge, No. 46, of Ancient Free and Accepted Masons, held its first meeting (under a dispensation from the Most Worshipful the Grand Master of Masons in Maryland) on Sunday, June 23, 1811, at Pipe Creek, Frederick (now Carroll) County. The members present on this memorable occasion were Jesse Cloud, Worshipful Master; William P. Farquhar, Senior Warden; William Slaymaker, Junior Warden; Enoch Taylor, Senior Deacon; Daniel Slaymaker, Junior Deacon; Moses Wright, Secretary and Treasurer; William McCollum, Tyler; and Moses B. Farquhar, an Entered Apprentice. The visiting brethren were William Knox, John Crapster, Israel Wright, and Isaac Lightner, of Philadelphos Lodge, No. 39, Taneytown, and John Cook, of Ireland. "An Entered Apprentice's Lodge was formed, a charge was read, and a prayer made to the Divinity for a blessing." Petitions were presented from Caleb Ogborn, Joel Pusey, and Thomas B. Franklin, "praying to be initiated into the mysteries of Masonry," which were referred to a committee appointed "to inquire into their characters, and to report the result of their inquiries." These, the first applicants for initiation in this lodge, received the degrees at subsequent meetings, and became, as the old record shows, active craftsmen. "A Fellow Craft's Lodge was then opened in due form, and Moses B. Farquhar was permitted to take the second degree of Masonry, and returned thanks accordingly." Where and when this brother was initiated there are no means of knowing, but his advancement to the degree of Fellow Craft was the first "work" performed in Door to Virtue Lodge. While working under a dispensation there were held eleven meetings, the last being on the 31st of October, when Jesse Cloud and Moses Wright were appointed the first representatives of this lodge to the Grand Lodge of Maryland, and during this period seven brethren were "raised" to the degree of Master Mason, among whom was the late venerable Thomas Shepherd, of Union Bridge.

On Sunday, November 10th, at a special communication, "the representatives appointed to the Grand Lodge, with the proceedings of this lodge, report that they have performed that service and obtained a warrant." The warrant was presented to the lodge, and, by virtue of the authority therein conferred, the officers already mentioned as acting during the period of dispensation were duly installed, and Door to Virtue took the rank and number (46) which it still holds among the Maryland lodges.

The charter or warrant referred to in the proceedings of Nov. 10, 1811, is the one under which the lodge is now working, and as a matter of interest to the membership an exact and literal copy of it is printed:

"John Crawford, M. D. and G. M. [L.S.]

"*To all whom it may concern:*

"We the grand Lodge of the State of Maryland of the most ancient and honorable Fraternity of Free and Accepted Masons, according to the Old Institution, duly established, constituted and organized for the said State by resolutions and authority of a Grand Convention held at Talbot Court House on the seventeenth day of April in the year of Masonry Five thousand Seven Hundred and eighty seven, Do hereby constitute and appoint our trusty and well beloved brethren, Jesse Cloud, Master, William P. Farquhar, Senior Warden and William Slaymaker Junior Warden of a new Lodge to be held in the neighborhood of Little Pipe Creek in Frederick County by the name of Door to Virtue Lodge, No. 46, and we do hereby authorize and empower our said trusty and well beloved Brethren to hold their Lodge at the place hereby appointed and directed at such times as they shall think necessary and convenient, and according to the constitution of Masonry, and to admit and to make Free Masons according to the most Honorable Custom of the Royal Craft in all ages and nations through out the known world and not to contrariwise. And we do further authorize and empower said Brethren and their successors to hear and determine all and singular matters and things relating to the Craft within the jurisdiction of the said Lodge No. 46. And lastly we do hereby authorize and empower our said trusty and well-beloved Brethren Jesse Cloud, William B. Farquhar and William Slaymaker to nominate, choose and install their successors to whom they shall deliver this Warrant, and invest them with all their powers and dignities as Free Masons and such successors shall in like manner install their successors, etc, such installations to be upon or near St John's the Evangelist day. Provided always, that the Master, Wardens and Brethren and their successors pay due respect to the Right Worshipful Grand Master, otherwise this Warrant to be of no force or Virtue. Given under our hands, and the seal of the Grand Lodge, this 4th day of November, A.D. 1811, A.L. 5811, at the City of Baltimore.

"George Keyser, *G. J. W.*

"John Wales, *G. S.*"

The lodge continued to hold its meetings at Pipe Creek until the autumn of 1813, the last recorded communication at that place being on the 25th of September of that year. The officers to whom was intrusted the management of the lodge during this period of its history were as follows: From December, 1811, to June, 1812, Jesse Cloud, W. M.; William P. Farquhar, S. W.; William Slaymaker, J. W.; Moses Wright, Sec.; and Moses B. Farquhar, Treas. From June, 1812, to December, 1812, Jesse Cloud, W. M.; William P. Farquhar, S. W.; Moses P. Farquhar, J. W.; Jacob R. Thomas, Sec.; and Joseph Wright, Treas. From December, 1812, to June, 1813, William P. Farquhar, W. M.; Enoch Taylor, S. W.; Daniel Slaymaker, J. W.; Jacob R. Thomas, Sec.; and Joseph Wright, Treas.

This lodge was located in the loft of a spring-house on Beaver Dam stream, a mile or two from Sam's Creek, on the property then owned by Alexander Slaymaker, but now owned by Nathan Englar.

The following is a list of persons aged seventy years and upwards in 1879 in New Windsor District:

Nancy Sanders (colored), 110; Katie Moore, 94; Daniel Coke, 85; D. W. Naill, 84; Moses Hayes (colored), 92; Mrs. D. W. Naill, 81; Jacob Shuster, 86; Boss Hammond (colored), 83; Moses Hammond (colored), 81; Joshua Warfield, 79; Stephen Gorsuch, 79; Miss H. Williams, 78; Thomas Horton, 73; David Engle, of P., 74; William Lewis (colored), 80; Jacob Lookingbill, 72; Mrs. Peter Naill, 90; John Riggler, 75; Abraham Nusbaum, 76; Lewis Kieffer, 79; Jacob Nusbaum, 73; Michael Zepp, 74; Mrs. Mary Devilbiss, 70; Mrs. Casper Devilbiss, 75; Daniel Wagner, 75; Peter Long, 82; T. Beal Porter, 80; Daniel and Lila Bowyer (colored), 72 and 76; Masheck Baker, 75; Peggy Porter, 79; Mrs. Emerata Franklin, 75; Mrs. Philip Snader, 71; Philip Nausbaum, 72; Daniel Nausbaum, 70; Michael Riggler, 75; Mrs. Nancy Chippey, 70; Nathan Franklin, 75; Lewis Green, 95; Perry Green, 70; Caleb Pike (colored), 70; Mrs. Mary Zepp, 78; Mrs. Sellman, 85; Mrs. Elizabeth Gillis, 90; Mrs. Elizabeth Doety, 88; Mrs. Mary Naille, 87; Singleton W. Harn, 77; Mrs. Maria Harn, 77; Mrs. Elizabeth Stocksdale, 75; Mrs. Susannah Barnes, 73; Rev. James Pearre, 70; Mrs. Sarah Lindsay, 70; Mrs. Rachel Buckingham, 76; Mrs. Annie Devilbiss, 75; Mrs. Sarah Miller, 78; Abraham Cole (colored), 79; Samuel Brown (colored), 80; Moses Haines (colored), 80. Total, 4633; average, 80. There are numerous others between 60 and 70.

The following is the vote for local officers from 1857 to 1861, inclusive:

1857.—Vote for Justices: Charles Denning 115, J. Smelzer 23, B. W. Bennett 225, F. H. Crabbs 224; Constables: P. M. Baile 47, Wm. Delphy 228; Road Supervisor: Moses Haines 237.

1859.—For Justices: Edwin A. Atlee 264, Israel Norris 228; Constable: Wm. Delphy 241; Road Supervisor: Wm. Ecker 269.

1861.—For Justices: Edwin A. Atlee 266, George P. Albaugh 257; Constable: Simon Bange 258; Road Supervisor: Wm. Ecker 249.

Below are given the public school trustees for 1881 and 1882, together with the teachers and number of pupils in each school:

1 and 2. New Windsor (Nos. 1 and 2).—Elkanan Engler, J. W. Engler, Jacob Frownfelter.

3. Park Hall.—Solomon Ecker, John W. Myers, Abraham Roop.

4. Baile's.—W. W. Naille, Henry Demmitt, Abram Albaugh.

5. Spring Dale.—Theodore Hibberd, John Geiger, Gustavus Barnes.

6. Wakefield.—David Baille, Jesse Eckard, Isaac C. Forrest.

7. Mount Vernon.—Jesse Haines, Jesse Baile, Dr. B. G. Franklin.

The teachers for the term ending April 13, 1881, were:

1, A. H. Zimmerman, 40 pupils; 2, Annie R. Yingling, 40 pupils; 3, G. T. Yingling, 36 pupils; 4, A. P. Albaugh, 57 pupils; 5, Laura I. Hooker, 44 pupils; 6, M. R. Lord, 43 pupils; 7, E. E. Lovell, 44 pupils.

The justices are Lewis Dielman, Wm. T. Smith, Ellsworth Loveall; Constable, Simon Bange; Notary Public, Dr. J. F. Buffington.

WESTMINSTER DISTRICT, No. 7.

The Seventh District of Carroll County, generally known as Westminster, is bounded on the north by Myers District, on the east by the districts of Manchester, Hampstead, and Woolery, on the south by Woolery and Franklin, and on the west by New Windsor and Uniontown Districts. Westminster is geographically the central district of Carroll County, and it is also the wealthiest, most prominent, and contains the largest number of inhabitants, the census of 1880 giving it a population of 5573. It is intersected by numerous streams, which furnish water-power for milling purposes, and the pure limpid element for farming and grazing lands, among which are the Patapsco Falls, Bear Branch, Morgan's Run, Pipe Creek, Cranberry Run, and Copp's Branch. It is bountifully supplied with turnpikes and excellent public roads, and the Western Maryland Railroad passes almost directly through the centre, furnishing admirable facilities for communication with Baltimore City and other commercial points. The people are intelligent, industrious, and enterprising, and it was in this district that the movement for the creation of a new county crystallized, and was moulded into such a shape as made its accomplishment a possibility. The commission appointed by the act of Assembly passed in 1837 to divide the county into election districts prescribed the following metes and bounds for the district of Westminster:

"Beginning at the 26th mile-stone, on the Reisterstown turnpike; thence to Richard Gorsuch's house; thence to the Patapsco Falls; thence to the forks of Hampstead and Richards' roads; thence with said road to the forks of Manchester and Hampstead; thence to the farm of Abraham Schaffer, leaving him in District No. 7; thence with the lane between Royer and Guyman's farm, on Baughman's county road, to Bixler's tanyard, leaving said Bixler in District No. 7; thence with the road to Andrew Angel's, leaving him in District No. 7; thence with the aforesaid road; thence on said road between the farm of Baughman's and Jacob Snyder; thence to Rinehart's mill-dam; thence to Rinehart's county road; thence to Rinehart's mill; thence on said road to Littlestown turnpike to the 33d mile-stone; thence with the stone road to Jacob Stoneseifer's; thence to Messing's mill; thence to Hesson's house, leaving said Hesson in District No. 2; thence with a straight line to Smith's old tavern, on the Taneytown and Westminster turnpike, leaving said house in District No. 7; thence to Morelock's tavern, leaving his house in District No. 7; thence through Michael Morelock's, Sen., farm, leaving him in No. 7; thence through Widow Haines' farm, leaving her house in District No. 2; thence to Haines' mill; thence down Pipe Creek to Turkey-foot Branch; thence up said branch to where the Howard road crosses said branch; thence with said road to the stone chapel; thence with the county road leading to the Washington road, to its point of intersection; thence with a straight line to the beginning."

Westminster was made the place for holding the polls. By an act of the General Assembly of Maryland, passed April 2, 1841, the substance of which is given in the history of Myers District, the boundary lines were altered to some extent.

The first settlers in the district were principally Germans from Pennsylvania or the Palatinate. As early as 1763 the following heads of families, all landowners, are recorded among the numerous settlers: Daniel Kober, John Greyder (Kreider), Peter Kraul, Valentine Fleigel, F. T. Dreyer, Valentine Bast, Henry Warman. The Everlys, Flickingers, Sullivans, Rinebarts, Reifsnyders, Jacob Heldenbridel, Henry Neff, Jacob Cassell, Peter Bender, David Shriver (then spelt Devaul Schreiber), Daniel Zacharias, Benedict Schwob (now Swope), Valentine Maurrer, Jost Runkel, Andrew Ruse, the Gists, Roops, Jacob Schaeffer, the Frizzells, Hoppes, Wentzs, Myerlys. There were also the Winchesters, Van Bibbers, Leigh Master, and Fishers.

The old Winchester mansion was on the land now owned by Judge John E. Smith, and the fine residence and seat of Col. William A. McKillip is a part of the original Winchester tracts. This mansion was built about 1800, and is still one of the finest in the county. In 1846, David Fisher bought it, with ten acres, of the Winchester heirs, and soon after it became the property of Jacob Fisher, and subsequently of John C. Frizzell. Col. McKillip purchased it in 1880.

The tract of land known as "Brown's Delight," situated on Cobb's Branch, was patented for 350 acres in 1743 to George Brown.

"On Aug. 16, 1698, John Young, of Frankelbach, and single state, was, after being regularly proclaimed, joined in wedlock with Anna Margarethe, the legitimate daughter of Hans Theobald Hess, of Altensborn, in the Electorate Palatine, Oberant Lantern. The above-named Margaretha was baptized in the church of Altensborn, Oct. 22, 1674, her father being Theobald Hess, and mother Margaretha, citizens and wedded persons of that place, and during her marriage with her before-mentioned husband (John Young) she had the following two children: Hans Theobald Young, baptized Feb. 21, 1699; sponsors, Hans Theobald Hess and Anna, the legitimate daughter of the late Sebastian Hess, citizens and inhabitants of said place; and Anna Magdalena, baptized Oct. 25, 1702; sponsors, Nicholas Speck and his wife Catharine."

After the death of the father (John Young) of these two children, the mother, Anna Margaretha, entered into wedlock as follows: "August, 1706, *Andrew Schreiber*, legitimate son of *Jost Schreiber*, citizens of Altensborn, was, after being regularly proclaimed, joined in wedlock with Anna Margaretha, the legitimate widow of the late John Young, who was a citizen of that place of the aforementioned Schreiber's birth." A protocol obtained from the said church certifies that Andrew Schreiber was born and baptized Sept. 7, 1673, the sponsors at the baptism being Andrew Fisher and his wife.

The protocol further shows that this Andrew Schreiber begat during his marriage with Anna Margaretha the following children:

1. Ludwig, born and baptized Oct. 14, 1709; sponsors, Ludwig Vollweiler and his wife, Anna Christiana.

2. Andrew (2), born and baptized Sept. 6, 1712; sponsors, Andrew Schram and Anna Barbara, legitimate wife of Nicholas Speck, citizens of that place.

3. Anna Margaretha, born and baptized July 25, 1715; sponsors, Jacob Gruger, legitimate son of Jacob Gruger, and Anna Margaretha, in the single state, citizens of the place. The following certificate shows the standing and character at home of Andrew Schreiber and his wife, Anna Margaretha:

"ALTENSBORN, May 13th, 1721, being in the Electorate Palatine Oberant Lantern.

[SEAL.] John Mueller, preacher of the word of God in the Reformed Congregation, Altensborn Circle.

That the bearer of (or person shewing) this, Andw Shriver, citizen and inhabitant of this place, and his wife Anna Margaretha, whom he has with him, confess themselves to be conformable to the pure word of God, of the Reform Church, and have until now assiduously observed the outward duties of Christianity in attending our public Worship, receiving the Holy Sacrament, and otherwise, as far as is known, have been irreproachable in their conduct, I attest. And whereas the said man and wife and their children, after having borne adversities, and about to turn their backs upon their country (God knows where), I would therefore recommend them to a willing reception by the preachers and elders of the said Reformed Church, wherever they may show this. Altensborn, oberant lantern, in the Electorate palatine, 13th May, 1721. [SEAL.]

"JOHN MUELLER, *Pastor*."

Andrew Schreiber (2),—now Shriver,—son of Andrew Schreiber and his wife, Anna Margaretha, who had been the widow of John Young (*i.e.* Jung), came to America in the fall of 1721 with his parents, and landed at Philadelphia, after which they moved into the country, to the neighborhood of Goshchappen, near "The Trap," on the Schuylkill, where his father soon died, having supported himself and family by labor. After his death his widow married John Herger, who lived in the same place. Andrew Shriver there learned the trade of tanner and shoemaker. He freed himself from his apprenticeship about 1732, and worked for one year, in which he received £18 ($78) in hand. In the spring of 1733 he married Ann Maria Keyser, and the following spring moved to Conewago, where, after paying for sundry articles with which to begin the world, he had left ten shillings. Ann Maria Keyser was a daughter of Ulrick Keyser and Fornica, his wife, who were both natives of Pfaltz, Germany. Fornica's father was a tanner, who lived five hours from Heidelberg (long. 48° E., lat. 49° 20′ N.), in a small village named Renche. Her eldest brother lived in a village called Schulughten, three hours from her father, and two from Holbron. Her father and mother came with her to America about the fall of 1721. They arrived at Philadelphia and moved into the country where Andrew Shriver lived, and her father soon dying she married Andrew Shriver. Andrew Shriver's step-brother, David Young, journeyed with him to Conewago and helped to clear three acres of ground, which they planted in corn, after which Young then returned home. During this clearing they lived under Young's wagon-cover, after which Andrew Shriver peeled elm-bark and made a temporary hut to keep off the weather, and by fall prepared a cabin. The wagon that brought him to this place passed through what is now known as "Wills' Bottom," and in the grass, which was as high as the wagon, left marks of its passage which were visible for several years. There was no opportunity of obtaining supplies for the first year short of "Steamer Mill," adjoining Lancaster. Shriver settled one hundred acres of land where he lived, but whether he squatted upon it or shortly after purchased is not known. It, however, cost him one hundred pair of negro shoes, this being the price agreed upon with Mr. Diggs, the owner, of whom he soon after purchased more land, which was paid for in money. At the time of his settlement in Conewago the nearest neighbor Andrew Shriver had was a family of the name of Forney, living where the town of Hanover now is. For a long time the public road from the south came by Andrew Shriver's house, and at the time of his settlement Indians surrounded him in every direction. About this period and for several years after, the Delaware and Catawba nations were at war; and each spring many warriors passed by after stopping at Andrew Shriver's water spring, a large flush limestone drinking-place, when they would display in triumph the scalps, hooped, painted, and suspended from a pole, which they had been able to obtain from the enemy. They demanded free quarters, but were very sociable, and smoked the pipe of friendship freely without any attempt at wanton injury. His brother Ludwig Shriver, David Young, Middlekunf, the Wills, and others followed in a few years and established a settlement. Ludwig Shriver's settlement must have been early, as he burned coal out of hickory-bark, and made the knife with which Andrew Shriver curried his leather, which was tanned in troughs cut out of large logs. Andrew Shriver's wife occasionally helped her husband in the tan-yard, and dressed deer-skins by night. Their son, David Shriver, wore deer-skin dressed as clothing, shirts excepted, until fifteen years old. Having but little cleared ground at this time, the stock was left to run at large in the woods; such as were wanted David, being the oldest child, had to collect every morning regularly, much to his discomfort; as the pea-vines and grass were nearly as high as himself, and covered with dew, they soon made his deer-skin dress so wet as to render it like unto his skin, adherent to his body. Deer and other game were at this time so abundant and destructive to grain-fields that hunting was necessary for self protection.

About 1685, John Ferree (or Verree) resided in the town of Lindau, not far from the Rhine, in the kingdom of France. His family consisted of himself, his wife, and six children,—three sons and three daughters. The names of the sons were Daniel, Philip, and John, and of the daughters, Catharine, Mary, and Jane. John Ferree, the father, was a silk weaver by trade, his religion Calvinistic, consequently he became one of the sufferers under the edict of Nantes. The Ferrees had no other resource left but flight, leaving behind them all their property except some trifling articles and some cash. They fled into Germany, not far from Strasburg, where they resided two years. On leaving France they were accompanied by a young man named Isaac Lefever, who stated to them that his family were nearly all or all put to death by the soldiers, but that he had escaped unhurt. He continued as one of the family until they arrived in America, and then married Catharine Ferree, one of the daughters, and from whom, as far as is known, all of the name of Lefever in this country have sprung. During their residence in Germany, John Ferree, the father, died, and it is singular that Mary Ferree, the widow, after she came to America, was not pleased to be called by any other name than that of Mary Warrinbuer, her maiden name. Whilst residing at Strasburg, hearing of a fine province called Pennsylvania, in North America, and that the proprietor, William Penn, lived in London, she set out for that city, determined, if she should receive sufficient encouragement from Penn, she would try to get to America. On her arrival in London she employed a person to conduct her to Penn's residence, and on their way her conductor pointed out to her Penn's carriage, which was just meeting them, and she being of a determined and persevering disposition, called to Penn, who stopped his carriage, and, being well acquainted with the French language, conversed with her freely.

Penn having learned the nature and object of her call, invited her into his carriage, as he was then on his way home. Penn told her he had an agent in Pennsylvania; that he would give her a recommendation to him, so that her business. he hoped, might be done to her satisfaction. They remained in London about six months, when a vessel sailed for North River (New York was then a small town), in which they took passage. On their arrival they moved up the river to a place called Esopus, where they remained about two years, and then moved to Philadelphia, and from thence to Piquea settlement, previous to which they had taken up three thousand acres of land. Before they sailed from London a variety of implements of husbandry were presented to them by Queen Anne, which they found to be of great use to them in cultivating and improving their lands. Philip, their oldest son, was now about twenty-one years of age, and evinced a desire to earn something for himself. Having formed acquaintance with several families of Esopus, he pushed for that place, where he lived for one year with a respectable farmer of the name of Abraham DuBois, and while in his service formed an attachment for Leah, the daughter of Mr. DuBois, whom at the expiration of the year he married and brought to his people in the Piquea settlement. There Philip and his wife commenced improving land on the north side of Piquea Creek, that had been previously taken up by his mother and family. Abraham DuBois, on May 17, 1717, took out a patent for one thousand acres in Lancaster County, Pa., which he subsequently gave to his daughter Leah. Their first labor was cutting grass in the woods for the purpose of making hay, no land having been cleared on that part allotted to them. They placed timbers in the ground, forked at the top, laid poles across them, and built their hay upon the *frame*, which served as a roof to their house, under which they lived for several months. During their stay in this rude shelter their son Abraham was born. They lived to raise eight children,—five sons and three daughters,—the names of the sons being Abraham, Isaac, Jacob, Philip, and Joel, and of the daughters, Lena, married to William Buffington; Leah, to Peter Baker; and Elizabeth, to Isaac Ferree. Abraham was married about 1735 or 1736 to a woman by the name of Elizabeth Eltinge, from Esopus, whose parents were Low Dutch. He lived on a part of the land taken up by his grandmother (Mary Ferree, or Warrinbuer) and her children. Their children were Cornelius, Israel, Rebecca, Rachel, Elizabeth, and Mary. Israel married a Miss Dickey, Cornelius settled in Virginia, and Rebecca married David Shriver. Abraham Ferree died at an advanced age, and was buried in a place now called Carpenter's graveyard, about one mile north of where he was born. This burial-place, near Paradise, was vested in trustees for the use of the settlement by Mary Ferree (Warrinbuer), who died in 1716, and was with several of her family interred in this graveyard. After Abraham's death his widow married one Curgus, and moved up the Susquehanna.

Sarah, daughter of Abraham Dubois, married Roeloff Ellsting, or Eltinge, who was therefore a brother-in-law to Philip Ferree.

It appears from a certain deed of partition (on record in Frederick County, Md.) made by sundry persons as devisees of Isaac Eltinge, dated April 18, 1771, that Isaac Eltinge was a resident of Frederick (now Montgomery) County anterior to March 13, 1756, the date of his last will and testament, and that he died without leaving issue, in which case he disposed of his estate in fee-simple to his sister Elizabeth (Eltinge) Ferree and the children of his sister Zachamintye Thompson. The will ordered it to be divided with three several parts, one of them to descend to his first-named sister, and the other two-thirds to the children of the last-named sister, namely, to William Thompson, Cornelius Thompson, John T. Thompson, and Ann McDonald. These appear to be the exclusive objects of the testator's bounty, but it is nevertheless known that he had one other sister, who married Isaac Hite, of Virginia. Of these sisters there are many descendants residing in Virginia.

Elizabeth Ferree had two sons and four daughters, viz.: Israel, Cornelius, Rebecca, Rachel, Elizabeth, and Mary. Israel married a Miss Dickey, by whom he had one son, who died without descendants. Cornelius married twice, and had a numerous family, who with himself emigrated to the Western country. Rachel resided near Bath, in Virginia, and was married to David Muskimmins. Elizabeth married William Miller. Mary first married a Mr. Graff, and on his decease Griffith Willett; and Rebecca married David Shriver. The latter couple continued to reside on their estate on Little Pipe Creek, in Carroll County, until their decease. They had nine children:

1. Andrew, born Nov. 7, 1762, married Dec. 31, 1786, to Elizabeth Shultz, of Baltimore, and died Sept. 20, 1847.
2. Elizabeth, born Nov. 23, 1764, died Feb. 18, 1766.
3. Rachel, born Jan. 7, 1767, married Adam Forney, of Hanover, Pa., and died Dec. 6, 1844.
4. David, born April 14, 1769, married Feb. 28, 1803.
5. Abraham, born May 5, 1771, married Feb. 18, 1803, and was for many years a judge of Frederick County Circuit Court.
6. Mary (Anna Maria?), born Nov. 29, 1773, and married John Schley, of Frederick City.
7. Isaac, born March 6, 1777, married April 22, 1802, and

died Dec. 22, 1856. His wife, Polly, born 1781, died March 1, 1859.

8. Jacob, born Dec. 13, 1779, died Oct. 15, 1841.

9. Susan (Susanna?), born Jan. 6, 1782, and married Samuel Frey, of Baltimore, Aug. 22, 1809.

In regard to Jacob Eltinge, it is not known whether he was father, brother, or son of the Eltinge family at the time of its settlement in Frederick County, or who the persons of the family were, further than is given in the deed above referred to. But it is evident that the settlement was at a very early date, and it is known to have adjoined the Potomac River at a time when much land along its banks was vacant, of which they secured considerable bodies by grants from the proprietary government. And from the manner in which the surveys were made, it would seem to have been anticipated that the navigation of that river would become highly improved, and that it would be controlled by running the lines of the tracts across the river, many of the tracts being thus located. It is known that the Eltinges migrated from New York, and that a number of the males fell victims to the bilious disease that prevailed with great malignity upon the banks of the Potomac. There were two branches of the Eltinge family in New York, one located with the New Paltz patentees in Ulster County, about sixteen miles from Kingston, the other at Kingston County. Of the latter, or Esopus family, some removed to New York City, some to Red Hook, in Dutchess County, and the others continued at Kingston.

The following is the history of the New Paltz branch: Two brothers, Josiah the elder and Noah the younger, were the patentees in the New Paltz patent, and had one sister, Zacamintye, who married in the Bivier family. Noah had no son, but one daughter, who married Dench Wynkoop and had two daughters. The eldest, Gurtyou Gitty, was married in the Colden family and left heirs. The youngest, Cornelia, was married to Isaac Eltinge, of the Kingston family, and left heirs. Zacamintye bore several sons and daughters. Josiah was married to Magdalena Dubois, and had four sons—Abraham, Ralp, Solomon, and Cornelius—and one daughter,—Cartrientye (Catharine). The latter married Jacobus Hardenbaugh, at Hurley, two miles from Kingston, and had one son—Jacobus—and three daughters,—Magdalena, Cartrientye, and Ann,—all of whom married and had heirs. Abraham was married in the Dubois family, and had five sons, viz.: Josiah, Noah, Philip, Henry, and Jacobus (who all had heirs), and two daughters, Jane and Magdalena, who left numerous progeny. Ralph married into the Lowe family, and had five sons, viz.: Josiah, Solomon, Ezekiel, John, and Ralph, and four daughters, viz.: Magdalena, Sarah, Catherine, and Mary, who all left descendants. The descendants of Ralph and Abraham lived about the New Paltz. Solomon married in the Vanderson family at Hurley, and had no heirs. Cornelius married in the Elmender family at Hurley, and had three sons, viz.: Wilhelms, Solomon, and Cornelius, and five daughters, viz.: Magdalena, Jane, Maria, Blandina, and Catharine, all of whom but Blandina married and left numerous offspring. The descendants of Cornelius and Cartrientye are settled at Hurley and Marbletown, near Kingston, excepting Cornelius and Wilhelms (descended from Cornelius), who were ministers and lived in New Jersey,—Cornelius in Sussex County, and Wilhelms at a point four miles from New York City, called Patterson Landing, whose Indian name was Unchquachinwick. Wilhelms had three children,—Cornelius Housman, Maria Blandina, and Jane Van Winkle. The eldest was married to Cornelius Van Winkle, and had a son, Wilhelms Eltinge. The New Paltz branch was probably more nearly related to the branch that settled on the Potomac, in Frederick County, Md., and in Virginia. Abraham, the eldest son of Josiah Eltinge, had land in an unsustained claim upon some of the tracts upon the Potomac as legal heir, and hence the inference is that Josiah, Noah, and Zacamintye were brothers and sister, either to Isaac Eltinge, resident of Frederick County (now Montgomery), and his sisters, Elizabeth Ferris, Zacamintye Thompson, and Mrs. John Hite, of Virginia, or they, Noah, etc., were brothers and sister to Abraham Eltinge, the father of Isaac and his sister.

Andrew Shriver, who came to America in 1721, when a boy nine years of age, with his parents, Andrew and Anna Margaretha Shriver, died Aug. 12, 1797, and was the grandson of Jost Shriver.

David Shriver, son of Andrew and Ann Maria (Keyser) Shriver, was born in York County, Pa., at Conewago, south of Hanover. His parents had been but a few years from Germany, and were recently married when they settled at that place in the woods surrounded by Indians. On account of his father's settlement on the frontier, remote from the centres of civilization, David Shriver, the first-born, grew up with scarcely any education, the opportunity and means being both wanting. The time of his minority was employed in aiding his father in his business of tanning and cultivating the soil. When he was twenty-one years of age he attracted the attention of Andrew Steiger, an enterprising business man and citizen of Baltimore. Mr. Steiger employed him as store-keeper in a country store, located not far from David's father. Here the want of education was immediately felt, and he so applied himself that in a short time he acquired a pretty good knowledge of figures. He also learned to write a fair hand, and otherwise improved himself in knowledge and address. At this time Lancaster, Pa., had become considerable of a town, and it was a custom there (continued to this day) to hold semi-annual fairs, which drew together vast numbers of people. At one of these fairs David Shriver first saw Rebecca Ferree, who had been sent to Lancaster to acquire a knowledge of ornamental needlework. He undertook to accompany her home, and was received with becoming respect by her father, but with much displeasure and indignity by her mother, who had imbibed high notions in consequence of the opulence and distinction enjoyed by her family in New York. Standing well, however, with the daughter and father, he persevered and succeeded in his suit. About 1759 or 1760, and previous to his marriage, which was in 1761, he had settled upon a tract of land provided for him at Little Pipe Creek, in Frederick County, Md. (now in Westminster District, Carroll County). The place of his location is the old "Shriver Homestead," some two miles southwest of Westminster, on Little Pipe Creek, where Copp's Branch joins it, now occupied by Mrs. Augustus Shriver, widow of a grandson of David. Here David had erected buildings and cleared land, and to this place he brought his wife. He then built a mill, which was of great importance to himself and neighbors at that early period when the settlement was in its infancy. Having experienced the want of education, he early sought to have his children taught, and for this purpose sent his eldest son abroad for some time, there being no school within reach of his home. His efforts were unceasing to promote education in the neighborhood, and he so far succeeded as to obtain for all his children a good English education. The community was much indebted to him for his exertions in this respect, and many persons afterwards enjoyed the receipt of useful knowledge which but for him they would not have acquired. Possessing an inquiring and discriminating mind, he added rapidly to his stock of information. As a self-taught mathematician, he made considerable advances, and was instructor to all his sons in the art of surveying, the compass and other instruments used being of his own manufacture. His mechanical talents were no less remarkable. He was carpenter, joiner, cooper, blacksmith, silversmith, combmaker, wheelwright; in short, he made everything that was wanting on the place, as well as the tools which occasion called for. He was, moreover, the umpire of the neighborhood in the settlement of controversies. Having a great aversion to lawsuits and litigation, he did much to preserve peace and harmony. His house was the resort of much company and the place where travelers regularly sought shelter and repose, and they were always received with kindness and hospitality.

The disputes between the colonies and the mother-country early attracted his attention, and he became an active and devoted Whig. So warm was he in the support of the rights of his country that his friends were alarmed for his safety, and his pastor emphatically warned him to beware, as the powers placed over him were of God, and that he would be hung for treason to Great Britain and his family made beggars. He treated the admonition with marked contempt, and persevered in taking an active part on the Committees of Vigilance and Public Safety and rousing his countrymen to vindicate their rights. He was in consequence elected a member of the Convention of 1776 to frame a constitution for the State of Maryland, and was afterwards continued, with the exception of a year or two, a member of one or the other branches of the Legislature for about thirty years, until the infirmities of age admonished him of the propriety of retirement. At the time of his death he had an estate valued at seventy thousand dollars. When he was married his wife's parents gave her a negro girl, from whom sprang a numerous progeny, more than forty in number, of whom about thirty remained in his possession at the time of his death, and whom he liberated by will. In the same instrument he divided his estate equitably among his children and provided for the inclosure of a family burial-ground, where his remains, those of his wife, and some of his children repose. He had two brothers and four sisters,—the former were Andrew and Jacob, of whom Andrew continued to reside on the home plantation and raised a large family. Jacob removed to Littlestown, Pa., and had one son, who died young, and his father passed away shortly afterwards. The four sisters married Henry and George Koontz, John Kitzmiller, and Jacob Will. They all lived to an old age within a few miles of their father and reared large families, except the wife of George Koontz, who had but three or four children and died in early life. David Shriver died Jan. 29 (or 30), 1826, aged ninety years and nine months. He was the oldest of his brothers and sisters, and survived them all.

His wife, Rebecca (Ferree) Shriver, was a noble Christian woman, of rare domestic qualities, and withal finely educated for the early pioneer days in which she grew up to womanhood. She was the oldest of her family. The home plantation being large enough for two places was divided between her brothers, Cornelius and Israel. The latter with his family having died, the former afterwards sold the places and went West. Rebecca Shriver died Nov. 24, 1812, aged seventy years, ten months, and three days.

Mordecai Gist, so distinguished in the Revolutionary struggle, was a son of Capt. Thomas Gist and Susan Cockey, and was born in Baltimore Town, Feb. 22, 1742. He was educated at St. Paul's Parish School, Baltimore City, and at the breaking out of the Revolution was a merchant doing business on Gay Street. The Gists were early emigrants to Maryland, and took an active part in the affairs of the province. Christopher Gist was of English descent, and died in Baltimore County in 1691. His wife was Edith Cromwell, who died in 1694. They had one child, Richard, who was surveyor of the Western Shore, and was one of the commissioners in 1729 for laying off Baltimore Town, and was presiding magistrate in 1736. In 1705 he married Zipporah Murray. Christopher Gist, one of his sons, because of his knowledge of the country on the Ohio and his skill in dealing with the Indians, was chosen to accompany Washington on his mission in 1753, and it was from his journal that all subsequent historians derive their account of that expedition. Christopher Gist, the son of Richard, married Sarah Howard, the second daughter of Joshua and Joanna O'Carroll Howard, and had four children,—Nancy, who died unmarried, and Thomas, Nathaniel, and Richard. Christopher, with his sons Nathaniel and Richard, was with Braddock on the fatal field of Monongahela, and for his services received a grant of twelve thousand acres of land from the King of England. It is said that Thomas Gist was taken prisoner at Braddock's defeat, and lived sixteen years with the Indians in Canada. Richard married and settled in South Carolina, and was killed at the battle of King's Mountain. He has descendants yet living in that State. Thomas, after his release from captivity, lived with his father on the grants in Kentucky, and became a man of note, presiding in the courts till his death, about 1786. Gen. Nathaniel Gist married Judith Carey Bell, of Buckingham County, Va., a grandniece of Archibald Carey, the mover of the Bill of Rights in the Virginia House of Burgesses. Nathaniel was a colonel in the Virginia Line during the Revolutionary war, and died early in the present century at an old age. He left two sons,—Henry Carey and Thomas Cecil Gist. His eldest daughter, Sarah Howard, married the Hon. Jesse Bledsoe, a United States senator from Kentucky, and a distinguished jurist, whose grandson, B. Gratz Brown, was the Democratic candidate for Vice-President in 1872. The second daughter of Gen. Nathaniel Gist, Anne (Nancy), married Col. Nathaniel Hart, a brother of Mrs. Henry Clay. The third daughter married Dr. Boswell, of Lexington, Ky. The fourth daughter, Eliza Violetta Howard Gist, married Hon. Francis P. Blair, and they were the parents of Hon. Montgomery Blair, ex-Postmaster-General, and Gen. Francis P. Blair, Jr. The fifth daughter married Benjamin Gratz, of Lexington, Ky. Mordecai Gist was a member of the Baltimore Town non-importation committee in 1774, and in December of the same year was captain of the first company raised in Maryland. He was three times married. His first wife was a Miss Carman, of Baltimore County, who died shortly after marriage. His second was Miss Sterrett, of Baltimore, who died in giving birth to a son. His third was Mrs. Cattell, of South Carolina. She also bore him a son. One of the boys was named "Independent," the other "States." Gen. Mordecai Gist died at Charleston, S. C., Aug. 2, 1792.

GEN. MORDECAI GIST.

On Jan. 1, 1776, the Maryland Convention appointed Mordecai Gist second major of Col. Smallwood's First Maryland Battalion. In the battle on Long Island, in August, 1776, the Maryland regiment, not numbering more than four hundred and fifty, was commanded by Maj. Gist, as Col. Smallwood and Lieut.-Col. Ware were in New York attending the court-martial of Lieut.-Col. Zedwitz. On Washington's retreat through New Jersey, Maj. Gist's Marylanders were reduced to one hundred and ninety effective men, who with Lord Stirling's and Gen. Adam Stephen's brigades covered the retreat. Maj. Gist's (formerly Smallwood's) regiment, on Dec. 1, 1776, re-enlisted for three years. In February, 1777, Gen. Smallwood sent Col. Mordecai Gist with a detachment against the Somerset and Worcester County Tories and insurgents, who were put to flight, many captured, and the others forced into obedience by his stern measures, and the disaffection quieted by overawing and quelling the insurgents. The battle of Brandywine was fought Sept. 11, 1777, when Col. Gist was at home attending his sick wife, but on learning of its disastrous termination, by a special express he instantly rejoined the army with reinforcements collected at home. In May, 1779, when Maryland was threatened with British invasion, on the application of its Governor, Col. Gist was ordered to that State, and assumed command of its defenses. Gen. DeKalb, who died on the third day after he was wounded, near Camden, S. C. (Aug. 16, 1780), in his last moments dictated letters to Gens. Gist and Smallwood expressive of his affection for them and their men, who had so nobly stood by him in that deadly battle. In this battle DeKalb led a bayonet charge with Col. Gist's Second Maryland Brigade, drove the division under Rawdon, took fifty prisoners, but fell exhausted after receiving eleven wounds. Congress voted thanks to Gens. Gist and Smallwood and their men. In June, 1781, Gen. Gist joined Lafayette's army on the march to Yorktown with the Maryland levies. On Nov. 21, 1783, at a meeting of the officers of the Maryland Line to form a State Society of the Cincinnati, Gen. Otho H. Williams presided, and Lieut.-Col. Eccleston was secretary. Maj.-Gen. Wm. Smallwood was made permanent president; Brig.-Gen. Mordecai Gist, vice-president; Col. Nathaniel Ramsey, treasurer; and Brig.-Gen. Otho H. Williams, secretary.

Joshua Gist, one of the early settlers in Carroll County, was a brother of Gen. Mordecai Gist, and was born in Baltimore Town, Oct. 16, 1743. His parents were Capt. Thomas and Susan (Cockey) Gist. His grandfather was Richard Gist, son of Christopher, the emigrant. During the administration of John Adams, near the close of the last century (1794), an excise duty was laid on stills. This created what was then known as the "Whisky Insurrection" by those opposed to the tax. The rebellion became so formidable, particularly in Western Pennsylvania, that Washington, at the request of President Adams, took the field in person as commander of the forces raised to suppress it. The excitement extended to what is now Carroll County, and the "Whisky Boys" marched in a band into Westminster and set up a liberty-pole. The people of the town became alarmed and sent out for Col. Joshua Gist, who then commanded a regiment of the militia. The colonel, who was known to be a brave man, mounted his horse, rode into town, drew his sword, ordered the pole to be cut down, and placing his foot on it, it was cut to pieces, when the Boys left. He died Nov. 17, 1839, aged ninety-one years, one month, and one day.

The Gist family graveyard in Carroll County contains the graves of the following members of the family:

Col. Joshua Gist, died Nov. 17, 1839, aged 91 years, 1 month, and 1 day.

Harriet Dorsey, wife of Nicholas Dorsey, and daughter of Col. Joshua Gist, died June 25, 1804, aged 74 years and 18 days.

Sarah (Harvey) Gist, wife of Col. Joshua Gist, died June 6, 1827, aged 72 years, 7 months, and 4 days.

Sarah (Gist), wife of Lewis A. Beatty, died March 30th, in her 27th year.

Rachel, wife of Independent Gist, died May 2, 1830, aged 50 years, 1 month, and 15 days.

Independent, son of Gen. Mordecai Gist, died Sept. 16, 1821.

Richard Gist, died Aug. 6, 1844, aged 23 years.

Mary G., wife of States Lingan Gist, and daughter of States Gist, of Charleston, S. C., died Feb. 8, 1847, aged 30 years.

Bradford Porcher Gist, born May 28, 1842, died Jan 2, 1865. He was a soldier of the Union, and died from disease contracted while a prisoner.

Richard Milton, infant son of Mordecai and Elizabeth (Orndorff) Gist, died Sept. 13, 1871.

Maggie, only child of George W. and Mary Owings, died Sept. 21, 1863, aged 3 years, 1 month, and 8 days.

Elizabeth (Gist), wife of Joseph Woods, born June 8, 1844, died Dec. 3, 1873; and her daughter, Mary, died Oct. 15, 1877, aged 3 years, 4 months, and 26 days.

Rachel, infant daughter of Mordecai and Elizabeth (Orndorff) Gist, died 1873.

The Gists were of English descent, and took an active part in the affairs of the province. Christopher Gist married Edith Cromwell, sister of Richard Cromwell, a son or brother of Oliver Cromwell. Christopher Gist died in Baltimore County in 1691, and his wife, Edith, in 1694. Their only child, Richard Gist, married Zipporah Murray, by whom he had three sons—Christopher, Nathaniel, and Thomas—and four daughters,—Edith, Ruth, Sarah, and Jemima. Christopher married Sarah Howard, Edith was married to Abraham Vaughan, Ruth to William Lewis, Sarah to John Kennedy, and Jemima to Mr. Seabrook. Thomas Gist married, July 2, 1735, Miss Susannah Cockey, daughter of John and Elizabeth Cockey, by whom the following children were born:

1, Elizabeth, born Dec. 24, 1736; 2, John, Nov. 22, 1738; 3, Thomas, March 30, 1741; 4, Gen. Mordecai Gist, Feb. 22, 1742; 5, Richard, Nov. 1, 1745; 6, Joshua, Oct. 16, 1746; 7, Rachel, Sept. 17, 1750; and, 8, David, April 29, 1753.

Thomas Gist died May 24, 1787, aged seventy-four years and nine months, and his children died as follows: Elizabeth, March 6, 1826; John, July 16, 1800; Thomas, Nov. 22, 1813; Gen. Mordecai Gist, Sept. 12, 1792; Richard, Nov. 1746 (an infant); Rachel, Sept. 8, 1825; Joshua, Nov. 17, 1839; and David, Aug. 3, 1820. Of these, as we have stated, Gen. Mordecai Gist first married a Mrs. Carman, of Baltimore County, who died shortly after marriage; his second wife was Miss Sterrett, of Baltimore, who died Jan. 8, 1779, in giving birth to a son (Independent); and his third wife was Mrs. Cattell, of South Carolina, who bore him a son named States. These were his only children.

Col. Joshua Gist, son of Thomas and Susannah (Cockey) Gist, and brother of Gen. Mordecai Gist, married, March 21, 1772, Sarah Harvey, who was born Nov. 2, 1755, and died June 2, 1827. Their children were:

1. Anna, born Feb. 24, 1774, died Aug. 26, 1790.
2. James Harvey, born Dec. 29, 1775, died Dec. 7, 1823.
3. Susannah, born March 21, 1778, married Joshua Jones, and died Oct. 8, 1817.
4. Rachel, born March 17, 1780, died May 2, 1830.
5. Mordecai, born June 20, 1782.
6. Polly Julia, born June 3, 1784.
7. Thomas, born April 1, 1786.
8. Sarah, born June 17, 1788, married Lewis A. Beatty, and died March 31, 1815.
9. Harriet, born June 7, 1790, married Nicholas Darsey, and died June 25, 1864.
10. Joshua Cockey, born Sept. 15, 1792, died March 27, 1878.
11. George Washington, born Dec. 18, 1795, died Nov. 20, 1854.
12. Federal Ann Bonaparte, born Aug. 14, 1791, and is the only one surviving of the above twelve children.

Independent Gist, eldest son of Gen. Mordecai Gist, married, Jan. 8, 1807, Rachel Gist, daughter of Col. Joshua Gist, his own cousin. He died Sept. 16, 1821, and his wife May 2, 1830. Their children were:

1. Mary Sterrett, born Sept. 1, 1808, and living.
2. Joshua Thomas, born Sept. 15, 1810, and living.
3. States Lingan, born July 31, 1812, died Nov. 9, 1879.
4. Mordecai, born Oct. 16, 1814, and living.
5. Independent, born Aug. 15, 1816, died June 29, 1859.
6. George Washington, born July 10, 1819, fought in the Union army under Gen. Sheridan in late war, and still living.
7. Richard, born Sept. 1, 1821, died Aug. 6, 1844.

Of the above children, States Lingan married Mary G. Gist, June 13, 1836, who died Feb. 8, 1847. Their children were:

1. Mary, born April 7, 1837.
2. Mordecai Joseph, born May 29, 1838.
3. Independent, born June 10, 1840.
4. Bradford Porcher, born May 28, 1842, died Jan 2, 1860.
5. Elizabeth Sarah, born June 8, 1844, married Joseph Woods, and died Dec. 3, 1873.
6. Richard Joshua, born Sept. 14, 1845, died July 21, 1864.

States Gist, second and youngest son of Gen. Mordecai Gist, married Sarah Branford Porcher and lived in Charleston, S. C.

The subject of this sketch, Mordecai Gist, son of Independent Gist, and grandson of Gen. Mordecai Gist, was born Oct. 16, 1814, in Frederick County, four miles from Taneytown. After his father's death, when but two years of age, his mother removed to Western Run, in Carroll County, and when he was about sixteen years old his mother moved to the farm on which he now resides, then the property of her father, Col. Joshua Cockey. Col. Cockey before the Revolution, about 1765, had removed from Baltimore Town and entered or purchased two tracts of land containing about four hundred acres. He built a log

MORDECAI GIST.

house which burned down in 1795, when he erected part of the present mansion. He subsequently made an addition to it, as did afterwards Mordecai Gist, the present owner. Part of these lands belonged to the tract known as "Fell's Dale," patented to Edward Fell in 1742. Mordecai Gist was educated in the old brick school-house still standing in Westminster in the cemetery near the "Old Union Meeting-House." Among his teachers were Mr. White and Charles W. Webster. His place now consists of one hundred and eighty acres of land, lying a mile and a half south of Westminster, on which he has resided for the past sixteen years.

He was married Nov. 7, 1848, to Elizabeth, daughter of Joseph and Mary (Byers) Orndorff, by whom he has had the following children:

Joseph Independent, born Nov. 18, 1850, and married, March 5, 1878, to Debbie F. Nelson.

Rachel, born Dec. 28, 1852, died Jan. 2, 1853.

Harriet Ann, born April 27, 1854, and married to Silas H. Gaitskill, Oct. 4, 1876.

Joshua, born Nov. 22, 1856, and married to Susie E. Naill, Nov. 7, 1878.

William Mordecai, born Aug. 10, 1859.

Mary Alverda, born March, 1862.

George Washington, born Sept. 27, 1864.

Robert, born July 24, 1868.

Richard Milton, born Nov. 24, 1870, died Sept. 13, 1871.

Mr. Gist is one of the best practical farmers in the county, and pays special attention to dairying, selling his milk, save in the winter, when it is made into butter. He belongs to the Methodist Episcopal Church, and for thirty-five years has been a member of Carroll Division, No. 42, Sons of Temperance. During the late civil war he was a strong supporter of the Union. In his spacious parlor hang elegant oil-portraits of his paternal and maternal grandfathers, Gen. Mordecai Gist and Col. Joshua Gist, with their wives. While Gen. Gist, of the Maryland line, was fighting the British in many battles, his brother, Col. Joshua Gist, was effectively sustaining the Continental cause at home, holding the Tories in check by his bold measures, which made him the terror of the disaffected and the idol of the Revolutionary Whigs.

The Van Bibbers were an ancient Holland family, its progenitor in this country being a Capt. Isaac Van Bibber, a native of Amsterdam, who came to America in command of a vessel belonging to Lord Baltimore's fleet, and settled in Cecil County, Md. From him descended Isaac Van Bibber, a native of Bohemia Manor in that county, who very early located in what is now Baltimore County, and was a famous sea-captain and voyageur, owning the ship he commanded. He married a Chew, of Philadelphia. His son, Washington Van Bibber, born in Baltimore, was one of the defenders of that city in 1814. He became an extensive farmer in Westminster District, and owned part of the old Leigh Master estate, Avondale, where the Master furnace was established in 1762 to 1765. The Van Bibbers were members of the Protestant Episcopal Church, and "Ascension church" in Westminster was largely built by their contributions and active support. His son, Dr. Washington Chew Van Bibber, was born near Avondale, July 24, 1824, and married, in 1848, Josephine, youngest daughter of Dr. Peter Chatard, an eminent physician of Baltimore. His success and ability in the medical profession of Baltimore, where over a third of a century he has been in practice, places him alongside of the most honored of its members.

St. Benjamin's (Kreiger's) Union Lutheran and Reformed Church, the joint place of worship of the Lutheran and Reformed congregations, was organized in 1763. On April 14, 1763, the members of each congregation entered into articles of agreement to build a church. Those signing it on the part of the Reformed denomination were Jost Runkel, Valentine Maurrer, Benedict Schwob, Daniel Zacharias (the four elders), David Shriver (there signed as *Devault Schrieber*), Peter Bender, Jacob Cassel, Henry Neff, Jacob Heldenbeidel, Henry Warman, Valentine Bast, F. T. Dreyer, Valentine Fleigel, Peter Kraul, John Greyder (afterwards corrupted into *Kreider*), Daniel Kober.

In 1763 was erected the first church, a story and a half log structure, which stood until 1807, when the present building, a two-story brick structure of ancient architecture, was erected on the same site. It was built on a tract of land called "Brown's Delight." The first four baptisms were in 1763, by Rev. William Otterbein, a German Reformed missionary of Baltimore, who for six years previous had been traveling through Frederick County (of which this section was then a part) preaching and holding religious services. The four children baptized were those of John Greyder (Kreider), viz.: John Peter (born May 25, 1754), John, Jacob, and Elizabeth. On May 8, 1766, this pioneer church had thirty-six communicants, nearly all heads of families. It is located on the Gettysburg turnpike, on the left side going from Westminster, and a mile and a half from that town. Its first Reformed preacher was the Rev. Jacob Lichey, and Rev. Jacob Wiestling was pastor before 1813. Since 1819 its pastors have been:

1819–41, Jacob Geiger; 1842–44, William Philips; 1844——, John G. Wolf; William F. Colliflower, W. Wissler, John W. Hoffmeier; 1868–76, William C. Cremer; 1876–82, J. G. Noss.

Adjoining the church is perhaps the oldest burying-ground in the county, which is still in an excellent state of preservation. It was laid out in 1763, in which year the first interments were made in its grounds. The inscriptions on the earliest stones are in German, and for about the first thirty years are illegible, owing to the corrosion of time. The dates of the births and deaths of many here buried are given:

John Schweigart, born in Berks County, Pa., Dec. 2, 1785, died Jan. 30, 1853.

Christian Schweigart, born in March, 1762, died June, 1846; and his wife, Dorothy, born Dec. 6, 1763, died Dec. 10, 1838.

Jacob Marker, born March 11, 1786, died Dec. 8, 1879; and his wife, Catharine, born Dec. 26, 1797, died Feb. 5, 1859.

Mary Myerly, born June 1, 1792, died Jan. 8, 1817.

Jacob Grammer, died March 13, 1815, aged 66.

Johannes Schnauffer, born Nov. 13, 1752, died Sept. 3, 1776; and his wife, Christina, born in 1756, died Oct. 15, 1818.

John Diffenbough, born Nov. 24, 1766, died April 16, 1814; and his wife, Eve Catharine, born Sept. 22, 1766, died April 26, 1842.

Catharine Klein, born Dec. 1, 1760, died May 19, 1819.

Larnice Farmwalt, born March 9, 1743, died July 8, 1807.

Susanna, wife of George Zacharias, and daughter of Conrad Sherman, born April 2, 1786, died Feb. 5, 1852.

William H. Editor (editor of *American Sentinel* many years), died Jan. 11, 1862, aged 39.

Jacob Schaeffer, died Feb. 2, 1854, aged 70; and Susan, his wife, born March 24, 1781, died March 28, 1852.

John Schaeffer, born June 11, 1755, died March 11, 1828; and his wife, Mary, born Sept. 5, 1765, died May 12, 1831.

Mary Magdalene, wife of Abraham Kurtz, born Nov. 5, 1783, died Dec. 8, 1827.

Jacob Utz, Sr., died Nov. 5, 1826, aged 61.

Jacob Utz, Jr., died Aug. 1, 1826, aged 27.

Jacob Henry, born March 15, 1791, died May 22, 1861.

George Henry, born Feb. 25, 1791, died Sept. 30, 1860; and his wife, Margaret, born Jan. 20, 1781, died Feb. 5, 1858.

George Crowl, born Oct. 26, 1795, died Feb. 4, 1865; and his wife, Rebecca, born Jan. 1, 1798, died July 29, 1862.

Hannah, wife of Michael Sullivan, born July 23, 1790, died Nov. 5, 1840.

Peter Lantz, died Nov. 22, 1840, aged 70.

Anna Maria Keller, wife of Jacob Keller, died Aug. 1, 1841, aged 79.

Elizabeth Krise, born July 20, 1781, died Oct. 24, 1850.

Micajah Stansbury, died July 14, 1858, aged 85; and his wife, Mary M., Nov. 18, 1861, aged 78.

James Beggs, born in County Antrim, and Parish Carulla, Ireland, 1752, died Feb. 12, 1829.

John Beggs (native of same place), died Feb. 28, 1875, aged 71.

Andrew Reese, died April 14, 1794, aged 84; and his wife, Barbara, Sept. 15, 1794, aged 71.

Frederick Boyers, born Oct. 10, 1781, died Feb. 26, 1815.

Barbara Angel, daughter of John Schaeffer, born March 10, 1786 (married to Frederick Boyers, 1807, by whom she had three sons and two daughters; married to Andrew Angel, 1816, by whom she had six children), died Jan. 18, 1832.

Jacob Flickinger, born July 25, 1742, died June 17, 1807; and his wife, Barbara, born July 25, 1745, died aged 73 years.

John Reese, born Jan. 26, 1793, died March 5, 1858; and his wife, Susan, died Nov. 30, 1875, aged 67.

Cornelius Sullivan, died 1816, aged 67; and his wife, Catherine, born 1753, died 1824.

David Sullivan, born June 1, 1788, died aged 25.

Margaret Everly, born 1743, died March 3, 1814.

Daniel Zacharias, born April 6, 1777, died April 24, 1813.

George Peter Rinehart, born Oct. 13, 1787, died May 1, 1845.

Mary Kuhn, died July 18, 1811.

George Daniel Zacharias, died Aug. 24, 1807, aged 61.

Jacob Schaeffer, born Feb. 6, 1723, died February, 1800.

Wesleyan Methodist Episcopal Church (colored) is one and a half miles from Westminster, due west, and its pastor in 1881 was Rev. R. J. Williams.

In the cemetery adjoining are buried

Jesse Cromwell, died Feb. 28, 1874, aged 74.

Ann Hays, died July 2, 1880, aged 78.

D. Woodward, aged 85.

Rebecca Cross, born Sept. 5, 1818, died Feb. 15, 1858.

Maria Buchanan, died Dec. 31, 1869, aged 75.

Dinah Smith, aged 78.

The following graves, among others, are found in the German Baptist cemetery, situated in Westminster District, between Westminster and Frizzelberg:

Polly Roop, born May 29, 1808, died Feb. 1, 1811.

Sarah, wife of Israel P. Haines, died July 11, 1835, aged 35 years, 3 months.

Catharine, wife of John Roop, Sr., died Dec. 17, 1837, aged 61 years, 4 months, 10 days.

John Roop, born Nov. 12, 1770, died June 24, 1852.

Ann R., wife of Jacob Petry, born Nov. 4, 1829, died Feb. 5, 1859.

John Roop, died Sept. 1, 1868, aged 58 years, 2 months, 24 days.

Lydia, his wife, died Feb. 4, 1879, aged 61 years, 6 months, 21 days.

Rebecca Reese, died Oct. 16, 1872, aged 68 years, 11 months, 18 days.

Chas. B. Stoner, died Oct. 26, 1878, aged 22 years, 8 months, 11 days.

Lovina, his wife, died, aged 17 years, 11 months, 9 days.

David Roop, born Dec. 21, 1795, died Nov. 19, 1878.

Mary, wife of Abraham Cassell, born April 5, 1822, died July 28, 1879.

Abraham Cassell, died Aug. 30, 1877, aged 60 years, 1 month, 3 days.

David Petry, born Feb. 25, 1821, died Aug. 16, 1878.

Peter Benedict, born May 1, 1797, died Feb. 12, 1859.

John Hoffman, died April 25, 1823, aged 80 years.

Dolly, his wife, born May 23, 1755, died Sept. 4, 1818.

Isaac Kurtz, born Sept. 27, 1811, died March 22, 1831.

Richard Belt, died March 28, 1865, aged 57 years, 2 months, 21 days.

Anna C. Miller, died Sept. 2, 1862, aged 32 years, 8 months, 15 days.

John P. Kauffman, born May 31, 1818, died Jan. 10, 1872.

Margaret, wife of George Kauffman, born March 13, 1776, died Sept. 2, 1858.

Louisa, wife of Peter Myers, born April 5, 1769, died Aug. 20, 1858.

Anna A. Miller, died Jan. 3, 1857, aged 22.

J. G. Miller, died Feb. 28, 1863, aged 29 years, 1 month, 20 days.

Mary, wife of John N. Harman, died April 18, 1865, aged 50 years, 3 days.

Elizabeth Diffenbough, died April 18, 1868, aged 60 years, 11 months, 14 days.

George Decker, born Jan. 11, 1794, died Dec. 30, 1872.

Eli G. Butler, died April 4, 1880, aged 63 years.

Sarah Routson, died March 19, 1878, aged 88 years, 7 months, 19 days.

Frederick Tawney, died Dec. 29, 1871, aged 53 years, 8 months, 23 days.

Catherine, wife of R. Beggs, died Nov. 5, 1877, aged 56 years, 2 months, 24 days.

Rebecca, wife of Samuel Myers, born June 12, 1793, died March 19, 1863.

Elmira F. Tawney, born May 5, 1815, died Oct. 9, 1861.

George Harman, born May 28, 1783, died March 11, 1858.

Eliza Harman, born April 8, 1814, died Nov. 11, 1860.

Lucinda Royer, born May 5, 1820, died May 28, 1840.

Peter Royer, born Aug. 17, 1775, died July 22, 1842.

Anna, his wife, died Jan. 7, 1858, aged 83 years, 6 months, 26 days.

Anna Weybright, died Dec. 17, 1855, aged 52 years, 1 month, 2 days.

Mary, daughter of Peter and Ann Royer, wife and widow respectively of Jacob Mering and John Burgord, died Jan. 21, 1879, aged 73 years.

John Royer, died Oct. 22, 1865, aged 52 years, 9 months, 10 days.

Amos M. Royer, died Oct. 27, 1865, aged 27 years, 7 months, 21 days.

Christian Royer, died March 11, 1870, aged 70 years, 14 days.

Louisa, wife of David Englar, died Sept. 29, 1870, aged 59 years, 9 months, 2 days.

Polly Schaeffer, born Sept. 27, 1792, died Jan. 2, 1880.

Elizabeth Schaeffer, born Feb. 6, 1795, died March 15, 1880.

Catharine Schneffer, died December, 1878, aged 81 years, 6 months, 10 days.

David, son of Jehu and Margaret Royer, "who was wounded in the battle of the Wilderness, Virginia, May 5, 1864, and died in the morning of the following day," aged 20 years, 7 months, 4 days.

Catharine, wife of John Wentz, born Sept. 28, 1848, died March 9, 1880.

Isaac Myers, born Aug. 20, 1797, died Jan. 2, 1880.

David Myers, born Dec. 27, 1802, died Jan. 23, 1879.

Lewis Myers, died Aug. 2, 1876, aged 66 years, 3 months, 28 days.

Mary A., his wife, died Dec. 2, 1873, aged 53 years, 11 months, 27 days.

Michael Petry, Sr., died April 25, 1857, aged 59 years, 6 months, 26 days.

Mary, wife of C. Albert Sproudon, died Nov. 19, 1865, aged 48 years, 2 months, 8 days.

John Tawney, died Jan. 18, 1862, aged 76.

Elizabeth, his wife, born Jan. 11, 1781, died May 1, 1863.

Nancy, wife of Francis Matthias, born Aug. 19, 1796, died May 10, 1866.

Mary Piper, died Dec. 31, 1866, aged 40.

Larkin McGomas, died May 10, 1848, aged 40.

Louisa Gearing, died March 6, 1878, aged 55 years, 9 months, 26 days.

Henry Williams, born Dec. 20, 1824, died Dec. 22, 1853.

Mary L. Jones, died May 30, 1874, aged 79.

That portion of Western Maryland now known as Carroll County is filled with legends and romances, but none is remembered so well by the oldest inhabitant, or believed in so firmly by the superstitious, as "The Ghost of Furnace Hills." Leigh Master came to this country from New Hall, Lancashire, England, in the early part of the eighteenth century. He was then quite a young man, full of enterprise and energy, and had come to "the new country" for the purpose of unearthing the hidden treasures and making a fortune therefrom. No place presented more promising inducements than that portion of Maryland situated a few miles west of Westminster. When Leigh Master took possession of the Furnace Hill property, now known as "Avondale," and owned by Thomas E. Van Bibber, he set to work to build furnaces and dig out the ore which he found in such profusion. Hence the name of "Furnace Hills." He not only owned a furnace, but also large tracts of land, some five or six thousand acres, about Avondale, New Windsor, Linwood, and Pipe Creek. He owned at one time the following tracts of land:

	Acres.
Long Valley, containing	101
Part of Arnold's Chance	506
Wilson's Delight	49
Indian's War	100
Jack's Purchase	50
Part of Cobb's Choice	50
Beauty Spot	30
Part of Edward's Fancy	21
Red Bud	21
Narrow Bottom	21
Part of Bond's Meadow, enlarged	110
Part of Bottom and Top	50
Part of Content	
Part of Wilson's Chance and Mistake	18¼
Part of Gabriel's Choice	80
Part of York Company's Defense	1000
Firelock	14
Part of Brown's Plague and Mine Bank	11¼
Neglect	65¼
Cold Evening's Stone Quarry	25
The Increase	5¼
Hug me Snug	10¾
Discovery	50
The Parable	5½
Strawberry Mead	12½
The Oblique Angled Triangle	1½
Leigh Castle	2686
The Resurvey on Look About	1443¼
Stoney Hollow	

He was a man of means and an enterprising citizen, and also aspired at one time, in 1786, to represent Frederick County in the State Legislature, but he was not successful as a politician. He was rather "inclinable," to use the expressive word of that day, to the British side of public affairs, which was not the popular side at that time. He owned considerable mountain land, and old Ben Biggs used to tell a queer story about his wrapping himself up in a white sheet and going through the woods at night, crying, "Stick, stuck," which scared a great many timid people, and secured for him an unsavory reputation. He was a great wag. One poor fellow, a little superstitious, in going through a woods from a neighbor's house, with a long pole balanced over his shoulders and hung full of shad and herring, ran against Master's ghost, and hearing his voice shouting "Stick, stuck," was so frightened at the strange apparition that he took to his heels, and dropped all his fish on the ground in his rapid flight, hallooing to his old woman, as he came in sight of the house, for God's sake to open the door, as Leigh Master's ghost was after him.

Much of his land was surveyed and recorded in the old books of Frederick County Court in the days before the Revolution, and during the reign of George III., when John Darnall was clerk and George Scott sheriff.

He employed a number of hands, bought negroes to work the furnaces and plantation, and in a short time the mines were in a promising condition, and the name of Leigh Master was known throughout the country. Among the slaves who worked the furnaces at "Furnace Hills" was one "Sam," an object of special dislike to his master, the owner of the property. From what cause his violent dislike sprang tradition does not tell, but Sam disappeared very mysteriously one dark night, when the furnaces were in full blast, and from that time Leigh Master was never known to mention his name. Years rolled by, and after a long life he died, on the morning of the 22d day of March,

1796, in the eightieth year of his age. In all probability his name would have perished also but for the vague rumors concerning the sudden and mysterious disappearance of the ill-fated negro, and the strange scenes and extraordinary sounds which followed so closely upon his death, accounts of which have been handed down from father to son through all these years, and have probably gathered strength in their travels. Suspicions of a desperate deed committed by Leigh Master during his lifetime began to be whispered about, and old men remembered, or thought they did, a scared and haunted look in his eyes, which they attributed to the constant dread of the discovery of his miserable secret. And thus the rumor spread, gathering as it went, until it was told that Leigh Master had taken the life of his despised slave, and had cast him into the furnace, that he might hide all traces of his crime.

To show that people were at least as superstitious in those days as at the present time the following unique fable is given: One dark night as a workman was returning home from a neighbor's house, he heard a rustling, hurried sound at the edge of the woods skirting the Furnace Hill, and in an instant Leigh Master rode past him, crying and begging for mercy upon his miserable soul. The terror-stricken man was rooted to the spot, and stood trembling like a leaf, when suddenly the vision appeared the second time, urging his horse to its utmost speed, while the rattling of chains and horrible groans were heard in the distance. A third time the spirit of Leigh Master appeared with agony on its face, and a third time the noises were heard. Thus night after night strange sounds and scenes were witnessed in the furnace woods. Sometimes the spirit was followed by three little imps carrying lanterns, and creeping stealthily along as if in search of some object. Sometimes Leigh Master would appear at one portion of the hill, as if he was seeking to hide something, but always on a gray horse, emitting flames and smoke from his nostrils.

And thus the story passed from mouth to mouth, till at length the sound of human footsteps in the haunted woods was a thing unknown after nightfall, and the ghosts held undisputed possession.

Whether Leigh Master got tired of roaming around, or whether the three little imps found what they were seeking, is not known; but the ghosts of Furnace Hill disappeared with the furnaces and the superstition of the people, and nothing is left now but an old gray stone, marking the resting-place of the once famous owner of Furnace Hill, and bearing the following inscription:

"Leigh Master, Esquire,
late of
New Hall, Lancashire,
England,
Died the 22d day of March,
1796.
Aged 79 years."

In 1876, Rev. Isaac L. Nicholson, Jr., of the P. E. Church (Ascension), had the remains of Mr. Master removed to the parish cemetery at Westminster. He was a member of a notable English family, but a roving disposition forced him to leave his native home in early life and migrate to America. The ruins of the furnace are still standing. To Master is attributed the unfortunate introduction of the white blossom, or daisy, into this country, the bane of farmers to this day. It is related that he sent to the old country for English clover-seed, and that this daisy-seed was sent him by mistake, and that he sowed the seed far and wide before the irretrievable error was discovered. They are known as "Caroline pinks," or "Leigh Master's clover," in the neighborhood where he lived. Some of the descendants of the Master family are still living in England, among them Rev. Charles Shreyusham, Vicar of Wiltshire, Salisbury.

The tradition as to Leigh Master's slave and his imagined untimely taking off only obtained credence with the ignorant and superstitious, for careful investigation shows that while Leigh Master was a rough man in manners,—no uncommon thing in early days,—he was an honest, charitable, and public-spirited citizen, and the very soul of honor and manliness. He left by will all his Carroll County real estate to his son Charles, living in England (where his mother had died before her husband, Leigh Master, came to America), with this condition precedent, that he became a naturalized citizen of the United States. Charles came to Maryland, sold this realty, and returned to England without ever becoming a naturalized citizen of this country. Though often threatened, the will of Leigh Master has never as yet been disturbed by litigation.

The death of August Shriver, which occurred July 28, 1872, was quite sudden, and a severe shock to his numerous relatives and friends. Mr. Shriver occupied the position of president of the Western Maryland Railroad in the early stages of its history, and contributed much to the building of the road by his efficient management. At the time of his death he was president of the First National Bank of Westminster, which office he had filled with great credit since its establishment. He dispensed unbounded hospitality at his mansion in Carroll County, and his heartfelt courtesy and suavity made him many friends.

He was well known in Baltimore by reason of his banking connections. He was president of the Carroll County Agricultural Society, and a successful farmer on a large scale. The news of his death caused much regret, not only in the community in which he lived, but also in other portions of the State, where he was well known. His public spirit and usefulness were exhibited in many undertakings in which he was concerned, and his death caused a loss in this respect which was widely felt. In all his acts he elicited the confidence and esteem of those who were brought into association with him, and he enjoyed the reputation of a worthy gentleman and a faithful and efficient officer. At various periods of his life he filled a number of positions of importance, in all of which he gave entire satisfaction to those whose interests were in his charge. Faithfulness in the discharge of duty and an unswerving adherence to correct principles were the leading characteristics of a more than ordinarily successful life.

The Hon. Jacob Pouder died Sunday, Feb. 13, 1870, at his residence near Westminster, in the seventy-eighth year of his age. Mr. Pouder had filled many prominent positions in his native county, and was much respected for his gentlemanly demeanor and courtesy towards all with whom he had business transactions. At the time of his death he was the chief judge of the Orphans' Court of Carroll County, a position which he filled with great satisfaction to the people. He was on several occasions a member of the State Legislature.

The Spring Mills Lead-Mine is on the property of John T. Hill, one mile south of Westminster, on the Western Maryland Railroad. Mr. Hill discovered the deposits in March, 1878. The ore is said to be very rich, assaying about eighty-five to ninety per cent. Upon the same property has also been discovered a good quality of iron ore, the vein being from twenty to thirty feet in width. Gilberg & Lilly, of Philadelphia, in 1879, leased the mineral right to this property, and explored it to learn its real value in lead and iron. An engine from the Taylor Manufacturing Company was taken to the scene of operations, and is used in hoisting out ore and draining the mines.

John C. Frizell, of Westminster, had several springs on his estate which he supposed contained medicinal properties, as a number of his friends had derived considerable benefit from the use of the water, and at their suggestion he had it analyzed. The water had also been highly recommended by physicians as anti-dyspeptic. During the first part of July, 1870, he placed some of the water in the hands of Prof. William E. Aiken, of the University of Maryland, Baltimore, who sent him the following analysis:

"UNIVERSITY OF MARYLAND,
"July 7, 1870.

"JOHN C. FRIZELL:

"*My dear Sir*,—I have just completed the qualitative analysis of the sample of mineral water you sent me, and herewith send results: a gallon of water contains 15.76 grains of saline matter. This quantity, taken in connection with the character of salts present, will fully entitle the water to the name of a mineral water. The contents of the water are

"Hydrochloric acid.
Sulphuric acid.
Carbonic acid.
Silicic acid, of the last a trace.
Lime.
Magnesia.
Soda.
Iron.
Alumina, a trace.
Organic vegetable matter.

"The above substances, arranged in their order of the well-known combinations, may be considered as representing the following compounds, which give the mineral character and medicinal value of the water:

"Bicarbonate of lime.
Bicarbonate of magnesia.
Bicarbonate of iron.
Sulphate of lime.
Sulphate of soda.
Sulphate of magnesia.
Chloride of sodium.
Alumina, }
Silicic acid, } of each a trace.
Organic vegetable matter, }

"Respectfully, etc.,
"WILLIAM E. AIKEN.

"P.S.—The copious deposit that falls when the matter stands for a time consists almost wholly of oxide of iron."

Westminster, the commercial centre of the district, is the county-seat of Carroll County, and contained in 1880 a population of 2507 inhabitants. Though not the oldest it is the largest and most important town in the county. It is situated on Parr's Ridge, at the head-waters of the Patapsco, about thirty-three miles from Baltimore. The town was laid out in 1764 by William Winchester, and the principal street was called King Street, showing that at the time it was founded its proprietor was loyal to the mother-country. William Winchester was born in London, England, Dec. 22, 1710. He came to America and settled in Maryland, March 6, 1729, and married Lydia Richards, July 22, 1747. He died Sept. 2, 1790. The town was first named Winchester, in honor of its founder, but the name was subsequently changed by an act of the General Assembly to Westminster because of the number of towns bearing the same name, notably Winchester in Virginia, which was a source of endless confusion. As it now stands Westminster is built on six different tracts of land. The east end, or original Winchester, is on the tract known as "White's Level," granted to John White in 1733, for 169½ acres. The west end is on the tract called "Fanny's Meadow," granted to James Walls in 1741. A portion of the town is on "Bond's Meadow," granted to John Ridgley in 1753, for 1915 acres. "Timber Ridge" and "Bedford," the latter Winter's addition, form the site of a part of Westminster; "Kelley's Range" takes in the Western Maryland College grounds, and "Bond's Meadow Enlarged" covers the ground upon which the court-house stands. Its situation on the main turnpike from Baltimore to the West gave the town great advantages in early days. Long trains of wagons were constantly passing back and forth, all of which selected Westminster as a favorite halting-place for rest and refreshment, and the town, what there was of it, probably presented a more animated and business-like appearance then than now. Business methods have undergone such a complete transformation since then that no just comparison can be instituted.

The Westminster of to-day is very interesting. It is perhaps the longest city for its width in America, which is mainly due to its early location along the pike, the great highway of travel, and the anxiety of those who had business interests to place themselves in direct communication with the unceasing trade and travel encountered at that point. The surroundings of the city are exceedingly picturesque. The view from College Hill is very fine. A beautiful, undulating country spreads out for many miles, and on very clear days the eye can take in an expanse of territory stretching from the Potomac to the Susquehanna. The population of the town is now 2507, with a number of handsome church edifices, at least forty stores, three banks, a college, and several large manufactories and warehouses. Some of the older residences in Westminster, handsome in themselves, possess that mellow tint so attractive to persons of taste, and which time alone can give, while those recently built are embodiments of the culture and refinement of their owners. The country in the vicinity is well watered by the Patapsco and other streams, which furnish abundant power for manufacturing purposes. It is a very healthy, rich, and productive agricultural region. The Western Maryland Railroad passes directly through the centre of the town, and the numerous trains passing over the road leave nothing to be desired in the way of communication with distant points.

Iron and copper ore abound in large deposits, and are successfully mined and shipped to Pennsylvania and New York. Quarries containing the finest varieties of marble have been opened, and are worked in the vicinity. The town contains the usual number of county buildings, commodious, and well adapted to the purposes for which they were erected.

The Western Maryland College, a fine four-story brick building, is located upon the highest site around the town, and is admirably arranged for educational purposes. The *Democratic Advocate* building, corner of Main and Centre Streets, forty by eighty feet, is a fair exhibit of the enterprise and energy of the conductor of this sterling journal.

The I. O. O. F. Hall is an imposing structure, and on its first floor is the large and elegantly-arranged office of *The American Sentinel*, the Republican organ of the county.

Among the earliest settlers up to the year 1800 were the Winchesters (William and his sons), the Fishers (John and David), McHaffies, Wamplers, Harners, Stansburys (Caleb, Sr. and Jr., and Joshua), John Miller, Andrew Reese, Sr., Ulerick Eckler, Mordecai Price, Jacob Feterling, Jacob Pouder, John McComb, Jacob Sherman, Isaac Shriver, Nimrod Frizzell, Jacob Crouse, Jacob Righter, Thomas Ward, Joseph Shreev, Jacob Fringer, the Yinglings, the Neffs, Adelspergers, Lockards, Smiths, Dells. The oldest house standing in town is that occupied by Peggy Adelsperger. It is a log structure on Main Street, nearly opposite the "City Hotel," and was erected between 1777 and 1780. It is yet a substantial dwelling, comfortable and neat. Her sister Elizabeth died a few years ago. Their parents, Thomas and Betsey, went to this old house to live after their marriage, about a century ago.

The oldest living person in town is William Crouse, who was born in Myers District in 1792, but came to Westminster in 1794 with his parents, and has resided here ever since. He and his wife (Catharine Shaeffer, aged eighty-three years) have lived in happy wedlock sixty-three years, since Feb. 15, 1818. His father, Jacob Crouse, was one of the first blacksmiths here, succeeding a Mr. Myers, whom he bought out in 1794. He was born Oct. 30, 1766, and died Jan. 1, 1846, and his wife, Elizabeth, born in 1773, died Sept. 12, 1820. About the first storekeeper was David Fisher, and after him Mr. Yingling, and then a Mr. Utz. The earliest schoolmaster remembered was Mr. Gynn, who held forth with an iron rule on the plat where Charles T. Reifsnider now resides. Jacob Sherman, who was born in Lancaster County, Pa., March 7, 1756, and married Elizabeth Wagner, Feb. 23, 1779, kept the first hotel or tavern, where the City Hotel is now, until 1807, when he was succeeded by Isaac Shriver. He died July 7, 1822, but his widow survived till June 28, 1842. Afterwards, taverns were kept by Mr. Winterow and Mr. Wampler. Jacob Wolf at an early period manufactured clocks, many of which are still in use over the country. When Westminster was made the county-seat of the new (Carroll) county in 1837, the town had about five hundred inhabitants, but immediately thereafter it began to increase in population and business. It received its greatest impetus, however, upon the completion of the Western Maryland Railroad to its limits. New additions were made and new streets laid out to accommodate the increasing population and the wants of trade and awakened enterprise.

The following legend of early days in Westminster is well authenticated : " Many years ago, in the northwestern part of Maryland, there stood a little village bearing the proud English name of Winchester, now the beautiful city of Westminster. For a long time peace and plenty had smiled upon its inhabitants, and they dreamed not of coming evil. It was in the midst of summer when God saw fit to send a mighty drought upon the land. For many days the scorching rays of the sun looked down upon the earth, burning and blighting the vegetation, and threatening to bring famine upon its track. Flowers drooped and died, and water—one of God's best and most necessary gifts to man—began to fail. In vain the people prayed and cried for rain. The citizens of Winchester became alarmed, and many of them locked their pumps, and refused even a cooling drink to the thirsty traveler or the famished beast, lest they should not have enough for themselves. Near the eastern end of the village dwelt two maiden ladies, aged and respected, who believed God would not forsake them in their time of need. Unlike their neighbors they did not refuse water to any, but unlocking their gate, placed a placard near the well bearing the following words, 'Free admittance to all,—water belongs to God!' In those ancient days railroads were unknown, and all traveling was done by stages or wagons. Emigrants were seen passing daily on their road to the great West, and the demand for water was constant. The doubting citizens advised these two Christian ladies to tear down their notice and close the entrance to prevent the water being carried away, or they would be left without, but their answer was always the same, 'The Lord is our Shepherd, we shall not want. We have no right to refuse, for water belongs to God.' Soon all the wells and springs in the village began to fail, and only two remained to supply the demands of the famishing citizens. One of these was the well which had been free to all. The other belonged to an old gentleman, who, as soon as he saw how great was the demand for water, guarded it and refused even a drop. All flocked to 'God's Well,' as it was now called, and its old-fashioned moss-covered bucket was never idle. And still the sky was cloudless, and the unrelenting rays of a July sun scorched and burned the earth. A few more days passed, and he who had so cruelly refused to give a cup of cold water from his plenteous store was obliged to go and beg for himself from the unfailing fountain of 'God's Well.' The demand on this well became greater day by day, but still its sparkling waters refreshed the thirsty traveler and the famishing beast. At length a small dark cloud was seen in the sky, and how eagerly it was watched! Larger and larger it grew, till at last the whole sky was overcast. The thunder pealed, the lightning flashed through the heavens, and the floodgates were opened. The clouds rolled away, and once more the whole face of nature smiled, and the grateful citizens of Winchester thanked God for the glorious rain, which had come just in time to save them from perishing. Time has passed rapidly, leaving many traces of its flight. Little Winchester is now a promising and thriving city, bearing the name of Westminster. The two noble-hearted Christian ladies, who in the time of need trusted in the Lord and shared with their suffering neighbors, have long since found their reward in heaven. Their old home has been torn down, but the 'well' still remains on the old lot of Mrs. Col. James M. Shellman, and though now covered over and out of repair, has never been known to fail, but to this day is filled with excellent, pure water."

The elegant mansion of Mrs. James M. Shellman on Main Street, opposite the City Hotel, was built in 1807 by Col. Jacob Sherman. He gave it to his daughter, the wife of David H. Shriver, who subsequently removed to Wheeling, W. Va. Col. Sherman was a native of Lancaster County, Pa. He was born March 7, 1756, and married Elizabeth Wagner, Feb. 23, 1779. He died July 7, 1822, and his wife, June 28, 1842. His son-in-law, David H. Shriver, who occupied the house in Westminster, was born April 14, 1769, and married Miss Sherman, Feb. 28, 1803.

Mrs. Shellman, the owner of this mansion and the old well to which reference is made, is a great-granddaughter of Philip Jones, Jr., who surveyed and, with three commissioners, laid out Baltimore Town in 1730. He was born in Wales, Oct. 25, 1701, and came to this country about 1720. Oct. 2, 1727, he married Annie Ratteenbury, whose ancestors came from the Isle of Wight in 1624 and settled in Virginia. They had nine children, all of whom died young except Thomas and Hannah. Hannah married William Worthington, of Maryland. Philip Jones, Jr., died Dec. 22, 1761, aged sixty years, three months, and six days. His widow became the second wife of John Eager, and died shortly after her marriage. Thomas, the only surviving son of Philip Jones, Jr., was the first register of wills of Baltimore, and afterwards became judge of the Court of Appeals. He married Elizabeth McClure, widow of David McClure, of Carlisle, Pa. He had three sons and three daughters. The oldest daughter married Maj. Beall, of the United States army; the second married Mr. Dallam, of Harford County, and the third Mr. Schley, of Baltimore. While on a visit to his daughter, Mrs. Beall, at Fort McHenry, Judge Jones was taken ill and died, Sept. 27, 1812, aged seventy-seven years. Of his three sons, Harry, the youngest, remained a bachelor. Thomas married and lived in Patapsco Neck. He had ten children, one daughter being Mrs. William Fenby, living near Westminster.

Philip also married, and lived for some time on his farm, "Gallipot," Baltimore County. He was one of the Old Defenders of Baltimore in the war of 1812. He came to Westminster in 1818, where he lived until within a few days of his death, and where he was one of the first merchants. He had ten children, one of whom is Mrs. James M. Shellman. The old Jones homestead in Patapsco Neck is still standing in a state of good preservation; has broad halls, large rooms, and very high ceilings. It is surrounded by magnificent walnut-trees, which gives the name of "Walnut Grove" to the place, and has a lawn running to the bank of the Patapsco River. It has always been in the possession of the Jones family, having been granted by royal patent through Lord Baltimore. This patent is still held by the family at "Walnut Grove," which is at present occupied by John T. Jones, two sisters and a brother, children of Thomas, and great-grandchildren of Philip Jones, Jr., surveyor of Baltimore Town.

When the Confederates under Maj. Harry Gilmor and Gen. Bradley T. Johnson made a raid into Westminster in 1864, they occupied Mrs. Shellman's mansion as their headquarters, and when Gen. J. E. B. Stuart was here with his command he caught up and carried in his front through town, on the saddle, Miss Mary M. Shellman, then a little lass, but the bravest Union girl of the place.

About the first year of this century Dr. Umbaugh practiced his profession in Westminster. He was a German physician of note, and rode over a vast territory to see his patients. After his location here Dr. Beringheit came, and remained several years. Dr. George Colgate died May 1, 1822, in the prime of life and a martyr to the noble profession he adorned. Dr. William Willis was, on the organization of the county, made the first clerk of the court in April, 1837, and was succeeded by Dr. William A. Matthias. The oldest physician here (if not in the county) is Dr. James L. Billingslea. He was born in Abingdon, Harford Co., in 1804. He was first educated in the common schools, then attended the Belair Academy, and afterwards St. Mary's College, Baltimore, where he completed his classical studies. He graduated in medicine at the University of Maryland in 1827, and located the same year in the practice of his profession at Uniontown, in Carroll County. He remained there twenty years, and then removed to Baltimore. He subsequently settled at Long Green, in Baltimore County, where he practiced for ten years, and in 1860 he came to Westminster and continued the practice of his profession for many years, but has now retired. He was in the State Senate from 1864 to 1867. He married Susan Harris, of Frederick County, in 1832, of the Society of Friends, for his first wife, and in 1867, Elizabeth Cove for his second wife. When he came to Westminster, in 1860, the physicians here were Drs. J. L. Warfield (now of Baltimore), Matthias, and J. W. Hering. The latter is still in practice, and is also cashier of Union National Bank. Dr. Frank T. Shaw has been clerk of the court since 1873.

The Corporation and Officers.—The General Assembly incorporated the town of Westminster by an act passed April 6, 1839, supplementary to the first act of Feb. 14, 1830, enacting that the adjoining towns, then called and known by the names of Westminster, New London, Winter's Addition, and New Elenburgh, together with Pigman's Addition, and all that space lying between Winter's Addition and Pigman's Addition, should forever thereafter be called and known by the name of Westminster. This act provided for the election on the first Monday in May of a burgess and five commissioners, and for annual elections of said officers thereafter. The act designated Andrew Pouder, Jacob Yingling, and Michael Barnitz as the judges to hold the first election.

By the act of Feb. 28, 1850, the town was erected into a city, and Michael Barnitz, Horatio Price, and Otho Shipley appointed judges to hold the first election under the city charter. The city limits were thus established:

"Beginning on the southeast at a stone planted near the Baltimore and Reisterstown turnpike, formerly a boundary stone between Baltimore and Frederick Counties, and running northeasterly at a right angle with said turnpike four hundred yards; thence westerly and northerly, and running parallel with the course of said turnpike, and four hundred yards therefrom, to the line of Adam Gilbert's land, located at or near a public road leading from said turnpike to Abraham Wampler's mill; thence westerly and southerly with the outlines of said Gilbert's lands to a point four hundred yards southwest of the turnpike leading from Westminster to Uniontown; thence easterly and southerly and parallel with the last turnpike and the aforesaid Baltimore and Reisterstown turnpike, and four hundred yards from each, to the line formerly dividing Baltimore and Frederick Counties; and thence with the last line to the place of beginning."

The following persons have been elected to the office of burgess and mayor:

Burgess.—1839, James M. Shellman; 1840, William Shipley, Jr.; 1841–44, George Trumlo; 1844, David Keiffer.

Mayor.—1850, Dr. Elisha D. Payne; 1851, Abner Neal; 1852, Jacob Grow; 1853–58, R. R. Booth; 1859, John M. Yingling; 1860, Samuel L. Swanstead; 1861–64, Michael Baughman: 1864, Jacob Grove; 1865, Emanuel Gernand; 1866, Hashabiah Haines; 1867, A. Reese Durbin; 1868, David Fowble; 1869–71, Jacob Knipple; 1871, David H. Leister; 1872, Henry H. Herbaugh; 1873, E. K. Gernand; 1874–76, David Fowble; 1876–82, P. H. Irwin.

The other officers are given as far as the corporation records show them:

1860.—Jacob Shaffer, Levi Evans, Michael Baughman (president), Reuben Cassell, Joshua W. Hering; Clerk, Otho Shipley.

1861.—Joshua Yingling, Henry Warner, William Reese, Samuel Myers, Wm. H. Grammer; Clerk, Otho Shipley.

1862.—George F. Webster, Joshua Yingling, Henry Warner, Samuel Myers, Denton Gehr; Clerk, Thomas J. Lockard.

1863.—Samuel L. Myers, Henry Warner, Edwin K. Gernand, Asbury F. Sharer, Joshua Yingling; Clerk, Thomas J. Lockard.

1864.—E. K. Gernand, S. L. Myers, J. Yingling, Jeremiah Yingling, Ira E. Crouse; Clerk, Thomas J. Lockard.

1865.—George Webster, Wm. H. Harman, F. R. Buell, John W. Gorsuch, David Fowble; Clerk, Thomas J. Lockard.

1866.—F. A. Shearer, E. K. Gernand, A. R. Durbin, W. A. Cunningham; Clerk, Albert Billingslea.

1867.—John H. Yingling, W. A. Cunningham, E. K. Gernand, J. H. Bowers, F. A. Shearer; Clerk, C. J. Yingling; Bailiff and Collector, G. W. Sullivan; Counselor, J. E. Pearson, Sr.

1868.—J. W. Perkins, M. B. Mikesell, G. W. Matthews, George S. Fouke, S. P. Everhart; Clerks, J. A. Dillar, P. B. Mikesell; Treasurer, Dr. George S. Fouke; Counselor, E. F. Crout.

1869.—George E. Wampler, David Wentz, John Bernstine, Elias Yingling, W. H. Harmans; Clerk, W. L. W. Seabrook; Collectors, William Baker, George Stouck.

1870.—John Bernstine, G. W. Matthews, J. W. Perkins, D. H. Leister, Joseph Woods; Clerks, W. L. W. Seabrook, W. H. Bidenhover.

1871.—J. W. Perkins, Samuel Everhart, Jeremiah Yingling, William Yingling, Dr. Francis Butler.

1872.—H. E. Morelock, Reuben Cassell, A. Shearer, Jesse Yingling, W. H. Harman; Clerk, L. F. Byers.

1873.—Henry Vanderford, Joshua Yingling, Edward Lynch, Elias Yingling, J. W. Hering; Clerk, George M. Parke.

1874.—E. O. Grimes, George M. Parke, William Lawyer, H. E. Morelock, James Rippard; Clerk, W. H. Rippard.

1875.—Henry E. Morelock, E. O. Grimes, William Lawyer, James Rippard, George M. Parke; Clerk, W. H. Rippard; Treasurer, E. O. Grimes; Counsel, J. M. Parke; Bailiff, Israel Zieber.

1876.—N. J. Gorsuch, William B. Thomas, Jesse Yingling, G. W. Sullivan, J. W. Perkins; Clerk, John Matthews.

1877.—N. J. Gorsuch, J. W. Perkins, W. B. Thomas, G. W. Sullivan, Jesse Yingling; Clerk, John Matthews.

1878.—Same board as for two previous years; Clerk, John Matthews.

1879.—W. B. Thomas, E. J. Lawyer, G. W. Sullivan, Orlando Reese, N. J. Gorsuch; Clerk, John Matthews.

1880.—Same board and clerk.

1881.—Same board; Clerk, C. H. Baughman; Bailiff, Street Commissioner, and Collector, Israel Zieber; Counsel, Joseph M. Parke; Council Committees: Streets, W. B. Thomas, O. Reese; Gas, G. W. Sullivan, N. J. Gorsuch; Finance, W. B. Thomas, N. J. Gorsuch.

Western Maryland College is located in the city of Westminster, on the line of the Western Maryland Railroad, about midway between the cities of Baltimore and Hagerstown.

The buildings stand on a commanding eminence at the "West End," overlooking the city and many miles of the surrounding country. The main building is five stories high, and affords ample accommodations for chapel, recitation-rooms, halls for the societies, professors' apartments, and dormitories. The grounds belonging to the college contain eight acres, allowing sufficient range for the exercise of students during the time not allotted to study. The institution is conducted on a modern basis. Young men and women are entered under the same corps of professors and instructors, enjoying all the advantages extended by the college. The course of study, however, is not precisely the same for both sexes, the young ladies completing theirs in three years, and the gentlemen graduating in four, although both sexes have the same instructors; the two departments are kept entirely separate, the sexes meeting only at chapel service and in the dining-room with members of the faculty.

The Western Maryland College was established under the auspices of the Maryland Annual Conference of the Methodist Protestant Church. A charter was obtained for the institution from the Legislature of Maryland in 1864, which contemplated its establishment in the city of Baltimore, but subsequent events led to the selection of Westminster as the site of the new college, and a more favorable location could scarcely have been chosen. In 1866, Rev. James Thomas Ward purchased a homestead in Westminster, which being made known to Rev. Rhesa Scott Norris, negotiations were entered into which resulted in a meeting between Fayette R. Buell, the original projector, and J. T. Ward. The

Conference of that year gave in its adhesion to the plan for making Westminster the place for the establishment of the enterprise, and an appeal was made to friends for money to erect suitable buildings. The responses were neither numerous nor large, and a loan was obtained from John Smith and Isaac C. Paile, which enabled F. R. Buell to commence building on the site he had purchased. The first stone of the building was laid Aug. 27, 1866, and the corner-stone was laid Sept. 6, 1866, by Door to Virtue Lodge, No. 46, A. F. A. M., in the presence of a large number of citizens of Westminster and friends from other places. At the session of the Maryland Annual Conference in March, 1867, an advisory board of directors was appointed, as follows: Revs. J. T. Ward, J. J. Murray, D. Bowers, P. L. Wilson, and R. Scott Norris, and on the part of the laity, J. W. Herring, John Smith, M. Baughman, A. Zollickoffer, John S. Repp, and Samuel McKinstry. This board in July announced F. R. Buell as proprietor of the college, and J. T. Ward principal of the faculty. College exercises were begun Sept. 4, 1867, and continued regularly thereafter. Some difficulty of a financial character was experienced in 1868, but the friends of the institution came forward and relieved the embarrassment, and a second charter was obtained from the Legislature, placing the college under the direction of a board of trustees. John Smith was elected president of the board, J. T. Ward, secretary, and J. W. Herring, treasurer. It was determined at their first meeting to purchase the property from F. R. Buell for twenty thousand dollars. The Conference in March, 1869, at the suggestion of J. T. Ward, appointed Rev. P. Light Wilson agent of the association on behalf of the college. During this year the female students formed the "Browning Literary Society," whose first anniversary was celebrated during commencement week, June 14, 1869. The career of the college since then has been prosperous and useful. In June, 1871, the first college degrees were conferred upon a class of four young men and three young girls. On the 19th of July, 1871, the first stone of the foundation of an additional building was laid, rendered necessary by the increased patronage of the college. In January, 1870, the State Legislature granted an appropriation out of the academic fund for Carroll County for the free tuition of one student from each election district in the county, and in 1878 an appropriation was made by the General Assembly of Maryland, enabling the college to furnish board, fuel, lights, washing, tuition, and the use of books free to one student, male or female, from each senatorial district of the State. This appropriation was continued by the Legislature of 1880. During the twelve years of its existence the college has had an average attendance of 116 pupils, 73 of whom were males and 43 females. There have been altogether under its care and training 1509 pupils, of whom 950 were males and 559 females. They have pursued the various branches of an English and classical education. Of this number 94 have been graduated with the degree of A.B., and 45 have studied with a view to the Christian ministry. The faculty of the male department is as follows:

Rev. J. T. Ward, D.D., President, Professor of Mental and Moral Science; Rev. H. C. Cushing, A.M., Vice-President, Professor of Belles-Lettres; R. L. Brockett, A.M., Professor of Physical Science and the French Language; Rev. James W. Reese, A.M., Ph.D., Professor of Ancient Languages and Literature; G. W. Devilbiss, A.M., Professor of Belles-Lettres; D. W. Herring, C.E., Professor of Mathematics; Charles T. Wright, Principal of Preparatory Department, and Professor of German Language; Rev. Augustus Webster, D.D., Professor of Theology; J. W. Herring, M.D., Lecturer on Anatomy, Physiology, and Hygiene; R. B. Norment, Esq., Lecturer on Civil Law and Political Economy; DeWitt C. Ingle, A.B., Tutor in Latin, Greek, and Mathematics.

Female Faculty.—Rev. J. T. Ward, D.D., President, Professor of Moral and Mental Science; Rev. H. C. Cushing, A.M., Vice-President, Professor of Belles-Lettres (resigned); Miss Lottie A. Owings, Preceptress of Female Department, and Teacher of Ornamental Branches; R. L. Brockett, A.M., Professor of Physical Science and the French Language; Rev. James W. Reese, A.M., Ph.D., Professor of Ancient Languages and Literature; G. W. Devilbiss, A.M., Professor of Belles-Lettres; D. W. Herring, C.E., Professor of Mathematics; J. W. Herring, M.D., Lecturer on Anatomy, Physiology, and Hygiene; Charles T. Wright, Professor of the German Language; Mrs. S. F. Jones, Teacher of Vocal and Instrumental Music.

List of Graduates.

Class of 1871: Mrs. Imogene L. Mitter Ensor, Charles H. Baughman, Mrs. Mary M. Ward Lewis, Rev. Thomas O. Crouse, A.M., Anna R. Yingling, William S. Crouse, A.M., Henry E. Norris, A.M., M.D.

Class of 1872: Lizzie B. Adams, Mary E. Johnson, Mrs. Annie Price Hoe, Annie G. Ridgely, H. Dorsey Newson, William P. Wright.

Class of 1873: Alice A. Fenby, Mary N. Nichols, Mrs. Clara Smith Billingslea, Ida T. Williams, B. Franklin Crouse, A.M., Joseph B. Galloway, A.M., M.D., Frank W. Shriver, Truman C. Smith, LL.B., Thomas B. Ward.

Class of 1874: Annie W. Birckhead, Janie M. Bratt, A.M., May Brockett, A.M., Mrs. Louisa D. Hooper James, Mrs. M. Emma Jones Willis, Mollie E. Jones, Mrs. Julia A. Lens Fowler, Sarah L. Whiteside, Rev. Charles S. Arnett, A.M., James A. Diffenbaugh, A.M., Rev. Philip T. Hall, A.M., George B. Harris, Samuel R. Harris, Philemon B. Hopper, A.M., William Hogg, Rev. Walter W. White, A.M.

Class of 1875: Ida Armstrong, George W. Devilbiss, A.M., Rev. Thomas H. Lewis.

Class of 1876: Drucilla Ballard, Mrs. Laura A. Edie Devilbiss, Laura K. Matthews, Mrs. Mary A. Miller Hering, Maggie E. Rinehart, Martha Smith, Louis L. Billingslea, A.M., LL.B., Richard B. Norment, Jr., A.M., M.D.

J. T. Ward

Class of 1877: Florence M. Devilbiss, Alice E. Earnest, M. Ada Starr, M. Virginia Starr, Maggie E. Woods, Lilian N. Young, Winfield S. Amoss, A.M., LL.B., C. Berry Cushing, A.M., LL.B., Wilson R. Cushing, Thomas J. Wilson.

Class of 1878: Lulu E. Fleming, Mamie V. Swornstedt, Alice V. Wilson, De Witt Clinton Ingle, J. Weldon Miles, Frank H. Peterson.

Class of 1879: Mollie J. Lankford, Mamie M. McKinstry, Mary Rinehart, Clara L. Smith, Lizzie Trump, Lou B. Wampler.

Class of 1880: Lizzie L. Hodges, Linnie C. Kilmer, M. Emma Selby, Florence E. Wilson, Edward S. Baile, William H. DeFord, Lewis A. Jarman, Rev. Frederick C. Klein, William R. McDaniel, Joseph W. Smith.

Class of 1881: Hattie Ballinger, Bettie Braly, Loulie Cunningham, M. Kate Goodhand, Hattie V. Holliday, Bessie Miller, H. May Nicodemus, Katie M. Smith, Laura F. Stalmaker, George Y. Everhart, J. Fletcher Somers, George W. Todd.

James Thomas Ward, the president of the Western Maryland College, was born in Georgetown, D. C., Aug. 21, 1820. His father, Ulysses Ward, born near Rockville, Montgomery Co., Md., April 3, 1792, being the youngest of eight children of John Ward (born in London, England, Aug. 1, O. S., 1747) and Mary Ann Eustatia (maiden name Forbes), born in London, Jan. 1, 1752, who came to America in 1770, and settled first in Prince George's Co., Md., whence they removed to Montgomery County in 1776. The ancestors of John Ward had resided during the sixteenth and seventeenth centuries in Yorkshire, England, being farmers by occupation. About the beginning of the eighteenth century the branch of the family from which he more immediately descended removed to London. On the mother's side the ancestors of Mr. Ward were of Scottish origin. Ulysses Ward, his father, was married Sept. 26, 1816, to Susan Valinda Beall, daughter of James Beall, (died 1821), son of James Beall, of the same family with George Beall, one of the first settlers of Georgetown, D. C., and son of Ninian Beall, who emigrated from Scotland towards the close of the eighteenth century, and died in Maryland at the great age of one hundred and seven years. Of the seven children of Ulysses and Susan Valinda Ward, James Thomas was the second. At the time of his birth his mother was a member of the Protestant Episcopal, and his father of the Methodist Episcopal, Church, which latter his mother also subsequently joined, and by a minister of which (the Rev. John Davis) he was baptized. His parents then resided in Georgetown, as before intimated, and continued there until the spring of 1822, when they removed to Prince George's County, and thence, after a brief stay in Georgetown, to Washington City, April, 1826, which became their permanent place of residence until the death of the father, March 30, 1868, in the seventy-sixth year of his age. Ulysses Ward was a most industrious, enterprising, and useful man. As a local preacher in the Methodist Church he became quite popular because of his earnest labors. He was extensively known as a business man: first as a master-workman in his trade, and afterwards as a merchant, and, when he had acquired wealth, as a benefactor in church and city by the judicious and liberal bestowment of his means. In the schools of Washington Mr. Ward received his first lessons in the common branches of an English education, his principal instructors being the well-known John McLeod and Joseph H. Wheat. The advantages thus afforded during the week-days were supplemented by excellent home training, and on the Sabbath by the teachings imparted in the Sabbath-school. Thomas from his infancy had been feeble physically. He gained knowledge rapidly, and was scarcely beyond the period of childhood when he made a public profession of his faith in Christ, and developed a fondness for learning and usefulness. At the age of sixteen he entered the Classical Academy of Brookville, in Montgomery County, Md., at that time under the superintendence of Elisha J. Hall, where he had fine opportunities, which were so well improved that when he left for home, in 1838, he bore with him the classical prize. He returned to Washington, and for a time was employed in business with his father, in the mean time devoting much of his time to study, and taking a deep interest in the Sabbath-school work. Still, he had no definite purpose of a professional career.

In the summer of 1840 he decided to consecrate his life to the work of the gospel ministry. In his preparations for this work he studied under the advice and counsel of Rev. A. A. Lipscomb and Rev. A. Webster. His parents were now, and had been since 1832, connected with the then recently organized church known as the Methodist Protestant. In this church he began his career as a preacher of the gospel, being licensed Aug 30, 1840, by the Ninth Street Methodist Protestant Church, of Washington City. After preaching in various places for many months, he was called to serve a church in the eastern part of the city until the meeting of the Maryland Annual Conference in the spring of 1841. The session of that Conference was held in the city of Philadelphia, in the Methodist Protestant church there which had been organized by the Rev. Thomas H. Stockton, and of which Mr. Ward became years after the pastor, succeeding that distinguished and eloquent divine.

Mr. Ward's first regular appointment was to Pipe Creek Circuit, embracing part of Frederick County, Md. He was then in his twenty-first year. He was associated with an elder minister, the Rev. Dr. John S. Reese, a man of great wisdom, learning, eloquence, and piety. Mr. Ward became very popular in all the churches of the circuit, embracing parts of Washington County, Md., and Berkeley County, Va. He had signal success in his work there, and during his term built a new house of worship and organized the church at Little Georgetown, Va., besides being instrumental in adding largely to the membership of the churches which had been established. During these years he also traveled very extensively in other portions of the Conference territory, preaching to large congregations, especially at various camp-meetings on the Eastern as well as the Western Shore of Maryland. His next appointment was the city of Cumberland, 1854, in the spring of which year he married Miss Catharine A. Light, of Beddington, Va., a lady of great piety and Christian devotion, who was held in the highest respect and esteem by her husband's parishioners. This year Mr. Ward's health, always feeble, gave way, and, by advice of his friends, he asked the Conference to leave him without an appointment. His request was complied with, and he spent three months in suitable recreation, a portion of the time in leisurely travel northward.

He returned to his father's house in Washington so much renewed in health as to warrant him in applying to the president of the Conference for an appointment for the remainder of the year, and being informed by the president that there was then no suitable field for him until the next meeting of the Conference, he accepted a position offered him by his father, who was then engaged in publishing a temperance journal called the *Columbian Fountain*, to assist in editing the same. Thus he became linked with an enterprise from which he found no opportunity to disconnect himself until the close of the year 1847, at which time also the regular close of the volume of the journal expired. He then received a unanimous invitation to take charge of the church in Philadelphia which Rev. Thomas H. Stockton had served nine years, but which he had recently left to take charge of a church in Cincinnati, Ohio. He accordingly obtained a transfer from the president of the Maryland Annual Conference, which was accepted by the president of the Philadelphia Conference, who appointed him to the pastorate of the church referred to. A condition of affairs arose by which the subsequent sessions of the Philadelphia Conference were broken up and the church he served caused to assume a position of independence, and he, not having any reasons for abandoning his charge, compelled, as he viewed the case, to remain and serve it so long as pleasant relations existed between it and himself.

This was the case until the close of 1856, when, feeling it his duty to sever his connection with that charge, he returned to the Conference in Maryland, was received by his brethren and associates of former years, and was again appointed to Pipe Creek Circuit, which he had served sixteen years before, embracing, however, not so large a field as when he was first appointed to it. His colleague was the Rev. J. Thomas Murray, and they were both continued on the circuit for three successive years. During these years nearly four hundred members were added to these churches. Mr. Ward's next appointment was Alexandria, Va., in the spring of 1860. During this year he visited Fredericksburg, Va., by request, and organized a Methodist Protestant Church in that city, where he continued for two years. The Conference of 1863 sent him to the Liberty Circuit, where he labored with success. From Liberty he was sent by his Conference to the church in Washington City from which he had first received his license to preach, and of which his parents, grown old by this time, were still members. His pastorate there continued for two years, when, on account of failing health, he asked the Conference to relieve him from pastoral charge, and retired in the spring of 1866 to a little suburban home which had been provided for him by his parents at Westminster, which had been one of his regular preaching-places in the years when he traveled Pike Creek Circuit the second time. His health being restored he became a teacher in the Westminster Academy, and afterwards president of Western Maryland College, to which position he has been re-elected from year to year since by the board of trustees, the appointment being confirmed by the Maryland Annual Conference, under whose auspices the college was founded, and under whose patronage it has been from the time of its incorporation by the General Assembly of Maryland in 1868. Western Maryland College was organized in September, 1867, and incorporated by an act of the General Assembly of Maryland, approved March, 1868. There have been about 1500 students, of which one tenth of the number have graduated, besides a score of young men educated with the view to entering the sacred office of the ministry, and others who are now in positions of prominence and usefulness. About the time of his entrance upon the duties of the presidency of the college Mr. Ward inherited from his father some considerable means, all the available portion of which he devoted to the college enterprise, fulfilling the duties of his office at a salary far below his actual and necessary expenses in such a position. Mr. Ward has great reason to rejoice at the success that has crowned his pastoral services, and deserves the heartfelt sympathies and aid of his church in his efforts to promote the success and prosperity of the college over which he presides.

Westminster Academy was incorporated by an act of the General Assembly of Maryland, passed Feb. 6, 1839. The incorporators were

Jacob Reise, Isaac Shriver, Jesse Reifsnider, Nicholas Kelly, John McCollum, Joshua Smith, Jr., Hezekiah Crout, Francis Shriver, John Baumgartner, Basil Hayden, John S. Murray, Otho Shipley, John Fisher, Charles W. Webster, Wm. P. Maulsby, A. H. Busby, George Shriver, Conrad Moul, James Keefer, Samuel Orendorff, Michael Barnits, Emanuel Gernand, S. D. Lecompte, Wm. Shreev, Joshua Yingling, Wm. Yingling, Benjamin Yingling, Elias Yingling, Levi Evans, David Keefer, John Fermwalt, John Swigart, Wm. Shipley, Jr., Wm. Zepp, Jacob Hartzhell, John M. Yingling, Jacob Grove, Samuel I. Dell, Lawrence Zepp, David Burns, George Sheets, George Ramby, Wm. Grumbine, John Baurgett, Nelson Manning, Jesse Manning, John A. Kelly, Nimrod Beck, Jacob Jease, Henry Geatty, N. H. Thayer, B. F. Fowler, Mordecai Price, David Hedidebridler, Amos Lightner, Ephraim Crumbacker, Joseph Shafer, John F. Reese, John K. Longwell, James M. Shellman.

The "Old Union Meeting-house" was erected in 1818. Rev. Charles G. McLean preached the dedicatory sermon. It is a two-story brick structure, and is now fast falling into decay. Its windows are shattered, its steeple tumbling to pieces, and its interior crumbling away. Here the Rev. Lorenzo Dow, the famous and eccentric revivalist and exhorter, preached eleven different times, once beginning his services at four o'clock in the morning. This edifice stands on an elevated site in the centre of the Westminster Cemetery. The pulpit, with a high stairway leading to it, and the old-fashioned galleries are all that is left of its interior. For the last third of a century it has not been used for religious services. It was built as a union church by contributions from various Protestant denominations, and was open for all Protestant sects. For nearly a quarter of a century it was the only Protestant meeting-house in the town, and in that period many of the ablest clergymen of the State or country have preached from its old-fashioned pulpit. Before its erection a log structure, built about 1790, was used, and at the entrance to the cemetery, on the right, is the old brick school-house.

The first burial-ground in Westminster was on the land now owned by George E. Crouse, where interments were made from about 1764 to 1790, in which year the ground adjoining that on which the "Old Union Meetting-house" was built was used as a graveyard, and the former cemetery abandoned. It was occupied as an ordinary burying-place until 1864, when the Westminster Cemetery was organized and incorporated. This corporation has added to the grounds, making about thirteen acres, and has greatly beautified them by walks, terraces, and other valuable improvements. The officers of this corporation for 1881 are Joseph M. Parke, president, and John K. Longwell, John E. Smith, H. L. Norris (treasurer), Ira E. Crouse, and Edward K. Gernand (secretary), directors. In this cemetery the graves of soldiers in the late war are numerous, and it is also the last resting-place of many prominent citizens of Westminster. There is one old stone, about a foot high, on which the only inscription is 1707, but whether it refers to some person who died that year or to some one born at that date cannot be determined. The oldest interment is that of Christian Yingling, born Oct. 13, 1788, and who died Jan. 24, 1790, the year the meeting-house was built and the graveyard first laid out. The most prominent grave is that of the colonial proprietor of the town, who laid it out in 1764 and called it Winchester, which name it bore until superseded by the no less English name of Westminster. By his remains lie those of his wife and descendants.

The epitaphs on the tombstones are as follows:

"In Memory of William Winchester,
who was born in London
on the 22d December, 1710.
Arrived in Maryland
on the 6th March, 1729.
Intermarried with Lydia Richards
on the 22d July, 1747,
And departed this life on the
2d September, 1790,
In the 80th year of his age."

"In Memory of Lydia Winchester
(widow of William Winchester),
Who was born in Maryland on the
4th of August, 1727,
And departed this life on the
19th of February, 1809,
In the 82d year of her age."

There is still standing against the old church the first tombstone erected to Mr. Winchester, but which was taken down from the head of his grave after his wife's death, when the two above mentioned were put up. The old tombstone is somewhat different in phraseology, and makes a variance of two days in the time of his birth. It is as follows:

"In Memory of William Winchester, Born in the City of London on the 24th of December, Anno Domini 1710 (O. S.). Intermarried with Lydia Richards the 22d July, 1747, and Departed this Life 2d of September, 1790, aged 79 years, 8 months, and 2 days."

The Winchester descendants' graves are those of Lydia

Moore, eldest daughter of William Winchester the second and Mary, his wife, born Feb. 24, 1774, died Dec. 4, 1821; David Winchester, born April 18, 1769, and died Jan. 13, 1835; Elizabeth Winchester, born April 19, 1763, and died June 17, 1847; and Lydia Winchester, born Dec. 27, 1766, died April 19, 1849.

Among other graves of old or distinguished people are the following:

Catharine Fisher, born June 9, 1750, married David Fisher, June 3, 1776, and died Nov. 15, 1793; and her husband, David Fisher, died Oct. 15, 1815, aged 61. His second wife, Elizabeth, died April 16, 1849, aged 80.

John Fisher, born in Westminster, Jan. 7, 1780, died April 11, 1863.

John C. Cockey, born Feb. 1, 1794, died Dec. 16, 1826; and his wife, Ellen, born Oct. 23, 1797, died July 21, 1858.

James McHaffie, born March 31, 1779, died Jan. 3, 1818; and his wife, Eleanor, born Jan. 7, 1777, died April 6, 1815.

Jacob Sherman, born in Lancaster County, Pa., March 7, 1756, married Elizabeth Wagner, Feb. 23, 1779, and died July 7, 1822; and his wife, Elizabeth, died June 28, 1842, aged 85.

Isaac Shriver, born March 6, 1777, died Dec. 22, 1856; and Polly, his wife, born April 14, 1781, died March 6, 1859.

Frederick Wagoner, born Feb. 7, 1794, died Dec. 22, 1855.

Rev. Isaac Webster, died Feb. 4, 1851, aged 63.

On one stone are Sarah E. Bennett, born April 12, 1841, died Oct. 23, 1870; and Josephine I. Bennett, born July 4, 1843, died Feb. 12, 1851.

"Sacred to the memory of R. H. Clarke, Co. B, Seventh Md. Volunteers, who was sunstruck on the march from Virginia to victory at Gettysburg. Brought in an ambulance to Westminster, and unable to proceed farther, he here died June 30, 1863, aged 24 years.

Toil-worn and faithful to his country
And her service to the last."

William Frazier, Co. F, 7th Md. Vols., died 1864.

William Horner, born Feb. 1, 1778, died Aug. 6, 1847; and Elizabeth, his wife, born March 18, 1793, died Jan. 12, 1849.

Sally Key, died Sept. 14, 1855, aged 84.

William Kung, born Dec. 27, 1790, died Aug. 6, 1851.

Caleb Stansbury, Sr., died Nov. 17, 1845, aged 90.

Caleb Stansbury, Jr., died Aug. 21, 1860, aged 66.

Joshua Stansbury, died July 28, 1867, aged 75.

John Powder, born April 6, 1791, died Nov. 10, 1814.

Andrew Powder, of Jacob, born Dec. 23, 1798, married Elizabeth John, Jan. 3, 1822, and died Jan. 28, 1830.

Jacob Powder, died March 2, 1842, aged 80.

Jacob Powder, born Oct. 20, 1794, died Feb. 13, 1870; and his wife, Elizabeth, died Aug. 6, 1873, aged 74.

Andrew Powder, born July 25, 1793, died Oct. 28, 1856.

John Mitten, died March 21, 1808, aged 72.

Susanna Mitten, born Feb. 29, 1789, died Aug. 6, 1868.

Henry Mourer, born Oct. 17, 1796, died Oct. 20, 1862.

Hannah Neff, died Jan. 18, 1826, aged 90.

Andrew Reese, Sr., born Dec. 12, 1759, died March 14, 1822.

Andrew Reese, born May 18, 1791, died Sept. 26, 1826.

John Wampler, born Nov. 19, 1773, died July 27, 1831; and his wife, Elizabeth, born Jan. 26, 1780, died Nov. 12, 1859.

Abram Wampler, born Sept. 22, 1791, died July 6, 1853.

Dr. S. L. Swarmstedt, born in Calvert County, April 4, 1801, died March 1, 1872; and his wife, Margaret, died Nov. 8, 1848, aged 43.

"Sacred to the memory of J. Thomas Manning, who served in the United States army against Mexico. At peace he returned in ill health, and after much suffering as a Christian he died. His virtues endeared him to many, and his youthful companions, to honor his patriotism and preserve his memory, have erected to him this testimonial of their affectionate regard. Requiescat in pace."

On the reverse side the monument reads: "Died February 28, 1849, aged 23 years, 13 days," "Born February 15th 1826."

Jacob Righter, born July 25, 1782, died March 21, 1852; and his wife, Rachel, born June 1, 1788, died March 12, 1846.

Dr. George Colgate, died May 1, 1822, aged 39.

Elizabeth, wife of John Winters, died Oct. 15, 1858, aged 75.

Thomas Ward, died Feb. 10, 1852, aged 79.

Martha, wife of Thomas Weirel, died Aug. 12, 1860, aged 74.

Dr. Jesse J. Utz, died July 4, 1849, aged 28.

Joseph Shreev, died Sept. 10, 1858, aged 84; and his wife, Comfort, died Nov. 26, 1862, aged 82.

Wm. Shreev, born Aug. 16, 1805, died Feb. 27, 1861; and his wife, Margaret, born May 16, 1802, died Jan. 24, 1863.

Levi Shreev, born March 6, 1807, died March 13, 1875.

"Sacred to the memory of Charles W. Oursler, a member of Co. B, First Maryland Potomac Brigade, who fell in the defence of his country on Maryland Heights, Sept. 13, 1862, aged 21 years and 11 months."

Rachel Oursler, died Dec. 5, 1811, aged 20.

Catharine Keefer, born March 5, 1776, married to David Keefer, May 18, 1795, died Sept. 11, 1809.

Polly Keefer, born Dec. 26, 1796, died Oct. 1, 1862.

Ulerick Eckler, died Aug. 27, 1832, aged 67; and his wife, Elizabeth Eckler, died Sept. 6, 1865, aged 100.

Catharine, wife of Mordecai Price, died Feb. 24, 1875, aged 80.

"John W. Grogg. He was O. S. in Co. A, 6th Md. Vol. Infantry. Died in Washington Hospital, July 11, 1864, from the effects of a wound received in the battle of the Wilderness, Va., aged 24 years, 9 months, 9 days."

Jacob Feterling, born Nov. 2, 1745, died Jan. 2, 1830.

John Grout, born April 7, 1788, died April 14, 1826.

John McComb, a native of Scotland, died Oct. 25, 1830, aged 74.

Joshua Smith, born March 18, 1803, died July 24, 1868; and Julia A., his wife, died April 24, 1880.

David H. Shriver, born Jan. 8, 1807, died Sept. 16, 1880; and his wife, Mary, born March 17, 1811, died Aug. 25, 1879.

Nimrod Frizzell, died Oct. 13, 1842; and his wife, Anna, Oct. 31, 1865, aged 72.

Jacob Crouse, born Oct. 30, 1766, died Jan. 1, 1846; and Elizabeth, his wife, died Sept. 12, 1820, aged 47.

Jacob Fringer, Sr., died June 22, 1834, aged 74; and Margaret, his wife, April 12, 1841, aged 74.

Catherine Yingling, born Nov. 20, 1790, died Dec. 29, 1866.

Mary Dell, died Aug. 17, 1821, aged 55.

Thomas Lockard, born Jan. 24, 1791, died April 29, 1835; and his wife, Sarah, Feb. 12, 1874, aged 80.

Lewis Trumbo, born Oct. 15, 1802, died Feb. 14, 1869; and his wife, Sarah, Feb. 18, 1870, aged 68.

Jacob D. Hoppe, died Feb. 24, 1868, aged 34.

"Rev. Jonathan Monroe, 1801–1869; a Gospel Herald 44 years."

"Matilda Monroe, 1803–1872; the Itinerant's Bride for 43 years."

Jacob Fisher, born Aug. 28, 1783, died July 1, 1865.

E. F. Crout, born Sept. 5, 1818, died Nov. 26, 1875.

Ann Morthland, died Sept. 16, 1868, aged 83.

Michael Baughman, born Sept. 23, 1820, died Jan. 2, 1876.

George Webster, born May 12, 1812, died Aug. 22, 1868.

Andrew W. Durbin, died March 13, 1873, aged 50; and his wife, Mary J., March 22, 1875, aged 52.

Capt. George W. Shriver, born Aug. 7, 1835, died Feb. 5, 1870.

Margaret Shriver, wife of Joshua Yingling, born July 2, 1813, died June 3, 1880.

Maria L. Wampler, born Jan. 20, 1811, died Sept. 14, 1875.

James L. Wampler, born March 20, 1815, died Dec. 4, 1876.

Miles Mitten, died Aug. 1, 1854, aged 67; and his wife, Rachel, Feb. 11, 1859, aged 65.

Sophia Shockey, born Jan. 10, 1808, died May 8, 1869.

Rebecca Catharine Sparklin, with her two little daughters, Eva and Lottie, instantly killed, Oct. 10, 1879, on the Michigan Central Railroad by a collision. She was born April 28, 1852.

Isaac Stansbury, died Jan. 23, 1873, aged 81.

Daniel P. Goodwin, died April 24, 1876, aged 61.

John Kuhn, died Aug. 13, 1870, aged 67.

Mahala Shue, wife of Daniel Shue, died Aug. 27, 1826, aged 33.

Dr. George Shriver, died Dec. 10, 1859, aged 31.

John Thomas Burns, born March 2, 1839, died from a kick by a horse, April 20, 1857.

Deborah D. Norris, died May 1, 1858, aged 44.

John M. Yingling, died July 19, 1873, aged 43.

Mary J., wife of H. L. Norris, died Oct. 21, 1852, aged 28.

William Metzger, born April 25, 1793, in Hanover, Pa., died Nov. 29, 1872.

William Yingling, born March 13, 1810, died March 13, 1876.

Annie L., daughter of Joshua and Julia A. Smith, and wife of Col. William A. McKellip, died May 1, 1880, aged 39.

Sarah J., wife of Wm. Reese, died Jan. 21, 1873, aged 47.

Gabriel Hannemann, died March 1, 1854, aged 65.

Abraham Shafer, died Dec. 13, 1872, aged 76; and his wife, Mary, Nov. 29, 1864, aged 65.

Mary Adrian, wife of John T. Diffenbaugh, born Jan. 22, 1828, died Feb. 6, 1877.

Miranda, wife of Richard Manning, died May 28, 1865, aged 41.

Jacob J. Leister, died Feb. 11, 1878, aged 67.

Alfred Troxel, born Nov. 25, 1816, died Feb. 27, 1867; and his wife, Louisa, Jan. 23, 1850, aged 30.

Absalom Riall, born Jan. 1, 1795, died March 15, 1839.

Sallie H., wife of Dr. Charles M. Martin, died Jan. 26, 1872, aged 28.

Abraham H. Busby, born Sept. 4, 1805, died Aug. 5, 1867.

Rebecca M., wife of Solomon Zepp, died March 18, 1875, aged 58.

David Fisher, died April 10, 1827, aged 32.

Thomas Smith, born June 14, 1797, died Feb. 15, 1877; and his wife, Mary, born Oct. 25, 1807, died June 2, 1862.

Joshua Smith, died Dec. 13, 1841, aged 80; and his wife, Susanna, May 3, 1832, aged 63.

Joseph Smith, born March 10, 1801, died Nov. 6, 1860; and his wife, Elizabeth, born March 7, 1806, died Feb. 17, 1881.

Isaac E. Pearson, born November, 1811, died March 18, 1877; and his wife, Maria, born May 12, 1821, died Feb. 19, 1873.

Emanuel Herr, born December, 1799, died July, 1860.

George R. Rhodes, born in Nottingham, England, Nov. 5, 1805, died March 8, 1859.

Dulcie Berry, wife of Rev. H. C. Cushing, born in Fauquier Co., Va., Oct. 18, 1826, died Sept. 7, 1874.

This cemetery corporation was organized June 17, 1864, under a charter passed by the Legislature of previous winter. The first officers were:

President, George E. Wampler; Secretary, E. K. Gernand; Treasurer, H. L. Norris; Directors, William Reese, Dr. J. L. Warfield, Joseph M. Parke, John K. Longwell, J. Henry Hoppe, Alfred Troxell.

After the Revolutionary war, John Logston gave four acres of ground in Westminster to the Catholic Church, and on it was erected the first church about 1785. It was a frame structure, which in 1805 made way for a neat brick edifice called "Christ Church." This stood until 1872, when it was taken down and part of the materials used in building that year St. John's Parochial School. The third, St. John's church, was dedicated on Wednesday, Nov. 22, 1866, according to the impressive and solemn rites of the Catholic Church. There were fifteen priests in attendance, among them Rev. John McCaffery, D.D., president of Mount St. Mary's College; Rev. John McClusky, D.D., vice-president of the same; and Rev. Thomas Foley, D.D., secretary to the archbishop. The dedicatory sermon, which was able and interesting, was delivered by the latter in a very chaste style. Solemn high mass was celebrated, Rev. John Dougherty being the celebrant, Rev. Henry McMurdle, deacon, Rev. Father Kronenberg, sub-deacon. The music was grand, there being present thirteen members of the Cathedral choir of Baltimore, under Prof. Leinhardt, who presided at the organ. It is estimated that eleven hundred people were present in the church. Rev. John Gloyd was then and is now the pastor in charge.

The first pastor was Father Nicholas Zacchi, who came to Taneytown in 1804. Through his efforts the second church edifice was erected in 1805. He had charge of the church until his death in 1845. His successor was Father Thomas O'Neill, from 1851 to 1862, there having been an interregnum of six years. The next pastor was Father John Gloyd, who came in November, 1862, and is the present able and beloved pastor. He removed here from Taneytown in 1869, and this then became the headquarters of the mission until its division in 1879. Father Gloyd has charge of this church, St. Bartholomew's, at Manchester, and attends St. Mary's chapel, at Uniontown, at the residence of Mrs. William Shriver. St. John's school since its establishment, in 1872, has been under the charge of F. A. McGirr.

Many years ago Rajenia Grand Adams left thirty acres of land adjoining the town to the Catholic Church, which was leased, and its rents are applied, one-fourth to the church and the remainder to the priest in charge. John Orendorff, father of Francis H. and Josephus Orendorff, was mainly instrumental in rearing the present handsome church, having given five hundred thousand bricks, the quantity necessary for its construction. Father Glowd's assistants on the mission until its division, in 1879, were Richard Haseman, from 1871 to 1873; from 1873 to 1874, Casper Schmidt; and from 1874 to 1879, John T. Delaney.

The following persons are buried in the Catholic cemetery:

Francis Anderson, died Oct. 28, 1842, aged 44.

Thomas Adelsparyer, died Nov. 28, 1822, aged 71; Eleanor, his wife, died Aug. 1, 1846, aged 87.

Mary A., wife of John H. Logue, died June 2, 1865, aged 38.

G. W. Fowler, died Dec. 21, 1858, aged 75; Rachel, his wife, died Jan. 8, 1864, aged 81.

Mary Fowler, died Jan. 30, 1851, aged 77.

Richard Fowler, died Dec. 4, 1850, aged 87; Mary M., his wife, died June 15, 1866, aged 68.

John A. Hirsch, died Sept. 1, 1872, aged 83 years, 4 months, 22 days; Anna M., his wife, born Sept. 10, 1790, died May 15, 1868.

Lydia C., wife of John Coker, died June 7, 1851, aged 34.

Elias Weaver, born Feb. 27, 1805, died Oct. 3, 1828.

John Beaner, died Jan. 2, 1815, aged 56.

Frances Conly, died Nov. 16, 1841, aged 79.

Robina M. Anderson, died Jan. 2, 1869, aged 75 years, 3 months, 12 days.

Ellen Weaver, born 1778, died April 28, 1851.

Christian Orendorff, died Jan. 24, 1816, aged 55.

Polly, wife of John W. Coker, died April 20, 1861, aged 70.

Kate Orendorff, died Aug. 13, 1869, aged 31.

Elizabeth Wells, died Sept. 3, 1829, aged 58.

Wm. Orendorff, born July 6, 1826, died Aug. 9, 1847.

John Orendorff, died Feb. 18, 1869, aged 74.

Joseph Orendorff, died April 6, 1821, aged 16 years, 7 months, 24 days.

Hannah Williams, died Oct. 21, 1831, aged 62.

Hannah Fowler, died 1824.

John Fowler, died 1825.

Catharine E., wife of Jeremiah Lockard, born May 8, 1824, died Dec. 25, 1869.

John Feltz, died April 11, 1802, aged 1 year, 4 months.

Joseph Arnold, died April 10, 1815, aged 70.

Mary Arnold, died March 20, 1835, aged 71.

Joseph Arnold, died Feb. 8, 1858, aged 76.

Wm. Hayden, died June 4, 1802, aged 48.

Honor Fowler, died May 7, 1862, aged 59 years, 1 month, 14 days.

Rebecca Fowler, died Nov. 8, 1863, aged 75 years, 10 days.

Comfort Durbin, died June 4, 1855, aged 83.

Benjamin Durbin, died Aug. 6, 1811, aged 30 years, 1 month.

Benjamin Durbin, born March 30, 1748, died Nov. 20, 1815.

Susannah Durbin, died Dec. 24, 1836, aged 84.

Catherine Durbin, died Dec. 9, 1849, aged 58.

Dr. Wm. Matthias, born March 8, 1821, died April 17, 1864; Adelaide E., his wife, born May 10, 1832, died Nov. 10, 1868.

Rebecca Orendorff, born Oct. 26, 1818, died Dec. 24, 1868.

Eleanor Hayden, died April 19, 1844, aged 37.

Catharine Hayden, died Oct. 10, 1857, aged 85.

Anna, wife of Patrick Hanrat, died May 3, 1817, aged 50.

Wm. Hayden, Jr., died March 12, 1817, aged 35 years, 6 months, 24 days.

Thomas Durbin, died April 3, 1810, aged 77 years, 9 months.

Daniel Arter, born Aug. 4, 1742, died Feb. 13, 1813.

Wm. Arnold, born Oct. 6, 1758, died Feb. 20, 1832.

Henrietta Arnold, died April 9, 1828, aged 66.

Mary Logsdon, died April 17, 1829, aged —.

Elizabeth A., consort of W. Loyd, died June 22, 1854, aged 74.

Philip Cleary, born Oct. 18, 1797, died Oct. 20, 1860.

Dr. W. S. Shipley, died June 21, 1870, aged 27.

John Matthias, died Aug. 6, 1817, aged 67.

Catharine, his wife, died Nov. 7, 1818, aged 59.

Regina Grenadam, died May 25, 1817, aged 80.

Francis Grenadam, born Feb. 15, 1728, married to Regina Brechbeal, 1754, died Feb. 18, 1806.

Catharine Matthias, born Nov. 22, 1785, died Sept. 4, 1807.

Margaret Matthias, born June 20, 1796, died Sept. 7, 1807.

Anthony Arnold, died Aug. 19, 1824, aged 47 years, 4 months, 5 days.

John Lockard, died May 8, 1874, aged 86 years, 5 months, 8 days; Elizabeth, his wife, died May 5, 1843, aged 55.

Edward Fowler, died Nov. 21, 1863, aged 86 years, 4 months, 21 days.

Catharine Corban, died Sept. 6, 1844, aged 47.

Basil Hayden, died Feb. 2, 1863, aged 79; and Apprillah, his wife, Feb. 6, 1864, aged 79.

John Matthias, wife of Jacob, born Nov. 15, 1791, died June 8, 1872.

Michael Lynch, died Nov. 20, 1860, aged 67.

Mary Lynch, died Oct. 5, 1868, aged 65.

Mary Ann Snider, died Sept. 20, 1862, aged 32.

Chryostom Burke, born Feb. 29, 1827, died Dec. 18, 1863.

Mary E., wife of Wm. H. Grumbine, born Feb. 10, 1825, died Sept. 14, 1863.

Anna Doyle, died Nov. 28, 1859, aged 50.

John A. Matthias, born June 18, 1821, died Dec. 22, 1860.

Cornelius Buckley, died May 12, 1877, aged 39 years, 2 months, 2 days.

Eliza J. Buckley, died Nov. 3, 1876, aged 41 years, 10 months, 6 days.

Joseph Eckenrode, died Sept. 18, 1868, aged 54 years, 8 months.

Regina Frankhouser, died August, 1853, aged 74.

Christina Obold, died Feb. 6, 1851, aged 89.

John Wise, died July 27, 1860, aged 68 years, 7 months, 4 days.

Susan, his wife, died April 19, 1861, aged 68.

Benjamin Fowler, died Jan. 7, 1862, aged 58 years, 9 months.

Charlotte, wife of Bernard Kean, born Oct. 21, 1801, died July 17, 1845.

Sephero N. Awald, died Jan. 31, 1855, aged 39.

Geo. Strawheaffer, died April 2, 1855, aged 43.

Catharine Riccle, died Feb. 16, 1858, aged 62.

Eve Awald, died April 4, 1856, aged 76.

Henry Hilzkamp, died Jan. 5, 1853, aged 54.

John Ore, died June 17, 1865, aged 63.

Anthony McConwell, a native of County Armagh, Ireland, died July 11, 1865, aged 50.

Adam Bowers, died Nov. 2, 1864, aged 72 years, 11 months, 23 days; Catharine, his wife, died Jan. 3, 1874, aged 84 years, 11 months, 8 days.

Anastace A., wife of John Ore, died March 4, 1876, aged 77.

Catharine, wife of Aquilla Bowers, died June 26, 1869, aged 70 years, 11 months, 14 days.

John Yingling, died Jan. 15, 1880, aged 95.

Eliza Lovell, died Jan. 10, 1870, aged 57 years, 6 months, 10 days.

Theresa, wife of J. W. Zentgraf, "born in Larbock, Ger'y," Aug. 7, 1767, died in Westminster, Dec. 6, 1818.

John Powers, died Aug. 7, 1876, aged 40.

Thos. Lynch, died March 2, 1870, aged 81.

Patrick O'Brien, "a native of the parish of Castletown-Rock, County Cork, Ireland," died Oct. 7, 1873, aged 80.

Margaret, his wife, born in Ireland, died Oct. 1, 1868, aged 72.

Helen M., wife of William J. Case, died Feb. 22, 1878, aged 39 years, 10 months, 15 days.

Sarah Haase, died June 27, 1876, aged 76.

John Roberts, born Aug. 12, 1804, died Oct. 25, 1870.

Ann, wife of William Roberts, died June 27, 1860, aged 85.

Daniel H. Roberts, born Sept. 18, 1840, died July 19, 1871.

Catharine G. Roberts, died April 26, 1855, aged 52.

Catharine Hook, died Oct. 27, 1873, aged 74.

John Sinnott, died May 12, 1880, aged 75.

Andrew J. Beaver, died May 8, 1879, aged 53 years, 5 months, 15 days.

Paul Case, born May 8, 1806, died Sept. 5, 1875; Helen, his wife, born Sept. 5, 1810, died Nov. 4, 1875.

Rose E. Neal, born July 8, 1807, died March 4, 1875.

Elizabeth Manydier, wife of John Brook Boyle, died Feb. 6, 1876, aged 64 years, 6 months.

Mary A., wife of Joshua Corban, died April 6, 1880, aged 70.

Michael O'Brien, a native of Cork County, Ireland, died Dec. 12, 1862, aged 40; Rebecca, his wife, died March 9, 1881, aged 60 years.

John Everheart, died Dec. 7, 1876, aged 84 years, 11 months, 24 days.

Anne Smith, born March, 1829, died February, 1877.

Mary Myers, died Nov. 8, 1878, aged 76 years.

Philip Keller, died July 15, 1867, aged 70 years, 9 months, 20 days.

John Koontz, died Sept. 27, 1872, aged 70 years, 6 months, 27 days.

Thomas Hurley, died April 22, 1869, aged 67 years.

Morris Hurley, died Oct. 21, 1878, aged 32 years, 9 months, 9 days.

Christopher Rooney, died Oct. 23, 1865, aged 46. "Served in the U. S. Navy for fifteen years. When the Rebellion broke out enlisted as a private in Company C, Sixth Regiment Md. Vol., U. S. Army, and served as chief musician of the regiment until the close of the war, receiving an honorable discharge Oct. 3, 1865."

Elizabeth Buchman, a native of France, born March 16, 1776, died March 24, 1855.

Elizabeth Koons, died March 26, 1851, aged 76.

Matthew Denning, died Feb. 4, 1865, aged 93; and Hannah, his wife, March 14, 1858, aged 78.

"Jim," "as a recognition of his services and fidelity to the family," J. T. Matthias.

Martin Whiteleather, died Nov. 29, 1876, aged 63 years, 1 month, 16 days.

Joseph Hawn, died Feb. 16, 1875, aged 81 years, 1 month, 27 days; Catharine, his wife, died March 23, 1864, aged 66 years, 5 months, 2 days.

Nicholas Zentgraf, born in Larbach, Germany, Jan. 10, 1810, died Oct. 12, 1872.

Joseph Shanaborough, died June 2, 1872, aged 75 years, 5 months; Patience, his wife, born Oct. 26, 1797, died July 26, 1853.

William Coghlan, born Dec. 31, 1774, died March 27, 1854.

Grace Lutheran Church was organized in 1846, and on August 5th of that year the corner-stone of its church edifice was laid with imposing ceremonies. Before that time the members of this new congregation had worshiped at St. Benjamin's church (Kreiger's), about a mile and a half from town. Occasionally Lutheran services were held in the "Old Union Meeting-house." The first preaching in this section of the country was by Lutheran and German Reformed preachers and missionaries, as far back as 1747 and 1748. Its pastors have been:

1842–53, Rev. Philip Williard (preaching before the building of the church at Kreiger's); 1853–60, Rev. Samuel Henry; 1860–63, Rev. J. Martin; 1863–67, Rev. H. C. Halloway; 1867–69, Rev. P. A. Strobel; 1870–78, Rev. John A. Earnest; Aug. 28, 1878, to the present time, Rev. Henry W. Kuhns.

It has a flourishing Sunday-school, of which Henry B. Grammer is superintendent, and William Seabrook, assistant. This church, an outgrowth of St. Benjamin's, forms with it and St. John's (Leister's), near Mexico, a charge under Rev. Mr. Kuhns. From 1846 to about 1857 Borst and Winters' churches were united with these three in one charge.

Adjoining the fine church is a neat parsonage owned by the congregation.

St. Paul's Reformed Church is a child of the old mother-church, St. Benjamin's (or Kreiger's), a mile and a half distant in the country. Its separate church organization was formed in 1868, when was laid the corner-stone of its elegant edifice, which was completed in 1869. Before that time its members worshiped at Kreiger's, though occasional Reformed preaching was heard in the "Old Union Meeting-house" from 1790 to 1840. The church was organized and its building erected under the auspices of Rev. W. C. Cremer, who continued as pastor until 1876. His successor was Rev. J. G. Noss, who is the present incumbent, and was installed in December, 1876. The Consistory is composed of Peter B. Mikesell, John H. Bowers, John L. Reifsnider, Andrew N. Stephan, elders; and J. Brinkerhoff, J. T. Orndorff, Theodore A. Evans, William H. H. Zepp, deacons. The superintendent of the Sunday-school is William B. Thomas. The elegant parsonage adjoining the church was built after the latter's erection. The site of this church, on the corner of Green and Broad Streets, is one of the most beautiful and desirable in the city. The main building is forty-six by seventy feet on the flank wall, with a pulpit recess of six by eighteen feet, making the entire length of the building, from the outside wall of the tower to that of the pulpit-recess, eighty-three feet. The building has a basement ten feet high, and an audience-chamber eighteen feet deep on the flank wall and thirty-one and a half in the centre. The style of architecture is modern Gothic, with traces of a composite nature. The front and tower are supported by pilasters, capped with the Gettysburg granite. The brick-work is adorned with pinnacles, and a spire sixty feet in height, making the entire height of tower and spire one hundred and twenty-six feet. The windows are Gothic, with stained and frosted glass. The audience-chamber has a chancel, with a beautifully-designed pulpit, reading-desk, and baptismal font. The pews are scroll, front and back, and the ceiling is ornamented with panel, stucco, and fresco-work. The building committee were David H. Shriver, Augustus Shriver, S. L. Myers, A. Long, Jesse Crowl, Josiah Crowl, and Rev. W. C. Creamer. The architects were Sharb & Leister; master-carpenter, George Lease; master-mason and bricklayer, Christian Awalt.

The Westminster Society of the Methodist Protestant Church was organized in 1829. It was originally included in the association of churches constituting Pipe Creek Circuit. In 1837 it was made a separate charge, and so continued until 1840, when it became a part of Baltimore Circuit. In 1844 it was again united with Pipe Creek Circuit, and continued to hold that relation until 1871, at which time it became again a district church under the title of Westminster Station.

Its pastors have been:

1829, D. E. Reese, Sr.; 1830, F. Stier, J. Hanson; 1831, F. Stier, J. Ibberston; 1832, Isaac Webster, C. Jacobs; 1833, Isaac Webster, W. Sexsmith; 1834, Josiah Varden, H. Doyle; 1835, J. W. Everest, H. Doyle, A. A. Lipscomb; 1836, John S. Reese, J. W. Porter; 1837, T. G. Clayton; 1838, Josiah Varden; 1839, J. W. Porter; 1840, Eli Henkle, James Elderdice; 1841, J. Keller, J. Hisore; 1842, J. Whitworth, J. Hisore; 1843, Eli Henkle; 1844, W. Collier, T. L. McLean, J. D. Brooks; 1845-46, W. Collier, P. L. Brooks, J. K. Nichols; 1847, J. Morgan, T. D. Valiant; 1848, J. Morgan, W. Roby; 1849, D. E. Reese, W. Roby; 1850, D. E. Reese, T. L. McLean; 1851, H. P. Jordan, J. Roberts; 1852, H. P. Jordan, H. J. Day; 1853, T. M. Wilson, H. J. Day; 1854, T. M. Wilson, J. A. McFadden; 1855, F. Swentzell, J. A. McFadden; 1856, F. Swentzel, N. S. Greenaway; 1857-59, J. T. Ward, J. T. Murray; 1860, D. E. Reese, J. B. Jones; 1861, D. E. Reese; 1862-64, P. L. Wilson; 1865-68, R. S. Norris; 1868-71, D. Wilson; 1871-74, W. S. Hammond; 1874-77, H. C. Cushing; 1877-81, S. B. Southerland; 1881, March, J. T. Murray, present incumbent.

The present church edifice was built upon the site of the former, and was dedicated August, 1868, Rev. Daniel Wilson being the pastor, when the dedicatory sermon was preached by Rev. J. J. Murray, D.D.

The superintendent of the Sunday-school is Dr. Charles Billingslea. The church trustees are E. O. Grimes, Joshua Yingling, Dr. J. W. Hering; and the stewards, Dr. C. Billingslea, R. S. Narment, Isaac Baile, Jesse Shreeve, Elias Yingling, Dr. W. H. Rippard, and M. L. Lantz.

The church edifice owned and occupied by the German Baptists, or Brethren (Dunkers), is situated on Bond Street, fronting Belle Park. It was erected by the Baptists, assisted by friends of its pastor, Rev. Dr. Cole. The congregation was small, and the sale of the building became advisable. It was purchased by the Brethren, they paying therefor the sum of two thousand two hundred dollars. They were materially assisted therein by the citizens of Westminster not connected with their denomination. The building is a handsome brick structure. The congregation is a part of that very considerable body known as the "Pipe Creek Congregation." Its bishop or elder is Solomon Stoner, who resides at Uniontown. The associate ministers are William H. Franklin, Ephraim W. Stoner, Joel Roop, Amos Caylor, and Uriah Bixler.

The original trustees were Henry Warner, John Englar, D. D. Bonsack, Uriah Bixler, and Dr. Lewis Woodward. To these, in trust for the use of the Brethren, were conveyed the buildings by Rev. Isaac Cole, Julia J. Cole, George W. Matthews, Charles L. Morgan, Isabella M. Matthews, trustees of the Westminster Baptist Church, by deed dated May 9, 1879.

In November, 1880, a Sunday-school was organized, numbering at present about one hundred and fifty scholars. Its superintendent is Dr. Lewis Woodward.

The Protestant Episcopal Church (Ascension) was organized in 1842 by Revs. David Hillhouse Buell and C. C. Austin, but Episcopal services had been held at various times previously. The corner-stone of the church edifice was laid Aug. 27, 1844, with appropriate ceremonies, by the Rt. Rev. Bishop Whittingham, assisted by other clergymen. It was erected on one of the court-house lots. It was built of stone, under the superintendence of R. Carey Long, an eminent architect of Baltimore. It was consecrated by Bishop Whittingham, May 19, 1846. The first record of baptism is that of Fannie C. Shellman, now the wife of Isaac E. Pearson, Oct. 16, 1842, by Rev. Charles C. Austin. Its rectors have been:

1842 or '43 to 1847 or '48, David Hillhouse Buell; 1848-51, Samuel Chalmers Davis; 1851-53, Thomas James Wyatt; Feb. 26, 1854, to 1857, Oliver Sherman Prescott; 1857 to Sept. 27, 1861, Edward H. C. Goodwin; April 20, 1862, to Jan. 20, 1864, James Chrystal; Jan. 20, 1864, to March 8, 1870, James W. Reese, A.M.; April 10, 1870, to July 10, 1871, John H. Converse, A.M.; Aug. 1, 1871, to April 1, 1875, Julian E. Ingle; Oct. 1, 1875, to Dec. 1, 1879, Isaac Lee Nicholson, Jr., A.M.; Jan. 7, 1880, James Stuart Smith, B.D.

The church officers in 1881 were: Wardens, Henry Vanderford, Charles T. Reifsnider; Vestrymen, Dr. George Fouke, Hugo E. Fiddis, George Sharer,

Chapman Johnson, Dr. Columbus M. Brown. Rev. Mr. Smith, the rector, is superintendent of the Sunday-school, and has also a colored congregation in connection with his parish. "The Guild of the Holy Child" has been in successful operation for several years. The new chapel was begun June, 1876, and completed in September of that year, and was opened September 29th, on the festival of St. Michael's. The new communion plate was procured at Easter, 1876, and consecrated in August succeeding. The commodious parsonage was commenced in October, 1879, and completed the ensuing year, and occupied on St. Barnabas' day, June 11th. An English ivy covers the entire façade of the church, which is a pure model of Gothic architecture. In the rear is the parish burying-ground, where lie at rest many who were prominently connected with the church. An interesting tomb in this cemetery is that of Leigh Master, the inscription on which is as follows:

"Legh Master, Esquire,
Late of New Hall, in
Lancashire, England.
Died the 22d day of March, 1796,
Aged 79 years."

In the corner of the yard lies the body of Capt. William Murray, who fell in a skirmish at Westminster, June 29, 1863, during the civil war, between a company of Delaware Federal cavalry and the advance-guard of Gen. J. E. B. Stuart's Confederate command, where six or seven others were killed. The names of all other persons in this cemetery to whom stones are erected are here given:

Betty G. Van Bibber, born May 18, 1816, died Oct. 24, 1853.

Sally F. Van Bibber, died Sept. 21, 1852, aged 16.

Isaac Van Bibber, born Jan. 27, 1810, died Sept. 28, 1847.

Washington Van Bibber, born Feb. 15, 1778, died April 8, 1848; and Lucretia Van Bibber, died May 10, 1867, aged 80.

Abraham Van Bibber, died Feb. 12, 1861, aged 39. George L. Van Bibber.

Isaac Van Bibber, Ann Neilson (both on one stone). Marcher, son of G. L. and H. C. Van Bibber. Mary Emory, died June 7, 1874, aged 82.

Elizabeth S. Perry, born March 31, 1817, died Oct. 7, 1861.

James M. Shellman, born in Louisville, Ga., Sept. 8, 1801, died Jan. 14, 1851.

Jacob Reese, born Jan. 31, 1798, died April 19, 1872; and his wife, Eleanor, born Oct. 5, 1798, died Nov. 20, 1871.

John F. Reese, born Feb. 17, 1808, died April 15, 1859.

Catherine F., wife of Edwin F. Reese, born Jan. 23, 1834, died Sept. 7, 1860; Fannie, her daughter, aged 3 months; and Ella, another daughter, died July 11, 1863, aged nearly 5.

Dr. Elisha D. Payne, born Nov. 11, 1796, died Jan. 19, 1855.

Gazelle, daughter of Joseph M. and Margaret Newson, died July 24, 1872, aged 16.

Anna Mary, daughter of D. W. and Mary A. Hunter, died Sept. 3, 1870, aged 8 months. Samuel Lantz.

Samuel Butler, of Company C, Thirty-second Regiment, U. S. C. T., died April 28, 1868, aged 45.

George Ann Buyer, aged 13.

Dr. Bernard Mills, died May 19, 1869, aged 38.

Eliza, wife of Francis Dorsey, born April 16, 1801, died March 14, 1865.

Clara V., daughter of George S. and Mary J. Fouke, died May 29, 1863, nearly 3 years of age.

Fannie, daughter of William and Mary A. Moore, aged 1 year.

R. T. D. Rosan, died Feb. 25, 1852, aged 1 year.

The Centenary Methodist Episcopal church was built in 1869. Methodist preaching was held at private dwellings in Westminster as early as 1769, and among the local or traveling preachers who held services were Hezekiah Bonham and his son Robert, Robert Strawbridge, Paul Hagarty, John Hagarty, Robert Walker, and Freeborn Garrettson, who came at irregular intervals and preached in this new settlement. After the building of the "Old Union Meeting-house" service was occasionally held until 1839, when the regular church organization took place. In this year was erected the first Methodist Episcopal church, a brick structure, on the site of the present edifice. In 1865 the parsonage was built. The present church building was begun in April, 1868. Its corner-stone was laid in August following, and the edifice was completed and occupied in March, 1869. It is a Gothic structure, twenty-nine feet high in the clear on the inside, and is thirty by eighty feet in size. It has an audience-room and basement, the latter one of the finest in the State outside of Baltimore. The building, with its furnishings, cost nearly sixteen thousand dollars. It has three organs. Its site was formerly owned by John Fisher. When erected its pastor was Rev. J. Edwin Amos, who was admitted to the Conference in 1859. Since it was made a station, in 1869, its pastors, with dates of their admission into the Conference, have been:

1869, John W. Hedges, adm. 1845; 1870–72, C. P. Baldwin, adm. 1866; 1872–74, C. H. Richardson, adm. 1869; 1874–76, George V. Leech, adm. 1856; 1876–78, E. E. Shipley, adm. 1862; 1878-81, J. D. Still, adm. 1859; 1881, John Edwards, adm. 1871.

Its Sunday-school superintendent is H. L. Norris, and the assistant is Miss Sue Castle. The number of scholars is 100.

The Union National Bank of Westminster (usually styled the "Old Bank") was removed in April, 1868, from the building it had occupied as a banking institution for more than half a century to the fine building erected by Dr. Hering in the central part of the town, which was fitted up in handsome style with all the necessary appurtenances for banking. This is one of the oldest institutions in the State.

The Commercial and Farmers' Bank of Baltimore

established a branch in Westminster in 1814. At that time the cities on the Chesapeake were threatened by the British army. It was located in the building then owned by Jacob Krouse, where the vaults were prepared and the specie and the other funds of the Commercial and Farmers' Bank were removed for greater security. The branch was under the management of Mr. Thomal, one of the clerks of the parent bank.

As this was intended merely as a temporary arrangement, after the war was over the branch was withdrawn.

An act of incorporation was obtained for the Bank of Westminster in 1816, with a capital of three hundred thousand dollars. The books of subscription for stock were opened in Westminster and Middleburg by commissioners, one of whom was Joshua C. Gist. The first election for directors was held in March, 1816, when the following-named gentlemen were elected, viz.: James McHaffie, John Fisher, Jesse Slingluff, Isaac Shriver, Joshua Delaplane, Jacob Shriver, John Wampler, Dr. George Colegate, Joshua Cockey, and Francis Hollingsworth. Mr. Hollingsworth declined serving, when Wm. Durbin, Sr., was chosen.

At the first meeting of the board, in April, 1816, James McHaffie was elected president, and at a subsequent meeting John Walsh (a clerk in the Union Bank of Baltimore) was elected cashier, and John Wampler appointed clerk.

A considerable amount of the stock of the bank having been subscribed at "Frederick Town," the stockholders then asked for a branch, styled the "Office of Pay and Receipt," which was granted in 1817, under control of a board of managers, with the venerable Dr. William Tyler at its head.

This was the origin of what afterwards became and is now known as the Farmers' and Mechanics' Bank of Frederick County.

In 1818, Jesse Slingluff was elected president in place of James McHaffie, deceased.

In 1819 the directors elected were as follows: Jesse Slingluff, president; William Durbin, Ludwick Wampler, Henry Kuhn, George Colegate, Benjamin Rutherford, John C. Cockey, Gideon Bantz, Thomas Boyer, John Fisher, Joseph Swearingen.

In 1820, John Wampler was chosen cashier in place of Mr. Walsh.

In 1821, Mr. Slingluff resigned the presidency and was succeeded by John C. Cockey; Mr. Slingluff continued as director until his death.

In 1828, Mr. Cockey died; Joshua Jones acted as president *pro tem.* until April, 1827, when Isaac Shriver was elected president, and at the same time John Fisher was elected cashier in place of Mr. Wampler.

In 1827 the stockholders at Frederick demanded a change, and the Legislature granted their request by changing the title from the "Bank of Westminster" to that of the "Farmers' and Mechanics' Bank of Frederick County," with the parent bank at Frederick and the branch at Westminster. Dr. William Tyler as president, and William M. Beale as cashier, were the officers at Frederick; and Isaac Shriver as president, and John Fisher as cashier, were continued at the branch.

In 1829 the Frederick stockholders attempted to abolish the branch, which was resisted, and finally resulted in a separation in 1830 of the two institutions, the bank here resuming its original title of "Bank of Westminster," with a capital of $100,000, one-third of the original stock remaining here and two-thirds in the Farmers' and Mechanics' Bank of Frederick County.

In 1857, John K. Longwell was elected president in place of Isaac Shriver, deceased, who had served in that capacity for thirty years.

In 1863, John Fisher died, after having been cashier of the bank for thirty-six years, and having served as director or cashier from the creation of the bank in 1816 to the period of his death, and was succeeded by the election of John C. Frizzell as cashier.

On April 27, 1865, the bank was robbed, as the following account of the same will show:

"About two o'clock on Thursday evening the cry of fire was raised in the town. John Frizzel, the cashier, and the clerk were both in the bank at the time. Mr. Frizzel locked the outer door of the building, leaving the vault open, and proceeded to the scene of the conflagration, which proved to be the barn of Mr. Frizzel, which had been set on fire, and which the citizens succeeded in extinguishing. On returning to the bank it was discovered that the front door had been forced, and the institution robbed of eleven thousand dollars in greenbacks and ten thousand dollars in the issues of the bank, consisting of twenty and fifty-dollar notes. A large package of ten-dollar notes was dropped on the floor of the vault in the hurry of the thieves to get away. The whole affair was executed in a few minutes, and was remarkably well planned."

In 1866 the institution was changed from the State Bank of Westminster to that of the Union National Bank of Westminster, when John J. Baumgartner was elected cashier in place of Mr. Frizzell, resigned.

In 1867, Mr. Baumgartner resigned, and Dr. J. W. Hering was elected cashier.

In 1869 the officers of the bank were as follows:

Directors, John K. Longwell, president; Jacob Powder, Daniel J. Geiman, Abraham Shafer, William Reese, John Roberts, J. Henry Hoppe, Lawrence Zepp, David Roop, David Geiman; Cashier, J. W. Hering; Teller, Hugo E. Fiddis.

In 1881 the directors were:

John K. Longwell, president; Daniel J. Gieman, William Reese, David Gieman, Lawrence Zepp, Charles B. Roberts, Francis H. Orendorff, William P. Maulsby, Dr. Frank T. Shaw, Dr. J. Howard Billingslea; Cashier, Dr. J. W. Hering.

The committee of directors of the Farmers' and Mechanics' Bank appointed to secure an eligible location for the erection of a banking-house reported, Oct. 25, 1850, that they had purchased the house and lot of ground then in the occupancy of Capt. John McCollum. This property was situated in the central part of the town, and was bought for $2300. The stockholders connected a banking-house with the main building, eighteen feet front, and running back thirty feet, on the side next to A. W. Dorsey's drug-store. This building was erected by Wampler & Evans, and completed in January, 1851. In November, 1850, the president, Jacob Matthias, selected the plates for printing notes of the denominations of 1's, 5's, 10's, 20's, and 50's. The third installment of five dollars on each share of subscribed stock was called for to be paid in by Jan. 4, 1851.

This bank has from the beginning done a large amount of business, and is under judicious management. The office of president has been filled by Jacob Matthias, John Smith, Dr. J. L. Warfield, Joseph Shaeffer, and that of cashier by Jacob Reese and A. D. Schaeffer. In 1876 the directors were William Bachman, Andrew K. Shriver, John Babylon, Benjamin W. Bennett, George Schaeffer, William A. McKellip. In 1881 they were Joseph Schaeffer, Benjamin W. Bennett, George Schaeffer, William Bachman, William A. McKellip.

The First National Bank of Westminster was established in 1860, under the new national system of banking, and the result of its operations is considered a decided success by its stockholders and customers. Up to 1881 its officers have been: Presidents, Alfred Troxel, Augustus Shriver, Granville S. Haines; Cashiers, William A. Cunningham, George R. Gehr; Directors, Joshua Yingling, David Englar, William Lawyer, David Cassell, Samuel McKinstry, Philip H. L. Myers, David J. Roop, Henry Baile.

The Mutual Fire Insurance Company of Carroll County was chartered and began business in 1869. Its first directors were Augustus Shriver (president), Richard Manning (secretary and treasurer), John Roberts, Alfred Zollickoffer, Dr. Henry E. Beltz, Edward Lynch, Dr. J. W. Hering, Dr. Samuel Swope, Granville S. Haines, David Prugh. The directors for 1881 were:

Dr. J. W. Hering (president), Richard Manning (secretary and treasurer), Granville S. Haines, Edward Lynch, David Fowble, Dr. Samuel Swope, Charles B. Roberts, David Prugh, Granville T. Hering, Alfred Zollickoffer.

The above comprises all who have been directors from its organization save Daniel H. Roberts, deceased.

The Westminster Savings Institution was organized in 1869. In 1876 its officers were:

President, Jesse Reifsnider; Treasurer, B. W. Bennett; Secretary, J. T. Diffenbaugh; Directors, Dr. Charles Billingslea, Luther H. Norris, Nathan I. Gorsuch, James W. Beacham, Ezra S. Stouffer, Charles T. Reifsnider.

Its officers in 1881 were:

President, B. W. Bennett; Secretary, John T. Diffenbaugh; Treasurer, Jesse Reifsnider; Directors, H. L. Norris, Dr. Charles Billingslea, E. L. Lawyer, E. O. Grimes, Mordecai McKinstry, Charles T. Reifsnider.

It was incorporated Oct. 4, 1869. Its incorporators and first officers were:

President, Jesse Reifsnider; Secretary, John T. Diffenbaugh; Treasurer, Nathan I. Gorsuch; Directors, Benjamin W. Bennett, John Englar, Josephus H. Hoppe, H. L. Norris, James W. Beacham, Chas. T. Reifsnider, Wm. L. Beggs.

A mass-meeting of the citizens of Westminster was held April 27, 1876, to consider the advisability of an additional water supply for the municipality. An act of Assembly had been passed authorizing the levy of a tax for this purpose, coupled with a proviso that it should not be levied unless approved by a vote of the next city council of the town. The meeting was enthusiastically in favor of the improvement. Mayor David Fowble presided, and Dr. William H. Rippard and W. H. Vanderford acted as secretaries. A ticket ignoring politics and in favor of the water-works was chosen, as follows: for mayor, P. H. Irwin; for councilmen, Jesse Yingling, Nathan Y. Gorsuch, and M. B. Grammer. The ticket was elected at the subsequent election, to carry out the necessary measures to furnish the city with a supply of pure water.

There was a meeting March 24, 1870, of the stockholders of the Westminster Gaslight Company, and the following officers were chosen to direct the affairs of the company: President, John L. Reifsnider; Directors, C. Oliver O'Donnell, C. Hart Smith, George C. Hicks, Joshua Yingling, Charles B. Roberts, and Edward Lynch. Dr. James L. Billingslea was chairman of the meeting, and W. A. Cunningham, secretary. The progress of the company from this time was rapid. The necessary buildings were begun and hurried to completion, and in September the city was lighted with gas. The work of construction was superintended by R. A. Holmes, of Baltimore The officers of the company in 1876 were: President, John L. Reifsnider; Directors, Charles B. Roberts, Edward Lynch, Joshua Yingling, C. Hart Smith, George C. Hicks, Charles E. Savage; Secretary and Treasurer, William A. Cunningham.

Joseph M. Parke, one of the most estimable citizens of Westminster, and the subject of this sketch, was born Feb. 6, 1810, in Sadsbury township, Chester Co., Pa., about one mile north of Parkesburg. His

Jos. M. Parke

father, George W. Parke, was born Oct. 18, 1780, and died Feb. 25, 1860. His mother was Mary, daughter of John Fleming, of the neighborhood of Coatesville. She died in February, 1817. His maternal grandmother was a Slaymaker, of Pequea, Lancaster Co., Pa., and his paternal grandfather was Joseph Parke, who was born in Chester County, Pa., Dec. 21, 1737, and died near Parkesburg, July 2, 1823. His paternal grandmother was Ann Maxwell, of Lancaster County, Pa. His great-grandfather was John Parke, who died July 28, 1787, and his great-great-grandfather was Arthur Parke, who came to this country with his family from Donegal County, Ireland, some time prior to 1724, and settled in West Fallowfield township, Chester Co., Pa., and died there in February, 1740, as stated in Everts' "History of Chester County, Pa.," published in July, 1881. The Parke family is of the Scotch-Irish Presbyterian stock, and went to North Ireland at an early period from Scotland or England. Joseph Maxwell Parke has several brothers and a sister still surviving, viz.: Samuel S., George W., Jr., and Dr. Charles R. Parke, all of Bloomington, Ill.,—the latter a half-brother by his father's second marriage,—and Caroline, wife of Evan Jones, now residing near Winchester, Va. In 1823, at the age of thirteen years, he left home to attend a classical school started by his uncle, Rev. Samuel Parke, a Presbyterian clergyman, at Slate Ridge, now the town of Delta, York Co., Pa., near the Maryland line. After a few years spent in studying the Latin and Greek languages and other studies, preparatory to entering college, he was employed by his uncle as a teacher in the same academy. He had a number of pupils of about his own age, some from Harford County, Md., and among them was Dr. F. Butler, now of Westminster. In 1829 he left Slate Ridge to attend college at Canonsburg, Washington Co., Pa., then in considerable repute, under the management of Rev. Matthew Brown, and graduated in 1831, at the age of twenty-one, in a class of thirty-one students. Having his mind fixed on the profession of the law, and with a view of assisting himself thereto, as well as improving his education, he determined to engage for a time in teaching. Seeing an advertisement in the Philadelphia *Saturday Evening Post* that a classical teacher was wanted at Manchester (then Baltimore), Carroll Co., he visited that place, and became the *first* principal of Manchester Academy, about Dec. 1, 1831. He continued as such until 1839, with an intermission of a year. In April, 1835, he was married to Amanda, second daughter of George Motter, of Manchester. They have had a large family of children, of whom five survive, viz.: Frances H., wife of Edwin K. Gernand, merchant; George Motter Parke, the present deputy register of wills; Mary Letitia, widow of the late Prof. J. Mortimer Hurley; Josephine Amanda, wife of J. Edwin Taylor, of the Taylor Manufacturing Company; and John Fleming, in the employ of said company,—all now of Westminster, Md.

As we have stated, in 1837 the new county of Carroll was established, and embraced Manchester within its limits. Dr. Jacob Shower, of that town, was one of the representatives of the new county for the first two sessions of 1837 and 1838, and having declined a re-election, Mr. Parke was nominated on the Democratic ticket, and elected in 1839 to the House of Delegates of Maryland. For some years he had devoted his spare time to the study of law under the direction of the late Charles F. Mayer, of Baltimore, and after the adjournment of the Legislature in the spring of 1840 he was admitted to the bar in Baltimore City by the Baltimore County Court. In April, 1840, he removed to Westminster, Md., the new county-seat, where he has ever since resided. About the same time he purchased the *Democrat and Carroll County Republican*, which had been started at Westminster by William Shipley in February, 1838, and had been conducted by him for about six weeks more than two years. The editing of that paper, with some practice of the law, occupied his attention for about eight years, until 1848, when he disposed of his interest in it to J. T. H. Bringman, who had purchased a half-interest in it two years before.

During the eight years of his editorial control there were three memorable Presidential campaigns: in 1840, between Harrison and Van Buren; in 1844, between Clay and Polk; and in 1848, between Taylor and Cass. Though an ardent politician and devoted to his party, his course was always fair and honorable, and commanded the respect of his political opponents. With him patriotism was superior to party, and there were occasions on which he did not hesitate to rise above mere party influences when he conceived its objects did not correspond with the public good. For many years he strenuously supported the cause of reform in Maryland. The present generation has but little idea of the difficulties encountered by Reformers in breaking the hold of the minority upon the legislative power of the State. The constitution was the mere creature of the Legislature, and as each county had four delegates and the cities of Annapolis and Baltimore two each, without regard to size or population, the smaller counties had entire control of the government, and the minority was naturally inclined to hold to power with a firm grip. After the fright caused by the refusal of the "glorious nineteen" senatorial electors to enter the college and elect State senators, thus leaving the other twenty-one without a constitutional quorum, it was perceived that the State was on the verge of a revolution, and the Legislature undertook to make the changes of 1836 in the constitution, conceding the right of the people to elect their Governor and State senators by a direct vote, and a moderate increase to Baltimore City and the larger counties in legislative influence. Still it was far from satisfactory, and the Reformers continued to press the call of a convention. In the western counties, especially in Carroll and Frederick, very many Reformers, both of the Democratic and Whig parties, perceiving that party feeling tended to defeat reform measures, agreed to combine without distinction of party, and accordingly, when the call for the convention of 1851 was obtained from the Legislature, a ticket was made up for the convention and triumphantly elected in Carroll County composed of three Democrats—Dr. Jacob Shower, Hon. Elias Brown, and Joseph M. Parke—and two Whigs,—Mordecai G. Cockey and Andrew G. Ege. In Frederick County three of each party were elected. In the convention Mr. Parke supported the most advanced measures of reform, including representation strictly according to population and the election of nearly all officers by the people.

John Baumgartner, the first register of wills of Carroll County, and the first elected under the constitution of 1851, died early in 1853, and Mr. Parke was appointed by the Orphans' Court to fill that vacancy. He held the office from Jan. 31, 1853, until the next election in the fall, when he was nominated by his party and elected for six years. In 1859 he was re-elected and served another term of six years. In 1865 he declined to be a candidate for that office, because, as he conceived, the Union party, with which he had acted during the civil war, had become merged into the Republican party, and he had supported Gen. McClellan, the Democratic nominee for President in 1864. In 1866 he purchased the *Democratic Advocate*, a newspaper started in November, 1865, by William H. Davis in the place of the old *Carroll County Democrat*, destroyed by a mob in April, 1865, and by its aid contributed to the success of the Democratic and Conservative party in the county and State. Under the constitution adopted by the convention of 1867, a new election of register of wills became necessary, and he was again nominated and elected to that office for another term of six years. On his election he sold the *Democratic Advocate* to W. H. Davis, who soon afterwards sold it to Henry Vanderford and his son, William H. Vanderford. He held the office of register of wills for nearly nineteen years, retiring therefrom in December, 1873, since which time he has not aspired to political station, but has quietly devoted himself to the practice of his profession. In 1860 he was a strenuous supporter of the late Stephen A. Douglas for the Presidency, and of the compromises introduced into Congress to heal the breach between the North and South. When the war broke out he adhered to the Northern Democracy, and warmly supported the cause of the Union, carefully discriminating between the government and the party conducting it; believing, in fact, that the South, by its factious rejection of Senator Douglas, one of its truest friends, and its secession from the Northern Democrats, had caused Mr. Lincoln's election.

When the war was over, Mr. Parke favored the policy of President Andrew Johnson, to restore the era of good feeling between the sections, and to admit the Southern States at once to their rights in the Union. He believed that there were mutual errors, and that the North was not so clear of blame as to entitle her to demand humiliating terms of the South. He has always maintained and expressed an exalted idea of the future of our great republic, and of its providential mission, and predicts that as soon as the sore places caused by the late war shall have been healed our entire people will combine to make the country what Providence designed it to be,—an illustration of the ability of the people to govern themselves, allowing the maximum amount of freedom, and securing the greatest prosperity to all.

The Farmers' and Planters' Live-Stock Mutual Aid Association of Carroll County was incorporated May 9, 1881, with the home-office in Westminster, for the sole insurance of live-stock. Its officers are Samuel Roop, president; Theodore F. Englar, vice-president; Charles H. Baughman, secretary; Charles Schaeffer, treasurer; B. F. Crouse, attorney. Board of Trustees, Samuel Roop, Theodore F. Englar, Milton Schaeffer, Charles H. Baughman, Dr. George S. Yingling, Charles Schaeffer, B. F. Crouse.

The State Mutual Benefit Association of Carroll County was incorporated in 1879. Its officers are: President, Jesse Reifsnider; Vice-President, Granville S. Haines; Secretary, Dr. George S. Yingling; Treasurer, George R. Gehr; Counselor, Charles T. Reifsnider; Medical Director, J. G. Keller, M.D. The board of trustees are Jesse Reifsnider, Granville S. Haines, Joshua Yingling, Philip H. L. Myers, Andrew N. Stephan, George R. Gehr, Charles T. Reifsnider, Josiah G. Keller, George S. Yingling, M.D.

The corner-stone of the engine house of the Westminster Fire Department was laid Monday, April 14, 1879, in the presence of a large number of people. Members of Door to Virtue Lodge and George Washington Masonic Lodge met at the Odd-Fellows' Hall, and preceded by the Silver Run Band marched to the lot opposite the Catholic church, formed a square, and at once performed the ceremonies. Dr. William H. Rippard, W. M., called the brethren to order. Prayer was offered by Rev. J. D. Still, pastor of Centenary Methodist Episcopal Church. The Master of the lodge, assisted by I. H. Miller, S. W., and Edward Ziegler, J. W., then laid the corner-stone, the members making the necessary responses. Hon. John E. Smith, the orator of the occasion, was absent, owing to indisposition. Dr. Rippard, president of the fire company, made a statement giving in brief a history of the fire department, what they had accomplished, and what they had every reason to expect from the citizens. The customary box was placed in the stone. It contains two copies each of the *Democratic Advocate* and *American Sentinel*, fractional currency, constitution, by-laws, and names of the members of the fire company, letters from Charles T. Holloway, fire inspector, and from the fire commissioners of Baltimore, and an autograph album containing the names of the business men of Westminster and others to the number of about one hundred and fifty, and an account of the "Walking Match." The stone was made by A. J. Beaver, marble-cutter, of Westminster, and is seven by twelve inches. It has inscribed on it, A.D. 1879. The officers for 1881 were:

President, Dr. William H. Rippard; First Vice-President, Chas. V. Mantz; Second Vice-President, E. J. Lawyer; Secretary and Treasurer, Denton S. Gehr; Assistant Secretary and Treasurer, Frank W. Shriver; Chief Foreman, Frank K. Herr; Assistant Chief Foreman, J. C. Mobley; Foreman of Truck, Wm. H. Shaeffer; Assistant Foreman of Truck, A. M. Warner; Foreman of Engine, J. Frank Brinkerhoff; Assistant Foreman of Engine, Edward L. Smith; Marshal, John H. Mitten; Librarian, W. L. Seabrook; Janitor, Charles Hill.

At a very early date in the history of Carroll County a decided interest was manifested in the organization and development of branches of the noted secret societies for the encouragement of brotherhood and benevolence among the people, and especially was this noticeable among the Masons, and doubtless much of the vigorous growth of sound principles and reciprocity of feelings and sentiments which characterize the people of that county in a marked degree are due to the benign influences of these orders.

Door to Virtue Lodge, No. 46, of Ancient Free and Accepted Masons, was chartered Nov. 4, 1811, to hold its meetings at Pipe Creek, where it had held its first meeting on Sunday, June 23, 1811, under a dispensation from the Most Worshipful the Grand Master of Maryland. Its last meeting at Pipe Creek was held Sept. 25, 1813, when it was removed to Uniontown, where, Nov. 7, 1813, the first meeting at that place was held. The question of the removal of the lodge from Uniontown to Westminster had occupied the attention of the brethren for several months, and it was finally resolved, on the 11th of July, 1824, "that Door to Virtue Lodge, No. 46, be removed, so that the lodge may be opened and held at Westminster on the fourth Sunday in this month (the 25th inst.), at ten o'clock A.M., and thereafter forever." A committee, previously appointed (June 20th) for that purpose, had entered into an agreement with Jacob Pouder, whereby the use of suitable rooms in his house was obtained for the meetings of the lodge at the rent of thirty dollars per annum. The first communication of the lodge at Westminster was accordingly held on the 25th of July, 1824, and the record shows it to have been a very busy one indeed. First the honorary degree of Past Master was conferred upon Jacob Pouder and John C. Cockey, the latter of whom was then duly installed senior warden, after which John Gilbert and Joseph Arthur were raised to the degree of Master Mason. Petitions for initiation also were received from George Warner and Henry Geatty. The officers from December, 1824, to December, 1825, were John C. Cockey, W. M.; Benjamin Yingling, S. W.; Jacob Pouder, J. W.; W. H. McCannon, Sec.; and M. Barnitz, Treas. On the 19th June, 1825, a resolution was adopted, changing the time of meeting to the third Saturday of each month "at early candlelight." The officers for December, 1825, to June, 1826, were J. C. Cockey, W. M.; B. Yingling, S. W.; Joshua Sundergill, J. W.; A. McIlhenny, Sec.; and Jacob Pouder, Treas. For the term ending December, 1826, no election appears to have been held, but on the 19th of November the following officers were selected to serve from St. John the Evangelist's day until June, 1827, viz.: J. C. Cockey, W. M.; Dr. William Zollickoffer, S. W.; J. Sundergill, J. W.; A. McIlhenny, Sec.; and J. Pouder, Treas. Mr. Cockey died, however, before the new term began, and his funeral, Dec. 12, 1826, was long remembered, not only for the unusually imposing Masonic solemnities with which it was attended, but also for the expressions of respectful sorrow which it elicited from the entire community. At the election held June 17, 1827, the officers chosen were Dr. William Zollickoffer, W. M.; J. Sundergill, S. W.; John S. Murray, J. W.; Dr. James Fisher, Sec.; and Joseph Arthur, Treas. The lodge, however, seems at this time to have lost much of its original vigor, and to have succumbed to adverse influences, many of which are to-day merely conjectural.

Prominent among them was doubtless the anti-Masonic excitement growing out of the alleged abduction of William Morgan, of Batavia, N. Y., in the autumn of 1826, for his alleged exposure of the secrets of the craft, and the organization in the following year of a political party avowedly hostile to Freemasonry. At all events, at the meeting held Oct. 21, 1827, it was resolved, "that Brothers Pouder and Murray settle and close the account of rent for the lodge," and the record of that date closes as follows: "No further business appearing to claim the attention of this lodge, it was, in accordance with a previous resolution, in harmony and love, *closed forever*. Signed, James Fisher, Sec."

Door to Virtue Lodge, it will be remembered, started with nine original or charter members, and held its first meeting on the 23d of June, 1811. In the course of the sixteen years and four months from that date till the surrender of its charter on the 21st of October, 1827, the number initiated was ninety-four, passed eighty, raised seventy-two, affiliated ten, while the honorary degree of Past Master was conferred upon forty-three members.

For more than thirty-eight years Door to Virtue's surrendered charter reposed in the archives of the Grand Lodge, and it seemed as if the old entry in the record was true, and that the lodge was in reality *closed forever*. But it was not so. As the result of a petition presented to the Grand Lodge at the November communication, 1865, and signed by twenty-five Master Masons, among whom were a due number of the old members of the lodge, the original charter was restored by Grand Master John Coates, Jan. 29, 1866, to Hon. John E. Smith as W. M., Rev. James W. Reese, S. W., and William H. H. Geatty as J. W., on behalf of the petitioners. The first meeting under the restored charter was held in Odd-Fellows' Hall, in the city of Westminster, on Tuesday evening, Feb. 6, 1866, when the officers just named, as well as A. D. Schaeffer and William A. McKellip, who had been elected respectively secretary and treasurer, were duly installed by Daniel A. Piper, P. M., Concordia, No. 13, Grand Tyler, proxy for the M. W. Grand Master; Bro. E. T. Shultz, W. M., Concordia, No. 13, and Grand Inspector for Baltimore City, as Senior Grand Warden; Bro. William D. Jones, P. M., Warren, No. 51, as Junior Grand Warden; John Van Tromp, W. M., Mystic Circle, No. 109, and Grand Inspector for Baltimore City, as Senior Grand Deacon; and David Martin, of Concordia, No. 13, as Junior Grand Deacon. On this occasion five petitions for initiation were received, and the first degree was conferred on William Hammett, Jr. Thus happily resuscitated, Door to Virtue Lodge became at once the centre of a vigorous and healthy Masonic activity, and applications from the best citizens were so numerous that for several years weekly communications were necessary in order to keep abreast of the "work" which came crowding in on the busy craft. On the 7th of April the lodge accompanied to the grave the remains of their veteran brother, Henry Geatty, who was "entered" Aug. 8, 1824, "passed" September 26th, and raised Jan. 9, 1825, and who died April 5, 1866, aged seventy-three years.

The officers from June to December, 1866, were Rev. James W. Reese, W. M.; William H. H. Geatty, S. W.; William A. McKellip, J. W.; A. D. Schaeffer, Sec.; and William A. Cunningham, Treas.

On the afternoon of September 6th the Master, assisted by his wardens, and surrounded by seventy-five of the brethren, laid the corner-stone of "Western Maryland College."

On Tuesday, November 20th, the lodge formed part of the immense procession which celebrated the laying of the corner-stone of the new Masonic Temple in the city of Baltimore. From December, 1866, to June, 1867, the officers were James W. Reese, W. M.; Wm. A. McKellip, S. W.; A. D. Schaeffer, J. W.; E. K. Gernand, Sec.; and W. A. Cunningham, Treas. The festival of St. John the Evangelist, Dec. 27, 1866, was appropriately observed by a banquet, a reunion of all the Masons of the county, and an oration by the Worshipful Master. On the 6th of June, 1867, the "Committee of Southern Relief" reported that they had collected and forwarded to the Masonic authorities of Georgia the sum of one hundred dollars, "to relieve the distress of our suffering brethren in that State." The officers from June to December, 1867, were J. W. Reese, W. M.; A. D. Schaeffer, S.W.; J. E. Pierson, Jr., J. W.; Joseph A. McKellip, Sec.; and W. A. Cunningham, Treas. The lodge, August 22d, participated in a most enjoyable picnic, given by Freedom Lodge, No. 112, during which, at the request of the latter, the Master of Door to Virtue delivered an oration on the "characteristics of Freemasonry." From December, 1867, to June, 1868, the officers were J. W. Reese, W. M.; J. E. Pierson, Jr., S. W.; Michael W. Sullivan, J. W.; Henry B. Grammer, Sec.; and W. A. Cunningham, Treas. On Wednesday, Feb. 26, 1868, the remains of Jacob D. Hoppe, an esteemed brother, ex-sheriff of the county, were consigned to the earth with Masonic ceremonies. On the occasion of the marriage of Worshipful Master Reese to Miss Mary Pauline Perry, of Westminster, on the 12th of February, the members of the lodge had prepared a beautiful present for him, consisting of an ice-pitcher, a pair of goblets, and a waiter, all of silver and suitably inscribed. On the evening of the 27th, says the record, "the Tyler was sent to summon the Master, who was unavoidably absent. The Worshipful Master, on his entrance into the lodge, was received with the grand honors, and was at once presented by P. M. John E. Smith, in the name of the lodge, with the gift abovenamed. The Worshipful Master, as well as his surprise would permit, responded with much feeling and cordial thanks." On the 6th of May a special communication was held at Union Bridge for the purpose of laying the corner-stone of the Methodist Episcopal church at that place. The officers from June to December, 1868, were J. W. Reese, W. M.; C. N. Kuhn, S. W.; David H. Zepp, J. W.; H. B. Grammer, Sec.; and Michael Baughman, Treas. From December, 1868, to June, 1869, J. W. Reese, W. M., J. W.; S. A. Leister, Sec.; and W. A. Cunningham, Treas. The festival of the nativity of St. John the Baptist, June 24, 1870, was observed in the afternoon by a procession and the solemn consecration of the burial lot belonging to the lodge in the Westminster Cemetery, and, at night, by the public installation of officers and an eloquent address by P. M. John E. Smith on the principles and tenets of Freemasonry. From June to December, 1871, the officers were J. W. Reese, W. M.; Wm. Coon, S. W.; S. A. Leister, J. W.; Wm. Moore, Sec.; and W. A. Cunningham, Treas., who were publicly installed June 22d, in the presence of a large assembly, including many ladies. The music, which was of a high order, was furnished by a volunteer choir and by the "Amphions," and the address, owing to the absence of Grand Master John H. B. Latrobe, who had been invited and expected to perform that duty, was delivered by the Worshipful Master of the lodge.

At a special meeting held October 14th the sum of eighty-five dollars was contributed by the members present for the relief of sufferers by the great fire at Chicago.

The officers from December, 1871, to June, 1872, were J. W. Reese, W. M.; S. A. Leister, S. W.; A. D. Schaeffer, J. W.; Wm. Moore, Sec.; and W. A. Cunningham, Treas.; C. N. Kuhn, S. W.; George Leas, J. W.; Wm. A. McKellip, Sec.; and M. Baughman, Treas. The festival of St. John the Evangelist, December 27th, falling on Sunday in 1868, the lodge observed the day by proceeding in a body to Ascension (Protestant Episcopal) church, of which the W. M. was a rector, where they participated in divine service and listened to a sermon on the life and character of "that beloved Disciple."

On the 18th of February, 1869, by a unanimous vote, the lodge gave its recommendation to a petition of a number of Baltimore County brethren to the Grand Master for a dispensation to open the lodge at Reisterstown, now so well and favorably known as Ionic, No. 145. June 8th was devoted by the lodge to the laying of the corner-stone of the Centenary (M. E.) church in Westminster. From June to December, 1869, the officers were J. W. Reese, W. M.; George Leas, S. W.; William Coon, J. W.;

Francis D. Sanford, Sec.; and W. A. Cunningham, Treas. On September 27th the funeral of Michael W. Sullivan, a faithful and zealous brother, took place.

The officers from December, 1869, to June, 1870, were J. W. Reese, W. M.; George Leas, S. W.; William Coon, J. W.; S. A. Leister, Sec.; and W. A. Cunningham, Treas. From June, 1870, to June, 1871, J. W. Reese, W. M.; William Moore, S. W.; William Coon.

On Sunday, April 14, 1872, Dr. Lewis Kelley was buried with the honors usually paid by the fraternity to the memory of a deceased brother.

The officers from June to December, 1872, were J. W. Reese, W. M.; S. A. Leister, S. W.; L. F. Beyers, J. W.; William Moore, Sec.; W. A. Cunningham, Treas.

On the 3d of October the lodge received and accepted an invitation from Friendship Lodge, No. 84, Hagerstown, to participate in the laying of the corner-stone of the new court-house in that city.

From December, 1872, to June, 1873, the officers were J. W. Reese, W. M.; S. A. Leister, S. W.; F. D. Sanford, J. W.; William Moore, Sec.; and W. A. Cunningham, Treas.

At a special communication, June 18th, on the eve of the departure of the Master for Europe, the members of the lodge presented to him, through Brother John E. Smith, an envelope containing one hundred dollars, "as a tribute of love and respect." An elegant repast then followed, attended by toasts and speeches, and many expressions of good wishes for a happy termination to the European tour on which the Worthy Master and Brother William A. McKellip were to sail on the 21st.

The officers from June to December, 1873, were J. W. Reese, W. M.; W. A. Cunningham, S. W.; George R. Gehr, J. W.; William Moore, Sec.; and James Rippard, Treas. From December, 1873, to December, 1874, J. W. Reese, W. M.; George R. Gehr, S. W.; Wm. O. Liggett, J. W.; William Moore, Sec.; and James Rippard, Treas. On St. John's (the Baptist) day, June 24, 1874, the officers-elect were installed by Jacob H. Medairy, R. W. G. S. of the Grand Lodge of Maryland, after which a banquet was served in the Town-Hall, all the lodges of the county being present as guests. On September 2d the Master, assisted by the wardens and brethren, laid the corner-stone of the Baptist church in Westminster.

From December, 1874, to December, 1876, the officers were J. W. Reese, W. M.; G. R. Gehr, S. W.; E. J. Lawyer, J. W.; William Moore, Sec.; and James Rippard, Treas. On Jan. 4, 1876, the lodge consigned to the tomb with Masonic honors the body of Brother Michael Baughman, ex-treasurer, and on the 26th of the following month a special communication was held at New Windsor for the purpose of performing the same sad service for Brother Washington W. Naill.

At the meeting of Dec. 21, 1876, J. W. Reese, after expressing his high appreciation of the honor so repeatedly conferred upon him, respectfully but positively declined to be a candidate for re-election to the office of Worshipful Master. From that date to December, 1877, the officers were George R. Gehr, W. M.; E. J. Lawyer, S. W.; Dr. W. H. Rippard, J. W.; William Moore, Sec.; and James Rippard, Treas. At a special communication, Jan. 11, 1877, Past Master Rev. James W. Reese was presented by his successor, Worshipful Master George R. Gehr, on behalf of the members of the lodge, with a beautiful Past Master's jewel as a slight token of their appreciation of his continuous and valuable services as Master from June 21, 1866, to Dec. 21, 1876.

On Nov. 26, 1877, Brother James Lippard, the treasurer of the lodge, was buried with the customary Masonic solemnities. The officers from December, 1877, to June, 1878, were George R. Gehr, W. M.; E. J. Lawyer, S. W.; W. H. Rippard, J. W.; William Moore, Sec.; and J. W. Reese, Treas. From June to December, 1878, George R. Gehr, W. M.; W. H. Rippard, S. W.; I. A. Miller, J. W.; William Moore, Sec.; and J. W. Reese, Treas.

Aug. 23, 1878, a venerable brother, Joseph Hesson, was buried by the lodge. From December, 1878, to June, 1880, the officers were Dr. William H. Rippard, W. M.; I. Amos Miller, S. W.; H. E. Ziegler, J. W.; William Moore, Sec.; and J. W. Reese, Treas.

On April 17, 1879, Worshipful Master Dr. William H. Rippard officiated at the laying of the corner-stone of the new engine-house belonging to the Westminster Fire Department; and on December 26th following he read the solemn Masonic burial service for the burial of the dead at the grave of Brother Jeremiah Robertson.

Door to Virtue Lodge held its first meeting under the restored charter Feb. 6, 1866, with twenty-four members on its roll. From that date to June 1, 1880, fourteen were admitted to membership by affiliation, eighty-two candidates were initiated, seventy-two "passed" to the degree of Fellow Craft, and seventy-one "raised" to the degree of Master Mason; the number of deaths were eighteen, and of applicants rejected, eighteen. The lodge now (July, 1881) has on its register: Master Masons, sixty. From June to December, 1880, its officers were Dr. W. H. Rippard, W. M.; J. A. Miller, S. W.; George

Lease, J. W.; William Moore, Sec.; E. J. Lawyer, S. D.; C. V. Wantz, J. D. From January to July, 1881, the officers were Dr. W. H. Rippard, W. M.; J. A. Miller, S. W.; George Lease, J. W.; William Moore, Sec.; J. W. Reese, Treas.; E. J. Lawyer, S. D.; C. V. Wantz, J. D. From July to January, 1882, the officers were J. Amos Miller, W. M.; George Lease, S. W.; E. J. Lawyer, J. W.; William Moore, Sec.; J. W. Reese, Treas. Of those members of the lodge when its charter was surrendered in 1827, Dr. James Fisher was the last survivor, and he died at Springfield, Mo., in the spring of 1881.

George Washington Lodge, No. 94, A. F. and A. M., was instituted some thirty years ago, but is not now in working order. From 1866 to 1881, Dr. Winfield K. Fringer was Worshipful Master, and J. W. Perkins was the last secretary.

The Independent Order of Odd-Fellows, a much younger association, has in many instances made up in zeal and works for the lack of antiquity. The attention of the order was directed to Carroll County soon after its formation, and some of its most active and flourishing branches are to be found there.

Salem Lodge, No. 60, I. O. O. F., was instituted in May, 1848, by a charter bearing date of May 12th of that year, and signed by E. P. Holden, M. W. Grand Master; N. T. Durbin, R. W. Deputy Master; G. D. Tewsbury, R. W. G. Sec.; Wm. Bayley, R. W. G. Treas.; and W. Fitzsimmons, Grand Warden. The charter members were C. W. Webster, Richard Manning, C. A. Smeltzer, Charles A. Poole, John W. Durbin, J. Q. Baugher, Joshua Yingling, D. Mitten. Its first officers were: N. G., J. L. Baugher; V. G., Joshua Yingling; Sec., J. W. Durbin; Treas., Richard Manning. In the first term of 1849, C. W. Webster was N. G.; William Wolf, V. G.; and George E. Wampler, Sec. The officers for the second term of 1849 were: N. G., William Wolf; V. G., John Matthias; Sec., George E. Wampler; Treas., Richard Manning; Per. Sec., Joseph Shaeffer. Its fine hall was dedicated on the second Thursday of November, 1858, the interesting ceremonies being performed by Hon. Joshua Vansant, Grand Master of the Grand Lodge of Maryland. William H. Young, Esq., Deputy Grand Master, delivered the address on the occasion.

The officers for the second term of 1881 were:

N. G., Samuel Hughes; V. G., W. L. Brown; Rec. Sec., H. L. Norris (for 14 years); Per. Sec., E. K. Gernand; Treas., F. A. Sharer; Marshal, John Bernstine; R. S. to N. G., F. C. Sharer; L. S. to N. G., John J. Reese; Warden, John Bernstine; Conductor, W. H. Rippard; R. S. to V. G., S. P. Everhart; L. S. to V. G., S. B. Fowler; R. S. S., W. J. Beaver; L. S. S., A. F. Fowler; O. G., E. L. Zahn; I. G., Geo. A. Zahn.

Number of members, 145; value of real estate, $10,000.

The charter of Columbia Encampment, No. 14, was granted Dec. 6, 1850, and signed by James P. Merritt, Grand Patriarch. The charter members were D. Evans Reese, J. L. Baugher, James Brewster, William Shreev, Joshua Yingling, John Matthias, Joseph Shaeffer, Levi Shreev.

The officers for 1881 were:

C. P., George P. Albaugh; H. P., H. L. Norris; S. W., Lewis A. Koontz; J. W., Charles H. Henneman; Sec., Joshua Yingling; Treas., H. B. Grammer; Trustees, H. L. Norris, John Bernstein, G. P. Albaugh.

The Independent Order of Red Men appears to have been a favorite association with the inhabitants of Carroll, as some of its lodges were instituted in the county at an early period, and have steadily grown in strength and influence.

Conowaga Tribe, No. 71, I. O. R. M., was instituted in Westminster, Jan. 11, 1881, with twenty-four members.

The officers are:

P., Milton Schaeffer; S., Charles H. Baughman; S. S., B. F. Crouse; J. S., James Humphreys; C. of R., F. W. Shriver; Ass't to C., George Batson; K. of W., J. Frank Brinkerhoff; Sannaps, F. S. Wright, John Keene; Warriors, Jacob Thomson, John A. Little, John Warner, Henry Harman; Braves, O. D. Gilbert, Milton Senpt, John Mitten, John Cassell; G. of W., J. B. Barnes; G. of F., James Sheets; Rep. to Grand Council, Milton Schaeffer.

The tribe meets every Tuesday night in I. O. O. F. Hall.

The dispensation for organizing Charity Lodge, No. 58, Knights of Pythias, was granted June 14, 1870, by Samuel Read, Supreme Chancellor, and J. M. Barton, Supreme Secretary and Corresponding Scribe. The charter members were John W. Yingling, J. Wesley Perkins, William Moore, Jacob Leister, J. M. Weller, John T. Oursler, Charles J. Yingling, Edward L. Bachman, Francis K. Herr, Michael Baughman. Its regular charter was dated Nov. 14, 1871, and signed by M. A. Steiner, V. G. P.; M. Schmidt, G. B.; G. N. Dickinson, G. C.; John P. Hudson, G. G.; J. F. Lewis, V. G. C.; Robert Sullapsey, G. I. S.; O. H. Vaughan, G. O. S; Thomas S. Upperci, G. R. S.

The lodge officers for 1881 were:

C. C., John H. Keene; V. C., Milton Schaeffer; Prel., R. C. Matthews; K. of R., Clinton S. Spurrier; M. of F., John G. Shank; M. of E., Edwin J. Lawyer; M. at A., Jesse Mitten; Trustees, E. J. Lawyer, John H. Hilton, John F. Shade, J. Wesley Pool, John M. Black; Representative to Grand Lodge, J. H. Mitten. Number of members, 65.

The officers of the lodge of Independent Order of Mechanics were in 1881:

W. M., Milton Shaeffer; J. M., James Humphreys; F. S., George Batson; R. S., C. H. Baughman; Chaplain, Benj. Franklin; Treas., Joseph Hunter; Conductor, Wm. J. Sheets; O. S., Fletcher A. Baile; I. S., Jesse Mitten; R. G. to W. M., F. A. Knight; L. G. to W. M., Harry Harman; R. G. to J. M., Philip Hunter; L. G. to J. M., Curtis A. Brown; Representative to Grand Lodge, Abraham Long.

J. Henry Hoppe was born near Bowers' church, now called Bachman's, in Bachman's Valley, Feb. 17, 1801. His father was Ferdinand Frederick Hoppe, and was born in Stuttgart, Germany. His mother was Catharine Snouffer, of Frederick County. Mr. Hoppe received a common-school education, after which he taught school for five years, studying surveying in the meanwhile, in which he became very proficient. On attaining his majority he united with the Democratic party, and always remained a stanch follower of "Old Hickory."

In 1825 he was appointed a magistrate, and, with the exception of a few years, he held the position until twelve months before his death. He became so thoroughly versed in testamentary law that he was frequently appointed to settle the estates of deceased persons, several of which were very large. In 1842 he was elected sheriff of this county, at which time there were fifteen candidates in the field. He received one hundred and forty-six votes more than Lewis Trumbo, Whig, who was the next highest. The incidents of that campaign he was fond of repeating.

Mr. Hoppe was a charter member of the Western Maryland Railroad, was elected secretary and treasurer, and was also a director in the road. He was for a number of years director of the Union National Bank of Westminster, and was also a charter member of George Washington Lodge, A. F. A. M., of that city. He was elected county surveyor for four consecutive terms. Mr. Hoppe always resided in Carroll County, though the place of his birth was then in Baltimore County. In 1829 he was united in marriage to Rachel Myerly, daughter of Jacob Myerly and Eve Bishop. They had only one child, Josephus H., who died Dec. 27, 1877. Squire Hoppe was a member of the Lutheran Church for over sixty years. No man in Carroll County was more generally or more favorably known. He died Jan. 5, 1881, after an active and busy career of nearly eighty years.

Carroll Division, No. 42, of the Sons of Temperance, was instituted Feb. 12, 1847, and has been in continuous and successful operation to the present time. Its charter was signed by the State grand officers, William Young, Grand Worthy Patriarch, and W. H. Gobright, Grand Scribe. Its charter members were Isaac Shriver, Thomas W. Durbin, Rev. Theodore Gallandet, Joshua Sundergill, Horatio Price, John Malchorn, Francis Shriver, William Zepp, Alfred Troxel, John Miller, James Keefer, Emanuel L. Kuns, Henry H. Wampler. It first met at Isaac Shriver's residence, and afterwards held its meetings over the *Sentinel* office, and later over Joshua Yingling's East End store. Since 1852 the society has met in its own elegant hall, completed in that year. Its officers for 1881 were:

W. P., F. K. Herr; W. A., George Lease; R. S., H. L. Norris (held this office for twenty-six years); A. R. S., C. H. Baughman; F. S., Dr. Charles Billingslea; Treas., Jesse F. Shreev; C., J. W. Pool; A. C., Thomas Bankert; I. S., George Arbaugh; O. S., George Litsinger.

Its motto is "Love, Purity, and Fidelity," which are the respective names of its three degrees, subsequently founded on this motto, adopted in 1847. It is a beneficiary association, and pays sixty dollars to the family of each deceased member. It also pays sick benefits of three and a half or four dollars per week. Its membership is forty-five. The corner-stone of the hall was laid July 4, 1850, and it was built by L. Evans and H. H. Wampler, at a cost of two thousand dollars.

The Taylor Manufacturing Company, of Westminster.—The property of a city is aptly illustrated by the number of its public buildings and its manufacturing establishments. "The Union Agricultural Works" of Westminster were opened in the summer of 1852, and were carried on under the management of William H. Harman & Co. The buildings, which had been from time to time enlarged and improved, consisted of a large two-story machine-shop, moulding-shop, blacksmith's shop, saw-mill, and sheds. They occupied nearly an acre and a half of ground. Their new mould-shop, which was finished in 1868, was one hundred feet long by fifty wide, and gave employment to fourteen hands. The machine-shop employed five iron and ten wood workers, and the blacksmith's shop and saw-mill four; a total force of thirty-three. These works turn out every season about three hundred plows, three hundred spring-tooth rakes, and sixty horse-powers, besides numerous other agricultural machines in less numbers. In 1872, in its place, was formed "The Taylor Manufacturing Company of Westminster," by J. A. Taylor, who was then president of the company. It was an incorporated company, composed of J. A. Taylor, G. A. Taylor, Edward Lynch, David Fowble, and O. B. Baile. It was a repair foundry, and manufactured agricultural implements.

In January, 1879, it was reorganized under the name of "The Taylor Manufacturing Company of Westminster, Md." It is still a stock company, distributed among a few stockholders, with a capital stock paid in of twenty-five thousand dollars. Its members are

J. A. Taylor, president; G. A. Taylor, secretary and treasurer; R. N. Beck, superintendent; Directors, Michael Shaw, York, Pa.; Thomas F. Shephard, Union Bridge; and W. N. Wise, Baltimore.

It is largely engaged in the manufacture of engines and other machinery, and employs one hundred and fifty hands.

The people of Westminster have from the creation of the county manifested an enterprising disposition and a desire to keep abreast of the great practical discoveries of the century. The question of railroad transportation engaged the attention of the inhabitants at an early date, and the extraordinary advantages to accrue to the county by rail and steam communication were thoroughly appreciated.

The citizens of Carroll County convened at the court-house, April 7, 1847, to take into consideration the propriety of extending the Westminster Branch Railroad through Carroll County. Mr. Evan McKinstry was called to the chair, assisted by Mr. Isaac Slingluff, and John Switzer and William Reese as secretaries. Col. James M. Shellman stated the object of the meeting, and introduced G. Gordon Belt, Esq., of Baltimore, who addressed the meeting in favor of the contemplated road. Cols. Shellman and James C. Atlee offered resolutions which were adopted, that a committee of ten be appointed to correspond with the president and directors of the Baltimore and Susquehanna Railroad, and urge upon them the necessity of early action under the act of 1845, so that the speedy building of the proposed road would follow.

The committee selected were James C. Atlee, William C. Roberts, Samuel McKinstry, John Clemson, Isaac Slingluff, William N. Hayden, David W. Naille, Augustus Shriver, John K. Longwell, John B. Boyle, and John McCollum.

A town-meeting was held at Westminster on the 16th of November, 1850, for the purpose of devising ways and means for connecting the Baltimore and Susquehanna Railroad with some point in the interior of Carroll County. The meeting was addressed at some length by R. M. Magraw, Esq., president of that road, upon the advantages that might be expected to be derived from the road. He was followed by Mr. Taggart and Dr. Cole. A series of resolutions were adopted, one of which appointed an executive committee of nine persons, whose duty it was to collect information in regard to the best probable route and cost of construction of said road, together with the amount of revenue likely to accrue therefrom, which information was to be submitted to an adjourned meeting to be held in Westminster on December 2d. There were two projects entertained,—one to continue the road from Owings' Mills, and extend it into the county, instead of stopping at Westminster, and the other was to branch off at Cockeysville by way of Reisterstown to Westminster.

On December 2d a large and enthusiastic meeting was held to further consider the project of building the proposed railroad. Mr. Magraw was again present and furnished abundant facts to prove the importance of the road, which he estimated would not cost more than two hundred and ten thousand dollars, pledging himself as one of two hundred to furnish the means to build it. Four routes were proposed,—one from Cockeysville to Ely's Mill, one from Love's Switch to Black Rock, one from Cockeysville to Hampstead, and another from Owings' Mills, Reisterstown, etc. Committees to examine and report as to right of way of each of these routes were appointed. A committee was also appointed to secure a survey of the different routes.

A convention was held for the same purpose at Westminster, Feb. 26, 1851, and was composed of citizens from Frederick, Carroll, Washington, and Baltimore Counties. The meeting was largely attended, but the surveys of the various routes not being complete but little was done. Resolutions were adopted to appoint committees and take up subscriptions to make the road from some point on the Susquehanna Railroad through Westminster to Hagerstown, which route was to be in the meanwhile surveyed. The subscriptions and surveys completed, they were to be forwarded to the executive committee, who would then call a general meeting and consider the same.

The engineers of the Baltimore and Susquehanna Railroad Company deputed to survey the route of the contemplated railroad arrived at Westminster Feb. 22, 1851. Their course was *via* Owings' Mills, Reisterstown, Ely's Mills, and up to the falls of Westminster.

A large meeting of those interested in the construction of the Baltimore, Carroll and Frederick Railroad was held in the court-house in Westminster on Sept. 1, 1852. Delegates were in attendance from the whole line of the proposed road, as also from Washington and Frederick Counties, through which it was calculated to extend the road to Hagerstown, where it would connect with the Franklin Road leading to Chambersburg. The meeting was organized

J K Longwell

by the appointment of Col. Jacob Matthias, of Carroll, as president, Col. W. Fell Johnson, of Baltimore, vice-president, with Mr. Bradenbaugh, of Washington County, and Joseph M. Parker, as secretary. A resolution was offered by Jervis Spencer, looking to additional legislation in regard to the charter of the company. Among those in attendance at the meeting, and who participated in the discussion of the propositions submitted, were Jervis Spencer, Alexander Neill, and others, of Washington; Wm. P. Maulsby, A. G. Ege, W. Hayden, J. K. Longwell, and Jos. Raymond, of Carroll County. The citizens of Westminster seem to have been greatly elated on hearing that the mayor of Baltimore City had signed the ordinance passed by the City Council indorsing five hundred thousand dollars' worth of eight per cent. Western Maryland Railway bonds. On July 28th the event was celebrated by the firing of cannon, and at night a large meeting was held and speeches were made by John E. Smith, C. W. Webster, and Joseph M. Parker, attended with music by the Westminster Band. Another meeting of general rejoicing was held at New Windsor on July 31st.

Carroll County Lyceum was incorporated by an act of the Legislature, March 30, 1839. The incorporators were Jacob Mathias, John McCollum, A. H. Busby, John F. Reese, John K. Longwell, Dr. George Shriver, John Baumgartner, H. Crout, James M. Shellman, Nicholas Kelly, Dr. Wm. Willis, A. F. Shriver, Isaac Van Bibber, Thos. E. Van Bibber, N. H. Thayer, Thomas Hook, C. W. Webster, James Raymond, Jacob Grove, Horatio Price, James Keefer, Samuel Orendorff, Jacob Reese, S. D. Lecompte, George Webster, John S. Baurgelt.

Maj. A. G. Enge, formerly of this county, died at his residence in Kansas in December, 1876. He represented Carroll in the House of Delegates in 1854, and in the Constitutional Convention of 1851. During his residence here in Carroll County he was frequently and prominently spoken of as a Whig candidate for Governor of the State. He was a brother-in-law of Col. John K. Longwell, and emigrated to Kansas about twenty years prior to his death.

James Raymond, who was a well-known member of the Carroll County bar, and who was admitted to practice at the first term of the court in April, 1837, died at his home in Westminster in January, 1858, in the sixty-second year of his age. He was a native of Connecticut, a graduate of Yale College, and for twenty-one years a citizen of Westminster. Several years prior to his decease he represented Carroll County in the Legislature, and was the author of a work known as "Raymond's Digest of Chancery Cases."

In the past half-century no man has been more closely identified with the financial, political, and material history of Carroll County than Col. John K. Longwell. He was born in the historic town of Gettysburg, Pa., in October, 1810, and was the son of Matthew and Jane (Klinehoff) Longwell. His father, a reputable merchant in that town, was of Scotch-Irish descent, whose ancestors at a very early period emigrated from the north of Ireland and settled in Pennsylvania. His mother was of Hollandish extraction, and from a race noted for their thrift and rare domestic qualities. Col. Longwell was educated in the academy of his native town, and learned the printing-business in the office of the *Adams Sentinel*, now the *Star and Sentinel*, of Gettysburg. In 1832 he removed to Taneytown, of this county, and established *The Recorder*, which paper was the successor of *The Regulator and Taneytown Herald*, a journal published for a year or two. He printed this paper about a year, and in the spring of 1833 came to Westminster and established *The Carrolltonian*. This journal was chiefly devoted to the interests of the formation of a new county with the county-seat at Westminster. Its first issue appeared June 25, 1833, and even the opponents of the measure acknowledged the zeal, ability, and fidelity with which it was conducted, until in four years afterwards the efforts of its editor and friends were crowned with success. He edited, published, and was connected with this paper for about eighteen years, and it was finally merged into the *American Sentinel*. He was married in 1840 to the youngest daughter of Maj. John McCaleb, of Taneytown, who came when only nine years of age with his father, Joseph McCaleb, from the north of Ireland. The McCalebs were early settlers around Taneytown and large landed proprietors. By this union Col. Longwell has one surviving daughter. Originally a Whig in politics, he has acted with the Democratic party for over twenty years. He was elected a State senator in 1850, and served four years in the Senate. In 1867 he was elected one of the delegates to the Constitutional Convention, and assisted in the framing of the present organic law of Maryland. In 1871 he was again chosen State senator for a term of four years. In 1879 he was prevailed upon to accept a nomination for the office of county commissioner,—the most important office in the State to the farmers, business men, and tax-payers,—and was triumphantly elected and made president of the board. He was the author of the charter of the Western Maryland Railroad, and secured its passage by the Legislature, and when this railroad was put under contract he was one of its board of directors, and is now a member of the board. He became a director in the Westminster Bank (now Union National), and has been its president for twenty-five years. Since 1858 he has been president of the Baltimore and Reisterstown turnpike, a road built in 1805, and for many years the great national thoroughfare from Baltimore to Pittsburgh for travel and freight. At the centennial celebration of July 4, 1876, in Westminster, he prepared and read a history of the county, with which no person in its limits is more familiar. He is a member of the Piney Creek Presbyterian Church, organized in 1763. His home, "Emerald Hill," at Westminster, is one of the most elegant private residences in the county. Col. Longwell contributed more than any single individual to the organization of Carroll County, and since its erection has been constantly associated with its progress, and the many public and fiduciary positions conferred upon him show the esteem in which he is held by the community.

The Carroll Rifle Association, for recreation and improvement in marksmanship, was organized June 28, 1879, by the election of the following officers: President, Dr. W. H. Rippard; Secretary and Treasurer, J. S. Weavers; Captain of Team, John T. Beard; Committee on Grounds, J. A. Miller, Joseph Pulis, and C. W. Knight. The following is a list of members: Col. McKellip, William B. Thomas, Dr. Swarmstedt, Frank Shriver, Ed. W. Shriver, Ed. H. Shriver, Denton Gehr, Henry Troutfelter, Michael Shuey, James Humphreys, Milton Wagoner, E. J. Lawyer, Samuel Roop, Willis R. Zumbrum, John C. Weaver, A. H. Wentz, B. F. Crouse, William Myerly, Jesse Smith, J. E. Crouse, J. Shunk, P. Callaghan, J. Winfield Snoder, J. J. Baumgartner, Peter Woods, John T. Anders.

At the celebration of Easter Monday in 1879 the most prominent event of the day was the eight-hour go-as-you-please pedestrian contest on the grounds of the Carroll County Agricultural Society, which was nearly an all-day affair. Large representations from every section of the county were present.

The contest was for a purse of $50: $25 to the first, $15 to the second, and $10 to the third. Half of the gate-money was also to be added in the same proportion. The entrance fee was two dollars, and the following entered, drawing positions in the order named: William Copenhover, John Groff, G. H. Walter, William H. Bell, Benjamin Gist, R. Palmer, Jacob Reinaman, Samuel Groff, Henry Himler, S. H. Blakesly,—all residents of this city and vicinity, except Copenhover, who was from Silver Run, and Blakesly, from Mexico.

Below we give the distance made by each contestant in each of the eight hours:

	1	2	3	4	5	6	7	8	Total.
John Groff	7½	6¼	6	5½	6	6	4½	5	47
Copenhover	6	6	4½	5	off	...	...	...	23½
Walter	5	4½	4½	off	...	...	...	...	15
Bell	6	6½	6	5½	5½	5½	5	5	45
Gist	6	7½	6	5	5	6	4½	4	44
Palmer	5½	5½	5	5½	4½	4½	5	4	39½
Samuel Groff	6½	6	4	3½	off	...	...	...	20
Himler	6	5½	6	5½	6	5½	off	...	35
Blakesly	6	6	4½	4	off	...	...	...	21½
Reinaman	5½	6	5	5	4½	off	...	...	26

John Groff, the winner, was a native of Westminster, and for nine years previous was engaged in a brickyard. He was seventeen years of age, five feet four inches high, of slender build, and weighed one hundred and ten pounds.

W. H. Bell was also a native of the city of Westminster, twenty-one years old, and weighed about one hundred and thirty pounds. He was a blacksmith by trade.

Benjamin Gist was a son of Samuel Gist, residing near this city, nineteen years old, and accustomed to farm-labor.

The Fourth of July, 1876, the centenary of American independence, was universally and enthusiastically celebrated in the United States, and Westminster was no exception in this respect. There were doubtless more imposing demonstrations at other points, but few that were more sensible and useful, or that exhibited a profounder appreciation of the benefits derived from a hundred years of self-government, or a more grateful sense of the value of the inheritance bequeathed to their successors by the founders of the republic. At an early hour the streets were thronged by an immense concourse of people, who were speedily formed into line by the chief marshal of the day, Hon. Wm. P. Maulsby, and his aides.

The order of the procession was as follows:

Chief Marshal and Aides.

Hanover Drum Corps.

Capt. A. D. Kohler, George Crumbine, G. K. Metzer, Kervin Smith, Lewis I. Renant, Jacob Bonge, John A. Cremer, M. H. Naill, Robert Stahl, Zachary Taylor Bonge, Franklin Kahle.

Surviving soldiers of the war of 1812; among them were Col. Joshua C. Gist, Michael Byers, Sterling Galt, and John Uhler. These were followed by the survivors of the first officers of the county, invited guests, the reverend clergy, the historian of the day, the readers of the Declaration, Washington's Farewell Address, and of the poem,—all in carriages.

Thirteen young ladies, in appropriate costumes, on horseback, each bearing a banneret, representing one of the original thirteen States, each horse led by a colored groom, dressed in white jacket and flowing pantaloons, with red cap of Nubian pattern, each lady with an attendant guard of honor. The names of the young ladies on horseback were Hattie Gist, Maryland; Ella Fringer, Pennsylvania; Alice Miller, New Jersey; Alreta Zepp, North Carolina; Mary Spellman, Georgia; Katie Miller, Massachusetts; Virginia Reese, Virginia; Ella Beachman, Delaware; Mollie Wheeler, South Carolina; Jennie Wilson, New Hampshire; Ella Shrieve, Connecticut; Jennie Golden, Rhode Island; Cordelia Miller, New York. The place of honor was given to Miss Hattie Gist, the young lady who represented Maryland, who is a great-granddaughter of Col. Mordecai Gist, of the old Maryland Line.

Mount Pleasant Band.

Platoon of four Mounted Guards.

Thirty-seven young ladies, representing the different States of the Union, all dressed in white, with crimson caps, with the name of the State in gilt letters on the sash in a corner, appropriately festooned with flags and banners, and decorated with a portrait of Washington in front. The car was drawn by six black horses; each horse was led by a colored groom in Nubian costume. The car was driven by Mr. John Tracy. The names of the young ladies were Hattie Bollinger, Louisa Zahn, Fannie Bloom, Flora Buell, Sallie Gernand, Jennie Malehorn, Emma Fowble, Carrie McElray, Estelle Marsh, Ida Fringer, Mollie Shawer, Ella Miller, Katie Baumgartner, Nannie Miller, Fannie Ebaugh, Mattie Ebaugh, Maggie Horner, Jennie Gist, Mary C. Wheeler, Lizzie Buckingham, Estelle White, Laura Smith, Ada Zepp, Ida Koontz, Ida Tracy, Amanda Poole, Rena Wagoner, Mattie Hull, Nicy Hull, Grace Bowers, Hannah Bowers, Annie Earnest, Jennie Fowler, Mollie Hoppe, Emma Heagy, Anna Haines, Emma Wright.

There was a Guard of Honor, composed of one hundred young men in rich and appropriate costumes, mounted upon fine horses, and commanded by F. I. Wheeler. Some of these flanked the representatives of the States, and the remainder rode in solid column in the rear of the car. Each guard had an eight-foot spear, with streamer on the point.

National Grays' Band.

Representatives of Chili and Cuba, Arturu Leke and P. M. Lamothe, mounted and bearing their national ensigns. The first named was dressed in a rich Chilian uniform, prepared expressly for the occasion.

Frizzelsburg Band.

Salem Lodge, No. 60, I. O. O. F., of Westminster. Sons of Temperance Encampment. Charity Lodge, No. 58, Knights of Pythias, of Westminster, in full uniform,—a very handsome display. United Order of American Mechanics. Trades, Granges, and Industries.

Fairview Brass Band (Colored).

Sentinel Job Printing Press, on a wagon, driven by steam. Handsome Portable Engine from the Taylor Manufacturing Company, Westminster. Reaping Machines in motion, from the shops of Mr. Elijah Wagoner, Westminster. Then followed a long line of visitors and citizens in carriages and on horseback, which brought up the rear.

The procession moved from the West End through Main Street to the Carroll County Agricultural Society's Fair Grounds, where a vast assemblage had already gathered. The number present was variously estimated from three to five thousand. The multitude were called to order by Col. William A. McKellip, chairman of the committee on exercises, who announced the following officers: President, Col. William P. Maulsby; Honorary Presidents, Hon. William N. Hayden, Nimrod Gardner, J. H. Hoppe, Hon. C. B. Roberts, Col. Joshua C. Gist, Col. John Lamott, Hon. John E. Smith, and Stirling Galt; Vice-Presidents, John Thompson, Rogers Birnie, A. K. Shriver, Daniel Stull, David Prugh, Hon. J. Shower, David Englar, Talbot Hammond, Henry Bussard, J. H. Winemiller, Thomas Smith, Granville S. Haines; Secretaries, William H. Vanderford and William H. Rippard. The order of exercises at the stand was as follows:

Singing of the "Star-Spangled Banner" by the choirs of Westminster, led by Mr. Buell; Miss Fanny Buell, organist.

Prayer by Rev. J. T. Ward, president of Western Maryland College.

Music by the Mount Pleasant Band.

Reading of the Declaration of Independence, by Dr. F. T. Shaw.

Music by Fairview Band.

Reading of Washington's "Farewell Address," by Dr. Charles Billingslea.

Singing, "Hail Columbia," Choir.

History of the County, prepared and read by Col. John K. Longwell.

Music by the National Grays' Band.

Ode, by Emma Alice Browne (Mrs. Capt. J. L. Beaver), read by A. H. Huber, Esq.

Singing, "America," by choir.

Prayer, by Rev. William C. Cremer.

Doxology, by choir and audience; and benediction, by Rev. Dr. Ward.

The procession reformed and marched into the city, and was dismissed by the marshal.

At the intersection of Main and Centre Streets, Messrs. John Faber and J. W. Perkins erected an arch over Main Street, which was decorated with the national colors, Chinese lanterns, and a number of small flags. The bells of the churches rang a merry peal in the morning, and again in the evening. The "Centennial Bell," erected by Messrs. Schenthall and Frank King, was rung almost incessantly through the night of the 3d, and also on the 4th.

Salutes were fired at morning, noon, and night by a detachment of artillery from Fort McHenry, under the charge of a sergeant and seven men. As the evening salute was being fired a thunder-storm prevailed, and the booming of artillery upon terra firma was answered by the electric batteries of the skies with peal on peal, which seemed to mock the impotence of man. At night there was a grand illumination throughout the city, which closed the observances of Centennial Day.

Judge William Nicholas Hayden, one of the presidents on this memorable occasion, is a lineal descendant of the Hayden family that came over with Lord Baltimore and settled in St. Mary's County. The family faithfully represented the Irish Catholic gentry, and took an active part in the first settlement of the province. On March 17, 1768, John Hayden removed from St. Mary's County to within a mile of Westminster, where he purchased a tract of land of one hundred and sixty-four acres, called "Friendship Completed," from Isaac Dehaven for one hundred pounds. The land was all in woods, but Mr. Hayden cleared it up, together with other tracts he subse-

Wm. N. Hayden

quently bought. He had eight daughters and one son. The latter, William, married Catherine Ensey. He died in 1802, and his wife in 1838. They had three daughters and seven sons, most of whom emigrated West and South and settled in the new countries. Of the sons, Basil married Apparilla Buckingham, daughter of Obadiah Buckingham, of a well-known Baltimore County family, by whom he had seven daughters and one son. He removed from his father's farm to Westminster in 1807, about the year of his marriage. He had learned the trade of hat-making with Mr. Kuhn, and carried on this business many years. He was a public-spirited citizen, and held several positions of honor and trust, from constable up to the judgeship of the Orphans' Court, having occupied the latter from 1848 to 1851. He died in 1863, and his wife two years later, both aged seventy-nine years.

Judge William N. Hayden was born Sept. 23, 1817, in Westminster, in the house his father had purchased ten years previously, on his removal to this city, and in part of which his father had his hat manufactory. His early education was obtained in the subscription schools of the city. In 1835 his father removed to Frederick County and engaged in farming for several years. While there William N. attended for a few months the school near Johnsville, after which he went to the Reisterstown (Baltimore County) Academy, then under the charge of his brother-in-law, Prof. N. H. Thayer, at present (1881) librarian of Baltimore City College. Here he pursued for a while his academic studies, and imbibed a great passion for historical literature, the reading of which induced him to turn his attention to the law. As a preparatory measure to the study of the legal profession, and to obtain means for the prosecution of his studies, he taught school. His first school was near McKinstry's Mills for three successive winters of six months each. He then attended Prof. Lauver's academy for four months at Uniontown, after which he taught school another winter.

In 1842 he came to Westminster and began reading law with Hon. James Raymond, then an eminent practitioner at the Carroll County bar. He was admitted to practice as an attorney-at-law Sept. 2, 1844, and on Dec. 8, 1846, was appointed by Hon. George R. Richardson, attorney-general of Maryland, deputy attorney-general for the county, to conduct the criminal prosecutions. He held this position for two years, until his increasing practice forced him to resign, to give his sole attention to other parts of his profession more congenial to his tastes. He then formed a law partnership with John J. Baumgardner, which continued until 1865, when the latter became connected with the old Westminster Bank (Union National).

In the spring of 1867, Judge Hayden was elected one of the members from Carroll County to the Constitutional Convention, in which he served on the judiciary and legislative committees, the most important in that body. In the fall of the same year he was elected for the term of fifteen years as an associate judge of the Circuit Court for the Fifth Judicial District, composed of Carroll, Howard, and Anne Arundel Counties. His term on the bench will expire Jan. 1, 1883.

He was married, May 31, 1859, to Eugenia Elizabeth Scott, daughter of Hon. Upton Scott. Her grandfather, John Scott, came from the north of Ireland at an early day and married a daughter of Normand Bruce, one of the first settlers near Bruceville, and sheriff of Frederick County before the Revolution Upton Scott was born in 1810, in Annapolis. He represented Carroll County in the House of Delegates in 1846, and died in 1881 in Baltimore.

Judge Hayden has one son and two daughters. On his father's side he is of Irish extraction, and on his mother's of English, while his wife is of Scotch-Irish descent. The Hayden homestead, where his great-grandfather, John Hayden, settled in 1768, remained in the family until 1838, when it was sold and subsequently divided.

Judge Hayden is a member of the Catholic Church, with which his ancestors were connected from time immemorial. Originally a Whig in politics, on the dissolution of that party in 1853 he attached himself to the Democratic organization, with which he has ever since affiliated. When engaged in a large and lucrative practice at the bar, he was noted for the ability and fidelity with which he conducted his causes, in which he won distinction and enjoyed the esteem of the court and community. On the bench he has made an able and upright judge, enjoying the respect of the bar and court officers and the confidence of the people, he being fearless in the discharge of his duties, but genial and affable in social life.

Jacob Marker, another prominent citizen of Westminster District, died Dec. 8, 1879, in the ninety-fourth year of his age. His father was a Hessian, and came over to this country during the Revolutionary war. He is believed to have been one of the fifteen hundred men stationed at Trenton, N. J., under the British Col. Rawle, when Washington crossed the Delaware amid floating ice to attack them, on the night of Dec. 25, 1776, nine hundred of whom were captured by him next day. Some of these Hessians, at the close of the war, returned to Europe with the British army, while others remained and settled in this country. The father of Mr. Marker was of the latter number. He settled at Littlestown, Pa., and married a Miss Reigel, of Myers District. Jacob Marker was born in Uniontown District, and was married when he was twenty-eight years of age. He was confirmed in the Lutheran Church when about fourteen years of age, and lived a consistent member of it for nearly eighty years. When a boy he helped to haul the stone to build the foundation of Kreider's church. His house was always open to ministers, and he was well known for his kindly disposition and charitable deeds.

The *Republican Citizen*, now published in Frederick City by the Baughman Brothers, was established in Westminster in March, 1821, under the auspices of the late Judge Abraham Shriver. A few years subsequently it was removed to Frederick. George W. Sharp was its first editor.

The *American Trumpet*, devoted to the promulgation of sentiments and news in the interest of the then called "Know-Nothing," or American, party, was established Nov. 16, 1854, by Hon. John E. Smith. After the May election in Virginia in 1855 it was sold to the Democrats. When sold its outside had been put to press, and the paper appeared with the outside zealous, as before, in its advocacy and support of the Know-Nothings, while the inside was a vigorous and uncompromising champion of the Democrats.

The Carrolltonian, a paper established and edited by Col. John K. Longwell, made its first appearance June 28, 1833. It was mainly devoted to the erection and organization of the new county, which followed in four years, and was largely due to its potent voice and influence. Before this paper was started three others had been published here by George Keating, a Mr. Burke, and George W. Sharp The *Carrolltonian* was published up to Jan. 1, 1850, its last editor and publisher being George D. Miller. It was then merged into the *American Sentinel*, with William H. Grammer as editor, publisher, and proprietor. He conducted it several years and sold it to F. H. Kerr. The latter afterwards sold it to George H. Miller, who in turn sold it to William H. Grammer. After the latter's death, Jan. 11, 1862, it was edited by Harry J. Shellman, and published by Thomas J. Lockwood, for Mr. Grammer's estate. It was then, from Sept. 10, 1868, to 1874, owned, edited, and published by W. L. W. Seabrook & Co., who sold out the office to E. J. Rippard & Co., the present publishers and proprietors, under whom Dr. William H. Rippard is editor. Both the editorial and business management of this paper have been characterized by great ability and energy. It has a very large circulation, and enjoys a lucrative advertising business.

It is the organ of the Republican party of the county, and has great influence in the counsels of that party in the State, of which it is a fearless exponent.

William L. W. Seabrook, who edited this paper from 1868 to 1874, during the two important Presidential campaigns of 1868 and 1872, was born near Fairfield, Adams Co., Pa., Oct. 9, 1833. The death of his father when he was four years of age left his mother in rather straitened circumstances with three children, of whom the eldest was nine years of age. Six years afterwards she returned with her children to her native place, in Frederick County, Md., at which time Mr. Seabrook was ten years of age. During the succeeding ten years he resided with a maternal uncle, and was employed alternately in tilling the soil and selling miscellaneous merchandise in his uncle's store, varied by attendance at the village primary school during the winter months, where he obtained a fair education in the English branches, American history, geography, and the rudiments of mathematics. At the age of seventeen he entered the office of the *Adams Sentinel*, at Gettysburg, Pa., where he continued about eighteen months and became a practical printer. On account of failing health he then abandoned the case for a period of six months, but at the age of nineteen resumed the occupation and became assistant foreman of the *Frederick Herald*, a newspaper published in Frederick City. At the age of twenty-one years he became one of the proprietors and leading editor of the paper referred to, a connection which continued about three years.

During this time, and subsequently, he has taken an active part in political movements, and has frequently discussed political issues on the public rostrum. In 1857, at the age of twenty-four, he was elected commissioner of the Land Office of the State of Maryland for the term of six years, having been a candidate on the American State ticket with Thomas Holliday Hicks, who was elected Governor at the same election. At the expiration of his term of office he was re-elected without opposition, having received the unanimous nomination of both radical and Conservative Union State conventions of that year, 1863. The adoption of the State constitution of 1867 cut short the tenure and vacated all the offices in the State except that of Governor. At the election of that year Mr. Seabrook was the Republican candidate for clerk of the Court of Appeals, but, with the other candidates on the ticket for State offices, was defeated. He was a delegate to the National Republican convention of 1864, at which Mr. Lincoln was renominated for the Presidency, and was a member of the committee which conveyed the action of the convention to the nominees. He was also elected a delegate to the National Convention of this party which renominated President Grant in 1872, but was unable to attend its sessions. Upon retiring from the Land Office in 1868 he became connected with the *American Sentinel* newspaper at Westminster, Md., as one of its proprietors, and as sole editor and manager, and so continued until Jan. 1, 1874.

In 1873 he was appointed superintendent of public stores in the Baltimore custom-house, and filled that position until Dec. 1, 1876, when he became chief United States weigher at that port. He has been prominently connected with the order of Ancient Free and Accepted Masons, having been Senior Grand Warden from 1861 to 1862, and Deputy Grand Master of the Grand Lodge of the State of Maryland from 1862 to 1864. He was married Sept. 4, 1855, in Frederick, Md., to Miss Harriet P. Thomas, a native of that city. He has been a member of the Evangelical Lutheran Church since 1851, and later has been actively identified with the work of the Young Men's Christian Association.

The Democrat and Carroll County Republican was published by Joseph M. Parke, Jan. 1, 1844, at the rate of two dollars per annum. The first page was devoted to political and miscellaneous matter, and the fourth page had twelve insolvent debtors' notices, while Hance's patent medicines occupied nearly the remainder of the page. Michael Sullivan, Benjamin Yingling, Lewis Trumbo, Jesse Manning, and Samuel Moffet announced themselves as candidates for the sheriffalty. The inside pages were filled with editorial, foreign news, and advertisements. The paper contained the following information:

The semi-annual meeting of the Carroll County Temperance Convention was held on the 26th of December. Rev. Daniel Zollickhoffer was president, and Jacob H. Christ, secretary; Rev. Hezekiah Crout opened the convention with prayer. Reports were read from the societies of Uniontown, Warfieldsburg, Westminster, Franklin, Bethesda, and Salem. Resolutions were offered by C. Birnie, Jr., asking that a committee of three be appointed to wait upon the commissioners of tax and solicit their aid in forwarding the temperance cause. Messrs. Birnie, Willard, and McCollum were appointed. Capt. McCollum offered a resolution asking that petitions be sent to the Legislature asking that each election district be allowed to say, by ballot, whether or not it would have a license issued to taverns or grog-shops. At the afternoon session the resolution was adopted. Rev. W. Harden offered a resolution inquiring into the absence of the Freedom societies and why they were not present. He was appointed to inquire into the causes. On motion of Rev. E. Henkle, the following persons were appointed to address the several societies, viz.: Revs. W. Harden, T. Gallaudet, P. Willard, J. P. Carter, E. Henkle, and Jacob Holmes, and J. McCollum, Isaac Cox, J. H. Christ, C. Birnie, Jr., J. J. Baumgardner, O. Cox, J. Lindsay, A. Gorsuch, C. W. Webster, E. T. Curry, E. F. Crout, Jere Malehorn, S. Murray, W. H. Grammer, F. H. Zollickhoffer, W. Zollickhoffer, I. N. Storr, and W. Holmes. The convention adjourned to meet at Westminister on Whit-Monday, May 12th. The members of the Westminster choir attended and "gave conclusive demonstration of their proficiency in sacred music."

Mrs. Susanna Morelock, wife of Jacob Morelock, died on the 19th ultimo, in Uniontown District; Elizabeth, wife of Jacob Beam, died in Baltimore on the 25th ultimo.

List of Letters Remaining in the Post-office at Westminster, Md., Jan. 1, 1844.—Thomas Ashton, John Abbot, John Buckingham, George Cox, J. G. Capito, J. B. Chenowith, Daniel Dimaen, James Davis, Maria Frieling, John G. Frick, Haner Green, John Gross, Samuel Harding, Richard Harris, Francis Keiser, Licrouse, Mr. Michael Ludwig, John Mile, Adams, David Pugh, Mrs. Rachel Poulson, Mr. Stanisfer, Michael Shaffer, Noah Stansbury, Miss Mary Stevenson, Diana Smith, William Stonebraker, Elmira Sherfy, Samuel Shade, John or Jacob Seel, Peter Woods, Mr. Winpiper, Nimrod Woolery, Peter Zentz, Henry Zimmerman, Christiana Zimmerman.—Joshua Yingling, Postmaster.

Basil Rook was clerk to the county commissioners.

Dr. William A. Mathias gave notice that he had located himself in Westminster, opposite the store of Samuel Orendorff.

Charles Rix advertised stoves and tinware.

Samuel Bennett, trustee of the late William Beam, advertised two farms for sale, situated near Marriottsville.

Elijah Wagner advertised cabinet-making and machine-shops.

Henry Saltzgiver advertised a price-list of hats, which he said were the best and cheapest in the State.

Joshua Smith, trustee, advertised a lot of ground and a brick brewery, occupied by Solomon Zepp, situated on the alley running from Court Street to Stone Alley.

Basil Root offered at private sale a farm on the Washington road, adjoining lands of Jacob Groves and others; also two unimproved lots situated at the Forks, in Westminster, fronting on the Littlestown road.

Joseph Stout advertised lime at nine cents per bushel. His kiln was on the Joseph Orendorff farm, now occupied by S. Meyerly, one and one-fourth mile from Westminster.

Jesse Manning offered for sale or rent his tavern-stand, situated on the turnpike six miles below Westminster; also forty acres of land.

The *Carroll County Democrat* of Oct. 2, 1851, contained the valedictory of Josiah T. H. Bringman, who retired from the editorship, and also the salutatory of Augustus C. Appler, who assumed control of the paper.

At that time a warm political contest was going on, the Democratic ticket being:

First Judicial District: For Judge of the Court of Appeals, William P. Maulsby; for Commissioner of Public Works, John S. Gittings. *Democratic State Nominations:* For Comptroller of the Treasury, Philip Francis Thomas; for Commissioner of Land Office, James Murray; for Lottery Commissioner, Thomas R. Stewart. *Democratic County Ticket:* For House of Delegates, Daniel Stull, John E. H. Liggett, Elijah F. Crout; for Judges of Orphans' Court, Michael Sullivan, George W. Monro, Levi Buffington; for Clerk of Circuit Court, John B. Boyle; for Register of Wills, Joseph M. Parke; for State's Attorney, Daniel L. Hoover; for County Surveyor, J. Henry Hoppe; for Commissioners of Tax, James Crouse, Thomas Smith, George L. Little, Jacob Wickert, Julius B. Berrett, George Crouse, Jacob Grove, George Richards, Jr., Bennett Spurrier.

On the Thursday night previous a large meeting of voters of Hampstead was held at Scarff's tavern, and was addressed by Dr. Liggett and Maj. Ege. Mr. Crouse was absent, owing to ill health. In behalf of the Whigs, Drs. Booth and Cox spoke.

On Saturday there was a large meeting at Union Bridge, which was addressed principally by Daniel L. Hoover and Charles W. Webster, candidates for prosecuting attorney; also by Messrs. Hook, Crout, Booth, Liggett, Cox, and Ege. The Union Bridge Brass Band, under Prof. Burke, enlivened the occasion.

On the 1st of October an election for Congressmen and school commissioner was held. The returns from only Westminster and Myers Districts were given: For Congress, Edward Hammond received 60 majority in Westminster District over Dr. A. A. Lynch. In Myers District he received 131 over the doctor. For school commissioner, John B. Summers received 67 majority over William Baughman in Westminster District, and in Myers District, J. William Earhart received 85 majority over Peter B. Mikesell.

The marriage of James W. Lantz and Eleanor Hyde, of Uniontown District, by Rev. J. Winter, was announced.

A political meeting was advertised to be held in Middleburg, October 11th, at which time all the candidates for the various offices were requested to attend.

Robinson & Eldred's circus was advertised to exhibit on October 6th.

Kettlewell & Cox advertised the Clover Hill farm, in Finksburg District, at public sale, October 25th.

William P. Maulsby and W. C. Van Bibber advertised the farm of George L. Van Bibber, part of the Avondale estate, two and one-half miles from Westminster, for sale on the 10th of November.

A statement of the expenditures of the county for the fiscal year ending July 6, 1851, is given, viz.: Outdoor pensioners, $3202.60; public roads, $3111-25; bridges and repairs to bridges, $553.16; judges and clerks of election for September and October, 1850, and June, 1851, $320; county commissioners, $625.50; colonization fund, $439.52; tax collector, $340; printing, $101.75; public buildings, $1000; clerk to commissioners, $200; preparing book for collector of State taxes, $50; counsel to commissioners, $50; judges of the Orphans' Court, $379.50; janitor, $25; inquests, $18.25; register of wills, $5;

stationery and postage, $18.50; wood for jail and commissioners' room, $56.50; grand and petit jurors for September, 1851, and April, 1852, $867.62; bailiffs and talesmen for same terms, $103.50; prosecuting attorney, $146.66; crier of the court, $59.95; clerk of the court, $395.50; sheriff, for fees and board, $431; State witnesses, $300; costs in removed cases, $56; constables, $65.55; miscellaneous, $255.34. Total amount of expenditures, $13,555.27. The assessment was $6,777,636, on which there was a levy of 20 cents on the $100.

Candidates were plentiful, as will be seen by the announcements:

For Judge of the Circuit Court, Madison Nelson, William M. Merrick, Richard H. Marshall, and Joseph M. Palmer; House of Delegates, Richard R. Booth, E. G. Cox, Abraham Lamott, and Thomas Hook; John McCollum as a candidate for clerk of the court; Register of Wills, John Baumgartner and John M. Yingling; State's Attorney, Charles W. Webster; Judges of the Orphans' Court, Jacob Mathias, Horatio Price, David B. Earhart, and Basil Hayden; County Commissioners, William Reese and James Smith; County Surveyor, J. Henry Hoppe and James Keely; Sheriff, Wm. S. Brown, Samuel J. Jordan, and Otho Shipley.

The issue of Oct. 16, 1851, is lively and exciting. The editorials are full of personal allusions, and the communications spicy. It also contains a long article from Col. William P. Maulsby. Political meetings are called for Uniontown District, at Crumrine's Hotel, four miles above Manchester, Finksburg, Franklinville, and at Little's Tavern, Freedom District.

The issue dated Nov. 6, 1851, was put in circulation on the 4th, two days before the election. Some of the articles are more forcible than polite.

The marriages of William Cornell and Elizabeth Kregelo, Emanuel Sell and Elizabeth Dotzour, George Gerhart and Lydia Black, William H. Angel and Geronda C. E. Everhart, and Samuel Messinger and Miss Frownfeller are published.

The issue of Jan. 1, 1852, contains very little of interest. It announces itself in favor of Stephen A. Douglas for President. By the census of 1850, Carroll takes rank as the fifth county in the State for the production of wheat.

The Democratic Advocate, now owned and published by William H. and Charles H. Vanderford, under the firm-name of Vanderford Bros., is the regular successor or continuation of *The Democrat and Carroll County Republican*, which was established by William Shipley, in February, 1838. Mr. Shipley continued its publication until April, 1840, when he sold out to Joseph M. Parke. Josiah T. H. Bringman bought a half-interest in it on March 12, 1846. The name was then changed to *The Carroll County Democrat*, and in 1848 Mr. Bringman purchased the remaining half-interest from Mr. Parke. Mr. Bringman published the paper until Oct. 2, 1851, when Augustus C. Appler became its owner, and he sold it to George H. Randall, on May 15, 1855. In July, 1856, Joseph Shaw became its publisher and editor. It was merged into a new paper called the *Western Maryland Democrat*, in May, 1861, of which W. Scott Roberts was editor. Joseph Shaw shortly afterwards again owned and controlled the paper. On April 15, 1865, on the reception of the news of the assassination of President Lincoln, the most intense excitement prevailed in Westminster. A large mass-meeting of its Republican citizens was held at the court-house in the evening, at which resolutions were adopted to notify Mr. Shaw, of the *Democrat*, "that the publication of his paper would no longer be permitted," on account (as alleged) of its containing articles abusive of the late President and Andrew Johnson, the Vice-President. At midnight, long after the meeting adjourned, the office of the *Democrat* was visited, and the type, cases, printing paper, and in fact all the material, were taken into the street and burned, and the presses, etc., in the building broken with axes, crowbars, and other means. On Nov. 22, 1865, *The Democratic Advocate* was established by W. H. Davis, who sold it to Joseph M. Parke in 1866, and on Nov. 28, 1867, Mr. Parke sold it to Mr. Davis again. In March, 1868, W. H. Vanderford, one of its present proprietors, purchased the establishment. He assumed control on March 12th following, and in connection with his father, H. Vanderford, published it until November, 1878, when he disposed of a half-interest to his brother, Charles H. Vanderford, H. Vanderford then retiring almost entirely from editorial duties.

In November, 1868, at the beginning of the fourth volume, W. H. Vanderford enlarged and otherwise improved the paper, and increased its subscription price from $1.50 to $2.00 per year. Under the management of himself and father the *Advocate* began to prosper rapidly. Its circulation increased, its advertising and job patronage expanded, and new material was added from time to time as necessity required.

At the beginning of the eighth volume, in November, 1872, when Charles H. Vanderford, who remained with the paper six months, became half owner, the paper was enlarged to its present size, a Cottrell & Babcock power-press and an entire outfit of new type was put in the office, including a large amount of job type.

The *Advocate* continued to prosper, and its patronage necessitated constant additions to its stock of material. The need of additional room became apparent, and its energetic proprietor purchased the lot on the corner of Main and Centre Streets, and erected the present *Advocate* building. It was finished in October, 1877, and the part occupied by the printing establishment is twenty by eighty feet, two stories high. The other part, twenty by forty feet, is occupied by James M. Shellman as a stationery store and news depot.

The building is of a very substantial character, well lighted and admirably adapted for the printing business. The first floor front is occupied as a business office, and the back room, fifty-six by eighteen feet, as a press and job room. In the second story is the editorial room, nicely carpeted and furnished and containing a library. It is connected with the office below by a dumb-waiter and speaking-tube. Back of the editorial room is the composing room, the same size as the press and job room. Under the latter room is a large cistern, from which, by means of a pump running up into the printing-office, water is obtained for the uses of the establishment.

The four presses—two new Universals, a Washington, and a Cottrell & Babcock—are run by steam, and the four rooms of the office are heated by steam.

The *Advocate* office in its appointments and equipments, and all the appurtenances necessary to a first-class establishment, is unequaled in Maryland outside of Baltimore, and the labors and enterprise of its proprietors have been generously appreciated by the people of Westminster and the county.

Henry Vanderford, editor and journalist, the father of the present editors and proprietors of the *Advocate*, was born at Hillsborough, Caroline Co., Md., Dec. 23, 1811. He is of Welsh descent, and was educated at Hillsborough Academy. He acquired a knowledge of the printing business in the office of the Easton *Star*, which he continued to publish after the death of Mr. Smith, the proprietor. He was subsequently employed on the Easton *Whig*. From 1835 to 1837 he published the *Caroline Advocate*, Denton, Md. The press and type he transferred in 1837 to Centreville, Queen Anne's Co., Md., and founded the *Sentinel*, which, though independent in politics, took a very decided part in the reform movement of 1836 and '37. He removed to Baltimore in 1842, and published *The Ray*, a weekly paper, and also the *Daily News* and the *Weekly Statesman*. In February, 1848, he bought the *Cecil Democrat*, enlarged the paper, quadrupled its circulation, and refitted it with new material. In 1868 he founded the *Middletown Transcript*, which was transferred in 1873 to his youngest son, Charles H. Vanderford. From 1870 to 1878 he was associated with his eldest son, William H. Vanderford, in the publication of the *Democratic Advocate* of Westminster. In 1870 he was elected to the House of Delegates from Carroll County, and re-elected in 1875, and in 1879 was elected a member of the State Senate, which office he still holds.

Mr. Vanderford married, June 6, 1839, Angeline Vanderford, a distant relative of his father. She is still living, being the mother of twelve children,—eight sons and four daughters. Only three of the sons are living, the eldest and youngest of whom are journalists, the former being William H. and the latter Charles H., late publisher of the *Old Commonwealth*, at Harrisonburg, Va. They are now the publishers of the *Advocate*. The second son, Dr. Julian J. Vanderford, is a dentist, and at present pursuing the practice of his profession in Stuttgart, Germany. Henry Vanderford and his wife are communicants of the Protestant Episcopal Church. He is a member of the Masonic order, and was formerly a member of the I. O. O. F.

The following is a list of persons living in Westminster in 1879, and within a radius of five miles thereof, who had attained to the age of seventy years and upwards. The list comprises one hundred and twenty-one persons, ranging from seventy to ninety-five years of age. There are omitted from the list the names of twenty-six persons above seventy years of age whose exact ages could not be obtained. The oldest inhabitant died at the almshouse, aged one hundred and twelve years.[1]

Jacob Stone, 95; Ruth Frizzell, 95; John Yingling, 94; Jacob Marker, 93; Joanna Biggs, 92; Henry Stonesifer, 90; Mrs. John Biggs, 89; James C. Graham, 89; William Crouse, 87; Miss Snider, 86; Mrs. D. Baumgartner, 85; Mary Beaver, 85; John Abbott, 84; James Williams, 84; Mrs. Jacob Snider, 84; John Crouse, 84; Mary Burke, 83; Mary Grammer, 83; Betsey Adelsperger, 83; James Hook, 82; Mrs. Wm. B. Crouse, 81;

[1] Becky McCormick, colored, familiarly known as "Old Becky," died on Sunday, March 9, 1879. It is impossible to give her exact age, but as far as can be ascertained, she was about one hundred and twelve years old. She had been an inmate of the almshouse for twelve or fourteen years prior to her death, and was a religious monomaniac. The most of her time was spent in singing and praying, intermingled with pleadings that her Good Master would take her home. She had been anxious to die for some years, saying that she wanted to go home to her people, and would sometimes get in paroxysms of excitement when any one would tell her that she would not die soon.

The "Beck" McCormick who was hanged in 1859, and who was the first to suffer death upon the scaffold in this county, was a granddaughter of this old woman. She was hanged for the murder of a colored boy belonging to William Orndorff, residing about one mile and a half from Westminster.

M. Baumgartner, 80; Samuel Young, 80; Joshua Sellman, 80; Joseph Keller, 79; Daniel Stultz, 79; Andrew Reese, 79; Wm. Stansbury, 79; Julia Gallandette, 79; Rev. T. Gallandette, 78; J. Henry Hoppe, 78; Isaac Meyers, 78; Mrs. Mary Beaver, 77; George Barbour, 77; Thomas Monahan, 77; Mrs. Andrew Reese, 77; Samuel Snider, 76; James Blizzard, 76; Sarah Kuhns, 76; Rebecca Roop, 76; Nancy Blizzard, 76; Henry Dell, 76; H. H. Harbaugh, 76; Jacob Babylon, 75; David Wentz, 75; Dr. J. L. Billingslea, 75; Thomas Williams, 75; Mr. Brown, 75; Elizabeth Shaeffer, 75; Mrs. Isaac Meyers, 75; Susan Gist, 75; John Babylon, 74; Sarah Leckins, 74; Henry Shreeve, 74; George Blizzard, 74; John Smith, 73; Catharine Stonesifer, 73; Mary Williams, 73; Mrs. Sarah Fringer, 73; Peggy Adelsperger, 73; David Wantz, 72; David Zepp, 72; Samuel Unger, 72; Mary Royer, 72; Catharine Meyers, 72; Daniel J. Geiman, 72; Polly Shaeffer, 72; Margaret E. Gerke, 72; Charles Meyers, 72; Joseph Newson, 72; Thomas Goodwin, 72; David H. Shriver, 72; Mrs. Horatio Price, 71; Daniel Shaeffer, 71; J. W. Swartzbaugh, 71; Henry Weiman, 71; Dr. Francis Butler, 70; B. W. Bennett, 70; Mrs. Mary Shriver, 70; Harry Baille, 70; Jesse Yingling, 70; Elizabeth Price, 70. *Colored People.*—Samuel Robinson, 90; Philip Briscoe, 88; Philip Leman, 87; Robert Bell, 83; Henry Anthony, 82; Serena Parker, 82; Samuel Thompson, 79; Wm. Parker, 79; Rev. J. B. Snowden, 77; Grace Paraway, 76; Elizabeth Harden, 72; Charlotte Troupe, 71; Ellen Robinson, 70.

John L. Reifsnider, a prominent merchant in Westminster, Carroll Co., Md., was born in Taneytown, Oct. 19, 1836. He has been twice married,—Dec. 10, 1861, to the eldest daughter of Dr. J. L. Billingslea, and Jan. 12, 1871, to the eldest daughter of Augustus Shriver. Mr. Reifsnider began business at a very early age, and at the age of eighteen was a member of the well-known firm of Reifsnider & Son, of Westminster. He is the president of the Westminster Gas Company, the success of which is due more to him than any other man. He has accumulated large wealth by his own industry, intelligence, and business judgment, and has retired from business, and lives in an elegant mansion in Westminster.

The traveler along the Westminster and Meadow Branch turnpike will find his attention pleasantly invited, at a point about two miles from Westminster, to "Meadow Brook," the comfortable-looking and attractive home of Samuel Roop. The house (a semi-Gothic structure) stands upon a gently-sloping eminence close to the highway, and is approached by a sweeping drive from either side. A prettily kept lawn makes a charming foreground to the picture. Mr. Roop's great-grandfather, Christian Roop, came from Switzerland to Lancaster County, Pa., during the eighteenth century. Four of his sons (Joseph, Christian, David, and John) removed to Carroll County at different periods soon after the Revolution to find new homes. John located upon the present Samuel Roop place, on which stood a small frame house when he purchased the property. About 1805 he built a brick house,—the one now occupied by Samuel Roop, who has by material improvements and tastefully-contrived embellishments made it a bright, cheerful-looking abode. Of the large land tract owned by his grandfather John, Mr. Roop is now the possessor of two hundred and fifty acres of as fine farming land as can be found in the county. The barns, outbuildings, and general equipments are well constructed, and are kept with an eye to their appearance. Since 1878, Mr. Roop has devoted considerable attention to the breeding of short-horned cattle, with highly encouraging results. The Westminster and Meadow Branch pike, which passes his place, was built largely through his efforts. Mr. Roop's farm is one of the best managed and most inviting estates in this section of the county, and he is justly regarded as one of Carroll's most useful and substantial citizens. He is an energetic and progressive agriculturist, and takes a keen interest in everything pertaining to his occupation.

Stonersville is three and a half miles from Westminster, thirty-two from Baltimore, and near the Patapsco Falls. It takes its name from the Stoner family. George W. Stoner is postmaster. The storekeepers are Noah Stansbury and D. H. Crouse.

Cranberry is on the Sullivan road, five miles from Manchester, and six from Westminster. Samuel Snyder is postmaster, and Snyder & Gummell, storekeepers.

Avondale is on the Western Maryland Railroad, three miles from Westminster, and thirty-four from Baltimore. James W. Beacham is postmaster.

Tannery is on the Western Maryland Railroad, one mile from Westminster, and takes its name from the leather manufactory of A. P. Baer & Co., of Baltimore, which is here located. James S. Baer is postmaster. The Methodist Episcopal Church has a neat chapel.

Warfieldsburg is three miles from Avondale, and four from Westminster, and near Morgan's Run. The merchants are J. W. Sellman and J. B. Allison; the latter is postmaster. The resident physician is Dr. J. P. Somers. Of the Church of God located here, Rev. Lewis Selby is pastor. David Baile and Washington Nicodemus are millers. The village takes its name from the Warfield family, one of the first to settle in the county.

The following is the vote for local officers from 1851 to 1861 inclusive:

1851.—Vote for Primary School Commissioner: Jacob Matthias 225, Francis Shriver 137, William Bachman 122, John B. Summers 189.

1853.—For Justices: Jesse Manning 317, J. H. Hoppe 287, James Keefer 217, F. O. Franklin 246, Otho Shipley 217, Wm. Sullivan 244, Washington Barnes 169, Wm. A. Wam-

RESIDENCE OF SAMUEL ROOP, WESTMINSTER, CARROLL CO., MD.

pler 320; Constables: Wm. Oursler 240, J. T. Diffenbaugh 294, Emanuel Gernand 355, Wm. H. Mourer 151; Road Supervisor: Michael Lynch 266, Geo. Shade 199, William Koontz 174.

1855.—For Justices: H. B. Grammer 269, E. Gernand 289, Jesse Manning 278, W. A. Wampler 295, Wm. Crouse 336, J. H. Hoppe 312, Joseph Matthias 318, F. O. Franklin 291; Constables: J. Diffenbaugh 302, Geo Webster 287, Thos. B. Gist 299, John Blizzard 303; Road Supervisor: Wm. Miller 312, Wm. Koontz 299.

1857.—For Justices: W. A. Crouse 382, Joseph Matthias 371, F. O. Franklin 350, J. H. Hoppe 317, W. A. Wampler 289; Constables: S. M. Gist 283, John Blizzard 330, J. T. Diffenbaugh 280, G. Sheets 105; Road Supervisor: M. Lynch 344, Noah Mitten 249.

1859.—For Justices: Joseph Matthias 428, Wm. Crouse 369, Chas. Denning 286, Jesse Manning 193, W. A. Wampler 350, James Keefer 178, Emanuel Tuni 187, J. Henry Hoppe 400; Constables: J. M. Yingling 335, Levi Evans 278, R. W. Stem 366, David Kuhn 351; Road Supervisor: Jacob Beaver 356, J. Shanebruch, Jr., 308.

1861.—For Justices: J. Matthias 467, J. H. Hoppe 415, E. Gernand 424, W. A. Wampler 455, W. J. Mitten 53, William Crouse 256, Daniel Byers 259, Jesse Manning 224, J. B. Summers 243; Constables: G. W. Plowman 416, R. W. Stem 459, Ira E. Crouse 206, J. M. Yingling 249, David Kuhn 76; Road Supervisor: J. L. Wampler 450, Philip Turfle 264.

The public school trustees for 1881 and 1882 are given, together with the names of teachers and number of pupils:

1. Grammar School.—Elias Yingling, F. A. Sharer, Geo. W. Miller.
2. Primary, No. 1.—David Fowble, Wm. B. Thomas, A. H. Huber.
3. Primary, No. 2.—Elias Yingling, F. A. Sharer, George W. Miller.
4. Primary, No. 3.—Same as Primary, No. 2.
5. Primary, No. 4.—David Fowble, Wm. B. Thomas, A. H. Huber.
6. West End, No. 1.—B. F. Crouse, E. J. Lawyer, Milton Schaeffer.
7. West End, No. 2.—Same as No. 1.
8. West End, No. 3.—Same as No. 1.
9. Warfieldsburg, No. 1.—Joshua Sellman, David Owings, Albinus Poole.
10. Warfieldsburg, No. 2.—Same as No. 1.
11. Shades.—Jesse Sullivan, A. Gieman, Charles Schaeffer.
12. Mexico.—No trustees.
13. Mountain View.—David Warchine, Uriah Bixler, John Baust.
14. Meadow Branch.—John D. Roop, David Reese, Ezra Bisch.
15. Cranberry.—Noah Schaeffer, William H. Reese, Lewis Schaeffer.
16. Friendship.—William Fenby, Frederick N. Hook, Joshua Stevenson.
17. Wm. Bachman's.—E. Bixler, Wm. Leas, William J. Biggs.
4. West End (African).—Alfred Bruce, J. M. Snowden, Reuben Woodyard (all colored).

The teachers for the term ending April 15, 1881, were:

1, C. H. Baughman, 32 pupils; 2, C. H. Spurrier, 31 pupils; 3, Belle M. Matthews, 29 pupils; 4, F. W. Shriver, 36 pupils; 5, Maria Pearson, 37 pupils; 6, George Batson, 51 pupils; 7, Mattie W. Beaver, 34 pupils; 8, Laura K. Matthews, 37 pupils; 9, Stanley R. Still, 36 pupils; 10, C. Belle Poole, 30 pupils; 11, Henry L. Shriver, 29 pupils; 12, Geo. H. Gist, 19 pupils; 13, G. W. Sullivan, 45 pupils; 14, D. L. McSwiney, 52 pupils; 15, Laura A. Everhart, 24 pupils; 16, F. A. Diffenbach, 55 pupils; 17, H. B. Burgoon, 42 pupils; 4 (African school), Fannie E. Balls, 58 pupils.

UNION BRIDGE DISTRICT, No. 12.

The Twelfth District of Carroll County, generally known as Union Bridge, is bounded on the north by Middleburg District, on the east by the districts of Uniontown and New Windsor, on the south by the latter and Frederick County, and on the west by Frederick County. It is the youngest district in the county, having been created by an act of the General Assembly of Maryland, passed March 14, 1872, out of portions of the territory embraced by the districts of Middleburg, New Windsor, and Uniontown. In area it is also smaller than the other districts, but it is by no means the least important. It is magnificently watered by Sam's Creek, which forms the western boundary line between the district and Frederick County, and by Little Pipe Creek, which flows directly through the centre of the district from east to west, and by a number of smaller streams which are tributary to those just mentioned. The soil is exceedingly fertile, and the Western Maryland Railroad, within easy reach from all parts of the district, furnishes ample facilities for the disposal of produce and communication with trade centres. The population in 1880 was 1235. It contains within its limits one of the largest and most prosperous towns in the county, and a large share of the manufacturing establishments of this portion of Maryland. The metes and bounds of the district, as prescribed by the act of Assembly which created it, are as follows:

"Beginning at Sam's Creek, the boundary line between Carroll and Frederick Counties, and at the point in said Sam's Creek where the tail-race from McKinstry's mills empties therein, and running thence by a straight line to intersect the middle of the public road from McKinstry's mills to Linwood, and at a point in said public road opposite the stone house now occupied by D. F. Albaugh and brother; thence by and with the centre of said public road to the bridge over Little Pipe Creek, near Linwood, being a corner of Election District No. 2; thence through said district by a straight line to Reuben Haines' dwelling-house, excluding said premises; thence by a straight line to intersect the public road from Union Bridge to Union Town, at a point in said road opposite the centre of a lane leading off therefrom towards the public school-house, being between the house and premises of Abraham Harris and the premises of Abraham Stoner; thence by a straight line to the spring at the head of Log Cabin Branch, being at a corner of Election District No. 10; thence down Log Cabin Branch to the centre of the road leading from Union Town to Middleburg; thence along the middle of said public road towards Middleburg until opposite a lane known as Haines' lane, being now between the lands of Abraham Shirk and Joseph Roop; thence down said lane to the south end thereof; thence by a straight line running by Lewis Haines' dwelling-house, and including said premises, to Pipe Creek, the boundary line between Carroll and Frederick Counties; thence up said creek and Sam's Creek to the place of beginning."

The first survey was that of "Kilfadda," for a large tract of land patented in 1729 to John Tredane, and afterwards to Allen Farquhar, being then in Prince George's County. This land embraces a part of "Union Bridge" and the farm of E. J. Penrose.

E. G. Penrose was born in the township of Washington, York Co., Pa., the 10th of the 9th month, 1817, the second in a family of four children of Josiah and Rachel (Garretson) Penrose. The family in this country spring from two brothers, who emigrated from England with Wm. Penn at his second voyage. They settled in Pennsylvania, and have scattered to different States, mainly Ohio, Illinois, Iowa, and Kansas. The only one who settled in Maryland is the subject of this sketch.

Thomas Penrose, his grandfather, born 4th day of the 1st month (old style), 1749, married Abigail Cadwalader; the latter was born the 18th of the 1st month, 1752. To this worthy couple were born seven children,—five sons and two daughters,—viz.: Amos, Thomas, William, Hannah, Ann, Josiah, and Cyrus.

Thomas moved to Illinois, and died there; William lived and died in Bedford County at the homestead; he raised a large family; Hannah married Jesse Kenworthy, a farmer near Brownsville, Washington Co., Pa.; she died there, leaving two daughters; Ann and Cyrus did not marry; lived and died at the homestead; Amos married and raised a family of eight children, he resided at the homestead and died there; Josiah, father of E. G., was born in York County, Pa., 28th of 3d month, 1790; married Rachel, daughter of John and Mary Garretson, 18th of 5th month, 1815. Her father was born 5th of 4th month, 1741; his wife, Mary, 16th of 10th month, 1745. They were married 9th of 6th month, 1763, at a public meeting of Friends at Huntington. He died 15th of 12th month, 1810; his wife, 3d of 7th month, 1827.

Rachel G. Penrose was born 8th of 12th month, 1788. When E. G. Penrose was seventeen years of age his father moved with his family to Menallen township, Adams Co., Pa., and settled on a farm; both himself and wife died in Adams County, the latter 25th of 12th month, 1824, the former 7th of 1st month, 1860.

Eliakim Garretson Penrose lived at home until he was nineteen years of age. His education was limited to an attendance at a private school. In 1836 he went to Baltimore, where he was employed as clerk in the grocery-store of Isaiah B. Price, with whom he remained four years. He then engaged on his own account in the meat business on Hillen Street, near the Belair Market, and continued in it four years, making it a success.

For the next three years he was engaged in the coal trade, in company with James Johnson; firm, Johnson & Penrose. In 1847, in company with Jonathan Shoemaker,—firm, Penrose & Co.,—he carried on a grocery on Pennsylvania Avenue, corner of St. Mary Street. At the end of three years the firm was dissolved. He then engaged in his own name in the grocery and produce business corner of Franklin and Eutaw Streets, first renting and subsequently purchasing the store; remained there from 1850 to 1855. In the latter year he entered into partnership with Thomas Russell, and for three years, under the firm-name of Penrose & Russell, carried on a store at 153 North Howard Street. At the end of that time he purchased Russell's interest, and took into partnership Wm. A. Simpson, under the firm of E. G. Penrose & Co., which partnership continued for twelve years. Upon its dissolution he took as partner John Russell, brother of former partner, the firm-name continuing as before. In 1878, Russell withdrew, and a partnership, under the firm-name of Penrose, Nelker & Co., was formed; his associates in this partnership are J. F. Nelker and A. H. Nelker, which partnership still exists, the business being carried on in the old place. From all his business transactions intoxicating liquors have been excluded.

In politics he has been identified with the Whig and Republican parties. He is a member of the Society of Friends, and although living in a slave State, has always been opposed to slavery. During the late war he was a stanch friend of the Union cause. He married, 24th of 2d month, 1853, Susan, daughter of Abel and Elizabeth (Roberts) Russell. Mrs. Penrose was born in Frederick County, Md., 7th of 1st month, 1828. They have had three children, viz.: Lizzie, born 5th of 10th month, 1860, died 25th of 3d month, 1866; William, born 16th of 6th month, 1862; now engaged with the firm at Baltimore; Mary, born 22d of 1st month, 1869.

In 1868, Mr. Penrose purchased the well-known Shepherd farm, one hundred and eighty-one acres, near Union Bridge, Carroll Co., Md., and moved there in 1869. Up to 1879 few men enjoyed better health or possessed a more vigorous constitution, and none who gave closer application to business. At that time he withdrew from active participation in the

E. G. Penrose

business of his house in Baltimore, retaining, however, as a general partner, his interest in the same.

During the time he has been engaged in business in Baltimore his house has passed successfully through three severe panics, which sufficiently attests his prudence and excellent judgment as a business man.

Many members of the Society of Friends settled in Union Bridge District prior to the war of the Revolution, and formed a "particular meeting," but the society never gained a strong foothold. Some of the descendants of the first Friends who settled here are yet living in this region.

Among the early settlers were the Farquhars, Wrights, Rineharts, Wolfes, Shepherds, Thomases, Husseys, and Benedums. These pioneers were men of unusual energy and intelligence, and they gave an impetus to this section which it has ever since maintained. Their experiences, some of which will be found in the introductory chapter of the history of this county, were very interesting. They evidently appreciated the natural advantages which the country offered, and availed themselves of them without loss of time. Mills, factories, and other necessary improvements were speedily erected, and many older settlements in Maryland might have profitably imitated their example. The first nail-factory in the State, probably, was established in this district, and the first reaping-machine was invented by John B. Thomas, in Union Bridge, the machine which Hussey used as his model, and from which all others generally in use on this side of the Rocky Mountains derived their origin.

The first Farmers' Club in Carroll County of which there is any knowledge was formed in 1817, in the vicinity of Union Bridge, at that time a portion of Frederick County, by Thomas Shepherd, Daniel Haines, Ulrich Switzer, Samuel Haines, David Englar, Philip Englar, Henry Rial, and Israel Rinehart (whose son, Israel C., is still a member of the organization). It was a society of producers for their mutual benefit and protection against the middlemen, and was the germ of the organization now known as the Patrons of Husbandry, which has recently reached out with its Briarean arms and embraced the whole United States. The plan of the club, or, as it was more generally styled, "the company," was to produce a first-rate article and deliver it directly to the consumer. They made "gilt-edged" butter, and got fancy prices for it. A person who did not make a good article could not be a member of the club, and they established a first-class reputation.

The club ran a wagon, which conveyed the produce to the Baltimore market every week. The members took turns in going: the one accompanying the wagon furnished a horse his week, and acted as agent for the association in selling their produce and buying goods for them. At their annual meetings they settled their financial business, and had no commissions to pay to agents at a distance.

The club is still in existence, and is sending produce to Baltimore every week. The excellent character established for its members enables them to command the highest prices for their produce.

A second, or Junior Club, was established in or about 1853, similar to the older company of 1817. It has been in successful operation ever since.

In 1864 there was an association organized at Union Bridge, under the name and title of "The Union Bridge Agricultural and Scientific Club." The first permanent officers were elected Feb. 20, 1864, as follows: President, Granville S. Haines; Recording Secretary, Joshua Switzer; Treasurer, Daniel Wolf; Librarian, Thomas W. Russell; Executive Committee, Warrington Gillingham, Solomon Shepherd, and Pemberton Wood. The meetings were held on the first and third Saturday of every month, at seven o'clock P.M. In 1868 there were other features introduced which materially enhanced the usefulness of the society. The club now meets at a member's house every month, and half the membership are ladies. The farmer's wife is as much a member of the club as he himself, with the same rights and privileges.

The first duty after organization is usually to examine the farm, buildings, fencing, work, etc., criticising and answering questions, after which they return to the house, where essays are read and questions discussed, after which they repair to the table bountifully supplied with the products of the farm, nicely prepared to suit the palate. The company having partaken of the feast, select the subject for their next meeting, and adjourn to meet again next month at the house of some other member. The plan of holding circular meetings has been adopted by all the wide-awake neighborhoods in the country.

The town of Union Bridge has a population of 576, and in both a commercial and social sense is the focal point of the district. It was to this spot that the early settlers flocked, a hardy, energetic, and remarkably intelligent race of people, who have given a distinct character to the community. The country in the vicinity of the town was very fertile, but in many places it was swampy, the woods and undergrowth were almost impenetrable, and ravenous wolves, made dangerous by hunger, were constantly prowling about the clearings to pick up the unguarded produce or the stock, and even to attack the unwary passer-by. The remarkable fertility of the soil had evidently attracted the notice of man long before the settlement of the whites. Upon the site of the present town large quantities of stone arrows, hatchets, and other implements referable to the stone age have been picked up, as well as numerous skulls and other human bones, indicating that sanguinary conflicts had taken place for the possession of this favored spot. William Farquhar and his wife Ann, with their children, an interesting account of whose settlement in the district has already been given, were probably the pioneers of Union Bridge. They settled upon a tract of land given them by Allen Farquhar, upon which much of the town now stands. On Aug. 7, 1747, a tract of land called "Forest in Need," containing one hundred and twenty acres, was granted to William Farquhar, in which is included all that part of the town south of Elgar Street. That portion of the town west of Main Street and north of a line struck from the intersection of Elgar Street with Main Street to the intersection of Broadway and Canary Streets was Moses Farquhar's. All that part south of the above line belonged to Samuel Farquhar. The portion east of Main Street and north of Elgar Street was Allen Farquhar's. The dividing line between the property of Samuel and William Farquhar became a road, which was subsequently placed on the county, and eventually became "Main" Street in the town of Union Bridge. During the Revolution and for some time afterwards the neighborhood was known as the "Pipe Creek Settlement," the word Pipe Creek being a translation into English of the Indian name "Apoochken." The inhabitants at that time were mainly Quakers, whose tenets were opposed to war; but their enthusiasm in many cases prevailed over their peaceful principles, and they contributed largely of their means in aid of the patriot cause, and not a few officers and soldiers were recruited from their number.

Benjamin Farquhar, a grandson of William, at the close of the last century, was the first to make use of the abundant water-power of the town by building a saw-mill and an oil-mill to utilize the seed of the flax which was grown in the neighborhood. This was on the site of what is now the Union Bridge Hotel, and is the same water-power used by the Western Maryland Railroad Company in operating its machine-shops. Peter Benedam, an enterprising German from Lancaster County, Pa., came to Union Bridge at the beginning of the present century and purchased five hundred acres of land, which included all of the town site north of Elgar Street and west of Main Street, a large portion of which he cleared off, drained, and brought under cultivation. He appears to have been, from all accounts, a thoroughly useful man in the community, and gave a healthy impetus to farming and other industries. He constructed at his own cost an elaborate, costly, and durable footway across the creek, which remained as a monument to his judgment and skill and proof against the ravages of time and floods for more than half a century. His residence was the premises now owned by Granville S. Haines. Joseph Elgar was the first merchant and manufacturer by machinery on the site of the town. He also built the first brick house in the town, in which Joseph Wilson now lives. The pioneers did not pass away without leaving their "footprints on the sands of time." A well-paved wagon-road was made across the swampy ground northward from the town, and a substantial bridge was built across the creek, done by the united labor of those who lived on either side of the stream. After its completion, while the builders were still assembled, it was proposed that the bridge be called by some name to distinguish it from other similar structures. "Union Bridge" was suggested, and its peculiar appropriateness secured its unanimous adoption. The bridge gave the name to both the town and the district. Peter Benedam sold out in 1814 and removed to the Valley of Virginia, and Jacob Switzer, the father of Joshua Switzer (the very able centennial historian of the district, to whom the author of this work is indebted for valuable material), purchased one hundred and thirty-eight acres of his land, embracing that part of Union Bridge west of Main Street and north of Elgar Street. The war with Great Britain created a demand for agricultural products, and Union Bridge and its vicinity enjoyed a season of great prosperity. All that part of the town west of Main Street was a clover-field, which, plowed up and put in a crop of wheat and followed with a crop of rye, would produce enough to pay for the first cost of the land. At this period the village contained but four houses,—one upon the site of Hartsock's Hotel, which was taken down to make room for the hotel in 1870; one near the site of Capt. Isaiah Lightner's dwelling-house, which was removed in 1814, and is now the central part of the dwelling-house of William Stultz; one on the present site of William Wilson's store, afterwards for a long time used as a shop, and taken away about fifteen years ago; and the brick house built by Joseph Elgar. All save the last were built of oak logs, and, though not strictly ornamental, were comfortable and durable. The brick cabinet-maker's shop, in which the first reaper was constructed by Jacob R. Thomas,

JOS. MOORE.

was subsequently converted into a dwelling-house. George Cox succeeded Elgar as a merchant, and took butter, eggs, and other produce in exchange for goods. He started a huckster-wagon and created a local market, and from the quality or quantity of butter sold here the town was called "Buttersburg," a name which has clung to it and by which it is sometimes known today. There was no post-office nearer than Taneytown. The growing condition of the "settlement" required better postal facilities, and in or about the year 1820 a post-office, with a weekly mail, was established between this point and Frederick City. In the selection of a name that might also designate its locality, the name of Union Bridge was chosen, after which time the village began to be called "Union Bridge Post-office," and then only "Union Bridge," and the name of Buttersburg was disused. In 1821, Jacob Switzer removed the old oil-mill, and built upon its site a brick four-story grist and merchant-mill, forty by forty-two feet, the stone basement of which is now the basement of the "Union Bridge Hotel." A part of the brick dwelling-house now the residence of Joseph Wolfe had also been built. But very little progress was then made in buildings for the two succeeding decades. In 1846, Joseph Moore, having become the owner by purchase of all that part of the town site west of Main Street, laid out a series of lots along the whole length of said street, fronting thereon and running about fourteen and a quarter perches, which he afterwards sold from time to time, and building then first began on the west side of Main Street, the first dwelling-house being that now owned and inhabited by Reuben Sayler.

Joseph Moore was born in Taneytown District (now New Windsor), Frederick Co. (now Carroll), Md., Sept. 26, 1802. His grandfather, John Moore, was a native of West Caln township, Chester Co., Pa. He married Hannah Hollingsworth, of Birmingham township, same county, April 13, 1749. Their children were David, Joanna, Enoch, John, Jehu, Mary, and Abigail. David married and settled and died in Petersburg, Va. Enoch and John were neither married; both were soldiers in the war of the Revolution. Enoch died at his father's residence, at Union Bridge. John died at his father's residence, near Westminster. Mary married a Mr. Stephenson, moved to Illinois, and died there. Soon after his marriage John Moore moved to Baltimore, where he carried on milling. About the time of the Revolution he moved to Westminster, and subsequently purchased a farm about two miles from that place; he died there. Jehu Moore, fourth son of John, and father of Joseph, was born in Baltimore, Oct. 8, 1757, married Hannah, daughter of Joseph and Jane Hibbard, of Pipe Creek, March 23, 1796. Mrs. Moore was born in Willets township, Chester Co., Pa., March 3, 1768. Their children were Ann, born Feb. 3, 1801; Joseph; and Mary, born Aug. 9, 1804. Ann died June 22, 1822. Mary, widow of Isaac Dixon, is a resident of Baltimore.

Jehu Moore settled in Union Bridge District (then Taneytown) in 1794, and engaged for several years in merchandising in company with Solomon Shepherd. Selling out his interest in the store about 1808, he purchased a farm east of the village, which he carried on to the time of his death, which occurred Dec. 11, 1841. His wife lived to the advanced age of ninety-six years, and died May 3, 1863. Both are buried in the Friends' burying-ground at Pipe Creek.

Joseph Moore lived on the home-farm from his birth to 1865. His education was limited to an attendance in summers at the common school of his neighborhood. In 1837 he purchased of David Switzer the tract of land known as the "Rich Indian Garden," consisting of forty-one acres, a portion of which he allotted, and upon which all that portion of the village of Union Bridge lying west of Main Street has been built up. The home-farm, which came into his possession by will, he sold in 1865, taking up his residence in the village of Union Bridge, where, with the exception of two years spent in Baltimore, he has since resided. He built his present residence, a fine brick mansion, on a site commanding a fine view of the village and surrounding country, in 1879 and 1880. In religion Mr. Moore belongs to the Society of Friends; in politics, first a Whig, then a Republican, and took an active interest in securing the construction of the Western Maryland Railroad, which has been the means mainly of building up the village of Union Bridge. He married, June 8, 1871, at Troy, N. Y., Hannah P., daughter of Elias and Mary (Bryant) Lord. Mrs. Moore was born Oct. 3, 1837, in Colchester, Chittenden Co., Vt. She received her education at Burlington Female Seminary and Mrs. Wooster's Ladies' School, Burlington, Vt. They have had two children,—Mary Hannah, born July 3, 1873, and Archer Joseph, born July 20, 1876, died May 23, 1877.

About this time the railroad which is now called the Western Maryland Railroad first began to be talked of (previous to which a connection with the Baltimore and Ohio Railroad had been supposed to be the most feasible after the unsuccessful attempt to secure the passage of its main stem through the place), but it was not until ten years afterwards, or in 1855–56, that work was actually begun on it, and in the month of May, 1862, the first passenger-trains came to Union Bridge. During this period but little additional building had been done in the town, other than the brick depot and warehouse built by Moses Shaw and David Hiltabidle, and some buildings by the railroad company preparatory to the opening of the road. On the completion of the railroad to this point, which remained its western terminus for six years, and the erection of the company's machine-shops here, an active demand sprang up for dwelling-houses for its employés and their families. That part of the town nearest and most convenient to the depot and machine-shops, being east of Main Street and bounding on Elgar Street, could not be obtained either by purchase or lease for the purpose of building thereon by reason of the occupants having a life estate therein. On Tuesday, June 30, and Wednesday, July 1, 1863, the Second and Fifth Army Corps, forming the central column of the Army of the Potomac, passed through the town on their march towards Gettysburg, being about the only local incident to recall the memories of the great civil war, and in this the town did not suffer, but rather prospered. In 1864 a telegraph company located an office here, which has since been maintained. In the same year Moses Shaw and Joseph Moore opened that part of the street since known as Broadway Street from Main Street westward, and this gave access to the remaining portion of Joseph Moore's premises, a great part of which he has since sold by the acre or fractions of an acre, in such quantities as were desired by the purchaser. About the same time the first public primary school-house was built. In 1865 all that part of the town south of Elgar Street and east of Main Street which could not heretofore be procured was brought into market, and it was laid out into lots and sold by the executor at public sale, Feb. 3, 1866, and purchased by Jesse Anders, Jasper C. Shriner, and Thomas T. Norris, who have from time to time sold the lots upon which the dwelling-houses are built. The town now made a more decided progress in improvement. In 1868 the Methodist Episcopal church was built, and also Anders & Lightner's store and public hall. On the 3d day of December, 1868, at eight o'clock P.M., the machine-shop, carpenter-shop, blacksmith-shop, and all the other buildings and local improvements (except the engine-house) of the Western Maryland Railroad Company took fire and were burned. The fire originated in the oil-house, and so rapid was the conflagration that the tools of the workmen, the books of the railroad company, and all the finished and unfinished work, including a new locomotive engine in process of construction, therein were destroyed and lost, but by extraordinary labor and vigilance all other contiguous buildings in the town were saved. This was the first experience of a loss by fire in the town, and was severely felt by the railroad company, then in its infancy, and was also felt as a public local calamity by the inhabitants of the town and vicinity, the mutual character of which being manifested by the local and substantial pecuniary aid contributed and the energy and enterprise of the railroad company, which being combined, all of the said shops and other buildings were forthwith rebuilt in a better and more substantial manner. In the same year the railroad began to run its trains westward from Union Bridge, and about that time much of the building on Benedam and Farquhar Streets was done. A "Building Association" was formed, by the aid of which twelve of the dwelling-houses in the town were erected.

An act of the General Assembly of Maryland passed in 1872, to incorporate the town of Union Bridge, in Carroll County. An election was held on the first Monday in April ensuing for a mayor and Common Council, and Reuben Saylor was elected the first mayor of the town, and John Hartsock, Philip B. Meyers, Joseph Wolf, and J. Calvin Wentz were the first elected councilmen, and John B. Eppley was its first bailiff, and Joshua Switzer its first clerk, and also treasurer; and what had been prior to that time a "settlement," a "burg," and a "village," at once rose to the dignity of a town, clothed with a municipal government.

At a session of the mayor and Common Council, held March 31, 1874, the same mayor and Council mentioned above, except that John M. Furney had been chosen in place of Joseph Wolf (who declined to serve), the following preamble and resolution were passed:

"*Whereas*, The streets in the town of Union Bridge have heretofore had no legal name, and some of the said streets have been called by different names, causing much ambiguity and misunderstanding in their location and description,

"*Therefore Resolved*, That the principal thoroughfare through the said town, being the Liberty and Pipe Creek turnpike road, be called Main Street; and that the street next westward thereof and running parallel therewith from the county road No. 80, at the southwest corner of the school-house grounds, past the premises of William H. Rinehart (the American sculptor) and Thomas Russell, Philip B. Meyers, and others, be called Whyte Street; and that the street next eastward from Main Street, and running nearly parallel therewith from the ground for the track of the Western Maryland Railroad, past the premises of G. T. Grumbine, Margaret Spurrier, Joshua Switzer, and others, to intersect the said county road No. 80 (the southern boundary of the town), be called Benedam Street; and that the street near the eastern boundary of the said town, and running parallel with the said eastern boundary from the ground for the track of the Western Maryland Railroad, along past the premises of Capt. Isaiah Lightner, J. Calvin Wentz,

Edward Kelly, and others, to intersect the said county road No. 80, be called Farquhar Street; and that the street running from Main Street eastward at the corners of the premises of John W. Diehl and Howard D. Hartsock, crossing Benedam Street at the corner of G. T. Grumbine and others, and crossing Farquhar Street at the corner of J. Calvin Wentz, Isaiah Lightner, and others, to the eastern boundary of the town, be called Elgar Street; and that the wide street crossing Main Street at the residence and stores of Jesse Anders, Anders & Lightner, William Wilson, and John N. Weaver, and running through the town from east to west, be called Broadway; and that the street next southward from Broadway Street, and running parallel therewith from Main Street at the corner of the premises of Jesse Anders and E. O. Mannakee (now M. C. Kinstry), and crossing Benedam Street to Farquhar Street, be called Thomas Street; and that the short street next westward from Whyte, and running parallel therewith and connecting the west end of Broadway Street with the aforesaid county road No. 80, as the same is marked and laid down on the plat, but not yet opened, be called Canary Street. And that the clerk be and he is hereby directed and authorized to write, mark, and designate the names of the said streets on the plat of the said town, and also cause the same to be written on the records of the said plat in the office of the clerk of the Circuit Court for Carroll County, in Liber J. B. B., No. 42, folio 241; and the aforesaid names shall be the established names by which the aforesaid streets shall be respectively known, called, and described; and the clerk is hereby directed and ordered to enter upon the records of the proceedings of the mayor and Council a brief synopsis of the meaning of the said names, or the reasons why the said local names were given or chosen and applied to the streets of the said town."

All of which has been duly done, and the general answer is, because they are historic and intended to perpetuate the local history of the town. "Main" Street, because it is the oldest, and is the principal traveled thoroughfare through the town; "Broadway," fifty feet wide, although not wider than Benedam and Whyte Streets, because it was the first wide street opened through the town; "Farquhar," "Benedam," "Elgar," and "Thomas," for the obvious reasons given in the preceding pages; "Whyte," so called for the Hon. William Pinkney Whyte, who was Governor of the State, and who approved of and signed the charter at the time of the incorporation of the town, whilst His Excellency vetoed all other town charters except one passed by the General Assembly of Maryland at the same session; "Canary," so called for the first railroad locomotive that came into the town of Union Bridge. It was a small engine with only two driving-wheels, but did all the work in the construction of the railroad to this place. It was called the "Canary" because of its diminutive size and its restless and constant activity; and while the town of Union Bridge is largely indebted to the railroad for her growth and prosperity, the railroad is also indebted to the town and country immediately surrounding it for the very large and liberal stock subscriptions which were made and paid up, thus making the construction of the road at that time a possibility.

In 1875 a separate passenger-house and depot was built by the railroad company, the town contributing $100 as a corporation, and private individuals $500 additional. In the same year another produce and freight depot was built by William Zimmerman and H. D. Hartsock, on the west side of Main Street.

In September, 1875, Messrs. Nock & Snyder introduced a printing-press and materials, and began the publication of the first newspaper in the town, called the *People's Voice*, which supplied a very important link in the chain connecting the town with the more advanced civilization of the age. On the 4th of July, 1876, the centennial year of independence was celebrated with imposing ceremonies in the town of Union Bridge. Hon. Joshua Switzer delivered an address which embodied the history of the town. It was admirably prepared, replete with valuble information, much of which has been utilized by the author of this history, and exceedingly interesting.

In April, 1875, John Hartsock was elected mayor, and John W. Furney, J. C. Wentz, P. B. Meyers, and Jesse Anders, members of the Council; J. Switzer, secretary and treasurer. In 1876, D. Rinehart was elected mayor, and M. C. McKinstry, Jesse Anders, P. B. Meyers, and Peter Hollenberger were chosen members of the Common Council; J. Switzer, secretary; John Hartsock, treasurer. In 1877, John Hartsock was elected mayor, and Moses Shaw, Jos. Wilson, D. R. Fogle, and William Kelley, councilmen; and John B. Eppley, secretary and treasurer. In 1878, John Hartsock was elected mayor, and Moses Shaw, Joseph Wilson, William Kelley, and D. R. Fogle, common councilmen; John B. Eppley, secretary and treasurer. In 1879, John Hartsock was elected mayor, and Moses Shaw, Jesse Anders, William Kelley and John N. Weaver, Common Council; John B. Eppley, secretary and treasurer. In 1880, John Hartsock was elected mayor, and Moses Shaw, Jesse Anders, D. Rinehart, and J. C. Wentz to the Common Council; John B. Eppley, secretary and treasurer. In April, 1880, a new act of incorporation was granted by the Legislature, to take effect June 1, 1880, when under its provisions John N. Weaver was elected a member of the Common Council, making five in that body. In 1881, D. Rinehart was elected mayor, and Jesse Anders, P. B. Meyers, J. C. Wentz, and E. O. Mannakee were chosen as the Common Council; John B. Eppley, secretary and treasurer. Jesse Anders and P. B. Meyers refused to qualify, and a new election was called, resulting in the selection of C. F. Reck,

Thomas Grumbine, and E. W. Leeds, who compose the present Council.

Strawbridge Methodist Episcopal Church was formed under the supervision of Rev. Thomas Slicer. A few years prior to 1868 they held their services in the public school-house until the erection of their church, which occurred in 1868. The church was named in honor of Robert Strawbridge, one of the pioneer Methodists of the county, and is a very neat frame structure, capable of holding about four or five hundred people. Rev. Thomas Slicer was succeeded by Rev. Montgomery, who was followed by Rev. William Ferguson in the year 1870. Mr. Ferguson occupied the pulpit only for one year, when the Rev. C. D. Smith was chosen as pastor. He remained in charge of the congregation until 1872, when he was succeeded by Rev. Reuben Kolb, whose pastorate expired in 1874. Rev. Edwin Koontz was the next pastor, and served in that position for three years, and was succeeded by Rev. J. J. Sargent until 1881, when their present pastor, the Rev. Wright, took charge.

The present trustees of the church are Edward Kelly, A. L. Beard, Joseph F. Snavely, E. Ingleman, Jesse T. Cleary, David Ogle, Dr. J. McK. Norris.

Steward, Edin Ingleman; Leader of Class and Exhorter, Jos. F. Snavely.

The church numbers about thirty-eight members, and it formerly belonged to the New Windsor charge, but is now in the Linganore Circuit. A very prosperous Sunday-school, numbering about one hundred and sixty members, is under the control of the church.

Through the united efforts of Capt. Isaiah Lightner and James M. Hollenberger, a dispensation was granted to Plymouth Lodge, No. 143, A. F. A. M., on Jan. 12, 1869. On that date an organization was effected, the lodge working under the charge of A. T. Geatty, W. M.; Isaiah Lightner, S. W.; John J. Derr, J. W.; and D. E. Bucky, S. D. *pro tem.*; A. L. Beard, J. D. *pro tem.*; J. M. Hollenberger, Sec. *pro tem.*; J. T. Hedrick, Treas. *pro tem.*; John M. Furney, Tyler.

At a meeting held Feb. 12, 1869, the first application for membership was received, the applicant being Ephraim B. Repp.

February 10th, E. B. Repp was received in the lodge and initiated at this meeting.

March 23d, E. B. Repp was raised to the degree of Master Mason.

On May 10th the charter was granted, empowering Isaiah Lightner, W. M.; J. M. Hollenberger, S. W.; John J. Derr, J. W. D. E. Buckey was elected secretary, and J. T. Hedrick, treasurer. These officers were publicly installed June 30, 1869, by Brother William H. Moore, of George Washington Lodge, Westminster.

The officers from December, 1869, to July, 1870, were Isaiah Lightner, W. M.; John J. Derr, S. W.; A. L. Beard, J. W.; D. E. Buckey, Sec.; Abraham Stoner, Treas. During this term Mr. Buckey removed from the town, and A. T. Geatty was appointed to fill the vacancy. From July to December, 1870, the officers were Isaiah Lightner, W. M.; John J. Derr, S. W.; John M. Furney, J. W.; A. Stoner, Treas.; A. Geatty, Sec. From December, 1870, to July, 1871, Isaac Lightner, W. M.; E. O. Mannakee, S. W.; J. M. Furney, J. W.; A. Stoner, Sec.; John D. Myers, Treas. From July to December, 1871, the officers were Isaiah Lightner, W. M.; E. O. Mannakee, S. W.; C. Kimball, J. W.; A. Stoner, Treas.; J. M. Hollenberger, Sec. The officers from December, 1871, to July, 1872, E. O. Mannakee, W. M.; J. M. Furney, S. W.; J. D. Myers, S. W.; J. M. Hollenberger, Sec. From July to December, 1872, Isaiah Lightner, W. M.; E. O. Mannakee, S. W.; J. M. Furney, J. W.; A. Stoner, Treas.; A. T. Geatty, Sec. From December, 1872, to July, 1873, J. M. Furney, W. M.; J. M. Hollenberger, S. W.; L. W. Partridge, J. W.; A. T. Geatty, Sec.; E. O. Mannakee, Treas. From July to December, 1873, the officers of the lodge were J. M. Hollenberger, W. M.; J. D. Meyers, S. W.; Isaiah Lightner, Sec.; L. W. Partridge, J. W.; and E. O. Mannakee, Treas. From December, 1873, to July, 1874, the officers were J. D. Meyers, W. M.; L. W. Partridge, S. W.; Wm. J. Crabbs, J. W.; A. L. Beard, Sec.; E. O. Mannakee, Treas. From July to December, 1874, John M. Furney, W. M.; A. L. Beard, S. W.; George W. Love, J. W.; J. M. Hollenberger, Sec.; John D. Meyers, Treas. From December, 1874, to July, 1875, J. M. Furney, W. M.; A. L. Beard, S. W.; Wm. J. Crabbs, J. W.; J. M. Hollenberger, Sec.; J. D. Meyers, Treas. From July to December, 1875, J. M. Furney, W. M.; J. D. Meyers, S. W.; W. J. Crabbs, J. W.; J. M. Hollenberger, Sec.; A. L. Beard, Treas. From December, 1875, to July, 1876, the officers were J. M. Furney, W. M.; J. D. Meyers, S. W.; W. J. Crabbs, J. W.; J. M. Hollenberger, Sec.; A. L. Beard, Treas. From July to December, 1876 J. D. Meyers, W. M.; W. J. Crabbs, S. W.; A. L. Beard, J. W.; J. M. Hollenberger, Sec.; J. M. Furney, Treas. From December, 1876, to July, 1877, J. D. Meyers, W. M.; Wm. J. Crabbs, S. W.; W. T. Penrose, J. W.; J. M. Hollenberger, Sec.; J. M. Furney, Treas. From July to December, 1877, the officers were J. D. Meyers, W. M.; A. T. Beard, S. W.; Wm. J. Crabbs, J. W.; J. M. Hollenberger, Sec.; J. M. Furney, Treas. From December, 1877, to July, 1878, J. D. Meyers, W. M.; Oscar Stiner, S. W.; Granville Crouse, J. W.; J. M. Hollenberger, Sec.; J. M. Furney, Treas. From July to December, 1878, they were J. D. Meyers, W. M.; Oscar Stiner, S. W.; G. Crouse, J. W.; J. M. Hollenberger, Sec.; J. M. Furney, Treas. From December, 1879, to July, 1880, the officers were J. M. Hollenberger, W. M.; G. W. Love, S. W.; Henry Crook, J. W.; M. C. Stoner, Treas.; J. M. Furney, Sec.

The lodge holds its meetings in the Mechanics' Hall, and their members in good standing number sixteen. The present officers, for 1881, are John D. Meyers, W. M.; Harry Crook, S. W.; George W. Love, J. W.; John M. Hollenberger, Sec.; E. O. Mannakee, Treas.

Olive Council, No. 50, of United American Mechanics, was organized and received their charter on March 31, 1875.

The charter was issued to W. H. Morningstar, John M. Furney, H. Clay Devilbiss, J. M. Hollenberger, J. H. Hooker, J.

C. Wentz, P. B. Meyers, David G. Ogle, Clinton Maynard, Theodore Clay, Wm. Kelly, Basil Metz, John Delaplane, Eli Hiltbidle, John D. Meyers, Edward Kelley, L. L. Wiler, James W. Ogle, S. J. Garber.

Their first officers were elected in July and served to December, 1875, and were:

Jr. Ex C., P. B. Meyers; C., W. H. Morningstar; V. C., Eli Hiltbidle; R. S., H. Clay Devilbiss; Treas., J. C. Wentz. From December, 1875, to July, 1876, Jr. Ex C., W. H. Morningstar; C., R. C. Billmeyer; V. C., E. H. Hooker; R. S., H. Clay Devilbiss; Treas., J. C. Wentz. From 1876 to 1877, Jr. Ex C., R. C. Billmeyer; C., E. H. Hooker; V. C., Basil Mentz; R. S., H. C. Devilbiss. January, 1877, to July, Jr. Ex C., E. H. Hooker; C., Basil Mentz; V. C., D. E. Little; R. S., J. M. Hollenberger. July, 1877, to January, 1878, Jr. Ex C., Basil Metz; C., D. E. Little; V. C., M. C. Stoner; R. S., J. M. Hollenberger. From January to July, 1878, Jr. Ex C., D. E. Little; C., M. C. Stoner; V. C., Benjamin Philips; R. S., J. M. Hollenberger. July, 1878, to January, 1879, Jr. Ex C., M. C. Stoner; C., Benj. Philips; V. C., J. M. Furney; R. S., J M. Hollenberger. From January to July, 1879, Jr. Ex C., Benj. Philips; C., Basil Metz; V. C., John Delaplane; R. S., J. M. Hollenberger. From July, 1879, to January, 1880, Jr. Ex C., W. H. Morningstar; C., Basil Metz; V. C., J. M. Furney; R. S., J. M. Hollenberger. From January to July, 1880, Jr. Ex C., Benj. Philips; C., Basil Mentz; V. C., J. M. Furney; R. S., J. M. Hollenberger. From July, 1880, to January, 1881, Jr. Ex C., W. H. Morningstar; C. Basil Mentz; V. C., M. C. Stoner; R. S., J. M. Hollenberger. January, 1881, Jr. Ex C., W. H. Morningstar; C., Basil Metz; V. C., D. E. Little; R. S., J. M. Hollenberger, who are the present officers.

J. M. Hollenberger and W. H. Morningstar were two of the original members, and have been very active in its management since that time.

The Union Bridge Brass Band and Orchestra is under the leadership of S. R. Garver, musical director, and has sixteen pieces. It has a handsome band-wagon, and is one of the best-drilled organizations in that State.

In the year 1735 the Friends, William Farquhar and Anna, his wife, removed from Pennsylvania and settled at Pike Creek. In process of time other members of this denomination settled there, and held meetings for worship at the Farquhar residence by permission of Fairfax Monthly Meeting. They were allowed to build a house for worship by Chester Quarterly Meeting, held at Concord in the 5th month, 1757, and a preparative by the Western Quarterly Meeting, held at London Grove on the 8th month, 1759, which continued and increased.

In the 9th month, 1746, came the Friends, Thomas and Joseph Plummer, from Patuxent, in Prince George's County; and in 1750 and 1751, Richard Holland and William Ballenger, with their wives, Ruth and Casandra, who settled at Bush Creek, and for some time were members of Monocacy Meeting. In 1755 they were allowed to hold meetings on First days for the winter season in Thomas Plummer's house, and in the year following week-day meetings, which continued until a house was built and a meeting for worship allowed by the Western Quarterly Meeting, held at London Grove in the 11th month, 1764. This house was erected near the locality now called Muttontown, but has long ago been torn down. They were then members of the above Preparative Meeting, which was held Circular, answerable to Fairfax Monthly Meeting.

After considerable time, the number at each meeting increasing, they petitioned for a Monthly Meeting in the 7th month, 1767, which was again renewed in the 4th month, 1768, and being sent to the Quarterly Meeting in the 8th month, 1771, was granted accordingly at the 11th month Quarterly in the year following.

About this time the meeting-house was erected, which is situated close to the town of Union Bridge.

At a meeting on the 19th of the 12th month, 1772, the representatives present on behalf of the Preparative Meeting were William Farquhar, William Ballenger, Richard Holland, and William Farquhar. Allen Farquhar was chosen clerk.

On the 16th of the 1st month, 1773, Samuel Cookson, a widower, and Mary Haines, a widow of Daniel Haines, were united in marriage, being the first wedding in that old edifice. Joseph Wright was appointed overseer of Pipe Creek.

At Bush Creek, 20th of 2d month, 1773, Joseph Talbott (afterwards keeper of the "Washington Hotel" in Frederick) produced a certificate for himself and wife, Anna, from West River, Md., Meeting.

Ruth Holland was appointed a minister to the meeting of ministers and elders.

In 1774, Joel Wright was chosen clerk.

In 1777, William Matthews was chosen clerk, and Joseph Wright, Sarah Miller, elders for Pipe Creek Particular.

Friends' cemetery is situated immediately in the rear of the meeting-house, and contains the graves of the following persons:

Beulah, wife of Nathan Haines, died 6th of 11th month, 1869, aged 56 years.

William Hughes, died 7th of 4th month, 1866, aged 67 years.

Eliza H. Moore, born in Petersburg, Va., Sept. 25, 1787, died Oct. 10, 1866.

Susan S., wife of Granville S. Haines, died Aug. 4, 1873, aged 53 years.

Elisha Janey, died 1876, aged 82.

Lydia Hughes, died 10th of 7th month, 1867, aged 74.

Harriet, wife of Thomas F. Shepherd, died Feb. 15, 1869, aged 47 years, 1 month, 9 days.

Mary G. Plummer, born 11th of 1st month, 1813, died 23d of 2d month, 1880.

Rebecca Russell, born 9th of 3d month, 1817, died 22d of 12th month, 1879.

Mary Wood, born 29th of 1st month, 1791, died 7th of 10th month, 1875.

Edith P. Wood, born 12th of 1st month, 1853, died 17th of 5th month, 1870.

Susanna S. Russell, born 21st of 7th month, 1821, died 26th of 4th month, 1868.

William Russell, born 22d of 10th month, 1812, died 17th of 12th month, 1877.

Ephraim Haines, died 26th of 2d month, 1868, aged 71 years, 4 months, 10 days.

Ann, wife of Moses Shaw, died July 16, 1866, aged 53.

Stephen Haines, died Feb. 16, 1879, aged 79 years, 11 months, 14 days.

Samuel Haines, born 25th of 4th month, 1763, died 15th of 2d month, 1833.

Lydia Haines, born 29th of 6th month, 1768, died 22d of 11th month, 1850.

William Haines, died 1830, aged 67 years.

Joanna McKinstry, born 1788, died 1842.

Esther, wife of Stephen Haines, died Dec. 16, 1845, aged 33 years, 3 months, 6 days.

Job C. Haines, born 21st of 3d month, 1790, died 29th of 11th month, 1853.

Sarah Cox, wife of George C., died 26th of 1st month, 1878, aged 82 years, 3 months, 15 days.

George Cox, born in Harford County, 17th of 6th month, 1789, died 2d of 6th month, 1857.

Ann Shepherd, died 1858.

Samuel Haines, died 1856, aged 77.

Ruth Anna Hibberd, died 1855.

Evan McKinstry, died 24th of 11th month, 1852, aged 73.

Thomas Shepherd, died 12th of 11th month, 1875, aged 87.

Portia H., wife of W. J. Smith, died 10th of 9th month, 1864, aged 27 years, 11 months, 2 days.

Rachel K. Hibberd, and M. Hibberd.

Elias F. Hibberd, died 1850.

Esther Hibberd, died 1850.

Hannah Moore, died 2d of 5th month, 1863, aged 96.

John Moore, died 2d of 12th month, 1841, aged 86.

William Shepherd, died 14th of 2d month, 1862, aged 76.

Ruth Shepherd, died 31st of 1st month, 1854, aged 65.

Mary S., wife of Nathan Smith, died 22d of 9th month, 1879, aged 64 years.

John A. Shugh, born Oct. 5, 1814, died Aug. 9, 1877.

Mary, wife of Samuel Haines, died 1852, aged 67.

Esther Haines, died 1851, aged 84.

Nathan Haines, died 3d of 2d month, 1862, aged 73.

Sarah Haines, died 13th of 2d month, 1863, aged 51.

Elizabeth M. Fisher, died July 22, 1860, aged 51.

In the Union Bridge Cemetery the following persons are buried:

John Davis Clemenson, born Jan. 24, 1816, died July 10, 1880.

John B. Norris, died May 9, 1874, aged 34 years, 2 months, 24 days.

Ephraim H. Hooker, died April 6, 1880, aged 37 years, 7 months, 9 days.

Clementine, wife of George W. Crabbs, and daughter of R. and S. Hollenberger, born Nov. 13, 1842, died June 25, 1863.

George W. Crabbs, born March 22, 1836, died Dec. 7, 1865.

Adam Willard, born Sept. 26, 1790, died March 26, 1877.

Catharine Anders, died April 17, 1866, aged 42 years, 9 months.

Joshua Switzer, born Jan. 16, 1811, died Feb. 14, 1877.

Thomas T. Shepherd was born Oct. 10, 1815, near Union Bridge, Frederick Co. (now Carroll), Md., of Scotch-Irish ancestry. His great-grandfather, William Farquhar, and his wife, Ann, moved from the province of Pennsylvania to the province of Maryland in 1735, and settled near the present town of Union Bridge, Carroll Co. He was the first white settler in that part of the State, and there being no roads, except the paths made by the Indians and wild beasts, he was obliged to move his family and goods on pack-horses. He was a tailor by trade, and made buckskin breeches and other clothing for the settlers when they came. His father, Allen Farquhar, gave him two hundred acres of land, and he took up and patented from time to time, as he acquired means, different tracts of land, until in January, 1868, he owned two thousand two hundred and fifty-six acres, including all of the site of the town of Union Bridge, which he divided among his seven children, some of which is still owned by his descendants. His grandfather, Solomon Shepherd, was the oldest son of William and Richmonda Shepherd, of Menallien township, county of York, Pa. He married Susannah Farquhar, daughter of William Farquhar, October, 1779, and built a fulling-mill upon a part of his wife's land. He subsequently built a woolen-mill on the same site, which is still owned by some of his descendants. Solomon Shepherd had four daughters and two sons. His eldest son, William Shepherd, was born Feb. 2, 1786. He married Ruth Fisher, daughter of Samuel Fisher, of Baltimore. They had four sons and four daughters. Thomas F. Shepherd was the oldest son and second child. Solomon, one of the brothers, and Mary Stultz, his sister, are living near Union Bridge. James, the oldest brother, lives in Iowa City. Thomas F., being the oldest son, in his youth was needed in the factory, and all the education he received was obtained at a district school and the business training he got by managing the factory and keeping its books. His brothers were more highly favored in this particular. William H. studied medicine, practiced in Maryland and Wisconsin, went to Australia in 1857, and thence to California, where he practiced his profession until his death in 1864. Solomon carried on the woolen-factory for a few years after Thomas left it, then moved to Wisconsin, where he engaged in farming for a few years, returned to Maryland, and is now farming near Union Bridge. James was farming in Iowa until his health failed; he then sold his farm and moved to Iowa City, where he now resides. In October, 1842, Thomas F. Shepherd married Miss Harriet Haines, born Jan. 6, 1822, near Union Bridge, and daughter of Job C. Haines, a farmer, and sister of G. S. Haines, president of the First National Bank of Westminster. In 1846, Mr. Shepherd withdrew from the factory on account of his health, and removed to his farm on which he now resides, containing about two hundred acres. In January, 1860, he was elected a director of the Mutual Fire Insurance Company of Montgomery County, Md., which position he still holds. In May, 1861, he was appointed postmaster at Uniontown, and still holds that office, though never attending personally to its duties, on account of the remoteness of his residence from the office. In November, 1861, he was elected county commissioner, and held the office six years, having been re-elected in 1863 and 1865, and was legislated out of office by the constitution of 1867. He was president of the board most of the time.

The First National Bank of New Windsor was organized in 1865, and Mr. Shepherd was chosen president, to which position he has been re-elected every year since. His wife died in February, 1869, leaving two daughters. During the same month the bank was robbed by burglars of about one hundred and thirty-eight thousand dollars, over one hundred-thousand of which was recovered. The stockholders expressed their confidence in the integrity of the officers and the management of the bank by immediately making good the entire loss, each one paying his proper proportion. Mr. Shepherd, with his whole family, were Old-Line Whigs. He joined the Know-Nothings, but did not approve of some of their principles. During the civil war he was a strong Union man, and was active in calling and conducting the first Union meeting held in the State. He was for many years a member of the State and County Republican Central Committees, also the Executive Committee of the National Council of the Union League of North America. At the first annual meeting of the State Grange, March, 1874, he was elected chairman of the executive committee, and re-elected at every election since. Mr. Shepherd's parents were members of the Society of Friends, of which he is also a member. Rev. Thomas Shepherd, of Boston, Moses Shepherd, of Baltimore, founder of the Shepherd Insane Asylum, and Col. Shepherd, of the Revolutionary army, were all of the same family.

The following is a list of public school trustees in this district for 1881 and 1882, together with the names of the teachers and number of pupils:

1. Priestland.—Peter Shriner, John E. Sensency, Jasper Shriner.

2 and 3. Union Bridge (Nos. 1 and 2).—Joseph Wolfe, Granville Haines, Samuel Wolfe.

4. Union Bridge (No. 3).—Joseph Wilson, Keener Billmyer, Daniel J. Saylor.

5. Middletown.—William Getsendofner, Edmond Yingling, Abram Harris.

1. African school, near Union Bridge.—Joseph Dunson, Benjamin Jones, Harper Brightwell (all colored).

The teachers for the term ending April 15, 1881, were:

1, R. L. Rinehart, 29 pupils; 2, John S. Repp, 44 pupils; 3, Maggie E. Repp, 42 pupils; 4, Lizzie S. Wolfe, 43 pupils; 5, Jesse F. Billmyer, 41 pupils; 1 (African school), Julia B. Battles, 42 pupils.

WASHINGTON COUNTY.

CHAPTER XL.

INTRODUCTORY.

General Character — Agriculture — Education — Finances — County Created—Soils and Climate—Land Grants and Surveys—Indian Antiquities.

WASHINGTON COUNTY, which is the next oldest in point of settlement in Western Maryland, was created on the 6th of September, 1776, by an act of the Provincial Convention of Maryland. Montgomery County was also created by the same act. Originally Washington was part of Frederick, and embraced the present counties of Washington, Allegany, and Garrett. As now constituted it is bounded on the north by Pennsylvania, on the east by the South Mountain, which separates it from Frederick County, on the south and southwest by the Potomac River, dividing it from Virginia, and on the west by Sidling Hill Creek, which separates it from Allegany. It is nearly triangular in shape, and its southern and southwestern boundary, running with the course of the Potomac River, is extremely irregular. The surface, like that of Frederick, is undulating and picturesque. Along the eastern edge extends the South Mountain, with a spur at its southern extremity known as Elk Ridge. In the northern portion, in what is known as the Clear Spring District, are the East Ridge, North Mountain, and Blair's Valley Mountain. Farther to the westward, in Indian Spring District, are Bare Pond Forest Mountain and Hearth Stone Mountain. There are also several other small ranges in the same district. In Hancock District, west of Clear Spring, are the Sidling and Tolonoway Hills. Round Top is a spur of the latter. The county is abundantly watered by the Antietam, Beaver, Conococheague, Israel, Indian, and other creeks tributary to the Potomac. The county-seat is Hagerstown, besides which are the thriving villages of Williamsport, Hancock, Clear Spring, Smithsburg, Leitersburg, Boonsboro', Funkstown, Keedysville, Sharpsburg, Cavetown, and others. Agriculturally, Washington ranks as one of the most flourishing counties of Maryland, and its population is remarkable for intelligence, prosperity, and thrift. Its area is five hundred and twenty-five square miles, and its population, according to the census of 1880, is as follows:

First Election District (Sharpsburg), including town of Sharpsburg		2311
Sharpsburg	1260	
Second Election District (Williamsport), including town of Williamsport		2625
Williamsport	1503	
Third Election District (Hagerstown), including part of the town of Hagerstown		4031
Hagerstown (part of)	3188	
Fourth Election District (Clear Spring), including town of Clear Spring		2715
Clear Spring Town	721	
Fifth Election District (Hancock), including town of Hancock		2233
Hancock Town	931	
Sixth Election District (Boonsboro'), including the following places		2262
Boonsboro' Town	859	
Mount Pleasant Village	165	
Seventh Election District (Cavetown), including the following places		1665
Cavetown Village	221	
Smithburg	433	
Eighth Election District (Pleasant Valley), including the following villages		1304
Brownsville Village	68	
Rohrersville Village	106	
Ninth Election District (Leitersburg), including village of Leitersburg		1546
Leitersburg	308	
Tenth Election District (Funkstown), including village of Funkstown		1534
Funkstown	600	
Eleventh Election District (Sandy Hook), including village of Sandy Hook		1585
Sandy Hook	373	
Twelfth Election District (Tilghmanton), including village of Tilghmanton		1580
Tilghmanton	171	
Thirteenth Election District (Conococheague), including village of Fairview		1630
Fairview Village	59	
Fourteenth Election District (Ringgold), including village of Ringgold		823
Ringgold	199	
Fifteenth Election District (Indian Spring), including hamlet of Millstone Point		1736
Millstone Point Hamlet	62	
Sixteenth Election District (Beaver Creek)		1199
Seventeenth Election District (Antietam), including part of the town of Hagerstown		4591
Hagerstown (part of)	3439	
Eighteenth Election District (Chewsville), including village of Chewsville		973
Chewsville Village	110	
Nineteenth Election District (Keedysville), including the town of Keedysville		1205
Keedysville	389	
Twentieth Election District (Downsville)		1013

The population of Hagerstown, situated partly in the Third and partly in the Seventeenth Election Districts, is 6627.

The total population is 38,561, of whom 19,068 are males, 19,493 females, 37,942 native, 619 foreign, 35,497 white, 3004 colored.

The population of the county since and including the census of 1790 has been as follows:

White.		*Free Colored.*	
1870	31,874	1870	2,838
1860	28,305	1860	1,677
1850	26,930	1850	1,828
1840	24,724	1840	1,580
1830	21,277	1830	1,082
1820	19,247	1820	627
1810	15,591	1810	483
1800	16,108	1800	342
1790	14.472	1790	64
Slave.		*Aggregate.*	
1860	1,435	1870	34,712
1850	2,090	1860	31,417
1840	2,546	1850	30,848
1830	2,909	1840	28,850
1820	3,201	1830	25,268
1810	2,656	1820	23,075
1800	2,200	1810	18,730
1790	1,286	1800	18,659
		1790	15,822

The agricultural products of the county, as reported in 1880, were: Buckwheat, 183 acres in cultivation, yielding 1506 bushels; Indian corn, 31,910 acres, 1,090,972 bushels; oats, 2874 acres, 52,497 bushels; rye, 1818 acres, 21,750 bushels; wheat, 56,923 acres, 1,024,769 bushels; tobacco, 5 acres, 7050 pounds.

The following interesting statistics give the figures of the yield of corn and wheat per acre in Maryland in 1879. It will be seen that Harford takes the lead in raising corn, the yield being 38¼ bushels per acre. Frederick follows with 34½, Washington 34, Baltimore 33¾, Cecil 33, the lowest being Worcester, 8½ bushels.

In the production of wheat, however, Washington is far above any of her sister counties, the average yield per acre being 25¾ bushels. Montgomery, next in order, with 17¼ bushels, is followed closely by Frederick with 17. Harford is fourth in the list, with 16½ bushels, Howard being the same. The average yield in Cecil 16, and in Baltimore County 13¾. Worcester shows the lowest average yield, namely, 7 bushels. The average yield of wheat in the State is about 14½ bushels.

The following is the yield of corn and wheat per acre in each county of the State:

Counties.	Corn per Acre.	Wheat per Acre.
Allegany	28	9
Anne Arundel	23¼	9
Baltimore	33¾	13¾
Calvert	20	7½
Caroline	17	11
Carroll	31½	14½
Cecil	33	16
Charles	16	8
Dorchester	16½	7½
Frederick	34½	17
Garrett	24½	11
Harford	38¼	16½
Howard	29	16½
Kent	26¾	15
Montgomery	29	17¼
Prince George's	22½	9
Queen Anne's	24½	13½
St. Mary's	15¼	8¼
Somerset	17	10¼
Talbot	26½	14
Washington	34	25¾
Wicomico	11	7¼
Worcester	8½	7

Public Schools.—The public schools of Washington County have long enjoyed a high reputation for thoroughness and regularity of attendance. Following are the statistics for 1881, as returned by P. A. Witmer, county superintendent, for the term ending Nov. 15, 1881:

No. of Election District.	No. of School.	TEACHERS.	FALL TERM, 1881.		WINTER TERM, 1881.	
			Pupils Enrolled.	Average Attendance.	Pupils Enrolled.	Average Attendance.
1	1	John E. Kelly	41	32	34	25
	"	Sue D. Johnson	59	42	62	45
	"	John P. Smith	68	57	68	50
	"	Alice V. Gower	75	60	72	50
	"	Lizzie Alder	49	29	109	64
	2	A. D. Warfield	54	25	49	22
	3	R. E. Borden	22	13	39	17
2	1	I. T. Beard	34	20	48	29
	"	E. W. Byees	38	25	63	39
	"	Cora Shawen	42	30	55	36
	"	Mamie Hawken	52	37	72	48
	"	Ella Hollman	73	52	88	65
	2	F. L. King	46	32	53	35
	3	S. A. Poffenberger	42	23	50	34
	4	A. M. Lynch	34	20	42	31
High	School.	George A. Harter	50	43	35	31
3	1	J. A. Zeigler	37	33	40	35
	"	F. J. Halm	35	27	38	31
	"	Bettie Braly	54	43	38	25
	"	Annie Cook	52	44	48	36
	"	Nettie Baker	45	33	44	34
	"	Mary Bundel	59	42	48	36
	"	Ella Taggart	50	39	52	40
	2	George B. Cummings	48	27	60	35
	3	D. F. Newcomer	43	29	37	24
	4	S. J. Baker	35	25	38	30
4	1	Isaac Sprecher	38	31	38	26
	"	W. S. Richardson	23	20	31	21
	"	Kate Staughenhaupt	27	22	38	26
	"	A. E. Snyder	44	38	48	31
	2	John Q. Miller	26	20	33	20
	3	George S. Fockler	38	24	42	28
	4	John J. Kreps	54	40	63	32
	5	B. F. Angle	39	25	41	27
	6	Cora Seiss	24	17	28	13
	7	Wm. H. Angle	34	25	36	24
	8	Joshua Phillips	27	23	41	26
	9	John M. Smith	34	17	44	24
5	1	George C. Pearson	27	22	34	26
	"	Milton Spessard	29	12	34	26
	"	Pleasant Johnson	42	30	51	32
	"	Mary B. Stuart	76	60	70	41
	2	N. McKinnery	29	18	51	23
	3	James S. Grant	24	16	34	14
	4	Annie Ambrose	38	24	29	20
	5	Clara Shepherd	25	14	20	13
	6	Sadie Carter	32	12	29	16
	7	George H. Seigman	21	15	25	18
	8	Scott Battenfield	2[illegible]	15	23	17
6	1	D. H. Staley	29	25	29	22
	"	J. Harlan Smith	36	28	35	27
	"	Harry Davis	33	28	45	32
	"	Amanda Barr	37	30	38	30
	"	Effie Grossnickle	63	49	63	47
	2	C. A. Newton	44	30	55	42
	3	T. H. Smith	32	21	54	32
	4	George M. Stover	43	21	47	21
	5	L. L. Grossnickle	16	11	29	16
	6	S. B. Shoop	45	37	51	46
7	1	George Pearson	25	19	21	20
	"	J. D. Seigman	27	22	22	19
	"	Haidee Poe	36	32	41	35
	"	Maggie Bingham	66	54	58	41
	2	Dillon Weagley	24	18	49	37
	"	D. H. Garver	51	44	57	44
	3	Emma Bachtel	26	16	27	22
	4	L. A. R. Kohler	40	19	41	15
8	1	Eugene Brown	57	43	49	26
	2	O. M. Snyder	21	16	20	13
	3	A. W. Leslie	32	24	48	32
	"	Thalia Boteler	42	34	45	23
	4	W. C. Zahn	49	29	55	43
	5	A W. Reeder	20	17	39	27
	6	Jacob Smith	24	14	24	19
9	1	Frank Leiter	28	23	29	26
	"	Emma Barnhart	38	36	35	31
	1	Linna Bell	43	39	47	40
	2	Orville Long	29	22	40	29
	3	T. F. Diffendal	38	24	49	35
	4	Robert Lamar	48	33	46	31
	5	John F. Kayhoe	46	28	45	37
	6	T. Harry Davis	41	27	51	36
	7	Preston Vogle	30	21	34	22
	8	James P. Harter	48	41	44	37
10	1	M. Emmett Cullen	21	18	29	24
	"	Charles W. McDade	37	27	35	26
	"	Sallie Gower	44	37	48	40
	"	Martha D. Stuart	73	54	58	47
	2	M. L. Keedy	22	16	20	15
	3	Marene Lamar	37	25	41	24
	4	Ambrose Reed	30	18	33	21
11	1	Anna Carter	43	25	47	30
	2	James Smith	38	21	36	16
	3	O. M. Yrumkins	40	22	65	39
	"	Emma M. Virtz	51	30	40	30
	4	Lind F. Currie	36	19	48	23
	5	D. D. Keedy	43	22	64	30
12	1	Amanda Shoop	41	29	45	30
	2	Laura Grossnickle	39	29	34	28
	3	M. L Schmucker	45	28	61	34
	4	Peter Schamel	25	19	41	31
	"	Alfred Betts	61	49	49	37
	5	T. J. Fahrney	39	21	44	28
13	1	George W. Hicks	56	38	57	43
	2	Samuel Hicks	39	25	33	39
	3	George H. Uhler	45	27	58	39
	4	Jos. M. Keeny	39	23	53	38
	5	Thos B Rice	50	37	64	51
	6	D. S. Pittinger	35	23	35	22
	7	J. E. S Pryor	29	19	37	23
	8	Wilfred Rice	39	21	47	31
14	1	L F. Benchoff	54	34	70	44
	2	J. V. Shank	30	21	39	27
	3	John Masters	36	22	38	24
	4	Maggie Bachtel	19	12	16	10
	5	A. F. Diffendal	42	28	45	32
15	1	W. F. Humbert	24	12	47	30
	2	M. L. Bachtel	32	16	48	28
	3	A. W. Culler	26	17	32	15
	4	Rebecca Boyd	26	12	36	22
	5	A. Shaeffer	52	47	41	32
	6	E. G. Kinsell	39	24	41	27
	7	George M. Draper	27	22	43	25
	8	H. S. Smith	30	14	36	27
	9	O. J. Zittle	26	15	38	19
	10	J. L. V. Cook	42	22	47	28
16	1	Cyrus D. Harp	53	29	49	28
	2	John Wagaman	22	13	39	20
	3	J. M. Kreidler	66	43	75	48
	4	A. G. Irvin	44	30	32	29
	4	A. J. Harsh	19	15	38	23
	6	M. Newcomer	25	19	26	17
17	1	Wm. D. Piper	36	25	21	18
	"	Mary Rowland	41	30	35	30
	"	Mary Dunlap	30	23	31	25
	"	Mary Hurley	37	30	38	32
	"	Daniel A. Thomas	40	30	41	21
	"	Blanche Wagoner	50	45	50	30
	"	Mary Rouskulp	41	36	40	19
	"	Margaret Newcomer	57	46	52	42
	"	Emily Walsh	71	58	48	38
	2	Cyrus Simmons	48	35	56	37
	3	Wm. Anthony	30	19	33	24
	4	A. Huntsberger	34	24	32	24
	5	Thos. Parmer	36	25	43	34
18	1	Chas. A. Santee	47	35	49	24
	2	John P. Fockler	30	25	45	37
	"	R. E. Brown	50	43	49	35
	3	Fred. K. Sykes	46	34	47	34
	4	J. H. Brewer	19	15	21	15
	5	A. M. Walfinger	46	35	56	44
19	1	Ezra Schildknecht	31	28	32	30
	"	E. E. Hertzell	19	18	27	22
	"	Ella Kelsey	29	24	32	24
	"	Agnes Stevenson	44	39	48	37
	2	D. W. Wyand	46	33	47	30
	3	C. W. Reichard	32	25	48	34
	4	Asa Lamar	45	29	38	24
20	1	C. A. Waynant	38	22	50	27
	"	Geary S. Betts	56	42	49	37
	2	D. E. Wolf	32	26	44	29
	3	O. V. Middlekauff	49	26	46	18
	4	Wm. H. King	50	28	24	20

COLORED SCHOOLS.

No. of Election District.	No. of School.	TEACHERS.	FALL TERM, 1881.		WINTER TERM, 1881.	
			Pupils Enrolled.	Average Attendance.	Pupils Enrolled.	Average Attendance.
1	4	J. F. Samons	22	16	22	13
2	5	C. W. Trusty	46	26	51	29
4	10	W. T. Williams	39	31	57	38
5	9	John Truman	29	16	52	22
6	6	John Newman	18	14	17	12
10	5	Louisa Jacobs	17	16	16	12
11	6	Wm. B. Hill	23	19	30	18
12	6	Wm. E. Nelson	42	25	23	14
16	7	F. V. Williams	23	17	23	15
17	6	George W Braye	50	30	65	43
"	"	Mary Russell	72	38	72	37
19	5	Truelove McDaniel	26	20	31	20

The following are the school district trustees for the year ending May, 1882:

Election District 1.—School District 1, J. C. Wilson, R. E. Hugg, J. McGraw; 2, J. Frees, E. Marker, E. Easterday; 3, S. J. Piper, Moses Cox, D. Coffman; 4, N. Zimmerman, Levi Porter, S. Wagoner; 5, H. Watson, George Tyler, D. B. Samons.

Election District 2.—School District 1, J. Farrow, J. Hawken, A. Schnebley; 2, J. D. Byers, J. Halbeck, G. Bussard; 3, D. Summer, C. D. Sprecher, W. Middlekauff; 4, Peter Kauffman, L. Trone, Joseph Rowland; 5, T. Barnum, C. Brown, Eli Keys.

Election District 3.—School District 1, J. W. Story, Peter Graey, W. S. Stover; 2, J. E. Johnson, Eli Summer, J. Hebb; 3, P. Wingert, J. J. Hershey, C. McDade; 4, J. M. Startzman, E. Baker, M. Startzman.

Election District 4.—School District 1, S. Reitzell, J. Bain, J. T. Snyder; 2, John Woolford, Eli Heller, D. Cowton; 3, J. C. Brewer, S. Mitchell, J. Lindsay; 4, G. Sprecher, L. A. Spickler, J. A. Miller; 5, John Strite, George Ruch, M. Schnebley; 6, D. Seibert, Israel Reiff, E. McLaughlin; 7, J. P. Blair, D. Clopper, Thomas Corbett; 8, T. Charlton, S. Davis, W. Cushwa; 9, J. M. Smith, Frank Ellis, A. Snyder; 10, Israel Dorris, Henry Miles, T. Dorsey.

Election District 5.—School District 1, Dr. W. H. Perkins, S. Crown, J. W. Baxter; 2, Emory Pelton, J. O'Farrell, R. Shives; 3, R. Murray, Henry Stine, Samuel Dignan; 4, S. Summer, Harvey Taylor, Alfred Watts; 5, J. Sheppard, John Henlin, C. Harvey; 6, H. Spicer, J. McAvoy, Joseph Exline; 7, T. E. Norris, Charles Norris, M. Yonker; 8, William Poole, D. Mann, Nathan Hartley; 9, N. Proctor, L. Robinson, John Thomas.

Election District 6.—School District 1, Dr. H. B. Wilson, J. L. Nicodemus, M. Bomberger; 2, D. O. Hammond, D. Foltz, D. F. Stouffer; 3, E. Miller, D. Poffenberger, R. Mumford; 4, J. W. Smith, H. St. Clair, J. P. Summers; 5, B. F. Brinham, G. Wallack, W. Fahrney; 6, J. Gaylor, D. Stull, Benjamin Foltz; 7, Lloyd Ridout, J. Shorter, Guy Butler.

Election District 7.—School District 1, H. Lyday, A. C. Hildebrand, J. D. Slaughenhaupt; 2, D. W. Blessing, J. Weagley, J. Little; 3, S. Smith, John Grey, Daniel Burns; 4, J. M. Brown, Josiah Taggert, J. Brown.

Election District 8.—School District 1, G. H. Brown, J. H. West, W. B. Kelley; 2, postponed; 3, J. H. Poffenberger, J. H. Mullendore, D. J. Holmes; 4, George Shiffler, D. D. Keedy, J. G. Hines; 5, L. Stine, G. G. Brane, John Slifer; 6, D. Baker, Henry C. Holmes, D. Glass.

Election District 9.—School District 1, S. Strite, Upton Bell, Solomon Hartle; 2, J. Trovinger, W. Crum, D. Sheeler; 3, Peter Smith, Isaac Jacobs, Isaac Heiks; 4, Abram Strite, Joseph Strite, S. Martin; 5, J. M. Bell, Benjamin Newcomer, U. Clopper; 6, D. W. Durburrow, H. Martin, J. Fahrney; 7, Abram Shank, Joseph Shank, D. G. Krouse; 8, D. Shumaker, P. K. Harter, W. M. Lantz.

Election District 10.—School District 1, V. Newcomer, R. Cushen, Isaac Hanna; 2, J. Keedy, William South, Peter Kesselring; 3, Abram Hamburg, J. Young, J. Huffer; 4, D. Doub, J. W. Murdock, D. Harshman; 5, Levi Grant, William Bell.

Election District 11.—School District 1, Warren Garrott, W. McDuell, C. W. Fry; 2, J. H. Elgin, G. E. Stonebraker, C. Virtz; 3, P. Higgins, C. Cole, John McCormick; 4, John Heskett, William Thompson, D. Reed; 5, James Ingram, M. T. Holmes, John Best; 6, R. Anderson, H. Duckett, R. Edemy.

Election District 12.—School District 1, T. J. Warfield, S. Reichard, C. Barr; 2, D. Wolf, N. Mumma, Jacob Leatherman; 3, T. Wolford, George Eakle, E. Davis; 4, Simon Coffman, John Petre, E. Yourtee; 5, A. Highberger, J. Fahrney, A. Hammond; 6, B. Oldwine, E. Whiting, W. Wade.

Election District 13.—School District 1, L. R. Schnebley, F. T. Spickler, Joseph Hershberger; 2, J. Keller, J. McDonald, J. Buchanan; 3, H. Strock, S. Wolfensberger, S. Cearfoss; 4, J. Maugans, S. Weaver, H. St. Clair; 5, John Strite, Henry Strite, S. Foltz; 6, J. F. Neibert, G. W. Hamilton, Frank P. Spickler; 7, J. Summer, J. Emmert, E. Clarkson; 8, D. Ankeney, G. W. Kretzer, D. Carl.

Election District 14.—School District 1, L. Barkdoll, J. Reecher, L. Teesinger; 2, J. L. Newcomer, J. Martin, Jr., J. W. Cable; 3, E. J. Wade, John Gladhill, Henry Crider; 4, A. Shrockey, J. Rhineheart, H. Socks; 5, T. B. Coyle, H. V. Schull, H. M. Stouffer.

Election District 15.—School District 1, T. H. Moore, J. H. Martin, Dennis Cain; 2, J. Houck, J. McCormick, S. Weller; 3, J. Cameron, L. Eichelberger, D. Dick; 4, A. Ditto, D. G. Holland, H. Starliper; 5, S. Penner, A. J. McAllister, J. Sponseller; 6, L. Shank, William S. Cook, S. Lauchbaum; 7, J. D. Tice, M. Whitson, David Myers; 8, A. Flory, John Kuhn, J. B. Martin; 9, G. Eichelberger, G. W. Bowers, William Gehr, Jr.; 10, E. S. Zimmerman, S. Beckley, W. Ernst.

Election District 16.—School District 1, Jonas Huffer, William C. Gray, J. L. Harp; 2, Benjamin Doyle, William Funk, Leonard Detrow; 3, H. Funk, J. Faulders, E. Stover; 4, J. M. Newcomer, J. Funk, M. Witmer; 5, G. Adams, J. Middlekauff, T. Kaylor; 6, C. Landis, J. R. Adams, George Orrick; 7, T. Williams, James Sewell, H. Williams.

Election District 17.—School District 1, M. L. Byers, J. L. Bikle, J. I. Bitner; 2, H. C. Loose, Joseph Itnyre, J. Snyder; 3, J. Clare, D. Downin, Abram Martin; 4, G. Cressler, J. Eschleman, D. Martin; 5, J. Wallick, A. C. Miller, D. Bostetter; 6, William Russell, T. J. Hopkins, J. F. Wagoner.

Election District 18.—School District 1, J. Houck, John Oster, Silas Alsup; 2, John H. Harp, L. D. Betts, D. Spessard; 3, G. L. Harbaugh, D. Stover, D. P. Spessard; 4, Jacob Stouffer, J. H. Michaels, D. Snyder; 5, J. B. Bausman, S. Bachtel, William Rohrer.

Election District 19.—School District 1, J. Thomas, G. W. Snavely, L. Poffenberger; 2, F. T. Hagan, W. C. Snavely,

J. L. Clopper; 3, G. Line, C. Snavely, C. M. Poffenberger; 4, A. C. Huffer, N. G. Thomas, S. Thomas; 5, G. Fisher, Henry Keats, William Summer.

Election District 20.—School District 1, S. Long, B. Hoffman, L. O. Downs; 2, J. Cromer, Ezra Nally, A. Middlekauff; 3, W. Hagerman, E. Jacobs, J. Cunningham; 4, T. Downin, William Barnhart, R. Hurleghe.

The educational statistics of the county for 1880 were:

126 elementary schools, 12 schools for colored children, 129 school buildings, of which 1 has more than one study-room; 9562 seats provided; total seating capacity of schools, 10,689; 108 schools reported in good condition, 21 reported in bad condition; 122 male teachers, 44 female ditto; total, 166; 9 male colored teachers, 4 female colored ditto; total, 13; whole number of teachers, white and colored, 179; of whom 73 were educated at high schools or academies, 16 were educated at normal schools, 25 at colleges or universities, and 65 held certificates other than the preceding. The average of teachers' salaries per month was $33.44; average number of months employed, 7.10.

The county commissioners fixed the rate of taxation for 1881 at 83 cents on $100 for county tax, which, added to the State tax of 18¾ cents, makes an aggregate taxation of 101¾ cents on the $100, which rate of taxation produces $148,570.25.

The following are the several appropriations:

Condemnations, etc.	$1,129.14
Constables	941.85
Printing	1,196.37
Collector	2,450.00
Court-house and jail	1,594.33
Coffins and graves	180.75
Magistrates	380.48
Registers and Orphans' Court	1,542.65
Sheriff's office	5,191.60
Commissioners' office	1,873.60
Bellevue	8,777.42
Attorneys	2,304.68
Clerk of court	1,662.76
Court-house and school bonds and interest	12,384.00
Fire department	266 64
McCausland debt	240.00
Interest R. R. and bounty bonds	34,422.00
Jurors and State witnesses	8,000.00
Roads	9,000.00
Bridges	2,500.00
Fox-scalps	19.50
Miscellaneous	542.30
Judges and clerks of election	803.00
Inquisitions	296.14
Pensioners	5,691.00
Schools	34,000.00
Registers	1,020.90
	$138,411.11
Amount of levy	148,570.25
Surplus	$10,159.14

The rate of assessment on the $100 is as follows:

For county purposes	27½ cts.
Court-house and school bonds and interest	7 "
Court expenses	4½ "
Bellevue Asylum	5 "
R. R. and bounty interest	19½ "
Schools	19½ "
	83 "
State tax	18¾ "
	101¾ "

The levy includes enough to pay off $9600 of court-house and school bonds.

The taxable basis has been increased over half a million of dollars by the new assessment of the railroads. The whole basis for 1881 was about $17,900,000, against $17,375,000 for 1880. The assessment of the Washington County Railroad, 24¼ miles, has been increased from $75,225 to $276,750. The Western Maryland road has been raised from $80,250 to $277,000. This includes $8000 for the portion of the Baltimore and Cumberland Valley road lying in this county. The Cumberland Valley road has been increased from $50,879 to $134,000, and the Shenandoah Valley road has been assessed at $69,000.

The schools get $2810 more for 1881 than 1880, which increases the rate 1½ cents on $100. The almshouse rate and rate for bonds is decreased, offsetting the increase for the schools, which makes the rate the same as for 1880, although, on account of the increase in the basis, the amount produced is increased $4100.

The bonded indebtedness of the county in 1880 was $693,475, and its floating debt was $5450, making the gross debt $698,925. The net debt per capita was $18.13.

Early History.—The county was established by an act of the Provincial Convention, passed on Friday, Sept. 6, 1776. Previous to that time, from the organization of Frederick County in 1748, it had been a portion of that county. The first mention we have of a separate representation of that portion of Frederick now called Washington County in the legislative proceedings of the province was on July 26, 1775, when the Provincial Convention, sitting at Annapolis, enacted the following:

"That for the ease and convenience of the people of Frederick County there be three different places of election; that the said county be divided into three districts, to wit: upper, middle, and lower; the upper district (now Washington County) to be divided by the South Mountain, and the lines of the county westward of the South Mountain; the middle district to be bounded from the mouth of Monocacy with Potowmack to the South Mountain, with that mountain to the temporary line, with the lines of the county to the head-waters of Patuxent, and with the lines of the lower district to Potowmack; the lower district to be bounded with Potowmack to the mouth of Monocacy, then with Monocacy to the mouth of Bennett's Creek, and with the creek to the head-waters of the Patuxent; that there be elected in the lower district one delegate, two persons to act as a committee of correspondence, and seventeen as a committee of observation; that in each of the other districts there be elected two delegates and eighteen persons to act as a committee of observation; and that three persons be elected in the middle district to act as a committee of correspondence; that the elections for the upper district be held at Elizabethtown (now Hagerstown), those for the middle district at Fredericktown, and those for the lower district at Hungerford's; and that no person residing or voting in one shall be admitted to vote in either of the other districts."

The convention proceedings further show that on Monday, Dec. 18, 1775, William Baird, a member for the upper district of Frederick (now Washington County), appeared and took his seat in the convention. On Jan. 6, 1776, the convention elected the following officers for the militia in the upper district of Frederick County:

"*First Battalion.*—Mr. John Stull, colonel; Mr. Andrew Kench, lieutenant-colonel; Mr. Henry Shyrock, first major; Mr. George Woltz, second major; Mr. Elie Williams, quartermaster. *Second Battalion.*—Mr. Samuel Beall, colonel; Mr. Joseph Smith, lieutenant-colonel; Mr. Richard Davis, first major; Mr. Charles Swearingen, second major; Mr. James Chapline, quartermaster."

On Friday, May 24, 1776, the convention again met, with all the members present, "as on yesterday," except Mr. Rumsey, Mr. Baird, Mr. Handy, and Mr. Stull, and transacted the following business:

"On hearing Mr. Daniel Hughes as to the execution of the contract made by Samuel Hughes, on the behalf of himself and the said Daniel Hughes, for the casting and furnishing cannon for the public,

"*Resolved,* That the inquiry be made what is the standing proof of cannon contracted for on account of the continent, and that the same proof be had of the cannon to be furnished by the said Hughes on their contract.

"*Resolved,* That notwithstanding the said Hughes have not furnished the public with cannon within the time they contracted to do the same, that on their pursuing the work with diligence the council of safety for the time being take the whole number contracted for on the account and for the use of the public."

On Monday, July 1, 1776, the convention met and passed the following:

"*Resolved,* That for the encouragement of Daniel and Samuel Hughes to prosecute their cannon-foundry with spirit and diligence, the council of safety be empowered, on their application, to lend and advance to them any sum not exceeding two thousand pounds common money out of the public treasury, they giving bond with good security to interest, and apply the same in prosecuting the said cannon-foundry, and repaying the same into the public treasury by the 10th day of April next."

The Hugheses were residents of Washington County, and were among the earliest organizers of the new county.

At a convention of delegates chosen by the several counties and districts, and by the city of Annapolis and town of Baltimore, of the province of Maryland, at the city of Annapolis, on Aug. 14, 1776, there were present as delegates from the upper district of Frederick (now Washington County) Samuel Beall, John Stull, and Henry Schnebly.

On Thursday, Aug. 15, 1776, the convention again met, and the Committee on Elections reported

"That by the return for the upper district of Frederick County (now Washington County), Samuel Beall, Samuel Hughes, John Stull, and Henry Schnebly, Esqrs., were duly elected delegates to represent that district in the convention."

As originally constituted, Frederick County was a vast and sparsely-settled tract, and the people living west of the South Mountain were put to great inconvenience in traveling to and from Frederick, the county-seat. Consequently, in response to their petition, the Provincial Convention, at a session held at Annapolis on Saturday, Aug. 31, 1776, granted leave for the introduction of an ordinance for the division of Frederick County. Later, on the same day, Mr. Wootton brought in and delivered to the president of the convention (Matthew Tilghman) an ordinance for the division of Frederick County into three distinct and separate counties, which was read and ordered to lie on the table.

On Friday, Sept. 6, 1776, the ordinance for the division of Frederick County was read the second time, and, on motion, the question was put, "That the consideration thereof be postponed till the next session of convention? Carried in the negative." Those voting in the negative were Messrs. Barnes, Semmes, Parnham, Fitzhugh, J. Mackall, Bowie, Hall, Sprigg, Marbury, Hammond, Paca, Wootton, Bayly, Williams, Sheredine, Edelen, Beall, Hughes, Stull, Schnebly, Ridgely, Deye, Stevenson, J. Smith, H. Wilson, Love, Archer, Brevard, T. Ringgold, and Johnson; those voting in the affirmative being Messrs. Hooe, Dent, Carroll, W. Ringgold, Earle, T. Smythe, Goldsborough, Murray, Gus Scott, J. Wilson, Fischer, Schriver, Bond, Ewing, T. Wright, S. Wright, Edmondson, Gibson, George Scott, Lowes, Mason, and Chaille. The convention then proceeded to take the same into consideration, which was agreed to. The bill, so far as it relates to Washington County, is as follows:

"*Whereas,* It appears to this convention that the erecting two new counties out of Frederick County will conduce greatly to the ease and convenience of the people thereof;

"*Resolved,* That after the first day of October next such part of the said county of Frederick as is contained within the bounds and limits following, to wit: beginning at the place where the temporary line crosses the South Mountain, and running thence by a line on the ridge of the said mountain to the river Potowmac, and thence with the lines of the said county so as to include all the lands to the westward of the line running on the ridge of the South Mountain, as aforesaid, to the beginning, shall be and is hereby erected into a new county by the name of *Washington* County.[1]

* * * * * * * * *

"*Resolved,* That the inhabitants of the said counties of Washington and Montgomery shall have, hold, and enjoy all such rights and privileges as are held and enjoyed by the inhabitants of any county in this State.

[1] The second resolution describes the boundaries of the new county of *Montgomery*. See history of that county.

"*Resolved*, That Messrs. Joseph Sprigg, Joseph Smith, John Barnes, Andrew Rench, Daniel Hughes, William Yates, and Conrad Hogmire shall be and are hereby appointed commissioners for Washington County; and they, or the major part of them, shall be and are hereby authorized and required to buy and purchase in fee a quantity of land not exceeding four acres, at or adjoining such place as a majority of voters within the limits of the said county, qualified as this convention, shall hereafter direct, the election to be held at the place heretofore appointed for the choosing of delegates in this convention (the said commissioners giving ten days' notice of the place and time of voting), for the purpose of building thereon a court-house and prison for the said county; and shall cause the said land to be laid out by the surveyor of Frederick County with good and sufficient boundaries, and a certificate thereof to be returned and recorded in the records of the said county; and the said commissioners, or a major part of them, shall draw their order on the sheriff of Washington County to pay such sum as shall be agreed upon for the said land, and the sheriff is hereby directed and required to pay the said order out of the money hereafter mentioned, to be collected by him for that purpose; and such payment for the land shall invest the justices of Washington County and their successors with an estate in fee-simple therein, for the use of the said county forever; and if the said commissioners, or the major part of them, and the owner of the said land shall differ about the value of the said land, in such case the commissioners, or the major part of them, shall be and they are hereby authorized and empowered to order the sheriff of Washington County to summon twelve freeholders upon the said land, who shall be empowered and sworn as a jury to inquire the value of the said land; and the said commissioners, or the major part of them, shall draw their order on the sheriff of Washington County to pay the said valuation; and the said sheriff is hereby directed to pay the said order out of the money hereafter mentioned to be by him collected for that purpose; and upon his payment of the said order the fee-simple in the said land shall be invested, as aforesaid, in the justices of Washington County and their successors for the use of the said county forever.

* * * * * * * * *

"*Resolved*, That the justices of Washington and Montgomery Counties, or the major part of them, respectively be and they are hereby authorized to contract and agree for a convenient place in each of the said counties to hold the courts for the said counties, and to contract and agree for a convenient place in each of the said counties for their books, papers, and other records, and also for a fit building for the custody of the prisoners; and the said courts shall be held and records kept at such places respectively until the court-house and prison for the said counties respectively shall be erected and built; and the charge and expense of such places shall be defrayed by the said counties respectively, and assessed with the public and county levy.

"*Resolved*, That the justices of the said counties respectively shall be and they are hereby authorized and required to assess and levy on the *taxable* inhabitants of the said counties respectively, with the public and county levy, as much money as will pay for the purchase on valuation of the land aforesaid, together with the sheriff's salary of such per centum as may be hereafter allowed for collection of the same, which said sum shall be collected by the sheriffs of the said counties respectively from the inhabitants of the said counties respectively, in the same manner as other public and county levies may be by law hereafter collected; and the said money, when collected, shall be paid by the sheriff to such person or persons as the commissioners aforesaid, or the major part of them, shall order and direct.

"*Resolved*, That the justices of Washington County shall be and they are hereby authorized and required to assess and levy, by three equal assessments, in the years 1777, 1778, and 1779, with their public and county levy, any sum not exceeding thirteen hundred pounds common money in and upon the inhabitants of Washington County, together with the sheriff's salary, of such a per centum as may be hereafter allowed for collection of the same; which said sum, so to be assessed and levied, shall be collected by the sheriff of Washington County from the inhabitants thereof, in the same manner as other public and county levies shall be hereafter by law collected, and the said money, when collected, shall be paid by the said sheriff to the commissioners of Washington County aforesaid, and shall be by them applied towards building the court-house and prison in the said county.

* * * * * * * * *

"*Resolved*, That the commissioners of the said counties respectively, or the major part of them, shall be and they are hereby authorized and required to contract and agree for the building of the said court-house and prison on the land to be purchased as aforesaid.

"*Resolved*, That all causes, pleas, process, and pleadings which now are or shall be depending in Frederick County Court before the first day of December next shall and may be prosecuted as effectually as they might have been had these resolves never been made; and in case any deeds or conveyances of land in Washington County or Montgomery County have been, or shall be before the division aforesaid, acknowledged according to law in Frederick County, the enrollment and recording thereof within the time limited by law, either in the County Court of Frederick County or in the County Court of Washington or Montgomery County, shall be good and available, the division aforesaid notwithstanding.

"*Resolved*, That executions or other legal process upon all judgments had and obtained, or to be had and obtained on actions already commenced, or to be commenced before the first day of December next, in Frederick County Court, against any inhabitant of Washington or Montgomery County, be issued and enforced in the same manner as if these resolves had not been made; which said writs shall be directed to the sheriff of the said counties respectively, and the said sheriffs are hereby authorized and directed to serve and return the same to Frederick County Court, with the body or bodies of the person or persons, if taken, against whom such writ or writs shall issue for that purpose; and during the attendance of the sheriff of Washington or Montgomery County at Frederick County Court he shall have a power to confine in Frederick County jail, if he shall think it necessary, such persons as he shall have in execution; but after his attendance shall be dispensed with by the said court, he shall then, in a reasonable time, remove such persons as he shall have in execution to his county jail, there to be kept till legally discharged.

"That the public and county levy now assessed or levied, or to be levied and assessed by the justices of Frederick County Court, at their Levy Court for the present year, shall and may be collected and received by the sheriff of Frederick County, as well of the inhabitants of Frederick as of Washington and Montgomery Counties aforesaid, and collected, accounted for, and applied in such manner as the said public and county levy would have been collected, accounted for, and applied had these resolves never been made.

"*Resolved*, That the County Court of Washington County shall begin and be held yearly on the fourth Tuesdays of those months in which other County Courts are held, and shall have equal power and jurisdiction with any County Court in this State."

The new county was named Washington, in honor of Gen. Washington, then conspicuous before the country as commander-in-chief of the Continental forces. The men who passed the ordinance creating it were the sturdy patriots who drafted the Declaration of Rights and adopted the first constitution of Maryland.

On the 11th of September, 1776, on motion of Mr. Hughes, it was

"*Resolved*, That the qualification of voters in Washington County for the purpose of fixing on the most convenient place for a court-house and prison in said county be the same as of voters for representatives in this convention." A few days later it was resolved that the elections for Washington County be held at Hagerstown, and that "Joseph Smith, Noah Hart, and Elie Williams, Esquires, or any two of them, be judges of and hold the elections for Washington County."

The people residing west of Sidling Hill, however, were dissatisfied with the provisions of the resolution,—*i.e.*, naming Hagerstown as the place for holding the election,—and in consequence they immediately petitioned the convention to establish a voting precinct in the western part of the county. On Monday, Oct. 21, 1776, the following action was taken by the convention:

"On reading and considering the petition of sundry inhabitants of Washington County, setting forth that by a late resolve of convention the election for fixing the place for the court-house of Washington County was to be held at Hagerstown, which would be so distant from many of the inhabitants of the said county that it would be very inconvenient for them to attend, and praying that the election might be held for one or more days at Skipton or Oldtown, thereupon the question was put, That for the ease and convenience of the inhabitants of the upper part of Washington County the election for fixing the place for the court-house of the said county shall be held two days at Skipton, beginning on the sixth day of November next, and that Andrew Bruce, Lemuel Barrett, and Thomas Warren, or any two of them, be judges of the said election, and give due notice to the inhabitants of the said county; and that the judges appointed to hold the election at Hagerstown and those appointed to hold the election at Skipton meet together as soon as conveniently may be at Hagerstown, and there examine the said polls and declare the said election according as the majority of voters may appear to be on both the said polls? Resolved in the affirmative."[1]

On Thursday, Nov. 7, 1776, on motion of Mr. Johnson, the convention

"*Resolved*, That all justices of the peace and other officers who were such of Frederick County shall continue and may exercise the same power and authority as if the resolutions of this convention for dividing Frederick County into three counties had not passed; and the justices of the County Court of Frederick, to be held in the month of November in this present year, or by adjournment, shall have cognizance of, and may proceed to hear and determine, all causes, matters, and things, criminal and civil, although the same have arisen or shall arise in Washington or Montgomery County, in the same manner and as fully as the same court might or could have done if the said resolutions had never been made; and the justices aforesaid may appoint constables and overseers of the highways, as well in the said counties of Washington and Montgomery as in Frederick County.

"That the County Court for each of the said counties of Washington and Montgomery shall be first held, as for separate and distinct counties, in the month of March next, and where any defendant against whom any original writ or process shall, after the first day of December next, issue resides in Washington or Montgomery County, the writ or process shall issue out of Frederick County Court, directed to the sheriff of the county where the defendant resides, if such county shall then have a sheriff qualified to act in the county separately, and if not, to the sheriff of Frederick County, and shall be returnable and returned to the next March court to be held for the county where the defendant resides.

"That the justices of Frederick County Court aforesaid may, at their November court aforesaid, assess and levy on the taxable inhabitants of Washington and Montgomery Counties, separately and respectively, such money or tobacco as the justices of the same counties might respectively have assessed at their November courts in this year had the same been held."

In 1789 a new county, Allegany, was formed out of Washington County, which had become sufficiently populous even at that early day to make the division a matter of necessity. Joseph Scott, the geographer, writing about 1807, says that Washington

"is a rich, fertile county, forty-nine miles long and twenty-seven broad, but at Hancock, on the Potomac, not more than two. It contains 317,126 acres. It is divided into the following hundreds, viz.: Upper Anti-Etam, Lower Anti-Etam, Elizabeth, Marsh Manor, Sharpsburg, Salisbury, Conococheague, First (Fort?), Frederick, and Linton. Washington County lies principally between the North and South Mountains, and includes the fertile and well-cultivated valley extending on each side of Conococheague Creek. The lands are esteemed equal if not superior in fertility to any in the State. All that part of the county northwest of the South Mountain, extending in breadth about twenty miles to the Pennsylvania line, is chiefly limestone land, interspersed with some slate land. That part of the county between the North Mountain and Allegany County is hilly and mountainous, and mostly slate and stony land, except the bottoms on the Potomac and the tributary streams which fall into that river. Many of these bottoms are exceedingly fertile in all kinds of productions peculiar to the climate. Wheat, rye, Indian corn, oats, potatoes, hemp, flax, with a great variety of vegetables, are chiefly cultivated by the farmers. Large quantities of flour are manufactured, particularly on the Anti-Etam, and transported to Baltimore. In some seasons considerable quantities are sent down the Potomac to Georgetown and Alexandria. Large quantities of whisky are distilled latterly and sent to the different seaports. It contains mines of iron ore, for the manufacturing of which three furnaces and three forges have been erected, which manufacture pig, hollow-ware, bar-iron, etc. There are about fifty grist-mills in the county, several saw-mills, fulling, hemp, and oil-mills. The water of the Anti-Etam turns fourteen mills. It is the largest and most constant stream in the county, and where the largest quantities of flour are manufactured. There are very few quarries of any other kind of stone than those of limestone, which are very abundant. It is the stone almost entirely used in building. In the North

[1] All of the members present voted in the affirmative, except Messrs. Stull and Beall, who voted No.

Mountain are quarries of freestone, but so hard that they are not used for any purpose, nor has any quarry been opened. In the South Mountain is a remarkable cave."

The Valley of the Antietam, or Hagerstown Valley, as it is sometimes called, is remarkable for its fertility, and the wheat grown here is of the finest quality, and is manufactured into superior brands of flour. The valley was the scene of the military operations during the war which culminated in the great battle of Antietam. The county is penetrated by the Washington County Branch of the Baltimore and Ohio, the Western Maryland, the Cumberland Valley, and the Shenandoah Valley Railroads, and the Chesapeake and Ohio Canal extends along its entire southern and southwestern boundary. It is thus abundantly supplied with transportation facilities. The county roads are numerous and excellent, and the general condition of the county is that of a high degree of prosperity. The principal products are wheat, corn, oats, hay, potatoes, wool, rye, live-stock, butter, and honey.

Lying at the foot of the Alleganies, Washington County has a pure, healthful, invigorating atmosphere, an industrious and numerous population of the most progressive American type, unusual facilities for manufactures, a fine soil, and, in fact, all the advantages necessary to enable it to maintain its position as one of the leading agricultural communities of the United States.

A spur of the Blue Ridge, named Elk Mountain, extends through the southeastern part of the county, between which and the South Mountain on the east is included a very charming and beautiful valley, whose qualities are but faintly expressed in the name of Pleasant Valley. Looking westward from Hagerstown, the eye, after wandering over some twenty miles of hill and dale, rests upon the bold crest of the old North Mountain, and still farther beyond that other spurs of the Alleganies. These mountains of Washington County do not need "distance" to "lend enchantment to the view," but afford, whether far or near, the most beautiful and picturesque scenery, and at the same time yield large returns for the skillful cultivation bestowed on them to their very summits. The surface of the remainder of the county is rolling, and in many instances very charming to the eye. The soils are very fertile, being for the most part of the very best quality of clay and limestone lands, with occasional varieties of shaly soil, all susceptible of high and easy improvement. Agriculture is conducted in a scientific manner; the implements in use are of the very best, and as a result unusually large crops are produced. Live-stock has been improved with the best foreign breeds, and the care, skill, and attention bestowed on this branch of husbandry has met with most gratifying rewards. The abundance of clover and the other cultivated grasses affords a large supply of dairy products. Quarries of excellent limestone, suitable for the manufacture of lime and for building purposes, are numerous in various parts of the county, and some also of the kind used for making hydraulic cement. Good iron ore exists in considerable quantities, and superior brick clay is found in almost every locality. This region has long been famous for the distillation of whisky, the excellence of which has been attested by good judges in every section of the country. The best fertilizers, paper, and iron are manufactured to a very large extent.

The Potomac River, the Antietam and Conococheague Creeks, and their tributaries afford fine water-power privileges in almost every neighborhood. These, since the first settlement of the county, have been utilized to a large extent, and their surplus waters have turned the wheels of many flour, grist, paper, and saw-mills, and various other manufactories.

The original settlers of Washington County were composed principally of Germans, English, Scotch, Swiss, and French, the latter from the border provinces of Alsace and Lorraine.

It is impossible to state exactly when and where the first settlement within the present boundaries of Washington County was made, but from the fact that the Lords Proprietary caused surveys to be made, and began granting lands (situated on the west side of the Blue Ridge or South Mountain, in Prince George's County) to individuals as early as 1732, it is safe to assume that a number of families were established in the present county of Washington as early as 1735, and that from about 1740 onward their numbers rapidly increased. They were Germans chiefly, the friends and relations of those who were then cleaning away the forests of Frederick, Montgomery, Carroll, and the lower counties of Pennsylvania.

A few families among the early settlers, however, usually of English origin, and the proprietors of "manors," or large tracts of land, lived in lordly style, and dispensed a generous hospitality. But the hardy pioneers who settled the country were a simple, industrious people, who ate out of wooden trenchers and platters, sat upon three-legged stools or wooden blocks upon a dirt floor, used bear's grease for lard and butter, and cut up their food with the same sheath-knife which they used in dressing the deer killed by their rifles. Westward of the Conococheague the country was in possession of the savages, with a few isolated exceptions, for a number of years, and not until the close of the French and Indian war was it fully opened up to settlers. But when peace was declared there was a great influx from the North and East, and flourishing settlements were speedily established at numerous points west of South Mountain.

Washington County began the year 1800 with a population of 16,108 whites, 342 free colored, and 2200 slaves, being a gain of but 2828 over the total number reported in 1790.

Hagerstown and Williamsport were already commercial and manufacturing centres of considerable importance; many saw, grist, and woolen-mills dotted the banks of the Conococheague and Antietam, and besides those of the villages numerous taverns were established at short intervals along the route of the principal highways, and almost invariably at the cross-roads.

Comparatively, the county at that early date was an old, settled region. Indeed, many considered it as already overstocked with human occupants, and a large number moving on to the westward sought homes in Kentucky.[1]

There has been no partition of the county since Allegany was taken off in 1789, though efforts have been made from time to time to procure a redivision. As late as the winter of 1851 there was a movement in favor of creating a new county out of the southwestern portion of Frederick and the southeastern portion of Washington County, and meetings were held at various places within the territory of the proposed new county, both in favor of and in opposition to the project. The movement came to nothing. Allegany County was divided in 1872, and the new county of Garrett created from territory which had once belonged to Washington County.

Land Grants, Surveys, Etc.[2]—Prior to the Revolutionary war grants of land were made by the Governor of the province on behalf of the Lord Proprietary, and subsequently by the State government. Following is a list of the principal grants prior to 1800:

Name of Lot.	To Whom Granted.	Date.	Acres.
Addition	R. Prather	Oct. 25, 1748	30
Addition to Black Oak Land	Charles Carroll	May 11, 1750	22
Addition to Jack's Bottom	Dr. David Ross	Sept. 29, 1761	395
Addition to Lawrence's Disappointment	Richard Barnes	April 3, 1794	103½
Addition to Locust Swamp	F. Hersh.		
Addition to Sly Fox			50
" to Spear	John Hoover	April 14, 1794	13
" to Stoney Batter	Jonathan Hager	March 9, 1763	82
Agreed to have it Shared	Benjamin Bowman	April 14, 1784	7½
All Meadow	Henry Toms	Sept. 2, 1761	4½
All that's Left	Peter Sheese	April 23, 1765	597
Allemaugh's	" "	Sept. 26, 1750	100
All we can get	Surveyed.	May 6, 1784	195
Annandale	Joseph Chapline	Feb. 21, 1764	50
Anything	Thomas Johnson	Feb. 23, 1763	84
Avey's Delight and Resurvey	John Avey	Aug. 19, 1751	450
Avey's Good Luck	" "	June 2, 1769	453
Balsher's Misfortune	Christian Burkhart		50
" Resurveyed	George French	Nov. 9, 1763	115
Badham's Refuse	Joseph Chapline	May 12, 1759	50
Bald Barren	John Beard	Feb. 8, 1759	20
Bachelor's Delight	John Feltigraw	Nov. 11, 1752	818½
Beall's Fort	Evan Shelby	Aug. 30, 1741	50
Beall's Neglect	Samuel Chase	Feb. 8, 1764	44
Beam's Purchase	Jacob Beam	Sept. 9, 1786	325¾
Belt's Buckle	Benj. Belt	April 23, 1762	690
Berkhead's Dispute	Jacob Lighter	Feb 2, 1762	50
Berkett's Folly	George French	Nov. 9, 1763	190
Biteley's Delight	Samuel Bitely	April 12, 1765	379
Big Spring	Evan Shelby	Nov. 14, 1741	150
Black Oak Level	John Bowling	July 6, 1761	50
Black Oak Land	Charles Carroll	April 10, 1750	225
Blind Man's Choice	Michael Miller	Oct. 31, 1760	50
Blue Hanch	Isaac Baker	Sept. 29, 1762	200
Blue Rock	Lawrence Bomberger	July 1, 1758	25
Boyle's Fancy	John Myers	Feb. 12, 1761	242
Boie Range	Robt. Twigg	May 26, 1743	50
Brightwell's Choice	Jonathan Hager	March 3, 1763	50
Brooks' Blunder	John Shockey	Sept. 7, 1769	9
Brookfield	Daniel Hughes	May 13, 1765	45½
Broster's Request	Ignatius Perre	May 1, 1744	500
Burns' Justice	Jonathan Kershner	Aug. 3, 1793	24
Carr's Quasey	John Carr	Dec. 25, 1758	60
Chance	Jacob Brumbaugh	May 11, 1765.	
"	Dr. Henry Sneavly	May 30, 1765	112
"	Isaac Shelby	April 29, 1772	48
"	Joseph Cheny		142
Charlton's Victory.			
" Resurveyed	John Scott	July 29, 1762	187
" Forrest			275
Chapline's Neglect	John Gronon	Aug. 10, 1753	22½
Cheney's Delight	Ezekiel Cheney	Aug. 10, 1761	135
" Choice	Zachariah Cheney	April 2, 1760	27
" Lot	Charles Cheney, Jr	March 25, 1755	98
Clear Spring	George Easter	Sept. 6, 1754	100

[1] After the close of the war of 1812 many Washington County people removed to Ohio, Indiana, Illinois, and Missouri, and in years quite recent the same restless spirit has carried large numbers of them to the Pacific Slope and to various Western States.

[2] The Hagerstown *Mail* of Sept. 9, 1870, gives the following description of one of the early land patents:

"Dropping into the sheriff's office a day or two since, we found Mr. Sol. B. Rohrer, of our place, overhauling some very memorable parchments belonging to his family, of which he is the only remaining representative, and which, along with the Hagers, were the pioneers of civilization in the valley of the Conococheague and Antietam. We selected a conveyance to which was dangling, as to a treaty between nations, a ponderous seal in wax, with the present coat of arms of our State impressed on one side and 'St. George and the Dragon' on the other. The document bore date Jan. 16, 1739, being, as was recited, 'the twenty-fifth year of our dominion,' and was issued by 'Charles, Absolute Lord and Proprietary of the Province of Maryland and Avalon, Lord Baron of Baltimore,' etc. It recites that 'Whereas Jacob Roarer, of Prince George County [how very few persons living here know that they occupy a portion of what was once Prince George's County !], by his humble petition to our agent for *transagment* of our land affairs within this province,' etc., 'did sell fifty acres of vacant land lying in and being in county aforesaid, about a mile from *Anteatam* Creek and about three miles from Shirk's mill,' etc. The whole document, as well as the other deeds, are quite curious and interesting, and to future historians may prove valuable. It was issued by Samuel Ogle, Lieutenant-Governor of the province.

"Rohrer's Addition to Hagerstown, of which the new academy is now the most conspicuous object, was made by a collateral branch of this family, which is still perpetuated in some of the Western States. The old family graveyard, at the roots of the familiar old walnut tree near the Potomac Extension of the Franklin Railroad, is all that remains of that family, and soon that solitary souvenir will be obliterated by the plow."

Name of Lot.	To Whom Granted.	Date.	Acres
Clift Spring[1]	Norman Bruce and Jno. Ross	April 20, 1787	
Clydesdale	Joseph Chapline	Feb. 21, 1764	243
Colier's Amendment	Frederick Nicodemus	Oct. 8, 1768	448
" Original.			
Conquest	James Bedeford	July 11, 1739.	
Contentment	Joseph Chapline	Feb. 21, 1764	1153
Continuation of Friendship	Samuel Hughes	Jan. 2, 1771	51
Crackle Hook	J. Houser	April 1, 1760	12
Cumberland	John Stoner	Oct. 13, 1750	100
Darby's Defeat	Arthur Charlton	Aug. 2, 1755	60
Darling Sale	John Charlton	July 24, 1745	420
Davis' Bargain and Resurvey	Roger Davis	March 25, 1750	122
Deal Bargain	Charles Friend	Dec. 18, 1741	25
Discovery (Original)			100
" (Resurvey)	Thomas Beatty	Dec. 5, 1769	275
Discontent (and Resurvey)	Resurveyed	April 27, 1754	1050
Doe Little	John Lewis	Nov. 3, 1743	50
Dolphin			25
Done in haste	Henry Pitman	April 22, 1752	50
Dorothy	C. Hogmire	June 16, 1767	119
Downey's Lott	Robert Downey	Dec. 4, 1741	100
" "	" "	July 13, 1743	50
Dry Plains	Daniel and Walter Dulany	Sept. 29, 1765	200
Dry Spring	F. Fogler	Aug. 26, 1762	129
Ducket's Misfortune	John Bond	March 19, 1744	200
Dunkard's Folly	John A. Dory	Dec. 14, 1774	235
Dutchman's Request	William May	June 18, 1750	151
Dutch Folly	Thomas Wells.	July 2, 1739	100
Dutch Lass	Francis Deakins	Aug. 8, 1771.	
Edinburgh	George Stuart	Sept. 18, 1762	50
Edmund's Lott	Edmund Lynn	July 19, 1797	11½
Egypt	Rudolph A——	March 11, 1762	1935
Exchange	Jonathan Hager	July 4, 1762	24
"	Christopher Burkhead	No date	17½
"	William Good	Nov. 5, 1783	20
Fairest Virgin	John Ingram	Jan. 14, 1755.	18
Fairly Got	William Griffith.	Feb. 1, 1749	200
Father's Good Will	John Stoner	Aug. 18, 1767	1365
Fellowship	Dr. Chas. Carroll	No date	140
Finest Coronalopus	Daniel Miller	Feb. 18, 1765	435
First Addition	Z. Cheyney	Feb. 5, 1755	60
First Choice	F. Powell	1752	50
Flaggy Meadow	H. Waggoner	Sept. 29, 1748	474
Forrest's Purchase	John Flora	Dec. 1, 1792	250
Found it Out	Capt. Jonathan Hager	May 13, 1763	62
Four Springs	Peter Rench		200
French's Contrivance	William Deakins, Jr	Aug. 11, 1770	30
Friendship	Philip Key, Esq	Oct. 18, 1750	206
"	John Ulrick	Feb. 16, 1768	10
"	John Webb		106
Funk's Last Bit	John Funk	July 15, 1805	6
Gaming Alley	John Butler	Aug. 27, 1744	100
Garden Spot	William Adams		16½
Garron's Loss	Henry Doyle	Nov. 13, 1739	150
Geo. Lambert's Land			200
" " Delight			15
George's Discovery	George French	April 11, 1764	1387
" Venture	" "	Dec. 1, 1747	50
George the Second	Samuel Chase and Thos. Johnson	Feb. 8, 1764	73
Germany	H. Waggoner	May 24, 1751	435
Gillespie's Bargain	George Gillespie	June 28, 1767	957
Good Friendship	Dr. Henry Schnebly	Feb. 26, 1765	74
" Hope	" "	Feb. 21, 1766	40½
" Luck	Richard Lilley	April 27, 1767	258
" Neighbor	Stephen Ulrick	Sept. 29, 1767	694
" Will (Original)	Christopher Reaves	Jan. 19, 1767	158
" "	Chase & Johnson	Feb. 2, 1764	268
Great Rock	Daniel Dulany	April 5, 1750	50
Greenwood	H. Toms	No date	50
Green Castle	James Sharp	Feb. 7, 1745	620
Hager's Defence	David Hager	May 17, 1760	22
Hampton Forrest			20
" Plains	Richard Lilley	March 23, 1764	200
Harrod's Profit	Michael Funk	Oct. 16, 1762	150
Harry's Grave			140
" Last Shift	M. Ridenour	April 18, 1769	505½
Hartel's Lott	Hartel	April 10, 1762	50
Help to Hall's Sale	George Coler	Nov. 3, 1768	46½
Humpfield	Bartholomew Booth	June 3, 1776	20
Hermit's Fancy	John Lilley	March 13, 1762	374
Hermitage	H. Stultz	No date	50
Hickory Swamp	William Wiles	None	50
Hidel Barrack	John Houser	July 27, 1754	50
Hit the Mark	David Startzman	Feb. 10, 1768	19
Hogmire's Made Over	Conrad Hogmire	Nov. 21, 1757	160
Hole in the Rock	John Bowling	July 6, 1761	58
Hoover's Last Chance	John Hoover	Feb. 11, 1799	83
Hunt for Timber	George Keeler	Nov. 24, 1755	100
I am glad it is no worse	Adam Roughsong	Aug. 24, 1776	362
Ill Nature	James Murdoch	March 31, 1755	60
Ill Will	Sebastian Shoap	June 24, 1761	123½
Ingram's Delight	John Ingram		100
Israel's Lot			75
Jack's Bottom	Jeremiah Jack	Dec. 12, 1739	175
Jacob's Delight	Jacob Shockey	Sept. 6, 1769	25
Jacob's Well	Jacob Rice	Feb. 5, 1760	152½
Jerico	Robt. Twigg	Nov. 10, 1745	44
Jerico Hills	John Ridout	March 10, 1775	922
John's Lott	John Bond		244
Jonas' Discovery	Mary Brooke	Dec. 11, 1752	60
Jones' Delight	William Jones		104
Joseph's Chance	Joseph Belt, Jr	June 23, 1752	40
Jonah's Last Bit	Moses Chapline	Oct. 12, 1761	67
Kelly's Delight	Wm. Kelly	June 28, 1753	1035
Kent's Chance	Joseph Cheny		70
Kilmore	Charles Carroll	April 19, 1750	190
Kindness	Dr. Charles Carroll	Aug. 10, 1753	3716
Kyser's Landing	John Summers	May 6, 1763	110
Kyser's Inheritance	Frederick Kyser	Nov. 28, 1792	160½
Lads and Lasses	Simon Bowman	Aug. 24, 1792	366½
Lambert's Delight	Geo. Lambert	April 24, 1755	15
Lambert's Park	" "	Feb. 17, 1742	200
Lambert's Stripe	" "	June 9, 1760	25
Lane's Folly			100
Lawrence's Disappointment	John Johnson	Aug. 10, 1770	279
Leather Button	Chris. Eversole	Feb. 11, 1755	20
Leesy			50
Lilley's Discovery	Samuel Lilley	April 19, 1764	30
Lilley's Discovery Resurveyed	" "		36½
Lilley's Industry	" "	Aug. 27, 1764	40
Limestone Land	John Howard	Feb 14, 1753	20
Link's Foundling	Andrew Link	May 3, 1759	50
Linton	Thomas Cresap	Aug. 2, 1742	155
Little Enlarged	Dr. H. Sneavely	June 12, 1765	83
Little Friendship	Joseph Chapline	July 1, 1760	200
Little Timber	Geo. Hartley	Nov 6, 1769	9½
Littleworth	Denton Jacques		64
Locust Swamp	Frederick Horse	Sept. 29, 1759	100
Locust Thicket	N. Nesbitt	May 5, 1761	93
Long Hill	Henry Sneavly	Feb. 18, 1766	83
Long Life to Lord Baltimore	Capt. George Beall	Oct. 16, 1739	150
Long Bottom	Frederick Horse		50
Love in a Village	Joseph Chapline	Oct. 19, 1785.	30½
Lanafield (and Resurvey)	Peter John	April 24, 1767	1020
Magdalin's Fancy	Ludwick Young	June 8, 1765	595
Maiden's Choice	Evan Shelby	Aug. 7, 1739	1000
Maid's Fancy	Thomas Claggett	April 26, 1749	100
Manhim	Henry Frederick	May 22, 1754.	
Marlboro' Fields	C. Hogmire	Nov. 21, 1757	240
McCoy's Delight	Dr. Chas. Carroll	Nov. 6, 1752	100
McCoy's Discovery	Daniel McCoy	April 23, 1755	44
McLaughlin's Chance	McLaughlin	June 19, 1776	50
Meadow Green	John Ingram	June 23, 1785	246
Meek's Neglect	Thomas Bowles	June 3, 1761	170
McShack's Garden	Geo. Bond, Jr	Feb. 19, 1760	553
Miller's Chance	Michael Miller	June 13, 1760	50
" Fancy	" "	March 9, 1754	36
" Range			50
Mine Bank	Richard Lucas	Jan. 6, 1764	50
Mouldepone	Evan Shelby	Nov. 30, 1741	593
Mount Ætna	Daniel and Samuel Hughes	Resurveyed Nov. 30, 1787	4482
Mountain of Wales	Evan Shelby	Oct. 13, 1740	200
Mountain Foot	Conrad Hogmire	Nov. 21, 1768	31
" Lott	Richard Prather	Dec. 23, 1760	10
Mount Misery	Fasnacht	Dec. 6, 1770	78½
" Pleasant	Hoover		50
" "	Henry Darby	July 25, 1762	60
" "	John Darby	Oct. 6, 1788	226
Mumma's Lott	Jacob Mumma	Jan. 7, 1812	10¼
Nanny	Geo. Mong	April 7, 1769	290
Neal's Bottom	Christopher Burkhead	Sept. 29, 1759	50
Near the Navel	Joseph Chapline	Dec. 20, 1761	100
Need Not	Daniel Dulany	Surveyed Feb. 11, 1742	200
Neglect	H. Keedy	Dec. 1, 1764	10
"	John McCoy	Nov. 9, 1742	150
"	Geo. Miller	Oct. 5, 1761.	75
Neighbors' Neglect	Owen Davis	July 20, 1749	52
New Work	Jonathan Hager	May 6, 1765	714
Nicholas' Contrivance	Edward Nichols	Oct. 28, 1740	75
" "	Edward Nichols	No date	110
Nicholas' Contrivance Resurveyed	James Downey	April 10, 1760	690
No More Left	Isaac Baker	Feb. 21, 1765	10
None Left	Jacob Friend	May 16, 1780	3¼
None Such	James Davis	July 21, 1752	300
North Point	William Toms	April 11, 1769	9
Not Much	William Good	Nov. 6, 1783	11
Nottingham	Isaac Brooke	July 20, 1754.	
Obid	John Stull	Sept. 28, 1769	104
Old Plott	Christian Yost	April 20, 1762	36
Paradise Regained	Philip Key	Oct. 19, 1750	530
Part of Chestnut Hill Resurvey	John Stull	Sept. 3, 1761	393
Part of Dutch Folly Resurvey	Joseph Wolgamott	March 18, 1746	112

[1] This land was purchased by Philip Barton Key in 1794, and sold to Wm. Bayly in January, 1797.

Name of Lot.	To Whom Granted.	Date.	Acres
Part of Third Resurvey on Sarah's Delight	Dan. and Sam. Hughes	February, 1771	770
Part of Third Resurvey on Sarah's Delight	Dan. and Sam. Hughes	Feb. 15, 1787	637
Pattison's Resurvey	James Pattison	April 10, 1755	411
Paul's Travels	Paul Rhodes	June 7, 1769	40
Pearce Well	John Pearce	Nov. 13, 1769	21
Pelican		Oct. 27, 1759	95
Perry's Retirement			100
Philadelphia	George Gillespie	July 5, 1768	283½
Peirpoint's Content			100
Pleasant Bottom			226
Pleasant Bottom, and part of the resurvey on the Mountain of Wales	Isaac Baker	Aug. 10, 1770	1130
Pleasant Hill	James Wardrope	July 9, 1744	49
Pleasant Spring	John Rench	March 10, 1760	100
Pleasant Valley	I. Houser	Sept. 2, 1747	50
Poor Chance	Daniel Burget	Jan. 7, 1814	1 7/10
Poor Robin's Almanac	Richard Wooten	April 23, 1765	187
Prevention	James Walling, Jr.	Dec. 10, 1770	20
"	Thomas Boyd	Sept. 29, 1763	104
Purchase	Arthur Charlton	June 4, 174-	100
Ravine Spring	William Borland	Sept. 8, 1760	145½
Resurvey on Balsher's Misfortune	George French		115
Resurvey on Chester			388
" " Jerico Hills	John Ridout	March 10, 1775	829
Resurvey on Joseph's Heritage	Henry Stultz	May 1, 1786	129
Resurvey on Lilley's Discovery	Samuel Lilley	Oct. 29, 1776	45
Resurvey on Nicholas' Mistake		Sept. 21, 1752	1025
Resurvey on part of Burkett's Lott	John Scott	April 4, 1770	298
Resurvey on part of Burkett's Lott	Christian Hyple	April 1, 1785	208¾
Resurvey on part of Cadiz	E. Cheny	Aug. 5, 1766	169¾
Resurvey on part of Well Taught	George Hartley	June 16, 1773	183
Resurvey on Pleasant Valley	I. Houser	May 31, 1769	242
Resurvey on Root's Hill		Dec. 31, 1760	300
Resurvey on Saint Patrick	Isaac Houser	May 20, 1762	722
Resurvey on Saint Patrick's Lott	Isaac Houser	Dec. 7, 1752	587
Resurvey on Smith's Lott	Mathias Otto	Sept 9, 1762	350
Resurvey on Summit of Policy	Samuel Hughes	Nov. 14, 1785	852½
Resurvey on Webb's Discovery	Margaret Webb	Oct. 24, 1788	451
Resurvey on White's Lott	James White	Nov. 20, 1762	104
Rich Barrens	Paul Rhodes	Nov. 25, 1759	100
Rich Barrens Resurvey	Peter Sheese	June 13, 1765	1154
Richard's Choice	Thomas Prather	Oct. 25, 1748.	
Rocky Hill	Joseph Miller	March 29, 1792	5
Rocky Land	John Ridenour	Nov. 28, 1792	40
Rocky Neck	Lancelot Jacques and Thomas Johnson	Feb. 11, 1764	548
Rutter's Delight	John Rutter	March 7, 1738	100
Rutting Spring			26
Saint Patrick	Isaac Houser	Nov. 1, 1743	50
Saint Patrick's Lott	Isaac Houser	Feb. 1, 1747	127
Save All	Andrew Rench	Nov. 29, 1759	50
" "	Philip Davis	July 12, 1745	50
Scant Timber	Vindal Sight	Feb. 20, 1766	5210
Scared From Home	Nicholas Baird	Feb. 7, 1760	1373
Scotch Lott Resurveyed	Henry Avey	March 19, 1746	202
Scotch Lott Original	Evan McDonald	Dec. 4, 1740	150
Scotch Lott and Resurvey	Henry Avey	March 19, 1746	202
Scott's Grief	William Douglass	Feb. 12, 1752	100
Scruple	Jacob Friend	May 26, 1764	40½
Search well and you will find	Anthony Bell	June 20, 1788	20¼
Second Addition	H. Toms	June 15, 1765	50
Settled in Time	Resurveyed for Joseph, John, and Andrew Rench	Dec. 5, 1785	2227
Shoe Spring and Resurvey	James Spencer	Sept. 4, 1740	150
Shockey's Part of Third Resurvey of Sarah's Delight	Jacob Shockey	Oct. 2, 1769	112
Shockey's Mistake	Jacob Hoover	Dec. 3, 1787	50
Sink Hole	Matthias Lizer	Dec. 8, 1764	50
Skipton in Crafen	Thomas Cresap	Nov. 27, 1740	100
Slay	Thomas Beatty	Dec. 10, 1769	92
Sly Fox			42
Small Bit	John Snevely	Jan. 31, 1761	10
Small Bit to David			40
Small Hope	Martin Rohrer	Aug. 19, 1769	4
Small Spring	Andrew Rench	March 10, 1760	50
Smithfield	Patrick Murphy	Sept. 29, 1757	155,
Smith's Choice	Peter Slusser	Jan 7, 1764	50
Snowden's Friendship	George Moore	May 23, 1739	84
Spring Garden	Jacob Stoner	Sept. 9, 1767	313
" " Original			200
Spring Head	Dr. Charles Carroll	May 30, 1750	96
Stokey	Joseph Chapline	Feb. 27, 1787	47½
Stone Walls	Lancelot Jacques and Thomas Johnson	Dec. 6, 1763	434
Stoner's Luck	John Stoner	Sept. 11, 1764	55
Stoney Glade	James Smith	Feb. 23, 1761	450
Stoney Hill	Daniel Ulrick	April 26, 1754	16
Stoney Ridge	Peter Slusser	Jan. 7, 1764	73¾
Stoney Run	George A. Quaranfleck	May 23, 1754	80
Stoney Valley	Devalt Mong	May 21, 1787	45
Strawberry Bottom	Richard Macklefish	July 1, 1760	51
Strife	Edward Dawson	Aug. 7, 1739	150
Struggle	John Ulrick	Aug. 12, 1767	176
Stull's Forest	John Stull	Jan. 12, 1764	1891
" "	" "	Feb. 13, 1761	756
Stoney Ridge	John Measter	July 18, 1761	100
Sugar Bottom	John Boyd	1739	37
Sweed's Delight	Charles Friend	Aug. 13, 1738	260
Taken in Time	James Walling, Sr.	Nov. 26, 1763	96
Tetrick's Folly	David Ross	May 22, 1766	212
The Addition to Catherine's Part	Matthias Musselman	Feb. 25, 1754	50
The Adventure	James Walling, Jr.	Aug. 15, 1762	1165
" Original			50
The Amendment of Dawson's Strife and Hickman's Meadows	Peter Rench	March 10, 1767	1915
The Barren Hills	Dr. Charles Carroll	May 11, 1750	55
The Barrens	James Wardrope	May 11, 1744	100
The Chance	John Bowland	Aug. 11, 1753	110
The Conquest	James Bedeford	July 11, 1739	275
The Forrest	Conveyed by Geo. Bond to Peter Hoover	Jan. 17, 1774	100
The Four Springs	Peter Rench		200
The Hartman	George Hartman	March 1, 1744	100
The Hazzard	Evan Shelby	Oct. 23, 1739	200
The Long Meadow	Jacob Kermemen	Feb. 1, 1747	25
" "	Thomas Cresap	June 16, 1739	550
The Mistake	Daniel Dulany	March 3, 1742-43	100
"	George French	Dec. 4, 1747	100
The Narrow Meadow	Henry Sneibly	Dec. 22, 1760	18
The Notch	Dr. Charles Carroll	May 11, 1750	18
The Old Fox Deceived	James Walling	Sept. 9, 1757	1367
The Russian Boatswain	—— Deakins		52
The Saw Pitt	George Bond	Oct. 22, 1744	150
The Steeple	Walter Dulany	Sept. 29, 1763	100
The Storm	Henry Prather	May 21, 1755	104
The third time of asking	Charles Cline	Sept 20, 1797	640
The Venture	Reverdy Ghesline	Aug. 11, 1761	25
The White-Oak Lick	Walter and Daniel Dulany	Sept. 29, 1765	238
The Wife's Choice	Michael Hallam	May 1, 1767	20
The Resurvey on Addition to Marshhead	Jacob Funk	Feb. 17, 1761	219½
The Barney's Venture	Barnabus Swope	Aug. 24, 1788	5½
The Castle Plains	William Boyd	Sept. 20, 1755	450
The Clegland's Contrivance	Jacob Brumback	Dec. 10, 1759.	
The Dickson's Pleasure	Michael Kirkpatrick	Sept. 4, 1764	688
The Discontent	Mathew Clarke	April 27, 1754	1050
The First Choice	Thomas Powell	Feb. 15, 1756	212
The First Choice, second resurvey	" "	Dec. 13, 1768	282
The French's Vineyard	Andrew Grim	Dec. 10, 1759	940
The Gaming Alley	John Rutter	Nov. 2, 1752	178
The Garron's Loss	Daniel McCoy	June 23, 1749	220
The George's Mistake. George's Venture, and the Barrens	George French	Dec. 20, 1753	1462
The Harrod's Profit	Michael Funk	March 25, 1767	311
The Hartman Place		Feb. 19, 1765	69
The Hazzard	Hugh Gilliland	Oct. 25, 1749	790
The Hazzard and Locust Thicket	Nathaniel Nesbitt	May 5, 1761	443
The Jerico	Robert Twiggs	Sept. 20, 1753	956
The Lilley's Discovery, second resurvey	Samuel Lilley	Oct. 29, 1776	45
The Locust Thicket	Nathaniel Nesbitt	May 5, 1761	443
The Ogle's Friendship			270
The Resurvey on part of Bachelors' Delight	Joseph Chapline	Sept. 19, 1763	443½
The Resurvey on part of Cadiz	Ezekiel Cheny	Aug. 5, 1766	169
The Resurvey on part of Kindness	Evan Shelby	March 12, 1771	424¾
The Resurvey on part of Simmons' Racket	I. Simmons		472
The Resurvey on part of Mountain of Wales	Evan Shelby	April 23, 1767	3342
The Resurvey on part of Pleasant Bottom and part of Mountain of Wales	Isaac Baker	March 7, 1768	1130
The Resurvey on part of Paw's part of Well Taught	Jacob Lighter	April 13, 1763.	
The Resurvey on part of Sarah's Delight	Charles Carroll	March 10, 1753	500
The Resurvey on part of Sarah's Delight (Third Resurvey)	Charles Carroll	June 1, 1766	1820

Name of Lot.	To Whom Granted.	Date.	Acres.
The Resurvey on part of Simmons' Racket	Isaac Simmons	Oct. 1, 1748	545
The Resurvey on part of Strong Corner	Francis Rohrer	Dec. 27, 1763	83
The Resurvey on part of Mountain of Wales	Evan Shelby	Feb. 22, 1763	9860
The Resurvey on part of Well Done	Moses Chapline	Feb. 1, 1764	1822
The Resurvey on part of Well Taught	George Poe		1300
The Resurvey on part of White Oak Grove	Conrad Hogmire	Feb. 3, 1755	354
Third Addition	Henry Toms	Oct. 16, 1766	18½
Three Friends and Resurvey	John Jones	Sept. 9, 1759	951
Timber Bottom	J. Bromback	Sept. 3, 1763	260
" Hills	Wm. Norris	Jan. 27, 1764	205
Time Elapsed	Chase & Johnson	Feb. 17, 1764	1417
Toddy Lane	John Stull	Jan. 9, 1767	41
Township	Isaac Houser, Jr	May 27, 1790	8½
Tressel's Good Will	Martin Ridenour	Dec. 30, 1785.	
Trifle	Jacob Friend	Aug. 8, 1781	22¾
Tryal	Daniel Hughes	April 15, 1770	24½
Tuckett	Joseph Chapline	Sept. 24, 1759	75
Tweedale	" "	Feb. 21, 1764	42
Ulrick's Lott	John Ulrick	April 18, 1755	50
Upper Farm	Thomas Bowles	Oct. 26, 1767	826
Upper (and Lower) Indian Bottom	John Hamilton	Aug. 10, 1741	100
Very Cold			50
Virgin Fair	Bambarger		58
Walker's Welcome to Antietam	Samuel Hughes	April 15, 1770	48
Walls' Neglect	William Deakins	July 9, 1768	197
Walnut Bottom	Jacob Bowman	Jan. 30, 1764	587
Warm Weather	John Snevely	Sept. 5, 1769	313
Webb's Discovery (and Resurvey)	Margaret Webb	Oct. 3, 1759	451
Welcome Home	Evan Shelby	Nov. 22, 1766	11¼
Well Done (Resurvey)	Moses Chapline	Feb. 1, 1764	1822
Well Phased	Duval Ankeny	June 19, 1773	500
Whisky (Original and First and Second Additions)	John Stull.		
Whisky, with First and Second Additions Resurveyed	John Stull	Oct. 27, 1744	580
Whisky Alley	James Dickson	Nov. 21, 1752	115
White Oak Grove	Conrad Hogmire	April 16, 1753	50
" Plains	Thos., David, & George Peters	Nov. 3, 1812	654
" Stump	John Leman		50
Wine Hill	Bambarger		50
Wolf Lodge	Thomas Mills	May 15, 1765	50
" Spring	Nicholas Beard	March 15, 1762	50
Woodstock	Robert Owen	April 6, 1762.	
Woodwall	Michael Hollum.		
Heister Borough	Daniel Heister	April 12, 1784	1434¼
Ash Swamp	Joseph Perry	Jan. 12, 1739	200
Hager's Delight	Jonathan Hager	Aug. 10, 1753	1780
Green Bottom	Wm. Williams	Nov. 17, 1741	250
Stony Batter	Jonathan Hager	March 20, 1762	118
Williams' Chance	George Williams	Feb. 24, 1752	150
Farewell	Thomas Gatterell	Dec. 14, 1739	50
Plumb Yard	Charles Lucas	Oct. 22, 1739	300
Leeds	Col. Thomas Cresap	May 1, 1752	160
Little Thought	Joseph Chapline	Feb. 2, 1763	6352
Huckleberry Hall	Daniel Dulany	Dec. 5, 1742	100
The Three Springs	George Stewart	Oct. 26, 1739	225
Hager's Fancy	Jonathan Hager[1]	Dec. 16, 1739	200
Iron Mountain	Dr Charles Carroll	April 24, 1749	50
Shelby's Misfortune	" "	April 10, 1749	250
Hanover	" "	June 10, 1750	1010
Marro Point	Nicholas Crist	Sept. 18, 1739	50
Walnut Level	Richard Snowden	Dec. 14, 1739	50
The Hurry	Daniel Dulany	July 24, 1744	100
Monican	Cornelius O'Neal	Sept. 7, 1741	50
Hills and Dales	Joseph Chapline	June 26, 1749	50
Perrin's Adventure	John Perrin	Nov. 20. 1739	100
Burrel's Bower	Francis Burrell	Aug. 20, 1742	50
Elting's Right	Cornelius Elting	Oct. 25, 1742	325
Caledonia	Geo. Frazier Hawkins	Oct. 31, 1765	3910
Park's Hall	William Parks	Nov. 24, 1732	1550
Pile's Delight	Richard Sprigg	Dec 14, 1742	724
The Addition to Pile's Delight	Col. Edward Sprigg	Aug. 9, 1743	117
The Resurvey of the addition to Pile's Delight	Col. Edward Sprigg	Jan. 30, 1750	2617
Lafferty's Lott	Daniel Dulany	Oct. 15, 1739	100
Scott's Comfort	Andrew Simson	June 27, 1765	143
The First Snow	Peter Ridinzover	Aug. 10, 1753	190
The White Oak Land	Robert Clark	Jan. 21, 1777	47½
Addition to Second Tryal	John Wolf	Sept. 24, 1763	50
The Resurvey on part of Sideling Hill	Richard Henderson	April 17, 1787	154¾
New Design	John Know	Feb. 1, 1791	12
Hunting Ground	Joseph Chapline	May 19, 1795	368
Elwick's Dwelling	John Elwick	Aug. 4, 1742	180
" "	Joseph Smith	Feb. 1, 1747	270
Smith's Purchase	" "	May 1, 1747	65
Hopewell	Joseph Chapline	Aug. 11, 1753	104
Porto Sancto	James Smith	July 15, 1756	23
Welch's Lott (resurvey)	Jacob Koontz	May 17, 1788	154
" "	Wm. Welch	Sept. 29, 1760	26
Coun's Lott	George Coun	March 5, 1762	25
Freagon's Disappointment	Jas Walling	March 8, 1755	30
Walling's Mistake	Alex. McCullum	" "	25½
Manhim	Henry Kendrick	Oct. 17, 1755.	
Penny Pack Pond	Peter Rench	March 19, 1753	50
The Resurvey on Freestone	Joseph Wolgamott	June 27, 1763	520
The Adventure	James Walling	Nov. 10, 1752	50
Long Meadow	Thos. Cresap	June 18, 1739	550
Addition to Long Meadow	Thos. Cresap	July 30, 1742	110
The west addition to Long Meadow	Thos. Cresap	Aug. 8, 1743	100
Long Meadow, enlarged	Daniel Dulany, Jr.	Nov. 5, 1751	2131
" " "	Col. Henry Boquett	Sept. 16, 1763	4163
Whiteman's Prospect	Henry Ridenour	Feb. 21, 1776	1076
The Resurvey on Deceit	Joseph Perry	Feb. 17, 1761	658
Darling Sale	John Charlton	Oct. 26, 1752	420
Stiffee's Home	Andrew, Nicholas, George, Michael, Peter, Catharine, Aug., and Elizabeth Stiffee	May 12, 1801	361½
Sawers' Lodge	Jacob Mills	Aug. 10, 1754	50
Table Stone	John Williams	July 13, 1752	50
Luck	Isaac Baker	Aug. 11, 1767	12½
Painter's Range	Daniel Painter	Feb. 1, 1787	30
The Resurvey on Round Meadow	Henry Rhodes	July 17, 1763	375
The Resurvey on Timber Land	Dr. Upton Scott	July 7, 1795	205
Liberty	Francis Deakins	Dec. 6, 1763	46
Antietam Hills	John J. Hays	Sept. 29, 1764	159
Number Five	John M. Jordon	Nov. 3, 1768	1735
Garden of Eden	Leonard Marbury and Otho H. Williams	June 3, 1788.	
Shippey's Neglect	Joseph Graybell	Aug. 21, 1749	74
The Resurvey on Canoe Bottom	Robert Wells	Oct. 19, 1754	290
Aguid in Peace	Jacob Rowland	Jan. 11, 1788	725
Walnut Grove	Redmond Follar	Aug. 31, 1741	175
Timber Wood	Jos. Graybell	May 14, 1752	50
Black Oak Bushes	" "	" "	50
Trouble Enough	Jacob Funk	July 13, 1786	2053
Secret Bottom	James Dickson	July 18, 1752	104
Paul's Delight	" "	Jan. 7, 1761	200
Salsbury	Hugh Parker	Feb. 27, 1750	4119
Hager's Fancy	Jacob Rohrer	March 19, 1747	507
The Resurvey on Walnut Point	Wm. Downey	Aug. 10, 1753	30
The Resurvey on Dawson's Strife	Peter Rench	June 17, 1757.	
Cousin's Obligement	Andrew Hoover	Feb. 14, 1755	51
The Chance	Jacob Brumbaugh	May 11, 1765	25
Brumbaugh's Lott	" "	Feb. 20, 1755	50
Joe's Lott	Joseph Chapline, Jr	Sept. 7, 1770	2127
Hunting the Hare	Joseph Chapline	Nov. 13, 1747.	
Abston's Forrest	Thos. Abston	Nov. 29, 1742.	
Dorsey's Risque	Edward Dorsey	Dec. 14, 1754	158
Water Sink	Joseph Tomlinson	Aug. 27, 1750	522
The Resurvey on Hopewell	Joseph Chapline	1755	717
Loss and Gain	" "	April 11, 1765	1168½
Addition to Loss and Gain	" "	Oct. 18, 1773	1484
Long Sought	John Wilson	Aug. 10, 1753	125
Lawwell	Philip Keywaughover	April 10, 1760	90
Whisky Alley	Caleb Touchstone	March 18, 1746	67
The Resurvey on Whisky Alley	Philip Keywaughover	Sept 14, 1768	567
Chew's Farm	Samuel Chew, Jr	June 23, 1736	5000
Dear Bought	James Wardrobe	Oct. 30, 1752	500
The Resurvey on Sprigg's Delight	Peter Rench	July 27, 1752	387
Hallum's Lookout	William Hallum	Nov. 13, 175[illegible]	215
Hard Fortune	John Mackentire	April 6, 1761	50
Search Well	James Smith	Sept. 29, 1763	584
Mistaken Friend	Edward Ricketts	Oct. 2, 1753	116
Content	Ralph Higginbottom	Jan. 14, 1760	114
Spring Hill	James Smith	Oct. 12, 1770	811
Mill Place	John House.	Dec. 1, 1747	25
The Dutch Loss	John Vandever	Sept. 29, 1761	100
Gaither's Luck	Henry Gaither	Oct. 21, 1784	56
The Resurvey on Dry Land	Andrew Link	July 6, 1768	136
Chase	Samuel Hughes	April 15, 1770	46½
Long Looked for	Robert Harper	July 28, 1763	10
Grandfather's Gift	Henry Holland Hawkins, Jr.	Nov. 13, 1741	305
The Resurvey on part of Park's Hall	Andrew Grim	July 28, 1766	510
Snowden's Friendship	George Moore	May 23, 1739	84

[1] This lot began "at a bounded white-oak standing on the side of a hill within fifty yards of the said Hager's dwelling-house," which shows that he was a resident in 1739.

Name of Lot.	To Whom Granted.	Date.	Acres.
Cheney's Neck	Charles Cheney	Sept. 29, 1754	52
Sweed's Delight	Charles Friend	July 11, 1739	260
Addition to Jack's Bottom	Dr. David Ross	Sept 29, 1761	395
Keep Trieste	John Sample	Sept. 29, 1764	10,202
Smith's Hills[1]	James Smith	April 17, 1745	208
Funk's Run	Michael Funk	Feb. 19, 1755	50
Shadrack's Lott	G. Atkinson	May 8, 1754	262
Nancy's Fancy	Joseph Prigmore	March 13, 1764	341
Draper's Chance	John Draper	Dec. 24, 1754	20
The Shoe Spring	James Spencer	Sept. 4, 1740	150
The Resurvey on the Shoe Spring.	John Stull	Oct. 3, 1755	510
Rogue's Harbor	William Stroope	Aug. 10, 1753	110
Duckett's Misfortune	Richard Duckett	March 19, 1744	200
Mill Place	William Yates	Dec. 13, 1764	50
Chance	Dr. Henry Schnebly	March 10, 1776	112
"	Henry Shryock	June 10, 1771	425
Long Look'd for.	John Perry	Nov. 2, 1754.	150
Colmore's Ramble	Colmore Beans	Feb. 28, 1743	66
Darling's Delight	Thomas Hargiss	Oct. 23, 1739	150
Conoloway's Lick	James Dickson	Aug. 24, 1747	100
Poalk's Meadow	Charles Poalk	Jan. 11, 1748	100
Boston	David Ross, Richard Henderson, and Samuel Beall, Jr.	July 25, 1769	8025
Johnson's Lott	Peter Johnson	April 7, 1745	139
Turkey Hill	Michael Mills	April 16, 1754	87
Skie Thorn	Col. Thomas Cresap	June 16, 1739	370
Strife	William Chapline	July 20, 1740	100
Bachelors' Hall	Thomas Mills	April 1, 1748	100
The Widow's Last Shift.	Anne Keishner	July 31, 1749	100
The Ash Swamp	John George Arnold	Jan. 16, 1739	150
Pleasant Bottom	William Boyd	Nov. 12, 1739.	160

Indian Antiquities.—The antiquities of the county are very interesting. In the vicinity of Sharpsburg there are mounds and earthworks, some of which have been destroyed, and others of which having been excavated were found to contain numerous interesting archæological specimens. Tradition says that a most bloody affair occurred on the Antietam Creek near its mouth (which is distant three miles south of Sharpsburg) more than a century ago, between those hostile and warlike tribes, the Catawbas and Delawares, who, it is said, were engaged in a strife when this section of the country was first known, and so continued for a long period subsequent. This event occurred some time between the years 1730 and 1736. The evidences of this conflict are still apparent in the skeletons which from time to time are exhumed.

On the farms of the heirs of William Hebb, distant two miles west of Sharpsburg, and near the Potomac River, vast quantities of arrow-heads, pestles, skinning-knives, and tomahawks of superior workmanship have been found.

On the farm of Lafayette Miller, about a mile and a half from Sharpsburg, and adjoining the lands of the last-mentioned farm, an abundance of stone implements have been brought to light. These implements were found in the fields, and were particularly numerous on the hills. Some curiously-wrought stones, varying from three to six inches in diameter, and about two inches in thickness, have been found from time to time on this farm. They are perfectly flat on both sides, and polished. A short distance from this farm, and bordering on the Potomac River, is the farm of Samuel Beeler, where two small stone mounds have been discovered, one of them about twelve feet in length and six in width. They were composed of small stones. One had been opened years ago, the other was excavated recently. After working for several hours in throwing off the loose stones, a grave was found ingeniously constructed beneath it. The bottom was laid with flat stone, the sides and ends composed of the same set up in a slanting position, and the covering was of large flat stone, built in the form of a comb-roof of a house. In this mound were found the remains of a skeleton, some broken pieces of pottery, and the part of a stone knife.

On the farm of the heirs of the late Jacob Miller, two miles south of Sharpsburg, on a high bluff bordering on the Potomac River, are two extensive stone mounds, which had been partly explored some twenty years ago, but on a more recent examination were found to contain bones, pottery, flints, etc. These mounds were about twelve feet long, six feet high, and were composed entirely of stone. The bones were so much decayed that they crumbled into atoms on being handled. A few years ago a skeleton was found near this mound buried in a perpendicular position. At the head was a small vessel of pottery, holding about a quart, which fell to pieces on being handled.

About a mile and a half from this point, on the farm of William Blackford, several articles of pottery have been unearthed. Traces of some earth mounds still exist, and beautifully-finished arrow-heads are still to be found.

On the lands of James Marker, three miles southeast of Sharpsburg, is a cave, which tradition says was used both as a dwelling and a burial-place. This cave is about twenty feet in diameter, and about six feet in height, and contains two rooms. The outer room has been partially explored. The opening to the inner room is so small that it would be difficult of access. In digging in this cave a year or two ago, a quantity of ashes and burnt bones were found, buried underneath large flat stones. There were also bead ornaments, arrow-heads, and flints, and a pipe of exquisite workmanship. On a bluff of land opposite the Antietam Furnace building, on the left-hand side of the creek, is a small stone mound. While some workmen were putting up a fence, which came directly over the mound, they found a skeleton apparently in a good state of preservation. In Cedar Grove, near Rohrersville, are several small earth mounds, which it is said are the burial-places of the aborigines. On every farm within a radius of three miles round Sharpsburg are to be found numerous specimens of implements of war very ingeniously made.

[1] Originally surveyed for Dr. George Stewart, Dec. 27, 1739.

When the Chesapeake and Ohio Canal was being constructed, tomahawks, arrow-heads, and ornaments were found in its bed. On the canal, near a place called Mercerville, is an old burial-ground, containing half an acre, which no doubt belonged to the Indians. On this spot are found pottery, bones, ornaments, and stems of pipes, etc. About two feet below the surface the bodies were buried. Ashes and burnt bones were found in the graves.

At the coke-yard at the Antietam Furnace, bordering on the Chesapeake and Ohio Canal, three miles south of Sharpsburg, is an Indian burial-ground. At this point, tradition informs us, a fierce battle was fought between the Catawbas and Delawares, which resulted in the destruction of the Delawares.

At Reynolds' Dam, on the Potomac River, Maryland side, one mile south of Shepherdstown, W. Va., an abundance of fragments of pottery have been found from time to time, which plainly indicates that this point was the site of an ancient aboriginal pottery. At Eakles' Mills, one mile south of Keedysville, at what is known as the limestone quarries, belonging to the Baltimore and Ohio Railroad, some singular indentations are to be seen in the rocks, and no doubt were the work of the Indians. They are of the shape of a basin, varying from the size of a basin to that of a tea-cup. These might have been used for pounding hominy, mixing paint, etc., as several pestles were found near these rocks. In quarrying the workmen came upon several caves and fissures in the rocks, which led a considerable distance under the hill, and which, no doubt, were used by the aborigines. In a few of the rocks were impressions like footprints, and also singular characters like letters or hieroglyphics. In various other portions of the county are similar memorials of the original occupants of the soil.

CHAPTER XLI.

PUBLIC OFFICIALS.

As Washington County was part of Frederick until 1776, the names of many of the officers selected by the people of Washington from time to time or appointed by the executive are comprised in the list of Frederick County officials. The same is true of their representatives in the Continental army. At the session of the Provincial Convention held at Annapolis, Dec. 7, 1775, there was no delegate present from the upper district (now Washington County) of Frederick, but on the 18th of December, "Mr. William Baird, a member of the upper district of Frederick County, appeared and took his seat in the House." About this time Charles and Thomas Beatty were prominent among the patriots of Frederick County, and their names are mentioned on several different occasions in the proceedings of the convention. On the 14th of August in the following year the convention again assembled at Annapolis, and among its members were Samuel Beall, Samuel Hughes, John Stull, and Henry Schnebly, as delegates from the upper district of Frederick. On the 6th of September the new county of Washington was formed by act of the convention, and since that date the following is a list of citizens of the county who have either been elected or appointed to office:

Governor of Maryland.

Wm. T. Hamilton, elected 1879.

United States Senator.

William T. Hamilton, term of service, 1869 to 1875.

Congressmen.

Thomas Sprigg, 1793–96; Daniel Heister, 1800–4; Roger Nelson, 1805; Samuel Ringgold, 1810, 1812, 1816, 1818; John Thomson Mason, 1840; J. Dixon Roman, 1846; William T. Hamilton, 1848–54.

Presidential Electors.

Samuel Hughes,[1] 1793; Martin Kershner, 1801; Frisby Tilghman, 1805; Nathaniel Rochester, 1809; Daniel Rentch, 1813; John Buchanan, 1817; William Gabby, 1821; William Fitzhugh, Jr., 1829; William Price, 1833, 1837, 1845; J. D. Roman, 1849; R. H. Alvey, 1853; J. D. Roman, 1857; Isaac Nesbit, 1865; J. Thomson Mason, 1869.

State Senators from Washington County.

1781–83, Samuel Hughes, May 9th, to fill the vacancy caused by the death of Charles Carroll, barrister; 1786–90, Samuel Hughes, December 2d, in place of Thomas Johnson, who did not accept; 1801–6, Samuel Ringgold; 1806, John Thomson Mason; 1811–14, Moses Tabbs; 1815–18, William T. Mason; 1821–24, William Price; 1836, William Price; 1838, Robert Wason; 1840–45, John Newcomer; 1846–50, William B. Clark; 1852–53, George French; 1854–57, George Schley; 1858–61, John G. Stone; 1862–64, Lewis T. Fiery; 1865–67, Elias Davis; 1868–70, James H. Grove; 1872–74, Z. S. Claggett; 1876–78, David H. Newcomer; 1880–82, Joseph H. Farrow.

Members of the House of Delegates from Washington County.

1777.—Joseph Sprigg, John Barnes, Samuel Hughes, Henry Schnebely.

1779–82.—John Stull, John Barnes, Joseph Sprigg, James Chapline.

1783.—John Stull, James Chapline, Nicholas Swingle, John J. Jacob.

1784.—John Stull, John Cellars, Nicholas Swingle, Thomas Hart.

1785.—John Stull, John Cellars, Jacob Funk, Henry Snavely.

[1] Mr. Hughes was not present at the election, and consequently did not cast his vote. George Washington was unanimously elected President, and John Adams, Vice-President.

1786.—John Cellars, Jacob Funk, John Stull, Rich'd Cromwell.

1787.—Jacob Funk, Andrew Bruce, John Cellers, Ignatius Taylor.

1788.—Thomas Sprigg, Henry Shryock, Ignatius Taylor, John Lynn.

1789.—Henry Shryock, John Stull, Adam Ott, John Lynn.

1790.—Adam Ott, Nathaniel Rochester, John Cellars, Lancelot Jacques, Jr.

1791.—Adam Ott, John Cellers, William Clagett, Benoni Swearingen.

1792.—Adam Ott, Benoni Swearingen, Richard Cromwell, Lancelot Jacques, Jr.

1793.—Benoni Swearingen, Matthew Van Lear, Robert Hughes, William Clarke.

1794.—Henry Schnebly, Martin Kershner, Robert Hughes, William Clarke.

1795.—Samuel Ringgold, Richard Cromwell, John Barnes, Lancelot Jacques.

1796.—John Cellers, Thomas Bowles, James McClain, Robert Douglass.

1797.—Martin Kershner, Cephas Beall, Ambrose Geohogan, John Buchanan.

1798.—Martin Kershner, John Cellers, Ambrose Geohogan, John Buchanan.

1799.—John Buchanan, Ambrose Geohogan, James McClaine, John Cellers.

1800.—John Cellers, Robert Smith, Ambrose Geohogan, Richard Cromwell.

1801.—Robert Smith, John Cellers, Frisby Tilghman, Adam Ott.

1802.—Martin Kershner, Richard Cromwell, Robert Smith, Frisby Tilghman.

1803.—Martin Kershner, Jacob Zeller, Robert Smith, William Yates.

1804.—John Bowles, William Yates, Tench Ringgold, Benjamin Clagett.

1805.—John Bowles, Robert Smith, Tench Ringgold, William Yates.

1806.—John Bowles, Tench Ringgold, Martin Kershner, David Schnebly.

1807.—John Bowles, David Schnebly, Moses Tabbs, Upton Lawrence, William Gabby, *vice* Lawrence, resigned.

1808.—Frisby Tilghman, William Gabby, William Downey, John Bowles.

1809.—John Bowles, George Celler, Moses Tabbs, William L. Brent.

1810.—John Bowles, Thomas B. Hall, Dr. William Downey, Dr. William B. Williams.

1811.—John Bowles, Thomas B. Hall, Dr. William Downey, Charles G. Boerstler.

1812.—John Bowles, Henry Lewis, William B. Williams, William O. Sprigg.

1813-14.—Frisby Tilghman, John T. Mason, Martin Kershner, William Gabby.

1815.—Martin Kershner, Jacob Schnebly, John Bowles, Edward G. Williams.

1816.—Edward G. Williams, John Bowles, Jacob Schnebly, Christian Hager.

1817.—Henry Sweitzer, William Yates, Jacob Schnebly, Thomas Kennedy.

1818.—William Yates, Thomas Keller, Thomas Kennedy, Jacob Schnebly.

1819.—Jacob Schnebly, Thomas Keller, Joseph Gabby, Thomas Kennedy.

1820.—Joseph Gabby, Thomas Kennedy, Andrew Kershner, John Bowles.

1821.—John Bowles, Joseph Gabby, Andrew Kershner, Caspar W. Weaver.

1822.—Thomas Kennedy (author of the bill abolishing the religious test in Maryland), Ignatius Drury, Elie Williams (died before taking his seat), Thomas Keller, Benjamin Galloway, *vice* Williams.

1823.—Andrew Kershner, Joseph Gabby, James H. Bowles, Joseph I. Merrick.

1824.—James H. Bowles, Henry Fouke, Isaac S. White, Joseph I. Merrick.

1825.—Joseph I. Merrick, Andrew Kershner, Lancelot Jacques, Jr., Thomas Kennedy.

1826.—Thomas B. Hall, Kobert M. Tidball, Jonathan Newcomer. William H. Fitzhugh.

1827.—William H. Fitzhugh, John Wolgamot, Daniel Rench, William Yates.

1828.—Jonathan Shafer, Benjamin F. Yoe, Jacob Miller, Robert H. Beatty.

1829.—Benjamin F. Yoe, David Brookhart, John Witner, and Daniel Donnelly.

1830.—Andrew Kershner, Benjamin F. Yoe, David Brookhart, Joseph I. Merrick.

1831.—David Brookhart, Joseph Hollman, John Hall, William H. Fitzhugh.

1832.—John H. Mann, Joseph Hollman, Thomas Kennedy, John D. Grove, Joseph Weast, *vice* Kennedy.

1833.—John H. Mann, John O. Wharton, John D. Grove, Frederick Humrickhouse.

1834.—Joseph Weast, John O. Wharton, Andrew Kershner, John Weltz.

1835.—John V. Wharton, Michael Newcomer, David Brookhart, Jacob Fiery.

1836.—John H. Mann, Michael Swingley, Andrew Rench, Andrew Kershner.

1837.—John H. Mann, Michal Swingley, Andrew Rench, John Witmer, Jr.

1838.—John O. Wharton, John T. Mason, Frederick Byers, John D. Grove.

1839.—John Thompson Mason, Michael Newcomer, Frederick Byer, William McK. Kepler.

1840.—David Claggett, Lewis Zeigler, Isaac Nesbit, Joseph Weast.

1841.—Samuel Lyday, Jacob H. Grove, Jervis Spencer, Joseph Hollman.

1842.—Jonathan Nesbit, Jr., Jacob H. Grove, William Weber, Horatio N. Harne, Edward L. Boteler.

1843.—Warford Mann, William Weber, Henry Wade, Edward L. Boerstler, Joseph Hollman.

1844.—Wm. B. Clarke, Hezekiah Boerstler, Isaac Motter, John D. Hart, Charles A. Fletcher.

1845.—George W. Smith, Elie Crampton, John Cushua, of D., Lewis Trittle, Henry W. Dellinger.

1846.—Wm. E. Doyle, George French, Joseph Leiter, Benjamin Reigle, Wm. T Hamilton.

1847.—George French, Hezekiah Boteler, George L. Zeigler, Robert Fowler, James Biays.

1849.—Elias Davis, Andrew K. Stake, Jacob Smith, Elie Crampton, Jeremiah S. Besore.

1852-53.—George Cushwa, John Wolf, George Strause, Edward M. Mealey, Wilfred D. McCardell.

1854.—Solomon Helser, T. H. Crampton, Daniel L. Grove, Andrew K. Syester, Denton Jacques.

1856.—Lewis P. Fiery, Benjamin Witmer, David Reichard, William Loughridge, John Corby.

1858.—George C. Rohrer, John Wesley Summers, John F. Gray, Andrew R. Schnebly.

1860.—James Coudy, Martin Eakle, John C. Brinning, George Freaner, Andrew K. Stake.

1861.—December Session, George Pearson, Samuel Rohrer, John J. Thomas, F. Dorsey Herbert, John V. L. Findlay; April Session, Martin Eakle, John C. Brinning.

1862.—Jno. V. L. Findley, Samuel Rohrer, George Pearson, Jno. J. Thomas, F. Dorsey Herbert.

1864.—Wm. Cushwa, Jacob B. Masters, Jacob A. Miller, Henry Gantz, Frederick Zeigler.

1865.—E. F. Anderson, Henry S. Eavey, Henry S. Miller, Frederick K. Ziegler, Benjamin F. Cronise.

1867.—R. C. Bamford, A. R. Appleman, Jonathan Tobey, Jacob Hoffhine, Joseph P. Bishop.

1868.—A. K. Syester, James Coudy, F. Dorsey Herbert, Elias E. Rohrer, David Seibert.

1870.—Alex. Neill, John Welty, John Murdock, J. Monroe Sword, David Seibert.

1872.—Augustus H. Young, Moses Whitson, David H. Newcomer, Charles Ardinger.

1874.—Alonzo Berry, George Freaner, W. H. Grimes, A. K. Stake.

1876.—J. McPherson Scott, Lewis C. Smith, Joseph H. Farrow, Henry E. Ranger.

1878.—Joseph H. Farrow, Nathaniel Fiery, Joseph Harrison, Wm. H. Perkins.

1880.—Henry Funk, Thomas H. Crampton, Dr. J. E. Holmes, Dr. J. McPherson Scott.

1882.—Wm. B. Kelly, George A. Davis, George W. Pittman, Peter J. Mayberry.

Members of the Conventions of Maryland.

Convention of 1776.—Samuel Beall, Samuel Hughes, John Stull, Henry Schnebly.

Convention to Ratify Constitution of the United States, 1788.—John Stull, Moses Rawlings, Thomas Sprigg, Henry Shryock.

Constitutional Convention of 1851.—George Schley, Lewis P. Fiery, Alexander Neill, Jr., John Newcomer, Thomas Harbine, Michael Newcomer.

Constitutional Convention of 1864.—Peter Negley, Henry W. Dellinger, James P. Mahugh, John R. Sneary, Lewis B. Nyman, Joseph F. Davis.

Constitutional Convention of 1867.—Andrew K. Syester, R. H. Alvey, Joseph Murray, S. S. Cunningham, William Motter, George Pole.

Officers in 1777.

Justices of the County Court, Samuel Beall, John Stull, Joseph Sprigg, Samuel Hughes, Henry Schnebly, Joseph Chapline, John Rainor, Richard Davis, Andrew Bruse, Andrew Rench, William Yates, Lemuel Barrett, Thomas Cramphin, Christopher Crune, John Cellar; County Surveyor, Thomas Brook; Register of Wills, Thomas Sprigg; Coroners, James Waring, William Baird; Judge of the Court of Appeals, John Thomson Mason, appointed January, 1806; Richard Sprigg, appointed later in the same month, and John Buchanan, in place of Mr. Mason, who did not accept.

Attorney-General.

John Thomson Mason, appointed July 12, 1806, to succeed William Pinkney; Mr. Mason resigned in October of the same year; Andrew K. Syester, elected November, 1871.

Judges of the Circuit Court.

John Buchanan, appointed for Fifth District, January, 1806; Thomas Buchanan, appointed for Fifth District, May 5, 1815; William Claggett, associate judge, appointed for Fifth District, May 5, 1815; Daniel Weisel, qualified as associate judge for Fourth District, November, 1861; Daniel Weisel, qualified as associate judge for Fifth District, November, 1864; George French, qualified as associate judge for Fifth District, January, 1865; R. H. Alvey, qualified as associate judge for Fourth District, November, 1867; W. Motter, qualified as associate judge for Fourth District, November, 1867.

State's Attorney for Washington County.

1859, W. Motter; 1863-64, F. M. Darby; 1869, H. H. Keedy; 1871, John C. Zellin; 1873, H. H. Keedy; 1875, Edward Stake; 1879, John F. A. Remley.

In 1838, Edward A. Lynch was appointed deputy to the attorney-general of Maryland for the counties of Washington and Allegany, to succeed James Dixon, deceased.

County Commissioners.

1830, David Claggett, Henry Firey, M. Van Lear, Jr., Henry Lyday; 1832, John Witmer, David Claggett, Robert Wason, Samuel M. Hill, Andrew Rench, Henry Firey; 1834, Thomas Hammond, Benjamin Oswald, Jonathan Shafer, David Rohrer, Nathaniel Swingley, David Claggett, John Sheppard, Andrew Rench; 1835, John Miller; 1836, W. H. Grove, George Sprecker, Frederick Dorsey, Henry Ankeney, John Sheppard, John Ringer, David Rohrer; 1838, W. H. Grove, Andrew Rentch, John C. Dorsey, Michael Smith, James Cendy; 1840, Horatio N. Harris, Eli Crampton, Samuel Lyday, Robert Fowler; 1842, John Otto, John Ash, Daniel South, Solomon Helser, James Cendy, John Horine, Jacob Adams, Emery Edwards, George Poe; 1844, Samuel Coes, John Ash, John C. Dorsey, Jereh Mason, J. Snively, John Horine, John Oswald, Wm. Easton, Wm. E. Doyle; 1846, John Newcomer, Michael Smith; 1847, John C. Dorsey; 1848, Lewis Watson; 1849, Wm. B. McClain; 1850, Jacob Funk, A. Leiter, John Shafer, Frederick Rohrer; 1853, Martin Eakle, Daniel Startzman, Jacob Newcomer, Joseph H. Piper, David Cushwa; 1855, J. J. Bowers, John Wachtel, Jonathan Schindel, Jacob Nicodemus, John Kretzer; 1857, Joseph Garver, Daniel Mentzer, John Kretzer, John Feidt, Jonathan Middlekauff; 1859, John Newcomer, David Cushwa, John Welty, Samuel Doub, A. Leiter; 1861, John Richard, Michael Newcomer, Daniel Startzman, William Rulett, Lancelot Jacques; 1863, John Reichard, William Rulett, Lancelot Jacques, John Zeller, Elias E. Rohrer; 1864, John Reichard, William Rulett, Lancelot Jacques, John Zeller, Elias E. Rohrer; 1865, John Zeller, John Riechard, George T. Heyser, Henry Adams, Frederick Bell; 1867, David Cushwa, David Hoover, Jr., B. F. Byers, John Shifler, John Ash; 1869, J. G. Brown, Elias Eakle, J. J. Moore, F. T. Spickler, S. Bowles; 1871, Theo. Embry, Henry F. Neikirk, Samuel Strite, H. W. Lyday, John H. Harp; 1873, John Fessler, Joseph Seibert, Henry Funk, Elias Young, G. W. Brown; 1875, John Harp, J. W. Stonebraker, Isaac Ankeny, Jonas S. Deaner, P. R. Doub; 1877, J. W. Stonebraker, Isaac Ankeny, John J. Hershey, John M. Newcomer, Joseph Newcomer; 1879, J. W. Stonebraker, Joseph Newcomer, William T. Hassett, William Creager, John Heflebower.

Clerks of Circuit Court.

1845-64, Isaac Nesbitt; 1865, Lewis B. Nyman;[1] 1867, Wm. McK. Keppler; 1873-79, George B. Oswald.

The present deputy clerks are George F. Burkhart, O. B. Ridenour, P. J. Adams, and George T. Leiter.

[1] To fill vacancy occasioned by death of clerk Isaac Nesbitt.

County Surveyors.

Jonas Hogmire was appointed county surveyor by the Governor and Council, January, 1815, and was succeeded by Marmaduke W. Boyd in June, 1818. Prior to Hogmire, Joseph Sprigg had held the office some twenty-five or more years. The succeeding surveyors have been:

1848, S. S. Downin; 1853, Thomas Taggart; 1855, Isaac H. ——; 1857, George W. Bowers; 1859, Isaiah S. Poe; 1862–65, James Brown; 1867–73, S. S. Downin; 1875, Isaac H. Durborow. S. S. Downin, the present surveyor, qualified in November, 1877, and in November, 1879.

Judges of the Orphans' Court.

1806, Ignatius Taylor, Elie Williams, Jacob Harry, Jacob Schnebly; 1807, Ignatius Taylor, Elie Williams, Jacob Schnebly, Frisby Tilghman; 1808–11, Elie Williams, Jacob Schnebly, Frisby Tilghman; 1812, Jacob Schnebly, Frisby Tilghman, Thomas B. Hall; 1815–16, Matthew Van Lear, Alexander Neill, Richard Ragan; 1817–19, Alexander Ragan, Eli Beatty; 1820, Jacob Schnebly, Frisby Tilghman, Thomas Kellar; 1821–24, Jacob Schnebly, Thomas Kellar, William Gabby; 1855, Charles G. Lane, Michael H. Miller, Charles Embrey; 1859, Peter B. Small, Wm. McK. Keppler, Joseph Rench; 1863–64, Peter B. Small, A. Shoop, Joseph Rench; 1867, John W. Breathed, William H. Knode, James I. Hurley; 1870, James I. Hurley, Josiah F. Smith; 1871, Josiah F. Smith, William H. Knode, John L. Smith; 1875, John Reichard, John L. Smith, Samuel Strite; 1879, William McK. Keppler, A. D. Bennett, James Findlay.

Sheriffs.

1804, Nathaniel Rochester; 1806, Isaac S. White; 1809, Matthias Shaffner; 1812, Henry Sweitzer; 1815, Daniel Schnebly; 1818, Thomas Post; 1821, John V. Swearingen; 1822, Thomas Post; 1824, Alexander Neill; 1827, George Swearingen; 1828, Christian Newcomer, Jr.; 1831, William H. Fitzhugh; 1833, Daniel Malott; 1839, John Carr; 1842, Thomas Keller, David T. Wilson; 1845, Thomas Martin; 1848, Daniel South; 1851, Christopher Hilliard; 1853, William Logan; 1855, Benj. A. Garlinger; 1857, J. M. Hauck; 1859, E. M. Mobley; 1861, Henry Gantz; 1863–64, Samuel Oliver; 1865, Jonathan Newcomer; 1867, George W. Grove; 1869, Daniel White; 1871, R. C. Bamford; 1873, Jacob Marker; 1875, Peter J. Mayberry; 1877, B. F. Reichard; 1879, F. K. Zeigler.

Tax Collectors.

1839, Christian Sheppard; 1841, George Shief; 1842, Joseph Weash; 1844, William Dellinger; 1845–46, Joseph P. Mong; 1847, William E. Doyle; 1851, L. R. Martin (deputy); 1852–53, Horatio N. Harne; 1854–55, Joseph O'Neal; 1856–57, Joseph G. Pratzman; 1859, Henry Gantz; 1860, David Oswald; 1864, Samuel F. Zeigler; 1862–63, Benjamin A. Garlinger; 1864–65, Samuel F. Zeigler; 1866–67, Ed. M. Mobley; 1874, William N. Keller; 1876–77, W. M. Lantz; 1878–80, C. W. Miller.

Justices of the Levy Court.

1806.—Thomas Sprigg, Samuel Ringgold, Adam Ott, William Yates, Robert Smith, Josiah Price, and Jacob Schnebly.

1807.—Thomas Sprigg, Samuel Ringgold, Adam Ott, William Yates, Robert Smith, Josiah Price, and Nathaniel Rochester.

1808–9.—The same were reappointed by the Governor.

1810.—Samuel Ringgold, Adam Ott, William Yates, Robert Smith, Josiah Price, Martin Kershner, and Jacob Rench.

1811.—Adam Ott, Robert Smith, Josiah Price, Martin Kershner, Jacob Rench, William B. Williams, and William Yates.

1812.—Adam Ott, William Yates, Robert Smith, Josiah Price, Martin Kershner, William B. Williams, and David Schnebly.

1813.—William Fitzhugh, John Harry, Lancelot Jacques, John Wagoner, John Hershey, George Smith, and William Van Lear.

1814.—John Harry, Lancelot Jacques, John Wagoner, John Hershey, George Smith, William Van Lear.

1815.—William Fitzhugh, John Harry, Lancelot Jacques, John Wagoner, John Hershey, George Smith, and Edmund H. Turner.

1816.—Those of 1815 reappointed.

1817.—The same; but in March of that year Matthew Van Lear was appointed, *vice* Col. Wm. Fitzhugh, resigned.

1818.—Matthew Van Lear, John Harry, Lancelot Jacques, John Wagoner, John Hershey, George Smith, and Edmund H. Turner.

1819.—The same as previous year.

1820.—William Gabby, Frederick Dorsey, Daniel Reichard, John McClain, William Fitzhugh, Jr., Edward G. Williams, and Jacob Miller.

1821.—Frederick Dorsey, Daniel Reichard, John McClain, William Fitzhugh, Jr., Edward G. Williams, Jacob Miller, and Jacob Zeller.

1822.—Frederick Dorsey, Daniel Reichard, John McClain, William Fitzhugh, Jr., Samuel Ringgold, Jacob Zeller, and Jacob Miller.

1823.—Frederick Dorsey, John McClain, William Fitzhugh, Jr., Samuel Ringgold, Jacob Miller, David Schnebly, Joseph Gabby, Peter Seibert.

1824.—Frederick Dorsey, John McClain, William Fitzhugh, Jr., Samuel Ringgold, Jacob Miller, David Schnebly, and Peter Seibert.

1825.—Frederick Dorsey, John McClain, William Fitzhugh, Samuel Ringgold, Jacob Miller, David Schnebly, and Peter Seibert.

1826.—John McClain, William Fitzhugh, Jr., Samuel Ringgold, Jacob Miller, David Schnebly, Peter Seibert, and Frederick Dorsey.

1827.—Frederick Dorsey, John McClain, Peter Seibert, Jacob Miller, Daniel Rentch, and David Brookhart.

1828.—Henry Firey, David Rohrer, Thomas C. Brent.

1829.—I. S. Swearingen, Thomas Hammond, Joseph Gabby.

1830.—George Brownbaugh, James Grimes, John H. Mann, Joseph West, Jacob Miller.

Commissioner State Board of Education.

1874–82, P. A. Witmer.

School Commissioners.

1864, Thomas A. Boulet, John A. Miller, Joseph Garver, Jacob Funk, Isaac Garver, P. S. Newcomer, Samuel I. Piper, William Davis, John J. Hershey, Samuel Mason, Jonathan Tobey, I. P. Mayhugh, Samuel Baker; 1865, Thomas A. Boullt, Joseph Garver, John Kretzer, Jacob Funk, John S. Hedding, Samuel Rohrer, John J. Hershey, John A. Miller, Albert Small (secretary and treasurer); 1867, Edward Stake (secretary and treasurer); 1868, G. W. Smith, J. V. Fiery, G. W. Brown, John D. Houck, Warren Garratt, A. W. Lakin, Moses Poffenbarger, Edward Ingram, Charles Hiteshew, Edward Smith, H. T. Spickler, William Jones, O. W. Johnson, Warford Mann, Henry Eakle, P. W. Witmer (secretary, treasurer, etc.), James Cullen; 1869, W. S. Williamson, Alexander Neill, William H. Armstrong,

Henry Strock, George T. Leiter, David H. Flory; 1870, J. V. Fiery, Moses Poffenbarger, Warren Garratt, G. W. Brown, Henry Eakle, Benjamin F. Fiery, William H. Armstrong, Samuel Knode, Isaac Garver, Henry Strock, J. Johnson, Denton G. Gehr, Solomon Jenkins, J. D. Slaughenhaupt, W. A. Riddlemoser, P. A. Witmer (secretary, treasurer, etc.); 1872, William Ragan, Benjamin A. Garlinger, H. S. Eavey, William B. McClain, Thomas H. Crampton; 1874, William Ragan, William B. McClain, Benjamin A. Garlinger, Thomas H. Crampton, H. S. Eavey; 1876, William Ragan, Thomas H. Crampton, William B. McClain, B. A. Garlinger, H. S. Eavey, P. A. Witmer (examiner, treasurer, and secretary); 1878, William Ragan, William B. McClain, B. A. Garlinger, H. S. Eavey, Thomas H. Crampton; 1879, William Ragan; 1880, B. A. Garlinger, William L. Stonebraker, H. S. Eavey, William B. McClain, P. A. Witmer (examiner and treasurer).

Register of Wills.

1857-64, William Logan; 1804, Thomas Belt; 1806, George C. Smoot.

Justices of the Peace.

1802-6.—Thomas Crampton, Robert Douglass, George Nigh, Adam Ott, William Webb, John Hunter, William Van Lear, William Yates, John Good, John Langley, George Scott, Sr., Jacob Schnebly, William S. Compton, Philip Mains.

January, 1806.—Thomas Crampton, Adam Ott, Samuel Ringgold, John Good, John Hunter, Thomas Sprigg, William Yates, Robert Douglass, William Webb, Daniel Weisel, Robert Smith, Josiah Price, George Scott, George Nigh, Henry Ankeny, James McClain, Thomas Kennedy, William S. Compton, George Smith, Jacob Schnebly, Martin Kerschner, Philip Mains, John Langley, John Bowles, and James Prather.

1807.—The appointments of 1807 were the same as the preceding year, except that the name of Daniel Weisel was dropped and John T. Mason added to the list.

1808.—The same were reappointed in 1808, except Webb, deceased, and the addition tc the list of William Gabby and Robert Hughes.

1809.—Appointments same as preceding year.

1810.—The only changes made in 1810 were occasioned by the death of Gen. Sprigg and appointments of Matthew Collins and Henry Lochner, Jr.

1811.—Thomas Crampton, Adam Ott, Samuel Ringgold, John Hunter, Wm. Yates, Robert Douglass, Robert Smith, Josiah Price, James McClain, Thomas Kennedy, William S. Compton, George Smith, Jacob Schnebly, Martin Kerchner, Philip Mains, John Langley, John Bowles, James Prather, William Gabby, Robert Hughes, Matthew Collins, and Ezra Slifer.

1812.—In January, 1812, the same were reappointed, except that Langley was dropped, and John Blackford, William B. Williams, John Wolgamott, Charles Heseltine, and William Fitzhugh, Jr., added.

1813.—No record.

1814.—Adam Ott, William Yates, James McClain, George Smith, Jacob Schnebly, John Bowles, James Prather, Robert Hughes, John Blackford, Edward Boteler, George Nichols, James D. Moore, John Witmer, John Barr, Christopher Burkhart, John Hershey, William Van Lear, William Fitzhugh, Jr., Isaac Hauser, Jr., Alexander Grimm, Edmund H. Turner, Jonas Hogmire, Joseph Ingram, Matthew Van Lear, Frederick Grosh, David Newcomer, Lancelot Jacques, Cornelius Ferree, Jeremiah Mason, Ephraim Davis, and John Adams.

1815.—George Smith, John Blackford, Edward Boteler, George Nichols, Alexander Grimm, Edmund H. Turner, Jonas Hogmire, Isaac Hauser, Jr., Joseph Ingram, Matthew Van Lear, Robert Hughes, John Witmer, John Barr, Christopher Burckhart, John Hershey, Wm. Fitzhugh, Jr., Frederick Grosh, David Newcomer, James McClain, John Bowles, James Prather, James D. Moore, Lancelot Jacques, Wm. Yates, Cornelius Ferree, Jeremiah Mason, Ephraim Davis, John Adams, Jacob Schnebly, Archibald M. Waugh, Joseph C. Keller, Seth Lowe, and Robert McCulloh.

1816.—The same as 1815, except James Prather, deceased, and the additions of Dr. Christian Boerstler, John Young, Septimus Stephens, and George Brumbaugh.

1817.—George Smith, John Blackford, Edward Boteler, George Nichols, Alexander Grimm, Edmund H. Turner, Isaac Houser, Jr., Joseph Ingram, Matthew Van Lear, Robert Hughes, John Witmer, John Barr, Christopher Burckhart, John Hershey, William Fitzhugh, Jr., Frederick Grosh, David Newcomer, John Bowles, James D. Moore, Lancelot Jacques, William Yates, Cornelius Ferree, Jeremiah Mason, Ephraim Davis, John Adams, Jacob Schnebly, Arch. M. Waugh, Joseph C. Keller, Seth Lane, Robert McCullough, Dr. Christian Boerstler, John Young, Septimus Stevens, George Brumbaugh, John Davis, Thomas C. Brent, and Ezra Slifer.

1818.—George Smith, John Blackford, Edward Boteler, George Nichols, Alexander Grimm, Isaac Houser, Jr., Matthew Van Lear, Robert Hughes, John Witmer, John Barr, Christopher Burckhart, John Hershey, William Fitzhugh, Jr., David Newcomer, John Bowles, James D. Moore, Lancelot Jacques, William Yates, Cornelius Ferree, Jeremiah Mason, Jacob Schnebly, Arch. M. Waugh, Seth Lane, Robert McCulloh, Christian Boerstler, John Young, George Brumbaugh, John Davis, Thomas C. Brent, Ezra Slifer, and Elie Baker.

1819.—The same were appointed in 1819, with Milton H. Sackett, James H. Bowles, David Stephens, and Edmund H. Turner as additional justices.

From and including the year 1820 the names of those only are given who qualified according to law, and as shown in the test books on file in the office of the Circuit Court clerk.

1814, A. M. Waugh; 1815, Robert McCulloch, Jacob Schnebly, Seth Lane; 1816, Christian Boerstler, John Jung, John Adams, George Brumbaugh; 1817, George Nichols, Ezra Slifer, M. Van Lear; 1818, Thomas C. Brent; 1819, Milton H. Sackett; 1820, Benjamin Yoe, Thomas Compton, Andrew Kershner, John McClain, Thomas Kennedy, Edward G. Williams, William Fitzhugh, Jr., John Rench, Dennis Burns, George Shafer, Jacob Miller, Michael Iseminger, William Webb, James Hemphill, John McKee, John Smith, Frederick Dorsey, William Gabby, Daniel Reichard, George Lochner, Stewart Herbert, Philip Means; 1821, Charles Heseltine, William S. Compton, John D. Moore, Henry Schnebly, Benjamin F. Hickman, Joseph Gabby, Jacob Zeller; 1822, Ezra Slifer, John Bowles, Ignatius Drury, Nathaniel Summers, Samuel Bayley, John Horine, James H. Bowles, Benjamin Boteler; 1823, Thomas B. Hall, Daniel Malott, Jonathan Shafer, Daniel Donnelly, Robert Clagett, David Rohrer; 1824, William Kreps, Jacob Kissinger, John M. Rohrer, Marmaduke W. Boyd; 1825, James Leggett, Joseph Gabby, Samuel Ringgold, George H. Lambert, John Baker; 1826, David Brookhout, John A. Cavan, William Eakle, William Boulto, Henry Firey, John M. McIlheny, Nicholas Lowe, John Hany; 1827,

Thomas Post, Isaac S. Swearingen; 1829, Washington W. Hitt, Charles Nourse, Henry Crosby, William Webb; 1830, Henry Lewis, Jacob Kessinger, J. M. Welch, Henry C. Schnebly, Anthony Snyder, Thomas Johns, Van S. Brashear, George Seibert, John Hall, William Booth, Samuel Dietrick, Jacob Baker, Henry Wade; 1831, S. Herbert, Benjamin Oswald, Jr., Joseph West, John A. Wagoner; 1833, Jacob Kausler, John D. Kiefer, Richard M. Harrison, John Lambert; 1834, John Newcomer, Daniel Grim; 1835, David Hughes, Watkins James, Jr.; 1836, Joseph Gabby, John Horine, Jacob Lambert, Lewis Tuttle.

Among other justices who qualified in years prior to March, 1839, but the date of whose qualification is not shown on the records, were:

Samuel Mitchell, Patrick Byrne, John Herr, Charles Rounse, David Schnebly, Peter Seibert, George Shafer, Solomon Sherfy, Andrew Smith, Samuel Claget, Perry Prather, George M. Elliott, John D. Ridenour, Joseph Gray, Alex. H. Laffon, Wm. H. Handey, John D. Dutton, William Downs, Isaac Nesbitt, D. H. Keedy, Thomas Boteler, John J. Keedy, James P. Mills, Abel Dunham, George Stubblefield, David Smith, David Showman, Elias Davis, Thomas D. Grim, H. Dyron, George Shafer, G. W. Rodgers, William S. Morrison, Abraham Witmer, Thomas Patterson, James Maxwell, Jonathan Newcomer, A. Macbride, David Brumbaugh, George Shief, James Hurley.

Subsequent justices of the peace to date, who have exercised their duties, are as follows:

1839.—George W. Smith, Jacob Powles, Daniel Gieshart, Samuel S. Prather, Daniel Flory, Daniel South, Daniel Hance, Emanuel Knodle, Anthony Snyder, Michael Iseminger, Jacob Reichard, D. Osler, Goorge Feidt, Jacob Smith, John Witmer, John M. Rohrer, Wm. McK. Keppler, George Sprecher, John Beard, Henry Wade, Daniel Grim, Eli Mobley, John Cook, Hugh Logan, John Cunning, Jacob Miller, E. S. Boteler, D. Keedy, B. Beam, Andrew Smith, William Webb, Benjamin Hartman, David T. Wilson, Nathaniel Summers, John D. Dutton, Solomon Helser, H. C. Schnebly, David Newcomer, Eli Crampton, George Brown, Ethelbert Taney, Arthur Blackwell, Joseph Knox, Conrad Wolf, William McAuley.

1840.—C. F. Gelwick, Geo. W. Smith, Samuel Blecher, Henry Mills, John Baker, John J. Grim, Abel Williams, Daniel Root, Hiram G. Reese, John L. Grow, Roger E. Cook, John Weis, Conrad Wolf, George Gerty.

1841.—Alexander H. Lappon, Jacob A. Miller, John B. Bachtell, Jonathan Keller, Wm. McK. Keppler.

1842.—John Johnson, F. A. Grim, Joseph A. Skinner, Joseph Unger, John R. Curtis, John Ringer, H. Snyder, James Mongan, William Kreps, Christian Sheppard.

1843.—John K. Smith, Jacob R. Martin, Jacob Shoop, Elijah Swope, Samuel Blecher, George Colliflower, M. W. Boyd, H. Downie, Philip Meade, Wm. C. Webb, William Hunter, Samuel H. Smith, Samuel Lyday.

1845.—George Hill, Wm. H. Boyd, Wm. H. Handey, S. L. Ditwiler, Henry Ridenour, Stewart Herbert, Jacob Shanebyer, Wm. R. Hughes, Daniel Flory, W. M. Tice, John Herr, W. W. Bucher, C. F. Gilwick, Robert Wilson, H. H. Snyder, Joseph Brewer, John Brown, John A. Wagoner, Abraham H. Ganer, Jacob Lambert, Jacob Kansler, Peter Springfield, William H. Miller, David Reichard, William Eakle, David Newcomer, Henry C. Welty, John M. Rohrer, Isaac Garver, James Waters, John D. Ridenour, O. H. Williams, D. Brumbaugh, Washington McCoy, Nathan M. Darnell, James Brown, George W. Grosh, Wm. McAuley, Charles G. Lane, John L. Smith, John J. Keedy, Samuel Brown, Matthew McClannahan, Jesse Blair, Peyton Skinner, Andrew Newcomer, Elias O'Neal, J. P. Stephey, Thomas Boteler, David Hughes, Jonathan Smith, Daniel Donnelly.

1846.—John W. Heard, Lewis Fletcher, Isaac H. Allen, Joshua C. Price, Elisha C. Wells, Elias J. Ohr.

1847.—Francis C. Shief, Joseph Cunningham, Solomon Florry.

1848.—C. Sheppard, John Cook, Wm. McK. Keppler, Joseph A. Skinner, Samuel Lyday, Moses Dillon, Jacob Bleacher, Jacob Smith, John Corby, D. H. Keedy, John Weis, George Long, Samuel Houser, J. P. Mayhugh, O. McClain, Charles W. McMinn, Jeremiah Kuhn, Joseph Knox, George W. Smith, S. S. Dounin, John R. Williams, R. E. Cook, D. E. Price, W. H. Fitzhugh, Hugh Logan, George Knodle, Joseph D. Price, Chas. W. Bigham, Henry Gray, Martin Eakle, John Hershberger, D. Haner, John Snyder, Eli Crampton, D. H. Myers, Wm. C. Kirkhart, Thomas Clingan, F. A. Grim, Jacob Powles, Jacob Shoop, Josiah Buck, Jonathan R. Humphries, John B. Bachtell, J. A. Miller, Michael Iseminger, Jr., William Trefoot, John Moore, James Cassidy.

1849.—Geo. T. Hawken, Thomas H. Crampton, David Fortney.

1850.—Daniel Grim, W. T. Aniba, Thos. E. Schleigh, Horatio N. Harne, William Morninger, Jacob Funk, G. W. Brown.

1851.—James Mongan, Absalom Eakle, John Snyder, John S. Wolf.

1852.—C. Sheppard, J. P. Mayhugh, John Cook, T. E. Schleigh, Daniel Grim, George Knodle, John Hershberger, D. H. Keedy, J. R. Humphries, Joseph A. Skinner, Jacob Blecker, Jeremiah Kuhn, George T. Hawkens, John Corby, Samuel Houser, George Long, John Wachtell, Martin Eakles, Absalom Eakles, G. W. Brown, John Snyder, Jacob Shoop, Henry L. Teatian, Owen McClain, R. Ellsworth Cook, Jonathan Hawer, Michael Iseminger, Jr., D. Haner, Hugh Logan, Joseph D. Price, David E. Price, Lewis Bell, Daniel H. Myers, David Fortney, Alex. Neill, Jr., William Monninger.

1853.—John Knodle, William Miller, F. Humrichouse, James Mongan, Samuel Houser, William M. Tice, William H. Handey, John Cook, John L. Smith, M. Iseminger, Jr., Daniel Grim, F. C. Shief, George T. Hawkens, J. P. Wolfersberger, Elias O'Neal, Samuel Boyd, Benjamin Schamel, David Reichard, Daniel Flory, J. R. Humphries, George M. Knode, George Hill, Isaac Garver, Thomas Watkins, Joseph Brittain, John Corby, John D. Hart, R. E. Cook, Elias J. Ohr, George Wolf, James Mongan.

1854.—John Troxell.

1855.—Josiah Buck, Otho B. Castle, John Troxell, Thomas Watkins, John W. Drenner, Jeremiah Kuhn, Samuel Boyd, Josiah Buck, Jacob Powles, J. R. Humphries, M. King, J. Cook, Tacitus V. Halley, David Wilhelm, Joshua Dayhoff, William Kreps, George Pearson, James W. Leggett, David M. Hoover, Elias O'Neal, Daniel H. Myers, George Hill, Owen McClain, John L. Smith, M. Iseminger, Jr., Solomon Davis.

1856.—Peter Mutersbaugh.

1857.—Jeremiah Kuhn, James Mongan, David Wilhelm, Samuel Nigh, Thomas Curtis, David Hughes, Owen McClain, J. Cook, William Kreps, James P. Hays, Ezra Munson, Elias O'Neal, John Savin, John Troxell, D. G. Potter, Tacitus V. Halley, James Proutzah, Elias Sprecker, M. King, Isaac Garver, Thomas Boteler, Peter Hull, James Hurley, J. R. Humphries.

1858.—Otho B. Castle, George T. Hawkens, Hiram Buhrman.

1859.—J. R. Hode, C. F. Gelwick, Thomas Curtis, B. F. Keller,

M. King, John McKing, John Stonesifer, Solomon Calklesser, J. R. Hode, George Caswell, Samuel Boyer, William Kreps, R. E. Cook, Owen McClain, Joseph Green, Joseph Harrison, Robert Shives, David Hughes, George W. Bowers, J. O. Fiery, Isaac Garver, B. F. M. Hurley, Thomas Boteler, David G. Potter, Joseph S. Grim, Tacitus N. Halley.

1860.—Jeremiah Kuhn.

1861.—William Biershing, John Cook, William M. Tice, William Phreaner, James Mongan, Thomas Watkins, Cornelius Virts, Samuel Houser, Frederick Harmon, James P. Hays, Adam Devilbiss, John Hershberger, Jacob Good, D. G. Potter, M. Iseminger, Jr., John Stonesifer, George Fulton, George Hill, John T. Wolverton, Joseph Harrison, Peter Ardinger, Isaiah S. Poe, Joseph S. Grimm, J. R. Hode.

1862.—James Dorrance, Samuel Boyd.

1863.—Jacob Craig, Moses Poffenbarger, Jacob Good, J. O. Firey, Lewis L. Mentzer, D. G. Potter, Jacob C. Thompson, Frederick Harmon, Tacitus Halley, J. Cook, Samuel Meredith, John Troxell, Samuel Houser, J. R. Hode, William M. Tice, Andrew J. McAllister, W. Biershing, James Dorrance, George Fulton, M. Iseminger, James R. Myers, Peter Ardinger, Thomas Watkins, James Mongan, Adam Devilbiss, George Hill, Joseph S. Grimm.

1864.—James Dorrance, Jacob Good, William M. Tice, John Cook, Samuel Meredith, Adam Devilbiss, William Beirshing, D. G. Potter, Samuel Houser, George Fulton, Tacitus V. Halley, Frederick Harman, Michael Iseminger, Samuel Boyer, J. R. Hode, Jacob C. Thompson, Peter Ardinger, D. J. Pittenger, Joseph S. Grimm.

1865.—Jacob Craig, Lewis L. Mintzer, George Hill, Thomas Watkins, David Pennel, James Dorrance, David Pennel, William Beirshing, Josiah Knodle, John Cook, Tacitus V. Halley, Thomas Watkins, Frederick Harman, George Fulton, Samuel Houser, William M. Tice, Samuel Boyer, Adam Devilbiss, M. Iseminger, Peter Ardinger, D. G. Potter, John J. Thomas, N. McKinley, Jacob C. Thompson.

1866.—George Hill, J. R. Hode, James Hurley, James W. Leggett, David S. Ledy, John Snyder.

1867.—William Beirshing, William M. Tice, George Long, O. McClain, Jacob Blecker, John H. Lakin, Thomas Taggert, Elijah Swope, M. H. Clarke, Joseph C. Hershberger, Joseph Harrison, J. A. McCool, George W. Hicks, John J. Watson, John Snyder, B. F. Keller, Samuel B. Preston, Josiah Buck, Jacob Craig, James A. Skinner, David M. Hoover, Tacitus V. Halley, James W. Leggett, Jacob Motz, James R. Myers, John G. Hine, John G. Ernst.

1868.—Daniel H. Myers, John G. Hine, Joseph Harrison, W. H. Grove, Dennis Cain, John Snyder, O. McClain, George H. Shafer, Josiah Buck, John H. Lakin, Jacob Blecker, Jacob Craig, Elijah Swope, Tacitus V. Halley, Thomas Taggart, Wm. M. Tice, Wm. Beirshing, M. H. Clarke, Solomon Davis, James A. Skinner, John Clark, Andrew R. Schnebly.

1869.—John Long, J. R. Hode, John H. Read, Samuel Boyer.

1870.—H. F. Perry, John H. Lakin, John Murdock, George Long, Jacob Craig, James A. Skinner, John Snyder, Wm. H. Grove, Tacitus V. Halley, Thomas Taggart, Josiah Buck, William M. Tice, Joseph Harrison, Wm. Biershing, Owen McClain, Joseph C. Hershberger, John G. Hine, G. W. Hicks, Elijah Swope, M. H. Clarke, T. E. Schleigh, John Long, James W. Leggett, Samuel Boyer, Thomas Watkins, James H. Harne, Thomas Boteler, Jonathan Bowser.

1871.—Hiram R. Stickel.

1872.—William H. Myers, G. W. Smith, Wm. H. Lowe, Thomas Boteler, Wm. H. Hawken, Charles Harvey, Wm. M. Tice, Peter Middlekauff, John Murdoch, Joseph A. Skinner, Morgan Miller, W. H. Grove, Jacob Craig, Elijah Swope, Samuel Boyer, W. H. Lowe, John F. Gray, Thomas Watkins, G. W. Smith, Wm. H. Myers, John S. Hine, Thomas Taggart, George W. Hicks, John Long, Joseph Hershberger, Thomas E. Schleigh, Josiah Buck, Hiram R. Stickel, Jacob Losey, James W. Leggett, Tacitus V. Halley, George Long, John H. Lakin, A. A. Cook, F. D. Claggett, H. F. Perry.

1874.—John Buck, W. H. Grove, J. A. Skinner, W. H. Lowe, Aaron F. Baker, John Murdock, J. A. Wright, W. V. Harne, Samuel Boyer, John F. Gray, Jacob Fiery, Wm. H. Myers, Morgan Miller, Jacob Craig, Thomas Watkins, William M. Tice, Thomas Taggart, S. Colklesser, Thomas Boteler, John H. Lakin, Wm. H. Hawken, Josiah Buck, R. E. Cook, James W. Leggett, John W. Hine, Peter Middlekauff, Elijah Swope, T. E. Schleigh, H. F. Perry, H. R. Stickler, Robert Shives, John Long, Jacob Motz, D. S. Pittinger, Tacitus V. Halley, Joseph C. Hersberger, J. R. Cushwa.

1875.—J. Irvin Bitner, M. H. Clarke, J. Snively, J. R. Anderson, Albert C. Tice.

1876.—John Buck, Christian G. Brezler, J. A. Skinner, Thomas Taggart, S. Colklesser, J. Irvin Bitner, R. E. Cook, Joseph H. Dreimer, J. A. Wright, John H. Lakin, W. H. Grove, John Murdock, H. F. Perry, Wm. H. Myers, Elijah Swope, Daniel W. Blessing, W. H. Lowe, Josiah Buck, John G. Hine, W. V. Harne, Morgan Miller, Otho Oliver, J. Snively, Peter Middlekauff, Robert Shives, Tacitus V. Halley, Wm. H. Hawken, Thomas Boteler, J. H. Wade, John Long, Charles Harvey, D. S. Pittenger, Thomas Watkins, John H. Fiery, Joseph C. Hershberger, M. H. Clarke.

1877.—John S. Wolf, Charles H. Dickel, James W. Leggett.

1878.—T. Belt Johnson, Allen A. Nesbitt, James R. Myers, Joseph Harrison, A. D. Sagar, J. Irvin Bitner, John Buck, James L. Elgin, Peter Middlekauff, Allen A. Nesbitt, John H. Lakin, John H. Wade, Elijah Swope, George H. Weld, R. W. Grove, C. G. Brezler, Wm. H. Myers, T. Belt Johnson, J. Snively, Otho Oliver, J. A. Wright, H. V. Harne, R. E. Cook, Jacob Lakin, John G. Hine, C. H. Dickel, J. A. Skinner, S. Summers, John E. Brown, Thomas Taggart, Joseph C. Hershberger, Lancelot Jacques, John Long, S. Cocklesser, Wm. H. Hawken, Josiah Buck, D. W. Blessing, John Murdock, John S. Wolf, Eli Stemm, Jr., John Lambert.

1880.—L. Colklesser, John Buck, Wm. H. Myers, R. W. Grove, T. Belt Johnson, J. I. Bitner, Philip Sprecker, C. G. Brezler, H. H. Long, John H. Lakin, Morgan Miller, Peter Middlekauff, P. Oswald, John Lambert, Elijah Swope, S. Summers, David Dick, John Long, Thomas Taggart, John Clarke, Aaron Sager, Joseph C. Hershberger, J. Snively, R. E. Cook, W. V. Harne, J. L. Evessole, Lancelot Jacques, Silas Wolfersberger, George H. Weld, J. A. Skinner, J. L. Elgin, Allen A. Nesbitt, John Murdock, John S. Wolf, Wm. H. Hawken, Josiah Buck, John G. Hine, J. A. Wright, John E. Brown, C. H. Dickel, Joseph Harrison, Garey S. Betts, Thomas J. Halley, Scott Palmer.

The judges of elections in 1822 for the county were:

District No. 1, Sharpsburg.—Jacob Miller, Robert Clagett, John D. Grove.

District No. 2, Williamsport.—Isaac S. Swearingen, Milton H. Sackett, Ignatius Drury.

District No. 3, Hagerstown.—Peter Humrickhouse, John Wolgamott, Henry Shafer.

District No. 4, Clear Spring.—Michael Bovey, David Cushwa, Jacob Dunn.

District No. 5, Hancock.—William Yates, James H. Bowles, Anthony Snyder.

District No. 6, Boonsboro'.—John Shafer, Matthias Shaffner, Michael Piper.

District No. 7, Cavetown.—William Gabby, William H. Fitzhugh, Peter Seibert.

Col. Henry Lewis was appointed coroner by the Governor in 1822.

CHAPTER XLII.

INTERNAL IMPROVEMENTS.

Roads — Bridges — Turnpikes — Stage-coaches—Mails—Railroads.

WASHINGTON COUNTY is better provided with transportation facilities than any other county in the State. Some of its far-sighted and enterprising citizens at a very early period inaugurated a system of turnpike roads which not only has given the county most admirable roads where they were most needed, but has also resulted in bringing, from their tolls, large revenues into the county treasury. The county is also traversed by several railway lines. The Chesapeake and Ohio Canal passes through the whole extent of its southern border, giving all necessary transportation to this section of the county, and full intercourse with the coal-fields in Allegany County. The main stem of the Baltimore and Ohio Railroad passes through the southeastern border, at the foot of Pleasant Valley, while the Washington County Branch of the same road, beginning at Weverton, on the Potomac, passes northward through Bartholow's, Brownsville, Claggett's, Beeler's, Summit, Rohrersville, Eakle's Mills, Keedysville, and Breathed's Stations to Hagerstown, a distance of twenty-four miles.

The Shenandoah Valley Railroad, beginning at Hagerstown, its northern terminus, passes through St. James, Grimes, and Sharpsburg Stations, or a distance of about fourteen miles in Washington County. The Cumberland Valley Railroad, which extends from Harrisburg, Pa., to Martinsburg, W. Va., has as stations in this county State Line, Morgantown, Hagerstown, and Williamsport, while the Western Maryland Railroad in its route from Baltimore passes that picturesque locality known as Pen-Mar, also Edgemont, Smithsburg, Cavetown, Chewsville, and Hagerstown to Williamsport. These roads all converging at Hagerstown, which is centrally located and the county-seat, have contributed greatly to its business activity and wealth, as well as to the prosperity of all parts of the beautiful and rich agricultural region surrounding it. In turnpike roads this county is better provided than any other in the State.

Rumsey's Steamboat.—Washington County may also claim to no inconsiderable share in the construction of the first steamboat ever built in the United States. This was the vessel built by James Rumsey, of Shepherdstown, W. Va., in 1785. Blasco de Garay in 1543, the Marquis of Worcester in 1655, Deuys Papi in 1695, Savery in 1698, and others had prophesied, proposed, or tried steam navigation, and various experiments with rude vessels had been made in Europe from time to time. It was not, however, until the experiments of Fulton in 1807, and his trip up the Hudson, that the practicability of propelling vessels by steam was fully and finally demonstrated. But Fulton had been anticipated by Rumsey, who as early as 1785 constructed a boat at Shepherdstown, and had it fitted up with machinery partly manufactured at the Catoctin Furnace of the Johnson Brothers, near Frederick. The boiler, two cylinders, pumps, pipes, etc., were manufactured in Baltimore by Christopher Raborg and Charles Weir. Some portions of the works were made at the Antietam Iron-Works. March 14, 1786, a public experiment was made on the Potomac River (the first of the kind ever undertaken in this country), and Rumsey succeeded in attaining a speed of four miles an hour against the current. The boat was eighty feet long, and propelled by a steam-engine working a vertical pump in the middle of the vessel, by which the water was drawn in at the bow and expelled through a horizontal trunk at the stern. She achieved the speed above stated when loaded with three tons, in addition to the weight of her machinery,—one-third of a ton. The whole of the machinery, including the boiler, occupied a space but little over four feet square. A newspaper account of the vessel, under date of April 25, 1793, gives the following description of her, viz.:

> "The vessel of the late lamented Mr. Rumsey to sail against wind and tide has lately been tried, and was found to sail four knots an hour. The following is the principle upon which it moves: A pump of two feet diameter, wrought by a steam-engine, forces a quantity of water up through the keel. The valve is then shut by the return of the stroke, which at the same time forces the water through a channel or pipe of about six inches square, lying above and parallel to the keelson out at the stern, under the rudder, which has a less dip than usual, to permit the exit of the water. The impress of the water forced through the square channel against the exterior water acts as an impelling power upon the vessel."

Gen. Washington and Governor Thos. Johnson, of Maryland, were patrons of Rumsey's experiment, which was made in the interest of the proposed Chesapeake and Ohio Canal. His demonstration that a boat could be propelled up stream against the current was regarded by them as being very satisfactory. Thus we find that the first steamboat was propelled on the Potomac, and the first machinery was made in Western Maryland, twenty years before Fulton's experiment on the Hudson. Rumsey's claim to priority was disputed by John Fitch, a Philadelphia watch-maker, but the evidence in favor of Rumsey is very clear and convincing. Fitch did not make public his plan until 1786. It consisted in "paddling a ship by steam," the device resembling vertical paddles, six on each side, working alternately. The vessel was launched at Philadelphia in 1788, and proceeded to Burlington, N. J., twenty miles distant, where she burst her boiler. She was floated back to Philadelphia and repaired, and made several subsequent trips. The cylinder was twelve inches in diameter and three-feet stroke. Rumsey, who was a native of Cecil County, had petitioned the Maryland Legislature for the passage of an act vesting in him "the sole and exclusive right, privilege, and benefit of constructing, navigating, and employing boats, constructed upon a model by him newly invented, upon the creeks, rivers, and bays within this State." It was read and referred to Messrs. McMechen, O'Neale, and James Scott, who on the same day reported that they had "examined the allegations therein contained and find them true, and are of opinion that the said invention will be of great utility to facilitate the inland navigation of this State, and that a law pass agreeably to the prayer of said petition." At the same session the Legislature passed an act to invest Rumsey "with an exclusive privilege and benefit of making and selling new invented boats on a model by him invented." The experiment which preceded this application took place in September, 1784, and had been witnessed by Gen. Washington, who was highly gratified, and gave Rumsey the following certificate, viz.:

> "I have seen the model of Mr. Rumsey's boats constructed to work against stream, examined the powers upon which it acts, been eye-witness to an actual experiment in running water of some rapidity, and give it as my opinion (although I had little faith before) that he has discovered the art of working boats by mechanism and small manual assistance against rapid currents; that the discovery is of vast importance; may be of the greatest usefulness in inland navigation; and if it succeeds, of which I do not doubt, that the value of it is greatly enhanced by the simplicity of the works, which when seen and explained may be executed by the most common mechanic."

The boat appears to have been propelled by paddles and setting-poles, the power being communicated by hand. But soon afterwards Rumsey turned his attention to the possible application of steam as the motive-power. He worked hard all that fall and winter, and was fortunate enough to secure the assistance and patronage of Governor Thomas Johnson. The latter was part proprietor, with his brothers, of the Catoctin Iron Furnace. The boat itself was built at Shepherdstown, and in December, 1785, was brought down to the mouth of the Shenandoah, and at Harper's Ferry a trial was made with successful results, as previously stated. In 1786, Benjamin Franklin and Oliver Evans suggested substantially the same method of propulsion, namely, the power of steam upon a column of water received at the bow and ejected at the stern on a line with the keel. The plan has been lately revived, and several vessels have been built in England to test it. In 1788 the Rumsey Society, of which Franklin was a member, was formed in Philadelphia to aid the Maryland inventor. He went to London, where a similar body was formed, a boat and machinery built for him, and patents obtained in Great Britain, France, and Holland. A successful experiment was made on the Thames in 1792, and he was preparing another when he died, December 23d of that year. In 1839 the Legislature of Kentucky presented a gold medal to his son, "commemorative of his father's services and high agency in giving to the world the benefits of the steamboat." There was an acrimonious controversy between Fitch and Rumsey, growing out of the latter's having charged the former with appropriating his idea of a steamboat from a description of Rumsey's boat given him by a Capt. Bedinger. Rumsey published a number of affidavits to prove that he was the original inventor of the steamboat, and among the other documents exhibited by him was a letter from Gen. Washington to show that he had spoken to him (Washington) of employing steam as a motive-power. In January, 1786, after Rumsey's experiment, John Fitch petitioned the Maryland Legislature for assistance in "bringing his theory of the elastic force of steam to experiment," but although the Legislature could not advance any money, owing to the condition of the public funds at the time, it passed a resolution stating that it was "strongly inclined to believe the probability of the success promised by the theory." Rumsey and Fitch were followed by many experimenters, but, as stated, Fulton's steamboat, the "Clermont," achieved in 1807 the first decisive and permanent success.

Public Roads.—As early as 1666 the Assembly of Maryland began the work of expediting intercommunication between the different parts of the colony, and for this purpose passed an act for "marking highways and making the heads of rivers, creeks, branches, and swamps passable for horse and foot;"

and in 1704 the width of roads was established at twenty feet, and provision was made for marking their route by notching trees and branding them with marking-irons; and in 1774, Isaac Griest, Benjamin Griffith, Jesse Hollingsworth, and others were appointed commissioners to direct the expenditure of nearly eleven thousand dollars to construct the three great roads leading to Baltimore. The Frederick, Reisterstown, and York roads were laid out in 1787.

The inhabitants about the Monocacy River and to the northward of the Blue Ridge petitioned, May 14, 1739, that a road be cleared through the country to Annapolis, to enable them to bring their grain and other commodities to market. The petition was laid over until the next session.

On the 1st of September, 1796, a number of the citizens of Elizabeth Town (Hagerstown) met at the court-house to discuss the utility of a turnpike road to the seaboard. Thomas Sprigg was appointed chairman of the meeting, and resolutions were unanimously passed to the effect that while agricultural prosperity depends on good markets and the best prices for the produce of the land, the interests of the citizens demand that every possible avenue of communication with the seaport towns, by land or by water, be opened, and that intercourse with them should be as cheap, easy, and convenient as possible. The resolutions further declared that it was very much within the power, disposition, and means of those present to provide such a road to Baltimore Town as would enable the farmers to make use of that season of the year in which they were unable to work upon their farms for the transportation of their produce to market. After calling attention to the advantages of the road to the State of Maryland, to the counties through which it was proposed to have it pass, and especially to Washington and Allegany Counties, the furthest removed from the seaboard, the resolutions proposed an address to the Washington County delegates in the Assembly, requesting them to use their efforts in obtaining a charter for the constructing of a turnpike road from Baltimore Town to Elizabeth Town and Williamsport, giving to Washington County the right to assume one-eighth of the whole expense, and to Allegany County a specified portion, provided this privilege was availed of within two months after the opening of the subscription-books. It was also determined that if the law should provide for only one commissioner from each county to lay out the road, that Gen. Heister was the choice of the convention; but if more than one was provided for, that the delegates should themselves appoint the other or others. Elie Williams, William Clagett, Samuel Ringgold, Daniel Hughes, Nathaniel Rochester, and Adam Ott were appointed to form and present the address to the delegates in the Assembly, and Cephas Beall, Robert Hughes, Abraham Woning, Jacob Schnebly, James Kendal, Benjamin Clagett, George Price, Jacob Myers, John Clagett, and Dr. Henry Schnebly to open petitions for signature by the citizens of Washington County, to be presented by their delegates to the Assembly of Maryland. The committee having in charge the address to the Washington County delegates on December 2d submitted the proceedings and resolutions of the convention as directed, and in addition thereto stated that it was the general sense of those present that it should be left to the Legislature to decide whether or not the road should fork on the upper side of the South Mountain, one fork to extend to Hagerstown and the other to Williamsport; if but one road should be thought necessary, then it was desired that the same should extend to Hagerstown, and thence to Williamsport.

An act was passed by the Assembly in March, 1797, to lay out a turnpike road from Baltimore "through Frederick Town in Frederick County to Elizabeth Town and Williamsport in Washington County." Another public meeting was held on the 19th of September of the same year to aid in the work, at which Nathaniel Rochester acted as chairman, and Elie Williams, Daniel Heister, Samuel Ringgold, Charles Carroll, and Nathaniel Rochester were appointed a committee to carry out the object of the meeting.

On the 8th of October, 1797, Samuel Newcomer, Christian Newcomer, John Snavely, Christian Martin, Henry Martin, and Jacob Martin gave notice that they intended to petition the next General Assembly to pass an act empowering the justices of the Levy Court of Washington County to make such alterations in the public road leading from Newcomer's mill to the South Mountain, and passing through the petitioners' land, as the justices may deem necessary for the public good. In the year 1801 the shares of stock issued for the purpose of building a bridge over the Eastern Branch of the Potomac were subscribed for immediately upon their being offered to the public. The company was authorized to call for forty-five thousand dollars, if necessary. Notice was given, Sept. 14, 1801, that certain of the inhabitants of Washington County intended petitioning the General Assembly for a law to remedy the errors in the returns of the commissioners in laying out and straightening the road from Christian Newcomer's mill to the top of South Mountain towards Frederick Town, and to authorize the taking of the best ground on said road and going up said mountain. The Westminster and Hagerstown turnpike road was the first pike projected in Washington County, and formed part of the line of the grand national road. It was built in 1812–16, the managers being John Welty, Walter Boyd, Robert Hughes, and William Gabby.

John Scott was treasurer of this company in 1814, and it was then proposed to commence work at the foot of South Mountain, on the west side, provided sufficient subscriptions could be obtained in Washington County to build five miles of the road.

In 1805 the Baltimore and Frederick Town Turnpike Company was incorporated, and in 1815 it was empowered to extend its road from Boonsboro' as the beginning of the Cumberland turnpike road. In 1813 the presidents and directors for the time being of the several incorporated banks in the city of Baltimore, of the Hagerstown Bank, of the Conococheague Bank, and the Cumberland Bank of Allegany were incorporated as the president, managers, and company of the Cumberland turnpike road. In 1821 the presidents and directors of the banks in Baltimore, except the City Bank, and the president and directors of the Hagerstown Bank were incorporated as the president, managers, and company of the Boonsboro' Turnpike Company.

The Baltimore, Liberty and Hagerstown turnpike road was chartered during the winter of 1815–16. The commissioners of Washington County appointed to receive subscriptions to the stock were Henry Lewis, Martin Kershner, Richard Ragan, Wm. Heyser, John Witmer, and Daniel Hughes, Jr.

From 1816 to 1825 a fever for turnpike companies seems to have raged. They were mostly stock companies, authorized by special acts of the State.

In 1817, John Kennedy, Jacob Zeller, Upton Lawrence, O. H. Williams, David Schnebly, Henry Witmer, William Heyser, Alexander Neill, and Henry Lewis were appointed commissioners to receive subscriptions to the stock of the Hagerstown and Conococheague Turnpike Company. In the same year John Davis, who had a store at the time at Hancock, contracted to construct the turnpike road from the Big Conococheague to Cumberland.

On the 27th of January, 1818, the Hagerstown and Conococheague Turnpike Board entered into a contract with Messrs. Kincaid, McKinlay, and Ramsay for turnpiking the whole of their road from the court-house in Hagerstown to the Conococheague Creek, to the point near Witmer's where the Cumberland turnpike road, then in course of construction, commenced.

The road, according to the contract, was to be completed by the 1st of January, 1820, in a style not inferior to the United States road west of Cumberland.

The board also contracted for a first-class stone bridge across the Conococheague, two hundred and ten feet long, including abutments and wing-walls. This bridge was intended to connect the road with the Great Western turnpike, thus bringing the latter down to Hagerstown, where it intersects with the Westminster and Hagerstown and the Baltimore and Frederick turnpike roads. The completion of the Westminster and Hagerstown road to Hagerstown lessened the distance from Baltimore to that town four miles.

The turnpike from the west side of Conococheague to Cumberland was located in 1818, and completed a few years later. This road, together with the United States road, furnished a turnpike road from Wheeling to Baltimore (with the exception of eleven miles between Hagerstown and Boonsboro'), two hundred and eighty-two miles long, one hundred and twenty-seven of which were free of tolls.

About this time the Legislature of Pennsylvania passed an act constituting a company whose purpose it was to open a turnpike road from Gettysburg to the division line between the States, thence to connect with a road to be constructed in Maryland, which, when completed, would furnish a direct turnpike communication between Philadelphia and Wheeling *via* Hagerstown, a distance of three hundred and thirty-three miles.

The subscription books of the Gettysburg and Hagerstown Turnpike Company were opened on the 21st of April, 1828, and the following commissioners were appointed to receive subscriptions: John Herch, Sr., Bernhart Gilbert, Andrew Marshall, James McKesson, William McMillan, Lewis Ripple, and Alexander Gordon.

Messrs. Thomas Cresap, Michael Cresap, James Wood, Jonathan Hagar, John Swan, James Caldwell, John Caldwell, and Richard Yeates were in 1773 appointed managers of a lottery to raise thirteen hundred and fifty dollars for repairing the road from Connoltoway to the Winding Ridge. There were three thousand tickets at two dollars each, and ten hundred and forty prizes.

A proclamation was issued by Governor J. H. Stone, Sept. 22, 1797, offering a reward of five hundred dollars for the arrest and conviction of any one committing highway robbery.

The following notice was issued on the 28th of February, 1799:

"All persons who may for the time to come have occasion to pass flour or other articles at the toll-places of the Potomac Company are required to pay the tolls fixed by law before the same shall be allowed to pass; it being understood that at Watts' Branch and the Great Falls tolls will not be exacted when the above-mentioned articles are deposited in the Company's stores, until they are taken therefrom."

This notice was signed by James Keith, president, and by John Mason and Isaac McPherson, directors.

Thomas Kennedy informs the public, Feb. 27, 1799, that the tolls leviable at the mouth of the Conococheague will continue to be received by him.

Pursuant to public notice a number of the citizens of Hagerstown and Funkstown convened at the Town Hall in Hagerstown on Saturday, the 3d of November, 1827, for the purpose of making arrangements for planting trees along the sides of the turnpike road between the two towns.

Frederick Grosh having been called to the chair and William D. Bell appointed secretary, the following resolution was offered and unanimously adopted:

"*Resolved*, That Dr. C. Boerstler, Frederick Grosh, H. Shafer, J. D. Keifer, Elias Davis, John Kennedy, Daniel Heister, John Wagoner, Samuel Steele, and William D. Bell, be and they are hereby appointed a committee with full power to make every arrangement necessary to carry into effect the desirable objects of this meeting, and that they be requested to obtain the consent of the landholders and such pecuniary aid as may be requisite from all persons disposed to afford it.

"FREDERICK GROSH, *Chairman*.
"WILLIAM D. BELL, *Secretary*."

The Hagerstown and Sharpsburg turnpike was finished about the year 1860, at a cost of twenty-six thousand dollars, or two thousand dollars a mile. Before the building of the pike it cost the county two hundred and forty dollars per annum to repair the mud road, yet the county commissioners were reluctant to subscribe to the stock of the company, fearing that it would not pay. Three thousand five hundred dollars were, however, subscribed, and the dividends received by the county from 1860 to 1880 on this amount of stock aggregated four thousand one hundred and forty-seven dollars.

In 1822 steps were taken by certain gentlemen to ascertain the proper location for the turnpike road from Hagerstown to Boonsboro'. The construction of this road was of importance to those interested in the Cumberland or Bank road, as its completion materially increased the value of the Bank road, in which the banks of Baltimore, the Hagerstown Bank, the Conococheague Bank, and the Cumberland Bank had together invested $486,170.71.

The Westminster and Hagerstown turnpike, *via* Herman's Gap, was incorporated by an act of the Legislature, Jan. 10, 1810, and Charles Carroll, Upton Lawrence, William Heyser, William Downey, and Robert Hughes were named as commissioners to receive subscriptions for the road in Washington County. A citizen of the county, writing March 21, 1810, said, "Let this road be once completed to Hagerstown and a good, common, well-graded road be extended thence through Hancock Town to Fort Cumberland to meet the Great Western road, now making by Congress from Cumberland to Wheeling, and through the State of Ohio, and then Hagerstown will become most certainly the thoroughfare for the whole of the Western wagons and travelers, and will without doubt become one of the very first and most flourishing inland towns in Maryland, or perhaps in the United States."

In 1821 the road from Hagerstown to Boonsboro' was the only portion of the distance from Baltimore to Wheeling that was not turnpiked, and in winter the stages were generally from five to seven hours passing over this space of ten miles.

Two stone bridges over Antietam Creek, one at John Shafer's mill, and another at or near Frederick Ziegler's ford on the road leading from Hagerstown through Nicholson's Gap to Gettysburg, were built by James Lloyd in 1824; and one over the same creek, on the road leading from Boonsboro' to Sharpsburg, at Mumma's mill, was erected by Mr. Silas Harry in the same year. A stone bridge was also built by Jabez Kenney over Beaver Creek, on the road leading from Boonsboro' to Williamsport, during the year 1824.

In 1881 the officers of the Hagerstown and Conococheague Turnpike Company were James W. Troupe, president; Joseph Kausler, secretary and treasurer; Directors, Joseph B. Loose, Frederick Fechtig, D. C. Hammond, P. H. Wingert, and Joseph Kausler.

In 1819 the roads in Washington County were the following:

District No. 1.—From Henry Keedy's to the top of South Mountain by Thomas Crampton's; from the forks of the road near Hogg's old place to Mackey's stone mill on the Potomac River; from the maple swamp until it intersects the main road leading by Mumma's mill to Fox's Gap; and from Harper's Ferry to the Frederick County line. Distance, twenty miles; Daniel Brown, supervisor.

No. 2.—From the turnpike at Mumma's mill to the Frederick County line at Fox's Gap; from George Geedy's store to Antietam bridge at Hess' mill. Distance, nine miles; John Shuey, supervisor.

No. 3.—From Swearingen's ferry to Sharpsburg. Distance, three miles; John Blackford, supervisor.

No. 4.—From Sharpsburg to the cross-roads at Stover's; and from the cross-roads at Carey's to Smith's bridge on Antietam Creek. Distance, eleven miles; Christian Middlekauff, supervisor.

No. 5.—From Hagerstown to Peter Newcomer's mill on Little

Beaver Creek. Distance, seven miles; Jacob Knode, Jr., supervisor.

No. 6.—From Newcomer's mill on Little Beaver Creek to Boonsboro'. Distance, four miles; Samuel Hager, supervisor.

No. 7.—From the cross-roads at Stover's, by Booth's mill, to where the road from John Shafer's mill intersects the Boonsboro' road. Distance, three and a half miles; William Booth, supervisor.

No. 8.—From the lower end of Samuel Ringgold's lane on the Williamsport road, by John Shafer's mill, until it intersects the aforesaid road, and from thence to Boonsboro'; from John Shafer's mill to Petry's school-house. Distance, seven miles; John Shafer, supervisor.

No. 9.—From E. G. Williams' lane near Williamsport to the cross-roads at Carey's. Distance, seven miles; Daniel Rench, supervisor.

No. 10.—From Williamsport to the cross-roads at Stover's. Distance, five miles; Thomas Kennedy, supervisor.

No. 11.—From the manor cross-roads to the corner of Christley Rohrer's fence, where it intersects the road from Hagerstown to Sharpsburg. Distance, four miles; John Dusing, supervisor.

No. 12.—From Williamsport to Hagerstown until it intersects the Sharpsburg road; and from Williamsport to Miller's mill on the Conococheague. Distance, eight miles; Jacob Hershey, supervisor.

No. 13.—From the cross-roads at Stover's to Wise's smithshop at the south end of Potomac Street, in Hagerstown. Distance, six miles; Frisby Tilghman, supervisor.

No. 14.—All the streets in Williamsport, including the road to the ferry; Joseph Hollman, supervisor.

No. 15.—From the Frederick County line at Orr's Gap to Funk's mill on Beaver Creek. Distance, four miles; Samuel Funk, supervisor.

No. 16.—From Hagerstown to the Antietam bridge on the Charlton's Gap road. Distance, two miles; David Middlekauff, supervisor.

No. 17.—From Cavetown to the Frederick County line. Distance, four miles; Conrad Mentzer, supervisor.

No. 18.—From Hagerstown to Antietam Creek below Lantz' mill on the Nicholson Gap road. Distance, six miles; Joseph Miller, supervisor.

No. 19.—From Antietam Creek below Lentz' mill to the Pennsylvania line. Distance, six miles; George Shiefs, supervisor.

No. 20.—From the Pennsylvania line near Peter Baker's until it intersects the Charlton's Gap road near Robert Hughes'. Distance, seven miles; John Mentzer, supervisor.

No. 21.—From Hagerstown, by David Schnebly's, to the Pennsylvania line. Distance, six miles; Henry Schnebly, supervisor.

No. 22.—From the forks of the road near Hagerstown, on the Mercersburg road, until it intersects the Greencastle road. Distance, five miles; Daniel Reichard, supervisor.

No. 23.—From the Greencastle road to the Pennsylvania line, in the direction of Mercersburg. Distance, three miles; Josiah Price, supervisor.

No. 24.—From the forks of the road near Upton Lawrence's plantation, on the broad fording road, to John Long's crossroads. Distance, 4 miles; Henry Stitzell, supervisor.

No. 25.—From Miller's mill on the Conococheague, by Kershner's cross-roads, near the turnpike, until it intersects the roads at Long's from Miller's mill to Ashford's, and from the forks of the Williamsport road near Wolgamott's, by Huffer's mill, until it intersects the road to the Broad Ford. Distance, six miles; Henry Garlock, supervisor.

No. 26.—From the Broad Ford on Conococheague Creek, by Nicholas Krig's, to the Pennsylvania line. Distance, 4 miles; Nicholas Krig, supervisor.

No. 27.—From the forks of the road at Henry Ford's to Jacques' furnace. Distance, five miles; James D. Moore, supervisor.

No. 28.—From Williamsport until it intersects the road from Hagerstown to Hancock by the Big Spring; from Ash's ford on the Conococheague to Lick Run, thence until it intersects the Williamsport road near Baltzer Moudy's old place. Distance, six miles; John McClain, supervisor.

No. 29.—From Jacques' furnace to the turnpike road near Licking Creek. Distance, five miles; John O. Moore, supervisor.

No. 30.—From the Big Tonoloway, by Henry Davis' mill, to the Pennsylvania line, and from Hancock Town, by Jeremiah Stillwell's, to the Pennsylvania line near Samuel Graves'. Distance, nine miles; John Ressley, supervisor.

No. 31.—From Little Tonoloway to Sideling Hill Creek, near Goulding's. Distance, ten miles.

No. 32.—From near Christian Shepherd's saw-mill, by George Rizer's, to Sideling Hill Creek. Distance, three miles.

No. 33.—From the Pennsylvania line on the Little Cove road, near Elie Williams' saw-mill, until it intersects the main road leading from Hagerstown to Cumberland, near Jacques' furnace. Distance, eight miles; Henry Bragonier, supervisor.

No. 34.—From the forks of the road near the Widow Robey's, by Wolgamot's mill, until it intersects the Sharpsburg road, and from thence until it intersects the Williamsport road near Booth's mill. Distance, three miles; Andrew Hogmire, supervisor.

No. 35.—From the east end of Washington Street, in Hagerstown, by Stull's old mill, to Funk's mill on Beaver Creek; from Funkstown till it intersects a road near David Hershey's. Distance, five miles; David Hershey, supervisor.

No. 36.—From Jonathan Street, in Hagerstown, to the Williamsport road. Henry Dillman, supervisor.

No. 37.—The streets of Hagerstown. Commissioners of Hagerstown, supervisors.

No. 39.—From the new bridge on the Charlton's Gap road to Cavetown. Distance, five miles; Levi Housely, supervisor.

No. 40.—From the north end of Jonathan Street, Hagerstown, to the Pennsylvania line. Distance, five miles; David Brumbaugh, supervisor.

No. 41.—From Henry Snyder's mill to the turnpike road near Summer's house. Distance, three miles.

No. 42.—From the Pennsylvania line, in Jacob Sears' field, where the new road from Mercersburg to that point ends, to McCoy's ferry on the Potomac River. Jonathan Nesbitt, supervisor.

No. 43.—From near Nicholas Parrott's, by Leopard's, to Tries'. Distance, ten miles; Paul Summers, supervisor.

No. 44.—Streets of Sharpsburg. Jacob Miller, supervisor.

No. 45.—From the west end of Salisbury Street, in Williamsport, to the Potomac River. Peter Ardinger, supervisor.

No. 46.—From Funkstown to David Hershey's. Jacob Knode, supervisor.

No. 47.—From John Long's to the new bridge on the Conococheague near Union Mills; from thence until it intersects the old road near Henry Ridenour's, and from Long's road to the Pennsylvania line. Jacob Zeller, supervisor.

No. 48.—From the old Harman's Gap road near Robert Hughes' to the top of the mountain at the Frederick County line, where it meets a public road leading through Frederick County to Frederick Town. Distance, one and a half miles; Jacob Ridenour, Jr., supervisor.

No. 49.—From the Opecken road near Nicholas Swingley's, by Clagett's mill, to intersect the road from Funkstown to Boonsboro'. Distance, four miles: David Clagett, supervisor.

No. 50.—From Sharpsburg to Antietam Forge. Distance, three miles; Jacob Miller, supervisor.

No. 51.—From the Broad Ford until it intersects the road from Hagerstown to Hancock, near Jacques' furnace. Distance, six miles; Daniel Gehr, Jr., supervisor.

Laws Passed by the Legislature for the Laying Out of Roads in Washington County.—In 1801–2 a road was authorized to be opened from Hancock-town, by Tong's mill, to intersect a road from Cumberland, in Allegany County, to Sidling Hill Creek. In 1801 a road from Elizabeth-town by Barrett's Ford to the Pennsylvania line. In 1801 part of a road from Turner's Gap to Williamsport to be reviewed. In 1801 the road by Bainbridge's and Newcomer's mill to Elizabeth-town to be reviewed and laid out. In 1801 a road to be laid out from Williamsport to the Pennsylvania line. In 1801 an act respecting a road from Elizabeth-town (Hagerstown) to the Pennsylvania line, in Nicholson's Gap. In 1803 the Levy Court authorized to change the direction of the road from Hagerstown towards Hancock-town. In 1803 a road to be opened from Bennett's ferry to intersect the old road from Hancock-town to Fort Cumberland. In 1804 a company incorporated for making a turnpike road from Baltimore, etc., to Boonsboro'. In 1804 the road to be extended to Hagerstown and Williamsport. In 1806 the direction of the road from Ashe's ford on Conococheague Creek to the intersection thereof with the main road from Hagerstown, etc., to be altered.

In 1806–7 a road to be laid out from the State line (where a road from Greencastle joins the same) to intersect the main road from Hagerstown to Baltimore through Charlton's Gap. In 1806 the road from Hancock-town to Cumberland to be laid out and improved. In 1809–11 the road from Baltimore through Frederick-town, etc., to Boonsboro' confirmed. In 1809 the Levy Court authorized to open a road to intersect a road from Hagerstown to Williamsport. In 1809 a road to be laid off from Boonsboro' to intersect the Sharpsburg road, and to Blackford's ferry on the Potomac. In 1812–13–16 a company incorporated to make a turnpike road from Westminster to Fredericktown, through Harman's Gap to Hagerstown. In 1809 a road to be opened from Little Tonoloway Creek, at the ford near Hancock-town, to intersect the road from Bedford towards Hancock-town at the Pennsylvania line. In 1810 a road to be laid off from the Pennsylvania line on the Little Cave road, etc, to intersect the main road from Hagerstown to Cumberland, near Jacques' old furnace. In 1810 the act of 1809, to clear and make public a road in Washington County, repealed. In 1810 the road from Hagerstown to Hancock-town to be straightened. In 1811–12 a road to be laid out from Snider's mill to intersect the turnpike road between the foot of the mountain and Boonsboro'. In 1811 a road to be laid off from a point on the road from Hagerstown to Sharpsburg, as therein directed, to intersect the road to Baltimore, etc. In 1811 the road from Boonsboro' to Funkstown to be straightened, etc. In 1811 a road to be laid out from the Charlton's Gap road to the divisional line between Frederick and Washington Counties. In 1812 a road to be laid out from Shairk's mill to intersect the main road from Hagerstown to Hancock-town. From McShain's, or Taylor's ferry on the Potomac, or Crampton's Gap on the South Mountain. In 1812 the road from Hancock to Cumberland, as located by Williams and Moore, declared to be a public road. In 1813 the old road from Hagerstown to Mercersburg, etc., to be straightened and amended.

In 1814 a road to be laid out from the Pennsylvania line, where the new road from Mercersburg ends, and thence to the Potomac River. In 1814 a company incorporated to make a turnpike road from Boonsboro' to Swearingen's ferry on the Potomac. In 1815 a road to be laid out from Jonathan Street, in Hagerstown, towards Greencastle, as far as the Pennsylvania line. In 1815 a company incorporated to make a turnpike road from Baltimore through Liberty-town to Hagerstown.

In 1815 the Washington and Frederick Turnpike Company incorporated. In 1815 a road to be laid out from the farm of N. Parrott, near Hancock-town, to intersect the old public road near W. Sedburn's. In 1816 a company incorporated to make a turnpike road from Hagerstown to intersect the Cumberland turnpike road on the west bank of the Conococheague. In 1817 companies incorporated to make a turnpike road through Montgomery County to Crampton's Gap in South Mountain and thence to Williamsburg. In 1817 a company incorporated to make a turnpike road from Boonsboro', through Williamsport, to intersect the road then making from Cumberland to the west bank of the Conococheague. In 1818 a company incorporated to make a turnpike road from the west bank of the Conococheague Creek at Williamsport to intersect the Cumberland turnpike road at or near Stone Quarry Ridge. In 1818 a company incorporated to make a turnpike road from Hagerstown to intersect the turnpike road leading from Gettysburg through Nicholson's Gap to the Pennsylvania line. In 1818 a company incorporated for making a turnpike road from Hagerstown to Boonsborough.

In 1821 a company incorporated to make a turnpike from Boonsborough to Hagerstown. In 1825 alteration authorized to be made in the location of the road from Sharpsburg to Hagerstown.

In 1849 an extension of Adams' Express Company's services from Baltimore through Frederick and the intervening towns to Hagerstown was effected by E. M. Mealey & Co.

Early Stage-Lines.—In 1781, Gabriel Peterson Vanhorn ran his "carriage" from Daniel Grant's

THE FOUNTAIN INN, BALTIMORE.

Fountain Inn, Market Space, Baltimore, at eight o'clock, to Capt. Phillips', "where the passengers may dine," and thence to Harford Town, where they remained overnight, and proceeded next morning to the Susquehanna for breakfast at Capt. Twining's, meeting there the stage from Philadelphia and exchanging passengers, returning by same route to Baltimore, "fare, four dollars specie, and the like sum for one hundred and fifty weight of baggage." Nathaniel Twining and Gershon Johnson, of Philadelphia, ran the stages connecting with Vanhorn's line, and assured the passenger leaving "Baltimore on Monday morning of completing his journey to Elizabeth Town by Friday at two o'clock." Letters were carried by this line,—for "every letter one-eighth of a hard dollar to be paid by the person sending the letter."

A bi-weekly line of stage-coaches ran in 1783 between Baltimore and Frederick Town, William Davey and Richard Shoebels, proprietors, "stopping for the entertainment of passengers at Mr. Hobbs', Mr. Simpson's, and Mr. Ricketts', where good fare may be had for fifteen shillings."

A weekly passenger stage from Elizabeth Town to Baltimore was announced Aug. 1, 1797. Leaving Elizabeth Town on Tuesdays, and passing through Frederick Town and New Market, it arrived in Baltimore on Wednesdays. After remaining there one day, it returned to Elizabeth Town by the same route, arriving on Saturdays.

John Ragan in 1797 ran a stage three times a week from Baltimore to Hagerstown.

An announcement dated Dec. 18, 1797, stated that proposals for carrying the public mails would be received at the General Post-office on the following routes: From Yorktown (now York, Pa.), by Hanover, Petersburg, Taneytown, and Frederick Town, to Leesburg, Va., once a week.

Leaving Yorktown on Monday morning at eight o'clock, the stage arrived at Frederick Town at five o'clock P.M. on the following day, and at Leesburg on Wednesday at two o'clock P.M. Returning, it left Leesburg at noon on Friday, and arrived at Yorktown at six o'clock P.M. on Sunday.

From Yorktown, Pa., by Abbottstown, Gettysburg, Fairfield, Elizabeth Town, Williamsport, Martinsburg, Winchester, Stevensburg, and Strasburg, to Woodstock once a week.

The stage on this line left Yorktown at noon on Sunday, and arrived at Martinsburg at eleven o'clock A.M. on Tuesday. After an hour's pause the journey to Woodstock was resumed, and was finished on Wednesday at six o'clock P.M. Returning, the stage left Woodstock at six o'clock A.M. on Thursday, arriving at Martinsburg on Friday at eleven o'clock A.M., and in Yorktown at the same hour on Sunday.

From Baltimore, by Frederick Town, Elizabeth Town, Greencastle, and Chambersburg, to Shippensburg, Pa., once a week.

The stage left Baltimore on Friday at eleven o'clock A.M., and arrived at Frederick Town at ten o'clock on Saturday morning, at Elizabeth Town in the evening of the same day, and at Shippensburg on Monday at seven o'clock P.M. Returning, it left Shippensburg on Tuesday morning at nine o'clock, arriving in Elizabeth Town in the evening at eight o'clock, in Frederick Town the next day at noon, and in Baltimore at five o'clock P.M. on Thursday.

From Elizabeth Town, by Hancock and Old Town, to Cumberland once a week.

Leaving Cumberland at six o'clock on Saturday morning, the stage arrived at Elizabeth Town on Monday morning at eight o'clock, and arriving in Cumberland on the return trip at six o'clock P.M. on Tuesday.

Basil Brooke & Co. announced to the public on the 24th of May, 1798, that they had commenced running a stage for the accommodation of passengers on the road leading from Hagerstown to Baltimore. The stage left Hagerstown on Tuesdays, and passing through Middletown, Frederick Town, and Liberty Town, arrived in Baltimore on Wednesdays. Remaining there until Friday morning, it then started on the return trip, pursuing the same route, and arriving in Hagerstown on Saturdays.

The same parties also announced that hack-stages from Hagerstown to Bath and from Liberty Town to the Sulphur Springs, in Frederick County, could be had during the season.

An announcement is made by Henry Winemiller, May 16, 1799, that the Frederick and Georgetown mail-stage starts from the house of Mrs. Kimball every Thursday morning at three o'clock, and arrives at Georgetown the evening of the same day, stopping at the Union tavern. Starting the next morning at three o'clock, it returned to Frederick Town, arriving there in the evening.

The stage of Messrs. Scott & Barrick also started from Mrs. Kimball's house, leaving on Saturday morning at five o'clock, and arriving at Lancaster on Sunday evening, where it stopped at Mrs. Ferree's tavern. The return trip was commenced at five o'clock on Tuesday morning, Frederick being reached on Wednesday morning.

The stage of Messrs. Peck & Coale started at five o'clock every Tuesday from Mr. Peck's, in Hagerstown, arriving at Frederick Town at noon. It there stopped at Maj. Henry Butler's tavern, leaving which it arrived at Liberty Town the same evening. The stopping-place in this town was Mr. Orndorff's tavern, whence it started on Wednesday morning at five o'clock, and arrived in Baltimore in the evening of the same day. Mr. Evans' tavern was the stopping-place in Baltimore, and there the stage remained until Friday morning at five o'clock, when it started to return by the same route, arriving at Frederick Saturday morning, and reaching Hagerstown the same evening. The announcement of these lines concludes with statements to the effect that passengers going to Georgetown, York, Lancaster, Philadelphia, Baltimore, or Hagerstown may, by taking the Georgetown stage on any one of these routes, arrive at his destination without longer detention on the road than is necessary to feed and change horses. The fares charged were three dollars from Georgetown to Frederick, four dollars and a half from Frederick to Lancaster, fourteen pounds of baggage being allowed to be carried by each passenger free, and one hundred pounds weight being considered equivalent to an additional passenger and charged for accordingly. It was further announced that the public-houses on these roads were excellent, and the charges as reasonable as any on the continent.

H. Peck announced on the 25th of July, 1799, that he would run a hack-stage during the eusuing season for the accommodation of passengers going to Bath or elsewhere, furnishing "a good comfortable stage, active horses, and steady, sober, and attentive drivers," all at reasonable prices.

On the same day John Home announces that his hack-stage will run as usual to Bath, applications to be made to Mr. Henderson at the Fountain Inn, on the corner of the Public Square, near the court-house, in Hagerstown.

In 1801, Peter Orndorf ran a line of stages between Frederick and Hagerstown.

On June 2, 1802, George Griffinger informs the public that he continues to keep a good stage and horses, which may be had at the shortest notice and on the most reasonable terms by applying to his house or at Mr. Stoner's tavern, near the court-house.

In an announcement made June 9, 1802, Peter Orndorf informs the public that as many inconveniences have arisen from there being but one stage a week between Baltimore and Hagerstown, he has gone to a very considerable expense and trouble to arrange for running in future two stages a week. He announced that stages would leave the Indian Queen Stage-office, Baltimore, every Tuesday and Saturday at four o'clock A.M., and arrive in Frederick at six P.M., leaving there the next morning at four o'clock A.M., and arriving at Hagerstown at four P.M. Returning to Baltimore, the stages were to leave Hagerstown on Tuesdays and Saturdays at eight o'clock A.M., stopping at Frederick during the night, and arriving in Baltimore at six o'clock in the afternoon of the next day.

In 1803, Messrs. George Crissinger, of Hagerstown, and John Geyer, of Frederick Town, established a line of mail-stages from Hagerstown to Baltimore, which left Jonathan Hager's tavern, at the "Sign of the Ship," near the court-house, Hagerstown, every Tuesday and Saturday at ten o'clock A.M., and arrived at Mrs. Kimball's, Frederick, the evening of the same day, and at the Columbian Inn, Baltimore, the next afternoon at six o'clock. Returning, they left Baltimore on Tuesdays and Saturdays at four o'clock A.M., and stopping at Frederick during the night, arrived in Hagerstown the next evening. The fare charged on this line was two dollars to Frederick, and from Frederick to Baltimore, three dollars and a half.

George Crissinger further announces that he will, if necessary, run an additional stage on Thursday, arriving in Frederick in the evening, and returning to Hagerstown next day.

On the 29th of March, 1805, George Crissinger and Joseph Boyd informed the public that they had commenced running a line of mail-coaches from Frederick Town, *via* Middletown, Boonsboro', Hagerstown, and Greencastle, to Chambersburg twice every week to and from the above places.

Starting from Mrs. Kimball's every Tuesday and Saturday at five o'clock P.M., they arrived at Hagerstown the same night, stopping at the house of George Beltzhoover (late Ragan's), and leaving the next morning at four o'clock, they arrived at the house of Thomas Hetich, in Chambersburg, by eleven o'clock A.M.

They left Chambersburg on their return trips on Sundays and Wednesdays at one o'clock P.M., and reached Hagerstown at six P.M., and leaving Hagerstown on Tuesdays and Thursdays at six A.M., they arrived in Frederick Town by one P.M. This line met at Frederick Town Mr. Scott's line from Philadelphia *via* Lancaster, Columbia, York, Hanover, and Petersburg, and also Mr. Winemiller's from Washingtan City *via* Georgetown, Montgomery Court-house, and Clarkesburg, and Mr. Orndorff's from Baltimore *via* New Market. At Chambersburg it met the line of Mr. Tomlinson & Co. from Philadelphia *via* Lancaster, Elizabeth Town, Middletown, Harrisburg, Carlisle, and Shippensburg; also theirs from Pittsburgh *via* Greensburg, Somerset, Bedford, and McConnellstown. The fare charged from Frederick Town to Hagerstown was two dollars, and thence to Chambersburg two dollars additional, with the usual allowance for baggage. A line of stages from Baltimore to Pittsburgh and Wheeling, *via* Frederick Town, Hagerstown, Cumberland, and Brownsville, commenced running Aug. 1, 1818; starting from Gadsby's Hotel, in Baltimore, every Sunday, Tuesday, and Thursday, it arrived at Hagerstown at eight o'clock P.M. same day; left Hagerstown Mondays, Wednesdays, and Fridays at three o'clock A.M., arriving at Pratt's tavern same evening at six P.M.; left Pratt's Tuesdays, Thursdays, and Saturdays at two A.M., and arrived at Uniontown, Pa., at nine P.M., leaving there at four A.M., and arriving at Pittsburgh and West Alexandria the same evening; thence at four A.M., arriving in Wheeling at seven A.M., through in four days.

A new line of post-coaches from Gettysburg to Hagerstown, for the accommodation of passengers from Philadelphia to Wheeling or Pittsburgh, was started in 1821, Stockton & Stokes being the proprietors.

On the 2d of April, 1822, it was announced that the Hagerstown and Gettysburg line of stages had recommenced running three times a week, connecting with the Philadelphia mail line at Gettysburg. The journey from Wheeling to Philadelphia, a distance of three hundred and forty-six miles, was accomplished in little more than four days, and the fare charged was twelve dollars.

The Hagerstown and Boonsboro' Turnpike Company was incorporated by the Legislature during the session of 1822–23.

In 1823 a new line was started by A. Lindsay between Hagerstown and McConnellsburg, Pittsburgh, Chambersburg, Bedford, and Greensburg. Travelers by these routes were conveyed from Pittsburgh to Baltimore or Washington in three days.

The following announcement is dated March 28, 1823: "The United States Mail Stage for Wheeling *via* Frederick Town, Hagerstown, Cumberland, etc., leaves the office, adjoining Barnum's Hotel, on Sundays, Tuesdays, and Thursdays, at four o'clock A.M., arriving at Wheeling in three and a half days. where boats are always in readiness to convey passengers down the river. On the 1st of April next an accommodation stage will leave the same place for Frederick Town and Hagerstown on Mondays, Wednesdays, and Fridays at four o'clock A.M., dining at Frederick Town, and lodging at Hagerstown, affording a conveyance to the two latter places six days in the week." An announcement dated Feb. 7, 1826, said, "The extra mail or accommodation line leaves Baltimore on Mondays, Wednesdays, and Fridays at four o'clock in the morning, and reaches Wheeling on the fourth afternoon, except the Friday stage, which arrives there on the fifth day after leaving Baltimore. The old mail line runs as usual on Sundays, Tuesdays, and Thursdays, going through in three and a quarter days." A line to run only during the day (except at special instance of the passengers) is also announced to commence running on the following 1st of March, making the trip to Wheeling in five and a half days. The fares charged were, from Baltimore to Hagerstown, $5.50; from Hagerstown to Cumberland, $5.00; from Cumberland to Uniontown, $4.00; from Uniontown to Wheeling, $4.25; making the total charge for the trip from Baltimore to Wheeling, $18.75. To Emmittsburg, *via* Union and Taneytown, a bi-weekly line was run in 1826, and in the same year a line to Chambersburg was running every Thursday and Saturday.

A new line of stages commenced running Jan. 1, 1827, between Boonsboro', Md., and Winchester, Va., by way of Shepherdstown, Martinsburg, etc., Mr. Humrickhouse, of Hagerstown, being part contractor.

The Hagerstown and Winchester mail line, *via* Williamsport, Falling Waters, Martinsburg, and Bucketstown, was run by Maxwell & Ringer in 1839, leaving Hagerstown on Tuesdays, Thursdays, and Saturdays, and leaving Winchester on Mondays, Wednesdays, and Fridays.

The Good Intent and Pilot lines to Pittsburgh and Wheeling and Cincinnati in 1838 ran *daily*, with United States mail.

In their "day and generation" these were the fast lines of our fathers, but they have passed away forever, leaving behind them only their advertisements for travelers to show who were the men of energy and enterprise that preceded the "railway kings" of the present time.

Mails.—The first protection to public and private letters in Maryland was given by an act of Assembly passed at the session of 1707, by which the opening of letters by unauthorized persons was made a penal offense.

Letters at that time were generally, in the absence of post-roads and post-offices, deposited in public-houses, to be sent by the first conveyance of which the landlord could avail. There was very little correspondence at that time between the towns along the coast, as most of the trade was direct with England from each port. Letters on business, sometimes containing bills of exchange on Liverpool and London merchants, were left at the public-houses, and forwarded by the hands of the captains of vessels sailing from the particular port to England, but were accessible, as well as the answers, to any designing person about the inn. In this way protests to bills of exchange were frequently intercepted, and it became necessary to protect such communications by law. This act was repealed and re-enacted at the session of the Assembly in 1713; the protecting clauses and penalties for breaking open letters by unauthorized persons were re-enacted, and additional clauses enacted making it the duty of the sheriff of each county to convey all public letters to their destination within his county, but if beyond, to the sheriff of the next county on the route. The sheriff of each county was allowed for this service so many pounds of tobacco annually.

The first regular post-office established in the colonies was by an act of the Parliament of England passed in 1710. By its provisions a general post-office was established in North America and the West Indies, and in 1717 a settled post was established from Virginia to Maryland.

It was not until 1753 that the practice of delivering letters by the penny post or letter-carrier and of advertising letters on hand commenced. Newspapers were carried by mail free of charge until 1758, when, by reason of their great increase, they were charged with postage at the rate of ninepence each year for fifty miles, and one shilling and sixpence for one hundred miles.

At this time the postal routes were few and far between, and did not afford sufficient facilities for the convenience of the public. Gentlemen of a town or a neighborhood were in the habit of making up a purse to supply a regular mail-rider, generally going to the single post-office of the province, as in Maryland to Annapolis, and depositing all letters they were intrusted with, and on their return bringing letters and papers to remote correspondents and subscribers. Stage-shallops were sometimes used between important places to carry passengers. The stage-shallop resembled a dug-out rigged upon wheels, at that time a very essential combination, as it often became necessary on these routes to cross streams that were not fordable and without a ferry.

The new post-rider between Frederick and Hagerstown made an announcement, Dec. 29, 1786, that he had made Mr. Steel's tavern, the "Sign of Gen. Hand," in Market Street (opposite Mr. William Stenson's), his stopping-place, where letters for and from those places would be received and carefully delivered.

The mails of Western Maryland, in March, 1792, were carried as follows: From Baltimore to Fredericktown, Sharpsburg, and Hagerstown, and thence to Chambersburg, once a week, the mail leaving Baltimore on Saturday at three o'clock in the afternoon, and arriving at Chambersburg the following Monday at seven in the evening, or on Tuesday at seven in the morning. Returning, it left Chambersburg on Wednesday morning at five o'clock, and arrived at Baltimore on Friday at four in the afternoon.

In 1815, William Kreps, postmaster, advertised for a letter-carrier. A daily mail for Washington City, Baltimore, and Wheeling was first made up at Hagerstown in May, 1822.

In June, 1869, the location of the Hagerstown Post-office was changed from the old stand on North Potomac Street to the new building erected by Postmaster Logan on West Franklin Street, north side, a short distance east of Jonathan. The building is one story high, is commodious, airy, light, and high-ceiled, and is sufficiently large to accommodate the business of the post-office for some years to come.

The following is a list of the postmasters of Hagerstown from the establishment of the office to the present time:

Oct 1, 1803, Nathaniel Rochester;[1] October, 1804, Jacob D. Dietrick; April, 1807, William Kreps; March 18, 1822, Daniel Schnebly (predecessor died); Aug. 23, 1826, Thomas Kennedy; July 8, 1827, O. H. W. Stull; Nov. 17, 1829, Howard Kennedy; April 5, 1838, Frederick Humrickhouse; Feb. 23, 1843, under Mr. Humrickhouse, the office became a Presidential appointment; March 2, 1847, Christopher Hilliard; June 21, 1849, George Updegraff; April 11, 1853, Samuel Ridenour; May 29, 1861, John Schleigh; April 21, 1869, William Logan; Sept. 5, 1878, Margaret Logan, who is the present incumbent.

Cumberland Valley Railroad extends a distance of seventy-four miles, from Hagerstown to Harrisburg, Pa., in one direction, and to Martinsburg, Va., in the other, only a small portion of the road being in Maryland. This road was chartered on the 2d of April, 1831. The work of construction was commenced in January, 1836, and the road was completed from Chambersburg to the Susquehanna River, opposite Harrisburg, in December, 1837, a distance of forty-nine miles. The company obtained leave, by an act of the Legislature approved Feb. 2, 1836, to construct a bridge over the Susquehanna, and to extend the road through Harrisburg three miles to the Pennsylvania Canal, and also to connect with the other roads centering in Harrisburg. That portion of the road extending from Chambersburg to Hagerstown was originally the Franklin Railroad, and was constructed under charters obtained from the Legislatures of Pennsylvania and Maryland in the year 1832. The road was built in 1838, and after passing through

[1] Col. Rochester was postmaster for years previous to 1803. He was appointed an associate judge of the Washington County Court in 1793, and his nephew, Robert Rochester, succeeded him as postmaster.

the hands of several owners, was finally transferred, in 1859, to the Cumberland Valley Railroad, by which it is now operated. The road was opened to Martinsburg in 1874. During a flood in the latter part of 1877 the Cumberland Valley Railroad bridge across the Potomac River was destroyed, the superstructure of wood, covered with tin, being entirely washed away. A ferry across the river was improvised, and trains were run as usual, the only interference with travel resulting from the disaster being an addition of thirty minutes to the regular time consumed in travel between Hagerstown and Martinsburg. The Cumberland Valley road is managed by the Pennsylvania Railroad Company.

Western Maryland Railroad.—Of all the railroads that centre at Baltimore, the Western Maryland was the last to be completed. Although projected in 1830, its trains did not enter the city on its own track till 1873. It is difficult for those who pass over the road to understand why its building was delayed so long. Fully fifty years ago the people of Baltimore were most anxious to establish communication by rail with the fertile and populous region which it traverses. The Baltimore and Ohio road would have been located upon this line if the engineers could have found a practicable route across the South Mountain. Railroad building was in its infancy when these explorations were made. After the Baltimore and Susquehanna Company (now the Northern Central) had completed eight miles of its main stem it turned to the west and built nine miles of road through the Green Spring Valley, with the intention of continuing the line to the Blue Ridge. The completed portion of this branch was opened for travel May 26, 1832. When work was resumed on the main stem, the western extension of the Green Spring branch was suspended, and nothing further was done for twenty years.

An act was passed May 27, 1852, incorporating the Baltimore, Carroll and Frederick Railroad Company. The corporators were George Brown, Robert M. Magraw, Zenus Barnum, William F. Johnson, Charles Painter, Richard Green, Richard Worthington, Nicholas Kelly, Edward Remington, Jacob Reese, John Fisher, Jacob Mathias, David Roop, Joshua Smith, J. Henry Hoppe, David H. Shriver, John Smith, Samuel Ecker, Joseph Moore, Reuben Haines, of W., Daniel P. Saylor, John Cover, Peregrine Fitzhugh, Joshua Motter, Robert Annan, David Rinehart, Jervis Spencer, Isaac Motter, and John Baker. This company was authorized to build a railroad to the "headwaters of the Monocacy River," with the option of beginning at Baltimore or at the terminus of the Green Spring branch of the Baltimore and Susquehanna road (Northern Central). In the following year the corporate name was changed to "The Western Maryland Railroad Company," and an act was passed at the same session of the Legislature authorizing the company to issue bonds to the amount of $1,000,000, and to extend the road to Hagerstown. Robert M. Magraw was the first president of the new company. Nothing was done for five or six years except that it was decided to begin building at the terminus of the Green Spring branch, and to use the main stem of the Northern Central Railway from Lake Roland to the city. The road was opened to Owings' Mills Aug. 11, 1859, and to Westminster June 15, 1861. One year afterwards trains began to run to Union Bridge, twelve miles beyond Westminster, and this place remained the terminus of the road until Jan. 9, 1871, when it was opened to Mechanicstown, fifty-nine miles from Baltimore.

The construction of the road on the west side of the Blue Ridge was begun in 1866. In that year the Legislature passed an act authorizing the county commissioners of Washington County to subscribe $150,000 to the capital stock of the Western Maryland Company, the money to be expended in grading the road from the western slope of the mountain to Hagerstown. The commissioners of Washington County subsequently indorsed the bonds of the Western Maryland Company to the amount of $300,000. There was some delay in getting over the mountain, and the eastern and western divisions were not united until June 6, 1872, when trains began to run to Hagerstown. The Williamsport "extension" and the "short line" from Baltimore to Owings' Mills were built simultaneously, and the road was opened to the Potomac River Dec. 17, 1873. After the completion of the direct line from Owings' Mills to Baltimore, the nine miles of track between the Green Spring Junction and Lake Roland reverted to the original owners, and this division is again operated as the Green Spring branch of the Northern Central Railway.

Baltimore City and Washington County furnished the greater portion of the capital used in building the Western Maryland Railroad, and the board of directors and the officers of the company were subject to the mutations of municipal politics. A great deal of money was wasted, and although the route presented no extraordinary difficulties, the cost of construction per mile far exceeded that of any other railroad in Maryland. The funded debt amounts to $4,205,250, or something more than $48,000 for every mile of the main stem. To this must be added the capital paid in by the stockholders. Bonds representing the funded debt to the amount of $2,375,000 are indorsed by the city of Baltimore, and bonds amounting to $300,000 are indorsed by Washington County.

Early in 1874, Col. J. M. Hood, a practical engineer of large experience, was elected president of the company and general manager. With his administration began a new era in the history of the Western Maryland Railroad. The management was completely divorced from municipal politics, and the president became in fact, as well as in theory, the chief executive officer of the company. The net earnings of the road increased from year to year, new sources of revenue were developed, the floating debt was paid, the overdue interest on the mortgage debt was funded, and the liquidation of the principal provided for on terms satisfactory to the bondholders. The old portion of the main stem was rebuilt, additional passenger-trains were put on the eastern division, and special inducements were held out to summer excursionists to visit the romantic spots on the line of the road. The increased facilities for getting to and from the city attracted a large number of people to the suburban towns on the line of the road, and the movement of population in this direction is seen in the constantly increasing receipts from passengers on the eastern division. A summer resort was established at Pen-mar, on the summit of the Blue Ridge, which was visited by more than one hundred thousand persons last season. In 1874 a contract was concluded with the Baltimore and Potomac Railroad Company, under which the trains of the Western Maryland Company enter Baltimore through the Baltimore and Potomac Railroad tunnel and run direct to Hillen Station. This fine depot was built in 1875 with funds loaned by the city. Early in 1880 the Baltimore and Hanover Railroad was completed to Emory Grove Station, nineteen miles from the city, where it connects with the main stem of the Western Maryland road. Its trains run to Hillen Station on the Western Maryland track, and the business drawn from the section of country traversed by the new road has added considerably to the revenues of the Western Maryland Company.

The projected line of the Western Maryland Railroad ran through Emmittsburg and Waynesboro' in all the old surveys, but in the multitude of counsels which prevailed between 1867 and 1870 the route was changed to its present location. It then became necessary to reach these two important towns, each lying five miles north of the main stem, by means of lateral branches.[1] The Emmittsburg branch, which diverges from the Western Maryland road at Rocky Ridge, fifty-four miles from Baltimore, and connects the road with Emmittsburg, was completed in 1875. The Waynesboro' branch, which has developed into the Baltimore and Cumberland Valley Railroad, leaves the main stem at Edgemont, on the western slope of the Blue Ridge, and extends to Waynesboro', seven and a half miles; thence to Shippensburg, by way of Chambersburg, twenty-six miles, the whole length of the road being thirty-three and a half miles. This, in fact, is an extension of the Western Maryland road into the very heart of the Cumberland Valley. The Baltimore and Cumberland Valley road was opened on the 5th of September, 1881, to Chambersburg, and has since been completed and opened to Shippensburg. The Cumberland Valley of Pennsylvania, which is brought into close connection with Baltimore by this road, extends from the Susquehanna River on the north to the Potomac on the south, a distance of eighty-one miles, and is an extremely rich and thickly-populated section. The land is well watered by small streams, and the North Mountain on the west, and the Blue Ridge on the east, protect the valley from violent storms in winter. Every product of the soil known to this climate is successfully raised. By this route Chambersburg is ninety-seven and a half miles from Baltimore, while it is one hundred and fifty miles from Philadelphia by way of Harrisburg; and Shippensburg is one hundred and eight and a half miles from Baltimore, and one hundred and forty miles from Philadelphia. It is confidently expected that this difference in distance in favor of Baltimore will have a marked influence upon the course of trade. The Frederick and Pennsylvania Railroad, completed in 1872, connects Frederick City with the Western Maryland Railroad at Bruceville Station, and extends northward into Pennsylvania to Littlestown, where it connects with the Pennsylvania system. The Hanover Junction, Hanover and Gettysburg Branch Road, recently extended, taps the Western Maryland at Glyndon, nineteen and a half miles from Baltimore.

The Western Maryland Railroad is one of the most attractive in the country for the variety and picturesqueness of the scenery along its route. From the deep cut at Fulton Station until the traveler reaches the terminus of the road at Williamsport, on the Potomac River, a constant succession of beautiful

[1] A company was chartered in 1865 called the Gwynn's Falls Railroad. A sufficient amount of stock having been subscribed, a company was organized on October 8th by the election of the following officers: George Slothower, president; and John Weathered, J. T. Myers, J. Howard McHenry, Mr. Harris, and Theodore Mottu, directors. Notwithstanding an earnest spirit was manifested, nothing more was done under the charter. It was estimated the road would cost $250,000.

J. M. Hood

pictures meet the eye. After passing the elegant country residences along the Liberty and Hookstown roads, the first point of interest reached is Greenwood Park, a fine grove of shade-trees situated on elevated ground, which is used as a public resort for excursions, picnics, etc. Leaving Greenwood Park, the train passes Owings' Mills, Reisterstown, Emory Grove, Westminster, and Union Bridge, where the company's shops are located. The country from Owings' Mills to Mechanicstown is beautifully diversified and undulating, and embraces one of the richest agricultural sections of the State. Numerous handsome farms in the highest state of cultivation, with thrifty-looking homes and huge barns and stables, dot the landscape in every direction on either side of the road. Ascending the Blue Ridge from the east, the road makes a complete semicircle around the town of Sabillasville, which is familiarly known to excursionists as the "Horse-shoe Curve." Here a lovely view of the beautiful Harbaugh's Valley is obtained. Several years ago the station "Penmar" (the word being a contraction of Pennsylvania and Maryland) was established, where passengers alight for High Rock, a point one mile distant, and situated near the summit of the mountain, whence a view is had of the Cumberland and Shenandoah Valleys on the north, west, and south, covering an area of two thousand square miles of the most charming scenery. High Rock is about two thousand feet above the sea-level, and fourteen hundred above the base of the mountain. The panorama of the Cumberland Valley is without doubt one of the grandest to be seen in any portion of the country east of the Mississippi. Of course there are loftier mountains and bolder effects, but for variety, richness, and sublimity combined it is scarcely equaled in any other portion of the Union. As far as the eye can reach the valley is thickly studded with towns, villages, hamlets, and farm-houses, and the landscape consists of undulating plains, silvery streams, projecting mountain peaks, and, in the distance, the blue crests of the loftier ranges. An observatory has been erected on the Rock, from which the spires of churches in Chambersburg, twenty-four miles away, can be seen. Monterey Station is a near point, where the road passes over a corner of Pennsylvania, for which no charter has ever been granted by the State. In order to obviate the necessity of applying to the Legislature for one, the railroad company purchased the farm through which the intended route was to pass, and built the road without a charter. From Monterey, where a view of Monterey Springs is obtained, to Waynesboro' the grade is on a descending scale. From Waynesboro' Station to Hagerstown the scenery is charming, and though its character is changed after leaving Hagerstown, it is none the less attractive. When the Potomac is reached the view from Williamsport is one of the handsomest to be found anywhere along the banks of that beautiful stream.

President John Mifflin Hood, through whose exertions and under whose personal direction these important extensions have been made, is one of the youngest of the prominent railroad men of the country. He was born at Bowling Green, the old family residence, near Sykesville, in Howard Co., Md., on the 5th of April, 1843. His father, Dr. Benjamin Hood, was the son of Benjamin and Sarah Hood, and was born at Bowling Green in 1812, and died in 1855, in the forty-third year of his age. His mother, Hannah Mifflin Hood, was the daughter of Alexander Coulter, of Baltimore, where she was born. Young Hood was educated in Howard and Harford Counties, completing his course at Rugby's Institute, Mount Washington, in 1859. He then commenced the study of engineering, and in July of the same year secured employment in the engineer corps engaged in the extension of the Delaware Railroad. The same corps was next employed in the construction of the Eastern Shore Railroad of Maryland, Mr. Hood soon becoming principal assistant engineer, and for part of the time having sole charge of the operations. In August, 1861, he went to Brazil, but finding the field for engineering unpromising, returned to Baltimore in January, 1862, and after studying marine engineering, ran the blockade, and reported to the Confederate authorities at Richmond, Va., for service. He was at once assigned to duty as topographical engineer and draughtsman of the military railroad then building from Danville, Va., to Greenboro', N. C. (since known as the Piedmont Railroad), and upon the completion of his work declined a commission offered in the Engineer Corps, and enlisted as a private in Company C, Second Battalion Maryland Infantry. He served with distinction in the Maryland Infantry until the spring of 1864, when, owing to the scarcity of engineers, he accepted a lieutenant's commission in the Second Regiment of Engineer Troops, in which service he continued until surrendered at Appomattox. Mr. Hood was several times slightly wounded, and at Stanard's Mill, in the Spottsylvania battles, had his left arm badly shattered above the elbow. While still incapacitated for duty he ran the blockade, and, wading the Potomac at night, visited his family, and came to Baltimore, where he had his wound treated by Prof. Nathan R. Smith, returning to his command before Richmond with a large party of recruits for the Confederate service. In September, 1865, he was employed by the Philadelphia, Wilmington and Baltimore Railroad to make surveys for the extension of the Philadelphia and Baltimore Central line between the Susquehanna River and Baltimore; he was next placed in charge of the construction of the Port Deposit branch of the Philadelphia, Wilmington and Baltimore Railroad, and made chief engineer of the Philadelphia and Baltimore Central Railroad, and constructed its line through Cecil County to the Susquehanna River. He was soon afterwards elected engineer and superintendent of the same company, and in April, 1870, became general superintendent of the Florida (now Atlantic, Gulf and West India Transit) Railroad. His health failing, in November, 1871, he accepted the position of chief engineer of the Oxford and York Narrow-Gauge Railroad, in Pennsylvania, and while holding this position he became also chief engineer of a new line, known as the Baltimore, Philadelphia and New York Railroad, the construction of which was stopped by the panic of 1873. On the 14th of January, 1874, Mr. Hood was elected vice-president and general superintendent of the Western Maryland Railroad, and on the 24th of March following he was made president and general manager of the road, including the office of chief engineer, in which position he continues to the present time. On the retirement of Mr. Keyser in 1881, Mr. Hood was tendered the office of second vice-president of the Baltimore and Ohio Railroad, but declined the office. Mr. Hood married on the 17th of July, 1867, Florence Eloise Haden, of Botetourt County, Va., and has five children. The presidents of the Western Maryland Company and the dates on which they were respectively elected are given in the following list:

	Elected.
Robert M. Magraw	Feb. 21, 1853.
Nathan Haines	1854.
William Roberts	June 23, 1858.
Augustus Shriver	June 12, 1860.
Nathan Haines	October, 1861.
John Smith	Nov. 6, 1862.
Robert Irvin	Jan. 6, 1863.
John Lee Chapman	Nov. 8, 1866.
Wendell Bollman	April 2, 1868.
George M. Bokee	May 17, 1870.
Robert T. Banks	Oct. 18, 1871.
James L. McLane	Nov. 21, 1871.
Alexander Rieman	Dec. 2, 1873.
John M. Hood	March 24, 1874.

Classification of Tonnage Receipts on Western Maryland Railroad for the Year ending Nov. 30, 1880, compared with Two Previous Years:

	1880. Tons.	1879. Tons.	1878. Tons.
Lumber and bark	11,808	10,154	11,016
Coal	31,123	10,081	9,955
Miscellaneous	47,882	39,037	42,225
Live-stock	7,890	3,081	3,530
Grain and feed	30,986	27,999	26,395
Lime and limestone	5,115	4,554	4,111
Wood	646	1,052	786
Ores	12,863	93,692	914
Flour, barrels	64,820	92,562	89,891
Net tonnage	154,795	108,906	....

Distances on Western Maryland Railroad.

	Stations.	Miles.
	Baltimore	.0
	Fulton	3.0
2.8	Oakland	5.8
1.0	Arlington	6.8
1.4	Mount Hope	8.2
0.9	Howardville	9.1
1.6	Pikesville	10 7
1.3	Greenwood	12.0
1.7	Junction	13.7
1.1	Owings' Mills	14.8
2.9	Timber Grove	17.7
1.8	Glyndon	19.5
0.4	Emory Grove	19.9
2.8	Glen Falls	22.7
3.4	Tank	26.1
2.7	Carrollton	28.8
1.5	Gorsuch Road	30.3
3.4	Westminster	33.7
2.9	Avondale	36.6
2.8	Wayside	39.4
1.7	New Windsor	41.1
2.4	Linwood	43.5
1.8	Union Bridge	45.3
2.5	Middleburg	47.8
1.4	Frederick Junction	49.2
0.1	York Road	49.3
1.7	Double Pipe Creek	51.0
3.1	Rocky Ridge	54.1
1.6	Loy's	55.7
1.7	Graceham	57.4
2.0	Mechanicstown	59.4
4.3	Deerfield	63.7
2.2	Sabillasville	65.9
3.1	Blue Ridge	69.0
2.4	Penmar	71.4
3.7	Edgemont	75.1
2.5	Smithsburg	77.6
3.4	Chewsville	81.0
5.0	C. V. Crossing	86.0
0.6	Hagerstown	86.6
6.4	Williamsport	93.0

Distances on Baltimore and Cumberland Valley Branch of the Western Maryland Railroad.

	Stations.	Miles.
	Edgemont	.0
3.4	Midvale	3.4
3.9	Waynesboro'	7.3
3.6	Five Forks	10.9
3.1	Altenwald	14.0
3.3	New Franklin	17.3
4.5	Chambersburg	21.8
4.9	Green Village	26.7
3.1	Southampton	29.8
3.8	Shippensburg	33.6

Washington County Branch of the Baltimore and Ohio Railroad.—The first action looking to the construction of a railroad connecting Hagerstown with the main stem of the Baltimore and Ohio was taken by the citizens on the 17th of March, 1857, when a convention from the various districts was held at Hagerstown. Resolutions were adopted petitioning the State Legislature to pass an act enabling the county to issue two hundred and fifty thousand dollars' worth of bonds for the construction of the road, and a committee, consisting of J. Dixon Roman, T. G. Robertson, Dr. Thomas Maddox, William Dodge, and James Wason, was appointed to confer with the authorities of the Baltimore and Ohio Railroad Company. Andrew Rench presided at the meeting, and George F. Heyser acted as secretary. Addresses were made by Judge Weisel, William Motter, Elias Davis, David Reichard, William Price, and Robert Fowler. On the 10th of March, 1864, the Legislature passed an act incorporating the Washington County Railroad, and naming Isaac Nesbitt, George S. Kennedy, Jacob A. Miller, Johns Hopkins, Galloway Cheston, Peter B. Small, and Robert Fowler as commissioners and first directors. The capital stock was fixed at one million dollars, with permission to increase it to a million and a half. The shares were to be of the value of twenty dollars each. The commissioners of Washington County and the mayor and Council of Baltimore were also empowered to subscribe each two hundred and fifty thousand dollars to the work, to be raised by issuing bonds.

In September, 1865, the county commissioners, William Rulett, Elias E. Rohrer, and John Reichard, accompanied by their clerk, John L. Smith, and by George S. Kennedy, Jacob A. Miller, Peter B. Small, Dr. Thomas Maddox, Thomas A. Bolt, Dr. Biggs, and A. Appleman, had a conference with the Baltimore and Ohio authorities at Camden Station, and were informed by Mr. Garrett that the company had decided to make a liberal subscription to the work. The county commissioners then subscribed $150,000, and the following additional subscriptions were recorded: Johns Hopkins, $12,000; Robert Garrett & Sons, $10,000; Robert Fowler, $10,000; A. Gregg & Co., $4000; Samuel Wilhelm, $2000. The work of construction was begun soon afterwards, and the first president under the original incorporation was E. W. Mealey.

The second board of directors was composed of Robert Fowler, Galloway Cheston, Johns Hopkins, Jacob A. Miller, Peter B. Small, and Walter S. Kennedy, Sr. P. B. Small was the secretary and treasurer.

It was not long, however, before it became apparent that the work could not be accomplished under the original management, and the Baltimore and Ohio came to the aid of the president and directors and finished the construction. The last rail was laid on Wednesday, Nov. 21, 1867, and arrangements were at once completed for running regular passenger and freight-trains between Hagerstown and Baltimore, beginning with Monday, November 25th. Until the opening of this road the large travel from Hagerstown and its vicinity which reached the Baltimore and Ohio Railroad at Martinsburg and Frederick was conveyed in stage coaches. The first shipment over the new road was a consignment of wheat, a car-load of which reached Baltimore on the 22d of November, 1867. The grain belonged to Samuel Emmart, and was consigned to A. W. Goldsborough. Mr. Mealey was succeeded in the presidency by Robert Fowler, who retained the position until his death, after which the corporation was merged into the Baltimore and Ohio. The road extends from Hagerstown to Weverton, on the main stem of the Baltimore and Ohio Railroad, a distance of twenty-three miles, and passes through the districts of Funkstown, Tilghmanton, Keedysville, Rohrersville, and Sandy Hook.

LOCAL RAILWAY STATIONS, BALTIMORE AND OHIO RAILROAD.

MAIN STEM—OLD LINE.

Stations.	Miles.	Stations.	Miles.
Camden Station, Balto..	0	Brady's	185
Relay	9	Rawling's	191
Ellicott City	15	Black Oak	194.5
Hollofields	18.7	Keyser	201
Elysville	20	Piedmont	206
Woodstock	24.5	Bloomington	208.2
Marriottsville	27.2	Frankville	212
Sykesville	31.5	Swanton	217.2
Gaither's	33	Altamont	221
Hood's Mill	34.2	Deer Park	223.7
Watersville	40	Oakland	230
Mount Airy	42.5	Hutton's	235
Plane No. 4	46	Snowy Creek	238
Monrovia	50	Cranberry	240
Hartman's W. S.	54	Rodemer's	245
Frederick Junction	58	Rowlesburg	251
Adamstown	64	Buck Eye	252.5
Doub's	65	Tray Run	253
Washington Junction...	68.7	Tunnelton	258.5
Point of Rocks	69	West End	259.5
Berlin	75.2	Newburg	265
Weverton	78.5	Independence	266.2
Sandy Hook	80	Thornton	272.2
Harper's Ferry	81	Grafton	277.7
Duffield's	87.5	Fetterman	279.5
Hobb's	89.2	Valley Falls	285.7
Kerneysville	92	Texas	292.2
Vanclevesville	95	Benton's Ferry	295
Opequon	97	Fairmont	299.5
Martinsburg	100	Barnesville	302
North Mountain	107	Barracksville	305
Cherry Run	113	Farmington	310.5
Miller's	115.5	Mannington	317.5
Sleepy Creek	117	Glover's Gap	324.7
Hancock	122.5	Burton	329.2
Sir John's Run	128	Littleton	335.2
Great Cacapon	132	Board Tree	337.5
Orleans Road	138.5	Bellton	342
Doe Gully	140.5	Cogley's	345.7
No. 12 W. S.	148.5	Cameron	349.2
Paw Paw	153.5	Easton's	354
Little Cacapon	156.5	Roseby's Rock	360
French's	161	Moundsville	366.2
Green Spring	163.7	McMechen's	372
Patterson's Creek	170.5	Benwood	373
Cumberland	178	Wheeling	377

MAIN STEM *via* WASHINGTON TO ST. LOUIS.

Stations.	Miles.	Stations.	Miles.
Baltimore	0	Rowlesburg	267
Relay Station	9	Tunnelton	275
Laurel	22	Newburg	281
Bladensburg	34	Thornton	288
Washington	40	Grafton	294
Metropolitan Junction	41	Bridgeport	311
Rockville	56	Clarksburg	316
Barnesville	73	Salem	330
Washington Junction	83	Long Run	335
Weverton	93	West Union	343
Sandy Hook	94	Central	346
Harper's Ferry	95	Pennsboro'	356
Shenandoah Junction	103	Ellenboro'	361
Kerneysville	106	Cairo	369
Martinsburg	114	Petroleum	376
North Mountain	121	L. F. Junction	378
Hancock	137	Kanawha	388
Sir John's Run	142	Parkersburg	398
Paw Paw	168	Athens	435
Green Spring	178	Chillicothe	495
Cumberland	192	Cincinnati	593
Keyser	215	North Vernon	666
Piedmont	220	Louisville	721
Altamont	237	Seymour	780
Deer Park	240	Vincennes	785
Oakland	246	Odin	868
Cranberry	256	St. Louis	933

HARPER'S FERRY AND VALLEY BRANCH.

Stations.	Miles.	Stations.	Miles.
Harper's Ferry	0	Strasburg Junction	51
Halltown	6	Tom's Brook	55
Charlestown	10	Maurertown	57
Cameron	14	Woodstock	61
Wadesville	23	Edinsburg	66
Stephenson's	27	Mount Jackson	74
Winchester	32	New Market	81
Kernstown	36	Broadway	88
Newtown	39	Linville	94
Middletown	44	Harrisonburg	100
Cedar Creek	46	Pleasant Valley	105
Capon Road	50	Fort Defiance	117
Strasburg	52	Staunton	126

METROPOLITAN BRANCH.

Stations.	Miles.	Stations.	Miles.
Washington	0	Gaithersburg	21.5
Metropolitan Junction	1	Germantown	26.5
Queenstown	3.2	Boyd's	29.5
Terra Cotta	4	Barnesville	33.2
Silver Spring	7	Dickerson	35.7
Knowles'	11	Tuscarora	39
Rockville	16.2	Sugar-Loaf	41.7
Washington Grove	20.7	Washington Junction	42.7

WASHINGTON BRANCH.

Stations.	Miles.	Stations.	Miles.
Camden Station	0	Savage	20.2
Camden Junction	4.5	Laurel	22.2
Relay	9	Contee's	24.5
Elk Ridge	9.5	Beltsville	28
Hanover	11.5	Paint Branch	31.7
Dorsey's	14.2	Alexandria Junction	34
Jessup's	16.5	Bladensburg	34.2
Bridewell	16.7	Metropolitan Junction	39
Annapolis Junction	18.6	Washington	40

BALTIMORE, COLUMBUS AND CHICAGO LINE.

Stations.	Miles.	Stations.	Miles.
Baltimore	0	Mount Vernon	520
Washington	40	Frederick	527
Harper's Ferry	95	Lexington	549
Martinsburg	114	Mansfield	557
Cumberland	192	Shelby Junction	569
Piedmont	220	Plymouth	577
Deer Park	240	Chicago Junction	583
Oakland	246	Manroeville	596
Grafton	294	Sandusky	611
Fairmont	316	Tiffin	607
Mannington	334	Fostoria	620
Cameron	365	Bloomdale	627
Moundsville	382	Deshler	645
Benwood	389	Holgate	657
Bellaire	391	Defiance	671
Wheeling	393	Hicksville	691
Quincy	406	Auburn Junction	708
Belmont	410	Garrett	711
Barnesville	418	Avilla	716
Spencer's	425	Syracuse	744
Cambridge	443	Milford Junction	749
Concord	452	Walkerton Junction	782
Zanesville	469	Wellsboro'	796
Pleasant Valley	478	Alida	804
Newark	495	Michigan Central Junc	820
Columbus	528	Kingston	842
Louisville	504	Chicago	854
Utica	509		

WASHINGTON COUNTY BRANCH.

Stations.	Miles.	Stations.	Miles.
Weaverton	0	Rohrersville	8
Bartholow's	4	Eakle's Mills	11
Brownsville	5	Keedysville	13
Claggett's	6	Breathed's	18
Baler's Summit	7	Hagerstown	24

BALTIMORE, WASHINGTON AND PITTSBURGH LINE.

Station.	Miles.	Station.	Miles.
Baltimore	0	Connellsville	284
Washington	40	Broad Ford	287
Washington Junction	83	Dawson	290
Harper's Ferry	95	Oakdale	293
Martinsburg	114	Layton	297
Sir John's Run	142	Jacob's Creek	301
Cumberland	192	Smithton	303
Mount Savage Junction	196	Port Royal	305
Cook's Mills	201	Snyder	307
Hyndman	206	West Newton	309
Sand Patch	225	Suter	313
Keystone	227	Shaner	317
Meyersdale	229	Guffey	318
Garrett	234	Ellrod	324
Rockwood	241	McKeesport	327
Casselman	245	Port Perry	331
Pinkerton	249	Braddock	332
Ursina	256	Glenwood	337
Confluence	258	Hazlewood	338
Ohio Pyle	268	Pittsburgh	342
Indian Creek	277		

The Shenandoah Valley Railroad was started as a local work, with home capital and home talent to guide it, and was finished by the Shenandoah Construction Company, the headquarters of which were at Philadelphia. Upon taking charge of the road, the company determined to extend it to Hagerstown, Md., and Waynesboro', Va. On the 4th of September, 1880, the first train from the Valley of Virginia entered Hagerstown, and the last spike in the track between the towns named was driven in March, 1881. The Construction Company is no longer in existence, having been succeeded by the Shenandoah Valley Railroad Company. The stations on this road and their distances from Hagerstown are as follows:

Stations.	Miles.
Hagerstown, Washington Co., Md	0
St. James', " "	5.9
Grimes', " "	9.0
Sharpsburg, " "	13.6
Shepherdstown, Jefferson Co., W. Va	16.9
Shenandoah Junc., " "	23.1
Charlestown, " "	28.4
Ripon, " "	33.9
Fairfield, Clark Co., Va	36.2
Berryville, " "	39.9
Boyceville, " "	46.2
White Post, " "	49.2
Ashby, Warren "	53.2
Cedarville, " "	56.4
Riverton, " "	59.2
Front Royal, " "	62.1
Manor, " "	66.4
Bentonville, " "	72.9
Overall, Page "	75.6
Ryleyville, " "	79.8
Kimball, " "	85.1
Luray, " "	88.8
Marksville, " "	95.6
East Liberty, " "	101.9
Grove Hill, " "	104.0
Shenandoah Iron-Works, Page Co., Va	106.7
Elkton, Rockingham Co., Va	112.5
Port Republic, " "	127.2
Weyer's Cave, Augusta Co., Va	129.1
Patterson, " "	132.1
Crimora, " "	136.9
Waynesboro', " "	143.7

CHAPTER XLIII.

REPRESENTATIVE MEN AND FAMILIES OF WASHINGTON COUNTY.

WASHINGTON COUNTY has been the mother of a long line of distinguished men in every walk of life. Although one of the youngest of the counties of Western Maryland, she has enriched the bench, the forum, the pulpit, the medical profession, and the halls of legislation with earnest and able men, whose lives have been conspicuous and honorable far beyond the small confines of their native county and State.

Many of those eminent men have contributed to the glory of their country on the field of battle, in literature, and in art, and some of them are a part of the history of the county itself, and probably no county in Western Maryland has been more prolific of men of force and character in private life than Washington. Her sons have held high and honorable positions in every section of the State, and some of them have left her bounds to find fortune and found honorable names in other States.

The Hughes family. Barnabas Hughes, the ancestor of the Hughes family in Maryland, emigrated from the county of Donegal, Ireland, in 1750 and settled at Lancaster, Pa. He married Elizabeth Waters, of Elizabethtown, Pa., and after residing some years at Lancaster removed to Baltimore. After a short stay in that town he decided to remove to Western Maryland, and finally located himself in a portion of Frederick County which afterwards fell within the boundaries of Washington County. Here he engaged in the iron trade, and built Mount Etna and other furnaces near the Black Rocks, above Beaver Creek. He died in 1780. His eldest son, Daniel, was born in 1730, and his second son, Samuel, was born in 1741. Both the brothers became conspicuous in the Revolution for their zeal in behalf of the patriot cause, and from the fact that many of the cannon used by the Continental army were cast at their forges. Besides Daniel and Samuel, one son and five daughters were born to Mr. and Mrs. Barnabas Hughes, but all of them died in infancy. On the 9th of August, 1759, was born another son, John Hughes, who afterwards became a captain in the Revolutionary army. He married Miss Chamberlaine, of the Eastern Shore. After John were born Elizabeth, who married Hon. Richard Potts, of Frederick; Margaret, who died single; and Barnabas, who married Miss Beltzhoover, of Hagerstown, and died aged twenty-three.

Daniel, afterwards colonel, married Rebecca Lux, of Baltimore. His children by this marriage were Robert, born in July, 1767; William, born March 2, 1769; Nancy, or Ann, born in April, 1771; Samuel, born in July, 1773; and James, born in 1775. The latter died unmarried. Both James Hughes and his mother, first wife of Col. Daniel, were buried in the Lutheran church at Hagerstown. Rebecca Lux, second daughter of Daniel Hughes, died in 1800, aged twenty-three. In 1780, Col. Daniel Hughes married Susannah Schlatter, of Germantown, Pa., whose father, Rev. Michael Schlatter, was one of the early missionaries to the German Reformed Church in this country. The children of Col. Daniel Hughes and Susannah Schlatter were Susannah, who died single, in 1826, and was buried in the Episcopal Cemetery, Hagerstown; Mary Ann (who married Joseph I. Merrick, the well-known lawyer, of Hagerstown, and had two children,—Daniel, who died in infancy; Mary, who died in 1824); Esther, born July 4, 1794 (who married Amasa Sprague, of Rochester, N. Y., and died in January, 1868); Daniel, who died single, in 1824; John Henry, who married Nancy Lyon. John Henry Hughes left one son, William Schlatter Hughes, who now resides in San Rafael, Cal. William S. Hughes married Mary Ashberry, and has seven sons and one daughter. At the age of seventy, Col. Daniel Hughes married his third wife, Mrs. Ann Elliott, of Carlisle, Pa., mother of Commodore Jesse D. Elliott, U.S.N. By this marriage he had one daughter, Rebecca Lux, who married Dr. Joseph Martin, of the Eastern Shore, and died leaving no issue. Both Mrs. Martin and her mother were buried in the Presbyterian graveyard at Hagerstown, but Col. Daniel Hughes and the other members of his family were interred in the Episcopal graveyard at the same place.

Robert Hughes, eldest son of Col. Daniel Hughes, married Susannah Purviance, daughter of Samuel Purviance, of Baltimore. Mrs. Hughes' brother, John Henry Purviance, was in the diplomatic service of this country, and for twenty years was the bearer of dispatches between this country and France. He accompanied the commissioners who contracted the treaty of Ghent. Another brother, Henry Purviance, studied law with Henry Clay. Mrs. Hughes' father left Baltimore in 1780, accompanied by Nicholas Raguet, of Philadelphia, and Samuel Ridout, of Annapolis. They traveled westward by way of Fort Pitt, now Pittsburgh, their purpose being to take legal possession of one hundred thousand acres of land owned jointly by Samuel and Robert Purviance. While descending the Ohio River in a flat-boat they were attacked by Indians, near the site of the present city of Cincinnati. Purviance and Raguet were murdered, but Ridout escaped, and returned to Annapolis, where his descendants still reside. Mr. and Mrs. Robert Hughes had six children,—Elizabeth Isabella, Henrietta Frances (who married Dr. Horatio Nelson Fenn, of Rochester, N. Y.), Henry C., Rebecca L., Letitia Purviance (who married Dr. H. H. Harvey), and Henry Courteney, who died in 1862. William Hughes, second son of Col. Daniel Hughes, married Margaret Coale, of Cecil County, and had the following children: William, Joseph, Samuel, Barnabas, Emily, Ann, Rebecca Hollingsworth, Augusta, and Helen. William and Joseph died early in life. Emily married George Clarke, of Baltimore, and lived many years in Louisville, Ky., where her descendants still remain. Rebecca H. married Nathaniel Ruggles, of Boston. Augusta married Dr. Alvas, of Henderson, Ky., and Helen married a Mr. Taylor, and still resides at Paducah, Ky. William Hughes removed to Henderson, Ky., after his marriage, and he and his wife died there. Samuel Hughes, third son of Col. Daniel Hughes, married Miss Holker, and had five sons, his eldest being John Holker; second, James; third, Napoleon; fourth, Henry; fifth, Lewis; and four daughters,—Marie Antoinette, Louisa, Adelaide, and Catharine. Marie A. Hughes married Col. William Fitzhugh; Louisa married Dr. John Claggett Dorsey, of Hagerstown; Adelaide married John Savage, of Philadelphia; Catharine married William Coleman Brien, and afterwards Rev. Tryon Edwards. John Holker Hughes died unmarried; Napoleon B. Hughes married Nancy Thompson, sister of Gen. Thompson, of Baltimore; Dr. Henry Hughes died unmarried; and Lewis Hughes married Laura Gray, of Baltimore.

Ann, or Nancy, daughter of Col. Daniel Hughes, married Col. William Fitzhugh, of Prince George's County, and they had seven sons and five daughters. The Fitzhugh family removed from their mansion, "The Hive," four miles from Hagerstown, to Genesee, N. Y., where Col. Fitzhugh assisted in founding the city of Rochester.

The eldest son of William Fitzhugh and his wife, Ann Hughes Fitzhugh, was William, who married, March 10, 1818, his cousin, Marie Antoinette Hughes, daughter of Samuel Hughes, of Mount Alto.

The second son, Daniel Fitzhugh, married Anna Dana, a second cousin. Her mother was the daughter of Peregrine Fitzhugh, who was a brother of the elder Col. Fitzhugh. She married Mr. Dana, an English gentleman. Anna was the only child.

John Henry Hughes, who married Nancy Lyon, of Philadelphia, died at Mount Etna Furnace. His widow married Thomas Curtis, of Mount Holly, Pa. The first furnace of the Hughes brothers was built at Black Rocks, near South Mountain, in partnership with Mr. Buchanan, of Baltimore, before the Revolutionary war. The second furnace, now known as Mount Etna, was about a mile lower down. After these were built, Col. Daniel Hughes formed a partnership with Col. Wm. Fitzhugh and built a forge and nail-furnace, now known as the "Old Forge," between Hagerstown and Leitersburg, on the Antietam. The fourth and last furnace was built by Col. Daniel Hughes and his two sons, Samuel and Daniel Hughes, both lawyers of Hagerstown, at Mont Alto, Franklin Co., Pa., now known as Mont Alto Park, a summer resort. It was sold by the Hugheses to Col. Weistling, of Harrisburg. John Horine purchased Mount Etna Furnace. The Mount Pleasant Furnace, near Havre de Grace, in Harford County, Md., was built by Samuel Hughes, son of the first Barnabas, and brother of Col. Daniel Hughes, of Antietam. There are cannon now in existence in the Boston Navy-Yard cast at this furnace during the Revolutionary war.

Capt. John Hughes, the youngest son of the first Barnabas Hughes, was in the Revolutionary war, and was a great friend of André, and attended him during his last confinement, and received letters and his picture with a request that they should be sent to his affianced in England. He performed all of André's bequests with scrupulous exactitude, and corresponded with André's intended bride, giving her all the particulars of his confinement and death.

Richard Stockton, formerly of Baltimore, married a daughter of Capt. John Hughes. Another daughter married Mr. Stokes, his partner. Stockton & Stokes were the great stage-men in the days before railroads were invented. Mr. Stokes also lived in Baltimore. His son is Dr. W. H. Stokes, of Mount Hope Institution, near Baltimore.

The Lawrence family. Among the leading citizens of Washington County in the early part of the present century, and one of the most conspicuous figures in the social, legal, and political circles of Hagerstown, was Upton Lawrence, a gentleman of exceptional talents and of a high standard of moral and intellectual attainment. Mr. Lawrence's father was John Lawrence, of Linganore, Frederick Co., who married Martha, a daughter of Sir Stephen West. Sir Stephen was the son of John West, of Horton, Buckinghamshire, England, and emigrated to this country at an early date. He settled in Anne Arundel County and left six children, of whom Martha was the fourth. Upton Lawrence, son of John Lawrence and Martha West, married Elizabeth, daughter of Col. Jonathan Hager, and granddaughter of Jonathan Hager, founder and proprietor of Hagerstown. Mrs. Lawrence, like her mother, the gifted Mary Orndorff, was lovely in person and in character, and was one of the belles of Hagerstown. About that time the Messrs. Buchanan, afterwards learned jurists,—one of them becoming a member of the Court of Appeals and the other a circuit judge,—were regarded as being among the most attractive and entertaining beaus of Washington County, which was famous for the culture and refinement of its early society. Miss Heister, daughter of Gen. Daniel Heister, and niece of Jonathan Hager, Jr., in writing of one of them, said briefly but impressively, "I like Mr. Buchanan and think him a gentleman." Mr. and Mrs. Upton Lawrence were married by the Rev. George Bower, rector of St. John's Episcopal Parish, a genial parson of the old school, who is said to have frequently danced the first cotillon at the gay assemblies in his parish. Mrs. Lawrence's grandfather, Christopher Orndorff, was of German extraction, and lived in great state on his plantation near Sharpsburg. He was a handsome man of commanding presence, and very free and genial in his manners. He kept open house, and dispensed a generous but by no means ostentatious hospitality. He reared twelve children, all of whom were educated with unusual care. Mr. Orndorff served as an officer in the Revolutionary army, attaining the rank of major, and all the officers of the Continental army passing to and fro from the theatre of war were received and entertained at his house with the utmost cordiality. Upon one occasion, when Gen. Horatio Gates was a guest of Maj. Orndorff's, Mary Madeline, a daughter of his host, passed him in the hall without seeing him, and entered the parlor to view herself in the large mirror there. She was very young and had on a new cap of the latest style, and doubtless wished to discover if it was becoming. As she passed him Gen. Gates turned to her father and exclaimed, "Who is that lovely creature?" Maj. Orndorff replied, "That is my youngest daughter." At Gen. Gates' request she was placed at the tea-table so that he could see her. A few days afterwards Gen. Gates proposed, through her father, to make her his wife; but as she was of a somewhat romantic temperament, she could not reconcile herself to a marriage with a person as old as her father, and promptly rejected him. In the same manner, while stopping at Maj. Orndorff's house on his way from the scene of military operations, Col. Jonathan Hager met Mary Orndorff and surrendered at discretion. He was, however, more fortunate in his suit than Gen. Gates, for he paid his addresses one day and was married the next. Their only child was a beautiful girl, Elizabeth Hager, who when only seventeen years of age married Upton Lawrence, who afterwards became a distinguished lawyer, and whose house was frequented by many of the leading people of Maryland. Among them was Luther Martin, the famous lawyer, who was at one time engaged to be married to Mrs. Lawrence's mother, the beautiful widow of Jonathan Hager. The match, however, was broken off because Mrs. Hager became convinced that Mr. Martin was intemperate.[1] Mr. Martin, however, appears to have been sincere in his expressions of admiration and esteem, and always treated her daughter, Mrs. Lawrence, with the utmost affection, making Mr. Lawrence's house his home whenever business called him to Hagerstown. Roger B. Taney and John Thomson Mason were also frequent guests at Mr. Lawrence's mansion. Mr. and Mrs. Lawrence had five children,—two sons, Jonathan and Upton, who are dead, and three daughters, one of whom is Mrs. Robert J. Brent, whose daughter is Mrs. William Keyser, wife of one of the former vice-presidents of the Baltimore and Ohio Railroad Company. The other two daughters remain unmarried and continue to reside in Hagerstown, occupying the building erected by the late Dr. John Reynolds, upon land owned by their father. It is situated on Prospect Hill, West Washington Street. The Misses Lawrence are now the sole representatives in the third generation of the original proprietor of Hagerstown, and preserve with creditable pride many rare and curious relics of the Hager family.[2] They reside in

---

[1] Mrs. Hager afterwards married Col. Henry Lewis, of Virginia.

[2] Following are copies of some of the letters addressed by Mr. Martin to Mrs. Hager during his courtship:

(No. 1.)

"May 12, 1800.

"MY DEAR MADAM,—I twice called at Mr. Wyant's yesterday to see you, and you were not at home. Being obliged to leave town this morning, I take the liberty of expressing to you in writing those sentiments which I should have been happy to have done in person. You have a charming little daughter who wants a father. I have two who stand in need of a mother. By doing me the honor to accept my hand our dear children may have the one and the other; and I promise you most sacredly that in me you shall ever find a tender, indulgent, and affectionate husband, and your present little daughter shall find in me everything she could wish for in a father. My fortune, my dear madam, is not inconsiderable. I have a large landed estate in Maryland and Virginia, and my practice brings me more than twelve thousand dollars a year. Our estates united will enable us to live in a style of happiness equal to our wishes. And so far am I, my dear madam, from wishing my little girls to be benefited by your estate, that if we should not increase our family, your fortune, whatever it may be, shall be your own if you survive me, or if you should not survive me, your daughter's. Forgive, my dear madam, the liberty I have taken in thus laying before you my wishes and my hopes, and do me the honor to write to me and treat me with the same candor. Should your answer be favorable, I will fly to you the

the old mansion in unostentatious but liberal style, and dispense a generous but charming hospitality. The atmosphere of their household is quaintly antique, and there is everywhere apparent a tender reverence for the traditions and associations of the past. Both ladies enjoy the confidence and respect

first moment in my power, and express my gratitude at the feet of her on whom, from that time, I shall depend for my happiness. With the most perfect esteem and affection, I am, my dear madam, your sincere friend and lover,

"LUTHER MARTIN."

(No. 2.)

"AT MRS. WYANT'S (no post-mark),
"ANNAPOLIS, May 14, 1800.

"MY DEAR MADAM,—Believe me when I assure you that I feel for you the most perfect respect, and it would give me infinite pain should you consider my letter to you as being in any manner wanting therein. It was the apprehension that you would leave Baltimore before I could return from this place that caused me to lay before you in the manner I have done those wishes which I otherwise intended to have declared personally, and which have not been hastily formed, for though I have not had the happiness of much personal acquaintance, I am no stranger to your merit. I wish to obtain for myself a kind and amiable companion for life, and for my two little daughters a worthy mother. You, my dear madam, are the lady who for some time past I had selected from your sex, as far as depends on myself, to supply that place, and I regret that I did not sooner know of your visit to Baltimore. Permit me once more, my very dear madam, to assure you most solemnly that if you can prevail on yourself to accept my hand and consent to my wishes, the unremitted study of my future life shall be to render you happy and to promote the interest of your amiable daughter.

"Permit me also most respectfully to solicit that you will honor me with an answer, and that you will not forbid me to hope that to you I may be indebted for my future happiness.

"With the sincerest esteem and affection, I am your friend and lover, and ardently wish you may honor me so far as also to give me a right hereafter to sign myself your tender and affectionate husband,

"LUTHER MARTIN."

[No. 3.]

"BALTIMORE, July 26, 1800.

"MY VERY DEAR AMIABLE MRS. HAGER,—Unless you have experienced something like it yourself, you cannot imagine the vacancy in my existence which your absence hath occasioned. I feel quite a solitary being, and shall so feel until I am blessed with the animating presence of my other, my better half. With what solicitude do I look forward to that period, and how tedious will be each hour until that time pass away. To you, my dearest, best of women, I have avowed my love and affection. Will you not then bestow on me the dear delight, by way of softening the pains of absence, of an assurance that you can, without a sacrifice of your own wishes, reward my love and affection by reciprocal affection on your part? You know not with what anxiety I shall on my return from New York fly to the post-office for a letter. Do not, dearest madam, disappoint me. . . .

"I have been told since you left town that on last Sunday week, in the evening, I was at your lodgings. Of this I had no recollection. I doubt not I made a very foolish figure, but I think it impossible that I should have behaved with rudeness or impropriety. Was that the reason, my very dear Mrs. H., of the coldness and reserve you appeared to me with on the Monday morning when I called on you before I went to Annapolis? If so, I will not blame you; but be assured you shall never see me again in a situation that I know not what I do, unless it should proceed from the intoxication of love! In the heat of summer my health requires that I should drink in abundance to supply the amazing waste from perspiration, but having found that I was so unexpectedly affected as I was by cool water and brandy, I have determined to mix my water with less dangerous liquors; nay, I am not only confining myself to mead, cider, beer, hock, mixed with soda-water, but I am accustoming myself to drink water alone. Thus if we live to see each other again, you will find me most completely reformed and one of the soberest of the sober. I hope, my dearest madam, that you arrived at your home in health, and that you remain so. The heat was so great that it is impossible you could have traveled with much satisfaction. Be so good as to express my affectionate regard to our amiable daughter, and be assured that the first wish of my heart is that her very amiable mother will give an undisputed right that she should be so called to her sincere and affectionate friend and lover,

"LUTHER MARTIN."

(No. 4.)

"BALTIMORE, Sept, 4, 1800.

"MY DEAR MADAM,—I returned from Richmond, in Virginia, on last Monday. I was one week gone. I returned much fatigued but in good health. But alas, alas, what is health to me? To a poor wretch, who, before you hear of him again, will most probably be tucked up, swinging from the limb of some convenient gallows-formed tree, something like those figures a little resemblant of the human shape which some prudent farmers hang up in their corn-fields to scare the birds from their corn. Yes, my dearest madam, be not alarmed should you hear that your swain, in a fit of despair, has in the French style given you the slip by sticking his neck into a noose; for alas! my dearest madam, I have been this day informed that some time past at Mr. Peck's tavern, some of the company having introduced our names, for you know impertinent people will take these liberties, some wight of great self-consequence, but whose name I cannot yet learn, most solemnly pledged himself that our union should not take place, and that he would undertake to prevent it. Nay, further, that some kind friend, who would be eternally miserable should you throw yourself away upon such a miscreant as myself, has sent you a cautionary letter, in which are enumerated all my sins and indignities. Now, my very dear madam, can you wonder should you after this hear that I had hung myself in despair? But to be serious, I have infinitely too good an opinion of your understanding and judgment to believe that you will suffer any person to put you, like a child, in leading-strings and compel you to move only subservient to their wills, and I have infinitely too good an opinion of the candor and generosity of your heart to believe that you will ever suffer your conduct towards me to be influenced by the cowardly attacks of an assassin in the dark. I have no doubt there are persons who would go half-way to the devil to prevent our union, and who can lie and misrepresent almost equal to their old master; but as I feel a consciousness that there is nothing in my situation in life, in my fortune, in my character, in my past or present life, which ought to justify to deprive me of that happiness I solicit, or render me unworthy of that blessing, I only ask that I may have an opportunity of explaining or falsifying any suggestions to my prejudice before they shall be supposed to influence your conduct towards me. Having thus discussed that subject, permit me to thank you, of the entire community of Hagerstown, which regards them with affectionate pride as the oldest representatives now living in the town, of the original proprietor, Jonathan Hager.

From memoranda in their possession, it is evident that eighty or ninety years ago Hagerstown was the centre of an exceptionally refined and highly cultivated society. In addition to the intelligent German families who had settled in the vicinity or in the town itself, it had received valuable accessions from the wealthiest and most aristocratic of the leading Southern Maryland and Eastern Shore families, such as the Ringgolds, the Tilghmans, the Buchanans, the Spriggs, the Belts, the Fitzhughs, etc. The period was one of fine dress and courtly equipage, of lace and ruffles, of powdered hair and silken hose, of "routs" and other entertainments of the most elaborate and lavish character. A gentleman's full dress at that time consisted of long silk stockings, short-clothes, embroidered vest, cut low in order to display

my dearest madam, for your favor of the 1st instant. You are so good as to receive the trifles I send you and express your thanks for them. I am equally actuated in sending them, as they may give pleasure in the enjoyment to yourself and our dear child, and as they are proofs of my affectionate attention to you,—another proof of which be so good as to accept in the few watermelons and cantaleups which will accompany this. The moment, my dearest madam, I receive from you the promised papers I will address the most immediate measures for your interest, and will give you my services in the execution of those measures. Why have you not mentioned to me my dear Elizabeth? I hope my sweet girl is well, and that she doth not hate me; present to her my sincerest wishes for her happiness. Promise me, my dearest Mrs. H., a longer letter by the return of the stage or post. Oh, my dearest madam! let me hope that you will throw off that unaccountable reserve which you have so long assumed, and which I am willing to suppose you mean as a trial of your power and of my patience. Indeed, my dearest madam, you have had proof sufficient of both, now be so very good as on your part to bless me with the assurance that you can without a sacrifice of your own wishes promise to receive as an affectionate, indulgent, tender husband him whom you have found a sincere and affectionate friend and lover.

"Yours, L. MARTIN."

(No. 5.)

"BALTIMORE, Dec. 17, 1800.

"It was, my dearest Mrs. H., with inexpressible delight that I once more received your handwriting. Indeed, you had been very cruel in so long neglecting me, and I felt it most sensibly. Were you really impressed with the belief that I love you with that tenderness and sincerity which is truly the case, I think you have too much generosity of disposition and goodness of heart intentionally to give me pain. But I will not, my dear madam, trouble you with complaints at present, whatever injustice I may have to charge you with. I will defer the charge until we are so happy to be 'by ourselves' in one of our habitations in Baltimore, where I shall demand personal satisfaction, which, I hope, you will not refuse me. And so my charming widow has really taken a house in Baltimore, and is coming to spend the winter there. Indeed, indeed, my dear, I will try hard to turn you out of possession in a very little time, and you must consent to have me a very constant visitor until that event takes place, for I shall not be able to live out of your company. Why, my ever dear, my tenderly beloved Mrs. H., did not you condescend to assure me that I should not be an unwelcome visitor on the approaching Christmas? With what joy would I have accepted the hint! Why, my best beloved, do you defer your consent to our mutual happiness, a consent which I must hope you intend to bestow on your sincere lover. Why, dearest of women, will you not name the day from which we both may date the happiest period of our lives? Is there anything in my situation of life which you wish to have explained? If so, inform me. I will explain anything you wish to know that concerns me in any respect whatever with truth, with candor, with sincerity; I will make you my judge.

"Let me entreat my dearest Mrs. H. to free me from the suspense she at present keeps me in. Tell me that you will be mine. Name the happy day that shall crown all my wishes, and my future life shall speak my joy, my love, my gratitude to you. Though you have been so unkind that you would not ask me to dine with you on Christmas-day, nor permit me to wait you on that day with a license and a ring as I wished to have done, yet, my dearest Mrs. H., permit me to increase your enjoyments at that period. By Joseph I send you a box containing some excellent raisins and currants as ingredients for mince-pies, which is generally a dish at that season, and I also send a jug of as good Madeira wine as this city can furnish. In return sometimes think of me, and think of me as one of those who delights and who always will delight in showing his approbation and affection for you, and on Christmas-day and the day after, exactly at half-past two o'clock, drink a glass of the wine to the health of your lover, exactly at which time I also will drink a glass to the health and happiness of my dearly beloved mistress. Thus we, though absent, shall have the pleasure of knowing that at that moment our thoughts are fixed on each other. Adieu, best, most beloved of women. Do not forget, do not neglect, but bless with another dear letter

"Your MARTIN."

(No. 6.)

"ANNAPOLIS, June 12, 1801.

"MY DEAR MADAM,—I have at length received and had deposited in the Chancery office all the exhibits in your case and Kershner's; as soon as I have a moment's leisure I will compare them with the depositions and proceed to do whatever may be necessary in the case. That I will render you and your daughter every service in my power, from *motives of friendship*, you may be assured. I once flattered myself you would have given me an *additional motive* for so doing. I have been for this eighteen days past engaged, without interruption, every day in the trial of causes. You may easily judge I have not had time to attend to anything else, and that my fatigue has been great. My daughters, with their friend Anna Maria Thompson, are at Governor Ogle's. They still love you, and frequently ask me when you and I are to be married. What answer can I give to that question? To my dear Betsey give my sincerest wishes for her happiness, and accept for yourself the same from your friend,

"L. MARTIN."

[Evidently, Mr. Martin had not yet abandoned hope, but the tone of his letter indicates a fear that his cause was a desperate one, and so it proved, for Mrs. Hager afterwards married Col. Henry Lewis, as we have before stated.]

the elaborate stock with its brooch of brilliants, velvet or satin coat, and pumps with enormous buckles. A lady's dress was even more costly and elaborate. On one occasion Mrs. Jonathan Hager wore plum-colored satin trimmed with fine black lace and cord and tassels. Her wardrobe also included a bewildering assortment of silk and satin costumes, the colors comprising "old gold," black, bronze, sage, and other hues which the English "renaissance" has made fashionable once more; light blue satin scarfs with trimming of lace and ribbon; capes trimmed with down; a green camel's-hair shawl, with green bonnet to match; brocades of light blue and deep pink, embroidered with bunches of flowers, etc. All the dresses were "gored," so as to set close to the figure, and all of them had long "trains." Upton Lawrence appears to have been a model entertainer of the old-fashioned type, and was noted for his handsome parties, fine dinners, and well-trained servants. He did not, however, neglect his profession, but was an eloquent and able lawyer and enjoyed an extensive practice. He also managed several farms, and was a gentleman of liberal cultivation and enlarged ideas.

The Tilghman family. Of the prominent Eastern Shore families represented among the early settlers of Washington County the Tilghmans were among the most conspicuous. Col. Frisby Tilghman, son of Judge James Tilghman, of Queen Anne's County, removed to Washington County prior to 1800 and settled on the estate known as "Rockland." His father, the third son of Susanna and Richard Frisby Tilghman, was a member of the Revolutionary conventions of Maryland of 1774, 1775, and 1776, a member of the Council of Safety throughout the war, and afterwards chief judge of the judicial district composed of Cecil, Kent, Queen Anne's, and Talbot. He was the first attorney-general of Maryland, and was a judge of the Court of Appeals from 1804 to 1809. On the 29th of June, 1769, he married Susanna, daughter of Dr. George Steuart, of Annapolis. One of their sons, Frisby, was born Aug. 4, 1773, and died on the 14th of April, 1847.

Col. Frisby Tilghman married, on the 24th of March, 1795, Anna Maria Ringgold, daughter of Gen. Samuel Ringgold, and had children,—Mary, born on the 8th of February, 1796; George, born on the 11th of May, 1797; Thomas Edward, born April 15, 1800; Susan Ann, born March 31, 1801; Frisby, born Oct. 23, 1807; and Ann Chester, born Feb. 20, 1810 (who married William Hollyday). Mrs. Anna Maria Tilghman died on the 21st of February, 1817. Her husband (Col. Frisby Tilghman) survived her, and on the 23d of September, 1819, married Louisa, daughter of Col. William Lamar, of Allegany, and had children, viz.: Louisa (who married William Hollyday), Margaret Ann (who married Gen. Thomas J. McKaig), and Sarah Lamar. Col. William Lamar married Margaret Worthington, daughter of John and Mary Todd Worthington, of Baltimore County. Their children were Mary, who married Hon. Michael E. Sprigg; William L. Lamar, who married Maria Briscoe; Richard Lamar, who died single; Louisa, who married Col. Frisby Tilghman; Ann, who married George Tilghman; and Sarah, who died single. Mary, daughter of Col. Frisby Tilghman and Anna Maria Ringgold, married Dr. William Hammond and had children,—Ann, Richard Pindell, Mary, William, Caroline, George, and Rebecca Hammond.

Richard Pindell Hammond entered West Point Military Academy in 1837, and graduated in 1841. After graduating he was assigned as brevet second lieutenant to the Third Artillery. On the 10th of September of the same year he was made a full second lieutenant. From 1841 to 1842 he served in garrison at Fort McHenry, Baltimore. For some years afterwards he served at various military stations in the South, and when the war with Mexico broke out was ordered to the front, and participated in nearly all the important engagements. Both at the storming of Churubusco and Chapultepec he distinguished himself by his intrepidity and coolness, and was brevetted major. After the war he served on the Coast Survey, and in May, 1851, resigned to engage in the practice of the law at Stockton, Cal.

George Tilghman (born on the 11th of May, 1797, died Aug. 25, 1831) was the son of Col. Frisby Tilghman, and married twice. His first wife was Ann E. Lamar, by whom he had children,—Anna Maria and Mary Tilghman, who married Phineas Janney. His second wife was Anna B. Lynn, daughter of Capt. David Lynn, of Allegany. Their children were Fanny Lynn, Susan, who married W. Bowene; George, and Frisby L., who married Anna, daughter of Col. Bolling, of Petersburg, Va.

Thomas Edward Tilghman, born on the 15th of April, 1800, was the son of Col. Frisby Tilghman, and married Rebecca Hammond. His children were Edward Sommerfield, born Jan. 21, 1827; William Frisby, born Feb. 23, 1828; Thomas Hammond, born Jan. 7, 1830. His second wife was Sarah Bugbee, by whom he had the following children: William Ridgeley, Anna Maria, Sarah, Charles Ringgold, Antoinette, Ida, and Henry.

Dr. Frisby Tilghman, son of Col. Frisby and Anna Maria Ringgold Tilghman, studied medicine in Pennsylvania, and practiced in Annapolis and Hagerstown.

He married his cousin, Henrietta Maria Hemsley, daughter of Alexander Hemsley and Henrietta Maria Tilghman. Alexander Hemsley was the son of William Hemsley, of Queen Anne's County, a member of the Continental Congress from the Eastern Shore, and Henrietta Maria Tilghman was the daughter of Lloyd Tilghman, son of Matthew, the youngest son of the second Richard Tilghman, of the Hermitage. Dr. Frisby Tilghman died, leaving no children.

Nathaniel Rochester was one of the earliest residents and most influential business men of Hagerstown. His father was John Rochester, son of Nicholas, who emigrated from England to Virginia, and settled in Westmoreland County, where he died, leaving two sons,—William and John. John married a daughter of William Thrift, of Richmond, Va., and died in 1754, leaving three daughters and two sons,—John and Nathaniel. The latter was born on the 21st of February, 1752, in Westmoreland County, Va. He was only two years old when his father died. Two years afterwards his mother married Thomas Critcher, and in 1763 the family removed to Granville, N. C. Mrs. Critcher died the same year, and Thomas Critcher died in 1778. Nathaniel's opportunities for education in early life were of the most limited description, but he possessed a vigorous mind and great energy of character, and whenever and wherever he could obtain it never failed to store his mind with information that might prove useful in later years. His youth was spent in mercantile business, and at the age of twenty he engaged in business with Col. John Hamilton, who afterwards held the consulate of the British government for the Middle States. When the Revolutionary war broke out he entered the Continental service, and by his gallantry and good conduct attained the rank of lieutenant-colonel at a very early age. After the war he again engaged in mercantile pursuits, first in Philadelphia and afterwards in Hagerstown, where he associated himself with Col. Thomas Hart, who in 1793 removed to Lexington, Ky. Two of Col. Hart's daughters married, respectively, Henry Clay and James Benton, father of the celebrated Thomas Hart Benton.

The names of Hart & Rochester, of N. & R. Rochester, of Thomas Hart & Son, and of William Fitzhugh are constantly recurring in the brief "notes" of the early enterprises and business of Hagerstown. Thomas Hart, N. Rochester, and William Fitzhugh were citizens of Hagerstown at the end of the last and the beginning of the present century. The following old advertisement sets forth alike their kind of business and the prices that ruled at that time:

"HART AND ROCHESTER
Have, and will constantly keep, for sale a
LARGE QUANTITY OF
NAILS, BRADS, AND SPRIGS,

of their own manufacturing, in Hager's-Town, at the following Prices:—Twenty-penny nails and flooring brads, at nine-pence per pound, or thirteen shillings and six-pence per thousand; sprigs of different sizes, in proportion (the quality of these nails being far superior to those imported from Europe, they have not a doubt of the preference being given to them at the above-mentioned prices); Twelve-penny, or shingle-nails, at nine-pence per pound, or eleven shillings three-pence per thousand; ten-penny nails at nine-pence per pound, or ten shillings per thousand; eight-penny nails at ten-pence per pound, or eight shillings and four-pence per thousand; six-penny nails at eleven-pence per pound, or seven shillings per thousand; four-penny or case nails, at four shillings and six-pence per thousand.

Hager's-Town, August 20, 1790."

Nathaniel Rochester, the other member of the firm, was well known to the old inhabitants of Washington County as a distinguished merchant, politician, and agriculturist. He was a candidate, and elected, on the electoral ticket in 1808 (in connection with Dr. John Tyler, of Frederick Town) in favor of the election of James Madison to the Presidency,—Frederick, Washington, and Allegany Counties constituting the district. In 1810 he removed from Washington County, Md, to the Genesee country in Western New York, and settled in what is now known as Monroe County. He purchased land on which the city of Rochester (named after him) is now built *at a pound of bacon for an acre of land.*

Col. Rochester, June 25, 1794, "declined the mercantile business in this place" (Hagerstown), and earnestly requested "all those indebted to him or to the late concern of Nathaniel & Robert Rochester, to make immediate payment, that he may be enabled to continue and enlarge his nail and rope manufactories." In October, 1804, he was elected sheriff, and resigned then the office of postmaster, having been the first postmaster of Hagerstown. Nov. 20, 1810, Col. Rochester advertised for sale his Hagerstown residence,—"a brick dwelling-house sixty-eight by twenty-two feet," with rope-house and rope-walk. On the 13th November, 1800, Mr. William Fitzhugh advertised for sale his residence and seven hundred acres, four miles from Hagerstown; and on November 4th, Col. Charles Carroll advertised his estate of one thousand and fifty acres adjoining Hagerstown. Whether the sales were then effected is not stated, but the three gentlemen emigrated to the Genesee Valley in New York.

Col. Rochester married Sophia, daughter of Col. William Beatty, of Frederick County, Md., on the 20th of April, 1788, and died on the 14th of May,

1831, in Rochester, N. Y., in his eightieth year. His widow died in the same place. They had twelve children. Col. Rochester was the first president of the Hagerstown Bank, and his portrait, painted while he held that position, is now in possession of the bank, and is highly prized by the officers of that institution. Col. William Beatty's wife and Mrs. Rochester's mother were the daughters of John Conrad Grosh, a respectable German immigrant, who settled in Frederick County about 1750. Col. Rochester removed to the Genesee country early in the present century, in company with Charles Carroll, of Bellevue, and Col. William Fitzhugh. He left his home in Hagerstown when over sixty years of age, and with his family and household goods journeyed across the State of Pennsylvania, in wagons and carriages, to the site of the city of Rochester. At his death he had amassed great wealth.

Col. Rochester's sons were William, who was lost at sea; Thomas, a judge of the court at Rochester, died a few years since; Nathaniel, a lawyer; Henry E.,[1] now living at Livingston Park, near Rochester; Mrs. Childs (Sophia); Mrs. Dr. Montgomery (Mary); Mrs. Bishop (Caroline); Mrs. Dr. Pitkin (Louisa); and Mrs. Coleman (Anna).

The Carrolls. Charles Carroll, who was one of

[1] The Hagerstown *Mail* of June 10, 1881, gives the following account of a visit of Henry E. Rochester, son of Col. Rochester, to that place in 1881:

"In 1810, Col. Nathaniel Rochester, one of the pioneers of the Genesee Valley in Western New York, and co-founder of the great city there which bears his name, left his home in Hagerstown at the mature age of sixty-one years, and, with his family, started, in carriages and wagons, across the State of Pennsylvania, taking with him most of his household goods, for his new home in the rich wilderness, now one of the garden-spots of the American continent. Of that cortege the youngest member was Henry E. Rochester, the youngest son, then four years old, and who on Wednesday last, seventy-one years after he had left the place of his birth, returned to it a father and a grandfather, in the full possession of health and of a mind and heart capable of taking in the full enjoyment of such a return. A few weeks before we had taken the liberty of publishing, with his initials, a private letter, in which was shown the deep interest which remained with him in matters pertaining to his old home, and it was with exceptional pleasure that we greeted him on Wednesday morning, and walked with him through the streets so familiar to and so much cherished by both.

"One of the first persons encountered in the stroll was Governor Hamilton, who was about to get into his buggy, on his way to his farms on the northern borders of Hagerstown, one of which was, when Mr. Rochester left here a child, owned by his mother's brother, Elie Beatty, and the other by Maj. Charles Carroll, who, with Col. Rochester and Col. Fitzhugh, were the co-partners in the pioneer enterprise of opening the Genesee country to agriculture, and in locating and founding the city which bears the name of 'Rochester,' and has to-day a population of one hundred thousand souls. That this ride with the Governor of the State and present proprietor of those farms was a pleasant one to the visitor we can readily imagine, and in addition have his own assurance. . . . That portion of the valley was seventy years ago, as it is now, noted for its fertility, and many changes, which are improvements, have been made, particularly in respect to the private macadamized roads by which those farms are approached, and in additions to the original mansions; but the old Beatty house was still on 'Oak Hill,' as the place was then called, and the old Carroll house still stands on the Bellevue farm, almost unchanged from what it was when Charles Carroll, of Bellevue, left it nearly seventy years ago to join his partners in the Genesee Valley.

"Later in the day, and after his return on Wednesday from those old scenes, we accompanied Mr. Rochester to East Franklin Street, to see one of the oldest of the old men of Hagerstown,—Mr. William Miller, now in his eighty-ninth year, and with a memory as accurate as it was at twenty-nine,—between whom and Mr. Rochester a mutual desire to meet had been expressed. Mr. Miller had previously, in conversation with us, shown a perfect recollection of the persons, characters, peculiarities, and homes of both Col. Rochester and Maj. Carroll, and could describe the latter as he rode from his estate into Hagerstown, around the corner at the Catholic church, seventy years ago, with as much precision as if it were but yesterday. His courtly manners and genial bearing made an impression upon the boy which survives in the nonogenarian. Mr. Miller's recollection of Col. Rochester was equally vivid, and when he and Mr. Henry E. Rochester met they at once launched out into reminiscences of the past, which showed how vivid was their recollection, and how deeply they had been impressed as youths. Mr. Miller spoke of the time when Col. Rochester lived in the stone house on North Potomac Street, now owned by Mr. William S. Williamson, and Mr. Rochester asked if that place was not then called 'Potato Hill,' to which Mr. Miller replied, 'Yes; and is so called now.' . . . At a later hour, as we passed the old stone house, now owned by Governor Hamilton, and occupied by Mr. Daniel White as a saloon, next the Antietam House, Mr. Rochester paused, and pointing out the alteration in the doorways, which now reach to the pavement, and in front of which there was once quite a high porch, said that he well recollected, though but a child, the vendue of his father's effects before leaving for New York, which took place in front of the porch, and especially did he recollect the man with a bell, who stood on the porch ringing it to bring the bidders to the sale. It is hardly necessary to say that it is in that very same spot every week farms and stocks and bonds are sold by thousands, just as Col. Rochester's household effects were seventy years ago.

"In a subsequent conversation with our friend, Mr. Rochester, we had a description of the passage of the emigrant family across the State of Pennsylvania, with the farmers' six-horse covered wagons to convey the effects and carriages the family, attracting attention wherever they passed, and this movement being followed by other families from this section, whose descendants are now among the prominent people of Western New York. Particularly did he recollect that a Mr. Schnebly, who afterwards kept the 'Globe Hotel,' and was for many years register of wills of our county, then a young man, had permission of Col. Rochester to go along with the party, he acting as driver of the family carriage, in order that he might see the country, which then attracted such interest. But it is hardly necessary to add that this young adventurer returned to his old home and died here at a ripe old age.

"Yesterday, Mr. Rochester had set apart to dine with some friends and to revisit the bank, to see his father's portrait, which is still preserved there, he being the first president of that institution."

Col. Rochester's associates in settling the Genesee country in New York, was one of the wealthy men of Washington County about 1800. He owned a tract of eleven or twelve hundred acres of the best land in the county, on the northern border of Hagerstown, now in part the property of Governor Hamilton and in part the site of Bellevue Asylum, erected several years ago by Washington County. Mr. Carroll's residence was a large stone mansion, one hundred and fifty feet in length. It is still standing, and is now occupied as a country-seat by Hon. William T. Hamilton. The property has been improved by Mr. Hamilton by the construction of a macadamized road from the turnpike, with a substantial stone fence on either side, and in many other ways. Mr. Carroll left three sons,—Charles, a man of great wealth and prominence, who remained in New York, William, who removed to Washington, and David. Charles H. Carroll, born in Washington County, was a representative in Congress from New York from 1843 to 1847, and a member of the Assembly in 1836, a State Senator in 1837. He was a lawyer by profession, but devoted his whole time to the management of a large estate in Genesee County. He died at Groveland, Livingston Co., N. Y., in 1865, aged seventy-one.

The Wetzels. The celebrated Indian-fighters, Lewis and Jacob Wetzel, were natives of Lewistown District, in Frederick County. They were born a quarter of a mile from Lewistown Village, on a farm now owned by George Eisenangle, and when young removed with their parents to near Wheeling, W. Va., where their father and mother were, with their brothers and sisters, cruelly massacred by the Indians. The boys Lewis and Jacob swore eternal vengeance against the savages, and roamed the forests killing Indians whenever and wherever they met them. Belmont County, Ohio, was the scene of two of the daring adventures of Lewis Wetzel, the far-famed borderer, whose exploits alone would fill a volume.

The road along what is now the Cincinnati waterfront, leading from Storrs' to Delhi, crossed what was in early days the outlet of a water-course, and notwithstanding the changes made by the lapse of years and the building improvements adjacent, the spot still possesses many traces of original beauty. At the period of this adventure, Oct. 7, 1790, Jacob Wetzel had been out hunting, and was returning to town, which at that time consisted of a few cabins and huts collected in the space fronting the river. He had been very successful, and was returning to procure a horse to bear a load too heavy for his own shoulders. At the spot mentioned he sat down on a decaying tree-trunk to rest himself. While seated thus he heard the rustling of leaves and branches, and silencing the growl of his dog, who sat at his feet and appeared equally conscious of danger, he sprang behind a tree and discovered the dark form of an Indian half hidden by the body of an oak, who had his rifle in his hands ready to fire. At this instant Wetzel's dog spied the Indian and barked, thus informing the Indian of the proximity of an enemy. Discovering Wetzel behind the tree, he took aim and fired, and the crack of the two weapons was almost simultaneous. The Indian's rifle fell from his hands, the ball of the hunter having penetrated and broken his left elbow, while Wetzel escaped unhurt. Before the Indian could reload, Wetzel rushed swiftly upon him with his knife, but not before the Indian had drawn his own. The first thrust was parried by the Indian with the greatest skill, and the hunter's knife was thrown some thirty feet from him. Nothing daunted, he threw himself upon the Indian and seized him around the body, at the same time grasping the right arm in which the Indian held his knife. The savage, however, was very muscular, and the conflict was a doubtful one at first. In the struggle their feet became interlocked, and they both fell to the ground, the Indian uppermost; this extricated the Indian's arm from the iron grasp of the hunter, and he endeavored to stab Wetzel, but the latter forced him over on his right side, and consequently he could have no use of his right arm. By a desperate effort, however, he succeeded in getting Wetzel underneath him again, and raised his arm for the fatal plunge. Just at this moment the hunter's faithful dog sprang forward and seized the Indian by the throat, and caused the weapon to fall harmless from his hand. Wetzel then made a desperate effort and threw the Indian from him. Before the prostrate savage had time to recover himself the hunter had seized his knife, and rushing upon him, plunged the weapon into his breast, killing him instantly.

As soon as Wetzel had possessed himself of his rifle, together with the Indian's weapons, he started on his way again, but had gone but a short distance when his ears were assailed by the startling war-whoop of a number of Indians. He ran down to the river, and finding a canoe on the beach, near the water, was soon out of reach, and made his way in safety to the town.

Lewis Wetzel roamed through the Ohio Valley, and Belmont County, Ohio, was the scene of two of his daring adventures. While hunting he fell in with a young frontiersman who lived on Dunkard's Creek, and who persuaded him to accompany him to his home. On their arrival they found the house in ruins and all the family murdered except a young woman who had been raised with them, and to whom the young man was ardently attached. She had been carried off alive, as was found by examining the trail of the enemy, who were three Indians and a white renegade. Burning with revenge they followed the trail until opposite the mouth of the Captina, where the enemy had crossed. They swam the stream and discovered the Indian camp, around the fires of which lay the enemy in careless repose. The young woman was apparently unhurt, but was making much lamentation and moaning. The young man, hardly able to restrain his rage, was for firing and rushing instantly upon them. Wetzel, more cautious, told him to wait until daylight, when there would be a better chance of killing the whole party. At dawn the Indians prepared to depart. The young man selecting the white renegade and Wetzel an Indian, they both fired simultaneously with fatal effect. The young man then rushed forward knife in hand to release the girl, while Wetzel reloaded and pursued the two remaining savages, who had taken to the woods. Wetzel, as soon as he was discovered, discharged his rifle at random, in order to draw them from their covert. The ruse took effect, and taking to his heels, he loaded as he ran, and suddenly wheeling about discharged his rifle through the body of his nearest enemy. The remaining Indian, seeing that his enemy's rifle was unloaded, rushed forward in eager pursuit, but Wetzel led him on, dodging from tree to tree, until his rifle was again ready, when suddenly turning he fired, and his remaining enemy fell dead at his feet. After taking their scalps Wetzel and his friend with their rescued captive returned in safety to the settlement. A short time after Crawford's defeat, in 1782, Wetzel accompanied Thomas Mills, a soldier in that action, to obtain his horse, which he had left some distance away. They were met by a party of about forty Indians at the Indian Springs, two miles from St. Clairsville, on the road to Wheeling. Both parties discovered each other at the same moment, when Lewis instantly turned and fired, killing an Indian. A shot from the Indians wounded his companion in the heel, and the savages overtook and killed him. Four Indians pursued Wetzel, who wheeled on one of them and shot him. He then continued his flight, and less than a mile farther a second Indian came so close to him that as Wetzel turned to fire he caught the muzzle of his gun. After a severe struggle Wetzel succeeded in pointing it at his chest, and firing his opponent fell dead. Wetzel still continued on his course pursued by the two Indians; all three were pretty well fatigued, and often stopped and "treed." After going something more than a mile, Wetzel took advantage of a piece of open ground over which the Indians were passing and stopped suddenly to shoot the foremost, who thereupon sprang behind a small sapling. Wetzel fired and wounded him mortally. The remaining Indian then turned and fled. About 1795 Wetzel went farther west, where he could trap the beaver, hunt the buffalo and deer, and occasionally shoot an Indian.

The Poes. In the present tavern of George H. Clem, situated in Lewistown District, Frederick County, were born the two brothers, Adam and Andrew Poe, the noted Indian-fighters. Their father had the old mill on Fishing Creek, the first ever built in the district. When these brothers were small their father removed to near Wheeling, W. Va., and throughout that section and portions of Pennsylvania the Poe boys became the terror of the savages. Adam finally settled in Columbiana County, Ohio, and in that and Portage County of the same State are found many of his descendants. The following is a narrative of the celebrated fight of these two brothers with the Indians nearly opposite the mouth of Little Yellow Creek, in Columbiana County, Ohio.

In the summer of 1782 a party of seven Wyandots made an incursion into a settlement some distance below Fort Pitt, and several miles from the Ohio River. Here, finding an old man alone in a cabin, they killed him, packed up what plunder they could find and retreated. Among their party was a celebrated Wyandot chief, who, in addition to his fame as a warrior and counselor, was a giant in size and strength. The news of the visit soon spread through the neighborhood, and a party of eight good riflemen was collected in a few hours for the purpose of pursuing the Indians. In this party were the brothers Adam and Andrew Poe. They were both famous for their courage, size, and activity. This little party commenced the pursuit of the Indians, with the determination, if possible, not to let the murderers escape, as they usually did on such occasions, by making a speedy flight to the river, crossing it, and then dividing themselves into small parties to meet at a distant point in a given time. The pursuit was continued the greater part of the night. In the morning the party found themselves on the trail leading to the river. When they arrived within a short distance of the river, Adam Poe, fearing an ambuscade, left the party, who followed directly on the trail, and crept along the river-bank, under cover of the weeds and bushes, to fall on the rear of the Indians should he find them hidden there. He had not gone far before he saw Indian rafts at the water's edge. Not seeing any Indians, however, he stepped softly down the bank with his rifle cocked. When about half-way down he discovered the Wyandot chief with a small Indian within a few steps of him. They were standing with their guns cocked and looking in the direction of the party, who by this time had gone lower down into the bottom. Poe took aim at the large chief, but his rifle missed fire. The Indians hearing the snap of the gunlock instantly turned and discovered Poe, who, being too near them to retreat, dropped his gun and instantly sprung from the bank upon them. Seizing the large Indian by the cloths on his breast and at the same time embracing the neck of the small one, he threw them both down on the ground and fell with them. The small Indian soon extricated himself, and running to the raft procured his tomahawk and attempted to dispatch Poe while the large Indian held him fast in his arms. But Poe watched the motions of the smaller Indian, and when he was in the act of aiming his blow at his head, by a vigorous and well-directed kick with one of his feet staggered the savage and knocked the tomahawk out of his hand. This failure on the part of the smaller Indian was rebuked by an exclamation of contempt and disgust from the large one. In a moment the Indian caught up his tomahawk again and approached more cautiously, brandishing and making a number of feints at his intended victim. Poe averted the real blow from his head by throwing up his arm and receiving it on his wrist, in which he was severely wounded, but not so much so as to lose entirely the use of his hand. In this perilous moment Poe, by a violent effort, released himself from the Indian, and snatching up one of the guns shot the smaller Indian through the breast as he ran up the third time to tomahawk him. The large Indian, who was now upon his feet, grasped Poe by a shoulder and leg and threw him down on the bank. Poe instantly disengaged himself and got on his feet again. The Indian then seized him again, and a new struggle ensued, which, owing to the slippery state of the bank, ended in the precipitation of both combatants into the water. In this situation it was the object of each to drown the other. Their efforts to effect their purpose were continued for some time, until Poe at length succeeded in grasping the savage's scalplock, with which he held his head under the water until he supposed he was drowned. Relaxing his hold too soon, Poe instantly found his gigantic antagonist still living and ready for another combat. While struggling they were carried into the water beyond their depth. In this situation they were compelled to loose their hold on one another and swim for mutual safety. The Indian being the best swimmer reached the land first. Poe, seeing this, immediately turned back in the water to escape being shot by diving. Fortunately, the Indian caught up the rifle with which Poe had killed the other warrior, and which therefore was unloaded. At this juncture Andrew Poe, who had missed his brother from the party, and supposing from the report of the gunshot that he was either killed or engaged in a conflict with the Indians, hastened to the spot. On seeing him Adam called out to him to kill the big Indian on shore. But Andrew's gun, like the Indian's, was empty. The contest was now between the white man and the Indian as to who should load first and fire. Very fortunately for Poe, the Indian in loading drew the ramrod from the stock of the gun with such violence that it slipped out of his hand and fell a little distance from him. He quickly caught it up and rammed down his bullet. This delay gave Poe the advantage. He shot the Indian as he was taking aim at him. He then leaped into the water to assist his wounded brother ashore, but Adam, thinking more of the honor of carrying the big Indian home as a trophy of victory than his own safety, urged Andrew to go back and prevent the struggling savage from rolling himself into the river and escaping. Andrew's solicitude for the life of his brother prevented him from complying with this request. In the mean time the Indian, jealous of the honor of his scalp even in the agonies of death, succeeded in reaching the river and getting into the current, so that his body was never obtained. Just as Andrew arrived at the top of the bank for the relief of his brother, one of the party who had followed close behind him, seeing Adam in the river and mistaking him for a wounded Indian, shot at him and wounded him in the shoulder. He recovered, however, from the wound. During the contest between Adam Poe and the Indians the party had overtaken the remaining six of them, and a desperate conflict had ensued, in which five of the Indians were killed. The loss of the whites was three men killed and Andrew Poe badly wounded.

The slaughter of the Indians, especially of their chief, caused great excitement among the Wyandots, the chief with his four brothers, all of whom were killed at the same place, being among the most distinguished warriors of their nation. The chief was magnanimous as well as brave, and, more than any other individual, contributed by his example and influence to the good character of the Wyandots for lenity towards their prisoners. He would not suffer them to be killed or mistreated. On learning the result of the conflict with the Poes and their companions the Wyandots determined on revenge. Poe then lived on the west side of the Ohio River, at the mouth of Little Yellow Creek. They chose Pohn-yen-ness, one of their warriors, as a proper person to murder him and then make his escape. He went to Poe's house, and was met with great friendship, Poe not having any suspicion of his design. The best food in the house was furnished him, and when the time came to retire for the night Poe made a pallet on the floor for his guest. He and his wife went to bed in the same room. Pohn-yen-ness afterwards said that they soon fell to sleep, and there being no person about the house but some children he thus had the desired opportunity to execute his purpose. But the kindness they had shown him worked on his mind, and he asked himself how he could kill an enemy who had taken him in and treated him like a brother. On the other hand, he had been sent by his nation to avenge the death of some of their most valiant warriors, and their ghosts would not be appeased until the blood of Poe was shed. He continued undecided until about midnight, when the duty he owed to his nation and the spirits of his friends aroused him. He seized his knife and tomahawk, and crept to the bedside of his sleeping host. Again the kindness he had received from Poe recurred to him, and unable to execute his crime he crept back to his pallet and slept until morning. His host then repeated the kindness of the previous night, and told him they were once enemies, but he had buried the hatchet and were brothers, and hoped they would always be so. Pohn-yen-ness returned to his tribe, and subsequently became a convert to Christianity.

Maj.-Gen. Perry Benson, of Washington County, was another of the distinguished soldiers whom Western Maryland gave to the country during the Revolutionary struggle. He displayed conspicuous gallantry at the battles of Cowpens and Guilford Court-house, at Hobkirk's Hill, and at Ninety-Six, where he led the forlorn hope. At Hobkirk's Hill Capt. Benson commanded the picket-guard, consisting of about two hundred and twenty men, and checked the advance of the whole British army until the American forces, which were separated and unprepared for an attack, could be concentrated and formed for battle, and did not retire until his command had poured six deadly volleys into the enemy, and he had lost in killed and wounded all but thirty-three of his men. In the attack on Ninety-Six Capt. Benson commanded the forlorn hope, and was shot down within a few yards of the enemy's works, while encouraging his command. He did not recover from the effects of this wound for many years, and even to the end of his life was occasionally a sufferer from it. During the Whisky Insurrection he joined the army with the rank of colonel, and in 1812, in spite of the infirmities of advancing age, he took an active part in the defense of the State as brigadier-general of militia, on one occasion handsomely repulsing a British attack on the town of St. Michael's with a small body of raw militia. Previous to the war of 1812 he had represented his county in the Lower House of Assembly, which was the only civil office he ever held. He died on the 2d of October, 1827, in the seventy-second year of his age, and was interred in the family burial-ground.

The Williams family. There is scarcely any family of Western Maryland that has played a more conspicuous *rôle* in its early history than did the Williamses. Otho Holland and Elie Williams were sons of Joseph Williams and Prudence Holland. Their father was of Welsh ancestry of gentle blood. In 1750 he removed to what was then Frederick County, near the mouth of Conococheague Creek. Otho Holland Williams was appointed at a very early age to a position in the clerk's office of Frederick County, which he held for several years, after which the office was given entirely into his charge. He subsequently held the position of Collector of the Port of Baltimore. At the breaking out of the Revolutionary war he enlisted in the colonial service, and became a distinguished officer.[1] Gen. Williams died July 15, 1794.

His brother, Col. Elie Williams, who died at Georgetown, D. C., in 1823, in his seventy-third year, was also conspicuous during the Revolution, and in the latter part of his life was an ardent advocate of internal improvements, especially the Chesapeake and Ohio Canal, in which he retained an active interest up to the time of his death.

Col. Elie Williams left two sons, Col. John S. and Gen. Otho H. Williams. Col. John S. Williams, who died at Washington, D. C., June 14, 1868, served as major in the war of 1812, and published an interesting narrative of the battle of Bladensburg. He lived for many years in Washington, and was president of the Association of Oldest Inhabitants of that city.

Gen. Otho Holland Williams, the younger, was born in 1784, and died Oct. 24, 1869. He was appointed clerk of Washington County Court in 1800, and continued to hold this office until February, 1845, a period of nearly forty-five years, during which time he discharged his duties to the entire satisfaction of the public. He was also at one time a judge of the

[1] For a sketch of Gen. Otho H. Williams, see the history of Williamsport District, in this county.

Orphans' Court of Washington County. Mr. Williams was an ardent Whig, and the intimate friend and warm personal admirer of Henry Clay.

He derived his military title from his appointment by the Governor of Maryland as brigadier-general of militia. Mr. Williams was a very active politician in his earlier years, and enjoyed great personal popularity throughout his career.

Gen. Samuel Ringgold was the son of Thomas Ringgold and Mary Galloway, and was born in Kent Co., Md., about 1770. The Ringgolds were among the earliest settlers of that section of Maryland, and the family in subsequent generations maintained a conspicuous position among the landed gentry of the State. On the 3d of May, 1792, Samuel Ringgold married Mary, daughter of Gen. John Cadwalader. Soon afterwards he removed from Kent to Washington County, and located himself at "Fountain Rock," near Hagerstown. He owned an immense estate, containing, it is said, some seventeen thousand acres of land in one of the most fertile and attractive sections of the State, and known as "Ringgold's Manor." He was also interested in an extensive tract in Pennsylvania.[1]

At Fountain Rock, Gen. Ringgold erected a splendid mansion, which in later years was converted into St. James' College. It was decorated with stucco-work and wood-carving executed with great taste and care. Many of the doors of the mansion were of solid mahogany, and the outbuildings, appointments, etc., were of the handsomest character. The architect was the distinguished Benjamin H. Latrobe, who was also one of the architects of the National Capitol at Washington. It was Gen. Ringgold's practice to drive to Washington in his coach and four with outriders, and to bring his political associates home with him. Among his guests were President Monroe and Henry Clay. Gen. Ringgold lived in great elegance and state, and is said to have squandered a large fortune. One local tradition even has it that he was wont to light his cigars with bank-notes. He was famous for his hospitality and for his pleasant genial manners. Towards the latter part of his life he became financially embarrassed, and died at the residence of his son-in-law, William Schley, in Frederick, on the 18th of October, 1829, aged about sixty years. Gen. Ringgold, who was very popular with all classes, was one of the most successful and influential politicians of his day. He was a member of Congress from 1810 to 1815, and again from 1817 to 1821, and held various local offices from time to time. He was also very active in organizing the militia of his section of the State, and was appointed brigadier-general. Probably no man ever lived in Western Maryland who exerted a wider influence or enjoyed a more unqualified popularity. "Fountain Rock" was sold to liquidate his debts, and went into the possession of the Hollingsworth family.[2]

When Rev. Dr. J. B. Kerfoot, afterwards Bishop of Pittsburgh, purchased the building for the use of St. James' College, it was in a very neglected and dilapidated condition. In the family graveyard at "Fountain Rock" the following persons are buried:

Samuel Ringgold, died Oct. 18, 1829, aged sixty.

Maria Ringgold, his wife, died Aug. 1, 1811, aged thirty-five.

---

[1] The following advertisements afford some idea of the extent of his landed possessions:

"ENCOURAGEMENT FOR SETTLERS.

"The subscriber wants to engage with a number of persons to settle a large quantity of land situated in the back part of Pennsylvania, about 45 miles above Pittsburgh, on the Allegany River, which is navigable to Pittsburgh, and from thence down to New Orleans. The terms are as follows. Apply to the subscriber near Williamsport.

"SAMUEL RINGGOLD.

"WASHINGTON COUNTY, June 16, 1795."

"TO THE CITIZENS OF WASHINGTON COUNTY.

"I shall offer at the next election to represent this county in the next General Assembly, and would thank you for your suffrages should you think me a proper character to fill so important an appointment. I am, Gentlemen,

"Your obedient servant,

"SAMUEL RINGGOLD.

"September 22, 1795."

In October, 1799, Tench Ringgold advertised that he would sell one thousand acres of land, lying in Washington County, within a mile and a half of Hagerstown. Following is a copy of the advertisement, viz.:

"I will sell one thousand acres of land, lying in Washington County, State of Maryland, within one mile and a half of Hagerstown.

"The above land is one of the reserves of Ringgold's Manor, well known for its fertility and advantageous situation; and it being presumed that those willing to purchase will view the premises, it will only be necessary to add that its distance from Baltimore is 70 miles, from George-town and the Federal City the same, from the Potomac six miles; and the greater part lying on Antietam Creek, having four merchant mills within one mile.

"The land will be shewn and the terms of sale made known by applying to Samuel Ringgold, esquire, at his seat, near the premises, or the subscriber, living in George-Town, on the Potomac.

"TENCH RINGGOLD.

"September 19, 1799."

[2] Sophia Givens, a former slave of Gen. Ringgold's, who was sold from the steps of the mansion, died in 1877. It was asserted that she had attained the age of one hundred and six years.

Edward Lloyd Ringgold, son of Samuel Ringgold, died July 28, 1822, aged sixteen.

Charles Ringgold, son of Samuel Ringgold, died May 28, 1817, aged six.

Charles Anthony Ringgold, son of Samuel Ringgold, died Sept. 25, 1825, aged fifteen.

Benjamin Ringgold, brother of Samuel Ringgold, died in August, 1798, aged twenty-five.

Thomas Ringgold, brother of Samuel Ringgold, died in March, 1818, aged forty.

The children of Gen. and Mrs. Samuel Ringgold were Anna Maria, born on the 10th of July, 1793, and died on the 4th of March, 1828; John Cadwalader, born 15th November, 1794, died young; Samuel, born 16th October, 1796; Mary Elizabeth, born Dec. 18, 1788, died March 9, 1836; Ann Cadwalader, born Jan. 10, 1801, and married William Schley, of Frederick; Cadwalader, born Aug. 20, 1802; Cornelia, born Jan. 27, 1809; and Charles and Frederick, twins, born 22d and 23d of July, 1810. Gen. Ringgold married in Washington at the Executive Mansion, a second time, Maria Antoinette Hay, granddaughter of President Madison, and had children, viz.: George H. Ringgold, U.S.A.; Fayette Ringgold, at one time United States consul at Peru; Virginia Ringgold, who married John Ross Key; and Rebecca Ringgold, who married Dr. Hay, of Chicago.

Three of Gen. Ringgold's sons entered the military service, viz.: Samuel, Cadwalader, and George H.

Maj. Samuel Ringgold was born October 16, 1796, and in 1814 entered West Point Military Academy. On the 24th of July, 1818, he was appointed second lieutenant of artillery. Upon his entrance into the army he received the appointment of aide to Gen. Scott, and repaired to Philadelphia, where that officer had his headquarters. After three years' service in this capacity he was detailed as an engineer under Maj. Bache to make an examination of a part of the Southern coast. At a later period he performed the duties of ordnance officer at New York. His improvement on the percussion cannon-lock, which was perfected while he was stationed in New York, brought his name prominently before leading military officers and inventors throughout the world. The lock at that time in use, not only in our own country but elsewhere, was peculiarly liable to injury from the unyielding manner in which the hammer fell upon the cap at the breech of the gun. The recoil was so great as frequently to throw the hammer from its position, and thus disable the piece. After much time and labor Maj. (then Lieut.) Ringgold succeeded in imparting a lateral motion to the hammer by means of a spring which drew it sideways and backward the moment after it gave the blow by which the cap was exploded. This invention formed the basis on which all the modern improvements were made. The military saddle was also an invention of Maj. Ringgold's.

MAJ. SAMUEL RINGGOLD.

On the 21st of May, 1821, Lieut. Ringgold was assigned to the Second Artillery, and on the 21st of August of the same year to the Third Artillery. In May, 1822, he was promoted to a first lieutenancy. In May, 1832, he was breveted captain for ten years of faithful service. In August, 1836, he was promoted to the captaincy, and on the 15th of February, 1838, was breveted major "for meritorious conduct in activity and efficiency in war against Florida Indians." He was appointed major in 1843, was mortally wounded in the battle of Palo Alto, in Mexico, and died on the 11th of May, 1846, at Point Isabel, Texas. The action of Palo Alto was a very spirited one, and Maj. Ringgold behaved with remarkable gallantry. Fire was opened by the Mexican batteries, and was responded to by Maj. Ringgold's battery. Maj. Ringgold pointed the guns with his own hands, directing the shot not only to groups and masses of men, but to particular individuals in the line. He saw them fall in numbers, and their places occupied by others, who in turn were shot down. Maj. Ringgold continued his fire for several hours, until he was shot through the thighs by a cannon-ball, passing from right to left, and carrying with it a mass of muscle and integuments, and tearing off a portion of the saddle and the withers of the horse which he was riding. He fell slowly, and before he reached the ground Lieut. Shover came to his assistance and supported him. While doing this the lieutenant called for aid to carry him to the rear. "Never mind, sir," said Maj. Ringgold, "you have work to do; go ahead with your men; all are wanted in front." Finally, however, the lieutenant persuaded him to allow him to carry him from the field. His body was taken to Baltimore, and buried there with civic and military honors on the 22d of December, 1846.[1]

[1] The following account of the death of Maj. Ringgold is taken from a letter published in the Washington *Union*. The letter is as follows:

"CAMP ISABEL, NEAR THE MOUTH
"OF THE RIO BRAVA DEL NORTE, May 9, 1846.

"The numerous friends of Maj. Ringgold will doubtless be anxious to know the particulars attending his melancholy end,

Soon after notice of Maj. Ringgold's death was received at Hagerstown a public meeting was held for the purpose of giving expression to the deep sense of popular regret at the unfortunate end of the gallant officer. Gen. O. H. Williams was appointed president, and Col. Charles Macgill and Capt. W. B. Clarke, vice-presidents, and John A. Wagoner and Andrew Kershner, secretaries. On motion of John T. Mason, the following resolutions were adopted:

---

and I hasten to give them to you. The engagement of the 8th was entirely in the hands of the artillery, and Maj. Ringgold took a most active and important part in it. About six o'clock he was struck by a six-pound shot. He was mounted, and the shot struck him at right angles, hitting him in the right thigh, passing through the holsters and upper part of the shoulders of his horse, and then striking the left thigh in the same line in which it struck him. On the evening of the 9th he reached this camp, under the charge of Dr. Byrne, of the army. He was immediately placed in comfortable quarters and his wounds dressed. An immense mass of muscles and integuments were carried away from both thighs. The arteries were not divided, neither were the bones broken. I remained with him all night. He had but little pain, and at intervals had some sleep. On dressing his wounds in the morning they presented a most unfavorable aspect, and there was but little reaction. During the night he gave me many incidents of the battle, and spoke with much pride of the execution of his shot. He directed his shot not only to the groups and masses of the enemy, but to particular men in the line; he saw them fall, and their places occupied by others, who in their turn were shot down. He said he felt as confident of hitting his mark as though he had been using a rifle. He had, he said, but one thing to regret, and that was the small number of men in his company. He said that he had made use of all his exertions to have his company increased to one hundred men, but without success. From the small number of his men, as they were disabled at their guns he was without others to take their places. During the day he continued to lose strength, but was free from pain and cheerful. He spoke constantly of the efficiency of his guns, and of the brave conduct of his officers and men. He continued to grow worse, and a medical officer remained constantly by his side. Dr. Byrne remained with him during the night, using every means which could be devised to save his valuable life, but without effect. He continued to grow worse until one o'clock last night, when he expired. He survived his wounds sixty hours. During all this time he had but little pain, and conversed cheerfully, and made all his arrangements for his approaching end with the greatest composure and resignation. He will be buried to-day at three o'clock P.M., lamented by the whole camp. The wounded are generally doing very well.

"I am your obedient servant,

"J. M. Faltz,

"*Surgeon United States Navy.*"

A letter from a young officer of Baltimore gives the following account of the wounding of Maj. Ringgold:

"About twenty minutes after the commencement of the action poor Maj. Ringgold was struck by a six-pound shot and mortally wounded (he has since died). I had lent him my pistols on going into the fight. The shot struck one holster, cut it and the pistol in two pieces, cut all the flesh off the upper part of the major's thigh, passed through the shoulders of his horse, cut the other pistol in two, and the flesh off the other thigh."

"*Resolved,* That while we unite in the general feeling of sorrow that pervades the whole nation at the loss of the noble and gallant officers and men who lately fell in Texas in defense of their country, we feel that in addition to our national bereavement we have sustained in the death of Maj. Samuel Ringgold the loss of one who was united to us by the ties of friendship, by the associations of youth, and by the relation of a companion and fellow-citizen.

"*Resolved,* That though we regret the death of the gallant Ringgold, yet we rejoice in the character and manner of that death, crowned as it was by the heartfelt joy which the patriot feels in the consciousness of dying in support of the dignity, the freedom and happiness of his country.

"*Resolved,* That it is a source of pride and congratulation to know that Washington County has not only furnished for the nation's defense the officer whose distinguished services we are called at present to commemorate, but that she has given a number of the flowers of her youth, who now fill the ranks of her country's noble army, and that the names of Sergt. John Anderson, Privates David Anderson, Jeremiah Carey, Calvin Bowers, Thomas Philips, and Upton Wilson will always be cherished as faithful citizens and well-tried soldiers.

"*Resolved,* As the sense of this meeting, that in time of actual war, regularly and constitutionally declared by the United States, it is too late to hesitate and inquire into the causes of hostilities, but that it is the duty of every American citizen on such an occasion to sustain his country, 'right or wrong.'

"*Resolved,* That the State of Maryland has nobly sustained on the plains of Texas her character for gallantry and patriotism by the conduct of her sons, Cross, Ringgold, May, Walker, Ridgely, and the many others who aided in the achievement of our late victories, and that she has shown that though small in territory, she can vie with the largest of her sisters in spirit, patriotism, and effective service."

On motion of Capt. W. B. Clarke, it was

"*Resolved,* That each citizen here present will lend his aid in encouraging the formation of a volunteer corps of sixty-four men, to attach themselves to the regiment now forming in this State under the organization of the President of the United States."

On motion of Isaac Nesbitt,

"*Resolved,* That this meeting heartily concur in the suggestion and movement of the Hagerstown Horse-Guards, on the 28th instant, respecting the erection of a monument to the memory of the gallant Ringgold, and will co-operate with them in carrying out the object set forth in their proceedings in relation thereto.

"*Resolved,* That a committee of three be appointed by the chair to unite with the committee of the 'Horse-Guards' in maturing the necessary plan and arrangements for the erection of the monument."

The Potomac Dragoons, being represented in the meeting, appointed Maj. Thomas G. Harris, Lieut. Hays, and Lieut. Grimes a committee to act with the committee appointed by the meeting and the committee on the part of the "Horse-Guards" for the erection of the monument.

At a meeting of the Hagerstown Horse-Guards, held at Hagerstown on the 28th of June, 1846, Capt. William B. Clarke, after referring to the triumphs of the American forces on the Rio Grande, submitted the following resolutions, expressive of the feelings of the corps in receiving the news of the death of Maj. Samuel Ringgold, of the Third Artillery.

The resolutions were prefaced by appropriate remarks upon the life and services of this distinguished officer, and were as follows:

"*Resolved*, That this corps will cause to be erected in Washington County, the place of his birth, a suitable monument as a mark of respect to his memory, and that the several volunteer corps of the county be requested to co-operate in carrying out this resolution."

The above resolution being unanimously adopted, a committee to consist of the commissioned officers of the corps was selected to report the design for the monument, and to take the necessary steps to insure its erection. The monument, however, was never erected.

Cadwalader Ringgold, son of Gen. Samuel Ringgold, was a distinguished officer of the United States navy, and died with the rank of rear-admiral. He was born at Fountain Rock in 1802, and was appointed midshipman on the 4th of March, 1819, and was promoted to a lieutenancy May 17, 1828. He was made lieutenant-commander July 16, 1849; captain, April 2, 1856; commodore, July 16, 1862; and rear-admiral in March, 1867. While a lieutenant-commander he was for a short time in charge of the surveying and exploring expedition to the North Pacific and China Seas. At the breaking out of the civil war he was transferred to the command of the frigate "Sabine." On Friday, Nov. 1, 1861, the blockading fleet to which the "Sabine" was attached encountered a terrific storm. The steamer "Governor," which had on board a battalion of marines, was seen to be in a very dangerous condition, and Capt. Ringgold went to their assistance. He succeeded in rescuing the marines and the crew, and shortly afterwards the steamer sank.

Admiral Ringgold rendered the Federal government valuable service in blockading the Southern ports, and in the operations against Port Royal and other ports on the Atlantic. He was made a rear-admiral in 1867, and died in New York City on the 29th of April in that year.

George Hay, son of Gen. Samuel Ringgold and his second wife, Marie Antoinette Hay, was born at Hagerstown in 1814, and was educated at the West Point Military Academy. He was appointed brevet second lieutenant of the Sixth Infantry on the 1st of July, 1833, and served on frontier duty at Jefferson Barracks, Mo., Fort Jesup, Fla., and Camp Sabine, La. On the 15th of August, 1836, he was promoted to a second lieutenancy, and on the 31st of May following resigned, in order to engage in agriculture and in the manufacture of flour. Subsequently, from 1842 to 1846, he served in the United States Ordnance Bureau at Washington. On the 4th of August, 1846, he was reappointed in the army, with the rank of additional paymaster. During the Mexican war he served as paymaster, with the rank of major, and during the civil war as deputy paymaster-general, with the rank of lieutenant-colonel. He died on the 4th of April, 1864, at San Francisco. Col. Ringgold was a gifted scholar, an accomplished draughtsman, and an amateur poet, and in 1860 published a volume of poetry entitled "Fountain Rock, Amy Weir, and other Metrical Pastimes."

The Fitzhughs. Among the early families of Washington County there was scarcely any which had a wider connection or enjoyed greater influence than did the Fitzhughs. The founder of the Western Maryland branch of the family was Col. William Fitzhugh, an officer in the British army, who threw up his commission at the beginning of the Revolutionary war and retired to his estate in Prince George's County. Towards the latter part of his life he removed to the residence of his son, Col. William Fitzhugh, known as "The Hive," in Washington County, and there spent the remainder of his days. His remains are buried in the Episcopal cemetery at Hagerstown.

Col. Fitzhugh's wife was Anne Frisby, the daughter of Peregrine Frisby, of Cecil County, who was born Sept. 5, 1757. Her first husband was John Rousby, and their only daughter married John Plater.

On the 7th of January, 1759, Mrs. Rousby was united to Mr. Fitzhugh, a colonel in the British service. Col. Fitzhugh had won considerable distinction in his military career in the West India expedition. At the commencement of difficulties between the colonies and the mother-country he was living on his half-pay. The large estate, highly improved, on which he resided lay at the mouth of the Patuxent River, and he had in operation extensive manufactories of different kinds.

When discontent ripened into rebellion, though he was advanced in years, in feeble health, and had almost entirely lost his sight, neither the infirmities of age nor any advantage to be derived from adhesion to the government prevented his taking an open and active part with the patriots. On account of his influence in the community he was offered a continuance of his half-pay if he would remain neutral, but he at once declined the offer, resigned his commission, and declared in favor of the colonies. Unable himself to bear arms, he furnished his two sons—Peregrine and William—for the army, and dismissed them with the command to be true to the interests of their country. They were both officers, and served with distinction under the Continental standard. Their father took his seat in the Executive Council of Maryland, giving his vote and influence to the debates till the political opinions of that body were no longer wavering. Not only thus did he render service, but he was seen and heard at every public meeting, going from place to place through the county, haranguing the people in stump-speeches, and devoting all his energies to the task of rousing them to fight for their rights. This active zeal for American freedom did not fail to render him obnoxious to the British. He was often apprised of danger, but no risk could deter him from the performance of duty. At one time, when he had disregarded a warning from some unknown hand, Mrs. Fitzhugh was surprised in his absence by news of the near approach of a party of British soldiers. She instantly decided to collect the slaves, whom she furnished with such arms as could be found. Then, taking a quantity of cartridges in her apron, she led the way out to meet the enemy, resolved that they should have at least a round of shots by way of welcome. Finding preparation for resistance where they probably expected none, the British party retired from the grounds without doing any damage. At another time, when they received information of a design on the enemy's part to attack the house that night, take the colonel prisoner, carry off what plunder could be found, and lay waste the premises, Col. Fitzhugh was dissuaded by his family from making any attempt at defense. Perhaps thinking that, meeting no opposition, they would be content with plunder, he reluctantly consented to leave the place with his household. Next morning nothing remained of the mansion but a heap of smoking ruins. The family then removed to Upper Marlboro', where they continued to reside until the close of the war.

In the fall, before peace was declared, a detachment of British soldiers having landed on the Patuxent, marched to the house of Col. Fitzhugh. It was about midnight when he and his wife were roused from sleep by a loud knocking at the door. The colonel raised a window and called out to know who was there. The reply was, "Friends." He asked, "Friends to whom?" "Friends to King George," was shouted in answer, with a peremptory order to open the door. Knowing that remonstrance or resistance would be useless, and that delay would but irritate the intruders, the colonel assured them that his wife—he being blind—would immediately descend and admit them. Mrs. Fitzhugh did not hesitate. Her dismay was great when, parting the curtains for an instant, she saw the court-yard filled with armed men. Hastily lighting a candle and putting on her slippers, she went down-stairs, stopping only for a moment to give her sons, who happened to be in the house, their pistols, and warn them that they must lose no time in making their escape. They left the house by the back door as their mother with difficulty turned the ponderous key which secured the front door.

The British soldiers instantly rushed in, touching her night-dress with their bayonets as she turned to leave the door. She walked calmly before them into the parlor, and addressing the officer said she hoped they intended to do the inmates of the house no harm. He replied that they did not, but he must see Col. Fitzhugh at once. Then, his attention being suddenly attracted by some articles of military dress, he demanded quickly, "What officer have you in the house, madam?" "There is no one here but our own family," answered Mrs. Fitzhugh.

The men spoke together in a low voice, and then the question was repeated, to which the same reply was given. She noticed a smile on the countenance of the officer as he said, "We must take these," pointing to the cap, holsters, etc. Nothing else was touched in the house, although the supper-table, with silver plate upon it, was standing as it had been left at night, and the sideboard contained several other valuable articles. Mrs. Fitzhugh, in obedience to the order that her husband should come down, went to assist him in dressing, and returned with him, unmindful in her anxiety that she had taken no time to dress herself. The officer informed him that he was his prisoner and must go with them to New York, then in possession of the British. Col. Fitzhugh replied that his age and want of sight made it scarce worth their while to take him, as he could neither do harm nor service, being unable indeed to take care of himself. Such arguments, however, availed nothing, and he was hurried off. Mrs. Fitzhugh had made no preparation for a journey. Walking up to her husband, she took his arm, and when the officer endeavored to persuade her to remain, saying she would suffer from exposure, she answered that Col. Fitzhugh was not able to take care of himself, and that even if he were she would not be separated from him. The officer then took down a cloak and threw it over her shoulders. With only this protection from the cold and rain she left the house with the rest. Their boat lay about half a mile away, and in going to the shore they had to walk through the mud, the ground being soaked with rain.

When they reached the boat, however, the officer

consented to permit Col. Fitzhugh to remain on his parole, which was hastily written.

On their return to their residence, the colonel and Mrs. Fitzhugh were much surprised to find all the negroes gone except one little girl who had hid in the garret. They had evidently been taken or persuaded to go off in their absence, and there was ground for the suspicion that the enemy's real object had been to obtain possession of the slaves without any resistance that might alarm the neighbors. Many of those missing returned to their master of their own accord, the fair promises made to allure them from his service not having been kept. Miss Plater, the granddaughter of Mrs. Fitzhugh, displayed much courage upon this occasion. After her grandparents had left the house in charge of the soldiers, one or two of the men came back to obtain some fire, and in carrying it from the room let some of it fall on the carpet. The young girl started forward, put her foot upon it, and asked if they meant to fire the house. They answered kindly that the house should stand and no harm come to her. They then asked for wine, which she ordered to be set before them. They would not drink, however, fearing it might be poisoned, till she had tasted each bottle. This young lady was afterwards the wife of Col. Forrest. Capt. Peregrine Fitzhugh, one of the sons already mentioned, who was for some time aide to Gen. Washington, married Elizabeth Chew, of Maryland, and removed in 1799 to Soders' Bay, on Lake Ontario, where he spent the remainder of his days. Col. William Fitzhugh married Ann, daughter of Col. Daniel Hughes, of Hagerstown, and removed to the vicinity of Genesee, Livingston Co., N. Y., in company with Messrs. Carroll and Rochester, and assisted in founding the city of Rochester.

Col. Fitzhugh's family consisted, in part, of seven sons: William H., three times sheriff of Washington County, and owner of "The Hive;" Dr. Daniel, one of the wealthy men of Western New York; Samuel, a judge in New York; James, who moved to Kentucky; Henry, of New York; Richard, killed on the railroad by an accident; and Robert. His daughters were the wife of the Rev. Dr. Backus, a celebrated divine of the Presbyterian Church; the wife of James Birney, once Abolition candidate for the Presidency; the wife of the late Gerritt Smith, philanthropist and abolitionist, of Petersboro', N. Y., whose son, Green Smith, was married to the youngest daughter of his uncle, Col. William H. Fitzhugh, and died at Petersboro'; Mrs. Tallman, of Rochester; and Mrs. Swift, wife of Commodore Swift, of Geneva, N. Y.

William H. Fitzhugh, eldest son of Col. William, married Mary Hughes, daughter of Samuel Hughes, and granddaughter of Col. Daniel Hughes, his own cousin. Dr. Daniel Fitzhugh married Ann Dana, his cousin. Judge Samuel Fitzhugh married Ann Addison, and had one son, who died unmarried. James Fitzhugh married a lady of Kentucky. Henry Fitzhugh married a daughter of Charles Carroll, of "Bellevue," Washington County, cousin of Charles Carroll of Carrollton. He went with the Fitzhughes, Rochesters, Hogmires, and others to Genesee. Robert married Maria Carroll, daughter of Daniel Carroll, son of Daniel Carroll, of Duddington. She has a son living, Carroll Fitzhugh, now of New York. Richard married a Miss Mary Jones, of Mount Morris, Livingston Co., N. Y.

Jesse Duncan Elliott[1] was born at Hagerstown on the 14th of July, 1782. He was descended from an Irish family of Fincastle, County Donegal, and his parents were Pennsylvanians. In 1794 his father, Col. Robert Elliott, was killed by a party of Indians on the Muskingum, whilst on the way to join Gen. Wayne's army.[2] The death of Col. Elliott rendered the family destitute, but through the efforts of John Thomson Mason, Congress granted a small pension to the widow, and President Jefferson forwarded commissions as midshipmen in the navy to the two brothers, St. Clair and Jesse D. Elliott. The latter had been educated at Carlisle, Pa., and had studied law. The warrants were dated April 2, 1804, and were accompanied by orders attaching St. Clair to the "President," Commodore Samuel Barron, and Jesse to the "Essex," Commodore James Barron. The two vessels proceeded to the Barbary States, and having humbled them, negotiated a treaty with Tripoli, and brought home the crew of the "Philadelphia," who

[1] On the 24th of November, 1843, Messrs. J. J. Merrick, O. H. Williams, Jervis Spencer, Charles Macgill, John Thomson Mason, and George Schley addressed a note to Commodore Jesse D. Elliott, conveying the request of a number of their fellow-citizens that he would accept the compliment of a public dinner on the following day. The commodore replied that he had come to Hagerstown for the purpose of visiting the graves of his mother and sister, who were buried there, and for that reason, and because he had an appointment at Baltimore, he was constrained to decline. The committee, however, prevailed upon him to make an address to his early companions and friends at the court-house, and from the speech delivered on that occasion, and from "A Biographical Notice," by a citizen of New York, the accompanying sketch was compiled.

[2] Col. Robert Elliott was an army contractor, and while traveling with his servant from Fort Washington to Fort Hamilton, was waylaid and killed, in 1794. Being somewhat advanced in life, the colonel wore a wig. The savage who shot him hurried forward to scalp him, but when, having drawn his knife, he seized him by the hair, the scalp, to his astonishment, came off. The Indian looked at it and then exclaimed, "Damn lie!" His companions were much amused at his discomfiture, and made a good deal of sport among themselves with the wig.

had been confined in the dungeons of that city. Having remained on shore until 1807, Jesse was attached to the ill-fated "Chesapeake," Capt. J. Barron, and on the 22d of June departed for the Mediterranean. She had scarcely cleared the American coast before she was attacked by the British ship of the line "Leopard," of greatly superior force, and such was the defenseless condition of the "Chesapeake," owing chiefly to her ignorance of the intended attack of a vessel belonging to a nation with which the United States were then at peace, that in a short time she was compelled to strike her flag. Commodore Barron was court-martialed on his return to the United States, but Commodore Elliott declared that he did all that a brave and skillful officer could have done under the circumstances. Commodore Elliott was so zealous in defense of Commodore Barron that he was challenged to fight a duel by one of Barron's detractors, and accepted. His antagonist fell, badly wounded, but afterwards recovered, and became a warm friend of the commodore's. Young Elliott was appointed, about this time, acting lieutenant on the "Enterprise," and subsequently was promoted, and commissioned to a lieutenancy on the "John Adams," and bearer of dispatches to the United States minister, William Pinkney, at the Court of St. James.

COM. JESSE D. ELLIOTT.

While in London he was insulted by "a person having the appearance of a gentleman," who took a seat near him in a coffee-house, and to whom he handed his card, expecting that a duel would follow. The man had mistaken him for a British officer, and "lavished all manner of abuse against the Yankees and their country," whereupon Elliott informed him that he was a Yankee, and when he made no sign of apologizing or handing Elliott his card, the future commodore, to quote his own language, "stepped to the person in waiting and observed, 'Sir, you put a scoundrel instead of a gentleman in the box with me; he has grossly insulted me. There's my card; give it to him and tell him I demand his.'" By this time, however, the man had disappeared, and Elliott never heard of him again. Mr. Pinkney, hearing of the affair, advised Elliott not to appear on the street in his uniform, since otherwise he would be subjected to many annoyances and insults. Elliott took his advice, and besides exchanging his uniform for a private dress, procured quarters where he was not likely to be the object of curiosity or suspicion. Returning to the United States, he shortly afterwards married. Immediately succeeding this event, war having been declared against Great Britain, he parted with his wife in order to join his ship at New York, but the vessel had sailed before his arrival in that city. Having learned that the British Admiral Sir John Borles Warren had information of the instructions to Commodore Rodgers to rendezvous in the Chesapeake, he volunteered to bear the news to the American fleet, hoping that he might be able to join the "Argus," of which he was the first lieutenant. For this purpose he hired a small pilot-boat called the "Patriot" (the ill-fated schooner on which Aaron Burr's daughter Theodosia was afterwards lost at sea), put one gun and thirty men on board, and cruised forty days, during which he was chased by two British gun-brigs and narrowly escaped. He then returned home and was ordered to report for service. Commodore Chauncey invited him to join his command, and he accepted. He was ordered to proceed to Genesee Falls, on Lake Ontario, and to Black Rock and Buffalo, on Lake Erie, there to communicate with Gen. P. B. Porter, Mr. Granger, the Indian agent, and Gen. Van Rensselaer upon the subject of obtaining vessels for operations on the lakes. Soon afterwards, Commodore Elliott, assisted by Capt. Nathan Towson, of Baltimore, effected the capture of the British vessels "Detroit" and "Caledonia." In his official report to the Secretary of the Navy he states that on the morning of Oct. 8, 1812, the "Detroit," formerly the United States brig "Adams," and the "Caledonia" came down the lake and anchored off Fort Erie, under the protection of its guns, and that he determined to attempt their capture. Accordingly, with two boats, each containing fifty men, he put off from the mouth of Black Rock (where he was engaged in the construction of an American fleet) at one o'clock on the following morning, and at three was alongside the vessels. In less than ten minutes he had captured both vessels and secured their crews. Being exposed to the fire of Fort Erie he beached the "Caledonia" under the protection of one of the American batteries, and succeeded in getting the "Detroit" out of range of the fort, but the pilot having deserted her, the vessel ran ashore on the American side. She had been so roughly handled by the guns of the fort and

GEN. NATHAN TOWSON.

the flying artillery that she was incapable of being floated again. The "Caledonia" was loaded with furs worth two hundred thousand dollars. The crew of the "Detroit" consisted of fifty-six men, and that of the "Caledonia" of twelve men. Commodore Elliott's loss was two men killed and five wounded. Elliott encountered the first man on boarding, and opposed three of the enemy with no other weapon than his cutlass. He captured nearly one hundred prisoners, and released forty of his own countrymen belonging to the Fourth Artillery who were confined on board. Congress voted Elliott a sword, and appropriated twelve thousand dollars as prize-money to the lieutenant and his crew. He then joined Commodore Chauncey on Lake Ontario, and assisted in driving the enemy into the harbor of Kingston. Subsequently he accompanied Gen. Dearborn and Gen. Pike in the operations against York, in Canada, and against Fort George, both of which were captured. He then joined Capt. Oliver H. Perry on Lake Erie, and took a conspicuous part in the famous naval engagement known as the Battle of Lake Erie, which was fought on the 10th of September, 1813. Capt. Elliott commanded the "Niagara" in that engagement until she was boarded by Perry, and the latter did not hesitate to say that he owed the victory to Elliott's coolness and skill. Elliott himself gives a very spirited and interesting account of the action. "At this time," he says, "the 'Lawrence' (Capt. Perry's ship) ceased her fire entirely, and no signal being made after the first to form in the order of battle, I concluded that the senior officer was killed. The breeze now freshening, I observed that the whole British fleet drew ahead, cheering along their entire line. I then set topgallant-sail, fore and aft mainsail and foresail, and passed within twenty yards of the 'Lawrence,' still not seeing Capt. Perry. Having now exhausted nearly all my twelve-pound round-shot, I ordered Mr. McGrath with a few bracemen to proceed in my boat to the 'Lawrence' and bring me all hers, and immediately steered directly for the head of the British line, firing continually my whole starboard battery on them as I passed. When I reached within two hundred and fifty yards of the beam of the 'Detroit,' and ahead of the 'Queen Charlotte,' I luffed on a wind and commenced a most deadly fire, the 'Niagara' then being the only vessel of our fleet in what I call close action. The British were just before cheering for victory, but their cheers were now turned into groans, and the blood ran from the scuppers of the 'Detroit' and 'Queen Charlotte' like water from the spouts of your houses in a moderate rain." While thus engaged the "Niagara" was boarded by Capt. Perry, who was much agitated. Elliott asked him what was the result on board his brig. He answered, "Cut all to pieces; the victory's lost, everything's gone! I've been sacrificed by the d——d gunboats!" To this Elliott replied, "No sir, victory is yet on our side. I have a most judicious position, and my shot are taking great effect. You tend my battery, and I will bring up the gunboats." "Do so," said Perry, "for heaven's sake!" Elliott then got into Perry's boat and passed down the line exposed to the enemy's fire, and ordered the gunboats to cease firing at the small vessels and to press up to the head of the line. He then took command of the foremost gunboat, the "Somers," and led the squadron into action. The "Detroit" and "Queen Charlotte" fouled at this juncture, and the "Niagara" and the gunboats rushing in upon them, the British were whipped and compelled to surrender. As soon as the firing had ceased Elliott went on board the "Detroit," and so slippery were the decks with blood that he slipped and fell, his clothing becoming completely saturated and covered with gore. Capt. Barclay, commanding the "Detroit," handed Elliott his sword, but the latter refused it, assuring him that every kindness would be shown him and the other prisoners. On meeting Capt. Perry that officer said to Elliott, "I owe the victory to your gallantry." The British flag on the "Detroit" was nailed to the mast, and Commodore Elliott, having had the nails extracted, afterwards presented them to the distinguished statesman Henry Clay. Mr. Clay was a warm friend of Elliott's, and was closely identified with the people of Hagerstown, having married Lucretia Hart, of that place.[1]

After the action on Lake Erie Elliott returned to Lake Ontario, designing to act as flag-captain on Commodore Chauncey's ship "Superior." On his arrival, however, he found a vacant brig, the "Sylph," a fast sailer of twenty guns, and by agreement accepted that vessel for the purpose of bringing on an action with the British fleet. Late in the summer he met a British brig and attacked her, but the captain ran her ashore and blew her up.

In 1818 began an acrimonious controversy between Commodore Oliver H. Perry and Commodore Elliott, which ended disastrously for the latter. Commodore Elliott appears to have been of a bluff, outspoken temperament, and to have made numerous enemies, partly on

[1] In his memoir Commodore Elliott speaks in high terms of the brave Israel, another Washington County boy, who threw himself on board the "Intrepid" at Tripoli for the purpose of destroying the Tripolitan fleet, and who, when discovered, rather than yield himself a prisoner, with his brave companions applied the torch to the magazine, and "went in one common wreck to the other world."

this account and partly owing to his pronounced political views. His troubles commenced with the battle of Lake Erie, it being asserted by those unfriendly to him that he had not behaved well in that engagement. When this assertion came to his ears he at once wrote to Capt. Perry, who replied that he was indignant that such a charge should be brought, and declared that Elliott's conduct had been such as to merit his warmest approbation, and to contribute largely to the victory. Notwithstanding this, however, the accusation was persisted in, and subsequently gave the commodore no little annoyance. After some service on Lake Ontario he proceeded to Baltimore to take command of the sloop-of-war "Ontario." That vessel sailed for New York, and while she was fitting out at the latter port Commodore Elliott received information that doubts were being circulated as to his conduct at the battle of Lake Erie. He thereupon asked for a court of inquiry, which was granted, and he was acquitted with honor. His enemies, however, continued to persecute him with defamatory publications, and Fenimore Cooper, the novelist, having given a correct account of the engagement in his "Naval History of New York," was assailed by R. S. Mackenzie, author of a "Life of Perry," whom he sued for libel. Cooper won his suit, and demonstrated the truth of his narrative. Sectional prejudice against Elliott was skillfully excited, and the Legislature of Rhode Island "gratuitously and by proceedings wholly *ex-parte* considered the circumstances of the battle, and pretended to decide the relative merits of the parties concerned." Mackenzie's "Life of Perry," which was grossly unfair to Elliott, was admitted into the libraries of the public schools of New York. Elliott challenged Perry to fight a duel, but Perry did not accept. Elliott next proceeded, in command of the "Ontario," as one of Commodore Decatur's squadron to the Mediterranean against Algiers, and contributed to the capture of a large Algerian frigate by pouring a heavy fire into her. Three days afterwards a brig of twenty-four guns and three hundred men was taken by the squadron. Peace being concluded with Algiers, the fleet proceeded to Tunis, and compelled the Bey to surrender a large amount of property belonging to the United States, captured from the British by American privateers. In a negotiation with the Bey, the American consul, M. M. Noah, went to the palace accompanied by Capts. Gordon and Elliott. The Bey's son was very insolent, whereupon Capt. Elliott observed, "We did not come here to be insulted. This interview must be cut short. Will you or will you not pay for these vessels? Answer nothing but that." Mustapha was furious, but the Bey finally consented to make the payment. During the interview thirty Mamelukes entered the room with drawn cimeters. Perceiving that the intention was to intimidate them, Capt. Elliott placed his back against the wall and, drawing his sword, declared that he would sell his life dearly. This action and his peremptory manner had a salutary effect on the Bey. Capt. Elliott returned home, and in 1817 was appointed a commissioner, with Gen. Bernard, Gen. Swift, Capt. Warrington, and Cols. Armistead and McCrea, to examine the coast of the United States for selecting sites for permanent dock-yards and fortifications, and for lighting the coast of North Carolina. In this position he continued until 1824.

Whilst discharging its duties he was informed by Mr. Crawford, then Secretary of the Treasury, that owing to the supposed danger of locating a light-ship and occupying it during a gale, no person could be found willing to perform such service. Capt. Elliott at once volunteered to locate one, and successfully accomplished the task in a storm, thus demonstrating the practicability of using the light-ships at dangerous points during a high wind. March 27, 1818, he was promoted from the rank of master commandant to that of full captain. On the termination of the Coast Survey Commission, in December, 1823, he received a highly complimentary and friendly letter from the chief, Gen. Bernard, afterwards French Minister of War. In 1825 he was sent in the frigate "Cyane" to the coast of Brazil, where, in the presence of a greatly superior force, he boldly asserted and maintained the right of an American war-vessel to enter a blockaded port. Before leaving Brazil he was offered by the emperor the post of admiral, with the highest salary paid to any Brazilian naval officer, but declined the offer. On his return from Brazil he was, in 1829, appointed to the command of the naval forces in the West Indies and Gulf of Mexico. On arriving at Pensacola he found a letter from Hon. J. R. Poinsett, United States minister to Mexico, stating the difficulties by which he was surrounded, and advising a demonstration of the squadron at Vera Cruz. Accordingly the squadron proceeded to the Mexican coast, and having taken Mr. Poinsett on board at Tampico, returned to the United States. While in Mexico the commodore was entertained by Gen. Santa Anna at his hacienda or farm. Having returned from the West Indies in 1831, his aid was asked in suppressing an insurrection of slaves in Southampton County, Va. Accordingly he ordered a force of one hundred seamen and sixty marines under Capt. J. S. Newton, of the sloop-of-war "Natchez," to proceed to Jerusalem, the scene of disturbance. Commodore Elliott, with the fleet-surgeon, accompanied them. They arrived in time to succor the terrified inhabitants, who were assembled at Jerusalem in such numbers that they were obliged to sleep in stables and outhouses. In this connection Commodore Elliott records an act of remarkable gallantry on the part of a child. "The hero," he says, "was a youth of less than thirteen years of age, the son of an aged and diseased gentleman of Southampton, Dr. Blount, who could not be removed to a place of safety on account of his extreme illness. His little son, the lad spoken of, assured his father that he, with the overseer and his two sons, could defend him; and accordingly when night came he barricaded the doors, opened the windows, gathered all the arms he could find about the house, consisting of a few old pistols, etc., and awaited the attack. About two o'clock in the morning the insurgent negroes to the number of two hundred and fifty, well mounted and armed, rode up, and were in the act of dismounting when the little fellow commenced a slow and steady fire upon them, which had the effect to intimidate them, and they went off, leaving their dead and wounded on the ground. It was the last attack the negroes made." Commodore Elliott procured the boy, S. F. Blount, an appointment as midshipman, and he afterwards became a distinguished officer. During the nullification troubles in South Carolina, Commodore Elliott was in command of the naval forces at Charleston, and afterwards took charge of the navy-yard at Boston. In 1835 he was deputed to take the Hon. Edward Livingston, United States minister, to France in the frigate "Constitution." This duty was performed, but on the return voyage the vessel narrowly escaped being wrecked during a heavy storm in the English Channel. Capt. Elliott's daring and skill in handling the vessel alone prevented her from being dashed on the Scilly Rocks, in which event her destruction was inevitable. Subsequently he took command of the Mediterranean squadron, and on returning home from that duty in 1839 found that reports derogatory to his professional character were again being circulated by his enemies. The charges were based on the commodore's conduct at Lake Erie and during the nullification troubles, and his treatment of certain midshipmen who had been engaged in a duel. He was also accused of using the ship's stores, receiving presents, and harsh treatment to sailors. He immediately demanded a court of inquiry, which was granted. The result was that the commodore was subjected to a court-martial. At the trial he claims he was deprived of some of his important witnesses, upon the ground that they were under sailing orders and could not be detached from their vessels. A verdict against him was rendered, and he was suspended from the service until the 6th of July, 1844, with loss of pay. The latter, however, was remitted by President Van Buren. After living in retirement for nearly four years, he succeeded in obtaining a rehearing of his case, with the result of being reinstated in the navy with his former rank of commodore. During his suspension, which lasted from the 22d of June, 1840, to the 18th of October, 1843, he resided near Carlisle, Pa., and was engaged chiefly in farming.[1] He devoted much time and attention to the breeding of fine sheep and swine which he had imported. He was a man of indomitable energy and courage, and though suffering keenly under the ignominy of an unjust sentence, applied himself bravely to the work which lay next his hand. At the age of fifty-five he learned how to plow, and boasted that he could "plow as good a furrow as any man in Pennsylvania."

While stationed in the Mediterranean, Commodore Elliott, in company with Gen. Lewis Cass, minister to France, visited various places in Europe, and along the African and Turkish coasts. At Rome he was cordially thanked by the Pope for the protection which he had given to the Sisters of the Ursuline Convent, near Boston, after the burning of the convent by the anti-Catholic mob, while he was in command of the Boston navy-yard. At Athens the King and Queen of Greece were entertained on board the "Constitution," and afterwards gave a ball in honor of the commodore and his officers.[2]

Commodore Elliott was a rigid disciplinarian and an earnest political partisan, and to this fact doubtless he owed much of the persecution to which he was so relentlessly subjected. He was a firm friend and admirer of Gen. Jackson, and during a period when

[1] His restoration to the service was due to President Tyler, who, having read a statement prepared by the commodore, instructed the Secretary of the Navy to place him on waiting orders. The letter restoring him is as follows:

"NAVY DEPARTMENT, Oct. 19, 1843.

"SIR,—The President of the United States having carefully considered the facts in your case in connection with evidences recently furnished, and considering also the long period of your suspension from the public service, and the gallantry exhibited by you on more than one occasion during the late war with Great Britain, has thought proper to remit the remaining period of your suspension, and to restore you to the public service. You will accordingly consider yourself as waiting orders, your restoration dating from the 18th inst.

"Your obedient servant,

"DAVID HENSHAW.

"COMMODORE J. D. ELLIOTT, U. S. Navy."

[2] Among his officers Elliott mentions Lieut. Cadwalader Ringgold, of Washington County, "a fine young officer," whom he had contributed to place in the navy.

the general was very unpopular in Boston insisted on adopting a statue of the old warrior as the figure-head for the "Constitution," then lying at the Boston navy-yard. The figure was placed on the ship despite a furious popular outcry, and during the night was sawed off and carried away by some one who obtained admission to the navy-yard. Commodore Elliott attributes much of his undeserved misfortune to the resentment of Hon. J. K. Paulding, Secretary of the Navy, who, he declares, was his bitter enemy while professing to be his friend. There seems little reason to doubt that his conviction by court-martial was brought about by unfair means, and that he was absolutely guiltless of the charges preferred. Many of these charges were so trivial as to have been unworthy of notice, but they seem to have been considered serious by a court-martial which was evidently determined to find the commodore guilty, and to humiliate him as much as possible. There does not appear to have been one of them which was not refuted by the most conclusive testimony. Commodore Elliott himself compared his conviction to the treatment of Commodore James Barron, and of the unfortunate Admiral Byng, and the comparison would seem to be fully justified by the records.

Commodore Elliott was appointed to the command of the Philadelphia navy-yard, and died there Dec. 10, 1845.

Commodore Elliott had a brother Wilson, who was captain in the Nineteenth Regiment United States Infantry, and one of those who accompanied Col. Campbell in the Mississineway expedition, in which there was so much suffering from hunger and cold. He was also one of the four captains who successfully charged the left flank of the British batteries when they had invested Fort Meigs. He contracted disease at Fort Meigs, which continued to weaken him until it caused his death.

The Kennedy family. Among the earliest and most successful business men of Hagerstown were the Kennedy brothers, John and Hugh. The Kennedys were a Scotch-Irish family, and were rigid "Covenanters" of the Cromwellian type. Their home was in the county of Derry, Ireland, where they occupied a respectable position. John Kennedy, the first immigrant, was born at Ballyavlin, a small farm near the town of Newton-Limavaddy, in the county of Londonderry, June 13, 1767. His parents were James Kennedy, Jr., born Nov. 23, 1739, and Rachel, whose maiden name was George. Their children were John, Hugh, Priscilla, James, Joshua, and Rachel. John Kennedy received a good education, and being of an adventurous disposition, left his home at the age of nineteen to sail for America. He landed at Philadelphia, and thence proceeded to New Castle, Del., where he taught school. Subsequently he removed to Hagerstown, where he was befriended by a fellow-countryman, James Ferguson, a merchant, who transacted a large miscellaneous business in Hagerstown. Ferguson employed him as clerk, and young Kennedy finding that a knowledge of the German dialect spoken in Pennsylvania and Maryland was indispensable to success in business, set to work to master it, and made such progress that he was soon enabled to render valuable service to his employer. As soon as he became firmly established in Hagerstown he sent over to Ireland for his brother Hugh, who came to this country and joined him in business. Mr. Ferguson being desirous of relinquishing the business, offered it to the Kennedys on condition that they would take into partnership with them Richard Ragan, also a clerk in Ferguson's employ. This they consented to do, and the firm became Kennedy & Ragan. For many years the firm practically divided the business of the county with another thriving house, that of Stonebraker & Co., at Boonsboro'. Both the Kennedys succeeded in thoroughly mastering the German dialect, and to this fact much of their success is doubtless to be ascribed. John married on Christmas-day, 1804, Mary Wagoner. Hugh remained a bachelor. Mary (Wagoner) Kennedy was the daughter of John Wagoner, who lived on the old "End Strife" farm, now "Ravenswood," nearly equidistant between Hagerstown and Funkstown. Mrs. Kennedy's mother (wife of John Wagoner) was the daughter of Peter White and Margaret Stull. Peter White was the son of John White, an Englishman, who settled in New Jersey. Peter White took up large tracts of land on both sides of the Antietam, called "End the Strife," "Whisky," and "Toddy." Eight children were born to Mr. and Mrs. White. They were Sarah, who married John Wagoner, who was sheriff of Washington County for two terms; Margaret, who married Mr. Geary, and was the mother of the late Governor Geary, of Pennsylvania, and of Rev. Edward Geary, a Presbyterian minister, now living in Portland, Oregon; Isaac Stull White, who was also sheriff of Washington County, and who married a Miss Rench; John, who was afterwards the father of Mrs. Judge Carson, of Mercersburg, Pa.; two sons who died single; and two daughters who also remained unmarried. Mrs. Peter White (Margaret Stull) was the niece of Judge Stull. Mrs. White's sister Susan married Col. Jack Swearingen of racing fame. In May, 1818, Mrs. John Kennedy died, leaving four children,—Sarah Anne, who married Benjamin Price, the lawyer of Frederick, and afterwards of Hagerstown; Louisa Margaret, who married Hon. James Dixon Roman; John Wagoner, who married Mary Elizabeth McPherson, only daughter of Dr. William Smith McPherson, of Prospect Hall, Frederick County; and James Hugh, who married Lydia, second daughter of Col. Jacob Hollingsworth, of Hagerstown.

On the death of their parents in Ireland, the Kennedys sent for their younger brother, James, who had remained at home to take care of his mother and father. He came over to this country with his wife and eight children and settled on a farm near Greencastle, Pa., which his brothers had purchased and stocked for him. On this place still resides the eldest son (John) of James Kennedy. After continuing for a number of years, the firm of Kennedy & Ragan dissolved, the Kennedys retaining the old stand, at the southeast corner of the public square, in the centre of which stood the court-house. Mr. Ragan established a new store two doors away. John and Hugh Kennedy then took into partnership two young men, James O. Carson, of Greencastle, Pa., and John McCurdy, of Mercersburg, Pa. Mr. Carson married Rosanna White, daughter of John White, and a cousin of Mrs. Kennedy. Mr. McCurdy married Rachel McClelland, a niece of John Kennedy. The firm continued in business for some twenty years, when Mr. McCurdy established a store in Hagerstown, and Mr. Carson removed to Mercersburg. Hugh Kennedy also retired from business, in favor of his nephew, John Wagoner Kennedy, and the firm became John Kennedy & Son. Hugh Kennedy died in 1835, aged sixty-six, and John Kennedy died in 1847, aged eighty. James Kennedy died in November of the same year, aged seventy-three. Of John Kennedy's children, Sarah Anne, widow of Benjamin Price, who died in 1840, still survives with two children,—Louisa Kennedy, who married Francis M. Darby, a lawyer of Hagerstown, and died about two years ago, and Kennedy, now living in Siskyou County, Cal. Mrs. James Dixon Roman (Louisa Margaret Kennedy) died on the 1st of August, 1878, having had the affliction to survive the death of her entire family,—her younger daughter Louisa, her husband, her daughter Sallie, wife of C. C. Baldwin, of New York, and her son, James Dixon Roman. John W. Kennedy and his wife and two children are still living. One of their children, John Wagoner Kennedy, died when seven months old. The other children are McPherson Kennedy, of New York, who married Esther Walden Tomlinson, of that city, and has two children,—McPherson and Esther Walden; and Antoinette Kennedy, who married Malcolm Crichton, of Baltimore. Mr. and Mrs. Crichton have six children,—William, Nettie, Malcolm, McPherson, James, and Mary Elizabeth.

James Hugh Kennedy, youngest son of John Kennedy, was attacked by a mob in Carlisle, Pa., while seeking to recover some runaway slaves, and so badly injured that he died. He left a wife and two daughters. His widow married Rev. Dr. William Jackson, at that time rector of St. John's Parish, Hagerstown, and died in Jacksonville. His eldest daughter, Nannie Hollingsworth Kennedy, married Dr. Lehman Adams Cooper, of Baltimore, who died recently in New Mexico. Mrs. Cooper died in Hagerstown in 1872, leaving a son, Lehman Adams Cooper, and a daughter, Marie Louise Cooper, both of whom survive her. James H. Kennedy's youngest daughter, Lydia Hollingsworth Kennedy, married Tryon Hughes Edwards, a lawyer practicing in Hagerstown. Their children are Catharine Hughes, Lydia Hollingsworth, and Tryon Pierpont. They have lost one daughter, Nannie Kennedy, about one year old.

All three of the Kennedy brothers were strict members of the Presbyterian Church. John Kennedy was a ruling elder, and for many successive years was a delegate to the General Assembly from the Presbytery of Carlisle. He was an uncompromising believer in and advocate of the orthodox Presbyterian doctrine, but at the same time was very tolerant, and enjoyed the friendship and confidence of Fathers Dubois and Duhamel, of Emmittsburg, in whose society he took great pleasure. Both the brothers were earnest Whigs, but neither took any active part in politics. They restricted their energies to their business and to promoting the interests of their church. Both of them amassed considerable property, and both led sober, well-balanced lives, whose influence upon all who came in contact with them, and upon the community at large, was of the most wholesome and beneficial character.

The Beatty family. Col. William Beatty, one of the earliest settlers of Washington County, was a man of remarkable energy and force of character. He married Mary Dorothy, daughter of John Conrad Grosh, one of the pioneer German immigrants of Western Maryland. They had twelve sons and four daughters, as follows:

1. William, born 1758; killed at the battle of Hobkirk's Hill, near Camden, S. C., April 25, 1781.
2. Henry Beatty, born 1760.
3. Elizabeth Beatty, born 1762.
4. John Conrad Beatty, born 1764.
5. Cornelius Beatty, born 1766.
6. Sophia Beatty, born 1768; married Col. Nathaniel Rochester, April 20, 1788; she died in Rochester, N. Y., Dec. 5, 1845.

7. Mary Beatty, born 1769.
8. George Beatty, born 1771.
9. Otho Beatty, born 1773.
10. Eleanor Beatty, born 1774.
11. Elie Beatty, born 1776.
12. Adam Beatty, born 1777.
13. John Michael Beatty, born 1779.
14. Daniel Beatty, born 1780.
15. William Beatty (2), born 1782.
16. Lewis Augustus Beatty, born 1784.

Peter Grosh's second daughter, Catharine, married William Kimball. His son Michael married Christiana Raymer. His daughter Anna B. married Elie Williams. His son Adam was killed at the battle of Germantown.

William Beatty, son of Col. William Beatty and Mary Dorothy Grosh, was born in Frederick County, Md., on the 19th of June, 1758. He was the eldest of twelve sons. In stature he was erect and stately, and in person vigorous and athletic, capable of enduring the greatest fatigue and of suffering the utmost privation. His attachments were warm and permanent, and his patriotism ardent and almost romantic.[1]

The venerable Frederick Humrichouse, one of the best-known citizens of Washington County, died on the 5th of October, 1876, at the age of eighty-five years, two months, and twenty days, and his remains were laid beside those of his ancestors, who were among the earliest citizens of Hagerstown, in the graveyard of the Old Reformed Church. Mr. Humrichouse removed to Hagerstown with his father in 1798, when nine years old, and continued to remain in the same spot for the remainder of his life.

The father of Frederick Humrichouse enlisted as a private in the Revolutionary army two months before the Declaration of Independence was signed, and on the 1st of July, 1776, was commissioned as an ensign. He participated in the great battles of the war, was at Valley Forge, and did not lay down his sword until the struggle was ended. He then lived in Philadelphia until the yellow fever epidemic, when he removed to Hagerstown. The maternal grandfather of Frederick Humrichouse was the Rev. Christian Frederick Post, of the Episcopal Church of England, who came to this continent first to Labrador as a missionary, where he remained twenty-two years. His second mission was to the then wilderness of which Pittsburgh is now the centre, and his third mission, to the same locality, to quiet the hostile Indians, was upon a commission issued by William Denny, the Governor of the province of Pennsylvania, and bears date Oct. 23, 1758.

Frederick Humrichouse represented the county in the General Assembly of Maryland, filled the office of postmaster at Hagerstown, was a director in most of the banking and other companies, and was, up to within a few months of his death, one of the most active and experienced working directors of the Hagerstown Bank and the Washington County Mutual Insurance Company. He "died in harness," with a mind as clear and strong as at any previous period of his life,—a useful man and earnest Christian.

William Heyser, who died on the 15th of January, 1875, aged eighty-four years and four months, was the son of William Heyser, for many years president of the Hagerstown Bank, and grandson of Capt. William Heyser, who was an officer in the Revolutionary army.

William Heyser, the great-grandfather of John H. Heyser, of Cold Spring, was the original settler of the family in Hagerstown Valley, and was contemporary with Hager and Funk, the first settlers. The first Heyser commenced the building of the German Reformed church of Hagerstown, whose "centennial" was celebrated in 1874, and it was with his means mainly that that building was erected. The finishing of it was suspended for a few years by the absence of Capt. Heyser with the army.

The following letter from his son William, aged nine, written to the captain during the Revolutionary struggle, provides a signal illustration of the universality of the patriotic and martial spirit of that period. The letter is as follows:

"*To Capt. William Heyser, at the American Camp, Philadelphia.*

"DEAR FATHER

"Through the mercies of almighty God, I my Mamma, my brother and Sisters are well, in hopes these may find you enjoying these Felicities, which tend to happiness in life, and everlasting Happiness in Eternity your long absence and great distance is the only matter of our trouble, but our sincere Prayers, is for your Welfare and Prosperity, begging that God may prosper you, and your united Brethren, in your laudable undertaking, and in the end crown you with the laurels of a Complete victory, over the Enemies of the inestimable Rights, Liberties, and Privileges of distressed America, and hand them down inviolate, to the latest Posterity. My Dear father, my greatest Grief is, that I am incapable of the military Service, that I might enjoy the company of so loving a father, and serve my country in so glorious a cause, but tho' absent from you yet my constant prayer is for your Safety, in the Hour of danger, your complete victory, over the Enemies, of the united States of America, and your Safe Restoration to the government of your family. I and my brother Jacob Continue at School, and hope to give a full Satisfaction, to our parents, and friends in our regular conduct, and Progress in learning, my Mamma, my

[1] A brief sketch of him is to be found among the distinguished men of Frederick County in this work.

brother and Sister do join me in their Prayers and well wishes for you.

"HAGERS TOWN October 12th 1776 } I am Dr. Father your most dutiful and obedt Son,

WILLIAM HEYSER"

William Heyser, grandson of Capt. William, was born in Hagerstown, and resided within a mile of that place. He was a man of powerful physique, indomitable energy, and great self-control. He built a number of houses,—the large stone house and buildings on the Heyser farm, and subsequently the houses for his son John, his grandson, Oscar Bellman, and his daughter, Henrietta Snyder. His remains were interred in Rose Hill Cemetery.

Mary Wolgamot, wife of Col. David Schnebly, attained the remarkable age of one hundred and three years, nine months, and two days.

The family Bible in which the record is kept is of the edition of 1807, Philadelphia, Mathew Carey. At the head of the list of "births" are recorded those of Col. David Schnebly and Mary Wolgamot, husband and wife, as follows:

"BIRTHS.

"David Schnebly, born May the 8th, 1770.

"Mary Wolgamot, born Feb. the 15th, 1773.

On the opposite page is recorded the marriage of the above:

"MARRIAGES.

"David Schnebly, married to Mary Wolgamot, May 7th, 1793."

And on the last page of the family record we find the death of Col. Schnebly thus recorded:

"DEATHS.

"October 4, 1842. This day Col. David Schnebly died, aged 72 years, 4 months, and 22 days."

After the death of her husband, whose remains were buried in the Reformed church, Hagerstown, Mrs. Schnebly continued to reside at the farm "Garden of Eden," lying near the Cumberland Valley Railroad, five and a half miles north of Hagerstown. Here Col. David Schnebly was born. Mrs. Schnebly's birthplace was the farm afterwards owned by Joshua Emmert, and at the time of her birth the property of her father, Col. John Wolgamot, about four miles southwest of the "Garden of Eden," near the Conecocheague. At this place Mrs. Schnebly was married, and on the 8th of May following removed to the "Garden of Eden" farm, where she resided for eighty-two years. Her father was a soldier in the Revolutionary war, and died when she was a little child. Mrs. Schnebly was last seen in public at the centennial celebration of the Reformed Church, which took place in Hagerstown in the spring of 1874.

From an account published in the Hagerstown *Herald and Torch* in February, 1873, of a visit to Mrs. Schnebly, we make the following extracts, viz.:

"The aged and venerable lady, seated erect as in early life in her arm-chair, received the congratulations of every visitor, and expressed in strong, unshaken voice her thanks and her happiness at seeing them all. Her portrait, taken in her prime by Eichholtz (whose colors never fade), was suspended near her on the hall, and all could mark the contrast between the youthful beauty and the beauty of serene age.

"Mrs. Schnebly's vision is impaired, and her hearing somewhat dulled, but her voice is strong, and she converses with wonderful facility for one of such extreme age. She told several amusing incidents of her life, and joined heartily in the merriment produced. Being in her fourth year when the Declaration of Independence was adopted, she was well grown when Gen. Washington visited this county, and she saw him and has a vivid recollection of him. She was born and reared within four miles of the residence to which she was transferred in her twentieth year by her marriage with the late Col. David Schnebly, whom she has survived about twenty-eight years. And there she has lived during her long life; her husband during his life in the peaceful occupation of agriculture, and she the dutiful, frugal, industrious, domestic wife, dispensing as oft they did a welcome hospitality. The carpet which now adorns her parlor, in colors bright as if new, was laid in 1812,—sixty years ago,—a beauful Brussels. The white, beautiful table-linen which covered the festal board on this occasion was made by her own bridal hands in 1790,—eighty years ago. Since the death of her husband she has been conducting the farm (and that not a small one) herself, with the aid of a worthy citizen, who attends to the out-door employments.

"On the anniversary here referred to her board was plentifully supplied with the good things of her household, and all partook, she herself being seated at the head of the first table and partaking liberally of the food she had so bountifully spread for her guests. After all had dined the entire party reassembled in the parlor for religious services. Appropriate passages were read from the Bible by the Rev. Dr. Kieffer, of Greencastle, Pa. The assembly then rising, the Creed was repeated by all. Then kneeling, a very touching prayer was offered up by that gentleman, and the benediction pronounced. During all these services and entertainment this aged and most interesting lady manifested no fatigue whatever."

Col. Jacob Hollingsworth, who died from a pistol wound inflicted accidentally by himself, in March, 1868, was about seventy-eight years of age, and was one of the prominent citizens of Washington County. About 1835 he purchased "Fountain Rock," the former residence of Gen. Samuel Ringgold, and removed from Anne Arundel to Washington County. Soon after he established his residence in Hagerstown, and invested his means, after selling the Ringgold property, in a sugar plantation in Mississippi. The war inflicted heavy loss on him, and in his later years he led a very retired life. He had an extensive family connection, among them the late Dr. Gibson, an eminent surgeon of Philadelphia, Gen. Charles Sterett Ridgely, and Dr. John B. Morris. The manner of Col. Hollingsworth's death was a great shock to his relatives and friends. When discovered, he was lying alone in his room, across the foot of the bed and insensible, the blood oozing out of a small wound a little behind and above the left ear. Under his body was found a Colt's revolver of the smallest size, loaded with the exception of a single charge. The report of the pistol had been heard by one of the colonel's daughters, about eleven o'clock, but it excited no alarm at the time. But the colonel's wife, whose mind has been enfeebled by age, entered the parlor about noon and told her daughter, Mrs. Watts, that something was the matter with her father. Mrs. Watts, on discovering the prostrate form of her father, called to her husband, Maj. Edward Watts, when the facts above related were developed.

The first impression was that the act might have been designed; but later in the day this impression was changed into the belief, among those persons who attended the bedside of the wounded man, that it was the result of accident. The Rev. Henry Edwards, former pastor of St. John's Parish, called at the bedside of the dying man, Drs. Regan and Dorsey, Maj. Hughes, Judge French, Maj. Watts, John W. Kennedy, and several ladies, friends of the family, were also present. The impression having rapidly gone abroad that the act might have been one of attempted suicide, Mr. Edwards felt it to be his duty to inquire into the circumstances of the case. Mr. Edwards subsequently stated that Col. Hollingsworth, both on the occasion of this visit and of a subsequent visit three hours later, was entirely conscious; that he answered the questions put to him knowingly and intelligibly; that he pronounced his (Mr. Edwards') name, as well as those of Maj. Hughes and Mr. Kennedy, when pointed out to him, quite distinctly; and that, although suffering severe pain which caused moaning, while Mr. Edwards was reading the church service he remained perfectly still and attentive. Mr. Edwards, again and again, in various forms, propounded the questions, "Had he done it on purpose?" "Was it accidental?" To the first he received the consistent answer "No!" and to the latter "Yes!" Mr. Edwards was satisfied, as fully as it was possible to be under such circumstances, that the act was one of accident, and in this view the other gentlemen present concurred. For a long while Col. Hollingsworth had been in a highly nervous state, mentally as well as physically. He had fancied that he was threatened by robbers, and one of his idiosyncrasies was that he must have a pistol constantly about him for his defense.

Among the thrifty and enterprising Swiss emigrants who crossed the ocean to America in the early part of the eighteenth century were the parents of Wolfgang Newcomer, who came to Pennsylvania with their son about 1720, and settled in the city of Philadelphia. They probably belonged to that large class of artisans and mechanics who poured into Pennsylvania in a steady stream at this period from Germany and Switzerland, and proved such valuable acquisitions in a land where skilled labor and steady workmen were difficult to obtain. The son, Wolfgang, was a carpenter by trade. He was twice married. His first wife, a Miss Baer, only lived about a year after their marriage; and about two years after her death he married Elizabeth Miller, by whom he had three sons—Henry, Christian, and Peter—and five daughters.

The three brothers removed from Lancaster County, Pa., where their father settled, to Washington County, Md., and became owners of large landed estates in the vicinity of Beaver Creek, near Hagerstown. All three of them soon took prominent positions in their new homes. Christian became a noted minister of the German Reformed Church, and eventually a bishop of that denomination, while Henry and Peter made their influence felt for good in more private walks of life. Among the descendants of Henry was John Newcomer, who was born on the 18th of December, 1797, in Washington County, Md., where he died on the 21st of April, 1861. John Newcomer would seem to have inherited in a special manner all the highest virtues and best qualities of the sturdy, honest stock from which he sprung. Although naturally quiet and retiring, his strong character and no less strong intellect made him a man of prominence all through his life, and in spite of his own personal tastes and wishes kept him almost constantly before the public, so that, even when permitted to escape the burden of official responsibilities, he still occupied by general consent a semi-official position, and as a sort of business oracle of the community in which he lived, was made by his friends and neighbors the judge and arbiter of their business disputes. His strict integrity and veracity, his frankness, sincerity, and disinterestedness, gave to these decisions the weight of law with the contending parties, and procured for him the genuine and universal respect of the community.

In 1836 he was elected sheriff of the county, and in 1840, after the expiration of his term, was sent to the State Senate, where he served his constituents with credit to himself and satisfaction to them for the period of six years. In 1846 he was elected county commissioner, serving until 1849, and in 1850 was elected a member of the convention which framed the constitution adopted in that year. In 1859 he reluctantly consented to become a candidate for county commissioner, and was the only one of the five candidates on the ticket with him who was elected to that office, which he held at the time of his decease. While thus holding many political offices of trust and honor, he never sank to the level of the politician, nor lost in public station the virtues which adorned and beautified his private life.

His wife, Catharine Newcomer, was a lady of the most admirable and excellent character, and to her loving and judicious training her eldest son, Benjamin Franklin Newcomer, who has won such well-merited distinction in the business world, attributes much of his success. Born on the 28th of April, 1827, at the old homestead of his great-grandfather, Henry Newcomer, which is still in possession of the family, Benjamin F. Newcomer was educated at the Hagerstown Academy with a view to civil engineering as his future calling, for which he seemed peculiarly adapted by his strong natural talent for mathematics. In the year 1842, however, his father formed a connection with Samuel Stonebraker and establishing in Baltimore the house of Newcomer & Stonebraker, wholesale dealers in flour and grain, sent his son, then but sixteen years of age, to represent his interests in the business. In a short time the firm stood among the leaders in the flour and grain business of Baltimore, and for many years their sales aggregated one-tenth of all the flour sold in that city. Two years after he had entered upon his business career, at the youthful age of eighteen, B. F. Newcomer purchased his father's entire interest in the establishment, having at that period sole charge of the correspondence and financial department of the house. In the mean time, however, anxious to complete, as far as practicable, the education which had been interrupted by his call to the pursuits of active life, he had become a member of the Mercantile Library Association, and very soon afterwards a director in that institution, spending his evenings in reading, study, and attending lectures, including several courses in philosophy, astronomy, and chemistry. In 1862 the firm of Newcomer & Stonebraker was dissolved and the present house of Newcomer & Co. established in the same line,—a house which stands second to none in the country for business enterprise, careful management, and financial integrity.

While laying the foundations of a great business house and building up an enviable reputation for himself personally, Mr. Newcomer was not indifferent to the calls of benevolence, and at the early age of twenty-five, in connection with Judge John Glenn, Jacob I. Cohen, William George Baker, J. Smith Hollins, J. N. McJilton, and David Laughery, became one of the incorporators of the "Maryland Institution for the Instruction of the Blind." Mr. Newcomer is now the only survivor of the original incorporators, but his interest in the institution has only increased with time, and with its development and progress. Since its establishment, a quarter of a century ago, it has done a noble work in the education of the blind, and it is indebted to Mr. Newcomer, who was for many years its treasurer and is now its president, for much of its past success and present prosperity. In 1854, Mr. Newcomer was elected a director in the Union Bank of Maryland (now the National Union Bank of Baltimore), and during the whole of his connection with it was the youngest member of the board, upon which he continued to serve until 1868, when the increasing pressure of private business compelled his resignation. He was also one of the original promoters of the Corn and Flour Exchange, organized in 1853, which has become one of the most important mercantile institutions in Baltimore. In 1861 he was elected a director in the Northern Central Railway Company, and was soon afterwards made chairman of the finance committee, holding that position until his resignation in 1875. His services were so highly appreciated that at the annual meeting of the stockholders in February, 1878, he was strongly urged to again become a member of the board. Yielding to this imperative solicitation, he was again elected chairman of the finance committee, and was also made a member of every committee of which the board is composed. He is also a director in the Philadelphia, Wilmington and Baltimore Railroad. In association with William T. Walters he served as one of the finance commissioners of the city of Baltimore from 1867 to 1869, and discharged the duties of the position with signal judgment and ability. After the close of the war he acquired large interests in various railroads in North and South Carolina, and assisted with capital and energy in the development of the railway system which has opened up a new era of prosperity in the South. He is vice-president of the Wilmington and Weldon Railroad, and a director in the various roads constituting the Coast Line, the management of which is in the hands of himself and his associates. In 1868, Mr. Newcomer was elected president of the Safe Deposit and Trust Company of Baltimore,—a corporation chartered for the safe-keeping of bonds, stocks, and valuables of every description, and for the purpose of acting as trustee, executor, guardian, etc. The Safe Deposit building is the most complete structure of its character in the country, and is unsurpassed by any similar building anywhere either in security or finish. It is strictly fire-proof, and the great burglar and fire-proof vault is a master-piece of strength and beauty.

The company has supplied a real need in Baltimore and its vicinity, and under the able management of Mr. Newcomer it is daily growing in public appreciation. The authority given it in its charter to act in a fiduciary capacity has proved as valuable to the public as to itself, and trusts of all characters are administered not only with fidelity, but with more than ordinary intelligence, owing to Mr. Newcomer's thorough familiarity with the laws and the business details connected with their management. Mr. Newcomer still retains the presidency of the company, is also a director in the Baltimore and Potomac Railroad Company, in the Chamber of Commerce Building Company, and in the Savings-Bank of Baltimore, and was formerly a director in the National Exchange Bank and in the Third National Bank.

While courteous and kindly in his intercourse with all with whom he is brought into contact, Mr. Newcomer is firm and independent in his business transactions, ready to receive suggestions, but relying largely, like all men of strong character who have carved out their own way in the world, upon his own judgment and experience,—guides, it may be added, which rarely lead him astray. With all his business capacity and talent, he possesses the rare virtue of modesty, shrinking from notoriety and prominence, and of all the positions he has been called upon to fill not one was ever sought by him. His attachments and affections are strong and ardent, and he has frequently declared that whatever success he has achieved in life can be attributed to a good mother and a good wife, in both of whom he has been peculiarly blessed.

When a little over twenty-one years of age, Mr. Newcomer married Amelia, daughter of John H. Ehlen, one of the earliest stockholders and for many years a director in the Baltimore and Ohio Railroad Company, as also in the Chesapeake Bank and in the Firemen's Insurance Company, a gentleman noted for his business integrity, genial manners, and kindness of heart. In the spring of 1870, accompanied by his wife, Mr. Newcomer joined at Paris their eldest daughter, who had been sent there to complete her education. Together they made the tour of Southern Europe and Great Britain. In 1877, accompanied by his wife and two younger daughters he made another and more extended tour, embracing France, Italy, Germany, part of Austria, Switzerland, Holland, Belgium, England, and Scotland.

Mrs. Newcomer, whose death occurred on the 20th of October, 1881, was a lady more than worthy of the love and esteem in which she was held by all who enjoyed the privilege of her acquaintance. Hers was a life spent in deeds of love and charity. In all the relations of her home circle, and in labors for the relief of suffering, she was true, devoted, and self-sacrificing. The beauty and nobility of her character were illustrated by the quiet exhibition of those virtues which best adorn womanhood, and she ever blessed and cheered with voice and hand. Her death was no ordinary loss, and the regret which it occasioned was widespread and sincere.

Mr. Newcomer has four children,—three daughters and one son. The eldest, Mary L., is the wife of James M. Maslin, of the house of Henry, Maslin & Co., wholesale merchants, of Baltimore; the second, Nannie, is the wife of F. H. Hack, a member of the Baltimore bar; the third, Hattie, and her younger brother, Waldo, reside with their father.

Christian Newcomer, a bishop of the German Methodist Society, was born in Lancaster County, Pa., Feb. 1, 1749. His father, Wolfgang Newcomer, emigrated from Switzerland and settled at Philadelphia. His occupation was that of carpenter. He first married a Miss Baer, who lived only one year after marriage, and after being a widower about two years he married Elizabeth Weller, by whom he had three sons and five daughters. Of the sons, Henry Newcomer was the eldest, Christian the second, and Peter the youngest. Both the parents were members of the Mennonite denomination. At a very early age Christian became deeply interested in religion, and was baptized into the Mennonite Society. He learned the trade of carpenter, which he continued to practice until the death of his father, when he took charge of the homestead. On the 31st of March, 1770, he was married to Elizabeth Baer. In the winter following he had a serious illness, but recovered. During this illness, and subsequently, he was assailed by many doubts and scruples concerning religion, and fearing to yield to the temptation to become a minister, sold his plantation in Pennsylvania and moved into Washington County, Md. During the Revolution he was considerably embarrassed by the conflict between his patriotism and the rule of his society forbidding any of the members to take up arms. Subsequently, during a visit to his old home at Lancaster, he rose in a meeting, and having related his mental vacillation, earnestly recommended "to them the grace of God in Christ Jesus." Some time before he had made the acquaintance of William Otterbein and George Adam Geeting, two preachers of the German Reformed Church, whose sermons produced a powerful impression upon him and caused him to withdraw from the Mennonites and attach himself to their communion. He soon afterwards entered fully upon the work of preaching and ministering, and often traveled a hundred miles and more to fill appointments. He preached both in German and English, though unable to speak the latter with fluency. His service extended over the whole of Western Maryland, and into portions of West Virginia, Pennsylvania, and Ohio. He continued to labor with wonderful activity and diligence, keeping a daily record of his work, until eighty-one years of age. In this year he was elected, with Henry Kumler, a bishop of the society. His health now began to fail, but he continued nevertheless to discharge the duties of his office with wonderful punctuality and vigor until his death, which occurred on the 12th of March, 1830, in his eighty-second year. The last entry in his journal reads:

"March 1st.—This day I rode to Boonsborough and lodged with brother Michael Thomas. 2d. My intention was to ride to Virginia to-day, but finding the weather rather disagreeable this morning I returned home. 3d. This morning I was very well satisfied that I had returned home; during the past night I was very ill and had but little rest. O God! stand by me for Jesus' sake; true, I am unworthy of all Thy mercies, but I am so needy; Lord, bless me, and Thine shall be all the glory. Amen. Some time in the day my son Andrew sent for a physician. 4th. This forenoon I tried to write in my journal, but, alas! I find that I am not able to perform the task, so I lay down my pen. The Lord alone knows whether I shall be able to resume it again. The Lord's will be done. Amen, Hallelujah!"

Shortly before his death, Bishop Newcomer rose from his pillow without assistance, and, with those present, offered an earnest prayer. He then lay down, and, "reclining his head on his pillow, drew breath but a few times and calmly expired." His funeral was attended by a vast concourse. Bishop Henry Kumler preached in German, and Dr. John Zahn in English.

Robert Fowler, State treasurer of Maryland, was a native of Montgomery County, but removed to Washington County in early life, and married there. He pursued the various avocations of hotel-keeper, merchant, contractor, and politician, and in all these relations enjoyed the respect and confidence of the community in which he lived. His first office was that of county commissioner, in which position he displayed, although a very young man, the same qualifications for business and the management of public affairs that distinguished him in after-life. In 1846, when party excitement was unusually high, Mr. Fowler was nominated as a Whig for the House of Delegates in opposition to Hon. Wm. T. Hamilton. The contest was a very exciting and extremely personal one, and resulted in the election of Mr. Fowler. After the expiration of his senatorial term he was engaged in projecting and building various turnpike roads. He also strenuously exerted himself to procure the construction of the Washington County branch of the Baltimore and Ohio Railroad, and the successful prosecution of that enterprise was largely due to his efforts in its behalf. He was elected treasurer of Maryland for several consecutive terms, and at the time of his death was regarded as one of the most influential politicians in the State. The greater portion of his life was spent in Washington County, but for some years previous to his death he resided in Baltimore County. The funeral took place from Barnum's Hotel, and was very largely attended. The Rev. C. R. Haines, rector of St. Timothy's Church, at Catonsville, of which Mr. Fowler was a member, and the Rev. Fleming James, rector of St. Mark's Church, were the officiating clergymen.

After the funeral service had been read the cortege was formed, the clergy leading. Then came the honorary pall-bearers of the Legislature, viz.: Senators Walsh, Spencer, Tuck, and Steiner, and Representatives Grimes, Leonard, Merryman, and Annan. Then followed the casket, borne by the following gentlemen, who acted as pall-bearers: Hon. Wm. T. Hamilton, Hon. Isaac M. Denson, Daniel Dorsey, A. S. Abell, Dr. J. Hanson Thomas, J. B. Brinkley, F. K. Zeigler, Wm. B. McLaughin, Henry James, John King, Jr., and Joseph Judick. After the family and friends had been seated the members of the Legislature and city officials took carriages in the rear, and the cortege proceeded to Loudon Park Cemetery. Among those present were Hon. Reverdy Johnson, Senator Whyte, and Mayor Vansant.

Luke Tiernan, importing and shipping merchant of Baltimore, was born in the county of Meath, Ireland, in 1757, and came to the United States in 1787 and settled in Hagerstown, Md. He married, in 1793, Ann Owen, a descendant of Col. Cresap. Mr. Tiernan removed to Baltimore in 1795 and went into the business of importing dry goods, and was also largely interested in ships. His house was on Baltimore Street, where the warehouse of Hamilton Easter & Sons is situated. In politics he was a Whig and a warm admirer of Henry Clay, who frequently stopped at his house, and always spoke of him as the patriarch of the Whig party of Maryland. He was a Presidential elector for John Quincy Adams; he was the head of the list of the founders of the Hibernian Society. He was one of the committee appointed in 1826–27 to urge upon the Legislature the incorporation of the Baltimore and Ohio Railroad. The "Herald," one of his ships, brought the first locomotive for that road from England. He was one of the organizers and president of the Screw Dock Company; he was one of the trustees of the Catholic Cathedral, and one of the committee at the inauguration of the Washington Monument. He died Nov. 10, 1839, aged eighty-three, and left eleven children. He was greatly respected and beloved in the community, and strongly attached to the people and government of his adopted country.

Adam I. Glossbrenner was born in Hagerstown, Md., Aug. 31, 1810. His school was the printing-office, to which he was apprenticed, and at seventeen he became foreman of the *Ohio Monitor*, and afterwards of the *Western Telegraph*. In 1829 he returned to Maryland, and afterwards removed to York, Pa., where he published the *York Gazette*. In 1849 he was elected sergeant-at-arms to the House of Representatives for the Thirty-first Congress, and was re-elected for four Congresses. In 1861 he was private secretary to President Buchanan; in 1863 he founded the *Philadelphia Age*, and in 1864 was elected to the Thirty-ninth Congress, and served on the Committee on Public Lands, and on Engrossed Bills. He was re-elected to the Fortieth Congress, serving on the Committees on Expenditures in the Navy Department and Executive Mansion.

Edward Merryman Mealey was born in the New Market District of Frederick County about 1810. His mother was a native of England, and his father a native of Ireland. On attaining his majority he removed to Hagerstown, where he became a clerk for Stockton & Stokes, the stage proprietors. The latter sold out to Dr. Howard Kennedy and James Cowdy, of Hagerstown. Dr. Kennedy afterwards sold his interest to Mr. Cowdy and George Sinn, of Hagerstown. In 1865 the proprietors sold their rights to Pretzman & Appleman, and in 1849, Mr. Adams, who was then endeavoring to organize the express company which now bears his name, visited Hagerstown and gave the elder Mealey a certain portion of the stock in payment for combining the express business with his stage-lines. Mr. Mealey was elected to the House of Delegates on the Whig ticket in 1858, and was president of the Washington County Railroad from commencement to completion, and director in the Hagerstown Bank.

In 1841 he married Elizabeth Frances Windsor, of Kentucky, and had one son, Edward W. Mealey, who was born on the 23d of August, 1846. E. W. Mealey, Jr., was educated at the College of St. James, where he graduated in 1864, and at Harvard College, where he graduated in 1867. He studied law, and on the 1st of June, 1876, married Gertrude Parks, of New York City, whose father was rector of Trinity Church. Mr. Mealey is a director of the Western Maryland Railroad, Hagerstown Steam-Engine and Machine Company, Mutual Insurance Company, and Washington County Water Company, and is one of the owners of the Baldwin House at Hagerstown.

George C. Washington was born in Westmoreland County, Va., Aug. 20, 1789, and died in Georgetown, D. C., July 17, 1854. At the time of his death he was the oldest and nearest surviving relative of his grand uncle, Gen. Washington. He represented Western Maryland in the Congress from 1827 to 1833, and from 1835 to 1837. He was also president of the Chesapeake and Ohio Canal and a commissioner for the settlement of Indian claims. He was spoken of for Vice-President on the ticket with Gen. Scott.

Frederick Bodmann, who died on the 29th of July, 1874, was born at Hannan, near Frankfort-on-the-Main, July 16, 1801, and was therefore at the time of his death a little more than seventy-three years of age. His father, Louis Charles Bodmann, was a judge of the Superior Court of a German principality near Frankfort. Ferdinand graduated with honor at Bamberg College in 1817, and subsequently received a liberal commercial education in a large banking-house in Frankfort. In 1822 the father, with three sons, Ferdinand among the rest, arrived in Baltimore, Md., and soon after settled in Hagerstown, where Ferdinand was engaged in commercial business until the death of his father, which occurred about six years after the immigration to this country. In a short time after the father's death Ferdinand disposed of his business and went to Cincinnati and engaged in the tobacco business, which he followed until his death.

Mr. Bodmann had considerable means,—about thirty thousand dollars, it is said,—and on this as a foundation he amassed a great fortune. Immediately on his arrival in Cincinnati he commenced the erection of a tobacco-factory on Main Street, between Sixth and Seventh. Remaining in this place a few years, he removed across the street, to what is now No. 273, and there remained in business until he died.

He was married Dec. 14, 1825, to a daughter of George M. Popline, of Baltimore. Of the six children born three survive, they being Charles, one of the largest tobacco dealers in Cincinnati; a younger son, George, engaged in business in Brussels, Belgium; and Lauretta L., widow of the late Joseph Reakirt, the wholesale druggist.

Mr. Bodmann was for ten years Master of Cincinnati Lodge, No. 133, Free and Accepted Masons, a member of McMillian Chapter, of the Cincinnati Council and Cincinnati Commandery of Knights Templar, and an honorary member of Hanselmann Commandery. Upon his arrival in this country he was made a Mason in Baltimore.

At the old business stand, No. 273 Main Street, Cincinnati, where he remained for about forty years, Mr. Bodmann at one time did a large wholesale and retail business in tobacco, considering the extent to which the trade was carried on in those days.

He lived with his family in a very unpretentious manner over the store until he moved to Mount Auburn, about twenty-six years before his death.

The vast property which he gathered was not the result of speculation. He never entered into a speculation in his life. His wealth, consisting of about a million of dollars' worth of real estate and other possessions, swelling his fortune to a million and a half or two millions of dollars, was the slow accumulation of years through industry, economy, and sagacious investment. Thus the years made him the oldest, and the product of his toil the wealthiest, German citizen of Cincinnati. To his estate belonged the tan-yard at the Great Western Stock-Yards, the carrying on of which was his principal business for the last few years of his life. He owned a large amount of real estate in the vicinity of his store on Main Street. At an early day, with John Groesbeck as president, he was a director of the Franklin Bank, in which he owned considerable stock.

Mr. Bodmann had many strong eccentricities of character, some of which were admirable. In his business investments he would not, under any circumstances, purchase a building unless he could own in fee-simple the ground upon which it stood. When real estate came into his possession he held on to it permanently. The only property of this kind he was ever known to part with was some eighty thousand dollars' worth on Fifth Street, which he sold to the government for room upon which to erect the new custom-house. He frequently afterwards regretted the sale. He was never known to give a note or a due-bill. When he purchased a piece of property upon which there were to be deferred payments, he invariably refused to give his notes for these payments. He simply had made on his books an entry of the amounts due, which, as he always had the cash ready when pay-day came around, was deemed perfectly satisfactory to the other parties. He was a man whose word was as good as his bond.

He often spoke of his native land, but never went back to see it. Indeed, with a residence of nearly half a century in Cincinnati, it is said that during all that time he was never outside of the city, except in the immediate vicinity. He was fond of hunting game, and occasionally, in early times, went out for sport in the neighboring woods and fields. He never trusted himself on board a steamboat or railroad cars. A friend relates that he was once urged to take the cars for Dayton to attend a Masonic meeting there. Though he answered that he had property in that city which he had not seen for thirty years, he could not be induced to make the trip.

Mr. Bodmann was most remarkably methodical in his habits. Though a millionaire, he until the last attended his plain little tobacco store, with unplastered walls, on Main Street. He made this his office, where he loaned large sums of money and transacted the business connected with his large estate, but at the same time he did a share in waiting on customers, and with alacrity weighed out small quantities of tobacco, snuff, etc., for them. He took pleasure in it, for with him his simple habits appeared a pleasure.

Mr. Bodmann was quite a bird-fancier, and in nothing else were his eccentricities more strongly marked than in this particular. He is said to have intimated that one great inducement for moving on Mount Auburn was the comfort of his pets. He had a large number of singing birds in his store, and at his home was a much larger collection, which in point of size and variety was one of the finest in the country. In this were about six hundred pairs of pigeons of all varieties and colors. The master fed the birds and animals from his own hand, and they became much attached to him. Only the morning before he died, against the advice of friends, who regarded his health too precarious, he went out early to feed and fondle his pets.

The Neill family. William Neill, the great-grandfather of Alexander Neill, was born in 1754 in County Antrim, Ireland, and emigrated to America, in company with his two brothers, about 1770. He landed in Baltimore, and engaged in business there, becoming one of the leading merchants of that town. His son Alexander was born in Baltimore, Dec. 22, 1778, and married Sarah Owen about 1803. He removed to Hagerstown the same year and entered into business. He was elected sheriff in 1826, and subsequently retired from business. He was for a long series of years president of the Hagerstown Bank. He had ten children, four girls—Sarah, Rebecca, Mary Chandler, and Isabella Callender—and six boys,—William Kennedy, Robert Callender, William, Alexander, Kennedy, and Luke Tiernan.

Alexander, father of Alexander Neill, now a prominent member of the Hagerstown bar, was born in Hagerstown, Dec. 5, 1808. He married Mary Sim Nelson, of Frederick, daughter of John Nelson, who was attorney-general under President Tyler.

Mary Sim Nelson was born March 22, 1819. She was the grandniece of William Burrows, commander of the United States sloop-of-war "Enterprise," to whom Congress awarded a gold medal for gallant conduct in destroying the British brig "Boxer" during the war of 1812.

The fruits of this marriage were eight children: Alexander, John Nelson, William, Sally, Harriet Burrows, Mary Chandler, Isabella, and Rose Nelson.

Alexander Neill, Jr., was born Aug. 5, 1844. He was educated at St. James' College, graduating in 1863, and commenced studying law with his father. After the death of his father he pursued his studies in the office of Judge William Motter. He was a member of the Legislature in 1870 and also a school commissioner, and was auditor of Washington County Court in 1876. Besides his public services, he has held numerous positions of trust in connection with private corporations, among them the treasurership of the Washington County Savings Institution in 1871, and a directorship in the Mutual Insurance Company of Washington County, for which company he was also attorney.

He married, April 27, 1871, Ellen, daughter of William Loubridge, of Baltimore, and has four children.

William Neill married Grace Kennedy, sister of Dr. Howard Kennedy.

Jonathan Hager's brother, George Hager, was born at Hagerstown, July 24, 1787, and settled in Terre Haute, Ind., in 1835. He was an active, enterprising business man, and contributed much to the growth and prosperity of Terre Haute. His character was a kindly, benevolent one, and he was extremely popular among his fellow-citizens. He died in April, 1870, in his eighty-third year.

J. Philip Roman was a native of Cecil County, of Quaker descent, and removed in early life to Washington County, where he studied law with his elder brother, Hon. J. Dixon Roman. Mr. Roman took a conspicuous part in the politics of Western Maryland, although, with the exception of representing Allegany County (in part) in the Constitutional Convention of 1867, he never held public office. In 1852 he was the Whig candidate for Congress, but was defeated by Hon. William T. Hamilton. In 1868 his name was before the convention which nominated Hon. Patrick Hamill for Congress, but after two days of ruitless balloting it was withdrawn. Mr. Roman was a man of unusual energy and decision of character, and was extremely popular with the masses. In the course of a long and active business life he amassed a handsome fortune. He owned several large tracts of valuable coal-lands, a shipping wharf to Locust Point, Baltimore, and other remunerative property. Mr. Roman was so engrossed in his business enterprises that he was not able to give much attention to his profession, the law. Soon after being admitted to the bar (1843) he removed to Cumberland, where he resided until his death. Mr. Roman married Miss Louisa Lowndes, daughter of Lloyd Lowndes, of Cumberland, who survived him.

Lieut. Louis M. Hughes, of the United States army, was killed on Feb. 14, 1870, by falling into a shaft at "Miners' Delight," a small town in the Sweetwater mining district of Wyoming Territory. He was a native of Hagerstown, and was appointed a second lieutenant from Maryland in the Thirty-sixth Infantry, July 28, 1866. On Feb. 22, 1869, he was promoted to a first lieutenancy, but as the consolidation of regiments about that time left him unassigned, he was at his own request continued in active service, and was attached to the Second Cavalry, then about to march to Montana. Subsequently he was assigned temporarily to the Seventh Infantry, and was ordered on duty in the locality where he was killed. Hearing that a notorious character who had stolen a number of government animals was concealed in a neighboring cabin, he obtained permission to try and capture him. With a detachment of soldiers he visited the place where the outlaw was supposed to be secreted. This proved to be the covering of a mining-shaft, through which Lieut. Hughes accidentally fell and received fatal injuries. His remains were brought to Hagerstown, where his mother resides, and were there interred.

Among the officers of the Army of Northern Virginia none were more celebrated for courageous daring, military gallantry, or affective aid to the "lost cause" than Maj. James Breathed, of Stuart's celebrated horse artillery, and in the civil war he won a reputation that will live for generations to come with those whose ancestors were sympathizers with the South in that sectional struggle. Maj. James Breathed was the eldest son and child of John W. Breathed, the founder of Breathedsville, Washington Co., and was born Dec. 15, 1838, in Morgan County, Va. In his infancy his father removed to Washington County, and James was educated at St. James' College. Upon concluding his studies he graduated as a medical doctor in Baltimore City and went to Missouri, where he settled near the city of St. Joseph. In his new home he soon became distinguished in his profession, which he abandoned at the breaking out of the war, and came East to cast his fortunes with those of his native State. On the journey he had for a traveling companion Gen. Stuart, who was afterwards his commanding officer in the Army of Northern Virginia, and whose errand was identical with that of young Breathed; but neither knew at that time of the mission of the other. Young Breathed first proceeded to the home of his parents to await the result of the action of the Maryland Legislature, which was about to convene in extra session. About this time, while in Chambersburg, Pennsylvania, he was suspected by the Federal authorities, who seized and searched his baggage, but released him after a short delay. Finding that the Legislature hesitated about the future course of the State, young Breathed, against the wishes of his parents, who counseled further deliberation, departed for Virginia and joined a company of cavalry commanded by J. Blair Hoge, of Martinsburg, afterwards known as Company B, First Virginia Cavalry. It was, together with other companies, placed under the command of Gen. J. E. B. Stuart, who was charged with the duty of retarding Gen. Patterson's advance upon Martinsburg. Recognizing in young Breathed his traveling companion of a few weeks previous, Gen. Stuart assigned him to scouting duty and other detached service, in the fulfillment of which he more than met the expectations of his commander. It was at this time that young Breathed displayed the elements of courage and daring which afterwards led to his rapid promotion.

Early in 1862, when Gen. Stuart organized a battalion of horse artillery, young Breathed was selected as first lieutenant of the first battery, of which John, afterwards Maj., Pelham was made captain. With this battery Maj. Breathed passed through the Peninsula campaign, Fair Oaks, the seven days' fighting around Richmond, Antietam, Gettysburg, and other celebrated engagements, in all of which he was more or less conspicuous. At the battle of Antietam the guns of this battery, commanded by him, opened the engagement. His guns were also the last to cross the Potomac at Shepherdstown on the occasion of Lee's retreat, and were constantly employed at the front of the Federal army as it moved on to Richmond. Just before the battle of Fredericksburg Lieut. Breathed was promoted to a captaincy. At the battle of Chancellorsville Capt. Breathed especially distinguished himself and won encomiums of praise from his commanding general, and at Gettysburg his company was in the fiercest of the fight and lost heavily.

Passing near his father's house on the return from Gettysburg, Capt. Breathed made it a visit, and while there was surprised by a company of Union cavalry and narrowly escaped capture.

On Sept. 25, 1863, Capt. Breathed, while in camp near Orange Court-House, tendered his resignation to Hon. James A. Sedden, assigning as a reason, "I am tired of my arm of service, and know that I can do better service in another arm of service."

Brig.-Gen. Wickham, in forwarding it, said, "Strongly disapproved." "Capt. Breathed is the best man for the management of a battery of horse artillery that I ever saw."

Brig.-Gen. Fitzhugh Lee indorsed it, "Disapproved." "Capt. Breathed is an excellent officer. He can do no better service in another arm of the service."

Maj.-Gen. J. E. B. Stuart, in his indorsement, said, "Respectfully forwarded disapproved." "I will never consent for Capt. Breathed to quit the horse artillery, with which he has rendered such distinguished service, except for certain promotion, which he has well earned."

The resignation of Capt. Breathed was also "disapproved" by Gen. Lee and the Secretary of War, and on April 22, 1864, he was promoted to major of artillery, to rank as such from Feb. 27, 1864. On the 26th of April following he was assigned by Gen. Lee to duty with the battalion of horse artillery serving with the cavalry corps of the Army of Northern Virginia.

Maj. Breathed's commission as lieutenant of artillery was dated April 1, 1862, and signed by Governor Fletcher, to rank from March 23, 1862, in the provisional army of the State of Virginia. His commission as captain in the provisional army of the State of Virginia, to rank from Aug. 9, 1862, was dated Sept. 22, 1862, and his commission as major was for "the provisional army in the service of the Confederate States."

After his last promotion Maj. Breathed went into winter quarters near Charlottesville. During this encampment he was surprised by a portion of Custer's brigade, then on a secret raid on Charlottesville. He drew two pieces on a neighboring hill, and as the first companies of the enemy charged through his camp fired upon them, and then with a small band of artillerists, under cover of the confusion created by the guns, charged them and drove them back, and chased and harassed them for many miles. For this daring act he received the thanks of the residents of Charlottesville, and the ladies of the town presented him with a stand of colors. In the campaign of '64, during Grant's march on Richmond, Maj. Breathed's battalion occupied the Confederate flank, and was fighting almost incessantly, sometimes as cavalrymen, again as artillery, and always with the dash and courage for which he was noted. Early in May of that year Fitzhugh Lee was endeavoring to hold the Federal columns in check at Spottsylvania Court-House, and received information that Longstreet's first division was hurrying to his relief. He was urged by Gen. Stuart to hold out at any sacrifice. At a moment of great importance, when the advance had been held at terrible cost, Fitzhugh Lee called on Maj. Breathed to check the advance of a fresh column of the enemy. The result Gen. Lee told afterwards, as follows:

"Maj. James Breathed, by my order, placed a single gun on a little knoll, and as we were falling back, disputing the enemy's advance towards Spottsylvania Court-House, we knew the enemy's infantry were marching in column through a piece of woods, and the object was to fire upon the head of the column as it debouched, to give the idea that their further advance would be contested and to compel them to develop a line of battle, with skirmishers thrown out, etc. Under Maj. Breathed's personal superintendence shells were thrown, and burst exactly at the head of the column as it debouched; the head of the enemy's advance was scattered, and it was only with some difficulty a line of battle with skirmishers in front was formed. I was sitting on my horse near Breathed and directed him to withdraw his gun, but he begged to be allowed to give the enemy some more rounds. He fired until their line got so close that you could hear them calling on him to surrender the gun. Breathed's own horse had just been shot. The cannoneers jumped on their horses, expecting, of course, the gun to be captured, and retreated rapidly down the hill. Breathed was left alone. He limbered the gun up and jumped on the lead-horse. It was shot from under him. Quick as lightning he drew his knife, cut the leaders out of the harness, and sprang on a swing-horse. It was also shot from under him just as he was turning to get into the road. He then severed the harness of the swing-horse, jumped upon one of the wheel-horses, and again made a desperate trial for life. The ground was open between the piece and the woods; the enemy had a full view of the exploit; and Breathed at last dashed off unharmed, almost miraculously escaping through a shower of bullets."

Many such exploits are told of the young officer, but one especially at "High Bridge," on the Appomattox, illustrated his reckless indifference to danger and dauntless courage. Breathed was sent with Gen. Rosser to prevent the Federals from obtaining possession of it, and finding them already there he gave battle. The fighting was so intense and close-handed that Gen. Reid, of Philadelphia, in command of the Federals, was killed by Brig.-Gen. Deering, a young Confederate officer, and Gen. Deering, Col. Boston, and Maj. Thompson had fallen on the Confederate side. When the fight was at its height and the result was doubtful, Maj. Breathed was commanded to lead a dismounted charging column. He went to the front and ordered the advance, but the men faltered and refused to move. Breathed galloped about forty paces and called upon his men again. At this moment two captains left the ranks of the enemy and came galloping upon him. Breathed received them with extended sabre, killed the first, and in the effort to avoid the stroke of the second was dismounted. This would have been fatal had not a soldier reached the spot and shot his antagonist. Maj. Breathed was dangerously wounded early in July, 1864, and Gen. Robt. E. Lee, commander-in-chief of the Confederate forces, on hearing of this, dispatched to him the following:

"MAJOR,—I heard with great regret that you were wounded and incapacitated for active duty. I beg to tender you my sympathy, and to express the hope that the army will not long be deprived of your valuable services. The reports I have received from your superior officers of your gallantry and good conduct in action on several occasions have given me great satisfaction, and while they increase my concern for your personal suffering, render me more desirous that your health will soon permit you to resume a command that you have exercised with so much credit to yourself and advantage to the service."

Gen. J. E. B. Stuart, commander of the cavalry of the Army of Northern Virginia, in a letter to Maj. Breathed, dated March 21, 1864, said,—

"I am sensible of the distinguished gallantry which you have always displayed when brought in contact with the enemy, and can also assure you of its appreciation by the commanding general. I feel confident that you will soon be promoted. Labor to get your battery in fighting and flying trim as soon as possible. Your conduct in the late attempt of the enemy at Rio Mills to seize your guns was in keeping with the heroism which has distinguished your career as a soldier, and I regret that necessary absence from my headquarters prevented me from seeing you on your recent visit, and expressing to you in person, as I wished, my congratulations upon your achievement, as well as my high appreciation of your gallantry."

Many were the similar tributes received by Maj. Breathed for his merit, valor, and personal attributes, and the regard in which he was held in the army was continued in private life when, after the declaration of peace, he settled down again in the pursuit of his professional calling. Maj. Breathed died Feb. 16, 1870, in his thirty-second year, and was interred in St. Thomas' Graveyard, at Hancock, Md.

Necrology.—Following is a list of persons either born in or at some time resident in Washington County who have died since 1791. Owing to the impossibility of collecting sufficient material, it is necessarily imperfect, but it contains a large number of the representative people of the county:

At West Conecocheague, February, 1799, Capt. John Ankeny.

May 28, 1872, Capt. David Artz, aged 78. Capt. Artz was among the most active and enterprising of the business men of Hagerstown for fully half a century, and was also an earnest member of Trinity Lutheran Church. He received his title of captain from commanding a local company of militia, but he had also seen real service under Capt. George Shryock in the war of 1812. His remains were interred in Rose Hill Cemetery, having previously been taken to Trinity church, where the usual exercises were held by the Revs. Lepley, Eyester, Hill, and Luckenbach, the latter, as pastor of the church, delivering an appropriate discourse.

May, 1804, Christopher Alter.

Jan. 1, 1814, Frederick Alter, overseer of the almshouse, aged 73.

In June, 1814, William Adams, who lived six miles from Hagerstown, aged 87.

May, 1810, at West Conecocheague, Henry Ankeny.

Feb. 14, 1820, Capt. John Ashbury, near Ringgold's Manor.

Mrs. Bowman, at Brownsville, Pa., Dec. 19, 1822, in the 79th year of her age. She was one of the earliest settlers of Washington County, and had resided at Hagerstown from its founding to 1816.

At the Globe Tavern, in Hagerstown, Dec. 3, 1823, Thomas Belt, aged 83. An obituary notice said of him, "He was almost one of the last of the good old fathers of Washington County who have rendered it ever memorable for its ancient hospitality."

Sept. 9, 1821, at Shepherdstown, Va., in the 20th year of his age, Samuel Bell, youngest brother of the editor of the Hagerstown *Mail.*

Dec. 12, 1822, at the residence of Alex. Kennedy, near Boonsboro', Bartholomew Booth, son of John Booth.

March 30, 1879, Lily, wife of Frank O. Baush, of Cumberland, and daughter of Hon. A. K. Syester, of Hagerstown.

November, 1870, at Mobile, Col. Daniel Beltzhoover, son of the Mr. Beltzhoover who kept the Globe Tavern at Hagerstown. The deceased graduated at West Point in 1845, served through the Mexican war with gallantry, and resigned his commission in 1856, when he was appointed professor of geometry and the higher branches of mathematics at Mount St. Mary's College, Emmittsburg, Md. When the war between the States broke out, though not a native of the South, he offered his services to the Confederacy, and was appointed on Gen. Twigg's staff at New Orleans, and was afterwards made captain of the famous Watson's battery, and for gallant conduct under Sidney Johnston was breveted major, afterwards lieutenant-colonel; was chief of artillery at Vicksburg, and whilst in command there received his commission as colonel of artillery. During the siege of Fort Powell, in Mobile Bay, he rendered further important services. After the war he devoted himself to the instruction of youth. He was a proficient in music, and the composer of many pieces of much instrumental merit.

Feb. 16, 1870, Maj. James Breathed, at Hancock. Maj. Breathed was a distinguished officer in the Confederate service, but after the war engaged in the practice of medicine at Hancock.

In May, 1877, John Boswell, an old resident of Hagerstown.

May 10, 1877, near Bakersville, Otho Baker, in his 68th year.

July (Monday prior to July 25), 1873, Dr. John Beckenbaugh, son of John Beckenbaugh, aged 30. He had acquired an extensive practice at and near Sharpsburg, but his health failed, and he was forced to retire. His wife was the daughter of the Rev. Robert Douglas. Mr. Beckenbaugh was a brother-in-law of Hon. John A. Lynch, of Frederick.

April 10, 1873, Mrs. Sallie Roman Baldwin, daughter of the Hon. J. Dixon Roman, of Hagerstown, and wife of Columbus C. Baldwin, of New York. She was a very estimable lady.

Dec. 6, 1878, David Brumbaugh, aged 76 years, 6 months, and 11 days. Mr. Brumbaugh was a thorough business man, as also an ardent politician and a devoted member of the Presbyterian Church. He also took a deep interest in agriculture, and for many years was president of the County Agricultural Society.

April, 1879, Rachel, widow of the late Henry Biershing, in the 80th year of her age. She was a Miss Steele, born in Hagerstown, of a family which was among the original settlers. Her husband, Henry Biershing, was a prominent and influential citizen of Hagerstown, of vigorous intellect, strongly marked character, and in his political convictions an original and decided Democrat. He was one of the leading citizens of the town, and as a watchmaker and silversmith acquired a very handsome independence for those days. He died in April, 1843.

July 29, 1874, in Cincinnati, Ohio, Ferdinand Bodmann, a former resident of Hagerstown. Mr. Bodmann had amassed a large fortune, and was a very influential citizen.

September, 1876, John Bowman, of Beaver Creek, in his 87th year.

May, 1881, David Brewer, of Clear Spring District, aged 83.

January, 1879, David Brumbaugh, vice-president Washington County Agricultural Society.

Oct. 19, 1854, in Leitersburg District, John Barr, in the 78th year of his age.

March 22, 1853, Henry Brumbaugh, aged 77.

In 1806, Samuel Bowles, an old resident of Hagerstown.

In February, 1808, Sebastian Baker, for many years crier of the Washington County Court.

June, 1812, near Williamsport, Nicholas Baker, a native of Germany.

Jacob Brosius, for many years a resident of Hancock, Dec. 6, 1822, in the 78th year of his age.

At the Globe Tavern, Hagerstown, on Wednesday, Aug. 3, 1823, Thomas Belt, in the 83d year of his age.

At his residence, in Washington County, May 25, 1852, John Breathed, aged 73. Mr. Breathed, who was a man of considerable means, was noted for his liberality in aiding deserving relatives and friends.

In 1844, Judge John Buchanan.

Near Hagerstown, suddenly, of apoplexy, Sept. 27, 1847, Judge Thomas Buchanan.

At Wheatland, Oct. 2, 1827, Maj.-Gen. Perry Benson, in the 72d year of his age.

Near Hagerstown, on the 23d of August, 1800, Mrs. Eleanor Beall.

On the 27th of August, 1800, Mrs. Margaret Baird, relict of the late Maj. William Baird.

On his plantation in Washington County, in the latter part of June, 1800, Col. John Barnes.

Near Hagerstown, Feb. 27, 1799, Martin Baer.

Nov. 20, 1801, Harriet R. Beatty, wife of Col. Cornelius Beatty, of Hagerstown.

At Williamsport, May 2, 1801, Rudolph Brill, merchant.

May 5, 1859, Elie Beatty, aged 83.

April 23, 1859, Rev. James Brown, aged 84, a colored preacher. He had been a slave of Benjamin Galloway, and at the time of his death was one of the oldest colored preachers in the county.

June 7, 1851, Henry J. Bentz, aged 52.

Oct. 7, 1841, William D. Bell, aged 49, the founder and proprietor of the Hagerstown *Torchlight.*

May 11, 1791, Maj. Wm. Baird, of Hagerstown, at an advanced age. He was an officer at Braddock's defeat, magistrate for many years, and coroner for Washington County from the time it was separated from Frederick.

Feb. 28, 1873, George Beard, a descendant of one of the earliest settlers of Hagerstown Valley.

At New Orleans, Nov. 21, 1817, Maj. Charles Boerstler, late of the U. S. army, and son of Dr. Christian Boerstler, of Funkstown.

March 14, 1828, in Blair's Valley, James Blair, in his 93d year. Mr. Blair was one of the earliest settlers of this portion of Washington County, and was engaged in many skirmishes with the Indians.

In Frederick Town, May 8, 1819, Richard Brooke, formerly of Hagerstown, in his 44th year. Mr. Brooke was a distinguished member of the Maryland bar, and a consistent member of the Catholic Church. At a meeting of the bar of Frederick, Hon. Abraham Shriver presiding, and Frederick A. Schley acting as secretary, it was resolved that those present wear crape on the arm for one month as a mark of respect for the deceased.

Feb. 12, 1870, J. F. Broderick, merchant, of Hancock.

February, 1872, Robert J. Brent, the distinguished lawyer, suddenly, at Baltimore.

September, 1794, Robert Elliott, surveyor, killed by Indians in the West. He was the father of Com. Elliott, U.S.N.

June 12, 1851, at the residence of his son-in-law, John R. Sneary, in Hagerstown, William Eakle, in his 65th year. Mr. Eakle had long been a useful and highly-respected citizen of Funkstown.

In October, 1878, at Williamsport, Charles Embrey, in his 71st year, formerly judge of the Orphans' Court of Washington County.

May 7, 1878, Martin Eakle, aged 63. Mr. Eakle in 1857 was elected county commissioner, and served as the president of the board for two years, and in 1859 was elected to the House of Delegates, of which body he was a useful member. He also was extensively known as a business man. Up to the time of his death he conducted the flouring-mill at Eakle's Mill, and was the agent of the Baltimore and Ohio Railroad at that place, and the senior member of the mercantile firm of Eakle & Son, and at one time was the active member of a firm which conducted the Antietam Iron-Works.

February, 1854, at Frederick, Md., at an advanced age, George M. Eichelberger. Maj. Eichelberger served in the war of 1812, and contributed much to the result by his patriotic and courageous example.

April 27, 1822, John Eichelberger, in the 69th year of his age.

At Hagerstown, on the 31st of August, 1825, aged 65, Mrs. Ann Hughes, widow of Robert Elliott, and mother of Com. Elliott, of the U. S. navy.

April 11, 1856, Daniel Creager, a soldier of 1812, aged 65 years, 6 months, and 2 days.

At his residence in Libertytown on the 14th of November, 1825, Maj.-Gen. Robert Cumming, commander of the Second Division of Maryland Militia, in the 72d year of his age.

At Hagerstown, on the 25th of March, 1810, after a lingering illness, William Clagett, an associate judge of the Fifth Judicial District of Maryland.

May 12, 1802, James Coombs, son of Coleman Coombs.

July 21, 1801, Jeremiah Callahan, an overseer for Charles Carroll, fell from a stairway outside a still-house, and was almost instantly killed.

March, 1859, in Funkstown, David Claggett, aged 79. He had been engaged in farming and milling for more than half a century.

Near Clear Spring, Sept. 9, 1857, George Cushwa, at one time a member of the House of Delegates. He was in his 54th year.

At Sharpsburg, Dec. 25, 1827, John Clarke, aged 61.

March 6, 1819, at his residence in Washington County, Col. John Carr, an officer of the Revolution.

At his residence in Pleasant Valley, May 20, 1819, Thomas Crampton, in his 84th year.

Dec. 6, 1875, Mrs. Mary Claggett, widow of Dr. Horatio Claggett. Dr. Claggett, who died in 1850, was among the most eminent men in the State.

May, 1881, Dr. Charles Macgill, at the residence of his son-in-law, Dr. S. D. Drewry, of Chesterfield County, Va., in the 75th year of his age.

March 29, 1879, at Chicago, Joseph P. Clarkson, formerly professor at St. James' College, and afterwards a member of the Hagerstown bar. Mr. Clarkson, who was a brother of Bishop Clarkson, of Nebraska, was killed by the accidental discharge of a pistol.

Dec. 5, 1878, Daniel Cearfoss, an active citizen, and a member of the Maryland House of Delegates during the civil war.

At Williamsport, in May, 1874, Daniel W. Cyester.

February, 1874, Thomas Curtis, aged about 82 years. Mr. Curtis was a teacher at the Hagerstown Academy for a number of years, and after he gave up teaching he held a number of local offices, embracing those of magistrate, collector of town taxes, registrar of voters, etc., the duties of all of which he discharged with care and fidelity.

February, 1870, Capt. Wm. Colklesser, in his 40th year. He resided in Hagerstown when the war commenced, and when Company A of the Seventh Maryland Regiment (Mobley's) was formed Capt. Colklesser was elected first lieutenant, and subsequently, when Capt. Mobley was promoted, he took charge of the company, and remained in the service to the close of the war.

March, 1794, Denton Jacques, of this county; and Robert Clarke, of Allegany, formerly of Hagerstown.

April 14, 1855, Wm. B. Clarke, aged 38. Mr. Clarke represented Washington, and afterwards Baltimore County, in the State Senate, and was a highly esteemed and distinguished citizen of Washington County.

January, 1827, Joseph Cresap, at an advanced age, at the residence of his daughter, Mrs. James Scott, in Cumberland.

At Williamsport, in December, 1824, William S. Compton, in his 67th year.

January, 1825, Dr. Zachariah Clagett, of Pleasant Valley, in his 65th year.

June 12, 1824, David Cooke, founder of Marietta, Pa., aged 74.

Jan. 12, 1803, in Baltimore, Frances, wife of Hezekiah Claggett.

Dec. 25, 1803, Richard Cromwell, a member of the House of Delegates.

Dec. 28, 1803, George Crumbaugh, in his 67th year.

At Vincennes, Ind., Dec. 11, 1802, William Clarke, first judge of the Territory of Indiana, and formerly a member of the Hagerstown bar. In 1795, Mr. Clarke was appointed United States attorney for the District of Kentucky, which position he retained until the organization of the Territory of Indiana.

At the residence of her son-in-law, Thomas Martin, on Beaver Creek, June 5, 1855, Mrs. Margaret Carnes, aged 90. She was a sister of George Doyle, who died aged 82, and her father was one of the original settlers of Hagerstown Valley.

Dec. 7, 1840, near Clear Spring, Mark Coyle, aged 86. Deceased was a soldier in the Revolutionary war, and participated in the battles of Monmouth and Princeton and in other important engagements.

June 11, 1821, Alexander Clagett, aged 77. Mr. Clagett was a zealous and earnest patriot during the Revolution, and for three years was sheriff of Washington County. He removed from Hagerstown to Baltimore in 1818.

September, 1808, John Clagett.

March 25, 1810, William Clagett, associate judge of Washington County.

May, 1819, at his residence in Pleasant Valley, Thomas Crampton, aged 84.

Feb. 23, 1822, Mrs. Catharine Carla, aged 109. She was a native of Germany, and had been a resident of Hagerstown since 1761.

At Williamsburg, Livingston Co., N. Y., Oct. 28, 1823, Maj. Charles Carroll, who prior to 1815 resided near Hagerstown.

Aug. 31, 1821, Capt. Joseph Chaplin, in the 75th year of his age. Capt. Chaplin was a soldier of the Revolution.

March 17, 1809, Rezin Davis, aged 53. Col. Davis served in the Revolutionary war, and also filled the offices of sheriff and coroner for a number of years.

Oct. 9, 1824, Rev. Patrick Davidson, minister of the Presbyterian Church at Hagerstown.

Nov. 1, 1813, Dr. Wm. Downey, in his 33d year. He was highly respected, and had filled a number of important trusts.

December, 1806, John Dagy and wife, living at the foot of South Mountain, were murdered.

Feb. 7, 1856, Rev. Robert W. Dunlap, in his 41st year, pastor of the Presbyterian Church of Hagerstown.

May 30, 1829, Dr. James Dixon, aged 32.

Oct. 26, 1858, Dr. Frederick Dorsey, Sr., in his 83d year. Dr. Dorsey was one of the oldest practitioners in the country, and was widely known and highly respected for his professional skill and attainments.

Aug. 10, 1823, William Dillehunt, in his 58th year.

At Hancock, Dec. 24, 1879, James B. Ditto, Sr., one of the oldest and most respectable citizens of the place.

Near Fort Smith, Ark., July 12, 1851, Col. William Duvall, aged 67.

Aug. 2, 1872, near Keedysville, Samuel Doub, a leading farmer. He was a man of considerable means, and had served as county commissioner.

February, 1801, Joseph Downey, innkeeper at Hagerstown.

July 26, 1801, Capt. Richard Davis, aged 53.

At his residence in the Williamsport District, early in March, 1859, Jacob Dellinger, at an advanced age.

Sept. 25, 1858, Col. Daniel Donnelly, for many years commander of the Fifty-fourth Regiment Maryland Militia. He was buried at Williamsport with military honors.

Near the College of St. James, Jan. 28, 1859, Daniel Reichard, Sr., aged 78. Mr. Reichard had been a bishop of the Tunker denomination for a number of years.

Jan. 10, 1858, at New Market, Frederick Co., Rhoderick Dorsey, brother of Dr. Frederick Dorsey, aged 73.

Feb. 6, 1818, at Mount St. Mary's College, Rev. Charles Duhamel, formerly of Hagerstown.

Dec. 27, 1875, Dr. Thomas Buchanan Duckett, aged 75. Dr. Duckett was nephew of the Judges Buchanan, and was married to a daughter of Joseph Gabby, in the olden time a leading man, and once a member of the Executive Council of the State before the formation of the first popular constitution. The deceased had two sons, one of whom, Joseph Gabby Duckett, was shot in the early days of the war while crossing the Potomac River to join the Southern cause.

Aug. 25, 1799, Maj. David Funk.

Feb. 16, 1791, Helena, wife of Michael Fackler.

May 21, 1829, at Hagerstown, Wm. Fitzhugh, Jr., in his 43d year. He was an elector on the Jackson Presidential ticket.

April 12, 1870, William Freaner, aged 79. Mr. Freaner served in the war of 1812, and was one of the most valuable citizens of Hagerstown.

Nov. 10, 1878, Maj. George Freaner, aged 47.

March —, 1875, Ann Carroll Fitzhugh, daughter of Wm. Fitzhugh, of Hagerstown. She was born on the 11th of January, 1805, and was consequently in her 71st year at the time of her death. In 1822 she was married to Gerrit Smith, of New York, the famous abolitionist. One of her sisters was the wife of James G. Birney, the Liberty party candidate for President in 1840 and 1844.

In the spring of 1881, Dr. Daniel H. Fitzhugh, of Rochester, N. Y., aged 87. Dr. Fitzhugh was the son of Col. Wm. Fitzhugh, who emigrated to New York in the early part of the century, and assisted in founding the city of Rochester.

Dec. 19, 1813, Henry Fiery, aged 48, at his residence, nine miles from Hagerstown.

March 24, 1813, at Big Springs, Dr. Emanuel Francis, aged 64.

In September, 1823, at Washington, D. C., Rev. Louis R. Fechtig, son of Christian, a native of Hagerstown, aged 36. At the time of his death he was presiding elder of the Baltimore District, Methodist Episcopal Church.

On Christmas-day, 1869, John Fiery, aged 64, a wealthy and highly-respected citizen of Washington County. Mr. Fiery was drowned accidentally in the Conococheague Creek.

June, 1872, Mrs. Fox, widow of George B. Fox, aged 102 years and 6 months. She was born in Frederick County, where she was married, and shortly afterwards removed to Hagerstown, where she resided up to the time of her death, through a period of probably seventy-five or eighty years. She had fourteen children, fifty-six grandchildren, and sixty-seven great-grandchildren. When she first lived in the village it had just begun to assume its new name of Hagerstown, it having been known as Elizabethtown up to that time, and nearly the whole of that portion of it now covered by the block bounded by Washington, Potomac, Franklin, and Jonathan Streets was a marsh filled with stagnant water and weeds, the centre of which was the present Oak Spring, and the stream flowing therefrom, that now passes under the Wingert buildings on Potomac Street, then flowed through what is now the Public Square.

Jan. 10, 1870, Abram Freaner, youngest brother of William Freaner, of Hagerstown. Mr. Freaner was born in Hagerstown, and at an early age located in Pennsylvania. After passing a number of years at Lebanon, Annville, Hummelstown, and Spring Creek, he removed to Harrisburg, where he resided for many years. In 1848, Mr. Freaner was elected recorder of deeds and clerk of the Orphans' Court of Dauphin County, Pa., which position he filled with so much credit that he was honored with a re-election, serving six years in all. At the time of his demise he was tax collector of the First and Second Wards of Harrisburg, and had reached nearly seventy years of age.

September, 1878, Jeremiah Funk, aged 37, son of Jacob Funk, and brother of Henry Funk, late president board of commissioners of Washington County.

August, 1878, George French, ex-judge Circuit Court.

April 28, 1881, Sophia Van Lear Findlay. Mrs. Findlay was the daughter of Matthew Van Lear, one of the leading men of Western Maryland in days of yore, of most pronounced character, and a decided Federalist of the old school. He contested the western district of the State for Congress with Gen. Samuel Ringgold, as decided a Democrat, by whom he was defeated, and who generally sold a farm in the "Manor" which still bears his name to sustain his bountiful expenditures in

Congress each term. The father of the deceased had a large family, the oldest of the sons being John Van Lear, for many years at the head of the Washington County Bank, and a man of as marked character as any in Western Maryland in his day. Matthew and Joseph were also brothers, and conspicuous among the sisters of Mrs. Findlay were Mrs. Ramsay, whose daughters were pre-eminently beautiful, and Mrs. Irwin, connected with the family of Gen. Harrison, over whose household, while President of the United States, members of this family presided. The husband of the deceased was Mr. Archibald Findlay, of the Chambersburg bar, son of William Findlay, Governor of Pennsylvania, and during one term United States senator from that State, whilst at the same time two of his brothers—Col. John, of Pennsylvania, and Gen. James, of Ohio—were members of the House of Representatives. At this period of her life Mrs. Sophia Van Lear Findlay spent much of her time at the national capital, and was an active participant in the social enjoyments of those times, when Henry Clay, whose personal relations with the Findlays were the most intimate, was particularly conspicuous in the Senate and in society. Mrs. Findlay was a woman of remarkable decision of character, conspicuously so in advocacy of what she believed right and in adhesion to principle. In the late struggle between the North and the South she entered with her whole soul into the cause of the former. She was a sturdy Unionist, and supported the government during the war neither as a Republican or a Democrat, but as a patriot, concerned not so much about this or that principle of constitutional construction as the maintenance of the Union in all its territorial integrity. Guided and governed by this sentiment, she was active in promoting the Union cause in every way she could, and there were few Union officers stationed at Williamsport and vicinity who were not at one time or another partakers of her generous hospitality.

Jan. 15, 1845, Peter Feigley, aged 97, a soldier of the Revolution. Mr. Feigley participated in a number of important battles, and was present at the surrender of Lord Cornwallis at Yorktown. The remains were buried with military honors, being escorted to the grave by the Hagerstown Cadets, commanded by Capt. Schley, and the Union Riflemen, Lieut. Helfelfinger, accompanied by the Hagerstown Mechanics' Band.

At Beaver Creek, Aug. 16, 1840, Samuel Funk, aged 65.

August, 1854, Jacob Fechtig, in his 52d year.

In Hagerstown, on Aug. 18, 1831, in the 79th year of his age, Benjamin Galloway, a native of Anne Arundel County, and for more than thirty-five years a resident of Washington County. He was appointed soon after the adoption of the constitution of Maryland the first attorney-general of the State.

Aug. 6, 1820, at the residence of Andrew Ramsey, Washington, D. C., Hon. John Graham, formerly minister to Brazil.

April, 1799, William Gordon, a highly-respected citizen of Hagerstown, at an advanced age.

Near Leitersburg, on the 4th of September, 1841, William Gabby, aged 78. Mr. Gabby had frequently been a member of the State Legislature, and was a judge of the Orphans' Court. For more than half a century he had been a communicant of the Presbyterian Church, and for forty years an elder of that denomination.

Dec. 29, 1857, John Gruber, founder of the well-known Hagerstown Almanac, aged 91 years.

About Dec. 1, 1877, Sophie Goens, a colored woman, said to be 103 years old, who claimed to have been born in the family of Mrs. Arthur Nelson, mother of Gen. Roger Nelson, of Revolutionary fame. She also asserted that she was present at the funeral of Gen. Washington at Mount Vernon. She was sold as a slave to Gen. Samuel Ringgold, of Fountain Rock, and when the estate became involved she went to Canada, whence she returned on the emancipation of the slaves. Subsequently she lived in Hagerstown, being cared for by the descendants of the Nelson family and others.

At Atchison, Kan., Feb. 17, 1877, Dr. William H. Grimes, formerly of Hagerstown, aged 74.

January, 1874, Jacob H. Grove, of Sharpsburg District, aged 75. Mr. Grove was a county commissioner about 1834, and served in the Maryland Legislature with the Hon. John Thomson Mason and William T. Hamilton.

July 7, 1881, George W. Grove, ex-sheriff of Washington County, aged 72. For many years he had been one of the directors of the County Agricultural and Mechanical Society, and always took an active part in its development. He was also connected with other institutions, and was one of the first selected as a director of the Washington County Water Company.

Nov. 15, 1824, Mrs. Christian Gruber, in her 87th year.

Oct 10, 1812, Henry Gaither, a prominent citizen.

November, 1823, Henry Goweding, inn-keeper at Hancock.

November, 1856, Joseph Gabby, at his residence near Leitersburg, aged about 78 years. Mr. Gabby for many years in succession represented Washington County in the Legislature of Maryland; was a member of the Governor's Council, and a very prominent and useful citizen.

April 22, 1856, in Hagerstown, Henry H. Gaither, in the 62d year of his age. Mr. Gaither was a prominent citizen, and for many years an active and successful member of the bar.

December 31st, at Hagerstown, John M. Hauck, aged 52. In 1859, Mr. Hauck was elected sheriff of Washington County, and served his full term. In May, 1870, he was appointed weigher of hay at Baltimore, and occupied that position at the time of his death.

At Mount Alto, Franklin Co., Pa., in the latter part of March, 1877, Col. Napoleon B. Hughes, son of Samuel Hughes and brother of Col. Holker Hughes, aged 74.

Friday, July (next to 25th), 1873, Mrs. Hager, relict of the late Jonathan Hager, at the residence of S. D. Straub, her son-in-law, on South Potomac Street, Hagerstown, in the 78th year of her age. Mrs. Hager was a daughter of Jonas Hogmire, Esq., one of the first surveyors of the county, and a very prominent, wealthy, and influential citizen in its early days, and was his last surviving child.

April (Friday preceding) 11, 1873, Isabella Hughes, daughter of Robert Hughes, one of three brothers (Robert, Samuel, and Daniel) who took up vast tracts of land, one of which covered almost the entire western face of the South Mountain, from a point near the Black Rock to a point far within the limits of Pennsylvania, above Mount Alto. Three other brothers located farther west, in Kentucky and elsewhere. Isabella, daughter of Robert, was born at the old homestead at the foot of the mountain, a mile east of Smithsburg, known as Oswald's tannery. The Hughes tract of land, which originally covered not only the mountain-side, but extended as far down into the valley at least as the Antietam, was a princely estate, and upon it were located by the members of that family the old furnace of Mount Ætna (now in ruins), Mount Alto (still in full blast), "The Forge," near the Antietam, and the tannery, which was sold a short time since to David Winter. The iron establishments were run by the two brothers Samuel and Daniel, Samuel having been at the same time a leading member of the Hagerstown bar, whilst the tannery and farm attached were conducted by the elder brother, Robert.

March 22, 1843, David Harry, aged 93, an ex-soldier of the Revolutionary war.

At the residence of his son, Jacob Huyett, near Cavetown, about May 1, 1828, Ludwig Huyett, aged 90.

Jan. 13, 1873, Overton C. Harne, aged 92 years, 3 months, and 28 days; said to be at that time the oldest printer in Maryland.

March 20, 1868, Col. Jacob Hollingsworth, aged 78, from a pistol-wound supposed to have been accidentally inflicted by himself.

Oct. 5, 1876, Frederick Humrichouse, aged 85 years, 2 months, and 25 days.

Jan. 15, 1875, William Heyser, aged 84 years and 4 months.

July, 1871, Capt. George F. Heyser, in his 56th year. Death resulted from an accidental fall on the railroad track.

April 24, 1880, Hannah Humrichouse, daughter of Jacob Harry and wife of Frederick Humrichouse. Mrs. Humrichouse was 83 years old.

April 25, 1880, Rebecca, widow of Stewart Herbert, and daughter of George Doyle, members of two of the original families of the county, aged 80.

In March, 1870, at Terre Haute, Ind., George Hager, in his 83d year. Mr. Hager was a brother of Jonathan Hager, Jr., and one of the descendants of the founder of Hagerstown. He was born in that town July 24, 1787, and was most active and energetic in promoting the interests of Terre Haute.

Nov. 6, 1878, Solomon Helser, aged 76. Mr. Helser had served as county commissioner and also as a member of the House of Delegates in the Maryland Legislature. He left two sons, John and Henry Helser.

May, 1870, John Harrington, aged 88, a soldier of the war of 1812.

June, 1879, Jonathan Harbaugh, of Ringgold's, aged 75.

June, 1793, Mrs. Hughes, mother of Col. Daniel Hughes.

Oct. 3, 1795, James Hughes, son of Col. Daniel Hughes, in his 19th year.

Sept. 13, 1826, at Williamsport, John Hogg, aged 70.

March 2, 1826, Daniel Hughes, of Hagerstown.

At his farm near Reading, Pa., Sept. 3, 1826, Gabriel Heister, in his 76th year.

Aug. 6, 1824, Anna, widow of the late Jonathan Hager, in her 68th year.

Sept. 27, 1823, Job Hunt.

November, 1802, Mr. Hanna, aged 106; his wife, who died six months before him, had reached the age of 102 years.

August, 1803, very suddenly, Michael Helfley.

November, 1853, Nathaniel Harmison, run over by cars at Cumberland. He imagined himself a successful politician and candidate for Congress, his head being turned by the fact that many years previously he had really been a candidate.

In Hagerstown, June 30, 1828, Susan Hughes, daughter of Col. Daniel Hughes.

June 4, 1881, W. W. Hoffman, founder of the banking-house of Hoffman, Eavey & Co., Hagerstown, aged 46.

In Washington, D. C., March 14, 1804, Gen. Daniel Heister, representative in Congress from Maryland. He resided in Hagerstown, whither his remains were carried.

In May, 1802, Mrs. Hanna, aged 102. Her husband, with whom she had lived for eighty years, died in the following November at the age of 105 years.

In June, 1854, Capt. John D. Hart, of Hancock.

March 16, 1853, Esther, widow of Christian Hoover, aged 74 years, 4 months, and 23 days.

March 3, 1818, Dr. Arnold Havenkamft.

Aug. 1, 1808, Thomas Helm, inn-keeper of Williamsport.

July 14, 1806, Jacob Harry, aged 50, a merchant of Hagerstown.

Dec. 5, 1818, Col. Daniel Hughes, in his 74th year.

In January, 1819, Jacob Hose, a Revolutionary soldier, aged 79.

Jan. 16, 1819, at Sharpsburg, Dr. John Hartman, in his 75th year.

In July, 1823, near Sharpsburg, Dr. John J. Hays.

Sept. 8, 1821, at Williamsport, in the 32d year of her age, Catharine, wife of John Herr, Jr.

Aug. 20, 1856, at the residence of Mrs. Susan Harry, in Hagerstown, the Rev. William Lane, pastor of the Presbyterian Church at Sykesville, Md. He was born in the town of Roamalton, in the north of Ireland, on the 29th of October, 1818, and was educated and graduated at the college in Belfast, Ireland. He emigrated to this country in 1839, and entered the theological seminary at Princeton, N. J. His first services as a pastor were in the Presbyterian Church of Hagerstown.

March, 1829, Robert Hughes.

April 6, 1846, Susan, wife of Robert Hughes.

—— ——, Henry Courtenay Hughes, son of Robert and Susan Hughes.

April 4, 1873, Elizabeth Isabella Hughes.

Feb. 24, 1880, Letitia Purviance Hughes, wife of Dr. H. H. Harvey.

March 21, 1879, Henrietta Frances Hughes, wife of Dr. Horatio N. Fenn.

Aug. 29, 1825, at her residence in Hagerstown, Mrs. Ann Hughes, widow of Col. Daniel Hughes.

On the 17th of October, 1825, the Rev. Daniel Hitt, in the 58th year of his age, and the 38th of his itinerant ministry in the Methodist Episcopal Church. For many years he filled the station of presiding elder, and for eight years the position of book-agent for the Methodist Church.

On the 3d of May, 1845, at his residence at Mont Alto Furnace, Samuel Hughes, in the 71st year of his age. Mr. Hughes was formerly a resident of Hagerstown, and was long known as one of the most distinguished lawyers of this State.

Jan. 31, 1873, at Memphis, Tenn., Julia P. M. Halm, daughter of Prof. and Mrs. R. Halm, of Hagerstown. Miss Halm was born near Vienna, Austria. Both her parents were accomplished musicians, and their daughter was thoroughly educated as a pianist. At ten years of age she was placed by her father under the instruction of competent teachers in Paris, where she remained five years, in which period she acquired a thorough mastery of the instrument. She gave concerts in New York and Baltimore, which were very successful. Subsequently she returned to Paris, and was admitted as one of five members to the famous Conservatory of Music, being chosen after a competitive examination of one hundred applicants. She was in Paris during the Prussian war, and performed at several concerts there with great success. At the close of the war she returned to Hagerstown and performed with Strakosch, and for Nilsson in Baltimore. Strakosch engaged her to play at his concerts if she were strong enough, but her health, which had been precarious, now grew worse, and she was forced to go South for its benefit. She seemed to improve, but in January, 1873, grew suddenly worse and died. Miss Halm had many friends in Hagerstown, to whom she had endeared herself by an amiability and sweetness of disposition which greatly enhanced the effect of her wonderful proficiency as a musician.

In Hagerstown, April 8, 1853, Stewart Herbert, aged 62. Mr. Herbert was the son of the founder of the Hagerstown *Spy and Herald*, and worked in that office as a compositor.

In December, 1798, Jonathan Hager, "proprietor" of Hagerstown and son of the founder.

April 9, 1799, William Hanshaw, county magistrate.

In Smithsburg, Dec. 24, 1841, Maj. Thomas Hollingsworth, in his 42d year.

June 11, 1791, Mrs. Catharine Hughes, widow of Bernard Hughes, in her 19th year.

Sept. 11, 1822, in Washington, D. C., Leonard Harbaugh, aged 74. Mr. Harbaugh was a large contractor for works of internal improvement, including those on the Potomac and the Shenandoah.

Jan. 16, 1819, at Sharpsburg, Andrew Hines, aged about 50.

Jan. 15, 1818, Rev. Thomas Pitt Irving, aged 48, principal of the Hagerstown Academy. A funeral sermon was preached at the Lutheran church by the Rev. Mr. Hatch, of Frederick, from the 4th and 12th verses of the 102d Psalm,—"My days are like a shadow that declineth," etc.

Near Big Spring, April 15, 1818, Denton Jacques, in the 70th year of his age.

Jan. 21, 1820, John Julius, an old and respected citizen of Hagerstown.

Nov. 10, 1881, Watkins James, in his 71st year. Mr James was thrice married, first to Miss Louisa Baker, daughter of the late Maj. Baker, from whom Bakersville derived its name; second, to Miss Maria Davis, sister of Wm. Davis, now residing in Fairplay; and third to Miss Maria Reynolds, sister of the late Wm. and John Reynolds. The deceased was a man of more than ordinary activity and was engaged in various pursuits. For a number of years he was chief clerk and manager for John McPherson Brien's iron-works, three miles from Sharpsburg. He was also employed at the Catoctin Iron-Works for a time. He moved from Washington County to Woodstock, Va., and resided there some nine years. After the war he was United States internal revenue assessor in that district, after which he returned to Washington County.

At Hancock, in the latter part of July, 1824, Hon. John Johnson, chancellor of Maryland.

Aug. 1, 1845, Arthur Jacques, aged 62.

April 1, 1859, Thomas Keller, aged 73.

At his residence, near Hagerstown, Oct. 6, 1857, Andrew Kershner, aged 70 years, 5 months, and 22 days. On the 8th he was buried in the German Reformed church at Hagerstown, his remains being followed to the grave by a large number of persons. He had represented the county in the Maryland Legislature seven times, and was a man of wide-spread influence and popularity.

Nov. 19, 1817, at his residence, near Hagerstown, Maj. Martin Kershner, aged 74. Maj. Kershner had several times represented the county in the State Legislature, and had also served acceptably as justice of the peace.

At Boonsboro', Aug. 18, 1876, Daniel Keedy, father of H. H. Keedy, of the Hagerstown bar, and Rev. C. L. Keedy, principal of the Hagerstown Female Seminary, aged 76. Deceased was a farmer of considerable means, and resided for a number of years on his estate in Rohrersville District, at the head of Pleasant Valley.

July 26, 1881, Howard Kennedy, eldest son of Dr. Howard Kennedy, aged 35. He was employed on the United States Coast Survey, and afterwards settled in Southern California for his health.

In April, 1873, Jacob Kaylor, at his residence on Beaver Creek, in the 81st year of his age. Mr. Kaylor was a soldier in the war of 1812.

Jan. 20, 1874, Mrs. Catharine Kausler, aged 84, daughter of Capt. George Shawl, and widow of Jacob Kausler. The deceased was the mother of eleven children, forty-eight grandchildren, and twelve great-grandchildren.

April 17, 1807, Catherine, widow of Englehard Kuther, aged 89. She was a native of Germany, and had resided in Hagerstown over forty years.

Feb. —, 1827, William Kreps, postmaster at Hagerstown, in the 51st year of his age.

September, 1878, John Kendall, aged 73. Mr. Kendall was an enthusiastic farmer, although during part of his life he was a member of the firm of Huyett, Kendall & Co., bone-mill, Hagerstown. He was also for fifty years an earnest member of St. John's Lutheran Church.

July, 1881, Rev. John Barrett Kerfoot, D.D., bishop of the Protestant Episcopal diocese of Pittsburgh, and professor in and rector of the College of St. James from 1842 to 1863.

October, 1880, Rev. Levi Keller, from an amputation rendered necessary by a fall. Mr. Keller, who belonged to the Lutheran denomination, entered the ministry in 1849, at Strasburg, Va.

July 26, 1824, Daniel Keedy, farmer and miller, in his 59th year.

Aug. 15, 1823, Joseph Kershner.

September, 1804, Michael Kapp, for many years an inn keeper at Hagerstown.

Feb. 17, 1867, in Boonsboro', David H. Keedy, aged 71 years, 5 months, and 2 days.

June 12, 1855, Dr. Howard Kennedy, in his 47th year. Deceased, who was a son of Hon. Thomas Kennedy, was at one time postmaster at Hagerstown, and afterwards for a number of years special agent of the Post office Department. He was also an extensive stage contractor, a member of the express firm of Adams & Co., and a State director of the Baltimore and Ohio Railroad Company.

June 25, 1847, James Hugh Kennedy, from injuries received at the hands of a mob in Carlisle, Pa., while attempting, in company with G. Howard Hollingsworth, to rescue some slaves that had absconded. Mr. Kennedy was very popular in Hagerstown. He was buried from the residence of his father-in-law, Col. Hollingsworth, and his remains were followed to the grave by the Hagerstown Horse-Guards, the Antietam Fire Company, and an immense concourse of citizens.

Dec 28, 1827, at the mill of John Kennedy, near Hagerstown, Lewis, the "old Antietam fisherman."

In October, 1816, a colored woman known as "Mammy Lucy," and said to be 130 years old. Her son is said to have been a servant of Col. Thomas Cresap.

March 2, 1818, Abraham Leiter, aged 78.

May 21, 1827, Capt. William Lewis, of the Revolutionary army, in the 72d year of his age. Deceased was in the battles of Trenton, Princeton, Brandywine, Germantown, and Monmouth, and engaged in several skirmishes. He also served under Gen. Wayne in the Indian campaigns, and was at the battle of Miami in 1793.

At Boonsboro', May 12, 1820, Abraham Lemaster, aged 78.

September, 1872, Mary, aged 84, widow of John Lushbaugh, a soldier of the war of 1812.

May 16, 1873, William P. Lavely, in his 67th year.

August, 1878, William Logan, postmaster at Hagerstown, aged 58. Mr. Logan devoted his earliest years to business, and was recognized in that capacity, as he was afterwards in others, as a man of remarkable popularity. This led, in 1849, to his appointment as collector of State and county taxes, when he removed from Leitersburg to Hagerstown. In 1853 he was elected sheriff of the county by a large majority, and in 1857 register of wills, at the head of his ticket. He was re-elected to this office in 1863, and held it until 1869, when a change of parties took place under the new constitution, and M. S. Barber was his successful competitor. In 1869 he was appointed postmaster at Hagerstown; was reappointed in 1873, and filling both of those full terms, was reappointed for a third term in 1877, and died in harness.

Sept. 20, 1824, Rev. John Lind, pastor of the Presbyterian congregations at Hagerstown and Greencastle, Pa.

April 30, 1824, Upton Lawrence, aged 45, a distinguished lawyer, and one of the most prominent citizens of the county.

In July, 1823, at Conococheague, John Long.

At Hagerstown, on Thursday, Dec. 31, 1846, Joseph Little, Sr., in the 81st year of his age.

July 21, 1873, Rev. Henry Myers, pastor of St. Vincent's Roman Catholic Church, aged 67.

May, 1871, Maj. Edward M. Mealey, aged 60. Mr. Mealey was for many years a prominent citizen of Hagerstown, taking an active part in local, State, and national affairs, and always maintaining intimate connections with the leading men of other portions of the State, by whom he was much respected for his sound judgment and sterling integrity. He was for two sessions a member of the Legislature, for several years president of the Washington County Railroad, and also a director of the Baltimore and Ohio Railroad Company.

February, 1874, John Mentzer, of Ringgold District, aged 79.

Nov. 6, 1797, Maj. Alexander Monroe, at an advanced age; a native of North Britain, and formerly an officer in the English service.

Near Smithsburg, November 22d, James McKissick, in his 65th year.

In 1803, William McIntosh, leaving a widow and five children.

Oct. 26, 1843, Thomas McCardell, aged 67.

Oct. 25, 1853, Susan, widow of John Gettillng, aged 77.

In November, 1853, at the residence of his son-in-law, Joshua P. Crist, Dr. Frederick Miller, in his 82d year. Dr. Miller, who settled in Hagerstown in 1797, established the first drug-store in that place.

March 13, 1848, at Camp Mier, Lieut. Edward McPherson, of Washington County. Lieut. McPherson was an officer in Capt. Merrick's company of dragoons, U.S.A., and fought a duel with Lieut. Maddox, of St. Mary's County. Two rounds were fired with dueling pistols, after which McPherson called for his horse-pistols. At the first fire he fell mortally wounded, the ball passing through the hip and loins. He died in about an hour. Upon falling he called for Lieut. Maddox, took him by the hand and said that he (Maddox) was a brave man.

In January, 1852, Daniel Middlekauff, a leading farmer of Washington County.

June 19, 1854, Joseph I. Merrick, an old citizen of Washington County, aged about 65. Mr. Merrick, who was a prominent lawyer, resided in Washington, D. C., for some years before his death.

In June, 1854, Thomas Mills, a substantial farmer of Clear Spring District, and a veteran of the war of 1812. Mr. Mills was chosen several times a member of the Maryland House of Delegates, and also held other offices of trust and honor.

April, 1817, Capt. Charles McCully, aged 64.

Aug. 28, 1822, Rev. Colin Macfarquhar, a native of the Highlands, Scotland, in his 91st year, at the residence of his son-in-law, David Cook, Hagerstown. He came to America in 1774, and before coming to Hagerstown lived over thirty years in Lancaster County, Pa.

Oct. 20, 1822, Jacob Myers, in the 64th year of his age.

March 5, 1804, Walter Machall, at his seat in Washington County. His remains were taken to Calvert County to be buried in the family burial-ground there.

June 3, 1836, at Washington, D. C., in the 35th year of his age, Horatio McPherson, cashier of the Washington County Bank.

Feb. 3, 1802, Rev. Thomas McPherrin.

Nov. 6, 1841, James Maxwell, aged 44. Mr. Maxwell was the original editor and proprietor of the Hagerstown *Mail*.

At Clear Spring, Sept. 28, 1849, Rev. Jeremiah Mason, in the 64th year of his age.

At Elkton, Maryland, March 28, 1873, Hon. John Thomson Mason, a native of Washington County and a prominent jurist of Maryland.

At the residence of Col. Daniel Malott, Nov. 16, 1827, Thomas McQuinney, aged 89, a soldier in the Revolutionary war. He was a native of Ireland, and enlisted at Elkton, Md., in the 5th Maryland Regiment, serving under Maj. Lansdale. Capt. Muse and Capt. Lynn, of Allegany, Monday before.

Dec. 7, 1877, Isaac Motter, of Williamsport, aged 72. Mr. Motter was one of the best-known farmers of that section, and was always prominent in movements for the development of the natural wealth of the county. He was a director in the Western Maryland Railroad, the Washington County Bank, and the two turnpike companies leading from Hagerstown to Williamsport and to Greencastle, Pa. In 1844 he was a delegate to the State Legislature.

Aug. 20, 1877, Joseph Middlekauff.

September, 1872, Mrs. Martin, widow of Nathaniel Martin, aged 97.

In May, 1872, Joseph P. Mong, aged 62. Mr. Mong was widely known both in business and in local politics. His remains were interred in the Dunkard burial-ground at Beaver Creek, Rev. Leonard Emmert delivering the funeral discourse.

June 24, 1843, Sarah, wife of Alexander Neill, president of the Hagerstown Bank, in the 62d year of her age.

July 20, 1807, Nathaniel Nesbitt, aged 82.

Jan. 4, 1826, at his residence on Beaver Creek, Rev. Peter Newcomer, aged about 73.

Jan. 22, 1826, Mrs. Isabella Neill, mother of Alexander Neill, in her 69th year.

In Hagerstown, June 17, 1856, Isabella Neill, aged about 75 years.

At his residence, near Clear Spring, on the 3d of April, 1856, Jonathan Nesbitt, Sr., aged 86.

On the 19th of June, 1856, at his residence, near Kenton, Hardin Co., Ohio, Jacob Nesbitt, aged 84 years and 50 days. The deceased was born in Washington County, Md., and in 1813 moved to the State of Ohio, and settled on Beaver Creek in 1814.

March 12, 1830, Rev. Christian Newcomer, bishop of the German Methodist Society, in his 82d year.

Aug. 2, 1858, Alexander Neill, Sr., aged 82.

Aug. 28, 1877, Jonathan Nesbitt, in the 73d year of his age. He was a farmer by profession, but took an active part as a writer and a politician in national and State affairs. He was at one time a member of the Maryland Legislature. He left two sons, C. J. Nesbitt and Jonathan Nesbitt, who emigrated to the West.

Aug. 29, 1879, at his home near Boonsboro', John Nicodemus, in his 79th year. Mr. Nicodemus was a leading farmer and miller, and amassed a handsome competence, which he did not hesitate to employ freely in acts of benevolence.

April 2, 1881, Michael Newcomer, aged 81, at his residence on Beaver Creek. He was born within half a mile of where he died, and passed his whole life in that district. His family was, and is perhaps, the largest connection, by blood and intermarriage, in Washington County, and has always been prominent in political and industrial affairs, the deceased taking a leading part at all times. He was a Democrat, and in 1836 was elected to the Legislature, serving one term. In 1839 he was re-elected to the House of Delegates. He was elected to the Constitutional Convention of 1851, and served in that body. During the war he was elected to the board of county commissioners, in which capacity he served a term. At all times he took an active part in local politics. He was a farmer and miller during the greater part of his life, his father being a miller. John Newcomer, former sheriff of the county, who was his colleague in the Legislature on the opposite side of politics, was an elder brother.

August, 1880, Mary Sim Neill, widow of Alexander Neill, and daughter of Hon. John Nelson.

August, 1878, Lewis B. Wyman, ex-clerk Circuit Court and corresponding clerk Baltimore custom-house.

June 8, 1803, Abraham Neff, an old and respected citizen of Hagerstown.

Aug. 10, 1827, Col. Adam Ott, a Revolutionary soldier, in his 74th year. He was commissioned an officer of the Pennsylvania Line in January, 1776, and served with credit in the war. Afterwards he became sheriff of Washington County, in addition to which he occupied other civil positions of honor and trust.

Oct. 3, 1824, Capt. Christian Orndorff, in his 67th year. Capt. Orndorff served in the Revolutionary army, and was present at the surrender of Fort Washington.

Sept. 14, 1823, in Logan Co., Ky., Christopher Orndorff, formerly of Hagerstown, in his 72d year.

In February, 1812, near Hughes' furnace, John Oswald.

Aug. 17, 1827, near Cadiz, Ohio, Neale Peacock, formerly of Washington County, and for many years a soldier in the Revolutionary Maryland Line.

In Hagerstown, on the 7th of May, 1877, Charles Poffenberger, in his 32d year. Mr. Poffenberger was a Federal soldier during the war, and was buried with honors by Reno Post, No. 4, of the Grand Army of the Republic.

Feb. 13, 1879, Dr. William S. Pittinger, of Fairview, Conococheague District, in his 60th year.

Aug. 4, 1794, Mrs. Eliza Pindell, wife of Dr. Richard Pindell, and daughter of Col. Thomas Hart, of Hagerstown.

Aug. 28, 1804, near Hancock, Rev. Joseph Powell.

Dec. 18, 1825, Col. Josiah Price, at an advanced age.

In Baltimore, Nov. 25, 1868, William Price, aged 75, a native of Washington County, and a prominent member of the Maryland bar.

November, 1840, Benjamin Price, a distinguished lawyer.

At Annapolis, Nov. 8, 1803, Allen Quynn, in his 77th year, long a resident of that city, and for twenty-five years a member of the House of Delegates.

July 25, 1826, at Tammany Mount, the residence of Mrs. Van Lear, Matthew Van Lear Ramsay, aged 21, son of Col. John Ramsay, of Pittsburgh.

About Aug. 31, 1798, Benjamin Ringgold.

At St. Joseph, Mo., on the 1st of February, 1860, David Reichard, aged 52. Mr. Reichard was a member of the Maryland Legislature from Washington County in 1856.

May 4, 1816, at his residence in Hagerstown, in his 86th year, Col. John Ragan. He was appointed a captain in the United States army in 1808, and served in that capacity at New Orleans and Camp Terre au Bœuf about eighteen months. In 1810 he returned to his native place, and upon his marriage resigned his commission. He was afterwards appointed by the Governor of Maryland lieutenant-colonel of the Twenty-fourth Maryland Militia.

Aug. 8, 1811, Maria, wife of Gen. Samuel Ringgold, and daughter of Gen. Cadwalader, of Philadelphia.

April 3, 1807, Capt. John Ritchie, for many years manager of the Antietam Iron-Works.

September, 1823, at his residence, five miles from Hagerstown, John Rice, an old inhabitant of the county.

Jan. 28, 1826, at Newcomer's Hotel, Hagerstown, John Rohrer, Sr., of Pleasant Valley, aged 65.

At Fountain Rock, July 28, 1822, in the 16th year of his age, Edward Lloyd Ringgold, son of Gen. Samuel Ringgold.

On the 9th of April, 1822, in Hagerstown, Jacob Rohrer, in the 76th year of his age.

At Frederick Town, on the 31st of January, 1823, Rev. James Redmond, aged 47 years, pastor of the Catholic congregations of Washington and Allegany Counties.

At Hagers Town, Tuesday, Aug. 26, 1856, John D. Ridenour, aged 53 years. Mr. Ridenour was a merchant and a deputy in the sheriff's office, and subsequently clerk in the Hagerstown Bank.

At Centreville, Md., Feb. 6, 1804, Rev. Elisha Rigg, formerly rector of the Episcopal Church, Lancaster, Pa., and well and favorably known in Western Maryland.

Sept. 29, 1804, David Ridenour, in the 55th year of his age.

Oct. 13, 1804, Jacob Rohrer, in the 63d year of his age.

July 27, 1853, Maj. Jacob Rohrback, a soldier of 1812.

Dec. 23, 1840, Dr. John Reynolds, in his 59th year.

Oct. 18, 1829, at the residence of his son-in-law, William Schley, in Frederick Town, Gen. Samuel Ringgold, in the 60th year of his age.

October, 1804, Jacob Rohrer, an old resident, near Hagerstown.

At Greensburg, Pa., Sept. 21, 1823, Frederick Rohrer, aged 81.

Oct. 7, 1823, at his residence, near Mount Ætna Furnace, William Reynolds, son of a wealthy farmer of Washington County, who was one of the first persons to purchase lands in Kentucky. The elder Reynolds was killed by the Indians while descending the Ohio. His family were captured and carried to Canada, but subsequently were permitted to return to Washington County, where his son, William M., settled and acquired considerable property, which he lost shortly before his death through his own generosity.

Sept. 23, 1817, Rev. Jonathan Rehauser, pastor of the German Reformed Church in Hagerstown, in his 53d year.

In February, 1828, while visiting friends in Frederick, Maria, eldest daughter of Gen. Samuel Ringgold.

Near Cavetown, Sept. 21, 1827, Jacob Ridenour, a soldier of the Revolution.

In June, 1875, aged 21, J. Dixon Roman, son of the Hon. J. Dixon Roman, and grandson of John Kennedy. The deceased had attained his majority only a few days before, and was about to graduate from Harvard University. His remains were interred in the old Presbyterian churchyard, and were followed to the grave by a large concourse of citizens, among whom he was extremely popular.

March, 1881, at Smithsburg, Dr. Riddlemoser.

At Cumberland, in April, 1878, John Rabold, a veteran bricklayer and builder, formerly of Hagerstown. He had the reputation of being the best workman in his section of country, and was the builder of most of the brick houses on Prospect Hill, Hagerstown, from 1832 to 1836, which stand as monuments of admirable workmanship. He it was who built Dr. Reynolds' house, now owned by the Misses Lawrence, that of Gen. Williams, now owned by Dr. Fahrney, and that of Maj. Yost, now the property of the Hon. W. T. Hamilton.

In September, 1879, Joseph Rench, at one time a judge of the Orphans' Court, and the senior of the Presbyterian Church at Hagerstown, aged 72. There was an immense attendance at the funeral, and an appropriate discourse was delivered by the Rev. Mr. Rondthaler.

March 16, 1875, Magdalena Rohrer, mother of Solomon Rohrer, in the 84th year of her age. She was the only surviving child of Martin Rohrer, who moved into Washington County, then a portion of Frederick County, about 1740, and who located near Hagerstown, on what is now known as the Brian farm, lying on the Antietam Creek, and near the Cavetown turnpike. Martin Rohrer had seven daughters, all of whom married and gave rise to a large connection, extending among the Hammonds, the Renches, and the Newcomers. Mrs.

Rohrer was a member of the Reformed Church, and was known in the neighborhood in which she lived as a most kind and charitable woman.

February, 1874, Martin Rickenbaugh, aged 81.

Feb. 1, 1870, Rev. John Rebaugh, in his 69th year. In 1831 he became pastor of the Boonsboro' charge, Washington County, Md., which then consisted of four congregations, namely, Boonsboro', Sharpsburg, Cross-Roads, and Pleasant Valley. In this field he labored until 1837, when he removed to Greencastle, Franklin Co., Pa., and took charge of the Reformed Church in that place, and of several other congregations in the vicinity. In 1851 he resigned the pastorate of the Greencastle congregation, which was then constituted a separate charge. He continued to serve the congregation at Middleburg, five miles south from Greencastle, in connection with other congregations, until he became disqualified through disease for the further prosecution of the work of the ministry in 1863. During the greater part of this latter period he preached regularly to the congregations at Clear Spring and St. Paul's Church, Washington County, Md.

November, 1794, John Rench and Martin Ridenour.

At Fredericktown, Sept. 22, 1824, Robert Ritchie, editor of the *Political Intelligencer and Republican Gazette.*

May 8, 1846, in the battle of Palo Alto, Mexico, Maj. Samuel Ringgold, of Washington County.

May 8, 1853, Dr. Andrew P. Ringer, in his 45th year. Deceased was a native of Hagerstown, but emigrated to Iowa, in which State he died. For some years he was a minister of the Christian or Campbellite Church, but later in life was actively engaged in the practice of medicine.

July 21, 1801, Christiana Rohrer, aged 53, wife of Jacob Rohrer.

March 22, 1842, David Rohrer, aged 63, an influential and worthy citizen.

In Baltimore City, on the 16th of June, 1850, Rev. James Reid, a former resident of Hagerstown. Mr. Reid was a minister of the Methodist Episcopal Church, and was in his 71st year at the time of his death.

Nov. 24, 1857, in the Clear Spring District, Martin Reckert, aged 106 years, 11 months. He was a native of Germany, and came to this country in company with the Rev. George Schmucker, father of the Rev. S. S. Schmucker, D.D. He settled in Lancaster County, Pa., but removed to Washington County towards the close of the last century. He voted for George Washington and for every succeeding President down to and including the election preceding his death.

At his residence, Green Spring Furnace, on the 2d of January, 1863, B. Franklin Roman, brother of the Hon. J. Dixon Roman. Mr. Roman was a partner in the firm and manager of the furnace.

Oct. 18, 1791, Susan, wife of Col. Moses Rawlings, of Washington County, in her 46th year. She left no issue.

Jan. 19, 1867, Hon. J. Dixon Roman, a distinguished lawyer and ex-member of Congress.

November, 1878, Louisa, wife of the Hon. James Dixon Roman. Mrs. Roman was the daughter of John Kennedy, one of the early settlers of Western Maryland, and a leading business man in Hagerstown. Her life was clouded by the death of her husband, daughter, and son, the latter just arrived at manhood, and with every promise of a highly honorable and successful career before him. Mrs. Roman resided during the winter months with her son-in-law, Columbus C. Baldwin, in New York.

Near Hagerstown, in the latter part of May, 1853, John Shafer, president of the board of county commissioners, aged 53.

Sept. 6, 1801, Elizabeth Schnebly, wife of Leonard Schnebly.

Nov. 28, 1801, Mrs. Magdalena Steidinger, mother-in-law of Col. A. Ott, aged about 80.

September, 1793, at an advanced age, Elizabeth Schnebly, wife of Dr. Henry Schnebly.

Dec. 7, 1858, John W. Summers, a former member of the State Legislature, drowned by accidentally falling into a canal-lock near Hancock.

At Augusta, Ga., Nov. 20, 1858, William Schley. Mr. Schley was at one time Governor of Georgia, and was a brother of Frederick A. Schley, of Frederick.

March 16, 1843, Nicholas Swingley, aged 94. He had been a citizen of Washington County ever since its formation, and is presumed to have been at that time the oldest person within its boundaries.

Dec. 20, 1807, John Shepherd, Sr., of Hancock District, aged 77 years and 6 months.

1791, Dec. 25, Frederick Steidinger, one of the oldest inhabitants, in the 64th year of his age.

April 9, 1791, Col. John Stull, president of the County Court, and formerly representative of the county in the General Assembly. Rev. George Bower preached his funeral discourse.

July 26, 1818, Col. Charles Swearingen, in his 83d year. Col. Swearingen was one of the most influential and respectable men in the county.

July 15, 1819, John M. Smith, principal of the Hagerstown Academy, aged 25.

Oct. 14, 1818, at his residence, near Sharpsburg, Robert Smith, aged 81 years. Mr. Smith served several terms in the State Legislature, and was a popular and influential citizen.

April 15, 1876, Col. A. K. Stake, aged 57. His father was a captain in the Revolutionary war. Col. Stake, the youngest of a large family, learned the trade of a joiner or carpenter, and before he was 21 went to the Western States and spent several years there. In 1840 he returned to Washington County, and was appointed to a responsible position on the Chesapeake and Ohio Canal. Up to the time of his death he was employed in various capacities on that work. In 1854–56 he was general superintendent of the entire line from Georgetown to Cumberland, and his administration was remarkably efficient and prosperous. He served in the State Legislature during the sessions of 1850, 1860, and 1874.

November, 1809, at the residence of her son, A. K. Stake, in Hagerstown, Mrs. Rosanna Stake, aged 102 years and 3 months. At the time of her death her descendants numbered over one hundred persons.

May 19, 1814, at his residence, in Shenandoah County, Va., Col. Henry Shryock, aged 78. He was a soldier for many years in the wars preceding the Revolution, and also during that period. In politics he was a follower of Washington. After the Revolution he settled at Hagerstown, Md., and filled various offices, being several times high sheriff of Washington County. Though at one time rich, he died poor.

In 1858, Daniel H. Schnebly, an old and respected citizen of Washington County.

April 9, 1791, at Hagerstown, Col. John Stull.

Oct. 24, 1879, John R. Sneary, in his 61st year.

Nov. 17, 1876, Mary Wolgamot, widow of Col. David Schnebly. Mrs. Schnebly was born Feb. 15, 1773, and was therefore 103 years, 9 months, and 2 days old.

In April, 1880, Peter Stouffer, of Funkstown District, in the 80th year of his age.

March 6, 1879, at St. Charles, Mo., where he had settled after removing from Funkstown, Oliver Stonebraker, aged 61.

In September, 1877, near Williamsport, George Shafer, aged 80. At one time Mr. Shafer was engaged in driving various important business operations at the extensive mills of the family in Funkstown, which many years ago were destroyed by fire and were by this circumstance still more generally advertised through a lottery granted by the State to replace them but never drawn. Of late years Mr. Shafer has lived a wholly retired life, and left behind him descendants highly esteemed and respected.

In April, 1877, John W. Stouffer, in his 76th year. Mr. Stouffer was a substantial farmer, an active politician, and a man of general influence and popularity.

In November, 1879, Richard Scheckles, a popular auctioneer of Hagerstown. The deceased had a host of devoted friends, and was exceptionally conspicuous as a leader and founder of beneficial and other associations in Hagerstown. He was one of the original members and highest officer in both the Masonic and Odd-Fellows' lodges, and was particularly conspicuous in the latter order.

At Funkstown, in April, 1873, Thomas South, aged 91, a veteran of the war of 1812.

May, 1874, Conrad Semler, of Hagerstown.

May, 1874, Daniel Shank, Sr., of Leitersburg, aged 81.

May 31, 1869, Jacob Snyder, Sr., in the 93d year of his age.

Sept. 11, 1879, between Des Moines and Grand Junction, Ia., Daniel Strite was shot and killed in some manner unknown. Mr. Strite was born near Leitersburg, and was a brother of Samuel Strite, associate judge of the Orphans' Court. He was 39 years of age, a man of liberal education and fine business qualities, and before removing to Iowa had filled the important posts of teller in the Washington County Bank, book-keeper of the Hagerstown Bank, clerk in the office of register of wills, and collector of internal revenue under President Johnson.

June, 1870, D. Sprigg, cashier Merchants' Bank of Baltimore, aged 81. Previous to 1830, Mr. Sprigg had been for several years the cashier of the Hagerstown Bank. In 1830 he became cashier of the Branch Bank of the United States at Buffalo, N. Y., and subsequently cashier of the Merchants' Bank.

Aug. 2, 1871, Eliza Schnebly, aged 81. She was the daughter of Dr. Jacob Schnebly, and granddaughter of Dr. Henry Schnebly, who in the year 1762 built the house in which she died, which is yet in a perfect state of preservation, and one of the most desirable pieces of property in Hagerstown. The elder Schnebly was one of the early settlers of Washington County, then a part of Frederick County, and was one of the framers of the first constitution of the State of Maryland. At various times members of this family have filled the most important offices of the county. One of the first, if not the first, departures from the old Ramage printing-press, and an invention which preceded the present power-press, was the invention of Thomas Schnebly, a brother of Miss Eliza.

At the residence of his son-in-law, James M. Schley, in Cumberland, on the 23d of July, 1867, O. H. W. Stull, in the 84th year of his age. This venerable gentleman was a native of Washington County, and the son of John Stull, of Revolutionary memory. He was in 1814 associated with the late William D. Bell in the editorship of the *Torch-Light*, and during Gen. Harrison's administration was secretary of the Territory of Iowa.

Dec. 22, 1873, Geo. W. Smith, aged 63. In 1838 he was appointed a justice of the peace, and for many years served in that capacity. Subsequently he was appointed a judge of the Orphans' Court, and for a number of years filled that position with exceptional ability. About this period he became editor of the *Washington County Democrat*, a Democratic newspaper, printed for several years in Hagerstown. In 1844 he was a candidate for the Legislature on the Democratic ticket and was defeated, but in 1845 he was again nominated and elected by a handsome majority, and served one term in the House of Delegates. In 1850, Mr. Smith was admitted to the bar of Washington County Court, at which he continued to practice, particularly as advising counsel, up to a few months previous to his death. He was one of the founders of the Franklin Debating Society, and also a director of the Washington County Bank.

February, 1881, Peter B. Small, cashier First National Bank of Hagerstown. Mr. Small was also a director of the Washington County Railroad, and of the Agricultural and Mechanical Association of the county. He also served a term as judge of the Orphans' Court.

Aug. 5, 1794, Peter Shugert, of Hagerstown, at an advanced age. At one time he was sheriff of York County, Pa., and held several other offices of trust.

Jan. 21, 1794, Mrs. Mary Shugert, wife of Peter, in her 68th year. She left nine children and thirty-nine grandchildren.

In the latter part of January, 1803, Nicholas Smith, in the 71st year of his age.

Aug. 30, 1804, Mrs. Schnebly, wife of Dr. Henry Schnebly.

In April, 1855, J. Henry Shafer, of Funkstown. Mr. Shafer was born in Pennsylvania, Jan. 11, 1766, but removed to Washington County at an early age, and settled at Funkstown, then called Jerusalem, in 1790. He resided there up to the time of his death. He was received into the German Reformed Church by the Rev. Jacob Weimer, at Hagerstown, about 1797. He afterwards united with the church at Funkstown, and was a member of the church council for half a century.

On the 2d of January, 1844, in Montgomery County, Ohio, Henry Schlenker, aged 68, a former resident of Washington County.

January, 1854, Henry Shriver, aged 73.

Aug. 16, 1853, Thomas Shaw, aged 66.

Dec. 13, 1809, Gen. Thomas Sprigg, aged 62. Gen. Sprigg resided in Washington County, and was conspicuous both in the Revolutionary war and as a member of Congress.

On Conococheague Manor, Oct. 27, 1820, Susanna, widow of Col. Charles Swearingen, in her 82d year. Col. and Mrs. Swearingen lived together harmoniously for upwards of fifty-nine years, and left numerous descendants in various parts of Maryland, Virginia, Kentucky, and Illinois.

Gerard Stonebreaker, at Funkstown, in June, 1813, at the age of 70.

Rev. Solomon Schaeffer, pastor of the Hagerstown Lutheran Church, March 30, 1815, aged 25.

Robert Smith, aged 81, at his residence, near Sharpsburg, Oct. 14, 1818. He had served several terms in the State Legislature, and for a number of years was a member of the county Levy Court.

Oct. 5, 1856, at his residence, near Chambersburg, John Shryock, in the 85th year of his age. Mr. Shryock was born at Hagerstown, on the 17th of October, 1771. His paternal ancestors immigrated to this country from Prussia between the years 1715 and 1730, and settled in what is now York, but which was at that time included in Lancaster County, Pa. His maternal grandfather was a Lutheran minister from Hanover, who came to America in company with Dr. Muhlenberg, and preached throughout Pennsylvania previous to the year 1755.

July 10, 1808, Jacob Shever, farmer.

Sept. 2, 1809, George Scott, of Boonsboro', formerly an associate judge and a justice of the peace.

Feb. 15, 1810, Jacob Seibert, at his residence, West Conococheague.

July 24, 1805, Dr. Henry Schnebly, aged 77. Dr. Schnebly was prominent during the Revolution, and was one of the most highly-respected citizens in the county.

At Kaskaskia, Ill., Dec. 5, 1821, Joseph Sprigg, aged 62, who removed to Illinois in 1816.

At Williamsport, May 23, 1822, Capt. Peter Stake, aged 57.

At Hagerstown, Aug. 12, 1823, Dr. Samuel Sherman.

Dec. 1, 1825, Lucy, widow of Thomas Sprigg, in the 74th year of her age.

Oct. 29, 1822, near the Maryland Tract, Frederick County, John Slifer, Sr., aged 79 years, 5 months, 3 days.

On the 9th of September, 1821, Nicholas Smith, farmer, near Williamsport.

Jan. 10, 1823, James W. Steele, formerly of Hagerstown, near Lake Champlain, New York.

In Hagerstown, October, 1802, John Byers Taylor.

Feb. 6, 1830, Rebecca Tilghman, wife of Thomas Tilghman.

Jan. 14, 1820, John Teisher, aged 73.

Dec. 6, 1818, Jonathan Turner, aged 28.

July 19, 1819, Jonathan Tutweiler, a Revolutionary soldier.

Aug. 4, 1872, Hugh Taggart, aged 87.

November, 1871, Rev. Septimus Tustin, D.D., for several years pastor of the Presbyterian congregation in Hagerstown. Dr. Tustin, although for a considerable period in the latter portion of his life engaged in a secular pursuit as clerk in some of the departments at Washington, had occupied many prominent positions in his church, the most conspicuous of which, probably, was that of chaplain to the Senate of the United States. Dr. Tustin was a brother-in-law of Maj.-Gen. Macomb, those gentlemen having married daughters of the late Rev. B. Balch, D.D., of the District of Columbia. He was also chaplain of the University of Virginia in 1836, chaplain to the House of Representatives of the United States in 1840, chairman of the Committee of Foreign Correspondence of the General Assembly, and was the first clergyman to initiate the measures for reunion, and president of the board of trustees of Lafayette College, Easton, Pa., as well as pastor of several churches in Pennsylvania and Maryland.

March, 1824, Ann Eliza, wife of George Tilghman, and daughter of Col. Lamar, of Allegany.

Sept. 30, 1840, Thomas Trice, editor Williamsport *Banner*, in the 51st year of his age.

Oct. 5, 1853, Dr. Frisby Tilghman.

In September, 1807, Ignatius Taylor, judge of the Orphans' Court, and a man of exceptionally high character.

In Hancock, on the 16th of March, 1856, George Thomas, in the 59th year of his age.

In December a colored woman known as "Aunt Tabby," said to be 104 years old, was burned to death at the home of her son-in-law, Hilary Wilson, in Sharpsburg.

Aug. 10, 1869, George Updegraff, aged 70 years, 11 months, and 29 days.

July 20, 1801, John Van Lear, aged 77.

July 5, 1822, Matthew Van Lear, a prominent citizen of the county.

At his residence in Williamsport, on Friday evening, April 24, 1859, in the 71st year of his age, John Van Lear, Jr., cashier of the Washington County Bank. Mr. Van Lear was connected with the bank from its organization, first as its president for four years, and afterwards as its cashier, which position he held from the year 1836. He was also a strong friend of African colonization, and in support of this, as well as other schemes of Christian benevolence, he gave liberally in money, and furnished constant encouragement and example.

Feb. 11, 1815, Col. William Van Lear, in his 58th year. Col. Van Lear served as brigade-major under Gen. Wayne, and inspector of the Marquis de Lafayette's division shortly before the surrender of Cornwallis. He was wounded at the battle of Green Springs, but afterwards returned to active service. At the close of the war he settled in Washington County.

Died at the farm of Matthew Van Lear, near Williamsport, Sept. 1, 1816, Dr. Matthew Simms Van Lear, in the 28th year of his age.

July 15, 1794, Gen. Otho Holland Williams.

At Georgetown, D. C., in 1823, Col. Elie Williams, in the 73d year of his age. Col. Williams was an ardent patriot during the Revolution, and in the latter portion of his life was deeply interested in the Chesapeake and Ohio Canal, being elected to the Legislature from Washington County with the special object of promoting the interests of that great enterprise.

June 13, 1819, Daniel Witmer, Jr., inn-keeper at Hagerstown, aged 60 years.

May 11, 1852, Gen. O. H. Williams, for many years clerk of the Washington County Court, in his 78th year.

July, 1854, Col. George C. Washington, formerly a representative in Congress from Maryland, and at one time president of the Chesapeake and Ohio Canal, in the 65th year of his age. The deceased was a relative of the great Washington, and a man highly esteemed for his elevated character, public spirit, and social and generous qualities.

At Washington, D. C., June 14, 1868, Col. John S. Williams, aged 84. Col. Williams was a brother of Otho H. Williams, so long a clerk of Washington County Court, and a nephew of Gen. O. H. Williams, of Revolutionary fame. Col. Williams was born in Maryland in 1785, and when a young man resided for several years in Georgetown, but again removed to Maryland, and after a residence of several years again removed to Washington, where he resided for many years. He was a major in the war of 1812. At the battle of Bladensburg he was an adjutant, and published an interesting history of that battle. He was vice-president of the Association of the Oldest Inhabitants of Washington, and the presiding officer of the soldiers of the war of 1812.

In March, 1879, Benjamin Witmer, of Beaver Creek, in the 71st year of his age. Mr. Witmer was elected a member of the State Legislature in 1855, and was an active and influential citizen.

May 5 (?), 1880, John Weltz, aged 67.

Oct. 24, 1869, Otho Holland Williams, in his 86th year.

At Williamsport, Sept. 25, 1880, Judge Daniel Weisel, aged 77.

July, 1804, John George Weiss, aged 83, who had been a teacher in Hagerstown upwards of thirty years. His death was followed by that of his widow within a week.

Oct. 20, 1811, at his residence, near Hughes' furnace, Col. James Walling.

Aug. 5, 1806, Dr. T. Walmsley. Dr. Walmsley removed to Hagerstown from Philadelphia in 1805, and was extremely popular.

In January, 1807, William Webb, for many years magistrate at Hughes' forge.

Archibald M. Waugh, died May 23, 1823, aged 47. He was a man of great integrity of character, and respected by all who knew him.

July, 1823, at Cavetown, Samuel Webb.

May 6, 1880, John Welty (nephew of John Welty), farmer and distiller. His farm was one of the richest and most carefully improved in Cumberland Valley. On it was a trout-pond which had quite a local celebrity. Mr. Welty was at one time a member of the State Legislature, and also a county commissioner, director of the Western Maryland Railroad, etc.

April 19, 1856, Robert Wason, at the residence of his nephew, James Wason, in Hagerstown, in the 68th year of his age.

Mr. Wason served in both branches of the Legislature of Maryland, and was an influential politician as well as successful business man.

At Charleston, Va., April 5, 1852, Richard Williams, a former resident of Hagerstown, and editor of the *Farmers' Repository* from 1802 to 1807. He was the first apprentice in the Hagerstown *Herald* office, having commenced work in that establishment in 1790.

At his residence in Hagerstown, April 5, 1842, Rev. Richard Wynkoop, pastor of the Associate Reformed congregation.

March 16, 1843, Joseph Weast, aged 53. Mr. Weast was a member of the first board of county commissioners, and a man of considerable local influence and standing. He had served three times in the State Legislature, and was county collector at the time of his death.

March 16, 1843, Samuel Wolfersberger, aged 24.

At Charleston, S. C., March 16, 1818, Otho H. Williams, of Baltimore, youngest son of the late Gen. Otho H. Williams, in the 23d year of his age.

January, 1872, Dr. Samuel Weisel, in his 63d year.

At New Orleans, on the 8th of May, 1875, Dr. John O. Wharton, at the residence of his son, Col. Jack Wharton, aged 70.

Feb. 2, 1876, Matilda, wife of Judge Daniel Weisel.

March 26, 1791, Jacob Young, in his 39th year.

April 26, 1793, Rev. George Young, aged 51 years, who for about nineteen years officiated as minister of the gospel in the German Lutheran Congregation of Hagerstown. He was a man of great piety and learning. He left a young wife and a number of children. After the funeral was over an appropriate sermon was preached by the Rev. Yunck from 2d Epistle of Paul to the Corinthians, 8th and 9th verses.

At Sharpsburg, Feb. 6, 1829, Henry Young, a Revolutionary soldier, in his 97th year. After the war he was a teacher of English and German, and resided in Sharpsburg for upwards of thirty years.

July, 1878, Barnett Young, aged 80 years.

Feb. 24, 1803, Rev. John Young, in his 40th year. Member of the Associated Reformed Synod, and pastor of the united congregations of Greencastle, West Conecocheague, and Great Cove.

June 8, 1803, Dr. John R. Young, at a comparatively early age.

March 3, 1863, Lewis Zeigler, a former member of the Maryland Legislature.

In the latter part of November, 1875, Rev. W. H. Zimmerman, in his 56th year. Mr. Zimmerman studied for the ministry under the late Rev. Dr. Zacharias, and upon the completion of his studies went to Clear Spring, in Washington County, where he preached for several years, but owing to physical disabilities he retired to his farm in this county, where he resided until his death.

At Frederick, March 31, 1873, Rev. Daniel Zacharias, D.D. "Dr. Zacharias was a native of Washington County, having been born near Clear Spring. His classical education was received at the Hagerstown Academy and Jefferson College (Canonsburg, Pa.). His theological studies were prosecuted at the Theological Seminary of the Reformed Church (then located at Carlisle, Pa.), under Rev. Dr. Lewis Mayer. During this time he attended some of the lectures in Dickinson College, which was then in charge of Dr. Nesbitt. Shortly after the completion of his theological studies he was chosen as pastor of the Reformed Church of Harrisburg, from which place he was called to Frederick in 1835. He was one of the most prominent ministers in his denomination, and was frequently selected by the preference of his brethren to preside over their ecclesiastical assemblies. In 1833 he was associated with Rev. Dr. Wolff in the preparation of the appendix to the church hymnbook. At a later date the German hymn-book was chiefly compiled by the Rev. Dr. Schneck and himself. In the preparation of the 'Liturgy of the Church,' and its revision, known as 'An Order of Worship for the Reformed Church,' he was a prominent member of the committees appointed by the Synod, and he likewise took a part in the preparation of the edition of the Heidelberg Catechism in German, Latin, and Greek, which was published by the church in 1863."

Sept. 27, 1823, Mrs. Elizabeth Zeller, aged 57.

At his residence near Leitersburg, on May 31, 1857, Frederick Zeigler, Sr., aged 79 years. Mr. Zeigler was one of the wealthiest and most respectable citizens of Washington County.

CHAPTER XLIV.

HAGERSTOWN.

The First Settler—Jonathan Hager—Cresap's Fort—Incorporation of the Town—The First Officers—Reminiscences—Prominent Events.

HAGERSTOWN, the county-seat of Washington County, is beautifully situated near Antietam Creek, eighty-seven miles from Baltimore, and lies five hundred and sixty-six feet above tide. It is located in the midst of the charming Hagerstown Valley, and is one of the most attractive and thrifty towns in the country. The streets are regular and in good condition, and the buildings substantial, and in many instances unusually handsome. Stores and shops of various kinds are numerous. The railway lines which centre here are the Washington County Branch of the Baltimore and Ohio, the Western Maryland, the Cumberland Valley, and the Shenandoah Valley. These roads drain a magnificent section of country, decidedly the richest in Maryland, and embracing also some of the fairest portions of Pennsylvania, Virginia, and West Virginia. From an elevated position in the town may be seen for miles the fertile fields of the Hagerstown Valley, while on the south lies the bleak battle-field of Antietam, and on the eastward that of South Mountain. From a point northwest of Hagerstown the line of intrenchments thrown up by Lee's army in his last invasion of Maryland extended in a southerly direction to the Potomac. At some points the intrenchments were not more than three-quarters of a mile or a mile and a half from the town, which was completely covered by the Confederate guns. The Union fortifications were also very extensive. In fact, Hagerstown was the theatre of some of the most important events of the war, and the vestiges of the havoc wrought by both armies are by no means effaced even yet. In addition to its railroad facilities, the town enjoys the advantage of being the point of convergence for a number of admirable turnpike roads, which have largely contributed to building up its flourishing trade. It is abundantly supplied with water-power, which, with the richness and productiveness of the surrounding country, has contributed to give it not only the appearance but the reality of remarkable prosperity and enterprise.

Looking eastward, towards the South Mountain ridge, the scenery is of the most imposing character. Splendid farms, teeming with richness of soil and all under perfect cultivation, are within visual range in every direction, whilst blue mountains rise up in the distance, making altogether a panorama that has few equals anywhere. Beautiful springs gush forth from limestone rocks at frequent intervals, and sparkling streams are seen winding through the rich fields like threads of glittering silver. To all this rural beauty is added a pure, salubrious atmosphere. One of the most attractive features of the town itself is the number of beautiful gardens and green inclosures attached to private residences.

The town is divided into five wards. The principal streets are Washington and Potomac. Washington runs nearly east and west, and Potomac north and south. Each is divided by the other into two sections, thus making East and West Washington and North and South Potomac Streets. The streets running parallel with Washington Street, beginning on the north, are North, Bethel, Church, Franklin, Antietam, and Baltimore. Those running parallel with Potomac Street, beginning on the east, are Mulberry, Locust, Jonathan, Walnut, Prospect, and High. Green Lane is an extension of West Washington Street, and Pennsylvania Avenue is a continuation of Jonathan Street. The Washington Branch of the Baltimore and Ohio Railroad enters the town from the south, passing between Potomac and Jonathan Streets. The depot is situated at the intersection of South Jonathan and West Antietam Streets, a short distance northwest of St. John's Lutheran church, which fronts on Potomac Street near the intersection of Antietam Street. The Cumberland Valley Railroad passes through the western portion of the town, along Walnut Street. The depot is situated at the intersection of South Walnut and West Washington Streets. For some distance the course of the Western Maryland Railroad is parallel with and westward of that of the Cumberland Valley, which, however, curves suddenly to the northward and intersects the Western Maryland in the northwestern section of the town. The depot is situated on West Washington Street.

The principal buildings in Hagerstown are the court-house, on West Washington Street, at the corner of Jonathan, near which stands the banking-house of Hoffmann, Eavey & Co.; the Baldwin House, a handsome new hotel, located on Washington Street, diagonally opposite from the court-house, to the eastward; the market-house, on the east side of Potomac Street, at the corner of Franklin; county jail, on Jonathan Street, at the corner of West Church; Hagerstown Female Seminary, located in the extreme southeastern portion of the town, and the Hagerstown Academy, which is situated in the southwestern portion, near Walnut Street. The town hall is situated at the corner of Franklin and Potomac Streets, with market-house under it.

The churches are located as follows: Catholic, Washington and Walnut Streets; St. John's Episcopal, Antietam and Prospect Streets; St. John's Lutheran, Potomac Street near Antietam; Presbyterian, corner of Washington and Prospect Streets, and another on South Potomac near Baltimore Street; Methodist, Jonathan Street near Franklin; Trinity Lutheran and the Reformed churches, on Franklin Street between Jonathan and Potomac; Bethel Methodist Episcopal church, on Bethel Street near Potomac; Colored Methodist church, on Jonathan near Church; United Brethren, at the corner of Locust and Franklin Streets; and St. Matthew's German Lutheran church, on the corner of Antietam and Locust Streets. Besides these there is another Reformed church on Potomac Street near Church. The handsomest and most conspicuous church in Hagerstown is St. John's Protestant Episcopal, a beautiful structure of graystone, with an imposing tower. The court-house is a spacious building of brick, with tower, and is one of the finest structures of the kind in the State. The Baldwin House is the principal hotel, and is a new, roomy, and well-appointed structure. The other hotels are the Franklin House, on Potomac Street; Antietam House, on West Washington Street; Hoover House, corner Franklin and Potomac Streets; and the Mansion House, near the depot of the Cumberland Valley Railroad. The Hagerstown Bank, one of the oldest institutions of the kind in Western Maryland, is situated on Washington Street, opposite the Baldwin House, and the First National Bank is now erecting a new building on Washington Street, opposite the court-house.

The sidewalks are paved with brick, and the streets are substantial turnpike-roads. The site of the old court-house, which stood at the intersection of Poto-

S. WALNUT ST.

N WALNUT ST.

S. JONATHAN ST

N JONATHAN ST

PUBLIC SQUARE

S. POTOMAC

N. POTOMAC ST.

W. ANTIETAM ST.

E. ANTIETAM ST.

W. WASHINGTON ST.

E. WASHINGTON ST.

W. FRANKLIN ST.

E. FRANKLIN ST.

W. CHURCH ST.

E. CHURCH ST.

ORIGINAL PLAT OF HAGERSTOWN.

mac and Washington Streets, is now used as a public square. It is a great rendezvous for market people. The finest private residences are situated on Prospect, and at the head of West Washington and North Potomac Streets, but there are also a number of others scattered about in different localities. The houses are mostly of brick, but some graystone is also used with handsome effect.

Hagerstown was laid out as a town in 1762 by Capt. Jonathan Hager, and its site is said to have been in the main a dreary, uneven swamp. Capt. Hager came from Germany about 1730 and settled in what is now Washington County, about two miles west of the present site of Hagerstown, on a tract of land which was known as "Hager's Delight," and which was owned recently by the late Samuel Zeller. The earliest information of Jonathan Hager, Sr., is found in the statement that he received a patent of certain land on which a portion of the city of Philadelphia now stands. He was a man of much independence and force of character, and pushed on to Maryland. Having obtained patents for extensive tracts of land in Washington County, he settled, as stated above, in the vicinity of Antietam Creek. On this farm was built the first two-story log house, with an arched stone cellar so constructed that if the family were attacked by the Indians they could take refuge there. Capt. Hager was frequently assailed by the savages, and his family found the cellar a most useful asylum. It was often necessary to protect the dairy-maids with armed men while engaged in milking the cows. As a rule, however, Capt. Hager generally managed to keep on pretty friendly terms with the Indians of the vicinity.

Jonathan Hager was not, however, the first settler in the neighborhood of Hagerstown. He was no doubt preceded several years by Capt. Thomas Cresap, the famous Indian-fighter, and other fearless settlers. Capt. Cresap at a very early period built an Indian fort of stone and logs over a spring at "Long Meadows," on the farm now owned by George W. Harris, about three miles from Hagerstown, which was known for many years as "Old Castle Cresap." During the Indian wars Cresap's fort was an important point, as it afforded protection to those who fled to it for safety. It was also a general rendezvous for the rangers established in the county for the protection of the back settlements. When the inhabitants increased and the Indians were driven farther into the interior, Cresap abandoned his castle near Hagerstown and erected a more formidable one at his new home at Skipton, or Old Town, in Allegany County. Some of the ruins of his old fort are yet visible; indeed, the old stone barn, on the farm of Mr. Harris which was purchased by him in 1868 from the executors of the late Richard Ragan, was built out of the stone of Castle Cresap, which stood on that farm. "Long Meadows" was the favorite abode of the early settlers of Washington County, and within the memory of many living the farms in that locality were owned by the Harts, Spriggs, Thomas B. Hall, and other names once familiar, but now extinct.

Jonathan Hager was attracted to Washington County by the fertility of its soil and the great abundance of pure and wholesome water, and was not disappointed in the hope of speedily accumulating a comfortable maintenance.

About 1740 he married Elizabeth Kershner, who lived in the same neighborhood. They had two children, Rosanna and Jonathan. Rosanna married Gen. Daniel Heister, and Jonathan married Mary Madeline, daughter of Maj. Christian Orndorff, who lived near Sharpsburg. Maj. Orndorff's house was the headquarters of the Revolutionary officers who passed that way to or from the scene of military operations in the North or South. Mrs. Jonathan Hager, Jr. (Mary Orndorff), was a great belle and beauty in her day, one of her suitors being the famous Gen. Horatio Gates. She rejected him, however, and when fifteen years of age accepted Jonathan Hager, Jr., and was married to him. They had one daughter, Elizabeth, who married Upton Lawrence. Nine children were born to Mr. and Mrs. Lawrence, and their descendants are very numerous. Among them are the two Misses Lawrence, who reside in the Lawrence mansion, and who have many interesting relics of the Hagers in their possession. Among them is the original plat of the town, as shown in the cut. They also have Jonathan Hager, Sr.'s, old-fashioned silver watch of the "turnip" pattern, the massively engraved silver shoe-buckles worn by Jonathan Hager, Jr., and the latter's suspender-buckles of silver, with his initials engraved on them. Among the other articles in their collection is a handsome silver stock-buckle set with brilliants and attached to a stock of black lace and blue satin, a brooch of brilliants for the shirt, a gold ring set with a ruby and diamonds, and a full-dress suit with lace and ruffles. This costume consists of two vests,—one of them of white satin embroidered with spangles and colored silks, and the other of apple-green silk embroidered with spangles, gold thread, and colored silks. The spangles and embroidery are still as bright, probably, as when they were first put on. They also have Mr. Hager, Jr.'s, silver shoe-buckles, magnificently set with brilliants, and retain possession of all the old silver and plate.

The elder Jonathan Hager named the new village

Elizabeth Town in honor of his wife, Elizabeth, but in after-years it came to be written Elizabeth (Hager's) Town, and gradually the Elizabeth was discarded and it was denominated solely Hagerstown. Capt. Hager laid off the town in about 520 lots of 82 feet front and 240 feet deep, making half an acre each, which were leased for £5 consideration money, $1, or 7 shillings and 6 pence, per annum as a perpetual ground-rent. He reserved all the lots outside the town which were not numbered in the original, but these were afterwards sold by his heirs. There are still in the possession of his descendants about 300 ground-rents of the original town lots. A large square was laid out, and a market-house was erected in the centre, at the intersection of what is now Washington and Potomac Streets. Afterwards a court-house and market-house combined was built, the market-house being below and the court-house above. When Washington County was created out of Frederick in 1776, Mr. Hager, we are told, "rode down to Annapolis and had his town made the county town." This must have been Jonathan Hager, Jr., as the date of his father's death is given as being 1775.[1] In the previous year (1773) Jonathan Hager, Sr., had been returned as a delegate to the General Assembly of Maryland from Frederick County, but not being a native subject of the English crown nor descended from one, but naturalized in 1747, was declared ineligible by the House. The act created a considerable stir, and the Governor and Council declared it unprecedented. He was also a member of the House of Delegates in 1771. The course of the Assembly in 1773 was predicated on a petition from Samuel Beall setting forth that a number of voters in Frederick County had not produced certificates of their naturalization, and on account of their religious tenets had refused to take the oaths required by law. The old Hager residence, a massive stone building on the eastern side of the public square and fronting on Washington Street, was torn down a few years ago in order to make room for a store. In this ancient structure the Hagers resided for a number of years, and after them Col. Henry Lewis, who married Mrs. Mary Hager, widow of Col. Jonathan Hager, Jr. Mrs. Mary Hager was still a very beautiful woman, and still young when Col. Hager died. At one time Luther Martin, the great lawyer, was an ardent suitor for her hand, but she rejected him and married Col. Lewis. Both the Jonathan Hagers, father and son, were very popular with the citizens of Hagerstown, and enjoyed almost unbounded influence. The elder Hager was accidentally killed on Nov. 6, 1775, in his sixty-first year, at a saw-mill near the site of Hager's mill, by a large piece of timber rolling upon and crushing him. The timber was being sawed for the German Reformed church, which Mr. Hager was very active in building. Jonathan Hager, Jr., entered the Revolutionary army, and served through the war. After his marriage he resided in Hagerstown, and died in December, 1798. In its issue of the 20th of that month the Hagerstown *Herald* paid him a warm tribute as a worthy citizen and an affectionate husband and father. His daughter, Elizabeth, married Upton Lawrence, a distinguished lawyer of Hagerstown.

In 1791, Henry Shryock, Matthias Need, and Martin Harry were appointed commissioners, with power and authority to lay out a portion of ground in Elizabeth Town for the purpose of building a market-house thereon not less than fifty feet in length and thirty in breadth. By the act of 1793 all the powers to these commissioners were transferred to the commissioners of the town. By an act passed by the General Assembly in 1791 "to improve the streets," etc., Elizabeth Town was incorporated. By this act Thomas Hart, Ludwick Young, William Lee, John Shryock, John Geiger, Peter Heighley, and Baltzer Gole were appointed the first commissioners.

The preamble of the act sets forth that the citizens of the town petitioned for the act of incorporation, stating in their petition that the streets of the town were frequently rendered almost impassable by means of many of the inhabitants raising the ground before their own houses, and turning the water with a view to their private convenience only, and that disputes often arose respecting boundaries of lots by filling up the streets and alleys, etc. The commissioners were

---

[1] Extract from the family Bible of Jonathan Hager, translated from the German:

"I entered into marriage with my wife, Elizabeth Grischner, in the year 1740. On the 21st of April, 1752, in the sign of the Lion, there was born to us a daughter, who was named Rosina.

"On the 13th of December, 1755, there was born to us a son, who was named Jonathan.

"We lived together until the 16th of April, 1765. Then it pleased the Lord to call her, after severe suffering, out of this world. 'What God does is well done.' Her funeral text is recorded in 2 Tim. i. 12. The hymn was sung, 'Lord Jesus Christ, true man and God;' also the hymn, 'Think ye, children of men, on the last day of life.' O, my child, lay rightly to heart the words of this hymn, and do right and fear God and keep His commandments. And if you have anything, do not forget the poor, and do not exalt yourself in pride and haughtiness above your fellow-men. For you are not better than the humblest before God's eyes, and perhaps not as good. And so, if you have no fear of God within you, all is in vain. My child, keep this in remembrance of your father, and live according to it, and it will go well with you here while you live, and there eternally."

empowered to levy a tax not exceeding three shillings on one hundred pounds, to dig wells, purchase a fire-engine, etc.

The commissioners were also made a body corporate by the name of the Commissioners of Elizabeth Town, and to have a common seal and perpetual succession. Additional powers were conferred on the commissioners by the act of 1792. At this time the lower part of the town was built on very low and swampy land, the streets have been raised many feet above the original level, and were often in a very bad condition. The marsh at the southern edge of the town accounts for the bend in South Potomac Street, as it was bent east of the straight line to avoid it. In the year 1802 the General Assembly authorized a lottery for the purpose of raising money to repair the streets. About 1810, Samuel Rohrer made an addition to the original town.

The first census of Hagerstown of which any record remains was taken in 1810. At that time the population numbered 2342, of which 1951 were whites, 297 slaves, and 94 free negroes.

In 1820 the population was as follows: Whites, males, 1161; whites, females, 1137; total whites, 2298; slaves, males, 147; slaves, females, 133; total slaves, 280; free colored persons, males, 55; females, 57; total, 112; total population, 2690.

For the censuses of 1850, 1860, 1870, and 1880, the only years we have been able to obtain the official figures, the returns were as follows:

	Total.	Native.	Foreign.	White.	Colored.
1850	3879	......	.....	3261	618
1860	4132	......	.....	3623	509
1870	5779	5442	337	4910	860
1880	6627	......	.....	......	.....

A writer describing Hagerstown in 1822 says:

"There are perhaps few towns in this county which have risen more rapidly in importance within the last few years than this town. Nor are its advantages in other respects less important. The arrivals and departures of stages in one week amount to forty-two,—seven arrive from Wheeling, seven from Washington, Georgetown, and Baltimore *via* Frederick; three from Baltimore *via* Westminster, Taney Town, and Emmittsburg, which line is intersected twenty miles from this place by a direct line from Philadelphia *via* Gettysburg; three from the respective sections of Pennsylvania *via* Chambersburg; and one from Virginia *via* Winchester, Martinsburg, and Williamsport, making twenty-one arrivals from, and the same number of departures for, the respective places above named. . . . An idea of the progress of improvement may be gathered from the fact that a court-house equal, perhaps, in elegance and taste, to any in the country has just been completed, and that there are now in progress a market-house, connected with a town hall and Masonic Hall, independent of a large Episcopal church and several private dwellings. The number of well-conducted public-houses is not, perhaps, surpassed by those of any inland town in the country, the enterprise and activity of our mercantile men are proverbial, and the industry and perseverance of our mechanical population give life and energy to the various branches of active business."

In connection with the town hall and market alluded to an animated discussion arose. It seems that the steeple of the old market-house was surmounted by a little old man of tin, with a rotund abdomen, who was popularly known as "Old Heiskel," doubtless from his resemblance, real or fancied, to some well-known resident of the town. The citizens generally wanted to have "Old Heiskel" placed on the steeple of the new building, but the Freemasons desired a compass and square to indicate the character of the edifice. Neither party would give way at first, and a violent controversy in and out of the newspapers was the result. The Masons finally triumphed, however, and the compass and square were placed on the vane.

Early Residents.—Among the residents of Hagerstown and its immediate vicinity from 1800 to 1805, inclusive, were the following:

Arnold, Henry, weaver.
Alter, Frederick, overseer of almshouse.
Adams, Nathan, farmer.
Artz, Christian.
Beatty, Elie, the first cashier of Hagerstown Bank.
Bower, Rev. George.
Beltzhoover, Melchor, tavern-keeper.
Brazier, William, bridle, bit, and stirrup-maker.
Bower, Abraham.
Bowers, Mrs., owner of brick-yard.
Belt, Thomas, register of deeds.
Blaire, L., classical teacher.
Byers, John, tailor and habit-maker.
Bailie, John, stocking-weaver.
Bender, George, wheelwright.
Bender,[1] John, laborer.
Baker, Sebastian, crier of Washington County Court.
Boreoff, Adam, blacksmith.
Coffroth, Conrad, merchant.
Crissinger, George, proprietor hackney stage.
Clagett, Alex., merchant.
Clapsaddle, Daniel, farmer.
Compton, Thomas, justice of the peace.
Clagett, William, associate judge.
Crumbach, John, potter.
Cake, Henry.
Conrad, John.
Crumbach, Conrad, potter, also brewer.
Clagett & Miller, merchants.
Clagett, Benjamin.
Carroll, Charles, farmer.
Coburn, A., teacher of music.
Cook, John, tavern-keeper at stone house, "Sign of Gen. Washington."
Carlos, Francis, barber.
Douglass, Robert, weaver.
Doyle, Dorris.
Dunn, William, tailor and habit-maker.
Devine, John, tailor and habit-maker.
Dietrick, Jacob D., merchant, also bookbinder.
Diffendorfer, Mrs., milliner.

[1] His wife gave birth to three children in July, 1803.

Devine, Mrs. John, milliner and mantua-maker.
Dorsey, Frederick, physician.
Dunnington, James, merchant.
Donaldson, John, whitesmith.
Dietz, J., bookbinder.
Davis, Samuel B., teacher and bookbinder.
Davis, Col. Rezin, a veteran of '76.
Eichelberner, Devalt.
Fechtig,[1] Christian, potter.
Ferguson, James, & Co., merchants.
Forman & Keller, merchants.
Foutz & Stucky, hatters.
Gibbs & Westover, who had carding-machines on the Antietam.
Galloway, Benj., politician.
Greiner, John, brass-founder.
Geiger, John, tanner.
Grieves, Thomas, publisher and bookseller.
Geiger & Harry, merchants.
Green, Wm., proprietor of grist-mill situated near the town.
Garrett, Thomas, weaver.
Gruber, John, printer and publisher.
Gilberts, Wendel, farmer.
Grubb, George, cooper.
Hughes, Daniel, Jr.
Harry, Jacob, merchant.
Harry, David, wagon-maker.
Hawken, Capt. Christian, gunsmith.
Hawken, George, gunsmith.
Hogmire, Conrad, dealer in flour, corn-meal, etc.
Haynes, Richard.
Hughes, Samuel.
Heyser, Wm., coppersmith and fire department chief.
Henderson, George, miller.
Heddinger, ——, auctioneer and market clerk.
Hager, Jonathan, proprietor tavern, "Sign of the Ship."
Hefleich, Peter.
Hose, Jacob, Revolutionary veteran.
Heister, Gen. Daniel, member of Congress.
Hawkin, William, gunsmith.
Hess, William.
Horndige, Philip, candle-maker.
Herr, John P., tailor and lumber-dealer.
Hisshen, J., teacher of private school.
Hartshorn, D., teacher of dancing.
Heffley, Michael, farmer.
Hilliard, James, farrier.
Heddington, James.
Herbert, Stewart, printer.
Hershey, John, tanner.
Hart, Thomas, merchant.
Johnson, Arthur, clock and watchmaker.
Kershner, Martin.
Kennedy, John, merchant.
Kreps, William, merchant.
Kreps, George, gunsmith.
Kreps, Martin, carpenter.
Kemmelmeyer, F., limner and portrait-painter.
Kealhofer, Jacob, boot and shoemaker.
Kelly, John V., fuller and dyer at Bechtel's mill.
Kendall, James, attorney-at-law and deputy county clerk.
Kapp, Michael, tavern-keeper.
Keller, Christian.

[1] The pottery business then carried on by Christian Fechtig and George Vogelsang, near the court-house, had formerly been controlled by Eichbaugh, and afterwards by Leisinger & Bell.

Keller, Philip, blacksmith.
Light, Benjamin, tavern-keeper.
Light, John.
Lewis, Henry, farmer.
Little, P. W., firm of Little & Miller.
Little & Miller, merchants.
Lawrence, Upton, attorney-at-law.
Lane, Seth, cabinet-maker.
Middlekauff, Henry.
Monahan, Timothy, plasterer, and captain of militia.
Miller, Frederick, firm of Little & Miller.
Miller, James, weaver.
Miller, John, weaver.
Miller, Peter, tavern-keeper.
Miller, Jacob, tavern-keeper, house, "Sign of the Indian Queen."
McNamee, George and Job, dealers in plaster, etc.
McCloskey, Stephen, who charged $1 per year for water taken from his well.
Mahony, Mr., scrivener.
Mahony, Mrs., teacher of private school.
Middlekauff, David, tavern-keeper, house, "Sign of the Swan."
McCoy, John, merchant.
Miller, Peter, merchant.
McCardell, James.
McIntosh, William, scrivener.
McDonald, Richard.
McKinley, Josiah, painter and glazier.
McIlhenny, John, merchant.
McIlhenny, Joseph, merchant.
McCardell, Thomas.
Neill, Alexander, merchant.
Nead, Capt. Daniel, tanner.
Nigh, George, justice of the peace.
Nichol & George, gunsmiths.
Oldwine, Barney, Revolutionary veteran.
Ott, Col. Adam, justice of the peace.
Oldwine, Charles, plasterer and bricklayer.
O'Neill, John.
Orndorf, Peter, stage proprietor.
Pindell,[2] Richard, physician.
Parsons, Daniel, tailor and habit-maker.
Pinkley, George, & Co., merchants.
Pinkley & Middlekauff, merchants.
Pinkley, George, blue dyer.
Pinkley, Jacob, blue dyer.
Price, George, collector of revenue.
Quantrill, Thomas, blacksmith.
Quantrill, Thomas, Jr., blacksmith.
Rochester & Beatty, merchants.
Rochester, John C.
Rochester, William B.
Rahp, John.
Ragan, Richard, merchant.
Reed & Byers, tailors and habit-makers.
Ragan, John, tavern-keeper, house,[3] "Sign of the Indian King," also stage proprietor.
Ragan, John, Jr., an officer of the war of 1812.
Ridenour, David, tavern-keeper.
Ridenour, Samuel, tanner.

[2] Dr. Pindell served as surgeon in the Continental army. He removed to Kentucky in 1814.

[3] On the 20th of July, 1803, Hon. John Randolph, M.C. from Virginia, was banqueted at this house by the citizens of Hagerstown.

Rohrer, Samuel.
Rahauser, Rev. Jonathan, pastor German Reformed Church.
Reynolds, Capt. John, clock and watchmaker.
Reynolds, William, spinning-wheel and chair-maker.
Robardet, James (of Baltimore), teacher of dancing.
Ridenour & Binkley, merchants.
Rochester, Col. Nathaniel, postmaster.
Rohrer, Frederick, farmer.
Schmucker, Rev. George, Lutheran pastor.
Smith, Peter, shoemaker.
South, Gera, shoemaker.
Steele, Benjamin, stocking-weaver.
Schnebly, Dr. Jacob, sheriff 1802 to 1804.
Stoner, Michael, tavern-keeper.
Stonebreaker, George, shoemaker.
Shupe, Peter, farmer.
Shall, George.
Simpson, Alexander, jeweler, watch and clock-maker.
Smoot, George C., scrivener.
Sharkey, George, carpenter.
Smith, George, painter and glazier.
Shane, Henry, tavern-keeper.
Shank, George.
Shuman, Thomas, tinman and tavern-keeper, house, "Sign of the Golden Swan."
Sleigh, Samuel, plasterer.
Sleigh, John, blacksmith.
Sharine, Samuel, school-teacher.
Stull, Capt. Daniel, mill-owner.
Stumple, Christian, blacksmith.
Strause, Henry, dealer in mill supplies.
Shryock, Samuel, saddle, cap, and harness-maker.
Stull, John I.
Stull, Otho H. W.
Stull, William B.
Townshend, Henry, tailor and habit-maker.
Tabbs, Capt. Moses.
Vogelsang, George, potter.
Williams, Otho H., clerk of Circuit Court.
Watt, John.
Worland, Charles, saddler.
Woltz, Dr. Peter.
Waugh, Archibald M., scrivener.
Woltz, Samuel, clock and watchmaker.
Woltz, William, cabinet-maker.
Wamsley, T., physician.
Young, Samuel, physician.
Young,[1] John R., physician.
Young, P. C., teacher.
Young, John, teacher.
Yerger, Michael, saddle and harness-maker.
Yakle, Jacob, tin-plate worker.

Besides the inhabitants just named, who represented a population of at least three hundred and fifty white inhabitants, and there were probably nearly as many more whose names cannot now be gathered, Hagerstown of that day boasted of four church edifices, viz.: Protestant Episcopal, German Reformed, Lutheran, and Roman Catholic,[2] the newspaper offices of the *Maryland Herald* and *Elizabethtown Advertiser*, *Elizabethtown Gazette*, and the *German Western Correspondent*, the court-house, jail and market buildings, Dietrick's Circulating Library, Mount Moriah Lodge of F. and A. M., a military company termed the Washington Blues, and a well-equipped fire company (The United).

Referring to the files of the *Maryland Herald* and *Hagerstown Advertiser*, we find that the following were residents of Hagerstown during the years from 1805 to 1815, inclusive:

Anderson, Franklin, attorney-at-law.
Ashcum, Mr., teacher.
Artz & Emmert, merchants.
Adams, Henry, earthenware manufacturer.
Armor, William, tailor.
Aniba, William, manufacturer of blacking.
Albert, John, butcher.
Brent, William L., attorney-at-law.
Bayly, Samuel, conveyancer, afterwards an inn-keeper.
Brumbaugh, George, tavern-keeper and brewer.
Beall, John L., classical teacher.
Brown, William, editor of the *Hagerstown Gazette*.
Bowart, George, brick-maker.
Brendle, George, master-cordwainer.
Barr, David, tanner.
Brinkley, George, merchant.
Beecher, William, grocer.
Barnes, Samuel W., house-painter.
Brown, Jesse, inn-keeper.
Bovey, Jacob.
Bell, William D., editor of the *Torch-Light*.
Beelor, Samuel.
Buchanan, Judge John.
Bean, George, tavern-keeper, house "Sign of the Rising Sun."
Beltzhoover, George, tavern-keeper.
Beecher & Nead, merchants.
Beigler, George, baker.
Bradshaw, John, wheelwright and chair-maker.
Bell, Peter, earthenware manufacturer.
Creager, Henry, saddler.
Creager, John, saddler.
Cake, John, brewer.
Cezerone, Mr., dancing-teacher, also painted portraits at ten dollars each.
Cramer, Peter, farmer.
Crissinger, John, proprietor of hack.
Cromwell (Nathan) & Martin (A. B.), merchants.
Downey, William, physician.
Doyle, George, saddler.
Dixon, William, farmer.
Dickey, W., agent Antietam Woolen Manufacturing Company.
Dillman, Henry, market clerk.
Edwards, P., teacher.
Ebert, John, comb-maker.
Embich, Philip, blue-dyer.
Eichelberner, Theobald, carpenter.
Eichelberner, Mrs. T., milliner and mantua-maker.
Emmert, George, merchant.
Edwards, Thomas, tavern-keeper.
Force, Abraham, hatter.
Freaner, John, master-cordwainer.
Fechtig, Frederick, master-cordwainer.

[1] Son of Dr. Samuel Young. He died June 8, 1804, at the age of twenty-four years.

[2] A sect known as the German Imperialists also had a meeting-house in 1806.

Fechtig, Christian, tavern-keeper, the "Coffee-House," "Sign of Columbus."
Fechtig, L.
Feague, Mr., tavern-keeper.
Funk, Henry B., merchant.
Gelwick, Charles, brewer.
Gear, John, proprietor of livery-stable.
Glossbrenner, Peter, tavern-keeper, house,[1] "Sign of the Billiard-table."
Greiner, William, gunsmith.
Generes, William, Jr., dancing-teacher.
Geisendorffer, Mrs., milliner.
Groff & Kausler, cordwainers.
Glassbrenner, Adam, carpenter.
Hilliard, Christopher, merchant.
Humrickhouse, Peter, blacksmith.
Hall, Thomas B., attorney-at-law.
Hanenkamft, Arnold, physician.
Howard, John, tailor.
Harry, John and George, merchants.
Hoffman, John, master-cordwainer.
Hammond, William, physician.
Harry, David, Jr., wagon-maker.
Harman, John, cordwainer.
Harbaugh, Thomas, agent Antietam Woolen Manufacturing Company.
Hughes, John H., & Co., merchants.
Hawken, Jacob.
Hunt, Job, coppersmith.
Herr, Samuel, carpenter.
Henneberger, John and Christian, cabinet-makers.
Hatfield, A., & Co., shoe-manufacturers.
Hager, George and Jonathan, merchants.
Humrickhouse, Frederick, silver-plater.
Humrickhouse, John.
Hager, Samuel, saddler, also tavern-keeper.
Harry, John & Co., tanners.
Hefleich & Nead, merchants.
Irving, Rev. Thomas P., pastor Episcopal Church.
Irwin, G. H., tavern-keeper, "White Swan Inn."
Irwin, Joseph, barber and umbrella-maker.
Justus, Peter, teacher.
Kissinger (J.) & Artz (P.), merchants.
King, Abraham, blacksmith.
King, John, wagon-maker.
Kausler & Graff, merchants.
Kissinger & Emmert, merchants.
Kennedy, Hugh and John, merchants.
Kay, James, teacher.
Keen, Kaighn & Ragan, hatters.
Kreps, George, cabinet-maker.
Kitchen, Uriah, teacher of penmanship.
Kinsell, Frederick, barber.
Kuhn, Leonard.
Kealhofer, John and Henry, saddlers, etc.
Klink, George.
Keller & Rohrer, merchants.
Kurtz, Rev. Benjamin.
Lighter, Abraham.
Little, David, tailor.
Little, Joseph, plow and wagon-maker.
Lantz, Christian, tavern-keeper.
Lee, William.
Linton, Joshua.

[1] A three-story log structure.

Lynes (James) & Fuct (Thomas I.), coach-makers.
Lantz, Christian, & Co., merchants.
Leopard, Adam, tailor.
Lewis, Capt. William, a veteran of '76.
Langnecker, Christian.
Lawrence, Otho, attorney-at-law.
McComas, Zaccheus.
Miller (Geo.) & Gibbs (Edward A.), cotton-spinners.
McCall, J., teacher.
McLaughlin, E., teacher.
McCleery, John, teacher.
Martin, Samuel, blacksmith.
Martiney, George.
Mayer, Michael F.
Mayer & Irwin, merchants.
Martin, Anthony B., & Co., druggists, etc.
May, Daniel, son-in-law of John Gruber.
Middlekauff & Julius, merchants.
McCardell, William.
Mason, William T. T.
Martiney, John, spinning-wheel and chair-maker.
Mendenhall, E. B., teacher.
Nead, Matthias, grocer.
Post, Thomas.
Post, Rev. Frederick.
Posey, Nathaniel, hatter.
Price, L., tavern-keeper.
Perrin & Sweitzer.
Pettit, Samuel, tavern-keeper, "Sign of Wheat-sheaf."
Price (Samuel D.) & Hussey (George), merchants.
Ringgold & Boerstler, merchants.[2]
Rawlins, Mrs. Ann, teacher.
Richard, Daniel, earthenware-manufacturer.
Rohrer & Barr, tanners.
Roushkulp, Samuel, hatter.
Robertson, William, instructor of military school.
Ragan, John, Jr., lumber-dealer.
Rea, Aaron P., teacher of penmanship.
Rohrer & Motter, tanners.
Strause, Henry, inn-keeper, "Sign of the U. S. Arms."
Seitz, John, inn-keeper, "Sign of the Buck."
Shaffner, Charles and Matthias, tanners.
Smith, George, inn-keeper.
Sholl, Jacob, rope-maker.
Scoggins, John, harness-maker.
Stallsmith, John, cordwainer.
Smith, George, merchant.
Schaeffer, Rev. Solomon.
Smith, Peter, auctioneer.
Snyder, Anthony, bridle, bit, and stirrup-maker.
Saylor, Jacob, inn-keeper.
Snavely, John, earthenware-manufacturer.
Sweitzer, Benjamin.
Sholl & Butler, rope-manufacturers.
Shank, George, Jr., harness-maker.
Schiller, Christopher, painter and glazier.
Shryock, Col. Henry.
Shryock, Capt. George, pump-maker.
Sprigg, D.
Troxell, Peter, weaver.
Tutwiller, Jonathan, auctioneer.
Watterson, George, attorney-at-law.

[2] They removed their stock of goods to Col. Samuel Ringgold's mill in February, 1809, where they continued the business for some years.

Welch, Maxwell, teacher.
Weis, George, cabinet-maker.
Wakenight, Philip.
Waugh, Arch. M., tobacco-manufacturer.
Whitney, A., auctioneer.
Williams (O. H.) & Ragan (John, Jr.), rope-manufacturers.
Willis, William, cordwainer.
Wells, John, druggist.
Wayman, Perry, harness-maker.
Weis, John, blacksmith.
Willis & Crawford, cordwainers.
Willis (L. C.) & Fechtig (F., Jr.), ladies' shoemakers.
Weitzel, John.
Worley, John, sickle-maker.
Worster, Frederick, butcher.
Yoe, Benjamin, tailor.
Young & Van Lear, physicians, druggists, etc.
Zimmerman, Gotlieb, pump-maker.

On Jan. 26, 1814, the Legislature passed an act "to alter and change the name of Elizabeth Town, in Washington County, to Hager's Town, and to incorporate the same." By this act Elizabeth Town was changed to Hagers Town and made an incorporated town. The body corporate consisted of a moderator and four other commissioners, who were elected annually from among the "free white male citizens of the town." They were to be not less than twenty-five years of age and have a freehold estate in the town. They were empowered to elect a clerk and assign him his duties, and to allow him a salary not exceeding sixty dollars per annum. The commissioners were entitled to receive two dollars per day for every day that they met to transact the business of the town. They were to meet upon the business of the town at least four times in every year,—on the third Monday in April, in June, in September, in December,—and oftener if they deemed it necessary. The commissioners were also authorized to appoint a treasurer of the corporation and to affix his salary. The ordinances were orderd to be published at least once in some German and English newspaper printed in the town. The commissioners had power to regulate by ordinance all the public affairs of the town, and to levy on all taxable property in the town and its additions a sum annually not exceeding twenty-five cents on every hundred dollars' worth of taxable property in any one year, and apply the taxes so collected to the expenses of the corporation. The act of 1814 was amended by an act passed Jan. 18, 1815, Feb. 1, 1817, and Jan. 23, 1818, which gave additional powers to the commissioners.

The following have been the corporate officers of Hagerstown since 1814:

Moderators.—1814–15, Henry Lewis; 1816, Archibald M. Waugh; 1817, George Shryock; 1818, Seth Lane; 1819, John Hershey; 1820, Thomas Quantrill; 1821–22, Daniel Schnebly; 1823–24, John Hershey.

Clerks.—1814–18, George Bower; 1819–23, George Brumbaugh; 1824, Joseph Graff.

Commissioners.—1814, Henry Lewis, Richard Ragan, George Brumbaugh, Charles Shaffner, and John McIlhenny; 1815, Henry Kralhoffer, Henry Lewis, David Harry, G. H. Irwin, and George Emmert; 1816, David Harry, Archibald M. Waugh, Charles Shaffner, John Kennedy, and Peter Humrickhouse; 1817, George Shryock, Charles Shaffner, John Hershey, Archibald M. Waugh, and John Schleigh; 1818, John Kennedy, John Hershey, Peter Humrickhouse, Thomas Shuman, and Seth Lane; 1819, George Brumbaugh, John Kennedy, William Kreps, John Hershey, and Theobald Eichelberger; 1820, John Reynolds, George Brumbaugh, John Schleigh, Thomas Quantrill, and George Martiney; 1821, William Heyser, Daniel Schnebly, Theobald Eichelberger, Charles Shaffner, and George Brumbaugh; 1822, Thomas Post (First Ward), Daniel Schnebly (Second Ward), Charles Shaffner (Third Ward), George Brumbaugh (Fourth Ward), John Reynolds (Fifth Ward); 1823, John Albert (First Ward), George Bean (Second Ward), John Hershey (Third Ward), George Brumbaugh (Fourth Ward), George Martiney (Fifth Ward); 1824, John Albert (First Ward) George Bean (Second Ward), John Hershey (Third Ward), George Brumbaugh (Fourth Ward), John Freaner (Fifth Ward).

On the 22d of March, 1848, the Legislature passed an act which changed the corporate body of the town to a mayor and five councilmen, "to be styled the Mayor and Council of Hagerstown," with all the powers heretofore granted to the moderator and commissioners. The mayor was to be elected for two years, and the councilmen (one from each ward) for one year. The compensation was to be the same as formerly allowed to the moderator and commissioners. By the act passed Feb. 4, 1850, Hagerstown is mentioned for the first time as "Hager's City." The mayors of Hager's City since 1859 have been as follows:

1859, D. G. Mumma; 1860, J. Cook; 1862, William Ratcliff; 1863, William Beirshing; 1864–65, John Cook; 1866, William Beirshing; 1868–70, William M. Tice; 1872, E. W. Funk; 1874, C. E. S. McKee; 1876–78, William S. Swartz; 1880, John D. Swartz.

Members of Common Council.—1865, Thomas A. Boult, William Hall, Wm. H. Protzman, M. S. Barber, R. Sliker; 1866, M. S. Barber, Thomas A. Boult, William Hall, R. Sliker, Wm. H. Protzman; 1868, George S. Miller, Thos. A. Boult, M. J. Kinyon, Daniel White, Robert Warner; 1869, M. A. Berry, Upton Rouskulp, M. J. McKinnon, John D. Swartz, Jonathan Middlekauff; 1870, George Fechtig, George Lias, Upton Rouskulp, John D. Swartz, M. L. Bowman; 1871, George Fechtig, Joseph B. Loose, Upton Rouskulp, John D. Swartz, M. L. Bowman; 1872, M. A. Berry, Lewis Schindle, Lewis Delamater; 1878, Joseph H. Firey, J. W. Monath, D. F. Hull, John D. Swartz, John W. Boward; 1879, Joseph H. Fiery, D. F. Hull, Lewis Delamater; 1880, Charles M. Futterer, Henry Doanberger; 1881, J. C. Roulette, Joseph H. Firey, D. F. Hull.

Early Notes and Reminiscences.—In 1805 there were about two hundred and fifty houses on Washington, Potomac, Antietam, Locust, and Franklin

Streets. They were nearly all built of logs, very substantial and roomy, and a very few were of brick. Upton Lawrence, Samuel Hughes, Mr. Brent, and John Thomson Mason, the elder, were the principal lawyers. Brent and Otho Stull, who succeeded Mr. Beltzhoover as the proprietor of the Washington Hotel, fought a duel in 1805, in Virginia, and Brent was shot in the knee. Old Dr. Frederick Dorsey attended them as their surgeon. Joseph I. Merrick removed to Hagerstown soon after, and was a very brilliant lawyer.

Two of the oldest houses in Hagerstown are Kirschtenfeter's, on Potomac Street, built by the elder Knapp in 1778, and the stone house now occupied as the office of the Hagerstown Agricultural Works, on South Washington Street, which was built in 1781.

From time immemorial Tuesday has been observed as "public day" in Hagerstown. The same custom prevails in most of the other county towns of Maryland, but in Hagerstown it has always been marked with peculiar observances. Even at the present day the people from the surrounding country assemble from miles around in order to transact their business and discuss the political situation. On these occasions peripatetic "fakers" ply a thriving trade in "thimblerigging" and other games shrewdly calculated to deceive the unwary and ease them of their cash, and the whole town is full of bustle and excitement.

Harry Cookus was one of the oddities of Hagerstown about seventy years ago. He was a large, corpulent man, weighing considerably over two hundred pounds, and was always strolling about, apparently waiting for something to turn up. He had been a recruiting sergeant and a soldier in the war of 1812. His favorite occupation, like many other prominent citizens in the town, was cock-fighting, and his elation or depression as his favorite chicken conquered or was vanquished is described as having been manifested by the most ludicrous writhings and contortions. Jacob Yeakle, who carrried on the business of tinsmith in a log house on West Washington Street, was also a most peculiar character. He kept several fine horses, and rode with the practiced ease and skill of an Arab.

When the post-office became vacant by the death of William Krebs, who had been postmaster for many years, there was quite an exciting contest among a number of applicants for the vacancy. As there was then no direct travel between Hagerstown and Washington City, except on horseback, each of the candidates started themselves or dispatched couriers to the capital to procure the possession of the desired vacancy. Yeakle was employed by Daniel H. Schnebly to carry his application to the seat of government. Some of them got the start of Yeakle, but he overtook them on the banks of the Monocacy beyond Frederick Town, and while they were waiting to be ferried over he plunged his horse in, swam the river, arrived in Washington first, and procured the appointment for his employer, and came back triumphant ahead of them all. Charles Ohlwein also achieved a local reputation by his bluntness in discharging the rather delicate duties of a constable. On one occasion he had a bill against a certain "very respectable" gentleman to collect, and instead of approaching him privately, blurted out one day in the street, "Say, Mr. ——, I've got a warrant for you." The "very respectable" gentleman was, of course, highly indignant, and the constable, concluding that he was the wrong man for the place, gave up his position and returned to his trade, that of a stonemason. Maj. Benjamin Galloway, who lived on the southwest corner of Washington and Jonathan Streets, in the house now occupied by E. W. Mealey, was another man of peculiar characteristics. He was a graduate of Eton College, England, and often prided himself upon that fact. He was quite a politician, and was always in his element when there was any political excitement. He was somewhat erratic, but always honest. He was frequently desirous of a seat in the Legislature, but having but few of the elements of popularity about him, he was often defeated or ruled out. On one occasion, however, after the death or resignation of a member of the Legislature, he was returned to fill the unexpired term. He was a man of strong prejudices, and vented his feeling against his opponents in placards and in doggerel verse, which he read aloud in the streets whenever he could obtain an audience to listen.

Considerable excitement was created one day in Hagerstown, about 1805, by the announcement that the old Episcopal church was haunted. The report arose from the fact that a large black dog got into the building on Sunday and went to sleep without being observed. When he awoke the door was locked, and his howls and frantic efforts to get out alarmed the neighborhood. It is a curious evidence of the prevalence of superstition at the time that the people generally jumped to the conclusion that the church was inhabited by ghosts. It was also gravely asserted that when the door was opened the dog sprang over the heads of twenty men.

An even more significant illustration of the superstition then prevailing is found in the conduct of the people immediately after the execution of the three Cotterills,—the father and his two sons. Some of the spectators, we are told, struggled fiercely for fragments of the ropes with which the men were hanged. Their object in striving to get possession of them was to wear them as "charms" against disease or misfortune. It is asserted that the bodies of the executed men were stolen from their graves by resurrectionists and dissected by local physicians. Upton Lawrence, the principal lawyer for the defense of the criminals, is described by Dr. W. H. Grimes as having been a genial, whole-souled man, of medium size, with dark complexion, piercing black eyes, black hair, and very pleasing address.

Old "Oak Spring" has been a famous local resort in Hagerstown for a great many years. It is situated on West Franklin Street, and the water flows from beneath the roots of an ancient oak, which is the only one remaining of the original forest. It is related that an aged Indian, who passed through Hagerstown about 1816, recognized the spring as the one at which he had often slaked his thirst in his boyhood. The water is famous for its sweetness and purity. In 1856 the town authorities inclosed the lot in which it stands with a substantial brick wall. The bowl of the spring was deepened and enlarged and a stone wall was thrown up around it.

One of the local features of Hagerstown was the general muster of the county militia, which was held in October of every year. There were sometimes over two thousand men in line.

A peculiar custom, by no means indigenous to Hagerstown, however, was the suspension, on the eve of St. Patrick's day, in some conspicuous place, of a dummy figure, popularly denominated a "Paddy," with the view of annoying the Irish residents of the town and vicinity. On several occasions this foolish practice provoked serious disturbances, which, however, ended without bloodshed.

In 1805, George Strouse built about the first of the large brick houses. It was located at the corner of Locust and Washington Streets. About this time there was a race-track out Locust Street on the Funkstown road, and races were run in four-mile heats. Among those most active in getting them up were Alfred Kline, Jonathan Hager, John Ragan, Maj. Bailey, Thomas McCardell, and William Fegley. Purses of five hundred dollars were contested for, and the meetings were held every fall. Horses from distant points, such as New York, Virginia, and Kentucky, as well as horses nearer home, from many different localities, took part in them. Betting was very heavy. Lafayette and White Stocking were famous winners. White Stocking slipped, while running one day in a light rain, and broke his leg. Gen. Samuel Ringgold had fine horses, but he was unlucky, and never won more than two races. Gen. Williams had a course at Springfield, and used to train his horses there. Gen. Williams was very fortunate in his races.

Stone's tavern, on Potomac Street, was a notorious gambling resort about 1805. George Stone is described as having been very gentlemanly and pleasing in his manners, but was always determined to win his intended victim's money, whether by fair means or foul. It is related that on one occasion a woman entered the tavern and "collaring" her husband, picked up his hat and forced him to leave with her. The tavern was the scene of many fierce brawls and violent deeds.

The old jail stood in an alley between Washington and Franklin Streets, and was an old log house, looking very much like a stable. There were little peep-holes for windows, and the door was thickly studded with huge spikes. Elbert, the jailer, was shot previous to 1805, by a prisoner named Orndorf, while the latter was endeavoring to escape.

About 1805 both town and country people were very sociable, and balls were frequently given at the Globe Tavern. No man was asked to an apple-butter boiling, which was one of the favorite amusements, unless he would consent to dance.

"Fourth of July" was always celebrated at Hagerstown in early days with a good deal of enthusiasm. In 1810, for instance, it was observed with a parade, volleys of artillery, and a dinner at the Cold Spring, south of the town. The cannon used was a large one, which lay unmounted on the hill just east of the town. It subsequently burst, killing one man, George Bower, and so seriously wounding another, George Gelwig, that his leg had to be amputated.

In olden times there was a singular custom prevalent among the people of designating a person by the trade or occupation followed, or from some particular habit or act done or committed. For instance, an old man who drove a two-horse team and did most of the local transportation about town was known everywhere by the pseudonym of "Bopple Miller," from a habit he had of talking a great deal in a loud and rapid manner. He had small bells attached to his horses' necks, so that any one having hauling to do knew by the tinkling of his little bells that "Bopple Miller" was about. A man residing in West Washington Street, who supplied his customers with bread and cakes, was always known as "Berker Hanus." So a man who had appropriated some bacon not legitimately his own was ever afterwards known as "Speck Martin."

"Cold Spring," situated about half a mile from

Hagerstown, near the Williamsport road, was a very popular resort in early times. The water gushes forth from the rock in a pure and limped stream, and the surroundings are of a charming character. The spring is situated in a sequestered dale, and was the favorite resort for picnics, etc.

Negro "runaways" appear to have been very numerous about 1817, as we find in a single number of the Hagerstown *Herald*, under date of Sept. 17, 1817, four advertisements of rewards for slaves who had disappeared. The rewards offered were ten, twenty, and fifty dollars.

In the Hagerstown *Herald* of Feb. 7, 1799, Samuel Hughes, Jr., advertised for sale "the house wherein I now keep my office, with a valuable lot belonging thereto."

Fishing in the Antietam was a favorite sport in the latter portion of the last century; so much so that, in 1798, John Booth, Elijah Cheney, George Powell, John Shafer, Jeremiah Cheney, Nicholas Broadstone, Matthias Springer, Nicholas Frankhauser, John Smith, Joseph Cheney, Stephen Foller, Edward Breathed, Elizabeth South, Christian Binckley, Jacob Sharer, and John Claggett advertised that as very great inconvenience had arisen from sundry persons fishing in the creek, they would not thereafter allow any persons to fish in the creek unless they first obtained permission.

On Wednesday afternoon, at two o'clock, Oct. 20, 1790, the approach of President Washington was announced in Hagerstown. Capt. Rezin Davis, of the light-horse, with a number of the prominent citizens of the place, met the distinguished visitor about three miles from town and escorted him to its environs, where they were met by a company of infantry commanded by Capt. Ott. The Presidential escort was then conducted through Washington Street amid the welcoming shouts of the inhabitants who lined the sidewalks and filled the windows, doors, etc., along the route of the procession. The bells of the city were also rung during the march. President Washington was conducted to Beltzhoover's tavern, where "an elegant supper was prepared by direction, of which the President and principal inhabitants partook." In the evening the town was illuminated, bonfires appeared in all quarters, and every demonstration of joy and enthusiasm was indulged in. At the close of the banquet the following toasts were drunk, accompanied with a discharge of artillery and volley of musketry to each:

1. "The President of the United States."

To this toast Gen. Washington responded in a few fitting remarks, and proposed the toast, "Prosperity to the inhabitants of Elizabeth-Town."

2. "The Legislature of the United States."
3. "The land we live in."
4. "The river Potomac."
5. "May the residence law be perpetuated, and Potomac view the Federal City."
6. "An increase of American manufactories."
7. "May commerce and agriculture flourish."
8. "The National Assembly of France."
9. "The Marquis de Lafayette."
10. "May the spirit of liberty liberate the world."
11. "The memory of those who fell in defense of American liberty."
12. "The memory of Dr. Franklin."
13. "May America never want virtuous citizens to defend her liberty."

The feast terminated before ten o'clock, and on the following morning, at seven o'clock, Gen. Washington resumed his journey to Williamsport, where, after a short stay, he took his passage down the river to his home at Mount Vernon. During his visit at Hagerstown the following address was presented to him by the citizens:

"To the President of the United States:

"Sir,—We, the inhabitants of Elizabeth Town and its vicinity, being deeply impressed with your illustrious character, and sensibly awake to your resplendent and innumerable virtues, hail you a hearty welcome!

"We are happy to find that, notwithstanding your perils, toils, and guardianship, you are still able to grant us this first, this greatest of all favors,—*your presence*.

"We felicitate ourselves on your exploring our country, and as you already reign in our hearts, so we should think ourselves doubly blessed could we have the honor to be included within your more especial command and jurisdiction,—within the grand centre of virtues.

"Our beloved Chief! Be pleased to accept our most grateful thanks for this honor conferred on us. And may the disposer of all things lengthen out your days, so that you may behold with satisfaction the virtue and prosperity of the people whom you have made free! And when you come to close the last volume of your illustrious actions, may you be crowned with a crown not made with hands!

"Thomas Sprigg,
"Henry Shryock,
"William Lee,
"In behalf of the whole."

The President returned the following reply:

"Gentlemen,—The cordial welcome which you gave me to Elizabeth Town, and the very flattering expressions of regard contained in your address, claim and receive my grateful and sincere acknowledgments.

"Estimating as I do the affection and esteem of my fellow-citizens, and conscious that my best pretension to their approbation is founded in an earnest endeavor faithfully to discharge the duties which have been assigned me, I cannot better reply to their confidence than by assuring them that the same impartiality which has heretofore directed, will continue to govern my conduct in the execution of public trusts.

"I offer sincere wishes for your temporal happiness and future felicity.

"G. Washington."

Washington Street, Hagerstown, was so named because Gen. Washington and his escort passed down that thoroughfare in proceeding through the town.

June 8, 1791, the editor of the Washington *Spy*, at Hagerstown, announced that he had been disappointed in receiving any papers from Baltimore by the last post. "The reason assigned by the person who came as post was that owing to a horse-race at Baltimore the post-office was shut."

On the 28th of December, 1792, the commissioners of Hagerstown prohibited the firing of guns and pistols in the town.

In March, 1792, by direction of the town commissioners, the Hagerstown market was ordered to be opened at sunrise on each market-day, of which notice was to be given by ringing the court-house bell.

On the 4th of May, 1801, Albert Gallatin, then recently appointed Secretary of the United States Treasury, stopped at Hagerstown with his family, on his way to Washington to assume the duties of his office.

In 1794 the following advertisement appeared in the Washington *Spy*:

"100 DOLLARS REWARD.

"Whereas, some evil-disposed person or person set up at the Market-House in this Town, last night, an advertisement in the German Language, charging us with having cut down the pole lately erected in this town, termed by the deluded authors of its erection a liberty-pole, and commanding us in menacing terms to erect another in its stead, or that we shall surely be put to death by the sword. And as the authors of said dangerous threats ought to be brought to condign punishment, We hereby offer a reward of One hundred Dollars to any person or persons who will give such information of the author or authors of the said advertisement, or of the person or persons who set up the same, that he or they may be brought to justice; to be paid on conviction.

"HENRY SHYROCK,
"REZIN DAVIS,
"ALEXANDER CLAGETT,
"ADAM OTT,
"JOHN GEIGER,
"JACOB SHRYOCK,
"WILLIAM WILLIAMS."

This pole had been erected by the whisky insurrectionists, but was cut down at night, and, as shown above, a placard was posted ordering some of the principal inhabitants, mentioning them by name, to put up another pole, but the threat was not regarded except by the publication of the above reward.

One of the earliest celebrations of the Fourth of July was that which took place in 1796. The Washington Blues, commanded by Capt. Jacob Schnebly, the mechanics of the town, and other citizens took part in the parade. A public dinner was given, and toasts were drunk, accompanied by discharges of artillery. Thomas Sprigg was chairman of the meeting, and Daniel Heister was vice-president. In the following year, on the same anniversary,

"a number of citizens, and the Washington Blues, Capt. J. Schnebly, met at Mr. Hager's, at Fountain Inn. After the usual evolutions they proceeded to Mr. Smith's tavern to dinner, where a number of toasts were drunk."

On the 15th of June, 1798, the companies of light infantry commanded by Capts. Rutledge and Davis held a meeting at Hagerstown, and adopted an address to the President concerning the threatened troubles with France. The correspondence which resulted was as follows:

"TO THE PRESIDENT OF THE UNITED STATES:

"Permit us, sir, the companies of infantry commanded by Capts. Rutledge and Davis, of Washington County, and the State of Maryland, to join the general voices of our countrymen in addressing you upon the present important and critical situation of our national affairs; to express our sincere affection for the government of our choice, and our firm determination at every hazard to support it. While we contemplate with the liveliest emotions of sorrow the unhappy issue which your late attempts to accommodate our differences with France are likely to experience, we cannot but derive peculiar consolation from the belief that nothing has been left undone on your part to have insured them a very different fate, and we are persuaded, sir, if the friendly disposition manifested by your instructions to our envoys at Paris had been met with a similar disposition on the part of the present rulers of that nation, the two republics would ere now have been reunited in the closest bonds of amity and friendship. Under this impression, and with full confidence in the wisdom, patriotism, moderation, and energy of our united councils, we deem it our duty to declare that we will support with promptitude and firmness such measures as they may find themselves indispensably called upon to adopt for our mutual defence and security. We hope, sir, that this address will not be less acceptable because a majority exercising the rights of freemen have not only indulged, but freely expressed their opinions, in opposition to certain measures of government. It ought, we conceive, rather to enhance its value, inasmuch as it offers to the world an animating proof that the American people, however they may differ in their sentiments as to their interior arrangements and regulations, will always be found ready to unite and defend with their lives and fortunes, the honor, dignity, and independence of their country, whenever they shall be assailed by any foreign power on earth.

"Signed by desire and in behalf of said companies.

"ABRAHAM RUTLEDGE,
"DENNIS DAVIS,
"*Captains.*

"June 15, 1798."

The following was President Adams' reply:

"TO THE COMPANIES OF INFANTRY COMMANDED BY CAPTS. RUTLEDGE AND DAVIS, OF WASHINGTON COUNTY, IN THE STATE OF MARYLAND.

"GENTLEMEN,—I thank you for this address, presented to me by your representative in Congress, Mr. Baer.

"The sincere affection you express for the government of your choice, and determination at every hazard to support it, are the more acceptable, because a majority of you, exercising the rights of freemen, have not only indulged, but freely expressed their opinions in regard to certain measures of government. I cannot, however, upon this occasion, forbear to lament the gross misrepresentations which have misled so many citizens in their opinions of many measures.

"JOHN ADAMS.

"PHILADELPHIA, June 25, 1798."

In the Hagerstown *Herald* of Feb. 14, 1799, the following advertisement appeared:

"To be rented, for one or two years, and possession to be given the 1st of April next, the house and lot where George Diffenderfer now lives, three doors above Mr. Shall's tavern.

"This stand is well calculated for a tradesman, as there is a convenient back building adjoining the house very suitable for a store. For terms apply to

"HENRY HOOVER.

"HAGERSTOWN, Feb. 14, 1799."

In the same paper of July 7, 1802, appeared the following:

"All persons are hereby forewarned from taking assignments on certain bonds given by me to Capt. Peregrine Fitzhugh, late of Washington County, in consideration of a tract of land called Chew's Farm, which I purchased from him, he not having complied with his agreement concerning the same. I am, therefore, determined not to pay said bonds, or any part thereof, until he shall have complied with his contract, unless compelled by law.

"HENRY LOCHAR.

"WASHINGTON COUNTY, July 5, 1802."

On the Fourth of July, 1799, Capt. Schnebly's troop of Washington Blues, after parading and going through various evolutions, repaired to Peck's Garden, in Hagerstown, where they had dinner and drank a number of toasts. The garden was handsomely illuminated, and was visited by a number of citizens. On the same day "a respectable number of the citizens," together with a company of the Twenty-fourth Regiment of militia, assembled "at the usual place of parade," before Maj. Ott's, "to celebrate the national anniversary." Maj. Ott presided, and Capt. Douglass acted as vice-president. After appropriate addresses, etc., they marched to "Mr. Rohrer's Spring, near town, where a handsome entertainment was prepared for them." Having refreshed themselves, "they withdrew to an adjoining eminence and drank a number of toasts, accompanied with cheers and discharges of cannon and small-arms."

Gen. Washington's death was announced by the Hagerstown *Herald* in the following extract from the *Rights of Man*, published at Frederick:

"FREDERICKTOWN, Tuesday evening,
"9 o'clock, Dec. 16, 1799.

"Disagreeable as the talk is to me, I think it is my duty to announce to the public the Dissolution of his excellency George Washington, who died at Mount Vernon (of a few hours' illness) on Sunday morning last, about 5 o'clock.

"This intelligence was received by two honest countrymen, who left Georgetown yesterday at 12 o'clock, and stopped at Maj. Miller's tavern about four this evening. A third person arrived from Alexandria near the same hour, who corroborates the melancholy circumstance, and leaves us to lament it is but too true.

"PRINTER OF THE RIGHTS OF MAN."

As soon as the news reached Hagerstown a meeting was held, at which it was resolved to have a funeral procession in Washington's honor on Friday of the following week. Elie Williams occupied the chair, and Nathaniel Rochester acted as secretary. The following resolutions were adopted:

"*Resolved*, That Messrs. Elie Williams, Adam Ott, N. Rochester, Jacob Schnebly, George Waltz, William Fitzhugh, Samuel Ringgold, David Harry, Josiah Price, Thomas Sprigg, and Daniel Heister be appointed a committee to make the necessary arrangements for, and to superintend, the said Procession, and that they or a majority of them meet at the Court-house, on Saturday next, to make the arrangements.

"*Resolved*, That the Committee consult the Rev. Mr. Smucker, Rev. Mr. Rauhauser, and Rev. Mr. Bower on the oration to be delivered on the occasion.

"*Resolved*, That the Military and other citizens of Washington County be, and that they are hereby invited to attend and join the said Procession.

"*Resolved*, That the secretary have these proceedings published in the papers of this town to-morrow.

"By order.

"N. ROCHESTER, *Secretary*."

In May, 1800, while the Tenth Regiment United States troops, commanded by Col. Moore, were stopping at Hagerstown on their way from Carlisle to Harper's Ferry, a duel was fought between Capt. Gibbs and Lieut. Franklin, in which the former was wounded in the side, but not seriously.

In January, 1807, a duel was fought in Shepherdstown, Va., between Wm. L. Brent and Otho H. W. Stull, both of Washington County. Mr. Brent was wounded in the leg.

Early in July, 1801, ten prisoners broke out of the jail. They were Wm. Dunn, John Johnson, James McDeid, Michael Ward, J. McCreery, Andrew Dawd, John Johnson, Wm. Harvey, John Lynch, and William Jolly.

Five Indian chiefs of the Pottawotamie tribe passed through Hagerstown in December, 1801, on their return from Washington City, accompanied by a Capt. Wells, who acted as their interpreter. Among them were the powerful chiefs "Little Turtle" and "The Toad." In January of the following year the "kings" of the Delaware and Shawnee tribes, nine chiefs and two attendants, passed through Hagerstown. In March of the same year fifteen Indians of the Seneca tribe passed through Hagerstown. Among them was the well-known chief Cornplanter. Doubtless many similar delegations passed through Hagerstown from time to time.

John Randolph of Roanoke visited Hagerstown

in July, 1803, and was tendered and accepted a dinner at John Ragan's tavern.

In 1804 the Fourth of July was celebrated with the usual artillery salute and the parade of the Washington Blues, under the command of Capt. Otho H. Williams. A public dinner was also served at Ragan's tavern. Gen. Thomas Spring was president of the day, and Capt. Otho H. Williams vice-president. The Declaration of Independence was read by Benjamin Galloway, after which a number of toasts were drunk. On this occasion Sebastian Fink was severely wounded in the thigh by the bursting of a swivel.

George Clinton, Vice-President of the United States, visited the town in June, 1809, while on his way to New York.

In 1821 it was proposed to erect a statue to Gen. Washington in the public square, but no further action appears to have been taken in the matter. The monument was to have been of Washington County marble, and was to have included a fountain, etc. At the November election of that year the sum of one hundred and six dollars was contributed by the voters in the different districts towards the completion of the Washington monument at Washington City, D. C.

During Lafayette's visit to this country in 1824 it was proposed that he should visit Hagerstown among other places in Maryland. In September of that year a public meeting was held at the court-house in Hagerstown, at which Willian Gabby presided, and J. Schnebly acted as secretary. The following resolutions were adopted:

"The citizens of Hagerstown and Washington County, participating in the general joy of the American people on the appearance among them of the distinguished and gallant Gen. Lafayette; deeply impressed with the importance and value of his services in their eventful and glorious struggle for independence; and being desirous of manifesting in a suitable manner their veneration for his person and character, have therefore

"*Resolved*, That Col. O. H. Williams, Col. F. Tilghman, the Hon. John Buchanan, William Price, and V. W. Randall, Esqs., be appointed a committee on behalf of this meeting to wait on Gen. Lafayette on his arrival in the city of Baltimore, tendering him their hearty congratulations, and inviting him to visit their county.

"*Resolved*, That the proceedings of this meeting be published.

"WILLIAM GABBY, *Chairman*.

"JACOB SCHNEBLY, *Secretary*."

At a subsequent meeting the committee reported their proceedings, as follows:

"That they repaired to Baltimore upon the arrival of the general at that place, and on Friday, the 8th inst., were introduced to him, at his quarters in Light Street, by the city authorities.

"Col. Williams, as chairman of the committee, then addressed him as follows: 'General, the spontaneous burst of grateful enthusiasm which has been elicited by your recent return to the United States is without parallel in the history of any modern people; it is not confined to our populous cities, but has diffused itself to the remotest borders of our country.

"'The citizens of Washington County, Md., largely participating in this general feeling, have deputed us to wait on you, and directed us to tender to you their warm and heart-felt congratulations on your return to a country whose rights you defended and whose liberties you greatly assisted to achieve. They have also directed us to present to you an invitation to visit them so soon as it may suit your convenience. Although we cannot compete with our brethren of the great commercial cities on the sea-board in the reception we shall give you, yet so far as the pure incense of grateful hearts, and the frank and cordial hospitality of republican manners, can supply the deficiency of pomp and splendor, we can affirm there shall be nothing wanting.

"'We feel proud, general, of the distinction conferred on us, in being made the organ of a community of freemen, through which this slight tribute of respect is presented to the champion of liberty in both hemispheres, the early and strong advocate of America, and the bosom friend of the illustrious father of our country. Be pleased to accept the assurance of our great personal esteem and affection.'"

To this address the general replied that he felt highly gratified by an invitation from the citizens of Washington County, and that he would, with great pleasure, pay them a visit at the earliest opportunity.

At a meeting of the citizens of Washington County at the court-house in Hagerstown, on Wednesday, the 27th of October, 1824, Col. David Schnebly was called to the chair, and R. M. Tidball was appointed secretary. The following resolutions were proposed and adopted:

"*Resolved*, That the following citizens be appointed a committee to make such arrangements and adopt such measures as they may deem necessary for the reception and entertainment of Gen. Lafayette in Hagerstown, viz.: John Hershey, Dr. F. Dorsey, Richard Ragan, Frisby Tilghman, William Heyser, P. Humrickhouse, Col. William D. Bell, Joseph Graff, Stewart Herbert, George I. Harry, George Brumbaugh, Alexander Neill, Jacob Schnebly, John Robertson, John Harry, Charles Shaffner, John Albert, F. Anderson, John Curry, A. Johnston, Samuel Hughes, Henry Kealhofer, Eli Beatty, Dr. J. Reynolds, T. Eichelberger, John Ragan, George Shryock, Jacob Motter, Daniel Schnebly, Maj. J. Reynolds, John Gruber, J. V. Swearingen, David Artz, Dr. W. D. Macgill, M. Rickenbaugh, Henry Dillman, Frederick Stover, David Clagett, William Gabby, George Shiess, John Witmer, Peter Seibert, William Webb, Col. D. Schnebly, Thomas Keller, Andrew Kershner, John Bowles, Henry Ankeny, John Barnett, Arthur Jacques, B. Kershner, Thomas C. Brent, James H. Bowles, Robert Mason, Benjamin Bean, Anthony Snyder, Dr. M. A. Finley, Daniel Weisel, Dr. W. Van Lear, William Dickey, Col. J. Blackford, Dr. Joseph C. Hays, Jacob Miller, Dr. T. Hammond, George Hedrick, William P. Stewart, Dr. Ezra Slifer, Jonathan Shafer, M. Stonebraker, Alexander Mitchell, Dr. C. Boerstler, Henry Shafer, W. Fitzhugh, Jr., Elias Davis, Jacob I. Ohr.

"*Resolved*, That the members composing the Committee of Arrangements be notified by the chairman and secretary of their appointment, and be requested to meet at the town-hall on Saturday, the 6th of November, at four o'clock A.M., for the purpose of entering on the duties of their appointment.

"*Resolved*, That the Military Committee be respectfully requested to communicate with the Civil Committee of Arrangements on the object in contemplation."

On motion of D. G. Yost, it was

"*Resolved*, unanimously, that a committee be appointed to address the representative in Congress from this District in behalf of this meeting, and to request him to use his influence in procuring a suitable appropriation from our government for Gen. Lafayette for his meritorious services in our Revolutionary struggle. David G. Yost, William Price, and Frisby Tilghman, Esqs., were appointed the committee.

"*Resolved*, That the above proceedings be published in the several newspapers of the place for the information of the citizens generally.

"DAVID SCHNEBLY, *Chairman*.
"R. M. TIDBALL, *Secretary*."

At a meeting of the officers attached to the Second Brigade, Maryland Militia, convened at the town hall in Hagerstown on Saturday, the 30th inst., Gen. Samuel Ringgold was appointed chairman, and Capt. V. W. Randall secretary. The following preamble and resolutions were adopted:

"*Whereas*, The acceptance by Gen. Lafayette of the invitation given him by the citizens of Washington County will soon afford them an opportunity of testifying their respect and affection for our illustrious guest, it becomes necessary that arrangements should be made forthwith for receiving and welcoming him in such a manner as will evince an attachment to the benefactor and friend of our country. Therefore

"*Resolved*, That the following officers be a Committee of Ways and Means: Col. Wellier, Col. Fouke, Lieut.-Col. Wolf, Majs. Rohrback, Hall, and Sprecker, Capts. Barr, Swearingen, Beall, Funk, Kessinger, Grosh, Brookhartt, Donnelly, Fletcher, Baker, Barnett, Lieuts. Hallman, H. Shafer, and J. Zwisler.

"*Resolved*, That the Committee of Arrangements and the Committee of Ways and Means assemble at the town hall on Saturday next at 10 o'clock A.M., to confer with the committee appointed on Wednesday last by the citizens, and to co-operate with them in making the necessary arrangements for the reception of Gen. Lafayette."

At the reception in Frederick a company of riflemen from Hagerstown, commanded by Capt. V. W. Randall, was present, and elicited the warmest commendation for its drill and evolutions.

Gen. Lafayette was unable to visit Hagerstown, but we give the foregoing account as a curious picture of the times and of the spirit then pervading the counties of Maryland.

On the 15th of July, 1826, it was resolved "that the citizens of Washington County be requested to meet at the court-house at Hagerstown on Saturday, July 22d, to arrange for a public tribute of respect to the memory of John Adams and Thomas Jefferson." In accordance with this resolution "a large and respectable meeting" was held at the court house in Hagerstown on the 22d of July, 1826. David Schnebly was elected chairman, and Thomas Kellar secretary. The following resolutions were adopted:

"Having heard with the deepest sorrow and most unfeigned regret of the deaths of Thomas Jefferson and John Adams, and desirous to evince to the world in common with our fellow-citizens of these United States the great veneration and respect we entertain for the characters of those illustrious patriots of the Revolution, for their pure and exalted worth, pre-eminent talents, and long and faithful public services, we therefore resolve as follows, viz.:

"1st. *Resolved*, That there be a public procession in Hagerstown on Tuesday, the first day of August next.

"2d. *Resolved*, That the citizens of this county be requested to wear crape on their left arm for sixty days, and the ladies be solicited to wear badges of mourning for the same period.

"3d. *Resolved*, That the clergymen of the different congregations of this county be requested to preach an appropriate sermon in their respective churches at such times as may be convenient.

"4th. *Resolved*, That in order to impress the minds of the rising generation with the virtues and characters of those illustrious dead, the teachers of the public schools in this county be requested to read at least once a week for two months obituary notices of those benefactors of mankind.

"5th. *Resolved*, That the committee of arrangements request their fellow-citizens to deliver an eulogium on the above solemn occasion; also request two clergymen to address the Throne of Grace.

"6th. *Resolved*, That the citizens of Hagerstown be requested to abstain from all business during the procession.

"7th. *Resolved*, That the chairman of this meeting, together with such other persons to be named by him, constitute the committee of arrangements, who shall have power to carry the foregoing resolutions into full effect, and make all other arrangements which the occasion may require.

"8th. *Resolved*, That the bells in the different churches in this county be tolled for one hour on the morning and evening of the day of the procession."

The following persons composed the committee of arrangements: "David Schnebly, chairman, Samuel Ringgold, William Gabby, Frederick Dorsey, Thomas Kennedy, George W. Boerstler, Otho H. Williams.

The committee held a meeting soon afterwards and agreed on the following order of procession:

Chief Marshal.
Revolutionary officers and soldiers in carriages.
Committee of arrangements.
Choristers.
Orator and officiating clergy.
Clergy of the county.
Moderator and commissioners.
Judges and officers of the court.
Judges of Orphans' Court.
Judges of Levy Court.
Members of the bar.
Physicians.
Students of divinity, physic, and law.
Teachers, with their pupils.
Representatives in Congress.
Delegates of the General Assembly.
Officers of the United States army and navy.
Militia officers.
Band.
Masonic brethren.
Citizens.

The procession rested with its right near the court-house, at the intersection of Washington and Jonathan Streets, and moved up Jonathan to Franklin Street, down Franklin to Potomac, up Potomac to the "stone" church, then countermarched down Potomac Street to the Lutheran church, which it entered in the same order. The officers of the army, navy, and militia appeared in uniform with crape on the left arm, and the usual badges of mourning on their side-arms. The ladies of the choir and the young girls attached to the different schools were dressed in white with a black ribband around the waist. One gun was fired at dawn, another at twelve o'clock, and a third at sundown, and the bells of the different churches tolled during the procession, which was under the direction of a chief marshal on horseback, with his assistants on foot, all of whom were designated by white sashes and wands.

A public meeting was held at the court-house, in Hagerstown, on the 24th of July, 1827, at which a committee was appointed to meet the engineers employed in surveying the proposed route of the Baltimore and Ohio Railroad and give them all the information in their power. William Gabby was selected as chairman, and William D. Bell was chosen secretary. After remarks by Dr. John Reynolds and Col. Otho H. Williams, the committee was appointed, as follows:

District No. 1, Col. John Miller, Robert Clagett; No. 2, Joseph Hollman, Col. Daniel Malott; No. 3, Gen. Samuel Ringgold, Col. Henry Fouke; No. 4, Lancelot Jacques, Henry Fiery; No. 5, John Johnson, Anthony Snider; No. 6, David Brookhartt, Elie Crampton; No. 7, M. W. Boyd, John Welty.

In December, 1827, the Hagerstown *Torch-Light* announced that Lieut. Dillehunt and a party of engineers had examined the route through Harman's Gap to the Antietam, thence down the stream to a point below Funkstown, and thence to Williamsport.

On the 4th of July, 1828, a number of gentlemen from Hagerstown repaired to the Black Rocks on South Mountain and celebrated the day in festive fashion with a good dinner, toasts, etc., and encamped there all night.

In the Hagerstown papers of April 7, 1841, there appeared an advertisement of Wise's twenty-sixth balloon ascension, announced to take place on the afternoon of the 24th day of that month from the prison-yard in Hagerstown.

During the performance of the circus company of J. M. June & Co., in Hagerstown, one evening early in October, 1850, some persons outside pulled down part of the canvas, and a conflict ensued between the circus people and the aggressors. The combatants fought for some time with dirks and clubs, and a number of persons were injured more or less severely.

On the 22d of May, 1872, Alexander Smith, Wesley Finnegan, and Frederick Fridinger were crushed to death by the falling of a wall of the court-house, which they were engaged in taking down. Smith was forty years of age, and lived on the Cavetown turnpike near Hagerstown. He served through the civil war, and was at the battle of Gettysburg. Finnegan was thirty-six years old, and had also been a Federal soldier. Fridinger was about seventeen years of age, and his father lost his life when the court-house was burned during the previous fall. On the Sunday following the catastrophe the three funerals took place, and the bodies were borne to the grave in a procession of Odd-Fellows, the Fire Department, and many citizens.

Hagerstown, like many other communities throughout the country, was invaded by the centennial epidemic, and a Martha Washington tea-party was the result. The entertainment was given on the evenings of the 18th and 19th of March, 1875, at Lyceum Hall. The following ladies were appointed on the various committees which managed the affair:

President, Mrs. Louis F. McComas; Vice-President, Albert Small; Treasurer, Miss Agnes McAtee; Secretary, Miss Nellie Gibson. Members of Committees: Mrs. J. E. McComas, Mrs. P. A. Brugh, Mrs. J. H. Seymour, Miss Lizzie Hagerman, Miss J. E. McComas, Mrs. Kate Fechtig, Mrs. Charles Bechtel, Miss Laura Kepler, Mrs. P. A. Brugh, Mrs. E. C. Bushnell, Mrs. P. B. Small, Mrs. N. B. Scott, Mrs. George Freaner, Mrs. S. D. Straub, Miss M. Robertson, Miss Lily Syester, Miss Ada McComas, Mrs. J. H. Van Lear, Mrs. David Zeller, Miss S. Thompson, Mrs. F. M. Darby, Miss Minnie Moon, Miss Cephie Herbert, Miss Nannie Cushwa.

In addition to these ladies the following gentlemen took part: Messrs. W. S. Herbert, C. A. Small, Albert Small, W. Harry, and Samuel Ogilby.

The executive committee consisted of Messrs. Straub, Small, Brugh, Kendall, and Rev. J. C. Thompson. Mrs. P. A. Brugh, Mrs. John H. Seymour, and Miss Nannie F. Little had charge of the fancy table. Among the interesting articles exhibited were the following: An oil-painting of Gen. Washington when forty-five years old, painted by Charles W. Peale, by order of Congress while the army was encamped at Valley Forge in 1777, which now belongs to Gen. T. J. McKaig; also a head of Washington woven in silk at Paris on a Jacquard loom (which was shortly afterwards destroyed), as fine-lined as a steel-engraving; also an engraving of Gen. Otho Holland Williams, the founder of Williamsport; a portrait of Commodore Jesse Duncan Elliott, born in Hagerstown in 1780; a portrait of John Henry Purviance, secretary to President Monroe, with an autograph letter from Samuel Purviance; also Robert Parker's certificate of membership in The Society of the Cincinnati, dated 1785, signed by George Washington. On the right of the stage was an oil-painting of Mrs. Gen. Heister, the only daughter of Jonathan Hager, painted in 1780.

On the east side of the stage was an Indian wigwam, in front of which was a table containing a number of articles of Indian workmanship. On the left of the stage there hung an engraving of President Monroe, taken from an original painting by I. Van der Lyn. On the stage was a chair one hundred and seventy-five years old, which belonged to Mrs. Dr. Bates; and a pair of arm-chairs, imported by Col. Daniel Hughes, of Antietam, in 1770, and another which belonged to Mrs. Murdock, of Frederick, one hundred and fifty years old; also a memorial picture, worked in silk by Rev. Mrs. Thompson's grandmother, Mrs. Hannah Upham, in 1797; a fac-simile of Washington's headquarters at Valley Forge; an autograph receipt from Gen. Washington to Mr. William McAnulty, dated Jan. 25, 1774; two auto_raph notes to Capt. Van Lear, inviting h m to dinner; a copy of "John Drane's Poems," published in 1560, and a number of other ancient volumes. In addition to these were the watch of Jonathan Hager (founder of Hagerstown) and the watch of Mrs. Gen. Heister, his daughter, together with articles worn by Capt. Jonathan Hager, of the Revolutionary army, including two embroidered vests, shoe-buckles, knee-buckles, suspender-buckles, stock-buckle, brooch, saddle ornaments, and Mrs. Hager's shoe-buckles. Besides these the exhibits comprised a copper kettle used by Lafayette while in the Revolutionary army, presented by him to Col. John Holker, of his staff; a medallion on satin of Louis XVI. and Marie Antoinette, presented to the Marquis de Lafayette, and given by him to Col. John Holker, agent of the French government during the Revolution; a pair of brass candlesticks, one hundred years old; a pair of solid silver goblets, one hundred and fifty years old, which belonged to Col. Hughes; a set of teaspoons and sugar-tongs, which were brought from Switzerland one hundred and twenty years before; an amber bead bracelet, which had been worn by six generations in succession; a set of tablespoons made in Hagerstown from Spanish half-dollars in 1785.

Among the china was a water-pitcher with the coat of arms of the thirteen original States, painted in 1778; a butter-dish and cup and saucer which were used in the family of President Monroe; a small box made out of the table on which the Declaration of Independence was written; a pitcher made the year after Washington died, to commemorate his death, which has on it a quaint picture; three dishes which were used in the Mitchell family when Maryland was a colony; an old set of china, used in the Price family over a hundred years; a set of spoons sent during the reign of George III. to Mrs. Kealhoffer's great-grandfather, then a missionary on the island of Jamaica.

The various supper-tables were ranged around the sides of the room, each table having the name and motto of the State it represented on the wall above it. The ladies in charge of the tables were:

Virginia, Misses Lily Cushwa and Lily Syester; New York, Misses Rene Boullt and Ada McComas; Connecticut, Misses Lily Seymour and Lottie Croynin; South Carolina, Misses Eva Foulke and Maggie Keller; Rhode Island, Misses Lily Scott and Nannie Ogilby; Massachusetts, Misses Kate Marshall and Sue Love; North Carolina, Mrs. Allan Yingling and Mrs. W. H. A. Hamilton; Delaware, Mrs. S. D. Straub and Miss Sue Herbert; Pennsylvania, Misses Bettie Zeller and Cephie Herbert; Maryland, Misses Emma Herbert and Mary McComas; New Jersey, Misses Nannie Cushwa and Lily Ogliby; New Hampshire, Mrs. E. C. Bushnel, Mrs. P. B. Small, and Misses Nellie Gibson, Eliza Keller, Annie Campbell, V. Dunn, and Mary Small; Georgia, Mrs. Kate Fechtig, Mrs. A. K. Syester, Mrs. C. Bechtel, Mrs. Joseph B. Loose, and Misses Louisa Johnson and Laura Keppler.

On the 6th of June, 1872, the first passenger-train over the Western Maryland Railroad from Baltimore arrived in Hagerstown. The run was made from Baltimore, 86 miles, in three hours and twenty minutes with seven stoppages. The train comprised the locomotive, which was tastefully decorated with flowers and flags, the baggage-car, and a new passenger-car. The latter contained a number of officials and invited guests, among whom were the president of the company, James L. McLane, and his predecessor in that office, George F. Bokee; Robert Hooper, secretary and treasurer; J. T. Rigney, general superintendent; B. H. Griswold, agent at Hagerstown; Mr. Hutton, chief engineer; Col. Longwell, of Carroll County; ex-Senator Briggs, of Frederick; John Welty, one of the Washington County directors; Col. Fred. Raine, of the *German Correspondent*, of Baltimore, and others. The conductors in charge of the train were Messrs. Besler and R. Stoner. The train was met by the mayor of Hagerstown and other municipal officers, together with a large assemblage of citizens. After being entertained at the residence of Mr. Harris, one of the directors, near the town, the visitors inspected the site of the depot, not then erected, and the officers of the company concluded the negotiations for its purchase with its owner, Richard Wise. In the afternoon they took dinner at the Washington House with the mayor and a number of other citizens of Hagerstown, after which they returned to Baltimore.

The Fourth of July, 1876, was observed in Hagerstown with elaborate and appropriate ceremonies. Two platforms were erected,—one in the southwest angle of the public square and the other in front of the court-house. The former was erected for the school of Joseph Updegraff, and the latter by the citizens of the town,—a spacious structure, which nearly covered one-half of the pavement in breadth, and was nearly the full length of the building.

Bunting was extensively displayed all over the town, and banners of all nations were flung to the breeze. The eve of the Fourth was celebrated by the school of Joseph Updegraff on their platform on the square, which was brilliantly festooned, and illuminated with Chinese lanterns interspersed among American flags. The exercises consisted of music led by Prof. Mentzer, and orations, recitations, and songs by members of the school, which continued until after ten o'clock, and were attended by a very large concourse of citizens.

At midnight the bells sounded a simultaneous peal, which was accompanied by the steam-whistles of the Agricultural Works on Washington Street. Next morning the procession formed as follows:

Chief Marshal, R. C. Thornburg.

Aides, M. M. Gruber, H. A. McComas, Oliver Ridenour, Dr. J. McP. Scott, and L. Delamarter.

The line moved up West Washington Street in the following order:

Hyser's Silver Cornet Band.

Omnibus containing thirteen of the oldest citizens, representing the thirteen original States of the Union, as follows: Frederick Humrickhouse, Samuel Newman, Samuel Ridenour, B. Costenbeder, D. Zeller, W. V. Heard, Frederick Fechtig, Geo. Crissinger, Michael Friese, Wm. Miller, George Hayes, Charles Martin, Elie Mobley.

Choir of young ladies,

representing the thirty-eight States, dresed in white, red, and blue, and seated on platform drawn by six horses.

Judges of Circuit Courts.

Hon. R. H. Alvey, Hon. D. Weisel, Hon. William Motter, Hon. George French, in carriage.

Orator and reader of the Declaration, in carriage.

Judge of the Orphans' Court, president and members of the board of county commissioners, and mayor and councilmen, in carriages.

Army of the Republic—Reno Post—on foot.

Parrott gun, mounted and officered and manned by Lieut. S. Martin, Dr. Crowther, George Kline, and William Crissinger. This piece fired one hundred rounds during the day,—thirteen at sunrise, thirty-eight at noon, and balance at sundown, at the rate of four rounds to the minute, from Cannon Hill, east of the town.

Boys' and Girls' Reading Association.

Winter's Band.

Boys in red, white, and blue.

Western Enterprise Fire Company,

in full force, dressed in uniform, red shirts, engine caparisoned and decorated, drawn by four grays, and truck decorated with a picture of Washington.

Field-piece on wheels, cast at Mount Ætna Furnace in 1774, under command of Capt. Wm. Sands.

Junior Engine,

trimmed with flags, and drawn by four grays.

First Hagerstown Hose Company,

upon whose engine was erected a temple of liberty, with appropriate canopy, under which was seated the goddess (Miss Sophie Updegraff), with the four corners guarded by Continental officer (Master Leah Cooper), Continental soldier (Master Fred. Ways), naval officer (Master Max Ways), and sailor (Master Walter Mobley). in the uniform of the Revolution.

First Hagerstown Hook-and-Ladder Company, with truck and equipments.

Gumbert & Mobley carriage in wagon, and attended by workmen.

"Centennial Band."

Willhide's cigar-works on wheels, and in full operation.

Hopple's pottery-works on wheels, and in full operation, turning out pots, and distributing them to the crowd in passing.

McComas' coal-wagon with load of coal.

Hagerstown foundry, represented by a pyramid of castings, drawn by two horses.

Singer's sewing-machine on wheels.

Bone-meal in bags

From the manufactory of Ames, Manning & Ames, at the old Hager mill, the bags packed in large hay-wagon and drawn by a full team.

Hagerstown Agricultural Implement Manufacturing Company,

led by the president, vice-president, treasurer, and secretary, in carriage drawn by two bays. Following this, drawn by distinct teams, were: 1. Cutting-machine; 2. Cutting-machine; 3. Cutting-machine; 4. Reaper; 5. Drill; 6. Drill; 7. Clover-huller in motion; 8. Workmen with their implements of labor appropriately festooned, and numbering in all forty men.

Schindle & Co.'s leather-works,

fitted up in three large wagons, with all of the hands performing their respective labors: 1. Working out the leather and shaving it down; 2. Pegging shoes; 3. Sewing leather by machinery.

Hagerstown Steam-Boiler Company,

with a separator decorated and in working order.

McKee & Bro.'s

wagon decorated with hardware.

Wm. Schlotterbeck,

wagon with emblems of his trade in stoves, etc.

Citizens in wagons with appropriate banners.

The procession having marched through the streets of the town according to programme, drew up in front of the court-house, when the officers of the day, the choir, and leading participants in the procession took their seats upon the platform, the Hon. Daniel Weisel having been called upon to preside. The young ladies and other musicians under Prof. Mentzer occupied the eastern division of the platform, the judges of the courts and other officials the western side, and in the centre were the aged men who represented the original States. The music was rendered with effect, the Declaration of Independence was read by W. H. A. Hamilton, of the Hagerstown bar, prayer was offered by the Rev. S. W. Owen, of St. John's Lutheran Church, and the oration was delivered by Hon. A. K. Syester.

In the afternoon there was a procession of the different Sabbath-schools, which concluded the day's proceedings. The heat of the day had gradually intensified until five o'clock, the hour fixed for this parade, when rain fell for half an hour, delaying and interrupting the proceedings. The ceremonies advertised had to be dispensed with on account of the rain, with the exception of the procession, which was formed in the following order by William H. Seidenstricker, chief marshal, with his aides, consisting of the superintendent of each Sunday-school in line, as follows:

First Reformed School.—William Gassman, superintendent, 200 in line. Left resting on Householder's corner.

Presbyterian School.—W. H. Herbert, superintendent, 75 in line. South side Washington Street.

St. John's Lutheran School.—John Bikle, superintendent, 350 in line. East side South Potomac Street.

United Brethren School.—Mr. Worst, superintendent, 75 in line. Right resting on Beachley's corner.

Methodist Episcopal School.—J. S. McCartney, superintendent, 150 in line. Right resting on Byers' corner, north side West Washington Street.

German Lutheran School.—Mr. Brey, superintendent, 75 in line. East Washington Street, right resting on Martin & Stover's corner.

Second Reformed School.—John Gassman, superintendent, 65 in line. North Potomac Street, right resting on Gassman's corner.

Trinity Lutheran School.—Jacob Roessner, superintendent, 250 in line. North Potomac Street, right resting on J. D. Swartz' corner.

Updegraff's Practical School.—Preceded by a drum-corps, and each scholar wearing upon his breast a shield emblazoned with the "Stars and Stripes."

In all the procession numbered about twelve hundred and fifty scholars and teachers. The line of procession shone brightly with numerous banners and flags, and various expressive devices and mottoes. One of these was a large bell, a representation of Independence Bell, made entirely of natural flowers, which was borne by children of the German school.

The line of march was from the public square to Antietam, Locust, Franklin, Walnut, Washington Streets to Square, headed by the drum-corps and the Heyser Band, and thence by countermarch to the court-house.

The display of fire-works was the finest, probably, ever witnessed in the town. The illumination and decoration of houses was also very effective, though not so general as might have been desired.

On the 31st of December, 1880, an entertainment was given at the Baldwin House by the gentlemen connected with the Shenandoah Valley Railroad, who had previously been entertained by the citizens at a banquet. The men from the company's shops at Shepherdstown were brought over to decorate the large dining-room of the hotel, and succeeded in making the apartment look very handsome and attractive. The colors used were chosen with a view to represent the signals employed in the running of the trains, and the head-light of a locomotive was also introduced in the decoration with striking effect. Over the entrance were the words "Welcome, 1881," and bunting and evergreens were tastefully draped from the walls, ceiling, and chandeliers. A locomotive was stationed so as to appear to be in the act of approaching, and on its head-light was the monogram "S. V. R. R." On the front of the engine the figures 1880 were so arranged that on the expiration of the old year the figures 1881 would instantly appear. At midnight the engine-bell struck and the whistle sounded, announcing the arrival of the new year, and from the smoke-stack a banner representing smoke, and bearing the inscription "1880," floated out and then disappeared, only to be followed by another bearing the inscription "A Happy New-Year." About two hundred persons were present, and between ten and eleven o'clock dancing commenced. A handsome supper was provided, including roast venison, olio, oysters, sweet-breads, turkey, and desserts. Music was furnished by John Ziegler's band from Baltimore, and the dancing continued until a late hour.

CHAPTER XLV.

RELIGIOUS DENOMINATIONS.

As in Frederick County, the honor of having first introduced the Christian religion into the then wilds of Washington County cannot be definitively accorded to any one denomination, but the probabilities are that the Episcopalians were first on the field as an organized body; for it seems to be very clear that the English settlers from Southern Maryland anticipated the Germans and the Scotch-Irish by some years, and most of the Southern Marylanders belonged to the Established Church, though many of them were Catholics.

Besides, the Episcopal Church was established by law, and started out with everything to facilitate its proper organization. Churches of other denominations were founded irregularly and in various localities as circumstances dictated, but the growth of the Episcopal Church was in a logical order of development, and its history may be termed almost identical with that of the county itself. The Lutherans and the German Reformed and Presbyterian denominations also established permanent congregations in many localities at a very early period, while the Methodists, though considerably later on the field, developed rapidly into strong and flourishing communities.

Originally Washington County was part of All Saints' Protestant Episcopal, or, as it was then, Anglican, Parish, which was an offshoot of St. John's, or Piscataway Parish. The latter began at the mouth of the Mattawoman Creek, on the Potomac, and ran up the said creek and the branch thereof to the utmost limits of Charles County, and thence ran with the county line to the line of the province, separating it from Pennsylvania; thence westward with that line to the boundary line separating Maryland and Virginia, and southward with that line to the Potomac River; down that river to the mouth of the Mattawoman, its beginning. In 1695 Prince George's County was created, embracing all the territory north of the Mattawoman Creek and the main branch of Swanston's Creek; or, in other words, all between the Potomac and the Patuxent Rivers. St. John's accordingly fell into Prince George's County. In 1696 the Rev. George Tubman was rector. He was presented in 1698 for bigamy and "sotting," and was suspended. Abraham Ford was made lay reader in his place, but in 1700, Mr. Tubman was reinstated in the ministry, and in 1702 again became rector of the parish, and died soon afterwards. He was succeeded by the Rev. Robert Owen, who did not continue long in charge. In 1704, Hickford Leman was employed as lay reader. Mr. Owen, however, officiated in the church every other Saturday during part of the year. These services were continued some four years, if not longer. In October, 1708, it was ordered that a new church be built. On the 23d of June, 1710, the Rev. John Fraser presented his appointment as rector. In 1726 a new parish, Prince George's, was erected out of St. John's Parish. It was eighty miles in length and twenty in breadth. Mr. Fraser died in November, 1742. Prince George's Parish embraced all the territory included in the then Prince George's County west of the Eastern Branch and East Fork of the Eastern Branch of the Potomac, Washington City, Georgetown, and the rest of the District of Columbia, Montgomery County, part of Carroll, and all of Frederick, Washington, and Allegany Counties. It was a frontier parish, and at the time of its formation had not more than two thousand four hundred inhabitants. The first rector (1726) was the Rev. George Murdoch, afterwards rector of All Saints', Frederick, which was created in 1742. The latter parish embraced all the territory north of Great Seneca Run River, and west of a line drawn from its head in the same direction to the head of one of the draughts of the Patuxent, comprising part of Carroll and Montgomery and all of Frederick, Washington, and Allegany Counties. At this time Washington County constituted part of All Saints' Parish, and was known as Antietam Hundred, or District of Frederick County. A chapel of ease was built in this district soon after that date, but in 1761 it was represented in a petition to the General Assembly that it was decayed, and built on so narrow and contracted a plan as not to be capable of holding one-third of the congregation willing and desirous to attend divine service there, and could not be enlarged with profit or convenience, so that it was absolutely necessary to rebuild it upon a better plan and with more durable materials. It is supposed that this was done, though without any legislative aid so far as can be ascertained. This was a frame building, situated about five and a half miles west of Hagerstown, and about a mile from the present site of St. James' College. A graveyard still remains there. At a comparatively recent period the structure was transformed into a dwelling, and the late Rev. Ethan Allen narrates that the "elder Dr. Dorsey" (probably Dr. Frederick Dorsey, Sr.) told him that he remembered the old chapel well.

In 1770, by an act of Assembly of that year, the Antietam District of Frederick County was created a separate parish, to become such on the removal of the then rector, Rev. Bennett Allen. The latter resided in Hagerstown, opposite the old chapel, and a curate officiated for him in the parish church at Frederick Town. Another curate had charge of St. Peters' Church, in the Monocacy District. In the fall of 1776 the new county of Washington was created by act of the Provincial Convention, and the legal provision for the maintenance of the clergy was abolished. Thereupon Mr. Allen relinquished the rectorship and returned to England. In accordance with the law of 1770, Antietam District now became Frederick Parish, and in 1806 the Diocesan Convention changed the name to St. John's Parish, embracing the whole of Washington County, except the portion comprised in St. Mark's Parish. In 1819 a number of Episcopalians residing at Sharpsburg petitioned the Diocesan

Convention for leave to establish a separate congregation at that place. This leave was granted and the new parish created. Similiar petitions were presented from St. Thomas' Church, Hancock, in 1835, and from St. Andrew's, Clear Spring, in 1839, and in both instances parishes were allowed to be formed. Two years later the Episcopal College of St. James was founded, the site being the old mansion of Gen. Samuel Ringgold. Congregations were also formed at Williamsport, Funkstown, Lappon's Cross-roads, and other thriving points.

According to the journal of the Diocesan Convention for 1881, the register of the Episcopal Churches in Washington County at present is as follows: St. John's Parish: St. John's Church, Hagerstown; St. Ann's Chapel, Smithsburg; Rev. Walter A. Mitchell, rector.

College of St. James: St. James' Chapel; Rev. Henry Edwards, chaplain.

St. Andrew's Church, Clear Spring; Rev. Coupland R. Page, rector.

St. Mark's Church, Lappon's Cross-roads; Rev. Henry Edwards, rector.

St. Paul's Church, Sharpsburg; Rev. Henry Edwards, missionary.

St. Thomas' Church, Hancock; Rev. Henry Wall, S.T.D., rector.

Hagerstown is a city of churches, and no community of its size in Maryland can boast of as many handsome church edifices. In point of architectural excellence, it is doubtful if its churches would not bear off the palm in competition with any of the rural cities in the whole country. Especially beautiful and even imposing is St. John's Episcopal church, belonging to the strongest religious congregation in the city, but several of the other churches are striking enough in their appearance to render any very marked distinction impossible. The Lutherans, the Presbyterians, the Catholics, and the Methodists all have fine church buildings, which are really models of style, and finished in a uniformly handsome manner.

The records of "The Vestry of Washington County" were begun on April 21, 1787, when "a number of the inhabitants of Washington County professing the Protestant religion of the Episcopal Church" met at the court-house in Elizabeth Town (Hagerstown) and elected as vestrymen John Stull, Daniel Hughes, Alexander Claggett, Thomas Sprigg, Richard Pindell, Nathaniel Rochester, and Elie Williams. On May 19th the vestry contracted with Henry Bowart for twenty-six thousand bricks for the church, and on June 2d they awarded to John Willar, at forty-five pounds, the contract for the carpenters' and joiners' work. The church stood near what is now the southern end of Locust Street, and was a substantial brick edifice. On June 21, 1788, the following accounts for materials furnished for the edifice were submitted to the consideration of the vestry and were settled:

	£	*s.*	*d.*
William and John Lee, 600 shingles and 25 pounds white lead	2	5	0
Hart & Rochester, scaffold, poles, hauling, etc.	2	11	0
Rezin Davis, for nails and white lead	4	10	9
Alexander and Hugh Claggett, for hauling	15	12	3
Alexander Claggett, for hauling	10	4	3
John Willar, for joiners' work	60	0	0
Frederick Alter, for mason-work	43	16	0
Total	138	19	3

On June 25th the vestry examined and passed the following accounts against the church:

	£	*s.*	*d.*
Dr. Richard Pindell, for part of his account	2	8	3
Elie Williams	9	6	10
Alexander and Hugh Claggett, for 3800 bricks of Charles Heffley	4	15	0
Henry Bowart, for bricks	37	10	0
John Scott, per account		7	6
Total	193	6	10

On April 13, 1789, "a number of inhabitants of Washington County" again met at the court-house, and elected as vestry Rev. George Bower, Alexander Claggett, Thomas Sprigg, Daniel Hughes, Elie Williams, Richard Pindell, and Hezekiah Claggett. The church-wardens appointed were Rezin Davis and Wm. Gordon. Col. John Stull was allowed £24 16*s.* 3*d.* for "lyme, scantling, and hauling;" Alexander Claggett £1 16*s.* 3*d.* for sundries for the use of the church; Alexander and Hugh Claggett, for sundries advanced for the use of the church, £6 8*s.* 4*d.*, and Frederick Alter ten shillings for altering a window in the church. At the meeting of the vestry on May 11th of same year the collectors of subscriptions were directed to proceed by legal process against the subscribers who had not paid the amounts for which they had set down their names. To collect actual money seems to have been rather difficult at that time, and when, on May 18th, the vestry contracted with John Willar to erect a pulpit and lay floors for the sum of £25, in case the parish did not pay him, Alexander Claggett, Daniel Hughes, Hezekiah Claggett, Elie Williams, Thomas Sprigg, and Richard Pindell made themselves responsible for the money. Hezekiah Claggett was appointed "to represent this parish as a lay deputy in convention to be held in Baltimore Town on the first Tuesday in June next." On Oct. 5, 1789, the vestry meeting drew up a subscription paper "for the purpose of employing Rev. George Bower to officiate for the term of one year" from Dec. 1, 1789. On April 5, 1790, the next meeting at the court-house was held, when the same vestry were re-elected, except that Mr. Bower was dropped and John Ingram was elected. Nathaniel Rochester was elected register of the vestry, and Daniel Hughes the lay delegate to the Diocesan Convention. Capt. Rezin Davis was appointed "to confer with a person to execute the duty of sexton; also to direct the grave-digger in what manner the graves are to be dugg (*sic*) in future." At the next meeting, June 7th, Rezin Davis informed the vestry that he had not been able to collect "any of the monies subscribed for furnishing the church;" and Samuel Finley was appointed collector, and Rev. Mr. Bower was requested "to make use of every endeavor to induce those in arrears to discharge the sum due by them, and that he inform such as use further delav that necessity will prevent the vestry from granting further indulgence." On August 2d, Capt. Rezin Davis reported that Titus Rynhart had agreed to act as sexton in return for the privilege of digging the graves in the churchyard. Benjamin Claggett was appointed to collect moneys due the church and one-half the salary of Rev. Mr. Bower, which had been for some time in arrears, but at the vestry meeting on November 1st it was still unpaid, and Rezin Davis was appointed to assist Mr. Claggett in raising subscriptions both for the pastor and the clerk, the salary of the former being now fixed at one hundred pounds per annum. Charles O'Neal accepted the position of clerk, and the vestry agreed to pay him twenty dollars for his services for eight months, from April 1st to November 30th. On Feb. 7, 1791, Henry Gamwell was appointed to collect the pastor's salary and the balance due on the old subscription papers, for which he was to receive five pounds.

The fourth vestry was elected by public meeting May 2, 1791, as follows: Daniel Hughes, Alexander Claggett, Elie Williams, Richard Pindell, Hezekiah Claggett, William Gordon, and William Reynolds, who chose Rezin Davis and William Prather to be church-wardens. On September 19th, John Willar submitted to the vestry his account of forty-five pounds for erecting pews, additional gallery, glass-rack, platform with steps, etc. He was debited with £19 4*s*. 8*d*. already paid him, leaving the balance due £25 5*s*. 4*d*. Willar's family was in distress for the necessaries of life, but up to November 8th the vestry could pay him but £3 5*s*. of the money due him, and William Reynolds was commissioned to collect the arrearages of subscriptions. Solomon Rawlings was made sexton, and was allowed £3 yearly, in addition to the usual compensation for digging graves. Of the latter he was to have a monopoly, the resolution of the vestry declaring that he shall "dig *all* graves that may be necessary in the English Protestant Episcopal churchyard." Hezekiah Claggett and William Reynolds were directed to procure bags in which a collection shall be taken up by the church-wardens each church Sunday. At the meeting on November 28th, Rev. Mr. Bower consented to remain as rector another year at the same salary, and it was decided to pay £7 10*s*. to the clerk, and £5 to a collector of subscriptions. On Feb. 6, 1792, the vestry settled up Mr. Bower's salary for 1790 and 1791, it appearing that they owed him £112 18*s*. On Easter Monday, April 1, 1793, the meeting for the annual election of vestry, previously held at the court-house, was convened in the church, and Elie Williams, Richard Pindell, Hezekiah Claggett, William Gordon, William Reynolds, Samuel Finley, and Rezin Davis were chosen, who elected as church-wardens Alexander Claggett and Cephas Beale. Rezin Davis was continued as treasurer, and Nathaniel Rochester as register. Solomon Rawlings was voted £3 yearly for taking care of and cleaning the church, and Titus Rynhart was continued as grave-digger. The treasurer was ordered to pay Mr. Bower £20 as soon as it could be collected, to enable him to finish his house. On October 14th, Turner Gor was appointed clerk, and it was ordered that "no person attempt to assist him in the clerk's desk but such as he shall invite for that purpose." As the register was directed to serve a copy of the order upon a certain Mr. Jones, it is probable that that gentleman had been intruding himself into the position. There is no record of the election of vestry in 1794. On June 14, 1795, *The Spy* contained an advertisement of "a lottery to be held at Elizabeth (Hager's) Town, Washington Co., to erect a church for the Episcopal congregation. There were two thousand tickets at two dollars," the prizes amounted to three thousand dollars, and eight hundred dollars was raised. The managers were Daniel Hughes, Thomas Hart, Elie Williams, Henry Schryock, Frederick Rohrer, Alexander Claggett, and Michael Fackler.

July 6, 1795, the regular meeting of parishioners elected Elie Williams, Richard Pindell, Rezin Davis, John Claggett, Cephas Beale, Charles Ogle, and William Gordon.[1] The record here speaks of All Saints' Parish for the first time. On July 21st, Alexander Claggett and Cephas Beale were appointed trustees to superintend the building of an addition to the church. In June, 1796, a corpse was stolen from the churchyard, and the vestry offered a reward of thirty dollars

[1] For complete roll of church officials, see the appended list at the conclusion of the history of this church.

for information leading to the arrest and conviction of the offender. On Aug. 13, 1797, the church and graveyard were consecrated by Bishop Claggett, who also on the same date confirmed the following persons: Mary Stull, Sophia Rochester, Ann Miller, Lucinda Bower, Catherine Swearingen, Matilda Stull, Elizabeth Rawlings, Rebecca Hughes, Susanna Hughes, Elizabeth Hall, Margaret Taylor, Otho Williams, Joseph Williams, Holland Stull, Prudence Williams, Allen Dowlas, Phœbe Grieves, Sarah Owen, and Sarah Dowlas. On November 6th the pews were sold to the highest bidders, as follows:

		Price.	Annual Rent.
No.	1. Daniel Hughes	$58	$30
"	2. Ignatius Taylor, Thomas Belt, and Charles Carroll	52	"
"	3. John Claggett	45	"
"	4. Samuel Ringgold	60	"
"	5. Elie Williams	58	"
"	14. Richard Pindell	26	15
"	15. Benjamin Claggett	30	"
"	16. William Elliott	26	"
"	17. Rezin Davis and Kennedy Owen	21	"
"	18. Nathaniel Rochester and Daniel Stull	15	"
"	20. John Ragan	20	"
"	21. Thomas Sprigg	25	"
"	22. Alexander Claggett	30	"
"	23. William Fitzhugh	30	"
"	9. George Bean	4	10
"	10. William Gordon	10	"
"	11. William S. Compton	12	"
"	12. Edmund Rutter	12	"
"	13. Maurice Baker	14	"
"	24. William Fitzhugh	20	"
"	25. Peter Miller	12	"
"	26. Perry McCoy	11	"
"	27. John Dowlas	11	"
"	19. James and Griffith Henderson	...	"

Accounts of John Hooper for £104 3*s.*, for joiners' work, and of Cephas Beale for £11 3*s.* 6*d.*, for the addition to the church, were passed. In 1798, Mr. Bower's salary as rector was increased to £150.

The act of Assembly for the establishment of vestries in the parishes required that members of the Protestant Episcopal Church should be enrolled on the parish-books a month before they could become eligible as vestrymen or electors of vestrymen. The earliest enrollments made were on April 8, 1799, as follows: Alexander Claggett, William Fitzhugh, Rezin Davis, Thomas Belt, John Carr, Griffith Henderson, Charles McCauley, Nathaniel Rochester, Otho Holland Williams, Eli Beatty, and Thomas Hallam. Daniel Hughes, Sr., Robert Hughes, and John Claggett were enrolled on April 19th. From November 6th, Mr. Bower's salary was cut down from one hundred and fifty pounds to four hundred dollars per annum. On Sept. 21, 1801, the vestry gave notice that they would prosecute delinquent pewholders who did not promptly settle up their arrearages. Still there was a deficiency in the finances.

In 1803, although the records do not mention the fact, a lottery scheme was successfully carried out for the benefit of St. John's congregation, which was superintended by the following commissioners, who had been authorized by the Legislature to conduct the drawings: Col. N. Rochester, R. Pindell, J. Taylor, R. Hughes, and O. H. Williams. The amount of money to be raised was five hundred dollars, "to finish the church edifice of the Episcopal All Saints' Parish in Hagerstown."

On Feb. 28, 1805, it was resolved to abandon the system of pew-rents and to resort to the old plan of soliciting subscriptions to meet the expenses of the parish. Rev. Thomas P. Irving was appointed rector Sept. 22, 1813, at a yearly salary of four hundred dollars, of St. John's Church, All Saints' Parish, as the title then appeared in the records, and on Nov. 13, 1814, he was authorized to charge five dollars for officiating at funerals, and four dollars for each christening. From this year onward the name appears as St. John's Parish. Mr. Irving resigned the pastorate in February, 1816, because of ill health, and on August 27th, Rev. Joseph Jackson was appointed his successor, but on July 26, 1817, the vestry rejected a resolution to reappoint him, and on October 1st refused him the use of the church to preach a charity sermon for the benefit of the Female Society for Instructing Poor Children. In a letter to Levin Mills, church-warden, in reference to Mr. Jackson's request, the vestry say that they "have determined, on account of the conduct of that gentleman on Sunday last, to hold no communication directly or indirectly with him." On Oct. 25, 1817, Rev. Jehu Curtis Clay was chosen rector, his incumbency to date from Jan. 1, 1818. At the vestry meeting Aug. 31, 1818, it was resolved to raise by subscription a fund for the building of a new church, the subscribers to have the choice of pews according to the amount of their subscriptions. On May 10, 1819, the pastor's salary was increased to one thousand dollars per annum. On May 12, 1821, one-fourth of the subscriptions for the new church edifice were called in, and Otho H. W. Stull was appointed to solicit aid in Baltimore. On July 2d, Eli Beatty, George Bear, Otho H. Williams, and Franklin Anderson were appointed the building committee, and a lot on Jonathan Street was bought for six hundred dollars from Christian Fechtig for the site of the new church. The committee were authorized to contract with Daniel Sprigg for one hundred thousand bricks, with George Bear for stone for the foundation, with Mr. Stout for the stone and brick-work, and to purchase all the requisite materials. Rev. Mr. Clay resigned the pastorate on Nov. 28, 1821, and on December 16th the vestry notified him that they would regret to lose his services, and would make any possible exertions to retain them. Mr. Clay removed to Pennsylvania, and Rev. Mr. Shaw filled the pulpit for a few months, until the election of Rev. George Lemmon on Oct. 12, 1822. The salary was fixed at eight hundred dollars, and on June 17, 1823, the pews in the new church were sold, as follows:

		Price.	Annual Rent.
No. 54.	Frisby Tilghman	$545	$50
" 55.	Benjamin Galloway	450	45
" 56.	Frederick Dorsey	302	40
" 3.	Otho H. Williams	300	50
" 2.	Thomas Belt	300	45
" 26.	Richard Ragan	212	30
" 53.	Eli Beatty	211	30
" 32.	John Reynolds	200	"
" 4.	Samuel Ringgold	"	"
" 33.	Thomas Buchanan and John R. Dall	"	"
" 25.	Upton Lawrence	"	"
" 24.	Samuel Hughes, Jr	"	"
" 34.	Daniel Sprigg	150	"
" 31.	David G. Yost	151	"
" 23.	John B. Claggett	152	"
" 30.	Thomas Grieves	150	"
" 22.	Franklin Anderson and John Ridout	"	25
" 27.	George Bear	"	30
" 9.	John T. Mason	125	20
" 48.	Henry C. Schnebly	"	"
" 47.	John Booth	105	16
" 46.	John Buchanan	"	"
" 45.	Susan and Esther Hughes and J. I. Merrick	80	12
" 35.	Levin Mills and William Fitzhugh, Jr	150	25
" 12.	Henry Barnett	76	12
" 48.	George C. Smoot	125	20
" 10.	William Price and Otho Lawrence	100	16
" 21.	Otho H. W. Stull	100	16
" 36.	William O. Sprigg	125	25

The new church was consecrated June 18, 1825, by Bishop James Kemp, assisted by Rev. William Armstrong. On Dec. 4, 1827, Rev. Mr. Lemmon tendered his resignation, and on the following June 26th, Rev. Robert B. Drane was called to the pastorate, and in 1834 he opened a school to increase his income. He was permitted to officiate every other Sunday in the church at Williamsport, and on April 20, 1835, the vestry ordered that a parsonage be built. He resigned April 26, 1836, and in reply to a question from the vestry, he wrote that it would be impossible for him to remain because "of the malicious and vindictive conduct of some who had set themselves to destroy my reputation and influence as a minister of the gospel"; and that such a course on his part "would involve a sacrifice of the happiness of one too near and dear to me to be thus destroyed." On July 29th the vestry extended a call to Rev. Mr. Coleman, of Cecil County, Md., but he declined it, and Rev. John Wiley became Mr. Drane's successor. In March, 1838, Mrs. Henrietta Johns was engaged "to play upon the organ" for fifty dollars per annum.

On March 24, 1840, the vestry passed a resolution dissolving their contract with Rev. Mr. Wiley from April 1st, but permitting him to occupy the rectory, and receive a salary at the rate of seven hundred dollars annually for six months from that date, and in case he claimed possession of the church after April 1st, they would not hold themselves liable to him for his emoluments, and would proceed to expel him by law. Joseph I. Merrick, as counsel for Mr. Wiley, addressed a letter to the vestry denying their legal right to terminate the contract, or reduce the salary without the rector's consent, and Mr. Wiley himself refused to accept the terms offered him, declaring that he would do nothing which might be construed into an acknowledgment of their right "thus summarily to cast a minister of the gospel with his family upon the world." The vestry, however, proceeded to elect Mr. Wiley for six months from April 1st, thus reaffirming their theory that they had no authority to install a pastor for an unlimited time. Eli Beatty, Otho H. Williams, David G. Yost, William H. Fitzhugh, Richard Ragan, and Thomas Schnebly voted for the resolutions, and Dr. Frederick Dorsey against them. At the election for vestry on Easter Monday, April 20, 1840, the pastor's party were victorious, choosing Dr. Frederick Dorsey, John S. Hamilton, Peregrine Fitzhugh, Joseph I. Merrick, and Col. Frisby Tilghman, and the controversy was terminated by the passage of a resolution declaring Mr. Wiley to be the lawful rector of the church; but he stated that as he had vindicated the right of the position which he had taken he offered his resignation, to take effect in September. The contention had done much harm to the church, and the vestry requested Rev. Dr. Whittingham, then recently elected Bishop of Maryland, to make his residence in Hagerstown, and act as rector of St. John's until it could be restored to peace and prosperity. The bishop declined the proposition, and recommended for the vacancy Rev. Theodore B. Lyman, who was elected on Oct. 12, 1840, but the vestry stipulated that the contract should only run from year to year, and might be terminated by either of the parties at six months' notice. Mr. Lyman accepted the conditions, although the bishop regretted that they had been imposed. By vigorous effort the church was relieved of the worst of its embarrassments, and on Nov. 14, 1842, Rev. Russell Trevett was made assistant rector. In 1843 a fund of over seven hundred dollars was raised and repairs made on the edifice, which was dedicated anew by Bishop Whittingham on October 26th. In December, Col. Tilghman and Charles Macgill resigned because of their inability to agree with the other vestrymen concerning the position of the furniture in the chancel, and they, together with Otho H. Williams, Richard

Ragan, Jervis Spencer, Alexander Neill, Jr., M. W. Boyd, Eli Beatty, and William B. Nelson, withdrew from the church. On April 5, 1845, Mr. Trevett resigned as assistant rector, and Dwight E. Lyman was chosen in his place. The gentlemen above named as having separated themselves from St. John's founded Christ Church, and on Oct. 29, 1845, the rector of St. John's wrote to their vestry suggesting a union of the churches, and avowing a willingness to arrange the chancel furniture as they desired, although he assured them that they were wrong in supposing that doctrinal innovations were concealed in the plan which he had adopted, and which had given offense to them. They, however, refused to entertain the proposition.

On July 18, 1848, Rev. R. G. H. Clarkson was elected assistant rector, to succeed Rev. Dwight E. Lyman, who had resigned, and in 1849, Mr. Clarkson was followed by Rev. Joseph C. Passmore. In the latter year Christ Church ceased to exist, and most of the Separatists returned to St. John's, in what was called by Eli Beatty "a nominal membership." On April 1, 1850, Rev. Theodore B. Lyman resigned to go to Trinity Church, Pittsburgh, and at the same time Mr. Passmore gave up the assistant rectorship. Rev. Mr. Wheat filled the pulpit temporarily, until the election of Rev. William G. Jackson, on April 22d, who did not take charge until September, having spent the summer in Europe, and in January, 1851, he was again compelled to accept an indefinite leave of absence on account of his health. He resigned in December, 1852, and Rev. George C. Stokes declining the call that was extended to him, Rev. Walter N. Ayrault was elected on March 23, 1853, who continued until Sept. 1, 1856. Rev. William W. Lord was offered the position, but could not accept it, and in December Rev. Henry Edwards was chosen. Gas was introduced into the church in May, 1857, and in April, 1859, Mr. Edwards was able to announce that the church had been freed from debt. On May 21, 1866, the building was damaged by fire, and was repaired at a cost of eleven hundred and fifty dollars. Mr. Edwards resigned Jan. 18, 1867, and on February 23d, Rev. Claudius B. Haines was elected On Nov. 17, 1869, a portion of the church property, at the corner of Jonathan and Antietam Streets, was sold to Thomas H. Grove for two thousand five hundred dollars. A protest against the legality of the election of A. S. Mason, Frederick Dorsey, Henry Bell, and Frank Kennedy as vestrymen in April, 1870, having been made, they resigned, and a new election took place in June. Mr. Haines tendered his resignation Dec. 26, 1871. The church was burned to the ground on the night of December 6th, and Benjamin Reigle, George W. Harris, George A. Gambrill, Buchanan Schley, and Dr. William Ragan were appointed a building committee for the erection of a new edifice, and they recommended that it should occupy the site of the destroyed church. Rev. Walter A. Mitchell entered upon the rectorship in February, 1872, and the congregation worshiped in the chapel of the Reformed Church. In May it was decided to sell the old church property for not less than seven thousand five hundred dollars and buy a new site on Prospect Street for two thousand three hundred dollars.

Since the formation of Frederick Parish in 1777 the rectors have been:

1777-85, Rev. Bartholomew Booth; Dec. 1, 1786, to 1812, Rev. George Bower; Sept. 22, 1813, to 1815, Rev. Thomas P. Irving; Aug. 27, 1816, to Aug. 1, 1817, Rev. Joseph Jackson; Oct. 25, 1817, to December, 1821, Rev. Jehu Curtis Clay, D.D.; Feb. 27, 1822, to July, 1822, Rev. Samuel B. Shaw, D.D.; Oct. 12, 1822, to April, 1828, Rev. George Lemmon; June 28, 1828, to June, 1836, Rev. Robert Brent Drane, D.D.; April 2, 1837, to 1840, Rev. John Wiley; 1840-49, Rev. Theodore Benedict Lyman, D.D.; September, 1850, to 1852, Rev. William Gooden Jackson, D.D.; June, 1853, to 1856, Rev. Walter Ayrault, D.D.; January, 1857, to Jan. 18, 1867, Rev. Henry Edwards; April 27, 1867, to 1871, Rev. Claudius B. Haines; Jan. 1, 1872, Rev. Walter A. Mitchell.

The vestries of St. John's Church have been:

1787.—John Stull, Daniel Hughes, Alexander Claggett, Thomas Sprigg, Richard Pindell, Nathaniel Rochester, and Eli Williams.

1789.—Alexander Claggett, Thomas Sprigg, Daniel Hughes, Eli Williams, Richard Pindell, and Hezekiah Claggett.

1790.—Alexander Claggett, Thomas Sprigg, Daniel Hughes, Richard Pindell, Hezekiah Claggett, Eli Williams, and John Ingram.

1791.—Daniel Hughes, Alexander Claggett, Eli Williams, Richard Pindell, Hezekiah Claggett, William Gordon, and William Reynolds.

1793.—Eli Williams, Richard Pindell, Hezekiah Claggett, William Gordon, William Reynolds, Samuel Finley, and Rezin Davis.

1795.—Eli Williams, Richard Pindell, Rezin Davis, John Claggett, Cephas Beall, Charles Ogle, and William Gordon.

1798.—Alexander Claggett, Eli Williams, John Claggett, Rezin Davis, William Fitzhugh, Ignatius Taylor, and Thomas Belt.

1799.—Alexander Claggett, Thomas Belt, Rezin Davis, Eli Williams, William Fitzhugh, Griffith Henderson, James Kendall, and Benjamin Claggett.

1802.—Nathaniel Rochester, Alexander Claggett, Ignatius Taylor, Robert Hughes, Samuel Ringgold, Frisby Tilghman, Benjamin Claggett, and Otho H. Williams.

1805.—Rezin Davis, Otho H. Williams, Robert Hughes, Frisby Tilghman, Benjamin Galloway, John Ragan, Sr., and Nathaniel Rochester.

1807 —Daniel Hughes, Thomas Belt, Rezin Davis, William Fitzhugh, Nathaniel Rochester, Eli Williams, Otho H. Williams, and Thomas Grieves.

1809.—William Fitzhugh, Thomas Belt, Thomas B. Hall, Nathaniel Rochester, William Fitzhugh, Jr., Otho H. W. Stull, Otho H. Williams, and Daniel Hughes, Jr.

1810.—William Fitzhugh, Thomas Belt, Thomas B. Hall, Upton Lawrence, Thomas Grieves, William Fitzhugh, Jr., Otho H. W. Stull, Otho H. Williams, and Daniel Hughes, Jr.

1813.—Daniel Hughes, Sr., William O. Sprigg, Otho H. Williams, Frisby Tilghman, John Ragan, Jr., Thomas B. Hall, Henry Lewis, George C. Smoot, and William Fitzhugh.

1814.—Otho H. Williams, Frisby Tilghman, Thomas B. Hall, William Fitzhugh, Daniel Hughes, Henry Lewis, Eli Beatty, and George C. Smoot.

1815.—Benjamin Galloway, Thomas Belt, Otho H. Williams, William Fitzhugh, George C. Smoot, Eli Beatty, Thomas B. Hall, and Frisby Tilghman.

1816.—Benjamin Galloway, Eli Beatty, Thomas Grieves, Daniel Sprigg, Anthony B. Martin, Levin Mills, Thomas Compton, and Franklin Anderson.

1817.—Same vestry, except that Rev. Thomas P. Irving and Otho H. W. Stull took the places of Levin Mills and Franklin Anderson. Mr. Irving resigned, and his place in the vestry was filled by Frisby Tilghman.

1818.—Eli Beatty, Daniel Sprigg, Thomas Grieves, Richard Ragan, Franklin Anderson, Otho H. W. Stull, Frisby Tilghman, and A. B. Martin.

1819.—Frisby Tilghman, Eli Beatty, Thomas Grieves, Otho H. W. Stull, Daniel Sprigg, Otho Lawrence, George Bear, and Franklin Anderson.

1820.—Frisby Tilghman, George Bear, Richard Ragan, Levin Mills, Thomas Belt, Daniel Sprigg, Edward Gaither, and Franklin Anderson.

1821.—Daniel Sprigg, Thomas Grieves, Otho H. W. Stull, Eli Beatty, Frisby Tilghman, George Bear, Richard Ragan, and Franklin Anderson.

1822.—Same vestry, except that Levin Mills took the place of Mr. Stull.

1823.—Eli Beatty, Daniel Sprigg, Thomas Grieves, John B. Claggett, Frisby Tilghman, George Bear, Richard Ragan, and Franklin Anderson.

1824.—Same vestry, except Otho Lawrence in place of Frisby Tilghman.

1825.—Same vestry, except Henry Barnett in place of Otho Lawrence.

1826.—Otho Lawrence, Eli Beatty, Daniel Sprigg, John B. Claggett, George Bear, Thomas Grieves, Joseph Martin, and Franklin Anderson.

1827.—Same vestry, except Richard Ragan in place of Thomas Grieves.

1828.—Vestry of 1827 re-elected.

1829.—Re-elected as above.

1830.—Re-elected as above.

1831.—Same vestry, except that Frisby Tilghman took the place of George Bear.

1833.—Richard Ragan, Otho Lawrence, J. B. Claggett, Marmaduke Boyd, Joseph Martin, Frisby Tilghman, J. P. Dall, and Eli Beatty.

1834.—Eli Beatty, Frisby Tilghman, Joseph Martin, Jr., Richard Martin, Horatio McPherson, Richard Ragan, and Otho Lawrence.

1835.—Frisby Tilghman, J. R. Dall, H. McPherson, Otho Lawrence, Richard Ragan, Eli Beatty, F. Tilghman, Jr., and Barton Bean.

1836.—F. Tilghman, Sr., F. Tilghman, Jr., Otho Lawrence, O. H. W. Stull, Horatio McPherson, John R. Dall, Richard Ragan, and John B. Claggett.

1837.—Richard Ragan, William H. Fitzhugh, O. H. W. Stull, Otho Lawrence, Thomas Schnebly, John B. Claggett, Frederick Dorsey, and William R. Abbott.

1838.—Otho H. Williams, Eli Beatty, Fred. Dorsey, Jacob Hollingsworth, John B. Claggett, Thomas Schnebly, John R. Dall, and William R. Abbott.

1839.—Eli Beatty, John B. Claggett, William Fitzhugh, Thomas Schnebly, William R. Abbott, Fred. Dorsey, Otho H. Williams, and Jacob Hollingsworth.

1840.—Frisby Tilghman, Joseph I. Merrick, John S. Hamilton, Peregrine Fitzhugh, Fred. Dorsey, William H. Fitzhugh, Thomas Schnebly, and Jacob Hollingsworth. Two members resigned, and their places were filled by John Thomson Mason and Charles F. Keerl.

1841.—Same vestry, except Jervis Spencer and James R. Jones, in place of P. Fitzhugh and Fred. Dorsey.

1842.—Same, except John R. Dall in place of Joseph I. Merrick.

1843.—Jervis Spencer, John Thomson Mason, James R. Jones, Fred. Dorsey, Charles Macgill, W. H. Fitzhugh, Frisby Tilghman, and John R. Dall.

1844.—William H. Fitzhugh, James R. Jones, Jacob Hollingsworth, Thomas Schnebly, J. T. Mason, Edward Gaither, and Fred. Dorsey.

1845.—Same, except John R. Dall in place of James R. Jones, and a vacancy filled by John Ingram.

1846.—Same, except William Motter, *vice* John Ingram.

1847.—No change.

1848.—Same, except Charles Macgill in place of John R. Dall.

1849.—Jacob Hollingsworth, William Motter, J. R. Jones, Fred. Dorsey, William H. Fitzhugh, J. T. Mason, and Charles Macgill.

1850.—Same, except John D. Reamure in place of J. R. Jones.

1851.—Jacob Hollingsworth, John D. Reamure, Wm. Motter, Fred. Dorsey, Charles Macgill, Joshua P. Crist, Edward Gaither, and Richard Ragan, Jr.

1852.—Same, except Benjamin Pendleton in place of Richard Ragan.

1853.—Wm. Motter, Jacob Hollingsworth, Edward Gaither, Fred. Dorsey, Chas. Macgill, John D. Reamure, J. P. Crist, and Robert Fowler.

1854.—Same, except Z. L. Claggett in place of Robert Fowler.

1855.—Same, except W. S. Berry in place of Z L. Claggett.

1856.—No change, except Z. L. Claggett in place of Edward Gaither.

1857.—Jacob Hollingsworth, Fred. Dorsey, Charles Macgill, Wm. Motter, John D. Reamure, Joshua P. Crist, Washington Berry, and Eli Beatty.

1858.—Same, except Charles F. Keerl and Dr. Wm. Ragan in place of Washington Berry and Charles Macgill.

1859.—No change.

1860.—Jacob Hollingsworth, W. Berry, James H. Grove, Charles F. Keerl, Charles Macgill, Joshua P. Crist, John D. Reamure, and Wm. Motter.

1861.—No change.

1862.—No change.

1863.—No change.

1864.—Frederick Dorsey, John D. Reamure, Jacob Hollingsworth, Edward Watts, James H. Grove, W. Berry, Wm. Motter, and Chas. F. Keerl.

1865.—No change.

1866.—Jacob Hollingsworth, Chas. F. Keerl, James H. Grove, W. Berry, D. G. Huyett, Wm. Motter, T. W. Simmons, and Wm. Ragan.

1867.—No change, except Richard Ragan in place of W. Berry.

1868.—Same, except Frederick Dorsey in place of Jacob Hollingsworth.

1869.—W. Ragan, Richard Ragan, T. W. Simmons, Charles F. Keerl, D. G. Huyett, George W. Pole, James H. Grove, and Wm. Motter.

1870.—Henry Bell, George W. Pole, D. G. Huyett, B. Riegle, Wm. Motter, Frederick Dorsey, T. W. Simmons, and Charles F. Keerl.

1871.—No change.

1872.—B. Riegle, Geo. W. Pole, Wm. Ragan, Wm. Motter, D. G. Huyett, Geo. W. Harris, Alonzo Berry, and B. H. Griswold.

1873.—Wm. Motter, Geo. W. Harris, Alonzo Berry, B. H. Griswold, Wm. Ragan, J. P. Crist, D. G. Huyett, Buchanan Schley.

Following are brief sketches of the rectors of St. John's: The Rev. Bartholomew Booth, who is put down as the rector of St. John's from 1777 to 1785, was born and ordained in England, and came over to this country about 1776. He was famous as an instructor, and a sketch of him is given in another place. There is no record of his officiating in the church, but as there is no mention of any other minister being there from the time of Mr. Allen's departure in 1777 to that of Mr. Bower's arrival in 1786, it is to be presumed that Mr. Booth performed all the functions of a minister.

The first record of the Rev. George Bower is that of his arrival, Dec. 1, 1786, and his employment at a salary of one hundred pounds, equal to two hundred and sixty-six dollars per annum. During this year a subscription was raised for building a church in Hagerstown, then called Elizabeth Town. The first records now known date from April, 1787, when the first vestry were elected. Mr. Bower still continued rector. In 1788, however, he left and became rector of Queen Caroline Parish, Anne Arundel County, now in Howard, where he continued a year, at the expiration of which he returned to Hagerstown. The Diocesan Convention met on the 2d of June, 1789, in Baltimore. Mr. Bower was present, and Mr. H. Claggett represented the parish as lay delegate. The first convention met June 22, 1784, but that of 1789 was the first in which St. John's Parish was represented. In the certificate of appointment of the lay delegate it is stated "that the upper part of the parish [of All Saints', which this had been] has for some time been considered a separate and distinct parish;" and so the act of 1770 had made it. This the convention recognized, and accordingly Mr. Bower and Mr. Claggett were admitted to seats from Frederick, now St. John's, Parish. Mr. Bower acceded to this, and ratified the constitution and canons for himself and Mr. Claggett in behalf of the parish.

Town commissioners were appointed in 1791, and in the same year Mr. Bower appears to have officiated part of his time in Frederick Town. It is possible that he had officiated there before. In 1795 an addition was made to the church. The following letter from Mr. Bower to Bishop Claggett gives an interesting picture of the condition of the parish at that time:

"HAGERSTOWN, July 11, 1797.

"REV. AND DEAR SIR,—It was out of my power to attend the convention this year, as it has been for some years past, owing to the delicate state of Mrs. Bower's health.

"Our congregation in Hagerstown has become very respectable. The addition we have made to our church is not yet completed. I attend here every other Sunday, at Fredericktown every fourth Sunday, and at Taneytown every fourth Sunday. Next Sunday, which is the fifth Sunday after Trinity and the 16th day of the month, I am to officiate here. The Sunday after, which is the 23d of the month, I am to officiate at Taneytown. The Sunday after that, which is the 30th, I stay here, and the Sunday after that, which is the 6th of August, I go to Fredericktown. And so on regularly through the whole year.

"Should we be favored with the pleasure of your company this fall, you will be so good, sir, to keep this letter, and you will know where to meet me. I have kept a constant register of the marriages, births, funerals, and communicants. But the adults I have found it impossible to make out. They are so scattered about in this extensive parish, which contains three counties, and is, I believe, near one hundred and fifty miles in length, reaching from Baltimore County to the end of the State.

"You would oblige me greatly to write a few lines by the post, to acquaint me with the time you think you can come up.

"I am, reverend and dear sir, with great respect,

"Your very humble servant,

"GEORGE BOWER."

In the following August the bishop visited this parish, and on the 13th of that month consecrated the church. In 1799, Mr. Bower's salary was four hundred dollars; in 1805, two hundred; in 1806, four hundred; in 1807, five hundred and fifty for half his services.

In 1806 a petition was presented to the convention from sundry inhabitants of All Saints' Parish, in Washington County, praying to be allowed to constitute a separate cure by the name of St. John's Parish, Washington County. An act was passed making the whole of the county St. John's Parish except that part of said county which forms a part of St. Mark's Parish. It would have been proper, doubtless, if desirable, to have granted a change of name and defined its bounds, but it had been made a separate parish before.

Very soon after May, 1813, Mr. Bower died, after a ministry of twenty-seven years. He had been placed on the standing committee five times, and in 1801 preached the convention sermon.

The only time when the number of communicants was reported was in 1808. The number then was ten. At more than half of the conventions he was absent. He left a widow, three sons, and a daughter. One of the sons died in Frederick. The others of the family went West, but in July, 1815, Mrs. Bower was living in Hagerstown.

Rev. Thomas P. Irving became rector Sept. 22, 1813, at a salary of four hundred dollars. He also taught a school. Mr. Irving was a native of Somerset County, but came into the diocese from the South, having been ordained by Bishop White in North Carolina, where he was principal of an academy at Newbern. In November, 1814, the vestry ordered five dollars to be paid for burial, and four dollars for a christening. In July, 1815, Mr. Irving had formed a Bible Society. Under date of May, 1816, Mr. Irving writes Bishop Kemp that he had been compelled on account of his health to resign his church, though not his academy. He is said to have died in 1817, at the age of forty-one years.

Rev. Joseph Jackson was elected rector Aug. 27, 1816. By birth Mr. Jackson was an Englishman. He was ordained deacon by Bishop Claggett in 1794, and in 1796 was rector of St. Peter's, Talbot, and for fifteen years of William and Mary, St. Mary's. He moved to Hagerstown in 1811, but remained only a year. In 1820 he went as a missionary to Kentucky, where he died that year. He had been twice on the standing committee, twice the convention preacher, and once deputy to the General Convention. His savings formed the nucleus of St. James' College.

Rev. Jehu Curtis Clay was elected rector Oct. 25, 1817, to commence Jan. 1, 1818. He was the son of the Rev. Slater Clay, of Pennsylvania. In giving notice of his becoming a candidate for holy orders, Jan. 16, 1812, he says he had lived with the Rev. George Dashiell since 1809, except a few months spent in the University of Pennsylvania, "under whose direction I have pursued and am still pursuing the studies preparatory to ordination." He was ordained deacon by Bishop White, June 13, 1813, being just twenty-one years of age, and went to North Carolina, whence he removed to Hagerstown. He continued there four years, and resigned Dec. 18, 1821. He returned to Pennsylvania in 1822. In 1831 he became the rector of Gloria Dei Church, Philadelphia, where he died Oct. 20, 1863, in his seventy-second year.

Rev. Samuel B. Shaw was elected rector Feb. 27, 1822. He came from Massachusetts, his native State, having been ordained deacon by Bishop Griswold in 1821. He remained at Hagerstown but six months, and then returned to Massachusetts.

Rev. George Lemmon was elected rector Oct. 12, 1822, with a salary of eight hundred dollars. He was a native of Baltimore, and was ordained deacon by Bishop Claggett in 1813. He became the minister of Queen Caroline Parish, in Anne Arundel County, but in 1816 removed to Virginia, where he married. From thence he removed to Hagerstown. In 1823 the new church recently built was consecrated by Bishop Kemp.

Hitherto the parochial reports on the convention journal had been merely statistical; but in 1825 Mr. Lemmon reports that two Sunday-schools had been put into operation, one white and the other for colored children. The congregation had much increased, and some had become the subjects of "spiritual change of heart." In 1826 he speaks of a lecture delivered on every Thursday evening. On the 1st of April, 1828, Mr. Lemmon resigned, after a six years' pastorate, and returned to Virginia, where he died, aged sixty. When Mr. Lemmon resigned Rev. Ethan Allen was invited to the charge, but declined.

Rev. Robert Brent Drane was elected June 26, 1828, but took charge on the 31st of August. He was a native of Rock Creek Parish, a graduate of Harvard College, and was ordained deacon by Bishop Griswold, of Massachusetts, May 3, 1827. Returning to the Diocese of Maryland, he became the rector of Addison Chapel Parish, Prince George's County, and thence removed to Hagerstown. In his report Mr. Drane mentions (1830) the reorganization of the Sunday-school and the formation of an Auxiliary Missionary Society. In 1832 he reports a weekly meeting for prayer and the exposition of Scripture. About this time he officiated once a month at Williamsport, and occasionally at a place seven miles east of Hagerstown. In 1833 he reports that he was continuing to officiate regularly at Williamsport, and also to a congregation then recently formed in Funkstown. In 1834 he reports having officiated every other Sunday at Williamsport from May 10th. During the year 1835 a parsonage was built for St. John's Church, and Mr. Drane had a school. In 1836 he preached the convention sermon. In June, 1836, after a ministry of six years, he resigned, and removed to North Carolina, to the rectorship of St. James', Wilmington. In 1843 he became the president of Shelbyville College, Kentucky, and received the degree of D.D., but at the end of the year he returned to Wilmington, where he continued till his death, in October, 1862. He died of the yellow fever, after a ministry of thirty-five years, and left a wife and children. On Aug. 1, 1836, Rev. John Weleyman was elected, but declined.

Rev. John Wiley was elected rector April 2, 1837.

He was a native of Delaware, and a graduate of the General Theological Seminary, and was ordained deacon July 5, 1829, by Bishop Hobart, of New York, and coming to Maryland, became the minister of St. James' Parish, Baltimore County. In 1833 he became ector of All Hallows and Worcester Parishes, Worcester County, and in 1836 of St. Peter's, Talbot, whence he removed to Hagerstown. Mr. Wiley's convention reports are all merely statistical. In 1840 he was the convention preacher. In 1841 he resigned this parish and went to North Sassafras Parish, Cecil County. In 1853 he removed to Trinity, Charles County; in 1866 to Labyrinth, Montgomery County; in 1872 to Sherwood Parish, Baltimore County. He has been a deputy to the General Convention twice.

Rev. Theodore B. Lyman became the rector of this parish in 1840, having been ordained deacon by Bishop Whittingham, Sept. 25, 1840. He was a native of Connecticut, and graduate of the General Theological Seminary. In 1841 St. James' College was founded under his auspices. In his convention report of 1842 Mr. Lyman mentions that since October he had been assisted by the Rev. Russell Trevett, deacon, that the church had been open on all holy days and Wednesday and Friday mornings, and that he had a Bible-class, a Sunday-school, a weekly service for the colored people, and weekly offerings. In 1844 the church had been enlarged and repaired, giving it a Sunday-school-room and a vestry-room. In 1848 two silver chalices and two large silver alms-dishes had been presented. About 1849, Mr. Lyman removed from St. John's Parish to Columbia, Pa. In 1857 he was in Pittsburgh; in 1857 he received the degree of D.D.; in 1863 was residing in Paris, France; in 1865 in Rome, Italy; in 1871 in San Francisco; and in 1874 became assistant bishop in North Carolina.

Rev. William G. Jackson took charge of the parish in September, 1850. Mr. Jackson was a native of England, the son of Rev. Thomas Jackson, rector of All Saints', Frederick, from 1830 to 1836. He graduated at the Virginia Theological Seminary, and was ordained deacon by Bishop Moore, of Virginia, in 1833. He became rector in 1850, and was married in 1852 to Lydia E. Kennedy, daughter of Col. Jacob Hollingsworth. In January, 1851, on account of ill health, he was absent a while, and his place was supplied by the Rev. W. W. Lord. Before the convention of 1853, Mr. Jackson had removed to South Carolina. In 1855 he had returned, and had become rector of Grace Church, Howard County. In 1870 he received the degree of D.D., and afterwards became dean of the Convocation. Rev. Walter N. Ayrault entered on his charge in June, 1853. He was a native of New York, and was ordained deacon in 1846 by Bishop De Lancey, and removed from Western New York. In 1856 he returned to Western New York. In 1868 he received the degree of D.D.

Rev. Henry Edwards became rector in January, 1857. He was born in Connecticut, and was ordained by Bishop Brownell in 1853, but came to Maryland from New York, and became assistant in Emmanuel Parish, Allegany, whence he removed to St. John's. In 1858 he reported that the daily service had been continued with increasing congregations, and that services had been held in two villages a few miles distant. In 1859 the old church debt had been entirely paid off. In 1860 were reported a parochial school and a ladies' sewing society of ten years' standing, and a new organ. During the civil war Washington County was often the scene of extensive military operations, and the parishes suffered greatly. Mr. Edwards resigned his charge in January, 1867, and became the rector of St. Mark's. He also assumed missionary charge of St. Andrew's, St. Luke's, Pleasant Valley, St. Mark's, and St. Paul's, in Frederick County.

The Rev. Clandius R. Haines commenced his rectorship April 29, 1867. In that year he reported that the church, which had been very much injured by a fire more than a year before, had been repaired at the cost of over three thousand dollars, and that two beautiful stained-glass windows had been presented for the chancel. In October, 1861, he became the minister of Christ Church, Anne Arundel County, but received his letters of transfer from Virginia in 1866, and from thence removed to Washington County. On the 1st of October, 1869, the vestry declared the church free. Its revenue increased, and in 1871 it had proved a great success. In that year he became the rector of St. Timothy's, Catonsville, Baltimore Co.

Rev. Walter A. Mitchell became rector January, 1872. He is the son of the late Rev. Richard H. B. Mitchell, so many years in St. Mary's County. He was ordained deacon by Bishop Drane, of New Jersey, in 1856, and in 1857 became rector of St. Paul's, Calvert County. In 1860 he was a missionary in Baltimore, and in 1866 became rector of St. John's, Howard County, whence he removed to Hagerstown.

Upon Mr. Mitchell's arrival, in the spring of 1872, he at once turned his attention to rebuilding the church. It was determined, as soon as the matter had been sufficiently discussed, that the wisest plan would be to sell the old site and erect the new church in another part of the town. A lot was accordingly purchased on the west side of Prospect Street, near "the Dry Bridge." The lot is ninety-two by two hundred and forty feet, and the position one of the most commanding in the town.

The foundations of the church were laid in August of 1872, and it was ready for occupancy on Nov. 3, 1875, although not absolutely complete until August 18, 1881, when the capstone of the spire was laid, and the cross which surmounts the whole was set up in its place by Geo. W. Stover, superintendent of the contractors, M. Gault & Son. As completed, the edifice is one of the most beautiful and convenient in the country. It is Gothic in style, and is built of limestone, broken range rock-work, laid in strong lime mortar. It presents a front of seventy-three feet, and is one hundred and nine feet deep. The tower is fifteen feet square, and the top of the steeple one hundred and ten feet from the ground, surmounted by a gilt cross four feet five and a half inches high, the whole steeple structure being of hewn stone, and is graceful and imposing in appearance. The native limestone is generously relieved by trimmings of brownstone and massive granite over the doorways of the tower. The tower and steeple were contributed by C. C. Baldwin as a memorial to his wife, and he has since ordered to be cast a magnificent peal of bells, which will soon be in place. The church building proper was erected under the superintendence of W. H. Hurley. The corner-stone was laid on September 4th by the rector, Rev. W. A. Mitchell, assisted by the following clergymen: Rev. Dr. Grammer, Rev. A. J. Rich, M.D., Rev. Wm. T. Johnson, Rev. Henry Edwards, Rev. Julian Ingle, and Rev. James B. Averitt. Rev. John D. Easter, Ph.D., delivered the address. The wardens, vestry, and building committee were prominently engaged in the ceremonies. They were as follows: Wardens, William Kealhofer and Buchanan Schley; Vestry, Hon. Wm. Motter, George W. Pole, Dr. William Ragan, Daniel G. Huyett, Geo. W. Harris, Alonzo Berry, and R. Howell Griswold; Building Committee, Geo. W. Harris, Dr. Wm. Ragan, Geo. Gambrill, and Buchanan Schley. Ember C. Little, of New York, the architect, was also present. At the time of its completion, in 1875, the building committee was as follows: Rev. W. A. Mitchell, Dr. Fred. Dorsey, Geo. W. Harris, and Geo. W. Pole, Esqs. The main auditorium will comfortably seat four hundred and fifty people, and its plan and decorations are very handsome. The walls are of a neutral drab, wainscoted four feet from the floor with alternate beaded walnut and chestnut planks oiled. The church is finished with walnut, and the furniture is of the same wood, the pews being richly upholstered. A magnificent organ furnishes the music for the congregation. The windows are exceedingly handsome and rich in their coloring. The central light of the chancel window is a figure of St. John, the two side lights figured stained glass, the three upper circular windows are figures of adoring angels with trumpet, lute, and harp. There are three handsome windows in the south transept, one, the subject of which is the Annunciation and Nativity, contributed by the Sunday-school of the church, costing about one hundred and sixty dollars; another, representing the presentation in the Temple and our Lord among the doctors, is a memorial of the late Maj. Holker Hughes; and a third, in memory of Miss Anna Fitzhugh, is triangular, and represents the adoration of the wise men. In the north transept is a large circular window representing the Ascension. The other windows are of diamond-shaped buff and white stained glass.

The opening services of the church were held on Oct. 11, 1875. The following clergymen were present: The Right Rev. Theodore Lyman, Assistant Bishop of North Carolina, a former rector of the parish; Rev. C. W. Rankin, of St. Luke's Church, Baltimore; Rev. Fred. Gibson, assistant rector St. Luke's Church, Baltimore; Rev. Dr. J. Stephenson, of Frederick County; Rev. Dr. S. C. Thrall, of Cumberland; Rev. Jas. Mitchell, Centreville, Queen Anne's Co.; Rev. Henry Edwards and Rev. Jos. B. Trevett, of Washington County; and the rector, the Rev. Walter A. Mitchell. The procession was headed by thirty choristers of St. Luke's Church, Baltimore. While marching up the aisle the hymn "Holy, Holy, Holy," was sung. The sermon was preached by Bishop Lyman.

The graveyard of St. John's Church contains the remains of the following old residents:

Col. Isaac Nesbitt, born Nov. 30, 1804, died June 1, 1865; and his wife, Ann Jane, died June 17, 1861, aged 50 years.

Capt. Alexander H. Nesbitt, of the Union army, died March 9, 1863, aged 29 years.

Alexander Neill, born Dec. 5, 1808, died July 18, 1865; and his wife, Mary S., born March 22, 1819, died Aug. 23, 1880.

Isabella Neill, born March 8, 1785, died June 16, 1856.

Mary Chandler, wife of Dr. Wm. Chandler, of Philadelphia, died May 28, 1862, aged 86 years.

Mary Macgill, daughter of Rev. James Macgill, first rector of Queen Caroline Parish, Anne Arundel Co., Md., born March 25, 1749, died Aug. 18, 1824.

Dr. Wm. D. Macgill, born Jan. 6, 1801, died March 22, 1833.

Dr. N. Carroll Macgill, born May 13, 1804, died Sept. 14, 1839.

Henry Howard Gaither, born March 11, 1793, died April 22, 1856; and his wife, Catherine K., born Jan. 17, 1793, died March 8, 1857.

Elizabeth Gaither, died June 30, 1845, in her 83d year.

Matilda, wife of George C. Smoot, died March 7, 1844, aged 68 years.

Rezin Davis, born April 29, 1753, died March 17, 1800; and his wife, Eleanor, born April 5, 1737, died March 28, 1815.

Eliza Schnebly, born July 16, 1791, died Aug. 2, 1871.

Mary McCardell, died Sept. 14, 1834, in her 72d year.

Mrs. Mary Pottinger, died March 7, 1854, in her 88th year.

John Williams, born in Badnearshire, South Wales, Feb. 2, 1757, died March 4, 1843.

Martha Stewart, wife of William Stewart, and daughter of Isaac Foury, of Londonderry, Ireland, died April 8, 1845, aged 70 years.

Gottleib Basler, a native of Germany, died Dec. 13, 1831, in his 76th year; and his wife, Mary, died Feb. 28, 1850, in her 86th year.

John Nibert, a native of Germany, born May 1, 1750, died Jan. 20, 1828.

Alexander Neill, Sr., died Aug. 2, 1858, aged 80 years; and his wife, Sally, died June 24, 1843, aged 62 years, 11 months.

Mrs. Isabella Neill, died Jan. 22, 1826, aged 69 years, 8 months.

Barton Bean, born March 24, 1780, died Aug. 24, 1835.

Benjamin Galloway, died Aug. 19, 1831, aged 77 years, 7 months.

Henrietta Galloway, died April 21, 1847, aged 89 years.

Wm. Fitzhugh, died May 14, 1829, aged 45 years, 8 months.

Dr. Samuel Young, born in County Down, Ireland, May, 1739, died July 23, 1838, aged 99 years, 2 months.

John McLaughlin, died Sept. 13, 1804, in his 65th year; and his wife, Susan, died Dec. 21, 1834, in her 92d year.

Jacob Harvard, died Feb. 18, 1867, aged 75 years, 1 month.

Stewart Herbert, died March 13, 1795, aged 40 years, 11 months.

David C. Newcomer, born in 1802, died in 1852; and his wife, Elenora, born in 1806, died in 1833.

Mary, wife of James Inglis, Sr., of Baltimore, died Aug. 9, 1829, in her 85th year.

Otho Holland Williams Stull, born March 7, 1784, died July 23, 1867; and his wife, Letitia, died Oct. 2, 1862, in her 75th year.

Otho Holland Williams, born Sept. 27, 1776, died July 11, 1852; and his wife, Elizabeth Bowie, died Nov. 14, 1816, aged 34 years, 6 months.

Thomas Belt, died Dec. 3, 1823, aged 82 years, 1 month; and his wife, Elizabeth Lawson, died July 30, 1816, aged 62 years.

Margaret Capito, born in 1789, died Jan. 23, 1878.

William Beverley Clarke, born Sept. 4, 1817, died April 14, 1855.

Sally, wife of William Price, born June 2, 1797, died Oct. 26, 1837.

Thomas Sprigg, died Dec. 15, 1809; and his wife, Elizabeth, died July 28, 1808.

John Reynolds, died Dec. 3, 1845, aged 59 years; and his wife, Maria Eliza Sprigg, died March 9, 1851, aged 60 years.

William O. Sprigg, son of Thomas and Elizabeth, died July 29, 1836, aged 63 years.

Thomas Curtis, born in 1783, died Feb. 15, 1874; and his wife, Ann, born Aug. 3, 1791, died March 19, 1851.

Elie Beatty, died May 6, 1859, in his 84th year.

John D. Reamure, died March 15, 1866, aged 49 years, 7 months.

Samuel Hughes, born July 6, 1773, died May 2, 1845; and his wife, Catherine, born March 29, 1781, died Oct. 29, 1857.

John Holker Hughes, born Sept. 19, 1798, died Jan. 15, 1871.

Napoleon Hughes, born Dec. 23, 1806, died March 29, 1877.

Ann Hughes Fitzhugh, died March 5, 1870.

Washington L. Berry, died May 15, 1866, aged 40 years.

William H. Fitzhugh, died March 13, 1851, aged 57 years.

Marie Antoinette Fitzhugh, died April 26, 1864, aged 63 years.

William H. Handy, died April 7, 1863, aged 77 years; and his wife, Catherine, died July 2, 1866, aged 68 years.

Judge Thomas Buchanan, born Sept. 25, 1768, died Sept. 28, 1847, aged 79 years; and Rebecca Maria, his wife, died Feb. 9, 1840, in her 70th year.

Harriet Rebecca Anderson Buchanan, born Oct. 13, 1803, died Feb. 11, 1872.

John Robert Dall, born Nov. 1, 1798, died May 5, 1851; and his wife, Meliora, daughter of Judge Thomas Buchanan, born Dec. 24, 1800, died April 2, 1879.

Jacob Hollingsworth, born Aug. 6, 1790, died March 19, 1868; and his wife, Nancy, born Sept. 10, 1793, died Aug. 24, 1872.

Hezekiah Claggett, died April 3, 1866, aged 79 years, 7 months; and his wife, Ann, died March 26, 1867, aged 66 years, 4 months.

St. John's Lutheran Church, Hagerstown, was organized in 1770, its constitution being signed by sixty members. Its first pastor was the Rev. Mr. Wildban, and within one year after its organization it had one hundred and sixty communicants, and a year later two hundred and seventy-one. From 1772 to 1779 the pastor was the Rev. Mr. Young, and it is believed that the first church edifice was built during his pastorate. In 1782 a collection, amounting to £127 19*s.* 6*d.*, was taken to purchase an organ. There are no records in existence of the proceedings for the ensuing eleven years, except that in December, 1791, the congregation held a lottery for raising nine hundred and sixty-five dollars. There were two thousand two hundred tickets at two dollars, with seven hundred and forty-one prizes and fourteen hundred and fifty-nine blanks. The trustees and managers were: Trustees, Peter Hoeflich, Henry Shryock, Peter Woltz, Baltzer Goll, David Harry, and Jacob Harry. Managers, William and John Lee, Rezin Davis, Alexander Claggett, Nathaniel Rochester, Henry Schnebly, William Reynolds, Melcher Beltzhoover, John Geiger, John Protzman, Adam Ott, Michael Kapp, George Woltz, John Ragan, Abraham Leider, Robert Hughes, Henry Shroder, Henry Eckhart, William Van Lear, Jacob Miller, F. T., Frederick Stemple, Peter Whitesides, Andrew Kleinsmith, Philip Entler, John Ney. In 1793 the Rev. J. G. Schmucker, D.D., became pastor. Dr. Schmucker was educated at Halle, Germany, and was twenty-two years of age when he came to Hagerstown. Previous to his acceptance of the charge of St. John's he had been engaged in religious work in York County, Pa., among his charges being "Quickel's." An old sermon contains a graphic picture of the condition of religious society at the time of his first appearance in Hagerstown. The Presbyterians were described as leisurely waiting God's time, while the Episcopal minister was "much more at home in the ball-room and on the turf than in the pulpit," and the Methodists only were fighting the devil with any vigor. The new pastor of St. John's entered vigorously into the work which was before him, and made a great impression and was very successful. In 1795 another building was erected. The congregation numbered one hundred and eight members at this time, and ten years afterwards it had increased to two hundred and eleven. A new constitution was adopted in 1806. Dr. Schmucker resigned in 1810, and was succeeded by the Rev. Solomon Schaeffer, who died young and was buried beneath the church. A marble tablet in the aisle near the chancel marks his resting-place. In 1815, Rev. Benjamin Kurtz, D.D., became pastor. He also supplied the congregations at Funkstown, Williamsport, Beard's, and Smithsburg. In 1816 there were one hundred and seventy-nine communicants; in 1800, three hundred; and in 1822, four hundred and two. In 1825 a second bell was purchased, the congregation having paid off an indebtedness of thirteen hundred dollars in the previous year. During Dr. Kurtz's pastorate, which lasted sixteen years, preaching in English and protracted prayer-meetings were introduced. During Dr. Kurtz's absence in Europe in 1825, for the purpose of securing assistance for Gettysburg Theological Seminary, the pulpit was supplied by the Rev. F. Ruthrauff and the Rev. J. Medtard.

In 1827, Mr. Kurtz returned from Europe and resumed his pastoral relations with the church, Rev. F. Ruthrauff removing to Pennsylvania, while Rev. J. Medtard took charge of the church at Martinsburg, Rev. Winter being called to Williamsport—an associate charge of St. John's—upon Mr. Medtard's removal therefrom to go to Martinsburg.

Dr. Kurtz was succeeded at St. John's by Rev. Samuel K. Hoshour in 1831, who was followed in 1834 by Rev. C. F. Schaeffer, D.D. The latter resigned in 1840. At the last communion of the latter three hundred and eight names were recorded. Rev. Ezra Keller, D.D., succeeded Dr. Schaeffer, and during his pastorate, lasting four years, the number of communicants increased to four hundred and sixty. Rev. F. W. Conrad became pastor in May, 1844, and resigned in October, 1850. During his pastorate two hundred and nineteen persons were admitted, one hundred and ninety-two buried, two hundred and fifty baptized, and the sum of seven thousand seven hundred and fifty dollars was raised for various objects. Four Sabbath-schools were organized in the county, which with that in Hagerstown numbered more than five hundred scholars. In the fall of 1850, Rev. F. R. Anspach, D.D., became pastor, and was succeeded by Rev. R. Hill in 1857, who was followed by Rev. J. Evans in December, 1860. Mr. Evans remained until 1866, and was succeeded in 1867 by Rev. T. T. Titus, who resigned in October, 1869, in order to become pastor of Trinity Lutheran Church, an offshoot of St. John's. During several intervals the pulpit was supplied by Rev. W. F. Eyster and Rev. C. Martin, while acting as principals of the female seminary. In November, 1869, the Rev. S. W. Owen (the present pastor) took charge. He preached his last sermon in the church in its old form on the last Sunday in May, 1870, and the first one in its remodeled form on the third Sunday of April, 1871. During the century and more of its existence this congregation has had fourteen regular pastors and four temporary supplies. Of the regular pastors six are still living, viz.: Revs. S. K. Hoshour, C. F. Schaeffer, F. W. Conrad, Reuben Hill, T. T. Titus, and S. W. Owen; and eight have died, viz.: Revs. Wildban, Young, J. G. Schmucker, Solomon Schaeffer, Benjamin Kurtz, Ezra Keller, F. R. Anspach, and J. Evans. Of the temporary supplies, Revs. C. Martin and W. F. Eyster are still living, while Revs. F. Ruthrauff and J. Medtard are dead. The original field covered by the pastors of St. John's has been divided into half a dozen charges, supplied by as many ministers. The older pastors took a prominent part in the organization of the General Synod, and in St. John's Church the delegates from the Pennsylvania, Maryland, and North Carolina Synods met on the 20th of October, 1820, to adopt its constitution. Here also the committee met to determine the location of the General Theological Seminary, and the congregation of St. John's subscribed the largest *bona-fide* sum, two thousand five hundred dollars, to secure it. Three of its pastors became editors of the *Lutheran Observer*, while others have been prominent in educational works. It has furnished a number of ministers, among them Dr. W. M. Reynolds, Prof. F. Springer, and Rev. Messrs. C. Startzman, J. H. A. Kitzmiller, H. J. Watkins, and J. Forthman. Its Ladies' Benevolent Association has aided a number of clergymen in obtaining their education. The congregation numbers three hundred and twenty-five members, and recently expended seventeen thousand dollars in remodeling its church edifice. The old church, built in 1795 and 1796, stood on South Potomac Street. Its pulpit was shaped like a wine-glass, and had six sides. It was twenty feet high, and entered by a door from a circular stairway, which led down into a latticed room which was used by the minister. Above the pulpit was a sounding-board, on which was emblazoned a large eye. There was no carpet on the floor, and the church was unheated, it being considered improper that the congregation should enjoy the comfort of a fire while listening to the minister and performing their devotions. The collection-bags were attached to rods about ten feet in length, and had a silken tassel and a bell, which was used to attract the notice of inattentive or sleepy members. At this period the attendance was not as large or as regular as might have been desired, cock-fighting at Big Spring or Yellow (now Ladle) Spring, horse-racing, bull-baiting, and similar sports proving attractions too strong to be resisted by some of the members.

In March, 1870, the old church was remodeled, so that the internal dimensions became seventy-five by sixty feet, and commodious access was afforded by means of two spacious stairways to the chief hall of worship on the upper floor. The lower floor was fitted up with new seats, and was used by the Sunday-school, then containing five hundred scholars and teachers. The auditorium on the upper floor was fitted up with the newest style of seats, very handsomely upholstered in crimson damask and soft cushions. The old organ gave way to a new one of later pattern and better tone, which cost sixteen hundred dollars. The old pulpit and chancel were taken out and replaced, the new ones being of solid curled walnut. Previous to this, in January, 1870, the two old bells had been taken down, both being cracked so badly as to render them useless. One of these bells had been cast in London in 1788, and the other in Boston in 1824. The inscription upon the older bell, although in English, had the German spelling.

Previous to 1834 the charge of St. John's embraced Williamsport, St. Paul, Clear Spring, and Martinsburg. At these places the church buildings were inconsiderable, there being only a log building even at Williamsport, which was the most considerable of them all. When Rev. Benj. Kurtz returned from Europe in 1827, Rev. Mr. Winter took charge of the church at Williamsport, and during his pastorate, in 1829, the present brick church was built.

In September, 1834, Rev. S. W. Harkey took charge of Williamsport, St. Paul, Clear Springs being served by Rev. Winter. After serving the charge one year and a vacancy of eleven months Rev. Daniel Miller became pastor, and continued to sustain this relation for one year, when, after a vacancy of one year and four months, Rev. Christian Startzman became pastor, and remained eleven years. During this period Clear Spring was reunited to the charge, but when Rev. Henry Bishop was called to be pastor in 1850, Clear Spring withdrew a second time from the charge. In 1855, owing to the removal of Rev. Mr. Bishop, Rev. Wm. F. Greaver was chosen as his successor. He is represented as having been "very much esteemed and beloved by the whole congregation, and under his ministry the church was prospering, but he died Oct. 16, 1857.

His successor was Rev. Jos. Barclay, late of Baltimore, during whose ministry the church edifice was enlarged and beautifully frescoed. In August or September, 1859, he resigned, and was followed on the 20th of October of the same year by Rev. Christian Lepley, who remained until October, 1864. After a vacancy of about a year Rev. S. Jesse Berlin was called to assume the pastoral care on Nov. 1, 1865, but owing to failing health he removed Feb. 1, 1867, when he was succeeded by Rev. M. L. Culler, who remained until 1869, when he removed to Martinsburg, W. Va. In 1870 another division took place in the pastorate by the union of St. Paul's with the Clear Spring charge. In 1871, Rev. W. D. Strobel became pastor, and after a ministry of about three years he resigned. The congregation was now supplied with preaching by Rev. J. McCrow, of the Hagerstown Female Seminary, and in April, 1874, Rev. J. B. Keller was called to become the pastor. During this period the membership has been considerably increased, numbering now about one hundred and forty. The church has for the second time been freed from debt, the contributions have been largely increased, a "Dime Society," averaging ninety members, who pay ten cents monthly, has been kept in successful operation for three or four years, the Sunday-school numbers on its roll one hundred and thirty-five pupils and twenty-two teachers, and the church has been lately repaired at a cost of about three hundred dollars.

One of the leading members of St. John's and a pillar of the church for many years was Capt. George Shryock. George, son of John and Mary (born Teagarden) Shryock, was born in 1783 on the manor in Washington County. In 1787 the family removed to Hagerstown, and resided on Franklin Street opposite the Oak Spring. In 1796 he accompanied his father and brother John to Westmoreland County, Pa., where they built a log house in the woods. The rest of the family followed them in the same year, the wagon conveying their goods being the first ever seen in that portion of the country. Heavy wooden sledges were used for hauling and pack-horse trains for transportation between more distant points. In 1803, George Shryock returned to Hagerstown and commenced the manufacture of pumps. He was a leading member of St. John's Lutheran congregation, which his father had furnished with a portion of the building materials for the church edifice, erected in 1796. In 1808 he married Elizabeth Lewis, daughter of Capt. James Lewis, and in the same year both himself and his wife became communicants of St. John's Church. In 1820 he was a lay delegate to the first General Synod of the Lutheran Church in America, which met in Hagerstown, and was the last survivor of that body. In 1813 he served as captain in Ragan's regiment, Stansbury's brigade. David Artz was first lieutenant of his company, —— Posey was second lieutenant, and Christian Fechtig was ensign. After the repulse at Bladensburg the company was detailed to support Commodore John Rogers' battery at Fort McHenry, Baltimore, and was present at the famous bombardment on the night the "Star-Spangled Banner" was written. Capt. Shryock was one of a family of eleven children, of whom seven reached the age of eighty years and over, one that of seventy, and two that of sixty years and over.

COMMODORE JOHN ROGERS.

Among those buried in the old St. John's Lutheran graveyard are the following residents of Hagerstown and vicinity:

Samuel Eichelberger, died July 22, 1863, aged 73.

Philip Householder, died Jan. 26, 1860, aged 78 years, 5 months; and his wife, Barbara, died April 8, 1863, aged 77 years, 3 months.

George McNamee, born March 27, 1775, died April 17, 1838.

David Startzman, died March 8, 1854, aged 70 years, 1 month.

Thomas Thirston, died Dec. 6, 1843, in his 51st year; and his wife, Sarah, died Dec. 9, 1876, aged 82.

Susan, wife of William H. Hager, born Oct. 8, 1820, died Dec. 16, 1875.

Henry Kealhapper, born Jan. 28, 1776, died Oct. 31, 1851; and his wife, Elizabeth, born Sept. 6, 1782, died Jan. 31, 1852.

George Gittinger, died Nov. 9, 1844, aged 80 years, 6 months.

Barbara, wife of John Eckstein, died Sept. 2, 1850, aged 73.

George Bowman, born Jan. 12, 1793, died April 28, 1870; and his wife, Mary, born Jan. 13, 1801, died Jan. 27, 1870.

Mary Hinkle, born May 15, 1817, died Jan. 8, 1871, aged 53.

Peter Jacob Creek, died April 3, 1838, aged 72 years, 6 months; and his wife, Margaret, died April 8, 1857, aged 78.

Valentine Glass, died Oct. 29, 1857, aged 83; and his wife, Mary Barbara, born April 4, 1781, died Aug. 25, 1843, aged 62.

Elizabeth Gelwicks, born March 15, 1775, died Feb. 26, 1841.

Thomas Wright, died March 22, 1841, in his 50th year.

Henry Freaner, died July 7, 1863, in his 66th year; and his wife, Sarah, died Jan. 17, 1847, in her 43d year.

Susannah Stewart, born Feb. 14, 1767, died March 31, 1842.

Joseph Trovinger, born Dec. 11, 1790, died May 17, 1851.

John Albert, died April 28, 1860, aged 81 years, 2 months.

Jacob Semler, Sr., died Oct. 29, 1853, aged 61 years, 1 month.

John Kealhoffer, died Oct. 17, 1856, aged 72; and his wife, Mary, died March 22, 1863, aged 73.

Sophia Smith, died July 28, 1868, aged 72 years, 1 month.

Samuel Rouskulp, died July 31, 1865, aged 81 years, 2 months; and his wife, Sarah, died Aug. 12, 1849, aged 57 years, 8 months.

Catharine Smith, daughter of Peter and Ann Maria Heiflich, born Oct. 22, 1771, died April 22, 1847.

Jacob Bragunier, died June 14, 1851, in his 57th year; and his wife, Mary, died March 17, 1859, aged 63 years, 7 months.

Jacob Zimmerman, born in Lebanon County, Pa., Oct. 19, 1770, died Dec. 11, 1868; and his wife, Elizabeth, born in Dauphin County, Pa., April 8, 1803, died April 14, 1871.

George C. Gelwicks, born March 16, 1784, died March 31, 1853; and his wife, Mary, born Feb. 15, 1788, died March 10, 1868.

James Hawthorn, died Feb. 17, 1853, aged 84.

Samuel B. and Ann Harris. The former died March 19, 1844, in his 79th year; the latter, June 15, 1844, in her 70th year. Their tombstone records that "they were wedded more than fifty years."

Eliza Woltz, born Sept. 23, 1797, died May 2, 1867.

Daniel Gearhart, born Feb. 14, 1791, died June 3, 1842.

Nancy Lutter, died July 5, 1865, aged 79 years, 7 months.

Peter Kuntz, born March 2, 1779, died Nov. 4, 1844; and his wife, Maria, born Nov. 14, 1786, died Nov. 14, 1853.

Susannah Brown, died June 22, 1862, aged 82 years, 6 months.

Thomas Phillips, born March 22, 1788, died Feb. 19, 1844.

Jacob Huyett, of Henry, born April 25, 1784, died Feb. 2, 1842; and his wife, Mary, died Jan. 25, 1851, aged 60 years, 9 months.

Jacob Firey, born Nov. 25, 1767, died May 10, 1831.

Susan Firey, died Sept. 15, 1872, aged 90 years, 5 months.

John N. Zimmer, born Aug. 20, 1781, died March 8, 1856.

Sergt. David L. Smith, Co. A, 7th Maryland Regiment, died June 21, 1865, aged 30 years, 1 month.

Daniel Willard, born Oct. 5, 1784, died Nov. 14, 1846.

George B. Brumbaugh, born Sept. 9, 1785, died May 22, 1837, aged 53; and Mary L., his wife, born Aug. 11, 1778, and died March 29, 1840, aged 61.

Joseph Newman, died May 7, 1862, aged 43.

Joseph A. File, died July 9, 1845, aged 48.

John G. Laisey, died Nov. 7, 1849, aged 57.

Rebecca A. Newcomer, wife of Jacob, born Aug. 15, 1813, died Nov. 1, 1850, aged 37.

Richard Rowe, born May 5, 1805, died Dec. 5, 1858, aged 53; and Ann Maria, his wife, born Sept. 23, 1805, died May 5, 1839, aged 33.

Thomas Lowery, died Feb. 25, 1844, aged 42.

Abraham Cushwa, died Aug. 25, 1859, aged 43.

Eliza, wife of Jacob Mumma, died Feb. 12, 1851, aged 52.

Jacob Semler, Sr., died Oct. 29, 1853, aged 61.

John Moyer, died March 27, 1871, aged 68.

Gottlieb B. Laiger, born April 22, 1806, died July 9, 1853, aged 49.

William Baker, born May 6, 1800, died Feb. 22, 1853, aged 52.

Catharine Smith, daughter of Peter A. and Ann Maria Heiflich, born Oct. 22, 1771, died April 22, 1847, aged 75.

Magdalena, wife of John D. Middlekauff, died May 29, 1858, aged 45.

Ann Maria Smith, daughter of Nicholas and Catharine Smith, born May 18, 1792, died April 20, 1844, in her 53d year.

Daniel Bragunier, died in September, 1858, in his 55th year.

Rosanna Bragunier, died Sept. 16, 1860, in her 55th year.

Elizabeth Startzman, born Aug. 15, 1803, and died May 15, 1856.

Jacob Zimmerman, born in Lebanon County, Pa., Oct. 19, 1790, died Dec. 11, 1868, aged 78; and Elizabeth, his wife, born April 8, 1803, died April 14, 1871, aged 68.

Christiana, wife of Jonathan Late, born Dec. 11, 1811, died July 6, 1864, aged 52.

Michael Rudisill, died June 28, 1868, aged 53.

Francis C. Reed, died Feb. 26, 1872, aged 64; and his wife, died Aug. 7, 1863, aged 52.

Susan Coal, died May 27, 1852, in her 47th year.

John Bentz, died June 9, 1847, aged 58.

Peter Wright, born May 16, 1806, died May 1, 1868, aged 61; and his wife, Susan, died Feb. 6, 1853, aged 41.

Mrs. Elizabeth Hostetter, born Jan. 27, 1808, died Jan. 25, 1844, aged 35.

Thomas Phillips, born March 22, 1788, died Feb. 19, 1844, aged 55.

Dr. Thomas P. Phillips, born Sept. 25, 1813, died Nov. 29, 1841, aged 28.

Susan, wife of James Kridler, died Aug. 18, 1856, aged 49.

Daniel Willard, born Oct. 5, 1784, died Nov. 14, 1846, aged 62.

Jacob Newcomer, died April 8, 1859, in his 58th year.

Henry Weise, born June 30, 1809, died Sept. 11, 1864, aged 55; and Elizabeth, his wife, died Aug. 4, 1840, aged 27.

Trinity Evangelical Lutheran Church.—The project of forming a new Lutheran society and erecting a new church edifice in Hagerstown took definite shape in the spring of 1868, the first meeting of those favorable to the enterprise being held in May of that year. The circumstance which led to the new church project was the refusal of a majority of the members of St. John's to remodel their old edifice. After numerous efforts on the part of some of the most enterprising of St. John's members to remodel the edifice had failed, about sixty or seventy withdrew from the mother-church and proceeded to organize another congregation. Before their withdrawal an equitable division of the common church property was proposed, and a committee was appointed to value the property, which they did, and reported the value to be sixteen thousand dollars. No division, however, was ever made.

On May 13th the friends of the new enterprise held a meeting, and a committee of arrangements was appointed, and other preliminary steps taken. At subsequent meetings the following committees were appointed: On subscriptions, Martin Startzman, Jonathan Schindel, and John E. Herbst, M.D., and to this number Philip Wingert, Jacob Roesner, and A. J. Weise were subsequently added; for procuring a lot and selecting a site, David Artz, Sr., Otho Swingley, and William H. Protzman; on constitution and by-laws, A. J. Weise, William H. Protzman, Otho Swingley, Wilson L. Hays, and John Byers; in procuring designs, Dr. J. E. Herbst and William Householder. Subsequently the following members of the building committee were chosen by ballot: Dr. J. E. Herbst, Otho Swingley, George W. Stover, Lewis L. Mentzer, and Jonathan Schindel. The following were named trustees of the new congregation: M. Startzman, W. L. Hays, and F. J. Posey.

The lot on which the church now stands, on West Franklin Street, was purchased for three thousand five hundred dollars from E. M. Reche. The architect of the present "Trinity Lutheran Church" was C. S. Witzel, of Danville, Pa. Ground was broken for the foundation on Oct. 1, 1868, and the ceremony of laying the corner-stone occurred in the presence of a large concourse of people on Nov. 7, 1868, Rev. Joel Swartz officiating. The church cost thirty thousand dollars, not including the furniture, which was put in at a cost of two thousand dollars, and when completed ten thousand dollars of debt remained against it. The congregation was formally organized on the 29th of August, 1869, with about one hundred and twenty members; the building committee, under whose superintendence the church edifice was erected, were as follows: Dr. J. E. Herbst, chairman; L. L. Mentzer, secretary; F. J. Posey, treasurer; and Messrs. Jonathan Schindel, Otho Swingley, and Geo. W. Stover.

The church was dedicated on the 3d of October, 1869, on which occasion Rev. F. W. Conrad, D.D., preached the dedicatory sermon. The congregation at once elected Rev. T. T. Titus, of St. John's, pastor of their new church, a call which he at once accepted, and began his ministry. In 1870 a chime of bells was placed in the steeple at a cost of fifteen hundred dollars, and a splendid organ placed in the church. The total cost of the church has been thirty-six thousand dollars, and although a parsonage has been recently purchased at a cost of three thousand dollars, the congregation only owes five thousand dollars. On the 3d of April, 1870, Rev. T. T. Titus, in consequence of the impaired condition of his health, was compelled to resign as pastor, and the church was without a pastor until Feb. 25, 1872, when Rev. W. H. Luchenbach was elected and served until August, 1874. On the 13th of June, 1875, Rev. John R. Williams, the present pastor, was elected.

Rev. T. T. Titus, first pastor of Trinity Lutheran Church, was born in Loudon County, Va., on the 4th of March, 1829. He was the son of poor parents, and the youngest of ten children. He manifested an eager desire for learning when quite young, and was carefully instructed by his mother in the principles of religion. At sixteen years of age he became a teacher, to which occupation he devoted some years of his life. Being very poor, however, he was often obliged to labor with slaves in the field. He was converted at a protracted meeting led by the Rev. P. Willard in 1847, and not long after united with the Lutheran Church. In 1848 he went to Gettysburg, and commenced his studies for the ministry in the preparatory department of the General Theological Seminary. His extreme poverty made it necessary for him to leave college several times in order that by teaching or selling books he might obtain the money needed to continue his education. In 1853 he was rewarded by graduating as valedictorian of his class. In the following year he took a class in the preparatory department, and at the same time continued his studies for the ministry. The double labor, however, was too much for his strength, and he was compelled to go abroad for the benefit of his health. He was then ordained, and served in the ministry for eighteen years. In 1867 he succeeded the Rev. J. Evans as pastor of St. John's Church, Hagerstown, and in October, 1869, became the pastor of Trinity Church. He labored with the greatest zeal, until at last his voice grew so weak that he could no longer be heard from the pulpit. As a writer he was vigorous and pointed, and was a valued contributor to the *Lutheran Observer*. He was also the author of a useful "Explanatory Question Book for Sunday-schools." Mr. Titus was very active in temperance work, and was twice elected to the office of G. W. C. T. in the order of Good Templars in Ohio. A memorial service was held at Trinity Church, conducted by Rev. Dr. McCron and Rev. W. H. Luckenbach, who preached the sermon.

The St. Matthew's German Lutheran Church, which stands on Antietam Street, was founded in 1871, and the congregation was organized on June 19th of that year. Work was commenced on the church during the next fall, and the edifice was completed in the spring, the dedication of the church occurring on May 26, 1872. The first church council was as follows: Lewis Heist, Y. Maisack, William Schlotterbeck, Christian Thomas, Jacob Schneider, Wolfgang Brey, Henry Darnberger, Peter Rauth, G. Grebner, John Brey. The first pastor was Rev. J. J. Dietrich, who was succeeded by Rev. C. Steinhauer. After him came Rev. J. G. Reitz, who immediately preceded the present pastor, Rev. G. H. Brandon. The present church council is constituted as follows: Christian Krohberger, George Rauth, Jacob Rettberg, Gottlob Schmidt, Frederick Baumbach, Jacob Wuensch, Justus Heinel, Christian Bretzler, Jacob Schlotterbeck.

The Reformed Church.—Although the Reformed Church was founded even prior to 1776, there are no authentic records of the church previous to that year, when the first regular church organization was effected. Its first regular pastor was Rev. Jacob Weymer, who was first put in charge of the congregation in 1770, and who continued to serve it until his death, which occurred in 1790. During his pastorate the oldest church edifice now standing in Hagerstown was erected, in the year 1774, more than a century ago. The congregation elected William Heyser, a member and deacon of the congregation, building-master, who was assisted in the construction of the church by his colleagues, Philip Osten, Peter Wagner, and Jacob Hauser, who carried the work on to the laying of the corner-stone.

On this occasion Rev. Frederick Ludwig Henop, Reformed pastor at Frederick Town, who had been invited to be present, preached on the words contained in Colossians iii. 17, "And whatever ye do in word or deed, do all in the name of the Lord Jesus, giving thanks to God and the Father by Him." At this service, which was held on the ground on which the church was to be built, there was likewise present Jacob Weimer, Reformed pastor in Elizabethtown, Rev. George Young, Lutheran pastor, and Rev. —— ——, also Lutheran pastor of Fredericktown; William Heyser, builder, and Philip Oster, Peter Wagner, Jacob Hauser, deacons. The following were the members of the first congregation: William Baker, Ernst Baker, Yost Wegand, Isan Guadig, Johannes Karr, Frantz Greilich, Herman Greilich, Andreas Link, Eustagines Jung, Wilhelm Courath, Henrich Doutweller, Jacob Fischer, Johannes Steinscyfer, Frantz Wagner, Ernst Ditz, Rutholple Bley, Johannes Oster, Michael Eberhart, Matthaus Saylor, George Herdii, George Clampert, Johannes Nicholas Schister, George ——, Hanadam ——, Valentin ——, Jacob Hauser, Peter Diller, George Frey, Johannes Frey, Conrad Eichelberger, Philip Klein, Ernst Kremer. The corner-stone of this venerable structure was laid on the 10th of August, 1774. The ground occupied by the church was given by Jonathan Hager, founder of the town, and a member of the congregation who was killed by a rolling log while engaged in cutting timber for the church edifice.

No record has been preserved of the date of consecration. It is known that after the building had been placed under roof the congregation, for want of means to complete it, worshiped in it for four years with the interior unfinished. The dedication probably took place about 1778. The succession of pastors is as follows: Rev. Jacob Weymer, 1770, who continued to serve the congregation and to preach at St. Paul's, near Clear Spring, at Salem Church, at Beard's Church near Cavetown, at Besore's, near Waynesboro', and at Apple's, in Frederick County, until the 12th day of May, 1790, when he died, at the age of sixty-six years, and was buried in the graveyard attached to the church, no stone, at his own request, marking his last resting-place. Two years afterwards the Rev. Jonathan Rahauser succeeded him in the charge of these congregations, and served them for a period of twenty-five years, performing an immense amount of labor, and proving an effective preacher and a popular pastor. He died Sept. 25, 1817, in the fifty-third year of his age, and was also buried in the graveyard attached to the church. Rev. James R. Reily was the third pastor, who entered upon the discharge of his duties on the 1st of January, 1819, having on that day preached his introductory sermon. He seems to have been a very popular preacher, as well as pastor, and drew immense congregations. He resigned on the 25th of April, 1825. Although there was an occasional English sermon preached during Mr. Reily's ministry, it was so rare that it might almost be said that the German was the only language used in the services of the church for fifty-five years of its existence. With his successor the transition from German to English fairly commenced. Mr. Reily's successors were Rev. Mr. Brunner, 1827-32; Rev. W. A. Good, 1833-36; Rev. Albert Helffenstein, 1837-43; Rev. M. Kieffer, 1844-49; Rev. D. Gaus, 1850-55; Rev. S. H. Giesy, 1855-60; and Rev. J. H. Wagner, 1861-64. Rev. J. S. Kieffer became pastor of the congregation in 1868, and still continues to serve in that capacity, being the eleventh in a succession of pastors covering one hundred and eleven years.

Improvements in the church building were made from time to time, and the entire structure was remodeled and placed in its present condition in 1867-68. About the same time a chapel was erected beside the church, on the site of the old lecture-room. Two or three years afterwards the tower of the church, which had been left unchanged when the remodeling took place, was replaced by a new one. The new spire, however, was blown down by a violent tornado in June, 1878,—a heavy loss to the congregation, which it has not as yet been able to repair. The Sunday-school connected with the church numbers thirty odd teachers and over two hundred scholars.

The Consistory of the congregation consists, in addition to the pastor, of six elders and four deacons. These are at present the following:

Elders.—D. C. Hammond, H. K. Tice, M. A. Berry, A. D. Bennett, Wm. Gassman, E. M. Recher.

Deacons.—W. H. McCardell, J. T. Seiss, W. D. Troxell, George Shaver.

In the cemetery of the Reformed Church are buried the following:

Philip Wingert, born Jan. 11, 1784, died Aug. 30, 1861, aged 77; and Martha Wingert, died Jan. 20, 1833, aged 40.

Gen. Daniel Heister, "the patriot, the soldier, and the statesman," died March 7, 1804, in his 57th year; and his wife, Rosanna, daughter of Jonathan Hager, died Jan. 11, 1810, in her 58th year.

John Henneberger, died Sept. 11, 1859, aged 74; and his wife, Catharine, died Aug. 11, 1869, aged 80.

John McNamee, died Aug. 11, 1858, aged 51; and his wife, Margaret, died Dec. 26, 1873.

John Bragunier, died Feb. 11, 1879, aged 70; and his wife, Susan, died April 24, 1871, aged 73.

Sarah, wife of George Thornburg, born Dec. 17, 1796, died Dec. 9, 1830.

Daniel Burgesser, died March 14, 1865, aged 80.

Philip Keller, died Sept. 19, 1846, aged 73 years; and his wife, Ann, died Jan. 7, 1841, aged 64.

Samuel Bragunier, born May 30, 1788, died Jan. 16, 1838; and Elizabeth, his wife, died Nov. 22, 1875, aged 82.

Samuel Beecher, died Oct. 8, 1821, aged 53.

Jacob Knode, born Sept. 26, 1751, died Feb. 2, 1828, aged 76; and his wife, Margaret, born April 10, 1750, died July 15, 1824, aged 74.

Peter Humrichouse, died Feb. 13, 1837, aged 84 years; and his wife, Mary Ott, died Oct. 7, 1839.

Elizabeth Hager Lawrence, only grandchild of Jonathan Hager, founder of Hagerstown, and the wife of Upton Lawrence, born Aug. 1, 1785, died Aug. 5, 1867.

Alexander Armstrong, born Sept. 8, 1798, and died Oct. 29, 1870.

Ann, wife of William Williamson, died Aug. 16, 1857, aged 78.

Frederick Bryan, died July 26, 1871.

Martin Rickenbaugh, born April 3, 1793, died Feb. 16, 1874.

Jacob Stahl, born Feb. 2, 1762, and died Sept. 6, 1831, aged 69.

John Tice, Sr., born Nov. 26, 1770, died July 27, 1833.

John S. Barr, died July 6, 1856, aged 63.

Daniel Middlekauff, born Aug. 6, 1794, died Oct. 23, 1855.

Benjamin Leight, died Oct. 14, 1848, aged 74.

Jacob Gruber, died Sept. 16, 1875, aged 86.

Michael Hammond, died Nov. 13, 1857, aged 81.

Jonas Cramer, born Oct. 14, 1755, died Aug. 14, 1835.

William Heyser, died Sept. 10, 1836, aged 67.

John C. Ulrich, died March 4, 1848, aged 69.

Johannes Weller, died Jan. 1, 1800, aged 25.

John Gruber, died Dec. 29, 1857, aged 89; and Catharine, his wife, died Sept. 15, 1859, aged 82.

Jonathan Rahauser, pastor of the church, born Dec. 14, 1764, died Sept. 23, 1817.

John S. Rahauser, born Feb. 23, 1794, died June 29, 1818.

Daniel Rench, died Dec. 2, 1831, aged 61.

Andrew Kershner, born April 12, 1787, died Oct. 6, 1857; and his wife, Elizabeth, born Oct. 31, 1791, died Sept. 10, 1860.

Frederick Wolfersperger, born May 8, 1780, died Dec. 6, 1821.

Frederick Humrichouse, born July 6, 1791, died Oct. 5, 1876; and his wife, Hannah, born Jan. 29, 1791, died April 25, 1880.

William Freaner, died April 12, 1870, aged 80.

Andrew Wagoner, died Aug. 22, 1872, aged 78.

John Gottleib Mittag, born March 7, 1776, died Nov. 4, 1828, aged 52; and his wife, Susan, died Oct. 18, 1853, aged 76.

Alexander McCammon, died April 6, 1869, aged 75.

Margaret, wife of Rev. Christian F. Post, died March 7, 1810, aged 77.

Ludwig Carl Bodman, born Nov. 29, 1752, died April 1, 1828.
John Seitz, died March 30, 1831, aged 63.
Elizabeth, wife of Peter Wingert, and daughter of David Hager, died Dec. 12, 1806, aged 57.
George Ross Beall, born April 10, 1796, died May 14, 1843; and his wife, Ellen, born July 8, 1809, died Jan. 18, 1840.
Isaac S. White, Sr., died in 1844, in his 73d year.
Henry Middlekauff, born Oct. 18, 1766, died March 13, 1837.
Col. David Schnebly, youngest son of Dr. Henry Schnebly, born May 8, 1770, died Oct. 4, 1842; and Mary, born Feb. 15, 1773, died Nov. 17, 1876, aged 103 years.
John E. Hoffman, born Oct. 23, 1789, died March 6, 1870; and his wife, Catharine B. Hoffman, born Aug. 28, 1793, died Dec. 12, 1877.
Wm. Kreps, died Feb. 28, 1822, aged 50.

Christ Reformed Church.—During 1852 religious meetings were held in the lecture-room of the First Reformed Church, in Hagerstown, for the benefit of those who desired services exclusively in the German language, and were attended by Germans, members of the German Reformed and Lutheran Churches, and others not members of any church. Rev. Carl Kast, a minister of the German Reformed Church, ministered to the special wants of the new congregation for several years. No organization was, however, effected at this time, although measures were taken to build a Reformed church in which those who desired German services exclusively might worship. A location was ultimately selected on Franklin Street, and the work of building went forward. In March, 1855, the Germans assembled in the First Reformed church and organized a Reformed congregation, after which they proceeded in a body to the new church, where the corner-store was laid, and the church received the name of "Christ Church," and was popularly known as the Second Reformed Church. The church was completed in 1856, and was dedicated in the spring of the same year. Among the ministers present were Rev. Samuel H. Giesy, D.D., pastor of the First Reformed Church, Rev. Philip Schaff, D.D., and Rev. Dr. George Wolff. The following were the officers of the congregation: Henry Winter, Leonard Maisack, Mark Benner, Jacob Gruber, Theobald Kiefer, William Beslard, and George Steinmetz. Rev. Mr. Kast continued to serve the congregation for a number of years, and was succeeded by Rev. John B. Poerner. Rev. Dr. George Seifert followed Mr. Poerner. In 1868, Rev. Henry Louis G. Micnard became pastor, and served for one year. He was succeeded by Rev. Casper Scheel, who was in turn succeeded by Rev. Theobald Heischman, who was a member of the Lutheran Church, and the only Lutheran minister that ever served its congregation. It appears that he was not installed as pastor of the congregation. During his brief term of service difficulties arose, and the Reformed Classis of Maryland, which held jurisdiction over Christ Reformed Church, at its next meeting took into consideration the difficulties and complaints made by the Reformed portion of the congregation, and by resolutions declared its unwillingness to have under its jurisdiction a congregation served in so irregular and unsatisfactory a manner. As a result of this action the German Lutheran portion of the congregation left the church and proceeded to build a German Lutheran church. Rev. William F. Colliflower succeeded Rev. Heischman in 1872.

During his pastorate there was practically a reorganization of the congregation. Quite a number united with the church by confirmation and certificate who were not familiar with the German language, and in consequence there were only occasional German services, and in a short time German services were discontinued. This change from German to English services rendered necessary a change in its constitution, and on Sept. 18, 1877, such changes and alterations as were necessary were made. Rev. Mr. Colliflower continued pastor of the congregation for about three years and three months, and his successor, Rev. C. H. Coon, was installed in the fall of 1876, and was succeeded on Oct. 1, 1878, by Rev. Leighton G. Kremer, the present pastor. The officers of the congregation are: Elders, George Fridinger, Charles Fridinger, C. G. Boryer, Henry Haltzapple; Deacons, George G. Solliday, John Gassman, Solomon Baker, Theodore Weagley. The present number of communicants is ninety-seven, and Sabbath-school scholars one hundred and sixteen. Extensive improvements were made in the audience-room of the church in the fall of 1878, and the congregation possesses a neat and comfortable place of worship. The basement of the church has lately been fitted up for a Sabbath-school and lecture-room.

The Presbyterian Church.—Traces of the Presbyterian Church are found as far back as 1774, when Rev. Thomas McPherrin was called by the united congregations of Conococheague and Jerusalem, the latter being known as "Hagerstown charge," to the pastorate of the Presbyterian congregations west of the South Mountain. In 1788 it is mentioned that, in compliance with a "supplication" from Falling Waters, Hagerstown, and Williamsport, Rev. Mr. Caldwell was appointed by the Presbytery "as a constant supply for those places for one year." There are, however, no known records of the church earlier than 1817, when the society was organized.

Previous to this, from about 1809, John Lind divided his time between Greencastle and Hagerstown. He was a son of Rev. Mathews Lind, and came from Ireland in 1774, and shortly afterwards organized the Associated Reformed Church, his church being erected in Greencastle. Under the pastorate of the younger Lind the first church on South Potomac Street was erected. Before this, service was held in the German Reformed church.

On Nov. 15, 1817, Robert Douglas, John Kennedy, Joseph Gabby, and John Robertson were ordained to the office of ruling elder, and the church was known as the Associated Reformed Church. On the following day the sacrament of the Lord's Supper was administered for the first time by an English Presbyterian minister. The society thus formed comprised thirty-seven members. The church had just been completed at a cost of $9149.17. This included also the price of the lot.

The lot upon which the church was erected was purchased for fifteen hundred dollars from Gotleib Zimmerman. Of the one hundred and sixty-seven contributors to the church fund, only one, Frederick Humrickhouse, was alive in 1875. It is mentioned that two of the subscriptions to this first Presbyterian Church amounted to six thousand dollars. From the organization of the church until the end of 1824 there were added to its membership fifty-seven persons. In 1824, Rev. Mr. Lind died, and was succeeded by Rev. Matthew L. Fullerton. The church, together with that of Greencastle, united in the spring of 1825 with the Presbytery of Carlisle. Mr. Fullerton was installed as pastor Sept. 28, 1825, and ministered to the congregations of Hagerstown and Greencastle upon alternate Sundays. He died Sept. 17, 1833, and was succeeded by Rev. Richard Wynkoop, who was installed June 25, 1834, when the severance from the Greencastle Church became final. In January, 1836, the Session having determined upon the election of three additional elders, on the 26th of that month Messrs. Joseph Rench, Samuel Steele, and John McCurdy were elected. In the opposition to the ordination of Mr. McCurdy was begun a difference which ultimately resulted in a division of the church. The pastorate of Rev. Mr. Wynkoop continued until his death, April 6, 1842. He was succeeded by Rev. Herman Douglas, and he by Rev. John F. McLaren, whose pastorate continued until it became evident that a reunion could be accomplished, when he and Rev. Mr. Love, the pastor of the other church, resigned in order to further it. The pastors of the seceding portion of the congregation were Rev. Mr. Davies and Rev. William Love. Under the corporate name of the First Presbyterian Church of Hagerstown they perfected and maintained an organization, worshiping in the court-house, the Session consisting of Elders William Stewart, Nathan McDowell, and William M. Marshall. This congregation was admitted to connection with the Synod of the Associate Reformed Church Jan. 26, 1838, notwithstanding the Presbytery of Carlisle did not release it nor recognize its withdrawal. The reunion of the congregations was effected April 10, 1846, and September 14th, Rev. Septimus Tustin, D.D., was called, and came in response to the call, but was not installed until the following year. John Kennedy, the founder of the church, died April 27, 1847. Dr. Tustin having resigned, Rev. R. W. Dunlap was next called, and began his ministry in the latter part of 1851 or early in 1852. He died Feb. 17, 1856, and was succeeded by Rev. Robert A. Brown, who was called early in the year 1858. During the summer of 1861, Victor Thomson, who had long been an attendant of the church, died and devised to it the sum of five thousand dollars, which was applied, in accordance with his will, first in placing a substantial iron fence in front of the church; the balance being invested with its annual increment, made it possible to indulge the idea of remodeling the church building, but the war occurring, dissipated the project, the ultimate result being the erection of the new structure.

In the spring of 1862, Rev. Mr. Brown resigned, and the pulpit was afterwards filled and until Sept. 24, 1866, by Rev. W. C. Stitt, first as stated supply and then as pastor. Feb. 18, 1867, Rev. Tryon Edwards, D.D., was called and entered upon the ministry. He resigned Oct. 29, 1872. In April following the congregation, at the annual meeting, directed the building of the new church. July 24, 1873, Rev. J. C. Thompson was called, and he was installed November 18th of that year.

Mr. Thompson resigned in 1879, and was succeeded by Rev. J. A. Roundthaler, the present pastor. The old church on South Potomac Street was sold to the Christian Church in 1878, but the last service held in it by the Presbyterians was on Sunday, Dec. 18, 1875. The sacrament having been a part of the opening services of the church fully eight years before, it was deemed proper that the final services should be also completed with the sacrament. There was not, however, a single person who was present on both occasions. The new church was dedicated on Sunday, Dec. 25, 1875, the sermon being preached by Rev. J. T. Smith, of Baltimore. Rev. George P. Hayes, D.D., president of Washington College, preached in the evening, and raised four thousand dollars with which to help pay off the debt of ten thousand dollars. The edifice, which was designed by E. G. Lind, of Baltimore, is of graystone, and is simple but imposing in style. The main auditorium is forty-three by seventy-five feet, and is entered from a vestibule nine by forty-five feet, which opens on Washington Street. A tower occupies the northwest corner, and faces both Washington and Prospect Streets. When completed this tower will be one hundred and twenty-five feet high. The finish of the audience-room is of black walnut oiled, the seats being cushioned in crimson terry, the floor carpeted in crimson and drab. The triple window in the front is a memorial in stained glass to Victor Thomson, whose bequest formed a valuable part of the building fund. The windows upon the sides are also of stained glass in simple style. The ceiling is broken by heavy white mouldings running across, and is of a lavender tint. It is lighted artificially by four large reflectors, circular in pattern, and neat and ornamental in design.

In the Presbyterian graveyard on Potomac Street the following are buried:

John McIlhenny, died Oct. 15, 1832, aged 51.

Susan, wife of W. D. Bell, born Dec. 3, 1799, died Feb. 22, 1870.

Mary Bell, died July 10, 1870, aged 67.

Thomas Sturr, died April 10, 1858, aged 72.

Thomas Kennedy, born Nov. 29, 1776, died Oct. 18, 1832; and Rosamond Kennedy, born May 10, 1774, died March 30, 1837.

James Ferguson, died March 24, 1832, aged 79.

John Wagoner, died Nov. 21, 1831, aged 76; and Sarah Wagoner, died July 13, 1832, aged 81.

Edith Kellar, died March 14, 1843, aged 60.

In the Roman family lot, which is marked by a simple pedestal and shaft of white marble, are buried the following: James Dixon Roman, born Aug. 11, 1809, died Jan. 19, 1867; Louisa Margaret, widow of James Dixon Roman, born May 7, 1809, died Aug. 1, 1879; Sallie Roman, wife of C. C. Baldwin, born Nov. 4, 1843, died April 3, 1873; James Dixon Roman, born June 8, 1854, died July 1, 1875.

Elizabeth, wife of Joseph McIlhenny, died Nov. 3, 1857, aged 73.

William D. Bell, born Sept. 20, 1763, died Oct. 7, 1841.

William Gabby, born April 25, 1762, died Sept. 5, 1841; and Emily Gabby, died July 9, 1833, aged 59.

Hannah Kellar, born Dec. 20, 1779, and died Sept. 13, 1857.

John Kennedy, born in Ireland June 13, 1767, died April 27, 1847; and Margaret Kennedy, died May 30, 1818, aged 35 years.

Hugh Kennedy, died March 11, 1835, aged 66.

Joseph Rench, died Sept. 6, 1879, aged 73.

Mrs. Rebecca L. Martin, daughter of Col. Daniel and Ann Hughes, died March 20, 1833, aged 25.

A monument marking the grave of the Rev. Mr. Fullerton bears the inscription: "A memorial of their late beloved pastor, Rev. Matthew Lind Fullerton, erected by his congregation. He was born Oct. 22, 1801, ordained and installed pastor of the Presbyterian Church in Hagerstown, Sept. 28, 1823, and departed this life Sept. 17, 1833."

Another memorial reads: "Dedicated to the memory of the Rev. Richard Wynkoop, pastor of this church, who died after a short illness on April 6, 1842, aged 43 years."

Rev. Colin MacFarquhar, a native of Scotland, and for thirty years pastor of the Presbyterian Church of Donegal, Lancaster Co., Pa., died Aug. 22, 1822, aged 93.

Mrs. Daniel Hughes, died Aug. 29, 1823.

Methodist Church.—The section of country surrounding Hagerstown was visited by Strawbridge, Owen, King, Asbury, and other pioneer preachers. In 1776, Asbury wrote, "It seemed as if Satan were the chief ruler there; the people were very busy in drinking, swearing, etc." In 1812 he revisited the place, and says that he "preached in the neat, new Methodist chapel to about one thousand hearers." It was for a number of years included in the Chambersburg Circuit, but in 1822 appears as a separate circuit, with John Emory, subsequently bishop, as pastor. As early as 1793 the Methodists had a congregation in Hagerstown, for they are mentioned in connection with Dr. Schmucker's first appearance, which was in that year. They held camp-meetings at Enoch Jones', five miles from Hagerstown, about 1807, of which Rev. Hambleton Jefferson had charge. They had built a church in the town early in the present century, and Rev. William Rylan preached there as early as 1810. A new church was dedicated in 1867, and on Sunday, Dec. 14, 1879, the present Asbury Methodist Episcopal church was dedicated. It is situated on North Jonathan Street, and was completed during the pastorate of Rev. J. W. Waters. The structure is of brick, and is built upon the site of the old building, in which the Rev. James Brown led in worship for so many years. Its gable front abuts upon the street. The main auditorium is on the second floor, and is quite plain in its appearance, a single motto in an arch upon the wall back of the pulpit being its only ornamentation.

The church lecture-room is upon the ground-floor. Thurston & Beck, contractors, commenced work on the edifice in July, 1879, and it was dedicated on Sunday, December 14th. Rev. N. M. Carroll, of Baltimore, preached the dedicatory sermon, and the services were conducted by Presiding Elder H. A. Carroll. Sermons were also delivered during the day by Rev. James Thomas, of Baltimore, and Rev. Robert Steel, of Baltimore. On the Sunday of the dedication Presiding Elder J. H A. Johnson, of the African Methodist Episcopal Church, and Rev. Mr. Wayman, bishop of the African Methodist Episcopal Church, participated in the ceremonies. The following members of the congregation conducted the collection, which amounted to a considerable sum: John Harden, H. W. Dorsey, Benjamin Myers, H. Dorts, C. Dorsey, P. Moxley, G. Miller, and J. T. Wagner.

The colored people of Hagerstown had maintained a Methodist Church organization for many years previous to the building of their church, in July, 1879. Their church edifice was completed in the fall following, and is a commodious and convenient place of worship.

Catholic Church.—The Catholics, although they had a congregation in Hagerstown previous to that time, built their first church in the spring of 1794. Proposals for this church, or "stone chapel," were received at the house of John Worland on the 29th of January. The walls of this chapel were fifty feet long, thirty-five feet wide, and nineteen feet high. The advertisement soliciting proposals for the building of this church was signed by William Clark, who stated that he would show the plan for the chapel upon application, and proceeded to say that the person undertaking to build the walls must find stone, lime, clay, sand, and all other materials, laborers, etc., "so that the whole work may be done within himself, and the walls delivered by him ready built. His proposals must mention what he will do it for by the perch of the wall,—that is, sixteen feet and one-half of a foot in length and one foot in height of the whole thickness of the wall. Stone can be had on the lot where the house is to be built, and the quarry is already opened, which will save a great deal of expense in hauling."

In 1804, Rev. Charles Duhamel was pastor, and Patrick Edwards was parish teacher of the congregation. In 1828 a new church was built, and dedicated on October 5th of that year. On June 9, 1837, Rev. T. Ryan, who had been for many years pastor of the church, died. After this, for twelve years, Rev. Henry Myers was pastor of the Hagerstown Church, it being embraced in his parish, comprising all of Washington County. Father Myers was one of the most highly-esteemed pastors of the church. He was born in Conewago, Adams Co., Pa., in 1806, and studied at St. Mary's Seminary, Baltimore. He was ordained in 1830, and prior to his pastorate at Hagerstown was stationed at St. Patrick's, Washington, D. C., and afterwards at Cumberland, Md., where he built a church. He went to Pikesville, Baltimore Co., after twelve years of labor at Hagerstown, and in 1860 succeded Rev. Leonard Obermyer as pastor of St. Vincent de Paul's, on Front Street, Baltimore City, where he remained until the time of his death, in July, 1873.

The old Catholic church in Hagerstown was repaired in the fall of 1870, and was re-dedicated on January 29th of that year. The improvement to the church, which was already large, consisted in the erection of a tower thirteen feet square and the building of a beautiful spire, the height of which from the ground to the summit of the cross is one hundred and twenty feet. The length of the church is one hundred and nine feet, and it is forty-eight feet wide. These improvements were made from designs furnished by George A. Fredericks, of Baltimore, under the direction of Mr. Hurley, Mr. Wright, and Mr. Cushwa. The total cost was seven thousand dollars, of which all but fifteen hundred had been paid on the day of dedication. The dedication services were conducted by Rev. Henry Myers, who was then pastor of St. Vincent de Paul's, Baltimore. The Very Rev. Dwight Lyman, of Baltimore, delivered the dedicatory sermon.

The Catholic cemetery at Hagerstown embraces four acres of land on West Bethel Street. Among the interments are the following:

Susan McLaughlin, died Dec. 1, 1846, aged 70 years.

Elizabeth Brooks, died ———, in her 85th year.

William Conden, born in Queen's County, Ireland, died March 14, 1822, in his 52d year.

Francis McBride, died Feb. 25, 1874, in his 60th year.

Bridget, wife of Francis McMullin, died Nov. 20, 1863, in her 75th year.

Thomas McCardell, died Oct. 26, 1843, aged 66 years, 8 months; and his wife, Ann, died March 24, 1861, aged 84 years, 3 months.

Joseph Reel, died Jan. 17, 1831, aged 76 years, 30 days.

Elizabeth Reel, died Feb. 16, 1822, aged 54 years, 4 months.

Hugh McKuskerd, died Dec. 14, 1867, aged 64 years, 9 months; and his wife, Margaret, died March 13, 1879, aged 74 years, 1 month.

James Adams, died in 1836, aged 56 years; and his wife, Elizabeth, died Feb. 5, 1836, aged 52 years.

Patrick Mooney, died Nov. 24, 1838, aged 65 years.

Margaret Adams, died Aug. 21, 1846, aged 63 years, 3 days.

Patrick Donnelly, died May 27, 1837, in his 54th year; and his wife, Margaret, died March 29, 1852, in her 59th year.

Richard Welsh, died Nov. 9, 1828, in his 61st year.

James McGonigle, native of Londonderry, Ireland, died Oct. 13, 1838, aged 70 years.

Jeremiah Lyons, died May 16, 1876, in his 75th year.

Mary Roach, native of Limerick, Ireland, died Sept. 6, 1876, aged 80 years.

Philip Bradley, native of Londonderry, Ireland, died March 1, 1875, aged 63 years.

Hugh Murphy, born in County Carlow, Ireland, died March 9, 1878, in his 71st year.

George Moore, died March 8, 1865, aged 77 years, 7 months.

William E. Doyle, died June 28, 1865, in his 64th year; and his wife, Margaret, died Dec. 15, 1860, in her 57th year.

Thomas Shirvan, died Oct. 17, 1868, in his 84th year; and his wife, Isabella, died July 29, 1867, aged 67.

Caper Schwab, died Feb. 22, 1855, aged 77 years.

Rev. Joseph J. Maguire, died Sept. 18, 1852, in the 36th year of his age.

Susan McLaughlin, died Dec. 1, 1846, aged 70.

Christopher Murphy, born in Armagh, Ireland, aged 61.

Adam Crist, died Aug. 13, 1852, aged 50.

Margaret, wife of Richard Barry, of County Limerick, Ireland, died Feb. 11, 1858, aged 68.

Thomas Drinen, a native of Queen's County, Ireland, died Oct. 17, 1857, aged 51.

Martha, wife of Isaac Rowland, born Dec. 17, 1808, died June 4, 1869, aged 60.

Julia, wife of Robert Lewis, died Dec. 20, 1856, in her 47th year.

Joachim Shilling, died March 8, 1859, in his 52d year; and his wife, Francesca, died Feb. 11, 1852, aged 42.

Jacob Butts, died May 16, 1861, aged 54.

The Church of the Disciples was dedicated on Jan. 1, 1859, by Bishop Glassbrenner, the Rev. Mr. Coursy, and the Rev. Mr. Lowber. The only debt on the church at that time was four hundred and ninety-four dollars, which amount was contributed upon the day of dedication. Among those buried in the church of the Disciples are the following:

Melville R. Smith, adjutant 6th Maryland Volunteers, U.S.A., wounded at Cedar Creek, Va., Oct. 19, 1864, died Nov. 17, 1864, aged 19 years, 11 months.

Nathan McDowell, born Aug. 5, 1803, died Oct. 30, 1860.

Capt. Lodovick Leeds, born in Groton, Conn., Sept. 14, 1776, died Sept. 7, 1863; and his wife, E. M., died July 10, 1848, in her 65th year.

Ann, wife of Andrew Thomson, of Belfast, Ireland, died April 23, 1844, aged 71.

Francis C. Thomson, born in Belfast, Ireland, July 24, 1800, died Nov. 20, 1876.

Victor Thomson, born in Belfast, Ireland, March 18, 1810, died July 17, 1860; and his wife, Margaret, died Jan. 9, 1842, in her 33d year.

Nathaniel Martin, died Oct. 7, 1863, aged 93; and his wife, Elizabeth, died Sept. 7, 1872, aged 97.

Thomas Keller, died April 1, 1859, aged 72.

Capt. James Biays, born in Baltimore, died Sept. 29, 1865, aged 74 years, 4 months; and his wife, Margaret, born in Philadelphia, Feb. 8, 1797, died near Hagerstown, March 21, 1871, aged 74.

George L. Harry, died March 19, 1847, aged 64; and his wife, Susan, died Jan. 13, 1873, aged 74.

John McKee, born Feb. 21, 1787, died January, 1871; and his wife, Isabella, died Dec. 17, 1851, aged 62 years, 7 months.

Sally McKee, died May 2, 1871, aged 81 years, 8 months.

Ann, wife of Gabriel Nourse, died Aug. 16, 1853, aged 80.

Charity Hagerman, died Dec. 3, 1852, aged 81.

Wm. Pott, died Dec. 4, 1848, in his 80th year; and Sarah, his wife, died Feb. 10, 1852, aged 59.

Dr. Thomas Buchanan Duckett, died Dec. 27, 1875, in his 76th year.

Joseph Taylor, born in Charlton, Saratoga Co., N. Y., Aug. 26, 1775, died in Hagerstown, June 3, 1829, while on a journey for his health. He held several prominent offices in his native State, and at the time of his death held one in the General Post-office Department at Washington.

Dr. Howard Kennedy, born Sept. 15, 1808, died June 12, 1855.

Jane Carroll, died Jan. 9, 1854, aged 75 years, 11 months.

Joseph Gabby, born April 25, 1779, died Nov. 30, 1856; and his wife, Ann, born April 25, 1777, died Jan. 6, 1852.

Susanna, mother of Rev. Septimus Tustin, died Aug. 22, 1817, aged 78.

Leander McKee, died April 5, 1854.

William Robertson, died June 8, 1847, aged 55.

Jane, wife of Dr. James Johnson, born Sept. 28, 1807, and died in 1839.

Sarah Johnston, wife of A. Johnston, died March 12, 1831, aged 47.

The Christian Church.—The youngest religious organization in Hagerstown is the congregation of the Christian Church, which began in 1876, with eighty members. The original officers were John D. Newcomer, J. H. Wagoner, elders, and Abraham Corbett and Alfred Stouffer, deacons. At first worship was conducted in Hoffman Hall, but in a short time the old Presbyterian church on South Potomac Street was purchased. In March, 1877, Elder Louis H. Stein, of Kentucky, was called to the pastorate of the church, being its first regular minister. He remained but a little more than a year, during which time Elder John H. Wagoner resigned his eldership, and Henry S Eavey was elected in his place. In September, 1878, Elder S. B. Moore, of Iowa, became the second pastor of the church. In the summer and fall of 1879 the old Presbyterian church building, recently purchased, was remodeled and repaired, making it one of the neatest and most comfortable church edifices in the city. The congregation has had an uninterrupted and steady growth, until it now numbers one hundred and sixty-eight communicants, and owns a church property valued at nine thousand dollars, free of debt. The present officers are: Elders, John D. Newcomer, Henry S. Eavey, A. M. Wolfinger; Deacons, Abraham Corbett, Alfred Stouffer, John W. Newcomer, George D. Keller. The pastor is S. B. Moore, and the treasurer Levi Middlekauff. The Sunday-school numbers one hundred, including officers and teachers. Superintendent, J. Irvin Bitner; Assistant Superintendent, Levi Middlekauff. In connection with the church is a "Ladies' Aid Society," the object of which is to raise money by weekly contributions for the aid of the poor in the congregation, and for other purposes.

Rose Hill Cemetery was incorporated March 16, 1866, Governor William T. Hamilton being one of the original incorporators. The others were B. H. Garlinger, W. M. Marshall, David Zeller, Chas. T. Nesbitt, Geo. F. Heyser, William Updegraff, W. H. Protzman, Samuel T. Zeigler, William McKeppler, N. I. Magruder, Chas. Knodle, and Geo. B. Oswald. Governor Hamilton was made president. The cemetery grounds were purchased from the wife of T. H. Norman, and consist of twenty-six acres, beautifully situated on the southern borders of the town, facing the Sharpsburg turnpike and the Washington County Railroad. The cemetery is one of the ornaments of the town. The grounds were laid out by Jno. Wilkenson, of Baltimore, and were dedicated in September, 1867, the Rev. T. T. Titus, of the Lutheran Church, delivering the address. The present officers of the cemetery are: President, Governor W. T.

Hamilton; Secretary and Treasurer, W. Updegraff; Directors, D. B. Sath, L. D. Herbert, D. W. Ragan, James I. Harly, M. E. Barber, B. A. Garlinger, C. W. Humrickhouse, William Updegraff, E. M. Mealey.

The following are among those interred in Rose Hill Cemetery:

Rev. Robert W. Dunlap, pastor of the Presbyterian Church, born in Lancaster District, South Carolina, in September, 1815, and died in Hagerstown, Feb. 17, 1856. He was a graduate of the theological seminary at Princeton, N. J., was ordained in April, 1838, and was called to the congregation at Hagerstown in 1851. A marble monument with a brownstone base was erected to his memory by the people of his charge.

Benjamin Price, born Jan. 5, 1799, died Nov. 16, 1840.

Mary McCardell, died Sept. 14, 1834, aged 72.

William McCardell, died Aug. 21, 1870.

Christian Fechtig, born Feb. 6, 1794, died Sept. 7, 1835.

Isabella Fechtig, born Feb. 26, 1800, died Aug. 1, 1866.

Christian Fechtig, born Feb. 18, 1759, died Jan. 14, 1834.

Susan Fechtig, born July 12, 1765, died April 9, 1840.

John Fechtig, born March 14, 1799, died April 10, 1869.

Jonathan Hager, died April 16, 1864, aged 72; and his wife, died July 18, 1873, aged 78.

John F. Heyser, died July 14, 1871, aged 55.

Joseph Emmert, born April 1, 1799, died Sept. 25, 1853: and Elizabeth, his wife, born July 25, 1799, died Sept. 17, 1866.

Catharine Wagner, wife of William, died Sept. 10, 1877, aged 30. Her grave is marked by a handsome monument, surmounted by an urn.

Zaccheus McComas, born March 31, 1792, died May 13, 1867.

Susan F. McComas, born Jan. 7, 1796, died Sept. 7, 1859.

T. G. Robertson, born April 17, 1823, died June 28, 1869.

Both these graves are marked by tasteful monuments.

Francis Diederick, died Feb. 25, 1878, aged 86.

Margaret Kriech, wife of William, died Nov. 28, 1864, aged 66.

Timothy Monohan, died Oct. 15, 1806, aged 41.

Francis McKiernan, died June 18, 1859, aged 86.

Eliza T. Monohan, born Feb. 12, 1803, died Nov. 15, 1874.

Martin Speck, Sr., born Nov. 15, 1789, died March 24, 1852, aged 62; and his wife, Ann, born July 24, 1790, died Oct. 21, 1858, aged 68.

Martin Speck, Jr., born Jan. 3, 1817, died April 11, 1877; and his wife, Isabel, born Oct. 28, 1824, died Jan. 3, 1878.

George G. Middlekauff, died Aug. 6, 1877, aged 43.

J. E. Rowland has a very handsome lot, with a monument of marble. Two children are interred in it.

Dr. Frederick Dorsey, died Oct. 26, 1858, aged 82; and Sarah, his wife, died Oct. 5, 1860, aged 75.

Catharine Kuntz, aged 63.

Christiana, wife of Michael Miller, died Aug. 3, 1880, aged 54.

Philip Schindel, died Aug. 15, 1854, aged 72; and Mary A. C., his wife, died April 28, 1869, aged 82.

Elizabeth, wife of Daniel Dunn, died April 8, 1861, aged 49.

William M. Tice, born Sept. 23, 1813, died June 25, 1875; Ann C., his wife, born March 22, 1818, died June 9, 1850.

Catharine, wife of James Hockley, born Oct. 18, 1801, and died Dec. 11, 1863, aged 62.

Jane S. P. Rench, wife of Andrew, born May 15, 1802, died March 15, 1861.

David Johnston, died Oct. 12, 1855, aged 57.

John Gambert, born Sept. 5, 1815, died June 21, 1862, aged 46; and his wife, Christiana, died May 24, 1861, aged 40.

Solomon Fiery, died Sept. 7, 1876, aged 66.

D Artz, died May 28, 1872, aged 78; and his wife, Catharine, died May 20, 1832, aged 41.

Lewis Heist, died Jan. 18, 1877, aged 69.

Archibald McCoy, died Sept. 10, 1868, aged 65.

Charles Ulrich, Sr., died Jan. 12, 1879, aged 64.

Isaac Motter, born Oct. 28, 1805, died Dec. 3, 1877. A fine monument of marble with granite base, and with a cross carved on it, marks Mr. Motter's grave.

Henry Stonebraker, born July 21, 1815, died Feb. 21, 1877.

John Zeller, died Feb. 16, 1873, aged 60.

Philip Neibert, died Nov. 23, 1859, aged 66; and his wife, Elizabeth, died Feb. 23, 1880, aged 73.

George Buch, died July 8, 1878, aged 71; and his wife, Anna Eve, died Oct. 17, 1870, aged 58.

Marinda Etta, wife of Elias Brumbaugh, died Aug. 26, 1878, aged 61.

Samuel Schindel, born Dec. 23, 1791, died Aug. 14, 1863, aged 72; and his wife, Julia Anna, died Oct. 19, 1858, aged 61.

B. Franklin Roman, born Dec. 29, 1819, died Jan. 3, 1863, aged 45.

Lewis K. Fouke, died Nov. 17, 1872, aged 82.

Edward B. Murray, died July 16, 1860.

Elizabeth, wife of Blakiston Lynch, died July 23, 1872, aged 45.

George W. Smith, born Jan. 12, 1810, died Dec. 22, 1873.

Melissa, wife of H. G. Wiles, born April 17, 1828, died Feb. 13, 1878.

Capt. Henry Clopper, died March 1, 1879, aged 77.

Sarah Ann, wife of George W. Martin, aged 64.

Jacob S. Huyett, died April 23, 1877, aged 56.

Jacob Yeakle, born in Hagerstown, Sept. 26, 1779, and died Jan. 7, 1844; and his wife, Elizabeth, aged 95.

Amelia, wife of Jacob K. Harry, died Sept. 27, 1874, in her 62d year.

Adam Andreas, born in Hesse-Cassel, Nov. 17, 1804, died Sept. 29, 1873.

William Cramer, born Oct. 4, 1806, died March 2, 1874, aged 67.

Frances, wife of Jonathan Schindel, died Aug. 13, 1871, aged 50.

Daniel Startzman, died March 17, 1863, aged 62; and his wife, Anna, died Dec. 19, 1872, aged 73.

John Booth, Sr., died Jan. 18, 1872, aged 51.

John Booth, Jr., died April 13, 1865, from wounds received in the civil war, aged 20.

Overton C. Hame, born Sept. 15, 1780, died Jan. 13, 1873, aged 92; and Susannah, his wife, born July 6, 1784, died July 29, 1873, aged 89.

Alexander Mitchell, Sr., died Nov. 29, 1860, in his 61st year.

Eliza Carr, died Sept. 30, 1852, in her 52d year.

Benjamin Riegle, born May 31, 1798, died Jan. 11, 1876.

Joseph G. Protzman, born March 24, 1803, died June 11, 1862, aged 59.

Simon G. Knode, died May 3, 1868, aged 57.

Mary, wife of Rev. S. W. Hartsock, died March 5, 1867, aged 24.

John Noel, died July 19, 1866, aged 71; and his wife, Catharine, died Sept. 1, 1868, in her 71st year.

Benjamin Harris, born Oct. 27, 1813, died Dec. 30, 1870, aged 57.

Thomas Hagerman, died Oct. 5, 1865, aged 68; and his wife, Hannah, died June 27, 1879, aged 74.

Esther, wife of William A. Hagerman, died March 17, 1872, aged 49.

Upton H. Bragunier, died Dec. 22, 1879, aged 57.

Christian Winter, born April 22, 1807, died Feb. 18, 1858.

Sophia M. Mobley, born Oct. 25, 1806, died Jan. 21, 1863, aged 56.

Clara, wife of Jacob Griffe, died Sept. 5, 1870, aged 75.

Abraham Crum, died Sept. 1, 1856, aged 60; and his wife, Mary, born Sept. 4, 1799, and died Aug. 10, 1875, aged 75.

John W. Boswell, died May 10, 1877, aged 68.

John S. Middlekauff, died Feb. 20, 1873, aged 78.

John Beck, died May 3, 1878, aged 83; and his wife, Ann, died June 4, 1873, aged 73.

Mary Born, died Nov. 30, 1863, aged 73.

Mary F. Helmar, died April 28, 1876, aged 51.

Sarah, wife of Geo. H. L. Chrissinger, died Feb. 10, 1873, aged 50.

Frederick Peters, died July 9, 1875, in his 70th year; and his wife, Mary, died Aug. 28, 1871, in her 54th year.

John Figeley, died June 8, 1862, aged 82.

Margaret Figeley, died April 19, 1850, aged 65.

Charles Brengler, died Feb. 13, 1879, aged 71; and his wife, Margaret, died Nov. 7, 1853, aged 42.

John C. Most, died Jan. 11, 1865, aged 65.

Anna Margaret Most, died Sept. 28, 1878, aged 72.

Zacharias Humrich, died Dec. 21, 1871, aged 43.

Sarah A., wife of Philip D. Blair, born April 25, 1825, died Jan. 6, 1874, aged 49.

Henry Schubert, born March 16, 1824, died Sept. 10, 1880, aged 56.

John Smith, born Feb. 15, 1827, died June 6, 1878, aged 51.

John Smith, born March 1, 1800, died Jan. 4, 1875, aged 74; and his wife, Catharine B., born Feb. 12, 1798, died July 6, 1871, aged 73.

Barbara, wife of John Masel, born Feb. 18, 1801, died July 16, 1876, aged 69.

Elizabeth, wife of Christian Krohberger, died Aug. 23, 1879, aged 53.

Mrs. George Sommar, died Sept. 23, 1880, aged 70.

Jacob Ridenour, born Feb. 9, 1791, died Dec. 21, 1876, aged 85.

Thomas Boyd, Sr., died Nov. 8, 1869, aged 55.

Stewart Herbert, died April 8, 1853, aged 61 years, 11 months, and 1 day; and his wife, Rebecca, died April 26, 1880, aged 80 years, 3 months, and 3 days.

Frederick Stover, died Oct. 24, 1864, aged 80; and Magdalene Stover, died April 30, 1872, aged 80.

George French, born Dec. 8, 1818, died Aug. 1, 1878.

Bernard B. Smith, died Feb. 16, 1841, aged 36; and Elizabeth G., died March 19, 1875, aged 67.

George Brundel, died Aug. 6, 1855, aged 81; and Maria Brundel, died Jan. 13, 1868, aged 66.

David Barr, born Oct. 17, 1788, died April 14, 1846.

Matilda S., wife of Daniel Weisel, died Feb. 1, 1876.

John S. Hamilton, born Oct. 20, 1801, died March 25, 1869.

Henry Schriver, died March 4, 1872, aged 65; and his wife, Barbara, Aug. 18, 1854, aged 46.

Samuel Yeakle, born Oct. 15, 1806, died Nov. 22, 1876.

Johanna Kutzherbst, died Oct. 17, 1878, aged 84.

G. Henry Hargis, died Dec. 31, 1874, aged 73; and his wife, Sabilla, died Feb. 10, 1852, aged 50.

John Tice, died Nov. 16, 1868, aged 73.

Henry Winter, born Aug. 31, 1815, died March 13, 1874.

Corp. Henry A. Gyer, killed in battle in front of Petersburg, Aug. 21, 1864, aged 26.

David Beeler, died Sept. 11, 1874, aged 70.

William Brazier, died Sept. 27, 1861, aged 78; and Mary Brazier, died May 9, 1872, aged 83.

John Appleman, born June 29, 1793, died Dec. 25, 1862.

Mary Swingley, died Sept. 8, 1867, aged 78.

George Boyd, born Jan. 8, 1812, and died June 16, 1871.

John Hagerman, died May 13, 1878, aged 74.

Sarah Hagerman, died Sept. 30, 1870, aged 58.

Daniel Carver, born July 28, 1796, died Feb. 9, 1872.

John Cook, died Feb. 5, 1874, aged 68; and Eleanora Cook, died Nov. 28, 1872, aged 57.

Rev. H. C. Fouke, died July 15, 1879, aged 45.

Barbara, wife of Christian Negley, died Sept. 17, 1869, aged 75.

Richard Ragan, Sr., died Nov. 13, 1850, aged 75; and Elizabeth Ragan, died July 20, 1835, aged 52.

Barbara Sellner, died Aug. 3, 1873, aged 67.

Michael Graybill, died April 26, 1875, aged 93; and Esther Graybill, born Aug. 24, 1785, died June 17, 1846.

Christian Thomas, died Dec. 13, 1880, aged 77.

Magdalene Neff, died Nov. 28, 1808, aged 77.

J. Conrad Simler, died April 28, 1874, aged 70.

William Kitzmiller, died Dec. 23, 1860, aged 55; and Catharine Kitzmiller, died Feb. 13, 1869, aged 55.

Charles E. Gelwicks, died May 14, 1875, aged 65.

George Shryock, died May 21, 1872, aged 83; and Elizabeth Shryock, died Feb. 7, 1865, aged 81.

Anthony W. Lewis, born Nov. 20, 1801, died March 27, 1876.

William Bester, died Sept. 28, 1859, aged 57.

Susan Beck, born May 30, 1793, died Aug. 11, 1855.

William Knodle, died Nov. 16, 1851, aged 65; and Rebecca Knodle, died March 6, 1828, aged 43.

Jacob Winter, died March 6, 1877, aged 72.

Charles G. Lane, born March 17, 1804, died Jan. 4, 1873; and Maria Lane, born July 4, 1806, died April 13, 1869.

Seth Lane, born Feb. 1, 1774, and died Dec. 7, 1824; and Catharine Lane, born June 17, 1777, and died April 20, 1825.

Margaret A. Black, died July 4, 1879, aged 83.

Catharine, wife of J. Q. Smith, died May 14, 1873.

Joseph Fiery, born Jan. 15, 1807, died Nov. 27, 1866.

John R. Sneary, died Oct. 24, 1879, aged 60.

Barbara Rowland, died Aug. 2, 1861, aged 71.

M. C. Humrichouse, born Aug. 7, 1804, died Feb. 5, 1878.

Joseph Ignatius Merrick, born Sept. 20, 1790, died June 19, 1854; and Sophia Buchanan Merrick, born Aug. 11, 1790, died June 14, 1873.

Rebecca Snider, died March 22, 1854, aged 70 years.

Elizabeth Perry, died June 27, 1878, aged 79.

Elizabeth, wife of Allen Glassbrenner, born Feb. 18, 1790, died March 18, 1880.

Daniel C. Miller, born July 19, 1794, died March 23, 1860; and Rachel, died Sept. 16, 1874, aged 76.

John Ringer, died March 20, 1869, aged 77; and Magdalene S. Ringer, died Nov. 19, 1868, aged 64.

Susan Miller, died Nov. 14, 1880, aged 83.

Mary McDaniel, died Sept. 6, 1845, aged 65.

Andrew Swartz, died Jan. 15, 1867, aged 63 years.

Eleanora, wife of Leonard Maisack, born July 6, 1797, died April 26, 1869.

Andrew Schwinger, born Feb. 3, 1802, died Feb. 28, 1869.

H. H. Harvey, died Nov. 22, 1875; and his wife, Letitia Purviance Harvey, died Feb. 2, 1880.

Henry Courtenay Hughes, died Feb. 23, 1862.

Isabella Hughes, died April 4, 1873.

Among the conspicuous lots in the cemetery are the following:

The Hughes lot, containing the bodies of Robert Hughes, who died March 26, 1829, and his wife, Susan Purviance, who died April 6, 1846. In the lot of D. H. Wiles is a monument in marble to his only child, Frederick M. Wiles. The lot of the Mealey family is marked by a monument of granite with a marble figure of Hope. The monument at the lot of the Dillon family is elaborately carved and surmounted by a cross. The Russell family monument is a tall granite shaft; on the panels at the base are the names of the family. A handsome monument of granite, polished and carved and surmounted by a draped urn, marks the grave of Elizabeth, wife of Samuel Goheen, who died Nov. 27, 1857, aged 73, having been a member of the Methodist Episcopal Church for fifty-four years. The grave of F. Dorsey Herbert is also marked by a fine marble monument. A monument erected by Potomac Lodge, No. 31, I. O. O. F., bears the inscription, "To Our Dead," and is decorated with emblems of the order on the panels. Another monument is dedicated to the memory of Charles E., son of John Gale, who was murdered by a mob "while in the fearless discharge of his duty as a member of the Hagerstown police force, Oct. 20, 1866, aged 24 years."

Washington Cemetery.—In 1870 the Legislature appropriated five thousand dollars to pay the expense of removing the bodies of the Confederate dead from

CONFEDERATE MONUMENT.

the battle-fields in this section, and the commission appointed selected a portion of Rose Hill as the most suitable place. The removals began in September, 1872. On Feb. 28, 1877, a beautiful monument was erected by the managers of the cemetery and dedicated to the Confederate dead. The body of the monument is of Scotch granite of Aberdeen, of a beautiful brown, dappled with varied hues; the base is a solid, heavy stone of American granite from Richmond; upon the top is a marble figure more than five feet in height, representing Hope leaning upon her anchor, with flowing robes, and upon her brow is set a star (perhaps the "single star of the Confederacy"). Upon the front of the die facing the cemetery is the inscription, "The STATE OF MARYLAND has provided this cemetery and erected this monument to perpetuate the memory of the Confederate dead who fell in the battles of Antietam and South Mountain." On the right side we read, "The State of Virginia has contributed toward the burial of her dead within this cemetery," and on the left the same of West Virginia.

On Tuesday, the 15th of June, 1877, the Washington Confederate Cemetery, near Hagerstown, was dedicated and decorated for the first time. The weather was very fine, and there was an immense concourse of people within the grounds. The arrangements were under the direction of Col. H. Kyd Douglas, president of the board of trustees of the cemetery, seconded by Mr. P. A. Witmer. The first arrival occurred about eight o'clock in the morning, when a train from Martinsburg, *via* the Cumberland Valley road, reached Hagerstown with over six hundred excursionists. Among these was Capt. Charles J. Faulkner's company of the Berkeley Light Infantry, numbering eighty men. About the same time the two regular trains of the Baltimore and Ohio Railroad came in, bringing about two hundred people from the lower districts of the county. At half-past eight o'clock a delegation from Shepherdstown, headed by Col. W. A. Morgan, trustee of the cemetery on behalf of West Virginia, and accompanied by the Shepherdstown Cornet Band, arrived on the scene, and shortly before noon a special car of the Baltimore and Ohio Railroad bearing Gen. Fitzhugh Lee reached Hagerstown, and was met by Maj. George Freaner, Col. H. Kyd Douglas, and Dr. A. S. Mason, who conducted Gen. Lee to Maj. Freaner's residence, where he was entertained. Maj. Freaner had been a member of Gen. Lee's staff during the war. At noon a train arrived from Baltimore, *via* the Western Maryland Railroad, and soon after two trains of the Baltimore and Ohio Railroad came in, one of them from Washington, and the other from Baltimore. The excursionists from Frederick returned home on learning of a railroad accident which had occurred at Point of Rocks. Among them was James Gambrill, one of the trustees of the cemetery. In Hagerstown the day was universally given up to the celebration. Many of the citizens kept open house and invited persons to lunch or dine with them. Although it was Tuesday, the county "public day," very little business was transacted. It is thought that at least six thousand people visited the cemetery during the day, and that there were five thousand present at one time.

At two o'clock P.M. the procession formed in the

public square at Hagerstown, with Col. R. E. Cook, chief marshal, assisted by Marshals A. J. Schindle, A. K. Syester, Jr., Edwin Schindle, George M. Stonebraker, Frank Emmert, and Upton Brumbaugh. In half an hour the different organizations had taken their proper places and the march to the cemetery was commenced. At the head of the column, preceded by the Martinsburg Band and Drum Corps, were the Berkeley Light Infantry, Capt. Charles J. Faulkner, who were followed by the mayor and City Council of Hagerstown, Gen. Fitzhugh Lee, Hon. D. B. Lucas, Gen. I. R. Trimble, and others in carriages. After these came the delegation from the Society of the Army and Navy of the Confederate States and other citizens of Baltimore, accompanied by the Fifth Regiment Band, and commanded by Capt. McHenry Howard, president of the society. Next in order came the Fire Department of Hagerstown, their engines handsomely decorated with flowers, and accompanied by the Keedysville Band. These companies were followed by the delegation from Shepherdstown, W. Va., commanded by Col. W. A. Morgan, assisted by Capts. J. S. Melvin and Lee H. Moler, and led by Criswell's Cornet Band. After the Shepherdstown delegation came various other delegations from Washington County and elsewhere. Those from Williamsport, Funkstown, and Sharpsburg were noticeably large, and carried masses of beautiful flowers. On the route from Hagerstown to the cemetery the different bands played lively and spirited airs, but when the inclosure was reached they were succeeded by solemn marches and dirges.

At the cemetery the light infantry were drawn up in line facing the graves and near the speaker's stand. The bands were stationed at various points. The mayor and Council, the speakers, and the guests were then conducted to the stand by the trustees of the cemetery. A choir of sixty persons, with an organ, were placed in front of the stand, and the engines of the Fire Department were stationed along the main drives, upon a conspicuous eminence.

The exercises began with prayer, which was offered by the Rev. Levi Keller, of Funkstown. He thanked Almighty God for the restoration of love and unity between the late contending armies, and offered an earnest supplication for the President and other civil functionaries of the United States. After music by the Fifth Regiment Band, Maj. George Freaner, secretary and treasurer of the cemetery association, delivered a historical sketch of the cemetery. The burial of the Confederate dead who fell in the battles of Antietam and South Mountain in an appropriate place was, he said, the result of a series of efforts made by the State of Maryland. Less than eighteen months after the battles were fought the Legislature passed an act organizing the Antietam National Cemetery. This act, which was amended and re-enacted at the succeeding session of 1865, provided for the purchase of ten acres of land, "a part of the battle-field of Antietam," as a burial-place for the soldiers who fell in that battle. These acts made it the duty of the trustees of all States joining the corporation to remove the remains of all the soldiers who fell in the battles of Antietam and have them interred in this national cemetery, the remains of the soldiers of the Confederate army to be buried in a portion of the ground separate from that in which the bodies of the soldiers of the Union army were interred. To carry out this scheme the sum of fifteen thousand dollars was appropriated and expended in the purchase of the grounds, etc., near Sharpsburg, now the National Cemetery. Many thousands of dollars were contributed by fourteen other States, but, in violation of the law, the remains of the Confederate soldiers were not reinterred, but were permitted to remain where they had been hastily buried. In many instances the trenches were so washed by the rain that their bones were laid bare and were turned over by the plow.

In a letter dated Dec. 3, 1867, Governor Fenton, of New York, called the attention of the trustees of the Antietam National Cemetery to the sad condition of these Confederate dead, and to the requirement of the Maryland acts of Assembly, which they had disregarded, viz., that the remains of Confederate as well as Federal soldiers should be removed to their cemetery. In this connection, Governor Fenton said, "The hostility of the generous and heroic ends with death, and brief as our history is, it has furnished an early example. The British and Americans who fell at Plattsburgh sleep side by side, and a common monument on the Plains of Abraham attests the heroism of Wolfe and Montcalm." Influenced probably by this appeal and the earnest entreaties of Thomas A. Boullt, secretary and treasurer of the board, the trustees passed a resolution designating and setting apart for the burial of the Confederate dead who fell in the battle of Antietam, in the first invasion of Lee, the southern portion of the grounds, not occupied, and separate from the ground devoted to the burial of the Union dead. At the next session of the Maryland Legislature five thousand dollars was appropriated to the cemetery, presumably for the reinterment of the Confederate dead. But the trustees in 1868 finally postponed any further action towards the removal of these remains. The five thousand dollars appropriated by Maryland still remained in the State treasury, and at the January session of the Legislature of 1870 an act was passed organizing the Washington Cemetery and appropriating the five thousand dollars to its use. The charter provides for the burial of the dead of both armies remaining unburied at the date of that instrument, and for the appointment of three trustees from Maryland and one from any State which may join the corporation. It gives the trustees full power to accomplish the work intrusted to them, and enables them to receive and hold all contributions by way of gift, devise, bequest, etc.

During the summer of 1870, Governor Bowie appointed as trustees on behalf of the State of Maryland Col. H. K. Douglas and Maj. George Freaner, of Washington County, and James T. Gambrill, of Frederick County. The first meeting of the trustees was held in the fall of 1870, and Col. Douglas was elected president. The summer of 1871 was consumed in seeking sites for the cemetery. The charter required that it should be located within one mile of Hagerstown, and the trustees finally purchased two and a half acres and ten perches of land from the Rose Hill Cemetery Company for two thousand four hundred dollars. The Rose Hill Cemetery Company agreed, in making the sale, to keep the grounds in the same condition as their own. After securing the ground, the trustees commenced the removal of the dead, first from the fields of Antietam, about twelve miles south of Hagerstown. With the aid of H. C. Mumma, of Sharpsburg, the trustees disinterred and removed from the battle-fields of Antietam seventeen hundred and twenty-one bodies. The remains when known were placed in single boxes, and when unknown were deposited two in a box. They were removed to Washington Cemetery and buried at an average cost of one dollar and a half per head. This closed the work for 1872 and nearly exhausted the money appropriated, leaving the dead of South Mountain and in isolated parts of the county unburied.

A further appropriation of five thousand dollars, however, was made by the Legislature of Maryland at its January session in 1874, and the Legislatures of Virginia and West Virginia each appropriated five hundred dollars. On receiving these appropriations, the trustees elected Col. W. A. Morgan, of West Virginia, and Maj. R. W. Hunter, of Virginia, to represent their respective States in the board of trustees. In 1874 the trustees resumed work, and buried two thousand four hundred and forty-seven dead, of whom two hundred and eighty-one were identified. The graves were sodded and the grounds decorated as far as the funds of the trustees permitted, after they had set apart a sum (two thousand dollars) which, invested, would yield an income sufficient to keep the cemetery in good repair. A monument was also erected, the work of A. Steinmetz, of Philadelphia, at a cost of fourteen hundred and forty dollars. At the close of his remarks Maj. Freaner said, "It is our intention to make this cemetery a beautiful spot, worthy of an annual pilgrimage from those whose friends and kindred lie here buried, as well as all those who may wish to render homage to a race of men who were willing to die rather than submit to humiliation."

The dedication dirge (words by Col. H. Kyd Douglas, music by F. J. Halm) was then sung by the choir, led by Prof. Halm, with organ accompaniment by Mrs. John Cretin. During the singing Capt. Faulkner's company stood at "present arms." The dirge and music were dedicated to Gen. Fitzhugh Lee. Gen. Lee, the orator of the day, was then introduced, and delivered an eloquent address, in which, after giving rapid sketches of the conspicuous Southern generals, he said that the people of the two sections now had a common country, and that it behooved his hearers to love and cherish it, and to banish discord and strife. After Gen. Lee's address there was music by the Martinsburg Band, which was followed by a poem delivered by its author, Hon. Daniel B. Lucas; then music by the Keedysville Band, after which a letter was read from Brevet Maj. Gen. J. W. Crawford, of the Federal army, then living at Chambersburg, Pa., in which he said that he would most willingly add his testimony to the bravery and devotion of the gallant men who rest at Washington Cemetery. "In their devotion to principle," said he, "and in those high qualities which enabled them to die for it, they have the respect of every true American." After the reading of this letter the graves were strewn with flowers, the monument was decorated with roses and evergreens, and a handsome magnolia was placed at the base. On the mound whereon the monument stands and in front of the monument stood a shield, with the ground in white roses and a St. Andrew's cross in red roses; and on the three remaining sides the words, in large letters, Gettysburg, Antietam, South Mountain, in red, white, and pink roses respectively. Besides these there was a great profusion of flowers and of floral decorations placed on the green turf near the monument. During the ceremony of strewing the graves with flowers the different bands played funeral marches and requiems. When the decoration was finished Harry Greenwood, of Shepherdstown, aged five years, performed a "solo" on the drum, accompanied by his father with the fife. The choir then sang "Farewell," with the words as arranged by A. D.

Merrick, and the long metre doxology, with accompaniment by the Hagerstown Band, after which the Rev. Walter A. Mitchell, rector of St. John's Protestant Episcopal Church, pronounced the benediction. The Berkeley Light Infantry then discharged three volleys over the graves of the dead soldiers, after which the procession formed again and marched back to Hagerstown, and the visiting delegations took the trains for their respective homes.

The following committees made the necessary arrangements for the occasion:

Committee of Arrangements.—P. A. Witmer, Alexander Armstrong, William Weller, Buchanan Schley, Christ. F. Bikle, A. J. Schindle, J. C. Lane, George Lias, George W. Grove.

Committee of Reception.—Col. Geo. Schley, Dr. A. T. Mason, Charles W. Humrickhouse, Lewis C. Smith, Alexander Neill, T. J. C. Williams, Dr. C. B. Boyle, William Kealhofer, W. McK. Keppler, W. H. Armstrong.

Committee on Music.—John H. Heyser, F. J. Halm, A. D. Merrick, Dr. M. W. Allison, Thomas E. Hilliard, Henry Winters, Mrs. John Cretin, Miss Mollie Schley, Miss Cora Heffinger, Mrs. H. C. Koehler.

Committee on Decoration of Monument.—Edward W. Mealey, Mrs. W. T. Hamilton, Mrs. H. H. Keedy, Mrs. Alonzo Berry, Miss Minnie Moon, Claggett D. Spangler, Frank Kennedy, Mrs. C. E. Ways, Miss Ida Hammond, Miss Eliza Stanhope, Miss Lizzie Ragan, Mrs. Nannie Beckenbaugh, Mrs. William Martiney.

Committee on Flowers.—Dr. William Ragan, Mrs. A. K. Syester, Miss Mamie Motter, Mrs. George Phreaner, Miss Alice Boyd, Mrs. George D. Keller, Mrs. B. Y. Fechtig, Miss Adelaide Berry, Miss Blanche Shindle, Miss Bessie Roman, Miss Ella Taggart, Miss Ella Smith, Mrs. J. C. Cookerly, Miss Susie Fiery, Miss Leila Cushwa, Miss Sepha Herbert, Miss Bettie Barber, Mrs. W. T. Williamson, William Bester, D. A. Peters.

DISTRICT COMMITTEES.

1. *Sharpsburg.*—George M. Stonebraker, Jacob Marker, Henry C. Mumma, Rentch Miller, W. F. Blackford, Mrs. Dr. Russell, Mrs. Jacob McGraw, Miss Julia Grove, Miss Savilla Miller, Miss Lutie Grove.

2. *Williamsport.*—J. L. McAtee, J. M. Sword, I. L. Motter, William E. Taylor, D. O. Witmer, Dr. Booth, Miss Mary Clark, Miss Nannie Motter, Miss Maria Hollman, Miss Mary Gruber, Miss Annie Miller.

4. *Clear Spring.*—David Seibert, Lewis Brewer, J. H. Wilson, William Smith, J. T. Cushwa, Mrs. Samuel Reitzell, Miss Seibert, Miss Creigh, Miss Cushwa.

5. *Hancock.*—Joseph Murray, Dr. Delaplane, Robert Bridges, Samuel Rinehart, Miss Mary Broderick, Mrs. Henderson, Miss Bridges.

6. *Boonsboro'.*—O. B. Smith, John L. Nicodemus, J. S. Henry, Henry Wade, Kennedy Wilson, William Welck, Mrs. A. W. Lakin, Mrs. George W. Hoffman, Mrs. Dr. Gaines, Misses Brining, Miss Annie Ringer, Miss Rachel Smith.

7. *Cavetown.*—Dr. Riddlemoser, Joseph H. Wishard, T. Harry Davis, David Winters, Mrs. Joseph Winters, Miss Emily Bishop, Miss Ida Riddlemoser, Miss Santee, Miss Nettie Little, Miss Emma Fiery.

8. *Rohrersvillle.*—Augustus Young, George W. Brown, John S. Miller, Josiah Buck, Mrs. John Shifler, Mrs. Joshua C. Miller, Mrs. Ezra D. Miller, Miss Jane Gouff.

9. *Leitersburg.*—Dr. Charles Harper, Daniel Beck, Henry Schriver, Jr., Miss Ground, Miss Middlekauff, Miss Leiter.

10. *Funkstown.*—Charles South, William H. Myers, Nathaniel Fiery, Joseph Williams, Henry Eyler, Charles Keller, Miss Libbie Keller, Miss Laura Shafer, Miss Ella Keller, Miss Sallie Knode, Miss Carrie Brewer, Miss Sallie Gower.

11. *Weverton.*—H. Clay Elgin, Edward Garrett, George H. Stonebraker, Marlow Thresher, Mrs. Warren Garrett, Mrs. Samuel B. Preston, Mrs. J. H. Elgin, Miss Moore.

12. *Tilghmanton.*—Thos. J. Warfield, J. H. Beeler, H. A. Poffenberger, George Eakle, J. W. G. Beeler, Mrs. Dr. Grimes, Miss Sue Booth, Mrs. John Henry Reynolds, Mrs. Dr. Duckett, Miss Nannie Maddox.

13. *Conococheague.*—F. T. Spickler, George W. Beckenbaugh, David C. Byers, Philip Neibert.

14. *Ringgold.*—Dr. F. Barkdoll, Jacob C. Reecher, Lewis Barkdoll, A. H. Schockey, Miss Sue Shockey, Miss Barkdoll

15. *Indian Spring.*—Alexander Flora, E. G. Kinsell, John D. Tice, Tom Moore.

16. *Beaver Creek.*—A. B. Martin, J. J. Bitner, John M. Newcomer, Elias Rowland, Miss Ella Newcomer, Mrs. James Kridler, Mrs. Elias Martz.

18. *Chewsville.*—John B. Baechtel, John H. Hartle, Jacob Huyett, Mrs. Emma Huyett, Mrs. Jacob Wolf, Mrs. Abner Betz, Miss Martha Hoover, Miss Ida Baechtel.

19. *Keedysville.*—Dr. Keedy, Daniel Neikirk, Frisby Doub, George W. Miller, George Snively, Miss Minnie Eakle, Miss Susan Hoffman, Miss Fannie Deaner, Mrs. Otho Miller, Miss Kate Hammond, Miss Barbara Neikirk, Miss Susie Snively.

The managers of the cemetery are H. Kyd Douglas, George Freaner, and James H. Gambrill.

CHAPTER XLVI.

THE BENCH AND BAR OF WASHINGTON COUNTY.

The Court-house—Early Trials and Executions—Jails—Early Court Notes—Distinguished Judges and Lawyers.

WASHINGTON COUNTY has erected three court-houses since the formation of the county in 1776. The first building was a quaint-looking brick structure, standing in the centre of the public square, and was erected soon after the establishment of the county.

The court-room was on the second floor, and was reached by a flight of steps on the outside. For a time all elections were held in this room, the voting being *viva voce.* The elections lasted several days, and were conducted in a very primitive manner. All the candidates sat in a row behind the sheriff, who took the votes. As each elector approached the candidates would take off their hats, bow politely, and solicit his vote. When the contest was very spirited there were, of course, some animated scenes, and not infrequently disturbances took place. The windows on one side of the court-house were protected with wire from random balls, there being a public alley for ball-playing on that side of the building. The lower story was open, and was used as a market-house.

At a regular session of the General Assembly of the State of Maryland, held in Annapolis during the winter of 1815–16, an act was passed and approved authorizing the inhabitants of Washington County to levy a tax and erect a new court-house. This was done in accordance with the wishes of a majority of the tax-paying citizens, who in their petition represented

"that the existing court-house of said county is in a state of ruinous decay, and the Public Records deposited therein are considerably endangered; that it is too contracted in its plan to accommodate a court and its officers; and that, standing in the Public Square, directly on the intersection of the two principal streets, it greatly injures the appearance of Hagerstown."

The chief provisions of the act were these:

"SEC. 2. *Therefore be it enacted by the General Assembly of Maryland,* That John Blackford, Samuel Ringgold, William Gabby, John Bowles, and Thomas C. Brant be and they are hereby appointed commissioners to select and purchase such lot or lots of ground within the limits of Hagerstown, or the additions to said town, as in their judgment they or a majority of them shall consider the most eligible and proper site for a new court-house for the county aforesaid.

"SEC. 3. *And be it enacted,* That the commissioners hereinbefore named, or a majority of them, be and they are hereby authorized and empowered to contract for and superintend the building of a new court-house, with suitable apartments for the court and juries, clerk's, sheriff's, and register's offices, and fire-proof places of deposit for the public records, on the site as above by them to be selected and purchased, upon such terms and in such manner as to them shall seem most advantageous to the community.

"SEC. 4. *And be it enacted,* That the commissioners hereinbefore named, or a majority of them, shall have power to appoint some capable person to superintend and direct the erection of the building aforesaid, under the order of the commissioners aforesaid; and that they be and they are hereby empowered to allow such person so employed such compensation as they or a majority of them may deem adequate to his services.

"SEC. 5. *And be it enacted,* That the Levy Court of Washington County be and they are hereby authorized and required to assess and levy upon the assessable property of said county, in five successive, equal annual installments, a sum not exceeding thirty thousand dollars, the first installment to be assessed by the said court at the second annual session which, after the passage of this act, they shall hold for the purpose of laying the county levy, and to be collected by the sheriff of said county.

* * * * * * * *

"SEC. 9. *And be it enacted,* That when the said court-house shall be completed and finished, the said commissioners or a majority of them may pull down the old court-house and sell the materials of the same, the proceeds of which may be applied to discharge any debt contracted for the building of the new court-house, over and beyond the sum hereinbefore mentioned.

* * * * * * * *

"SEC. 11. *And be it enacted,* That the public ground on which the court-house now stands shall be condemned as a public street of Hagerstown, not to be built upon or used but as one of the streets of the said town.

"SEC. 12. *And be it enacted,* That the commissioners aforesaid shall meet at the court-house in Hagerstown on the first Monday in April next (1816), and may proceed to the discharge of the several duties provided by this act, and may adjourn from time to time, as may be convenient and necessary; and each commissioner shall be entitled to receive two dollars for each day in which he may be engaged in the discharge of the duty imposed by this act."

Thomas Harbaugh was employed as architect and contractor, and work was commenced soon afterwards to erect a new court-house at the corner of Washington and Jonathan Streets, on the site of the present edifice, the greatest care being taken in building the walls. The court-room was originally on the ground-floor, and extended up to the dome, and was hung around with red tapestry. The effect of this was very handsome, but it was impossible for a speaker to make himself heard in it. Subsequently an upper floor was built, and the court removed up-stairs, but being still under the dome, its acoustic properties were as bad as before. The floor was removed and the hall brought back to its original position, and the next improvement attempted was a floor made directly beneath the dome, in which position it remained until a back building was constructed by R. C. Thornsburg, the contractor, in 1859. The floor in the old building was then restored, and the space above was fitted up for offices. The court-hall was then removed to the back building, and no further change was made until the whole building was burned on the night of the 6th of December, 1871.

In 1821, soon after the completion of the second court-house, the subject of erecting a statue to George Washington upon the site of the old building in the public square was agitated, but the movement never reached a satisfactory result. Washington's name is honored in the town, however, by being given to the most prominent street and the public square. After the fire in 1871 steps were taken for the erection of a new court-house, and a committee was appointed by the court to select temporary accommodations until the completion of the new building. The committee consisted of Hon. George French, George W. Smith, Jr., H. H. Keedy, Edward Stake, L. C. Smith, L. E. McComas, and J. C. Zeller. After examining a number of proposed locations, it was concluded to select the basement story or lecture-room of the Methodist church, which is but half a block distant from the record office, on North Jonathan Street. The term for which this room was rented began March 1, 1872, and ended March 1, 1873, with privilege of renewal at the rate of four hundred dollars a year. In the mean time preparations were made for the erection of the new building. The county commissioners intrusted the selection of the plan to a committee of lawyers, consisting of A. K. Syester (chairman), Col. George

Schley, John C. Zeller, F. M. Darby, Albert Small, Henry K. Douglas, and George W. Smith, Jr. The corner-stone was laid in October, 1872, by the Masonic order at the invitation of the county commissioners, the ceremonies being conducted by Friendship Lodge, No. 84, of Hagerstown, assisted by representatives of lodges from Westminster and other points in the surrounding country. The building was dedicated in the spring of 1874, and the charge of Chief Judge Alvey was listened to by an audience that filled the spacious hall. The new building has given satisfaction in all particulars, the acoustic properties being excellent. The building occupies the site of the old court-house, at the corner of Washington and Jonathan Streets, fronting ninety-one feet on the former and running back about one hundred and twenty feet. This includes a back building, which is sixty-two and a half feet long by fifty-nine and a half wide. The material is brick, unpainted, and pointed with black mortar, and the building is surmounted by a mansard-roof. Over the main entrance is a large iron plate bearing the coat of arms of the State, and at the angle on Jonathan Street, where the main and back buildings join, is a small belfry, which is about the same height as the highest point in the roof of the main building.

In this tower, facing on Jonathan Street, is a brownstone tablet bearing the names of the county commissioners by whom the building was erected, the architects, and the contractor.

The sides of the building are relieved by pilasters surmounted by urns. A great deal of brownstone has been used in the structure, and the cornice, which is of galvanized iron, is painted and sanded in imitation of stone. The entrance-doors are of paneled oak, varnished, and are quite handsome. On the right of the main entrance, going in, is the register's office, and on the left the clerk's office, and in the rear of each is a commodious fire-proof vault in which to keep the records of the respective offices. Going down the passage, on the right-hand side, is the county commissioners' room and the main stairway, which is of solid oak. On the left-hand side of the passage are the rooms of the school commissioners, the sheriff, and collector, and a private stairway for the use of the court and members of the bar, leading to a door which opens inside the bar of the court-hall.

The court-hall occupies the whole of the second floor, with the exception of a library and a witness-room at the eastern end, and is lighted by large and well-proportioned windows. About one-half of the hall is taken up for the court and the bar. The petit jury box is on the left of the bench, and the grand jury box faces the petit jury. The hall is seventy-two feet long by fifty wide. The ceiling is coated with plaster of Paris, as are those of the other rooms, and ornamented with stucco; all the walls throughout the building are left unpainted and unwashed. Near the centre of the ceiling is a large circular opening, which is designed by the architect to secure ventilation; it has two semicircular lids, which can be raised or lowered at pleasure. When both of these lids are raised, the heated air will ascend on one side of them and the cool air descend on the other. The rooms on the second floor of the back building are occupied by the State's attorney and the grand and petit juries. All of the rooms in the building have the purpose for which they are designed painted on the doors. The vaults are furnished with iron window-shutters and double iron doors with patent combination locks. Outside of the private entrance to the court-hall is a stairway leading to the roof, from which point there is a grand view of the town and the surrounding country.

Jail.—The first jail was a small rough building of round logs, and occupied the lot where the tannery of the Washington County Leather Company stood. It was used for a number of years, and then the building afterwards occupied by Richard Sheckles was erected for that purpose. Thence it was removed to the jail building, which was destroyed by fire in 1857. The building of this jail became necessary, and was authorized by the Legislature in 1818. The commissioners having in charge the erection of the structure were S. Ringgold, William Gabby, O. H. Williams, William Heyser, and Henry Lewis, the same who erected the second county court-house. This jail was built of limestone, rough-casted outside, and was inclosed by a wall on the north, west, and south. The approach to the entrance was through a neat plastered house, which was generally occupied as a residence by the sheriff and his family.

In passing through the hall of the sheriff's house, the visitor approached the outer door of the prison. This door was large and massive, being constructed of oak, and traversed in all directions by spikes and screws, and lined between the bars of wood with substantial sheet-iron.

This building was destroyed by fire in April, 1857, the entire wood-work of the jail proper being consumed. The sheriff's house, separated by a few feet from the prison, escaped destruction. The old jail was erected in 1826, at a cost of twelve or fifteen thousand dollars.

Steps were immediately taken to provide a new prison for the use of the county, and work on the building was commenced under the direction of John B. Thurston. The structure is seventy-three by forty-seven feet, and is one story high. It is roofed with tin, covered with Childs' elastic cement roofing, and is heated by a furnace placed in the cellar. It is fire-proof throughout. The cost of the building was about seven thousand dollars. The transfer of prisoners, some eight or nine in number, to this jail was made by Sheriff Hauck in May, 1858, each of them being placed in a separate cell.

Notable Early Trials and Executions.—In early days in Maryland the penalty even for misdemeanors was excessively and cruelly severe, our ancestors acting upon the idea that the greater the punishment the more effective the check to crime. Even imprisonment for debt was used as a means of private malice. An instance of this is afforded by the case of a colored barber, who had a tipsy customer imprisoned for a debt of six and a quarter cents, and paid three pounds in fees before his malice was satisfied. Persons offending against the somewhat puritanical laws of the province were imprisoned during the pleasure of the court, not exceeding one year. Among other punishments were banishment, boring through the tongue with a red-hot iron, slitting the nose, cutting off one or both ears, whipping, branding with a red-hot iron, in the hand or on the forehead, with the initial letter of the offense for which the sufferer was punished,—"S L" for seditious libeler, on either cheek, "M" for manslaughter, or "T" for thief, on the left hand, "R" for rogue, on the shoulder, and "P" for perjury, on the forehead,—"flogging at the cart's tail," when the criminal was tied to the end of a cart and flogged on his naked back while the cart was driven slowly through the town. At the Baltimore County Assizes in 1748 an old, gray-haired man was convicted of blasphemy, and his tongue was bored through, and he was sentenced to remain in jail until he paid a fine of twenty pounds. The pillory and whipping-post were also used as a sort of preliminary punishment to the more severe penalties to follow. In 1819 the pillory was used for the last time in Maryland for a revolting crime. The last man whipped in the State was a postmaster, for tampering with the mails in Annapolis. He was tied to one of the pillars of the portico of the State-house and whipped, while Judge Chase was holding court in the Senate chamber.

On the morning of April 12, 1799, two negroes, known as Emanuel and Jack, sentenced to death for the murder of their overseer, Mr. Todd, were taken from the jail at Hagerstown, about nine o'clock, to the place where they had committed the murder, and at twelve o'clock were hanged in the presence of a great multitude of spectators.

On the 3d of December, 1799, John Jacob Werner, an old man living with his family in the vicinity of Hagerstown, entered the room where his four children were sleeping, and with a tomahawk proceeded to butcher them, fracturing their skulls by repeated blows upon the backs of their heads. When he had completed the work of destruction he left the room to search for his wife, whom he found gathering wood in the yard. Telling her that he had something very extraordinary to say to her, he called her into the house, and, as she was entering the door, assaulted her with the tomahawk, and fractured her skull in several places. Leaving her for dead, he returned to the room where his first victims lay, locked the door, and, seizing a razor, cut his own throat from ear to ear, and fell down and expired. Two of the children died instantly. The wounds of the mother and of the two other children were of a desperate nature, but they survived.

The cause of the deed was supposed to have been despair, engendered in the mind of the perpetrator by apprehensions that a law suit in which he was engaged, and which was then pending in the County Court, would be decided against him. His wife stated that for eight or ten weeks previous to the catastrophe he had been subject to fits of insanity.

On the 15th of April, 1803, John McDaniel was executed, in pursuance of his sentence, for breaking open and robbing the house of Jonas Stevenson. The execution took place back of the new jail at Hagerstown. The condemned man acknowledged having committed many crimes, but utterly denied the crime for which he was to be hung, as well as three others, for which he was tried and sentenced to hard labor.

On the 24th of August, 1803, Peter Light was arraigned at the bar of Washington County Court, charged with making counterfeit dollars. He was tried and found guilty, and was sentenced to be whipped, pilloried, and cropped, which sentence was duly executed by the sheriff.

Thomas Burk (colored), who had been sentenced to death by Judge J. Buchanan for rape, committed in 1808, on Maria Branner, under twelve years of age, escaped from the Washington County jail July 4, 1809.

In 1811, Elizabeth Cope was tried and convicted of having cut off the ears of a boy about six years of age, for which she was sentenced to the Maryland Penitentiary for nine years, and to be kept in a cell on low diet for eighteen months of that time.

One of the most notable murder trials that ever took

place in Washington County was that of the Cotterills, father and two sons, for the murder of James Adams, in Allegany County, on the 9th of May, 1819.

The circumstances attending the murder were as follows: William Cotterill, Sr., and his two sons, William and John, in company with their victim, sailed from Liverpool for Baltimore about the 1st of February in the ship "Ceres," Adams having in his possession a considerable sum of money and a check on a mercantile house in Baltimore for a further amount. Arriving in Baltimore in the latter part of April, the four took lodgings together, and remained in the city a few days, when, not finding employment, they determined to seek their fortunes in the West. Reaching Allegany County, they contracted on Thursday, the 6th of May, with Messrs. Wood & West for employment as laborers on the turnpike road. They continued to work for them until the following Saturday evening. On Sunday morning Adams, believing that he had lost the check which he had brought with him from England, determined to return to Baltimore in search of it, and if unsuccessful in this, to stop payment upon it and return to England. He started down the road in pursuance of this determination, accompanied by the two younger Cotterills, the father remaining at the house of Messrs. Wood & West. Two or three hours later the Cotterill brothers returned, not by the road, but through the woods, having their pantaloons wet up to the knees. Their father, who had manifested much uneasiness and agitation during their absence, met them as they approached the house, and a short conversation ensued, during which one of the sons was heard to say, "Father, we have done it."

They immediately applied for the wages due them, announcing their intention to return to England, and in about three-quarters of an hour after the return of the two sons the three left the house, going through the woods in the same direction in which they had come. One week afterwards the dead body of Adams was found in Fifteen Mile Creek, a short distance below the road. The head and breast were terribly mangled, the clothing torn, and the pockets rifled of their contents.

The place was a secluded spot, situated between two mountains, and the surroundings were dreary and wild. Men seldom ventured to intrude upon its solitude, and only accident revealed the dark deed that had been perpetrated there. The murdered man was known in Baltimore, and was said to have been a respectable farmer from Cadworth, England. Circumstances strongly indicated that the three Cotterills were the authors of the murder, and they were pursued to Baltimore, where they were found on the point of embarking for England in the ship "Franklin." Their trunk was searched, and in it were found a watch, clothing, and other articles known to have belonged to Adams, and also some money believed to have been a part of that which Adams was known to have possessed. Upon this evidence they were committed to the Baltimore City jail, where they remained until the session of the Allegany County Court was convened. At the request of the prisoners the trial was removed to Washington County. The prosecution was conducted by Roger Perry, and the two younger prisoners were defended by Beal Howard, Samuel Hughes being associated with him in the defense of the elder. The trial was conducted with great ability and ingenuity by the counsel engaged in the case, and after a patient hearing the three prisoners were found guilty of murder in the first degree. The case of each of the three murderers was tried before a different jury. The one which convicted William Cotterill, Jr., was constituted as follows: Jacob Zeller (foreman), John Barr, John McLain, Theodore Mills, Michael Smith, Ignatius Drury, William Gabby, Jeremiah Mason, Archibald Ritchie, Alexander Grim, William Dillehunt, and Frederick Fishaugh.

John Cotterill's jury was composed of the following: John Johnson (foreman), John Neff, Michael Smith, John Hedrick, Daniel Rench, John Ragan, Isaac S. White, William H. Fitzhugh, John Schnebly, Adam Myers, John Hall, and Thomas Brent.

The following were the jury which tried William Cotterill, Sr., viz.: Daniel Schnebly (foreman), Jacob Zeller, William Gabby, Isaac S. White, Theodore Mills, John Hedrick, Archibald Ritchie, Daniel Rench, William Fitzhugh, Jr., Frederick Fithzugh, John Neff, and William H. Fitzhugh.

Friday, February 25th, the day appointed for the execution, was wet and cheerless, yet thousands were gathered in the streets of the town, and along the roads leading into it from the surrounding country. Various estimates have been made of the number present at the execution, ranging from ten thousand to forty thousand. At half-past ten o'clock a wagon left the jail door, bearing the three criminals and their spiritual advisers, guarded by the troops of horse of Capts. Barr and Swearingen, and the foot companies of Capts. Dewey and Bell. Preceded by the coffins of the doomed men, the procession passed on to the place of execution. On reaching the scaffold, the Rev. Messrs. Allen and Kurtz ascended the platform and conducted religious services. The criminals then ascended, accompanied by the Rev. Mr. Clay, who offered prayer, the prisoners kneeling and joining with apparent earnestness in the devotions. Several hymns were then sung, after which the youngest son, John, addressed the vast crowd present. He confessed that he and his brother had murdered Adams, and that they suffered justly the penalty of death, but he strongly denied that his father had participated in the crime. William, the elder son, also declared the innocence of his father, and the father himself asserted to the last that he was not guilty. The condemned men continued to pray until the drop fell.

The trial of George Swearingen for the murder of his wife, which was another celebrated case, commenced Aug. 11, 1829, and lasted eight days. The accused was one of the most popular young men in Washington County, and had been elected sheriff in 1827. He married in Allegany County, and in that county was committed the crime for which he suffered death. The testimony during the trial tended to show that Swearingen had married his wife from mercenary motives, and his conversations not only indicated that this was true, but also that his affections were engaged and were reciprocated in another quarter. Evidence of his indifference towards his wife was produced, and it was also stated during the trial that in June or July, 1827, he had upset her in a gig on Martin's Mountain, injuring her severely. It was proven that in August or September, 1827, just previous to his election, he formed an intimacy with a lewd woman, Rachel Cunningham, whom he took to a camp-meeting in Washington County in a barouche, and for whom he built a house in Hagerstown which is still standing. His connection with the woman becoming notorious, he was threatened by a mob, who intended to demolish the house, but, arming himself, he declared that he would kill the first man who approached him, and thus deterred the rioters. After this he sent the woman Cunningham to Virginia, and finally removed her to a farm which he held in his wife's name in Allegany County.

His wife left him, but subsequently consented to live with him again on condition that he gave up his intimacy with Rachel Cunningham. After this his conduct towards her underwent a change. He treated her with more attention, and promised to reform his habits. One Sunday he left Cumberland with his wife, traveling as far as Mrs. Peggy Cresap's, where they spent the night. Next morning they started for the house of another Mrs. Cresap's. Upon arriving at a point opposite his farm, Swearingen and his wife left the road just as a drove of cattle came up, at the head of which was a young man named Hillary. This man swore that he saw the accused leave the road, he leading the way and carrying the baby, while his wife followed a short distance in the rear. Traveling about two hundred yards in this direction, they reached the foot of a steep hill, where he dismounted, put down the child, and fastened his horse. He then took his wife's horse by the bridle and led him up the hill, where Hillary lost sight of them. The drover had gone about three-quarters of a mile when Swearingen, riding at a moderate gait and carrying the child in his arms, overtook him, inquired his name, where he was from, etc., and then informed him that his wife had been thrown from her horse, and that he feared she was dead. He requested him to take his horse and ride to Cresap Town and send Robert Kile to him immediately. This Hillary did. Kile received the message and started for the scene of the catastrophe. While passing along the road leading to Swearingen's farm he heard a whistle, and looking in the direction from which it came, discovered Swearingen sitting by the dead body of his wife. This spot was about a mile from the main road, and about a quarter of a mile from the place where Swearingen said the horse had fallen with her. The coroner's inquest, held the next day, rendered a verdict that the deceased came to her death by an act of Providence. Two days after the death of Mrs. Swearingen the ground was carefully examined from the point where Hillary lost sight of the party to the place where Kile found Swearingen by the side of the body.

The track of a horse was traced by some persons through a laurel thicket, over the hill, from the former of these points to a point in the road about fifty yards above where the corpse was first seen, and a place was discovered where a hollow had been formed by the leaves having been pressed down. Beside this depression was a log, and upon the log a stone. Not far off was a place where a horse had evidently been hitched, and a club was found, which had apparently been cut in a hurry.

Some of the witnesses testified that the leaves were spotted, as they thought, with blood, although others considered this as not being certain. There were also some who did not think that the tracks discovered were those of a horse, and one witness stated that there were, in his opinion, no tracks at all. The statements of the accused were very contradictory. He asserted on one occasion that his wife's fall from the horse had killed her at once; on another, that he had placed her again on the horse after her fall to take her to a place of safety, and that she had again fallen, being killed by the second fall. To some he stated that the drove of cattle came in view when she fell, and to others that the accident occurred just as the drove was out of sight.

Another inquest was held, and several physicians were called upon to examine the body. Its advanced state of decomposition rendered it apparently impossible to obtain any evidence from the examination, and the physicians so stated in writing. They afterwards, however, came to the conclusion that the deceased had suffered death from suffocation. This latter conclusion was based upon the swollen state of the neck, but some of the physicians contended that this was not sufficient evidence upon which to establish death by suffocation, and that an examination of the lungs and brain should have been made to render the judgment conclusive. No such examination was undertaken. After this second inquest Swearingen fled, and a summons was issued for him by the coroner. The knees of the horse ridden by the deceased were examined, and several witnesses swore positively that the injuries had been inflicted by some sharp instrument, and could not have been produced by a fall. While Mr. Price was making the closing argument a letter from the accused to Rachel Cunningham, written by him in the jail, was produced and read by the prosecuting attorney. Within ten minutes after the case had been given to the jury a verdict of murder in the first degree was rendered. The case was tried before Judges John Buchanan, Abraham Shriver, and Thomas Buchanan. Mr. Dixon appeared for the State, and the defense was conducted by Messrs. William Price, J. V. L. McMahon, and Bushkirk. The report states that Mr. Price argued five hours before the jury, and Mr. McMahon seven hours and a half.

On Monday Judge John Buchanan sentenced him to be hanged, and October 2d was fixed for the execution. The place selected was on the west bank of Will's Creek, in the vicinity of Cumberland. The condemned man was taken from the jail precisely at ten o'clock, and proceeded to the scaffold on foot, escorted by five companies of infantry from Somerset and Bedford Counties, Pa., and by a troop of horse from the former of these counties, under command of Capt. Forward. Swearingen was attended to the scaffold by the sheriff and by Revs. Messrs. John Miller, C. B. Young, N. B. Little, L. H. Johns, and H. Haverstick, who conducted religious services. The rope was then adjusted and the cap drawn by the sheriff. A few moments before the platform fell Swearingen assured the sheriff and the Rev. Mr. Little "in the presence of the Judge of all the earth," that certain particulars previously communicated to them were true. A full confession was made by the prisoner to the Rev. Mr. Little, and the particulars mentioned above are supposed to have been connected with the crime for which he died. About twenty minutes before twelve o'clock the sheriff told the doomed man that his last moments had arrived, and let the platform fall from under him. His death was comparatively easy.

Rachel Cunningham, his mistress, died a pauper in Bayview Asylum, Baltimore, several years ago.

On Friday, April 10, 1863, Frederick Smith was hung at Hagerstown for the murder of Agnes Tracy. It is estimated that from six to eight thousand persons were present at the execution.

Early Court Notes.—In December, 1793, Nathaniel Rochester was appointed one of the associate judges of Washington County. In April, 1800, the justices of the Washington County Court appointed Otho H. Williams clerk of the court in place of Elie Williams, resigned. In 1802, William Clagett was appointed chief justice of the Washington, Frederick, Montgomery, and Allegany Courts. The justices of the Levy Court were Thomas Sprigg, Samuel Ringgold, Adam Ott, Richard Cromwell, John Good, Charles Carroll, and William Yates. In the same year Ignatius Taylor, Elie Williams, and Jacob Harry were appointed judges of the Orphans' Court, and Thomas Crampton, Adam Ott, Richard Cromwell, Lancelot Jacques, John Downey, Samuel Ringgold, Thomas Brunt, William Van Lear, John Good, John Hunter, Isaac Baechtel, George Kennedy, Thomas Sprigg, William Yates, Charles Carroll, Robert Douglass, William Webb, Benjamin Clagett, Henry Shroeder, Daniel Weisel, and Jacob Harry were appointed justices of the peace for Washington County. In an advertisement dated Feb. 23, 1802, Nathaniel Rochester announced that, having observed in the newspapers a notice calling the attention of the voters to the next election for sheriff, in which it was stated that a poll would probably be opened in his favor, he felt called upon to make known his intentions. He therefore informed the voters of the county that he was a candidate, and would thank them for their votes.

In 1804 the Governor and Council appointed Martin Kershner to be associate justice of the Washington County Court in place of Benjamin Galloway, resigned.

Distinguished Jurists and Lawyers of Washington County.—The bench and bar of Washington County has always sustained the lofty character that has been accorded to the Maryland bar in two hemispheres. Its high professional honor has never been questioned, and to-day among leading jurists and counselors it ranks with any county in the State. Among those citizens of Washington County who have achieved conspicuous reputation in the pleadings and practice of the law we have selected a few of the most prominent.

One of the most brilliant intellects that the bar of Western Maryland has ever boasted was that of Frederick A. Schley. Mr. Schley was the fourth son of John Jacob Schley, and was born at Frederick, Md., on the 14th of May, 1789, and died there on the 5th of February, 1858. His grandfather, Thomas Schley, the progenitor of the Schleys of Western Maryland and Georgia, was born in the Palatinate, in Germany, in 1712, came to America in 1745, and selected the site of Frederick City as his permanent home. He there erected, in 1746, the first house of the future town, and died there in 1790, aged seventy-eight years. He had the reputation of being a gentleman of polished and refined manners, of extensive and varied learning, and the possessor of ample means. One of Thomas Schley's sons, John Jacob Schley, married Ann Maria Shelman, and there were born to them while they lived in Frederick Michael, John, Ann Maria, William, Frederick Augustus, and George. About 1793, John Jacob Schley removed from Frederick to Louisville, Ga., where were born Philip Thomas and Catharine Schley. Michael died early in life. John was a lawyer, and for years prior to his death was a judge. William was a lawyer, a member of Congress, judge, and afterwards Governor of Georgia. One of the counties of the State was named after him. George was an insurance lawyer. Philip Thomas was also a lawyer, amassed a fortune, and retired from the bar. The above all died in Georgia, leaving numerous descendants, of whom five have been lawyers. One of them, ex-Judge William Schley, resides in New York. Another member of the family is a judge, and several of them have been physicians.

Frederick Augustus Schley, the special subject of this sketch (born as stated, May 14, 1789, and died Feb. 5, 1858), removed to Georgia with his father, John Jacob Schley, but the climate not agreeing with him, he left the University of Georgia when seventeen years of age and returned to Frederick, his birthplace, in the hope that the change would benefit him. Finding that his health improved he remained in Frederick, and completed his education at the Frederick Academy. While a student at the academy his tall figure, genial manner, and bright intellect attracted the attention of Roger B. Taney, future chief justice of the United States, who was then a leading member of the Frederick bar. On completing his studies, at the invitation of Mr. Taney he entered the latter's office to prepare himself for the bar. In 1809 or 1810 he was admitted to the bar, and decided from considerations of health to remain in Frederick instead of returning to Georgia. He soon achieved success, and gradually built up an extensive and lucrative practice. Mr. Schley was a gentleman of commanding

FREDERICK A. SCHLEY.

stature, being over six feet in height, refined and polished in manner, profoundly versed in his profession, a close and accurate reasoner, and possessed of great oratorical powers. The latter talent was enhanced by reference to a treasury of poetry and literature which was ever at his command, and which was used with rare and striking effect in his addresses to the jury. He possessed in a pre-eminent degree the "*fortiter in re et suaviter in modo*." His knowledge of law was full and precise, and in the argument of difficult and abstruse points his clearness of statement and aptness of illustration always elicited admiration, while his reasoning seldom failed to convince. The late John Nelson, at one time Attorney-General of the United States, and William Schley, of Baltimore, his relative and former student in his office, were often his opponents at the Frederick bar, where both those gentlemen practiced law for many years.

Like all lawyers of a past generation, Mr. Schley is now known only by his arguments in the Court of Appeals, reported in the Maryland Reports. Whoever will examine them will find there some record of his learning and research, the imprint of a vigorous and thoroughly disciplined legal mind, and the evidence of a comprehensive knowledge of law, and rare skill in its application. But, of course, the personality of the orator, the pleasant and graceful manner, the eye beaming with intelligence, and the charm of elocution, which formed such important factors of his success at the bar, are not to be found on the formal records of his achievements, nor can they be perpetuated in words. Mr. Schley's reputation was not confined to Western Maryland, but extended throughout the State. He was often urged to remove to Baltimore, where he would have had a wider and more promising field for his talents, but he preferred to remain in Frederick. Mr. Schley left four sons, of whom three are distinguished lawyers, George and Buchanan Schley, residing in Washington County, and James M. Schley, residing in Allegany County.

John Thomson Mason, father of the late Judge Mason, was for a long time a prominent lawyer and country gentleman of Western Maryland. He moved there in early life from Georgetown, D. C., while in active practice, owing to his impaired health, and a large and influential family grew up around him. He was a son of the well-known Thomas Mason, of Virginia, and nephew of George Mason, of Virginia, whose statue in Richmond perpetuates his great memory and deeds as one of the country's distinguished men, and a signer of the Declaration of Independence.

The subject of this sketch lived at "Montpelier," which place originally belonged to John and Richard Barnes, and here were received many prominent guests from all parts of the country,—Thomas Jefferson used to drive there in his coach to visit Mr. Mason.

As a brilliant lawyer and orator he was accorded a high place, but his singular modesty and impaired health prevented him from seeking or accepting any political office, though any were at his disposal. In this respect he was much like the late John V. L. McMahon. He was tendered the office of attorney-general under President Jefferson, but declined it.

The early Maryland Reports and legislation bear the impress of Mr. Mason's legal and literary ability and statesmanlike mind.

The following letter from William Price, the distinguished lawyer, to Judge Mason supplies some interesting reminiscences of John Thomson Mason, viz.:

"Baltimore, Aug. 26, 1863.

"My dear Sir,—My recollections of your father are all of the most agreeable kind. He was the object of my youthful admiration, and I sought his society constantly and eagerly.

"I was married at the age of twenty-three, and a week or two afterwards Mr. Mason came to my house, sent for my wife and self, and gave us a lecture upon the conduct of life, business, etc., the substance of which was that I was to study hard, my wife to be economical; we were to give no entertainments, and live as much at home as possible. We had occasion long to remember his good advice and the kind feeling which prompted it.

"His last case at the bar was my first. It was a prosecution against a man named Duncan for purchasing wheat from his negroes. I have no doubt the fellow was guilty, but the proof was very scant, and I got him off.

"He was in the habit of settling the disputes which arose among his neighbors. If one party came to him he would send for the other, then hear patiently all they had to say, examine their papers if they had any, and finally give his decision, which was generally final. On one occasion Henry Fiery and a person with whom he had a dispute came to Mr. Mason. They made their statements, and during the investigation Fiery produced a receipt, which the other party snatched up and put into his pocket. Your father deliberately arose from his chair, caught up the poker, and advancing to the person, said to him, 'Lay down that receipt, you d—d rascal, or I will break your head.' The receipt was at once produced, and the settlement proceeded.

"Col. John Barnes, your father's uncle, occupied the Montpelier estate to the time of his death, shortly after which event Richard Barnes, of St. Mary's, died, leaving the estate to your father. It was a magnificent property, which my father estimated at three hundred thousand dollars. Your father had been laboriously engaged in his profession, until one bright morning, finding this on his table, he determined to remove upon the estate, and never entered a court-house afterwards, except to prosecute Duncan. It was perhaps unfortunate that he ever acceded to this immense estate, as he gradually thereafter lost his knowledge of the law and perhaps the vigor of his intellect.

"He was an admirable lawyer. Many a time have I, a mere child, played truant to hear him speak. His explanations and reasonings were so plain that I, even at that early age, could understand everything he said. I once heard Luther Martin say that he had practiced law with him for forty years and never knew him once to be taken by surprise.

"He once remarked to me that Blackstone was a great misfortune to the profession,—that it made the law too easy. He thought that knowledge acquired without labor did not stick by one, nor was it so well understood as that which was dug out by incessant toil and then arranged for yourself.

"I was once dining at Montpelier, and your father, seeing my glass remaining untouched, though nearly full of wine, called out to me, 'Will, drink your wine; come, sir, you poured it out. If I had helped you, you would not be bound to drink more of it than you pleased; but it is not so when you have helped yourself.' Of course I turned off the whole whether I liked it or not.

"I take it for granted you have heard of what occurred between your father and Judge Stull in relation to the trial of a man who was indicted for stealing a horse. The proof was very strong, and the theft clearly proven, but in the course of the evidence the fact was disclosed that the horse was stolen in Pennsylvania, and never was in possession of the thief on this Maryland side of the line. Your father, therefore, made the point that the court had no jurisdiction of the case,—that the stealing of a horse in Pennsylvania was no violation of the laws of Maryland. The judge, however, seemed to be incredulous, and said, in his broken English, 'I ton't know 'pout dat, Mishter Mason.' 'But,' rejoined your father, 'you have no authority to try him. If you convict him, and punish him, he may still be punished for the same offense in Pennsylvania.' 'Vell, Mishter Mason, ve'll see about dat.' Your father then obtained permission to go to his office for the books, to show that he was right. The court-house was above the market-house, and the whipping-post was in the centre of the latter. And as your father was ascending the steps with an armful of books he heard an outcry in the market-house, and looking under the arch, saw that his client was lashed to the whipping-post and the sheriff was diligently engaged in giving him the benefit of the law of Moses on his bare back. Your father went into the court-house in a towering passion and commenced a fracas with the court. He found the judge, however, perfectly satisfied with what he had done, who remarked in a very business style, 'Dat de man had stole de horse, and was whipped for it, and te ting was now over.'

"It was said that while the altercation between your father and the judge was in progress the man, who had come into court, asked what his lawyer was doing with the court, and was answered that he was applying for a new trial. 'Oh, for God sake!' said he, 'I don't want any more trials. I've had one trial too many already.'

"But this last was the improvement of some one who was fond of adding to history his own embellishments. The story, I think, properly closes with the scene at the whipping-post and the remonstrance of your father in court.

"Your father honored me with his confidence, and spoke to me always with the freedom which might characterize the intercourse of persons more nearly approaching the same age. On one occasion at Montpelier he said to me, 'Will, avoid the horrible vice of gaming. I should have been ruined by it but for a vow I made never to play after I had lost all my cash. Frederick,' he continued, 'was the worst place for excessive play I ever saw. I have lost as much as five thousand dollars at a sitting, but when my money was gone I have said, "Well, gentlemen, you have now got all I had to lose, and I suppose my company is no longer agreeable to you."' And he quit the table.

"Judge Stull was a remarkable man. He had certainly no pretentions to legal knowledge, yet his services as president of the Committee of Observation for Elizabeth (now Hagerstown) District during the years 1775-77, which committee assumed and exercised all powers of government, legislative, judicial, and executive, during a period of great difficulty and disorder,—and his will, owing to his excellent judgment and extraordinary force of character, was received as law,—were regarded as sufficient to insure him a place of especial dignity and trust in the community which he had served so faithfully. He was on the bench, therefore, from the habit of the people to look up to him for advice, and he was not the man to suffer the forms of law to stand in the way of what he considered the justice of the case.

"Many amusing stories were told of him, one of which, on account of your father being connected with it, I will mention. Judge Claggett was the chief justice of the court, and was a man of ability. On one occasion the term of court commenced, and in the absence of the chief justice, who had not arrived, Judge Stull was forced, much against his will, to address the grand jury. It was his duty, however, and he was not the man to shirk from it. Addressing them as 'Shentlemens of te Grand Inquesht for te pody of Washington Gounty,' he went through the whole list of crimes, which by the aid of your father he defined as he proceeded. Some of the definitions were a little extraordinary, but were, nevertheless, propounded with a very grave face. At last they came to 'burglary.' 'Wat te tevil is dat pooglary, Mason?' 'Oh,' said your father, 'that is selling liquor by the small.' And the judge gave that explanation of 'pooglary' to the jury.

"Your father acquired great distinction by the ability displayed by him in the case of Harper *vs.* Hampton. It was long before my time,—the suit being instituted in the old General Court in the year 1803, but I have frequently heard the old people talk about it. Robert Goodloe Harper was the plaintiff, and Gen. Wade Hampton, of either Georgia or South Carolina, the defendant. Your father, William Pinkney, and John Johnson, the father of Reverdy Johnson, an admirable *nisi prius* lawyer, were for the defendant, and Luther Martin, Philip Barton Key, and Alexander C. Magruder for the plaintiff. The prominence of the parties, the great distinction of the counsel, and the large amount involved in the controversy gave to the trial an uncommon degree of interest. Mr. Harper took part in his own case, and, although not so well trained as lawyers of his standing at the Maryland bar, was notwithstanding a very formidable man to encounter. Your father and he came in contact early in the trial, in a manner which made it extremely difficult to avoid personalities of the most pointed character. And it was said that your father, who was very competent to hold his own in such a quarrel, made the trial an extremely unpleasant one to Mr. Harper. There were some letters of Mr. Harper which were given in evidence, and which offered free scope for sarcasm and invective, and your father did not feel himself particularly called upon to spare either.

"After I had been reading law for a year or more I went home for about six months, and had the use of your father's books. I was of course frequently at Montpelier, and had very frequent conversations with him about the course of study and the practice of the law. He has frequently said to me that I had better be a respectable mechanic than a second-rate lawyer, and admonitions of this character coming from him stimulated me to greater exertions, that without them I should not have used. He was a very good talker: possessed an even flow of spirits which I never saw ruffled. It was said that at the bar he was remarkable for calmness and equanimity; that nothing was ever permitted to put him out of temper, and although his adversary might be furious, he was perfectly cool, and would say the most cutting things with a smile on his countenance.

"My engagements are such that I cannot continue these reminiscences. I began intending to write a short letter, but the matter has grown under my hand, and I must here stop for want of leisure.

"Very truly yours,

"WILLIAM PRICE.

"HON. JOHN THOMSON MASON."

Judge John Thomson Mason, son of John Thomson Mason, was born at the family-seat, "Montpelier," Washington County, May 15, 1815. He was one of a large family, whose home was a resort of many prominent persons of this and other States.

After a preliminary course at Mount St. Mary's College, Emmittsburg, Judge Mason entered Princeton College, where he graduated in 1836 with high honors and the valedictory. Returning to Hagerstown, the county-seat, and about ten miles from the Mason family home, he entered the law-office of the late William Price, one of Maryland's most prominent lawyers. After passing the bar he at once began a successful and active life, both professionally and soon politically. In this latter field it was his happy portion, and for which he received the just tribute and love of both personal and political friends and those opposed, to have honors seek him, and to have kept himself pure and retiring in all contests, successes, and defeats.

Retaining to the day of his death an ardent love for agricultural pursuits, his attention was frequently diverted to his farms lying near Hagerstown.

In 1845 he was sent to Congress from the district in which Hagerstown then belonged, and after one term returned to his profession. In 1851 he was elected one of the judges of the Court of Appeals of Maryland, under the old constitution, which then provided for only four judges for that tribunal. He then removed to Annapolis permanently. His associates were Judges Tuck, Legrand, and Eccleston. After six years' service, during which time his decisions were marked and his labors conspicuous (the case of Ware *vs.* Richardson, 7 Maryland, demonstrating the applicability of the rule in Shelley's case in Maryland, being one of his important opinions), he resigned, upon the accession of Mr. Buchanan to the Presidency, to accept the position of collector of the port of Baltimore under that Executive. Upon the breaking out of the war Judge Mason, whose sympathies were warmly with the South, retired to private life, and during the exciting scenes of our civil war he quietly yet firmly gave his time and counsels as he thought best to those of his friends and such measures as demanded his attention. He was imprisoned twice, once in Western Maryland while upon his farm, and also in Fort McHenry with many other prominent gentlemen.

At the close of the war Judge Mason, whose residence was still in Annapolis, resumed the practice of law in Baltimore, associating himself with the late Maj. Thomas Rowland. When Hon. William Pinkney Whyte was elected Governor, he appointed Judge Mason his Secretary of State, which position he held to the day of his death, which occurred very suddenly on March 28, 1873, at Elkton, Md. His busy professional life would not admit of his sparing himself, even with the duties above mentioned, and he may be said to have literally "died in harness." At the close of a long and important case in Elkton (Mow *vs.* McHenry), and just as he sat down to his dinner and was receiving the congratulations of his friends and brother attorneys upon his able speech in the case, and before hearing the verdict in his favor, a few minutes previously announced, his head fell back, and he died peacefully, in a moment, a victim to apoplexy. He was buried in the county and near the mountains he loved so well. He was a man of large and liberal views, of great experience and learning both as judge, lawyer, and politician; and, withal, possessing a large, warm heart, simplicity of manner, and a zealous and devout religious nature, he was equally loved and admired in public and private life, and the humblest citizen seemed to know and feel his loss, as did his companions everywhere throughout the State.

At the close of the war Judge Mason espoused the Catholic religion, and soon, with his hearty, zealous nature, became an important and prominent member. He delivered the address at the Cathedral upon the occasion of the twenty-fifth celebration of the pontificate of Pope Pius IX., and in many ways gave prominence to the lay representation of the church.

He died in the fifty-eighth year of his age, in the full vigor of manhood and intellectual brightness, and his loss was one that the "new school" cannot perhaps supply. He leaves a widow, two married daughters, and one son, the latter bearing his name (the third in succession), and now a member of the bar of Baltimore.

Judge John Buchanan, a brother of Judge Thomas Buchanan, was the second son of Thomas and Anne Buchanan, and was born in Prince George's County in 1772. Losing his parents quite early in life, he was sent to Charlotte Hall Academy, Charles County, where he received the usual education of that day, and when still but a youth was sent to Winchester, Va., to read law with Judge White, a learned jurist of that place, but soon afterwards was transferred to Washington County, where he continued his studies with John Thomson Mason, the elder, at that time one of the most distinguished lawyers in the State. After a successful practice of a few years, he married the daughter of Col. Elie Williams (niece of Gen. Otho H. Williams), and shortly afterwards was placed on the Supreme Bench of Maryland. He continued to occupy and adorn this conspicuous office for a period of forty years and up to his death, winning, as a jurist of remarkable profundity, the admiration and respect of such legal minds as those of Luther Martin, Pinkney, Roger B. Taney, Reverdy Johnson, and many others. In personal appearance and manners he was regarded as being one of the most elegant men of his age, and his public worth may be measured by the many valuable decisions which he rendered from time to time throughout the long period of his official career. Judge Buchanan died in November, 1844.

The family is descended from the Buchanans of Loch Lomond, Scotland, one of whom, George Buchanan, was tutor to the royal Earl of Murray, and another, Alexander Buchanan, distinguished himself at the battle of the Boyne.

Judge Buchanan's death was announced to the court of Baltimore County by I. Nevett Steele, deputy attorney-general, in the following words:

"May it please the court: I rise to discharge the melancholy duty of announcing to the court the death of the Hon. John Buchanan, chief judge of the Court of Appeals. For nearly forty years he has adorned the judiciary of our State, and in his death he has left behind him, in the reported decisions of our highest legal tribunal, the most enduring evidences of his profound learning and great judicial ability. Without attempting here any eulogy upon his private character, Mr. Schley has most truly observed that the announcement of Judge Buchanan's death would be the occasion of the deepest regret to the court. He has filled for thirty-eight years the station of chief judge of the district in which he resided, and has presided for upwards of twenty years as the chief justice of this State. The report of the decisions of our court evince his learning, and will pass his name to succeeding generations, as long as our free institutions and the principles of the common law are respected. Few men, in any age or country, have lived who possessed more generous feelings, a kinder heart, or a wiser head. It has been my good fortune to have lived in intimate friendship with him, and to have acted with him for more than one-half of his judicial career, and I can say, with truth and sincerity, that in all my intercourse with the world I have met with no man of a more scrupulous sense of honor, of a better-regulated judgment, or of more urbane manners. He had lived beyond the age allotted to our race, but he quit our earthly and temporary habitation for his eternal abiding-place with an intellect unimpaired by age, leaving behind him a character distinguished for virtue and for every quality which could adorn our nature."

In announcing the death of Judge Buchanan the Hagerstown *Torchlight* said,—

"It is with feelings of the most profound sorrow that we announce the death of his Honor John Buchanan, chief justice of the State of Maryland, in the seventy-first year of his age. He expired at Woodland, his late residence, on Wednesday last, at eleven o'clock. Judge Buchanan was appointed associate justice of this judicial district in 1806, and in 1825 took his seat as chief judge of the Court of Appeals, from which time to the present he has presided in such a manner as to have conferred upon himself the reputation of one of the ablest jurists in the country. During this period, notwithstanding his precarious health, he has labored with indefatigable perseverance in his vocation, and has bequeathed to his State a series of decisions which will always be looked upon as one of the proudest monuments, and from which her sons, so long as she exists, will continue to reap the wholesome and vivifying fruits. Deeply do we deplore his decease, and most deeply do we sympathize with his bereaved family in the loss which not only they, but the public, have sustained."

Judge Thomas Buchanan was the eldest son of Thomas Buchanan and Anne Cooke, of Chester, England, and was born Sept. 25, 1768, on his father's plantation near Port Tobacco, Md. He graduated in the law quite early in life, and practiced in the courts of Anne Arundel and St. Mary's Counties until his marriage with Miss Anderson, granddaughter of Samuel Ogle, Governor of Maryland, in April, 1797, when he removed to Baltimore, and afterwards to Washington County, where he had large landed estates. He succeeded the Hon. Roger Nelson as judge of the Circuit Court, May 5, 1815, and died Sept. 27, 1847, of apoplexy, with which he was seized while returning home from court at Hagerstown. During his long career at the bar and on the bench Judge Buchanan was noted for his learning, integrity, and lofty sense of professional honor.

In announcing his death a Hagerstown paper said:

"We have the melancholy duty to perform this week of announcing the sudden death of this very distinguished citizen of our county. Never before have we felt ourselves so utterly incompetent to the right performance of any duty as that which devolves upon us in briefly portraying in suitable and becoming language the merits of this able and profound jurist. The circumstances immediately surrounding his last moments are sad and deeply afflictive. He had come to town in the forenoon of Tuesday last, and opened a court for the purpose of hearing an argument in chancery of considerable importance; and the near approach of the election brought to town some fourteen or fifteen persons, to avail themselves of his presence to become naturalized. This duty he performed with more than usual strictness, as we are told, and then listened with his usual patience to the arguments of the case just alluded to for about three hours, during all of which time he exhibited no symptoms of indisposition, nor did he at all complain. After a session of some five hours he rose from his seat, and having appointed Monday following for the meeting of the court again, in order to dispatch some other pressing business before he should leave for the court in Allegany, he took leave of those who were present with his usual kind manner, and in company with his amiable daughter and an old valued servant, he started for his residence, some ten miles distant. On the way, as we learn, he seemed very well, and conversed with cheerfulness, until within about two miles of his home, when he was suddenly seized in his carriage with apoplexy, and died instantly, without a groan or struggle. Thus passed from earth to heaven the late venerable and venerated senior associate judge of this judicial district, the Hon. Thomas Buchanan. But few are the men indeed, if any, who have ever descended to the tomb in Western Maryland whose death was more deeply mourned, or whose loss was more severely felt.

"He was the very model of a judge, and has left behind him an ermine of spotless purity, which but few could wear and not soil. For upwards of *thirty-two* years—having been commissioned on the 5th of May, 1815—he sat upon the bench, dispensing justice alike to the rich and to the poor; administering the laws of the land with an impartiality that knew no friend; with a judgment that seldom erred, and with a dignity, yet easy grace, entirely free from ostentation, that would at once have made insolence stand rebuked in his presence. And although in him was found the stern and upright judge, yet for the misfortune of a fallen fellow-creature no one possessed a more kindly heart, as all who knew him can bear witness. As a citizen he was equally exemplary, discharging the duties of neighbor, and the nearer relation of family, in a way that secured the love and esteem of all, and in these varied relations, whether as a public minister of the law or as a private citizen, he has left a vacuum that we fear will not be easily filled. His remains were, on Thursday following his demise, brought to this place, and interred in the Episcopal burying-ground, amidst the tears and regrets of a vast assemblage of his neighbors, friends, and acquaintances."

At a meeting of the bar of Washington County Court, convened at the clerk's office, in Hagerstown, on the 29th day of September, 1847, R. M. Tidball was called to the chair, and Jervis Spencer appointed

William T. Hamilton

secretary. The following preamble and resolutions, submitted by Daniel Weisel, and prefaced by him with some remarks, were unanimously adopted:

"*Whereas*, This meeting has learned with equal surprise and sorrow the sudden death of Hon. Thomas Buchanan, late the senior and associate judge of the Fifth Judicial District of Maryland, which occurred yesterday evening in his carriage on his way home from this place, where he had on that day mingled with us, in health, in the discharge of official business.

"*And whereas*, The pure and elevated character, private and judicial, of the deceased, the relation which he bore to us, and his long, able, and faithful service to the public, demand from us a suitable expression of the sentiments with which we have received the intelligence of this mournful dispensation of Providence. Therefore

"*Resolved*, That this event, so sudden and affecting, and depriving us and the community of one so endeared and distinguished as was the late Judge Buchanan, has impressed us all with the most profound sorrow.

"*Resolved*, That we recognize in the deceased the true gentleman, the valued and valuable citizen, the pure, learned, and upright judge, and a public benefactor, whom any community might have been proud of and blessed to call its own, and whose loss cannot but be most sensibly felt and deplored.

"*Resolved*, That the members of the bar have by this event been deprived of a valuable friend, society of a highly respected and venerated member, the bench of an ornament, and the cause of public justice of a firm and noble pillar."

William T. Hamilton, the present Governor of Maryland, was born at Hagerstown on the 8th of September, 1820. His father was Henry Hamilton, who resided at Boonsboro', where his son, William T., received the rudiments of his education from James Brown, at one time surveyor for Washington County. His (William T.'s) mother died when he was about six years old, and his father about two years later. Left thus unprotected, he was received into the family of one of his uncles on the maternal side, who was noted for his devotion to the principles of the old Jefferson school and for his strict attention to business. The future Governor and senator was placed at the Hagerstown Academy, where he remained for some time, making for himself an honorable record as a close and diligent student. He then entered Jefferson College, at Canonsburg, Pa., and after completing his studies returned to Hagerstown, and entered the law-office of Hon. John Thomson Mason as a student of law. In 1843 he was admitted to the bar, and in 1846 was nomimated upon the Democratic ticket and elected to the House of Delegates; the ticket, after a hard-fought contest, being divided, with William Beverly Clarke, a Whig, elected to the Senate. One of the most prominent topics before the Legislature was the question as to whether the interest upon the State debt should be paid or not. Mr. Hamilton advocated its payment with great earnestness and ability. In 1847, Mr. Hamilton was renominated, but, although he led his ticket by a large majority, he was defeated by his Whig opponent.

In 1848 he was placed upon the Cass electoral ticket, and in 1849 was nominated by the Democratic party for Congress. After a close and exciting contest he was elected, although in the previous year the county had given a large majority for Gen. Taylor, the Whig candidate for President. The absorbing issue of the day was the tariff question, and Mr. Hamilton did not hesitate to affirm and demonstrate in the most forcible manner the theories of the Democratic party looking to a tariff for revenue only, although many of his constituents were strongly tinctured with Protectionist ideas. His opponent was Thomas J. McKaig, who received 7191 votes against 7307 for Hamilton. During his first term in Congress, Mr. Hamilton distinguished himself by the ability and eloquence with which he supported and advocated the Clay Compromise Bill. In 1851 he was again elected to Congress, receiving 6863 votes against 6626 cast for Mr. Roman, the Whig candidate. At the expiration of his second term Mr. Hamilton determined to retire from politics, but being urgently pressed by his friends, consented to be placed in nomination in 1853. His opponent, Hon. Francis Thomas, was an independent candidate, and in the contest which ensued the two candidates were pitted against each other in joint discussions. The result was a larger majority for Hamilton than at either of the two preceding elections, the vote being, Hamilton, 7545; Thomas, 6429. During his third term in Congress, Mr. Hamilton gave an energetic and loyal support to the administration of President Pierce. As chairman of the Committee on the District of Columbia, he took a leading part in the prosecution of the vast work by which the city of Washton is now supplied with water from the Great Falls of the Potomac. At the expiration of his term Mr. Hamilton again announced his desire and intention to retire to private life, but his constituency demanded that he should continue in the field, and he was obliged to yield to their wishes. In 1855, therefore, he was for the fourth time a candidate for Congress; but the Know-Nothing, or "Great American," party having suddenly gained phenomenal, though temporary strength, he was defeated. Thenceforward Mr. Hamilton devoted himself assiduously to the practice of his profession, in which he achieved the most gratifying success, demonstrating in a variety of cases remarkable argumentative powers and a thorough and comprehensive knowledge of the law. During his career as Congressman Mr. Hamilton was assisted in his legal practice by R. H. Alvey, now an eminent judge of the Court of Appeals. In 1861 he was strongly urged to accept the Democratic nomination for Governor, but declined the honor. In 1868 he consented to stand as a candidate for the United States Senate, and was elected for six years from the 4th of March, 1869. His predecessor, Governor Whyte, had been appointed to fill the unexpired term of Reverdy Johnson, who had been sent by President Johnson as United States minister to England. The vote stood: Hamilton, 56 (exactly the number necessary for a choice); Swann, 46; and Merrick, 7. In the Senate Mr. Hamilton proved himself to be a fluent and forcible debater, and made a marked impression upon that body at a period when it was exceedingly difficult for a senator of his political persuasion to obtain even a respectful hearing. His term expired in 1875, in which year the Democratic convention met to nominate a candidate for Governor of Maryland. In an eloquent and forcible speech Hon. John Ritchie, of Frederick, presented the name of ex-Senator Hamilton, but Mr. Hamilton failed to receive the nomination, and Hon. John Lee Carroll was chosen by the convention and elected by the people. On the 7th of August, 1879, however, Mr. Hamilton was unanimously nominated by the Democratic State Convention to succeed Gov. Carroll, and in the following autumn was elected, his majority over his Republican opponent, James A. Gary, being 22,208. His inauguration was the occasion of an enthusiastic popular demonstration, and the ceremonies at the State-house were of an exceptionally interesting and impressive character. Governor Hamilton devotes much time and attention to the management of his farms, which are considered to be among the most intelligently and carefully tilled and among the most productive in Washington County. He has a handsome residence in Hagerstown, besides his country-seat about two miles distant, and alternates between these two points and Annapolis. He has six children,—four daughters and two sons,—the latter being Richard and William T. Hamilton, Jr. Governor Hamilton is a man of remarkable force of character, strict integrity, and a lofty appreciation of the duties incumbent upon a public official. As an executive, he has shown invariably an earnest disposition to prevent and reform abuses, and to reduce the burden of taxation to the lowest possible point. As a lawyer, he ranks among the foremost members of the bar of Western Maryland; and in all matters of business or of agriculture he is quoted by his neighbors and friends as an authority from which there should be no appeal.

William Price, one of the most distinguished lawyers that Maryland has produced, was a native of Washington County, his father being an officer of the Revolution, and died Nov. 25, 1868. He was educated at Dickinson College, and studied law with Judge Cooper, of Carlisle, Upton Lawrence, of Hagerstown, Judge Nicholas Brice, of Baltimore, and John Thomson Mason, the elder. While a resident of Washington County he was elected a member of the State Senate by the electoral college about 1825. He was afterwards a candidate for Congress. He moved to Cumberland, Allegany Co., and after a few years removed to Baltimore. He was elected a member of the State Legislature from Baltimore in 1862, and was afterwards appointed United States District Attorney by President Lincoln, which office he held for one term. Mr. Price was one of the commissioners appointed by the Legislature to simplify the forms of pleading and practice in Maryland. He was a prominent member of his profession, by whom his social qualities and personal character were held in high regard. The courts of Baltimore, in which tributes of respect were paid to his memory, all adjourned to attend his funeral.

In the Superior Court George M. Gill announced the death of Mr. Price. He spoke of the deceased in becoming terms, and moved that the court adjourn in respect to his memory.

Hon. J. Thomson Mason rose to second the motion. He gave a sketch of the life of the deceased, and said his abilities as a lawyer were generally recognized, and his high personal character was as well known as his professional abilities.

In response to the remarks of the members of the bar Judge Dobbin said,—

"The whole bar of Maryland will unite with us in mournful regret at the death of our brother Price. Enjoying in his younger life a large practice in the western counties of the State, Mr. Price followed his cases to the Court of Appeals, where all remember how his majestic presence, his genial urbanity, and his rich colloquial gifts adorned the professional circle which assembled at Annapolis. Mr. Price possessed also an extensive and varied scholarship, which he so gracefully blended with the severer labors of his vocation that he was always an engaging and instructive orator. The liberal view which he took of the science to which he was devoted carried him ahead of most of his contemporaries in those simplifications of the law now so apparent upon our system of conveyancing and pleading; and he was the first, under legislative appointment, to get rid of many of the technical embarrassments of the older law. After his removal to Baltimore, and in the late trouble of the country, William Price became the law officer of the general government in this district; and while he faithfully discharged his duty to the public, he made what was often a painful exercise of office as little offensive as possible to those of his fellow-citizens who differed from him in opinion. He belonged to a generation of lawyers fast passing away, and when our younger professional brethren shall look back in the forensic annals of the State to find a type of the old Maryland gentleman and lawyer, none will be more likely to furnish the example than the late Mr. Price.

"Out of respect for his memory, and in order that we may attend his remains to the grave, I shall now order the court to stand adjourned."

Mr. Price once appeared as a writer of romance, and produced the novel entitled "Clem. Falconer, or the Memoirs of a Young Whig." It was not a success, and was his only attempt. He also at one time contemplated the publication of work on chancery practice, which no doubt would have met a different fate from the novel, for the inclination of Mr. Price was law, in which he was profoundly versed. He also frequently essayed politics, but without a success commensurate with his natural ability; and was also once connected with an edge-tool manufacturing company, which proved a failure. His sphere was emphatically the law, and nothing else appeared to suit him. He was an enthusiastic Union man at the commencement of the war, and while in the Legislature introduced the "Treason Bill," with which his name became familiarly associated, and which, owing to peculiar circumstances, subjected him to severe animadversion. Towards the conclusion of the struggle he became pre-eminently conservative, and before his death those estrangements which sprang from his zeal at a more early stage of the war, were entirely removed.

In a letter to the Hagerstown *Mail*, correcting certain misstatements, the late Judge Mason gives the following interesting reminiscences of Mr. Price:

"It would be unnecessary to refer to the prominent incidents in the life of Mr. Price, as the recollection of them is still fresh in the minds of most of your readers. His urbane manners, his commanding personal appearance, his fascinating powers of conversation, his earnest, distinguished, and apostolic style of public speaking are all well remembered by his former friends and neighbors. Of his father, who was no less remarkable in his way, little is now known. Col. Price lived and died on the banks of the Conococheague, and was distinguished no less for the vigor of his intellect and personal integrity than for his great eccentricities. His history and peculiarities, of which I heard so much when a child, have passed, amid the changes and vicissitudes of Washington County, almost entirely out of the memory of the people. In many respects he was a wise man. He showed this in the course he pursued towards his four sons. Having but a moderate estate, he summoned his sons before him, and after a thorough explanation of his purpose, their consequences, etc., to the effect that his means would not enable him to give to them all a complete and polished education and leave them property besides, he proposed to those of his sons who preferred that they should receive such an education, but at his death should get no part of his estate, while the others, who might be content with the common education which the neighborhood could furnish, should have his property. William and Benjamin selected the education, and the other two the property; but by a strange decree of Providence the two last referred to died while young, and their surviving brothers thereby succeeded to the property as well as to the education. In regard to this compact, Col. Price carried it out in perfect good faith, for he spared no pains in affording his two sons, William and Benjamin, every advantage of education which his judgment could suggest and his means furnish, and they in turn no less appreciated these advantages, as was abundantly shown in the highly-cultivated state of their minds, evinced as well in legal attainments as in general literary tastes and acquirements. But they commenced life without a dollar.

"I have heard one anecdote of Col. Price, which is so well vouched for and so creditable to his good nature and neighborly feelings, if it even does not reflect much honor upon his loyalty (as now understood), that I think it worthy of public notice.

"During the famous 'Whisky Insurrection,' in Washington's administration, Col. Price held a military position under the government. The spirit of rebellion was not confined to Western Pennsylvania, but it extended to other parts of the country, and even in the secluded region where Col. Price lived it had taken strong hold. A public meeting of Republicans, as they were then called, which was composed of many of the most substantial and respectable of Col. Price's neighbors, had been held at Rockdale to express sympathy with the Pittsburgh insurgents. The movement had assumed such proportions that the government determined it should be thwarted. Accordingly a body of soldiers was ordered to report to Col. Price, with instructions that some fifteen or twenty, whose names were furnished, of those who had participated in the meeting should be arrested. The soldiers reached his house early in the afternoon and delivered their instructions. He received them with his usual hospitality, but instead of proceeding at once to the execution of the orders, he insisted they should remain with him till morning, when he would see that their mission was fulfilled. They accordingly did so, and early the next day, accompanied by a guide, they started on their assigned duty. Late in the evening they returned with but one prisoner, and that was Philip Kriegh, a man well known in his day for respectability, probity, and frankness, in all of which qualities he is well represented by his son William, still living in Washington County. Col. Price met him at the gate in the most cordial manner, and inquired 'where the rest of his neighbors were?' Mr. Kriegh seemed a little surprised at this question, and with more frankness than prudence presently responded, 'Didn't you send your son all through the neighborhood last night to tell us to run away, that the soldiers were after us?' And he then explained that the reason he did not run with the others was that, being sick, he had not been able to attend the Rockdale meeting. At first the colonel was a little confused and discomfited at this unexpected public disclosure of disloyalty, but he soon recovered his presence of mind, and turning to the commanding officer, said, 'What can my good, harmless neighbors do to injure this great government? Come in! come in! and let us drink the health of Gen. Washington.' Greatly given to conviviality, as well as hospitality, it may be well imagined that Col. Price and his friends had a merry night. It was sufficient at all events to forever obliterate from the mind of the government all memory and resentment for the Rockdale treason."

In August, 1840, Mr. Price fought a duel with the Hon. Francis Thomas, which caused no little excitement throughout the State. The Baltimore *Sun* in its issue of Aug. 6, 1840, said,—

"Our city was thrown into considerable excitement yesterday by a painful report, said to be brought by passengers in the railroad cars, that a hostile meeting had taken place somewhere on the Virginia shore of the Potomac between the Hon. Francis Thomas, member of Congress from this State, and president of the Chesapeake and Ohio Canal Company, and William Price, Esq., an eminent member of the Hagerstown Bar."

On the following day the same paper added,—

"In a part of our edition yesterday morning we added a postscript containing authentic intelligence of the result of a duel between Mr. Thomas and Mr. Price, and we must now repeat it for the benefit of those who did not see it. The parties met on Wednesday morning in Morgan County, Va., between Bath and Hancock, Md.; one shot was exchanged without effect, and the difficulty was then compromised on the interference of friends. We rejoice exceedingly at the result. Mr. Thomas is a gentleman well known in this State, and as a politician throughout the country, and few men have had greater share of the confidence of their immediate constituents than he. He now, besides his place in Congress, holds a responsible situation in the Chesapeake and Ohio Canal Company, that of president. From this his position in society may be inferred. In Congress he was looked upon by his party as a man of more than ordinary discrimination and talent, having been placed at the head of the Judiciary Committee, one of the most important committees in the House. The distance at which the gentlemen fought was twelve paces."

The particulars of the affair, as given in the Hagerstown *Mail*, were these:

"The difficulty originated in a speech delivered by Mr. Price at Cumberland some time since. There are various rumors afloat about the rise, progress, and settlement of the affair, but we have not been able to obtain a statement that could be relied upon, because, as we understand, it was agreed among the friends of the parties that no publication should be made except the following:

"'A Card.—Understanding that the public are aware that a misunderstanding between William Price, Esq., of Washington County, and Francis Thomas, Esq., of Frederick County, in this State, has resulted in a hostile meeting, the undersigned, who acted as the respective friends of the parties upon the ground, take pleasure in stating, with a view to correct all error upon the subject, that after an exchange of shots, at our instance the difficulty was adjusted to the entire honor of both gentlemen.

"'Wm. H. Norris,
"'John McPherson,
"'J. Hollingsworth.

"'Hancock, Aug. 5, 1840.'"

Robert J. Brent, one of Maryland's most gifted lawyers, was born in Louisiana, and died in Baltimore City in February, 1872. Mr. Brent married a daughter of Upton Lawrence, of Hagerstown, and was otherwise identified with the people of Washington County. His grandfather, Mr. Fenwick, was for many years a member of the Maryland State Senate from Charles County, and his father practiced law in Louisiana and in Washington, D. C. Robert J. Brent studied law in the office of his father, and in that of Gen. Walter Jones, of Washington, and was admitted to the bar in 1834. After practicing a short time in the courts of Washington he removed to Frederick City, and thence to Hagerstown, where he married. A few years later he removed to Baltimore, where he soon acquired a large practice. He also frequently appeared before the Court of Appeals, and in the courts at Washington. His associate and intimate friend was the Hon. Henry May.

Mr. Brent was originally of the old Whig school of politics, but becoming dissatisfied with the party during the administration of Gen. Harrison, allied himself with the Democrats, and afterwards remained an active and influential member of that party. Although he was never a seeker for office, he was on several occasions chosen delegate to the Presidential Nominating Conventions, served several terms in the State Legislature, and was a member of the Constitutional Convention in 1850 and 1851. While in the latter body he was appointed State's attorney for Baltimore City, on the death of George R. Richardson, by Governor Lowe. Mr. Brent was engaged in a number of the most important cases, not only in Baltimore, but in the various counties in the State, in the Court of Appeals and in the Superior Court. As an advocate he was fearless and faithful, so devoted to the interests of his client that he sometimes failed to see the imperfections of the cause in which he was engaged. To his associates he was always polite and courteous, and to the younger members of the profession he was kind and considerate. In social life he was genial and entertaining, never, however, carrying any pleasure or sport to excess. During his leisure hours in summer he indulged his love of aquatic sports, and his yacht "Minnie" was well known in the Patapsco. The last time Mr. Brent appeared as counsel was for the defendant in a civil suit in the Superior Court, and during the trial complained of a pain in the heel, which finally became so acute as to cause him to retire to his home. The disease was finally pronounced acute rheumatism, which, extending to vital parts, terminated his life. Mr. Brent left a widow, several daughters, and one son, who was associated with his father in the practice of law.

Hon. Richard H. Alvey, chief judge of the Fourth Judicial Circuit, and judge of the Court of Appeals, was the eldest child of George and Harriet (*née* Wicklin) Alvey, and born on the 6th of March, 1826, in St. Mary's County, Md. Both of his parents were of English descent, and belonged to families which were among the oldest and most distinguished in Southern Maryland. Straitened family circumstances, however, did not permit them to give their eldest son a liberal education, and his early intellectual training was confined within the unpretentious limits offered by the curriculum of a county school taught by his father. In 1844, when only eighteen years of age, he entered the clerk's office of Charles County, where he held the position of deputy clerk for several years, and while thus employed began the study of law, which he prosecuted principally at night, after the daily routine of regular duties had been brought to a close. In 1849 he was admitted to the bar in

Charles County, and in the early part of 1850 removed to Western Maryland and settled in Washington County, where he has ever since resided. He commenced his professional career in partnership with the late Judge John Thomson Mason, and was subsequently associated for a time with the present Governor of Maryland, Hon. William T. Hamilton.

He had been at the bar but a short time when he discovered (as the great majority of young lawyers soon discover), that it was necessary to supplement his previous preparation by thorough reading and a systematic course of study. He did, however, what so few young lawyers do on discovering their deficiencies, --set at once and energetically to work to supply them. Law-schools and learned professors to make smooth the road of professional knowledge were not so abundant as at the present day, and aspirants for legal honors were forced to rely to a large extent upon their own judgment as to the best method of mastering the unarranged material which was to be digested and assimilated. The subject of this notice had the good sense to appreciate the necessity for systematic and intelligent study, and commencing anew on a comprehensive plan, pursued a regular course from the foundation up, beginning with Littleton and Coke. This course, in connection with his practice, which was meantime steadily increasing, occupied him for several years, and when completed gave him a professional soundness and thoroughness of which few young lawyers can boast. His natural aptitude for the law, his conscientious and thorough preparation of his cases, his fidelity to the interests of his clients, his marked ability, and his spotless integrity rendered anything but success impossible, and he soon stood in the front rank of his profession in Western Maryland.

Although Judge Alvey came of a strong Whig family, he became an earnest disciple of the political principles of Mr. Jefferson at the very outset of his career. His political opinions were formed in rather an accidental way. Just before he arrived at manhood he happened to become the owner of a copy of Prof. Tucker's "Life of Jefferson," and as he was not then the owner of many books, he read and reread this with great care. He thus became thoroughly acquainted with Jefferson's doctrines with respect to questions of civil government, national policy, and constitutional law, and the opinions then formed have been only strengthened and confirmed by the experience of succeeding years. In addition to the influence exercised in the formation of his political views by the work already mentioned, one of the earliest law-books which fell into his hands was an old copy of that now much neglected but still valuable treasury of political and constitutional law, Tucker's "Blackstone." He not only read carefully the text of Blackstone, but Judge Tucker's admirable appendix, wherein are discussed most clearly the questions of the sources of sovereignty and the power of legislation, the forms of government, the various provisions of the Constitution of the United States, and the sources of the unwritten or common law as it has been introduced and practiced in this country. The theory that pervades Mr. Tucker's discussion of these subjects is that of Mr. Jefferson, and it made a very deep and lasting impression upon the mind of the youthful reader.

Thus Judge Alvey commenced life with views upon political and constitutional questions which were the result of independent investigation, not of training or prejudice, and brought to the discharge of his duties as a citizen an amount of information on these subjects that is rarely possessed by much older men. His familiarity with the political history of the country, and his thorough and clear comprehension of the great principles of constitutional government enunciated by Mr. Jefferson, soon brought him into notice, and the year after his removal to Washington County he was induced to become the Democratic candidate for the State Senate, the opposition candidate being the late Judge French. The county was then strongly Whig, and the Democratic candidate was a comparative stranger, but, nothing daunted by the discouraging prospect, he canvassed the county in company with his Whig opponent, and the result, to their mutual surprise, was a tie vote. The Whigs, however, grew alarmed, and, redoubling their efforts, succeeded in defeating Judge Alvey in the second election by a few votes only. Probably this defeat was the most fortunate circumstance for the State that could have occurred, as it doubtless prevented his being tempted from the severer duties of his profession to the more seductive sphere of political life,—a result which would have given the country a profound constitutional lawyer and a great statesman, but would have lost to Maryland one of the brightest ornaments of her bench. In 1852, Judge Alvey was nominated as one of the Pierce electors, and with several of his associates canvassed the greater portion of the State, which they carried triumphantly for the Democratic candidate.

While Judge Alvey, in common with a very large majority of the people of Maryland at the beginning of the sectional troubles in 1860, felt that many of the grievances of the South were well founded, and that there was no constitutional authority for a war of coercion, he never believed in the doctrine of secession, and never advocated the extreme and unwise measures adopted by the Southern States. The idea of hostile invasion of one section of the country by another seemed to the great majority of the people of Maryland at that time as nothing less than the total subversion of the fundamental principles of the union of States. Judge Alvey did not hesitate to proclaim his opinions, which in his view were entirely consistent with his obligations to the general government, and his known opposition to the war soon made him a marked man. On the 2d of June, 1861, immediately after the arrival of the Union army at Hagerstown, he was arrested in his office at night by a military squad upon the charge (which was totally unfounded) that he was holding communication with the enemy, and taken to the headquarters of the army, where he was treated with great rudeness and indignity. After being closely confined in Hagerstown for several days he was sent to Fort McHenry, at Baltimore, from there to Fort Lafayette, New York, and thence to Fort Warren, in Boston Harbor, where he was detained, with the other Maryland State prisoners, until the following February, when he was allowed to return home upon parole.

The close of the war found a large portion of the people of the State disfranchised and otherwise deprived of their rights as citizens, and Judge Alvey was among the first in Western Maryland to move for the restoration of their liberties. A large number of the best citizens had been excluded from the juries, and one of the first measures deemed essential to rectify this evil was the adoption of a new jury system. Judge Alvey, accordingly, drafted the present jury law in force in the counties, with the exception of some slight changes recently made, and attended the Legislature at the session of 1867 to procure its passage. The bill was passed as he prepared it first, as a local law applicable only to Washington, Frederick, and Carroll Counties, but before the session closed it was converted into a general law, and passed for all the counties in the State.

The same Legislature which passed the jury law passed the act calling the Constitutional Convention of 1867, which framed the present constitution of the State. Judge Alvey was sent to that convention as a delegate from Washington County, and was made chairman of one of the principal committees of that body,—that on representation. He took an active and influential part in all the proceedings of the convention, and contributed greatly to the satisfactory completion of its labors by his large experience, broad views, and profound knowledge of political and constitutional questions. Under the new constitution he became a candidate for chief judge of the Fourth Judicial Circuit, embracing the counties of Allegany, Washington, and Garrett, and judge of the Court of Appeals of Maryland, and was elected in the fall of 1867. He has held these positions ever since, participating in the decision of many important cases, some of them affecting most deeply the welfare of the entire State, and has discharged the duties of his high office with honor to himself and to the universal satisfaction of the people of Maryland. Few men have ever been upon the bench in Maryland who have graced it more, who have better sustained the dignity and strict impartiality of the judicial office, or have brought to the discharge of its important duties a richer store of legal knowledge, a more discriminating judgment, or a clearer and more vigorous intellect.

Judge Alvey was first married in 1856, to Mary Wharton, eldest daughter of the late Dr. John O. Wharton and niece of Judge Mason. She died in 1860, leaving one child surviving her. In the fall of 1862 Judge Alvey married Julia I. Hays, only daughter of the late Dr. Joseph C. Hays, of Washington County, by whom he has had a large family of children.

George Freaner was born on the 20th of January, 1831, and was a member of one of the oldest and best-known families of Washington County. His death, which occurred on the 10th of November, 1878, was rather sudden, and was a sad shock to his large circle of friends and acquaintances. Mr. Freaner was educated at Dickinson College, read law in the office of Alex. Neill, Sr., and was admitted to the bar in 1853. Later in the year he emigrated to the Pacific coast, and it was there that one of the most adventurous portions of his life was passed. Among the first and most prominent of the daring spirits who laid the foundation of American empire on that coast were two of his cousins, natives also of Hagerstown,—James L. and John A. Freaner. The former had become world-famous as "Mustang," of the New Orleans *Delta*, during the Mexican war, having in an extraordinary ride from the City of Mexico to Washington brought on the treaty which attached California to the United States. James L. Freaner directed his energies and his influence to the opening of a line of communication through the unexplored wilds of Northern California infested by the most savage of Indian tribes, then known as the "Pitt River Indians," and still later as the "Modocs." The California Legislature granted to James L. Freaner and his associates the charter of a wagon-road through the northern portion of California to the Oregon line, with extraordinary privileges. It was in exploring this route, accompanied by a single companion, that James L. Freaner was lost. Years after captured Indians told how desperate was the struggle of a single white man at the crossing of Pitt River, when, in the middle of the stream, he was beset by foes on all sides and literally crushed by numbers, many of whom fell before he perished. The gold filling in his teeth, which were preserved by the Indians, established his identity as James L. Freaner.

Upon his arrival in California in 1853 the first impulse of George Freaner was to commence the practice of the law in San Francisco. As that bar was then crowded, he was compelled to locate instead at Oakland, which sustains pretty much the same relation to San Francisco as Brooklyn does to New York. After practicing his profession for some time with indifferent success, he accepted a position as associate editor of the Oakland *Times and Transcript*. Subsequently he was tendered and accepted the editorship of the leading Democratic organ at Yreka. In this capacity he at once took a commanding position, particularly in his advocacy of the principles of law and order as opposed to the practice of the vigilance committees. Mr. Freaner was chosen a delegate to the Democratic Convention of 1856, and was selected as one of the candidates for Presidential electors. The ticket was successful, and Mr. Freaner was delegated to be the bearer of the Electoral College vote to Washington. After being in that city some time he concluded a partnership in the practice of the law with James Wason and George W. Smith, Jr. In 1859 he was elected a member of the House of Delegates from Washington County, and at once took a commanding position in that body.

He was made chairman of the special committee appointed to investigate the alleged frauds in the Baltimore election, that city having fallen under "Plug-Ugly" domination, and so searching was the investigation under his direction, accompanied by a report that was conclusive of the controversy, that the entire delegation was expelled from their seats. Following immediately upon this triumph was the discovery that Mr. Freaner himself was not, under a strict construction of the constitution of the State, eligible. The constitution required a continuous residence of three years in the State, and Mr. Freaner's sojourn in California had broken this, and, as was believed, rendered him ineligible. Mr. Freaner, upon having his attention called to the matter by a friend, arose in his seat, and upon the impulse of the moment tendered his resignation. His resignation was accepted with regret.

Returning to Hagerstown, Mr. Freaner pursued his profession in connection with Messrs. Wason and Smith until the breaking out of the war, when he cast his lot with the South. During the whole war, from the fall of 1861 to the capitulation at Appomattox, Maj. Freaner was in the saddle and field, participating in nearly all the great battles of the Army of Northern Virginia. Gen. J. E. B. Stuart very soon discovered his high qualities as a soldier, and he was solicited to become one of the aides upon the staff of that distinguished cavalry officer, which position he filled up to the time of the death of Stuart. Maj. Freaner was then attached to the staff of Gen. Fitzhugh Lee. At earlier periods of his military career he filled the positions of adjutant of the First Virginia Cavalry, commanded by Col. L. Tiernan Brien, and that of assistant adjutant-general of the brigade to which that regiment belonged. He also for a time served on the staff of Gen. Wade Hampton, in command of the Confederate cavalry, and was by the side of that distinguished officer, who then commanded a division, when one of his sons was killed and another wounded in one of the fiercest battles of the war, and personally assisted in their removal from the field.

Upon the re-establishment of peace, Mr. Freaner returned to Hagerstown. His former law-firm had been dissolved, and he entered in 1866 into permanent connection with A. K. Syester, then one of the leading members of the bar of Washington County, and afterwards attorney-general of Maryland. From that day to the day of his death the law-firm of Syester & Freaner held a commanding position in Western Maryland.

In 1867 he was appointed auditor of the Circuit Court for Washington County. In 1874 he was again elected on the Democratic ticket to the House of Delegates, where he at once assumed a leading position, both in debate and on committees.

Mr. Freaner was noted for his lofty purity of character, as well as for acuteness and force of intellect. Mr. Freaner left a widow, daughter of the late George Fechtig, of Hagerstown, and two daughters. His remains were attended to the grave by an unusually large concourse. The funeral services were conducted by the Rev. Mr. Thompson, of the Presbyterian Church, assisted by the Rev. Mr. Hank, of the Methodist Episcopal Church. An escort of honor, consisting of eight ex-Confederate soldiers, walked on either side of the hearse to the grave, and the pall-bearers were the following members of the bar: H. H. Keedy, H. Kyd Douglas, F. M. Darby, Alex. Neill, Edward Stake, and G. W. Smith, Jr.

At a meeting of the members of the bar and officers of the Circuit Court for Washington County, held at the court-house, Nov. 11, 1878, on motion of Hon. Wm. T. Hamilton, the Hon. Daniel Weisel was called to the chair, and Geo. B. Oswald was appointed secretary.

The chair stated that the object of the meeting was for the purpose of taking suitable action upon the death of the Hon. George Freaner, a member of this bar and auditor in chancery.

On motion of Hon. A. K. Syester, a committee of three was appointed to draft suitable resolutions, when the chair appointed Hon. A. K. Syester, H. H. Keedy, and Louis E. McComas, Esqs., as the committee.

The committee then prepared and presented the following preamble and resolutions, which were upon motion unanimously adopted:

"*Whereas*, The sudden death of Maj. George Freaner, a member of this bar, and for eleven years auditor of this court, cut down in the strength of his days and the maturity of his intellect, has affected his brothers of the bar with a sad and painful bereavement, therefore,

"*Resolved*, That we have heard with feelings of deepest grief of the sudden and untimely death of our friend and brother, Maj. George Freaner, cut off in the prime of a useful and distinguished life, which gave abundant promise of still greater usefulness and honor in the future.

"*Resolved*, That in the death of our brother the whole community have lost one of its most honorable, active, and useful citizens; the bar of Washington County one of its brightest ornaments and ablest advocates; his more intimate friends and associates a warm-hearted, generous, and devoted friend; his afflicted family a tender and considerate husband and father, and the State itself one of her most promising and honored sons.

"*Resolved*, That whether in the walks of public or private life, or the practice of the arduous and responsible duties of his profession, the community generally has sustained no ordinary loss in the sudden and unlooked-for death of one who was at all times and under all circumstances an attractive and instructive companion, an eminent, honorable, and upright lawyer, and in all the varied pursuits of life a dignified, polished, and courteous gentleman, without fear and without reproach.

"*Resolved*, Whether as a gallant soldier in the field, an eloquent orator on the hustings, or a faithful advocate in the forum, or above all as a citizen of spotless integrity, his name will not soon be forgotten, and his memory will long be especially cherished by this bar for his many manly, generous, and winning social traits, and for his lofty standard of professional conduct.

"*Resolved*, That we tender to his afflicted family, to whom most especially the loss is indeed an irreparable one, our most heartfelt and deepest sympathy in this dark hour of their distress.

"*Resolved*, That a copy of these resolutions be sent to his family, and that the chairman of the committee be instructed to present the same to the Circuit Court at its next session, with a request that they be entered on the minutes of the court.

"*Resolved*, That as a further mark of respect we attend the funeral in a body and wear the usual badge of mourning for thirty days.

"D. WEISEL, *Chairman*.

"GEORGE B. OSWALD, *Secretary*."

At this meeting eloquent tributes of respect to the memory of Maj. Freaner were paid by ex-Attorney-General Syester, ex-Senator Hamilton, and Judges Weisel, Motter, and Pearre.

Andrew K. Syester, ex-attorney-general of Maryland, and one of the leading lawyers of the State, was born on the 11th of March, 1827, in Berkeley County, Va. His father, Daniel Syester, was a native of Berkeley County, and his mother, Sarah Moudy, was born in Washington County, Md. A. K. Syester was educated at Franklin-Marshall College, Mercersburg, Pa., where he graduated in 1849. He removed to Hagerstown in 1850, and during the following winter was a committee clerk in the House of Delegates of Maryland. In January, 1852, he was admitted to the bar, and in the autumn of the following year, 1853, was elected to the House of Delegates. In 1854 he was elected State's attorney, which office he held for four years from the 1st of January, 1855. In 1859 he was nominated by the Whig party for judge of the Court of Appeals in opposition to Jas. L. Bartol, Democrat, and was beaten by seven votes, after a very

close and exciting contest. At that time the judicial district comprised Allegany, Washington, Frederick, Carroll, and Harford Counties. In 1864, Mr. Syester was a candidate for Congress against Hon. Philip Francis Thomas, and was defeated in common with all other Democrats at that period. In the spring of 1867, however, he was elected a member of the Constitutional Convention, and in the following autumn to the House of Delegates. In 1872 he was nominated by the Democratic party and elected attorney-general of Maryland. During his tenure of the office, Mr. Syester was called on to assist James M. Revell, of Annapolis, State's attorney for Anne Arundel County, to which the case was removed from Baltimore, in the prosecution of Mrs. Mary E. Wharton for the murder of Gen. Ketchum, of the United States army, by poisoning, and for attempting to poison Eugene Van Ness. Mrs. Wharton was acquitted on the charge of murder, but on the charge of attempting to poison Mr. Van Ness the jury failed to agree. During this trial Mr. Syester, who was pitted against I. Nevett Steele, John Thomas, and Herman Stump, exhibited a legal acumen and shrewdness in cross-examination, as well as oratorical power, which placed him in the foremost rank of Maryland's trial lawyers. Among the witnesses in this celebrated case was Gen. W. S. Hancock, Democratic candidate for President of the United States in 1880. Another famous trial in which Mr. Syester was engaged as counsel for the prosecution was that of Rousby Plater, who was tried at Cambridge for the murder of his wife. Plater was a man of good family, and the circumstances of his wife's death were of a most peculiar and extraordinary character. Plater was found guilty of manslaughter, and was sentenced to a term of years in the penitentiary. Mr. Syester also conducted the prosecution of Joseph Davis for the murder of Lynn, in Carroll County. Davis was convicted. Probably the most interesting and difficult case in which Mr. Syester has ever been engaged was that of Harry Crawford Black, charged with the murder of William McKaig. Black shot McKaig in Cumberland, but the case was removed to Frederick County, and tried there in May, 1872. The result of the trial depended on Mr. Syester's introduction of testimony showing that Black's sister had been betrayed by McKaig. At first it seemed very doubtful whether he would be allowed to introduce this testimony, but he finally succeeded in getting it before the jury and secured the acquittal of young Black. The progress of the case was watched with the keenest interest throughout the State, and Mr. Syester's eloquent and able defense of the accused assisted greatly in obtaining him the nomination for the attorney-generalship. In 1880, Mr. Syester defended Mrs. Mary E. Rowland, charged with the murder of her husband. This was a most remarkable case. In Washington County the tide of public opinion ran so strongly against Mrs. Rowland that two hundred and ninety-three jurors disqualified themselves. The case was removed to another county, and Mrs. Rowland was acquitted after a very brief deliberation on the part of the jury. In the course of his professional career Mr. Syester has been engaged in thirty-two cases of homicide. In one case he secured the acquittal of a lad accused of the murder of a canal-boat captain who had brutally maltreated him, although the evidence as to the homicide was perfectly clear and positive. Some years ago Mr. Syester received a deed for one hundred and sixty-two acres of valuable land from the accused, who, having settled in the West, had succeeded in business and had secured the confidence and respect of his neighbors. From his earliest experience as a lawyer Mr. Syester has always had a large trial practice, and is generally regarded as being one of the ablest criminal lawyers in the State. His civil practice has also been very large, and is now heavier than ever before. Mr. Syester has always been an industrious, busy lawyer, and is in the full bloom of intellectual vigor. Reared in a Whig family and surrounded by Whig influences, he nevertheless cast his fortunes wholly and unequivocally with the Democratic party, and during the war was an earnest sympathizer with the South. Mr. Syester was raised in the family of Andrew Kershner, whose wife was his aunt. Mr. Kershner was a leading Whig in Washington County for many years, representing it in the House of Delegates continuously from 1818 to 1832, but notwithstanding the training which he received in Mr. Kershner's household, Mr. Syester adhered to the Democratic party at an early age, and continues to be one of its most earnest, consistent, and eloquent exponents. Mr. Syester resides in Hagerstown, where he is engaged in the practice of the law, and is regarded as being one of the most influential and popular citizens of Washington County.

Daniel Weisel was born at Williamsport on the 25th of September, 1803, and died on the 25th of September, 1880, aged seventy-seven. He was educated at Princeton, graduating in 1824, and having read law and been admitted to the bar (in 1826), began the practice of his profession in Hagerstown and Williamsport. On the 2d of January, 1830, in connection with Mr. Tice, he established at Williamsport the *Republican Banner*, a Whig organ, which they conducted for several years at Williamsport. Early in life he married Matilda Davis, a niece of

Gen. O. H. Williams. In 1838 he removed to Hagerstown, where he obtained a lucrative practice. In 1847, Judge Weisel was appointed by Governor Pratt associate justice of the judicial district then composed of Frederick, Washington, and Allegany Counties, to fill the vacancy occasioned by the death of Thomas Buchanan. This position he retained until the constitution of 1852 vacated it by establishing the single judge system. In 1861 he was elected judge of the Fourth Judicial Circuit, then composed of Washington and Allegany Counties, and in 1864 was elected a judge of the Court of Appeals, but went out of office with the change of the judicial system under the new constitution of 1867.

Judge Weisel assisted in founding and promoting the Hagerstown Lyceum and the Hagerstown Female Seminary. He was founder of the Williamsport Bank, and its president for many years. In 1868 he was the Republican candidate for Congress in the Sixth District, and reduced the Democratic majority from 2800 to 480. In 1872 he was delegate-at-large from Maryland to the National Republican Convention which nominated Grant and Wilson. During the closing years of his life he was weighed down by physical infirmities and financial embarrassments. He was a man of sturdy independence of character, sincere convictions, and great earnestness of purpose.

For a long period Judge Weisel was a member of the board of visitors at the Deaf and Dumb Asylum at Frederick, and always manifested a keen interest in the working of that institution. At a meeting of the bar of Washington County, immediately after his death, Judges Alvey and Motter presiding, and George B. Oswald acting as secretary, a committee, consisting of Z. S. Claggett, A. K. Syester, F. M. Darby, George Schley, L. E. McComas, H. Kyd Douglas, and D. H. Wilds, was appointed to draft resolutions, and after retiring, presented the following, which were unanimously adopted:

"The bench and bar of Washington County having met together to give formal expression of their regret at the death and their respect for the memory, and of their sense of the worth of Hon. Daniel Weisel, LL.D., their senior brother, who for more than fifty years was a member of this bar, a judge of this court for two terms,—from 1847 to 1851, and from 1861 to 1864,—and a judge of the Court of Appeals of this State from 1864 to 1867, do present the following:

"1. In the death of the Hon. Daniel Weisel the bar of Maryland has lost one of its oldest and wisest members, one who, in a long professional life, was always the personification of gentlemanly bearing and professional courtesy, qualities which, both in his official administration upon the bench and as a practitioner at the bar, endeared him in a peculiar manner to the profession.

"2. To diligence in study there was added practical legal learning, gained from experience, which enabled him to elucidate difficult legal subjects with that force and precision which attested a well-disciplined mind stored with the varied and exceptional learning of his profession.

"3. In the discharge of his professional duties he was ever characterized by amenity of manner and profound respect to the court and jury, and for his uniform courtesy to his brothers of the bar, especially to the younger and more inexperienced, whether as associates or opponents, he will be held in tender remembrance by us all.

"4. The elements which made up his professional character and achieved his success were simplicity of style, directness of thought, patience, industry, and perseverance, both in his office and at the trial table.

"5. His life was not lighted up by occasional brilliant displays of ability, but he used his powers steadily and earnestly, adding something by each year's study and experience until he was fitted to fill with honor to himself and the State every professional and public position in which he was tried.

"6. As a citizen, he was for more than half a century the first and foremost in all the undertakings in our midst which encouraged and fostered the culture and education of the people. He was prominent and foremost in all the enterprises which in later days have so wonderfully enlarged the business and industrial activities, and developed the natural resources of our town and county, and his name will continue to be associated with all the various public improvements in our midst which his early and indefatigable exertions so largely contributed to establish.

"7. A life devoted to belles-lettres and congenial studies, apart from the labors of the law, endowed him with an excellent style as a writer, made him a favorite lecturer before literary and other societies, and decorated his general learning.

"8. Ordered, that a copy of these resolutions be sent to the kinsfolk among whom Judge Weisel died, and that the chairman of this committee present them to the Circuit Court at its next session, with a request that they be entered upon the minutes of the court; also that the proceedings of the meeting be published in the county papers, and that the members of the bar attend the funeral of the deceased in a body, and wear the usual badge of mourning for thirty days."

Among other eulogistic addresses was that of Mr. Z. S. Claggett, who, in the course of his remarks, said,—

"His reputation as a *nisi prius* judge was of the highest order of excellence. His acknowledged legal learning and ability, and his large experience in the discharge of circuit duties, designated him for a position of more extended usefulness, and in the year 1864 he was elected to the bench of the Court of Appeals. The opinions of the court delivered by him furnish abundant evidence that he possessed judicial talents and capacity of a high order. They show great care and labor in their preparation, and are characterized by purity and perspicuity of style, elaborate research, lucid arrangement, vigorous argument, and ardent love of justice. They are an enduring record of his learning, and have secured to him the reputation of a faithful, able, upright, and impartial judge."

Personally, Judge Weisel was one of the warmest-hearted and most benevolent of men. He was extremely hospitable and fond of social recreation, and enjoyed an extensive popularity.

At the funeral the pall-bearers were Judges Alvey, Motter, and Pearre, of the Circuit Court, and Findlay, of the Orphans' Court, George B. Oswald, clerk of the Circuit Court, and Messrs. William Updegraff, Jonathan Late, and Jacob Roessner. The funeral services were held in Trinity Lutheran church, and were conducted by Rev. J. R. Williams, pastor, and Rev. Mayberry Goheen, of the Methodist, and Rev. J. A. Rondthaler, of the Presbyterian, Church.

George French was a native of Washington County, and was born in 1818, and died on the 4th of August, 1878. He was reared as a farmer, but while serving a term in the House of Delegates his mind was powerfully attracted to the law, and, having sold his farm, he entered the office of Judge Weisel as a student.

After Judge Weisel's first judicial term had ended he formed a partnership with Mr. French, with whom he continued for ten years. During this period Mr. French was a close student, especially of the decisions by the Maryland courts. When Judge Weisel was elected a member of the Court of Appeals a vacancy was created in the Circuit Court, which was filled by the appointment by the late Governor Bradford of Mr. French as associate judge. Judge Weisel once said that, so far as he knew, not one of Judge French's decisions was ever reversed by the Court of Appeals.

In 1867 he retired to private life. It was one of Judge French's prominent traits of character that he never took part in a trial before a jury if he could help it, his modesty and timidity causing him to shrink from public exhibition of any kind. In an address at a meeting of the bar called to take action on Judge French's death, Hon. William T. Hamilton said,—

"He was a schoolmate in our early boyhood days, and we were in the same class. In our early manhood we were competing candidates for the Legislature, and were both elected. In that body he was respected for the faithful and intelligent discharge of his public duties. Upon the leading measure of State policy at that session, although differing in political opinion, we were in full accord. His career in the Senate and House of Delegates was marked by a conscientious desire to perform his duty.

"He was engaged in farming for many years, but having a liberal education he after some time directed his attention to the study of the law, and became a member of this bar. His reclusive nature and diffident disposition repelled him from entering into the strifes of the law, but his daily attendance upon the sessions of the court and his diligent and extensive reading gave him many of the acquirements of a lawyer.

"He became the judge of this court during our late civil commotions. Some feared that here he would fail. They were happily mistaken. Our venerable friend Judge Weisel being removed to a higher sphere, the Court of Appeals, says that he cannot so particularly speak from personal observation and experience of Judge French's course upon the bench. I can. During that gloomy period when turbulence and violence afflicted our people, in every case involving the passions of the day we turned to him as our safe anchorage, and though of a timid and apprehensive nature he never failed in giving to all the impartial benefit of the law just as it was. He was a just judge.

"He possessed all the amenities of life. He was distinguished for integrity and Christian deportment, and he left the world with an unblemished name behind him."

William B. Clarke was born in Washington County in 1817, and died at the Eutaw House, Baltimore, on the 14th of April, 1855, in his thirty-eighth year. Mr. Clarke was a native of Washington County, and one of the most distinguished men in Western Maryland. He was elected to the State Senate from Washington County, and was the Whig candidate for Governor in opposition to the Hon. Enoch Lewis Lowe, but was defeated. During the four years preceding his death he resided in Baltimore. His remains were taken to Hagerstown for interment, but the funeral service of the Protestant Episcopal Church was read before the departure from Baltimore by the Rev. H. V. D. Johns. Mr. Clarke made a will in which he bequeathed two thousand dollars, to be invested in some safe and judicious manner, and the interest thereof to be annually appropriated to the poor of Hagerstown; one thousand dollars for the improvement of the Episcopal graveyard in that town; one thousand dollars for the use of his negro boy Cato; and five thousand dollars for the support of an aged and infirm aunt. Mr. Clarke having subsequently disposed of a large portion of his real estate, or exchanged it for other property, it became necessary to revoke his will; and before he had time to make another, in which all the above bequests would have been continued, he was overtaken by death.

Mr. Clarke removed to Washington County in 1836, and entered the law-office of William Price, whose daughter he afterwards married. He had scarcely attained his majority before he became locally prominent and influential. In the campaign of 1840 he was one of the most conspicuous of the Whig debaters, and in 1844 he was nominated for the House of Delegates. In 1846 he was elected to the State Senate, and retained his seat until the adoption of a new constitution changing the mode of electing the officers. In 1850 he was nominated by the Whigs for Governor, but was defeated. Mr. Clarke was not only a successful lawyer, business man, and politician, but he was also in private life a most attractive and amiable gentleman. His remains were interred in the Episcopal graveyard at Hagerstown.

Among the many distinguished families of Western Maryland none have been more prominently or honorably identified with its history than the Schleys. They were among the earliest settlers in Frederick County, and from the first took a leading part in the development and adornment of the western section of the State. One of the earliest representatives of the family in Western Maryland was John Thomas Schley, who built the first house in Frederick Town, now Frederick City, in 1746.

Among other early representatives of the family was John Jacob Schley, who married Ann Maria Shelman. They were both natives of Frederick, but removed to Georgia, where they spent the remainder of their lives. Frederick Augustus, the son of John Jacob Schley, was one of the most distinguished lawyers that have adorned the Maryland bar. He was born in Frederick, May 14, 1789, and studied law in the office of Chief Justice Taney, whose friendship he enjoyed throughout his entire life. He soon acquired a very large and lucrative practice in Frederick, Washington, and Allegany Counties, and a reputation which extended far beyond the limits of his native State. Severely logical in legal argument; easy, graceful, and forcible before a jury; gifted with a wonderful memory, and possessing a richly-stored intellect, he illustrated in a striking manner the "*suaviter in modo, fortiter in re.*" He was a man of fine presence and commanding stature, being six feet two inches in height, and though, unfortunately, many of his addresses and orations have been lost to us, the earlier volumes of the Maryland Reports contain evidences of his professional ability which fully entitle him to be classed with the great legal minds with which he was contemporary. His wife, Eliza Asbury, daughter of James McCannon, of Baltimore, was born Sept. 10, 1794, and died suddenly in 1816, leaving two sons to the care of their father.

George, the elder, was prepared for college at the Frederick Academy and at a private school near Frederick, kept by the late Rev. Jonathan Woodbridge, of Massachusetts. In 1829 he entered the sophomore class of Yale College. His father accompanied him and the late John J. Steiner to the college, and was present at their examination for admission by Profs. Kingsley and Silliman. Both of the young men, being very ambitious and to a certain extent rivals, were at first a little nervous, but were relieved by Prof. Kingsley's interrupting the examination, on the reading of the words in the first book of the Æneid—"*et mens sibi conscia recti*,"—to tell the story of two rival shoemakers, one of whom had hung up a new sign with these words upon it, given to him by a friendly scholar, whereupon his competitor, not meaning to be outdone, got up his new sign also, with the words "*mens and women's conscia recti*" upon it.

This pleasantry restored the equilibrium of the young men, and the examination proceeded to the satisfaction of all concerned. After remaining at Yale a year young Schley spent two years and a half at the University of Virginia, where, in 1833, he graduated in the schools of ancient and modern languages. Thereupon, simply in pursuit of science, he

studied and practiced chemistry at Baer's chemical-works, in Carroll County, Md., for six or seven months. He then read law in his father's office in Frederick, was admitted to the bar in 1836, and commenced the practice of law in Frederick. Within a very few months after he opened his office he was much astonished by the announcement to him that he had been nominated for the Legislature. His astonishment may be imagined when it is stated that he did not even know that a political convention was being held, or that his name had even been mentioned in that connection. That year, however, the party (Whig) was defeated; the next year he was renominated and elected. After the adjournment of the Legislature, in May, 1839, he removed to Hagerstown, Washington Co., where he has since resided. In 1850 he was elected a member of the Constitutional Convention of Maryland, and took an active part in its proceedings. In 1852 he was elected to the State Senate, serving during the sessions of 1854 and 1856. He was chairman of the most important committees of that body, and chairman of the joint committee of the two houses upon the reform of conveyancing, civil proceedings, and pleadings. In 1862 he was nominated for Congress, but declined the nomination. Since that time he has confined himself to the practice of his profession. In 1872 he was nominated for judge of his circuit, but failed of election, owing to pride of county feeling in one of the counties composing the district. In 1873 he was elected president of the First National Bank of Hagerstown, a position which he still holds.

As a lawyer Mr. Schley has won a deservedly high reputation throughout the State. He possesses many of the intellectual characteristics of his father, is a graceful and forcible advocate, a clear and logical reasoner, and an impressive and eloquent public speaker. His legal attainments are varied and profound, and are supplemented and strengthened by a rich culture and a wide reading which raise even the dryest of professional efforts far above the ordinary level of legal argument. He has been connected with some of the most interesting and important cases that have come before the Court of Appeals during his professional career, and has frequently been associated with the best legal talent of Maryland. He is now the senior member of the Hagerstown bar. Mr. Schley is extremely popular, and by his kindly nature and generous qualities of heart and character has won the strong esteem and affection of all who know him.

In June, 1839, he married Mary Sophia Hall, daughter of Thomas B. Hall, and grandniece of Chief Justice John Buchanan and Associate Judge Thomas Buchanan, her grandmother being Mrs. Mary Pottenger, widow of Dr. Pottenger, of Prince George's County, Md. Mrs. Schley died suddenly in Boston, in January, 1880, while on a visit to a daughter, Mrs. Eliza M. Stellman. Mr. Schley's only son, Frederick, graduated in medicine at the University of Maryland in 1866, and immediately thereafter was elected clinical assistant by the faculty. In the discharge of his duties he contracted malignant typhus fever, and died after five days' sickness. His eldest daughter is married to Washington Bowie, and his youngest to Joseph F. Stellman, who resides in Brookline, Mass., but is engaged in business in Boston. His second daughter is unmarried and resides with her father.

William Motter, associate judge of the Fourth Judicial Circuit of Maryland, was born at Emmittsburg, Frederick Co., on the 29th of March, 1817. After one year's attendance at Pennsylvania College, Gettysburg, he entered Princeton College, and after graduating in 1836, studied law with William Schley and afterwards with Edward A. Lynch, at Frederick City. After finishing his legal studies he was admitted to the bar at Hagerstown. For six months he practiced law in Cumberland in partnership with Judge Pearre, who had been his fellow-student. He then retired from practice and went to Wheeling, W. Va., from which place he removed in 1845 to Hagerstown, where he has since remained. In 1857 he was a candidate for the State Senate, but was defeated. In 1859 he was elected State's attorney. In 1867 he was a member of the State Legislature, being a member of the committee on judiciary and printing, and was regarded as being one of the most active and useful members of the Convention. At the first election for judges under the new constitution in 1867, he was elected associate judge of the Fourth Judicial Circuit of Maryland. Judge Motter is universally recognized as a jurist of unusual learning and strict impartiality, and enjoys the confidence and esteem not only of the community in which he resides, but of the people of his entire district.

Henry Kyd Douglas, born Sept. 29, 1840, at Shepherdstown, W. Va., is the son of the Rev. Robert Douglas and Mary, daughter of Col. John Robertson. He was educated at the Franklin-Marshall College, Pennsylvania, and graduated in 1859, after which he studied at the law-school of Judge Brockenborough, at Lexington, Va., graduating in 1860. He continued his studies under the instruction of Judge Weisel, and was admitted to the bar at Charlestown, W. Va. Before he entered fairly upon the practice of the law, however, the civil war broke out, and he entered the Confederate army as a private, enlisting at Harper's Ferry in the Shepherdstown company of the Second Virginia Infantry, "Stonewall" Brigade. He rose rapidly through the grades of non-commissioned officer, lieutenant, and captain of the same company. Subsequently he was promoted to the position of adjutant and inspector-general of the "Stonewall" Brigade, from which he was transferred to a post as aide-de-camp on Gen. Jackson's staff. He was afterwards made assistant inspector-general of Gen. Jackson's corps, and occasionally acted in the capacity of adjutant-general. After Jackson's death he served as adjutant-general to Maj.-Gens. Edward Johnson, John B. Gordon, Jubal A. Early, and others, commanding the "Stonewall" division and Jackson's corps. He was made colonel of the Thirteenth and Forty-ninth Virginia Regiments consolidated, and was assigned to the command of the light brigade formerly commanded by Gen. Early and Gen. A. P. Hill. While in command of this brigade he assisted in the assault on the salient hill of the Federal lines at Petersburg. On the retreat of Gen. Lee from Petersburg and Richmond he was placed in command of the rear-guard, and was engaged with the enemy several times during the retreat, especially at High Bridge, where he lost forty-five per cent. of his command in two hours and was shot twice, his wounds being severe but not dangerous. After Gen. Lee surrendered he was engaged for half an hour on the extreme right of the line, not knowing that Lee had been defeated. During the war Col. Douglas was wounded six times, once very seriously at Gettysburg. After the war he went to Winchester, Va., where he practiced law for two years. In 1868 he removed to Hagerstown, and has been practicing there ever since. Col. Douglas was a member of Governor Carroll's staff, and during the railroad strike of 1877 was placed in command of the department of Western Maryland, with his headquarters at Cumberland. Here he superintended the movements of the troops who opened the Baltimore and Ohio Railroad, and afterwards moved his headquarters to Sir John's Run and opened the Chesapeake and Ohio Canal. While thus engaged Col. Douglas arrested fifteen of the rioters and handed them over to the civil authorities. Upon the organization of the Hagerstown Light Infantry in the fall of 1880 he was unanimously elected captain, and subsequently, in 1881, was appointed, with the rank of lieutenant-colonel, to the command of the First Maryland Infantry, composed of the militia of Washington and Frederick Counties, with assigned companies from Baltimore County. In October, 1881, Col. Douglas was present at the celebration of the Yorktown Centennial, in command of the First Regiment, and was one of the three field-officers of the day for the encampment appointed by Gen. Hancock. Col. Douglas represented the Southern troops; Gen. De Russey the regular army; and Gen. E. Burd Grubb the Northern volunteers. Col. Douglas has devoted himself since the war to the practice of the law, but has also contributed a number of articles, chiefly military sketches and reviews, to the press. He has also delivered a number of lectures and addresses, and has taken the "stump" in every campaign for President and Governor since he has been in Hagerstown. In 1875 he was a candidate for the State Senate on the ticket with Governor Carroll, and was defeated, but ran ahead of the ticket in Washington County by nine hundred votes.

Francis Moore Darby, one of the leading members of the Hagerstown bar, was born near Monrovia, Frederick Co., Md., on the 11th of March, 1838. He is the son of Charles A. and Martha (Chandler) Darby, and was educated principally at Rockville Academy. His grandparents were of English descent, and were among the earliest settlers of Montgomery County. After completing his education he at once began the study of law in the office of the Hon. James Dixon Roman, and in November, 1858, was admitted to the bar. Since then he has been actively and profitably engaged in the practice of the law in Hagerstown. In 1859 he was married to Louisa Kennedy, daughter of Benjamin Price, and granddaughter of John Kennedy. Mrs. Darby died on the 5th of July, 1879. In 1863, Mr. Darby was elected State's attorney for Washington County on the Republican ticket. He was a Union man throughout the war, and has been a Republican ever since. Mr. Darby's personal popularity is such that he has been appealed to by the party on a number of occasions to accept nominations when defeat seemed inevitable. In 1859 he ran for State's attorney, but was not elected. In 1869 he was a candidate for the State Legislature, but the Democratic majority was so large that, in common with his ticket, he was defeated. In 1871 he ran for the State Senate under similar circumstances and with a similar result. In 1879 he was the Republican candidate for attorney-general of the State, and led the ticket. Mr. Darby has been a director in the Hagerstown Bank since 1859, and is president of the Washington County Mutual Insurance Company. He has been elected several times as a member of the Republican State Central Committee, and has taken an active part in all the national and State campaigns since his first appearance in the political arena. Mr. Darby is a fluent and graceful speaker, and is one of the leading members of his party. On the 25th of October, 1881, he was married to Ella V., daughter of John S. Leib, treasurer of the Northern Central Railway.

John F. A. Remley was born in Greencastle, Pa., Nov. 12, 1843. His earlier education was obtained in the public schools, after which he attended the Allegany Seminary, in Bedford County, Pa., the high school in McConnellsburg, Fulton Co., Pa., and the Iron City Commercial College, in Pittsburgh. In 1859 he began teaching. He removed to Washington County in 1862, and was principal of Antietam Grammar-School for six years. He was also for two years principal of the Hagerstown Academy. He commenced reading law with Judge Weisel and Louis E. McComas in 1873, and was admitted to the bar in 1876. He was elected State's attorney in 1879, and now holds that office.

Jervis Spencer, who was elected State's attorney of Baltimore County in the reform movement of 1875, is a native of Washington County, and a son of Jervis Spencer, the well-known lawyer, who died at Catonsville in 1875. Mr. Spencer is about thirty-six years of age. He was in the Confederate army, and served all through the war in Company C, First Maryland Battalion of Infantry. He was captured when Bradley T. Johnson was surprised at Moorefield, remained a prisoner some time, was exchanged, and rejoined the battalion before the Appomattox surrender. After this event he went with the battalion to join Joseph E. Johnston in North Carolina, and, when that command surrendered, returned to Baltimore and commenced the study of law. He afterwards removed to Baltimore County, and in the beginning of the campaign of 1875 he came before the people before the reform ticket was decided upon as an independent candidate, and, being endorsed by the reformers, was elected. Mr. Spencer was married to Miss Elder, of Baltimore County, in 1875.

The following is a list of attorneys who have qualified in Washington County from an early period:

Prior to 1805, William Clagett, Daniel Hughes, Jr., Samuel Hughes, James Kendall, Upton Lawrence; prior to 1815, Franklin Anderson, William L. Brent, Thomas T. Hall, Otho Lawrence, George Watterson; established in 1816, Joseph I. Merrick, William Price; established in 1822, Henry H. Gaither, Thomas Kennedy (the poet), R. M. Tidball, W. V. Randall; dates not given, John A. G. Kilgour, Colin Cook, Dennis Hagan, George Chambers, John Nelson, Wm. Price, William Ross, Joseph M. Palmer, Thomas C. Worthington, Roger Perry, David G. Yost, Isaac Howard, Zadok Magruder, Robert Mackey Tidball, Almon Sortwell, Frederick A. Schley, Henry H. Gaither, Benjamin Price, J. Dixon, J. Reynolds, William Wirt, W. Jones, V. W. Randall, Geo. Swearingen, Singleton Duval, Robert P. Henger, John A. McKesson, John T. Brooke, James Raymond, Thomas Anderson, William Schley, Calvin Mason, Thomas Van Swearingen, John R. Key, Samuel M. Semmes, Jonathan H. Lawrence, Edward W. Beatty, Edmond J. Lee, Jr., Richard J. Bowie, R. V. Hollyday, J. Dixon Roman, Mountjoy B. Luckett, Wm. Henry Daingerfield, David H. Schnebly, C. Schnebly, George C. Patterson, William Pitts, William I. Ross, William B. Clarke, George Schley, William Motter, A. H. Pitts, Thomas J. McKaig, John Thomson Mason.

	Qualified.
John V. L. McMahon	1824.
Francis Thomas	1825.
Benjamin F. Yoe	1826.
D. Weisel	1826.
Calvin Mason	1827.
John H. McElfresh	1827.
John D. T. Custer	1827.
Richard M. Harrison	1827.
Clement Cox	1828.
John Davis	1829.
C. Ringgold	1829.
Richard Henry Lee	1831.
Robert James Brent	1833.
John Thomson Mason	1834.
J. B. Hall	November, 1839.
M. Swartzwelder	" "
Joseph S. Dellinger	" "
Richard H. Marshall	March, 1841.
Robert I. Taylor	" "
George H. Hollingsworth	April, 1842.
Edwin Bell	" "
Thomas Perry	November, 1842.
Wm. Meade Addison	" "
James Wason	" "
Joseph Rowland	" "
W. B. Nelson	March, 1843.
James McSherry	" "
John Miller	April, "
Zachariah S. Clagett	November, 1843.
J. Philip Roman	" "
William T. Hamilton	December, "
Luther Martin	March, 1844.
James M. Spencer	November, 1844.
Samuel Martin, Jr	" "
Joseph Hullman, Jr	March, 1845.
Rufus H. Irwin	" "
S. Addison Irvin	" "
Joseph Chambers	April, "
Thomas Harbine	" "
William F. Brannon	" "
Daniel O'Leary	October, 1846.
J. Manhold	March, 1847.
A. H. Melown	November, 1847.
W. G. Van Lear	" "
Daniel Negley	" "
J. W. Heard	" "
C. B. Thurston	" "
M. Tapham Evans	December, 1848.
George A. Pearre	" "
George French	" "
Peter Negley	April, 1849.
R. H. Allen	May, "
John F. Tehan	November, 1849.
R. H. Lawrence	" "
Wm. M. Merrick	" "
Bradley T. Johnson	April, 1851.
Joseph P. Clarkson	July, "
Andrew K. Syester	November, 1851.
T. E. Buchanan	" "
J. M. Schley	" "
J. J. Merrick	February, 1852.
J. Spencer	" "
R. H. Allen	" "
Thomas Harline	" "
J. Dixon Roman	" "
H. H. Gaither	" "
George Schley	" "
Peter Negley	" "
Z. L. Claggett	" "
R. M. Tidball	" "
D. Weisel	" "
G. H. Hollingsworth	" "
Wm. F. Brannan	March, "
A. H. Melown	" "
Wm. F. Morgan	" "
John M. Smith	" "
G. W. Smith	April, "
Alex. Neill, Jr	" "
Edward E. Cheney	July, "
Richard R. Macgill	" "
Alfred D. Merrick	November, "
Marshall McIlhenny	December, "
George French	" "
Grayson Eichelberger	" "
William J. Ross	March, 1853.
George Freaner	" "
Henry May	September, 1853.
J. Willie Price	March, 1854.
G. A. Hanson	" "
James W. Shank	" "
J. T. M. Wharton	July, "
David H. Wiles	August, "
Jerome D. Brumbaugh	December, 1854.
James H. Groove	August, 1855.
A. N. Rankin	November, 1855.
George W. Smith, Jr	August, 1856.
William P. Maulsby	December, 1857.
Kennedy Price	April, 1858.
Francis M. Darby	November, 1858.
F. S. Stumbaugh	March, 1859.
Snively Strickler	" "
Eli Day	November, 1859.
Charles J. Nesbitt	December, "
James D. Bennett	" "

	Qualified.
John A. Lynch	December, 1859.
George K. Shillman	“ “
Samuel M. Firey	March, 1860.
E. L. Lowe	“ “
George W. Brown	August, “
J. H. Gordon	December, 1860.
Thomas Devecmon	“ “
Joseph A. Skinner	January, 1861.
J. Mortimer Kilgour	March, 1861.
John V. L. Findlay	“ “
William Walsh	March, 1863.
C. B. Thurston	“ “
J. E. Loughridge	“ “
Albert Small	November, 1863.
James Murdock	December, “
Fred. J. Nelson	“ “
J. E. Ludden	“ “
William McK. Keppler	March, 1864.
J. Addison McCool	“ “
R. Wilson, Jr.	September, 1864.
George A. Thruston	December, “
James P. Mathews	March, 1865.
William Kealhofer	“ “
Albert Small	June, “
James H. Grove	“ “
Alexander Neill	“ “
George W. Smith, Jr.	“ “
William Kealhofer	“ “
A. K. Syester	“ “
D. H. Wiles	“ “
F. M. Darby	“ “
William T. Hamilton	“ “
R. H. Alvey	“ “
George Schley	“ “
W. Motter	“ “
James P. Mathews	“ “
William McK. Keppler	“ “
Z. S. Claggett	“ “
Peter Negley	“ “
G. W. Smith	“ “
E. F. Anderson	July, “
W. B. Downey	“ “
H. H. Keedy	“ “
Albert L. Levi	November, 1865.
J. Addison McCool	December, “
Alexander Neill	“ “
Edward Y. Goldsborough	March, 1866.
B. F. M. Hurley	July, “
J. C. Zeller	“ “
Thomas W. Berry	November, 1866.
T. Cook Hughey	April, 1867.
John Williams	July, “
Alfred D. Merrick	“ “
R. H. Jackson	“ “
George Freaner	“ “
A. K. Syester	November, 1867.
William T. Hamilton	“ “
D. H. Wiles	“ “
George French	“ “
Alfred D. Merrick	“ “
James P. Mathews	“ “
George W. Smith, Jr	“ “
H. Kyd Douglas	“ “
James H. Grove	“ “
F. M. Darby	“ “
H. H. Keedy	“ “
Albert Small	“ “
Z. S. Claggett	“ “
George Freaner	“ “
Wm. Kealhofer	“ “
G. W. Smith	“ “
J. C. Zeller	“ “
H. C. Kizer	“ “
John Thomson Mason	“ “
Edward Stake	“ “
George Schley	“ “
Alex. Neill	“ “
Thomas W. Berry	“ “
D. Weisel	December, “
Thomas H. Grove	March, 1868.
Peter A. Witener	April, “
Louis E. McComas	August, “
James A. Skinner	“ “

	Qualified.
Lewis M. Blackford	November, 1868.
R. P. H. Staub	December, “
Lewis C. Smith	“ “
W. D. B. Motter	March, “
Edw. W. Mealey	“ “
J. H. McCauley	“ 1869.
Richard T. Semmes	“ “
S. A. Cox	November, 1869.
C. P. Hikes	March, “
E. J. Lee	April, “
Albert Ritchie	March, “
F. Watts	“ “
A. B. Marten	August, 1870.
James M. Sherry	December, 1870.
John S. Grove	March, 1871.
J. Thomas Jones	July, “
C. V. S. Levy	“ “
Alexander Armstrong	November, 1871.
Buchanan Schley	“ “
T. I. C. Williams	March, 1872.
Tryon Hughes Edwards	“ “
C. S. Devilbiss	“ “
Wm. J. Read	“ “
John E. Smith	September, 1872.
J. A. C. Bond	“ “
N. B. Norment	“ “
S. L. Heffenger	November, “
Stephen H. Bradley	“ “
Wm. P. Maulsby	“ “
Thos. Donaldson	December, “
Wm. A. Fisher	“ “
T. C. Kennedy	August, 1873.
John K. Cowen	“ “
Wm. McK. Keppler	“ “
J. W. G. Beeler	“ “
Fred. F. McComas	March, 1874.
Reinhold J. Halm	“ “
William H. A. Hamilton	July, “
J. Clarence Lane	“ “
W. P. Lane	November, 1874.
W. M. McDonell	March, 1875.
J. M. Mason	May, “
Charles Davis	“ “
W. M. Price	“ “
R. Chew Jones	“ “
B. F. Winger	August, “
V. R. Martin	November, 1875.
Frederick J. Halm	February, 1876.
N. S. Cook	“ “
A. F. Munsell	March, “
Isaac Motter	May, “
Charles Negley	“ “
S. B. Loose	“ “
Charles G. Biggs	November, “
John F. A. Remley	December, “
George W. Graham	February, 1877.
A. Hunter Boyd	May, “
H. W. Hoffman	June, “
William Brace	“ “
Benjamin A. Richmond	“ “
Ferdinand Williams	“ “
James D. Butt	“ “
John C. Motter	May, 1878.
John L. McAtee	June, “
John D. McPherson	“ “
William Shepard Bryan	“ “
George A. Davis	December, 1878.
John Ritchie	“ “
Clayton O. Keedy	“ 1879.
James E. Ellegood	November, 1880.

CHAPTER XLVII.

MEDICINE AND PHYSICIANS.

As early as Nov. 21, 1785, attention was called, through the columns of the *Maryland Gazette*, to the necessity of forming in Washington County a “medical society for the suppression of quackery," and proposing a State board of medical examiners appointed and paid by the State, which might be the nucleus of a future medical school. "Physic, Thoughts on Reform in the Practice of," is the title of a paper in the *Maryland Gazette* of Dec. 13, 1785, suggesting a plan for the better regulation of the profession.

A public meeting of the inhabitants of Hagerstown, held Oct. 13, 1793, with Col. Henry Shryock in the chair, established quarantine against "Philadelphia or other places supposed to be infected with that contagious fever now raging in Philadelphia." By the meeting a board of health was established, composed of Drs. Samuel Young, Peter Woltz, and Jacob Schnebly, and Thomas Hart, William Lee, George Schall, Rezin Davis, John Geiger, George Woltz, Andrew Levy, Jacob Harry, David Harry, and Wm. Reynolds, who were empowered to take such measures to secure the town from infected persons as their judgment might suggest. The magistrates of the county were earnestly requested to vigilantly execute the powers given to them by the Governor's proclamation of the 12th of September, 1793, and it was also

"*Resolved*, That the clothing from Philadelphia sent forward to the troops now in this place shall not be received in this town, or suffered to come within seven miles thereof."

"Quackery" was not by any means suppressed, for Dr. Robinson, practitioner of animal electricity and magnetism, was in Hagerstown Jan. 17, 1794, and William Kerr continued every day to instruct ladies and gentlemen in the curious and definite arts of animal electricity and magnetism for three pounds each, with a written promise not to teach or cause to be taught any other person whatsoever for the next twelve months.

Dr. Richard Pindell removed from Hagerstown to Lexington, Ky., with Thomas Hart, in 1793, and was Mr. Clay's family physician for twenty-five years. Dr. James Scott in 1793, Dr. Henry Schnebly in 1794, Dr. Samuel Young in 1797, Dr. J. Schnebly in 1798 were practicing medicine in Hagerstown. Dr. B. Fendall, surgeon dentist (the same who advertised in 1779 that "those who have had the misfortune of losing their teeth may have natural teeth transplanted from one person to another, which will remain as firm in the jaw as if they originally grew there," and who also "grafted natural teeth on old stumps") was in Hagerstown in 1797; Dr. Runkel in 1799; Mr. Hayden, dentist, from Baltimore, in 1804; Drs. Pindell and Dorsey in 1803; J. Wamsley, John R. Young, Wm. Downey, Arnold Hennenkemph, Wm. Hammond, Young & Van Lear, from 1800 to 1818; Samuel Showman, J. Reynolds, —— Ridout, from 1818 to 1821; J. Fitzhugh, A. F. Belzer, Joseph Martin, Charles H. Goldsborough, Wm. Macgill, and T. B. Duckett to 1824. Dr. Wm. Macgill in 1825 performed the first operation for lithotomy "ever performed in the county."

From the constitution and by-laws of the Washington County Medical Society, we find that the following were members of the society in 1866: District No. 1, Augustin A. Biggs, Benjamin D. De Kalb; District No. 2, J. Johnson, S. Weisel, H. Zeller, J. A. Croft; Hagerstown, J. B. McKee, N. B. Scott, M. J. McKinnon, T. W. Simmons, John E. Miller, Frederick Dorsey, Joshua Jones, R. H. Kealhofer, William Ragan; District No. 4, H. F. Perry, Fred. C. Doyle, W. W. Shapely; District No. 5, J. B. Delaplane, Jas. Breathed, Edward Borck; District No. 6, H. B. Wilson, Otho J. Smith, J. F. Smith, J. D. Keedy, and N. D. Tobey; District No. 7, E. Bishop, E. Tracey Bishop, W. A. Riddlemoser; District No. 8, James H. Claggett; District No. 9, Samuel M. Good, O. M. Muncaster; District No. 10, Wm. Booth, R. H. E. Boteler; District No. 12, Thomas Maddox, Wm. Grimes, R. J. Duckett.

The County Medical Association was formed July, 1881, with the following officers: President, Dr. William H. Perkins; Vice-Presidents, Drs. William Ragan and E. Tracy Bishop; Secretary, Dr. J. W. Humrickhouse; and Treasurer, Dr. T. W. Simmons.

Drs. A. S. Mason, E. T. Bishop, William Ragan, J. McP. Scott, and H. B. Wilson were appointed a committee to prepare rules and regulations.

The County Board of Health was organized March 10, 1881, and is composed as follows:

No. 1. Hagerstown, Funkstown, and Conococheague Districts.—Mayor John D. Swartz, State's Attorney J. F. A. Remly, Dr. A. S. Mason, Dr. T. W. Simmons, Dr. J. McP. Scott, Dr. O. H. W. Ragan, Dr. J. W. Humrickhouse, Dr. Victor D. Miller, and Dr. H. B. Gross.

No. 2. Sharpsburg, Keedysville, and Tilghmanton.—Dr. C. W. Russell, Dr. Thomas Maddox, Dr. William Grimes, Dr. R. Duckett, and Messrs. Thomas Smith and Albert G. Lovell.

No. 3. Sandy Hook and Rohrersville.—Dr. J. E. Holmes, Dr. Boteler, Dr. Yourtee, and Messrs. George H. Weld and Augustus Young.

No. 4. Boonsboro' and Beaver Creek.—Dr. John M. Gaines, Dr. H. B. Wilson, Dr. S. S. Davis, and Messrs. Albert B. Martin and A. Will Lakin.

No. 5. Chewsville and Cavetown.—Dr. E. T. Bishop, Dr. John Ames, Dr. Baldwin, and Messrs. John H. Harp and L. D. Betts.

No. 6. Leitersburg and Ringgold.—Dr. F. Barkdoll, Dr. C. W. Harper, and Messrs. Josephus Ground, Abraham Frick, and Samuel Strite.

No. 7. Hancock, Indian Spring, and Clear Spring.—Dr. Gale, Dr. W. H. Perkins, Dr. F. C. Doyle, Dr. Broderick, and Moses Whitson, Esq.

No. 8. Downsville and Williamsport.—Dr. H. Y. Zeller, Dr. Lesher, and Messrs. Victor Cushwa, Henry Onderdonk, and August Shorb.

Dr. Frederick Dorsey, one of the earliest physicians of Washington County, and one of the most distinguished, was born in Anne Arundel County, Md., on the 4th of May, 1776, and was the son of Nicholas and Mary B. Dorsey. He was well educated, and in 1795, before he was of age, removed to Washington County, where he spent the rest of his life in the active pursuit of his profession, that of physician, and of Thomas Jefferson. Dr. Rush was his instructor and friend, while among his early associates are to be found the familiar names of Henry Clay, Col. Nathaniel Rochester, the Fitzhughs, the Barneses, the Ringgolds, the Tilghmans, the Masons, the Lawrences, the Hugheses, the Spriggs, the Carrolls, the Buchananses, and the Kershners,—men who like himself made an indelible impression upon the history not only of their county, but the whole of Western Maryland. When he first arrived at Hagerstown (then Elizabethtown) Dr. Dorsey considered himself to

Fre Dorsey

died Oct. 26, 1858, in the house in which he had lived since his marriage, aged eighty-two. He continued in active practice up to the last hour of his illness, a period of nearly seventy years, and was associated in practice at the time of his death with his son and grandson. He left behind him also great-grandchildren. Dr. Dorsey lived through the American Revolution, was a witness from afar of the bloody Revolution in France, and watched with more intelligent eyes the brilliant and afterwards disastrous career of Napoleon from beginning to end. He had shaken hands with Washington, and was a personal admirer have reached almost the farthest point of Western civilization; but before the close of his long and eventful life he witnessed the settlement of all those vast tracts of fertile land between the Alleganies and the Pacific coast which are now known as "the West." Probably no man ever lived who was more thoroughly identified with a community than was Dr. Dorsey. He was well known to every man, woman, and child, his peculiarities making him a most conspicuous personage, while his benevolence and generosity gave him an enviable pre-eminence. In his profession he could scarcely have been surpassed. Prof. Nathaniel

Potter, an eminent authority, pronounced him as good if not the best judge of the pulse he ever knew. "A single touch of that mysterious fibre was for him sufficient to know whether it beat the cheerful notes of life or the sad, muffled toll of death. His predictions of life and death were almost superhuman. He could fix with miraculous precision the last moment of a sinking patient, and in his own case he foretold with as much calmness and precision as Wolsey had done of himself the very moment when his spirit would take its flight."[1]

In the department of midwifery he was admitted to stand in the front rank of his profession. He entered upon this branch of medical science at the age of seventeen, and before he died officiated in upwards of eleven thousand occurrences. The great secret of Dr. Dorsey's success, as revealed by himself, was to secure the confidence of the patient first, and in order to accomplish this he would seem to humor any and all of their whims, but if questioned he would generally reveal minutely his theory and treatment of the case. Dr. Dorsey was also a skillful surgeon, and performed a number of extremely difficult operations with rare success. Although indifferent to popular approval, and scorning to make the slightest effort to secure it, Dr. Dorsey was one of the best-known and, in the popular judgment, most eminent physicians in the country, his death being mentioned with terms of compliment "in almost all the papers from Maine to Texas."

Dr. Dorsey had been a student of the famous Dr. Rush, and continued throughout his career an ardent disciple and admirer of that great man. He was among the first American physicians to adopt etherization in surgical operations, but he held steadfast to the Rush doctrine of calomel and blood-letting for certain forms of disease, although extremely careful to use these remedies only in cases of absolute necessity. His skill in the treatment of children's diseases was very remarkable, as was also his intuitive perception of the real character of a disease. Thus, for instance, on one occasion, when a gentleman who had been treated by other physicians for consumption came to him, he bluntly told him that "a pound of calomel" would cure him, as his liver, and not his lungs, was diseased. Calomel did cure him. His ingenuity was no less remarkable than his professional skill. Upon one occasion he was called in to prescribe for a hypochondriac who imagined that he had swallowed a spider. Knowing that argument would be useless, Dr. Dorsey procured a blue-bottle fly, and having had the room darkened and the patient's eyes bandaged, bade him open his mouth, and passed the fly several times before his face, at the same time exclaiming, "I see him!" "He's coming!" etc. The fly was finally exhibited to the man, who believed firmly that it was the insect which had tormented him.

Dr. Dorsey was not a regular graduate of any medical college, though he attended one or two courses of lectures. In 1824, however, the honorary degree of Doctor of Medicine was conferred on him by the University of Maryland. Twenty years previously (1804) he had received a diploma of honorary membership in the Philadelphia Medical Society, of which he was at the time of his death the oldest honorary member. Dr. Dorsey's practice was probably as extensive as any ever obtained by a physician, either in this country or in Europe. It is said that he often made a circuit of eighty miles in twenty-four hours. On a single day he visited and prescribed for one hundred and eighty-six patients. On his last birthday he rode on horseback upwards of twenty-five miles. For some forty days preceding his mother's death he saw her every day, although she lived thirty-two miles from Hagerstown, besides attending to his other practice. During this period, too, he had a patient at Chambersburg, twenty miles distant, whom he occasionally saw.

In his private character Dr. Dorsey was an earnest hater of hypocrisy and sham, so much so that he often strove to make himself appear worse for fear he might seem better than he was.[2]

He was, however, a profound respecter of religion and a prominent member of the Protestant Episcopal Church. And yet he could not resist a fondness for such sports as fox-hunting, horse-racing, and chicken-fighting, and though never a gambler, his love for these out-door sports continued to be an absorbing passion with him, and after he was sixty years of age he went all the way to New York to attend a main of famous cocks.

"He would often," says Judge Mason, "economize his time so that he could make the same visit from home subserve both

[1] Address upon the life and character of Dr. Frederick Dorsey, by John Thomson Mason.

[2] To listen to some of the sentiments he would utter you would suppose him a monster, while to witness his unobtrusive acts of benevolence and virtue you would esteem him a model of goodness. I have known him in apparent seriousness to advocate the burning of all Christian churches, and the hanging of all Christian ministers. Yet who contributed more liberally and cheerfully to the support of both? He would denounce certain persons at one moment, and yet in the next quietly heap upon them the most substantial benefits. You would hear him recommend the most cruel punishment to slaves, yet he was proverbially one of the kindest of masters."—*John Thomson Mason's Address.*

an Episcopal convention and a chicken-fight." His peculiarity in this respect was the result not of any moral obliquity, but of an uncontrollable vivacity and zest for lively amusements. He had, we are told, the spirits of a boy to the end of his days, and "his long life was one unbroken season of youthful enjoyment and sunshine." His generosity was so great that, it is asserted, he perhaps lost more money by securityship and long indulgence than any man who ever lived in Washington County. He was the main support of his church in Hagerstown, and was a member of its vestry for half a century. At times he was "president, secretary, treasurer, collector, and . . . everything else," and even made the fires and rang the bell. Dr. Dorsey was the leader of the High Church party in his vicinity, and by his vigorous and aggressive course succeeded in carrying the day at the church elections. He was also a warm and steadfast friend of St. James' College, and was one of its trustees from the first organization, and among the earliest and most liberal contributors. In all business transactions his integrity was unquestioned. In his personal habits and dress he was scrupulously simple and unaffected, and often boasted of having worn certain articles of clothing for a number of years.

"His hospitality was proverbial, and his conversation extremely interesting. He was a famous talker, and somebody once said of him that he had an assortment of stories for his journeys, which varied from one to twenty miles in length. When he had no one to narrate them to he would talk to his horse. "On one occasion," we are told, "for *nine* days and nights, so pressing were his professional engagements, he never went to bed. On the *tenth* he presided as chief judge at the great race between the famous horses Industry and Bachelor, and was the merriest man on the ground."

In an obituary notice the *Herald and Torch*, of Hagerstown, in its issue of Wednesday, Nov. 3, 1858, said of him,—

"Dr. Dorsey was personally known to almost every citizen of the county. Far and near his fame had spread, and it will be long before the recollection of his great usefulness, his remarkable activity and endurance, his wonderful and untiring energy, and above all his great benevolence and his generous sacrifices, shall fade away from the memory of those among whom he lived and died. As a citizen he was distinguished for his love of justice and reverence for law. Possessed of a sound and enlightened judgment, enlarged and comprehensive views, enterprising, and eminently useful, his large influence and honored position suffered no abatement with his declining age. He filled as large a space in the community under the weight of many years and the infirmities of age as he did in the full strength and vigor of ripened manhood. No man was ever more honored in the confidences and affections of a people, none more venerated and beloved, and few so richly deserving it all. He lived to an unusual age, and the flower of his youth, the strength and vigor of his manhood, and the unequaled and matured experiences of his old age were given to his profession with a constancy and devotion seldom if ever equaled.

"He loved his profession for its own sake, and the blessings which its proper practice would confer on others; he devoted all the energies of his remarkable life to its practice, not with a view to the accumulation of wealth, but with the high and noble purpose of mastering its complex and delicate principles, and faithfully discharging its momentous and solemn responsibilities. He was eminently successful. Faithfully, completely, amply, to the full extent of human ability and the farthest stretch of human endurance, did he discharge the heavy responsibilities and delicate duties of his laborious calling. No call was ever unanswered. Heat and cold, darkness and light, cloud and sunshine, the dashing fury of the storm, the blackness of the midnight hour found him, up to the moment when he was prostrated on his bed of extreme suffering, exposed to their perils and inclemencies. He never stopped to inquire, in the midst of his heaviest practice, concerning the pecuniary ability of his patient. He gave his services alike to the rich and the poor. He never pressed the needy or unfortunate. To them his acquirements, his skill, experience, and labor were ever a gratuity. Even in extreme old age, endowed as it was with an unparalleled power of endurance, when others claim that immunity and repose from service and labor so much needed and so cheerfully given, in the face of the fiercest and bitterest storms that howl around us, and under the darkness of the blackest midnight sky, he was on his errands of benevolence, his aged and welcome form bent over the bedside of the dying and unfortunate, or carried hope and health to the wasted frame of the poor and neglected. The gratification of having relieved the afflicted, of having restored strength and health to the homes of want and suffering, was the only reward he ever asked, and to him that reward was a treasure which money could not buy. In the cherished affections and lasting remembrances of thousands of our people this rare and noble characteristic of his nature will live enshrined. It will embalm his name in the purest impulses of our hearts, and passing down from parent to child will perpetuate his memory, and long survive that ephemeral fame which waits on the unsubstantial gratification of wealth or the uneasy and unstable honors of a public life.

"In the course of his long and active life he was never known to occasion distress or embarrassment to any one, though he was schooled in misfortune himself, and was called on frequently to endure anxieties and make heavy sacrifices for others, owing to the confiding generosity of his nature. He chose to suffer himself rather than cause others distress. In the midst of cruel perplexities and severe embarrassments he was always cheerful, self-possessed, and just, and difficulties which would have bent others to the earth, or have dashed their temper with a shade of sullen and morose bitterness, seemed only to nerve him with increased energy and a firmer resolution, or develop in bolder relief the innate strength and manliness of his character, and illustrate the great superiority of his nature."

On the morning after his death all the church-bells of the town were tolled in honor of the deceased. Friday morning at ten o'clock was the hour fixed for the funeral, but at that time it was raining in torrents, as it had been from an early hour. A postponement until two o'clock in the afternoon was then announced, at which hour, though still raining, the body was borne to the Episcopal church, followed by an immense concourse of people. Arrived in the church, an anthem was chanted and the service read, after which an appropriate discourse was pronounced by the Rev. Dr. Kerfoot, rector of the College of St. James. The remains were then taken and deposited in their last resting-place.

On the 17th of March, 1859, an address upon Dr. Dorsey's life and character was delivered by the late Judge John Thomson Mason in the Lutheran church at Hagerstown.

At a meeting of the vestry of St. John's Parish, Washington County, held at the parsonage, on Wednesday, Oct. 28, 1858, the following preamble and resolutions were unanimously adopted:

"WHEREAS, It has pleased Almighty God, in His wise providence, to remove from this world Dr. Frederick Dorsey, Sr., one of the oldest and most useful citizens of our county, and one who has, for many years, been a member of this vestry, and has also filled the offices of warden, treasurer, and register in this parish; therefore,

"*Resolved,* That while we desire to bow in submission to the will of Him who doeth all things well, we feel that, in the removal hence of our associate, we have lost one in whose wisdom and experience we have learned to confide, and one who was always ready to the extent of his ability to aid in everything which he supposed would promote the material prosperity of the parish; and, therefore, we know that we express the feelings of the parishioners in general when we say that in his death the parish has to mourn the loss of one of its truest friends, and the Church of God a faithful servant.

"*Resolved,* That in our estimation a great and a good man has been taken away: a great man, because in his prominence and success in his profession we recognize talents and abilities which would have fitted him for any station in life to which, in the providence of God, he might have been called; a good man, because in all the relations of life, whether as a citizen of the State, a member of the social circle, or in the practice of his profession, we have always found him faithful in the discharge of his duties. But we desire to record our sense of his worth particularly in reference to the special business of his calling,—the practice of the medical profession. In skill he was proficient, and in the bestowal of his services he was altogether disinterested, for the relief of suffering humanity seemed to be the aim of his life; and the lowly and the poor were as sure of his assiduous attentions, when called for, as those who from their circumstances and position in life were able to command them.

"*Resolved,* That we sympathize most deeply with the family of Dr. Dorsey in their bereavement, but more especially with her who has been so long associated with him in affairs of love.

"*Resolved,* That we will wear the usual badge of mourning for thirty days, in token of our respect for the memory of the deceased.

"*Resolved,* That these resolutions be entered upon the records of the parish, and that a copy of them be sent to the family of Dr. Dorsey, and also that they be published in the newspapers of the town.

"HENRY EDWARDS, *Rector.*

"WM. MOTTER, *Register.*"

The board of trustees of the College of St. James having been specially convened to take some action in regard to the decease of Dr. Dorsey, it was unanimously

"*Resolved,* That this board, in common with the public in general, has sustained an irreparable loss in the death of that venerable physician who for more than sixty years has been actively engaged in the practice of his profession, whose eminent skill has always been freely given to the destitute, and whose great goodness of heart has secured him a multitude of friends in all ranks of the community.

"*Resolved,* That as a trustee of the College of St. James from its beginning, the deceased has always been one of the most useful and unwavering of its friends; this board therefore desires to acknowledge that, for the space of sixteen years, his labors, his counsel, and his friendship have been to the college of inestimable value.

"*Resolved,* That the surviving members of this board will ever cherish an affectionate remembrance of their venerable associate and beloved friend; as one who, having been in his generation a prominent benefactor to his fellow-men, has in a good old age been 'gathered to his fathers, in the communion of the Catholic Church, in the confidence of a certain faith, in the comfort of a reasonable, religious, and holy hope, in favor with his God, and in perfect charity with all the world.'

"*Resolved,* That a copy of these resolutions be sent to the family of the deceased, to the diocesan church paper, and to the county newspapers.

"A true copy from the minutes.

"J. C. PASSMORE, *Secretary of the Board.*"

At a meeting of the medical faculty of Washington County, Oct. 29, 1858, Dr. Thomas B. Duckett in the chair, the following resolutions, reported by Dr. Charles Macgill and Dr. Thomas Maddox, were unanimously adopted:

"*Resolved,* That we have heard with deep regret of the death of the venerable Dr. Frederick Dorsey, Sr., a distinguished member of the medical profession for more than half a century, and that we sympathize with his family and friends in the loss they have sustained.

"*Resolved,* That in testimony of our respect to the memory of the deceased, the usual badge of mourning shall be worn by the faculty for thirty days.

"T. B. DUCKETT, *President.*

Dr. Dorsey married Miss Sally Claggett, of Hagerstown, daughter of John and Ann Claggett, by whom he had three sons and one daughter, viz.: Richard Pindell Fitzhugh, Freeland, John Claggett, and Lucy. Richard P. Fitzhugh and Freeland died young, and Lucy in infancy. John Claggett Dorsey married Louisa Hughes, daughter of Samuel Hughes, in 1828. Dr. J. C. Dorsey was born Oct. 6, 1805, and educated at Washington College, Pennsylvania, where he graduated. He then studied medicine with his father, and entered the University of Maryland at Baltimore, where he also graduated. He then practiced medicine with his father, and entered into partnership with him, continuing in this relation until 1856. His son, Dr. Frederick Dorsey, Jr., entered into partnership with him in that year, continuing until his father's death, July 30, 1863. Dr. Dorsey, the elder, acted as consulting physician to his son and grandson until his death, Oct. 26, 1858. Thus representatives of three generations of the same family practiced medicine together. At one time Dr. John Claggett Dorsey was a member of the board of county commissioners. A peculiarity of the Dorseys was that they never put out a sign and never had an office. The people knew them so well that there was no necessity for resorting to such advertisement. The patients were always received in the parlor. Some of the old families of

Hagerstown never had any physician except a Dorsey for three generations.

Dr. Lancelot Jacques, of Washington County, was a native of England, and emigrated to this country in early life. He was educated at Newark School, served a short time as surgeon in the American army during the Revolution, was three times elected to the General Assembly, and filled several other official positions with honor and credit to himself and general satisfaction to the public. He died at his residence near Hancock on the 29th of October, 1827, in the seventy-second year of his age.

Dr. James Dixon was the son of English emigrants, and was born in St. Mary's County, Md., on the 7th of January, 1797. After receiving a suitable education he studied medicine under the direction of Dr. Dorsey, of Hagerstown; and, after attending the customary lectures in Philadelphia, he commenced the practice of medicine in 1818 in Hagerstown. For ten years he continued to advance in practice, and at the time of his death was regarded as being one of the best physicians in the county. In 1824 he married a daughter of Judge King, by whom he had a son and daughter.

Dr. Charles Macgill, who died at the residence of his son-in-law, Dr. S. D. Drewey, near Richmond, Va., May 5, 1881, was a lineal descendant of Thomas Jennings, who filled the position of king's attorney under the colonial government of Maryland, and of Rev. James Macgill, of Scotland, who settled in Maryland in 1728. He was educated at the old Baltimore College, completing his studies in 1823. He became a student of medicine under Dr. Charles G. Worthington, of Elkridge, Md., and subsequently at the Baltimore Hospital, and graduated from the Maryland University in 1828, and entered upon the practice of medicine at Hagerstown, Md., in 1829. He married a daughter of Richard Ragan, of that place. In 1840 deceased was Presidential elector on the Van Buren ticket. He assisted in establishing the Hagerstown *Mail* in 1828, and subsequently the Martinsburg *Republican*. He was appointed by Governor Francis Thomas lieutenant-colonel of the Twenty-fourth Regiment Maryland Militia; subsequently commissioned colonel, and later promoted to the rank of major-general, Fourth Division Maryland Militia. In 1861, Dr. Macgill was arrested by order of the government on account of his Southern sympathies. He was sent to Fort McHenry, thence to Fort Lafayette, and afterwards transferred to Fort Warren, Boston harbor. The doctor was several times offered his release during his imprisonment if he would take the oath, which he declined. In 1862 he was released and returned to his home, where he resumed practice. In 1863, when Lee invaded Maryland, he established a hospital at Hagerstown. When the Confederate army fell back Dr. Macgill went to Virginia with it, and was appointed a full surgeon by President Davis, which position he held till the close of the war. After that time he settled in Richmond and practiced his profession.

In its issue of May 7, 1881, the Baltimore *American* gave the following sketch of his life:

"The death of Dr. Charles Macgill, in Richmond, Va., Thursday, which was announced in yesterday's *American*, caused general regret in this city and State, where he lived for many years, and was widely known and respected. Messrs. R. G. and P. H. Macgill, of the firm of C. A. Gambrill & Co., and Mr. Oliver P. Macgill, of Baltimore County, are nephews of the deceased, and he also leaves a niece, Mrs. James Gittings. From inquiries among his friends in this city further details as to the career of the deceased were learned yesterday, and will doubtless prove a source of regretful interest to all who knew him personally, as well as the many who can recall his political and professional standing in this State when the present generation was in its infancy.

"Dr. Macgill was educated at the old Baltimore College, and completing his collegiate studies in 1823, entered the office of Dr. Charles G. Worthington, of Elkridge Landing, Howard Co., Md., where he remained two years. Subsequently he became a student of the Baltimore Hospital. He graduated with high honors in the University of Maryland in 1828, and entered upon the practice of his profession in Hagerstown, Md., in connection with his brother, Dr. William D. Macgill. This partnership continued up to the fall of 1828, when he removed to Martinsburg, Va. In 1829 he married the daughter of Richard Ragan, Esq., of Hagerstown, Md., and returned to Hagerstown in 1833, where he was active in many public undertakings. He assisted in establishing the Hagerstown *Mail* in 1828, and subsequently the Martinsburg *Republican*.

"His decease recalls to mind an era in the political history of the State in which he was a leading actor. The State Senate in 1836 was not then, as now, elected by the people, but by electors, each county and the city of Baltimore being entitled to two electors, who convened at the capital and selected the Senate. In the year named, after an exciting contest, twenty-one Whigs and nineteen Democratic electors were chosen.

"Upon attempting to organize the latter insisted that their party should be recognized as the dominant one, inasmuch as it had received a popular majority. To this the Whigs refused to consent, upon which the Democrats, or 'the glorious nineteen,' as they called themselves,—two of whom, Hon. Joshua Vansant and Maj. Sprigg Harwood, still survive,—seceded from the convention, came on to Baltimore, and organized by electing Dr. Macgill president. The excitement throughout the State was intense, and a riot was only averted by Governor Veazy threatening to call out the militia. Shortly after several members of the 'glorious nineteen' returned to the main body, thus forming a quorum, which elected the Senate. Dr. Macgill, however, held aloof, and would never recognize their authority. In 1839 he was appointed a visitor to West Point by President Van Buren, and was in 1840 a State elector on the ticket of Martin Van Buren in the Presidential contest of that year. He was appointed by Governor Philip Francis Thomas lieutenant-colonel of the Twenty-fourth Regiment Maryland Militia, and was subsequently commissioned colonel. His rank was afterwards raised by the Governor to that of major-general of the Maryland Militia, Fourth Division.

"In September, 1861, while Dr. Charles Macgill was at home with his family at Hagerstown, the rattling of sabres and the tramp of soldiers were heard. In a moment a squad of soldiers entered his house. The leader said, 'Dr. Macgill, you are my prisoner.' 'By whose order?' inquired the doctor. The reply was, 'By order of Col. Kenly, who has instructions from the Secretary of State.' Dr. Macgill asked permission to visit his wife, who was ill, up-stairs, and started on his way, when the command was given to stop him. A number of privates advanced to seize the prisoner, when he turned upon them and dashed two of them down the stairway. This provoked a desperate struggle.

"Dr. Charles Macgill, Jr., went to the assistance of his father, and Miss Macgill, a daughter, who had returned from riding, and was equipped in a riding-habit, and carried in her hand an ivory-headed riding-whip, bravely defended her brother, who had received a sabre cut in the neck.

"At this juncture the soldiers drew their sabres and pistols on Miss Macgill, and but for the timely interference of their captain the consequences might have been serious. The father and son were both arrested, and were carried to Camp Banks, near Williamsport. The colonel commanding ordered the release of the son, and Dr. Macgill was sent to Fort McHenry. From Fort McHenry he was transferred to Fort Lafayette, and afterwards was removed to Fort Warren, in Boston harbor.

"The doctor was offered his release several times during his imprisonment upon the condition of his taking the oath, which he emphatically refused. In 1862 he was released, and returning to his home, quietly resumed the practice of his profession.

"In 1863, when Gen. Lee invaded Maryland, Dr. Macgill established at Hagerstown a hospital for the sick and wounded Confederates, which he superintended in person. When Gen. Lee was compelled to fall back, Dr. Macgill went to Virginia with him, and was appointed by President Davis a surgeon in the army of Northern Virginia, a position which he held until the surrender, after which event he settled in Richmond, and built up a lucrative practice.

"The following document, now on the records of the parish of 'Queen Caroline,' at Elkridge Landing, will be read with interest:

"'*By the honorable Benedict Calvert, Captain General and Commander-in-Chief, &c. To the gents of the vestry of Queen Caroline Parish, in Anne Arundel county greeting:* Whereas, the Rev. Mr. James McGill, clark, has been sent and recommended by the Right Rev. Father in God Edmund, Lord Bishop of London, &c., diocesan of this province, to officiate as minister of the Church of England, I do hereby appoint said James McGill minister of your parish, wishing and requiring you to receive him as such; and I do strictly command you to be aiding and assisting unto him, to the intent that he have the full benefit of the forty pounds of tobacco per poll raised for the support of the minister of your parish, and other rights, dues, and perquisites to his said office belonging.

"'Given at Annapolis this 13th day of May, in the 3d year of the reign of our sovereign Lord, King George the Second, and the sixteenth of his Lordship's dominion, anno Dominie 1730. 'BENEDICT LEONARD CALVERT.'

"The Rev. James McGill referred to was the ancestor of Dr. Charles Macgill, and consequently of the present well-known Maryland family of that name."

Dr. John A Wharton, who died at the residence of his son, Col. Jack Wharton, in New Orleans, on the 8th of May, 1875, was son of the Hon. Jesse Wharton, formerly United States senator from Tennessee, and was born about the year 1805, near Nashville, in that State. At about the age of twenty-five, having studied medicine there, he left his home with a view to complete his education at Edinburgh, Scotland. On arriving in Baltimore *en route* for Europe, he ascertained that the lectures at the Edinburgh University had commenced, and that he would lose no time by remaining in Baltimore for the season, which he did, and there resumed his studies under Dr. Potter of that city. Whilst living in Baltimore he had made the acquaintance of Miss Mason, daughter of John Thomson Mason, of Montpelier, who subsequently became his wife. The Edinburgh trip was abandoned, and his medical studies were completed at Baltimore, where he graduated after a residence of two years. Dr. Wharton then returned to Nashville, where he commenced the practice of medicine, and after establishing himself there returned to Maryland for his bride, was married at Montpelier about the year 1828 or '29, and returned to Tennessee to live. After the residence of a year in her new home it was found the climate did not agree with Mrs. Wharton, and the doctor and his wife returned to Maryland and took up their abode on one of the farms of the Montpelier estate, "Avondale," where the former abandoned his profession and devoted himself to agriculture, and where he continued to reside for a number of years.

But farming, though entirely congenial to his tastes, was not the natural bent of his mind, and in a short time Dr. Wharton became deeply immersed in politics, and for the balance of his life he made the politics of his county a study, almost as long as he continued to be a citizen of Maryland, and up to a late period of his life. His first appearance as a candidate was in 1833, when he was elected to the Legislature, with Messrs. Man, Grove, and Humrickhouse, on the regular Democratic ticket, he having received a majority of fourteen hundred and fifty-four votes over Zwisler, the highest on the opposition ticket. This was the year in which Dixon beat Thomas in Washington County. In 1834 he was again elected to the Legislature, the only one on his ticket, with Messrs. Andrew Kershner, John Welty, and Joseph Weast, and was one of the most active members of that memorable session. That year his colleagues on the Jackson ticket, who were defeated, were Robert Wason, Joseph Hollman, and Dr. J. C. Hays. Dr. Wharton beat Joseph I. Merrick, the lowest man on the anti-Jackson ticket, twenty-nine votes. Again, in the fall of 1835, he was a third time a candidate on the Jackson Republican ticket for the Legislature, and was elected at the head of his ticket, his colleagues being Michael Newcomer, David Brookhart, and Jacob Fiery. The opposition ticket consisted of Isaac Nesbitt, Joseph Weast, John Horine, and E. Baker.

Some years later Dr. Wharton was the Democratic candidate for the State Senate, and was defeated by the Hon. William B. Clarke by a few votes. This completed his legislative career, but for the rest of his life he continued to take a keen and active interest in politics.

Whilst a member of the House of Delegates the great "Indemnity" question, growing out of the demolition of the residence of John Glenn and Reverdy Johnson, in Baltimore, by a mob, was brought before that body. The House was Whig by a majority of one, and the payment of an indemnity was chiefly urged by the Whig party of that day, and opposed by the Democratic party in the Legislature. The Republican newspaper of Baltimore, the then recognized organ of the Democratic party of the State, edited by Gen. Richardson, desperately resisted the passage of the appropriation, and as the final day for the vote drew near it was ascertained that a majority of one in favor of the indemnity existed in the House. There were three Whigs who were opposed to the bill and three Democrats in favor of it. Among the latter was Dr. Wharton, whose position was boldly defined, and who in consequence thereof brought down upon himself personally the censure of the leading organ of his party, as well as of many of the leading men of his party.

In 1847, Dr. Wharton was in the Democratic State Convention which nominated the Hon. Philip Francis Thomas for Governor, and it was in a great measure through his personal exertions that that gentleman was nominated. By Governor Thomas he was appointed lottery commissioner at Baltimore, one of the most lucrative offices in the State. Upon the election of Gen. Pierce, Dr. Wharton received at his hands the appointment of surveyor of the port of Baltimore, which he held until the installation of the Buchanan administration. He then originated the Agricultural College, near Washington City, which was established and endowed by the State Legislature, and of which Dr. Wharton was register of the board of trustees. This position he held until the close of the war, making the college his place of residence. After peace was established and order restored at the South, he was induced by his son, Col. Jack Wharton, to remove to Mississippi and become a planter. He accordingly located himself near two of his brothers, in the vicinity of Jackson, and there he was living with his only surviving daughter three weeks before his death, when he was induced by his son, the colonel, to pay him a visit at New Orleans. In that city he was attacked with a gastric fever, subsequently ascertained to have been accompanied by organic disease of the heart, and there he died, attended by his daughter Elizabeth and his son, the colonel. Besides these, his only other child is William F. Wharton, a member of the Towson bar, Baltimore County, Md.

Dr. Wharton's remains were transported to Hagerstown and interred at the Episcopal burying-ground at that place. The pall-bearers were Hon. W. T. Hamilton, Col. George Schley, Hon. William Motter, Hon. Z. S. Claggett, Dr. J. F. Smith, Frederick Humrickhouse, J. P. Crist, and J. I. Hurley. The funeral cortege was preceded by Rev. Walter A. Mitchell, rector of St. John's Church. who officiated.

Dr. Samuel Weisel was born in Williamsport on the 16th of May, 1810, and died on the 26th of January, 1872. His father having died when he was still a mere lad, his training devolved upon his brother, Judge Daniel Weisel, and after a course at the Hagerstown Academy he began the study of medicine under the direction of Dr. Michael A. Finley, of Williamsport. In April, 1832, he graduated as a doctor of medicine at the University of Maryland, and at once commenced the practice of his profession in his native town, and there remained for the rest of his life, a period of forty years. Dr. Weisel maintained throughout his career a lofty character as a Christian gentleman and careful, laborious physician. His funeral was very largely attended, and the services were conducted by Rev. Mr. Smith, Presbyterian, and Rev. Mr. Strobel, Lutheran.

Joseph Edward Claggett, M.D., was born in Pleasant Valley, Washington Co., Md., Sept. 5, 1830. He attended the course of medical lectures at the Winchester Medical College of Virginia, and subsequently in Baltimore, Philadelphia, New York, Richmond, and Charleston. After his health failed he visited the Southern States, and having recruited his health returned and settled in the drug business at Harper's Ferry, where he remained from 1855 to 1861. He was at Harper's Ferry during the John Brown raid, and knew John Brown very well. In 1861, when the Confederate army retired from Harper's Ferry, he abandoned his home and business and went to Richmond, and was appointed a full surgeon, and remained with the army of Gen. Lee until the surrender at Appomattox. He was chief surgeon of the receiving and forwarding hospital of the Army of Northern Virginia. He was, in 1866, elected professor of materia medica and therapeutics of the medical department of the Washington University, Baltimore. He is a member of the Medico-Chirurgical Faculty of Maryland. He married, in 1850, Sidney C. Lindsay, daughter of Lewis Lindsay, of Winchester, Va.

Dr. James Thomas Notely Maddox was born at Chaptico, St. Mary's Co., Md., April 3, 1810. He is the son of Samuel and Sarah Fowler Maddox, and a descendant of Thomas Notley, Proprietary Governor of Maryland. Dr. Maddox was born on the farm "Green Spring," which has been in the Maddox family since a few years after the settlement of the State. In 1832 he graduated at the University of Maryland, school of medicine, and a few years later removed to Louisville, Ky., then a small town, and there engaged in the practice of medicine. He was in that town during the prevalence of the Asiatic cholera. In 1840 he returned to St. Mary's on a visit, and in consequence of his father's ill health remained. In 1846 he married Mary Claggett, of Frederick County, a granddaughter of the Right Rev. Thomas John Claggett, Bishop of the Protestant Episcopal Diocese of Maryland. Two years later he removed to Washington County and purchased a portion of the Tilghman estate, upon which he now resides. At that time it was a rough and unpromising tract, but skillful farming has converted it into one of the most productive properties in the State. Dr. Maddox gradually became so absorbed in farming that he abandoned the practice of medicine and devoted himself to agriculture exclusively, carrying into that occupation a zeal, sound judgment, and intelligence which not only accomplished important results in the improvement of his own farm, but communicated to his neighbors a spirit of emulation in the improvement of their lands and stock, which has borne most valuable fruit. He was probably the first farmer in the county who made any practical application of agricultural chemistry, and although his use of chemical fertilizers was the subject of much good-natured banter upon the part of his neighbors, they were not slow to follow his example when they saw the results of his methods. It is believed also that Dr. Maddox was the first farmer of his section to use a drill in sowing his wheat. It may here be stated that Mrs. Maddox's grandfather, Bishop Claggett, conferred a great boon upon the farmers by the introduction of clover, the seed of which he brought from England. Dr. Maddox steadily refused to be a candidate for office, and the only public position he has ever held was that of school commissioner. In politics he was originally a Whig, and during the war was a "Union" man, but since then he has been a Democrat. He is a zealous member of the Episcopal Church, and has been a vestryman for forty years. He has raised five children,—two sons and three daughters. One of his sons is a member of the Washington (D. C.) bar, and the other is a surgeon in the United States army.

CHAPTER XLVIII.

THE PRESS OF HAGERSTOWN.

UNTIL 1790 the inhabitants of Washington County, but more particularly Hagerstown, were entirely dependent on Annapolis, Baltimore, and Frederick Town for the current news of the day and a medium for advertising their merchandise or wants. On the 1st of January, 1790, the first number of the *Washington Spy*, the first newspaper published in Hagerstown, was issued and distributed throughout the town. It was handsomely printed on stout paper, fifteen and one-half inches by ten, in good clear type, and contained four pages, with three columns to the page, without rules. The last line in the first column of the fourth page contained the publisher's notice, as follows: "Elizabeth (Hager's) Town, Printed by Stewart Herbert." The *Spy* was published weekly by Mr. Herbert, and at his death was continued by his widow.

Newspapers were not edited at this time, but only printed, and all comments upon affairs came from the outside, in the shape of communications, or, as they were styled, "letters," to the printer, signed by "Manlius," "Home," "Junius," and the like. Herbert made a success of his new enterprise at the start. He was full of work, and at once established posts to all principal points. The *Spy* was furnished to subscribers at fifteen shillings per annum. Mr. Herbert died in April, 1795, but the paper was continued by his wife, Phebe Herbert, and John D. Cary. This partnership was dissolved in March of the following year, and Mrs. Herbert assumed the management, which she continued until she married Thomas Grieves, when he published the paper.

The *Spy* was not the only newspaper enterprise in Hagerstown at this time. John Gruber, whose name has since been inseparably connected with the famous almanac which he founded, and which has become a household word in Western Maryland and Southwestern Pennsylvania, came over from Philadelphia in 1795, where he had been engaged in the printing business, and, at the solicitation of Gen. Ringgold, started a paper, which was printed in the German language, and was called *The German Washington*

Correspondent. This German paper was continued for a number of years, but it was not a permanent success. While Mr. Gruber was printing his German sheet Gen. Ringgold suggested that he should establish an English paper, and, for the purpose of encouraging and supporting the venture, a supper was given by Gen. Ringgold and his political friends. The paper was to sustain the policy of the Republican (anti-Federal) party, and was published under the title of *The Sentinel of Liberty.* It was not at all successful, and in a very short time was discontinued. Mr. Gruber continued his German paper for some years afterwards, and it was at one time published under the management of his son-in-law, Samuel May. The paper was finally discontinued. With this enterprise off his hands Mr. Gruber planned and projected his famous almanac, which has made his name locally famous with all generations since, and which has been widely known throughout the country.

The almanac was first published in the German language in quarto form, and was called "The German Almanac." The material and press used in printing the almanac were made and purchased in Philadelphia, and were used and in good condition up to 1857. The workmanship upon the almanac was Mr. Gruber's up to the last three years of his life. It finally became "The Hagerstown Town and County Almanac," by which title it has appeared every year since. It was first published in English and German in 1812. It had at once a wide circulation. There were then as now cuts on the title-page, with borders around them, representing pictures of farm labors from January to December. Selections for fireside reading, wise sayings of sages and philosophers, homely common-sense quotations from Franklin, and kindred matter filled up the pages not taken up with the almanac proper. Many elaborate almanacs have been printed since, but none of them have been able to supplant Mr. Gruber's publication, of such homely associations and practical value among a large circle of readers. After Mr. Gruber's death the almanac passed into the hands of his heirs, and its publication was continued by them until it was transferred to its present publishers, M. A. Berry & Co.

John Gruber, the founder of "The Hagerstown Town and County Almanac," was born in Strasburg, Lancaster Co., Pa., on Oct. 31, 1768, and lived to be eighty-nine years of age. Mr. Gruber was of German descent, his family record dating back as far as 1555, and locating his ancestors at Marburg, in Hesse. His paternal ancestors were highly respectable and honorable, several of them being learned divines and pastors, one of whom (Andreas Gruberus) was in one parish for forty-eight years, and had lived fifty-two years, as the record says, "in connubial felicity." On the maternal side his lineage is traced from noble blood. His grandfather, John Adam Gruber, emigrated to Philadelphia in 1726, and settled in Germantown, Pa., where several of his children were born, and among them the father of John Gruber, in 1736, whose name was John Everhard Gruber. His great-grandmother died at the age of seventy-six; his grandfather (J. Adam Gruber) at the age of seventy. His father, John Everhard Gruber (a physician by profession), was married to Christiana Pain, of Philadelphia, in 1763, and he and his wife both spent the concluding years of their lives with their son in Hagerstown, the former dying in 1814, aged seventy-eight, and the latter in 1824, aged eighty-six.

John Gruber, the subject of this sketch, was apprenticed to the printing business in the city of Philadelphia, and served six years in learning his trade. Being in feeble health, he visited the island of San Domingo, and while there was engaged as a compositor upon a French paper. The insurrection broke out during his stay upon that island, but he escaped its horrors. He came to Hagerstown in 1795, at the suggestion of Gen. Ringgold, then a young and active citizen and influential politician of the county. His connection with the publication of several newspapers late in the eighteenth and early in the nineteenth centuries has already been shown. The most important of these enterprises, of course, was the founding of "The Gruber Almanac," which still has the imprint of John Gruber.

Besides the regular publications which have been spoken of, Mr. Gruber was from time to time engaged in other literary works. He published the first edition of the psalms and hymns of the German Reformed Church, under the supervision of the Synod of that church, in 1831. Under his care and instructions many young men were trained at the printing business, who afterwards had honorable and successful careers in life. The sergeant-at-arms of the House of Representatives of the United States in 1857, Adam Glossbrenner, served an apprenticeship to him. Mr. Gruber was never a violent politician. He calmly formed his opinions and consistently adhered to them, without the prospect or desire of political preferment. He voted at every Presidential election, beginning with that of Washington, and was a disciple of the Jefferson school of Republicanism. In later times he joined the Democratic party, and held office once (that of notary public), forced upon him by his friends, and which he refused to take until the incumbent, his predecessor, insisted upon his accepting it.

Through a long life Mr. Gruber was distinguished by marked and uniform quietude and equanimity of temper. Strictly industrious and attentive to his business and concerns, he was never known to speak ill of any human being. He had a heart and a hand for every one in affliction and distress that came within the range of his charity; but so quiet and unostentatious were his deeds of benevolence that generally none but those whom he relieved knew of them. He died on Dec. 30, 1857, and his remains were interred in the burying-ground of the German Reformed church in Hagerstown, on the morning of the last day of that year, in the presence of a very large number of friends, the religious services being performed by the Rev. Mr. Giésy, pastor of that church.

The *Spy* was published until the early part of 1797, and was succeeded in March of that year by the *Maryland Herald*, under the direction and control of Mr. Grieves, the first issue bearing date of March 2, 1797. On the beginning of the year 1804 the publisher of the *Herald* discontinued the use of the old fashioned letter s, and two months later changed the title of his paper to that of the *Maryland Herald and Hagerstown Weekly Advertiser*. The price of the *Herald and Advertiser* in 1806 was $2.25, which was payable " half-yearly, in advance," as the publisher's notice announced, and its advertisement rates were one square three times for one dollar, and one-fifth of a dollar for every subsequent insertion.

Files of the old *Herald and Advertiser* from March, 1802, to January, 1826, are preserved. The earliest number is Vol. VI., and is dated " Elizabeth (Hager's) Town (Maryland), Wednesday, March 31st, 1802." The same heading also informs the reader that it was " Printed by Thomas Grieves, near the Court-House." Beneath the heading " Elizabeth-Town Weekly Advertiser" appeared the motto, " Open to All Parties—Influenced by None." There is nothing to show, however, upon what terms it was delivered to subscribers, or what were the publisher's rates for advertising.

The size of the *Herald and Advertiser* was that of a four-column folio, each page of printed matter occupying a space of nine and one-half by sixteen and one-half inches. The absence of local news and editorials was characteristic of all the newspapers of that period, and, indeed, for some thirty years later, but they usually contained considerable home and foreign news of a general character. Thus the issue in question contained the proceedings of the United States Congress during the last days of March, 1802; " Both Sides of the Gutter," or two political articles copied from the *Monitor* and *Aurora*, which respectively controverted and coincided with the positions assumed by President Jefferson; letters from Gen. Samuel Ringgold and Matthew Van Lear, then engaged in a bitter newspaper war regarding some business transactions; and news of the troubles between the French and negroes in San Domingo.

In 1809 a newspaper was started in Hagerstown, which was called the *Gazette*. Its first issue was dated May 23d. It was published until June, 1813, when its brief life closed. At the time of its collapse the paper was the property of William McPherrins, who in December, 1814, made an assignment to Henry Switzer for the benefit of his creditors, under which the paper, press, type, etc., were sold.

It is somewhat curious to observe the amenities of journalism in Hagerstown in the early part of the present century. In September, 1809, for instance, in an editorial paragraph, the *Herald* speaks thus of the editor of its only English contemporary, the *Gazette*: " Billy Brown is certainly a poor thing. He neither knows how to write, spell, print, or talk. Although a friend of order, good government, and religion, it appears from his last paper that he does not look at his catechism even on the Sabbath." It would seem that soon after this Mr. Brown was the victim of some violent person who had been offended by his paper, and the *Herald* of Sept. 20, 1809, thus exclaims, " Halloo, Billy! how do you feel after the caning you got last evening!!!"

In February, 1813, upon the beginning of the thirteenth volume of the *Herald*, Mr. Grieves associated with himself in its management his step-son, Stewart Herbert, the son of the founder of the *Spy*. Mr. Grieves was a strong Democrat of the old school, who, had he supposed that there was a drop of Federal blood in his veins, would have had it drawn out. His step-son and partner was very popular, and was a gentleman of warm heart and generous impulses. Between the two the old *Herald* became a power in its day. Until 1813 the *Herald* was the only newspaper in the English language published in Hagerstown. It was not, however, to remain without a rival, and in that year O. H. W. Stull and a few other prominent gentlemen put their capital together and started the *Torch-Light*, its first editor being William D. Bell, whose industry and ability made the paper a complete success. It was a weekly issue, of course, a daily paper being something unknown in Hagerstown at that early day. The *Torch-Light* flourished and was prosperous. It met with a misfortune some little time after its birth, when the office—a part of Mayor William Lewis' house, on the northeast corner of the public square—

was burned, and a removal was made to the brick house, which it occupied for a number of years, near the Hagerstown Bank.

The *Torch-Light* in a few years got possession of the old *Herald* through Dr. John Reynolds, who had purchased it of Mr. Grieves and transferred it to W. D. Bell. The *Torch* thus came in the regular line of succession, and could claim to be the continuation of the oldest paper in Washington County. The old *Spy* was first presented to the public in January, 1790. For some time afterwards the *Spy* stood in the front rank of American newspapers, and was very far in advance of any of its contemporaries in Maryland. It is a curious fact worthy of mention that as late as 1854 the *Torch* had in its office and successively used some of the very type used in the printing of the first issue of the *Spy*.

After selling the *Herald* Mr. Grieves, who had been for so long a time its publisher, moved away from Hagerstown. He had been for thirty years connected as proprietor and editor with the paper. His parents were natives of Scotland, and he was himself born in that country. He died at Cumberland in 1840. His old partner and step-son, and the son of the founder of the *Spy*, Stewart Herbert, died on April 13, 1853. Mr. Herbert remained in Hagerstown after the *Herald* had been purchased by the *Torch*, and occupied a number of local public offices. He was for years justice of the peace, and was elected to the State Legislature. He was a man of great equanimity of temper and composure of mind, and his manner was very dignified and impressive. He was one of the most prominent and influential men in Washington County up to the time of his death.

Mr. Herbert's father was not only the first editor but the first printer in Hagerstown. On the 5th of April, 1852, Richard Williams, who was Mr. Herbert's first apprentice, died at Charlestown, Va. Mr. Williams, after leaving the business in the office of the *Spy*, became the editor of the *Farmer's Repository* in 1802, and remained in that position until 1827. He was a lieutenant in the war of 1812.

In 1816 the *Herald* felt justified in putting on a little more style as well as four more columns of space. On the 14th of August of that year the following announcement was made by the publishers:

"We have this week the pleasure of presenting our readers with the *Maryland Herald and Hagerstown Advertiser* on a super-royal sheet and on new type. By this arrangement we shall in future be able to enrich our columns with a greater variety of news, both foreign and domestic, and at the same time accommodate our advertising friends, whose liberality we cannot sufficiently acknowledge. The terms, our readers will observe, are the same as heretofore."

The enlargement consisted of a change from a four-column to a five-column folio.

The *Torch-Light* continued to be controlled by W. D. Bell, its first editor, until the time of his death, in 1841, twenty-seven years after he had founded the paper. Mr. Bell was a Whig, and was an able advocate of his political faith. At the time of his death the *Torch-Light* was a widely-circulated and widely-read journal. He left a widow and a number of children.

For nearly a decade after the death of his father, Edwin Bell, a son of the founder of the *Torch-Light*, and now one of the editors and proprietors of the Hagerstown *Mail*, continued to edit the paper with ability and success. His health, however, was not good, and in the spring of 1850 he permanently settled in California, and Mrs. Susan Bell, his mother, announced that she had formed an association with Otis W. Marsh, formerly of the office of the Washington *National Intelligencer*, and that he would edit the paper. Mr. Motter, who for a year had been filling the editorial chair for his friend Mr. Bell, took graceful leave of the readers of the *Torch*. Marsh did not for some reason remain long at the helm. On Jan. 4, 1851, a second change was announced, when Mrs. Bell, the proprietress, stated that she had made such an arrangement for the conduct of the journal as she trusted would make it "hardly less welcome to its readers than it had been for the thirty-eight years of its existence." Mrs. Bell discovered in the end that she could not manage her property so satisfactorily as she anticipated, and the result was that in the August following the paper was sold to Messrs. Mittag & Sneary, who had successfully re-established the *Herald of Freedom*. The consolidation of these two papers by Messrs. Mittag & Sneary has transmitted to the present generation the Hagerstown *Torch-Light*. Mittag & Sneary had taken possession of the *Herald of Freedom* in 1839, soon after James Maxwell, after a brief and not successful experience, had given it up in despair. The *Herald of Freedom* had been established by Mr. Maxwell early in 1839 for the purpose of making it the organ of that faction of the Democratic party in Western Maryland which had fallen out with President Van Buren, and which was known as the Conservative party. The failure of "the Conservative Democrats" of that period is historic; it soon fell to pieces, and with it fell the hopes of Mr. Maxwell and others. On the 10th of December, 1839, the firm of Mittag & Sneary was formed, and the moribund organ was put on its feet as a "simon pure" party paper.

The *Torch-Light and Herald* was published by

PETER NEGLEY.

Mittag & Sneary until it was sold to Carridan & McCurdy, who did not, however, continue its publication for a very long time. Subsequently the old partnership was revived, and the paper was published by them until August, 1879, when Mr. Sneary sold his interest to Charles Negley, and retired finally from the editorial desk. He was the first of the old firm to succumb to old age and disease. He died of dropsy of the heart on the 24th of October, 1879. His career was almost entirely confined to the printing-office. He began life in the composing-room of the *Torch-Light and Advertiser* when seventeen years of age, and before he had reached his majority, in 1839, entered into the partnership, which existed for over forty years. He was a member of the State Constitutional Convention in 1867, and was a director in the First National Bank of Hagerstown, which was the only official position he ever held.

In 1880, Mr. Mittag, on account of failing health, also retired from his long connection with the *Torch-Light*, and sold his interest to Peter Negley, who, with his son, Charles Negley, has since conducted the paper.

Peter Negley, although by birth a Pennsylvanian, has resided nearly all his life in Washington County. He was born Aug. 29, 1818, on Welsh Run, in Franklin County, Pa., to which place his father, Christian (a native of Cumberland County, Pa., where he was born Oct. 19, 1791), removed when a lad with his father, Eliab, in 1800. Eliab Negley was a native of Lancaster County, Pa. His father was one of the pioneers in that county, and one of the founders of the first Seventh-day Baptist Society, organized at what is now known as Ephrata Springs.

Christian Negley, the youngest of four sons, inherited from his father a farm on Welsh Run, and in 1832 exchanged it for a place near Hagerstown, where he passed the rest of his life in the pursuits of agriculture, dying there May 18, 1880, in his eighty-ninth year. In 1814 he was married in Washington County to Barbara, daughter of Peter Newcomer, who with his three brothers moved to Beaver Creek from Lancaster County, Pa. The ancestors of the Newcomers were immigrants from Switzerland. Peter Newcomer died about 1825. From the four brothers sprang the numerous family of Newcomers of Washington County, a name that represents much wealth, intelligence, and influence. Mrs. Christian Negley, who was born in Washington County in 1793, died Sept. 17, 1869. Three daughters and one son (Peter) were born to Mr. and Mrs. Christian Negley. The only surviving daughter is Mrs. George I. Foulke, of Washington County.

Peter Negley remained upon his father's farm until he reached his seventeenth year, attending school meanwhile at the Salem school-house. He then entered a store at Greencastle, Pa., and continued to serve as a clerk about two years and a half, at the expiration of which he was placed in the preparatory department of Dickinson College, Carlisle, of which Rev. Dr. Durbin was then president. Rev. Stephen Asbury Rossell was principal of the preparatory department. In the spring of 1839 young Negley was transferred to the preparatory department of Marshall College, at Mercersburg, Pa., Rev. Dr. Rauch being then president, and in the fall of 1839 he entered the freshman class. Ill health compelled a cessation of his studies for a year, at the end of which he returned, and graduated in 1844. In that year he commenced the study of the law with James Dixon Roman, of Hagerstown, and in 1848 was admitted to the bar. He located himself in Hagerstown, and at once began the active practice of his profession. In 1851 he was brought forward as the Whig candidate for prosecuting attorney against Thomas Harbine (Democrat), by whom he was defeated by one hundred and thirty-seven votes. In 1852 continued ill health led him to abandon his law practice for an appointment as treasurer of the Hagerstown Savings Institution, and when, in 1854, that institution was chartered as a State bank, he was chosen its cashier. In 1864 he was elected a Republican member of the State Constitutional Convention.

Mr. Negley and H. W. Dellinger, of Clear Spring, are the survivors of the six Republican delegates on the Union ticket. In 1866, Mr. Negley purchased a half-interest in the *Herald and Torch-Light* newspaper, and became one of its editors. He is still the editor of that journal, and with his son Charles owns the establishment. He maintained his connection as cashier with the Hagerstown Savings-Bank until it was rechartered as the First National Bank in 1865, and until 1870 was the cashier of the latter institution. In June, 1870, when the United States depository at Baltimore was made a sub-treasury, Mr. Negley was appointed by President Grant assistant treasurer in charge, and he thereupon resigned his place as cashier to take possession of his new office, which he first occupied Aug. 1, 1870. In 1874 he was reappointed by President Grant, and in 1878 by President Hayes, and still holds the position under the last appointment. His residence is and has been since 1844 at Frederick. During 1878 and 1880 he was president of the Hagerstown Agricultural Implement Manufacturing Company, and later was chosen its treasurer. On the 8th of May, 1849, Mr. Negley married Laura, daughter of Martin Rickenbaugh, of Washington County, by whom he had three sons and one daughter, all of whom survive. Of the sons, Walter and Charles graduated at Amherst, and William was educated at Cornell. Walter and William are now extensively and prosperously engaged in sheep-raising in Texas. Charles is associated with his father in the proprietorship of the *Herald and Torch-Light*. Mr. Negley's first wife died Feb. 12, 1859. In October, 1861, he married, at Cambridge, Mass., Mrs. Brooks, a native of Massachusetts.

The *Torch-Light* maintains under its present management the high reputation which it has so long enjoyed as a carefully-conducted, vigorous, and intelligent journal. Its editorials are ably written and always pertinent to the leading issues of the day, while its news columns every week are filled with interesting local intelligence and news presented in a condensed and attractive form from all quarters of the globe. Its miscellany is notably fresh, interesting, and varied, and in fact the *Torch-Light* may be said to be a model county newspaper.

Its former editor, Mr. Mittag, is living in Hagerstown, in the enjoyment of vigorous health, and is one of the best known and most popular members of the fraternity in Maryland. The author is greatly indebted to Mr. Mittag for much valuable assistance and many important suggestions in collecting historical material; but more especially for a nearly complete file of the *Torch-Light*, which he kindly loaned for the preparation of this work.

Numerous journalistic enterprises have been started in Hagerstown. In June, 1828, a weekly paper called *Our Country* was published, and continued to be printed until the Presidential election in the fall. It was run in the interest of Mr. Adams, and was discontinued as soon as the election was over. The *Maryland Free Press* was a venture made by Andrew G. Boyd, who had been the editor of the *Weekly News*. The *Free Press* was first issued in November, 1862; it was not a permanent success. The *Bloomer* came out in August, 1851, and its name tempted the Baltimore *Sun* to express the hope that the paper would make its way in the world faster than did the costume of its name. The *Bloomer* was published by Blair & Rayan, but the hope of its Baltimore contemporary was not realized. The Hagerstown *Times and Farmers' Advertiser* was published as far back as 1827, at two dollars a year, by Reynolds & May, and was another failure. In 1850–57 and afterwards the *Chronicle* was published by Mr. Marshall, and then by M. Brittingham; it did not long survive. The *Weekly Times* appeared in November, 1826, but the *Torch-Light* was too much for it, and the *Times* did not get along, and was finally suspended. In 1852, John C. Wise purchased the Clear Spring *Whig* and removed it to Hagerstown, where he published it for a little while, but it did not pay, and was also discontinued.

In April, 1842, John A. Freaner and John W. Boyd launched the weekly and semi-weekly *News*. The paper was continued by Boyd after 1846, when his partner sold out and became one of the publishers of the *Mail*. The *News* was subsequently sold to A. G. Boyd, who published it until 1851, when he disposed of the office to S. M. E. Cook, who kept it afloat until 1854, when it finally suspended.

The *Odd-Fellow* was first issued in Boonsboro', on Dec. 17, 1841, its first publisher and editor being Josiah Knode, a self-made printer, never having served an hour's apprenticeship in any office. He was something of an inventor, and his first press was of his own construction. In a short time the success of the enterprise warranted the purchase of a "Ramage press" from the *Torch-Light*, of Hagerstown. Mr. Knode continued in control of the *Odd-Fellow* until November, 1855, when he sold out to Isaiah Wolfensberger and retired from business on account of failing health. Mr. Wolfensberger only published the paper for two years, and in April, 1860, F. H. Irwin took possession, and after a short time associated with himself in the management of the enterprise Rev. L. A. Brunner, of the Reformed Church at Boonsboro', who in July, 1860, became sole proprietor, but retired after a brief experience. Mr. Irwin, in February, 1861, resumed entire control. He was a strong Union man, and during the civil war his office was raided and his type destroyed by Confederate soldiers, on account of the strong Northern sentiments expressed in the paper. The *Odd-Fellow*, however, survived all the vicissitudes of the war, and Mr. Irwin in 1866 sold out to Capt. John M. Mentzer, of Franklin County, Pa., who made the tone of the paper intensely Republican. So bitter was the feeling which his editorials created in the community that his office was several times assailed with stones, etc. He, however, was not intimidated, and continued to advocate the views which he had professed at first. In July, 1880, the *Odd-Fellow* was removed from Boonsboro' to Hagerstown, and published on South Jonathan Street, in the "Remley Building." So favorably was the paper received in its new home that an enlargement was necessary, which was made in October, 1881, and on the 6th of that month the first issue of *The Hagerstown Odd-Fellow* was published. The enlargement makes it a handsome thirty-two-column paper, twenty-seven by forty inches. Capt. Mentzer continues to be its editor and publisher. He was born in Franklin County, Pa., near Fayettesville. The paper is ably managed, and its editorial page commands general attention and respect.

The *Hagerstown Mail* is the oldest paper published under the same title in Western Maryland. For some years prior to the election of Gen. Jackson the Democratic party had no mouth-piece in Washington or the adjoining counties. Party spirit ran high. Jackson was pressed for the Presidency and was bitterly opposed by the Whigs. It was in this exciting campaign that a number of citizens of Washington County got together and made up a sum of money to start a Jackson paper. It was accordingly established, with James Maxwell, of Martinsburg, Va., as editor, and the first number was issued on the 4th of July, 1828. The following is an extract from the prospectus of the paper:

"PROPOSALS *for publishing in Hagerstown, Washington Co., Md., a weekly newspaper, under the title of* THE HAGERSTOWN MAIL.

"The *Mail* will convey 'news from all nations,' particularly those most interesting to our own country, and will be conducted so as to give early and correct information of affairs generally, of political occurrences in the different States, of the rise and fall of American produce in our principal cities, and the prices in foreign markets.

"The political principles of this paper will be as purely Republican as those contained in the Declaration of Independence, and the rights of the people shall be at all times zealously, firmly, and fearlessly supported, whoever may be in power. The establishment is intended to be a permanent one, and as such every endeavor will be used to render it a first-rate country paper deserving of public patronage.

"With regard to the Presidential question which now agitates the whole Union, the *Mail* will decidedly and openly advocate the election of ANDREW JACKSON. And when it is considered that there is only one press in Baltimore, and only one between Baltimore and Cumberland that espouses his cause, it will readily be allowed that in so large an extent of country there is room for at least another, more particularly as all the other presses in this rich and populous county, where he has so many disinterested friends, are against him. The times, too, emphatically demand the establishment of such a press, for at no period of our political history has such *unfair* and *unjustifiable* means been resorted to in order to destroy the character of a public man as have been, within the last year, to injure the well-earned fame of the hero of New Orleans, and merely because he is a candidate before the people for a high and important office, although he was brought out by the people themselves; but the *Mail* will never leave him until he safely arrives at Washington, and receives from the hands of the people the honors justly due to one whose whole life, in peace and in war, has been devoted to his country's liberty, welfare, and happiness.

"*Terms of Subscription.*—For a single paper, three dollars per annum; but this may be discharged by two dollars in *advance*, or two dollars and fifty cents in six months. Persons obtaining ten subscribers, and becoming responsible for the money, shall have a paper *gratis*.

"HAGERSTOWN MAIL, *printed and published by James Maxwell, between the bank and court-house, West Washington Street.*

"The *Hagerstown Mail* will be published every Saturday morning, at three dollars per annum, but this may be discharged by two dollars paid in *advance*, or two dollars and fifty cents in six months. No subscription will be received for less than six months, and no paper discontinued until all arrearages are paid up.

"Advertisements not exceeding one square inserted three weeks for one dollar, longer ones in the same proportion, and twenty-five cents for every subsequent insertion."

The following is an extract from its salutatory editorial:

"And on this day, and in this State, the only surviving signer of that memorable state paper, Charles Carroll of Carrolton, instead of the pen with which he inscribed his name, pledging his life and fortune and sacred honor to the cause of his country's independence, will be seen with spade in hand breaking ground in a great work,—the Baltimore and Ohio Railroad: a work which, from his letter to a citizen of this county, published in this day's paper, he considers as only second in importance, to Maryland, to the Declaration of Independence.

"And on this day another, and, in our estimation, a still greater, a still nobler national work will be commenced,—we mean the Chesapeake and Ohio Canal,—a work which is destined to bind the East and the West in indissoluble ties; a work first patronized by our beloved Washington; a work which through life and until death was with him a favorite public work, and which has at last been rendered certain of completion. It, too, commences this day, and an attempt to revoke and annul the Declaration of Independence would now be as likely to succeed as any efforts to impede the progress of the Chesapeake and Ohio Canal. It will go on."

The paper as first published had six columns to the page, and was well printed on good paper. The news it contained was mainly European, and its columns were well filled with communications upon national politics. The paper immediately secured a wide circulation and a valuable patronage. It was first published in a room of the Indian Queen Tavern, on West Washington Street, a few doors east of the court-house. In 1831, Mr. Maxwell published a number of articles which were distasteful to the proprietors of the paper. His future services were therefore dispensed with, and on the 1st of April in that year Mr. Thomas Kennedy, postmaster of the town, was appointed editor. The printing-office was then removed a few doors farther west on the same street, and from there to South Potomac Street, next door to the post-office. Mr. Kennedy was nominally editor of the paper until Jan. 9, 1835, but the paper was conducted by his son, Dr. Howard Kennedy. In the issue of Nov. 11, 1831, John D. Ott's name appears at the head of the paper as "Printer." On the 9th of January, 1835, John D. Ott and William Weber took control of the paper, and published it under the firm-name of Ott & Weber for many years. In the mean time, when James Maxwell left the *Mail*, he bought up a little literary or neutral paper called the *Courier and Enquirer*, which was published in a building which stood where the *Mail* office now is. He changed its name, and endeavored to keep up an opposition Democratic paper, but it failed in a short time. The next change in the firm was that occasioned by the sale of William Weber's interest to John A. Freaner. The firm then continued for some years to be Ott & Freaner. Mr. Weber is now living in Cumberland, Md., and Mr. Freaner in Oakland, Cal., of which he is a prominent citizen. About the year 1847 or 1848, Mr. Ott sold his interest in the paper to William F. Brannon, and for a time the publishers were Freaner & Brannon. Mr. Brannon left after a short editorship, and became one of the public school teachers of this county. In 1851 he was appointed by Judge Perry auditor of the Circuit Court. After Brannon left the paper it was published by Mr. Freaner alone until 1849, in which year he sold out to John Robinson, who was a brother-in-law of Col. Kunkel, of Frederick. In 1855, Daniel Dechert bought a half interest in the paper, and some time afterwards bought the other half from Mr. Robinson, or rather from Mr. Kunkel, into whose hands it had passed as Mr. Robinson's trustee. In 1856 the first cylinder press, a Hoe, was put into the office. In the night of May 24, 1862, the *Mail* office, then situated at the northwest corner of the square, above J. D. Swartz's present store, was destroyed by a mob. The presses were broken and the type and other materials were destroyed or scattered broadcast in the square. The files of the paper from 1828 were all burned. The mob consisted of a number of men and boys variously estimated from fifty to three hundred, who had been wrought up to a high state of excitement by a report that the First Maryland Regiment of the Federal army had been massacred at the battle of Front Royal, and Col. Kenly had his throat cut. In consequence of this destruction the publication of the *Mail* was suspended for the only time in its career. Publication as a smaller paper was resumed in the fall of 1863, having been stopped about eighteen months.

In December, 1868, the trial of a suit for damages, entered by Daniel Dechert, representing the *Mail*, against the mayor and City Council of Hagerstown, was commenced, and afterwards decided in favor of the plaintiff, the damages being assessed at seven thousand five hundred dollars. The original counsel in the case for plaintiff were Judges Alvey and Motter and Hon. Wm. T. Hamilton. These gentlemen becoming disqualified, they were succeeded as counsel by Hon. Wm. M. Merrick, Z. S. Claggett, H. K. Douglas, and Geo. W. Smith. The defendants were represented by Hon. A. K. Syester and Judge John Thomson Mason. The facts of the riot as testified to by Daniel Dechert, proprietor of the *Mail*, were as follows:

"Daniel Dechert testified that he was the editor and proprietor of the Hagerstown *Mail* in the year 1862; that his printing-office was located on the northwest corner of the public square, in Hagerstown; that on the night of the 24th day of May, 1862, his establishment was destroyed by a mob, and all the printing materials, presses, type, etc., were scattered about and thrown out of the windows, also a large lot of stationery, cards, and paper was destroyed and carried off; his ledger and subscription book were burnt; all his furniture, consisting of two desks, a table, sideboard, lounge, chairs, etc., with a lot of miscellaneous books, were destroyed. That he was paying one hundred and thirty dollars a year rent for the rooms he then occupied for his printing-office; that his printing-office, with all the materials, was worth, in the aggregate, ten thousand dollars, and by the destruction of his books of accounts he sustained a further loss of four thousand dollars, not being able to collect the accounts therein from memory; collected a very small proportion from persons who came and told him that they owed him. On the evening his property was destroyed he was working in his garden, when he was told that there was considerable excitement down street, and that he had better see about his office; that he immediately went down street and found his office-door closed, and thought there was considerable evidence of coming trouble; that he went to see the mayor, Mr. Radcliff, whom he met on the street between five and six o'clock, on said evening, and there told him, the mayor, that there was great apprehension that there would be a riot and destruction of property, and that the property of plaintiff was in danger, and asked that the same should be protected by the authorities of the town; the mayor in reply said that the plaintiff was entitled to no protection whatever, and that he should look to his disloyal articles for protection; that on returning home he called to see Mr. Biershing, and asked him to go and see the mayor and use his influence to have his property protected.

"On cross-examination, he testified that there was considerable excitement in town on the evening before the mob, growing out of a report that a Maryland regiment had been slaughtered in the valley, and that Col. Kenly had his throat cut. There had been threats made frequently before to destroy the office, and had been some demonstrations, and he therefore asked the mayor, in his official capacity, to protect his property on this occasion. That he came to the county in the year 1855, and bought one-half of the Hagerstown *Mail* printing-office for fifteen hundred dollars, and afterwards bought the other half from Mr. Kunkel, at the rate of six thousand dollars for the whole; that he purchased the Hoe power-press in 1856, and afterwards made additions of material to the office from time to time. That the presses in the office at the time of the mob were a power-press worth eighteen hundred dollars, hand-press worth four hundred dollars, and others; that he paid eleven hundred dollars on the power-press, and the balance, seven hundred dollars, was owned by citizens of the county, who held stock in it. The next morning after the mob he went down and undertook to gather some of the material together and save what he could, but was run and chased off by a part of the mob still there. That he thinks it cost three hundred or four hundred dollars to repair the power-press so that he could use it; that he had two other presses, one worth about five hundred dollars, and proof-press worth about fifty dollars. That he left town on Tuesday after the mob, and did not return till June 17th following, and was then warned to leave for his personal safety, and did leave on the 18th. In his absence Mr. Boyd took the office and printed the *Free Press*."

No effective measures appear to have been taken by the town authorities for the suppression of the mob, which is said to have been maddened by intoxicating drink. A short time after the mob of 1862, Charles J. Nesbitt, now of Missouri, purchased a half-interest, and for a while the proprietors were Dechert & Nesbitt. Mr. Dechert again became sole proprietor.

On the 27th of January, 1867, the old Eagle Tavern, which stood on the square and partly occupied the ground now covered by the *Mail* building, took fire and was consumed, together with the *Mail* office. Scarcely anything was saved, and the files from the date of the mob were destroyed with the rest. Owing to the courtesy of the proprietors of the *Herald*, not a single issue was missed by reason of the fire. For four weeks the *Mail*, in rather a diminutive form, was issued from the office of the *Herald*. At the expiration of that time a new office was fitted up in the old Hagerstown Hotel building, nearly opposite the old office, and a new outfit and presses procured. In October, 1866, James Wason purchased a half-interest in the paper. He died on the 14th of August, 1867. On the 9th of August, 1867, a steam-engine was first erected in the *Mail* office. On Oct. 4, 1867, Edwin Bell and Robert Wason (a son of James Wason) each purchased a third-interest in the paper. Several changes followed in quick succession. C. P. Hickes, a member of the bar, was for some years a partner in the firm. In August, 1874, F. J. C. Williams, a member of the bar, who had lately come to Hagerstown from Calvert County, Md., purchased an interest in the business, and since that time Messrs Bell & Williams have been the proprietors and publishers of the paper.

In March, 1880, the *Mail* office was provided with entire new type and new machinery, and made a new departure in the publication of country papers, in that it condensed its matter into the smallest possible space, and while increasing the matter published, decreased the size of the paper. This involved the throwing out of all large type and "display" advertisements. This plan proved successful and popular, and has since been adhered to, and fine book-paper has been used.

The *Mail* is generally regarded as being one of the ablest country papers in the State. Its editorials are well written, outspoken, and aggressive, and its columns are abundantly stocked with the freshest news and carefully-selected miscellany.[1]

Edwin Bell, the senior editor of the *Mail*, is the eldest son of William D. Bell, founder of the Hagerstown *Torch-Light*, now the *Herald and Torch*. W. D. Bell established the old paper at the close of the war of 1812, and Edwin Bell entered his father's office at the age of sixteen years. He studied law in Hagerstown, under the instruction of William Price, and was associated with his father as editor of the *Torch-Light* in 1841, and conducted the paper as sole editor until 1849, when he went to California, and the paper was conducted by his brother-in-law, Judge William Motter, until it was sold to the proprietors of the *Herald of Freedom*. In California, Edwin Bell was connected with the San Francisco *Daily Herald*, published by John Nugent, first as reporter of legislative proceedings, and then as city editor for nearly two years. He resigned this position to become joint editor and proprietor of the San Francisco *Daily Placer*, *Times*, *and Transcript*, with B. F. Washington and Joseph E. Lawrence, with whom he continued for nearly two years, after which, until his retirement from the Pacific coast, he was on the staff of the Sacramento *Daily Union* as general editor. In 1858 he organized, and conducted until the war broke out in 1861, the correspondence by "pony express" and telegraph of the San Francisco *Alta California* and Sacramento *Union*, which thus had a monopoly of Eastern news. In 1867 he purchased a third-interest in the Hagerstown *Mail*, which experienced several changes of proprietors, with the exception of Mr. Bell, who remained in the different firms, and who is now associated with T. J. C. Williams in its publication.

Mr. Bell is a fluent and vigorous writer, and has succeeded in placing the *Mail* in the front rank of Maryland journalism. His influence in the community has always been of a healthy and beneficial character, and he is entitled to great credit for having steadily maintained a high standard of excellence in the matter admitted for publication into the columns of the *Mail*. In politics he has strenuously advocated retrenchment and reform, and has never hesitated to point out party abuses wherever they existed, although at the same time he has been a steady and consistent member of the Democratic organization. In all public enterprises for the promotion of the interests of Hagerstown and of Washington County generally he has always been

[1] Through the courtesy of the proprietors, Messrs. Bell & Williams, the author was enabled to obtain a mass of invaluable historical material from the columns of the *Mail*, which had published from time to time many important contributions to the history of Washington County in general and of Hagerstown in particular. For their kindly efforts to aid him in his work, as well as for the material furnished, the author desires to return his grateful acknowledgments.

among the first to lend a helping hand, and the columns of his paper show that he is keenly alive to all opportunities for development and growth as they present themselves from time to time. He is now in the full vigor of his intellectual faculties, and is one of the most active and energetic citizens of Hagerstown. Mr. Bell's brother, Gen. George Bell, graduated at West Point Military Academy in 1853, and after serving in the West and in Florida was assigned to garrison duty and on the coast survey. During the civil war he served in the Manassas campaign, and was afterwards appointed to a position in the commissary department. In March, 1865, he was made brevet lieutenant-colonel for meritorious service, and subsequently brevet brigadier-general. He now has the rank of major in the regular army, and is chief commissary of the Department of the Missouri, with headquarters at Fort Leavenworth.

Thomas John Chew Williams, junior editor and proprietor of the Hagerstown *Mail*, was born in Calvert County, Md., Aug. 6, 1851. His father, the Rev. Henry Williams, was a native of Hagerstown, of a family which came to that town from South Carolina. He was a clergyman of the Episcopal Church. He left Hagerstown when quite young, and after having parishes in two other counties took charge of All Saints' Parish, Calvert County, of which he was rector for fifteen years, up to his death in 1852. Soon after going to Calvert he married Priscilla Elizabeth Chew, daughter of Col. John H. Chew, who became the mother of T. J. C. Williams and four other sons. Her family, the Chews, have long been prominent in the State, and their lineage is traced back in England for many generations. Chief Justice Benjamin Chew, of Pennsylvania, came from a younger branch of the same family,—the branch which owned the celebrated Chew house, which was stormed at the battle of Germantown. Mrs. Williams was a granddaughter upon her mother's side of the Right Rev. Thomas John Claggett, the first Bishop of Maryland, Delaware, and Kentucky, and the first Episcopal bishop ever consecrated in America. He also came of an English family of great prominence.

Thomas J. C. Williams attended the public schools of Calvert, and for a while Columbian College, Washington, D. C. He left there before his sixteenth year, and at that early age became a teacher in the public schools. While engaged in this occupation he studied law under the direction of his oldest brother, Henry Williams, now agent of the Weems line of steamers in Baltimore, but then practicing law at Prince Frederick, Md. At the age of nineteen he entered the bar, having passed his examination before the late Judge Brent, of the Court of Appeals, and Judge D. R. Magruder. In January, 1872, he removed to Hagerstown, his father's native town, and established himself in the practice of law. In less than a year he had obtained a fair practice, and placed himself in friendly relations with a large number of the leading citizens of the county. In June, 1874, he was married to Cora Martin Maddox, daughter of Dr. Thomas Maddox, one of the best-known and most highly-respected citizens of the county. Miss Maddox was distantly related to Mr. Williams, being, like him, a descendant of Bishop Claggett. A little previous to this Mr. Williams had commenced contributing articles to the Hagerstown *Mail*, and in October, 1874, he purchased a one-third interest in the establishment. For some time he still devoted himself entirely to the law, but in a year or two purchased an additional interest, becoming joint proprietor with his present partner, Edwin Bell. From this time he devoted his whole attention to the paper, managing the business part of the concern with vigor and success, which, with Mr. Bell's rare accomplishments and many years' experience as an editor, placed the paper upon a substantial basis. Mr. Williams is a member of the Episcopal Church, and has been a vestryman for seven or eight years.

The first attempt to start a daily paper in Hagerstown was made in 1873, the projector of the enterprise being M. E. Fectig, a native of the town, who made an arrangement with A. G. Boyd, then editor of the *Free Press*, to use his press and material for the purpose. The paper appeared on the 1st of February, 1873, its adventurous proprietor spending his last nickel to buy candles to assist his first night's work. The *News* was published under many disadvantages by Mr. Fectig for about a month, when, owing to some disagreement with Mr. Boyd, of the *Free Press*, he was compelled to suspend for want of a press and material. Mr. Boyd issued the Hagerstown *Daily* in place of the *News*, Mr. Updegraff being the ostensible editor and proprietor. Mr. Fectig, however, soon made arrangements to continue his paper, and Mr. George H. Nock was taken in as a partner, and a hand-press with barely sufficient type to print the paper was put in the Hoffman building on the public square. A large box was used as an editorial desk, and with two chairs comprised the entire furniture of the room. The paper came out again on February 25th, under the firm-name of Fectig & Nock. It was a twenty-column paper, and has never failed to make its appearance since that time. Its early days were full of trouble, and often the little venture was in danger of being summarily evolved, but it survived all adverse circumstances, and is now firmly established as one of the institutions of the town. In May of the first year of its publication a new press and additional material were purchased from Jacob Bomberger, of Cumberland County, Pa., and the paper was at last placed on its feet. On June 10, 1873, Mr. Fectig retired from the paper, and Mr. Nock became sole editor and proprietor, but in a few days John M. Adams was taken into partnership by Mr. Nock, and the *News* was continued by the firm of Nock & Adams. Upon completing its first volume the *News* was enlarged to a twenty-four-column paper, and the columns were considerably enlarged.

The great panic of 1873 and 1874 was cleverly weathered by the enterprise and sagacity of the management of the *News*, and, although a little crippled, it came out with fair prospects for future success, which have been fully realized. On July 19, 1875, Mr. Nock retired from the *News*, disposing of his interest to W. S. Herbert, a native of Hagerstown, and a descendant of the founder of the *Spy*, and the paper was published by Adams & Herbert. In October, 1880, the *News* was enlarged to a twenty-eight-column paper, its present size. On Sept. 1, 1881, Mr. Herbert retired from the paper, disposing of his interest to Peter A. Witmer, and the present proprietors of the paper publish it under the firm-name of P. A. Witmer & Co. It is the only morning daily in the town, and commands a generous patronage. The *News* is edited with tact and discretion, and is a remarkably bright and enterprising journal, representing most creditably the community for which it is printed. Its contents are fresh and varied, and its editorials always thoughtful and well considered.

Peter Augustus Witmer, its chief editor and proprietor, was born March 28, 1834, in the Clear Spring District of Washington County, Md. His paternal ancestor, Benjamin Witmer, emigrated from the canton of Berne, in Switzerland, in 1716, and settled in the Conestoga Valley, Lancaster County, Pa. In 1805 his great-grandfather, Henry Witmer, moved from Lancaster County, Pa., to Washington County, and bought property on the Beaver and Conococheague Creeks. In 1820 his father, John Witmer, married Rosanna Brewer (formerly written Brua), of a family of Huguenot extraction, which was one of the largest and most influential in the western portion of Washington County. His father died in 1847, at the age of forty-eight, leaving a widow and six children,—four sons and two daughters,—Peter A. being the second son.

On the death of his father he was placed in a country store, where he remained two years, and then attended the Clear Spring Academy for one year. During the following year he taught school in the neighborhood of his home, after which he again attended school at Williamsport for nearly two years. On leaving school he returned to his former occupation of teaching. In 1856 he accepted a position as

P. A. Witmer

tutor in a private family in Prince George's County, Md. While thus occupied he read law with the late Judge Samuel H. Berry, of that county, but before being admitted to the bar he returned to Washington County, in 1859, and engaged in farming and teaching. In 1862 he was nominated by the Democratic party as a candidate for the Legislature, but was defeated. In 1866 he removed to Hagerstown, and entered the law-office of Hon. William T. Hamilton. In 1867 he married Mary Kate, second daughter of John A. K. Brewer, and was admitted to the Hagerstown bar at the March term of court, 1868. In May, 1868, he was appointed secretary and treasurer of the board of public school commissioners and examiner of public schools for Washington County, which office he still holds, having been reappointed for seven successive terms. In 1872 he was appointed a member of the State board of education by Governor Whyte. He has been reappointed by successive Governors, and still holds the office. On the 1st of September, 1881, he became joint proprietor and editor with J. W. Adams, of the Hagerstown *News*, a daily and weekly paper. Mr. Witmer has two sons, aged respectively thirteen and four, and a daughter aged eleven. He is a member of the Lutheran Church, and his family are connected with the same denomination. His public life is best known in connection with, and has been most closely identified with, State and county educational work. He has been secretary of the Agricultural and Mechanical Association of Washington County since 1870. He is a member and Grand Vice-Dictator of the Grand Lodge, Knights of Honor, of Maryland, and a member of the Grand Council, Royal Arcanum, of Maryland.

Mr. Witmer ranks among the foremost educators in Maryland, and is a thoroughly progressive and enterprising man. He is a sound scholar, and having had considerable experience in teaching, knows exactly what should be done in order to accomplish the most desirable educational results. He enjoys the additional advantage of being a forcible and interesting speaker, and is thus enabled to emphasize his opinions, and to draw to himself that outside help and co-operation which are indispensable to the successful prosecution of his work. Mr. Witmer is possessed of fine business capacity and great executive ability. When Mr. Witmer was first appointed the task before him was an exceedingly difficult one. Party spirit ran high, and there was doubt and discontent on every hand. He was, however, the man for the emergency. He examined all the teachers, visited all the schools, talked with the leading men in all their districts and enlisted their aid, restored the finances to a proper condition, and finally succeeded in putting the school system of the county upon a permanent and prosperous basis. New school-houses sprang up in every election district; competent teachers took the place of those who had failed to give satisfaction; the country schools were systematized according to a schedule of graded work; and the old Hagerstown Academy, which for years had been dragging out a feeble and uncertain existence, was remodeled as a county high school. Although he was obliged to combat old prejudices and to advocate new theories, he soon acquired the sympathy and respect of the teachers, the approval of the school commissioners, and the confidence of the public. So great has been Mr. Witmer's success that there are now very few private schools of a primary grade in Washington County, the public schools being of such a character as to render private schools superfluous. As a member of the State board of education his influence has been as marked and as potent for good as it has been in the county school board, and his intimate practical knowledge of the working of the system was of great assistance to the State board in the important and difficult task of enacting by-laws for the uniform administration of the school law. His thorough knowledge of law and clear judgment have found full scope and exercise in the decision of many important and intricate cases which were brought before the board for adjustment. No decision of the board has as yet been reversed by a court of law. Few men as young as Mr. Witmer, and in his line of work, have made so good a record, or can look forward to a future so full of promise.

The *Globe* job printing-office was established by Ira W. Hays in November, 1876, and continued to be a job office merely, with frequent increases in the facilities of the office, until February, 1879, when a daily evening paper was attempted. At first the paper was printed upon a treadle press, but the encouragement proving so liberal, steam was at once supplied. In May, 1879, the *Weekly Globe* was started under the same proprietorship and in connection with the *Daily Evening Globe*. In May, 1880, the daily was enlarged to a twenty by thirty folio, which it still retains. Both publications are independent in all things except politics, and in that they are neutral.

The *Globe* is a bright, spicy paper, and has contributed largely to the advancement of the material interests of Hagerstown and of Washington County generally. It is very enterprising in gathering news, which it presents in attractive shape, and its columns are always filled with interesting matter.

One of the best-known printers and journalists of Western Maryland was Overton C. Harne, who died on Jan. 13, 1873, at his home on the Williamsport pike, at the ripe age of ninety-two years and three months. Mr. Harne was born near Elk Ridge Landing. His family was of old Revolutionary stock, his father having fought as an officer in the Continental army. When an infant he was left to the care of Robert Johnson, tobacco inspector at Elk Ridge Landing, who sent him at an early age to the printing office of the Baltimore *American*. After serving his apprenticeship on the *American* he went to Winchester, Va. He did not remain there long, and after his return to Maryland lived with John Thomas, the father of ex-Governor Francis Thomas. He married a daughter of Rev. Jonathan Forrest and removed to Frederick City, where he published for a year the *Republican Citizen*, in connection with Matthias Bartyn. In 1812 he was connected with the *Federal Gazette* and the *Republican Gazette*. He afterwards removed to Pipe Creek, taught school, and as deputy sheriff, took the census; being engaged in all these occupations at one time.

He was the man who arrested the negro who

murdered Mrs. Baker, a crime which excited the whole of Western Maryland for a long time. As a lieutenant he was engaged in the defense of Baltimore, being the only man of his company, formed at New Union, who went to the defense of the city. He was honorably discharged on Chinquapin Hill and returned to Hauver District, and became a junior judge of the District Court, justice of the peace, etc. He raised seven sons and one daughter. All of his children, except one son, live in Washington County.

CHAPTER XLIX.

SCHOOLS AND LIBRARIES.

THE first school-teacher engaged in active educational efforts in Washington County was the Rev. Bartholomew Booth, who taught school in the county as early as 1776–77. In 1779 he was especially authorized by the Legislature to teach and preach the gospel, and to teach and educate youth in any public or private school. At that time he resided on the banks of the Antietam at his home, which was known as Delamere, or "Booth's Mills," and was about a half-mile from what is now Breathedsville, on the Washington County Branch of the Baltimore and Ohio Railroad. This property is still in possession of the descendants of this illustrious man. Mr. Booth had come over to this country from England as early as 1770. In 1754 he was a member of the University of Oxford. He was ordained deacon by Edmund Keene, Bishop of Chester, in 1755, and was ordained a minister in July, 1758, and on the same day licensed curate in charge of the chapel of Marple, and the next day an adjunct curate in the chapel of Derby. He removed to Washington County, then a part of Frederick County, in the early part of 1776, and settled at Delamere, at which place he remained up to the time of his death, which occurred Sept. 13, 1785. His county-seat, where also was his school, contained nearly eleven hundred and fifty acres Previous to his removal to Washington County he had been residing in Annapolis, and it is supposed for a short time in Georgetown, D. C., and in Virginia. His fame as a teacher appears to have been very great, and his school was patronized by some of the most prominent men of the historic days in which he lived, and he was in frequent communication with them.[1]

No record appears to have been kept of the early history of education in Hagerstown, and until the publication of the first paper—the *Spy*, in 1790—

[1] Among the letters which have been preserved which he received during his first years at Delamere were the following, the first one from Robert Morris, the first Secretary of the Treasury:

"YORK IN PENNSYLVANIA, Nov. 25, 1777.

"SIR,—The high reputation you have acquired by your institution for the education of youth must naturally create a desire in many parents to have their sons admitted into so promising a seminary, and I am amongst the number of those who admire your character and wish my son to partake the advantages of instruction from so accomplished a gentleman.

"I expect none but the customary terms, and without inquiring what those are I shall readily comply with them. My child reads and writes English tolerably for a boy not yet eight years old; he is just entering on Latin with a master in this place, but we are at a loss for school books, as none are now in the shops for sale. I shall write to Europe for some, as soon as possible. Understanding that you limit the number of scholars, I address you now to know if my son can be admitted, and if he can, I will bring or send him as soon as convenient. With respect and esteem, I remain, sir, your obed't humble servant,

"ROBT. MORRIS.

"To BOOTH, ESQ., Near Frederick Town, Md."

The following is from a medical man holding a high position in the Revolutionary army, and a relative—either father or brother—of the wife of Benedict Arnold, who was a Miss Shippen:

"PHILADELPHIA, May 29, 1779.

"SIR,—From the character you bear, and the very favorable account I have had from some of my friends of your plan of education, I have been very anxious to have my son admitted to a share of your instruction, but till lately have had no expectation of it, from a belief that your number of pupils was complete. However, on consulting with Mr. Robert Morris and Mr. Purviance, I have reason to expect there is still a vacancy, and they both encourage and advise me to send my son by this opportunity. Relying, therefore, on their recommendation and opinion that he will not be rejected, I take the liberty of sending him in company with Gen. Arnold's son and a son of Col. Plater, and at the same time have inclosed in a bundle in my son's trunk the like sum of money which other gentlemen have agreed to pay you. I hope, sir, you will have no difficulty in taking him. His age is about thirteen, and considering the unfavorable state of the times he has made some progess in his learning. If I am not partial you will find him a boy of good dispositions and easily controlled. I am told you have sent a bond to the other gentlemen. I am, sir, with much respect, your most obed't humble servant, EDW. SHIPPEN."

Another of later date was from the traitor Arnold. The handwriting is very distinct, although now darkened by age, and its execution is remarkably precise. It reads as follows:

"PHILADA, May 25th 1779.

"DEAR SIR

"Being in daily expectation of sending my Sons to you, has prevented my answering your favor of the 2d April before; I am extremely happy in Commiting the Care of their Education to a gentleman so universally Esteem'd, and admired, not in the heart doubting your Care and attention to them in every particular. Let me beg of you my Dear Sir to treat them in the same manner as you would your own; when they deserve Correction, I wish not to have them spared. They have been for sometime in this City which is a bad School, and my Situation has prevented my paying that attention to them I otherwise should have done. If they have Contracted any bad Habits no traces of the methods or means of mental and mechanical instruction in the town can be found. In 1791, Miss Ann Rawlings had a school in which she taught children "reading, sewing, flowering, marking, and open work," and Mr. Spicer taught "the rules and practice of vocal music" in the court-house on Thursdays and Fridays in the afternoon. There were other schools in Hagerstown, and probably a free school of some sort, but of them there has been left no record, and these are the first two teachers of the town mentioned. Two years later, in 1793, Mr. and Mrs. Jones came from Annapolis and opened a boarding-school for young ladies, in which were taught

"Reading, writing, and arithmetic, Tambour and Dresden, English, and French embroidery, drawing and painting in water colors, geography, filigree and riband work, plain and colored needle-work of all kinds, instrumental music, seed, shell, and paper-work." Mr. Jones taught in a separate house a few "gentlemen, English grammar, reading, writing, arithmetic, and book-keeping."

In September, 1795, an academy for the education of young men was opened, in which the various branches of science and literature were taught by the president, Mr. McDonald, and his assistants. The thirst for knowledge in Hagerstown seems to have grown wonderfully after this, for it justified Mr. Barrett in establishing, in October of the same year, a school for the special instruction in "that agreeable and necessary branch of learning,—French." O. H. Williams was his assistant, and in a public announcement he refers his students to the firm of Ogle & Hael for such books as they would need. "The Academy" appears to have been very successful, and to have commanded the respect and admiration of the *Spy*, for on December 24th, in giving an account of the public examination held by President McDonald, that paper used the following complimentary language:

"The young gentlemen were eminently distinguished for the proficiency and knowledge they discovered in the different branches of their education since the commencement of their instructions. The general satisfaction they have given the visitors, as well as examinators, in the pertinency and propriety of their answers to the various questions of their examination, sufficiently indicates the justness of their claim to merit, and gives an early presage of their future success in those studies which are either necessary or ornamental."

An announcement was soon afterwards made that Thomas Grieves would open an evening school at "The Academy," for the instruction of such young gentlemen as could not conveniently attend day lectures, in writing, arithmetic, and merchants' accounts. The hours of instruction were from seven to nine o'clock, and this, the first night-school of Hagerstown, was opened on Jan. 18, 1796. There was also an English teacher—Thomas Kirby—at that time in Hagerstown, who apparently was successful, for he advertises for an assistant to teach the rudiments of English.

On the 1st of January, 1796, Mrs. Levy announced that she had opened a boarding-school for the reception and instruction of young ladies in every branch of useful and ornamental "needle-work, tambouring, with the art and elegancy of shading and taste in the arrangement of patterns." She designed the work and executed the drawings herself without additional expense. Mrs. Levy did not, however, confine herself to teaching needle-work alone, but gave instruction in reading and writing.

Mr. Grieves' night-school must have given him a firm hold upon the confidence of the people, for, in September, 1796, he opened a day-school, and declined to take more than twenty pupils, to whom he gave lessons in French, English, the classics, and writing. It is probable that Mr. Kirby did not remain long at the English school which he established, for on October 5th an advertisement appeared in the *Spy* announcing that a schoolmaster was wanted im-

---

they are not of a long standing, and I make no doubt under your Care they will soon forget them. I wish their Education To be useful rather and learned. Life is too Short and uncertain to throw away in speculation on subjects that perhaps only one Man in Ten thousand has a genius to make a figure in,—you will pardon my dictating to you, Sir, but as the Fortunes of every Man in this Country are uncertain I wish my Sons to be Educated in such a Manner that with prudence and Industry they may acquire a Fortune (in Case they are deprived of their Patrimony) as well as to become useful Members of Society.

"My Taylor has disappointed me and sent home their cloths unfinished I am therefore under the necessity of sending them undone or detaining the Waggon, I cannot think of doing the latter and must beg the favor of you to procure their cloths finished and some new ones made out of my old ones. I must beg you to purchase any little matters necessary for them I have Inclosed three hundred Dollars for their use out of which you will please to give as much to spend as you think Proper, with this Condition that they render to you a Regular account as often as you think necessary of their Expenses, a Copy of which I shall expect they will transmit to me, this will teach them Economy, and Methord so necessary in allmost every thing in Life.

"If there is any Books wanting I beg you to purchase them, and whenever you are in want of money to Draw on me.

"I shall expect they will write me frequently—of this they will doubtless want reminding.

"I have the honor to be with great Respect and Esteem

"Dear Sir

"Your most obedient

"Humble Serv't

"B Arnold

"Rev'd Mr. Booth"

Other letters are preserved written to him by Gen. Chas. Lee and Mrs. Hannah Washington.

mediately, and that any one willing to engage would meet with liberal encouragement. The president of the school board, George Smucker, and the trustees, Jacob Harry, Frederick Alder, and John and Jas. Geiger, stated that the candidate for the place must furnish testimonials of good moral character, but that they will be the judges of his ability.

The advertisement was signed by Jacob Shryock. In November, Mr. Grieves, in connection with his day-school, again opened a night-school, in announcing which he said he

"hopes none may apply but such as will conduct themselves with propriety and decent deportment. Impressed with gratitude for the favors he has already received, he trusts it will ever remain a first object of his ambition, by advancing the literary and moral improvement of his pupils, to deserve the public confidence."

There is a gap in the history of the schools after 1795, and P. Edwards' English school, established in May, 1798, is the first mentioned after the former year. Mrs. Levy seems to have been quite successful with her mental and industrial school, for she continued it after 1794, and is mentioned by the paper and in several private records in very flattering language. A new French teacher, Boiseau, had taken the place of Mr. Barrett in 1798. In April of that year Mr. Edwards removed his school to the house formerly occupied by Mr. Hoover, on Main Street. In September, 1799, Mrs. Ragan announced that she would open a school for the instruction of young ladies in needle-work at the two-story brick house belonging to Mrs. Heyser, on Main Street. She was particular to mention that if any young ladies applied she would find suitable accommodations at her house for board.

In the early part of 1800 the first attempt was made to found a seminary for higher education, and a subscription-paper was circulated for the purpose of raising the necessary funds. The *Maryland Herald*, which had succeeded the old *Spy*, strongly indorsed and advocated the movement, Mr. Grieves, the editor of the paper, having been, as we have seen, a teacher in the town himself.

It was maintained that such an institution was a positive necessity; that it would attract a large number of students from abroad, who would give tone and standing to the town and enlarge its fame and fortune; that it would enable the young men of Hagerstown to obtain a full education without being subjected to the temptations and dangers of school life far away from home, and that the establishment of such a school would be an inducement to wealthy people, who had children to educate, to move in the neighborhood and settle in and about the town. The effort was, however, unsuccessful, and the Hagerstown youths for ten years more obtained all their home instruction through the medium of private schools and the Hagerstown Grammar School, which was under the direction of William L. Kelley, and the trusteeship of Col. Nathaniel Rochester,—the postmaster of the town,—P. Miller, and D. Heister. P. Edwards was still one of the instructors of the town at this time, carrying on both a day and night-school. There was also a school maintained by the Lutheran Church. It does not appear that there were any other schools in the town except these. In March, 1802, J. Hisshen announced that he had opened a school, in which he would teach the English branches, mathematics, etc., and would charge for readers, three dollars per quarter; for writers, three dollars and a half; and for arithmeticians, four dollars. In April following L. Blaire, who was acting under the advice of "prominent gentlemen," published a prospectus of his "institution of learning," which he had established at the house of Col. Rochester, about a quarter of a mile from Hagerstown. This was the first attempt to establish a classical school in Hagerstown, and Mr. Blaire's announcement was that he would teach Greek, Latin, English, and French. It was stated that the number of scholars would be limited unless such a number were obtained as to enable him to employ an usher. Mr. Blaire also offered to take as boarders a few boys, the conditions of boarding to be ascertained "by sending him a letter free of postage." He had taught two years at the academy of Lower Marlborough, Calvert County.

While these efforts were being made to train the minds of the young people of Hagerstown, their deportment was not neglected. A Frenchman named Gabaude was the first dancing-master of Washington County, and modestly announced in the *Maryland Herald* of May 5, 1802, the opening of his dancing-school at Col. Daniel Hughes' country-seat at Antietam Forge. In July, 1803, D. Hartshorne announced to the ladies and gentlemen of Hagerstown, through the advertising columns of the *Herald*, that he would open a school at Mrs. Jonathan Hager's long room, for the purpose of instructing them in the rules of dancing and other graceful deportments which are ornamental to society. He also proposed to devote three hours on the days of his tuition in teaching vocal music. This was some weeks after James Robardet had made a similar announcement.

From 1803 until 1806 the names of the following teachers appear as giving mental instruction to the students of the town: Samuel B. Davis, L. Blaire, J.

Hisshen, Mrs. Mahony, P. C. Young, John A. Coburn. In 1807 the Hagerstown Library Company was formed, being a subscription stock company.

The names of the following teachers appear as having been engaged in educational efforts in Hagerstown from 1815 to 1820: Mrs. Ashcum, John L. Beall, P. Edwards, James Kay, Uriah Kitchen, J. McCall, E. McLaughlin, John McClurg, E. B. Mendenhall, Mrs. Ann Rawlins, Aaron P. Rea, Maxwell Welch, Patrick Devine, Edward Bennett, D. C. Roscoe.

In the spring of 1822, Dr. Horwitz, who had made a great reputation in teaching Hebrew, paid a visit to Hagerstown and gave some lessons. It was claimed that he gave his pupils a critical and grammatical knowledge of Hebrew in thirty lessons of one hour each, which a writer in the *Maryland Herald* said he would be inclined to doubt if it were not for the many certificates which he brought with him.

Hagerstown Academy.—In 1810 the attempt to establish an academy for higher education was revived. On May 15th a meeting was held, at which Dr. Richard Pindell was chairman, and Elie Williams secretary. The meeting was addressed by Samuel Hughes, who detailed the advantages to be derived from an institution of this character. After which the following gentlemen were appointed by the chairman to carry the object of the meeting into effect: John T. Mason, John Bowles, William Yates, Thomas Brent, John Ragan, Sen., Matthias Shaffner, Upton Lawrence, John Kennedy, Otho H. Williams, Alexander Neill, Dr. F. Dorsey, Robert Hughes, Dr. Frisby Tilghman, Samuel Ringgold, Jacob Towson, John Ashbury, Benjamin Tyson, John Brien, Dr. Claggett, and Henry Locher. The committee had obtained up to September 8th three thousand seven hundred dollars, at which time Samuel Ringgold, O. H. Williams, Frederick Dorsey, Upton Lawrence, and John Ragan were appointed a special committee to inquire as to the best site, and to prepare plans, etc., for the building. In December the Legislature passed an act incorporating the academy, and the following incorporators were by the act made the trustees of the institution: Richard Pindell, John T. Mason, Samuel Ringgold, Samuel Hughes, Jr., Charles Carroll, Upton Lawrence, Frisby Tilghman, Otho H. Williams, Moses Tipps, William Huyser, John Kennedy, John Harry, Jacob Zeller, Christian Hager, John J. Stull, Jacob Schnebly, Thomas B. Hall, John Ragan, Sr., Matthias Shaffner, Alexander Neill, and Frederick Dorsey. The capital stock was placed at six thousand dollars, divided into twelve hundred equal shares. On Jan. 29, 1811, the trustees elected the following officers: O. H. Williams, president; William Hughes, secretary; Thomas B. Hall, treasurer. Subscription books were opened at George Beltzhoover's early in March, 1811. A sufficient amount of stock had been subscribed to go on with the enterprise, the subscriptions being made payable in four equal installments of twenty per cent. each, the first twenty per cent. being paid in cash. A site was selected on a pleasant eminence near the town, and on the spot where the present academy now stands. The erection of the building was not rapid. The last installment of the capital stock was not called in until May 10, 1812, and the academy was not finished until a year afterwards, when Thomas B. Hall, the secretary, made the announcement in the public print that the institution was completed in a capacious and handsome manner, calculated for the reception of at least one hundred and fifty scholars, and that the patronage rendered the institution "will enable the trustees to grant liberal salaries to professors in the different branches of education, which it is deemed best by them at this time to have adopted and taught." They solicited applications for the situation of a president, a teacher of the Latin and Greek languages, and a teacher of the English language, mathematics, and geography; "the known healthiness of this country," continues the secretary, "the local situation of the academy, and the reasonable price of board, etc., must offer great inducements to professors, as well as to parents and guardians, to select this place as one highly eligible for the purposes of education. Applications to fill the above stations in the academy may be made by letter to me in Hagerstown."

After the academy had been put in operation the following legislation was passed in regard to it. In 1811 the Legislature directed the treasurer of the Western Shore to pay $800 annually to the Hagerstown Academy. Two years later permission was granted this academy to hold a lottery to raise a sum not exceeding $10,000. In 1816 the Legislature passed a bill directing the treasurer to pay the Levy Courts of Frederick, Washington, and Allegany Counties their proportion of the school fund. This fund was created by act of Assembly in 1812. A supplement to the act of 1810 was passed in 1818 providing for the sale of part of the real estate of the Hagerstown Academy, and in 1819 an act to enable the trustees to acknowledge conveyances of any real estate. In 1825 Hagerstown Academy was included among those schools declared by the Legislature to have forfeited their donations, but in 1826 a bill was passed for the relief of the academy.

The first academic year commenced on June 7, 1813. One of the departments was a military school, in which William Robertson instructed the pupils in the use of the sword and the manual of arms, and James Robaudet taught fencing with the short sword and cutlass. The corporation continued to be kept alive by annual meetings of the stockholders in March and the election of a board of trustees, of which for a number of years O. H. Williams was president. A lottery scheme was organized, and successfully carried out in 1814, to help the institution out of financial difficulty, and the following gentlemen were engaged in the enterprise: O. H. Williams, William Fitzhugh, Sr., Frisby Tilghman, John Buchanan, Jacob Schnebly, Thomas Buchanan, Thomas B. Hall, and Upton Lawrence. Among the professors during the first years of its existence was Daniel McCurtin, of Baltimore, who taught belles-lettres after June, 1814. It is a matter of record that Mrs. Philbern was engaged by O. H. Williams, who was the first president of the academy, to superintend the household department, that John N. Smith succeeded Mr. Irving as principal, and Cyrus Blood was engaged to take charge of the English department in the early part of 1819, but Mr. Smith died in July, 1819, and Andrew Craig, of Long Island, was chosen to take his place.

In 1820, Daniel Wilson succeeded Mr. Craig, and under his management the tuition per quarter was six dollars; boarding and washing per quarter, thirty-one dollars and fifty cents. The State some time after this made appropriations to the institution to the amount of eight hundred dollars per year, and thus assumed a *quasi* control. In 1828, when W. A. Abbot was at the head of the classical department, there were about thirty classical students. It became an institution of considerable fame, and could boast with truth that it had graduated some of the most distinguished men in Western Maryland. After about 1855, however, it began to decay, and in 1867 the building was discarded as being little more than an unsightly mass of bricks and other useful building material. It was situated west of what is now Walnut Street, and south of the present depot. The old building remained standing until 1877. Efforts had been made to establish and sustain a private academy for years under the management of the trustees, but the academical fund having been transferred, by act of the Legislature in 1864, to the board of school commissioners, the school languished, became involved in debt, was finally sold on May 1, 1877, and purchased by the school commissioners for six thousand dollars. The old academy building was at once torn down, and the present handsome Washington County High School was erected in its place, and on Sept. 1, 1877, the institution was opened under the management of the board of school commissioners. Prof. R. S. Henry was chosen principal, and under his direction, in spite of opposition, the school soon won the favor of the people of the county. For four years Prof. Henry devoted his energies to the building up of the school, and before he retired had the satisfaction of seeing all his opponents forced to acknowledge the school a complete success. Prof. Henry resigned the position of principal at the close of the school year of 1880–81, and George A. Harter, A.M., a native of Washington County, was chosen his successor. The prospects of the school are excellent. The number in attendance at the High School is now larger than ever before, there being fifty-four pupils enrolled as high-school pupils.

Hagerstown Charity School.—In 1815, Miss Isabella Neill, of Hagerstown, while in Philadelphia became deeply interested in the "Ragged Schools" which had been established there, and which were doing so much for the education of the destitute. Free schools were then unknown, and she determined to attempt the establishment of a charity-school at Hagerstown. Three other ladies, Misses Susan Hughes, Jane Milligan, and Betsy Harry, joined her in her benevolent undertaking, and "a school for the education of poor children" was soon in active operation. The first officers were elected on the 14th of January, 1815, as follows: President, Susan Hughes; Treasurer, Isabella Neill; Secretary, Rebecca Fitzhugh; Managers, Betsy Harry, M. Humrickhouse, Maria Sprigg, Jane Milligan, Eliza Schnebly and Jane Herbert.

The first trustees were Rev. J. C. Clay, John Kennedy, and Alexander Neill. The school was opened with twenty-five pupils. The report of the managers for the first year showed that the receipts had been, from ladies, $395; from gentlemen, $278; from the Masonic lodge, $50. Total, $723. The expenses were: for teachers, $300; for clothing, $199.90; stationery, $16.50; rent, $20: sundries, $8. Total, $557. During the year thirty children had been thus instructed and taken care of. At first the ladies taught the children themselves, but as their work began to be appreciated by the public contributions flowed in, and they were enabled to hire a room in the back building of a house still standing on North Potomac Street, and employ a teacher. A sermon on behalf of the charity was preached in some one of the churches every year, and a subscription was taken up for its benefit. Singing societies also gave concerts in its behalf, and efforts of various kinds were made to increase its funds. In 1827 a statement was made showing that the institution had educated for the thirteen years of its existence between thirty and fifty pupils each year.

The managers then, as now, were two from each church. For many years two of the ladies met the children at the school-room on Sunday morning and proceeded with them to church. The children were neatly attired, and wore blue bonnets and capes. In 1818 the school was incorporated; thus being enabled to receive legacies and funds from its friends. In 1832, Miss Susan Hughes left it a legacy of three hundred dollars. Since then it has received the following bequests, viz.: 1833, by Mrs. Dr. Martin, $50; 1835, Hugh Kennedy, $100; 1838, Dr. Young, $100; 1842, Martin Hammond, $1700, which was applied to the erection of a school building; 1850, Mrs. Pott, $200; 1852, Mrs. Tutwiler, $50; 1856, Mrs. Dr. Reynolds, $100; 1861, Victor Thompson, $1000. The last legacy was bequeathed by Samuel Eichelberger, and amounts to $74. These legacies have been invested, and the school is supported by the income derived from them. From the books it appears that over two thousand children have been educated by this noble charity. The present teacher, Miss Eliza Keller, has had charge of the school for a number of years. The children are taught spelling, reading, writing, arithmetic, geography, and plain sewing. Two of the ladies visit the school once a week to instruct the children in needle-work, and the garments made by them are given to the needy ones.

Washington County Public Schools.—There is no history of the public schools of Washington County previous to the organization of the free public schools under the act of the General Assembly of 1865, known as the Van Bokkelen system. Under this act the free public school system of Washington County was organized July 11, 1865, with Thomas A. Boullt as president, Albert Small, secretary and treasurer, and the following board of commissioners: Samuel I. Piper, John J. Hershey, John A. Miller, John S. Hedding, Peter S. Newcomer, Joseph Garver, and Jacob Funk. The number of teachers for the fiscal year ending June 30, 1866, was 118,—schools open seven and a half months; number of different pupils for the year, 6689. There was no county levy, the revenue derived from the State being $25,203.04. The school law was changed by the Legislature of 1868, and under it a new board of school commissioners was appointed by the county commissioners, consisting of one member from each election district, as follows: Moses Poffenberger, Dr. Jerry Johnson, George W. Smith, Sr., John D. Houck, Warford Mann, Dr. A. Will Lakin, Edward Ingraham, George W. Brown, Edward Smith, Jacob Fiery, Warren Garrott, Mr. Jones, F. T. Spickler, Charles Hitechen, James Cullen, and Henry Eakle.

This board met and organized on the 5th of May, 1868. George W. Smith, Sr., was elected president, and Peter A. Whitmer, secretary, treasurer, and examiner. For that year the receipts were, from the county levy $26,500, and from other sources $62,832; total receipts, $88,332. The expenditures were $85,832, of which amount $26,505 was for the erection of new houses. There were employed 138 teachers, and the number of different pupils was 8352.

The board, composed of members elected by the people, was reorganized under this law on the 1st of January, 1870, with Jacob Fiery as president, and Peter A. Witmer as secretary, treasurer, and examiner.

The law was again changed by the Legislature of 1870, which authorized the Circuit Court to appoint the members of the several boards in the counties of their respective circuits. Under this law the court appointed as commissioners for Washington County Dr. William Ragan, Thomas H. Crampton, Henry S. Eavey, B. A. Garlinger, and William B. McLain, who met and organized on Jan. 2, 1872, by electing Dr. William Ragan president, and P. A. Witmer, secretary, treasurer, and examiner. This organization is still maintained, with the exception of Thomas H. Crampton, who retired in January, 1880, and was succeeded by Dr. William S. Stonebraker. The following are the statistics for 1880: Receipts from State, $22,731; from county, $36,487; total from all sources, $60,656; number of school-houses, 129; number of teachers, 179; number of different pupils, 8822; average attendance, 5396,—schools open seven and a half months; value of school property, $140,000. In 1877 the board purchased, at a cost of six thousand dollars, the building erected by the Hagerstown Academy trustees, with ten acres of ground attached, and converted it into a county high school. The building is eligibly located on a commanding position in the western section of the town, between the Western Maryland, Cumberland Valley, and Shenandoah Valley Railroads. Since the organization of the high school it has been under the charge of Professor R. S. Henry. During the past year there has been at the institution an average attendance of thirty-five pupils, eight of whom graduated in June last. In the county there are eighteen graded schools, having from two to ten teachers each. The average cost per pupil in average attendance at the public schools in the county for the year 1880 was three dollars and thirty-three cents per term, or ten dollars per year, which statistics show to be the lowest in the State.

HAGERSTOWN SEMINARY,

MARYLAND.

Hagerstown Female Seminary.—This institution was projected and built by the Maryland Synod of the Evangelical Lutheran Church. Trustees were chosen and a charter was obtained from the Legislature of Maryland, and the first scholastic session was commenced in September, 1853. The first class was graduated in June, 1857. Rev. Mr. Baughman was the first principal, and had charge of the school for nearly seven years. He was succeeded by Rev. W. Eyster, who remained in charge for two terms of three years each. Between the two terms Rev. Ch. Martin, A.M., was principal for three years. After Mr. Eyster's second term, Rev. J. McCron, D.D., became principal for three years. In June, 1875, Rev. C. L. Keedy, A.M., M.D., the present able principal, took control. In consequence of heavy liabilities incurred in the building and management of the institution, Messrs. C. W. Humrickhouse and J. C. Bridges purchased the property and paid off its indebtedness in 1865. A few years after this Mr. Humrickhouse became sole owner and proprietor, until April 1, 1878, when the present principal purchased it, and has continued to improve it until it has become one of the most beautiful and attractive places in any of the Middle States. The seminary stands upon a commanding eminence just east of Hagerstown, from which may be had a magnificent view of hill and dale and of the town outstretched below. The main edifice is an imposing brick structure, four stories in height, and built in the Romanesque style. There are three wings of equal height with the main building. The grounds, comprising an area of eleven acres, are thickly set with upwards of one hundred handsome evergreens, and about five hundred trees of other varieties. Choice shrubbery marks in graceful lines numerous picturesque divisions of the inclosure, and over the entire surface is spread a bright carpet of rich green-sward. Near the seminary stands the residence of the president, a handsome brick edifice. Under the administration of President Keedy the seminary has continued to be a widely-known and flourishing school. Since its foundation it has received upwards of two thousand pupils and graduated one hundred and fifty. In 1881 the whole number of pupils was one hundred and ten; the graduates, thirteen; and the boarders, sixty. The curriculum of the institution is practical and thorough rather than showy and superficial, provided parents allow their daughters to remain sufficiently long to be graduated. The study of one ancient and one modern language, a complete knowledge of all the English branches, together with some degree of musical culture, are required before a diploma is given. The library, literary society, and athenæum are valuable and highly appreciated adjuncts to the seminary. The Hagerstown *Seminary Monthly*, founded in 1876, and conducted solely by the pupils, under the supervision of the president, is a prosperous and profitable element in the course of practical experience sought to be developed by the school. The library and apparatus are complete, and the furniture of the buildings is modern and neat in appearance. The school deservedly enjoys a high reputation, and is in a very flourishing condition.

Linden Seminary is comparatively a young institution, having been established in 1878, and was at first known as "Hagerstown Select School," but the name was changed in 1880, since when it has been known as Linden Seminary. It is a strictly private institution, governed and controlled by D. M. Long, the principal. Its beginning was not a favorable one, and the first year it had only nine scholars. The president now congratulates himself on the fact that its roll contains the names of seventy-four students. It is pleasantly situated on South Potomac Street. The institution is intended to be a preparatory school for students who intend completing a collegiate course, but a great many of the pupils are engaged in such studies as they select themselves, without regard to a collegiate course.

The Hagerstown Lyceum, a joint-stock company, was chartered by the Legislature of Maryland on the 5th of February, 1848, and was organized on the 25th of the same month by the election of Wm. M. Marshall as president, and James R Jones, Jas. I. Hurley, John Robertson, William Stewart, and H. P. Aughenbaugh as managers, who subsequently appointed Edwin Bell secretary and treasurer. The object of the incorporators was to purchase a lot and erect a building mainly for literary and scientific purposes, the whole not to cost over ten thousand dollars. A building committee was appointed, who commenced preparations for the erection of the building on the south side of West Washington Street, Hagerstown. The corner-stone of the building was laid on Tuesday, Sept. 12, 1848, with Masonic ceremonies. A procession was formed, preceded by the Mechanics' Band, consisting of the members of the Masonic and Odd-Fellow lodges of Hagerstown, together with a number of their brethren from other lodges in the county. The Independent, Junior, and the First Hagerstown Hose Companies, the scholars attached to the Hagerstown Academy, the workmen and builders of the lyceum, the officers of the association, ministers of the gospel, etc., the whole under the direction of Col. George Schley and his aides, Mathew S. Barber and Dr. William Ragan. After marching through the principal streets of Hagerstown the procession halted in front of the lyceum, and the ceremony of laying the corner-stone was performed by the Masons. The exercises were followed with prayer by the Rev. Mr. Conrad. The procession then moved to the court-house, where an oration was delivered by the Hon. Daniel Weisel. The structure was put under roof and the lower story finished by the 1st of April, 1849. The upper story or hall was finished during the ensuing summer. Hon. Daniel Weisel presided at the preliminary meetings of the stockholders, of whom he was one of those who were most active and energetic, and accepted an invitation to act with the board of managers. The amount of stock subscribed fell considerably short of the expense incurred for the erection of the building and for furnishing the hall. The net annual revenue, therefore, from 1849 to 1855 was applied to the liquidation of the remaining indebtedness. In 1856 a dividend of seven per cent. was paid the stockholders. Since that time regular annual dividends have been paid of from eight to ten per cent., and on several occasions as much as twelve and a half per cent., on a basis of eight thousand dollars, which is about the first cost of the building and furniture.

William M. Marshall was elected the first president, and was re-elected until 1852, when Thomas Harbine was elected, and re-elected in 1853. Mr. Marshall was again elected president in 1854, and re-elected annually thereafter until 1868, when James I. Hurley was elected, and re-elected for 1869 and 1870. In 1871, F. D. Herbert was chosen president, and has been re-elected annually, and is now president. James Wason was elected secretary and treasurer in 1850, and retained annually until 1862, when H. K. Tice was appointed, who served until 1865. F. J. Posey was appointed in 1868, and served until 1876, when H. K. Tice was re-elected, and holds the office at present.

The father of Henry K. Tice was John Tice, who was born in 1770 in Lebanon County, Pa., and married Elizabeth Keisicher, who was born near Hagerstown in 1778. Their ancestors emigrated to this country from Switzerland at a very early date. Henry K. Tice was born near Hagerstown, Oct. 17, 1810, and married, in 1838, Mary McCardell, daughter of William McCardell, of Hagerstown, whose wife was Margaret Powless, of the same place. Mr. Tice has had eight children, six of whom are living,—four daughters and two sons. He was educated at the county schools, receiving the rudiments of an English education. He is a member of the Reformed Church, and in politics was a Henry Clay Whig, but is now a Democrat. The industries which Mr. Tice has aided and promoted are many and various. He was one of the founders of the Washington County Agricultural Society as early as 1852; trustee and secretary of the Hagerstown Female Seminary when it was built, and its chief promoter, and the first to subscribe to the stock of the Hagerstown Gas Company. He was the principal originator of that enterprise, of which he was for many years a director. The Mutual Insurance Company of Washington County owes to Mr. Tice much of its success. For over a quarter of a century he was the treasurer of the company, and indeed nearly every enterprise of Hagerstown for the last twenty-five years has been aided with his means and promoted by his intelligence and energy. The Antietam Paper Company was at one time the property of Mr. Tice and John W. Stonebraker. In 1836 he was in the hardware business in Hagerstown, in which he continued until 1881 in partnership with David C. Hammond. Thus his life has been one of usefulness, energy, and enterprise.

The Thursday Club, composed of ladies of Hagerstown, having, through its dramatic, literary, and other entertainments, accumulated a sum of money, applied it to the formation of a library for general circulation and use in the community, and, as preliminary and auxiliary, determined, if possible, to secure as a nucleus the library of the Belles-Lettres Society of the College of St. James, which had not been in use for several years. This object was accomplished in 1878, and the club received from the trustees of the college the library. It consisted of about two thousand five hundred volumes of standard and popular works, selected with great care through a period of eighteen or twenty years by members of the society. These works comprise all standard histories, novels, reviews, all the English poets, and works of general interest.

In order to hold the library thus loaned, and make it a permanent institution, in the advantages of which the citizens might participate, it became necessary to incorporate the club, which was done, with the following ladies as incorporators: Mrs. W. T. Hamilton, Mrs. E. W. Mealey, Mrs. Peter Negley, Mrs. Albert Small, Mrs. Mary Hays, Mrs. H. H. Keedy, Mrs. Alex. Neill, and Miss Anna H. Kennedy. The next step was to secure a proper and permanent place for the accommodation of the library, and accordingly the two large rooms on the second story of Mr. Crist's building, West Washington Street, formerly used as the clerk's office, were rented and devoted to this purpose. The annual subscription is three dollars, and the books now number about three thousand.

Henry K Rice

CHAPTER L.

PUBLIC INSTITUTIONS OF HAGERSTOWN.

Market-houses—Almshouse—Water-works—Telegraph—Street Lighting—Street Paving.

Market-Houses.—A market was established by an act of the Assembly as early as June, 1783. It appears from the language of the act that the public labored under many great inconveniences for want of a market-house in Elizabethtown; that a large and commodious space of ground was laid out for that purpose in the centre of said town; and that the petitioners proposed to build thereon at their own expense. Permission was therefore granted to Henry Shryock, Matthias Need, and Martin Harry, as commissioners, to contract for the building of a house not less than fifty feet by thirty feet, to be used for a market-house. Wednesdays and Saturdays were the market-days, and all victuals and provisions brought to town for sale, "except beef by the quarter or large quantity and pork by the hog or hogs," had to be sold in the market-house. The following is the eleventh section of the act:

"*And whereas,* It has been practiced by people coming in from the country to tie their horses in said market-house, which is very indecent and offensive to the inhabitants of said town, *Be it enacted,* That any person or persons who shall put their own or any other person's horse, mare, or gelding into or under the said market-house, on any pretense whatsoever, he shall pay or forfeit two shillings and sixpence current money, etc."

In the old market-house, as almost every family had its own vegetable-garden and poultry-yard, there was little else to be seen save the different kinds of meat, butter, and eggs. The rules of the market required the butter to be printed in one-pound lumps exactly. If a lump lacked even one-half ounce of full weight it was confiscated and taken by the market-master. An act of the Legislature, passed at the session of 1818–19, authorized the erection of a new market-house. Peter Seibert, Joseph Gabby, and Henry Shafer were named in the act as commissioners, and it was further provided that when the new court-house should be completed the moderator and commissioners of the town should cause the old one to be pulled down and the materials applied to the building of the market-house.

On the 5th of September, 1820, Frisby Tilghman, William O. Sprigg, and William H. Fitzhugh were appointed by the Levy Court commissioners to select and purchase a site for the market-house. These commissioners purchased in October Stump's lot, known as Lot No. 7. It had a front of eighty-two feet on North Potomac Street and two hundred and forty feet on East Franklin Street. The price paid for this site was one thousand dollars. In the following year the first installment of the market-house tax was levied, and the building was opened to public use in December, 1822. Daniel Schnebly was then moderator, and George Brumbaugh was clerk. By an amendment to the original act, the commissioners were authorized to erect a town hall over the market-house, and Mount Moriah Masonic Lodge, No. 33, were to have the privilege of providing quarters for their use in the building at their own expense. This last provision gave rise to a controversy which was conducted with singular bitterness and venom, although the subject at issue was of a very trivial nature. The Masonic fraternity, as heretofore stated, had been permitted to erect a portion of the building for their own use, and at their own expense, but the lower story of the building, the portion used as a market-house, was built and paid for by the town corporation. A cupola was also added at the expense of the town, and the dispute arose concerning the character of the vane to be placed thereon.[1]

[1] The nature of the dispute and the manner in which it was conducted can be best illustrated by the insertion here of one of the numerous anonymous communications published in the Hagerstown newspapers during the progress of the affair:

"To the Public.

"The excessively ridiculous clamor which has been raised by some persons against the moderator and three of our town commissioners [the commissioners at that time were John Albert, George Bean, John Hershey, George Brumbaugh, and George Martiney] makes it necessary to acquaint the public with some facts in relation to the affair. It is generally known that an agreement was entered into between the town and Mount Moriah Lodge, by which the latter secured the privilege of building a hall over the market-house. The contract between the parties guarantees to the lodge the right of constructing their part of the edifice according to their plan, and of carrying it up to the base of the cupola, and no farther. The cupola, then, is to be considered as not under the control of the lodge, nor can it be presumed for a moment that the agreement gives them any power to construct or ornament it. It is not our intention to enter into the details of the compact between the parties, and we refer all those who wish for precise information to the instrument itself. The fraternity contains in its body several members of the law, and we take it for granted that however ignorant they may be in the black letter, they know how to interpret plain English.

"As well might it be contended that the lodge had a right to plan the market-house beneath this hall as to interfere with the cupola above, but, in fact, the commissioners were indifferent what vane was placed on the cupola, and they were willing that the lodge should construct the whole of it if they bore the expense, but this was refused. It can also be stated, and proved, if necessary, that the commissioners did not take the vane down.

"Whence, then, comes this disgusting and silly clamor which has disturbed the public feeling? The commissioners never

Bellevue Almshouse.—The relief of the poor was the subject of early consideration in Hagerstown. On the 28th of March, 1799, the trustees of the poor for Washington County advertised for proposals to erect a brick building in Elizabethtown (Hagerstown) for the poor of the county, thirty-six by sixty feet, two

originated it, nor have they done any precedent act to give rise to it; they have, nevertheless, been industriously attacked, lampooned, and bespattered by a host of petty scavengers, all anxious who should throw the most mud and slime, and this course they pursue, forsooth, by way of ridicule they term it. Really, the Masonic brethren must be miserably deficient in the knowledge of mankind if they do not perceive the effect of the silly plan they have adopted. If they were anxious to cover their craft with dishonor and bring it into disrepute, they could not have adopted a better expedient than the outrage they have committed. Do they think the feelings of good citizens can be sported with with impunity?

"The scorpion lash of ridicule which they pretend to wield with so much effect will surely recoil upon themselves, and devour the hand that brandishes it. Put the moderator and commissioners in one scale and as many of the Royal Arch fraternity in the other, and which will kick the beam? Reader, you know both parties; look at them and then decide; give them in the bargain all their reputation for charity which the trumpet-tongue of fame has proclaimed from the house-top. The commissioners are not afraid of the opinion of their townsmen, and they invite an investigation of their acts in a judicial manner, conscious that they have done nothing affecting the privileges of any one in the smallest iota. They defy the brotherhood from A to Z, with their compass, square, trowel, and every implement, jewel, or signet of their mystic art. Let them go on with their childish and harmless mummery, and do all the good they can; but let them respect the rights and persons of others.

"We wish not to be personal, or to retaliate in their own style, but certain it is that if they go on with their unprovoked and silly warfare they may have occasion to wish that their slang had been permitted to slumber in its parent brain. Everybody knows who the commissioners are; they affect no mystery, and they act under the responsibility of their names. The press is free and, although they may not gain admittance into the *Torch-Light*, which appears to be the willing vehicle of all the ribaldry engendered against them, they know that truth and plain facts will not be excluded from the *Herald*.

"We cannot conclude these observations without a word to Mr. Mechanic, the last writer in the *Torch-Light*, and, we presume, the champion of the confederacy. Judging from his style and invective, his elegant punctilio and pertinacities, we presume he intends to flourish his *goose-quill* against the moderator and commissioners in the potent manner that he intends shortly to flourish his glittering steel in the air. He is read in Roman history, too, we perceive, and he concludes his philippic with the threatening prophecy of a ghost who made a considerable figure in the older times.

"We also have to inform this phantom that we heed not his bravado. We will meet his nothingness when and where he pleases. We have come reluctantly before the public; but if it be rendered necessary by the temper of our assailants, we shall be constrained to sift the affair to the bottom and expose everything to the eyes of our fellow-citizens. We want neither truce nor quarter.

"Many Citizens.

"Hagerstown, June 9, 1823."

stories high. The advertisement further stated that the plan could be seen in the hands of William Heyser, who would receive proposals for the mason, bricks, and carpenters' and joiners' work upon the building. The trustees signing this notice were Henry Schnebly, William Heyser, and George Ney. The building was completed and was occupied by the poor in 1800.

In March, 1827, a meeting was held at the Charity School-room, on East Antietam Street, to give practical shape to the ideas of those who favored the establishment of a society in the town for the relief of the sick poor, and an organization was soon after effected, the fruits of which were extremely beneficial.

The old county almshouse was situated in the suburbs of Hagerstown, and consisted of two brick buildings, respectively two and three stories high. These buildings for years supplied shelter to the indigent of the county, but in later years their proximity to the town and their situation on one of the principal routes of travel were felt to be serious evils, as the effect of town influence upon the institution was generally acknowledged to be bad, and the public location rendered it a convenient lodging-place for tramps and other idlers. The reports of the grand juries year after year called attention to these facts, and recommended the selection of a more remote site, and the erection of a building better adapted to the purposes of an almshouse. The recommendation was at length submitted to a vote of the people, but on account of the financial condition of the county at the time it was rejected. The subject continued to be agitated, and at a meeting of the Farmers' Club, in 1873, Dr. Maddox read an essay upon the condition of the almshouse, in which he strongly urged that the buildings then in use be sold, and that a farm, remote from the influences and associations of the county-seat, be procured as a site for the institution. These suggestions met with the unanimous approval of the large body of influential tax-payers present, and a committee, consisting of Dr. Maddox and A. K. Stake, secretary of the club, was appointed to draw up a paper for presentation to the county commissioners, in which the opinions of the meeting should be urgently expressed. After a full consideration of the matter the passage of an enabling act was secured from the State Legislature, and the erection of a new building upon a new site was determined upon. In 1878 the generosity of John Nicodemus, of Boonsboro', placed at the disposal of the county a valuable farm, situated north of Hagerstown, on the Hagerstown and Middleburg turnpike. This farm, embracing one hundred and twelve acres, was purchased by Mr. Nicodemus from Thomas Spickler at a cost of twelve thousand five hundred dollars, and was presented to the county commissioners to be used "for the accommodation of the poor and indigent of the county, and for an almshouse and the general uses of like character which the interests of the county and its people may require." The gift was made free from any embarrassing conditions, the commissioners being empowered, if at any time another location might seem to them more desirable, to sell the land and purchase a farm elsewhere with the proceeds of the sale. The public-spirited generosity which inspired the gift was the subject of universal commendation, but some fears were expressed lest the location of the farm might prove to be too close to the town to do away with the evils connected with the location of the old almshouse. The county commissioners determined to rent out the farm for one year, and to submit the question of removal to the people at the congressional election in the November following. In the mean time the clerk was directed to advertise for proposals to furnish the county with one hundred cords of wood to be used in burning bricks for the new building. Dr. C. W. Chancellor, secretary of the State Board of Health, submitted plans for the institution, and was invited by the commissioners to visit and inspect the new location, which invitation he accepted, and pronounced the situation healthy and possessed of many other advantages. The final determination was that the site presented by Mr. Nicodemus should be used for the new building, and work was commenced in 1879. The farm is a compact body of good limestone land, easily drained, and sloping gently towards the east.

Near the northern boundary, and running through the entire length of the farm, is a stream of water, along which are rich bottom-lands, well adapted to the raising of the vegetables necessary for the use of the inmates of the asylum. A good barn and a comfortable dwelling-house were on the farm at the time of its purchase. The land adjoins the estates of Hon. William T. Hamilton and Andrew J. and Jacob Schindle. The new building is situated about three hundred and fifty yards from the pike, on which it fronts. It is a plain brick structure, two stories high, and of irregular shape. The only attempt at ornamentation in the design is on the front or gable end of the portion in which the main entrance is situated. This has a heavy ornamental cornice and a handsome porch, which is approached by a wide flight of steps. In this front are placed three tablets; upon the one in the centre is inscribed the name of the asylum, "Bellevue," and the date of its erection; on another are the words, "John Nicodemus gave this farm to be a home for the poor;" and on the third are the names of the board of county commissioners, their clerk, J. C. Dayhoff, and the architect, Frank E. Davis.

The whole length of the building from the end of one wing to that of the other is one hundred and fifty-two feet, and the extension back is one hundred

BELLEVUE ASYLUM.

and thirty-three feet. It contains seven hundred thousand bricks, which were burned on the spot, out of clay dug from the foundation. The basement is high, built of stone quarried within a short distance. There are in the building seventy-four apartments, which will comfortably accommodate one hundred and fifty inmates. The apartments are divided as follows: in the keepers' department fourteen, insane department twenty-seven, in each wing nine, and in the centre building fifteen.

The keepers' department is in the main front of the building. It faces the turnpike, and is forty-one feet in width. The main entrance is in this wing, and opens into a large hall, upon either side of which is a fine apartment, the one on the right being the parlor and that on the left the office. The dining-room is a spacious and lofty room, well lighted and neat in all its appointments. A tower surmounts the front wing and commands a fine view of the surrounding country. There are separate rooms for the sick and for the harmless insane, who are thus cut off from contact with the violent. The latter occupy a wing which has only one means of communication with the rest of the building by means of a single door in the basement. Surrounding this wing is a tower, which extends one story higher and has a mansard-roof. This is the highest point of the building, and in its roof is placed a boiler-iron tank with a capacity for five thousand gallons. Water is supplied to this tank from the stream near the building by means of a water-ram worked by the stream itself. This tank supplies the bath-rooms, etc., in various parts of the building, and also the hose connections for use in case of fire. The arrangements for securing good ventilation are very complete. Over each wing of the building is an iron ventilator, and each room is provided with a register near the ceiling. In addition to this there is a shaft built through the centre of the building, and large ducts lead from this to air-chambers formed by making the floors of the rooms double. These air-chambers communicate with the rooms by means of openings in the chair-boards, by which arrangement floor-ventilation is secured. The roof of the building is of slate, the brick-work is unpainted and unornamented, and the sills are of wood, except those of the basement story. The windows are large and numerous, and are all hung with weights so that the upper sashes can be lowered. The situation of the building is on the side of a gentle hill, which affords excellent drainage. A number of tile pipes are used for carrying off waste water, etc.

The height of the ceilings on the first floor is thirteen and a half feet, and of those on the second floor thirteen feet. The removal of the last of the inmates from the old almshouse to the Bellevue Asylum took place during July, 1880, Dr. Chancellor being present to assist in the classification of the cases. The total cost of the building, as stated in the official estimate of the county commissioners, was twenty-six thousand dollars, a portion of which was provided for from the sale of the old almshouse property.

In December, 1877, a meeting was held at the court-house, at which Hon. A. K. Syester presided, and J. F. A. Remley acted as secretary. The object of the meeting was to provide some means for the relief of the poor of Hagerstown. A committee, consisting of A. K. Syester, chairman; A. R. Appleman, William Updegraff, M. M. Gruber, George Lias, F. A. Heard, E. M. Mobley, H. H. Keedy, P. J. Adams, J. F. A. Remley, Edward Stake, Michael McDonald, and H. A. McComas, was appointed to carry into practical effect the benevolent purpose of the meeting. The committee held a meeting shortly afterwards and passed the following resolutions:

"*Resolved*, That for the purpose of fairly and impartially distributing relief to the actual distress and needs of the unfortunate the following rules and regulations will be observed:

"1st. All applications for relief must be presented to this committee in writing signed by the applicant, and giving references.

"2d. Applications will be considered by the committee, and if upon investigation the object is worthy, the committee will furnish such relief as the exigencies of the case may require.

"3d. Cases of distress arising from sickness or disability to earn a living shall have precedence.

"4th. Contributions in money will be given only in the most extreme and exceptional cases.

"5th. No relief will be granted except to *bona-fide* residents of the town and vicinity."

Mr. William Updegraff was appointed treasurer of the fund to be raised, and store-keeper of the articles which may be contributed, and the following gentlemen were appointed as a committee in each ward to solicit contributions of goods, provisions, money, and fuel:

Ward No. 1.—Andrew J. Schindel, William S. Swartz, Dr. J. F. Smith, David Zeller, and Rev. John M. Jones.

Ward No 2.—H. H. Keedy, F. A. Heard, Joseph S. McCartney, H. S. Eavey, and Rev. S. W. Owen.

Ward No. 3.—J. Roessner, Albert Heil, M. L. Byers, George B. Oswald. and Rev. J. C. Thompson.

Ward No. 4.—Lewis Schindel, William S. Williamson, John L. Bikle, Henry Colliflower, and Rev. J. S. Kieffer.

Ward No. 5.—D. S. Boyer, Samuel L. King, M. M. Gruber, William S. Herbert, and Rev. John R. Williams.

Water-works.—For a long time previous to the establishment of the water-works the subject of introducing this improvement into Hagerstown was agitated among the citizens. Early in 1872 a public meeting relative to the subject was held in Junior Hall, at which it was elicited that the tax-payers of the town were practically a unit as to the necessity of constructing them. A committee, consisting of William McK. Keppler, George W. Harris, F. M. Darby, B. Schley, and Henry Bell, was appointed "to procure counsel to prepare a law to be submitted to the Legislature, the said law to authorize the mayor and Council of Hagerstown to make the necessary appropriations for the introduction of water into the town." Another committee was appointed to form an estimate of the cost of sinking an artesian well, the construction of a reservoir, the laying of pipes, and the other expenses of supplying the town with water. This committee consisted of the following: H. H. Keedy, Alexander Neill, William Updegraff, D. C. Aughinbaugh, David Zeller, and W. M. McDowell. On the 22d of November, 1880, the Washington County Water-works were incorporated for thirty-nine years, the incorporators being William T. Hamilton, William Updegraff, Alexander Armstrong, Edward Stake, Henry H. Keedy, George R. Bowman, Jacob Roessner, David C. Aughinbaugh, George W. Smith, John B. Thirston, P. A. Brugh, and Joseph Kausler. The capital stock was fixed at $66,600, divided into 6600 shares of $10 each. The number of directors was eleven; the first board, to serve for one year, being named in the articles of incorporation, as follows: William T. Hamilton, William Updegraff, Charles W. Humrichouse, George R. Bowman, Edward W. Mealey, Edward Stake, Henry H. Keedy, David S. Boyer, William Gassman, George W. Harris, and George W. Grove. At the first meeting of the board of directors, held one week later, Edward Stake, William Updegraff, and H. H. Keedy were appointed a committee to draft by-laws and propose a plan of operations. The source of supply selected was the South Mountain water-shed, and it was deemed advisable at this time to provide for all contingencies by increasing the capital stock from $66,000 to $80,000.

To increase the stock a new charter was filed, and the old one, not yet consummated, was withdrawn, and the name of the company was changed by the omission of the word "Works" to that of "The Washington County Water Company." By this company a tract of fourteen acres of land, the property of William Wagley, at the base of the South Mountain, between Cavetown and Smithsburg, and seven and a half miles from Hagerstown, on the line of the Western Maryland Railroad, upon which is a saw-mill, with capacious dam and dwelling-houses, has been secured in fee-simple. The dam is upwards of two hundred feet above the highest point in Hagerstown. It covers a natural basin, and on the tract immediately above the dam nature has carved out a natural reservoir, which may at will be converted into a storage dam capable of retaining a supply for six months' demand by the present population of Hagerstown, without receipts from any auxiliary source. But in the mountain and above this natural reservoir is a cluster of from seven to ten other distinct springs, most of which have never been known to fail, which in an emergency or extraordinary growth of the demand for water in the future could in turn be utilized, indefinitely increasing the supply.

It is believed that by care in the collection and utilization of the Wagley stream, and by the cleaning out and opening of fountains now filled up, and the preservation of the water thus lost by diffusion over a large surface, all those persons below the Wagley property through whose farms the stream passes will in no manner be interfered with in the matter of water-supply. So copious is the Wagley stream that within half a mile above the Wagley mill two other mills are turned by it. The water is as pure as crystal, and bursts from the rocks in the gulch in which the mill stands. The spring on the property bought by the company from Wagley is believed to be alone sufficient to supply the town, and the stream from above passes about one hundred yards from the Wagley dam, which is used as the reservoir of the company, so that in case of freshets all the surface water will be carried around the dam, and none of it will enter into the supply of the town. At all times this supply will be pure spring-water, without mud or sediment, equal to the best and purest water on the continent. Should the requirements of the future call for an increase of the volume, two plans are open: first, a storage reservoir can be constructed on the company's property; or, second, the supply can be indefinitely increased by tapping other fountains and running as many additional springs as may be needed into the dam on the company's property, which is judiciously located on a level below them all. The right of way for the water company was procured from the directors of the Western Maryland Railroad Company, which authorized them to use the track for the laying of pipes from their property at the mountain to Hagerstown.

The reservoir is in charge of the company's tenant, who attends to turning off the surface water and keeping things there in order. From the dam to Hagerstown, seven and a half miles, a ten-inch pipe conveys the water, under ground, along the railroad track to the distributing pipes and hydrants within the town. There is no reservoir at Hagerstown, the distribution being direct from the mountain dam. A clear fall of more than two hundred feet to the highest point in town carries the water by its own pressure to every point, for fire or other purposes, that may be needed. A greater altitude and pressure could have been reached, but it was not desired, as a corresponding increase of strength and cost of pipe would have been needed, and the pressure now secured is all that could be desired.

A ten-inch pipe will supply 1,134,000 gallons in twenty-four hours, or 47,555 gallons per hour. The largest quantity consumed in large cities, where every one uses hydrant water, is fifty gallons to each individual, and in those which have a population of twenty thousand or less the quantity required for each person is thirty gallons per day. Upon this basis over seven thousand population would require a supply of two hundred and ten thousand gallons daily. The ten-inch pipe in five hours will supply 236,275 gallons, or in a little more than the fifth part of a day will furnish all the water needed by Hagerstown for a whole day. The money to construct the water-works was subscribed promptly by the people of the town, and a contract was entered into with William H. Allen & Co., of Baltimore, to furnish the iron pipes, plugs, and hydrants, and to do the complete work, furnishing everything, excavating and restoring streets, etc., to their proper condition, and handing over the work with the insurance of its successful operation for thirty days, for the sum of $90,875. A. H. McNeal, of Burlington, N. J., stipulated on the foregoing contract with Allen & Co. to furnish the iron, and accepted an order on the water company from Allen & Co. in payment thereof. The work is to be completed by the 1st of May, 1882, and the laborers employed are as far as practicable to be residents of the county. The pipes are twelve inches diameter instead of ten inches as at first intended, and are to be laid along the Hagerstown and Smithsburg turnpike.

This increase in the diameter of pipe will secure fifty per cent. of an increase in the volume of water supplied, and will involve an additional expenditure of about twelve thousand dollars. This increase in expenditure and capacity of the pipe was incurred after great deliberation by the company, and after it had been ascertained to be the almost universal wish of the stockholders and others interested, who desired to supply a sufficiency of water-power for the rapid development of the manufacturing interests of the town. The entire cost of the works when completed is not expected to exceed $100,000. The work of laying pipes, constructing the necessary works at the reservoir, etc., is being carried forward with all possible speed.

Hotels and Early Inns.—Hagerstown has long been noted for the excellence of its hotels and taverns, or inns. Situated on the great national highway from the North and East to the West and South, it was at one time an important stopping-place for politicians, office-seekers, etc., on their way to and from the national capital. Some of its early taverns attained a wide-spread celebrity; such, for instance, as the Globe, the Indian King, the General Washington, and many others. The Globe was the great rendezvous for the huge wagons in which in those days the produce of the surrounding country was transported. It occupied the site of the present Baldwin, formerly the Washington, House, and was kept for many years by George Beltzhoover, brother of Daniel Beltzhoover, the proprietor of the Fountain Inn, Baltimore. Beltzhoover was succeeded in turn by Daniel Snively, John Cline, and John Young.

The Indian King Tavern was one of the oldest in Hagerstown, and its hospitalities were dispensed by many different landlords during the long term of its existence. On the 28th of October, 1797, John Ragan, who had kept this noted tavern for some time, sold out, and was succeeded by Thomas Crabb. In 1799 we find John Ragan again in charge. On the 31st of October in that year he announced that having resumed his old stand, at the sign of the Indian King, on the Main Street leading from the court-house to Bath and the Western country, he was prepared to entertain travelers in the best manner, etc. In 1812, under the proprietorship of Samuel Bayly, the name was changed to the Hagerstown Hotel. It was then the principal tavern in the town. In 1818 the old name had been restored, and Christopher Griffith was proprietor.

In 1797, Melchior Beltzhoover was proprietor of a tavern on the corner of the public square, near the court-house. In 1798, George Scholl kept a tavern at the sign of the Black Bear. This house was situated at the corner of Walnut and Franklin Streets, on the present site of the Eyler House. In 1799, H. Peck announced that he would open a house of entertainment in his gardens, near Col. Rochester's, in Hagerstown. In the same year he was landlord of the Columbian Inn, in Baltimore. In 1818, George Witmer was proprietor of the White Swan, and George Bromet of the Black Horse. The Bell Tavern, now the Newcomer House, stood nearly opposite the court-house in 1821, and was owned by Wm. Hammond. In that year John McIlhenny was proprietor of the Eagle Tavern on the public square, George Beltzhoover was landlord of the Globe, opposite the bank, formerly kept by O. H. W. Stull, and John Schleigh kept the Swan Tavern on Potomac Street, formerly kept by Ridenour and by George C. Hamilton. In 1827, Thomas H. Rench took charge of the hotel on North Potomac Street, Hagerstown, formerly kept by Martin Newcomer. In the same year Daniel H. Schnebly announced that he had rented the Bell Tavern, opposite the Hagerstown court-house, where he intended opening a house of entertainment.

Another popular hostelry was the Swan Tavern, on North Potomac Street, near the public square, now owned by Philip Wingert, and occupied with stores. Contemporaneous with it was Enstein's General Washington Inn, situated near the present Hoover House, which is on the corner of Franklin and Potomac Streets. Nearly opposite the General Washington Inn was a tavern kept by Mr. Cook, a famous resort in its day. Stover's tavern, kept for many years by Frederick Stover, is now the Mansion House, kept by John Riley, opposite the depot of the Cumberland Valley Railroad. It has recently been refitted and enlarged. At the corner of Baltimore and South Potomac Streets was another well-known tavern, kept by Michael Treiber, which is now used as a private dwelling and store. The old Eagle Tavern was located on the present site of the Hagerstown *Mail* office, at the corner of Washington Street and the public square. In this building Henry Clay was married to Letitia, daughter of Col. Thomas Hart, of Hagerstown, uncle of Thomas Hart Benton, the famous Western senator.

At present the leading hotels of Hagerstown are the Baldwin, the Franklin, the Newcomer, the Antietam, the Mansion, and the Hoover House. The Baldwin is a handsome brick structure, and is one of the largest and finest hotels in Maryland outside the city of Baltimore. It is situated on Washington Street, near Potomac, and is managed by Messrs. McLaughlin and Herbert. Its site is that of the Washington House, which was burned on the 29th of May, 1879. The construction of the Baldwin was commenced on the 1st of November, 1879, and it was finished and opened to guests on the 1st of September, 1880. During the year ending September, 1881, it entertained 16,176 persons. The arrivals by months were as follows: September, 1880, 1680; October, 1460; November, 1175; December, 1126; January, 1881, 964; February, 1132; March, 1221; April, 1311; May, 1618; June, 1440; July, 1318; August, 1731. Total for the year, 16,176. Its principal owners are C. C. Baldwin, president of the Louisville and Nashville Railroad, who represents the heirs of the late James Dixon Roman, one of the leading proprietors of the Washington House, E. W. Mealey, Dr. Josiah G. Smith, David C. Hammond, and William T. Hamilton. Originally the site of the Baldwin House was occupied by the famous Globe Tavern. James I. Hurley and Mrs. Harbine bought the property from Dr. Frederick Dorsey, and sold it to a company of which the directors were J. Dixon Roman, president, Peter Swartzwelder, George W. Smith, William B. Chaney, James Wason, and James I. Hurley. The new management tore down the old structure and erected a large brick hotel, which they named the Washington House. The new hotel was kept at first by a Mr. Stitson, then by Joseph P. Morig, who was followed by Henry Yingling. The latter was succeeded by a Mr. Wiles, afterwards proprietor of the Howard House in Baltimore, who in turn was followed by John Anderson, Stanhope & McLaughlin, and George Middlekauff. On the death of the latter his widow undertook the management of the property, and was in charge when the fire broke out.

The origin of the fire has never been discovered. The alarm was given by a guest, who was awakened by the smoke, and the local fire companies repaired at once to the scene. In the mean time, however, the flames had made such headway that it was impossible to rescue some of the inmates. Of those in the house at the time, J. C. Taylor, of Adams, Buck & Co., Baltimore, escaped with slight bruises; Wm. Middleton, of New York, uninjured; J. F. Stine, Philadelphia, uninjured; Mrs. Melville Patterson, daughter, and nurse, of Baltimore, and Miss Josephine Gerry, of Portland, Me., rescued by S. H. Dorsey and Wm. Stake; C. F. Manning, uninjured; T. J. Wallace, of York, Pa., uninjured; Judge Geo. A. Pearre, uninjured; also Henry Swartzwelder, of Cumberland, Md., Walter Bray, of Philadelphia, J. W. Showaker, of Baltimore, and T. J. Kyle, of Baltimore. Isaac Wyman, of New York, engaged in the flour, grain, and commission business, escaped down the main stairway to the office, thence to the veranda, and thence to the pavement. He was badly, but not seriously, burned. A Mr. Little, of Philadelphia, escaped by the back stairway, as did also R. J. Stewart, of Oneida, N. Y. Edward Watts and his son, Edward C. Watts, also succeeded in escaping. Edward C. Watts, however, returned and extricated Mr. Exline, of Hancock, who was in imminent danger.

The following also escaped: Wm. K. Benner, Middletown, Pa.; Harry B. Keiper, Lancaster, Pa.; C. L. Jackson, Baltimore; George and Henry Rinker and John Rippon, Cumberland, Md.; M. Shannon and C. Hoenicka, of Cumberland, badly hurt; Solomon Jenkins and J. H. Exline, of Hancock; Col. E. Ames; A. O. Dillingham, agent of the Singer Sewing-Machine Company; Mr. and Mrs. Hill and two children; August Tabler, Charles M. Valentine, W. G. Haller, and Joseph Hughes; Geo. A. Davis, J. M. Landis, severely burnt about the head and on the hands; J. H. Hannis, of Renovo, Pa.; D. S. Wolfinger, F. F. Burgess, of Baltimore; Wm. Gibson, J. W. Yost, H. Hillbruner, of Philadelphia; Col. D. Bruce, of Cumberland; W. H. Zorus, of Philadelphia; S. Jacques, William Stake, R. H. Groverman, of Baltimore; Wm. M. Price and Jesse Korns, of Cumberland; W. T. Barth, of Baltimore; Mr. and Mrs. T. B. Cushwa, J. M. Knodle, A. B. Almony; and Dr. W. Macgill, of Cumberland. J. E. Troxell, of Hancock, who occupied room No. 25, was fatally burned. F. B. Snively, of Shady Grove, Pa., was terribly burned and died a few hours later. J. H. Exline and Solomon Jenkins were both severely, but not seriously, injured. A number of other persons were more or less severely hurt. The building was insured for twenty-one thousand dollars. Immediately after the fire a stock company was formed for the erection of a new hotel, and the result is the Baldwin,—a carefully-constructed edifice, with elegant furniture and all the appurtenances of a first-class hotel in one of the larger cities. Attached to the Baldwin House proper, in the same building, is the Academy of Music, located on the site of Christian Winters' restaurant, a noted establishment in its day. The length of the Baldwin House is one hundred and fifteen feet, and its depth one hundred and fifty feet. It is seventy feet in height, is furnished throughout with solid walnut furniture of one pattern, and handsome Brussels carpets, and is supplied with hot and cold water and gas throughout. There are in all one hundred and ten rooms, of which eighty-eight are sleeping apartments. Besides the Academy of Music, which seats eight hundred persons, the building contains the offices of the Adams Express Company, Baltimore and Ohio Express, and the American Union Telegraph Company. The rooms of the Baldwin House are spacious and well appointed, and the general appearance of the establishment, as well as the food and service, does full justice to the business activity and enterprise of the progressive and thriving community in which it is situated. Messrs. McLaughlin & Herbert, the present courteous and enterprising proprietors, have had long experience in hotel management, and to their tact, good judgment, energy, and unfailing politeness to their guests, the remarkable success of the Baldwin House is chiefly due. Their staff of employés was selected with great care, and is diligently kept up to the original standard, while all the appointments of the house are of the best description.

The Franklin House, which now ranks next to the Baldwin, was known for many years as Wright's Hotel. It is owned and managed by Philip Yahn, and has recently been enlarged and improved. It stands on North Potomac Street, near the public square.

The Antietam House, situated at the corner of Washington and Jonathan Streets, is one of the oldest landmarks in the town. Many years ago it was a tavern, kept by Benjamin Light, who was succeeded by Martin Newcomer and a number of others. At one time it was known as the "Southern and Western Hotel," and as such was kept by a Mr. Pollard, who was afterwards a contractor for the construction of the Cumberland Valley (then the Franklin) Railroad. Subsequently, during the management of Mr. Powers, its name was changed to the "City Hotel," and afterwards to the "Antietam House," kept by Wm. E. Doyle. Its present manager is John Cretin, and the proprietors are Wm. T. Hamilton, Dr. N. B. Scott, Z. S. Claggett, and James I. Hurley. The Antietam House is believed to be at least one hundred years old, and is certainly the most ancient tavern property in Hagerstown. Part of the lot on which it stands was occupied during the official term of its first president, Col. Nathaniel Rochester, by the old Hagerstown Bank.

The Newcomer House, formerly the Bell Tavern, is now owned by Dr. N. B. Scott, and managed by Jonathan Newcomer. Alfred Cline, a noted character in Hagerstown, was at one time proprietor of the Newcomer House.

Paving.—By the act of Assembly, November session of 1791, Thos. Hart, Ludwig Young, Wm. Lee, John Shyrock, John Geiger, Peter Heighfly, and Baltzer Goll were made commissioners to improve and repair the streets in Hagerstown, and April 28, 1801, John Heddinger, clerk of the market, "by order of the commissioners," gave notice "to the inhabitants of Elizabeth Town" that, "whereas it was ordered by the commissioners in the month of May, 1794, and public notice thereof given, that the ditch from the public spring to the foot of Frederick Brentlinger's lot should be made three feet wide and two feet deep, and the sides of the said ditch done with stone or logs by the owners of each lot through which the water runs," and that "at the same it was ordered that the inhabitants of Elizabeth Town should have their footways paved and posted; and whereas little attention has been given to the above orders," the commissioners gave notice that unless these orders are obeyed by the 1st of September, they will employ workmen at the expense of the owners, and complete the work of ditching and paving. On the following 5th of April, 1802, the same commissioners, by their clerk, issued the following notice:

"To the Inhabitants of Elizabeth Town.

"Whereas, notice has heretofore been given by the commissioners of Elizabeth Town to the inhabitants of the town to have their footways paved and posted, this is therefore to give notice that the commissioners will meet at the court-house on Monday next, the 12th inst., when they are determined to make such arrangements as will compel the inhabitants aforesaid to post and pave the footways of the said town, agreeably to law, and will appoint some day when they are to commence. Any of the inhabitants who have not as yet complied with the former notice of the commissioners are requested to attend at their next meeting, at the time above appointed, when they shall receive the necessary instructions. Those persons who own lots which the water from the public spring runs through are requested to attend.

"By order of the commissioners.

"John Heddinger,

"April 5, 1802. *Clerk of the market.*"

The work of paving the streets was resumed the following year, Feb. 16, 1803, when by an act of Assembly, Nathaniel Rochester, Adam Ott, Otho Holland Williams, Jacob Harry, and William Heyser were appointed commissioners for a scheme or schemes of a lottery for raising a sum of money not exceeding two thousand dollars, to be used in improving the streets of Hagerstown, in Washington County. Under this authority the following advertisement from the *Hagerstown Herald*, Feb. 16, 1803, offered fortunes and footways to the good people of Hagerstown:

"STREET LOTTERY.

"Authorized by law to raise two thousand dollars for improving the streets in Elizabeth (Hager's) Town, in Washington County, Maryland.

"All Prizes.

"*Scheme.*

"1 prize of 400 dollars	$400
2 prizes of 100 "	200
4 " 50 "	200
8 " 25 "	200
40 " 10 "	400
104 " 5 "	520
1 " 4 "	4
3170 " 2½ "	7925
3 last drawn of $50 each	150
3333 tickets at $3	$9999

"All prizes, subject to a deduction of twenty per cent., will be paid immediately after drawing by Jacob Harry and William Heyser, with whom the money arising from the sale of tickets will be lodged for the purpose.

"Those prizes not demanded within six months after drawing will be considered as relinquished for the benefit of the streets.

"The lottery will be drawn as soon as the tickets are disposed of, and public notice given of the time and place of drawing.

"Tickets at $3 each ($1 only to be paid at the time of purchase) are to be had of the following commissioners:

"N. ROCHESTER, JACOB HARRY,
"ADAM OTT, WILLIAM HEYSER."
"O. H. WILLIAMS,

The people of Hagerstown were actively engaged in paving and improving the streets, and from April, 1814, to March, 1815, there was expended on streets $692.20.

The Telegraph.—On the 3d of May, 1854, I. Dixon Roman organized a company for the construction of a telegraph between Hagerstown and Frederick City, of which he was president, with William M. Marshall, M. S. Barber, Peter Swartzwelder, Howard Kennedy, and George W. Smith as directors. The line was speedily constructed and opened, bringing Hagerstown into connection with the then existing telegraphic communication of the country.

Street Lighting.—While it is quite certain that Hagerstown had no street-lamps in December, 1827, when the question of light or no light was decided is not very clear. Gas-lights were authorized by a vote of the people, Jan. 20, 1858, with a majority of 24 votes out of 448 polled. The Hagerstown Gas-Light Company was organized and chartered in the summer of 1854. The enterprise was inaugurated by Leander McKee, H. K. Tice, and Thomas G. Robertson, whose object at the start was to have gas furnished to light up only the stores, hotels, and business rooms generally, between the square and the court-house, on West Washington Street. The projectors had no hope at the time of securing the co-operation of citizens living or doing business outside of these limits to an extent that would justify the erection of works of sufficient capacity to furnish gas for any considerable portion of the town. As soon, however, as it became manifest that these gentlemen, with a large proportion of the business men in their district, were determined to carry out their purpose, a number of those outside, first from one section, then from another, proposed to subscribe for an additional amount of stock necessary to build works of sufficient capacity to supply their respective portions of the town. These propositions were accepted, and the company was organized by the election of James Dixon Roman as president, who was re-elected every succeeding year until 1859, when George Kealhofer succeeded him, with an entire new board of directors.

The amount of capital was fixed for the present at $6000, with the privilege of increasing it to $10,000. A contract was entered into with the "Maryland Portable Gas-Light Company" for the building of the works, at a cost of two thousand dollars, and for laying down all main pipes at a cost of 80 cents, $1.35, and $1.65 per foot for two-inch, three-inch, and four-inch pipes respectively. The works were erected in the rear of Lyceum Hall, and were constructed to manufacture gas from rosin oil, under Longbottom's patent. The result of the first year's operation was unsatisfactory, having fallen far short of the Baltimore company's guarantee, and at the end of three years it was discovered that the company had not paid expenses. The Baltimore company then proposed to build new works to manufacture gas from coal. The capital stock was increased to $15,000, with the privilege of a further increase to $25,000. The new works were built on South Locust Street, and gas was made from coal, and at the end of the year 1859, notwithstanding the company charged five dollars per thousand feet of gas, its receipts were far short of its expenses. A meeting of the stockholders was held, when the president and directors all resigned, and a new board was elected. The Baltimore company, at the same time, proposed to lease the works for ten years, and pay the stockholders five per cent. per annum for the first five years, and six per cent. per annum for the next five years, which was readily accepted, as hitherto they had received nothing, and were now compelled to pay a considerable debt that had been accumulating from the time that the company commenced operations. The Baltimore company paid promptly during the period of their lease out of the net earnings of the works, and at its expiration had a handsome surplus. The home company having now paid its entire indebtedness, again took charge of the works, electing F. I. Posey president. The capital stock was increased to $22,500, the works at the same time, and subsequently, were greatly improved and extended, and from that time to the present semi-annual dividends of five per cent. have been regularly paid. The present officers are F. I. Posey, president; James I. Hurley, H. K. Tice, Dr. Smith, Albert Small, D. C. Hammond, and Edward W. Mealy, directors.

CHAPTER LI.

TRADE AND INDUSTRIES OF HAGERSTOWN, AND FINANCIAL INSTITUTIONS.

THE earliest industries of a community are always interesting, however humble they may appear to succeeding and more prosperous generations. The mill of John Stull, on the Antietam, near Hagerstown, as early as 1752, may not have been a very pretentious structure, yet to those early settlers it was an important institution. Capt. Charles Higgenbotham lived on "Secret Bottom," near this mill, which probably takes precedence in the industries of Hagerstown. Then Antietam was written Anti-Eatam, according to the *Maryland Gazette* of 1757. Capt. Tobias Stansbury, in 1763, obtained a patent for sixteen hundred acres of land, called "Fellfoot," at Anti-Eatam, in Frederick (now Washington) County, upon which was situated a noted place of entertainment called "The Hickory Tavern," and near by lived at that time Joseph Chapline and James Smith. It was offered for sale in October, 1763, by Joseph Euser, and it was stated that there was every appearance of iron ore upon it, and a stream to work the furnace. Capt. Stansbury's home-place was called "Hallam's Look," which was offered for sale in October, 1767, by his wife, Mary Stansbury. Fort Frederick Furnace was conducted by Jacques & Johnson in 1771; and Daniel Hughes manufactured patriotic cannon and small-arms at Antietam in March, 1776. Samuel Beall, Jr., was at that time the proprietor of the Frederick Forge, situated at the mouth of the Antietam. Mount Ætna Furnace, six miles from Hagerstown, manufactured cannon and shot in 1781. In 1773, William Bailey, coppersmith, living at York Town, Pa., informed "the public in general, and his old customers in particular, that he has, for the convenience of the inhabitants of the back part of this county, fixed a coppersmith's shop in Hagerstown, Frederick Co., next door to Baltzer Goll, hatter, where he makes for sale all sorts of copper-work, such as stills, brewing coppers, wash and fish-kettles, tea-kettles, sauce-pans, coffee and chocolate-pots, which he will sell as low as any imported in the provinces of Pennsylvania, Maryland, or Virginia. He still carries on the same business where he formerly lived in York Town, Pa., two doors below the sign of the Buck." Thus we learn from the enterprising coppersmith, spreading his business from Pennsylvania to Maryland, that chocolate was drank in Western Maryland one hundred and nine years ago. The Great Rock Forge, belonging to Daniel and Samuel Hughes, stood, in 1786, on Antietam Creek, within eight miles of Mount Ætna Furnace, with "two hammers, four fires, a substantial dam, and considerable head of water." The Messrs. Hughes advertised both the Great Rock and Mount Ætna Furnaces for rent in 1786. Hart & Rochester had for sale at their nail-factory, in Hagerstown, July 3, 1789, "all kinds of nails, brads, and sprigs," which they offered for sale on "lower terms" than those imported from Europe. To journeymen nailers they offered "good wages, paid at the end of every week."

In 1790, Hart & Rochester were in the dry-goods and grocery business, in the house formerly occupied by Messrs. M. & W. Van Lear. Fulling, dyeing, and coloring of all kinds was the business of John Rohrer (son of Jacob), in Hagerstown, in 1790. Daniel Nead was engaged in tanning in the same year, carrying on the business at the tan-yard previously owned by his father, Matthias Nead. William Downey, Nathaniel Morgan, Lawrence Protzman were dry-goods dealers, while Frederick Rohrer dealt in Kentucky lands, and Alexander and Hezekiah Claggett dissolved a dry-goods and grocery partnership, and Alexander and Benjamin Claggett formed a new firm for the same business Feb. 10, 1791. May 4th of the same year Jacob T. Towson kept a store near the house of Maj. Van Lear; May 21st, John & Hezekiah Claggett advertised a dry-goods and grocery trade. Jacob Ott was a hatter, and Daniel Linebaugh, driven from Greencastle, Pa., by the burning of his house, was a tailor; Lawrence Protzman was a reed-maker and blue-dyer; Geiger & Harry were in the dry-goods and grocery business at the southeast corner of Court-house Square; and James Ferguson, on Court-house Square, next door to Christopher Adler, had a general assortment of merchandise. In 1792, Henry & Jacob

Hoover were dealers in French burr millstones; Baltzer Goll was a merchant; Mrs. and Miss Aull conducted the millinery and mantua-making business; Robert Aull was a joiner and cabinet-maker; and William and John Lee, having dissolved their partnership, were in business, each on his own account,—William in the dry-goods line, and John had a "good assortment of groceries, bar-iron, and castings" at the "Sign of the Sugar-Loaf." May 1st, Nathaniel Rochester, having dissolved the partnership of Hart & Rochester, admitted his nephew, Robert Rochester, as a partner, and kept a general assortment of dry-goods and groceries at the old stand, under the name of N. & R. Rochester. April 25th the firm of Rezin Davis & Co., then composed of David Mitchell and Rezin Davis, in Skipton and Hagerstown, was dissolved, the latter continuing business at the old stand in Hagerstown, and the former in Skipton. May 16th, Thomas Hart & Son, opposite the market-house, commenced the dry-goods business; John Boggs was a printer; Davan & Luke Tiernan, in the dry-goods business; Thompson & Kean, also in the dry-goods trade; John Steikleader and Hyatt Lownes made watches and clocks. August 8th, Frederick Rohrer offered his town house with sixteen and a half lots for sale; William McIntosh was a conveyancer. In 1793, Henry Hoover, stone-cutter, dealt also in French burr millstones, Andrew Gordon was a tailor, and John T. Mason a distiller. An "elegant harpsichord" was offered for sale by Joseph M. Jones.

Rezin Davis, in 1794, offered for sale nails from the factory of Hughes & Fitzhugh, and clover-seed from Lancaster County, Pa. Wm. Reynolds, coppersmith and tinner, sold his property April 18th, and removed to Baltimore. Leonard Stright was a blacksmith; John Heddinger, a hatter; Christian Hawken, a gunsmith; Ogle & Hall, dry-goods and grocery merchants; Peter Hoeflich, a merchant; John Smur sold drums; and John Byers was a tailor.

On the 9th of April, 1794, Nathaniel Rochester announced that he had purchased Col. Thomas Hart's rope-walk in Hagerstown, and that he would keep constantly on hand a supply of mill and well-ropes, bed-cords, leading lines, hatters' cords, etc. As he proposed to live at the rope-walk, he offered for sale the house and ground in which he had resided. In May, 1794, Charles Ogle announced that as he had given up the Mount Etna Company's business at Mount Etna Furnace, all accounts would be settled by his successor, Daniel Hughes. The company appears to have consisted of Daniel Hughes, Samuel Hughes, and Charles Ogle. In the following June, Col. Rochester abandoned the business of general merchandise, in which he had been, in order to devote himself to his rope and nail manufactories. In 1795, Isaac Woodcock was the gold and silversmith; Jacob Rohrer, a brewer; John Rohrer, a fuller; Levy Andrew Levy, a conveyancer; James Ferguson and John Short, merchants, who dissolved August 31st, as well as Basil and Richard Brooke, on September 15th.

William Fitzhugh advertised for an overseer at fifty pounds per year on December 17th. James Ferguson opened his new store next to Christopher Atler's, Jan. 21, 1796. K. Owen & Co. opened in the store formerly occupied by Luke Tiernan, January 14th. Alexander Kennedy was in the dry-goods, hardware, and grocery trade, and William Heyser was a coppersmith and brass-founder. Claggett & Forman succeeded John and Hezekiah Claggett, April 7th. Jonathan Tutweller was a cooper; Jonas McPherson, a merchant; Frederick Miller & Co., apothecaries.

On the 29th of June, 1796, Daniel Hughes advertised that bar-iron of the finest quality was being made at Antietam Forge. In 1797, Leonard Billmire was a coach-maker; Henry Wingart, a hatter; John Reynolds, a watchmaker; John Leight manufactured gunpowder at a mill near the town, and conducted a tinware business in the town; Jacob Earhart was a merchant, and John McJilton made boots and shoes; John Greiner was a brass-founder; Peter Miller, as well as Francis Forman & Co., was a dry-goods merchant; John McNeill, a boot and shoemaker; Thomas McJilton and Hugh Carry, boot and shoe manufacturers; Wm. Bridlinger, barber and hair-dresser; Doris Dozel, tanner; Alexander Kennedy, merchant, opposite the Fountain Inn; Keller & Co., merchants; Conrad Coffroth.

In 1799, James Downey finished, January 3d, his hemp-mill at the forks of the Antietam, one mile above Rock Forge, and two miles below Nicodemus' mill. Alexander Simpson, clock-maker and mathematical instrument maker, conducted his business in the house of David Cook, next door to Mr. Kapp's tavern, and opposite the German Lutheran church. George Henderson advertised plaster of Paris for sale at Col. Stull's old mill on Antietam, near Hagerstown. John A. Donaldson, living "near the public spring next door to Mrs. Bird's," advertised for two or three whitesmiths and the same number of apprentices. About the same time Nathaniel Rochester announced that he would give a generous price in cash for about twenty bushels of good, clean hemp-seed. Philip Myers "followed the house-painting business" at the house next door to Devalt Lefinger's, formerly occupied by Henry Werley. John Byers, the tailor, removed, April 18th, to the stone house opposite Adam

Cooke's tavern, and next door to Col. Ott's. Jacob Cooke removed to Mr. Reinhart's house, nearly opposite Maj. Adam Ott's, where he manufactured saddles, saddle-bags, bridles, coach-harness, all kinds of wagon gear, which he was determined to sell at reduced prices for cash or country produce. John Baker had for sale, August 30th, ten hogsheads of tobacco, good and sound. Keller & Forman, at their new store, lately occupied by Claggett & Forman, received, August 1st, from Philadelphia and Baltimore a general assortment of dry-goods, ironmongery, cutlery, and groceries, which they were determined to sell at reduced prices for cash or country produce only. George Shall continued the boot and shoe business. The subscribers to the Hot Pressed Bible Works in Hagerstown were respectfully informed, October 10th, that it is completed and ready for delivery at the English printing-office, and the proprietors hoped "with deference that they shall be excused in requesting the subscribers to call at the office,—their only motive for it is that their friends may have a choice, the copies being differently bound." In the same year Henry Peck advertised a garden and lot for sale, announcing at the same time that he intended to remove to Baltimore. Subsequently Mr. Peck established the "Columbia Inn" at the corner of Market (now Baltimore) and Howard Streets, Baltimore, in the house previously kept by Lewis Pascault. John Reynolds, Jan. 9, 1800, in announcing that he would continue the watch and clock-making business, returned his grateful thanks for past favors. Jacob Rohrer, Jr., resumed, January 30th, the business of brewing, before conducted by Messrs. Jonathan Hager & George Shall, and advertising for good barley hops, promised a "generous price." Robert Douglass having removed from Stull's Addition, in Hagerstown, to the stone house opposite the Lutheran church, next door to Mr. Capp's tavern, on the main street leading to Williamsport, assured, April 3d, his friends and former customers that he has made arrangements for carrying on weaving in all its branches more extensively than ever, particularly plain linens, woolens, striped cottons, coverlets, diapers, and table linen of every pattern and figure required." Charles Worland commenced, April 10th, the business of making saddles and harness, holsters, and light horseman's caps, "in the neatest and most fashionable manner," at the new brick house, the property of Nicholas Smith, two doors from Dr. Schnebley's, and nearly opposite Mr. Price's inspection-office. George Beigler continued, March 27th, the comb-making business in all its branches. April 11th, Lawrence Owen had just received from Philadelphia and Baltimore at his store, lately occupied by Alexander Kennedy, and next door to Peter Miller's, a large assortment of dry-goods, hardware, queens and glassware, Morocco and kid shoes, and a number of other articles in the grocery line too numerous to mention, which he offered for cash or merchantable wheat. B. Claggett invited, June 12th, all those who wish to lay out their money to advantage to call and examine in his store, at the "Sign of the Golden Sheaf," a very handsome assortment of seasonable dry-goods, linens, hardware, queens and glassware. Michael Yerger carried on the saddling business in all its branches at the late dwelling-house of Baltzer Goll, next door to Mr. Neill's store, and nearly opposite Mr. Reidenour's tavern; he sold for "cash, or on short credit." July 10th, Samuel and David Claggett commenced the dry-goods, ironmongery, and grocery business in the dwelling-house of Gen. Heister, in the store-room formerly occupied by Benjamin Claggett; they were also engaged extensively in the milling business. August 14th, William Hughes "wanted a person who will contract to build the stock and store-houses of a furnace; he must employ eight hands, and begin work in ten days, at Mount Etna Furnace." November 13th, Jacob D. Deitrich removed from Chambersburg to Hagerstown and engaged in the business of ironmongery, paint, books, and fancy goods; his store was in the Diamond, and nearly opposite Jonathan Hager's inn.

Archibald Watt, March 10, 1801, carried on the business formerly conducted by his father, John Watt, of wheelwrighting and chair-making. Lawrence Owen continued the dry-goods, hardware, queens and glassware business, March 12th. Frederick Miller, at the "Sign of the Golden Mortar," received fresh drugs and medicines from Philadelphia and Baltimore, March 26th. Claggett & Miller—Benjamin Claggett and Peter Miller—had a general assortment of dry-goods and groceries, March 31st. John Fry was a shoemaker, Seth Lane was a cabinet-maker, and William Kreps, hatter, wanted two or three apprentices of reputable connections, to be taken to the business on liberal terms. John Finley was a house and furniture-painter and glazier. John Reynolds continued the watch and clock-making business, May 25th. John McCoy was in the dry-goods and grocery business, July 15th; Fouts & Stuckey were hatters, and gave the highest price for wool and furs, Aug. 12th; Alexander Simpson continued the business of clock, watch, and instrument-making, September 9th; James Garret, a weaver, commenced business, October 15th, at the house where Devalt Leisinger formerly lived, next to Mr. Ranhauser's house, in the back street leading to the Western country, where he weaved linen, linsey, woolen cloth, striped cottons and bed-tick, and other plain work. Henry Townsend, tailor and habit-maker, commenced business October 20th, in the stone house "lately occupied by Mr. Deitrich," where clothes of every description and ladies' riding-habits, in a neat and genteel fashion, and long cloaks for ladies, could be obtained. Henry Dillman was a reed-maker, at his shop near the Catholic chapel, "on the road leading to Jacob Rohrer's, in the vicinity of this town." P. W. Little & F. Miller conducted the mixed business of new medicines and fresh groceries at their store, at the house formerly occupied by James Ferguson, where there was "a large and general assortment of medicines, fruits, paints, groceries, queensware, and twenty thousand Spanish segars."

James Miller commenced the business of weaving, Jan. 28, 1802, at the house formerly occupied by Doris Doyle, "in the street where the jail stands," where linen, linsey, woolen-cloth, striped cottons, bed-tick, and other plain work was done for cash or country produce. Little & Miller, March 6th, received from John Lee & Co., patent and family medicine store, Baltimore, a fresh supply of the "following valuable medicines": Dr. Hamilton's Elixir, Grand Restorative, Worm Destroying Lozenges, Genuine Essence and Extract of Mustard, Dr. Hahn's Anti-Bilious Pills, True and Genuine German Corn Plaster, Genuine Persian Lotion, Restorative Powder for the Teeth and Gums, Genuine Eye-Water, Tooth Ache Drops, Sovereign Ointment for the Itch, Anodyne Elixir, Damask Lip Salve, Infallible Ague and Fever Drops, etc." Jacob D. Dietrich also advertised "valuable medicines" from Lee & Co.'s patent and family medicine store, Baltimore, and adds, "take notice, for sale at no other place in Hagerstown." Michael Yerger removed, March 16th, to the "red house," adjoining Jonathan Hager's tavern, the fourth door above Mr. Ferguson's store, and nearly opposite the sheriff's office. Mathew Treacy, March 29th, warned all persons from taking an assignment on a note given by him to James McCoy for £23 17*s.* 6*d.*, for a certain house and lot in Funkstown, as he was determined "not to pay the same until he received a sufficient title or was compelled by law."

George and Job McNamee offered ground plaster of Paris at Stull's old mill, and Little & Miller had for sale, by the barrel, a quantity of Indian Spring or Seneca Oil, now known as crude petroleum. Pinkleys & Middlekauff carried on the dry-goods business at the stone house opposite Mr. Stoner's tavern. September 1st, Mr. Hayden, dentist, from Baltimore, was in Hagerstown ready to perform every necessary operation on the teeth of the people of that town and vicinity. His stay in the place was only for two weeks. George Stonebraker, boot and shoemaker, from Baltimore, opened a store, October 13th, next door to Capt. John Reynolds, watch and clock-maker. Jonathan Wickersham, at the Tuscarora Fulling-mill, informed the "inhabitants of Maryland" that he still continued to carry on the fulling and dyeing business at Edward Beesom's fulling-mill, Martinsburg, Berkeley Co., Va., and that at the request of his customers he had fixed a store at Peter Light's tavern, at the ferry crossing to Williamsport, where raw cloth will be received, and carefully returned when dressed.

John Geiger associated John Harry with him in the dry-goods business, Feb. 23, 1803, and of the same date Jacob Harry opened his dry-goods business in the store-room formerly occupied by Samuel and David Claggett. Joseph Kennedy was, March 30th, in the dry-goods business at Williamsport. The pottery business was conducted by Fechtig & Voglesang, —Christian Fechtig and George Voglesang. John Bailie, stocking-weaver, commenced business May 4th, in the house lately occupied by Frederick Atler, next door to the Rev. Mr. Schmucker. Boerstler & Harry dissolved May 24th, and Charles G. Boerstler continued the grocery and flour business at the old stand. "Francis Pie, from Georgetown, Potomac," opened, September 7th, at John Ragan's tavern, "Sign of the Indian King," a handsome assortment of millinery and jewelry, and proposed to stay only three days. George C. Smoot commenced the business of scrivener in the clerk's office of Washington County, November 30th. In 1804, Rochester & Beatty opened, May 30th, a handsome assortment of spring goods at the house lately occupied by Christian Keller, and adjoining the Court-house Square Peter Bell carried on the pottery business at the stand formerly occupied by Conrad Crumbach, next door to John Miller and opposite to Henry Arnold's, on the street leading to Cumberland. Thomas Shewman carried on the trimming business at the house lately occupied by John McCoy, nearly opposite to Middlekauff's (formerly Ridenouer's) tavern. Simpson & Johnson dissolved their clock and watch-making business September 19th, and Arthur Johnson continued the business at the "well-known shop" in the public square, next door to Mr. Heiser's. John Geiger and John Harry became the sole agents for the sale of all the iron manufactured by Col. Daniel Hughes.

Among the mills in the early part of the present century in Washington County were the following: Wolgamott's mill, on Conococheague Creek, a stone building standing in 1800; Michael Hoffer's mill, five miles from Hagerstown, in operation in 1812; and John T. Mason's mill, near Hagerstown. Denton Jacques and Peter Fite were neighbors of Mr. Mason, whose estate was known as "Montpelier." Near Hughes' forge was Mayer's mill. At Kershner's mill, on the road from Hagerstown to Hancock, and four miles from Hagerstown, Jacob Dunn and Andrew Kershner had a carding-machine in 1812. John Cushwa's mill was distant about two miles from John T. Mason's. The cooper at Cushwa's mill in 1813 was Jacob Troxell. Joseph Sprigg also had a mill at some point on the Potomac in 1810. In January, 1810, Geo. Muller and John Julius advertised for sale a paper-mill, grist and saw-mill on Antietam Creek, about one and a half miles from Hagerstown, on the road leading to Harman's Gap. The paper-mill was three stories high, sixty feet long, thirty-six feet wide, with a vat-house on each side two stories high and eighteen feet square.

The mill was used as a woolen-factory by George Miller from 1815 to 1820. Mr. Miller also built a mill for cleaning clover-seed at the same place in 1818.

Benjamin Galloway, a famous local politician, had a mill on the Potomac River about 1814.

In 1815, John Freaver had the right for selling wooden pegged shoes in Washington County. The proprietors of the patent were Samuel B. Hitchcock and John Bement. John and Joseph McIlhenny first offered stoves for sale (square, oval, and round-end stoves from Harriet Furnace) in October, 1812. In 1813, Daniel Reichard, Peter Bell, John Snavely, and Henry Adams manufactured earthenware.

In his reminiscences, published in the Hagerstown *Mail*, Dr. W. H. Grimes presents the following interesting picture of business habits in Hagerstown in the early part of the nineteenth century:

"I recollect," he wrote, "seeing every winter, when there was much snow on the ground, numbers of two-horse sleds coming into town from quite a distance, bringing wheat, rye, oats, green and dried apples, feathers, and beeswax, honey, venison, hams, etc. This was a harvest for the merchants of the town, who all kept extensive apartments of every kind of merchandise, dry-goods, groceries, queensware, shoes, and boots,—more shoes than boots, as the extensive boot-factories of New England had not then been established. The merchants who did the most extensive business at that time were James Ferguson, who was afterwards succeeded by the Messrs. Kennedy, John and Hugh, the Harrys, John and George, Richard Ragan, and the McIlhennys, John and Joseph. James Ferguson realized a handsome fortune by merchandising, and so did the Kennedys who succeeded him. These gentlemen had both been school-teachers in their early lives, and being men of honesty and integrity, and of considerable business capacity, were taken as clerks by Mr. Ferguson, and afterwards had his business transferred to them. Hugh never married, and contributed more to the Bible Society every year than any other citizen. The Presbyterians owe the erection of their church as much, or perhaps more, to his generous munificence than to any one else's. Counterfeit money must have been extensively circulated in those days, for I recollect of seeing the window casings in Kennedy's store pasted over with bank-notes, and upon inquiring what that meant, I was told by Jonathan Rahawser, one of the clerks, that they were counterfeits. Archibald M. Waugh carried on the manufacture of tobacco and snuff just south of Kennedy's store, on Potomac Street. You could then purchase six cigars for *one* cent; now, you pay ten cents for *one* of the same kind. '*Tempora mutantur!*' Richard Ragan, a little northeast of the Kennedys, in the square, was also extensively engaged in the business of merchandising. George and John Harry kept store on the east corner of the square, on Washington Street. I think they were succeeded by the Hagers, George and Jonathan. Of this, however, I am not certain. On the opposite corner north, in the large three-story stone building, Maj. Henry Lewis held forth. Beyond him, farther north, on the corner of Potomac Street, George I. Harry kept a store. He married a Miss Amelia Knode, of Funkstown, who was the belle of that ancient village at that time. John and Joseph McIlhenny kept store on the northwest corner of the square and Washington Street.

"Comb-making was carried on in East Franklin Street by a man named Deitrick. The manufacturing of hats was an extensive and lucrative business, or it would not have supported so many shops. Henry Middlekauff, on the southwest corner of Potomac and Franklin Streets, John Julius, on North Potomac Street, and John Crumbach, at the extreme west of Washington Street, were all extensively engaged in hat-making. Cut nails had not yet come into general use, and Peter Suter made and sold *wrought* nails on the northwest corner of Franklin and Jonathan Streets. Immediately west of him, on Franklin Street, John Crenger made curled-hair mattresses, while just beyond him Mr. Brentlinger made gloves and buckskin breeches for all who wanted that kind of goods. I recollect his sign was a pair of buckskin short-clothes and a wild deer *courant*.

"Stocking-weaving was another of the institutions carried on in the town at that time. A Mr. Baily, on Antietam Street, near the corner, and a Mr. Crawmer, on West Franklin Street, wove stockings for the good people of the town and neighborhood. George Marteny, on West Franklin Street, made saddle-trees, while John Cramer, on Jonathan Street, plated them. A Mr. Brasier, a whitesmith, manufactured bridle-bits and stirrup-irons on Jonathan Street, in a small brick shop. Not far off was the residence of the Rev. Mr. Rahauser, the pastor of the German Reformed Church, on North Potomac Street. The upper story of this shop was subsequently turned into a meeting-house. Methodism was in its infancy then in and about Hagerstown, and very enthusiastic meetings were frequently held in this small meeting-house, and no doubt many an old pious Methodist can date his conversion from this humble locality. Capt. George Shryock, on West Washington Street, made pumps for the people. They were large and unwieldy, not at all like those of the present day, but they answered the purpose of their construction, and were quite an improvement on the old rope and windlass. Mrs. Shryock was the daughter of Capt. William Lewis, a soldier, who had been out with Wayne in his Northwest campaign in 1794. He was court crier for many years before his death. He was a man of large proportions, of a generous disposition, of a kind heart, and universally respected by all who knew him. I very well recollect with what sudden timidity the boys slunk out of sight in the court-house when they heard his stentorian voice crying out, 'Silence in court!'

D. W. REICHARD & CO., Hardware and Cutlery.

LOWENSTEIN BROS., Clothiers and Tailors.

W. F. FINGER & CO., General Fancy Goods.

HUMRICHOUSE BUILDING, HAGERSTOWN, MD.

"Blue-dyeing and coverlet-weaving was another trade carried on in East Washington Street by a Mr. Binkly. The farmers' wives and daughters were very industrious in those days, and usually spun and wove and made most of the articles worn by themselves, their husbands and brothers. The yarn when spun was carried to the blue-dyers and colored blue, part was then wove into coverlets, and the remainder was taken home and made into *homespun* goods. John Shugert, who lived and carried on his trade of wheel-maker on the southeast corner of Franklin and Potomac Streets, where the market-house and Masonic Hall now stand, had for a sign of his occupation a small spinning-wheel set upon the top of a post in front of his shop, which indicated to the country folks and others where they could purchase new spinning-wheels or have their old ones mended. Job Hunt, a very worthy citizen, conducted the business of a coppersmith on the opposite corner north. Whisky-distilling was not then thought such a disreputable calling as some people think it now, and many worthy people who engaged in that pursuit bought their stills of Job Hunt. Job was a member of the church, and certainly did not think his calling of still-making incompatible with his profession of Christianity, or he would not have followed it. But, besides whisky stills, he manufactured large copper kettles, used for domestic purposes generally, but more particularly for boiling apple-butter. In the fall of the year butter-boiling was a great source of pleasure and amusement to the young folks in and around the town, and I have but little doubt but that many a contract entered into at these meetings was afterwards ratified at the hymeneal altar."

In 1817, James Earengey advertised in the Hagerstown *Herald* that he had commenced the business of cabinet-making on Antietam Street, two doors east of Daniel Shnebly's dwelling, nearly opposite the residence of the Rev. George Schmucker. He added that he had laid in an extensive stock of mahogany, which he would dispose of low for cash. In the same paper is an announcement that "Kennedy's Poems," by Thomas Kennedy, of Washington County, were for sale at Anthony B. Martin's store. On the 27th of March, 1828, John Lambert advertised that he would soon remove from Creagerstown, Frederick Co., and that he had rented that "well-known stand" formerly occupied by Martin Newcomer.

Located in a country of remarkable fertility, Hagerstown offers advantages for manufacturing enterprise equaled by no city in Maryland. Abundant water-power, close proximity to the coal-fields of Virginia, Maryland, and Pennsylvania, railroad connections reaching into every State, with a climate of unequaled salubrity and exempt from all miasmatic influence, her future as a great manufacturing centre is assured. Already very great progress has been made in that particular, and with increased capital her men of enterprise, of whom there are many, will make the great advantages of the town known and recognized as the centre of busy industry in every branch. A very great revolution has of late years taken place in the manufacturing business of the country, and instead of the heavy work being done in the large cities, it has to a very great extent been transferred to the towns of the interior. By this change the towns adjacent to New York and Philadelphia have become great manufacturing centres for those cities, and the same influences must exert like results in Maryland. Hagerstown, with five intersecting lines of railroads connecting her directly with Baltimore, Washington, Philadelphia, and New York, with the East and the West, the North and the South, exempt from the heavy taxation of large cities, and wanting no one of the great elements of manufacturing success, is now increasing her enterprises with greater rapidity than any city in Maryland. As her people accumulate wealth, its re-investment in enterprises in their own midst will still further augment the business capital of the town.

One of the conspicuous features of Hagerttown is the large number of spacious and handsome business-houses which it contains. Its leading merchants transact an extensive business with the rich farmers of the surrounding country, and their stock of goods is always large, well assorted, and of a superior grade. Among the buildings more recently erected for business purposes is the large and elegant row of stores on Washington Street, nearly opposite the Baldwin House, erected in 1881 by C. W. Humrichouse, and occupied by Lowenstein Brothers, clothiers and merchant tailors, who have the central portion, and D. W. Reichard & Co., hardware and cutlery, and W. F. Finger & Co., general fancy goods. It is known as "the Humrichouse Building," and consists of three large warehouses, four stories high, with a handsome cornice and a rich and tasteful façade. The windows are large and of fine plate glass, and the building has all the modern improvements. In fact, this is one of the most important, as it is one of the handsomest, recent improvements in Hagerstown.

From the earliest period the town has been noted for the number and variety of industries prosecuted by its inhabitants. From the foregoing notes it is evident that from its infancy no community in Maryland could boast a larger percentage of skilled labor in the various branches of trade. Manufactures in this country previous to the Revolution were heavily weighted with the restrictions imposed by Great Britain, but about the beginning of the nineteenth century they began to make rapid progress.[1]

[1] An article in the Hagerstown *Herald* of Oct. 4, 1809, says, "Since the infamous policy now pursued in Europe commenced we have in this county made rapid progression towards supplying ourselves with clothing of our own manufacture. There have been erected within the last eighteen months *fourteen carding-machines* for wool and cotton, all of which find constant employment. Besides, there has lately been erected a

Dec. 22, 1841, the matter of home manufactures was brought directly before the people of Hagerstown by the following call:

"WHEREAS, the undersigned having viewed with regret a rising disposition manifested by many of our citizens to give a preference to articles of foreign manufacture, and as we believe this disposition to be detrimental to the interest of the whole American community, and particularly to the manufacturing and mechanical portions thereof, and as we feel a deep interest in the prosperity and advancement of home manufactures and the sustenance of our American operatives, will meet at the court-house on January 1st (New Year's day), for the purpose of forming a 'Home League.' There will be several addresses delivered on the occasion. The citizens generally are invited to attend.

"W. H. Handy, John Weis, Samuel Gettinger, George A. Bender, Thomas Schnebly, William Brazier, Jonathan Kershner, J. Buchanan Hall, Richard Ragan, Jr., George W. Hartly, Charles F. Gelwicks, John W. Boyd, Martin Startzman, John Bradshaw, W. Waltz, Henry Weis, John Swartzwelder, Joseph Boyd, William Thomas, M. W. Boyd, William Faulkler, William Allen, Thomas E. Mittag, W. McK. Thompson, John R. Sneary, W. H. Boyd, Charles G. Lane, Martin King, George Updegraff, Edward Watkins, Samuel Eichelberger, Henry Metcalf.

"Dec. 22, 1841."

In 1865, William Updegraff, trading under the firm-name of Geo. Updegraff & Son, commenced the manufacture of gloves in their retail store on West Washington Street. They employed but *one* hand, and designed manufacturing gloves only for their retail department, and particularly for persons having odd-sized or chapped hands, who could not be fitted from a regular stock. After several years, they succeeded in perfecting a new system of cutting by measurement, which induced them in 1870 to enlarge their business facilities. The excellent make, fit, and durability of their gloves could not fail to attract attention of dealers in the glove trade. In 1872 their trade demanded still larger room, and fifteen hands were soon employed. In 1874 another enlargement of quarters and a further increase of hands became necessary, until fifty hands in 1878 were employed in the production of their gloves. The quarters on West Washington Street no longer sufficed for their enlarged business. The old brewery property on East Franklin Street was purchased, and upon the lot, one hundred and twenty by eighty-two feet, the present factory was erected in 1880. Their trade is confined to retail dealers, and their goods are sold mostly to first-class dealers in large cities. They make seventy-two different styles and grades of gloves. The materials used are kid, castor, buckskin, and leather, also fine otter and beaver-skin. The system under which their gloves are made is entirely different from other glove-manufacturers, and no less than fourteen different hands work upon each pair of gloves, each hand having only a small portion of the labor to perform, and thus by continual work on one part perfection of execution is obtained.

The name of Updegraff is and has been for many years prominently identified with the business interests of Hagerstown. Peter Updegraff removed to Hagerstown from York County, Pa., and for many years carried on in the town a prosperous business as baker and confectioner. He died in 1835. His son George, born in Hagerstown, Aug. 12, 1798, was a well-known hatter, and served as postmaster of Hagerstown from 1848 to 1852. His business career began in 1824, and until 1848 he was steadily employed as a journeyman hatter. He married Eliza, daughter of Joseph Boyd, an early settler in Hagerstown, and proprietor of the National Line of coaches, running over the National pike between Baltimore and Wheeling. Mr. Boyd died in 1869, in Hagerstown, where his daughter (widow of George Updegraff) still lives at the age of eighty. Her surviving sons and daughters are Joseph, William, and Mrs. D. C. Aughinbaugh. William Updegraff was born in Hagerstown, June 22, 1832. He attended school in Hagerstown under Isaac Allen until reaching his eleventh year, when he was placed in a store, and after serving three years returned to his studies in the Hagerstown Academy. At the age of seventeen he was apprenticed to H. J. Downey, a Hagerstown hatter, and at the age of twenty went to Baltimore, where he was employed as a journeyman hatter for two years. In 1854 he formed with others in Baltimore the firm of Updegraff, Deveau & Co., for the purpose of manufacturing silk hats. From 1852 he had been a partner with his father in the manufacture of hats in Hagerstown; and when in 1856 the elder Updegraff was compelled by illness to relinquish the active management of business, William sold out his interests in Baltimore to

spinning-machine, having about three hundred spindles, and others are about to be erected. That enterprising and ingenious mechanic, Mr. E. Gibbs, who has made and actually has an interest in the most of them, now has it in contemplation to erect a set of mules in the same building with the spinning-machine. Several of our weavers, who carry on their business pretty extensively, have brought in use the *flying shuttle*, the advantages of which are incalculable. There appears to be a general preference among our citizens to domestic products, which, although not as superb and gaudy as the enervated European might think *stylish*, yet they are all comfortable, and suitable to republican manners.

"We have also a manufacturer of bridle-bits and stirrup-irons, some of which, for beauty, utility, and cheapness, will bear comparison with any of those from Europe. We now know and men of every political sect agree that we have resources within ourselves which will amply supply the want of that commerce denied by the belligerents of Europe."

William Updegraff

take full charge of affairs at Hagerstown. Since that date William Updegraff has been steadily engaged in the hat trade in Hagerstown, although the firm ceased to manufacture when the introduction of hat-making machinery at the close of the war crowded the hand-made goods out of the market and ended that kind of manufacture. It was to supply the vacancy thus made in their business enterprises that George Updegraff & Son resolved to embark in the manufacture of gloves; and although beginning in an humble way, they gradually expanded the business as the excellence of their work became known, and enlarged their trade. In 1867, William bought out his father, and in 1870 materially enlarged the sphere of his manufacturing department. In 1879 he still further increased it to its present capacity, which is about six thousand dozen pairs of gloves and mittens annually, in the production of which one hundred hands are employed. The style of the firm has ever remained George Updegraff & Son. Besides William Updegraff, the members are his sons, George F., William M., and Edward M. While pushing the affairs connected with his private business, Mr. Updegraff has been among the foremost in his native town in the work of promoting and encouraging general manufacturing industries. In 1867, as a member of the firm of Miller, Protzman & Co., he founded the Hagerstown Agricultural Implement Manufacturing Company, with which important enterprise Mr. Updegraff was connected until 1875, first as president and later as treasurer. In 1859 he assisted in organizing the Mechanics' Loan and Savings-Bank, of which corporation he has been the president since 1866. He was one of the projectors of Rose Hill Cemetery, and from 1867 to the present has been secretary and treasurer of the cemetery association. In 1879 he succeeded after persistent efforts in organizing the Hagerstown Spoke-Works Company. These works are now in the full tide of success, and employ upwards of eighty hands. In 1870, Mr. Updegraff began to agitate the subject of a system of water-works for Hagerstown, and in the winter of 1871–72 obtained the passage through the Legislature of a bill submitting to the people the question of water-works or no water-works. The question was answered at the polls in the negative, but despite this result Mr. Updegraff still worked for the project, and in the spring of 1881 enjoyed the satisfaction of seeing it emphatically indorsed at the popular election. The company (in which Mr. Updegraff is a director) is fully organized, and contemplates the completion of the works in May, 1882. In 1855, Mr. Updegraff married Laura A., daughter of Eli Mobley, of Hagerstown. Of their seven children, three sons and three daughters survive. Mr. Updegraff is one of the busiest, as he is one of the most progressive and enterprising, men in Hagerstown. No scheme for public improvement or industrial development which had a reasonably substantial basis has been inaugurated in the town in recent years of which he has not either been the originator or the earnest and energetic promoter. He recognizes fully his responsibilities as a citizen of means, and instead of shrinking from expenditure for the general good has gone out of his way repeatedly to invite and incur it. In short, Mr. Updegraff is never better satisfied than when hard at work pushing forward some new enterprise, and his influence and example have been of inestimable value to Hagerstown.

The Washington County Leather Manufacturing Company was organized in 1867, with Daniel Schindle, president; William M. Marshall, Daniel Dunn, F. M. Darby, M. J. McKinnon, J. E. McComas, and A. Small, directors. The capital was $50,000. The main building is eighty-four by forty-five feet, with a wing sixty by thirty feet, and contains seventy-two vats.

The Hagerstown Manufacturing Company, for sash, doors, shutters, and blinds, was organized Jan. 15, 1867, with John H. Cook, president; L. Delamater, vice-president; B. F. Kendall, secretary and treasurer. The capital was $30,000, working 25 hands. The Hagerstown Agricultural Implement Manufacturing Company was incorporated Jan. 1, 1869, with A. Miller, Wm. Updegraff, A. R. Appleman, J. W. Cook, and Wm. H. Protzman, incorporators and directors. The first president was A. Miller, and Wm. H. Protzman was the first treasurer. The officers, Jan. 1, 1880, were A. R. Appleman, president; N. G. Thomas, vice-president; P. Negley, treasurer; J. M. Knodle, secretary. The manufactured product of the first year was $35,000; that for 1880 amounted to $280,000. The number of hands employed the first year was 18, and the number for 1880 ranged from 150 to 200. The company manufactures clover-hullers for the market of West Virginia, and grain-drills and hay-rakes for States both North and South. The capital invested is $100,000, and the horse-power used is 60. The company shipped, Jan. 2, 1881, *via* Baltimore and Ohio Railroad, eleven car-loads of agricultural implements, consisting of twenty-two Victor double clover-hullers. This consignment was worth ten thousand dollars and over, and went to John McKee, Jr., & Co., of Kalamazoo, Mich., and to Morris & Son, of Warsaw, Ind. The works employ from 140 to 150 men, and the weekly pay-roll amounts to

$1200 per week. The gross product of the works daily is from $2500 to $3000. A. Miller is the general superintendent, and John Kailor is the assistant superintendent, and each department is run by a foreman who has charge of the men in his department.

The organ-factory of M. P. Möhler manufactures both reed and pipe-organs. These organs combine all the late improvements and new designs of cases, and are very elegant in finish. A novel construction of Möhler's choral pipe-organs, which is patented, is built with five sets of pipes with independent pedal base, that can be shipped to any distance without removing a single pipe, and ready for use. The reed-organs manufactured by Mr. Möhler are in very general use, and stand deservedly high, and are unsurpassed in sweetness and perfection. There is one of these pipe-organs in the German Reformed and one in the Lutheran churches, Greencastle; one in the Presbyterian church, Mercersburg; and in the First Reformed chapel, Hagerstown, and other places of worship.

The enterprise of Mr. Möhler was greatly aided by an advance of capital made by Wm. Updegraff, Philip Wingert, Hon. Wm. T. Hamilton, M. L. Byers, S. M. Bloom & Co., A. D. Bennett, Hagerstown Manufacturing Company, E. M. & B. H. Griswold, Henry K. Tice, George W. Harris, Martin & Stover, Gassman & Bro., J. M. Bayer, J. H. Beachley, William Schlotterbeck, Jacob Roessner, L. E. McComas, F. C. McComas. The terms upon which the advance was made were the use of the money for ten years without interest, secured by a mortgage upon the property.

The Hagerstown Spoke-Works were established in 1873 by Charles W. Sebold, and were transferred to a stock company in 1880. The factory is a large brick structure, thirty by one hundred feet in size, containing all of the most modern machinery for the prosecution of a large business. The manufactures of the establishment are all kinds of foreign and domestic spokes from second-growth white-oak and hickory. The officers of the company are Charles W. Sebold, president; J. H. Beachley, vice-president; and J. A. Richardson, secretary and treasurer. The trade of the company extends over many parts of the United States, Canada. Great Britain, France, Germany, and other European countries. The spoke and rim-works of Lutz & Reynolds are among the leading industries of Hagerstown. The machinery is complete in every particular, combining all the latest improvements. A powerful new engine drives all the machinery; the saw-mill has all the latest improvements applied to it; the turning-lathes and other machinery are of the latest patents, and the machine for bending the rims is as powerful as it is curious, and works with remarkable force and precision. The buildings are roomy, light, and airy, and everything is so arranged that an air of permanency and efficiency pervades the whole establishment.

Large quantities of timber, in the rough and already worked up into rims and spokes, attest the extensive business with which the establishment commences operations, and with heavy orders far ahead, it will be kept running to its utmost capacity in the indefinite future. This timber consists of white-oak and hickory. The machinery consists of a complete saw-mill, where white-oak and hickory timber are cut up for spokes and rims, and other timber sawed to order. The spoke machinery comprises two lathes, tenoning, throating, facing, and sand-belt machines, which are used in the order named. The combined average daily capacity of the two lathes is one thousand spokes. The rims are first planed smooth on a machine on the ground-floor, then hoisted on a steam-elevator to the second floor, where they are steamed for about half an hour in a steam-chest, from which they are carried to the bending-machine near by, which latter is new in construction and design, of great strength, and bends with perfect uniformity. With sufficient number of steel bands, from sixty to one hundred and twenty rims can be bent in one hour, according to the size of the rims, since three large or six small rims are bent at one time, and twenty bendings can readily be made in one hour. Water is obtained from the Hagerstown Manufacturing Company's cistern, through a pipe recently laid, and drawn by either of two pumps in the engine-room. The number of hands employed is 17.

The Hagerstown Steam-Engine and Machine-Works, formerly the machine-shops of Garver & Flanagan, were organized in 1874, by John H. Garver, Wm. Flanagan, Wm. T. Hamilton, Jos. J. Smith, E. W. Mealey, Chas. B. Doyle, Henry H. Keedy, John Welty, and Charles W. Humrickhouse, with a capital stock of $40,000, which was increased in 1881 to $70,000. John W. Garver and William E. Flanagan, the original proprietors of the works, bought the lot on which they are situated from George Lias on the 5th of October, 1867. They formed a partnership under the name of Garver & Flanagan. By the middle of January, 1868, they were ready for work. For the season of 1868 they finished the castings for five hundred grain-drills, built fifty drills and twenty-eight horse powers, and a large amount of grist and paper-mill machinery. The works continued in successful operation, and in 1874, as stated, were transferred to a stock company.

J. W. Stonebaker

The old Hagerstown foundry was purchased in 1881, and converted into a factory for portable and stationary engines and boilers. The company has been awarded premiums for its manufactures at the Montgomery County Fair, and at Gettysburg, Carlisle, York, Frederick, and Chambersburg.

The manufacture of cigars in Hagerstown and vicinity for the last six months of 1881 amounted to 1,642,500 cigars, and gave employment to 70 men, at average wages of seven dollars per week. J. K. Baker, G. W. Earnshaw, J. H. Grove, J. F. Leggitt, I. B. Sweeney, Geo. Shaver, J. H. Timms, and Samuel Urich, in Hagerstown, and J. C. Adams, at Williamsport, and Chas. L. Small, at Boonsboro', are the principal manufacturers of cigars.

The spoke-works of Hoopes Brothers & Darlington is another important industry of Hagerstown. The firm is composed of William Hoopes, Thomas Hoopes, Stephen P. Darlington, Jerome B. Gray, Edward Darlington, Thomas Jackson, and David Allen. The industry was originally started by the Hoopes brothers on their farms near West Chester, Pa., where they now have a large factory, which is operated in conjunction with the Hagerstown factory. They procure their timber in Virginia and Maryland and transport it to Hagerstown, where it is prepared for the West Chester factory. O. W. Reagan is foreman of the mill, and J. R. Smith is the agent in Hagerstown. The works began operation in Hagerstown in March, 1881.

Among the most extensive and enterprising manufacturers of Washington County is John W. Stonebraker. He is a descendant of one of Washington County's oldest families, traces his ancestry in Western Maryland as far back as 1730, when his grandfather, John Stonebraker, came to America from Sweden with his two brothers and located in what is now Funkstown District, Washington County. The letters patent for his land, dated 1730, are still in the possession of his descendants, while the home-farm has since then been continuously in the possession of one of his lineal descendants,—its present owner being John W. Stonebraker. Upon that place John Stonebraker and his wife passed their days. His son, Girard, was born there in 1780, and died there in 1855, aged seventy-five. During the war of 1812 he raised a company at and near Hagerstown, of which he became captain, and served with it during that campaign. His wife was Catharine, daughter of Frederick Schroeder, of Washington County, and formerly of Germany. She died in 1849. They had seven children, two of whom survive,—John W. Stonebraker, of Hagerstown, and Sophia Beeler, of the same place,—they being respectively the youngest and the oldest of the children. John W. Stonebraker was born on the old farm Sept. 28, 1828, and resided there until 1859, except when attending the Pennsylvania College at Gettysburg. He assisted his father on the farm and in conducting the Funkstown woolen-mill, which was founded by his father, until the latter's death in 1855, when the property descended to him. Mr. Stonebraker was married in 1849 to Laura L., daughter of William McCardell, of Hagerstown, of which place he was a native. In 1859, Mr. Stonebraker removed his residence to Hagerstown,—still continuing, however, the woolen-factory and farm,—and in the year named erected a paper-mill in Funkstown. The latter enterprise was put in operation in 1860 for the manufacture of book and news paper. In 1864 he sold the paper-mill property and built a new mill two miles east of Hagerstown. In 1867 he leased his woolen-mill.

In 1873 the new paper-mill was destroyed by fire, and by the following year it was succeeded by a larger and materially improved establishment, in which Mr. Stonebraker has as a partner John A. Dushane,—the firm being Stonebraker & Dushane. It is known as the "Antietam Paper-mill," and manufactures the finer grades of book and news paper. It has a capacity of six thousand pounds per twenty-four hours. Seventy hands are employed. The main building is sixty by one hundred feet, and the wing forty by one hundred and thirty feet. In 1879, Mr. Stonebraker entered into the manufacture of fertilizers at Funkstown with his son, J. E. Stonebraker, and his son-in-law, George Keller, under the firm-name of J. W. Stonebraker & Co. In politics he has always been a Republican, and from 1875 to 1879, and in 1881, served as a member of the board of county commissioners. During his incumbency he was the advocate of and active in many measures looking to the advancement of the public interests, and with his co-laborers established a record for the faithful discharge of public trusts that was highly indorsed by the citizens of the county. It was during his terms of service that the removal of the almshouse from within the city limits and the erection of the present fine structure was accomplished. Mr. Stonebraker is still in the prime of life, and is one of the influential men of the county. Of his four children, three are daughters, and his son, J. Ellsworth Stonebraker, is associated with him in business.

Banks and other Financial Institutions.—The Hagerstown Bank was organized March 12, 1807. Previously to that date it had transacted business as an association, with Col. Nathaniel Rochester as president. He was the founder of the bank, and his portrait in water-colors, which his numerous descendants, it is said, have repeatedly tried to purchase, adorns the walls of the present bank, the president and directors having refused to give it up on any terms. The bank was organized in the stone house of Col. Rochester, situated opposite the court-house, which had been fitted up for the purpose. This building is now owned by Hon. A. K. Syester, and is used as a restaurant. The capital stock of the institution under its charter was limited to $500,000, in 10,000 shares of $50 each, of which one-tenth was "reserved for the use and benefit of the State of Maryland." The remaining 9000 shares were allotted as follows: Hagerstown, 5000 shares, represented by Jacob Schnebly, Matthias Shaffner, Martin Kershner, Henry Shafer, and Jacob T. Towson; Baltimore, 2000 shares, represented by Luke Tiernan, James L. Hawkins, Christian Keller, William Matthews, Clement Brooke; Frederick, 1000 shares, represented by John Schley. At the first meeting there were present Nathaniel Rochester, Elie Williams, Thomas Sprigg, William Fitzhugh, Charles Carroll, Jacob Zeller, and William Heyser. These gentlemen "took the oath prescribed by the charter of the association before Thomas Sprigg, who took the same before Elie Williams." The capital stock was then fixed at $250,000; it is now $150,000. The business was conducted at this place until 1814, when the new banking-house (of which an engraving was used on the bank-notes until the National Banking Act came into force, and is still printed on the drafts) was finished. This building was erected on the lot opposite the present Baldwin House, which had been purchased from a Mr. Hawken for five thousand dollars, and the old building was offered for sale in the following year. The first officers were Nathaniel Rochester, president, and Elie Beatty, cashier. The latter received a salary of five hundred dollars per annum, and also performed the duties of book-keeper and teller. At that time Col. Rochester was postmaster of Hagerstown, and Mr. Beatty was his assistant. In 1809 the bank paid a dividend of eight per cent. on its capital stock. In 1810, Col. Rochester removed from Hagerstown to Western New York, where he founded the beautiful city which bears his name. William Heyser was thereupon elected president, and Elie Beatty continued as cashier. In May of this year the stock of the bank commanded a twenty-five per cent. premium and was in great demand. Mr. Heyser died in 1831, and Elie Beatty became president, and Daniel Sprigg cashier. In 1833, Mr. Sprigg was appointed cashier of a bank at Rochester, but soon afterwards was tendered a similar position in the Merchants' Bank of Baltimore and removed to that city. Otho Lawrence was then elected president of the Hagerstown Bank, and Mr. Beatty went back to his position as cashier. In 1840, Alexander Neill, Sr., was elected president, and in 1851 was succeeded by the Hon. J. Dixon Roman. Mr. Beatty, the cashier, died in 1859, and his place was filled by William M. Marshall, who had been teller of the bank for many years. In 1866 John H. Kausler succeeded Mr. Marshall, and in 1867 the death of Mr. Roman occurred, and Hon. William T. Hamilton was elected president.

Among the many bright ornaments of the legal profession in Western Maryland in the middle of the present century there were none more prominent or able, and none who were more respected in public and private life, or who exerted a greater or more useful influence than Hon. James Dixon Roman, born in Chester County, Pa., Aug. 11, 1809. He removed to Cecil County, Md., with his parents the year following, and after receiving a practical education entered the law-office of his uncle, James Dixon, in Frederick, at which place he was admitted to the bar. Shortly thereafter the death of his uncle threw him upon his own resources, and nothing daunted he removed to Hagerstown and began the practice of the law. His natural talents, high moral character, and gifted mind brought him at once into prominence, and he was soon a leader in the Whig party of that district, and was elected to the House of Representatives in 1847. Two years later he was an elector for Taylor and Fillmore, and in 1857 for Buchanan and Breckenridge. In Congress he participated in the exciting debates of that period, and was an ardent supporter of the tariff laws. At the national capital he earned the reputation of an able statesman and constitutional lawyer, and enjoyed cordial relations with Clay, Webster, Tyler, Adams, and men of like character.

At the end of his term in Congress he declined a renomination and returned to the bar. Afterwards he was persuaded to accept a nomination for the State Senate, but was defeated. Mr. Roman's ability as a financier was recognized in 1851 by his being elected the successor of Alexander Neill, Sr., as President of the Hagerstown Bank. On vacating this position he directed his energies to financial affairs, invested in real estate, and was largely identified with public enterprises in his section, in the management of all of which he was very successful. He was a member of the Peace Convention held in Richmond, Va., in 1861, and labored earnestly to prevent hostilities. His experience on that occasion served to enlist his sympathies with the South, and he was strong in his advocacy of peace measures.

In 1837, Mr. Roman, on September 2d, married Louisa Margaret, daughter of John Kennedy, who was one of the founders and elders of the Presbyterian Church in Hagerstown. The fruits of this marriage were three children,—Louisa, Sallie, and James Dixon, all of whom are now dead. Louisa died in childhood, James died while at the Harvard University, and Sallie, who married C. C. Baldwin, head of the firm of Woodward, Baldwin & Co., of New York, died in April, 1873.

Mr. Roman died in 1866, at the age of fifty-six years, from a spinal affection of long standing. Mrs. Roman lived in Hagerstown until 1878, when she also died.

In 1873, John H. Kausler resigned the office of cashier of the Hagerstown Bank, and Joseph Kausler was chosen in his stead. The present officers of the bank are: President, Hon. William T. Hamilton; Directors, Messrs. Frederick Fechtig, Dr. Josiah F. Smith, Matthew S. Barber, F. M. Darby, William Newcomer, David S. Boyer, E. W Mealey, and H. H Keedy; Cashier, Joseph Kausler; Teller, John H. Kausler. The last annual statement of the condition of the institution, published Jan. 3, 1881, showed a surplus fund of $60,000.

The Citizens' National Bank of Hagerstown was removed to Washington, D. C., under a special act of Congress, and commenced business Aug. 1, 1874, with a capital stock of $200,000, which has since been increased to $300,000. The stock is held by some of the most substantial men of the District and of Maryland. The largest stockholder is Hon. Jacob Tome, of Port Deposit, Md., who is now president of three banks, viz.: Cecil National Bank, Port Deposit, Md., capital $300,000; National Bank of Elkton, capital $100,000; Fredericksburg National Bank of Virginia, capital $100,000. The remainder of the stock is owned by the officers and directors of the bank and other citizens of the District of Columbia. The bank is in the building formerly occupied by Jay Cooke & Co. and the First National Bank, which they purchased and had remodeled, making it the finest banking-house in the District of Columbia.

The First National Bank of Hagerstown had its origin in the "Hagerstown Savings Institution," which was incorporated by the act of 1846, ch. 266. P. B. Small was the first president, and H. P. Aughinbaugh secretary. Upon the resignation of Mr. Aughinbaugh, Peter Negley was elected secretary. When Hon. George Schley was a member of the Maryland State Senate he succeeded in securing the passage of the act of 1854, ch. 109, by which the institution was transformed into the Hagerstown Savings-Bank, a bank of issue and deposit. P. B. Small was its president, and Peter Negley its cashier. In 1865 the Hagerstown Savings-Bank was converted into the "First National Bank of Hagerstown, Maryland," with the same president and cashier. In 1870, Mr. Negley resigned to accept the position of assistant United States treasurer at Baltimore, and P. B. Small was elected cashier (resigning the presidency), and so continued until his death, Feb. 25, 1881. When Mr. Small resigned the presidency, Charles G. Lane was elected president in his stead, and continued so to act until his death in 1873. On the 21st of January, 1873, George Schley was elected president, and was re-elected in January, 1882. Upon the death of P. B. Small, cashier, John D. Newcomer was elected cashier, and A. B. Almony book-keeper and teller. The *personnel* of the bank at present, therefore, is George Schley, president; John D. Newcomer, cashier; and A. B. Almony, book-keeper and teller. The capital of the bank is $100,000, and its dividends, paid semi-annually, are five per cent. A very handsome bank building is now in course of construction on Washington Street opposite the court-house, and will soon be completed. Meanwhile the bank is occupying temporary quarters near at hand. The new building will contain all the improved facilities for transacting business and every possible safeguard against fire and burglars.

The Washington County Savings-Bank was incorporated under an act of 1860 by George W. Smith, Jr., Samuel E. Schindel, Henry Bell, M. S. Barber, Ephraim Funk, George W. Pole, Alex. Neill, Louis Heist, William Ragan, M. J. McKinnon, T. G. Robertson, John D. Swartz, Thomas A. Boullt, and F. Dorsey Herbert. It was organized in April, 1868, by the election of George W. Smith, Jr., president; Alex. Neill, secretary and treasurer; and the following board of directors: George W. Smith, Jr., Thomas A. Boullt, Henry Bell, Louis Heist, Matthew S. Barber, William Ragan. In December, 1869, Alex. Neill resigned as secretary and treasurer, and was succeeded by Edward W. Mealey, who in turn resigned in May, 1872, and was succeeded by Thomas Taggart. The regular and special deposits of the bank, according to its last annual statement, June 15, 1881, amounted to $35,718.39; surplus and profit, $1284.04. The present officers are George W. Smith, Jr., president; Thomas Taggart, secretary and treasurer; George W. Smith, Jr., James I. Hurley, M. M. Gruber, John Curran, J. J. Monath, Justus Heimel, directors.

John Duval Swartz, who was one of the incorporators of the Washington County Savings-Bank, and who took a very active part in the organization of the institution, is now (1881), the mayor of Hagerstown. He is of German origin, and was born in Hesse-Darmstadt, Aug. 26, 1831. He was but one year old when his parents emigrated to America and settled at Smithsburg, in Washington County. John Swartz, his father, was by trade a tailor, and remained at Smithsburg three years, when he removed to Hagerstown, where, until about 1871, he continued in active service as a "cutter." He still resides in Hagerstown with his aged wife. John D. Swartz obtained his early mental training under Mr. Hoffman and Mr. Beyers, two well-known Hagerstown tutors of their day, and at the age of twenty entered the employment of J. D. Reamer, then one of the leading tailors of Hagerstown. At the age of twenty-six Mr. Swartz left Reamer's service to engage in the merchant tailoring business with his brother, William Swartz, under the firm-name of J. D. Swartz & Brother. In 1862 the firm was dissolved, and in that year John D. Swartz engaged in business on his own account at his present place of business, where he has continued uninterruptedly to the present as merchant tailor and dealer in furnishing goods. On Feb. 2, 1852, he married Mary E., daughter of Charles Spangler, long a resident of Hagerstown, but a native of Pennsylvania. Twelve children were the result of this union, ten of whom are now living. Mr. Swartz's only son is associated with his father in business and represents the third generation. In 1867, Mr. Swartz was appointed one of the board of almshouse trustees. For four years he served in that capacity, and earned an enviable record for zealous performance of duty and watchful administration of the public trust. In 1869 he was elected a member of the City Council, and remained in that body for seven terms, acting meanwhile as its treasurer for two years. In 1879 he was elected mayor of Hagerstown on the Democratic ticket over Thomas J. Walker, Republican. During his administration the material interests of Hagerstown have received his careful supervision, and the city has greatly prospered.

The Mechanics' Loan and Savings Institution of Hagerstown was organized April 5, 1860, with Leander McKee, William Updegraff, Warfield Staley, Henry Freaner, Charles A. Cranwell, and Henry Gantz as directors; Thomas A. Boullt, president; and George W. Smith, Jr., secretary and treasurer. On Aug. 4, 1862, Mr. Smith resigned, and B. F. Kendall was chosen to fill the vacancy. On April 30, 1866, William Updegraff was elected president. Mr. Kendall resigned as secretary and treasurer Aug. 25, 1873, to take effect October 1st of that year, and William Wallace Stover was appointed assistant treasurer. On Mr. Kendall's retirement Mr. Stover succeeded him.

The annual statement of the institution, July, 1881, showed weekly demand and dime deposits amounting to $129,190.80; surplus fund, $10,000. The present officers are William Updegraff, president; William Wallace Stover, secretary and treasurer; George E. Stover, assistant treasurer; Directors, Joseph H. Firey, George B. Oswald, Wilson L. Hays, F. A. Heard, J. S. McCartney, Samuel Ulrich.

W. W. Hoffman commenced the business of banking in 1869, and was soon joined by his brother, Joseph T. Hoffman, under the firm-name of W. W. Hoffman & Co. They purchased a large building on the northwest corner of the public square, known as the Hager building, where the business was conducted until 1874, when Messrs. Henry T. Eavey and Chas. T. Lane became partners, and the firm was changed to Hoffman, Eavey & Co. The growth of the enterprise necessitating the acquisition of a larger and more convenient banking-room, they removed to the building on West Washington Street formerly occupied by the Washington County and Citizens' National Bank, where the business now continues, and the firm has grown to be one of the leading private banks of the State. W. W. Hoffman retired in 1879 on account of failing health, and transferred his interest in the business to the remaining partners. This establishment is purely a home enterprise, founded and conducted by gentlemen natives and residents of Washington County, themselves widely known and thoroughly acquainted with its interests. It is the only private banking establishment in Hagerstown, and employs a capital of about $60,000.

W. W. Hoffman, founder of the banking-house of Hoffman, Eavey & Co., was drowned in the Antietam Creek, near Hagerstown, on the evening of Saturday, June 4, 1881. His remains were interred in Rose Hill Cemetery, the Rev. S. B. Moore, pastor of the Christian Church, officiating, and H. H. Keedy, Albert Small, J. J. Funk, S. D. Straub, Charles S. Lane, and Joseph H. Firey acting as pall-bearers.

Mr. Hoffman was born in Washington County, Md., April 19, 1835, and died June 4, 1881, aged forty-six years, one month, and fifteen days. He left a wife and adopted daughter, one brother, J. T. Hoffman, of the banking firm of Hoffman, Eavey & Co., and one sister, the wife of Henry S. Eavey, of the same firm.

In early life he and his brother engaged in farming in the Beaver Creek District, Washington County,

John A. Swartz.

and about the commencement of the late war they also conducted a successful mercantile business in connection with their farming operations. He retired from this business about the close of the war, and in 1869 commenced the banking business in Hagerstown, under the name of W. W. Hoffman & Co. His career as a banker has already been narrated. After his retirement in 1879 he gave his attention largely to the introduction of fine-bred sheep into the States of Maryland, Pennsylvania, and Virginia, in which business he was engaged at the time of his death.

He was a man possessed of good business qualifications, and by honesty, industry, and upright dealing was successful in all his enterprises, and succeeded in accumulating a large amount of property.

In his social and church relations his life was blameless. He was a highly-respected and influential member of the Christian Church, and was largely instrumental in securing the permanent establishment of that denomination in Hagerstown.

The Mutual Insurance Company of Washington County was incorporated Jan. 22, 1846, for the purpose of doing a general fire insurance business. The incorporators were Daniel Weisel, Alexander Neill, Jr., George W. Smith, George Fechtig, George A. Bender, William McAtee, George Shafer, George Schley, William H. Boyd, Daniel Schindel, Marmaduke W. Boyd, Edwin Bell, Joseph Rench, Samuel Eichelberger, Jacob Swope, Richard Ragan, Sr., Jervis Spencer, James H. Kennedy, Victor Thompson, William Brazier, John Robertson, Frederick Miller, D. M. Middlekauff, David Artz, William Robertson, Jr., and D. Willard. On the first Monday of May, 1846, the first-named twelve persons were elected directors of the company, with William B. Clark as president, and Edwin Bell, secretary. Since its organization the company has received in fire premiums $101,060.92, and has paid out in losses $42,012.74, an average of but 42½ per cent. against the general average of 60 per cent. which insurance authorities give as the experience of leading companies for the past half-century. During the same period the stockholders have received in cash dividends $39,584.27, and the present assets of the company amount to $104,070, in mortgages, stocks, and judgments. The several presidents of the company since its organization have been Wm. B. Clark, James I. Hurley, Isaac Nesbitt, E. M. Mealey, George Fechtig, Matthew S. Barber, and F. M. Darby. The present directory is as follows: President, F. M. Darby; Secretaries, Messrs. Armstrong and Bitner; Treasurer, Henry K. Tice; Attorney, Alex. Neill; Directors, James I. Hurley, E. W. Mealey, H. H. Keedy, F. Dorsey Hubert, P. A. Brugh, Alex. Neill, Matthew S. Barber, Henry K. Tice, A. D. Bennett, Jos. B. Loose, F. J. Posey, Dr. M. A. Berry.

The following is a statement of the condition of the several banks of Western Maryland, compiled from the official reports of the year ending July 1, 1880:

Name.	Capital.	Surplus and undivided Profits.	Deposits.	Last Dividend.
1st National, Cumberland...	$100,000	$69,000	$315,000	July, 1881, 5 %
2d National, Cumberland....	100,000	81,000	421,000	" " 6 %
3d National, Cumberland.....	100,000	8,000	247,000	" " 3 %
Central National, Frederick.	200,000	56,000	183,000	April, " 4 %
Farmers' and Mechanics' National, Frederick............	125,000	55,000	156,000	May, " 6 %
1st National, Frederick.......	100,000	31,000	229,000	July, " 7 %
Frederick County National, Frederick	150,000	52,000	156,000	June, " 6 %
1st National, Hagerstown....	100,000	50,000	207,000	July, " 5 %
Hagerstown, Hagerstown....	150,000	60,000	439,000	May, " 6 %
1st National, New Windsor..	55,000	14,000	80,000	July, " 4 %
Farmers' and Mechanics' National, Westminster.........	50,000	5,000	72,000	Jan., 1880, 3 %
1st National, Westminster...	125,000	38,000	148,000	" 1881, 4½ %
Union Nat , Westminster.....	100,000	25,000	205,000	June, " 4 %
Washington County National, Williamsport........	150,000	37,000	47,000	June, " 6 %

CHAPTER LII.

MISCELLANEOUS SOCIETIES AND EVENTS.

Fire Companies.—The earliest means employed in Hagerstown for extinguishing fires were the fire-buckets, which were very generally distributed among the householders. Long lanes of citizens extending from the scene of conflagration to the nearest supply of water were organized whenever a fire broke out, and these buckets were passed from hand to hand along the line, and their contents poured upon the flames. In 1791 a meeting of the fire company of Hagerstown was held at the court-house, to which the citizens had been notified to bring their buckets, that they might have them registered, and that their safety might be thus assured. A call was issued in 1802 inviting all citizens who were desirous of becoming members of the fire company to attend a meeting at the court-house on the first Saturday in April. This call was signed by J. Schnebly, clerk. On Saturday evening, Feb. 5, 1803, the United Fire Company met and adopted resolutions dividing the town into two fire districts, and organizing the service upon a more efficient basis. The first district embraced all the south side of the town, including the south side of Main Street. The northern portion, including the north side of Main Street, constituted the second district. The fire-engines Nos. 1 and 2 were attached to their respective districts, and the following officers were selected for the proper management of the system: One director-general and one assistant director-general; one director of furniture and goods, one assistant, and six men; one director of hook-and-axe men, one assistant, and ten men; one director of ladders, one assistant, and twelve men; one director, one assistant director, one lane director, four assistants, and twenty-four engine-men for Engine No. 1; one director, one assistant director, one lane director, four assistant lane directors, and thirty-six engine-men for Engine No. 2. Three axes, twelve buckets, and four additional fire-hooks of a small size were directed to be procured for each engine-house. The general offices named above were filled by the fire company, and the offices attached to each engine were filled by the vote of the citizens enrolled in the volunteer companies of each district. If, however, the election was not held within three months of the meeting, the right to appoint persons to fill the vacancies was given to the fire company. Officers and members of the companies were required to meet and exercise at least four times a year, on days appointed by the director-general. The badges of office were a black and white staff about eight feet long for the lane director and his assistants, and a white staff of the same length for the director of furniture and goods and his assistants. In case of neglect of duty a majority vote of the fire company could remove any officer and order a new appointment.

As previously stated, it was the practice in early days to have regular trials of the fire company.

Agreeably to a resolution of the fire company, reads a notice in the Hagerstown *Herald*, "Adam Ott, Richard Pindell, John Ragan, David Harry, George Woltz, Robert Douglass, Frederick Alter, George Shall, Samuel Young, George Shank, Nathaniel Rochester, Alexander Clagett, Charles Gelwicks, William Hess, Henry Cake, Peter Hefleich, Conrad Coffroth, Peter Miller (hatter), Peter Woltz, William Clagett, Thomas Grieves, Peter Miller (merchant), Henry Middlekauff, and James Ferguson are directed to attend at the court-house square, on Saturday, the 17th inst. [Oct. 17, 1807], precisely at 3 o'clock in the afternoon, for the purpose of working the fire-engines: those who do not attend or furnish persons in their places will be fined twenty-five cents, agreeably to said resolution. The engine directors are requested to attend under the penalty of one dollar each. (Signed) WM. HEYSER, *Director-General*."

On the 2d of July, 1808, the same authority called out Leonard Kuhn, John Hershey, John Wise, Christian Hawken, George Binkley, Philip Kellar, Wm. Kreps, John Miller, John Reynolds, Christian Langenecker, Alexander Neill, John Cook, Peter Humrickhouse, Samuel Beeler, Geo. Kreps, Henry Lewis, John P. Herr, Seth Lane, John Conrad, Frederick Miller, Jonathan Hager, Devalt Eichelberner, Geo. Crissinger, and Frederick Dorsey for the purpose of working the engines. The same penalties were to be incurred by a failure to comply with the order of Wm. Heyser, the director-general.

The "United Fire Company," as it was called, continued in existence until during or just after the war of 1812–14, when, in consequence of the unsettled condition of affairs generally, it, like the County Agricultural Society, expired through lack of interest on the part of its members. With the commencement of the year 1817, however, a number of the citizens convened in public meeting for the purpose of organizing themselves into companies for the more effectual protection of property against fire. Archibald M. Waugh was chosen chairman, and Richard Ragan, secretary. It was resolved that J. Kennedy, Geo. Brumbaugh, Otho H. Williams, Richard Ragan, and William Heyser be appointed a committee to draw up such by-laws, ordinances, etc., "as to them shall seem conducive to the interests of the Hagerstown Fire Company;" and further, Peter Humrickhouse, David Harry, Arthur Johnson, and J. A. Donaldson were appointed a committee to examine and make report upon the "present condition of the fire-engines." Joseph McIlhenny, Alexander Neill, William Kreps, Theobald Eichelberner, S. Martin, John Hershey, D. Sprigg, John Seitz, Henry Lewis, and A. M. Waugh were members of a committee appointed "to receive the names of citizens who were willing to become members of the company."

At an adjourned meeting of the citizens of Hagerstown, held at the court-house, Feb. 1, 1817, an organization was effected, composed of the following members: Otho H. Williams, president; William Heyser, director-general; Richard Ragan, assistant director-general; John Kennedy, treasurer; Thomas Grieves, secretary; John A. Donaldson, keeper; Samuel Hager, collector.

Director of Engine No. 1, Henry Kealhofer; Engine-men, Jacob Miller, Peter Glossbrenner, Jacob Butler, John H. Hughes, Fred. Humrickhouse, John Bradshaw, John Currey, John Stallsmith, Daniel May, Michael Kapp, Henry Protzman, John Gruber, Frederick Miller, Jacob Moyer, Peter Suter, John Kramer. Director of Engine No. 2, George Shryock; Engine-men, Frederick Stover, John Dussing, Frederick Rohrer, Samuel Hager, John Miller, Jr., Jacob Kinkle, Jacob Motter, Gera South, Adam Kinkle, John Lorshbaugh, Jacob Shaffner, Michael Bowart, Jacob Burckhartt, Jacob Bowart, Henry Biershing, Henry Adam, John Ebert, John Marteny, Moses McNamee, Gottlieb Mittag; Lane Directors, William Kreps, John McIlhenny; Assistant Lane Directors, Frederick Dorsey, Daniel Sprigg, Eli Beatty, Andrew Johnson, A. M. Waugh, Daniel Schnebly, Upton Lawrence, Geo. C. Smoot; Property Director, David Harry; Property Guards, John Weis, Jonathan Hager, Joseph McIlhenny, Peter Humrickhouse, George Brumbaugh, Charles Shaffner; Director of Ladders, Jacob Renner; Ladder-men, Andrew Beck, John

Billmeyer, Samuel Martin, Jacob Kraft, John Figeley, George Emmert, John Weitzel, William Brazier, Henry Diehl, John Cook, John Freaner, Martin Showaker; Axe Director, Henry Lowry; Axe-men, George Hager, Jacob Sturr, William McCardell, Jacob Little, John Seitz; Hook Director, Thomas Quantrill; Hook-men, Seth Lane, George Smith, Theobald Eichelberner, George I. Harry, Benjamin Yoe, David Barr, Joseph Little, Philip Kellar; Standing Committee, Otho H. Williams, David Harvey, John Hershey, Thomas Grieves, William Kreps, John P. Herr, Archibald M. Waugh.

In 1820 a third engine company was formed, and soon after the town was divided into three fire districts. The citizens residing in South Potomac and Antietam Streets were attached to Engine No. 1; those residing in Franklin and Church Streets, and in North Potomac north of Franklin Street, were attached to Engine No. 2; and those residing in Washington Street, and in North Potomac south of Franklin Street, were attached to Engine No. 3. An order from the commissioners directed that the citizens in each district repair to the respective engine-houses and assist in conveying them, in case of fires; also requesting all the inhabitants of the town to place lighted candles in their windows if fires should occur at night.

The office of the *Torch-Light* and other buildings standing on and near the northeast corner of the public square were burned April 1, 1822, and it seems that the people then experienced difficulties by reason of not having an organized hose company, for at a meeting held at C. C. Frechtig's tavern, April 17, 1822, the "First Hagerstown Hose Company"[1] was formed, its officers and other members being named as follows:

George F. Kreps, president; Charles C. Frechtig, vice-president; H. J. Rahauser, secretary; Wm. C. Drury, treasurer; Engineers, John Weis, Jr., Stewart Herbert; Directors, Thomas Post, Chas. Humrickhouse, George Fechtig, David T. Wilson, William Wise, William Bender; Hose Guards, William Robertson, Martin Kershner; Hose-carriage Guards, Samuel J. Downey, John Reynolds, Jr.; Engine-men, James Davis, George Emmert, John May, William Miller, John A. Doyle, William Good, John H. Fechtig, John V. Swearingen, Geo. Swearingen, Luther Ainsworth, Mandeville Miller, Levin C. Willis, John M. Kreps.

The charter members of the company were George F. Kreps, C. C. Fechtig, H. J. Rahauser, William C. Drury, John Weis, Jr., Thomas Post, George Fechtig, William Bender, Martin Kershner, John Reynolds, Jr., James Davis, George Emmert, William Miller, George Kealhofer, Luther Ainsworth, George Swearingen, Peter Shank, John A. Doyle, Stewart Herbert, David T. Wilson, William Wise, William Robertson, Samuel J. Downey, Mandeville Miller, John H. Fechtig, John M. Kreps, George Lorshbaugh, James Zwisler, Jr., John V. Swearingen, Levin C. Willis, and Daniel H. Middlekauff. The records of the company have been lost from the date of organization to Jan. 15, 1853, at which date Edward M. Mobley was president. The succeeding presidents were Gottlieb Simler, elected 1857; John D. Smart, 1862; Elie Mobley, 1864; John H. Blake, 1868; Oliver B. Ridenour, 1874; Dr. J. McP. Scott, 1880; and George F. Burkhart, 1881, who is the present incumbent. The other officers elected in 1881 were Rufus Hays, secretary, M. L. Byers, treasurer, and George B. Oswald, O. B. Ridenour, John H. Blake, Mark H. Fellheimer, and Alexander Armstrong, standing committee. This company is now erecting a new engine-house on South Potomac Street, which, it is estimated, will cost, with the lot, about fifteen thousand dollars.

On the 27th of May, 1827, an ordinance was passed dividing the town into two fire wards. The first comprised all taxable limits and additions south of Washington Street, and all houses fronting on that street and on the public square. The second ward contained all the taxable limits and additions north of Washington Street and of the public square. All taxable white male persons within the limits of these wards, except persons already enrolled in the First Hagerstown Hose Company, were directed to assemble at the town hall on the 29th of May, 1824, and enroll and organize themselves into a fire company for the ward in which they resided. They were required to exercise at least twice a year, on the second Saturday in June and on the first Saturday in November. The organization formed in pursuance of this ordinance in Fire Ward No. 1 was called "The Washington Mechanic Fire Company;" that formed in Fire Ward No. 2 took the name of "The Franklin Union Fire Company." The owner of every dwelling-house, or in case of neglect on the part of the owner, the tenant or occupier, was required to provide two "well-made leather buckets, painted black, and marked with the owner's name," provided he was assessed for more than three hundred dollars. If assessed for seventy-five dollars and for not more than three hundred dollars, one bucket of this kind was required. The use of these buckets for any other than the purpose for which they were provided was punishable by a fine of fifty cents, one-half to go to the informer. One hundred dollars were at the same time appropriated for repairs, for procuring apparatus, and for incidental expenses, to

[1] The company was incorporated by an act of the Legislature passed in December, 1822.

be dispensed under the direction of the moderator and commissioners of Hagerstown.

The meeting of the citizens of the First Fire Ward, at which the Washington Mechanic Fire Company was organized, was presided over by John Kennedy, and Joseph I. Merrick acted as secretary. The citizens proceeded to enroll themselves as members, and Messrs. O. H. Williams, John Harry, Otho Lawrence, William Heyser, and Joseph I. Merrick were appointed a committee to prepare a constitution and by-laws. The citizens residing within the limits of the Second Fire Ward met, in pursuance of the ordinance passed May 24th, and organized the Franklin Union Fire Company. P. Humrickhouse was called to the chair, and Seth Lane was appointed secretary. After the enrollment of those present as members, Messrs. P. Humrickhouse, John Curry, John Freaner, Seth Lane, and George Brumbaugh were appointed a committee to draft a constitution and by-laws for the company.

On the 26th of January, 1827, a committee was appointed to wait upon the citizens of the different wards to solicit subscriptions for the purchase of a new hose and suction-pump. The committee was constituted as follows: For the First Ward, James Zwisler and Stewart Herbert; Second Ward, William Bender and William Weise; Third Ward, William Robertson and William Moffett; Fourth Ward, George Updegraff and William Miles; Fifth Ward, C. C. Fechtig and John Anderson. The record of the organization of the Antietam Fire Company was destroyed at the time of the court-house fire in 1871, but upon the most reliable information it appears that the company applied for a charter in 1834. The charter was granted by the Legislature March 9, 1835, the incorporators being William D. Bell, William Holliday, Daniel Carver, Roberdeau Annan, William Johnson, John W. Kennedy, Jacob Swope, Jacob Bachelder, William Weber, Alexander Armstrong, Peter Swartzwelder, Victor Thompson, and William S. Brown. On Whit-Monday, 1852, the Independent Junior Fire Company laid the corner-stone of their new building, on North Potomac Street. The announcement of the programme drew a large number of strangers to town to witness the parade and ceremonies. The procession was formed in the public square, under the direction of Joseph P. Mong, chief marshal, assisted by William Logan, Andrew K. Syester, Samuel Schindel, and Jacob Cramwell on horseback, and others on foot. The Martinsburg Band occupied the right, and was followed by the First Hagerstown Hose Company, dressed in white shirts, black pantaloons, and red hats. Next came a delegation of the United Fire Company from Frederick City, in red uniforms; these were followed by the Independent Order of Odd-Fellows in regalia. Next came a delegation of Juniors, another body of fine-looking firemen, from Frederick, in red uniform; the rear being brought up by a very long line of Independent Juniors, preceded by the Mechanics' Band, with their engine drawn by eight gray horses, which were led by as many colored grooms. There was also a carriage in the line containing Messrs. Jackson, Anspach, and Gans, a portion of the clergy of Hagerstown. On reaching the site of the new building the procession halted, and the corner-stone was laid with Masonic ceremonies by Mr. Entler, of Shepherdstown, Va. The assemblage then proceeded to the market-house, where a rostrum had been erected and seats prepared for their accommodation. After music from the two bands, and remarks from Z. S. Claggett, an oration was delivered by Hon. Daniel Weisel, after which a benediction was pronounced by the Rev. Mr. Jackson. The procession then reformed and marched to the public square, where it was dismissed.

The day's entertainment concluded with a free concert at the lyceum by the two bands. The Independent Junior Company is a sort of continuation of the old Franklin Company. In 1859 the Antietam Fire Company contracted with the Western Hose Company, of Baltimore City, to purchase their suction-engine, which was rendered useless to the latter company by the introduction of steam fire-engines. The price named for the engine was eight hundred dollars, its original cost having been fifteen hundred dollars. The committee appointed to visit Baltimore in connection with the purchase consisted of William McKeppler, William Devy, and Benjamin A. Garlinger.

In May, 1880, the company adopted a new constitution and by-laws, the old ones having been lost. The present membership is one hundred and ten, representing all trades and professions. The officers are Maj. F. Dorsey Herbert, president; D. Kontz Middlekauf, first vice-president; Franklin M. Wroe, second vice-president; John L. Wroe, treasurer; and Dixon N. Garlinger, secretary.

The Pioneer Hook-and-Ladder Company was organized Aug. 15, 1872. The first officers elected were William H. Armstrong, president; William Ulrick, vice-president; John Biershing, secretary; Ellsworth Stonebraker, treasurer; Cornelius Artz, chief director; Thomas Colklesser, first assistant director; and John Martin, second assistant director. This company has been in active and constant service since the date of its organization.

In August, 1874, the Western Enterprise Fire

Company tested a steam-engine which had been brought from Wilmington, Del., in accordance with a contract made between the fire company and parties in Wilmington, in which it was provided that if the engine should accomplish certain work at a public trial it should be purchased by the company. The test took place in the public square, and was entirely satisfactory in its results. The engine was of the Amoskeag make, and weighed about three thousand nine hundred pounds. The various fire companies gave a torchlight procession in honor of the addition of the steamer to the department, which was witnessed by a large number of people.

Fires.—About 1796, George Scott's farm-house, near Boonsboro', was destroyed by fire, and his two sons, John and Jacob, perished in the flames. In February, 1822, an alarm of fire drew the citizens of Hagerstown to the public square, where it was found that the shop of Mr. Shank, cabinet-maker, was in flames. Within a few minutes from the giving of the alarm the fire had enveloped the shop, and had communicated to the adjoining brick building, occupied by the *Torch-Light* newspaper. Still continuing in its course, it soon reached the large stone house adjoining the *Torch-Light* office, on the corner of the square. The fire burned fiercely, fanned by a breeze, and, despite the vigorous exertions of the firemen, but for the fact that the wind was blowing in the direction of the open square, a much more extensive conflagration would probably have resulted. The stone building was not materially damaged, but the brick office of the *Torch-Light* was considerably injured. The larger portion of the type and other articles belonging to the newspaper establishment were preserved, though somewhat injured. A large edition of a work, in sheets, just completed, was nearly destroyed by being thrown into the street from the third-story windows of the house. Mr. Shank, the proprietor of the cabinet-maker's shop, lost all his tools, and Col. Lewis' loss was also considerable. On this occasion the ladies of Hagerstown came to the assistance of the firemen, working in the lines and assisting materially in the preservation of property and goods. A destructive fire occurred on Sunday evening, July 26, 1840, at half-past nine o'clock. The fire was of incendiary origin, and was started in the hay-loft of a large stable belonging to the Messrs. Knodes, merchants, in the rear of the two-story brick building known as Hager's Row, east of the Hagerstown Bank, on Washington Street. The cry of fire and the ringing of bells assembled the firemen and citizens generally; but such was the combustibility of the material in which the fire was started that it had enveloped several back buildings in flames before the engines could be brought to bear upon it. The west end of the row, occupied for many years as the office of the *Torch-Light*, was first reached by the flames from the back buildings. From this point the fire rapidly extended eastward, and was not arrested until it had consumed a portion of the building occupied by the *Torch-Light*, *Our Flag*, and the *Herald of Freedom*, the barber-shop occupied by E. Brown, the hat-store of Mr. Ainsworth, the book-store of Mr. Stewart, the saddler-shop of Mr. Kealhofer, and the painter's shop of Mr. Hurley. The roof on the back extension of the bank, which was near the origin of the fire, caught from sparks, but the flames were speedily extinguished. The front body of the building was covered with slate, upon which the fire made no impression. The Globe Inn and several other buildings on the opposite side of the street were for some time in imminent danger, the sparks having fired the roofs; but these were saved from serious damage by water poured upon them by the engines. The furniture and merchandise in the buildings consumed were generally removed, except the books, stationery, and other valuable articles in the second story of Mr. Stewart's book-store, which were destroyed. Mr. Stewart, who was absent at the time, sustained a heavy loss.

On the 17th of April, 1857, the Washington County jail was destroyed by fire. The alarm was given about twelve o'clock, and the firemen and citizens immediately repaired to the burning building. The scarcity of water in the vicinity, and the difficulty experienced in getting at the fire until it had burned through the roof, rendered the efforts made to save the building futile. The entire wood-work of the jail proper was destroyed, but the sheriff's house, only a few feet from the burned structure, escaped. Only the walls of the jail were left standing when the fire subsided. The sheriff was out of town when the fire occurred, but his wife displayed great presence of mind in the emergency, holding the keys and refusing to open the doors of the jail until the proper officers arrived to take charge of the prisoners. These, seven in number, were placed in the grand jury room temporarily. When the sheriff returned next day, he caused a room in his residence to be fitted up for them. The origin of the fire remained a mystery. It was at first supposed to be the work of an incendiary, but the theory was afterwards abandoned; the fire originated in the garret, immediately under the roof,—a point inaccessible to the prisoners. It is more probable that a spark from one of the chimneys caused the fire.

At ten o'clock on Wednesday night, Dec. 5, 1871, a fire was discovered by the watchman at the Washington County Railroad Depot in the agricultural implement warehouse of Messrs. Burbank & Rollins, immediately opposite. The building was a frame one. When Mr. Burbank left the office, early in the evening, the fire in the stove—the only fire about the premises—was quite extinguished. The conflagration was the work of an incendiary, and although first seen in the forepart of the building, it was in an instant observed elsewhere, and in a few minutes burst out of the roof. The first alarm was given by the cry of the watchman and the whistle of the locomotive attached to the train just arrived.

A fierce gale from the south was blowing at the time and had been for several days, and the location of the fire, on the extreme southern limits of the heart of the town, was well calculated to sweep the most valuable portion of it.

It was only the sudden cessation of this storm at the most critical juncture that saved the greater part of Hagerstown from destruction. It was feared at one time that the fire would extend across Washington Street, and many of the householders removed their goods; but the lull in the gale enabled persons to saturate the roofs with water, thus averting the threatened extension of the fire.

By reason of a shingle roof and the impossibility of reaching it in time, the Episcopal church, not long before partially destroyed in the same way, was at this time wholly destroyed, along with its organ. From this roof to the roof of the new part of the court-house (the whole of which was, most unfortunately, covered with shingles) the sparks were communicated to that building.

All about the church were small frame structures, —many of them stables filled with straw,—which were intact, even to the straw, the next morning, and even the old fencing was uninjured. The brick dwelling-house of Frederick Fechtig, but a few feet from the warehouse, was much damaged by fire, but not destroyed; and besides the outbuildings mentioned, the parsonage occupied by Dr. Mason, the dwelling of Dr. Fechtig, the dwelling of Mrs. Post, and the new Antietam engine-house, and offices of Messrs. Hamilton & Smith and Syester & Freaner were preserved from the flames. The house of Mrs. Post adjoined the court-house, but, having a tin roof, was saved along with the adjacent buildings. Dr. Mason, with a few friends, saved the parsonage and its contents, with the stable, by the application of water in buckets. The Antietam House was carefully guarded upon the roof by the Washington County Railroad men, aided by the engine companies and the efforts of citizens. It was at this point the firemen and citizens arrested the progress of the conflagration by saturating the roofs of the Bowden House, Mrs. Mealey's dwelling, and that of Mrs. Sturr. During the height of the conflagration, and after the cupola of the court-house was in flames, a number of citizens and firemen, with the pipe of the Junior Company, were in the great hall, second story, and were at work when the cupola (fifty feet from the floor) fell in with a frightful crash. John Fridinger (mason), one of those engaged in holding the ladder upon which Henry Bester was opening the half-moon window of the dome, to enable William Gould, engineer, to bring the pipe to bear on the roof, was crushed under the fallen burning beams and pinned fast. John Smith made the last effort to save him by pitching a bucket of water over him; but trying to draw him out, found he was pinned in fast. The few remnants of the charred remains of Mr. Fridinger were recovered next morning. Henry Bester was dreadfully injured by a fall from the dome to the floor, exclaiming, as the dome fell, "God save us!" John Smith and Joshua Wise were severely burned, and Col. Cook suffered a contusion of the arm.

Among those present in the building at the time of the catastrophe were Charles Spangler, William H. Armstrong, Joshua Wise, William Davis, William Gould, Surveyor Downin, and E. W. Funk. The last two gentlemen succeeded in securing a number of papers. There were also others, whose names are unknown, in different parts of the building. Alexander Armstrong, Col. Cook, and several others made their escape by means of ladders from the window, while Charles Spangler, W. H. Armstrong, and others ran down the stairs, and nearly fainting, escaped. Charles Shank fell from the Antietam House, and was dreadfully injured. Robert Grove, of Sharpsburg, was injured by a falling window of the same house. A great deal of loss was occasioned by the removal of goods, some of which were stolen. The chief loss was that sustained in the burning of the court-house, which was not insured. Most of the records, papers, and valuable documents were removed, and two office vaults were found almost intact on the morning after the fire; a few papers in the clerk's office were injured. The walls of the court-house were left standing, but those of the Episcopal church were in such a condition as to preclude any use being made of them, and accordingly were torn down. The church was insured for $3000, and the organ for $500; Messrs. Burbank & Rollins held an insurance for $8500; and the losses of the Antietam House and of H. Bell were covered by policies in the Washington County Mutual Insurance Company.

It was scarcely after dusk on a March evening

in 1872 when smoke was seen issuing from a stable situated on the lot of Philip Wingert, formerly the Hagerstown Hotel stable. The building was occupied as a stable by Pilkington & Schlotter, dealers in stoves and tinware, and by Alexander Cook, one of the Hagerstown policemen. The cause of the fire is unknown. Mr. Cook, it is said, was in the building ten minutes before the alarm was given, and saw no indications of fire. When the fire broke out a fierce gale was blowing, but the direction of the wind was fortunately away from the centre of the town, and towards the almshouse, or a point south of it, where the buildings were comparatively few and low. The supply of water was inadequate, and the flames soon crossed the alley which separated the stable from the tannery of the Washington County Leather Manufacturing Company. Once there they were uncontrollable, and it was not long before the bridge across the other alley had conducted them to that portion of the works which were on the opposite side of that alley. The burning of the immense piles of bark continued a day or two afterwards, though a fire-engine was kept on the ground by the Fire Department to prevent damage.

Apart from the leather company, the losses were comparatively trifling. Upon that building the loss was estimated variously at from $50,000 to $75,000. The Manufacturing Company was insured for $10,000 in the Farmers' and Mechanics' Mutual Insurance Company of Washington County. In the Mutual Insurance Company of Washington County the leather company was insured for $4000.

At two o'clock on Sunday morning, July 4, 1872, an alarm was sounded in the heart of the town, the rear of the Lyceum building having been discovered to be in flames. The edifice was rather old and inflammable, and besides the hall, which occupied the entire second story, and was used for purposes of exhibition, two spacious store-rooms, one on either side of the wide entry which ran the full length of the long building, were occupied as the grocery-store of Maj. F. D. Herbert & Son and the merchant tailoring establishment of Mr. Felheimer. The fire companies were soon aroused, and the flames were extinguished without serious loss.

On the 29th of May, 1879, occurred the disastrous conflagration by which the Washington House was destroyed, accompanied by loss of life. An account of this catastrophe is given in the sketches of the hotels and early inns of Hagerstown.

Military.—Nowhere in the colonies was the martial spirit more active and energetic than among the frontier settlers on the Antietam and the Conococheague. Led by the intrepid Cresaps, the pioneers of Washington County repeatedly marched against the French and Indians, and contributed materially to the final success of the British operations against Fort Du Quesne. In 1757 nearly all the able-bodied men residing west of the South Mountain were mustered into the military service. Among them were Lieut.-Col. Joseph Chapline, Capt. Evan Shelby, Lieut. Prather, John Harewood, John Patten, Adam Heath, Hallam Dick, William Rich, Abram Enoch, George Reed, Nicholy Veace, Henry Cramer, Moses Chapline, Leven Wiley, Daniel Wiley, Thomas Wiley, John Springer, Ezekiel Chaney, John Swearingen, John Marshall, William Anderson, George Robbenott, John Nicholy, Richard Dean, James Black, Joseph Nack, John Chaney, and John Wolgamott.

The position occupied by Western Maryland in the war for the independence of the American colonies has been treated in a general manner in the chapter on the Revolutionary war; and the appended notes, referring particularly to Washington County before and during that period, are of special interest in connection with the history of Hagerstown. As illustrating the feeling over the unjust duty imposed on tea imported from the mother-country, it is interesting to know that "on the 26th of November 'the committee for the upper part of Frederick County' met at Elizabethtown—now Hagerstown—and compelled John Parks to walk bareheaded and with torch in his hand and set fire to a chest of tea which he was accused of having imported, contrary to the non-importation resolutions of the colonies."

The first military company organized for the Revolutionary war in Hagerstown was mustered in January, 1776, the members whose names are appended subscribing to the following obligation:

"We whose names are subscribed do hereby enroll ourselves into a company of military, agreeable to the resolution of a Provincial Convention held at Annapolis on the 26th of July, 1775, and we do promise and engage that we will respectively march to such places within this province and at such times as we shall be commanded by the convention or the Council of Safety of this province, or by our officers in pursuance of the orders of said convention or Council, and there with our whole power fight against whomsoever we shall be commanded by the authority aforesaid. Witness our hands the 6th day of January, 1776.

"Joseph Chapline, James Chapline, Thomas Crampton, James Stewart, John Duncan, Robert Cockburn, John Banks, William Roberts, William M. Gathy, Frederick Waitenberger, William Codd, Adam Deeds, John Hill, Hasias Crampton, William Easton, John Grimes, James Dean, Thomas Shepherd, Nicholas Innes, James Graham, James Martin, Thomas Newel, Jacob Shuff, James Black, William Renwicks, John Grub, Jesse Burns, George Myers, Hugh Cain, Richard King, William Gilson, Thomas Maddors, Isaac Keepers, Clement Peace, James McKay, Jr., Henry Haun, John Berger, Thomas Leonard, Richard Moore,

Peter Burrel, Benjamin Burrel, Thomas Dean, Thomas Wiles, Jr., Edward Power, Francis Adams, William Mercer Smith, Andrew Crummy, Hugh McNamee, Jeremiah Chapline, Samuel Dean, Alexander McNutt, Jr., William Hamor, David Miller, David Meek, Robert McNutt, James McNutt, Joseph Morrison, Barnett McNutt, Charles Mager, Robert Work, William Patterson, Thomas Stewart, John McCoy, David Burcham, Peter Grabel, William Newel, Joseph Newel, John O. Donaldson, Jr., William Patrick, Michael Marker, John Wilkins, Thomas Murrow, Thomas Night, Andrew Flick, Samuel Donaldson, Robert Huffman, Jacob Tussy, Peter Wise, Philip Strider. Michael Forx, and Philip Grove."

There was also a company from Washington County commanded by Capt. William Heyser, consisting of eighty-seven persons, who participated in several of the most important engagements of the Revolution. The *personnel* of this organization was as follows:

Captain, William Heyser; First Lieutenant, Jacob Kotz; Sergeants, David Morgan, Jacob Hose, John Jaquet, Jacob Miller; Corporals, P. Revenacht, Bernard Frey, William Lewis, John Breecher; Privates, George Buck, David Morgan, John Michael, Andrew Fuller, Frederick Switzer, James Duncan, John Etnier, William Lewis, Henry Stroam, Melcher Bender, John Breecher, George Wise, Otzen Reeger, Jacob Bishop, George Harmony, John Crafft, Peter Fisher, Mathias Dunkle, Stuffle Beever, John Mettz, Henry Tomm, George Gitting, Alexander Seller, Peter Getting, James Fournier, Jacob Pifer, Jacob Klein, John Smithley, John Flick, John Robertson, Thomas Cliffton, Nicholas Biard, Henry Stadler, Martin Pifer, Jacob Lowre, Jacob Hoover, John Oster (drummer), Maurice Power (fifer), George Wilhelm, Phillip Greechbawn, Christian Sides, Jonathan Hecket, Henry Omer, Philip Revenacht, Francis Myers, Jacob Miller, Michael Weaver, Jacob Gross, Conrad Hoyt, John Fogle, Frederick Fuller, Thomas Burney, Jr., Daniel Jaquet, Michael Yeakly, Barnard Frey, Everheart Smith, Michael Gambler, Jacob Beltzhoover, John Smith, Peter Shuse, Henry Wagner, Frederick Locher, Tobias Friend, George Miller, John Kibler, Godfrey Young, John Rhods, Wentle Strayley, Adam Lieser, Mathias Gieser, Simon Fogler, Stuffle Waggner, John Crapp, John Shoemaker, Jacob Hose, Philip Fisher, Henry Benter, John Hattfield, Jacob Heefner, George Biggleman, Robert Hartness, Jacob Greathouse, Adam Stonebraker, John Armstrong, Henry Michael.

The original roster of the company, enlistment-papers, pay-rolls, and other souvenirs of its existence are now in the possession of Capt. Heyser's grandchildren. Many of his descendants still live in Washington County, where the family names of Heyser, Miller, Oster, Lewis, Stonebraker, Boward, Myers, Smith, Wise, Wagner, Frey, Robertson, Friend, and a very few others in the above list are familiar at the present day.

The following returns of grain purchased by order of the General Assembly will prove interesting to many persons in Washington County:

By Henry Schnebly, April 16, 1780, from John Barns, Ludwig Cameron, Frederick Showenfield, Valentine Ebert, Jacob Zeller, Jacob Hofferd, Henry Rittenower, Jacob Seibert, Jonathan Mayer, Casper Schneider, Martin Seider, Martin Rittenower, John Gabrall, Jacob Brombach, James Downey, David Rittenower, Nicholas Martin, George Shaffer, John Shweitzer, Phyllin Krick, John Galloway, Col. John Stull, Jacob Weymer, Martin Kershner, Henry Schnebly, Jacob Hauck.

By Henry Shryock, from Martin Harry, Martin Kershner, Daniel Gorman, Jacob Martin, David Barr, David Smith, John Stull, Jeremiah Chaney, Paul Wertzberger, Jacob Yakle, Peter Reed, Cunrad Eichelbeaner, Rudolph Hasse, Christian Miller, Henry Startzman, Sr., Henry Startzman, Jr., Jacob Funk, Alexander Clagett, Frederick Stydenger, James Winders, Samuel Downey, John Gabby, Peter Baker, Adam Ott, Jacob Shaver, Frederick Rohrer, Ludwick Ridenour, Leonard Swingle.

By Joseph Chapline (per order of Assembly 28th April, 1780), from Elisha Larklin, Joseph Haines, Selvanus Barnes, Nathan Peticoat, George Frederick Wartsbarger, Thomas Smith, Rignal Prather, William Paterson, Abraham Hauver, Tobias Brothers, Posthumus Clagett, Jacob Pence, William Booth, Richard Davis, Jr.

Among the signers of the constitution of the Maryland Society of the Cincinnati in 1783 were Brig.-Gen. Otho H. Williams, Lieut.-Col. Moses Rawlings, Capt. Benjamin Price, Capt. Rezin Davis, Lieut. John Linn, Lieut. John J. Jacobs, and Richard Pindell, surgeon and physician.

Among the surviving veterans of the Revolutionary war who were granted pension certificates in August, 1820, according to an act of Congress of March 18, 1818, were the following residents of Washington County:

Michael Altigh, Jacob Albert, William Bower, John Barnheizer, George Bradshaw, Anthony Balzar, Hugh Connolly, Mark Coyle, John Eichelberger, James Fanning, John Wm. Helmer, Robert Hewitt, Michael House, Frederick Mittag, Philip Studer, William Stewart, Esau Bicknell, James McIssick, Thomas McQuinny, Jonathan Mayhew, Jesse Massey, John Newman, Melchor Painter, Solomon Rawlings, David Wilson, John Winn, Henry Young, Caspar Shirtzer, Andrew Willis, Henry Tomm, Barney Oldwine, Barclay Holmes, Nicholas Fitzgerald.

This act was amended May 1, 1820, and, according to the provisions of the amendment, applicants for pensions had to go before the judges of the Circuit Courts and make oath as to the amount, kind, and value of their real and personal estate, provided their applications were considered at all. In other words, it was necessary that the veterans of '76 should be in the enjoyment of a certain degree of *poverty* in 1820 to be enabled to become pensioners of the government they had created.

Speaking of the objectionable features of the law, the *Maryland Herald*, in its issue of April 8, 1818, said,—

"During the late term of the County Court at Hagerstown a number of those *veterans* appeared in order to verify their claims to a pension under the late act of Congress, and it called forth mingled sensations of pity and respect to behold those worthy characters, bowed down by age and infirmity, and some of them scarcely able to crawl along.

"Among them were men who passed through many of the memorable scenes of the Revolutionary war, from the year 1775 until the year 1783, men who were with Montgomery at Quebec, at Saratoga with Gates, and with Washington when Cornwallis surrendered at Yorktown.

"Many of them have hitherto been justly entitled to pensions, but for want of the proof required by law have never been able to substantiate their claims, and several of them have been compelled to take refuge in the poor-house at Hagerstown. When we reflect on these facts we are involuntarily compelled to exclaim, 'Why have these worthies been so long neglected? and why are they now asked to make oath "*that from their reduced circumstances they stand in need of their country's assistance for support?*"' a declaration that the proud heart of a patriotic soldier, though ever so poor, shrinks from with disgust, and they protest against this *new test*, and with downcast looks ask their countrymen, 'Does justice require this humiliating acknowledgment? Does the law require it?' We have no hesitation in saying that the act of Congress does not require such a declaration to be made upon oath; that, above all, neither justice nor sound policy demand it, and we trust the Secretary of War will review and alter his instructions on this point, for we have strong evidence that he, too, is the friend of the old soldier. We have a late instance of the attention of the War Department to a militia-man of Washington County. David Palmer marched to Baltimore in the detachment commanded by the late Col. Ragan, in the year 1814. One of his eyes was at that time defective, and he might have plead legal disability and stayed at home, but his friends and neighbors were going, and he could not stay behind. During the campaign he received a wound which deprived him of the sight of the other eye, and he is now totally blind. During the late session of Assembly at Annapolis a resolution passed the House of Delegates in his favor, granting him half-pay (about forty dollars per annum) for life. This resolution was rejected by the Senate. It was then sent back to them by the House of Delegates, accompanied with a message asking the Senate to reconsider the same. They reconsidered and again rejected it. Documents in Palmer's case having been presented to the War Department of the United States, the Secretary of War has ordered him to be placed on the pension list at the rate of eight dollars per month for life.

"Acts of generous justice like this will be of incalculable service to the government in future wars, and wars will come let the policy of the government be what it may. For what is it in the hour of danger and in the hour of death which *damps* the spirit of the brave? It is not the fear of danger, it is not the fear of death, but it is friends at home,—a helpless wife and suffering children that cling to the heart and awaken feelings of melancholy and sorrow. Now, every soldier and every militia-man will know that if he falls his family shall not be forgotten. If he is wounded he shall not suffer the pangs of bitter poverty."

Of the Revolutionary pensioners the official returns only gave five in the county in 1840, as follows: Third District, Peter Feighly and Polly Lewis; Fourth District, Mark Coil and Francis Krick; Fifth District, Anthony Belsor.

For many years succeeding the Revolutionary war the military spirit continued to be very vigorous in and around Hagerstown. Capt. John Lee commanded a company in Washington County in 1795, and in November, 1797, the volunteer troop of Federal Blues of the same county, commanded by Capt. Samuel Ringgold, unanimously offered their services to the Governor in the event of a war with France, which then seemed imminent.

The news of the burning of Washington in the war of 1812 was carried to Hagerstown by horse express, as there was then no quicker mode of conveying intelligence. Horsemen were at once dispatched throughout the county to spread the news and summon volunteers for the defense of Baltimore, against which the British were moving. On the same day Capt. Quantrell's company was enrolled and paraded in the public square, opposite Barker's building, on the east side. Next day it marched to Boonsboro', where it arrived one hundred and forty strong. On the following morning the line of march for Frederick was resumed, the company then numbering seventy. Exactly one-half had reconsidered their determination to fight the "red coats," and looking upon home as the dearest spot on earth, returned to enjoy its felicities and admire the courage of their more daring companions. These seventy reached Baltimore to a man, and took up their quarters at the corner of South Street and Lovely Lane. The captain was compelled to impress provisions, and in one instance seized a dozen barrels of flour concealed in the house which they occupied, and which had been represented to contain nothing. It was accidentally found concealed in the garret. None of the members of the troop are living at the present time. E. W. Lewis was captain of the Warren Rifle Corps at Hagerstown in 1826, and in the same year D. Oster and John Miller, of Hagerstown, were adjutant of the Eighth Regiment and colonel of the Tenth Regiment State Militia, respectively.

In 1840 the military spirit ran high, there being in the county the Hagerstown Horse-Guards, Capt. Wm. B. Clark; Clear Spring Horse-Guards, Capt. Cushwa; Potomac Dragoons (Sharpsburg), Capt. T. G. Harris; Potomac Riflemen (Williamsport), Capt. Magruder; Washington Riflemen (Funkstown), Capt. P. L. Huyette; Hagerstown Cadets, Capt. George Schley; and Hagerstown Union Riflemen, Capt. L. O. Harn. The members of these companies manifested great interest in keeping them up to a first-rate standard. They frequently visited each other and similar organizations in Frederick County, and held annual encampments and conventions, in which the military of the two counties united.

In June, 1844, there was a military encampment near Hagerstown composed of the following companies: Frederick Hussars, Capt. E. Schley; Potomac Dragoons, Capt. Harris; Clear Spring Horse-Guards, Capt. Cushwa; Hagerstown Horse-Guards, Capt. Clarke; National Guards, Capt. E. Shriver; Maryland Light Infantry, Capt. Small; Hagerstown Cadets, Capt. G. Schley; Potomac Riflemen, Capt. Magruder; Washington Riflemen, Capt. Huyette; Lafayette Guards, Capt. Lappon; Union Riflemen, Capt. Harn; St. Thomas Artillerists, Capt. McCalister. At the present time there is but one military organization in Hagerstown, the Hagerstown Light Infantry, commanded by Maj. H. Kyd Douglas, captain, with the following officers and men:

First Lieutenant, Samuel F. Croft; Second Lieutenant, Alexander M. Roberts; Orderly Sergeant, P. A. Witmer; Second Sergeant and Ordnance Sergeant, D. W. Crowther; Third Sergeant, John L. Bikle; Fourth Sergeant and Quartermaster, M. H. Fellheimer; Fifth Sergeant and Commissary, W. P. Lane; Corporals, J. C. Roulette, James Hammond, S. A. Suter, G. N. Harbaugh, J. U. Adams, A. E. Hoover, E. Highbarger, E. M. Schindle.

Agricultural Societies, etc.—The first agricultural society in Washington County was established under the act of 1807, and the founders were from among the Williamses, Tilghmans, and other prominent families. The organization was called the Washington County Agricultural Society, and the officers elected in 1808 were Thomas Sprigg, president; Frisby Tilghman, secretary; and Charles Carroll, treasurer. William Fitzhugh, Sr., Samuel Ringgold, Charles Carroll, John T. Mason, and Martin Kershner were appointed a committee to devise a scheme for a lottery by which to raise two thousand dollars for the use of the society. Its members in 1812 were Frisby Tilghman, William Fitzhugh, William Heyser, Martin Kershner, Upton Lawrence, Jacob Zeller, Gen. Samuel Ringgold, David Clagett, Daniel Hughes, John Buchanan, H. W. Stiell, and John T. Mason. The society met at Bayly's farm, near Hagerstown, Sept. 3, 1812, and discussions of a lengthy nature, relating to the raising of crops, stocks, etc., occupied the time of the members. The transactions of the society seem to have been interrupted during the war of 1812–14, but the society subsequently revived and gained a State reputation. The members were among the best-known agriculturists in Western Maryland, and owned fine estates. After several years the society went out of existence, and in November, 1827, another organization was formed; this, too, was short-lived, its existence lasting only a few years.

The next attempt, and the most successful, was the organization of the Agricultural and Mechanical Association of Washington County, which was incorporated under the provision of the act of Assembly of Maryland passed 1854, ch. 60, with David Brumbaugh, John Ash, Lewis P. Fiery, James Coudy, Jacob Fiery, Martin Startzman, John H. Heyser, Henry K. Tice, Marmaduke W. Boyd, and others as incorporators.

The association leased a tract of land containing several acres, and located just outside the corporation limits of Hagerstown, on the Williamsport turnpike road. Here the annual exhibitions of the association were held until 1872, when fourteen acres, located near Hagerstown, on the Cearfoss turnpike, were purchased of Richard Wise for two thousand five hundred dollars, and buildings erected the same year. These continued to be the grounds of the association until 1880, when a new site was selected upon the lands of George W. Harris. Twenty-eight acres were purchased, and improved with a track and suitable buildings, the whole cost, including land and improvements, amounting to fifteen thousand dollars.

The first president of the association was David Brumbaugh, who continued to hold the office until January, 1872, when he was succeeded by George W. Harris, who was followed in 1874 by B. A. Garlinger. In 1881, Mr. Garlinger, who had presided over the association through great trials and vicissitudes for six years, was compelled by his engagements to decline re-election, and was succeeded by Charles W. Humrickhouse. The other officers elected in the same year were William Updegraff, vice-president; Benjamin F. Fiery, treasurer; P. A. Witmer, recording secretary; Albert Small, corresponding secretary; and H. A. McComas, George W. Stonebraker, P. B. Small, Benjamin F. Rench, Dr. John T. Grimes, George W. Harris, B. A. Garlinger, Charles Emmert, C. F. Manning, and A. C. Huffer, directors. At the same time it was determined to open the annual fair on the 11th of October, 1881. The capital stock is limited to five hundred shares of twenty-five dollars each, which is held by about four hundred and fifty members. The first annual fair of this association was held in 1854, commencing October 13th, and lasting three days. The exhibition was markedly successful, the collection of cattle and horses being very extensive, and embracing a variety of breeds, both imported and domestic. The field, orchard, garden, and domestic exhibits were also of a very interesting character. At the January meeting of the society in 1855 officers were elected for the ensuing year, as follows:

David Brumbaugh, president; Samuel E. Stonebraker, John Snively, George S. Kennedy, Frederick Rohrer, George Thomas, William Loughridge, George C. Rohrer, Henry Eyerly, Dr. W. A. Riddlemoser, Dr. Thomas Maddox, and W. L. Berry, vice-presidents; Dr. F. Kennedy, John Tice, James Condy, John Graves, Joseph Ground, Daniel Rohrer,

John Kendle, David Cushwa, A. R. Snively, Daniel Startzman, John W. Breathed, and Andrew Rench, executive committee; L. McKee, Jacob Fiery, P. B. Small, Martin Startzman, John Heyser, and William Hall, managers; H. K. Tice, treasurer; E. M. Moberley, recording secretary; and T. G. Robertson, corresponding secretary.

On the 17th of September, 1873, the members of the society, with a number of farmers from Washington County and their families, made an excursion to Druid Hill Park, Baltimore. The party numbered twelve hundred persons, and spent the greater part of the day at the park. At first the intention was to hold simply the September monthly meeting, but the project became so popular in time that invitations were extended to the farmers generally of Washington County, and hence the large attendance.

One of the main objects of the excursion was a social reunion to afford an opportunity for conference and interchange of opinions in regard to the common interests of agriculturists. The several sites occupied by the Agricultural Society as fair-grounds have been already mentioned. The location occupied previous to 1872 was a lot belonging to Richard Wise, situated about one-quarter of a mile to the northeast of the town, at the point where the Mercersburg and old Greencastle roads branch off. This lot contained ten acres, and was leased of the owner with the privilege of purchasing in fee. The grounds were improved by a small house at the northeast angle, containing the offices of the secretary and treasurer, by refreshment booths, stalls for horses, cattle, sheep, and hogs, a carriage-way, and a trial course twenty-six feet in width and about a half-mile in length. The track inclosed a natural mound, raised above it some twenty feet, which commanded a fine view of the whole inclosure, and of the South and North Mountains, and the rich valley between them. On this hill were the judges' stand and an amphitheatre intended for the reception of the more valuable and perishable articles. The entire exhibition was within the circle formed by the track. In May, 1873, a meeting of the stockholders of the society was held at the office of the secretary, P. A. Witmer; B. J. Byers acting as chairman, and Mr. Witmer, secretary.

The meeting was called for the discussion of the question of removing the society's grounds from the location then occupied to another on the east side of the town, containing between twenty and thirty acres, and known as the old race-course. The advisability of the change was universally admitted, although, from a financial point of view, a difference of opinion prevailed. After a lengthy discussion it was decided, by a majority of 22 in a total of 122 votes, to make the change in location. Immediately after this decision of the question the work of improvement was commenced. Such of the property of the association as could be transferred was removed from the old grounds, and steps were taken to dispose of those grounds as soon as it could advantageously be done. The new location possessed many advantages over the old; and its greater area was a matter of much importance, as the restricted limits of the latter had been a source of much inconvenience to visitors. In addition to the advantages of accessibility and beauty of location, the new grounds were also near a running stream, from which they could be copiously watered. In 1880 another change of location was made, the association purchasing what were known as the Summers and Harris grounds. These grounds are located in the northeastern suburbs of the town, and consist of a rectangular lot containing about twenty-nine acres.

The location is elevated and commands an extensive view. The buildings and other improvements are of a character unsurpassed by those of any similar association in the country, while the proximity of the location to the city limits enables visitors to walk to the gates upon good pavements. The exhibition hall is one hundred and fifty feet long, and consists of a main building and wings, the main building being three stories high and the wings two stories. This hall is similar to, but larger than, the one built upon the old fair-grounds. The machinery hall is one hundred feet by thirty feet, and the restaurant and dining-rooms seventy feet by thirty feet. The grand stand has a seating capacity of twelve hundred, and from it a full and unobstructed view of the whole track can be had. The stalls provided for stock of all kinds are of the very best character, and are ten by six feet each, well lighted and well ventilated, and the stables all have shingle roofs. The track is a full half-mile long, nearly elliptical in shape, with easy curves, and mostly level, the steepest grade being one foot eight inches in the one hundred feet. There are, in addition to these improvements, ladies' and gentlemen's reception-rooms, a poultry-house, carriage-shed, and telegraph-office. At the fairs of the association prizes are offered in all the various branches of farm produce, stocks, agricultural machinery, household products, etc. The amount of stock before a new issue was made at the time of the purchase of the new grounds was $7500, and the additional two hundred shares then subscribed increased the amount to $12,500.

The fair of 1880 was celebrated as the "Silver Exhibition" of the association, it being the twenty-fifth year of the association's existence. The largest assemblage ever gathered at an agricultural fair in the valley witnessed the display of exhibits and the special exercises in honor of the event. The accessories to the silver exhibition were the processions of the I. O. O. F. on Tuesday, under Dr. J. McP. Scott as chief marshal, and of the fire companies under J. U. Adams as chief marshal, on Wednesday. Both parades were brilliant affairs, and were conducted with perfect system and the most gratifying success. The procession of Odd-Fellows through the streets was very imposing, but that of the visiting and home fire companies was the most numerous and one of the most interesting ever seen in the vicinity of Hagerstown. The music of more than a dozen bands and several drum-corps gave animation to a scene otherwise brilliant, and the gay uniforms of seventeen visiting companies, in addition to two at home, with numerous streamers and other paraphernalia, made up a handsome picture. The procession, which consumed half an hour in passing a given point, was composed of the Frederick Riflemen and cornet band of Frederick, escorted by Reno Post, No. 2, G. A. R.; Fame Hose and Water Witch Hose, of Wilmington, Del., with the Washington Grays and Brennan Bands, of Philadelphia; Washington Independents, of Sunbury, Watsontown Band; Always There Hook-and-Ladder Company, of Waynesboro', with cornet band; Good Will Company, of Harrisburg, and City Grays' Band; Good Will and Friendship, of Chambersburg; Junior Cornet Band; Rescue, of Greencastle; drum-corps; Friendship, of Greencastle; drum corps; Washington, Mechanicsburg; Singer Cornet Band; Friendship, of Newville; Vigilant and Shawnee, of Columbia, with Mountville and Ironville Bands,—all of Pennsylvania; the Martinsburg fire department; Criswell's Cornet Band; Westminster fire department; Emmittsburg drum-corps; Friendship, of Shippensburg; the Junior and First Hose Companies, of Hagerstown.

The dedicatory exercises on Tuesday by the I. O. O. F. consisted of an address by the chief marshal, Dr. Scott, and a response by the secretary of the Grand Lodge of Maryland, John M. Jones, of Baltimore. On Wednesday the procession of firemen was formed in the grounds and massed in front of the grand stand, where the visitors were received with an address of welcome by Governor W. T. Hamilton, to which, on behalf of the firemen, A. K. Nebinger, of Harrisburg, responded.

Each day's proceedings closed with racing. Wednesday night was one of unusual brilliancy. A number of houses were beautifully dressed and illuminated, and a pyrotechnic display in the public square added greatly to the enjoyment of the occasion. A bountiful supper was served in the evening to the firemen. The feast took place in the market-house, and tables were spread for five hundred guests, until three times that number had been fed.

The society was not the only agricultural association in Washington County, there being several others of a more local character. Chief among these was the Manor Agricultural Society, composed of gentlemen living in the neighborhood of Ringgold's Manor. The Ringgolds were a very old Washington County family, one of them, Gen. Samuel Ringgold, being a prominent member of the first agricultural society in 1812, and they were the possessors of the manor which later passed into the hands of the Reichard family. The Manor Agricultural Society, at its January meeting in 1855, elected the following officers for the ensuing year: Andrew Rench, president; Andrew Hogmire and Isaac Motter, vice-presidents; John Reichard, recording secretary; and Dr. Thomas Maddox, corresponding secretary.

Washington County has always possessed an enviable reputation for the culture of farm, orchard, and garden products, and the raising of cattle, sheep, and horses. One of the earliest records at Hagerstown, dated 1799, refers to the high-bred imported stallion Herod, owned by Wm. Hylton, of Retreat, near Bath, Berkeley Co., Va., which stood in the spring of 1799 at Retreat, Hancock, and Hagerstown. Some very fine horses were the offspring of this stallion, and the breed still exists in Washington County. There were also some very excellent specimens of sheep owned in the early part of the present century. Hon. John Johnston, who possessed a fine estate on the Conococheague, within three miles of Kershner's ford, had merino sheep for sale in 1813, and in 1823, Gen. Samuel Ringgold owned a flock of splendid sheep, numbering over one thousand. In the last twenty years Washington County has gained quite a reputation as a grape-growing district, and it is commonly said that at no point in the United States east of the Sierra Nevadas are grapes grown in greater perfection than on the banks of the Antietam. The extensive vineyards of the Messrs. Heyser, on the western boundary of Hagerstown, and that of Dr. Harvey, on West Washington Street, present ample evidence of that fact. In Dr. Harvey's grapery there were in 1870 every variety known in the latitude, including the "Rogers" and "Muscats." The Reichards established a nursery of pear, apple, and peach-trees about 1840 in Ringgold's Manor, and plants were sold all over the county, thus distributing the varieties far and wide.

The agitation of the subject of pisciculture, which at the present time is assuming great importance in this country, had its origin, as far as can be learned, in Washington County about 1824. The project of stocking the Antietam with fresh-water fish originated in that year, and was taken up by prominent citizens, who called a meeting in the town hall, Jan. 18, 1824, to ascertain what could be done to promote the objects of the movement. Col. Frisby Tilghman was called to the chair, and George W. Boerstler was elected secretary. Col. Otho H. Williams, William Fitzhugh, Jr., William D. Bell, John Harry, and G. W. Boerstler were appointed to draft a resolution expressive of the sense of the meeting. The resolution recommended that a petition be sent to the Legislature, then in session, asking for a State law for the protection of fresh-water fish in Antietam Creek, and a committee, consisting of Col. Frisby Tilghman, John Harry, William Fitzhugh, Jr., George W. Boerstler, Peter Sailer, David Clagett, Edmund McCoy, William Booth, Samuel M. Hitt, J. Neff, Daniel Boerstler, Joseph Graff, George Sheip, and Seth Lane, was appointed to present a suitable memorial to the Legislature. The petition was duly prepared and sent, and a law was passed. The gentlemen who originated the project formed a company and stocked Antietam Creek with fish. Washington County is one of the most prosperous and enterprising agricultural communities in the United States. The soil is peculiarly adapted to the growth of wheat, and the crops of that cereal raised there are larger per acre, as a rule, than in any other county of Maryland. Added to the natural advantages of the soil and climate, the traditional economy and thrift of the Washington County farmers have secured the county a phenomenal reputation for the superiority and the abundant yield of its agricultural productions. No community in the State takes a greater interest in all topics relating to agriculture, and none is more ready to adopt improvements, or to experiment in new agricultural methods that are likely to yield substantial results. The superiority of Washington County farming is shown in the fact that, according to the census returns of 1880, the average yield of wheat per acre in that county was 25¾ bushels, or 8½ bushels in excess of that of the next best wheat-producing county, Montgomery, where the average yield was 17¼ bushels per acre.

Secret Societies.—On St. John's day, June 24, 1815, the members of Mount Moriah Lodge, No. 33, marched to the German Lutheran church to listen to a Masonic discourse, delivered by Rev. Thomas P. Irving, a member of the order. Thomas Compton was at that time secretary of the lodge. It is evident from this that Mount Moriah Lodge had been in existence for some time. In 1821 Masonic lodges were in operation in Frederick, Hagerstown, Sharpsburg, and Boonsboro'. On St. John's day, June 24, 1822, the corner-stone of a new building to be devoted to the purposes of a Masonic hall, town hall, and market-house was laid in the presence of a large gathering of Masons and others. The committee of arrangements for the occasion was composed of the following members of Mount Moriah Lodge: Samuel Ringgold, O. H. Williams, Henry Lewis, William Price, William D. Bell, George F. Kreps, and Samuel Rohrer. The programme embraced a procession from the court-house to the site of the new building, and back to the court-house after the laying of the corner-stone, and thence to the Wabash Spring, where a dinner was served. The following was the order of exercises at the laying of the corner-stone. First, the choir sang "Hail, Mystic Art!" Second, the stone was raised, and a short prayer offered by Rev. Mr. Shaw. Third, music by the band. Fourth, ceremony of laying the stone. Fifth, music by the band. Sixth, oration. Seventh, "Hail, Masonry Divine!" by the choir. The procession then moved to the German Lutheran church, the choristers in the rear, and upon arriving at the church the procession halted, opened to the right and left, and the choristers preceding, the whole line moved in reversed order into the church. The ceremonies at the church were commenced by the choir with an appropriate hymn, after which prayer was offered by Rev. Mr. Kurtz. The hymn "Lord, what an entertaining sight," was then sung by the choir, after which a sermon was preached by the Rev. Mr. Clark. After a collection the hymn "When darkness brooded o'er the deep" was sung, followed by a Masonic ode by John Pattison, composed for the occasion; the services ended with prayer by Rev. Mr. Clark. In the corner-stone were placed among others the following memoranda and articles:

"This foundation stone was laid on St. John's day, the 24th of June, A.D. 1822, by the brethren of Mount Moriah Lodge, No. 33, assisted by several members of the Grand Lodge of Maryland, and of the subordinate lodges of the State and adjoining States, in the presence of a large concourse of people. The officiating clergymen on the occasion were Rev. John Clark, of Greencastle, Pa., and Rev. Samuel B. Shaw and Rev. Benjamin Kurtz, of Hagerstown.

"*Officers and Members of Mount Moriah Lodge.*—Otho H. Williams, W. M.; Henry Lewis, J. W.; William D. Bell, S. W.; George F. Kreps, Sec.; John V. Swearingen, Treas.; John W. Main, Tyler; George Strause, Frisby Tilghman, Samuel Ringgold, Sr., John Harry, William Hammond, Matthew Murray, George C. Smoot, John Reynolds, Edward G. Williams, Charles Hesletine, Archibald M. Waugh, William Price, Daniel Malott, John M. Diffenbaugh, Andrew Hogmire, William Booth, George Foreman, James Brotherton, Colin Cooke, William Albert, David Morrison, William Boullt, James Davis,

John May, Samuel Rohrer, Jacob Wolf, Joseph Hollman, Henry H. Gaither, Otho H. W. Beall, Peter Ardinger, Joshua Murray, Thomas Hammond, Thomas Post, Samuel Ringgold, Jr., Robert M. Tidball, George Swearingen, Thomas B. Duckett, George Ross Beall, George Brumbaugh, John R. Dall, John J. Hayes, L. W. Stockton, Jacob Powles, William McCardle.

"*Washington County Court.*—John Buchanan, chief judge; Abraham Shriver, Thomas Buchanan, associates; Otho H. Williams, clerk; John N. Swearingen, sheriff; William Lewis, crier; Jacob Myers, auditor, Court of Chancery.

"*Washington County Orphans' Court.*—Jacob Schnebly, chief justice; Thomas Keller, William Gabby, associates; George C. Smoot, register; William Lewis, crier.

"*Washington County Levy Court.*—Frederick Dorsey, Jacob Miller, Samuel Ringgold, William Fitzhugh, John M. Clain, Jacob Zeller (one vacant); Otho H. Williams, clerk; Charles Oldwine, crier.

"*Postmaster at Hagerstown.*—Daniel Schnebly.

"*Commissioners of the Tax for Washington County.*—David Harry, George Smith, John Shafer, Joseph Gabby, John Bowles; Jacob Myers, clerk.

"*Trustees of the Poor for Washington County.*—Thomas Grieves, Peter Humrickhouse, Charles Shanner; Christian Fechtig, Sr., overseer.

"*Hagerstown Academy.*—Frisby Tilghman, president; Elie Beatty, Upton Lawrence, Richard Ragan, Alexander Neill, Frederick Dorsey, trustees; David Wilson, principal; John Murray, teacher; Thomas Kennedy, steward.

"*Hagerstown Bank.*—William Heyser, president; Elie Beatty, cashier; Daniel Sprigg, teller; directors, Alexander Neill, Frederick Dorsey, David Clagett, John McIlhenny, Daniel Schnebly, John Buchanan, Andrew Kershner, John Wolgamott, John Harry, Otho Lawrence.

"*Moderator of Hagerstown.*—Daniel Schnebly.

"*Commissioners of Hagerstown.*—Thomas Post, George Brumbaugh, Charles Shaffer, John Reynolds; John Anderson, collector.

"*German Lutheran Church.*—Rev. Benjamin Kurtz, pastor; elders, who serve eight years, Samuel Ridenour, George Brendel, George I. Harry, Anthony Howard, Martin Showecker, Peter Suter, Peter Artz; wardens, who serve three years, John Albert, Jacob Knodle, David Bish, Jacob Hammer, Samuel Roushkulp.

"*German Reformed Church.*—Rev. James R. Reily, pastor; elders, Peter Humrickhouse, Daniel Middlekauff, Jacob Knode, Philip Keller, David Middlekauff, John Tice; deacons, Michael Hamman, Martin Rickenbaugh, Frederick Humrickhouse, Daniel May.

"*English Presbyterian Church.*—Rev. John Linn, pastor; Elders, John Kennedy, Robert Douglass, John Robertson, Joseph Gabby.

"*Episcopal Church.*—Rev. Samuel B. Shaw, pastor; Vestry, Elie Beatty, Frisby Tilghman, Richard Ragan, Franklin Anderson, Daniel Sprigg, Thomas Grieves, George Bear, Levin Mills.

"*Methodist Church.*—Rev. J. Emory, pastor; Stewards, Job Hunt, Zacharias McComas, Archibald M. Waugh, John Wright, George Fechtig, Enoch B. Kinsell.

"*Catholic Church.*—Rev. James M. Redmond, pastor.

"*Female Charity School.*—Mrs. Ellen Duncan, president; Miss Elizabeth Harry, secretary; Miss Isabella Neill, treasurer; Managers, Miss Jane Milligan, Miss Nancy Douglass, Miss Eliza Carr, Miss Margaret Hillard, Miss Amelia Rahauser, Miss Mary S. Grieves.

"*Hagerstown Union Missionary Society, auxiliary to the Foreign Missionary Society of New York.*—Rev. Benjamin Kurtz, president; Dr. Jehu Reynolds, vice-president; John Kennedy, treasurer; Wm. D. Bell, secretary; Managers, Rev. James R. Reily, Rev. Jehu Curtis Clay, Daniel Schnebly, Dr. John Ridout, John Robertson, Arthur Johnston, George Shryock.

"*Teachers in Hagerstown Schools.*—Miss Anna Maria Inglis, Female Academy; Mrs. Ann Rawlings, school in East Franklin Street; Mrs. Ann Philingem, school in North Potomac Street; Elijah B. Mendenhall, Union Academy; Cyrus Blood, school in West Franklin Street; John Hoffman, school at German Presbyterian church; Henry Rixacre, school at German Lutheran church."

In addition were the names of State and national officers, copies of newspapers, coins, bank-notes, etc. The hall was dedicated two years later, on St. John's day, the 24th of June, 1824. The committee of arrangements on this occasion was composed of Otho H. Williams, Frisby Tilghman, Thomas Kennedy, William D. Bell, William Hammond, Henry Lewis, George Brumbaugh, David Morrison, George F. Kreps. A few days previous to the opening of the new Masonic Hall, Mount Moriah Royal Arch Chapter, No. 11, was organized. The procession moved from the court-house to the Rev. Mr. Kurtz' church, where it halted, closed files, faced inward, and opened ranks fifteen feet to permit the Grand Master, the Grand Lodge, and the rest of the procession in reversed order to pass into the church. After prayer had been offered the choir sang an anthem composed by C. Merricks. The Grand Master, Gen. B. C. Howard, then delivered an address, and the installation of the Grand Warden of Maryland took place, the exercises closing with the benediction. When the services at the church were finished the procession moved to the new hall. When the front of the procession reached the door of the hall it halted, faced inward, and opened ranks as before to admit the Grand Master, who, preceded by a band of music, the Grand Sword-Bearer, the two Grand Stewards, and the Grand Banner, and followed by the two Grand Deacons, moved forward through the ranks, the members uncovering as he passed. Then closing from the rear the main body entered the hall, where the ceremony of consecration took place.

Friendship Lodge, No. 84, A. F. and A. M., was originally chartered by the Grand Lodge of Maryland to work at Williamsport, but was removed to Hagerstown in 1843. The charter bears date May 22, 1827, and the charter members were Meredith Helm, W. M.; Daniel Malott, S. W.; and Joseph Hollman, J. W. The officers of the Grand Lodge whose names are signed to the charter are B. C. Howard, G. M.; William Stewart, D. G. M.; O. H. Williams, S. G. W.; Dennis Claude, J. G. W.; Thomas Phenix, G. S.; and J. G. Woodyear, G. T. There are now about seventy members in the lodge, and its officers are A. A. Mobley, Worshipful Master; Charles W. Henneberger, Senior Warden; William Gumbert, Junior Warden; E. M. Mobley, Secretary; and M. L. Myers, Treasurer.

The lodge-room is in the old town hall over the market-house.

Following is a list of the officers of other organizations in Hagerstown, chosen in 1881:

Valley Lodge, No. 70, Knights of Pythias.—C. C., D. K. Middlekauff; V. C., George B. Oswald; Prelate, William M. Weller; M. at A., O. B. Ridenour; Trustee, F. A. Heard.

Antietam Lodge, No. 25, Ind. Order Mechanics.—S. M., John D. Ridenour; W. M., Peter Breitweiser: J. M., John P. Wagoner; R. S., David Summer; F. S., William B. McCardell; T., Philip P. Warfel; C., Thomas Colklesser; Con., Charles E. West.

Antietam Tribe, No. 46, Ind. Order Red Men.—Prophet, David Wolf; Sachem, George N. Frederick; Sen. Sagamore, John H. Slick; Jun. Sagamore, Thomas A. Nock; C. of R., John D. Ridenour; K. of W., William S. Davis.

Antietam Fire Company.—President, F. Dorsey Herbert; First Vice-President, D. Koontz Middlekauff; Second Vice-President, Frank M. Wroe; Secretary, Dixon M. Garlinger; Treasurer, John L. Wroe; Chief Director, Wm. McK. Keppler; First Assistant Director, William B. Oliver; Second Assistant Director, John H. Middlekauff; Finance Committee, Lewis Cass Smith, Lewis E. McComas, Edward W. Mealey; Standing Committee, F. D. Herbert, D. Koontz Middlekauff, Frank M. Wroe, Dixon N. Garlinger, John L. Wroe; Chief Pipeman, T. Bomstead Oliver; Assistant Pipemen, John H. Bitner and Frank Largent; Torch-Bearers, Stewart H. Braley, Samuel S. Jones, J. A. Mason, F. Cook, C. S. Richards; Property Guards, John D. Middlekauff, John H. Lorshbaugh, John H. Cook, Dr. A. S. Mason, P. J. Mayberry, B. F. Fechtig.

Amateur Musical Circle.—President, Mr. P. A. Brugh; Vice-President, Mr. R. J. Halm; Secretary, E. E. Braly; Treasurer, J. Winter.

About May, 1819, an organization was formed under the title of the Union Sabbath-school Society of Hagerstown. The officers elected to serve the first year were:

John Kennedy, president; Elie Beatty, vice-president; Joseph Graff, secretary; George I. Harry, treasurer; Richard Ragan, Franklin Anderson, George Shryock, George Hamner, John Hershey, Job Hunt, Peter Humrichouse, John Robertson, Alexander Neill, committee.

A meeting of the citizens of Hagerstown was held Oct. 17, 1827, for the purpose of forming an auxiliary organization to the American Colonization Society.

At a meeting of the Washington Beneficial Society of Hagerstown, held in the town hall on the 2d of September, 1829, the following officers were chosen for the ensuing term:

Rev. B. Kurtz, president; James Zwistor, vice-president; Elliott W. Hillerd, secretary; and Thomas Martin, treasurer; Samuel Protzman, Marmaduke W. Boyd, and James Davis, committee of investigation; Charles G. Lane, Ignatius Dillon, Martin King, stewards; William Hawkins, John Martiney, Anthony W. Lewis, directors; Henry Fraener, messenger.

At the first annual meeting of the Hagerstown Beneficial Society, on the 22d of March, 1830, the following officers were elected:

Rev. Benjamin Kurtz, president; James Zwistor, vice-president; E. C. Fechtig, secretary: John Martiney, treasurer; William M. Boyd, Thomas Martin, Anthony W. Lewis, committee of investigation; John King, David Gilbert, Martin King, Ignatius Dillon, stewards; J. Boyer, messenger.

The first meeting of the Washington County Temperance Association was held in the Lutheran church in 1830. The officers were Daniel Reichard, president; Samuel M. Hitt, secretary; and Daniel Sprigg, treasurer. Addresses were delivered by Franklin Anderson and Rev. Benjamin Kurtz.

In August, 1868, the Potomac Lodge, I. O. O. F., having purchased several lots in Rose Hill Cemetery, and set them apart for such of its brethren, strangers, or others as might have no burial-place of their own, and having erected a beautiful marble monument some fifteen feet in height upon these lots, held dedicatory services in the cemetery, which were witnessed by a large concourse of people. The lodge attended in full regalia and was accompanied by Heyser's Silver Cornet Band from its hall in Hagerstown to the cemetery. The exercises upon the ground consisted of music by the band, the singing of an ode by the order, prayer by Rev. T. T. Titus, an address by Hon. A. K. Syester, dedicatory services by Samuel L. King, William H. Protzman, and William L. Hays, and the benediction pronounced by Rev. Mr. Titus. An election of officers for Potomac Lodge was held at their hall on Tuesday night, July 5, 1881, and the following were elected:

P. G., D. K. Middlekauff; N. G., M. H. Fellheimer; V. G., Charles C. Fechtig; R. S., George B. Oswald; W., George Garlock; C., Alexander M. Roberts; O. G., Ed. H. Wareham; I. G., Joseph M. Bayer; R. S. N. G., Jacob H. Powles, L. S. N. G., J. H. Kridlor; R. S. V. G., Jacob A. Zeigler; L. S. V. G., William M. Lowman; R. S. S., John Wareham; L. S. S., Clare McComas; Finance Committee, W. S. Williamson, B. F. Beck, O. B. Ridenour; School Committee, P. J. Adams, J. S. McCartney, John F. A. Remley.

Washington Lodge, No. 333, Knights of Honor, was instituted at Hagerstown, Md., Aug. 7, 1876, with the following charter members: Dr. C. E. S. McKee, J. H. Kridler, C. W. Henneberger, H. H. Beeler, C. N. Snyder, Wm. A. Weller, A. A. Mobley, Levi Stone, M. L. Byers, Daniel Stover, John L. Bikle, James B. Warner, D. M. Brenner, George Lias, Samuel D. Martin, and Wm. D. Troxell.

The following were the officers for the first term:

P. D., Dr. C. E. S. McKee; D., M. L. Byers; V. D., J. N. Kridler; A. D., Daniel Stover; G., C. W. Henneberger; R., John L. Bikle; F. R., H. H. Beeler; Treas., Wm. M. Weller; G., C. N. Snyder; S., A. A. Mobley.

Washington Lodge now has one hundred members. The following are Past Dictators: Dr. C. E. S. McKee, M. L. Byers, Dr. D. W. Crowther, A. A. Mobley, Dr. J. McP. Scott, John L. Bikle, Prof. R. S. Henry, P. A. Witmer, E. C. Mobley, and Alexander Neill.

This lodge has lost by death one member, Dr. Albert Hammond, and within thirty days his heirs received the death benefit,—$2000.

This lodge has a Past Grand Dictator, Vice Grand Dictator, Grand Reporter, Past Grand Chaplain, Past Grand Trustee, and Grand Chaplain of the Grand Lodge of Maryland. Washington Lodge elected the following officers on the 24th of June, 1881:

P. D., Alexander Neill; D., James B. Warner; V. D., John L. McAtee; A. D., Rev. J. R. Williams: R., John L. Bikle; F. R., C. E. S. McKee; C., J. A. Reed; G., William T. Mittag; Gd., William S. Davis; Sec., George Fridinger; Treas., Joseph H. Fiery; Med. Ex., Dr. O. H. W. Ragan; Hall-keeper, Wm. S. Davis.

Penmar Council, No. 440, of the Royal Arcanum, was instituted at Hagerstown, Feb. 18, 1880, with the following charter members: Dr. C. E. S. McKee, P. A. Witmer, Dr. D. W. Crowther, Prof. R. S. Henry, James Hammond, Wm. Gassman, John L. Bikle, John D. Swartz, Daniel Stover, Samuel D. Martin, Dr. A. S. Mason, Dr. O. H. W. Ragan, Chas. E. Ways, Thos. J. Warfield, James B. Warner, M. L. Byers, C. W. Henneberger, J. W. Monath, John W. Schock, C. G. Boryer, E. M. Recher, and John C. Simler. The officers of the present term are:

P. R., P. A. Witmer; R., Dr. D. W. Crowther; V. R., Prof. R. S. Henry; O., Albert Sewall; Chapl., Wm. Gassman; G., Jno. C. Simler; Sec., John L. Bikle; C., M. L. Byers; Treas., B. F. Fiery; W., Samuel F. Croft; S., George W. Rouzer.

The Council now has forty-two members. The Past Regents are Dr. Dr. C. E. S. McKee and P. A. Witmer.

Amusements.—The early amusements of the people of Hagerstown and vicinity were horse-racing, cock-fighting, bowling, and occasional theatrical performances by strolling companies, with now and then a picnic excursion to some popular resort in the vicinity. Hagerstown enjoyed a peculiar pre-eminence as a chicken-fighting centre, and its game-cocks were renowned all over the country, from New York to New Orleans, for their expertness, daring, and endurance. Many "mains" were fought between the Hagerstown cock-fighters and the sportsmen of Virginia, while some of the most celebrated contests at New York and in other leading cities were participated in by Washington County chickens. The breed is still preserved at Funkstown and elsewhere. One of the most enthusiastic patrons of the sport was the elder Dr. Frederick Dorsey, who would ride many miles and encounter almost any obstacle in order to witness a first-rate "main." The great cock-fights generally took place on Easter Monday. Peripatetic bands of actors, like those whom Théophile Gautier describes so vividly in "Captain Fracasse," or a circus, or troupe of jugglers and acrobats, would often visit the town, and the appearance of these performers was probably much more frequent than in our own day; the multiplicity of places of amusement and the easy accessibility of the towns to the large cities having greatly reduced the chances for profit of the minor traveling combinations.

"Cold Spring," south of the town, and the banks of the Antietam, between Hagerstown and Funkstown, were the favorite resorts of the youthful portion of the inhabitants, and, doubtless, in these localities many troths were plighted and mutual vows exchanged. Parties were also formed to visit the "Black Rock" or the Cave at Cavetown. There were no beer-gardens in those days, and the only approach to a modern garden was a place on East Franklin Street, where cakes and beer that would not intoxicate might be had. Another place of popular resort on the warm summer evenings was the "soda fountain" kept by "Apothecary Miller," on North Potomac Street.

There was a cock-pit at Ladle Spring, where a large portion of the population spent much of their time. Bullet-playing, or long-bullets, was another favorite amusement. This game consisted in throwing a four-pound ball nearest to a given point in the fewest possible number of throws. The usual place for the game was on North Potomac Street, from "Wayside," Mr. G. W. Harris' place, to the market-house. As the population increased, however, the game became so dangerous that in 1819 it was suppressed by an act of the General Assembly, which imposed a fine of fifty dollars upon all who engaged in the sport. A curious custom of the day was the manner in which weddings were celebrated. Couples in the country generally came to town upon horseback to get married, accompanied by a numerous cavalcade of friends. After the ceremony was performed the whole party would repair to Mr. Cook's tavern, on North Potomac Street, and the one adjoining, where an entertainment would be awaiting them. The party would dance all night, and have, frequently, an uproarious time. In the morning they would again form in line and proceed homewards. When they reached the edge of town all would halt, and one of the groomsmen would return to the tavern and buy a bottle of wine, with a waiter and two glasses. After giving each, the bride and groom, a glass of wine, the bottle, glasses, and waiter would all be thrown down in the road. The party would generally proceed but a short distance ere they encountered a high, strong fence built across the road by the neighbors and acquaintances who had not been invited to the wedding, and who invariably took this method of revenging themselves for the slight they had received.

Theatrical entertainments appear to have found favor in Hagerstown at a very early day, and in 1791 there seems to have been a regular theatre there. The following advertisement in the Washington *Spy* affords us an idea of the character of the performances in those days:

"THEATRE—ELIZABETH-TOWN.

This Evening, Wednesday, April 13th [1791], *will be Presented*
THE COMEDY OF
THE CONTRAST,

Written by a Citizen of the United States, and performed with universal applause at the Theatres of Philadelphia, New York, Baltimore, Alexandria, Georgetown, and Fredericktown.

The original Prologue to be spoken by Mr. McGrath.

At the end of the Play, 'The New Address to the Play-House, or Belles Have-At-Ye-All,' to be delivered by Mrs. McGrath.

To which will be added A FARCE, called
LIKE MASTER LIKE MAN,
OR THE WRANGLING LOVERS.

The Doors to be opened at 6, and the Curtain to rise at 7 o'Clock precisely.

CHARLES McGRATH."

The *Spy* said that "a crowded and respectable audience evinced their entire satisfaction by the warmest plaudits and bursts of approbation." Among the performances during the season were Dr. Young's tragedy of "Revenge," Fielding's comedy of "The Miser," Foote's comedy of "The Devil upon Two Sticks," and a farce called "The King and Miller of Mansfield," the whole concluding with a farewell address to the ladies and gentlemen of the town and its vicinity by Mrs. McGrath.

A "concert of music" was given in the "great ball-room at Mr. Crabb's" on March 16, 1792. Tickets 25 cents. Thomas Schley, manager.

In 1793 the following announcement was made in the *Spy:*

"(*To the curious.*)
[Large cut of camel two columns wide.]
A MALE CAMEL

From the deserts of Arabia. To be seen at Mr. Beltzhoover's tavern in Hagerstown, on Tuesday and Wednesday next, the 7th and 8th instant (May, 1793).

This stupendous animal is most deserving the attention of the curious, being the greatest natural curiosity ever exhibited to the public on this continent. He is twenty-one hands high, his neck is four feet long, has a large high hunch on his back, and another under his breast in the form of a pedestal, on which he supports himself when lying down. He has four joints in his hind legs, will travel twelve or fourteen days without drink, and carry fifteen hundred-weight. He is remarkably harmless and docile, and will lie down and rise at command."

On the 30th of December, 1794, a concert was given at "Ragan's great ball-room" by Thomas Schley, music-master of Hagerstown.

The "old theatrical company of Hagerstown," we are told, "met at Mr. Stoner's tavern on Thursday, March 30, 1801," for the purpose of determining as to how it should appropriate the money acquired by the performances of the company. There were present Messrs. C. Keller, Hughes, McPherson, Kelly, Ragan, D. Keller, Young, Boerstler, and Forman. Mr. Young moved that the money be presented to the German Lutheran congregation, and Mr. Kelly that it be appropriated to the construction of causeways from the different corners of the square. Mr. Young's motion was carried, and the money was ordered to be paid to the German Lutheran Church. From this it would seem that there was a regular theatrical organization in Hagerstown at a very early period. In August, 1803, the arrival was announced of Mr. Ramie, "the justly celebrated" ventriloquist. From 1810 to 1825, Durang's Theatre Company frequently performed in Hagerstown, the "Forty Thieves" being one of the favorite pieces. In 1822, Herbert & Williams announced that they had converted the long room at Mr. Newcomer's hotel into a theatre, "with new and splendid scenery, dresses, and decorations," and that it would open on Saturday, the 13th of July, with "Cherry's" much-admired play, "The Soldier's Daughter." Mr. Herbert was announced as being from the Baltimore and Philadelphia theatres, and the other members of the company from New York, Boston, Montreal, and New Orleans theatres. In addition to the play, songs were announced by Mr. Page, from the Charleston theatre, and Mr. Williams, from the Baltimore theatre, and a farce entitled "Lovers' Quarrels." Tickets for the "boxes" were fixed at 75 cents, and for the "pit" at 50 cents. The tickets were for sale at the bars of Beltzhoover's and Newcomer's taverns. About the same time Mr. and Mrs. Richardson, "from Philadelphia, Baltimore, and Virginia theatres," and Mr. Taylor, from the Charleston and New Orleans theatres, were advertised to give a performance of ventriloquism. In the Hagerstown *Torch-Light* of Aug. 3, 1826, it was announced that "Mr. Brown, the proprietor of an equestrian corps, has erected a pavilion circus in Hagerstown."

When it was decided to erect a new hotel in place of the Washington House, destroyed by fire, it was also determined to incorporate with it a handsome and well-appointed theatre. Accordingly, in the same building with the Baldwin House was constructed an Academy of Music, a spacious and handsome structure, which is provided with all the scenery, mechanical appointments, etc., required in giving a first-rate theatrical or operatic performance. The academy was opened to the public on Monday evening, Oct. 18, 1880, under the direction of S. W. Fort, manager of the Baltimore Academy of Music. The entertainment comprised the reading of a prologue by Prof. R. S. Henry, principal of the Hagerstown Academy, and the opera "Chimes of Normandy" by a selected company from New York and Baltimore. The engagement lasted throughout the week, and a variety of pieces were rendered.

Horse-racing was a very popular pastime not only at Hagerstown, but also at Sharpsburg, Williamsport, Hancock, and other points in the county. The Hagerstown course was just outside the town, and appears to have been under the charge, for a number of years, of John Ragan and Jonathan Hager, two noted inn-keepers of Hagerstown. On the 2d of May, 1780, two races were announced to take place on the "Commons" of Hagerstown. Adam Ott and Hezekiah Claggett were the managers, and the horses were to be entered with Col. Henry Shryock. Subscribers were to pay $100 entrance-money for the first day, and $50 for the second. Non-subscribers were to pay $200 for entrance-money for the first day, and $100 for the second day. In 1792 the following announcement was made in the Hagerstown *Spy*:

"On Wednesday, the 5th day of September next (1792), will be run for, over a handsome course adjoining the town, a purse of fifty pounds; free for any horse, mare, or gelding; four-mile heats; aged horses carrying one hundred and twenty-six pounds weight, with a deduction of seven pounds for every year under age. On Thursday, the 6th, will be run for, over the same course, another purse of twenty-five pounds; three-mile heats; free, and carrying weight as aforesaid, the winning horse of the preceding day excepted.

"The horses to be entered with Messrs. Peter Shaffner and John Ragan, and entrance (one shilling in the pound) paid the day preceding each race, or double at the post. No person will be permitted to ride without being dressed in a silk jacket and cap. Four horses to start each day, or no race.

"And on Friday, the 7th, will be run for, over the same course, two-mile heats, a sweepstake of the entrance-money of the two preceding days; free, the winning horses of the two preceding days excepted. Proper persons as judges will be appointed, and the purses paid at the post.

"JOHN RAGAN."

Three horses belonging to Mr. Duvall, named Trimmer, Spot, and Matchhim, won the three days' races. Similar races were run over this course on September 25th, 26th, 27th, entries being made with John Ragan and Jonathan Hager.

On the 30th of July, 1793, John Ragan and Jonathan Hager announced another meeting at the Hagerstown course, as follows: Wednesday, September 25th, a purse of £50; Thursday, September 26th, a purse of £30; Friday, September 27th, a purse of £10; the first a four-mile heat, the second a three-mile heat, the third a two-mile heat. In 1794, Jonathan Hager and George Shall, inn-keepers, were named as the persons with whom the horses were to be entered for the fall races of that year. No person was to be permitted to ride who did not wear a silk jacket and jockey-cap. In 1796, John Ragan and George Shall had charge of the races, which lasted three days, beginning Wednesday, September 14th. The same persons announced another series of races at the same course in 1797. In the following year Jonathan Hager and George Shall had charge, the purses being $100, $48, and $24. In 1799, Griffith Henderson and John McMunn announced that races would be run on the 9th and 10th of October for purses of $100 and $50 respectively. In August, 1800, John Ragan and Jonathan Hager advertised races for the 17th and 18th of September, and on the 6th of April, 1801, Daniel Gehr announced a race for a purse of $20 on Thursday, April 24th, and another for $10 on Friday, April 25th. In September, 1802, races were run at "Rohrer's old course near this town," under the direction of Michael Stoner and Jonathan Hager, who gave notice that no person would be allowed to erect a booth or stand on or near the race-ground without permission from the managers. In July, 1804, a similar announcement was made by John Ragan and Jonathan Hager, the purses being $150, $100, and $50. Hagerstown continued to be a noted racing centre until 1817. As indicated above, the tavern-keepers were chiefly instrumental in getting up the races, and reaped a rich harvest from them. In 1817 the grand jury, David Schnebly, foreman, called the attention of the community to the abuses which they had engendered, such as gambling, drunkenness, profanity, etc., and advised that the races be discontinued, which appears to have been done.

Floods and Storms.—On the 10th of November, 1810, a heavy rain fell in Washington County and the adjacent country drained by the Potomac River and Conococheague Creek. Everything that opposed the progress of the flood was swept away. The bridge which had been built but a short time before over the Conococheague at Williamsport was entirely destroyed, and Mr. Towson's warehouse in that town was washed away, together with a quantity of tar and coal. In August, 1872, a sudden and unexpected freshet did much damage to the crops, stock, and fences in portions of Washington County. The rain all fell in the northern part of the county, but the principal damage was done farther down the courses of the Conococheague and Antietam, where not a drop of rain fell. Smithsburg and other points to the eastward, as well as Hagerstown on the south, were not visited by rain, but in the marshes and about Leitersburg the rain fell in torrents, and both Marsh Run and the Antietam were much swollen. Along their banks the destruction of property was very great. The meadow-lands were swept over and submerged, and the fencing and stock carried away by the flood. The farmers and millers along Marsh Run suffered great loss, the width of the stream having been swollen to half that of the Antietam River. It is said that persons coming from Leitersburg to Hagerstown that night were compelled to turn back and go around by way of Funkstown. Along the Antietam, from Strite's farm to Funkstown, the flood inflicted great damage. It swept down that stream by Hager's mill, and the accumulation of logs, fencing, and débris at the two islands below Funkstown backed the water to a height of eight feet, completely submerging all the low grounds, highly cultivated about Funkstown, and causing great damage to individuals.

As an evidence of the suddenness of the rise in the streams, it is said that some persons who had been fishing with hook and line, not meeting with success, had fallen asleep on the banks, and, awakened by the rising waters, were compelled to wade through water quite deep to the shore. What the full extent of the damage was could not be accurately determined, but every one along the line of the two streams suffered more or less loss.

The year 1877 witnessed the greatest flood that has occurred in the history of Western Maryland. The rain commenced falling one Thursday afternoon in November, and continued to fall, with temporary interruptions, until the following Monday. On Saturday the Potomac, the Antietam, and the Conococheague began to rise rapidly, and reached a height unprecedented in the recollection of any one then living. It was along the Potomac and Antietam that most of the damage in Washington County was done. The chief loss fell upon the Chesapeake and Ohio Canal and two of the railroad companies. The Baltimore and Ohio was washed and injured to such an extent between Martinsburg and Cumberland that travel was suspended on that portion of the main stem. The destruction of the bridge over the Potomac on the line of the Cumberland Valley Railroad compelled the company to again make Hagerstown the western terminus of the road. The destruction of this bridge entailed upon the road a loss of between thirty and forty thousand dollars.

The water in the Potomac during the great flood of 1852, according to a mark at Embrey's warehouse in Williamsport, was three-quarters of an inch higher than the flood of 1877 reached, but this mark is not looked upon as accurate, and according to all other marks the water rose higher in the latter year than in the former. Along the entire line of the river great damage was done; not only fencing, grain, hay, fodder, stock, and lumber being swept away, but several houses, and quite a number of stables, hog-pens, chicken-coops, and different sorts of outhouses were seen passing down the river at Williamsport and other points. Many visitors from Hagerstown and the surrounding country were in Williamsport on Sunday, viewing the surging river and watching the débris brought down with the flood. At Embrey & Cushwa's warehouse the damage was but slight, but Mr. S. Culbertson, on the west side of the Conococheague, lost between forty and sixty thousand feet of lumber.

At the junction of the Conococheague and the Potomac there was a vast lake, covering canal, aqueduct, and everything except the tops of the trees. Ardinger's mill was in the middle of the Conococheague, and the water was pouring into the windows of the upper story, leaving but a few feet of the stone walls visible between the waters and the eaves of the roof. The stone bridge at this point and the aqueduct on the canal were submerged, but were not materially injured. The most serious damage near Williamsport was the injury done to the Cumberland Valley Railroad bridge. The superstructure of this costly work went about five o'clock on Sunday afternoon. Its danger was appreciated, and six car-loads of coal, railroad and pig-iron were sent out from Hagerstown to hold down the capping of the bridge and track. T. J. Nill, the agent there, accompanied the train, and it was run to the Virginia side, which was in greatest danger, and there stationed. But a slight space remained between the surface of the stream and the track on the bridge, so that its destruction by the heavy bodies coming down the stream was inevitable. Three canal-boats in turn, which had broken loose from Williamsport, struck the bridge. Two passed under and went down the stream, while the other blocked the stream. Then came an immense float of drift-wood, which cut off a large willow-tree as with a knife, and, striking the bridge with a concussion which sounded like the discharge of artillery, and was heard in Williamsport, bore off with it the whole superstructure save only that which spanned the canal, and the canal-boat which was held in suspense was thus released and went down the stream with the moving mass. At this juncture it was Mr. Nill's good fortune to escape in a manner that may be termed almost miraculous. He was the last upon the bridge, some fifteen or twenty men having just left it, when he saw the impending danger and started in a run for the Maryland side. The first concussion knocked his feet from under him and he fell; but recovering just as the portion of the bridge behind him was swept away, and whilst that upon which he ran was coiling up and moving under his feet, he succeeded in reaching the shore uninjured, and almost at the instant the bridge disappeared. The leading officials of the road, President Kennedy, General Superintendent Lull, and General Agent Boyd, were all present on the bridge a few minutes before it went down, with fifteen or twenty other persons. A little engine had been trying to haul out the canal-boat that had lodged to the Virginia shore, but without effect. Col. Kennedy and Col. Lull had walked off towards the Maryland side, leaving Gen. Boyd and Mr. Nill. The former started a few minutes before the latter, and was about fifty yards ahead of him when he saw the drift approaching and started in the manner above described.

Only a small portion of the fine "Dam No. 4," the best on the river, having cost almost a half-million dollars, was washed away. This dam was between the Cumberland Valley bridge and the Shepherdstown bridge, one span of which was washed away. This span was one of four, each one hundred and fifty feet long, and was secured and made fast some distance below. A canal-boat loaded with coal, belonging to George McCann, was the first to strike this bridge, and was followed by two others, which were empty, belonging to Lawson Poffenberger and Mr. Boyer.

These were the first boats to strike the Harper's Ferry iron bridge, which was supposed for some time to have been in great danger, but withstood the terrific shocks and pressure brought against it in a wonderful manner, it having been struck by no less than fifteen canal-boats, besides the Powell's Bend bridge, houses, logs, and all kinds of floating missiles. Mr. Ways, agent of the Baltimore and Ohio Railroad Company, stated that but a single span of the bridge—that over the current—was affected, and that only in the bending of some of the irons.

The damage to the canal was very great, causing the suspension of its operations for the season. The locks at Harper's Ferry and several other locks were washed out and greatly damaged. From Sandy Hook past Harper's Ferry, a distance of four miles, the tow-path was wholly destroyed.

In places the bed of the canal was filled with mud, and all the locks were choked up with accumulations of various kinds. The canal company's buildings were all of them either damaged or washed away, and the total injury to the property of the company amounted to five hundred thousand dollars. The only fatal disaster in Washington County was the drowning of Charles Little, of Hancock, which took place Saturday evening, below Dam No. 4, below Williamsport. Mr. Little, who was a boatman, was proceeding up the canal. When the water got deep on the tow-path his driver refused to go any farther. Mr. Little got on one of the mules to drive. In a short time the current was too strong, the mules were swept down in the flood, and Mr. Little was drowned. The two mules scrambled to the bank, some distance below, and were saved.

At Powell's Bend, opposite Falling Waters, the dwelling-house of Andrew Pope, a well-known farmer of that neighborhood, was taken up, carried away, and deposited upon the land of one of his neighbors. David Straw, of the same vicinity, lost a corn-crib. Mrs. Louisa Davis, another neighbor, lost seventy-five barrels of corn, a buggy, sleigh, and other articles. The house of John Snyder, a small building, was carried away, as was also a small house owned by John H. Gattrell, and occupied by a man named Price. Mr. Gattrell's saw-mill was also injured, and was moved about four inches. Everything between the canal and the river, from Williamsport to Hancock, that could be carried off by the storm was swept away, and the canal and railroad were greatly damaged. The upper part of Hancock was under water, and along the flats and slopes beyond that town many houses were swept away. All the bridges between Hancock and Indian Spring on the turnpike were carried off or rendered impassable. The Antietam rose to a point higher than was ever before known. Bridges were destroyed all along the line of the creek,—among them the one at the Forks, midway between Leitersburg and Waynesboro', Pa., and the one at the Little Antietam, near Hartle's. Among the numerous losses suffered along this stream were the washing away of Mr. Walter's stable, the partial destruction of Frisby M. Stouffer's saw-mill, and the washing away of outhouses, fences, etc. The substantial bridge over the Antietam on the National road was not injured, but the other bridge, built by the county over this stream at Funkstown, was materially damaged. At Rose's paper-mill, an old frame structure sixty feet long, used as a bleach-house, was washed away.

At the Roxbury mill the whole dam was swept away and the stone bridge injured. A portion of the dam at Myers' mill was also destroyed. The Antietam Iron-Works, at which every preparation had been made by the Messrs. Ahl for starting work, were damaged to the extent of several thousand dollars, about eight hundred tons of coke having been washed away. The Conococheague, like the Antietam, rose to a higher point than had ever been reached before, but except the damage done at Williamsport no great loss was suffered, the principal injury being the washing away of fences and fodder, and the submerging of the lower stories of buildings. This storm was widely extended, and carried great destruction with it along the Atlantic coast, inflicting death and loss of property all along its line of advance. It was in this storm that the United States steamer "Huron" was lost on the North Carolina coast, with about one hundred of her officers and crew.

On the 12th of July, 1878, Hagerstown was visited by a terrific storm, which inflicted considerable damage. Its ravages were confined almost entirely to the corporate limits of the town. All the neighboring villages escaped with only a strong wind and some rain, and one mile south of Hagerstown Mr. Straub, a farmer, was not even compelled to stop hauling wheat. In other portions of the county trees were blown down and wheat-shocks scattered, but the storm was not serious. In Hagerstown, however, it was so severe as to cause general consternation, and the destruction of property was greater, so far as known, than at any previous period. The wind burst upon the town about five o'clock in the afternoon. It struck the steeple of the old Reformed church, on Potomac Street, and hurled it to the ground. In falling the steeple knocked off a corner of the roof. The church had celebrated its centennial anniversary in 1875, and a few years previously the steeple had been erected in place of the old one. It had been fastened on to the old timbers, which were so badly decayed that its demolition under the circumstances was not surprising. The old bells which were brought from Germany in 1791 were heard to toll when the blast struck them, a moment before the steeple fell. They were dug out of the débris, and were found to be unharmed. Fortunately no one was passing at the time, nor was there loss of human life in any other portion of the town. The rear of the Junior engine-house was struck, and the gable and a large portion of the roof were demolished. The roof was carried over the back building of Mrs. Artz' house without injuring it, along with a lot of bricks and mortar, and deposited in Franklin Street. A tin roof on Mr. Orndorf's house, on Potomac Street, was coiled up, and a house on Baltimore Street, occupied by David McCall, was unroofed. The front half was blown out into the middle of the turnpike, and the other half was carried into the back yard of Mr. Bell, two lots off, and lodged upon the pump. The front wall was cracked, and the house shook so during the storm that the family took refuge in the cellar, where they remained unhurt. The sheet-iron smoke-stack of the Agricultural Implement Works, on East Washington Street, was blown across into Locust Street, and the roofing of the engine-house of the Western Maryland Railroad was torn off and precipitated upon the track. About one-fourth of the roof of the Cumberland Valley engine-house was also blown away. The engine-house of the steam flouring-mill at the Cumberland Valley Railroad depot was badly damaged, the smoke-stack being blown down and the roof torn off and wrecked. The zinc capping on the roof of the Presbyterian church was also blown off in places, and a number of shade and fruit-trees were uprooted.

WASHINGTON COUNTY DISTRICTS.

CHAPTER LIII.

SHARPSBURG DISTRICT, No. 1.

SHARPSBURG, or Election District No. 1, is situated in the southern portion of the county, and borders on the Potomac River. On the north is

Tilghmanton District; on the east, the districts of Keedysville and Rohrersville; on the south, Sandy Hook District; and on the west, the Potomac River. Its original boundaries were:

"Beginning at the mouth of the Great Marsh Run, at the river Potomac, and running from thence up the said run to the road leading from Williamsport at Eversole's mill; thence down the said road, by Carey's, to the Antietam Creek, at the bridge lately built by Robert Smith; thence up the creek to Booth's bridge; thence down the road to the Eleven Mile tree, where the road forks to Williamsport and Funkstown; and thence by a line to the top of the mountain, to include the town of Boonsboro' and the plantation of Jacob Petry, in District No. 1; thence with the county line on the top of the mountain to the river Potomac; and thence with the river to the place of beginning: this district to be called No. 1, and the election to be held at the house of Andrew McCloy, in the town of Sharpsburg."

In 1822 the boundaries were:

"To commence at the Potomac River, at the point where the Frederick County line intersects the said river, and near the stone mill; thence with the Frederick County line till it is intersected by the road leading from Crampton's Gap to Casper Snavely's; thence with said road by Casper Snavely's to Keedy's store; thence with the road by Keedy's store to the Sharpsburg and Boonsboro' turnpike road; thence with said road to the road leading from Hess' mill to Cary's Cross-roads; thence with said road by Cary's Cross-roads to the Great Marsh Run near Houser's mill; thence down and with said run to the Potomac River; thence down and with said river to the place of beginning."

These boundaries were established by commissioners appointed under an act of the Legislature passed at the November session of 1821. The population of the district, according to the census of 1880, and including the town of Sharpsburg, which has 1260 inhabitants, is 2311.

Running from north to south a little east of the central portion of the district is Antietam Creek, from which the famous battle of Antietam, fought at Sharpsburg, between the armies of McClellan and Lee, derived its name. In addition to the Antietam and the Potomac the district is watered by numerous small streams which flow into both those rivers. The country is traversed in every direction by substantial roads, and two turnpikes pass through Sharpsburg, one leading to Hagerstown and the other eastward into Keedysville District. The only town of importance in the district is Sharpsburg, but there is a small village at Antietam Iron-Works, and one also at the Canal Lock, in the extreme western portion of the district. Among the well-known families of the district are the Renches, Poffenbergers, Newcomers, Eichelbergers, Mummas, Nicodemuses, Cramptons, Groves, Knodes, Remsburgers, and Stonebrakers.

Samuel Stonebraker was born April 11, 1801, on the old homestead near Bakersville, which has been owned by four generations of Stonebrakers, and is now in the possession of George M. Stonebraker. Michael Stonebraker, the father of Samuel, died May 6, 1815, aged fifty-six years, and his wife, Esther S. Wolgamot, the mother of Samuel, was born Dec. 27, 1769, and died Feb. 17, 1827, aged sixty-four years. Samuel Stonebraker married Margaretta Pennel, who was born in Pennsylvania, May 15, 1812, and died in Baltimore, Dec. 20, 1852. They were married in Washington County in 1836, and had four children. The eldest, Elmira, married F. W. Cassard at Baltimore; the second, a boy, died in infancy; the third, Mary J., married John T. Foster, of Baltimore; and the fourth, George M., married Florence V. Benton, and is now living in Hagerstown. Samuel Stonebraker was educated in the country schools of his neighborhood. He is a member of the Reformed Church, and was one of the founders of the Third Reformed Church, at the corner of Paca and Saratoga Streets, Baltimore. He was a farmer until 1839, when he removed to Baltimore and engaged in the grain and flour commission business, on South Howard Street, with Jacob Meixell, under the firm-name of Meixell & Stonebraker. In 1842 the firm was dissolved, and Mr. Stonebraker continued, under the name of Newcomer & Stonebraker, in partnership with John Newcomer, of Washington County, the father of the present B. F. Newcomer, who in a short time purchased his father's interest and became a member of the firm, which retained the same name. They continued in partnership until 1862, when the firm was dissolved, and the new firm of Stonebraker & Co. was formed, with Dr. H. F. Zollickoffer, of Baltimore, as partner. The firm continued until dissolved by the death of Mr. Stonebraker, Jan. 17, 1873, aged seventy-one years. Mr. Stonebraker was continuously in business on Howard Street, and was also at the time of his death a member of the firm of Stirling, Ahrens & Co., sugar-refiners and importers. He was one of the founders and originators of the Corn and Flour Exchange of Baltimore, and during his whole life took an active interest in everything tending to advance the growth and prosperity of Baltimore.

George M., the only son of Samuel Stonebraker, was born in Baltimore, Aug. 3, 1846, and was educated at Midfield, Baltimore Co., and at Rugby Institute, Mount Washington, Baltimore Co. He married Florence V. Benton, March 23, 1873, and has two sons,—George Benton and Levin. Mr. Stonebraker has been a member of the Town Council of Sharpsburg.

The ancestors of nearly all these old families were

among the earliest settlers of that portion of the province. Sharpsburg District has been the theatre of more stirring events than any other portion of Maryland, having been the scene, besides other military operations, of the bloody battle of Antietam, one of the most stubbornly contested, as it was one of the most eventful, engagements of the civil war.

The town of Sharpsburg, which has a population, according to the census of 1880, of 1260 persons, was laid out in 1763 by Joseph Chapline, a gentleman from England, and was named in honor of Governor Sharpe. Horatio Sharpe was one of the most distinguished of the provincial Governors of Maryland. He was appointed to the position by Lord Baltimore after the death of Governor Ogle, in 1752, and arrived in the colony on the 10th of August, 1753. His administration was very energetic, and his conduct throughout the French and Indian war gave evidence of high military and administrative capacity. In 1755 he was appointed commander of the forces at Fort Cumberland in place of Col. George Washington, and afterwards commander-in-chief of the colonial forces against the French and Indians. When Gen. Braddock arrived Governor Sharpe was superseded, but after Braddock's defeat he was again appointed commander-in-chief. Governor Sharpe erected Fort Frederick, and greatly improved and strengthened Fort Cumberland, besides contributing in many ways to the prosecution of the French and Indian war. On the 1st of August, 1768, he was succeeded by Governor Eden. In 1755, Governor Sharpe descended the Potomac from Fort Cumberland, a distance of two hundred and fifty miles, in a boat, accompanied by Gen. St. Clair. This was some eight years before Sharpsburg was settled. Mr. Chapline, who was an officer in the French and Indian war, appears to have arrived in the neighborhood some time before. He took up all the lands on and about the site of the future town of Sharpsburg for a distance of three miles.

The records now in possession of Mrs. Mary T. Hays, of Hagerstown, Md, whose husband was a descendant of the Chapline family, contain the following, viz.: "Joseph Chapline, of the county of Frederick, province of Maryland, has laid out a town at a place called the Great Spring, Frederick Co., province of Maryland, July 9, 1763." Sharpsburg was to have been the county-seat of Washington County, and was laid out for that purpose. An election, however, was held, which resulted in the choice of Hagerstown, or Elizabethtown, as it was first named, Sharpsburg being defeated by one vote. Prior to the formation of Washington County all the county business was transacted at Frederick Town, as it was then called, and many deeds, etc., relative to Washington County are still on record there. The spot where Sharpsburg now stands was once a vast forest full of undergrowth of hazel and chinquapin bushes, and abounding in all kinds of game, and was well watered by the Great Spring. It is said to have been the favorite hunting-ground of the Delaware Indians, and mounds in which are numerous arrow-points, tomahawks, etc., have been found in and around the town. John P. Smith, of Sharpsburg, possesses a very interesting collection of these relics.

John P. Smith was born at Sharpsburg on the 2d of September, 1845. His parents are John H. and Sarah Smith. Mr. Smith adopted the profession of teaching, and took charge of the first intermediate department of the public school at Sharpsburg, which position he has occupied for fifteen years. He was married on the 24th of August, 1880, by the Rev. J. A. Rondthaler, pastor of the Presbyterian Church at Hagerstown, to Kate V. Snively, of Greencastle, Pa. In 1878, Mr. Smith wrote a historical sketch of the town of Sharpsburg, which was published in the Sharpsburg *Enterprise*, and to which the author of this work is greatly indebted for much valuable material. He is a diligent collector of historical material of a local character, and, as above stated, possesses a valuable collection of Indian relics and antiquities unearthed near Sharpsburg and in other portions of Washington County. He is a careful and painstaking teacher, and occupies a deservedly high position in the confidence of the community in which he resides.

Tradition informs us that a bloody affair occurred on the Antietam near its mouth between 1730 and 1736, between the Catawbas and Delawares. The few particulars known are as follows: The Delawares had made an incursion far to the south, and in returning had committed some gross outrages on the Catawbas, and on their retreat were overtaken near the mouth of the Antietam by the exasperated Catawbas. A terrible conflict ensued, which resulted in the slaughter of all the Delawares with the exception of one man, who escaped after the battle was over. It was, however, only for a time. Every warrior among the Catawbas showed a scalp with the exception of one. He felt this to be a disgrace, and set out in pursuit of the fugitive, whom he did not overtake until he reached the Susquehanna River, where he killed and scalped him. This battle took place on what is now known as the coke-yard of the Antietam Iron-Works, three miles from Sharpsburg. Numerous skeletons and implements of war have been found there from time to time. About a mile up the Antietam, on the lands of James Marker,

GOV. HORATIO SHARPE.

is a cave, which tradition informs us was a burial-place of the aborigines.

In what year Joseph Chapline arrived in Washington County there is nothing on record to show. That it was some time prior to 1757 is evident from the fact that his name appears on a muster-roll of the French and Indian war. Joseph Chapline is said to have been noted for his many excellent qualities of head and heart. He bequeathed to the Lutheran Church at Sharpsburg a burial-ground and site for a church. Many of his descendants are now living. He reached a good old age, and was buried in the family burying-ground on his farm, two miles west of Sharpsburg, on the Potomac River. The tombstones were destroyed during the late war, and it is therefore impossible to learn anything definite as to his age or the time of his death. In this graveyard lie the remains of an aged Episcopal minister. The headstone bears the following inscription :

> "To the memory of the
> Revd. Samuel Thompson,
> Born in the year 1687, departed this life
> April 29, 1787. Aged 100 years.
> Also his wife,
> Mary Thompson,
> Born 1724,
> And departed this life March 6, 1801,
> Aged 77 years."

Near by lie the remains of Capt. Alexander Thompson, an officer of the Revolution, who was born in 1753, and died on the 24th day of December, 1815, aged sixty-two years.

These, no doubt, were relatives of the Chapline family. The burial-ground is on a hill overlooking the Potomac. The fence has been destroyed, the place has grown up into a wilderness, and cattle roam at will over the graves. The tombstones of Joseph Chapline and wife are broken in pieces, and the entire yard is neglected.

The first settlers were principally of English and German descent. They emigrated to this country about the time the settlement took place. Some of them were the Chaplines, Hays, Crusses, Needs, Sams, Hawkers, Flicks, Graffs, Bartoons, Tyrones, Millers, etc. The descendants of some of these settlers are living in Sharpsburg at the present time. One of them is in possession of a German Bible of Martin Luther's translation, printed in 1748. It is a quaint, old-fashioned book, having oak boards one-quarter of an inch thick, and bound in stout leather, with brass clasps. It was brought from Wittenberg by one of the settlers.

When the town was founded there were only four houses in it. The first house was the old log and weather-boarded building standing on the site of the brick building afterwards owned by Samuel Show. This house, we are told, was used for a long time as a trading-post between the Indians and whites. It was a building of very peculiar construction, and attracted much attention when the workmen were tearing it down. The second house was the one next to the Methodist church, and was torn down by J. F. Shamel, who erected a new one on the site. The third was the old log house now encased with brick, and owned by Samuel Michael, and the fourth the weather-boarded portion of the house belonging to the heirs of the late Jacob Miller. The first hotel was kept by a Mr. Harvey. After that hotels were kept by Matthias Knode, William Rohrback, and many others. In 1791, Conrad Shutz kept store and tavern "at the place previously occupied by John Salmon." In the same year Rosa Orendorff was a local celebrity, and not less than fifty or sixty persons are said to have passed through Shepherdstown, Va., daily to visit her, some of them coming a distance of two hundred miles. In 1800, Peter Deterlt had a tavern at the "Sign of the Fountain," on the public square, Sharpsburg.

The first store in the place was kept by David B. Miller, in 1768. Calicoes and muslins were then imported goods. The former were fifty cents a yard, and the latter were fifty cents and one dollar a yard. In very early times Mr. Miller would ride to Baltimore on horseback, carrying with him a pair of saddle-bags, which he would bring back full of dry-goods and groceries. Very little calico and muslin were used, as the inhabitants raised flax and hemp and made their own goods. Coffee was only used on Sunday, owing to its high price. In after-years goods were brought in wagons from Baltimore. Philip Grove and Benjamin Tupson had stores in Sharpsburg in 1808, and George Cronise and Samuel Ruckle in 1809. The first school-house was a log one, and was erected on the corner of the lot adjoining the lot of Judge David Smith, on the site where the carriage-house now stands. The first teacher was named Young. In 1808 the German language was taught. The English language was taught in another log school by a man named Clayton. Afterwards a Mr. Legget taught there. In those days the boys did all the cutting of the wood for fire in the school-house. Two of the girls were detained every evening to sweep the room, and on Saturday of each week the girls and boys assembled and swept the room. Each boy was required in his turn to make the fires during the winter months. Some time after, a brick school-house was built on the site where the jail now stands. This was occupied for many years. In 1870 this was torn down and the new building erected.

Dr. Rich was the first physician. He practiced in 1775. Then came Dr. Nathan Hays, in 1783, Dr. George W. Hays, in 1811, Dr. Hartman, in 1816, Dr. Rubel, in 1818, Dr. John Jones Hays, in 1821, Dr. Joseph C. Hays, in 1824. These were followed by Drs. Hammond, Buchanan, Stubblefield, Biggs, Kennedy, Chapline, Hays, Grove, Smith, Tobey, De Kalb, Kretzer, J. M. and J. H. Beckenbaugh, A. A. Biggs, Russell, J. J. Coffman, and J. E. S. Baker. For some time after the settlement of the town there was no resident physician, and in cases of severe sickness the people were obliged to go to Frederick, twenty-two miles, for a physician. In 1816 a market-house was erected. It stood between the hotel and the dwelling of George M. Stonebraker. It appears to have been used chiefly as a refuge for intoxicated persons and as a shelter for swine. Some time after its erection it was torn down and the material hauled away. In 1820 the census of Sharpsburg was: White males, 298; white females, 280; total whites, 578. Slaves, males, 19; females, 33; total slaves, 52. Free colored persons, males, 12; females, 14; total free colored persons, 26. Total population, 656.

The town had a post-office in July, 1813, and the postmaster, Gabriel Nourse, advertised the following letters remaining in the post-office July 7, 1813: Benjamin Burrell, William Baker, Henry Bampford, Elisha Chambers, Elisha Easton, John Furry, Peter Holmes, Martin Hosinest, Amos Heakle, Catharine Jones, John Lancaster, Christian Poffenberger, Henry Shamel, J. Speilman.

At a meeting held at Philip Myers' tavern in May, 1812, Robert Smith, chairman, and Henry Locher, clerk, Philip Hammond, George Shafer, Henry Schnecter, Matthew Collins, John Smith, Conrad Nicodemus, and Ephraim Davis were appointed the local Republican committee. These meetings were generally held at the tavern. In May, 1826, for example, we are told there was a meeting of the Sharpsburg friends of the administration at John M. Knode's tavern, "Col. John Blackford in the chair."

Sharpsburg at one time enjoyed an extensive celebrity for its races. On the 9th of October, 1799, John Good and Jeremiah Chapline announced that races would be run for over the course near the town for purses of seventy and thirty dollars and a handsome sweepstake, the races to last three days. In September, 1800, Andrew McCoy advertised races at Sharpsburg, under the rules of the Annapolis Jockey Club. Two years later, Mr. McCoy and Basil Beall advertised races for purses of sixty and forty dollars.

Among the early residents of Sharpsburg were the following:

John L. Hovermeal (in 1812).
Michael Carey.
Andrew McCoy, tavern-keeper.
Basil Beall, tavern-keeper.
Conrad Knode.
B. Tyson, merchant (in 1804).
Dr. Henry Boteler (in 1804).
Gibbs & Westover (who had a carding-machine at Jacob Mumma's mill, near Sharpsburg, in 1806).
Capt. John Ritchie, manager of Antietam Iron-Works.
Capt. John Blackford, of the "Independent Blues."
Samuel D. Price, merchant (in 1811).
Philip Myers, tavern-keeper (in 1812).
Baker & Ziglar, merchants.
Alexander Montgomery, tailor.
Mr. Miller, merchant.
Dr. John Hartman (who established his office in 1800, and died there in 1819).
Dr. J. J. Hays, who established his office in 1819.

The Boonsboro' turnpike was organized Sept. 24, 1815. In 1820 a dyeing and weaving establishment was carried on by Jacob Miller, which gave employment to many people. Mr. Miller is entitled to the credit of having woven the first seamless bags ever woven in the United States, for which he took out letters of patent. Some years later a hat manufactory was carried on by Andrew Fraher, and afterwards by James Early. At a very early day a number of people in the town and on the farms in the neighborhood had distilleries and manufactured their own liquors. The mill now owned by Jacob A. Myers was built in 1783, the residence in 1743, and the bridge in 1828. This was the first mill known in the neighborhood. In 1853 a printing-office was established, and a paper edited by the Rev. J. H. Ewing, a Methodist minister and public school-teacher, was issued from it. Christopher Cruss, whose name appears in the deed to the vestrymen of the Lutheran Church, was a German chemist, and was one of the first settlers. He lived on the farm, two miles north of Sharpsburg, now owned by Col. John Miller. He (Christopher Cruss) leased this land from Joseph Chapline for ninety-nine years. While living on the farm, it is said, he became interested with Rumsey in building the first steamboat constructed in America. He also conceived the idea of putting up machine-mills, and sent to England for the machinery. Gen. Washington is said to have visited Sharpsburg twice, once during the French and Indian wars, and once later, when he made a short speech in the public square of the town.

In January, 1810, Edward Bran was committed to the Washington County jail, charged with having murdered Elizabeth Murphy, a child eleven years of age, near McPherson & Brinn's iron-works, four miles from Sharpsburg.

The only paper published in Sharpsburg in recent years was the Sharpsburg *Enterprise*, George E. Woody and John W. Snyder, which was started early in the fall of 1878 and expired in 1881.

The present Town Council of Sharpsburg is composed of the following: Burgess, Moses Poffenberger; Assistant, Jacob Lakins; Bailiff, Peter Mose; Councilmen, Wm. H. Cronise, Jr., Wm. F. Blackford, John P. Smith, Jacob McGraw, B. F. De Lanney.

Churches and Cemeteries.—The oldest church in Sharpsburg is the Mount Calvary Evangelical Lutheran, which was established soon after the settlement of Chapline and others. An old deed is recorded in Liber L, folio 179, of the land records of Frederick County, at the request of Christopher Cruss, March 16, 1768, as follows:

"This indenture, made this 5th day of March, 1768, between Joseph Chapline, of Frederick County, province of Maryland, on one part, and Christopher Cruss, Matthias Need, Nicholas Sam, and William Hawker, vestrymen and church-wardens of the Lutheran Church in the town of Sharpsburg, in the county aforesaid, of the other part,

"Witnesseth, that the said Joseph Chapline, for and in consideration of the religious regard he hath and beareth to the said Lutheran Church, as also for the better support and maintenance of the said church, hath given, granted, aliened, and enfeoffed and confirmed, and by these presents doth give, grant, alien, and enfeoff and confirm to the said Christopher Cruss, Matthias Need, Nicholas Sam, and William Hawker, vestrymen and church-wardens, and their successors, members of the above church, for the use of the congregation that do resort thereto, one lot or portion of ground, No. 149, containing one hundred and fifty-four feet in breadth and two hundred and six feet in length, with all profits, advantages, and appurtenances to the said lot or portion of ground belonging or appertaining, to have and to hold, to them, the said Christopher Cruss, Matthias Need, Nicholas Sam, William Hawker, vestrymen and church-wardens, and to their successors forever, to them and to their own use, and to no other use, intent, or purpose whatever, yielding and paying to the said Joseph Chapline, his heirs and assigns, one *pepper-corn*, if demanded, on the 9th day of July, yearly. . . . And if the above-named vestry . . . do not build or cause to be built a church on said lot in a term of seven years, then the above lot to revert to the said Joseph Chapline, his heirs and assigns."

The witnesses to the deed were Joseph Smith and Samuel Beall, Jr. Joseph Chapline's wife, Ruhannah Chapline, at the same time relinquished her right of dower to the land and premises, and on the same day one half-penny sterling was paid to Lord Baltimore for an alienation fee, in accordance with the order of Edward Lloyd, his lordship's agent for the province of Maryland.

The receipt for the half-penny was signed by Christopher Edelen, clerk of Frederick County.

The first church edifice was a log house, thirty-three by thirty-eight feet, situated in the northwest corner of the old graveyard. It was a quaint, old-fashioned building. The bell, which was supposed to be over a hundred years old, swung for a long time on a pole outside the church. Afterwards a cupola was built. The interior of the church was very antique in appearance, and the pulpit was lofty, and was entered by a flight of ten or twelve steps. A "sounding-board" of wood, shaped like an open umbrella, was suspended some distance above the head of the speaker. The pews were rudely constructed, and had very high backs. The elders and deacons were seated on a platform. There is nothing upon record to show that a corner-stone was ever laid, or that the church was ever dedicated. Joseph Chapline is said to have occupied a pew in this church till he died. In 1849 the church was rough-casted and the interior remodeled. During the battle of Antietam, in 1862, the church was shelled, and the Federal troops used it for a hospital. It was so much damaged as to be unfit for use, and was pulled down. The ground was exchanged for the site of the present church. The corner-stone of the latter was laid Sept. 15, 1866, and the church was dedicated May 23, 1869. The early records of the church have been either lost or destroyed. It seems evident, however, that it was supplied by ministers from Hagerstown and Frederick. The preaching up to 1831 was done in German. It was the custom in those days when the minister called to see his members for them to indulge in an old-fashioned toddy. The following is a list of the ministers who have officiated since 1814: Revs. Schaeffer, Ravenock, Bachey, Little, Sway, Winter, Rigen, Ozwald, Diehl, Hunt, Unruh, Martz, Sunger, Stine, Startzman, Buhrman, Weills, Beckley. In the old graveyard of the Lutheran church the following early residents are interred:

David Showman, died March 4, 1858, aged 68 years, 4 months; and his wife, Kezia, died Aug. 13, 1864, aged 68 years, 10 months.

Elizabeth Myers, died Nov. 8, 1821, aged 57 years, 3 months.

Wm. Roullett, born March 10, 1774, died Oct. 5, 1826; and his wife, Charity, born March 1, 1773, died Feb. 14, 1826.

John Jones Hays, M.D., born March 5, 1796, died July 16, 1823.

Dr. Joseph C. Hays, died Jan. 8, 1841, aged 42 years.

Dr. Nathan W. Hays, died Oct. 9, 1812, aged 55 years; and his wife, Theodocia Chapline, born March, 1760, died March, 1844.

Sarah Chapline, died July 31, 1834, aged 81 years.

Jane Chapline, died May 24, 1837, aged 80 years.

Frederick Hovermale, born July 25, 1764, died April 15, 1815.

Matthias Spong, Sr., died Oct. 8, 1846, aged 75 years; and his wife, Catherine, died Sept. 4, 1845, aged 73 years.

Nancy Davis, died Jan. 28, 1846, aged 76 years.

George Stiffler, died Nov. 21, 1855, aged 66 years, 8 months; and his wife, Salome, died Nov. 8, 1850, aged 57 years, 5 months.

John Renner, died Aug. 26, 1850, aged 65 years.

John Hine, died April 14, 1856, aged 69 years; and his wife, Mary, born March 14, 1788, died Jan. 14, 1845.

John Benner, died Dec. 14, 1825, aged 83 years; and his wife, Magdalene, died Dec. 23, 1825, aged 75 years.

Daniel Benner, died Dec. 20, 1853, aged 87 years; and his wife, Catherine, died Feb. 15, 1853, aged 77 years.

Daniel Funk, born Oct. 4, 1798, died Aug. 12, 1854.

Regina Fortney, died April 20, 1847, aged 89 years.

James McGrath, died Dec. 19, 1856, aged 87 years; and his wife, Sarah, died Oct. 10, 1875, aged 84 years.

Raphael Gray, born May 14, 1786, died March 26, 1853.

Col. Jacob Rohrback, born March 16, 1787, died July 30, 1853; and his wife, Mary, died Aug. 24, 1866, aged 66 years.

Jacob Gardenour, born Jan. 28, 1764, died April 10, 1846; and his wife, Zelinda, died Aug. 26, 1842, aged 66 years, 8 months.

Julia Sheeler, born April 22, 1764, died Dec. 7, 1812.

Elizabeth Harman, born July 28, 1763, died April 16, 1836.

In the new graveyard of Mount Calvary Church the following are buried:

David Reel, died Sept. 21, 1848, aged 69 years, 10 months; and his wife, Annie M., died Jan. 19, 1859, aged 38 years.

Elias Knodle, died Sept. 12, 1869, aged 51.

Samuel Cramer, died July 19, 1873, aged 77 years.

George Peterman, died March 10, 1874, aged 48.

Elizabeth, wife of Henry Rye, died Oct. 17, 1873, aged 64 years, 6 months.

Jacob Nichols, died July 22, 1880, aged 64.

Elizabeth, wife of William Gloss, died Dec. 28, 1871, aged 71 years, 11 months.

Elizabeth, wife of John W. Peyton, died July 18, 1878, aged 44.

John Hill, died March 13, 1879, aged 83 years; and his wife, Rosanna, died Jan. 19, 1878, aged 65 years, 2 months.

Hester, wife of Samuel Cramer, died May 5, 1877, aged 75 years, 1 month.

Barbara, wife of John Mullen, died Dec. 2, 1869, aged 72 years, 11 months.

Richard W. Johnson, died Feb. 15, 1870, aged 60.

Jacob Miller, died Dec. 6, 1865, aged 92 years, 11 months.

Hilliard F. Hebb, died May 13, 1875, aged 67 years, 7 months.

John S. Bender, born March 20, 1806, died Aug. 8, 1874, aged 68.

Catharine Kretzinger, died Feb. 21, 1871, aged 77 years, 5 months.

Christian Dibert, died July 2, 1856, aged 77 years, 6 months.

Nancy Dibert, died Oct. 8, 1858, aged 55.

Mary Jane, wife of William A. Ecton, died March 5, 1881, aged 54.

Margaret, wife of Noah Putman, died May 24, 1880, aged 59.

Jerusha, wife of William Wickers, died July 22, 1880, aged 45.

John Mullender, died June 9, 1875, aged 73.

John Himes, died Feb. 27, 1860, aged 61 years.

Jacob H. Rohrback, born Nov. 19, 1812, died July 4, 1864.

Henry Bamford, died Nov. 22, 1868, aged 77 years, 6 months; and his wife, Sarah, died May 4, 1874, aged 84 years, 1 month.

Samuel Reel, died Jan. 29, 1879, aged 70 years, 4 months; and his wife, Maria, died March 2, 1857, aged 48 years, 11 months.

Adam Michael, died May 18, 1873, aged 82 years, 15 days; and his wife, Nancy, died Nov. 24, 1862, aged 65 years, 6 months.

Henry Reel, died Jan. 12, 1873, aged 59.

Jacob Shay, born Sept. 15, 1785, died Jan. 15, 1866, aged 80.

Timothy Coin, died March 10, 1866, aged 52.

William Gloss, died Nov. 8, 1864, aged 66 years, 7 months.

Henry Wade, died Dec. 9, 1847, aged 45.

Catharine, wife of Jacob Brenner, died March 1, 1867, aged 72 years, 9 months.

Elizabeth, wife of Adam Myers, died April 3, 1868, in her 72d year.

John Mullender, died June 9, 1875, aged 73.

Ann M., wife of David Wilhelm, died Aug. 8, 1875, aged 64.

Elizabeth Bowers, died Dec. 6, 1880, aged 60.

Catharine Saylor, died July 24, 1863, aged 59.

David Wilhelm, died March 20, 1859, aged 48.

Elizabeth, wife of Daniel Poffenberger, died Feb. 20, 1858, aged 46.

David Pennel, died March 9, 1874, aged 60; and his wife, Barbara C., died Jan. 19, 1866, aged 52.

Henry S. Blackford, died July 19, 1870, aged 51.

Levin Benton, died July 4, 1868.

Dorcas, first wife of John Otto, born Nov. 29, 1804, died Dec. 24, 1845, aged 41.

Catharine, second wife of John Otto, born Oct. 18, 1805, died May 6, 1867, aged 61.

Mary, wife of Samuel Benner, died April 25, 1877, aged 56.

Amanda H., wife of Henry W. Shamel, died June 18, 1879, aged 50.

Rebecca, wife of John Zimmerman, died Aug. 11, 1856, aged 51.

Catharine Rohr, died Sept. 7, 1869, in her 84th year.

As all the old records of the Reformed Church have been either lost or destroyed, there is nothing to show definitely when it was organized or when the first church was built. From the recollections of the oldest inhabitants of Sharpsburg, however, it is known that a small church was built in the inclosure of the old German Reformed graveyard, facing B. A. Edmunds' stable, prior to 1775. It was then known as the "Old Ironside" Presbyterian Church, and was served by a Mr. Matthews, stationed at Shepherdstown, W. Va. When it fell into the hands of the German Reformed congregation is not known. It was a small brick building, surmounted by a cupola, in which hung a small cast-iron bell. Some years later an addition was put to the church. This addition was built in the form of a half-circle, and the church had the appearance of a jews-harp. It was called the "Jews-harp" church until it was torn down. The interior was somewhat similar to that of the old Lutheran church, except that the aisle and space in front of the altar were paved with brick. The preaching and singing up to the year 1821 were in German. It is not improbable that the word "Presbyterian," as applied to it, was a misnomer, as we find in the *Maryland Gazette* of June 8, 1769, that six hundred dollars had been raised by lottery to complete the

Reformed Calvinist church and build a school-house in Sharpsburg. The managers of this lottery were George Strecker, Christian Orndorff, Joseph Smith, William Good, Abraham Lingenfelder, John Stull, Michael Fockler, George Dagon, and Benjamin Spyker. The inference is that the building was erected for the Reformed Church and always used as such. The first minister of this church of whom there is any account was the Rev. Samuel Helffenstein, Jr. He was there in 1824; in the same year Rev. James N. Reilly took charge. After him followed the Rev. Mr. Dennis. In 1832 the edifice was torn down, a piece of ground on Main Street was purchased from Mrs. Mary Ground, deceased, and the present church was built. For a long period this and the Lutheran were the only churches in the place. The new church was finished and dedicated in 1833, during the ministry of Rev. John Rebaugh. Rev. Mr. Hoffmier succeeded him in 1837; after whom came the Rev. Messrs. Dole, Douglass, Shuford, Gring, and A. C. Geary.

In the Reformed churchyard the following persons are buried:

Capt. David Smith, born Jan. 5, 1796, died Aug. 7, 1869.

Jacob Middlekauff, died Jan. 25, 1834, aged 75 years, 9 months.

John Kretzer, died Feb. 26, 1828, aged 46 years, 9 months; and his wife, Mary, died in 1869, aged 93 years.

Leonard Kretzer, born April 23, 1777, died Jan. 18, 1841.

John Ritchie, died April, 1807, aged 65 years.

Jacob Graf, born June 4, 1737, died Aug. 13, 1819.

Catherine Grove, died Sept. 25, 1823, aged 84 years.

David Miller, born Dec. 5, 1734, died May 14, 1811.

Catharine Miller, died Dec. 21, 1829, aged 77 years.

Mary M., wife of Col. John Miller, born Oct. 10, 1787, died Aug. 22, 1863.

Elizabeth, wife of William F. Hebb, died Feb. 27, 1875, aged 69.

Julien Smith, born March 13, 1771, died June 3, 1852, aged 81.

George Smith, died March 3, 1834, aged 66.

Hannah Kretzer, died Nov. 27, 1860, aged 78.

John Beard, died March 26, 1827, in his 63d year; and Elizabeth, his wife, died Dec. 7, 1837, in her 84th year.

Mary, wife of John Myers, died Feb. 28, 1823, in her 77th year.

Josiah Good, Sr., died July 25, 1848, aged 80.

William Good, born Feb. 20, 1799, died Sept. 4, 1868, aged 69.

Elizabeth, wife of Samuel Bender, died June 18, 1878, aged 63.

Jacob Bender, died Dec. 24, 1861, aged 59; and his wife, Rosanna, died June 20, 1871, aged 65.

Esther, wife of Jacob Middlekauff, died May 11, 1854, aged 91.

William Rohrback, died July 2, 1859, aged 74.

Daniel Piper, died March 3, 1857, aged 77; and Martha, his wife, died July 8, 1851, aged 76.

Elizabeth Dillon, died Feb. 2, 1855, in her 79th year.

The Protestant Episcopal congregation at Sharpsburg (now known as St. Paul's Church) was organized in 1818 by the Rev. Benjamin Allen, then rector of St. Andrew's Parish, Shepherdstown, W. Va. In 1819 a petition was presented to the Diocesan Convention of Maryland, "from a number of Episcopalians residing in St. John's Parish," for permission to establish a separate congregation at Sharpsburg. The convention granted the desired permission. For some time the congregation worshiped in the Lutheran church, but on the 31st of May, 1819, the corner-stone of a church edifice was laid. An address was delivered by the Rev. J. C. Clay, and the ceremonies ended with prayer by the Rev. Mr. Allen. After some years the structure was rough-casted and a spire built. The bell was purchased in England and presented by the wife of Joseph Chapline, Jr., who was a zealous member of the church. After the battle of Antietam the church was used as a hospital by the Confederate army. A large number of the soldiers died and were buried in the lot adjoining the church. The latter was so badly wrecked that it was unfit for use. Some time after the war the old building was torn down and a new one erected. The Rev. Mr. Thompson, who is buried in the Chapline graveyard, is said to have preached to this congregation in the Lutheran church before they had one of their own, and before Mr. Allen began his ministrations. The rectors after Mr. Allen were Revs. Adams, Hedges, Jones, Andrews, Wilcoxon, Kehler, and Adams. After Mr. Adams' pastorate the church was without a rector for some time. Finally the Rev. H. Edwards took charge. To this church belongs the honor of having established the first Sunday-school in Sharpsburg, which was done in 1818, by the Rev. Mr. Allen. In 1828, Mr. Allen's health failed and he was obliged to take a sea voyage. He was in England a little while, and then sailed for this country in very delicate health, and died and was buried at sea.

The rectors have been:

1819–21, Rev. Benjamin Allen; 1822–29, vacant; 1829–30, Rev. R. B. Drane; 1830–33, Rev. J. A. Adams; 1833–35, vacant; 1835–36, Rev. C. S. Hedges, of Virginia; 1836–38, vacant; 1838–40, Rev. L. H. Johns; 1840–42, ——; 1842–43, Rev. R. Trevett; 1843–45, Rev. R. H. Phillips; 1846–49, vacant; 1849–53, Rev. A. S. Colton; 1853–54, vacant; 1854–69, Rev. J. H. Kehler, Rev. J. A. Adams (assistant); 1865–69, Rev. J. A. Adams; 1869–82, Rev. H. Edwards.

The Methodist congregation of Sharpsburg was organized in August, 1811. The circumstances were these: Some of the members of the Beeler family attended a Methodist camp-meeting at Liberty, Frederick County, and were converted and united to the Methodists. Shortly after their return to Sharpsburg a minister visited the place and organized a congregation, the Beelers being the first members. Having no church, they worshiped in a barn belonging to Christian Beeler in summer, and in winter met in private houses. For some time they used the old Reformed church. Their first minister was Lawrence Everheart, the famous Revolutionary soldier. Everheart was a very enthusiastic preacher, and would often during his sermon cry out, "I fought for Gen. Washington, glory be to God!" The first circuit preachers were Revs. Hammond and Towne, after whom followed Revs. Swartzwelder, Leakins, Reed, Mathers, and Askens.

The Methodists at Sharpsburg are said to have been much persecuted in various ways, but persevered, and in 1818 a piece of ground was purchased and a church built. It was a plain brick edifice. The dedicatory sermon was preached by Rev. William Monroe. The following is a list of ministers in charge since 1831: Revs. Givens, Bear, Lyon, Parker, Monroe, Young, Goheen, Reese, Myers, Brooks, Bradds, Dyson, Prettyman, Parkerson, and Cullum. In 1856 the old church was declared to be unsafe and was pulled down, and the corner-stone of a new church on Main Street was laid Oct. 20, 1856. The first sermon was preached by the Rev. William Monroe before the church was completed, the occasion being the funeral of Elizabeth, widow of George Cronise. Mr. Monroe lived to a green old age, and was buried at Boonsboro' by La Grange Lodge, I. O. O. F. The church was completed in August, 1858. During the battle of Antietam, Sept. 17, 1862, the building was used as a hospital by the Federal troops, and the benches were torn out to make coffins to bury the dead soldiers. In 1864 it was renovated and rededicated, and a cupola and bell were added. Following are the ministers who have officiated in the new church since 1857: Rev. Messrs. Hall, Downs, Foust, Akers, Buckley, Montgomery, Cook, Osborne, Herbert, Case, McDaniel.

Dr. A. A. Biggs, of Sharpsburg, possesses an old English Bible which bears the inscription:

"The legacy of Bishop Asbury
To
Augustin Asbury Biggs,
Search the Scriptures."

The Methodist graveyard was laid out by Christian Beeler, who gave the ground, and was the first person buried in it. Among those interred there are the following:

David Sprong, born Oct. 12, 1793, died Feb. 18, 1869.

Sarah, wife of Frederick Myers, died June 13, 1860, aged 69 years, 10 months.

Daniel Grim, died Dec. 18, 1858, aged 80 years; and his wife, Sarah, died April 29, 1864, aged 77 years, 7 months.

George Cronise, died June 13, 1859, aged 77 years, 3 months; and his wife, Elizabeth, died Aug. 2, 1858, aged 71 years, 10 months.

Christian Beeler, died April 29, 1828, aged 65 years; and his wife, Susan, died Jan. 7, 1856, aged 89 years, 7 months.

Catharine Bash, died Nov. 29, 1851, aged 79.

Margaret Dureff, died Sept. 24, 1858, aged 48.

Jacob Eavey, died Oct. 12, 1863, aged 72; and Catharine, his wife, died July 14, 1870, aged 76.

James Clayton, born Sept. 7, 1807, died Aug. 19, 1865, aged 57.

Sarah, wife of Gabriel Mose, died Sept. 10, 1873, aged 73.

Robert Wilson, died Sept. 12, 1879, aged 79; and Eleanor, his wife, died March 4, 1879, aged 73.

Peter Beeler, died June 7, 1872, aged 82.

Christianna Wise, died Sept. 21, 1879, aged 84.

The corner-stone of the Colored Methodist Episcopal church was laid Oct. 20, 1866, and the church was dedicated October, 1867. The ground on which the church is erected was given by Samuel and Catharine Craig (colored). The congregation numbers about thirty-five members. The following is a list of the ministers who have officiated from the dedication of the church to the present time: Revs. Jarret Bowman, J. R. Tolson, D. Aquilla, H. Kennedy, J. Armstrong, J. Grose, Samuel Brown, Henry Williams, and G. W. Jenkins, and the present pastor, Rev. Benjamin Brown.

The Tunker or German Baptist church is situated one mile north of the town of Sharpsburg, on the turnpike leading to Hagerstown, and on the ground occupied by the left wing of the Confederates at the battle of Antietam. During the battle the church was used as a sort of fort by the Confederates, and was shelled by the Federal forces. The church was built in 1850 and 1851. The ground was given by Samuel Mumma, a member of the church. The building committee were Daniel Miller and Joseph Sherrick. The dimensions of the church are thirty-five by forty feet, and it is a plain brick building. The ministers who have officiated from the building of the church to the present time are Elders Daniel Reichard, Jacob Highbarger, Michael Emmert, David Long, and Daniel Wolf. The Tunkers have four churches within a scope of eight miles, having a membership of three hundred.

Belinda Springs.—Two miles southeast of Sharpsburg are the Belinda Springs. In 1818 these springs were in full operation and had many visitors from the cities, who were attracted by the medicinal qualities of the springs and the romantic character of the scenery in the vicinity. The springs were then owned by Jacob Gardenhour, who named them "Belinda," in honor of his wife, Belinda. A number of cottages were built for visitors; also billiard-houses, ten-pin alleys, bath-houses, drinking saloons, and barber-shops.

Antietam Creek flows near the spring, and rocky cliffs are seen in all directions. About two hundred yards distant from each other are the springs, one of which contains pure limestone water; the other, according to an analysis made by Dr. Hartman, one of the first physicians of Sharpsburg, contains sulphur, iron, and magnesia. The latter spring is about six feet in depth, and is surrounded by a stone wall capped with marble. The grounds were neatly and tastefully laid out with carriage-roads and gravel walks, and adorned with trees and ornamental shrubbery. In 1832, when the cholera epidemic broke out, Daniel Schnebley, of Hagerstown, was the proprietor of the hotel at Belinda Springs. Since then the buildings have fallen into decay, and some of them have been pulled down. Two acres of ground are attached to the springs. In 1826, at a meeting of citizens of Sharpsburg, Daniel Donnelly chairman, and Jacob H. Grove secretary, the following committee was appointed to arrange for a celebration of the fiftieth anniversary of American independence at Belinda Springs:

Col. John Miller, Maj. Jacob Rohrback, Jacob Miller, of Sharpsburg; Philip H. Hunter, of Shepherdstown; John T. Edwards, of Boonsboro'; Thos. B. Dunn, of Antietam Iron-Works; Samuel Gardiner, of Belinda Springs.

At this time a Mr. Thomas had charge of the springs.

Military Notes.—A muster-roll of the French and Indian wars, in the possession of John P. Smith, of Sharpsburg, reads as follows:

"An Exact Muster Roll or List of a part of the Militia that served with Joseph Chapline in June and July, 1757, in Frederick County."

The roll has nearly fallen to pieces from age, but among the names that have been deciphered are those of Joseph Chapline, lieutenant-colonel; Evan Shelby, captain; —— Prather, lieutenant; John Harewood, John Patten, Adam Heath, Hallam Dick, William Rich, Abram Enoch, George Reed, Nicholy Veace, Henry Creemer, Moses Chapline, Levin Willey, Daniel Wiley, Thomas Willey, John Springer, Ezekiel Chaney, John Swearingen, John Marshall, William Anderson, George Robbenott, John Nicholy, Richard Dean, James Black, Joseph Nack, John Chaney, and John Wolgamott. On the 12th of October, 1758, Lieut. Prather was killed. Some days later Capt. Evan Shelby, of Col. Chapline's regiment, had a personal combat with one of the principal Indian chiefs and slew him. Col. Chapline is believed to have played a conspicuous part in the war.

In 1813, Capt. John Miller marched to Baltimore with seventy-three men who had enlisted at Sharpsburg. Capt. Miller was afterwards promoted to the rank of colonel for gallant conduct. His company was part of the regiment commanded by Lieut.-Col. Richard K. Heath, which was attached to Gen. Henry Miller's brigade. The company entered the service on the 28th of April, 1813, and was discharged on the 3d of July of the same year. Following is a list of the officers and men:

John Miller, captain; Ignatius Drury and Jacob Rohrback, lieutenants; William Rohrback, ensign; N. W. Hays, William Carr, T. Nicholson, and John Beckley, sergeants; J. Clayton, drummer. Privates: David Highbarger, Charles Cameron, Rezin Beel, James Corwarder, Luke Baker, Joseph Barrick, William Brashears, William Boon, Ignatius Barber, Martin Barnhind, Henry Buck, Kelly Cox, James Crandle, Benjamin Carnes, Moses Crampton, John Connelly, Hugh Conner, Israel Churchhelt, Henry Dick, Henry Dibert, Samuel Durff, Christian Dibert, Christian Ensminger, Daniel Edwards, Jacob Emrick, Christian Farber, William German, Thomas Griffien, Thomas Higgs, George Huffmaster, Henry Hoffman, George Hine, Joseph Hedrick, Jacob Holfield, Joshua Hammond, Peter Hill, John Jones, Henry Nichols, John Schroy. Of the remaining twenty-five whose names are not included in this list, some died, some were discharged, and others deserted.

Attached to the brigade was an artillery company consisting of two guns, one a twelve and the other a twenty-four-pounder, commanded by David Smith, father of G. F. Smith, druggist. After the battle of Bladensburg the guns were taken back to Sharpsburg. One of them burst on the hill above the town while being fired on a Fourth of July celebration, and the other was captured by the Confederates during the war.

Beneficial Societies, etc.—The first Masonic lodge organized in Sharpsburg was the Washington Lodge of Free and Accepted Masons, established in May, 1821, in the attic of the house formerly owned by William Rohrback, deceased. The following entry of the fact is found on the records:

"We, the Master, Officers, and members of the most ancient and honorable fraternity of Free and Accepted Masons, are duly constituted under a dispensation from the Right Worshipful Grand Lodge of Maryland, bearing date at Baltimore City, the 15th day of May, 1821, A.L. 5281."

The first officers were: W. M., James Leggett, Jr.; S. W., Josiah Curtis; Treas., David Spong; Sec., Henry Gilna; S. D., Elias Baker; Tyler, Joseph Snively. This lodge assisted in laying the corner-stone of the first Episcopal church at Sharpsburg. Some years later the lodge went out of existence, but was reorganized in 1858 under the name of Eureka Lodge, No. 105. George Strause, David Pennel, and Jacob Grove were the charter members.

In June, 1841, a lodge of the Independent Order of Odd-Fellows was organized at Sharpsburg. The early meetings were held in the house owned by

George Stonebraker. Afterwards the lodge removed to the house of John Kretzer, where it continued to hold its meetings for some time. It was known as La Grange Lodge, No. 36. In 1845 the lodge removed to Boonsboro'.

Some years afterwards, Cherokee Tribe of the Improved Order of Red Men was organized, and purchased a hall in which they have since held their meetings. Antietam Lodge, No. 4, Independent Order Good Templars, was established on the 25th of February, 1868. Jehu Tent, Independent Order of Rechabites, was organized on the 25th of November, 1868. Magnolia Lodge, Knights of Pythias, was established Jan. 28, 1871.

The first fire company of Sharpsburg was organized prior to 1818, for we find in the Hagerstown *Torch-Light* of Feb. 17, 1818, the announcement of a lottery of two thousand dollars to raise money for the purchase of a fire-engine for Sharpsburg. The managers were George Smith, John Miller, Philip Grove, Jacob Miller, Mathias Spong.

Antietam National Cemetery.—About half a mile to the eastward of Sharpsburg is Antietam National Cemetery, in which lie buried the remains of Federal soldiers who perished in the memorable battle of Antietam, Sept. 17, 1862.

During this terrible conflict Sharpsburg was almost deserted by its inhabitants, who fled to the country. Those who remained hid themselves in their cellars, hoping thus to escape the hurtling storm of shot and shell. Others sought refuge in "Killingsburg Cave," two miles west of the town, on the Chesapeake and Ohio Canal. Buildings were riddled with bullets and cannon-balls, and the streets were choked with débris. During and after the battle the churches and many of the private dwellings were filled with the wounded. On the following day, Sept. 18, 1862, the Confederates retreated across the Potomac, at a point one mile south of Shepherdstown, W. Va., leaving behind them most of their dead and a number of wounded. No steps were taken to procure a proper interment of the slain until the session of the Maryland Legislature in 1864, during which Hon. Lewis P. Fiery, senator from Washington County, introduced a resolution appointing a joint committee, consisting of three members on the part of the Senate and an equal number on the part of the House,—

"to inquire into the expediency of purchasing on behalf of the State a portion of the battle-field of Antietam not exceeding twenty acres, for the purpose of a State and national cemetery, in which the bodies of our heroes who fell in that great struggle, and are now bleaching in the upturned furrows, may be gathered for a decent burial, and their memories embalmed in some suitable memorial."

Soon afterwards the committee, consisting of Governor Bradford, State Treasurer Robert Fowler, Gen. Shriver, Col. Harwood, and others, visited the battle-field and selected as the site for the cemetery a lot of ground at about the centre of the battle-field, and "upon the right of the road leading into Sharpsburg."

At the same time they obtained from the owner of the land a positive offer of sale upon favorable terms. Upon their return to Annapolis they recommended the purchase of ten acres of ground for the uses and purposes of a State and national cemetery. March 10, 1864, the Legislature passed unanimously an act appropriating five thousand dollars for the purchase and inclosure of a portion of the battle-field not to exceed ten acres. It was also provided that those who fell in the army of Gen. Lee should be buried in a separate portion from that set apart for those who belonged to Gen. McClellan's forces. In accordance with the provisions of the act, Govornor Bradford, with several other gentlemen, subsequently visited Sharpsburg and purchased ten acres for one hundred dollars per acre. Afterwards, however, it was discovered that the title to the land was defective, and considerable delay was experienced on this account. In the winter of 1865 a supplementary act was passed incorporating the cemetery, and naming Augustine A. Biggs, of Sharpsburg, Thomas A. Boullt, of Hagerstown, Edward Shriver, of Frederick, and Charles C. Fulton, of Baltimore, as trustees for Maryland. The trustees held their first meeting May 25, 1865, at Hagerstown, and elected Dr. A. A. Biggs president, and Thomas A. Boullt secretary and treasurer. After inspecting the grounds they decided that an acre and a quarter of additional land, situated on the east side of the original lot, should be purchased.

This was accordingly done and the ground was inclosed. Initiatory steps were taken at the same meeting to secure a list of the dead and to make a registry of the names. In the attainment of this object Aaron Good and Joseph A. Gill, residents of Sharpsburg, rendered valuable aid, having previously collected a large number of the names. The board decided to employ Mr. Good to complete the list which he had commenced, by going over the battle-field and making careful notes of all the information he could obtain. Under the act of incorporation it was provided that the land occupied by the cemetery was to be held by the State of Maryland in fee-simple in trust for all the States that should participate therein, and that the same should be devoted in perpetuity as a burial-place for the remains of soldiers who fell at the battle of Antietam, or at other points north of the Potomac River, during the invasion of

Lee in the fall of 1862. Arrangements were made by the board for grading the grounds and inclosing them with a stone wall, and Dr. A. A. Biggs, the president, was made superintendent of the cemetery. Dr. Biggs at once entered upon the discharge of his duties, and employed a large force of men, principally ex-Union soldiers, in quarrying stone for the wall. A modification in the original programme was made at the suggestion of the quartermaster-general, in accordance with which the remains of all those who fell and who were buried in the counties of Washington, Frederick, and Allegany were removed to the cemetery. Appropriations were made by the different States to the amount of $62,229.77, of which Maryland contributed $15,000. The other States contributing were New York, Indiana, Connecticut, New Jersey, Illinois, Minnesota, Maine, Rhode Island, Pennsylvania, Ohio, Wisconsin, Michigan, Vermont, Delaware, West Virginia, New Hampshire, and Massachusetts. The whole number of bodies interred in the cemetery was 4667, a number exceeding those interred in Gettysburg Cemetery by 1103. The removal of the dead was commenced in October, 1866, by the United States Burial Corps, detailed by the general government, under the superintendence of Lieut. John W. Sherer. They continued their work until January, 1867, up to which time 3000 bodies had been removed, and resumed in April, 1867, finishing in September of that year. The bodies were exhumed, placed in coffins, and reburied in the cemetery. Every coffin was numbered, and a corresponding number entered in a book kept for this purpose, with the name, company, regiment, and State, where they could be ascertained. The dead were buried under the immediate supervision of the superintendent, Dr. Biggs, who held the tape-line over every coffin deposited, and entered the name, number, and company in his field-book before any earth was replaced. By this record, therefore, any body can be identified at any time when called for. The trenches for the reception of the bodies were six feet in width and three feet in depth, and one-third of them were quarried out of the solid rock which to a great extent underlies the ground of the cemetery. Two feet in width were allowed for each body. The coffins were furnished by the general government. A person occupying a position about the centre of the grounds, with his face turned to any point of the compass, can with a good field-glass read the inscription on every head-board in the cemetery. At a meeting of the board in September, 1866, a design for an iron fence and gateway for the front line of the grounds was adopted, and a contract for the work was subsequently made with Robert Wood & Co., of Philadelphia, who erected a neat and tasteful fence and gateway, the latter twenty-six feet in width. A massive stone wall surrounds the inclosure.

The cemetery is located on a gentle elevation, from which may be had a view of nearly the entire battlefield, with South Mountain in the background. In the far distance looms up the continuous chain of hills known as the Maryland Heights, the rendezvous of John Brown prior to his raid on Harper's Ferry. A short distance from the foot of the cemetery grounds flows the Antietam Creek. The plan of the cemetery is that of a semi-ellipse divided into segments of circles, sections, and parallelograms of varying size according to the number of the dead from different States. Every division is marked by a letter, and the graves are numbered in regular order. That portion of the grounds devoted to this purpose begins at a point about one hundred and thirty feet from the main entrance to the cemetery, thus leaving a large open space between it and the wall which extends along the line of the Sharpsburg and Boonsboro' pike in front. A main carriage-drive about sixteen and a half feet in width leads from the entrance through the grounds, from which extend in every direction subordinate roads and walks, macadamized and graveled, leading to every portion of the cemetery. The grounds are thoroughly drained, and are kept in the neatest possible order. Near the entrance to the cemetery stands a lodge, which is occupied by the keeper, and is also used for the comfort and convenience of visitors. In the centre of the grounds, in the midst of an open space, stands the colossal statue of an American soldier keeping guard over the dead who lie buried there. The following of Maryland soldiers are buried in the cemetery:

Section 19.

Lot A, grave 13, Corp. Robert Barr, Co. F, 1st P. H. B. Inf.; died Aug. 28, 1864; removed from Weverton.

Lot A, grave 16, David Barnes, Co. K, 1st Cav.; died Aug. 5, 1864; removed from Weverton.

Lot A, grave 26, Fisher Bagunier, 1st P. H. B.; removed from Point of Rocks.

Lot B, grave 45, J. H. Brunce, Co. H, 2d; died June 13, 1864; removed from Frederick; residence Eastern Shore.

Lot B, grave 59, Corp. George Brown, Co. I, 1st P. H. B.; died Aug. 4, 1864; removed from Frederick.

Lot C, grave 64, Edward Bufler, Co. B, 1st Art.; removed from Williamsport.

Lot B, grave 68, John Barker, Co. E, 3d P. H. B. Inf.; died July 9, 1864; removed from Frederick.

Lot B, grave 73, James O. Byrne, Co. K, 1st Inf.; died Feb. 20, 1862; removed from Frederick.

Lot C, grave 89, James Boyd, Co. H, 1st P. H. B. Inf.; removed from Boonsboro'.

Lot A, grave 25, W. P. Coldwell, Co. A, 1st P. H. B. Inf.; removed from Point of Rocks.

Lot A, grave 38, W. Clasy, Co. F.; died April 2, 1864; age 32; removed from Frederick.

Lot B, grave 53, Charles Coleman, Co. H, 5th Inf.; died Oct. 1, 1862; removed from Frederick.

Lot B, grave 74, Enoch Clark, Co. A, 4th P. H. B. Inf.; died Feb. 17, 1862; removed from Frederick.

Lot A, grave 4, Corp. William Deshields, Co. K, 1st P. H. B. Cav.; died Aug. 5, 1864; killed in action at Keedysville.

Lot A, grave 19, Daniel Dorsey, Co. K, 1st P. H. B. Inf.; died March 8, 1864; removed from Weverton.

Lot C, grave 63, Henry Dove, Co. B, 7th Inf.; died Jan. 23, 1863; age 24; removed from Hagerstown.

Lot B, grave 76, David H. Deniker, Co. A, 2d P. H. B. Inf.; died Sept. 30, 1864, at Clarysville of wounds from his own gun.

Lot B, grave 77, Daniel Delaney, Co. B, 1st P. H. B. Cav.; died Jan. 5, 1865; removed from Clarysville.

Lot A, grave 32, Sergt. George L. Flinton, Co. A, 5th; died Oct. 24, 1862; removed from Frederick.

Lot A, grave 33, F. A. Frieand, Co. D, 3d P. H. B. Inf.; died Dec. 23, 1862; removed from Frederick.

Lot A, grave 35, Joseph Fessmyer, Co. K, 6th; died July 8, 1863; age 40; removed from Frederick.

Lot B, grave 78, Elijah Friend, Co. A.; died Aug. 24, 1864; removed from Clarysville.

Lot C, grave 84, Jonathan Frare, Co. I, 2d; removed from Cumberland.

Lot C, grave 86, William Fashbaker, Co. G, 2d; removed from Cumberland.

Lot B, grave 46, Moses A. Gosnell, Co. C, 1st P. H. B. Inf.; died June 24, 1864; removed from Frederick.

Lot B, grave 55, Martin Van Buren Gift, Co. A, 1st P. H. B. Inf.; removed from Antietam.

Lot B, grave 71, John E. Grant, Co. F, P. H. B. Inf.; removed from Frederick.

Lot B, grave 72, William H. Glass, Co. K, 1st P. H. B. Inf.; died Jan. 21, 1862; removed from Frederick.

Lot A, grave 3, John Hippard, 3d; removed from Antietam.

Lot A, grave 10, —— Hergins, Co. K, 1st P. H. B. Inf.; removed from Boonsboro'.

Lot A, grave 14, Sergt. Edward Hanson, 2d Eastern Shore; removed from Weverton.

Lot A, grave 21, Mathias Hayde, Co. E, 2d; removed from Weverton.

Lot A, grave 36, George Henderson, Co. G, 3d; died Feb. 28, 1863; age 32; removed from Frederick.

Lot B, grave 49, J. T. Harrison, Co. E, 1st P. H. B. Inf.; died Sept. 6, 1864; removed from Frederick.

Lot B, grave 50, Robert Heavawa, Co. I, 3d P. H. B. Inf.; died Sept. 11, 1864; removed from Frederick.

Lot B, grave 67, John Homer, Co. F, P. H. B. Inf.; died 1861; removed from Frederick.

Lot B, grave 69, A. E. Heardy, Co. H, 1st; died April 29, 1864; removed from Frederick.

Lot C, grave 87, Charles Hitchengs, Co. C, 2d; removed from Cumberland.

Lot B, grave 66, David Jenkins, 3d; died March 18, 1863; removed from Frederick.

Lot A, grave 20, Henry Kubier, Co. E, 2d; died 1862; removed from Weverton.

Lot A, grave 31, Sergt. John J. Kerns, Co. B, Cole's Battal.; died June 10, 1866; age 32; removed from Clear Spring.

Lot A, grave 34, John Kabb, Co. C, 3d P. H. B. Inf.; died Dec. 31, 1862; removed from Frederick.

Lot B, grave 56, William Kelley, 2d; removed from Antietam.

Lot C, grave 81, James Kennedy, 3d; removed from Cumberland.

Lot A, grave 9, James Love, Company E, 19th Inf.; removed from Boonsboro'.

Lot B, grave 42, L. Luderz, Co. A, 9th; died May 3, 1864; removed from Frederick.

Lot B, grave 47, F. Lutz, Co. K, 1st P. H. B. Inf.; died June 22, 1864; removed from Frederick.

Lot B, grave 58, Christian Lukehart, 2d; removed from Antietam.

Lot C, grave 88, Abraham Locquay, Co. D, 2d P. H. B. Inf.; removed from Bloomington.

Lot A, grave 2, John Means, 3d; removed from Antietam.

Lot A, grave 22, Joseph Maloney, Co. K, 1st P. H. B. Inf.; removed from Antietam.

Lot A, grave 24, —— McQuoy; removed from Berlin.

Lot A, grave 27, —— Michael, Cole's Cav.; removed from Point of Rocks.

Lot A, grave 37, Otto C. Murry, Co. H, 1st Inf.; died May 29, 1864; age 19; removed from Frederick.

Lot B, grave 41, M. Mauley, Co. K, 1st P. H. B. Cav.; died May 3, 1864; removed from Frederick.

Lot B, grave 44, D. McAllister, Co. G, 3d; died July 12, 1864; removed from Frederick.

Lot B, grave 52, George Meterling, Co. G, 9th Inf.; died Sept. 20, 1862; removed from Frederick.

Lot B, grave 75, E. McKeldan, 11th Inf.; removed from Frederick.

Lot C, grave 82, Patrick Murphy, Co. A, 2d Inf.; died Oct. 18, 1864; removed from Clarysville.

Lot A, grave 18, George L. Noble, Co. E, 8th Inf.; died Jan. 9, 1863; age 25; removed from Weverton.

Lot B, grave 70, Lewis W. Neibergal, Co. K, 1st P. H. B.; died 1864; removed from Frederick.

Lot A, grave 40, William Pollman, Co. H, 1st P. H. B. Cav.; died March 25, 1862; removed from Frederick.

Lot B, grave 48, A. Powell, Co. B, 3d; died June 26, 1864; removed from Frederick.

Lot A, grave 8, Michael Rooney, Co. F.; died Sept. 1862; removed from Smoketown.

Lot C, grave 85, William Rose, Co. E, 2d P. H. B.; removed from Cumberland.

Lot A, grave 7, Frederick Swartz, Co. A, 6th Inf.; died Feb. 28, 1863; removed from Smoketown.

Lot A, grave 30, John Shepard, Co. G, 7th Inf.; died March 26, 1862; removed from Clear Spring.

Lot A, grave 39, Sergt. John A. Simmons, Co. F, 3d; died Aug. 16, 1864; removed from Frederick.

Lot B, grave 43, T. Setzler, 1st P. H. B. Cav.; died July 5, 1864; removed from Frederick.

Lot B, grave 54, John Sullivan, Co. A, 1st P. H. B. Inf.; removed from Antietam.

Lot B, grave 57, Sergt. —— Stewart, 2d; removed from Antietam.

Lot A, grave 12, Alexander Turner, Co. B, 8th; removed from Boonsboro'.

Lot A, grave 17, S. Tucker, Co. A, 2d; died Oct. 31, 1863; removed from Weverton; from Eastern Shore.

Lot B, grave 51, R. H. Turner, Co. E, 1st; died Sept. 3, 1862; removed from Frederick.

Lot C, grave 60, John Thomas, Co. K, 1st P. H. B. Inf.; died Aug. 5, 1864; killed in action at Keedysville.

Lot C, grave 90, G. Trott, Co. C, 6th, drummer; died June 30, 1864; killed at Maryland Heights; from Baltimore.

Lot A, grave 5, Frederick Ulrick, 1st P. H. B. Inf.; removed from Antietam.

Lot A, grave 11, unknown, 1st P. H. B. Inf.

Lot A, grave 23, unknown, 1st P. H. B. Inf.

Lot A, grave 28, unknown, 1st.
Lot A, grave 29, unknown, 1st.
Lot C, grave 62, unknown, 1st.
Lot B, grave 65, unknown, 1st.
Lot A, grave 1, Sergt. James Watson, Co. K, 1st Cole's Cav.; died Aug. 5, 1864; killed in action at Keedysville.
Lot A, grave 6, Frederick Wengert, Co. E, 1st Cole's Cav.; died July 26, 1864; killed in action at Falling Waters.
Lot A, grave 15, Jacob Wiles, P. H. B. Inf.; removed from Weverton.
Lot C, grave 61, Robert Watson, Co. A, 1st Art.; removed from Antietam.
Lot B, grave 79, E. Van William, Co. B, 1st Art.; died March 6, 1865; removed from Clarysville.
Lot B, grave 80, John Whitaker, Co. B, 2d; removed from Cumberland.
Lot C, grave 83, Andrew Warnick, 3d P. H. B. Inf.; removed from Cumberland.
Lot A, grave 20, Lieut. —— Moltrie (com. officer), 5th; removed from Keedysville.

Of the dead thus interred, 3261 were volunteers, 1377 were unknown United States "regulars," and 29 were unknown soldiers, making 4667 in all. The cemetery was dedicated on the 17th of September, 1867, and the corner-stone of the monument was laid in due Masonic form. The committee of arrangements for the occasion consisted of Dr. J. E. Snodgrass, of New York; Gen. James S. Negley, of Pittsburgh; Hon. G. L. Cranmer, of Wheeling, W. Va.; Gen. Edward Shriver, of Baltimore; John J. Bagley, of Detroit, Mich.; Henry Edwards, of Boston; and Henry A. Boullt, of Hagerstown, Md. The day was the fifth anniversary of the battle. There was a very large attendance, including many distinguished men, and the exercises were of a very interesting character. President Andrew Johnson was present, accompanied by Secretary of State Seward; Hon. Hugh McCulloh, Secretary of the Treasury; Hon. Gideon Welles, Secretary of the Navy; and Hon. Alexander Randall, Postmaster-General. Hon. Montgomery Blair and the ministers from France, Russia, Spain, Italy, Austria, Nicaragua, Mexico, and Turkey were also present. From Maryland there was a very large representation, including Governor Swann, ex-Governor Bradford, Mayor Chapman, and members of the City Council of Baltimore, Adjt.-Gen. John S. Berry, Lieutenant-Governor C. C. Cox, the Grand Lodge of Masons in Maryland, John Coates, Grand Master, and an encampment of Knights Templar. Besides these there were representatives of the Grand Lodge of Pennsylvania. At noon a procession was formed on the turnpike, composed of the military organizations, the Masons, Knights Templar, and others. The chief marshal was Lieut.-Col. James M. Moore, United States army. The military consisted of the Gray Reserves and the National Guards of Philadelphia. The order of procession was the military, the President and cabinet and other prominent visitors, and the Masons and Knights Templar. On arriving at Antietam the military formed a line near the cemetery gate and presented arms while the President and his party were passing into the inclosure. An immense multitude had assembled at the cemetery, and much enthusiasm was manifested. On a temporary platform were placed the President, the orator of the day, the ladies, and a number of prominent guests. The exercises were begun with an address by Hon. Thomas Swann, Governor of Maryland, which was followed by a prayer delivered by the Rev. Hiram Mattison, D.D., of New Jersey. A hymn composed by the Rev. Henry Myers, of Pennsylvania, was then sung by the assemblage under the leadership of William E. Donaugh, of New York. During the intervals various selections were given by the bands. After the hymn the corner-stone of the monument was laid by Grand Master Coates, of Baltimore, after which Hon. A. W. Bradford, ex-Governor of Maryland, delivered the oration. Another hymn, by Rev. Edward Myers, was then sung, after which the dedication poem by Clarence F. Buhler, of New York, was read. When it was finished Governor Swann introduced to the assembly Hon. Andrew Johnson, President of the United States, who delivered a brief address. The benediction was pronounced and the assemblage then broke up, the President and his party being escorted back to the train by the military present. The officers of the cemetery at the time were as follows:

President, Gibson L. Cranmer, Wheeling, W. Va.; Vice-President, Gen. Edward Shriver, Frederick, Md.; Secretary and Treasurer, Thomas A. Boullt, Hagerstown, Md.; Executive Committee, J. H. B. Latrobe, chairman, John J. Bagley, Henry Edwards; General Superintendent, Augustin A. Biggs, M.D.; Keeper of the Cemetery, Hiram S. Siess; Trustees, Maj.-Gen. H. W. Slocum, New York; Maj.-Gen. Edward Shriver, Maryland; John H. B. Latrobe, Maryland; Hon. R. B. Carmichael, Maryland; Thomas A. Boullt, Maryland; Hon. James G. Blaine, Maine; Col. W. Yates Selleck, Wisconsin; Gibson L. Cranmer, West Virginia; Henry Edwards, Massachusetts; Gen. E. A. Carman, New Jersey; Col. Gordon Lofland, Ohio; Hon. Alex. Ramsay, Minnesota; John J. Bagley, Michigan; Maj. William Rounds, Vermont; Maj.-Gen. James S. Negley, Pennsylvania; Hon. H. D. Washburne, Indiana; B. Lapham, Rhode Island; Hon. Harry H. Starkweather, Connecticut.

The trustees who have died, resigned, or been appointed since the organization of the board have been:

Maryland: Thomas A. Boullt, original trustee named in charter; term expired Jan. 1, 1868; succeeded by James H. Grove; Augustin A. Biggs, M.D., original trustee named in charter; first president of the board; term expired Jan. 1, 1868; succeeded by Gen. Charles E. Phelps; Gen. Edward Shriver, original trustee named in charter; term expired

Jan. 1, 1866; reappointed for three years; term expired Jan. 1, 1869; reappointed; Charles C. Fulton, original trustee named in charter; term expired Jan. 1, 1867; succeeded by John H. B. Latrobe; James H. Grove (to succeed Thomas A. Boullt), resigned and succeeded by Thomas A. Boullt; Gen. Charles E. Phelps (to succeed Dr. A. A. Biggs), resigned and succeeded by Hon. R. B. Carmichael. *New York:* Gen. John B. Van Petten and Dr. J. E. Snodgrass; terms expired Sept. 17, 1867; succeeded by Hon. John Jay, second president of the board, who resigned and was succeeded by Maj.-Gen. Henry W. Slocum. *Pennsylvania:* Gen. John R. Brooke, resigned; succeeded by Maj.-Gen. James S. Negley. *Connecticut:* A. G. Hammond, died; succeeded by William S. Charnley, resigned; succeeded by Hon. Henry H. Starkweather. *Massachusetts:* William Dwight, resigned; succeeded by Henry Edwards.

At a meeting of the cemetery association held on the 17th of June, 1868, on motion of the Hon. B. Lapham, of Rhode Island, the following resolution was adopted:

"*Resolved*, That the superintendent, Dr. A. A. Biggs, be and he is hereby authorized to remove all fixed rocks from the cemetery grounds which project above the surface at least one foot below the surface, which work shall be done and completed before the next meeting of the board."

This resolution, though general in its character, was, it is stated, designed to secure the removal of "Lee's Rock," as there were no other fixed rocks in the cemetery. "Lee's Rock" was a rock from which the Confederate general, Robert E. Lee, is said to have watched the progress of the battle of Antietam. Before its removal it was the common practice of visitors to chip off pieces of it and carry them away as relics. After the adoption of the Lapham resolution it was demolished and the remaining fragments covered up with earth. On the 24th of January, 1880, the monument known as "The Private Soldier" was completed, and on the 17th of September, 1880, the anniversary of the battle of Antietam, it was unveiled in the presence of an immense assemblage. The monument is composed of twenty-seven pieces. The base course consists of eight pieces, making a square of twenty-two feet, and two feet high; the second course consists of four pieces, making a square of seventeen feet, and two feet high; the third course consists of eight pieces, and occupies a square of fifteen feet, six feet and six inches high. The die-course, which stands upon the third course, occupies a square of nine feet three inches, and consists of four pieces ten feet and seven inches high. The cap-course is one stone eight feet and six inches square and two feet high. These five courses constitute the pedestal, which is surmounted by a colossal granite soldier, standing twenty-one feet and six inches high. The whole structure stands forty-four feet and seven inches, weighing in all about two hundred and fifty tons. It is entirely of granite from the "Westerly Granite Quarry," of Westerly, R. I.

The figure is that of a private soldier at "parade rest," with the cape of his overcoat thrown back from his left shoulder. The soldier is gazing wistfully towards

MONUMENT IN ANTIETAM NATIONAL CEMETERY.

the north, as if anticipating the fierce struggle in which he is soon to become a prominent actor. The monument bears the simple inscription, "Not for themselves but for their country,—Sept. 17, 1862." On the base are carved designs of crossed swords, a wreath of laurel, draped colors, a drum, a cartridge-box, and a canteen. It stands in the centre of the cemetery, which is the highest point in the inclosure, upon an embankment four feet high, and upon the site selected by the chief engineer of the Quartermaster's Department, United States government. It is a commanding spectacle from the entire surrounding country.

The artist was James G. Batterson, of Hartford, Conn., and the entire cost of the work was thirty-five thousand dollars. The setting of the monument was done by D. C. Hutchinson, of Boston, assisted by George Hezlett, of Cambridge, Mass., and John Flannigan, of Meriden, Conn. The ceremonies attending the unveiling of the statue were of a very imposing character, and were participated in by a number of prominent persons and various military organizations. At two P.M. a procession was formed in the public square of the town of Sharpsburg, composed of the

Fifth Maryland Regiment, Col. W. H. S. Burgwyn, with band and drum-corps, Wilson Post and Dushane Post, with cadets of the Grand Army of the Republic, accompanied by bands, the Anderson Guards, of Woodstock, Va., John A. Rawlins Post, No. 2, Lincoln (colored) Post, No. 2, Reno Post, No. 4, and Kit Carson Post, No. 3, all of the Grand Army of the Republic, National Guards of Chambersburg, Pa., Warren Light Guards, of Front Royal, Va., and Light Battery A, Third Regiment United States Artillery. On reaching the cemetery the military formed on the outer walk, near the fence, stretching in a half-circle around the veiled monument. When everything was in readiness Miss Helen Wright, daughter of Gen. George B. Wright, of Ohio, was driven in an open barouche to the statue, which was guarded by the Warren Light Infantry, and at a given signal, which was answered by a salute from the artillery company, she pulled the string, and the figure of "The Private Soldier" stood revealed.

After the statue had been unveiled the Fifth Regiment and the Grand Army formed in front of the speaker's stand, which is built partly of brick, so that it may be used on Decoration Day or at short notice. The cadets seated themselves on the ground in front of the soldiers. The Fifth Regiment Band was stationed near one corner of the stand and played frequently. The other companies taking part in the procession scattered about the grounds, going wherever it pleased them. The stand was decorated with flags and was thronged with ladies and gentlemen, among the latter being Gen. W. E. W. Ross and staff, Adjt.-Gen. J. W. Watkins, Gen. James R. Herbert and staff, Col. Burgwyn, Gens. Wright, of Ohio, Carman, of New Jersey, and Shriver, of Maryland, who, together with Dr. A. A. Biggs, represented the trustees of the cemetery, Col. H. Kyd Douglas, Gen. John A. Steiner, Col. Vernon, Henry Stockbridge, Peter Negley, George Savage, Capt. Walker, of Hagerstown, and others. Rev. Henry Edwards, of the Protestant Episcopal Church, Hagerstown, and chaplain of Reno Post, who was introduced by Gen. Ross, offered an impressive prayer. An oration was delivered by Marriott Brosius, of Lancaster, Pa., after which Col. Wm. H. Lambert, of Philadelphia, paid an eloquent tribute to the dead interred at Antietam. The benediction was then pronounced by the Rev. B. K. Miller.

In 1877 the cemetery was transferred to the United States, and Capt. W. A. Donaldson was appointed superintendent.

Since it passed into the hands of the government the cemetery has been greatly improved and beautified. Over the rostrum which was erected for the use of the speakers at the unveiling of the statue vines have been trained, making a very pretty effect, and a number of handsome trees, mainly Norway spruce, maple, and hemlock, have been planted, and a hedge of American arbor vitæ surrounds the burial sections. The superintendent is also engaged in taking out all poor and common trees, and is otherwise rapidly improving the grounds. At the entrance to the cemetery is a thirty-two-pound cannon, which was captured by the Southern troops at Harper's Ferry, and recaptured by Gen. Geary at Williamsport and taken to Antietam, where it was abandoned. It was afterwards removed to the cemetery grounds and placed in position by Capt. Donaldson.

Augustin Asbury Biggs, M.D., a prominent citizen of Sharpsburg District, was born near Double Pipe Creek, in what was then Frederick County, and now

Augustin A. Biggs

in Carroll County, on the 27th of December, 1812. He resides in Sharpsburg District. His parents were Joseph and Mary Biggs, both natives of Frederick County, Md. His children are Charles G., Edward C., William N., and Stella M. He was graduated in medicine at Jefferson Medical College in the spring of 1836. He is trustee of the State of Maryland of Antietam National Cemetery, one of the charter members and first president of the board of trustees, and was general superintendent during its construction and up to the time of its transfer to the United States. He was the originator of the plan upon which the cemetery was laid out and of the order of the graves, and was secretary and treasurer to the board of trustees prior to its transfer to the United States. He has been a member of the Masonic fraternity and of the Odd-Fellows for about thirty years, and has filled various offices in both orders several times. He has been a successful practitioner of medicine in Sharpsburg since 1836. In politics he was a Whig prior to the late war, during which he was a stanch Union man, and since has always been associated with the Republican party.

Antietam Iron-Works.—These locally famous works are situated on the Antietam, about three miles south of Sharpsburg. They were erected by Wm. M. Brown about sixty years ago, and were operated by Ross, Bell & Henderson, of Baltimore. They were afterwards sold to John McPherson Brinn, and were known for some time as Brinn's Iron-Works. The water-power was furnished by the Antietam Creek, and the works comprised rolling and slitting-mills, a sheet-iron mill, a shingle-mill, saw-mill, puddle-mill, and an extensive nail-factory. Near the works is a large bed of iron ore. As far back as 1853 quite a village had sprung up near the works, and in addition to the dwellings for the operators there was a large grist and saw-mill, a blacksmith-shop, a store and office, and a handsome mansion for the proprietor. About five hundred operatives were employed at the works. The property was sold by Mr. Brinn in 1853 to Samuel Horine and William B. Clarke, of Hagerstown. Subsequently David Ahl purchased Horine's and then Clarke's interest, and operated the works for nearly three years, after which they remained idle for three years longer. In 1879 operations were renewed, and continued up to February, 1880, the works producing from eight to ten tons per day. In February, 1880, the works suspended operations for a while. The ore for the mills is obtained both on the Virginia and Maryland sides of the river.

The Grove family. Jacob Groff, the ancestor of the large and influential Grove family of Washington County, removed to Sharpsburg in 1760. He was the grandson of Hans Groff, who was born in Switzerland in 1661, and who fled to Alsace, Germany, during the prosecution of the Mennonites in his fatherland. In Alsace he bore the title of Baron von Weldon, and several copies of his coat of arms are in the possession of his descendants. Whether the original is in existence or not is unknown. After remaining in Alsace for some time he emigrated to America with his family and household goods. One of the articles which he brought over with him, and which is now in the possession of Levi W. Groff, of Lancaster, Pa., is a family Bible printed in 1585. It is a large and weighty tome, with thick covers protected by plates of iron, and stands on four small iron feet. Hans Groff arrived in Pennsylvania about 1695, and moved westward to a stream now known as Groff's Run, in Lancaster County, where he established a trading-post with the Indians, exchanging blankets for furs, which he hauled to Philadelphia in a stout wagon drawn by six powerful horses. Subsequently he purchased from the sons of William Penn a tract of land containing some fourteen or fifteen hundred acres, and laid out Earl township, so named from his title of nobility, upon the banks of Groff's Run. The locality is now known as East Earl and West Earl, Lancaster County. He lived to be a very old man, and was buried in the graveyard attached to Groff's meeting-house. His grave was marked with a rough sandstone slab, on which the letters "H. G." are still decipherable.

By his wife, Susanna, Hans Groff had the following children: Samuel, Marcus, Daniel, John, David, Peter, Hannah, Fanny, and Mary. John married and had sons,—Jacob and Henry. It was this Jacob, the grandson of Hans Groff, from whom sprang the Grove family of Washington County, Md. He came to Sharpsburg from Lancaster previous to the laying out of the town, 1765, and, as near as the oldest inhabitants can remember, is thought to have engaged in the practice of medicine. He lived in a stone house on one of the side streets, which is still standing, and died at the age of eighty-two. A slatestone slab with the inscription, "Jacob Groff, born June 4, 1737, died Aug. 15, 1819," marks his resting-place in the old Reformed graveyard; and engraven upon the tombstone of his wife, who lies beside him, is, "Catherine Grove, born March 3, 1742, died Sept. 25, 1823." The fruit of this marriage was nine children,—Catherine, Philip, Stephen, Henry, Peter, Jacob, Paul, John, and Elizabeth.

His second-born, Philip, embarked in the mercantile business, and was one of the early merchants of Sharpsburg. His superior business tact soon gave him advantage over his competitors, and by thrift and economy he became, before he died, owner of large estates in and around Sharpsburg. He married Catharine Hess, by whom he had Jacob H., Mary, Elias, Samuel, Joseph, Lavenia, and by his second wife, a Mrs. Susan Hess,—maiden name Susan Locher,—there were born to him Daniel, Stephen, and Catharine. At the age of sixty-seven Philip Grove died, and was buried in the family burial-ground at Keedysville. Jacob H., his eldest son and child, succeeded him in business, and inheriting his father's business capacity, met with like success. He was an energetic and public-spirited man, and was an active member in the Democratic party. He served as a director in the Canal Board, was twice a candidate for county commissioner,—defeated once,—and served as representative in the Legislature in 1842. He married Mary Hite, daughter of Col. Thomas Hite, of Virginia. Mary, daughter of Philip Grove, married Jacob Locher and removed to Lancaster, Pa. Elias married Mary Smith, of Sharpsburg, and located on a farm near that town. Samuel married Lavenia Houser, of Sharpsburg, and remained in that town. Joseph married Susan Houser of the same place, and also located there. Lavenia married Dr. Joseph Hayes, of Sharpsburg. Daniel Locher, the eldest son by the second wife, married Margaret C. Shafer, daughter of Jonathan Shafer, of Boonsboro', and having purchased his brother's, Jacob H., stock of goods, remained at Sharpsburg several years, doing business in his father's old stand. Mr. Grove was very genial and popular, and was noted for his kindness to the poor. Without any solicitation on his part he was put upon the Democratic ticket and elected to the Legislature of 1853. Jan. 1, 1857, in Buchanan's administration, he was appointed to a position in the custom-house, Baltimore. When the administration expired he engaged some six or seven years in the mercantile business, and then retired with his family to the village of Liberty, Frederick Co., Md., where he died Feb. 4, 1868. Stephen P. married Mrs. Norman Robinson,—maiden name Maria Dillon,—of Sharpsburg. He resides upon the old home place, one of the finest farms of the county, handsomely improved and beautifully located about one mile south of Sharpsburg, near the main county road and Shenandoah Valley Railroad, which run parallel before his house. Mr. Grove is a man of many excellent traits, and stands very high in the estimation of the people of his county. He is the only one living of his generation. Catharine married Christian Reinhart and located in Jefferson County, W. Va.

Jacob Miller was born near Waynesboro', Franklin Co., Pa., Dec. 31, 1782, and emigrated with his parents to Washington County, Md., at the age of nine years. His parents were of German descent. He was twice married, and raised a family of eleven children, nine of whom are living. He was a weaver by trade, and in 1828 wove the first two-ply carpet on a loom of his own invention. In 1832 he wove the first seamless bags. He also manufactured woolen and cotton goods. He served as county commissioner on two different occasions, and on one occasion helped to assess the entire county. He was once elected to the Legislature by the Democratic party, of which he was a stanch member, and was one of the charter members of the Boonsboro' and Sharpsburg Turnpike Company. In 1833 he was contractor for a section on the Chesapeake and Ohio Canal. In these various positions he was faithful and industrious, and enjoyed the general confidence and respect of his neighbors.

He lived to the old age of ninety-two years and eleven months, dying on the 6th of December, 1875. His remains are buried in the Lutheran graveyard of Sharpsburg.

WILLIAMSPORT DISTRICT, No. 2.

Williamsport District, No. 2, is the second in importance in Washington County, and its chief town, Williamsport, is, next to Hagerstown, the largest and most flourishing town. The population of the district, including Williamsport, is 2625. As a rule, the face of the county is rolling, although there are several ranges of high hills, and the country about the town of Williamsport is somewhat uneven, being cut up by an environment of hills of considerable magnitude. The quality of the soil is rich and the land is under a high state of cultivation, and is thickly dotted with fine farm-houses and extensive farm buildings for storage and stock purposes. The district extends almost due north and south, and is exceedingly irregular in shape. The Potomac River forms almost its entire western boundary, making a sudden curve from its last point of contact with Clear Spring District, and cutting a segment of a circle out of Maryland. Clear Spring, Conococheague, and West Hagerstown Districts are on the north, the three forming a sort of triangular boundary. West Hagerstown, Funkstown, and Tilghmanton Districts are on the east, and Downsville District on the south. The district is about five miles in length and three and a half in breadth. Conococheague Creek winds a serpentine course through the northern part of the district, emptying into the Potomac River at the town of Williamsport. The Chesapeake and Ohio Canal follows the Potomac River along its entire course on the eastern boundary of the district. The Western Maryland Railroad has its terminus at Williamsport, traversing about three miles of the district, and the Cumberland Valley Railroad runs south of the Western Maryland, about three miles of the road being within the boundary of the district. Two turnpike roads enter the town of Williamsport, the one marking almost the course of a straight line from Hagerstown, and the other entering the district from Conococheague District.

Numerous public roads, leading to every point of importance, traverse the district, and, together with the turnpikes, the two railroads, the canal, and the navigation of the Potomac River, furnish the people of Williamsport District with the most abundant facilities for transportation and travel. The land is well cleared off, and most of it under constant and intelligent cultivation, and readily produces from ten to thirty-five bushels of wheat, from twenty-five to thirty bushels of oats, from thirty to fifty bushels of corn, and from fifty to one hundred and fifty bushels of potatoes.

The boundaries of Williamsport District in 1822 were officially described as follows:

"Commencing at the Great Marsh Run, where it empties itself into the Potomac River; thence with the lines of District No. 1 to Cary's Cross-roads; thence with the Sharpsburg and Hagerstown road to the road leading from Clagett's mills to Williamsport; thence with said road till the same passes the cleared land of Nicholas Swingley; thence still with the said Williamsport road till it intersects the road leading from Hagerstown to Forman's ferry; thence with said road till the Williamsport road intersects said Forman's ferry road; thence with said road towards Williamsport till it intersects a line of Salisbury; thence with a line of Salisbury north to the end thereof; thence due west with another line of Salisbury till it intersects a road heretofore laid off from Sprecket's mill to the Hagerstown and Conococheague turnpike road; thence with said road to the aforesaid turnpike road; thence with said road to the stone bridge on the Conococheague Creek; thence down said creek to the road at John Ash's fording; thence with said road till it intersects the road leading from Williamsport to the Big Spring; thence run along the lane and wagon road leading through Moudy's old place, and with said road, between the place that Charles Potts now lives on and Samuel Gruber's, to the high rocks on the Potomac River; thence with the said river to the beginning."

Previous to this, in 1800, it had been thus officially described:

"Beginning at the mouth of the Great Marsh Run at the river Potomac, and running thence with No. 1 to the top of the mountain, thence up the mountain with the county line to where the road from Hagerstown crosses the mountain near George Orr's tavern; thence with the said road by Newcomer's mill to where it forks near Hershey's; thence with the road by Stonebraker's to John Clagett's mill on the Antietam Creek; thence with the road from said mill to where it intersects the road from Hagerstown by David Hammett's to the mouth of Opecken Creek; thence with the manor lines to where the east line of said manor intersects the road leading from Swingley's mill by Matthew Van Lear's; thence with the said road to said Swingley's mill on the Conococheague Creek; thence down the creek to the river Potomac; and thence with the river to the place of beginning. This district to be called District No. 2, and the election to be held at the house of Henry Heckrotte, in the town of Williamsport."

Williamsport, its chief town, is situated at the confluence of Conococheague Creek and the Potomac River, and has a population of 1503. It is a healthy and agreeable place of residence, and its business is quite extensive. The Western Maryland road has its terminus at Williamsport, and its depot is in the town. The Cumberland Valley Railroad depot is within a short distance of the town limits. There are four fine churches,—the Lutheran, the Catholic, the Presbyterian, and the Methodist. The Washington County National Bank has been in business at Williamsport for a long time, and is a prosperous institution, with a fine building. The present officers of the bank are A. S. Cunningham, president; E. G. W. Stake, cashier; J. L. Motter, teller. The town officers are: Burgess, Peter Ardinger; Assistant, W. H. Loy; Commissioners, Michael Kreps, John Barry, Caleb Goodrich, Charles Ardinger, M. V. B. Harsh; Bailiff, Simon Poffenberger. Until May 11, 1881, there was still standing in Williamsport a building which was one of the first houses built in the town in 1787. On that day it was entirely destroyed by fire, being occupied at the time as a store by Thomas J. Lemen. It stood on the corner of Potomac and Conococheague Streets. The building was of stone, its walls being two feet in thickness. It was used as a tavern in the early history of the town, and was visited by President Washington in 1791, when he was at Williamsport.

There are still left, however, many points of historic interest in the town, although the old landmarks are fast disappearing. No spot attracts more attention than the old cemetery overlooking the Potomac River and all the approaches to the town, as well as the town itself. In this city of the dead are the graves of two of the most distinguished men of Maryland. One of the most venerable tombs within the inclosure, and fast crumbling to ruins, is that of the founder of the town, the friend of Washington, and one of the most brilliant soldiers of the Revolution, Otho Holland Williams. The monument was constructed of sandstone in box form, and the inscription will in a few years become illegible. The slow but sure ravages of time are washing away each letter. On the north side of the tomb the inscription reads: "Dedicated to the memory of Gen. Otho Holland Williams (founder of Williamsport in 1787), a distinguished patriot and hero in the armies of the United States, in which he attained, by meritorious service, the rank of brigadier-general during the war that terminated in establishing the independence of his native country." On the south side of the crumbling tomb is the inscription: "A devoted, tender, and excellent husband, father, and brother; a refined, generous, and steadfast friend; an enlightened citizen; a virtuous, benevolent, and accomplished man." On the west end of

POTOMAC RIVER AND CANAL AT WILLIAMSPORT.

the tomb is the simple inscription: "He died in 1794, aged forty-five years, beloved, honored, and deplored."

Near this grave is that of Judge John Buchanan. The tomb stands within a small, dilapidated inclosure of brick walls, not over eight feet square, nor more than forty inches high, with the gateway broken down and mouldering into ruins. There is no stone to mark the spot, nor any inscription to show who lies buried there.

In the same cemetery are interred the remains of Capt. Alexander Patrick, of the United States army, born at Windsor, Vt., 1794, died at Williamsport in 1834. The marble slab which marks his resting-place records that he was "detached from Fort McHenry, with his company, for the security of this place, and died, after a short illness, beloved and lamented." The occasion referred to was riots on the line of the canal, which troops were called out to suppress. In addition to these the cemetery contains the remains of Daniel Syester, father of Hon. Andrew K. Syester, and of members of such old families as the Towsons and the Chews.

The descendants of Gen. Williams have a fine marble monument in another section of the cemetery. It bears the following inscriptions:

Otho Williams, born April 12, 1785, died Oct. 22, 1869.

Agnes McDowell, wife of Otho Williams, born March 23, 1798, died June 29, 1870.

Mary Emma Williams, born May 20, 1826, died Jan. 6, 1871.

Catharine McDowell, wife of Otho Williams, born Jan. 17, 1793, died Oct. 24, 1821.

Anna McPherson, Anna McDowell, Helen Margaret, infant children of Otho and Agnes M. Williams.

Another stone tablet is inscribed: Consecrated to the memory of Edward Green Williams, by his affectionate and bereaved wife, died Feb. 7, 1829, aged 59.

Among others buried in this cemetery are the following:

Dr. Michael A. Finley, died March 25, 1848, aged 62 years, 3 months.

Rev. Jonathan Dickerson, born March 16, 1798, died Sept. 28, 1842.

Susan Van Lear, born June 17, 1800, died Dec. 28, 1855.

James Van Lear, born Dec. 16, 1796, died July 20, 1820.

Horatio Nelson Van Lear, born Sept. 6, 1798, died Aug. 20, 1823.

William Van Lear, born Jan. 27, 1794, died May 7, 1836.

Mary Van Lear Finley, born Feb. 9, 1790, died June 14, 1818.

Matthew W. Van Lear, died July 5, 1823, in his 68th year; and his wife, Mary, died June 28, 1828, in her 68th year.

Lieut. Wm. H. Irwin, First Maryland Cavalry, born July 28, 1842, died April 9, 1863.

John Cyester, died Sept. 24, 1854, aged 58 years, 10 months.

Rev. Cæsar Peters, born Jan. 1, 1790, died Jan. 25, 1876.

Peter Light, Sr., born Aug. 16, 1758, died Aug. 22, 1821.

Rev. Robert Wilson, of Augusta County, Va., born June 23, 1788, died March 2, 1849.

Prudence Davis, died Feb. 11, 1837, aged 54 years.

George Lefevre, died April 20, 1850, aged 70 years.

Daniel Kretzer, born June 11, 1794, died March 30, 1860.

Joseph Hollman, died March 7, 1848, aged 57 years, 9 months.

Daniel Weisel, Sr., born April 10, 1765, died May 19, 1825.

Jacob Weisel, born Aug. 5, 1753, died Oct. 31, 1812.

George Moudy, born June 14, 1764, died Oct. 14, 1835; and his wife, Eva, died Dec. 13, 1861, aged 85 years.

Robert Culbertson, died June 4, 1851, aged 81 years.

Jacob T. Towson, died Dec. 12, 1841, aged 78 years, 11 months; and his wife, Jane, died Aug. 24, 1794, aged 32 years.

Lydia Irwin, died Nov. 6, 1869, aged 80 years, 8 months.

Andrew K. Stake, born March 18, 1819, died April 15, 1876, aged 57.

Elizabeth Hawken, his wife, died July 22, 1873, aged 57 years.

John Herr, died Jan. 29, 1855, aged 65 years.

Sarah Herr, his wife, died April 29, 1870, aged 72 years.

Isaac Rohrer, died March 20, 1873, aged 55 years.

Wm. T. Ensminger, died April 26, 1873, aged 50 years.

Daniel W. Cyester, born Feb. 29, 1828, died May 5, 1874, aged 46 years.

Charles B. Dellinger, died April 9, 1873, aged 62 years.

Peter Garling, died March 9, 1876, aged 54 years.

Nancy Bear, wife of Peter Garling, born July 17, 1828, died May 8, 1873, aged 44 years.

Wm. H. Wolf, died July 1, 1876, aged 64 years.

Abraham Leiter, born June 3, 1806, died March 31, 1864, aged 57 years.

Charles G. Downs, died June 1, 1857, aged 63 years; and his wife, Sarah, born Sept. 17, 1801, died Nov. 21, 1869, aged 68 years.

George Sellers, died Oct. 20, 1856, aged 60 years; and his wife, Elizabeth, died Jan. 12, 1876, aged 68 years.

John Parker, died June 27, 1853, aged 54 years.

John Hahn, died June 30, 1853, aged 45 years.

John T. Miller, born Nov. 22, 1794, died March 22, 1854.

Michael Krebs, born May 28, 1784, died Dec. 9, 1835, aged 51 years.

His second wife, Mary, died Sept. 28, 1867, aged 67 years.

.John Grimes, died Nov. 25, 1836, in his 47th year; and his wife, Rebecca, died Jan. 14, 1858, aged 59 years and 23 days.

Thomas Powell, died Oct. 9, 1849, aged 61; and his wife, died July 31, 1831, aged 47 years.

Samuel Poffenberger, died Sept. 3, 1860, aged about 52 years.

James Watkins, born Sept. 21, 1815, died Nov. 16, 1865.

Henry Friend, died May 13, 1873, aged 72 years.

Horatio Watkins, died 20th of March, 1858, aged 61 years.

Elizabeth Friend, died April 14, 1846, aged 79 years.

Eleanor Friend, died May 13, 1859, aged 66 years.

Eleanor Hammond, died Dec. 15, 1877, aged 77 years.

Daniel Syester, born May 14, 1788, died May 10, 1828, aged 33 years.

Robert Kimble, died Feb. 17, 1872, aged 66 years.

Sarah, his wife, died May 12, 1867, aged 57 years.

George O. Hazeltine, died Dec. 19, 1861, aged 51 years.

John Kendle, died Sept. 13, 1878, aged 72 years.

Theobold Kendle, died April 14, 1842, aged 63 years; and his wife, Elizabeth, died June 1, 1853, aged 88 years.

John Boyers, died Oct. 16, 1844, aged 74 years.

David Boyers, born July 20, 1797, died April 21, 1846.

Martha Byers, died March 15, 1875, aged 74 years.

William Boullt, died Nov. 30, 1845, aged 70 years.

Elizabeth Boullt, died Sept. 31, 1830, aged 57 years.

Philip Sprecher, died March 27, 1844, aged 84 years.

Mary Sprecher, wife of Col. George, died April 29, 1841, aged 44 years.

William Dickey, a native of Ireland, died Oct. 17, 1831, aged 43 years.

Joseph Byers, died March 6, 1856, aged 47 years; and his wife, Elizabeth, died Dec. 4, 1856, aged 40 years.

John Davis, died April 3, 1858, aged 65 years; and his wife, Matilda, died Nov. 24, 1852, aged 50 years.

Henry Lefevre, died July 6, 1852, aged 41 years; and his wife, Catharine E., died Oct. 22, 1859, aged 48 years.

Jacob Sprecher, died May 26, 1873, aged 66 years; and his wife, Margaret, died Dec. 4, 1857, aged 49 years.

Christian King, died June 5, 1859, aged 87 years.

Isaac Thompson, died Feb. 23, 1852, aged 55 years.

Henry Stinemitz, born Nov. 16, 1792, died Nov. 7, 1859.

John Baker, died Feb. 28, 1854, aged 58 years; his wife, Mary, died Aug. 30, 1874, aged 75 years.

John Springer, died July 20, 1854, aged 74 years.

Frederick Dellinger, died Aug. 2, 1871, aged 84 years; his wife, Elizabeth, died July 23, 1854, aged 68 years.

David Sprecher, died May 20, 1856, aged 53 years.

Martin Bear, died Jan. 3, 1872, aged 77 years; his wife, Elizabeth, died Dec. 3, 1875, aged 80 years.

Adolphus H. Melown, died May 12, 1855, aged 33 years.

Mary Melown, died Sept. 3, 1870, aged 70 years.

George Sprecher, born April 10, 1791, died May 30, 1870.

Charles Wallace, born Oct. 27, 1833, died Oct. 16, 1876.

Philip Sprecher, died Dec. 17, 1856, aged 37 years.

Isaac Ridenour, died Sept. 29, 1878, aged 70 years.

James Neal, died Sept. 29, 1862, aged 63 years.

Joseph Artz, died July 11, 1863, in his 33d year.

David Sprecher, died Aug. 2, 1872, aged 67 years.

Jesse Long, died April 3, 1857, in his 65th year.

John F. Dellinger, died June 11, 1856, aged 47 years.

Lewis H. Dellinger, died Aug. 19, 1854, aged 4 years.

Henry Monninger, died June 24, 1853, aged 44 years.

Peter Sword, died Dec. 6, 1847, aged 62 years.

Mary A. Sword, died Jan. 30, 1867, aged 68 years.

John Monninger, died Oct. 1, 1837, aged 59 years; his wife, Eve C., died March 31, 1844, aged 60 years.

John Henderson, died Oct. 30, 1836, aged 77 years; his wife, Susanna, died Aug. 22, 1830, aged 72 years.

Eve Crow, died Nov. 25, 1870, aged about 60 years.

Philip Crow, died Feb. 5, 1847, aged about 64 years; his wife, Elizabeth, died May 8, 1840, aged about 50 years.

Robert Anderson, died July 13, 1853, aged 58 years.

Miss Mary Dubois, died Aug. 19, 1853, aged 63 years.

Jane Elliott Crozier, wife of Edmund C. Dubois, died July 24, 1848, aged 45 years.

Wm. Towson, died Feb. 17, 1869, aged 71 years; his wife, Louisa, died June 27, 1860, aged 60 years.

Maria, wife of Benj. Crow, died Sept. 24, 1857, aged 46 years.

Christiana Lefevre, wife of John, died May 15, 1863, aged 85 years.

Nancy, wife of Jacob Bomberger, died Oct. 12, 1873, aged 69 years, 2 months, 11 days.

Matilda B., wife of Samuel Culbertson, aged 69 years.

John P. Chaney, died April 12, 1873, aged 54.

Catharine Stake, died Aug. 27, 1871, in her 62d year.

The town of Williamsport was founded by Gen. O. H. Williams shortly after the close of the Revolutionary war. After having served through the war with gallantry and distinction, and being especially complimented by Congress, Gen. Williams returned to Maryland and became collector of the port of Baltimore, which position he held until his death. The duties of that position did not occupy his time so completely that he was unable to engage in other enterprises, and in 1787 he was busily engaged in founding upon the banks of the Potomac the town which bears his name, and where he now lies buried, beneath a tomb bearing this inscription, "Dedicated to the memory of the Founder of Williamsport." The act of incorporation recites that "it is represented to the General Assembly that Otho Holland Williams possessed a tract of land called Ross' Purchase, and a tract adjoining thereto called Leeds, contiguous to the mouth of Conococheague Creek, and that, from the advantages of navigation from the head branches of 'Potowmack' River to the mouth of Conococheague, and the great prospect of the navigation of the said river being extended to tide-water, on the application of many citizens of Washington County he hath been encouraged and induced to lay out part of the said tracts into a town, and both contracted with the commissioners of the said county to build a warehouse on the said land and to furnish scales and weights for the inspection of tobacco, and an inspector is already appointed, and prayed to lay out and erect a town on the said lands and to secure the purchasers of lots in the said town." The act created a board of commissioners, consisting of Thomas Hart, Thomas Brooke, Moses Rawlings, Richard Pindell, and Alexander Clagett, who were authorized to lay out a town not to exceed one hundred and fifty acres, which was to be known as Williamsport, on the lands mentioned in the preamble to the act. The main streets of the town were not to be less than eighty feet wide, and the cross streets not less than sixty feet wide. The commission was authorized to levy a tax of ten pounds a year to pay a clerk. This act of incorporation was passed in November, 1786.

In a few years Williamsport was a thriving village, and in 1791 Thomas Dobbins, a merchant of the town, writing to some friend, appears to have been highly delighted with the prospects. He thought that it bade fair to be the first town on the river, "as many thousand bushels of wheat come down the river in boats and are unloaded at the bank, and many boats loaded with above one hundred barrels of flour are sent down to Georgetown from the banks of Conococheague." Dobbins was engaged in buying hog bristles and horse-tails for the purpose of making brushes. He also manufactured "ink powder," guaranteed to make ink in one minute, and which he advertised as equal to "anything ever imported from England, Paris, Amsterdam, Rotterdam, or any other dam wheresoever." He likewise advertised extensively "shining blackball and pomatum." During the previous year an effort had been made to establish the national capital at Williamsport. The matter was indeed seriously considered, and President Washington, much to the delight of the busy but patriotic townspeople, paid them a visit in order to see what the advantages of the situation were as a suitable location for the capital. Before his visit the following petition had been circulated and numerously signed, to be presented to the State Legislature then in session:

"The subscribers, citizens of Washington County, most respectfully represent that the law of Congress respecting a district for their permanent residence presents us with an occasion to hope that the said district may be located in this county; and as we are willing to make every contribution towards the necessary accommodation of Congress that can reasonably be expected or that our circumstances can afford, we pray that the General Assembly will be pleased to pass an act agreeably to the aforesaid law of Congress and the Constitution of the United States, to appropriate a district ten miles square within this county, wherever it may please the President to make the location. And we will ever pray, etc."

Of course the President's visit was a great event for Williamsport. He arrived on the evening of the 14th of October, and a Hagerstown paper, in a brief account of the visit, states that he was in most excellent health, and was received with every demonstration of affection and gratitude. Every house in the town was brilliantly illuminated, and bonfires burned at every street corner. He remained for the night in Williamsport, probably stopping with Gen. Williams' brother, Elie Williams, at Springfield farm, the homestead near the village, and left the next morning on his way up the river as far as Cumberland. This was not, however, Washington's first visit to the locality. More than thirty years before, during Braddock's war, when the place was a wilderness, he had visited the spot. He pointed out to his host, as they stood at the fountain on Springfield farm, an old hut, which he said was the only improvement to be seen on the face of the country thirty years before. This hut had been the dwelling of the noted Col. Cresap. Elie Williams was very hopeful that Washington would select Williamsport as the site of the capital, and so wrote his brother in Baltimore. One of these letters has been preserved, and is of great length and detail, giving an account of the President's movements and observations, with speculations in a confident strain upon the prospects. The old general did not, however, share his brother's rose-colored views, and treated the matter with indifference if not contempt, for he wrote on the back of the letter "All a Hum," and so it proved. Washington in a few weeks reported in favor of the present site of the capital.[1] The same newspaper which announces the visit of the President at Williamsport also records the election to Congress of Thomas Sprigg for the district embraced in Washington, Allegany, and a part of Frederick Counties, the vote standing as follows: Thomas Sprigg, 1758; R. Nelson, 1030. Dr. Henry Schnebly, Martin Kershner, Robert Hughes, and William Clark were elected to the House of Delegates.

Two years after the President's visit, on Oct. 18, 1793, George Bishop announced that he had opened a house of entertainment on the main street of the

[1] The bateau in which Washington made his first surveying trip up the Potomac above where Williamsport now stands was built of a large yellow poplar, and was constructed at Catoctin Furnace, under the direction of a brother of Governor Johnson, and hauled to Williamsport. Among those who accompanied him was Governor Johnson. One of the latter's nephews, writing in 1827, says,—

"It was necessary after the fatigues of the survey to have quarters prepared at some planter's or farmer's house for the night, and it was at one of these hospitable mansions that at supper, after they had taken coffee, my father asked the lady of the house for a bowl of milk. The servant immediately brought in a bowl of rich cream, which he told her to take away. 'Stop, stop, colonel!' exclaimed the general; 'give it to me; it is not too rich for me.' His constitution was remarkably good at that time, and no doubt his appetite was increased by the labors of the day. When the hour of retirement arrived, the general, Governor, and my father were shown into a room with two beds. 'Come, gentlemen,' said the general, 'which of you will sleep with me?' They both declined the polite invitation."

town, "at the Sign of General Washington." After that and until 1800 the following business changes are recorded in Williamsport: In March, 1793, Jeremiah Evans and Charles Shanks, merchants, dissolved partnership, and in May of the next year James Brown & Co. also dissolved, and Shanks, Osburne & Co. went out of business. Dr. James Forbes came from Pennsylvania to practice medicine in 1795. Benjamin Tyson, of Sharpsburg, was married to Miss Peggy Morgan in the same year. In April, 1796, P. Devecmon and Randolph Brill each had a store in the town, and in 1797, Samuel Porter kept an inn, Christian Ardinger was the ferryman, P. and L. Henop & Co. general merchants, and John Kennedy & Co. sold dry-goods, hardware, and groceries. In 1798, William Didenhover had a hemp and gunpowder-mill near Conococheague Creek, six miles above Williamsport. The last Fourth of July in the eighteenth century was celebrated with a great flourish by the citizens of the thriving young town, and the Hagerstown *Herald* correspondent gives the following quaint account of the ceremonies:

"The day was celebrated at this place by a respectable collection of the citizens of this town and its vicinity, among whom was a detachment of militia in uniform, and composed of cavalry and infantry, who led the procession of citizens from the town to Federal Spring, where the means for regaling the party was furnished upon a well-spread table, displaying a variety and abundance, well prepared and neatly adjusted. The countenance of the company bespoke a lively sense of the interesting event under which our country assumed a national position, and the mirth and pleasantry that prevailed declared for the citizens that they had left their cares at home, and that political prejudices were not suffered to intrude upon the pleasantness of the day. After a cheerful repast a number of toasts were drank, and in the evening the party returned in procession to the town, and was dismissed, highly gratified by the proceedings of the day."

The next "Fourth," being the first of the new century, was also appropriately celebrated much in the same manner as the previous one had been. The celebration was held at Federal Spring.

In February, 1801, the Kennedy firm was dissolved, the notice being signed by John and Thomas Kennedy. The latter at the same time announced that he would commence to keep store in the brick house, corner of the public square, where "goods will be sold on moderate terms for cash or country produce." During the first decade of the nineteenth century the following were among the business men and firms of Williamsport:

Tavern-keepers, Henry Cyester, Abram Hibbling, James Kendall, Henry Funk, Samuel Porter, John Langley, William McCoy, Thomas Edwards, Thomas Helm, John Russell Milton H. Sackett (who kept the Columbian House); merchants, John Hogg, Thomas Kennedy (who boated flour from that place to Georgetown for one dollar per barrel in 1802, was also merchant, poet, etc.), Rudolphus Brill (died in 1802), Basil Carricoe, Jacob T. Towson, Ringgold & Brothers, Joseph Kennedy, Jacob Brosius, John Irwin, John Weisel, Henry Heckrotte, William Bayly, John Wolfkill; Jacob Bowles (blacksmith), Christian Ardinger (who boated on the river between Williamsport and Georgetown); Col. William Van Lear and Dr. Scott were physicians; Thomas Williams and William B. Williams were distillers; James Walker was a wood-corder.

In 1804 the Legislature was asked to pass a bill to authorize a lottery for the purpose of raising funds for the erection of a market-house, and in January, 1805, the petition was granted, and the following commissioners were appointed: Jacob T. Towson, William McCoy, Thomas Helm, John Hogg, Daniel Weisel, and William L. Compton. The amount of money to be raised was four hundred dollars, and the commissioners were required to give bond to the amount of twelve hundred dollars. Advantage was not, however, taken of the act for some years. News came to Williamsport about this time of the terrible death of young Israel, a midshipman in the navy, an orphan nephew of Elie Williams. He was a youth of manly and enterprising spirit, and gave promise of a brilliant future. He was much esteemed in Williamsport, and the intelligence of his death was received with great sorrow. He was killed in the awful gunboat explosion in the harbor of Tripoli, having fired the magazine in order to prevent himself and companions from falling into the hands of the enemy. After languishing for some time the market-house enterprise assumed definite shape, the lottery was held with entire success, and the new market-house was opened on Wednesday, April 18, 1810, the commissioners being Jacob T. Towson, Daniel Weisel, and Thomas Edwards. Wednesdays and Saturdays were fixed on as market days, and the market hours were from sunrise and three hours thereafter. A penalty of ten shillings was imposed for selling before the ringing of the bell, and twenty shillings for buying provisions, except beef by the quarter or pork by the hog, during market on any day in town or within a mile, except at the market; penalty for selling in like cases, ten shillings; penalty for butcheries in or near the market-house, one dollar; for putting a horse into the market-house, two shillings and sixpence. In the fall, after the building of the market, there was a heavy fall of rain along the entire Atlantic coast. On November 10th the rainfall in the section of country through which the Potomac and Conococheague flowed was tremendous. Both rivers rose to a great height. The bridge, but recently built across the Conococheague at Williamsport, was entirely swept away. Everything that in-

Theodore Embrey

terrupted its course, such as distilleries, saw-mills, haystacks, fences, etc., became a prey to its ravages and fury. Mr. Towson's warehouse at Williamsport, which contained a quantity of tar and coal, was also carried away, his loss being estimated at more than twelve hundred dollars.

The trade of Williamsport at this time was largely with Georgetown, D. C., and Washington, by means of river boats, but the only boat-owner whose name is mentioned in connection with freight business up to 1820 is that of Joseph Holland, who had a line of boats in 1819. The census of the town in 1820 was as follows:

White males, 318; white females, 317; total whites, 635. Slaves, males, 66; females, 53; total slaves, 119. Free colored persons, males, 42; females, 31; total, 73. Total population, 827.

Among the prominent names which appear in the records of the second decade of the nineteenth century as inhabitants of Williamsport are the following:

Nicholas Baker, who died in 1812; James Nowell; James Muir, tavern-keeper (1812); Weisel (Daniel) & Humrickhouse (Albert), merchants; James Sterret, tanner; John Gelwick, brewer (1813); Charles Heseltine, merchant (1810); Willis & Frankenberry, shoemakers (1813); Mr. Kreps, hatter; Jacob Miller, weaver; Turner & Heseltine, merchants; Robert McCullough & Son, tanners; Samuel Ross, shoemaker; George Saunders; Michael G. Kessinger, merchant; Jacob Wever, who purchased Gelwick's brewery (1817); Rev. Mr Jackson, who was there in 1817; George Bowman; William Melone; Richard Pool, tailor (1817); Dr. Smith; Joseph G. Brown, shoemaker; Lane & Cramer, merchants, in 1819.

Theodore Embrey, retired merchant, was born in Washington, D. C., Jan. 13, 1832. His paternal ancestry belongs to the history of Fauquier County, Va., to which place the first Embrey of the family in America was sent from England as a tax-gatherer for the Crown. He became a large landholder, and by entailment his large possessions passed through successive generations of descendants. In 1831, Charles Embrey married Elizabeth, daughter of Richard and Elizabeth Merriman, of St. Mary's County, Va., and in 1833 removed from Virginia to Williamsport. He occupied himself at first as a canal contractor, was subsequently appointed superintendent of the Williamsport division of the Chesapeake and Ohio Canal, and when he resigned the appointment he engaged in mercantile business in Williamsport. From 1868 to 1872 he was judge of the Orphans' Court, and for several years prior to his death (1878) was extensively occupied as a canal forwarder. His widow survives him, as do six of his children. Theodore Embrey attended school in Williamsport until his twentieth year. At the age of twenty-one he was superintendent of the Williamsport division of the Chespeake and Ohio Canal, and after continuing two years under the appointment gave it up to engage in business with his father as merchant and shipper. In 1874 the elder Embrey retired, and in 1875, Theodore took in Victor Cushwa as a partner. In 1880 the firm of Embrey & Co., canal forwarders, was dissolved. Since then Mr. Embrey has lived in retirement. He was a heavy shipper by canal for several years, and during the late war did a great business. Political honors never tempted him into giving much attention to their pursuit, although he did serve one term as county commissioner, and during that term gave much time and concern to the work of constructing the new Washington County court-house. He has ever taken a lively interest in the promotion and encouragement of home industries, and among other efforts of a like nature assisted in founding in 1880 the Williamsport Manufacturing Company, of which successful corporation he is and always has been the president. Dec. 28, 1871, he married Irene, daughter of John Buchanan, of Williamsport, a native of Baltimore County, a settler in Williamsport in 1808, and in his day the director of valuable interests. Mr. Buchanan died in 1873.

In 1822, Thomas Kennedy, the poet, removed to Hagerstown, and Henry H. Gaither was practicing law in Williamsport, the first lawyer whose name appears on the records of the town.

Thomas Kennedy came to America from Scotland in 1777 in his twentieth year, and first settled near the Great Falls of the Potomac River. He was the son of William and Grizzel (Lindsay) Kennedy, both of whom belonged to educated Scottish families. He was the youngest of eleven children. Thomas had a brother who died in the English service in the East Indies, and one in the same service in the West Indies. In 1797 he married Rosamond Harris Thomas, daughter of William and Amelia (Selby) Thomas, of Welsh extraction, and whose ancestors were of the Thomas family that first settled on the site of Philadelphia, Pa. After leaving Great Falls he settled in Williamsport, Washington Co., and became the leading merchant of that region, selling merchandise that went to Fort Cumberland on pack-horses. He had nine children, of whom the only survivor is Grace Amelia Neill, widow of William Neill, whom she married in 1833. She was born Nov. 14, 1799, in Williamsport, and after her marriage lived several years in Sandusky City, Ohio, and in 1841 came to Frostburg, in 1843 to Cumberland, and in 1846 to "Alpine Cottage," one mile east of Cumberland, where she resides at the present time. Her husband died March 18, 1862.

Although over eighty-two years of age she is very active, mentally and physically, more so than most ladies of sixty-five. She remembers all the old society people of Annapolis and Washington over half a century ago, when she was one of the belles at those two capitals, and relates with great zest her meetings with "Aunt Rachel," the wife of Gen. Jackson, who died a few months previous to the general's inauguration as President. Her brother, Howard Kennedy, was the leading merchant of his day at Hagerstown, and a large stage and express proprietor. Another brother was Lieut. John Francis Kennedy, of the United States army, who served in the Florida war, and died of exposure incurred there, at Charleston, S. C., May 19, 1837. In 1807, Thomas Kennedy removed from Williamsport to his farm, "Wooburn," five miles distant, and in 1809 removed back to "Mount Liberty," his beautiful seat in Williamsport.

In 1812 he removed to "Roslin Castle," his place, one mile away, and next year to his farm "Ellerslie," three miles from Williamsport and six from Hagerstown. In 1828 he established the Hagerstown *Mail*, which he edited until his death, by cholera, Oct. 18, 1832, when his son, Howard Kennedy, and William Weber purchased it.

Mr. Kennedy served many years as senator and delegate from Washington County in the Legislature, and after seven years of hard work secured the passage of a bill of which he was the author, giving to the Jews the same rights as other citizens in voting, holding and owning real and personal property, and other franchises before then denied by the Maryland statutes. Such was his persistence in its advocacy for seven years that the bill got to be finally known as "Kennedy's Jew Baby," but its final passage into an enactment secured him a national reputation and the lasting friendship of the Jewish residents of Maryland, and, in fact, of the whole country. His wife died March 1, 1837, aged sixty years. She was a cousin of Col. Jack Thomas, the father of Governor Frank Thomas.

Mr. Kennedy was not only a successful merchant in early life, and an able editor and distinguished legislator in subsequent years, but he was a poet whose reputation was at one time coextensive with the Federal Union. His poems were published by Daniel Ropine, in Washington City, in 1816, in a neat volume of three hundred and thirty-four pages. It was dedicated to his parents, one of whom was descended from the noble house of Cassillis, and the other—his mother—from the ancient house of Lindsay and the illustrious though ill-fated family of Stuart.

Many of these poems were patriotic ballads relating to the war of 1812, and descriptive of war scenes in Maryland, Virginia, and at the national capital, and on the lakes and borders of New York. There were also love sonnets and satirical verses, not a few of the latter being local in character. Perhaps his finest poem and the one which gave him a world-wide celebrity was his "Speech of Logan," the Mingo chief, founded on the speech said to have been made to Lord Dunmore, Governor of Virginia. His most humorous production was an ode, occasioned by reading in the newspapers a sketch of J. T. Callender's trial at Richmond, Va., for sedition, in which the extraordinary behavior of Judge C—— served to awaken his muse.

His "Old Soldiers' Petition to the General Assembly of Maryland" was a popular production with the survivors of the "Maryland Line" of the Revolution. Quite a large number of the poems were elegies, hymns, etc., for burials of distinguished patriots of 1776 and the war of 1812. In 1817 he published, in a volume of over one hundred pages, his "Songs of Love and Liberty," the first of which was "Oh, Were She Mine." The scene of this poem was located at the little village of Matildaville, at the Great Falls of the Potomac, his first home in America. His "Mary's a Mason," to the tune of "Kate Kearney," had a great run as a ballad about 1810. In the war of 1812–14 the American tars sang on every United States vessel his "Impressed Seaman" (tune of "Galley-Slave"), and in political campaigns a favorite song was his "Jackson is the Boy" (tune of "Malbrook").

In 1821–22, Michael Kreps was proprietor of the "White Swan Tavern," formerly occupied by David Harry, Jr., afterwards by James Shoaf. David Harry, Jr., was proprietor of the Globe Tavern, once occupied by Joseph Hollman, while James Shoaf kept the Golden Swan, on Main Street.

The following school commissioners were appointed under the act of 1821 for the management of the school fund of Williamsport District: Jacob Towson (president), Charles Heseltine, Ignatius Drury, Daniel Rench, and Isaac Rowland.

On the 5th of July, 1823, Matthew Van Lear died, and was buried with considerable state.

Between 1820 and 1830 the following names appear as active in the affairs of the town:

Robert T. Friend, inn-keeper, 1820; Charles Heseltine kept the "Bell Tavern" in 1822; John Crawford kept the Spread Eagle Tavern in 1822; J. W. Sterrett was a cabinet-maker, in

J. H. Farrow

1823; Rev. Mr. Ruthrauff was there in 1823; Charles H. Lee, brewer, in 1823; Col. John Carr, a veteran of the Revolution, and a very prominent citizen, was one of the residents of Williamsport at this period; Dr. William MacGill, in 1824, removed to Hagerstown.

As the years went on Williamsport continued to prosper and grow, and in 1851 the town appeared to be developing at a more rapid rate than any other inland town in the State. Through the public spirit of its citizens a turnpike road was in progress and soon to be completed from Martinsburg, Va., to the bank of the Potomac opposite the town, and a company had a competent person in Williamsport making observations with a view to the construction of a bridge over the river to connect the turnpike with the town. Another turnpike was afterwards built, and the Western Maryland Railroad was finished in 1873. Other improvements had been made in the town, including an Odd-Fellows' hall, which was dedicated on July 27, 1860, at which addresses were made by Grand Master W. H. Young, of Baltimore, and Rev. M. Riley, of Frederick. Several churches had been built.

The following were the burgesses of Williamsport from April, 1860, to 1875:

Jonathan Spellman, 1860; W. H. Wilson, 1860–61; Daniel W. Cyester, 1864–68; Henry Artz, 1866; J. H. Farrow, 1870; Addison Munsell, 1870; Matthew McClanahan, W. H. Beard, Addison T. Munsell, 1872–75; E. Bomberger, from March, 1876, to 15th of March, 1879; P. Ardinger, from 1880 to the present time.

Joseph Henry Farrow, State senator, and for many years the leading druggist of Williamsport, Washington Co., was born in Washington County, near Hagerstown, Feb. 11, 1831. His father (Nathaniel) and mother (Mary McCall) were natives of Maryland, and were descended respectively from French and German ancestry. Nathaniel Farrow was a cooper, and followed his trade in Williamsport many years. In that place he died in 1859. His widow resides now in Garrett City, Ind., with her son, Henry Clay Farrow. Of her nineteen children, thirteen were sons. The living sons and daughters number now but five. Young Joseph was early bred to the necessity of working for a livelihood, and his educational advantages were therefore limited. His actual attendance at school did not cover more than a year, but such was his ambition to acquire knowledge that he sat up many a night after a hard day's work and taught himself as best he could. When but fourteen years old he worked as tow-boy on the Chesapeake and Ohio Canal, and stuck to the task for about two years. Part of the time he toiled in his father's cooper-shop, and from his sixteenth to his nineteenth year plied the adze constantly. In 1850 he took other service, as a clerk in C. T. Porterfield's drug-store in Williamsport, but at the end of a year returned to the coopering business. In 1861 he was appointed a boss on the canal, and acted in that capacity until 1865, when he engaged in the drug business in Williamsport, having, however, meanwhile been a United States revenue agent at Williamsport from 1863 to 1864. Since 1865 he has remained steadily in the drug trade. In 1869 he was chosen to the mayoralty of Williamsport, being the only Republican chosen that year to office in his section, and upon the expiration of his term was re-elected. He was twice elected a commissioner of the town board, and in 1875 was elected a member of the House of Delegates. In 1877 he was re-elected, in the latter contest leading his ticket handsomely. During his legislative terms he lent his energies steadily to the passage of a bill providing for equal taxation, and opposed all exemptions save for churches and burying-grounds, while he labored also with much zeal for the success of the measure providing for the increase of homestead exemptions from one hundred to five hundred dollars. In 1879 he was nominated by acclamation as a Republican candidate for the Senate, despite his previous announcement that he would not be a candidate. His opponent was George W. Smith, the law partner of Hon. William T. (now Governor) Hamilton, whom he defeated by a majority of one hundred and thirty-one. Mr. Farrow was in early life an Old-Line Whig, cast his first vote for Winfield Scott, later joined the Know-Nothings, was a strong Union man during the war, and in 1864 gave his allegiance to the Republican party. Sept. 3, 1853, he married Mary S., daughter of John Nitzel, of Washington County. They have five living children, —three sons and two daughters. He has been an active member of Friendship Lodge, F. and A. M., since 1862, and a member of Potomac Lodge, Knights of Pythias, since 1875. He is in every sense a self-made man, and after a life of pretty hard knocks and persistent energy enjoys the satisfaction of knowing that his labors and his determination to win have brought him a gratifying reward.

Religious Denominations. — The early church history of Williamsport is so closely woven into that of Hagerstown that it is almost impossible to make a distinct narrative of either; the Williamsport congregation, whether Episcopal, Lutheran, Catholic, or Methodist, being under the supervision of Hagerstown pastors. In the history of the Lutheran Church at Hagerstown the history of the congregation at Williamsport is given up to 1834. The old log church which had been in use until 1829 was torn down, and the corner-stone of the present church edifice was laid in June of that year, the sermon on the occasion being preached in the woods (now the Matt farm) adjoining the tower. In eleven weeks from the laying of the corner-stone the dedicatory sermon was preached by the Rev. Mr. Hoshour. Rev. Mr. Winter was succeeded in the charge by Rev. S. W. Harkey in 1834, at Williamsport and St. Paul, but retained Clear Spring, and thus this pastorate was divided. In two years Mr. Harkey left, and was followed by Rev. Daniel Miller in 1836, who remained only one year; his successor being Rev. C. Startzman, in December, 1838, who remained eleven years, the longest pastorate since the building of the church.

In 1840, Clear Spring was reunited to Williamsport, and in 1850, Rev. Mr. Bishop was called to the pastorate from Indiana, Pa., when Clear Spring withdrew a second time. In 1855, Mr. Bishop removed, and Rev. Mr. Sreaver was his successor. He died in October, 1857.

His successor was Rev. Joseph Barclay. During his ministry the church edifice was enlarged and tastefully frescoed. He was succeeded by Rev. C. Leply in 1859, who remained nntil 1864, when he resigned, to be followed by Rev. Mr. Berlin in the same year. He remained until 1867, and was succeeded by Rev. M. S. Culler, who resigned in 1869, and accepted a call to Martinsburg, W. Va.

St. Paul's left the charge in 1870 and joined Clear Spring, when Williamsport was left alone to constitute an independent charge. The pulpit was filled for a time by Rev. Dr. Strobel, who was finally chosen pastor, but resigned in 1872 to remove to New York. The pulpit was then supplied by the Rev. Dr. McCron, in charge of the Female Seminary at Hagerstown, until 1874, when the present pastor, Rev. J. B. Keller, was called to the charge.

The Presbyterian Church of Williamsport was organized about 1829, by Revs. Daniel Elliott and James Buchanan, of the Carlisle Presbytery. Dr. Michael A. Finley was the first ruling elder, and the first board of trustees was as follows: Matthew Van Lear, John Hogg, Joseph T. Towson, and Dr. A. Finley. The records of the church up to 1838 have been lost. At that time the members were

Dr. M. A. Finley, Mrs. Isabella Finley, Mrs. Rachel Sterrett, Mrs. Louisa Towson, Mrs. Susan Van Lear, Otho Williams, Ann Williams, A. M. Cramer, Mrs. Emily Cramer, Miss Elizabeth Whiteman, Mrs. Mary Rhodes, Miss Sarah Wilson, Samuel Culbertson, Mrs. Culbertson, Miss Annie Porterfield, Mrs. Adelaide Zellers, Mrs. Amanda Anderson, Mrs. Mary Weisel.

Prior to 1831 the Presbyterians bought the German Reformed church, and in 1838, Rev. Isaac Keller, of the German Reformed Church, was pastor. After him were Rev. John O. Proctor, 1842; Rev. J. K. Cramer, 1855–58; and Rev. Jos. H. Russell, 1858–60, who early in the war went into the Union army. After Mr. Russell resigned, Rev. Mr. Marr supplied the pulpit for fifteen months. After that, until 1868, there is no record of the pastors. Rev. George G. Smith was pastor from 1868 to 1874, and was succeeded by Rev. John S. Foulk, who remained until 1876. Rev. C. Williams succeeded him, but resigned in 1879, since when there has been no regular pastor, Rev. Mr. Downly, of Martinsburg, and Drs. Jelley and Woodruff, of New Windsor College, supplying the pulpit from time to time. The elders of the church now are S. S. Cunningham, Washington Barrett, Caspar Shunk, and Samuel Culbertson.

The church, on the east side of Conococheague Street, near the Western Maryland depot, is a plain brick building, and has a seating capacity of three hundred.

The first Catholic church was consecrated in 1851, by Rev. Henry Myers, who had been pastor of the congregation and of the church at Hagerstown for some years, and who subsequently moved to Baltimore, and died while serving as pastor of St. Vincent de Paul's in that city. The present church was built in 1876, the corner-stone being laid on May 18th of that year. The edifice is sixty feet long and thirty feet wide, and occupies a commanding position. The ceremonies of the laying of the corner-stone were performed by Father Jones, the pastor, and Father Ryan, of Cumberland. In the deposit-box were placed the names of the President of the United States, of the pastor, and of Eli Stake, the superintendent of the building; also a bottle of holy water, the Bible, prayer-book, and several coins. The church was consecrated April 30, 1877, as "St. Augustine's." The dedicatory services were conducted by Right Rev. John J. Kain, Bishop of Wheeling. Mass was sung by Rev. D. De Wolf, of St. Matthew's Church, Washington, D. C., assisted by Rev. Stanislaus Ryan as deacon, and Rev. Thomas Flemming as sub-deacon. Revs. J. O. Sullivan, Charles Danun, and John M. Jones were also within the chancel during the services. The mass was Mercadante's, in B flat, the principal singers being the Misses Cretin and Nettie Hurley, and Messrs. Merrick and Conduy, of Hagerstown. Mrs. J. H. Cretin was organist. The church building is a neat structure of brick, capable of seating two hundred persons. It cost two thousand dollars, although much of the material was given and a great deal of the work was done gratuitously.

The Methodists were among the pioneers of Williamsport, and had a congregation there almost as soon as the town was founded. The present church was greatly damaged during the war, but was refitted and repaired immediately afterwards. It was re-dedicated on Oct. 13, 1867, Rev. T. D. Valiant, of Baltimore, Rev. Crouse, of Virginia, and others officiating.

In April, 1816, it was proposed to build a Protestant Episcopal church in Williamsport on the lot owned by the original proprietors of the town. A writer then said that "Hagerstown and Williamsport, jointly, are surely able to support two preachers in the English language—the one a Presbyterian, the other a Protestant Episcopal."

Newspapers.—There is a flourishing weekly paper in Williamsport, the *Pilot*, edited by G. W. McCardell. In 1829 a paper was started, and continued to run for many years, called the *Republican Banner*, its original editor being Daniel Weisel, and its publisher Thomas Tice. In 1847 the *Times* was an opposition paper. In 1852 the *Scott Banner* made its appearance, the publishers being Williams & Allen, but was afterwards discontinued.

Williamsport Banks.—The Conococheague Bank of Williamsport was incorporated by the State Legislature Jan. 7, 1814. The original capital stock was to be $250,000. Samuel Ringgold, Thomas Buchanan, John Bowles, Matthew Van Lear, Charles Heseltine, Jacob T. Towson, Peter Miller, and John Irvine were elected directors to serve for the first year. Samuel A. Chew was elected cashier, and the bank went into operation immediately. In April, 1815, Jacob T. Towson, Thomas Buchanan, Dr. William B. Williams, Charles Heseltine, John Bowles, Matthew Van Lear, Michael A. Finley, and John Hogg were elected directors. The bank started successfully, and paid a dividend of twelve per cent. the first year. The directors of the bank elected in 1817 were William Williams, Jacob T. Towson, Edward G. Williams, Thomas Buchanan, Thomas C. Brent, Daniel Rench, Daniel Schnebly, Robert Wilson. The bank was examined in December, 1819, and found to be perfectly solvent. Frederick A. Schley, Alex. Mill, Richard Ragan, Frederick Dorsey, and James S. Lane, the examiners, found that the bank had in circulation of its own notes $23,785, to redeem which it had in its vaults specie and United States six per cent. stock amounting to $26,569. In 1823, Jacob T. Towson was president of the bank, when its affairs were being settled prior to a final winding up, and the bank closed in 1824, after satisfying all claims.

The Williamsport Bank was first incorporated on the 22d of February, 1832, under the title of the Washington County Bank, the capital stock authorized being $250,000, divided into 10,000 equal shares. The commissioners named in the act to establish the bank were John R. Dall, Daniel Weisel, Matthew S. Van Lear, James Grimes, Michael A. Finley, Charles A. Warfield (of A.), and Robert Wason. The original place of business was at the corner of Conococheague and Potomac Streets. In 1865 it became a national bank, under the name of the Washington County National Bank, under the national banking laws.

The following have been the presidents and cashiers of the bank since its incorporation in 1832:

Presidents, John Van Lear, Jacob T. Towson, John R. Dall, Daniel Weisel, S. G. Cunningham, James Finley; Cashiers, G. R. Mosher, Horatio McPherson, John Van Lear, E. C. Dubois, S. S. Cunningham, E. G. W. Stake.

The present officers of the bank are:

James Finley, president; E. G. W. Stake, cashier; Joseph L. Motter, teller; Directors, James Finley, S. P. Cunningham, John A. Miller, John H. Snavely, John Troup, J. C. Ankeny, E. G. W. Stake, Samuel Lefever, Alonzo Berry.

The bank is now located on the south side of Potomac and Conococheague Streets. An exhibit of its affairs on Aug. 2, 1881, showed that its assets amounted to $369,727.05, consisting of bills and notes discounted, $124,912.64; bonds and stocks United States, $175,000; mortgages, $19,998.18; other securities, $194,998.18; due from other banks and the United States Treasurer, $26,844; specie, $6841.31; legal tenders, $9906; cash items, $334.82; costs paid and current expenses, $200.27; real estate, $3500; taxes paid, $2186.83. Its liability column showed that its capital stock amounted to $150,000; surplus fund, $30,000; discounts, $4027.20; profit and loss, $445.46; national circulation, $131,142; deposit, $445,605.13; dividends unpaid, $2633.11; due other banks, $1865.15.

Early Transportation Notes.—The question of water transportation was an interesting and serious one from the earliest period of Williamsport's existence. The Potomac Company announced on Jan. 6, 1802, that "the locks at the Great Falls being now completed, and boats consequently being enabled to pass without interruption to tide-water, the president and directors have established toll-gatherers at Williamsport, Hooker's Falls, and at the Great Falls, who will receive the respective tolls authorized by law as per table subjoined, and they require all persons who use this navigation to observe the following regulations, which have been deemed indispensably necessary for the interest of the institution and the accommodation of the public."

Efforts were made from time to time to improve the transportation facilities on the river, and at a meeting of the president and directors of the Potomac Company, held in Georgetown on the 4th of February, 1804, it was resolved that a premium of one hundred dollars "will be paid by the president and directors of the Potomac Company to such persons as shall, in their judgment, during the present year, bring down the river Potomac the boat, on an improved construction, best calculated for interior navigation, the conveyance of produce," etc., etc. In adjusting the premium the following considerations were announced as governing the award:

"The safety of the cargo, the gunwale not to be less than six inches above the water when fully loaded; the burden of the vessel, which shall not be less than one hundred barrels of flour; the least draught of water, the beam on the fork not exceeding eight feet; and the strength and workmanship of the boat and its capability of ascending the stream.

"And also a premium of fifty dollars will be paid by the president and directors to such person as shall, during the present year, bring down the boat exhibiting the cheapest effectual covering to secure the cargo from the weather, and also the best means and devices for keeping the cargo clean and free from damage by water.

"Persons who wish to be candidates for either of these premiums will show their boats, when at Georgetown, to Mr. Joseph Carleton, treasurer of said company, who will notify the directors thereof."

It appears that no entirely satisfactory craft was ever constructed, and the question of the Chesapeake and Ohio Canal was taken hold of in a practical manner on Sept. 22, 1827, when a meeting of citizens of Washington County favorable to the enterprise was held at Williamsport, and it was decided to form the Washington County Canal Association, and to appoint a committee to collect subscriptions. The following were the members of the committee:

First District, John Miller, Daniel Donnelly, Elias Baker, John Dunn, Peter Beeler; Second District, Jacob Wolf, A. M. C. Cramer, Joseph Hollman, John R. Dall, Daniel Malott; Third District, William Price, Otho H. Williams, Thomas Kennedy, Jacob Zeller, George Shafer; Fourth District, Lancelot Jacques, Jr., Jonathan Nesbit, David Cushwa, Henry Ankeny, Daniel Harbine; Fifth District, Thomas Brent, James H. Bowles, Robert Wason, Anthony Snyder, John Johnson; Sixth District, Samuel M. Hitt, Ezra Slifer, William Booth, John A. Bentz, David Bookhart; Seventh District, William Gabby, Marmaduke W. Boyd, Peter Seibert, John Horine, John Welty.

John R. Dall, J. Wolf, and A. M. C. Cramer were appointed a committee of three to draw up and forward subscription papers to the committees.

The first passenger train which ever came into Williamsport bore a party of gentlemen—officers of the Western Maryland Railroad—and a few guests, who were on a trip of inspection, and arrived in the town on the afternoon of November 27th. A large throng of citizens met the train, and greeted its advent with cheers and other demonstrations of joy. The party consisted of President Alexander Rieman, George Bokee, Wm. A. Boyd, Jr, J. D. Hipsley, Samuel Adams, D. J. Foley, A. P. Gorman, M. Bannon, Mr. Fawcett, James Webb, F. A. Hack, S. H. Myers, R. A. Snowden, Hon. J. K. Longwell, John Welty, Hon. Joshua Biggs, and George W. Harris; Hon. W. T. Hamilton, United States senator; Hon. A. K. Syester, attorney-general of the State; Hon. A. K. Stake, member-elect to the House of Delegates; E. M. Mobley, and other influential gentlemen. They remained for several hours in the town, and left late in the evening for Baltimore.

The celebration upon the completion of the road was a great event in Williamsport. At three o'clock in the afternoon of Dec. 17, 1873, a train of six handsomely-decorated passenger-coaches arrived in the town from Baltimore. The cars contained a distinguished party, including Governor William Pinkney Whyte, a deputation from the City Council of Baltimore, the officers of the road, and a number of invited guests. The party had been met at Union Bridge by a reception committee comprised of the following: Wm. H. Beard, burgess of Williamsport; E. McCoy, assistant burgess; Charles Ardinger, Lewis Wolf, Theodore Embrey, and Joseph H. Farrow, Town Council; Alonzo Berry, S. S. Cunningham, James Findley, John L. McAtee, Robert Lemon, Jesse Thompson, John Buchanan, Jos. Buchanan, Isaac Gruber, Henry Grosh, and Samuel Lefever.

The arrival of the train was announced by the ringing of church-bells and other demonstrations of welcome. Business in the town had been suspended, flags were floating from every window, and the train was met at the terminus, near the canal, by a canal-barge, decorated with garlands, drawn by six mules, with bannerets hanging from every part of the harness. The boat contained a band of music. When the four or five hundred visitors had alighted, Attorney-General Syester delivered an address of welcome, at the conclusion of which a procession was formed, and the guests were escorted to the public school-house, where a banquet had been prepared, under the direction of Mrs. John Ensminger, Mrs. John Long, and Mrs. Jacob Masters, Alonzo Berry, S. S. Cunningham, Joseph Motter, John Ensminger, Matthew McClanahan, A. J. Hanning, Jacob Masters, Daniel Syester, Joseph Ervin, and Dr. William Booth. At the table Mr. Beard, the burgess of Williamsport, extended to the guests a hearty welcome, to which Governor Whyte responded, saying that he had been early associated with the scenes and inhabitants of the town. Mr. Syester proposed the health of the officers

Samuel Lefever

of the canal, to which Mr. A. P. Gorman, the president of the board of directors, responded. President Rieman, when asked to reply to the toast "The Western Railroad," called upon Hon. J. K. Longwell to respond, which he did. Hon. Montgomery Blair replied to the toast, "The President of the United States." The toast, "To the city of Baltimore" was responded to by Mr. Joseph S. Heuisler. After dinner Governor White and a number of other gentlemen visited the houses of Isaac Motter, C. W. Humrichouse, Alonzo Berry, James Finley, and J. L. McAtee, at which places they were handsomely entertained. At five o'clock the excursionists re-embarked, and the train went back to Baltimore. Samuel Lefevre, who was very active in securing the extension of the Western Maryland Railroad to Williamsport, is a retired merchant and manufacturer of Williamsport, and was born near that town May 20, 1815, upon the farm whereon also his father, John, was born, about the year 1770. The land was taken up and first improved by Samuel Lefevre's grandfather, David Lefevre, who came hither from Lancaster County, Pa. The land in Washington County thus settled and improved by him some years before the beginning of the war of the Revolution remained in the possession of a Lefevre until 1865, or for more than a hundred years. David's father, Abraham, a French Huguenot, emigrated from France to America in 1707 and settled in New York State, at the place now known as Kingston, where two brothers Lefevre, doubtless Abraham's uncles, had made a settlement in 1660, or forty-seven years before. Abraham moved from Kingston to Lancaster County, Pa. There David was born and there his father, Abraham, died. For two hundred and twenty-two years, therefore, as has been seen, the name of Lefevre has been connected with the history of America.

Samuel Lefevre's father (John) married Christianne Householder (whose father and grandfather were identified with Washington County's early history). They had eight children. The daughters—numbering four—are dead. The sons, of whom Samuel is the youngest, are all living. John Lefevre died in 1815, the year his son Samuel was born, and in 1823 the widow removed with her children to Williamsport. She continued to reside there until her death, in 1862, aged eighty-five. When but a lad young Samuel was apprenticed to the trade of a carpenter, but he did not pursue it after his apprenticeship was ended. His first inclination was towards a mercantile occupation, and in that branch of business he early passed a brief experience. In 1842 he saw a wider field for advancement in a new departure, and in that year accordingly established a tannery in Williamsport, which he conducted successfully for ten years, or until 1852. His next business venture involved the combination of lumber and coal dealing and general merchandise, and the conduct of a saw-mill and planing-mill. In these enterprises, calling for the exercise of much industry, and exerting an important influence as factors of local business prosperity, Mr. Lefevre was associated with Mr. A. Shoop. The firm carried on their store, mills, etc., without interruption until 1876, when Mr. Lefevre retired from active business pursuits, and has since then enjoyed a season of well-deserved rest.

In 1854 he married Ann W., daughter of John Herr, a native of Pennsylvania, but then a resident of Washington County. Their children have been three sons, —John W., Samuel Franklin Grever, and Benjamin Constant,—all of whom are living. Mr. Lefevre has been a lifelong Democrat. During the late war he was a stanch Union man, but was nevertheless called upon to witness the spoliation of much of his property during the conflict, and to suffer losses of considerable magnitude, for which he received no subsequent recompense.

Early Sports of Williamsport.—At an early period horse-racing was a favorite amusement among the Williamsport people, there being as early as 1791 a fine race-course near the town, and on October 26th of that year a race was run for a purse of fifteen pounds, three-mile heats, free for any horse, mare, or gelding. Aged horses carrying nine stone, half a stone allowed for every year to the younger horse. On the day following a purse of seven pounds ten shillings was run over the same course, free for any horse, mare, or gelding, "the winning horse of the first day's purse excepted, carrying weight as above, the best of two-mile heats." On the 28th there was a handsome sweepstake race, catch-riders, two-mile heats, for every horse, mare, or gelding, the winning horse of the first two days excepted. Two days' races were held at the same course on Oct. 11 and 13, 1791. The first race on the first day was for ten guineas, the second was for a purse of six guineas. The horses were entered with Amos Davis and George Bishop, at Williamsport. The highest purse in October, 1792, was twenty pounds. The judges were John Orbison, John Blair, and Charles Shanks.

In September, 1793, the Hagerstown *Spy* announced that races would be run over the Williamsport course October 22d. The first race was for a purse of sixty dollars, free for any horse, mare, or gelding, four-mile heats, each horse carrying one hundred and twenty-six pounds weight, with a deduction of seven pounds for every year under age. On the next day there was run over the same course a race for a purse of thirty dollars, three-mile heats, free, the horses carrying weight as on the day before, and the winning horse of the preceding day excepted. And on Thursday, the 24th, was run a sweepstake race for the entrance-money of the preceding days, the winning horse of the two preceding days excepted. The horses were entered with George Gittinger and Thomas Worley. These races continued for many years to be one of the chief attractions of Williamsport. In 1797 the managers were Christian Ardinger, John Dugan, and Lewis Bryant. In the year previous the races occurred on the 26th, 27th, and 28th of October, owing to the fact that the Martinsburg races had been for the 19th, 20th, and 21st. It was announced by Nicholas Lynch and Samuel Ross that no person would be permitted to erect a stand or booth at or near the race-ground without paying four dollars to the races.

Representative Men of Williamsport District.—The Williams Family. Gen. Otho Holland Williams, after whom Williamsport was named, was born in Prince George's County in March, 1749. His family came from Wales, and was highly respectable. Otho Holland was of the third generation of their settlement in Maryland. His parents, Joseph and Prudence Williams, lived in Prince George's County, but in 1750 they removed to Frederick County and settled at the mouth of the Conococheague, in what is now Washington County. At the age of thirteen Otho was placed with Mr. Ross in the clerk's office of Frederick County, where he remained several years, when he removed to Baltimore to take a similar position there. He was then about eighteen years old and of fine appearance, being six feet in height, elegantly formed, and of pleasing manners and address. In the spring of 1774 he returned to Frederick Town, and entered into mercantile business there. On the 14th of June, 1775, Congress asked for soldiers, and young Williams marched to the American camp at Boston as first lieutenant of Capt. Price's company of Frederick riflemen. Soon after reaching Boston he was promoted to the command of his company. In 1776 a regiment was formed of the several rifle companies from Virginia and Maryland. Stevenson, of Virginia, was appointed colonel, Moses Rawlings, of Maryland, lieutenant-colonel, and Williams, major. At the fall of Fort Washington, on the Hudson River, the colonel was absent, and the lieutenant-colonel, Rawlings, was wounded early in the action. The command thus devolved upon Maj. Williams, who, after a desperate struggle, was compelled to surrender to the British. He was sent to New York and permitted at first to go about, while his troops were cooped up in sugar-houses and prison-ships, but on account of some trumped-up charges he was seized and thrown into a filthy cell, together with Ethan Allen, where he suffered terribly for seven or eight months. Williams' health was seriously impaired, and he never fully recovered from the effects of his imprisonment. Finally, however, he was exchanged for Maj. Ackland, of the British army. During his imprisonment Williams had been appointed to the command of the Sixth Regiment of the Maryland Line, and on being released joined his command in time to be present at the battle of Monmouth. In a letter urging his promotion, Hon. John Hanson wrote to the Governor and Council testifying in the warmest manner to the conspicuous military abilities of Maj. Williams, and recalling the fact that he had been elected colonel of the Flying Camp, but had declined the honor. Another argument used was that, next to Lieut.-Col. Rawlings, for whom another place was vacant, he was the oldest field-officer in the State. On the 16th of March, 1778, Col. Williams wrote to the Governor that the regiment he was to command did not number above one hundred effective men, and these indifferently clothed. However, it was soon considerably augmented and equipped, and Williams ultimately brought it up to a high state of efficiency and discipline. Soon after the reduction of Charleston by the British, the Maryland and Delaware Lines were detached and ordered South, under the command of the gallant Baron De Kalb. Williams accompanied De Kalb, and when Gates took command of the army he was appointed deputy adjutant-general. Gen. Williams took a conspicuous part in the battle of Camden, and commanded the rear-guard at the battle of Guilford Court-house, in which position he displayed great coolness, courage, and military talent. Gates was displaced and Gen. Greene appointed in his stead. Greene promoted Williams to be adjutant-general instead of deputy. His record throughout the Southern campaign was a brilliant one, and he gained great honor for the skill with which he covered the retreat of the army through North Carolina. At the battle of Eutaw he led the famous bayonet-charge which swept the field and secured the victory. To-

GEN. OTHO H. WILLIAMS.

S. S. Cunningham

wards the close of the war he was sent North by Gen. Greene with dispatches to Congress, which promoted him to the rank of brigadier-general. After the war he was appointed navy officer of the Fourth District, to succeed Mr. Sellers, but in a few years he settled in Baltimore, and was appointed collector of the port, which office he retained for the balance of his life. He was married in 1786 to Mary, the second daughter of William Smith, a wealthy merchant of Baltimore. He acquired considerable property, and was enabled to purchase the old home of his father in Washington County. On this property, in 1787, he laid off the town of Williamsport, which takes its name from him. In 1792, on the score of ill health, he declined the appointment of eldest brigadier-general in the army and second in command, and in 1793 he made a voyage to Barbadoes for the benefit of his health, which improved somewhat. In 1794, however, his malady returned, and continued to gain upon him until, on the 15th of June, he died, in the forty-sixth year of his age, while on his way to the Sweet Springs of Virginia.

Gen. Williams' sister Mercy married Col. John Stull, and died Feb. 6, 1787; and his sister Priscilla, who married James Chapline, died in December, 1788.

Gen. Otho H. Williams had four sons,—William Elie, Edward Green, Henry Lee, and Otho Holland.

His son William Elie married Susan Cook, daughter of the late William Cook, an eminent lawyer of Baltimore. William Williams, dying, left four children,—two sons, William and Otho H., and two daughters, Mary and Elizabeth, who married Col. Richard Tilghman, of the Hermitage.

Edward Green Williams married a daughter of the late William Gilmor. He served as captain of horse in the war of 1812. He died early in life, leaving one daughter, who married John White, son of Joseph White, and grandson of the late William Pinkney and Dr. John White. Henry Lee and Otho H. died unmarried.

Col. Elie Williams, brother of Gen. Otho Holland Williams, second son of Joseph and Prudence Williams, was born in Prince George's County, Md., and raised in Frederick County. He was commissioned in the Continental army with the rank of colonel, and was afterwards appointed clerk of Washington County Court, which office he held until the year 1800. He was also a contractor with Robt. Elliott, under the firm of Elliott & Williams, during the campaign of Harmer, St. Clair, and Wayne against the Indians. He died in Georgetown, D. C., in 1823, in the seventy-third year of his age, leaving two sons and three daughters,—Otho Holland Williams, of Hagerstown, Md., late clerk of Washington court, and afterwards brigadier-general in the second brigade and fourth division of the Maryland militia; John S. Williams, formerly of Howard District, Anne Arundel Co., Md., but afterwards of Quincy, Ill.; Maria Sophia, the eldest daughter, married the Hon. John Buchanan, late chief justice of the Maryland Court of Appeals, which office he held until his death; Prudence Holland, married Col. John I. Stull, cashier of the Farmers' and Mechanics' Bank of Georgetown, D. C.; and Catharine Kimball, married Henry H. Gaither, attorney-at-law. The coat of arms of the Otho Holland Williams family is a wild boar with a spear through the neck.

Samuel Shields Cunningham was born in Berkeley County, Va., April 13, 1810, and now resides in Williamsport, Washington Co., Md., where he has lived for more than fifty-six years. His father was Samuel Cunningham, born in Lancaster County, Pa., Feb. 6, 1765, and emigrated to Berkeley County, now West Virginia, with his parents in the year 1785. He was of Scotch-Irish parentage, and was a successful farmer. He died in 1824, in the sixtieth year of his age. Hugh Cunningham, the grandfather of Samuel S., was born of Scotch-Irish parentage, in Lancaster County, Pa., in 1741. He was an only child, and died in 1817. The grandmother, Agnes Cunningham, died in 1812.

Samuel S. was twice married,—in February, 1835, to Eliza A. Youtz, of Shepherdstown, Jefferson Co., W. Va., who died in June, 1860. By this marriage there were six children, all of whom died in infancy except one daughter, who is the wife of John S. Payne, and living at the old homestead in Berkeley County. In January, 1869, Samuel S. married Sallie Long, of Fauquier County, Va., and of this marriage only one daughter was born, who died in infancy. With only a common-school education, he enjoyed no college advantages. The religious connection of himself and family is with the Presbyterian Church, in which both himself and his father have held the office of ruling elder. In politics he has never sought or desired office; his first vote for President was cast for Andrew Jackson in 1832, and he has voted for every Presidential candidate of the Democratic party except Gen. Hancock, sickness preventing his attending the polls at that election. In 1855 he was nominated by the County Convention to represent Washington County in the Legislature, but was defeated on the Know-Nothing issue. In 1867 he was elected a member of the Constitutional Convention from Washington County, which met at Annapolis,

May 8, 1867, and framed the constitution of the State. His early life was passed in mercantile pursuits, from 1825 to 1831, in Williamsport, Md. In the latter year he was appointed executor of his late employer, and in 1832 entered into partnership with J. F. Dillinger, to conduct the dry-goods, grocery, and general variety business. This business continued until 1838, when he formed a partnership with John Baker in the same line of business, which continued until 1843, when he became, by the purchase of his partner's interest, the sole proprietor, and so continued until 1854, when a partnership was formed with Isaac Gruber, which continued until 1860, when he sold out his interest and retired from the mercantile business. He has been successful in all his enterprises. In December, 1859, he was elected cashier of the Washington County Bank of Williamsport, Md., which position he held until the bank was changed, in 1866, into a national bank, when he declined re-election as cashier, and was elected unanimously president of the Washington County National Bank, which office he resigned April, 1880, on account of ill health.

The Van Lear family. Among the oldest families of Western Maryland are the Van Lears, who for nearly a century have occupied the well-known Tammany plantation, near Williamsport, on the turnpike connecting that town with Hagerstown. According to " Foote's Historical Reminiscences," and well-established traditions in the family, its founder, John Van Lear, of sturdy Calvinist stock, emigrated from Holland in the early part of the eighteenth century and settled in Philadelphia, where he took an active part in the building of the first Presbyterian church erected in that city. His son, also named John, afterwards settled in Lancaster County, Pa. The descendants of John Van Lear separated into two branches, one of which, represented by Matthew and William, located first in Hagerstown. Matthew and William Van Lear engaged in trade with the West, and afterwards purchased a large tract of land in the vicinity of Williamsport, upon part of which the descendants of Matthew still reside. The other branch of the Lancaster family removed to Augusta County, Va., where its representatives are to be found. One of the Augusta Van Lears was present at the siege of Yorktown and the surrender of Cornwallis. One of the Maryland family, too, was only prevented from being present upon that memorable occasion by a serious wound received just previous to its occurrence. This was William Van Lear, who at the outbreak of the Revolutionary war joined the army, rose to the rank of major, and was frequently the guest at Gen. Washington's table, as autographic invitations preserved by the family still attest. Maj. Van Lear was wounded in a skirmish just prior to the surrender at Yorktown, which prevented him from witnessing that event. He carried the enemy's ball until his death, which his wound was supposed to have hastened. He was an original member of The Society of the Cincinnati. The other brother, Matthew, married Mary Irwin, of the well-known family of that name in Franklin County, Pa., and abandoning commercial pursuits about the close of the Revolutionary war, purchased a tract of land which he called "Tammany," after a well-known Indian chief of that name, and, after erecting the mansion so well known in the county, he settled there, and became an intelligent and successful farmer. There were born to him twelve children, many of whom, however, died young. Those who lived to a sufficient age, with one exception, were educated at the best seminaries and colleges in the country. He was a man of strong intellect, of sterling principle, and of unswerving convictions. In religion he was a Presbyterian, both by birth and by conviction, and to the forms and tenets of this church he clung with unyielding tenacity. In politics he was a Federalist, and was once the candidate which that party brought forward to contest congressional honors with Gen. Ringgold, the candidate of the Jeffersonian Republicans, who so long represented the district. He was defeated, and was thus left free to pursue his chosen occupation as a tiller of the soil until his death, which occurred on the 5th day of July, 1823. He is buried in the family lot at Williamsport.

John Van Lear, his oldest son, was born Nov. 18, 1786. He went to Baltimore when quite a youth, and afterwards achieved great success as a merchant, the firm of Finley & Van Lear, of which he was a partner, on Howard Street, being still remembered by very old citizens. Meeting with reverses, however, he returned to Williamsport, and subsequently became, first, president, and afterwards cashier, of the Washington County Bank, which institution he faithfully and acceptably served for more than a quarter of a century, dying in its service on the 24th of April, 1857. For public life he had little taste, although at one time he was a member of the Board of Public Works. Indeed, he had little time for such service, for although a bachelor, he had reared, as he afterwards said, more children than any head of a family in Washington County.

This feature of his life deserves special mention, and is much more worthy of being recorded and commemorated than the empty honors of Congress and the Legislature. At the time of his mother's death, the estate his father left behind him, although large, was somewhat involved, and not in a condition to be advantageously divided, and in consequence was held together, John Van Lear and his brothers, Dr. William, Joseph, and Matthew, undertaking to pay off the debts and to support and educate the children of the deceased heirs out of a common fund, which might be sufficient for the purpose, but which, if divided so that each one received the share to which he was entitled, would prove entirely inadequate. Matthew afterwards married and withdrew from the compact, and William having died in the service some years before, John and Joseph remained single, and for a period of nearly forty years, terminating only with death, devoted themselves to the task of rearing and educating nephews and nieces and grandnephews and grandnieces. Joseph, who was the youngest son, was born April 10, 1800, and had about completed his medical studies when this singular arrangement was entered into; but, abandoning all thoughts of professional reputation and emoluments, for which he had a fair chance, threw himself into the work with an energy of purpose and resolute self-denial as if he had been specially consecrated to it. He undertook the management of the outside affairs of the estate, which by additions soon amounted to nearly twelve hundred acres of land, besides a large commercial flouring-mill, in which many thousands of barrels of flour were annually manufactured. This was a large trust, but day and night, summer and winter, in cold and heat, his steady hand was never absent from the helm during all these long years of self-denial until its grasp was enfeebled by disease and finally loosened by death. He died on the 21st of October, 1859. John Van Lear managed the finances of the estate, and the two brothers were singularly well adapted for their respective positions, as the large estate, notwithstanding its original incumbrances and the heavy charges upon it in the mean time, left at their death, amply attests. It was finally divided in 1862.

Both the brothers were stanch Whigs in politics. Joseph Van Lear was born to lead a forlorn hope, and it can be written of him with perfect truth that he did not know what fear was. Dr. William was distinguished by the same intrepid spirit, dignity of character, and sterling worth which characterized all the members of this family. At the time of his death he was the most popular and successful physician in all the country surrounding Williamsport, in the town itself, and across the Potomac in Berkeley County, Va. He was born on the 29th of January, 1794, and died in May, 1837. Two of his sons still survive,—the Rev. Matthew, a minister of the Presbyterian Church, now settled at Winchester, Ky., and Maj. John Van Lear, at present paymaster of the Marietta and Cincinnati Railroad.

The eldest daughter and oldest child of Matthew Van Lear married Col. John Ramsey, of Pennsylvania, and became the mother of what were called forty years ago in Washington County the "beautiful Ramseys." There were three or four of these girls, distinguished for their exquisite grace of manner and person, who constituted a part of the orphan flock that the old bachelor uncles referred to took in charge. At the time they formed part of the household Tammany was a favorite resort of the yonng gallants of the county from far and near. Among others who was a constant visitor, was the late Hon. John V. L. McMahon, a first-cousin of their mother and bachelor uncles. Mr. McMahon was the son of William McMahon, of Cumberland, and of his first wife, who was a sister of Matthew Van Lear, the founder of Tammany. It may not be out of place here to state that his maternal uncle had the sagacity to foresee that a large city was the only fit arena for the display of his very remarkable talents, and when temporarily discouraged by his want of success in Baltimore, and about to return to Cumberland, and, indeed, on his way back, put money in his purse and told him to try the city again. The time of Mr. McMahon's visits was made the occasion of much merriment, and many were the pranks and tricks which still linger in the traditions of the old house. Mr. McMahon was baptized John Van Lear, after his maternal grandfather. The Misses Ramsey died young and unmarried, with the exception of Sarah, who married William Irwin, of Cincinnati, by whom she had a family of six children, all of whom at his death, with their widowed mother, subsequently returned to the old roof-tree at Tammany. There were, besides the daughter of Matthew Van Lear who married Col. Ramsey, twin sisters, married to two of the Finley brothers, John and Dr. Michael, sons of Ebenezer Finley, a prominent merchant in his day in Baltimore. One of these brothers, Dr. Michael, was long an able and successful physician in Williamsport, where he is buried. The other, John Finley, was a merchant in Baltimore. He had one daughter, who died young. Dr. and Mrs. Finley had no children. There was a fourth sister, the youngest of the twelve children of Matthew Van Lear. Her name was Sophia, and she married, in October, 1829, Archibald Irwin Findlay, a lawyer practicing in Chambersburg, Pa., a man of fine literary tastes and attainments. He was the son of William Findlay, who had been for years treasurer, then Governor of Pennsylvania, and afterwards United States Senator from that State, filling that position at the same time that his two brothers were members of the House of Representatives,—one of them, Col. John Findlay, from Pennsylvania, and the other, Gen. James Findlay, from Ohio. It is believed that the only other instance of the kind in the history of the country was the case of the three Washburn brothers. They, however, were members of the same House.

The only sister of Mr. Findlay was married to Francis R. Shunk, who, after filling many distinguished positions in Pennsylvania, died while serving his second term as Governor of the State and on the highroad to further promotion. A brother, James Findlay, became Speaker of the House of Delegates and Secretary of the Commonwealth under Governor Wolf, and at the time of his death was one of the leading lawyers of the bar at Pittsburgh. Another brother, John King Findlay, graduated at West Point, and after a short service in the army took up the profession of the law, and afterwards became judge in Philadelphia, and at Allentown and Easton. Still another brother, Samuel, who declined steady work and application, was recognized in all circles in which he entered as the most brilliant conversationalist of his time. Archibald I. Findlay died Oct. 8, 1839, in the forty-first year of his age, leaving his wife Sophia a widow with two children, James and Nancy I. Findlay. A third son was born some two months after his death, John V. L. Findlay. This family was taken into Tammany and carefully watched, tended, and educated by the same fostering care which had been extended to so many before. After the death of the old uncles, in the partition of the estate in 1862, the Tammany place was apportioned to Sophia, she being the last survivor of the old Van Lears. She died afterwards in the house in which she was born, on the 21st day of April, 1881, in the seventy-eighth year of her age. Mary Irwin, the wife of Matthew Van Lear, was born near Mercersburg, Franklin Co., Pa. She was a devoted, tender, and Christian mother, for whom all her children felt and expressed the deepest veneration to the last day of their lives. One of her sisters married Gen. James Findlay, and another William Findlay, Governor of Pennsylvania, before referred to. She had a brother Archibald, whose first wife was a sister of the Col. Ramsey before mentioned. One of his daughters married a son of Gen. Harrison, and during his short administration was the lady of the White House, and was distinguished for her grace and beauty. She had a brother, Capt. James Irwin, a graduate of West Point and Gen. Scott's quartermaster during the Mexican war, and at whose death of fever in the city of Mexico the general is said to have exclaimed "that the army wept." A sister of Mrs. Harrison married John Scott Harrison, another son of Gen. Harrison, and became the mother of the Hon. Benjamin Harrison, one of the senators of the United States from Indiana. "Tammany," the centre of these associations, was built of brick made on the place soon after the termination of the Revolutionary war, and now, after having witnessed many changes of ownership of the surrounding estates, can claim the distinction of still remaining in the same family. There are about four hundred and fifty acres in the tract, part of it wooded and generally well watered. The soil is limestone, well adapted to the growth of wheat, the staple crop of the country. There is a spring near the house which was once shaded by a magnificent elm, and tradition has it that Gen. Braddock on his fateful march rested for a while beneath its shade. "Tammany" is easily reached by rail and turnpike, and there is no house in the county, perhaps in the State, which has entertained so many guests, or sheltered so numerous a family. During the late war a battle was fought in its fields, all fencing was destroyed, and its crops and live stock were either consumed or driven off by the contending forces, but with the renovating hand of art and the gentle touch of time the old place has resumed its wonted thrift and order. One thing has, however, never faded or changed,—the undying devotion of the children who have been reared beneath its roof not only to the memory of their own parents, but to the two noble brothers who sheltered and protected them.

John Van Lear Findlay, a distinguished lawyer and public speaker of Baltimore, was born on the 21st of December, 1839, at Mount Tammany, near Williamsport, Washington Co., Md. His father, Archibald Irwin Findlay, was a sound lawyer and a man of excellent literary taste and accomplishments; his mother, Sophia Van Lear, the daughter of Matthew Van Lear, was born on the 12th of February, 1804. She was possessed of an unerring judgment and common sense which was never at fault, a lofty and intrepid spirit, and gifted with the most gracious and winning manners.

The paternal grandfather of the subject of this sketch was William Findlay, at one time Governor of Pennsylvania and also a senator from that State in the United States Senate.

John V. L. Findlay first married Mary C. Mackenzie, a daughter of Dr. John P. Mackenzie, one of the

oldest and most successful physicians of Baltimore. She died March 28, 1868, leaving one child, which subsequently died. His second wife was Mary Keesey, the daughter of a prominent lawyer of York, Pa. They were married 23d of January, 1878, and have two children living. He was educated by James Allen, a famous instructor of that day, in the "three Rs" at Williamsport, and also by John McCarthy, a graduate of Maynooth, by whom he was grounded in the classics. He was graduated from Princeton in 1858.

While very liberal in his views of religion, he inclines to the Presbyterian Church. In politics, he was reared by his mother's brothers, strong and violent Whigs, but at a time when the Whig party was more a memory than an active political force in shaping the politics of the country. His paternal ancestors were Jeffersonian Republicans, and during the late war he was an uncompromising Union man, belonging to the Unconditional Union party, and advocating the prosecution of the war until the unconditional surrender of all opposing forces. After the surrender at Appomattox, he was opposed to extreme and violent measures of reconstruction, and was in favor of restoring the Union to what it had been before the conflict, as near as the altered circumstances of the country would admit. Never a Republican in politics, he opposed the Congressional scheme of reconstruction.

In State politics he has been prominent and active, favoring the abolition or modification of the registration, which at the close of the war disfranchised so many citizens. These sentiments carried him and many other Union men into that wing of the Democratic party known as the Conservative, and it was in deference to these men and their sentiments that the compound name of "Democratic Conservative Party" was adopted in Maryland. He was a member of the Union Legislature of 1861–62, and chairman of the committee on militia. He drafted the bill for the relief of the families of Maryland volunteers in the service of the United States, and was also the author of the measure appropriating $7000 for the relief of the families of those men of the Sixth Massachusetts Regiment who suffered on the 19th of April. He was appointed by both Houses of the Legislature to deliver an address on the 22d of February, 1862, in commemoration of Washington's birthday. In that Legislature were the Hon. Reverdy Johnson, Allen Bowie Davis, John A. J. Creswell, R. Stockett Mathews, and many other distinguished lawyers and public men of the State. Yet among so many leading men Mr. Findlay took and held a prominent place. In his profession of the law he occupies a position among the first rank of lawyers at the Baltimore bar, having been the city solicitor for two years from March, 1876. As a political speaker he rendered great service to the Democratic party as well as to the Union party during the war. He has been called upon by the committees of his party to speak in Pennsylvania, Indiana, Virginia, and Maryland, and many of his speeches have been published. He was a prominent leader in the protest of the people of Baltimore against Sheridan's administration in Louisiana, and with Reverdy Johnson, S. T. Wallis, Thomas Donaldson, and William Pinkney Whyte, addressed the people of the city at the Masonic Temple, in February, 1875. He was commissioned and sworn into the military service of the United States, and authorized to raise a company in Washington County, in which effort he was foiled by the approach of Stonewall Jackson, which prevented all work of that kind. He visited and made the tour of Europe in 1873, in company with Andrew Sterret Ridgley. Mr. Findlay is a fluent and forcible speaker, quick at reply, and often eloquent. He has on many public occasions, and notably on the 19th of October, 1876, at the Centennial Exposition at Philadelphia, and before the Teachers' Association of Hagerstown, in August, 1869, delivered addresses which bore the stamp of great research and investigation.

Charles William Humrichouse was born March 13, 1824, at Fredericktown, Md., and resides at Springfield farm, near Williamsport, Washington Co., Md. He was the son of Charles Humrichouse, who was born in Philadelphia, Nov. 19, 1796. His mother's maiden name was Catherine Levy, born in Fredericktown, Md., Aug. 7, 1804. Mr. and Mrs. Humrichouse were married Sept. 4, 1821.

Peter Humrichouse, the paternal grandfather of Charles W., was born in York County, Pa., Oct. 10, 1753. At the age of eighteen he moved to Germantown, Pa., and May, 1776, entered the army as a private in a volunteer company under the command of Capt. Duning. He was commissioned ensign, with the rank of lieutenant, July, 1776, and was officer of the day when Washington crossed the Delaware and captured the Hessians at Trenton, N. J. His term of service expired shortly afterwards. He married on the 20th of February, 1777, and remained at home until September of the same year, when he re-entered the army, in the Second Battalion of Philadelphia troops, and continued in service until the close of the war. In 1798 he moved to Hagerstown, Md., and died there in 1836, aged eighty-four years. The wife of Peter Humrichouse was Mary Post, the only daughter of Rev. Christian Frederick Post, who came to this country as a missionary from the Church of England, and died in Germantown, Pa., May 14, 1785, aged seventy-five.

Charles W. married Mary Hawken, daughter of William and Sarah Hawken, of Hagerstown, Md., on May 6, 1846, and their children are William H., of the firm of Humrichouse & Baylies, of Baltimore; James Walker, a practicing physician in Hagerstown; Sarah Maria, the wife of Louis E. McComas, a lawyer of Hagerstown, Md.; and Mary, who died Dec. 4, 1872. He was educated at Frederick Academy and in Hagerstown. In religion he is a Lutheran, and in politics a Democrat.

One of the earliest friends of the Western Maryland Railroad, he is a director of that company, and president of the Agricultural Society of Washington County, and director in the Hagerstown Steam Engine and Machine Company of Hagerstown. From 1839 to 1847 he was engaged in the printing business, and in the latter year commenced the grocery business in Baltimore, in which he was engaged until 1879, when he retired to his present residence. Mr. Humrichouse has long been one of the most prominent and enterprising citizens of Washington County, and has done fully as much as any other single individual to advance its general prosperity and to promote its industries and trade. Mr. Humrichouse is a gentleman of large wealth, of great public spirit, kindly and benevolent in character, and of sound business judgment. His opinion is often sought by friends and neighbors before taking an important step or embarking in any doubtful enterprise, and he enjoys the warm esteem and unreserved confidence of the entire community. Mr. Humrichouse recently erected a fine block of buildings in Hagerstown, opposite the Baldwin House, occupied by Lowenstein Brothers, and has been the chief promoter of many important public improvements. In fact, it would be difficult to estimate too highly the benefits conferred by his exertions not only upon Hagerstown, but upon Washington County generally.

It falls to the lot of very few professional men to reach the period of forty-five years of uninterrupted practice in one locality. Such a record, however, has been achieved by Dr. Henry Zeller, of Williamsport, who in 1837, fresh from college, located in that town as its village doctor, and who has in that period steadily pursued his calling there, and has risen from comparative obscurity to be known and appreciated the county over as one of its most skillful physicians. Of the grown people of the place resident therein when he came to it in 1837, the survivors, he remarks, do not number more than a score.

Dr. Zeller comes of German ancestry, his great-grandfather having emigrated from Switzerland to America, and founded a new home in the then wilderness of Washington County. His son John entered the Continental service for the war of the Revolution as a member of the Maryland Line, and was killed at the battle of the Cowpens. He left four children,—Jacob, Martin, Otho, and Mary. Jacob was a man of some local mark in his day, and was once chosen to the House of Delegates. Otho, father to Dr. Zeller, was born in 1781, upon the old Zeller place, near Hagerstown, known now as the Red-Pump farm. On that farm Jacob Zeller kept the Red-Pump Tavern before the day of the railway, and at no point on the road between Philadelphia and the West was there a more popular or inviting roadside inn than the old Red Pump. Until 1856 the property had remained continuously in the hands of a Zeller from the time the first of the name cleared away the forest that encumbered it. Otho married, in 1807, Barbara, daughter of Nicholas Spichler, a native of Washington County. His wife dying in 1817, Mr. Zeller married for his second consort Elizabeth Bollinger, of Bedford County, Pa. Otho Zeller died in 1840. His widow survived him three years. By the first marriage there were three sons. Of these Dr. Zeller is the only one living. The only child of the second marriage is dead. Dr. Henry Zeller was born Aug. 17, 1810, in Washington County, six miles from Williamsport. He attended school at the Hagerstown Academy, studied medicine with the famous Dr. Frederick Dorsey, of Hagerstown, and graduated in 1837 at the Jefferson Medical School of Philadelphia. As already narrated, his first field of practice was Williamsport, and at Williamsport he has resided ever since. Being a country doctor in that day meant hard work about twenty hours out of each twenty-four, long rides, sleepless nights, and little pay. Dr. Zeller encountered all these experiences, and bravely bearing them, won enduring success at last. In 1839 he married Eleanor, daughter of James Anderson, of Alexandria, where the latter was a prominent merchant. She died one year after marriage, leaving one child. In October, 1844, he married Margaret E., orphan daughter of John Corcoran, a native of Delaware. She died in 1853. The children were three daughters and one son. The latter, John C., was at one time district attorney at Hagerstown, and died in 1873, while in office. Dr. Zeller's third marriage took place in 1871, with Mary, daughter of Henry Lefevre, of Washington County. By the last marriage there has been one son. Dr. Zeller was an Old-Line Whig, and is now a stalwart Republican. He

H. ZELLER.

has always taken a lively interest in the progress of political events, but judging that the faithful pursuit of his profession would not permit the indulgence, he has studiously held himself aloof from the business of the politician or the occupancy of any public office.

The College of St. James was founded and opened Oct. 3, 1842, under the title of St. James' Hall, as the diocesan school, in what had been the manor-house of Gen. Samuel Ringgold, at Fountain Rock (Indian name, Bai Yuka). The property was purchased by money raised by subscription, largely in Washington County, of members of the Protestant Episcopal Church, and devoted by them to the purposes of a church school. The active spirit in the matter was the Rev. T. B. Lyman, at that time rector of St. John's Church, Hagerstown, now bishop of the diocese of North Carolina. The charge of the school was placed in the hands of Rev. John Barrett Kerfoot, at the time one of the faculty of St. Paul's school, Flushing, N. Y. Dr. W. A. Muhlenberg had established St. Paul's, the first school of the kind in this country. Its success in forming the character and producing good men as well as good scholars had attracted the attention of the bishops, and Bishop Whittingham was the first to establish a school to be governed by the same principles, and to have the same ends in view. The more certainly to secure this he procured as the head master one who had been trained as scholar and teacher in that school. The interest of Dr. Muhlenberg was secured by making him joint adviser with the bishop. This latter arrangement, however, was soon abandoned by the withdrawal of Dr. Muhlenberg from all official connection. During the second year of its existence, February, 1844, a successful effort was made to obtain a college charter, and on the 9th of April the institution was reorganized under its legal title and character as "The College of St. James." The trustees of the college must, by the charter, be always members of and attached to the Protestant Episcopal Church. No endowment came with the charter; none was asked or expected. In 1845 it was found that the original buildings were not sufficient to accommodate the pupils, and an enlargement was made by extending one of the wings. In 1851 another enlargement was made by the building of Kemp Hall. This was a large five-story brick building, containing study-hall, dining hall, dormitories, lavatory, etc. In 1857, however, this building was completely destroyed by fire. In consequence of this calamity it was decided to remove the college proper to a more accessible place, as at this time there was no railroad nearer than Frederick. A site was selected in Baltimore County, near the present St. James' Post-office. A subscription was started, and it was determined to raise an endowment of one hundred and fifty thousand dollars, in addition to the nearly one hundred thousand dollars already raised for building, etc. The work of raising the money and erecting the buildings was progressing favorably when it was stopped by the breaking out of the civil war. The original buildings at Fountain Rock were intended to be retained as the grammar-school.

As the patronage of the college was chiefly from the South, it was greatly crippled in its resources. After a manful struggle for its existence it succumbed after the battle of Gettysburg, and was closed and the faculty scattered. Dr. Kerfoot, the president, was elected president of Trinity College, Hartford, Conn., but was subsequently elevated to the bishopric of Pittsburgh. He died in 1881. Under President Kerfoot's administration the college was prosperous, and was fully carrying out the expectations of its founders. It numbers among its graduates many men prominent at the bar and at the pulpit. Many of the clergy of this and other States owe their education to St. James', and among the prominent laymen who have been educated at the college may be mentioned such men as Hon. Ferdinand Latrobe, late mayor of the city of Baltimore, and Bernard Carter, the eminent lawyer of that city.

After the battle of Gettysburg, when Gen. Lee took possession of the grounds on his return to Virginia, the college was abandoned. The furniture was sold, and the library and apparatus removed to a place of safe-keeping. The following were the officers of the college at the time it was closed, in 1863: Board of Trustees, the Rt. Rev. W. R. Whittingham, D.D., Baltimore, Md. (since deceased); the Rev. John B. Kerfoot, D.D., Fountain Rock, Md. (since deceased); W. G. Harrison, Baltimore; the Rev. Jos. C. Passmore, Fountain Rock, Md. (since deceased); J. Mason Campbell, Baltimore (since deceased); Geo. W. Coaklay, LL.D., Fountain Rock, Md.; Frederick W. Brune, Jr., Baltimore (since deceased); Samuel G. Wyman, Baltimore; Rev. A. Cleveland Cox, Baltimore. Dr. Whittingham was president of the board, and Joseph C. Passmore was secretary. The vacancies in the board have since been partially filled by the appointment of Bishop William Pinkney,

GEORGE WILLIAM BROWN.

D.D., LL.D., of Washington, D. C., and Bernard Carter and Judge George William Brown, of Baltimore. The faculty and other officers of the college and grammar school were:

The Rev. John B. Kerfoot, D.D., Rector, Professor of the Evidences and Ethics of Christianity; the Rev. Jos. C. Passmore, M.A., Vice-Rector, Professor of Rhetoric, Intellectual Philosophy, and Political Economy; George W. Coaklay, LL.D., Professor of Mathematics, Analytical Mechanics, and Astronomy; the Rev. Julius M. Dashiell, M.A., Professor of the Latin and Greek Languages; Alexander Falk, Ph.D., Associate Professor of the Latin and Greek Languages and Professor of History; the Rev. Joseph H. Coit, M.A., Librarian, Professor of Physics and Natural History; M. S. V. Heard, Assistant Professor of the Latin and Greek Languages; George C. Shattuck, M.D., Lecturer on Anatomy, Physiology, etc.; Hugh Davey Evans, LL.D., Lecturer on Civil and Ecclesiastical Law, and on History; Lewis H. Steiner, M.D., Lecturer on Physics and Chemistry; Herman Vistris, M.A., Instructor in the French and German Languages; Rev. John K. Lewis, B.A., Instructor in Mathematics, and in charge of the Grammar School, etc.; Henry A. Skinner, B.A., Tutor in English; J. Thorne Clarkson, B.A., Tutor in History; Hall Harrison, B.A., Tutor in Latin and Greek; Max Lenzberg, Instructor in Instrumental Music; J. W. Breathed, Secretary of the College and Curator for the Students.

Up to the time of the closing of the college the following trustees had been connected with the management of the institution:

By charter, Feb. 29, 1844: Frederick Dorsey, M.D., Hon. Thomas Buchanan (resigned 1844), John R. Dall, (resigned 1845), Right Rev. W. R. Whittingham, D.D. (deceased), Rev. Theodore B. Lyman (resigned 1845), Rev. John B. Kerfoot, D.D. (died 1881), Rev. Reuben Riley (resigned 1845), Rev. Russell Trevett, Rev. Dwight E. Lyman (resigned 1848), Hon. John Buchanan, elected 1844, died 1844; William G. Harrison, elected 1845; Rev. Joseph C. Passmore, elected 1845, dead; J. Mason Campbell, elected 1846, dead; George W. Coakley, LL.D., elected 1848, resigned 1863; Rev. William G. Jackson, elected 1850, resigned 1854; Rev. Julius M. Dashiell, elected 1854; Frederick W. Brune, elected 1855, dead.

The degree of LL.D. was conferred in 1850 upon Hugh Davey Evans and John Henry Alexander, and in 1852 upon James Alfred Pearce. The building was going to ruin when it was taken in hand by the present management, under a lease from the trustees, and conducted as a grammar-school. While it retains its character as the diocesan school for boys, it is in reality a private enterprise.

The first rector of the college, as has already been mentioned, was the late Bishop Kerfoot, of Pittsburgh, who remained at the head of the college until it was closed in 1863.

John Barrett Kerfoot was born in 1816, in Ireland, but came to this country in early boyhood. He received his education from that eminent teacher, the Rev. Wm. Augustus Muhlenberg, of St. Paul's College, New York. Of all Dr. Muhlenberg's scholars, Mr. Kerfoot, as he was one of the first, was also one of the most distinguished. About the year 1842, Mr. Kerfoot married Eliza, daughter of the late Abel T. Anderson, of New York. In the same year, 1842, occurred another event, which may justly be regarded as one of the most important in his life. Bishop Whittingham, who had lately been called to preside over the diocese of Maryland, was exceedingly anxious to obtain a suitable principal and rector for the new school which he was about to found, and which afterwards became the College of St. James.

After looking about unsuccessfully in various quarters, he decided to apply to the man who was the most eminent educator at that time in the Episcopal Church, the Rev. Dr. Muhlenberg. After some correspondence Dr. Muhlenberg consented to give up to Bishop Whittingham his old pupil and friend, Prof. Kerfoot, who removed to Maryland and became the head of the new establishment. His twenty-two years' labor at St. James' College forms no unimportant chapter of the unwritten history of the diocese of Maryland. The college went on quietly and unobtrusively, but growing in importance and usefulness year by year until in 1864 the desolations of war and the tramp of hostile armies brought to an untimely end the work to which the Bishop of Maryland and his rector had devoted the best years of their vigorous manhood. The situation of the College of St. James, on the border line between North and South, made the effort to carry on the institution very difficult, and at times even perilous. But it was not at once abandoned. The students were mostly from the Southern States. These soon took their departure, many of them to join the Confederate army. Most of those from Maryland who remained sympathized with the Southern cause. Dr. Kerfoot was known to be an earnest adherent of the Union, and it is one of the strongest proofs of his transparent honesty and firmness, and yet generous consideration of the views of others, that he was able without loss of respect to continue the head of such an institution at a time of such unparalleled excitement.

At length, however, the prospect of successfully continuing the institution became manifestly hopeless. In the summer of 1864, Gen. Early with a Confederate army crossed the Potomac and proceeded through Maryland to Chambersburg, in Pennsylvania. The students of the college were hastily dismissed by the only route which remained accessible, and not long after a portion of the army encamped upon the beautiful grounds of the college. The officers were accommodated in the buildings, some of them in the rector's own house. One morning, while Dr. Kerfoot was sitting at breakfast with some of these officers, an orderly rang the bell, and presented a dispatch from Gen. Early, who was a few miles distant. It proved to be an order to the officer in charge to place under close arrest the Rev. Dr. Kerfoot and another clergyman, one of the professors of the college. The officer, Maj. H. Kyd Douglass, was unable to give any reason for the unpleasant duty which had been laid upon him of arresting the host who was at that very time hospitably entertaining him. There was, however, no help for it, and the mystery was soon explained by the arrival of Gen. Early in person. Gen. Early, with many regrets, informed Dr. Kerfoot that orders had been received from Richmond to arrest two of the most prominent clergymen he could lay hands on, in retaliation for the imprisonment of the Rev. Hunter Boyd, a Presbyterian minister of Winchester, Pa., who had been arrested by Gen. Milroy. Dr. Kerfoot and his brother professor were then released on parole, under solemn promise to repair to Washington and obtain the unconditional release of Mr. Boyd. Failing to accomplish this, they were pledged to go to Richmond and surrender themselves to the Confederate authorities. Anticipating little difficulty, the promise was readily given. It proved, however, no easy task to untie the red tape of the War Department. There was no record or information attainable in Washington about Mr. Boyd's arrest, which appeared to have been wholly unauthorized. At last, after much running to and fro and sending many telegrams, an order was obtained from Secretary Stanton requiring the immediate and unconditional release of the prisoner, and Dr. Kerfoot and his companion, Prof. Jos. H. Coit, were restored to their friends. This was the end for the time being of the College of St. James.

Dr. Kerfoot died July 9, 1881, at Pittsburgh, Pa., having since the closing of St. James' College been made bishop of that diocese. He has been prominent before the church as a bishop during the fifteen years of his episcopate.

The following persons have been connected at different times with the faculty of St. James' College:

Russell Trevett, D.D., a native of New York, brought up a Congregationalist, was ordained by Bishop Onderdonk, of New York, in 1841. He removed to Maryland, and officiated as missionary and assistant in St. John's Parish. In 1843 he became Professor of Languages in St. James' College, and in 1855, Professor of Languages at St. John's College, Annapolis.

Reuben Riley, a native of Canada, brought up in the church, was ordained by Bishop Onderdonk, of New York, in 1843, and became vice-rector of St. James' College. In 1846 he accepted a call to the rectorship of St. Luke's, Baltimore.

Dwight Edwards Lyman, a native of Connecticut, and a brother of Dr. T. B. Lyman, was ordained by Bishop Whittingham in 1844. He was assistant teacher and adjunct professor in St. James' College, and became assistant minister in St. John's Parish, Washington County. In 1849 he removed to Pennsylvania, and in 1853 joined the Catholic Church.

Joseph Clarkson Passmore was vice-rector and professor of St. James' College about 1848, in which year he was ordained by Bishop Whittingham. He was also rector of St. Mark's, Washington County. He removed in 1862 to Racine, Wis., and died Aug. 12, 1866. He published a life of Bishop Butler, some of whose works he edited, and some poetry.

Robert Heber Clarkson, D.D., was the rector's assistant at St. James' College in 1848. On the 18th of June of that year he was ordained by Bishop Whittingham, and in 1849 removed to Chicago, Ill., where he became rector of St. James' Church. He continued there for seventeen years, and on the 15th of November, 1865, was consecrated Bishop of Dakotah and Nebraska.

In 1849, James Cole Tracey became a professor in St. James' College, and in 1850 was officiating in Troy, N. Y. He died in Baltimore in 1855. He was ordained by Bishop Whittingham in 1846.

Julius Matthias Dashiell, D.D., was ordained by Bishop Whittingham in 1852, and became assistant professor and afterwards vice-rector of St. James' College, Hagerstown, where he continued until 1863. Subsequently he became Professor of Ancient Languages at St. John's College, a position which he held until the summer of 1881, wnen he resigned to take charge of a parish.

Rev. Edward Augustus Colburn, a native of Baltimore, and brought up in the church, was a tutor in St. James' College about 1853 or 1854, and afterwards became assistant in St. Luke's, Baltimore.

Rev. Joseph Howland Coit, assistant professor in St. James' College, Hagerstown, was ordained by Bishop Whittingham in 1854. He afterwards became professor in the same institution, and in 1861 removed to Virginia.

Rev. James Kerfoot Lewis, a native of Pennsylvania, brought up a Methodist, and ordained by Bishop Whittingham in 1858, was also at one time a tutor of St. James' College.

Leonard John Mills, a native of Calvert County, and brought up in the church, was ordained by Bishop Whittingham in 1859. He was a tutor in St. James' College, and assistant at St. Mark's, Washington County. He removed in 1862 to Prince George's County, and died in 1867.

Robert John Coster, a native of Calvert County, was a tutor in St. James' College, of which institution he was a graduate. He was ordained deacon by Bishop Whittingham, March 1, 1863, and in 1866 removed to Pittsburgh.

In 1860, Rev. Meyer Lewin was appointed agent for St. James' College. Dr. Lewin, who is a native of Prussia, was ordained by Bishop Whittingham in 1844.

With St. James' College since its commencement there have been connected the following clergymen of the Episcopal Church: Rev. Drs. M. Kerfoot, Trevett, Passmore, and Falk, and the Rev. Messrs. J. Dashiell, Coit, Clarkson, Mills, and Lewis.

Some time after the close of the war Henry Onderdonk, the present principal of St. James', made a proposition to the trustees, which provided for the reopening of the grammar-school. His proposition was at once accepted, and in 1869 he began the work of repairing and improving the college buildings and grounds, and in a short time they were restored to their former condition. The site of the buildings possesses an historic interest as being the home for many years of Gen. Samuel Ringgold and the birthplace of Maj. Samuel Ringgold, the gallant artillery officer, who was killed at the battle of Palo Alto during the war with Mexico. The college grounds are beautifully situated, and are about five miles from Hagerstown by way of the Sharpsburg turnpike. The original college buildings were designed by the architect of the national capitol, B. H. Latrobe, father of J. H. B. Latrobe, of Baltimore, and grandfather of F. C. Latrobe, late mayor of that city. The centre building—Claggett Hall—was erected in Revolutionary times by Gen. Samuel Ringgold, who was one of the most distinguished public men of Maryland, and whose hospitality was famous. Among his guests was Gen. Washington before he became President. From a distance the college presents a striking appearance, its lofty mansard roof towering above the elms and willows which cluster around it. Very important additions have been made to the structure left standing after the war, which comprise a school-house, chapel, dormitory, play-room, bath-houses, etc. The library is quite extensive, and contains all necessary appliances for the purposes of the students at the college. Back of the college is the spring of water, gushing from a fissure of a rock, which gave the estate its name of Fountain Rock. This natural fountain was famous among the Indians before the settlement of the country. The commanding situation of the college, presenting a view for miles of a most beautiful and picturesque country, and its spacious grounds, handsomely laid out and tastefully decorated, render it one of the most attractive places in Washington County. The institution is now under the personal control and management of Henry Onderdonk, and is a grammar-school of high grade and a preparatory academy for students seeking a higher collegiate education. Its faculty consists of the principal and the following professors: of Mathematics, Henry M. Onderdonk, M.D.; Latin and Greek, John H. Chew; French and German, Bernard Auer; Chaplain, Rev. Henry Edwards; Tutor, Jas. R. Colburn. Its post-office address is St. James' College, Washington County, and the nearest railway station is within a few minutes' walk of its entrance.

WEST HAGERSTOWN DISTRICT, No. 3.

Hagerstown lies partly in in two election districts, West Hagerstown District, No. 3, and East Hagerstown District, No. 17. West Hagerstown District, including that portion of Hagerstown proper which lies within its boundaries (the population of which is 3188), contains 4031 inhabitants. The district is bounded on the north by Conococheague District, on the east by East Hagerstown, on the south by Funkstown and Williamsport Districts, and on the west by Williamsport and Conococheague Districts. It is traversed by numerous excellent roads, and by the Western Maryland and Cumberland Valley Railways. The Baltimore and Ohio Railway (Washington County Branch) crosses its southeastern corner. The Washington County Agricultural Society's fair-grounds are located in this district, just outside of Hagerstown, and the village of Pikeville is situated partly in the western portion of West Hagerstown District and partly in Conococheague. The history of the district is incorporated in the chapter on Hagerstown.

CLEAR SPRING DISTRICT, No. 4.

In 1800 the boundaries of Clear Spring Election District, No. 4, were thus officially described:

> "Beginning at Swingley's mill on the Conococheague Creek, and running thence with District No. 3 to the State line; thence with the State line to where it intersects the Green Spring Furnace Run; thence with the run to the river Potomac: thence down the river to the Conococheague Creek; and thence with the creek to the place of beginning."

The district was known as "Number Four," and the elections were held at the house of Joseph Fiery.

In 1821 the Legislature made some changes in the district, and it was then described as follows:

> "The boundary line to commence at the beginning of District No. 3 on the Conococheague Creek; thence down said creek and with the lines of District No. 2 to the high rocks on the Potomac; thence with the Potomac River to the mouth of Licking Creek; thence with the creek to the Pennsylvania line, and with said line to the place of beginning."

The Levy Court of Washington County at the same time designated the house of James Prather as the place for holding the elections in the district, and appointed the following commissioners to manage the school fund: James Bowles (president), Benjamin Cushwa, Michael Bovey, Jacob Dunn, John Barrett. Clear Spring District at present is bounded on the north by the Pennsylvania line, and extends south as far as the Potomac River. Conococheague Creek forms a part of the eastern boundary, dividing it in part from Conococheague and Williamsport Districts. Indian Spring District is on the west. The district contains two towns of considerable size, Conococheague and Clear Spring, which are situated on the great turnpike which extends entirely across it. Between these two towns is the little village of Shady Bower. Conococheague is situated upon a bend of the creek which gives the name to the town. Clear Spring is in the western portion of the district, at the foot of

North Mountain, and is a place of considerable historic interest. Little Conococheague Creek flows from among the mountains in the northwestern portion of the district, in a southeasterly course into Conococheague Creek proper, and one of the affluents of Little Conococheague, Tom's Run, passes from its source in North Mountain through Clear Spring. The Chesapeake and Ohio Canal extends through the southern portion of the district along the course of the Potomac River, and a little hamlet known as Two Locks is situated on the canal near the double locks, which were found necessary in order to utilize the Potomac River itself for the distance of about a mile. The population of the district (including the town of Clear Spring, which has 721 inhabitants) is 2715.

Clear Spring, naturally, is one of the most interesting sections in Washington County, the mountain scenery in the northwestern portion being surpassed in beauty by few spots in Maryland or Virginia. A cluster of mountains grouped above the town of Clear Spring form a magnificent vantage-ground, from which to view, to the utmost extent of vision, a far-reaching landscape of picturesque beauty, which it would be difficult to equal anywhere in the county. The North Mountain range is broken by a solitary peak, Mount Gilliland, at the northwest of which is Blair Valley Mountain, and on the northeast and south are the broken halves of North Mountain range. It has been maintained that valuable mineral deposits exist in these mountains, and efforts have been made to successfully locate coal-fields and iron strata. Experts have from time to time visited Blair Valley Mountain, and some of them have been fully convinced that such deposits of coal, as will some day be valuable, are hidden beneath its rugged surface.

During the fall of 1873 a survey for the extension of the Western Maryland Railroad was made through Ernst's Gap, and at that time, in order to encourage the extension into Clear Spring District, an effort was then made to show the existence of iron ore on the route. The gentlemen interested commenced digging, and conducted their experiments through a great many difficulties and discouragements. The first shaft cut through a carboniferous limestone rock filled with fossils, from which after exposing the outcrop of a vein of rich hematite ore, about nine feet thick, it came to a stratum of blue clay, containing carbonaceous matter and gas. Into this a shaft was sunk about thirty-five feet, but had to be stopped on account of surface water running in. A shaft was then started a little farther west to reach the underlying stratum. It is to be understood that all the strata in the valley, dip at an angle of about 65° to the southeast, and towards the northwest. This shaft was sunk vertically to the depth of seventy feet through coal shale. The water from a very heavy rain in August, 1873, drove the workers out, and they immediately started shaft No. 3, sixty-five feet farther west. At the depth of forty feet they struck a vein of what is known as shaken coal, which was not pure, because at that particular point of outcrop it had been disturbed, was saturated with water, and its mineralization stopped. They followed the strike of vein for about seventy-five feet, and though the coal was getting more solid, were induced to return to shaft No. 2 and drift westerly for vein, it being thirty feet deeper. They passed through shale, and then through eighteen feet of black laminated slate (which showed disturbance by being very much fractured), and struck the vein of coal which was shaken as above. They cut *into* the vein twelve feet, and then had to abandon both shafts, on account of the fall rains. They then selected a fourth locality (on the strike of strata) on the spur of Mount Gilliland, where the strata had *support* on the west. (This was not the case at shafts Nos. 2 and 3, a deep ravine being directly abreast on the west side of them, and the disturbance at this point was caused by the undermining of strata, etc.)

Here they found the alluvial cover to be about thirty-five feet deep at this point, and then struck a deposit of variegated sand strata, filled with fossil shell, etc., and in a position approaching verticality, showing that they were unquestionably in a land slide from the mountain-top.

At the depth of seventy-four feet, thinking they were low enough to strike the outcrop of vein by drifting, the workers started westward and soon found that the vein had been washed off to that level. Keeping on, however, at the end of about forty feet in drift they struck a vein of heavy brown hematite about six feet thick; then at seventy feet in drift they reached the coal formation, the stratum being a grayish slate clay, and this they cut into about ten feet, when they stopped in drift and started down again in shaft. At the depth of one hundred and fifty-eight feet from surface, a two-foot vein of clay iron stone (common in the coal measures) was struck, and from that into fire-brick clay intermixed with thin seams of almost pure anthracite. This proved the land slip to be one hundred and fifty-eight feet deep. They worked on down to the depth of two hundred and two feet in all, or forty-four feet in the coal formation, and without having struck a drop of water *in shaft*. At the end of only eight feet in, they pierced a solid ore rock, and the water came in such quantities as to make it impracticable to keep on.

Nothing daunted, they resumed work again in drift above for other veins in the deposit. They advanced one hundred and sixty feet in the gray slate, and the length of the drift from the shaft is about two hundred and thirty feet. The material changed considerably in the last ten feet. They were at least one hundred feet from surface at the end of drift.

Nothing of importance, however, came of these explorations, and the question of coal and iron deposits is still an interesting one. The railroad extension was never made, and no railroad touches any portion of the district, the nearest station being Cherry Run, W. Va., on the Baltimore and Ohio road. The land in Clear Spring District, which is below the mountains in the northwest, is well cleared, and principally limestone, is well cultivated, and very productive. It readily yields from ten to fifty bushels of wheat, forty to sixty bushels of corn, and two tons of hay per acre, and is worth from ten to one hundred dollars.

Clear Spring.—The town of Clear Spring was a sparsely-settled neighborhood in the beginning of the nineteenth century, but grew into a small hamlet during the first decade, and soon became the voting-place of the district. Of its very early history little is known. A post-office was established there in 1823, of which Nicholas Lower was made postmaster. Among the early residents of Clear Spring were the following tavern-keepers: Thomas Geogegan, Barton Carricoe, Daniel Harbine, James Kirkpatrick, Denton Jacques. Dr. Emanuel Francis died there in 1812, and letters addressed to the following persons were left at Martin Myers old tavern-stand in April, 1821: James Ashkettle, Wm. Blackmore, Joseph Charles, Andrew Krick, George Miller, Peter Nead, Jacob Snyder, William Wools.

At a meeting of the voters of the district, held at the house of Henry Fiery, in May, 1812, Dr. Emanuel Francis was chairman, and John T. Mason was secretary. The following district representative committee was appointed: Nicholas Ridenour, John McClain, John Adams, John Johnson, John Cushwa, Emanuel Francis, and John Wolgamot.

Among the residents of Clear Spring in the next decade were Dr. S. R. Beatty, who practiced in 1824; Dr. Thomas Hammond, who was in practice there in 1823; and Dr. James J. Beatty, who was there the same year. The following were inn-keepers: Daniel Brewer, Andrew Brewer, and George Lowe. Benjamin Beem had been a tavern-keeper at the stand known as "Carlisle's," near Green Spring iron-works, in 1805. The first sale of lots took place in 1822, and the town in 1825 consisted of forty-seven dwelling-houses, some of which were large and commodious brick dwellings. It contained four stores, three taverns, two doctors, a school-house, a post-office, and two hundred and ninety inhabitants, of whom fifteen were carpenters, nine shoemakers, six tailors, four masons, three cabinet-makers, three wheelwrights, three wagon-makers, three saddlers, two tanners, two blacksmiths, two plasterers, two physicians, one clergyman, one barber, and one butcher.

At present Clear Spring has a population of about one thousand, contains seven churches, Lutheran, Reformed, Presbyterian, Methodist, Protestant Episcopal, Catholic, and Methodist Colored, and several schools. The town officers are Burgess, John Switzer; Assistant, Amos Spielman; Commissioners, Isaac Sprecher, John T. Peterman, Samuel Bayard, James Lohr, and John Powers. Solomon Steinmetz is postmaster. The practicing physicians of the town are Drs. F. C. Doyle, G. N. Richardson, and Adam A. Shank.

Dr. Frederick Charles Doyle, for seventeen years a practicing physician in Clear Spring and vicinity, was born near Hagerstown, Nov. 24, 1839. His paternal ancestors were among the pioneers of that section of Pennsylvania known as Path Valley, and, according to tradition, were more than once compelled to abandon their homes for the shelter of Fort Carlisle, by reason of Indian incursions into the settlement. Dr. Doyle's great-great-grandfather was a captain under Gen. Braddock, and assisted in founding the pioneer Catholic Church of Path Valley. His maternal grandfather, John Byer, was a captain in the war of 1812. The Byers came from Prussia at an early day, and located in Lancaster County, Pa., where the family became widely prominent. William E. Doyle moved from Path Valley to Washington County, Md., when a young man, and after an extended experience as a farmer, miller, and distiller, became the landlord of Doyle's Hotel, now the Antietam House of Hagerstown. For fifteen years he conducted that hostlery with much success, and made it a famous place of resort. He was a strong Henry Clay Whig, served one term as legislator, one term as county commissioner, several terms as tax collector, and was one of the best-known men in the county. In 1863 he retired from business. He died in Hagerstown in July, 1865. His wife was Margaret, daughter of Capt. John Byer, of Leitersburg. She died in Hagerstown in 1860. Their two surviving sons are Dr. Doyle, of Clear Spring, and John E. Doyle, of California.

Dr. Doyle received his early education at Mount St. Mary's College, attended a course of medical lectures at the University of Maryland, and graduated at that institution in March, 1859. His first field of practice was Bradford County, Pa., where he remained from 1860 to 1865, when he changed his location to Clear Spring, where he has been in active practice ever since. His circuit in Pennsylvania was

H. C. Doyle. M. D.

a large one, and embraced portions of Bedford and Fulton Counties. Journeys of from sixty to seventy-five miles were frequent experiences in his early professional career. By unflagging energy and skill in his profession Dr. Doyle has risen to a conspicuous place among the physicians of Washington County. He was married, April 19, 1871, to Laura, daughter of Henry McLaughlin, of Franklin County. He has never held a public office and has never aspired to one, his professional duties engaging all his time and attention.

The two hotels are kept by Samuel Bovey and F. Fellinger & Son. T. B. Johnson and Allen A. Nesbitt are justices of the peace. Clear Spring is one of the most compactly built towns in Western Maryland. It is nestled at the foot of North Mountain, and the country about is uneven and irregular. The National turnpike runs directly through the town, in which it takes the name of Cumberland Street, which is the principal thoroughfare, and is solidly built up on either side. Market Street, which intersects it at right angles, is the next most important street. Mill Street, running parallel with Market and to the east of it, contains a number of fine residences. The Episcopal church and St. John's Reformed church are both on Cumberland Street, the former west of Market and the latter east of Mill Street. St. Michael's Catholic church, the Presbyterian church, and the Lutheran church are on Market Street below Mulberry, which runs parallel with Cumberland and to the south of it. The Methodist church is on Mill Street. One of the chief enterprises of the town is M. L. Beard's large tannery on Mulberry Street. In 1849 a weekly newspaper was started in Clear Spring under the management of L. Jewett Grove, and was known as *The Clear Spring Sentinel,* and in 1850 *The Whig* was issued by Charles E. Lewis, which was three years later supplanted by *The Fountain of Health.* There is at present, however, no newspaper issued in the town.

Among the most prominent merchants, farmers, and business men in Clear Spring District are Isaac, John T., and David Ankeny, Wm. Cushwa, John T. Cowton, Milton, Joel, and Benjamin F. Charles, E. Frantz, L. I. Feidt, Chas. S. Goodrich, D. M. Grove, Rudolph Herr, Rudolph Kreps, A. J. Kershner, Fred. H. Luther, Jonathan Loose, Daniel Mason, John A. Miller, S. M. Reitzell, F. T. Spickler, Amos Spielman, W. E. Smith, Christian Shup, Peter J. Sowns, Cornelius Summers, David Seibert, Joseph Seibert, Abraham Shup, R. H. Wilson, J. D. Young, Samuel K. Yost, and B. S. Zeller.

William Cushwa, one of the prominent farmers of Washington County, was born Oct. 22, 1810, six miles from his present residence. His father (David) was born on the same farm in 1778. He was a captain in the war of 1812, and died in 1849 on the present David Cushwa place. His widow died in 1862. Two of his daughters (Mrs. Thomas Herbert and Catharine McLaughlin) and four sons (William, David, James, and John) still survive. The father of David Cushwa and grandfather of William Cushwa was one of Pennsylvania's early settlers, and in 1754 assisted in the construction of Braddock's road, in the southwestern part of the State. He migrated from Lancaster County, Pa., to Washington County, Md., and there passed the remainder of his life. He was in every sense a true pioneer, and with unflinching fortitude bore up against and overcame such obstacles as would have driven many men from the field. Of the wilderness he made a fruitful garden, and to his descendants transmitted that sturdiness of purpose and faithful energy which rarely fail to win success. William Cushwa, son of David, was reared as a farmer, and the little education he obtained was imparted by rural teachers near his home. At the age of twenty he left home and entered the store of Hammett & Ridenour, at Clear Spring, where he remained eight years. He was subsequently employed by George Edlen, of Clear Spring, with whom he remained three

years, and in 1841 he was appointed postmaster at Clear Spring. In 1845 he ended his term as postmaster, married, and settled on a farm at the foot of the mountain. In 1856 he moved to his present home, then barren of improvements. It is now a fine farm of two hundred and four acres, and among the best appointed in the county. In 1864 he was elected to the Legislature and rendered excellent service to his constituents. Always a devoted admirer of Henry Clay, he was a strong Whig until the party became extinct. He was a stanch Union man during the war, and now makes it a rule to be strictly independent,—in favor of men, rather than of political theories or opinions. As a farmer he has been very successful, and as a citizen he occupies a high position in popular regard. In the fall of 1845 he married Ann Elizabeth, daughter of Samuel Prather, of Clear Spring, whose grandfather, Richard, was among the earliest settlers of Washington County. Richard Prather patented a tract, called "Richard's Choice." Launcelot Jacques, grandfather of Richard Prather's wife, patented land in Washington County in 1740, having with other Huguenots fled from France in 1720. He was a partner with Governor Thomas Johnson in the Green Spring Furnace, and in 1776 carried on the work on his own account. Samuel Prather died in 1846. Three of his daughters are living. Of William Cushwa's children those living are two sons (William J. and Samuel) and two daughters (Elizabeth J. and Mary C.).

Churches at Clear Spring.—The Lutheran and German Reformed congregations worshiping at St. Paul's Church were first organized in 1773, and were then called "the Lutheran and Presbyterian German congregations on the west side of Conococheague bridge." They owned jointly a log church about seven miles west of Hagerstown and two miles east of the present site of St. Paul's, which was located in the "Cedars," half a mile south of Conococheague bridge, in which they continued to worship until the completion, in 1798, of the present church. The latter was built by the grandparents of those who worship there now. Having been jointly erected by the members of the Lutheran and German Reformed congregations, St. Paul's has ever since been held as a Union Church, with equal rights of worship and church government. It was incorporated under the general act of Assembly of Maryland, passed in 1800, and continues to elect biennially elders and deacons of both congregations, who, in connection with the pastors, form the joint council.

The principal Lutheran families during the early history of St. Paul's, and who aided chiefly in its erection, were the Brewers, Firys, Barkmans, and Stines; and among the families of the Reformed congregation were the Ankeneys, Millers, Garlocks, and Hellers, many of whose descendants still worship in the same church, and it was not until the pastorate of the Rev. Benjamin Kurtz, somewhere about 1820, that the increase in membership of the church was such as to make it necessary to form a separate charge of the congregations at Williamsport and St. Paul's. They continued to support the same pastor for forty-three years, when St. Paul's withdrew and united with the Clear Spring charge. In 1837, during the ministry of Rev. Christian Startzman, the interior of St. Paul's was thoroughly repaired and remodeled; the pulpit, which before had stood on the north side of the church, and was perched, like a hogshead, midway between the floor and the ceiling, was lowered to its present position, and placed at the west end of the building. The old pews, with high backs and devoid of paint, were removed, to give place to more modern seats, and, in short, the whole of the interior was reconstructed. Soon after the church had been remodeled a season of revivals ensued in the winter of 1841 and 1843, which surpassed in interest and extent any that had previously taken place in the church. The first Lutheran pastor of St. Paul's, and during whose ministry the church was built, was Rev. Dr. George Schmucker, who served the congregation longer than any of its pastors, viz., from 1795 to 1809. Rev. Solomon Schaeffer was the next pastor, and he served from 1809 to 1813; Rev. Henry Baughy served from 1813 to 1815; Rev. Benjamin Kurtz, 1816–25; Rev. Frederick Ruthrauff, 1826–27; Rev. John Winter, 1827–32; Rev. Simeon Harkey, 1832–35; Rev. Daniel Miller, 1836–39; Rev. Christian Startzman, 1839–50; Rev. Henry Bishop, 1850–53; Rev. Wm. Greaver, 1854–56; Rev. Joseph Barclay, 1857–59; Rev. Christian Lepley, 1860–64; Rev. C. Berlin, 1864–66; Rev. M. L. Culler, 1867–69; Rev. C. Startzman, 1869–73; Rev. David Swope began his ministry Nov. 1, 1875.

Rev. George Schmucker, the first pastor of the Lutheran congregation at St. Paul's, was a native of Germany, who emigrated to the United States when a young man and became the pioneer of the Lutheran Church in Southern Pennsylvania and Western Maryland. The oldest Lutheran church in Washington County was Beard's church, not far from Smithsburg, which is now in ruins. St. John's Lutheran church, in Hagerstown, and St. Paul's church are next in point of age, and were both built in 1795, although the latter cannot be said to have been entirely completed until 1798, three years later. They were both erected, however, during the ministry of Rev. George Schmucker and through his instrumentality, and they were both included in his pastoral charge. The whole territory of Washington County was at that time missionary ground, known familiarly as the "Black Woods," through which the young missionary (as he then was), George Schmucker, rode on horseback, and over rough roads, a distance of more than a hundred miles, often fording the swollen streams, and at the frequent peril of life and limb, to minister to the scattered congregations of his charge. The congregations at Hagerstown, Funkstown, Boonsboro', Beard's Church, and St. Paul's, were all embraced in his charge at that time, and for a period of fourteen years he labored with great zeal and success. In 1875 there was still living in Washington County, Peter Brewer, then eighty-eight years old, who received catechetical instruction from Dr. Schmucker. During the fourteen years of his ministry, Dr. Schmucker preached principally in the German tongue, as it was then the prevailing language in the settlement, and continued to be so for twenty years after. He died at York, Pa., in the eighty-sixth year of his age.

Rev. Solomon Schaeffer was the second pastor of St. Paul's congregation. He was a native of Pennsylvania, and like his predecessor conducted public worship in the German language. His ministry at St. Paul's terminated in an early death, after three years of faithful labor. He died in 1813.

Rev. Henry Baughy completed his studies for the ministry under the tutelage of Rev. Solomon Schaeffer, and, at the latter's death, Mr. Baughy succeeded him as pastor in 1814. His call to the congregation aroused opposition on the part of some of the members, which continued for a year and six months from his succession, when he was deposed for conduct unbecoming a minister.

Rev. Benjamin Kurtz was called to be pastor of the charge in the fall of 1815. He found the congregation much divided and demoralized, owing to the misconduct of his predecessor. The tact and ability of the new pastor soon reconciled all differences and restored harmony among the members, insomuch that the growth of the church was very apparent, and the increase of members so great that during the eight years of Mr. Kurtz' ministry it was found necessary to form a separate charge. Mr. Kurtz was for many years editor of the Lutheran *Observer*, and a minister of great ability and influence. He was also the founder of the Missionary Institute at Selin's Grove, Pa. He died Dec. 29, 1865, in Baltimore, in his seventy-first year. Rev. Frederick Ruthrauff was next chosen pastor of the Williamsport and St. Paul's congregation. He labored with success for two years, and resigned in 1825.

Rev. John Winter succeeded to the charge, and for a period of seven years labored with fidelity and success. The congregation at St. Paul's received large accessions during his ministry. He resigned the charge in 1832, and died in 1857. He was buried in the graveyard at Clear Spring.

Rev. Simeon Harkey followed Mr. Winter as pastor. He was then a young man, having just entered upon the active duties of the ministry, and, though without any experience in his chosen walk of life, he gave early evidence of the talent and ability which marked his subsequent life, and made him one of the leading ministers of that section. He was for several years president of the Illinois University, at Springfield, and is the author of several works, which form a valuable contribution to church literature.

Rev. Daniel Miller was called to succeed Mr. Harkey in the autumn of 1835. He resigned in October, 1836, much to the regret of the congregation. He spent most of his ministry at Greenwich, N. J., and died there.

Rev. Christian Startzman was the next minister of St. Paul's. He was called to the charge in 1837, and it was during his ministry that the church was first repaired and remodeled, and interesting revival services were held day and night for five or six weeks. He continued pastor until 1849, a period of eleven years, and for twenty years thereafter he ministered elsewhere. In 1868 he was recalled to the Clear Spring charge, of which St. Paul's forms a part, and continued for seven years, after which he retired to his old homestead, a few miles south of Hagerstown.

Rev. Henry Bishop accepted a call to St. Paul's in the autumn of 1849 to succeed Mr. Startzman, on his first resignation. His connection lasted four years, and his ministry was acceptable to the congregation. The early part of his ministry was mainly occupied in missionary labor in the Western States, whither he returned and located after completing his pastorate at St. Paul's. Upon leaving St. Paul's he changed his relation from the Lutheran to the Presbyterian Church.

Rev. William F. Greaver was installed pastor of the charge in 1855. He died in 1857, after a short ministry of two years. His funeral was attended by a large concourse of people of various denominations.

Rev. Joseph Barclay, afterwards pastor of the First Lutheran Church, Baltimore, succeeded Mr. Greaver in 1867. He was then a young man, having lately completed his ministerial studies at a seminary in Gettysburg, Pa. He gave early promise as a writer of the success which he subsequently attained as a pulpit orator, and his "Travels in Egypt, the Holy Land, and Europe" possesses high literary merit. He resigned from St. Paul's in 1859.

Rev. Christian Lepley succeeded Mr. Barclay in November, 1859. One year after his ministry began the slavery agitation, which had been brewing for more than thirty years, culminated in the civil war, and the churches, especially in the border States, were many of them riddled by cannon-balls or burned to the ground, and congregations were distracted by political discussion. Mr. Lepley's attitude was a very trying one, but he adhered unflinchingly to the Union cause. He resigned in May, 1864.

Mr. Lepley's successor was Rev. J. Berlin, who accepted the position of pastor to the charge in November, 1865. He soon contracted a distressing cough, which developed speedily into consumption, and in two years his life and ministry terminated. He died in Tremont, Pa., in 1867.

Rev. Martin L. Cullen, Mr. Berlin's successor, received a unanimous call to the charge in March, 1867. He ministered with general acceptability for two years, and made many warm friends. He resigned in 1869, and went to Martinsburg, W. Va., where he took charge of the Lutheran congregation. He was succeeded by Rev. Christian Startzman, before mentioned, who was recalled after twenty years' ministry elsewhere, and served until 1873.

Rev. David Swope succeeded to the charge Nov. 1, 1875, under favorable circumstances and with the cordial co-operation of the congregation. He presented his resignation Aug. 31, 1876, but it was not accepted until Jan. 6, 1877, and only went into effect April 1st of that year. He was succeeded by Rev. Victor Miller, who preached as temporary minister for a short time, and was followed in the fall of 1877 by Rev. Samuel M. Firey, who is now pastor.

While the Lutheran congregation worshiped at St. Paul's, and one minister succeeded another, the German Reformed congregation also held their religious meetings and had their separate pastors. The only reminiscences of the German Reformed pastors extant are those of the late Rev. Daniel Zacharias, of Frederick County, in newspaper correspondence. St. Paul's was to Dr. Zacharias a sacred spot. Here his father worshiped at a period when there was no other church within eleven miles, and his mother was buried in St. Paul's graveyard. In these reminiscences he mentions many facts of interest alike to history and the people of Washington County. The first German Reformed minister of St. Paul's was Rev. Jonathan Rahauser, who was called on the establishment of St. Paul's congregations, and before the church had been quite finished, in 1795. His ministry covered a period of twenty-two years, until 1817, a longer time than any of his successors to the charge. He entered upon the duties of the charge at a very youthful age, and his merits as a preacher and catechist, as well as a pastor, were of a high order.

At that time there was no turnpike leading from Hagerstown to St. Paul's or farther west to Cumberland, nor was there then a bridge across the Conococheague which might be used at high water. Mr. Rahauser was hence more than once exposed to accident or death by ferrying the stream at "Kershner's Ford," when the surging waters rolled through his vehicle. Dr. Zacharias, in his memoirs, says, "On such occasions we used to look with unusual anxiety for the top of his carriage, which was first seen as he rounded the hill in the road leading from the ford to the church, and as he drove up slowly to his wonted place near the church, the faithful and courteous deacons first helped their pastor out of his carriage, and then took care of his horse, whilst the elders gathered around him to express their joy at seeing his face once more." Mr. Rahauser died in 1817, and on the day of his burial an immense concourse gathered in Hagerstown. Rev. Jonathan Helfenstein, of Frederick, preached the funeral discourse.

Rev. Mr. Rahauser was followed as pastor of the Reformed congregation by Rev. Mr. Ebaugh, and the sermons, which were hitherto preached in German, were by Mr. Ebaugh preached in the English language. When he took charge Mr. Ebaugh was quite young, and dissatisfaction, especially in Hagerstown, soon sprang up. The trouble was carried before the Lutheran Synod, with the request that it would interfere and so determine that peace and harmony might again be restored. The Synod investigated the difficulty, and exonerated Mr. Ebaugh from blame, but advised him to withdraw from the charge. This he did in 1818, and shortly after Rev. James R. Reily was called. The congregation then regained its former status, and matters moved along with unexampled prosperity. At this time (in 1818) the charge consisted of Hagerstown, Salem, St. Paul's, and Funkstown (Salem was called Schnebly's, and St. Paul's, Conococheague), and in the succeeding year, 1819, Mr. Reily added Williamsport and Barth's to the congregations belonging to the charge. He was a very acceptable and popular preacher. Mr. Reily's ministry was brief. He began it in February, 1819, and preached his farewell sermon in 1825, leaving there to go to Europe, as well for his health as on an important mission for the church. During the six years of his pastorate he baptized 829 infants and 103 adults, and confirmed 519 persons. He preached 225 funeral sermons. Mr. Reily's successor was the Rev. Mr. Martin, of Frederick County, who served about six months, resigning in 1826. Rev. Mr. Keller, a Presbyterian, served from this time until 1827, and was succeeded by Rev. Mr. Bruner, who ministered for three years, and resigned in 1831. Rev. Daniel Bragonier followed Mr. Bruner as pastor of the Reformed congregation in 1831, and preached acceptably five years, until 1836. He died Oct. 25, 1869, and was buried at Shepherdstown, W. Va. Rev. David Leopold was the next pastor and served six months, having been deposed from the ministry for misconduct June, 1839. Rev. Charles Ewing, of Baltimore, supplied the charge for one year thereafter, and resigned in April, 1842. He was succeeded by Rev. Dr. Neill, who served nearly four years, and resigned in 1846. Rev. Mr. Callender followed, and ministered four years, until 1850, when Rev. Mr. Beck became pastor, and so continued for two years, resigning June, 1852. His successor was Rev. Jonathan Rebaugh, a popular pastor and successful minister, who was called in 1852, and who remained until 1864, when, becoming deranged, he was placed in the Pennsylvania Asylum for the Insane at Harrisburg, where he died in 1872. Rev. Mr. Goodrich received a call Nov. 1, 1865, and has labored with general satisfaction to the congregation.

The ground upon which St. Paul's church stands, including three acres lying around it, was originally vacant land without an owner, and so remained until taken up by John Ankeney, Sr., under a patent from the State, and conveyed by a deed in 1795 to the church for a public burial-place. In it are buried the dead of both the Lutheran and German Reformed congregations. The old graveyard, after the apportionment of the land by John Ankeney, Sr., for the purposes of a church edifice and a burial-place, embraced a little over an acre of ground, but having become filled with graves it was found necessary to enlarge it by the purchase of an additional acre on the north side, which was done in 1867. Another half-acre was procured by exchange and added to the east side, and the whole addition was laid out in family lots with walks between them. As early as 1857 there were no trees or shrubbery save a few lilac-bushes and an occasional flower planted upon some new-made grave. The rows of beautiful cedar-trees which now adorn the graveyard were there planted by William Firey, at his own expense, and the plan was also projected by him of building the stone wall which now incloses the church grounds on the south-east side and along the turnpike, so as to prevent the washing of the soil. In 1873, Rev. Victor Miller solicited and collected the sum of five hundred and six dollars in the neighborhood of St. Paul's, to be known as the graveyard fund of St. Paul's Lutheran and Reformed congregations in Clear Spring District, Washington Co., Md. This fund was placed under the control of the trustees of the congregations and invested by them in Washington County Bank stock, and the interest alone is expended annually in beautifying the grounds and in keeping the graveyard and its inclosures and adornments in as good condition as possible. The present Lutheran church edifice was built in the spring of 1875, the old stone church which had been built in 1828 having been burned down on Sunday, Feb. 12, 1875.

There are no records of St. John's Reformed congregation earlier than 1834, but little doubt exists that it was established about the beginning of the nineteenth century. In 1825 the congregation worshiped with the Lutherans at St. Peter's church. In 1860 they sold out their interest in the church edifice to the Lutherans. The pastors of St. John's have been Rev. D. G. Bragonier, 1834–40; Rev. George

H. Leopold, one year; Dr. B. T. Neal, 1842–45; Rev. S. W. Callender, 1846–48; Rev. John Beck, 1851–53; Rev. John Rebaugh, 1854–63; Rev. William Goodrich, 1865, the present pastor. The congregation numbers one hundred members, and the present church edifice was built in 1866. It has a parsonage connected with it, and a benevolent society, which has raised several thousand dollars for benevolent objects.

St. Michael's Catholic church was built in 1866, the corner-stone having been laid in July, and the church dedicated soon afterwards. The pastor of the church at Hancock serves the Clear Spring congregation.

In 1839 St. Andrew's Episcopal Church mission at Clear Spring made an application for permission to form a separate congregation, which petition was granted. The Rev. Joshua Peterkin entered on his ministry at Hagerstown, Dec. 22, 1839. Before this there had been no permanent church services. The church edifice was built in 1840. The rectors of St. Andrew's, Clear Spring, have been:

1840–41, Rev. Joshua Peterkin; 1843–46, Rev. James A. Buck; 1846–47, Rev. Philip Berry; 1848–54, Rev. Hanson T. Wilcoxon; 1855–58, Rev. George L. Machenheimer; 1858–60, Rev. William Scull; 1860–65, Rev. Alexander Falk; 1865, Rev. William A. Harris, who was succeeded by Rev. Henry Edwards, the present rector.

In 1846, Philip Berry, a native of England, who had come from North Carolina to Maryland in 1842, became rector of St. Andrew's, Clear Spring. In 1851 he removed to New York, and in 1857 died in Richmond.

In 1848, Hanson Thomas Wilcoxon became rector of St. Andrew's, Clear Spring, and in 1850 removed to Virginia. He was a native of Montgomery County, and was ordained by Bishop Whittingham in 1846. His first charge was Harriott chapel, Frederick County, whence he removed to St. Andrew's. In 1852 he became rector of St. Andrew's again. In 1854 he removed to Pennsylvania, but in 1856 returned in bad health, and died in Baltimore in 1858, aged thirty-six.

Rev. Alexander Falk, Ph.D., a native of Prussia, and brought up a Lutheran, was ordained by Bishop Whittingham in 1859. He was a tutor in St. James' College, Hagerstown, and officiated at St. Andrew's, Clear Spring, and at Williamsport. In 1862 he added St. Thomas', Hancock, to his charge, and in 1865 removed to Pennsylvania.

Cemeteries.—On the summit of the ridge immediately east of Clear Spring is Rose Hill Cemetery. The following are the most noticeable epitaphs:

Ruth, consort of Wm. Harrison, died Feb. 5, 1855, aged 84.

John Cowton, died Aug. 2, 1876, aged 77 years, 2 months; and his wife, Sarah, born July 24, 1801, died March 11, 1880.

H. F. Perry, M.D., born Oct. 20, 1823, died March 21, 1878.

Christian Conrad, died Oct. 15, 1876, aged 76 years, 11 months; and his wife, Eveline, died Nov. 2, 1874, aged 75.

Susan Middlekauff, born May, 1809, died Nov. 9, 1872.

The subjoined are the names of the old residents whose remains lie in St. Paul's Reformed Church cemetery:

Samuel Stauck, born July 26, 1792, died Oct. 1, 1840.

Frederick Spigler, died June 18, 1833, aged 69 years; and his wife, Mary B., died May 30, 1848, aged 82 years, 4 months.

Mary Elliott, consort of George W. Elliott, died Sept. 5, 1836, aged 52 years.

Susan Pinder, died 1846, aged 90 years.

Emanuel Brewer, born Oct. 30, 1795, died Jan. 22, 1839; and his wife, Catharine, born April 11, 1799, died Jan. 8, 1843.

Sarah, wife of Henry Masters, died April 24, 1852, aged 56 years, 8 months.

Capt. John A. Brewer, died Jan. 1, 1845, aged 59 years, 7 months.

John Witmer, Jr., died Aug. 24, 1847, aged 48 years, 5 months; and his wife, Rosanna, died June 4, 1861, aged 65 years, 2 months.

Jacob Jones, born July 23, 1779, died Feb. 4, 1847.

John Hamilton, born April 8, 1793, died Feb. 27, 1835; and his wife, Margaret, died June 18, 1872, aged 73 years.

Michael Seibert, died April 10, 1859, aged 71 years, 2 months; and his wife, Elizabeth, born Dec. 2, 1792, died April 13, 1875.

D. H. Newcomer, died Dec. 15, 1873, aged 65 years, 4 months.

Jonathan Ridenour, died March 3, 1875, aged 78 years, 4 months; and his wife, Sarah, died Jan. 19, 1862, aged 53 years, 11 months.

Phœbe, wife of William Reed, died July 9, 1852, aged 82 years, 2 months.

Daniel Hauer, died Feb. 9, 1860, aged 67 years.

George Hauer, born Aug. 9, 1787, died Jan. 20, 1855.

George Harsh, died April 9, 1855, aged 57 years, 11 months; and his wife, Sarah, died Aug. 13, 1861, aged 64 years, 9 months.

John Hicks, died Nov. 28, 1869, aged 63 years, 9 months.

Rev. Christian Startzman, died March 3, 1880, aged 70 years, 3 months.

George Ankeney, died Sept. 24, 1863, aged 76 years.

Henry Ankeney, died July 7, 1857, aged 69 years, 6 months; and his wife, Catherine, born Dec. 18, 1787, died Dec. 6, 1849.

Capt. John Miller, died April 24, 1804, aged 48 years. He was a soldier of the Revolution, and on his tomb is the inscription: "He fought for liberty and lived to enjoy it."

Joseph Firey, died July 24, 1833, aged 61 years; and his wife, Mary Magdalene, died July 10, 1832, aged 57 years.

Henry Firey, died Nov. 19, 1813, aged 47 years, 9 months; and his wife, Elizabeth, died Sept. 21, 1853, aged 83 years.

James Ashkittel, died Sept. 28, 1829, aged 47 years.

Henry Brewer, died April 24, 1837, aged 76 years; and his wife, Catherine, died May 10, 1827, aged 74 years.

John Firey, died Nov. 30, 1824, aged 60 years; and his wife, Sabina, born Oct. 7, 1779, died March 8, 1843.

Catherine Schnebly, consort of Jacob Tice, died April 1, 1825, aged 56 years, 4 months.

Ann Barbara Schnebly, born Aug. 2, 1749, died March 3, 1833.

Adam Troup, born May 13, 1771, died May 26, 1840; and his

wife, Mary Elizabeth, died Aug. 3, 1853, aged 76 years, 10 months.

Michael Moudy, born Aug. 1, 1779, died Sept. 28, 1844.

John Brewer, Sr., died June 5, 1832, aged 65 years, 10 months.

John Schnebly, born Feb. 3, 1750, died Jan. 17, 1838.

Daniel Heller, born Sept. 7, 1779, died Dec. 16, 1873; and his wife, Dorothea, born June 20, 1782, died Jan. 2, 1829.

Over the grave of George C. Beard, died April 23, 1880, aged 21 years, 5 months, is a superb marble monument upon an Ohio freestone base. Upon the shaft are carved the open Bible, the rising dove, the hands upraised to heaven, the sickle, and the garnered sheaf of wheat, the whole surmounted by the crown above the cross.

The grave of John Calvin Miller, born March 14, 1854, died Sept. 8, 1879, is marked with a marble octagonal shaft with Corinthian ornamentation.

In the Catholic cemetery the following persons are interred:

William Roach, born in County Cork, Ireland, died March 31, 1876, in his 49th year.

Catherine Drinner, born at Golden Gate, County Tipperary, Ireland, died Oct. 23, 1879, aged 70 years.

John Chambers, died Oct. 31, 1871, in the 50th year of his age.

In the churchyard of St. Paul's the following persons are buried:

John Wolferd, Sr., died Nov. 15, 1856, aged 62 years, 1 month.

Sarah Jacques, born Dec. 14, 1774, died March 13, 1837.

Martha, widow of Michael Roney, died July 4, 1842, aged 70 years, 9 months.

Henry Myers, died Aug. 12, 1864, aged 71 years.

Catharine Moyer, died April 10, 1866, aged about 85 years.

David Cushwa, born Aug. 10, 1777, died March 8, 1849; and his wife, Catherine, born Jan. 20, 1783, died Aug. 27, 1861.

George Cushwa, died Sept. 9, 1857, aged 54 years, 6 months.

Nancy Swisher, born July 27, 1770, died Jan. 15, 1862, aged 91 years, 5 months.

Michael Dillehunt, died March 13, 1848, aged 81 years.

Charles Potts, died Dec. 7, 1854, aged 87 years, 3 months.

Samuel Winders, died Nov. 13, 1878, aged 76 years, 2 days; and his wife, Susan, died May 28, 1864, aged 59 years, 4 months.

Margaret, wife of John Springer, died March 12, 1856, aged 66 years, 7 months.

Jacob Miller, born May 16, 1811, died Nov. 16, 1859.

Jacob Seibert, died May 20, 1864, aged 66 years, 4 months.

John Elliott, died Dec. 27, 1860, aged 59 years; and his wife, Mary, died May 1, 1876, aged 68 years.

Catharine Seibert, died Oct. 20, 1880, aged 84 years, 11 months.

Jacob Worley, born Sept. 3, 1787, died July 7, 1837.

Henry Farley, died Dec. 27, 1861, aged 68 years, 5 months; and his wife, Martha, died Aug. 30, 1871, aged 70 years, 5 months.

Sarah, wife of Peter Eichelberger, died Aug. 26, 1871, aged about 83 years.

William Ditto, born April 16, 1797, died Dec. 16, 1855; and his wife, Hannah, born Aug. 31, 1803, died Feb. 29, 1880.

Sarah E. Hitchcock, born Jan. 25, 1827, died July 19, 1880.

Elizabeth, wife of Jacob Brewer, born March 18, 1797, died Aug. 10, 1872.

George Bragonier, died Oct. 2, 1862, aged 61 years, 5 months.

Joseph Brewer, died March 9, 1863, aged 73 years, 3 months.

Frederick Nicodemus, died April 20, 1858, aged 52 years, 1 month.

Martha M. Schnebly, died Sept. 20, 1871, in her 89th year.

John Schnebly, died Feb. 19, 1876, aged 79 years, 4 months.

Elizabeth, wife of David Brewer, died Dec. 4, 1873, aged 71 years, 8 months.

George Kline, died Feb. 21, 1876, aged 76 years, 9 months.

Jacob H. Brewer, died Sept. 2, 1877, aged 62 years, 6 months.

Samuel Troup, born Oct. 15, 1809, died Feb. 27, 1862; and his wife, Elizabeth, born April 15, 1831, died Aug. 21, 1877.

Adam Troup, born March 6, 1806, died March 10, 1870.

Robert Gesford, died March 24, 1877, aged 76 years, 10 months; and his wife, Sarah Ann, died Feb. 8, 1877, aged 75 years, 10 months.

Jacob Holbrunner, died Dec. 20, 1872, aged 77 years, 9 months.

Rebecca Mong, born Aug. 29, 1792, died March 29, 1872, aged 79 years, 7 months.

Maria, wife of George Gomer, died Jan. 15, 1877, aged 85 years, 6 months.

Daniel Sprecher, died June 30, 1876, aged 80 years, 1 month; and his wife, Mary, born Aug. 25, 1800, died March 23, 1877.

Samuel Miller, died June 3, 1849, aged 65 years, 5 months; and his wife Mary, died Aug. 5, 1877, aged 81 years, 5 months.

Mary C. Sprickler, wife of Rev. Victor Miller, died Aug. 10, 1873, aged 35 years, 5 months. A beautiful monument is erected over this grave.

Michael Bargman, born Oct. 29, 1738, in Europe, died Dec. 17, 1818; and his wife, Eva Brockonier, born Nov. 30, 1752, in Hanau, Europe, died May 18, 1827.

George Mish, born March 13, 1772, died June 26, 1826; and his wife, Mary, died Aug. 21, 1854, aged 74 years, 2 months.

Peter Swope, born Dec. 20, 1750, died July 15, 1811.

HANCOCK DISTRICT, No. 5.

Hancock, or Election District No. 5, occupies the extreme westernmost position in the county, and extends from Indian Spring District, which bounds it on the east, to Allegany County on the west, and from the Chesapeake and Ohio Canal and the Potomac River on the south to the Pennsylvania State or Mason and Dixon's line on the north. The population (including the town of Hancock, which has 931 inhabitants) is 2233. The original boundaries of the district were fixed as follows:

"Beginning at the mouth of the Green Spring Run Furnace at the river Potomac, and running thence up the river to the Sideling Hill Creek; thence up the creek to the State line; thence with the State line to the Green Spring Furnace Run; and thence with Number Four to the place of beginning. This district to be called Number Five, and the election to be held at the house of John Donovan, in the town of Hancock, lately occupied as a tavern."

In 1822 the following boundary lines were fixed in conformity with an act of the General Assembly:

"To begin on the Potomac at the mouth of Licking Creek, and with said creek to the Pennsylvania line; thence with said line to Sideling Hill Creek; thence with said creek to the Potomac River, and with said river to the beginning."

It is a semi-mountainous territory, noted for deposits of limestone and slate, but has extensive tracts of fine farm-lands, and is well watered by numerous streams, among them the Big Tonoloway, the Little Tonoloway, and Sideling Hill Creeks. It is thickly populated. The community is intelligent and thrifty, and possesses an excellent public school system which is fully utilized. The Chesapeake and Ohio Canal, which skirts the southern limits, is a fruitful source of revenue to a large number of inhabitants, and several valuable industries in and near the town of Hancock add much to the value of the district. Among the older and more prominent family names are those of Hughes, Brent, Bowles, Delaplane, Resley, Phillips, Stiger, Creager, Myers, Miller, Houck, Bridges, Henderson, etc.

The only town of prominence in the district is Hancock, from which it derives its name. Hancock is situated on the National turnpike, one hundred miles from Baltimore and thirty-nine miles from Cumberland. The Baltimore and Ohio Railroad traverses the opposite or West Virginia bank of the Potomac, and a ford and ferry afford means of communication between the railway station and the town. Hancock, which has 931 inhabitants, is one of the oldest towns in the State, and was named after the first settler, whom history does not show was especially distinguished in any other direction. The buildings in the place, many of which are of brick, are of ancient architecture. In the matter of commercial importance, Hancock has no rival on the canal between Georgetown and Cumberland. It has a number of stores, several warehouses for traffic in grain and flour, etc., and among its inhabitants are many industrious and skillful mechanics, including boat-builders.

Hancock was incorporated at an early date, but after a number of years the charter was permitted to expire. About two years ago it was renewed, but has not been acted upon. John Donovan was among the earliest settlers, and kept a public-house in addition to conducting a farm. He owned an island in the Potomac immediately north of the town, and lived in a frame house now owned and occupied by John Hickson, at the intersection of Wason Street and the National turnpike. His tavern was immediately adjoining this house. The Barton Central Hotel is probably the oldest house in Hancock. Among the early residents of the town were Jacob Houck, druggist; John Johnson, an old farmer and merchant, who was an old settler; Rev. Joseph Powell, who died there Aug. 28, 1804, aged seventy; Leonard Shafer, merchant; James Saunders, tavern-keeper, "Sign of the Cross Keys," in 1805; John Watt, formerly of Hagerstown, was there in 1806; John Protzman, tavern-keeper, was there in 1800; Benj. Bean, tavern-keeper, house "Sign of the Green Tree," —prior to 1808 he kept tavern at Parkhead Forge and other places; Charles Worland, saddler; John Mathews, inn-keeper, house "Sign of the Seven Stars," stand formerly occupied by J. Protzman; William Yates, a prominent citizen, lived near there; Dr. Samuel J. Gregory; D. and C. Cartwright, merchants; John Davis, merchant, also in 1817 the contractor for making a turnpike from the Big Conococheague to Cumberland; John Brady, merchant; Robert Donavan, tanner; Capt. Jacob Stephens, innkeeper; Andrew Goulding kept the "Union Inn" in 1820, the house occupied formerly by Jacob Brosius; J. Reichard, postmaster in 1820; Col. David Stephens, inn-keeper; Henry McKinley, postmaster in 1822.

In 1790, Samuel McFerran kept store at Hancock. Col. Hynes, of Kentucky, formerly lived (before 1792) nearly adjoining Hancock, where he had a splendid mansion and several hundred acres of land. He removed thence to Kentucky with a large number of other settlers from this section of the State.

Mr. Donovan, in September, 1793, advertised his property and business for sale in the following terms:

"To be Sold.

"That well-known House & two lots of Ground, with all the improvements thereon, in Hancocktown, where John Donovan formerly lived, and where Capt. Casper Shaffner now lives; . . . the stand is so well known by the public that little need be said in its favour, and more especially as it is presumed the purchaser will view the premises before he deals.

"John Donovan.

"Hancocktown, Sept. 20, 1793."

And April 14th, three years later, "Casper Shaffner opened a public-house at the stand formerly occupied by John Donovan at Hancocktown." Previous to this, in 1792, he kept at the "Sign of the Ship."

Dr. Van Rohden settled in Hancock in 1804, and announced his presence there in the following advertisement:

"Doctor Van Rohden, lately from Germany, Gives notice that he intends to practice as Physician and Surgeon, in internal and external maladies; also as Man-Midwife, in Hancock Town, Maryland.

"He solicits the confidence of a generous public, with the assurance that on his part nothing shall be wanting to serve his patients with the utmost care and attention. He also keeps an Apothecary Shop in Hancocktown, where all kinds of Medicines may be had at reasonable rates."

Prior to the nineteenth century the citizens of "Hancocktown" were to a certain measure devoted to turf sports. A public advertisement of Sept. 7, 1797, gave notice that

"At Hancocktown, on the 18th of October next, there will be a race for a purse of 25 pounds, free to any horse; on the 19th, on the same course, another race for 15 pounds; and on Friday, the 20th, a handsome sweepstake. The horses will be entered with John Johnson and Casper Shaffner the day preceding each race. Horses to start each day at one o'clock."

The following copy of the list of letters in the Hancock post-office Dec. 31, 1820, will prove of interest:

James Anderson, Terence Bowen, Archibald Bryson, Richard Carr, John Craig, Isaac Catlett, Margaret Coady, Jacob Dunn, George Dunn, Pherus Eldridge, Jr., Thaddeus Fields, Jacob Fields, Robert Grady, Jonathan Gammels, Elizabeth Gaither, Abner Hess, John Kerr, Henry Kleppert, John Kenny, Jacob Leopard, Addis Linn, Jacob Lansinger, Mark McAfee, Jonathan Meyers, Patrick Mumfort, Joseph Orrin, Isaac Osmun, Denton Poole, Robert Patterson, William Reese, Jr., William Reese, David Rowland, Henry Resley, Alexander Reed, Henry L. Redburn, Edmond Richmond, William Rooby, John Stillwell, Frederick Snyder, Samuel Shriver, John Stigers, Ester Stahl, Anthony Snyder, Cornelius Vanderbelt, Col. Elie Williams, William Williams, James West.

The census of the same year (1820) showed a population of 266, of whom 219 were white, 3 free colored, and 44 slaves.

Cemeteries.—Hancock was originally laid out by Mr. Hancock, the first settler, alluded to above, but as the town grew in size and importance it was extended on the east by the annexation of territory which was subsequently known as Donovan's Addition, and on the west by Brent's Addition. John Donovan gave a portion of his property fronting on High Street for a public cemetery, and the citizens by general contribution acquired possession of an addition, making a lot two hundred feet wide by three hundred feet deep. In addition to this there is a cemetery attached to the Roman Catholic church, a fine large brick building; to St. Peter's Protestant Episcopal church, a commodious edifice, also of brick, and to the Presbyterian church.

In these several cemeteries and graveyards the following persons among others are buried:

Ann Bevans, born November, 1786, died Jan. 21, 1852, aged 63 years.

Thos. McAvoy, native of Queens County, parish of Clancy, Ireland, died March 29, 1850, aged 55 years.

Hugh McCusker, died Jan. 4, 1853, in his 69th year.

Dorothy Clingan, died Sept. 25, 1846, aged 54 years.

Margaret McCusker, died Feb. 26, 1846, in her 50th year.

Ethelbert Taney, born April 4, 1794, died June 17, 1863, aged 69 years; and Eliza M., his wife, died Jan. 1, 1847, in her 44th year.

Andrew Colvin, born in the parish of Dramgoon, County Cavan, Ireland, died March 14, 1844, aged 46 years.

Frank Bresler, died May 27, 1873, aged 52 years.

Francis McCormick, died Nov. 4, 1844, aged 80 years.

Margaret McCormick, died Aug. 2, 1842, aged 75 years.

Wm. McCormick, died April 26, 1856, aged 45 years.

Bernard Gorman, a native of the parish of Amatras, County Monaghan, Ireland, died Dec. 10, 1839, aged 38 years.

Hugh Egan, died June 7, 1857, aged 52 years.

Mary Egan, died Feb. 27, 1858, aged 75 years.

Michael Egan, died Feb. 8, 1875, aged 61 years.

Patrick Kelly, of Kings County, Ireland, died Oct. 6, 1836, aged 45 years.

Patrick Munday, died May 22, 1839, aged 46 years, a native of Fermanagh County, Ireland.

Charles Stewart, died June 26, 1872, aged 48 years.

Mary E., wife of Wm. T. English, died June 7, 1879, aged 35 years.

Augustin B. Taney, born April 27, 1829, died Oct. 2, 1865, aged 36 years.

Capt. James Hook, died June 21, 1837, aged 47 years.

Ann Murray, died Feb. 16, 1872, aged 83 years.

Michael Gartner, died May 21, 1876, aged 71 years.

Patrick Broidrick, born Nov. 12, 1808, died Jan. 16, 1878.

Margaret Broidrick, born April 1, 1811, died Aug. 1, 1874.

John T. Broidrick, died Feb. 12, 1870, aged 33 years; Ella, his wife, died Aug 12, 1866, aged 23 years.

Catherine, wife of Henry S. Barnett, died July 4, 1878, aged 57 years.

Richard Murray, died Jan. 14, 1852, in his 69th year.

James Dochenney, died Oct. 10, 1850, in his 39th year; Bridget, his wife, died March 16, 1862, in her 49th year.

Patrick Gilleece, native of County Cavan, parish of Dremrigen, Ireland, died Dec. 4, 1863, aged 56 years.

Patrick McDonnell, native of County Longford, parish of Templemichael, Ireland, died Aug. 15, 1863, aged 55 years.

Bridget McEvoy, born May 4, 1793, died May 11, 1874.

Daniel Baxter, died Aug. 25, 1865, aged 67 years.

Elizabeth Spicer, died Jan. 26, 1880, aged 72 years.

Patrick McAvoy, died April 5, 1879, aged 81 years.

Sophia Eliza, wife of Samuel H. Davis, died July 18, 1872, aged 43 years.

John A. Byers, died April 7, 1872, in his 67th year.

Elizabeth Hunter, born May 3, 1803, died Jan. 26, 1874.

John J. Bowles, died Oct. 11, 1868, in his 53d year.

Mary A., wife of Frederick W. Weddell, died Sept. 30, 1876, aged 58 years.

Theophilus Barnett, died Oct. 25, 1879, aged 49 years.

John Conradt, died Sept. 8, 1876, aged 80 years.

George Foster, of Company F, Second Maryland Cavalry, Home Brigade, died Sept. 18, 1863, aged 27 years.

Eliza C. Stephens, wife of Samuel McF. Stephens, born June 3, 1813, died Feb. 14, 1874.

James B. Ditto, born Dec. 4, 1809, died Dec. 24, 1879, aged 70 years; Elizabeth, his wife, born April 10, 1812, died Aug. 8, 1867, aged 55 years.

Mary, wife of Wm. Creager, died Feb. 14, 1862, aged 75 years.

John Coudy, native of Ireland, died Sept. 8, 1823, in his 48th year.

Joseph Beall, born July 12, 1822, died May 20, 1855.

Dr. Samuel J. Gregory, born March 18, 1793, died Oct. 20, 1835.

Lavinia Richmond Gregory, born March 3, 1798, died April 8, 1867.

Malcolm, son of S. and I. Gregory, born Feb. 19, 1832, died Dec. 25, 1872.

Richmond Gregory, born Sept. 25, 1825, died Sept. 26, 1865.

Ann Lou Gregory, born Oct. 7, 1828, died Sept. 22, 1875.

Henry Snider, born March 29, 1804, died Dec. 29, 1866, aged 62 years.

John Davis, died Nov. 13, 1866, in his 67th year.

Daniel Brosius, died Oct. 25, 1859, aged 53 years.

Eleanor, his wife, died Feb. 20, 1865, aged 57 years.

Kitty Reynolds, died Sept. 14, 1852, aged 64 years.

Jane Goss, died March 4, 1855, aged 74 years.

Rachel Pendleton, died June 14, 1866, aged 70 years.

Kelly Thomas, died March 22, 1848, aged 55 years.

Jane Thomas, died Nov. 30, 1851, aged 60 years.

George Thomas, died March 16, 1855, aged 58 years.

Martha, wife of Ethelbert Taney, died May 30, 1862, in her 60th year.

Catherine, wife of Joseph Graves, died Nov. 5, 1863, aged 69 years.

Mary C., wife of W. T. Bootman, died Sept. 25, 1879, aged 38 years.

Benjamin Pendleton, died March 14, 1853, in his 72d year.

Harriet Pendleton, born Dec. 24, 1788, died April 23, 1850.

Isaac Breathed, died Jan. 12, 1858, aged 77 years.

Kitty Breathed, died March 18, 1863, in her 70th year.

Elizabeth Snodgrass, died March 18, 1863, in her 43d year.

Rev. John Delaplane, "late rector of St. Mark's Parish, Frederick County," died Oct. 11, 1841.

Mrs. Jane B. Buck, widow of Rev. John Delaplane, and wife of Rev. James A. Buck, who died Aug. 24, 1847, in her 30th year.

James Henry, died Nov. 4, 1864, aged 51 years.

Lavinia R., wife of Dr. James B. Delaplane, born Nov. 10, 1840, died Sept. 26, 1867.

Dr. James Breathed, born Dec. 15, 1838, died Feb. 14, 1870, aged 31 years.

Alexander McFerran, died Nov. 2, 1823, aged 41 years.

Priscilla, his wife, died Jan. 10, 1869, aged 86 years.

Thomas Payne, born Dec. 18, 1793, died Nov. 20, 1874, aged 80 years.

John Stine, died Dec. 24, 1868, aged 78 years.

Robert T. Bridges, died Sept. 27, 1845, aged 49 years.

Rebecca, his wife, died June 24, 1878, aged 76 years.

Sarah M., daughter of the above, and wife of Rev. W. T. Thompson, died April 27, 1869, aged 31 years.

Mary Catherine, wife of William Cornelius, died Aug. 13, 1880, aged 26 years.

John Truxell, died April 4, 1848, aged 62 years.

Mary Truxell, born Oct. 25, 1815, died Jan. 30, 1872, aged 57 years.

Elizabeth Truxell, died Nov. 9, 1862, aged 66 years.

Mary A., wife of John H. Brady, died Oct. 3, 1854, aged 48 years.

Henry Jones, a native of Wales, died May 31, 1851, aged 65 years.

Hopewell Bean, died June 26, 1863, in her 75th year.

Henry Claggett, born April 24, 1814, died March 15, 1866, in his 51st year.

Mary A., his wife, died Oct. 9, 1880.

John S. Miller, died Sept. 5, 1847, aged 52 years.

Lloyd H. Barton, died March 30, 1862, aged 75 years.

Frances, his wife, died June 9, 1863, in her 68th year.

Susan Snow, died Jan. 13, 1850, aged 52 years.

Benjamin Bean, died April 8, 1847, aged 45 years.

Sophia Bean, died Aug. 4, 1850, aged 50 years.

Ruth Gano, died Dec. 27, 1844, in her 92d year.

Elizabeth, wife of Capt. John D. Hart, died Jan. 27, 1857, aged 62 years.

James H. Bowles, died Nov. 5, 1849, aged 68 years.

Martha, his wife, died Feb. 1, 1861, aged 62 years.

James Garaghty, died Aug. 17, 1854, aged 54 years.

Catherine, his wife, died Dec. 15, 1856, aged 40 years.

John Gano, died March 26, 1847, aged 46 years.

Nancy Gano, died Jan. 6, 1854, aged 59 years.

David Troxell, died Feb. 9, 1848, aged 40 years.

Louisiana Bowers, died April 9, 1869, aged 53 years.

William Bowers, died Sept. 3, 1848, aged 44 years.

Capt. David Barnett, died Aug. 6, 1842, in his 49th year; Ann, his wife, died Sept. 16, 1864, aged 67 years.

William Brady, died July 12, 1866, aged 59 years.

Edward Allen Gibbs, died Jan. 24, 1847, aged 63 years.

Mrs. Elizabeth Gibbs, died Jan. 15, 1847, aged 51 years.

Jacob Leopard, died March 14, 1853, in his 80th year; Delilah, his wife, died Jan. 16, 1866, aged 70 years.

Mary Scott, born Feb. 5, 1772, died Oct. 15, 1845.

Elizabeth Scott, born Oct. 23, 1791, died Aug. 19, 1842.

Cromwell Orrick, died Feb. 27, 1856, aged 62 years; Mary, his wife, born Jan. 24, 1861, died Nov. 24, 1842, aged 40 years.

Eve, wife of Jacob Brosius, died Nov. 24, 1846, aged 61 years.

Samuel Brosius, died May 15, 1856, aged 45 years.

J. W. Bortman, born June 16, 1818, died Aug. 22, 1860, in his 43d year.

Thomas Brooke, died Aug. 17, 1836, aged 39 years; Phebe, his wife, died Oct. 26, 1858, aged 63 years.

Catherine Snider, wife of J. H. Snider, born Feb. 27, 1795, died March 12, 1853.

Samuel Brosius, died April 4, 1849, aged 61 years; Mary, his wife, died May 5, 1854, aged 62 years.

John Protzman, born in Germany, Feb. 26, 1749, died July 4, 1804, aged 55 years.

David Smart, died Aug. 14, 1822, aged 26 years.

Sarah, wife of E. M. Wilson, died Jan. 29, 1832, in his 42d year.

John Clark, died April 22, 1838, aged 60 years; Eleanor, his wife, died Nov. 8, 1844, aged 67.

In the cemeteries and burial-grounds of Hancock there are numerous handsome monuments, and graves around which there are centred reminiscences of more than ordinary interest. Among the latter is the tomb of Chancellor Johnson. It is in the public cemetery, a simple thick white marble slab, resting on a substantial base of white sandstone, and shaded by a large cedar. The tablet bears the following inscription:

"Sacred
to the memory of
John Johnson, Esq.,
who was born at
Annapolis, Maryland,
Sept. 12th, 1770,
and died
Suddenly at Hancock,
July 30th, 1824.
At the time of his death he was
Chancellor of his native State."

On the day of his death Chancellor Johnson, who was on his way to Berkeley Springs, about six miles southward, on the Virginia side of the Potomac, reached Hancock, and stopped at the Light House, then kept by John Snively. He went to his room and was taken suddenly ill, and died in a short time.

He had recently been appointed by the Governor commissioner on the part of Maryland, to act with the Virginia commissioners in establishing a boundary line between the two States, and was prosecuting this mission when his demise occurred. On the 17th of August following, Hon. Theodorick Bland was appointed chancellor to succeed Mr. Johnson, and Hon. Reverdy Johnson, his son, was delegated as boundary commissioner in his father's stead.

Another notable monument in Hancock is a handsome marble one in the yard in front of the Presbyterian church, denoting the last resting-place of Robert Wason, who was one of the celebrated nineteen Van Buren electors. The inscription on the stone states that he was born April 3, 1787, and died April 17, 1856.

In the Episcopal burial-ground the tomb of Jacob Frey, Sr., who died Dec. 21, 1865, aged fifty-eight years, and Catharine Frey, his wife, who died Aug. 20, 1866, aged fifty years, is marked by a beautifully-carved monument, surmounted by carved urns. The lot of Daniel Cave in the Presbyterian graveyard, in which two of his children are buried, is also designated by a costly monument.

Early Reminiscences.—In 1823 there were no churches in Hancock, and an old log school-house, where David Neil taught the youth of the town and vicinage for thirty years, was used by all denominations as a place of worship.

Mason and Dixon's line is only one and a half miles from the town, and about the same distance west was the old Brent estate, which was held by the Brent family for more than a century. On the place is a prominent knoll, upon the summit of which, during the earliest period of settlement, the inhabitants of that section erected a stone block-house, which, in times of border peril, afforded them a refuge against the Indians. The property on which the fort was situated, the site of which is in full view from the Potomac River, is now owned by Singleton Whitmire.

In the Brent family graveyard the following persons are interred:

George Brent, died Jan. 11, 1872, aged 38.

T. C. Brent, died Dec. 25, 1831, aged 59.

Hannah Brent, died May 16, 1823, aged 56 years, 11 months, and 20 days.

James Tidball, died April 25, 1831, aged 72.

Eleanor Tidball, died Dec. 15, 1843, aged 70.

Mary, wife of Dr. C. H. Ohr, died Oct. 10, 1875, aged 74.

U. L. Blackwell, born March 1, 1805, died Feb. 27, 1855.

Arthur Blackwell, born April 30, 1787, died May 28, 1852.

Walter Blackwell, died Aug. 31, 1845, aged 61.

Elizabeth Bean, died Aug. 20, 1833, aged 75.

Benjamin Bean, died July 28, 1823, aged 64.

In 1828, May 26th, there was a meeting held at the house of Walter Blackwell in Hancock, Thos. C. Brent, presiding, at which Wm. Price and George Baltzell, who were pledged to vote for John Quincy Adams for President and Wm. Rush for Vice-President of the United States, were indorsed for Presidential electors.

In 1846 three strangers visited Hancock, and during the night succeeding their advent robbed all the stores in the town, securing from six to eight thousand dollars. About three years later three thousand dollars of the proceeds were recovered under the following singular circumstances. The thieves were in the act of loaning a sum of money to a purchaser of land near Harrisburg, Pa., when the magistrate, who was executing the mortgages, identified three one-thousand-dollar bills of the Williamsport, Md., Bank, which were, among other funds, advertised as having been stolen from Robert Wason, of Hancock, at the time of the robbery. The result was the arrest of the thieves and their conviction and sentence to the penitentiary by the Frederick County court.

Early in 1854, George Harvey, an eccentric resident of the Hancock District, died. He was a native of Prince George's County, but early in life, or about the year 1780, he removed to the Hancock District, where he resided to the day of his death. He had no family, and lived alone with his servants, isolating himself from society. He was a man of frugal habits, and left an estate valued at ten or twelve thousand dollars to relatives in Washington City. He was frequently asked during his lifetime what disposition he made of his money, to which his uniform reply was that he had deposited it in the bank; but after his death his administrator could not find any deposit to his credit in any bank. About a month after his death, as it was known that he had money, the premises were carefully searched, and the sum of seventeen hundred and ninety-one dollars and two cents was found stowed away in a powder-keg in one of the cellars. The money was all in silver coin, put up in small amounts and wrapped in paper. This was the bank, and these the deposits to which he alluded.

The *Weekly Gazette* was started in Hancock in August, 1854, by F. A. Williams, son of James Williams, of Hagerstown, and in 1858 E. & C. H. Day began the publication of the Hancock *Journal*. On the 25th of July, 1862, Lieut. George Shearer, of Gen. Bradley Johnson's First Maryland Confederate Regiment, was captured at Hancock, Md., together with a fine horse and equipments. He was taken to Hagerstown and committed to jail. It was alleged that he had been in Washington and Frederick Counties for three weeks recruiting for his regiment with poor success, and was about to return to Virginia when arrested.

Industries of Hancock.—Hancock has now one private and three public schools, five churches, and several private business enterprises of great importance. Among these are the hydraulic cement works of Bridges & Henderson, located at Round Top Hill, a short distance west of the town. The firm is composed of Robert Bridges and Charles W. Henderson, and they employ from seventy-five to one hundred men, and from sixteen to twenty in the cooper-shop, where the barrels in which the cement is shipped are made. The rock from which the cement is made is mined out of Round Top Hill, in the side of which are five tunnels, two of them running clear through the hill, and all of them are being worked constantly. The layers of argillo-magnesian limestone from which the cement is made crop out in several places on the north bank of the Potomac River, and were cut into in 1837 and the hydraulic character of the stone discovered, during the process of constructing the canal. The strata of cement rock are exceedingly crooked and tortuous, bending up and down, and doubling upon each other in a very singular and complex manner, forming a series of arches and counter-arches and concentrating a large quantity of the stone within easy and convenient reach. The aggregate thickness of the cement-producing stratum varies, in different parts of the quarries, from eight to twelve feet. Although it is, in fact, a single layer of that thickness, this thickness is in some places apparently doubled, and even trebled, in consequence of the peculiarly crooked condition in which the bed is found. There are six distinct outcrops of the same layer of cement rock exposed to view upon the slope of the hill, within a distance of about two hundred yards along the canal, and they are so located as to secure to the manufacturer every advantage which position can afford for many years to come. Shortly after the discovery of the rock a mill was erected upon the canal at the quarries, two and three-quarter miles west of Hancock, Md., by Mr. Shafer, who until 1863 manufactured under the brand "Shafer Cement." In 1863 it was purchased by the present company.

The stone is burnt at the works in eight perpetual kilns, each twenty-one feet deep and ten feet in diameter at the base. The aggregate daily capacity of the eight kilns, when running full, is about three hundred and twenty barrels of three hundred pounds each, or two thousand two hundred barrels per week, f the kilns be drawn down the same on Sundays as on other days. All labor is suspended at the works on the Sabbath-day. The mill for grinding the cement is driven by an overshot water-wheel, sixteen feet in diameter and sixteen feet width of breast, with buckets thirteen inches in depth. Water for turning the wheel is supplied by the Chesapeake and Ohio Canal, upon the tow-path of which the mill is located. The power of the wheel is considerably in excess of what is required for the works at their present capacity, and the flow of water, although restricted, is sufficient for manufacturing purposes. The grinding is done with four pairs of French burrstones, each five feet in diameter. Their aggregate capacity for grinding somewhat exceeds four hundred barrels of cement in twenty-four hours, by running night and day. After being barreled, the cement is run across the Potomac by cable and is shipped east and west *via* the Baltimore and Ohio Railroad. The firm have about three hundred acres of land on the West Virginia shore, on which is erected a warehouse for the deposit of the cement prior to shipment, and switches connect with the Baltimore and Ohio main tracks. The Chesapeake and Ohio Canal, on which the works are located, is also utilized as a shipping medium and for the reception of coal.

Samuel Rinehart, a leading merchant and manufacturer of Hancock, Washington Co., was born in Waynesburg, Greene Co., Pa., June 9, 1813. Greene County was likewise the birthplace of his father, Barnet Rinehart. On his father's side his ancestry was German, and on his mother's side Scotch. His grandfather, Bennett Rinehart, came from Germany and located in Greene County, where he was slain by the Indians. Barnet Rinehart, his son, was a colonel in the war of 1812, and married Sarah, daughter of James Hook, a colonel in the Revolution, and one of Greene County's earliest settlers. Barnet Rinehart died in Greene County in 1845, twenty-one years after the death of his wife. There were seven children. Those living are Samuel Rinehart and his sister, Mrs. Lucy Green, of Iowa. Samuel left home when he was but fifteen years of age, and with a pack upon his back journeyed on foot through the country, and at Point of Rocks, Md., found his first employment in hauling logs out of the Potomac. He "roughed it" in this way for four months, when John S. Washington, a store-keeper at Point of Rocks, gave the lad employment as clerk. At the end of six months he was made superintendent for a lumbering firm at Harper's Ferry, where he remained about two years. He was then appointed a division assistant superintendent on the Chesapeake and Ohio Canal, with headquarters at Sharpsburg. He continued for three years in this service, and engaged himself as clerk at the Antietam Iron-Works, under John McPherson Brinn. That business, however, did not suit him, and he soon returned to the canal as section "boss," four miles east of Hancock. After six months he changed his location to Cumberland, where for the

next year and a half he was a contractor's superintendent. By this time he had concluded to settle somewhere, and selecting a place on the canal twenty-five miles west of Hancock (at the tunnel), opened a store. He traded there about two years, when he removed to the mouth of Cacapon Creek, and traded another year. The suspension of the canal company inflicted upon him, as it did upon many, a heavy financial loss. A year later, 1842, he began business at Hancock, starting with a few goods obtained on credit. This small beginning was improved by close attention to business and untiring energy. Prosperity came in due time, and he gradually amassed a competence. He remained in Hancock until 1860, when he removed to St. Joseph, Mo., and engaged in banking with Thomas Harbine. In 1861 he sold out his interest in the bank, returned to Hancock, and resumed business as a merchant, in which he has since remained uninterruptedly. From 1856 to 1858 he was interested in a tannery in Fulton County, Pa., and in 1872 built at Hancock a sumac and citron-bark mill, which continues in a flourishing condition. In 1881 he attached to it a saw-mill. Mr. Rinehart's business undertakings include likewise canal contracting, warehousing, the control of a line of boats, and farming. He was an Old-Line Whig, and is now a Democrat. He was a candidate for county commissioner in 1881, but was defeated. In November, 1838, he married Eliza, daughter of Thomas and Ann Bevans, of Washington County. Of their seven children two sons and two daughters survive.

Mr. Charles W. Henderson, of the firm of Bridges & Henderson, owns the land in which the Hancock white-sand mines are located on the West Virginia side of the Potomac, one and a half miles above Hancock, the product of which is used in the manufacture of white glass. The mines are operated by Speer & Co., of Pittsburgh, Pa.

There are also in Round Top Hill extensive deposits of limestone, of which Prof. William E. A. Aiken, in a letter to Messrs. Bridges & Henderson, April 1, 1878, after examining a specimen of the mineral from this point, says, "It is a remarkably fine variety of carbonate of lime, its peculiar appearance being due to its crystalline form. The exact composition by analysis is as follows: In one hundred parts I find

Lime	56.20
Carbonic acid	43.70
Moisture and loss	.10
	100.00

"As it contains no valuable metallic matter, its value would be as material for making a perfectly pure lime in the ordinary manner by burning."

St. Thomas' Protestant Episcopal Church.—In 1835, St. Thomas' P. E. Church, Hancock, was created. At a meeting of the Diocesan Convention a petition from the minister, wardens, and vestry of the church was received, asking that they be recognized as a parish. It was referred to a committee, which reported that Jacob Brosius, Cromwell Orrick, Kelly Thomas, Dr. S. I. Gregory, John Breathed, Dr. R. G. Belt, Isaac Breathed, and George Thomas, and others associated with them, be permitted to form themselves into an Episcopal congregation by the name of St. Thomas' Church. The Rev. J. Delaplane, rector, reported that he entered on this field of labor Aug. 23, 1834. The erection of a church had been commenced, and he reported thirty communicants.

The delegates to conventions and communicants have been as follows:

1838–39, delegates, J. Schlegel and I. Graves; communicants, 1838, 40; 1839, 50; 1840–50, delegate, J. Schlegel; communicants, 1841, 42; 1842, 53; 1843, 57; 1844, 75; 1845,

76; 1846, 72; 1847, 64; 1848, 50; 1849, 54; 1850, 64; 1851–58, delegate, B. Pendleton; communicants, 1851–53, 63; 1854, 60; 1855, 54; 1856, 56; 1858, 65; 1859–60, delegate, John Brosius; communicants, 61; 1861–69, delegate, Mr. Lee; communicants, 1863, 38; 1864, 32; 1866, 47; 1869, 88; 1870, delegate, J. P. Delaplane; communicants, 102; 1871–73, delegate, C. W. Henderson; communicants, 1871, 104; 1872, 106; 1873, 103.

The rectors of St. Thomas' have been Rev. J. Delaplane, 1834–41; Rev. O. Bulkley, 1842–43; Rev. J. T. Hoff, 1844–45; Rev. J. A. Buck, 1845–47; Rev. A. J. Berger, 1848–50; Rev. J. N. Wattson, 1850–51; Rev. G. L. Machenheimer, 1854–57; Rev. W. Stull, 1857–59. Since the latter date Revs. Baird, Jones, Lee, W. A. Haines, and Williams have officiated.

In 1851 Rev. Alexander Berger became assistant in St. Peter's, Baltimore. He was originally a member of the German Reformed Church, but was ordained by Bishop Whittingham in 1843, and removed to Georgia, whence he returned to take charge of St. Thomas' Church. In 1854 he married Mary Anne Allport, of Clearfield, Pa.

David James Lee, M.D., a native of New England, was ordained by Bishop Meade; removed from Virginia, and became rector of St. Thomas', Hancock. In 1863, his church having been destroyed in the war, he returned to Virginia, and in 1863 took letters dismissory to California.

William Scull, a native of Pennsylvania, and a Lutheran minister, was ordained by Bishop Moore in 1836; came to Maryland from Louisiana in 1853, and became rector of St. Andrew's Parish, in St. Mary's County, and in 1867 of St. Thomas' and St. Andrew's, Washington County. In 1859 he removed to Florida. He died Oct. 6, 1871.

Representative Families.—The Breatheds are one of the leading families of Washington County. John Breathed immigrated from Europe to Maryland about the middle of the eighteenth century and settled in Washington County, where he married Jane Kelley, a member of a Scotch-Irish family, whose father owned large tracts of land which he bequeathed in the main to his grandchildren. Soon after his marriage John Breathed removed to Pennsylvania, and became the father of twelve children. There being no church in his neighborhood, Mr. Breathed read the services of the Episcopal Church in his own house, and the Bible and prayer-book used by him were preserved by his grandson until a few years ago, when they were destroyed by fire. Several of his sons never married, and lived and died in the rude old house, not allowing a stone of it to be touched, and prided themselves particularly upon their beautiful stock. After their death the house was torn down, and a new dwelling erected, which is now owned by a member of the family. The brothers largely increased their inheritance by surveying unoccupied lands, a portion of which is still in the possession of the family. As the brothers died they left the greater portion of their land to the survivors among the six. The last of them to die was John, at whose death the land and money were divided up among members of the family of the present generation. Four of the children of John Breathed—Edward, Ranney, James, and Frances—are buried on the farm near Hagerstown, George and Jane on a farm in Pennsylvania, and John at St. Mark's Church, near Breathedsville.

William Breathed married Miss Whitaker, of Virginia, and removed to Kentucky in the year 1800. The fruits of this marriage were eight children, of whom George became private secretary to Gen. Jackson, John Governor of Kentucky, Cardwell a farmer, James a lawyer, Susan never married, and Jane married Dr. Sappington, of Saline County, Mo. William Breathed died in 1817, and with the exception of Mrs. Sappington, who alone attained old age, all of his children died between 1830 and 1837.

Governor Breathed's son, Cardwell, removed to Arrow Rock, Mo., and is the only living representative of the name belonging to the Western branch of the family. Ellen Breathed married twice. Her first husband was Mr. Reynolds, and her second, Maj. Thomas. Her five children are buried in the Episcopal churchyard at Hancock.

Catherine Breathed married John Hunter, a merchant, who was a native of Ireland. Of the seven children of Catherine Hunter, only two are living,—Ranney Hunter, who resides near Hagerstown, and Mrs. Kitty Steiger, who lives near Hancock. The deceased members of this branch are buried on the Breathed farm in Pennsylvania.

Isaac Breathed, the grandfather of Maj. Breathed, married Kitty Lyles, daughter of Dr. Lyles, a surgeon in the Revolutionary army, and lived on a farm near Hancock. He died Jan. 12, 1858, aged eighty-eight years. He had three children, two of whom are dead. His daughter Jane was first married to Rev. James Delaplane, who died several years after his marriage, leaving two children. She subsequently married Rev. James Buck, who is pastor of the Soldiers' Home, and of a neighboring Episcopal Church, which position he has occupied for twenty-eight years.

Another daughter of Isaac Breathed, Elizabeth, married Steven Snodgrass, of Martinsburg, W. Va., and had seven children. The deceased members of this branch are also buried in the Episcopal church at Hancock. John W. Breathed is the sole survivor of Isaac Breathed's family who bears the family name. He married Ann McGill Williams, and had twelve children by this marriage. His second wife was Stella Cullen, daughter of Dr. Cullen, of Richmond, by whom he had six children. Of his children by his first wife, seven are still living, four of them in Maryland. Grafton is a clerk in the house of Anderson & Bro.; Edward is a farmer near Hancock; Priscilla Williams married Robert Bridges, of Hancock; Isaac is a sergeant in the regular army; Francis is a farmer, and married Eleanor Shelton, of Virginia; Elizabeth is unmarried, and lives with Edward; John Breathed married Caroline Breathed, of Missouri. Four of the children of John W. Breathed by his second wife are not yet grown, and live in Virginia. Seven of his children are dead, five of them being buried at St. Mark's church, near Breathedsville. Maj. Breathed is buried at St. Thomas' church, Hancock.

J. W. Breathed was born near Hancock in 1814. When sixteen years old, he was appointed by Gen. Jackson to a cadetship at West Point. His father wished to give him a classical education, but having caught the Western fever, he took a tour in that direction, but soon returned home. He married in 1837, and entered into mercantile pursuits in Virginia. While residing in that State he served in the State Legislature as a representative of Morgan County. In 1848 he left Virginia and returned to Maryland. He settled on the lands of his great-grandfather, and paid considerable attention to agriculture. Subsequently, wishing to educate his sons, he removed to St. James' College. He returned to Virginia in 1871, and now resides at Lynchburg. His only public positions have been those of judge of the Orphans' Court and president of a turnpike company.

Ann McGill Williams, daughter of John McGill Williams, and wife of John W. Breathed, was born in 1819, in Montgomery County, Md. Her father was a farmer, and Walter Williams, her grandfather, was of the same family as Gen. Otho H. Williams. Her grandmother, Ann McGill, belonged to an ancient family, the American head of which was Rev. James McGill, a native of Perth, Scotland, who settled in Maryland in 1728, and who was the first rector of Queen Caroline Parish, Elkridge, Anne Arundel County.

Rev. James McGill traces his pedigree to the year 1543, and to Sir James McGill, Viscount of Oxford. Ann McGill Williams' maternal grandfather was Dr. Lyles, of Montgomery County, Md., whose wife was a Miss Jones, of Prince George's County. She and her husband were first cousins, both having the same maternal grandfather, Dr. Lyles.

John Breathed, second son of John W. Breathed, was educated at St. James' College, Maryland. Before the war he conducted a farm for his father, but when Gen. Lee invaded Maryland, he embraced the opportunity of joining the Confederate army. On the way to Chambersburg, two or three of the company strayed away and were captured by a party of Federal troops. Mr. Breathed was one of the captured party, and was taken as a spy to Chambersburg, where he was fortunately recognized by one of the refugees, and identified before the authorities as a regular Confederate soldier. He was sent to Philadelphia, and was confined in company with a number of deserters. The morning following the provost-marshal ordered that all prisoners of war should be sent to Fort Delaware. His name, however, not being called until too late, he was left behind. In a few days he was sent to Fort Mifflin. He was again accused of being a spy, and was placed in close confinement. In about ten days, not finding any evidence against him, the authorities again treated him as an ordinary prisoner of war. Confinement soon affected his health, and he was finally seized with an attack of typhoid fever, which ended fatally.

BOONSBORO' DISTRICT, No. 6.

Boonsboro', or the Sixth Election District of Washington County, is situated along its eastern border, a little south of the centre, and is separated from Frederick County by the South Mountain range. It is bounded on the south by the Rohrersville District, on the west by the Keedysville and Tilghmanton Districts, and on the north by the whole of Beaver Creek and a portion of the Funkstown Districts. The historic Antietam divides it from Tilghmanton District. Beaver Creek crosses the northwestern portion of the district, and joins the Antietam a short distance below Delamere mills. The district is a most valuable agricultural section, being traversed by the celebrated Pleasant and Hagerstown Valleys, and penetrated by the Frederick and Hagerstown turnpike, a most important highway in that thickly populated and fertile portion of the State. The most prominent town within its borders is Boonsboro', but the villages of Mount Pleasant, Benevola, Zittlestown, and Mill Point add much to the wealth of the general community, and afford it many conveniences and facilities not possessed by other regions in the interior of the State. The entire country is one of great scenic beauty, passing gradually from the weird and rugged steeps of the South Mountains to the picturesque and pastoral landscape of the lowlands in the interior. The district was also the theatre of important military operations during the stirring days of 1861 to 1865, which are treated at length in a preceding chapter.

The population of the district (including the towns of Boonsboro', 859 inhabitants, and Mount Pleasant, 165 inhabitants) is 2262. Boonsboro' District is abundantly supplied with good county and public roads, which cross the country at all angles and afford convenient access to all points. The majority of these lead to and from the Frederick and Hagerstown and the Boonsboro' and Sharpsburg pikes. The latter is one of the best-kept thoroughfares in the State. It runs from Boonsboro' to Sharpsburg through Keedysville, passing over the celebrated Antietam battle-ground, and from it can be seen all of the prominent points on that historic and bloody field. In the rural community there are many families of age and prominence, and many fine estates and residences. Among the leading residents may be mentioned I. Q. A. Kemp, O. Williams, N. Keplinger, L. Baker, J. Hammond, D. H. Newcomer, George Cline, S. and A. Funk, L. Emmert, G. S. Kennedy, J. Newcomer, H. Nunamaker, William Shifler, B. Durnbaugh, J. Foltz, D. W. Foltz, E. Doub, S. Wissinger, J. S. Toms, H. B. Snively, William Sigler, C. Long, E. Moser, G. Goss, J. Kitsmiller, S. Roe, D. Beachley, O. B. Smith, J. Neikirk, P. Irvin, S. Thomas, E. Schlosser, I. H. Ringer, A. C. Huffer, S. Huffer, C. Nicodemus, A. U. Huffer, M. Davis, M. Line, J. Line, A. Keadle, I. Huntsberry, J. Nicodemus, J. Haupt, William Miller, J. L. Nicodemus, J. Huffer, George Shifler, D. Poffenberger, J. Hedrick, J. Neff, Mrs. Snyder, C. N. Mertz, J. Brown, P. Lepole, D. Green, J. Green, D. Easterday, M. Griffin, A. Philhom, F. Keefauver, T. Ford, Mrs. Mertz, W. Griffin, John Kline, M. Hoffman, Mrs. Norris, D. Martz, John Lepole, John Hoffman, J. Easterday, J. Smith, S. Young, I. W. Smith, I. Tine, D. Smith, J. Summers, P. Little, L. Emmert, William Miller, William P. Smith, S. Ringer, M. Nyman, S. Neikirk, John Shriver, G. Houpt, H. Nott, U. Emerson, Mrs. Emerson, J. Little, H. Frunkhouser, William J. Fletcher, J. Albaugh, A. Cadle, and others.

John Nicodemus was born at the old homestead, two miles southeast of Boonsboro', Washington Co., Md., on Nov. 14, 1800. His father was Valentine Nicodemus, who was born in Lancaster County, Pa., Nov. 21, 1763, and moved to Washington County in early life with his brother Conrad, and settled southeast of the present town of Boonsboro'. Early in life he was married to Anna Margaret Speilman, who was born Sept. 1, 1767, and died Feb. 28, 1826. The fruit of this union was three daughters, who died young, and two sons, the elder of whom is the subject of this sketch. His brother Jacob still lives at an advanced age. The grandparents of Mr. Nicodemus emigrated to this county from South Germany about 1720, and settled in Lancaster County, Pa. They died about the close of the Revolutionary war. John Nicodemus married Anna Maria Motter, whose father, Henry Motter, was born in Frederick City, Md., in 1758, and died near Middletown, Frederick Co., Md., Oct. 27, 1830, at the age of seventy-two. His wife was Catharine Smith, who was born April 28, 1766, and died Jan. 18, 1828. The grandfather of Mrs. Nicodemus was born in France, and belonged to the Reformed Church of France, then known as the Church of the Huguenots, and was driven to this country by the cruel persecutions that were waged against these earnest Protestants during the reign of Louis XV. The family name was Mottrie or Mottieur. Mr. and Mrs. Nicodemus were married near Middletown, Frederick Co., by Rev. Jonathan Helfenstein, pastor of the Reformed Church, June 13, 1826. Seven children were born to them, three daughters and four sons, all of whom have died save one son, John L. Nicodemus, of Boonsboro'. Their educational advantages were limited, such only as were afforded by public and private schools at home. The religious connection of both families was the Reformed Church in Europe and in this country. Mr. Nicodemus affiliated with the Whig party, and afterwards with the Republicans, but was in no sense a politician. He never sought and never held a political office. His choice of business was in early life farming and milling, which he followed successfully up to 1854, when he passed it over to his son, John Luther, and removed to Boonsboro', where he remained engaged in managing his large estate up to the time of his death, Aug. 29, 1879. He died after a short but painful illness, at a good old age. He was blessed with a strong constitution, which, together with careful habits, brought him with unusual health and unimpaired vigor to nearly fourscore years. Mr. Nicodemus possessed a benevolent disposition, as is shown in his liberal gift to the erection of the present handsome Reformed Church edifice in Boonsboro', and also by his generous support of the gospel, and his aid in other religious enterprises. About a year (July 1, 1878) before his death he gave a farm for which he paid $12,500 to his native county in fee-simple for the maintenance of the poor and homeless. On this farm, which is near Hagerstown, the board of county commissioners have since erected Bellevue Hospital, where for all time to come the poor, helpless, and

John Nicodemus

homeless will find rest, food, and raiment. His remains lie buried in Boonsboro' Cemetery. The spot is marked by a handsome monument of beautiful design, which is considered one of the finest in the county. The following resolutions of respect were adopted by the board of county commissioners at the time of his death :

"*Resolved*, By the county commissioners of Washington County, that we have heard with great regret of the death of John Nicodemus, a venerable citizen and benefactor of Washington County.

"*Resolved*, That as a manifestation of the respect and regard of the people of Washington County for the long and blameless life of this aged citizen we enter this expression of the public regret upon the minutes of this board, and hereby approve the stopping of all labor in 'Bellevue' on the day of his funeral.

"*Resolved*, That the healthful and ample domain given to the poor and afflicted of this county by his unexampled benevolence is his best eulogy.

"*Resolved*, That a copy of these resolutions be sent by the clerk to the family of John Nicodemus and copies be furnished to the public press."

Mr. Nicodemus was simple and unostentatious in character, but possessed a thoroughly sincere and generous disposition, and never tired of doing good. He was very active in promoting the interests of his church, and was remarkable for the scrupulous care and method with which he transacted whatever business was at hand, or discharged any trust that might be committed to him. His son, J. L. Nicodemus, inherited his father's large landed estate and other property, and manages them with the same judgment and sagacity which secured his father's success.

Under an act of the General Assembly, the boundaries of Boonsboro' District were fixed by a commission in 1822, as follows:

"To commence at the road leading through Crampton's Gap to the Frederick County line; thence with the lines of District No. 1 to Cary's Cross-roads; thence still with the lines of District No. 2 to the road leading from Claggett's Mills to Williams Port; thence with the lines of District No. 3, to the road leading from Hagerstown to Orr's Gap; thence with said road to the Frederick County line; thence with said line to the beginning."

The most important town in the Boonsboro' District is Boonsboro', which is situated near the west base of the South Mountains, on the Frederick and Hagerstown or old National pike, eight miles from Hagerstown and sixteen miles from Frederick. The site of the town was originally owned by William and George Boone, who are supposed to have been members of Daniel Boone's family. A tradition of the section has it that Daniel Boone, the Kentucky pioneer, was originally from this portion of the State, and emigrated to Kentucky, as did the Shelbys, one of whom was the first Governor of that State; the Hart family, into which Henry Clay married; and hundreds of other hardy Western Maryland people who opened up the wilds of the Blue Grass State during the latter part of the eighteenth century. Boonsboro' was originally a part of two tracts called Beall's Chance and Fellowship, and was first called Margaretsville, in honor of the wife of George Boone.

Wm. Boone resided here during his lifetime. He died in 1798 and was buried in the Salem, afterwards Trinity, Reformed Church graveyard. George Boone died in Reading, where he lived for many years. His house stood until the year 1800 in the rear of Salem church. Susannah Boone, wife of Wm. Boone, died in 1844, at the age of eighty-eight years. The first house erected in Boonsboro' is said to have occupied the site of the present residence of Mrs. Davis, widow of Senator Eli Davis, adjoining the Eagle Hotel. Christian Dagenhart came here in 1796, and has left a record that there were at that time five houses in the town,—P. Conn's Eagle Hotel, Boone's farmhouse, Jacob Craig's, Mrs. Short's log cabin, and a house at the spring. In 1829, when Henry Nyman came here, there were twenty-nine houses. Mr. Nyman's house was in 1798 the Eagle Hotel, and the residence now occupied by Dr. Gaines was put up in 1800. There was a post-route through this section in 1802, and Mr. Locker was postmaster at that time. Sept. 9, 1813, the land belonging to the heirs of Wm. Boone was sold to Henry Nyman and Mr. Petebenner, who laid it off in building lots. In 1810, Gen. Samuel Ringgold, of Fountain Rock, contributed a sufficient number of shingles to cover the old stone or Salem church. In 1786, Mr. S. Nyman kept store at Boonsboro', and Boone & Co. also had a store there during the latter part of the eighteenth century. In 1802, George Troutman had a store. Following him were the Stonebrakers, and by 1831 Boonsboro' had grown to be an important trade centre for the Middletown and Pleasant Valleys, and Loudon and Berkeley Counties, Va., one house alone selling ninety thousand dollars' worth of merchandise in a year. About this time Samuel Bentz built a paper-mill and subsequently converted it into a foundry, which is still being operated. Patrick Conn kept a store in the first building next the Eagle Hotel, which was torn down in 1828 or '29. A glance at Conn's books of that date would indicate that some of the early settlers were not especially ardent in the matter of local option. Some of the entries in his ledger were as follows:

"Sept. 22,	1802.	Two grogs at 5½*d*.....	11*d*.
March,	1804.	1 qt. beer................	11*d*.
"	"	1 grog....................	5½*d*.
" 9,	"	1 qt. spts................	11*d*.
" 4,	"	1 qt. beer................	11*d*.

Credit:

Looking-glasses and chairs in club...... 2*s*. 6*d*."

The first hotel in Boonsboro' was the Eagle, kept by Peter Conn, located at the corner of Baltimore and St. Paul Streets. Mrs. Scott's store, in the early history of the town, was in a log house on the site of the present United States Hotel, which was built in 1811. Another hotel, built about 1800, stood on the northwest corner of Baltimore and St. Paul Streets, and was torn down fifteen years ago. "Rose Hill," now the residence of John F. Horine, was formerly a hotel, erected by Dr. Ezra Slifer in 1814.

Dr. Meyer was the first physician in Boonsboro' (1806); Dr. E. Slifer in 1809. Henry Dick had a weaver's shop where the parsonage now stands as early as 1800, and probably before. "Chris" Dagenhart, Peter Baker (born 1762), and Peter Heck were in the same business. John House, Aaron Py, George and Anthony Baltzer were master-masons. Anthony Baltzer was a soldier in the Revolutionary war, and drew a pension. Henry Blessing, Jacob Myers, and John Stemple were chair-makers. Samuel Mowery and Andrew Sardinger were cabinet-makers, Mr. Wolf was a blacksmith, and Michael Brunett and Daniel Christian were shoemakers.

The National pike was finished as far as Boonsboro' in 1810. In 1806 it was feared that it would not be brought through to Boonsboro', and there was considerable indignation among the people. A public barbecue was held, at which Gen. Samuel Ringgold, Brien Ringgold, and Gen. Tilghman pacified the public.

A military company existed in Boonsboro' in 1802, of which Patrick Conn was captain. In 1810, John Petebenner organized an infantry company, and Henry Petebenner a rifle company. Capt. Lewis Fletcher and Abijah Smith, of Boonsboro', were soldiers in the war of 1812. The light-horse existed in the town in 1815–16, and in 1826 a rifle company commanded by H. Petebenner. In 1836 the Ringgold Riflemen were organized, George French, captain, John C. Brining, first lieutenant, and Jonathan Gelwicks, second lieutenant. A company was also raised in 1861, under John C. Brining, James W. Shank, and G. P. Strouse.

The people of this section always possessed a sterling martial spirit and a genuine admiration for the military heroes of the day. Washington was specially venerated, and in the excess of their regard for him they erected a monument on the top of South Mountain, at a point on "the Blue Rocks" overlooking the town. This act was consummated on the Fourth of July, 1827, and the Hagerstown *Torch-Light* of that time made the following report of that remarkable proceeding:

"WASHINGTON MONUMENT, NEAR BOONSBORO'.

"Pursuant to previous arrangements, the citizens of Boonsboro' assembled at the public square on the 4th instant, at half-past seven o'clock in the morning, to ascend the 'Blue Rocks,' for the patriotic purpose of erecting a monument to the memory of him whose name stands at the head of this article. This spot was selected in consequence of the great facility with which the materials were furnished. A little more than the foundation had been laid the day before, which enabled us to proceed without delay in the grand design before us. The men seemed actuated by a spirit of zeal and ardor almost bordering on enthusiasm. All except a few accidental visitors from the adjoining county (who ate and drank, but stood aloof from the work) seemed influenced by a vigorous principle of emulation that promised a speedy termination of that day's labor.

"Though the majority of the men were from that class of society who earn their bread by the sweat of their brow, yet I can say safely, and as proudly say, that not one of them returned home intoxicated, so much superior was their desire to accomplish the work undertaken than the love of self-gratification. About twelve o'clock we heard a very appropriate extempore address from the Rev. Mr. Clinghan, a gentleman of the Revolutionary period, whose warm patriotism, animating a constitution rendered infirm by age and bad health, induced him to bear all fatigue and danger to accomplish the purpose of his heart.

"About one o'clock we partook of a cold collation, as our object was not to gratify our pampered appetites; consequently no sumptuous arrangements had been made, neither were toasts prepared for the occasion, but we enjoyed more heartfelt satisfaction in partaking of our simple fare than the most costly or high-seasoned dishes would have afforded. Our thoughts and food were both highly spiced with the contemplation of our work, thereby needing no stimulants to excite an artificial appetite. At the conclusion of our labors, about four o'clock, the Declaration of Independence was read from one of the steps of the monument, preceded by some prefatory observations, after which several salutes of infantry were fired, when we all returned to town in good order.

"This monument is seated immediately upon what is called the 'Blue Rock.' It is fifty-four feet in circumference at its base and fifteen feet high (we contemplate raising it thirty feet after the busy season shall be passed). The wall is composed of huge stone, many weighing upwards of a ton, with the whole centre filled up with the same material. A flight of steps, commencing at the base and running through the body of the fabric, enables us to ascend to the top, from whence the most beautiful prospect presents itself that the eye can possibly behold. Shepherdstown, Hagerstown, and Cavetown are distinctly seen, with all the fertile fields of Jefferson, Berkeley, and Washington, affording a landscape teeming with life and wealth.

"To the summit of this mountain is a rugged path, but the view will afford a rich compensation for the labor. Twelve feet from the base, upon the side fronting Boonsboro', was inserted a white marble slab, with the following inscription:

"'Erected in memory of Washington, July 4, 1827, by the citizens of Boonsboro'.'

"At the laying of the monument several Revolutionary soldiers ascended and fired three rounds from its top."

The "Blue Rocks" upon which the "monument" was reared are twelve hundred feet above the valley, at the summit of the South Mountain, about two miles from Boonsboro'. They consist of immense quantities of loose rock, ranging in size from a pound to many tons, and are scattered over the top and down the slope of the mountain in confused masses. It does not appear that the Washington monument referred to above was ever completed according to the intention of the zealous projectors, and at the present day the novel structure is in ruins.

Among other early residents of Boonsboro' were the following:

Benjamin Clagett, J. P.; Capt. Peter Conn, merchant; George Scott, John Brandner, Henry Nyman, John Ludy, Henry Locher, Jr., George Troutman; Peter Baker, weaver; Dr. Ezra Slifer, who was a prominent citizen; John B. F. Benner, Daniel Christian, George Nichols, Ephraim Davis, George Shafer, Conrad Nicodemus, George Wordell, Mordecai Boone, Wendel Shechter; John Adams, tavern-keeper; Christian Artz, tavern-keeper and tinman; Dr. H. Clagett, who came there from Pleasant Valley, 1816; John Weast, shoemaker; George Fague, cabinet-maker; Charles Hallar, Michael Piper, John Dotro, George Fague, George Schott, and George Nikirk.

In 1818 the people of Boonsboro' advertised that "they stood in need of the following mechanics: one whitesmith, one silversmith, one gunsmith, one cabinet-maker, and one blue-dyer." The census of 1820, two years later, showed that the population consisted of 395 white persons, 7 free colored, and 26 slaves, or 428 in all.

Ira Hill was superintendent of the Boonsboro' Academy in November, 1825 and 1826. In 1828 "the friends of the administration convened at Edwards' Hotel, Boonsboro', Jonathan Newcomer, chairman."

Churches and Cemeteries.—Early in May, 1828, the corner-stone of a new church was laid in Boonsboro' with Masonic ceremonies, under the direction of Eureka Lodge. About one hundred and forty Masons were present. The Rev. Dr. Green delivered an appropriate address on the occasion, preceded and followed by prayer by the Rev. Mr. McCauley. The church was intended to be used by all denominations, but was principally erected under the auspices of the Methodist society.

On Jan. 21, 1830, a meeting of the citizens of Boonsboro' was called to consider the most effectual means to secure the location of the contemplated college of the Baltimore Annual Conference of the Methodist Episcopal Church in the town. Rev. E. Smith was called to the chair, and Washington W. Hitt was appointed secretary. The following resolutions were adopted:

"That the citizens of Boonsboro' and vicinity make every possible effort to obtain the location of the proposed college in or near this village, and that a committee be appointed to superintend the obtaining of subscriptions; also that the committee consist of three, who shall act in conjunction with the chairman and secretary in obtaining subscriptions, and that they shall be vested with discretionary power to appoint as many to assist them as they may in their judgment think proper."

George French, Joseph Weast, and Samuel Bentz were named as the committee, and they designated the following gentlemen to assist them, under the terms of the resolution: Jonathan Shafer, John A. Bentz, John Sharer, William Booth, Samuel M. Hitt, Jonathan Newcomer, Charles A. Warfield, Jacob Miller, Col. John Blackford, Daniel Sprigg, Dr. G. W. Boerstler, Franklin Anderson, Alexander Neill, John D. Ridenour, L. C. Willis, Robert Wason, David Rohrer, Robert Clagett, Rev. Jeremiah Mason.

The establishment of the Trinity Reformed Church, Boonsboro', dates as far back as 1750, nearly forty years before the laying out and settlement of the village of Boonsboro', which took place in 1788. The first church building was of logs, and stood on a rise of ground a half-mile to the northeast of the present town of Boonsboro'. Here the early settlers met and worshiped before the Declaration of Independence, and here also those of the faith of the Reformed Church worshiped for more than fifty years.

As early as 1802, when Boonsboro' had grown to be a considerable village for those times, the log church was found to be insufficient, and occasional services were held in the public school-house of the town. This was not, however, satisfactory to the zealous Christians of the Reformed faith, and public attention was called to the necessity for a new church edifice. The congregation were not as strong financially, however, as they were in their religious purposes. It was determined in view of all the circumstances to ask the Legislature for permission to raise sufficient funds by lottery, the following committee being appointed to present the petition: George Scott, John Brantner, Sr., Henry Locher, George Trautman, Henry Nyman, Sr., and John Lundey. The petition was granted, the scheme proved successful under the management of the same committee, and sufficient money was raised to build the church, at a cost of two thousand eight hundred dollars. It was completed in 1810, and was built of stone on a lot given by a citizen, and deeded to the trustees of the Reformed and Lutheran congregations. In 1812 a bell, made in England, was placed in the belfry at a cost of four hundred dollars. This bell still does service for the congregation, and is as good as when it was brought over, seventy years ago. The first sermon preached in this church was at its consecration in 1810, and was delivered by Rev. Jonathan Rahauser, pastor of the Reformed Church at Hagerstown. The church was dedicated as "Salem Church," but became better known as the "Stone Church."

The original church, the log structure of which mention has been made, was at this time still standing, a half-mile northeast of the town, and was known as Shouk's (German, Schwang's), and used by the United Brethren congregation until 1832, when it was deserted by them for a better church in the town. A few years afterwards the old building was taken down, and nothing remains to mark the spot except the little graveyard on the hill.

Salem church met the wants of the Reformed and Lutheran congregations until 1859, when the desire for a new and larger building was frequently expressed. The war interfered with carrying out the wishes of the congregation, but with the return of peace the desire for a new building again expressed itself. On Dec. 25, 1869, the Reformed congregation unanimously resolved to build a new church, and to this end purchased for sixteen hundred dollars the entire interest of the Lutheran congregation in Salem church The erection of the new edifice was superintended by the following committee: William Miller, John Shifler, John Nicodemus, Frisby J. Davis, David Schlosser, Samuel Knode, and Moses Bomberger, appointed Feb. 19, 1870. The plans, drawings, and designs were prepared by John L. Gettier, of Baltimore, and were adopted by the committee, May 20, 1870. In June and July, 1870, the old church was torn down, and the foundation of the new begun July 19th. On August 28th the corner-stone was laid with appropriate services, and on Sunday, May 14, 1871, the church was consecrated as the Trinity Reformed church. The style of the church is Gothic Romanesque. The dimensions are seventy-three by forty-three, with four feet for the front part of tower and four for a recess pulpit, making the length of the building eighty-one feet. The interior has a seating capacity for six hundred persons. The lecture-room for Sunday-school and prayer-meetings will seat about three hundred persons. The spire in front of the church is one hundred and twenty feet high, and is surmounted by a large gilded cross. The entire cost of the church and furniture was eighteen thousand dollars. It is a beautiful edifice, and one of the most attractive in the county. The congregation numbers about one hundred and forty communicant members, who are an intelligent and earnest people, made up of prosperous farmers, business and professional men. There is considerable wealth in the congregation, and perhaps no less than one million dollars is represented by the membership. As far as can be learned from reliable data, the following pastors have served this congregation:

1770–90, Rev. Jacob Weymer; 1790–92, Rev. J. William Runkle; 1792–1817, Rev. Jonathan Rahauser; 1817–21, Rev. Lewis Mayer; 1822–29, Rev. Solomon K. Denius; 1831–37, Rev. John Rebough; 1837–44, Rev. J. W. Hoffmeier; 1844–51, Rev. A. G. Dole; 1851–56, Rev. Robert Douglass; 1857–62, Rev. L. A. Brunner; 1863–67, Rev. M. L. Sherford; 1869–73, Rev. Jacob Hassler; 1874 to the present time, Rev. Simon S. Miller.

In conducting the lottery by which funds were realized to build the first Trinity church, as above referred to, the work of the managers was subjected to the inspection of a committee consisting of John B. F. Benner, Daniel Christian, George Nichols, Ephraim Davis, George Shafer, Conrad Nicodemus, George Wordell, Mordecai Boone, and Wendel Shechter, who, in February, 1812, certified that "the managers of the Boonsboro' church lottery had judiciously applied the money raised by the lottery in building the church edifice and churchyard fence." This is not the only instance in Boonsboro' history where lotteries were utilized as a medium for raising money for public purposes, as Charles Haller, Michael Piper, John Dotro, George Fague, George Shott, and George Nikirk were managers of "a lottery to raise money to finish the school-house and buy a bell in 1817."

In the yard of Trinity Reformed church are the graves of many of the Boone family. The spot where William Boone, the founder of the town, is buried, is known, but it is not marked by any stone. It is among luxuriant weeds and grass in a remote corner of the place, and is indicated only by a mound, which is now only a few inches above the surface of the surrounding ground. The stones in this burial-place bear the following inscriptions:

Susanna Boone, proprietress of Boonsboro', born Sept. 11, 1755, died Feb. 1, 1844.

Charlotte Boone, wife of Ephraim Davis, born June, 1783, died August, 1806.

Michael Stonebraker, died Jan. 25, 1826, in his 41st year.

Sarah Boone, died Sept. 7, 1874, aged 83 years.

Mary Retz, born Aug. 13, 1786, died Feb. 22, 1819.

Dorothea Hacken, born Jan. 23, 1760, died July 29, 1817.

Daniel Clary, born Feb. 25, 1768, died March 1, 1817.

Ann Maria Fritz, born June 18, 1767, died June 29, 1824.

Susanna Funk, born Feb. 18, 1753, died Sept. 22, 1830.

Peter Conn, born Aug. 24, 1758, died March 24, 1820.

Susanna Brandner, born May 9, 1767, died Jan. 25, 1830.

John Brandner, born Feb. 9, 1761, died Aug. 28, 1818.

Rachel Walker, born April 12, 1756, died May 26, 1822.

Ann Mary Summers, born Oct. 8, 1768, died Feb. 13, 1833.

William Cligen, D.D., born Dec. 4, 1753, died Oct. 28, 1833.

John Gelwicks, born May 6, 1786, died April 13, 1836; and his wife, Margaret, died July 30, 1860, aged 80 years.

John Hammond, Sr., born May 27, 1774, died Feb. 22, 1849; and his wife, Catharine, born Dec. 17, 1776, died Dec. 8, 1866.

Wendel Schichter, born December, 1754, died Jan. 29, 1845.

John B. Welty, born April 2, 1792, died Jan. 23, 1841.
Jacob Barnet, born Oct. 4, 1781, died Feb. 2, 1850.
John Montebaugh, died May 17, 1865, aged 75 years.
John Horine, died July 13, 1862, aged 76 years.
Jacob Hoffman, born July 3, 1760, died March 26, 1732; and his wife, Mary Barbara, born Oct. 23, 1763, died April 14, 1834.
Joseph Weast, Sr., born Jan. 24, 1791, died March 16, 1843.
Robert Ringer, born Aug. 12, 1762, died Jan. 18, 1835.
Elizabeth Shaw, born April 10, 1788, died Oct. 19, 1865.
Abijah Smith, died May 24, 1878, aged 82 years.

In the Methodist Episcopal Church graveyard the following old residents are buried:

Patrick Kearney, born 1778, died Aug. 5, 1832.
Isabella Shaw, died Jan. 14, 1875, aged 81 years.
Christiana Grubb, born Sept. 10, 1769, died March 13, 1843.
Martha Kearney, born Dec. 28, 1789, died June 26, 1845.
Martha Keadle, died May 1, 1850, aged 75 years.
Letitia Smith, died March 17, 1850, aged 74 years.
Sophia Baker, died July 20, 1862, aged 62 years.
Catharine Albaugh, died Oct. 3, 1858, aged 56 years.

The public cemetery at Boonsboro' is probably the prettiest in the State. It is situated on an incline back of the main street in the southern part of the town, and is especially distinguished for its fine location and arrangements, handsome lots and monuments, and attractive surroundings. Among those who are interred there are the following:

John Nicodemus, born Nov. 14, 1800, died Aug. 29, 1879.
Valentine Nicodemus, born Nov. 21, 1763, died Nov. 2, 1835.
Anna M. Nicodemus, born Dec. 1, 1769, died Feb. 28, 1826.
Henry Detrick, born Oct. 11, 1811, died May 20, 1870.
Joseph Fasnacht, died March 24, 1875, aged 64 years.
Daniel Keedy, died Aug. 13, 1876, aged 76 years.
William H. Gilbert, born May 3, 1827, died October, 1877.
Mary, wife of Jonas Davis, died June 23, 1875, in the 52d year of her age.
Jesse Morrison, died Oct. 27, 1874, aged 67 years.
Eliza Beard, died Sept. 25, 1872, aged 66 years.
Sarah Ann Brengle, wife of Charles Brengle, died Feb. 8, 1870, aged 69 years.
Eve Ann, wife of S. Ringer, born April 14, 1814, died Dec. 17, 1879.
Lloyd Davis, who died in Toledo, Ohio, Jan. 8, 1875, aged 53; also Frisby and Joseph Davis, brothers.
Jonathan S. Gelwicks, born Dec. 19, 1819, died Aug. 21, 1864.
Joel Schlosser, died Oct. 18, 1879, aged 68 years.
John Nikirk, born Dec. 25, 1807, died May 16, 1878.
Susannah, wife of John Nikirk, born Sept. 20, 1814, died May 16, 1866.
Joseph Lighter, born March 17, 1788, died May 8, 1875.
Magdalene E., wife of Joseph Lighter, born Dec. 28, 1794, died Aug. 14, 1866.
Jonas Keedy, born Aug. 5, 1820, died Feb. 17, 1879.
Andrew Hershey, died Dec. 27, 1822, aged 43 years.
Robert Smith, born Jan. 15, 1738, died Oct. 14, 1818.
Daniel Smith, died Sept. 25, 1878.
Caroline, wife of Daniel Smith, died Nov. 11, 1862, aged 19 years.
Absalom Itneyer, died Feb. 22, 1869, aged 49 years.
George Staubs, died May 11, 1874, aged 73 years.
Abraham Thomas, born May 16, 1794, died April 10, 1838.
Elizabeth, wife of Abraham Thomas, died April 28, 1871, aged 80 years.
Samuel Reynolds, died Feb. 5, 1879, aged 61 years.
Dr. William E. Davis, born Dec. 9, 1829, died Dec. 14, 1858.
Elias Davis, died Aug. 17, 1870, aged 71 years.
Phinehas Williams, died Nov. 3, 1850, aged 58 years.
Ann M. Williams, died July 8, 1875, aged 74 years.
Henry Muller, died Feb. 6, 1843, aged 76 years.
Susannah, wife of Henry Muller, died April 22, 1851, aged 71.
Mary Muller, wife of George Muller, of Washington City, died March 30, 1845, aged 73 years.
Emanuel Herr, died Dec. 30, 1856, aged 51 years.
Frederick Weckler, born in Würtemberg, Germany, March 6, 1818, died June 29, 1871.
Thomas P. Lynch, died December, 1866, aged 48 years.
Mary H., wife of Thomas P. Lynch, died Feb. 8, 1872, aged 51 years.
Magdalena Ordner, died Dec. 6, 1860, aged 82 years.
Peter Ringer, born Aug. 19, 1876, died Nov. 8, 1860.
Almira, wife of Peter Ringer, died Nov. 6, 1854, aged 37 years.
Matthias Green, died July 10, 1861, aged 46 years.
Barbara Ann, wife of Matthias Green, died April 13, 1873, aged 63 years.
Levi Meredith, died Feb. 17, 1872, aged 93 years.
Samuel Meredith, died April 13, 1868, aged 61 years.
Mrs. Elizabeth Meredith, died Aug. 16, 1860, aged 85 years.
John Castle, died April 7, 1877, aged 69.
Catherine Summers, died Feb. 3, 1879, aged 71.
Jos. H. Zepler, born May 26, 1827, died Nov. 19, 1876.
James Chambers, died May 18, 1875, aged 76.
Mary, first wife of James Chambers, died June 1, 1847, aged 53.
David H. Keedy, died Feb. 17, 1867, aged 71.
Joseph O'Neal, died Dec. 4, 1878, in his 76th year.
Fonrose H. Irwin, born Feb. 22, 1837, died April 10, 1878.
Wm. Stephens, died Jan. 30, 1867, aged 49.
Elizabeth, wife of Wm. Stephens, died Aug. 12, 1860, aged 40.
Septimus Stephens, born March 11, 1786, died March 17, 1855.
Amelia Stephens, died March 21, 1862, aged 79.
Rev. Wm. Monroe, born Sept. 8, 1783, died May 29, 1871, in the 88th year of his age and 62d year of his ministry of the Methodist Episcopal Church. His second wife, Mary Talbot, died Dec. 5, 1863.
James William, only son of Rev. Wm. Monroe, died Feb. 14, 1859, aged 36 years; his wife died Jan. 6, 1858, aged 31.
Henry Nyman, Sr., died April 16, 1876, aged 91. He was one of the original settlers of the town.
Susannah, wife of Henry Nyman, Sr., died April 20, 1836, aged 48.
Henry Newman, Jr., born Aug. 5, 1811, died Dec. 11, 1860.
Christian Deaner, born June 21, 1794, died Jan. 11, 1869.
Emory E. Deaner, born Jan. 1, 1835, died April 18, 1863.
Jacob Hammond, died May 29, 1845, aged 73.
Mary, wife of Jacob Hammond, died June 17, 1875, aged 75.
Rev. G. W. Weills, pastor of Trinity Lutheran Church, died July 7, 1868, aged 40.
Samuel Doub, died Aug. 2, 1872, aged 66.
Jacob S. Toms, died Aug. 22, 1879, aged 66.
Jacob Huffer, born March 16, 1806, died Dec. 31, 1868.
Geo. Staubs, died May 11, 1874, aged 73.
Edward E. Fague, died Aug. 14, 1871, aged 24.
Joseph B. Dehoff, died Oct. 2, 1872, aged 29.
Jacob Blecker, born June 5, 1807, died Nov. 29, 1871.
Joseph Knox, died Aug. 2, 1871, aged 77.
Nancy, wife of Joseph Knox, died Oct. 21, 1872, aged 59.

Lewis Watson, died March 25, 1869, aged 60.
Louis B. Nyman, born March 7, 1824, died Aug. 4, 1878.
Henry Horine, died Jan. 30, 1864, aged 53.
Samuel Horine, died Dec. 4, 1863, aged 55.
Dr. Samuel C. Troupe, died March 17, 1872, aged 26.
Hiram Weast, died Dec. 17, 1854, aged 39.
L. D. Welck, died Aug. 30, 1857, aged 49.
Wm. B. Cheney, born Nov. 9, 1791, died April 17, 1828.
Jacob Knode, died March 6, 1855, aged 67.
Robert Cheney, Sr., born March 8, 1767, died Aug. 21, 1830; his wife, died May 15, 1855, aged 85.
Robert Cheney, Jr., born Oct. 13, 1801, died Jan. 25, 1831.
Michael Funk, born Sept. 18, 1787, died Feb. 5, 1834.
Naomi Funk, born June 25, 1790, died Jan. 7, 1834.
John D. Heister, died July 20, 1841, aged 32.
Matilda C. Heister, died April 18, 1851, aged 40.
Maj. Peter Seibert, born Nov. 11, 1773, died Dec. 27, 1838.
Margaret Seibert, died June 19, 1835, aged 57.
George Strause, born Oct. 12, 1800, died March 5, 1860.
Philip J. Rickard, died April 15, 1874, aged 76.
Catherine Rickard, died Jan. 2, 1863, aged 64.
John P. Rickard, died Dec. 13, 1854, in his 30th year.
Benjamin Stone, died March, 1870, aged 61.
John T. Troup, born Nov. 6, 1826, died March 19, 1880.
Jacob F. Eckshire, died June 25, 1880, aged 72 years.
Ezra Houpt, died Aug. 16, 1880, aged 59.
Solomon Warrenfeltz, died Feb. 15, 1863, aged 40.
Michael Hoffman, died April 19, 1879, aged 77.
Mary, wife of Michael Hoffman, died March, 1881, aged 74.
Peter Wisman, born May 13, 1815, died March 26, 1878.
Lewis H. Smith, died Nov. 6, 1878, aged 59.
John M. Reapsomer, died June 4, 1858, aged 56.
Jacob Lime, died April 29, 1879, aged 83.
Leah, wife of Jacob Lime, died Feb. 1, 1852, aged 49.
Margaret Lime, died May 18, 1863, in her 68th year.
Solomon Eavey, died Oct. 26, 1879, aged 77.
Mary Ann, wife of Solomon Eavey, born Oct. 13, 1813, died Nov. 24, 1850.
Henrietta V. Wilson, died Feb. 18, 1860, in the 73d year of her age.
Michael Thomas, born May 5, 1779, died Jan. 23, 1839.
Elizabeth Thomas, his wife, born Nov. 25, 1756, died Sept. 22, 1823.
Conrad Nicodemus, born Jan. 10, 1777, died March 27, 1834.
Sophia Nicodemus, his wife, born Oct. 22, 1779, died Jan. 16, 1859.
Mary A. Clark, daughter of Conrad Nicodemus, died July 14, 1871, aged 72.
Elizabeth, wife of Jacob Easterday, died April 4, 1873, aged 72.
Mary M., wife of Michael Easterday, died April 3, 1874, aged 89.
Dr. O. J. Smith, born Jan. 13, 1810, died June 14, 1868.
Jeannette V. Smith, died June 27, 1842, aged 24.
Dr. F. J. Smith, born Sept. 13, 1841, died July 7, 1867.
George N. Snyder, died June 30, 1875, aged 69.
I. Miller Snyder, died Dec. 7, 1873, aged 24.
Conrad Thompson, died March 22, 1873, aged 80.
Mary Thompson, his wife, died Dec. 5, 1831, aged 41.
Margaret R. Direly, wife of Ezra, born May 24, 1820, died Oct. 23, 1878.
John C. Lane, born April 7, 1811, died July 15, 1855.
George Scott Kennedy, died April 2, 1878, aged 78.
Samuel H. Smith, died April 8, 1876, aged 65.
Henry Barkman, died Oct. 26, 1850, aged 56.
Elizabeth, wife of Abraham Zigler, died Jan. 15, 1879, aged 82.

Among the specially attractive and costly memorials in the public cemetery is a granite monument surmounted by the figure of an angel in marble, with a star on the forehead, and outstretched hand pointing to the sky, and a sprig of lilies resting gracefully on the left arm. The inscription on the shaft is "BARGER." The owner is a native of Locust Grove, and is now a resident of Cincinnati, where he built the Queen City water-works. Another is a magnificent marble monument surmounted by an urn with the figures of the Virgin and children carved on the front. This is situated in the Nicodemus family lot. The Keedy lot is also marked by a handsome monument surmounted by a cross, and the grave of Mrs. Mary Davis is marked by a fine arched tomb.

The United Brethren church, three miles from Boonsboro', was dedicated on Christmas day, 1858, and four hundred and seventy dollars were collected for the purpose of paying for the same.

La Grange Lodge, No. 36, I. O. O. F., was instituted at Sharpsburg under a dispensation of the Grand Lodge, dated July 16, 1841, and was located at Boonsboro', May 8, 1847.

The Boonsboro' *Odd-Fellow* of Feb. 22, 1849, annonnced that "a friend of ours has just informed us that he has discovered a silver-mine on Red Hill, three miles south of this place. A specimen of the ore has just been left at this office. It is very heavy, and resembles silver very much, but whether it is or not we are unable to decide."

In November, 1858, the Boonsboro' *Odd-Fellow* passed into the hands of Mr. Isaiah Wolfersberger. The retiring editor, Mr. Josiah Knodle, in announcing the change, said, "A little over eighteen years ago we established this office; and now we confess it is with reluctance that we take leave of our favorite calling, but a disposition to accommodate our young friend (with some other considerations) has caused us to yield our preference and retire to the shades of private life."

On Wednesday, Aug. 17, 1870, Hon. Elias Davis, a prominent citizen of Washington County, died at his residence in Boonsboro', in the seventy-first year of his age. Mr. Davis represented Washington County in the House of Delegates from 1849 to 1851, and was State senator from 1864 to 1867. He was assessor of internal revenue for the Fourth Congressional District from 1862 to 1864.

Boonsboro' of the present is one of the most important provincial trade centres in Washington County. Its situation on the old National pike, as the terminus of the Sharpsburg pike, and as a point from which the district roads radiate in every direction, places it

Robert J. Shafer

not only in a channel through which flows all the business of that section, but gives it the advantage of constant association with and the patronage of the wealthy agricultural community of the surrounding country. Boonsboro' has several general and special stores, a number of artisans and mechanics, mills, printing-office, several physicians, two hotels, and a community of intelligent, industrious, thrifty, and go-ahead inhabitants. In churches the denominations of Lutherans, Disciples, Methodist Episcopal, Catholics, Reformed, and United Brethren are all represented, and there is also an excellent public-school system. La Grange Lodge, I. O. O. F., and the South Mountain Encampment, are located in the town.

Robert John Shafer, of Boonsboro', is pre-eminently a self-made man. For thirty-eight years he has been a tanner in Boonsboro', and still follows that calling. About 1732, Alexander Shafer, who was then about twenty-one years of age, emigrated from the Palatinate, Germany, to America, and settled in Lancaster County, Pa., where he ultimately became the owner of twelve hundred acres of land. In 1745 he founded the town of Shaferstown, in Lebanon County, Pa. His only son, John, was a prominent farmer in that section, and became the father of five children. Two of them, John, Jr., and his sister, removed to Washington County and settled on Antietam Creek, six miles from Hagerstown. John was a farmer and miller, and built the mill now known as Rockboro' Mill. He acquired a handsome competence, and lived to be ninety-seven years old. He married Miss Miller, of Shaferstown, Pa., by whom he had five children. John, the eldest, married a Miss Hess, who died a few years after marriage, leaving a daughter, Elizabeth. Mr. Shafer's second marriage was with Angelica Troutman, by whom he had six children,—Jonathan, Catharine, Samuel, John, Mary, and Daniel. Jonathan, the eldest, born April 14, 1794, and still living, is the father of the present Robert J. Shafer, of Boonsboro'. He embarked in business at Boonsboro' early in life as a tanner, and followed it with success for many years, ultimately transferring the establishment to his son Robert, after which he removed to Georgetown, D. C., where he resumed trade as a leather-dealer. At the age of twenty-six he married Susan Ringer, of Ringer's Manor, near Boonsboro'. Three children were born to them,—Robert J., Margaret C., and John C. In 1826 his wife died, and in 1831 he married Mrs. Crebbs. By this union he had five children, of whom three are living. Jonathan Shafer was a public-spirited man, and for more than twenty-five years served as magistrate in his district. He was elected a member of the Legislature in 1829, and was largely instrumental in the passage of the act incorporating Boonsboro', of which he was the first burgess. He was successively re-elected to the latter office for several terms, until he emphatically declined to serve any further. To his administration of affairs the people of Boonsboro' are indebted for the town's excellent pavements.

Although often in office, it is his boast that he never solicited a nomination or an appointment. He was an ardent admirer of Andrew Jackson, and prided himself on his Democracy. In 1832 he was one of the first county commissioners chosen by the people. He is still in vigorous health, in his eighty-eighth year, and resides with his widowed daughter, Mrs. Daniel L. Grove, at Sharpsburg, Md. He is one of the few surviving veterans of the war of 1812, and is in receipt of a regular pension. Robert J. Shafer, his son, was born Oct. 6, 1821, in Boonsboro', in the house which is now his home and which was erected many years ago. He was carefully trained in the tanning business, and after being associated for some time with his father, succeeded the latter in 1843. Since then, from a small beginning and after severe trials, he has gradually developed an extensive business, which has yielded him handsome returns. He has been too busy with his own affairs to engage in politics, and, although frequently pressed to accept nomination to office, he has invariably declined. He was married, Oct. 21, 1851, to Mary E., daughter of James Chambers, then of Boonsboro', a native of Washington County, and in early life landlord of the Eagle (now Central) Hotel, in Frederick City. Mr. Chambers died in 1875. His first wife died in 1847, and his second wife lives in Nebraska. Five of his children are still living. Four children have been born to Mr. and Mrs. Shafer. Clarence E., one of the sons, is a merchant in Boonsboro', and Robert L., the second son, is at college.

Benevola, the next place in importance to Boonsboro', is a village of about one hundred inhabitants. It is seven miles from Boonsboro' on the old National pike, and has a public school, one church, the chapel of St. James' church, two flour-mills belonging to David H. and Joseph Newcomer, and one general store, and is the centre of a thriving farming community.

Mount Pleasant, at the foot of the South Mountain, to the northeast of Boonsboro', is a small but thriving village. The United Brethren and Disciples, of Boonsboro', have erected a chapel here, the corner-stone of which was laid in 1881.

Zittlestown is a small straggling village on the old National pike, near the summit of South Mountain, where a chapel, to be called St. John's mission, is being erected.

Mrs. Dahlgren's Mountain Home.—At the very summit of South Mountain, where the old National pike crosses through Turner's gap, Mrs. Dahlgren, widow of Admiral Dahlgren, has a handsome summer residence, which she purchased in 1876, together with considerable land in the vicinity known as the Keedy property, including the field near Crampton's Gap, where Gen. Reno fell in September, 1862, while forcing the Confederate hosts back towards Antietam. The house now owned by Mrs. Dahlgren was known for years as the "South Mountain House," or Smith's tavern, but has been remodeled and improved at a considerable outlay. Here the widow of the eminent naval officer spends the summer season, and varies the pleasing task of entertaining her friends with that of looking after the wants and supplying the necessities of the neighboring mountaineers' families. During last summer she began the erection of a handsome Gothic stone chapel nearly opposite her residence, on the north side of the pike, in order to afford her protégés facilities for worship and to assist her in the work she has voluntarily undertaken.

CAVETOWN DISTRICT, No. 7.

Cavetown, the seventh election district of Washington County, lies along the extreme eastern border, and but one remove from the Pennsylvania line, Ringgold District, which occupies the extreme northeastern position, intervening. The eastern line of Cavetown District follows the irregular course of South Mountain, extending along its summit. Chewsville District binds it on the south, and on the southwest; Leitersburg District on the west and north; and Ringgold District forms its northern boundary. Like the adjacent districts of Beaver Creek, Boonsboro', and Rohrersville, Cavetown District abounds in the wildly picturesque and charming pastoral scenery which so diversifies the eastern portion of the county. The face of the country in the interior is rolling, but the land is rich and fertile, and yields large crops. The district is thickly populated by an industrious, wealthy, and thrifty community, who enjoy the advantages of an excellent public-school system. The main line of the Western Maryland Railroad passes through the centre of the district, which is penetrated by numerous county and public roads, and the Cavetown and Hagerstown pike. Among the farmers and old residents of the district are D. Gaither Huyett and David Oswald, who have handsome estates near Cavetown; J. Diamond, S. Grove, J. Gouker, J. Grove, D. Wolf, S. Alsip, G. Burns, J. Alsip, J. Williams, William Grove, H. Delbert, William Jones, G. Lum, A. Grove, Mrs. Colliflower, H. Colliflower, Dr. W. A. Riddlemoser, Mrs. Waltz, W. F. Unger, B. Ridenour, D. Beard, O. Beard, A. Noles, S. Creager, G. Punt, H. Reynolds, J. D. Eibert, Mrs. D. Eibert, S. Lum, T. Davis, Mrs. Coyle, F. Miller, W. Null, J. Dayhooff, L. E. Davis, P. Hoffman, Mrs. E. George, D. Winters, J. Winters, D. Krouse, S. Bachtel, F. M. Deal, George Noles, Mrs. Barr, J. H. Bishop, L. Burkhart, Mrs. B. Bachtel, D. Hoover, J. Krouse, Mrs. Oswald, A. Oswald, T. Winters, S. Diffendal, A. Ridenour, J. G. Robinson, William Shoop, J. Weagly, J. Wishard, E. Ingram, D. Pike, A. Weagley, E. T. Bishop, B. Shank, J. Shank, A. Geiser, T. Clark, J. Adams, J. S. Besore, A. Lichtenberger, F. Bickle, John Flory, G. Gardenour, J. Stevenson, J. Barkdoll, C. Fogler, J. Mentzer, T. A. Brown. William Stevenson, William Shilling, D. Baer, Joseph Garver, J. Stoner, G. Diffenbach, T. Coyle, H. Harne, J. Fulton, P. Reynolds, E. Barkdoll, D. Fessler, J. Fessler, and others.

Under an act of Assembly of 1821 the following boundaries of Cavetown District were fixed a year later:

"To commence at the Pennsylvania line where the same crosses the road leading from Green Castle (Pa.) to Harman's Gap; thence with said line to the Frederick County line; thence with said line to the road leading from Hagerstown to Orr's Gap and Middle Town; thence with said road to the lines of District No. 3; and with the lines of District No. 3 to the beginning."

The population of the district (including the villages of Cavetown, 221 inhabitants, and Smithburg, 433 inhabitants) is 1665.

Cavetown.—The district derives its name from the village of Cavetown, which is eight miles directly east of Hagerstown, at the terminus of the Cavetown and Hagerstown pike, and near the line of the Western Maryland Railroad. Cavetown in turn received its title from a large natural cavern on the edge of the town, popularly known as Bishop's Cave. The village nestles at the foot of the South Mountain in a little valley, and is celebrated for its romantic and picturesque location and its health-giving atmosphere. In 1820 its inhabitants were 103 whites and two slaves. In 1822 the Levy Tax Court of Washington County designated the house of Thomas Johnson in Cavetown as the place for holding elections. The town is surrounded by limestone quarries, and has general stores, school, churches, and other elements pertaining to a healthful and growing country village.

The Reformed Church, Cavetown, has an interesting history. It is necessary to distinguish this denomination from that of the Dutch Reformed, the immigrants of the former coming principally from the Palatinate, in Germany, and from Switzerland and France, while those of the Dutch Reformed came from Holland and the Netherlands. These branches of the Reformed Church differed in language, but in their confession and church government they are alike. The immigrants from Holland and the Netherlands settled at New Amsterdam (New York) and in the eastern part of the State, and those from the Palatinate and Switzerland settled in Pennsylvania, Maryland, Virginia, and the Carolinas.

The Reformed Church, which used to be known as the German Reformed, in distinction from the Dutch Reformed, has a venerable history. She had her origin in the beginning of the Reformation period, and owes her existence to differences which existed among the Reformers, these differences finding expression on the Reformed side as early as 1563 in the "Heidelberg Catechism," the only symbolic book acknowledged by the church, and nearly one hundred years before the Westminster Confession was formed. As the tide of immigration from the fatherland commenced flowing to the New World, these early settlers brought with them their Bibles, hymn-books, and catechisms, and in their simple way served and worshiped God. They came to found homes for themselves and their children, and accordingly we find them scattered over large portions of Pennsylvania, Maryland, Virginia, and southward, as well as Southern New York. In the early history of the Reformed Church, these scattered families were visited by missionaries who came from Philadelphia, under the care of the Classis of Amsterdam, who gathered these scattered members together, preached to them the gospel, baptized their children, and in this way kept alive their faith until pastors could be settled among them.

At an early day were found Reformed members in Southern Pennsylvania and Western Maryland. The Reformed people living in Washington and part of Frederick Counties, true to their faith, first enjoyed the blessings of the gospel by making their way to Hagerstown, as far back as a century ago. Subsequently, as they increased in numbers, they had service at what was then known as Beard's church, where they enjoyed the ministrations of Rev. James R. Riley. He was the first minister of the Reformed faith who preached in this section of the State, and many members would walk for miles to take part in the services. But it was felt that the spiritual wants of the people could not be met nor adequately supplied by this arrangement, and then the question of building a church was agitated. To satisfy the members as to the location of a building, Cavetown, in Washington County, was finally selected as the most central point.

The first notice of building a house of worship for the Reformed people in this section is in a minute of a "meeting of the subscribers for the building of a Reformed church in Cavetown, held on Saturday, Nov. 11, 1826," when five trustees were elected, viz.: William Kreps, George Colliflower, Daniel Huyett, Henry Lyday, and Jacob Lambert, who were to have the oversight in the building of the house. They determined to build of brick, size fifty feet long by forty-five feet wide. At this time Rev. Henry Kroh was the pastor, and the congregation had no connection elsewhere. The corner-stone was laid Aug. 8, 1827, and has inscribed on it "Christ's Church," and on another stone in the front above the pulpit-window "German Ref^{d}. Church." In the meanwhile the pastor, Rev. Henry Kroh, was called to another field of labor, but the work of building went on, and in the following year (1828) Rev. J. C. Bucher had taken charge, and the church was so far finished that in the month of October, 1828, it was consecrated, at which time the pastor was assisted by his predecessor, Rev. Henry Kroh, Rev. James R. Riley, Rev. Martin Bruner, and Rev. Jacob Beecher. The church was now completed, and the congregation was fully organized and entered on its mission and work. Rev. J. C. Bucher was a faithful and energetic pastor, and it is a matter worthy of record that he, "aided by my Lutheran colleague," as he says, "was instrumental in organizing the first temperance society in Washington County, and in all Western Maryland." He says "it occasioned a very severe struggle and sore trial, but was attended with good success and usefulness." The ministry of Rev. J. C. Bucher came to a close in February, 1830, and, brief as it was, a great work was done for morals and religion. During this year the congregation was attached to those of Waynesboro' and Salem, in Pennsylvania, and Leitersburg, in Maryland, and now had settled over it as pastor Rev. G. W. Glessner, and as early as May 23, 1831, a record is made of a baptism he performed. His pastorate continued into the spring of 1840, about nine years, when he was called elsewhere, and was succeeded by Rev. J. H. A. Bomberger, who labored in the charge until the spring of 1845. After his removal the congregation called Theodore Apple, a student from the theological seminary, who took charge in the spring of 1845, which relation continued for two years, when a division of the charge was made, and Cavetown, Leitersburg, and a few points (one in Franklin County, Pa., the other in Frederick County, Md.) were constituted a charge, and Rev. Theodore Apple was called to serve it until December, 1850, when he resigned and removed to Mercersburg, Pa. The charge gave a call to the present pastor, J. W. Santee, then a student, who accepted it and entered on his pastorate in the spring of 1851, which relation continues to this day, over a period of thirty years, the longest pastorate in Western Maryland, and probably the longest in the State.

The building originally erected was substantial in every way, and is the same used by the congregation now. It is in good condition, and with proper care will last for many years to come. It has connected with it a beautiful cemetery, which is pronounced one of the neatest and best kept in the county. The church is the only one in the village, and has been doing good service for society; is an ornament to the place, and a blessing to the people. It has attached to it a parsonage and land containing two acres, with all the necessary buildings. The following is a list of the pastors and time of pastorate: Rev. Henry Kroh, probably a little over one year; Rev. J. C. Bucher, one year and a half; Rev. G. W. Glessner, nine years; Rev. J. H. A. Bomberger, five years; Rev. Theodore Apple, five years; Rev. J. W. Santee, present pastor, since April 28, 1851.

In the German Reformed cemetery at Cavetown the following persons among others are buried:

Catharine Gray, died September, 1879, aged 79 years.

John H. Bussard, born Feb. 14, 1794, died Aug. 11, 1868.

Susanna Bussard, born June 22, 1789, died March 24, 1869.

George Colliflower, died Feb. 13, 1868, aged 76 years, 7 months.

Maria, wife of David Spessard, born March 9, 1805, died Feb. 28, 1880.

Elizabeth, wife of Peter Hammacker, died Sept. 18, 1874, aged 79 years.

Anna Mary, wife of Jacob Krouse, born Nov. 5, 1795, died Nov. 27, 1867.

Joanna Gentry, wife of Thomas Hughes, died Oct. 23, 1861, aged 70 years.

Rachel Garlinger, died Oct. 3, 1862, aged 68 years, 10 months.

Frederick Harman, died May 19, 1870, aged 67 years, 7 months.

Daniel Smith, died May 16, 1868, aged 73 years, 7 months.

Thomas Swope, died Sept. 11, 1875, aged 86 years.

Samuel Creager, born Aug. 25, 1793, died April 28, 1879; and wife, Sarah, died July 5, 1871, aged 79 years.

Barbara, wife of John Shank, born Nov. 16, 1787, died Jan. 5, 1870.

George Lum, died Oct. 22, 1861, aged 76 years.

Jacob Bechtel, born Aug. 27, 1790, died Oct. 21, 1867; and his wife, Elizabeth, born Sept. 20, 1798, died Feb. 28, 1872.

Jacob Deibert, born Aug. 9, 1784, died Jan. 15, 1860.

Peter Akenberger, died Aug. 26, 1857, aged 71 years.

Catharine Wearick, died Jan. 7, 1856, aged 68 years.

Daniel Myers, born Jan. 10, 1780, died June 8, 1846; and his wife, Sarah, born Dec. 18, 1780, died Dec. 3, 1873.

Catharine Renner, died Nov. 1, 1875, aged 74 years, 10 months.

Elizabeth Kuhn, born July 24, 1764, died March 26, 1848.

Frederick Fishaugh, died Sept. 10, 1850, aged 83 years.

Rev. Wm. Webb, born Aug. 12, 1811, died Dec. 26, 1848.

Mary Knode, born May 12, 1788, died Jan. 22, 1845.

Elizabeth Renner, born May 20, 1794, died Feb. 14, 1839.

Jacob Sager, died March 15, 1837, aged 87 years.

Catharine Fishaugh, born Aug. 5, 1774, died May 18, 1853.

Catharine Colliflower, born April 19, 1758, died April 17, 1852.

Peter Colliflower, born Sept. 20, 1785, died Jan. 2, 1847.

Jacob Garver, born Jan. 20, 1784, died Oct. 4, 1859.

John Winters, died Oct. 6, 1835, aged 75 years; and his wife, Elizabeth W., died Aug. 19, 1855, aged 69 years.

Susanna, wife of Jacob Ridenour, died Feb. 20, 1837, aged 84 years, 8 months.

Mary M. Beard, died March 20, 1846, aged 84 years.

Ludwig Huyett, died April 17, 1828, aged 89 years; and his wife, Margaretta, died Feb. 21, 1833, aged 81 years.

Daniel Huyett, died May 14, 1869, aged 83 years.

Jacob Thomas, born Sept. 25, 1774, died Dec. 30, 1838.

Jacob Huyett, died Oct. 8, 1840, aged 57 years; and his wife, Elizabeth, born June 7, 1795, died April 15, 1878.

Henry Lyday, died Oct. 15, 1865, aged 84 years.

William J. Huyett, born Aug. 11, 1813, died July 4, 1879; and his wife, Catharine, born Sept. 28, 1807, died Feb. 28, 1875.

John Davis, died Nov. 25, 1873, aged 62 years; and his wife, Eveline, died April 1, 1880, aged 67 years.

Mary Unger, died June 17, 1859, aged 67 years.

In the Lutheran Church graveyard are the graves of the following among others:

Caroline V., wife of D. H. Stonebraker, died July 16, 1878, aged 36 years.

Solomon G. Krouse, born Dec. 4, 1835, died Aug. 14, 1863; Emma M., wife of Solomon G. Krouse, born Dec. 21, 1840, died June 10, 1863.

The large cave, or subterranean curiosity from which the town received its name, is located about three hundred yards from the village, on the property of Dr. Bishop. The mouth of the cave is fifty-eight feet wide, and is covered by an arch-like ceiling, leaving the entrance about six feet high. From the mouth the floor declines at an angle of forty-five degrees. The first of several chambers in the cave is about one hundred and forty feet long, nearly the same in width, and from fifteen to twenty feet high. At the rear of this room a narrow passage, about twenty feet long, descends at an angle of about sixty degrees and leads into another passage ten feet in height, with level floor, affording ingress to another chamber, somewhat smaller than the first apartment. Thence a third passage leads to the farthest extremity of the cave, which ends in a small lake of water, as clear as crystal and as cold as ice. Above the pool is an arched rocky roof. To what distance this chamber extends has never been ascertained, as it has never been explored.

Standing on the edge of the lake, the rays from the rude lamp carried by the visitor cast a lurid light over the waters, but failing to penetrate the darkness beyond, simply intensify the mystery, which has never proved of sufficient interest to encourage a full exploration of this portion of the cavern. The entire length of the cave is three hundred and sixty-three feet. From the lake chamber there is a side passage, about sixty feet long, running towards the entrance, and nearly parallel with the main avenue, ending in a small apartment which is called "the kitchen." A large spur of stalagmite occupies a form and position reminding the visitor of a cook-stove, while it requires but little imagination to perceive in numerous crevices and niches cupboards and similar kitchen furniture.

The ceiling of the cave is grand in a stalactical covering, eccentric and beautiful in form and general arrangement. It is fully fifty feet in height, resembling the interior of an old cathedral. There were probably in former years many beautiful specimens of stalagmites, but either vandal hands of curious visitors have destroyed this feature, or it has been eradicated by natural causes. The atmosphere of the cave is chilling in summer and temperate in winter. It is said that on one occasion a young man who was harvesting in a neighboring field left his work and entered the cave to enjoy its cool temperature, and the result of the severe and sudden change was an attack of fatal illness. Tradition has it also that nearly a century ago the cave was the retreat and hiding-place of a notorious robber who operated in that portion of the State. The Smithsonian Institution at one time sent an expert to the cave to investigate it, and in the researches then made remnants of knives, pottery, arrow-heads, and a number of other relics were unearthed, demonstrating that the cavern in the primitive history of this country had been inhabited or used by the Indians. The cave was owned at one time by Robert Hughes, who sold it to Dr. Elisha Bishop. Saltpetre was made out of the stalactites, and troughs and vats were placed in the cave to preserve drippings.

During the early part of the present century the cave was illuminated on various occasions. One of these was advertised in the local papers of Washington County in the spring of 1823, as follows:

"James Camper, having been at considerable expense in fitting up the cave for the accommodation of the public, most respectfully informs them and his friends that he will, in commemoration of the glorious independence of the United States of America, brilliantly illuminate it on the 4th, 5th, and 6th days of July next. That no one may be disappointed, he begs leave to state that he cannot admit any person into the cave on those days for less than 12½ cents. Any person throwing stone or any thing else in any part of the cave, particularly in the water at the extreme end of the subterraneous passage, will be fined one dollar. The cave will be kept in good order during the summer. Families or parties wishing to visit this wonderful work of nature can have it illuminated at any time by sending a letter (post-paid) to James Camper, Cavetown, or they will be admitted and provided with light for 6¼ cents each. For the accommodation of visitors and others, he will have a supply of good porter, beer, and ale."

A second cave was accidentally discovered at the same place in the latter part of May, 1881. In blasting a large rock with dynamite cartridges for Bishops' lime-kiln at Cavetown, a fissure in the rock was discovered, which opened into a cavern of considerable dimensions and of curious beauty. It is situated near the railroad station, on the opposite side of the track from W. Fockler's house, and extends under the large cave. The chamber into which the hole was made extends back about ninety feet, and a gallery which branches off at right angles is about the same length. The highest point of the ceiling is about fifteen feet. It has not yet been carefully explored, and it may be found to be of much greater extent. The stalactites and stalagmites are of delicate and beautiful color, and there are deposits of limestone sediment which have assumed curious and fantastic shapes.

A geological description of both of these caves will be found on page 34 of this work.

Smithsburg.—The most important town in Cavetown District is Smithsburg, situated directly at the foot of South Mountain, on the line of the Western Maryland Railroad, eight miles east of Hagerstown. It derived its name from its founder, Christopher Smith, who sold out the land in lots where the town now stands about the year 1813. It is one of the many villages to be found scattered over the country, affording a public convenience to the surrounding neighborhood, without which it would often be difficult to procure many of the necessaries of life. Its proximity to the mountain gives it a decided advantage over many of the villages farther distant, because lumber, wood, and all kinds of building materials can be had there very cheap. The houses at first were built principally of wood, but latterly there have been many very elegant brick buildings erected, not surpassed by any village in the State.

In 1820 its population consisted of 133 whites and 3 slaves. At that time Jacob Kissenger had a store there. In 1841 it had upwards of sixty houses. There were three retail dry-goods stores, two taverns, three blacksmith-shops, four tailor-shops, two wagon-shops, one whitesmith's shop, two cooper-shops, two cabinet-shops, two saddle and harness-shops, one tin and copper-shop, and a number of others. There were also two houses of public worship, one a Lutheran and the other a Methodist Episcopal; a school-house in charge of a very competent teacher, "which, unfortunately, in those days was seldom the case."

Christopher Smith, commonly known as "Stuffle" Smith, the founder of Smithsburg, was born in what was then Frederick, but is now Washington County, about 1750. His wife's name was Eve. Mr. Smith was a stone mason by trade. In 1813 he purchased from Samuel B. McClanahan, of Chester County, Pa., a tract of land known as part of "Shadrach's Lot," lying in Washington County, Md., and immediately thereafter laid the ground off into lots, the village being named Smithsburg. About 1820 he carried on the business of distilling, but, failing in business, his family consisting of six children—four sons and two daughters—moved to the West. These children are all dead with the exception of one son, who lives in Ohio. Christopher Smith did not accompany his family, but became an inmate of the almshouse of Washington County, where he died about 1831. His remains were buried in the old graveyard attached to the Lutheran Church in Smithsburg, but no stone marks his grave. He formerly lived on the west side of Main Street, near Water Street, and kept a store on the northwest corner of these thoroughfares. At one time there was a fountain in the bed of Main Street, which was fed by pipes from the spring of Jacob T. Towson, a quarter-mile from the town. The town was incorporated about the year 1846. After the battle of Gettysburg, in 1863, it was occupied by Kilpatrick's cavalry and was shelled from the mountain by the Confederate Gen. Stuart. There were two hospitals in the town in 1862 and 1863, for the treatment of soldiers from South Mountain and Antietam.

John H. Zittle started the first newspaper published in Smithsburg in September, 1852; it was entitled *The Trumpet*. He continued the publication until September, 1853 (one year), when he sold the plant to the office of the Hagerstown *News*, then published by Messrs. L. M. C. Cooke & Co. Mr. Zittle then purchased the Shepherdstown *Register* in West Virginia, in the year 1853, which paper he is still publishing.

St. Peter's, or "Beard's" Church, is the oldest of the Smithsburg, Lutheran charge. The first church, a log structure, was built in 1787. It had three galleries, and a goblet-shaped pulpit with a sounding-board. Being the only Lutheran Church east of Hagerstown, its membership extended over a very large territory, reaching even to the western portion of Frederick County, and including Wolfville and the neighborhood of the present Mount Moriah Church. It is impossible to ascertain who was the first pastor or by whom the first church was organized. To the record of a baptism and confirmation dated June 2, 1791, is subscribed the name of a minister written in German, but the characters are illegible. The first infant baptism of which a record is preserved is dated Oct. 15, 1789, but the name of the pastor is not given. A register of infant baptisms appears to have been regularly kept from that time up to 1814, but from some cause it was suspended until 1828; nor are the names of the pastors who administered the ordinance given until 1856 and afterwards. The constitution of the church is dated Nov. 18, 1798, and is signed by the Rev. John Ruthrauff, who was doubtless pastor of the church at the time, and whose name is the first on record. Tradition, however, names two pastors who preceded him, viz., Rev. Messrs. Schroeter and Hall, but the record makes no mention of them. The constitution was also signed by Andrew Beard, Michael Geiser, Franz Protzman, and John Young. The first register of communicants is dated May 22, 1808, and the number is stated to have been forty-seven. The act of incorporation is dated Aug. 14, 1808. It is written in English, and is signed by the Rev. J. George Schmucker. When Mr. Schmucker's labors commenced or terminated does not appear. The names of the Council who signed the act of incorporation were Francis Protzman, John Young, and Jacob Mong, elders; and John Beard, Leonard Schneider, and Peter Mong, church-wardens. Rev. George Schmucker was succeeded by Rev. Solomon Schaeffer, but there is no mention of Mr. Schaeffer upon the record. The name of the next pastor is Rev. Benjamin Kurtz, who also officiated at Hagerstown. Mr. Kurtz probably assumed the pastorate of St. Peter's Church in 1817. During his ministration he superintended the erection of the church at Smithsburg. From this period the pastors were the same as those of Trinity Church, with which it united, until Aug. 14, 1880, when a division of the charge was made, and St. Peter's united with St. Paul's at Leitersburg. Rev. V. Miller became pastor of the two churches, St. Peter's and St. Paul's, and has continued in that capacity ever since.

Attached to this church is a cemetery in which are the following interments:

Jacob Shank, born Aug. 8, 1786, died Feb. 2, 1867; and his wife, Catherine, born Jan. 10, 1793, died March 4, 1869.

Mary B., wife of Adam Shank, died Feb. 20, 1866, aged 76 years, 3 months.

Jacob F. Kimler, died Jan. 6, 1856, aged 70 years, 7 months; and his wife, Catherine, died Dec. 29, 1860, aged 68 years, 27 days.

Margaret, wife of John W. Miller, died Jan. 22, 1872, aged 70 years, 1 month.

Barnabas Dimond, died Dec. 27, 1853, aged 69 years, 6 months.

Barbara A., wife of Conrad Metzer, born Feb. 28, 1781, died Feb. 24, 1870.

Samuel Meisner, born Nov. 1, 1777, died April 5, 1874; and his wife, Margaret, born Jan. 1, 1782, died Oct. 22, 1856.

David S. Bachtell, born Dec. 2, 1810, died Jan. 10, 1873.

Martin Bachtell, born Oct. 26, 1783, died Oct. 30, 1849; and his wife, Eve, died Jan. 15, 1847, aged 58 years, 4 months.

Jacob Justice, born Jan. 2, 1801, died March 8, 1858.

Samuel Ridenour, died May 26, 1858, aged 54 years, 3 months.

Nathaniel Clary, died Sept. 5, 1874, aged 67 years, 1 month; and his wife, Cassandra, died Jan. 29, 1859, aged 57 years, 5 months.

Augustus L. Lesher, died April 1, 1859, aged 55 years, 10 months.

Samuel Reynold, died March 20, 1862, aged 70 years, 4 months; and his wife, Elizabeth, died Aug. 19, 1861, aged 69 years, 4 months.

Lieut. James L. Clary, Co. B, 3d Regiment Maryland Volunteers, died March 5, 1864, aged 29 years, 4 months.

John Stormeborn, born Nov. 18, 1799, died March 2, 1870; and his wife, Elizabeth, died Aug. 4, 1877, aged 78 years, 6 months.

Sarah Oliver, died June 17, 1839, aged 82 years.

Frederick Crown, died Dec. 14, 1842, aged 59 years, 9 months.

Isabella Hoover, died Nov. 13, 1864, in her 71st year.

Hannah Saylor, died July 11, 1825, in her 64th year.

Margaret, wife of Peter Flory, died Jan. 16, 1836, aged 68 years, 1 month.

Jacob Tritle, born Dec. 11, 1777, died Sept. 11, 1851; and his wife, Elizabeth, born Dec. 10, 1778, died March 6, 1827.

Luther Fogler, of Co. H, 6th Regiment Maryland Volunteers, wounded at Petersburg, April 2, and died April 10, 1865.

George Fogler, born February 28, 1790, died Feb. 27, 1867; and his wife, Hannah, died May 8, 1862, aged 64 years, 6 months.

Elizabeth, wife of Jacob Burkhardt, died April 4, 1862, aged 64 years, 1 month.

Susan, wife of Philip Beck, died Nov. 10, 1876, aged 74 years, 1 month.

John H. George, died Nov. 11, 1865, aged 60 years, 6 months.

Isaac Gehr, died Feb. 15, 1875, aged 73 years, 4 months; and his wife, Elizabeth, died July 1, 1876, aged 74 years, 3 months.

Jacob Harter, born March 17, 1786, died Nov. 10, 1870.

David Harter, died Dec. 18, 1872, aged about 73 years.

Daniel Snyder, died Sept. 23, 1871, aged 68 years, 9 months; and his wife, Elizabeth, died Dec. 21, 1862, aged 53 years, 2 months.

Christian J. Bickle, died Dec. 5, 1874, in his 72d year.

Trinity Evangelical Lutheran Church, Smithsburg, was organized in 1822. The first preliminary meeting was held on the 1st of January of that year, at which a building committee was appointed consisting of Christopher Flory, Peter Mong, Jacob Little, John Flory, and John Etnoyer. John Welty and John Sigler were appointed collectors to raise subscriptions. Jacob Slessinger was chosen permanent secretary, and Peter Hammaker treasurer. John Welty and Peter Hammaker were appointed a committee to purchase a lot on which to erect the proposed building. The corner-stone of the new structure was laid on the 27th of May, 1822. The ministers present were Rev. Benjamin Kurtz, under whose immediate supervision the work was being prosecuted, and Revs. Jacob Schnure, Jacob Medtart, and Peter Recksicker, the latter of the German Reformed Church. In the corner-stone were deposited a Bible, a German and English catechism, a memorandum with the names of the committees, builders, etc., and a proclamation indicating the purpose of the building and the name "Trinity," by which it was to be known. Coins then in circulation were also deposited. The church was dedicated on Whit-Monday, June 7, 1824. The ministers who took part in the services were Revs. Benjamin Kurtz, John Lind, from Greencastle, Pa., John Herbst, from Gettysburg, and Jacob Schnure, from Middletown. About the same time the congregation was regularly organized. The elders elected were Frederick Fishack, Conrad Mentzer, Peter Flory, and Conrad Flory. The deacons were Samuel Mackin, Jacob Castle, George Fogler, and George Sigler. The parsonage was built in 1829, and is the house now owned by Mrs. Martin. The first infant baptism of which any record remains was that of a daughter of Jacob and Catharine Sensebach. The ceremony was performed on the 17th of April, 1729, by Rev. S. K. Hoshour. The first communion was held some time in 1825, and the number of communicants was one hundred and one. The members who entered into the first organization had for the most part belonged to St. Peter's (Beard's) Church. Rev. Benjamin Kurtz, pastor of St. John's Lutheran Church at Hagerstown, served St. Peter's congregation, as well as other churches in the county. On the 26th of December, 1825, a plan of incorporation was adopted, but the records do not state when the church was legally incorporated. The first church was of stone, and becoming dilapidated and unsafe, was taken down a little over thirty years ago and replaced by the present brick structure, which was erected in 1851. Rev. Benjamin Kurtz, afterwards and for many years editor of the *Lutheran Observer*, was the first pastor, but he resigned soon after the dedication of the church. His successor was the Rev. S. K. Hoshour, who was pastor from 1828 to 1830, and who was followed by the Rev. John Reck. The latter remained from 1830 to 1832. After him came Rev. J. P. Cline, whose pastorate extended from June 3, 1833, to Dec. 1, 1846. He was succeeded by the Rev. J. J. Reimensnyder, who remained from 1846 to 1851, and whose successor, Rev. L. H. Bittle, continued for eighteen months, commencing in April, 1851. Rev. J. F. Probst took charge in 1853, and remained three years. Rev. John Heck became pastor on the 1st of January, 1857, and died on the 11th of March, 1861. Rev. W. F. Eyster succeeded him and served the charge until June, 1865. He was followed by the Rev. M. C. Horine, whose labors terminated in June, 1869. In May of the following year Rev. S. Henry commenced his ministrations. Rev. X. J. Richardson took charge on the 1st of September, 1872, and is still the pastor of the the church. Until the 14th of August, 1880, the church was one of a charge of four. On the date mentioned a division of the pastorate was made. Since then the present pastor has served only Trinity Church, Smithsburg, and Mount Moriah. The other two churches, St. Peter's, or Beard's, situated about three miles southwest of Smithsburg, and St. Paul's, at Leitersburg, united in extending a call to the Rev. V. Miller, who accepted and took charge in April, 1881. The Mount Moriah church was built and a congregation regularly organized in 1831, the corner-stone having been laid the previous year. The first communion was held on the 4th of June, 1831, the number of communicants being forty-one. At present the membership at Trinity is about two hundred and sixty, and at Mount Moriah eighty, making a total membership in the pastorate of about three hundred and forty. The only society connected with either of these churches is the Ladies' Mite Society of Trinity. The original parsonage was sold some twenty years ago, and the four congregations united in purchasing the present one. After the division of the charge, Trinity and Mount Moriah united in purchasing the interest of St. Paul's and St. Peter's, or Beard's, church in the parsonage, and still retain the building.

On the tombstones in the yard of Trinity Church are the following inscriptions:

John Fogler, born May 8, 1799, died Sept. 1, 1876; and his wife, Catherine, born Aug. 11, 1805, died Aug. 28, 1878.

Christian Schiller, born 1778, died 1861; and his wife, Rebecca Schiller, born 1790, died 1865.

Solomon Rohrer, Co. I, 7th Maryland Regiment, U.S.A., wounded at the battle of the Wilderness, May 8, 1864, and died June 6th.

Frederick Bowers, died Feb. 1, 1852, aged 70; and his wife, Margaret, died May 14, 1860, aged 75.

William McGowen, died May 20, 1852, aged 69; and his wife, Margaret, died Oct. 10, 1851, aged 66.

E. Gardner, died Aug. 31, 1850, aged 76.

Charles W. Bigham, died Sept. 27, 1849, aged 61; and his wife, Margaret, died July 8, 1849, aged 51.

John Fulton, born Aug. 28, 1729, died Jan. 11, 1849.

Jacob Bowers, died March 8, 1862, aged 81; and his wife, Esther, died Sept. 22, 1872, aged 84.

John Fleming, died Sept. 16, 1864, aged 74 years, 7 months.

Esau Bricknell, died July 25, 1834, aged 82 years, 6 months.

Capt. Thomas H. Hollingsworth, born Sept. 24, 1797, died Dec. 25, 1841.

Frederick Unger, born Feb. 29, 1776, died May 2, 1835.

Anthony Unger, born May 11, 1781, died in December, 1827.

Jacob Garlinger, born Sept. 8, 1796, died Oct. 29, 1824.

Hannah Taylor, died July 11, 1825, aged 64.

Margaret Oswald, born Oct. 20, 1742, died April 17, 1825.

Benjamin Oswald, born Oct. 3, 1784, died Feb. 14, 1844; and his wife, Sarah, born Aug. 17, 1792, died Oct. 20, 1859.

The Protestant Episcopal church at Smithsburg was built in 1873, the corner-stone being laid July 11th of that year. A number of prominent clergymen from Baltimore City were present,—Mr. Rankin, of St. Luke's; Dr. Leeds, of Grace Church; Mr. Leakin, of Trinity Church; and Mr. Dudley, of Christ's, among others. The service was conducted by Rev. Mr. Mitchell. A melodeon had been provided, and music formed quite an attractive feature of the proceedings. The corner-stone was laid by the rector of the parish, the Rev. Mr. Mitchell, as St. Anne's chapel, according to the form prescribed by the Book of Common Prayer. Rev. Dr. Leeds made an address, in which he said, "It was very meet that a church should be erected in this beautiful spot; in the place where was lately the sound of war now arises the anthem of praise. We are creatures of associations, and need our churches for the worship of God. The Christian delights in the cross, which was once the most ignoble of objects. I hope that as often as the cross shall be seen on this chapel, as often shall it be made on the forehead of the infant. All of you shall be consecrated to the service of God. A church is often looked upon as a place of worship merely, and not of itself a shrine. We have the privilege of drawing near to God in that place which is made sacred by all consecration. 'Where two or three are gathered together in God's name, there will he be among them.' To all minds there are some localities which suggest thoughts of communion with God." Dr. Leeds spoke of grand scenery suggesting thoughts of God. "More imposing than mountains and waterfalls is the sign that has been made upon us in baptism, impressed upon us in the presence of God." At the conclusion of Dr. Leeds' address the "Gloria in Excelsis" was sung, and the benediction pronounced by Mr. Mitchell. The services closed with the hymn commencing "Jerusalem the golden." Among those present were a large number of residents of Hagerstown.

The Methodist Church of Smithsburg was organized in 1831, and the corner-stone was laid in the same year. The church was consecrated in 1835. The first pastor was Rev. Robert S. Winton, who was succeeded by Rev. Henry Smith. The church was rebuilt in 1868, and consecrated in the same year. The only religious society cennected with the church is a Sunday-school, which dates back to 1840.

The cemetery at Smithsburg occupies a site of great natural beauty on a bit of meadow-land, rising gently

John Welty

from the roadside, while the mountains almost encircle it, and below it the pleasant little town is barely visible through the thick foliage of the woodland. It is surrounded by a hedge of boxwood, and contains some handsome monuments. Here rest the remains of the following:

Elijah Bishop, died April 4, 1870, aged 73 years. Over his grave is a tall shaft of granite, majestic in the severe simplicity of its outlines.

Paul Hoye, born March 26, 1736, died Oct. 13, 1816; and his wife, Miriam, died Nov. 13, 1811, aged 78 years.

George Kohler, died April 14, 1875, aged 88 years, 5 months.

Rebecca Houser, died Jan. 12, 1874, aged 69 years, 9 months.

Mary Ann Houser, died March 11, 1876, aged 65 years.

Peter S. Mong, died Aug. 24, 1863, aged 58 years, 6 months.

John Mong, died Sept. 20, 1863, aged 73 years, 10 months.

Jeremiah C. Funk, born July 27, 1841, died Sept. 13, 1878. This lot is ornamented with a very artistic monument of polished bluestone and marble, the contrast of the two stones forming a striking effect.

Smithsburg has now a population of about 433, and has several general stores, mills, schools, churches, a number of mechanics, etc., and is considered one of the most prominent and important places in that section of Washington County.

John Welty, who died upon his farm near Smithsburg, May 6, 1880, after a residence in Washington County of nearly fifty years, was one of the representative citizens and leading farmers of the county. He was born in Franklin County, Pa., near the Maryland line, May 24, 1813. His father, Jacob Welty, was a native Pennsylvanian, whose ancestors emigrated to America from Germany. There were five children in Jacob Welty's family, of whom John was the eldest son. His brother Samuel resides near Waynesboro'. One of his sisters is Mrs. James Wilson, of Trumbull County, Ohio, and a second, Mrs. Benjamin Cable, of Tuscarawas County, Ohio. Jacob Welty moved from Pennsylvania to Ohio, where he settled and passed the remainder of his life. John accompanied him, and remained upon his father's farm until 1834, when he went to Washington County, Md., to visit his uncle John. The latter, who was much attached to his nephew, proposed to adopt him as his heir, provided he would live with him. The arrangement was agreed to, and John, the nephew, accordingly made his home thereafter in Washington County. He assisted his uncle in the management of his farm, and upon the latter's death found himself in the possession of a liberal competence. He became in time a man of large means, and at his death was regarded as one of the wealthiest farmers in the county. On the 27th of October, 1845, he married Barbara Alice, daughter of John Funk, of Franklin County, Pa., whose father came to America from Switzerland at an early period and settled in Franklin County. The tract upon which he located has ever since been in the possession of his descendants. Mrs. Welty's mother was Alice, daughter of Jacob Barr, a native of Lancaster County, Pa. She was born July 6, 1787, and died in December, 1876, in her ninetieth year. She was the oldest of ten children (all daughters), and outlived them all. The only one of her living children besides Mrs. Welty is John Funk, a resident of Kansas. Mrs. Welty's father died July 1, 1844. In addition to his farming operations, John Welty was engaged for twenty years or more from 1846 in the tanning business, which he conducted with much success. He was, moreover, interested in business enterprises at Smithsburg, and in all his undertakings displayed a far-seeing judgment and shrewd management which yielded more than ordinarily profitable results. His estate was valued at his death at about one hundred and fifty thousand dollars, and included three fine farms in addition to his Smithsburg property.

Beginning with 1856, he occupied a conspicuous place as a representative man. In that year he was chosen a county commissioner on the Democratic ticket, defeating his opponent, Daniel Mentzer, by one vote. He took an active part in the project looking to the extension of the Western Maryland Railroad to the Potomac, and upon the completion of that enterprise he was chosen a director of the company. In 1870 he was elected to the State Legislature. He was one of the founders of the Hagerstown Steam-Engine and Machine Company, of which he was one of the directors at his death, and was also a member of the board of directors of the Baltimore and Cumberland Valley Railway Company. After his death the directors of the Hagerstown Steam-Engine and Machine Company adopted resolutions of respect to his memory, in which the following occurs:

"*Resolved*, That the simplicity of his character, his elevated principles, his integrity, his justice, his magnanimity and benevolence have endeared him to us in the ties of friendship, and have added to the deep sense of loss to us of one who, under all circumstances and in all places, was worthy of the highest praise."

Mr. Welty was unassuming in his deportment, steadfast in his friendships, benevolent towards the poor, and kind and attentive in his domestic relations. His widow still resides upon the old homestead.

Raven Rock.—Among the many points of interest in Cavetown District is "Raven Rock," about two and a half miles northeast of Cavetown. It is a famous resort for tourists, who visit it for the purpose of viewing the magnificent stretch of landscape visible from its summit. It is composed of solid limestone, with an ascent of four hundred feet to its summit, from which the eye takes in the surrounding country for a distance of forty miles, including the fertile valleys of the Conococheague, the Antietam, and the Potomac. From the top of Raven Rock the visitor can also look down a perpendicular cliff into an abyss over four hundred feet in depth. In 1841 arrangements were made to erect a monument on the top of Raven Rock to the memory of President Harrison, fifty feet high, on a Corinthian base, under the supervision of the following committee: William B. Clarke, chairman; J. C. Dorsey, George Updegraff, J. D. Roman, Martin King, Eli Kreigh, John Howard, William B. McAtee, Charles A. Fletcher, Hiram Weast, Watkins James, Lewis Zeigler, John G. Stone, Samuel Horine, Henry Landis, James H. Kennedy, Richard Wise, William H. Boyd, Samuel Bloom, S. Detwiler, Charles G. Lane, David Zeller, Capt. Samuel Clagett, Joseph S. Van Lear, Charles H. Ohr. The work was commenced, but never completed.

ROHRERSVILLE DISTRICT, No. 8.

Rohrersville, or Election District No. 8, extends farther south than any district of Washington County, with the exception of Sandy Hook. The population of the district is 1304, including Rohrersville, the principal village, which contains 106 inhabitants, and Brownsville, the next village in importance, 68 inhabitants. South Mountain extends along its eastern border, and Sharpsburg District on the west separates it from the Potomac River. Keedysville District lies to the west and north, and Boonsboro' District is also on the north. South of it is Sandy Hook District, which also intervenes between it and the Potomac. The Washington County Branch of the Baltimore and Ohio Railroad runs through the district from north to south, and there are five stations within its limits,—Clagett, Bartholow's, Bealer's Summit, Rohrersville, and Brownsville.

Elk Ridge Mountain extends from Rohrersville to the extreme southwestern portion of the district, with South Mountain on the east, inclosing a fertile valley through which the railroad runs, and in which are located the villages and farms of the district inhabitants. This valley has been well named Pleasant Valley, and is one of the most picturesque sections of the State. The land is rich and the country is thickly settled. Towns and villages dot the valley from end to end, and well-cared-for farm-houses meet the eye in every direction. Rohrersville, the chief town, is situated at the foot of Elk Ridge Mountain, in the northwestern portion of the district, within a mile of the point where the Baltimore and Ohio road enters the district. To the northeast of Rohrersville is the straggling but pretty little village of Locust Grove, and in the south of the district, a quarter of a mile from the railroad, is Brownsville. South Mountain is pierced, within about two miles of Brownsville, by Crampton's Gap, which is approached by a forked public road, one part of which leads to Rohrersville and the other to Brownsville. There is also a road leading from Brownsville, at the foot of South Mountain, below Crampton's Gap, directly across the mountain. The principal town is Rohrersville, which was named after David Rohrer, who lived about four hundred yards east of it, where the saw-mill now stands, and which is now owned by his son, Frederick D. Rohrer. The first house built in the town was erected by George Kefaufer, a son-in-law of old Frederick Rohrer, which was torn down to make way for the Lutheran church, a handsome structure.

The first church built where Rohrersville now stands was erected in 1842, on the public road leading east, where the cemetery now is, and about one hundred yards in the rear of the spot where Bethel United Brethren church now stands, the corner-stone of which was laid on July 24, 1871. The first church in the neighborhood was also built of logs, about 1800, and about a mile distant on the Harper's Ferry road. It was a free church for all denominations, and was torn down about 1867. After the first church was built in the town, in 1842, this old log church was used by the colored people.

St. Mark's Lutheran congregation of the town is an outgrowth of the Mount Zion Lutheran congregation of Locust Grove, and was permanently organized in June, 1879, under the pastoral care of Rev. George H. Beckley, then pastor of Boonsboro' charge. The corner-stone of St. Mark's was laid on the 12th of July, 1879, and the church was dedicated on the 21st of March, 1880, by Rev. Mr. Shull, of Baltimore, assisted by Rev. Mr. Bergstresser, of Waynesboro', Pa. This congregation was united with Boonsboro' charge, and Rev. George H. Beckley became pastor, and is still in charge.

The church of the United Brethren was built in 1842, the corner-stone having been laid on May 5th. It is a convenient and pretty church building. In the graveyard of this church are buried David Rohrer, the founder of the town, and Rev. Jacob Markwood, bishop of the United Brethren Church, who was born Dec. 22, 1818, and died Jan. 12, 1873. He was in the active ministry and a member of the Virginia Annual Conference for thirty-six years.

Frederick Rohrer, father of the founder of Rohrersville, who died at Greensburg, Pa., Sept. 21, 1823, had experienced many remarkable vicissitudes. He was a native of France, and was born July 28, 1742. During the war between France and England (1754 to 1763) he emigrated to America. In 1766 he married Catharine Deemer, in York County, Pa., and soon after removed to Hagerstown. The same year (1766) he visited the Western country, going as far as Pittsburgh, then composed of a few Indian huts. He took a number of cattle with him, which he exchanged with Gen. Arthur St. Clair for a tract of land in the Ligonier Valley. He still left his family at Hagerstown, and in 1767 took the first wheat over the mountains ever imported into that country. He cultivated it, together with other grain, on his farm in the valley, and prepared for his family, whom he removed there in the following fall. He took out a warrant for all that tract of land on the Conemaugh River on which the salt has since been made, and was the first to discover those immense springs of salt water. He boiled the first salt in an earthen pot, and traded it to the Indians, then the only inhabitants of Westmoreland County. In 1771, with his family, he returned to Hagerstown, being unable to live any longer among the hostile Indians. Here he remained until 1793, when he removed to Greensburg, where he remained until his death, at which time he had nine children, forty-two grandchildren, and seventeen great-grandchildren.

Locust Grove, which is about a mile north of Rohrersville, has a small Lutheran Church.

Among the well-known residents who have been buried in the graveyard of the United Brethren Church at Rohrersville are:

Mary Gardner, died May 27, 1865, aged 72 years.
Elizabeth Holmes, died Nov. 19, 1875, aged 75 years.
Rev. John Huffer, died July 23, 1842, aged 71 years.
Rachel Haynes, died March 17, 1846, aged 62 years.
Charlotte Gouft, died Nov. 19, 1862, aged 60 years.
George Keafauver, died April 17, 1862, aged 72 years; Mary Ann, his wife, died March 13, 1864, aged 81 years.
Jacob Mullendore, died Aug. 17, 1854, aged 59; Catharine, his wife, died Jan. 8, 1876, aged 69 years.
John Mullendore, died Sept. 23, 1869, aged 100 years.
Julian Mullendore, died Jan. 20, 1851, aged 79 years.
Samuel Clopper, died March 31, 1871, aged 66 years.
Jeremiah E. Rohrer, died July 21, 1877, aged 54 years.
George Bealer, died Nov. 17, 1854, aged 89 years.
Catharine Bealer, died Jan. 23, 1857, aged 56 years.
Rev. John Clopper, died June 13, 1852, aged 79 years.

LEITERSBURG DISTRICT, No. 9.

Leitersburg, or Election District No. 9, is on the Pennsylvania border, and is bounded by Ringgold District on the east, Cavetown on the south and east, Chewsville on the south, and East Hagerstown on the south and west. The population is 1546, including 308 inhabitants in Leitersburg Village. The district averages two miles and a half north and south, and about three and a quarter miles east and west. Antietam Creek flows from the north entirely through the district, forking below the town of Leitersburg, and a branch extending to the southeast. The turnpike road from Hagerstown enters the district directly from the southwest, strikes Leitersburg Town, and then takes almost a due northeastern course for the Pennsylvania line. The district contains a network of public roads, which are in good condition and well cared for. A valuable grist and saw-mill is situated upon the estate of W. Lighter, on Antietam Creek. The land of the district is almost entirely cleared up and cultivated, its average value being estimated at fifty dollars per acre, and it will readily produce eighteen bushels of wheat, thirty bushels of corn, and one ton of hay to the acre. As a general thing, the surface of the country is rolling, although some parts of it are nearly level. There are no mountains nor any hills of considerable size, and the nearest railroad station is Smithsburg, on the Western Maryland Railroad. The district takes its name from the town of the same name, situated near Antietam Creek, two miles from the Pennsylvania line. Leitersburg town was named after the Leiter family, of which Andrew Leiter was the first resident of Maryland.

Benjamin F. Leiter, a son of the founder of the town, was born in Leitersburg, Washington Co., Md., Oct. 13, 1813. He was educated by his father, and taught school in Maryland from 1830 to 1834, when he removed to Ohio and taught there until 1842. He was then admitted to the bar, and became very successful in the practice of the law. He was elected to the Legislature of Ohio in 1848, and was chosen temporary chairman by the Democrats, acting as such throughout the long contest of that year between his party and the Whigs, which is now spoken of in Ohio as the "days of the Revolution." In 1849 he was re-elected to the Legislature, and was chosen speaker, and in 1854 was elected to Congress. Among the early residents of Leitersburg were John Russell, who had a farm and grist-mill there in 1815; Michael Broonet, who opened a tavern (formerly kept by Jacob Howser) in 1819; Dr. E. B. Hibbard, there in 1824; Christopher Burckhardt, inn-keeper in 1824.

The town was incorporated about thirty years ago, but for years its charter has been allowed to go by default, and no town-officers have been elected for ten years. The first house at Leitersburg was erected in 1810, by Boughman, and was called "Boughman's house," after him. The village contains now several good public school-houses, two churches, United Brethren and Lutheran, good hotels, and a large cemetery. The town is pleasantly situated, and is built on two streets which intersect each other. Antietam Street runs northeast, and Main Street northwest.

Among the prominent farmers and merchants of Leitersburg District are Christian Lehman, H. Lehman, Abraham Lehman, W. M. Lantz, Jacob B. Lehman, Peter Middlekauff, W. A. Repp, David Strite, and Samuel Strite.

The first lodge of the Independent Order of Mechanics established in Western Maryland was at Leitersburg, in March, 1871. The lodge was instituted by W. V. G. Architect James M. Wilson, W. G. Supreme Recording Secretary Louis Schley, and W. C. Conductor W. T. Wilson. The following officers were installed:

W. S. M., James A. Hays; W. M., Henry Shurer, Jr.; J. M., John W. Nigh; R. S., David Sumner; Sec., H. T. Creps; Treas., Upton Clopper; Chaplain, Edward Smith; C., Samuel T. Nigh; I. S., William Shus; O. S., William F. Hose; R. G. to W. M., Daniel W. Lowman; L. G. to W. M., Abraham Hoover; R. G. to J. M., Solomon Stephey; L. G. to J. M., Samuel T. Lowman; Representatives to Grand Lodge of Maryland J. O. M., to Jan. 1, 1872, P. W. S. M.'s James A. Hays, Solomon Stephey, Samuel T. Lowman, and J. D. Slaugenhaupt.

St. Paul's Lutheran Church at Leitersburg was originally in Smithsburg charge, but in August, 1880, united with St. Peter's or Beard's Church. For many years it had been associated with St. Peter's, Trinity (at Smithsburg), and Mount Moriah. In April, 1826, the following advertisement was published:

"Proposals will be received until April 22d, at the house of Christopher Burckhardt, in Leitersburg, for building a church forty-five by sixty feet, two stories high, with gallery on three sides, to be built with brick or stone and rough cast, and finished in a plain, substantial manner."

The erection of the church was commenced in 1826, and on the 6th of August in that year the corner-stone was nominally laid. The following explanation was made concerning this date, by "a spectator," in the *Torch-Light* of Hagerstown:

"An impression has gone abroad that the corner-stone of the church about to be erected at Leitersburg was actually laid on Sunday, August 6th. This is not the fact. The religious ceremonies usual on such occasions were performed on that day, unaccompanied by any manual ceremony or labor."

The ministers who participated in the services were Revs. Frederick Ruthrauff, John Ruthrauff, Henry Kroh, and Jacob Medtart, all of whom made addresses. The building committee consisted of Christopher Burckhardt, Frederick Bell, Lewis Zeigler, Frederick Zeigler, and Joshua Grimes. The architect was Jacob Tanner.

The church was dedicated September 2d, the ceremonies being in both German and English. The first church council to whom the deed for the lot was given were Frederick Zeigler, John Byers, Jacob Bell, Lewis Trittle, John Bowers, and Henry H. Snider. As it was then part of St. Peter's or "Beard's" Church charge, its first pastor was probably the Rev. S. K. Hoshour. The first church book or register was prepared in 1831, by Rev. John Reck, who records 86 communicants. Rev. J. P. Cline, the next pastor, records three infant baptisms and confirmations on six different occasions, numbering 62. On the 26th of May, 1841, Mr. Cline installed Frederick Bell and Samuel Etnyer deacons; on the 8th of May, 1842, Jacob E. Bell and John Byers, Jr., elders, and Jacob Kissel deacon; and on the 6th of October, 1844, Samuel Creager, elder, and Thomas Atkinson, deacon. Mr. Cline was succeeded by Revs. J. J. Reimensnyder, L. H. Bittle, J. F. Probst, John Heck, W. F. Eyster, M. C. Horine, S. McHenry, and H. J. Richardson. When St. Paul's united with St. Peter's or Beard's Church, Aug. 14, 1880, Rev. V. Miller took charge and has ministered to it ever since. The records of the different ministers down to Mr. Miller's pastorate are extremely defective. The largest communion of which there is any mention was held on the 1st of May, 1859, during the ministration of Rev. J. Heck. There were 166 communicants, including 36 new members. For several years afterwards the condition of the church continued favorable, but subsequently the congregation declined until 1870, when the number of communicants was only 69. After that year the congregation began to grow again until the average attendance under Mr. McHenry was 106. Under Mr. Miller it has increased to 110. The whole number of communicants is something over 130.

The congregation erected the present church in 1878–79, the corner-stone being laid on Thursday, September 19th. In the corner-stone were placed interesting documents, containing important statistics, both of the Reformed Church and of the country in general, besides the papers of Hagerstown; also a history of the Reformed interest in the village and section of country, with the names of all the members connected with the congregation. The church was dedicated on March 16, 1879. The sermon was preached by Rev. J. O. Miller, D.D., York, Pa. The building is of brick, thirty-five by fifty feet, with a steeple built from the ground, forming the entrance. The exterior is neat and the edifice stands upon a commanding spot. The interior presents a neat appearance, with an arched ceiling, an end gallery, and a recess pulpit. The ceiling is white, and the walls are finished in sand. The room is lighted through eight large side windows, with two smaller in the front, and also two in the recess. The glass is beautifully stained, giving a fine, mellow light. The pews are of ash for back and front.

It may be related as a curious piece of church history in Leitersburg District that in March, 1849, the corner-stone of Jacob's church, eight miles north of Leitersburg, was quarried out and the contents stolen, including some coins and other valuables.

In St. Paul's churchyard are the graves of the following old residents:

George H. Lambert, died July 1, 1864, aged 80 years, 9 months.

John Frederick Dieterick, died Feb. 28, 1861, aged 80 years; and his wife, Maria E., died April 14, 1864, aged 80 years.

Joseph Leiter, born Dec. 13, 1805, died July 25, 1862; and his wife, Ann, born Oct. 16, 1805, died Dec. 18, 1863.

Julia Waggoner, died Oct. 24, 1863, aged 81 years.

Peter Bell, born Sept. 23, 1795, died June 4, 1880; and his wife, Julianna, died Sept. 11, 1871, aged 77 years.

John Lahm, born Feb. 4, 1781, died Nov. 6, 1838; and his wife, Elizabeth, born Aug. 12, 1784, died June 5, 1851.

Barbara Hoekman, born June 12, 1760, died July 11, 1832.

George Lowry, born June 10, 1780, died May 1, 1842.

John Bell, born June 29, 1794, died April 12, 1830; and his wife, Elizabeth, born Aug. 2, 1796, died Jan. 24, 1860.

Anna Mary Derr, died Dec. 4, 1864, aged 74 years.

John Mayhugh, died June 30, 1856, aged 77 years.

George Bell, died May 27, 1874, aged 62 years; and his wife, Mary, died Dec. 28, 1860, aged 47 years.

Elizabeth Bell, born May 25, 1793, died Feb. 17, 1870.

John P. Stephey, born Oct. 11, 1794, died Nov. 12, 1849.

Christian Drill, born Sept. 15, 1785, died June 20, 1851.

Adam Burkstrasser, died April 13, 1831, aged 67 years.

John Lowry, born March 16, 1794, died June 16, 1867; and his wife, Susan, born Sept. 27, 1796, died June 10, 1873.

John Clopper, died March 24, 1878, aged 83 years.

George Poe, born Oct. 7, 1791, died Feb. 14, 1869; and his wife, Catherine, born Aug. 5, 1797, died Jan. 11, 1861.

James Swailes, born Dec. 14, 1788, died Jan. 18, 1878.

Emanuel Springer, died Dec. 16, 1878, aged 89; Catharine, his wife, died Sept. 24, 1864, aged 71.

Mamie, wife of John Shilling, died Sept. 12, 1871, aged 82.

Jacob Shilling, died June 15, 1873, aged 61.

John Heck, minister of the Evangelical Lutheran Church, was born at Chambersburg, Franklin Co., Pa., Dec. 11, 1809, died at Smithsburg, Washington Co., March 11, 1861.

Anna Maria Beckman, died Sept. 19, 1866, aged 83.

George W. Bowers, died July 20, 1867, aged 43.

Mary W. Mayhugh, died Oct. 14, 1868, aged 82.

Anna, wife of James P. Mayhugh, died April 21, 1861, aged 35.

George Zeigler, died Sept. 15, 1862, aged 69 years.

Samuel Dougherty, born March 1, 1808, died 1852, aged 54.

Michael Wolfinger, died Jan. 1, 1863, aged 60.

Elias Hoover, died June 17, 1864, aged 51.

Nancy, wife of John Clopper, died May 4, 1859, aged 63.

Jeremiah Wampler, died June 5, 1859, aged 45.

Jacob Holbruner, died Aug. 5, 1856, aged 70.

Henry Lowry, died July 26, 1861, aged 70.

Margaret Johnson, died in 1860, aged 78.

Jacob Wolfinger, died May 1, 1857, aged 51.

Jacob Houser, died May 11, 1857, aged 72.

Catharine Houser, died Nov. 16, 1857, aged 73.

Susan White, died May 19, 1863, aged 72.

Jane Lambert, died Dec. 17, 1854, aged 74.

Barbara Zeigler, wife of George Zeigler, Sr., died April 13, 1853, aged 77.

Samuel Leiter, died Dec. 17, 1855, in his 66th year.

Dr. F. Byer, son of Capt. J. Byer, aged 49.

George L. Ziegler, died Dec. 9, 1866, in his 54th year.

Lewis Zeigler, died March 2, 1863, aged 75; Catharine, his wife, died Jan. 26, 1851, aged 58.

Benjamin Hartman, died Jan. 2, 1852, aged 63.

Samuel Lantz, died Jan. 10, 1844, aged 46; his wife, Elizabeth, died Jan. 16, 1867, aged 69.

Capt. John Byer, died Feb. 12, 1859, aged 82.

Elizabeth Lantz, wife of John Byer, died Jan. 27, 1841, aged 51.

John Barr, born 1777, died Oct. 19, 1854, aged 77; his wife, Catharine, died Oct. 28, 1845, aged 59.

Sarah Wolfinger, wife of Michael, died June 15, 1848, aged 76.

Anna Mary Derr, died Dec 4, 1864, aged 74.

James P. Mayhugh, died Dec. 28, 1865, aged 54; his wife, Rebecca, died June 21, 1842, aged 23.

Charlotte Kætzel, died June 27, 1872, aged 81.

Louisa H., wife of Joshua Sheley, died June 2, 1876, aged 66.

Joseph Clopper, died Aug. 6, 1876, aged 63; Margaret, his wife, died Jan. 26, 1871, aged 58.

Catharine, wife of Christian Rohrer, died March 11, 1875, aged 77.

Sallie Shiep, died Dec. 29, 1875, aged 69.

David Frey, died Oct. 2, 1878, aged 64.

Catharine, wife of Jacob Kahl, died April 24, 1880, aged 56.

Benjamin Hartman, died July 28, 1875, aged 62.

John Wolfinger, died Oct. 8, 1878, aged 74.

Among the interments in the churchyard of St. James are the following:

Samuel M. Price, died Oct. 27, 1880, aged 70; and his wife, Julian, died Jan. 7, 1880, aged 69.

Peter Hartle, born Jan. 15, 1835, died Sept. 24, 1879.

Benjamin Gerver, died May 24, 1875, aged 70.

George Miller, died March 14, 1857, aged 53.

Samuel C. Wengley, died June 25, 1861, aged 44.

Mary, wife of John Renner, died July 16, 1869, aged 75.

FUNKSTOWN DISTRICT, No. 10.

Funkstown, or Election District No. 10, adjoins East and West Hagerstown Districts on the north, and is bounded by Chewsville District on the northeast, Beaver Creek on the east, Boonsboro' on the southeast, Tilghmanton on the south, and Williamsport District on the west. The Washington County branch of the Baltimore and Ohio Railroad passes through its centre from north to south, the old National or Frederick and Hagerstown turnpike and the Sharpsburg and Hagerstown pike run almost parallel with the railroad, and on either side, the former bearing to the southeast to Boonsboro', and the latter southwest to Sharpsburg. Antietam Creek passes through it, preserving pretty much the same course. The district was named after the only town in it,—Funkstown,—and is a thickly-settled and fertile territory, well supplied with schools and churches, and numerous county-roads intersecting one another at all points. The population of the district is 1534, including 600 inhabitants in the village of Funkstown.

Among the well-known farmers and residents of the district are M. Lamar, F. Hildebrand, J. W. Huffer, J. C. Middlekauff, G. Clagett, J. H. Clagett, I. Croft, J. H. Baker, Mrs. Rowe, E. Young, A. Ball, J. Warden, W. Poffenberger, B. P. Fiery, I. Fiery, A. Rench, C. Stouffer, H. Eakle, Mrs. M. Shafer, C. Herr, J. Kendel, J. W. Stouffer, J. Johnson, Mrs. Ridenour, G. H. Stockslager, Dr. J. Mundey, Dr. Scott, D. Wareham, A. H. Suman, J. Morler, D. Doub, G. Steinmetz, B. Garlinger, H. McComas, J. Horn, D. Wolf, D. Beehler, Dr. I. E. Miller, J. W. Stonebraker, J. Hager, H. Beehler, F. B. Watts, Robert H. Cushen, A. Massilla, D. Eyrely, W. H. Knode, S. Shilling, W. Stouffer, N. G. Fiery & Co., C. Bloomanauer, J. Spessard, J. G. Miller, C. Fleming, Mrs. Anderson, J. Harp, D. Schindel, E. Rowland, J. Hunter, D. South, Dr. F. Dorsey, R. L. Rose, Mrs. Welsh, E. Young, J. Talbott, J. Bentz, G. H. C. Bentz, H. Ranger, I. Stouffer, D. Stockslager, L. Rep, S. Hoover, S. Baker, J. Krotzer, George Kemp, H. McCauley, D. Alter, J. Alter, C. Hamilton, R. G. Thornburg, W. Hager, and others.

The village of Funkstown is two miles and a half south of Hagerstown, on the old National pike, on a neck or body of land in a bend of the Antietam, which flows around three sides of it in the form of a horseshoe. This tract is a portion of eighty-eight acres called Black Oak Ridge, granted in 1754 by Frederick Calvert to Henry Funk, who settled here, and who, tradition says, was the same Funk who established Funkstown or Hamburg on the present site of the city of Washington about 1790. The old town was a failure owing to the proximity and growth of Carrollsburg, established by Daniel Carroll. Funk is said to have removed to Washington County, and to have established Funkstown, but here again his venture was outstripped by a rival enterprise, the village of Elizabethtown, now Hagerstown, two miles away. There is no memorial to Henry Funk in Funkstown, and George Alfred Townsend based an amusing poem on his failure to find any trace of the man who gave to the town his name. The town was originally called Jerusalem, and was incorporated under this title, but the inhabitants have never acted under the charter. The oldest house in the town was built of logs, near the site of the present cemetery, and is owned by Mrs. Mary Iseminger. Another old house, a two-story stone, owned by Samuel Baker, was built in 1769, it is supposed by the original settler.

Among the early residents of Funkstown were:

Martin Funk, who had a wool-carding machine; Henry Beckley, tavern-keeper; Dr. Christian Boerstler, proprietor of powder-mill, 1804; John F. Shrader, tavern-keeper, house "sign of Cross-Keys;" Isaac Patrick, weaver; Jacob Knode, tavern-keeper; Daniel Boerstler, who manufactured rifle, gun, and common powder there in 1808; George and Michael Stonebreaker, merchants there in 1808; Frederick Kehler, Jacob Moyer, and Martin Funk, proprietors of carding-mill, 1810; John Shafer, Henry Shafer, merchant; Henry Bentz, Abraham Schmutz, Frederick Grosh, Jacob and Michael Conradt, woolen-manufacturers; Gerard Stonebreaker, who died there in 1813, aged seventy years; Daniel Stover, weaver and dyer; Henry Lowrye, carpenter; Thomas Fleming, weaver; Peter Miller, blue dyer; Thomas Mulhall, cooper; Henry and J. H. Ohr, Dr. G. W. Boerstler, established a woolen-factory in May, 1815; A. Degroff and W. Wilen, merchants, 1815; Henry Shafer, president Antietam Woolen-Manufacturing Company; M. Stonebraker & Co., merchants; Henry Whisner, inn-keeper; Jonathan Irvin, who owned the building occupied by Whisner; Dr. G. W. Boerstler began practice in 1820; John Knode, tavern-keeper in 1820.

Many of the earlier residents at Funkstown were Germans, and their immediate descendants, some of them, directly from the "Vaterland." Many of these people had brought the customs and habits of the old country with them and introduced them here. The cultivation of flowers was a passion with them, and a considerable emulation existed among them as to who should have the greatest variety, the rarest and most beautiful. The Shafers, Knodes, Shroeders, Boerstlers, Beckleys, Stonebreakers, and others, all vied with each other, and the result was some of the most lovely and fragrant gardens in the county. They also introduced the culture of the vine in Funkstown. In 1809, Frederick Kehler manufactured two barrels of wine, which was the first made from cultivated grapes in the county. He sold it for four dollars per gallon. A newspaper published at that time said that there were then eighteen vineyards in the county, the eldest being three and one-half years old.

Tho people of this ancient village were also remarkable for their observance of the old-established customs. They always colored the eggs at Easter and hid them in the garden, so that the children were really induced to believe that the rabbits had laid them. They put themselves to a good deal of trouble and were quite lavish in their expenditures in providing Christmas trees for the amusement of the young folks, and upon these was hung almost every conceivable thing that could be made out of sugar which could please and gratify the youthful members of the family. There was one custom among them which some considered of doubtful propriety,—that of telling frightful stories to the children about ghosts and witches, thus exciting the fears of the young ones to such an extent that they could not, for any consideration, be induced to go out at night, or in the dark, unless accompanied by some older member of the family. "Bellsnichol" and "Kriskringle" were always in their glory about Christmas times, and woe be to the urchin that was found out in the streets after a certain hour in the night! Bellsnichol was a character in his day, or rather in his night, for he was rarely seen in daytime. He always wore a mask, and, besides his bell, he carried nuts and cakes to reward the good children, and a raw-hide to punish the bad ones.

March 22, 1791, families to the number of about fifty persons in and about Funkstown took their departure for Kentucky; also "that good old man, Mr. Funk, late a representative of the county, went with his baggage."

In 1797, Adam Iseminger was a spinning-wheel maker in Funkstown. That the earlier residents of the town were admirers of horseflesh is demonstrated in the following announcements at the beginning of the present century. The first one is of date of 1800, as follows:

"On Thursday, the 9th, will be run for, over the same course, a purse of thirty dollars and a complete saddle. On Friday, the 10th, a handsome sweepstake, free to all, the winning horses of the preceding days excepted. The horses to be entered with Henry Beckley or Jacob Brunner the day preceding the race. Four horses to start each day at twelve o'clock or no race."

The second one, in the following year, says,—

"On Wednesday, the 18th of November, a purse of forty dollars, on Thursday, the 19th, twenty dollars, and on Friday, the 20th, forty dollars." Signed by Henry Beckley and George Beigler.

Again, in October, 1802, Henry Beckley, of Funkstown, announced that

"On Wednesday, the 27th of October, will be run over a handsome course near this town for a purse of fifty dollars. On Thursday, the 28th, will be run for, over the same course, a purse of twenty dollars. And on Friday, the 29th, will be run for, over the same course, a purse of forty dollars. The horses to be entered with Henry Beckley the day preceding each race. Four horses to start each day at eleven o'clock A.M. or no race. Proper persons will be appointed as judges, who will determine any disputes."

In 1810, Jacob Knode, George Stonebraker, John Shafer, Henry Shafer, Henry Bentz, Abraham Schwartz, and Frederick Grosh were managers of a lottery for repairing a church in Funkstown.

In the same year Philip Pitry had a powder-mill a half-mile from Sherer's mill and two miles from Funkstown.

Boerstler & Son also had a powder-mill in Funkstown in 1812. In that year, Jacob and Michael Conradt erected and put in operation a woolen-factory there, and Martin Funk had a wool-carding machine at the same time. Henry Shrader lived there in that year. The Conradt mill turned out cassimeres, kerseys, flannels, and blankets.

Rev. James Reid preached in the old school-house in Funkstown in August, 1813.

The people of Funkstown celebrated Gen. Harrison's victories in Canada in October, 1813, on which occasion Frederick Grosh, Jacob Ohr, Jacob Bruner, Abraham De Graft, and Capt. Henry Lohra were conspicuous figures.

In June, 1814, the Antietam Woolen Manufacturing Company, Henry Shafer, president, advertised for a bookkeeper. The following year the company opened a store in Hagerstown, of which W. Dickey was agent.

In 1816, Boerstler's factory was operated by the Jerusalem Manufacturing Company, and the Antietam factory was running at the same time, with Henry Shafer and Gerard Stonebreaker as managers.

The population of Funkstown in 1820 consisted of white males, 261; white females, 245; total whites, 506. Male slaves, 13; female slaves, 9; total slaves, 22. Free colored males, 4; females, 6; total free colored, 10. Total population, 538.

While building the Boonsboro' and Hagerstown turnpike the laborers at work thereon inaugurated a riot on St. Patrick's day, 1823, which was suppressed by the military of Hagerstown.

In 1827 the Jerusalem inn in Funkstown, Md., was "taken by William C. Bowen for the accommodation of travelers, drovers, wagoners, etc."

In 1828 the Antietam woolen-factory was operated by Henry Shafer & Sons, and during Christmas night, 1835, it was destroyed by fire. It is now running as a fertilizer factory by Stonebraker & Keller, who employ twenty men. After the war the Antietam Manufacturing Company bought the mill, but subsequently failed. It was then converted into a paper-mill, and in 1879 was bought by John W. Stonebraker, who restored it to its original purpose,—a woolen-mill.

John Brown was at Funkstown on several occasions while hauling arms from Chambersburg to Harper's Ferry. There was a skirmish at Funkstown, July 10, 1863, between the Union and Southern troops.

In April, 1873, Thomas South died at his residence in Funkstown, in the ninety-second year of his age. The chief mourner was his widow, ninety-one years old. The deceased was, as well as his wife, a native of Washington County. His parents, who were among the very first settlers in the wilderness bordering the Antietam, came from England. His father entered a piece of land on the west bank of the Antietam, just below Rose's paper-mill, with a view to its advantages as a hunting-ground rather than for agricultural purposes, and built his house on the spot where the house, which has never passed from the family, now stands. The property was known as "the Crook," and is owned by David South. Here the first of the Souths reared his three sons (Thomas, Geary, and William), and here Thomas lived and reared a family of eight children,—Daniel, former sheriff of Washington County; Joseph, now dead; and David and Benjamin, who reside in Funkstown; together with Mrs. Kline, Mrs. Zimmerman, Mrs. Shilling, and Mrs. Crawford. When the war of 1812 broke out, Thomas South, the deceased, was living at "the Crook," and volunteering his services as a private in one of the companies from Washington County, took part in defense of his country at both Bladensburg and North Point. He was a man of powerful physique. In mid-life he purchased a property in Funkstown, upon which he lived during the residue of his life, and from which his remains were removed to Funkstown Cemetery. His widow, who was originally a Miss Tracy, was the widow Wolf when she was married to Mr. South, and had a sister married to his brother William.

On Wednesday, Feb. 4, 1880, Mr. and Mrs. Elias Emmert, of Fairview, near Funkstown, celebrated their golden wedding, on which occasion there was a grand reunion of the Emmert and Newcomer families and the descendants of the aged couple.

The Churches of Funkstown.—The Evangelical Lutheran and the German Reformed congregations were incorporated as a body in 1803, and worshiped together in the old church until 1851, the Evangelical Lutherans having withdrawn and created a church of their own. The corner-stone of the new edifice was laid in 1850, and in the year following the church was consecrated. It was built of brick, and had a seating capacity for four hundred persons. The old church was located near the public cemetery, and was destroyed by fire in 1857. The new edifice was located on Main Street, and was named St. John's Evangelical Lutheran church. The combined charges were served by Rev. Solomon Schaeffer, Rev. Benjamin Kurtz, Rev. Charles F. Schaeffer, Rev. Ezra Keller, and Rev. C. C. Culler. After St. John's was built, the following pastors served the congregation: Rev. C. C. Culler, Rev. John N. Unruh, Rev. A. Copenhauer, Rev. M. W. Fair, Rev. Levi Keller, and Rev. D. S. Lentz, the latter the present pastor.

The Dunker church, a brick structure, was built in 1859, and will seat two hundred persons. Elder Joseph Wolf, Leonard Emmert, Andrew Curt, Daniel F. Stauffer, and others, have served this charge in the capacity of pastors.

The graveyard of the Dunker church contains the tombs of the following persons:

Christian Stouffer, died Aug. 15, 1873, aged 59 years, 5 months.

John W. Stouffer, died April 20, 1877, aged 75 years, 8 days; and his wife, Margaret, died July 25, 1873, aged 67 years, 5 months.

Elizabeth Roe, died April 27, 1873, aged about 86 years.

Jacob Moyers, died Dec. 22, 1866, aged 69 years, 6 months.

Samuel Resh, died June 2, 1877, aged 63 years, 7 months; and his wife, Mary, born April 18, 1810, died March 21, 1863.

John S. Rowland, born March 22, 1798, died May 2, 1878.

John Maysilles, died Oct. 27, 1862, aged 57 years, 2 months.

The corner-stone of the Methodist Episcopal church was laid in 1842, and the edifice was dedicated in 1843. It is a brick building, with seating capacity for two hundred persons. Its pastors have been Rev. William Hurst, Rev. Elisha Phelps, Rev. George Brooks, Rev. James Brand, Rev. Dr. Cullums, Rev. John P. Hall, Rev. Wilford Downs, Rev. Mr. Osbourn, Rev. Mr. Parkerson, Rev. Franklin Dugson, Rev. William Forrest, Rev. John Lloyd, Rev. John Butler, Rev. Mr. Montgomery, Rev. Watson Case, Rev. William Herbert, Rev. Samuel Alford, and Rev. John D. Hall.

The corner-stone of the American Methodist Episcopal church was laid in 1879, and the church was dedicated in 1881. The pastor is Rev. Mr. Jones.

The majority of Funkstown's dead rest in the public cemetery in the southern part of the town, and among the graves there are the following:

Gottleib Grosh, died Oct. 27, 1868, aged 96 years, 5 months; and his wife, Catharine, died June 16, 1863, aged 90 years, 5 months.

John H. Claggett, died Sept. 18, 1877, aged 56 years, 6 months.

Richard Welsh, died Sept. 9, 1863, aged 57 years, 10 months.

John Beckley, died April 29, 1862, aged 65 years, 3 months; and his wife, Anna, died Oct. 13, 1879, aged 73 years, 11 months.

George Cridler, died Jan. 8, 1875, aged 75 years, 11 months.

Samuel Stouffer, born Sept. 25, 1796, died Aug. 18, 1871; and Mary Stouffer, died May 17, 1862, aged 73 years, 11 months.

Catharine Stock, died Aug. 9, 1864, aged 68 years, 2 months.

Joseph Flora, died June 1, 1877, aged 66 years, 9 months.

Sarah Ann, wife of David Fisher, died Aug. 5, 1876, aged 72 years, 8 months.

Samuel Craley, died July 8, 1866, aged 53 years, 5 months.

Joseph South, died Oct. 29, 1863, aged 49 years, 5 months.

John Snyder, died Dec. 8, 1863, aged 64 years, 7 months; and his wife, Nancy, died June 5, 1873, aged 72 years, 11 months.

Rev. William Tryday, of the Lutheran Church, died Jan. 25, 1876, aged 55 years, 11 months.

Sarah, wife of Gera South, died Nov. 25, 1869, aged 85 years, 10 months.

William Bower, died Dec. 26, 1873, aged 77 years, 2 months.

Catharine Stockslager, died Feb. 18, 1866, aged 66 years, 7 months.

John Stockslager, born Jan. 18, 1763, died May 9, 1863, aged 100 years, 3 months, and 21 days; and his wife, Barbara, died Sept. 28, 1849, aged 74 years, 5 months.

Mary Stockslager, died June 7, 1869, aged 74 years, 6 months.

Jacob Stockslager, died Aug. 5, 1867, aged 57 years, 7 months.

Henry J. Bentz, born Nov. 10, 1797, died June 7, 1857; and his wife, Christiana, born Sept. 2, 1811, died Jan. 10, 1862.

Sophia Karn, died March 14, 1864, aged 72 years, 3 months.

Dr. Samuel H. Rench, died Aug. 23, 1853, aged 52 years.

Elias Chaney, Sr., died March 7, 1859, aged 63 years, 11 months.

Margaret Bowman, died Nov. 12, 1878, aged 83 years, 1 month.

Samuel McCauley, died May 4, 1848, aged 81 years, 4 months; and his wife, Elizabeth, died Sept. 10, 1867, aged 66 years, 10 months.

Michael Iseminger, died June 2, 1863, aged 84 years, 4 months; and his wife, Catherine, died Sept. 17, 1866, aged 87 years, 11 months.

Elizabeth Boerstler, born Feb. 15, 1788, married Feb. 4, 1810, died March 27, 1823.

Dr. Christian Boerstler, and his wife, Dorothea, 1833.

William Eakle, born Aug. 11, 1786, died June 12, 1851; and his wife, Elizabeth, born Aug. 29, 1787, died April 21, 1850.

Henry Bentz, died July 30, 1835, aged 73 years, 4 months; and his wife, Maria, died Sept. 13, 1848, aged 81 years, 5 months.

Gerard Stonebreaker, died March 1, 1855, aged 75 years; and his wife, Catherine, died Dec. 14, 1840, aged 66 years.

John Cook, died Feb. 3, 1857, aged 71 years, 25 days; and his wife, Hannah, died June 26, 1847, aged 49 years, 8 months.

John Knode, born March 2, 1780, died May 23, 1848.

Ann, wife of John Sharer, born Nov. 27, 1783, died Aug. 22, 1842.

Daniel Moyer, born May 17, 1772, died Aug. 13, 1853; and his wife, Margaret, died March 31, 1854, aged 88 years.

John Shafer, died April 22, 1861, aged 97 years.

Ann Maria Winn, died June 29, 1850, aged 81 years, 14 days.

George Lacher, born March 17, 1789, died March 25, 1831; and his wife, Elizabeth, died Dec. 9, 1861, in her 69th year.

John Shafer, born Aug. 12, 1789, died Sept. 1, 1873.

Peter Baflichs, born in 1741, died Oct. 20, 1796.

Christiana Trautman, born Oct. 17, 1745, died Sept. 10, 1804.

Angelica Trautman, wife of John Shafer, born May 4, 1773, died May 29, 1806.

Henry Shafer, born Jan. 11, 1766, died April 14, 1855; and his wife, Anna Rosina, born Feb. 24, 1774, died March 27, 1842.

John Shafer, died May 18, 1853, aged 53 years, 8 months.

John Henry Fritch, died Sept. 12, 1850, aged 70 years, 1 month.

Samuel Knight, died Jan. 9, 1872, aged 75 years, 3 months.

Barnett Young, born May 28, 1798, died July 12, 1878; and his wife, Sarah, died Dec. 14, 1848, aged about 53 years.

Elizabeth Westenberger, died March 20, 1846, in her 61st year.

Jacob Reed, died Oct. 21, 1872, aged 85 years, 7 months; and his wife, Mary, died Dec. 12, 1861, aged 71 years, 4 months.

John Adams, died March 4, 1843, aged 62 years, 3 months; and his wife, Catherine, died Dec. 24, 1862, aged 73 years, 10 months.

Catharine Hyett, died April 15, 1846, aged 68 years, 5 months.

Catharine Printzin, born 1737, died Sept. 29, 1807.

Elizabeth Printzin, born in 1704, died in 1784.

Henry Prunce, died Jan. 23, 1828, aged 89 years.

Anna Maria Conrad, died Nov. 30, 1817, in her 81st year.

John Conrad, born Dec. 25, 1727, died April 2, 1787.

John Smith, born April 20, 1776, died Sept. 28, 1829; and his wife, Sophia, born Oct. 5, 1778, died April 25, 1859.

Henry Schrader, born in Prussia, April 15, 1754, emigrated to the United States in 1776, died Aug. 19, 1824.

Catharine C. Schrader, born Dec. 26, 1772, died Feb. 26, 1838.

Frederick Grosh, born Oct. 28, 1774, died June 17, 1862; and his wife, Anna Maria, born Feb. 11, 1781, died Oct. 3, 1823.

Daniel Shriver, born Nov. 11, 1790, died July 27, 1854.

John Riddle, born Nov. 21, 1751, died Sept. 25, 1845, aged 93 years, 10 months, 4 days; and his wife, Catharine, born Aug. 3, 1757, died Oct. 21, 1824.

Edward Silvers, born April 18, 1797, died Oct. 8, 1837; and his wife, Mary, born April 22, 1799, died Feb. 10, 1833.

Wm. South, died Feb. 28, 1827, aged 49 years, 1 month; and his wife, Martha, died Nov. 6, 1871, aged 84 years, 1 month, 19 days.

Thomas South, died April 5, 1873, aged 91 years, 2 months; and his wife, Barbara, died April 5, 1874, aged 90 years, 6 months.

Daniel South, born May 5, 1806, died April 14, 1858; and his wife, Eliza, born Dec. 5, 1804, died May 24, 1848.

Susanna Winder, wife of John Orr, died April 11, 1844, aged 84.

Catharine Kaler, born Aug. 16, 1788, died June 28, 1867.

Gerard South, died May 27, 1855, aged 81 years, 7 months; and his wife, Rachel, died Aug. 24, 1828, aged 42 years, 5 months.

John Maysilles, died Dec. 10, 1850, aged 78 years, 3 months; and his wife, Elizabeth, died May 6, 1831, aged 59 years, 1 month.

Catharine Arts, died May 26, 1852, in her 75th year.

David Betz, born Jan. 12, 1791, died Dec. 9, 1840; and his wife, Elizabeth, born May 3, 1795, died Nov. 21, 1856.

Jacob Stouffer, died July 17, 1869, aged 76 years, 6 months; and his wife, Catharine, died April 22, 1851, aged 53 years, 2 months.

George Pinkley, born Sept. 17, 1790, died Nov. 2, 1829.

Susan Pinkley, born Feb. 17, 1757, died April 25, 1837.

John Hebb, died April 2, 1875, aged 81 years, 2 months; and his wife, Catharine, died Aug. 7, 1866, aged 65 years, 10 months.

John Tracy, born Oct. 19, 1792, died Feb. 8, 1859.

Thomas Flemming, died April 4, 1863, aged 78 years, 9 months.

David Shilling, died March 10, 1860, aged 69 years, 7 months.

Margaret D. Kendle, died Oct. 14, 1866, aged 76.

Conrad Hildebrand, died Sept. 4, 1854, aged 77 years, 2 months.

Isaac Hildebrand, died Jan. 15, 1879, aged 80 years, 1 month.

James D. Kendle, born March 19, 1799, died Sept. 5, 1865.

Catharine Shoneberger, died Sept. 8, 1849, aged 73 years, 6 months.

Andrew Kemp, born Sept. 30, 1781, died Dec. 16, 1866; and his wife, Catherine, died Aug. 12, 1857, aged 70 years, 10 months.

Jacob Gower, died Feb. 6, 1852, aged 53 years, 11 months.

George Gower, died April 9, 1854, aged 52 years, 2 months.

Hugh R. Hughes, born May 15, 1804, died July 9, 1857.

James Winder, died July 17, 1782.

Alexander Winder, born Nov. 26, 1765, died Oct. 30, 1789.

Martin Waltz, born July 2, 1815, died Dec. 9, 1873.

Barbara A. Fiery, died Feb. 16, 1875, aged 64 years, 7 months.

L. A. Grosh, born Nov. 27, 1808, died Feb. 23, 1874.

Amelia, wife of Michael Weltz, died Oct. 28, 1867, aged 50 years, 7 months.

Peter Friese, died Aug. 30, 1872, aged 50 years, 4 months.

Sarah A., wife of Wm. South, died in 1872, aged 43 years, 7 months.

Wm. Shilling, born March 27, 1826, died Sept. 12, 1872.

Mary A., wife of Hiram Roger, died July 4, 1874, aged 45 years, 8 months.

Benj. South, of G., died Nov. 9, 1866, aged 46 years, 9 months.

John Stockslager, died Jan. 1, 1875, aged 48 years, 3 months; and Mary, his wife, born Nov. 18, 1824, died April 19, 1859.

Charlotte Sager, died Feb. 16, 1878, aged 59 years, 1 month.

Lydia Karns, died Feb. 25, 1878, aged 52 years, 8 months.

Peter Stockslager, born Dec. 4, 1807, died Jan. 23, 1861.

Henry Eyerly, died Aug. 16, 1856, aged 58 years, 3 months; and Elizabeth, his wife, died Nov. 7, 1862, aged 58 years, 3 months.

John E. Knode, died Sept. 16, 1875, aged 60 years, 8 months.

Maria, wife of Geo. Kemp, died Nov. 4, 1881, aged 67 years, 8 months.

Amelia Iseminger, born Jan. 8, 1806, died July 24, 1870.

Jacob Shaneberger, died March 16, 1862, aged 63 years, 1 month.

Leah S. Shafer, wife of Alexander Shafer, died March 3, 1848, aged 32 years, 9 months.

Joseph Kretsinger, died Jan. 22, 1852, aged 47 years.

Catherine E. Huyett, wife of Peter L. Huyett, born Jan. 14, 1813, died April 20, 1838.

Sophia Alter, wife of Elias O. Neal, born July 9, 1809, died Aug. 30, 1852.

Catherine, wife of Samuel Knight, died March 25, 1859, aged 56 years, 3 months.

Samuel Bender, died Aug. 27, 1845, aged 46 years, 1 month.

Catherine Grosh, died Nov. 17, 1865, aged 59 years, 3 months.

Ann E. Crawford, died May 30, 1880, aged 57 years.

George Bloom, born June 18, 1824, died Jan. 4, 1878.

Elizabeth Morgan, died March 16, 1852, aged 50 years, 9 months.

Elizabeth, wife of James McCoy, died May 24, 1851, aged 59 years, 10 months.

Jeremiah Robinett, died Aug. 13, 1853, aged 40 years, 5 months.

Mary A. Lancaster, born May 16, 1818, died Aug. 9, 1863.

Margaret Miller, died Sept. 4, 1843, in her 49th year.

Sarah, wife of James Tennet, born Oct. 1, 1801, died Feb. 25, 1858.

Israel Thomas Beckley, died Aug. 29, 1857, aged 31 years, 11 months.

Christiana, wife of Benj. South, died April 13, 1858, aged 33 years, 1 month.

Mary, wife of Thos. Fleming, died Jan. 8, 1858, aged 64 years, 6 months.

Cinderella, wife of Wm. F. Morgan, died June 26, 1852, aged 19 years.

Barnett Young, born May 28, 1798, died July 12, 1878; and Sarah, died Dec. 14, 1848, aged about 53 years.

Elizabeth, wife of Samuel C. Stouffer, died April 29, 1873, aged 64 years, 1 month.

Eliza, wife of David Troup, died Feb. 15, 1863, aged 54 years.

Elizabeth, wife of Isaac Hildebrand, died Oct. 4, 1848, aged 47 years, 7 months.

Rebecca, wife of John Knode, born March 5, 1803, and lived 45 years.

Mary E., wife of Peter S. Funk, died April 9, 1871, aged 31 years, 10 months.

Funkstown now has 600 inhabitants, among whom are B. F. Fiery, Mrs. Hughes, J. Fiery, Mrs. McCoy, J. Garver, W. Dellinger, Mrs. Shanaberger, H. Shilling, O. H. Snyder, M. Williams, D. W. McCoy, B. South, D. South, C. B. South, J. W. Stockslager, Mrs. Welsh, S. J. Keller, Mrs. Crawford, J. Bierly, D. Bowers, J. Williams, G. Kendle, Mrs. Winkfield, Mrs. Duke, N. Paris, G. Peydon, W. Troxell, Mrs. Erick, R. H. Cushen, J. Flora, Mrs. Shilling, L. Troxell, H. Fritsch, J. Gross, J. Weller, S. G. Mill, William Farray, F. Shilling, P. Strode, G. Kemp, A. Bowman, E. Williams, C. Stacks, L. Gaunt, M. W. Harman, M. Iseminger, G. Gares, H. Dusang, Dr. R. E. Butler, Mrs. Shafer, S. Williams, Mrs. Frieze, Mrs. Sager, V. H. Newcomer, Mrs. Keller, P. Rumberger, W. H. Myers, E. Schieldknecht, M. H. Clark, C. T. Hamilton, W. H. Knode, I. Hannah, Mrs. Hughes, A. McCoy, D. Valentine, Mrs. Grosh, George Dusang, W. Harper, J. Armes, O. Iseminger, J. Gumple, T. McCoy, W. Fisher, Mrs. L. Grosh, J. Bowman, W. S. Knode, F. Knode, D. Schindel, S. Baker, B. Marks, H. Stouffer, E. Stouffer, H. Gower, Mrs. Riddle, H. Iseminger, P. Stouffer, L. Stouffer, G. Shafer, W. Bowman, and others.

SANDY HOOK DISTRICT, No. 11.

Sandy Hook, or Election District No. 11, is the extreme southern district of Washington County, and the greater part of its surface is covered by mountains, Elk Ridge and Maryland Heights and their spurs occupying more than one-half the entire district, and South Mountain extending along its entire eastern boundary. "Huckleberry Hill," an offshoot from Maryland Heights, fills up the little peninsula formed by a curve in the Potomac on the southwest. The Potomac extends along the entire western and southern boundary of the district, separating it from Virginia. Rohrersville District is on the north. Sandy Hook is about two and three-quarter miles from north to south, and three miles from east to west. The population of the district is 1585, including the 373 inhabitants of Sandy Hook Village. The Washington County Branch of the Baltimore and Ohio Railroad runs through the district from north to south and connects with the main stem at Weverton. The main stem of the road runs along the southern portion of the county. Sandy Hook and Weverton are the only two towns in the district. "Harper's Ferry," one of the most historic spots in Virginia, is nearly opposite Sandy Hook Village, and is connected with it by the Baltimore and Ohio Railroad and its bridges. On the summit of Maryland Heights is a historic fort and a redoubt of seven guns. A relic of Sullivan's famous battery still remains upon the farm of James Beck, one of the oldest settlers of Sandy Hook. The house occupied by John Brown as his headquarters is in Semple's Manor, three and a half miles from Harper's Ferry, at the foot of Maryland Heights, about one and one-half miles from the Potomac. It is a two-story log house. William Cult was the first settler at Maryland Heights, and his neighbors were Josiah Hayne and George Yertee Baker. John Brown's log school-house was built by John Beacher about 1848, but was torn down during the war. The spot is now inclosed, and is owned by James Patten. A curious duel occurred near the Maryland Heights in the summer of 1800, in which two army officers in the cantonments—Lieuts. Swan and Elliott—were engaged.

The cause of the difference is said to have originated in Elliott's arresting Swan, in consequence of his having come on parade out of uniform. At this arrest Swan took umbrage and sent a challenge, which was accepted by Elliott. On receiving the word Elliott fired, his ball entering the thigh of his antagonist, who fell to the ground; on observing which he walked up and inquired of Swan if he was badly hurt, who, without giving any answer, ordered him back to his post and said that he must also have his fire. He went back, and Mr. Swan, being unable to stand, discharged his pistol in a sitting posture. His ball penetrated the right breast of Elliott and lodged in the left shoulder. The life of Elliott was for some time despaired of, but both finally recovered.

Sandy Hook obtained its name from a quicksand pool in which a teamster lost his team on the road to Frederick City. Fifty years ago there were but two houses there, in one of which Mr. Grow, one of the early settlers, lived. The town now contains 373 inhabitants and a comfortable Methodist church, built of brick, nicely finished, and capable of seating two hundred and fifty people. Rev. S. M. Alvord, who lives in Harper's Ferry, is the pastor.

Weverton was named after Casper Wever, a celebrated engineer connected with the Baltimore and Ohio Railroad, who built the first bridge at Harper's Ferry, laid out Pennsylvania Avenue, Washington, D. C., in Jackson's time, and was at one time secretary of the United States Senate. Mr. Wever, attracted by the possibility of utilizing the water-power of the Potomac at this point, purchased five hundred acres of land with the water-right all the way from where Weverton now is to Harper's Ferry. A substantial dam had been thrown across the river, at a cost of thirty-three thousand dollars, by the Weverton Manufacturing Company, and the Potomac Company purchased machinery and put up three hundred feet of fronting and built a mill. Five years ago the old mill building was torn down. For thirty years it remained idle, its affairs having become so tangled up that it never could get fairly started. The Henderson Steel and File Manufacturing Company commenced operations about 1846, and was worked only a few years, remaining idle until a few years ago, when its works were bought by Chapman & Stewart, who have, however, made no use of them as yet.

Wm. Loughridge owned a small marble-works of twenty horse-power, under the Weverton Company, about 1846. All the enterprises started as a part of Mr. Wever's scheme finally fell through. Mr. Wever died just before the war. His family have since all moved west. Jasper Kindell now owns the water-power all the way up from Weverton to Harper's Ferry, estimated at about two hundred thousand horse-power. A flour-mill is run by David Rinehart. The file-factory once managed by Gen. Henderson and a large cotton-factory belonging to the Potomac Company were sold to the canal company five years ago, after having been badly injured by floods. There is fifteen feet fall between Weverton and Harper's Ferry, a distance of two and a half miles. Much of the property of the place is now for sale at low prices. A hotel once stood at Weverton, which was burned. It was owned by Kindell & Caldwell, and was managed by Gen. Stewart, a brother-in-law of Col. Thomas Scott. The house was built in 1796, and near it was a Lutheran church, which was also built in 1796, which was moved to Knoxville in 1875. Mason Kindell was a music-teacher, whose attention was attracted to the property going to ruins at Weverton while he was teaching music in Waynesboro'. Great floods have been of frequent occurrence at Weverton. The most destructive were those of 1852, 1870, and 1877. In the latter year the river rose thirty-two feet above low-water mark and caused immense damage. At present Weverton is a town of about two hundred inhabitants. The postmaster is J. Rice Garrett, also a merchant. Dr. Robert H. E. Boteler is the resident physician; John Marquett, railroad agent; Samuel Garber, hotel-keeper; Warren Garrett and David Rinehart, millers; and J. W. Himes, builder.

In the graveyard on the Vert property between Weverton and Sandy Hook the following are buried:

William S. Elgin, born April 28, 1809, died Feb. 8, 1855; and Mary Elgin, born March 19, 1807, died Jan. 18, 1863.

John Reel, died March 28, 1856, aged 64.
Elizabeth Goldsborough, died Jan. 2, 1866, aged 54.
John W. Peters, died Nov. 1, 1867, aged 38.

TILGHMANTON DISTRICT, No. 12.

Tilghmanton, or Election District No. 12, is east of Williamsport District, south of Funkstown, west of Boonsboro', and north of Keedysville and Sharpsburg Districts. The Potomac River forms a portion of its southern boundary. It is about the size of the Beaver Creek and Funkstown Districts, and like the latter possesses the advantage of being penetrated by the Washington County Branch of the Baltimore and Ohio Railroad, which passes through the eastern portion of it, as also does the Sharpsburg and Hagerstown pike. Like the majority of the districts in Washington County, Tilghmanton is thickly populated, and is equipped with a network of good county and private roads. It has within its borders the villages of Tilghmanton, after which the district is named, Fair Play, Bakersville, Jones' Cross-roads, and Breathedsville, the latter on the Washington County Railroad. The Antietam flows along the entire eastern boundary of the district, and Marsh Run crosses it from north to south, a little west of the centre, supplying water-power for numerous flour and saw-mills, among them Delamere and Roxbury Mills. The population of the district is 1580, including Tilghmanton Village, which contains 171 inhabitants. Among the residents of the district are C. Schnavely, William P. Remsburg, C. Schnebly, L. C. Remsburg, J. Brill, Mrs. Shaw, S. Boyer, J. H. Gatrell, D. Marmaduke, N. Bowers, E. Harper, O. Baker, J. H. Heck, E. J. Herrington, B. F. Middlekauff, J. Wright, E. Eakle, J. James, A. Kroon, E. Davis, T. H. Davis, George Stonebraker, D. Coffman, J. Mondel, D. Rhoads, A. Schnebly, D. Schlosser, S. Schlosser, J. Eakle, J. Poffenberger, J. Warnranfeltz, H. Poffenberger, E. Burtner, S. Motes, D. Wolf, H. Motes, J. Doub, I. Emmert, S. Smith, I. Wilson, J. Reynolds, J. Schnebly, G. W. Long, N. Motes, J. Miller, U. Morin, J. Petre, C. Palmer, J. W. Stouffer, J. Middlekauff, Mrs. Rench, Mrs. S. Schnebly, J. Speilman, William H. Banks, T. M. Haley, John Reichard, V. Riechard, R. L. Cross, D. Long, L. N. Rowland, S. Cross, J. Fauny, J. Monigan, J. Barber, J. Emmert, E. Emmert, B. Oldwind, S. Artz, Mrs. Welty, J. Motes, Mrs. South, B. Palmer, C. Fahrney, O. Showman, A. Showman, W. Jones, G. W. Anderson, E. Smith, J. F. Rowland, William James, J. Ensminger, J. Friend, Mrs. Price, T. J. McKaig, M. Miller, J. Leatherman, P. Monroe, P. Sweeny, C. Jacobs, J. Wade, J. Bloom, Mr. Boot, Dr. Maddox, I. Warfield, Dr. J. P. Cheney, William Jones, George W. Kline, J. M. Cook, P. Middlekauff, T. J. Warfield, William McKnee, G. W. Kennedy, A. Miller, J. M. Grow, J. O. A. Kemp, William Booth, Dr. William H. Grimes, and others.

Dr. William Henry Grimes, who resides at Grimes' Station, near Bakersville, is one of Washington County's best-known physicians. His professional career began in 1842 at his present home, where he has practiced ever since. His father, James Grimes, was born in Jefferson County, Va., in 1787, and after his marriage to Margaret, daughter of James Strode, of Jefferson County, removed, at the age of twenty-one, to Washington County, and settled on a farm within five miles of Dr. Grimes' present home. Here he continued to reside until his death, in 1859, thirty-seven years after the death of his wife. Of his six children, those living are Dr. William H. Grimes, John A. Grimes, and Mrs. James Beler, of Washington County. Dr. Grimes' grandfather fought in the Revolutionary war, and his uncle, John Grimes, served through the campaign of 1812.

Dr. Grimes resided upon his father's farm until he was sent to Marshall College, Mercersburg, Pa. He subsequently studied medicine at the University of Maryland, where he graduated in 1842. In that year he made his home upon his farm, called "Marshton," where he has ever since resided. On the 15th of May, 1855, he married Sarah E., daughter of Andrew Rench, of Washington County. Mr. Rench has for many years enjoyed the distinction of being the largest landholder in Washington County, and is still living at the age of eighty-two. He is a native of Washington County. His father, Daniel, came to America from Germany in the latter part of the eighteenth century. Dr. Grimes devoted himself exclusively to his medical practice from 1842 to 1851, and in the latter year engaged in farming upon an extensive scale. As medical practitioner and farmer he has been equally successful, and as the result of his arduous labors in both occupations he has secured a bountiful competence. His field as a physician has covered a wide area, and few men in his county are better known or more highly respected.

In 1874 he was elected a member of the State Legislature, and made a record as a capable and diligent representative. Although for forty years a vigorous worker he is still in the full enjoyment of his physical strength and vigor, and is as active and useful as at any period of his career.

The village of Tilghmanton is situated in the centre of the Tilghmanton District, on the Sharpsburg and Hagerstown pike. It was named after Col. Frisby Tilghman, who came there before the beginning of

Wm H Grimes

the present century from the Eastern Shore of Maryland and laid out the town into lots for poor people. Col. Tilghman lived where Gen. Thomas J. McKaig now resides, and in 1807 was appointed judge of the Orphans' Court of Washington County. The first resident of Tilghmanton was John Smith, who removed from the neighborhood of Hancock about the year 1810. The Morgan family were next, among them Catherine Morgan, afterwards Mrs. John Smith, and Catharine Poffenberger, who is still living in the town, and is over eighty-one years old. Among the present residents are M. Motes, Mrs. Groff, H. Motes, J. Smith, L. Dietrick, H. Burgan, H. Wright, Mrs. Palmer, J. Miller, B. Smith, H. Smith, David Smith, H. Mannigan, O. Mannigan, F. Mannigan, D. Mannigan, A. Smith, J. Bloom, J. Wade, J. Shaw, Mrs. Reynolds, F. Fitch, George Bloom, J. Bloom, P. Sprecher, Mrs. Robbins, D. Eckman, S. Rohrer, A. Roberts, Mrs. Roberts, George Motes, D. Beeler, A. Kennedy, T. Hennesy, H. N. Cross.

There are several fruit-tree nurseries in the vicinity of Tilghmanton. Arch Spring Nursery, belonging to John Reichard, started in 1844, is a large concern, as is also that of H. M. Cross & Coffman, at Tilghmanton.

Churches in Tilghmanton District.—The Dunker church in Tilghmanton District is nearly a mile southeast of the village, on a cross-road leading towards the Antietam. The stones in the graveyard bear the names of the following persons:

Daniel Emmert, died Oct. 27, 1879, aged 72 years, 4 months; and his wife, Margaret, died Sept. 15, 1863, aged 53 years, 3 months.

Eleanor Brown, died March 16, 1879, aged 72 years, 6 months.

John Long, born Oct. 22, 1798, died Dec. 1, 1865; and his wife, Margaret, died May 28, 1878, aged 83 years, 11 months.

Elizabeth Slifer, died Sept. 7, 1862, aged 68 years, 30 days.

Jacob Newman, died April 4, 1876, aged 76 years, 3 months; and his wife, Catharine, died Nov. 24, 1862, aged 60 years, 9 months.

Jacob H. Barr, died Feb. 20, 1862, aged 53 years, 2 months.

Joseph Long, died Sept. 22, 1852, aged 60 years, 3 months; and his wife, Nancy, died Sept. 6, 1865, aged 73 years, 10 months.

David Wolf, died April 17, 1846, aged 52 years, 8 months; and his wife, Susannah, died Oct. 16, 1839, aged 41 years, 7 months.

Rev. Emmanuel Long, died Dec. 6, 1866, aged 38 years, 7 months.

Elizabeth, wife of Emmanuel Long, Sr., died Aug. 24, 1863, aged 57 years, 6 months.

Of the old residents buried in the graveyard attached to Emmert's church are the following:

Barbara Reichard, born Jan. 15, 1770, died Aug. 15, 1841, aged 71 years.

Lewis Burkhardt, born July 12, 1782, died April 2, 1846; and his wife, Catherine, died April 18, 1878, aged 82 years and 7 months.

John Newport, born Feb. 13, 1788, died July 24, 1843; and his wife, Mary, died June 15, 1859, aged 76 years and 9 months.

Peter Miller, died Feb. 14, 1856, aged 64 years and 3 months.

Elias Moats, died April 28, 1872, aged 64 years; and his wife, Rebecca, died April 15, 1875, aged 67 years and 2 months.

Eli Eckman, died March 25, 1876, aged 73 years and 2 months.

Catherine Poffenberger, died June 1, 1877, aged 85 years and 6 months.

Lydia, wife of David Coffman, born April 15, 1809, died April 28, 1873.

John H. Welty, born Jan. 16, 1806, died Aug. 6, 1860.

Magdalene Welty, died Aug. 11, 1862, aged 81 years and 3 months.

David Palmer, died April 18, 1855, aged 63 years and 10 months.

George Buser, born Feb. 28, 1792, died April 22, 1852; and his wife, Susannah, died June 29, 1850, aged 48 years and 7 months.

Salem Evangelical Lutheran church, built in 1854, is near Bakersville, in the southern section of Tilghmanton District, and is the most prominent religious structure in that neighborhood. It is a large brick edifice, occupying a commanding elevation, and surrounded by forests, which form a conspicuous feature of that section of the country. In the burial-ground are interred the remains of the following former residents of the vicinity:

John H. Grove, died Oct. 31, 1877, aged 52 years, 1 month.

George B. Middlekauff, died March 27, 1881, aged 33 years, 5 months.

John W. Avey, died Oct. 4, 1877, aged 59 years, 4 months; and Elizabeth, his wife, died Aug. 3, 1874, aged 54 years, 11 months.

Samuel A. Stonebraker, died Aug. 1, 1880, aged 62 years, 10 months.

Otho Baker, died May 10, 1877, aged 67 years, 2 months.

William Reynolds, Sr., born Aug. 25, 1771, died Dec. 4, 1839; and his wife, Susan, born Jan. 4, 1781, died Feb. 19, 1849.

Lucy Reynolds, died in 1826, aged 84 years; and her daughter, Lucy, died in 1864, aged 80 years.

William Reynolds, died July 2, 1876, aged 66 years, 5 months; and his wife, Elizabeth, died Feb. 5, 1858, aged 43 years, 1 month.

John Reynolds, died Feb. 7, 1879, aged 72 years, 4 months.

Amelia Stauffer, wife of Jacob Poffenberger, born April 21, 1804, died Jan. 13, 1872.

Henry Poffenberger, born Feb. 2, 1760, died Dec. 14, 1836; and his wife, Elizabeth, died Dec. 9, 1835, in her 64th year.

Jonathan Slifer, died May 7, 1880, aged 57 years, 1 month.

John Line, died March 16, 1836, in his 44th year.

Hiram Showman, died June 2, 1879, aged 61 years, 10 months.

William Hammond, died Jan. 16, 1872, aged 65 years, 11 months.

Christian Eakle, died May 24, 1861, aged 73 years, 2 months.

James Grimes, died Jan. 10, 1860, aged 74.

Thomas Albert, born June 20, 1804, died May 18, 1865; and his wife, Hannah, born April 5, 1801, died Aug. 17, 1868.

Henry Lowman, born July 5, 1791, died Dec. 14, 1848; and his wife, Mary, died Jan. 17, 1873, aged 80 years, 8 months.

Daniel Middlekauff, died Jan. 26, 1856, aged 55 years, 3 months; and his wife, Catherine, died Sept. 18, 1849, aged 47 years, 10 months.

Elizabeth McDade, died Feb. 10, 1842, aged 74.

Watkins James, Sr., died April 2, 1849, aged about 87; and his wife, Sarah, born Oct. 20, 1771, died Feb. 17, 1842.

Susannah Moats, died Jan. 17, 1849, aged 81 years, 16 days.

Jacob Moats, died April 28, 1842, in his 84th year.

John Poffenberger, died July 8, 1874, aged 77 years, 5 months; and his wife, Nancy, died Nov. 13, 1842, aged 38 years, 1 month.

Mrs. Jane Knodle, died Jan. 23, 1865, aged 76.

Jesse Banks, born Oct. 4, 1800, died March 18, 1866.

Henry C. Welty, died May 30, 1850, aged 63 years, 6 months; and his wife, Elizabeth, died March 8, 1860, aged 77 years, 6 months.

Levi R. Shaw, died June 26, 1851, aged 42 years, 1 month.

Mary A. Davis, born Feb. 10, 1814, died July 24, 1873. A very handsome marble shaft marks the lot of the Davis family.

John B. Eakle, born May 17, 1795, died Oct. 25, 1866; and his wife, Sarah, born Aug. 28, 1795, died Nov. 11, 1875.

Peter Showman, died Jan. 3, 1857, aged 62 years and 9 months; and his wife, Catharine, died Feb. 18, 1863, aged 68 years.

Elizabeth Binkley, died Sept. 2, 1878, aged 83 years.

Cyrus Zuck, died Nov. 22, 1865, aged 50 years.

Elizabeth, wife of Jacob Middlekaupf, died April 11, 1880, aged 82 years.

Courtney, wife of William H. Marmaduke, died Dec. 4, 1856, aged 59 years, 9 months.

Elizabeth Show, died Nov. 12, 1855, aged 75 years.

Margaret Dovenbarger, born Dec. 25, 1744, died Jan. 31, 1826.

John Dovenbarger, born April 25, 1788, died Jan. 13, 1865; and his wife, Mary, born Jan. 8, 1793, died Dec. 26, 1854.

Ralph Ormiston, born May 20, 1756, died Jan. 8, 1834.

John Knodle, died Jan. 13, 1862, aged 82 years; and his wife, Susannah, born Jan. 10, 1790, died Feb. 22, 1831.

Barbara Hoffman, died Aug. 10, 1831, aged 72 years.

Christian Middlekauff, born Sept. 30, 1769, died Aug. 1, 1828; and his wife, Rosanna, born Nov. 24, 1772, died Feb. 8, 1832.

Michael Stonebraker, died May 6, 1815, aged 56 years.

Eve A., wife of Francis Davis, died Feb. 2, 1857, aged 85 years.

George Garey, born March 6, 1735, died May 8, 1813.

Sarah, wife of John Stiffler, died Nov. 1, 1865, aged 100 years, 5 months, and some days.

Samuel Stonebraker, born April 11, 1801, died Feb. 17, 1873; and his wife, Margaretta, born May 15, 1812, died Dec. 20, 1852. Over their remains is erected an elegant marble monument, elaborately carved and decorated.

John Stonebraker, born March 2, 1786, died Feb. 6, 1848.

Elizabeth Stedman, died July 4, 1849, aged 58 years.

Peter Hammond, born Jan. 4, 1761, died Oct. 18, 1836; and his wife, Catharine, born July 19, 1769, died March 13, 1838.

In 1849 a Protestant Episcopal congregation was organized at Lappon's Cross-roads, near Breathedsville, six miles from Hagerstown, and a stone edifice was erected there. It was called St. Mark's, and the same year a petition was granted to Hezekiah Claggett, George S. Kennedy, T. Tilghman, Thomas Maddox, John Breathed, John Booth, M. C. Clarkson, and Daniel Donnelly, Sr., to form a separate congregation. The congregation was first collected the fall before, and worshiped three miles from St. James' College. Rev. Joseph C. Parsons became rector July 24, 1849. The following year he reported the new church finished. The delegates to conventions and the number of communicants from that time to 1873 were as follows:

Delegates: 1850–53, G. S. Kennedy; 1854–58 and 1860–66, Dr. Thos. Maddox; 1859, A. Falk: 1865–66, Dr. Maddox; 1867, J. W. Breathed; 1868, Dr. Maddox; 1869, W. S. Kennedy; 1870–73, H. Onderdonk. Communicants: 1850, 14; 1851–53, 13; 1854–56, 12; 1857, 11; 1858, 10; 1859, 12; 1860–63, 8; 1864, 11; 1867, 16; 1868–71, 17; 1872, 20; 1873, 6.

Prior to the building of St. Mark's church John Breathed, after whom the town of Breathedsville was named, conducted services in his own house.

Among those buried in the graveyard attached to St. Mark's are:

Jane, wife of Ezekiel Chaney, died Aug. 6, 1865, aged 64 years.

Elizabeth, wife of Daniel Donnelly, died Sept. 1, 1856, in her 58th year.

Legh Richmond Keech, son of Samuel and Eleanor Keech, of St. Mary's County, born Oct. 2, 1831, died July 28, 1856.

The Breathed family have a lot in this churchyard inclosed by an iron fence and marked by a handsome brownstone monument. Among the inscriptions there are:

John Breathed, died May 25, 1852, aged 72 years, 1 month, 19 days.

Ann McGill Breathed, died March 11, 1862, aged 42 years, 11 months, and 22 days.

CONOCOCHEAGUE DISTRICT, No. 13.

Conococheague, or Election District No. 13, borders on the Pennsylvania line, which forms its northern boundary. On the east is East Hagerstown District, on the southeast West Hagerstown District, which also bounds it on the south, and on the west Clear Spring District, from which it is partially separated by Conococheague Creek, which, trending to the east, then north, then east, then north again, extends across the western portion of the district into Pennsylvania, where it has its source. The population of the district, including the village of Fairview (which has fifty-nine inhabitants), is sixteen hundred and thirty. There are four towns in the district,—Fairview, Cearfoss, Mangansville, and Pikesville. The Cumberland Valley Railroad runs through the northeastern section, passing by Mangansville. From north to south Conococheague Creek winds a tortuous course, doubling upon itself twice and forming a clearly-defined letter S. Well-cared-for public roads extend in all directions through the district, and numerous saw and grist-mills run by water-power are distributed along the water-courses which abound in the eastern section. There are two Tunker churches in the district, each near one of the bends of Conococheague Creek. Mount Tabor church is in the southeast, and there is also a Mount Tabor church near Fairview. Mount Zion church is on the road leading from Cearfoss north, and there is a Mennonite church within a quarter of a mile of the town. Mount Salem church is two miles and a quarter from Cearfoss. The surface of the county in Conococheague is generally rolling, and the land is good. The average production per acre is about twenty-five bushels of wheat, forty-five bushels of corn, and three tons of hay to the acre, and the average price of land per acre is seventy-five dollars. The district was one of the earliest settled in the county, and contained a portion of Lord Baltimore's reserved lands and manors.

On Nov. 9, 1767, the commissioners empowered by him offered these lands for sale at the house of Col. Thos. Prather, in Frederick County. The manor contained over eleven thousand acres. The ancestors of the immortal author of the "Star-Spangled Banner" were residents of Conococheague District, and Edmund Key owned "Paradise," an estate of three hundred and thirty-five acres, "Good Hope," of three hundred acres, and "Friendship," of two hundred and six acres. He died in 1766. In January, 1807, Michael Tice and his four horses were drowned in attempting to cross the dam at Hoffer's mill, near the broad ford on Conococheague Creek. John Hershey owned the mills on Conococheague Creek, six miles from Hagerstown, and died in 1812. Among other early residents were Henry Ankeny and John McClain, who lived on the west side of Conococheague Creek, eight miles from Hagerstown. It is also related that John Downin managed John Hershey's cloth-factory, half a mile from Michael Hoffer's mill, in 1814. Among the volunteers in Capt. David Cushwa's company in 1812 were Philemon Cromwell, Robt. Chambers, Geo. Steinemetz, David Stoltz, Stephen Cromwell, Jas. Myers, Philip Troxell, and Abraham Watson, all of Conococheague District. The largest town in the district is Fairview, which is six miles from Mason and Dixon's line and nine miles from Hagerstown. It was settled by the Kreight and Fiery families. Mount Tabor church was built in 1858 by Jacob Reed and John Fiery. The land all about was originally called "Kreight's Establishment," after the family who had taken it up. John Fiery, the last of the family in the neighborhood, was drowned in the Conococheague in the winter of 1868. F. T. Spilker is postmaster. Mount Tabor Lutheran church, near the town, is a comfortable and pretty church edifice, and the congregation is quite large.

Cearfoss is four miles from Hagerstown, and is situated almost directly in the centre of Conococheague District. Originally it was Stearn's Tavern, on the Williamsport and Chambersburg pike, and was subsequently known as Cunningham's Cross-roads. John Cunningham, who lived there early in the century, died in 1850. Daniel Cearfoss began to reside there in 1852. He came from Pennsylvania, and improved the place by erecting new buildings, including a large store-house. The town was named after him on account of the enterprise which he displayed in pushing its fortunes. He was a farmer, store-keeper, and drover, and was made postmaster when Cearfoss was made a post-town, in 1877. The population of the town is now about 200, and it contains a German Reformed, Evangelical, German Baptist, Winebrennarian, and Mennonite church. The postmaster at present is J. M. Boyer. Mangansville takes its name from Jonathan and Abraham Mangan, who settled on the spot early in the present century. In 1820 they owned two hundred acres of land in the neighborhood. Abraham Mangan died in 1830, and was buried in a private graveyard. When the Mangans arrived the land was all a dense forest of timber. The first buildings of importance were erected in 1835 by Jonathan Mangan. The Cumberland Valley Railroad depot now stands on the old Greencastle road.

Churches of Conococheague District.—Salem German Reformed church, in Conococheague District, is located four miles southeast of Cearfoss post-office. It is a stone building of moderate dimensions, and in the churchyard are buried the following persons:

Daniel Brumbaugh, Sr., died Aug. 24, 1824, aged 52 years; and his wife, Elizabeth, died Dec. 12, 1860, aged 81 years, 11 months.

John Long, died Aug. 10, 1856, aged 72 years, 7 months; and his wife, Pamelia, died Nov. 30, 1857, aged 62 years, 13 days.

Susannah Brumbaugh, born May 28, 1799, died Feb. 6, 1861.

Andrew Rentch, died Oct. 7, 1792, aged 60 years; and his wife, Elizabeth, died Sept. 4, 1812, aged 73 years.

Barbara, wife of George Gross, died Dec. 24, 1842, aged 56 years, 8 months.

John Felker, died Aug. 1, 1846, aged 90 years, 6 months; and his wife, Catherine, died Feb. 3, 1847, aged 83 years, 11 months.

John Cunningham, died June 28, 1851, aged 42 years, 9 months; and his wife, Mary, died Aug. 13, 1843, aged 36 years, 1 month.

Daniel Zeller, died Oct. 12, 1865, aged 72 years, 7 months; and his wife, Rachel, died Jan. 13, 1862, aged 43 years, 9 months.

John McLaughlin, Sr., born June 9, 1780, died Nov. 22, 1853; and his wife, Ruth, born July 8, 1783, died Sept. 8, 1878.

Masham Metcalf, born May 16, 1781, died April 26, 1836.

Samuel Weaver, born June 27, 1799, died Aug. 14, 1839; and his wife, Elizabeth, born June 13, 1805, died June 4, 1875.

Michael Strock, died May 30, 1837, aged 47 years, 6 months; and his wife, Rebecca, died Aug. 8, 1859, aged 67 years, 4 months.

Samuel Zeller, born Aug. 5, 1797, died April 2, 1869; and his wife, Mary, died Feb. 9, 1864, aged 50 years.

George Wolfenberger, died Sept. 22, 1862, aged 54 years, 7 months.

John Neikirk, died July 15, 1852, aged 63 years, 3 months; and his wife, Barbara, died Oct. 1, 1865, aged 71 years, 3 months.

Eve Kuhn, died July 28, 1870, aged 62 years, 2 months.

Philip B. Bingaman, died May 28, 1870, aged 62 years, 3 months.

Barbara Moyer, died June 29, 1872, aged 79 years, 3 months.

Samuel Zeller, of Jonas, died Sept. 24, 1868, aged 70 years; and his wife, Margaret, died March 4, 1853, aged 46 years, 3 months.

Joseph Gabriel, died Oct. 16, 1845, aged 53 years, 21 days.

Daniel Kershner, born April 21, 1798, died Aug. 23, 1851.

David Cunningham, died April 15, 1853, in his 73d year; and his wife, Ann, died Sept. 20, 1852, aged 66 years, 15 days.

Joseph Cunningham, died Dec. 10, 1875, aged 63 years, 3 months.

Margaret, wife of Jacob Rummel, died Jan. 30, 1837, aged 75 years.

Jacob Schnebly, died July 23, 1858, aged 72.

John Schnebly, born Aug. 15, 1785, died Oct. 23, 1818.

Daniel H. Schnebly, died Aug. 3, 1858, aged 69 years, 7 months; and his wife, Ann Maria, born Oct. 25, 1795, died Oct. 17, 1846.

John Seibert, died Sept. 4, 1841, aged 48 years, 9 months.

Col. Henry Fouk, born Aug. 10, 1787, died March 5, 1867; and his wife, Henrietta B., born Jan. 11, 1798, died Aug. 8, 1870.

Perry B. McLaughlin, died Nov. 11, 1875, aged 61 years, 3 months.

John McLaughlin, born Aug. 11, 1806, died Jan. 8, 1877.

Henry McLaughlin, born March 28, 1776, died July 20, 1837.

Jacob Rench, died July 15, 1811, aged 50 years; and his wife, Margaretta, died Nov. 2, 1846, aged 75.

Henry C. Miller, died Nov. 2, 1865, aged 85 years, 6 months; and his wife, Mary, died April 1, 1871, aged 80.

John Rench, died Nov. 20, 1794, aged 68 years; and his wife, Margaret, died April 30, 1806, aged 75.

Peter Rench, died Sept. 24, 1796, aged 42.

John Rench, died Jan. 7, 1798, aged 42.

John Schnebly, died May 20, 1833, aged 84 years; and his wife, Catharine, born July 31, 1768, died May 13, 1835.

John Rench, born March 1, 1784, died April 18, 1814.

John Barnett, died Feb. 17, 1828, aged 40 years; and his wife, Sally, died Nov. 13, 1862, aged 69 years, 4 months.

David Newcomer, died March 19, 1856, aged 76 years, 10 months; and his wife, Mariah, died Nov. 1, 1826, aged 49.

Otho Zeller, died April 18, 1841, aged 58 years; and his wife, Eve, born Dec. 10, 1794, died April 19, 1833.

Mount Zion Evangelical church is a short distance north of Cearfoss post-office. It is a brick structure, and was erected by the Evangelical Association in September, 1852. In the graveyard attached the remains of the following persons are interred:

David Baker, died Sept. 2, 1876, aged 71 years, 9 months; and his wife, Lydia, died Jan. 29, 1859, aged 29 years, 7 months.

Elizabeth Magowen, born Aug. 31, 1803, died Dec. 17, 1879.

Yost Strock, born April 30, 1788, died Oct. 4, 1865.

Peter Rummell, died Feb. 26, 1877, aged 87 years, 15 days; and his wife, Margaret, died Dec. 23, 1871, aged 74.

Peter Frounfelter, died Oct. 16, 1869, aged 68 years, 9 months; and his wife, Margaret, born May 4, 1807, died March 29, 1867.

Susan, wife of Jacob Hershberger, died March 16, 1863, aged 67 years, 11 months.

Samuel Spileker, born May 8, 1795, died Dec. 23, 1857; and his wife, Nancy, born Feb. 26, 1801, died Aug. 5, 1860.

Jacob L. Middlekauff, died Aug. 30, 1870, aged 77 years, 9 months; and his wife, Mary, died July 14, 1855, aged 61 years, 11 months.

A small brick church belonging to the Mennonite denomination is located within a mile of Mangansville. In the graveyard attached to it the following persons are buried:

Susan Snively, wife of Samuel Burkley, born June 4, 1821, died Aug. 25, 1877.

Mary Kilhofer, died Jan. 5, 1870, aged 64 years.

Elizabeth, wife of Christian Hoover, died Sept. 7, 1864, aged 74 years, 8 months.

John Witmer, born March 23, 1798, died April 2, 1872; and his wife, Susanna, born Jan. 29, 1804, died Feb. 12, 1862.

Samuel Weber, born Dec. 2, 1806, died April 26, 1872; and his wife, Susanna, born Jan. 8, 1805, died July 9, 1868.

Christian Eshelman, died Nov. 23, 1853, aged 56 years, 4 months; and his wife, Lydia, died Aug. 20, 1878, aged 66 years, 8 months.

Jacob Witmer, Sr., died Sept. 6, 1856, aged 66 years, 10 months.

John Ebersole, born Feb. 4, 1788, died July 25, 1862; and his wife, Fanny, born Oct. 17, 1787, died July 12, 1871.

Rev. John Summers, died Oct. 13, 1858, aged 57 years, 10 months; and his wife, Sarah, died Jan. 31, 1881, aged 75 years.

Benjamin Eby, born Oct. 5, 1797, died April 16, 1866.

Catharine Eby, born Dec. 17, 1789, died March 14, 1869.

John Horst, born Dec. 11, 1801, died April 15, 1875; and his wife, Elizabeth, died Dec. 22, 1865, aged 64 years, 2 months.

Jacob Hufferd, born Jan. 16, 1798, died Aug. 16, 1849.

Michael Carl, died June 15, 1860, aged 70 years, 5 months.

Christian Niswander, Sr., died March 14, 1856, aged 72 years, 4 months; and his wife, Elizabeth, died Feb. 8, 1846, aged 62 years, 4 months.

John Plum, died Oct. 7, 1855, aged 58 years, 21 days; and Magdalena Plum, died Oct. 19, 1846.

Andrew S. Witmer, born Feb. 1, 1819, died Sept. 15, 1863.

Susan Snively, wife of Samuel, born June 4, 1821, died Dec. 25, 1877.

Mount Tabor United Brethren church is in the southwestern corner of Conococheague District, and is a small frame edifice. In the churchyard the following persons are interred:

John Stine, born Dec. 6, 1792, died Dec. 19, 1873.

Josiah Kershner, died March 12, 1855, aged 54; and his wife, Catharine, died March, 1855, aged 57 years, 9 months.

Peter Gingrich, died March 10, 1855, aged 78 years, 5 months; and his wife, Catharine, died Dec. 28, 1857, aged 70 years, 3 months.

Martin Bopp, died Aug. 15, 1860, aged 69 years, 8 months.

Mary, wife of John D. Troup, died Jan. 8, 1867, aged 81.

David Needy, died April 26, 1876, aged 69 years, 2 months; and his wife, Sarah, died Jan. 28, 1871, aged 61 years, 5 months.

John Resh, died Jan. 10, 1879, in his 73d year.

Sarah Miller, died June 26, 1874, aged about 51.

Henry Byers, died March 18, 1879, aged 66 years, 11 months; and his wife, Sarah, died Feb. 8, 1877, aged 50 years, 8 months.

John Seigman, died Aug. 11, 1862, aged 60 years, 3 months; and his wife, Hannah, died Dec. 5, 1875, aged 72 years, 7 months.

Mount Tabor Lutheran church, near Fairview, is a wooden edifice on a stone foundation. The corner-stone is dated May 18, 1858. In the graveyard are interred the following former residents of the vicinity:

John Cook, died May 8, 1859, aged 53 years, 8 months; and his wife, Nancy, died July 2, 1868, aged 62 years, 6 months.

Jacob Fox, died Jan. 18, 1861, aged 51 years, 7 months; and his wife, Catharine, died Dec. 2, 1862, aged 52 years, 4 months.

Jacob Wisherd, Sr., died June 1, 1861, aged 77.

John Firey, died Dec. 25, 1868, aged 68.

Priscilla Davis, died Feb. 1, 1869, aged 75.

Mary, wife of Daniel Angle, born Sept. 16, 1786, died Nov. 17, 1873.

In the Tunker churchyard, in the southeastern section of the district, the following persons have been buried:

Rosanna Black, died Sept. 4, 1862, aged 75 years.

David W. Deaver, died Feb. 26, 1861, aged 56 years.

Susan, wife of John Kayser, born May 9, 1806, died Feb. 24, 1876.

John Bear, died April 1, 1863, aged 67 years, 4 months.

John Sword, died March 1, 1860, aged 55 years; and his wife, Mary, died Aug. 5, 1871, aged 61 years, 6 months.

Christian Sheller, born April 30, 1798, died Nov. 18, 1872.

Jacob Funk, born April 16, 1810, died Aug. 27, 1875.

John Showalter, died April 12, 1869, aged 79 years; and his wife, Christina, died Sept. 8, 1866, aged 72 years, 10 months.

Henry Jacobs, died Aug. 27, 1865, aged 73 years, 9 months; and his wife, Nancy, died March 31, 1876, aged 81 years, 9 months.

There is a small Winebrennarian church at Cearfoss, in the cemetery of which the bodies of the following persons have been buried:

David T. Wilson, died Oct. 11, 1861, aged 75 years.

Elder Daniel Woolford, died Dec. 27, 1875, aged 52 years.

Jacob Shafer, died June 6, 1847, aged 64 years.

Mary Willis, died Dec. 28, 1852, aged 56 years.

Catherine Moates, died March 30, 1844, aged 72 years.

John Hershberger, died Oct. 13, 1863, aged 67 years.

RINGGOLD DISTRICT, No. 14.

Ringgold, or Election District No. 14, has for its northern boundary Mason and Dixon's line, separating it from Pennsylvania. On the east is South Mountain, separating it from Frederick County. Directly south of it is Cavetown District, and on the west is Leitersburg District. The Western Maryland Railroad, after crossing the South Mountain at Blue Ridge Summit, descends a curve down the mountain-side, and then crosses the eastern portion of the district along the base of the mountains. The country here is very irregular, consisting of a range of hills extending up and down the eastern portion of the county. In the central and western part of the district there are many valuable tracts of fertile land in a high state of cultivation, and the section is thickly settled. The district was named after Ringgold Village, situated in the northeast portion, which is the only town in it. The population of the district (including the village of Ringgold, which contains 199 inhabitants) is 823. Among the residents of the district are I. H. Durburow, J. Martin, J. Stoner, J. N. Newcomer, G. K. Byer, D. Creager, B. Newcomer, A. Wingert, C. Shank, A. Frick, J. Wiles, J. Addlesparger, Wm. Stewart, J. Rinehart, J. Shockey, A. Shockey, G. Gardnour, J. Motz, C. Hoffman, E. Shockey, J. Hess, John Welty, L. A. R. Kohler, Mrs. Wolf, J. Kohler, E. Vogle, J. Miller, J. Crosby, J. Kohler, J. Martin, J. F. Lantz, G. Bachtell, I. Bachtell, B. Shull, George Fulton, G. Masters, G. Deffenbaugher, D. Guiser, J. Law, Mrs. Shelley, A. Stouffer, J. Stouffer, J. Shelley, D. Row, J. A. Hoover, W. De Losier, J. B. Loose, A. Shank, D. Fesler, H. Harbaugh, H. Baer, S. Frantz, H. Shindledecker, H. Krider, T. Vance, J. H. Chapman, J. Gladhill, and others.

The town of Ringgold is situated in the northwestern corner of Ringgold District, adjacent to the State line. It was first settled by John Creager, who built a log house there in 1825, and was originally called Ridgeville, owing to its position on the knob of a ridge. At the time it was made a post-office the name was changed to Ringgold, in honor of Maj. Samuel Ringgold. The change occurred in 1850, and John H. Besore was appointed postmaster. The town has now a population of about 200, and has never been incorporated. Among the inhabitants are John Barkdoll, Joseph Barkdoll, C. Hoffman, Mrs. Motz, C. Barkdoll, J. Motz, M. Hoffman, Dr. F. Barkdoll, Mrs. Hoover, S. Kohler, L. Barkdoll, J. Harbaugh, D. P. Protzman, S. G. Martin, J. C. Reecher, C. Hoffman, J. Wise, Nancy Flory, D. Barkdoll, Mrs. Rush, D. M. Hoover, Mrs. Knode, E. Euhler, J. P. Hoover, C. Dayhoof, Wm. Stewart, J. Addlesberger.

In the village of Ringgold is the only church in Maryland of the River Brethren, as they are commonly termed, although the name they have given themselves is Brethren in Christ. They have also the privilege of preaching once in every four weeks at a union church at Beaver Creek post-office.

The church at Ringgold was built in 1871, and is a brick structure 40 by 65 feet in size. It cost six thousand dollars, and will seat six hundred persons. The congregation numbers sixty-nine male and female members. The pastor, who is styled the bishop, is Aaron C. Wingert, who has held that office ever since the church was erected. Joseph Hess was the first assistant, and was succeeded upon his death by the present incumbent, Laban W. Wingert. The deacon is Daniel Hollinger, and he and the bishop are the trustees. In the graveyard of the church are buried the following persons:

Samuel Dayhoff, born May 19, 1799, died April 19, 1877; and his wife, Maria, born Nov. 1, 1813, died March 13, 1876.

Elizabeth Welty, died July 6, 1877, aged 53 years.

Magdalena Strite, born March 4, 1781, died April 16, 1864.

Rev. Christian Lesher, born April 26, 1775, died Sept. 6, 1856; and his wife, Catharine, born Aug. 21, 1779, died Feb. 15, 1865.

Henry Lesher, died Nov. 7, 1821, aged 81 years.

Solomon Shockey, died March 23, 1871, aged 65 years, 2 months; and his wife, Ann Elizabeth, died Dec. 27, 1875, aged 73 years, 5 months.

Margaret, wife of William Rogers, died Nov. 22, 1874, aged 73 years, 16 days.

Elizabeth Pass, died March 7, 1876, aged 75 years, 1 month.

Margaret Stouffer, died June 16, 1875, aged 83 years, 6 months.

David Shockey, died Dec. 30, 1875, aged 57 years, 9 months.

Rev. Joseph M. Hess, born Jan. 21, 1838, died Dec. 20, 1876.

On the Ringgold and Waynesboro' road, near the Pennsylvania State line, which passes five yards north of it, is the New Mennonite or Franzite church, the only one of that denomination in Maryland. The doctrines of the sect, whose founder is buried in this churchyard, are described in the article upon religious denominations in Washington County. The church is a large brick building, and its neatness and the elegance of many of the monuments in the churchyard testify to the wealth of the congregation. Among those whose remains are here interred are the following:

Daniel Resch, born Nov. 30, 1798, died May 15, 1875.

Magdalena Resch, born July 29, 1796, died Jan. 28, 1864.

John Stewart, born Dec. 27, 1799, died Sept. 7, 1870.

Jacob Reecher, born Jan. 8, 1788, died Aug. 13, 1866; and his wife, Catharine, born Sept. 7, 1797, died Feb. 24, 1870.

Jacob Kendig, born Jan. 14, 1793, died Oct. 30, 1876; and his wife, Elizabeth, born Dec. 19, 1803, died Nov. 13, 1868.

Mary B., wife of Abraham Groff, died Sept. 23, 1853, aged 61 years, 9 months.

Rev. Jacob Frantz, born Oct. 13, 1815, died Feb. 25, 1880; and his wife, Fanny, born June 1, 1816, died Aug. 30, 1854.

Maria Frick, born Dec. 18, 1797, died March 8, 1861.

Christian Frick, born June 2, 1764, died Dec. 15, 1851.

Barbara Frantz, born Nov. 9, 1784, died Sept. 12, 1874.

John Frick, born April 7, 1799, died April 27, 1878; and his wife, Anna Kelso, born Jan. 1, 1800, died Jan. 20, 1876.

John Welty, born May 24, 1813, died May 6, 1880.

Abraham Barr, died Sept. 24, 1869, aged 57 years, 10 months.

John Funk, Sr., born March 25, 1786, died June 27, 1844; and his wife, born July 6, 1787, died Dec. 19, 1876.

Henry W. Funk, died March 27, 1870, aged 52 years, 9 months.

Adam Morgal, born Feb. 3, 1793, died Oct. 16, 1873; and his wife, Maria, died May 1, 1880, aged 82 years, 2 months.

Emanuel Miller, born Feb. 23, 1794, died Feb. 6, 1864; and his wife, Mary, born July 29, 1791, died Aug. 5, 1864.

Jacob E. Miller, born Oct. 15, 1813, died Feb. 28, 1877.

Frederick Oppenlander, born Jan. 3, 1793, died Feb. 11, 1868; and his wife, Frederica, born Oct. 26, 1796, died July 6, 1873.

Abraham Frick, born May 8, 1793, died Feb. 4, 1879; and his wife, Catharine, born Jan. 20, 1793, died Sept. 7, 1872.

Samuel Bearer, born Dec. 19, 1799, died Oct. 7, 1856; and his wife, Frenny, born Jan. 27, 1805, died Sept. 1, 1875.

John Frantz, died March 4, 1877, aged 65 years, 6 months; and his wife, Ann, died Sept. 1, 1845, aged 20 years, 1 month.

Samuel Barr, born Dec. 14, 1784, died July 10, 1824.

Maria, wife of Wm. Scott, born June 30, 1772, died July 17, 1856, aged 84 years, 17 days.

David Rohrer, born Jan. 25, 1801, died Feb. 3, 1875.

Martin Rohrer, died Sept. 20, 1843, aged 69 years, 7 months; and his wife, Anna, died Nov. 10, 1832, aged 58 years, 1 month.

Christian Franz, minister of the gospel and bishop of the Mennonite Church, born Dec. 17, 1786, died Feb. 7, 1862; and his wife, Anna, born Oct. 12, 1787, died April 8, 1836.

Welty's Tunker church, on the Ringgold and Smithsburg road, was built by the late John Welty and made a free gift to the Dunkards. It is a brick edifice in the plain and substantial style common to all the churches of the denomination. A graveyard is attached to it, in which are buried the following old residents of the neighborhood:

John Barkdoll, born Feb. 27, 1804, died Sept. 22, 1877; and his wife, Susan, born Aug. 15, 1804, died Dec. 13, 1875.

Joseph Garver, born June 12, 1803, died April 24, 1870; and his wife, Mary, born July 28, 1804, died Aug. 27, 1869.

William Welty, born April 24, 1780, died Sept. 25, 1844; and his wife, Susanna, born April 9, 1785, died Sept. 6, 1871.

John Geiser, born Nov. 2, 1784, died March 25, 1849; and his wife, Mary, born July 12, 1792, died Jan. 16, 1852.

Catharine Fesler, born Nov. 22, 1782, died Aug. 2, 1857.

Mary Boman, died Feb. 7, 1867, aged 91 years, 8 months.

Mary, wife of Christian Newcomer, born Oct. 17, 1806, died Sept. 5, 1877.

Christian Snively, born Jan. 18, 1788, died March 15, 1855.

Jacob Hise, born Feb. 5, 1805, died Jan. 6, 1878.

Joseph F. Rohrer (elder), born Jan. 3, 1810, died Oct. 9, 1873.

Elizabeth, wife of John Rohrer, died May 24, 1866, aged 77.

Solomon Newcomer, died Jan. 12, 1867, aged 33.

Abraham Stouffer, died April 8, 1869, in his 69th year.

John Miller, born July 18, 1788, died April 26, 1870.

Nancy, wife of John Miller, born March 16, 1794, died Oct. 10, 1873.

INDIAN SPRING DISTRICT, No. 15.

Indian Spring, or Election District No. 15, lying between Clear Spring District on the east and Hancock District on the west, Pennsylvania on the north, and the Potomac River on the south, is historically one of the most interesting and naturally the most picturesque sections in Washington County. Its average length is about four and a half miles, and its average width about three miles. The face of the country is very mountainous, but between the ranges are valleys of exquisite loveliness. The views in nearly every direction are of the most romantic and beautiful character. The Potomac River winds along its southern boundary, passing beyond the district at the foot of Pigskin Mountain Ridge, which extends just within the district line, in a northeasterly direction. Above the northern extremity of Pigskin Ridge, Licking Creek cuts its way through a rocky bed, and flows with many a turn through the mountain passes to the Potomac, which it enters two miles south of Millstone Point. From the northeastern corner of the district a range of rugged mountains, beginning with Hearthstone Mountain and extending to North Mountain, half of which is in Clear Spring District, runs through the entire eastern portion of the district, terminating in a group of mountains in the southeast, clustering about Green Spring Furnace and Indian Spring Village. The population of the district (including the hamlet of Millstone Point, which has 62 inhabitants) is 1736. A little town called Four Locks, in the southeast, obtains its name from the four canal locks which are located there. The Chesapeake and Ohio Canal extends along the southern border of the district. Besides those in the towns there are several churches in the district, one a short distance north of Fort Frederick, and Union church, at the point where Licking Creek flows into the Potomac. The National turnpike crosses the mountains at Fairview, through the town of Indian Springs, and continues southwest along the Potomac to Millstone Point. Lane's Run, an affluent of Licking Creek, flows from northeast to southwest, and forms a part of the eastern boundary of the district. The district is very sparsely settled, owing to the mountainous nature of the country, although in the southeast, about Green Springs Furnace and Four Locks, there is a moderately populous section.

Naturally the most interesting spot in Indian Spring District is Fairview Mountain. The National turnpike crosses the mountain two miles north of Four Locks. Near the summit of Fairview is the Mountain House, kept by John W. Kinsell. Here the weary climber rests before making the final ascent to "Fairview" itself, a point from which a landscape unrivaled in picturesque beauty spreads in every direction, — a veritable fair view indeed. Seven-eighths of a circle is visible to the eye, and portions of four States can plainly be seen. On the north and south are the rugged brows of North Mountain, a wild and dreary background to a picture of entrancing beauty. Stretching as far as the eye can reach eastward is the fertile Cumberland Valley, dotted with villages, farm-houses, and patches of glistening water. To the south of the Potomac is the Shenandoah Valley, and beyond for miles after miles the blue Appalachian range. Within this vista can be seen Hancock, Hedgesville, Martinsburg, Harper's Ferry, the battle-grounds of Antietam, Boonsboro', South Mountain, Crampton's Gap, Williamsport, Clear Spring, Fort Frederick, Cavetown, Smithsburg, Waynesboro', Funkstown, Greencastle, and Chambersburg. The Potomac circles like a huge snake six times before it is lost in the distance, and Conococheague and Antietam Creeks wind their devious ways from north to south.

The historic family of Indian Spring District are the Jacqueses. The first of the name was Launcelot Jacques, who patented the manor, which included Fort Frederick, Green Springs, and Indian Springs. In later years the executors of Arthur Jacques sold the Green Spring property to J. Dixon Roman. In 1864 it was purchased by Moses Whitson, and Jeremiah and Mark Haines.

Moses Whitson is a native of Pennsylvania, and was born in Sadsbury township, Chester Co., Jan. 24, 1840. His father, Moses, son of Thomas and Hannah, was born in the same township Aug. 24, 1798, and died there Feb. 14, 1853. Thomas Whitson was also a native of Chester County. The Whitsons came to this country from Scotland, and locating first on Long Island, moved subsequently to Pennsylvania. They intermarried with the Jacksons, whose ancestor, Isaac Jackson, settled in Londongrove township, Chester Co., in 1725. Isaac Jackson was also the progenitor of the Confederate Gen. "Stonewall" Jackson. The father of the present Moses Whitson married Elizabeth, daughter of Jacob and Elizabeth Taylor, of Chester County. Both Mr. and Mrs. Taylor lived to be very old, he dying in 1865, aged ninety-three, and she in 1868, at the same age. Moses Whitson, Sr., was a strict member of the Society of Friends, and his occupation was that of surveyor and conveyancer. He lived and died in Chester County, his death occurring in 1853, nine years after the decease of his wife. Their children were two sons and two daughters, all of whom are living. Young Moses resided at the home of his father until the latter's death, when he was sent to school in West Chester. When fifteen years of age he entered as clerk the store of George W. Taylor, of Philadelphia, and after remaining there a short time was placed in the Millersville Normal School, near Lancaster, Pa., where he studied through three terms, and was a member of the senior class when he left to attend the Normal School near Chester. He remained at the latter school one term, and on leaving took charge of a school, at which he remained until, in the following year, he became a teacher in the grammar-school at Chester. At the close of the term he gave up this position to enter the employment of his brother Jacob, a forwarding merchant at Christiana, Lancaster Co., Pa., with whom he remained until August, 1862,

Moses Whitson

when he enlisted in the Federal service as second sergeant of Company C, One Hundred and Twenty-second Regiment Pennsylvania Volunteers, Col. Emlin Franklin. He was subsequently made sergeant, and remained with this regiment until it was mustered out of service in the following May, having meanwhile participated in the battles of Chantilly, Fredericksburg, and Chancellorsville. In June, 1863, he re-enlisted as captain of Company C, Fiftieth Regiment Pennsylvania Volunteers, Col. Franklin commanding. The term of enlistment was for one hundred days, or as long as needed, and at the end of four months' service the regiment was disbanded, without having taken part in any general action. In the fall of 1863 Mr. Whitson entered Duff's Commercial College at Pittsburgh, and having graduated in twenty-two days, was employed as a teacher in the institution. In the spring of 1864 he resigned this position and went West. In November, 1864, in company with Jeremiah B. Haines and Mark Haines, he purchased the Green Spring Furnace property in Washington County, Md., and established his residence. The firm of J. B. Haines & Co. carried on the furnace successfully until 1874, manufacturing about eighteen hundred tons of pig-metal annually. Since 1874 the furnace has been idle. It is owned by Mr. Whitson, in company with the sons of his deceased partners, who with Mr. Whitson are also the proprietors of three fine farms in the vicinity, which they operate in common.

On the 13th of October, 1869, Mr. Whitson married Mary C., daughter of Isaac H. and Cecilia Gehr, of Washington County. Of their three children two survive. Mr. Whitson has been prominently identified with the local interests of the Republican party since 1864. In 1871 he was chosen to the Legislature, and in 1874 was renominated by acclamation, but with the rest of his ticket was defeated at the polls. In 1879 he was an unsuccessful candidate for the office of clerk of the county courts. During the past six years he has been a member of the Republican State Central Committee, has frequently been a delegate to county conventions, and was the presiding officer at the last county convention.

Among the relics of the Jacques family which have been preserved is an old Bible, which, as is shown by the inscriptions, was a gift from Jonathan Jacques to his nephew, L. Jacques, in 1763.

Indian Springs was not named until the post-office was established, when the pike was opened, in 1819. There was then a hotel there, which is still standing and which is used as a store. The first settlers were probably the Hellers, who located themselves on the Jacques and Johnson lands, and George and Daniel Gehn bought some of the property. Boyd's ferry was below the present McCoy's ferry, and here Braddock was joined by the Virginia troops who came up from Winchester. Millstone Point was owned by Dr. L. Jacques, who was a surgeon in the Revolutionary army and was with the army at Valley Forge. He owned six hundred acres at Green Springs, and lived, died, and is buried there. He settled at Millstone Point after the war, and the house in which he lived before removing to Green Springs was burned down within a few years. The estate now belongs to William Moffet, Millstone Point, and is now and has been for many years a post-town, and probably received its name from boatmen and hunters. Green Springs Furnace was built by Launcelot Jacques, who came over from France as agent, and obtaining letters patent to an extensive manor, put up the furnace about 1750. In 1848 the property was bought by J. Dixon Roman & Co., and was rebuilt by J. B. Haines & Co. in 1866, by whom it was worked until 1874. It has not been in operation since. The furnace was intended to work up the native ores, brown hematite, etc., of which there is an abundance in the mountains. The Jacqueses abandoned the furnace on account of the scarcity of the ore, but the trouble was that they did not know where to look for it. The old Jacques residence was situated on the hill a few hundred yards from the furnace. It was a log and plaster clapboarded structure, one story high, with a huge stone chimney and a high hip roof. Its location is evidence of the excellent taste which characterized the French emigrants. There were other old buildings at the furnace, which were erected previous to 1750. The old furnace stood at the foot of the hill, but when Roman & Co. bought it there was no trace of it left except the crumbling ruins of the stack.

Launcelot Jacques was a Frenchman who came from England as an agent for English planters and settled at Annapolis in 1720 or 1721. He took up fifteen thousand acres of land in Indian Spring District in 1750, and had as his partner Thomas Johnson, afterwards first Governor of Maryland. In 1765, Launcelot Jacques settled at Green Spring, and Jacques & Johnson established Green Spring and Catoctin Furnaces. They dissolved partnership in 1776, Jacques remaining at Green Spring, and Johnson taking Catoctin. Launcelot Jacques died in 1791, in his seventy-fifth year. He was married, but had no children, and made Denton Jacques his heir, having brought him over from England when he was but twelve years of age. An old resident of Green Spring, Mrs. Brewer, who is now seventy-three years old, can recall some of the stories of John Forsythe, who died thirty years ago, at the ripe age of ninety-five, and who remembered the time when the inhabitants went to preaching in the old fort, where there was a Governor's house. John Forsythe was the last of the generation which had witnessed the old wars.

Years ago a block-house stood on what was the Thomas J. Jacques farm, now owned by William Loose. Denton Jacques carried on the Green Spring Furnace until 1806, when it was stopped. There was also a forge on Licking Creek, which belonged to the Jacqueses. Denton Jacques had two sons—Arthur and James Jacques—and two daughters, Catherine and Elizabeth. At the present time Green Spring Furnace is a flourishing village, and contains Pleasant Grove church, two schools (combined), of which E. G. Kinsell is teacher, and a post-office, of which M. S. Haines is postmaster.

Fort Frederick.—This last visible vestige of ante-Revolutionary times owes its existence more to the animosity existing between England and France than to any hatred between the white and red races in America. After the disastrous failure of Braddock's expedition against Fort Du Quesne, in the summer of 1755, the western districts of the three provinces, Pennsylvania, Maryland, and Virginia, were devastated by bands of savage raiders, some of which penetrated as far as Carlisle, Fredericktown, and Winchester. These incursions were accompanied with all the horrors and atrocities which have been among the familiar experiences of our frontier settlements from the time of Capt. John Smith. After that disaster they were the more persistent and formidable, as they were instigated and directed by the French, for the purpose of annihilating the English settlements in the disputed territory. The protecting military arm was for the time completely paralyzed. The land was filled with terror, and all the more advanced forts and block-houses were crowded with fugitive settlers and their families. The panic extended even to the shores of the Chesapeake, and planters who had grown old in peace and dignity abandoned their estates and sought refuge in Baltimore and Annapolis. But even here terror had preceded them, and frightened citizens were planning to escape by sea with their families and household goods into Virginia, while others believed there could be no safety short of England.

The stouter-hearted citizens of Annapolis set about fortifying the town, and in Green's *Gazette* of Nov. 6, 1755, there is a call on the neighboring country gentlemen to come in with their forces and assist in expediting the work. Every day fresh stories of murders and scalpings and burnings were retailed on the street corners, while still more disquieting rumors of the propinquity of lurking savages sent many a mother shuddering to a sleepless bed. When there happened to be a dearth of outside reports, the gobemouches and wondermongers imagined all sorts of absurd impossibilities, which served to keep up the alarm and excitement. At length some scouts who had scoured the country westward nearly to Fort Cumberland returned with the report that they had seen but one Indian in their route, and he was perfectly quiet and inoffensive. This was reassuring, especially as it afterwards leaked out the savage was stone dead. The effect of this grim joke was to throw ridicule on the panic at Annapolis, which presently subsided. Meanwhile there had been a convention of provincial Governors in the city of New York to devise measures for the present protection of their people and prospective offensive operations against the common enemy. Horatio Sharpe, Governor of Maryland, was among them, and on his return home the General Assembly of his State promptly responded to his recommendations by voting a supply of forty thousand pounds, of which eleven thousand were to be applied to the building of a fort and block-house on the western frontier and keeping them garrisoned. Relating to this event there seems to be a discrepancy of dates between the historians of Maryland. McSherry dates this act of the Legislature March 22, 1756, while McMahon treats it as an immediate consequence of the Governor's return from the council in New York, in the fall of 1755, and goes on to say, "The erection of an extensive and powerful fortification was immediately begun, and so far completed before the close of the year as to receive a garrison," etc.

The date of an address of the House of Delegates, "December, 1755," alluding to the fort as "now constructed," would seem to sustain McMahon's statement, and furnish proof of the fact (otherwise almost incredible) that this extensive and massive work was begun and completed within the space of two or three months.

On the other hand, McSherry's statement, giving the day of the month and year fully, would appear to have been taken from the official record of the House, and better comports with our modern experiences of legislative promptness, as well as our practical estimates of the amount of time necessary to collect and put solidly together so vast a mass of material.

The letter from Governor Sharpe defending his work against legislative strictures is dated Aug. 21, 1756, and circumstantially inclines to the belief that on this point McMahon's chronology may be inaccurate. The importance of establishing the exact date of its authorization and construction has been recognized by every historian of Maryland, but without any one of them being able to fix upon the exact date for either. The weight of evidence is in favor of the year 1754–55, having most probably been begun in the former and completed in the latter year.

Governor Sharpe in his letter to Mr. Calvert, dated Annapolis, the 21st of August, 1756, speaking of Fort Frederick, says,—

"I thought proper to build Fort Frederick of stone, which step I believe our Assembly will now approve of, though I hear some of them, some time since, intimated to their constituents that a stoccado would have been sufficient, and that to build a fort of stone would put the country to a great and unnecessary expense; but whatever their sentiments may be with respect to that matter, I am convinced that I have done for the best, and that my conduct therein will be approved of by any governor and by every impartial person. The Fort is not finished, but the garrison are well covered, and will, with a little assistance, complete it at their leisure. Our Barricks are made for the reception and accommodation of two hundred men, but on occasion there will be room for twice that number. It is situated on the North Mountain, near the Potomac River, about fourteen miles beyond Conococheague and four miles on this side of Licking Creek. I have made a purchase in the Governor's name, for the use of the country, of one hundred and fifty acres of land that is contiguous to the Fort, which will be of great service to the garrison, and, as well as the fort, be found of great use in case of future expeditions to the westward, for it is so situated that the Potomac will be always navigable thence almost to Fort Cumberland, the plats and shallows of that River lying between Fort Frederick and Conococheague."

All authorities agree in representing the situation in 1755 as extremely critical, and all unite in commending the zeal and promptness with which the public guardians, and especially Governor Sharpe, met the emergency. Brave Capt. Dagworthy, with a small but devoted band, still stoutly held the fort at Cumberland, but that post was too isolated and too far advanced to afford any protection to the feeble and scattered settlements behind it. The Governor, therefore, fixed upon a point near the river, about fifty miles east and in the rear of Cumberland, and fourteen miles west of Conococheague, in Washington County.

Here he purchased one hundred and fifty acres of land, and, after a plan furnished by himself and under his personal supervision, he proceeded to build his fort. So zealously was the work prosecuted that in August, 1756, six months after the authority and means had been furnished by the Assembly, it was sufficiently advanced to receive a garrison, and was named Fort Frederick, in honor of Frederick, the last Lord Baltimore.

Its garrison consisted of three hundred men, commanded by the trusty Capt. Dagworthy, of Fort Cumberland fame. Of these, one-third were kept on scouting duty to guard the settlements against stealthy attacks from small parties of the enemy, and to fire their zeal a bounty of thirty pounds was offered for every Indian scalp or prisoner brought in by the rangers. While thus engaged in securing his people against the enemy in front, the Governor himself was assailed by a fire in the rear. The tremor having subsided, certain economical legislators began to grumble at the cost and to criticise the character of the work, the gist of which complaints appears in the address of the House of Delegates, December, 1755, as follows:

"When from the incursions and horrid dèpredations of the savage enemy in the neighboring colonies an opinion prevailed that force was necessary for the defense and security of the western frontier of this colony, it was thought most likely to be conducive to these ends to have it placed somewhere near the place Fort Frederick is now constructed, because from thence the troops that might be judged proper to be kept on foot for the security of the frontier inhabitants might have it in their power to range constantly in such manner as to protect them against small parties, and in case any considerable party of the enemy should appear, or the fort should be attacked, the troops might at a very short warning be assisted by the inhabitants. Near the sum of six thousand pounds has been expended in purchasing the ground belonging to and constructing Fort Frederick, and though we have not any exact information what sum may still be wanting to complete it (if ever it should be thought proper to be done), yet we are afraid the sum requisite for that purpose must be considerable, and we are apprehensive that the fort is so large that in case of an attack it cannot be defended without a number of men larger than the province can support purely to maintain a fortification."

The fall of Fort Du Quesne, Nov. 22, 1758, virtually ended the war in this region, and removed the frontier line of the colonies beyond the Ohio River, while in 1762 the peace of Fontainebleau forever settled the contest for supremacy between the French and English races in North America.

About 1720 the hardy hunters and trappers roamed this region in search of furs and peltries, and there is a multitude of legends still extant of their deadly combats with the Delaware Indians, whose favorite hunting-grounds were along the river and on the slopes of the North Mountain. Twenty years after the pioneers had blazed the trails across these noble hills and uplands came tenants of the patentees, who held their grand manors of scores of thousands of acres in extent under the grants of the Calverts and their lieutenant-governors at Annapolis. Sometimes even a patentee, ruined in fortune and with but this single chance for financial recuperation, would locate on his lands, and clear them or set up an iron-furnace, but he was the exception to the rule of the gentlemen who preferred the luxuries of the Governor's court at Annapolis in pre-Revolutionary days. Old Launcelot Jacques, for instance, was one of the few who had the energy and courage to move out on to what were the frontiers of civilization, just about the time when Baltimore was first feeling proud of being a town. His history and that of his descendants seems to blend naturally into the narrative of the middle years of the eighteenth century, Fort Frederick, and the decline of the families once possessing these great manorial estates, until now a few pitiful acres are all remaining to their descendants, while their roomy mansions long ago passed into the hands of strangers to their blood and pride. It was in this neighborhood that the original Launcelot Jacques and Governor Thomas Johnson had fifteen thousand acres of land patented to them about 1740. Jacques was a descendant of French Protestant refugees who had settled in England after the revocation of the Edict of Nantes, and in 1720 he came to this country to purchase tobacco on English account. Besides this land in Washington County,—it was then all Frederick County,—he and the Governor owned another vast tract on the Catoctin Mountain. They established the Catoctin Furnace on one tract, and the Green Spring, or Fort Frederick Furnace on the other, and were very successful in working the hematite ores that abound hereabouts. In 1776 they dissolved partnership, and Jacques took the Green Spring Furnace and grant for his share. His great-grandnephew and nieces, who are living at Indian Spring, have records which indicate that he combined French vivacity with English pluck, and was just the sort of a man for opening up a new country. The last traces of the furnace that he built vanished years ago, but his dwelling-house still stands on the hill, and is a specimen, in most excellent preservation, of rural architecture, masonry, and carpentering of one hundred and forty years ago. Its location, on a gentle eminence, in the midst of a lovely dale, with a brook babbling through, and the mountains walling it up on the eastward, proves that the old settler had a nice taste for the beauty of nature. When the furnace was in blast, and the hillside dotted with the cabins of his numerous slaves, the scene must have been one full of life and animation.

Launcelot Jacques, great-grandnephew of the patentee of the manor, resides at Indian Spring, three miles from Fort Frederick, with his two sisters, the eldest of whom, Mrs. Brewer, is seventy-three years of age. She remembers well John Forsythe, who died about 1850, and as he was then ninety-five years old, the chronicles of affairs in and around Fort Frederick came to him at first hands. Early in this century she went to attend religious services in the fort, which was then a favorite stopping-place for Methodist itinerants bound to the West. At that time, not later than 1820, the barracks, which were substantial stone structures, were still standing, and the largest of them was known as the Governor's house. John Forsythe lived in the fort, and was the last survivor of the generation who had known it in the days of the war. He was in possession of all his faculties up to his death, and his narratives were received as entirely credible. A most thrilling one related to a woman named Sanders, who lived near McCoy's ferry on the Potomac. She had left her house to call her children, when a roving band of Indians captured her and took her up into the North Mountain, where they had an encampment at Indian Spring. A party of hunters, who had followed them up, had a sharp encounter with the savages, but they succeeded in recapturing her and returning with her to the fort, where their victory was made the occasion of an impromptu jubilee. Frequently there have been six hundred to seven hundred people within the fort when the news of an Indian foray would be spread throughout the country, and the settlers would abandon their homes and farms and rush to its walls for shelter. They came from all points along the Potomac and Conococheague Creek for a distance of twenty-five miles; and they were safe enough at the fort, for there is no record that the Indians were ever rash enough to attack its to them impregnable defenses. It was also useful as a rendezvous for sallies against the enemy. We read in the *Maryland Gazette* of 1758 that "in July our forces evacuated Fort Frederick on their march to the front, and the Governor ordered Capt. Butler's, Capt. Middaugh's, and Capt. Luckett's companies of militia to garrison it and to parade on the frontiers for the protection of the inhabitants." And again, in October, 1764, that "Capt. William McClellan marched from Fort Frederick with his company of volunteers, consisting of forty-three brave woodsmen, besides officers, all of them well equipped with good rifles, and most of them born and bred on the frontiers of Frederick County. They serve without pay, and intend to go against our enemy in the Indian towns." These were not the only Indian-fighters of the day, for tradition preserves the name of Michael Mills, who had a cave on Licking Creek, near the fort, where he would take several days' provisions and ambush himself, picking off any Indians who came within his sight. He is remembered as a famous marksman, whose aim was sure death.

The old records, Feb. 3, 1759, show that "Lieut. James Riley, of the Maryland forces, who often distinguished himself by his bravery in defense of his country, died in Fort Frederick of smallpox, much lamented by all who knew him;" and that Capt. Evan Shelby's house in Frederick County, near Fort Frederick, together with his furniture and a large store of provisions, was accidentally destroyed by fire early in December, 1763. Denton Jacques offered for sale, Dec. 14, 1792, ten thousand acres of land and furnace called Fort Frederick; the land extended along the Potomac for nine miles; this is now known as Green Spring.

The old fort occupied an acre and a half of ground, and its massive walls of hard magnesian limestone are four feet thick at the bottom, and two feet at the top. The stone, which is mostly in large, irregular blocks, was brought from the mountain three miles distant, and is laid in such an excellent mortar that nothing but an earthquake or the hand of man will ever shatter the walls. These are seventeen and a half feet in height at the highest point, and are very fairly preserved. The greatest damage that has been done was the cutting of a wagon-gate through the west curtain sixty years ago, and now Nathan Williams, its present

OLD FORT FREDERICK.

owner, has pulled down the west bastion to make room for his barn. The fort is square, with a bastion at each angle. The south bastion is the best preserved, but the whole structure is very far from being a ruin. The huge gates, one having a small postern, were in the east wall. The portal was twelve feet wide, and the immensity of the gates may be judged by the fact that one of the iron hinges, which Williams kept until a few years ago, weighed forty-two pounds. There is not a piece of the old wood-work left, some curiosity-seekers having carried off the last bit in 1858. Gen. Kenly's First Maryland Regiment occupied the fort in 1861, and knocked a hole in the wall through which to point a gun for taking pot shots at the Confederates across the Potomac. The original armament of the fort was a gun in each bastion, worked *en barbette*, and within the inclosure, where Nathan Williams' potatoes and tomatoes now ripen under the summer sun, were barracks.

Before the fort was abandoned and became a military nullity the following affectionate and diplomatic letter was written by a Cherokee chief to Governor Sharpe:

"Fort Frederick, April 29, 1757.

"To the Governor of Maryland:

"*Brother of Maryland*,—This day I came into your Province, with a company of our nation, on our way to war against the French, Shawanees, and all their Indians, hearing they had killed some of our brothers, not knowing when we set off from Winchester but the murder was committed in Virginia; but coming to this Fort, found we were in another Province; and on being informed by Capt. Beall that our brother, the Governor of this Province, had a real love for our nation, and that he had provided clothes for our nation, though unacquainted with us, I have just now held a council with my young warriors, and have concluded to write you, to acquaint you, our brother, our design of coming into this country was, hearing from our good brother, the Governor of Virginia, that it was the desire of our father, King George, that we should join the English in War against the French and the Indians. On hearing this news we immediately took up our hatchet against the French and their Indians, and hold it fast till we make use of it, which I expect will be in a few days. We intend to set out immediately from this Fort, and immediately on our return expect to meet you, our brother, here, to make ourselves acquainted with you. If you cannot come yourself, you will send one of your beloved men with your talk, which we will look upon as from your own mouth. I hope you will let the Province of Pennsylvania know that I am come this length to war, and if they are in need of our assistance. I have men plenty at home, and will not think it troublesome to come and fight for our brothers. I set off from home with one hundred and fifty men, part of which are gone to Fort Cumberland; forty more by this are come to Winchester. Our people will be so frequent among you that I wish you may not think us troublesome. Our hearts ache to see our brothers' bones scattered about the country, but you will hear in a short time we have got satisfaction for our brothers, and in confirmation of what I have spoke I have sent you these few white beads to confirm my regard to this Province. Likewise I have sent you these black beads, to convince you that I have taken up the hatchet against all the English enemies. We intend to stay as long amongst our brothers as there is use for us. I hope our good brother will not be backward in providing necessaries for us. I have sent you a list of what is useful for us, and I have got our good friend, Mr. Ross, to carry this letter to you, whom we shall always acknowledge as a particular friend to us. As we expect to see you soon, we will add no more at present, but remain your loving brother,

His
"WAHACHY ╳ OF KEEWAY."
mark

John Ridout, the Governor's secretary, and Daniel Wolstenholme were sent as commissioners with a wagon-load of presents and two hundred pounds in goods, and received the scalps of four hostile Indians in return.

Fort Frederick was a source of constant dispute between the House of Delegates and Governor Sharpe; the bill for reducing the number of men in the pay of the province and restraining those employed to the frontier around Fort Frederick was "for these and about a hundred other reasons returned to them with a negative." The House of Delegates, Dec. 15, 1757, returned the Governor's assault upon their privilege, and retorted as well upon the cost as upon the manner of construction. For this contumacy Loudon quartered five companies of Royal Americans upon the citizens of Annapolis. The change made by Mr. Pitt by the recall of Lord Loudon and superseding Abercrombie by the appointment of Gen. Forbes drew from Governor Sharpe to Sir John St. Clair a sarcastic letter, in which it is said, "It is well Capt. Dagworthy and the rest of our officers taught their men to live without victuals last summer, otherwise they might not have found it so easy a matter to keep them together six months without pay in the winter."

The treaty of Paris, Feb. 10, 1763, gave to Great Britain all the territory east of the Mississippi, from the Gulf of Mexico to Hudson's Bay, and brought peace to the American colonies with the Indians on their western frontier. The Ohio River soon became the western boundary between the white and red races, and with the departure of the Indians Fort Frederick ceased to have any military significance.

In 1777 the British prisoners of war were confined in Fort Frederick, and during Tarleton's raids in Virginia the prisoners of war at Winchester were, by order of Gen. Lafayette, removed to Fort Frederick and placed in charge of Maj. Rawlings, deputy commissary-general of prisoners.

In 1790 the Legislature directed the sale of the land and fort. After passing through various owners, the property now belongs to Nathan Williams, a well-to-do colored citizen, who, born in slavery, emancipated himself long before the abolition of slavery. He bought the fort property in 1857, and has made a thriving farm of it. The fine features of his bronze face, set in a circle of white hair, give him an honorable appearance, which closer acquaintance proves to be the truthful index of his character. There is no better point from which to approach Fort Frederick than the lane which conducts you to Mr. Williams' residence. The fort stands on a spur of the North Mountain, a hundred feet above the level of the Potomac, and a third of a mile away from its banks. The "Big Pond" of the Chesapeake and Ohio Canal —a sheet of placid water whose setting should earn for it a better descriptive name—is almost at your feet. Just beyond, the pools and rapids of the Potomac stretch away to the Virginia shore; and to the west and south, the mountains towering peak on peak fill up a panorama so irresistibly attractive as to compel one to forget that he is in search of a relic of the past. But here in the foreground of this wonderful picture of mountain, valley, and stream it sits, its high gray walls sharply outlined against the vivid green of a pine forest.

BEAVER CREEK DISTRICT, No. 16.

Beaver Creek, or Election District No. 16, is about the central one of the six districts in Washington County which extend along its eastern border from the Potomac River on the south to Mason and Dixon's line at the western base of the South Mountain. It takes its name from Beaver Creek, which flows through it, and which was so called because it was formerly a great resort for beavers. Boonsboro' District bounds Beaver Creek District on the south, Funkstown District is on the west, Chewsville District on the north, and the Frederick County line on the east. Within the district are the villages of Beaver Creek, the most important, Beaver Creek Post-office, and Smoketown. The scenery in Beaver Creek District is very fine and diversified, the land, rich and fruitful, commands a very high figure, and is thickly settled. The population of the district is 1199. Among the residents of the district are the following: M. Maysilles, S. Maysilles, Mrs. Snyder, J. R. Martin, J. Avey, J. D. Wisherd, J. Turnbaugh, J. Grossnickle, Mrs. Stouffer, J. Bowman, P. Gayler, I. Hildebrand, C. Rowland, Mrs. J. Kahler, N. Fahrney, C. B. Kaylor, J. Thomas, George Adams, J. M. Middlekauff, H. Adams, P. Gray, M. Newcomer, P. R. Doub, D. Troup, S. Funk, J. Stotelmyer, J. Adams, H. Eakle, J. Funk, J. Doub, G. Newcomer, E. Roland, J. I. Bitner, Mrs. J. Newcomer, A. Harrison, Dr. Fahrney, Mrs. Adams, J. H. Newcomer, D. R. Doub, J. L. Harp, H. Landis, J. Shiffler, C. McCauley, A. Sager, Rev. S. Matthews, B. Witmer, Mrs. Witmer, Dr. E. L. Mackey, Wm. Newcomer, H. Fultz, Dr. Smith, D. Harbaugh, J. Ross, Mrs. Horine, George Hartle, George Hartle, Jr., S. Rice, L. Shoup, T. Hartle, A. Funk, J. F. Miller, J. Bowman, Mrs. A. Fahrney, A. Funk, J. Hahn, E. Bowman, J. Shoup, J. Bishop, H. Welty, E. T. Reese, H. Funk, W. Moore, L. Taylor, L. Reese, B. F. Stouffer, I. Shealy, J. T. Kinsey, Wm. Kinsey, Wm. Irvin, Jr., S. Faulder, John Reese, George Folker, Mrs. Dirben, J. Bargett, D. Bowman, D. Kline, G. W. Kline, Wm. Gallian, Mrs. Kinsey, D. B. Cramer, J. A. Winders, Rev. A. Cost, E. Keplinger, C. Stotelmyer, E. Stouffer, J. Stotelmyer, S. Wagner, J. Bowers, B. Doyle, J. Hoffman, M. James, P. R. Doub, S. Krotzer, J. Marsh, K. Newcomer, C. Gates, D. Witmer, E. Marts, S. Ramsey, M. Snively, P. Phœnix, Mrs. E. Davis, J. Funk, G. Funk, L. Dutrow, D. Troup, R. A. Hanna, J. Lechty, H. Williams, H. Walker, H. Huntsberry, J. Long, W. Troxel, J. Swisher, I. Clevidence, Dr. Smith, C. Fowler, and others. Among the business enterprises are the Woodside Mills, of P. R. Doub, at Beaver Creek. There are several churches in the district. Among them the Tunker church, near Beaver Creek, the Lutheran and Christian churches, at Beaver Creek, the Fahrney meeting-house, south of Smoketown, and the Union church, at Smoketown.

The congregation of the Disciples of Christ, or Christian Church, at Beaver Creek, was organized in 1833, and continued to meet for several years once a week for social intercourse and for the observance of church rites. They met in the old school-house, being served occasionally by visiting pastors until 1845, when they began to meet in the present edifice. In 1848 the first regular pastor was employed, and from that year until 1852 the pastors were Robert Ferguson, of Virginia; John R. Frame, of Ohio; George Caldwell, of Pennsylvania. The next regular pastor was E. Adamson, whose services continued from May, 1858, to 1864. From 1864 to 1869, Jesse H. Berry was employed. In 1870, Thomas Hillock served about six months. John Mitchell, of Pennsylvania, preached from 1871 to 1874, and Samuel Matthews from 1874 until 1877. The charge was then vacant until 1878, when the present pastor, Samuel F. Fowler, of St. John's, New Brunswick, was employed. There are no religious societies except a Sunday-school connected with the church.

The churchyard of the Disciples Church contains the graves of the following old citizens:

Yost Cox, died June 27, 1874, aged 72 years, 6 months.

Daniel Root, died Nov. 15, 1872, aged 67 years, 11 months; and his wife, Susannah, died Feb. 20, 1879, aged 76 years.

Marzilla Hemsworth, born Oct. 6, 1781, died March 7, 1872.

Jacob Doyle, died Jan. 25, 1862, aged 69 years, 2 months.

David Witmer, died April 29, 1862, aged 57 years, 2 months.

Jacob B. Rohrer, died Nov. 2, 1860, aged 58 years; and his wife, Elizabeth, died Dec. 6, 1860, aged 62 years.

Elder Samuel Matthews, born June 8, 1818, died April 10, 1877.

Jacob Snavely, born July 20, 1792, died March 28, 1846.

Christian Brown, died Sept. 22, 1869, aged 70 years, 2 months.

Elizabeth, wife of John Bowers, died Jan. 7, 1863, aged 68 years.

The corner-stone of the Lutheran church in Beaver Creek, a brick structure, was laid April 12, 1845, and the edifice was finished the same year. In the graveyard of this church are interred the following old residents:

Barbara Arhlborn, born Dec. 7, 1804, died April 29, 1857.

Robert G. Albert, died Sept. 22, 1871, aged 43 years.

Joseph Gray, died Sept. 20, 1876, aged 80 years.

Margaret, wife of George Hill, died March 14, 1875, aged 72.

Charles W. Bowser, died March 22, 1876, aged 30 years.

Margaret, wife of Samuel Faulder, died Nov. 27, aged 63 years.

Daniel Welty, died Feb. 2, 1856, aged 42 years.

Daniel Gearhart, died June 28, 1867, aged 74 years.

Jacob Coy, died March 12, 1855, aged 75 years.

Mary Lichty, died Nov. 20, 1864, aged 72 years.

Henry Ruch, died June 30, 1857, aged 52 years.

Catherine, wife of George Hartman, died June 19, 1851, aged 74 years.

John Brinkham, died March 17, 1855, aged 80 years.

Mary Brinkham, died April 21, 1869, aged 83 years.

John Loudenslager, died April 5, 1852, aged 62 years.

Jacob Harbaugh, died July 15, 1877, aged 56 years.

George Hartle, born Dec. 10, 1826, died May 16, 1878.

Peter Corbett, died Aug. 29, 1876, aged 65 years.

Martin Ridenour, died Feb. 28, 1873, aged 64 years.

Jacob Funk, born Jan. 19, 1793, died Oct. 14, 1856.

Susanna, his wife, born Oct. 18, 1809, died May 1, 1869.

Conrad Horine, born July 16, 1784, died Sept. 16, 1857.

John Doub, died Sept. 15, 1880, aged 65 years.

Jonathan Doub, died Aug. 24, 1863, aged 51 years.

Catherine, his wife, died Aug. 30, 1863, aged 45 years.

The Tunker church is situated on the turnpike, near Beaver Creek. On the tombstones in this churchyard are the epitaphs of the following persons:

Mary A., wife of Henry Newcomer, died April 1, 1876, aged 64 years, 7 months.

Jane, wife of George Winders, died Feb. 20, 1876, aged 74 years, 11 months.

Benjamin Witmer, born Sept. 15, 1808, died March 19, 1879.

Joseph P. Mong, died June 27, 1872, aged 63 years, 10 months.

Catharine, wife of John Petre, born July 6, 1784, died Dec. 11, 1846.

Susan Rohrer, born April 10, 1784, died Feb. 20, 1852.

Mary Rohrer, born July 17, 1807, died July 20, 1878.

John Wolf, died March 13, 1849, aged 58 years, 6 months.

John Gray, died May 17, 1853, aged 59 years, 2 months; and his wife, Mary, died May 5, 1875, aged 75 years, 4 months.

Jacob Kailer, died March 21, 1873, aged 80 years, 11 months.

Nancy, wife of Samuel Clevidence, born March 22, 1800, died May 19, 1859.

John Bovey, born Oct. 24, 1774, died Nov. 16, 1838; and his wife, Susan, died Dec. 12, 1836, aged 54 years.

Jacob S. Snyder, died Aug. 30, 1864, aged 70 years, 10 months; and his wife, Elizabeth, born Aug. 17, 1794, died Aug. 4, 1858.

Henry Fultz, died Dec. 2, 1862, aged 69 years, 10 months; and his wife, Nancy, died Jan. 26, 1868, aged 71 years, 6 months.

Jacob Maysilles, born Aug. 23, 1801, died Jan. 18, 1878; and his wife, Nancy, died March 28, 1865, aged 53 years, 7 months.

John Newcomer, born Dec. 18, 1797, died April 21, 1861.

Jacob Middlekauff, died Feb. 21, 1859, aged 69 years, 9 months; and his wife, Elizabeth, born Dec. 6, 1795, died Sept. 21, 1845.

Rev. John Funk, died April 16, 1851, aged 60 years, 10 months; and his wife, Susan, died April 7, 1860, aged 66 years, 10 months.

Jacob, son of John and Elizabeth Newcomer, a member of Co. H, 6th Maryland Regiment, U.S.V., wounded at the battle of the Wilderness, and died May 27, 1864, aged 20 years, 3 months.

John Funk, died Oct. 24, 1877, aged 88 years; and his wife, Catherine, died Jan. 28, 1867, aged 67.

Isaac Bowman, died Aug. 30, 1853, aged 86 years, 3 months; and his wife, Mary, died Nov. 4, 1867, aged 88 years, 3 months.

Christian Stouffer, born Feb. 27, 1767, died June 20, 1827.

John Whitmer, died Aug. 11, 1858, aged 84 years, 3 months; and his wife, Barbara, died May 1, 1837, aged 63 years.

Henry Newcomer, died March 15, 1828, aged 56 years; and his wife, Elizabeth, born April 1, 1776, died March 17, 1854.

Mary, wife of Abner Williams, born July 17, 1801, died Jan. 28, 1880.

Joseph M. Wolf, born June 9, 1816, died May 3, 1873; Catherine, his wife, died Dec. 5, 1876, aged 61 years, 2 months.

Theresa, wife of Andrew Cost, died March 20, 1876, aged 50 years.

Jacob Adams, died Oct. 16, 1837, in the 69th year of his age.

Brittana Thorp, died May 26, 1852, aged 61 years, 6 months.

John Snyder, died Sept. 12, 1877, aged 68 years, 1 month.

Jacob Winders, died July 25, 1863, aged 59 years, 8 months; Sarah, his wife, died July 3, 1879, aged 50 years, 11 months.

John Winders, died Feb. 22, 1828, in his 49th year; he married Sarah Adams, who died April 28, 1830, in her 51st year; they had nine children,—five sons and four daughters.

Samuel Newcomer, died May 1, 1811, in his 42d year.

Mary Winders, born Sept. 15, 1744, died Dec. 12, 1794.

Barbara, wife of Henry Newcomer, born Dec. 25, 1746, died Feb. 1, 1818.

Nancy, wife of Christian Stouffer, born July 21, 1778, died Oct. 5, 1828.

Mary Warner, born Nov. 18, 1749, died Nov. 14, 1817.

Jacob Warner, born March 17, 1748, died March 2, 1838.

Henry Landis, Sr., died Oct. 11, 1853, aged 70 years, 6 months.

Joel Newcomer, died March 6, 1852, aged 78 years, 10 months; Elizabeth, his wife, died Jan. 26, 1867, aged 81 years, 9 months.

Henry Newcomer, died May 7, 1876, aged 65 years, 4 months.

Sarah Newcomer, died May 13, 1871, aged 57 years, 4 months.

Jacob L. Funk, died Sept. 7, 1863, aged 43 years, 4 months; Caroline, his wife, died Aug. 11, 1863, aged 36 years, 4 months.

Michael Newcomer, died April 10, 1879, aged 66 years, 8 months.

John Keller, died Feb. 4, 1854, aged 53 years, 2 months; Elizabeth, his wife, died Dec. 16, 1879, aged 71 years.

Christian F. Newcomer, died May 4, 1880, aged 78 years, 7 months; Sarah, his wife, died Dec. 29, 1875.

Andrew Newcomer, died Aug. 14, 1847, aged 70 years; Elizabeth, his wife, died Feb. 10, 1854, aged 75 years, 7 months.

John G. Miller, died March 19, 1877, aged 77 years, 9 months; Catherine, his wife, died Oct. 31, 1873, aged 64 years, 9 months.

Daniel Newcomer, born June 15, 1779, died June 16, 1829; Elizabeth, his wife, born July 5, 1783, died Nov. 8, 1818.

Mary Foley, born Oct. 7, 1762, died Oct. 7, 1849.

The following persons are interred in the graveyard of Fahrney's church, a building used by various denominations, and situated in Beaver Creek District, near Smoketown:

Robert C. Cross, died May 22, 1858, aged 57.

David Stouffer, died July 17, 1855, aged 86 years; and his wife, Julia, died Dec. 27, 1872, aged 96.

John Loughridge, son of George and Martha, born in Cumberland County, Pa., Nov. 5, 1775, died Aug. 3, 1827, aged 51.

John Phelony, born July 16, 1793, died Dec. 3, 1864, aged 71.

William McAllister, died March 31, 1873, in his 71st year; and Catharine, his wife, died Oct. 28, 1868, aged 64.

Nancy, wife of Jacob Betts, died Oct. 18, 1866, aged 75.

Daniel Wolf, born Nov. 15, 1780, died Nov. 26, 1864, aged 84; and Magdalena, his wife, born Nov. 23, 1779, died May 13, 1860, aged 80.

Elizabeth, wife of John Rice, died March 24, 1866, aged 65 years, 5 months, 11 days.

John Bomberger, died Oct. 22, 1862, aged 71; Catharine, his wife, died March 20, 1862, aged 65.

John Bomberger, born Dec. 11, 1763, died Jan. 24, 1848, aged 84 years, 1 month, and 13 days; and Anna, his wife, died June 28, 1842, aged 72 years, 10 months, and 15 days.

Abraham Fasnacht, died Dec. 29, 1842, in his 53d year; and Catharine Fasnacht, died March 20, 1843, in her 58th year.

Jacob Eavy, died Oct. 1, 1828, aged 45 years, 9 months, and 27 days; and his wife, Susan, died Jan. 27, 1852, aged 61 years and 1 month.

John Fasnacht, died June 11, 1853, in his 64th year; and his wife, Rosanna, died May 13, 1865, aged 74.

George W. Betts, died Jan. 14, 1880, aged 55 years.

Catharine, wife of David Buhler, died Sept. 11, 1863, aged 53.

John Emmert, died Aug. 18, 1858, aged 54 years, 7 months, and 8 days; and Elizabeth, his wife, died Nov. 9, 1879, aged 70 years, 8 months, and 11 days.

Barbara Emmert, died Aug. 22, 1860, aged 51 years, 7 months, 9 days.

Dr. Daniel Fahrney, died Feb. 25, 1867, aged 47 years, 6 months, and 4 days.

John Bowman, died Sept. 16, 1878, aged 87 years, 3 months, and 18 days; and Mary, his wife, died Jan. 12, 1867, aged 74 years, 1 month, and 3 days.

Samuel Fahrney, died Aug. 2, 1863, aged 40 years, 10 months, and 24 days.

Samuel McKey, died May 3, 1853, in his 66th year.

Nancy Faulders, born Oct. 30, 1803, died Jan. 20, 1869, aged 65 years, 2 months, and 20 days.

George Young, born May 24, 1784, died Nov. 10, 1848, aged 64 years, 5 months, and 16 days.

Henry Bowman, born Nov. 14, 1785, died Jan. 24, 1853, aged 67 years, 2 months, and 10 days; Christianna, his wife, died Aug. 15, 1861, aged about 80.

Henry Maysilles, died March 16, 1854, aged 57 years, 6 months, and 3 days; and Amelia, his wife, born Dec. 24, 1800, died Dec. 14, 1842, aged 41 years, 11 months, and 10 days.

Henry Bowman, died July 5, 1836, in his 83d year.

Jacob Bowman, born Nov. 10, 1781, died Aug. 12, 1837, aged 55 years, 9 months, and 2 days.

Elizabeth Bowman, born Jan. 8, 1790, died April 11, 1844, aged 54 years, 3 months, and 3 days.

Jacob Bowman, died May 26, 1866, aged about 55.

Peter Hoover, died April 1, 1815, aged 46; Sarah, his wife, died Aug. 28, 1844, aged 66 years, 5 months, and 5 days.

John Miller, died March 28, 1862, aged 75 years, 9 months, and 17 days; and Mary, his wife, died May 31, 1866, aged 77 years, 8 months, and 24 days.

Sarah, wife of George Ambrose, died Dec. 21, 1866, aged 51 years, 7 months, and 18 days.

Leonard Emmert, died Aug. 12, 1876, aged 59 years, 9 months, and 4 days.

Elizabeth Emmert, died March 19, 1850, aged 70 years, 10 months, and 29 days.

Dr. Andrew Emmert, died Oct. 29, 1865, aged 37 years, 10 months, and 18 days.

Bishop Newcomer died at Hagerstown on Friday, March 21, 1830, in his eighty-second year. Rev. Christian Newcomer was for fifty years bishop of the German Methodist society. Nine days before his death he left home for ecclesiastical duty, when his horse took fright and threw him, and broke several of his ribs. The accident resulted in his death. On Sunday, March 23d, his remains were taken to the family burial-ground, near Beaver Creek, attended by a large concourse of people. A full sketch of Bishop Newcomer will be found in the chapter on "Representative Families of Washington County."

EAST HAGERSTOWN DISTRICT, No. 17.

East Hagerstown, or Election District No. 17, includes part of Hagerstown and a considerable section of farming country. The population of the district (including part of town of Hagerstown, which has 3439 inhabitants) is 4591. East Hagerstown District is bounded on the north by Pennsylvania,—a section of it also being bounded on the north by Leitersburg,—on the east by Leitersburg and Chewsville Districts, on the south by Chewsville and Funkstown Districts, and on the west by West Hagerstown and Conococheague. The only town in the district outside of Hagerstown is Fiddlersburg, situated on both sides of the public road, about two miles northeast of Hagerstown. There is also a small hamlet on the west side of Antietam Creek, opposite Antietam Paper-Mill. Antietam Creek flows along the southern boundary of the district, and Marsh Run crosses the eastern portion of the district, running from north to south. The fine country residence of Hon. Wm. T. Hamilton is situated in this district, just outside of Hagerstown and west of the turnpike which extends through the district in a northeasterly direction from Hagerstown. The history of this district is incorporated in the chapter on Hagerstown.[1]

[1] **Early Marriage Notes.**—1791. December 27.—By Rev. George Bower, Dr. Lancelot Jacques, magistrate, "to the amiable Miss Sally Rose," of Washington County.

1792. January 6.—By Rev. Mr. Cahill, Luke Tiernan, merchant, to Miss Nancy Owen, daughter of Mrs. Owen, of Hagerstown.

1793. June 9.—William Clarke, attorney-at-law of Hagerstown, "to the beautiful and accomplished Miss Harvey, of Sharpsburg."

June 11.—John Wolgamott, of Washington County, "to the very agreeable Miss Betsy Rench, daughter of the late Andrew Rench, Esq."

In the same month, Jacob Shryock, eldest son of Col. Henry Shryock, of Hagerstown, married in Virginia "that celebrated and engaging beauty Miss Amelia Heiskel, eldest daughter of Frederick Heiskel, now of Virginia, merchant."

June 23.—By Rev. Mr. Rahauser, Jos. Reynolds, son of Capt. Reynolds, of Washington County, "to the amiable and sprightly Miss Betsy Heyser, daughter of the late Capt. Heyser," of Hagerstown.

November 10.—By Rev. George Bower, Benjamin Clagett, son of Alexander, "to the amiable and truly accomplished" Miss Jeannette Lee, daughter of William Lee, merchant, of Hagerstown.

1794. January 14.—By Rev. Mr. Rahauser, Jacob Heyser, of Hagerstown, "to the amiable and agreeable Miss Kitty Otto," of Washington County.

1794. February 9.—Jacob Orendorff, of Washington County, "to the amiable and agreeable Miss Sukey Miller, daughter of Jacob Miller, of Franklin County, Pa."

March 30.—By Rev. George Bower, Samuel Price, attorney-at-law, "to the amiable, beautiful, and highly accomplished Miss Sukey Hart, daughter of Col. Thomas Hart," of Hagerstown.

April 27.—Thomas Johns "to Elizabeth Shryock, daughter of Leonard Shryock."

In December, in Greensborough, Pa., Capt. Shindle, of the New Jersey Line, "to the amiable and beautiful Miss Betsy Rohrer, daughter of Frederick Rohrer, late of Hagerstown."

December 22.—Stephen McCloskey "to that amiable and uncommonly active widow lady, Mrs. Catharine Belch."

1796. June 14.—By Rev. George Bower, James Kendal, merchant, "to Mercy Stull, daughter of the late Col. J. Stull, both of Hagerstown."

August 21.—By Rev. George Bower, Alexander Kennedy, merchant, to Margaret Stephen, daughter of Robert Stephen, of Berkeley County, Va.

CHEWSVILLE DISTRICT, No. 18.

Chewsville, or Election District No. 18, Washington County, was established in 1872. It is situated in the northeastern part of the county, and is bounded on the north by Leitersburg District, on the south by Beaver Creek, on the southwest by Funkstown, west and northwest by East Hagerstown, and on the east by Cavetown District, excepting a small tapering strip which runs out to the Frederick County line, between Cavetown and Beaver Creek Districts. The district is crossed in the centre, east and west, by the Western Maryland Railroad and the Hagerstown and Smithsburg turnpike. It is a fine agricultural country, and is more sparsely settled than any of those surrounding it. It is prominent as having been the original residence of Col. Wm. Fitzhugh, who had a large and valuable estate near the present village of Chewsville, known as "The Hive," now owned and occupied by F. A. Baker. The population of the district (including the village of Chewsville, which has 110 inhabitants) is 973. Among the present residents of the district are M. Stockslager, D. F. Harper, M. Funk, C. Bryant, W. Myers, David Rhinehart, Daniel Rhinehart, S. Miller, G. Bowers, G. Myers, J. Balsman, C. Rowland, J. Wolf, J. Funk, W. Wolfinger, H. Poffenberger, J. McGruder, J. Faltz, E. Smith, H. B. Rhinehart, H. Bovey, J. Dibert, S. McCauley, J. H. Huffer, D. Swope, J. Hoffman, S. Funk, J. Stotler, W. W. Hoffman, H. Huyett, W. Huyett, Mrs. Wolf, Wm. H. Rohrer, G. Bowers, M. Thomas, J. Swope, J. Stover, J. H. Harp, D. D. Spesard, N. Beard, N. Sener, I. Brown, S. Haus, Mrs. E. George, J. Oster, D. G. Huyett, Wm. J. Huyett, J. Rohrer, A. Cohler, D. Null, Mrs. Kinney, L. Thomas, F. Thomas, G. Powles, B. Bell, S. Thomas, I. Green, H. Burns, J. Waltz, B. H. Flory, J. Burns, A. Bachtel, F. Unger, J. Doub, Wm. Stotler, John

---

1797. May 9.—By Rev. Mr. Phalan, Richard Brooke, to Lydia Ragan, daughter of John Ragan, of Hagerstown.

1798. April 22.—By Rev. George Smucker, John Hefleich, son of Peter, merchant, to Magdalen Alder, both of Hagerstown.

1799. February 7.—At Chambersburg, Pa., by Rev. Mr. Stock, Dr. Runkel, son of Rev. Dr. Runkel, of Fredericktown, to Hannah Little, of Hagerstown.

September 26.—By Rev. Mr. Bower, John Ragan, inn-keeper, to Barbara Orndorff, both of Hagerstown.

1800. February 13.—By Rev. George Bower, David Hammett, of Hagerstown, to Ann Funk, daughter of Maj. David Funk, of Washington County.

April 13.—By Rev. Dennis Craighill, P. Edwards, schoolmaster in Hagerstown, to Theresa Smith, daughter of Henry Smith, of Washington County.

May 1.—By Rev. George Bower, Alexander Simpson to Nancy Sly, both of Hagerstown.

June 7.—By Rev. Mr. Rahauser, Christian Orndorf, of Shepherdstown, Va., to Mrs. Mary Wireman, daughter of Jacob Rohrer, near Hagerstown.

October 9.—By Rev. Mr. Bower, O. H. Williams, clerk of the Washington County Court, to Elisa Bowie Hall, of Washington County.

December 11.—By Rev. Mr. Bower, Alexander Neill, merchant, to Sally Owen, of Hagerstown.

1801. April 15.—By Rev. Jonathan Rahauser, Henry Barnet, son of Jacob Barnet, to Catherine M'Laughlin, daughter of Capt. John M'Laughlin, both of Washington County.

1801. May 7.—By Rev. George Bower, Robert Friend to Nancy Porter, daughter of Samuel Porter, inn-keeper in Williamsport.

1802. February 14.—At Geneva, N. Y., William Dana to Ann Fitzhugh, eldest daughter of Capt. Peregrine Fitzhugh, previously of Washington County.

May 26.—By Rev. George Bower, Henry W. Lewis to Mrs. Mary Hager, of Hagerstown.

1803. January 25.—By Rev. Mr. Rahauser, Maj. Martin Kershner to Mrs. Magdalena Ankeny.

January 26.—By Rev. George Bower, Dr. Frederick Dorsey to Sally Clagett, daughter of John Clagett.

November 23.—By Rev. Mr. Rahauser, James Redgrave to Elizabeth Dalrymple, both of Hagerstown.

November 23.—By Rev. Mr. Rahauser, Thomas Begole to Ann Bowles, both of Washington County.

1804. January 5.—By Rev. George Bower, A. Waugh to Catherine Hager, only daughter of Jonathan Hager.

May 8.—By Rev. George Bower, Dr. Grafton Duvall to Elizabeth Hawkins, daughter of Thomas Hawkins, of Frederick County.

1811. June 25.—By Rev. Mr. Schaeffer, William Brown, editor of the Hagerstown *Gazette*, to Sally Protzman.

1814.—William Hammond to the daughter of Dr. Frisby Tilghman.

1819. December 21.—At Cumberland, by Rev. J. C. Clay, George Tilghman to Ann Eliza Lamar, daughter of Col. William Lamar.

1824. April 15.—By Rev. Mr. Henshaw, Vachel W. Randall, of Hagerstown, to Jane Claggett, of Baltimore.

September 28.—By Rev. Mr. Lemmon, William Schley, of Frederick, to Ann Cadwalader, third daughter of Gen. Samuel Ringgold.

1825. June 7.—By Rev. M. Kellar, Thomas G. Clagett, of Baltimore, to Elizabeth B., daughter of Col. O. H. Williams, of Hagerstown.

At Richmond, Va., in April, 1879, the fiftieth anniversary of the wedding of Dr. and Mrs. Charles Macgill was celebrated in the presence of their children and grandchildren, there being eighteen of the latter and about one hundred invited guests. The invitation to their wedding read: "Mr. and Mrs. Richard Ragan respectfully request your attendance at their residence, April 16, 1829, at 8 o'clock P.M., to witness the marriage ceremony of their daughter, Mary Ragan, to Dr. Charles Macgill, of Hagerstown, Md."

Among other relics displayed at the golden wedding celebration was Mrs. Macgill's wedding dress. The presents were numerous, consisting of nine hundred and fifty dollars in gold coin, besides a profusion of gold jewelry and flowers.

The husband, who had reached the age of seventy-three, would have readily passed for a man of sixty, and the wife, seventy years of age, was equally fresh-looking. Dr. and Mrs. Macgill's children are Mrs. Ellen Swan, Dr. Charles St. G. Macgill, William D. Macgill, Mrs. S. D. Drewry, Davidge Macgill, Miss Mollie Macgill, James Macgill, Mrs. C. C. Bridges, and Francis Macgill.

Neff, J. Warvle, J. H. Stouffer, D. Stouffer, Mrs. Haus, S. K. Oswald, F. A. Baker, J. Lunnenecker, Wm. Cooper, J. Barkdoll, Mrs. B. Bachtel, D. M. Good, Geo. Bowers, S. Coss, P. Beck, D. Hoover, Jr., and others.

Among the early settlers of this district, which derived its title from the town of Chewsville, was George Beard, who died on the 28th of February, 1873. He was the only son of Andrew Beard, and was a descendant of one of the earliest families that settled in the valley of Maryland. Before the red man was fairly ousted from his hunting-grounds in Hagerstown Valley, Nicholas Beard, the father of Andrew, emigrated hither. He was a native of Germany, and first settled in Pennsylvania, but afterwards removed to this locality, the then backwoods of America. This place, by common consent, received the name of "Beard's Church" and "Beard's Church Settlement," from the fact that at an early day the settlers made provision for some sort of a house of worship, and pitched upon this locality as a site for their church.

George Beard was born and lived and died at or near the old homestead of the Beard family. He was the last and only survivor of the name in whose possession remained any portion of the patrimony obtained by inheritance.

The first church building, known as "Beard's," was merely a block-house, which has long been demolished. A house was subsequently built of the logs of the old church on a high bluff along the Antietam. It was in this old church that Zuliphen and Schrader and others held forth immediately succeeding the war of the Revolution. Some of them, it is said, practiced exorcism.

The old building was replaced by a new block-house, built in 1787, which served as the Beard's Church for successive generations. The interior of the old church was remodeled; the stem-glass pulpit, the old organ and gallery,—indeed, the entire interior,—were removed, and the structure rearranged after the newer style of churches. This state of things, however, did not long endure; the material of which the house was built was going to decay. The congregation some years ago resolved to take down this house too, and replace it with a more substantial brick building. The material of the old house was sold, and from it was built a church standing not very far from the forks of the roads leading to Hagerstown and Funkstown, and not a great distance from the site of the old building above mentioned.

Nicholas Beard, the grandfather of George, took up and patented a large tract of land, on which he and his posterity for generations lived. The patent name for this land was "The Dutch Lass." The old surveyors, who usually named these lands, were very fruitful in the choice of names, generally selecting one from some circumstance or cause connected with the peculiar parcel in question, and doubtless "The Dutch Lass" was suggested in this case because Beard was a German.

Nicholas Beard selected a very oddly-shaped piece of land for his possessions. He employed a surveyor to run it out for him, as was the custom at that day. They started out, Beard in advance, and the surveyor following after, and whenever they came to a place that did not suit him he would run it out of his parcel, and whenever a place suited he would run it in. It is said that when they were running lines in the vicinity where the Western Maryland Railroad now cuts through the ridge at Waltz's he thought they were approaching the mountain (at that time the country was a wilderness), so he turned off short and made a very sharp point of land at that place, which he afterwards corrected by trading with the owners of the adjoining lands.

Those adjoining lands had been subsequently patented by Johnson and Chase under the name of "Gleanings." This, likewise, was a significant name, as it was intended to include all that was left in the field over which land-gatherers had been reaping a harvest.

Chewsville is the only village in the district. It is situated on the Western Maryland Railroad and on the Hagerstown and Smithsburg turnpike, five miles east of Hagerstown. It has two general stores, blacksmith-shop, wheelwright-shop, and other conveniences, and is a point for shipments of cereals grown in the surrounding country. The town was named after the Chew family, which once owned large tracts of land in the vicinity. Samuel Chew, Jr., patented five thousand acres of land in this locality June 23, 1736. Col. Fitzhugh at one time operated a furnace on the Antietam, two and a half miles from the town, now called the Old Forge.[1] The first house erected in Chewsville was built by John Bowers, and is now occupied by Mr. Betts.

The most prominent church at Chewsville is that of the United Brethren, which was built in 1868, and was dedicated on Sunday, November 15th of that year, when the attendance was regarded as the largest religious gathering ever known in that community, probably not more than one-half being able to gain ad-

[1] A sketch of the Fitzhugh family will be found in the chapter on "Representative Families."

mittance. The dedicatory sermon was preached by Bishop Glossbrenner, of Baltimore. After which an appeal was made to the people for fifteen hundred dollars to liquidate the debt remaining on the church, which was promptly responded to, the whole amount being secured. The church was then dedicated by Bishop Glossbrenner, and among the ministers present and assisting were Messrs. Russell, Lower, Stern, and Baltzell. The church is a substantial brick building, forty by fifty-six feet, with cupola and bell. The whole cost was four thousand three hundred dollars. The old church was built in 1834, and stood a little west of the Hagerstown road. It is now used as a dwelling-house. In the graveyard attached to the old stone church of the United Brethren, at Chewsville, are the following inscriptions:

Christian Spesard, born in 1755, died July 1, 1831.

Michael Spesard, born December, 1750, died April, 1825.

John Spesard, Sr., born March 27, 1791, died May 13, 1878; and his wife, Catherine, born Aug. 5, 1792, died Feb. 10, 1851.

Peter Stotler, died Jan. 28, 1835, aged 73 years; and his wife, Elizabeth, born Aug. 24, 1763, died Oct. 12, 1827.

John Stotler, died June 22, 1860, aged 70 years.

Henry Yessler, born Sept. 13, 1782, died Feb. 25, 1839; and his wife, Catherine, born Aug. 24, 1787, died June 6, 1845.

Ellen Sanderson, died Sept. 3, 1865, aged 52 years.

Elizabeth Stottler, born June 15, 1788, died March 12, 1838.

Elizabeth, wife of Jonathan F. Doup, born May 24, 1819, died June 3, 1879.

A picturesquely-situated cemetery is among the features of the town of Chewsville. In it are buried the following persons:

Deborah Weller, died Dec. 6, 1875, aged 55 years, 4 months.

Amelia, wife of Jacob D. Warbel, died Jan. 27, 1881, aged 73 years, 3 months.

Jonathan Rinehart, died Aug. 7, 1872, aged 77 years, 6 months.

John Yepler, died March 7, 1869, aged 57 years, 1 month.

John P. Stotler, born March 8, 1789, died Sept. 23, 1874; and his wife, Anna, born Nov. 27, 1805, died Aug. 29, 1868.

John Miller, died July 19, 1866, aged 51 years, 7 months; and his wife, Mary, died Jan. 1, 1874, aged 59 years, 7 months.

Elizabeth, wife of Christian Stotler, died Dec. 29, 1862, aged 35 years, 10 months.

Elizabeth Catherine, wife of Christian Stotler, died June 8, 1868, aged 25 years, 3 months.

David Stotler, died Aug. 1, 1876, aged 55 years, 7 months; and his wife, Eliza Jane, died April 23, 1876, aged 51 years, 2 months.

Mary, wife of David A. Betts, died Dec. 14, 1877, aged 34 years, 6 months.

Martha, wife of Wm. Twigg, born Sept. 14, 1826, died June 7, 1867.

KEEDYSVILLE DISTRICT, No. 19.

Keedysville, or Election District No. 19, is situated in the southern part of the county, on the narrow strip of land lying between the South Mountain and the Potomac, and one remove from the mountains on the east and the river on the west. Tilghmanton District is on the southwest, Boonsboro' on the northeast and east by north, Rohrersville on the east and south, and Sharpsburg on the southwest and west. The Washington County Branch Railroad, extending from Hagerstown to Weverton, on the main line of the Baltimore and Ohio Railroad, passes through the centre of the district, north and south, and affords an outlet to the thickly-populated territory within its borders. The face of the country is irregular, and is formed by a line of hills extending from the South Mountain to the Antietam, which passes through the western part of the district on its way to the Potomac. Keedysville District was a most important field for military operations prior to and during the battle of Antietam. Both armies passed through the district on their way to the field of strife, and formed on or just beyond its western borders. During the fight at Antietam, Gen. McClellan had his headquarters in the district, a short distance from the town of Keedysville, on the Boonsboro' and Sharpsburg pike, which crosses the district from northeast to southwest. There are large tracts of finely-cultivated land in all parts of Keedysville District, and its value is well appreciated by its possessors, many of whom have been residents in that section for many years. The population of the district (including the town of Keedysville, which contains 389 inhabitants) is 1205.

Among the inhabitants of the rural districts are A. Griffith, H. Griffith, J. Wolf, J. Toy, H. Hopewell, L. Wright, T. Griffith, M. Lewis, A. Thomas, J. Dunn, C. Zimmerman, B. Zimmerman, N. Zimmerman, J. Rohrer, A. Wyand, J. Keafauver, E. Snyder, M. T. Snyder, A. C. Wyand, M. Eakle, Joseph Keedy, C. Nicodemus, Mrs. Eversole, W. Snively, A. Keedy, Dr. John D. Keedy, J. Miller, A. T. Baker, J. Snively, H. Buck, H. Gelmocher, E. Geeting, S. Drenner, Mrs. King, S. Ray, M. Rohrer, D. Wyand, C. Wyand, J. Thomas, J. Eckart, Mrs. Ecker, George Keedy, P. Thomas, H. F. Neskirk, J. H. Cost, D. Bovey, Mrs. S. Hoffman, M. Line, A. Hammond, E. H. Hoffman, George Line, J. Leiter, J. Miller, J. H. Myers, George Morter, D. Schlosser, J. Schlosser, N. G. Thomas, J. Line, S. Wagoner, E. Baker, A. M. V. B. Deaner, E. Snively, J. Snyder, J. Buck, and others.

The district received its name from the town of Keedysville, which is eight miles south of Hagerstown, on the Washington County Branch Railroad, and half-way between Boonsboro' and Sharpsburg. Keedysville was settled by John J. and Samuel Keedy, sons of Jacob H. Keedy, who lived one mile southeast of the town. When John J. Keedy settled there he purchased all the land from the Hess heirs, who owned what was known as the mill property on the Little Antietam, which now runs through the centre of the village. The Hesses and Rineharts were the original owners of the land, and had lived on it for years. Samuel Keedy purchased the land on the northwest side of the Boonsboro' and Sharpsburg pike from his brother. He subsequently purchased the place he now lives on from his brother-in-law, Samuel Cost. Mr. Cost contributed the ground upon which the Mount Vernon Reformed church is built. There were three or four houses in the neighborhood before the arrival of the Keedy brothers. They were located close to the mill, were built of logs, and were owned by the Hesses. Samuel Keedy built the first brick structure in the town about 1836, at the intersection of the Harper's Ferry road, which is now occupied by a brother-in-law of Samuel Keedy. The latter prior to this built a stone dwelling-house on a site opposite that occupied by the brick building, and which is now owned by Josiah Thomas.

Samuel Keedy kept a store in the brick building for thirty-four years, and then sold out to his father, Jacob H. Keedy, and built another large brick store and dwelling a short distance to the northeast, towards Boonsboro', now owned by Dr. P. D. Fahrney. At this time the town was known as Centreville, from its relative location to Boonsboro' and Sharpsburg. The inhabitants applied to the Post-office Department for a post-office, but without success. This was repeated several times, and an immense petition signed by everybody in the neighborhood with their occupations was forwarded to Washington without avail. Finally Samuel Keedy applied to Thomas Snively, the publisher of the Hagerstown *Pledge*, who wrote a letter to the Postmaster-General, and a new post-office was at once established. The postal authorities designated Keedysville after Samuel Keedy, as there was another Centreville post-office in the State. On the mill property, near the little Antietam, there is an old stone building, which from 1842 to 1852 was used as a woolen-factory by Hiram Riley and David Jones, who afterwards emigrated west. Andrew Sigler built a brick house in Keedysville about 1832, adjoining the Wyand house, which is owned by David Bell. Keedysville was incorporated in 1872, and the town officers since then have been as follows:

1872.—Burgess, C. M. Keedy; Assistant Burgess, George W. Miller; Commissioners, Ezra Lantz, Washington Kitzmiller, Lewis E. Suman.

1873.—Burgess, George W. Miller; Assistant, Ezra P. Rohrer; Commissioners, Ezra Lantz, Josiah Thomas, George W. Keedy.

1874.—Burgess, George W. Miller; Assistant, George W. Keedy; Commissioners, Ezra Lantz, John A. Grossnickle, William Lantz.

1875.—Burgess, George W. Miller; Assistant, Hiram Snyder; Commissioners, Ezra Lantz, John A. Grossnickle, William Lantz.

1876.—Burgess, George W. Miller: Assistant, George W. Keedy; Commissioners, John A. Grossnickle, Josiah Thomas, F. Wyand.

1877.—Burgess, James P. Waddell; Assistant, George W. Keedy; Commissioners, F. Wyand, Ezra Lantz, W. O. Baker.

1878.—Burgess, George W. Miller; Assistant, Jeptha Taylor; Commissioners, Ezra Lantz, W. O. Baker, Josiah Thomas.

1879.—Burgess, Jacob A. Keedy; Assistant, Jeptha Taylor; Commissioners, T. J. Keedy, John Hoffman, Aaron Rudy.

1880.—Burgess, Mahlon Knadler; Assistant, Alfred Cost; Commissioners, John Cost, Michael Stine, Jacob Eavy.

1881.—Burgess, George W. Miller; Assistant, Jacob Keplinger; Commissioners, John Cost, D. H. Wyand, Josiah Thomas.

Fairview Cemetery.—This burial-ground, covering about five acres, is a public cemetery, with the exception of about one acre in the centre, which belongs to the Mount Vernon Reformed Church, and a portion held by the Hess and Rinehart heirs. The cemetery company was organized at Dr. Fahrney's office, May 18, 1872. The first president was Jonas S. Deaner. He was succeeded by Christian M. Keedy, who was in turn superseded by Jonas S. Deaner, the latter being president at the present time. The managers are Josiah Thomas, Ezra Baker, George W. Keedy, F. Wyand, D. H. Wyand, and Aaron F. Baker; F. Wyand, treasurer; and D. H. Wyand, secretary. Among the persons buried in Fairview are the following:

Christina, wife of Rev. John Russell, born March 22, 1800, died Jan. 8, 1881.

Lavena, wife of Samuel Grove, born March 15, 1811, died Sept. 28, 1855.

Philip Grove, died June 13, 1841, aged 66 years.

John Hess, born Feb. 9, 1778, died March 1, 1815.

Susan Grove, died Sept. 10, 1827, aged 45 years.

John Hess, died Nov. 18, 1825, aged 21 years.

Samuel Grove, born March 10, 1806, died Dec. 11, 1847.

David Hess, died Dec. 20, 1855, aged 70 years; Anna, his wife, died Nov. 12, 1863, aged 71 years.

Jacob Hess, Sr., died July 1, 1815, aged 75 years; Margaret, his wife, died Oct. 9, 1814.

Jacob Hess, born March 27, 1771, died June 6, 1848; Elizabeth, his wife, died Dec. 19, 1829, aged 64 years.

Ellen Jane, wife of Rev. Levi Hess, died Aug. 12, 1859, in the 34th year of her age.

Andrew Rinehart, died March 25, 1848, aged 80 years; Margaret, his wife, born Feb. 8, 1780, died June 1, 1849.

Catherine, wife of Samuel Wagner, died April 22, 1872, aged 61 years.

David Keplinger, died Feb. 12, 1872, aged 59 years.

John Thomas, died March 26, 1880, aged 79 years; Eliza, his wife, died May 31, 1878, aged 76 years.

Nancy Thomas, died Aug. 19, 1878, aged 76 years.

Jacob Lantz, died Jan. 3, 1880, aged 58 years.

John Kitsmiller, died Nov. 9, 1862, aged 63 years; Margaret, his wife, died Dec. 16, 1869, aged 69 years.

Susan C., wife of Washington Kitsmiller, died July 22, 1880, aged 55 years.

Tracilla, wife of John H. Nicodemus, died Oct. 3, 1874, aged 31 years.

John Hoffman, born Nov. 8, 1788, died Nov. 8, 1859, aged 71.

Jacob Nicodemus, of C., died Jan. 4, 1875, aged 55 years.

J. Clinton Newcomer, aged 20, killed in C. S. army.

Henry J. Keedy, died April 10, 1859, aged 56 years.

Nicholas Stine, died Nov. 19, 1877, aged 86 years; Nancy, his wife, born Aug. 6, 1794, died May 15, 1868.

Philip Pry, born 1760, died May 1, 1828, aged 68 years; Susannah, his wife, died Sept. 4, 1856, aged about 85 years.

Samuel Cost, died Oct. 19, 1868, aged 74 years; Barbara, his wife, died Nov. 6, 1854, aged 48 years.

Frederick Cost, died July 14, 1848, aged 76 years; Madeline, his wife, died July 14, 1823, aged 50 years.

Eve Cost, died Sept. 29, 1850, aged 74.

Jacob S. Cost, died Jan. 9, 1880, aged 79 years; Catherine, his wife, died June 1, 1876, aged 66 years.

John J. Keedy, founder of Keedysville, born Jan. 2, 1805, died April 19, 1868.

Elizabeth Valentine, died Nov. 24, 1864, aged 65 years.

John A. Buck, Sr., died June 15, 1864, aged 71 years; Mary, his wife, born 1790, died Oct. 18, 1861.

Sarah Ann, wife of John Buck, died Nov. 19, 1863, aged 48.

Peter Smith, died July 17, 1863, aged 67 years; Mary, his wife, died Feb. 19, 1860, aged 69.

Elizabeth Smith, born Aug. 15, 1790, died Nov. 5, 1855.

Sarah, wife of Peter Thomas, died Dec. 6, 1870, aged about 65.

Susan Thomas, died May 2, 1869, aged 66.

Edward Reilley, died May 13, 1870, aged 59.

John H. Lantz, born Jan. 26, 1785, died Oct. 11, 1859.

Ann Maria, wife of Henry Lantz, died Aug. 23, 1852, aged 59.

Mary C., wife of John Keafauver, died April 17, 1876, aged 58.

Sarah C., wife of Rev. J. Renbush, died March 18, 1878, aged 48.

Martin Eakle, died May 7, 1878, aged 61.

Joseph Snively, died Aug. 27, 1872, aged 59; Mary A., his wife, died Sept. 5, 1860, aged 43.

Susan W. Snively, wife of Joseph Snively, died Sept. 20, 1879, aged 55.

George Snively, died Sept. 2, 1872, aged 64; Eliza, his wife, died July 1, 1864, aged 53.

Philip Mades, died March 5, 1872, aged 57.

Jacob Rohrer, died Aug. 14, 1868, aged 68; Rosanna, his wife, died Aug. 12, aged 66.

Fredk. Baker, died Jan. 27, 1857, aged 27.

Mary Ann, wife of J. D. Smith, died Dec. 9, 1872, aged 58.

Wm. Cost, died Nov. 17, 1873, aged 81; Elizabeth, his wife, born Nov. 4, 1791, died Feb. 7, 1868.

Nancy Thomas, died Aug. 19, 1878, aged 76.

Henry C. Rohrer, died Dec. 9, 1874, aged 47.

Ann M. Speilman, died May 9, 1878, aged 53.

Wm. H. Buxton, died Oct. 6, 1877, aged 68.

Christian Wyand, died April 24, 1878, aged 78.

In this cemetery is a costly monument of artistic design erected in memory of Daniel Mullendore, who was born Nov. 2, 1807, and died July 19, 1880. It is a marble shaft with a sheaf of wheat in front pierced by a sickle. On the base is carved an open Bible with the inscription: "I am the Way, and the Truth, and the Life."

Churches in Keedysville District.—The first church in the neighborhood of Keedysville was built in the last century of logs, and stood on the site of Mount Hebron United Brethren church, about one-half mile southwest of the town. The stone church, now Mount Hebron, was erected about 1845. It was subsequently sold by the congregation to Elias Snively, and is used by the Tunker denomination. The corner-stone of the German Reformed church was laid on Aug. 28, 1852. Among those interred in the Mount Hebron United Brethren graveyard at Keedysville are the following:

John Orork, died Sept. 4, 1869, aged 88 years, 2 months; and his wife, Margaret, died March 2, 1875, aged 74 years, 3 months.

Casper Snively, died Oct. 18, 1839, aged 77; and his wife, Mary, died Dec. 7, 1832, aged 62 years, 6 months.

Jacob Russell, died Feb. 7, 1798, aged 71.

Sarah Russell, died Jan. 1, 1878, aged 78.

Jacob C. Snively, died Oct. 17, 1862, aged 87 years, 5 months; and his wife, Susan, died Dec. 31, 1857.

Adam Snively, born June 7, 1769; died Sept. 7, 1846; and his wife, Catherine, born July 4, 1775, died Aug. 16, 1847.

Rev. John Russell, born March 18, 1799, died Dec. 21, 1870.

Frederick Welty, born June 25, 1767, died Sept. 19, 1814; and his wife, Catherine, born Oct. 18, 1769, died April 1, 1808.

Catherine, wife of Y. Benner, born Sept. 8, 1759, died April 26, 1826.

Catherine Thomasin, born Sept. 18, 1782, died March 31, 1818.

Martin Billmyer, died April 12, 1812, aged 65 years, 10 months.

George Thomas, died Oct. 30, 1857, aged 64 years, 6 months.

Yost Deaner, born Jan. 20, 1762, died Aug. 15, 1824.

Valinda, wife of Andrew Ullum, died July 24, 1862, aged 53 years, 5 months.

Elizabeth, wife of Jacob Detwiler, died April 25, 1852, aged 56 years, 1 month.

Benjamin Zimmerman, died Nov. 1, 1877, aged 75 years, 9 months; Mary, his wife, died Oct. 10, 1838, aged 42 years, 9 months.

Jacob Snyder, died May 31, 1869, aged 92 years, 3 months; Catherine, his wife, died Sept. 30, 1871, aged 87 years, 1 month.

Simon Wyand, died July 23, 1872, aged 68 years; Rebecca, his wife, died Feb. 15, 1866, aged 59 years.

Amelia Wyand, died Nov. 6, 1853, nearly 100 years old.

Christian Wyand, died in 1812.

Elizabeth Thomas, born March 23, 1773, died Nov. 12, 1853.

Conrad Thomas, born March 11, 1761, died Nov. 4, 1836.

George Thomas, of Concord, born Nov. 29, 1799, died Dec. 7, 1823.

George Thomas, born March 11, 1761, died June 11, 1835.

Susannah, wife of Jacob Thomas, born June 24, 1755, died Nov. 28, 1824.

Jacob Thomas, died Sept. 10, 1811, aged 64.

George Bealler, died Dec. 13, 1834, in his 78th year.

Rev. George A. Geeting, minister for 34 years, died Feb. 5, 1814, aged 60 years, 11 months.

Barbara Ann, wife of G. Geetting, died March 28, 1848, aged 67.

John Speilman, died July 30, 1850, aged 50.

Samuel Deaver, born Dec. 3, 1801, died Jan. 19, 1865.

Benjamin Witter, born July 26, 1807, died June 3, 1840.

Elizabeth Snyder, born Sept. 3, 1790, died June 24, 1820.

Keedysville is the most important town on the Washington County Branch Railroad, and is the centre of a thriving section, from which it draws a valuable patronage. Its location on the railroad and pike is a most advantageous one. It has a broom-factory, hotel, general and special stores, grist and saw-mills, three churches, public school, etc., and the moral atmosphere of the town is above the average. Among its inhabitants are E. Lantz, S. Lantz, Samuel Keedy, J. Snyder, Mrs. Hoffman, Mrs. Deaver, William Lantz, Jos. Criswell, Sr., George Snively, J. Thomas, J. Jones, J. Hoffman, J. Snively, William F. Carr, L. E. Suman, Dr. P. D. Fahrney, J. A. Grossnickle, A. Cost, E. Baker, H. F. Neikirk, E. Rohrer, S. Rohrer, S. Barks, C. M. Keedy, J. Keplinger, S. Eversale, H. Snyder, R. Domer, J. Baxter, D. Kretzer, D. Bell, F. Wyand, D. H. Wyand, G. W. Keedy, A. F. Baker, M. Knadler, J. Eavey, C. Nicodemus, J. Lantz, A. Smith, J. Taylor, E. Mades, T. J. Keedy, S. Buck, G. W. Reiley, L. Snyder, W. Kitzmiller, and others.

DOWNSVILLE DISTRICT, No. 20.

On the 7th of August, 1878, at the request of the commissioners of Washington County, a new election district was made by cutting off the southern part of Williamsport District, to which was given the title of Downsville District, No. 20. The boundaries of the new district were laid by survey as follows:

"Beginning for the outlines of the said District No. 20 on the southwest margin of the public road leading from Williamsport to Boonsboro', a short distance westward from the mouth of the college lane, and at the mouth of Reichard's private road, and running thence along Reichard's private road south thirty-seven and a half degrees west two hundred and fourteen perches to a point in said private road about three perches southwest from William Wade's (colored) house; thence south nineteen and a half degrees west five hundred and eighty perches to intersect A. N. Schnebly's private road on the farm now occupied by Jeremiah Cromer, and passing east of Mrs. Francis Schebly's tenant-house and east of Mrs. Daniel Schnebly's house, and to intersect the said private road about twenty perches southwest from the Downsville and Bakersville road; thence along said private road and by a straight line south eight and a half degrees west nine hundred and ten perches to the Potomac River, passing east of the premises on Andrew Rentch's farm now occupied by Show; then bounding on the Potomac River the distance of fourteen miles and eighty perches more or less to the Cumberland Valley Railroad bridge at Powell's Bend over the Potomac River; thence by a straight line running north seventy-nine degrees east eight hundred and seventy perches to the centre of the cross-roads leading from Williamsport to Boonsboro', and from Downsville to Hagerstown; thence along the road leading from Williamsport to Boonsboro' south fifty-six degrees east two hundred and eighty-six perches to the beginning."

This leaves the Downsville District inclosed by the Williamsport District on the north, Tilghmanton District on the east, and the remainder by the Potomac River and Chesapeake and Ohio Canal, which follow in an irregular course on the west and south. The district is a populous one, and enjoys an extended canal traffic. The population of the district is 1013. Among its residents are A. Pope (who has a warehouse on the canal), Mrs. Davis, D. Stroh, J. Snyder, A. Snyder, Rev. Mr. Seccard, William Christman, J. Lefever, E. McGill, W. Barnett, A. Stonebraker, J. F. Dellinger, Dr. H. Zeller, B. Crow, M. Baughley, B. Long, I. Long, J. R. Long, D. Neikirk, Mrs. Francis Schnebly, William M. Miller, S. Long, William Elliott, D. Heighberger, D. Rhodes, William Avis, H. Poffenberger, J. Slifer, J. Reynolds, W. Reynolds, William Hagerman, D. Zeller, Mrs. Lynch, P. Coffman, Dr. W. H. Grimes, Mrs. J. W. Berry, A. Berry, Andrew Rench, and others.

Andrew Rench is one of Washington County's oldest and worthiest citizens. Indeed, it would be difficult to find one who has been longer resident in the county, for he has lived in it and been identified with its progressive interests all his life, measuring now the extended span of eighty-two years. He was born April 8, 1799, on his father's farm, near Hagerstown. His father, Daniel Rench, emigrated from Germany to America, and late in the eighteenth century settled in Washington County. In 1814 he moved from the vicinity of Hagerstown to the farm tract known as "Bellevue," lying near Williamsport. On that farm young Andrew was reared and trained to the life of an agriculturist, and on that farm he has had his home since first he set foot upon it in 1814. The tastes of the youth inclined him strongly towards the path which his father had trod before him, and he became and has remained a true son of the soil,—wedded to the cares of his landed estates, and so wise and prudent in the management and development of his interests that he ranks to-day as one of the largest landholders in Washington County—and indeed, in Maryland. The rugged honesty and stern integrity that were conspicuous qualities in the character of the father descended in full measure upon the son, and in all his business intercourse with his fellow-men they have been the principles he served. His ambition to become a man of mark as a landed proprietor was skillfully fostered, and favored by a shrewd capacity for business and a more than ordinarily intelligent administrative ability. He acquired prosperity rapidly, and is now the owner to-day of thirteen farms in Maryland, besides a tract of thirteen hundred acres lying near Richmond, Va. Mr. Rench was married in 1826 to Jane Scott, daughter of Col. Josiah Price, himself a native of Washington County,

who lived on Welsh Run (sixteen miles west of Hagerstown), where Jane, his daughter, was born in 1802. Col. Price's father came from Wales, and with other emigrants from that country founded new homes on Welsh Run, at a time when the primeval forests covered that region, and when the Indians roamed at will and gave the little colony of Welshmen no little cause for apprehension. Col. Price's father was a man of considerable property when he came to the New World, and on Welsh Run the Price estate was long afterwards known as a large and valuable tract.

The only descendants of Col. Josiah Price still bearing the family name are supposed to be Benjamin Price and Thomas B. Price, of Baltimore, and Kennedy Price, of California. Benjamin and William Price, sons of Col. Josiah Price, became distinguished members of the bar respectively of Frederick City and Hagerstown.

The union of Mr. and Mrs. Andrew Rench was blessed with six children,—three sons and three daughters,—of whom one son and three daughters are living. The son is Benjamin Rench, one of Washington County's sterling citizens. He occupies a fine farm near Hagerstown, is a director of the County Agricultural Society, and pursues the occupation of agriculture according to the most approved methods. The daughters are Sarah Elizabeth, wife of Dr. William H. Grimes, of Bakersville; Susan M., wife of Dr. J. M. Gaines, of Boonsboro'; and Alice Jane, wife of Dr. Victor Miller, of State Line, Md. One of Mr. Rench's sons, De Witt Clinton, was killed in Williamsport by a mob during the war because of his supposed connection with the Confederate army. Mrs. Rench died in 1860, and Mr. Rench married a second time, his wife being the widow of Elisha Miller, and daughter of David Newcomer, of Washington County.

Mr. Rench, as has easily been conceived, had no desire to cultivate a taste for public life, since he was devoted too earnestly to his business to suffer the intrusions of political distractions. Nevertheless, he was urged against his will to stand for the Legislature, and being elected, served one term. Again he allowed himself to be persuaded into a nomination as county commissioner, and was elected by a handsome majority. Although he had no liking for public office, he served the people zealously and vigilantly while representing the public trust, and gave such tokens of fitness as a true representative as to show how much his retirement to private life deprived the commonwealth of valuable services. He was one of the founders and stanchest supporters of the Williamsport Bank, and for many years one of its most valued directors. From the days of his early manhood he has stood unfalteringly up for the principles of the Democratic party, and holds to them to-day as rigorously as ever. His early religious teachings issued from the German Reformed Church, and from those counsels and that faith he has never departed. He has been a member of the church all his life, and for upwards of forty years an elder and deacon therein.

Andrew Rench's record is one of which he and the community in which he has spent his life may well be proud. His name has ever been the synonym for honorable principle and a strict advocacy of the spirit of fair dealing. Of him during the active days of his business career it was commonly observed, "Andrew Rench's word is as good as gold." To his farm tenants he is a generous and kindly considerate landlord, and in the esteem of those who have known him longest and best he holds an exalted place. More than fourscore winters have whitened his head, but he is still in the hearty enjoyment of health, albeit he has retired from active participation in life's busy cares and enjoys the tranquil ease and comfort that have been doubly earned through the well-directed efforts of a stirring career.

Daniel Huyett Stonebraker, another prominent citizen of this district, was born near Hagerstown, Washington Co., Md., Aug. 19, 1839, and resides near Downsville, Washington Co. His father was William Stonebraker, born in 1805, near Hagerstown, and who married, in 1827, Ann Eliza Huyett, who was born in 1810. The father of William Stonebraker was Gerard Stonebraker, born in Washington County. Ann Eliza Huyett, the wife of William Stonebraker, was the daughter of Daniel Huyett, who lived near Cavetown, Washington Co. He was formerly from Lancaster, Pa., and was among the first settlers of Washington County. He married Miss Swope, of Huntington, Pa. Gerard Stonebraker married Susan Schroeder. Daniel Huyett Stonebraker was married three times: his first wife was Ellen Winters, daughter of Joseph Winters, of Cavetown; they were married Jan. 18, 1864, and she died July 20, 1865, leaving one son, Joseph William Stonebraker, born Dec. 2, 1864, who is still living. Jan. 15, 1867, Daniel H. Stonebraker married Caroline Virginia Winders, of Clear Spring, who left two sons,—Benjamin Franklin, born April 18, 1869, and Samuel Eugene Santee, born Feb. 5, 1873. On Dec. 31, 1878, Daniel H. Stonebraker married Frances Marion, the widow of Jacob Schnebly. She was the daughter of Isaac Rowland, who was born March 13, 1785, and Susan Boyd, who was born Jan. 18, 1799. Frances Marion was born Dec. 29, 1840, and was married to Jacob Schnebly, Sept. 10, 1857, by the Rev. C. C. Russell. Jacob Schnebly died Dec. 11, 1872. By this marriage there were eight children,—Susan Maria, born July 2, 1858; Isaac Rowland, born May 18, 1860; William Grimes, born April 30, 1862, and

D. H. STONEBRAKER.

died July 28, 1863; Harry, born Feb. 6, 1854; Elizabeth Booth, born Nov. 15, 1865; Andrew Rench, born Feb. 26, 1868; Francis Marion, born June 26, 1870, and died Nov. 14, 1873; and Emma Gring, born Aug. 4, 1872.

By her marriage with Mr. Stonebraker there was but one child, George Edward Stonebraker, born May 28, 1881. Isaac Rowland, the father of the third Mrs Stonebraker, was first married to Elizabeth Smith, Sept. 11, 1808. On the 6th of May, 1819, he married Susan Boyd, by whom he had three children,—Samuel Updegraff, who died Dec. 26, 1828, Frances Marion, and Sallie. Daniel Huyett Stonebraker was educated at Smithsburg with Prof. George Pearson, and at Hagerstown with Prof. Blood. All the family belong to the German Reformed Church, and in politics Mr. Stonebraker is a Democrat. He is a successful farmer, is kind, sociable, and hospitable, and enjoys the respect and esteem of his neighbors.

Downsville, the only town in Downsville District, is situated along the upper eastern border, three miles from Williamsport, at the intersection of the Williamsport, Sharpsburg, and Hagerstown roads, and has a population of about 200. It was named after Charles Downs, who died in May, 1857, and whose sons are still living in the county. The first house was built in 1848, and is still standing. There are three churches in Downsville,—the Disciples', the Tunker, and German Reformed. The Disciples', or Christian Church, is named Bethany, and was built in 1869. The dimensions are thirty-five by forty-three feet. The present pastor is S. S. Fowler, living at Beaver Creek, who preaches at Downsville once a month. Among the residents of Downsville are M. Baughley, Mrs. Snively, J. C. Thompson, S. Pierce, Mrs. Roe, D. Long, C. Downs, George Mull, George Lydan, D. Bowers, Wm. Snyder, Mrs. Heighberger, M. Burkett, P. Long, George Taylor, and Mrs. Downs.

Samuel A. Stonebraker was born Sept. 26, 1817, near Fair Play, in Washington County. His father (John) was a native of this county, and his ancestors were of German origin. John Stonebraker died near Fair Play about 1850. His first wife was Lydia Avey, of Washington County, and by that marriage he had three sons and one daughter. The latter (Mrs. Susan Baker, of Bakersville) is the only one now living. His second wife was Elizabeth Davis, whose father was one of Washington County's old and prominent citizens. Their only child was a son, Francis, now living at Mount Morris, Ill. Samuel A. Stonebraker was a son by the first marriage. He lived on his father's farm and assisted in its management until his marriage, April 11, 1839, to Eleanora, daughter of John Rench, of Washington County. Her mother, Catharine Rench, aged eighty, still resides at Shepherdstown. Mrs. Stonebraker died March 20, 1840, within a year after her marriage, leaving one child, who died in infancy. On the 27th of May, 1845, Mr. Stonebraker married S. R. Knode, daughter of John Knode (born 1780, and died 1848), of Washington County, who was born Feb. 19, 1822, and survives her husband. Their children were six daughters and three sons, all of whom are living. Four of the daughters are married respectively to Rev. W. A. Gring, of Emmittsburg; Adrian McCardell, of Frederick; Rev. David Whitmore, of Bedford, Pa.; and Clarence Hoffman, of Washington County, near Downsville. After his first marriage, in 1839, Mr. Stonebraker rented a farm owned by his uncle, Samuel Stonebraker, and carried it on until 1855, when he took possession of the Cedar Hill farm, which he had purchased some time before, and upon which he continued to reside until his death, Aug. 1, 1880. Cedar Hill, where his widow now resides, is a fine estate of three hundred and fifty acres, and is regarded as being among the most valuable properties in the county. Mr. Stonebraker devoted all his energies to farming, and had

Samuel A. Stonebreaker

no taste for the turmoils of a public career. Although frequently urged, he would never permit his name to be used for any public office. He was a member and zealous supporter of the County Agricultural Society, and in many ways exhibited his attachment to agricultural pursuits. Although holding aloof from active participation in politics, he took great interest in the fortunes of the Democratic party. His worth as a citizen was widely recognized.

ALLEGANY COUNTY.

CHAPTER LIV.

INTRODUCTORY.

Topography—Geology—Coal Basin—Iron Ores—Clays—Names of Mountains—Manufactures of Cumberland.

ALLEGANY COUNTY is situated in the northwestern portion of Maryland. It is bounded on the north by Pennsylvania, on the east by Washington County and West Virginia, on the south by West Virginia, and on the west by Garrett County. The North Branch of the Potomac River passes along the southern, southeastern, and eastern limits of the county, and separates it from West Virginia. Mason and Dixon's line separates it from Pennsylvania on the north, and Great Savage Mountain divides the counties of Allegany and Garrett. The boundary between Allegany and Washington Counties is Sideling Hill Creek.

The face of the country is very much broken by numerous ridges of the Allegany Mountains, making an almost constant alternation of rugged hills and narrow defiles or valleys. Along the Potomac River there are large bottoms or flats formed by alluvial deposits from the mountains which surround it, which were formerly very productive in Indian corn and grass. One of the most striking and curious features of the surface of Allegany County is the "glades," large, level, flat, swampy bodies of land between the highest ridges of the Alleganies. These are famous grazing-places for large flocks of cattle, which are driven from the neighboring counties of West Virginia to be pastured in the summer months. They were doubtless at one time lakes, and have been filled up gradually by washings from the surrounding hills, and by the decay of plants and trees which grew on them. The soil to the depth of many feet contains a large proportion of vegetable matter, and from this cause is dark and loamy, resembling very much the black-gum swamp soils of the lower counties of the Eastern Shore of Maryland. The Little Savage Mountain, a ridge of the Alleganies, divides the eastern waters which flow into the Potomac from the western streams which flow to the Ohio River. The summit of the mountain is from fifteen hundred to two thousand seven hundred feet above tide-water, and though the temperature in summer is pleasant, the spring season is backward and the winters are of long duration and great severity. The crops most generally grown are oats, buckwheat, rye, Indian corn, and wheat. The alluvial bottom-lands grow principally corn and oats; buckwheat and rye are confined more especially to the mountainous parts of the country, whilst wheat is almost exclusively restricted to the clay limestone lands in the eastern and the Cove in the western part of the county. This county would not compare with some others in the State if compelled to depend solely on its agricultural resources. In some portions farming has made great advances, and in others lands if properly cultivated and manured will in time pay large profits, and Allegany County in the future may become as famous for its agricultural as its mineral wealth, but at present the latter is the paramount basis of prosperity. The soils may be divided into the red rock or red sandstone, the limestone clay, the shaly red sandstone, the Potomac bottom, and the loamy soils in the coal regions.

The red sandstone soils are formed by the disintegration or decay of the red sandstone, which is easily recognized by its color. These soils are light and porous, except where argillaceous sandstone and shales are mixed with them. They do not suffer from drought or moisture, and from their color they readily absorb heat, and belong to the class known as quick soils. These are found from Sideling Creek to Polish Mountain, and extend within the mountain ranges to the bottom-lands of the Potomac. The soil in some places is much more porous and light than in others, owing to its location on the side of the hills, all its fine particles as soon as formed being washed out by rain-water, which leaves the larger fragments of rock behind. Analysis shows the following:

	Per cent. per acre.	(Soluble.)
Silica	65.8	
Peroxide of iron	11.6	
" manganese	2.0	
Oxide of aluminum (clay)	7.0	
Humus	7.0	
Water	3.8	
Lime, as carbonate	0.8	
Manganese, as carbonate	1.6	
Oxide of potassium (potash)	0.26	about 100 lbs.
" sodium (soda)	0.52	
Phosphoric acid		about 30 lbs.
Sulphuric acid		under 6 lbs.
Chlorine		about 36 lbs.

The analysis above given is nearly an average of ten different examinations of this variety of soil taken from the different localities where it exists. On the eastern side of Polish Mountain we meet with the limestone and clay soils; for a short space on the eastern side of Martin's Mountain the red soil again appears, but gives way to the limestone clay on the western slope, which continues until the top of Evitt's Mountain is reached, where the shaly red sandstone occurs. The soil of the country between Savage River and Meadow Mountain is of this character, and it is found also in the Cove in a highly-cultivated state, producing fine crops.

The clay limestone soil is marked by the outcropping of limestone rocks running parallel to the mountain ranges. The surface soil, of variable depth, is a loam and of a darkish color; the subsoil is a tough, reddish clay, making fine brick, and with proper cultivation is very productive. These soils are so easily recognized as to render further description unnecessary. The difference in their fertility is due in part to the greater abundance of phosphoric acid in some localities than in others. On Merley's Branch they are very productive. This is due not less to their composition than to the excellent mode of their cultivation and management.

The following is a sample of soil taken from the west slope of Warrior Mountain, formed by the disintegration of shaly sandstone and limestone:

	Per cent. per acre.	(Soluble.)
Silica	73.6	
Peroxide of iron	8.8	
" manganese	......	
Oxide of aluminum	6.5	
Humus	3.8	
Water	1.8	
Lime, as carbonate	1.3	
Magnesia, as carbonate	1.6	
Oxide of potassium (potash)	0.08	about 20 lbs.
" sodium (soda)	0.26	
Phosphoric acid		about 15 lbs.
Sulphuric acid		None.
Chlorine		about 96 lbs.

The difference in the color of these limestone clay soils is due to the greater quantity and higher degree of oxidation of the iron in some than in other specimens.

The red shaly and sandstone soils are of a lighter color than the red sandstone soils, and have very nearly the same composition. They require thorough cultivation, and manuring with stable manure, straw, and litter as a top-dressing. The great disadvantage of these soils is their shallowness. Wherever the underlying rocks allow, thev should be plowed as deep as possible. This will enable them to retain moisture well, and prevent their washing from heavy rains, which is a serious injury to them. The soils of the coal-lands on George Creek and the neighborhood of Frostburg are clayey soils and very productive, though they have received but little in the way of cultivation and nothing from manures. The soils in the middle and western coal-fields are generally of a light and sandy texture.

The bottom-lands on the Potomac vary in proportion to their composition from the washings of the different varieties of soils named above, but some of them are very productive.

The following sample of soil is taken from Flintstone Creek bottom, composed of fine river sand and quartz:

	Per cent. per acre.	(Soluble.)
Silica	87.	
Peroxide of iron	3.8	
" manganese	0.4	
Oxide of aluminum (clay)	5.	
Humus	3.	
Water	0.9	
Lime, as carbonate	0.8	
Magnesia, as carbonate	0.6	
Oxide of potassium (potash)	0.15	about 30 lbs.
" sodium (soda)	0.12	
Phosphoric acid		about 20 lbs.
Sulphuric "		under 6 lbs.
Chlorine		under 6 lbs.

This analysis is nearly an average of ten different specimens of this soil, taken at various points from Piedmont to Oldtown. In many places these lands suffer from too much moisture from the springs of the adjacent hills. There is another soil here, covering but a small space of the country, tough, cold, clayey, and of a whitish character. The stable bulwark of this county is its mineral wealth. The effort to develop this and to afford facilities for its introduction into market has absorbed much of the legislation of the State for years. To effect this development the Chesapeake and Ohio Canal has been built, at a cost of many millions of dollars. The extent of this mineral wealth, its value to the State, and its importance to the country at large in its commerce and manufactures, fully justify the consideration which has been given to it.

Allegany Coal-fields.—The great Allegany coal measures consist of a deep series of strata, which include gray sandstones, shales, bituminous shales, slate-clay and fire-clay, carbonate of iron, and coal, aggregating in thickness about one thousand five hundred feet. The whole series has been curved downwards a few degrees, and hence the ends are uplifted on both sides of the basin, in Davis and the Great Savage Mountain. Its entire length from northeast to southwest is estimated to be about thirty miles, but this includes that part of the basin which crosses into West Virginia, as well as a portion in Pennsylvania. The surface has suffered such deep and wide-spread erosion since the deposit of the upper strata of coal that perhaps less than one-half of this important fuel now remains where formerly it constituted one continuous sheet over the whole expanse of the valley. It may be noticed that the two ridges of mountains bounding the basin run nearly parallel, and thus give the longest possible exposure of the strata along their flanks. Fortunately for mining, the forces which have operated to carry away such vast areas of the surface have also cut longitudinal deep troughs, through which the rivers and creeks now run, into the subjacent strata, and have thus laid bare the edges of all the seams of coal. Near the upper end of the basin a transverse ridge, nearly equaling the adjacent mountains in height, connects Davis Mountain with the Great Savage, and cutting off about one-fourth of the valley, turns the streams to the east, to be precipitated through the gap into Will's Creek. On the western part of this ridge also stands the town of Frostburg, from which this upper basin takes its name. The lower division of the great coal basin extends down with a gentle slope towards the Potomac River, and is traversed in nearly its whole length by George's Creek, which runs through a trough scooped out of the coal and hard rocks to a depth of more than twelve hundred feet. The Potomac River has likewise cut a deep and wide trough across the southern part of these measures, leaving the strata exposed in a section more than one thousand feet thick. Besides these, numerous creeks and brooks have cut across it from the mountain flanks on both sides, thus intersecting the coal-seams and dividing them into small areas. In the northern valley, Braddock's Run and Jennings' Run, with their tributaries, also cut deep into the coal-rocks and expose their ends. The former rises near Frostburg, receives the waters of Preston's Run, and after flowing eastwardly for about six miles, passes through a gap in Davis Mountain and empties into Will's Creek two miles northwest of Cumberland. Through this natural avenue the Cumberland and Pennsylvania Railroad finds a way up the heavy grades to Frostburg, and from thence transports the coal mined in this region; but the coal mined in the larger basin, farther south, finds a natural outlet in the direction of the Potomac River, and is accordingly carried by rail to Piedmont, to be transferred to the charge of the Baltimore and Ohio Railroad.

The great importance of these coal measures to the State and country at large seems to justify the detail which is necessary to a correct understanding of the resources of this region. Through the careful surveys made several years ago by the State geologist of Maryland, Philip T. Tyson, a section was drawn showing the whole series of strata included in these coal measures, and giving measurements of all the beds of coal in their order of succession from above downwards. For purposes of reference the table is here reproduced, which shows the altitude above the sea, the relative position and thickness of the coal strata and of all the intervening members of the series:

TABLE OF STRATA OF THE POTOMAC AND GEORGE'S CREEK COAL-BASIN.

Feet above Tide-level.		Ft.	In.
2065	Shale	1	6
	Coal	2	6
	Shaly sandstone	19	
	Shale	23	
	Coal	6	
2000	Limestone, with seams of shale	12	
	Fire-clay	13	9
	Undetermined	3	9
1950	Shale, with a few nodules of iron ore	27	3
	Shale	27	9
	Sandstone of fine grain	3	6
	Shale	2	6
	Coal, with two inches of shale	4	3
	Fire-clay	10	
1900	Coal	3	
	Fire-clay	3	
	Shaly sandstone / Micaceous sandstone / Coarse sandstone }	51	
1850			
	Shales, with unimportant nodules of iron ore	42	6
1800	Coal	4	6
	Shale	2	
	Coal	1	
	Shale	4	9
	Coal	0	10
	Shale	1	3
	Shaly sandstone	1	
	Ferruginous shale'	4	8
	Main coal-bed	14	
	Iron ore, in bands or layers	0	4
	Shale	11	8
	Fire-clay	3	
1750	Limestone	1	6
	Shale	15	6
	Sandstone, of fine grain	29	
1700	Shale	27	6
	Coal	2	6
	Shale	4	
	Coarse iron ore in shale	0	8
	Shale	16	
	Ferruginous shale	1	
	Coal	3	9
	Shale	1	
	Iron ore in shale	2	6
	Iron ore in fire-clay	3	
	Coal	1	6
	Shale with iron ore	0	7
	Fire-clay with iron ore	2	
	Shale	6	
	Coal	1	6
	Shale	2	6
	Fire-clay with iron ore	5	6
	Sandstone	1	6
	Iron ore in shale	6	6
	Shale with iron ore	6	6
	Iron ore	0	7
	Shale with iron ore	4	3
1650	Coal	0	6
	Iron ore	0	6
	Coal	1	6
	Shale	2	
	Coal with shale	2	3
	Iron ore in shale	2	2

Feet above Tide-level.		Ft.	In.
1600	Coal	2	1
	Shale	0	6
	Fire-clay with iron ore	2	8
1597	Shale with iron ore	4	10
	Iron ore in shale	2	6
	Blackband iron ore	1	6
	Coal	0	4
	Shaly sandstone	2	
	Shale	4	6
	Coal	2	6
	Limestone	3	
	Fire-clay	3	6
	Coal	0	8
	Shale	1	6
	Highly ferruginous shale	1	6
	Shale	1	
	Coal	1	3
	Shale	1	3
	Coal	1	6
	Shale	1	6
	Coal	1	6
	Shale	2	8
	Sandy shale with iron ore	5	
1550	Shaly sandstone	8	
	Shale	4	6
	Coal	1	6
	Fire-clay	7	4
	Ferruginous shale	2	
	Shale	1	
1500	Sandstone	39	
	Shale	15	
	Iron ore in fire-clay	3	
	Limestone	6	
	Iron ore in fire-clay	2	
	Shale	10	
	Sandstone	44	
	Coal	1	8
	Shale		10
	Limestone	2	2
	Sandstone	23	6
	Shale	6	
	Stratified iron ore	6	
	Ferruginous shale	6	
1350	Shale	4	6
	Coal	5	8
	Sandy fire-clay	4	
	Shaly fire-clay with iron ore	6	
	Limestone	6	
1300	Sandstone	33	
	Shale	9	6
	Shale containing iron ore, a layer of marine shells, and iron ore in the lower layers	11	
	Coal		2
	Shale	6	
	Coal	2	2
	Shale	14	
1250	Coal	4	
	Shales, fire-clay, and sandstone	25	6
1220	Coal	2	
	Strata consisting principally of sandstone	102	
1100	Shale, the upper layers ferruginous	24	
	Coal	6	
	Fire-clay	3	
	Shale with iron ore	6	
	Unexplored	27	
	Coal	3	
	Shale	0	4
	Sandstone	19	
	Shale and fire-clay	20	
	Coal	1	6
1000	Fire-clay	10	
	Sandstone	92	
900	Iron ore in shale	3	
	Shale	14	6
	Coal	2	6
	Shale		3
	Sandstone in thin layers	12	3
	Coal	2	
	Shale	2	6
850	Sandstones	42	6
	Iron ore in shale	7	6
	Principally sandstones, but little explored	83	
750	Coal	2	6
	Sandstone in thin layers	27	
	Coal	2	
	Shale	0	3
520	Principally coarse sandstone, the lowest rock of this coal-field	160	

From the above enumeration it will be observed that no less than thirty-six beds of coal have been originally laid down in this region. Some of these, however, range at present from only a few inches to a scarcely workable thickness of not more than two to two and a half feet. But, besides these more numerous beds, there is a grand aggregate in ten others which amounts to a total thickness of fifty-four feet of good coal. At the present time the great "Fourteen-foot Bed," as it was then called, is so accessible and easily mined that attention is almost entirely diverted away from the narrower and consequently more difficult ones. The system of mining is, however, still so wasteful that the narrower beds will no doubt be brought into use before the end of the present century. Greatly to the advantage of mining in this region is the order in which the strata have been laid down. They rest one above the other in regular layers, no faults or serious dislocations having been found in any part of their extent, and accordingly they can be excavated continuously without the hindrances occasioned by having to search for the broken ends thrown out of level. With regard to the mining of this great deposit, Prof. James T. Hodge reports,—

"At those mines now worked in the northern end of the basin, the real thickness of the bed is about eight and half feet, and still farther to the northeast the bed becomes thinner and poorer by increased intermixture of seams of slate. In the central portion of the basin, although its thickness may reach twelve feet, there is hardly a mine in which it can be said that more than ten feet of coal is worked to any extent, while the most of them save only about seven feet. Various reasons are given in explanation of this. In some mines the slate roof over the coal-bed when undermined is apt to fall in blocks or 'slips,' and endanger the lives of the miners. In these mines it is almost a necessity to leave the upper two or three feet of the coal-bed for a safe roof, and remove only the middle and lower portions. The roof coal, as it is called, is often more or less streaked with layers of 'bony coal,' a variety duller and more compact than the rest, but otherwise entirely unobjectionable. Merely on account of this appearance this portion of the bed is entirely lost, even when the overlying slates would make it as safe a roof as the coal itself. In some mines, as at the Borden Shaft, on George's Creek, where the roof coal is left to the thickness of about two feet, and from nine to nine and a half feet taken out below it, a portion of the upper coal is expected to be saved, when the pillars are finally removed and the whole roof is allowed to come down.

"But the roof coal is not the only part left unworked at many of the mines. Throughout the whole coal-field the lowest two or three feet of the bed contain one or two seams of slate, each half an inch or so thick and about a foot apart. In the destructive rivalry that has existed in the different companies many have allowed their 'bench-coal' to remain unworked, and have been willing to pick out the choicest middle part only and sacrifice all the rest."

This will suffice to show how imperfect the system of mining has been, even in quite recent times, but extended experiences suggest more exact methods, and the work of the future will be conducted with increased precision, as the laws governing the pressure, elasticity, etc., of the associated layers of rock and coal are more closely watched and studied. These coal-beds have been built, as others of similar character, by the slow accumulation during long periods of time of dense forests and thickets of trees and plants related to our present club-mosses and horse-tails. These plants in the age now current are of small size, scarcely any of them exceeding a foot in height, while most are but four or five inches; but, during the carboniferous epoch, they covered the marshes with examples as large as the great pines and swamp-cedars, and which, falling, left their huge bodies in deep deposits in the mud and water. These became covered by clay, sand, and decomposed rocks, as each stage of development was reached, and by the great pressure of the weight accumulated above, accompanied by slow, mild heat, were finally converted into the coal-layers now so useful as fuel. In the shale accompanying the more important part of the coal, vast numbers of impressions of the twigs, leaves, buds, etc., of the trees, plants, and ferns of the epoch remain imbedded, testifying to the form, proportions, and character of the flora which once tenanted the beds.

The main coal-field of Allegany County is embraced between Davis Mountain on the east, the slopes of Savage Mountain on the west, the Potomac River on the south, and Mason and Dixon's line on the north.

The whole extent of this area, called the eastern coal-field of Allegany, is about thirty miles in length by an average of four miles in breadth, making altogether one hundred and twenty square miles lying in Maryland. The figure of this coal-basin is slightly curved from north to south, and rises sometimes from its longitudinal axis to its eastern and western borders, resembling in shape an Indian's canoe, except that its sides are not so perpendicular. On the eastern side some of the smaller veins penetrate through Davis Mountain and overlook the Potomac River. On the west this coal-bed does not go to the summit of Savage Mountain, much less crop out on the eastern side of Savage Mountain, though maps are not wanting to show that even the Big Vein extends through and overlooks Savage River.

This coal-field is in one continuous bed at Frostburg, extending from one mountain to the other, and a little below the Big Vein is washed out by George's Creek for a short distance; it is then continuous from side to side until near Wright's mill, where George's Creek again cuts through it. From this point south the Big Vein is separated into two parts by the vallley of George's Creek, and serrated by the numerous small streams which are its tributaries. North of Frostburg the coal-vein is divided into three parts by the valley of Jennings' Run and Braddock's Run. The extent of the other veins, being much lower than this, embrace a much larger area, inasmuch as some are but slightly and others not at all injured by the denudations of George's Creek, Jennings' Run, and Braddock's Run.

The veins of this coal-basin amount to about fifteen, many of them, however, of no value. The chief veins are, first, a three-foot vein; second, the Big Vein, or fifteen-foot vein, as it has been called; third, the eight-foot vein, composed of two distinct veins of coal separated by a bed of fire-brick clay about two feet in thickness; fourth, the six-foot vein; fifth, the forty-inch vein,—this is about forty-four inches in thickness; and a vein of about two feet in thickness. There are others to the amount of five or six, perhaps more, lying at different depths below.

The only veins whose coal is worked for exportation are the Big Vein, the six-foot vein, and the forty-four-inch vein. In the valley of Jennings' Run several small veins are worked for the Mount Savage Company, and for domestic purposes in the immediate neighborhood. Mining operations were carried on here at one time for foreign use, but the Big Vein gradually absorbed the force at work on these ventures. The Big Vein is that which has given the high reputation to the Maryland coal, and constitutes to a great extent the real capital of most of the corporations in this county, and must be for a long time the basis for valuable tolls on the Chesapeake and Ohio Canal. The thickness of this vein, as we have stated, varies in different sections of the coal-field, being thinner on its northeastern border, on the extreme edge of which it is about nine feet. At Frostburg its workable thickness is about eleven feet, whilst in the middle and southwestern sections fourteen are claimed by those holding property there.

The average thickness of workable mercantile coal is about eleven feet. Neither the exact size of this coal-field, nor the extent of any of its seams can be determined save by a very accurate trigonometrical survey. The estimates made here are only approximations derived from detached surveys of different tracts belonging to different companies or individuals. The most reliable estimates agree in giving the number of acres of the Big Vein at about twenty thousand. It hardly exceeds that amount. This vein does not extend beyond the Withers property, northeast of Frostburg; and here it is extensively denuded by Jennings' and Braddock's Run. A short distance below the National road George's Creek washes it down. It then sinks below the level of George's Creek, but even here to what extent it suffers by insufficient covering has yet to be ascertained. It is probable that much of it between Frostburg & Wright's mill is unfit for mercantile purposes. This vein is impaired by the washing of the following streams, which are tributaries to George's Creek: Koontz's Run, Laurel Run, Bartlett's Run, Jackson's Run, and Moore's Run, on the south. At Wright's mill, George's Creek has formed a valley below the level of this seam, which widens until it reaches the Potomac. The Potomac River has also washed out the seam to a great extent, none of it being found to exist on the Maryland side above Bloomington, on the Baltimore and Ohio Railroad, though the eight-foot vein, the six-foot, and other small veins of the coal formation exist here. The six-foot and smaller veins embrace a much larger area than the Big Vein. They do not suffer so much by denudation, and comprise more than eighty thousand acres, cropping out on the eastern slopes of Davis Mountain; they lie much below the denudation of George's Creek, and extend far towards the summit of the Great Savage Mountain, and for miles up the Potomac above Piedmont. The veins which will for a long time to come furnish the country with Cumberland coal are the Big Vein, from which by far the largest quantity will come, the six-foot vein, and the forty-four-inch vein. According to an estimate by the State agricultural chemist, made in 1854, the Big Vein contained 354,933,333 tons of coal; deducting one-fourth for wastage of every kind, and there would be then expected from the vein 266,200,000 tons of mercantile coal. The six-foot vein contained in each acre 9680 tons of coal, equal to 774,400,000 tons; deducting as above, and it would be capable of furnishing 580,800,000 tons of coal. The four-foot contained in each acre 6050 tons of coal, and the whole vein ought, therefore, to produce 363,000,000, after making the same deductions.

These three veins then, according to the estimate of 1854, would furnish the following quantities:

Big Vein	266,200,000	tons.
Six-foot vein	580,800,000	"
Forty-four-inch vein	363,000,000	"
Total	1,210,000,000	"

This estimate is for these three veins alone, and is rather below than above their actual capacity. A very modest estimate by thoroughly competent persons has placed the available amount of mercantile coal in the Allegany coal-beds at 4,000,000,000 tons.

If the quality of an article be all that is necessary to insure its proper appreciation, the coal of Allegany would have no rival in many branches of industry. For the generation of steam or for manufacturing purposes it is unequaled. In fuel for the generation of steam three things are especially required,—quickness of combustion, continuance of combustion, and steady combustion. Fuel should take fire rapidly, it should burn for a long time, and its intensity should not be diminished by fresh additions of material. Any substance possessing all these qualities would be a perfect fuel, and the coal from this region is unapproachable in these qualities. In the chemical constituents are a large percentage of carbon, a small percentage of ashes, a trace of sulphur and nitrogen, very little water, and a moderate quantity of bitumen. This bitumen, if in excess, as in many of the bituminous coals, would give a very rapid fire, but one of short duration. If less than this, or none at all, as in the anthracite, it would be a very slow combustion, though it might last for a long time, but at every fresh addition of coal the fire would be deadened, and the amount of steam lessened until fuel combustion again took place. A coal then, for steam generation, should contain enough of bitumen to make it readily inflammable, so as to burn quickly and not deaden the fire with each fresh addition of it, and such a proportion of carbon as to maintain a uniform heat for a long time, and in these conditions the Cumberland coal stands without a rival. Use has fully confirmed the scientific deductions made from its chemical composition.

In the year 1844 a report was made to the Navy Department by Prof. Johnson, "on American coals, applicable to steam navigation and other purposes." Full and fair trial was given to all the American coals by an extended series of practical tests, which resulted in placing the coal of this field above that of every other *inevaporative power, both as to equal weights, and what in navigation is of the greatest consequence, equal bulks.* That is to say, a pound of coal or a bushel of coal from this region will generate more steam than the same amount of coal from any other mines in the country. Wherever this coal has had a fair trial the results have been the same. It is scarcely necessary to mention its unquestioned superiority for locomotives and stationary engines.

The tendency now is to concentrate the carrying trade of the world in long narrow ships of immense tonnage, propelled by steam, and swiftness is a paramount consideration, and the navies of all nations have discarded sailing-vessels. A man-of-war requires a fuel which can speedily generate and keep up a steady head of steam, whether in pursuit of, flying from, or in actual combat with an enemy, and the competition everywhere developed in the merchant marine of the world makes this a matter of no less importance to the shipping interests. The demand, therefore, for coal from Allegany must greatly increase with every year.

Cumberland coal has been carried around the Horn to stations on the Pacific, and despite the great cost of transportation its superior qualities have commended it to the shipping lines on that ocean. The completion of the many projected highways through Mexico and the Central American States and the construction of the Panama Canal will be the means of introducing this coal to this portion of the world for all industrial purposes, to the exclusion of that from other localities.

Cumberland coal, being remarkably free from sulphur, is admirably adapted for the smelting of iron and other ores. It makes a beautiful compact coke, and in this shape is unsurpassed for the manufacturing of all kinds of metal. For the forge or blacksmith-shop it is inestimable. It makes a cheerful, bright fire, gives out a steady heat, and resembles more nearly a wood-fire than that from any other variety of coal.

It has been urged by interested parties, and by others ignorant of its qualities, that Cumberland coal is dangerous by reason of its liability to spontaneous combustion. A more absurd or baseless hypothesis could not have been advanced. Careful analyses by the most skillful experts have effectually disposed of these invidious assertions, but as experience far outweighs the testimony of science, however positive may be its conclusions, careful inquiries instituted in the coal-fields along the Chesapeake and Ohio Canal, and at the depots where the coal is stored, have failed to disclose a single case of combustion without active extraneous interference. It has been exposed to the air in large heaps for several seasons, placed in damp cellars and piled on dry floors, stored away in barrels or in the holds of canal-boats, but it has invariably failed to gratify the anxieties of its enemies, whose inconsistency and eagerness have led them into the unpardonable error of asserting, at the same time that they urge its tendency to spontaneous combustion, that *it is not sufficiently combustible.*

The middle coal-field of Allegany is situated between Negro and Meadow Mountains. The coal approaches nearest in its composition to the Pittsburgh coal. It is a fine, compact mineral, and is only debarred from general use by lack of the means of transportation. There are three veins here, one of about forty inches in thickness, one of four feet, and another of about five feet. But comparatively a small portion of this coal-field lies in Maryland. The western coal-field lies in the valley of Youghiogheny River, and is destined to become an interest of great importance for the manufacture of the iron ores, which are associated with it in large quantities. It is very similar in quality to the coal in the middle field. As soon as a railroad shall penetrate this field, which is a matter of near accomplishment, a great industry will be developed. The coal veins in this region are a two-foot vein, a four-foot vein, a six-foot vein, and a five-foot vein. All these coal-fields, by reason of the peculiar formation of the country,—it being intersected by ravines,—can be very readily worked. Many of them drain themselves, and can be ventilated at a trifling expense. In the value of coal-lands this is a very important item, and materially lessens the cost of mining, while in the same measure it increases the profits.

On Town Hill, in the eastern section of the county, there is another coal formation, but the owners have as yet done but little in the direction of development.

The following represents the composition of the different veins of coal worked for exportation in the eastern coal-field of this county. They are the average run of the mine, where they are carefully worked. Average of five specimens:

Big Vein. Specific gravity, 1.32.	
Carbon	88.05
Hydrogen, Oxygen, Nitrogen, a trace, Sulphur, "	8.54
Ashes	3.41
Six-Foot Vein. Specific gravity, 1.34.	
Carbon	86.01
Hydrogen, Oxygen, Nitrogen, a trace, Sulphur, "	8.68
Ashes	5.31
Forty-four-Inch Vein. Specific gravity, 1.39.	
Carbon	74.24
Hydrogen, Oxygen, Nitrogen, a trace, Sulphur, "	7.13
Ashes	18.63
Oakland Coal. Specific gravity, 1.39.	
Carbon	73.34
Hydrogen, Oxygen, Nitrogen, a trace, Sulphur, "	12.54
Ashes	5.12

The following are the results of a chemical examination of the Lonaconing bituminous coal from the "Big Vein" of the George's Creek Company. The two results are by different analyses of the same sample:

Carbon	.900000	.902727
Hydrogen	.055556	.053334
Oxygen and nitrogen	.023072	.022567
Sulphur	.001372	.001372
Ashes (fawn-colored)	.020000	.020000
	1.000000	1.000000

Specific gravity, 1.3197.

The iron ore in this county may be divided into four kinds,—fossil, iron ore, red and brown hematite, and the clay iron-stone of the coal formation. At the head of Merley's Run, on the western slope of Warrior Mountain, there are found large quantities of red hematite ore. The vein is seen at intervals for a space of a mile and a half, and induces the belief that it exists there in very large quantities. This is strengthened by examinations made on the eastern slope of the same mountain, overlooking Town Creek. Here for several miles the red hematite shows itself, and at one opening made the bed disclosed a thickness of eighteen inches. It was opened far enough into the hillside to prove it to be a regular stratum lying between strata of brown shale. The ore, as far as penetrated, is a compact argillaceous oxide of iron, but has been changed by atmospheric agency. The quantity here is sufficient to justify the erection of furnaces on a large scale. The ore is of fine quality, and makes good malleable iron.

The abundance of large pieces strewn on the surface indicates the existence of other strata. There are good indications on a spur of Polish Mountain, near the Potomac.

Between Martin's and Evitt's Mountains, near the junction of the red shaly sandstone and the clay limestone soils, hematite ore also exists in considerable quantities.

The fossil ore and hematite are found in distinct veins on Dan's Mountain. As both of the ores in this locality have been worked for a long time, a particular description of them is deemed unnecessary. These veins have in a great measure supplied the furnaces in this part of the country with ore, and are of very great extent. In the valley of Jennings' Run and its tributaries there are also hematite and clay ironstone ores, but not in large quantities. The evidences of its existence greatly increase as we approach the Pennsylvania line. Near Frostburg there are found two veins on the head-waters of George's Creek, which are from ten inches to three feet in thickness. The ore is of fine quality, and extends over a large space.

There are also found large bodies of red hematite ore on the benches of Meadow Mountain and the heads of several of the branches of Savage River. At the Little Crossings there is an immense deposit of bog-iron ore, and associated with the coal veins found there is also clay iron-stone (carbonate of iron). The ore here of each kind is rich in quality and of very great extent.

By far the largest quantity of iron ore is found in Garrett County, in the coal-fields of Youghiogheny River and its tributaries, which lie in the coal basin. On either flank of Will's Mountain there are outcroppings of important strata of iron in the formation. It is called the *Clinton Group* in the New York reports, and *Sargent Shales* in Pennsylvania. There are several strata of ore, some of which are too thin to be profitably mined. The lower strata, called hard ore, contain much sand, and vary in composition considerably, but usually contain less iron than those higher in the series, called fossil ores, because of the numerous impressions of fossil shells which they contain.

There is an outcrop of hard ore five feet in thickness a mile and a half above Cumberland (on the Baltimore and Ohio Railroad), containing twenty-four and three-quarters per cent. of metal. The fossil ore varies in the proportion of iron from thirty-five to fifty per cent., and has been extensively used in the furnaces at Mount Savage and Lonaconing. Much of it contains sufficient phosphoric acid to affect injuriously the quality of the metal.

There are several varieties of the carbonate of iron in the coal-fields, differing in appearance as well as in their proportion of iron. They exist either in flattened nodules, called "balls" by the miners, or in stratified masses called bands. The balls vary in weight from two or three to ten, and sometimes twenty, pounds, and are imbedded in courses in either shale or fire-clay. The bands are interposed between beds of shale, and are called clay bands and black bands.

These ores usually contain from thirty to thirty-six per cent. of iron, but there are some bands containing only twenty-five per cent., which will be available because of the low price for which they may be mined and delivered to furnaces.

Among the clay bands there is a thick stratum, which examination made at a point on Laurel Run, three miles from Lonaconing, in the George's Creek region, proved to be six feet thick, and it was fouud to contain twenty-five per cent. of iron. It rests upon a bed of shale six feet thick, which, although highly ferruginous, does not contain a sufficient proportion of the metal to constitute a workable ore. Numerous other bands of ore of lesser thickness, but richer in iron, exist in this coal-field which need not be particularly described.

There is, however, a variety of black band of

sufficient importance to require special notice. This name was first applied by Mr. Mushett to an ore discovered by him in the year 1801, but which was not generally recognized until the year 1825, because it differed so materially in appearance from the ores formerly used in coal regions that iron-masters were slow to believe it to be an iron ore.

At its outcrops, the black band, owing to the action of atmospheric agents, crumbles down and becomes mixed up with the adjacent earthy matters, so as to give slight indications of its presence. The nodules and clay bands at their outcrops present themselves in larger pieces, which often resemble the earthy varieties of hematite, and indicate the proximity of the ores in their regular strata. The most important black band in the George's Creek coal-field lies about one hundred and seventy-seven feet below the main or fourteen-foot coal-bed, which was opened at several points during the progress of the explorations above referred to. It was ascertained that this valuable ore occupies an area of many square miles.

At one point on Mill Run, which flows into George's Creek, it was penetrated by a drift to the distance of forty-five feet, by which the unaltered ore was reached and its character fully investigated. The thickness of the one proved to be eighteen inches, and owing to its being underlaid by a seam of coal four inches thick, it was ascertained that it could be mined at a cost not exceeding seventy-five cents per ton. Iron of good quality can be produced from it—with the superior smelting coal of that region—at a very low price.

In order to determine accurately the proportion of iron, a sample was taken from the whole thickness of the bed, which was found to contain thirty-one per cent. of iron.

A great advantage possessed by this ore, in common with the Glasgow black band, consists in the fact that coal is mined with it. The mixture of iron and coal is placed in long hills or ricks, which, upon being fired, are found to contain sufficient fuel for roasting, which is necessary for all the carbonates of the coal regions. Before roasting, three and one-third tons of ore would be required for one ton of metal; but the roasted ore, owing to the loss of carbonic acid and water, is found to contain more than forty-two per cent. of iron, so that two and three-eighths tons only are needed for a ton of metal. There are many other deposits of ore, besides those above mentioned, that will prove valuable if properly worked.

The following is an analysis of iron ores from Allegany County, being an average of six specimens of each variety:

	Clay from Stones.			Hematites.		
	Dark-gray.	Light-gray.	Dark-gray.	Red.	Brown.	Brown.
	No. 1.	No. 2.	No. 3.	No. 4.	No. 5.	No. 6.
Carbonate of iron	77	74	89	......	......	......
Peroxide of iron	......	......	......	86	68	86
Phosphate of iron	trace.	trace.	none.	trace.	trace.	none.
Carbonate of lime / Carbonate of magnesia	1.2	3.1	trace.	trace.	trace.	trace.
Clay	1.6	0.9	1.4	1	1.5	1
Sand	17.6	13	8.8	3	18.6	11.5
Water and organic matter and loss	2.6	9.1	0.8	10	11.9	1.5
Produces of metallic iron	37	35.7	43	60	47.6	60

Immense beds of fire-brick clay accompany the coal formation, valuable for hearths, for furnaces of all sorts, fireplaces, stoves, etc. The demand for these bricks is greater than can be promptly supplied, owing to the limited capacity of the works engaged in their manufacture. The quantity of this kind of clay is sufficient in the coal-fields of Allegany to supply the demands of the country for many centuries to come.

One of the great natural resources of this county is its immense primitive forests of timber, consisting of white oak, red and black oak, black walnut, wild cherry, curly maple, red and white pine, yellow poplar, and locust. A feature worthy of note is the growth of locust timber, which springs up immediately on the destruction of the original forests. The growing scarcity of timber in this State, and indeed all along the seaboard, gives the timber resources of this county an intrinsic value that has been somewhat dwarfed by the coal and iron speculations in this region.

Accompanying the coal formation large quantities of bituminous limestone are found in parallel layers. On Martin's Mountain, between Evitt's and Polish Mountains, it is also found extensively imbedded. Indeed, the localities where limestone is found are so numerous in this county that a bare enumeration of them would occupy much space. There is more than will ever be used, whether for roads, buildings, ore-fluxes, or agricultural purposes. The limestones are all dolomites, containing from eight to forty per cent. of carbonate of magnesia. Recent developments have shown that the city of Cumberland occupies a position upon the great fossil or Clinton ore-belt, which is not only central, but really will give it the command of the iron trade in the near future.

Pittsburgh, the present iron-mart of this country, possesses cheap and ready fuel, but is compelled to range far and near for ores to feed her furnace-fires. An essay read before a meeting of the leading business men of that city (Pittsburgh) showed that a saving of millions of dollars per annum would result from the building of a line of railroad which should tap the ore-beds of West Virginia, some two hundred and fifty miles distant. These ores are found in vast profusion at a distance of about forty miles south of Cumberland, and at an elevation which will give an average grade of forty-five feet to the mile to the local railroad, whose construction is being rapidly arranged for at present date; this railroad will have its terminus in Cumberland.

It is a noticeable, and a very remarkable, fact that nearly all of the mineral wealth surrounding the city of Cumberland lies above its level, and in many instances can be handled by gravity alone from the mine to the furnace.

This fact will strike an interested mind at once as one well calculated to decide the location of new works, the more especially when, by referring to the map, it will be seen that the lines of natural drainage meet directly in the city, and it is upon or down such lines that heavy raw material can be handled to best advantage, and at least cost.

Among the available ores are those lying along the Pennsylvania Railroad, and which can be mined and handled at a very low rate.

The "Soft Fossil Vein" varies from one to two feet in thickness, and is separated only by a foot or more of sandstone from the "Hard Fossil," which ranges from six to twelve inches thick. The ore has the following composition:

Metallic iron	41.34
Silica	15.10
Water	6.92
Phosphorus	.51

Like all the fossil of this region, it contains only a trace of sulphur, and nearly sufficient lime to flux the silica in the ore. These ores, if mixed properly, can be relied upon to yield forty per cent. in furnace, and will cost about three dollars and fifty cents per ton delivered in Cumberland. The "Big Fossil Vein," also known as the "Levant," or "Black Ore," crops out near the city, and can be traced for twenty miles along the Potomac River and the Baltimore and Ohio Railroad, until it assumes the character of ferruginous sandstone. Specimens of this ore assay:

Iron	27.77
Phosphorus	.33
Silica	54.20

The lower leads are not exposed, but will yield about thirty per cent. in the furnace; its remarkable thickness and the low cost at which the ore can be quarried and shipped renders it valuable, as it can be delivered in Cumberland at but little over one dollar and seventy-five cents per ton. It can be mixed to advantage with the limestone fossils first mentioned, and can be worked to advantage along with the rich hematites and magnetites of Virginia. The measures lying immediately south of Cumberland yield over forty-three per cent. of iron, and are unusually free from silica. They are so situated that they can be mined easily and economically. The only effort towards bringing them into the market has been made through the medium of a single charcoal furnace, the product of which has held an excellent reputation.

In summing up, it may be said that the city of Cumberland occupies a position relative to three great parallel zones of fossil, hematite, and magnetic ores, which renders it highly probable that an early day will witness its development into one of the leading iron-working localities of our country. The following calculations are taken from the report of Arthur F. Wendt, M.E., upon cost of making iron in vicinity of Cumberland, Md.

A pair of modern furnaces, at least eighteen feet in the bosh, and seventy feet high, built with all labor-saving improvements, ample hot blasts, blowing engines, calcining kilns, and coke ovens, could manufacture iron at the following cost:

A cold, short iron, containing 1.3 per cent. phosphorus, made exclusively from 40 per cent. fossil:

2½ tons ore at $3.80	$9.50
1 ton limestone	.80
1½ tons coke at $2.80	4.20
Labor and salaries	3.50
Material and general expenses	1.00
	$19.00

A neutral iron containing 0.7 per cent. of phosphorus and some titanium, smelted from a forty per cent. stock of equal parts of the Levant and limestone fossil mixture and titaniferous magnetite, which stock will yield sufficient cinder to prevent any difficulty from the refractory character of the titanium ore:

2½ tons ore at $4.32½	$10.80
1¼ tons stone at 80 cents	1.00
1½ tons coke at $2.80	4.20
Labor	3.00
Materials	1.00
	$20.00

Estimating the average cost of North Mountain and Fredericktown hematites at five dollars and twenty cents per ton, and their yield at only forty-five per cent., and further allowing the make of the furnaces to increase eight per cent. on the calcined and richer stock, the cost of a strong mill iron containing, according to the ore used, from 0.10 per cent. to 1.71 per cent. phosphorus will be as follows:

2¼ tons ore at $5.20	$11.70
1⅕ tons stone at 80 cents	.96
1½ tons coke at $2.80	4.20
Labor	2.75
Materials	.92
	$20 53

Bessemer, soft foundry, or a red short forge iron made from various proportions of picked and calcined Virginia hematites and titaniferous magnetites, worth an average of $5.60 per ton:

2 tons ore at $5.60	$11.20
1 ton of stone	.80
1½ tons coke at $2.80	4.20
Labor	3.00
Materials	1.00
	$20.20

Iron made exclusively from African ores:

1⅗ tons ore at $11.50	$18.36
⅝ ton stone at 80 cents	.50
1¼ tons coke at $2.80	3.50
Labor	2.10
Materials	.60
	$25.06

The preceding estimates are based on the actual work done at a furnace near Cumberland, and represent the *maximum* cost of the iron in every instance, proving conclusively that Cumberland can manufacture iron from three dollars to four dollars per ton cheaper than Pittsburgh, where the cost of production from a mixture of mill cinder and lake ore is about twenty-four dollars at present. With a superior coal no more expensive, the excellent Mount Savage and Savage Mountain fire-brick from five to six dollars per thousand less costly, and labor a trifle lower than in Pittsburgh, wrought iron can be manufactured et a proportional reduction in cost. Estimating the loss of metal from pig to the finished product at fifteen per cent., the necessary fuel consumed in puddling and heating at two tons, and the fettling at two hundred and twenty-five pounds of one per net ton of merchant iron, its cost to a company owning mines and furnace will be approximately as follows:

Pig-iron at $20.00	$21.00
Coal	3.50
Fettling	1.00
Labor and superintendence	16 00
Materials and repairs	2.00
	$43.00

Leaving a margin of ten dollars per ton at present prices.[1]

The above calculations were made in 1875, and it is fair to presume that with the additional advantages derived from the completion of several new lines of railroads, chief among which is the securing to the local manufacturers of the lowest competitive freight rates upon both raw material and finished products, the manufacturer will be enabled to enter the market with full assurance of success.

Fire-Clay.—In all industries requiring the use of a higher degree of heat, and especially in the manufacture of glass and iron, the quantity, quality, and cost of such fire-clay as may be necessary are very important items.

The national reputation of the fire-brick manufactured in the vicinity of Cumberland obviates any necessity from going into the details of making it, yet it might be well to state that, under the improved methods now in use at the Union Mining and Manufacturing Company's works, located at Mount Savage, it is possible that cheapness in cost of production can now be added to that advantage of superiority in quality which causes the fire-brick made in this region to be sought for above all others.

The beds of pure fire-clay contained in the coal measures of this region comprise some eight veins, and in the aggregate measure about fifty-three feet in thickness.

It has been stated that a mixture of this fire-clay with the German clay now extensively used makes a pot for glass furnaces which is unequaled for strength and resistance to the action of the necessary intense heat.

Suitable clay for potting, tile, terra-cotta, and common brick can be had in inexhaustible quantities in different localities contiguous to the city, and sharing in its transportation facilities.

Limestone.—Cliffs of this rock, so necessary for the successful working of iron-ore silicates, tower far above the level of the river, canal, and the several railroads, whose lines cross each other in the very heart of the city,—in fact, the "Lower Helderberg" and "Water Line" formations are quarried and worked inside of the city limits; the latter material being the basis of one of the oldest and most thriving industries of the town. The Cumberland Hydraulic Cement Company has furnished for nearly forty years a hydraulic cement which yet stands highest in the records of civil engineering for energy of action, strength, and durability as compared with other American cements.

We append a table taken from "Trautwine's Hand-Book," showing weight sustained by cement mortars made into prisms two inches square by eight inches long, and broken on supports four inches apart by pressure in the middle.

The cements were kept in sea-water for the first twenty-four hours, and were three hundred and twenty days old when subjected to the test.

[1] The analyses in the foregoing article were made by Prof. C. F. Chandler, Ph.D., School of Mines, New York, and J. Blodgett Britton, Philadelphia.

TABLE OF TRANSVERSE STRENGTH OF CEMENT MORTARS, BREAKING WEIGHT IN POUNDS.

Designation of Cement.	Pure Cement. lbs.	Cement 1. Sand 1. lbs.
English Portland (artificial)	1536	1260
Cumberland, Maryland	**954**	**920**
Newark and Rosendale	841	560
Delafield & Baxter's Rosendale	836	692
Hoffman, Rosendale	849	607
Lawrence, Rosendale	777	......
Round Top, Maryland	......	720
Utica, Illinois	732	756
Shepherdstown, Virginia	747	618
Akron, New York	764	651
Kingston and Rosendale	720	556
Sandusky, Ohio	554	464
James River, Virginia	......	623
Roman cement, Scotland, injured	553	......
The following were broken when 1 year old :		
Lawrenceville Manufacturing Co., *Rosendale*	......	910
Sandusky, Ohio	802	......
Kensington, Connecticut	954	709
Lawrence Cement Co., Rosendale, Hoffman brand	875	91

The value of this material as used in the manufacture of drain and sewer-pipe, paving blocks, and artificial stone has yet to be tested to any definite extent, but it is evident that, owing to the close proximity of such markets as can be found in the chain of large cities encircling Cumberland, and the ease and cheapness with which this class of low-grade freight can be conveyed over the nominal intervening distance, there is an unusually promising opening in that particular line of manufactures, and one which must soon attract the attention of interested parties to the profit of all concerned.

Glass-Making Material.—Upon making a careful survey of the advantages of Cumberland it is an unavoidable conclusion that for the manufacture of glass there can be found no locality where are assembled together in greater abundance the varied materials, all adapted to such a purpose, than the city of Cumberland and its immediate vicinity.

Surrounded by vast deposits of sandstone of varied formations, by ample supplies of the finest lime, the cheapest of fuel, the most durable of fire-clay, and the material for making cheap charcoal, combined with a location insuring the greatest convenience in the matters of handling, working, and shipping, and a central position in relation to the different great distributing points, with a climate and social advantages which go far towards giving to the workman a healthy and happy home, it certainly seems that Cumberland is a favored spot, regarding it from an industrial point of view.

The Medina sandstone, which is of the greatest importance in the manufacture of glass, crops out in every mountain gorge, forming walls in some places over five hundred feet in height. It is a stone of an average fine grain, breaks easily under the hammer into sand which is composed of angular crystals, looking more like grains of glass than natural sand. This peculiar angular grain is of the utmost importance, as it leaves a certain space between each particle, by means of which the heat soon permeates the entire mass, causing a certain weight of sand to melt much sooner with a given amount of coal than if lying in finely powdered, pasty lumps in the pot. An analysis of this stone, of which millions of tons are lying along and above the different railroads, gives it more than ninety-eight per cent. of silica, and of sesquioxide of iron only forty-two one-hundredths of one per cent., this being the only real impurity.

The supply of this material is simply unlimited, and is obtainable in such varied localities and under such advantageous circumstances that there can be no question of its being procured at any time and at any quantity at but little above the mere cost of handling.

For the benefit of interested parties, we append a copy of the analysis and letter:

"LABORATORY SCHOOL OF MINES,
"COLUMBIA COLLEGE,
"NEW YORK, March 9, 1875.

"SIR,—The sample of Medina limestone submitted to me for examination contains: Silica, 98.35 per cent.; sesquioxide of iron (equivalent to 0.29 per cent. of metallic iron), .42 per cent. Bottle glass, which is dark green or black, contains from 3.8 to 6.2 per cent. of oxide of iron. Plate glass contains from 0.2 per cent. to 1.9 per cent. of oxide of iron. Assuming that the glass to be made of your sandstone will contain 75 per cent. of the sandstone, the glass would contain less than one-third of one per cent. of oxide of iron, which is too little to give it any objectionable color, or practically to color it at all. I am satisfied, therefore, that the *sandstone is in every respect well fitted for the manufacture of glass of the best quality.*

(Signed) "C. F. CHANDLER, Ph.D.,
"*Professor of Analytical and Applied Chemistry.*"

In manufacturing glass the only material needed from abroad in any appreciable quantity would be soda ash and crucible stock, which can be transported to the city at the very lowest rates, as there is but little if any return freight for the cars and boats of the different coal-shippers.

The various glass-works in the West which draw their supplies of the finest qualities of sand from points far eastward can find in this section material which, it is claimed, will equal in most respects the famous Berkshire sand of Massachusetts. Certainly the proprietors of different distant works can find here such combinations of advantages as will compel them to coincide with the declaration of one of the pioneers in the glass trade of America, which was that, in his estimation, "glass could be made in Cumberland at a cheaper rate than elsewhere in the States."

Derivation of Names of Mountains and Streams.[1] —The first white man who penetrated the wilds of the mountain region of Allegany County was an individual named Evart. Tradition says that he was an Englishman by birth, and a man of education who had seen much of civilized life. The Western settlements of the white man had not then penetrated farther into the forest than the Conococheague, and that fierce struggle for the possession of the country was going on between the white and the aborigines which in nearly every portion of our land has been marked by blood and cruelty. Evart, driven to desperation by disappointment in love, penetrated that part of the country which stretches some sixty miles west of the Conococheague, and built a cabin on the top of a mountain some seven miles northeast of the present city of Cumberland. The trail of the Indians, as they traversed the mountainous region lying between the Atlantic and the western waters, passed along the valley of the Potomac and crossed Dan's Mountain, some eight miles south of the spot where Evart built his cabin. There upon the top of a mountain, far from the habitation of civilized man, and even from the haunt of the red man of the forest, this singular individual took up his lonely abode. It is asserted that his disgust for civilized life was caused by the frailty, fickleness, or falsehood of a woman on whom he had placed his hopes of happiness. When these were wrecked he sought the wilderness. Neither the allurements of civilized life, nor the dangers of the forest, traversed only by the savage, were sufficient to deter him. Without expecting or desiring ever to see the face of civilized man, he fixed his habitation far in the wilderness, and on so rugged a spot that even to this day perhaps not a dozen individuals have ever visited the spot where his cabin was built.

Shortly after Gen. Thomas J. McKaig removed to Maryland he heard the story of the residence of "Evart the Englishman" from George Hughes, then some eighty years old, and one of the earlier settlers of this part of Maryland. In order to test the truth of the tradition, Gen. McKaig procured a mountain-guide and went in search of the spot where it was said Evart's cabin had stood. Traversing the side of the mountain now known as "Evart's" or Evitt's Mountain for some distance north of the point where the turnpike leading from Hagerstown to Cumberland crosses Martin's Mountain, Gen. McKaig and his guide left their horses, and with much labor reached the top of the mountain near the point where the stream called "Evart's Creek" breaks through the mountain. Here he found undoubted evidence that the spot where he then stood had been the residence of the hermit. Even then silence covered the mountain, and with the eloquence of Ajax among the dead served to tell the melancholy story of its former occupant. On the top of the mountain, or at least that which seemed the top, was a level piece of ground of about two acres, with good soil, that had been cleared and in cultivation. The mountain gradually rose to the north, for at the brow of the mountain in clear soil was a fine spring of mountain-water. The access to the top was so rugged that cattle seldom, if ever, reached it. The grass had grown up and fallen until it formed a sward as soft as a bed of down. The house or cabin was gone, but the chimney, of rude stone, some ten or twelve feet high, was still standing. There were scattered around some three or four apple-trees, two pear-trees, some sprouts from the peach-trees, and one plum-tree. Over the whole surface of that part which had been cultivated the English strawberry had spread, and was then growing in great profusion. Gen. McKaig brought down with him some of the roots, and had them transplanted in Cumberland, from which has been produced the finest quality of the English strawberry. Here, in this solitary spot, lived one whom neither the thirst for gold, nor the speculative spirit of adventure, nor the maddening zeal of religious enthusiasm had driven from civilization and home and friends, but a romantic disappointment which he had permitted to blight his life. His idea seems to have been to lose his identity and bury his name, but in this he failed, for his name still clings to the mountain on which he resided, and to the stream which flows at its base. George Hughes fixes his death prior to the year 1750, but when or under what circumstances it took place no human being ever knew, nor was there any friendly hand to close his eyes or perform the sad offices of sepulture.

Between the years of 1742 and 1745 there lived at Salisbury, near Williamsport, a family named Clemmer, consisting of the father, mother, three sons, and a daughter. The daughter was accidentally drowned. While returning with their neighbors from the funeral, one of the boys riding behind his father and another behind the mother, they were fired upon by a party of fifteen Delaware Indians. The men of the party, five in number, were all killed, and the horse on which the mother rode was killed. The two boys and the mother were captured. The mother on the day after the capture escaped, was retaken and murdered, and the two boys were brought by their captors to "Wills-

[1] The author is indebted to Gen. T. J. McKaig, formerly of Cumberland, for the information contained in the accompanying sketch of the derivation of names of mountains and streams in Allegany County.

town," which was situated just west of the gorge where Will's Creek bursts through Will's Mountain, one mile west of the present site of Cumberland. Indian "Will," the chief of a tribe, resided at this Indian village, and gave his name to the mountain immediately west of Cumberland, known as "Will's Mountain," and to the creek which passes through the town of Cumberland, known as "Will's Creek."

Here the young Clemmers, Lawrence and Valentine, were held prisoners for nine years. On the conclusion of peace with the Indians the boys were returned to the white settlements. Valentine, the younger boy, and who at the time of the capture was only five years old, married near Williamsport, and in 1802 removed with his family to Allegany County, the scene of his earliest recollections. His son, Jacob Clemmer, a man of great respectability, afterwards filled several important offices in the county.

Fort Cumberland, where the town of Cumberland now stands, was laid out about 1749, by the Ohio Land Company, and was then supposed to belong to the territory of Virginia. On the site of the old fort a beautiful church of Gothic architecture has been erected by the Episcopalian congregation of Cumberland. One of the first settlements made within the territory now embraced by the county of Allegany was made shortly after Fort Cumberland was located by Thomas Cresap, usually called the "English Colonel," at a place called by him "Skipton," now called Oldtown.

The house, or fort, as it was then called, built of stone, is still standing, and was afterwards occupied as a dwelling-house. Col. Thomas Cresap, the progenitor of the Cresap family, now a numerous and highly respectable family of Allegany County, was an Englishman by birth, a member and agent of the Ohio Land Company, and a man of great bodily strength, and of a high order of intellect. He had been the agent of Lord Baltimore, proprietor of the province of Maryland, and had built a fort on the banks of the Susquehanna for the purpose of taking possession and holding that part of the country, claimed as part of Maryland, against the family of Penn, the proprietors of Pennsylvania. Some of the Pennites came over, and after an obstinate resistance, in which they burnt his fort, they took him prisoner and carried him to Philadelphia. After his release he removed to Allegany, and settled at Skipton, where he reared a numerous family of enterprising sons. His house served as a fort for the protection of the white inhabitants who were settled around him, to which all fled in the hour of danger, and many a fierce combat was fought around that little house. Cresap was the master-spirit, and always took the command, and marshaled his little band of stout hearts when the alarm was given that a party of marauding Indians were in the neighborhood. A braver band of pioneers never pulled the trigger.

The sons of Col. Thomas Cresap were Daniel, Thomas, and Michael. He had also two daughters.

In one of the conflicts with the Indians, after the latter had come stealthily upon the settlement and had murdered a family and stolen some of their horses, Cresap mustered his clan, pursued them, and surprised them on the side of the second mountain beyond Fort Cumberland, Will's Mountain being the first. The Indians separated and fled. Daniel Cresap, one of the colonel's sons, a young man of humane disposition and of remarkable fleetness of foot, observed a young Indian separate from his comrades and take a southerly course along the side of the mountain. Not wishing to shoot him, he pursued, and after a severe race overtook him. The Indian, finding that Cresap was gaining on him, would spring behind a tree and raise his gun, as though about to shoot. Cresap would shelter himself behind a tree, and after watching each other for a minute or two, the Indian would again run. This was repeated several times, when Cresap concluded that the Indian's gun was not loaded, because he had had several opportunities to shoot and had not done so. When at length they came to an open space, and the Indian, looking back, found that Cresap would overtake him before he could reach a shelter, he whirled round, and raised his gun to shoot. Cresap saw at once from his motion that he was mistaken in supposing that his gun was unloaded. He instantly took aim, and both guns went off at the same moment. The ball of the Indian passed through Cresap's lungs, and Cresap's ball through the abdomen of the Indian. Col. Cresap, hearing the report of the rifles, started in pursuit. When he came up with them he found the pursuer and pursued, both mortally wounded, lying within a short distance of each other. The Indian in the agonies of death begged that they would kill him, which they did. Cresap died of his wound before they got him off the mountain. The mountain was called "Dan's Mountain" after him, and has been known by that name from that day until this. Young "Dan" Cresap, on account of his generosity of spirit, was a great favorite with the mountaineers, who in giving the mountain his name have perpetuated the memory of his dramatic death.

Dan's Mountain forms the eastern verge of the coal basin of Allegany County. The mountain immediately west of "Dan's," and running parallel with it

FORT CUMBERLAND, 1755.

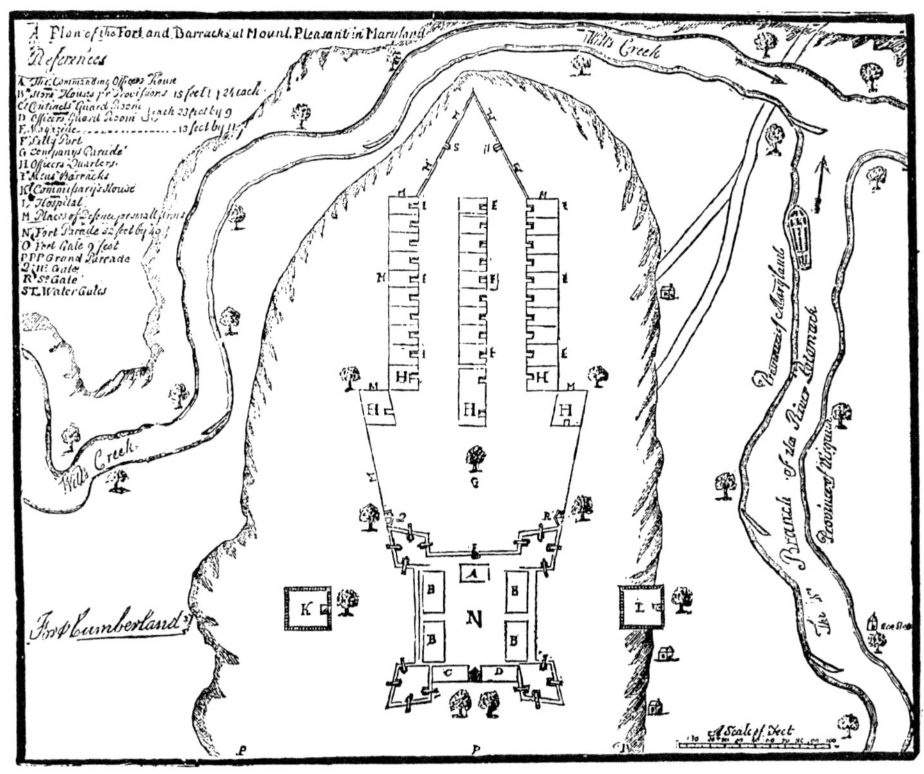

PLAN OF FORT CUMBERLAND IN 1755.

from south to north, is known as "Savage Mountain." It is a grand and noble elevation, rising some twenty-five hundred to three thousand feet above tide-water, is rough and rugged, and abounds in fine springs of pure sandstone water. Prior to the year 1760, and during the period when the habitations of the settlers were confined principally to "Cresap's Fort," or Skipton,—now called Oldtown, situated some fifteen miles below Cumberland, near the Potomac, opposite the present station of the Baltimore and Ohio Railroad, called "Green Spring Run,"—the Indian, who had been gradually driven westward, still held possession of this mountain. The whites, it is true, had located and then held Fort Cumberland, but they held but little save the inside of the fort.

The Indians who had been driven westward from the Conococheague, now within the present limits of Washington County, kept up a constant warfare upon this pioneer settlement. They would suddenly burst from the dense forest surrounding it, and sometimes would succeed in killing one or two of the inhabitants and driving off their cattle and horses. But as soon as they made their appearance and committed depredations, Col. Cresap, at the head of his pioneer band, would start in pursuit and generally succeed in chastising them, sometimes overtaking them on "Kobly" Mountain, sometimes on "Will's" Mountain, and sometimes upon "Dan's," but for many years never pursuing them as far as the mountain immediately west of the present village of Frostburg, called Savage Mountain. That mountain was left for years in the undisputed possession of the Indian. The grave of his father was there; it was the *ultima thule* to which he would retreat. There he made a desperate stand for many years; there he held his nightly war-dance, and recounted among the braves of his tribe the glorious war deeds of his father. In troublous times the deep glens of the mountain-passes and the dark lonely peaks of that grand old mountain were lighted by the beacon-fires of the savage foe. The white man, awed by the rugged grandeur of the lofty mountain and the deep and almost impenetrable forest which covered its side, halted when he had pursued his foe to its base, and called it the Savage Mountain, or the mountain belonging to the savage. Hence to this day the mountain is known by its original name,—"The Savage Mountain."

Years rolled on, and the tide of emigration flowed westward, and Col. Cresap's little colony at Skipton had become more than a match for the Indians. But one night the colony was aroused from sleep by the war-whoop of the savages. Col. Cresap, equal to every emergency, soon rallied his affrighted colonists, got them into the fort, and stood upon the defensive until the morning, when it was ascertained that a family had been murdered and some of the horses of the colonists taken. Pursuit was at once determined upon, and the colonel's order to that effect was given. In the morning, when the colonel came out of the fort, he found his body-servant, Nemesis, a large athletic negro, cleaning his rifle to be ready for the fray He said to him, "Well, Nemesis, are you ready for the fight?" Nemesis replied, "Yes, massa; but I don't come back." Col. Cresap jestingly said, "Well, Nemesis, if you are afraid of being killed, you can stay here with the women, and I will go without you." Nemesis hesitated a moment, and then replied, as he continued to clean his rifle, "Massa, you knows I's not afraid; where you go, I will go; where you fight, Nemesis will fight; but Nemesis will not come back." The colonel, feeling that he had wronged Nemesis, —for he was as brave a man as ever drew a trigger, —and touched also by the devotion of his servant to his person, said, "Nemesis, I did but joke; I know you are not afraid. You and I will keep together to-day; I will defend you with my life; and if I get into danger or difficulty, you will be by my side to aid me." With the morning light Cresap and his band of avengers were upon the Indians' trail. They pursued them over the Savage Mountain, and as far west as the next mountain, where they overtook them and had a severe battle, killing several of the Indians. Fighting bravely at his master's side, Nemesis was slain, and that mountain was named by his companions "Negro Mountain," and it is still known by that name.

Nemacolin, an Indian who was strongly attached to the Cresap family, and was employed by Col. Thomas Cresap to mark the route from Cumberland to Redstone, now Brownsville, on the Monongahela, performed his work so well that Gen. Braddock, who afterwards traversed the mountains in 1756, followed the path marked out by Nemacolin, and the present location of the National road varies but little from it. Nemacolin, after lingering for several years behind his brethren who had gone towards the setting sun, making his home with Daniel Cresap, followed his tribe; but before leaving he placed his son George with Daniel Cresap, and left him behind. George lived with the family for years, going occasionally on "the hunt," but always returning to Cresap's. He died at the family residence, in old age, cared for by the family of Thomas, the youngest son of Daniel, who resided in the family mansion, a stone house afterwards occupied by Moses Rawlings. This house is situated twelve miles above Cumberland by rail. "Indian George" for years had his hunting camp in the valley which lies between Dan's and Savage Mountains. The valley is traversed by a small stream which takes its rise at Frostburg, and running south empties into the Potomac at Westernport, opposite the village of Piedmont. The stream has been called "George's Creek" from this circumstance from that time to the present. The valley of George's Creek is the centre of the great coal region of Allegany County. The stream which takes its rise at the mines of the Cumberland Coal and Iron Company, east of Frostburg, and empties into Will's Creek immediately west of the point where Will's Creek finds a passage through the gorge of Will's Mountain, is called Braddock's Run, from the fact that Braddock's road passes along its banks during its whole course. The stream which rises north of Frostburg at the mines of the Frostburg Coal Company, and empties into Will's Creek four miles above Cumberland, was called "Jennings' Run" from the fact that a pioneer hunter by that name had his hunting station upon its banks. Thus we find that the mountains and the streams which flow at their base have received their names from the Indian or first white man who was known to have occupied or traversed them. The whole county from Town Creek, the stream dividing Allegany from Washington Counties, is traversed by mountains running from south to north from Town Hill to the "Big Back Bone," and geologically is a "transition formation," in which are usually found coal, iron, and lead. Coal and iron have long since been discovered in great abundance, but no lead has as yet been found, though there is a tradition, handed down from the earliest of the white settlers, that a very rich and productive lead-mine in the county or neighboring mountains of Virginia was known to the Indians. Out of this tradition a man named Paugh made some money by pretending to reveal the locality of the mine, as shown to him by Indian "George."

The city of Cumberland, the county-seat, is six hundred and forty-two feet above tide-water, at the junction of Will's Creek with the Potomac. The highest point of the National road is on "Kyser's Ridge," thirty miles west of Cumberland, two thousand eight hundred and forty-eight feet above tide, the highest peaks of the Alleganies in the county being about three thousand feet.

Of the early settlers one of the most noteworthy was Michael Cresap, the third son of Col. Thomas Cresap. Jefferson, in his "Notes on Virginia," calls him "Col. Michael Cresap." He was the first captain commissioned by Maryland in the Revolutionary war, and marched from Frederick County to Boston, where he joined the army under Gen. Washington. His health gave way under the hardships of a camp-life. He endeavored to reach home, but died in New York on the 5th of October, 1775. He was a man of great bravery, and one to whom all who knew him or lived within his reach looked as a leader in time of danger. This is shown by the fact that when it was known on the Ohio, among the frontier settlers where Capt. Cresap had lived, that Maryland had appointed him a captain in the Maryland Line, twenty of those daring spirits at once crossed the Alleganies, and joined his company and marched with him to Boston.[1]

[1] Jefferson, in his "Notes on Virginia," says, "Cresap was a man infamous for his many Indian murders." This charge was bitterly repelled by his son-in-law, Luther Martin, the great Maryland lawyer, and the charge has from that day to this been a source of annoyance to the numerous and highly respectable descendants of Capt. Cresap. In this connection Gen. Thomas J. McKaig furnishes the following: "Much has been written in defense of the memory of Capt. Cresap, but still the charge of Jefferson, owing to his high position and the exceeding beauty and eloquence of the speech put into the mouth of Logan, the Mingo chief, has gone far to fix the stain of that atrocious murder on the fair fame of Capt. Cresap. It may be asked of the writer, What do you know of the murder of the family of Logan? I answer, more than Jefferson ever knew, and more than any man now living. I was born in Steubenville, on the Ohio River, ten miles below Baker's Fort, where Logan's family were murdered, and have heard the story of these murders from Andrew and Adam Poe, who participated in the fight with these Indians on the Ohio, and 'Old Pugh,' all of whom lived in the neighborhood at the time of the murder, and I had the same identical story of the murder from Benjamin Tomlinson, of this county (Allegany County, Md.), after I came to this State to reside. I had therefore an opportunity of comparing the statements of the different individuals, all of whom knew personally the facts, but had no opportunity of comparing their statements with each other, and had no motive for misrepresenting the facts; and they all told the same story, or at least all agreed that Capt. Cresap had nothing to do with the murder, that he was not even present, and that he was at Wheeling, forty miles below Baker's Fort; that those who committed the murder did not even know Capt. Cresap, or that Capt. Cresap was at Wheeling, for he belonged to a settlement at the Flats of Grove Creek, now Moundsville, some twenty-two miles below Wheeling, and had gone up to the fort at Wheeling because of the disturbances then going on between the Indian and the white men,—the one struggling to maintain his frontier settlement on the Ohio, the other to stop the further progress of the white men.

"Jefferson wrote his 'Notes of Virginia' from papers collected and filed in the archives of the province at Richmond in 1787, some thirteen years after the murder of the family of Logan at Baker's fort, and it is fair to presume that he knew, personally, nothing of the transactions of which he wrote. I had the personal history of the matter from those who were present and saw who were present and what passed. Jefferson was not present, and therefore did not, nor does he pretend to, speak of the murder from any personal knowledge of his own; nor does he say that he had any knowledge of the transaction save what he got from the supposed speech of Logan, which he found filed among the papers connected with the war with the Indians at the time the Earl of Dunmore was Governor of Virginia. I had a history of the transaction from those who were present.

HEIGHT OF THE ALLEGANIES ABOVE TIDE-WATER.

	Feet.		Feet.
At Cumberland	537	At Barren Hill	2450
Wills Mountain	1003	Woodcock Hill	2500
Frostburg	1792	Laurel Hill	2412
Great Savage Mountain	2580	Munroe Village	1065
Little Savage Mountain	2480	Uniontown	952
Boruby Hill	2437	Conly Hill	1274
Red Hill	2437	Brownsville	833
Meadow Mountain	2550	Krebb's Hill	1040
Little Crossings	1999	Belleville	1010
Negro Mountain	2825	Hillsborough	1770
Keyser's Ridge	2843	Equars Hill	1532
Winding Ridge	2534	Washington, Pa.	1406
Smithfield	1405	Alexandria	1792
		Wheeling Hill	850
		Washington City	748

Early Roads. — Braddock's road was made in 1754, under the direction of the Ohio Company, aided by traders and Indians, and was the one that had been blazed by Nemacolin when he and Col. Cresap first chose a route over the mountains. It was subsequently followed by Braddock's army through the advice of Sir John St. Clair. It went from Will's Creek through the valley which is now Green Street. It was used as the only road to the West until 1818, when the National road was made, the latter crossing the former at various points. This old road is as visible to-day as a century ago, though in its bed in many places immense trees are growing. Just where the Cresaptown road leads off, about a hundred yards east of Mr. Steel's residence on the National road, the Braddock road bore a little to the north, and ran straight to almost the top of Will's Mountain at a steep grade, and then descended to the bed of the National pike at Sandy Gap. Here it crossed the valley of the present National road to the base of the hills. Near the "Five-Mile House" it crossed from the left to the right of the National road, and ran almost parallel with it to within two hundred yards of the "Six-Mile House." When Col. Bouquet proposed his expedition of 1758, Washington thought it would be made over the Braddock road. But the colonel announced his intention of building a new road from Raystown to the Ohio River, and of marching part of his army by that route, and the other portion by Braddock's road, the two bodies to form a junction on the Monongahela. He was induced to this course by the dispatches of Braddock, which led him to the belief that the old road was almost impassable, and by interested persons in Pennsylvania, who told him a new one with light grades could be easily made. Washington, who had used the old road in 1754 and 1755, wrote as follows to Bouquet:

"CAMP NEAR FORT CUMBERLAND, 25 July, 1758.

"DEAR SIR,—I shall most cheerfully work on any road, pursue any route, or enter upon any service that the general (Forbes) or yourself may think me usefully employed in or qualified for, and shall never have a will of my own when a duty is required of me. But since you desire me to speak my sentiments freely, permit me to observe that after having conversed with all the guides, and having been informed by others who have a knowledge of the country, I am convinced that a road to be compared with General Braddock's road, or, indeed, that will be fit for transportation even by pack-horses, cannot be made. I have no predilection for the route you have in contemplation for me, not because difficulties appear therein, but because I doubt whether satisfaction can be given in the execution of the plan. I know not what reports you may have received from your reconnoitring parties, but I have been uniformly told that if you expect a tolerable road by Raystown you will be disappointed, for no movement can be made that way without destroying our horses."

Gen. Forbes, however, determined upon the new route through Pennsylvania from Raystown.

Washington wrote again from Fort Cumberland on Aug. 2, 1758, stating the advantages of Braddock's over the proposed new road. The new road was made, but the sequel proved that Washington was right, for in the march over the obstacles were nearly insurmountable, and the army's progress greatly retarded, while, if Braddock's road had been taken, not half the time would have been consumed nor so many horses lost.

Road from Fort Frederick to Fort Cumberland. —In December, 1758, the General Assembly considered the state of the road between Fort Frederick and Fort Cumberland, with the object of constructing a shorter route between these two important forts which should be all in Maryland, and thus save the necessity of fording the Potomac River.

Col. Thomas Cresap, Joseph Chapline, E. Dorsey, Josias Beall, Francis King, and Capt. Crabb were ap-

"Benjamin Tomlinson went before a magistrate on the 17th of April, 1797, and made oath that he was present when Logan's family were murdered, and that Michael Cresap was not present, and that the murder was committed by a party of men from Buffalo. If, therefore, Benjamin Tomlinson is worthy of belief, the matter in controversy is settled. Then who was Benjamin Tomlinson? and was he worthy of credit on oath? I am free to admit that the question resolves itself into the query, 'Was Benjamin Tomlinson worthy of belief on oath?' He has sworn he was present at the time the murder was perpetrated, and that Cresap was not present. If he is worthy of belief, then is the charge false and the statement a cruel libel on the character of one who sacrificed his life in the cause of his country.

"When the writer came to reside in Allegany County, Benjamin Tomlinson was an old man of more than seventy years, residing within four miles of Cumberland. He was a man of high character, large property, and singularly pure life. No man stood higher as a man of truth and veracity than he. I will venture the assertion that there never was a man in this county who had a more enviable reputation. Benjamin Tomlinson was no ordinary man. He was, in point of intellect, one of the first men in the county, and filled all the prominent offices of the county, and that, too, at a time when no one was chosen to fill an office because of his party services."

pointed a committee to inquire into the feasibility of clearing up a new road between these points through the province of Maryland, and to estimate its cost. Their report was as follows:

"Your committee have made an inquiry into the situation of the present wagon-road from Fort Frederick to Fort Cumberland, and are of the opinion that the distance by that road from one fort to the other is at least eighty miles, and find that the wagons which go from one fort to the other are obliged to pass the river Potowmack twice, and that for one-third of the year they can't pass without boats to set them over the river.

"Your committee have also made an inquiry into the condition of the ground where a road may be made most conveniently to go altogether on the north side of the Potowmack, which will not exceed the distance of sixty-two miles, at the expense of £250 current money, as may appear from the following estimate, viz.:

"An estimate of the expense of clearing the road from Fort Frederick to Fort Cumberland, and the several different stages:

	£	s.	d.
For clearing a road from Fort Frederick to Licking Creek, 3½ miles	0	0	0
From Licking Creek to Prakes' Creek, 8½ miles	12	0	0
From Prakes' Creek to Sideling Hill Creek, 12 miles	16	0	0
For a bridge over Sideling Hill Creek	60	0	0
From Sideling Hill Creek to Fifteen Mile Creek, 4 miles	22	0	0
From Fifteen Mile Creek to Town Creek, 15 miles	140	0	0
From Town Creek to Col. Cresap's, a good road, 4 miles	0	0	0
From Col. Cresap's to Fort Cumberland, wants no clearing, 15 miles	0	0	0
	£250	0	0

"Your committee are of the opinion that a road through Maryland will contribute much to lessen the expense of carrying provision and warlike stores from Fort Frederick to Fort Cumberland, and will induce many people to travel and carry on a trade in and through the province, to and from the back country."

The road was finally built, and was of great use in settling up the western part of the province.

In compliance with an act of the Legislature incorporating a company to make a turnpike road from the Pennsylvania line, to intersect the road then making by the Somerset and Cumberland turnpike company, and thence in the direction of Cumberland, to intersect the National road, subscription books were opened at Slicer's hotel, in Cumberland, on the first Monday in August, 1833, by the commissioners,—Bene S. Pigman, William McMahon, Jacob Snyder, Gustavus Beall, John M. Buchanan, Joseph Everstine, George Blocher, Martin Rizer, Jacob Tomlinson.

"The Northwestern Turnpike Company, of Allegany," through its commissioners,—Alexander Smith, Frederick A. Castings, Jonathan W. Magruder, George Reinhart, John McHenry, and John Hoyer,—opened books for subscription Aug. 26, 1833, to make a turnpike road from the North Branch of the Potomac River, at the point where the "Northwestern turnpike of Virginia" crosses said river, which was near Alexander Smith's; thence through that part of Maryland lying between the North Branch of said river and the western boundary line of said State, to intersect the "Northwestern turnpike of Virginia" near George H. A. Kunst's, a distance of about nine miles.

In 1834 the Allegany County commissioners laid out a new road from the George's Creek road, that intersected the National road near Jesse Tomlinson's, to begin near Casper Hiller's, and from thence to intersect the Cherry-Tree Meadow road, near Christian Garlitz's.

They also made alterations on a road laid out four years previous, from the mouth of Mill Run, on George's Creek, to intersect the National road near Jesse Tomlinson's.

The following persons received contracts for making and repairing the National road (First Division):

1st Culvert Section, Jonathan Witt; 2d Culvert Section, R. A. Clements.

New Location, Section No. 2, Gustavus Beall; No. 3, Mattingly & Mulholland; No. 4, Edmund Bulger; No. 5, Cahone & Moore; No. 6, Miller, Baker & Co.; No. 7, Lonogan, O'Neal & Kennedy; No. 8, Thomas Feely.

Old Road, Section No. 9, R. A. Clements; No. 10, Hewes, Stewart & Howard; No. 11, John Neff; No. 12, Josiah Porter; No. 13, Hewes, Stewart & Co.; No. 14, Meshack Frost; No. 15, Joseph Dilley; No. 16, Isaiah Frost; No. 17, T. Beall & Coombs; No. 18, M. Meneer; No. 19, Adam Shooltre; No. 20, Michael McGaverin.

Mr. Fielding had the contract for building the second bridge.[1]

United States National Road.—In 1806 a road leading from Cumberland to the State of Ohio was laid out as follows:

"Beginning at a stone at the corner of lot No. 1, in Cumberland, near the confluence of Will's Creek and the north branch of the Potomac River; thence extending along the street westwardly to cross the hill lying between Cumberland and Gwynn's at the gap where Braddock's road passes it; thence near

[1] On June 24, 1831, for the summer season, the post-office adopted the following schedule of time for the opening and closing of mails:

For the West, every day at 9 o'clock A.M.

For the East, the same.

For Virginia, every Tuesday, Thursday, and Saturday at 9 o'clock A.M.

Old Town, every Sunday at 11 A.M.

Westernport, the same.

Berlin, every Thursday at 9 P.M.

Bedford, *via* Rainsburg, every Tuesday at 9 P.M.

The office was open for the delivery of letters during the week from 5 o'clock A.M. until sunset, except on Sunday, when it was open from 10 to 11 in the morning only.

Persons wishing to pay the postage on letters to go by mail when the office was closed inclosed the letter and amount of postage in an envelope and directed to the postmaster.

Persons having intercourse with the post-office observed the above arrangements, as they were strictly adhered to by the postmaster, Mr. Joseph P. Carleton.

Gwynn's and Jesse Tomlinson's, to cross the Big Youghiogeny near the mouth of Roger's Run, between the crossing of Braddock's road and the confluence of the streams which form the Turkey Foot; thence to cross Laurel hill near the forks of Dunbar's Run, to the west foot of that hill, at a point near where Braddock's old road reached it near Guest's old place, now Col. Isaac Mason's; thence through Brownsville and Bridgeport to cross the Monongahela River below Josias Crawford's ferry; and thence on as straight a course as the country will admit to the Ohio River at a point below the mouth of Wheelen Creek and the lower point of Wheelen Island."

This road was one hundred and seventeen miles in length, of which twenty-four passed through Maryland. It was laid out by Joseph Kerr and Thomas Moore. In July, 1813, thirty-four miles of it had been constructed from Cumberland to Brownsville, Pa., or at least worked upon. It was to have been thirty feet wide. The whole cut of timber was to be sixty feet wide, and the road-bed, to the width of twenty feet, to be covered with stone twelve inches deep, none longer than three inches, and the artificial stratum to be supported on each side by good and solid shoulders.

The National turnpike, which led over the Alleganies from the east to the west, is a glory departed, and the traffic that once belonged to it now courses through other channels; but it still lives in the memories of some of the aged citizens of Allegany County, and not infrequently a glow of excitement and enthusiasm will mantle their cheeks when mention is made of it. Those who have participated in the traffic over that renowned thoroughfare are loth to admit that there were ever before such landlords, such taverns, such dinners, such whisky, such bustle, or such endless cavalcades of coaches and wagons as could be seen between Wheeling and Frederick in the palmy days of the old National "pike." And it is certain that when coaching days were palmy, no other post-road in the country did the same amount of business as this fine old highway, which opened the West and Southwest to the East. The wagons were so numerous that the leaders of one team had their noses in the trough at the end of the wagon ahead, and the coaches, drawn by four or six horses, dashed along at a speed of which few have any conception. Besides the coaches and wagons, there were gentlemen traveling singly in the saddle, with all the accoutrements of the journey stuffed into their saddle-bags, and there were enormous droves of sheep and herds of cattle, which at times blocked the way for miles and elicited from the travelers expressions of disgust often "more striking than classic."

The old National road has echoed to the tread of great men. Clay, Jackson, Taylor, Harrison, Houston, Polk, Crockett, and a host of others were wont to pass over it on their way to the national capital.

The compactness of the traffic secured it from marauders to some extent, but the traveler by coach had his expedition spiced by the occasional assaults of highwaymen, or road agents, as they are more elegantly styled in modern times, and there are places along the pike whose very names bespeak the terrors they occasioned in the olden times. Nearly every mile had its tavern, and every tavern its pretty maid or jovial host.

There were rival lines of coaches, and the competition led to overdriving and many accidents. The passengers became partisans of the line by which they traveled, and execrated the opposition and its patrons. The threats of the disputants were often emphasized by an exhibition of bowie-knives and pistols, which more than once led to the verge of a battle. But among themselves the passengers in each coach were fraternally intimate, and the driver was usually an old hand, who could tell stories by the hour to beguile his companions on the box-seat.

The rival lines brought rival taverns into existence, and as the two opposition coaches drove into a town for supper, they pulled up before separate houses. The survivors of the old days are united in giving credit for the uniform excellence of all the taverns. They were clean, spacious, generously conducted, and in some instances so durably built that they are still in good condition. The gilded and glittering sign swung out from a pole or staff, and a moss-grown trough overflowed and trickled melodiously before the porch, at one end of which an archway led into the stable-yard. The interior was substantially furnished, without filigree or veneer. The floors were sanded, and the beams in the ceiling were uncovered. An hour before the coach was due the landlord was to be found in a little alcove of the tap-room transferring his liquors from demijohns to bottles, setting his glasses in single file, and bidding his servants make haste with the supper. The villagers appeared at their doors; for the arrival of the coach, although a very familiar event, acquired a fresh interest from day to day, and as they glanced towards the curve at the foot of the hill, their anticipations were soon fulfilled. Here it came, ahead of time, swaying and pitching perilously, the horses at full gallop, and the driver swinging his whip with a pistol-like snap over their heads. No sooner did mine host at the table hear it than, with a parting admonition to the kitchen, he hastened to the porch, and stood there with a smiling face, the picture of welcome, as the coach rounded up under the elms and chestnuts, and the driver threw his reins to the waiting hostlers.

Most of the travelers were the farmers, stock-raisers, and "merchandisers" of the West, dressed in homespun cloth and buckskin; but a few indicated familiarity with the usages of polite society by their costumes; and in the case of the statesmen bound to Washington, it was the custom to blend urbanity of speech with loftiness of manner in such discreetly measured proportions that the combination preserved the dignity of the representative, and satisfied the self-esteem of the constituent with a degree of success that might excite the emulation of politicians in our own time.

Although there was no unreasonable haste, ten miles an hour, including delays, was not an unusual degree of speed in the days of stage-coaches. According to John E. Reeside, of Washington, who drove over the road, four kinds of coaches were used on the "pike" at different periods. The first was built at Cumberland by Abraham Russell, and carried sixteen passengers; and when this was found too cumbrous, a lighter vehicle, almost egg-shaped, and built at Trenton, was adopted. The latter was succeeded by the Troy coach, carrying nine passengers inside and two outside, which was finally superseded by the familiar Concord.[1]

The traffic seemed like a frieze with an endless procession of figures. There were sometimes sixteen gayly-painted coaches each way a day; the cattle and sheep were never out of sight; the canvas-covered wagons were drawn by six or twelve horses, with bows of bells over their collars; the families of statesmen and merchants went by in private vehicles; and, while most of the travelers were unostentatious, a few had splendid equipages and employed outriders. Some of the passes through the Alleganies were as precipitous as any in the Sierra Nevada, and the mountains were as wild. Within a mile of the road the country was a wilderness; but on the highway the traffic was as dense and as continuous as in the main street of a large town.

The National road proper was built from Cumberland, Md., to Wheeling, Va., by the United States government, the intention being to establish it as far as St. Louis. It was excellently macadamized; the rivers and creeks were spanned by stone bridges; the distances were indexed by iron mile-posts, and the toll-houses supplied with strong iron gates. Its projector and chief supporter was Henry Clay, whose services in its behalf are commemorated by a monument near Wheeling. Henry Beeson, a former congressman, was also an advocate of it, and on one occasion he made a public speech, in which he showed the audience—so flexible are arithmetic and imagination combined—that from the number of horse-shoes it would necessitate, and the number of nails, it was better adapted to promote trade than any railway could be. This road, which was completed in 1821, is one hundred and twenty-one miles long. From Cumberland to Baltimore the road, or a large part of it, was built by certain banks of Maryland, which were rechartered in 1816, on condition that they should complete the work.[2] So far from being a

[1] When other diversions were lacking, when there was no opposition to storm at, when all the good stories had been told, and the current events discussed until they were threadbare, the passengers sometimes amused themselves by holding letters at arms'-length out of the windows, and beckoning to the villagers, who, supposing the missives were for them, would follow the coach for many a weary league. One day the trick was practiced upon Daniel Oster, who, to the gratification of the passengers, pursued the coach up a long and precipitous hill. The distance between him and them was so great that it did not seem likely that he could reach them. Oster was not to be trifled with, however. He knew that they had no letter for him, but he had a public-spirited ambition to make an example of the inconsiderate wag. "Who has a letter for me?" he fiercely demanded, when he had overtaken the coach, and ordered the driver to stop. None of the passengers answered, and Oster supplied himself with a variety of unpleasant-looking missiles. "If you don't confess which one it is, I'll pepper and salt the whole crowd," he said. Finding that the actual transgressor was willing to impose a vicarious sacrifice upon them, the passengers unimplicated surrendered him to Oster, who dragged him out of the coach and gave him a merciless thrashing. "Now," he said, "don't fool me any more." And it is said that, in his neighborhood, at least, the amusement soon became obsolete. He was well known along the "pike" for the force and integrity of his character. Though somewhat small in stature, he had great courage and determination. One day a high-handed traveler refused to pay toll at a gate kept by an unprotected woman, and Oster, learning the circumstance, persistently followed him for a whole day. He left the road and went into the woods; still Oster was at his heels; he drew his pistols and threatened to shoot, but Oster "got the drop on him." At last he offered to pay the toll, double, triple, quadruple. Oster was implacable. "I mean," he said, "to follow you into the next town and put you in the lock-up." He fulfilled his word, and only then was satisfied. The animosities between passengers by rival lines were intensified in the drivers, and an instance is on record of a race which was ended by a prolonged "set-to." The teams were so well matched that, strained to the utmost, one could not pass the other, and when the drivers had exhausted their prolific vocabulary of invective, they decided to settle their differences by a combat, a resolve that was gleefully abetted by the passengers. Their proficiency and strength seemed to be as well balanced as the speed of the horses, and they buffeted one another for an hour or more before a decisive point was reached.

[2] It was called the Cumberland or Bank road, the following banks having subscribed the amounts stated for its construction:

burden to them, it proved to be their most lucrative property for many years, yielding as much as twenty per cent.; and it is only of late years that it has yielded no more than two or three per cent. The part built by the Federal government was transferred to Maryland some years ago, and the tolls became a political perquisite; but within the past three years it has been acquired by the counties of Allegany and Garrett, which have made it free.

Before Braddock's road had been passed over by his expedition it was a mere pathway, by which the footman and an occasional horseman could reach the frontier in trafficking with the Indians. This now historic road when made was of sufficient capacity to pass vehicles; but it was simply a removal of timbers and rocks; there was no engineering, grading, or smoothing. Scarcely a wagon passed over it for the first thirty years. Such heavy articles as salt, iron, etc., were carried from the East to the West over the mountains on pack-horses.

As the eastern part of the country increased in wealth and population, its accretions moved to the opposite direction over this route, and in time it became the most important thoroughfare in the country to the inviting West. Its lines in many places, upon inspection, can still be identified. A full-grown cherry-tree stood a few years ago in the centre of Braddock's road, on the farm of Mr. Geo. F. Gephart. It was entirely abandoned over sixty years ago, and every tavern and building that once lined it has entirely disappeared. The Tomlinson Hotel, the most noted of all, built over a hundred years ago, was torn down about fifteen years ago. Its site is now a truck-patch.

After the organization of the general government, in 1789, the tide from the East to the West, mainly over this way, increased steadily, so much so that the road became worn out and utterly inadequate to the public necessities, and this decayed public artery was the first to receive national treatment.

As far back as 1806, the year in which Henry Clay was admitted into the United States Senate, the sum of $30,000 was appropriated to open and make the "Cumberland road" from Cumberland to the Ohio River. From this time on it was known as the "Cumberland" road. In 1810, $60,000 were appropriated to be spent between Cumberland and Brownsville, Pa. In 1811, $50,000 were appropriated to be applied between the same points; in 1812, $30,000, to be used within the same limits; and in 1815, $30,000; in 1818, the sums of $52,984 and $260,000 were appropriated for the Cumberland road generally.

In 1820, $10,000 were appropriated preliminary to its extension from Wheeling west. In 1823, $250,000 were appropriated for the road between Cumberland and Wheeling. This law for the first time authorized a superintendent to be appointed by the President. In 1825, $150,000 were given to be used between Canton and Zanesville, Ohio; in 1827, $30,000 between Cumberland and Wheeling; in 1829, $100,000 to extend the road beyond Zanesville, Ohio; in 1831, the aggregate sum of $244,915.85 was appropriated for the same object in Ohio, Indiana, and Illinois. In 1832, $150,000 were appropriated to be used east of the Ohio River. The law of 1833, ch. 79, is an assent to the act of Virginia, taking control of her part of the road. The act of 1834 appropriated $450,000 to be applied in Ohio, Indiana, and Illinois, and $300,000 east of the Ohio River. In 1835, $200,000 in Ohio, $100,000 in Indiana, and $346,186.58 were appropriated for the road east of the Ohio. This was the last money voted by Congress for the road east of the Ohio River. In 1836, $200,000 were given to Ohio's part, $250,000 to Indiana, and $150,000 to Illinois, and in 1838 the sum of $150,000 was appropriated to each of these rising States,—that is, for the road within the limits of each State, this being the last money voted by Congress for the National road.

Most of the sums spent east of the Ohio River came from the general funds of the government, but the money applied on the road in Ohio, Indiana, and Illinois was taken entirely from the proceeds of the sales of the public lands within these States.

The "Cumberland road" began on the west side of Will's Creek. Crossing Will's Mountain at Sandy Gap, it followed the general route of Braddock, rarely, however, using that road as a bed. It appears that Brownsville was the first objective point to be reached. The manner of construction was first to clear and grade the bed and then to closely overlay it with strong flat rock, and upon this face or foundation was placed a covering of well-broken stone and earth. It was officially styled the "Cumberland road," but popularly

Union Bank of Maryland	$142,353.49
Bank of Baltimore	75,413.53
City Bank of Baltimore	54,585.01
Mechanics' Bank of Baltimore	42,938.18
Commercial and Farmers' Bank of Baltimore.	41,059.63
Farmers' and Merchants' Bank of Baltimore.	31,197.27
Franklin Bank of Baltimore	27,842.72
Bank of Maryland	20,127.27
Hagerstown Bank	16,772.72
Marine Bank of Baltimore	15,766.36
Conococheague Bank	10,566.81
Cumberland Bank	7,547.72
Total	$486,170.71

it was known as the National road, because built by the government, and no man did as much for it as its great friend Henry Clay. He was affectionately called its father, and he passed over it many times in his forty-five years of public service. Its costly stone bridges and culverts are all to-day as sound and safe as when built, except the parapet walls, which have been thrown down by maliciously disposed persons. Although much repaired, these structures still have a despoiled appearance from such vandalism. Two of these, the Little and Big Crossings, about twenty miles apart, are quite different from the bridges now in use. The former, with its immense semicircular arch of great width and height, is a never-failing source of admiration to the engineer of to-day. Such a work can be built now with one-half the labor and cost, but in 1815 it was a triumph of engineering skill. In after-years the superintendent and engineer, David Shriver, told of the anxiety which consumed him. The great arch rested upon a strong wooden structure, which was so arranged as to be thrown down by taking away a key, somewhat after the manner of launching a vessel. The general impression was that when the wood-work was removed the magnificent archway would follow in a chaotic mass.

The time was fixed for the ceremony, for they had such things in those days. Failure would be ruin to the great work as well as himself, so the courageous superintendent had his misgivings. But the night before he and a few of his aids secretly removed the key, and in this way tested its safety. The day came, and the launch was made in safety and to the satisfaction of the assembled multitude.

Notwithstanding the large sums of money appropriated for and expended on the old National road, the year 1830 found it in a worn-out and almost useless condition. Traffic and travel on it had increased heavily. Little of it was left except the rough stone bed. The old patching system of repairing here and there with a few broken stone would not answer. It would wear and wash away suddenly. It was seen that a new plan had to be adopted. Macadamizing was decided upon, and carried into effect.

This great national enterprise was commenced about the year 1832, and was accomplished under the supervision of the War Department. Some of the most prominent and talented young men of the army were especially selected as engineers, such as Lieut. Mansfield, and Capts. Delafield, McKee, Bliss, Hetzell, Williams, Colquit, and Cass, all West Pointers. A word as to the fate of these young men: Mansfield fell at the battle of Antietam, a major-general in the United States army; Williams fell at the storming of Monterey, in Mexico, along with Lieut.-Col. William H. Watson, of Maryland; and Col. McKee at Buena Vista, in the same country; Maj. Hetzell died on his return from the Mexican war, at Louisville; Gen. Delafield and Col. Bliss died but recently; Gen. Colquit, of South Carolina, followed the fortunes of his State during the civil war, and died before its conclusion. George M. Cass, a nephew of the great statesman of that name, still survives, and is, or was not long since, president of the Pittsburgh, Fort Wayne and Chicago Railroad Company.

LIEUT.-COL. WM. H. WATSON.

During this reconstruction of the road its route by way of Green Street, Cumberland, and Sandy Gap was changed to Mechanic Street and through the narrows, and on to the "Old Burnt House," where it again connected with the former route. This change was made in 1834, and was a great improvement. Limestone was quarried wherever it could be obtained, and in some instances was hauled as much as ten miles by teams of four and six horses. When the stone was properly broken it was spread with a horse-rake over the bed of the road to a depth of about nine inches. The hardships of heavily-laden wagons in passing over such a bottom can be readily imagined. All sorts of stratagems were resorted to to compel vehicles to pass over these compact stones. No doubt there was as much swearing done in those days by the teamsters as the Dutch soldiers did in Flanders. However, in time the road became packed and solidified, and as smooth as some avenues in Washington City. From about 1834 to 1845 it was the finest road in America, and in all probability in the world, considering its length, reaching from Baltimore to or near St. Louis.

The line of the Baltimore and Ohio Railroad reached Cumberland from the east in the fall of 1842, and here it rested until 1849. During this interval the National road was a substitute for the present railroad to the Ohio River. The many warehouses in Cumberland in the spring and fall seasons would be choked with freight for the West. Sometimes weeks would elapse before it could be moved, on account of a deficiency in transportation. Many people in those days made wagoning a distinct and profitable business, and in the busy seasons a number of small teams called sharpshooters made their appearance on the pike, to the disgust of the regular carriers. No toll was charged upon this road until the act of the General Assembly of 1831, which authorized not more than two toll-gates in Maryland. This act also authorized the government to appoint a superintendent, with a salary of five hundred dollars, an office of great influence. The act of 1835 further regulated the tolls. The canal and the railway have superseded the old National pike, and it is not often now that a traveler disturbs the dust that has accumulated on it.

The dust, indeed, has settled and given root to grass and shrubbery, which in many places show how complete the decadence is. The black-snakes, moccasins, and copperheads, that were always plentiful in the mountains, have become so unused to the intrusion of man that they sun themselves in the centre of the highway. Many of the villages which were prosperous in the coaching days have fallen asleep, and the wagon of a peddler or farmer is alone seen where once the travel was enormous.

The men who were actively engaged on the road as drivers, station-agents, and mail-contractors are nearly all dead. The few that remain are very old and decrepit. But the taverns, with their hospitable and picturesque fronts, the old smithies, and the toll-gates have not entirely been swept away. Enough has been left to sustain the interest and individuality of the highway, which from Frederick to Cumberland is rich by dower of Nature, independently of its past.

A correspondent of *Harper's Monthly*, who made a journey over the road in 1879, writes: "We made Frederick our starting-point, and entered it from the fertile meadows basined in the Blue Ridge, which are as sunny and as tranquil as the description of them in Whittier's poem. We hired a team to Cumberland. The driver's whip cracked, and Frederick was soon invisible by reason of the foliage which engirths it. Placid meadows were on both sides of us; the Blue Ridge was like a cloud in the south, and ahead of us was the famous highway, dipping and rising by many alternations towards a hazy line of hills in the west, like a thread of white drawn through the verdant meadows. The chestnuts made arches over it, and divided its borders with tulip poplars and the blossoming locusts, which filled the air with fragrance. A Roman highway buried under the farm-lands of England could not be more in contrast with the activity of its past than this. The winding undulations revealed no travelers; some of the old taverns with windows out gaped vacantly, while a few others were occupied; a part of the toll-houses were abandoned, and those which do double duty find so little business that the keeper combines his occupation with that of the cobbler or blacksmith. Reaching the crest of the hill, we found the Middletown Valley below us,—as fair a prospect and as fertile and beautiful a reach of country as the world contains, and it was through here that Lee came 'marching down, horse and foot, into Frederick Town.' South Mountain was purple in the west; and the gap of Harper's Ferry gave an inlet to the valley on the southwest. Up here the Union artillery swept the meadows, reaping a different harvest from that which is now ripening; and every acre has known the anguish and fierce heat of war's arbitrament. Midway in the valley, and bordering the highway, which courses in a straight line, stands the sleepy little village of Middletown, embowered in the chestnuts, oaks, and locusts. All the visible inhabitants were loafing and yawning under the foliage at the doors of the shops, on the porch of the tavern, or under the wide eaves of the cottages. Then we toiled up the South Mountain, upon which the prolific growth of the chestnut forms endless zigzag lines, dotted with occasional pines: the grade is very heavy, but the coaches went up at a gallop, and came down without brakes. On the farther side is Boonsboro', and between Boonsboro' and Hagerstown the first macadam pavement used in the United States was laid. Hagerstown has suffered little by the withdrawal of the coaches; it is the busy and crowded seat of a Maryland county; but its old citizens lament the change, and cherish their reminiscences of the day when the 'pike' was in its glory.

"'From here to Boonsboro',' said Mr. Eli Mobley, an old coach-maker, to us, 'the road was the finest in the United States, and I have seen the mail-coaches travel from Hagerstown to Frederick, twenty-six miles, in two hours. That was not an unusual thing either, and there were through freight-wagons from Baltimore to Wheeling which carried ten ton, and made nearly as good time as the coaches. They were drawn by ten horses, and the rear wheels were ten feet high. Although there was so much traffic, the mountains were very wild, and sometimes you would find a bear or deer on the road. The snakes were powerful abundant. South Mountain was full of 'em,—black-snakes, copperheads, moccasins, and rattlesnakes, I've seen Clay and Jackson often; neither of them was handsome, and one thing that strikes me is the fidelity of all the likenesses I've seen of 'em. Jackson and his family came along quite often, the family in a private carriage and the general on horseback, which he changed now and then for a seat in the vehicle. He was very fond of horses, and his own were something to look at. Once I was in Wheeling when the general was expected to arrive, and a friend of mine, Daniel Steinrode, had purchased a team which he intended to present to him. Steinrode had a speech prepared, and the horses beautifully groomed. The arrival of the general was announced, and he went forth to meet him with the speech and the team; but when he reached the Ohio River, he found Jackson going down stream, and waving his hat to a crowd from the stern of the boat. Steinrode was very much crestfallen, and I had to laugh at him until my sides ached.' An echo of the mirth convulsed the old gentleman now, and when he recovered he spoke of Clay, who was 'courteous, but not familiar.' One time Clay was coming East on the mail-coach, which was upset upon a pile of limestone in the streets of Uniontown. After the accident he relighted his cigar, looked after the other passengers, and said, "This, gentlemen, is undoubtedly mixing the Clay of Kentucky with the limestone of Pennsylvania." Mr. Clay was a very witty man, and very clever, too. He bowed to every one along the road who bowed to him.' Another survivor of the old 'pike' is Samuel Nimmy, a patriarchal African, who played tambourine for Gen. Jackson and drove on the road for many years. He is an odd mixture of shrewdness, intelligence, and egotism. His recollections are vivid and detailed in point of names and dates, although he is eighty-six years old, and he describes his experiences in a grandiose manner that is occasionally made delicious by solecisms or sudden lapses into negro colloquialisms. He lives in a comfortable cottage at Hagerstown; the walls of his parlor are hung with certificates of membership in various societies, and with various patriotic chromos; the centre-table is loaded with books, principally on negro emancipation and the events of the civil war.

"West of Cumberland the road was bordered by an extraordinary growth of pines, the branches of which were so intermeshed that they admitted very little daylight, and from its prevailing darkness the grove was called the 'Shades of Death.'

Uncle Sam Nimmy and others declare that on the most effulgent day not a ray ever penetrated it, and that it was absolutely black, which is a piece of picturesque exaggeration. It was very dark, however, according to the statements of more exact observers, including Mr. B. F. Reinhart, the well-known painter, and it afforded a favorable opportunity for highwaymen. 'I had a very keen team, sir,' said Uncle Sam; 'a very keen team indeed, and nobody knows more about a horse than I do. I drove that team, sir, nine months without the least sickness to the horses, and I flatter myself that we had some rough service. Well, sir, one day I was driving through the Shades of Death with a few passengers. It was darker than usual; it was Cimmerian—Cimmerian, sir; and one said to me, "Don't you hear the sound of horses walking?" I listened. I did hear the sound of walking, and seemed to see—although it was so dark—several figures in the woods. Some one then opened the pistol-case and examined the weapons. The flint had been removed from each pistol, and about that time, sir, my hair began to get curly. The passengers did not like the way affairs were looking, and I thought that if big men were scared there was no reason why a little one shouldn't be scared too. I admit, sir, I was scared, and I just assure you, gentlemen, that I made every horse tell until we came to a tavern. But I wasn't naturally timid; I was puzzled as to how the flints came out of those pistols, and we never could unravel the mystery. I've had a varied life, sir, and always took an interest in general travel to see if any one was bigger than I was, sir. I started a company of volunteers in the war, and then started a lodge, and bought up all the blue cambric there was in town for sashes. We had a parade, and Hagerstown never seen the like since she became a tavern. Next I started the Sons of Freedom, and came in contact with the law, because it was supposed we had an underground railroad on hand. I was vindicated, of course, and was as big as a dog at hog-killing. I was born on the 29th of August, 1793, and I am just as bright as ever I was. I've been frozen on the box, but I never allowed anybody to compose upon me.'

"Beyond Hagerstown the road is level and uninteresting, save for the capacious taverns, mostly in disuse, the stables, and smithies which time has left standing. Some of the old forges are exceedingly picturesque, notably one near Fairview.

"Three brothers named Boyd, all of them veterans in the stage-line, formerly resided at Clear Spring, but they are all now dead. In a yard at Clear Spring we found the last of the coaches, a massive vehicle in faded grandeur, with paneled landscapes and a superabundance of gilt ornamentation, with springs so flexible that the pressure of as light a foot as you please sways it, and with a commodious interior upholstered in crimson damask, out of which all the brilliancy has been extracted by time. If the road between Hagerstown and Clear Spring is unattractive, between Clear Spring and Hancock it approaches in beauty the grandest passes of the Sierras. There is a salient resemblance between the scenery of the Alleganies and that of the Sierras. The two ranges have the same dusky and balsamic profusion of evergreens, the same deep and ever-silent glens imprisoned by almost sheer walls of pine, the same continuity and multiplicity of ridges, and in many other superficial points the similarity is sustained. The difference in altitude is not observable without instruments, and the affinity continues to the end with two exceptions. Above the evergreen ridges of the Sierras an occasional and perpetually snow-clad peak lifts a glistening apex to the azure: that is one difference; and while the majesty of the Western mountains is harrowing, the beauties of the Alleganies are invariably soothing and comprehensible. The road begins the ascent of the mountain at Clear Spring, and is overarched with oaks, chestnuts, and sugar-maples. As the grade increases the pines multiply, and near the summit the hardy evergreens are almost alone. The view expands, and throughout the tangled shrubs and loftier foliage, between which the road is cut, glimpses are revealed of pale-green valleys and mountain walls, singular even along their crests. At the summit of Sideling Hill there is an immense prospect of ridges beyond ridges visible along their whole length, which look like the vast waves of a petrified ocean. The basin disclosed is of extraordinary extent, and the mountains are crowded together with little more than gorges between, in which lie depths of blue and purple haze.

"The turmoil of traffic here, the beat of hoofs, the rumble of wheels, the tintinnabulations of the teamsters' bells, the bellowing of cattle, the bleating of sheep, and the cries of the drovers, once so familiar, would now sound strangely inappropriate; but even in the travelers of long ago a thrill of novelty must have been excited by the stream of commerce flowing through these mountain confines.

"From the crest we drove down the farther slope, which has a break-neck grade, through avenues of pines and over rushing little brooklets, spending their crystal force across the road. We passed Indian Spring, the site of a noted tavern, and many primitive log cabins, which shelter the few agriculturists of the region, and in about an hour we came into a long, narrow valley, with the Chesapeake Canal embanked between the road and the flashing Potomac, on the farther side of which we could see the Baltimore and Ohio Railroad traced in the mountain-side, with the oblique dip of the rock and the ferruginous color of the earth revealed. There was an old toll-house by the road, and not far beyond a swift curve is made around an embankment, which extends far below, and here, at Millstone Point, one of the many fatal accidents of the old times occurred. Either when the driver was intoxicated or asleep, he drove his coach down the embankment, and several persons were killed. Overfast and reckless driving often led to disasters, the liability to which was compensated for in the minds of many passengers by the speed and exhilaration of the journey. At Millstone Point, also, a committee from Hancock once came out to meet Gen. Jackson. Some excavations were being made in the neighborhood, and several blasts were fired in honor of the occasion as 'Old Hickory' approached. 'Didn't the detonations alarm your horse, general?' inquired a solicitous committeeman. 'No, sir,' said Jackson, emphatically; 'my horse and I have heard a similar sort of music before.'

"Hancock, which was one of the busiest villages on the road, is now lugubriously apathetic, and the citizens sit before their doors with their interest buried in the past. The main street is silent, and the stables are vacant. No one who ever traveled over the road can fail to remember the many excellences of Ben Bean's [tavern], which stood midway on the main street. The old house is still standing, in much the same condition that it was,—with a long white front shaded with chestnuts and locusts, with a trough of water rippling before the door, with a breezy and commodious porch, and with low-ceilinged apartments, cleanly sanded. But Ben Bean has long been gathered to his fathers, and the gayety and activity that made his tavern in a measure famous have left no echo.

"His successors are two elderly nieces. . . . . . The little alcove in the top room, where the glasses, flasks, and demijohns confronted the thirsty and exhausted traveler, is closed beyond appeal.

"Between Hancock and Cumberland the road is almost deserted, and there is no tavern in over forty miles. The isolation and wilderness of the region made it a favorite ground of the bushwhackers, where the Union soldiers suffered more than elsewhere during the late war. . . .

"It was intensely quiet and lonely on the mountain. A herd of tame deer browsed about the garden, and once or twice we heard the sound of a wild-cat in the dense wood surrounding. The old farmer talked about the 'pike.' 'The loss of it ain't very bad,' he said. 'When it was at its height all the people along here depended on it for a living, and now they are driv'n to farming, which is much better for them.'

"Cumberland profited largely by the 'pike,' especially when it was the western terminus of the Baltimore and Ohio Railway, and the point of transfer for passengers and freight going farther west or east.

"A paragraph in the local annals announces that 'the extent of passenger travel over the National road during 1849 was immense, and the reports of the agents show that from the 1st to the 20th of March the number of persons carried was 2586.' Four year later, in 1853, the same annals announce the completion of the railway to Wheeling. 'The effect was soon felt in Cumberland, as most of the stage lines were taken off, and the great business of transferring merchandise at this point was largely diminished.' But while Cumberland was the biggest depot on the 'pike,' when that route was suspended it continued to succeed through other resources, and it is now an active city.

"Among the old inhabitants is Samuel Luman, who was formerly one of the best-known drivers between Wheeling and Cumberland. One night, when he was coming through the 'Shades of Death,' he was attacked by highwaymen. He had an exciting quarter of an hour, which he will never forget, but he escaped without injury to himself or his passengers.

"West of Cumberland the National road proper extends to Wheeling, partly following the route of Gen. Braddock, who has left an interesting old mile-stone at Frostburg. The old iron gates have been despoiled, but the uniform toll-houses, the splendid bridges, and the iron distance-posts show how ample the equipment was. The coaches ceased running in 1853; the 'June Bug,' the 'Good Intent,' and the 'Landlord's,' as the various lines were called, sold their stock, and a brilliant era of travel was ended."

At what date coaches for the conveyance of travelers were introduced is not known, but it was somewhere about the year 1815. The institution, or whatever it may be called, in the beginning was very crude and imperfect. Coaches in those days were called "turtle-backs," on account of the roof resembling that reptile. They were very uncomfortable for travelers, but they were apace with the times. Stages were running between Cumberland and Baltimore some years before they commenced plying from Cumberland west.

The Troy and Concord coaches were very popular in after-times, and were called post-coaches. In their day they were thought to be as grand as Pullman's palace-cars.

The first coach of the Troy pattern was sent from Philadelphia, by James Reeside, in the winter of 1829. It had been won by the owner upon a bet on the Presidential election the previous year, and he intended President Jackson should be the first person to ride in it from Cumberland to Washington, to take his seat. Charles Howell, of Cumberland, was the driver. The President-elect came as far as Cumberland in his own private conveyance, and a poor one at that. No doubt he was pleased with the finest vehicle he had ever seen, but, "By the eternal!" he would not ride to Washington in a free conveyance, no matter how attractive and comfortable it might be. He would be under no obligations to anybody. So his old shabby two-horse carriage not only took him to the seat of government but back to the Hermitage, eight years thereafter. However, Old Hickory bent so far as to permit a portion of his family to "christen" the coach which had been won on his own election. These fine vehicles were built at Troy, N. Y., and Concord, N. H., and cost about five to six hundred dollars. They were very strong and durable, neatly upholstered inside, with three cross-wise seats, accommodating nine passengers inside and one or two outside with the driver. The springs for years were quite a desideratum among coach-builders. Thomas Shriver, who was largely interested in staging, brought his genius into play and invented the elliptical spring, which was a decided improvement. L. B. Stockton and James Reeside were the pioneers in the business. Farther on came the late Thomas Shriver, then Alpheus Beall, now a resident of Cumberland, and some others of a later day. The fare was about equal to the car-fare of the present time. There were opposition lines or companies at intervals, and the competition was quite spirited, riding almost free,—precisely like the railroad wars of our days.

In the traveling season it was not extraordinary for one hundred people to be sent west per day from Cumberland in these coaches. Stage-owners made money and grew rich.

The stage-drivers were a jolly set of men, proud of their situation, some of them of more importance in their own estimation than the congressman or cabinet minister riding in the coach below them. They were in some respects picked men, and their places much sought after,—politics no test, religion not expected; a reasonable amount of profanity and a sprinkle of "Piney Grove" no bar to employment. They were expected to be reliable, to possess a good share of knowledge in horse anatomy, and to use the long whip gracefully, but not too much. There are still a few of the veterans of the tin horn left. In addition to Howell we have Samuel Luman, the two Willisons, and Jacob Shuck, all respectable and successful in life, and also John Farrell, of Grantsville, now over eighty-four years of age, hale and hearty. He retired from the "box" at least forty-five years ago, and has been a farmer ever since.

Cass, Benton, Corwin, Douglas, Bell, and many other statesmen were familiar with this favorite highway. Four of the eight Western Presidents passed over it in coaches or private conveyances, viz., Jackson, Harrison, Polk, and Taylor.

President Taylor and his party were in 1847 conveyed over the road under the marshalship of that most indefatigable Whig, Thomas Shriver, who with some other Cumberlanders proceeded to the Ohio River and met the Presidential party. Among the party were statesmen, politicians, and office-hunters, notably Col. Bullet, a brilliant editor from New Orleans, who was to occupy a relation to President Taylor something like that of Henry J. Raymond to Lincoln. The road was a perfect glare of ice, and everything above ground literally plated with sheeted frost. The scenery was beautiful; to native mountaineers too common to be of much interest, but to a Southerner like Gen. Taylor, who had never seen the like, it was a phenomenon. In going down a spur of Meadow Mountain the Presidential coach with the others danced and waltzed on the polished road, first on one side of the road and then on the other, with every sign of an immediate capsize, but the coaches were manned with the most expert of the whole corps of drivers. Shriver was in the rear and in the greatest trepidation for the safety of the President. He seemed to feel himself responsible for the security of the head of the nation. Down each hill and mountain his bare head could be seen protruding through the window of his coach to discover if the President's car was still upon wheels. The iron-gray head of the general could almost with the same frequency be seen outside of his window, not to see after anybody's safety, but to look upon what seemed to him an Arctic panorama. After a ride of many miles the last long slope was passed and everything was safe. At twilight the Narrows were reached, two miles west of Cumberland, one of the boldest and most sublime views on the Atlantic slope. Gen. Taylor assumed authority and ordered a halt, and out he got in the storm and snow and looked at the giddy heights on either side of Will's Creek until he had taken in the grandeur of the scenery. He had beheld nothing like it before, even in his campaigns in Northern Mexico. The President-elect was tendered a reception on his arrival at Cumberland, and the next morning he and his party left in the cars for Washington. Tolls were abolished on the National road in 1878. The last stage-coaches disappeared from it about 1870. The venerable Sandy Conner, a veteran stage-driver of forty-five years' experience, can daily be seen perched on his one-horse spring-wagon, carrying the mail from Frostburg to Grantsville, with an occasional passenger by his side.

From 1818 to 1820, Col. Henry Lewis, of Hagerstown, and Jacob Sides ran a line of stages from Cumberland to Uniontown, Pa. Mr. Sides afterwards became sole proprietor. In 1824, Reeside, Moore & Stockton organized a line of stages to run between Baltimore, Washington, and Wheeling. The stages left Baltimore and Washington at two o'clock in the morning on Sundays, Tuesdays, and Thursdays, and arrived in Wheeling in seventy-eight hours *via* Cumberland. A special stage left on Monday, Wednesday, Friday, and Saturday, and made the time by daylight in four days. On March 10, 1825, Capt. John S. Dugan, proprietor of the Wheeling and Zanesville (Ohio) stage-line, was killed by the upsetting of the stage four miles east of Cumberland. In 1825 the mail stages departed from Cumberland eastward on Tuesdays, Thursdays, and Saturdays at six o'clock in the morning, and westward at four in the afternoon, on Mondays, Wednesdays, and Fridays. The fare rates were:

From Baltimore to Frederick	$2.00
" Frederick to Hagerstown	2.00
" Hagerstown to Cumberland	5.00
" Cumberland to Uniontown, Pa.	4.00
" Uniontown, Pa., to Washington, Pa.	2.25
" Washington, Pa., to Wheeling, Va.	2.00
Through fare	$17.25

April 1, 1839, Thomas Shriver, Daniel Hutchinson, John A. Woert, Alpheus Beall, and William H. Still purchased from James Reeside & Co. all the stage stock running on the National road, and known as the Good Intent and the Pilot lines of coaches. In August the firm adopted the name of T. Shriver & Co.

In 1843, the increasing travel from the east to the west over the National road, from Cumberland to Wheeling and other points, brought out the greatest enterprise in the supply of stages for public conveyance. The different lines were The National Road Stage Company of Stockton & Stokes; Good Intent Stage Company, owned by William H. Still, John A. Woert, Alpheus Beall, and Thomas Shriver; June Bug Line, of Reeside & Sons; Landlord's Line, owned by the tavern-keepers along the line, of whom John W. Weaver, William Willis, Joseph Dilley, and Samuel Luman were prominent stage-men; and the Pioneer Line, between Wheeling and Hagerstown, of Peters, Moore & Co., which was also a favorite line. So great was the cutting of rates that the June Bug Line was forced off the road, and the Baltimore and Ohio Railroad gave the two old companies an advantage of two dollars per passenger over the Landlord's

Line. This led to great excitement and discussions in the press, and finally the two old companies bought out the Landlord's Line, and for the next ten years the National and the Good Intent made large sums of money. The following from the Cumberland *Gazette* explains the stage competition:

"DELAY IN TRAVELING.

"Travelers from Baltimore to Pittsburg should be careful to obtain the best and most convenient route; at least to avoid being detained for non-payment of turnpike tolls, as the gate-keeper at Uniontown refused to open the gate to let the Good Intent and National Road Lines pass for non-payment of dues. The Express Line, in which I was a passenger, being behind, was consequently detained, the keeper refusing to open the gate, and was prevented thereby from arriving at its regular time. Eventually the tolls were paid, and we all passed on. When a line of stages cannot pay their toll, how is it that passengers are to get on? I should advise all persons traveling this route to take the Express Line from either the city of Pittsburgh or Baltimore. Many passengers can attest the truth of this statement.

"J. COLDER, a Passenger.

"PITTSBURGH, May 13, 1843."

In July, 1850, a daily line of stages were put on the road from Cumberland to Bedford, Pa. In 1842 the Baltimore and Ohio Railroad was completed to Cumberland, in consequence of which the stage business was greatly injured between Cumberland and Baltimore. In 1852 the lines began lessening their facilities, and soon there was no connection by stage with any cities, though stages were sent to neighboring towns, for the purpose of carrying the United States mails and passengers, and until about 1872 they were not entirely suspended. In 1877 the last of the old-line coaches was brought out by some young men to run between Cumberland and the fair-grounds at the time of the exhibition. Dingy, musty, shaky, its ancient symmetry, beauty, and strength could scarcely be traced beneath the mouldering hand of time, and in its creaking and groaning, as it went tottering through the streets, one could almost fancy the original of Dickens' admirable ghost story was before him. Mails are still carried to and from Flintstone by hack twice a week, but that has nothing to do with the old lines. In the days of staging two coaches were sent regularly every day from Cumberland by each company, and as many arrived. After the completion of the National road between Cumberland and Baltimore, the old "war road" was abandoned, and as the road was made west of Cumberland, coaches followed it up. Before the present road to Bedford was made, the road that led in that direction took its course over Shriver's Hill. Traces of it are yet visible on the hill-sides at the head of Bedford Street. Another road led through a wild, dismal country to Petersburg, Va., and the drivers and passengers were often startled in the night by the howling of wolves and the cries of panthers. Regular communication was kept up by coaches with Somerset, Uniontown, and Pittsburgh, and at Uniontown a coach-factory was operated for many years. The principal offices of the stage lines were in Baltimore, Frederick, Hagerstown, Cumberland, and Wheeling. The offices in Cumberland were at the National Hotel, corner of Mechanic and Baltimore Streets, and later at Barnum's House (now Weir's Hotel), and the United States Hotel (now the St. Nicholas). The stables of the Good Intent Line were situated on the east side of Centre Street, a short distance north of where Harrison Street now is, and just below there Thomas Shriver carried on the business of coach-making in a large factory that he had erected. He furnished the Good Intent Line with all their coaches, but the other companies generally got their supplies from the East. The stables of the other companies were located a little to the southeast of the corner of Baltimore and Centre Streets. The establishment of the first line between Cumberland and Wheeling took place in 1842. The time occupied in going from Cumberland to Baltimore, or Wheeling, was about eighteen hours. The horses were changed at the end of every ten or twelve miles, and the drivers relieved at the end of every thirty miles. The coaches were required to leave stations at a certain hour, though they often failed to make their time in bad weather. The Henry Clay (or National) road was kept up west of Cumberland by the government, and east of it, during a portion of the time, the road was maintained by a company.

Among the prominent persons who passed through Cumberland by stage were Henry Clay, Gen. Jackson, Gen. Harrison, Gen. Cass, James K. Polk, and the celebrated Indian chief Black Hawk, who was captured by Gen. Atkinson in a battle near the mouth of the Upper Iowa, in 1832. These were all carried by Samuel Luman. There was but one man employed on the stage-coaches of this section, and he was the driver. The drivers were all provided with a horn (which they blew on arriving at or departing from a station), and were armed with whatever weapons they chose to carry, and they generally chose to carry the best weapons they could get, as it sometimes happened that highwaymen attacked them, and on various occasions the mails were robbed. On Aug. 6, 1834, the United States "express mail," which was in charge of Samuel Luman, was attacked by highwaymen in the heavy pine-forest known by the name of the "Shades of Death," about seven miles west of Frostburg. The highwaymen had built a brush fence across the road, and had then withdrawn from it a short distance. When the coach came up, and as soon as it got between them and the brush, the robbers called for its surrender, but the veteran Luman, lashing his horses, drove safely over the obstruction and escaped. During the whole of the year 1841 two men, named Brady and McCormack, kept up a systematic robbery of the mails carried by the coaches, but they were finally captured, and, McCormack turning State's evidence, Brady was convicted and sent to the penitentiary, where he died.

The appropriation made by Congress for the construction of the National road was a matter of great moment to the people of Allegany County, and perhaps none more highly appreciated its importance than the citizens of Cumberland, as will appear from the following quaint account from a contemporary journal:

"The citizens of the town, on the 21st of May, 1832, in demonstration of their great joy, growing out of the appropriation made by the national government for the repair of the Cumberland road, made arrangements for the celebration of that event. In pursuance of that arrangement, Samuel Slicer, Esq., illuminated his large and splendid hotel, which patriotic example was followed by James Black, Esq. In addition to the illumination, Mr. Bunton, agent of L. W. Stockton, Esq., ordered out a coach drawn by four large gray steeds, driven by Mr. George Shuck. The stage was beautifully illuminated, which presented to the generous citizens of this place a novelty calculated to impress upon the minds of all who witnessed it the great benefits they anticipated by having the road repaired. There were also seated upon the top of the vehicle several gentlemen, who played on various instruments, which contributed very much to the amusement of the citizens, and gave a zest to everything that inspired delight or created feelings of patriotism. . . . They started from the front of Mr. Slicer's hotel, and as they moved on slowly the band played 'Hail Columbia,' 'Freemasons' March,' 'Bonaparte Crossing the Rhine,' 'Washington's March,' etc., together with a new tune composed by Mr. Mobley, of this place, and named by the gentlemen on the stage 'The Lady we Love Best,' and many others, as they passed through the principal streets of the town. On their return they played 'Home, Sweet Home,' to the admiration of all who heard it."

Bridges, Railroads, and Canal.—In a letter from George Washington, dated July 21, 1758, to Col. Bouquet, written from "Camp near Fort Cumberland," he says, "The bridge is finished at this place, and to-morrow Maj. Peachey, with three hundred men, will proceed to open Braddock's road." This bridge was across Will's Creek. In 1755, Braddock's men had prepared the timbers for it, but it is not known whether or not they completed it. They probably made a temporary structure during the fall and spring rises, when the creek was too high to allow the passage of wagons over the fords. The bridge alluded to by Washington was carried away by a flood after the town was laid out. In 1790 there was a small bridge built over Will's Creek, near the Baltimore Street bridge of to-day. In 1791, by order of the Levy Court, Alpheus and Thomas Beall repaired it at a cost of twenty pounds, and in the following year Joseph Kelly and William McMahon expended the same amount of money on it by the court's order. In 1795 the court selected Patrick Murdoch, John Graham, and David Hoffman to erect a bridge over Will's Creek for thirty pounds. They contracted with William Logsden in April, 1796, to rebuild the old bridge and finish it by September following. The specifications stipulated that it should be five feet higher than the old one, and sixteen feet in width, with a railing of three feet. Logsden contracted to preserve it for seven years, and to put it up again if carried off by floods, save when the water became so high as to float the bridge and thus sweep it away. His securities were Ralph and John Logsden. In 1799, £26 12*s.* 13*d.* were further levied to pay the remainder due and to improve it with extra additions. This bridge was originally built in 1790 upon wooden piers, and by occasional repairing did good service till 1804, when the high freshets injured it. The Legislature, in 1805, authorized by special act a lottery for raising two thousand dollars to erect a bridge over Will's Creek and to purchase a fire-engine for the town. The commissioners to manage the scheme were George Hoffman, William McMahon, Thomas Thistle, Upton Bruce, and David Hoffman. The bridge was built, but it was swept away by the great flood of 1810, which inundated Mechanic Street. A ferry was then substituted. A rope was run across the creek from the foot of Baltimore Street, the ends being fastened to large trees, and a boat was attached to a ring slipping along the cable. In a year or two a new wooden bridge was erected, which stood until 1820, when another flood swept it off. The county authorities then entered into an agreement with Valentine Shockey to build a chain bridge, an invention of James Finley, of Fayette County, Pa., in 1796. There were two piers at each end of single locust posts, braced together at the top. The span was one hundred and fifteen and a half feet in the clear. The deflection of the two chains stretched from one side of the creek to the other was one-sixth of the span. Trautwine's "Civil Engineer's Pocket-Book" says, "The double links, of 1⅜-inch square iron, were ten feet long. The centre link was horizontal, and at the level of the floor and at its ends were stirruped the two central transverse girders. From the ends of this central link the chains were carried in straight lines to the tops of the posts, 25 feet high, which served as piers or towers. The back-stays were carried away straight, at the same angle as the cables, and each end was confined to four buried stones of about half a cubic yard each. The floor was only wide enough for a single line of vehicles. All the transverse girders were ten feet apart, and supported longitudinal joists, to which the floor was spiked. There were no restrictions as to travel, but lines of carts and wagons, in close succession, and heavily loaded with coal, stone, iron, etc., crossed it almost daily, together with droves of cattle on full run. The slight hand-railing of iron was hinged so as not to be bent by the undulations of the bridge. Six-horse wagons were frequently driven across on a trot. The iron was of the old-fashioned charcoal, of full thirty tons per square inch ultimate strength. The united cross-section of the two double links was 7.56 square inches, which at thirty tons per square inch gives 227 tons for their ultimate strength, or say 76 tons with a safety of 3."[1] Associated with the contractor, Valentine Shockey, was Godfrey Richards.

In 1831, on the giving away of some of the piers, Jonathan Witt replaced them with new and larger locust posts. The bridge stood until April 25, 1838, when its western abutment gave way and the bridge fell into the creek. When it went down a boy and two men were on it, but escaped unhurt, the former walking over the débris, and the latter swimming ashore. On May 4th of that year the commissioners chosen to rebuild it, George Hoblitzell, George Blocher, and Gustavus Beall, advertised for proposals for a new bridge. A wooden bridge of two wooden arches from shore to shore, with a carriage-way in the middle, and a foot-walk on each side, was constructed. It was covered, had heavy lattice-work on the sides, and the floor was filled with tan-bark. Under Mayor Thomas Shriver's administration, in 1843, the Council erected new bridges over the race and paved them with stone. In the summer of 1853 the wooden bridge over Will's Creek became unsafe from its rotten timbers, and it had to be propped up. In 1854 it was replaced by an iron bridge of the Bollman pattern, erected by a Baltimore firm. It was built by the city and county jointly, the former paying one-fifth and the latter four-fifths of its cost. In 1872 the bridge over the Potomac River, connecting Cumberland with West Virginia, was erected, and subsequently two more bridges were built over Will's Creek.

[1] The author is greatly indebted to Lowdermilk's "History of Cumberland" for valuable information.

On the 1st of January, 1795, a post-office was established in Cumberland, and Charles F. Broodhog was appointed postmaster. He was succeeded in that capacity by Beene S. Pigman on July 1, 1802. Since that time the postmasters with dates of appointment have been as follows:

Samuel Smith, Jan. 17, 1807; Edward Wiatt, Dec. 21, 1819; Samuel Magill, Jan. 18, 1820; James Whitehead, Oct. 19, 1824; James P. Carleton, Dec. 11, 1827; Daniel Wineon, Feb. 16, 1841; William Lynn, March 5, 1842; Jacob Fechtig, Feb. 24, 1846; James C. Magraw, May 9, 1849; William A. Taylor, June 1, 1853; Samuel Taylor, Aug. 31, 1858; George A. Hoffman, March 27, 1861; John H. Young, April 11, 1865; Will H. Lowdermilk, May 13, 1869; and the present occupant, H. J. Johnson, appointed March 1, 1878.

In 1813, Samuel Smith kept the office in his store above Blue Spring. In May, 1849, James C. Magraw removed the office to a one-story frame building, about forty feet from the gutter, on Baltimore Street, next to the savings-bank, where now is Reynolds' Block. On July 27, 1853, W. A. Taylor removed it to No. 93 Baltimore Street, where it was kept until November, 1869. Under the direction of Will H. Lowdermilk, then postmaster, it was changed to its present location on Centre Street, between Baltimore and Frederick Streets.

Cumberland City is on the outer edge of the great coal-basin, and is connected with it by the Cumberland and Pennsylvania Railroad, which runs from Cumberland to Piedmont; by the Eckhart Mines Branch, which runs from Cumberland to Eckhart, and other mines on the eastern edge of the coal-fields, and by the George's Creek road, which runs from Cumberland to Lonaconing. It is the principal shipping-point for the celebrated Cumberland coal. It is near the centre of the main stem of that great national highway, the Baltimore and Ohio Railroad, two hundred and four miles from river navigation at Parkersburg and Wheeling, in West Virginia, and one hundred and seventy-eight from tide-water at Baltimore. The Pittsburgh and Connellsville Branch of the Baltimore and Ohio Railroad joins the main stem here, and connects it with Pittsburgh, one hundred and forty-nine miles, and the oil regions of Pennsylvania. The Bedford and Huntington Branch of the Pennsylvania Railway connects it with all important points in Central and Eastern Pennsylvania. The Chesapeake and Ohio Canal has its western terminus here, and connects it with tide-water at Georgetown, in the District of Columbia, and Alexandria, Va.

The inhabitants of Cumberland, as far back as 1827, were an active and progressive community. They were keenly alive to the wonderful resources their county possessed, the admirable location of the city, and the inestimable advantages to be derived from properly constructed lines of communication and transportation. The project for the construction of a railroad from Baltimore City to the Ohio River was hailed by them with the utmost enthusiasm, and every facility was extended to the company. An ill-grounded apprehension that the road was to be diverted from the line which would bring it to the city of Cumberland was the occasion of a mass-meeting, which was largely attended, and the proceedings of which were unanimously indorsed by the citizens. Wm. McMahon was chairman of the meeting, and Wm. Buskirk acted as secretary.

Resolutions were adopted urging an examination of the Cumberland route, and strongly commending it to the consideration of the railroad authorities. A committee was also appointed to meet and confer with the surveyors of the road. This committee was composed of the following: John Hoye, B. S. Pigman, David Lynn, William Reid, Martin Riser, Jr., James D. Cresap, Robert Cresap, Isaac McCarty, Thomas Greenwell. Their wishes were gratified, as the Cumberland route was chosen, and Nov. 1, 1842, the first regular passenger-cars arrived from Baltimore, and re'urned at six the next morning. The through fare was six and a half dollars. The schedule time arranged was: leave Cumberland at eight A.M., reaching Baltimore at six P.M., and leaving Baltimore at seven A.M., reaching Cumberland at five P.M. The express locomotive bearing President Tyler's message arrived at the Cumberland depot Dec. 5, 1842, at ten minutes before eight o'clock in the evening, making the run from the Relay House, one hundred and seventy miles, in the short space of *five hours and fifty minutes*, which was considered extraordinary speed and the subject of great discussion.

In 1867 Cumberland presented to the Baltimore and Ohio Railroad Company forty acres of ground in its southern limits, whereon to build rolling-mills. The gift was accepted, and the mills were built. The erection of the mills gave work to over six hundred men, and resulted in a rapid increase of population, with a great demand for dwelling-houses. There followed a large advance in real estate, and some two hundred new dwellings were built. The avenue and several other new streets east of the railroad were quickly built up. The Baltimore and Ohio Railroad Company completed its "Queen City Hotel," the pride of the city, in 1872, and tore down the old dingy depot at the Baltimore Street crossing and removed the station to its magnificent new hotel. Its mills are the finest in the country, and have largely added to the prosperity of the city, which gave twenty-eight thousand dollars for the land upon which they are built. They are in charge of the efficient superintendent of the company, William Robinson.

William Robinson was born in Baltimore City, May 14, 1819, and was the fourth in a family of six children of Thomas and Mary (Kelley) Robinson. The family are of Scotch-Irish descent. His father was a

Wm. Robinson

sailor, and died in Baltimore about 1829. All the family except William are dead. At the age of twelve William was employed in the store of William M. Johnson, with whom he remained four years. His education was limited to attendance at a private school in Baltimore. At the age of sixteen he was apprenticed to Wm. Jones, of Baltimore, for five years, to learn the shipsmithing trade. After the termination of his apprenticeship he worked for Mr. Jones at his trade eighteen months. For eleven years and eight months thereafter he was employed in the Canton Forge, having charge of the works during the later years of his connection with them. He was next employed as superintendent of the Baltimore Steam Forge Bar-Iron Rolling-Mill, which position he occupied twenty-two years and one month.

In October, 1878, he was appointed general superintendent of the Baltimore and Ohio Steel Rail-Mill at Cumberland, Md., which position he still holds.

QUEEN CITY HOTEL, CUMBERLAND, MD.

These works are the most extensive of their kind in Maryland, and their successful management requires a thorough knowledge of the business in all its departments and no small amount of executive ability. In politics Mr. Robinson was first a Whig, but has been identified with the Republican party since its organization. The only secret order of which he is a member is the Powhatan Order of Red Men. He has been twice married. His first wife was Mary Jane Collins, of Baltimore. By this union one child was born,—Susan, wife of John T. Calvert, of Baltimore. His second wife is Sarah J. Nicol, of Baltimore. Their children are William H., employed in charge of the bar-mill at the Baltimore and Ohio Steel-Works; Sarah Kate, living at home; and Thomas Albert, a commission merchant in Baltimore. Mr. Robinson still retains his residence and home at Baltimore.

On Thursday, Oct. 10, 1850, the opening of the Chesapeake and Ohio Canal for continuous navigation from Cumberland to Alexandria, was commemorated at Cumberland with appropriate ceremonies. On the day previous a number of gentlemen arrived in Cumberland to participate in the ceremonies. Among them were Gen. James M. Coale, president; and Messrs. John Pickell, William Cost Johnson, William A. Bradley, George Schley, and S. P. Smith, directors of the canal company; ex-Governor Sprigg, Gen. Tench Tilghman, and J. Vanclear, State agents; the Hon. William D. Merrick, late United States senator from Maryland; John L. Skinner, editor of the *Plough, the Loom, and the Anvil;* Henry Addison, mayor of Georgetown; and a number of others from various parts of Maryland and Virginia.

These gentlemen came by the invitation of the canal company, and were properly received and entertained by them. Col. John Pickell was accompanied by the band of the Independent Blues of Baltimore, who, soon after their arrival, made their appearance on the portico of the United States Hotel and rendered a variety of selections. About half-past eight on Thursday morning a large assemblage had collected in the street before the United States and Barnum's Hotels. About this time the Eckhart Artillery, Capt. Davidson, with a battery of two pieces, arrived and performed various military evolutions. At nine o'clock the procession was formed, the Eckhart Artillery in front, escorted by the band of the Baltimore Blues, and followed by the visitors, officers of the canal company, and State agents. Behind these were the mayor and Council of the town of Cumberland, and in their rear a large procession of the citizens of Allegany, preceded by the Mechanics' Band of Cumberland. The procession marched through the streets in the direction of the canal-locks, gathering numbers as it advanced, until, when that point was reached, there was an immense assemblage of all ages. When everything had been arranged, five canal-boats, laden with the products of the mines of Allegany, and destined for the Eastern markets, were passed through the locks amid the salvos of artillery from the Eckhart battery, accompanied by music from the bands. William Price, the distinguished lawyer, then ascended the deck of one of the boats, and delivered an eloquent address on behalf of the people of Cumberland. Gen. James M. Coale, president of the Chesapeake and Ohio Canal Company, arose and replied to the speech of Mr. Price. These ceremonies being concluded, the visitors, officers of the company, and a large number of citizens embarked on the canal-packet "Jenny Lind" and the canal-boat "C. B. Fisk," which had been fitted up for their reception, and proceeded down the canal, followed by the Eckhart Light Artillery with their pieces on another boat, the coal-boats "Southampton," "Elizabeth," "Ohio," and "Delaware," belonging to the Merchants' Line of Messrs. McKaig & Agnew, and the "Freeman Rawdon," belonging to the Cumberland Line of Mr. Ward, bringing up the rear. The passage down was enlivened by the music of the bands and the firing of cannon. Arrived at a large spring ten miles east of Cumberland, the boats halted, and the company having disembarked and viewed the surrounding country, returned on board to partake of a collation prepared by the committee,—Messrs. S. P. Smith, W. A. Bradley, and John Pickell. After luncheon the fleet of boats was again put into line, and started on their return to Cumberland, the coal-boats proceeding down the canal towards their destination. The return was accomplished by night-fall, and the whole affair passed off in the most agreeable manner.

Upon the return of the company to Barnum's, they were entertained by the citizens of Cumberland at a dinner prepared by J. A. Hefelfinger, proprietor of that establishment. After the cloth was removed a number of toasts were drunk. Hon. William Cost Johnson, who, as chairman of the Committee of Internal Improvements of the House of Delegates, at December session, 1844, reported the act under which the canal was completed, rose during the course of the evening, and after alluding in handsome terms to the recent courtesies extended to the officers of the canal company by the Baltimore and Ohio Railroad Company, offered the following sentiment, which was drunk with applause:

"The Chesapeake and Ohio Canal and the Baltimore and Ohio Railroad. The former has happily reached its ebony harvests amid the coal-fields of the Alleganies; may the latter journey vigorously on westward until it rejoices amidst the golden plains of far California!" Soon after the drinking of this toast the tables and chairs were removed, and the dining-room converted into a ball-room. The ball was a very brilliant entertainment, and was generally participated in by the ladies and gentlemen of Cumberland.

The magnitude of the business transmitted over the canal in the one article of coal alone can be estimated from the number of boats unloaded at the elevators in Georgetown every year. Last year six thousand boats unloaded at these elevators, averaging one hundred and twelve tons each, making the total number of tons received six hundred and seventy-two thousand. During some years it has amounted to over one million tons. The facilities for unloading are so perfect that at least sixty boats can be unloaded in a day. The freight from Cumberland is about eighty-five cents per ton, while the toll amounts to forty cents per ton. The collector's office for the company is at Georgetown, D. C., and William E. Porter is superintendent of the canal company. He was appointed from Cecil County in 1878. Previous to this he was with the Baltimore and Ohio Railroad twenty-seven years, twenty as assistant master and seven as supervisor of the road. During the war he had general charge of repairing and constructing bridges west of Harper's Ferry. Previous to the battle of Winchester, in March, 1862, Gen. Shields ordered him to construct a suspension bridge across Back Creek for the passage of his army, which he accomplished in three hours, and over which Gen. Shields and his army of sixteen thousand men crossed in safety. The collector is William Snowden, from Anne Arundel County. F. M. Griffith, who has been connected with the canal since 1870, is assistant collector, and is from Beallsville. James S. Kemp, of Clarksburg, is harbor-master, and is assisted by Frank Fisher, from near Darnestown.

CHAPTER LV.

EARLY SETTLEMENTS AND EDUCATION.

First Settlers, County Officers, and Public Buildings—Early Courts and Officials—Executions—Political Statistics.

THE ill-starred expedition of Gen. Braddock (an interesting sketch of which will be found elsewhere in this work, in the chapter on the French and Indian war) doubtless exerted a powerful influence in the early settlement of Allegany. The forces rendezvoused at Fort Cumberland, where they remained for a considerable time, and the expedition passed through the heart of the county both going and returning. Many of those attached to it remained in this section permanently, while others, attracted by the natural resources of the region, either returned later and settled in Allegany, or induced others to do so. An amount of exploration was accomplished, moreover, which would have required many years by the slower process of individual enterprise, and thus it will be perceived how benefits often spring from those events which at the time are regarded as unqualified misfortunes. The most available points for crossing the steep and rugged mountains were in many instances determined, and the shallow places in rivers and streams ascertained. Localities which have since become prominent in the history of the county were at that time brought into notice. "Little Meadows" and "Great Meadows," "Little Crossings" and "Great Crossings," figure prominently in Braddock's march through this portion of Maryland. The experiences of Washington and other engineers attached to the expedition doubtless laid the foundations for the great national highway which was subsequently constructed through this part of the State.

An Englishman named Evart was the first white man who penetrated the wilds of the mountainous regions of Allegany County, after whom are named Evart's, or as it is now generally written, Evitt's, Creek and Evitt's Mountain. Evart built his cabin on the top of Evitt's Mountain, at the point where Evitt's Creek rounds its steep and rugged point, some seven miles east of Cumberland, and about six or seven from the valley of the Potomac,—the Indian trail from Conococheague to the West. A portion of the rude chimney of his cabin is still remaining. He died before 1749, prior to which time the white settlements had not penetrated farther west than the Conococheague, now in Washington County, and even there the fierce struggle for the possession of the country was still going on between the whites and the aborigines.

Some difficulties were thrown in the way of *bona fide* settlers, moreover, by the action of the last proprietary of Maryland. He directed that no land warrants should be issued until ten thousand acres had been surveyed for himself in the territory west of Fort Cumberland. In the effort to gratify his wishes 127,680 acres were surveyed in different tracts. The board of judges of the Land Office was subsequently notified that the prohibition no longer existed, and, as sometimes happens in this enlightened age, a job was developed, or at least very strongly suspected. Notice that the Land Office was opened for the perfection of titles, was given in such a manner that those who had braved the toils and dangers of life to establish a home for themselves and their families could not possibly avail themselves of it in time to secure the fruits of their enterprise, while the wealthier class of speculators in the vicinity of the seat of government were enabled to pre-empt, to use a more modern term, the most valuable lands belonging to the public domain. Mr. Jenifer, the agent of the proprietary, fully exposed the injustice of the board, and a sharp controversy ensued, from which the agent emerged with flying colors, and rules were established for the governance of the whole subject which assured the rights of the early settlers. The previous instructions of the proprietary, however, doubtless had the effect of retarding emigration to this portion of the province.

The settlement of the county dates before the formation of the "Ohio Company." Col. Thomas Cresap, the bold pioneer and Indian-fighter, located himself at Oldtown, on the north fork of the Potomac, with his own and other families, in 1741. On Jan. 15, 1755, the proprietary Governor, Horatio Sharpe, accompanied by Sir John St. Clair, set out from Annapolis to visit the camp at Mount Pleasant, on Will's Creek, and returned February 2d. They found the settlement thriving, notwithstanding the threatened appearance of the Indians. In 1756 Fort Cumberland ("Mount Pleasant") mounted ten carriage cannon, and contained a garrison of four hundred men, and May 5th of that year Capt. Dagworthy was in command.

On Feb. 11, 1762, a communication was published in the *Maryland Gazette* calling the attention of the public to the great advantages that would arise from "the opening of the Potomac River, and making it passable for small craft from Fort Cumberland, at Will's Creek, to the Great Falls," which would facilitate the commerce of Maryland and Virginia, and asking for subscriptions, which were to be paid to Col. George Mercer and Col. Thomas Prather, treasurers.

The following were appointed managers and authorized to solicit subscriptions: in Virginia, George Mercer, Jacob Hite, William Ramsay, John Carlyle, John Hite, Joseph Watson, James Keith, James Hamilton, John Hough, John Patterson, and Abraham Hite; in Maryland, Rev. Thomas Bacon, Dr. David Ross, Christopher Lowndes, Thomas Cresap, Benjamin Chambers, Jonathan Hager, Thomas Prather, John Cary, Caspar Shaaf, Robert Peter, and Evan Shelby, any eight of whom were a sufficient number to proceed to business. The first meeting was held in Frederick Town, in May, 1762.

At the close of the French and Indian war the settlements rapidly increased until the Revolution, when immigration practically ceased. After the peace of 1783 new settlers flocked in from the old counties of the State, from Pennsylvania and Virginia, and from Europe. The population increased to such an extent that the inhabitants became tired and impatient of going so far as Hagerstown to transact their court and other public business, and agitated the question of a new county, with the county-seat at Cumberland.

The following is a list of settlers located in 1788 upon the lands lying in Maryland west of Fort Cumberland:

William Ashby, Anthony Able, George Anderson, Patrick Burnes, Charles Boyles, Thomas Baker, Philip Bray, Mallner Burnstredder, John Beall, John Blair, John Brendage, Peter Bonham, Norman Bruce, Daniel Cresap, Sr., Daniel Cresap, Jr., Robert Cresap, James Cresap, Joseph Cresap, John Durbin, Aaron Duckworth, Nicholas Durbin, William Durhane, John Doomer, Joseph Davis, Steven Davis, Levi Davis, Samuel Dawson, Sr., Samuel Elliott, Adam Eckhart, John Ervin, Herman Frazee, Joseph Frost, George Fegenbaker, Briant Gaines, Edward Grimes, Paul Grim, John Great, Benjamin Green, Sam. Humphreys, Edward Huston, James Henderson, John House, Ralph Adams, John Arnold, of A., John Arnold, of John, Andrew Bruce, William Barnes, Michael Beeme, Benjamin Brady, John Buhman, Ben. John Biggs, Frederick Bray, Thomas Barkus, George Barkus, Samuel Barrell, William Coddington, Peter Crawl, Thomas Cordray, Henry Crosley, John Cruise, Samuel Dawson, Jr., William Dawson, Sr., William Dawson, Jr., Edward Dawson, Sr., Edward Dawson, Jr., Thomas Dawson, Joseph Dye, Barney Dewitt, Terence Dyal, John Elbin, Samuel Ellison, John Eckhart, John Firman, John Friend, Gabriel Friend, Richard Green, Daniel Green, Thomas Greenwade, Salathiel Goff, John T. Goff, Andrew House, Elisha Hall, John Harshan, Moses Hall, Anthony Arnold, Moses Ayres, Sr., Moses Ayres, Jr., Robert Boyd, Matthew Ball, Frederick Burgett, Josiah Bonham, Micijah Burnham, Amariah Bonham, John Brufly, John Buckholder, Jacob Beall, Nathan Corey, Godfrey Corbus, Edmund Cutler, Ely Clark, Michael Corn, Benjamin Coddington, Samuel Durbin, James Denison, Peter Doogan, Samuel Durbin, Edward Davis, Jacob Duttro, Sr., Jacob Duttro, Jr., Peter Devecmon, David Eaton, George Eckhart, Charles Friend, Hezekiah Frazier, Joseph Friend, Harry Franks, George Fiddler, James C. Goff, Evan Gwynn, John Glasman, John Gaiey, John Glaze, Nicholas Holsbury, Charles Huddy, Richard Hall, George Harness, George Haver, William Howell, Paul Hoye, Robert Johnston, Evan James, Conrad Joleman, John Kevser, Henry Kite, John Lowdermilk, William Logsden, Daniel Levit, Jacob Lower, Rosemond Long, Joseph Lee, Stephen Masters, Gabriel McKinsy, John Matthews, Sr., John Magomery, Christopher Myers, James McMullen, Nathaniel Magruder, Josiah Magruder, Samuel McKinsy, Peter Nimirck, George Paine, Henry Porter, Moses Porter, George Preston, Henry Peters, John Purguson, Peter Poling, Stephen Pierson, Godfrey Richards, William Rideford, John Richards, John Rubast, Daniel Recknor, John Simpkins, Jacob Storm, George Sapp, John

Steyer, Garrett Snedeger, John Strickler, Matthew Singleman, John Stuck, John Trotter, David Troxell, Peter Tittle, Sr., Ezekiel Totter, James Utter, Sr., James Utter, Jr., John Vanbuskirk, Moses Williams, Adam Hicksenbaugh, Benjamin Hull, Richard Harcourt, William Jones, John Jonas, William Jacobs, Jacob Koontz, Henry Kemp, George Laporte, William Logsden, Ralph Logsden, Elisha Logsden, John Lynn, Zachariah Linton, Henry Mattingly, Henry Myers, Philip Michael, Moses Munro, Josiah McKinsy, John Metz, James McPipe, Thomas Matthew, John Neff, Johannes Paugh, Robert Parker, Gabriel Powell, Nicholas Pittinger, Henry Pittinger, Hezekiah Pound, Martin Poling, Sr., John Price, John Ryan, John Rhoads, John Ratton, David Robertson, Adam Rhoads, Peter Stuck, William Show, Joseph Scott, Simon Speed, Matthew Snooke, John Seyler, William Stagg, James Schimer, Peter Tittle, Jr., Michael Tedrick, Jesse Tomlinson, John Trimble, William Utter, Thomas Umbertson, David Vansickle, William Wells, Samuel Hatton, Abraham Hite, Jacob Hazlewood, Samuel Jackson, William Jones, Jacob Kreger, John Kelly, Leonard Stimble, David Lee, John Liptz, Breton Levit, Jacob Lee, James Montain, William Moore, John Matthews, Jr., Jacob Miller, Alexander Moore, Daniel Moore, Moses McKinsy, Daniel McKinsy, Conrad Millen, Elias Majors, John Nepton, Samuel Postlewait, Michael Paugh, Margaret Poling, John Porter, Samuel Poling, Martin Poling, Richard Poling, Charles Queen, Benjamin Rush, Enoch Read, Roger Robertson, Aaron Rice, Michael Raway, John Ragan, John Streets, Moses Spicer, Abel Serjeant, Adam Seigler, Jacob Seigler, Jacob Scutchfield, John Sibley, Frederick Thoxter, John Tomlinson, Jacob Trullinger, Moses Tilsonel, Richard Tilton, Charles Uhl, John Vincent, Henry Woodger, John Workman, Archibald White, Arthur Watson, Jesse Walter, John Wikoff, Alexander Wilhelm, George Wilhelm, Peter Wikoff, Jacob Wikoff, James Woodringer, Alpheus Wigwire, George Waddle, Isaac Workman, Joseph Warnick, William Workman, James Wells, Peter Wells, Samuel Wikoff, George Winters, Andrew Workman, Jacob Workman, Stephan Workman, Thomas Williams, John Whiteman.

The General Assembly in 1777, as is shown elsewhere, enacted that a bounty of fifty acres should be granted to every able-bodied recruit who should serve three years in the American army, and one hundred acres to each recruiting officer who enlisted twenty men. By the act of 1781 these lands were to be located in the State west of Fort Cumberland. By the act of 1787, Francis Deakins was appointed to survey these lands, and his report showed that forty-one hundred and sixty-five lots of fifty acres each had been laid off, and that three hundred and twenty-three families were settled on six hundred and thirty-six of said lots already improved and cultivated. By the act of 1788 these settlers were allowed to purchase their lots at prices varying from five to twenty shillings per acre, in three equal payments of one, two, and three years. By subsequent acts the Maryland officers and soldiers were secured in the lots to which they were entitled for military services. The following is from the *Maryland Journal* of Friday, July 3, 1789:

"Notice is hereby given to the officers and soldiers of the Maryland Line, that a distribution of land will be made to them at Upper Marlborough, in Prince George's County, on the 1st and 2d of August next, agreeably to an act of Assembly, and at the same time and place will be offered at public sale about one thousand lots of land, of fifty acres each, for ready money, or specie certificates of the State of Maryland. This land lies to the westward of Fort Cumberland. For a particular description thereof, apply to Capt. Daniel Cresap or Mr. John Tomlinson, who lives near the same.

"David Linn,
"Daniel Cresap,
"Benjamin Brookes,
"*Commissioners.*"

At the session of the Legislature in 1789 a petition was presented asking for the erection of a new county, and the following act was passed on the 25th of December of that year:

"An Act *for the division of Washington County, and for the erecting of a new one by the name of Allegany.*

"Whereas, A number of the inhabitants of Washington County, by their petition to the General Assembly, have prayed that an act may pass for a division of said county by Sideling Hill Creek, and for the erection of a new one out of the western part thereof, and it appearing to this General Assembly that the erecting such a new county will conduce greatly to the due administration of justice and the speedy settling and improving the western part thereof, and the ease and convenience of the inhabitants thereof,

"II. *Be it enacted by the General Assembly of Maryland,* That all that part of Washington County which lies to the westward of Sideling Hill Creek shall be and is hereby erected into a new county, by the name of Allegany County, and the inhabitants thereof shall have, hold, and enjoy all such rights and privileges as are held and enjoyed by the inhabitants of any other county in this State.

"III. *And be it enacted,* That the County Court and Orphans' Court for Allegany County shall be held at the town of Cumberland until the voters of said county, by election to be held as hereinafter provided, shall determine on some other place; and until a place may be fixed on by the said election, and a court-house shall be built, the justices of said county may contract and agree at the county charge for a convenient place in the said town to hold their courts, and for a convenient place in the said town for the keeping of their books, papers, and records.

"IV. *And be it enacted,* That all causes, pleas, processes, and pleadings which now are or shall be depending in Washington County Court before the first Monday in December, 1790, shall and may be prosecuted as effectually in that court as if this act had not been made; and in case any deeds or conveyances of land in that part of Washington County now called Allegany County have been or shall be, before the first Monday in December, 1790, acknowledged according to law, the enrollment or recording thereof in either of the said counties within the time limited by law shall be good and available.

"V. *And be it enacted,* That the county charge of Washington County heretofore assessed shall be collected and applied as if this act had not been made.

"VI. *And be it enacted,* That the County Court and Orphans' Court of Allegany County shall first be held on the first Monday in April, 1791, and the said County Court be afterwards held on the first Monday in April and September, yearly, and the said Orphans' Court shall be afterwards held on the second Monday in the months of June, August, October, and December, and the same courts shall have the same powers and jurisdiction respectively as other County and Orphans' Courts within this State.

"VII. *And be it enacted,* That all civil causes to be brought in Allegany County shall be determined within two courts from the Appearance Court, and none shall continue longer, unless under such circumstances as civil causes in other County Courts may be continued longer than three courts from the Appearance Court.

"VIII. *And be it enacted,* That the Governor and Council be authorized and required to commission fit and proper persons as justices of the peace, and fit and proper persons as the Orphans' Courts, as also surveyor and other officers, and that a fit and proper person be appointed by the Governor and Council sheriff of Allegany County, and be commissioned and qualified in the usual manner; to continue in office until a new appointment shall take place in the other counties of this State, under an election according to the constitution and form of government.

"IX. *And be it enacted,* That at the first election to be held in the said county for sheriff, the voters of said county shall and may, by a majority of votes, determine the place at which the courts of the said county shall be held after the said election."

Thus Allegany County was organized. It was created wholly out of the territory of Washington County, the latter parting with more than two-thirds of its superficial area, 672,000 acres, and a population of 5000 inhabitants. The act creating the county made no provision, as will be seen, for a voting-place, but elections were held until 1799 at Cumberland, which had been chosen by the people as the county-seat. Fortunately for the comfort of the citizens there were few officers chosen by ballot in those days, the only county officials being members of the Legislature and sheriff, or the electors would have been subjected to great inconvenience in traveling from Sideling Hill Creek on the one side, and Fairfax Stone on the other, to exercise their right as freemen. Many persons in those days were absolutely debarred from voting by the distance to be traversed, as was the case also in the other counties of Maryland, and in 1799 an act was passed by the General Assembly for the appointment of commissioners in every county of the State to lay off the counties into districts. The commissioners for Allegany were John B. Beall, David Hoffman, Thomas Stewart, William Shaw, George Robinet (of Nathan), and Jesse Tomlinson. Allegany was divided into six election districts, numbered from one to six, which were better known by their local names, as the Glades, Selbysport, Westernport, Musselanes, Cumberland, and Oldtown. The county remained districted as above from 1799 to 1817, in which year the Legislature passed an act for the redivision of the county into eight districts, and appointed the following commissioners for that purpose: Isaac Oyman, William Reid, William McMahon, George Newman (of Butler), and John Simpkins. The commission discharged its duty, and divided the county into the required number of election districts. The division of 1799 was generally adhered to, but a new district was established in the eastern end of the county, then and now known as No. 8, or Little Orleans; and in the west No. 3, or Little Crossings, as it was known till 1850, when the polls were removed from this place to Grantsville by an act of the Legislature. The latter is the largest district in Garrett County, both in point of territory and population, having over four hundred voters, double the number of the district (Selbysport) from which it was taken. A considerable amount of its jurisdiction and population were added to Frostburg in 1856.

The members of the board which made the division are now dead. McMahon was the father of the eminent lawyer John V. L. McMahon. Reed was a prominent man of the county, and died in 1848. Newman was a "Little Crossing's" man, and has been dead for fifty years. Simpkins lived in Selbysport District.

Since 1817 no general districting of the county has been made. As new districts were from time to time needed for the convenience of voters, they were authorized by acts of the Legislature, and laid off by three commissioners named in the act, who reported their proceedings to the County Court. By the act of 1835 Ryan's Glades, or No. 10, was established; 1849, Accident, or No. 11; 1852, Nos. 12 and 13; 1852, No. 14, or Song Run. In 1860 Nos. 15 and 16 were "surveyed and laid out." These two districts are now known as Oakland and Lonaconing respectively. In 1872 the 17th District was created for the benefit of the Barton voters.

The county of Allegany displayed a proper spirit of patriotism upon the breaking out of the last war between the United States and Great Britain. Her citizens volunteered promptly, and several large companies marched to Baltimore to defend that city from the threatened attacks of the British forces. The record will be found in the chapter on the war of 1812.

Early Court Proceedings.—The first court in the county met April 25, 1791, at John Graham's house. Andrew Bruce, on producing his commission as associate justice, was sworn in and opened court. The officers were John Beatty, clerk; John Lynn, clerk; and Jeremiah Willison, crier. On the third day, Richard Potts, chief justice, appeared and took his seat, as also did John Simpkins, the second associate judge. The following attorneys having paid the State license of three pounds each were admitted to practice law: William Claggett, John Johnson, Lenox Martin, George Magruder, and Samuel Selby, of whom Mr. Martin was prosecutor for the State, having received his appointment from the attorney-general of Maryland. The court continued in session five days, and the following were the first judgments rendered: The State of Maryland against John Hoge Bayard, a fine of one shilling for assault and battery; Normand B. Magruder *vs.* Peter Devecmon, wherein the judgment of the latter obtained before John H. Bayard, justice of the peace, was reversed; The State of Maryland *vs.* John Glassiner, Jr., who was fined one shilling three pence "for refusing to desist from quarreling when commanded by the constable;" Same *vs.* George Dent, for striking George Mattingly, was fined one shilling three pence; Harmon Parsons *vs.* Osborn Sprigg, wherein the latter's judgment before Daniel Cresap, justice of the peace, was reversed; The State of Maryland *vs.* Thomas Mattingly, for going on the plantation of Thomas Beall, of Ninian, and beating him, fined one shilling three pence; Same *vs.* Jesse Chaney, wherein the jury found him not guilty of an assault, and the court decreed he recover from the State all the costs and charges of his defense; Same *vs.* Richard Glover, "for breaking the Sabbath," who was fined three shillings nine pence and costs, and admonished to observe in the future the Lord's day. In the first year of the organization of the Levy Court it offered rewards for wolves' scalps, as follows: one pound for that of a young wolf, and five pounds for that of an old one. For several years preceding the completion of the court-house in 1799, the Circuit, Orphans', and Levy Courts and Tax Commissioners all met at Abraham Faw's tavern, on Green Street, west of Smallwood, on the site of the residence of the late William Landwehr, who yearly received £3 6*s.* 12*d.* for rent of his rooms for the public service, besides the perquisites of his bar and increased custom of his inn by having the courts at his hostelry.

The first six indentures, or deeds of conveyance, were recorded Jan. 1, 1791, by John Lynn, clerk of court. The first was from Jonathan Morris to John Lynn, dated Dec. 4, 1790, for lot No. 96 in Cumberland, consideration, £10; the next, from Thomas Beall, of Samuel, to Henry Kemp, dated Oct. 6, 1790, for lot No. 102 in Cumberland, consideration, £20; the third, from Edward Willson to Mark Brayfield, dated Oct. 7, 1790, for thirty-one acres ("Willson's Study"), consideration, £90; the fourth, from George Robinette to John Willison, dated Oct. 7, 1890, for twenty acres ("Addition to Two Springs"), consideration, £10; and the sixth, from Samuel Robinette and Mary Keve to Moses Robinette, dated Sept. 23, 1790, for one hundred acres ("Charles' Lot"), consideration, £90. At the April court of 1798 the grand jury were David Lynn (foreman), Peter Gephart, Samuel Poland, John C. Beatty, Josiah Beall, of Jonah, Frederick Sapp, John Brook Beall, John Brockenhart, Evan Gwynn, James King, John Graham, Benjamin Beckwith, John Matthew, Jr., Michael Collier, James Scott, William Hilleary, John H. Bayard, James Slicer, Jerard Dawson, Henry Mattingly, John Shroyer, William James, Edward Willson, Jr. At the same term the petit jury were William Shaw, Evan James, Elijah Robinson, Benjamin Morris, George Hoffman, Walter Selby, John Deakins, Jr., Conrad Creekbaum, Ralph Logsden, Aaron Duckworth, Thomas McElfish, Moses Robinette. At October court, 1798, the grand jury were William Shaw (foreman), Jacob Trullinger, John Seylar, William Davidson, Daniel Spencer, Griffith Johnson, Sr., James Wells, Godfrey Richards, Sr., Nathaniel B. Magruder, Obed McCrackin, Josiah W. Pigman, John Harness, George Rizer, John Wolf, Peter Lowdermilk, Thomas Dew, Michael Loyster, Nehemiah Barnett, John S. Hook. At same term the petit jury were Thomas Beall, of Samuel, John Bridenhart, Elijah Robinson, Andrew Harry, Robert Larrimore, Benjamin G. Vaughn, Dickinson Simpkins, Henry Winower, Jacob Neff, William Berton, Edward Ward, Daniel Lantz. At the April court, 1799, the grand jury were Thomas Blair, Benjamin Tomlinson, John B. Beall, James Slicer, John Tomlinson, Samuel Poland, Sr., Thomas Wilson, George Fouty, Ralph Logsden, David Lynn (foreman), Thomas McElfish, Robert Cresap, William Hilleary, Benjamin Coddington, Robert Tivis, Evan Gwynn, Henry Stitsman, George Hoffman, James Scott, George Hinkle, Sr., Samuel Selby, Sr. At the same term the petit jury were John Logsden, James Danison, Edward Ward, William Logsden, John Deakins, Sr., Conrad Creekbaum, Peter Gephard, Paul Purcy, George Fouck, James Bryan, J. H. Bard, E. Ward.

The following schedule of inn prices was fixed at the April term, 1799, and is the same as established for several preceding years:

	s.	*d.*
Lodging in clean sheets	1	10
" double "	0	9
" in sheets before used	0	6
Lodgings for Servants	0	6
A Hot Dinner for a Gentleman, with Beer or Cider	3	0
A Supper or Breakfast	2	0
Cold Dinner, per gentleman	1	10½
Supper and Breakfast, per servant	1	6
Dinner, " "	1	10
Hay, per night, for Horse	1	6
" for twenty-four hours	2	6
Corn and Oats, per quart	0	3

	s.	d.
French Brandy, per half pint	1	10
Peach " " "	1	3
Madeira and Claret Wine, per quart	10	0
Port, Sherry, or Lisbon Wine	7	6
Whisky, per gill	0	5½
Other Wine, per quart	5	0

The members of the grand and petit juries received in those days a levy of ten shillings per day. The judges received £1 per day each for their services. James Prather, Daniel Cresap, Jr., and John H. Bayard were the judges of the Orphans' Court. They drew fifteen shillings per day. The levy of 1791 was "made by the justices of Allegany County, pursuant to the direction of the act of Assembly." The justices who signed the proceedings were Daniel Cresap, Jr., Thos. Beall, of Samuel, Samuel Barritt, James Prather, and John Bayard, who each served three days, and received therefor £1 10*s.* The total amount of the levy was £286 7*s.* 7*d*, there being a deficit to meet of £37 13*s.* 1*d.* The rate of taxation was fixed at 7*s.* 3*d.* on every £100 of property in the county.

The next session of the court was more lengthy, as it took the jury three days to get through their business. In April, 1792, the session was prolonged to four days, and thus the service increased and the levy ran up, as will be seen from the fact that in 1791 it was £317 3*s.* 9½*d.*; and in 1793, £528 14*s.* 0*d.* For 1792 and 1793 the tax was 10*s.* on the £100. In 1794 the court lasted five days; the levy was £705, and the tax was 12*s.* 6*d.* In 1795 the court lasted six days, and witnesses having increased and other expenses augmented, the levy was £910 7*s.* 8½*d.*, and the tax 15*s.* on the £100. In 1796 the levy was £1235 8*s.* 11*d.*, and the tax £1 0*s.* 10*d.* In 1797 the April term lasted eight days; the levy was £1503 8*s.* 6*d.*, and the tax £1 2*s.* 11*d.* Eleven justices signed this return. In 1797, the levy ran down to £1183 15*s.* 7¾*d.*, and the tax to 16*s.* 8*d.* on the £100. In 1798 and 1799 the levy was only a few pounds more, and the tax the same. The tax of the April term, 1797, caused the yeomanry to complain, and hence the reduction for the August term, and in the years 1798 and 1799. In 1800 the levy was about the same as in the two preceding years, and the tax remained the same, being a good start for the new century. In 1801 the levy was £1469 18*s.* 8*d.*; the tax, 20*s.* 10*d.* In 1802 the levy was down a little again, being £1186 17*s.* 4*d.*; the tax, 16*s.* 8*d.* In 1803 the levy was £1410 5*s.* 5½*d.*; the tax, 20*s.* 10*d.* In 1804 the levy was £1617 5*s.* 3*d.*; the tax, 22*s.* 11*d.* The levy record of this year is signed by Justices William Shaw, Benjamin Tomlinson, Thomas Pratt, and U. Bruce. The levy of 1804 was the last in which the old English money designations, £ *s.* *d.*, were used in the Levy Court of Allegany County. In 1805 the columns of the records are headed with "$" and "cents." From that date forward, so far as the books of the court show, the new order was followed. Jurymen drew $1.50 per day. The foreman of the grand jury for the term in 1805 was Thomas Stewart; the associate justices were Hanson Briscoe and Robert Armstrong. The justices who signed the levy were William Shaw, Benjamin Tomlinson, Asa Beall, Thomas Pratt, U. Bruce, John Reid, and John Burbridge. The levy footed up $4224.50; the tax being $1.12½ on every $100.

The Orphans' Court, composed of Justices James Prather, Daniel Cresap, and John Hodge Bayard, met April 4, 1791. Its first business was to approve of the bond of William McMahon, register of wills, and its second to order a seal for the court. The bondsmen of the register of wills were John H. Bayard and John Lynn, in two thousand pounds. It then adjourned till the second Monday of June, when Jean Flora, by her attorney, made a motion to establish the validity of a verbal will made in her favor by John Pursley, and which was disputed by Dennis Pursley. The court sustained the will. The next court assembled on the second Monday of August, but no business appearing, it adjourned to October 10th, at which date there being still no business it again adjourned to December. At this term Elizabeth, the orphan daughter of George Brent, deceased, chose Daniel Cresap, Jr., as her guardian, who gave bond, with John Lynn and John Johnson as sureties. At the next term, in August, 1792, no business was transacted. At the October court following, citations were issued against Barbara Snook, Joseph Warnock, and Samuel Elliott, executors of the estate of Matthias Snook, against Elizabeth Alexander, administratrix of Patrick Alexander, against Margaret Arnold, executrix of John Arnold, and Elizabeth Brandstratter and John Simkins, executors of Matthias Brandstratter, deceased. At the April term of 1794, James Price, aged eighteen years, was apprenticed to Thomas Foster until he arrived at the age of twenty-one, during which time his master agreed to find him sufficient diet, lodging, and apparel, to give him six months' schooling, and to teach him the trade of a blacksmith, and when free to furnish him with a suit of clothes of the value of six pounds current money.

At the same time Isaac Warren, aged fourteen, was bound out to Spencer Cooper, to learn the trade of a painter. Michael Kesner was apprenticed to Joseph Ridenour to become proficient in the art of a blacksmith, and Nancy Meekin was bound to John Lynn, and to have three pounds at her majority.

The wills of the following decedents were proven and recorded up to 1800:

Matthias Snook, Dec. 29, 1790: Matthias Brandstetter, Feb. 15, 1791; John Arnold, April 26, 1791; Richard Hall, Nov. 24, 1791; Thomas Cresap, Jan. 21, 1790; James Burk; Ebenezer Davis, Jan. 13, 1794; Robert Clarke, April 9, 1794; Moses Porter, Jan. 3, 1795; George Payne, April 29, 1794; John Tuney, Jan. 31, 1795; Gilbert Whitney, June 3, 1795; John Wall, Aug. 25, 1795; Robert McMinn, Sept. 20, 1795; Zachariah Magruder, May 3, 1796; James Matthews, Aug. 9, 1796; Jerome Plummer, July 26, 1796; Michael Feile, Sept. 7, 1796; Jacob Bell, Aug. 21, 1795; John Parkison, Feb. 25, 1797; Balsor Shelhorn, March 18, 1797; Joseph Monntz, Dec. 28, 1797; Elizabeth Pitsen, June 22, 1798; Daniel Cresap, July 14, 1798; Lucy Beall, May 23, 1799; Cornelius Willison, Oct. 21, 1799; John Shelhorn, April 10, 1800.

The following is a list of marriage licenses up to 1800, granted under the act of Assembly entitled An Act Concerning Marriages:

1791.

Aug. 1. Godfrey Richards, Jr., to Temple Knight.
" 26. Robert Green to Barbara Chambers.
Sept. 14. George Jordan to Elizabeth Tetrix.
" 22. John Glanner to Mary Snediker.
Oct. 28. John Hagerman to Eleanor Gorman.
Nov. 14. Jacob Stever to Mary Bonham.

1792.

April 4. Jonathan Cox to Susanna Baillie.
" 24. David Beall to Mary Davis.
May 21. Elias Stillwell to Catharine Morgan.
Aug. 13. George Payne to Mary Sapp.
Sept. 27. Benjamin Morris to Rebecca Simpkins.
Oct. 23. Richard Moore to Sarah Moore.
Nov. 6. Peter McKean to Anna Hull.

1793.

May 9. Benjamin Durbin to Liddy Longe.
" 29. Jesse Reno to Prudence Randolph.
" 29. Samuel James to Frances Randolph.
June 24. Charles F. Brodhag to Elizabeth Alexander.
July 16. Caleb Godwin to Mary McMinn.
Aug. 20. Samuel Beckwith to Susanna Durbin.
Nov. 3. Richard Tomlinson to Phœbe Sliff.
" 20. John Knight to Nancy Davis.
Dec. 18. Nehemiah Barnett to Winey Cammins.

1794.

Feb. 6. Asa Beall to Elizabeth Beall.
" 6. Peter Iseminger to Rebecca Henderson.
May 24. John Coleman to Margaret Savage.
July 12. Michael Fisher to Margaret Savage.
" 16. Jacob Nagle to Mary Selby.
Aug. 20. Henry Boyles to Rebecca Barcus.
Sept. 6. Ezekiel Chaney to Mary Balzel.
" 11. Daniel Lovett to Polly James.
Dec. 13. William Stephens to Ann Pigman.
" 30. Aquila A. Brown to Sarah Cresap.

1795.

April 16. John Bridenhort to Mary Lowdermilk.
" 21. Thomas Chaney to Susanna Stockwell.
" 23. Alexander Grimes to Eleanor Pearel.
June 1. John Shryer to Christiana Letter.
July 15. Jacob Myers to Mary Payne.
Aug. 8. John Clarke to Abiel Shepherd.
Oct. 12. John Compton to Rebecca Clarke.
" 31. John Evans to Johanna Fitzgerald.
" 31. Ralph Logsden to Margaret Arnold.
Sept. 2. Daniel Loge Ellison to Ann Logsden.
Dec. 5. Josiah Beall, of T., to Ann Pullen.
" 31. William McMahon to Sally Van Lear.

1796.

Jan. 2. Thomas Pritchard to Nancy Titchenal.
Feb. 2. John McColm to Sarah Smith.
" 13. Samuel Selby to Jane Thistle.
" 26. Joshua Titchenal to Elsea Bevins.
March 2. Gavin Woodfield to Peggy Brawalt.
" 7. Cornelius Young to Catharine Sisler.
" 17. Robert Sinclair to Ann Cromwell.
April 7. Robert Armstrong to Elizabeth Cresap.
" 16. James White to Elizabeth Eping.
" 28. John Kimberly to Elizabeth Tomlinson.
May 2. Stephen Deakins to Elizabeth Freland.
" 14. Nicholas Coonce to Rebecca Danford.
" 26. William W. Hoge to Eleanor Slicer.
June 11. John D. Lucas to Jane Benick.
" 17. John Clisisman to Peggy Stonesaffer.
July 7. John House to Ann Harlewood.
" 19. Jeremiah Helley to Mary Cadey.
Aug. 31. William Taylor to Elizabeth Gocy.
Sept. 11. John Mattingly to Onea Arnold.
Oct. 1. Daniel Sapp to Mary Robison.
" 5. Hugh Graham to Sarah Lappins.
" 18. Bogue Pellem to Sarah Clarke.
Nov. 5. Patrick Conner to Polly Lannam.
" 9. William Craik to Hannah Hall.
" 21. Thomas Porter to Mary Logsden.
" 28. Daniel Cresap, Sr., to Elizabeth Dawson.
" 29. Edward Richardson to Hannah Durbin.
Dec. 9. John Bare to Sarah Piles.
" 17. Bennet Logsden to Abigail Lewis.
" 13. Moses Barcus to Nancy Thompson.
" 24. Thomas Selby, Sr., to Ann Harlewood.

1797.

Jan. 8. Edmund Crawford to May Poole.
Feb. 10. Zachariah Magruder to Ann Dawson.
" 14. William Michael to Rachel Brian.
" 26. David Duttro to Mary Crickbaum.
" 26. Nathaniel Price to Mary Eblin.
March 4. William Key to Sally Deakins.
" 25. Charles W. Selby to Elizabeth Selby.
April 26. Alexander Baillie to Mary Doyle.
" 28. George Bluhn to Rosanna Essing.
May 5. Daniel Cresap, Sr., to Hannah Longshore.
" 10. Gabriel M. Porter to Rebecca Frost.
" 23. Nath. B. Magruder to Mary Beavins.
" 23. Walter A. Murdoch to Sary Beavins.
June 3. George Barnes to Catharine Eigler.
" 8. John Deakins to Margaret James.
" 10. Robert Boyd to Mary Eckhart.
" 22. William Logsden to Susanna Williams.
" 23. George Sapp to Catharine Arnold.
Aug. 8. John Lindy to Elizabeth Catchall.
Sept. 27. William Rutherford to Elizabeth Harper.
Nov. 25. Peter Crickbaum to Mary McBride.

1798.

Jan. 18. John Smith to Mary Pritchards.
Feb. 14. Benjamin Foster to Catharine Prather.
" 19. Conrad Neff to Susanna Creightbaum.
March 6. George Fouty to Eve Sapp.
April 11. John Mitchell to Susanna M. Jacobs.

June 21. John Taylor to Hanna Casad.
" 21. Samuel Semple to Martha Idley.
Oct. 12. William Renick to Elizabeth Watton.
" 17. John James to Liddy Hays.
Dec. 3. Adam Grace to Barshaba Hinkle.
" 31. Angus McDonald to Anne Doyle.

1799.

Jan. 1. Thomas Cromwell to Ann Slicer.
" 14. Thomas Caiwell to Margaret Davidson.
March 7. John McClery to Sarah Hendrickson.
" 20. John Gilmore to Anne Price.
" 30. John Patterson to Elizabeth Wire.
April 18. William Winebrenner to Alice Smith.
May 23. William McLoughlin to Lina French.
June 4. Martin Rizer to Rosina Grephart.
" 6. Joseph Shepherd to Rebecca McDougal.
" 20. John Scott to Ann Hilleary.
Sept. 15. Dennis Maddon to Mary Canning.
Nov. 11. John Logsden, of Wm., to Patience Arnold.
" 14. Jacob Hoffman to Margaret Steck.
" 16. Andrew Polston to Susanna McCabe.
" 23. Abraham Rhodes to Mary Newmyer.
Dec. 21. John C. Beatty to Ann Beall.
" 21. William Osborn to Christiana Stonecser.
" 23. Valentine Shockey to Elizabeth Climer.

1800.

Jan. 29. David Smith to Elizabeth McCollum.
" 30. Jacob Showaker to Catharine Woodring.
Feb. 6. Joseph McDonald to Sinah Dew.
" 12. John Durbin to Sarah Clifford.
" 21. Daniel Johnston to Sarah Danison.
March 5. William Stidger to Sophia Davis.
" 8. John Graham to Elizabeth Brent.
June 2. Frederick Metz to Christina Keelan.
July 26. William Berry to Kesiah Ebling.
Aug. 27. Peter Counce to Polly Langshire.
Sept. 11. Joseph Crawford to Mary Plank.
William Stephens to Ann Pigman.
Oct. 2. Nottey Barnett to Elsie Ragan.
" 2. Mahlon Longshore to Sally Ragan.
" 2. William Naylor to Nancy Sanford.
Nov. 3. Frederick Young to Eliza Wall.
" 8. Davis Meredith to Ann Pritchard.
" 15. Scott Robinson to Ann Moore.
" 17. John Williams to Phœbe Smith.
" 24. William Moore to Margaret Robinett.
" 24. John Parker to Elizabeth Nepton.
" 27. James Bailey to Polly Fetter.
" 27. Amos Robinette to Darky Willson.

County Courts and Civil Officers.—The following is a list of officers who have served in the county since its organization as far as can be ascertained from the records:

JUDGES OF THE CIRCUIT COURT.

Chief Justices.—1791, Richard Potts; 1806, John Buchanan; 1845, Robert N. Martin.

Circuit Judges.[1]—1851, Thomas Perry; 1864, James Smith (died Aug. 14, 1865); 1865, George A. Pearre.[2]

Chief Justice.—Richard H. Alvey.

Associate Judges.—1791, Andrew Bruce, John Simpkins; 1797, Patrick Murdock, Hanson Briscoe; 1801, William Craik, *vice* Murdock; 1802, William Claggett, *vice* Briscoe; 1806, Abraham Shriver, *vice* Craik; 1810, Roger Nelson, *vice* Claggett; 1815, Thomas Buchanan, *vice* Nelson; 1843, Richard H. Marshall, *vice* Shriver; 1847, Daniel Weisel, *vice* Buchanan. Under constitution of 1867: 1867, William Motter, Thomas Perry; 1871, George A. Pearre, *vice* Perry, deceased.

JUDGES OF THE ORPHANS' COURT.

1791–95.—Daniel Cresap, John Hoge Bayard, James Prather.
1795–1802.—Evan Gwynn, John Hoge Bayard, A. A. Browne.
1802.—Ninian Cochran, Thomas Cresap, Andrew Bruce.
1803–10.—Andrew Bruce, Thomas Thistle, Thomas Cresap.
1810–12.—Upton Bruce, Thomas Cresap, Hanson Briscoe.
1812–14.—George Hebb, Lenox Martin, Thomas Thistle.
1814–17.—John Scott, Thomas Thistle, Lenox Martin.
1817–20.—John McHenry, John Scott, Thomas Thistle.
1820–22.—Edward Wyatt, Thomas Cresap, John McNeill.
1822–25.—William McMahon, Thomas Cresap, John McNeill.
1825–27.—Robert Swann, Thomas Cresap, John McNeill.
1827–29.—Robert Armstrong, Thomas Cresap, John McNeill.
1829.—Thomas Cresap, John Scott, John McNeill.
1830.—George Hoblitzell, John Scott, Thomas Cresap.
1831–33.—Thomas Cresap, John McNeill.
1833–37.—George Hebb, John McNeill, Thomas Cresap.
1837–39.—John Gebhart, Thomas Cresap, George Hebb.
1839–45.—John Hays, Moses Rawlings, Thomas Cresap.
1845–48.—Martin Rizer, Jr., John Gebhart, Isaac Beall.
1848–50.—John Hays, James Fitzpatrick, John Porter.
1850.—William Weber, John Hays, H. H. Ainsworth.
1851–54.—Jacob Fechting, E. Mullan, J. Robinette.
1854–56.—J. M. Buchanan, Patrick Hamill, J. Robinette.
1856–59.—Moses Rawlings, Patrick Hamill, Alexander King.
1859–64.—Moses Rawlings, Alexander King, Francis Mattingly.
1864–67.—J. B. H. Campbell, A. M. L. Bush, Douglass Percy.
1867–69.—Patrick Hamill, John Coulehan, John M. Buchanan.
1869–71.—Upton D. Long, John Coulehan, John M. Buchanan.
1871–74.—W. R. McCully, Upton D. Long, John Coulehan.
1874.—Upton D. Long, John Coulehan, Cornelius Slack.
1875–77.—Robert Bruce, John Coulehan, Cornelius Slack.
1877–79.—William Piatt, Robert Bruce, John Coulehan.
1879.—James D. Armstrong, John Coulehan (present incumbents).

REGISTERS OF WILLS.

William A. McMahon, from April 14, 1791, to July 10, 1798.
Thomas Cromwell, from July 10, 1798, to Feb. 12, 1805.
George Bruce, from Feb. 12, 1805, to Oct. 6, 1818.
Charles Heck, from Oct. 6, 1818, to May 25, 1841.
Daniel Blocher, from May 25, 1841, to Dec. 30, 1846.
Wm. R. McCulley, from Dec. 30, 1846, to Dec. 1, 1857.
John B. Widener, from Dec. 1, 1857, to Dec. 15, 1863.
Geo. W. Hoover, from Dec. 15, 1863, to Nov. 19, 1867.
Elijah Fuller, from Nov. 19, 1867, to 1873.

In 1873, C. C. Shriver was elected, and served until his death, in October, 1875, when he was succeeded by Howard Fuller, who served until the election in November, when John Rhind was elected, and began his term Dec. 1, 1875, and was re-elected in 1881 for six years from Dec. 1, 1881.

SHERIFFS.

1791, John Beatty;[3] 1797–1801, Robert Sinclair; 1801, John C. Beatty; 1804, Levi Hilleary; 1807, William Bruce;

[1] The constitution of 1850 provided for one circuit judge only, and made the office elective, whereas prior to this date the judges had been appointed by the Governor.

[2] The constitution of 1867 provided for a chief justice and two associate judges, to be elected for a term of fifteen years.

[3] No minutes of proceedings of court from 1791 to 1798 in clerk's office.

1810, William Hilleary; 1813, Thomas Pollard; 1816, William R. Dawson; 1819, George Bruce; 1822, Andrew Bruce; 1825, William McMahon; 1828, Richard Beall; 1831, Moses Rawlings; 1834, Lawrence O. Holt; 1837, Thomas Dowden; 1840, Michael T. Porter (one term of court), John M. Charlton; 1842, Norman Bruce; 1845, Moses Rawlings; 1848, John Barnard; 1851, George M. Blocher; 1853, Perry Shultz; 1855, Dr. John Everett; 1857, Hanson Willison; 1859, Henry R. Atkinson; 1861, Thomas G. McCulloh; 1863, Basil J. Garlitz; 1865, Daniel Duncan; 1867, Hanson Willison; 1869, George L. Layman; 1871, Richard Gross; 1873, James C. Lynn; 1875, John G. Bauer; 1877, Edward Manning; 1879, Henry Hanekane; 1881, J. William Shuck (present incumbent).

Clerks of Circuit Court.

1791, John Lynn; 1811, Hanson Briscoe; 1817, William McMahon (temporary), Asa Beall; 1845, Henry Bruce; 1851, Horace Resley; 1873, Theodore Luman (present incumbent).

Levy Court and County Commissioners.

1791.—Daniel Cresap, Thomas Beall, of Samuel, Samuel Barrett, James Prather, John H. Bayard.

1792.—John Orme, Samuel Barrett, James Prather, Gabriel Jacob, John H. Bayard, John Reed.

No records of meetings of the board from 1793 to 1813 can be found.

1813-16.—J. H. Bayard, James D. Cresap, George Hoffman, John Reid, John Templeman.

1816-22.—J. H. Bayard, J. D. Cresap, George Hoffman, Thomas Dawson, John Reid.

1822-24.—J. H. Bayard, J. D. Cresap, George Hoffman, Thomas Dawson, William Reid.

1824.—Benjamin Tomlinson, Samuel Coddington, John Burbridge, William Price, Walter McAtee, George W. Glaze, Meshac Frost.

1825.—George Rhinehart, Archibald Thistle, Benjamin Robinson, Valentine Hoffman, Walter McAtee, William Price, John Burbridge, Samuel Coddington, Benjamin Tomlinson.

1826.—Upton Bruce, Martin Rizer, Benjamin Tomlinson, Samuel Coddington, William Price, Benjamin Robinson, Archibald Thistle, William McLaughlin, Valentine Hoffman, Walter McAtee.

1827.—Francis Reed, Benjamin Tomlinson, Samuel Coddington, William Price, Valentine Hoffman, Archibald Thistle, William McLaughlin, Walter McAtee.

1828.—J. H. Bayard, George Hoffman, John Willison, Thomas Dawson, James D. Cresap.

1829.—John Miller, Martin Rizer, Upton Bruce, William McLaughlin, Archibald Thistle, Francis Reed, Valentine Hoffman, Walter McAtee, Samuel Coddington, Benjamin Tomlinson.

1830.—Jasper Robinette, Henry Myers, Walter Bevans, Joshua O. Robinson, Joseph Frantz, George Blocher, William McLaughlin, Jacob Holman, John Mattingly, Thomas D. Beall.

1831.—Joseph Frantz, George Hoffman, George Blocher, William Newman, Robert Lashly, George Devilbiss, George Bruce, Ezekiel Totten.

1832.—George Hoffman, George Bruce, Ezekiel Totten, Peter Preston, George Blocher, Robert Lashly, William Newman, Isaac McCarty, Joseph Frantz, John Devilbiss.

1833.—George Blocher, Jonathan Wilson, Joseph Frantz, John Wiley, Henry Myers, Peter Preston, Martin Rizer, William Newman, John Larew, Robert Lashly.

1834-35.—Daniel Woolford, Daniel Folck, William Newman, Martin Rizer, Thomas Dowden, Peter Preston, John Poland, John Slicer, Jonathan Wilson, John Wiley.

1836.—Cornelius Kight, Henry Brown, John Slicer, James D. Armstrong, Peter Preston, Burgess Magruder, John Cress, William Newman, Daniel Folck, Robert Lashly.

1837.—William Newman, Peter Preston, J. D. Armstrong, John Slicer, Henry Brown, Cornelius Kight, Robert Lashly, Burgess Magruder, John Cress, Daniel Folck.

1838.—Walter Bevans, George H. A. Kunst, John Slicer, Henry Brown, George M. Blocher, Martin Rizer, Burgess Magruder, John W. Mountz.

1839.—Martin Rizer, G. H. A. Kuntz, J. D. Armstrong, Henry Brown, Walter Bevans, J. W. Mountz, John Slicer, Cornelius Kight, Burgess Magruder, George M. Blocher, John Probst.

1840.—Martin Rizer, John Slicer, Henry Brown, Cornelius Kight, Elisha Combs, Burgess Magruder, Robert Lashly, Leonard Shercliff, J. W. Mountz.

1841.—John Probst, John Slicer, Godfrey Fazenbaker, John M. Twigg, William Conard, George M. Reid, Henry Smouse, James Twigg, Samuel Cessna, G. H. A. Kunst.

1842.—John Probst, John Slicer, Godfrey Fazenbaker, J. M. Twigg, James Twigg, George Bruce, Wm. Conard, George M. Reid, Henry Smouse, Samuel Cessna, Henry Bruce.

1843-45.—John Probst, John Frantz, Peter Yeast, G. Fazenbaker, Henry Kreighbaum, G. M. Reed, Alexander King, L. M. Jamison, H. Bevans, Robert Lashly, Henry Bruce.

1845-47.—John Probst, Richard Fairall, Peter Yeast, Henry Miller, Henry Kreighbaum, Daniel Wineow, Baptist Mattingly, John Daniels, H. Bevans, Robert Lashly, Jonathan Rinehart.

1847-48.—Jonathan Wilson, William Fear, George R. Bruce, Peter Bare, Henry Brotenmarkle, Samuel Soyster, Daniel Crabtree, John Bevans, Jasper Robinette, Israel Thompson.

1848-50.—G. R. Bruce, William Fear, Francis Mattingly, Peter Smouse, Levin Benton, Israel Thompson, Edward Hays, Robert Ross, of William, Daniel Wineow, James Twigg, George Robinette.

1850.—J. T. Edwards, N. Bruce, G. Beall, George Rizer, J. J. Hoffman.

1851.—H. D. Carlton, H. Brotenmarkle, Aquila Long, Archibald Chisholm, Jesse Wilson, Richard Fairall, F. L. Friend, John Frantz, Eli Engle, T. W. Dawson, George McCulloh.

1852.—John W. Browning, Eli McElfish, George Matthews, Eli Engle, T. W. Dawson, Charles A. Scott, N. D. Smith, Ashbel Willison, James Watson, J. McClure Mason, Perry Schultz, Jesse Wilson.

1853-56.—John Gephart, William Browning, Charles A. Scott.

1856-59.—Henry Brotenmarkle, F. Shultz, Elisha Willison, Peter Diffenbaugh, Jacob Hoblitzell.

1859.—Charles A. Hamill, William Combs, George Robinette, John Flewell.

1861-63.—William R. McCulley, Daniel Duncan, David Kent, Ashford Trail, David Compton.

1863-65.—John Bell, Charles Ridgeley, J. L. Townsend, John H. Stallings, Elijah Friend.

1865-67.—Robert McCulloh, Ashford Trail, R. S. Dayton, D. H. Friend, S. J. Beachy.

1867-69.—William Browning, Honorius Shircliff, Daniel Frazer, John Farrell, W. H. Barnard.

1869-71.—Israel Thompson, J. L. Browning, Michael Naughton, Adam Garringer, William McCulley.

1871-73.—A. C. Greene, Wm. R. Beall, J. L. Townsend, George Renschlein, Ashford Trail.

1873-75.—A. C. Greene, Ashford Trail, B. L. Turner, Wm. R. Beall, George Renschlein.

1875-77.—A. C. Greene, William R. Beall, George Renschlein, A. B. Shaw, Ashford Trail.

1877-79.—A. C. Greene, F. M. Cramlich, W. Y. McCulloh, Jonathan Willison, J. C. Cookery.

1879-81.—A. E. Hitchins, A. J. Clark, M. A. Frost, Martin Rouzer, Henry Hergot.

1881-83.—Robert Matheny, Nathan Loar, L. V. Alderton, John Kolb, A. M. L. Bush (present incumbents).

CLERKS TO COUNTY COMMISSIONERS.

1813-16, Levi Hillary; 1817-24, Thomas Pollard; 1824-31, John McNeill; 1831-37, Richard Beall; 1837-42, George W. Devecmon; 1842-43, John E. Offutt; 1843, J. M. Carlton; 1844, G. W. Devecmon; 1845-48, John T. Hoblitzell; 1848-51, G. W. Devecmon; 1851-55, F. M. Deems; 1855-60, Thomas A. Hopkins; 1860, William Kilgour; 1869, William McCulley; 1869-78, Thomas E. Gonder; 1878-79, F. M. Cramlich, Jr.; 1879, Levi T. De Witt (present incumbent).

MEMBERS OF CONSTITUTIONAL CONVENTIONS.

1776, Allegany and Washington Counties, as the Upper District of Frederick County.—Samuel Beall, Samuel Hughes, John Stull, Henry Schnebly.

1788, Allegany and Washington, as Washington County.—Moses Rawlings, John Stull, Thomas Sprigg, Henry Shryock.

1851.—William Weber, William M. Holliday, John Slicer, James Fitzpatrick, Dr. Samuel P. Smith.

1864.—Albert C. Green, Hopewell Hebb, Jasper Robinette, George A. Thruston, Jacob Wickard.

1867.—Thomas J. McKaig, Thomas Perry, Alfred Spates, William Walsh, Jacob Hoblitzell, J. Philip Roman.

STATE'S ATTORNEYS.

Since the adoption of the constitution of 1850 and 1851 the State's attorneys have been elected by the people as follows: 1851, Josiah H. Gordon; 1855, J. M. Schley; 1863, George A. Thruston; 1867, Charles B. Thruston; 1871, William J. Reed; 1875, A. Hunter Boyd; 1879, David W. Sloan.

JUSTICES OF THE PEACE, 1881.

Date of Commission.		District.
April 14, 1880	James Watson	No. 1.
" "	H. Shircliff	" 1.
" "	L. O. Piper	" 2.
" "	John Hartley	" 2.
" "	Lennox Perrin	" 3.
" "	Thomas McElfish	" 3.
" "	Alexander King	" 4.
" "	John R. Brooke	" 4.
" "	J. Wm. Jones	" 5.
Sept. 6, 1881	J. M. Strong	" 5.
April 14, 1880	Andrew Gonder	" 6.
" "	John B. Widener	" 6.
" "	Stanley Cresap	" 7.
" "	Geo. W. Sheetz	" 8.
" "	J. T. Facenbaker	" 8.
" "	Patrick Cadden	" 9.
" "	Uriah Duckworth	" 9.
" "	Cornelius T. Murphy	" 10.
Aug. 17, 1881	John O. Hanley	" 10.
April 14, 1880	O. J. Moat	" 11.
" "	Hy. R. Atkinson	" 11.
" "	Joseph M. Byrne	" 12.
" "	John Lavelle	" 12.
" "	James Warren	" 13.
" "	Jas. Forsyth Harrison	" 14.
Jan. 7, 1881	H. J. Flanagan	" 14.
April 14, 1880	John Ryan	" 15.
" "	John Mansfield	" 15.

Deputy Clerks of Courts, Percival Rowland, Will O. Hoffman, Julian H. Thruston, Frank E. McCulloh, Frank G. Luman.

State's Attorney, David W. Sloan.

Deputy Register of Wills, Howard M. Fuller.

Surveyor, John Schaidt.

Attorney to Commissioners, William Brace.

Almshouse Trustees, John Wiebel, Peter Smouse, John Wilson; Physician to same, Dr. Wardlaw McGill; Steward to same, James Reid.

County Treasurer, Daniel Annan.

Superintendents of National Road, Charles Getz, Henry Smeltz, John B. Wright.

Coroner, John M. Strong.

Collector of Taxes, A. M. Rush.

School Commissioners, George B. Fundenberg, Samuel Sonneborn, P. L. Burwell Secretary, Treasurer, and Examiner of Schools, J. W. S. Cochran.

Auditor to Court, Robert W. McMichael; Court's Standing Commissioners, G. T. Porter, James A. McHenry, Will S. Bridenholph.

Notaries Public (in Cumberland), J. L. Griffith, G. L. Wellington, James W. Thomas, J. S. Humbird.

United States Collector of Internal Revenue, Webster Bruce; Deputies, Henry H. Hartsock, Geo. H. Gilpin; Storekeeper and Gauger, John H. Young; Gauger, James C. Lynn.

REGISTRARS OF VOTERS.

Districts.	
Orleans, No. 1	James T. McKnight.
Flintstone, No. 3	Owen McElfish.
Cumberland (Canal), No. 4	O. M. Schindel.
" (Will's Creek), No. 5	J. Geo. Flurshutz.
" (River), No. 6	Sprigg S. Lynn.
Rawling's, No. 7	A. C. Rawlings.
Westernport, No. 8	John S. Miller.
Barton, No. 9	O. G. Barchus.
Lonaconing, No. 10	John Moran.
Frostburg, No. 11	J. L. Porter.
East Frostburg, No. 12	G. H. Arnold.
Mount Savage, No. 13	James Stephens.
Cumberland (Central), No. 14	John S. Craigen.
East Lonaconing, No. 15	Edward Shockey.

MEMBERS OF CONGRESS.

1824, Thomas C. Worthington; 1827, Michael C. Sprigg; 1831, Francis Thomas, ten years; 1845, Thomas Perry; 1847, James Dixon Roman, two years; 1849, William T. Hamilton, six years; 1855, Henry W. Hoffman, two years; 1857, J. M. Kunkel, four years; 1861, Francis Thomas, eight years; 1868, Patrick Hamill, two years; 1870, John Ritchie, two years; 1872, Lloyd Lowndes, Jr., two years; 1874, William Walsh, four years; 1878, Milton G. Urner, four years.

STATE SENATORS FROM ALLEGANY COUNTY.

1811-15, Upton Bruce; 1815-30, George Hebb; 1831-36, B. S. Pigman; 1836-37, Levi Hilleary; 1838-39, William Mathews; 1840-46, John Beall; 1846-51, Daniel Blocher; 1851-55, William Weber; 1855-60, Samuel M. Semmes; 1860-61, Thomas J. McKaig; 1862, John Everett; 1863-67, Charles H. Ohr; 1867-74, Alfred Spates; 1874-76, Thomas G. McCulloh; 1878, John S. Combs; 1882, William Brace.

MEMBERS OF THE HOUSE OF DELEGATES FROM ALLEGANY COUNTY.

1790.—Thomas Beall, of Samuel, John Tomlinson, John Simpkins, Daniel Cresap, Jr.

1791.—Thomas Beall, of Samuel, David Cresap, Jr., Benjamin Tomlinson, Gabriel Jacob.

1792.—Thomas Beall, of Samuel, John Hodge Bayard, John Johnson, Jesse Tomlinson.

1793.—John Johnson, John Hodge Bayard, Jesse Tomlinson, John Simpkins.

1794.—John Johnson, Thomas Beall, of Samuel, John Cresap, David Lynn.

1795.—John Johnson, David Lynn, James Cresap, Alpheus Beall.

1796.—John Conrad Beatty, Daniel Clark, Jr., Asa Beall, Benjamin Tomlinson.

1797.—Daniel Clark, Jr., Asa Beall, Benjamin Tomlinson, John Rice.

1798.—James Cresap, of Michael, James Cresap, of Daniel, Asa Beall, John Simpkins.

1799.—Roger Perry, John Tomlinson, Asa Beall, John Rice.

1800.—Joseph Cresap, James Cresap, A. Michael, John Simpkins, Peter Gebhart.

1801.—Jesse Tomlinson, Joseph Cresap, John Simpkins, Benjamin Tomlinson.

1802-3.—John H. Bayard, John Simpkins, Jesse Tomlinson, Joseph Cresap.

1804.—Upton Bruce, Benjamin Tomlinson, John H. Bayard, Jesse Tomlinson.

1805.—Upton Bruce, Benjamin Tomlinson, George Rizer, Thomas Cresap.

1806.—Upton Bruce, Hanson Briscoe, Asa Beall, George Rizer.

1807.—Upton Bruce, Benjamin Tomlinson, Thomas Greenwell, Hanson Briscoe.

1808.—William McMahon, Levy Hilleary, Jesse Tomlinson, John Reid.

1809.—Levi Hilleary, John H. Bayard, James Cresap, of Dare, John Reid.

1810.—Levi Hilleary, Roger Perry, John H. Bayard, Aquila A. Brown.

1811.—Thomas Blair, James D. Cresap, Beall Howard, Benjamin Tomlinson.

1812.—Roger Perry, George McCulloh, George Robinette, of Nathan, James D. Cresap.

1813.—William Hilleary, George Robinette, of Nathan, George McCulloh, Beall Howard.

1814.—Jacob Lantz, William Hilleary, William McMahon, Jesse Tomlinson.

1815.—William McMahon, William Hilleary, James Prather, Jr., Joseph Tomlinson.

1816.—James D. Cresap, William Ridgley, James Prather, Joseph Tomlinson.

1817.—James D. Cresap, Joseph Tomlinson, John Scott, James Tidball.

1818.—Joseph Tomlinson, William Shaw, Samuel Thomas, James Tidball.

1819.—Benjamin Tomlinson, William Price, Thomas Greenwell, Thomas Blair.

1820.—William Hilleary, John Scott, William Reid, Thomas Blair.

1821.—Michael C. Sprigg, John A. Hoffman, Thomas Greenwell, Edward Wyatt.

1822.—Thomas Greenwell, John A. Hoffman, Benjamin Tomlinson, Thomas Pollard.

1823.—George Bruce, Michael C. Sprigg, John V. L. McMahon, John McHenry.

1824.—John V. L. McMahon, Jacob Lantz, Lewis Klipstine, John A. Hoffman.

1825.—Roger Perry, William Reid, Thomas Blair, Robert Armstrong.

1826.—William Ridgley, Jacob Hoblitzell, William Shaw, Robert Armstrong.

1827.—John McNeill, Jr., John A. Hoffman, Jacob Hoblitzell, George McCulloh.

1828.—William McMahon, Joseph Dilley, William Price, William Buskirk.

1829.—William McMahon, Joseph Dilley, William Price, William Buskirk.

1830.—William McMahon, William Ridgley, William Shaw, William Reid.

1831.—George M. Swan, William Armstrong, Jacob Lantz, Thomas Blair.

1832.—Jacob Lantz, Moses H. Louthan, Andrew Bruce, John Slicer.

1833.—Normand Bruce, William Ridgley, Jeremiah Berry, Jr., Jacob Lantz.

1834.—Alpheus Beall, William McMahon, Normand Bruce, G. W. Devecmon.

1835.—William McMahon, William Matthews, Jeremiah Berry, Jr., Joseph Frantz.

1836.—George Smith, Robert Bruce, John M. Buchanan, Thomas Perry.

1837.—John Neff, Daniel Blocher, Jonathan Huddleston, Michael C. Sprigg.

1838.—John Neff, Jonathan Huddleson, Daniel Blocher.

1839.—Jeremiah Berry, Jefferson M. Price, Andrew Newman.

1840.—Michael C. Sprigg, Elisha Coombs, Ralph Thayer.

1841.—William V. Buskirk, John M. Buchanan, William Shaw.

1842.—William Buskirk, John Neff, John M. Buchanan, John Pickell.

1843.—William W. McKaig, Patrick Hamill, Samuel P. Smith, James Fitzpatrick.

1844.—Michael C. Sprigg, Patrick Hamill, John Neff, James Fitzpatrick.

1845.—Jeremiah Berry, James M. Schley, John H. Patterson, John Swan.

1846.—John Swan, John H. Patterson, Owen D. Downey, P. Roman Steck.

1847.—John Galloway Lynn, William Coombs, Henry Brown, George W. Kildow.

1849.—John Sands Fell, George B. M. Price, George W. Kildow, and Jacob Reel.

1852-53.—John Frantz, of Jos., Richard Fairall, John Everett, Jefferson M. Price.

1854.—J. J. Morrison, Isaac Kalbaugh, Thomas Devecmon, T. J. McKaig.

1856.—F. B. Tower, Joseph A. Wickes, George W. Kildow, William Frey.

1858.—Charles B. Thruston, William R. Barnard, William Kilgour, John D. Mountz.

1860.—Josiah H. Gordon, William R. Barnard, Asa Beall, David W. McCleary.

1861.—April Session: Josiah H. Gordon, William R. Barnard, David W. McCleary. December Session: George A. Pearre, Lloyd Lowe, Charles W. White, and A. Chamberlain.

1862.—George A. Pearre, Charles W. White, Lloyd Lowe, A. Chamberlain.

1864.—A. C. Greene, William Shaw, Henry Brown, Hopewell Webb.

1865.—Samuel P. Smith, Henry Brown, S. W. Wardwell, Michael Sherry, Mathias G. Dean.

1867.—William A. Brydon, W. R. McCulley, William Devecmon, D. C. Bruce, G. W. McCulloh.

1868.—George W. McCulloh, Anthony Kean, William Devecmon, Noah Trimble, E. G. Hall.

1870.—Anthony Kean, John M. Standish, Jacob Myers, George Percy.

1872.—G. E. Porter, John Coles, Charles Young, Jasper Robinette.

1874.—John Wier, C. B. Wack, James Park, William Brace.

1876.—George M. Rawlings, Henry R. Atkinson, William O. Sprigg, John R. Brooke.

1878.—J. B. Oder, Patrick Carroll, J. McMahon McKaig, William Brace.

1880.—J. J. Bruce, B. L. Turner, Reuben Anthony, and D. D. Shearer.

1882.—Benjamin L. Turner, Charles F. McAleer, Christian F. Hetzel, John Fatkin.

Attorneys Admitted to the Bar of Allegany County.

George Magruder	1791
John Johnson	"
Lenox Martin	"
William Clagett	"
S. Selby	"
Beall Howard	1801
John Hanson Thomas	1802
Robert C. Stone	1803
James Shair	1805
Robert J. Brent	
Otho Shrader	
P. Worthington	
Josiah Espy	
D. Weisel	
John McNeill, Jr	
Daniel Clarke, Jr	
John T. McBurbridge	
M. Brown	
John Taylor	
E. Gaither	
S. Hughes, Jr	
John Miller	
Roger Perry	
Joseph Wegley	
R. Semmes	
Samuel Price	
William Sprigg	
Jacob Nagle	
William G. Brown	
C. L. Sample	
T. Murdoch	
Patrick Magruder	
Silas Paul	
Thomas Thistle	
George Price	
Rezin Davis	
Beene S. Pigman	
Samuel G. Bartley	
Richard Brooks	
Cheston Ringgold	
D. Raymond	
Phil. B. Street	
James D. Roman	
Thomas D. Pottenger	
Upton S. Reid	
George B. Balch	
H. M. Brackenbridge	
James Carson	
George G. Ross	
John M. Fosdick	
Daniel Hughes	
Robert Swann	
James M. Riddle	
M. Wallace	
Moses Tabb	
William Magruder	
Brice W. Howard	1816
Arthur Shaaf	"
J. D. Yore	1817
James W. Russell	
John and J. Kilgour	
Joseph B. Fayes	
J. M. Palmer	
Samuel M. Semmes	
John Tod	
David G. Yost	
Zadock Magruder	
J. E. Barclay	
Wm. J. Ross	
D. Forward	
Thos. Perry	
C. Forward	
Loxley H. Thistle	
J. V. L. McMahon	
George Swearingen	
Cuth. Powell, Jr	
James Smith	
W. J. Naylor	
Wm. Matthews	
W. V. Buskirk	
V. M. Randall	
John Davis, Jr	
Edward McDonald, Jr	
Wm. W. McKaig	
William Thistle	
Wm. Matthews, Jr	
J. Dixon	1827
Jas. Wm. McCullough	1834
Edward Shriver	"
R. C. Hollyday	"
Wm. Lawrence	
Wm. Schley	1835
Frederick A. Schley	
Hanson B. Pigman	1836
Elisha C. Wells	
Benjamin P. Smith	1839
George A. Pearre	"
Jervis Spencer	"
William A. Pitts	"
William Motter	"
George Schley	
Charles H. J. Pigman	
George R. C. Price	1840
William Perry	"
Worthington Ross	1841
Thomas Mason	"
Wm. P. Webster	"
George A. Thruston	"
John F. Dilley	1842
W. M. Hollyday	"
Minor Gibson	"
Tall. P. Shaffner	1843
H. B. Tomlinson	
A. W. McDonald	
Edward Warner	1843
Upton Lawrence	
H. H. Gaither	
John Lynn, of B.	
John J. Stull	
T. J. McKaig	
James P. Carlton, Jr	
John C. Graff	
John M. Brewer	
M. Topham Evans	1843
Charles C. McCulloh	"
E. C. Guest	
J. P. Roman	1844
James H. Bevans	"
J. H. Gordon	"
J. Marshall	1845
N. Carroll Mason	1846
J. H. Clay Mudd	"
W. G. Van Lear	1847
Charles B. Thruston	"
George H. Hickman	"
Aurelius Steele	"
L. M. Barclay	"
R. Wilson, Jr	"
Andrew W. Kercheval	"
Thomas C. Green	1848
Thomas Devecmon	1848
Charles F. Mayer	"
A. S. Ridgely	"
G. B. M. Price	"
H. W. Hoffman	"
Jacob Brown	"
Alonzo Berry	1850
Asa Beall	"
J. M. Schley	"
Andrew E. Kennedy	"
William Baird	1851
Thomas A. Hopkins	1854
Daniel Blocher	1852
Henry Price	"
Michael Menbaugh	"
John A. Dilte	1853
Hopewell Hebb	"
Joseph A. Wickes	1854
Joseph A. Chaplain	"
Richard H. Alvey	1855
John McCarty	"
John L. Thomas	"
Theodore Brace	1856
Wm. Kilgore	"
Joseph Sprigg	
George Hebb	
F. S. Hoblitzell	
Peter Devecmon	1856
I. Frank Seiss	"
Charles B. Pearre	1859
Samuel Smith	"
Wm. McClay Hall	"
Joseph A. Cahill	1860
Richard T. Semmes	"
J. J. McHenry	"
S. W. Downey	1863
Darius W. Robinette	"
William Walsh	1865
Henry Bruce	"
Wm. J. Reid	"
Wm. Devecmon	"
Thomas J. McKaig, Jr	1866
Wm. M. Price	"
Ferdinand Williams	"
Jos. L. Vallandigham	"
T. Cook Hughey	1867
A. H. Blackiston	"
D. Jas. Blackiston	"
Maurice A. Healy	"
R. Chew Jones	1868
Lloyd Lowndes, Jr	1868
Claredon Tate	"
Wm. H. Cahill	"
Thomas E. Gonder	"
James M. Beall	"
Robert W. McMichael	"
S. A. Cox	1869
John B. Fay	"
W. H. Resley	"
A. B. Gonder	"
James F. Harrison	1870
Charles Brown	"
A. Beall McKaig	"
J. W. Wolf	1871
G. S. Hamill	"
A. Hunter Boyd	"
Wm. Brace, Jr	"
John M. Reed	1872
O. G. Getzendanner	"
B. F. M. Hurley	"
Wm. M. Goldsborough	1873
J. D. Ludwig	"
Robert H. Gordon	"
Dwight McCleave	"
Benj. A. Richmond	1874
John S. Grove	"
John E. Semmes	1875
James A. McHenry	"
David W. Sloan	1876
T. F. Chandler	1877
Johns McCleave	"
Will S. Bridendolph	1878
Robert McDonald	"
W. J. Ravenscroft	"
H. C. Brace	"
Jas. E. Ellegood	"
N. E. Fuller	"
J. W. Thomas	1879
George E. Price	"
H. Wheeler Combs	"
D. H. Reynolds	"
Austin W. Wilson	"
W. E. Balyston	"
A. McClure Rouzer	"
W. C. Clayton	1880
John L. Thrall	"
J. N. Willison	"
Charles C. Willison	1881
Edwin R. Johnston	"
Edward Macbeth	"

Magistrates, Constables, Election Judges, Etc.

The following justices of the peace were appointed for Allegany County in 1828:

Jesse Tomlinson, Thomas Cresap, William Price, Lenox Martin, George P. Hinkle, John Burbridge, Samuel Coddington, Robert Armstrong, John McNeill, Jacob Snyder, William Riely, John Porter, Henry Ingman, Henry Myer, John Irvin, Frederick Rice, of John, Archibald Thistle, John Piper, John Norris, John Warnick, Meshach Browning, Walter Bevans, William Shaw, Jesse Robinette, George Bruce, Thomas Greenwell, Jonathan Cox, Joshua O. Robinson, Jonathan Arnold, William Newman, Theophilus Beall, John North, Henry Korn, Joseph France, Valentine Hoffman, James Totten, Jr., Lewis F. Klipstone, Wm. R. Dawson, Joseph Biggs, Peter McClary, Peter Preston, Emanuel Custer, James Tidball, Leonard Shircliffe, John Easter, Jr., Frederick Castings, Isaac McCarty, James Amos, Joseph Dilley, John Uhl, Andrew Morrison, Jacob Clemmer.

The following appointments were made by the Governor and Council of Maryland for Allegany County in 1829:

Justices of the Peace, John Tomlinson, Thomas Cresap, Lenox Martin, George P. Hinkle, John Burbridge, Samuel Coddington, John McNeill, Jacob Snyder, Wm. Riely, John Porter, Henry Ingman, Henry Myer, Jonathan Cox, Joshua O. Robinson, Jonathan Arnold, Wm. Newman, Theophilus

Beall, John North, Joseph France, Valentine Hoffman, James Totten, Jr., Lewis F. Klipstine, Wm. R. Dawson, Joseph Biggs, Peter McCleary, John Irvin, Frederick Rice, of John, Archibald Thistlé, John Piper, Jr., John Norris, John Warnick, Meshach Browning, Walter Bevans, William Shaw, Jesse Robinette, Jasper Robinette, George Bruce, Thomas Greenwell, Emanuel Easter, Jr., James Tidball, Leonard Shircliff, John Easter, Jr., Isaac McCarty, James Amos, Andrew Morrison, Jacob Clammer, Frederick Houser, John A. Hoffman, George Tilghman, John McHenry, John Wright, George Devecmon, Adam Sigler, John H. Bayard, John Scott, Adam Gower, John Poland, Samuel Slicer, Geo. Layman.

The following were the judges of the several election districts of the county for 1829, appointed by the Levy Court:

District No. 1.—Joshua O. Robinson, Joseph Biggs, George W. Devecmon.
No. 2.—Zadock Bobey, Christian Mosser, Jos. Frantz.
No. 3.—Stephen Millholland, Jacob Holdeman, Benj. Payton.
No. 4.—George Layman, Joseph Rocknor, Geo. Smarr.
No. 5.—Isaiah Frost, John Combs, Samuel Mattingly.
No. 6.—Jacob Snyder, Geo. Rizer, Geo. Rice.
No. 7.—Samuel McBride, Charles Twigg, Thos. Greenwell.
No. 8.—Leonard Shircliff, Walter Bevans, John Norris, Sr.
No. 9.—John North, Amos Robinette, John Wilson.

The following appointments were made by the Governor and Council of Maryland for Allegany County in 1830:

Justices of the Peace, Thomas Cresap, Lenox Martin, Geo. P. Hinkle, John Porter, Henry Ingman, Henry Myer, Jonathan Cox, Joshua O. Robinson, Jonathan Arnold, John North, Joseph France, Valentine Hoffman, James Totten, Jr., Lewis F. Klipstine, Joseph Biggs, Peter McCleary, John Ervin, Archibald Thistle, John Warnick, Meshach Browning, Walter Bevans, Jesse Robinette, Jasper Robinette, George Bruce, Thomas Greenwell, Emanuel Custer, Leonard Shircliff, Isaac McCarty, James Amos, Andrew Morrison, Adam Sigler, John H. Bayard, Samuel Slicer, George Layman, John North, John McHenry, George Rinehart, Frederick A. Carstine, Jacob Welch, John Fike, Stephen Mullholland, Luke Bolden, Thos. Beall, Nottey Barnard, Wm. Ravenscraft, Peter Preston, John Combs, Chas. L. Shepherd, John Uhl, Moses Porter, Geo. Blocher, Henry Wineon, of G., Henry Horn, John White, Frederick Deems, William Shaw, Israel Mayberry, Wm. McLaughlin, Lionel M. Jamison, Joseph Mattingly, John Loren, David McElfresh, Geo. Slicer.

Coroners, Michael Lane, Robert McClary.

The following appointments of judges of elections were made by the Levy Court of Allegany County in 1830:

District No. 1.—George Rinehart, Thomas Wilson, Jos. Biggs.
No. 2.—John Fearer, Jacob Markley, John Fike.
No. 3.—Stephen Milholland, John Blocher, Wm. Stanton.
No. 4.—Joseph Reckner, Robert Ross, Cornelius Kight.
No. 5.—John Neff, Elisha Combs, Raphael Logsden.
No. 6.—Jos. Carter, A. D. Beall, Frederick Rice, of John.
No. 7.—Jacob Lantz, Isaac Ward, Israel Mayberry.
No. 8.—Joseph Mattingly, James Tidball, Chas. Norris.
No. 9.—Jeremiah Berry, Thos. McElfresh, John Willison, of Jeremiah.

The following were appointed constables:

District No. 1.—Adam Gower, Edward Barnard, Thomas Moore, Wm. Browning.
No. 2.—John Slicer, Thomas Drane.
No. 3.—Robert Ferguson, Peter Baker.
No. 4.—Godfrey Facenbaker, Daniel B. Layman, Wm. Ravenscraft.
No. 5.—John M. Porter, James Mattingly.
No. 6.—John Hayes, Wm. Houx, Theophilus Beall, Joseph S. Stafford.
No. 7.—James Twigg.
No. 8.—John Gouldrag.
No. 9.—Elisha Willison.

In 1836 the following magistrates were appointed by the Governor and Council:

Joseph Biggs, Meshach Browning, Robinson Savage, Frederick Houser, John Warnick, Joseph Frantz, Peter McCleery, Samuel Coddington, Jacob Clemmer, Archibald Thistle, George Bruce, James Totten, Jr., Thomas Wilson, Sr., George Layman, Wm. Shaw, Thomas Dawson, Sr., Jonathan Arnold, Valentine Arnold, Valentine Hoffman, John Mattingly, Sr., Elisha Combs, Thomas Cresap, George W. Devecmon, George P. Hinkle, Adam Sigler, Henry Korn, Wm. R. Dawson, John McNeill, Sr., John Wright, Jacob Snyder, Frederick Rice, of John, Lenox Martin, Israel Mayberry, Walter McAtee, William Newman, Walter Bevans, Leonard Sh rcliff, John North, Jasper Robinette, Cornelius Kight, Thos. Beall, James Prather, Truman West, Archibald Chisholm, Peter Uhl, Robert Lashley, George Smith, of Alexander, Jonathan Wilson, James Dawson, of Ed., Moses H. Louthan, Burgess Magruder, John M. Carleton, John Bomward, Ebenezer Vowell, Michael Porter, of Samuel, Wm Harvey, George Slicer, Daniel Wolford, Sr., Wm. Reily, John W. Mountz, John Layman, Charles Miller, George Hebb, Peter Kreighbaum, James D. Armstrong, Singleton Townshend, Joseph C. Cresap, Wm. Conrad, James Carter, Adam Gower, John Larew, Henry Yontz, Joseph Frantz, of Joseph, Wm. Thompson, Ezekiel Totten, Lewis F. Klipstine, John McHenry, Jonathan Rhinehart, John Baker, Wm. Ridgely, Andrew Bruce, John Neff, Wm. L. Lamar, John G. Hoffman, John Gephart, Wm. Reese, and Thomas Cromwell.

The justices of the District Courts in 1840 were:

District No. 1.—Meshach Browning, Murray Thayer, John Warnick.
No. 2.—John Frantz, of Joseph, Richard White, James Robison.
No. 3.—John Ogg, Daniel Blocher, George Layman.
No. 4.—Henry Miller, Cornelius Kight, Uriah Dockworth.
No. 5.—John Porter, Elisha Combs, George S Evans.
No. 6.—Daniel Blocher, John M. Buchanan, John Black.
No. 7.—John W. Mountz, John Hartley, Henry I. Crosson.
No. 8.—Jacob Reel, Samuel Cessna, Enos Childs.
No. 9.—George Slicer, John North, Jasper Robinette.
No. 10.—Jonathan Rinehart, John Hammond, John Gower.

COUNTY SURVEYORS.

1790–1803, George Dent; 1803–13, Ninian Cochran; 1813–21, Benjamin G. Vaughan; 1821–23, Ninian Cochran; 1823–43, Benjamin Brown; 1843–46, H. M. Pettit; 1846, Benjamin Brown; 1847, Denton D. Brown; 1848–58, Thomas F. White; 1858–62, Denton D. Brown; 1862–64, William Bruce; 1864–68, James Chisholm; 1868–70, William M. Owens; 1870–72, William Armstrong; 1872–76, Daniel Chisholm; 1876–81, John Schault.

Public Education in Allegany County received its first impulse in 1799, when, by an act of the General Assembly, the Allegany County School was established. The act of the 15th of January, 1799, provided that,—

"WHEREAS, It is reasonable that education should be extended to the several parts of the State, and that there should be a public school in Allegany County, therefore

"*Be it enacted by the General Assembly of Maryland*, That in order to the erecting and building a house and other conveniences for a county school, the persons hereinafter named shall have power to purchase one or more acres of land in or adjoining the town of Cumberland, in Allegany County, to wit: John Lynn, Evan Gwynn, Wm. McMahon, Joseph Cresap, David Lynn, Patrick Murdoch, Hanson Briscoe, John B. Beall, and John C. Beatty, who shall be visitors of said school, which persons so nominated visitors for Allegany County School, and their successors, appointed in the manner hereinafter declared, shall and are hereby declared to be one community, corporation, and body politic, to have continuation forever, by the name of The Visitors of Allegany County School, and by that name to sue and be sued, implead or be impleaded, and to make and have a common seal, and the same to break, alter, or renew when and so often as they shall see fit."

Under this act the lot now occupied by the school building of St. Peter and St. Paul's German Catholic Church was bought, and a building erected thereon for school purposes. Profs. Pierce and Benjamin Brown were the first principals. The sum of two hundred dollars per year was granted from the State treasury. The organization then established is maintained to this day. In 1849 the building was declared by the principal, Allen P. Weed, to be insufficient for the accommodation of the pupils, and the trustees secured from citizens subscriptions for the erection of a suitable building. For this purpose the county commissioners appropriated the lot occupied by the old clerks' offices, and upon this site the present academy building was erected and occupied June 8, 1850.

In 1828 the proposition to establish primary schools in the county was defeated by a vote of 1031 to 249. Nevertheless, the cause of education was promoted by the parochial and private schools.

In 1865 the public school system was established in Allegany County, and under it education has prospered and has been greatly extended. The greatest difficulty encountered has been the want of funds for buildings, apparatus, and teaching force. Taxes and a few gifts have been the only sources of revenue. The board of school commissioners at present is composed of R. L. Burwell, of Mount Savage; Samuel Sonneborn, of Cumberland; and John Douglas, of Lonaconing. The present examiner, J. W. S. Cochran, now in the fourth year of his service, was born on the Eastern Shore of Maryland, and was graduated from Dickinson College in 1874, with the degree of A.B. He taught in Accomac County, Va., and Frostburg, Md., in private schools, and in the public schools of the county until Jan. 1, 1881, when he was appointed secretary, treasurer, and examiner.

The trustees for the ensuing year are as follows:

Election District No. 1.—Orleans School, No. 1, Thomas Callan, Thomas H. Norris, William McDonald; Hartley's School, No. 2, J. T. Hartley, G. W. Price, B. D. Shipley; "Brickhouse" School, No. 3, Frederick Brinkman, Harman Brinkman, Daniel Kline; Shircliff's School, No. 4, Henry Shircliff, Jacob Lichty, William Lynn; Barnes School, No. 5, Silas Kifer, Hughey Ijams, Michael Kennard; Slider School, No. 6, Stephen Slider, Francis Troutman, Francis Twigg; Sulphur Spring School, No. 7, Randolph Sprigg, R. T. Seamon, Jacob Reckley; Tunnel Hill School, No. 8, B. T. Moreland, John Hudson, Daniel Gross.

Election District No. 2.—Oldtown School, No. 1, Dr. B. B. McElfish, George L. Wilson, William Foley; Town Creek School, No. 2, Daniel Diffenbaugh, Adam Barth, Upton Athey; Upper Green Ridge, No. 3, Peter Alderton, Aaron Athey, John Mathews; Lower Green Ridge, No. 4, Samuel Morgan, August Bender, Luke V. Alderton; Spring Gap School, No. 5, John A. Daniel, Amos Davis, Joseph Eyler.

Election District No. 3.—Flintstone School, No. 1, James Ash, Jeremiah Leasure, Isaac Wilson; Flintstone School, No. 2, James Wilson, Owen McElfish, John Davis; Fairview School, No. 3, H. F. Willison, Jonathan Wilson, Dennis Perrin; Murley's Branch School, No. 4, Henry North, Jesse Robinette, Samuel F. Wilson; Twiggtown School, No. 5, G. A. Robinette, Levi Rice, Thomas P. Rice; Bucey School, No. 6, Denton B. Bucey, Jasper Hoff; Lashley School, No. 7, Jeremiah Robinette, John Stewart, Jacob Lashley; Frazee School, No. 9, Daniel Frazee, F. C. Struckman, Edward Hartsock; Piney Plains School, No. 10, W. T. Rubey, Riley Twigg, Daniel Twigg.

Cumberland City Schools.—White, B. R. Edwards, W. A. Withers, C. F. Hetzel; Colored, Philip Hammond, John Howard, Andrew Banks.

Election District No. 4.—Pleasant Grove School, No. 3, Boyd Bowden, Morgan Hinkel, Moses Wilson; Wentling School, No. 4, Michael Naughton, Francis Twigg, Robert Christie; Iron's Mount School, No. 5, G. W. Weber, Oliver E. Rice, Michael Brotemarkle; North Branch School, No. 6, Adam Siebert, Charles Fisher, John Coleman.

Election District No. 5.—School No. 2, Little Valley, Owen Willison, John McElfish, Charles Keller.

Election District No. 6.—Corrigansville School, No. 2, Samuel Jenkins, George Clawson, M. Corrigan; Ellerslie School, No. 3, C. M. King, Joseph Johnson, Francis Naughton; Boettcherville School, No. 4, J. F. Seiss, D. R. Long, Barney Dilley; Everstine School, No. 5, John Walker, Josephus Everstine, Enoch McKenzie; Long's School, No. 6, Upton D. Long, W. Milner Roberts, Andrew Harman.

Election District No. 7.—Cresaptown School, No. 1, Martin Burns, Thornton G. McKenzie, Elijah Wigfield; Frost River School, No. 2, J. W. Wilson, M. A. Frost, Francis Elliott; Rawlings' Station School, No. 3, J. C. Cookerly, Newton Rawlings, Lynn Hudson; Ravenscraft School, No. 4, R. D. Ravenscraft, John Hart, J. F. Ravenscraft.

Election District No. 8.—Westernport School, No. 1, G. W. Sheetz, Maurice A. Miller, G. W. Spangler, Franklin Mines; No. 2, Joseph Logsdon, R. K. Snyder, Andrew Patrick; Dayton School, No. 3, R. S. Dayton, Philip Fletcher, George Carpenter; Duckworth Settlement School, No. 4, Samuel Miller, A. C. Duckworth, Henry Lenear.

Election District No. 9.—Barton School, No. 1, O. G. Barchus, John Pattison, John Shaw.

Election District No. 10.—Castle and Detmold Schools, John O'Hanley, Aug. Eichorn, James Little; Pekin School, No. 4, James Ryan, Frank McDermott, Jonathan Baker; Ocean Mines, No. 4, George Loar, Charles Keefer, Harrison Poland.

Election District No. 11.—Frostburg School and Sand Spring, Dr. J. Ruhl, Francis A. Maury, Levi Porter; Borden Mines, No. 3, C. A. Greene, Conrad Ort, G. M. Crow; Allegany Mines, No. 4, Cornelius Gill, Polk Stevens, John Lewis; Borden Shaft, No. 5, J. D Barnard, George Robb, George Tiffen; Midlothian Mines, No. 7, William Close, John Winters, William Conrad; Frostburg Colored School, William Jackson, Thomas Jackson, George Johnson.

Election District No. 12.—Eckhart Mines Schools, Nos. 1 and 2, William Parker, J. P. Kelly, Ransom T. Powell; Hoffman Hollow School, No. 3, August Kolinger, Christopher Maguire, Peter Cain; Pompey Smash School, No. 4, Philip McMahon, Walter Martin, James Tibbetts; Loarville School, No. 5, Elijah Loar, Nathan Loar, Jonathan Radcliff.

Election District No. 13.—Mount Savage Schools, Nos. 1 and 2, Thomas Malloy, Francis McNamee, Edward Casey; Barrellville School, No. 3, Jacob Rizer, Isaac H. Thorp, John C. Witt; Mattingly Settlement School, No. 4, Rinehart Shaffer, August Brailer, John Mattingly.

Election District No. 14.—Wilson Academy, No. 1, Peter Smouse, L. F. Gurley, Jesse Wilson; Pleasant Valley School, No. 2, William Yergen, John Fisher, Lemuel Bucey; Folck's Mill School, No. 3, H. D. Carleton, Joseph Brandt, John T. Beall; Bottle Run School, No. 4, Martin Rouzer, Richard Hendrickson, John H. Leasure.

Election District No. 15.—Rockville School, No. 1, and Jackson School, No. 2, Lonaconing, Peter Phillips, James Anderson, Patrick Hogan; Dye School, No. 3, John Dye, Benjamin Metz, Jacob Miller; Midland School, No. 3, Salem Koontz, John Llewellyn, P. P. Hansel.

The teachers for the county are as follows:

Cumberland City.—Union Street School: Principal, H. G. Weiner; Assistants, W. C. Handy, Miss S. A. White, Mrs. E. M. Clark, Miss H. Sterner, Laura M. Young, Belle Weiskittel, Claudia T. Pendleton, Estella Macbeth, Mary M. Hilleary. Lena Furnace School: Principal, Thomas N. Johnson, was born near Freeport, Harrison Co., Ohio, Jan. 4, 1848. In early life he was engaged with his father in agricultural pursuits, and having secured a good common-school education, he began teaching at sixteen years of age. He entered Denison University, Granville Co., Ohio, in 1871, and was graduated in 1875, receiving in 1878 the degree of A.M. He removed to Allegany County in 1877 as principal of Barton School, and has been the principal of Lena Furnace School for four years. The assistants are Mary S. White, Edith McCulley, Sallie Hetzel, Jessie G. Macbeth, Lillie C. Lougabaugh; German teacher, Rev. J. L. Eiseman. Maryland Avenue School: Principal, William A. Devemer; Assistants, Ella Scott, May Sibley. Green Street School: Principal, Victor Bridaham; Assistant, Maggie Rowe. Fair Ground School: Principal, Rev. F. Schwedes; Assistant, Ella X. Mulligan.

Frostburg: Principal, L. H. Gehman; Assistants, W. K. Wimbrough, Miss M. J. Flint, Helen Berkebile, Ida Keller, Jennie Scott, Lillie Burton, Estella G. Staples, Mrs. Adeline E. Brown, and Lillie B. Thrasher.

Rockville: Principal, D. O. Sullivan; Assistants, William Gunning, Rose E. Bevans, Ella Brady.

Lonaconing Castle School: Principal, R. H. Vanhorn; Assistants, Maggie R. Sloan, Maggie E. Shilling, Janet Maxwell, Fannie Bevans, Bettie L. Young, Alice McMichael.

Pekin School: Principal, William J. Bogan; Assistants, Mrs. Annie Collins and Lizzie Locke.

Mount Savage School: Principal, George G. McKay; Assistants, Ava Wheedon, Mary L. Sentf, Mary F. Campbell.

Barton School: Principal, J. E. J. Buckley; Assistants, Lida Stewart, Lida Duckworth, Kate E. Cadden, Sadie P. Carter.

Westernport: Principal, O. H. Bruce; Assistants, Eva McDonald, Kate Grannon, Althea Duckworth.

Eckhart Mines: Principal, Thomas F. Hill; Assistants, Mary A. C. Bevans and Una Woun.

Midland Mines: Principal, John T. Walsh; Assistant, Jessie F. White.

Pompey Smash: Principal, George M. Perduo; Assistant, Susie E. Hogan.

Detmold School: Principal, Magnus Reid; Assistants, Helen P. Sloan and Lizzie Hannon.

Franklin Mines: Principal, Dennis Bogle; Assistant, Minnie McKone.

Jackson Mines: Principal, James A. Maxwell; Assistant, Emma McKone.

Borden Shaft; Principal, Alexander W. De Witt: Assistant, Annie Kohl.

Borden Mines: Principal, John A. Smith; Assistant, Agnes T. Davis.

Flintstone, No. 1: Principal, Bridget A. Noon; Assistant, Kate Kildow.

Murley's Branch, John H. Fox.
Corrigansville, John L. Kelly.
Ocean Mines, E. O. McKinley.
Sand Spring, W. J. Ort.
Allegany Mines, John Walsh.
Midlothian, John W. Hunt.
Hoffman Hollow, Patrick O'Rourke.
Ebenezer, John Watkins.
Dutch Hollow, Sallie Campbell.
Wilson Academy, John F. Neff.
Pleasant Grove, Annie M. Beall.
North Branch, H. C. McGee.
Pekin Hill, Maggie Orr.
Loarville, Lizzie McCaughan.
Mattingly Settlement, Kate M. Sullivan.
Cresaptown, Joseph L. Enos.
Folk's Mills, Lena Uhland.
Flintstone, No. 2, John L. Hendrickson.
Charlestown, Ella McCaffree.
Little Orleans, Ella Gallagher.
Hartley's, Annie Daniels.
Higgins, James McDermed.
Barnes', Maggie Martin.
Shircliff, James L. Hopkins.
Spring Gap, Austin D. Twigg.
Upper Green Ridge, Ella C. McGill.
Sulphur Spring, Rebecca Syfes.
Tunnel Hill, Annie Galton.
Town Creek, Mary Bopst.
Lower Green Ridge, Kate T. McGill.
Pine Hill, Elsie Bridaham.
Lashley, M. Blanche Spencer.
Fairview, J. A. Hendrickson.
Twiggtown, Lycurgus M. Boon.
Ellerslie, Josie M. Young.

Everstine, Emma Everstine.
Ravenscroft, Mary E. Broderick.
Dayton, John B. Lee.
Bottle Run, D. W. Snyder.
Iron Mountain, Benton Twigg.
Frazee, Maggie McCulley.
Meese's, Mary J. Cavanaugh.
Boetcherville, J. P. Davis.
Frost River, Laura Howson.
Wentling, Annie Wise.
Barrelville, Jane S. Mulligan.
Dye Settlement, Mary Walsh.
Little Valley, Lizzie Deffenbaugh.
Long's, Belle L. Wilson.
Rawlings' Station, Mary A. McMichael.
Ducksworth Settlement, W. B. Stevens.
Pleasant Valley, M. C. Hendrickson.
Slider School, Agnes Sammon.
Warrior Mountain, Mary Smouse.

Private Schools.

Allegany County Academy, Court-house Square. William Johnston, principal.

Hebrew School, basement of synagogue, South Centre, corner Union.

SS. Peter and Paul's Parochial School, on Fayette Street near Smallwood. Under charge of Ursuline Sisters.

St. Edward's Academy for Young Ladies, North Centre, adjoining St. Patrick's church. Sister Mary Louise, superior.

St. Patrick's Male Parochial School (Carroll Hall), on North Centre Street. Joseph Smith, principal.

Trinity Church (Evangelical Lutheran) School, adjoining church edifice.

Miss Sallie McCleave's Select School, No. 61 Decatur Street.

The distribution of the school fund in Allegany and Garrett Counties for 1881 was as follows: white, $5065.70; colored, $151.02.

The school fund of Allegany County from 1820 to 1834 inclusive was as follows:

	Received.		Distributed.
1820	$782.78	1822	$241.00
1821	731.16	1823	278.03
1822	717.62	1824	499.03
1824	730.85	1825	484.10
1825	2100.00	1826	411.05
1828	1481.22	1827	394.09
1829	1091.04	1828	342.45
1830	642.31	1829	410.12
1831	979.83	1830	647.39
1832	671.01	1831	723.91
1833	668.55	1832	687.02
		1833	938.46
Bank transferred, 1819	3,824.03	1834	1,364.19
Bank transferred, 1834	4,050.00	Costs and commissions	241.90
Interest received on judgments	1,371.22	Deposited in Hagerstown Bank	180.23
Dividends on bank stock, etc	3,154.06	On judgments in Allegany County courts	13,862.04
Total	$22,996.13	Cash in hands of treasurer to commissioners	1,291.12
		Total	$22,996.13

The following is the manner in which the free school fund was distributed, with the number of schools, the amount allowed to each school, and the trustees appointed to each for the year 1831

Place of Schools.	Trustees.
District No. 1. One school.	
In Ryan's Glades	Alexander Smith.
In neighborhood of Henry Lower's	Isaac McCarty.
" " P. H. Bray's	Thomas Wilson.
" " Sanging Ground	John McHenry.
District No. 2. One school.	
Near Selby's Port	David Hoffman.
" Hazlet's Mill	John Fike.
On Ridge	Jacob Welsh.
Near Ash's Glades	Alexander Thomas.
" Jonathan Frantz's	Jonathan Frantz.
" Abraham Shockey's	Abraham Shockey.
District No. 3. One school.	
Near Jesse Tomlinson's	George Bruce.
At Grantsville	Archibald Thistle.
In forks Little Youghiogheny	Eli Ridgely.
Near Custer's	John Wiley, Jr.
In German Settlement	William Weitzell.
District No. 4. One school.	
Near Westernport	Silas Reese.
" Widow Shaw's	William Shaw.
" Thomas M. Dawson's	T. M. Dawson.
" Michael Wilts'	Charles Broadwater.
" James Totten, Jr	James Totten, Jr.
" John Barnes'	John Barnes.
District No. 5. One school.	
Near Jonathan Arnold's	Jonathan Arnold.
" William Ward's	William Ward.
" Swan's Mill	Peter Speelman.
" Frostburg	Meshach Frost.
" Peter Preston's	John Matthews.
District No. 6. One school.	
Near Henry Smouse's	Henry Smouse.
At Rocky Gap	Rezin Beall.
At Cresaptown	William R. Dawson.
At Peter Kreechbaum's	Peter Kreechbaum.
Three schools in Cumberland	George Blocher.
District No. 7. One school.	
Near Alkire's	Solomon Alkire.
" Lewis Crabbtree's	L. Crabbtree, Sr.
" Skipton	Lenox Martin.
" Peter Devenbaugh's	John Ash.
District No. 8. One school.	
Near Walter Bevans'	Walter Bevans.
" C. Norris'	John Devilbiss.
" Tidball's	Daniel Folck.
District No. 9. One school.	
Near Flintstone	Amos Robinette.
" George Robinette's	Jesse Robinette.
" Miller's Tavern	John Miller.
At the head of Murley Branch	Eli Wilson.

It was ordered that each school established by the above regulations be allowed twenty-five dollars per annum (with the exception of the school near A. Shockey's, which was allowed twelve dollars and fifty cents), to be drawn by the trustees appointed for each school from Asa Beall, the treasurer of the school fund, to be laid out for the best advantage on children whose parents were unable to have them taught.

The Allegany County Teachers' Association was formed in Cumberland, Jan. 9, 1875. The first officers, chosen on this day, were R. R. Sanner, president; A. A. Shaw and Miss A. White, vice presidents; William Grim, secretary; and Miss N. E. K. Palmer, treasurer. The rules usually governing deliberative bodies were adopted. Messrs. Hill, Byrne, and Shaw, Miss L. John, and Mrs. E. Clark were appointed a committee to prepare business for the association.

The following constituted the committees: committee on constitution and by-laws, Messrs. Sanner, Ambrose, and Hill, Misses Hartzell and Leigh; committee to draft memorial, Mr. Hughey, Misses Dorsey and John; special committee to present memorial, Messrs. Ambrose, Sanner, Higgins, Shaw, and Mrs. E. Clarke.

The statistics of the public schools of Allegany County, as returned by the census of 1880, are as follows: whole number of elementary schools, 78; schools for colored children, 3; whole number of school buildings, 78; number of buildings having more than one study-room, 19; number of buildings having two or more recitation-rooms, 19; whole number of seats now provided, 8000; number of schools reported in good condition, 68; number reported in bad condition, 10; number of white teachers, 124, of whom 60 are male and 64 female; colored teachers, 3, all males; whole number of teachers, white and colored, 127; number of teachers educated at normal schools, 3; number of teachers not educated at normal schools but holding certificates, 124; average of teachers' salaries per month, $36.50; average number of months employed, 7.11.

The statistics of illiteracy, as returned by the Census Department, are as follows: white population over ten years of age who cannot read, 2829; white population over ten years of age who cannot write, total white, 3423, of whom 2008 are native and 1415 foreign; total colored, 614; grand total of white and colored, 4037; white population who cannot write: from ten to fourteen years, male, 244; female, 231; total, 475: from fifteen to twenty years, male, 148; female, 165; total, 313: twenty-one years and over, male, 1031; female, 1604; total, 2635: total colored population who cannot write: from ten to fourteen years, male, 31; female, 37; total, 68: from fifteen to twenty years, male, 30; female, 27; total, 57: twenty-one years and over, male, 234; female, 255; total, 489. The whole number of pupils in attendance during 1881 was: white males, 3881; white females, 3194; total white, 7075; colored males, 95; colored females, 78; total colored, 173; making the grand total 7248. The average attendance daily was: white, 4500; colored, 123; total, 4623. Of the pupils 146 were under six years of age, and 507 were over sixteen years of age. The average number of days during which school was taught during the year was 165. The amount realized from State taxes was $17,545.08; from county, town, and city taxes, dog taxes, and other public funds, $32,000; from all other sources, $925.26; making the total $50,470.34. The expenditures amounted to $45,172.59, and the total value of school property was $305,800.

Population and Financial Statistics. — According to the census of 1880, the total population of Allegany County is 38,012, of whom 19,223 are males and 18,789 are females. The native inhabitants number 31,023, and the foreign 6989. Of the population 36,481 are white, and 1531 colored. The population by districts and towns is as follows:

First Election District (Orleans)		1016
Second Election District (Oldtown), including village of Oldtown		1194
Oldtown Village	180	
Third Election District (Flintstone), including village of Flintstone		1531
Flintstone Village	315	
Fourth Election District (Cumberland Canal), including part of city of Cumberland		4370
Cumberland City (part of)	3290	
(See Fifth, Sixth, and Fourteenth Election Districts.)		
Fifth Election District (Cumberland Mills Creek) including part of city of Cumberland		3168
Cumberland City (part of)	2761	
(See Fourth, Sixth, and Fourteenth Election Districts)		
Sixth Election District, Cumberland (River), including the following places		2508
Cumberland City (part of)	1523	
(See Fifth, Fourth, and Fourteenth Election Districts.)		
Ellerslie Village	126	
Seventh Election District (Rawlings'), including the following towns		2396
Cresap Town	50	
Westernport Town	1468	
Eighth Election District (Westernport)		676
Ninth Election District (Barton), including the following places		1937
Barton Town	1112	
Moscow Village	264	
Tenth Election District (Lonaconing), including the following places		2808
Frostburg Town (part of)	——	
(See Eleventh Election District.)		
Lonaconing Town	2147	
Pekin Village	505	
Eleventh Election District (Frostburg), including the following places		4057
Borden Shaft Village	289	
Frostburg Town (part of)	2471	
(See Tenth Election District.)		
Midlothian Mines Village	398	
Twelfth Election District (East Frostburg), including the following villages		3278
Boston Village	100	
Clarysville Village	99	
Eckhart Mines Village	822	
Grahamstown Village	498	
Hoffman Hollow Village	203	
Lowtown Village	91	
Parkersburg Village	100	
Pompey Smash Village	535	
Thirteenth Election District (Mount Savage)		1934
Fourteenth Election District (Cumberland Central), including the following places		3782
Bottle Run Village	93	
Cumberland City (part of)	3119	
(See Fourth, Fifth, and Sixth Election Districts.)		
Fifteenth Election District (East Lonaconing), including the following villages		3357
Midland Mine Village	276	
Miller Mine Village	100	
Ocean Mine Village	126	
Cumberland City, situated in the Fourth, Fifth, Sixth, and Fourteenth Election Districts		10,693

The part of Frostburg Town which is in the Eleventh Election District has been separated, but up to the time of going to press the enumerator of the Tenth Election District had failed to make the separation.

The population of the county since and including the census of 1790 has been as follows:

	White.	Free Colored.	Slave.	Total.
1790	4,539	12	258	4,809
1800	5,703	101	499	6,303
1810	6,176	113	620	6,909
1820	7,664	195	795	8,654
1830	9,569	222	818	10,609
1840	14,663	215	812	15,690
1850	21,633	412	724	22,769
1860	27,215	467	666	28,348
1870	37,370	1166		38,536

In 1791 the valuation of the taxable property in Allegany County was £78,978 1*s.* 11*d.*, and the rate seven shillings three pence on every one hundred pounds. In 1833 the assessed valuation of the real and personal property was as follows:

	Real.	Personal.	Total.
District No. 1	$120,662.58	$35,179.30	$155,807.88
" " 2	64,891.62	44,047.75	108,939.37
" " 3	107,891.38	28,681.50	136,572.88
" " 4	115,540.36	49,291.00	161,831.36
" " 5	105,344.62	44,579.00	149,923.62
Cumberland	136,952.44	36,830.00	173,978.44
District No. 6	170,652.17	48,066.00	218,718.17
" " 7	77,822 75	33,962.00	111,784.75
" " 8	65,187.73	18,527 50	83,175.23
" " 9	98,457.90	37,411.50	135,869.40
Aggregate values	$1,063,319.55	$373,575.55	$1,436,945,10

Valuation of orchard products	$6,714
" market gardens	$475
Number of tons of hay	10,896
" pounds of flax	1,517
" " honey and beeswax	6,457
" " maple sugar	47,740
" gallons of molasses	1,430
" " wine	65
Valuation of home-made manufactures	$9,397
Number of manufacturing establishments	24
Capital employed in same	$750,100
Number of employed hands in same	403
Average monthly wages of same	$9,284
Value of annual manufactures	$491,391

Of these manufactures two were of cabinet-ware, two of cigars, two of woolen goods, one of fire-brick, one foundry, one furnace, four saw-mills, three coal-mining establishments, one railroad machine-shop, and seven tanneries.

The total valuation of all property was	$4,205,453
The taxes for State purposes were	$10,514
" " county "	$26,915
Number of native paupers	44
" foreign "	6
Annual cost of the poor	$2,000
Number of native criminals convicted	1
" foreign " "	3
" native adults unable to read and write	389
" foreign " " " "	750
" private and public schools	109
" children attending same	3480
" " at other schools	105
" newspapers	3

The valuation of church property was $81,000, and there were 72 libraries with 55,467 volumes.

There were thirty churches with congregations numbering 13,900 persons, of which—

17 were Methodist, accommodating		5950
5 Catholic,	"	3000
4 Lutheran,	"	2000
2 Protestant Episcopal,	"	1400
1 German Reformed,	"	800
1 Presbyterian,	"	400
1 Baptist,	"	350

In 1847 the assessed valuation of property was $4,234,720; total taxes collected, $10,586.80. In 1850 the

Number of farms was	892
" acres improved land	72,577
" " unimproved land	144,695
Cash value of lands	$2,519,858
Value of farming implements and machinery	$60,368
Number of horses	2,902
" asses and mules	9
" milch cows	4,207
" working oxen	89
" other cattle	6,257
" sheep	12,439
" swine	7,877
Valuation of said domestic animals	$270,070
Wool produced, in pounds	25,240
Butter " "	231,038
Cheese " "	880
Value of animals slaughtered	$57,587
Wheat raised, in bushels	73,525
Rye " "	29,187
Corn " "	101,773
Oats " "	163,943
Barley " "	100
Buckwheat raised, in bushels	19,887
Beans and peas raised, in bushels	67
Potatoes " "	21,920

The total assessment of property for 1868 was	$16,000,000.00
Amount of levy	$125,989.31
Contingent fund in hands of collector	11,230.00
	$137,219.31
Collector's 5 per cent. on State tax	1,520.00
Collector's 5 per cent. on county tax	6,860.96
	$145,600.27
By 91 cents on $100 of assessable property	145,600.00

The State and county taxes amounted to $1.10 on the $100.

The assessed valuation of property for 1872 was as follows:

Real estate and personal property	$10,723,059.00
Capital stock	8,921,691.00
Total	$19,644,750.00
Ratio of county tax, 82 cents on each $100.	
Ratio of State tax, 17 cents on each $100.	
Ratio of State tax upon capital stock of corporations, 19 cents on each $100.	
Total amount of county tax, including $16,400 contingent fund on B. & O. R. R.	$161,086.95
Total amount of State tax	18,217.08
Total amount of State tax upon stock of corporations	16,951.21

The tax levy for 1881 and financial exhibit of the county were as follows: Entire levy of 1881, $131,-264.31, which, upon a taxable basis of $18,423,-033.60, places the county taxes at 71½ cents on the $100, which, added to the State tax of 18¾ cents on the $100, makes a total of State and county tax of

90 cents on the $100, or four cents less than 1880. The items of the levy are the following:

Almshouse	$5,900.81
Appropriations to corporations	3,500.00
Attorneys' fees	2,410.03
Clerk's office	3,705.29
Collectors' commissions	5,202.06
Contingent fund	6,883.89
Constables' fees	1,789.14
County commissioners	2,990.00
Court-house expenses	982.57
Court-house and jail fund	7,400.00
Coroner's juries	83.50
Election expenses	449.38
Fox and Cat Scalps	142.10
Jail expenses	449.38
Jury and witness fund	15,389.17
Magistrates' fees	2,091.33
Miscellaneous	3,120.48
New assessments	84.00
Orphans' Court	1,936.24
Outside pensions	3,567.67
Public schools	35,000.00
Registration officers	615.00
Removed cases	824.00
Road levies for 1881	7,800.00
Road balances	612.15
Road and bridge expenses	954.55
Sheriff's fees	5,424.62
Special road and bridge levies	7,750.00
Sundry charities	3,516.85
Taxes paid in error	129.53
Witnesses	214.66
Total	$131,264.11

Of the appropriations to corporations $500 was to Cumberland, $2000 to same, $750 to Frostburg, and $250 to Westernport. The bounties for animals and birds included foxes, hawks, cats, and owls. Up to and including the quarter ending Oct. 10, 1881, the receipts amounted to $102,147.38, leaving after expenditures, a cash balance of $36,861.31. The resources of the county on the 15th of October, 1881, amounted to $92,659.48, against which there were liabilities for the same amount. The bonded indebtedness of the county amounted to $41,000. The receipts for public school purposes in Allegany County for the year ending Sept. 30, 1881, amounted to $61,006.14; leaving, after disbursements, a cash balance of $156.10.

The yield of the cereals in Allegany County, according to the census of 1880, was as follows:

	Acres.	Bushels.
Buckwheat	1130	11,368
Indian corn	8661	206,949
Oats	3772	52,570
Rye	2832	19,165
Wheat	7549	67,458
Tobacco	2	1,115

The average yield of wheat and corn per acre was: wheat, nine bushels; corn, twenty-eight bushels.

Court-Houses, Jails, Almshouse. — When Thomas Beall, of Samuel, laid out the town of Cumberland, Oct. 4, 1784, he specially set apart four lots for the public buildings of the county, then expected to be shortly erected. In 1793 the Legislature, by a special act, appointed Benjamin Tomlinson, George Dent, William McMahon, John Lynn, and Thomas Beall commissioners to make the plans and contract for the erection of a court-house, and to have general supervision of the building of the same. In each of the years 1794, '95, and '96 two hundred pounds were levied on the taxable property of the county to pay for its construction. It was built on a lot adjoining the one on which now stands the academy, on the north side of Washington Street. The upper story, built of brick, was used for a court-room, and the lower part, made of stone, for a jail. It was finally completed in 1799 at a cost of £612 10*s*. Until it was finished a temporary jail was established in an old log house on the opposite side of the road from Abraham Faw's tavern and a little west of it, on Green Street. It was built in the French and Indian war, and had been a guard-house when the soldiers were at the fort. The courts met at John Graham's house, Mr. Faw's tavern, and at other places until the completion of the temple of justice. The General Assembly, in 1833, passed an act for the building of a new court-house, and the commissioners to have charge of its erection were John G. Hoffman, Bene S. Pigman, Martin Rizer, and John Hoye. A levy of five thousand dollars was made, of which one-fifth was to be collected each year. Strenuous exertions were made by some of the citizens to have the new edifice erected on the east of Will's Creek, but without avail. Digging of the foundations and the other preparatory work was begun in 1836. Work progressed very slowly, and in January, 1839, a petition signed by one hundred and forty-three citizens was presented to the Legislature praying for a change of its location to the east side of the creek. A counter petition against the change of site signed by three hundred and ninety persons was sent up, and the General Assembly decided against a removal. The new building was completed in the fall of 1839. The Legislature in 1850 passed an act for the purchase of land upon which to build an almshouse, and also for the rebuilding of the jail. In 1872 the court-house was enlarged and built over at an expenditure of some fifty thousand dollars, making it one of the finest and most commodious in the State. A new jail was also erected back of the old court-house, and the old prison, adjoining the academy, was subsequently torn down.

On Sept. 8, 1828, George Swearingen, then sheriff of Washington County, murdered his wife just above Cresaptown. Three days after her burial the body was taken up, and the verdict of the inquest was, "After a careful and full examination of numerous witnesses, we are of opinion that Mary C. Swearingen came to her death by the hands of her husband, George Swearingen." Before the disinterment of the body, Swearingen ran off with one Rachel Cunningham, with whom he had maintained a close intimacy. Mrs. Swearingen was an estimable woman, and the daughter of James Scott, of Cumberland. The Governor offered three hundred dollars reward for Swearingen's apprehension, and he was captured Feb. 17, 1829, in New Orleans, where he had arrived on a flat-boat, under the assumed name of Thomas Martin. He was brought to Baltimore on the brig "Arctic" on April 3d, and having been indicted for murder in the first degree, was tried at a special term of court in August, 1829. The court consisted of Chief Judge John Buchanan, and Associate Judges Abraham Shriver and Thomas Buchanan. The prosecuting attorney was James Dixon, and the prisoner's attorneys were William Van Buskirk, William Price, and William McMahon. The jury retired August 22d, and in a few minutes returned a verdict of guilty. He was publicly hanged October 2d following, on the west side of Will's Creek. Over four thousand people witnessed his execution, and two military companies from Bedford and Somerset, Pa., and the Washington Guards of Cumberland were present to preserve order.

On the 22d of July, 1843, William S. Chrise killed Abraham Frey, who resided near Selbysport. The former had been unduly familiar with the latter's wife, which caused Frey to send him word not to again visit his house. Chrise then threatened to kill Frey, and tried to carry off his wife. On July 22d, Chrise met him in the woods, and killed Frey by a blow with a hoe, crushing his skull. A few days afterwards the body was found secreted behind a tree. Chrise was apprehended, indicted, and his trial commenced October 16th following. H. B. Pigman and Wm. Van Buskirk were the lawyers for the State, and George A. Pearre and William Price for the prisoner. The case lasted four days, when the jury found him guilty. He was hanged by Sheriff Normand Bruce, in November, 1843, near Fayette Street, where the railroad now crosses. The Cumberland Guards, under Capt. Alexander King, preserved the peace. His body was dissected by the physicians, and "Old Joe Shumate," a curious old character, got a part of the skin and tanned it, and it is said the leather was exceedingly pliable. Thomas McLaughlin, in the employ of the Baltimore and Ohio Railroad, killed his wife in September, 1850, near Oldtown. He buried the body, which was discovered under the ground at a place being filled up to grade. At his trial Judge Weisel presided, at which John M. Bruver conducted the prosecution, assisted by Henry W. Hoffman. He was found guilty by the jury, and was publicly hanged March 7, 1851, in a hollow on the old turnpike, a little beyond the terminus of Green Street. An immense crowd of men, women, and children assembled to witness the execution, which took place amid the falling of a slight snow. Many of those in attendance came from Virginia and Pennsylvania.

ALLEGANY COUNTY COURT-HOUSE.

In the summer of 1855 a foreigner named Frederick Miller came to Cumberland from parts unknown. He became acquainted with Dr. J. F. C. Hadel, and on October 14th took a walk with the doctor through Sandy Gap. When near the Eckhart Railroad he shot the doctor, who died in a few moments. The villain then cut off the head from the murdered man's body and concealed both in the rocks and woods. He then returned to the doctor's office to rob it. Here he discovered Henry Groff, a friend of the doctor, and he persuaded him to go with him, taking the exact route the doctor had in the morning. When they got to the culvert on the old pike, Miller shot Groff and killed him. He placed the body in the culvert and covered it with stones. The absence of the two murdered men caused on the third day a general alarm, and the whole town turned out to look for them. The remains of the two murdered men were discovered, and Miller was arrested, indicted, tried, and found guilty. He was publicly executed Jan. 4, 1856, near the almshouse, by the sheriff, Dr. John Everett. Miller proclaimed his innocence to the last, but the testimony against him was overwhelming.

In July, 1864, Francis Gillespie, of Company B, Fifteenth New York Regiment, for shooting Lieut. William Shearer on the cars from Parkersburg to Cumberland, was hanged near Rose Hill Cemetery, after his trial by court-martial. Sept. 30, 1864, Joseph Provost, for murdering Christian Miller in Bath, Morgan Co., W. Va., was hanged by the military after his court-martial trial.

On Friday, Jan. 10, 1873, William Craig, a colored man, was executed by Sheriff Gross, assisted by Deputy Dowder. The crime for which Craig suffered the extreme penalty of the law was that of rape.

On the 26th of August, 1872, Craig, then in the employment of John F. Dayton, who resided in Allegany County, near Twenty-first Bridge on the Baltimore and Ohio Railroad, was returning from New Creek, whither he had gone on an errand for Mr. Dayton, when he was arrested on the charge of having committed an outrageous assault on Mrs. Lottie Dayton, an aged lady, grandmother of his employer. He was taken to New Creek, and after a hearing committed to jail by a magistrate. On the 27th of September, having received from the Governor a requisition for Craig, Sheriff Gross, of Allegany County, proceeded to New Creek, brought Craig to Cumberland, and placed him in jail. His case came up for trial in the Circuit Court for Allegany County on October 24, 1872, Judges Pearre and Motter on the bench. He was ably defended by J. H. Gordon and W. McMahon McKaig. The prosecution was conducted by William J. Reid, State's attorney for this county, the opening statement for the State being made by W. M. Welch, commonwealth's attorney for Mineral County, W. Va. On the afternoon of October 25th the jury, after a short absence, returned a verdict of "guilty." On October 26th he was sentenced by Judge Pearre. On November 27th the death-warrant was signed by the Governor and transmitted to Sheriff Gross, who read it to the condemned man on the afternoon of the 28th. The following is a sketch of his life as given by himself:

"My name is William Craig. I am about twenty-two years of age. I was born and matured in Winnsboro', S. C., working upon the plantation of Mr. James McConnell until Sherman's army came through the State. At the close of the war I joined an army-train and came to Washington, D. C. I was afterwards attached to another wagon-train, coming west over the National road. Tired of wagoning, I left the train near Flintstone (after being employed by several parties mentioned by him). I began working for Mr. Dayton at New Creek. At my trial Mr. Gordon and Mr. McKaig did all they could for me; Rev. H. Nice and my pastor, and the attendants of the jail have been very kind to me. I feel that I shall go to heaven."

His execution was strictly private.

The General Assembly, by an act of 1832, authorized the erection of an almshouse, which was built just below Old Town, fourteen miles from Cumberland, on the Chesapeake and Ohio Canal. At the January session of the Legislature of 1850 a new act was passed for the purchase of land and the erection of a new almshouse. The county authorities bought sixty acres in the little valley adjoining Cumberland, upon which was a building, which was temporarily used for the accommodation of the county poor. Since then two additions have been made to the main building. The present structure, adjoining St. Patrick's Cemetery, is of brick, some two hundred by thirty-five feet in dimensions, and two stories high, with a cellar under the whole building. It has eighty-five acres of land attached, which is farmed by the inmates. The average yearly number of inmates is sixty-five. It is managed by a board of trustees appointed by the county commissioners. The trustees for 1881 are John Wilson (president), Peter Smouse, John Wiebel (steward), James Reid, and Dr. Wardlaw Magill, physician. The accommodations are ample and the poor are comfortably cared for, and the institution is as economically managed as the wants of the inmates will allow.

Political Statistics.—On the 10th of January, 1796, at a large meeting of the citizens of Allegany County, held in Cumberland, President Washington's administration was indorsed and the Constitution of the United States approved as the sheet-anchor of the safety of the American people.

At a meeting of the Republicans of Allegany County, held in Cumberland in March, 1801, the following address was adopted and presented to the President:

"CUMBERLAND, March 4, 1801.

"THOMAS JEFFERSON, PRESIDENT OF THE UNITED STATES:

"SIR,—Truly sensible of the importance of the late political contest, and actuated by the most pure and unalterable zeal for the welfare of our country, we, the Republican citizens of Allegany County, in the State of Maryland, beg leave to offer you our most cordial congratulations on your election to the office of President of the United States, and bid you a sincere and unfeigned welcome to the chair as our chief magistrate.

"We freely commit, sir, to your management and direction the helm of our political affairs, under the most perfect reliance that that spirit which dictated the declaration of our independence, and that those sentiments which have so eminently distinguished you amongst the number of American patriots, cannot fail to produce an administration founded on the basis of the genuine principles of the Federal Constitution, and consonant with the true interests of Americans.

"We rejoice that, notwithstanding the deep-laid schemes of the enemies of our freedom to disunite us, there is a display of virtuous courage, and a manifestation of zeal for the support of our country's independence, dignity, and honor, which evidently pervade the United States, and fully proves that the citizens of America, so far from being dismayed by any efforts or threats hostile to their liberty, are animated to a degree that arouses their contempt as citizens and their spirit as soldiers.

"With unspeakable pleasure we anticipate the enjoyment of those blessings which necessarily result from the due administration of wise and wholesome laws, such as are warranted by the letter and spirit of our inestimable Constitution, and calculated to give peace and unanimity to citizens at home and respectability to our nation abroad.

"We draw, sir, the happiest presages in favour of your administration, fondly hoping that no imperious threats from abroad will draw your attention from wise and necessary domestic regulations, and firmly believe that nothing will be wanting on your part to promote and increase the prosperity, liberty, and true happiness of the United States. With best wishes for your good health and happiness, we beg leave, on the part of the Republican citizens of Allegany, to subscribe, with the most profound respect,

"Yours, etc.,

(Signed) "HANSON BRISCOE, *Chairman.*

"ROBERT SINCLAIR, *Secretary.*"

To this address the President made the following reply:

"WILLIAMSPORT, March 23, 1801.

"GENTLEMEN,—I am sensible of the kindness of the Republican citizens of the county of Allegany, in Maryland, in their cordial congratulations on my election to the office of President of the United States, and I pray you to be the organ of my acknowledgments to them. The confidence reposed in me in committing to my management the helm of our political affairs shall not be abused, but, to the best of my skill and judgment, I will administer the government according to the genuine principles of our inestimable constitution and the true interests of our country, sparing no effort which may procure us peace and unanimity at home and respectability abroad.

"I rejoice with them in the display of virtuous courage and zeal for the support of our independence, dignity, and honor which pervade the United States, and that our countrymen, undismayed by any efforts hostile to their liberty, will meet them with the animated courage of citizens and soldiers. The union of these characters is the true rock of our safety, and should be the pride of every man who is free and means to remain so.

"Accept, I beseech you, for yourselves and the Republican citizens of Allegany, the homage of my high consideration and respect. (Signed) "TH. JEFFERSON.

"HANSON BRISCOE, ESQ., Cumberland."

Universal suffrage was not as highly appreciated eighty years ago as now. Prior to 1801 a property qualification was required of every voter in Maryland. In that year, however, the General Assembly passed an act which abolished this restriction, and it was confirmed in 1802. There was great rejoicing all over the State, and nowhere perhaps was there more marked satisfaction exhibited than in Cumberland, where a mass-meeting was held, the proceedings of which are given below. But a majority of the voters in Allegany County do not appear to have considered the action of the Legislature an unmixed blessing, as at the following election for members of the Assembly the ticket nominated by the mass-meeting was defeated, the delegates elected being Joseph Cresap, Jesse Tomlinson, J. H. Bayard, and John Simpkins, who were not indorsed by the meeting.

At a meeting of a number of the Republican citizens of the town of Cumberland and its vicinity, held the 30th day of August, 1802, Hanson Briscoe chairman, and B. S. Pigman secretary, the following resolutions were unanimously agreed to:

"1st. *Resolved*, That the bill passed by the last General Assembly for the consideration of the people, intended to amend the Constitution and extend the right of voting to every male white citizen of twenty-one years of age, having resided one year in the county where he offers to vote next preceding every election (notwithstanding his want of property), is truly Republican, equitable, and just, and therefore meets our warmest approbation.

"2d. *Resolved*, That we highly censure and disapprove the conduct of Joseph Cresap and Jesse Tomlinson, our present representatives, in voting against the said proposed amendment, inasmuch as their votes strongly evince a desire to confine the right of suffrage to monied men only and disenfranchise the indigent though honest man, merely on account of his want of lands and tenements.

"3d. *Resolved*, That we hold it to be our duty, as well as our right, to support the general government as long as it is constitutionally administered, and that the officers of the present administration merit and possess our fullest confidence.

"4th. *Resolved*, That Benjamin Tomlinson, Thomas Cresap, John Rice, and George Rizer are fit and proper characters to represent Allegany County in the next General Assembly. That as such we are determined to support their election, and we beg leave to recommend them to the consideration of our fellows-citizens.

"5th. *Resolved*, That the proceedings of this meeting shall be published in the Maryland *Herald* and *Hornet*.

"HANSON BRISCOE, *Chairman.*

"BEENE S. PIGMAN, *Secretary.*"

In this county, by a vote of 596 for the Democrats to 593 for the Federalists, in 1814, three Democrats and one Federalist were *chosen by the people*, but by a small technical interpretation of the law the people of one district of the county were deprived of their suffrages, and the four Federal candidates declared elected. The presiding judge of the Fourth District was a justice of the peace. He qualified the other two judges and the clerks, and was then himself qualified by a judge instead of a clerk. After the election, when one of the three judges from each of the three districts of the county assembled to make the returns, it was contended that the election in the Fourth District was illegal, as the presiding judge had not been properly qualified. Four of the assembled judges, after rejecting all the votes cast in said district (which was Democratic), selected the four Federal candidates having the highest number of votes on the list and gave them a certificate of election, with a note stating an "irregularity" in one of the districts. The other two judges also made a return, giving credit to the whole number of votes received in the county, showing that three of the Democratic and one of the Federal candidates were elected. All the judges were Federalists. As the possession by either party of these three contested delegates would determine the election of the Governor, who was at that time chosen by joint ballot, great interest was manifested in the result of the contest.

The Legislature was convened on the 6th of December, and when the clerk of the House called the names of the four Federal delegates from Allegany County who had certificates of election, several objections were made by the Democrats to their admission. The Federalists, who were in the majority, contended that the returns of a majority of the judges of election were at least *prima facie* evidence that the persons named were duly and legally elected, and they had no right, therefore, to decide that they should not be qualified as members. There was nothing, they said, in the Constitution, or in the history of parliamentary proceedings, which would justify such an act. It was only after the House had been organized that they had the power to give any decision on the legality of contested elections, and to exclude members returned by the constitutional authority would be a course of proceeding altogether novel. On the other side the Democrats, through Messrs. John T. Mason, of Washington County, Thomas B. Dorsey, of Anne Arundel, and Tobias E. Stansbury, of Baltimore County, argued that as neither of the returns appeared correct, it would be better for the House to proceed in its organization and have the question come before them at another time. Mr. Mason said, as there was no case parallel to the one under consideration, they must be governed by what seemed most expedient. Mr. Stansbury seemed greatly alarmed for the dignity of the House, lest disorder should ensue before they were in a situation to meet it, or a Speaker had been appointed. As two returns had been made from Allegany, and one appeared equally correct with the other, he wished to know who was to decide which of the persons returned should be allowed to qualify and take their seats as members. Messrs. John C. Herbert (Speaker), from Prince George's, Ephraim K. Wilson, of Worcester, and J. Hanson Thomas, of Frederick County, said that these imaginary difficulties might be easily obviated, for they were bound to pay attention to the returns made by a majority of the judges until it should be made to appear that they had been illegally made.

In the course of the proceedings several attempts were made by the Democratic members to organize the House before admitting the Allegany members, but the grounds they took were regarded untenable, and they were overruled by the majority. Upon the reference of the whole subject to the Committee on Elections, they, on the 11th of December, made a report in favor of the Federalists who had the minority of votes but the certificates of election, and the House, by a strict party vote, adopted it, thus deciding that "it would be setting a dangerous precedent to admit collateral testimony to set aside the returns of the judges of election." The Monday following was the constitutional day for electing the Governor.

The question whether the Senate (who were all Democrats) should secede and refuse to go into the election of a Governor and Council unless the House of Delegates would consent to be controlled by their wishes and decide not to admit the Allegany delegates, which gave the controlling power to the Federalists, was fully discussed in caucus, not only by members of their own body, but by some of the most distinguished Democrats in the State, who were invited to attend. At the same time the Democrats of the House of Delegates exhorted the Senate with great warmth not to go into an election of the executive for the ensuing year. In fact, they threatened to resort to arms to maintain their opinion and to compel the Federalists to yield.

On the appointed day it was thought that the Senate would not meet the House in joint convention, but at a late hour the principle that each House should be judge of its own elections prevailed over what the Senate unanimously believed was a sacrifice of the rights of the people to a form, and Governor Levin Winder was re-elected Governor of Maryland for the following year. Seventeen of the members of the House of Delegates, however, refused to cast their ballots.

When, in 1824, John V. L. McMahon, who represented Allegany County in the General Assembly, declined being a candidate for re-election, owing to "the imperative calls and necessities of his profession, which forms his only support," *fourteen* candidates announced themselves for election.

The vote for Congress this year stood:

	Thos. C. Worthington.	John Lee.
Allegany County	669	510
Frederick "	1558	1533
Washington "	2095	1446
Total	4322	3489

In 1833, for congressman, the district gave James Dixon (Whig) 3421 votes, and Francis Thomas (Dem.) 4012.

In 1837 the county's vote for Congress was: Francis Thomas 732, W. M. Merrick 851.

On April 25, 1828, at a meeting of the friends of the administration, Col. Thomas Greenwell was called to the chair and Andrew Bruce appointed secretary. Resolutions were adopted sustaining the administration of John Quincy Adams, and advocating his re-election to the Presidency. The following committees were appointed:

Committee to Draft an Address, Benjamin Tomlinson, B. S. Pigman, B. W. Howard, R. Perry, H. B. Tomlinson, Martin Rizer, Jr., John McNeill, Sr., William Reiley, John Easter, Col. Walter Bevans, James Tidball, John W. Pratt, William Reid, Jonathan Arnold, George Bruce, Samuel Coddington, Jacob Clemmer, William Shaw, Upton Bruce, John McHeury.

Committee to appoint Corresponding Committees, Brice W. Howard, Dr. J. M. Lawrence, John Hoye, John A. Hoffman, Andrew Bruce.

Corresponding Committee in each Election District: District No. 1, Upton Bruce, John McHenry, Jonathan Magruder, William Armstrong, Meshach Browning; No. 2, David Hoffman, Benjamin Coddington, Jacob Clemmer, Samuel Jamison, Richard Drane; No. 3, Jesse Tomlinson, Eli Ridgely, Thomas Thistle, Jacob Sides, William Sutton; No. 4, Rev. John Miller, George Smar, William R. Dawson, Edward McCarty, Jacob Jacobs; No. 5, William Ridgely, Meshach Frost, Gabriel M. Porter, Col. Theodore Blair, Samuel Mattingly; No. 6, James D. Cresap, George P. Hinkle, Jacob Snyder, Jesse Tomlinson, of B., Dr. Samuel P. Smith; No. 7, James Prather, Samuel McBride, Lenox Martin, John Ash, Abel T. Crabtree; No. 8, James Tidball, Henry Bevans, Leonard Shircliffe, Walter McAtee, John Norris; No. 9, Capt. George Robinette, Walter Slicer, Francis Reid, John Piper, John Wilson.

June 28, 1828, a meeting of the administration party was held at Flintstone. Amos Robinette was chairman, and John Piper, Jr., was appointed secretary.

Messrs. Robert Lashley, Elie Wilson, Hugh R. Montgomery, Jesse Robinette, and Nathan Wilson were appointed a committee to prepare resolutions. They soon reported a series of resolutions complimentary to the administration, and also the following, which were adopted:

"*Resolved*, That by and with the individual consent of the parties, the following persons be named as a Committee of Vigilance, viz.: Ed. Montgomery, John W. Pratt, John Flake, Robert Lashley, John Piper, Jr., Samuel Bowden, Moses Willison, Ed. Montgomery, Jr., M. I. R. Montgomery, H. R. Montgomery, William I. Montgomery, Francis Reid, Amos Robinette, Henry Yautz, George Roberts, Robert Denison, Nathan Wilson, Elie Wilson, John Wilson, Elias Wilson, Amos Wilson, Jesse Robinette, Moses G. Robinette, Jarus W. Robinette, Thos. Cheney, of John, Egbert Willison, John Beall, George Slicer, Thomas Robison, Walter Slicer, Reuben Elben, Jr., Reuben Elben, Sr., William Newman, Elijah Collins, John Crock, Sr., John Crock, Jr., David Crock, Lorenzo Hobbs, Jacob Gross, Thomas Pratt, Amon Cheney, Eliphalet Robinette, Robert Edmeston, David Cheney, George Robinette, Jr., John Davis, Ezekiah Cheney, Sr., Jeremiah Robinette, Jr., Jacob Fletcher, John Davis, John McElfresh, Sr., Elijah Robinette, Sr.

July 19, 1828, a meeting was held in the Fifteen-Mile District, at the residence of Mr. Joseph Mattingly, Walter Bevans, chairman; James Tidball, secretary; Committee on Resolutions, Walter McAtee, Henry Bevans, Leonard Schircliff, John A. Hamilton, Esqs., and Capt. Daniel Folke. The following gentlemen were chosen as the vigilance committee, viz.:

Capt. Daniel Folke, John A. Hamilton, Henry Bevans, Leonard Shircliff, Walter McAtee, Thomas King, William Sherwood, John King, James King, Andrew Jenkins, Owen Tracey, Ludwick Roderick, John S. Power, Sandy Mills, William Hughes, William Carroll, John B. Shircliff, William Shircliff, John Norris, Sr., John Norris, Jr., William Norris, James Norris, John Devilbiss, Nicholas Fauver, Daniel Rine, Alexander Robinson, John Slider, Jacob Slider, J. D. Sherwood, Thomas Hartley, John Sherwood, Michael Morgan, Joseph Slider, Andrew Engal, James Tidball, Walter Bevans, Basil Bevans, John Bevans, Rudolph Price, Jeremiah Mecker, Benjamin Knight, Jacob Fouty, Stephen Fouty, George Fouty, James Paul, Peter Hardy, Basil Athy, Elijah Athy, Solomon Slider, Peter Null, Barnabas Fox, Henry Steed.

July 19, 1828, in pursuance of previous notice, a meeting of the voters of the Seventh Election District friendly to the re-election of John Quincy Adams to the Presidency of the United States was held at the house of William Riley, in Old Town. Col. Thomas Greenwell was called to the chair, and Samuel McBride appointed secretary. An address was delivered by John A. King. Messrs. John Reed, John Easter, Jr., William Riley, John Ash, and Lenox Martin were appointed a committee to draft resolutions.

It was also resolved that the following be a committee of vigilance for this district:

John Daniels, Isaac Sapp, John Alkire, Solomon Alkire, Elisha Huff, Benjamin Gamble, John Gamble, Nathan W. Tracy, Nathan Tracy, Jacob Shellhorn, James Prather, Jr., John

Easter, Jr., Andrew Dew, Jacob Stump, Sr., James Malone, Frederick Durn, Michael Hover, Samuel Albaugh, Thomas Perrin, Sr., Thomas Perrin, Jr., Hugh Nixon, Baltzer Crabtree, Thomas Hendrixon, Lenox Martin, J. M. C. Martin, Andrew Hiles, Richard Davis, Robert Morrow, George Morrow, William Morrow, Samuel Davis, Henry Wessman, George Shambaugh, Joseph Dean, Jacob Shambaugh, John Dean, John Athy, Lewis Shambaugh, Sr., Lewis Shambaugh, Jr., William Dean, John Shambaugh, Casper Yinger, David Yinger, William Athy, Martin Cabaugh, David Tracy, Alexander Robertson, Thomas Greenwell, John Ash, John Wilson, William Harness, Daniel Coones, William Riley, Samuel McBride, Peter Deffenbaugh, Thomas Talbert, Joseph Harness, John Deffenbaugh, George French, Brice Twigg, John Reed, William Matthews, Abel Crabtree, John Hook, Alfred Bowman, William Powell, Eli Reed, Thomas Largent, George Athy, Payton Ash, Lewis Crabtree, Sr., Lewis Crabtree, Jr., Francis Twigg, Simeon Twigg.

The result of the Presidential election in Allegany County in 1828 and 1832 was as follows:

Presidential Election, 1828.

	Adams.		Jackson.		
	Baltzell.	Price.	Taylor.	Fitzhugh.	Total.
Glades	90	90	40	40	130
Selbysport	76	76	94	94	170
Little Crossings	20	20	59	59	79
Westernport	49	49	154	154	203
Frostburg	88	88	140	140	228
Cumberland	208	208	218	218	426
Old Town	64	64	57	57	121
Flintstone	98	98	80	80	178
Fifteen-Mile Creek	48	48	14	14	62
Total	741	741	856	856	1597

Presidential Election, 1832.

Districts.	Henry Clay.	Andrew Jackson.
Glades	70	43
Selbysport	58	110
Little Crossings	27	68
Westernport	30	130
Frostburg	86	114
Cumberland	199	180
Old Town	44	60
Fifteen-Mile Creek	42	18
Flintstone	68	92
Total	624	815

Vote for Congressman, 1835.

Districts.	William Schley. (Whig.)	Francis Thomas. (Democrat.)
Youghiogheny Glades	65	56
Selbysport	66	121
Little Crossings	28	71
Westernport	54	92
Frostburg	169	79
Cumberland	205	208
Old Town	32	61
Fifteen-Mile Creek	38	19
Flintstone	65	80
Total	722	787

On Feb. 21, 1835, a called meeting of the Cumberland mechanics was held at the court-house to consider the grievances under which they labored and to adopt the best measures for their redress. A committee reported that it was unwise for the store-keepers of the town to send east for those articles manufactured here, and that it was the duty of all to encourage home manufactures and thus build up the place.

Forty-two persons signed the following pledge:

"We, the undersigned, members of the Farmers' and Mechanics' Union Society of Cumberland, mutually pledge ourselves to support each other by using, and causing to be used in our families, by ourselves and our servants, the manufactures of the mechanics of this community, and will give our undivided support to those who encourage us in like manner. To the faithful performance of which we individually pledge our sacred honor."

The delegates appointed by the districts of Allegany County to form a convention at Cumberland to nominate a ticket to be supported by the Harrison voters met in convention at the Masonic Hall, in Cumberland, on July 11, 1840, and organized by electing Col. Thomas Blair president, Thomas Thistle, Jonathan Frantz, and Jacob Clemmer, vice-presidents, and John Piper, Jr., and Ralph Thayer, secretaries. The delegates in attendance were as follows:

Glades, No 1, Clement Smith, Samuel W. Friend; Glades, No. 10, Normand Bruce, Jehu Gregg, Gwynn Read, William Patterson; Westernport, Joseph McCarty, James Hamill; Little Crossings, M. D. Cade, Isaac Beall, John Lamon, John Plucker, Joel Messetter, John McCurdy, Romulus Thistle, Samuel McCurdy, Michael Durst, Basil Gorlets, Henry Fuller, Samuel Custer, Thomas Thistle, Samuel Smith, John Luckmon, Eli Ridgely, J. H. Wagamon, John McDavid, Martin Stoner; Selbysport, William Drane, Jacob Clammer, John Fike, James Stoddart, Jonathan Frantz, John Mosser, Ralph Thayer; Frostburg, Robert McCulloh, Henry Kuntz, Jonathan Arnold, Geo. W. Bedford, L. Evans, Douglas Percey, Peter Gephart, Jesse W. George Chaney, Thomas Blair; Cumberland, C. M. Thruston, Daniel Wineow, Samuel M. Semmes, A. H. Gross, W. R. Lowdermilk, Joseph H. Hoblitzell, William L. Lamar, Daniel Folck, Jonathan Barkdoll, H. D. Black, A. King, Jacob Bargdoll, Sr.; Old Town, R. W. Watkins, A. W. Tracey, David Ellis, James Johnson, Solomon Alkier, William Hough, Joseph W. Offutt, N. P. Ryan; Flintstone, Elie Wilson, Thomas Cromwell, Robert Lashley, Gideon Butler, Allen House, Philip Fletcher, Thomas Twigg, Jr., John Piper, Jr.; Fifteen-Mile Creek, Thomas McCubbin, Lee Montgomery, J. J. Fenton, Thomas S. Conley, Anthony Loftus, E. H. Coleman, Joseph H. Bevans, Joseph C. Brannon, T. W. Wightman, Isaac Dunham.

The several delegations thereupon proceeded to vote according to rules, and it appeared from their reports that John Beall was nominated as candidate for senator, and that M. C. Sprigg, Ralph Thayer, and Elisha Combs were elected as candidates for the House of Delegates.

The committee of arrangements having in charge the "Harrison rally" in Allegany County, on Sept. 21, 22, and 23, 1840, were as follows:

Thomas Shriver, Samuel Athey, Daniel Wineow, William Lynn, Thomas Rizer, H. G. Grieves, John Gephart, Joseph H. Hoblitzell, H. B. Pigman, Thomas A. Healey, Michael

Wilson, George W. Haller, U. R. Lowdermilk, R. V. Hook, John Pickell, Joseph Shumate, J. J. Johnson, George Mattingly, Samuel Eckles, William Saylor, Abraham Russell, William R. McCulley, Matthias Rizer, Jonathan Butler, Aza Twigg, Gustavus Beall, Jacob Rizer, John M. Maguire, Patrick Crowley, Daniel Cresap, Benjamin Davis, Alexander King, George C. Perry, J. W. Magruder, Samuel Charles, Jacob Barkdoll, Alpheus H. Gross, J. M. McCleary, Thomas Reid, Harrison D. Black, Henry Hudson, Henry B. Osborn, William Copeeler, Frederick Shipley, Robert V. Craggs, William L. Lamar, Daniel Folck, R. Worthington, Isaac Rice, Jesse Hinkle, Joseph Shriver, Samuel P. Smith, Joseph Shuck, George Stubblefield.

"The people came together in their majesty," says a newspaper of that day, "and gave such a demonstration of public opinion that has never been yet equaled.

"The public speaking commenced on Monday night, at the stand erected near the great liberty-pole at Shriver's square. Mr. Bingham, the Buckeye stage-driver, first cracked his whip, and as he started out the Northern Lights commenced shooting and scintillating from the north, as if it had been the glorious news from Maine personified and embodied. This beautiful incident was remarked by the large and attentive auditory. At about nine o'clock the public square, with Baltimore Street leading east and west, and Mechanic Street north and south, became so densely thronged as to be almost impassable. The crowd extended even from Beall's mills to Shriver's mill, and from the covered bridge to Liberty Street. It was almost impossible to make any arrangement of the living mass, so perfectly unexpected was its size and numbers to the marshal of the day, Capt. John Pickell.

"The procession was headed by the inspiring brass-band of Wheeling. They were drawn by six beautiful horses, elegantly adorned and dressed up with covers of white and appropriate trimmings. They were followed by the Straightouts, about eighty of them in number. These were headed by a banner representing the American eagle sitting upon the constitution, around which the storm and waves beat in vain. In his proud beak he held the simple yet expressive motto, 'Straightouts.' They also carried several banners and transparencies. Next rolled in hugest dimensions the great ball itself. This the committee had designed to illustrate how the Harrison ball had gathered and accumulated since the great 4th of May convention, when the ball first started. How well the illustration succeeded every beholder could not but be struck with It was of vast size, twenty feet in diameter. It resembled, indeed, some mammoth animal resistlessly moving onward in its clear way. It was upon a broad rim in the middle, which had upon it a tire as upon a wagon-wheel. It could not be propelled, however, with the same facility as the Baltimore lion, because its axles could not be reached as that was by the ball-rollers, on account of its tremendous size. Shafts, however, were prepared to make the axles indirectly accessible, by means of which it was kept in 'the right track.' It was painted in alternate stripes of blue, white, and red, filled with appropriate mottoes, the poles being surrounded by a blue field studded with stars. The following are the mottoes: 'Old Allegany,' 'O. K.,' 'No Sub-Treasury,' 'No Reduction of Wages,' 'No Standing Army,' 'No Direct Taxation,' 'A Protecting Tariff,' 'A Sound Currency,' 'Hurrah for Old Tip!' and 'One Term,' each motto accompanied by a verse of odd rhyme.

"The ball-rollers were about sixty in number, of stout, athletic men, and many of them dressed in the genuine hunting-shirt.

"The Cumberland Tippecanoe Club marched next in order, followed by the Allegany County delegations. Next followed the delegation from Glades District, No. 1, with various transparencies and banners; then the following delegations in line, all of which had banners, streamers, and transparencies, bearing patriotic and enthusiastic mottoes: Glades District, No. 10, Selbysport, Little Crossings, Westernport, Frostburg, Flintstone, Old Town, Fifteen-Mile Creek, Washington County, Wheeling, and other Virginia delegations, Bedford, Somerset, and Uniontown (Pennsylvania).

"More than five thousand people were on the ground, and, after three-fourths of an hour for rest and refreshment, the following officers, reported by the nominating committee, were chosen by the convention by acclamation: President, John Gephart; Vice-Presidents, Normand Bruce, Jonathan Frantz, John Laymon, John Poland, George S. Evans, John G. Hoffman, Col. John Mitchell, Leonard Shircliff, Alexander S. Carlisle, James D. Armstrong; Secretaries, John Peter, Jr., Robert McCulloh, L. M. Cresap, Samuel Charles. The ball-rollers lighted up their immense ball, *and raised it upon the liberty-pole!* Their stand was splendidly illuminated, and the vast crowd assembled at the large open lot around it. On Wednesday the spirit had not yet abated. The people still lingered to hear the great political battles of the Whig cause.

"The great ball could not be got out of the barn where it was built. The owner thereof, who had just announced the news from Maine, assured them that it had begun to swell, and ordered the door-jambs to be cut away immediately, and to be quick, or it would soon be so large as to require the barn to be taken down!

"On the last evening this same patriot, at his mansion-house, gave to all parties a most agreeable 'winding-up' of this joyous convention."

The following article appeared in the advertising column of *The Civilian*, printed in Cumberland, after the election of Harrison:

"THE RIGHTS OF THE PEOPLE ARE NOT TO BE SOLD.

FOR SALT RIVER,

KINDERHOOK, AND INTERMEDIATE LANDINGS,

The Packet Ship Van Buren,

Only Four Years Old,

Commandant, Amos Kendall, will leave on the 4th of March next for Salt River *via* Kinderhook. For freight or passage, apply at the White House, Washington City, or at the captain's office.

"N.B.—All baggage, extra globes, and Glentworth Papers at the risk of the owners.

"Hypocrites will be in attendance to amuse the passengers, free of charge.

"B. F. Butler, Jesse Hoyt, E. P. Blair, Recorder Morris, and other choice spirits it is expected will be among the forward-deck passengers.

"☞ Gold and silver only received for *passage*."

The election returns of Allegany County in 1840 were as follows:

Districts.	Harrison.	Van Buren.
1. Armstrong's Glades	106	19
2. Selbysport	116	90
3. Little Crossings	113	48
4. Westernport	69	119
5. Frostburg	195	97
6. Cumberland	342	331
7. Old Town	90	139
8. Fifteen-Mile Creek	90	125
9. Flintstone	105	88
10. Ryan's Glades	45	37
Total	1271	1093

Vote for Congressman, 1855.

Districts.	H. W. Hoffman. (Whig.)	W. T. Hamilton. (Democrat.)
Glades, No. 1	87	57
" " 10	78	68
" " 14	66	27
Selbysport	113	94
Grantsville	172	126
Westernport	150	206
Frostburg	326	206
Cumberland, No. 6	257	254
" " 13	318	423
Old Town	86	61
Fifteen-Mile Creek	26	60
Flintstone	132	63
Accident	60	91
Mount Savage	58	236
Total	1929	1968

Presidential Election, 1856.

Districts.	Fillmore.	Buchanan.
Glades, No. 1	83	79
" " 10	79	60
" " 14	69	25
Selbysport	116	99
Accident	61	89
Grantsville	135	139
Westernport	179	260
Frostburg	352	292
Mount Savage	48	285
Cumberland, No. 6	253	255
" " 13	306	486
Flintstone	142	64
Old Town	84	61
Orleans	31	54
Total	1938	2248

Gubernatorial Election, 1857.

Districts.	T. H. Hicks.	Groome.
Glades, No. 1	72	87
" " 10	77	66
" " 14	62	36
Grantsville	127	137
Selbysport	117	104
Frostburg	276	337
Accident	40	118
Westernport	151	234
Cumberland, No. 13	273	460
" " 6	255	269
Old Town	95	59
Orleans	33	53
Flintstone	128	69
Mount Savage	68	272
Total	1774	2299

Congressional Vote, 1860.

	J. M. Kunkel.	H. W. Hoffman.
Allegany County	2288	2201
Frederick "	3718	3673
Washington "	2842	2842
Total	8849	8716

Vote for President and Governor, 1864.

Districts.	Lincoln.	McClellan.	Swann.	Chambers.
Glades	57	57	58	46
Selbysport	122	65	124	65
Grantsville	128	117	128	117
Westernport	200	192	191	192
Frostburg	444	244	421	239
Cumberland, No. 6	277	279	278	279
Old Town	79	56	80	56
Orleans	63	33	63	33
Flintstone	99	84	99	84
Ryan's Glades	61	24	61	21
Accident	46	102	48	102
Mount Savage	86	173	89	169
Cumberland, No. 13	506	367	509	363
Sang Run	78	10	78	10
Oakland	114	69	119	67
Lonaconing	95	118	95	118
Total	2455	1990	2439	1983

In 1864 the county's vote for congressman was: Francis Thomas, 2487; A. K. Syester, 1933.

In 1864, on the vote for calling a Constitutional Convention, the county voted aye, 2307; nay, 1135; and on its adoption, voted aye, 1839; nay, 964.

Vote on Constitutional Convention, 1867.

	Yes.	No.
Altamont	40	43
Selbysport	52	77
Grantsville	111	107
Westernport	187	104
Frostburg	183	296
Court-House	256	149
Old Town	51	42
Orleans	41	40
Flintstone	107	63
Glades	58	15
Accident	95	50
Mount Savage	187	54
Market-House	356	241
Sang Run	12	56
Oakland	49	78
Lonaconing	75	69
Total	1870	1481

County's Presidential Vote, 1860.—Bell, 1521; Douglas, 1203; Breckenridge, 980; Lincoln, 552.

Presidential Vote, 1868.

	H. Seymour.	U. S. Grant.
Altamont	80	67
Selbysport	102	106
Grantsville	142	170
Westernport	230	215
Frostburg	314	427
Court-House	418	239
Oldtown	87	58
Orleans	60	53
Flintstone	118	106
Ryan's	54	63
Accident	99	80
Mount Savage	226	98
Market-House	502	384
Sang Run	19	70
Oakland	115	97
Lonaconing	155	195
Total	2721	2428

Presidential Vote, 1872.—Grant, 3301; Greeley, 2695.

Vote in 1875.[1]

District.	Governor.		Atty.-Gen.		Comptroller.	
	J. Morrison Harris (Ref.)	John Lee Carroll (Dem.)	S. T. Wallis (Ref.)	C. J. M. Gwinn (Dem.)	Edward Wilkins (Ref.)	Levin Woolford (Dem.)
No. 1, Orleans	62	77	62	76	65	74
" 2, Oldtown	68	73	69	72	69	72
" 3, Flintstone	100	98	97	106	99	100
" 4, Cumberland, Canal	283	355	285	383	294	343
" 5, Cumberland, Will's Creek	311	262	315	263	319	252
" 6, Cumberland, River	163	251	167	246	185	225
" 7, Rawlings'	31	35	31	35	45	120
" 8, Westernport	124	157	120	159	131	148
" 9, Barton	212	88	210	92	214	85
" 10, Lonaconing	449	259	449	255	489	190
" 11, Frostburg	449	146	455	151	474	107
" 12, East Frostburg	185	195	185	195	189	175
" 13, Mount Savage	83	228	84	228	92	219
" 14, Cumberland, Central	366	250	359	257	377	236
Total	2904	2474	2861	2518	3042	2246

[1] Dem., Democrats; Ref., Reformers.

Sixth District Congressional Election, Nov. 5, 1872.

	Lloyd Lowndes, Jr.	John Ritchie.
Allegany County	3,611	2,646
Washington "	3,635	3,385
Frederick "	4,892	4,099
Montgomery "	1,920	2,213
Total	14,058	12,343

Lowndes' majority, 1715.

Vote for Congressman, 1876.

District.	Wm. Walsh.	Louis E. McComas.
Orleans	66	74
Old Town	96	62
Flintstone	122	114
Cumberland, Canal	522	286
" Will's Creek	344	349
" River	296	189
Rawlings'	53	43
Westernport	204	161
Barton	112	231
Lonaconing	369	516
Frostburg	179	506
East Frostburg	216	251
Mount Savage	167	151
Cumberland, Central	364	371
Total	3110	3304

District.	Wm. Walsh.	Louis E. McComas.
Allegany County	3,110	3,304
Garrett "	950	1,020
Washington "	3,893	3,986
Frederick "	4,921	5,305
Montgomery "	2,853	2,098
Total	15,727	15,713

County Vote for President in 1876.—S. J. Tilden, 3303; R. B. Hayes, 3217.

Gubernatorial Vote in 1879.—W. T. Hamilton, 2775; J. A. Gary, 2970.

Vote for Congressman and on Local Option, 1880.

	M. G. Urner.	J. M. Schley.	For License.	Against.
Orleans	67	86	93	48
Old Town	78	120	120	61
Flintstone	123	154	150	89
Canal (Cumberland)	310	509	486	258
Will's Creek (Cumberland)	308	337	418	182
River (Cumberland)	168	288	291	112
Rawlings'	46	56	43	54
Westernport	153	152	110	242
Barton	185	81	95	192
Lonaconing	249	120	293	102
Frostburg	502	170	312	362
East Frostburg	260	203	274	216
Mount Savage	140	220	242	97
Central (Cumberland)	407	393	396	352
East Lonaconing	333	178	303	172
Total	3329	3067	3026	2539

Urner's majority, 262; majority for license, 487.

Vote for President, 1880.—J. A. Garfield, 3338; W. S. Hancock, 3089. Garfield's majority, 249.

Congressional Vote of District, 1880.

	Urner.	Schley.
Allegany County	3,329	3,067
Frederick "	5,842	5,154
Garrett "	1,208	1,122
Montgomery County	2,564	3,066
Washington "	4,189	3,929
Total	17,138	16,338

Urner's majority, 800.

Allegany County Election Returns, Tuesday, Nov. 8, 1881.[1]

For Comptroller:

THOMAS GORSUCH	3092
Thomas J. Keating	2434
F. L. Morling	537

For Senator:

WILLIAM BRACE	2941
J. B. Oder	2614
Andrew Patrick	469

For House of Delegates:

B. L. TURNER	2788
C. F. MCALEER	2881
JOHN FATKIN	3026
C. F. HETZEL	3080
James Moriarty	2465
J. Smith Johnson	2405
James Wilson	2486
William Heffron	2284
James Barnard	420
R. W. Price	1161
William Whitfield	651
A. H. Herbert	503

For County Commissioners:

ROBERT MATHENY	3040
NATHAN LOAR	3116
L. V. ALDERTON	2757
JOHN KOLB	3131
A. M. L. BUSH	3048
John A. Daniels	2406
S. P. Harbaugh	2273
Martin Rouzer	2690
John W. Sanders	2290
John H. Patterson	2533
H. B. Elbin	531
Michael Hannon	525
J. P. Hanna	606
Alex. Recknor	713
C. V. Ogden	507

For Sheriff:

J. W. SHUCK	3199
Wm. J. Farrell	2349
Wm. B. Baird	446

For Register of Wills:

JOHN RHIND	3048
Horace Resley	2363
Thomas Rooney	584

For Surveyor:

JOHN SCHAIDT	2971
Charles E. Widener	2488
James Park	583

That portion of Allegany County in which the city of Cumberland is situated is divided into four districts, known respectively as Canal District, No. 4; Will's Creek District, No. 5; River District, No. 6; and Cumberland Central District, No. 14. These divisions have been necessitated by the rapid growth of population and the increase in the number and importance of the material interests which constitute the prosperity of that progressive portion of the State. The city of Cumberland lies in all of these districts, and that the reader may form an accurate idea of the localities their metes and bounds are given as follows:

Canal (Cumberland) District, No. 4.—The lines of this district were amended July 6, 1875, to read as follows:

"Beginning at the bridge over Will's Creek on Baltimore Street, and running thence with the centre of Baltimore Street and with the centre of the National pike to the line of Flintstone District, No. 3; then with the line of said Flintstone District, and with the line of the Old Town District, No. 2, to the Potomac River, nearly opposite a 'brick house' in Virginia known as 'Slogle's Old House;' then westerly with the Potomac River and Will's Creek to the place of beginning."

This district is bounded on the north by Central (Cumberland) District, No. 14, east by Old Town and Flintstone Districts, south and southwest by the Potomac River, separating it from West Virginia, and west by River (Cumberland) District, No. 6.

(Cumberland) Will's Creek District, No. 5.—"Beginning at the viaduct of the Baltimore and Ohio Railroad over Will's Creek, and running thence with the centre of said Baltimore and Ohio Railroad to Bedford Street, thence with the centre of

[1] Republicans in SMALL CAPS. Democrats in Roman. Greenbackers in *Italics*.

Bedford Street with the centre of the Bedford road to the Pennsylvania line, and with said line westerly to Will's Creek; thence down with said creek to the place of beginning."

It is bounded on the north by Pennsylvania, east by Central (Cumberland) District, No. 14, and west and south by River (Cumberland) District, No. 6.

(Cumberland) River District, No. 6.—"Beginning at the bridge over Will's Creek between Baltimore and Washington Streets, in Cumberland; thence up and with the meanderings of Will's Creek to the Pennsylvania line; thence with said Pennsylvania line west to the Mount Savage District line; thence with the eastern line of said district to the line of East Frostburg District, No. 12, and with a part of the eastern line of Lonaconing District to the intersection with the lines of Rawlings' Station District, No. 7, on the top of Davis Mountain; thence with a straight line to the head of Warrior Run: thence with said run eastwardly to the Potomac River, about one-half mile below Brady's mill, and nearly opposite Seymour's house, on the Virginia side of said river; thence down with the Potomac River to the mouth of Will's Creek; thence up with Will's Creek to the place of beginning."

It is bounded on the north by Pennsylvania; east by Will's Creek (Cumberland) District, No. 5; south by the Potomac River (separating it from West Virginia) and Rawlings' District; and west by East Frostburg and Mount Savage Districts.

(Cumberland) Central District, No. 14.—"Beginning at the bridge over Will's Creek on Baltimore Street, and running thence with the centre of Baltimore Street and with the centre of the National pike to the line of Flintstone District, No. 3, and with it to the Pennsylvania line, and with said line west to the Bedford road, and with the centre of said road to Bedford Street, and with the centre of said street to its intersection with the Baltimore and Ohio Railroad, and with the centre of said railroad to the viaduct of said Baltimore and Ohio Railroad over Will's Creek, and thence down with said creek to the place of beginning."

It is bounded on the north by the Pennsylvania line; east by Flintstone District; south by Canal (Cumberland) District; and west by Will's Creek (Cumberland) District.

The city of Cumberland is situated at the confluence of Will's Creek and the North Branch of the Potomac River. It lies on both sides of the former stream, and is surrounded by mountain peaks and lofty ranges of hills. On the north Will's Mountain forms an impenetrable barrier, and on the south the Knobleys rear their heads, while far in the distance the gloomy crest of Dan's Mountain looms up, giving to the town the appearance of being completely cut off from the outer world. Its natural barriers form at all times an absolute protection from the fierce winter storms which prevail in that portion of the State, and the inhabitants, owing to the elevation of the city and the pure, exhilarating breezes which sweep down from the neighboring hills, are exempt from many of the ills to which less favored localities are liable. About a mile west of the town Will's Mountain breaks away as though cleft in twain by some former convulsion of the elements, and Will's Creek glides tranquilly through the beautiful cañon thus made. The National road and the railway tracks of the George's Creek and Pennsylvania Companies occupy one bank of the stream, while the tracks of the Pittsburgh Division of the Baltimore and Ohio and the Cumberland and Pennsylvania Railroads monopolize the space between the frowning cliffs and the water's edge on the other. The gorge, or the "Narrows," is a mile in length, and is unsurpassed for beauty and sublimity. The mountain rises on either side almost perpendicularly for nine hundred feet, and it is easy to imagine that the battlements of some moss-grown castle are frowning down upon the innovations of modern invention and progress. The capping and strata of the rocks, a reddish sandstone, with the fantastic forms they assume, encourage the illusion. Westward from Cumberland there stretches one of the loveliest valleys vouchsafed to human vision. It is about one mile in width and nearly thirty in length, and lies between the Knobley range and Dan and Will's Mountains. The Potomac meanders through the centre, and on the banks of the river lies the track of the Baltimore and Ohio Railroad. The surrounding mountains are lofty and precipitous, and gracefully serpentine in their course. The location of Cumberland, in an amphitheatre formed by the ranges of the Alleganies, which surround it in all directions, has given it the name of the Queen City. Its geographical position is latitude 39° 39′ 14″; longitude, 78° 45′ 25″. Cumberland is 179 miles, by rail, west of Baltimore, 152 miles by rail from Washington, and is 639 feet above sea-level. Its natural advantages as a manufacturing, mining, and commercial centre fully equal its healthfulness and the magnificence of its scenery.

"The Ohio Company," a Virginia association, chartered by the British government in 1749 to trade with the Indians, engaged Christopher Gist to make explorations of the country west and northwest of Virginia. Gist arrived at Will's Creek in October, 1749, and on the last day of that month started west, whither he went as far as the Miami River, in Ohio and Indiana. In the following year the company erected a store-house of logs at Will's Creek, and sent to London for four thousand pounds of merchandise. This was the first settlement upon the site of the present city of Cumberland. In 1751, Col. Thomas Cresap, of Old Town, partially laid out a road from Will's Creek to the mouth of the Monongahela, now the site of Pittsburgh. In the following year the company built another and larger store-house at Will's Creek, on the Virginia side of the Potomac, on the site of Capt. Roger Perry's residence. Made of logs, it was large enough to hold the goods of the company, to serve as the home of its agents, and to be used as a resort for defense against any attacks the Indians might make. The first store-house, built two years prior to this time, was north of the Potomac, on the west of Will's Creek. Gen. Washington, who was a member of the "Ohio Company," was commissioned by Governor Robert Dinwiddie, of Virginia, to visit and deliver a letter to the commandant of the French forces on the Ohio.

Washington, in his report of that journey, says, "We pursued the *new* road to Will's Creek, where we arrived the 14th of November, 1753. Here I engaged Mr. Gist to pilot us out, and also hired four other servitors." In Gist's journal are the following entries:

"Wednesday, 14th November, 1753. Then Maj. George Washington came to my house at Will's Creek, and delivered me a letter from the Council of Virginia, requesting me to attend him up to the commandant of the French Fort, on the Ohio River. Thursday, 15th, we set out, and at night encamped at George's Creek, about eight miles, where a messenger came with letters from my son, who was just returned from his people at the Cherokees and lay sick at the mouth of the Conococheague. But as I found myself entered again on public business, and Maj. Washington and all the company unwilling I should return, I wrote and sent medicines to my son, and so continued my journey, and encamped at a big hill in the forks of the Youghiogany, about eighteen miles."

Washington's report that there was a new and an old road leading to Will's Creek, and that he succeeded in hiring five persons to accompany him across the Allegany Mountains, indicates that this frontier settlement, three years old, was of some importance. Gen. Braddock occupied "Fort Cumberland" (erected by Col. Innes in 1754) in 1755, when he passed with his army to disaster and death on the Monongahela River, July 9, 1755. When the site of Fort Cumberland was selected by the Ohio Company, at the junction of Will's Creek with the Potomac (or Cohougaroutan) River, it was believed to be in Virginia, which exercised jurisdiction over it and the adjacent regions. The white settlements, as late as 1758, extended but a short distance beyond the mouth of the Conococheague, which was at that time the extreme limit of civilization in the West. Every vestige of the fort has long since disappeared, and on its site has been erected a beautiful church edifice, of Gothic architecture, by the Protestant Episcopal congregation of Cumberland. As originally contemplated by the Ohio Company, the city is built on both sides of Will's Creek. The site of Fort Cumberland and the public buildings are upon a spur lying at right angles with Knobley and Will's Mountains, which appears to have been thrown up from the bottom of a lake or running water; for, as deep as it has been dug for cellars and wells and for the passage of the Baltimore and Ohio Railroad, the ground has been filled with what geologists call "traveled stone,"—that is, bowlders large and small, worn round and smooth by the action of the water.

In February, 1763, at the repeated solicitations of many persons, the Ohio Company agreed to lay off a number of lots for a town that was to be located at Fort Cumberland, near the mouth of Will's Creek, on Potomac River, in the province of Maryland. As an inducement and encouragement to purchasers of the said lots the company made the following announcement:

"That each purchaser may have an opportunity of attending and choosing the lots he may judge most convenient, they will be sold to the highest bidders on Friday, the 15th of April next. Any one who will consult the maps must see that Fort Cumberland, from its natural situation and contiguity to that very extensive and fertile country on the Ohio and its waters, must be the key to all that valuable settlement, it being the highest and most convenient landing-place for the inhabitants on the other side of the Allegany Mountains on all the river Potomac, which affords a water-carriage that with a very inconsiderable expense might be rendered safe, certain, and easy at all seasons of the year from the Great Falls to the spot now proposed for a town. It is about seventy-five miles land-carriage to the Monongahela, which is navigable to the Ohio for flat-bottom boats or battoes, and not more than sixty-five miles to the Yauyougaine, where the road, as it is at present cleared to Pittsburgh, crosses, to which place the Indians frequently, before the war, brought up their battoes loaded with skins. And all who are acquainted with the country agree that a very good wagon-road may be made to that very spot, or even a few miles lower down the river, which would reduce the distance from thence to Fort Cumberland at least fifteen miles. The land-carriage from Pimmette's ware-house, at the Little Falls, which is the highest tide-water of Potowmack, to the Great Falls does not exceed twelve miles, and the manufactures of Great Britain may be transported by the Potowmack to the Ohio, and its produce or furs remitted through the same channel, with only ninety miles land-carriage at the most. Fort Cumberland is about one hundred and fifteen miles from Pittsburgh, thirty from Fort Bedford, sixty from Winchester, land-carriage, good wagon-roads, and one hundred miles water-carriage from the mouth of Conococheague Creek, in Maryland. The day the lots are sold the Ohio Company will let to the highest bidder for a term of years two very good store-houses, opposite to Fort Cumberland, in Virginia, one 45 by 25 feet, with a counting-room and lodging-room at one end, the other 44 by 20 feet, with proper conveniences for a family to live in, two stories high each, besides garrets, with good dry cellars fit for storing skins the whole size of the houses, and a kitchen, stable for twelve horses, meat-house, and dairy. There are two good battoes, which will be given to the person who rents the houses, the whole entirely new, and will be completely finished and fit to enter upon immediately; and the person who takes the store-houses may also have a lease for a term of years of as much land adjacent to them as he chooses. Any one desirous to treat privately for the store-houses, etc., before the day of sale, or the town-lots, may know the terms by applying to the subscriber, who will attend at Fort Cumberland on the 15th day of April, before mentioned, to deliver the purchasers' deeds for their lots. There is great plenty of good timber and limestone on the lands on each side of the river, and the company are building a saw- and grist-mill within a mile of the spot proposed for a town."

On the 15th of April of the same year the Ohio Company sold at auction the lots at Fort Cumberland which they had laid off as a town. The town, however, existed only on paper, and never grew as its projectors anticipated, owing perhaps to the company's transformation that year into the "Grand Company." Thomas Beall, of William, on Monday, Oct. 4, 1784, laid out a town and sold the lots at public sale. Many of the lots were sold to persons in Baltimore, where Hezekiah Waters was Mr. Beall's agent. The town was located upon a survey named "Walnut Bottom," "beginning at two bounded white-oak trees standing on a cliff of rocks at the lower end of a bottom, near half a mile below the mouth of Will's Creek, near the river-side." Thomas Cresap surveyed "Walnut Bottom" June 1, 1745, for Governor Thomas Bladen, who owned many large bodies of land in this part of the province, then included in Prince George's County. Governor Bladen sold his right to "Walnut Bottom" to George Mason, of Fairfax County, Va., who obtained his grant therefor March 25, 1756. Oct. 25, 1783, Mr. Mason sold it with another tract, called "Limestone Rock," to Thomas Beall, of Samuel, for £1407 10*s*. Mr. Beall called his town "Washington Town." In 1787 the inhabitants of the new town petitioned the General Assembly for the legal establishment of the town, and desired that it should be named after the old fort erected in 1754 by Col. Innes, on the site of the proposed town.

On the 20th of January, 1787, the following act was passed by the Legislature, authorizing the erection of the town of Cumberland:

"An Act *for erecting a town at or near the mouth of Will's Creek, in Washington County.*

"Whereas, It is represented to this General Assembly by Thomas Beall, son of Samuel, that he is possessed of a tract of land called Walnut Bottom, contiguous to the mouth of Will's Creek, in Washington County, whereon, at the instance of many of the inhabitants of said county, he hath been induced to lay out ground for a town; and the said Thomas Beall hath prayed a law to appoint commissioners to lay out and erect a town on the said land and to secure the purchase of lots therein, reserving the right of the proprietors and their interest in said land; and this General Assembly are of opinion that the erecting of a town at the mouth of the said creek may be convenient and beneficial to the public.

"II. *Be it enacted by the General Assembly of Maryland,* That Andrew Bruce, Daniel Cresap, George Dent, John Lynn, and Evan Gwynn, or any three or more of them, be and are hereby appointed commissioners to survey a quantity of land, not exceeding two hundred acres, being part of a said tract of land called Walnut Bottom, contiguous to the mouth of Will's Creek, in Washington County, and the same, when surveyed, to lay out into lots, streets, lanes, and alleys (the main streets, running in the direction of the Powtomack River, not to be less than eighty feet wide, and the streets crossing the said main streets not to be less than sixty feet wide), to be erected into a town, and to be called and known by the name of Cumberland, and a correct and accurate certificate and plot thereof returned to the clerk of Washington County Court, who is hereby required to record the same among the land records of the said county, and to keep the original plot in his office, and a copy from the original, or the record thereof, shall be conclusive evidence as to the bounds and lines of the lots of the said town, and of the streets, lanes, and alleys thereof.

"III. *And be it enacted,* That the said commissioners, or a major part of them, shall cause the said lots in the said town to be substantially and fairly bounded and numbered, and they and their successors are hereby required, from time to time, to take care that the said boundaries be constantly kept up and preserved.

"IV. *And be it enacted,* That on the death, removal, or resignation of any of the said commissioners, the major part of the remaining commissioners shall appoint another to serve instead of such commissioner so dying, removing, or resigning.

"V. *And be it enacted,* That the said commissioners of the said town, or a major part of them, shall have full power to employ a clerk, who shall be under oath fairly and honestly to enter into a book to be kept for that purpose all of the proceedings of the said commissioners relating to the said town, in which book, among other things, shall be entered a copy of the plat and certificate of the said town, describing every lot by its number, and who the taker-up or purchaser was or shall be, and the said book shall always be open to the inspection and examination of the said commissioners.

"VI. *And be it enacted,* That the said commissioners, or a major part of them, are empowered to levy, assess, and take by way of distress, if needful, from the inhabitants of the town, by even and equal proportion, a sum not exceeding ten pounds current money yearly, to be paid to their clerk; and they shall have power to remove or displace their clerk as often as they shall think fit.

"VII. *And be it enacted,* That every purchaser of any of the lots of the said town in fee, and every lessee thereof, for years, or rent reserved, shall hold and possess the same against any person hereafter claiming title to the same, and shall not be disturbed in their possession, and if any person shall hereafter make claim to the land, or any part thereof, laid off in virtue of this act, and shall, by due course of law, make good title thereto, such person shall be entitled to recover from the said Thomas Beall, his heirs, devisees, executors, or administrators, any purchase-money or rents by him received from any of the purchasers or lessees of any of the said lots, and, upon any such recovery, the tenants holding under the said Thomas Beall shall hereafter hold under pay the rent reserved to the person making title to and recovering the same land.

"VIII. *And be it enacted,* That if any of the buildings already built on the land so as aforesaid to be laid out by the said commissioners and erected into a town should happen to interfere with, or to stand on any of the streets laid off in virtue of this act, the same shall be permitted to continue, but shall not at any time hereafter be repaired or rebuilt."

At that date there were but few houses in the town. The following persons were residents: George Blocher,

John Mustard, Henry Wineow, Elie Williams, David Harvey, James Slicer, George Simmons, John C. Beatty, John Lynn, Jeremiah Wilson, George Payne, Robert Clark, David Hoffman, John S. Hook, Thomas Stewart, Jonathan Cox, Jacob Lowry, George Lowdermilk, Evan Gwynn, David Lynn, Andrew Bruce, George Dent, Thomas Beall, George Calmes, Michael Kershner, James McCoy, David Watkins, George Hoffman, Charles Clinton, John Graham, Charles F. Broadhag, William Hoye, Dickeson Simkins, Peter Devecmon, and Benjamin Wiley. The town was located principally on the west side of Will's Creek, and the houses were generally built along "Braddock's road," now Green Street, but near Washington Street (on a bluff) several buildings had been erected. The first white child born after Cumberland had been incorporated was Frederick Dent, the father-in-law of Gen. Grant. George Dent and his wife lived in a log house on Green Street, where, in the fall of 1786, Frederick Dent first saw the light. The house is still standing, and is known as the "Dent" or "Devecmon" house. Frederick Dent removed when young to Pittsburgh, and in 1817 settled at St. Louis, Mo. He died at the Presidential mansion in 1873, aged eighty-seven years.

Washington's headquarters were on the site of O. C. Gephart's residence. The house was built about the time of the erection of Fort Cumberland, and was situated a short distance from the fort. It was occupied at different times by Mrs. Bridenhart, David Lynn, George Bruce, and John Kane. George Blocher purchased it in 1844, and removed it a mile distant to the Bedford road, where for over twenty years John Baker lived in it. It is yet standing on the land of Christian Eichner. Prior to 1784, George Lowdermilk put up a frame house a little west of Washington's headquarters, in which he resided eighteen or twenty years. On the southwest corner of Smallwood and Green Streets was erected in 1792 the McMahon house, attached to which was a storeroom. The building in the rear was put up afterwards, and was the first brick edifice in town. Henry Wineow, the first brick-mason in Cumberland, did the masonry work. Here was born John V. L. McMahon, the distinguished lawyer. About 1790, Michael Kershner built a frame house on the north side of Green Street. Abraham Faw erected a log tavern (two stories) where Mrs. W. Landwehr's residence is. In it were born Gen. E. O. C. Ord, of the United States army, and Hon. J. Galloway Lynn. George Dent, surveyor of the town, built in 1790 the Devecmon house, and his wife died eighteen years later at the house of Dickeson Simkins, corner of Valley and North Mechanic Streets. David Hoffman built the first house on the east side of the creek, which was of logs forty by twenty-five feet. It was just south of the Blue Spring.

Mr. Wyatt put up, in 1791, a log house on North Mechanic Street, above the Blue Spring. Samuel Smith occupied it in 1809 and 1810 for a store and post-office. In 1790, Dickeson Simkins built his house on the corner of Valley and Mechanic Streets and shortly afterwards his brother-in-law, Benjamin Morris, a shoemaker, built a house below Weyman's store, on Mechanic Street. After this John Snowden Hook removed from Washington County and built a log structure next to lot No. 215. In 1800, Jacob Neff built a house on lot No. 132 North Mechanic Street, and there carried on a pottery. He was succeeded by Emanuel Easter (Neff's first apprentice), who continued in this business till his death, in 1877. Jonathan Cox built a stone house on North Mechanic Street, and with David Cox had a tannery just above the site of Withers' tannery. George Shuck lived in a log house where Shipley's tavern stood. He came from York, Pa., about 1790. George Payne's house, in 1796, stood near Payne's Spring, on the Little Valley road. John Miller, in 1794, built a log house on the corner of Liberty and Bedford Streets, just opposite the City Hall, known as the Snyder property. Thomas Beall, of Samuel, the proprietor of the town, built, in 1785, a house on Liberty Street below the City Hall, on the other side.

The surveys, boundaries, and map of the town, as required by the act of Jan. 20, 1787, were not filed among the land records of either Allegany or Washington County. Hence, the General Assembly, Jan. 27, 1805, passed an act setting forth that

"*Whereas*, Thomas Beall, son of Samuel, and other persons, did lay off a parcel of their land contiguous to the mouth of Will's Creek, in Allegany County, into lots, a great part of which have since been purchased, and considerable improvements made thereon, and there being no record of the same, the titles of the proprietors thereof are precarious and uncertain; and it appearing right and proper that commissioners should be appointed to lay out and erect a town on the said lands, and to secure the purchasers of lots therein, reserving the right of the proprietors and their interests in said lands; therefore commissioners should be appointed to perform the work."

Under this act Roger Perry, Evan Gwynn, Jonathan Cox, George Hoffman, and Upton Bruce were appointed to make a new and accurate survey and minute plat of the town, giving the original location of the streets, alleys, lots, etc., and to file the same in the county clerk's office. The act required them to have the lots numbered consecutively from one upwards as in the original location, and made provisions for saving to purchasers their rights, and repealed the act of 1787. In 1806, George Dent, as surveyor, made his resurvey and carried out the requirements of the act by filing his plat in the land records of the county. The portion of the town on the north and east side of Will's Creek had been first surveyed and laid out in 1798.

The commissioners made the following report, which, with a minute description of each lot, was filed with the map or plat:

"The town of Cumberland had grown into considerable size before the passage of the law authorizing its being laid out; and as no correct plot had been preserved of its ancient location, or boundaries set up, by which it could be ascertained correctly, the commissioners for want of some guide of this kind met with considerable difficulty in assigning to each lot its due and proper situation, particularly so on the east side of Will's Creek, where the lots being of no given size, and the streets crooked and irregular, one lot became of little service in leading to the establishment of another; the conveyances or titles by which many of the lots were held were very imperfectly drawn, and many blunders committed, so that they frequently served to add to our perplexity than furnish us with correct information. The commissioners, nevertheless, trust they have produced as perfect a return as could be desired or expected, and that besides the advantage of every man knowing how and where to find the precise situation of his lot, many disputes will be quieted from the having a settled and determined record to refer to. Several additions have been made to the town as just laid off, and as each addition begins with number one, two, and so on, it follows that there are five lots thus numbered in the town of Cumberland, a circumstance it was impossible for the commissioners to avoid under the restriction of the law giving them their powers. At first glance of the plot this may seem like confusion, but which it will be easy to avoid if, where in searching for any number, due regard be had to the addition it is distinguished by as lying in. There are on the plot two lots numbered 219, which could not be avoided, as by some error conveyances had been made to two different persons for two adjoining lots by this number; but to distinguish we have called one the senior and one the junior lot. Occasionally on our approach to the neighborhood of some metallic substance, we found ourselves led astray from the attraction of the needle; sometimes we were unable to discover where the course lay, though the effect was quite plain. It was observable that in passing by where had been several years back a smith-shop the attraction from small particles of iron concealed under the ground was very considerable, and would have thrown us totally into confusion had it not been discovered in time. So that in any future running due caution ought to be paid to this circumstance. The commissioners ask for their intentions and their return a fair and liberal interpretation; and while they are confident strict and equal regard has been paid to each particular interest, express a hope that their labors will be found to have given order, form, and certainty to what was heretofore perplexed, confused, and doubtful; and that each proprietor of a lot in the town of Cumberland may discover its situation, extent, and limits by a reference to the plot, and without an appeal to the remedy at law, which is always attended with expense and delay.

"ROGER PERRY,
"EVAN GWYNN,
"JONATHAN COX,
"GEORGE HOFFMAN,
"W. BRUCE."

The original town of Cumberland was on the west side (now First Ward), and Thomas Beall, one of the wealthiest and most prominent men of the place, afterwards laid off a portion of his land on the east side, which was called "Beall's Addition." The first streets were Mechanic and Bedford, now Baltimore; next in order was Mill, now Bedford. The lots on Mechanic Street were laid off along the road from Will's Creek and other valleys, and Western Pennsylvania to Beall's Mill, which was a meandering route; hence the crooked Mechanic Street of to-day, and the several bends in Centre, which were necessarily made to give the lots between the two streets an average depth in the same squares or blocks, but not for the entire length of these thoroughfares. It was the tradition that this meandering road was made over the route taken by the cows when going to pasture, and it was known in old times as the "cow-path" road. Mr. Beall, the original "proprietor" of the town of Cumberland, was a kind-hearted man, who did good in many ways in his generation, and when he platted the ground and sold lots on Mechanic Street, he offered unusual inducements in the way of prices and terms to steady, reliable men with trades, but not possessed of much means. Men of this class became the purchasers of nearly all the lots on the new street, and from this fact it was named Mechanic Street. Before "Beall's Addition" was made to Cumberland, the whole stretch of valley land from the Payne Spring to Capt. John Black's place (now the property of Mr. Black) was called "Walnut Bottoms." From 1804 to 1810, among the leading citizens were William McMahon, merchant; John Lynn, county clerk, who settled here before the "Whisky Insurrection" of 1794; William Moore, Maj. Beatty, George Dent, John Rine, and Roger Perry.

Property Holders.—The following is a list of the names of the owners of real estate in "Cumberland Town" in the year 1813, and the amounts for which they were assessed that year, as taken from the assessment books. From this list it will be seen that the town was then owned by one hundred and fifty-nine persons, and the value of the property as assessed for the purpose of taxation amounted to only $22,829. In that year (1813) there were but one hundred and thirty-eight houses in the town.

John Anderson	$1080
Harmanus Alricks	25
Robert Armstrong	25
Christian Albright	100
Chas. F. Broadhag	290
John L. Bugh	15
Mary Ann Boyd's heirs	330
N. Basnett's heirs	450
Peter Bumwart	200
Margaret and Elizabeth Beard	$30
George Blocher	252
John Brideham	60
Daniel C. Brant's heirs	115
Jacob Blocher	360
John C. Beatty's heirs	225
Andrew Bruce	12
Upton Bruce and J. Cox	60

Name	Amount
Jeremiah Berry	$80
C. F. Broadhag and Geo. Magruder	15
Robert Beaver	100
Upton Bruce	700
Thomas Beall, of Samuel.	1815
Hanson Briscoe	175
Jonathan Cox	134
Dennis Corbett	20
George Clark's heirs	40
Absalom Chambers	50
David Cox	235
George Clice's heirs	100
Zadock Clark	40
Fred'k Christman	80
David Cook	15
Christian Deetz's heirs	125
Frederick Deems	60
Mary Davis' heirs	37
Francis Deakins	30
Grafton Duvall	25
Solomon Davis	80
Hannah Entler's heirs	40
Leonard Extine's heirs	50
Michael Fisher	100
George Funke	175
Abraham Faw	205
John Folk	240
Jacob Fair	75
James Glenn	25
John Graham	75
Peter Gephart	111
Peter Geary	70
James Hook	75
George Hebb	230
Jacob Hoblitzell	465
George Hoffman	230
David Hoffman, Sr	817
James Hendrixon	90
John L. Hook	71
John Hunter	30
John Hoblitzell	200
Daniel Haner	80
George M. Houx	15
Beall Howard	115
John G. Seiss	90
Robert Selby's heirs	10
Gilbert Strong	35
Henry Stantzman	208
Michael Soyster	151
John Shroyer	210
James Scott	270
Dickson Simpson	175
Patrick Sullivan	195
Walter Slicer	1025
John Scott	200
James Searight	40
Joseph Shumate	40
John Searight	120
Samuel Smith's heirs	230
John Shook	50
Benj. Stoddert's heirs	30
Geo. Thistle	270
John Hoye	485
George Hoblitzell	80
Jonathan Hendrixson	40
Clement Engle	15
Michael Kershner	65
Nicholas Koontz	105
L. Klemmer's heirs	50
Joseph Kelley's heirs	40
Christian Kealhoover	10
John Kime's heirs	$56
Jacob Korn	180
H. Korn and J. Witt	80
James Kinkead	200
S. Lowdermilk's heirs	6
Robert Larimore	15
John Lynn's heirs	55
Peter Lowdermilk	125
William Lamar	240
David Lynn	30
Patrick Murdoch	205
John McCleary's heirs	40
George Murrow	140
Mary Myers	30
Jacob Myers' heirs	96
William Moore	70
Robert McCleary, Sr	75
Wm. McMahon	699
Henry Mattingly	65
Henry McCleary	15
Nancy McIntosh	35
John Myers	50
A. McCleary's heirs	50
John McKim, Jr	80
Clement Masters	45
John Milbourn	50
Isaac Montz	25
Robert McCleary, Jr	120
Francis Madore	50
Henry McKinley	210
Mary Murdoch	285
James McIntosh	10
Jacob Neff	598
William Osborn	97
Richard J. Orms	15
John Patterson	85
Jos. Polson	65
George Payne's heirs	75
Thomas Price's heirs	10
Edward Pannell	15
Roger Perry	600
John Peter	80
Martin Rizer, Jr	135
Anthony Reintzell	15
Elnathan Russell	60
Thomas Reid's heirs	75
John Ryan	75
William Roberts	40
Martin Rogers' heirs	155
George Rizer, of M	200
Jas. Robardent's heirs	30
Martin Rizer, Jr	15
Jacob Shook	70
George Shook	120
James Timmons	140
John Tomlinson	10
Josiah Thompson	15
Samuel Thomas	15
Ebenezer Vowell	474
Benj. G. Vaughn	75
John B. Wright	65
Henry Wineow	170
John Walls	60
Samuel Walls	40
Sarah Willison's heirs	30
Michael Wire	125
Charles Worthington	20
Benjamin Wiley	70
O. H. and Eli Williams	20
John Wykart	50
George W. Yontz	10

In January, 1815, the General Assembly incorporated the town by passing an "Act to provide for the appointment of commissioners, for the regulation and improvement of the town of Cumberland, in Allegany County, and to incorporate the same." Under it five "judicious and discreet" persons residing in the town and owning real estate in its limits were to be elected on the first Monday of June, 1816, and on the same day in every succeeding year, at the court-house, by the legal voters of said town, and the five persons having the greatest number of votes were to be the commissioners. The latter were empowered to select one of their own number as chief burgess, and to meet for business at least four times a year. This act limited taxation for municipal purposes to one dollar for each one hundred dollars of valuation, and provided for the appointment of a bailiff and clerk. A subsequent legislative act of 1816 appointed John Scott, William McMahon, and Roger Perry commissioners to locate, mark, lay off, bound, and number into streets, lanes, alleys, and lots the ground between Chase and Smallwood Streets, exempting said lots, however, from town taxes until their improvement by building, etc. At the first town election in June, 1816, the following board of commissioners was elected: John Scott, John Hoye, Henry McKinley, George Thistle, and David Shriver, Jr., of whom the first was chosen chief burgess. Thomas Pollard was appointed clerk. Among the subsequent town officers were: 1822, Samuel Magill, chief burgess, and John McNeil, clerk; 1824, Commissioners, Roger Perry (chief burgess), Peter Garey, John Boose, Gustavus Beall, John Gephart, Jr.; Clerk, C. Heck.

In 1834 the Legislature passed an act amendatory of the act of 1815, incorporating Cumberland as a city. Its legal boundaries were fixed as follows: "half a mile all around the town, to be computed and measured from the town lots on the outer edge or confines of the town proper, as located and settled by law, and by the plat already recorded among the land records." The new incorporating act provided for the election annually of seven councilmen, who should each year elect one of their own number mayor.

The mayors have been:

1835, John Gephart; 1836, John Wright; 1837, Thomas J. McKaig; 1838, Frederick Deems, who resigned September 25th of the same year, when Peter Hoffman was elected in his place; 1839–40, Samuel Charles; 1841, James Smith; 1842, John Gephart; 1843–50, Thomas Shriver; 1850, Thomas F. White; 1851, Daniel Saylor; 1852, John Hays; 1853, F. B. Tower; 1854, A. L. Withers; 1855, W. W. McKaig; 1856, J. H. Tucker; 1857, J. W. Jones; 1858–59, D. W. McCleary; 1860, John Humbird; 1861, C. M. Thruston; 1862, C. H. Ohr; 1863, James Smith; 1864, C. H. Ohr; 1865, George Harrison; 1866–68, John Humbird; 1869–70, Lloyd Lowe; 1871, William Piatt; 1872, J. B. Widener; 1873, W. A. Withers; 1874, W. R. McCulley; 1875, John Humbird, elected to fill vacancy of McCulley, who died Dec. 4, 1874; 1876–78, W. A. Withers; 1878–80, W. J. Read; 1880–82, J. B. Walton.

In January, 1874, the Legislature passed a new charter for the city, under which the first election was held May 18, 1874, when two councilmen were elected from each of the six wards, one to serve one and the other two years. The mayors were by this act to be elected for two years.

The city of Cumberland was divided in January, 1874, into six wards, bounded as follows:

"For the First Ward, all that portion of the city lying on the west side of Will's Creek; beginning for the Second Ward at the intersection of Bedford (commonly called Mill) Street with Will's Creek, and running with said creek to the northwesterly limits of the city, and with said limits to the Cumberland and Pennsylvania Railroad to Bedford Street, and with the centre of Bedford Street to Will's Creek; beginning for the Third Ward at the intersection of the Cumberland and Pennsylvania Railroad with Bedford Street, and running thence with the centre of Bedford Street and the Bedford road northeastwardly to the city limits, and with said limits westwardly to the Cumberland and Pennsylvania Railroad, and with said railroad to the place of beginning; the Fourth Ward shall comprise all that portion of the city bounded on the west by Will's Creek, and lying between Bedford Street and Baltimore Street and the Baltimore turnpike to the eastern limits of the city; beginning for the Fifth Ward at the intersection of Baltimore Street and Will's Creek, and running with Baltimore Street and the Baltimore turnpike to the eastern limits of said city, and with said limits to the Williams road, and with said road to the Baltimore and Ohio Railroad, thence by a straight line with the centre line of said Williams road extended to the Potomac River, and with said river and creek to beginning; and the Sixth Ward shall contain all that portion of the city lying south of the Fifth Ward and east of the Potomac River."

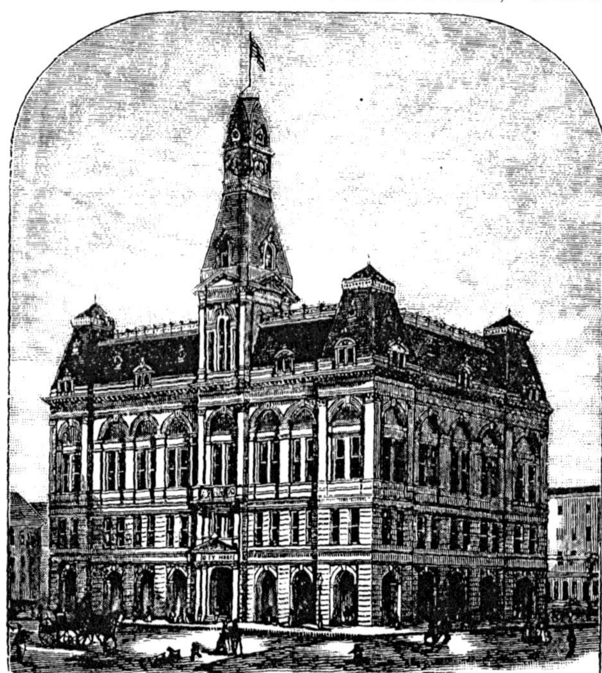

CITY HALL AND ACADEMY OF MUSIC AT CUMBERLAND.

The City Hall of Cumberland is the largest, finest, and most costly building of the kind in Maryland, outside of the city of Baltimore. It was commenced in 1874 and completed in 1876. The building stands upon the square bounded by Centre, Frederick, Liberty, and Bedford Streets, in the very centre of the city, and can be seen from all points outside the city, though the ground occupied is low, and the building is closely hemmed in by houses all around. When the erection of the City Hall was determined on, a committee of citizens, selected for their probity and enterprise, were appointed to put the project in shape and carry it out. The committee was composed of Messrs. J. B. H. Campbell, J. H. Gordon, Frank Haley, and Jesse Karns, with Hon. H. W. Hoffman as chairman. All of the committee took great interest in the work, and the chairman in particular, who gave a great portion of his entire time and to every detail his personal attention. The result of his labors—a complete public work, the admiration and pride of the citizens—is his reward. The architect of the building was Frank E. Davis, of Baltimore, and the builder John B. Walton, who agreed to do the whole work, excepting the putting in of the steam-boilers and fixtures and the decoration of the academy. The cost of the building was about ninety thousand dollars.

The edifice fronts on Centre Street a distance of one hundred and twenty-six feet, the Frederick side being one hundred and four feet, the Liberty Street side one hundred and fifteen feet, and the Bedford Street side one hundred and four feet. It is, with the market-house and mansard roof, five stories in height, though showing only four on the outside. It is built of Cumberland brick, and, on account of the many openings necessitated by the market-house and theatre, contains only a little over a million bricks. The distance from the ground to the mansard roof is sixty-two feet, and to the top of the roof seventy-eight feet. In the middle of the Centre Street front is a tower one hundred and forty-five feet in height, one hundred and twenty feet of which is brick-work. In the tower-roof is a space for a fine tower-clock and bell.

The ground-floor is occupied by the market-house, which includes the entire site of the building, excepting the tower and a small room under it. It is fitted up in modern style, with thirty-three butchers' stalls and fifty vegetable stalls. There are twenty-one entrances,—five on Centre Street, five on Bedford Street, six on Liberty, and five on Frederick Street.

The first floor includes the council chamber and municipal offices, and the lobby, dressing-rooms, and first-floor box-entrances, etc., of the theatre. The offices of the city government occupy the northern half of the floor. The council chamber, occupying the northwest corner, is a splendid room, fifty by forty feet, and eighteen feet high. In the rear of the council-chamber and next the lobby is an ante-room, twenty by twenty feet. On the northeast corner is the mayor's office, and adjoining it the city clerk's office, each twenty by twenty feet.

The second floor is a counterpart of the first, excepting one additional room over the council chamber.

The third floor is leased entirely by the Masonic fraternity. The main lodge-room is sixty by forty feet, and sixteen feet high. There are also chapter and banqueting-rooms, ante-rooms, and numbers of small rooms for the storing of regalia, paraphernalia, etc. The I. O. O. F. order has three rooms on the third floor.

The crowning feature, in point of size, beauty, and elegance, of the City Hall building is the theatre, which occupies the southern half of the building, above the market-house. After the Baltimore theatres, it has no equal in this State in seating capacity, and few or no superiors of its class in beauty and elegance, while for the convenience and completeness of its appointments of all kinds, and particularly those of the stage and its appurtenances, by the statement of several prominent theatrical managers, it is absolutely unsurpassed in this country. The stage has everything that is required by the leading companies, and is pronounced perfect in its appointments by those who know. It is the work of Mr. W. H. Fowler, stage-carpenter, Baltimore. The scenery is beautiful, and has been warmly commended by connoisseurs who have seen it. The auditorium is sixty-two by sixty-six feet. The seating capacity of the house is eleven hundred persons. The entire building, including the market-house, Masonic Hall, etc., contains four hundred gas burners.

The Academy of Music was opened March 7, 1876, with a performance of "The Big Bonanza," by Frederick B. Warde, under the management of John T. Ford, of Baltimore, which was followed successively by "The Two Orphans" and "Jane Eyre," under the same manager.

The Water-Works.—To the General Assembly of Maryland, early in its session of 1816, a petition was presented by the inhabitants of Cumberland praying for the incorporation of the "Cumberland Water Company," for introducing soft water into the town. The charter was granted, and the company authorized to raise ten thousand dollars by issuing five hundred shares of stock at twenty dollars each. David Shriver, Michael C. Sprigg, George Thistle, Samuel P. Smith, John Scott, and Peter Lowdermilk were the committee in charge of the subscription-books. After a year or so the company failed in its project, and the matter was dropped until the third year of the civil war, when the local authorities and citizens generally realized the necessity of obtaining an adequate supply.

The inadequate supply of good water for domestic and other purposes had long been a cause of much inconvenience, and oftentimes considerable loss to the inhabitants of Cumberland, and the subject of works to supply the city had been talked about for ten years or more, but no movement was made in the right direction until a few enterprising citizens had the matter brought before the Legislature of Maryland in 1864, and a charter was granted by that body on March 5th of that year for the erection of city water-works.

The charter gave the mayor and councilmen of Cumberland the authority to issue bonds to the amount of sixty thousand dollars, bearing six per cent. interest, for the purpose of realizing a fund for the introduction of water into the city for the use of the inhabitants thereof. For the purpose of carrying out the provisions of the charter, a board of water commissioners was named in the charter, comprising Messrs. Joseph Shriver, V. A. Buckey, Alpheus Beall, Hopewell Hebb, and J. B. H. Campbell. Surveys were made by Charles P. Manning, and also by William Brace, civil engineers, with a view of supplying the city with water by the reservoir system. It was designed to place a large steam-engine at the river, and to force water up into a large reservoir to be constructed upon the top of the hill immediately in the rear of J. Galloway Lynn's residence on Rose Hill, the height above the river being about one hundred feet. Estimates were made for the entire cost of this system, which was set down at eighty thousand dollars. This being twenty thousand dollars more than the sum named in the charter, the project was permitted to come to a "stand-still." Thus affairs remained for several years, until the question was again brought up in the Maryland Legislature in April, 1870, when a new bill was introduced, and passed on the 7th day of April, repealing certain sections of the act of 1864, and enacting certain others, authorizing the mayor and councilmen to issue bonds to the amount of one hundred thousand dollars, said bonds to bear seven per cent. interest, for the purpose of carrying out the intent of the charter and introducing a supply of water into the city. The following were named in the act to serve as a board of commissioners: Messrs. Horace Resley, Lewis Smith, James M. Schley, J. B. H. Campbell, Asa Willison, John Humbird, J. Philip Roman, Hopewell Hebb, and George Henderson, Jr. These gentlemen immediately thereafter set about carrying out the provisions of the water act. The reservoir system, as planned by the former board in 1864, was again revived, and that plan was about to be adopted, when the Holly system was brought to the attention of the commissioners. In the mean time surveys were being made by T. L. Patterson, civil engineer, whose estimate for the reservoir system, with all the mains as now adopted, was nearly the same as that made by Mr. Manning, being about eighty thousand dollars. Before operations had been begun on the reservoir plan, parties visited the city to lay before the board of commissioners the Holly system, claiming its superior merits over all others.

In the summer of 1870 a number of citizens, including several of the board, visited Dayton, Ohio, for the purpose of witnessing the operations of the Holly system just completed in that city. The result of their visit was so satisfactory to the committee that, on their return, they reported that the Holly system was far superior to anything of the kind they had ever witnessed, and they urgently recommended its adoption for the city of Cumberland. Negotiations were then had with the company, and a contract was finally entered into for the erection of a set of works in Cumberland.

A question of a suitable site for the works was settled by the purchase of the "old Pigman property" from John B. Widener, in July, 1870, and in August following the first ground was broken in the rear of that property for the erection of the buildings, Asa Willison having in the mean time been elected as superintendent of the work. The engineering for the line of mains, etc., was done by William Brace, and the general work was speedily put into active operation. A contract for the mains was entered into with Messrs. Gaylord & Co., of Cincinnati, Ohio, who agreed to furnish the mains, lay them in place, and guarantee them serviceable, at a pressure of one hundred and fifty pounds to the square inch, for five years from the date of commencement of use, and within a few weeks of the date of contract the pipe began arriving.

The mayor and councilmen had duly issued the bonds for one hundred thousand dollars, and they were placed in the banks of Cumberland for sale, and large amounts were readily disposed of at a discount of about five per cent. on par value, and money was at once realized to carry on the work. In October, 1870, the work of laying the mains was begun and continued for several weeks, when the work was discontinued until the following spring. In the mean time, the Holly Manufacturing Company was erecting its machinery in the building which had been built for that purpose. The management was under the superintendence of Mr. Edward S. Alexander, and by June, 1871, the Holly works were prepared to operate. After some deliberation as to the best mode of crossing Will's Creek with the mains, it was finally decided to lay a wrought-iron main in the bed of the stream to connect with the cast-iron mains at the two shores.

On the 7th of July, 1871, the first water ever thrown by the Holly works of Cumberland issued from the fire-plug on the hill in the rear of the court-house. On the 10th of August, 1871, the wrought-iron main was laid in the creek and attached to the shore ends.

On Saturday, Sept. 30, 1871, the grand trial was effected. It was under the management of Chief Engineer Wolvington and Mr. Anderson, the assistant, the whole under the charge of Mr. Alexander. The trial was a success in every particular.

On the 1st day of October, 1871, the city of Cumberland was first regularly supplied with water. In 1880, Mayor Read closed a contract with C. G. Helbreath, of the Holly Works Company, for improvements upon the water-works to the amount of eighteen thousand dollars. Joseph Zweng is the chief engineer.

Fire Companies and Fires.—The General Assembly, in January, 1805, passed an act for raising two thousand dollars to purchase a fire-engine for Cumberland, etc., and designated in it William McMahon, George Hoffman, Thomas Thistle, David Hoffman, Sr., and Upton Bruce as the commissioners to hold a lottery in furtherance of the project. The scheme was probably not carried out, for the Legislature in 1814 enacted a new law appointing George Thistle, Samuel Smith, John Scott, Jacob Lantz, John Folck, Peter Lowdermilk, and William Lamar, Sr., to have and conduct a scheme of lottery to raise two thousand dollars to procure a fire-engine.

At a meeting of the citizens, Dec. 10, 1830, at "Newman's Tavern," the "Cumberland Fire Engine Company" was organized and officers elected.

In February following another fire company was organized, and two of its ladders were kept on the turnpike, over the rack at Shriver's shed, and two at Hook's fence, corner of Frederick and Centre Streets. The town purchased in 1837 a forcing-engine, popularly known as the "Goose-neck," and a tax of thirty cents on the hundred dollars was levied for its payment. Its dimensions were about the size of a modern "Saratoga trunk."

In the spring of 1839 this unique engine was given to the "Cumberland," or "Canada Hose Company," by the authorities, along with four ladders, three hooks, and four axes, and thirty dollars toward erecting a house. A wagon carried the hose.

In the fall of 1849 the old engine-house was changed to the Bedford road from its former location at the Baltimore Street bridge. A competition between the fire companies in 1850 caused continued incendiarism and difficulties, and was finally stopped by prompt legislation of the local authorities. The "Mountaineer" and "Pioneer" Hose Companies participated in the great Baltimore firemen's parade of Nov. 2, 1851, the former being guests of the "New Market," and the latter of the "Vigilant" company. The "Mountaineers" carried a big buck, which was cooked for their dinner.

The "Pioneer" Company erected its new engine-house in 1853, on the corner of Frederick and Centre Streets, for which the city gave a thousand dollars.

Cumberland Hose Company.—The Cumberland Fire-Engine Company was organized Dec. 10, 1830, at Newman's Hotel, and was known afterwards as the "Canada Company." In 1831 the stations and duties of its members were:

Property-men and property guards, W. V. Buskirk, Robert McCleary, Charles Heck, John H. Bayard, James Sullivan, William Osborn, Samuel Charles; to form the line, Gustavus Beall, Samuel Blocher, Benc S. Pigman, John McNeil, William McMahon, John A. Hoffman, Henry Wincow, Sr., James Black, John Scott; Ladder-men, Richard Beall, Jonathan Witt, George Deetz, William Shryer, Joseph Shook, Samuel Hoblitzell, Joseph Hughes, John Miller, of Jacob; Axe-men, John J. Hoffman, John Cress, John Holtzman, John Cline; Hook-men, Martin Rizer, of M., Elnathan Russell, Solomon Stover, R. Worthington, George Hoblitzell, B. Magruder; Engine-men, Jonathan Butler, Thomas J. McKaig, Clement Smith, Samuel Shockey, Ephraim Shipley, George C. Perry, John T. Sigler, Jacob Rizer, Edward Sullivan, Isaac S. Hook, Daniel Blocher, John M. Buchanan, Baptist Mattingly, Henry Wineow, Wm. Roberts, James Moore, of George, John Lingo, John Deetz, Samuel Magill, Jesse Korn, Wm. Lynn, M. H. Louthan, J. M. Carleton, Dr. S. P. Smith, John Wright, R. T. Lowndes, Harmon Stidger, John Ambrose, Enoch Moore, James Siers, George M. Read, R. A. Robinson, D. B. Hoblitzell, R. P. Bayley, Wm. K. Newman.

The officers in 1832 were:

President, George Hebb; Vice-President, John McNeill; Secretary, S. P. Smith; Treasurer, R. T. Lowndes; Captain, James M. Smith; First Lieutenant, Martin Rizer, of M.; Second Lieutenant, George Blocher; First Engineer, John G. Hoffman; Second Engineer, Eli Moody; Third Engineer, Joseph Everstine; Directors, John Wright, Baptist Mattingly, Thomas Dowden, Joseph Shook; Property-men and Guards, David Shriver, Roger Perry, John H. Bayard, James Sullivan, Jr., William Osborn, Samuel Charles; to form the line, R. T. Lowndes, George Blocher, Sr., B. S. Pigman, Wm. McMahon, Gustavus Beall, John M. Lawrence; Ladder-men, Jonathan Witt, George Hoblitzell, Richard Beall, Joseph Hughes, Samuel Hoblitzell, John Miller, of J.; Axe-men, Burgess Magruder, Peter Hoffman, Solomon Stover, Elnathan Russell, Martin Rizer, of M., Reuben Worthington; Engine-men, Thomas J. McKaig, Thomas Perry, Jonathan Butler, John Miller, Jonathan McCleary, Charles Heck, George Deetz, John Holtzman, John M. Carleton, James Moore, of G., Samuel Shockey, William Roberts, John Lingo, Enoch Moore, John Deetz, John T. Sigler, Samuel Magill, John Cress, George M. Read, John Clise, Jesse Korn, Edward Sullivan, R. A. Robinson, Moore N. Falls, Isaac S. Hook, Moses H. Louthan, P. A. S. Pigman, Daniel Blocher, Theophilus Beall, John A. Hoffman.

It was reorganized in 1839 as Cumberland Hose Company, with the following members:

A. L. Withers, president; A. N. Barnitz, secretary; Joseph Hadel, treasurer; George Hughes, chief engineer; A. B. Simpkins, James Pew, Lewis Smith, Joseph Britten, Joseph Hughes, Joseph Shuck, Joseph Stewart, John Hadel, Wm. Heck, Peter McLaughlin, A. J. Walton.

The company was incorporated in 1840. Meetings were first held in a box-shed in Withers' tannery, on Mechanic Street, where the engine was kept. In 1845 the engine-house was erected on North Mechanic Street, at Blue Spring, to which the company then removed, and its headquarters have since been located there. Heretofore they had used the "Goose-neck" engine, but in 1850 an engine was purchased of Button & Co., of Waterford, N. Y., and was called the "Cumberland." It was more familiarly known as the "Dutch Chest." It was bought by the town corporation, and in 1852 a new engine was bought of the same firm, and paid for by the active members of the company. Its membership is one hundred.

The officers for 1881 were:

President, George Mortz; Vice-President, L. W. Thompson; Secretary, A. McGirr; Treasurer, William Himmler; Engine-Keeper, John Hadel; Chief Engineer, John Wegman; Assistants, John Bochman, John Taylor, A. H. Bond, and Harmon Kogel.

Mountaineer Hose Company.—At a meeting of the citizens held Dec. 15, 1838, this company was organized, with the following officers:

President, Alexander King; Vice-President, John Beall; Treasurer, John G. Hoffman; Secretary, John M. Carleton; Directors, H. G. Grieves, C. W. Gephart, Thomas Rizer, John J. Hoffman, Archibald McNeill; Chief Engineer, G. W. Haller; Assistant Engineers, George M. Read, Jacob Rizer, J. C. Laley; Standing Committee, William Saylor, Thomas Dowden, Thomas Reid, John McCleary, Upton R. Lowdermilk.

The next meeting was held at Thomas Reid's shop, Jan. 8, 1839. A grand parade of the company took place on New Year's Day. The town gave it a suction-pump worth seven hundred and fifty dollars.

The officers and men for 1840 were:

President, George W. Haller; Vice-President, Samuel Charles; Treasurer, John G. Hoffman; Secretary, John M. Carleton; Property Director, Archibald McNeill; Lane Director, Horatio G. Grieves; Axe, Hook-and-Ladder Director, John J. Hoffman; Chief Engineer, George M. Reid; Assistant Engineers, John Beall, Alexander King, John Skank; Hose Director, George W. Kephart; Engine Director, Thomas Rizer; Standing Committee, Samuel Soyster, John McCleary, Henry McKinley, Upton R. Lowdermilk, Thomas Reid; Property Guards, John Gephart, Sr., S. M. Semmes, Robert Read, Thomas J. McKaig, James P. Carleton, Thomas Perry, C. M. Thruston, R. T. Lowndes, Jonathan Butler; Axe-men, Jesse Korn, Abram Russell, Samuel Soyster, Matthias Rizer; Hook-men, John A. Chambers, Joseph Jordan, R. V. Craggs, John Lingo; Ladder-men, William Dowden, Thomas Reid, Martin L. Rizer, Henry Schuck; Hose-men, Upton R. Lowdermilk, S. M. Haller, H. B. Osborn, John B. Widener, Morgan Rizer, James Cyphers, William R. McCulley, Henry McKinley; Engine-men, John McCleary, Daniel Blocher, William Saylor, Thomas Schuck, G. S Lowdermilk, John T. Hoblitzell, Thomas Dowden, James Howe, J. L. Willoughby, William Craver, H. D. Black, James P. Wright, Hanson Lowdermilk, James W. Rye, John Windell, John M. Carleton, John Saylor, John Deetz, John G. Hoffman, John H. Miller, Jacob Rizer, William Walker, Joseph Bowden, John T. Edwards, William J. G. Hilleary, William L. Blocher, Hampton J. Long, Francis Madore, George Deneen.

The officers for 1843 were:

President, A. McNeill; Vice-President, George F. Shryer; Secretary, W. R. McCulley; Treasurer, Thomas F. White; Engine Director, Jesse Korn; Hose Director, U. R. Lowdermilk; Axe Director, John Skank; Lane Director, Thomas Reid; Property Guards, Joseph Shriver; Chief Engineer, George M. Reid; Assistants, H. B. Osborn, R. V. Craggs, J. Rizer; Executive Committee, D. Saylor, W. T. Peterman, J. B. Widener, Thomas Rizer, W. J. G. Hilleary; Engine-keeper, R. V. Craggs.

It disbanded in 1871.

Pioneer Hose and Hook-and-Ladder Company.—The original members of this organization were formerly members of the old Mountaineer Company, but upon the purchase of a new engine by that company, they withdrew and formed themselves into an independent company, under the title of the "Pioneer Hose and Ladder Company." Among these members were H. B. Black, Casper Cassin, H. W. Hoffman, Jacob Shuck, James Donnelly, Henry Shuck, Levi Shaw, Sr., and Henry Karns. Harrison B. Black was the first president, and was succeeded the following year by H. W. Hoffman. The first building occupied by them for the storing and keeping of their engine and property was on Liberty Street, and is now owned by James B. Walthon. The next was situated on Centre Street. In 1854 their present building was completed, having been commenced the year previous. It is situated upon the corner of Centre and Frederick Streets, is two stories in height, and contains, besides an engine-room, a large hall, in which the company hold their meetings. The first engine owned by the organization was the old "Mountaineer," the first suction-engine ever brought to Cumberland. They obtained possession of it when the Mountaineer Company purchased their new engine, the "Old Defender." The second engine was the "Mountaineer," remodeled and rebuilt after the drawings and specifications of H. W. Hoffman. It was used until a few years ago, when it was disposed of by the corporation. In 1851 the "Pioneer," or "Old Sioux" engine was purchased of Button & Co., of Waterford, N. Y. It was a side-lever engine, and was sold to the municipality of Harrisonburg, Va., upon the introduction of the Holly system of water-works in Cumberland. The "Pioneer" was constructed after a drawing by H. W. Hoffman. The company possess now only hooks, ladders, and a reel. The present board of officers are as follows:

President, Edward Walker; Vice-President, William Small; Secretary, George N. Hoover; Treasurer, George W. Crummel; C. H. Shoughter, chief engineer.

The company did valuable work at the Frostburg and Lonaconing fires.

Vigilant Hose Company.—This fire company was organized in 1873 at Washington Hall. It procured the loan from the city of an old reel, and kept it in the stable of Hon. William Walsh until the building of its engine-house. The first officers were:

President, George Rosswarm; Vice-President, P. G. Cowden; Secretary, Wm. Coleman; Treasurer, Gustavus Rizer; Chief Engineer, William Helderfer; Assistant Engineers, James McHugh, Jr., James Reagan, George Mallon, Frederick Mertens, Jr.; Reel Directors, Michael Rosswarm, Frederick Baer; Hall-keeper and Collector, Wm. Myer.

It had sixty active and eleven honorary contributing members. In 1874 it was incorporated, and its engine-house erected on Smallwood Street near Washington. The officers from 1874 to 1881 have been as follows:

1874.—President, George Rosswarm; Vice-President, B. O'Donnel; Secretary, Edward Schilling; Treasurer, Geo. B. Hargett; Chief Engineer, Wm. Coleman; Assistant Engineers, Michael Kean, Jesse Young, J. F. Caruthers, John Baer; Reel Directors, M. Rosswarm, Henry Weyman; Hall-keeper and Collector, Fred. Baer.

1875.—President, John B. Slattery; Vice-President, Wm. Coleman; Secretary, Edward Schilling; Treasurer, Geo. Rosswarm; Engineer, M. Rosswarm; Assistant Engineers, Wm. Nolan, Edward Caton, Thomas Kain, J. F. Caruthers; Reel Directors, J. McCormick, Frederick Baer; Hall-keeper, David McEvoy.

1876.—President, John B. Slattery; Vice-President, Wm. Coleman; Secretary, Edward Schilling; Treasurer, B. Kean; Chief Engineer, Thomas Kane; Assistant Engineers, Geo. Mallon, Wm. Nolan, Fred. Zink, John Zink; Axe-men, J. Kenney, J. F. Caruthers; Reel Directors, Wm. Broderick, M. Nolan; Collector, M. F. Kean; Hall-keeper, Patrick Broderick; Fire Police, P. Broderick, J. F. Caruthers, M. Gill, Chas. Keyser, P. Rosswarm.

1877.—President, John B. Slattery; Vice-President, Wm. Coleman; Secretary, Edward Schilling; Treasurer, B. Kean; Chief Engineer, Thomas Kane; Assistant Engineers, Geo. Mallon, Wm. Nolan, Fred. Zink, John Zink; Reel Directors, Wm. Broderick, M. Nolan; Hall-keeper, P. Broderick; Collector, B. Kean; Axe-men, James Kenny, John F. Caruthers; Fire Police, P. Broderick, J. F. Caruthers, Martin Gill, James Weibel.

1878.—President, Wm. Coleman; Vice-President, Geo. Mallon; Secretary, Daniel E. Kean; Treasurer, Geo. L. Landwehr; Chief Engineer, Thomas Kean; Assistant Engineers, Wm. Nolan, Fred. Zink, John Dugan, Jas. Keating; Reel Directors, Frank Fisher, James Keating; Hall-keeper, Patrick Broderick; Axe-men, John Gillen, John Ammon; Fire Police, John Zink, J. Kenny, F. Rosswarm, G. Baer.

1879.—President, Wm. Coleman; Vice-President, J. B. Slattery; Secretary, D. E. Kean; Treasurer, Thomas Kean; Chief Engineer, Jas. Caton; Assistant Engineers, Wm. Nolan, John Zink, D. Kenny, John Dugan; Reel Directors, Fred. Fisher; Hall-keeper, P. Broderick; Collector, P. Broderick; Axe-men, John Gillen, John Ammon; Fire Police, John Zink, John Baer, Geo. Kean, James Kean.

1880–81.—President, Wm. F. Coleman; Vice-President, J. B. Slattery; Secretary, D. E. Kean; Treasurer, F. Rosswarm; Hall-keeper, T. S. Kean (1880), M. F. Kean (1881); Chief Engineer, Frederick Gaubler; Assistant Engineers (1881), John Zink, John Fisher, Geo. A. Kean, D. Kenny; Reel Directors (1881), F. Fisher, M. Blunski; Axe-man (1881), Charles Baer.

South Cumberland Engine and Hose Company.—The South Cumberland Fire Company was formed in 1877 with the following officers:

President, Peter Kelly; Secretary, Chas. A. Judy; Vice-President, James Berry; Treasurer, Thomas Connolly; Chief Engineer, H. C. Hensel, and about two hundred active members.

The officers since have been as follows:

1878.—President, D. E. Haller; Vice-President, J. W. Stuff; Secretary, C. A. Judy; Treasurer, Thomas Connolly; Chief Engineer, H. C. Hensel.

1879.—President, E. M. Bynnon; Vice-President, Edward Keech; Secretary, C. A. Judy; Treasurer, Thomas Connolly; Chief Engineer, John McGinnis.

1880.—President, E. M. Bynnon; Vice-President, Isaiah Leberman; Secretary, C. A. Judy; Treasurer, Thomas Connolly; Chief Engineer, John McGinnis. In June, 1880, Bynnon resigned, and upon the reorganization of the company, in the same month, W. G. Haller was chosen president; J. W. Stuff, vice-president; C. A. Judy, secretary; Thomas Connolly, treasurer; and Benj. Job, chief engineer. Haller resigned in September, and J. W. Stuff served the unexpired term.

1881.—President, J. W. Stuff; Vice-President, E. J. Coony; Secretary, C. A. Judy; Treasurer, Thos. Connolly; Chief Engineer, Benj. Job.

Meetings were first held in a house which stood upon Wineow Street. They removed the house to a vacant lot on the Old Town road north of the Baltimore and Ohio Railroad. In 1878 their present building was erected, standing upon the Old Town road north of the railroad, and but a short distance from the old building. The reel they possess was given to them by the corporation prior to the organization. Their engine, the old "Cumberland" remodeled, and known to the members as the "Old Dutch Chest," was put into their hands by the corporation in 1878.

Cumberland, until 1833, enjoyed an uninterrupted career of exceptional prosperity. The immense traffic between the East and West had chosen the city as its entrepôt, and the numerous lines of stages to the commercial centres and the large towns of neighboring States had caused to spring up a busy and enterprising population and a number of industries almost out of proportion to the size of the town. Fine buildings for business purposes had been erected, elegant residences built, and some church edifices, which reflected credit on the taste and culture of the citizens. On the 14th of April, 1833, the city was visited by one of those terrible calamities which have grown unfortunately too familiar of late years, but which at that early date were almost unknown in America. About two o'clock in the afternoon a sea of fire swept over the town, and in a few hours the labors of a generation were in ashes, men of wealth were suddenly reduced to poverty, and hundreds of women and children were exposed to the vagaries of the elements with scarcely sufficient to stay the pangs of hunger. The following letter appeared in the Hagerstown *Herald and Torch-Light* several days after the conflagration:

"CUMBERLAND, April 15, 1833.

"Seventy-five houses, comprising the heart of our town, now lie in ruins. The fire originated in a cabinet-maker's shop, three doors north of the *Civilian* printing-office. Many citizens have nothing left. The *Civilian* office is burnt, except its account books. All the stores but one are burnt, Bruce & Beall's, Mr. Shriver's large three-story tavern, Mr. Fechtig's tavern, and the bank. The fire commenced at two o'clock, and the wind being high, the flames soon spread, leaving little time to move goods. Nothing now remains but parts of walls and chimneys, where once the principal part of the town stood. The *Advocate* office was also burnt, saving only the cast-iron press (badly damaged) and a few type. The ruins commence at Gustavus Beall's mills and extend down to Elnathan Russell's carriage-shop; the mill and Russell's house are saved, but on both sides of the street between these there is not one house standing, a distance of about one-fourth of a mile. The principal sufferers are:

"George Hoblitzell, three or four houses; James Everstine, three houses; Dr. Lawrence, one house; George Wineow, one house; B. S. Pigman, two houses; Mr. Lowndes, one store; John

T. Sigler, two houses; late John Scott, one house; bank property, three houses; Dr. S. P. Smith and R. Worthington, three houses; Henry Wineow, one house and fifteen hundred dollars cash; J. M. Buchanan, one house; George Hoffman, two houses; Shriver, three houses: Mrs. Gephart, one house: Dr. J. M. Smith, two houses; George Hebb, two houses; Samuel Hoblitzell, one house; Thomas Dowden, two houses; George Deetz, one house: S. Bowden, one house; John G. Hoffman, two houses; Butler's store, two houses; Capt. Lynn, one house; Robert McCleary, three or four houses; Adam Fisher, one or two houses; Martin Rizer, of M., one house; Robert Swann, two houses; Mrs. Saylor, one house; besides others, mostly brick houses, and two-story log buildings."

At a meeting at the court-house, in Cumberland, composed of the citizens of the town, the court, the bar, and the juries, assembled on the 15th of April, for the purpose of instituting an inquiry into the extent of the calamity occasioned by the fire, and of devising means for the relief of the sufferers, the following proceedings were had:

Upon motion of William Price, the Hon. John Buchanan, chief justice of Maryland, was appointed chairman, who in a feeling and appropriate address explained the object of the meeting. Upon motion of John Hoye, William Price was appointed secretary. Upon motion of Bene S. Pigman, the chair appointed the following committee to inquire into the extent of the calamity occasioned by the late fire, together with the number and description of sufferers, and to report thereon to the meeting, viz.: John McHenry, Thomas J. McKaig, A. W. McDonald, William Price, B. S. Pigman, David Shriver, George Hebb, Dr. Samuel P. Smith, John Hoye, Dr. John M. Lawrence, Dr. James Smith, David Lynn, Robert Swann, and Richard Beall, who having retired for the purpose, afterwards returned and submitted the following report:

The committee appointed to ascertain the calamity by which the town has been visited, together with the number and description of the sufferers, have, in the execution of the melancholy duty assigned them, ascertained the following particulars for the information of the meeting:

It is ascertained that the entire business portion of Cumberland has been destroyed. All the taverns and all the stores in the place but one are now in ashes; about thirty flourishing mechanics, all in prosperous business, have been reduced to ruin, and their families left without a shelter to cover them. The three physicians of the town have lost nearly all their property and medicines. It is believed that two-thirds of the inhabitants are homeless. The value of property destroyed and the description of citizens to whom it belonged, the committee have estimated and classed as follows:

Seven merchants, whose loss in real and personal property and goods is estimated at	$94,000
Three physicians	12,000
Three hotels, including the losses of the owners	50,000
Thirty mechanics (real and personal property, stock, etc.)	71,000
Citizens not included in above description	31,000
Citizens not residing in the town	14,000
Total loss	$272,000

Upon motion of Mr. Pigman a committee was appointed to draft an address to the people of the United States, inviting their aid in behalf of the Cumberland sufferers. Upon motion of Mr. Pigman it was resolved that the chairman of the meeting be the chairman of the said committee. The following gentlemen composed the committee: Hon. John Buchanan, Hon. Thomas Buchanan, Hon. Abraham Shriver, A. W. McDonald, John McHenry, William Price, James Dixon, Frederick A. Schley, and John King.

Upon motion the following residents of Cumberland, who were not sufferers by the fire, were appointed a committee to receive contributions and distribute them, and to conduct correspondence: John Hoye, Thomas J. McKaig, Richard Bell, Rev. L. H. Johns, William McMahon, and James P. Carleton. Upon motion of Thomas J. McKaig it was unanimously

"*Resolved*, That the thanks of the meeting are due the Hon. John Buchanan for the dignified and able manner in which he presided over its deliberations."

Upon motion of Mr. Buchanan it was

"*Resolved*, That the proceedings of this meeting be signed by the chairman and secretary, and published.

"JOHN BUCHANAN, *Chairman*.

"WILLIAM PRICE, *Secretary*."

There being then no press in Cumberland, the proceedings were forwarded to Hagerstown for publication.

The committee appointed by the above meeting for the purpose of drafting an appeal for aid to the people of the United States, after some consultation, issued the following address, which was published in all the Baltimore papers:

"AN ADDRESS TO THE PEOPLE OF THE UNITED STATES.

"The undersigned, being a committee appointed by the citizens of Cumberland to draft an address to the people of the United States, detailing the particulars of their late dreadful calamity, and the condition to which they are reduced, and of soliciting contributions in their behalf, are enabled from their own view and from their inquiries on the subject to make the following statement:

"The town of Cumberland is situated at the junction of Will's Creek and the river Potomac. The National road passing through the place has given it the advantage of a great amount of travel, and large sums were expended for its accommodation. The principal hotel was a splendid building, and cost the proprietor upwards of $25,000. There were two other large and commodious hotels, well kept and provided, upon the same square. Cumberland being the chief town of Allegany County and its seat of justice, the principal mercantile business was transacted at this place. Here also the coal from the mines is brought and deposited for transportation. The merchants, tradesmen, and mechanics were all in prosperous circumstances, and were located, as near as conveniently might be, in the vicinity of the hotels, which formed the centre of business.

"The calamitous fire which forms the occasion and subject of this address broke out about two P.M. on Sunday, the 14th of April last. It originated in a joiner's shop, and is said to have been occasioned by a lighted cigar, which a careless boy threw among some shavings This shop unhappily stood at the northwestern extremity of the business portion of the place, and a strong northwest wind prevailing at the time, the flames, burning shingles, and other combustibles were carried directly through the heart of the town. The citizens labored first to save the building, which was frame, adjoining the shop where the fire commenced, but this was soon abandoned as hopeless.

"The panic then became general and uncontrollable, and each endeavoring to save his own effects carried out store-goods, beds, bedding, clothing, and furniture into the streets, but the houses on both sides were now in a full blaze, the progress of destruction was rapid beyond conception, and those who had placed their effects in the streets were driven from them by a body of flame and scorching smoke that filled the entire space from side to side, burning up side-boards, chairs, tables, articles of male and female attire, beds and bedclothes before the eyes of their owners.

"The next effort of the citizens, where the flames had not yet reached, was to carry their goods to the houses of their friends at a considerable distance from what was supposed to be the scene of danger. In the midst of these labors, what was their consternation to behold these places of refuge (with all the intervening houses), even the most distant, on fire!

"The inhabitants now withdrew in despair to a distance from the raging elements. From right to left one unbroken sheet of flame, extending full a quarter of a mile, raging and roaring like a tornado, was the awful spectacle presented to the eye. The two sections of the town were completely separated from each other. To those on the west the fate and condition of their friends beyond the flames remained involved in mystery and apprehension. Mothers were separated from their children, and wives from their husbands, but fortunately not a single life has been lost.

"In two hours and a half seventy-five houses fronting on the principal street of the town, including the three hotels, all the stores save one, all the dwellings, shops, and material of the tradesmen and mechanics were burnt to the ground. The whole number of buildings destroyed, including the barns, stables, and other outbuildings, cannot, it is believed, be short of one hundred and fifty. In this brief space of time seven hundred people have been rendered houseless and otherwise deplorably destitute. The value of the property destroyed has been estimated at two hundred and seventy-two thousand dollars, and the undersigned believe this estimate to be rather below than above the truth. In appealing in behalf of the Cumberland sufferers to the generous sympathies of their countrymen, the undersigned cherish a lively hope that the appeal will not be in vain. The spectacle of a thriving village, daily increasing in all the comforts of life, reduced in so short a time to a melancholy waste of broken walls and naked chimneys cannot fail to call forth those principles of active benevolence that form a distinguished characteristic of the American people.

"The following gentlemen, residing in Cumberland, constitute the committee to receive contributions and distribute them among the sufferers, viz.: John Hoye, Thomas J. McKaig, Richard Beall, Rev. H. L. Johns, William McMahon, and James P. Carleton.

"They are not among the sufferers, and have been instructed and feel it their duty to apply all contributions received by them to the relief of those who are most destitute. The undersigned avail themselves of this opportunity to assure the public that all donations which may be intrusted to the care of these gentlemen, or either of them, will be faithfully applied and accounted for.

"John Buchanan, Abraham Shriver, Thomas Buchanan, A. W. McDonald, John McHenry, William Price, James Dixon, Frederick A. Schley, John King."

Below is given a complete list of the persons who sustained losses, with the amount annexed:

George Hoblitzell lost six houses, store-goods, and house-furniture; George Wineow, one house; William Shryer, stock and furniture; Joseph Everstine, three houses, furniture, shoes, and leather; Charles Howell, house furniture; John Gephart, two houses; Widow Saylor, one house; A. King and family, furniture and clothing; Widow Anders, furniture, etc.; Dr. J. Smith, two houses, medicines, etc.; John Rutter, house furniture and leather; Jonathan Butler, store-goods and furniture; Edward Johnson, household fnrniture; J. G. Hoffman, two houses, tinware, and furniture; Dr. S. P. Smith, two houses, medicines, and furniture; J. M. Buchanan, one house; G. S. Evans, furniture and $800 in money; Widow Frithey, one house and furniture; S. Bowden, one house; Robert Swann, two houses; David Shriver, six houses; John Murrell's heirs, two houses; E. Mobley, furniture, tools, and wagon-stuff; M. Rizer, of M., one house and furniture; Kershner's heirs, one house; George Deetz, one house and furniture; Widow Oglebay, furniture; George Lowdermilk, house furniture; John Deetz, house furniture; Widow Gephart, one house and furniture; R. McCleary, seven houses, tools, stock, and furniture; Blocher & Harry, one printing-press, type, and office furniture; John Cress, blacksmith tools and iron; Post-office, furniture and papers; David Lynn, one house; James Sires, furniture and tools; Widow Koontz, two houses; Sarah Koontz, furniture; M. Fisher, two houses, furniture, and stock; John Fisher, $500 in money; William Fisher, $100 in money; H. Wineow, one house, grain, furniture, and $1500; Thomas Dowden, one house, shop, furniture, and tools; Jos. Black, grain and furniture; the bank, six houses; Jacob Fechtig, furniture, etc.; S. Slicer, furniture, etc.; Widow Scott, furniture, etc.; John Scott's heirs, two houses; George Hebb, two houses, with furniture and goods; A. McNeill, tools and jewelry; John Wright, tools, jewelry, and furniture; R. Worthington, one house, furniture, and goods; Smith, Worthington & Co., one house; J. F. Sigler, one house, saddlery, and furniture; Dr. Lawrence, one house, medicine, and furniture; Messrs. Lowndes, one house and store-goods, furniture, and $700; S. Hoblitzell, furniture, etc.; B. S. Pigman, three houses; P. A. S. Pigman, furniture; S. Pritchard, tools and clothing; L. W. Stockton, two mail-coaches; J. W. Weaver, one mail-coach; H. D. Carleton, furniture, etc.; Eleanor Merryman, clothing; John Beall, clothing; John P. Lowdermilk, clothing; Sophia Johnson, clothing; Elizabeth Bevans, clothing; H. B. Wolfe, tools, books, and furniture; Samuel Charles, the *Civilian* office entire; J. Wolf, tools, leather, and shoes; J. Marr, tools, etc.; H. Smouse, one carry-all; T. Adams, furniture, etc.; B. W. Howard, furniture, etc.; W. V. Buskirk, furniture, law library, and papers; Bruce & Beall, part of stock of goods; Krebs & Falls, store-goods and furniture; S. & G. Shockey, hats, furs, and tools; John M. Carleton, clothing, etc.; Nancy Davis, clothing, etc.; Edmund

Hoffman, furniture, etc.; W. W. Weaver, furniture, etc.; William Hoblitzell, clothing, etc.; M. Rizer, Jr., a lot of bacon, etc.; J. B. Wright, money and clothing; Louthan & Offutt, stock of goods, etc.

At a meeting of the sufferers of Cumberland by the fire of the 14th of April, assembled at the court-house, agreeably to previous notice given, Dr. John M. Lawrence was called to the chair, and Dr. James M. Smith appointed secretary.

On motion of J. G. Hoffman it was "*Resolved*, That the entire accounts of the committee of distribution be submitted to this meeting."

The committee on distribution then reported as follows:

"The committee having made a distribution of the larger part of the money and articles of food and clothing sent from various parts of the United States for the relief of those who were sufferers by the late desolating fire, beg leave to report to those for whom they have acted the amount of money received and in what manner they have discharged the trust reposed in them.

"They herewith append a list of the donors and donations received in money, amounting to the sum of $20,684.98. The committee have also received a quantity of clothing, flour, bacon, etc., the amount in cash not known, as they were prinpally distributed to the most necessitous of the sufferers as they came to hand.

"Of the amount of money received, the committee distributed as it also came to hand, and as the necessities of the sufferers seemed to demand, the sum of $20,066.23½.

"The provisions of clothing, at a fair uniform value, to the amount of $273.02½, have been distributed to the necessitous, and a small balance remains on hand yet to be disposed of.

"The committee, considering themselves as trustees, have in the distribution endeavored to carry into effect the object of the donors. The intention of those who so generously contributed, as far as it could be ascertained from resolutions and instructions accompanying the donations, was to relieve the most necessitous. That class of sufferers was therefore the first object of the committee whose aggregate amount of loss was small compared with others, but which was 'their little all,' or so much of it as placed them in necessitous circumstances. They have been reinstated in some instances, as nearly as the committee were able to ascertain the amount of their loss, in others with the greater proportion of their loss, or so much of it as in the judgment of the committee the amount received and circumstances would permit.

"The residue was then to be apportioned among those whose amount of loss was greater, though various, and whose necessities were as various as their loss.

"To have given to this class a uniform percentage on the amount of loss the committee believed would not have met the approbation of the sufferers, nor fulfilled the intention of the donors. The committee therefore made an apportionment on the basis of loss and necessity combined.

"Acting as the agent of others, they believed that in this way the trust would best be fulfilled, although it involved more labor and much more responsibility. After availing themselves of all the information within their reach to ascertain the true situation of each and every sufferer, they made the distribution according to the circumstances of each particular case.

"The committee feel that in the distribution of this fund they had not only a laborious and difficult task to perform, but also a task in its very nature delicate and involving great responsibility. In making a distribution among sufferers whose wants and circumstances were various, and whose necessities were so far beyond the reach of the fund to be distributed, the committee cannot hope to have given satisfaction to every individual; but conscious of the purity of their own motives, they do hope that their well-meant endeavors as agents of others in bestowing a charity will secure an indulgent consideration for any errors in judgment.

"Respectfully submitted.

"JOHN HOYE, THOMAS J. MCKAIG, RICHARD BEALL, L. H. JOHNS, WM. MCMAHON, JAMES P. CARLETON, *Committee of Distribution.*

"*List of Donations.*

Maryland—Baltimore City	$6162.28
Hagerstown (besides $200 worth tools)	111.00
Williamsport	449.75
Frederick City and County	1546.86
Cambridge	26.00
Port Tobacco	70.00
Annapolis	286.25
Taneytown, Frederick County	150.00
	$9972.66
Pennsylvania—Philadelphia	$3595.19
Bedford (besides $100 in goods)	300.00
Uniontown (besides 3000 pounds bacon and 21 barrels flour)	369.00
Chambersburg	398.00
Washington	282.00
Gettysburg	164.00
Brownsville (besides 16 boxes glass, some bacon and flour)	318.75
Lancaster	465.29
Harrisburg	339.99
York	462.32
Huntingdon	258.00
Edensburg	50.00
McConnellsburg	90.00
Somerset County	147.75
	$7239.89
District of Columbia—Georgetown	$452.76
Washington	418.00
	$870.76
Virginia—Moorefield	$368.00
Winchester	457.50
Morgantown	75.00
Shepherdstown	181.00
	$1075 50
From Fayetteville, S. C	$363.75
Savannah, Ga	500.00
Springfield, Ohio	103.00
President of the United States	50.00
Postmaster-General	20.00
Andrew Bruce, Allegany County	50.00
John Reid, " "	5.00
John Piper, Jr., " "	5.00
George Watson, " "	5.00
John Waltz, " "	1.00
John J. Jacob, " "	1.50
Alex. Stuart, " "	2.00
F. A. Cortsings, " "	2.00
Leonard Smith, " "	15.00
Samuel Hamilton, " "	5 00
Wm. Reid, " "	40 bush. corn.
Matthew Wallace, " "	$50.00
A. Morrison, Somerset, Pa	20.00
Wm. Hartley, Bedford	20.00
C. C. Stuart, Philadelphia	30.00
John Davis, Baltimore	20.00
Wm. J. Ross, Frederick	10.00
R. Wallace, Dorchester	5.00
Miss E. Harry, Hagerstown	5.00
Dr. Martin, "	10.00

W. D. Bell, Hagerstown (printing-press and type)	$150.00
John Harry, Georgetown	10.00
A. Mellier, per S. Slicer	10.00
B. Morris, New Garden	5.00
Bishop Meade	5.00
Rev. J. Milnor, D.D., New York	5.00
Persons, names unknown, and one pair of shears sold	101.37

On motion,

"*Resolved*, That after an examination of the accounts of the distributing committee we believe that the committee have discharged the trust reposed in them impartially, and as far as they could ascertain, correctly, and that we have entire confidence in their integrity.

"*Resolved*, That the list of donations, with the names of the donors, together with the report of the committee of distribution, be published in the form of handbills and in the newspapers of the town.

"*Resolved*, unanimously, that the thanks of the sufferers be most respectfully tendered to the donors for their very liberal aid freely administered to our pressing needs, and that a copy of these proceedings be forwarded to them by the committee of distribution.

"*Resolved*, unanimously, that the thanks of the sufferers are due to the committee of distribution for their very prompt, efficient, and energetic discharge of the arduous, responsible, and laborious duties assigned them.

"JNO. M. LAWRENCE, *Chairman*.

"J. M. SMITH, *Secretary*.

"CUMBERLAND, MD., Nov. 21, 1833."

Fires are not always unmixed evils, as was proved in this instance. Old and worthless buildings were destroyed, together with an infinite amount of rubbish, the accumulations of years. Where there is energy and enterprise a town soon rises from its ashes. The fire of 1833 was necessarily a heavy misfortune to a city so small as Cumberland, but little time was given to vain repinings over vanished wealth. The citizens immediately set to work to repair the ravages of the flames, and Cumberland arose from the ruins in a more modern dress. The work of rebuilding was hurried forward to meet the demands of the growing traffic, and the new houses were more substantial, more durable, and more elegant in appearance. Opportunity was given for the introduction of modern improvements, and few would have recognized, in the city which rose upon the former site, the quaint town which existed prior to the conflagration. The Baltimore *Phœnix and Budget*, in April, 1841, says of Cumberland,—

"Cumberland was one of the earliest settlements in Maryland. It is situated on the North Branch of the Potomac River (about eighteen miles from its junction with the South Branch thereof), in a most wild and romantic region of country. In regard to population it is the fourth town in the State, having increased more than fifty per cent. within the last ten years. It now numbers nearly three thousand inhabitants. While the American colonies were yet in the possession of Great Britain a rude fort was erected here by the latter government. This has long since decayed, and where it once stood now stands a neat and commodious church belonging to the Protestant Episcopal congregation. It is to be regretted that much of the early history of this place has been suffered to sink into forgetfulness. Were it otherwise, many instructive and interesting tales might be told of its early settlement, and the many conflicts of its first inhabitants with the Indians, who then resided in the neighborhood. Little is now known of them, and all that can be gathered is a few vague rumors, in themselves uninteresting and uninstructive. . . .

"Cumberland seems to have been made the sport of the elements. It has been overflowed on several occasions by the rising of the waters in Will's Creek and the Potomac, by which considerable losses were sustained. It is peculiarly liable to disasters of this character from its low situation. In 1833 it was visited by a most destructive conflagration, in which nearly two-thirds of the town rose destroyed. It rose, however, 'like the Phœnix from his ashes,' and in a short time was built up with many improvements. It now has two printing-offices, an academy, female seminary, and several common schools.

"In addition to these should be mentioned two literary institutions, the Cumberland Lyceum and Mechanics' Library Society,—the latter a most excellent and praiseworthy institution. As before stated, Cumberland has more than doubled its population within the last ten years. There has also been erected many public buildings within a shorter time.

"Among these may be mentioned a new court-house, Masonic Hall, and three new churches, viz.: Catholic, Presbyterian, and Methodist Episcopal. The Methodist and Episcopal churches have undergone material repairs, the former being considerably enlarged. Many private residences have also been erected, adding much to the wealth and beauty of the town.

"Judging from various circumstances, Cumberland is destined to become a place of no little importance on the map of our country. When the canal and railroad shall have been completed, and the vast mineral resources of the country in which it is situated shall have been fully developed, Cumberland will have risen to a proud and eminent station, and will be justly entitled to be called the Sheffield of America."

On Sunday, Sept. 25, 1864, another fire occurred in the city, which destroyed twelve or thirteen buildings, involving a loss of from thirty to thirty-five thousand dollars. It broke out in the frame buildings connected with the foundry and machine-shops of Messrs. Taylor & Co., on George Street, which were soon in flames. The fire then communicated with two frame dwellings adjoining, one of them unoccupied, the other occupied by Mr. Hume, an employé of the Baltimore and Ohio Railroad Company. These also were consumed so quickly that Mr. Hume was unable to save any of his furniture. A high wind prevailed at the time, and swept a perfect shower of sparks and cinders upon the buildings on the opposite side of the street, and though the most strenuous efforts were made by the firemen, six engines being constantly and unremittingly kept at work, seven buildings also fell a prey to the flames. Three of them were occupied by Taylor & Co.,—two as machine-shops and pattern-rooms, the third as a store-room. The fourth building was used as a repair-shop and store-room of the Baltimore and Ohio Railroad. The contents of all these buildings were lost. The remaining three buildings were dwelling-houses,—two of them brick and one frame,—occupied respectively by Mr. Long, Mr. Alee, and Mrs. Cole. The old foundry buildings were owned by Lieut. Wise, of the United States army. The new stone and brick buildings used as the machine-shops of Taylor & Co. were the property of James W. Jones, and the dwelling-houses belonged respectively to T. J. and W. W. McKaig, William O. Sprigg, Dr. James Smith, and Vowoman's heirs. Mr. Jones' loss was partially covered by insurance. The remainder of the property was uninsured. The large hotels and other valuable property that fronted on Baltimore Street, near the locality, were in imminent danger, the progress of the fire only being checked by pulling down the frame work-shop that connected the burnt quarter with the rear of these buildings and the railroad depot. The city was again visited by fire March 22, 1874. The fire continued until late on the following morning, and was only controlled by the untiring efforts of the fire department. The losses were as follows: Anthony Kean and William Devecmon, City Hotel property, $10,000, insured for $6000; Mrs. Julia Adams, furniture, carpets, etc., of the City Hotel, $3000, partly insured; Ferguson & Cruzen, Dexter House, $12,000, including billiard-saloon, etc., no insurance; William Walsh, one building, $2000; Charles Miller, "Green House" saloon and restaurant, $1800, fully insured; T. T. Hause & Co., fruit and provision-store, $2000, insured for $1000; S. T. Little, Masonic Hall building, $300, his building and stock well insured for $5000; John May, proprietor of American House, $300; and a great many other smaller losses. At the great fire in Hagerstown, on May 29, 1879, when the Washington Hotel was burned to the ground, many citizens of Cumberland were occupying apartments in the hotel. Judge Pearre, who was holding court in Hagerstown, barely escaped with his life. He was forced to leave his clothing, money, chancery-papers, law-books, etc., to be destroyed by the flames, and reached the ground in his night-clothes. Messrs. D. C. Bruce and Jesse Karns were able to dress themselves and to save their effects. William M. Price, partially dressed, escaped by climbing down the posts of the rear porch. While he was descending a little girl fell from the fourth story, and, striking him on the shoulders, bounded off to the ground. Fortunately, she alighted on a newly-made flower-garden, and the yielding earth protected her from serious harm. Among the witnesses from Cumberland attending court were Thomas Troxell, Michael Shannon, and Christian Hoenica. Mr. Troxell was missed, and shortly afterwards a dead body was taken from the burning house which was recognized as his. Mr. Troxell was well known, and left a wife and six children in South Cumberland. Mr. Shannon, who jumped from one of the windows, was badly injured. Mr. Hoenica had one leg broken and was badly bruised and stunned.

Military Organizations.—In August, 1814, Capt. William McLaughlin and Capt. Thomas Blair's militia companies were at the defense of Baltimore. In the same year the Fiftieth Regiment of militia was recruited in Allegany County, of which Thomas Greenwell was lieutenant-colonel, John Folck, major, Thomas Porter, Joseph France, Conrad Carbus, Dennis Beall, John McElfish, captains, and Levi Hilleary, adjutant.

In 1824 the officers of the "Allegany Blues" were H. B. Tomlinson, captain, Thomas Dowden, first lieutenant, and S. M. Keene, ensign.

In 1828 the crack company was "The Washington Guards." In 1839 the "Allegany Horse-Guards" held a meeting at the National Hotel, Moses Rawlings, captain. The "Allegany Cavalry" and "Cumberland Guards" celebrated Feb. 22, 1841, by a dinner prepared by J. Hoover, at "Our House." The committee of the "Guards" were James H. Hoblitzell, Charles W. Gephart, and Tal. P. Shaffner, and of the "Cavalry," J. Mason Maguire, William O. Sprigg, and Reuben Worthington. In 1843, Capt. Alexander King commanded the "Cumberland Guards." In 1855, Capt. James M. Schley commanded the "Cumberland Guards," and Capt. Joseph H. Tucker the "Continentals," both companies having their armory on George Street.

In the fall of 1861 "The Second Maryland Regiment Volunteer Infantry, Potomac Home Brigade," was recruited in the county. Its roster was: Colonel, Thomas Johns, succeeded by Robert Bruce; Lieut.-Col., Robert Bruce, afterwards, G. Ellis Porter; Major, G. Ellis Porter, afterwards, Alexander Shaw; Adjt. Orlando D. Robbins, Qr.-Mr. K. H. Butler, Surg. Dr. Samuel P. Smith, Asst. Surg. Dr. P. A. Healey, Chaplain, Rev. J. H. Symmes. Co. A, Capt. Alexander Shaw, 1st Lieut. John Douglass, 2d Lieut. Andrew Spier. Co. B, Capt. J. D. Roberts, 1st Lieut. J. A. Marrow, 2d Lieut. A. S. Galion. Co. C, Capt. J. H. Huntley, 1st Lieut. John Weir, 2d Lieut. R. C. Sansom. Co. D, Capt. B. B. Shaw, 1st Lieut. Robert Powell, 2d Lieut. Mark Powell. Co. E, Capt. James C. Lynn, 1st Lieut. Theodore Luman, 2d Lieut. George Couter. Co. F, Capt. Lewis Dyke, 1st Lieut. Norval McKinley, 2d Lieut. George D Somers. Co. G, Capt. C. G. McCellan, 1st Lieut. Robert Cowan, 2d Lieut. Lloyd Mahaney. Co. H, Capt. George H. Bragonier, 1st Lieut. S. T. Little, 2d Lieut. George W. McCulloh. Co. I, Capt. J. F. McCulloh, 1st Lieut. J. M. Shober, 2d Lieut. John F. Troxell. Co. K, Capt. P. B. Petrie, 1st Lieut. Jason G. Sawyer, 2d Lieut. Moses Bickford. The promotions other than those given before were J. H. Huntley to be major, Theodore Luman to be adjutant, John Douglas, J. A. Marrow, John Weir, Norval McKinley, to be captains, Andrew Spier, Alexander Tennant, Lloyd Mahaney, R. C. Sansom, George Couter, to be first lieutenants, and James Thompson, G. W. Pelton, D. C. Edwards, George Wigley, Moses Bickford, to be second lieutenants. At the end of three years four of the companies re-enlisted as veterans, and were organized into a battalion, whose officers were Lieut.-Col. James C. Lynn; Capts. J. F. McCulloh, P. B. Petrie, H. H. Hartsock, Robert Cowan; 1st Lieuts. C. H. Thayer, J. A. Howard, L. N. Goudon, A. B. Lynn; 2d Lieuts. Levi Shaw, J. A. McKee, J. H. Buckey, and R. T. Browning. Capt. George D. Somers was killed in action at Summit Point, Va., Oct. 7, 1863.

In May, 1862, the "Third Maryland Volunteer Regiment

Infantry, Potomac Home Brigade," was sworn in. It was raised and recruited largely at Cumberland, with the remainder from Hagerstown, Ellicott's Mills, and Baltimore. Its roster was Lieut.-Col. Stephen W. Downey, Maj. C. L. Graflin, Adjt. N. M. Ambrose, Surg. C. E. S. McKee, Asst. Surg. Jesse Beerbrower. Co. A, Capt. J. S. Inskeep, 1st Lieut. John Coles, 2d Lieut. W. A. Cross. Co. B, Capt. W. F. Cardiff, 1st Lieut. M. Whitford, 2d Lieut. J. K. Whitford. Co. C, Capt. H. C. Rizer, 1st Lieut. W. R. Jarboe, 2d Lieut. C. F. McAleer. Co. D, Capt. Michael Fallon, 1st Lieut. J. L. Forsyth, 2d Lieut. J. M. Armstrong. Co. E, Capt. H. B. McCoy, 1st Lieut. J. W. Dodson, 2d Lieut. Theodore Goff. Co. F, Capt. Robert Maxwell, 1st Lieut. P. J. Mayberry, 2d Lieut. W. H. Foreman. Co. G, Capt. Jacob Sarbaugh, 1st Lieut. W. H. Hipsly, 2d Lieut. J. K. Pitman. Co. H, Capt. W. H. Falkenstine, 1st Lieut. Frederick Pringly, 2d Lieut. H. B. Friend. Lieut.-Col. Downey resigned September 1st, and was succeeded by Charles Gilpin the next day, who was promoted to be colonel April 16, 1864, having recruited two full companies, thus making a full regiment. He continued in service until the expiration of the three years' enlistment, when the regiment was transformed into a battalion commanded by Harry C. Rizer, promoted to be lieutenant-colonel. Its officers were Capts. W. A. Falkenstine, N. M. Ambrose, J. W. Dodson, J. E. Garrahan, G. Valois, Samuel T. Eck, Charles Pratt, 1st Lieuts. E. C. Hedding, J. W. Cook, W. J. Donahoe, J. W. White, W. H. H. Friend, B. F. Cook, Quartermaster F. A. Penny, Adjts. W. H. Foreman, Augustus Robinette, Daniel C. Shriver, 2d Lieut. Theodore Goff. On Jan. 16, 1863, Crawford Shearer succeeded C. L. Graflin as major of the regiment. Capt. Jacob Sarbaugh was killed Sept. 14, 1862, at Bolivar Heights.

In 1862 "The City Guard" was formed of three companies for home protection, and was commanded by Lieut.-Col. Horace Resley. Its officers were Capts. Casper Kassen, Jacob Wickard, Horace Resley, 1st Lieuts. Joshua Steiner, W. R. McCulley, J. J. McHenry, 2d Lieuts. J. A. Buckey, J. M. Koerner, J. F. Troxell, Ord. Sergts. D. B. Myers, Charles A. Seay, George M. Read.

On July 31, 1864, the following "Citizens' Organization" went out to meet the Confederates near Folck's mill in defense of the city: Commander, Gen. C. M. Thruston, Quartermaster William Wickard, Com. Sergt. Josiah Witt. Co. A, Capt. Samuel Luman, 1st Lieut. S. J. Edwards, 2d Lieut. J. J. Watkins, Ord. Sergt. E. A. Lingo, Privates J. M. Kearner, P. W. Hoblitzell, G. W. Hoblitzell, J. W. Hummelshime, William Wolf, R. W. McMichael, William Reid, M. Sibley, John Heck, John Ohr, Charles Shaw, Daniel Webster, Winfield Jordan, Walter Beall, William Reid, of William, William Brengle, W. W. Beall, Jacob Suter, William Anderson, Thomas Reid, Summerfield Speelman, S. Valentine (color-bearer), William Shepherd, Chauncey McCulloh, Lona Ward, J. T. Mahaney, Charles Rizer (drummer), Alonzo Smenner, Thomas Hays, Thomas Wickard, James Reid, James Wingard, John Madore, Arnor Keller, John Laney, F. Finnegan, Charles B. Madore, William Trieber. Co. B, Capt. J. J. Creighen, 1st Lieut. Joshua Steiner, 2d Lieut. G. F. Shryer, 1st Sergt. Henry Shriver, 2d Sergt. Robert Shriver, 3d Sergt. Charles A. Seay, 1st Corp. George T. Knorr, 2d Corp. C. B. Smith, 3d Corp. S. H. Fundenberg, Privates, A. M. Adams, Samuel Anderson, L. W. Brant, T. D. Davis, J. H. Doke, George F. Gephart, O. C. Gephart, George M. Gloss, William Hext, George A. Hoffman, E. M. Johnson, Thomas Johnson, John Morris, M Y. Rabold, Oliver Rice, John Schilling, Thomas Shuck, Josiah Shuck, Augustus Smith, Amos Stallings, J. Speelman, W. H. Wilkins, J. P. Wolf, J. H. Young. Co. C, Capt. Pat Morrisey, 1st Lieut. H. M. Carleton, 2d Lieut. John Winterstine, Ord. Sergt. John Wefer, Privates Henry Bersee, John Taffel, John Smith, John Reis, John Hart, John Sheiler, Frederick Minke, John Baker, George Zink, John Himmler, John Keogel, John Rhitter, Kuhnrod Hartman, John Willer, Thomas Leon, George Morgan, James Shaning, Joseph Schilling, Henry Willison, George Shuck, Jr, Benjamin Bakley, John Baker, Kuhnrod Waltz, William Smith.

Voltigeurs, Co. A, Second Battalion Infantry, Maryland National Guard, was organized in the month of August, 1879, with Capt. Henry J. Johnson, since promoted to be major, commanding the battalion; 1st Lieut. W. McKaig, since promoted to be colonel and aide-de-camp on the Governor's staff; 2d Lieut. Wm. Brace, since resigned. Present officers: 1st Lieut. W. O. Hoffman, commanding company; 2d Lieut. Edward Schilling. The company numbers about fifty members, and since its organization has attended the parades at Baltimore during the sesqui-centennial, and at Yorktown, and also two encampments at Oakland (1880 and 1881). The uniform is dark-blue frock-coat, light-blue trousers, dark-blue cap, all trimmed with light blue and buff.

Hamilton Light Infantry, Co. C, Second Battalion, Maryland National Guard, was formed in the latter part of the year 1879, only a few months after the organization of the "Voltigeurs." The original officers were Capt. Thomas F. McCardell, since resigned; 1st Lieut. J. F. Harrison; 2d Lieut. R. H. Gordon. Present officers commanding: Capt. R. H. Gordon, 1st Lieut. J. F. Harrison, 2d Lieut. B. Scott Rigger. It numbers fifty men, and the uniform is dark-blue frock-coats, light-blue pants, and dark-blue caps. It assisted in the parade at the Baltimore sesqui-centennial and at Yorktown, and participated in one encampment at Oakland (1881).

Among the young men who served in the Confederate army from Cumberland were Malcom G. Harrison, killed; Charles Bruce, killed; Albert Rice, killed; Edward Browning, wounded; C. James Dailey, wounded; William Armstrong, wounded; Thaddeus W. Clary, wounded; John McCafferty, wounded; Charles H. Blair, wounded; Roberdeau Annan, wounded; J. Henry Shriver, wounded; W. H. Cahill, wounded; Jacob Gassman, wounded; Sprigg S. Lynn, wounded; Peter Devecmon, John G. Lynn, Jr., David Lynn, J. B. Fay, W. W. McKaig, Jr., J. V. L. McKaig, Edward I. McKaig, Jr., Edward Bryan, John Palmer, Harry Osborn, Dr. Thomas A. Healey, M. A. Healey, James Taylor, Harry C. Black, Matthew Coffey, John Calvin, John D. Mountz, Lloyd L. Clary, John Hadley, John Dermody, H. A. Higgins, Joseph A. Cahill, John H. Shriver, Anthony Shriver, Lamar Sprigg, Van Lear Perry, Charles Nichols, Walter Bruce, James R. Annan, Roger Annan, Duncan McBlair, Capt. C. H. McBlair, Thomas M. Healey, William Lamar, James Pollock, Thomas Goldsborough, Richard L. Clary, Joseph Pennington, Jr., Mr. Winters, James Briscoe, Theodore Dawson, James A. Mason, Walter Chisholm, Harlan Tabb, Peyton Tabb, George Ritter, William D. Hoye, Samuel Hoye, Peter Chisholm, Fetter S. Hoblitzell, Thomas W. West, H. P. Tasker, James R. Higgins.

Local Events.—On the 4th of July, 1792, a number of citizens of the county celebrated the day at the house of John Simpkins, on the Allegany Mountains, where a dinner was provided and fifteen toasts drunk.

On April 19, 1793, Thomas Beall, of Samuel, navigated the Potomac with freight, etc., from Cumberland to Williamsport, and offered to give for good hands ten dollars a month, and forty shillings bounty to each hand that would work three months.

In June of that year a merchant in Cumberland sold and delivered in Hagerstown over one hundred pounds' worth of good maple-sugar, manufactured in Allegany County. It was said that five tons of this sugar were for sale in this county.

May 28, 1795, George Ebert opened a public-house at the stand formerly occupied by George Dent in Cumberland.

In 1794, preparatory to their march into the Westmoreland region of Pennsylvania to subdue the famous "Whisky Insurrection" of 1794, in the western part of that State, the militia of Virginia and Maryland assembled in Cumberland. On October 16th, President Washington arrived, and on the third day after his arrival held a grand review on the site of old Fort Cumberland. He passed several days inspecting the militia, who were encamped on the "Island" along Will's Creek. Gens. Richard Henry Lee and Daniel Morgan, of Virginia, were both at Cumberland, the former the commander of the expedition, and the latter in command of the Virginia troops. Daniel Cresap, John Lynn, and Gabriel Jacob, in a letter to Governor Lee, of Virginia, dated Cumberland, Sept. 2, 1794, informed His Excellency that the insubordination was not confined to Western Pennsylvania, but that there were insurgents near Hagerstown and at other points in Maryland, west of the mountains. The army marched in two divisions from Cumberland and Bedford (where the New Jersey and Pennsylvania militia were encamped), and the two wings formed a junction at Uniontown, Pa. On its approach the insurgents fled, and in a few months this formidable rebellion was merely an interesting topic of fireside gossip. The Virginia and Maryland military were encamped at Cumberland several weeks, and their fine reviews attracted the attention and commanded the admiration of the denizens of the then small village.

On Wednesday, Oct. 12, 1796, a purse of twenty guineas was run for on the race-course at Fort Cumberland, and on the following day a purse of sixty guineas. On Friday a sweepstakes was contested. The races were respectively four, three, and two-mile heats. The horses were entered with John Rine.

At a meeting held Oct. 20, 1828, at the house of Jesse Robinette, in Flintstone District, it was "resolved that the citizens of Allegany, Bedford, and Hampshire Counties be invited 'to turn out to a Grand Circular Hunt,' on Saturday, the 22d day of November, at eight o'clock A.M., and form a line for the purpose of encircling the grounds herein described:

"The line of the First Brigade to extend from the Narrows to the smith-shop at the mouth of Col. Lamar's lane, on the Old Town road; Generals, John Burbridge, Joseph Sprig; Captains, Burgess Magruder, from the shop downwards, Capt. Laban Wiley to join Magruder's company, Capt. Samuel House to join Wiley, and Capt. Daniel Cokely to extend to the Narrows; First Marshal, John G. Hoffman; Second Marshal, Joseph Everstine.

"Second Brigade—To extend from the smith-shop to Davidson's house on the middle road; Generals, Richard Beall, James Black; Captains, Christopher Stotter, Sylvanus Bennett, John J. Hoffman, Wm. Taylor, and Samuel Hoblitzell; Marshals, Thomas Dowden, Anthony Skimming, and Richard Lamar.

"Third Brigade—To extend to the top of Nichols Mountain; Generals, Paul Bussey and Isaac Rice; Captains, Andrew Rice, George Crow, Isaac Chapman, and James Beall; Marshals, Daniel Ball, Alpheus B. Hinkle, Brooks Beall, Alpheus Gross.

"Fourth Brigade—To extend from the top of Nichols Mountain to John Twiggs, deceased, on the Old Town road. Generals, Walter Slicer, John Wilson; Marshals, Simeon Twigg, Samuel Gillis; Captains, Jeremiah Cheney, Wm. Robinette, Jasper Middleton, Benjamin Walford, Elisha Willison.

"Fifth Brigade—From John Twiggs', deceased, to Isaac Ward's, on the Old Town road. Generals, Amos Wilson, Thomas Cromwell; Marshals, John North, Horatio Middleton, Amos Willison; Captains, Francis Reid, Nathan Wilson, James Moore, and Egbert Willison.

"Sixth Brigade—From Isaac Ward's to Old Town. Generals, James Prather, Jacob Lantz; Marshals, Wm. McLaughlin, Isaac Ward, Wm. Reilly; Captains, James Morton, Wm. Britain, David Tracy, Wm. Johnson, Henry Ward, James Keely.

"Seventh Brigade—To extend up the river to the head of Prather's Island, on the Maryland side. Generals, Isaac Baker, Mr. Pancake; Captains, Henry Tracy, Solomon Alkine; Marshals, Lionel Jamieson, J. W. Mountz.

"Eighth Brigade—To line the Virginia banks of the river, from the head of Prather's Island to the Narrows. Generals, Garrett Seymour, Thomas Dunn, Mr. Suckslogle, Isaac Sapp, Thomas Daniels, Benjamin Wiley; Captains, Samuel Brady, Charles Keller, Joseph Ketles, Jacob Wagoner, John Alkive, Mr. Johnson; Marshals, Inskeep and Houser.

"Committee to collect and sell game—Jesse Robinette, Walter Slicer, Jacob Lantz, Robert Read, Garrett Seymour, Mr. Slugsdale, Col. John A. Hoffman, James Stoddard, and Dr. Samuel P. Smith."

Col. John Folck, Jesse Robinette, Col. Thomas Greenwell, and Col. Wm. Lamar were appointed major-generals of the hunt; Jacob Hoblitzell, Jeremiah Berry, Samuel Charles, and Wm. Harness were their aides; and Drs. James Smith, J. M. Lawrence, and Clement Smith, surgeons. Owing to the inclement weather of November 22d, the day appointed for the hunt, it was postponed, and occurred on Dec. 6, 1828, proving a great success.

In 1832, when Asiatic cholera prevailed so generally over the land, Cumberland escaped a visitation from the plague, but during its prevalence in other towns the citizens held a public meeting October 22d, at the "Union Hotel," and resolved to arrange a building for hospital purposes, and solicit contributions for medicines, etc. In 1853, however, the epidemic broke out, the first case occurring August 17th. Thousands fled to the country, nearly all business was abandoned, and for three weeks the town was almost deserted. From August 1st to September 10th there were one hundred and four deaths in the town, of which seventy-two were adults and thirty-two children, and of these two-thirds died of cholera. In September the city authorities appropriated certain sums of money to Maria Shuck, Mrs. Bacon, Mrs. McGirr, W. H. Billmire, Asbury Simpkins, and J. H. C. Morrison for their devoted and unremitting labors to the sick who suffered from the prevailing disease. The cause no doubt of the visitation was the overflowing of the river and creek from the heavy rains which inundated the town, and which left in the streets, alleys, and lots large deposits of filth and débris, which decomposed during the summer and caused the disease.

At a meeting of the citizens of Cumberland and Allegany Counties, held at the court-house, Jan. 7, 1835, to devise means for relieving the sufferers by the destructive fire at Snow Hill, John Gephart presided, and H. M. Pettit was secretary. The following committees were appointed to solicit subscriptions:

Cumberland.—Robert Swan, Levi Hilleary, J. J. Hoffman, M. N. Falls, John McNeill, Sr., Joseph Schuck.

Glades.—George Rinehart, William Armstrong, Joshua Kight.

Big Crossings.—Joseph Frantz, John Slicer, Jacob Clemmer.

Little Crossings.—John Wiley, John Layman, Thomas Thistle.

Frostburg.—Moses Rawlings, Thomas Blair, Joseph Dilley, Robert McCulloh, Meshach Frost, George M. Swan.

Westernport.—George Lyman, William Shaw, William Ravenscroft, Henry Hamill.

Flintstone.—Jeremiah Berry, Jr., Jasper Robinette, J. Huddleson, S. Hamilton.

Fifteen-Mile Creek.—Leonard Shircliff, Walter Bevans, John Larew.

Old Town.—Lenox Martin, Jacob Lantz, William Rielly.

Aug. 28, 1829, a series of services began under the auspices of an association for religious exercises in the Protestant Episcopal church, and lasted one week.

Early on the morning of the Fourth of July, 1833, a large flag was seen waving upon the top of Will's Mountain, on the west side of the Narrows. It had been placed there by the workmen on the National road. Rev. Mr. Kehler delivered a discourse in the Lutheran church at eleven A.M. At half-past twelve the citizens again assembled in the church, when the Declaration of Independence was read by Lieut. Pickell, of the United States army, and an oration was delivered by James P. Carleton, Jr. The following were then chosen as officers of the day: Capt. David Lynn, president; Col. William Lamar and George Calmes, vice-presidents,—all veterans of the Revolution; James P. Carleton, standard-bearer; Thomas J. McKaig and H. M. Pettit, secretaries; and Lieut. Pickell, marshal. The procession formed in front of the church in the following order: musicians, officers and soldiers of the Revolution, national flag, orator of the day, officers of the day, and citizens. In this order the whole party proceeded to the "McCleary Hollow," about half a mile from the town, where, after resting in the shades of this retreat, the company sat down to a dinner prepared by James Black, after which toasts, regular and impromptu, followed, interspersed with patriotic speeches.

On the 30th of October, 1833, J. B. Green & Co. published a curious advertisement announcing that they would exhibit their menagerie and circus on Wednesday, November 13th. The advertisement was decorated with rude wood engravings of a zebra and a kangaroo, both regarded at that day as phenomenal curiosities. Among the attractions announced was the male elephant, Runjeet Sing, the Ethiopian zebra, the "gnoo," a fierce and untamable animal from the deserts of "Zahara," "positively the only one ever imported to or exhibited in this country," two kangaroos from New Holland, the "huanicas," or Peruvian camel, two African lionesses, etc. The circus comprised pony tricks, vaulting, tumbling, juggling, equestrianism, etc.

Miller, Mead & Olmstead advertised a circus about the same time to appear at Westernport, Frostburg, and Cumberland. One of the attractions was a stuffed ostrich, which had "unfortunately died in May last."

A large assemblage of the citizens of Allegany County convened at the court-house in Cumberland on Tuesday, April 26, 1836, for the purpose of appointing delegates to represent the county in the Internal Improvement Convention to be held in Baltimore on the 2d day of May following. William McMahon was called on to preside, assisted by Andrew Bruce and Isaac McCarty, and Joseph Shriver and James Smith were appointed secretaries.

Thomas J. McKaig, after stating the object of the meeting, moved the following resolution, which was unanimously adopted:

"*Resolved*, That this meeting, taking into consideration the great importance of the subjects proposed to be submitted to the convention intended to be held in Baltimore on Monday, the 2d day of May next; the large expenditure which has already been made on the Chesapeake and Ohio Canal, and on the Baltimore and Ohio Railroad; the interest which this county and State have at large in their early completion, as well as in the successful prosecution of a general system of internal improvement; do approve of the proposition to hold the said convention, and that a delegation of thirty persons be appointed to represent us therein."

The president of the meeting was, on motion of John Hoye, requested to appoint the delegates, which was done accordingly. Those selected were, viz.: John Hoye, David Shriver, Andrew Bruce, Isaac McCarty, Thomas J. McKaig, William Lynn, M. N. Falls, John Gephart, Alpheus Beall, Robert Bruce, Thomas Perry, James Smith, S. M. Semmes, William Ridgely, Joseph Dilley, George M. Swan, John Neff, Thomas Thistle, William Shaw, John Poland, Jonathan W. Magruder, Dr. L. F. Klipstine, William Carroll, Amos Robinette, H. A. Jamison, J. Huddleson, Dr. J. W. Mountz, John Ash, Daniel Raymond, Edward Armstrong.

The following resolution was then offered by James Smith, and unanimously adopted:

"*Resolved*, That Gen. Duff Green, Gen. R. C. Weightman, Virgil Maxey, J. L. Skinner, John A. Smith, and John H. Alexander, who have recently become deeply interested in the coal and iron mines of this county, as members of different chartered companies, be invited to attend the said convention as members from this county."

The Cumberland races occurred on Nov. 10, 11, 12, 1836. The races were conducted according to the general rules of racing, and the course run over was in excellent condition. The purses were, for the first day, one hundred dollars for three-mile heats; second day, seventy-five dollars, two-mile heats; third day, one mile and repeat, for a handsome sweepstake.

In the early history of the Chesapeake and Ohio Canal disturbances among the workmen were of frequent occurrence, and when they were paid off and fired with liquor the wildest scenes of excitement at times prevailed. On the 1st of January, 1838, a party of men at work on the tunnel made an attack upon Old Town, and "raided" the tavern of Nicholas Ryan. The sheriff of the county, Thomas Dowden, summoned a posse of citizens, and the military was called out, but the rioters, probably receiving intelligence of what was in store for them, had disappeared. These riots gradually became more frequent and serious as the laborers learned the helplessness of the inhabitants and their own impunity. At length the Governor of the State ordered out the militia and supplied them with arms, one hundred and eighty-nine muskets and one hundred and twenty rifles being dispatched to Cumberland. The Fiftieth Regiment of Maryland militia was organized, with C. M. Thruston, colonel; Thos. J. McKaig, lieutenant-colonel; Normand Bruce, major; Dr. H. C. Grieves, surgeon; Alexander King, captain; George M. Reid, first lieutenant; and John M. Carleton, second lieutenant. In obedience to the orders of the Governor all the available military force of Allegany responded, consisting of the "Cumberland Guards," an infantry company, the "Cumberland Grays," a rifle company, and the "Frostburg Grays," also a rifle company. Col. Thruston took command of the troops and marched to the scene of the disturbances. Here he was joined by some troops under Col. Hollingsworth, and a company of cavalry from Clear Spring commanded by Maj. Barnes. Both commands were from Washington County. The troops were skillfully handled, and their movements resulted in a complete surprise of the rioters, who threw down their arms and surrendered at discretion. Twenty-five of the ringleaders were captured and taken to Cumberland, where they were imprisoned in the jail, and many of them were subsequently tried, convicted, and sent to the penitentiary for terms ranging from one to eighteen years. Two hundred stand of arms were captured, sixty barrels of whisky were destroyed, and fifty shanties torn down. It is related of a lieutenant who accompanied the expedition that he was so incensed with the conduct of the rioters, and so unwilling to be foiled in his expectation of a fight, that he threw down his sword, doffed his regimentals, rolled up his sleeves, and went in whether or no, to the astonishment and dismay of the wilted rioters, who just previously had been defying the authority of the State of Maryland.

The celebration in Cumberland of the Centennial Fourth of July (1876) was one of the most interesting demonstrations that has ever taken place in that city. The day was ushered in at twelve o'clock on Monday night by a salvo of thirteen guns from a ten-pounder cannon, the ringing of church and engine-house bells, the blowing of whistles, etc. The cannon was in charge of Sergt. Wm. Hamilton, formerly of the regular army, assisted by Andrew Fink, formerly of Snow's battery, John Gannon, formerly of the regular army, and Wm. Love, formerly of the Fourth Virginia Battery. A company of minute-men, commanded by Capt. John Potts, joined in the salutes with volleys of musketry and beating of drums. At nine o'clock a procession was formed, and started from the City Hall in the following order:

Chief Marshal and aides, mounted.
Queen City Cornet Band.
Knights of Pythias.
Independent Order of Odd-Fellows.
Independent Order of Red Men.
Heptasophs, or S. W. M.
Young America Independent Order of Mechanics.
First German-silver Cornet Band.
St. Patrick's Temperance Society.
St. Patrick's Beneficial Society.
St. Edward's Beneficial Society.
Arion Singing Society.
St. Joseph's Beneficial Society.
SS. Peter and Paul's Beneficial Society.
Carriage with Capuchin Monks.
Rolling-mill Men.
Cumberland Hose Company.
Cooper's Band.
Star of the West Lodge of Masons (colored).
Laboring Sons' Society of Cumberland (colored).
Twelve Carriages containing Committees.
Speakers, Mayor and City Council, and Invited Guests.
Holly and Fisher's String Band in wagon.
Alleganian Boat Club in wagon.
Fantastics in wagon.
Holtzhu's advertising wagon.
Shertzer's advertising wagon.
Boatmen in row-boat drawn by seven mules.
Host's advertising wagon.
Citizens on foot, horseback, and in carriages.

The chief marshal was Jacob Brengle, assisted by Harvey Ladew, R. H. Gordon, T. P. Morgan, H. Gerdman, W. Kornhoff, John R. Brooke, Alexander McFerran, Jr., Caspar Reichart, Dennis O'Neill, Jr., Harman White, H. Swartzwelder, and Alexander King, Jr.

At 7.30 in the evening a mass-meeting was held on South Centre Street, at which an assemblage of over two thousand persons had collected to hear the addresses. On the stand were the speakers, Mayor Withers, the City Council, and clergy, Revs. E. B. Raffensperger, J. K. Dunn, W. S. Edwards, and H. J. Chandler, and Prof. J. P. Wiesel and his choir of fifty singers. After a prayer by Rev. E. B. Raffensperger, and the reading of the Declaration of Independence, Hon. Henry W. Hoffman was introduced and delivered an eloquent address. In the course of his address Mr. Hoffman said,—

"Had we been here at the close of the 14th of November, 1753, we might have seen two travel-stained horsemen descending the hill by the way of the Old Town road. In the younger of the two we recognize the youthful Washington, just passed his majority. In the other, Jacob Van Braam, the swordsman, and interpreter of the former. They cross Will's Creek at the foot of Green Street, and stop overnight at one of the two or three humble dwellings that then constituted a settlement at this point, then the extreme western frontier. In the following year, on the 20th of April, we again see Washington coming by the same road, at the head of one hundred and fifty men, *en route* to Fort Du Quesne, now the city of Pittsburgh. He stopped here for some ten days, resting and preparing his men for the arduous march that was before them, and it was during this time that the post at Will's Creek was erected into a fort, called Fort Cumberland, in honor of the Duke of Cumberland, then captain-general of the British army. Unsuccessful in this his first attack on Fort Du Quesne, Washington returned to Fort Cumberland, and passed here his 4th of July, 1754. About the middle of May of the year 1755 we find Braddock's army, more than two thousand strong, encamped on the spot where now rises that beautiful temple, the Protestant Episcopal church. Gen. Braddock, in his chariot, purchased from Governor Sharpe, of Maryland, makes his appearance upon the scene, attended by Washington, his aide, and is received with a salute of seventeen guns. Thus early were the echoes of the mountains around us stirred by salutes similar to those we have this day heard. Here were assembled to greet their approach the noted chiefs Scarooyadi, Silver Heels, and White Thunder, the latter attended by his daughter, Bright Lightning, a princess among her race, and, if history is not at fault, whose charms proved bright lightning among the hearts of the officers. As Braddock did not start out on his ill-starred and ill-fated march until June 10th, this locality was the scene of reviews and drills for nearly a whole month. Here, again, were they brought, on their retreat, by Washington, after the defeat and death of Braddock, July 17, 1755. Again, on July 2, 1758, we find him at Fort Cumberland, preparatory to the taking of Fort Du Quesne. He remained here nearly three months in getting his troops in such a state of proficiency as would authorize his advance. And still later, in 1770, we once more find him here, going to and returning from Fort Pitt. In view of these repeated visits, and the length of time spent here, we may safely conclude that not a rod of the soil on which our city now stands but has been pressed by the foot of him who was a few years later intrusted with the command of the Revolutionary army. Nay, more, I maintain that here was in great measure the training-ground, the military academy, where the youthful Washington was educated for the high service that was to be demanded of him. I hold, therefore, that the people of Cumberland could not afford to let this centennial pass without a proper observance."

At the close of Mr. Hoffman's address Hon. G. A. Pearre addressed the assemblage. He was followed by Hon. J. H. Gordon, and the benediction was then pronounced by Rev. H. J. Chandler, of the First Baptist Church.

The effects of the storm of the 22d, 23d, and 24th of November, 1877, were more severe in Cumberland than ever before known, except perhaps in 1810. Early on Saturday morning, the 24th, Frederick and parts of North Centre and Baltimore Streets to the mill-race were covered with swiftly-running water to the depth of about one foot. This water, which was the product of local rains, subsided, and about one P.M. Will's Creek, which had been rising rapidly for several hours, broke through to Mechanic Street at Dennis O'Neill's, and afterwards at John Morrissey's, farther up street, and poured down Mechanic Street a rapid stream about two feet in depth. Soon the water ran up Baltimore Street to Liberty, and up North and down South Liberty Street, and finally reached nearly to Centre Street, the highest point attained by a flood for many years. The water on Baltimore Street from Canal to Centre was of a uniform depth of about two feet. The one great point of interest and occasion of alarm, however, was the canal-bank at the foot of Canal Street. About an hour after the great rise in Will's Creek water was noticed trickling through the bank, and at once measures were taken to stop the leak, but little success attended the efforts at first. Finally, after a short consultation, it was decided to use a different method to secure the bank, which proved successful and allayed the growing excitement of the people. The extent of the averted disaster may be imagined when it is known that the surface of the water, which was within a few inches of the top of the bank, was nearly on a level with the pavement in front of the Queen City Hotel. The west side of Will's Creek was inundated by the waters of the Potomac, which was higher than ever before known. In South Cumberland many houses were inundated with from six inches to three feet of water. The canal was greatly damaged, and in some places the banks were obliterated, and there were many bad breaks on the Georgetown level, many boats and several lives being lost. The Baltimore and Ohio Railroad sustained great damages, their wires being torn down for miles, trestles washed out, and bridges destroyed, which caused a delay of trains for several days. The Cumberland and Pennsylvania also suffered heavy loss. A number of trestles be'ween Ocean and Westernport were washed out, and the track badly damaged in some places. The business of the inundated portion of Cumberland was suspended until the waters subsided.

Early Reminiscences.—The population of Cumberland in 1830 was only 1162, but it was then a lively town with bright prospects for the future. The town depended principally upon the through traffic between the sea-board and the interior, and was of importance as a transfer station. Judging from the price of provisions, Cumberland fifty years ago was an economical place to live in. Flour was selling at $3.50 to $4 per barrel, wheat from 65 to 70 cents per bushel, corn from 25 to 31 cents per bushel, oats 25 cents per bushel, and potatoes 25 cents per bushel, beef 2½ to 3 cents per pound, pork 3 to 4 cents, butter 9 to 10 cents, and whisky in barrels 31¼ cents per gallon. Among the members of the Cumberland Fire Engine Company, which was in existence in 1831, were Dr. Samuel P. Smith, Thomas J. McKaig, Jesse Korns, and John M. Carleton. Stages were running between Cumberland and Washington City, *via* Winchester, leaving Cumberland on Tuesdays, Thursdays, and Saturdays. In December of that year Hon. Henry Clay and family, of Kentucky, passed through Cumberland on their way to Washington. Thomas J. McKaig at that time was principal of the Allegany County Academy, and had an interview with Kentucky's great statesman when he stopped at one of the hotels to dine. Gen. Jackson was President at that time, and was afterwards renominated. Henry Clay was his opponent, but was defeated. Jackson carried Allegany County by 191 majority, and Clay carried the town of Cumberland.

The Fourth of July, 1832, was celebrated in Cumberland by the citizens generally and many persons from the country. At eleven A.M. they assembled at the English Lutheran church, where prayer was offered by Rev. Mr. Johns. The Declaration of Independence was read by George Hebb, and an oration was delivered by Thomas J. McKaig. Benediction was pronounced by Rev. Mr. Havenstock. The procession then moved to Fechtig's Union Hotel, now the boarding-house kept by Mrs. L. D. Cross. The Declaration was there read by John White, and an oration was delivered by James P. Carleton, Jr. At two o'clock dinners were served by Fechtig and Star at their hotels, of which between eighty and one hundred persons partook.

At the time of the great fire (1833) Cumberland was not a city of churches, as it is to-day, but a village of few places of worship, where one or two buildings were used to accommodate three or four different denominations. The Lutheran congregation was the largest, their church being situated on a lot which commenced on the corner of Baltimore and Centre Streets, and extended westward as far as the property now occupied by K. H. Butler's furniture manufactory. The Methodists occupied a building on the same spot where their new church now stands. There were no Protestant Episcopal or Catholic churches in the town at that time, and Fort Cumberland, where Emmanuel church now stands, was a vacant lot. The court-house stood on the lot now occupied by the old jail and the Allegany County Academy, while the academy, then presided over by Dr. Robert S. McKaig, stood upon the property now owned by the German Catholics, where a church and monastery were erected upon the completion of the Baltimore and Ohio Railroad and Chesapeake and Ohio Canal to Cumberland. The largest hotel in the city previous to the fire was what was known as Kreb's Hotel, kept by Samuel Slicer, which occupied the lot now owned by the Semmes family, extending on Main Street as far as the race, and on Mechanic Street nearly to Kelso's Hotel, which property at that time was owned and occupied by Dr. James Smith, who had an office where the barber-shop is now. The hotel had a large porch fronting on Baltimore Street, and a large yard fronting on Mechanic Street, where stages were kept belonging to the Stockton and Stokes line. The building now standing on the southwest corner of Baltimore and Mechanic Streets was a hotel kept by Samuel Slicer, the walls of which are still standing, the hotel having been rebuilt after the fire, and a few years afterwards raised half a story by Dr. Samuel P. Smith, who rented it to the United States government during the war as a hospital for wounded Union soldiers.

The other hotel, kept by James Black, was situated on the property now owned by Col. Alfred Spates and the Third National Bank. One part of the hotel was occupied by the Cumberland Bank of Allegany County, the walls of which were used in the erection of that part of the building now occupied by the Third National Bank, on South Mechanic near Baltimore Street.

The *Maryland Advocate*, in its issue of May 1, 1832, had an account of a paper balloon that was sent up in Cumberland a few evenings before. The balloon was eighteen feet in height. After ascending several hundred yards it took a northeastern course, and traveled some five miles. The next issue of the paper had a communication from a subscriber describing the effect the balloon had upon the country people, as follows: Some persons who were standing in a field when they discovered the balloon approaching began to conjecture among themselves what it was. One declared it was the comet, because he saw the fire issuing out of its mouth, and that it was young, but would grow to be as large as one-third of the world, and destroy many of the inhabitants of the earth. An old woman stepped to the door and caught a glimpse of it as it passed. She was badly frightened, and cried out, "Mercy, mercy on me! look at the roebuck flying across the field, and the fire flying out of his tail."

The following appeared in the same paper of the 19th of November, 1833: "On the night of Tuesday last, the 12th inst., a most alarming and awful sight was witnessed by many of the citizens of this city and county generally. The whole heavens were illuminated, as far as the eye could penetrate, with what is commonly called 'shooting-stars.' They flew in every direction, like snow in a storm, except from the earth. Some of them appeared as large as a half-bushel, with every variety of size from that down to a spark of fire, with brilliant tails, corresponding in size with the ball they followed. At times they were so thick that the whole atmosphere appeared in flames. Many of them came within a few inches of the earth before they vanished. There was no noise accompanying their explosion. It commenced about twelve o'clock, and only disappeared by the light of the sun after daybreak."

About the year 1837 the work of building the dam in the river at the foot of Lewis' alley was commenced. The foundation was laid and the dam built up until it was several feet above the bed of the river, but owing to the scarcity of funds it was abandoned for some years. The contractors were Sterret & Lockwood. That portion of the tow-path extending from the Cumberland lock up to Brengle's store was built about 1840. George Hoblitzell was the contractor. The ground was dug away some feet below the level of the creek and then filled in with clay, which was beaten down until it was hard and compact. Previous to that time the east end of Washington Street presented quite a different appearance near the bridge from what it does now. It was only a narrow road, and went up between two steep banks. John Hoye owned the ground and wanted to have it dug out and leveled, so he agreed with Mr. Hoblitzell that if the latter would take the earth from it for making the piece of tow-path mentioned he would furnish the "jiggers" for the men engaged in the work. Mr. Hoblitzell accepted the offer, and got all the earth required for the work from this spot. The old mill-race seems to have extended in the beginning past the present location of the Consolidation Coal Company's wharf, where there was, about 1800, a large mill. But the mill has passed away, and not a stone is left to mark the spot. It was at a later date that the "old mill" at the foot of Mechanic Street was built.

Mrs. Nancy Miller, *née* Rafter, who resides with her son, Henry Miller, on George Street, is without doubt the oldest person in Cumberland, and probably in the county. She was one hundred and one years of age on the 17th of June, 1881. She was born at Greencastle, Pa., June 17, 1780, and at the age of eight years removed with her parents to Cumberland; hence she is also the oldest resident of the city. The town at that time consisted of one brick and a score of log houses. When nineteen years old she married John Miller. The ceremony was performed at a place about five miles below Old Town, by a Methodist minister, Rev. Lenox Martin, there being no minister at that time in Cumberland. They lived happily together for thirty-one years, until Mr. Miller's death. They had eleven children, of whom nine are dead. The two still living are Henry Miller, with whom she resides, and John Miller, who lives in Illinois.

Mrs. Miller has resided in Cumberland almost continuously for ninety-three years. On the night of Mr. Miller's death there was to have been an illumination because of a decision to complete the Chesapeake and Ohio Canal, but it was deferred out of respect for the deceased.

Speaking of the early history of the city, on one occasion, Mrs. Miller said, "There was more real happiness and comfort in those days. The rich worked as well as the poor. Liquor was not sold except at the taverns, and there was little or no drunkenness. A lot with a comfortable log house of one room at first sold for about one hundred dollars. As soon as the National road, or old pike, was projected and in the course of building, the price rapidly advanced to one thousand dollars and over. The first church erected was the Lutheran, a plain log building, on the site of the present edifice, of which Rev. Jonathan M. Butler, grandfather of the present K. H. Butler, was the first pastor. The seats were boards laid upon stones, yet the congregations were large and attentive. There was no misbehavior in church in those days. At first there was preaching only occasionally, but the Sabbath was devoted to Bible reading by all the inhabitants. The greatest hardship in those days was imprisonment for debt. The creditor, after selling off the last article of his debtor, might have him put in jail for forty days, where, of course, he could do nothing to relieve himself. Although there was one mayor, Daniel Sayors, who favored it, the whipping-post was never established in Cumberland, the people being strongly opposed to it. The Indians used to come through the town on their way to Washington. They would always behave well, but would call at every house for something to eat, which was given to them without charge. They went on foot, the squaws having their children strapped to their backs. Wagons were not much used. Trains of thirty or forty pack-horses heavily laden with wool or flax used to pass through to Baltimore and the East, and return just as heavily laden with 'store-goods.'"

The *Columbian Magazine* of April, 1788, contained the following:

"To the Editor of the Columbian Magazine:

"Sir,—The following is an extract from the journal of an officer on Gen. Forbes' expedition against Fort Du Quesne (now Fort Pitt) in the year 1758:

'About one hundred yards from Fort Cumberland is a large square post with a pyramidical top, having a plate of lead with the following inscription nailed on one side of it, viz.:

To The Memory of
Sergeant William Shaw, Sergeant Timothy Shaw, Jeremiah Poor And James Cope, Soldiers Of The 1st Virginia Regiment; This Monument Is Erected, To Testify the Love And Esteem Paid Them by Their
Officers For Their
Courage And Gallant Behaviour,
Nov. 1756. They went with 11 Catawbas To
Gain Intelligence; And In The First En-
Counter With The Enemy Met With The
Success Their Courage Deserved—Incited
By this Advantage, and Fired with Noble
Ambition to Distinguish Themselves, They
Engaged A Party Of The Enemy, Hard By
Fort Duquesne, And Fell Gloriously, Fight-
Ing Bravely, Being Greatly Overpowered
By Superior Numbers.
'In Premium Virtutis Erigendum Curavit
'Adamus Stephen.'

. . . Some of these men afterwards returned, and are now officers in the Virginia service. B."

The region about Cumberland has, like so many other localities in America, its legend of buried treasure. Braddock's expedition is made to play a part in the legend, which is as follows:

A gentleman of Cumberland, traveling over the National road, some twenty or thirty miles west of that city, on a bright moonlight night in May, 1881, was terribly unnerved by a huge mass of stone rolling down the steep side of a mountain in front of him, and looking up he discovered a man with gray locks holding a huge crowbar in his hands. The strange man seemed to regret that he had scared the midnight traveler, and offered an apology as he came down towards the buggy. The traveler nervously twitched at his hip-pocket until he observed the decrepitude of his new acquaintance, who informed him that he lived three miles east and was on a "hunting" expedition. The traveler invited him to a seat in the vehicle, which he accepted, and the two drove eastward together. The old man's mind turned upon Braddock's defeat, when the traveler said he had an ancestor named Giles in Braddock's army. "Giles?" said the old man. "He was a messmate of my father, and the two were of the six guards who had charge of the treasure of Gen. Braddock, kept for the payment of the troops. They were so closely pursued by the French and Indians that, though they sought to reach Fort Cumberland, they were compelled to hide the money in a cave among the rocks, which an old hunter had pointed out to them on the march to Fort Pitt. I am glad to meet you. Stop with me overnight in my hut, beyond the gap to the right. Very few people ever come that way, and I have lived alone for years. My father was very young when he marched through here with Braddock, and after the battle he lived in New York until the Revolution, when he joined Gen. Washington's Virginia troops, and fought through the war, after which he married and came here, and in that hut I was born. It is dear to me, and I love it more than if it were a palace. Let me lead your horse through this woodland road to my house, and I will tell you a secret about Braddock's money."

On reaching the hut the traveler found it more inviting inside than out. When they were seated the occupant of the hut gave a history of the traveler's ancestor, Giles, which was pronounced correct. "My father," continued the recluse, "was in command of the guard who had charge of the money, believed to be about fifteen thousand dollars in gold, besides valuable ornaments of the officers. They were dispatched ahead of the troops in the line of retreat, and instructed to make for Fort Cumberland. It was expected that the Indians would harass the retreating army, but not that they would push ahead and intercept them after reaching the Meadows. The guard found to their sorrow, however, that there was danger ahead as well as in the rear. Just as the sun was setting they received a volley from behind a ledge of rocks which killed two and wounded a third. The fire was returned and horses whipped up. Another fire killed the third and wounded my father. The horses kept on, and the pursuit ceased at nightfall. Two were badly wounded, the third fatally. Arriving at a point where the run divided into two streams, flowing around a large rock, they buried the money, and the two who were worst wounded mounted the horses and started for the fort, leaving father to watch the treasure. Ten days after father was found wandering along the banks of Will's Creek, his wound having brought on a fever which deprived him of his reason. He was taken to the fort and properly cared for. On his recovery he learned that nothing had ever been heard of the two men. He started back with scouts to find the hidden treasure, but how far he had wandered, or which of the many points where the stream divided had been selected to hide the money, he could never determine. He was suspected of hiding it for his own future use, and this preyed upon his mind until he determined to go to New York. At the close of the Revolutionary war he returned here, and ever since I can remember he or I have been seeking for this hidden treasure. There is something tells me I shall find it yet before I die, though I have seen eighty winters. I have sought among the rocks that border Braddock's Run for a distance of twenty miles, wherever my father's rough description of the place seemed to locate it. Now, as you are a descendant of my father's messmate, you are equally entitled to share with me the treasure when found, and I invite you to make this your headquarters while we continue the search." The traveler concluded to remain over until the next day, but declined to join in the hunt. His host threw down upon the floor a lot of skins, upon which both lay down, and soon host and guest were dreaming of the hidden treasure.

The next morning the two men arose, and after partaking of breakfast, the traveler proposed starting for home, and invited the old hunter to ride to Cumberland with him, which was less than twenty miles distant. "I will ride to the junction of Will's Creek and the Run with you, and return by night," said the old man. "I desire that the spirit of my father may cease to wander and be at rest, and I know it will not be while this gold lies hidden from mortal eyes. I do not care for it myself, for I have plenty for my necessities, but I want it to get into circulation for my dead father's sake." Climbing into the vehicle they sped along rapidly, he peering into every cavity, and closely inspecting the bends in the stream. At the "Six-mile House" he observed a dry bed of Braddock's Run on one side of the road, and the running stream on the other side, with buried rocks at the dividing point. He said he would give that a closer inspection on his return. Continuing they came to the junction of the creek and run, where he stopped the vehicle and spent half an hour gazing around with wistful eyes, first to the right and then to the left. "It should be hereabouts, but I have closely inspected every crook and cranny, yet I shall give this another inspection on my return." Proceeding on their way, they entered the Narrows, and when they reached Sebastopol he looked across the creek to a pinnacle jutting above the precipice at a height of many hundred feet. "That is *Lover's Leap*," said he. "There is a romantic story connected with it, and as I shall go no farther, if you will seat yourself here I will narrate it." The traveler expressed a desire to hear it, and the old man began. "Jack Chadwick," said he, "lived in the wild country near Negro Mountain with his mother and little brother Jesse. He was a great hunter and feared nothing. In one of his excursions he came across an Indian chief who lived in the break in Will's Mountain, a mile or two up the creek, with his white wife and daughter, the latter just blooming into womanhood. The chief had sided with the whites against the protest of his tribe, and they forsook him. He took up his residence in the hollow. Jack fell in love with the daughter, and his attachment was reciprocated. But the chief wanted his daughter to marry an officer of the fort, and told Jack he was too poor. Disheartened, but still determined, Jack left for his home. Stopping at a spring to drink he turned over a stone and uncovered a glistening ledge of rock, which he found to be rich silver ore. Returning to the home of his sweetheart, he told the chief what he had found, and proposed to show him the mine if he would give him his daughter. The chief agreed, the silver mine was shown him, and the young man went home to prepare for the wedding. Returning, he brought his brother with him. The chief, however, had changed his mind at the instigation of the officer of the fort, and declined to give his daughter to young Chadwick. All day Jack protested, but the old chief was obdurate, and finally the lover seemed to acquiesce, and asked for a few moments' talk with the girl, which was granted. Sauntering among the trees and talking over the harshness of the parent, the lovers finally agreed to escape to the fort and get married. They soon slipped out of sight, but the old chief was watching, and when he missed them went in pursuit, overtaking them behind one of the cliffs. He was very angry, and attacked Jack with a club. The latter threw a stone at the chief and, unfortunately, killed him. The daughter loved her Indian parent dearly, and amid her wailing declared she could die with Jack, but could not live with him, now that he had killed her father. "Then let us leap off the cliff yonder together and end our trouble," said he. She consented, and arm in arm they walked to the cliff, where they clasped hands and leaped off together before little Jesse, who was near by, could comprehend their purpose. The mutilated remains were taken up by friends and laid away in a cave or grotto in the side of the mountain, and in my younger days I saw the bleached bones of the skeletons mingled together in the cave.

"There are three things," continued the old man, "which I want to find out, and hope to do so before I die. The first is, whether young Chadwick's father was the Chadwick who helped my father to bury the Braddock treasure; second, whether the mine found by Jack was not the buried treasure which he had evidently discovered through directions given by his father before dying; and, third, I want to find that treasure before I die and put it in circulation, so that my father's spirit may rest in peace." Here the old man rose, bade the traveler good-by, and walked slowly away, until he was lost amid the huge bowlders that covered the mountain-side at the mouth of the Narrows.

Finances of Cumberland.—In the fall of 1784, when the town was laid out, there were only thirty-five families in and near it, and in 1813 the assessment books showed 138 houses, and taxable property valued at $22,829. In 1824 the corporation taxes were twenty cents on every one hundred dollars. The population in 1830 was: white males, 522; white females, 475; slaves, 129; free colored, 36; total, 1162.

In 1832 the valuation of personalty and realty was $392,500.61. As late as 1835 the expenditures of the corporation were extremely modest, the receipts from May, 1835, to May, 1836, amounting to $291.70, leaving a balance after expenses were paid of $40.91.

In 1840 the population was 2428, and two years later the assessed valuations were:

Lands and lots	$452,229
Individual securities	200,273
Merchandise and trade stock	105,985
Bank and other stock	61,877
Slaves	40,100
Household furniture	32,440
Live-stock	23,327
Miscellaneous property	8,738
Gold and silver watches	3,661
" " plate	2,488
Total assessments	$931,118

The population in 1850 was 6067, of whom 224 were slaves and 267 free colored.

In 1860 the assessed valuation was $2,124,400. According to the annual report of J. B. Walton, mayor of Cumberland, dated May 2, 1881, the receipts, disbursements, assets, and liabilities of Cumberland at that date were as follows: receipts for the year, $232,276.50, leaving after disbursements a balance in the treasury of $13,291. The total resources of the city amounted to $33,881.69, leaving after current liabilities were satisfied a balance of $915.06. The sinking fund as reported April 4, 1881, amounted to $33,942.27. The following is a statement of expenditures as compared with appropriations:

	Appropriated.	Expended.
Water-works	$6,000 00	$6,425.92
Police department	4,050.00	4,213.94
Legal expenses	300 00	282.00
Printing and stationery	500.00	356 50
City Hall and market	1,800.00	1,806 00
Streets and bridges	3,500.00	2,804.06
Street lights	3,200.00	2,963.60
Fire department, $800; additional, $800	1,600.00	1,313.20
New assessment	300.00	305.50
Elections	75 00	75.00
Salaries, including collector's commission	3,925 00	3,819.94
Discount and interest	200.00	500 93
Sinking fund	5,000.00	5,000.00
Manufacturing company	1,500.00	1,500 00
Coupon account	27,000.00	29,411.75
Contingent account	894.00	275.71
Expenses for May, estimated		1,600.00
Balance		2,189 95
	$59,844.00	$59,844 00

The bonded indebtedness of Cumberland is as follows:

Bonds.	Amt. of Issue.	Interest Payable	Rate.	Amt of Interest	Matured.
Bridge bonds	$16,400	Feb. 1	6 %	$492	Dec. 1, 1881
" "		Aug. 1	6 "	492	" "
Penna. R. R. in Md	65,000	Feb. 1	6 "	1,950	May 1, 1908
" " "		Aug. 1	6 "	1,950	" "
Water bonds	100,000	June 1	7 "	3,500	June 1, 1890
" "		Dec. 1	7 "	3,500	" "
Water extension bonds	50,000	April 1	7 "	1,750	April 1, 1892
Water bonds		Oct. 1	7 "	1,750	" "
City debt bonds	20,000	April 1	6 "	600	" 1883
" " "		Oct. 1	6 "	600	" "
Consolidated debt bonds	30,000	April 1	6 "	900	Oct. 1, 1908
" " "		Oct. 1	6 "	900	" "
Water improvem't bonds	18,000	April 1	5 "	450	" 1910
" " "		Oct. 1	5 "	450	" "
Consolidated debt bonds	145,000	April 1	5 "	3,525	" 1908
" " "		Oct. 1	5 "	3,625	" "
	$444,400			$26,534	

POPULATION OF CUMBERLAND.

1830	1162	1860	7300
1840	2428	1870	8056
1850	6067	1880	10,693

John Rhind, register of wills for Allegany County, a native of Scotland, born Dec. 25, 1810, was the second son of Alexander Rhind and Ann Cook, of the parish of Duffus, Morayshire, Scotland. His father died when he was about four years of age, from the effects of an injury received in falling through the centre of a bridge, the construction of which he was superintending, near Exeter, in Devonshire, England. The family returned to Elgin, Morayshire, where, soon after their arrival, the father died, and was buried at Duffus, leaving his widow with two children,—Wm. and John, the youngest child, Alexander, having died in England. In 1816, Mrs. Rhind was married to James Laing, of Forres, Morayshire, a man in comfortable circumstances, to which place she removed with her two boys, who were sent to school and received a common English education. John, at the age of fourteen, left home and went south to Glasgow, where he served an apprenticeship to William

Campbell, of Kent Street, builder, and learned the trade of mason and stone-cutter. In 1832 he went to England, and found employment at the government buildings, then being erected near Plymouth. He returned and spent the winter of 1833–34 at home.

Jno l Rhind

Early in the spring he left for the United States, and arrived at New York in May, 1834. He went to Baltimore, where he found employment at his trade on the "Thomas Viaduct," near the Relay House, Baltimore and Ohio Railroad. In the fall of 1835 he was appointed assistant superintendent of masonry on the Chesapeake and Ohio Canal under A. B. McFarlane, and retained the position until the spring of 1837. When offered an interest in the contract for the building of the Tonoloway Aqueduct by Andrew Small, he accepted, and remained until the completion of the work. During this year, on the 13th of July, 1837, he married Eliza Snyder, born March 29, 1818, the youngest daughter of Anthony and Eleanor Snyder, of Parkhead, Washington Co., Md. The fruit of this marriage has been five boys and four girls. In 1840 he removed to Washington City, and was employed at the Patent Office building. He remained in Washington several years, finding employment at Fort Washington, Prince George's Co., Md., and in the city.

In 1845 he removed to Cumberland, Md., and was variously employed until 1848, when he was appointed superintendent of masonry on the Chesapeake and Ohio Canal, by Charles B. Fisk, chief engineer on T. L. Patterson's division. On leaving the canal he spent three years in Monongalia County, Va., at Woodgrove Furnace, with Messrs. E. A. and W. H. Clabaugh, in the capacity of clerk and general manager. On his return to Cumberland, in May, 1852, he entered the wholesale grocery establishment of G. W. Claubaugh, and remained until 1864, when he was admitted a partner, under the firm-name of Clabaugh & Rhind. He conducted the business successfully until 1873, when the firm sold out to James Clark & Co.

In 1875 a vacancy occurred in the office of the register of wills (owing to the death of C. C. Shriver). Being unemployed he became a candidate for that office, and after a severe struggle received the nomination from the executive committee of the Republican party, having been an Old-Line Whig until the dissolution of that party, and then an ardent Republican. He was elected register of wills at the November election of 1875 by the handsome majority of 379. During 1877 he had the misfortune to lose his wife, who had been in delicate health for several years. Mrs. Rhind left seven children. She died July 15, 1877. In the fall election of 1881, Mr. Rhind was again a candidate for the office of register of wills, and was nominated by the Republican convention which met in Cumberland, October, 1881, by acclamation ; he was elected Nov. 8, 1881, by the large majority of 685 over the most popular candidate the Democratic party could select, and the majority of 101 over both Democratic and Greenback-Labor party combined. Of five sons, three by his mother's first and two by her second marriage, John Rhind is the only survivor. His eldest brother, Wm. Rhind, died in Australia. James Laing, her eldest son by the second marriage, is buried at Linlithgow, Scotland, and Robert Laing, her youngest, at Canton, China. His mother is buried in Rose Hill Cemetery, Cumberland.

In religion Mr. Rhind is a firm believer in the doctrines of the Presbyterian Church. Courteous and accommodating to all who have business with his office, methodical and painstaking in the discharge of its duties, his selection for a second term sufficiently attests the estimation in which he is held by the community in which he has passed so many years of his life.

Cumberland Bar and Representative Men.—Owing to the multiplicity of legal controversies concerning coal, railroad, and other corporations which have arisen in Allegany County, Cumberland has for many years presented a specially inviting field for members of the legal profession. The questions involved have often been of a peculiarly abstruse and difficult character, demanding great research, close powers of analysis, and the highest type of legal talent. For these reasons the bar of Allegany has long enjoyed a distinctive reputation, and many of its members have attained the highest rank of the profession.

In making comparisons between the lawyers of the past and present, it must not be forgotten that much more is demanded of advocates nowadays than was the case a hundred or even fifty years ago. The rules and forms of practice have been greatly simplified, statutes codified, reports made more complete and comprehensive, and the profession wears much more the aspect of a science than formerly. But at the same time the sphere of the advocate has both widened and deepened enormously. Precedents and rulings have multiplied on all sides, and the *juris-consult* must nowadays be ready at a moment's warning to thread the intricate labyrinths of a dozen branches of science which had no existence in the times of Martin and Pinkney. Then expert testimony was almost unknown, now it is called in the majority of important issues. Patent law, railroad law, telegraph law, all open new and most arduous fields to the profession, and compel it to specialize itself more and more every day. Business law is assuming a thousand new shapes, each more complicated than the other, nor can the vast body of decisions, rapidly as it accumulates, keep pace with the ever-swelling volume of new issues daily coming up for adjudication. A lawyer who would embrace the whole scope of his profession nowadays must travel very far beyond Coke and Blackstone, Chitty and Greenleaf, Kent and the code. He must be an accountant, a civil engineer, an architect, a mechanician, a chemist, a physician, he must know the vocabulary and technology of all the arts and professions, he must be a theologian and a metaphysician, with the experience of a custom-house appraiser and the skill in affairs of an editor. And after all, with all these stores in his possession, so great is the competition that he may scarcely be able to hew out a living in his profession.

Hon. William Walsh, the leading member of the bar of Cumberland, and one of the most distinguished lawyers in Maryland, is a native of Ireland, having been born in Killennore, near Tullamore, King's County, on the 11th of May, 1828. John Walsh, his father, was also born in Killennore, and died there in 1844. His mother, whose maiden name was Sarah Doran, came to America after the death of her husband, and lived at Harper's Ferry with her brother, Richard Doran, who was successfully engaged in business at that place. Mrs. Walsh died Sept. 8, 1858. The Doran family had settled at Harper's Ferry early in the century, and some of the Walsh family were also among the early inhabitants of the neighborhood. William Walsh remained at his father's home in Ireland until he had reached his fourteenth year. He was all this time undergoing a thorough course of education, which laid the foundation of his future success in the profession in which he has achieved such prominence. In 1842, at the earnest solicitation of his uncle, Richard Doran, he left his home in Ireland and came to America, to carve out his future among the people of the republic, which he had been taught to love with only less affection than he felt for his own unhappy land. After his arrival in America he was engaged in business at Harper's Ferry with his uncle for about two years, after which he was admitted to Mount St. Mary's College, at Emmittsburg, where he remained for four years, applying himself with diligence, and left that institution to attend the law-school at Ballston, near Saratoga, N. Y. From this institution he returned to Virginia, and completed his law studies at Charlestown, Jefferson Co., under the direction of the distinguished lawyer, Andrew Hunter, in whose office he remained for two years after he had, in 1850, been admitted to the bar.

Mr. Walsh finally determined to establish himself in law practice at Cumberland, and in 1852 opened his office in that city, where he has remained ever since, and where he has achieved the foremost place in his profession, and in a long and busy life has won by his remarkable talents, lofty integrity, and rare generosity of character the affection and admiration of every class and condition. His career has been rather in the line of his profession than in the more turbulent course of partisan politics. It was not possible, however, that the sterling worth of such a man should fail to attract public attention, and had he been disposed to engage actively and persistently in the arena of politics, it is highly probable that no honor which could be conferred upon him by the people of Western Maryland, or of the State, would have been withheld. His disposition, however, has been to shrink from political entanglements and official responsibility, preferring to rest his fortune and his fame upon his accomplishments in a profession which has always been his pride, and in which he has gained so much distinction.

William Walsh

Mr. Walsh has not, however, been able to escape entirely from public duties. In 1874, when the Democrats felt the necessity of selecting a strong candidate for Congress against the Hon. Lloyd Lowndes, Mr. Walsh was nominated, and although, in 1872, Mr. Lowndes had been elected by 1700 majority, he was defeated by Mr. Walsh, who not only overcame the Republican majority of 1872, but was handsomely returned, and took his seat as a member of Congress on the 4th of March, 1874. In the next congressional campaign (1876) he was again a candidate, and was again elected, his opponent being Louis E. McComas, of Washington County. At the end of his second congressional term Mr. Walsh returned to the practice of his profession, declining to be a candidate for re-election, and although his name has been prominently mentioned in connection with the Democratic nomination for Governor, he has not filled any other official position of distinction.

Mr. Walsh served on the Democratic ticket in 1860 as elector, and was chosen a Presidential elector on the Democratic ticket in 1872, voting with the Electoral College for Horace Greeley for President. He was a member of the Constitutional Convention of 1867, and his legal attainments and abilities had full scope in the formation of the present constitution of the State, some of the most important provisions of that instrument having been suggested or formulated by his hand. His thorough knowledge of the law was in constant demand during the deliberations of the convention, and he took a prominent part in the discussions which arose from time to time. During his whole career Mr. Walsh has been a zealous Democrat, but, although he has been identified to some extent with politics, his distinction rests chiefly upon his record as a lawyer of commanding ability and upon his contributions to legal knowledge. He is a successful advocate as well as a safe counselor, and is one of the best-equipped lawyers in this or any other State. His comprehension of intricate points seems almost intuitive, while his fund of knowledge regarding abstruse questions is apparently inexhaustible. His mind is of an analytic character, and his judgment unusually accurate. He unites a generous temper with broad and catholic views, and is in every sense a nobleman whose patent comes from nature herself. His personal influence among his immediate neighbors is almost unlimited. He is trusted, respected, and loved by men of every type of character. The laboring classes equally with the wealthy and influential hold him in the highest esteem, and among them his word is law. The influence for good which he exerts among the miners especially has been of great value more than once to the community in times of trouble and distress.

In May, 1858, Mr. Walsh married Marian Shane, daughter of John and Margaret Shane, of Cumberland, and nothing has marred the happiness of their wedded life except the frequent presence of death within the family circle. Mrs. Walsh is a lady of great accomplishments and refinement, a devoted wife, and a most loving mother. Mr. and Mrs. Walsh are special benefactors of the Academy of the Visitation at Wilmington, Del., where their only daughter, Clara, is now being educated. Both are consistent and practical Christians,—kind, hospitable, and charitable to the poor and afflicted.

Seven of their children have died in infancy, but the severest blow was the death of their oldest daughter, Mary, an amiable girl of seventeen, with more than an ordinary share of brilliancy of intellect and high moral rectitude. She graduated with the highest honors at the Academy of the Visitation, Wilmington, Del., in June, 1880, but returned the following September to continue her music, painting, and French, in which branches she excelled beyond her years. Her early death was a great blow to her father, for whom she had a great fondness, and left a void in the hearts of her teachers and friends that cannot be filled.[1]

Clara, a younger daughter, is now pursuing her studies at the academy where her sister was educated. She is a bright, promising girl, and bids fair to rival her sister Mary's talent for music on the harp and piano, and in other fine and useful arts, and to become a brilliant ornament to society.

There are two children living, Clara Teresa, who

[1] The high esteem in which Miss Mary Walsh was held is touchingly displayed in the following paragraphs in the leading papers of Cumberland at the time of her sad death. The one thus testifies to her many virtues:

"While her mind and hand were trained in varied accomplishments, her heart was nurtured in Christian virtue, and she was as modest and unassuming as she was gifted. She was greatly beloved by all the members of her family and her friends, and particularly by her father, who almost idolized her, and feels his bereavement with much keenness. The sympathy expressed for the bereaved relatives yesterday was universal, and we express the hope that they may be able to bear the sad stroke with resignation."

The other said,—

"Brought up from childhood in the purest atmosphere of a pious academy, far from the dangers of the world, she had every opportunity to advance in piety and in literature. Nor was she wanting in either respect. With quick apprehension she learned all that was put before her; admirable in mathematics, skilled and tasteful in music, wanting in nothing,—to grasp a subject was with her to retain it always,—to see was the equivalent of learning."

was born Nov. 21, 1867, and of whom mention has already been made, and William Edward, who was born June 25, 1860, and graduated with honor at Mount St. Mary's College in 1879, at the age of nineteen. At college he was looked upon as exceptionally bright, and was the leading member of his class.

John Van Lear McMahon was a native of Cumberland, and was the only son of William McMahon, who for many years was a merchant of that city. His father was unfortunate in business, and his son was left to begin life without any resources other than his own industry, energy, and talents. He graduated at Princeton College with honor when only seventeen years of age, and studied law at Cumberland. He was admitted to the bar about 1820, and although a very young man his natural eloquence and intellectual abilities placed him at once in the foremost ranks. He continued the practice of the law in Cumberland until 1826, when he removed to Baltimore. Before leaving Allegany County, however, he was, in 1821, elected to the Legislature, in which his eloquence and pre-eminent legal abilities attracted general attention. By his able advocacy of what was known as "the Jew Bill" he greatly assisted its author, Thomas Kennedy, in securing the enfranchisement of the Hebrew residents of Maryland. Mr. McMahon was elected to the Legislature again in 1824. When in 1826 he commenced the practice of the law in Baltimore, the bar of that city was famous for the number of its able lawyers and eloquent orators.

Mr. McMahon, however, soon took rank among them, although his experience at first appears to have been rather discouraging. In 1831 he published the first volume of his exhaustive and able "History of Maryland," but professional duties intervening which absorbed all his time, he never finished this valuable work. Mr. McMahon gradually obtained an extensive and lucrative practice, and soon came to be regarded as one of the ablest lawyers in the State, especially on constitutional questions. His memory was remarkable, and his knowledge of the decisions in the courts of the various States is said to have been a never-ceasing source of astonishment to his brethren of the profession. His voice was of great volume and power, and as a political orator he had few superiors among his contemporaries.

In 1861 he was stricken with partial blindness, and was compelled to employ persons to read to him. So insatiable was his thirst for current information, as well as for general literature, that he would listen to his reader morning, afternoon, and night, day after day. His affliction was doubly painful from the nature of the disease from which he suffered. All shades and tints of colors were constantly flitting before his eyes, whether opened or closed, causing him continual irritation and distress. He bore his sufferings, however, with wonderful fortitude, and was cheered by the devoted attentions and tender ministrations of his family, who surrounded him with every comfort and consolation that the ingenuity of love could suggest. Mr. McMahon died on the 15th of June, 1871, at the age of seventy-one.

Thomas Jefferson McKaig was born at Steubenville, Ohio, on the 4th of November, 1804. His grandfather emigrated to this country from the north of Ireland in 1759, settling in Adams County, Pa. His father, Patrick McKaig, was born in Cork in 1758, and was but a few months old when he arrived in America. He married Rachel Star, a native of Adams County, and the granddaughter of Robert Stuart, who held a command under the Pretender at the battle of Culloden, escaping with him from Scotland to France, and subsequently emigrating to this country and settling in Adams County.

A few years after their marriage they removed to Steubenville, Ohio, and about 1806 moved to Columbiana County, in the same State, where they took up their residence upon the west fork of Beaver River, in the midst of an unclaimed forest, and in a region over which the Indians still held partial sway. Burdened with the maintenance of a family of thirteen children, and dwelling in a country where rapid accumulation of wealth was impossible, the father could do but little to assist the youthful ambition of young McKaig to obtain a liberal education. Aided, however, by one of his brothers, he succeeded in his object, graduating with the degree of Bachelor of Arts at Washington College in October, 1826, from which, as well as from Cannonsburg, or Jefferson College, he afterwards received the degree of A.M. He had now realized the first step of his ambition, but his resources were exhausted, and he left college with only ten dollars in his pocket. Too independent to ask further aid from his generous brother, he turned his face eastward, and taking the stage arrived in Cumberland, Md., on the 3d of October, 1826, with a capital of one dollar and twenty-five cents. But happily Fortune had guided his steps in the right direction, and he found at Cumberland the opportunity which he was seeking. The Allegany County Academy needed a principal, and Mr. McKaig secured the position, which he held for eight years. Under his management the institution, which had been fast falling into a decline, was infused with new life, so that when he resigned in 1834 the number of pupils had increased

Thomas J. McKaig

from seventeen at the beginning of his administration to one hundred and fifty, and was one of the best-regulated and most flourishing schools in the State. Mr. McKaig was a born teacher, and had his energies and talents not been devoted to wider fields, would have made a brilliant mark as an educator and instructor. But his ambition had not yet reached its goal, and in the intervals of scholastic duties he prepared himself assiduously for the bar, to which he was admitted in April, 1831. He continued his labors at the academy for several years longer, however, and only relinquished them at the imperative command of his physicians, who told him that he must either give up the academy, the law, or his life, and he therefore abandoned in October, 1834, what had become to him a labor of love, and devoted his entire energies to his profession.

His success at the bar was immediate. He argued a case alone on the day of his admission, receiving a fee of fifty dollars for his services, and on the second day tried another case unassisted, gained it, and received a fee of one hundred dollars. Some idea of his rapid success may be gathered from the fact that at the second court after his admission to the bar he had fifty-six cases out of one hundred and twenty-two on the docket. This early promise was followed by a professional career of exceptional success and brilliancy, and it is no exaggeration to say that when Mr. McKaig retired from the active practice of the law he stood in the very front rank of his profession. He was counsel for the Baltimore and Ohio Railroad at Cumberland for thirty-nine consecutive years, and argued many of the most important cases which came before the Maryland Court of Appeals. During the course of his long professional career he was frequently called upon to try cases of peculiar importance in Virginia, Pennsylvania, and Ohio, and was often employed in association with or against such men as John V. L. McMahon, John Nelson, William Schley, Charles F. Mayer, S. Teackle Wallis, and I. Nevett Steele during the brightest days of the Maryland bar. Gifted with a wonderful memory and an intellect of great natural strength, and possessing a mind which had been brought to a high state of discipline by his experience as a teacher, and which could utilize on the instant any of the large stores of knowledge which had been laid up in the early days of his professional life, he became a power in the legal forum, and in certain departments stood almost unrivaled. He excelled especially in the combination and presentation of the facts of a case before a jury, or in any argument which chiefly demanded the possession of logical force and clear statement. In 1872, after a long and honorable career of more than forty years, he retired from active practice, to the regret of the public and of his large and constantly increasing clientage.

Mr. McKaig began life as a Whig, but his connection with that party was due rather to early associations and his strong personal attachment to Mr. Clay than to actual belief in its political doctrines. In 1849 he ran as the Whig candidate for Congress against William T. Hamilton, the present Governor of the State, and was defeated by only one hundred and sixteen votes in a total vote of twelve thousand. After the death of Mr. Clay the only tie that bound him to the Whigs was severed, and under the belief that that party was becoming imbued with Abolition tendencies, he declined to act any longer with it, and supported Gen. Pierce against Gen. Scott. In 1854 he was elected to the Legislature to urge the completion of the Chesapeake and Ohio Canal to Cumberland, and in 1859 was elected to the State Senate from Allegany County, being a member of the memorable Legislature of 1861.

While an earnest Democrat, he was opposed to secession, and was placed at the head of the committee which visited President Davis at Montgomery, Ala., for the purpose of bringing about a peaceable adjustment of the difficulties of that period. He delivered an eloquent and forcible address before the Confederate President and cabinet, portraying the folly of resistance, and picturing in almost prophetic language the actual course of events.

The government considered his mission to Montgomery as an effort to take the State out of the Union, and Mr. McKaig was arrested after his return and imprisoned in Fort McHenry, where, however, he was kindly treated, and from which he was soon released. In 1867 he was elected and served as a member of the Constitutional Convention, and took a leading part in the proceedings of that important body.

Mr. McKaig served for several years as colonel of the Fiftieth Regiment, and was subsequently appointed brigadier-general of the Maryland militia. In 1879, in addition to the titles previously received from other institutions of learning, he was honored by St. Mary's College, at Emmittsburg, with the degree of LL.D.

Gen. McKaig was brought up as a Presbyterian, but has since become a member of the Catholic Church. Since his retirement from the profession his residence has been at "Rockland Farm," Washington Co., Md., one of the most beautiful country-seats in the State.

Gen. McKaig married Margaret Ann Tilghman,

youngest daughter of Dr. Frisby Tilghman, of Washington County, and granddaughter of Louisa Lamar, who was the daughter of Col. William Lamar, of Revolutionary memory. His children are Frisby Tilghman and Nina Lamar McKaig.

B. M. F. Hurley was born in Chewsville, Washington Co., Md., in 1839, and was educated at Rock River Seminary, Illinois, and at Franklin and Marshall College, Pennsylvania. He began life as a teacher, but afterwards adopted the profession of law, and was admitted to practice in 1861. From his twenty-first year he was a school commissioner, and a justice of the peace up to 1861, at which time he resigned to accept a clerkship in the Post-Office Department. During the same year he was transferred to the Attorney-General's office, and soon afterwards, at the request of Hon. S. P. Chase, then Secretary of the Treasury, he was appointed to a clerkship in the office of that gentleman. He was deputy surveyor of Kansas Territory in 1860. In August of the following year he was appointed Military State agent at Washington, D. C., and in June, 1863, was elected councilman for the Fourth Ward of the city of Washington. After this he was reappointed a clerk in the Second Auditor's office of the United States Treasury, and designated again as Military State agent by Governor Bradford. In 1864, Mr. Hurley was appointed by President Lincoln, upon the recommendation of ex-Governor Francis Thomas, Reverdy Johnson, and Henry Winter Davis, Secretary of Washington Territory, but declined on account of the meagreness of the salary attached to that office. In 1865 he was designated by Mayor Wallach, of Washington, D. C., as school trustee for the Third and Fourth Wards of that city, and resigned all his positions to accept that of assessor of internal revenue for the Fourth Congressional District of Maryland, which appointment was tendered him by President Johnson. In March, 1867, Chief Justice Chase, of the Supreme Court, appointed him register in bankruptcy for the Fourth Congressional District of Maryland. Mr. Hurley then removed to Frederick, Md., and entered upon the discharge of the duties assigned him. In 1871 the State of Maryland was divided into six congressional districts, and Mr. Hurley was transferred to the Sixth Congressional District, R. Stockett Matthews becoming his successor. From the city of Frederick Mr. Hurley was sent, in 1871, as a delegate to the National Commercial Convention which met in Baltimore. About this time he removed to Cumberland, where he has since resided. In 1876 he was appointed a commissioner to take testimony for the Alabama Claims Commission. In May, 1879, he was nominated by the Republicans of the Fifth Ward of Cumberland as their candidate for councilman, and was elected by the largest majority ever obtained by either a Democrat or Republican in the ward he represents. In 1880 he was elected president of the City Council, a position he still holds. Mr. Hurley was admitted to the bar of the United States Supreme Court in 1867, and still practices his profession.

Henry W. Hoffman, a distinguished lawyer of Cumberland, was a representative from Western Maryland in Congress from 1855 to 1857. He was subsequently sergeant-at-arms of the House of Representatives, and was appointed by President Lincoln collector of the port of Baltimore. Since his retirement from that position he has resided in Cumberland, engaged in the active practice of his profession. At the centennial celebration in Cumberland, on the 4th of July, 1876, he delivered a masterly oration, and on a number of occasions has delivered public addresses, which have been marked by unusual breadth of thought and attractiveness in delivery. Mr. Hoffman justly ranks as one of the most eloquent speakers in Western Maryland, and occupies a high position at the bar.

William Wallace McKaig was born in New Lisbon, Columbiana Co., Ohio, Jan. 2, 1806. His parents were among the original settlers of that section of Ohio, and owned an extensive landed property near New Lisbon, upon which they resided. At the age of nineteen he was matriculated at Washington College, Pennsylvania, from which institution he graduated three years later. He then removed to Cumberland and commenced teaching in the English Department of the Allegany County Academy, of which his brother, Thomas J. McKaig, was at that time the principal. In this occupation he was engaged about fourteen months, during which time he assiduously devoted every moment of leisure to the study of law, under the instruction of Brice W. Howard, then considered the ablest lawyer in Cumberland. Not satisfied with the progress he was making, and desiring to give his whole time to his legal studies, he returned to Ohio and entered the office of Hon. Andrew W. Loomis, the foremost lawyer of his day in that section of the State. He was in a short time called to Baltimore, to take the place of his brother in a select school in that city, and while there was admitted to the bar of Baltimore. He then returned to New Lisbon, and commenced the practice of his profession in April, 1831. In 1833, Mr. McKaig was elected prosecuting attorney of Columbiana County. While holding this position he was twice elected clerk of the Senate of Ohio, and was also appointed paymaster-general on the military staff of Governor Lucas. Upon the termination of his term of office as clerk of the Senate he was elected a member of that body, taking his seat as the youngest member. He was again nominated to this place, but declined, and was defeated by three votes for the nomination as the Jackson Democratic member of Congress. He successfully pursued his profession in New Lisbon until 1839, when he removed to Cumberland and entered into partnership with his brother, Gen. Thomas J. McKaig. For nearly forty years the firm of McKaig & McKaig enjoyed an exceptionally large practice, and maintained a reputation for legal ability and attainments unsurpassed in Western Maryland. In 1843, Mr. McKaig was elected a member of the Legislature of Maryland, and in May, 1855, immediately after the incorporation of Cumberland as a city, was elected its first mayor. These were the only two political offices he could be induced to accept. For seven years he was president of the Frostburg Coal Company, and was one of the principal owners of the Cumberland cotton-factory. He was also closely identified with other leading institutions of the city. He died June 22, 1880.

Josiah H. Gordon, the oldest practicing lawyer of the Allegany County bar, was born in 1816, near Chambersburg, Franklin Co., Pa. He read law with Gen. McKaig, of Cumberland, and was admitted to practice in 1844, since which time he has devoted himself uninterruptedly to his profession. He has tried twenty-two murder cases, and more ejectment suits than any attorney in the State. He was elected prosecuting attorney of Allegany County in 1852, and served five years, being the first person elected to this office under the new constitution.

Thomas Perry, son of the late Roger Perry, under whom he studied law, was admitted to the Allegany bar in 1828. In 1834 he was elected to the Legislature. In 1844 he served upon the electoral ticket of his party in the memorable Clay and Polk canvass, and in the following year was elected to Congress over Jacob Snively, and served for two years. In 1851 he was elected judge, and presided over the circuit composed of Allegany and Washington Counties for ten years. In 1861 he was a candidate for the same position, but was defeated by Judge Weisel, as the latter had been defeated ten years before by the former. After this, his only defeat, to use his own expression, " he returned to his first love,—the practice of the law." In the spring of 1867 he was elected a member of the Constitutional Convention of Maryland, and in the fall of that year, and for the second time, was elected to the bench as judge of the Fourth Judicial Circuit, in company with Judges Alvey and Motter. He died June 27, 1871.

H. G. Worthington was born in Cumberland, Md., Feb. 9, 1828, and having studied law, was admitted to the bar in 1851. He removed to Tuolumne County, Cal., where he remained until 1856. After spending some time in Central America and Mexico he resumed the practice of law in California. In 1861 he was elected to the State Legislature from San Francisco. In 1862 he removed to Nevada, and settled in Austin, and was elected the first representative in Congress from that State, taking his seat in the second session of the Thirty-eighth Congress. He was appointed in 1868 minister to Uruguay.

Among the leading lawyers of Western Maryland James M. Schley, of Cumberland, deservedly occupies a conspicuous place, both on account of his extensive legal attainments and his natural aptitude for the profession. He possesses a clear, logical mind, with unusual power of analysis, is deeply versed in the law, and is a forcible and eloquent speaker. James McCannon Schley was born at Frederick City, Md., and is the son of the late Frederick A. Schley, who, in the full vigor of his professional life, had no superior at the bar of Western Maryland. His mother was Eliza Asbury Schley, whose father was James McCannon, of Baltimore City. His father, Frederick A. Schley, was the son of John Jacob Schley, whose father was John Thomas Schley, the immigrant who built the first house in Frederick Town in 1746. The Schleys were among the earliest settlers of Western Maryland, and have contributed as largely as any other family towards building up that section of the State. James M. Schley's mother, who was born Sept. 10, 1794, died suddenly in 1816, leaving two sons,—George, afterwards a distinguished lawyer of Hagerstown, and James M. The latter was sent to Princeton College, and, after finishing the course at that institution, returned to Frederick City and began the study of the law. After being admitted to the bar, he commenced the practice of the law in his native county, and was elected a member of the House of Delegates in 1841. He subsequently declined a nomination for State senator, and in 1843 removed to Cumberland, where he has since resided. In 1845 he was elected to the House of Delegates from Allegany County, leading his ticket by one hundred and fifty votes. Shortly after the death of Attorney-General George Robinson, Robert J. Brent, who was appointed by Governor Lowe to fill the vacancy, made Mr. Schley deputy State's attorney of his county. In 1855 he was elected State's attorney. The same convention which nominated him for State's attorney first nominated him for the State Senate by acclamation, but for the second time he declined a nomination for that position. He served as State's attorney nine and a half years. After the death of Judge Thomas Perry, a Democratic delegation from Allegany to the nominating convention favorable to Mr. Schley as a candidate for the judgeship was chosen, but his brother, George Schley, received the nomination, and

was defeated by Hon. George A. Pearre. Since then Mr. Schley has devoted his time to the practice of law. He is president of the Third National Bank of Cumberland, and also of the Pennsylvania Railroad in Maryland. In 1880 he was the Democratic candidate for Congress in opposition to Hon. M. G. Urner in the Sixth District, but his party being in a minority he was defeated.

Mr. Schley has been prominently identified during the past thirty-five years with all the various public enterprises which have been inaugurated in Cumberland. He was largely instrumental in securing the construction of the water works, and in the erection of the new jail, the court-house, and the city hall, besides assisting in many other works of improvement which have contributed materially to the growth and advancement of the city. Mr. Schley married, in Hagerstown, Ellen N., daughter of Otho Holland Williams Stull, who is a member of the Protestant Episcopal Church at Cumberland. Mr. Schley himself is a Presbyterian. In addition to other public positions, Mr. Schley, who has always taken a warm interest in the maintenance of a creditable militia organization throughout the State, has commanded a rifle company of Frederick and the Allegany Guards, of Allegany, at the head of which company he was present at the inauguration of President Buchanan. Mr. Schley is a zealous Democrat, but at the same time liberal and tolerant in his political views. In the community in which he resides he possesses an enviable reputation for strict integrity, benevolence of disposition, and a kindly, genial temperament. He is one of the leading business men of Cumberland, as well as one of the ablest members of its bar, and enjoys the respect and good will of people of all classes and all shades of opinion.

William Brace was born in Allegany County, Md., Nov. 23, 1850, and was the eldest of seven children of William and Susan (Stafford) Brace. His grandparents emigrated from Wales and settled in Connecticut, and his father, who was a native of that State, was a soldier in the Mexican war. He was wounded a number of times, but served through the war. At its close he settled in Maryland, and was employed in the engineer corps in the construction of the Baltimore and Ohio Railroad. After closing his engagement with the railroad company he settled in Cumberland, where he followed civil and mining engineering and surveying, and devised and superintended the construction of many of the mining improvements now in use in the coal regions. He married Susan Stafford, of Virginia, and their children were William; Mary, who died in infancy; Charles H., a physician in Cumberland; Harry C., lawyer; Sue C., wife of Stanley Hitchins, a resident of Philadelphia; Thomas, died at the age of ten years; and Theodore, living with his mother at Cumberland. The father died at Cumberland in September, 1875.

William Brace (son of William) received his education at the Cumberland Academy, supplemented by a number of years of private instruction under the Rev. J. W. Nott. At the age of nineteen he commenced the study of law in the office of Judge Pearre at Cumberland. He was admitted to the bar Oct. 18, 1871, and at once entered upon the practice of his profession in the office of Judge Pearre, the latter having been elected to the position of associate judge of the Fourth Judicial Circuit of Maryland. From the first Mr. Brace took high rank in his profession, and has built up a constantly-increasing practice. In 1876 he formed a partnership with Benjamin A. Richmond, under the firm-name of Brace & Richmond. The firm has always done its full share of

William Brace

Saml P. Smith

the legal business of the locality. Mr. Brace is a Republican in politics, and has for a number of years been among its most active workers. In the fall of 1873 he received the nomination of his party for the House of Delegates, and was elected. He was renominated, but, with the entire delegate ticket, was defeated. He was again nominated in the fall of 1877, and was the only candidate on the Republican Legislative ticket who was elected. In the fall of 1881 he was nominated for candidate to the Senate, and was elected over J. B. Oder, a popular candidate of the Democratic party, after a hotly-contested campaign. These positions of honor and public trust to which Mr. Brace has been called sufficiently attest the confidence and esteem in which he is held by the community among whom his life has been passed.

Mr. Brace is a Past Master of Ohr Lodge, A. F. and A. M.; Past Grand of Chosen Friends' Lodge, I. O. O. F.; Past Chancellor of Cumberland Lodge, K. of P.; and is a member of the Knights of Honor, and also of the Legion of Honor. He married, June 17, 1879, Maggie, daughter of James B. and Margaret Thomas, of Frostburg.

Physicians.—The first resident physician remembered in Cumberland was Dr. Murray, who studied medicine in Annapolis. He settled in Cumberland about the time the town was laid out, and practiced as late as 1814. He was a fine physician of the old school, a thorough believer in calomel and jalap and phlebotomy, and a great favorite with the people. The next who located was Dr. John M. Reid. He was born in Montgomery County, and was the son of an Episcopal clergyman of some note. He died in 1822. After him came Drs. Price and Reese, and the latter was still in practice in 1813. The next to settle was Dr. Lawrence, who remained until after the fire of April 14, 1833, in which his house, furniture, and medicine were burned. He then left for Baltimore, and subsequently removed West. Dr. Samuel P. Smith came to Cumberland Feb. 20, 1820, and is still engaged in the practice of his profession. At that time Cumberland was a town of but eleven hundred inhabitants. Dr. Smith was born Dec. 21, 1795, near Frederick, Md. His father was Joseph Sim Smith, of Taneytown, Frederick Co., and his mother was Elizabeth Price, of Frederick. Joseph Sim Smith died about 1823, and his wife a year or two later. They had ten children,—John, Samuel P., Thomas, Benjamin, Clement, Eliza, Mary, Rebecca, Matilda, and one other. All the daughters are now dead except Matilda, who married Col. Henry Naylor, in Washington City. Rebecca married Reuben Worthington, of Montgomery County, and raised a large family of children. John, who was then mayor of Washington, married Miss Cox. Benjamin P. Smith married Miss Price, his cousin, daughter of Benjamin Price, of Leesburg, Loudon Co., Va. Dr. Samuel P. Smith was educated at the Leesburg Academy, and began the study of medicine in the office of Dr. Bradley Tyler, of Leesburg, who afterwards married Miss Murdock, of Frederick, and removed to the latter place. Dr. Smith went to Frederick, resumed his studies with Dr. Tyler, and subsequently removed to Baltimore, where Dr. Colin Mackenzie was his preceptor. He was for two years in the Maryland University Hospital in that city, and graduated in March, 1817. He then commenced the practice of medicine in Taneytown, where he remained three years, when he removed to Cumberland, where he has resided ever since. In 1814, Dr. Smith joined Capt. Kitzmiller's infantry company in Leesburg, and marched to the defense of the national capital. The company was without arms, and when they reached the chain bridge at Washington they found three thousand more volunteers in the same plight, all having expected to receive equipments there. Washington was already destroyed, and Capt. Kitzmiller's company marched to Rockville, Montgomery Co., and thence to Baltimore, where they were armed and stationed on Loudenslager's Hill, now Patterson Park, where Dr. Smith witnessed the bombardment of Fort McHenry. After the repulse of the British the command was ordered home, and Dr. Smith returned to Frederick and resumed the study of medicine with Dr. Tyler. In 1822 he married Margaret D. Watson, daughter of Dr. Wm. Watson, a distinguished practitioner of Bedford, Pa., who died in Cumberland in 1865, leaving no children. Dr. Smith has represented the Whig party three times in the Legislature; was a member of the Constitutional Convention of 1851, and was a director of the Chesapeake and Ohio Canal nine years, continuing as such until the work was completed to Cumberland. He has also been a director in the Second National Bank of Cumberland from its organization. Dr. Smith is a Republican in politics. He was warden of the Emmanuel Protestant Episcopal Church for a number of years, and is now a warden of the Reformed Episcopal Church. In August, 1861, he was commissioned a surgeon of the Second Maryland Potomac Home Brigade, Maryland Volunteers, and continued in service until October, 1864. During this period he had charge of two large hospitals at Keyser, W. Va. Dr. Patrick A. Healey, of Cumberland, was assistant surgeon in the same regiment. In 1864 he returned home and resumed the practice of medicine, in which he is still engaged.

When Dr. Smith came to Cumberland the National road was completed to Wheeling, and it was customary for the physicians to ride on horseback over the mountains to see their patients. Dr. Smith is the oldest physician in Maryland, and until quite recently has been in vigorous health. He stands undoubtedly at the head of his profession in Western Maryland, and has enjoyed an extensive practice. When he first settled in Cumberland the surrounding country was almost a wilderness, and Dr. Smith's practice has been co-extensive with the counties of Allegany and Garrett. No man in that region is more widely and favorably known, and his name is a household word in almost every family. He has long been identified with the material interests and the industrial and intellectual development of Allegany County, and has contributed largely of his time and means to aid the suffering poor of Cumberland and vicinity. He is a gentleman of warm, benevolent impulses, lofty integrity of character, uncommon professional attainments, and wonderful energy, tempered by an unfailing courteousness and geniality of disposition. When he reached Cumberland, Drs. John M. Reid and Lawrence were the only physicians in the place. Dr. Smith's father-in-law, Dr. William Watson, of Bedford, Pa., attended Dr. Reid during his last illness, in 1822. In those early days the Cumberland physicians had a practice extending into Pennsylvania for many miles, and nearly to Hancock, in Maryland, and Romney, in Virginia, a mountainous region with roads (if any) hardly passable.

In 1833, Dr. J. M. Smith was practicing in Cumberland. Oct. 14, 1855, Dr. J. F. C. Hadel, a popular physician, was murdered by Frederick Miller.

Drs. Samuel P. Smith, Patrick A. Healey, Thomas M. Healey, M. R. F. Carr, M. J. Craigen, C. H. Ohr, Wardlaw McGill, W. H. McCormick, E. Herman, W. F. Fundenberg (eye and ear), G. B. Fundenberg, J. A. Fechtic (homœopathic), John A. Doerner, G. C. Perry, J. Jones Wilson, W. W. Wiley, O. M. Schindel, J. M. Smith, and D. P. Welfley are the physicians now practicing in Cumberland.

C. H. Ohr, M.D., was born in Funkstown, Washington Co., Md., Oct. 19, 1811. He was the second in a family of six children of Jacob I. and Elizabeth (Boerstler) Ohr. His grandfather, with his wife and three children (Jacob I., Henry, and Elizabeth), emigrated from Germany, and settled in Frederick County, Md. Henry, the second son, moved to Indianapolis, where for many years he carried on a mercantile business, and died there at the age of ninety-two. Elizabeth was twice married,—her first husband was a Mr. Dean; her second, George Cost, by whom she had one child. She died near Burkittsville, Frederick Co., Md., aged ninety-two. Jacob I., the doctor's father, was a tailor by trade, but for the later years of his life was employed as a merchant at Burkittsville. He died in 1853 while visiting in Indiana. His wife died about 1820 at

DR. C. H. OHR.

Funkstown. Dr. Ohr received his education at a private academy in Hagerstown, and the Military Academy at Frederick. In 1827 he entered Gettysburg College, where he remained two years. He commenced the study of medicine with Dr. G. W. Boerstler, his maternal uncle; attended the sessions of the University of Maryland, Medical Department, in 1832, '33, and '34, receiving his diploma in March of the latter year, and the same year established himself in Hancock, Washington Co. Thirteen years later (1847) he removed to Cumberland, Md., where he has since remained. In July, 1847, he introduced the use of chloroform in his practice at Cumberland. During the cholera epidemic of 1853 he introduced the use of strychnia as the treatment for that disease. Out of six hundred violent cases he lost but one hundred and thirteen. He published an article at the time in the *American Journal of Medical Sciences* on "Epidemic Cholera in Cumberland." His articles on the "Public Institutions of Allegany County" and "Preventive Medicine" were published by the State Board of Health. At the present time he is preparing for the press an article upon "Genito-Urinary Nervous Reflexes." During the war he filled the positions of acting assistant surgeon and acting post surgeon at the Cumberland hospitals. He has filled for ten years the position of consulting physician to the board of health of Cumberland. He is a member of the Medical and Chirurgical Faculty of Maryland, and was its president in 1872. He is also a member of the Allegany County Medical Society, of which he was the first secretary and its president one year, and of the American Medical Association. The doctor has taken a leading part in local and State politics for a number of years. He has served as a member of the City Council three terms; as mayor from 1859 to 1866; and as a member of the Maryland State Senate during 1864, '65, '66, and '67. As a member of the Masonic fraternity he has filled the positions of Worshipful Master of the Tonoloway Lodge at Hancock, also of the Potomac Lodge at Cumberland; Junior Grand Warden of the Grand Lodge of Maryland, afterwards Grand Master; Grand High Priest of the Grand Chapter of Maryland; General Grand King of the General Chapter of the United States; and Eminent Commander of Knights Templar. He is also a member of the Independent Order of Odd-Fellows. He married, Feb. 17, 1835, Mary, daughter of Daniel and Ann Blackwell, of Prince William County, Va. Mrs. Ohr died Oct. 10, 1875.

D. P. Welfley, M.D., of Cumberland, Md., was born in Salisbury, Somerset Co., Pa., Feb. 27, 1832. His paternal ancestors were natives of Germany. His father, Peter Welfley, was born in Frederick, Md., in 1787. Having acquired his trade at Cumberland at an early age, he emigrated to Somerset County, Pa., and became one of the founders of Salisbury. Here he followed the occupations of potter and teacher, and continued to reside there until his death, which occurred in 1867. He married Eva, daughter of Martin Weimer, who had served in the Continental army during the entire period of the Revolutionary war, and was present at the surrender of Lord Cornwallis. Mr. Welfley was one of the early settlers, and located himself three miles north of Little Meadows, and within a mile of the place on which subsequently rose the village of Salisbury. Dr. Welfley received his rudimentary education at his father's school and that of Prof. J. J. Stutzman. He spent some time in teaching and assiduously prosecuting his studies. His success as teacher, coupled with his steady and diligent habits, won for him the respect and confidence of his acquaintances generally. In 1851 he entered upon a classical and scientific course in Pennsylvania College, Gettysburg. In the winter of 1855 he commenced the study of medicine, and after the usual preliminary course in the office of Dr. H. C. Stewart, and having attended two full courses of lectures, he received from the University of Pennsylvania his degree of Doctor of Medicine. Dr. Welfley at once entered upon the practice of his profession with great zeal and earnestness at Accident, then in Allegany County,

D. P. Welfley, M.D.

Md., where he was eminently successful. Returning at the expiration of four years to his native county and State, he established himself in the practice of medicine at Salisbury, and subsequently at Grantsville, Md., securing an extensive practice, and winning the esteem of the entire community as an able and successful physician.

Seeking a wider field of labor and usefulness, he settled in Cumberland in the spring of 1873. Though he has a large general practice, he has devoted himself especially to certain diseases, in the treatment of which he has achieved some remarkable successes. Dr. Welfley ranks high in his profession, and is a careful and at the same time progressive physician. In his practice, however, he scrupulously adheres to the well-established principles, and repudiates whatever savors of empiricism. He has been earnestly devoting a considerable portion of his time to the study of public and domestic hygiene and sanitary science, especially that branch of it pertaining to the microscopical examination and chemical analysis of drinking-water, and the sanitary examination of air and food. He adopted early in life the religious faith of his parents, who were members of the Lutheran Church. Dr. Welfley has acquired a considerable literary and scientific reputation, having contributed to the press numerous articles on the subject of health and the physical sciences. He has devoted much time to the study of geology, and has written a valuable series of papers on "The Origin and Formation of Coal," "The Origin and Formation of Limestone," etc. He has a fine professional and miscellaneous library, which he greatly enjoys. He was married in 1857 to Mary E., second daughter of the Hon. Richard Fairall, and has three children,—one a son, Dr. R. H. Welfley, a graduate of the University of Maryland, located at Romney, W. Va., where he is practicing his profession, and two daughters. Dr. Welfley, Sr., has three brothers living,—Hon. B. Welfley, member of the Maryland Senate from 1878 to 1882; the Rev. J. Welfley, Lutheran minister, now in Ohio; and Israel Welfley, farmer, residing near Confluence, Somerset Co., Pa.

Oscar Melvin Schindel, M.D., was born near Hagerstown, Washington Co., Md., Oct. 21, 1849. On his father's side he is a German, on his mother's of Scotch-Irish descent. His grandfather, Samuel Schindel, was a native of York County, Pa., who in 1816 settled on a farm near Hagerstown. He married a Miss Hade, of Franklin County, Pa., by whom he had thirteen children, eleven of whom—six sons and five daughters—are still living. All are married, and eight are settled in Washington County, Md., and three in Virginia. Samuel Schindel was a large landholder, and gave to each of his children a farm. George Schindel, the eldest of his children, was born at the homestead, Jan. 12, 1818, and married Camilla Winders, September, 1846. Their children are Wilford, superintendent and partner in the firm of Huyett & Schindel, manufacturers of bone phosphates at Hagerstown; Oscar Melvin; Norman, farmer near Hagerstown; Ida and Geneva, deceased. Mr. Schindel owns and lives on the homestead farm, and is one of the most successful farmers of Washington County.

Dr. Schindel spent his boyhood at home, receiving his primary education at the common school of his native place. He was three years in attendance at the Hagerstown Academy, where he prepared for college, and entered Mercersburg College, Sept. 18, 1867. He remained to the end of the junior year, and in 1870 commenced the study of medicine with Dr. N. B. Scott, of Hagerstown, with whom he remained one year. He matriculated at the University of Maryland in October, 1871, and received his medical diploma from that institution March 3, 1873. During his connection with the University he took a special course in anatomy and physiology. In May, 1873, he began the practice of medicine in company with F. C. Doyle, M.D., at Clear Spring, Washington Co., Md., where he remained eighteen months. He re-

moved to Cumberland in January, 1875, and has since continued in the practice of his profession there. In 1875 he was appointed by the mayor and council of Cumberland as smallpox physician, in an epidemic of that disease which occurred that year. For the past four years he has been the secretary of the Allegany Medical Society. Dr. Schindel is devoted to his profession, is thoroughly read in current medical literature, and is a successful practitioner. He is a member of Emmanuel Episcopal Church of Cumberland, and in politics is a Democrat.

Charles H. Brace, M.D., was born in Allegany County, Md., Sept. 11, 1855, and is the third child of William and Susan C. (Stafford) Brace. He received his education in the schools of Cumberland, and under the private tuition of the Rev. J. W. Nott. The course of studies was selected more especially with a view of following civil and mining engineering. He received from his father a practical knowledge of engineering in all its branches, and for a time followed that profession. When eighteen years of age he projected and surveyed the suburban village of Mapleside, for Messrs. Gleason & McBride, and drew a map of the water-mains of the city of Cumberland. In 1873 he entered the office of Dr. James A. Fechtig, at Cumberland, where he remained until

Charles H. Brace M. D.

September, 1875. He matriculated at the Hahnemann Medical College of Philadelphia, attending the sessions of 1875–76 and 1876–77, and received his medical diploma from that institution March 12, 1877. During the progress of his medical studies he took special courses of study, at Philadelphia, in surgery with Prof. Charles M. Thomas, in obstetrics with Prof. O. B Gause, and in practical and surgical anatomy with Prof. A. R. Thomas. He also attended a series of surgical and medical lectures and clinics at the Pennsylvania Hospital, receiving certificates for each branch. April 10, 1877, he opened an office in Frostburg, where he continued in the practice of his profession until Dec. 1, 1879. Having then purchased the practice and good will of his former preceptor, Dr. Fechtig, at Cumberland, he removed to that city, and has followed his profession there since that time. Though among the younger practitioners of the city, Dr. Brace has been eminently successful in building up a large practice. He is enthusiastically devoted to the profession, and a firm believer in the superiority of the homœopathic school of practice. In politics he is a Republican. He married, Dec. 14, 1880, Edith M., daughter of Barney and Rachel E. (Clary) Dilley. Mrs. Brace was born in Wellersburg, Pa., May 6, 1859.

Allegany Medical Society.—In accordance with a previous notice the following gentlemen met in the office of Dr. C. H. Ohr, in Cumberland, Feb. 28, 1867,—Drs. S. P. Smith, T. A. Healy, B. A. Dougherty, William H. McCormick, M. R. F. Carr, G. E. Porter, J. M. Porter, H. C. Stewart, C. H. Ohr, and George B. Fundenberg,—for the purpose of organizing a medical society. Dr. S. P. Smith was chosen chairman, and H. C. Stewart secretary. Committees were appointed to draft a constitution, report by-laws, etc., and the following permanent officers were elected: President, Dr. S. P. Smith; Vice-Presidents, Drs. J. S. Smith and M. R. F. Carr; Recording Secretaries, Drs. P. A. Healy and W. H. McCormick; Corresponding Secretary, Dr. C. H. Ohr; Treasurer, Dr. George B. Fundenberg. The society was incorporated in the spring of 1867; the officers from 1867 to 1881 have been as follows:

1867.—Pres., Dr. S. P. Smith; Vice-Pres., Drs. P. A. Healy and M. R. F. Carr; Cor. Sec., Dr. C. H. Ohr; Rec. Sec., A. P. Duval; Treas., G. B. Fundenberg.

1868.—Pres., Dr. S. P. Smith; Vice-Pres., Drs. J. M. Porter and M. M. Townsend; Sec. and Librarian, Dr. C. H. Ohr; Treas., Dr. G. B. Fundenberg.

1869.—Pres., Dr. S. P. Smith; Vice-Pres., Drs. A. F. Gerstill and J. M. Porter; Sec., Dr. C. H. Ohr; Treas., Dr. J. C. Chew.

1870.—Pres., Dr. S. P. Smith; Vice-Pres., Drs. G. B. Fundenberg and A. F. Gerstill; Sec., Dr. C. H. Ohr; Treas., Dr. W. H. McCormick.

1871.—Pres., Dr. S. P. Smith; Sec., Dr. C. H. Ohr; Cor. Sec., Dr. G. E. Porter; Treas. and Librarian, Dr. G. H. Fundenberg.

1872.—Dr. S. P. Smith; Vice-Pres., Drs. P. A. Healy and G. H. Fundenberg; Sec., Dr. S. M. Scott; Treas., S. H. Fundenberg.

1873.—Pres., Dr. S. P. Smith; Treas. and Librarian, Dr. S. H. Fundenberg.

1874.—Pres., Dr. S. P. Smith; Vice-Pres., Drs. A. F. Gerstill and G. E. Porter; Sec. and Treas., Dr. S. H. Fundenberg; Librarian, Dr. G. B. Fundenberg.

1875.—Pres., Dr. G. Ellis Porter; Vice-Pres., Drs. G. B. Fundenberg and Wm. H. Ravenscraft; Sec. and Treas., Dr. S. H. Fundenberg; Librarian, Dr. G. B. Fundenberg.

1876.—Pres., Dr. A. F. Gerstill; Vice-Pres., Drs. G. B. Fundenberg and J. M. Porter; Rec. Sec. and Treas., Dr. S. H. Fundenberg; Cor. Sec., Dr. W. McGill; Librarian, J. M. Greene.

1877.—Pres., Dr. G. B. Fundenberg; Treas. and Rec. Sec., Dr. S. H. Fundenberg; Vice-Pres., Drs. J. D. Skilling and A. B. Price; Cor. Sec., Dr. Wardlaw McGill.

1878.—Pres., Dr. C. H. Ohr; Vice-Pres., Drs. W. McGill and D. B. Price; Rec. Sec., Dr. O. M. Schindel; Treas., Dr. D. P. Welfley.

1879.—Pres., Dr. J. M. Porter, of Frostburg; Vice-Pres., Dr. D. P. Welfley; Rec. Sec., Dr. O. M. Schindel; Cor. Sec., Dr. J. A. Doemer; Treas., Dr. J. Jones Wilson.

1880.—Pres., Dr. S. P. Smith; Vice-Pres., Drs. J. Jones Wilson and Thomas A. Healy; Treas., Dr. W. W. McCormick; Cor. Sec., Dr. J. A. Doemer; Rec. Sec., Dr. O. M. Schindel.

1881.—Pres., Dr. Thomas A. Healy; Vice-Pres., Drs. P. Jones Wilson and W. W. Wiley; Rec. Sec., Dr. O. M. Schindel; Cor. Sec., Dr. J. A. Doemer; Treas., Dr. J. Jones Wilson.

The society numbers thirty-one members, and meets on the first Tuesday of every month. This organization is very flourishing, and is said to be the most progressive of its kind in the State. It possesses a fine library of two hundred and thirty-one volumes of the choicest medical works.

The Press.—The press soon followed the establishment of Cumberland. The town was situated in a wilderness of trackless mountains, but the people who possessed the fortitude to explore and settle such a region also had the enterprise which gives birth to journalism. As early as September, 1808, mention was made by the Baltimore papers of a newspaper printed in Allegany County, but its name and place of publication were not given.

In 1812 the *Allegany Freeman* was established in Cumberland by Samuel Magill, and devoted to the interests of the Democratic party, of which it was an able advocate.

The Cumberland *Gazette* was issued for the first time by William Brown, Jan. 13, 1814. In politics it espoused the cause of the Federalists. It was a four-page paper, with four columns to the page. The issue of July 21, 1814, contains, among other interesting items, a long account of the capture of the United States frigate "Essex," and among its advertisers were Hanson Briscoe, clerk of the court, Jonathan Hendrixon, William McMahon, Dr. Reid, Peter Lowdermilk, Roger Perry, Thomas Thistle, and William Hoblitzell, names still well known and popular in the community. The following advertisement has a familiar sound:

"Notice.—The friends of Peace, in Allegany County, are respectively invited to assemble in their respective Election Districts, as soon as convenient, and choose three delegates to represent them in General Committee; the Committee will meet at Cumberland, at the house of Walter Slicer, at eleven o'clock on the first Monday in August (it being the first day) to recommend four suitable persons to represent this county in the next General Assembly."

The following has an unfamiliar sound just now:

"For Sale.—A likely, active, and healthy negro girl, well acquainted with, and accustomed to, house work.—Enquire of Printer.

"July 6, 1814. tf"

The *Alleganian*, a Democratic paper well known in Western Maryland, was established in 1820. On the 20th of February, 1846, Wm. B. Lanahan, who had published it for some time, sold it to Wm. Weber. In April, 1859, Wm. Weber disposed of his interest in it to his son, Wm. Eldridge Weber. In July, 1860, it was purchased by the friends of Hon. Stephen A. Douglas, whose election to the Presidency it advocated.

In August, 1861, during the heated political Congressional campaign and amid the excitement of the civil war, its office was destroyed and its material thrown out of the windows by a mob. In May, 1864, its republication was commenced by O. F. Mattingly. W. E. Weber published it in 1866. It is now published by J. T. Taylor, 45 Baltimore Street. It is a weekly paper, of high standing with the press of the State.

The *Western Herald* was published by Joseph Smith in 1820.

The *Maryland Advocate* was established by John M. Buchanan, in September, 1823, on the discontinuance of the *Allegany Freeman*. It was Democratic in politics. Its issue of Sept. 6, 1824, contains on the first page a large cut of a coach-and-four, labeled "Line," and surmounted by a driver who flourished about the largest whip ever swung by a Jehu. The office of the "Line" was next door to "Barnum's Indian Queen Hotel," and just where S. T. Little's jewelry establishment now stands. The "Mail Coach" on the "Line" made the trip from Baltimore to Wheeling, or *vice versa*, in three and a quarter days, while the "Accommodation" made the run in four days. Messrs. Reeside, Moore, Stockton & Co. were proprietors of the "Line." On the next page Messrs. Wm. McMahon, Thomas Thistle, and Joseph Carter were announced as candidates for sheriff of the county, while Messrs. John McNeill, Jacob Lantz, John V. L. McMahon, John A. Hoffman, John C. Graff, Lewis F. Klipstine, Thomas Cresap, and Samuel Thomas were announced as willing to serve their constituency in the Legislature.

Dr. Samuel P. Smith announced in the columns that his health having been restored, he would continue the practice of medicine here.

The most interesting feature of this issue of the *Advocate* is a long account from the pen of the gifted John V. L. McMahon, of the visit of J. C. Calhoun, then Secretary of War, to the "contemplated summit level (as it was termed) of the Chesapeake and Ohio Canal." It will be remembered that the design long held in consideration was to run the canal to the Ohio River, and it was with the view of ascertaining the most practicable route that the excursion to the "summit level" was made. Secretary Calhoun made the tour in an official capacity, as the general government at that time was taking considerable interest in the canal.

From the account of Mr. McMahon it is learned that Mr. Calhoun's party, consisting of himself, Col. Roberdeau, Maj. Abert, Thomas Kennedy, and John Hoye, repaired on the 26th of August, 1824, to the waters of Deep Creek, in Allegany County. At that point they were joined by Capt. NcNeil, James Shriver, John McHenry, and Andrew Stewart. At Deep Creek, Little Youghiogeny, Crab-tree Run, and other streams, protracted observations and experiments were made to ascertain the flow of water, etc. Dams were constructed at different points, and the capacity of the various streams thus practically tested. Mr. McMahon wrote to the *Advocate* in glowing terms of the trip, describing minutely the routes pursued, detailing every movement in the progress of the party, and paying a high tribute to Mr. Calhoun for the active part he was taking in forwarding the great work.

Oct. 23, 1830, the paper was sold by Mr. Buchanan to Richard P. Bailey and Daniel Blocher. Oct. 30, 1832, Otho Harry became a half-owner, but sold back to Mr. Blocher, June 18, 1833. Sept. 10, 1833, Mr. Blocher sold it to S. C. Parker, but bought it back October 7th following.

The *Allegany Journal*, a weekly paper, was established September, 1827, by Samuel Charles & Co., its prospectus having been issued in the Hagerstown *Torchlight* of June 7th in the same year.

The Civilian was founded by Samuel Charles, Feb. 14, 1828, and took its name from the fact of its advocacy of Henry Clay, "The Great Commoner," to the Presidency, in opposition to Gen. Jackson, a military chieftain. In 1833, after the great fire, its office was located in a new building below the Cumberland Bank, and its name changed to the *Phœnix Civilian*. In November, 1846, it passed into the hands of A. Cary, formerly of Virginia. It continued to advocate Whig men and measures with renewed ability. On the 17th of March, 1858, it was united with the *Telegraph* under the name of *Civilian and Telegraph*, and its proprietors were Evans & Maupin. The *Civilian*, of which for many years Col. W. H. Lowdermilk was editor and proprietor, is now published on Sunday mornings by the *Civilian* Publishing Company, of which Arthur Shriver is business manager. It is Republican in politics, and is printed on Baltimore Street, at the corner of North Centre Street. On May 28, 1852, Henry W. Hoffman bought a half interest in it, and became associate editor with Archibald Carey. The *Civilian* has long enjoyed the reputation of being one of the ablest and most readable county papers in Maryland.

The *Maryland Gazette* was established May 3, 1843, by Steck & Smith, with P. Roman Steck, editor. Its office was on North Mechanic Street, one door above John Gephart's store. Its first issue presented the name of John C. Calhoun as its candidate for the Presidency. It was published on Wednesdays. From its columns it is learned that Eliza McElfish kept the Sand Spring Hotel one mile west of Frostburg, and that Samuel Cessna and John Black were innkeepers in Cumberland.

The following proposals for publishing a paper with the unique name of *John Smith* were published May 10, 1843:

"It is proposed by the undersigned to publish in the town of Cumberland, Allegany Co., Md., a weekly paper entitled the *John Smith*, to be devoted to news, literature, science, and the arts, and will contain many interesting, exhilarating, and burlesque tales, anecdotes, etc., of the *Great Smith Family* of the universe.

"The undersigned has been prompted to this undertaking by the most sanguine expectations that he will be adequately supported by the public and the 'Great Smith Family' of the world; and he respectfully asks the same of the public generally and the 'Smith Family' particularly.

"The *John Smith* will be a medium through which every member of the 'Smith Family' of the whole world—be his name *John* or not—may have the pleasure of expressing his sentiments.

"As the *John Smith* will not be one of those mammoth sheets extant, communications will be published in rotation,—first come first served,—so that every *Smith* and other person will have a fair chance to figure in his own cause, provided he does not touch upon political matters.

"Should the undersigned meet with the anticipated approbation of the public, and of that multifarious 'generation' whom he designs advocating, he will issue the first number about the first of August next at the unprecedentedly low price of *Seventy-Five Cents* per annum (or two copies for $1), invariably in advance; and he hopes that no one of the noted and numerous 'Smith Family' will fail to support a paper in which their inestimable rights will be amply vindicated and adhered to. He pledges himself to support no *Political Party*; but to support the 'UNIVERSAL SMITH FAMILY,' and hopes that the *Thirty Thousand* 'JOHN SMITHS,' the Smiths in general, the Smiths' relatives, and the major part of the inhabitants of the world, will forward their names forthwith.

"If sufficiently supported he will procure able pens as contributors, which will render the *John Smith* one of the best and cheapest weekly papers in Christendom.

"Any person obtaining ten subscribers and remitting $5 in current money, will be entitled to one copy gratis. Any person obtaining twenty subscribers and remitting $10 in current money, will be entitled to one copy for two years gratis. Any person obtaining double, etc., etc., of the above number of subscribers, will be entitled to the number of copies in proportion, gratis.

"☞ Editors throughout the world will please give the above a few insertions, for which the most sincere thanks will be given, and a return of the favor when the opportunity is offered, by

"H. K. GREGG.

"CUMBERLAND, May 10, 1843."

No copy of its issues can now be found.

The Mountaineer, a weekly independent journal, was first issued Dec. 31, 1846, by Callan & Sherry, and during its brief publication was an able and spicy paper.

The Unionist was established Jan. 2, 1851, by George W. Hoover and James Evans. It was not a party journal, but independent in tone.

The Cumberland *Telegraph*, a weekly, was founded in 1851 by Hilleary A. Ogden. On April 28, 1853, T. E. Ogden disposed of his half of the paper to A. Beall, who subsequently bought Hilleary's half, and thus became its editor and proprietor. On March 17, 1858, the *Civilian* and *Telegraph* were united under Evans & Maupin, and called the *Civilian and Telegraph*. Asa Beall died in Frostburg, March 8, 1863. He was an able editor, and had served in the State Legislature. Col. W. H. Lowdermilk bought the *Civilian and Telegraph* in the summer of 1865, and became its editor.

The *Cumberland Union and Allegany County Gazette* was established by George T. Knorr, Aug. 14, 1862. It was published weekly until 1868, and in that year was published by Tingley & Steiner as the *Cumberland Union*, and still later by Mattingly & Steiner, O. F. Mattingly, editor.

The *Mountain City Times* was established April 3, 1869, by John A. Murray, Jr., & Co., in the third story of Minke's new building, No. 96 Baltimore Street. May 7, 1870, Lloyd L. Clary became associate editor, and September 17th following, editor-in-chief. At this date A. Chamberlain & Co. became the publishers. In the spring of 1873, Broydrick & Clary became the editors, publishers, and proprietors. May 30, 1874, Thomas F. McCardell became the editor and publisher.

The *Transcript*, a daily paper, was founded in May, 1869, by Col. Will H. Lowdermilk. It was published for several months and then discontinued, owing to the ill health of the editor.

April 3, 1871, George Charles & Co. issued the first number of the *Daily News*. It was subsequently sold to George Charles and Henry J. Johnson. Afterwards they dissolved partnership, since which Mr. Johnson has been sole editor and proprietor. It is published daily, except Sundays, on Baltimore Street, corner of North Centre Street. It is Republican in politics, and is edited with marked ability. Its news columns always contain the latest local, domestic, and foreign intelligence, and in every department it is a thoroughly satisfactory and enterprising journal.

The Cumberland *Daily Times* was established May 1, 1872, and its first number was issued by Chamberlain & Co. (publishers of the *Alleganian*). Lloyd L. Clary was the editor. In the spring of 1873, Broydrick & Clary became the owners and publishers. After Mr. Clary's death (May, 1874), Thomas F. McCardell became editor, and was associated with John Broydrick in its publication until its discontinuance late in 1876.

On the 10th of January, 1876, the first issue of the *Daily Alleganian and Times* appeared, published by L. G. Stephens and T. B. Taylor. Subsequently Mr. Taylor became sole owner, and changed its name to the *Daily Times*. It is the Democratic organ of the county, and is published daily, Sundays excepted. Taylor & Co. are proprietors, and T. Buckey Taylor, editor. Its office is on Centre, near Baltimore Street. The *Times* is a bright, aggressive journal, and its editorials are well written and forcible. It devotes considerable space to local news, and its reading matter always presents an agreeable variety.

The Independent, a weekly paper, is published at No. 5 Baltimore Street. It was founded Feb. 22, 1880, by U. S. Lowdermilk and Thompson Wickard, whose office was at No. 5 Liberty Street. Its present publisher and manager, C. E. Hambright, took charge in April, 1880, two months after its establishment.

The Leader was established in 1880, by the Leader Publishing Company, and edited by T. F. McCardell. It was printed semi-weekly at No. 10 North Centre Street, at two dollars and a half per year, and was discontinued after a few months' publication.

CHAPTER LVI.

RELIGIOUS DENOMINATIONS — CHARITABLE AND BENEVOLENT ASSOCIATIONS — SECRET ORDERS AND SOCIETIES.

The Baptist Church.—The exact date of the establishment of the Baptist Church in Cumberland cannot be fixed by any existing record. The Rev. John I. Jacobs, of *The Methodist*, is of the opinion that there was as early as 1782 an organization which subsequently disbanded. Writing in 1831, he says, "Our Baptist brethren were, I think, a little earlier in the work in this section of the country than we (Methodists) were. They made some proselytes, but gradually declined and removed away, so that but few remain at this day." The first reliable record of this denomination is only as far back as 1847 or '48, when, with seven or eight making the congregation, they worshiped in the hall above the old Pioneer engine-house on North Centre Street. The Rev. Benjamin Griffith, D.D., secretary of the Baptist Publication Society of Philadelphia, was the first missionary and also the first pastor.

The corner-stone of the First Baptist church was laid June 18, 1849, on Bedford Street, between Front and Columbia Streets. The original trustees were Rev. Dr. R. Fuller, Rev. F. Wilson, Rev. B. Griffith, Joseph H. Tucker, and A. F. Roberts. The building was consecrated Nov. 4, 1849, by the Rev. Dr. Fuller. Owing to a defect in the title to the lot, the congregation have paid twice for their property. The officiating ministers have been as follows: Rev. Benjamin Griffith, 1849 to 1852; Rev. Philip Price, 1852, for a short time; Rev. John Bray, for a short time; Rev. Mr. Brown, for six months; Rev. J. B. T. Peterson; Rev. T. P. Warren, under whom the congregation disbanded. In 1871 the Rev. H. J. Chandler, missionary, arrived in Cumberland and organized the eighteen members then there, with five more subsequently baptized, and remained the pastor until 1880, when he was succeeded by the present pastor, the Rev. E. B. Watts. Mr. and Mrs. James Landrum Holmes were sent from this church as missionaries to China, where Mr. Holmes was murdered in an insurrection.

The Ebenezer Baptist Church was organized in 1875, by the Revs. H. J. Chandler, of the Bedford Street First Baptist Church, and James Nelson, of Georgetown, D. C. The number of enrolled members was at the organization about twenty, and they worshiped in Reynolds' Block, on Baltimore Street, with the Rev. Lewis Hicks as pastor, until the present edifice was completed. When the small number of the members is considered, the building of this church may be considered a work of great courage and energy. Business was prostrated, money remarkably scarce, and the members of the congregation dependent upon their daily labor for their bread, yet they undertook to build, and completed their church. The lot was purchased of George Henderson, Jr., and deeded to Lewis Hicks, Willie Johnson, Robert Trent, Simon Bolden, and John H. Thomas, as trustees of the Ebenezer Baptist Church of Cumberland. The building is of brick, two stories in height, and forty by twenty-eight feet. The officiating pastors have been the Rev. Lewis Hicks, 1875–77; Rev. Jacob Robinson, 1877–81; Rev. M. Johnson, 1881.

Methodist Episcopal Church.[1]—In the year 1787, Cumberland, then a village of humble pretensions, had but one log meeting-house, which had been built more particularly for the Lutheran congregation, but was used in common by persons of any other denomination, and occasionally an itinerant Methodist preacher would deliver a sermon there. About that time the five or six Methodist families living in the town concluded to form a congregation, and Cumberland was placed upon the circuit as a point to be visited once a month by the circuit preacher. The leading Methodists of that time in Cumberland were James Hendrixon, Thomas Leakins, Adam Seigler, Aquilla Brown, and Dickinson Simpkins, who formed the nucleus around whom gathered a faithful band. They successfully organized a congregation, and by the efforts of the men named, the first three of whom were "local preachers," a project was inaugurated to erect a church, and after some hard work by the zealous members in the cause, the first Methodist church in Western Maryland was built, about the year 1789. It was erected upon a lot of ground given for the purpose, situated on the hill west of Will's Creek, immediately in rear of Dr. Bruce's present residence, on what is now known as Smallwood Street. It was a one-story frame building, about thirty-two by forty feet. It was furnished with a plain plank pulpit, and long, narrow benches, without backs.

The young congregation flourished, and new members were added to the flock. Among the membership were the well-known names of Irvin, Wall, Hinkle, and Twigg. Regularly every fourth Sunday the preacher upon this circuit would make his rounds. Having a very large territory, it required four weeks' regular riding every day for him to traverse the circuit. In the intervals between the visits of the circuit preacher the "locals" would preach, and these early workers in the cause of Methodism were most zealous

[1] The almost entire absence of all historic record of the early history of Methodism in Cumberland makes an account of its rise purely traditional and often inferential. Bishop Asbury, John Haggerty, and Richard Owen are regarded as the true pioneers of Methodism in that part of Maryland, but which of them was first on the ground has not been determined. Their labors date about 1782. The Revs. Francis Paytheres and Benjamin Roberts, in 1783, Wilson Lee and Thomas Jackson, in 1784, Lemuel Green, William Jessup, and John Paup, in 1785, John I. Jacobs, in 1786, all shared in the establishment of Methodism in Western Maryland. The Rev. Enoch Watson labored in 1786 and 1787, and Philip Bruce's great revival, in 1788, is among the well-remembered incidents of early Methodism in Cumberland. From 1788 to 1802 the church languished, with little life and no progress, until revived and warmed into activity by Bishop Whatcoat, who, in 1803, added over one hundred to the little congregation, in which work he was most faithfully aided by the Rev. L. Martin, a local preacher. The Revs. James Ward and Louis R. Fechtig, in 1805, revived the church and infused new zeal into its members. Allegany Circuit first appears in the general minutes of the church in 1804, with J. Paynter, Joseph Stone, and James Read as preachers, and James Ward as presiding elder.

and faithful Christians. The earliest preachers were Revs. James Ward, Mr. Matthews, and James Reid. These were men of great power in the pulpit, and whenever their day would arrive to preach the church would be filled to overflowing, people coming in from the country for miles distant. An incident is related which shows the character of the Rev. James Reid. He was a large, robust man, of at least six feet two inches in height. His voice was very loud, but musical, and he had the power to move an audience to tears or laughter at will. One Sunday afternoon Rev. "Jimmy" Reid was preaching, and during the services, while the minister was in the midst of his sermon, there came up a terrible storm of thunder, lightning, and rain. The sky was so overcast that the noonday grew dark as twilight, and the lightning, with terrific flashes, would light up the gloomy heavens, to leave them the next instant more sombre than before. The thunder rolled and vibrated until it shook the earth, and the rain came pouring down in torrents, but still the impassioned preacher continued his discourse, waxing more eloquent as the rolling of the thunder increased. At a moment when the peals were so fearful that it seemed as if the heavens must be rent asunder, the fervent speaker raised his tall figure to its full height, upturning his flushed face, and, gazing heavenward, and in his loudest voice, with impassioned eloquence, exclaimed, "*Oh, God! Thou Great Jehovah! Thou who art thundering amongst the elements, let me, Thy humble servant, thunder amongst men!*" And thunder he did. The man seemed to lose his identity, and the audience trembled as he continued to preach on in the most impassioned manner. He became so powerful that many of his hearers fled from the church out into the rain. Many fell upon their knees, and then followed one of the greatest prayer-meetings that has ever been witnessed from that day to this.

The congregation continued to increase, and services were held nearly every Sunday, and prayer-meetings during the week. In 1795, when Gen. Lee was at Cumberland with his army to suppress the "Whisky Insurrection," the chaplains of the regiment held religious services in the meeting-house. The meetings were largely attended by the soldiers. When intelligence was received in Cumberland of the death of Gen. Washington, in December, 1799, funeral services in his honor were held in the old meeting-house. Upon that occasion a militia company, organized in Cumberland, turned out, and to the tune of the "Dead March," and carrying an empty coffin, repaired to the church, where old "Father Jacobs," a nephew of the famous Capt. Cresap of the "border times," preached a funeral sermon upon the death of Washington. Services were held in the church until the year 1816, when it was found to be too small for the congregation, and a lot of ground having been secured on the east side of Will's Creek, on Centre Street, the spot now occupied by the present handsome edifice, a new church was built. It was a one-story brick building, about forty by fifty feet in size, with a gallery on three sides. Peter Schultz, James Hendrickson, John Wright, and Jonathan Peterson were prominent in the church at this time. Of the preachers who officiated during the later years in the old church the records give only the following names: Revs. Harris, Hinkle, Hanson, James Reilly, and the never-to-be-forgotten Tobias Reilly. It was by the latter's efforts, assisted by Robert Cadden and Presiding Elder Gerard Morgan, that the second church was built, and by his exertions the congregation became the largest in Cumberland. Mr. Reilly was, like the Rev. Mr. Reid, a remarkable man, and a powerful and influential preacher. He devoted much of his ministerial labors to Cumberland, a place to which he was much attached, and where now, beneath the altar of the present church, his remains lie interred. Of the ministers officiating in the second church during its early years we have the following names: Revs. Hamilton, Willis, French, Codden, Reilly, and Miller. These all occupied the pulpit prior to 1829, from which date we have a perfect record, which we publish below. In the year 1837 the second church was considerably enlarged. In 1848 it was torn down, and the third church built upon the spot at a cost of six thousand dollars. This was considered a fine church, and served its purpose until 1871, when it too had to give way to the increasing demands of the large congregation, and in August, 1871, the corner-stone of the present imposing edifice was laid by Rev. A. R. Reilly, a nephew of Tobias Reilly. This church was erected upon a spot hallowed to Methodism by associations of the past.

The last services in the third church were held by Rev. A. R. Reilly, on Sunday, April 30, 1871, and on the following morning the work of demolition was begun to clear the spot for the erection of the fourth church, an edifice that stands to-day, an ornament to the city, a credit to the builders, and an honor to the Methodists of Cumberland. The present edifice is a beautiful structure, of the Romanesque style. It was designed by Frank E. Davis, architect, Baltimore. The contract for the erection of the entire church was let to Mr. James W. Sowders, of Cumberland, for the sum of twenty-three thousand five hundred dollars. The church was completed and dedicated in 1874-75. The Baltimore Conference met in the church in 1851 and 1878. The building committee consisted of Messrs. Jesse Korns, L. R. Fechtig, Robert J. Morris, Jacob Brengle, C. W. Brengle, William Weber, John H. Young, Charles A. Seay, L. W. Brant, and Samuel T. Little.

The following is a list of the ministers who have served in this charge from 1829 to the present date:

1829-31, Charles B. Young; 1831-32, T. H. W. Monroe; 1832-33, George Humphreys; 1833-34, Hezekiah Best; 1834-35, Basil Barry; 1835-37, P. D. Lipscomb; 1837-39, S. C. Parkinson; 1839-41, James Stephens; 1841-43, Edward Allen; 1843-45, W. Prettyman; 1845-46, John A. Henning; 1846-48, James Sewell; 1848-50, Thomas Myers; 1850-52, John M. Jones; 1852-54, John Lanahan; 1854-56, W. T. D. Clemna; 1856-57, Samuel Kepler; 1857-59, A. E. Gibson; 1859-61, Benjamin Crever; 1861-63, Thomas Barnhart; 1863-66, Samuel W. Sears; 1866-69, Edward Kinsey; 1869-72, Ashury R. Reilly; 1872-74, Samuel V. Leech; 1874-75, James H. Lightbourne; 1875-76, G. G. Baker; 1876-78, W. S. Edwards, D.D; 1878, Joel Brown, A. W. Rudisil.

The number of communicants is now about four hundred.

Protestant Episcopal Church.—It was not until the year 1803 that any steps were taken to establish the Protestant Episcopal Church in Cumberland. In the parish records for that year are the names of Lynn, Bruce, Perry, Lamar, Hilleary, Beall, Thistle, Briscoe, Cresap, and Burbridge. After divine service on Easter Monday of 1803 a provisional vestry was chosen, and John Kewley was selected as delegate to the Diocesan Convention, and recommended for holy orders. The first vestry was composed of Patrick Murdoch, Hanson Briscoe, David Lynn, Upton Bruce, Robert Tivis, George Hebb, John B. Beall, and Levi Hilleary. The Rev. John Kewley was the first minister of the parish; he had previously been lay-reader. He continued to officiate until 1804, and also to minister at Cresaptown, Morley's Branch, and Old Town. His salary was one hundred pounds, equivalent then to $266.66 United States money. The holy communion was administered for the first time on the 16th day of October, 1803.

The rectorship of Mr. Kewley ended in 1804, and for a quarter of a century the parish was without a pastor, and was served only by passing clergymen. It was not until 1829 that the combined efforts of the Episcopalians and Presbyterians secured a place of worship in a brick church on Fort Hill, when, under the rectorship of the Rev. L. H. Johns, Col. Lamar and Capt. Lynn deeded the property to Emmanuel Parish. The church was consecrated and used the first time in 1830. The rectors from 1829 have been the following:

1829, Rev. L. H. Johns; 1834, vacant; 1835, Rev. Thaddeus M. Leavenworth; 1836, vacant; 1837, Rev. Mathias Harris; 1841, Rev. Samuel Buell; 1847, Rev. D. H. Buell; 1854, Rev. Henry Edwards; 1856, Rev. William Wiley Arnett, died 1859; 1859, Rev. Dr. William W. Spear, died October, 1861; 1862, Rev. Orlando Perinchief, died February, 1864; 1864, Rev. E. Owen Simpson, died July, 1865; 1865, Rev. J. B. Henry, died February, 1868; 1868, Rev. Dr. Chauncey Colton, died July, 1872; 1872, vacant; 1873, Rev. Dr. S. C. Thrall.

The corner-stone of the present church was laid in May, 1849, and the building was consecrated in 1851. From the reorganization of the parish in 1853 there has been but one register, William Hopewell Webb, the present incumbent. The number of communicants is now about one hundred and fifty. The church is a handsome Gothic structure, and stands upon the site of old Fort Cumberland.

St. Patrick's Catholic Church.—Missionary work was probably carried on in Cumberland as early as 1790 by priests from the lower counties, and the first church was, according to the best obtainable date, built about 1794-95. The "Old Church" of the oldest citizens was torn down in 1850 to make room for Carroll Hall. "St. Mary's" was the name of the "Old Church," but the new edifice, built in Father Obermyer's time, was called St. Patrick's. The pastors in charge from 1833 have been as follows:

1833, Rev. Francis X. Marshall; 1837, Rev. Henry Myers, Rev. B. S. Piot, assistant, from Mount Savage mission, until 1842; 1842, Rev. Leonard Obermyer; 1853, Rev. John B. Byrne, assistant; 1854, Rev. John B. Byrne; 1854, Rev. P. B. Lenaghan; 1856, Rev. James Carney, Rev. Michael O'Reiley; 1859, Rev. George Flaut, Rev. Edward Brennan, assistant; 1860, Rev. Edward Brennan; Rev. Edmund Didier, assistant; Rev. Father Barry, assistant; Rev. James Casey, assistant; Rev. Charles Damur, assistant; Rev. F. S. Ryan; 1881, Rev. F. Brennan, Rev. J. Mattingly, assistant.

Carroll Hall was built in 1850, and has since been used as a parochial school building. In 1866, St. Edward's Academy was built and placed under the charge of the Sisters of Mercy. It is devoted solely to the education of young ladies, and many Catholics and Protestants have availed themselves of its advantages. The present handsome parochial residence was built in 1875.

St. Patrick's church, located upon Centre Street, is a handsome brick edifice of Ionic architecture, one hundred and forty by sixty feet, with a seating capacity of one thousand.

The Lutheran Church.—The organization and active work of the Lutherans in Cumberland dates as early as May 11, 1794, when Nicholas Leyberger, John Rice, George Rizer, Andrew Harry, Christopher Brotemarkle, George Shuck, Christian Kollhoefer,

Frederick Loch, Jacob Valentine, Jacob Gauner, and John Cramer organized the first Lutheran Church, with a constitution (still extant and well preserved) in the German and Latin languages, in which the rules of church government are expressed with simplicity and vigor. A log house served as their church, and was located near the site of the present building, on the northeast corner of Centre and Baltimore Streets. Its first pastor was the Rev. Frederick William Lange. In 1839 a congregation was organized from this church of purely German Lutherans, and the original congregation continued as the English Lutherans.

The corner-stone of the present imposing edifice was laid in 1842, under the pastoral charge of the Rev. Jesse Winecoff. It owes something of its architectural beauty to the prank of an irreconcilable vestryman, who, not being able to impress his ideas of proper proportions upon his fellow-committeemen, quietly in the dead of night removed the stakes to his ideas of proportion, and the change not being discovered the foundation was dug and the walls built to a considerable height, when the length of the timbers revealed the alteration. No change was made, and the building was completed in its present elegant proportions. The church has recently been renovated in every respect, and adorned with six memorial windows, —one to W. R. McCulley, by the members of his family; one to John Rabold, by M. Y. Rabold; one to W. R. Beall, by his daughter, Mrs. Watts, of North Carolina; one to Mrs. Peterman, by Mrs. I. G. Greenfield; one to Charles Troxell, by the French family; and one to Martin Luther, by Sunday-school Class No. 8. The pastors have been:

1794–1805, Rev. Frederick William Lange; 1805–16, Rev. John George Butler; 1816–19, vacant; 1819–25, Rev. C. F. Heyer; 1825–29, Rev. N. B. Little; 1829–32, Rev. Henry Haverstick; 1832–41, Rev. John Kehler; 1841–44, Rev. Jesse Winecoff; 1844–46, Rev. Samuel Finkle; 1847–52, Rev. Joseph A. Seiss, D.D.; 1852–57, Rev. John Francis Campbell; 1857–68, Rev. A. J. Weddell; 1868–79, Rev. H. C. Holloway; 1879, Rev. J. O. McAtee.

The Rev. C. F. Heyer, affectionately remembered as "Father" Heyer, revived and reinvigorated the Lutheran congregation of Cumberland. Energetic and enthusiastic, he gathered the scattered flock and re-established worship in the church. He removed to Somerset, Pa., and was sent as the first missionary of the church by the General Synod to India.

First Presbyterian Church.—Presbyterianism in Cumberland is probably as old as the place itself,—that is, there were perhaps among the earliest sett ers some persons holding that doctrine of faith, though so few in number that for many years they held no services as a body, but worshiped God according to their belief at the family altar.

There is no record, no tradition even, of the existence of congregational Presbyterianism in Cumberland up to the close of the last century or later. The only record of early Presbyterian worship that we can learn anything of is transmitted by the memory of one of the "oldest inhabitants," well known as a prominent and useful member of the church, and one of Cumberland's most highly esteemed citizens. He remembers that about 1810 or '11, Rev. Mr. Porter, who was principal of the old academy (which stood upon the Jones lot, corner of Fayette and Smallwood Streets), preached occasionally as a Presbyterian minister in the log church belonging to the Lutherans, located on the site at the corner of Baltimore and Centre Streets, now occupied by their present church. Of Mr. Porter or his congregation nothing is definitely known.

As the country was at war with Great Britain between June, 1812, and January, 1815, and a large proportion of Cumberland's then small population was engaged in the war in some capacity, it is not likely that churches or church organizations prospered greatly during that period. Certain it is that no one seems to have any knowledge of Presbyterianism as expounded from the pulpit from the time of the departure of Mr. Porter until the arrival of a Rev. Mr. Hayes in 1815. Mr. Hayes was also principal of the academy, was a man of fine natural and acquired abilities, and had been president of Carlisle College, Pennsylvania (then under the control of the Presbyterians). He removed to Cumberland on account of his health, which was fast failing, hoping that the pure mountain air would invigorate him and the change of climate prolong his life. He was relieved, but only temporarily; the "fell destroyer" had too firm a hold upon him, and he died in a year or more after taking up his residence. His widow married again, and became the second wife of William McMahon, and stepmother of John V. L. McMahon, the brilliant lawyer.

The successor of Mr. Hayes as principal of the academy and preacher to the small body of Presbyterians was Rev. Robert Kennedy, who came to Cumberland in 1817, and remained until the spring of 1825. During his labors the congregation increased in numbers and influence.

During Mr. Hayes' time the Presbyterians had worshiped in the Lutheran church on alternate Sundays with that congregation. This arrangement was continued during Mr. Kennedy's ministry. But in 1817 a subscription paper was circulated for the "building of a church in Cumberland for the joint use of the Presbyterians and Episcopalians of the town." Two thousand one hundred and twenty-two dollars in cash was subscribed, besides Thomas J. Perry's subscription of "lot No. 68 in the fort," valued at one hundred dollars (the present Episcopal church lot). The contributions to the subscription list were extremely liberal, and the list included the names of not only Episcopalians and Presbyterians, but of several other Protestant denominations, three Catholic gentlemen, one Hebrew, and several persons not connected with any church. Among the subscribers were Wm. McMahon, Samuel Thomas, Henry McKinley, Roger Perry, James Scott, John Hoye, David Lynn, Thomas J. Perry (a lot), George Thistle, Rev. Robert Kennedy, and Thomas Beall, of Samuel, one hundred dollars each. Mr. Beall (who was the original "proprietor" of the town) subscribed with the understanding that he was to have "choice of pews next to the pulpit." Among the other names on the list are those of John Hayes, Walter Slicer, J. William Hoblitzell, Samuel Smith, Robert McCleary, John Shryer, P. Lowdermilk, Hanson Briscoe, C. Tilghman, Martin Rizer, John Hoblitzell, Henry Koons, Elnathan Russell, John McHenry, William Hilleary, Jacob Hoffman, George Blocher, Robert Swan, George McCulloh, Jacob Seass, John Gephart, Valentine Hoffman, John Hoffman, George Shuck, John M. Read, Henry Wineow, and William Magruder.

The erection of the church was commenced during the same year (1817), but owing to some legal as well as financial difficulties it was not completed until after Mr. Kennedy left. The church then built was removed nearly twenty years thereafter to allow the erection of the present fine and imposing edifice of the Episcopalian congregation.

About the year 1832 or 1833 the Domestic Board of Missions of the church sent Rev. Mr. Raymond to Cumberland, thus recognizing the church there as a "mission." For a while during his labors "joint use" was made of the Fort Hill church. His stay was short,—between one and two years,—when he went to another mission in some part of Virginia, and it is believed is still living and preaching in that State.

Mr. Raymond was succeeded (in 1834, November 11th) by Rev. S. H. McDonald, also sent by the Domestic Board of Missions, and partly supported by the board. During his ministry (in 1837) the preliminary steps for a church organization were taken, and on December 9th the organization was perfected. We find in the minutes of the board of trustees that

"At a meeting of the members of the Presbyterian congregation in Allegany County, agreeably to previous notice, held in the town of Cumberland, for the purpose of forming themselves in a body corporate, according to the provisions of an act passed by the General Assembly of Maryland in the year of our Lord 1802, Chapter 3, the Rev. H. R. Wilson (of the Carlisle Presbytery) was appointed moderator, and Thomas J. McKaig secretary. Whereupon it was resolved, upon motion of Rev. S. H. McDonald, that the members of this congregation proceed to elect thirteen trustees, according to the provisions of the aforesaid act, when the following persons were elected and duly appointed trustees of the Presbyterian congregation of Allegany County, viz.: William McMahon, James Moore, of Geo., James M. Smith, John G. Hoffman, Thomas J. McKaig, Joseph B. Hayes, Alexander King, John J. Hoffman, John Boward, John A. Mitchell, William Harness, Jeremiah Berry, Jr., Charles Heck.

"After the election of the aforesaid trustees," the minutes go on to say, "the constitution (thereafter recorded) was unanimously adopted by the congregation, and after being signed, sealed, and delivered by aforesaid trustees, before John M. Carleton and John Wright, two justices of the peace, it was duly recorded in the clerk's office of said county."

Of the first trustees, only four are now known to be living,—Dr. James Smith, Gen. Thomas J. McKaig, Alexander King, and John Boward.

After the adoption of the constitution (at the same meeting), the following resolutions were unanimously passed by the congregation:

"*Resolved*, That the trustees be and they are hereby directed to proceed to the erection of a Presbyterian church in the town of Cumberland. To this end be it

"*Resolved*, That the trustees are hereby authorized to appoint a building committee, to consist of five persons."

At the first meeting of the board of trustees, Thomas J. McKaig was elected president of the board, Joseph B. Hayes, secretary, and John G. Hoffman (father of Hon. H. W. Hoffman and George Hoffman), treasurer, and the building committee was composed of Messrs. J. J. Hoffman, James W. Smith, John G. Hoffman, Thomas J. McKaig, and James Moore.

In 1836, Richard Beall, a citizen of wealth and prominence, left, at his death, among other bequests, a lot of ground to the Presbyterian congregation upon which to build a church, if they chose so to do. This piece of ground was on the west side of Will's Creek, fronting on the present Washington Street, and contained, singular to note, the lot upon which the new church is built. It also included the Minke residence lot and the corner below the church, upon which Messrs. Spier & Sinclair's business building stands. A subscription paper had been circulated before Mr. Beall's death, but the response was not sufficiently encouraging to justify the building of a church. When the lot was bequeathed, it gave a fresh impetus to the project, and the result was the action of the congregation as stated above.

The building committee, it appears, went actively

to work, and were successful in obtaining subscriptions of such an amount as justified them in proceeding with the erection of a church. The lot, however, willed to the church by Mr. Beall was not deemed a suitable location. The street was not graded; there were no sidewalks; the approach to it on every side was somewhat difficult, and in wet seasons very disagreeable, so the lot was sold to Samuel Semmes for four hundred dollars, and the one upon which the Liberty Street church stands was bought of Robert Swan for five hundred dollars.

We have no record of the building of the church, which was completed in 1840. The congregation, still small in numbers, responded liberally to the call of the committee, and were aided by different citizens. The paid subscriptions amounted to $2596.10, a very respectable sum in those days. The treasurer's report in January, 1841, showed (by balance due him of $14.70 and note unpaid $150) the cost of the building to have been $2760.27. The church then built was about two-thirds the size of the present old church (Liberty Street), main building.

In 1841, Messrs. Smith, Moore, McKaig, King, Hoffman, Boward, Mitchell, Heck, Wm. W. McKaig, Wm. P. Sterret, Alexander B. McFarland, and Abraham Russell were elected to serve as trustees the ensuing three years.

Rev. Samuel H. McDonald continued his labors until 1843, when he removed to another mission, and was succeeded in Cumberland by Rev. B. Wall, who was installed first pastor of the church the same year. He remained there two years.

In 1845, Rev. John H. Symmes was called, and was duly installed on the 14th of June in that year. He officiated as pastor of the church for a period of seventeen years.

It appears that through an inadvertence of the congregation the board of trustees elected in 1841 held over until 1846, when a new board was chosen at a congregational meeting on the 5th of February, as follows: Messrs. Hoffman (J. J.), Moore, McKaig, Smith, Russell, Boward, Hoffman (John G.), Alexander King, W. W. McKaig, of the previous board, and Messrs. A. M. C. Cramer, John P. Agnew, G. Beall, and Joseph Dilley, new members.

At the same meeting the question of the "expediency of enlarging the church and building a schoolroom" was considered. At the first meeting of the new board of trustees, Thomas J. McKaig, who had acted as such from the organization of the church in 1837, was re-elected president; John G. Hoffman, who had served as treasurer from the time of organization, was succeeded by J. B. H. Campbell; and John P. Agnew (whose predecessors were Joseph B. Hayes, elected in 1837, and W. W. McKaig, elected in 1841), was chosen secretary.

At a subsequent meeting of the committee a building committee, consisting of Messrs. W. W. McKaig, John Boward, A. Russell, A. M. C. Cramer, and G. Beall, was appointed. Under their charge improvements were made to the building to the amount of thirteen hundred dollars.

In 1851, Messrs. Smith, McKaig (Thos. J. and W. W.), Cramer, Gustavus Beall, Agnew (all re-elected), J. H. Gordon, John Beall, John Folck, J. W. Offut, Jacob Brognier, John Oliphant, and J. B. H. Campbell were chosen trustees. Gen. McKaig was re-elected president, and John Oliphant, secretary. In 1854 seven of them—Messrs. Smith, T. J. and W. W. McKaig, John Oliphant, John Beall, Gordon, and Campbell—were re-elected, with Messrs. John E. Russell, John Jones, H. W. Hoffman, George Shaffer, J. B. Walton, and A. H. Weld as new members. The officers of the previous board were re-elected, and J. B. H. Campbell was chosen treasurer. The election in 1857 resulted in the selection as trustees of Messrs. Campbell, Oliphant, W. W. McKaig, Walton, Smith, Shaffer, and John E. Russell, of the old board, and Messrs. Boward, A. Russell, John L. Thomas, Dr. C. H. Ohr, Dr. John Everett, and James Moore, of George, new members. W. W. McKaig was elected president, and John Oliphant and J. B. H. Campbell were re-elected secretary and treasurer. In 1860, Messrs. Shaffer, Walton, Campbell, and Russell were re-elected, the remaining seven being Messrs. Cramer, J. H. Gordon, Horace Resley, A. P. Shepherd, John Beall, Frederick Minke, and George F. Shryer. A. M. C. Cramer was chosen president. Three vacancies the following year, occasioned by the death of John Beall, removal of George Shaffer, and declination of Mr. Shepherd, were filled by the election of Drs. Smith and Ohr and John Rhind.

Early in the spring of 1862, Rev. John H. Symmes tendered to the session his resignation as pastor, which was accepted by the trustees on the 2d of April, who unanimously adopted a resolution tendering to Mr. Symmes their gratitude for the zeal, ability, and industry he had displayed during his pastorate.

Mr. Symmes remained and preached to the congregation until the 6th of November following, when pastoral relations were entirely dissolved by his removal.

From that time until early in 1867 no congregational services were held in the church, which was used a considerable portion of the time as a hospital for the Union troops.

In September, 1865, a committee appointed by the Carlisle Presbytery (to which the Cumberland Church yet belonged) visited Cumberland, the object of their mission, as stated at a meeting of the trustees, being "the establishment of the means of grace within the borders of the church here." Shortly afterwards services were renewed in the Baptist church on Bedford Street. In March, 1866, Rev. James D. Fitzgerald, by invitation of the congregation, began his ministerial labors there. The congregation worshiped in the Baptist church the remainder of the year, and in February, 1867, the old church was again occupied by them.

In October, 1867, Messrs. James W. Schley, Dr. W. H. McCormick, Jacob Brown, and J. C. Orrick were elected to fill vacancies occasioned by the resignation of Messrs. Ohr, Resley, Rhind, and Russell.

On the 22d of March, 1868, at a congregational meeting, Rev. J. D. Fitzgerald was elected pastor of the congregation, and a regular "call" extended to him through the Presbytery. He accepted the call, and was duly installed as pastor in October of that year. In April, 1868, the board of trustees were re-elected, excepting the following: Messrs. Brown, Cramer, Russell, Beall, and Shaffer; Messrs. J. B. H. Campbell, Dr. Smith, John B. Widener, and Augustus Cramer being elected in their stead. Subsequently Mr. Cramer resigned, and John Cowden was chosen; he resigned in 1870, and was succeeded by William Piatt.

On June 19, 1870, the congregation adopted the recommendation of the board of trustees in favor of the purchase of the "Devecmon lot," on Washington Street, as a site, and resolved to "proceed immediately to build a church." In August the trustees' committee, consisting of Messrs. Gordon, McKaig, and Minke, concluded the purchase of the said lot (fronting sixty-four feet on Washington Street), from G. W. Case and F. Minke, for the sum of five thousand dollars. A building committee, consisting of Messrs. J. B. H. Campbell, J. H. Gordon, F. Minke, William Piatt, and W. W. McKaig, was appointed, and a plan submitted by Mr. Frank E. Davis, architect, of Baltimore, was adopted.

In May, 1871, the old church property on Liberty Street was sold to the German Reformed congregation of Cumberland for the sum of five thousand five hundred dollars. The full transfer was not made until June, 1872. The building is now designated as "Zion's" church. The contract for the entire stone masonry of the new church building was awarded to William Kavanaugh, in August, 1871, and he shortly after commenced operations. He abandoned the work in February, 1872, and Moretz Raeder completed it. J. B. Walton was the builder of the church, superintending its entire construction.

The laying of the corner-stone of the new church took place on the Fourth of July, 1871. The stone was laid with the impressive ceremonies of the Masonic order, conducted by Ohr Lodge of Cumberland, assisted by others. The clergy present were Revs. Drs. Smith and Leyburn, of Baltimore; Rev. Dr. Hays, of Chambersburg, Pa.; and Revs. Fitzgerald and Leech, of Cumberland.

At the election of trustees, Jan. 13, 1873, W. W. McKaig, J. B. N. Campbell, J. C. Orrick, J. H. Gordon, Jacob Brown, F. Minke, J. B. Walton, Dr. James M. Smith, William Piatt, O. C. Gephart, S. F. McBride, M. Sinclair, and F. W. Shryer were chosen; W. W. McKaig, president; J. B. H. Campbell, treasurer; and T. W. Shryer, secretary of the board. In April, 1873, Rev. James D. Fitzgerald resigned, and the pastoral relation was dissolved by the Presbytery of Baltimore (to which the congregation now belongs) at its session the same month. On the 14th of July the congregation unanimously elected Rev. E. B. Roffensperger to the pastorate. The present pastor, the Rev. J. E. Moffat, began his pastorate in 1878. The membership of the church at present is two hundred and forty.

The Bedford Street Methodist Protestant Church was in 1836 a mission station, with the Rev. Dennis B. Dorsey as minister, and the names of John Gephart, Addison L. Withers, and William Haller are to be found upon the records of the church. The services were held in the basement of the English Lutheran church. The Rev. John Elderdice was next in charge of the congregation, and under his pastorate the congregation in 1838 erected a building on Bedford, then Blocher Street. Eleven years after, the building was found to be too contracted for the increased congregation, and the present edifice was erected at the corner of Front and Bedford Streets. The parsonage was built in 1852. The record of its ministers, as far as it can be traced, is as follows:

1836, Rev. Dennis B. Dorsey; 1838, Rev. John Elderdice; 1849, Rev. W. T. Eva, Rev. Mr. Courtenay; 1871, Rev. Henry Nice; 1875, Rev. T. H. Lewis; 1877, Rev. Francis T. Little; 1880, Rev. R. T. Smith.

In the fall of 1871 the pastor, the Rev. Henry Nice, and a part of the congregation desired to transfer their church relationship to the Methodist Episcopal Church, and the pastoral relation was severed, the property passing under the control of the Methodist Episcopal Church until 1875, when it was restored to the Methodist Protestant Church.

The German Lutheran Church.—The German Lutheran Church separated from the English Lutheran Church in 1839, and, under the ministration of the Rev. M. Kehler, continued to worship in the English church, at the corner of Baltimore and Centre Streets, with services once a month, until 1848, when, the English Lutherans requiring their church all the time for their own services, the German Lutherans began the erection of their present church on Bedford Street. This church, designed by Henry Smenner, is of the Etruscan style of architecture, and was finished and dedicated March 17, 1850. The corner-stone was laid in June, 1849, the ceremonies being participated in by the clergy, the Masons, the City Council, the Odd-Fellows, the Order of Red Men, and many professional gentlemen. The building is one hundred and thirty feet by fifty-five feet, with a steeple one hundred and fifty feet high from the ground, and extending one hundred feet above the roof.

The pastors of the church have been as follows:

1839, Rev. M. Kehler; 1843, Rev. M. Winecoff; 1846–47, Rev. Samuel Finkle; 1847–49, Rev. Peter Rizer; 1849–52, Rev. C. Schwankoosky; 1853–55, Rev. Mr. Bauman; 1855–58, Rev. Daniel Maier; 1858–66, Rev. G. H. Vosseler; 1866–67, Rev. "Father" Heyer; 1867, Rev. John Philip Conradi.

The present number of communicants is about six hundred.

The record of this church contains the following entry: "On the 10th of August, 1853, the cholera appeared in this town, and took away sixteen fathers of families and six mothers from this church. Many children also died, but, as the force of the epidemic was so great, the burials took place at night, and as I, myself, was for some time very ill, it was impossible to obtain names, ages, and dates of death." This record was made by the Rev. Mr. Bauman.

German Evangelical Reformed Zion Church was organized in May, 1867, and the corner-stone was laid in 1844. The dedicatory services were held in 1845. The church is located on North Liberty Street, and was purchased in June, 1872, for the sum of five thousand five hundred dollars. The officiating clergymen have been the Revs. A. Wauner, 1867–71; C. Cast, 1871–74; F. R. Schwedes, 1874. The congregation numbers one hundred and fifty confirmed and one hundred and twenty-five unconfirmed members. It has a flourishing Sunday-school, and Female Aid Society and Youths' Society, and owns Greenmount Cemetery, on the Baltimore pike.

SS. Peter and Paul's German Catholic Church.—Early in 1847 the few German Catholic families of Cumberland held their religious services in the basement of St. Patrick's church twice a month; a priest from Baltimore officiating at stated intervals. During the summer the members succeeded in collecting three hundred dollars towards building a church. Upon the approval of Father Newman, afterwards Bishop of Philadelphia, they purchased from the King heirs the lot of ground on Fayette Street, and began building thereon the present imposing edifice in 1848, the corner-stone being laid on the 4th of June, with ceremonies conducted by the Rt. Rev. Archbishop Eccleston, assisted by Fathers Obermyer and Helenbrecht. Joseph Noll was the architect, and Messrs. Francis Haley & Bros. the builders. The church was completed and dedicated in 1849. When first erected it was ninety by fifty feet, with altar recesses, but in 1872 it was lengthened twenty-four feet. In 1832 a seminary for the education of priests was erected on a part of the lot south of the church, and in 1856 this building was enlarged to furnish additional educational facilities. The present seminary is one hundred by forty feet, and six stories in height, built of brick in a most substantial manner.

The order of Redemptorists established a parochial school in the basement of the church, and afterwards purchased the old Allegany County Academy, and erected upon the lot west of the church a parochial school building. On part of the same lot, in the spring of 1870, the church erected a convent, and three sisters of the Ursuline order were employed to teach the children of the congregation.

The record of the officiating priests is imperfect. The following is correct as far as possible: 1849, Father Urbauzick; 1849, Father Krounnenberger; 1849–66, Redemptionist Fathers; 1866–75, Carmelite Fathers; 1875, Capuchin Fathers from Münster, in Westphalia, Germany. The number of communicants, including children, is nearly two thousand. Fathers Antonius and Francis are the present pastors.

The following inscriptions are found on gravestones in SS. Peter and Paul's (German) Catholic Cemetery:

Ferdinand Obeker, born 1794, died Jan. 16, 1876.

Henry Nieman, died Oct. 11, 1874, aged 62 years, 1 month, 26 days.

Seballa Hodel, wife of James Twig, Sr., born May 11, 1832, died Sept 11, 1874.

Adam Kerber, born Jan. 6, 1823, died Nov. 12, 1875.

Kuniguntha Diettrich, born May 7, 1823, died July 21, 1874.

Bernard Koleman, died April 9, 1875, aged 50.

Anna K. Schroder, born May 18, 1816, died Dec. 21, 1867.

Bernhortne Droll, born May 11, 1811, died April 3, 1870.

Eva E. Berkart, born Dec. 10, 1813, died Feb. 1, 1868.

Anna M., wife of F. H. Brockman, born May 1, 1803, died Feb. 19, 1867.

Nickolaus Berkart, born August, 1817, died Feb. 6, 1865.

Anna, wife of James Carloss, and daughter of Lawrence Gannon, a native of Ireland, Strokestown, Roscommon County, died May 22, 1851, aged 24.

Johannes Knopp, born March 19, 1796, died Feb. 13, 1874.

Heinrich Wigger, born 1799, died Feb. 27, 1871.

Andreas Stegmeier, died Feb. 20, 1873, aged 62.

George Amon, born May 8, 1816, died May 30, 1872.

George Brock, born Feb. 14, 1832, died Aug. 26, 1873.

John H. Bruckman, born January, 1817, died July 19, 1871.

Andreas Steinlein, born April 8, 1803, died July 9, 1871.

Sebastian Hulbig, born Jan. 1, 1800, died Jan. 7, 1871.

Joseph Krebel, died Aug. 23, 1871, aged 48.

Nicholas Lidchen, died Nov. 22, 1870, aged 66.

Wilhelm Becker, died Dec. 21, 1870, aged 44.

Lawrence Reglan, a native of County Westmeath, Ireland, died Sept. 23, 1859, aged 62.

John A. Oker, died May 18, 1866, aged 51 years; Dorothy, his wife, born Feb. 6, 1806, died June 11, 1863.

Gertrude, wife of Michael Kohlhepp, born Sept. 14, 1819, died Nov. 28, 1862.

Anna S. Brenker, born Nov. 11, 1783, died Nov. 11, 1862.

Heinrich Barloge, born July 17, 1806, died April 28, 1864.

Valentine Rohrig, born March 21, 1781, died Aug. 8, 1864.

W. Berk, born Oct. 20, 1813, died Dec. 23, 1863.

Arthur Coffield, Co. F, 153d Ohio Vol.

John Kerber, born Nov. 1, 1815, died May 31, 1866.

Wilhelm Hohring, born Sept. 24, 1822, died Oct. 25, 1864.

Juliana, wife of George Hart, born Feb. 24, 1813, died Jan. 12, 1865.

Rosna, wife of J. Krebel, died Feb. 25, 1863, aged 40.

John O'Keefe, "a member of Co. G, 23d Minn. Vol., or the Ohio Irish Brigade."

Karl Steppe, born Nov. 9, 1815, died Dec. 7, 1864.

Elizabeth, wife of Peter Miller, born Jan. 16, 1800, died Dec. 30, 1860.

Genofeva Kotz, born Dec. 29, 1828, died Dec. 23, 1866.

Anna M., wife of John Doemer, died Sept. 9, 1867, aged 62 years, 10 months, 11 days.

Nicholas Hodel, born Dec. 6, 1794, at Oldsberg, Switzerland, died Dec. 6, 1861.

John Jakel, died March 24, 1864, aged 65 years, 7 days.

Anna D. Petril, died Aug. 4, 1862, aged 54.

Maria T. Helmstetter, died Aug. 12, 1870, aged 56 years, 6 months, 28 days.

John Schellhous, born Aug. 18, 1791, died Dec. 8, 1862.

Anna Eve Forbock, born 1813, died aged 57.

A. T. Maria Gelhouse, born May 22, 1816, died June 28, 1878.

Michael Stropmenger, died March 12, 1871, aged 61 years, 4 months, 3 days.

Martha, wife of Carl Somribeard, born 1788, died Sept. 10, 1868.

Martin Ehrbar, born Nov. 11, 1808, died Oct. 18, 1865.

Maria Ehrbar, born June 25, 1813, died Jan. 21, 1875.

F. M. Gromlich, born April 6, 1818, died Sept. 20, 1869.

Anna M., wife of Michael Utter, died March 24, 1869, aged 61 years, 10 months, 16 days.

John S. Gromlich, died Jan. 16, 1839, aged 40.

Peter Schneer, died May 20, 1863, aged 81 years, 1 month.

Katharine, his wife, died Dec. 2, 1871, aged 83 years, 1 month.

F. Casper Reichert, born Dec. 22, 1812, died Nov. 20, 1877.

Margaret, his wife, born Aug. 10, 1814, died June 12, 1867.

Catharine, wife of Wm. Rest, died June 4, 1874, aged 40.

Frans. Xavier Feigel, born March 15, 1828, died Dec. 1, 1876.

Frank Von Wagner, died March 18, 1872, aged 62.

George Hummel, born April 24, 1802, died March 8, 1872.

John Meder, born 1799, died Sept. 20, 1877.

Margaretta Meder, born 1804, died November, 1874.

Daniel Keane, died April 30, 1864, aged 41.

Francis B. Wempe, died Jan. 19, 1855, aged 44.

John G. H. W. Knapp, died Feb. 28, 1867, aged 59.

Elizabeth G. M. Knapp, died Dec. 17, 1877, aged 66.

Francis Poulis, died Feb. 28, 1875, aged 61 years, 11 months, 22 days.

Harmon Brown, died Dec. 12, 1878. aged 72.

Theodore McCroy, died Sept. 12, 1875, aged 55.

Maria A. Helbig, born 1803, died October, 1880.

Johannes Horner, born Oct. 24, 1810, died Feb. 5, 1877.

Joseph Ahous, born Sept. 14, 1827, died Oct. 20, 1878.

Heinrich Schwanklaus, born Feb. 5, 1816, died Aug. 7, 1877.

Nicholl Lupe, born March 31, 1823, died Jan. 3, 1880.

Johannes Jekel, born Oct. 26, 1798, died Nov. 20, 1877.

Johannes Boch, born March, 1819, died March 12, 1877.

Wolfgang Hammersmith, died March 27, 1878, aged 50.

James Fitzpatrick, M.D., born in Carlow, Ireland, 1805; "came to America in 1821, and to Allegany County in 1835." He was distinguished as a physician, and discharged many public trusts with ability and integrity. Died March 14, 1865.

Bernhard Drebmann, born Sept. 24, 1814, died June 31, 1877.

Theresa, wife of John Oker, died Aug. 27, 1873, aged 38 years, 7 months, 17 days.

George Brinker, born Oct. 28, 1814, died Nov. 24, 1873.

William Gessner, died Oct. 19, 1863, aged 48 years, 10 months, 12 days.

John A. Reinhard, died Sept. 10, 1863, aged 47.

John P. Schellhous, born Aug. 10, 1818, died Aug. 11, 1873; and Barbara, his wife, died June 6, 1867, aged 46 years, 7 months, 29 days.

Henry Wriever, died Dec. 13, 1864, aged 57 years, 1 month, 6 days.

Thomas Brophy, "a native of County Kilkenny, Ireland," died Dec. 29, 1853, aged 42.

Ludwig Lippold, born Dec. 24, 1811, died Jan. 30, 1873.

James Callan, died Sept. 12, 1866, aged 76 years.

Margaret, his wife, died March 17, 1869, aged 82 years, 9 months, 23 days.

John Callan, his son, died June 17, 1861, aged 36 years, 4 months, 22 days; and David S. Callan, his son, died May 20, 1861, aged 38 years, 5 months, 24 days.

Johannes Jupe, born Jan. 18, 1823, died June 6, 1869.

Heinrich Brockman, born Jan. 1, 1800, died Jan. 3, 1864; and Elizabeth, his wife, died February, 1874, aged 78.

Wendeline Firle, died May 13, 1869, aged 59 years, 6 months, 12 days.

Eliza, wife of Thomas Gonder, died Aug. 22, 1853, aged 53 years.

Thomas Gonder, died Nov. 21, 1859, aged 79 years.

Ann, consort of Edward Mullon, died Feb. 26, 1856, aged 52 years, 19 days.

Thomas Coulehan, born in King's County, Ireland, died Oct. 18, 1853, aged 66 years.

Marguard Wolf, born April 6, 1815, died Dec. 27, 1879.

Elizabeth Wolf, born June 10, 1827, died July 24, 1862.

William Landwehr, born Aug. 28, 1829, died Aug. 9, 1875; and Catharine, his wife, died April 9, 1862, aged 37.

Heinrich Landwehr, born 1793, died Feb. 22, 1858.

Gerard W. Ludtman, born Feb. 5, 1787, died June, 1857.

Margaret Smyth, died Dec. 25, 1856, aged 63.

Clara, wife of Henry Landwehr, died Aug. 15, 1873, aged 74 years, 6 months, 12 days.

Francesca Stegmeier, died May 10, 1856, aged 92 years.

Anna Maria, wife of Michael Schnebel, died Sept. 21, 1853, aged 59.

Ellen, wife of Arthur McGirr, born Oct. 29, 1834, in County Clare, Ireland, died Jan. 29, 1857.

Maria Wigger, died July 17, 1855, aged 54.

Heinrich Wigger, died at Oldtown, April 10, 1857.

Peter Krigbaum, died May 15, 1857, aged 86.

Trinity Evangelical Lutheran Church.—The congregation of this church separated from the German Lutheran Church in 1852. The services were for some time held in the old court-house. The corner-stone of the present building was laid in June, 1854. The building is a neat, commodious brick structure, fifty by thirty feet, and was completed and dedicated in 1854. The pastors have been as follows:

1852, Rev. E. G. W. Keye, Revs. Mr. Nortmann and Mr. Sommer (irregularly); 1853, Rev. J. F. Beltz; 1860, Rev. Conrad H. Steger; 1862, Rev. W. Kaehler; 1865, Rev. Conrad Schawankoosky; 1871, Rev. Frederick Keugell; 1878, Rev. J. E. Möll; 1881, Rev. W. Hanewinchel.

The present number of church communicants is one hundred and fifty, with a parochial school of thirty-three members.

The Bair Chajim Synagogue.—In a room in No. 22 Baltimore Street, on the 27th of April, 1853, the few Israelites of Cumberland met and formed the Bair Chajim congregation for worship according to the Israelitish ceremonies and faith. In 1854 the place of worship was changed to the corner of Centre and Baltimore Streets, opposite the English Lutheran church; and again in 1858, to the west side of Will's Creek, opposite Emmanuel Episcopal church.

The organization had H. Rosenbach for president; A. Shields, vice-president; H. Adler, secretary; and S. Nathan, treasurer; with Samuel Sanneborn and S. Burgunder as trustees. A strict observance of the Sabbath and other holy days, according to the Mosaic dispensation, was enforced upon the members. The Rev. Judah Wechsler was engaged as reader, and at the end of one year he was succeeded by the Rev. Mr. Hermann, who remained two years, and was followed by the Rev. Isaac Strauss, who was succeeded by the Rev. Mr. Freundlich, who, after a year's service, was followed by the Rev. A. Laser. The latter, in 1860, was succeeded by the Rev. Isaac Gotlieb, who, after a service of four years, was succeeded by Rev. Isaac Baum. The present synagogue, corner of Centre and Union Streets, was erected in 1866, under the ministration of the Rev. Isaac Baum. The building, a neat brick structure, with a seating capacity of one hundred and fifty, has a school-room in the basement, with a school under the care of the pastor. The synagogue was dedicated March 2, 1867, by the Revs. B. Szold and H. Hochheimer, of Baltimore. In 1869 the Rev. A. Oppenheimer succeeded Mr. Baum, and died suddenly on the 24th of April, 1871. The Rev. A. Bonheim was the pastor until 1873, when he was followed by the Rev. G. Levi, who, in 1875, was succeeded by the Rev. M. Wurzel. In 1877 the Rev. L. Eiseman, the present rabbi, succeeded. He has greatly increased the membership. The congregation owns a cemetery on the Baltimore pike. The number of pew-holders is about eighty.

McKendree (African) Methodist Episcopal Church.—This organization of colored Methodists was formed by withdrawal from the Centre Street Methodist Episcopal Church in 1854. The present church was purchased in that year, and has been occupied for religious services ever since. The first trustees were Lewis Graham, Joseph Taper, James Tibbs, and Eli Robinson. The congregation then numbered about forty. Rev. Henry Matthews was the first pastor. There is a flourishing Sunday-school in connection with the church. The pastors have been as follows:

1854–56, Rev. Henry Matthews; 1856–59, Rev. W. S. Wilson; 1859–69, no record; 1869–72, Rev. M. Spreddles; 1872–73, Rev. E. Lawson, Rev. Thomas Davis; 1874–75, Rev. A. B. Wilson; 1875, Rev. Henry Cellers, Rev. W. S. Harris.

During the pastorate of Mr. Spreddles the church was enlarged and improved, and in 1881 it was again enlarged, renovated, and remodeled. The number of communicants is about one hundred.

The African Methodist Episcopal Church.—In 1848 the colored members of the Centre Street Methodist Episcopal Church organized a separate congregation and provided themselves their present house of worship on Frederick Street. The board of trustees was composed of Nathaniel Burgee, Philip Only, Jacob Mitchell, William Hamilton, John Page, John Murdock, and Henry Robinson. "Father" Golden, of Baltimore, greatly aided the congregation in the building of their church. In 1871 the building was enlarged, and again in 1875, to accommodate the increased membership. The pastors from 1848 have been as follows:

Revs. Golden, Thomas Henry, Dr. Watts, D. A. Ridout, James Sterrichs, Mr. Russell, R. A. Hall, John F. Lane, William Smith, C. Sampson, W. H. Waters, Joseph Thompson, James H. A. Johnson, J. B. Hamilton, J. M. Cargill, B. H. Lee.

Trinity Methodist Episcopal Church South.—Early in 1868, Rev. Williamson Harris, a clergyman from North Carolina, who was on his way to a Western town, where he intended to remain for some time for the benefit of the health of himself and family, was compelled to stop at Cumberland on account of the illness of his daughter. Owing to her slow recovery he was compelled to remain for a considerable time, during which he met several gentlemen of the city, at whose request he held services, which were attended by them and their friends. His first sermon was preached to only three persons, but in a few weeks the number of his hearers augmented to twenty-five or thirty, and in the month of May, 1868, eight of them, Messrs. John Humbird, Asahel Willison, Horace Resley, W. M. Price, John Longabough, Levi Wickard, and John E. Buck, held a meeting, at which they resolved to request Mr. Harris to remain in this city and gather around him a congregation to be connected at some future time with the Methodist Episcopal Church South, and pledged themselves to his support. Mr. Harris accepted their offer and continued to preach, holding services in the Market-house Hall, and afterwards at Pioneer Hall. On the 23d of August, 1868, the congregation was organized with twenty-four members as a charge of the Methodist Episcopal Church South, and connected itself with the Baltimore Conference, but on Oct. 9, 1868, withdrew from the Conference and organized an independent congregation, under the name of Trinity Independent Methodist Episcopal Church, with Rev. Williamson Harris as pastor.

At a congregational meeting on the same day the following gentlemen were elected stewards: John Humbird, John E. Buck, Asahel Willison, John Longabaugh; William M. Price, recording steward; and Levi Wickard, treasurer.

At another congregational meeting, Nov. 11, 1868, it was decided that, in view of the increasing membership, and consequent stability of the organization, a house of worship was needed, and it was resolved to build one, the result being the fine edifice now occupied by the congregation. The board of stewards were authorized to collect money by subscription, on which work they immediately entered, and so great was their success that on the 30th of the same month sufficient funds had been obtained to justify the selection of a suitable site and the making of further arrangements for the erection of the proposed building. The gentlemen composing the board of stewards were elected trustees of the church, and Messrs. John Humbird, J. B. Buck, and John Longabough were chosen as the building committee.

On the 5th of April, 1869, a lease was executed for a lot of ground fronting sixty-four feet on Centre Street, and running back seventy-six feet on Union Street. Ground was broken soon afterwards and the foundation laid.

On the 18th of August, 1869, the corner-stone was laid by Potomac Lodge, No. 100, A. F. and A. M., with appropriate ceremonies, assisted by Piedmont Lodge, No. 128; Hiram Lodge, No. 103; Ohr Lodge, No. 131; and Oakland Lodge, No. 133; Chosen Friends' Lodge, No. 34, I. O. O. F., was also present. The dedicatory sermon was preached by J. B. Williams, of Baltimore. The corner-stone is a beautiful piece of white marble, and bears the inscription, "Aug. 18, 1869." In it is deposited a copper box, containing the following articles:

The name of the lodge and assisting lodges of Masons laying the corner-stone, with the names of the officers of the Grand Lodge of the State; the date of organization of the church, name of pastor, etc.; the names of national, State, and county officials; and copies of the newspapers of the city. The work of building was rapidly pushed forward, and the edifice was under roof and the lecture-room on the ground-floor completed and furnished early in June, 1870. The lecture-room was dedicated on the 12th of June, Rev. Williamson Harris officiating, assisted by Rev. A. R. Reilly, of the Centre Street Methodist Episcopal Church.

This room was used for holding divine services up to Sept. 29, 1872, when the audience-room was completed, and dedicated by Bishop Kavanagh, assisted by Rev. Dr. Poisal, Rev. D. Thomas, Rev. H. C. Holloway, and others.

In March, 1871, Mr. Harris resigned the pastorate and Rev. James Higgins, of the Baltimore Conference of the Methodist Episcopal Church South, was shortly afterwards elected pastor of the church. On the 27th of September, 1871, the congregation, by a unanimous vote, again connected themselves with the Baltimore Conference of the Methodist Episcopal Church South, by which Rev. James Higgins was continued in the charge of the station. At the meeting of the Conference in March, 1872, Rev. James W. Duffey, of West Virginia, the present pastor, was appointed to the charge. The members at the date of organization, as stated above, numbered twenty-four. On Oct. 9, 1869, they numbered forty-five, and Sept. 29, 1872, about eighty-five.

Kingsley Methodist Episcopal Church.—The needs of Methodists living in South Cumberland induced Messrs. S. T. Little, John Kellenbeck, and Samuel Milford, in August, 1870, to lease a lot whereon the present building was erected, at a cost of one thousand dollars. It was dedicated by the Rev. J. E. Gray, then stationed at Frostburg, Md., on the 5th of December, 1870. The pastors since then have been:

1870, Rev. J. McK. Walsh; 1871, Rev. A. J. Gill; 1873, Rev. S. M. Alford; 1876, Rev. W. H. Reed; 1877, Rev. D. M. Browning; 1879, Rev. George E. Maydwell.

The number of communicants is about one hundred. A neat parsonage was built on part of the lot in the summer and fall of 1876.

Christ Reformed Episcopal Church.—The parish was organized May 16, 1876, at the office of George Henderson, Jr., on North Liberty Street, and the church established under the name of Christ Reformed Episcopal Church. The inaugural services had been held on the previous Sunday in Trinity Methodist Episcopal Church South, corner of Centre and Union Streets, when Bishop George D. Cummins, assisted by the Rev. John K. Dunn, officiated. The first vestry consisted of the following persons: Wardens, Dr. S. P. Smith and George Henderson, Jr.; Vestrymen, Thomas Johns, George S. Pearre, Jonathan W. Magruder, E. T. Shriver, C. J. Orrick, Dr. S. H. Fundenburg, J. W. Pearce, and W. H. Harrison. On the following Sunday, May 21st, services were held in the hall of the Young Men's Christian Association by the Rev. John K. Dunn, rector. A Sunday-school was established the same afternoon. The hall of the Young Men's Christian Association was used for services until March, 1877, when Trinity Methodist Episcopal Church building on South Centre Street was purchased, at the cost of five thousand six hundred dollars. The Rev. J. K. Dunn continued rector to 1880, and the Rev. G. W. Huntingdon is the present rector. The present number of communicants is about one hundred, with a Sunday school of two hundred.

Rose Hill Cemetery.—Among those buried at Rose Hill Cemetery are the following:

Charles W. Shaw, born Jan. 23, 1850, died Dec. 12, 1880.

James J. Shaw, born Oct. 23, 1840, died Nov. 2, 1878.

Charles Robb (a Mason), born Oct. 25, 1812, at Lanark, Scotland, died Aug. 23, 1878.

John F. Johnson, died Aug. 24, 1876, aged 64 years, 7 months.

Estelle F. Perry, wife of Capt. Roger Perry, U.S.N., died Nov. 10, 1867, aged 34 years, 9 months.

Rev. J. K. Cramer, born Sept. 24, 1824, died Dec. 19, 1869.

A. M. C. Cramer, born Oct. 18, 1797, at Downpatrick, County Down, Ireland, died Dec. 29, 1872.

Eleanor C. Stuart, daughter of Dr. David Stuart, of Virginia, died Sept. 30, 1875, aged 79.

Sarah Waite, daughter of Dr. David Stuart, of Virginia, died Sept. 1, 1870, aged 85 years.

Sarah C., wife of Horace Resley, and daughter of J. and R. McLanahan, died Sept. 3, 1872, aged 57 years.

Edward H. Campbell, died July 13, 1880, aged 47.

Henry Korns, died Feb. 28, 1878, aged 63 years, 2 months.

Wm. W. McKaig, Sr., born Jan. 21, 1806, died June 21, 1880.

Orlando D. Robbins, died Jan. 22, 1877, aged 48 years.

Jacob Saylor, died April 5, 1828, aged 34 years, 7 months.

Margaret, his wife, died Feb. 10, 1842, aged 41 years, 9 months, 5 days.

Frederick Deems, died Sept. 12, 1845, aged 71 years, 1 month, 18 days.

Catharine, his wife, died Nov. 12, 1849, aged 69 years.

Joseph Duley, died March 16, 1879, aged 86.

Elizabeth, his wife, died Jan. 23, 1873, aged 77.

Dr. John Everett, died May 21, 1870, aged 59 years, 11 days.

Armada, his wife, died October, 1866, aged 41 years, 2 months, 24 days.

Wm. A. Gross (a member of the Masonic society), died Nov. 18, 1874, aged 31 years, 8 months, 26 days.

William Lynn, born Sept. 9, 1801, died July 21, 1851.

Mary, wife of Geo. A. Pearre, born Aug. 4, 1823, died April 30, 1871.

M. C. Sprigg, died 1845; and M. L., his wife, 1862.

Hon. James Smith, judge Circuit Court for Allegany County, died Aug. 10, 1865.

Ann Eliza, his wife, died Aug. 11, 1859.

Kate Price, died at Washington, D. C., June 15, 1863.

Richard T. Lowndes, died April 24, 1844, aged 43.

J. E. Russell, died Jan. 3, 1872, aged 52.

Margaret, his wife, died Jan. 31, 1862, aged 45.

Anna F. Mertens, born in Hamburg, Germany, July 14, 1798, died June 8, 1876.

William Neill, died March 18, 1862, aged 55 years, 1 month, 21 days.

Edward G. Guest, died July 21, 1868, aged 44 years.

Samuel M. Semmes, died Oct. 14, 1868, aged 57 years.

Eleonora, his wife, died Jan. 14, 1875, aged 54 years.

George Lynn, died Dec. 8, 1860, aged 55 years, 4 months.

Virginia Moss Lynn, died Aug. 26, 1872, aged 58.

Mary, wife of R. H. Jones, and daughter of Hon. William Hunter, of Washington, D. C., born Dec. 7, 1837, died May 18, 1873.

Charles J. Thurston, died Dec. 6, 1868, aged 42 years.

R. Worthington, died Dec. 31, 1871, aged 72 years.

Rebecca P. Worthington, died July, 1879, aged 80.

John Hays, died Feb. 14, 1872, aged 86 years, 11 months, 5 days; Anna M., his wife, died Feb. 9, 1872, aged 78 years, 3 months, 24 days.

Burgess Magruder, born April 15, 1794, died April 23, 1865.

Margaret Magruder, born Dec. 23, 1799, died March 16, 1862.

Robert Morris, died Nov. 3, 1869, aged 68 years, 11 months, 6 days.

Fannie T., wife of A. F. Withers, born Sept. 18, 1802, died Jan. 6, 1868.

Harriet B., wife of Geo. H. Gassaway, and second daughter of M. and F. T. Mukers, born Oct. 7, 1831, died March 17, 1861.

Sarah Beall, died June 3, 1873, aged 84 years, 3 months, 26 days.

Joanna Holmes, died July 24, 1856, aged 74 years, 11 months, 21 days.

Samuel Eckles, died June 9, 1844, aged 49.

Joseph Shock, died March 18, 1873, aged 83 years, 8 months, 13 days.

Maria, his wife, died Dec. 19, 1851, aged 54 years, 11 months, 19 days.

Amos P. Shepperd, died May 8, 1875, aged 71 years, 2 months, 27 days.

J. Philip Roman, born Nov. 25, 1821, died Feb. 28, 1871.

Susanna, wife of A. P. Shepperd, died Dec. 9, 1873, aged 59 years, 10 months, 26 days.

Deborah R. Winegart, died Nov. 5, 1777, aged 67.

Daniel R. Long, died March 6, 1878, aged 45 years, 26 days.

Barbara Koontz, died Dec. 18, 1880, aged 56 years, 20 days.

G. B. Wagenroper, died April 23, 1874, aged 44 years, 2 months, 1 day.

John Deetz, died Sept. 16, 1868, aged 66; Maria, relict of John Deetz, died May 14, 1876, aged 65.

Rebecca Vrooman, died 1874, aged 56 years, 2 months.

Jacob Wickard, died Nov. 23, 1877, aged 59 years, 3 months, 5 days.

John H. Kehelenbeck, died May 25, 1877, aged 50.

Sarah, wife of Henry Brotenmarkle, died July 6, 1874, aged 69 years, 4 months, 1 day.

"Normand Bruce."

Charles Key Bruce, born May 23, 1816, died Nov. 10, 1875.

Henry Bruce, born July 10, 1808, died Sept. 15, 1865.

Isaac Rice, born March 24, 1791, died March 25, 1881.

Thomas Perry, died June 27, 1871, aged 62.

Elizabeth, wife of Charles Ridgely, born July 24, 1792, died July 1, 1871.

John Dowden, born March 17, 1809, died Feb. 16, 1877.

Fannie C., wife of William A. Withers, born July 3, 1841, died April 27, 1876.

David Taylor, died Jan. 16, 1871, aged 56 years, 9 months, 26 days.

William K. Newman, died Dec. 19, 1859, aged 56 years, 1 month, 23 days.

Elizabeth, wife of Rev. A. Bush, died Oct. 11, 1862, aged 42 years, 8 months, 20 days.

Smith Hurd, born in Southbury, Conn., died Dec. 14, 1858, aged 55.

John Ball, died Feb. 16, 1856, aged 53 years, 3 months, 8 days.

James Porcy, a native of Muirkirk, Ayrshire, Scotland, died Feb. 22, 1865, aged 64 years, 8 months, 5 days.

Margaret Rizer, died Dec. 4, 1858, aged 70.

George Rizer, died June 30, 1867, aged 82 years, 5 months, 3 days.

David Elliott, died June 18, 1872, aged 64 years, 9 months, 3 days.

Albert A. Rizer, died Dec. 15, 1869, aged 50 years, 9 months.

John Folck, died Jan. 19, 1879, aged 87 years, 10 months, 9 days.

W. P. Sterett, aged 63.

Nancy D. Sterett, aged 38.

L. H. Johns, died Oct. 27, 1863, aged 78.

Caroline M. Johns, aged 40.

Mary A. Towson, of Baltimore, died May 21, 1876.

George Hebb, died May 17, 1846, aged 69 years, 2 months, 14 days.

Susan Hebb, died June 7, 1872, aged 79.

Richard Gronswick, died Nov. 25, 1846, aged 73; Catharine, his wife, died Sept. 14, 1850, aged 76.

Abraham Russell, died Aug. 27, 1869, aged 59 years, 8 months, 6 days.

E. J. Russell, born April 16, 1834, died June 8, 1874.

Nancy, widow of Jason Phillips, died June 15, 1854, aged 78; and her daughter, Diana Phillips, died June 15, 1856, aged 56.

Ellen Willoughby, died July 20, 1844, aged 32 years.

Mary A. Gassman, died July 14, 1854, aged 45 years, 2 months, 11 days.

Martin V. Mull, Co. "C," 2d Md. P. H. B., died at Staunton, Va, July 19, 1864, aged 24 years, 4 months, 27 days.

Hampton Long, born Nov. 20, 1816, died May 17, 1874.

John A. Hoffman, died May 3, 1863, aged 84.

Margaret Miller, died June 31, 1867, aged 49.

Mary Miller, died May 12, 1867, aged 47.

Harriet Gleeholmes, died April 29, 1875, aged 84.

Sarah A., wife of John Lingo, died Dec. 18, 1865, aged 51 years, 10 months, 14 days.

Jacob Fechtig, born May 2, 1802, at Hagerstown, died at Cumberland, Aug. 1, 1854.

Matilda, daughter of William Hillcary, and wife of J. Fechtig, died May 16, 1873, aged 76 years, 10 months, 20 days.

Lavinia, wife of William Taylor, born April 22, 1809, died April 18, 1869.

James and Catharine Searight and three children.

Isabella, wife of J. H. Young, died Nov. 1, 1848.

Mary C., wife of L. W. Brent, died March 11, 1876, aged 50 years, 2 months, 7 days.

William Brace, died Sept. 15, 1875, aged 55 years, 1 month, 8 days.

James M. Rowe, died May 12, 1875, aged 57.

M. Asa Adams, died Jan. 14, 1870, aged 54 years, 3 months, 5 days.

Elizabeth, wife of A. S. Vrooman, died Aug. 26, 1857, aged 75 years, 10 months, 12 days.

Dr. John Little, died Sept. 8, 1853, aged 59; Ann Little, his wife, died June 8, 1865, aged 69 years, 9 months, 20 days.

Christian, wife of John Troxell, died Jan. 26, 1872, aged 53 years, 2 months, 24 days.

Elizabeth, wife of Charles Scott, died April 11, 1868, aged 89.

Edward F. Sommerkramp, died April 22, 1864, aged 61 years, 3 months, 16 days.

William R. Beall, died April 9, 1878, aged 60.

Obadiah Stillwell, died Feb. 11, 1877, aged 91 years, 9 months, 18 days; Sarah M., his wife, died July 5, 1870, aged 76 years, 7 months, 29 days.

Elizabeth, wife of Harmon Horton, born in Westmoreland County, Pa., March 20, 1791, died July 31, 1868.

Michael Criss, died June 23, 1870, aged 36 years, 7 months, 20 days.

Hale S. Wortzwelder, died Dec. 23, 1876, aged 46 years, 8 months, 20 days.

Elizabeth O'Neill, died June 27, 1871, aged 69 years, 11 months.

Thomas Edwards, died in 1833; Mary Edwards, died in 1863.

John T. Edwards, died May 27, 1871, aged 67 years, 9 months, 23 days; Elizabeth A., his wife, died July 25, 1863, aged 45.

George Stubblefield, died Dec. 26, 1867, aged 63 years, 10 months, 24 days.

Frederick Shipley, died April 16, 1860, aged 48 years, 16 days.

Ozias S. Crompton, died Feb. 18, 1859, aged 38 years, 5 months, 6 days.

Samuel Cessna, died Sept. 20, 1846, aged 45 years, 11 months, 4 days.

James Woffutt, died July 15, 1854, aged 38.

Christina, wife of Jacob Myers, died Jan. 8, 1865, aged 54 years, 4 months, 20 days.

Rev. John B. Henry, rector of Emmanuel Parish, Cumberland, born Jan. 10, 1832, died Jan. 31, 1868.

Samuel Charles, "editor and publisher of the Cumberland *Civilian* for seventeen years," died Jan. 15, 1845, aged 45.

B. S. Pigman, born Sept. 4, 1819, died Jan. 9, 1855.

Nathaniel Pigman, died May 10, 1865, aged 44.

Charles Pigman, born in 1818, died in 1842.

Hanson Pigman, born in 1815, died in 1847.

Bene S. Pigman, born Jan. 20, 1775, died July 20, 1845; Harriet Pigman, his wife, died April 16, 1863, aged 75 years.

Philip A. S. Pigman, born in 1812, died in 1840.

Thomas Wilkinson, a native of Newcastle-upon-Tyne, England, died Dec. 31, 1877, aged 67.

J. B. Campbell, died Feb. 18, 1876, aged 53; Ann W., his wife, died April 13, 1861, aged 44.

James Young, died April 11, 1880, aged 42 years, 11 months, 28 days.

Julia Young, died July 7, 1869, aged 65 years, 2 months.
John Young, died Dec. 10, 1863, aged 56 years.
Christina Beockler, died Jan. 2, 1860, aged 30.
J. W. Magruder, born Oct. 17, 1793, died March 13, 1817; Mary Galloway, his wife, born Nov. 12, 1799, died Feb. 7, 1879.
Harrison Startzman, died Feb. 23, 1867, aged 48 years, 9 months, 22 days.
Eliza Snyder, wife of John Rhind, born March 29, 1818, died July 15, 1877.
John Cole, died May 9, 1872, aged 39.
Andrew J. Boose, born July 29, 1827, died May 14, 1867.
Catharine Boos, died July 24, 1849, aged 37 years, 3 months, 19 days.
John Boos, died Feb. 11, 1837, aged 45 years, 9 months.
D. M. Tuthill, died Nov. 17, 1870, aged 45 years, 1 month, 8 days.
Jacob Meyers, died Dec. 16, 1872, aged 54 years.
Mary A., wife of John T. Shuck, died Jan. 25, 1867, aged 43.
Charles Heck, died May 8, 1841, aged 58.
Mary McCleary, died Jan. 27, 1865, aged 60 years.
Nathaniel Bryan, died July 28, 1861, aged 69 years, 7 months, 21 days.
J. J. Meister, born March 27, 1817, died March 28, 1858.
E. Catharine, wife of John Nold, died Dec. 18, 1858, aged 49 years, 11 months, 18 days.
Thomas McKee, died June 12, 1870, aged 78 years, 7 months, 26 days.
Benjamin Coats, died Feb. 8, 1873, aged 68; Ellen, his wife, died April 15, 1881, aged 66 years, 7 months.
Lemuel Willison, died March 7, 1879, aged 46 years, 11 months, 21 days.
David McKnight, died Nov. 27, 1871, aged 71 years.
John N. W., son of M. L. and M. C. Rizer, died April 23, 1864, aged 20 years and 1 day; he served his country in Company H, Second Maryland P. H. B., and "was sacrificed upon the altar of liberty and humanity."
Samuel Cooper, died Feb. 16, 1879, aged 36.
Edward D. Smith, died March 21, 1877, aged 42 years, 1 month, 11 days.
B. M. Lawder, born July 25, 1805, died Aug. 8, 1877.
H. Dollhope, born July 6, 1823, died Aug. 28, 1879; Margaret, his wife, born Jan. 25, 1827, died April 14, 1879.
H. Johnson, died Feb. 6, 1872, aged 39.
Alexander M. Scott, died Aug. 25, 1867, aged 67.
John W. Henrick (a member of the Masonic lodge), died Oct. 18, 1872, aged 36 years, 7 months, 18 days.
Malinda Bennett, born May 5, 1791, died March 8, 1879.
Nancy, wife of J. M. Flake, died Dec. 29, 1874, aged 42 years.
Sarah, wife of H. Jackson, died July 29, 1868, aged 40.
Susan, wife of A. Mitchell, died Dec. 2, 1874, aged 42.
James R. W. Moore, died March 18, 1866, aged 40 years.
Isabella Moore, died Jan. 22, 1864, aged 70 years.

Lodges of Odd-Fellows.—All the members of the Independent Order of Odd-Fellows meet in Odd-Fellows' Hall, City Hall building.

The charter of Cumberland Encampment, No. 23, was granted Nov. 17, 1868, and signed by Caleb W. Greenfield, Grand Patriarch, and John M. Jones, Grand Scribe. The charter members were William R. Beall, E. S. Zeberly, George Flurshut, R. Armbuster, John H. Young, W. A. Withers, J. H. Earlougher, and Hopewell Webb, of whom the last four are living. The officers for 1881 were:

C. P., F. M. Dernoss; H. P., Eli Shaw; S. W., J. J. Earlougher; J. W., J. B. Pritzer; Scribe, W. J. Harrison; Treas., George W. Davis; S., Henry Burchett; G., Harmon White; 1st W., George B. Hargett.

Number of members, thirty-six. Meets Monday evenings.

Chosen Friends' Lodge, No. 34, received its charter April 16, 1840, signed by A. G. Warner, M. W. Grand Master, and W. J. Cook, M. W. Grand Secretary. Its officers for the second term of 1881 were:

Sitting P. G., Harmon White; N. G., F. M. Dernoss; V. G., Matthias Eberle; Sec., A. M. Adams; Treas., W. J. Harrison; Chapl., H. Zelch; C., D. Walker, Jr.; W., George B. Hargett; S., R. S. Waters; Trustee, William Brace.

A. M. Adams has been its secretary for the past thirty years, and J. H. Earlougher was its treasurer for thirty-four years. Number of members, one hundred. Meets Friday evenings.

Herman Lodge, No. 51, was chartered March 16, 1847, by John A. Thompson, M. W. Grand Master, and G. D. Tewksbury, M. W. Grand Secretary. The charter members were Henry Boerner, M. Treiver, Ulrich Steilmann, Albert Holle, John Holtzman, M. Topham Evans. The officers for the second term of 1881 were:

N. G., Valentine Fralich; V. G., Henry Burchert; Sec., John Weible; Treas., Conrad Zelch.

Number of members, thirty-nine. Meets Wednesday evenings.

Buena Vista Lodge, No. 53, was instituted in 1847, but subsequently lost its charter, but was reinstated. It surrendered its charter in July, 1881, and is not now in operation. Its meetings were held Thursday evenings.

Masonic Order.—All the Masonic bodies meet at Masonic Hall, at eight P.M., on the days designated.

Antioch Commandery of Knights Templar, No. 6. This commandery was chartered by dispensation Aug. 28, 1871, by Grand Commander Charles H. Mann; Francis Lincoln, Grand Generalissimo; Michael Miller, Grand Captain-General; and F. J. Kugler, Grand Recorder. Its regular charter is dated Jan. 14, 1873. The Grand Commander for 1881 was Dr. D. P. Welfley. Meetings, first and third Tuesdays.

Salem Chapter, Royal Arch Masons, No. 18. This chapter was chartered Nov. 9, 1858, by Grand High Priest E. S. Courtney, Deputy Grand High Priest James Goszler, Grand King H. N. Steele, and Grand Secretary Joseph Robinson. Its first officers were H. P., G. W. Fuller; K., Charles H. Ohr; S., O. W. Lackey. In 1877 its officers were: H. P., J. H. Gebhart; K., G. M. Deitz; S., J. S. Turner; Treas., S. Rosenheim; Sec., Henry Shriver; Janitor, S. M. Haller; and it then had forty-three members. Its Past High Priests are S. M. Haller, J. H. Gephart. It meets on second and fourth Tuesdays.

Salem Council, Royal and Select Masters, No. 6, meets quarterly.

Potomac Lodge, No. 100, was chartered May 19, 1855, by Charles Webb, M. W. G. M.; E. T. Owens, D. G. M.; George B. Taliafero, G. S. W.; G. J. Kennedy, G. J. W.; and Joseph Robinson, G. Sec. Its first officers were: W. M., A. L. Withers; S. W., J. B. Widener; J. W., Horace Resley. Its Past Masters have been A. L. Withers, Benjamin Barrett, Harry Baker, Walter W. Court, John H. Gephart, Charles H. Ohr (and Past Grand Master of the State), James M. Schley, Charles A. Slay, Thomas Venners, Harry Venners, William A. Withers, George L. Wellington, Daniel Annan, Ernest Hartman, Dr. D. P. Welfley, C. F. McCulloh. In 1879 its officers were: W. M., Daniel Annan; S. W., Ernest Hartman; J. W., Duncan Sinclair; Sec., John H. Gebhart; Treas., William A. Withers. The officers for the second term of 1881 were W. M., C. F. McCulloh; S. W., William R. Wilson; J. W., J. N. M. Brandler; Sec., J. H. Gephart; Treas., H. G. Weimer; Tyler, Thomas N. Johnson. It has forty-eight members, and meets on the first and third Fridays.

Ohr Lodge, No. 131, was chartered May 13, 1867, by John Coates, M. W. G. Master; Thomas Burns, D. G. Master; Lawrence Sangston, G. S. Warden; S. Woolford, G. J. Warden; and Jacob H. Medairy, G. Sec. Its first officers were: W. M., William Darrow; S. W., George W. Deitz; J. W., William J. Taylor. In 1879 its officers were: W. M., H. B. Buck; S. W., Thomas F. Myers; J. W., W. C. Darrow; Sec., F. M. Flurshut; Treas., William E. Turner. Its Past Masters are William Darrow, H. B. Buck, William Brace, George M. Deitz, Thomas Johnson, W. E. Turner, H. W. Shuck. Its officers for the second term of 1881 were: W. M., Thomas Johnson; S. W., F. W. Flurshutz; J. W., R. H. Arnold; Sec., H. W. Schuck; Treas., J. T. Hill. It has thirty-six members, and meets on the second and fourth Wednesdays of each month.

On July 4, 1839, the corner-stone of the Masonic Hall was laid with imposing ceremonies. Cumberland Lodge, No. 61, paraded in full regalia, and was flanked by the Cumberland Guards, commanded by Capt. A. King. The address was delivered at the laying of the stone by G. W. M., W. G. W. Haller. Several eloquent and able speeches were also made by prominent Masons. The celebration closed with an elegant dinner prepared by J. J. Johnson, at which many toasts were drank by the guests.

The charter of Royal Arcanum, Potomac Council, No. 607, was granted July 28, 1881, by A. E. Keyes, Supreme Regent.

The charter members were C. J. Orrick, J. M. Strober, Thomas P. Morgan, Jr., L. A. Camp, L. F. Miller, H. O. Weimer, Kennedy Hoffman Butler, J. M. Spear, W. H. Shepherd, F. M. Offutt, Dennis Graves, A. S. Brennaman, Hopewell Webb, Daniel Annan, Sylvester Osbourn, Joel L. Griffith, Thomas Foster, George P. Hast, Charles E. Hambright, S. A. Walter, M. M. Fuller, L. M. Shepherd. It meets at I. O. O. F. Hall.

American Legion of Honor, Logan Council, No. 74, was chartered Jan. 16, 1880, by Davis Wilson, Supreme Commander, and Nettie F. Mosler, Supreme Secretary. The charter members were W. J. Craigen, J. S. Craigen, Malachi Rice, C. E. Schwartzenbach, Jacob Schuck, Charles A. Seay, A. M. H. Seay, Joshua Steiner, Levi Shaw, J. B. Humbird, Levi W. Brant, M. J. Brant, John T. Dixon, H. U. T. Hurshurtz, John A. Sills, Archie Scott, H. M. Treiber, W. A. Withers, Henry Weber, John C. Young, T. D. Gephart, William Armbuster, S. T. Little. It holds its meetings in the I. O. O. F. Hall.

Knights of Pythias, Cumberland Lodge, No. 60, was chartered Aug. 16, 1870, by J. N. Dickson, Grand Chancellor, and Thomas S. Uppercue, Grand Scribe. The charter members were W. H. Wilkins, J. W. Rhind, J. C. Lynn, John Weir, Henry Howard, Jesse Klinefelter, Richard L. Gross, John Gephart, of Charles, James F. Harrison. It was instituted July 7, 1870.

The officers for 1881 were:

P. C. C., Charles H. Woolford; C. C., C. L. Madore; V. C. C., T. G. Petermann; Prel., Jacob Koodor; K. of R. and S., John H. Gephart; F. S., James Buckey; M. of F., Benj. A. Richmond; M. at A., C. N. Witt; I. G., Adam Johnson; O. G., William Shaffer.

It meets at its hall (Castle Hall), No. 110 Baltimore Street, every Monday evening.

Dispatch Lodge, No. 11, Ancient Order of United Workmen, was instituted Nov. 25, 1879, and its charter granted Jan. 19, 1880. The charter members and first officers were:

P. M. W., J. F. Legge; M. W., W. R. Wilson; G. F., H. B. Woods; O., G. F. McCulley; Recorder, A. T. Brennaman; F., T. S. P. Bowers; Receiver, William Brace; G., Alexander Adams; I. W., S. W. Wise; O. W., William Shaffer.

The officers for the second term of 1881 were:

P. M. W., H. B. Woods; M. W., J. J. Miller; F., J. W. Hart; O., Daniel W. Einer; Recorder, A. T. Brennaman; F., W. R. Wilson; Receiver, H. H. Hartsock; G., W. Deetz; I. W., George Shuck; O. W., William Shaffer.

Number of members, forty-three. It meets every first and third Tuesday in Knights of Pythias' Hall, over Little's store.

Omicron Conclave, No. 15, of Heptasophs, meets every Wednesday evening, at No. 45 Baltimore Street.

Sigma Conclave, No. 18, meets every Wednesday evening, at No. 86 Baltimore Street.

The Cumberland Christian Temperance Union meets at different churches.

St. Patrick's Temperance Society meets on the second Sunday of each month, in Carroll Hall, North Centre Street.

Sheffer Lodge, No. 26, I. O. G. T., meets at Good Templars' Hall, No. 86 Baltimore Street, every Monday evening, and the Degree Lodge the second Monday evening of each month. Its charter, dated Feb. 12, 1867, was signed by J. A. Spencer, R. G. W. T., and Samuel Hastings, R. G. W. C. T. The charter members were V. A. Buckey, S. T. Little, M. N. Finigan, Charles Robb, J. M. Russell, Charles Madore, John Madore, Robert V. Vayler, R. J. Morris, Mrs. Brengle, Lizzie Madore, Dr. Hummelshine, Miss E. Russell, C. C. Shuck, C. T. Brengle, Dr. J. W. Ewing, Mrs. Steiner, Mollie McCullogh, Rev. E. Kinsey, John A. Cress, Anna Steiner, Mollie A. Davis, Annie E. Ash, Wm. Schilling, Eliza Lambee, Welfley Smith, W. J. Zimmerly, George F. Johnson. Although this lodge is not now in active operation, it still retains its charter.

Mountain City Lodge, No. 1, Amalgamated Association of Iron and Steel-Workers, was granted a charter Feb. 19, 1880, by Grand Officers Wm. Martin, secretary, John Jarrell, president, and Edward McGinnis, treasurer. The charter members and first officers were, President, John Lloyd; Vice-President, Richard Rowley; Recording Secretary, James Tyson; Financial Secretary, August Barrett; Treasurer, John C. Whalley; Guide, Thomas Finch; Inside Guard, Richard Fitzsimmons; Outside Guard, George W. Grindel. The lodge meets every other Saturday evening at Castle Hall, No. 110 Baltimore Street.

The charter of Mountain City Lodge, No. 27, I. O. M., was granted Nov. 8, 1872. The charter members were W. J. Boyd, W. J. Harrison, Thomas Bradshaw, E. N. Madore, A. W. Rowe, J. W. Bradshaw, Philip Nash, C. W. Caldwell, Alexander Vincent, James Carey, Joseph Hughes, Jacob Keiner, Albin Elder, E. P. Welty, Elias Graves, J. J. Angel, John J. Lygard, J. W. Cope, Dennis Graves, J. E. Turpin, Henry Painter, J. C. Cordry, Charles E. Hambright, and others.

It meets at Castle Hall, No. 110 Baltimore Street. The officers for the second term of 1881 were:

W. M., W. T. Allee; J. M., George W. Everstine; R. S., S. P. Welty; F. S., Thornton Poole; Treas., G. J. Everstine; Chap., C. D. Bopst; C., C. Haller; Trustee, S. P. Welty; W. S. M., Samuel Brant.

Crescent Lodge, No. 589, Knights of Honor, was chartered April 13, 1877, and organized on the same date. It is a beneficiary society, and holds its meetings above S. T. Little's jewelry-store, No. 106 Baltimore Street. The "Dictators," or presiding officers, have been J. C. Hughley, N. J. Craigen, W. J. Walker, D. P. Welfley, W. M. Price, J. M. Shober, T. N. Johnson, C. F. McCulley, C. J. Orrick, J. N. Bradler, and H. J. Weimer. But two members have died since the organization, viz., Charles Robb and E. H. Campbell, the widows of whom received the two thousand dollars agreed to be paid on the death of a member. A. F. Brennaman was succeeded as Reporter by T. S. P. Bowers.

The officers for the second term of 1881 were:

Dictator, J. N. M. Brandler; V. D., H. G. Weimer; A. D., T. P. Morgan; R., T. S. P. Bowers; F. R., A. T. Brennaman; T., Thomas N. Johnson; Guide, L. A. Camp; C., G. J. Everstine; Guardian, Sylvester Osborn; S., Dennis Graves.

The lodge meets every second and fourth Friday in Knights of Pythias Hall, over Little's store, No. 110 Baltimore Street.

St. George's Branch, No. 33, Catholic Knighthood of America, meets on the second and fourth Sundays of each month at school-house adjoining SS. Peter and Paul's church.

President, John Hart; Vice-President, John Griffin; Recording Secretary, A. H. Herbert; Financial Secretary, J. D. McEvoy; Treasurer, Joseph Zweing; Sergeant-at-arms, Peter Miller; Sentinel, Alex. Leisure; Trustee, Henry Heker.

The Society of the Holy Family (religious) meets at the same school-house.

The Cumberland Athletic Club was incorporated in 1878. Its gymnasium is in Hart building, No. 5, North Centre; club room open to members at all times.

The Allegany County Jockey Club has the following officers: President, James M. Schley; Vice-President, H. Willison; Treasurer, F. Mertens, Jr.; Secretary, James T. Hager. Headquarters, No. 6 North Centre Street.

The Tri-State Dental Association meets monthly at Dr. H. Virgil Porter's dental rooms, corner Baltimore and North Liberty Streets.

The convents are as follows: Capuchin Monastery, on Fayette below Smallwood Street, Father Joseph, Superior; St. Edward's Convent, on North Centre Street, Sister Mary Louise, Superior; Ursuline Convent, on Fayette near Smallwood Street, conducted by Ursuline Sisters; Sister Theresa, Superior.

Logue Council, No. 74, American Legion of Honor, was chartered by the Supreme Lodge, Boston, Dec. 18, 1878, and was organized Jan. 16, 1880. It is a beneficiary organization, and meets in the hall of the I. O. O. F. The names of the charter members are W. J. Craigen, M.D., J. S. Craigen, C. A. Seay, A. M. Seay, J. C. Young, Joshua Steiner, Jacob Sluch, Levi Shaw, J. B. Humbird, R. H. Cuthbert, J. A. Sills, Archer Scott, William Ambruster, W. A. Withers, Malachi Rice, C. E. Schwartzenbach, Levi Brant, M. J. Brant, H. M. Treiber, Henry Weber, John T. Dixon, C. W. Brengle, T. D. Gephart, H. W. Flurshutz, and S. T. Little. The first commander was C. A. Seay, and the present is Levi Shaw. Lewis R. Danner is the only member who has died since organization, and two thousand dollars insurance was promptly paid.

B'er Chajim Lodge, No. 177, of the I. O. B. B., was instituted Feb. 18, 1872, chartered March 3, 1872; the purposes are to relieve sick and distressed members, to provide for the care and protection of widows and orphans of deceased members, to foster and encourage fraternal feelings and courtesies between members, and to elevate their characters intellectually and mentally. The funds are provided by quarterly payments. The presidents have been Selig Adler, N. Coleman, I. Sonneborn, G. Dettelbach, S. Sonneborn, D. Lashshy, Charles White, E. Klinger, S. Rosenbaum, Isaac White, S. Rosenbaum, H. Adler, H. White, L. Greenbaum, I. L. Eiseman, Joseph Hirsh. The charter members were Samuel Sonneborn, N. Coleman, Reuben Lichtenstein, A. Katz, Charles Preiss, Ira Miller, M. Bonheimer, F. Sonneborn, S. Larshansky, Harmon White, G. Detterbach, G. Gamp, H. Adler, Joseph Hirsch, S. Hamburger, S. Adler, S. Hirsch, M. Gross, Isaac White, M. Lowenstein, Charles White, G. Eisenberg, J. Goldsmith, S. Gross, D. Larshansky. It meets at I. O. O. F. Hall, on the first and third Sundays of every month; Harmon White, secretary.

The Young Men's Christian Association was organized May 3, 1873. Its first officers were: President, E. H. Campbell; Secretary, W. H. Shepherd; Treasurer, J. C. Orrick; Recording Secretary, J. H. C. Pancake. The executive committee consisted of the above officers and the chairmen of the various business committees. Its first meeting was held in the basement of the Methodist Episcopal Church South (now Reformed Episcopal Church), where its headquarters were for a few months. Then it met in the building now occupied by the Telephone Exchange Company, and after that in the Hart Building, on North Centre Street, until December, 1879, when it moved to its present quarters on Bedford Street.

Its officers for 1881 are: President, John Wilson; Vice-Presidents, C. J. Orrick, L. B. Wilson; Corresponding Secretary, C. V. Derr; Recording Secretary, W. P. Campbell; Treasurer, C. T. Brengle. The board of directors consist of the above officers and J. W. Hadley and H. Weber. It has five hundred volumes, most of them presented to it. Its membership fee is one dollar per year, and three dollars including gymnasium. Its expenditures last year were about one hundred and ten dollars, including the secretary's salary. Its rooms are always open and free to all, where are found all the latest newspapers and current periodicals. At its "book receptions," at which the entrance-fee is a book given to the association, there are readings, recitations, music, etc., followed by refreshments, a social reunion, etc. It is one of the best institutions of the city, and productive of great good.

On Nov. 22, 1881, Willis A. Guernsey, a graduate of Middlebury (Vermont) College, assumed the duties of general secretary and superintendent. During the seasons previous he was likewise engaged for the Ogdensburgh (N. Y.) Young Men's Christian Association.

A meeting for the purpose of forming a "Temperance Society" was held in the Lutheran Church, Dec. 5, 1833, at which William McMahon presided, and of which Dr. Samuel P. Smith was secretary. Thirty-three persons signed the constitution then adopted, and the society, the first in Allegany County, was duly organized. The permanent officers were William McMahon, president; Thomas J. McKaig, vice-president; William Thistle, secretary; and Rev. John Kehler, Rev. H. Best, Samuel Eckles, Levi Hilleary, Emanuel Easter, John Miller, of J., John White, managers. Revs. John Kehler and H. Best were appointed a committee to wait upon the merchants of the town and solicit them to discontinue their traffic in ardent spirits, and also to wait on persons engaged in boating and solicit them to discontinue the practice of giving their hands ardent spirits. The society then adjourned to meet the second Saturday in February, at early candle-light, in the Methodist meeting-house.

The Ladies' Beneficial Society meets on the first Wednesday evening of every month in the lecture-room of Christ Lutheran church, on Baltimore, corner of North Centre Street. SS. Peter and Paul's Beneficial Society meets the first Saturday of each month in the school-house adjoining SS. Peter and Paul's church, on Fayette near Smallwood Street. St. Joseph's Beneficial Society meets the last Saturday of each month in the school-house above named. St. Patrick's Beneficial Society meets on the first Monday after the second Saturday of each month, at Carroll Hall, on North Centre Street. St. Edward's Beneficial Society meets at five P.M. every third Sunday at Carroll Hall.

The Arion Singing Society meets every Tuesday and Saturday evenings in Arion Hall, on South Centre, corner of Harrison Street. The Lorely Glee Club meets once a week in Wiesel's music store, J. P. Wiesel, conductor.

The Laboring Sons of Cumberland meet every Monday in McKendree Chapel, on North Centre Street. G. U. O. F., Queen City Lodge, meets in Reynolds' Block, on Baltimore Street, the first and third Tuesdays of each month. The I. O. G. T. meets in Reynolds' Block every Thursday evening.

Star of the West Lodge, A. F. and A. M., meets in Reynolds' Block every Wednesday evening.

Tyler Post, No. 5, Grand Army of the Republic, has the following officers: William E. Griffith, post commander; J. B. Winslow, adjutant. The charter was granted June 24, 1876, for the department of Maryland. The charter members were L. H. Dowden, J. B. Winslow, Joseph Reid, William E. Griffith, Henry J. Johnson, J. C. Lynn, John Weir, William S. Shuck, Henry Shriver, Harmon White, Levi Shaw, Jr., George B. Fundenburg, C. N. Madore, J. D. George, Richard L. Gross.

Saturday, April 11, 1840, members of the I. O. O. F. met at James Black's hotel and formed a lodge.

The Young People's Association meets on the second Tuesday of every month in the lecture-room of the First Presbyterian Church.

The Young Men's Lyceum, SS. Peter and Paul's Church, meets every Thursday evening at school hall on Fayette Street.

The Literary and Philharmonic Society of Centre Street Methodist Episcopal Church meets the second and fourth Wednesdays of every month.

Bayley Institute meets every Sunday evening in Carroll's Hall.

Cumberland Lyceum meets every Wednesday evening at Good Templars' Hall, No. 86 Baltimore Street.

Young Men's Literary Society of Kingsley Chapel meets at the chapel every Saturday evening.

Waverly Social Club meets Thursday evenings, on Prospect Street opposite court-house.

Arion Gesang Verein meets at Arion Hall, corner of South Centre and Harrison Streets, the first Wednesday of every month.

The Baptist Literary and Musical Society meets the third Tuesday of every month.

Luther Union meets first Tuesday evening of every month, in the lecture-room of Christ's Lutheran Church.

Excelsior Sextette Band meets Monday, Wednesday, and Friday evenings at Foreman's store, on North Centre Street. Thomas Halle, leader.

First Western Maryland Cornet Band (colored) meets Monday, Wednesday, and Friday evenings, at hall on North George Street. Number of men, 12. Thomas Males, leader.

Potomac Cornet Band meets every Monday, Wednesday, and Friday evening, in Gramlich's Hall, on North Centre Street. Number of men, 18. Chris. Scheermesser, leader; John Minnicks, president; George Herbick, vice-president; C. Loeber, corresponding secretary; G. Neal, financial secretary; H. Helker, treasurer.

Queen City Band meets Monday and Thursday evenings of each week in their hall, No. 8 North Centre Street. Number of men, 15. C. T. Hayden, leader.

Cumberland has the following public halls:

Academy of Music (City Hall building). Stage, twenty-eight by thirty-one feet. Complete set of choice scenery, with seating capacity to accommodate twelve hundred persons.

Arion Hall, South Centre, corner Harrison Street.

Belvidere Hall, No. 115 Baltimore Street.

Castle Hall (K. of P.), Little's Building, 110 Baltimore Street.

Carroll Hall, North Centre, adjoining St. Patrick's Church.

Good Templars' Hall, No. 86 Baltimore Street.

Gramlich's Hall, North Centre Street.

Hetzel's Hall, No. 47 Baltimore Street.

Reynolds' Hall, on Baltimore Street.

Terpsichorean Hall, No. 15 Washington Street.

Turner Hall Gardens, on Baltimore turnpike.

At a meeting held on Monday evening, Feb. 4, 1828, for the purpose of forming a Bible Society auxiliary to the Young Men's Bible Society of Baltimore, the following persons were chosen officers and managers:

President, Rev. Mr. Rhodes; Vice-President, Rev. N. B. Little; Secretary, Dr. S. P. Smith; Corresponding Secretary, William V. Buskirk; Treasurer, Jonathan Butler; Managers, from Cumberland, Rev. Mr. Berkley, John Wright, Maj. J. Bayard, Jacob Snyder, George Hoffman, William McMahon, B. S. Pigman, Elnathan Russell, Peter Baumward, Martin Rizer, of M., Martin Rizer, Jr., Peter Hoffman, John G. Hoffman; First District, John McHenry, Robert Swan, Mr. Koontz, Upton Bruce, Mr. Armstrong;

Second District, B. Coddington, Joseph France, John Fite, Jr., Jacob Clemmer, John Whitehead; Third District, Jesse Tomlinson, Edie Ridgely, Robert Hunter, Archibald Thistle, George Bruce; Fourth District, William Shaw, John Templeman, Thomas Dawson, Rev. Mr. Miller, John Brandt; Fifth District, Andrew Bruce, Valentine Hoffman, Peter Uhl, William Ridgely, Hon. M. C. Sprigg; Seventh District, Rev. James Taylor, John Easter, Jr., John Reed, Rev. Lenox Martin, Thomas Greenwall; Eighth District, James Tidball, Daniel Folck, Samuel Slicer, Walter McAtee, John Norris; Ninth District, Francis Reid, George Robinette, Thomas Cromwell, John Davis, Thomas Pratt.

April 7, 1828, Rev. N. B. Little's seminary was opened in the house of the Rev. N. B. Little, in Bedford Street, formerly tenanted by R. R. Robinson, for the reception and tuition of scholars, at the following terms: Children in their first rudiments, $2 per year; reading, writing, drawing, printing, arithmetic, etc., $2.50 per year; geography, projection of maps, and drawing upon globes, together with their use, composition and history, $3 per year. For higher branches terms were regulated accordingly.

The third annual meeting of the Association for the Relief of the Poor was held in the lecture-room of the English Lutheran church, Nov. 20, 1866, and the following officers were elected for the ensuing year:

President, W. R. McCulley; Secretary, John B. Shaw; Treasurer, J. B. H. Campbell; Board of Managers, First District, Joshua Steiner, A. Scott; Second District, A. L. M. Bush, Henry Bloomhower; Third District, C. A. Seay, E. Easter; Fourth District, William Weber, S. Adler; Fifth District, John Howard, S. M. Haller; Sixth District, Gustavus Rizer, Hopewell Hebb.

$189.86 were disbursed to the poor in the preceding year, leaving a balance in the treasury of $36.75.

The officers of the Agricultural and Mechanical Society of Allegany County are as follows: James M. Schley, president; S. H. Fundenberg, secretary; William M. Price, treasurer; Directors, Lloyd Lowndes, Horace Resley, Hanson Willson, G. Stucklauser, William Price. No exhibition was held in 1880 or 1881.

CHAPTER LVII.

RAILROADS, INDUSTRIES, ETC.

Railroads—Leading Industries—Coal Companies—Banks and Financial Institutions—Prominent Citizens—Necrology.

The railroads which centre at Cumberland are the Baltimore and Ohio, the Pittsburgh and Connellsville, which extends from the main stem of the Baltimore and Ohio to Pittsburgh, the Cumberland and Pennsylvania, the George's Creek and Cumberland Railroad, and the Pennsylvania Railroad in Maryland. The Pittsburgh and Connellsville Branch of the Baltimore and Ohio Railroad was opened to Cumberland on the 26th of June, 1871. The train arriving from Pittsburgh brought a large number of its citizens with the "Du Quesne Band," and a large delegation was present from Baltimore, headed by John W. Garrett, president of the Baltimore and Ohio Railroad. The address of welcome was delivered by Hon. Henry W. Hoffman, of Cumberland. The completion of the road was an important epoch in Cumberland's history, and brought into close connection two of the great coal marts of the country.

The Cumberland and Pennsylvania Railroad extends from Cumberland, Md., to Piedmont, W. Va., with several branches to such of the coal-mines as do not lie immediately upon its main stem. Its length, including branches, is fifty-five miles. Leaving Cumberland, the road runs along the left bank of Will's Creek, through the "Narrows," a pass through Will's Mountain, whose white sandstone cliffs rise almost perpendicularly from the banks of the creek to a height of six hundred feet, affording wild and picturesque scenery not surpassed in this country. At the west end of the "Narrows," near the mouth of Braddock's Run, the Eckhart Branch Railroad leaves the main stem; and at Kriegbaum's the State Line Branch leaves the main stem. By this last-named branch the Cumberland and Pennsylvania Railroad connects with the Pennsylvania Railroad, and over this latter line a portion of its coal traffic reaches South Amboy, a shipping-point within twenty miles of New York City, from which it is distributed along the Atlantic seaboard north and east. At Cumberland the Cumberland and Pennsylvania Railroad connects with the Baltimore and Ohio Railroad and the Chesapeake and Ohio Canal, and through these channels of transportation much of its large coal traffic reaches tidewater at Baltimore, Georgetown, D. C., and Alexandria, Va. The line passes through a beautiful and picturesque country, by the towns of Mount Savage, Frostburg, Lonaconing, Barton, Westernport, and a number of populous villages, to Piedmont, W. Va. From the busy populations of these towns and villages it draws a large passenger and general freight traffic. At Piedmont it again connects with the Baltimore and Ohio Railroad, sending over that line large quantities of coal to the States west of the Ohio, as well as east to Baltimore. The first section of the road built was called the Mount Savage Railroad, and was completed in 1846, connecting the Mount Savage Iron-Works with Cumberland. Owning no rolling-stock, this road was operated by the Baltimore and Ohio Railroad Company. Between 1846 and 1864, by successive extensions of the original Mount Savage Railroad (the title of which had been changed to the Cumberland and Pennsylvania Railroad), and the purchase of the George's Creek Railroad, running from Lonaconing to Piedmont, the Cumberland and Pennsylvania Railroad reached its present terminus. Having been built with inadequate means, the facilities the road offered the coal trade of the region through which it passed were very limited, but since 1864 large sums of money have been expended upon it in laying the entire line with heavy steel rails, ditching, stone ballasting, and thoroughly equipping it, and all that energy and enterprise could do to place the road in a state of thorough efficiency in every department has been done.

The chief traffic of the railroad is its coal transportation, which amounted in 1881 to 1,930,647 tons. It has also an active freight and express business in general merchandise, its express connecting with the Adams and the Baltimore and Ohio Railroad Expresses. Four passenger-trains run daily between Piedmont and Cumberland, two east and two west, offering excellent accommodations to the large travel of the busy communities through which the line passes. The mail is delivered twice daily to all stations upon the road. The company's large locomotive and car-shops at Mount Savage are completely equipped with the most approved modern machinery and every appliance necessary for the building of locomotives and cars. Besides the rebuilding and repairing of locomotives and cars for the company, these shops are now doing a large business in manufacturing for the general market, and have now contracts on hand sufficient to occupy them to their full capacity for the whole of the current year. The rolling-stock of the company consists of twenty-five heavy freight and passenger engines and four hundred and fifty-seven passenger, baggage, freight, and coal-cars. The officers are Charles F. Mayer, president; Charles F. Mayer, William F. Frick, Decatur H. Miller, Robert Garrett, William Whitewright, directors; Charles W. Keim, secretary and treasurer; P. L. Burwell, general superintendent.

The George's Creek and Cumberland Railroad was organized and incorporated in 1879, with a capital stock of $345,000, which is controlled by the American and Maryland Coal Companies. A bonded indebtedness of $500,000 was authorized, which will not be fully required to make the road complete in sidings and rolling-stock. The main line of the road is twenty-four miles long, extending from the centre of the George's Creek coal-field to the city of Cumberland, where it connects with the Chesapeake and Ohio Canal and the Baltimore and Ohio Railroad, and there are about three miles of sidings. The same parties control the connecting Pennsylvania Railroad in Maryland, which is six and a half miles long and has about one mile of sidings. This road has a capital stock of $35,000, and a first mortgage of $80,000, and a second mortgage of $65,000, which is held by the city of Cumberland and bears no interest for thirty years. These lines have been completed, and now a large portion of the George's Creek coal-field has outlets to the Pennsylvania Railroad and the Chesapeake and Ohio Canal, whereas in the past this district was depending on the Baltimore and Ohio Railroad alone. These roads form a line that extends from the heart of the George's Creek basin to the city of Cumberland, and to the Pennsylvania State line, where a connection is made with the Pennsylvania Railroad system, and they thus enter into competition with the Cumberland and Pennsylvania Railroad. The saving in distance by the new route is said to be about twenty per cent., while it is asserted that a reduction of twenty-five per cent. from the minimum rate (two cents per ton per mile) charged by the old roads will make the new enterprise a very profitable one. This road has a further advantage in the fact that it runs along at the mouths of the drifts of the several mines, and does away with the expensive planes. The economies aggregate what alone should be a good profit to the coal companies. Furthermore, the Chesapeake and Ohio Canal Company is under contract for a period of twenty-seven years to limit the tolls collected on all coal passing over this road to its canal to a maximum of forty cents per ton.

Shipments of coal over the Pennsylvania Railroad for transhipment into vessels at Philadelphia began June 1st, and shipments are now also making to the Chesapeake and Ohio Canal. The business over the new road for the current year is expected to amount to one million tons. In addition to the advantages which are to accrue to the trade from the building of this road, the Chesapeake and Ohio Canal is to make improvements which will both facilitate the transportation of coal and reduce the cost of delivering it at tide-water. It will double the length of half its locks this year, and next winter will complete the work. Steam canal-boats have been adopted with substantial advantages on this canal; and with the increased size of the locks, it will be but a few years before all of the carrying will probably be done by them. The present steam colliers carry but about ninety tons, and compete successfully with horse-boats carrying about one hundred and ten tons. Upon the completion of the enlarged locks, it is proposed to use boats of double the present length, with a capacity for carrying about two hundred and ten tons. The power required to move these will scarcely be ten per cent. greater than that required for the ninety-ton boats now in use. The result of all these improvements will be to enable the Cumberland mines to put coal on board vessels at tide-water at a lower cost than any other mining district in this country, and about as cheaply as any of the English mines. The subject is of special interest to the producers of both bituminous and anthracite coal, for besides exerting its influence on the prices of other bituminous coals, Cumberland will become, in a measure, the regulator of prices of anthracite steam coals, which are even now suffering from the competition with bituminous coal. While the policy of the companies which control the George's Creek and Cumberland Railroad will be not unnecessarily to depress the price of their product, yet with the economies which have been and are to be established they will be able to do a profitable business at prices which have heretofore been considered very low, and which otherwise would not be remunerative. The officers are: President, Henry Loveridge; General Manager, James A. Milholland; general office on North Centre, corner of Hays Street. The stock, which was subscribed on May 7, 1879, was taken by sixteen parties. The American and Maryland Coal Companies each hold one hundred thousand dollars worth of stock, and the balance is held by New England capitalists. On June 10, 1879, the stockholders selected the following gentlemen as directors of the road: Henry Loveridge, G. P. Lloyd, G. P. Bangs, C. E. Dana, G. L. Kingsland, A. J. Aiken, Sidney Witringham; and as officers, President, Henry Loveridge; Vice-President and Treasurer, Gardner P. Lloyd; Secretary, Samuel T. Ross. The directors on June 16th awarded the construction of the road to Willis and J. N. Phelps, of Springfield, Mass.

The Pennsylvania Railroad in Maryland was incorporated in 1868. The first rail laid upon the road in Maryland was placed in position May 20, 1879, by a committee consisting of the following gentlemen: John Humbird, J. H. Percy, William Hall, George Henderson, Rev. Dr. S. C. Thrall, F. Minke, William Brace, William Piatt, S. Luman, and L. M. Shepherd. Mayor Reed, of Cumberland, drove the first spike. The directors of the road for 1877–78 were M. A. Healy, J. F. Zacharias, F. Williams, Frank Haley, K. H. Butler, F. Minke, F. Laing, Jr.; President, M. A. Healy; Vice-President, J. F. Zacharias; Treasurer, F. Laing, Jr.; Secretary, G. G. McKay. May 6, 1879, the following directors were chosen for the road: Nelson Beall, F. Haley, M. A. Healy, Henry Loveridge, J. M. Schley, F. E. Brockett, and A. J. Clark, and on May 10th they chose the following board of officers: M. A. Healy, president; Henry Loveridge, vice-president and treasurer; F. Laing, Jr., secretary. Col. J. M. Schley, A. J. Clark, and F. E. Brockett were chosen as a committee to manage the road. The road was finished to the Narrows June 17th, and about this time Edward Manley, John Hummler, J. H. Percy, and Henry Loveridge were selected by the company and property-holders along the Payne Spring route to determine the valuation of land, and on June 20th they made the investigation. July 2d a change of management occurred in this company, and the following officers and directors were elected: Henry Loveridge, A. J. Clark, F. E. Brockett, J. F. Zacharias, F. Laing, Jr., F. Holley, J. M. Schley, directors; J. M. Schley, president; Henry Loveridge, vice-president and treasurer.

The Pennsylvania road lapped the disputed crossing of the Cumberland and Pennsylvania Railroad on July 19, 1879. The first train (a freight) that entered the city from this road arrived on December 2d, and proceeded down the track to Payne Spring Street. On December 15th passenger trains began running regularly. To the tact, foresight, and energy of ex-President Healy this road owes its construction. He originated the plan, obtained the necessary aid from the city of Cumberland and legislation from the State of Maryland, and with the assistance of Mr. Prevost, formerly superintendent of the Bedford Division, secured the co-operation of the Pennsylvania road.

The Western Maryland Railroad has an office at Cumberland, whence freights and cars are shipped over the Chesapeake and Ohio Canal to Williamsport, a distance of one hundred miles, and thence by this railroad to tide-water at Baltimore, the eastern terminus of the road. The first shipment from Baltimore to Cumberland over this road in connection with the canal was made Aug. 5, 1876, when it reduced the tariff rates to a lower figure than previously carried by the Baltimore and Ohio Railroad.

The road has a regular line of boats to carry its freight on the canal from Cumberland to Williamsport, where it is transferred to the cars. The railroad has a warehouse at the head of the basin in Cumberland, where it receives freight from or for boats. Jacob Brengle is the railroad's general agent at Cumberland.

Trades and Industries.—In 1811, Capt. Thomas Blair had a hat-factory on Green Street, near Water

Street, and nearly opposite James Glenn had a shop where he made nails by hand. Abraham Faw kept tavern west of Smallwood Street. On Bedford Street there was a blacksmith-shop near the banks of the creek and close to the bridge. Between Liberty and Centre Streets. John Shryer had his tan-yard. On the west side of Mechanic Street, Elnathan Russell had a blacksmith-shop, A. Rogers a butcher's shop, Nicholas Koontz and Michael Fisher cooper-shops, and Thomas Dowden a blacksmith-shop. Between Baltimore and Creek Streets, on Mechanic Street, were Wyatt's drug-store, the Cumberland Bank, and Slicer's tavern. Between Bedford and Baltimore Streets were George Hoblitzell's store, William Shryer's cabinet-shop, Peter and Samuel Lowdermilk's harness and saddlery-shops, E. Vowell's store, McGill's drug-store, and the old National tavern. Between Blue Spring and Bedford Streets were McDonald's shoe-shop, Adam Zeigler's store, James Simmons' butcher-shop, Jacob Neff's pottery, Robert McCleary's and Jacob Karns' blacksmith-shops. On the upper side of Blue Spring were Henry Korns' comb-factory, Samuel Smith's store and post-office, M. Soyster's tan-yard, and Jacob Soyster's saddlery-shop. Between Bedford and Baltimore were the taverns of Mr. Carrico and John Ryan, the stores of C. F. Broadhag, Jacob Hoblitzell, and Mr. Justice, the hat-shop of John Gephart, and the tailor-shop of Solomon Davis. Between Little Valley road and Bedford Street were Michael Wise's drug-store, George and Jonathan Cox's tan-yard, James Hook's wheelwright-shop, and the "Three-Butts" inn, kept by Dickinson Simkins. North of Little Valley road were Hector McIntosh's comb-factory, Stricker's tailor-shop, Crawford's shoe-shop, David Shultz's wagon-making-shop, and Jonathan Hendrixson's carpenter-shop. Henry Startzman's tannery was on the northwest corner of Bedford and Centre Streets, and on the northeast corner was Thomas Thistle's tavern. Patrick Murdock's grist-mill stood at the mouth of the race, where is now the wharf of the Consolidation Coal Company. It was built in 1800 by Peter Devecmon, and cost eight thousand dollars. John Gephart was an auctioneer, W. T. Pollock a saddler, William Houx chair-maker, John Milburn auctioneer, John Folck owner of a warehouse, Zadoc Clark hatter, Robert McGuire watch and clock-maker, and Miss Bradley, a teacher.

The following persons advertised in the Cumberland newspapers during 1832: D. D. Hoblitzell, property for sale; Union Sabbath-school, celebration of anniversary; Edward Mull, about to open an English school; B. S. Pigman, as trustee to sell James Black's tavern and the residue of the estate of the late James Scott, near Cresaptown; John Clarke, of Baltimore, announced a drawing of the Maryland State Lottery, of which the highest prize was $20,000; Moses Rawlings, sheriff, sale of interest of Agnes Morris and John Harness in property known as "Cresap's Prospect," etc.; Wm. K. Newman, removal to Pleasant Valley Inn; John Nead, barber; Robert Swantt, sale of lands in "The Glades"; John Brant, sale of lands and a coal-mine; William Norris, offering thirty dollars reward for "Negro Jim"; Moses Rawlings, sheriff, sale of property belonging to John Albright; James Clemmer, as trustee, sale of property belonging to William Coddington; Moses Rawlings, sheriff, sale of real estate and two slaves belonging to Wm. McMahon; James Hook, chair and spinning-wheel-maker; Thomas Reed, five thousand acres of land for sale in the mountains, four miles from "Paddy Town"; Martin Rizer, Jr., plow and wagon-maker; Thos. Dowden, Eli Mobley, and Sylvanus Bennett in the same business; Adam Yeast, sale of farm-lands; John Reed, merchant in "Old Town"; D. B. Hoblitzell, to rent the saw and grist-mill, two and three-quarter miles east of Cumberland, known as "Pleasant Mills"; James Moore, druggist; David Ellis, that he had opened a house of private entertainment, to be known as "Traveler's Rest," at the noted stand occupied some years before by Joseph Carter and afterwards by Nathan Nadenbush, on the main road leading from Winchester, Va., to Old Town; Miss Yeakle, that she had opened "a female seminary"; Krebs & Falls, removal of store to the brick house adjoining William H. Newman's hotel; Edward Johnson, barber; William Shryer and William W. Weaver, cabinet-makers. Reuben Worthington & Co. advertised in 1834 that they would receive from one thousand to two thousand dollars in Chesapeake and Ohio Canal scrip in payment of goods at their store.

S. Hamilton advertised for rent the "Central Inn" (late Pratt's), twenty miles east of Cumberland.

Thomas Beall, of Samuel, in December, 1807, owned several mills, and advertised to sell them as follows: a set of mills adjoining the town of Cumberland; a set at mouth of Town Creek, which had a good brick dwelling, miller's house, cooper's shop, and distillery; and a mill on Evitt's Creek, within two miles of Cumberland. All of these mills had excellent farms attached to them.

In 1829, Samuel Charles printed and published *The Civilian;* Mrs. E. Gayard kept a millinery-store on the west side of Will's Creek, opposite Stidger's store; James Black was the proprietor of a large grocery; Jonathan Butler kept dry-goods, hardware, queensware, groceries, and liquors; Joseph McCulloh was a clock and watch-maker, No. 3 McCleary's Row; Pratt Collins was a saddle and harness-maker on the public square; Philip Wengert had a wool-carding, fulling, and dyeing establishment on Jennings' Run, three miles from Cumberland; Samuel Shockey had a hat-manufactory on North Mechanic Street; J. J. Wells had a tailoring establishment; and Reuben Worthington opened his stock of dry-goods, groceries, etc., at his store on the public square.

On Feb. 3, 1841, Lockwood & Faxon opened the Cumberland Foundry and Machine-Shop, just erected by them. They manufactured bevel and spur-gearings for mills, and did all kinds of boring, turning, and fitting up such machinery. The castings were first-class, and their workmanship in moulding and finishing unsurpassed.

The Cumberland Cast-Steel Works, located near the Baltimore and Ohio Railroad, and directly on the Chesapeake and Ohio Canal, were started in 1873, and were erected by Thompson & Paxton. A company was afterwards organized and chartered under the title of Cumberland Cast-Steel Company, of which J. H. Grover was president.

The property consists of a machine-shop and hammer-room, containing two steam hammers, furnaces, a boiler and engine of twenty-five horse-power, a donkey-engine for hoisting coal, etc.; a blacksmith-shop, with all necessary tools for gas, etc.; a charcoal-house, converting-furnaces, oil-house, ingot-furnaces, gas-furnaces, melting-shop, pattern-shop, brick oven, and carpenter-shop. There is also a dwelling-house, of four rooms and a kitchen, with a well at hand, an office building of two rooms, with furniture and one Hall's safe, a stable, wagon, etc., all in good condition. Ten acres of ground belong to the works, the whole having cost fifty thousand dollars. The capacity is twelve thousand pounds of cast steel per day, and, if necessary, it could easily be increased to forty thousand by adding sufficient steam-hammers. Its location is admirable, having a wide frontage upon the canal and standing in immediate proximity to the railroad, thus giving most ample facilities for shipping by rail or water. It has not been in operation for several months.

The Cumberland Gaslight Company was organized in May, 1854, with the following stockholders composing the corporation: Joseph Shriver, E. T. Shriver, and Alpheus Beall, of Cumberland, and Pericardus & Hoye, of New York City. Its officers were: President, Joseph Shriver; Treasurer, E. T. Shriver; and Superintendent, Charles A. Seay, who have held these positions to the present time.

On Nov. 10, 1854, Cumberland was first lighted by gas, and on December 21st following the City Council enacted an ordinance for the erection of twenty iron lamp-posts on the leading streets, at an expense of twenty-five dollars each, which the Gaslight Company stipulated to light with gas for thirty dollars each per year. The office is No. 12 North Centre Street.

The "Basin Wharf" is owned by Walsh & McKaig. Its directors are John Walsh, W. W. McKaig, S. A. Cox, William Walsh, Thomas J. McKaig; general agent, M. Coulehan.

In the spring of the year 1816, Thomas and Roger Perry built their glass-works on the ground close to the lot on which now stands the residence of John B. Widener. Sand adapted to glass manufacturing was obtained near the Narrows, on Will's Mountain. The first glass was manufactured from a coal-fire, and was of a green color. They worked this blast up into green bottles, of which they turned out large numbers for so small an establishment. Afterwards they used wood for fuel and made a better quality. They sold their manufactured wares in the Eastern cities and Pittsburgh. Four or five pieces of glass made by the Perrys are yet preserved by Mrs. Grace Neall. The venture, however, did not realize the expectations of its projectors, and in 1819, after three years' trial, with severe pecuniary losses, they were compelled to cease manufacturing. Vestiges of this old factory are visible yet, and portions of it are still standing. The sand in this region is said to be the best in America for glass manufacture, and had it not been for the monetary depression following the war of 1812, from 1815 to 1822, there is no doubt these works would have become one of the greatest in the country.

In September, 1880, the Warren Glass-Works was erected and started in South Cumberland, of which Josiah Porter is president, A. V. Whiteman, secretary, and W. B. Whiteman, treasurer. L. P. Whiteman is superintendent. The general office is No. 39 Warren Street, New York. A temporary suspension of the works was caused Nov. 5, 1881, by the breaking of the last two of the eight pots. The stoppage necessarily occasioned a loss of several thousand dollars.

In April, 1853, Thomas J. McKaig, William W. McKaig, Alpheus Beall, J. H. Tucker, M. P. O'Hern, S. M. Semmes, M. O. Davidson, and A. T. Roberts organized a joint-stock company, and built and started a cotton-factory at the northern end of Centre Street. Ira Stambrough was the first superintendent and manager of the factory.

The Cumberland Hydraulic Cement Company was

established originally by Dr. Lynn in 1836, and in 1868 the present company was incorporated, comprising Dr. A. Thompson, of Mount Savage, as president, George F. Gephart, of Cumberland, as secretary, and Cornelius Stock, of Cumberland, holding the remaining interest. Mr. Stock died in 1877, and his interest was purchased by William Hall, of Cumberland. This gentleman, at the time of the organization, had secured the services of Thomas W. Evans, an expert in the practical manufacture of cement. From that date the works have been kept constantly busy in supplying the always-growing demand. The works are of course extensive, the mill proper covering sixty-five by eighty feet of space, with two stories and a basement. A one hundred horse-power engine drives four burrs, with a capacity of two hundred and fifty barrels per day. Forty men are employed.

The present officers of the company are as follows: President, A. Thompson; Superintendent, George F. Gephart; Secretary, Oliver C. Gephart; Directors, A. Thompson, O. C. Gephart, G. F. Gephart, William Hase, J. F. Zacharias. The works are on the west side of Will's Creek, near Lee. The original Lynn Cement-Mill was burned down June 30, 1859, and rebuilt two months later.

The Cumberland Telephone Company was established in the city of Cumberland under the rights and franchises of the Maryland Telephone Company of Baltimore on the 1st day of March, 1881. The central office or exchange building is situated on South Liberty Street, in the rear of the Second National Bank, and diagonally opposite the post-office. From this point, which is one of the most eligible, the wires of the company radiate in almost every direction, reaching the homes and business places of about one hundred persons. The construction work of the Cumberland Exchange building is of a superior character, and in the opinion of electricians compares favorably with that of some of the first exchanges in the country. Two switch-boards of fifty lines each are used in connecting one subscriber with another. Three operators are employed in relays of eight hours each, the service being continuous day and night. The central office has a capacity of five hundred wires, which can be readily handled whenever the demand arises. In addition to the city lines, this company has recently built a telephone line to Lonaconing, distant from Cumberland about twenty miles, *via* the George's Creek and Cumberland Railroad, and on its way the line taps the little village of Pompey Smash. Other lines beyond the limits of the city are contemplated, connecting it with Frostburg, Barton, and other points in the great coal regions of Maryland.

As above stated, the company is working under the franchises of the Maryland Telephone Company, and its present officials are John A. Blatton, superintendent, and Edward Deve, manager. The work of construction was begun and carried on successfully under the most disadvantageous circumstances, the chief of which was the unprecedentedly hard winter during which the greater portion of the work was done. Like all other enterprises of a progressive character, the establishment of the Telephone Exchange in Cumberland was a laborious task, and only accomplished by dint of unwearying labor and unflagging energy. The service in the exchange is of the best character, the connections being made in from three to four seconds after a party has been "rung up." The rates paid by the patrons of the exchange are lower than those charged in cities of the same size in the Eastern and Western States, while the most approved instruments of modern invention, including the Blake transmitter, are in use on every line. Up to the 30th of August, 1881, as many as eleven thousand five hundred calls and connections had been made through the switch-board at the central office, which shows that twenty-three thousand persons conversed by aid of the telephone, and numbers of these were many miles apart.

The Coal-Fields of Allegany County—Exhibits at Different Periods.—Three or four bateaux arrived at Washington, D. C., on April 20, 1826, laden with coal from the rich mines near Cumberland, on the Potomac. It sold twenty cents cheaper than the Richmond coal, and was of better quality.

The Baltimore *Sun* of Aug. 7, 1841, said,—

"The coal region is at present one of the unproductive regions of the State, and the most prominent adverted to about the commencement of this article. It lies principally in Allegany County, and is mostly of the bituminous description. The expense already incurred for providing means for bringing it to market, by opening a canal from the Potomac River at Georgetown, in the District of Columbia, denominated the Chesapeake and Ohio Canal, having exceeded the estimate of engineers previously employed in the service, and a yet further heavier expense to complete it to the coal beds being ascertained to be necessary before a profit can be realized, have placed the prospects of the party prosecuting very far in the background, at such a distance that under the existing circumstances it is quite uncertain when this work of internal improvement will be completed. The distance yet to be opened is about fifty miles, and unfortunately being the western terminus, the site is more than ordinarily broken, rocky, and even mountainous. That which is denominated the 'Frostburg Coal-Basin' is particularly noticed by Prof. Ducatel, the State geologist, and his remarks in reference thereto will show the character of the region to which it is intended the canal shall extend. This basin is forty miles long and five miles in width, and contains 86,847 acres, which at 8840 square yards to the acre, and fifteen yards in depth, as it is known the bed of the coal is, gives 6,305,137,287 cubic yards, and as one ton of coal occupies by estimate one cubic yard, there is in the basin named the number of tons of coal as expressed in the aforesaid figures. By a similar process the quantity of iron ore ascertained to be imbedded in what is termed the Lonaconing section in the same county amounts to 3,237,576,144 tons, enough to yield, as demonstrated by actual practice, 1,079,191,714 tons of crude iron. Notwithstanding the distant prospect in reference to time in making Maryland productive, or in other words, of converting the minerals into merchandise, there are twelve incorporated companies already within its limits, with a chartered capital of $6,700,000, ready to make a demonstration wherever the opportunity shall present, either by the canal aforementioned or by the Baltimore and Ohio Railroad, which will have reached within about twelve miles of the nearest coal-beds in about a year. One of the prominent companies which has already performed much in exploring, testing, analyzing, etc., the different minerals is the Maryland and New York Iron and Coal Company, whose capital is adequate to the enterprise in which it has entered. And another, the George's Creek Iron and Coal Company, have carried their plans so far into operation, for the purpose of testing the qualities of the material, and expense of operating, etc, that they have erected a furnace and foundry, the former fifty feet high, with boshes of four and a half feet, and when in blast the consumption of coal was twelve hundred tons a month. The campaign was nearly of four months' duration, during which time nine hundred tons of iron were made, the highest yield per week being ninety-two tons. The lump-coal at the opening of the drift was fifty cents per ton, and the iron ore two dollars and a half."

Prior, and up to 1842, it was the practice for merchants, laborers, and others who were employed in various pursuits during the spring, summer, and autumn of each year to engage in the coal trade during the winter, some as miners, some as teamsters, and some as boat-builders. But few mines (or coal-banks, as they were then called) were worked to any extent, the principal one being the old Eckhart mine, located along the side of the National road, nine miles west of Cumberland, from which coal was hauled in wagons, two, three, or four-horse teams, and unloaded on the bank of the Potomac River, at the place now occupied by the Holly water-works in Cumberland City, and farther up the river, where the end of the new bridge is. Coal would be piled up there in large quantities during every winter.

At the great freshet in the spring, the boats which had been built during the preceding winter would be brought into the river, to the points where the coal was piled, and then the work began. Hundreds of men and large boys, with wheelbarrows, would be engaged in loading the boats, often working in the rain, as all were anxious to take advantage of the earliest rise of water in the river to float off the boats. As soon as the boat was loaded, the crew having provided themselves with the necessary provisions, generally consisting of bread, bacon, and coffee, with a little whisky, would start down the river, carried along by the current usual at freshets. The other boats, as soon as loaded, would follow in rapid succession, until all the boats were gone or the large pile of coal exhausted. Frequently the boats would become wrecked by running against rocks in the river, if the water was not sufficiently high to float them over the obstruction; or, on the other hand, if the water should be so high and rapid as to render the boats unmanageable, a boat would be hurled against the bank of the river so violently as to dash it to pieces. In either case the boat and cargo would be a total loss, and occasionally part of the crew were drowned. Upon reaching its destination, the boat and cargo were delivered to the party who had engaged or purchased it, and the crew would immediately return on foot, traveling by the nearest routes, so as to reach home as soon as possible. Instances were common where the boatmen would walk sixty miles from early in the morning until bedtime, only stopping long enough to partake of a couple of frugal meals. The wages given averaged, for the time occupied in running a boat down the river and walking back home, about six dollars per day for steersmen, and two dollars per day for the other men.

The boats as then built contained from one thousand to fifteen hundred bushels of coal, according to size; some were called flat-boats, and others keel-boats. The flat-boats were not brought back, but occasionally a keel-boat would return with salt, fish, or other commodities. When this was done, it required great labor upon the part of the boatmen to push the boat up-stream with poles, and it could only be done at certain times, when there was but little current in the river to contend against. From fifty to sixty boats, carrying in the aggregate about seventy-five thousand bushels of coal, was the average shipment per year on the river by freshets, prior to the completion of the Baltimore and Ohio Railroad and the Chesapeake and Ohio Canal to Cumberland.

In November, 1842, the Baltimore and Ohio Railroad was completed to Cumberland, and but little coal was transported over it during that month and December, but in the year 1843 there were shipped over the road 10,082 tons of coal.

In 1850 the canal was completed to Cumberland, and 4042 tons of coal were shipped by that channel.

On Nov. 30, 1846, the failure of the Mount Savage Iron Company was announced.

In 1850 the Cumberland coal trade was conducted by the Maryland Mining Company, the Frostburg Coal Company, the Allegany Mining Company, and the Borden Mining Company only. The Maryland Mining Company shipped its coal to Cumberland by the Eckhart

Railroad, but the other companies' coal was hauled to Mount Savage by horse-power on a tram-road, and there transferred to the railroad cars. The canal was only opened for business in the latter part of that year, and the terminus of the Baltimore and Ohio Railroad was still at Cumberland. Except the Borden, all the coal companies of 1850 have disappeared. After long struggles and many vicissitudes they were at last all absorbed in the Consolidation Coal Company of the present day. The whole George's Creek region was as yet undeveloped. Only the mines of the George's Creek Coal and Iron Company were worked in a small way, merely to supply the little blast-furnace at Lonaconing, operated by Mr. Detmold, whose metal was sent to market by means of a wooden tramway, connecting with the Eckhart Railroad above Clarysville.

Frostburg was then a small and straggling village, confined almost wholly to the sides of the National road. Highland Hall, the principal hotel, large and commodious, was annually filled during the summer months by many of the leading families of Washington and Baltimore. The Franklin House, the Sand Spring Tavern, and the Stone House on the mountain were all prosperous establishments. In 1850 the founders of the town, Meshach Frost, George McCulloh, George Bruce, Thomas Beall, and Col. Thomas Blair, were living and daily seen on the streets.

Of those who were in the service of the Borden Company at the beginning, when Mr. Knode joined it, there still remain connected with it George Tennant, William Staples, Noah Skidmore, and James Dempster. The half-dozen miners of 1850 were succeeded by more than two hundred in 1872, and four hundred in 1881, and there are many among them, able-bodied men and good workmen, who were yet unborn when Knode weighed the first coal from the mine. The managers and superintendents of the coal trade of 1850 are no longer connected with the business, with the exception of Mr. Greene, of the Borden.

Mr. Williams, of the Allegany Company, died long since at the West, and his successor, Mr. Huntley, has been dead for many years. Mr. Davidson, of the Maryland Mining Company, died in 1872. Mr. Bruce, of the Frostburg Company, was collector of internal revenue in Cumberland for many years.

On Wednesday, Sept. 1, 1852, the large and valuable property of the Maryland Mining Company in Allegany County was sold at public sale in Cumberland for the sum of $500,100; the purchaser being D. Leavitt, president of the American Exchange Bank of New York. This property consists in part of two tracts of land, called "The Maryland Mining Company" and "Fountain Inn," located in one body, containing about nineteen hundred acres of land, a large part of which is underlaid by the great vein of coal fourteen feet in thickness, likewise by many other veins varying in thickness from two to four feet, the whole situated in the very heart of the great semi-bituminous coal-fields of Maryland, with mines opened at great expense. The property includes various lots of ground, and the village of Eckhart Mines, on the National road, near Frostburg, containing about one hundred houses, of which seventy are dwellings, the rest shops for carpenters, blacksmiths, engineers, etc; also two railroads, one nine and a quarter miles long, extending from the mines to the Mount Savage Railroad, which gives a continuous railroad connection to the Baltimore and Ohio Railroad depot at Cumberland; and another one mile long, extending from the Mount Savage road to the property of the Cumberland Basin Company at Cumberland. These two roads alone cost originally $250,000. In addition to all this property there was included in the sale a vast amount of personal property, such as locomotives, several hundred cars, horses, oxen, wagons, farming utensils, machinery, tools, mining implements, etc., all for the sum of $500,100; an insignificant sum when compared with the original vast outlay, which must have been several millions of dollars. The Maryland Mining Company had failed some time before, and its affairs had gone into the hands of trustees. Mr. Leavitt, it was believed, made the purchase for the Cumberland Coal and Iron Company, who owned the adjoining property.

William Cullen Bryant, the famous poet and editor of the New York *Evening Post*, made a visit in 1860 to the coal-regions of Allegany. In a letter dated Mount Savage he gives the following account of the mode of operating the mines, a sketch of the scenery to be witnessed, and other impressions:

"The railway (Baltimore and Ohio) which brought us to Mount Savage is one of the most picturesque in the United States. For more than one hundred and fifty miles it follows the course of the Potomac, winding as the river winds, making sudden turns around lofty crags, sweeping around the base of grassy hillsides, passing under old forests, now bright with their autumnal hues, and sometimes coming out into fair open valleys. Harper's Ferry, where the Shenandoah comes breaking through its rocky pass to pour itself into the Potomac, would be itself sufficient to give this railway pre-eminence were there nothing else worth looking at along the track. Here the train generally stops a few minutes, and the passengers alight to look at the majestic cliffs and to see the place which has recently acquired a new and memorable historical association by the strange adventure of John Brown. A hundred and eighty miles from Baltimore you reach Cumberland, one of the most beautiful sites for a town I ever saw. It lies on the north bank of the Potomac in a circle of lofty hills clothed with forests and divided by half a dozen deep gorges. The town has one or two pleasant streets, the rest are shabby and unsightly. At Cumberland you leave the Baltimore and Ohio Railroad, and enter a single passenger-car at the end of a long row of empty coal-wagons, which are slowly dragged up a rocky pass beside a shallow stream into the coal regions of the Alleganies. You alight among smoking furnaces and forges and vast heaps of cinders at Mount Savage, near the foot of the mountain-range of that name, a village of four thousand inhabitants, gathered from various nations, mostly employed in the iron-works and the mines, and living in cottages. As you ascend from the village you perceive more and more of the beauty of that region. You are among deep, winding valleys and broad mountain-sides, forests of grand old trees and grassy fields, and at every step some new charm of the prospect opens upon you. From the mouths of the coal-mines on the mountains short railways descend to the village, down which rattle trains of trucks loaded with coal.

" . . . Our party made a visit to a coal-mine some three miles distant from Mount Savage. From one of the black entrances flowed a lively little stream with yellow waters, into which I dipped my finger to ascertain their flavor. It was acidulous and astringent, holding in solution both alum and copperas. Leaving the Stygian rivulet we came to another entrance, out of which a train of loaded trucks was passing, every one of which was attended by a miner blackened from head to foot with the dust of his task, and wearing in the front a small crooked lamp to light his way. As they emerged from the darkness they looked like sooty demons of the mine with flaming horns coming from the womb of the mountain. We now entered, each carrying a lantern, attended by a guide. The vein of coal is from eight to ten feet thick, and the passage is of that height, with a roof of glistening slate, propped in some places by wooden posts. Here and there, on each side of the passage, yawned chambers cut in the veins of coal, and extending beyond the reach of the eye in the faint light of our lanterns. At length we heard the sound of sledges, and proceeding for some distance farther came to the end of the passage, where the workmen, each with a lamp in his cap, were driving wedges into the cracks and fissures of the coal to separate it from the roof and walls. We saw several large blocks detached in this manner, the workmen jumping aside when they fell, and then we retraced our steps. Before returning to the entrance, however, our guides took us into a branch of the main passage, in which, after proceeding a little way, we heard a roar as of flames, and then saw a bright light before us. A furnace appeared, in which a fierce fire was blazing; the blackened workmen were stirring and feeding it, and a strong current of air rushing by us went with the flames up the shaft, which reached above to the surface of the ground. This, we are told, was a contrivance to ventilate the mine. All the foul air and all the fire-damp and other noxious gases are drawn up and carried off from the passages and chambers by this method. On our way back to the entrance we perceived that the veins lay at just such an inclination as allowed the workmen to roll the loaded trucks by hand along an easy descent to the mouth, as I hear is the case with all the mines. When I was in this region, twenty-eight years since, they had not begun to work the mines of coal and iron. From the little town of Frostburg, where I then passed the night, a place lying high among the mountain-ridges, where the winter comes early and lingers late, you now look down upon several mining villages. There are twenty-five of them in this coal region, and they are adding greatly to the population. New mines are opened from time to time, so that the mountains ere long will be pierced from side to side with these artificial caverns. A curious effect is observed in some of them. The little veins of water in the earth are collected in the drifts or main passages, and issue noiselessly forth with a current of the color of a porter-bottle. Whether the soil derives any advantage from this sort of under-drainage we have not heard. The population of the mining villages, though to this remark there may be exceptions, does not appear to me to be of the most hopeful kind. They owe little to the schoolmaster, and know so little of the advantages, that they are not generally anxious to procure them for their children.[1] Some of them, however, are provident, invest their earnings in lands, and they and their children will ultimately pass into the agricultural class. They inhabit a region of considerable fertility, their fields yield good crops of wheat and other grains, the finest hay and sweet pasturage for their herds. These farmers are Catholics, and almost in sight of where I write, in one of the pleasantest and greenest nooks of the hills, stands their old church and the house of their priest surrounded by trees. From the point at which I write many interesting excursions may be made. The visitor may follow my example in a drive to the neighboring mines, or he may pass to the Glades, as they call the country west of Cumberland, on the railway, a tract of hills and dales covered with rich grass and grazed by numerous herds, or go on horseback to the pine woods of Mount Savage and lose himself, . . or, proceeding a few miles farther, and crossing the Pennsylvania boundary, find himself among the Dunkers, a primitive and friendly people living in the Dutch Glades, who never suffer the razor to pass over their chins."

The coal-fields are located west of Cumberland, in a basin between the Great Savage Mountain and Dan's Mountain. This basin has a breadth of about five miles, and a length of nearly twenty-five miles. Its axis trends nearly northeast, and near its northern end its floor has an elevation of about two thousand feet above mean tide, the southern range being drained by George's Creek, and the northern by Jennings' Run. The aggregate depth of the formation is eleven hundred feet, its base being the conglomerate, or mill-stone grit. The principal veins are the "Big Vein," the "Four-foot Vein," and the "Six-foot Vein." The "Big Vein" measures fourteen feet of coal, and lies eighteen hundred and sixty feet above tide. This is the vein from which most of the coal is now being mined. It underlies the surface of the valley at Frostburg and Borden shaft, but southward this vein and the measures above it have been carried away by erosion. The "Four-foot Vein" is next to the "Big Vein," and lies about eight hundred feet below it. Part of this vein has suffered from erosion, but on the hill-sides bordering the valley there are splendid opportunities for mining the vein, as it lies some sixty feet above the level from Barton southward down the George's Creek. The "Six-foot Vein" lies one hundred and sixty feet below the "Four-foot Vein." This vein is above water-level in the lower part of the valley only. The total acreage of coal-lands in this

[1] Since then there has been a great change, and Mr. Bryant, if alive, would find the miners intelligent, surrounded with pleasant homes, and their children attendants at the free and Sunday-schools, than which none in Maryland are better than those of the mining regions of Allegany County.

field is 44,132; of this, 17,300 acres contain the "Fourteen-foot Vein," and, of course, all contain the two smaller veins.

There are a number of smaller veins, but they have never received attention, and therefore are not taken into consideration. The output of the various mines reaches Cumberland *via* the Cumberland and Pennsylvania Railroad, which runs from Piedmont to Cumberland through the entire basin; the George's Creek Railroad, which also runs through the coal-fields; the Eckhart Branch, running from the mines of that name; and the main line of the Baltimore and Ohio Railroad, which crosses the George's Creek Valley at its junction with the valley of the Potomac River at Piedmont.

There is also an adjacent coal-field along the Pittsburgh and Connellsville Railroad, the product of which is very similar to that of the above-described region, and as its natural outlet is through the city of Cumberland, it assures the customers located in that city unlimited supplies of the best of fuel.

As will be seen by the following statement from a report made by a committee of naval officers and engineers appointed by the United States government, the average Cumberland, or George's Creek coal has no superior in the market for steam and forging purposes. With equal weights, it surpasses the anthracite in evaporative power by about 2.3 per cent.; with equal bulk, by 1.4 per cent. It surpasses the foreign bituminous coals 20 per cent., comparing equal weights, and 26 per cent., comparing equal bulk.

TABLE OF RELATIVE VALUES OF FOREIGN AND DOMESTIC COALS FOR STEAM GENERATING AND FIRE PURPOSES.

(*Compiled from Senate Doc., No. 386, 28th Congress, 1st Session.*)

DESIGNATION OF COAL.	Percentage of fixed carbon.	Pounds of steam to one of coal from initial temperature.	Pounds of steam furnished by 1 cubic foot of coal.	Steam from 212° from 1 foot of combustible matter.	Reducing power. Parts of lead from litharge by 1 part of coal.	Forge power. Number of links of chain cable 1⅜ inches by 60 pounds coal.	Total waste in ashes and clinker to 100 parts.
Beaver Meadows anthracite.....	91.47	8.76	556 1	10.592	33.29		6.74
Peach Mountain "	89 02	8.96	645.7	10.871	33.49		6.97
Lackawanna "	87.74	8 56	477.7	10.764	33.53		8.93
Lehigh "	89.15	7.73	494.0	9.626	28 92		7 22
Lykens "	83.84	8.43	459.6	10.788	32.60		12.24
Cumberland coal. Average of 5 samples..............................	75.05	8.77	530.1	11.624	33.60	20	9 94
Pennsylvania bituminous........	74.24	8.31	472 8	11.171	31.18	14	16.36
" "	73.11	8.64	515.9	10.956	32.54	15⅜	11.20
" Cambria County..	69.37	8.04	486.9	10.239	31 46		9.74
Virginia bituminous..............	53 01	7.30	448.5	9.741	29 03	14	14.83
Pittsburgh "	54.93	7.03	384.1	8.942	28.89		8 25
Indiana "block" coal..............	58.44	6.31	348 8	7.734	26.53	11	5.12
Pictou, N. S..........................	60.74	7.45	417.9	9.648	26 69	11	12.06
Liverpool	54.90	6.95	375.4	8.255	27 88	13	5.04
Newcastle	57.00	7.68	439 6	9.178	27 55	15	5.68
Scotch..................................	48.81	6.14	353.8	9.719	27.00	10	10.10

The Cumberland coal-fields are worked by seventeen companies, representing a total capital of about twenty-five millions of dollars. The coal is of the kind known as semi-bituminous, and is widely celebrated for its freedom from impurities of all kinds, especially sulphur. It therefore leaves a fine clear ash, without clinker. For heating qualities it is considered pre-eminent, and therefore where great purity and economy in the use of fuel is of importance, it is altogether the most valuable coal of any produced in the country. All the veins lie approximately horizontal, and are especially favorable for mining at the least expense. The "fourteen-foot," or "Big Vein," is the one generally used, although there have been many developments, and indeed, there are several mines in the smaller veins in actual operation. The peculiar locations of portions of the "Big Vein," with reference to points of access for mining without great expenditure or complicated mining machinery, the ease in getting this coal by the miner, the natural drainage of the mines, and many other valuable conditions, all conduce to the production of coal in the most economical manner. Hence it can be purchased in Cumberland, delivered in cars alongside factories, at prices ranging from one dollar to one dollar and a half per ton of two thousand two hundred and forty pounds, and even as low as eighty cents per ton for screenings, which latter, for many purposes in manufacturing, is quite as desirable as the most carefully mined or picked "lump" coal. In this coal-field there are computed to be at least fourteen thousand acres of the "Big Vein" alone remaining untouched. This, at the common production in mining of ten thousand tons to the acre, would indicate that the very large quantity of one hundred and forty million tons still remains to be taken out. This estimate will give some idea of the vast amount of coal in the region, irrespective of the smaller veins, which will ultimately be resorted to, and which are much more extensive than the "Big Vein" proportion.

From Cumberland coal is also made excellent coke, which was used for many years in iron smelting, both in this region and at a distance from it. Heretofore the supply of iron ore has not been sufficient to encourage an expansion of the business of iron manufacturing in the region, but with recent direct railroad connections with the fossil-ore region in the neighborhood of Bedford, Pa., and with connections soon to be made with the red and brown hematite iron-ore regions of West Virginia, the city of Cumberland will doubtless become an iron manufacturing centre of very considerable importance.

It may also be safely predicted that by reason of the extreme purity of the iron ores and of the coal the manufacture of steel, even to the finest cutlery, will be one of the chief industries. Railroad facilities for putting manufactured articles in the market are nearly all that could be desired. The Baltimore and Ohio Railroad runs directly through the city to the great West, and to the Eastern markets and the sea-board. It also reaches Pittsburgh by an important branch direct from Cumberland. The Pennsylvania Railroad Company has an independent line into and out of the city, connecting with all parts North, South, East, and West. The Chesapeake and Ohio Canal starts also from Cumberland, and reaches the sea-board *via* the city of Washington. There are two independent lines of railroad bringing coal from the neighboring coal region to the city, and thus competitive rates are secured for all supplies of that commodity. There is probably no point at present which has before it in the near future so promising a prospect for a busy manufacturing centre as the city of Cumberland. This is consequent upon the recent construction of competitive lines of railway, and the opening up of new regions noted for an abundance of iron ore, timber of a valuable description, and the products of husbandry.

The Blue Ridge Mountains constitute an abrupt and perfect line of demarkation between the ancient silurian and paleozoic formations, and west of a line drawn from Harper's Ferry to the Pennsylvania border there is a totally different geological formation. On the east of this line you leave the ancient formations referred to; on the west you enter immediately the permean and calcareous eras, the upper and lower chalks, and find yourself in the midst of the mesozoic age. The formations in Washington, Allegany, and Garrett Counties are almost totally limestone and sandstone, outcropping in strata in every exposed situation. After crossing the intermediate valley or plain between the Blue Ridge and the Alleganies, you enter at once into the mountain region of Maryland, the North Mountain forming the eastern confine of the great Allegany range. It is in Allegany County, next to Garrett, the extreme western part of Maryland, that one enters the intensely interesting regions of that great geological era in the wonderful and sublime cosmogony. It is here one is first introduced into the great coal-measures, and brought in contact with the ancient carboniferous formations. An abrupt and almost perfect line of demarkation exists, formed by the North Mountain, between the water-shed of the Blue Ridge Mountains, extending eastwardly to the sea, and the plain or valley interposed between the North Mountain and the Allegany range on the west. Geologically, the area east of Dan's Mountain or range is totally different from that west of it. On the east of Dan's Mountain all the geological formations and strata are limestone and sandstone, geologically comparatively recent. On the west of this mountain is to be found a more ancient formation, viz., the great coal-measures. In the coal-basin lying between Dan's Mountain and the Great Savage range flows George's Creek, a tortuous and shallow stream. In periods of drought nothing is to be seen but a dry, rugged water-bed, but in seasons of rain and melting snows this channel is flooded by a deep and turbulent torrent. The sources of George's Creek are near Frostburg, and after traversing this valley for seventeen miles it unites with the Potomac at Piedmont. On either side of this George's Creek Valley, for its entire length, the mountain-ranges are filled with coal to their very apices, and the coal-measures or beds underlying this valley and beds of the creek extend to the depth of one hundred and sixty-five feet. In this valley are innumerable mines, and from Mount Savage to Piedmont is one continuous street and town, twenty-four miles in length, inhabited by miners and their families, mostly of the Welsh and Scotch nationalities. One desirous of ascending Hampshire Mountain takes his position in the train of small cars which glide up the side of the mountain, reaching the first level or halting-place five hundred feet from the surface of the earth. On alighting, he is transferred to a small locomotive, and proceeds horizontally around the mountain when he arrives at the starting-point of another perpendicular ascent. Here on a train of small cars one starts on the upward journey of two thousand feet. At the top of the mountain, at the entrance of the shaft, the visitor starts with his guide, each carrying a torch elevated above their heads, and proceeds along the main avenues, but frequently turning off to explore some branch avenue and chamber. These tunnels through the mines are about fifteen feet wide by eight or ten in height, and are cut through the solid coal. The floor of each tunnel is laid with an iron railway, upon which the small coal-cars run. The cars are drawn by horses, and each car and horse has an attendant or driver, or is propelled by steam-power. To the cap of the driver and to the head of the horse small lamps are attached. Points under the mountains have been reached to the depth of fifteen hundred feet. Generally shafts are sunk into the earth in the measures underlying the valley to the depth of nearly two hundred feet. Where the mine is on top of the mountain the coal is transported down the mountain-side in small cars, regulated by a steam-engine.

OFFICIAL REPORT OF THE CUMBERLAND COAL TRADE *for the week ending November 12th, and for 1881 to that date.*

COMPANIES.	B. & O. R. R. Tons. Cwt.	C. & O. Canal. Tons. Cwt.	P. S. Line. Tons. Cwt.	Total for Week. Tons. Cwt.	Year to Date. Tons. Cwt.
Borden Mining	243 09	3,228 02	875 08	4,346 19	142,458 12
Consolidation Coal	11,500 16	5,492 09	44 14	17,037 19	628,063 14
Blaen Avon Coal	22 04	982 14	......	1,004 18	22,698 03
Hampshire and Baltimore	1,665 12	......	......	1,665 12	52,291 17
George's Creek Coal and Iron	5,309 14	878 04	......	6,187 18	213,002 12
New Central Coal	4,141 16	1,709 00	1,872 00	7,722 16	[1] 254,936 02
Maryland Coal	......	3,301 07	1,409 01	4,857 13	98,475 02
American Coal	......	2,645 18	1,853 01	4,565 04	98,375 12
Atlantic and G. C. Coal	1,542 00	......	......	1,542 00	48,395 15
Piedmont Coal and Iron	390 07	......	......	390 07	6,453 13
Swanton Mining	1,266 00	......	......	1,266 00	34,022 16
Potomac Coal	1,622 00	......	......	1,622 00	69,243 00
Maryland Union Coal	3,807 10	......	......	3,807 10	141,449 08
Davis Brothers' Virginia Mines	1,551 06	......	......	1,551 06	60,219 10
Union Mining	......	......	......	......	10 10
W. Va. Central and Pittsburgh Railroad	850 10	......	......	850 10	2,123 13
Total	33,913 04	18,237 14	6,054 04	58,418 12	
Previously	1,155,095 04	413,545 13	239,198 06	1,813,801 07	
Aggregate	1,189,008 08	431,783 07	245,252 10	1,872,219 19	1,872,219 19

[1] This includes 3,721 10 tons omitted from the report for the week ending November 5th.

STATEMENT OF COAL *transported over the Cumberland and Pennsylvania Railroad and branches during the week ending Saturday, November 12th, and during the year 1881 compared with the corresponding period of 1880.*

	WEEK.				YEAR.			
	C. & O. Canal. Tons. Cwt.	B. & O. R. R. Tons. Cwt.	P. S. Line. Tons. Cwt.	Total. Tons. Cwt.	C. & O. Canal. Tons. Cwt.	B. & O. R. R. Tons. Cwt.	P. S. Line. Tons. Cwt.	Total. Tons. Cwt.
1881	12,290 09	31,121 01	2,792 02	46,203 12	372,432 01	1,123,943 15	142,089 07	1,638,465 03
1880	22,310 06	18,209 03	5,194 11	45,714 00	571,025 11	1,040,562 15	197,130 12	1,808,718 18
Inc.		12,911 18		489 12		83,381 00		
Dec.	10,019 17		2,402 09		198.593 10		55,041 05	170,253 15

COAL TRANSPORTATION *of the George's Creek and Cumberland Railroad to close of week ending Nov. 12, 1881.*

SHIPPER.	To C. & O. Cn'l. Tons. Cwt.	To Pa. R. R. Tons. Cwt.	Local. Tons. Cwt.	Totals for Week. Tons. Cwt.	Year to Date. Tons. Cwt.
American Coal Co.	2,645 18	1,853 01	66 05	4,565 04	79,304 11
Maryland Coal Co.	3,301 07	1,409 01	147 05	4,857 13	85,653 02
Total for week	5,947 05	3,262 02	213 10	9,422 17	......
Previously for year	53,393 01	99,901 01	2,240 14	155,534 16	......
Year to Date	59,340 06	103,163 03	2,453 24	164,957 13	164,957 13

The Cumberland Coal Trade from 1842 to 1874 Inclusive, in Tons.

Years.	Total by B. & O. R. R.	Total by C. & O. Canal.	Total by Pa. R. R.	Aggregate.
1842	1,708	....	....	1,708
1843	10,082	....	....	10,082
1844	14,890	....	....	14,890
1845	24,653	....	....	24,653
1846	29,795	....	....	29,795
1847	52,940	....	....	52,940
1848	79,571	....	....	79,571
1849	142,449	....	....	142,449
1850	192,806	4,042	....	196,848
1851	174,701	82,978	....	257,679
1852	268,459	65,719	....	334,178
1853	376,219	157,760	....	553,979
1854	503,836	155,845	....	659,681
1855	478,486	183,786	....	662,272
1856	502,330	204,120	....	706,450
1857	465,912	116,574	....	582,486
1858	395,405	254,251	....	649,656
1859	426,512	297,842	....	724,354
1860	493,031	295,878	....	788,909
1861	172,075	97,599	....	269,674
1862	218,950	98,684	....	317,634
1863	531,553	216,792	....	748,345
1864	399,354	258,642	....	657,996
1865	560,293	343,202	....	903,495
1866	736,153	343,178	....	1,079,331
1867	735,669	458,153	....	1,193,822
1868	848,118	482,325	....	1,330,443
1869	1,230,518	652,151	....	1,882,669
1870	1,112,938	604,137	....	1,717,075
1871	1,494,814	850,339	....	2,345,153
1872	1,517,347	816,103	22,021	2,355,471
1873	1,718,710	778,802	114,589	2,674,101
1874[1]	1,576,160	767,064	67,671	2,410,895
	17,584,434	8,585,966	204,281	26,338,681

Since 1874 the total shipments from the Cumberland region have been as follows:

	Tons.
1875	2,342,773
1876	1,835,081
1877	1,574,539
1878	1,679,322
1879	1,730,709
1880	2,136,160

The total production up to 1881 was 37,637,268 tons.

Coal Prices, Freights, Etc., from 1861 to 1874.

The following table shows the average price of George's Creek coal at Baltimore, the freight thence to Boston, and the price at which it was delivered at Boston during a series of years:

	Average price for the year at Baltimore.	Average freight to Boston.	Average price delivered at in Boston.
1861	$3.44	$2.25	$5.69
1862	4.23	2.42	6.65
1863	5.57	3.28	8.85
1864	6.84	3.39	10.23
1865	7.57	3.79	11.36
1866	5.94	3.53	9.47
1867	4.97	2.68	7.65
1868	4.71	3.21	7.92
1869	4.97	2.83	7.80
1870	4.72	2.64	7.36
1871	4.72	2.73	7.45
1872	4.66	3.06	7.72
1873	4.84	3.17	8.01
1874	4.50	1.50	6.00

[1] This includes 38,100 tons used on line of Cumberland and Pennsylvania Railroad and its branches, and at Cumberland and Piedmont; also 484,580 tons used by Baltimore and Ohio Railroad in locomotives, rolling-mills, etc.

The total shipments of each of the seven heaviest shippers during 1880, with the increase as compared with 1879, is shown by the following table, which is carefully compiled from official reports:

Company.	1880.	Increase.
Consolidation	552,484	82,288
New Central	350,184	17,455
George's Creek	235,599	106,666
Borden Mining	157,534	2,560
American	124,901	26,327
Maryland	113,445	45,174
Maryland Union	102,821	538

Mining began in 1842, and since then nearly forty million tons of coal have been sent to the market by some twenty companies. This immense transportation has been chiefly done over the Baltimore and Ohio Railroad. In the two principal veins there are estimated to be now three hundred and ten million tons, besides several underlying veins not yet developed.

The Consolidation Coal Company.—Some years previous to 1828 some rude efforts at the development of the Allegany coal-fields had been made. But not until the incorporation, in that year, of the Maryland Mining Company, which, however, made no progress towards its ultimate object for several years, and the granting, ten years later, of the charter of the Maryland and New York Mining Company, can it be said that any organized effort to work the valuable coal deposit of this region was begun. The history of these two companies is the history of enterprise in advance of its time.

Each company set out to build a railroad, the one upon Braddock's, the other upon Jennings', Run. Under changed names and new auspices both of these roads were completed, and both finally united under the ownership of the Consolidation Coal Company. Indeed, the waters of the two streams, flowing naturally on the opposite sides of a mountain-range, have recently been united, as the water of the Eckhart mine, once pumped at great cost into Braddock's Run, now flows through the works of the Consolidation Coal Company into Jennings' Run; this achievement being one of the good results of the consolidation of these neighboring and once rival properties.

The Consolidation Coal Company of Maryland was incorporated in 1860, and in April, 1864, Frederic Walcott was elected its first president, and Wm. Aspinwall, Erastus Corning, David Hoadly, John M. Forbes, Henry Delafield, E. T. Woolsey, James B. Varnum, and David Stewart, its first board of directors. The lands of the Ocean Steam Coal Company, the Frostburg Coal Company, and the Mount Savage Iron Company, together with the iron-works, brick-yards, railroads, wharves, and other property belonging to these companies, were united by this arrangement.

At this time, and for several years subsequently, the Cumberland Coal and Iron Company was eking out a precarious existence.

In May, 1864, Chas. P. Manning, the distinguished civil engineer, was made superintendent of the Consolidation Coal Company. June 2, 1864, Fred. H. Wolcott resigned, and Alex. J. Centre was elected president, Henry T. Weld appointed shipping agent, and F. H. Delano elected a director. The coal shipments from the company's mines amounted to 33,641 tons in 1864.

Jan. 18, 1865, Alex. J. Centre was re-elected president, and the work continued under his management. Fifty-eight thousand and ninety-seven tons of coal were mined, and the whole region mined 903,495 tons.

Jan. 1, 1866, the late Jas. Millholland was elected general superintendent, and on the 17th of the same month, Mr. Centre having resigned, Mr. Millholland was elected president, and, with one or two exceptions, the old board of directors retained. During this and the two succeeding years great energy was displayed on the part of the management, and large sums of money were expended in improving the mines, iron-works, and railways. Especially was this the case with regard to the Cumberland and Pennsylvania Railroad, which transported not only the coal of the Consolidation Coal Company, but, with the exception of that mined by the Cumberland Coal and Iron Company, the coal of the whole region. Many miles of new rails were laid, and large sums of money expended in erecting machine-shops at Mount Savage, which were intended both to do work for the company's railroad, rolling-mills, etc., and to manufacture locomotives and cars for the general market. In 1881 these shops have for the first time been availed of for the last-named purpose, and a large force is now working night and day constructing locomotives and cars of superior character for several Western railroads. Coal shipments were as follows: in 1866, 93,570 tons; in 1867, 190,311; and in 1868, 183,477 tons.

March 29, 1869, James Millholland having resigned the presidency of the company, C. H. Dalton, of Boston, was made president. During this year J. T. Hodge, a distinguished mining geologist, made a careful survey of the coal region. He fixes the area of "Big Vein" coal, then owned by the Consolidation Coal Company, at 7833 acres.

It had become apparent that the iron-works of the company were unprofitable, and from this time forward the mining and transportation of coal occupied the whole attention of the company. Coal shipments in 1869 were 256,790 tons, this being the year in which the company took the leading place among the miners of Cumberland coal, a position which it has ever since maintained. During the next few years heavy expenditures were made for steel rails, iron having proved unfit for the hard service required by the steep grades and heavy locomotives, and gradually the road and its entire equipment were brought up to their present condition of thorough efficiency.

Jan. 19, 1870, the memorandum agreement under which the Cumberland Coal and Iron Company was united with the Consolidation Coal Company was signed, and it took effect March 1st of that year. By this arrangement there was added to the then Consolidation Coal Company the property of the next largest company in the region, comprising large bodies of unworked coal land, together with the railroad from Eckhart mines to Cumberland and valuable wharf property in Cumberland. The shipments during 1870 were 383,707 tons.

Dec. 29, 1870, the Consolidation Company acquired the coal under the Wright farm, one of the finest bodies of coal land in Allegany County, consisting of nearly five hundred acres of coal, without outcrop, and surrounded by land previously owned by the company. Shipments during 1871 were 505,523 tons. May 31, 1871, G. W. McCullough and wife conveyed to the Consolidation Coal Company the tract of land called "Paris," containing five hundred and fifty-seven acres. By this purchase the company not only acquired a large body of valuable coal, but from the position of this land in relation to the company's property it gained an outlet by natural flow for the water which had previously been pumped from the mines at great expense.

In 1872, Allan Campbell was elected president. In 1872 was completed the State Line Branch Railroad, which was built by and under the charter of the Consolidation Coal Company to give the Cumberland and Pennsylvania Railroad a connection with the Pennsylvania Railroad. By this route the Allegany coal-fields gained an all-rail route to South Amboy, a shipping port within twenty miles of New York City, and the shipment of coal to that port by that route at once commenced, and has continued ever since to a large amount annually.

The shipments in 1872 were 504,127 tons. In 1873, Allan Campbell was again elected president, with Messrs. Evarts, Neilson, Warren, Aspinwall, Delano, Norvil, Stewart, Roosevelt, Mott, and Whitewright, directors. The coal mined by the company during 1873 amounted to 548,414 tons, from which

Chs F. Mayer

high point the four subsequent years showed a steady decline. This decrease in the production of Cumberland coal was due to general depression in business consequent upon the crisis of 1873, to the continued high rates paid for mining, which were maintained at the prices prevailing prior to 1873, and to the active competition of the inferior coal mined in the Clearfield region of Pennsylvania, which had been recently developed.

No important event marked the years 1874, 1875, and 1876. The decrease of the coal trade in the region continued year by year to be greater. In February, 1877, a new president and board of directors were elected, consisting of Charles F. Mayer, of Baltimore, president; Messrs. Galloway Cheston, William F. Burns, William F. Frick, John Gregg, William Donnell, Decatur H. Miller, and Robert Garrett, of Baltimore, and William Whitewright, David W. Bishop, and George B. Warren, Jr., of New York, which board still manages the affairs of the company, with two exceptions, viz.: Mr. Cheston, deceased, and Mr. Bishop resigned; Edward de Rose occupying the place vacated by Mr. Bishop.

The chief office of the company was then removed to Baltimore, and the Consolidation Coal Company became in reality a Maryland corporation. In recording this fact it becomes necessary to make more extended mention of the gentleman who then assumed, and has ever since ably performed, the duties of chief manager of this great Maryland property, second only in importance in the State to the Baltimore and Ohio Railroad.

Charles F. Mayer is a Baltimore merchant by right of descent from Christian Mayer, his grandfather. Christian Mayer was for many years the principal member of the mercantile firm of Mayer & Brantz, which did extensive business with the East Indies and Europe, and was one of the firms which built up the ancient reputation of Baltimore for commercial enterprise. Later in life Christian Mayer became an authority upon statistics and the more intricate questions of marine insurance. He came to Baltimore from Amsterdam, Holland, in 1784, as the representative of a large commercial house in that city. He filled, until his death, the office of consul-general of Würtemberg for the United States, and was, during his life, the only representative of that country in the United States. He was the father of Lewis Mayer, Charles F. Mayer, the distinguished lawyer, and Col. Brantz Mayer, the well-known *littérateur*. The first named and eldest of these sons, Lewis Mayer, was the father of the Charles F. Mayer of this sketch. Lewis Mayer was educated at one of the best continental universities. He was a cultivated and accomplished gentleman, and an able man of business, and died in the prime of a brilliant manhood, shortly after he and members of his family in Pennsylvania had entered as the pioneers into the development of the anthracite coal region of Pennsylvania, in which they had been large landholders from colonial times. He was married in Lancaster, Pa., to his relative, Susan O. Mayer, daughter of Christopher Mayer, of that place, an opulent merchant, who represented his district for years in the Senate of his native State, and was one of its most trusted and respected citizens.

Charles F. Mayer has inherited in a marked degree the business characteristics of his ancestors. Without further reference to the details of the family genealogy, which shows the descent from Melchior Mayer, born in Ulm in 1495, until the emigration to America in 1752, it is sufficient to say that Charles F. Mayer is sprung from a race of men and women noted in their day for possessing the virtues as well as the accomplishments of generations of culture and education. Of Mr. Mayer's private and personal character it is unnecessary, as it would be inappropriate, to speak in this connection.

A man of actions rather than words, of remarkable business talents and untiring energy, he demonstrates his public spirit by actual achievements that advance the prosperity and welfare of the community. Whatever is undertaken by him he gives to it his whole soul, and lets none of the many interests confided to his care suffer for want of close and able attention and industry. Such men are indeed rare, and an honor to the community in which they reside. As president of the "Despard Coal Company" his enterprise and energy built up a large gas-coal trade against many obstacles. Known as a patient and intelligent compiler of statistics, he was selected to collect and digest the facts connected with the soft-coal trade of the country for submission to Congress, and for years the statement then prepared served to guide Congress in dealing with the intricate question of tariff upon foreign coals. In 1866 he was married to his cousin Susan Douglas, daughter of the late Hon. George May Keim, of Reading, Pa.

When it was resolved to make the Consolidation Coal Company a Maryland enterprise, Charles F. Mayer, then president of the Despard Coal Company, a director of the Western National Bank, and other institutions, and the head of the firm of Mayer, Carroll & Co., was at once chosen president. When he came into office the coal trade of the company and the region was in a very depressed condition, and it was further complicated by the labor troubles of that memorable year. With 1878 began the steady improvement in the company's affairs, which has continued until the present time. The history of the past four years has been one of ceaseless activity and anxiety to the management of the company. Its trade has been rapidly extended in the face of keen competition abroad, and in spite of serious labor troubles at home.

In 1877 the coal output of the company touched its lowest point for many years, as did that of the whole region. Every succeeding year has shown a steady increase of production, and as steadily has the ratio of increase of the Consolidation Company's trade to that of the whole region grown, until (1881) the region shows a total increase of over *forty* per cent. over the output of 1877, while the trade of the Consolidation Company has much more than doubled, and to-day this great Maryland property consists of 15,000 acres of land, whose surface is either covered with valuable timber or fertile farms, all of which is underlaid with workable veins of coal. More than 7000 acres of it hold the famous "Big Vein," yielding 10,000 tons to the acre, and lying nearer to market than the lands of any other company of the region. With excellent railroad facilities, which afford its own mines, and those of the rest of the region, ample means of reaching the Baltimore and Ohio Railroad at Piedmont and Cumberland, the Chesapeake and Ohio Canal, and the Pennsylvania Railroad, the company has assumed its proper place as the largest producer of semi-bituminous coal in America, and has plainly before it a long career of successful operation.

Important as is the work that has been accomplished by the Consolidation Coal Company in the development of the Cumberland region merely as a mining company, still more valuable has been the success of the same enterprising parties in providing railway facilities for the entire region, and in consolidating and perfecting what is now known as the Cumberland and Pennsylvania Railroad, a full sketch of which is given elsewhere.

The Borden Mining Company was chartered by the Maryland Legislature at the December session of 1846, and organized at Fall River, Mass., on the 30th of April, 1847, by the election of the following-named persons as directors: Richard Borden, Jefferson Borden, Joseph Durfee, Philip D. Borden, William S. Tisdale, and William Borden. Richard Borden was chosen president, and William Borden, secretary and treasurer. Arrangements were soon after made, in connection with the Frostburg Coal Company and the Allegany Mining Company, for the construction of a tram-road from the mines of the former company, and connecting with those of the latter, to Mount Savage, a distance of about three and a half miles, at which point connection was effected with the Mount Savage Railroad to Cumberland. This tram-way was completed and put in successful operation in 1849, and continued to be used until the month of October, 1852, when the extension of the Mount Savage Railroad, now called the Cumberland and Pennsylvania Railroad, was completed to the mines of the three companies, and the tram-road was abandoned. The Borden Company had decided to defer active operations in the coal business until the Chesapeake and Ohio Canal should be completed to Cumberland, which important event occurred in the fall of 1850, and on the 10th of October of that year the first boats loaded with Cumberland coal departed from Cumberland on the voyage to Alexandria, which port had been adopted by all the companies then engaged in the business as their depot and shipping-point.

In the mean time the Borden Company had been engaged in opening their mines, building miners' houses, tram-roads, etc., as well as a dump-house and sidings at Mount Savage, and generally getting in readiness to commence business when the canal should be fairly opened. They had, in connection with the same parties associated with them in building the tram-road to Mount Savage, constructed large and costly wharves at the outlet locks of the Alexandria Canal, in Alexandria, and this continued to be their principal canal depot until the breaking out of the civil war. At a meeting of the company on the 28th of November, 1849, William Carr was chosen a director in place of Joseph Durfee, deceased. In August, 1850, Albert C. Greene, of Providence, R. I., was chosen agent of the company, and in the following month he removed to Maryland and took charge of the property and business, and has remained the company's agent until this time. In the spring of 1851 the company built, at Cumberland, a line of twelve canal-boats, and placed them in service upon the canal. This beginning was followed up by the construction of others from time to time until the number so built by the company exceeded sixty, furnishing them with a daily line adequate to their wants. The completion of the Cumberland and Pennsylvania Railroad to the mines of the company, in October, 1852, added greatly to their facilities for shipping coal, though it involved the total abandonment of more than twenty thousand dollars invested in the tram-road to Mount Savage, and in the construction of dump-houses, offices, sidings, etc., at that place.

In April, 1852, a heavy freshet destroyed navi-

A. C. Greene

gation on the canal for the greater part of the season, and in the following two years the canal trade suffered greatly from droughts, interrupting, and finally suspending, traffic for about two months, in August and September. It was not until 1855 that the canal business began to assume a steady character and to show a rapid increase. In January, 1854, Albert C. Greene was elected a director in place of William S. Tisdale, who had retired from business. In August, 1856, the company purchased the farm of William Ward, two miles south of Frostburg, containing about five hundred acres, underlaid with two big veins of coal. In the summer of 1858 repeated freshets had destroyed Dams Nos. 4 and 5, and navigation was maintained only precariously by temporary expedients. The coal companies met the president and directors of the canal at Berkeley Springs in August, and concluded a contract with them by which it was agreed to advance the canal company one hundred and twenty-five thousand dollars, to rebuild, of stone, the broken dams, the sum to be reimbursed in tolls. The work was completed, and the money refunded in a few years. Since that time the canal has been comparatively exempt from damage suspending navigation.

In April, 1859, the ground was broken for sinking a shaft upon the Ward property, and, after some mishaps, the big vein of coal was struck at the end of December in the same year, and the putting up of steam pumping and hoisting-machines, from the Allaire Works, New York, was at once begun. In February, 1860, William B. Durfer was chosen director in place of William Carr. In August, 1860, coal was first hoisted and sent to market from the shaft on the Ward farm. During the four subsequent years the war between the North and South greatly interfered with the company's coal business, but they availed of every opportunity, when communications were open, to send down their coal, and, at the same time, secure the ventilation of the mine by proper air-courses and ventilating-shafts. In 1866, the influx of water in the shaft proving too great for the pumping machinery originally provided, a new shaft was sunk one hundred and eighty-four feet deep, and furnished with a steam pumping-engine of forty-inch steam cylinder, ten-feet stroke, and twenty-inch working barrels, ten-feet stroke, having a working capacity of seventy-two thousand gallons per hour. This pump, in connection with a twelve-inch by eight-feet plunger-pump at the hoisting-shaft, capacity of twenty thousand gallons per hour, has hitherto been adequate to the work of freeing the mines from water. On Sunday morning, April 12, 1873, the structure covering the hoisting-shaft, and containing all the machinery, was discovered to be on fire, and in a few hours the destruction was complete. The hoisting and pumping-engines, with all the machinery, were utterly ruined. The work of reconstruction was immediately commenced, and on the 6th of August following shipments of coal were resumed, and there has been no interruption since. On the 17th of February, 1875, Thomas J. Borden was elected a director in place of Richard Borden, deceased. On the same day William Borden became president, P. D. Borden, secretary, and L. N. Lovell, of New York, treasurer. On the 12th of February, 1881, Edward P. Borden was chosen director in place of P. D. Borden, and W. B. Durfer was made secretary. These are the only changes which have taken place in the administration of this corporation in an existence of thirty-five years. Its business has been carried on from year to year without any great variation in amount. The greatest extremes in its production are thirty thousand tons in 1861, the first year of the civil war, and two hundred and thirty thousand tons in 1875, after which the consequences of the great panic of 1873 began to tell upon the interests which use the Cumberland coal. Since going into active operation in 1851 it has marketed about three and a half million tons of coal, or an annual average of over one hundred and ten thousand tons, and its last year's production exceeded this average by fifty thousand tons. The prosperous condition of the mines at present is largely due to the administrative tact and energy of the superintendent, Albert C. Green, who is generally recognized as being one of the most capable and intelligent coal operators in the country. Mr. Green enjoys the reputation of being an undisputed authority on the Allegany coal region, of which he is said to possess a more accurate and comprehensive knowledge than almost any other operator. He is a gentleman of liberal education and cultured tastes, and is extremely popular with all classes.

Hampshire and Baltimore Company. — This company was organized about 1856, in Virginia, and has operated some eight years on its present mines. Its superintendents have been, first, John Elan; second, William A. Brydon; third, Malcolm St. Clair; fourth, Charles W. Shaw; and fifth, and present one, Robert Anderson. The latter has been one year superintendent, but six years with the company. Its officers for 1881 were: President, J. George Repplier; Vice-President, E. L. Bolles; Secretary, George D. Bond; Directors, E. L. Bolles, J. George Repplier, Henry S. Henry, George H. Potts, George B. Satterlee, James S. Merriam, Edward Oothout. Before 1874, Thomas Gammill was president. O. Tibbets is the shipping agent at the mines adjoining Westernport. It has a force of one hundred and twenty-five hands, and owns three mines, respectively of 300, 250, and 200 acres. Its office is No. 11 Washington Street, Cumberland.

Blaen Avon Coal Company.—Officers for 1881: President, Andrew Spier; Vice-President, Dr. G. E. Porter; Directors, Andrew Spier, Dr. G. E. Porter, J. K. Shaw, W. L. Shaw, John Sheridan, Frederick Mertens; Treasurer, J. J. Shaw (office, 13 Washington Street, Cumberland); Secretary, John V. Hart. Incorporated 1873. Capital, $200,000.

Barrelville Coal Mines.—Samuel B. Barrelville (founder of the village of this name) advertised in January, 1843, to deliver coal from his mines, which were situated near the forks of Jennings' Run, only seven miles from Cumberland. He had opened two veins of coal upon his lands,—one the old Parker vein, the other the Bluebaugh vein.

He sold the former at five cents per bushel at the mouth of the mine, and the latter at four. David Percy was superintendent of his mines. The coal was transported five miles over the Cumberland and Somerset turnpike to its intersection with the National road, two miles from Cumberland.

American Coal Company.—This company was organized in 1852 and '53, and has been actively working ever since. It owns some two thousand acres of coal lands, and is now operating its mine at Lonaconing. Its officers are: President, Gardner P. Lloyd; Secretary and Treasurer, George Sherman; General Superintendent, W. J. Boothe; Mine Superintendent, A. J. Clark (thirteen years). General office, No. 18 Mechanic Street, Cumberland.

Maryland Coal Company.—President, Henry Loveridge; Secretary and Treasurer, S. F. Ross; Superintendent, F. E. Brackett (three years); Assistant Superintendent, S. M. Petrie. Its general office is 104 Broadway, New York. It is now working one mine at Lonaconing, the "Kingsland," named after one of its directors. It owns three others,—the "Savage Mountain," and the old and new Detmold mines. Its coal-fields exceed one thousand acres of land. It employs two hundred men, and ships over the George's Creek and Cumberland Railroad to canal and to Philadelphia. The old Maryland Mining Company broke ground for beginning its railroad on April 7, 1845.

The Potomac Coal Company has two hundred and fifty acres in its mines at Barton, of which one hundred and fifty are of the big vein unworked, and the balance of the small vein. It employs one hundred and fifty hands. The superintendent has constructed a plane under the ground 1570 feet, that runs the coal down to the opening and saves the use of ten horses. The building of another plane is in contemplation. George L. Lyons has been superintendent eight years.

The Swanton Coal Company is managed by Stephen L. Lee & Son, who have controlled it over twenty years. They reside in Baltimore. Archibald McDonald is superintendent, and Paul S. H. Lee, clerk. It is not incorporated. It mines about fifty thousand tons a year, and employs at its mines at Barton some seventy hands. Its present opening has four miles of coal, and the distance up the plane to the opening is a half-mile. Stephen L. Lee opened the Franklin mine, and built its plane at a cost of thirty thousand dollars, and shipped from it the first car of coal.

New Central Coal Company.—President, William Jacques, of New York, and George H. Adams, secretary and treasurer; General Manager, Malcolm Sinclair, and Superintendent, Robert Boyd (six years). This company changed its name from that of the Lincoln Coal Company seven years ago. Its mine at Lonaconing has been worked ten years. It also operates the Koontz mine, just above Barton, and has three hundred and sixty hands employed. Its other two mines, "Johnson's" and "Midland," near Borden shaft, are being got ready to work, with James Thompson as superintendent. Mr. Boyd, superintendent, has been engaged in mining all his life, either in Great Britain or in this country.

Piedmont Coal and Iron Company.—This company's mine at Barton having been worked out, it is now working its new mine at Bloomington, Garrett Co. John Somerville, superintendent.

The George's Creek Coal and Iron Company was organized in 1835. Its first president was John A. Alexander, and its first secretary, Richard Wilson. John Douglas became connected with it in 1852, was mining boss eleven years, and since 1863 has been superintendent. Its president is A. H. Stump, of Baltimore; Secretary and Treasurer, Charles W. Millar; Mining Bosses, John Douglas and John Boyd. It has two mines at Lonaconing, and employs two hundred and eighty hands. It was formerly engaged also in making iron, but its furnaces are not now in operation. Its coal is shipped mostly to Baltimore. Its stock was originally nearly all held in England, and is yet to a large degree. Its superintendent, John Douglas, was born near Glasgow, Scotland, and in 1839 came to Nova Scotia, where he resided until 1851, when he removed, and in 1852 settled in George's Creek. This was the pioneer company in the mining of Cumberland coal, and founded the town

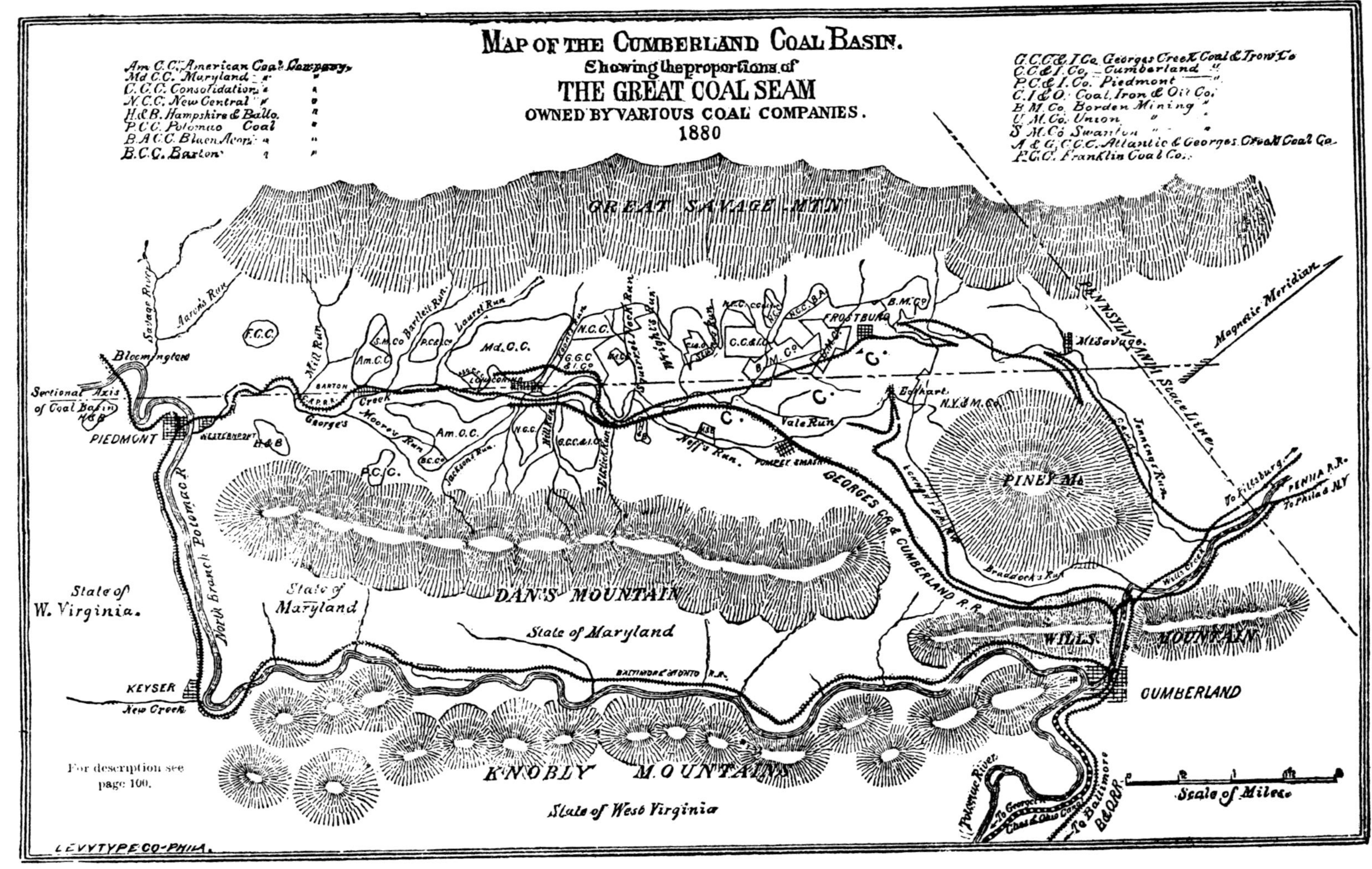
MAP OF THE CUMBERLAND COAL BASIN.
Showing the proportions of
THE GREAT COAL SEAM
OWNED BY VARIOUS COAL COMPANIES.
1880
Am. C. C. American Coal Company.
Md. C. C. Maryland " "
C. C. C. Consolidation " "
N. C. C. New Central " "
H. & B. Hampshire & Balto. "
P. C. C. Potomac Coal "
B. A. C. C. Bloomington "
B. C. C. Barton " "
G. C. C. & I. Co. Georges Creek Coal & Iron Co.
C. C. & I. Co. Cumberland " "
P. C. & I. Co. Piedmont " "
C. I. & O. Coal, Iron & Oil Co.
B. M. Co. Borden Mining "
U. M. Co. Union " "
S. M. Co. Swanton " "
A. & G. C. C. C. Atlantic & Georges Creek Coal Co.
F. C. C. Franklin Coal Co.
GREAT SAVAGE MTN
DAN'S MOUNTAIN
KNOBLY MOUNTAINS
WILLS MOUNTAIN
PINEY Mt.
State of W. Virginia.
State of Maryland
State of Maryland
State of West Virginia
PIEDMONT
KEYSER
New Creek
CUMBERLAND
FROSTBURG
Mt. Savage
Eckhart.
Bloomington
Sectional Axis of Coal Basin
North Branch Potomac R.
Savage River
Aaron's Run
Mill Run
Bartlett's Run
Laurel Run
George's Creek
Moore's Run
Jackson's Run
Hill Run
Elklick Run
Squirrel Neck Run
Wright's Run
Neff's Run
Vale Run
Jennings Run
Braddock's Run
Wills Creek
Potomac River
GEORGES CR. & CUMBERLAND R. R.
BALTIMORE & OHIO R. R.
PENNSYLVANIA State Line
Magnetic Meridian
To Pittsburg
PENNA R. R. To Phila & N.Y.
To Baltimore B. & O. R. R.
Chas. & Ohio Canal
Scale of Miles
For description see page 100.
LEVYTYPE CO. PHILA.

of Lonaconing. It also built the George's Creek Railroad from Piedmont to one mile above Lonaconing. George A. Hoffman is agent at its office, No. 11 South Liberty Street, Cumberland.

The Atlantic and George's Creek Consolidated Coal Company has its mine at Pekin, of which John Sheridan is superintendent.

George's Creek Valley Coal Company.—Its mines are near Westernport.

Grant Coal and Iron Company.—Its mines are at Pompey Smash, of which W. A. Montell is superintendent.

New Creek Coal Company.—Its mines, located near Piedmont, are owned by Davis & Co.

New York Mining Company.—Office, 36 Baltimore Street, Cumberland. Mine just southeast of Consolidation Coal Company's lands.

Franklin Coal Company.—Its mine is at Westernport, of which H. Crawford Black is superintendent.

Union Mining Company.—Mines at Mount Savage. President, James S. Mackie, New York. Office, 71 Broadway, and Warren Delano, Jr., superintendent, Mount Savage.

Banks and Insurance Companies.—The Legislature in 1811 incorporated and established "The Cumberland Bank of *Allegany*," with a capital stock of $200,000, divided into four thousand shares of fifty dollars each. The act provided for eight directors and a president, and exempted the stockholders from all liability beyond their individual stock. The engravers having spelled the word *Allegħany*, and the bank-notes having nearly all been put into circulation before the mistake was discovered, the June session of the Legislature of 1812 changed its corporate name to "The Cumberland Bank of Alleghany." Its first officers were: President, Upton Bruce; Cashier, Matthew Wallace; Directors, Thomas Greenwell, David Shriver, Jr., George Thistle, Benjamin Tomlinson, James Scott, John Scott, Samuel Smith, Patrick McCarty. On Sept. 17, 1814, as a result of the war, it, in common with all the banks, suspended specie payments. The bank resumed business (after the fire of April 14, 1833) on Jan. 13, 1837, with Joseph Shriver as cashier. In May, 1852, Joseph Shriver, for many years cashier, was elected president, and C. T. Shriver was appointed cashier in his stead. On Sept. 30, 1857, during the great monetary crisis, it temporarily suspended specie payments, as it had done May 13, 1837. On July 1, 1864, it was changed into the First National Bank of Cumberland, with the same officers as before,—Joseph Shriver, president, and Edwin T. Shriver, cashier.

The Mineral Bank, incorporated by the Legislature in 1836, opened its doors for business Jan. 3, 1837, George E. Dyson being its cashier. On May 16th following it temporarily suspended specie payments, owing to the financial panic then sweeping over the land. May 31, 1838, George E. Dyson, its cashier, was killed by being thrown from his buggy, and Jonathan W. Magruder was appointed in his place. Its president was then C. M. Thruston. June 19, 1848, Col. Thomas J. McKaig was elected president, but resigned on the 1st of January, 1854, and was succeeded by Joseph H. Tucker, formerly its cashier. A. F. Roberts, assistant cashier, was then elected cashier. On March 30, 1848 the bank closed its doors, owing to the failure of Joseph S. Lake & Co., of New York, but on April 10th following resumed business, having been secured by Lake & Co. The bank in the early part of this year (1848) had built and occupied its new building. On Oct. 5, 1857, during the great financial revulsion of that year, the bank ceased business, and appointed George A. Pearre and John Beall as trustees to wind up its affairs. Its liabilities were $199,681.33. The creditors received eighty-three and one-half cents on the dollar, clear of all the expenses attending the settlement.

On the 5th of June, 1848, the Cumberland Savings-Bank was established, and began business with J. R. Annan, president, and Robert Bruce, cashier. In May, 1858, its name was changed to that of the Cumberland City Bank, and new and beautiful notes were engraved to take the place of the old issues. On the 26th of November, 1858, it declined to redeem its notes and closed its doors, and J. R. Annan was appointed its trustee. In January, 1859, the trustee's report showed that the bank's liabilities were $24,693.31, of which $23,857 consisted of its notes in circulation, and $836.31 notes of bankers and depositors. Its assets were put at $29,497.04, of which $11,603.02 were doubtful and worthless, $3478.50 in cash, $12,803.07 considered good, and $1612.45 banks and bankers. The assignment made a preference in favor of note-holders and depositors. On Jan. 10, 1863, the new Cumberland City Bank, of which Alfred Spates was president and William E. Weber was cashier, was organized.

The Allegany County Bank was organized April 6, 1859, with a capital of $50,000. Its officers were Dr. George Lynn, president, and A. C. Whitmore, cashier. On the night of March 14, 1864, it was entered by means of false keys. The thieves on gaining an entrance commenced the work of excavating the vault. A considerable pile of brick and mortar was dug from the vault, but from some cause the robbers before going far enough into the wall to reach the valuables made a hasty retreat.

The First National Bank has its banking establishment at No. 121 Baltimore Street, and was incorporated in 1864. Its capital is $100,000, with $50,000 surplus. The officers are: President, Joseph Shriver; Cashier, E. T. Shriver; Directors, Alpheus Beall, George A. Pearre, Joseph Shriver, A. R. Lewis, Robert Shriver. Discount days, Tuesdays.

The Second National Bank is situated on Baltimore Street, at the corner of South Liberty Street. It has a capital of $100,000, and a surplus of $50,000. Discount days, Thursdays. The certificate of organization of this bank is dated Aug. 11, 1865. The first board of directors consisted of J. Philip Roman, Amos P. Shepherd, William W. McKaig, John Coulehan, Dr. Samuel P. Smith, Richard D. Johnson, and James H. Percy. J. Philip Roman was elected president, and continued at the head of the bank until his death, Feb. 28, 1871. Through his popularity, executive ability, and energy the bank became very successful. Shortly after the death of Mr. Roman, the directors elected E. L. Moore president. He had been the cashier from the commencement of the bank. Mr. Moore did not hold the position of president very long, and was succeeded by Amos P. Shepherd. Jan. 14, 1873, Lloyd Lowndes was elected president, John Coulehan vice-president, and Daniel Annan cashier. These gentlemen have continued in office from that time to the present.

The board of directors now are Dr. Samuel P. Smith, Douglas Percy, Nelson Beall, John S. Combs, L. M. Shepherd, John Coulehan, and Lloyd Lowndes, all of whom are energetic and successful business men of Allegany County. The following is the statement of this bank made to Hon. John Jay Knox, Comptroller of the Currency, under date of Dec. 31, 1881:

Resources.

Loans and discounts	$341,545.65
Overdrafts	4,096.11
U. S. bonds to secure circulation	100,000.00
U. S. bonds on hand	102,400.00
Other stocks, bonds, and mortgages	35,600.00
Due from approved reserve agents	33,939.90
Due from other National banks	109,476.24
Due from State banks and bankers	4,735.94
Real estate, furniture, and fixtures	8,632.63
Current expenses and taxes paid	2.13
Checks and other cash items	6,962.08
Bills of other banks	12,572.00
Fractional paper currency, nickels, and pennies	593.44
Specie	5,345.50
Legal-tender notes	55,578.00
Redemption fund with U. S. Treasurer (5 per cent. of circulation)	4,500.00
Due from U. S. Treasurer (other than 5 per cent. redemption fund)	2,959.00
Total	$828,938.62

Liabilities.

Capital stock paid in	$100,000.00
Surplus fund	50,000.00
Undivided profits	33,600.00
National bank-notes outstanding	89,000.00
Dividends unpaid	6,000.00
Individual deposits subject to check	540,426.43
Demand certificates of deposit	1,725.00
Certified checks	1,006.50
Due to other National banks	4,645.55
Due to State banks and bankers	720.18
Tax account	1,814.96
Total	$828,938.62

Hon. Lloyd Lowndes, the president of the Second National Bank, is a descendant of a distinguished Maryland family. Richard Lowndes, of Bostock House, Cheshire, England, was his great-great-grandfather. His great-grandfather, Christopher Lowndes, came from England, and was a successful merchant at Bladensburg before the national capital was located at Washington. He married Elizabeth Tasker, daughter of Governor Tasker, one of the prominent early colonial Governors of the State. His grandfather, Charles Lowndes, married Elizabeth Lloyd, daughter of Governor Edward Lloyd, one of the most distinguished of the early Governors of Maryland. Charles Lowndes was in early life a merchant at Georgetown, D. C., but husbandry being more to his tastes, he retired upon a neat estate in Jefferson County, the eastern outpost of the Valley of Virginia. On the 4th of July, 1800, before this event, Lloyd Lowndes, the father of the present Lloyd Lowndes, was born at Georgetown, D. C. When twenty-four years of age he and his younger brother, Richard T. Lowndes, settled in Cumberland, Md. They followed the family traditions and engaged in mercantile business. Very soon the firm of L. & R. T. Lowndes became one of the strongest in the State.

In 1831, Lloyd Lowndes moved to Clarksburg, Harrison Co., Va., and there established a branch house, under the name of Lowndes & Co. He gave to the new enterprise in this comparatively primitive section of the country the force of his best exertions and vigorous business ability. The twin houses acting in conjunction, controlled by the same business sense and integrity, became very prosperous. In 1840, Mr. Lowndes married Maria Elizabeth Moore, daughter of Thomas Moore, of Clarksburg. Four sons were the issue of this marriage, three of whom grew to manhood. Mr. Lowndes died on the 14th of March, 1879, in Clarksburg, after a remarkably successful career of more than half a century, the greater part of which was spent in that place. It can be said of him that he was one of the most careful business men, successful merchants, and valuable citizens of the State. He was the vice-president of the Mer-

Lloyd Lowndes.

chants' National Bank of Clarkesburg, and president of the Clarkesburg Gaslight Company. In addition to his large mercantile interests, his tastes attached him to farming. Lumbering and other pursuits also engaged his successful attention. He left a large fortune as the fruit of his industry and business tact. His name occupies a conspicuous place in the history of this section of West Virginia, not more for the successful monuments of his life's work than for the liberality, kind-heartedness, and untiring zeal with which he lent his name and force to the advancement of the section in which he lived.

Commodore Charles Lowndes was the only one of his direct family to leave the avenues of business. He served with distinction in the United States navy, and now resides on a beautiful estate on Miles River, Talbot Co., Md.

Of the three sons of Mr. Lowndes who grew up, two became professional men, and one succeeded to his father's business. The eldest son, Charles T. Lowndes, became a physician, and died in February, 1865, while serving as United States assistant surgeon. Richard T. Lowndes, the second son, has succeeded to and now manages the vast business interests of the estate which his father left. He is engaged in mercantile business, lumbering, milling, and railroading, in all of which he has displayed business sagacity and foresight similar to that which distinguished his father's career.

Hon. Lloyd Lowndes, the subject of this sketch, was born in Clarkesburg, Feb. 21, 1845. He laid the foundation of his early education at the academy in his native town. In early life he developed those qualities of mind and character which have since given him marked success at the bar, in politics, in business, and in social life. When sixteen years of age he entered Washington College, at Washington, Pa., where he remained for two years. He finished his education at Alleghany College, Meadville, Pa., graduating with distinction in 1865, when only twenty years of age. As he had chosen the profession of law, he set about preparing himself for the bar. Richard L. Ashhurst, of Philadelphia, was his preceptor. While pursuing his legal studies with this distinguished lawyer he attended the Law School of the University of Pennsylvania, and graduated therefrom in 1867. He at once settled in Cumberland, Md., where his father had begun business. He married Elizabeth T. Lowndes. His force of character, energy, talents, and probity won him almost immediate recognition and success. In the midst of a practice which almost immediately demanded a great part of his time, his ambition and tastes led him to the broader field of politics and state-craft. Public affairs tending to the advancement of the community in which he lived secured his early and eager attention, and gained him the opportunity for that distinction which he has since achieved.

In politics as well as in business life he soon took a prominent part. He is a Republican of earnest convictions, and forcible and aggressive in their expression. In 1872 he was nominated for Congress, his district at that time being largely Democratic, with but a single Republican county. So rapidly had he advanced in public favor that he carried the district by 1700 majority against the Hon. John Ritchie, of Frederick County, who had carried it by over 1500 majority two years before. A very spirited canvass followed Mr. Lowndes' nomination, and in his election he was the first to change its political complexion since the Hon. Francis Thomas had represented the district. His election was a reversal of 3200 votes.

Mr. Lowndes was only twenty-eight years of age when he entered the Forty-third Congress, and was its youngest member. He served on some of its most important committees during the sessions of that Congress, and advanced quite as rapidly in his congressional career as in the other pursuits in which he had met with such signal success. He was not a talker, but a worker. While his social qualities made him exceedingly popular with his fellow-members, his active energy won him the respect and admiration of his constituents. His courage in maintaining his convictions had a striking illustration in his vote upon the Civil Rights Bill. He lived in a district where there was a large colored constituency, who were directly affected by the bill. Out of the six Republicans who voted against the measure, he was the one whose political fortunes it jeopardized.

When the avalanche of 1874 struck the Republican party and swept away its majority in Congress, Mr. Lowndes was renominated, Hon. William Walsh being his Democratic opponent. A most memorable campaign followed. Although defeated, Mr. Lowndes showed scarcely less popularity and power in defeat than in victory. So active, exciting, and doubtful was the canvass that it required the official count to show the scant fifty majority by which his opponent was elected, while reversals by the thousands told the story in other strong Republican districts. Since this time Mr. Lowndes has not been in public life, although he has never ceased to take an active part in politics. In 1879 he was widely mentioned for the Governorship, and in the late Republican National Convention at Chicago he was a delegate-at-large from his State.

He is still regarded as one of the strongest men in the Republican party of Maryland.

In addition to his successful public life, he has filled and now fills various positions of trust and honor in the business world. Since 1873 he has been president of the Second National Bank of Cumberland, one of the largest financial institutions of Western Maryland. He is a director in the Cumberland and Elk Lick Coal Company, and vice-president of the Millville Milling Company. He is prominent in the Frostburg Gaslight Company, and is president of the Bar Association of Allegany County. He is a member and vestryman of the Episcopal Church, from which he has frequently been a delegate to the Diocesan Conventions, and no man in his section of the State has contributed more generously to public and private enterprises than Mr. Lowndes. His means are very large, and are freely expended in developing the city of Cumberland and Allegany County. Besides his large financial, coal, and milling interests, he has turned his attention somewhat to farming, and has one of the most fertile estates in the county, upon which he raises the choicest breeds of cattle. He has been president of the Allegany County Agricultural Society for several years. He is now but thirty-seven years of age, and enjoys a position and social popularity which make him one of the foremost men of his State.

The Fire Insurance Company of Allegany County has its office at No. 57 Hebb's Block, Merchants' Row, Baltimore Street, Cumberland. Its cash capital is $50,000. The officers are William R. Beall, president; Hopewell Hebb, secretary; J. B. H. Campbell, treasurer; Directors, William R. Beall, J. B. H. Campbell, William R. McCulley, Richard D. Johnson, Frederick Minke, Dr. J. J. Bruce, John H. Young, James Reynolds, A. M. L. Bush, James M. Shober, Kennedy H. Butler, Hopewell Hebb.

The Third National Bank was organized March 10, 1879, and the charter was granted March 6th. Its original officers were J. M. Schley, president; W. E. Weber, cashier; John Humbird, Jesse Korns, Frederick Mertens, A. Willison, J. B. Walton, D. C. Bruce, directors. The only change in the officers since organization has been the election of W. E. Weber as a director, to fill a vacancy caused by the death of D. C. Bruce. Its first place of business was South Mechanic Street, from which it removed to No. 77 Baltimore Street. It was originally established as the "Queen City Savings-Bank," an institution chartered by the State Legislature April 1, 1872. Its officers were those named above, who were continued after it was converted into a National bank.

Following is a report of the condition of the bank:

Resources.

Loans and discounts	$120,179.76
Overdrafts	17.25
U. S. bonds to secure circulation	100,000.00
Other stocks, bonds, and mortgages	25,600.00
Due from approved reserve agents	156,201.92
Due from other National banks	18,028.80
Due from State banks and bankers	553.93
Real estate, furniture, and fixtures	1,500.00
Protest account	8.12
Premiums paid	1,000.00
Checks and other cash items	282.33
Fractional paper currency, nickels, and pennies	367.15
Specie	16,453.30
Legal-tender notes	8,680.00
Redemption fund with United States Treasurer (5 per cent. of circulat'n)	4,500.00
Total	$453,372.56

Liabilities.

Capital stock paid in	$10,000.000
Surplus fund	8,000.00
Undivided profits	822.67
National bank-notes outstanding	89,500.00
Dividends unpaid	4,324.54
Individual deposits subject to check	247,682.44
Demand certificates of deposit	2,319.80
Certified checks	160.00
Due to State banks and bankers	563.11
Total	$453,372.56

The officers of the Mutual Benevolent Life Insurance Company of Allegany County are as follows:

President, John Humbird; Vice-President, James J. McHenry; Secretary, Hopewell Hebb; Treasurer, J. B. H. Campbell; Directors, J. S. Johnson, J. C. Orrick, K. H. Butler, Asa Willison, J. B. H. Campbell, Hopewell Hebb; General Agent, J. S. Johnson.

Building and Loan Associations.—Enterprise Building Association organized Nov. 3, 1865, with the following officers: President, W. R. McCulley; Vice-President, Valentine A. Buckey; Secretary, James T. Hill; Treasurer, E. T. Shriver; Solicitor, William Walsh; Directors, A. J. Clark, A. M. L. Bush, John Schilling, Robert I. Morris, Samuel D. Ways, Charles A. Seay.

Carroll Building Association. President, Frank Haley; Secretary, F. M. Gramlich, Jr.; Treasurer, John Coulehan; Solicitor, J. J. McHenry.

Equitable Building Association. President, R. D. Johnson; Secretary, F. Laing, Jr.; Treasurer, E. H. Campbell; Solicitor, William M. Price.

Fourth German Building Association. President, Harman Baake; Secretary, S. Petrie; Treasurer, John Wiebel; Solicitor, J. B. Widener.

Home Building Association. President, J. J. Shaw; Secretary, John Schilling; Treasurer, Alexander Adams; Solicitor, F. Williams.

Mutual Landlords' Association of the City. President (2d term), R. D. Johnson; Secretary, J. W. Jones; Treasurer, Daniel Annan; Solicitor, Jacob Brown.

People's Building Association. President, Hopewell Hebb; Secretary, J. Schilling; Treasurer, E. H. Campbell; Solicitor, Thomas E. Gonder.

Queen City Perpetual Building Association. President, Frank Haley; Secretary, F. M. Gramlich, Jr.; Treasurer, John Coulehan; Solicitor, J. J. McHenry.

Third German Building Association. President, John Riehl; Secretary, John Kolb; Treasurer, William Knierim; Solicitor, J. B. Widener.

Workingmen's Building Association. President, Frank Haley; Secretary, Thomas B. Griffin; Treasurer, John Coulehan; Solicitor, M. A. Healy.

Young Men's Building Association. President, Robert Shriver; Secretary, H. H. Hartsock; Treasurer, J. P. Weisel; Solicitor, R. W. McMichael.

Hotels and Early Taverns.—There was certainly one tavern, and not improbably more than one, on the present site of Cumberland before the establishment of the town, for we know that when Thomas Beall, of William, laid out the town on the 4th of October, 1784, Dickinson Simkins was keeping an inn at that point.

From 1791 to 1800, Abraham Faw had his two-story log inn on Green Street, where stood the residence of the late W. Landwehr, and the courts met there for many years. In 1812, Barton Carricoe opened a tavern. In 1813 the taverns were Slicer's, McKinley's (or Reeside's), Ryan's, Dickinson Simkins' "Three Butts," and Thomas Thistle's.

Henry McKinley kept an inn in 1815, and in 1819 James Reeside kept the "Cumberland Hotel," adjoining the chain bridge. In the spring of 1824 the tavern on Mechanic Street, near Will's Creek, was remodeled and named the "Columbian Inn." For many years after 1828, Jacob Fechtig was landlord of the "Cumberland Hotel," which was the headquarters of the stage-lines. In 1830, "Newman's Hotel" was in full operation and was a popular resort. In the great fire of April 14, 1833, all the taverns were burned, including Mr. Shriver's large three-story building and that of Jacob Fechtig's. On the 2d of January following the tavern of Mrs. Francis Bruce, on the National road, five miles from the town, was destroyed by fire. The occupants lost all their clothing, and only saved their lives by jumping from the second-story windows.

In pursuance of an act of the General Assembly of Maryland, entitled "An act to incorporate the Cumberland Hotel Company in Cumberland," passed at the December session, 1835, David Shriver, R. Worthington, M. N. Falls, and John Gephart, commissioners, opened their books and received subscriptions to the capital stock of the company, on Monday, June 27, 1836, at the office of James Smith, in Cumberland. The books were to be kept open from ten o'clock A.M. until one o'clock P.M. each day, for six successive days, and for such longer time as the commissioners should direct. The shares were twenty-five dollars each, five dollars to be paid on each share at the time of subscribing, and the balance in installments not exceeding ten dollars each, after thirty days' notice to the stockholders, at such time as should be directed by the president and directors of the company.

In 1837 the National Hotel had been rebuilt, and Joshua Johnson kept "Slicer's Tavern," a fine building, erected on the site of the present "St. Nicholas Hotel." In 1843, Matthew McCully kept the brick tavern formerly occupied by Mrs. Folck, six miles east of Cumberland. Eliza McElfish kept the "Sand Spring Hotel," one mile west of Frostburg, and in Cumberland, Samuel Cessna kept "Our House," adjoining the old bank. John Black was proprietor of the "Exchange Hotel," near the public square. In 1848 the leading hotels were the "National," kept by James Searight, and later by James Black; the "Virginia," kept by Washington Evans; "Barnum's," by Barnum & Stephens; and the "United States" (now "St. Nicholas"), kept by A. Cowton. In 1849 the city authorities caused the old tavern-stand near Baltimore Street to be torn down, as from its ancient and rickety condition it had become unsafe. In 1852, Washington Evans gave up the "Virginia Hotel" and became landlord of the "United States," whose former proprietor had removed to Baltimore. In June of the same year J. A. Heffelfinger gave up "Barnum's Hotel" and became landlord of the "Revere House," a large and commodious hostelry which had been recently built. April 1, 1853, Washington Evans became landlord of "Barnum's," and M. P. O'Hern opened the "United States," just rebuilt and refitted.

The Queen City Hotel is the principal hotel in Cumberland, and one of the finest in the State. It was erected by the Baltimore and Ohio Railroad for the double purpose of affording accommodations to travelers to and from the West and for persons visiting Cumberland; having been constructed with the special view of attracting summer travel. It would be difficult to imagine a more delightful summer trip than that from Baltimore to Cumberland, or a more attractive summer residence than the Queen City Hotel. After leaving the Relay House the road passes along the bed of the Patapsco River, through scenery which is scarcely rivaled anywhere in pastoral loveliness and picturesque beauty. In Carroll and Frederick Counties it traverses a prosperous farming country, and when the Potomac River is reached, approaches a region of wild and romantic beauty. All along the Potomac the views from the car-windows present a rapid panorama of varied scenery, now sombre and rugged, now charming in its indescribable variety and warmth of color. The route is doubly interesting as presenting a marvelous exhibition of human power and ingenuity in triumphing over apparently insurmountable obstacles. The rugged face of the country seems to bid defiance to the engineer, but the living reality of the railroad, with its trains thundering after one another in quick succession, is a vivid commentary on the capabilities of human intellect and human muscle. The section traversed by the road after reaching the Potomac is either mountainous or rolling. At Harper's Ferry the view is particularly fine, and the scenery of the Cheat River is famous for its variety and impressive beauty. The Queen City Hotel at Cumberland is a large and handsome structure, built of brick, and tastefully finished with mansard-roof and cupola. It consists of a large centre building two stories high and two wings, each four stories high. An ornamental piazza extends along the entire front and at the sides. The piazza gives a promenade of four hundred feet. The centre building is one hundred and forty feet in length, and the wings are each forty-seven by eighty-four feet. There is also a back building thirty-seven by ninety-seven feet and three stories in height, and a basement under the entire building. The hotel is heated by steam provided by two large tubular boilers, and all the appointments are of the most superior character. The building is handsomely furnished, and is supplied with all the modern conveniences. The grounds, which comprise several acres, are handsomely laid out, and are tastefully ornamented with fountains, evergreens, trees, and shrubbery. The hotel was completed in 1872, and its cost was two hundred and fifty thousand dollars.

The scenery at this point is grand and beautiful, and there is scarcely any spot in Maryland which is near so many points of historic interest. The surrounding country contains innumerable localities associated in local tradition, as well as in history, with romantic episodes in the unceasing warfare of the early settlers with the aborigines, in the disastrous Braddock campaign, and in the late civil war. The Queen City Hotel is a very popular resort in summer, and large numbers of persons visit it during the season.

The hotels in Cumberland are the Queen City, Baltimore and Ohio depot; St. Nicholas, Baltimore Street; Shipley House, North Mechanic Street; Mountain House, North Mechanic Street; City Hotel; Farmers' and Drovers', 141 Baltimore Street; and Centennial, South Mechanic Street.

Representative Men.—Among the business men of Cumberland contemporaneous with himself, there was none more energetic or successful than the Hon. J. Philip Roman. Mr. Roman was a native of Cecil County, Md., and was the brother of the Hon. James Dixon Roman and B. Franklin Roman, both of them leading business men of Washington County. After studying law with his brother, James Dixon, J. Philip Roman removed to Cumberland in 1843, when about twenty-four years of age, and engaged in business there, in which he was very successful. Mr. Roman married, in 1864, Eloise, daughter of Richard T. Lowndes.[1] Owing to his absorption in business pursuits Mr. Roman was unable to give much attention to the practice of his profession, but took great interest in politics, and, being very popular, achieved a conspicuous position as a political leader. He was a member of the Constitutional Convention of 1867, but with that exception never held any political office. In 1852 he was the Whig candidate for Congress, but was defeated by Hon. William T. Hamilton. In 1868 he was before the Democratic Convention for Congress, but after two days of balloting his name was withdrawn, and Hon. Patrick Hamill was nominated. Mr. Roman's local influence in politics, however, was very great, and throughout a long and active life his kind-heartedness, liberality, and enterprise not only attached to him a large following of true and earnest friends, but secured him the general respect and confidence of the community. It was in business rather than in politics, however, that Mr. Roman developed his capabilities. He was largely interested in coal lands and in mining, and owned valuable wharf property at Baltimore. He was president of the Second National Bank of Cumberland, which owed its success at the start in large measure to his personal popularity and business tact, and was the first to move in the project of providing Cumberland with an adequate water-supply. Mr. Roman also took great interest in agriculture, and was at one time president of the Agricultural Society of Allegany County. In all public enterprises he was invariably among the foremost, and his liberality not only in helping forward whatever tended to promote the interests of Cumberland, but in relieving distress and assisting merit, was proverbial. Mr. Roman died on the 28th of February, 1871.

Thomas J. Smith was born in Cumberland in 1806, and emigrated to Ohio in 1830, and subsequently held many responsible offices in that State, including the presidency of the Dayton and Michigan Railroad. He was a distinguished lawyer, and in 1860 was the Democratic candidate for judge of the Supreme Court. He died at Dayton, Ohio, in July, 1868.

James Reeside, the veteran stage proprietor of for-

[1] Not Louisa, daughter of Lloyd Lowndes, of Cumberland, as incorrectly stated in the chapter of this work on Representative Families of Washington County.

mer years on the old National road, and hotel-keeper in Cumberland's early days, died in Philadelphia, Pa., on Sept. 3, 1841. Few men were more extensively known in the Middle, Western, and Southern States than this old-time mail contractor, on whose coaches the greatest statesmen of the land were passengers to and from Washington.

Daniel Blocher was born in Cumberland in 1809. He learned the printer's trade under John M. Buchanan, of the *Maryland Advocate*, and in 1832 purchased that paper, and was its sole editor until about 1838, when Jacob Wickard became its editor and proprietor. Mr. Blocher in the mean time had studied law and had been admitted to the bar. In 1833, in the great fire of April 14th, his office was destroyed. Money was sent him from well-known citizens of Baltimore, such as John W. Garrett, Frank Burns, and Wm. Krebs, to buy new type and start his paper again. It was the organ of the Allegany County Democracy. Mr. Blocher was engaged in the brick business for many years, and at one time was farming with one of his sons in Charles County.

He was successively elected by the Democratic party to the House of Delegates for 1837 and 1838, with such men as John Neff and Jonathan Huddleston, the latter still living in Virginia. He was a candidate for State senator in 1840, but in the whirlpool of that year was beaten by the Harrison Whigs, who elected John Beall. In the following year Governor Grason appointed him register of wills, to fill the vacancy occasioned by the death of Heck, which position he held until 1846 (five years). He then resigned, and in the fall was elected State senator over Dr. Samuel P. Smith, the Whig nominee.

In 1854, Governor Ligon appointed him inspector of the cattle-scales in Baltimore. In 1861 he was made quartermaster in Col. Maulsby's regiment of the Potomac Brigade, and served three years. After the war he resided in Charles County, but returned to Cumberland in 1867, and was appointed a justice of the peace, which office he held up to the time of his death. He left a widow and nine children,—four sons and five daughters,—and quite a number of grandchildren. One son is a sergeant of police in Baltimore City. His son William, who was associated with his father while in charge of the cattle-scales, is also living in Baltimore. His other two sons live in Cumberland. All of his daughters but one are married. Mr. Blocher was always a prominent Democrat, and was able to be on the stage at the Academy of Music at one of the Democratic mass-meetings during the campaign of 1880.

John McHenry died at his residence in the Glades, Oct. 26, 1860, in his eighty-third year. In connection with Mr. Harris he was the first reporter of the decisions of the Court of Appeals of this State, and published four volumes known as "Harris and McHenry's Reports." He also published a book on the law of ejectment. In early life he was secretary of the American legation to France, and filled the same position at the Hague for two years. He was a member for one term of the House of Delegates from Allegany County.

Dr. James Fitzpatrick died in Cumberland, March 14, 1865, aged sixty years. He was once president of the Chesapeake and Ohio Canal Company. He was also for several years superintendent of that portion of the National road lying in Maryland, and represented Allegany County in the State Legislature.

Near the confluence of Song Run and the Big Youghiogheny lived until some twenty years ago Meshach Browning, a celebrated Maryland hunter, who "escheated" about one thousand acres of land in the latter part of his days, built a grist-mill, and left a name revered by a large posterity. He was the son of a subaltern English officer, who escaped after Braddock's defeat, and was born in Frederick County, Md., in 1771. He never saw his father, and his mother married again. A married aunt took him to Western Maryland, and his early childhood was spent in a cabin in Buffalo Marsh. After St. Clair's defeat his uncle fell back with some forty settlers to Blooming Rose, where the future hunter met his wife. He married her against the wishes of her father, who turned both of them out of doors. After this he hunted constantly, seldom wearing his hat on the hunt, and often killing bears, deer, and even panthers at close quarters with his hunting-knife. He began to hunt in 1795, and killed his last game in 1839. During that period he killed from 1800 to 2000 deer, between 300 and 400 bears, 50 panthers and catamounts, and scores of wolves and wild-cats. He had six sons, forty-four grandsons, seventeen great-grandsons, and five daughters, thirty-two granddaughters, and eighteen great-granddaughters,—in all one hundred and twenty-two descendants. At the time of the second war with England the old mountaineer was induced to join the army, an act which caused him the keenest regret to the end of his days, as he was opposed to shedding human blood. About 1814 he began to carry peltries and venison to Baltimore and Georgetown, and in 1824 put up his mill. In 1826 he visited Annapolis, and, although a Marylander all his days, tasted there the first crabs and oysters he had ever seen, which he heartily disliked.

Mr. Browning lived with his first wife forty years,

and with the second eighteen years. He was very feeble in his old age, but his frame bore evidence to the great strength and vigor he once possessed. He was a justice of the peace for Allegany County for many years, and was regarded by his neighbors with unbounded respect and reverence for his integrity and fine, manly qualities. He died in November, 1859, aged nearly ninety.

George Henderson was born in New York, July 3, 1828, and removed to Cumberland, Md., as agent and general superintendent of the Cumberland Coal and Iron Company, with his headquarters at Eckhart mines, in Allegany County, Md. The responsible duties of this trust he discharged with the utmost fidelity, and resigned in 1859 to become a partner with Newell, Sturtevant & Co. in the bituminous coal business in Philadelphia. In 1861 he entered the banking and stock commission business in Philadelphia. In 1866, and again in 1875, he made extended tours over Europe. While residing at Eckhart mines, in 1856, he married Rebecca E., daughter of Jonathan Magruder. In 1867 he removed his family to Cumberland, Md., where he still resides. He is a warden of Christ Reformed Episcopal Church, and is very active in promoting the interests of that denomination. Mr. Henderson is a generous, public-spirited citizen, and has long been prominently identified with the industrial development of Cumberland, to which he has contributed largely of his time, energy, and means. He extends a prompt and liberal encouragement to every measure or enterprise calculated to promote the interests of Cumberland, and is one of its most popular and useful citizens.

Gen. Charles M. Thruston was born in 1793, and graduated at West Point in 1814. In 1820 he was captain of Company C, Third Artillery, of the regular army. In the late war he attained the rank of brigadier-general. He was married Sept. 5, 1820, to Juliana Hughes, daughter of Christopher Hughes, Sr., of Baltimore. Her brother, Christopher Hughes, once represented the American government at Stockholm, and was one of the diplomatic corps at the treaty of Ghent in 1815. In 1837, Gen. Thruston and wife removed to Cumberland, where the former died in 1873, and the latter Nov. 14, 1881, in her eighty-third year. The only living child of this couple is Mrs. C. P. Manning, of Baltimore. The others were Col. George A. Thruston, who died May 3, 1874, aged fifty-three years; Charles B. Thruston, who died Dec. 6, 1868, aged forty-two years; William S. Thruston, accidentally drowned June 10, 1865, aged thirty-seven years; Dr. Henry Scott Thruston, a surgeon in the late war, who was killed in an explosion in a factory, June 15, 1868; and Julian Thruston, who died April 29, 1853, aged nineteen years.

James Espy, the renowned "Storm King," and author of the theory of producing rain, etc., by the explosion of gunpowder, was born in Allegany County. He was an old-time schoolmaster in Cumberland, and over twenty years ago went to Washington and made the acquaintance of Lieut. M. F. Maury, who perfected or adopted Espy's theory, and acquired a great reputation thereby in the scientific world. Mr. Espy published a book on the "Theory of Storms," which attracted great attention among the *savants* of Paris, Berlin, and London.

In 1850, Kennedy H. Butler, then a young man, commenced business as a chair-maker on Centre Street, Cumberland, near the spot where his warerooms now stand. He was unable to employ any assistance, but his industry, sobriety, and good workmanship soon made for him a name and a business, and in 1851 he built a small two-story shop, sixteen by thirty feet in size, which he was compelled in 1852 to increase to three stories, twenty-eight by fifty feet. and again in 1853 by the addition of a building twenty-eight by sixty feet. As his business grew he was enabled to employ labor and to purchase a six horse-power steam-engine, the first ever used in Western Maryland in the manufacture of furniture. This was replaced in 1856 by a twenty-five horse-power engine. During the next five years the business continued to expand until, in 1861, his establishment, with his entire stock in trade, was destroyed by fire. Owing to the unsettled condition of the country, and particularly of the border States, during the early part of the war, Mr. Butler did not rebuild his factory until 1864, when he erected the building now occupied by Public School No. 1, on Centre Street. His factory was again destroyed by fire about four years ago, and he was compelled to erect new buildings. The space now occupied by the works is fifty-four thousand square feet.

Henry Clay McAllister was born at Martinsburg, W. Va., in 1829. When about eighteen years of age he entered the service of the Baltimore and Ohio Railroad as a brakeman. He was soon promoted to be conductor. After the army left Cumberland he was ordered to that city, and assumed the duties of dispatcher of trains. He superintended the transportation of Sherman's army to the West, trains laden with troops starting every thirty minutes for four days. Not a single train missed its connection and not a man was injured. It was a feat which still remains without a parallel in the history of railroads in this country. During the whole of the four days Capt. McAllister neither rested nor slept. It was while acting in this capacity at Cumberland that he rescued Father Carey, then of St. Patrick's Catholic Church, from a horrible death by snatching him from the track in front of an engine which was running at full speed. After holding the position of dispatcher of trains at Cumberland for several years Capt. McAllister was appointed a passenger conductor on a train running between Cumberland and Wheeling. In 1868 he was made supervisor of trains on the Second Division of the Baltimore and Ohio Railroad, a position of great responsibility and trust. He died June 19, 1873, and was buried by the Masonic fraternity, Potomac and Ohr lodges participating in the services.

Frederick Dent, Sr., was born in Cumberland on the 6th of October, 1786, and died at Washington, D. C., Dec. 15, 1873, in his eighty-seventh year. He was the father of Mrs. Gen. Grant, and at the time of his death was the oldest native of Cumberland. He was the son of George Dent, who was the surveyor of the town of Cumberland and of Allegany County, and a grandson of Col. Thomas Dent, surveyor general of the State of Maryland before and after the war of the Revolution. The town of Cumberland was surveyed in 1805. The act authorizing the work also named Roger Perry, Evan Gwynne, Upton Bruce, Jonathan Cox, and George Hoffman as commissioners. On the 23d day of May, 1806, Messrs. Gwynne, Perry, and Bruce met at the court-house, and after qualifying appointed George Dent to be surveyor to the commission. Mr. Dent appointed Peter Gephart and Benjamin Riley as chain-carriers, and Elias Eckhart as pole-carrier, and made the survey. His report, with the map, is filed among the records of the county. In 1806, David Shriver, a prominent civil engineer, was appointed to locate the National road from Cumberland to Wheeling, the building of which had been ordered by the Congress of the United States. After his arrival in Cumberland he engaged a number of persons as members of the locating corps, and selected as his assistant Frederick Dent, then in his twenty-first year. The work of location, in which young Dent participated, occupied several months. In 1812, Mr. Dent removed to St. Louis, where he became engaged in business. He resided there until 1865, and after that year lived with his daughter, Mrs. Grant.

John Blair Hoge Campbell was born in Berkeley County, W. Va., and lived near Martinsburg until the age of twelve years, when he obtained employment with a druggist in Martinsburg. About 1840 he removed to Cumberland and opened a drug-store on North Mechanic Street, in which his former employer at Martinsburg was a partner. Shortly afterwards, Mr. Campbell purchased the latter's interest in the store, and a few years before his death associated with him his brother, E. H. Campbell, forming the well-known firm of Campbell Brothers. He was a member of the building committees of the city hall and the First Presbyterian church, and of numbers of other public buildings and improvements. At the time of his death he was a stockholder and director of the First National Bank, the Fire Insurance Company of Allegany County, and the Cumberland Steel Manufacturing Company. He was also an extensive real-estate owner. Mr. Campbell was a zealous member of the First Presbyterian Church, and aided largely, both financially and personally, in the erection of the fine edifice on Washington Street. He was first married about 1848, to Ann Richardson, of Frederick County, by whom he had two children. His wife and children died a number of years ago. About 1862 he married Ellen W., daughter of J. W. Magruder, the issue of which marriage was five children. Mr. Campbell had no immediate relatives in the county except his brother. He had three other brothers and one sister,—Dr. Newton Campbell, D.D., of Darnestown, W. Va., Lemuel Campbell, of Winchester, Va., Pendleton Campbell, of the firm of R. M. Proud & Co., of Baltimore, and Mary Campbell, of Darnestown, W. Va. Mr. Campbell died Feb. 13, 1876, in his fifty-fifth year.

Samuel Charles, the well-known newspaper editor and publisher, was born in Hagerstown in 1800, and died in 1845. He married Margaret Wincow, of Cumberland, by whom he had eight children, of whom but two are living, George Charles, of Cumberland, and Laura, married to A. C. Hoopman, of Harford County. Mr. Charles was a devoted friend of Henry Clay, to assist whom in his campaign for the Presidency he established the *Civilian* in Cumberland, issuing his first paper Feb. 14, 1828. He continued its publication until his death, a period of seventeen years, and the year following it passed into the hands of Archibald Carey. His son, George Charles, now a prominent citizen of Cumberland, established the Cumberland *Daily News*, April 3, 1871, and in the following year sold it to Henry J. Johnson, the present editor and publisher.

Jonathan W. Magruder was born in Montgomery County, Md., in November, 1793, and died in Cumberland, March 13, 1878. In September, 1820, while engaged in business at Clarkesburg, in his native county, he was married to Mary Lynn, daughter of

Capt. David Lynn. In 1826 he removed to a farm in that part of Allegany County which is now Garrett. In 1838 he returned to Cumberland, and became cashier of the Mineral Bank, a position he held until 1843, when he purchased a farm in Frederick County, upon which he lived for a year, after which he returned to Cumberland and engaged in the dry-goods business on North Mechanic Street. He continued in business in Cumberland until the breaking out of the late war, when he sold his store to Humbird & Long. Since that time he has not been actively engaged in business. He also held the position of treasurer of the Potomac Wharf Company. Mr. Magruder had six children,—five daughters and one son. The latter is Dr. David Lynn Magruder, a surgeon in the United States army. One of the daughters is the wife of Col. Thomas Johns, another the wife of George Henderson, Jr., and two others are the widows of J. B. H. Campbell and O. D. Robbins, respectively. The fifth daughter, who was unmarried, is dead.

Daniel F. Miller was born in Allegany County, Md , Oct. 4, 1814; studied law in Pittsburgh, and was admitted to the bar in 1838. He emigrated to Iowa in 1839, and the following year was elected to the Legislature of that Territory. In 1848 he was the Whig candidate for Congress, but his seat was contested, and a new election ordered, which took place in 1850, and he was elected for the term ending 1851. He was Presidential elector in 1856.

Necrology.—The following are among the citizens of Allegany County who have died from 1813 to the present time:

At the residence of Dr. McHenry, on March 18, 1813, Col. John Lynn, a soldier of the Revolution, and for many years clerk of the county.

Hanson Briscoe, clerk of the county courts of Allegany, Sept. 12, 1817, aged sixty-eight years. He was a native of St. Mary's County, and held a commission in the militia in the Revolutionary war.

Nov. 30, 1823, at his residence, near Old Town, James M. Cresap.

Jan. 20, 1827, Col. Joseph Cresap.

April 11, 1835, at Rose Hill, near Cumberland, in the 78th year of his age, David Lynn, an officer of the Revolution. At the close of the Revolution he removed from his native county, Montgomery, to Allegany. While but a youth, and shortly after the commencement of the war, he entered the army, and bore a commission first as a lieutenant, and soon afterwards as a captain, in the Continental service. He served throughout the war, and was present at Monmouth, Germantown, and other battles, and at the surrender of Cornwallis.

Jan. 26, 1838, Col. William Lamar, an officer of the Revolution, at an advanced age.

Nov. 27, 1838, at his residence, near Frostburg, Andrew Bruce, a member of the Senate of Maryland.

Hon. Michael C. Sprigg died suddenly at his residence in Cumberland, Dec. 18, 1845. He retired in his usual health, and about midnight he was seized with a severe pain in the head, and in a few hours breathed his last. Mr. Sprigg had been a member of Congress, and had repeatedly represented Allegany County in the Legislature. He was also at one time president of the Chesapeake and Ohio Canal Company, and had held other responsible positions.

April 21, 1859, Rev. W. W. Arnett, pastor of Emmanuel Parish (Protestant Episcopal) Church at Cumberland.

November, 1859, Meshach Browning, one of the early settlers of Allegany County, at the age of nearly ninety years.

Sept. 20, 1854, Archibald Carey, editor of the Cumberland *Miners' Journal.*

Dec. 21, 1864, Thomas Devecmon, a leading member of the Allegany bar. He had frequently represented his county in the State Legislature, and was one of the candidates on the McClellan electoral ticket.

Oct. 14, 1867, Samuel M. Semmes, a prominent lawyer, and formerly a member of the State Legislature. He was a brother of Capt. Semmes, of the Confederate navy.

May 24, 1868, at Frostburg, J. Hoblitzell, a member of the State Constitutional Convention of 1867 from Allegany County.

May 24, 1868, at Cumberland, George White, a well-known citizen.

May 21, 1870, Dr. John Everett, of Cumberland. He was about fifty-eight years of age, and was born and raised in St. Lawrence County, N. Y. He settled in Cumberland in 1835, and in 1851 was elected to the House of Delegates. In 1855 he was chosen sheriff of the county, and one of his first official acts was to execute Miller, the murderer of Dr. Hadel and Mr. Groff. In 1861 he was elected to the State Senate. In all these positions he discharged his duties faithfully.

Feb. 28, 1871, J. Philip Roman.

Oct. 27, 1873, Lloyd L. Clary. Mr. Clary was born in Frostburg in 1842, and lived there until the breaking out of the civil war, when he entered the Confederate army, and served under Capt. McNeill until the close of that struggle, after which he resided at Frostburg, and subsequently on a farm in Pennsylvania belonging to his father. In June, 1870, he removed to Cumberland, and took a position on the Mountain City *Times* (weekly), then managed by J. A. Murray & Co. In the fall of 1870 the paper passed into the hands of A. Chamberlain & Co., Mr. Clary receiving the position of managing editor. On the 1st of May, 1872, the proprietors of the Mountain City *Times* commenced the publication of the *Daily Times*, with Mr. Clary as its editor. On Feb. 21, 1873, Mr. Clary and John Broydrick, then foreman of the *Civilian* office, purchased of Messrs. Chamberlain & Co. both papers, and conducted them under the firm-name of Broydrick & Clary, Mr. Clary being managing editor. On the 27th of October, 1873, Mr. Clary was fatally shot in his office by John M. Resley. The trouble originated in an article published in Clary's paper reflecting upon the father of Mr. Resley. Mr. Clary only survived the shooting a few hours.

March 16, 1879, Joseph Dilley. Mr. Dilley was born in Botetourt County, Va., but in his boyhood removed to Somerset County, Pa., where he learned the blacksmith trade. After this he located where Frostburg was afterwards built, and for many years labored hard at the anvil and the bellows. His prosperity in this line in due time enabled him to embark in other enterprises, by which the foundation of a large estate was laid. He represented Allegany County in the Legislature, and at one time was superintendent of the National road. For a number of years Mr. Dilley was not engaged in any active business other than attending to his large estate. He left three children,—two living in Cumberland and one in Minnesota, who is a judge of one of the counties of that State.

Dec. 4, 1880, Daniel Blocher, a venerable citizen of Cumberland.

Oct. 1, 1881, John Galloway Lynn. Mr. Lynn was born and always lived in Cumberland. He built the Potomac Coal Wharf, and was superintendent of the wharf from 1840 to the time of his death. He left a widow, three sons, four daughters, and fifteen grandchildren. He was once elected to the House of Delegates as a Whig, voted for Douglas, and was a Democrat afterwards. He was nominated for sheriff in 1879 on the Citizens' ticket, and ran largely ahead of the ticket. He was a communicant and vestryman in Emmanuel (Protestant Episcopal) Church for many years.

ALLEGANY COUNTY DISTRICTS.

CHAPTER LVIII.

ORLEANS DISTRICT, No. 1.

THE metes and bounds of District No. 1, generally known as Orleans District, are as follows:

"Beginning at the mouth of Pusley Run, on the Potomac River; thence down and with the meanderings of said river to the mouth of Sideling Hill Creek; thence up and with Sideling Hill Creek to the Pennsylvania line; thence with the said Pennsylvania line west to the top of Green Ridge at the intersection with the line of Flintstone District; thence with the top of Green Ridge to the present division line between Oldtown and Orleans; thence crossing the Oldtown road leading from Hancock to Cumberland at Mrs. Cart's; thence down and with the Pusley Run to the Potomac River near Col. Thomas Greenwell's farm, the place of beginning."

It is bounded on the north by Pennsylvania, east by Washington County, east-southeast and south by the Potomac River, separating it from West Virginia, southwest and west by Old Town District, and west by Flintstone District. In the western part is Town Hill range of mountains, and in the northwest Green Ridge and another range of Town Hill. Among its early settlers were the Trails, Hallers, Hunters, Hartleys, Pottses, Norrises, Bodens, Barneses, Prices, Stiders, Bevanses, Sweitzers, Shipleys, Lynns, Shircliffs, Morgans, Mays, Brinkmans, Yonkers, Stormers, Creeks, Marns, Robys, Stotts, Watsons, Weavers, Benders, Higginses, Slyders, Kasacamps, Twiggses, Ziglers, Sniders, Robinsons, Linns, Ryans, Aldertons, Northcrafts, Rockwells, Keslers, Grosses, and Slottlemyers. Within its limits are four Methodist Episcopal churches and one Catholic church.

The village of Little Orleans is on the Chesapeake and Ohio Canal and Fifteen-Mile Creek. Orleans Road, forty miles east of Cumberland by rail, is reached by a good ford across the Potomac River, three-quarters of a mile in length. Fifteen-Mile Creek runs through the district for twelve miles, and takes its name from being fifteen miles from Hancock, in Washington County, and fifteen miles from Old Town, in Allegany County. The village is five miles from Sideling Hill Creek, the dividing line between Allegany and Washington Counties, twenty-seven miles from Cumberland by the county road, nine from the Pennsylvania line, and seven from the National road. Some very fine sulphur springs are found in the vicinity, among which the most noted is Carroll's Sulphur Spring. The post-office is Orleans Cross-roads, W. Va. Dr. William B. Beach is the physician of the town, M. L. Callan the merchant, H. Shircliff and James Watson are magistrates, John Carpenter is the village blacksmith, and Nathan Trail the miller. In 1811, Mrs. O'Queen kept tavern at the mouth of Fifteen-Mile Creek.

Piney Grove is situated in the eastern section of the county, near the Washington County line. Its shipping-point is at Orleans, and Orleans Road, on the Baltimore and Ohio Railroad, is the nearest station. E. V. Creek is the postmaster, Samuel Brady, carpenter, I. N. Watson, deputy sheriff, and John D. Watson, school-teacher.

Between the Green Ridge and Polish Mountain, on the property of William Carroll, there are several mineral springs, which have been examined and analyzed by two experienced chemists, Prof. William R. Fisher and George W. Andrews.

These springs are four in number, all issuing from a slate rock (containing fossils), which appears to constitute the substratum of the entire valley in which the springs are situated. Three of them have their openings near each other, within an area of thirty or forty feet in diameter, while the fourth is distant from these about two hundred yards, though flowing from the same kind of rock. As two of them take their rise in the bed of a small branch, they are liable to be overflowed, but this, however, seldom takes place during the summer months. One of the springs, situated thirty or forty feet from the margin of the branch, and at all times free from inundation, is more particularly described as rising from the slate rock and preserving a perfect transparency and limpidity in the small basin which has been excavated around it. It flows off through a channel, upon which, immediately after its leaving the basin, it commences to deposit the peculiar white material from which the characteristic title of white sulphur is derived. This deposit is found in great abundance in the bed of the stream proceeding from the spring. The taste at once indicates the character of the spring as a sulphur-water, which, corroborated by the appearance of the copious deposit, leaves no doubt upon the mind of the visitor that the spring before him is honestly entitled to the denomination of a "white sulphur spring." From this spring was obtained the water subsequently subjected to analysis, by which its constituents were determined. The physical condition and analysis of this spring are given as follows:

Temperature, 47° to 48° F.

Gaseous Contents.—Sulphuretted hydrogen, carbonic acid.

Solid Contents.—Sulphate of magnesia, muriate of soda, sulphate of lime, muriate of lime, carbonate of lime.

The Carroll White Sulphur Springs have decided advantages in that the temperature is so low that, besides furnishing a cool and refreshing draught, they are enabled to retain their gaseous contents much longer in a state of combination. These springs were all found to contain carbonic acid gas, which contributes its peculiar pungency to the water, and several glasses may be taken without any sense of oppression, such as is almost invariably experienced after drinking in succession two or three glasses of common water.

Each of the Carroll Springs is said to yield nearly twenty-four hogsheads per day, showing manifestly that no scarcity of water can ever be apprehended, however numerous the company of visitors may be.

It is asserted of these waters that they are found to possess all the medical properties usually met with in white sulphur springs.

The distance from Baltimore to the Springs is about one hundred and nineteen miles, one hundred and fifteen of which are on the present main route to Cumberland, and the remainder of the distance along the valley of Fifteen-Mile Creek.

A traveling mineralogist and watch-maker named Hoster, who stopped at Flintstone in the summer and fall of 1881, discovered in October of that year a mine or stratum of very valuable iron ore near Orleans, on the land of Harmon Brinkman.

In company with James Wilson, of Flintstone, Mr. Hoster leased a part of Mr. Brinkman's land, and they are now engaged with a force of men in opening the mine. The ore or metal is said to be of an extremely fine quality, and of the very desirable kind specially used in the manufacture of car-wheels.

The population of the First Election District, Orleans, was, by the census of 1880, 1016.

OLD TOWN DISTRICT, No. 2.

The metes and bounds of District No. 2 of Allegany County, generally known as Old Town District, are as follows:

"Beginning at the end of Nicholas Mountain (known as Martin's Mountain), on the bank of the Potomac River, opposite a brick house on the Virginia side, known as Slagle's old house; thence running down with the meanderings of the Potomac River to the mouth of Pusley Run, on Greenwell's farm, and including said farm; thence up and with said Pusley Run and crossing the old road at Mrs. Cart's, on Caspar Yngen's farm, and including said Mrs. Cart's; thence reversing the line of Orleans District up and with the top of Green Ridge to the Johnson Pack Horse road, and at the intersection with the lines of Flintstone District; thence with said Johnson Pack Horse road to where said road crosses Big Run; thence with a straight line to the top of Polish Mountain at the south end of a farm formerly belonging to Weaver Barnes, deceased; thence to Peters' Run, and with it to Town Creek; thence with Town Creek to Bear Wallow or Hollow, and with said Hollow to the head of the same; thence with a straight line to Lost Knob, or Warrior Mountain; thence by a straight line to where the Murley Branch road crosses Twigg's Hill; thence by a straight line to where the Williams road crosses Nicholas Mountain; thence with the top of said mountain to the place of beginning."

The district is bounded on the north by Flintstone District, east by Orleans District, south, southeast, and southwest by the Potomac River, separating it from West Virginia, and west by Canal (Cumberland) District, No. 4.

Old Town is appropriately named, as it was undoubtedly occupied by white settlers a number of years prior to any other locality in Allegany County. As early as 1741 the famous pioneer and Indian-fighter, Col. Thomas Cresap, established a frontier post at what is now known as Old Town, or Skipton, and which was then called Shawnee Old Town, presumably from the fact that a village of the Shawanese, or Shawnees, had once been located there. Here Col. Cresap built and lived in a stone house, situated on a high hill about one-half of a mile southeast of the town, and within four hundred yards of the Potomac River. The house had very thick stone walls, and only two rooms, each about twenty feet square. The building was known in early times as "Cresap's Fort," and often afforded shelter to the inhabitants of the country for miles around during the forays of the Indians. It was occupied as a dwelling for many years after it was abandoned by the Cresaps, and is now owned by Edward Ginneman. The treaty between the chiefs of the Six Nations and the Maryland commissioners of June 30, 1744, recites: "Beginning at about two miles above the uppermost fork of the Cohougarouton, or Potomac, on the north branch of said fork, near which fork Capt. Thomas Cresap has a hunting or trading cabin." From the fact that this treaty embraced Cresap's settlement, and did not include that portion where Fort Cumberland was afterwards located, and that there were no other settlements nearer than the Conococheague, it is evident that Cresap was the first actual settler of Allegany County. Col. Thomas

Cresap owned large tracts of land on both sides of the river. His son, Capt. Michael Cresap, also lived at Old Town, and his house is still standing, and is now owned by the heirs of Christopher Barth. Old Town was called by Col. Cresap "Skipton," after a little town in Yorkshire, England, from which he emigrated.

Thomas Cresap and Michael Cresap, in the *Maryland Gazette* of March 19, 1767, advertised that they

"have a piece of ground at the Old Town commodiously situated for a town, and lying on the main road that leads to Pittsburgh and Redstone from Virginia, Maryland, and Pennsylvania. A wagon-road may be made from the two last-mentioned places to Fort Cumberland without crossing any mountain. And whereas it is expected that the South Branch of the Potomac River will be the boundary line between Lord Baltimore and Lord Fairfax, by which means all the land to the north of the said branch, so far as the temporary lines, which is fifteen miles from this place, will be Maryland, and that the town now proposed is nearest the centre, therefore the most proper for a country town; and inasmuch as the river Potomac is for four months in a year, and at sundry other times, passable for battoes, and canoe-vessels also of ten and fifteen tons' burthen may pass and repass at some seasons in the year as far as Old Town but no farther, by reason of the South Branch's coming in there, unless at some particular time, when they may go as high as Cumberland with small loads. The lots laid out are half an acre each, to be sold to the highest bidder at public sale, May 12, 1767, paying a rent of half a dollar each for the first ten years and one dollar per year after. There are also five acre lots to be sold to such persons as shall think proper to buy; also a large quantity of good meadow land near the said town, which the subscribers would lease for twenty-one years or three lives. One lot will be given from any purchase-money to men of each of the following callings who will set up and carry on their respective businesses, viz.: a carpenter, a tailor, a hatter, a blacksmith, a weaver, a saddler, a tanner, and a shoemaker."

It is thought that silver is to be found in Alum Hill, which takes its name from the alum that impregnates the water coming from the hill. Luther Martin Cresap, now living in Old Town, is the son of James M. Cresap, and grandson of Michael Cresap, who lies buried in Trinity churchyard, New York City. He was born, Sept. 14, 1812, in Old Town. His father, James M. Cresap, died in Cumberland, and is buried there. His wife was the widow of Abraham Van Bibber, of Baltimore, whose maiden name was Mary Young. Luther Martin Cresap was an only child. He has in his possession a letter written in 1818, which states that a number of Spaniards explored the neighborhood of Old Town and found a silver-mine, which is said to be in Alum Hill, and that they erected a furnace and passed the ore through all the various processes until it was coined into money. The ore is said to be rich and plentiful. The neighborhood is particularly rich in minerals, and black band iron ore, surface and hematite ore are found. Old Town is bounded on the north by Bare Hill and Warrior Mountain, which in Pennsylvania is called Warrior Ridge, and on the south by the Potomac. In the early days of Old Town there was a spirited contest between it and Cumberland as to which should be made the county-seat. Efforts were also made to establish a bank there, but both movements proved fruitless. There is a small frame Methodist Episcopal Church north of the town, built about 1876. The frame Methodist church, built in 1812, was torn down in 1863 by the New York Lincoln Cavalry to build shanties. Old Town was frequently the scene of military raids during the civil war, and Imboden and McNeill, with Confederate cavalry, paid frequent visits to the town.

Luther Martin, the famous lawyer, married Miss Cresap, sister of James M. Cresap, by whom he had two children,—Maria Keene, who died in Baltimore, and Eleanora, who married Col. Richard Keene, a student under Mr. Martin. His descendants are all in the West. Lennox, the brother of Luther Martin, lived near Old Town, and married Elizabeth Cresap, the sister of the wife of Luther Martin. Lennox Martin had a large family, who went West, and are now all dead. He died in Old Town, and is buried on his farm, now owned by Henry Henry, about three miles from the town. Luther Martin Cresap, a hale, hearty old gentleman, well-to-do and very intelligent, with every appearance of the old stock, still resides at Green Spring Run, Hampshire Co., W. Va. Long years afterwards came the Twiggses, Wilsons, Atheys, Barths, Altertons, Wakefields, Wagoners, Stallings, Stumps, Beagles, Crabtrees, Daniels, Devenbergs, Fields, Eylers, Shryocks, Shotsens, Rubys, Reelys, Richambaughs, Fishers, Furlows, Hartlys, Harrises, Kelleys, Herricks, Kerns, Littels, Longs, Rises, Pipers, Myerses, Matthews, Conellys, and Ginnevans. John Deakins lived on the road between Hancock and Old Town in 1812.

As previously stated, Old Town, known as Skipton prior to 1744, is the oldest town in the county. It is on the Chesapeake and Ohio Canal, and the North Branch of the Potomac River. Green Spring, the beginning of the Second Division of the Baltimore and Ohio Railroad, is within one-fourth of a mile, and affords every convenience for receiving and shipping goods. The Lantz family settled here at an early date, and built, in 1811, a large brick house. The village has a good school and a Methodist Episcopal church. The North and South Branch Bank of the Potomac was incorporated by an act of Legislature in 1818–19, but was never established at Old Town. The post-office for the village is Green Spring,

W. Va. The resident physician is Dr. F. McElfish, and J. Mountz, Carder & Darky, and William McCully have stores. C. C. Showacre works a tannery, and L. M. Cresap a mill. The population of the district is 1194, including the village of Old Town, which contains 180 inhabitants.

FLINTSTONE DISTRICT, No. 3.

The following are the metes and bounds of District No. 3, generally known as Flintstone:

"Beginning at the Pennsylvania line on the top of Martin's Mountain; thence with the top of said mountain to the Williams road crosses Nicholas (known as Martin's Mountain); thence with a straight line to where the Murley Branch road crosses Twigg's Hill; thence with a straight line to the Lost Knob on Warrior Mountain; thence with a straight line to the head of Bear Hollow; thence with said Bear Hollow to Town Creek; thence with Town Creek to Peter's Run; thence with Peter's Run to the top of Polish Mountain, at the south end of a farm formerly owned by Weaver Barnes, deceased; thence with a straight line to where Johnson's Pack Horse road crosses Big Run; thence with said Pack Horse road to the top of Green Ridge, intersecting with the lines of Orleans District; thence with the lines of Orleans District and with the top of Green Ridge to the Pennsylvania line; thence with the Pennsylvania line west to the place of beginning."

It is bounded on the north by Pennsylvania, east by Orleans District, south by Old Town District, and west by Canal District No. 4, and Central, No. 5 (both Cumberland). The old village of Flintstone is in the northeastern portion of the county, near the State line of Pennsylvania, twelve miles from Cumberland. The first settlers in this region were the Robinettes, Wilsons, Chaneys, Ashes, Hartsocks, Beaders, Bottomfields, Buceys, Brownings, Twiggses, Willisons, Sliders, Turners, Smiths, Robossons, Perrins, Morgans, McElfishes, Lashleys, McCoys, Kifers, Elbins, Fletchers, Diffenbaughs, Dickenses, Dieberts, and Davises. There are two Methodist Episcopal churches in the town, and good public and select schools. The merchants are E. W. Ash & Son, J. Lashley & Co., J. W. Wilson & Co., J. B. Willison, R. R. Montgomery, and H. B. Elbin. Jacob Lashley is postmaster, and Dr. T. P. Robosson the resident physician. The industries are represented by B. F. Barkman and W. A. Davis, carpenters; L. T. Dickinson and J. B. Hoyt & Co., tanners; Filler & Browning, wagon-makers; Jeremiah Leasure and J. Steckman, blacksmiths; Wilson & Castle, lumber-dealers; and Hamberg Wilson, miller. Flintstone and Town Creeks supply an abundance of good water.

The early settlers of Murley's Branch (not given above) were the Flakes, Frazers, Woolfords, Rices, Norths, Middletons, Jamisons, Hinkles, Houses, Hamiltons, and Fletchers. This village is ten and a half miles east of Cumberland, its nearest shipping-point. Murley's Branch, a small stream, rises one-half mile west of the post-office from under an arched rock. The water is very cold in summer and warm in winter. Good limestone water, sulphur water, and warm spring water within twenty yards of each other can be seen two miles from the village. These springs—great natural curiosities—are annually visited by hundreds of tourists. Iron, coal, and various ores abound in this vicinity, and the mountains and fields are filled with game, and the waters with fish of several varieties. There are two Methodist Episcopal churches, and one English Lutheran church. Flintstone Grange, No. 111, of Patrons of Husbandry, is located here, of which Thomas P. Robosson is Master, and S. Hinkle, Secretary. Jesse Robinette is postmaster. The merchants are McElfish & Wilson and Willison & Robinette. G. W. Dean is a carpenter, M. V. Willey, blacksmith, and D. Pennell, wheelwright.

Mineral Lodge, No. 126, I. O. O. F., was instituted in July, 1870, with sixteen members, by the grand officers of Maryland.

On Jan. 8, 1875, the following officers were installed by Deputy Grand Master J. H. Gephart and Assistant Grand Marshal Harmon White:

N. G., J. B. Robinette; V. G., James Ash; Sec., B. T. Barkman; Treas., O. S. Wilson; Chap., D. A. Perrin; Trustee, Joseph Losaire; Representative to Grand Lodge, T. P. Robosson.

At this time the lodge had increased its membership to thirty-seven.

Population, according to the census of 1881, was, for the Flintstone District, 1531, and for Flintstone village 315.

Among the prominent citizens of this district is Hon. Benjamin L. Turner, who was born in the town of Olive, Ulster Co., N. Y., Jan. 29, 1842. Samuel Turner, his great-grandfather, a native of Connecticut, settled at Olive, Ulster Co., N. Y., in 1791. His (Samuel's) grandfather, Samuel Turner, emigrated from Holland, having fled thence from England during the persecution of the Puritans in the reign of Elizabeth. He emigrated to Casco Bay, Maine, some time prior to the year 1700. At the time of the King Philip (Indian) war he, with his son Samuel, removed to Connecticut. The second Samuel settled at Uniontown, Conn., where he married a Miss Choler and had four children,—Samuel, John, Richard, and Hannah. He was afterwards killed at the siege of Quebec, during the French war, while serving under Gen. Monk. The third Samuel lived at New Milford, Conn., and married Freelove Turrill, who was one of two daughters in a family of thirteen. Her brother Stephen joined the army in

1758, under Gen. Abercrombie, at the age of nineteen. He was afterwards in the Continental army, and was at the battles of White Plains, Valley Forge, Saratoga, the surrender of Burgoyne, and the surrender of Cornwallis at Yorktown, and died in Vermont, Feb. 28, 1848, at the age of one hundred and one

BENJAMIN L. TURNER.

years. The third Samuel Turner, the great-grandfather of the subject of this sketch, was also a soldier in the war of the Revolution, and was engaged in many of the principal battles. He settled in Olive, Ulster Co., N. Y., in the year 1791, and died Oct. 5, 1811, leaving seven children, the sixth being Benjamin, the grandfather of Benjamin L. Turner. Benjamin Turner served in the war of 1812, under Gen. Van Rensselaer, and married Polly Eaton, a native of Connecticut. Her father and grandfather were also soldiers in the war of the Revolution, and were both with Gen. Washington at the time of his evacuation of Long Island. The children of Benjamin and Polly (Eaton) Turner all married and settled in New York. Their father was a hatter by trade, but he purchased and carried on a farm in Olive, on Esopus Creek, during the latter portion of his life. He served as a soldier in the war of 1812, under Gen. Van Rensselear, and died at the age of eighty seven at the residence of his son Benjamin, in Olive. The latter, father of Benjamin L., was born in Olive, is a lawyer by profession, and has been a resident of Shokan, Ulster Co., N. Y., for the last sixteen years. He is a prominent citizen of the place, having served as magistrate, supervisor of his township, and a member of the State Legislature. He married Laura A., daughter of James and Rebecca Morton. She was a sister of Dr. William Thomas Greene Morton, the discoverer of etherization. Benjamin L. Turner passed most of his boyhood at his grandfather's. He was educated in the district school of his native place and at the Roxbury Academy, Delaware Co., N. Y. For a number of years he was clerk in the stores of George W. Cross and Hoyt Brothers at Shokan. On the 17th of October, 1861, he enlisted as a private in the Fourth New York Cavalry; was promoted to be quartermaster-sergeant, December, 1861; and subsequently first sergeant. On the 30th of August, 1862, he was severely wounded by a sabre-cut across the right shoulder in a cavalry charge at the second battle of Bull Run, and was left on the field for dead, being unconscious for twenty-four hours. While in this state he was stripped of all clothing except his pantaloons. His wound was dressed in a stone house at Centreville, and he was then taken to Carver Hospital, Washington, from which place he received an honorable discharge from the army Feb. 1, 1863. Returning to Olive, for four months he held the position of enrolling-officer at that place. In the fall of 1863 he was appointed assistant provost-marshal of the Thirteenth Congressional District of New York, which position he filled until November, 1864. On the 14th of that month he was commissioned by Governor Horatio Seymour first lieutenant in the Fifteenth New York Volunteers, and was acting captain during nearly the whole term of service. He remained in the army till it was mustered out at the close of the war, and was at the fall of Petersburg and Richmond, and with the army near Appomattox Court-House at the surrender of Gen. Lee. Upon returning home he engaged in the lumber trade at Shokan. In June, 1868, he moved to Flintstone, Allegany Co., Md., where, since that time, he has carried on a general merchandise business and farming.

In politics he is Republican, and has taken an active part in local and State politics. He was county commissioner in 1874–75, and was elected to the House of Delegates in 1879 and 1881. He is a member of the Masonic fraternity, and though not a member is a trustee of the Methodist Episcopal Church at Flintstone and a large contributor to its support. He married, Dec. 5, 1864, Mary E., daughter of Alexander and Mary A. Robinson, of Marbletown, Ulster Co., N. Y. Mrs. Turner was born near Stone Ridge, May 12, 1845. They have had one child, Louisa, born April 21, 1866, died July 21, 1868.

RAWLINGS' STATION DISTRICT, No. 7.

The metes and bounds of District No. 7, generally known as Rawlings' Station District, are as follows:

"Beginning at the mouth of Clay Lick Run, at the west end of Fort Hill, on the North Branch of the Potomac River; thence running westerly and with said Clay Lick Run to the top of Dan's Mountain; thence north with the top of Dan's Mountain to the line of Cumberland River District, No. 6, at the head of Warrior Run; thence with said run, and with the division line of District No. 6, easterly to the Potomac River, about one half-mile below Brady's Mill, and nearly opposite Seymour's house, on the Virginia side of said river; thence up and with the meanderings of the Potomac River to the mouth of Clay Lick Run, the place of beginning."

It is bounded on the north by the River (Cumberland) District, No. 6, east by the Potomac River, separating it from West Virginia, south by Westernport District, and west by Barton, East Lonaconing, and East Frostburg Districts. The Rawlings family was the first to settle in this district prior to the Revolution. The subsequent settlers were the Ravenscrafts, Wilsons, Welches, Biers, Carders. Cookerleys, Stottlers, Rodericks, Harts, Hudsons, McCartys, McKenzies, Frosts, Edward Cresap, the Wrights, Winters, Bradys, Darrows, Randalls, Longs, Elliotts, Burns, Atheys, Clises, Hemmings, Squires, and Martzes.

Moses Rawlings was commissioned, July 1, 1776, lieutenant-colonel of a Maryland rifle regiment. He commanded it at Fort Washington, and, after a brave resistance, was captured at the fall of that fortification, Nov. 16, 1776. At this time Washington said of him, "I entertain a very high opinion of the merits of Col. Rawlings and his officers, and have interested myself much in their behalf." His four companies of riflemen were joined to the Rifle Battalion, which was afterwards known as the Eighth Maryland Regiment. In 1779 he was ordered by Washington to Fort Pitt, and in consequence of the refusal of Washington to permit the German troops to accompany him, in April, 1779, he resigned. Capt. Beall took charge of his command at Frederick, and on May 7, 1779, marched with them to Fort Pitt. On Sept. 27, 1779, Col. Timothy Pickering placed Col. Rawlings in charge of the prisoners at Frederick, where he remained until the close of the war. He died in Hampshire County, Va., in May, 1809. His children were the first settlers in this, the Seventh, district, and many of their descendants still live there, one of whom, Moses Rawlings, was sheriff from 1831 to 1834.

Rawlings' Station was named in honor of the Rawlings family. It lies twelve miles west of Cumberland, and nine east of Keyser, W. Va. The situation is between two ranges of mountains, forming a beautiful valley for six miles. The Potomac River is the boundary on the east, and a range of the Alleganies bounds it on the west. C. M. Rawlings is postmaster; Middleton & McIntire, Hiram Albright, J. O. Dawson, and David Grove are merchants; and J. H. Dawson is the carpenter of the village. The new Methodist Episcopal church was dedicated Nov. 1, 1881. It was built of wood, after a plan drawn by Dixon & Carson, of Baltimore, and cost two thousand and fifty dollars. The preachers present were Revs. A. M. Courtenay, L. T. Widerman, and W. McKim Hammack. It took the place of the old structure built long ago.

Brady's Mill is located on the Baltimore and Ohio Railroad, near the North Branch of the Potomac River, seven miles west of Cumberland. Richard F. Bunce is postmaster, J. B Hudson, merchant, and John C. Brady, a cattle-dealer. The trades are represented by John Winters and R. F. Bunce & Son, blacksmiths; Robert Deremer and Jacob Shook, carpenters; Elijah Winters, gunsmith and miller; Nicholas McKenzie and Martin L. Roman, lime manufacturers. In the days of the French and Indian war a number of Indian depredations were committed in the vicinity, and several persons were carried off and killed by the savages. The old mill built by Mr. Brady gave the name to the place.

The population of the district, according to the census of 1880, including Cresap, 50, and Westernport, 1468, was 2396.

WESTERNPORT DISTRICT, No. 8.

The metes and bounds of District No. 8 are as follows:

"Beginning at the mouth of Clay Lick Run, at the west end of Fort Hill, on the North Branch of the Potomac River; thence up and with the Potomac River to the Garrett County line; thence with the Garrett County line to where said line crosses Mill Run; thence with Mill Run to the mouth thereof; thence south twenty-six degrees east through the lines of James Morrison, John Morrison's heirs, Emory Duckworth's heirs, and Alton C. Duckworth's lands to the forks of Stony Run; thence following the south fork of Stony Run and water-shed thereof to the top of Dan's Mountain; thence with the line of Rawlings' Station District and with Clay Lick Run to the place of beginning."

It is bounded on the north by Barton and Rawlings' Districts, east and south by the Potomac River, separating it from West Virginia, and west by Garrett County. The first settlers were the Devecmons, Morrisons, Siglers, Wilts, Ravenscrafts, Rosses, Powers, Polands, Michaels, Clarks, Broadwaters, Daytons, Colemans, Kights, Kookens, Groveses, Duckworths,

Hixenbaughs, Fazenbakers, Paxtons, Murrays, Murphys, and Jamessons.

Westernport is the southern terminus of the Cumberland and Pennsylvania Railroad, and is one-half mile from Piedmont, W. Va., on the Baltimore and Ohio Railroad. The first settler on the original site was Peter Devecmon. Subsequently James Morrison and Adam Sigler owned all the land, including the town and its contiguous territory, the former of whom laid out the town at the beginning of the century. But before the Revolution it was a straggling hamlet, and Washington's headquarters were once where Andrew Mullen lives on Main Spring. The place in early times was on the great thoroughfare from Winchester, Va., to Morgantown, Pa., over which salt, flour, and other merchandise were transported on horseback. The oldest house now standing is the post-office, a log cabin, built before 1810. The first stores were kept by James Morrison, William Price, and John Crawford. The first resident physician was Dr. Gerstell. Mrs. Burns kept the first hotel and Mrs. Brumney the second. When the Baltimore and Ohio Railroad was built to this point the town did not have over thirty houses, and Piedmont was an open field with not a building on it. The land on which the latter town is situated was the property of Mrs. Burns (the hotel proprietress), who sold it just before the building of the railroad. The town was originally called in popular parlance, "Hardscrabble." The old Burns Hotel was taken down in November, 1881, by Mr. Getty. The second generation of store-keepers were Samuel Brady and Mr. Dewittman. After the completion of the Cumberland and Pennsylvania Railroad the town increased rapidly in population.

The town was incorporated Feb. 23, 1859. Its officers have been:

1859.—Commissioners, A. Gerstell (Pres.), Stephen Fuller, W. T. Jamison, E. J. Frenlock, C. A. Pagenhardt; Clerk, A. Kalbaugh.

1860.—Commissioners, Martin Fusner (Pres.), M. Kalbaugh, Samuel Evans, H. Barnes, Isaac Clark; Clerk, G. W. Spangler.

1861.—Commissioners, George W. Jenks, Isaac Clark, H. Barnes; Clerk, G. W. Spangler. In this year the charter was suspended, and so continued until 1868, when a new one was obtained from the Legislature.

1868.—Commissioners, James McGlennon (Pres.), M. Kalbaugh, Henry Stine, Michael Gannon, Henry Hushman; Clerk, Owen Riordan.

1869.—Commissioners, James McGlennon (Pres.), M. Kalbaugh, James Hughes, J. S. Jamesson, Edward Evans; Clerk, Owen Riordan.

1870.—Commissioners, Edward Evans (Pres.), M. Kalbaugh, M. Foley, J. Kight, Patrick White; Clerk, W. A. Daily.

1871.—Commissioners, Stephen Fuller (Pres.), Martin Fusner, C. A. Pagenhardt, Ranson Tibbets, J. C. Clark; Clerk, William Duckworth.

1872.—Commissioners, Martin Fusner, Joseph Cramer, Maurice Miller, Joseph Nesbit, Michael Currie; Clerk, W. Montgomery.

1873.—Commissioners, Charles A. Pagenhardt, Maurice Miller, Henry Stine, Joshua Kight, M. Kalbaugh; Clerk, W. Montgomery.

1874.—Commissioners, Stephen Fuller (Pres.), Joshua Kight, Henry Rehs, J. C. Clark, M. Miller; Clerk, E. C. Lyons.

1875.—Commissioners, R. C. McCulloh (Pres.), James Hughes, J. C. Clark, S. Fuller, Henry Rehs; Clerk, W. Montgomery.

1876.—Commissioners, J. C. Clark (Pres.), G. W. Sheetz, C. A. Pagenhardt, J. S. Miller, James Brown; Clerk, W. Montgomery.

1877.—Commissioners, Martin Fusner (Pres.), Joseph Cramer, John Onthank, Austin Jones, C. A. Pagenhardt; Clerk, W. Montgomery.

1878.—Commissioners, Martin Fusner (Pres.), C. A. Pagenhardt, Austin Jones, John Onthank, J. C. Clark; Clerk, Owen Riordan.

1879.—Commissioners, Martin Fusner (Pres.), John Onthank, M. Kalbaugh, Josiah Kight, James Hughes; Clerk, Owen Riordan.

1880.—Commissioners, Martin Fusner (Pres.), James Hughes, Harmon Brown, Stephen Fuller, J. Kight; Clerk, Owen Riordan.

1881.—Commissioners, Martin Fusner (Pres.), G. W. Spangler, Conrad Nall, W. F. Mansfield, Patrick White; Clerk, Owen Riordan.

Since 1875 the bailiff has been William Bell. The expenditures in 1880 were nine hundred and five dollars and eighty-eight cents. G. W. Sheetz is police magistrate.

St. James' chapel (Protestant Episcopal) was built in 1878, and is part of Cumberland Parish. Rev. Dr. Thrall is rector. It is a fine brick structure, near the Potomac bridge.

The Lutheran church, a brick edifice, was erected in 1879, under Rev. Mr. Miller, of Washington County, the first pastor, who removed to Iowa, and was succeeded by the present pastor, Rev. Mr. Staffer.

The United Brethren church building was erected in 1875, and dedicated in the fall of the same year. Before this Rev. Mr. Underwood had services for six months in a hall and six months in private houses. It was built in the second year of his pastorate. After him Rev. Mr. Stinespring was pastor for two years. He was succeeded by Rev. J. W. Whitmeyer, for one year, who was followed by the present incumbent, Rev. Mr. Hicks.

As late as 1853 there was not a Catholic church within twenty miles of the village. At that time the few Catholics who resided in Piedmont and Westernport walked to Bloomington, Frankville, and Swanton in order to attend mass celebrated in a private house. In 1854, Father Slattery bought of Hamill & Combs, at Bloomington, an old warehouse (14 by 20 feet), which he used as a church until 1857, when he built the "Old St. Peter's," in Westernport. When Father Slattery dedicated "Old St. Peter's" his congregation named it the "Cathedral," so large did it appear to them. Father Slattery remained pastor until 1860, when he was transferred to Baltimore to take charge of St. Joseph's Church in that city, where he died in 1866.

From 1857 to 1868 the Catholics of Piedmont and Westernport were attended from Frostburg and Cumberland. In the latter year Father De Wolf was appointed resident pastor, and remained in charge two years, during which time he effected much for the spiritual and material welfare of his people. In 1871, Father De Wolf was transferred to the pastoral charge of Hagerstown, and was succeeded by Father Sullivan, under whose charge a new church was erected in 1873. The following clergymen have at different periods been stationed at St. Peter's: Revs. William Slattery, M. Carney, R. Browne, M. O'Reilly, Fr. Elchart, J. Wirth, Fr. O'Connor, W. H. Gross (Bishop of Savannah), Fr. O'Berle, Fr. Lewis, Fr. McDonald, D. De Wolf, M. Kelley, J. Andreas, and J. O'Sullivan. The present church edifice, which was built in 1873 and dedicated October 5th of that year by Most Rev. James Roosevelt Bayley, Archbishop of Baltimore, exceeds in size and appearance every other building in the immediate neighborhood. It is one hundred and twenty-one feet long, by fifty-three feet wide, with a tower and spire surmounted by a golden cross. The walls are of brick, and the roof is covered with the best quality of slate. In the interior are two beautiful stained-glass windows and a marble altar of exquisite workmanship. The building is in the Roman style of architecture. The entire cost of the edifice, including the cost of pews and altars, amounted to twenty-five thousand dollars.

A Methodist Episcopal congregation has no church edifice, but holds services in the halls of the town.

Philos Cemetery, a beautiful cemetery, is located on an elevated plateau overlooking the town. Among the persons interred are the following:

Mary Ann, wife of Stephen Powell, died March 31, 1873, aged 52.

Gertrude, wife of Robert Clague, died Dec. 8, 1878, aged 56.

B. B. Dawson, died March 14, 1872, aged 54; and his wife, Elizabeth, Sept. 18, 1867, aged 60.

E. T. White, died Dec. 22, 1872, aged 49.

Rebecca, wife of Joshua Kight, died Jan. 3, 1876, aged 35.

W. M. McNeall, died March 17, 1878, aged 48.

Mary, wife of G. Kerhule, died Jan. 30, 1872, aged 46.

Elizabeth, wife of C. D. Downey, died Feb. 17, 1876, aged 55.

Joseph Paxton, died Sept. 29, 1865, aged 71; and his wife, Susan, July 18, 1873, aged 71.

Catharine M., wife of J. Paxton, died Aug. 10, 1867, aged 19.

Rachel J., wife of Samuel Paxton, died Feb. 17, 1867, aged 40.

Thomas Paxton, born Oct. 13, 1822, died Dec. 29, 1873.

Anna M., wife of John Keys, died Jan. 23, 1865, aged 76.

Sarah, wife of John Kight, died May 4, 1874, aged 83.

Ignatius Middleton, died June 23, 1859, aged 36.

Alfred R. Carroll, died Jan. 2, 1876, aged 34.

Maria, wife of Samuel Ayers, died March 27, 1874, aged 68.

Margaret, wife of J. N. Barchus, died March 27, 1873, aged 36.

John Hartell, born in Goditz, Bavaria, Oct. 22, 1833, died May 11, 1875.

Nancy Murray, born Feb. 19, 1801, died Oct. 3, 1875.

James T. Ball, died April 26, 1869, aged 49.

Matilda, wife of Simon Roberts, died July 26, 1876, aged 37.

Joseph Martin, born in Kilbirnie, Ayrshire, Scotland, died May 11, 1875, aged 67.

Joseph Martin, born as above, Jan. 9, 1832, died July 19, 1879.

Mary A. Murphy, born Jan. 16, 1792, died Oct. 17, 1863.

Anna, wife of Rev. A. Baush, died Dec. 4, 1879, aged 56.

Harriet, wife of Charles Pagenhardt, died June 24, 1859, aged 68.

Eleanor F., wife of Joseph Hendrickson, died Feb. 5, 1876, aged 66.

William Connelly, born in Scotland, died Feb. 12, 1872, aged 44.

L. M. Jamesson, born Feb. 17, 1801, died Oct. 12, 1876.

Mary E., wife of Jacob S. Jamesson, died Dec. 24, 1875, aged 43.

William R. Davis, born Aug. 23, 1833, died April 22, 1879.

Nancy, wife of William Kight, died Nov. 6, 1871, aged 54.

John Ferguson, native of Scotland, died Feb. 29, 1876, aged 69.

George T. Sigler, died March 22, 1874, aged 43.

William Harris, died Dec. 6, 1872, aged 44.

Margaret S., wife of Alexander Kalbaugh, died Feb. 3, 1876, aged 46.

Anna L., wife of Edward Bice, died Dec. 20, 1873, aged 63.

Robert D., son of Edward and Anna L. Bice, died May, 1875, aged 44.

Eve B. Reitzel, died June 16, 1860, aged 41.

Henry Miller, died Aug. 24, 1859, aged 49.

Lucy C., wife of James B. Clarke, born Sept. 4, 1845, died Jan. 22, 1872.

George L. Wheeler, killed by the explosion of the boiler of his engine, No. 117, Dec. 21, 1869, aged 29.

Margaret, wife of Robert Duncan, born in Scotland, died July 13, 1872, aged 49; and her husband, Robert, native of Scotland, died Oct. 17, 1873, aged 51.

Elizabeth Klein, born in Loudon County, Va., April 28, 1789, died Aug. 2, 1879.

Louisa, daughter of Lewis and Elizabeth Klein, and wife of William B. Wright, died March 17, 1872, aged 65.

The teachers of the public schools in 1881 and 1882 were: Principal, O. H. Bruce; First Assistant, Annie Wedon; Second Assistant, Eva McDonald; Third Assistant, Katie Gannon.

Fire Department.—At a meeting of the citizens held Oct. 8, 1881, with M. C. Fuller in the chair, and Michael Ahern secretary, C. F. McCulloh, Charles Pagenhardt, and Capt. W. F. Mansfield were appointed a committee to draft the constitution and bylaws of the new fire department. The engine-house was erected on Main Street in 1881, and two fire-engines, reel, and hose purchased.

Newspapers.—The town has no journals, but in Piedmont, adjoining, the *Piedmont Observer* was established Sept. 3, 1881, by G. T. Goshorn. It is a Republican paper, largely devoted to local news, and giving much space to Westernport items. Another paper, called the *Potomac Herald*, was started in Piedmont in April, 1878, by W. Scott Lee, but was discontinued in September, 1880.

Orders and Associations.—Hiram Lodge, A. F. and A. M., No. 103, was instituted May 1, 1855. Its first officers were: W. M., Walter Moore; S. W., P. J. Bunnell; J. W., George S. Koontz; Sec., W. M. Elen; Treas., James Warren. This was under a dispensation. The charter members were E. C. Lyons, David Long, M. L. Gregory, N. Gerstell, B. B. Shaw, James Funk, James Graham, William Hall, Joel S. White, Gilmor F. Sims, Clement Lovett. Under the charter, in the fall of 1855, the first officers were: W. M., George S. Koontz; S. W., P. J. Bunnell; J. W., B. B. Shaw; Sec., Joel S. White; Treas., Walter Moore, of whom not one is now a member. In 1855 the following persons received the Entered Apprentice and Fellow-Craft degrees: Samuel Arnold, Edward Shockey, John Jones, and James Livers. The officers for 1881 were: W. M., J. G. Williams; S. W., James Brown; Sec., F. D. Beck; Treas., J. C. Kerhule; S. D., W. C. Johnston; J. D., John Jose; Tyler, John H. Fisher. It has twenty-eight members. Since its institution several new lodges have been organized in its territory, two of which are at Barton and Piedmont. The lodge meets on the first and third Tuesdays of each month. Its Past Masters are F. D. Beck, S. F. Ringgold, Wm. Klipstine, J. C. Kerhule, J. H. Fisher.

Samaritan Tent, No. 32, I. O. Rechabites. This tent meets at I. O. O. F.'s Hall every Saturday evening.

Potomac Lodge, No. 11, I. O. G. T., meets every Monday evening at Kildow Hall.

Order of United American Mechanics meets every Thursday evening.

Union Section, No. 12, C. T., holds weekly meetings.

St. Patrick's Catholic Temperance Society meets on the first Sunday of every month at one P.M.

St. Aloysius' Catholic Temperance Society meets on the third Sunday of every month at one P.M.

Sober Men's Union meets in Jamesson's Hall every Saturday night at eight P.M.

Father Mathew Temperance Society of young men meets on the third Sunday of every month.

Lafayette Lodge, No. 4, Knights of Pythias. The officers for 1881 were:

P. C., Maner Jenkins; C. C., John H. Jones; V. C., John M. Lewis; P., Worthy Montgomery; M. at A., N. B. Smouse; M. of E., A. J. Clark; K. of R. and S., Samuel C. Gilbert.

Meets every Monday evening.

Philos Lodge, No. 91, I. O. O. F., meets Wednesday evenings, and Mount Carmel Encampment, No. 7, on Friday evenings.

Canal Extension Convention.—On June 22, 1875, the convention held at Westernport to inaugurate measures looking to the extension of the Chesapeake and Ohio Canal to that place was largely attended by citizens of the surrounding country, as well as a considerable number from abroad. The meeting was held at Roh's Park, on the Westernport Heights, and was presided over by John Coles, of Barton, John Broydrick acting as secretary. Speeches in advocacy of the extension were made by Hon. Patrick Hamill, Hon. Montgomery Blair, Hon. A. P. Gorman, president of the Chesapeake and Ohio Canal, and by Messrs. Daniel Biser, A. K. Stake, and Michael Bannon, of the board of directors. The committee on resolutions reported the following, which were unanimously adopted:

"*Resolved*, By the citizens of Allegany and Garrett Counties of Maryland, and the County of Mineral, W. Va., assembled in mass-meeting, that the project of extending the Chesapeake and Ohio Canal, or improving the navigation of the Potomac River to the centre of the coal basin at the mouth of the Mount Savage River, is not only feasible, but the commercial, manufacturing, mining, and agricultural interests of the entire State now demand it.

"*Resolved*, That a committee of ten be appointed to draft a memorial requesting our representatives in Congress to secure national aid for the work.

"*Resolved*, That the thanks of the meeting are hereby tendered the Hon. Montgomery Blair, together with the president and directors of the Chesapeake and Ohio Canal Company, for their presence and able advocacy of the extension and completion to the mouth of the Savage River."

Under the resolutions adopted the following committee was appointed by the president: Allegany County, W. A. Miller, Owen Riorden, James Park, A. J. Clark; Mineral County, E. J. Fredlock, David Davis, John Broydrick; Garrett County, E. Kemp, Andrew Mullen, C. T. Abell. After the meeting adjourned, a banquet was served at the "Sims House," Piedmont, W. Va., at which speeches were made by Judge Patrick Hamill, Hon. Montgomery Blair, and others. Though the project failed, it is believed that the extension of the canal is only a question of time.

The population of the district was, by the census of 1880, 676.

BARTON DISTRICT, No. 9.

The following are the metes and bounds of District No. 9, generally known as Barton District:

"Beginning at Mill Run on the Garrett County line and running with said Mill Run to the mouth thereof; thence south twenty-six degrees east through the lines of James Morrison and heirs of John Morrison, heirs of Emory Duckworth and Alton C. Duckworth's lands to the forks of Stony Run; thence following the south fork of Stony Run and water-shed thereof to the top of Dan's Mountain; then with the top of Dan's Mountain to the present existing line of Lonaconing District; thence with said line westerly to the mouth of Laurel Run; thence up and with Laurel Run to the Garrett County line; thence with the Garrett County line southwesterly to the place of beginning."

It is bounded on the north by East Lonaconing and Lonaconing Districts, east by Rawlings' District, south by Westernport District, and west by Garrett County.

The town of Barton is located in the George's Creek Valley (extending to the hills upon both sides), about four miles from the Potomac River at Westernport, Md. It is named after the town of Barton, in England, the birthplace of the father of Maj. A. B. Shaw, the founder of the village. The town is situated on the line of the Cumberland and Pennsylvania Railroad, and its sole business is that of coal-mining, the surrounding hills all containing the rich veins of coal so abundant in the George's Creek coal-field. Some twenty-seven years ago, when this coal region was being opened up, and the George's Creek Coal and Iron Company was building a broad-gauge road up the creek from the Baltimore and Ohio Railroad at Piedmont to the company's coal lands at or near Lonaconing, M. O. Davidson removed to the place now occupied by Barton, and opened the "Swanton Coal Mines," the first in that vicinity. This was in the year 1854, and where Barton now stands there were only two farm-houses and three railroad shanties. By the time the George's Creek Railroad was ready to carry coal, Mr. Davidson had the Swanton mines ready for shipments, and from that day the growth of Barton commenced. The land where the town now lies was mostly owned by Maj. Shaw (above alluded to), a gentleman well known in the county. Town lots were sold, and houses erected, and the place named.

The "Swanton mines" continued in successful operation, and were soon followed by the opening of other mines,—the "Caledonia," "Pickel," "Piedmont," "Barton," and "Potomac." With the opening of each successive mine more miners and trades-people came to the place, and the little settlement made rapid progress. The coal-mines at Barton are situated high upon the hills on both sides of the town, and long, steep inclined planes, with railroad tracks half a mile in length, extend from the mines to the dump-houses on the railroad below, and mine-cars, holding about two tons of coal each, are let down by wire rope to the dump below. The coal is emptied into the cars and shipped East. The vein worked is the fourteen-feet, or "Big Vein." The coal-veins of the George's Creek region "dip" towards the north, and are at the head of the stream below the surface, while at Barton, about eight miles below, the veins are several hundred feet below the surface. Barton is on the Cumberland and Pennsylvania Railroad, five miles north of Piedmont, W. Va., and thirty three by Baltimore and Ohio Railroad and twenty-one by turnpike from Cumberland.

William Shaw was born in Barton, England, in 1768. He came to this country when a young man and settled near Cresaptown, and married Charlotte Trimble, near Frostburg. He was the first Methodist preacher in this region. His mother was a Miss Nameday, of London. His son, William Shaw, married Philadelphia Burns, of Westernport. William Shaw, Sr., built his house—a log structure—near the Swanton inclined plane. It was the first house on what is now the site of Barton, but was many years ago torn down. The next house was built by William Shaw, Jr. It now belongs to the Shaw estate, and is occupied by William Birmingham. William Shaw, Jr., laid out the town in 1853 into sixty-six lots, and in 1868 his son, A. B. Shaw, made an addition to it of fifty-one lots. This town, with Moscow and Pekin, were a part of the Shaw estate of some twelve hundred acres, composed of part of surveys "Flower Meads" and "Ball's Good Luck" and military lots. After the town was laid out in 1853 the first house erected was by Russell Bevridge, which subsequently burned down, and the lot is now owned by August Tribbet. William Shaw, Jr., kept the first store in the old Shaw log cabin, and after the laying out of the town, the first store was kept by William B. Shaw & Co. The first resident physician was Dr. Benjamin B. Shaw, and the first blacksmith, John Price. Mrs. William Sigler kept the first hotel. When the town was laid out in 1853 there were but two houses, both belonging to the Shaws. A. B. Shaw, son of William Shaw, Jr., married Mary Martha Dawson, of Springfield, Ohio, and resides just above the town, on his fine farm of five hundred and seventy-five acres.

Andrew Bruce Shaw, son of Maj. William and Patsey Ellicotte (Bevens) Shaw, was born at Moscow Mills, near Barton, Allegany County, Md., Nov. 4, 1837. His grandfather, William Shaw, was a son of George Shaw, of Barton-on-Humber, Lincolnshire, England. He was born in England, Dec. 3, 1757, and emigrated when quite young to America. He married Charlotte Trimble, who lived near Frostburg, Md., March 4, 1785. His father, William Shaw, was born near Cresaptown, Allegany County, Md., Dec. 2, 1794. He served with distinction in the war of 1812, and was an extensive land-owner in

George's Creek Valley. Andrew Bruce Shaw attended the schools of the county until about fourteen years of age, when he was employed as clerk in a general merchandise store in Barton, where he remained about eighteen months. He left the store to attend to his father's business, and after remaining with him a year or so attended several terms at the Fairmount Academy. He was again called home to take charge of his father's affairs, and remained with him until his death, which occurred May 2, 1867. He was chosen by the heirs executor of the estate, and upon the sale of the latter became its purchaser. Both the towns of Barton and Pekin are on the estate, and Mr. Shaw completed the work of laying them out, which was begun by his father. He has also laid out and built the village of Moscow, which is located almost in the centre of the estate. He has very much improved the homestead, having built on the place one of the finest dwellings in the county, a new barn, and a large steam saw and planing-mill, and has in successful operation a large flouring and grist-mill. Though a busy man, Mr. Shaw has found time to travel much, for his own gratification, through the States and Territories. He is fond of good reading, and his library shows excellent taste and judgment in its selection. In politics he is a Republican. He married, Sept. 15, 1868, Mary M., daughter of Theodore and Orpah (Totten) Dawson, of Springfield, Ohio. They have four children,—Willie Dawson, Alleda Orpah, Lloyd Bruce, and Margaret Ann.

The oldest person in Barton is William Warnick, who was born three miles above Westernport in 1797, and has lived all his life within a space of four miles. His father, Joseph Warnick, with John Sigler (near Hampshire Mountain), the Peters (on Dan's Mountain-side), the Duckworths, Barnards, William Howe, Roger Poland, Benjamin Brady, David Spencer, Philip Michael, and Daniel Rickoners were among the earliest settlers in this region. The Warnicks were of Irish descent. When he was a boy the only road from Westernport to "Frost's Town" was a horseback road. Dr. Lewis F. Klipstein was the first physician in the lower valley, and Rev. William Shaw the first preacher. A Mr. Bartley had a distillery on the mountain near Bloomington. The Shaws and Notley Barnard, at the time of the war of 1812, got out timber for gun-stocks for the Harper's Ferry armory, which they hauled to Westernport and then transported on flat-boats down the Potomac River. At the beginning of the century the people traded for their supplies at Romney, W. Va., then the port for Winchester. The first post-office in all this region was at Westernport, which received its mail once a week by horseback. The first mill was Morrison's, one and a half miles below Barton, on George's Creek, near which, on the old Morrison homestead, is the graveyard where lie interred the Morrisons and Shaws and a few other early settlers. Another aged resident is David B. Inskeep, who was born on New Creek, W. Va., in 1805, one mile above Keyser (formerly called Paddy Town). His mother was a Miss Fry, of Big Capon region. He moved to Allegany in 1840, and settled near Barton, which then had but two houses (those of the Shaws). His father, James Inskeep, was born and raised in Hardy County, W. Va., on the South Branch, where his grandfather was one of the pioneers. When he arrived there were three coal-mines, viz., the Neff mines, Moore mines, and Philip Sigler's mines. The physicians who then practiced in the valley were Drs. Lewis F. Kleinstine, Samuel P. Smith, and Lawrence. The New York capitalists first bought coal-lands at Frostburg, and afterwards in this locality. A one-fifth interest of the Myers estate, where the Swanton mines are, was sold by its owner for an old rifle, and eleven hundred dollars only was paid for the Caledonian (now American) mines. George Lee paid fourteen hundred dollars for the Linn property, some two hundred acres, and now part of the Swanton mines. Cowan, Perry & McMullen purchased of Joseph Reckener some land, now part of the American mines, for eleven hundred dollars, and fifty acres ol John A. Duckworth for eight thousand dollars, now part of same company. In 1840 the county road up the George's Creek Valley was rough and hardly passable for carriages. William Jones, an old Revolutionary soldier, lived where Mr. McFarland now resides. Mr. Inskeep married Catherine, a sister of William Shaw, Jr., and when he was a lad the only buildings at Keyser, W. Va., were one dwelling and a store (kept by a Mr. Mosely). In early times John Hoyt, of Cumberland, owned large tracts of land around Barton.

John Piper, the progenitor of the Piper family in America, came from Yorkshire, England, in 1680, and settled at Alexandria, Va., then the stopping-point for British vessels. He married in Virginia, and his son John became a sailor. John Piper, Jr., also had a son named John, who was a planter. His descendants have nearly all been engaged in agricultural pursuits. His son John was the father of John Piper, born in 1796, who died June 19, 1874. The latter was in the militia in the war of 1812, and his company was ordered to the defense of Washington, but before marching the order was countermanded, as it was supposed that enough troops had arrived to defend the national capital. He married Sarah, daughter of Jesse and Dorcas (Johnson) Robinette. The Robinettes were of French extraction, and came over with (or about the time of his arrival) Count De Rochambeau. In 1819 he removed to Flintstone District, Allegany County, from Hancock, Washington County, whither his father had removed a few years previous from his native county of Jefferson, Va. His wife, Sarah Robinette, was a daughter of the Robinette who settled in Allegany County, and who had two brothers, one of whom located in Philadelphia, and the other in New York State. Watson J. Piper, son of John and Sarah (Robinette) Piper, was born Aug. 17, 1842, and received the usual advantages of the country schools. He afterwards attended the Greensburg, Pa., Academy, then a noted institution under Prof. W. W. Brim. In 1861 he went to the Western plains, and was for several years employed by Gen. O'Conner on special duty as a military scout, and was a comrade of William Comstock. He scouted in all the Territories and to the extreme Pacific slope, was in several Indian fights, and was captured by the red men at O'Fallon's Bluff, in Nebraska, near the junction of the North and South Platte Rivers, but was surrendered the evening before O'Conner's treaty at Fort Laramie. On his return from the Western frontier he read medicine with Dr. Samuel P. Smith, of Cumberland, and attended lectures at the University of Maryland,

at Baltimore, from which institution he graduated March 9, 1865. He was appointed assistant surgeon in the United States army, and was assigned to duty in the Fifth Military District of Texas and Louisiana, in charge of the post hospital at Baton Rouge, La. He was thirteen months in the military service, and resigned his commission. He then located (1866) at Barton, where he has since resided in the active practice of his profession, in which he has been most successful, and eminently so in the department of surgery. He is a member of the County and State Medical Associations, and of the Potomac Lodge, A. F. and A. M., No. 100, of Cumberland, Salem Royal Arch Chapter, No. 18, and Salem Council of Royal and Select Masters of the same city, and De Molay Commandery of Knights Templar of Frederick City. From the latter he changed, in January, 1881, his membership to Baltimore Commandery, No. 2. He was one of the charter members of Allegany Lodge, A. F. and A. M., No. 157, at Barton, and its first Worshipful Master for three years. In 1870 he became a member of Philos Lodge, I. O. O. F., No. 91, and Mount Carmel Encampment, No. 7, of Westernport. He belongs to Monterey Lodge of Knights of Pythias, No. 90, in Barton, and is Past Chancellor, and a member of the Knights of Honor. He is a Democrat in politics, but has refused to be a candidate for public positions, though often urged by his friends to be, when it was thought that he alone of his party could be elected in the county. He was married May 11, 1870, by Rev. Alexander T. Rankin, to Miss Clementine Hurley, of Allegany County, who was born Feb. 12, 1848, and died Dec. 23, 1874. He was married the second time, Nov. 1, 1877, to Mary J. Elliott, of Allegany County. By his first wife he has one son, John Kemp Warfield Piper, born Sept. 23, 1871, and by his second wife one child, Claude Lorraine. One son by his first wife, William Watson Piper, born Aug. 12, 1874, died Feb. 4, 1875. Dr. Piper resides at his beautiful seat overlooking the town, from which a charming view is had of the magnificent scenery up and down the famous George's Creek Valley.

Allegany Lodge, No. 157, A. F. and A. M., was chartered Nov. 7, 1871, under a warrant signed by John H. Latrobe, G. M.; Francis Burns, D. D. G. M.; L. A. C. Gerry, S. G. W.; Geo. L. McCahan, S. J. W.; and Jacob H. Medary, G. Sec. The officers named in the charter were Dr. Watson J. Piper, W. M.; James Goodwin, S. W.; and Archibald McDonald, J. W. The first meeting was held May 22, 1871, under a dispensation, when the following officers were present: W. M., Dr. Watson J. Piper; S. W., James Goodwin; J. W., Archibald McDonald; S. D., James Tibbitt; J. D., Richard Phillips; Sec., John Wilson, Jr.; Treas., John Somerville; Tyler, Joseph Pearce. The first degree was conferred June 19, 1871, and was that of Entered Apprentice on James Herron, John Somerville, Jr., and George W. Porter.

The Worshipful Masters have been:

1871-74, Dr. Watson J. Piper; 1874, Archibald McDonald; 1875, Jacob W. Daily; 1876-77, J. T. Pearce; 1878-80, Archibald McDonald; 1881, John Somerville, Jr.

The secretaries have been:

1871, John Wilson, Jr.; 1872, John Somerville, Jr., Albion Coles; 1873, John Somerville, Jr., and John Wilson, Jr.; 1873, E. Creutzburg; 1875 and '76, John Somerville, Jr.; 1877, Albion Coles; 1878, D. R. Porter; 1879, Albion Coles; 1880 and '81, James Dick.

The officers for the second term of 1881 are:

W. M., John Somerville, Jr.; S. W., Hugh Thomson; J. W., Anthony Reese; Sec., James Dick; Treas., John Somerville, Sr.; S. D., Richard Phillips; J. D., Charles Edwards.

It has thirty-three members, and meets the second and fourth Mondays of every month in I. O. O. F. Hall.

Dr. Watson J. Piper, from 1875 to May, 1881, was Grand Inspector of Garrett and Allegany Counties.

The charter of Barton Lodge, No. 94, I. O. O. F., was granted July 22, 1856, and contains the names of Simon Arnold, John Jones, J. R. Berkepile, Thomas W. Morgan, and Edward Shockey. On Jan. 3, 1857, it was instituted by D. G. M. John Douglas, and at this meeting the following officers were chosen: Simon Arnold, N. G.; John Jones, V. G.; Thomas W. Morgan, Sec.; and Edward Shockey, Treas. Seven members were at this meeting admitted by card, viz.: John W. Parker, William Shaw, Thomas Herron, Isaac N. Johnson, William Combs, J. W. Kalbaugh, and John H. Patterson. The Noble Grand appointed the following subordinate officers: Thomas Herron, R. S. N. G.; William Shaw, L. S. N. G.; Warden, J. W. Parker; Conductor, Z. W. Kalbaugh; O. G., J. H. Patterson; I. G., J. N. Johnson; L. S. V. G., William Combs.

William Alexander and George Williams were the first two members received by initiation, both of whom were afterwards killed in the mines. Below are given the Noble Grands, Vice-Grands, secretaries, and treasurers who served from 1857 to 1860 and from 1875 to the present time:

July, 1857, to Jan., 1858.—N. G., William Combs; V. G., Z. W. Kalbaugh; Sec., John W. Parker; Treas., D. Yost.

Jan. to July, 1858.—N. G., Z. W. Kalbaugh; V. G., H. C. Getty; Sec., Samuel Ferrell; Treas., Thomas Herron.

July, 1858, to Jan., 1859.—N. G., H. C. Getty; V. G., Thomas Herron; Sec., Samuel Fernell; Treas., P. Y. Perkepile.

Jan. to July, 1859.—N. G., Thomas Herron; V. G., John Barnes; Sec., S. T. Facenbaker; Treas., Robert Cowan.

July, 1859, to Jan., 1860.—N. G., John Barnes; V. G., Robert Cowan; Sec., J. K. Perkepile; Treas., J. S. Jamison.

Jan. to July, 1860.—N. G., R. Cowan; V. G., Joseph Andrews; Sec., S. Fernell; Treas., W. Shaw.

July, 1860, to Jan., 1861.—N. G., Joseph Andrews; V. G., Robert Orr; Sec., Thomas Herron; Treas., Wm. Shaw.

Jan. to July, 1875.—N. G., J. M. Murrie; V. G., John Sommerville; Sec., Albion Coles; Treas., Henry Crentzburg.

July, 1875, to Jan., 1876.—N. G., John Sommerville; V. G., Alexander Week; Sec., Albion Coles; Treas., Henry Crentzburg.

Jan. to July, 1876.—N. G., Alexander Meek; V. G., George H. Shaw; Sec., Theophilus George; Treas., Henry Crentzburg.

July, 1876, to Jan., 1877.—N. G., G. H. Shaw; V. G., Joshua Langham; Sec., Albion Coles; Treas., Henry Crentzburg.

Jan. to July, 1877.—N. G., Joshua Langham; V. G., Theophilus George; Sec., Albion Coles; Treas., Henry Crentzburg.

July, 1877, to Jan., 1878.—N. G., Theophilus George; V. G., Joseph Jones; Sec., Albion Coles; Treas., Henry Crentzburg.

Jan. to July, 1878.—N. G., Wm. Penman; V. G., Richard

Woodward; Sec., Albion Coles; Treas., Henry Crentzburg.

July, 1878, to Jan., 1879.—N. G., R. Woodward; V. G., J. J. McDonald; Sec., Albion Coles; Treas., Henry Crentzburg.

Jan. to July, 1880.—N. G., Wm. Orr; V. G., Richard Woodward; Sec., Albion Coles; Treas., Henry Crentzburg.

July, 1880, to Jan., 1881.—N. G., R. Woodward; V. G., H. Ayres; Sec., Albion Coles; Treas., Henry Crentzburg.

Jan. to July, 1881.—N. G., Henry Ayers; V. G., D. H. Walsh; Sec., Albion Coles; Ass't Sec., Theophilus George; Treas., Wm. Orr.

July, 1881, to Jan., 1882.—N. G., D. H. Walsh; V. G., Joseph Jones; Sec., Albion Coles; Treas., Wm. Orr.

The original members of the order organized themselves into a building association prior to the establishment of the lodge, and erected a hall, which was purchased by the lodge upon its institution. This hall is now owned by Mrs. James Major. Meetings were held in this building until the erection of their present edifice in 1869, which was dedicated by Joseph B. Escavaelle, G. S., in 1870, assisted by Dr. Cox, G M. Their hall stands upon Hall Street, a few blocks northwest of the railroad. The membership of the order at present is 78.

Since the institution of the lodge to date there have been 263 initiations, 24 reinstatements, 24 admitted by card, 182 suspended for non-payment of dues, 26 died, 24 withdrawn, 8 suspended for cause, 3 expelled, and 76 rejected, and the financial statement for twenty-one years ending in 1877 is as follows:

Paid the Grand Lodge dues	$846.38
" weekly benefits for the sick	3,972.65
" funeral benefits	1,714.98
" " expenses	67.00
" for education of orphans	224.19
" donations	193.50
Total receipts of the lodge from all sources..	17,756.00

Monterey Lodge, No. 90, Knights of Pythias, was organized by dispensation granted July 30, 1874, to O. C. Hayslett, W. J. Piper, T. B. Powell, Jacob Dailey, Charles O. Miller, P. Kight, Samuel Santymeyer, Alexander S. Small, W. L. Dick, James Campbell, A. J. McCulloh, Edward Sexton, James N. Small, John W. Murrie, Theophilus George, J. F. Pierce, John Sexton, Benjamin Harris.

The charter was obtained Jan. 28, 1875, appointing W. J. Piper, P. C.; Jacob Dailey, C. C.; J. N. Small, V. C.; T. B. Powell, P.; James Campbell, M. of E.; Theophilus George, M. of F.; C. O. Miller, K. of R. S.; W. L. Dick, M. of A.; Samuel Santymeyer, I. G.; C. Hayslett, O. G.

The officers from the organization until January, 1881, were as follows:

Jan. to July, 1875.—C. C., T. B. Powell; V. C., John Waxler; K. of R. S., J. W. Murrie; M. of E., J. Campbell.

July, 1875, to Jan., 1876.—C. C., J. T. Waxler; V. C., J. W. Beller; K. of R. S., J. N. Small; M. of E., Charles O. Miller.

Jan. to July, 1876.—C. C., Jas. W. Beller; V. C., James McDonald; K. of R. S., James N. Small; M. of E., Charles O. Miller.

July, 1876, to Jan., 1877.—C. C., James Campbell; V. C., J. W. Murrie; K. of R. S., J. N. Small; M. of E., John T. Waxler.

Jan. to July, 1877.—C. C., J. W. Murrie; V. C., William J. Bacon; K. of R. S., James N. Small; M. of E., Theophilus George.

July, 1877, to Jan., 1878.—C. C., Alex. Williams; V. C., David Penman; K. of R. S., Theophilus George; M. of E., Jas. Campbell.

Jan. to July, 1878.—C. C., David Penman; V. C., J. H. Jarboe; K. of R. S., Theophilus George; M. of E., James Campbell.

July, 1878, to Jan., 1879.—C. C., J. H. Jarboe; V. C., James McDonald; K. of R. S., Theophilus George; M. of E., James Campbell.

Jan. to July, 1879.—C. C., James T. McDonald; V. C., Arthur Stewart; K. of R. S., Theophilus George; M. of E., James Campbell.

July, 1879, to Jan., 1880.—C. C., Arthur Stewart; V. C., David Clark; K. of R. S., Theophilus George; M. of E., James Campbell.

Jan. to July, 1880.—C. C., David Clark; V. C., Joseph Bradley; K. of R. S., Theophilus George; M. of E., James Campbell.

July, 1880, to Jan., 1881.—C. C., Joseph Bradley; V. C., William Russell; K. of R. S., Theophilus George; M. of E., James Campbell.

The officers in 1881 were William Russell, C. C.; Robert Russell, V. C.; Theophilus George, K. of R. S.; James Campbell, M. of E.; having been elected in January, 1881, and re-elected in July of the same year. Their meetings are held in the I. O. O. F. Hall, and the membership numbers fifty-six.

Good Hope Lodge, No. 187, I. O. G. T., was instituted in February, 1880. The charter was issued Feb. 6, 1880, to John Wilson, Jr., N. Sommerville, W. T. Barnes, Anderson Cohn, Silas Kight, H. Warbach, D. W. Santymeyer, Hugh Montgomery, J. H. Barnes, Eliza Wilks, Sarah F. Kight, Robert Carr, D. H. Welsh, John H. Jarboe, Samuel N. Inskeep, H. J. Sommerville, J. P. McDonald, B. B. L. Santymeyer, Lizzie Harris, Annie McClain, Lydia Stewart, Robert McDonald, Laura Sommerville, and Rachel Kirk.

The officers for the year 1881 were:

J. H. Jarboe, W. C. T.; Annie McClain, M. V. T.; Wm. T. Barnes, W. Chap.; James P. McDonald, W. Sec.; John Willison, Jr., W. A. S.; B. B. Santymeyer, W. F. S.; Robert Carr, W. Treas.; John H. Barnes, W. M.; Laura Sommerville, W. D. M.; Lizzie Harris, W. I. G.; J. A. Inskeep, W. O. G.; Lydia Stewart, M. R. H. S.; Rachel Kirk, W. L. N. S.; N. J. Sommerville, P. W. C. T.

I. O. O. F. Cemetery is situated on Laurel Run, about one mile from town. It comprises four and a half acres, and was purchased of John Shaw in 1876. It was immediately laid out by the order into lots, and is nicely shaded and fenced.

The Barton Circulating Library, which is doing so much for the literary advancement and culture of the town, was established in 1880. It has copies of the works of the standard authors, and keeps files of many of the principal newspapers of the country. Its first and second president was James Campbell, and third, James S. Roberts. Its first secretary was Ernest Crentzburg; second, Alvin Coles; and third, William Cribb. From its organization John Major has been treasurer.

Its admission fee is one dollar and ten cents, and monthly dues fifteen cents.

Court Liberty Lodge, No. 1, Independent Order of Foresters, meets every Wednesday evening at Foresters' Hall.

Olive Lodge, No. 4, Ancient Order of Free Gardeners, meets every Tuesday night at Foresters' Hall.

Considerable attention has been bestowed upon musical culture. The Barton Cornet Band, David Penman, leader, meets in Foresters' Hall, Mondays and Fridays.

James Howard is leader of the Barton Orchestra.

Churches. — In 1856 the congregation of the Methodist Episcopal Church was gathered together by an English minister of some renown. Worship was held at first in an old log house which stood in the public cemetery at Moscow. This house was used by the several different denominations as a union meeting-house, and was a one-story log building. They worshiped here until about 1864, when they erected a frame church in the town of Barton, which is now unoccupied and belongs to John Barnes. This structure was used by them until 1869, and in that year, under the auspices of Rev. Austin M. Courtenay, the corner-stone was laid and the erection of a new church begun. The laying of the corner-stone was attended by Masonic ceremonies, and the sermon was delivered by Rev. Samuel S. Cummins. In 1870 the building was completed and dedicated by the Rev. Edward Gray, then pastor of Frostburg Church, and now president of the Williamsport Dickinson Seminary. It is a neat frame building, two stories high, with a seating capacity of three hundred persons, standing upon the Barton and Frostburg road, at the corner of Latrobe Street. The second pastor of the church was Rev. Mr. Deem, who was succeeded by Rev. Mr. Calphous. His successors were Rev. Mr. Schaeffer, from 1865 to 1867; and Rev. Samuel Shannon, from 1867 to 1869. Rev. William Mullen took charge of the church in 1869, but served only a short time, and was followed by Rev. A. M. Courtenay, who acted as minister of this congregation until 1872. Rev. Ezekiel Richardson served from 1872 to 1873; Rev. B. P. Reese, from 1873 to 1876; Rev. J. L. Walsh, from 1876 to 1878; Rev. Solomon German, from 1878 to 1879; Rev. Alexander Bielaski, from 1879 to the present time, 1881.

In 1865 among the prominent members were Silas Kight, Joseph Andrew, M. Dawson, Henry Trenear, John Pattison, George Buckle, and William Harris. The church then numbered one hundred and fifty persons, and now numbers about the same. The deacons for the year 1881 were William J. Kribb; Stewards, John Yan, Francis Herron, and Aaron Poland; Trustees, A. B. Shaw, J. W. Young, Aaron Poland, Silas Kight, Charles M. Inskeep.

Prior to 1868 the congregation was connected with the Piedmont Circuit, which comprised Lonaconing, Bloomington, Firm Rock, Barton, and Piedmont.

From 1868 to 1876 it was connected with the Lonaconing Circuit, which comprised Barton and Lonaconing Churches. Since 1876 it has been a charge by itself. The present pastor's father, Capt. Bielaski, was born in Poland, served under Gen. Grant, and was killed at the battle of Belmont.

St. Paul's German Lutheran congregation was organized in 1860, by Rev. Mr. Steagle. Among the original members were Valentine Creintzburg, Valentine Lintz, Henry Schram, Henry Creintzburg, Gottleib Miller, Conrad Wingfelt, George Schram, and Christian Fier. At its formation it numbered about fifteen members. After occupying the old schoolhouse for a year as the meeting-house, it removed to the Presbyterian church, where services were held until the erection of the church in 1872. The church has always been supplied by preachers from the Maryland Synod, and was connected with the Frostburg Lutheran Church in these supplies. In 1870 the church was begun, and at the same time some misunderstanding occurred among its members, which resulted in the division of the congregation and the formation of two different societies. The church was completed in 1872. It is a neat frame structure, twenty-five by forty feet. The elders are Ernest Geintzburg, Christian Fier, and the Sunday-school superintendent, Henry Schram.

On the division of the congregation about 1870, the German Lutheran (Missouri Synod) congregation was formed, comprising among its members George Miller, August Tribbet, John Longlet, August Frenzeny and wife, and Samuel Phoebe. They worship occasionally in the Presbyterian church. Among the ministers who have served them are Rev. Mr. Shancovie, Rev. Mr. Keglie, Rev. Charles Louderbach, and Rev. Ernest Sander. The congregation is now connected with the Lonaconing Church.

Meetings of members of the Presbyterian church were frequently held prior to its organization in 1860, in the old school-house, a carpenter-shop, and various other places. In 1859 the church was erected, the building committee comprising Messrs. James Spark, John Sommerville, John Wilson, Sr., Peter Goodwin, and William Orr. The lot upon which it stands was presented to the congregation by Maj. William Shaw. The building cost nine hundred and eighty dollars, is a frame structure, and has since been improved at twice the original cost. The organization of the congregation occurred in February, 1860. Dr. Foote, of Romney, and Rev. Woodruff were the ministers who had it in charge, being appointed by the Synod of Baltimore to organize this congregation. Among the original members were Peter Goodwin and wife, Mrs. Mary Park, Mrs. John Sommerville, Mrs. John Wilson, William Orr and wife, and John Wilson, Jr. At the first meeting several were admitted into the church. The congregation was transferred in 1870 from the Presbytery of Carlisle to the Presbytery of Baltimore. The parsonage was purchased in 1880 of John Wilson, Jr.

The following is a list of pastors who have served the congregation and the dates of their terms:

Feb. 24, 1861, to Sept., 1861, Rev. James Donaldson; Sept., 1862, to Sept., 1863, Rev. W. A. Flemming; March, 1864, to April, 1866, Rev. Benjamin Merrill; July, 1867, to Dec., 1868, Rev. W. G. Hillman; Dec., 1868, to Dec, 1872, A. T. Rankin, D.D.; Jan., 1873, to Dec., 1876, Rev. J. K. Black; April, 1877, to May, 1878, John A. Bower; Jan., 1880, Rev. A. S. Leonard, the present incumbent.

The elders for 1881 were Archibald McDonald, Peter Goodwin, John Wilson, Jr.; Deacon, John Sommerville, Jr.; Trustees, John Sommerville, Jr., Mr. Park, and John Bowles.

The fine frame edifice of St. Gabriel's Catholic Church was erected in 1867. It was a missionary church until 1875, when Father Mahony took charge and remained two years. It was then attended for two years by Father Finney, who was succeeded for the same period by Father McCall, and it is now supplied from Westernport. It has a large parochial school and elegant brick residence. One of its leading laymen is Patrick Caddan, who arrived in 1854, and has been active in the mining business. He has served many years as a magistrate, and is one of the pioneers of the town.

The spacious and beautiful cemetery of the Catholic church lies below the town, on the west bank of the creek, on high and well-located grounds. The following are interred in it:

Patrick Connahan, born in County Donegal, Ireland, and died Aug. 23, 1879, aged 39.

Elizabeth Atkinson, born in County Wicklow, Ireland, and died Feb. 16, 1880, aged 66.

George Clark, died Jan. 5, 1877, aged 45.

Edward Donohue, born in County Donegal, Ireland, died Aug. 24, 1879, aged 39.

Andrew Mooney, died March 7, 1872, aged 46.

Sarah, wife of John Coleman, died Dec. 30, 1870, aged 23.

Joseph Murray, born in County Wicklow, died May 4, 1878, aged 37; and his wife, Elizabeth, born in same county, died March 22, 1877, aged 22.

Mary, wife of Charles Mulvy, born in Grave, County Roscommon, Ireland, died Jan. 28, 1857, aged 29.

Anna Nevin, wife of John Locke, born in Craughwell, County Galway, died July 1, 1869, aged 35.

Jeremiah Sullivan, born in the parish of Ballyfeard, County Cork, Ireland, died Dec. 20, 1869, aged 63.

Bridget, wife of Charles O'Tool, born in Queen's County, Ireland, died May 14, 1872, aged 37.

Thomas O'Meara, born in Ireland, died Oct. 5, 1874, aged 35.

W. M. Foster, died March 29, 1878, aged 22.

John O'Connell, born in parish of Mallow, County Cork, Ireland, died June 23, 1873, aged 46.

Thomas, son of P. and C. Hobam, born in parish of Killinam, County Galway, Ireland, died Jan. 6, 1877, aged 27.

Joseph Logsdon, died March 13, 1871, aged 72.

Martha, wife of Patrick Griffin, died Feb. 14, 1872, aged 29.

Elizabeth, wife of Edward Louth, born in Ireland, died Oct. 28, 1871, aged 76.

Mary J., wife of P. Mullen, born in Ireland, died Jan. 26, 1872, aged 31.

The Baptist church was dedicated Sept. 27, 1872. Rev. James Nelson, D.D., delivered the dedicatory address, and was assisted in the services by Rev. L. Llewellyn, Rev. A. M. Courtenay, and Rev. William Harris. The cost of the edifice was over nine hundred dollars, of which one-third was contributed at the dedication.

Rev. Samuel N. Eltroth is the pastor.

Among the old citizens of the district is Uriah Duckworth, born near Westernport in 1799, where he has resided all life except a short time spent in Virginia when a boy. He is hale and hearty, with unimpaired mental faculties, and is remarkably well preserved for one so aged. He still fills the office of justice of the peace, which he has occupied for the past forty years, with two displacements, one of two years, by the Whigs, and another of four years, during the administration of Governor Carroll. He is probably the oldest justice in the State, and much respected for his integrity and worth.

The population of the district is 1937, including Barton Town, 1112, and Moscow Village, 264.

LONACONING DISTRICT, No. 10.

The following are the metes and bounds of Lonaconing Election District, No. 10 :

"Beginning at a point on the Garrett County line where said line crosses Laurel Run, and running thence down with the meanders of said Laurel Run to George's Creek ; thence up with the centre of said George's Creek to the lines of Frostburg District, No. 11, at the mouth of Wright's Run ; thence up with said Wright's Run to the Garrett County line, and with said line to the place of beginning."

It is bounded on the north by Frostburg District, east by East Lonaconing District, south by Barton District, and west by Garrett County. Population, 2808.

FROSTBURG DISTRICT, No. 11.

The following are the metes and bounds of Frostburg, or Election District No. 11 :

"Beginning on the Garrett line at the northwest corner of Lonaconing District, No. 10, and running with the lines of said Lonaconing District and with Wright's Run easterly to the centre of the so-called Legislative, or New County road, leading from Barrelville to Westernport; thence with said road northerly to its intersection with Bowery Street, in the town of Frostburg ; thence with the centre of said Bowery Street to the National turnpike ; thence with the centre of the National turnpike westerly to its intersection with the aforesaid Legislative road leading from Barrelville to Westernport ; thence with said Legislative road northerly to the present existing line of Mount Savage District; thence with the line of Mount Savage District to the Garrett County line ; thence with said Garrett County line to the place of beginning."

It is bounded on the north by Mount Savage District, east by East Frostburg District, south by Lonaconing District, and west by Garrett County.

Borden Shaft is a station on the Cumberland and Pennsylvania Railroad just below Frostburg. The Borden Mining Company erected this shaft in 1854, and after it burned down, in 1873, immediately rebuilt it with improved machinery. The place is fast increasing in size, has good schools and one church.

Frostburg, lying in Frostburg and East Frostburg Election Districts, is the second town in importance in Allegany County. It is situated near the head-waters of George's Creek, on a plateau between the Great Savage and Dan's Mountains of the Allegany range, seventeen hundred and ninety-two feet above tide. The location and climatic conditions are eminently healthy, and the town is favorably known as a summer resort.

The town is near the centre of the Great George's Creek semi-bituminous coal region, and midway between Cumberland, Md., and Piedmont, W. Va., on the line of the Cumberland and Pennsylvania Railroad, and enjoys quick connections with the great trunk-line railways, east and west. It is fourteen hundred feet above Cumberland, eleven miles distant, and two thousand three hundred feet above Baltimore. The town is completely undermined, all the coal having been removed from beneath it, with the exception of the columns of coal left as supporting pillars. The Cumberland and Pennsylvania Railroad passes under the town through a tunnel. In going from Cumberland to Frostburg, eleven miles distant, the whole road is up the mountain, and to accomplish the ascent the railway is constructed in the form of "Y's" ; the locomotive and train climb one Y switch, and then another, backwards and forwards, until Frostburg is reached on the top of the mountain.

A view unsurpassed for panoramic character and grandeur is obtainable within two miles of Frostburg, from the summit of the Great Savage Mountain.

BRADDOCK'S GRAVE.

On the Braddock road, south of and adjacent to Frostburg, stands a dark-gray slab or tablet, about two feet wide by three in height. On the reverse of the tablet is inscribed in old English characters, "11 miles to Fort Cumberland, 29 miles to Capt. Smyth's Inn and Bridge—Big Crossings. The best road to Red Sandstone, Old Fort 64 miles." On the other side is inscribed in the same character of letters, "Our Country's Rights we will defend."

Either the iconoclast or memento-lover has chipped off the angles and edges of the venerable tablet. A short distance west of this Braddock received his mortal wound. The accompanying sketch portrays the locality supposed to be the grave of Gen. Braddock, situated in Wharton township, Fayette Co., Pa.

About seven miles west of Frostburg, on a plateau upon the summit of the Great Savage range, and skirting the old National road, is a locality called "The Shades of Death," which takes its name from the dense growth and deep gloom of a white-pine forest, which formed an impenetrable shade at this point.

Excepting Virginia City, Nev., Frostburg probably lies higher above tide than any town of equal size in the United States. This altitude affords a view in all directions, rarely excelled for beauty and sublimity. Eastward, Dan's Mountain, running northward, breaks off into a defile traversed by the National pike and Eckhart Branch of the Cumberland and Pennsylvania Railroad. Here nestles the picturesque town of Eckhart, one and one-half miles from Frostburg, with a large population.

Southward, the Great George's Creek Valley, flanked on the west by Dan's Mountain, and on the right by Big Savage, stretches seventeen miles away to the Potomac, and is traversed by the Cumberland and Pennsylvania Railroad and George's Creek Railroad, both of which are lined with dwellings, making nearly a continuous town the whole way. Aside from its material significance, the tourist cannot fail to be impressed with the scene, every element of nature and handiwork of man contributing to lend grandeur and diversity to the prospect. On the west the rugged, precipitous Great Savage Mountain stands like a bulwark, as it is, against the storms of winter. Continuing northward, the mountain maintains its altitude, breaking off to the right in hills and general declivities, until the bed of Jennings' Run is reached. Here another valley opens to view, quite as rich in landscape perspective as the George's Creek. To the right a ridge rises diversified with fertile farms and picturesque groves.

The eye glances from the hills of Pennsylvania across Maryland over to the mountains of West Virginia. A great part of the town is here spread out at the feet of the spectator. Six miles by air line to the southeast Dan's Rock towers high and rugged, overlooking the most extended and varied landscape in all this section. From this point Frostburg and Cumberland are plainly seen, the mountains in all directions, the Potomac and its magnificent bottom-lands, farm-houses, and railroad, making a panorama which cannot be easily forgotten. The tourist to this section who has not visited Dan's Rock has no conception of the wonderful features in which this region abounds. In short, no town of the size and prominence of Frostburg enjoys in its surroundings a more unique topography; and no part of this array of imposing projections furnishes a more interesting outlook than Dan's Rock. If to these are added the novelty of its industrial avocations, the salubrity of its atmosphere, and the purity of its water, we have a series of conditions which, properly estimated, must, sooner or later, give the town a commanding prominence as a summer resort.

The inhabitants of Frostburg and vicinity are mainly miners of foreign birth or extraction, made up of English, Welsh, Scotch, Irish, and Germans; they comprise an industrious, thrifty, and intelligent population, of good morals and studious habits. To them the town owes its extraordinary growth since the war, and the coal region its immense development. The original name given to the town, and one which is duly recorded in the land records of this county, is "Mount Pleasant." It dates back to 1800, when there were but three houses on the hill, occupied respectively by Meshach Frost, Joseph Dilley, and Dennis Beall, and all the surrounding land was owned by George McCulloh, Meshach Frost, and Isaiah Frost, the former two of whom may be said to be the founders of the town, and who not only left a goodly number of descendants to stock the town with, but for their numerous offspring to share.

When the National road was first opened, some time in the year 1812 or thereabouts, Mount Pleasant was laid off into a town, and building-lots were offered for sale by Meshach Frost, and brought from twenty-five to fifty dollars per lot. Mr. Frost kept a tavern upon the spot where the Catholic church now stands, and his house was a very popular resort for teamsters engaged in the transportation of goods from Baltimore to Brownsville, Pa., and Mount Pleasant was soon better known along the road as "Frost's Town," or Frost Town, which was easily converted into Frostburg. Frost Town was a small village for many years. Its sole dependence for support was upon the traveling public over the National road, but it continued to grow slowly but steadily until the development of the coal business, which gave it a wonderful impetus.

The first coal ever mined in this region was taken from the "Sheetz farm," then owned by John Hoye, of Cumberland, and located a mile and a half east of Frost Town. The coal was mined under the direction of John Hoye and Roger Perry, and wagoned to

Cumberland for use there at the glass-works. Other mines were soon opened at Eckhart, and at Frost's mine, nearer the town, and coal was transported to the river-banks at Cumberland, and shipped to Washington and Georgetown, D. C., by the spring freshets of the Potomac River. Upon the completion of the railroad and canal to Cumberland, Frostburg began to assume considerable importance. Other mines were opened, and the Cumberland Coal and Iron Company was organized, and largely carried on the mining business. The Mount Savage Railroad was first built, and then the Cumberland Coal and Iron Company's road. The coal trade steadily increased, and Frostburg waxed strong and prosperous. It then had two sources of revenue,—its coal-mines and the travel over the National road. Cumberland being then the terminus of both the Chesapeake and Ohio Canal and the Baltimore and Ohio Railroad, a great traffic was carried on over the pike.

But in 1852 the railroad was extended to the Ohio River, and the National road declined. However, the constantly increasing coal trade kept up the business of Frostburg, and the town, despite its loss of travel on the pike, continued to grow, and has steadily increased to the present time.

One of the most influential and energetic of the business men of Frostburg was William Ward, who was born near Frostburg, Feb. 13, 1812, and was the son of William and Mary E. (Miller) Ward. His father was a native of Frederick County, Md., married there, and about the year 1790 moved to Allegany County, where for a number of years he was employed as overseer for Normand Bruce. Subsequently he purchased the land now known as the Old Boston Mine, situated about one and a half miles east of the village of Frostburg. He farmed it in summer and mined the coal in winter, being one of the first to mine coal in this now extensive coal region. In 1838 he sold the farm to Samuel B. Barrell, reserving a lease of it for farm purposes only, and about that time purchased a house and lot in Frostburg, where he died in April, 1839. His wife survived him, and died in January, 1871, aged ninety-four. His children in order of birth were Sarah, Mary, Elijah, James, Abner, William, and Elizabeth. All are now dead. William Ward spent his childhood on the Old Boston Mine farm, and his education was limited to about six months' attendance at the common school. At the age of fifteen he commenced hauling coal from his father's farm to Cumberland, and for six years was so employed. He married, March 26, 1833, Anna M., daughter of John and Sarah Easter, of Fayette County, Pa. After his marriage he continued to carry on the old homestead until 1842. In 1841, in company with his brother Abner, he purchased of the heirs of Thomas Swan the Swan Mill property, about six hundred and twenty-five acres, now known as the Borden Shaft Mines. His brother Abner died in 1844, and he

purchased his interest in the property. To a grist-mill, which had already been built upon the property, he added a saw-mill. In 1858 he sold the property to a coal company, retaining the use of it for farm purposes, free of rent, and moved to Frostburg, where, after renting a place for two years, he purchased and improved the village property owned by his mother, where he resided until his death. For a number of years after moving to Frostburg he continued in the oversight of the Borden Mine farm. For the last twelve years of his life he had withdrawn from active participation in business. Mr. Ward was a slave-holder, and was a kind and considerate master. To his twenty-nine slaves, set free by President Lincoln's emancipation proclamation, he gave a new suit of clothes and a dinner to commemorate the event. He was thoroughly devoted to his business and family, and neither sought nor desired official position. In politics he was first a Whig and afterwards a Democrat, and was a member of the Evangelical Lutheran Church of Frostburg. He died at his residence in Frostburg, March 2, 1877. His children were Ellen V., born Jan. 17, 1836, wife of R. H. Pitman, O'Fallon, St. Charles County, Mo.; Sarah C., born May 19, 1838, wife of J. J. Morrison, both deceased; Mary Elizabeth, born Sept. 18, 1840, wife of J. M. Standish, both deceased; George W., born Feb. 17, 1843, married Missouri Hartman, of Berlin, Somerset Co., Pa., and is a farmer near Oakland, Garrett Co., Md.; James H., born June 17, 1845, married, May 11, 1864, Isabella M. F. Clara; the latter died Dec. 6, 1866, and he married, Dec. 31, 1877, Alice A., daughter of Barney and Rachel E. Dilley, of Cumberland; by the latter marriage there have been two children, Lilabel A. and Alice D.; John E., born April 18, 1848, died Aug. 9, 1848; Anna M., born Sept. 9, 1855, wife of Rev. Wesley Hammond, now living at Lexington, Va.

The Frost Monument.—Upon the death of Mrs. Catherine Frost, July 24, 1876, the remains of Mr. Frost, the founder of Frostburg, buried at Mount Savage, were removed to Frostburg, and reinterred by the side of his wife in the St. Michael's Church Cemetery. The original intention of the heirs was to place a monument over their grave in the cemetery, but on a subsequent consideration of the matter it was determined to secure a location for the graves and monument in the front yard of the church. To this the pastor, Rev. V. F. Schmidt, consented, and in accordance with this conclusion preparations were commenced Nov. 19, 1877, under the supervision of Nathan S. Frost, for the location of the monument and the removal of the remains, the latter being accomplished on the 20th. The foundation of the monument was laid by James Fuller, who had all in readiness for the structure when it arrived on Wednesday morning, the 21st. Mr. Sinenner, the builder of the monument, then completed the work in a few hours.

The base is a square granite block with an octagon champ. This is covered with a sub-base, on which is laid a round die with moulded cap, supporting a round tapering column five and a half feet high. This column is covered with a cap, forming also the base of a large, heavy, solid urn, which crowns the structure. The monument is about thirteen feet high, and made of Italian marble highly polished. The inscriptions are as follows, beginning at the top:

The
Founders
of
Frostburg,
1812.

In memory of Meshach Frost, Died Oct. 9, 1863, aged 76 years.	In memory of Catherine Frost, Died July 24, 1876, aged 84 years.

Just above the first inscription four crosses appear on the column. At the foot of each grave a marble grave-marker is placed, representing a scroll, the lower edge slightly turned, bearing the initials, respectively, "M. F." and "C. F."

The late Meshach Frost may be justly regarded as the pioneer of Cumberland coal production and trade. When quite a young man he developed coal on his property in and around Frostburg, and hauled it to Cumberland in road-wagons.

He was the owner of 881 acres of coal land, and his brother, Isaiah Frost, the owner of 474 acres, making jointly 1355 acres. On the 30th day of January, 1845, they applied to the Legislature of Maryland for an act incorporating the Frostburg Coal Company, with a capital of $500,000, which was granted. Early in the spring of the same year the company was organized, and the building of a narrow-gauge or tram-road was immediately commenced, leading from the mines at Frostburg to Mount Savage,—a distance of about four miles,—and connecting with the road just completed, then known as the Mount Savage Railroad, but now a part of the Cumberland and Pennsylvania Railroad. At Cumberland a connection was thus formed with the Baltimore and Ohio Railroad, affording a direct transportation from the mines to tide-water at Baltimore. Early in the spring of 1846 all the necessary arrangements for forwarding coal were completed, and shipments began on the 6th day of April of that year. These were pressed and augmented as rapidly as the then limited demand would allow. Mr. Frost was for many years the president of the company, but owing to the growing debility which came with advancing years, he relinquished the responsibilities of presiding officer and accepted those of a director. In the performance of the duties of the latter position he gave his personal attention daily to the business of the company until the 23d day of September, 1863, when he was taken ill, and on the 9th day of the succeeding month of October he died, aged seventy-six years.

Thus ended the career of one of Allegany's most useful and enterprising sons, and one whose honor and integrity were never questioned. Born within the sound of the church-bells under the shadow of whose lofty tower he sleeps at last, it is eminently fitting also that he and his beloved wife should rest side by side, in the ground on which they erected their first home. Here in the bosom of the great community they founded, and in the home of numerous descendants, their graves and their memories will be kept alike green and fragrant.

It is well to mention in this connection some of

the outgrowths of Mr. Frost's energy and enterprise. The completion of the Frostburg Coal Company's road to Mount Savage afforded an outlet for all the coal along the Jennings' Run Valley. Taking advantage of this, the Allegany Mining Company soon followed the Frostburg Coal Company by opening what is known as Allegany mine, a short time after the Young mine was opened in the immediate vicinity of the New Hope slope. In 1850–51 the Borden Mining Company commenced the development of their property, which completed the principal coal enterprises in the Jennings' Run Valley.

In the spring of 1864 the personal and real property of the Frostburg Coal Company was sold to the Consolidation Coal Company, and still constitutes a rich portion of the very valuable coal estate of that company.

Meshach Frost was born on the farm near town where Mr. Thomas lives, now the property of the Consolidation Coal Company. His wife was a Catherine Magers, born in Mount Savage, and a sister of Mrs. Logsden, of that town. Meshach Frost and wife were married June 20, 1812, and immediately moved to what is now Frostburg, where he erected a log cabin on the site of St. Michael's church. He at first kept a tavern, and boarded the laborers then working on the National road. In after-years his hotel became a favorite stopping-place for the congressmen on their route from the West and Southwest to Washington. At his hotel Henry Clay, Col. Richard M. Johnson, Gen. Jackson, and other distinguished personages often stopped overnight. Meshach Frost was the son of Josiah Frost, who came to Allegany County from New Jersey at the close of the last century. Catherine, his wife, was the daughter of Nathan Magers, who came from Harford County at an early period, and who was one of the pioneers of Mount Savage. Meshach had two brothers, Isaiah and Josiah, who both lived in this vicinity. The children of Meshach Frost were:

1. Elizabeth, who died unmarried. She was the first female child born in Frostburg.
2. Ann, married to Daniel C. Bruce, and still living in Cumberland.
3. William, the first male child born at Frostburg, and still living eight miles from the town on the National road, in Garrett County.
4. Josiah, yet living.
5. Thomas, residing in Pittsburgh, Pa.
6. Nathan S., the only son now living in Frostburg.
7. Meshach A., a farmer, living in the county, on the Potomac River.
8. Catherine, married to C. H. Hamill, and residing in Frostburg.
9. Arman H., living on the National road, nine miles below the town.

There was another girl (Betsey), who died in infancy. Meshach Frost was the first postmaster, and on his appointment the government changed the name of the town from Mount Pleasant to Frostburg, as there was another post-office of the former name in the State.

The Steyer, McCulloh, and other families. Tobias Steyer was born Nov. 7, 1730, in Berdeshofer, Upper Alsace, Germany, and emigrated to Pennsylvania. His son, John Tobias, was born in Manheim, York Co., Pa., June 20, 1762, and moved to Allegany in 1780, when eighteen years old. He was married, June 30, 1789, to Elizabeth Eckert, and had the following children: Sarah, born May 5, 1790; John, March 9, 1792; Absalom, April 29, 1794; George, Dec. 6, 1796, and married to Lydia Uhl, Dec. 14, 1823; Elizabeth, April 18, 1799; Margaret, Sept. 20, 1801; John Jacob, Oct. 28, 1803; and James, Jan. 28, 1806.

George McCulloh, the ancestor of the well-known McCulloh families of the county, settled at Frostburg at the beginning of the century. Between 1812 and 1813 he built his house where Dr. J. M. Porter's residence is, and there his son George W. was born, April 4, 1815. Mr. McCulloh was, with Meshach and Josiah Frost, Joseph Dilley, and Dennis Beall, among the earlier settlers, and owned large tracts of land. William H. Moore, otherwise known as "Boggy Moore," yet living in town, carried the mail on horseback over threescore years ago between Frederick City and Washington. Sandy Conner, still residing in Frostburg, is the last surviving veteran of the oldest stage-drivers on the old National road, on which he drove for nearly fifty years.

James M. Porter, M.D., was born at the "Rose Meadows" farm, about three miles from Frostburg, April 14, 1817, the seventh in a family of eight children of John and Catharine (Glissan) Porter. His father, the seventh son of John Porter (an extended account of whom is given in the biography of Dr. G. Ellis Porter), was born in Pennsylvania, June 24, 1783, and was a farmer from early youth. He died at the residence of his son-in-law, Judge Douglas Percy, in Frostburg, Feb. 5, 1863. Dr. J. M. Porter spent his boyhood at the "Rose Meadows" farm, receiving his primary education in the common school of his native place and at the private school in Frostburg, taught by E. K. Huntley, which he attended two years. He was also a pupil for two years at the Cumberland Academy. April 10, 1838, he commenced the study of medicine in the office of Drs. Samuel P. Smith and T. A. Healey, at Cumberland. He attended his first course of lectures at the University of Maryland, session of 1839–40, his second at the University of New York, 1841–42, and received his medical diploma March 10, 1842. After his graduation he at once commenced the practice of his profession as an assistant in the office of his former

J. M. Porter

preceptors, Drs. Smith and Healey. In December, 1843, he located at Frostburg, and with the exception of a short time in Mount Vernon, Ohio, has continued in the practice of his profession there ever since. Living in a mining region demanding special skill in reparative surgery, the doctor has had an extensive experience in that department of practice. He is a member of the American Medical Association, of the Maryland Medico-Chirurgical Society, and also of the Allegany County Society, and was the president of the latter for 1879. In politics he has been a life-long Democrat, but has been too thoroughly devoted to his chosen profession to take an active part in political affairs. His life has been spent almost entirely in the relief of suffering, and his good offices have been extended to the poor with no stinted hand. Pay for services rendered has with him always been a secondary consideration. In the building of its churches and schools, and in all matters looking to the prosperity of Frostburg, he has taken a lively interest. Dr. Porter married, Aug. 1, 1848, Mary Ellen, daughter of Minor and Elizabeth Gibson, of Rappahannock County, Va. By this union there were two children, viz.: Glissan T. Porter, a lawyer in Cumberland, and Lucy Elizabeth, living at home. His wife died Oct. 3, 1853. May 22, 1857, he married Rebecca, daughter of Isaac McCarty. She died March 17, 1858. His third wife, whom he married Jan. 28, 1864, is Sally A., daughter of William and Elizabeth French, of Wheeling, W. Va.

In 1823 there were only seven houses in Frostburg, viz., Meshach Frost's "Highland Hotel," the McCulloh house, the building now occupied by Shaeffer's store, the house now occupied by Mr. Porter, the building now known as the "St. Cloud Hotel," where Fielding R. Shepherd then kept a hotel and store, and three houses near the present Methodist church.

In 1841, Lowndes & Clary had a general merchandise store, and occupied the building that stood upon the site of Beall's hardware-store. J. Henry Hoblitzell kept store on the lot where now is Hutchins' store.

Fielding R. Shepherd had his store in the house now owned by Peter Payne.

The hotels were the "Highland Hall," "Franklin," and the "St. Cloud" (now kept by C. Lynch). The town began to develop and grow upon the organization of the coal companies and the working of the mines with increased force and capital.

Braddock, on his march to Fort Du Quesne, encamped near Frostburg upon that piece of land situated to the northwest of "Allegany Cemetery." While here some of his soldiers and officers died, and were buried by his order. The graves were marked only by a plain head-stone. In 1854 a party of Englishmen visited the town. They comprised some English gentlemen of prominence, and they had with them the directions or the location of the graves written upon paper, and without any difficulty discovered the spot where the soldiers were buried, although it was not known to the inhabitants of the town. There were five graves near the house of Mr. Preston, which was recently burned. The Hill Street road runs directly over them. Washington, on his return from Braddock's ill-fated expedition, encamped here also. An old tavern and tan-yard stood upon this field, and was built very early in the present century.

By an act of the Legislature of Maryland of 1870 the town of Frostburg was incorporated and granted the right to elect a mayor and councilmen. The limits of the town were set as follows:

"Beginning at a stone standing on the south side of the National road, south forty-five and a quarter degrees, east three hundred and ninety-four feet from the southeast corner of the

German Lutheran church, and from thence running south nineteen degrees, west twenty-three hundred and forty-one feet to a stake on the east side of the Cumberland and Pennsylvania Railroad; then with said road south thirty-two and a half degrees, west nine hundred and seventy-five feet, north fifty-nine degrees, west eight hundred and fifty feet to a bounded red-oak, north forty-six and a half degrees, west four hundred and seventeen feet to a red-oak at the southeast corner of Sonnenberg's lot; thence north twenty-three degrees, west thirty-eight hundred and sixty-six feet to a large white-oak in a lane leading from Mrs. Frost's house; thence north seven degrees, east twenty-five hundred feet to a chestnut-tree; thence north eighty-one and a quarter degrees, east two hundred and eighty-four feet, south fifty-five degrees, east twenty-three hundred and seventy feet, south thirty-one degrees, east eight hundred and fifty feet to a stake in the centre of the road leading to the Cumberland and Pennsylvania depot, and with said road south eight degrees, west three hundred and sixty feet, to a stake standing north sixty-three and a half degrees, east ten feet from the northeast corner of Holley's brewery: thence north eighty-four degrees, east eleven hundred and forty-nine feet, south five degrees, west fifteen hundred and fifty feet, to the point of beginning."

The following gentlemen have served as mayor and councilmen of the town since its organization:

1870.—Mayor, N. S. Frost: Councilmen, Wm. Warn, Douglas Percy, Henry Bepler, L. M. Gorsuch, James J. Hoblitzell, William Thomas. Henry J. Wade was chosen clerk to the Council and of the Corporation, and Michael Sherry, bailiff.

1871.—Mayor, L. M. Gorsuch; Councilmen, Reuben Anthony, John Johns, L. B. Porter, Daniel Krappf, John B. Wright, John D. Koontz; Clerk, H. J. Wade; and Bailiff, William Conrad.

1872.—Mayor, Fred. Johnson; Councilmen, James D. Armstrong, Conrad Sapp, Jabez Jeffries, Frederick Gross, Wm. Noel, Philip Michael; Clerk, H. J. Wade; and Bailiff, Owen Evans.

1873.—Mayor, Henry Bepler; Councilmen, Hanson Jordan, William Noel, Abnor Riggs, J. B. Wright, Wm. Bowen, Owen Price; Clerk, H. J. Wade, and Owen Evans, bailiff.

1874.—Mayor, Aden Cleary; Councilmen, George Boettner, James D. Armstrong, Wm. H. Evans, R. C. Paul, Jacob Baker, William Warn; Clerk, John S. Grove; Bailiff, Owen Evans.

1875.—Mayor, L. M. Gorsuch; Councilmen, O. Price, John L. Porter, Conrad Sapp, John D. Koontz, R. R. Sauner, A. Griffith; Clerk, John S. Grove; and Bailiff, A. Smeltz.

1876.—Mayor, Joseph Jandorf; Councilmen, Conrad Sapp, Mr. McCulloh, A. Griffith, Owen Price, John D. Koontz, Alexander Recknor; Clerk, John S. Metzgar; Bailiff, George Ort.

1877.—Mayor, Dr. William H. Ravenscraft; Councilmen, Richard Brace, Wm. Y. McCulloh, Enoch Clise, L. C. Burgemeister, George Boettner, John Nash; Clerk, John S. Metzgar; Bailiff, George Ort.

1878.—Mayor, John S. Metzgar; Councilmen, Enoch Clise, William Payne, William Oats, John Vogtman, David Armstrong, James Dundo; Clerk, T. G. Mason; Bailiff, James P. Smith.

1879.—Mayor, John L. Porter; Councilmen, J. D. Armstrong, R. C. Paul, Henry Williams, William Crump, A. T. Stewart, John Price; Clerk, James Hanson; Bailiff, J. P. Smith.

1880.—Mayor, J. B. McCulloh; Councilmen, George Hoskins, Andrew Willison, John S. Grove, Peter Kneireim, Philip Michael, B. J. Thomas; Clerk, T. J. Mason; Bailiff, G. H. Eisfeller.

1881.—Mayor, Noah Skidmore; Councilmen, John Preston, George Johnson, George Lemmart, Benj. J. Thomas, James Taylor, William Beane; Clerk, Frederick Bepler; Bailiff, Jacob Baker.

The Frostburg *Mining Journal*, a weekly newspaper, was established by J. R. Grove and J. B. Oder, and its first number issued Sept. 30, 1871. It was from the beginning a four-page sheet, each of seven columns. On Feb. 24, 1872, C. H. Walker succeeded Mr. Grove, and continued as part proprietor until 1873, when C. W. Oder purchased his interest. Since then the paper has been published by J. B. Oder & Brother, the former being the editor. It is one of the best edited papers in Maryland, specially devoted to local news, and independent on all subjects.

J. Benson Oder, editor of the *Mining Journal*, was born in Page County, Va., in August, 1841, and served during the late war in the Confederate army, being present at Cold Harbor, Malvern Hill, Chancellorsville, Winchester, and Gettysburg. He removed to Maryland, and was elected to the House of Delegates in 1877. He has attained great local influence as an editor, and was an efficient and pains-taking member of the Legislature.

The Frostburg *Republican* was established in 1876 by Meshach Frost, who was editor and proprietor. It was published about one year, and the office was removed to Lonaconing, where Mr. Frost started the *Valley Times*, which he still conducts.

In 1834 Frostburg Circuit of the Methodist Episcopal Church comprised all that portion of Garrett and Allegany Counties outside of the city of Cumberland (which was a charge by itself). The first church in Frostburg was erected in 1834 on ground deeded from Isaiah Frost and wife to the church trustees, who were Peter Uhle, John Combs, James Amos, Jesse Chaney, John Neff. This ground is the site of the present edifice. The congregation had an existence prior to 1834, but worshiped in Neff's meeting-house, a log building, which was situated about two miles from Frostburg. The first church was a small stone structure. The second, which was built in the year 1855, was a neat frame building, and was removed to Keyser upon the erection of the present church in 1870. Below is given a full list of the pastors from 1839 to the present day:

1839, Josiah Forrest, preacher in charge, Joseph Morris, assistant pastor; 1840, Francis M. Miles, Andrew Jameson, John Moorhead; 1841, F. M. Miles, Robert Gier; 1842, S. M. L. Conser, Tobias Riley, John Lanahan; 1843, George W. Deems, William Gwinn; 1844, George W. Deems, William Crawford; 1845, P. McNally, A. E. Morris; 1847, David Trout, David Shouff; 1848, J. C. H. Dosh, David

Trout; 1849, Thomas Switzer, Henry Hoffman; 1850, Thomas Switzer, Cambrig Graham; 1851, Elisha Buttler, William Steel; 1852, Elisha Buttler; 1853, Rev. Richey, J. P. Hall; 1854, Rev. Richey, Rev. Leatherberry; 1855, Samuel Dunlap, B. F. Stevens; 1857, William Memmeryer, Rev. Conner; 1858, William Memmeryer, Rev. Ockerman; 1859, Daniel Shoff, Rev. Hartsock; 1861, Wilford Downs; 1862, '63, '64, '65, Nathan Buckingham; 1866, '67, '68, J. N. Cooper; 1869, Edward Rensey; 1870, '71, E. J. Gray; 1872, '73, '74, L. T. Widerman; 1875, L. M. Gardner; 1876, '77, '78, N. Y. Edward; 1879, '80, '81, J. P. Wilson.

The church since the Rev. Mr. Wilson began his duties has wonderfully improved. Judge Armstrong has been the recording steward for thirty-four years. Only one of the trustees of the church of 1834 is now living, Jesse Chaney, who resides in Garrett County. The Methodist Episcopal Church is the pioneer church organization of the town. It is worthy of note that two of its members—Mrs. Elizabeth and Mrs. Susan Wright, twin sisters, who married brothers, and whose maiden names were Neff—are still living at the advanced age of ninety-two, and both have been members of the Methodist Episcopal Church for over sixty years.

The dedication of the present church occurred Dec. 17, 1871. Among the eminent ministers in attendance were Bishop E. R. Ames, of Baltimore, Rev. R. L. Dashiell, D.D., president of Dickinson College, Carlisle, Pa., Rev. W. Holliday, P. E., Winchester District, Revs. George W. Cooper and Wilford Downs, of Baltimore, Rev. Austin Courtenay, of Lonaconing, Rev. Durbin Miller, Rev. John Edwards, Rev. E. J. Gray, Rev. G. H. Humphrey, Rev. D. L. McKenzie, and Rev. L. Llewellyn, the latter four ministers of Frostburg. Bishop Ames delivered the dedicatory sermon. The style of the church is decorative Gothic, with a tower in the centre of the front, which, with the spire, reaches an altitude of one hundred and sixty-seven feet. The main walls are built of good Cumberland brick. The building is eighty-five by fifty-two feet, with a recess in the rear eleven by twenty-one feet. The masonry was done by James Fuller, and the stone-cutting by Henry Williams, of Frostburg, the whole being under the supervision of J. B. Walton, of Cumberland. P. Hanson & Co., of Baltimore, furnished the house, and Lankan & Kruger did the frescoing. Mr. Davis, of Baltimore, was the architect.

Mr. Neff, one of the trustees, who attended the dedication, had also been in attendance at the dedication of three churches which successively stood upon the site of the present edifice.

The following financial exhibit was approved on the day of dedication:

Dr.	
Cost, additional ground	$2,020.00
" church edifice	37,261.00
" furnishing church	1,405.62
Interest thus far paid	1,550.62
	$42,236.62
Cr.	
Subscriptions and shares in building associations	$26,306.00
Sale of old church	825.00
Collected by ladies	1,205.62
" in Sunday-school	200.00
Balance	13,700.00
	$42,236.62

Of the above balance there was at the dedication subscribed and paid:

Morning service	$6002
Evening "	2148
Since	170
	$8320
Balance unpaid on December 18th	$5380

In 1872, Dr. Wm. H. Ravenscraft, John Myers, Joseph Yates, John Lewis, John Davis, and others withdrew from the Welsh Baptist Church, and under the charge of Rev. Mr. Llewellyn united themselves into an English Baptist congregation. Services were held for several months in the Southern Methodist Episcopal church, until a formal organization occurred, when arrangements were made for the erection of a church. John B. Reese, John Davis, and David Griffith constituted the building committee. The corner-stone was laid and the church edifice erected in 1872, and in June, 1873, the church was dedicated by Dr. J. W. M. Williams, of the First Baptist Church, Baltimore. The building is a frame structure, costing two thousand dollars, and standing upon a lot purchased of Thomas McCulloh for one thousand dollars. It is situated immediately above the Lutheran church, on Main Street. In 1874, Rev. J. T. Bradford became the pastor, and acted in that capacity until the year closing December, 1876. For two years the pulpit was vacant, and in the early part of the year 1879, Mr. William Q. Petty began his pastorate. The church still retains him in that position. According to the minutes of the Maryland Baptist Union Association of 1880 the church "enjoyed a reasonable degree of prosperity during the year; the pastor regular and faithful in all his duties; and finances conducted with system and satisfactory results."

The following members have served the church as deacons since its establishment: Dr. William H. Ravenscraft, Henry Williams, John Lewis, and Joseph Meyers. The original members of this congregation were mainly of Welsh and English nativity, and after a few years a number of the Welsh members withdrew and returned to the mother-church. Notwithstanding this loss of members the church now numbers over fifty persons. The clerk of the congregation is Charles Crook; Treasurer, George Keedy.

The following statistics connected with the church for the year 1880 are appended: Members received by baptism, 3; received by letter, 1; restored, 1; dismissed by letter, 1; excluded or erased, 6; pastor's salary and church expenses, $600; Maryland Union Baptist Association, $11.65; foreign missions, $10.60; building fund, $1.25; miscellaneous, $9.01. Total, $632.51.

Grace Methodist Episcopal Church South, of Moorefield District, Baltimore Annual Conference, was organized in October, 1869, at the home of Mr. Ward, on Main Street, under the administration of Rev. M. Y. Balthis, preacher in charge of Piedmont station. The entire membership at this time was only five, as follows: Mrs. Anna M. Ward, Evaline Johnson, John D. Barnard, James Barnard, and Mrs. Nancy Ryland.

In 1870, Rev. G. H. Zimmerman became pastor. In this year the church was erected, and formally dedicated on December 19th, under the name of Wesleyan Chapel. Rev. Dr. W. E. Munsey delivered the dedicatory sermon. The board of trustees at the building of the church consisted of John D. Barnard, James Barnard, Josiah McKenzie, William Ward, Nelson Beall. The last three, although not members of the church, took quite an active interest in its erection, Messrs. Ward and Beall contributing very liberally. In 1871 this charge was severed from Piedmont station, West Virginia, to which it had been previously attached, and was converted into a station with seven members, under the charge of Rev. Lemuel W. Haslup. During his four years of service he added Emmanuel Church, in Garrett County, and developed a work in and around Listenburg, Somerset Co., Pa., which was separated at the session of the Baltimore Annual Conference, March, 1875, into an independent circuit, leaving Frostburg a station, with Emmanuel Church connected, having a membership in all of 36. In 1875, Rev. Charles E. Semmes occupied the pulpit, and Rev. Thomas G. Nevitt in 1876 and 1877.

Rev. J. R. Andrew, the present pastor, succeeded Mr. Nevitt in March, 1878. At this time the membership had increased to sixty. During Mr. Haslup's pastorate the title of the church was changed to "Grace." In 1881 the church was enlarged, remodeled, and refurnished at almost its original cost. It is heated with a furnace, and has a seating capacity of two hundred and seventy-five, and is entirely free from debt.

The committee who had this improvement in hand comprised the following gentlemen: J. R. Andrews, chairman and treasurer; Nottey Barnard, O. C. Deffenbough, William Hawkins, George Layman, and James Yoste.

The present board of trustees are John D. Barnard, James Barnard, Charles Barnard, Rev. E. M. Davis, George S. Robb, George L. Layman, and Thomas Layman.

Stewards, Notley Barnard, James Yost, John D. Barnard, George Layman, George Robb, William Davis, O. C. Deffenbaugh.

Class-leaders, John D. Barnard, Rev. E. M. Davis, James Hanne, William Hawkins, Rev. J. R. Andrew.

Average congregation, 240; classes sustained, 5; prayer-meetings, 3; membership, 165.

Sunday-school, William Davis, superintendent, 140 members.

This territory, previous to 1867, was supplied with occasional preaching by missionaries of the Reformed Church from the churches at Cumberland and Baltimore. The earliest of these was Rev. J. Johnson, then Rev. Aaron Warner, who after a short while organized the congregation, evidently believing that much effective work could be done by banding together. They held their worship in the Presbyterian church. Among the original members who assisted Rev. A. Warner in forming the Reformed Church in 1867 were John Vogtman, John Wiegand, Ludwick Harpel, Peter Knierien, Daniel Brod, Harman Krowl, John H. Shuckart, Philip Wink, Philip Hartig. At the same time Philip Wink, Philip Hartig, Henry Offman, George A. Laemmert were chosen deacons, and Lewis Harpel and John H. Shuckart elders. The deacons and elders combined constituted a board of trustees. These gentlemen at once purchased of Nelson and Caroline Beall a piece of property designated as lot No. 3, Frostburg, situated on Broad Street, in Beall's Addition to Frostburg, for which they paid one hundred and seventy-five dollars. Immediately they began the erection of their present frame edifice, which was completed at a cost of five thousand five hundred dollars. Mr. Warner's pastorate expired in 1869, and in May of that year Rev. J. Ruhl was installed as the pastor. At the time of Mr. Ruhl's formal installation the congregation numbered forty members, and the sermons were delivered only in the German language. Rev. J. Ruhl soon began the practice of preaching both in English and German, which has proved very successful. In 1873 the trustees purchased of Nelson Beall the parsonage, for the sum of three thousand dollars. The membership now numbers over three hundred persons, an increase of two hundred and sixty since Mr. Ruhl's succession to the pulpit. The deacons of the church for 1881 are John Roop, Conrad Youngerman, Frederick Wink, Peter Knierien, and the elders, Conrad Ort, Sr., and Henry Smelse. Connected with the church is a society for the relief of the poor, known as the Ladies' Benevolent Society, which has been in existence since 1870, and has done much to promote the interests of their organization. Mrs. J. Ruhl is its president, and Mrs. Eliza Wineberg, secretary, Mrs. Mary Wiegand, treasurer. The church has also under its supervision two Sunday-schools, German and English. John Wiegand is the superintendent of the English, and Peter Knierien of the German. The English school numbers one hundred scholars, and the German one hundred and fifty-five.

Mr. Ruhl during his pastorate has baptized one hundred and sixty persons, and confirmed one hundred and sixty-five members.

At the suggestion of some of the citizens of Frostburg, the Committee of Missions of the Winchester Presbytery took measures in the fall of 1857 to have occasional preaching by the Presbyterian denomination in Frostburg, the Synod of Baltimore having requested the committee to attend to the destitute places in the county. The Rev. John Phillips visited the place and commenced preaching regularly in the early part of the summer of 1858, in the hall of the Independent Order of Red Men. In September of that year the communion was administered according to the order of the Presbyterian Church, the services on the occasion being held in the Methodist church. The ministers were Revs. William Henry Foote and John Phillips. Before the close of the meeting a petition to be regularly organized as a Presbyterian Church was drawn up and signed by a number of persons who had been members of the Presbyterian Church in other places, and most of them from the Presbyterian Church of Scotland. The petition was directed to Winchester Presbytery, and was laid before that body at its stated meeting at Mount Zion church, Hardy County, Va., commencing Sept. 16, 1858. The Presbytery expressed their approbation, and directed the Rev. W. H. Foote to lay the matter before the Presbytery of Carlisle at the meeting of the Baltimore Synod in Carlisle, Pa. The Presbytery of Carlisle (in whose jurisdiction Allegany County then was) approved the petition, and requested the Presbytery of Winchester to proceed in the matter if the way was clear, to organize the church and receive it under its care. The Synod also notified the Winchester Presbytery of their approval of the same. Whereupon the latter Presbytery appointed Rev. Messrs. Foote, Woodworth, and Phillips, with Mr. J. C. McCarty, elder, to organize the church in due form. On Saturday, the 11th of December, 1858, Messrs. Foote and Woodworth met the congregation in the hall in Frostburg. After sermon, at night, due notice having been given, the names of the petitioners were called and fourteen answered and presented their credentials, or gave satisfactory evidence of their membership in a distant church, or of their desire now to become members of the Presbyterian Church, and all having made a profession of their faith publicly, they were united in the bonds of church fellowship, to be under the care of Winchester Presbytery, and to be known as the Presbyterian Church of Frostburg. The names of these fourteen original members were Archibald McDonald, George Tennant, James Percy, Anna Percy, James Patton, Jane Patton, Alexander Patton, Maria Tennant, John McDonald, Jane Russell McDonald, William McIndor, Mary McIndor, Hugh Sampson, Margaret Sampson. Archibald McDonald, James Patton, and George Tennant were chosen elders. The pulpit was supplied at intervals by Revs. William H. Foote and M. W. Woodworth until November, 1859. From July, 1864, to March, 1867, Rev. William R. Sibbet was pastor, and from March, 1868, to October, 1869, Rev. D. L. Rathburn.

From about the end of the year 1869 to 1871 there were no regular pastors and no services held, nearly all of the members having removed from the town. From 1871 to 1873 the church edifice was occupied and services held by a mixed congregation, composed principally of Congregationalists and Calvinistic Methodists. The pulpit at this time was supplied by Rev. G. H. Humphrey, a Presbyterian minister. On April 8, 1874, a portion of the congregation became identified with the Presbyterian Church, and appeared before the Session, which met at the house of Alexander Rankin at the Borden mine. The Session was ruled over by Rev. J. K. Black, of Lonaconing, who acted as moderator, and Elders Alexander Sloan, of Lonaconing, and Alexander Rankin, of Frostburg. The members of the new organization were Thomas O. Evans, Morgan Reese, Thomas A. Evans, Francis Reese, Gushon Anthony, John H. Thomas, Reuben Anthony.

Thomas A. Evans, Thomas O. Evans, and Reuben Anthony were elected elders, and were regularly installed. On April 26, 1876, the Session met at the church, and was composed of Thomas A. Evans, R. Anthony, and Thomas O. Evans, elders, and Rev. John Thomas, moderator. At this meeting the following persons were received into the church: William Phillips, John Henry, Mrs. Sarah Gunter, Mrs. Mary Evans, Mrs. Ann Jones, Mrs. Hannah Jones, Miss

Mary A. Anthony, Mrs. Ann Lewellyn, Mrs. Elizabeth Cramp, Mrs. Elizabeth Anthony, Mrs. Ann Evans, Mrs. John H. Thomas, Mrs. Ann Reese, Mrs. Rachel Anthony, Mrs. Ruth Evans, William H. Evans, Daniel Reese, Mrs. Daniel Reese, Mrs. Martha Thomas, Mrs. Mary Price, Mrs. Jacob Lewellyn, Miss Lizzie Evans, Miss Lea Anthony, Miss Dina Anthony, Simon Evans, Mrs. Simon Evans, John Thomas, Jr., and Miss Maggie Thomas. On July 14, 1874, Rev. John Thomas, formerly of the Presbytery of Lackawanna, Pa., was installed pastor. The committee which performed this duty were Revs. Robert H. Williams, of Frederick, J. K. Black, of Lonaconing, and Edward B. Roffensberger, of Cumberland. Mr. Thomas was pastor of this church until the close of the year 1876. From 1876 to 1879 the pulpit was supplied by different ministers, most of that time by Rev. Mr. Fitzgerald. From May, 1879, to July, 1881, Rev. William A. Powell was pastor. The church was erected in 1860. The lot on which it is situated was purchased of Alfred Newlon and wife, Oct. 15, 1859. The parsonage and lot on which it stands were bought of Sarah Wright.

The dedication of the English Baptist church occurred Oct. 20, 1872. The sermons were delivered by Rev. Dr. J. W. M. Williams, of Baltimore; and by Rev. H. J. Chandler, of Cumberland. The English Baptist church is a neat structure, situated upon a slight eminence in the eastern part of the town, adjoining the properties of James Kane and the McCulloh heirs. The audience-room is twenty-eight by forty feet in dimensions.

The English Lutheran Church is the pioneer church organization of the town, dating back to the year 1812, when the people of this denomination were gathered together in the old Neff meeting-house by the Rev. G. Butler, and there formed themselves into a congregation of the English Lutheran Church. Among these original members were Jacob Muzzleman, George Orter, John Neff, John Tobias Steyer, Jacob Loar. These men were very active in the interests of the church and greatly assisted Mr. Butler in his duties. Great revivals were held here, and many were the converts that Mr. Butler brought into the church. He was a very popular minister, and scattering members of the different denominations soon became regular attendants at his preaching, but after some years Mr. Butler retired from the pulpit on account of his advanced age, and was followed by Rev. C. Heyer. After a while the congregation began to fall off, and for some time it was small compared with the former large membership. At this time and during Mr. Butler's pastorate services were held but once in two weeks. This charge was then connected with that of Cumberland, and the ministers had regular posts of duty. Beginning at Cumberland, they would preach all along the National road to a point about ten miles beyond the "Glades" (now Oakland), and on their return would preach at the same points. This work was very fatiguing to the ministers, as it required them to be constantly upon horseback and exposed to all kinds of weather.

The Neff meeting-house, referred to above, was given for worship to all congregations and denominations by John Neff, and it stood upon the lot adjoining the residence of Wm. Wright. This log building was afterwards hauled to the property given by John Eckard, at the east end of Frostburg, and there used as a place of worship by this denomination.

Rev. Mr. Heyer was succeeded by Rev. Mr. Keller, and services were held in the old log school-house which stood over the hill on the National road. Rev. Mr. Winecoff became pastor about the year 1839, and again the place of worship was changed, this time to the log building above mentioned; the ground upon which it stood is now owned by the Consolidation Coal Company. In 1841 about thirty-five members worshiped regularly in the church, and only two were residents of the town. At the beginning of Mr. Winecoff's term, as this church was connected with the Cumberland charge, he was the pastor for both congregations, but upon the division of the Cumberland charge and the establishment of Frostburg Church as a separate and distinct charge he became pastor of the latter.

Among the members of the church in 1841 were William Ward, George Steyer, Jacob Steyer, John Steyer, Henry Loar, Jacob Loar, Jacob Winter. During this year worship was held but once a month. Rev. Christian Lepley followed Rev. Mr. Winecoff, and in 1846 the congregation erected the church which is now owned by the German Reformed congregation. This, upon its completion, was the finest edifice in the town. About 1855, Rev. Winecoff was again called and took charge of the congregation, which position he held for three years, when Rev. Frederick Benedict became pastor.

In 1858 one-half of a lot upon the corner of Union and Water Streets was given to the church by Jacob Steyer, and the other half was purchased of him. In the mean time the old church was sold to the German Lutheran congregation. In 1860 the corner-stone of the new edifice was laid. The church was completed and dedicated some years afterwards, the war retarding somewhat its construction. Rev. A. J. Wendel, of Cumberland, delivered the dedicatory sermon. Rev. A. H. Aughe succeeded Mr. Benedict in the latter part of 1860, and served for about four years He was followed by Rev. Henry Bishop. At this time the congregation had increased in number to one hundred and forty.

Rev. A. L. McKenzie was selected as the pastor in 1870, and during his term the church was refurnished, remodeled, and otherwise improved, and finally rededicated by Rev. T. W. Conrad, of Philadelphia, who is now the editor of the *Lutheran Observer*. In September, 1874, the church was totally destroyed by fire, but was immediately rebuilt, and the lower room, or basement, was soon ready for the use of the congregation. This basement-room was formally dedicated by Rev. S. W. Owen, of Hagerstown. This was used as the place of meeting until the pastorate of Rev. O. G. Harrison, when the upper portion of the edifice was finished. The church now numbers over one hundred and eighty members. The elders are Douglas Percy, Joseph Knode; Deacons, Robert Scott, Joseph Robbins, William Staples, Martin Whitney.

The church was dedicated on Sunday, April 20, 1879. Rev. S. W. Owen, of Hagerstown, preached the dedicatory sermon. Rev. P. L. Harrison, pastor, and Revs. R. Smithson and J. R. Andrew also took part in the services. At the conclusion about five hundred dollars were contributed, and at the evening service over one hundred dollars more were realized, or altogether a small sum in excess of the amount asked for,—six hundred dollars.

Before 1851, Revs. G. S. Tracy and Wm. Green held Episcopal services in Frostburg and at Eckhart mines. At the latter a stone church was built in 1850, and its interior finished in 1852. The land was leased from the coal company. This church was never consecrated, and has not been used for worship for twenty years. In 1851, Rev. John W. Nott (now of St. George's Protestant Episcopal Church, at Mount Savage) came to Frostburg and held services in a school-house, which with the lot was subsequently purchased for the use of the Protestant Episcopal Church in 1853. Since then the room has been enlarged, but has never been consecrated.

Since 1874 the rectors have been Rev. S. H. Griffith (now of Pittsburgh), Rev. George S. Tracy, Rev. John Atkinson (now of Ohannock, Va.), and the present incumbent, Rev. C. S. M. Stewart.

The beautiful structure of St. Michael's Catholic Church stands on the old "Highland Hall" property, where, in the palmy days of the old National road, was kept a noted hotel, from which daily departed over thirty-six stages. It was on these lots that the first house in town was built in June, 1812, by Meshach Frost. The Catholics of the town and vicinity attended the Catholic church at Mount Savage, and afterwards a house was rented in Frostburg on the lot where Mary Wineland now lives, in which services were held until 1852. In November of that year Father Slattery, who had been appointed pastor, purchased the "Highland Hall" hotel, which had been a great summer resort, and was large enough to accommodate nearly three hundred guests. He bought it of the stage company, and fixed up one wing for a church. Besides his duties here he attended congregations at Lonaconing, Barton, Oakland, Piedmont, Westernport, Blooming Rose, and Johnstown. He was the pioneer priest in the mining regions, and traveled great distances on horseback to attend his flocks. The territory under his charge now comprises some six flourishing churches with separate residences. He formed St. Michael's congregation, and labored from 1852 until 1860, when his failing health compelled him to cease his labors, and he removed to St. Joseph's church, in Baltimore, where he died in 1866.

After his departure Fathers Carney and Brown, from Mount Savage, attended the church. They were succeeded by Father Riley as resident pastor, who remained two years. He was followed by the Redemptorist Fathers from Cumberland, who attended for two years, and until October, 1866. Then Father L. A. Morgan was appointed resident pastor. He was very energetic and greatly beloved. He began the foundation of the present church structure. Owing to continued ill health he left in August, 1868, and was succeeded, Aug. 18, 1868, by Father V. F. Schmitt, the present incumbent. Under his direction the old hotel property was torn down and removed, and the present church edifice erected. The corner-stone was laid Aug. 2, 1868, and the church consecrated and dedicated Aug. 15, 1870. It is built of brick, is a Gothic structure, and has a set of chimes. Its steeple is one hundred and sixty-five feet, the highest in the town. The seating capacity of the building is over six hundred. It has a large organ, a marble altar, and a handsome font. The congregation has grown from small beginnings to a large parish, and now numbers over fifteen hundred. The church, residence, and other church property are valued at sixty thousand dollars. The basement is used for a parochial school, but a large lot adjoining the church is reserved for the erection, in the near future, of an academy. All the improvements in buildings and elegant gardens and lots have been made under the auspices of Father Schmitt. He was born in Bavaria, where he was partially educated, but completed his studies at St. Mary's Seminary, in Baltimore. He also attends St. Anne's church, in Garrett County, erected by him in 1874, and holds occasional services in Grantsville in that county.

The Baptist Welsh Church was formed in 1867 with about twenty members, and services were held at the private residences of the members. The church edifice was erected in 1868, and dedicated the following year. In 1872 the English Baptist Church was organized out of its membership. Its pastors have been H. L. Llewellyn, E. Morddal Evans, Morris Evans, D. R. Jones, D. H. Jones.

The Evangelical German Lutheran Church was built in 1846 by Rev. C. Lepley as an English Lutheran Church. In 1853 and 1854 the German Lutheran Reformed congregation met in the church under Rev. Joseph R. Focht, and soon after bought the property. In 1867 a separation took place, the Reformed members erecting their own edifice at Broadway, and leaving the German Lutheran element in possession of the property. A number of pastors succeeded each other, some only staying a brief period. On Nov. 1, 1879, Rev. A. Homrighaus being called from Schenectady, N. Y., took charge of the congregation, under whose administration the old edifice was remodeled at an expense of six thousand five hundred dollars. The dedication of the remodeled edifice took place on July 24, 1881. Revs. F. P. Henrighausen, of Baltimore, Samuel C. Yingling, of Harrisburg, and P. L. Harrison, of Frostburg, were present and participated. Henceforth a new departure was taken. There having been only one German service in the morning since the organization of the church, an English service was introduced by the pastor at night.

Among the pastors preceding Rev. Homrighaus were Rev. M. During, Rev. B. Sickle, and Rev. Mr. Stump. The parsonage, which is a neat structure, standing by the side of the church, was purchased in 1865 of Hon. Thomas McCulloh. The membership now numbers about one hundred and sixty-five. At the beginning of Mr. Homrighaus' pastorate there were only ninety members, showing an increase of seventy-five members in two years' service. A lot of ground was purchased of W. McCulloh and laid out as a cemetery for the church, to be known as the German Lutheran Cemetery. A Sunday-school is in existence under the supervision of the church, with 100 scholars. The church has a chime of bells.

Percy's Cemetery.—Prior to the year 1850 one acre of this ground was donated for public use by Josiah Porter. Afterwards, David Percy, deceased, made an addition, and disposed of the lots by sale. Among the graves to be found here are those of

George Bruce, died Nov. 3, 1853, aged 73 years; and Helen, his wife, born July 28, 1772, died May 19, 1841.

Gerard Clary, died Aug. 24, 1850, aged 74.

John Chaney, of N., died April 6, 1846, aged 72; and his wife, Elizabeth, March 11, 1851, aged 64.

Conrad Oesterling, born Jan. 2, 1815, died Sept. 26, 1864.

Sarah Ann, wife of William Taylor, died Aug. 14, 1856, aged 44.

John Wood, a native of Riccarton, Ayrshire, Scotland, died Jan. 5, 1848, aged 30.

William Wright, died Jan. 10, 1857, aged 71.

Rachel, wife of William Frost, died Aug. 30, 1864, aged 30.

Mary Ann, wife of Josiah Englar, died Sept. 15, 1848, aged 24.

Lewis B. McMillan, a native of Ayrshire, Scotland, died Oct. 28, 1870, aged 60.

Jane, wife of David Lewis, died Oct. 8, 1869, aged 22.

Sarah, wife of William Yates, born in England, Jan. 25, 1818, died Oct. 14, 1869.

Anna M., wife of G. J. Conner, died Dec. 11, 1863, aged 63.

Catherine, wife of Nelson Beall, died Jan. 11, 1872, aged 46.

Elizabeth P. Beall, died July 11, 1867, aged 72.

Daniel Sease, died Dec. 15, 1859, aged 58; and his wife, Elizabeth, April 17, 1870, aged 68.

William Humerston, died Sept. 6, 1875, aged 62.

David T. Jones, a native of Llansamled, Carmarthen, South Wales, died March 18, 1870, aged 55.

Mary Ann, wife of William B. Davis, died Aug. 10, 1854, aged 19.

Mary, wife of David Thomas, a native of Wales, died Jan. 11, 1851, aged 40.

Sarah Waner, died March 8, 1856, aged 60.

Conrad Lapp, born Nov. 7, 1812, died April 17, 1855.

Susan, wife of Amos Willison, died April 8, 1879, aged 73.

John Combs, died Nov. 1, 1854, aged 94; and Margaret, his wife, died Jan. 11, 1859, aged 79.

Margaret, wife of William Gunter, a native of Blaenavon, Wales, died June 5, 1863, aged 57.

William Thompson, died Aug. 8, 1857, aged 70; and Mary Thompson, died Feb. 24, 1879, aged 42.

Thomas Davis, died Jan. 27, 1847, aged 34.

Charles Bepler, died Jan. 30, 1877, aged 32.

John P. Porter, died Feb. 19, 1853, aged 34.

Thomas Wright, died March 10, 1867, aged 85.

John Neff, died Oct. 16, 1878, aged 86; and Harriet A., his wife, died Jan. 15, 1875, aged 75.

David Percy, a native of Ayrshire, Scotland, died March 20, 1858, aged 52.

A. T. Percy, born in Muirkirk, Ayrshire, Scotland, died March 9, 1858, aged 25.

William Williams, a native of Blaenyvant, Carmarthenshire, Wales, died April 4, 1866, aged 31.

William Calmes, died Nov. 3, 1849, aged 58; and Catherine Calmes, Oct. 18, 1857, aged 62.

J. H. Huntley, born Nov. 23, 1839, died Oct. 6, 1877; and E. K. Huntley, died Dec. 18, 1862, aged 51.

August F. Schull, died Oct. 20, 1851, aged 63; and Johanna A. C., his wife, March 3, 1874, aged 64; and George Schull, born 1852, died 1872.

Ada M. Poff, born September, 1817, died June, 1870.

August Schneider, died Sept. 2, 1873, aged 64; and Anna Maria, his wife, born March 15, 1809, died Jan. 25, 1871.

Herman Seiffer, died Dec. 21, 1868, aged 58.

Jacob Steyer, died Oct. 24, 1878, aged 74.

Lydia, wife of George Styer, died Dec. 13, 1867, aged 62.

Moses Matheney, died Oct. 16, 1869, aged 68.

Jacob Miller, died May 4, 1860, aged 48.

Elizabeth, wife of Joseph E. Carter, died Dec. 4, 1848, aged 57.

Allegany Cemetery.—This property originally belonged to the I. O. O. F. Lodge, Frostburg, No. 49, who laid it off and gave it its title in 1864. In 1879 it became the property of W. H. Evans and Thomas G. McCulloh.

The graves of the following persons are within the limits of this cemetery:

John Cowan, who died April 28, 1876, aged 75 years, 6 months, 25 days; Clementine, his wife, died Feb. 1, 1842.

Agnes C., wife of James Shearer, died April 14, 1842, aged 68.

Agnes, wife of R. Beveridge, died Sept. 3, 1860, aged 32 years, 1 month, 2 days.

Catherine, wife of J. W. McLeyne, died Oct. 15, 1864, aged 28 years, 22 days.

Elizabeth, wife of Thomas Pierce, died Oct. 23, 1868, aged 33 years, 7 months, 24 days.

Janet, wife of John Hurley, died Dec. 30, 1874, aged 41 years, 8 months, 29 days.

James Shearer, died May 21, 1874, aged 30 years, 5 months, 16 days.

Jacob Hoblitzell, born June 3, 1822, died May 24, 1868; and Elizabeth J., his wife, born March 29, 1827, died April 21, 1869.

Minor Gibson, born April 7, 1797, died June 14, 1877; Elizabeth, his wife, born June 14, 1800, died Feb. 8, 1874; Lucy E., their daughter, born May 13, 1821, died Feb. 13, 1874.

Susanna Wright, wife of Curtin W. Graham, died April 13, 1878, aged 49 years, 8 months, 24 days.

Catherine E., wife of Joseph Knode, died June 21, 1878, aged 55.

Marcia A. Gifford, died Dec. 14, 1876, aged 50 years, 2 months, 16 days.

John W. Taylor, born March 18, 1827, died Aug. 26, 1865.

Sarah, wife of William Morgan, a native of Gloucestershire, England, died Aug. 20, 1875, aged 52.

Benjamin Bowen, born Oct. 17, 1847, died Jan. 29, 1881.

Margaret, wife of Thomas Elias, died Aug. 9, 1875, aged 30 years, 6 months.

Henry Ellis Anwye (member of Masonic lodge), died Sept. 16, 1877, aged 29 years, 5 months.

Elizabeth Beall, died July 5, 1876, aged 53.

Aza Beall, died March 8, 1863, aged 39.

Mrs. Thomas Beall, died Jan. 9, 1860, aged 63 years; and Thomas Beall, died March 18, 1864, aged 69.

Thomas Williams, born June 16, 1812, in Wales, died Aug. 1, 1864.

George McCulloh, born March 6, 1782, died Dec. 27, 1854; Mary C., his wife, born April 20, 1790, died Feb. 9, 1876.

Moses Rawlings, died Feb. 7, 1867, aged 62.

Conrad Ort, a native of Germany, died May 7, 1876, aged 73 years, 8 days.

George Holmes, died May 15, 1872, aged 66 years, 3 months.

Wife of Digory Noel, died Feb. 8, 1875, aged 53 years, 2 days.

Methuselah Phillips, died March 4, 1877, aged 71 years, 11 months, 24 days; Elizabeth, his wife, died Aug. 9, 1864, aged 55 years.

Mary P., wife of Robert McCulloh, died March 26, 1872, aged 55.

William Ward, born Feb. 13, 1812, died March 2, 1877.

Mary, wife of J. J. Keller, died Dec. 5, 1856, aged 36 years, 1 month, 26 days.

John M. Standish, born at Plattsburgh, N. Y., Jan. 6, 1829, died at Frostburg, Md., Nov. 30, 1874. "He was a lineal descendant in the eighth generation of Capt. Miles Standish, 'The Puritan.'" Mary E., his wife, died Oct. 15, 1877, aged 37 years.

Matthew R. Sloan, died June 26, 1863, aged 46.

Missouri E., wife of A. J. Willison, died Aug. 17, 1876, aged 39 years, 6 months, 25 days.

Susannah, wife of George S. Gunther, died Dec. 17, 1868, aged 23.

Alexander Sloan, a native of Ayrshire, Scotland, died Sept. 6, 1874, aged 54 years, 5 months, 2 days.

Jane Hawkins, died Sept. 28, 1866, aged 64.

Mary C., wife of George Boettner, died Aug. 18, 1877, aged 54 years, 10 months, 8 days.

Clements Reidler, died Oct. 4, 1878, aged 70 years, 8 months, 28 days.

Evan Rees, died 1879, aged 48.

David Gelly, died 1879, aged 35.

John Stokes, died 1875, aged 60 years, 9 months, 15 days.

William Leatham, died Sept. 4, 1874, aged 20 years, 11 months, 18 days.

Ann Beall, died Sept. 10, 1867, aged 67.

Ann, wife of John Smith, died July 29, 1879, aged 27 years, 11 months.

John Whitefield, born Sept. 18, 1816, died March 16, 1880.

John Barnard, died Dec. 21, 1863, aged 62 years, 4 months, 25 days.

Susan J. Barnard, died Feb. 14, 1871, aged 58 years, 6 months, 3 days.

Rev. V. F. Schmidt has purchased a lot of ground upon the plateau which forms the summit of "McCulloh's Hill," to be used as a Catholic cemetery. It is beautifully located, and possesses natural advantages which can be readily improved.

The graves of the following persons are within the limits of the old Catholic cemetery:

John Beane, born June 12, 1808, died May 18, 1869, born in Queen's County, Ireland.

Lloyd L. Clary, died Oct. 27, 1873, aged 30 years.

T. M. Clary, died April 20, 1874, aged 33.

Joseph McKenzie, died Jan. 23, 1879, aged 62.

Cyrus McKenzie, died Feb. 15, 1869, aged 27.

Ellen C., wife of James Casserly, a native of Roscommon County, Ireland, died Jan. 10, 1877, aged 60.

Elizabeth Flynn, died May 22, 1877, aged 30.

Sarah Lanhady, died Sept. 14, 1877, aged 55.

Ann, wife of Thomas Rooney, died June 30, 1877, aged 39.

Joseph Winner, died April 7, 1872, aged 43.

Margaret, wife of John R. Yan, a native of Galway County, Ireland, died Oct. 20, 1869, aged 75 years.

Mary, wife of John Dooley, died March 16, 1870, aged 23.

Michael Baxter, died Nov. 2, 1867, aged 48 years.

Joseph G. Lint, died June 21, 1868, aged 41 years, 2 months, 27 days.

Patrick D. Ward, died June 18, 1859, aged 36 years, 3 months, 5 days.

Sarah, wife of Robert Walsh, died Oct. 28, 1857, aged 36.

Richard Harvey, died April 19, 1855, aged 60 years.

John Harvey, killed Oct. 31, 1875, aged 40 years.

J. W. Harrigan, died Feb. 24, 1855, aged 22 years.

John D. McMullan, died Aug. 18, 1860, aged 36, a native of Killkove Parish, Armagh County, Ireland.

Martha, wife of Peter Scalley, died Feb. 7, 1878, aged 43.

Hugh Rowan, a native of County Mayo, Ireland, died June 4, 1862, aged 61.

Mary, wife of Patrick Mansfield, a native of Parish Tamour, County Mayo, Ireland, died Oct. 21, 1868, aged 31.

Maria M., wife of A. Stemmer, died May 1, 1856, aged 42 years, 11 months, 22 days.

Rebecca Eckhart, died Jan. 28, 1858, aged 26.

John Kirby, a native of Lisle Parish, Cork County, Ireland, died June 12, 1870, aged 60.

James Byrne, of County Wicklow, Ireland, died Sept. 29, 1878, aged 25.

J. Nelson, died Dec. 1, 1860, aged 56 years.

John Donahoe, died Aug. 15, 1862, aged 42.

James Kelly, a native of Kilkenny County, Ireland, died July 23, 1860, aged 42.

Mary, wife of John Carroll, a native of Westmeath County, Ireland, died Dec. 8, 1865, aged 56 years, 5 months, 4 days.

Owen Leddy, a native of Cavan County, Ireland, died March 8, 1879, aged 37 years, 3 months, 8 days.

Henry Betz, died Nov. 12, 1873, aged 51 years, 19 days.

Elizabeth, wife of James O'Malley, a native of County Dublin, Ireland, died Feb. 8, 1881, aged 70 years.

James O'Malley, died Jan. 15, 1879, aged 73 years.

Thomas F. Higgins, a native of St. John's Parish, Roscommon County, Ireland, born Dec. 15, 1845, died March 30, 1878.

John Powers, a native of Parish Ballyroy, King's County, Ireland, died May 31, 1855, aged 52.

Patrick Casey, died May 15, 1859, aged 51.

Mary Baxter O'Conor, a native of Scotland, died June 4, 1866.

Ann, wife of James Powers, died April, 1866, aged 53.

Michael Ryan, died April 6, 1876, aged 35.

Margaret Murphy, died Aug. 23, 1880, aged 60.

John J. Hicken, died Oct. 17, 1871, aged 26 years, 6 months.

Ellen Sullivan, died May 24, 1872, aged 36 years.

Joseph Brunner, died Oct. 26, 1873, aged 32 years, 9 months, 19 days.

Thomas Cain, a native of Kildare, Ireland, died April 5, 1877, aged 76 years.

Joseph Hartman, a native of Prussia, died aged 67 years.

Frostburg Fire Department.—This organization was effected March 18, 1878, at a meeting of young men of the town, presided over by George B. McCulloh, with R. K. Mason as secretary. The first officers of the department were, inside: President, George McCulloh; Vice-President, Thos. G. Mason; Secretary, R. K. Mason; Treasurer, Frank Maury; Sergeant-at-Arms, John Jeffries. Outside: Chief Engineer, George H. Wittig; Assistants, John B. McCulloh and John A. Spades; Nozzlemen, Wash. McCulloh, Frank Maury, Charles Sourbough, and Alfred Jeffries; Assistants, John Jeffries, Charles Merrill, Walker Keller, and T. S. Preston; Plugmen, George B. McCulloh, D. Skelly, John Donahoe, and Henry Albright.

The charter was granted the same year to the following persons: George H. Wittig, George B. McCulloh, Francis W. Maury, Madison Gunnett, John Zimmerly, Richard K. Mason, Benjamin Bower, Worthington McCulloh, Silas Duggan. The managers for the first year appointed by the charter were George H. Wittig, Benjamin Bower, William Carson, Daniel Sealy, Francis Maury. In August, 1878, by order of the Town Council, the company purchased a steam-engine. The cost of it was $650. This engine was afterwards sold to the fire company at Greensburg, Pa.

Savage Mountain Fire-Brick Works.—A comparison of Frostburg in 1839 with the busy, enterprising town of to-day exhibits a marked contrast. Forty-two years ago it could boast of only two stores; now it contains more than half a hundred. The coal output for the year 1839 would hardly equal that for a day now. Elegant business blocks stand upon the sites where the rude log huts of the first settlers withstood the rough winds of winter. Handsome churches with towering spires have supplanted the primitive meeting-houses and places of worship. Two large and elegant opera-houses afford accommodations for public meetings and amusements. The coal-mines have all the modern machinery to facilitate the transit of the black diamonds from the bowels of the earth to the sea-board; railroads traverse the valleys and mountains, and the coal trade gives employment to many hundreds of miners.

Among the industries which have developed into large proportions since 1839 is the Savage Mountain Fire-Brick Works. This enterprise was started in 1865 by its present owner, L. M. Gorsuch. The capacity of the works is ten thousand standard bricks per day, in the making of which Mr. Gorsuch employs about forty men and boys, who receive good wages and are kept constantly at work the year round.

The fire-clay is procured from the banks on Savage Mountain, and in manufacturing, one-fourth of the soft clay to three-fourths of the hard is used. The *Pittsburgh Brick, Tile, and Metal Review* has the following to say about this clay:

"One of the best-known articles of fire-clay used to-day is procured from Savage Mountain, in Maryland. We herewith give an analysis of this clay, as made by Dr. George Hay, of Allegany City, for the information of our readers, many of whom are deeply interested in this subject: Silica, 59.590; alumnia, 30.097; protoxide of iron, 00.903; oxide of manganese, trace; lime, 00.074; magnesia, 00.66; water, etc., 08.890; alkalies, 00.327; loss, 00. 053; total, 100.000."

At this clay-mine a number of men are employed mining the material from which the bricks are made. Great care is exercised by the superintendent, Thomas Humbertson, to prevent accidents to the men, as fire-clay, unlike coal, gives no warning whatever when it is going to fall, and props every few feet are absolutely essential to safety. The clay is blasted out. After it has been brought out of the mine it is carried in cars on a tram-road to the dump, where it is put in the wagons and conveyed to the works in the lower part of the town.

The first process is crushing the clay in a large crushing-pan with two rollers weighing three thousand three hundred pounds each; a stream of water is thrown into the pan continuously from a pipe overhead, which serves to reduce the mass to a putty-like condition, so that it can be easily handled. It is then taken in wheelbarrows to a side room and thrown up in piles, where it stays twenty-four hours to settle and solidify before moulding. From thence it is taken to the moulding-tables, where it is moulded into bricks; the bricks are then left on the floor long enough to dry, after which they are removed to the presses, where they are shaped, and then laid back again on the floor for twenty-four hours.

After they have become thoroughly dry and hard they are carried to the kilns, of which there are three large ones, and burned so as to give them body and strength. They are then carried to the cars, where they are packed for shipment to points all over the United States.

Thos. H. Paul & Sons' Iron-Works.—This establishment was first started on the site now occupied by the Presbyterian church, on Broadway, in 1855, by the senior member of the firm, who came originally from Baltimore. Business increasing rapidly compelled Mr. Paul to remove, in 1867, to the lot near the depot, upon which he has erected a foundry thirty-three by seventy feet, and also a handsome residence, with commodious outhouses adjoining.

This has proved to be one of the most successful enterprises in Allegany County. The firm have supplied and built all the inclined-plane machinery for the American, Maryland, Hampshire, Franklin, and Atlantic Coal Companies, and have also furnished a number of narrow-gauge engines for the mines in this region. They have a reputation for building locomotives equal to that of the larger locomotive-builders of the East. This firm have also a branch foundry on the corner of Davidson and Front Streets, Cumberland, and turn out excellent work therefrom. The pattern-room of the foundry is in the second story over the machine-shop, and has all the appliances necessary to such a department.

The moulding department, where the castings are made, is an interesting feature of the establishment. The first process here is placing the patterns in loam sand and making the moulds, into which the metal is poured. The castings are taken out, when cold, and conveyed to the machine-shop, where the rough edges are knocked of, polished, and fitted up. In the machine-shop are lathes, planers, and drills of the latest and most improved machinery; these help to fit castings for the work they are intended. In the boiler-room are the punches, rolls, etc., for the purpose of bending the iron and forming it into proper shape for boilers. Annexed to the boiler-room is the blacksmith-shop. This of itself is a most necessary adjunct to such an industry. The proprietors employ in Cumberland and in their foundry about sixty men, all of whom are expert workmen. They receive orders for engines from some of the most prominent railroads in America, as well as from foreign countries.

Thomas H. Paul was born in New York City, March 10, 1820, the third in a family of nine children of Alexander and Agnes (Haig) Paul. His father was born in Edinburgh, Scotland; his mother in Melrose. They were married in Scotland, Jan. 1, 1815, emigrated to America in 1818, and settled in New York City, where they lived five years. They then moved to Paterson, N. J. Alexander Paul was a millwright and machinist by trade, and established an enviable reputation as a mechanic. He carried on his trade in Paterson, N. J., under the firm-name first of Paul & Hogg, and subsequently of Paul & Beggs. The latter firm, in the winter of 1834–35, built the first locomotive-engine constructed in New Jersey, and manufactured all descriptions of heavy factory machinery. Their factory was totally destroyed by fire in 1835. In the spring of 1838, Mr. Paul purchased the machine-shop of William Winans, brother of the celebrated Ross Winans, at Baltimore, where he remained in business until his death, which occurred March 17, 1851. His wife survived him many years, and died in Baltimore, July 28, 1880. They had nine children: two born in Scotland, one in New York City, and six in Paterson. Four are living, viz.: Thomas H.; Ann F., wife of Alexander Russell, residing in Baltimore; Robert C., machinist, living in Frostburg; and Agnes A., living in Baltimore. Having received a good common-school education, Thomas H. Paul, at the age of fifteen, commenced to learn the trade of machinist in his father's shops at Paterson in the same year the factory was burned. He was then employed for seven months as engineer on the Paterson and Hudson River Railroad, and it is claimed was the youngest engineer who was ever put in charge of a locomotive. Upon leaving the railroad he was employed in Rogers' Locomotive-Works at Paterson, N. J., where he remained until 1837.

He then became associated with his father in carrying on the works at Baltimore, and for ten years prior to the death of the latter was the general manager.

In the fall of 1850, on account of his health, he took a journey to Paraguay, South America, and remained there about seven months. He then visited England, and returned to Baltimore in 1852, where, for about a year, he continued at his trade. In the spring of 1854 he received the appointment of master mechanic of the Cumberland and Pennsylvania Railroad, whose shops are located at Mount Savage. He held this position until the fall of 1855. The same year he built his machine-shops at Frostburg. These works have been devoted principally to the manufacture of steam-engines and all classes of mining machinery, though for the past year the business has been confined, for the most part, to the construction of locomotive-engines.

The first narrow-gauge locomotive-engine built in America was constructed by Mr. Paul at these works in 1864, and placed on the Potomac Company's road June 19th of that year.

Mr. Paul is a member of the Masonic fraternity, and has contributed liberally towards improvements in Frostburg, taking an active interest in all enterprises which promise to aid in the development of the place. In politics he is a Republican. Nov. 7, 1854, he married, at Reading, Pa., Marian M., daughter of John and Joanna (Smull) Neff. Mrs. Paul was born in Berks County, Pa., May 31, 1834. Their children are John T. H., born Jan. 30, 1856, and Ella Marian, born April 23, 1857.

The Frostburg Gaslight Company was organized in 1870, and the charter was obtained April 22d of the same year. The following were the incorporators: J. M. Standish, Douglas Percy, Nelson Beall, Thomas H. Paul, A. E. Hitchins, James Kane, Marx Wineland, Joseph Jandorf, and Lloyd Lowndes, Jr.

At the first meeting officers were elected, as follows: President, John M. Standish; Vice-President, Douglas Percy; Secretary, John C. Weis; Treasurer, Nelson Beall; Directors, Thomas G. McCulloh, Lloyd Lowndes, Jr., A. E. Hitchins, Thomas H. Paul, William Ward, Aden Clary.

The capital was fifty thousand dollars, and operations were commenced at once, and by Feb. 17, 1871, the works were finished. R. G. Jordan, of Wheeling, W. Va., had the building of them. The first manager was Joseph Keller, with Watson Carr as general superintendent. The works cover about one-half acre, and have a large tank, three retorts, and about five miles of pipe, reaching to all parts of the town. Two years ago the large gasometer became useless, and R. C. Paul made a new one, much stronger and better in all respects.

This enterprise has not paid the stockholders as it should have done, having yielded only about four per cent. on the money invested.

In the manufacture of this gas only pure bituminous and gas-coal are used. The latter is obtained from the Despard mines of Clarksburg, W. Va. The company has had many obstacles to overcome since it was started, but now seems to be on a solid foundation.

The following are the officers elected at the last meeting in 1881, to serve during the ensuing year: President, James Kane; Vice-President, Adam E. Hitchins; Secretary, Charles A. Greene; Treasurer, Davisson Armstrong; Directors, Lloyd Lowndes, Richard Beall, Joshua Johnson, Douglas Percy, James H. Ward; Collector, John N. Benson. C. H. DeMoss, formerly of Cumberland, is manager of the works.

A. J. Willison's Steam Planing-Mill and Sash-Factory.—This industry is one of the oldest in Frostburg, and the proprietor is one of the largest builders in Allegany County.

He is a native of the county. In February, 1864, Messrs. John D. Koontz (now in Iowa) and A. J. Willison formed a partnership for the purpose of conducting the lumber business in all its branches. In two years' time business had increased to such an extent with them that it was found necessary to erect an annex to the original building, the latter being sixty by one hundred and eighty feet, and the dimensions of the original building being fifty by one hundred feet. Mr. Koontz withdrew from the firm in 1876 and went West, leaving Mr. Willison sole proprietor.

The machinery used in this large establishment is of the latest and most approved pattern. The engine-room is on the northwest side of the building.

Mr. Willison has an immense trade and patronage, and during the past few years has built many handsome houses in the town, which, for architectural finish, can hardly be excelled. He is an energetic and progressive business man, and much esteemed in the community. He is an ex-member of the City Council, and has given employment to a large number of men, many of whom have established themselves as master-mechanics in their several branches.

Mr. Willison deals in white and yellow pine, oak, poplar, spruce, chestnut, walnut, and other varieties of lumber; he also manufactures sashes, doors, window-shutters, mouldings, brackets, and flooring, and makes a specialty of useful and ornamental carpentering.[1]

[1] A Wonderful Clock.—H. W. Wegman, of this town, after years of labor, has completed a clock which, for curious and ingenious mechanism, has seldom been surpassed. The body

Paul's Opera House is a valuable addition to the business centre of Frostburg. It includes four store-rooms and a public hall, besides offices. The main building is three stories high, flanked by two two-story wings. The dimensions of the main building are forty feet front, with a depth of one hundred feet; the wings are eighteen by fifty; a cellar extending under all. The foundation walls are twenty-two inches thick, and furnish ample support for the numerous divisions above. A twenty-five horse-power steam-boiler provides heat for the entire building. This, together with the fixtures and gas apparatus, was put in by Mr. Paul himself. The first floor is laid off in four rooms, two sixteen by fifty feet, two eighteen and a half by eighty feet. On the second floor are three rooms sixteen by seventeen, sixteen by thirty-five, and sixteen by forty feet in dimensions. On the third floor is a room sixteen by forty feet, and the opera hall, the latter's size forty by eighty feet. The stage in this hall is twenty-five by forty feet, and is properly equipped with all the necessary conveniences for traveling companies. Five hundred chairs furnish seating accommodations. J. T. H. Paul, son of the proprietor, was the architect, and has succeeded in giving to the city a very creditable building.

Centennial Hall was projected during the spring of 1873, and was begun a year later. The excavations for the basement story were accomplished by the voluntary labor of the members of Frostburg Lodge, I. O. O. F. The building was completed in 1876. The stone for the foundation walls was contributed by the Borden Mining Company—A. C. Greene, agent—and the Consolidation Coal Company,—James B. Thomas, superintendent. The first story is divided into three store-rooms, all large and well arranged. The public hall is forty-eight by forty-four feet, and twenty-four feet high. Four huge iron columns support the spacious gallery and the uppermost floor. The auditorium affords seating capacity for seven hundred persons.

The stage and orchestra-stand are properly arranged and convenient. The drop-curtain, representing a scene entitled "A dream of Arcadia," is very beautiful. On the third floor is the lodge-room, sixty-one and three-quarters by forty-six feet, which is supple-

of the clock is made of ash, with the trimmings of walnut, and the carving was done with a penknife. It stands twelve feet in height, and is five feet in width. On the base is a representation, carved in wood, of "Death and his victim," and on each side is a pyramid of cannon-balls. Immediately above them are two sheaves of wheat, which support the front of the structure. The front is a shield, in the centre of which is an astronomical dial, showing the revolutions of the heavenly bodies. Over each side of the upper part of the shield are accurately carved in wood two large American flags, and immediately over the centre of the shield is a small clock showing Washington time. Above this are fortresses with parapets, from which protrude the black muzzles of cannons. On either side of these are two doors, through which a figure emerges every five minutes and walks across the platform of the clock.

On the stage at the base of the monument are two figures, one a drummer-boy, dressed in blue, who, with every revolution of the second hand, taps his drum, and at each quarter-hour beats a tattoo. The other figure represents Mars, the god of war, holding a spear in his hand, who records the number of wars the United States has been engaged in by striking a bell which hangs in front of him. In the background of these figures are carved representations showing the rapid strides America has made since its discovery in arts, sciences, mechanical industries, and literature. Immediately above these are the two goddesses, Liberty and Justice, holding a streamer in their hands, bearing the words "In God we Trust."

Over the fortress on the right is a specimen of Athenian architecture in miniature, on which are three dials, showing the day of the week and month, also the changes of the moon. On the top of this building is a dome, on which is the statue of Washington in wood. The building over the fortress on the left is of the same style of architecture, in which is a full band of musicians, representing nine different nationalities, viz.: Chinese, German, Irish, English, American, Negro, Indian, French, and Scotch, over whom are the words "Welcome All." On the top of this building is the figure of Lafayette.

On the stage is erected a fac-simile of Bunker Hill monument, and proudly perched on the top is a large eagle, holding in his left claw the emblematic olive branch and spears, also the scroll of "E Pluribus Unum." In his right claw is the pendulum, fifteen inches in diameter, which has on it the face of the clock. At every hour the eagle whistles. On the pendulum are classical and historical emblems, among which are the heart, anchor, and cross,—Faith, Hope, and Charity,—a snake encircling the hour-marks, and around all the thirteen stars and national colors. Hanging to the bottom of the pendulum is a globe representing the earth, showing its revolutions on its axis, and also the cause of night and day.

Just above the face of the clock are the figures Time and Death, which guard four figures representing the march of life from the cradle to the grave.

At every stroke of the quarter-hour small doors, on which are painted scenes of American history, open and show movable figures. The first quarter is a representation of the Americans disguised as Indians throwing the tea overboard in Boston Harbor.

The second quarter shows a scene from the war of 1812,—captured American seamen disembarking, while in the foreground is Johnny Bull inducing the Indians to take up arms.

A Mexican war scene, with Gens. Scott and Taylor politely doffing their hats, whilst behind them are tents, cannon, etc., shows the third quarter.

The fourth and last quarter is a scene from the late war,—a soldier from each of the eleven Confederate States walks in and turns his back on a negro, who is perched upon an auction-block in the background; these are followed by a figure of Lincoln, who faces the negro and hands him the Emancipation Proclamation.

At the end of the hour the band of musicians strike up a lively air, with Uncle Sam in the centre as leader.

This clock was commenced in 1869. The inventor is a native of Allegany County. By trade Mr. Wegman is a tanner, but is now engaged in painting.

mented in the east end by four regalia and paraphernalia rooms allotted to the lodges which meet there.

The building committee was as follows: George Hosken, chairman; Thomas Hill, secretary and treasurer; R. W. Mason, George Boettner, Henry Robinson, Robert Tennant, Jr., Andrew Fox.

The members of Frostburg Lodge, No. 49, I. O. O. F., carried out a hope cherished alike through unfavorable and prosperous times, and it is to be regretted that they could not continue in the possession of the property. In 1880 the building was sold, and John Ravenscraft became the purchaser. Perhaps no member of the order exceeded George B. McCulloh in close attention, practical interest, and constant assistance in whatever capacity he was employed by the lodge. No other building in the town equals it in size, and no other can be applied to so many uses. It is Frostburg's greatest achievement in the line of benevolent enterprise, and was completed in the centennial year of American independence. In 1878, the name was changed to the "Odd-Fellows' Opera House."

Mountain Lodge, A. F. and A. M., No. 99. Its charter was dated Nov. 22, 1854. Its first officers were: W. M., Samuel M. Haller; S. W., David Percy; J. W., Robert Tennant. Its charter was granted by Grand Master Charles Webb, Deputy Grand Master Edward T. Owens, Grand Warden George H. Kennedy, and Grand Secretary Joseph Robinson. Its Past Masters have been Samuel M. Haller, William Warn, James Reid, C. M. McCulloh, James H. Ward, Frederick Johnson, and John Davies. Its officers for 1881 were: W. M., John Davies; S. W., J. B. Oder; J. W., D. Armstrong; Sec., John N. Benson; Treas., R. J. Thomas; S. D., C. M. McCulloh; J. D., G. W. Zeller; Tyler, Robert Puder. Its members in 1881 were

Davisson Armstrong, J. N. Benson, A. J. Clark, James Campbell, John Davies, W. H. Evans, Thomas W. Frost, Josiah Ford, Frederick Gross, S. M. Haller, A. E. Hitchins, John Hitchins, Owen Hitchins, Wm. Hoblitzell, Hugh Howland, Frederick Johnson, James Jacobs, C. M. McCulloh, T. B. McCulloh, Thomas McNeill, J. B. Oder, Thomas Phillips, Robert Puder, Robert Pasco, W. H. Ravenscraft, James Reid, Walter B. Spill, D. Stewart, Alexander Tennant, B. J. Thomas, J. P. Tibbits, James H. Ward, William Warn, G. W. Zeller.

The lodge meets on the second and fourth Thursday evenings of each month.

Frostburg Lodge, No. 49, I. O. O. F., is the pioneer lodge of Odd-Fellowship in the city, and was chartered Oct. 26, 1846. The original five members, those who applied and received the charter, were Asa Ricketts, Edward Thomas, George Armstrong, Sr., George Armstrong, and J. B. Quigley. This charter was signed by Archer Roones, who was then Grand Master of the State, and also by E. P. Holden, R. W. D. G., G. W. Tewksbury, Grand Secretary, and William Boylen, Grand Treasurer.

The lodge since its institution has seen two new lodges spring up in the city, and has met regularly in the old hall on South Water Street with the exception of a few years, when it occupied the lodge-room in the hall which was erected by it and the other two lodges conjointly. The officers in 1881 were:

N. G., Henry M. Boettner; V. G, Adam Wagner; Sec., J. W. Fallon; Treas., G. B. McCulloh; P. G., Harry Odgers; W., Thomas S. Parker; Trustees, George B. McCulloh, J. W. Fallon, P. P. Mason.

The lodge numbers over one hundred and fifty members.

Frostburg Encampment, No. 29. Upon application from the following parties, Levi B. Porter, James L. Tennant, George B. McCulloh, Alexander F. Reckner, Thomas J. Thomas, John Smith, and Joseph Jones, the Grand Lodge granted a charter May 20, 1872. The meetings are held in the hall on Water Street. The officers elected for 1881 were:

C. P., James Prout; S. W., Thomas Hill; J. W., George P. Tennant; H. P., Philip Oss; Scribe, Robert Tennant, Jr.; Treas., George Boettner; Trustees, L. B. Porter, George Boettner, and George B. McCulloh.

L. B. Porter, through whose indefatigable efforts the charter was obtained, has occupied the position of Deputy District Grand Master for thirty-one years.

Heine Lodge, No. 127, I. O. O. F. Grand Master William Kirk and Grand Secretary John M. Jones, I. O. O. F., visited Frostburg, Oct. 2, 1874, for the purpose of instituting two new lodges of the order. In the evening of that day these officers, assisted by District Deputy Grand Masters Gephart, of Cumberland, and Sheets, of Westernport, and Mason, of Frostburg, instituted a German lodge under the style and title of the above, with fifteen charter members.

After the usual ceremonies of institution were completed the lodge elected their officers, as follows: N. G., August Eickhorn; V. G., Daniel Kropf; Sec., B. Stern; Treas., C. Lapp. These officers, after being installed in proper form, appointed their subordinates, and were then proclaimed by the Grand Master to be a regular working lodge of Odd-Fellows of Maryland. The officers elected for the second term of 1881 were:

S. P. G., Andrew Lapp; N. G., John Rupp; V. G., Conrad Miller; Sec., Frederick Mitchell; Treas., John Peffer.

They were installed by District Deputy Grand Master Levi B. Parrier.

Savage Mountain Lodge, No. 128, I. O. O. F. This lodge was instituted Saturday evening, Oct. 3, 1874, with a membership of twenty-five members. The officers were chosen as follows: N. G., Reuben Anthony; V. G., William Noel; Sec., Gershon Anthony; Treas., Owen Price. These gentlemen were installed by Grand Master William Kirk, Grand Secretary John M. Jones, and District Deputy Grand Masters Gephart and Sheetz. The officers elected in June for the second term of 1881 were:

S. P. G., Alexander T. Reckner; N. G., Owen Lewis; V. G., Owen England; Sec., Thomas Bath; Treas., Gerson Anthony; Rec. Sec., John B. Rees.

Frostburg Lodge, No. 590, Knights of Honor, was instituted in Frostburg, April 17, 1877, by District Deputy Dictator P. L. Teeple, of Ohio. The first officers elected were as follows:

P. D., Dr. G. Ellis Porter; D., Charles D. Johnston; V. D., Robert Matheney; A. D., Alex. B. Johnston; C. W., H. McGiffert; G., C. E. Chipley; R., Duncan J. Sloan; F. R., James Murray; T., A. J. Clark; Guard, R. M. Boyd, Jr.; S., James W. Nicklin; Trustees, Joseph Myers, James R. Anderson, M. F. Cline.

The charter which was granted to this organization bears the date of Oct. 18, 1877, and contains the names of the following persons: Charles Walker, Walter Edwards, Thomas Hill, Josiah Ford, John S. Kidwell, Philip Michael, Joseph Jandorf, B. Stern, Conrad Lapp, George A. Winegart, George M. Crow, Conrad Ort, Jr., Daniel Krapf, J. B. Oder, George Ort, C. F. Hartzell, C. W. Oder, Louis Kreiling, John F. Ort, Horace Beall, William H. Koch, William H. Ravenscraft, C. H. Getzendanner. The lodge has always held its meetings in the Odd-Fellows' Hall on South Water Street.

The first officers elected under the charter were:

P. D., W. H. Ravenscraft; D., C. H. Walker; V. D., Joseph Jandorf; A. D., Walter Edwards; Chaplain, Daniel Kraff; Guide, C. W. Oder; Rep., Thomas Hill; Fin. Col., Horace Beall; Treas., W. H. Koch; Guardian, G. M. Crow; Sentinel, J. S. Kidwell; Trustees,—long term, J. B. Oder; intermediate term, Philip Michael; short term, Conrad Lapp. The officers elected in December, 1880, for 1881, were: D., George Ort; V. D., Lewis Kreiling; A. D., B. Stern; Chap., Rev. J. P. Wilson; Guide, J. S. Kidwell; Fin. Rep., Josiah Ford; Rep., Thomas Hill; Treas., C. W. Walker; Guardian, Conrad Ort, Jr.; Sentinel, A. A. Rogers; Med. Examiner, Dr. W. H. Ravenscraft; Trustees, George B. McCulloh, George A. Winegart, J. B. Oder; Representative to Grand Lodge, A. A. Rogers; Alternate, Philip Michael.

A branch of the Irish Land League was formed in the basement of St. Michael's church, Jan. 2, 1881, with the following temporary officers: President, Michael Carney; Vice-President, Peter Cordial; Rec. Sec., James Sloan; Fin. Sec., J. P. Moody; Treas., Andrew Carney. The object was to alleviate the condition of the tenantry of Ireland, and all persons, irrespective of creed, condition, or nationality, were requested to become members. The following were the permanent officers:

President, J. P. Moody; Vice-Presidents, John Burns, Joseph O'Connor, and Michael Carney; Rec. Sec., G. Robert Cooper; Cor. Sec., P. Hoye; Fin. Sec., Charles Henry; Treas., Edward Donohue; Executive Committee, James Sloan, John McCaughn, W. N. Broderick, John O. Winter, and P. McCaffery.

The League numbers about one hundred and fifty members.

St. Joseph's Benevolent Society meets the first Sunday of every month in the basement of St. Michael's church.

St. Michael's Temperance and Beneficial Society meets the third Sunday of every month at the same place.

St. Michael's Total Abstinence Society meets the fourth Sunday of each month at the same place.

McPherson Post, No. 20, G. A. R., was formed Sept. 8, 1881, by Gen. Ross, assisted by Adjt.-Gen. Suter, Inspector Johnson, and Graham Dukehart, A.D.C., National staff. The officers elected were:

C., John Douglas; S. V. C., William Atkinson; J. V. C., G. L. Bennett; O. D., Samuel Nichols; Q., William McIndoe; O. G., John Martin; Chaplain, C. C. Shockey.

Thoburn Post, No. 21, G. A. R. Gen. William E. W. Ross, commanding Department of Maryland, Grand Army of the Republic, on Sept. 9, 1881, admitted this post into the organization. Gen. Ross was assisted by Adjt.-Gen. Suter, Inspector Johnson, and Graham Dukehart, A.D.C., National staff. The officers elected were:

C., William H. Koch; S. V. C., Thomas Hill; J. V. C., Jacob Keller; O. D., L. T. Dewitt; Q., William Thomas; O. G., Lewis Skidmore; Chaplain, James P. Smith.

This post was named in honor of the late Col. Joseph Thoburn, of the First Virginia Regiment, U.S.A.

About twenty members of Tyler Post, of Cumberland, accompanied by their drum-corps, attended the institution of the post.

The Orion Literary Sociable meets every Thursday evening at places of weekly appointment.

The Welsh Literary Class meets every Thursday evening in Welsh Congregational church.

Mount Pleasant Lodge, No. 3, of the Independent Order of Foresters, was instituted Sept. 30, 1874, being the third lodge organized in the State of Maryland. The special dispensation was granted to David

Griffiths, Levi B. Porter, Abraham E. Bennett, Rees Harris, Wm. Lewis, Thos. Lewis, Charles C. Cleveland, George Gunnett, Joseph Huston, Charles B. Michael, Wm. John, John Powell, Wm. Thomas, Samuel Meyers, John Richards. The charter was obtained Oct. 20, 1875. The lodge has always since its formation met in the Odd-Fellows' Hall, on South Water Street. It meets every Monday evening.

Ancient Order of Free Gardeners. Adam Lodge, No. 5, was organized in 1877, and its by-laws were approved Jan. 24, 1877, by Joseph Graham, R. W. G. M., John Gedder, D. G. M., G. Walker, G. T., and W. H. Steen, Grand Secretary. It meets every Monday evening.

Court Wincland Rangers, A. O. F., meet every Friday evening at Foresters' Hall, Bowery Street.

Light of Wales Lodge, Ivarites, No. 20, Class E, meets first and third Saturdays of every month in a room over D. Thomas' store.

Fraternity Council, American Legion of Honor, was instituted in Odd-Fellows' Opera House on Friday evening, July 22, 1881, by Dr. W. J. Craigen, Deputy Supreme Commander, of Cumberland. The order is similar to the Knights of Honor in the benefits arising from it. About fifty-five persons joined the order, and the following officers were elected:

C., C. H. Walker; V. C., R. W. Mason; O., William Brace; P. C., L. T. De Witt; Sec., George M. Perdeu; C., J. S. Metzger; Treas., G. B. Wack; Chap., Rev. J. P. Wilson; G., B. J. Thomas; W., Alfred Jeffries; Sentry, John Jeffries; Trustees, P. Michael, Enoch Clise, J. J. Keller; Representative to Grand Council, L. T. De Witt.

The officers remain unchanged at the present time, with the exception of George M. Perdeu, who was succeeded by John M. Zimmerly as secretary, and T. G. Mason was the successor of J. S. Metzger.

Knights of Pythias, Frostburg City Lodge, No. 88, was instituted under a dispensation granted April 18, 1874, with the following officers:

P. C., Charles H. Getzendanner; C. C., John Fiddy; V. C., R. J. Harvey; P., Robert R. Stevens; M. of E., E. J. Hitchins; M. of F., F. D. Thomas, Jr.; K. of R. S., O. G. Getzendanner; M. at A., A. J. T. Lewis; I. G., H. Reidler; O. G., G. D. Noel.

The charter, granted Jan. 28, 1875, named the above officers, except that Clement Riddler was made M. of A., A. J. T. Lewis made M. of F., and F. D. Thomas, Jr., made M. of E. The officers for 1881 were:

P. C., John B. Rees; C. C., Thomas J. Williams; V. C., Thomas A. Evans; P., Jabez Warn; K. of R. and S., George M. Perdeu; M. of E., John T. Lewis; M. of F., Thomas Bath.

Mountain Spring Lodge of Good Templars, No. 12, now numbering nearly three hundred members, was organized March 2, 1880. The officers for three terms of 1881 were:

First Term—P. W. C. T., T. G. Mason; W. C. T., W. S. Burton; W. V. T., Miss Agnes Davis; W. R. S., W. H. Carson; W. F. S., J. A. Wagner; W. T., George Conner; W. M., Wm. Kennedy; W. C., W. B. Baird; W. D. M., Miss Kate Bath; W. A. R. S., Miss Lucy Kalbaugh; W. I. G., Miss Annie Thomas; W. O. G., A. B. Largent; W. R. H. S., Miss Annie Williams; W. L. H. S., Miss Mary J. Taylor.

Second Term—W. C. T., John E. Johns; W. V. T., Mrs. Alcinda Thomas; W. R. S., Wm. Dande; W. F. S., A. B. Largent; W. T., Miss Emma Bath; W. M., W. Kennedy; W. C., Joseph Morris; W. D. M., Miss Kate Bath; W. A. R. S., David Hill; W. I. G., Miss Lizzie Fuller; W. O. G., Lincoln Warn; W. R. H. S., Miss Maggie Davis; W. L. H. S., Miss Bertha Biddington.

Third Term—W. C. T., R. P. Mason; W. V. T., Miss A. R. Hartzel; W. R. S., David Hill; W. F. S., Joseph Bear; W. T., Miss Rosa Martin; W. M., Lincoln Porter; W. C., John Conner; W. D. M., Miss Maggie Jeffries; W. A. R. S., Miss Mary Shaw; W. I. G., Miss Mary Davis; W. O. G., Thomas G. Mason; W. R. H. S., Miss Annie Bailey; W. L. H. S., Miss Jane Phillips.

The Representatives to the Grand Lodge for 1881 were Wm. H. Carson, J. A. Daily, J. M. Zimmerman.

The Young Men's Christian Association was organized in July, 1873, with the following officers and committees:

President, Dr. Wm. H. Ravenscraft; First Vice-President, William Staples; Second Vice-President, John McKinley; Recording Secretary, Reuben Anthony; Corresponding Secretary, R. P. Mason; Committee on Library and Reading-room, R. W. Mason, R. R. Sanner, Gilmore Wade; on Lectures and Reading, Rev. L. T. Widerman, Owen Hitchins, Gershon Anthony; Finance, Davisson Armstrong, Thomas Hill, John W. Griffin; Tract Distribution, John Meagher, George Richardson, Moses Evans; Prayer-meetings, Douglas Percy, George Richardson, John James; Membership, Reuben Anthony, Thomas Hill, R. P. Mason; Visitation, Rev. S. H. Griffith, Henry Morgan, Richard Bond; Music, Gilmon Wade, Thomas Hill, Henry Schumacher; Temperance, J. W. Gilbert, Douglas Percy, J. S. Metzger; Open-air Meetings, John McKinley, John W. Griffin, Davisson Armstrong.

They first held their meetings in the lecture-room of the Methodist Episcopal church, but afterwards leased the hall over Hartman's shoe-store. In 1875 a reorganization took place, and the following were chosen officers for that and succeeding years:

1875.—President, John T. Smith; Vice-President, D. L. McKenzie; Treasurer, J. W. Berry; Recording Secretary, George M. Perdeu; Corresponding Secretary, R. P. Mason.

1876.—President, R. P. Mason; Vice-President, Douglas Percy; Treasurer, Miss Sue Armstrong; Corresponding Secretary, A. R. Hatzell; Recording Secretary, George M. Perdeu.

1877.—President, George M. Perdeu; Vice-President, John Harris; Treasurer, Wm. Oats; Corresponding Secretary, J. H. Mason: Recording Secretary, R. P. Mason.

1878.—President, Thomas Rowe; Vice-President, Edward Howell; Treasurer, Walter B. Sprill; Corresponding Secretary, R. P. Mason; Recording Secretary, J. H. Mason.

1879.—President, Wm. McLuckie; Vice-President, Joseph Morris; Treasurer, Wm. B. Spill; Recording Secretary, Wm. Johns.

1880.—President, John A. Thomas; Vice-President, John Conrad; Recording Secretary, William Johns; Corresponding Secretary, Thomas Rowe; Treasurer, R. P. Mason.

1881.—President, John Conrad; Vice-President, William E. Walsh; Recording Secretary, John E. Johns; Treasurer, A. A. Rogers.

In the year 1878, under the charge of C. F. Nickel, a band was organized. The officers are as follows: President, Thomas Gunter; Secretary, F. W. Maury; Treasurer, Philip Pfieffer. The band comprises nineteen pieces at present, although when they were in attendance at the Sesqui-Centennial in Baltimore twenty-four musicians were in the organization. The members of the band are as follows: C. F. Nickel, leader; John Roop, bass; Adam Krouse, bass; Joseph Kauffman, bass; Peter Pressman, E. B.; John Miller, E. B.; Philip Pfieffer, clarionet; William Wink, alto; Wm. Horchler, alto; F. W. Maury, alto; Thomas Lewis, B flat; Thomas Gunter, B flat; George Vogtman, tenor; George Ort, tenor; George Horchler, clarionet; Wm. Wink, bass drum; Peter Dailey, tenor drum; John Marbach, cymbals.

Building Associations.—Frostburg: President, William G. McMillan; Secretary, Thomas Hill; Treasurer, Nelson Beall; Solicitors, Brace & Richmond.

Frostburg Mutual: President, H. W. Mason; Secretary, Thomas Hill; Treasurer, William B. Thomas; Solicitors, Brace & Richmond.

Frostburg Perpetual: President, William Staples; Secretary, J. B. Oder; Treasurer, James Kane; Solicitors, Brace & Richmond.

St. Joseph Society's Band, John A. Roop, leader, meets on Main, near Bowery Street.

The natives of Scotland in Frostburg and vicinity annually celebrate the anniversary of the patron saint of their native land (St. Andrew's Day) on November 30th, at which, after a supper, the songs of Scotland are sung and her traditions related.

The executive committee for 1881 were Peter McDonald, David Hartley, James Dumpster, James Hokkess, John Brinlow, George Chapman, David Frew, Hugh Duncan, Robert S. Harvey.

Fire of 1874.—At about twenty minutes past one o'clock on Saturday, Sept. 5, 1874, a fire broke out in the loft of the store of Beall & Koch, on Main Street, nearly opposite St. Michael's Catholic church. The flames gaining headway soon extended to the adjoining roofs of Keller and the old Franklin Block. This row of buildings, including Marx Wineland's extensive store, next caught fire, and being very dry wooden structures, were in a few minutes a sheet of flames. From the Franklin Block the fire moved southward on Broadway, and crossed Mechanic Street to a large stable owned by the Hoblitzell heirs. From Mechanic Street the fire swept around on Water Street, in both directions. The Cumberland fire-engines arrived about three o'clock, and after a sharp struggle conquered the flames.

The losses on Main, or Union, Street were as follows: Beall, Koch & Co., dry-goods dealers, building and goods, $30,000; J. J. Keller, grocer, building and goods, $15,000; Marx Wineland, dry-goods dealer, building and goods, $45,000. These establishments were insured to the value of two-thirds of the property destroyed. John Huntley, hardware dealer, $3000, said to have been uninsured; Madame Van Klaiser, millinery, $1500; T. S. Metzger & Co., stationery, $1000, insured; August Theopil, confectioner, $1500. These four establishments were in what was known as the Franklin Block, owned by the Hoblitzell heirs, loss in building about $6000. English Lutheran church, damaged to the amount of $10,000, insured; Lutheran parsonage, some $1000, insured; Hitchins Bros., dry-goods dealers, damage to stock by removal, $300; Frostburg *Mining Journal* office, damage to stock by removal, $100; Peter Payne, damage to property, $300.

On Broadway the following losses occurred: L. M. Gorsuch's stable, owned by Hoblitzell heirs, $1500, insured; L. B. Porter, liquor-dealer and grocer, Porter's Hall building, containing Porter's establishment, barber-shop, and saloon, $15,000, insured; Douglas Percy, damage to buildings, $600, insured; William R. Percy, grocer, damage to building and goods, $600, insured.

The losses on Mechanic Street were Hitchins Bros., three tenement-houses, $1800, insured; Mrs. Joseph Keller, two tenement-houses, $1000, insured, $700; Philip Michaels, blacksmith and wagon-maker, $1000, insured; McCormick & Locke, wagon-makers, loss $1200; Nelson Beall, small dwelling and office, $800; Dr. Englar's stable, $800, insured.

On Water Street the following property was destroyed: Mrs. Joseph Preston, corner Mechanic and Water, saloon and bowling-alley, $500; Hoblitzell heirs, three double dwelling-houses, $4500, insured; J. W. Tomblinson, wagon-maker, shop and stock, $1000, no insurance; Mrs. Sarah Taylor, brick residence, $2000; Levi Taylor's residence, $1200; Geo. Humbertson, three dwellings, $1800, no insurance.

Totals, Main, or Union, Street, $114,700; Broadway, $17,600; Mechanic, $6600; Water, $11,000. Aggregate loss, $149,900.

EAST FROSTBURG DISTRICT, No. 12.

The metes and bounds of the Twelfth District of Allegany County are:

"Beginning at a point on the so called Legislative, or New County road, leading from Barrelville to Westernport, at the southeast corner of District No. 11, and on the line of Lonaconing District No. 10, and running thence with the lines of said Lonaconing District by a straight line to the mouth of Matthew's Run; thence up and with Matthew's Run easterly, and with the line of said Lonaconing District to the top of Dan's Mountain; thence with the top of Dan's Mountain northerly to the Red, or Rock Hill on the National turnpike; thence with the top of Piney Mountain to the present existing line of Mount Savage District; thence with the line of said Mount Savage District westerly through the lands of Josiah Porter, and on the north side of Hansell's old mill to the centre of the aforesaid Legislative road from Barrelville to Westernport; thence with the centre of said road southerly to the centre of the National turnpike, nearly opposite the McCulloh house in Frostburg; thence with the centre of said National road to its intersection with Bowery Street; and with the centre of Bowery Street by a straight line to the centre of the aforesaid Legislative road from Barrelville to Westernport; and with the centre of said road southerly to the place of beginning."

It is bounded on the north by Mount Savage District, east by River (Cumberland) District and Rawlings' District, south by East Lonaconing District, and west by Frostburg District.

The mining village of Eckhart Mines is near Frostburg, on the Eckhart Branch of the Cumberland and Pennsylvania Railroad. It is picturesquely situated in a basin formed by Dan's and Great Savage Mountains, making it one of the most interesting mining villages in the Cumberland coal-fields. The place has grown up in the past twenty years. There are four stores of general merchandise and several groceries. Dr. M. M. Townsend is the resident physician. It has two churches,—the Baptist, Rev. William P. Fortney, and the Methodist Episcopal.

Clarysville and Parkersburg are small mining villages east of Frostburg. They have recently sprung into existence owing to the unprecedented increase of the coal traffic.

Pompey Smash is a small village on the side of Dan's Mountain. It is the home of several hundred miners of Welsh, Scotch, and Irish extraction. The habits and customs of their native countries are very generally preserved. They are an honest, hard-working class, whose wants are few and easily supplied. Near the town are the Consolidation and Grant coal-mines, which furnish employment to the residents. Population in 1880, 535.

Near the residence of Mr. John Kirby, between a quarter and a half-mile from Pompey Smash, on the Consolidation Coal Company's "Vale Farm," stands a beautiful granite monument, about ten feet high, mainly dedicated to the "memory of Col. William Lamar, a soldier of the Revolution." A lengthy inscription on two sides of the quadrangular shaft details his gallant and faithful services as a soldier and amiable qualities as a gentleman, supplemented by a tribute to his excellent wife. The third side is given to the names of his infant grandchildren buried on the same spot, brothers and sisters of William O. Sprigg, of Cumberland, who is the only surviving son of Michael C Sprigg, and grandson of Col. Lamar. During his long and eventful life Col. Lamar was a stirring, active man. He went wherever duty called him, and flinched from no hardship which its performance entailed. At an advanced age he braved the rigor of a winter day in search of lost cattle. He was subsequently found dead on the "Workman Farm," near Frostburg.

The inscription on Col. Lamar's tombstone reads as follows:

"In memory of Col. William Lamar, a soldier of the Revolution. At the tap of the drum in his native State (Maryland) to the standard of his country he flew, nor left until she was acknowledged free and independent amongst the nations of the earth. At the battles of Harlem Heights, White Plains, Germantown, Monmouth, Staten Island, in the North; at Guilford Court-house, Eutaw, Camden, the capture of Forts Mott, Granby, Waterel, and the siege of '96,' in the South, he was present and actively engaged and by his coolness, bravery, and skill he rendered most signal and important services to the army. At Guilford, the desperate charge of the American troops which turned the scale of victory in their favor was ordered at his suggestion, which was communicated to Gen. Greene through Maj. Anderson, and the plan of firing Fort Mott, which was successfully adopted, and which occasioned the immediate surrender of that fort by the British, originated exclusively with him. In the disastrous battle of Camden he was present in the fight, and was by the side of De Kalb when that brave officer fell. In the siege of '96' the immortal Kosciusko was his fellow-soldier, and served under him for a while. The noble conduct of this brave Pole was the fond theme of his admiration and praise through life. Entering the army at the commencement of the Revolution, he continued in it, engaged in active services, until the close of the war. During the contest he made but one visit home. He married early, had sons and daughters, the most of whom he lived to see begirt with glowing infancy. Possessing a heart full of kindness and a temper almost proof against anger, he was respected in all the relations of life. He was born in Frederick County, but for thirty years previous to his death resided in Allegany, where he died Jan. 9, 1838, aged eighty-three. Also sacred to the memory of Margaret Lamar, his wife. She was beloved and esteemed by all who knew her for the many virtues that adorn her character. She died, universally lamented, March 17, 1821, aged fifty-four years."

Col. Lamar's wife was Margaret Worthington, daughter of John and Mary (Todd) Worthington. Ann, a sister of Col. Lamar's wife, married Dr. John Cradock, son of Rev. Thomas Cradock. One of

Col. Lamar's daughters, Louisa, was the second wife of Col. Frisby Tilghman, Col. Tilghman's first wife being Anna M. Ringgold, a sister of Gen. Samuel Ringgold. Another daughter of Col. Lamar, Mary, married Hon. Michael C. Sprigg, a former member of Congress.

Minor Gibson was born in Fauquier County, Va., on the 7th day of May, 1797. He was the eldest son of Moses Gibson, a prominent planter and merchant, who removed to Culpeper County, Va., shortly after the birth of Minor. Mr. Gibson adopted the profession of law, was educated at William and Mary College, Williamsburg, Va., and continued his studies in the law-office of Hon. John Shackelford, at Culpeper Court-house. In June, 1819, he married Elizabeth, the eldest daughter of his tutor and partner. In 1842, Mr. Gibson removed with his family to Allegany, and in 1851 returned to his old home in Virginia. After the war he again removed to Allegany County. In 1874 he lost his wife and eldest daughter. He died June 14, 1877, leaving four sons and one daughter, viz.: Rev. Isaac Gibson, Norristown, Pa.; Dr. John St. P. Gibson, who practices his profession at Staunton, Va.; Moses Gibson, a merchant in Louisville, Ky.; and James Gibson, who is in business at Lonaconing. His daughter is Mrs. Dr. G. E. Porter, of Lonaconing. Mr. Gibson was a gentleman of culture and decided literary tastes, and was much esteemed by the community in which he lived.

George W. McCulloh was born, reared, and passed his life in Frostburg. His career has been intimately and prominently associated with the town. He was stricken with paralysis, which terminated in death on Wednesday, Nov. 11, 1874. He was born at the McCulloh homestead, which occupied the ground where Dr. J. M. Porter's residence now stands, April 4, 1815. His age was therefore fifty-nine years, seven months, and seven days. During his life he occupied a number of positions with credit. He was postmaster some twenty-nine years ago, and subsequently president of the Frostburg National Bank. He was also a prominent member of the Maryland House of Delegates in 1867.

Dr. J. T. Getzendanner was born near Rockville, Montgomery Co., Md., on the 4th day of May, 1817, and was in the fifty-ninth year of his age when his death occurred, on Sept. 19, 1875. He began the study of medicine under the late Dr. Somers. To this instruction he added a course in Jefferson Medical College, Philadelphia, where he graduated. He moved to Frostburg about the year 1840, and pursued his profession with great perseverance and success. He was thrice married. By the second wife he had four children, three of whom are living. Of these, Charles H. is a resident physician in Staunton, Va., and Osborn G. is practicing law in Cleveland, Ohio. The other, a daughter, also resides in Virginia.

MOUNT SAVAGE DISTRICT, No. 13.

The metes and bounds of the Thirteenth District of Allegany County, generally known as Mount Savage District, are as follows:

"Beginning on the Garrett County line and at the northwest corner of Frostburg District, No 11, and running thence with the lines of Districts No. 11 and 12, crossing the so-called Legislative road leading from Barrelville to Westernport on the north side of Hansell's old mill, easterly to the top of Piney Mountain; thence with the west line of Cumberland River District, No. 6, northerly, crossing the Cumberland and Somerset plank-road on the east side of the old red house to the Pennsylvania line; thence with the Pennsylvania line west to the Garrett County line; thence with the Garret County line to the place of beginning."

The district is bounded on the north by Pennsylvania, east by River (Cumberland) District, south by East Frostburg and Frostburg Districts, and west by Garrett County. The early settlers were Jonathan Arnold, the Mattinglys, Logsdons, Carters, McKenzies, Durhams, Deans, Porters, Martins, Gareys, Kimmels, Magers, Yateses, Workmans, Welds, Wilhelms, Smiths, Trimbles, Thomases, Shaffers, Pratts, Malins, Monaghans, Rooneys, Brailers, Cramps, Combses, and Bluchbaughs.

The town of Mount Savage is situated on the Cumberland and Pennsylvania Railroad, nine miles northwest of Cumberland, and located on hills from one to three hundred feet above the railroad tracks, which are in a valley, making the altitude over fifteen hundred feet above sea-level. At the beginning of the century it was a little hamlet, and in 1825 had become a village of some note. In 1839 it became widely known by the erection of a rolling-mill, and in the subsequent year two blast-furnaces were established. The first operations were carried on by a company of English capitalists, but afterwards the property changed hands and was operated by the "Mount Savage Iron Company," an essentially American concern. In the Mount Savage mill were rolled the first rails made on the Western Continent, in honor of which a medal was awarded by the "Franklin Institute." For a number of years these iron-works, alternately prosperous and struggling against adverse circumstances, gave employment to a large number of operators. The population of the town was then over four thousand. The mill closed in 1868. At the blast-furnace several subsequent attempts were made to compete with more modern furnaces. Of the rolling-mill scarcely a trace is now visible, as it has been dismantled to make room for other works. The present industries from which the town derives its life are the manufacture of "Mount Savage" fire-brick (begun as early as 1842), iron and brass-foundries, and the mining of coal and fire-clay, all operated by the Union Mining Company.

In 1812, Mount Savage was visited on several occasions by Father Ryan, of Hagerstown, an aged priest, who came on horseback, and said the first mass ever celebrated here. It was subsequently visited by Father Moloway, and afterwards by Father Ryan, a young priest, in 1819. The latter was the first priest temporarily stationed there, and only came three or four times a year, remaining a week or so at a time. His successors were Fathers Marshall and Obermier, also temporarily stationed there until 1845, when the Rev. Charles C. Brennan took permanent charge of the parish, which included the western part or half of Allegany County. He remained until 1855, and his successor, Rev. James Carney, was pastor until July, 1861. Rev. Richard Browne then had charge until June, 1868, and was succeeded by Rev. Jeremiah Henricks, who died there July 27, 1875. He was buried in front of the present new church edifice, and a beautiful marble monument twenty feet high was erected to his memory by his parishioners. He was the only priest who died there. Rev. Father Patrick Thomas O'Conor, the present popular pastor, took charge in September, 1875. St. Ignatius', the first church, was built about 1825 by a few early settlers. Among these was Jonathan Arnold, who gave the lot on which to erect it, and contributed a good part of the funds for building it, and also gave the original graveyard, the Mattinglys, Logsdons, Carters, McKenzies, Durhams, Hagans, Deans, Porters, Magers, and others assisting. These were all Catholic farmers. It was a small brick building, but was ample until 1840. When iron-works and coal-mines were started there was a sudden influx of iron-workers, miners, mechanics, and laborers to this place. Three-fourths, at least, of these were Catholics, which necessitated an addition to the old church. It stood until September, 1863, before which time the old church became dilapidated, rendering it necessary to make costly repairs. As it was inconveniently located for nine-tenths of the congregation, Father Browne, then the priest in charge, with the consent of the archbishop, determined to build a new edifice in the town. The Mount Savage Iron Company gave him half an acre of ground for this purpose, and the building was commenced in 1862, and the corner-stone laid in 1863. It was dedicated Oct. 5, 1873, by Archbishop Bayley, of Baltimore. It is now one of the neatest churches in the diocese in appearance and inside finish. Its dimensions are one hundred and eight by forty five feet, with a steeple one hundred and seven feet high to the top of the cross, and cost thirty thousand dollars. When Father Brennan was the pastor he had for several years to visit a number of mission churches, among which were George's Creek, Grantsville, and Blooming Rose, and also to attend different stations on the Baltimore and Ohio Railroad, during its extension from Cumberland to Wheeling in the years 1849 and 1850. He traveled on horseback over rivers and streams, over rough and wild hills and mountains, and in all kinds of weather. These labors he zealously performed until Frostburg was formed into a parish and put in charge of Rev. Michael Slattery in 1852. About 1878, Hon. John S. Combs, then State senator, presented to the church a lot of ground for an addition to the old graveyard. The church is built of white stone, and its marble altar cost six hundred dollars.

The Methodist Episcopal Congregation, until the erection of their church in 1870, worshiped in a log building situated at the head of Jelly's Row, and now the property of the Union Mining Company. Mount Savage was a part of Frostburg Circuit until the spring of 1870, when it was set apart as an independent charge. The following have been the pastors of this church since its separation and establishment as a distinct charge:

1870-71, Rev. G. W. Hobbs; 1871-74, J. C. St. Clair Neal; 1874-75, G. A. Threlkeld; 1875-76, Reuben Kalb; 1876-78, H. Clay Smith; 1878-80, J. N. Ryland; 1880-81, W. W. Van Arsdale; 1881, Page Milburn, the present pastor.

The church, which is a fine frame structure, was erected in the spring of 1870 by Rev. G. W. Hobbs, the pastor in charge. The officials of the church for the year 1881 are Josiah Rodenbough, Samuel S. Munn, Peter Kimmel, W. W. Crow, William Lowery, J. H. Close. The membership is now one hundred and thirteen, of which sixty-eight have united with the church since Mr. Milburn's succession to the pulpit. The Sunday-school has one hundred and thirty scholars, and is superintended by William Lowery, assisted by Josiah Rodenbough.

The following are buried in the Methodist Episcopal cemetery:

Ann C. Eisel, born Sept. 9, 1799, died Dec. 21, 1875.

William Facenbaker, died March 26, 1870, aged 41 years, 9 months, 25 days.

Henry Lewis, born March 8, 1838, at Bristol, Reckley Parish, Somerset County, England, died Aug. 27, 1866.

James Price, died June 16, 1863, aged 28.

John James, a native of Wales, died March 6, 1864, aged 63.

Esther, his wife, died Aug. 5, 1860, aged 64.

Robert Laird, a native of Scotland, died Nov. 17, 1856, aged 42 years, 7 months.

Thomas Wheatley, died Aug. 10, 1859, aged 51 years, 3 months, 10 days.

Ann, his wife, died March 17, 1859, aged 56.

Elizabeth Carney, died Nov. 8, 1844, aged 54.

The first recorded movement for establishing an Episcopal Church was in 1841, when Bishop Whittingham visited the place and held service. In 1843 the Rev. M. Kehler held bi-monthly services, first in a small room, then in the machine-shop. A large union Sunday-school was in operation that year. In 1844 the church was begun, finished, and paid for. In September of the same year it was consecrated by Bishop Whittingham. In 1845 the Rev. Mr. Kehler and the Rev. Mr. Johns officiated. The Rev. Mr. Tracy became rector in 1847, and resigned in the spring of 1849. In 1849, Rev. William Greene took charge of the parish. In 1850 the bell was purchased, and in the spring of 1851 Mr. Greene resigned. The Rev. Mr. Pryse had charge of the church from early spring in 1852 to some time in 1853. Rev. P. Manning Styher was rector in 1853 and 1854. The Rev. James Chipchase was rector in 1855 for a few months. Rev. James Young was rector from August, 1856, to the summer of 1858. The Rev. Octavius Perinchief became rector in March, 1859, and resigned Aug. 18, 1861. He became rector again in 1864, and resigned 1866.

In June, 1867, Rev. P. Wilson Styher became rector, and resigned in 1869. On Sept. 15, 1870, Rev. C. C. Penick (now missionary bishop at Cape Palmas, Africa) became rector. He left in the spring of 1872. The Rev. J. W. Nott, the present rector, began his services on Sunday, Oct. 26, 1873. In 1875, May 29th, the congregation was established as a parish known as St. George's, with metes and bounds, by an act of the Diocesan Convention. The metes and bounds are those of the Election District of Mount Savage. At various times improvements have been made in the church building during the last eight years.

The following are buried in St. George's Episcopal Cemetery:

John Hoskins, died June 16, 1874, aged 38 years.

Alexander McDonald, died June 19, 1854, aged 57 years.

William Ridgely, born Dec. 2, 1775, died Sept. 23, 1847, aged 71 years, 9 months, 21 days.

Peter Shafer, died Jan. 13, 1855, aged 56 years, 4 months, 13 days; Catharine, his wife, died Oct. 18, 1872, aged 72 years.

John Guest, a native of England, died at Annapolis, April 3, 1865, aged 46.

Richard Harvey, died July 16, 1877, aged 70 years, 2 months, 12 days.

John B. Swanger, died April 19, 1880, aged 42 years, 1 month.

Peter Scheetz, born in Prussia, Aug. 23, 1813, died Jan. 3, 1877.

David Thomas, died Sept. 5, 1850, aged 67.

Elizabeth, wife of John T. Taylor, died June 20, 1857, aged 29.

Janet, wife of Joseph Thomas, died Nov. 21, 1855, aged 20 years, 8 months, 16 days.

Margaret, wife of Eph. Davis, died Aug. 7, 1873, aged 32 years.

Margaret, wife of William Findlay, died May 12, 1879, aged 68.

Joseph McCuen, died Aug. 6, 1878, aged 66 years.

Robert Graham, died Sept. 18, 1853, aged 47 years.

John Bray, died June 4, 1853, aged 22 years, 1 month, 14 days.

James Graham, died Feb. 5, 1853, aged 20 years, 10 months, 12 days.

Mary Ann, wife of David Evans, died Aug. 23, 1881, aged 60 years.

Stewart McMullen, died Sept. 27, 1852, aged 24.

Lewis G. Pritchard, died Feb. 17, 1876, aged 68.

Nancy Martin, died Feb. 9, 1873, aged 22 years.

Christina, wife of James Lancaster, died Jan. 14, 1871, aged 77 years, 10 months, 29 days.

John Blume, born May 10, 1848, was killed Dec. 8, 1870, by a railroad accident at Mount Savage.

Mary Jones, wife of George Rushton, died March 6, 1866, aged 24 years, 6 months, 27 days.

Margaret, wife of John D. Jones, died May 28, 1862, aged 40 years.

Esther Thomas, died Aug. 13, 1855, aged 67.

Richard Sanson, died Feb. 4, 1851, aged 45 years, 1 month, 14 days.

William D. Clifford, born at Fagely, near Tamworth, England, Sept. 23, 1853, died March 6, 1880.

Ann, wife of John R. Davis, died Feb. 5, 1862, aged 28 years.

Ann, wife of John Lewis.

Ann, wife of Theophilus Lewis, died March 13, 1874, aged 41 years.

On Feb. 19, 1844, the following persons met in the school-house to organize an I. O. O. F. lodge: George Armstrong, Dr. A. Bruce, J. Morgan, W. Mose, Moses Stevens, Charles Wood, Thomas Pritchard, Thomas Philips, Thomas Kinstry, Thomas Seyland, J. Jenkins, Solomon Jones, D. Reese, George Armstrong, Jr., John Richards, Charles Thomas, Walbert Wilkins, A. Jones, and William Lewis. At this meeting measures were taken to secure a charter, which was granted by the Grand Lodge of Maryland, and dated May 24, 1844. On June 4th following Past Grands William Bayley, of Washington Lodge, Baltimore, and member of the Grand Lodge, and Past-Grand Vroomans and Holtzman, and Vice-Grands Ricketts, Edward Thomas, John Gephart, Jr., Christian Renninger, O. S. Crampton, Thomas B. Kirk, B. M. F. Lander, and Van Neider, all members of Chosen Friends Lodge, No. 34, I. O. O. F., of Cumberland, met at the house of Dr. Andrew Bruce and instituted Mount Savage Lodge, No. 43. Its charter members were Past Grands Thomas Pritchard and Charles Thomas, and Brothers William Mose, David Jones, and John M. Carleton. Its first officers were: N. G., Charles Thomas; V. G., Parker Pennington; Sec., Dr. Andrew Bruce; Treas., George Armstrong, Sr. The first members initiated were George Armstrong, Jr., Solomon Jones, Thomas Philips, Moses Stevens, and Herbert Watkins. At the same meeting Lazarus Watkins and E. Morris, members of Allentown, Pa., Lodge, deposited their cards.

Aug. 31, 1844, the following committee was appointed to build a hall: George Armstrong, Sr., John H. Jones, Joseph Collins, Charles Thomas, and William O. Bryan. The hall was erected and dedicated in 1845. Present membership, ninety. Officers for 1881, second term: N. G., John M. Mason; V. G., Charles Evans; Sec., John Kleine; Treas., H. Hergot. Its meetings are held Saturday evenings.

Eureka Encampment, I. O. O. F., No. 32, meets on first and third Thursday evenings in the month.

Kemp Lodge, A. F. and A. M., No. 154, whose records were burned, meets on the first and third Tuesday evenings of every month.

Its officers for the second term of 1881 were:

W. M., A. B. Turner; S. W., Charles Witt; J. W., M. W. Howson; Sec., J. Kline; Treas., H. J. Kennah.

Its Past Masters are A. B. Turner, W. F. Walker, E. L. Parker, Jr., Jeremiah Reagan, John Hinkle.

The population of the district, according to the census of 1880, is 1934.

EAST LONACONING DISTRICT, No. 15.

"Beginning at the mouth of Laurel Run where said run empties into George's Creek; thence up with said George's Creek to the line of Frostburg District, No. 11; thence with the southern lines of Frostburg District, No. 11, and East Frostburg District, No. 12, eastwardly to the top of Dan's Mountain; thence with the top of Dan's Mountain southwest to the line of Barton District, No. 9; thence with the line of said Barton District, No. 9, westerly to the mouth of Laurel Run to the place of beginning."

It is bounded on the north by East Frostburg District, east by Rawlings' District, south by Barton District, and west by Lonaconing District.

The flourishing and important mining town of Lonaconing is located in Election Districts 10 and 15, in the heart of the coal-measures, and offers as a future site for manufacturing purposes very considerable advantages. The water-power of George's Creek is ample, and can be readily utilized. It flows through the town from east to west. Lonaconing is the first important station on the Cumberland and Pennsylvania Railroad, eight miles from Piedmont, W. Va., its western terminus, and eight miles southwest from Frostburg, twenty-four miles by rail, and eighteen by macadamized pike, from Cumberland. It is also a station on the George's Creek Railroad, thus affording competing rates in freight to all points by the latter company's connection with the Pennsylvania Company's system of railroads. The location for a city is picturesque in the extreme. The valley of George's Creek narrows to a beautiful glen, and the two parallel mountain ridges tower a thousand feet above the level of the creek on either side. Four companies, operating nearly a dozen openings, control the greater portion of the coal deposits, from which they can mine more than thirty thousand tons per week.

Years before coal was discovered in Allegany County, an Indian named George dwelt on the present site of Lonaconing. He was of a tribe whose chief was called Lonacona, the signification of which is "where many waters meet," and from this chief the name of the town is derived. "Indian George," as he was called, was always a welcome guest at the house of Capt. Michael Cresap, then living below Fort Cumberland. Before the National road was built an old State road, known as the "Braddock's road," ran from Cumberland to "Froststown," and another from the latter place to Westernport. In this valley, now almost a continuous town from Frostburg to Westernport, there were not in 1830 more than a dozen houses. At Moscow there was a mill owned and run by William Shaw, the father of the present proprietors. From there to the present site of the old Brady house it was an unbroken forest. William Davidson had a log mill about where the Savage Mountain trestle-work now is, which was washed away in the freshet of 1823, caused by the melting of the largest fall of snow known to the oldest inhabitants, it having fallen to the depth of three feet four inches in one morning. He substituted a more substantial mill, the stone for which was furnished by Henry Koontz and James Dye. This, however, followed the steps of its predecessor, although portions of the foundations could be seen when the country began to be populated. The log mill was probably the oldest in the valley, and when washed away was upwards of a hundred years old. The first settlers who came to the valley were the Groves, Trollingers, Jacksons, and Tottens, from New Jersey, and the Broadwaters, Hahns, and Duckworths, from Goose Creek, Loudon Co., Va., the Ayers, Shaws, aud Polands. Tracts of lands upon which these families lived and bearing their names are still familiar to many on the creek.

In November, 1810, the largest freshet ever witnessed in this region completely stripped the earth from the banks of Guinea Run, leaving bare the coal on what is now known as the Barton property. The neighbors from three or four miles distant assembled to see the "mountain of coal." For some time it was mined with mattocks, the covering being stripped off as in mining ore, and hauled to Winchester and Romney for blacksmithing purposes, and in later years shipped on flats to Washington. In 1814 or 1815, when making the National road, coal was found at Eckhart mines, and hauled in wagons to Cumberland or Baltimore. It proved to be so profitable that capitalists from the Eastern States were attracted thither, and made investments. The George's Creek Coal and Iron Company was the first to develop the coal-fields west of Frostburg. In 1835 parties came on from New York, and after making purchases, began preparations to erect an iron-furnace. Iron-ore drifts were opened on Scotch Hill and on the mountain opposite, just above where the New Central Company's stable now stands. The fourteen-feet vein of coal was opened on the point of Scotch Hill a few yards below the cut, on the Koontz tram-road. Limestone was procured from the mountains in the vicinity of the coal-bank. The George's Creek Coal and Iron Company began the excavations for their furnace in 1836, but the work of erecting it was not begun until the following year. Above the arch of the furnace there still remains a small stone bearing the following inscription:

"G. C. C. & I. Co.
No. 1.
J. N. Harris,
1837."

which demonstrates that part of it was completed in that year. In 1838, J. H. Alexander, C. S. Alexander, and P. T. Tyson came on to manage the affairs of the company. Under their directions the stone house, "Mansion" as they called it, now occupied by Judge Douglass, their successor, was erected. They brought with them Charles R. Shaw, a Welshman, as superintendent of the mines, and several officers of lower degree, among whom was David Hopkins, whose descendants still remain in the county. To accommodate the laborers then at work a number of pole-houses were thrown together on the flat opposite the stone house, and many a gallon of apple-jack was smuggled into these primitive quarters despite the vigilance of the bailiff and his patrol. In the same year the foundation of the stone store-house was begun, and also the saw-mill, but neither was finished until the following year. The abutments for the dam above Rockville was built by "Uncle Billy" Combs early in the summer, and he says, "It was the dryest summer I ever saw. There was no rain to speak of from the 4th of July until the following May." Fords on the Potomac that were usually impassable in the winter could be waded with ease. The charter of the Coal Company conferred powers on the superintendent similar to those exercised by justices of the peace, with additional authority to appoint bailiffs and to call out the military in case of a riot. By it he was authorized to draft, vote on, and adopt ordinances without the intervention of a refractory council. The following extracts from orders issued will give an idea of how the town was governed:

"The superintendent of the works of the George's Creek Coal and Iron Company, of Lonaconing, has prescribed the following rules for the government of all persons in the service of the company:

"Every department of the works, whether mining, carpentering, blacksmithing, masonry, or digging of any kind, is under the charge of a particular manager, by whom all the hands in the respective departments are immediately superintended, and to whom every hand in his particular department will be required to pay entire respect and obedience. These managers are selected in the discretion of the superintendent, and report to him the state and progress of the work in their particular charge. They also report the time and wages of the hands in their employ, by which report the payment of wages is governed.

"Every person in the employment of the company will be required to be present at work every day in the year, except Sundays and Christmas day; and the hours of employment, excepting in special cases, which the superintendent allows in his discretion, shall be from sunrise to sunset, with such intermission for meals as shall from time to time be appointed.

"Signals are given by tolling the great bell of the company of the hour of beginning and leaving work.

"No distilled spirituous liquors shall be sold on the ground of the company, nor shall any distilled liquors be used by any person while he is actually engaged at work for the company. The managers of the several departments are required to enforce the strict observance of this rule by dismissing immediately from the service any person or persons under their respective charges who may be guilty of a violation thereof. The superintendent requires its observance also on the part of the managers themselves.

"Monthly settlements will be made with every individual in the regular employment of the company. From the sum due him for the labor will be deducted the amount of the accounts against him at the store, mills, and post-office, and his contribution for the school fund and the doctor, as heretofore mentioned, and the balance will be paid him in money or a check on Baltimore or Cumberland, at the discretion of the superintendent.

"For the promotion of the general health a physician is settled at Lonaconing. Every able-bodied man in the employment of the company who will contribute out of his wages a monthly sum of fifty cents for the support of a physician will be entitled to medical advice and assistance for himself and family without further charge.

"Every tenant of the company is expected to preserve neatness and cleanliness about his premises, and more especially to pay attention to the stye or other places where he may keep his hogs and pigs. The superintendent will assist in the observance of this rule, and will prohibit the keeping of hogs and pigs by any person who may disregard the same.

"After the first day of January next no dog shall be allowed on the company's grounds without special permission of the superintendent, who may withdraw the same at any time in his discretion."

The "great bell" referred to is the one which hung on the store previous to its destruction by fire a few years ago.

The State road not being in a condition to haul the heavy material necessary for the construction of the furnace, advertisements for the letting of contracts for a turnpike to a point on the National road were inserted in the *National Intelligencer* (Washington), Baltimore *American*, Frederick *Herald*, and Cumberland *Civilian* on the 1st of October, 1838. On the 22d of the same month M. Frost and G. S. Evans came from Frostburg to make propositions in reference to the point of the junction of the turnpike with the National road. They were requested to reduce them to writing, and the following Thursday (25th) Maj. Powell wrote to Mr. Alexander that at a meeting of the citizens of Frostburg, of which he was chairman, it was resolved that they would insure the right of way for the northern five miles of turnpike and contribute fifteen hundred or two thousand dollars if they would terminate the road at that point. This proposition was accepted, and the road was finished within a year and a half after, under the superintendence of Mr. Serpell. The mails were carried from Frostburg on horseback for many years by Mr. Rupert, father of a former collector of Cumberland. On the 26th of November he returned without any mail, and reported that the Eastern mail had arrived at twelve o'clock that morning, but the deputy postmaster had neglected or refused to get up to receive it, and it had journeyed on towards Uniontown. Tradition does not state whether he was reprimanded, removed, or allowed to receive mails when he pleased. This mode of conveyance was continued until the completion of the railroad to Piedmont. Rupert continued to carry it until he fell dead from his horse in an apoplectic fit near Knapp's Meadow. Notwithstanding the powers delegated to the superintendent, Mr. Shaw, to summon force to assist in "quelling insurrections," disturbances frequently arose at the "Residency," a record of one of which is still extant, and is as follows: "The peace of the previous night (Sept. 29, 1838) having been broken by a riotous assembly at and before the house of William Konig, resulting in the demolition of the windows of said house by some person or persons unknown, the entire day was given to examination by Mr. William Shaw (magistrate) of sundry witnesses to the transaction, who, however, could give no satisfactory information as to the person or the individual active in the outrage. The result of the evidence was that William Konig was guilty of selling spirituous liquors on that night to several parties; that William Zimmerman was guilty of fighting, but whether as attacker or attacked could not be made out satisfactorily; that another was guilty of fighting; that a certain individual was guilty of being manifestly drunk; and that a party who had been discharged was probably the active agent in the mêlée. At night, by way of flourish, eight guns were brought to the house, loaded, and stacked up, and a scout-patrol perambulated the streets and byways to assure quietness, and if possible to meet with the rioters of the preceding night."

The stone store-house was subsequently re-opened, under the supervision of R. Graham, who succeeded Mr. Shaw as superintendent of the George's Creek Company. The management of the store was, however, in the hands of Mr. Zacharias. Trade at William Combs' store, in Jackson, was enlivened with the opening of the furnace, although he had not closed his doors at any time during the stoppage. The year following he associated with him his son, John S. Combs, who two years later became sole proprietor. Between the latter and Mr. Detmold a lasting intimacy sprang up, and proved highly beneficial to both parties. When Mr. Detmold had occasion to go to New York, he left Mr. Combs in charge of the furnace, and the year his lease expired Mr. Combs had entire charge. The mail, as before mentioned, was carried on horseback from Frostburg by Mr. Rupert, at the expense of the company, and was distributed usually by the clerk of the store, but as Mr. Graham and Mr. Detmold could not agree in reference to provisions in the lease and other matters concerning his management of the furnace, the latter did not wish to have his letters pass through the hands of an officer of the George's Creek Company, and therefore determined, if possible, to get a post-office at Lonaconing. Petitions numerously signed praying that a post-office be established were forwarded to the department at Washington. Both the Detmold and George's Creek factions were unanimously in favor of the proposition, but which of them should control the office was an important matter to be yet determined. Mr. Graham, a stanch Whig, supported Mr. Smith, afterwards his successor. Mr. Detmold selected his friend, John S. Combs, and strained every nerve to secure for him the appointment. The announcement of the success of the first part of the project, the establishment of mail facilities, was received with great satisfaction, but the failure to announce the postmaster created great anxiety. J.

Dixon Roman, then a prominent Whig politician, wielded great influence at the national capital. From him Mr. Combs got a letter of recommendation, and also one from the editor of the Cumberland *Civilian*, and on the next day started for Washington, where he obtained his commission as postmaster. On his return the contract was let for carrying the mails from Frostburg. All the expenses over $190 were defrayed by Mr. Detmold, and in after-years by Mr. Combs, until a change of administration placed the office in other hands. A desk, containing a number of pigeon-holes, still in the possession of Mr. Combs, constituted the first post-office establishment. On his return from Washington Mr. Combs had it made in Baltimore and sent to Cumberland by rail, from which place it came by the usual conveyance—a wagon.

About 1847, Mr. Detmold constructed a tram-road from Lonaconing to Detmold's Switch, near Clarysville, to connect with the Maryland Mining Company's Railroad, running from Cumberland to Eckhart mines. Over this route he received his supplies of ore, from what is now called Bucherville, and points still farther east, and on the return trip shipped the iron produced at the furnace to market. The eastern end of the road afterwards afforded transportation for the coal from Percy's mine at Pompey Smash. Much of the western end has been converted into a county road, the ballast proving of great service in making a substantial foundation for wagons to rumble over. When the Baltimore and Ohio Railroad was in course of construction westward of Cumberland, Mr. Detmold repeatedly expressed his regret at ever having constructed a road to the "Switch," and said if he had thought an attempt would have been made to reach the Ohio River at a point other than Pittsburgh (which he considered a proper one), he would have built a broad-gauge road to Piedmont. Since then the broad gauge road (of which mention is made later) has been built, and the proper point on the Ohio River reached, although had the order of building the two roads to the Ohio been reversed, this country would probably not have derived more benefit from the Pittsburgh route than it has received from that leading to Wheeling. In the fall of 1848 an unusually large freshet swept all the bridges from the creek. Large portions of the country road were washed out, cutting off communication from east to west. The creek was swollen so much that the horses could not be taken through it for nearly a week. G. Berkeybile, of Frostburg, who was visiting the family of Wm. Combs, intended to return home on the day the rain began to descend, but was obliged to remain until the waters subsided. There are many persons still living who remember the "flood" as being much greater than that of 1860. The completion of the George's Creek Railroad to its junction with the Baltimore and Ohio Railroad at Piedmont, in 1852, added materially to the growth of the town.

The George's Creek Company, after the expiration of Detmold's lease, made a siding from the main track to the foot of the "old incline," near the top of the furnace. From the opening at the top of the plane the first George's Creek coal was shipped to the Baltimore and Ohio Railroad. The Swanton Coal Company, under the management of M. O. Davidson, made strenuous efforts to put the first coal in market, but the George's Creek Company having control of the road refused to carry freight until it was well ballasted, although they sent a train of their own coal down when the track was but a series of "hills and hollows."

Dr. Atkinson succeeded William H. Smith as superintendent of the George's Creek Company in 1835, and opened a mine on the hill above where the Koontz mine load-house is now standing. This continued to be worked as late as 1867, when the present superintendent, John Douglas, Sr., made another opening farther east, which is now known as the old mine. Again, in 1872, he opened the new mine on the opposite side of the creek, and it is from the two last named that the George's Creek Company get all their coal. In the old mine a light locomotive has been substituted for horse-power, and is found to work well.

The railroad enhanced the value of property in the valley, and large speculations were made in the immediate vicinity.

The Perceys purchased the old Jackson farm for a few hundred dollars, and had the coal opened by Alexander Sloan and Alexander Tennant, of Frostburg. They sold to M. P. O'Hern for a sum considered by the citizens as almost fabulous.

Mr. O'Hern organized the Westernport Coal Company, under which the present opening and plane were made. From the Westernport Company it passed to the well-known Packervein Company, and was subsequently transferred to its present owners, the American Company. The duties of superintendent and mine-boss were performed by Andrew Patrick at the outstart, but the following year (1853) the increasing business warranted the company's employing a mine-boss in the person of Andrew Main, now filling that position for the Atlantic Company, who remained in their employ twenty-one years.

In 1855, Mr. Patrick was superseded by William C. Darrow, who, after remaining five or six years, went to Cumberland as shipping agent, and Alonzo Chamberlain, at one time the proprietor of the Mountain City *Times*, was appointed to fill the vacancy. He resigned after a few years. A. J. Clark, then their shipping agent, was transferred to the mines as superintendent, where he still remains.

About 1856, Mr. Detmold returned, and, having purchased, opened the Ravenscraft property, which he worked until it fell into the hands of the Central Coal Mining Company, with Maj. Alexander Shaw as superintendent and John Love mine-boss. About this time they opened the new mine, a short distance below the other, which is probably the first planed mine on the creek, and from which as much coal to the acre has been taken as from any mine in the region.

In 1869 the Savage Mountain Company was organized by M. P. O'Hern, and its property was afterwards sold to the Maryland Coal Company.

In 1869 the Maryland and Central consolidated, under the name of the former, with O. D. Robbins as superintendent, and in 1873 opened the Kingsley mine, about a mile northeast of the "Old Detmold," from which the coal is taken to the top of the plane on a narrow-gauge road by an engine. The company is now doing the largest coal trade in the region. Their facilities for shipping, with the exception of the Consolidation, are unsurpassed by any in Allegany County.

In May, 1870, the Davis Brothers purchased a tract of land nearly opposite the old furnace, upon which was opened the Big Vein mine. They sold out the following year to the New Central Company, under whose control it now is.

In 1858 the Cumberland and Pennsylvania Railroad having been extended from Frostburg to this place, gave an outlet for coal by canal. In 1863 the same company purchased the George's Creek Railroad, which does as heavy a coal traffic in proportion to its length as any road in the country. At first a single passenger-car attached to the rear of a coal-train carried all the passengers to and from Cumberland; now there are two trains daily, in which at times it is difficult to get a seat.

In 1851, C. E. Detmold operated the old furnace on the property of the George's Creek Coal and Iron Company, whose superintendent was W. H. Smith. The number of coal-diggers was fifteen, who received thirty cents for lump-coal and twenty for fine. They had to divide it, which made about twenty-five cents per ton for average digging. Their output was thirty trips a day, or sixty tons. The cars held one ton each. The population of the town was then small, depending on the furnace, and was composed chiefly of German, Welsh, and Irish, with a sprinkling of English, besides the natives. The election district was formerly part of Frostburg, which was the voting-place. The first Sunday-school, a union school, was established in 1852.

The George's Creek Coal and Iron Company built the George's Creek Railroad from Piedmont to one mile above Lonaconing, which it finished in 1853, and it sold this road in 1863 to the Cumberland and Pennsylvania Railroad Company, which had built the road from Cumberland to its terminus above Lonaconing. This coal and iron company gave the lots for all the churches. The town contains the workmen's houses of the Maryland Coal Company and of the George's Creek Coal and Iron Company, and lots leased or sold by the latter. In 1853 the George's Creek Company built the houses and leased them. In 1852 there were but five houses between Westernport and Lonaconing. In the latter there were then but eighteen dwellings, the oldest of which was the old frame building now opposite the residence of Judge Douglas. The first store was kept by the company up to 1858, when Mr. Hoblitzell rented it. The first brick used by the company were brought from Baltimore. In 1853, on the opening of the mines and renewal of work, the company had to build houses for its workmen. After the war closed the coal operations largely increased, and the town grew rapidly in population and wealth. The company sold lots to the amount of over fifty thousand dollars. Many of the workmen own the houses in which they reside. The purchasers (miners) built double houses on the lots purchased by them, living in one and renting the other. The first resident physician in the town was Dr. Herman, a German, who subsequently removed to Oregon. The first boarding-house or hotel was the frame house nearly opposite the Presbyterian church. In Lonaconing, on the 19th of April, 1861, upon the arrival of the news that the Massachusetts troops, while passing through Baltimore, had been attacked, the first speech was made in Maryland in favor of the Union. Dr. G. E. Porter, mounted on a store-box, addressed an immense assemblage of citizens wholly in sympathy with his subject, calling upon them to take up arms in defense of the old flag. When he suggested that immediate steps be taken to form a company of soldiers to go to the front, cheer after cheer rent the air, and before the expiration of two days a company was formed, with Dr. Porter as captain, and a letter offering their services was dispatched to Mr. Cameron, the Secretary of War. The men were regularly and carefully drilled until May 23d, when an answer was received saying no more men were needed, upon which the company disbanded. In August, when national affairs were assuming a more threatening aspect, another company was organized to form a part of the Maryland Potomac Home Brigade. Its officers were: Captain, Alexander Shaw; first lieutenant, John Douglas, Jr.; second lieutenant, Andrew Spear; orderly sergeant, James Thompson. Dr. G. E. Porter was major of the regiment, and O. D. Robbins, adjutant.

G. Ellis Porter, M.D., was born near Frostburg, Allegany Co., Md., July 9, 1830. He is a descendant in the fifth generation of John Porter, a native of Gloucestershire, near Bristol, England, who had made himself obnoxious to the party in power by singing a song of his own composition at a gathering of his farmer neighbors which was very uncomplimentary to the reigning monarch, George the First, on which account he was obliged to flee the country. He came to America about the year 1715 and settled in Baltimore County. John Porter, his son, and great-grandfather of the doctor, was born in Baltimore County, and married a Miss McKenzie, and was the first of the name who settled (1782) in Allegany County. He first purchased a farm near Mount Savage, which he supposed was located in Maryland; but upon the establishment of the boundary line between the States it was found to be in Pennsylvania. On this account he sold it and purchased the farm near Mount Savage now owned and occupied by Henry Weld. He subsequently sold this farm and settled on one near the Eckhart mine, where he died in 1810. His children were Michael, Samuel, Thomas, Gabriel, Henry, Moses, John, and Nellie. The first six were born in Baltimore (now Carroll) County, the two latter while he was living on the farm in Pennsylvania. Gabriel McKenzie Porter, his fourth son, born September, 1776, married, first, Rebecca Frost, of Frostburg, by whom he had five children, viz.: Jane, Josiah, John, Moses, and Margaret, all of whom were married and settled in Allegany County. He died at the residence of his son Moses, April 20, 1842. Moses Porter, his fourth son, born at the homestead, Jan. 10, 1804, married Amy Wade, of Frostburg, April 20, 1826. She was born in Allegany County, April, 1810. Fifteen children were born to them, eight of whom are living, viz.: Margaret Rebecca, wife of John Keyser, a farmer living in Tyrone township, Fayette Co., Pa.; G. Ellis, the subject of this sketch; Samuel Smith, teacher and farmer in Westmoreland Co., Pa.; James Dennis, farmer in Tyrone; George Westley, farmer in Westmoreland Co., Pa.; Elisha, a farmer in Tyrone; Lydia, living at Tyrone; and Lutellus Lindley, physician in Moingona, Boone Co., Iowa. In 1836, Moses Porter moved to Tyrone township, Fayette Co., where he carried on a farm, and died there June 9, 1880. His wife survives him, living at Tyrone with her daughter Lydia.

Dr. G. Ellis Porter received his primary education in the common school at Tyrone, his academic at the Connellsville and Uniontown Academies. He began the study of medicine with Dr. James M. Porter, of Frostburg, in 1848, with whom he remained eighteen months. He continued his studies in the office of Dr. Lutellus Lindley, of Connellsville, Pa., until September, 1850, after which he attended lectures at Jefferson Medical College during the years 1850–51 and 1852–53, receiving his diploma from that institution in March of the latter year. In April following he entered upon the practice of his profession in company with his former preceptor, Dr. J. M. Porter, at Frostburg, and was associated with him till September, 1856. He then located at Lonaconing, where he built up a large practice, and was its only physician until the breaking out of the war, in 1861. From the first the doctor took a decided stand on the side of the Union, and made the opening speech at a mass-meeting called at Lonaconing for the purpose of raising volunteers in response to the President's call for 75,000 men. A company was raised for the three months' service, and Dr. Porter was elected its captain. Upon the organization of the Second Maryland, Potomac Home Brigade, August, 1861, he was appointed major. In January, 1862, he was promoted to lieutenant-colonel, and from December, 1863, to the time of its being mustered out of service, Oct. 2, 1864, had command of the regiment. The doctor was appointed in October, 1864, acting assistant surgeon and post surgeon in charge of the hospital at Cumberland, which position he held till the close of the war. In October, 1865, he returned to his old field of labor at Lonaconing, where he has since continued in the practice of his profession.

The doctor has made a specialty of surgery, and, located as he is in the centre of the coal-mining region, has been called to do more than ordinary work in that branch of his profession. He has published in the *Medical and Surgical Reporter* of Philadelphia articles upon the "Sub-Periosteal Excision of the Tibia," "Anterior Extension Splint for Fractures of the Lower Limbs," and "Wire Extension Splint for Fracture of the Forearm." He is a member of the Medical Society of Allegany County, and was its president in 1876; and a member of the Medical and Chirurgical Faculty of Maryland, of which he was second vice-president in 1880. Though enjoying one of the most extensive practices in the region in which

Eng'd by A H Ritchie

G. Ellis Porter M.D.

he resides, the doctor has always taken an active interest in politics. He was elected to the Legislature in 1871 on the Republican ticket, and was the candidate of his party for comptroller of the treasury in 1876, but was defeated. He is a member of the Masonic fraternity, of the subordinate and Encampment lodges of the Independent Order of Odd-Fellows, and of the Knights of Honor. Of the latter he has been twice a representative to the Grand Lodge of Maryland. He is a member of the Presbyterian Church of Lonaconing. Dr. Porter married Oct. 18, 1853, Alcinda, daughter of Minor and Elizabeth Gibson. Mrs. Porter was born in Rappahannock County, Va., Feb. 20, 1830. They have had nine children, viz.: Muscoe Shackelford, Francis Gibson, Emma E., Elizabeth Pendleton, Minor Gibson, Alexander Shaw, John St. Pierre, Robert Bruce, and Lindley. Muscoe S., John St. Pierre, Robert Bruce, and Lindley are dead.

At the time the coal in the hills began to be developed the population increased rapidly, and houses were erected for the accommodation of the newcomers. The Scotch Hill and Pink Row houses were built in 1852 and 1854 by the George's Creek Company. The Jackson "Log Row" was built in 1852, and those on the hill in 1853 or 1854 by the American Company. The Detmold houses were built in 1856 by the person whose name they bear, and the new Detmold row was erected by the Central Company in 1866.

In 1867 the Odd-Fellows built their large hall, the lower portion of which was used for some time as a store-room by the Lonaconing Co-operative Society.

In 1865 the population of Lonaconing was about 800, and the places of business numbered four. In 1870 the population was 3003. Now (1881) there are over thirty-four houses doing business, and a population of about 5000. Among the men who have been identified with the coal interests of this region from its earliest history there remain in the town Andrew Main, John Douglas, Sr., and Alexander Sloan.

Mr. O. D. Robbins came to the region at the age of nineteen with M. O. Davidson. Four years later the Swanton plane was constructed under his management. He opened the first slope mined (Eckhart) in the region, and has located the majority of the inclined planes and all the tram-roads in the valley. It was by his advice that the first narrow-gauge engine was built by Thomas H. Paul, at Frostburg, and placed on the Barton Company's tram-road. So complete was the success that all the coal companies having tram-roads have placed engines thereon. After Mr. Robbins' return from "the wars," he accepted the position of superintendent from the Central Company (now Maryland), with which he still remains.

Mr. Douglas came to Lonaconing in 1851 and engaged with his present employers, the George's Creek Company. He was several years postmaster and justice of the peace.

Mr. Main came as boss miner for the American Company in 1853, which place he held until March, 1874, when he accepted the same position with the Atlantic Company.

Mr. Sloan has been in the employ of the Percy, Miller, and Midlothian companies, was one of the proprietors of the Spruce Hill mine, and is now superintendent of the New Central Company.

John Ryan was born in Ireland, June 24, 1827, and was the youngest of the six children of John and Margaret Ryan. His father died when he was but

JOHN RYAN.

two months old, and the children were left to the care of the mother. Three of them died in Ireland, and three emigrated to America. Catharine, married and living in New York City, is the only child except John now living. Their mother came to America and lived with her son John, dying at his residence at Lonaconing, Oct. 4, 1870. John Ryan emigrated in 1848, and settled at Eckhart, Allegany Co., Md., where for about two years he was employed in the mines, and for the following two years in the mines at Barrelville. In 1853 he moved to Lonaconing, where until 1860 he was in the employ of the American Coal Company. For the next eleven years he was weigh-master for the George's Creek Coal and Iron Company. In 1871 he commenced a general merchandise business, which he has continued ever since. He was chosen justice of the peace in 1862, and has filled the position continuously since that time. He married, May 9, 1849, Mary, daughter of Daniel and Ann Nolan, and they have had eight children,—James A., John F. X., Margaret C., Daniel A., Bridget M., Francis P., Thomas J., and Michael A. Mr. Ryan is a member of the Catholic Church, and is a Democrat in politics. He is regarded by his friends and neighbors as a man of unusual business capacity and unsullied integrity.

In July, 1865, the George's Creek Company sold the first lots to John Bell, being those on which Ryan's and Muir's houses stand. The two then brought three hundred and sixty dollars, and could not now be bought for three thousand dollars. Purchasers became numerous and the value of real estate increased rapidly, until now the demand far exceeds the supply. Houses are being built on the steep hills and far back in the ravines. Since 1865 the population has almost quadrupled, and continues to increase in the same ratio.

With the growth of the town the congregation of the Methodist Episcopal Church has steadily increased. Soon after the village was established services of the church were held, the first class being led by John Nast, of Frostburg, the only remaining member of the church being Mrs. John Broadburn, of Lonaconing. Mr. Nast at the same time held a union Sunday-school in what was known as the "Old Castle," the present site of the public school building.

About the year 1862, when Rev. Dr. Lanahan was preaching in this county, his circuit embracing Frostburg and Westernport and the country between,—he occasionally preached in Lonaconing in the "Old Castle." The village at that time contained only a few persons.

In 1865 the Methodist congregation, feeling the want of a suitable place of worship, determined on the erection of a church building. A lot of ground was leased from A. H. Stump, president of the George's Creek Coal and Iron Company, and the church built during that year. It was a plain but neat frame structure, with a capacity of seating perhaps two hundred persons. Rev. Mr. Sheffer was the pastor of the congregation at the time. This building is now used as a place of worship by the German Lutherans. Previous to 1865 all denominations worshiped in the old school-house, a building erected by the Lonaconing Coal Company.

On account of the rapid increase in the size of the congregation the then resident minister, Rev. A. M. Courtenay, conceived the project of the erection of a larger and better church building, both in plan and construction. By his exertions, ably seconded by Dr. Porter and A. J. Clark, sufficient financial encouragement was obtained to warrant the commencement of the work upon the church. Several sites were suggested, with strong advocacy of each, but it was finally agreed to build upon the meadow between Douglas Avenue and Savage Mountain plane. The land—one-half acre—was given by A. J. Clark. The building committee was composed of Dr. G. E. Porter, A. J. Clark, J. Bradburn, John Perry, Robert Anderson, C. C. Shockey, and Thomas Engelby.

The architect was G. E. Frederick, of Baltimore, and the contractor for the work George Schaidt. The church was erected, and was dedicated Dec. 30, 1873. Rev. W. H. Chapman, of Baltimore, Rev. E. Richardson, then the pastor of the congregation, Rev. A. M. Courtenay, the former pastor, Rev. James H. Black, of the Presbyterian Church, officiated in the dedicatory services. The trustees at that time were T. Engleby, C. C. Shockey, Robert Anderson, William Thomas, and A. J. Clark.

The church is a frame structure, one story high, with a basement under the Sunday-school room. The dimensions of the main or audience-room are thirty-eight feet by sixty-five feet, with walls twenty-two feet high. The entire building is heated by a furnace in the basement.

At a stated meeting of the Presbytery of Carlisle, held in New Bloomfield, Pa., October, 1860, a committee, consisting of Revs. J. H. Symmes and R. F. Sample, ministers, and Archibald McDonald, ruling elder, were, at the request of a goodly number of persons residing in and around Lonaconing, appointed to visit that place at their convenience, and if the way was clear, to organize a Presbyterian Church; and in pursuance of this appointment the said committee, with the exception of Rev. Mr. Sample, who was unable to attend, repaired to this place, and commenced services there on Jan. 4, 1861, preparatory to the organization of the church. The committee was also assisted by Rev. M. W. Woodworth. On January 5th twenty-three persons met in the old school-house, and under the direction of these ministers formed themselves into a Presbyterian congregation. These twenty-three pioneer members were James and Ellen Stephenson, John Muir, Mary Muir, Agnes Craig, Janet Smith, William McWinn and wife, John Love and wife, Thomas Wilson and wife, John Connor and wife, Joseph Laird, Sr., and wife, Archibald Hutchinson and wife, William Reed, Thomas Gemmell,

Agnes Dobbie, and John Fisher and wife. Thomas Gemmell was chosen elder, being the first elder of the Lonaconing Presbyterian congregation.

Oct. 18, 1861, nineteen persons were received into the church.

On the 26th of October, 1865, was made the first movement towards the erection of a church. In the summer of 1867 the church was built, costing about four thousand dollars. The site of the building was given to the church by the George's Creek Coal and Iron Company. The dedication occurred on Sunday, Nov. 17, 1867, Rev. J. M. Maxwell, of the Twelfth Presbyterian Church, Baltimore, being present and assisting in the ceremonies. The articles of incorporation were adopted April 29, 1868, the following persons being the incorporators: William Reed, John Muir, Sr., Isaac Collins, J. D. Skilling, and John Fisher.

Since the change in the constitution of the church in 1876, and the adoption of the rotation system by this congregation, the following persons have served as elders: J. D. Skilling, W. McFarland, James Main, James Jackson, Isaac Cochrane, John Abbott, William Murphy, and Robert Samson.

The pastors who have served the congregation and the dates of their services are as follows:

James Donaldson, Feb. 24, 1861; W. A. Flemming, Sept. 1, 1862. The charge was vacant for some months. The term of Rev. Benjamin Merrill began Sept. 11, 1863, and ended March, 1864; W. G. Hillman, July 7, 1867, to Nov. 15, 1868; A. T. Rankin, Nov. 29, 1868, to December, 1872; J. K. Black, January, 1873; W. McLeffert, Jan. 23, 1877, to September, 1878; and Rev. Mr. Rutherford, October, 1879, to April, 1880.

The board of elders under the present pastor, Rev. William H. McGifford, are John Abbott, James Jackson, Andrew Walker, William Murphy, J. D. Skilling, M.D., Robert Samson, James Bernard, Isaac Cochrane.

Rev. Mr. Donaldson, the first minister, was from the Church of Scotland, and Rev. Mr. Merrill was a licentiate of the Presbytery of New York, but afterwards became connected with the Carlisle Presbytery. Two hundred and eighty members worship at this church, and the Sunday-school, under the superintendence of Andrew Walker, has over four hundred scholars. The parsonage was built in 1867 with the church, and cost two thousand two hundred dollars.

In 1871 about fifteen members of the Lutheran denomination united themselves together under the charge of Rev. Charles Lauderbach and adopted the title of "The German Lutheran Church." This congregation worshiped in the Presbyterian church until January, 1873. In the fall of 1872 they purchased the old M. E. church, and immediately remodeled and repaired it at a great expense. In January of 1873 they began holding services in their own church, which were continued until the time of its destruction. Among the fifteen original members were Henry Zehner, August Reichold, George Richter, George Scheall, George Soher, Henry Shafer, Adam Lichtenhahn, Charles Longlatz, Lawrence Rank, Nicholas Lonreash, Leonard Coleman. Rev. Mr. Lauderbach was succeeded by Rev. Ernest Y. Sander, Rev. M. M. Moll, and Rev. Ernest Hanewinkle. In September, 1881, the church edifice was totally destroyed by fire, causing a loss of some $4000. The trustees are Lawrence Rank and Leonard Coleman.

The number of members is five. The preaching is only occasional, and by pastors from Cumberland.

Prior to the year 1859, Father Slattery, of Frostburg, held services and ministered to about one dozen families in the town and its vicinity. These services were held in an old stone house situated on "Knapp's Meadow." In 1859, Father Slattery laid the foundation for the erection of a frame church, now known as "St. Mary's." The war retarded the work, and several years elapsed before its completion. The lot upon which the church stands was given by the George's Creek Coal Company, of which Dr. Atkinson was then superintendent. Dr. Atkinson was very active in assisting Father Slattery in the erection of the church. The edifice was dedicated in 1869. Until 1868 the church was attended by Redemptorist fathers from Cumberland. On Sept. 1, 1868, Father De Wolfe was permanently located, and was the first resident pastor of the church. He was succeeded in 1870 by Father J. W. O'Brien, who has remained ever since. The church was remodeled and enlarged in 1876, and at present about eleven hundred persons are connected with it. This station was always attached to the Frostburg Church until Father De Wolfe came, it being then only a small station. Since that time it has been a distinct charge.

The Protestant Episcopal Church erected its first house of worship in Lonaconing in 1859. Rev. Mr. Gould was pastor for several years, but since he left no regular services have been held in the building. It is of Gothic architecture, is large and commodious, and finely finished inside.

Rev. C. Louderbach is pastor of the German Evangelical Emmanuel Church.

The Independent Primitive Baptist Church has no regular pastor.

The Primitive Methodist Church holds its services in Perry's Hall, but has no regular pastor.

Orders, Societies, and Organizations.—Rising Sun Lodge, No. 81, Knights of Pythias, meets every

Friday evening at Myers' Hall. Its officers for 1881 were:

P. C., John Crichton; C. C., Thomas Gardner; V. C., James Picken; P., Henry A. Atkinson; M. of E., John E. Beveridge; M. of F., Thomas Dunn; K. of R. S., Thomas Fisher; M. at A., D. L. Shue; I. G., William Fulton; O. G., William Hamilton; Representative to Grand Lodge, Alexander Dick.

Lonaconing Lodge, No. 85, I. O. O. F. The officers for the second term of 1881 were:

N. G., James Ingles; V. G., Joseph Graham; Rec. Sec., John McIndoe; Per. Sec., James Hotchkiss; Treas., Robert Boyd, Jr.

The lodge holds its meetings on Monday evenings.

George's Creek Valley Lodge, No. 161, A. F. and A. M. The officers for 1881 were:

W. M., James Frew; S. W., H. Muir; J. W., Thomas Dunn; Sec., William B. Bradley; Tyler, J. Martin.

Meetings are held on Wednesday evenings. Past Masters, John Culbertson, Andrew Main, Joseph Graham.

Lincoln Lodge of Good Templars. The officers in 1881 were:

W. C. T., William Boyd; W. V. T., Bella Kirkwood; R. S., David Lochead; F. S., Alexander Dick; Treas., Ella Duckworth; Chaplain, M. Walker; Marshal, Joseph Laird; I. G., Jennie McAlister; O. G., Burk Greer; R. H. S., Mary Cook; L. H. S., Janet Philips; Representatives to Grand Lodge, John Story, Alexander Dick.

The officers of the Lonaconing Cornet Band in 1881 were:

President, David Baillie; Vice-President, Richard Mooney; Musical Conductor, Henry Rank; Leader, Frank Stevenson; Secretary, Henry Schaidt; Treasurer, Harry Thomas; Trustees, Richard Thompson, J. Schuyler, H. B. McMillan.

Court Purity Lodge, No. 2, I. O. Foresters, meets every Monday night at Rechabite Hall. The officers elected in July, 1881, were:

C. R., J. Whitford; V. C. R., Robert Gardner; Rec. Sec., J. Garnold; Fin. Sec., Harmon Albright, Jr.; Treas., Samuel Nightingale; S. W., John Spiker; J. W., Alexander Nichols; S. B., F. B. Eichhorse; J. B., Edward Wilson; Chaplain, Mungo Walker.

The officers of the Perpetual Building Association in 1879 were:

President, Walter Ireland; Vice-President, J. W. Bishop; Treasurer, Dr. J. D. Skilling; Secretary, W. S. Douglas; Solicitor, D. W. Sloan; Directors, J. R. Anderson, J. Rankin, Jr., Robert M. Boyd, Jr., Robert White, Jacob Nairn, William Murdie.

I. O. O. F., Jackson Encampment, No. 26, meets the second Saturday evening in the month.

Lonaconing Thistle Lodge, No. 87, Ancient Order of Free Gardeners, meets every Friday evening at Odd-Fellows' Hall.

The following bands are an evidence of the musical tastes of the community: Riordan Cornet, John O. Hanley, leader; St. Mary's Cornet, John C. Douglas, leader; Stevenson's Cornet, Frank Stevenson, leader.

St. Mary's Benevolent Society meets every second and fourth Wednesday in each month at Myers' Hall.

Salem Tent, No. 28, Rechabites, meets every Thursday evening in Rechabite Hall. Degree meetings are held on the first Tuesday in every month.

Lonaconing Lodge, No. 591, Knights of Honor, meets every second Wednesday evening at Myers' Hall.

Tuscarora Tribe, No. 62, Improved Order of Red Men, meets every Thursday evening in Myers' Hall.

There are in addition to the above the Lonaconing Literary Society, National Total Abstinence Society, and Ancient Order of Hibernians.

Newspapers.—The first paper established in Lonaconing was the *George's Creek Press*, a sprightly weekly journal started in June, 1873, by Meshach Frost and J. R. Grove. It was published nearly a year, and discontinued.

In 1878, Meshach Frost began the publication of the *Valley Times*, a weekly Republican journal, which, on Oct. 8, 1881, was changed into a semi-weekly paper. Mr. Frost is the grandson of Meshach Frost, the founder of Frostburg, and is a gentleman of rare editorial ability. His paper is the recognized organ of the Republican party in George's Creek Valley, and is a bright and forcible journal.

The Weekly Review is a large four-page sheet, whose first number was issued Oct. 21, 1881, by Harry H. Robinson. It is an independent journal, largely devoted to local news and the general interests of the people of the valley, and is conducted with notable tact, discretion, and judicious enterprise.

The Fire of 1881.—The conflagration which occurred at Lonaconing Sept. 7, 1881, destroyed all that business portion of the town extending from the Merchants' Hotel on Bridge Street, near the Cumberland and Pennsylvania depot, to Main Street, and on both sides of Main Street to Castle Run, taking in about ten acres of ground. Eighty-three persons were burned out of homes and business places, and the total loss was estimated at from $100,000 to $150,000, upon which there were $65,000 insurance. The fire started in a stable in rear of P. T. Tully & Co.'s store, on the east side of Main Street, about 12.15 P.M., just as the family of Mr. Hanlon, one of the firm, were sitting down to dinner. Had the fire broken out at night there would have been a terrible loss of life, so rapidly did the wooden structures, which were built very close to each other, burn. After the stable caught, the fire extended to the store, and there being a wind blowing, which shifted several times, the fire swept along Main Street as far north as the buildings extended, and as far south as Bridge Street, where Brady's Hotel stood. It then swept down Bridge Street to the railroad, where it destroyed several buildings on the west side, the last building burned on that side being the Merchants' Hotel, kept by William Atkinson, who also kept a store adjoining. Here the fire stopped. Among the lucky merchants whose property was saved was Peter Peebles, who kept a general merchandise store opposite the Merchants' Hotel; W. E. Henshaw, John S. Combs, and John Ryan, in the same line of business. One hotel only escaped, that kept by Mr. Jackson, near the depot.

The largest and most valuable buildings burned were those of D. R. Sloan & Co., Rechabite Hall, the German Lutheran church and parsonage, Dixon's Hotel (on Main Street), the Merchants' and Brady's Hotels (on Bridge Street), and Joseph Meyers' row of buildings on Bridge Street.

Within one hour after the fire started the Westernport fire department arrived and did good service with a little hand-engine called "The Old Defender," which, up to a short time prior to the fire, belonged to the Pioneer Engine Company, of Cumberland, and which did valuable service in the Cumberland fire of April 14, 1833. It was sold to the town of Westernport for three hundred dollars. The steamer from Cumberland would not work, and the Cumberland firemen, who were willing and anxious to do anything in their power, were obliged to return home after a short stay on the scene. Had there been an engine of any kind in Lonaconing at the breaking out of the fire, much valuable property could have been saved. Fortunately, the principal loss fell upon those who were able to rebuild, although many lost everything. The list of buildings burned, with estimated losses and insurance, so far as can be ascertained, is as follows: the large stable, two-story frame building, and general merchandise store of P. T. Tully & Co., loss $10,000, insurance $6000; Mr. Hohinghall, loss $4500, insurance $3000; Sampson's double block, valued at $5000; H. Edwards & Co., general clothing establishment, $5000; Thomas Engleby, general merchandise, loss $12,000, insurance $6000; McKenley, butcher, loss not known; Williams' butcher-shop (the last two in buildings belonging to G. H. Fresh), Sowder's bakery, a barber-shop, and Dean's saddlery, loss $7000, insurance $2000; Scott, a shoemaker, Margin's confectionery, Baughman's wholesale liquor house, David Davidson's grocery, and Joseph Myers' row of buildings, valued at $20,000, insurance $5000. In this row were Mr. Eichorn, furniture saved; Samuel Barber, tin-shop; Jack Williams, barber-shop; Mr. McCousland, jeweler. These were all on one side of Main Street. On the opposite side were Samuel Barber, Jr., tin-shop, loss $1000; James Bogan, confectionery; Brady's Hotel, stable-house, carriage-shed, and Kavanaugh's saloon, loss $10,000, partly insured; then west to James Dickinson, confectionery; David Dickson, hotel, corner Bridge and Main Streets, loss $5000, partly insured; D. R. Sloan & Co., two-story brick (the only brick store burned), loss $18,000, insurance $12,000; Sloan & Douglas' drug-store, $2500 loss, insurance $1700; O. T. McDonald, dentist, loss $1000, no insurance; Lloyd Durst, butcher; Stafford's saloon, loss $350; Lizzie Bell & Brother, general merchandise, loss $15,000; H. R. Kimmel & Co., furniture, loss $2000 in goods and $2200 in cash; John Perry & Son's residences and general merchandise store, loss $2000, insurance $9000. On Douglas' Avenue Dr. Williams' two-story frame, W. Mongan's two-story frame, and Mrs. Bell's, John and David Peebles', and John Bell's houses were destroyed; also a building used as a school-house belonging to the George's Creek Coal and Iron Company. Crossing the bridge, the flames swept up Bridge Street and up the railroad, consuming the Merchants' Hotel, loss $12,000, insurance $6000; W. McIndoe, post-office, loss $2500; David and Solon Koontz's four houses, $3200, and Mrs. Donaldson's dwelling, $600, belonging to M. Bannon.

James Carrigan, a tailor from Baltimore, located in Frostburg, had his arm cut off in jumping from the special train containing the Cumberland engine when it arrived at Lonaconing. David Dickson was badly burned, being forced in one instance to pass through the flames to save his life; James Hohing had his wrist burned by a falling joist; Edward Lewis, of Frostburg, had his arm and neck burned, and Robert Sommerville, of Barton, had his foot badly sprained. Hector Bell lost five hundred and twenty-five dollars in hair material and hair-work; insurance, two hundred dollars.

During the fire the streets were filled with intoxicated men, and there were numerous fights. There was a great panic, and whisky-barrels were broken open and their contents drank by boys and men. The Cumberland and Pennsylvania depot had a narrow escape. The Cumberland Telephone Company lost several hundred dollars in poles and wires. The disaster was the most serious that has happened in the county since the Cumberland fire of 1833.

Among the leading citizens of Lonaconing is Dr. John M. Williams, who was born in Neath, Glamorganshire, Wales, Oct. 1, 1840. His parents were John and Hannah Williams, and he was the third of five children. His father and mother both died in Wales, his father, Dec. 5, 1880, and his mother, Dec. 24, 1866. Their children were William W., David M., John M., Mary A., and Daniel W. All but Mary A., who is the wife of the Rev. J. E. Griffiths, of Wales, emigrated to America. William W. is a

builder, and holds the office of county commissioner of Lackawanna County, Pa. David M. died in Lucas, Iowa, July 22, 1881, and Daniel W., a physician, resides at Shenandoah, Schuylkill Co., Pa. Dr. John M. Williams emigrated to this country in 1867, having obtained a primary education at Ruthin, North Wales, and his medical education at the London University Hospital, from which institution he received his medical diploma. For three years he practiced his profession at Maesteg, Glamorganshire, Wales, and upon his arrival in this country settled in Scranton, Pa., at which place he continued in practice from 1867 to 1877. In the latter year he moved to Lonaconing, where he has built up a large and lucrative practice. In politics he is a Republican, and in religion a Congregationalist. He married at Maesteg, Wales, March 6, 1865, Margaret, daughter of Thomas and Susanna Miles, by whom he has six children,—Amy Maud, Hannah M., Albert C., Sarah Edith, Mary Ella, and Alfred.

Ocean is a station on the Cumberland and Pennsylvania Railroad, on George's Creek, a few miles south of Frostburg. It is located in the celebrated Cumberland coal-fields, and all the land in this vicinity is owned by the Consolidation Coal Company, now most actively at work on its mines. James B. Thomas is superintendent of the mines, James M. Sloan postmaster, Drs. Price and Smith physicians, Sloan & Sloan merchants, John Ford mine-boss, and Wesley Ford clerk. The Consolidation Coal Company, in October, 1881, began an improvement on the Ocean mine which will greatly increase its capacity. Nearly all the coal that could be reached through its previous opening had been taken out. In consequence of this the company decided to make a new opening, which gave access to a large acreage of coal lying on the left side of George's Creek, and which will increase this (the largest) company's production millions of tons. Population of Ocean, 126.

Pekin is on the Cumberland and Pennsylvania Railroad, ten miles from Frostburg and six from Piedmont, W. Va. It is located in the mining regions. The Atlantic and George's Creek Consolidated Coal Company has its mines here, of which John Sheridan is superintendent. The merchants are Edward Kelly, Ryan & Hoban, Sloan & Bro., and Mrs. Sarah M. Yost. The latter is postmistress. The Methodist Episcopal denomination and the Primitive Methodists both have churches in this village. This town was laid out in 1859 by William Shaw into forty-nine lots. Population, 505.

Moscow is one mile below Pekin, and on the same railroad. It has a good school, and supports a Presbyterian church, a frame edifice built about 1856, whose preacher is the pastor of Barton Church. The people get their post-office matter at the Pekin or Barton offices. A. B. Shaw, one of the leading farmers of the county, has an elegant residence here on his large and productive farm, and also operates an extensive saw-mill. This is one of the many villages that dot George's Creek from Frostburg to Piedmont. It was laid out by A. B. Shaw into one hundred and thirty lots. The I. O. O. F. Cemetery was established in 1876.

Shaw's Cemetery, so called in honor of William Shaw, who died in 1847, has among others the following interments:

Helen Burrell, wife of John F. Dobbie, born in Scotland, Feb. 16, 1819, died Dec. 12, 1870.

Henry Petters, died Sept. 20, 1818, aged 92; and his wife, Sarah, died Nov. 21, 1825, aged 89; their daughter, Mary, died Aug. 19, 1811, aged 38.

Rachel, wife of Ezra Totten, died Aug. 3, 1827, aged 79.

Cecilia Smith, died Oct. 2, 1838.

Margaret, wife of James Totten, died Aug. 12, 1834, aged 37.

William Buckell, died July 5, 1873, aged 68.

Margaret P. D., wife of Wm. McKenly, born in Scotland, died Aug. 4, 1874, aged 30.
John W. Kooken, died Sept. 4, 1848, aged 40.
Wm. Alexander, died July 23, 1848, aged 47.
Ann, wife of Benjamin Davis, died March 23, 1880, aged 61.
John F. Beresford, died May 1, 1875, aged 36.
Catherine, wife of John Miller, died Feb. 14, 1844, aged 53.
Daniel Yost, died Oct. 21, 1876, aged 56.
Wm. J. Miller, died Dec. 1, 1845, aged 25.

The population of the district, according to the census of 1880, is 3357.

Carrigansville is four miles northwest of Cumberland, and one-half mile west of Mount Savage Junction. The Cumberland and Pennsylvania, Pittsburgh and Connellsville, and Pennsylvania Railroad in Maryland, pass here. Its healthy location, in a narrow valley, formed by Will's and Short Mountains, makes it an attractive site, and its scenery is grand and sublime. Jennings' Run and Will's Creek supply good water. It contains a good school and a Methodist Episcopal church. The place was named in honor of its postmaster, Matthew Carrigan. John Martin operates a saw-mill there. The principal farmers in the vicinity are John Bancord, A. Bukey, Reuben Taylor, Henry Logsdon, Manuel Jenkins, George Clawson.

Ellerslie is on the Pittsburgh and Connellsville Branch of the Baltimore and Ohio Railroad, near the State line, six miles northwest of Cumberland. The situation is in a valley of Will's Creek, between two ranges of the Allegany Mountains, making it a beautiful and picturesque location for a town. There are two churches—Methodist Episcopal and Presbyterian—and a public school. Mrs. J. Delano is postmistress, and F. A. Buckholtz assistant. D. Delano has a store. Henderson & Gibson are butchers. John H. Clark, miller, and Gardner Brothers have a store, and also manufacture fire-brick. This place and Carrigansville are in River (Cumberland) Election District, No. 6.

GARRETT COUNTY.

CHAPTER LIX.

GARRET COUNTY AND DISTRICTS.

Garrett County was created from portions of Allegany County by an act of the General Assembly of Maryland, approved April 1, 1872. It constitutes the extreme northwestern section of the State, and is bounded on the north by Pennsylvania, on the east by Allegany County, and on the south and west by West Virginia. Mason and Dixon's line is the boundary between the county and the Commonwealth of Pennsylvania on the north, and the North Branch of the Potomac River separates it from West Virginia on the southeast. The county was named in honor of John W. Garrett, the distinguished president of the Baltimore and Ohio Railroad, to whose enterprise is mainly due its prosperity. John W. Garrett was born in the city of Baltimore on the 31st of July, 1820. His childhood was spent in the old family mansion where his father and mother dwelt so long,—the large three-story house, with windows close down to the ground, on the south side of Fayette Street, between Eutaw and Howard Streets, afterwards made the ladies' entrance and ladies' parlor of the Howard House (or, as it was formerly known, the Wheatfield Inn). Mr. Garrett, with his elder brother, Henry S. Garrett, the only sons of their father, Robert Garrett, attended several private schools in Baltimore, then went to Lafayette College, Pennsylvania, to graduate and finish their education, which being done, they were received into partnership with their father, and the house of Robert Garrett & Sons was founded. This was in 1849, when John W. Garrett was only nineteen years of age. The elder Mr. Garrett had long been successfully engaged in business, and his house enjoyed an extensive commercial reputation. In his father's counting-room John W. Garrett obtained a thorough business education and a practical knowledge of the vast resources of that Western country towards the development of which he was afterwards to contribute so largely in brains and money. From his earliest manhood he had the conviction repeatedly confirmed and emphasized that Baltimore possessed remarkable advantages of location as a port of shipment and market for the West. His house transacted a large Western business, and Mr. Garrett was thus enabled to obtain a mastery of all the intricate details of Western transportation, which has been of incalculable value to him as a railroad president. He also improved the opportunity provided by the relations of Robert Garrett & Sons as correspondents with the house of George Peabody & Co., and other large European firms, to acquaint himself with the theory and practice of finance on a large scale, and to establish close relations with foreign capitalists.

The house was a survival of the once productive wagon-trade of Howard and Franklin Streets, groceries and dry-goods one way, "Western produce" the other. In a little city directory of 1853, under the head of "Wholesale Grocers and Commission Merchants," we find the entry: "Robert Garrett & Sons, 34 n. Howard." The building is there still,—solid, broad, three floors and a garret, with deep cellar, and much space for storage. The door-sill was flush with the street, the window-sills only two feet higher, and the space you entered was often nearly empty. Yet all this space was needed, for the business often required storage for months before an entire Western consignment was sold. The firm dealt in all varieties of Western produce, and transacted a large business in the sale of choice clover, timothy, orchard grass, and other seeds. On the first floor of the warehouse, just to the left as you entered, was the counting-room, where Mr. Robert Garrett, Sr., was always to be found during business hours,—a tall gentleman, erect, largely framed, not corpulent, with white hair, a kindly eye, a firm yet sweet mouth, and his smooth-shaven skin hale with the uniform roseate tint of healthy old age. He wore only black clothes, with sometimes a white neck-tie; and the low-quartered, well-blacked shoes in which he dressed his shapely feet suggested that he had given up pumps, silk stockings, and small-clothes with reluctance. There was the appearance of the gentleman *debonair* in Mr. Garrett as he rose to meet you, holding his spectacles in one hand, his newspaper in the other; yet there was a touch also of business-like promptitude in his manner, which was characteristic of the race from which he sprung. For Mr. Garrett was of that stern, yet mobile, daring, energetic Scotch-Irish race which contributed so much invaluable material to the early business population of Baltimore. He had immigrated from the north of Ireland with his parents when he was already eight years old, and it was not until 1820 that he finally established himself in Baltimore. The counting-room was severely plain in its equipments and narrow in its proportions,—so narrow that when Henry and John W. acceded to the firm they furnished up another for themselves farther east in the building. It is worth while to compare the accommodations and appearance of the old house on North Howard Street with those of the present banking-house on South Street. The other was a banking-house, too, and the "Western produce" business that had once enriched it was drying and dwindling up. But Mr. Garrett, Sr., was the correspondent of Peabody's London house, and did, besides, a large business in real estate and ground-rents. Upon the latter his authority was acknowledged by every one in the business, and none knew better than he the conditions which constituted "a first-class" ground-rent, or stood more ready to buy one when offered. The firm was already rich, and the two sons did the banking business; the elder brother, Henry S., a tall, handsome man, being noted for a fine knowledge of general finance, and as an operator of dash and spirit.

This (1853) was a speculative period; the connections with the West were rapidly developed; railroad bonds were largely offered at low figures in blocks, and many wealthy houses and persons were taking them in great quantities. The Baltimore and Ohio Railroad had got to Wheeling in 1852, but lay there on the river's brim panting, palpitating, exhausted, almost inanimate from its great effort, and it seemed as if its rivals meant to pass round it on every side. The road was not well equipped nor well connected. It had bought ground for the depot on Camden Street, but still used the depot on Pratt Street, while the company's general offices were still at 23 Hanover Street, where, in a handsome parlor up stairs, the treasurer, J. I. Atkinson, received you and confessed the company's impecuniosity,—the blandest, most courteous, most genial gentleman of the old school who ever bowingly acknowledged notice of a protest or a judgment. "The road will make its way through, never fear," was his daily remark; and the road did make its way through,—by other means and in other hands than those contemplated by Mr. Atkinson. It was at this period that the names of "Central Ohio" stocks and bonds, "Mariettas," and "Parkersburgs" began to be heard in the Baltimore market. They represented money subscribed by local capitalists towards the building of roads and branches, by means of which it was sought to connect the Baltimore and Ohio Railroad with Cincinnati. The house of Robert Garrett & Sons was among the largest of the large subscribers. So much had they put into these various enterprises that when the panic of 1857 came, every *quid nunc* of the stock market thought they must go down. "They are in for millions of Central Ohio seconds!" "They are elbows deep in income bonds!" So the busy gossip of the street ran on, while hundreds of supposed fortunes vanished as quickly as the breath from the surface of a looking-glass.

Meanwhile a crisis had come, early in 1857, in the affairs of the Baltimore and Ohio. The road had gone on in an easy, gentlemanly way, living upon the interest of its debts and its relations to the city of Baltimore and the State of Maryland, doing very little real work, and calmly disregarding the interests of individual stockholders. It was rapidly lapsing into helpless imbecility, while its rivals on every side were growing, developing, and taking trade away from Baltimore. The stockholders were split up into factions, and the rallying-cry of "State interest" was met by that of "Stockholders' interest." There was a meeting of friends of the road in 1857, at which John W. Garrett was present, and these questions were mooted as usual. Mr. Garrett, with characteristic decision, cut the Gordian knot by boldly declaring for "stockholders' interest" as the only way to secure "State interest." The State and the city, he said, being equally stockholders with individuals, there could be but one interest, that of the stockholders, and this could take but one direction, that of making the property productive by increasing receipts and reducing expenses. This was true, and it was unconditionally agreed to, but the means of putting it in force were still in active dispute. In October, 1857, Mr. Garrett went into the directory of the company, and those means were soon found. It took ten years, however, to enforce them finally. The charter had originally given the management of the road and the majority of directors to the individual stockholders. The road's embarrassments and many appeals to both State and city for aid had left it finally in 1857 with twelve directors to represent the subscribers, and eighteen to represent the city and State. This was what continually baffled the development of the road as an industrial enterprise, and continually threatened to make it a political catspaw. Mr. Garrett went into the board in October, 1857, as the champion of the stockholding interest and of the policy of conducting the road as a business enterprise on strictly business principles. He formulated and offered to defend the scrip dividend policy, and as the avowed champion of these two lines of policy he was elected president Nov. 17, 1858, and has remained president ever since. He had a hard and bitter fight of it,—one that must have disheartened any man less tenacious of his ground, less capable of bearing the weight of versatile and sometimes unscrupulous opposition,—but he won. In 1862 the scrip dividend policy was carried through all the courts. In 1867 the adoption of the new constitution, by enabling the State of Maryland to sell out its shares and reduce its representation in the company, restored to the stockholders their majority in the board of directors.

Since then there has been no dispute, even, about the wisdom of the policy which Mr. Garrett carried through. There have been rubs, some of them severe ones. There were the four years of war, with the road lying between the two hostile lines, the Confederates eager to destroy it, and the Unionists by no means friendly. Thomas A. Scott, afterwards president of the Pennsylvania Railroad, was Assistant Secretary of War, and every day, like Cato of old, Simon Cameron, the most influential senator of the Republican party, and the bitterest enemy of the Baltimore and Ohio, used to go into the Senate chamber and give an English version of "*Delenda est Carthago.*" But after all, the war did not hurt the road. Every new battle revealed how indispensable it was to the country, and every year of the war strengthened the country's appreciation of Mr. Garrett's talents as a railroad manager in a situation where tact was the only possible resource against force, and where any mistake must needs have been fatal. There were rubs also with the Legislature and the City Council on the old familiar question of discriminative rates, and with the Legislature on the capitation tax and the gold premium. All these have finally been settled on the general basis of business principles. The people of Baltimore know that the Baltimore and Ohio cuts rates not against their city, but for it, and the people of Western Maryland fully understand that in every case where the through rate has been reduced lower than the local one the final object is to preserve the local traffic from extinction. Every one knows what a metropolitan thoroughfare the Baltimore and Ohio has become under its present management. The *principles* by which this has been brought about and the road saved for its owners are what we have sought to set forth here. Essentially the road's present circumstances are due to the assertion and maintenance of those principles; to John W. Garrett, in other words, who enunciated and championed them from the beginning to the end.

A few words personal to the man who has had the power, during such extraordinary times, to direct men, money, and so many moral and material forces through such broad channels to such comprehensive and satisfactory ends. He is a man of large, commanding frame, more portly than his father. His face, full, with large forehead, heavy eyebrows, and a firm mouth, is one we might look for in the man who, as he once said, "stood by Stanton's side for thirty-six hours, watching the click of the telegraph instrument without rest during the pursuit of Lincoln's assassins." It is a face full of keen intelligence, the listener's attitude natural to it; full also of benevolence and appreciative human kindliness. Mr. Garrett's address is good; he never speaks without having something to say, and revealing the capacity to say it broadly. He takes a thinker's interest in the leading concerns of our society, religion, education, art, and has given largely to promote each in its kind. He converses much with men of comprehensive minds, and reads always with an eye to leading topics. When he was in Europe during his last visit it was curious to note how often some of the local press of

Baltimore would receive journals from him with marked articles, and clippings, and extracts of something which he thought illustrated the temper of the times, or might be of use to work up for Baltimore. For this railroad king is like a child in his affection for his native city. He fights for it fiercely; he loves it tenderly; his sense of duty towards it is almost a religion in itself.

It is impossible within the limits to which we are necessarily restricted to do full justice to Mr. Garrett's achievements as a railroad manager and financier. As previously indicated, up to 1857 the directory of the Baltimore and Ohio Railroad had been anything but harmonious, and the enterprise was then staggering along under heavy burdens. The capital stock of $3,000,000 was found insufficient to carry the road through to the Ohio River; and while there was no denial of the fact that more money must be raised, there was much contention over the respective representation of the State of Maryland and the private stockholders in the board of directors. Mr. Garrett, who had been elected president in place of Chauncey Brooks, on the 17th of November, 1858, listened patiently to the discussion, and then laid down the only true solution of the difficulty, namely, that there was but one common interest to be subserved; that it was the same with all parties, and that the obstacles could be overcome if the board would put economical business principles into practice in handling the property. The practical wisdom of the policy inaugurated by Mr. Garrett was shown at the close of his first year, when the increase in the aggregate comparative net gains of the company was over seven hundred thousand dollars above the yield of the preceding twelve months. It is needless here to say that the gains have steadily increased, or to trace the stages through which the stock quoted at forty-six dollars per share in 1858 rose to a stiff holding price of two hundred and twenty-five dollars in June, 1881. Such results are at least witnesses to the sagacity of Mr. Garrett's administration.

He soon succeeded in harmonizing conflicting interests, and gathered around him a staff of officials who were in full sympathy with his views. When the civil war broke out the road was on the flood-tide of prosperity, and throughout that trying and difficult period Mr. Garrett piloted in safety the mighty corporation which had been committed to his charge. His responsibilities and the difficulties which beset his path on every side were enormous; but he met them with a courage and wisdom that rose superior to all emergencies. His energy seemed unbounded, and it was soon demonstrated that he possessed a will and nerve of iron. The road ran through the theatre of the principal military operations of the war. For four years contending armies swept across it, and frequently miles of track were torn up and valuable engines and rolling-stock destroyed. And even with the road thus constantly threatened or crippled, Mr. Garrett was frequently called upon by the national authorities for assistance in moving troops at critical periods.

This was the case when men were hurried from the Virginia Valley to Washington after the battle of Bull Run; again when Banks had to be reinforced to stay the march of "Stonewall" Jackson; again when a whole army corps was shifted from the army of the Potomac to Tennessee, after the battle of Chickamauga; again when Early had conquered at Monocacy and was menacing Washington; and once more when Sheridan needed the Nineteenth Corps at Winchester. Mr. Garrett during these troublous days was in frequent consultation with President Lincoln and Secretary Stanton, who expressed in the warmest terms their appreciation of the aid which he rendered them. With the conclusion of the war he, more than any other single individual, aided in the establishment of the European steamship lines, the fostering of the grain trade, the building of the elevators, and the construction of the splendid dry-dock.

After the war he was tendered by the directors an increase of salary from $4000 to $10,000 per annum, but refused it, though offered about that time a salary of $50,000 by another corporation. Mr. Garrett has made several trips to Europe, from the last of which he returned in June, 1881, when he was welcomed home with an enthusiastic reception at the hands of the business men of Baltimore. While his European tours have mainly been taken in search of health, he has nevertheless made them of much value to his native city by consultations with steamship owners and capitalists, to whom he has presented the great advantages of Baltimore as a commercial centre. Although refusing to accept any public office other than that which he has occupied for twenty-four years, his solicitude for the best interests of the city is known to all its people. Since his return from Europe Mr. Garrett has taken an active part in the management, but for the last year the chief burden of responsibility has devolved upon his son, Robert Garrett, first vice-president of the company, who has attained that position by the remarkable ability which he has displayed as an executive railroad officer in recent years.

In his official connection with the Baltimore and Ohio Railroad, Robert Garrett has exhibited many

John W. Garrett

sterling business traits, as well as popular characteristics, to the advantage not only of the railroad corporation, but of the city of Baltimore. He combines with the sagacity and prudence of a veteran the enterprise and courage of a young and vigorous manhood, and he may be trusted to make prompt and profitable use of every opportunity as it arises to promote the interests of the company. Endowed with a remarkable capacity for hard work, a quick intelligence, and a positive genius for railway management, and enjoying, moreover, the advantage of his father's vast experience, he is peculiarly well fitted to assume the grave responsibilities which will rest upon him as the executive of the company. Doubtless as long as his health permits John W. Garrett will remain at the head of the road; but it must be a source of satisfaction to him, as well as the general public, to know that a succession at any time would involve no interruption of the company's policy, and jeopardize none of its interests. If any evidence were needed to show the comprehensive business intelligence of Robert Garrett, a recital of a few of the prominent features from the fifty-fourth annual report of the company would demonstrate beyond question the enormous work the road has accomplished in the last year of his management. It proves also that Baltimore's trunk-line is the line of the country,—in fact, the most important in the world. The revenues for the fiscal year ending September 30th aggregated no less than $18,317,740.10, an increase, as compared with 1879, of $4,123,759.67, and an increase, as compared with 1878, of $4,552,460.11. In other words, the revenues were greater by about 25 per cent. The net earnings were $5,172,980.76, or $831,735.67 more than in 1879. Compared with the great increase in revenues this shows at first sight a disappointingly small gain, large as the figures are; but he who reads the report carefully will find an explanation much more than satisfactory. Twenty-four engines of the largest class (the "Consolidated" or "Mogul" engines) and two engines for switching purposes have been built at the cost of $211,733.61; 334 cars of largely-increased capacity have been built; 697 iron hopper-cars have been raised from 20,000 to 30,000 pounds capacity per car; 297 house and 727 gondola-cars have been increased in capacity from 20,000 to 40,000 pounds; 50 additional refrigerator-cars have been built; 501 hopper-gondolas, 115 stock, and 1012 house cars, each of 40,000 pounds capacity, have been constructed, besides 5 passenger-coaches and other miscellaneous cars. The cost of 1690 cars was $716,881.32. A very large amount was also expended upon steel rails. Seven hundred and fifty miles of track are now laid with steel rails. The whole of this has been charged to *repairs*. In other words, over a million of dollars of the revenues has been applied to the construction of new rolling-stock alone, and instead of the sums being charged against "construction account," they are entered against "repairs." The dividend is provided for, a splendid surplus is left, and the stockholders find themselves possessed of a fuller and better equipment by far than ever before in the history of the corporation, and with the roadway in splendid condition. The increase in the tonnage is most remarkable. In 1871 the aggregate of through merchandise east and west was 435,207 tons; in 1876 it had reached 1,093,393 tons; in 1879 it was 1,425,629 tons; in 1880 the total was 1,980,397 tons. This increase of about 33 per cent. is almost unprecedented in railroad history. In this aggregate enter the following items: 598,992 barrels of flour, 25,962,696 bushels of grain, and 54,530 tons of lumber brought to Baltimore; 165,454 tons of live-stock transported, and 4,388,856 tons of coal, an increase for the year of 997,881 tons of coal.

But the half is not yet told. The indebtedness of the corporation was decreased in the fiscal year by the sum of $2,830,815.98. And the profit and loss account shows an increase of $2,356,984.44, the surplus fund, which represents invested capital derived from net earnings, and which is not represented by either stock or bonds, now amounting to $40,561,642.37. With all this accomplished, the condition of the tracks, engines, and cars has been brought to a very high standard, and the hotels owned by the company have been placed in superior order.

As regards the branch lines, the Washington road reports an increase in net earnings of $22,822.88, the Parkersburg branch an increase of $176,250.49 (1862 tons of steel rails were laid), the Pittsburgh division an increase of $279,545.04, the Central Ohio of $38,754.21, the Chicago of $72,142.93, the Lake Erie of $19,739.76, and the Straitsville of $42,598.54. The improved result on all the lines worked by the company aggregated $652,849.71. The condition of the Pittsburgh and Connellsville road is very satisfactory, the net earnings being $1,011,827.09, and the excess of net earnings, after paying $678,858.40 for interest on mortgage indebtedness, $332,968.69.

John W. Garrett has proved his devotion to Baltimore and Baltimore interests in many ways. In addition to the time and labor bestowed on the development and solidification of the city's representative corporation, he has extended generous aid to all local enterprises which he considered as likely to yield substantial results, while his hand has been ever open for the encouragement of worthy charities and the assistance of such institutions as contribute to the general welfare of the community. His liberality is large and unostentatious. Among the few of his gifts that have been made public is that of fifteen thousand dollars to the art-gallery of the Peabody Institute, and a public fountain costing the same amount, which he has authorized to be purchased and presented to the city. A handsome bridge over a picturesque ravine in Druid Hill Park, erected at his expense, is another monument of his generosity and good taste. He has also given largely to the Boys' Home and to the Young Men's Christian Association, and no general movement of a public character has been inaugurated in Baltimore in recent years to which he has not been among the most liberal contributors, if not the most liberal. At the meeting of the citizens of Baltimore called to raise funds for the erection of the new hall of the Young Men's Christian Association, which was held on the 22d of December, 1870, he was elected chairman, and delivered a forcible address, in which he vividly depicted the perils which threaten young men in all large cities, and warmly indorsed the association's work. Mr. Garrett has made valuable contributions to the art collection of the Peabody Institute, and has established a library and reading-room at Mount Clare for the benefit of the apprentices of the machine-shops. His own mansion contains many fine specimens of foreign and American art, and no man takes a keener interest in or derives more pleasure from literature and art than does Mr. Garrett. In his capacity as president of the Baltimore and Ohio Railroad Company he has in recent years been call upon to direct several memorable contests with rival corporations, and, notwithstanding the enormous power and influence arrayed against him, has come out from every conflict with greater substantial gains and far less loss than have any of his antagonists. He now has the satisfaction of knowing that the great railroad which he has served so long and so faithfully is on a more solid and prosperous basis than ever before, and that its future promises to be one of continuous and vast development.

His last visit to Europe greatly improved Mr. Garrett's health, and his capacity for thought and work is not less than it was twenty years ago, notwithstanding that he was sixty-one years old July 31, 1881, and has undergone incessant labor from his early youth.

The banking-house of Robert Garrett & Sons is still continued under the original firm-name, Mr. Garrett having some years since taken into partnership with him his sons, Robert and T. Harrison Garrett. As Robert Garrett is now closely identified with the management of the Baltimore and Ohio Railroad as its first vice-president, the banking business is directed almost exclusively by T. Harrison Garrett. The firm not only operates largely in stocks and bonds, but does a large foreign business, the great London firm of Morgan & Co. being among its correspondents. J. W. Garrett's brother, Henry S. Garrett, for many years a member of the firm, died on the 10th of October, 1867, aged fifty years, deeply and generally lamented in business and social circles. The banking firm of Robert Garrett & Sons still transacts an extensive and lucrative business under the able management of T. Harrison Garrett, who not only possesses great business tact and administrative capacity, but is also a gentleman of cultivated tastes, and possesses the largest, and probably the choicest, private library in Maryland.

Garrett County contains six hundred and seventy square miles of territory. It is crossed through its entire length, north and south, by the Great Savage Mountain. Two-thirds of the territory of the county lies west of it. On the east is the Maryland coal-basin, one-third of which is in Garrett County, and on the west, flowing north from the south end of the county, are the Youghiogheny and Castleman Rivers, draining, with their tributaries, other valuable but undeveloped coal and iron regions. The streams flowing from the west side into the Youghiogheny are Laurel River, Snowy Creek, Harrington Creek, Muddy Creek, and Buffalo Creek, and on the east are Cherry Creek, Little Youghiogheny, Deep Creek, Lazy Run, Bare Creek, and Mill Run. The Savage River has its source and tributaries here, and empties into the North Branch of the Potomac at the extreme eastern end of Garrett County. The geological formation is sandstone, limestone of fine quality, and stone-coal. The elevated table-lands on the western side of the Savage Mountain, and between that and Meadow Mountain, covering an area of four hundred square miles, at an elevation of two thousand five hundred feet above tide, and comparatively level, are about one-third glades, interspersed regularly by ridge or timber-land, and are admitted to be the best grazing portions of Maryland. They are only partially settled, and offer superior advantages for farming and stock-raising. Immense forests of timber cover large portions of the county. Pine, oak, maple, and all hard woods found in high latitudes exist of the best quality and growth. The products are wheat, corn, rye, buckwheat, oats, potatoes, wool, and butter. Grass grows naturally on the glades, and timothy and clover in abundance follow cultivation. The Baltimore and Ohio Railroad passes from east to west, a distance of thirty miles, through the southern end of the county, and the National road through the northern portion a distance of over twenty miles. In August, 1871, *The Glade Star*, a paper published at Oakland, Allegany Co., advocated the erection of a new county, to be formed from the eastern portion of Allegany, of which the Savage River should be the eastern boundary. It said the required constitutional elements of ten thousand population and an area of four hundred square miles existed in the proposed new county. Among other reasons for its organization the *Star* pointed to the erection of Wicomico County, which had given the Eastern Shore an additional senator and delegate in the Legislature, and which, it seemed to think, had disturbed the political equilibrium of the two sections of the State. It reviewed the extraordinary resources of the contemplated new county, especially the Youghiogheny coal-basin, which it expected to see properly developed under the influence of the Connellsville Railroad. The paper also mentioned other extensive coal deposits, and alluded to the agricultural capabilities of the beautiful "glades," and as an unanswerable argument pointed out that the territory proposed for a new county was paying twenty-eight thousand dollars a year under the county levy, and only receiving eighteen thousand six hundred and four dollars and fifty-six cents in the county's (Allegany) appropriations. It concluded by saying that Allegany County was one hundred miles in length, which was inconvenient for the transaction of the county business. The people took hold of the subject in earnest; public meetings were held all over the projected county, speeches were made in every nook and corner, and the matter thoroughly canvassed. In January, 1872, petitions were presented to the Legislature praying for a division of Allegany and the formation of a new county, which should comprise all of Allegany lying west of a line extending from the middle of Savage River, where it empties into the Potomac River, north twenty-six miles to a point on the top of Savage Mountain, where said mountain is crossed by Mason and Dixon's line.

The Legislature, by act of April 1, 1872, created the county. The first section of the act is,—

"That all that part of Allegany County lying south and west of a line beginning at the summit of Big Backbone, or Savage Mountain, where that mountain is crossed by Mason and Dixon's line, and running thence by a straight line to the middle of Savage River, where it empties into the Potomac River; thence by a straight line to the nearest point or boundary of the State of West Virginia; then with the said boundary to the Fairfax stone, shall be a new county, to be called the county of Garrett; *provided* the provisions of this act as to taking the census of the people and the area of the said new county, and the sense of the people therein, shall be complied with in accordance with the constitution of this State."

The second section provided for taking the vote as to whether the new county should be created, and also for designating the people's choice for a county-seat. The following commissioners were appointed by the eleventh section to take the census in the districts of Allegany County comprised in the proposed division:

District No. 1, James Z. Browning; No. 2, Elijah M. Friend; No. 3, Charles Bell; No. 10, J. McClure Mason; No. 11, William Hinebaugh; No. 14, D. Harrison Friend; No. 15, Ralph Thayer; No. 4, William H. Barnard; No. 16, James Poland; No. 5, George W. Blocker.

It was further provided that all justices, constables, and road supervisors residing in the limits of Garrett County who received their appointment as such for Allegany County should be continued in office, and that three county commissioners be elected. Many other provisions were made for the complete organization of the county, to take effect when the people voted in favor of the new county, and when the new county-seat was chosen and confirmed by an act of a subsequent Legislature.

Under the above act the election was held Nov. 5, 1872. The proposition to create the new county was carried by a vote of 1297 yeas to 405 nays.

At the same election the vote for designating the county-seat resulted as follows: for Oakland, 653; for Grantsville, 590; for McHenry's Glades, 456. So Oakland became the "shire town" by the bare plurality of sixty-three votes, and the Legislature, by an act of March 10, 1874, confirmed the people's choice by declaring Oakland the future county-seat of the new mountain county. In this confirmatory act the last preamble is, "*Whereas*, If this General Assembly should pass an act authorizing the holding of another election for the purpose of locating the county-seat, it is not likely that any one of the points which were voted for would receive a majority of the whole vote; therefore, in order to prevent unnecessary taxation, and to stimulate the prosperity and material growth of the new county," etc. Then followed the closing enactment making Oakland the seat of justice.

Mountjoy Bayley, appointed by the Governor for that purpose, sold, April 16, 1792, the State's lands west of Fort Cumberland, which embraced a large part of Garrett County.[1] In the fall and winter of 1875 a movement was made to create another county by a division of Garrett. Two public meetings were

[1] The history of these lands will be found at the end of the chapter on the war of the Revolut on.

held in furtherance of this scheme,—one, Dec. 8, 1875, over which Dr. J. M. Porter presided. Among those present were Senator McCulloh and delegates-elect Sprigg and Rawlings. Resolutions were adopted in favor of the proposed division, and a committee appointed to prepare a memorial to the Legislature, and another to confer with the residents of the neighboring districts. The other meeting was held December 4th at Grantsville, the leading citizens of which section were making an earnest effort to separate themselves from Garrett. The project, however, failed, the Legislature concluding that further sub-divisions of the territory of the State were not necessary at that time.

For the perfecting of the county's organization the Legislature in 1874 passed acts authorizing the State librarian to furnish the Garrett Circuit Court with the decisions of the Court of Appeals, fixing the mileage of members and officers of the county, regulating the terms of its Circuit Court, granting appropriations to academies and schools in Garrett, regulating the number of justices of the peace and constables in the county, providing for the county commissioners taking the census, creating it a part of the Sixth Congressional District, providing for the appointing of registration officers, authorizing the Governor to have a survey made of Garrett and Allegany Counties, for the protection of birds, for regulating the sheriff's fees, and for regulating fences in the county. Another act authorized the county commissioners to erect a court-house and jail at a cost not exceeding thirty thousand dollars, and to borrow on the county's credit the necessary money by issuing bonds of not less than a hundred or more than a thousand dollars each, or to borrow such sums as were needed for this purpose, and levy upon the assessable property in such installments annually as might be deemed proper. Another act of the same Legislature created nine election districts in the county by making the districts previously known in Allegany County as numbers one, two, and three, the corresponding districts in Garrett, by consolidating numbers four and sixteen into a single district as number four, by changing the numbers of eleven, fourteen, fifteen, and ten into numbers five, six, seven, and eight, respectively, and by consolidating numbers five and twelve into a single district, number nine.

Garrett County was thus firmly established with all the necessary machinery for proper government. It is the youngest county in the State of Maryland, but the enterprise and intelligence of its people have secured it already a prominent place among the other counties. An unusually large portion of its soil is fertile, and much of it is covered with a splendid growth of timber. The mineral deposits are rich, the county is abundantly watered, and the power supplied by the rushing mountain streams has been largely utilized for mills and manufactures. Grist and saw-mills, distilleries, woolen-mills, and tanneries are located at different points in Garrett, and for the most part are in a prosperous condition, while the pick and the shovel are penetrating the bowels of the earth in many directions, wresting from them their treasures, the demand for which is increasing rapidly with the advance of civilization and settlement.

The early settlers were sturdy men, who possessed the requisite qualifications for grappling with the obstacles which lay in their way. This section of the State, so remote from the centres of population, was beset with peculiar hardships and dangers. Wolves, bears, and wild-cats abounded, and the inhabitants at this late day can point to the trophies of the chase hanging in the halls of their mansions as a proof that hunting is not yet deprived of that spice of danger which creates such a strong attraction for the true sportsman. In 1760, John Friend, then well stricken in years, and who is supposed to have been one hundred and three years of age at the time of his death, moved from a point on the Potomac River east of Cumberland to the Youghiogheny, though the location selected by him there is not now definitely known. He was accompanied by his six sons,—Nicholas, Gabriel, John, Charles, Joseph, and Augustine. Nicholas and a number of other young men of the "Crossing neighborhood," enlisted in the British army to fight against the French and their Indian allies. He and his associates fell on the field of battle. Joseph and Gabriel remained where their father settled until they died, the former at the age of one hundred and four, and the latter one hundred years old. John and Charles removed some miles farther up the Youghiogheny, near what is now known as Sang Run. John died at the age of eighty-six years. Charles emigrated to Missouri, where, after visiting once or twice his native State, he died at the age of fifty-five. Augustine, in 1774, moved down the Youghiogheny, and selected a tract of land near Bear Creek, which he surveyed and called "Friends' Choice." Augustine ultimately sold "Friends' Choice," and it has changed hands often since, and is now owned by George N. Williams, of Baltimore. Like his brother Charles, Augustine emigrated, finally settling in Missouri, where he died at the age of eighty. He leaves descendants in Garrett County to the number of several hundred, and they and their connections number over one thousand, despite the fact that a considerable number of them emigrated to other States. A large proportion of the inhabitants of Garrett are the descendants of the Friends or of the following settlers: Paul Dewitt, Benjamin and William Coddington, John Rutan, Thomas Casteel, Jacob Vrooman, Jacob Welch, and Browning, Van Sickle, Frantz, and Frazee. The manner in which names are sometimes given to tracts of land is worthy of note.

On one occasion when Col. Hoffman was surveying a tract of land, his men asked a holiday to go merry-making in the vicinity. Their request was refused, as the old colonel was anxious to finish his work. Not to be baffled, however, they raised a cry of "Indians!" a word that struck deadly terror into the heart of every white man. Consternation prevailed, and Col. Hoffman hastily collected his men and retired into a fort or block-house. After a while the pleasure-seekers went out on a scout—after Indians. When they returned at midnight and found Col. Hoffman and his companions still in the block-house, they told him of the ruse that had been practiced, and he was furious at first and made the wildest threats of vengeance on the jokers, but was finally induced to laugh and forgive them. In token of the deception he named the tract of land they were surveying "False Alarm," which name it retains to this day. It was at this same fort that a very romantic incident occurred three-quarters of a century ago. A small company were assembled, among them a Mr. Harrington, of Harrington's Creek, and Miss Moore, of Crossing neighborhood. After a five minutes' conversation Mr. Harrington proposed and Miss Moore accepted, and on the next day they were married.

One of the most conspicuous of the early settlers was Meshach Browning, the famous hunter, whose eventful career is narrated elsewhere in this work in the history of Allegany County. He was entirely free from vice, honest and direct as any man could be, and greatly respected. He was very positive and strong in his nature, as every line in his rigid face clearly indicated. He was a powerful man, and occasionally had a combat with a man of known metal when it would not be manly to avoid it. He had a noted battle in early life at Selbysport with a man by the name of Shannon. The contest began in an old-fashioned saw-mill, and ended below among the water-works. The ducking they received in the race had the good effect of cooling the ardor of the contestants. But no man more despised the ruffian and the bully than he. His fondness for his rifle and the woods remained with him as long as he could follow the tracks of the game, but long and severe exposure finally compelled him to relinquish the sport.

Francis P. Blair, Sr., Edward Stabler, and other Eastern people became acquainted with him, and were in the habit of visiting him annually in the summer season. They were delighted with his anecdotes and hunting stories. It is said that these old men would sit together whole nights at the plain but comfortable house of Browning, and listen to what appeared to many to be the wildest of romances. They insisted that Browning should write a book. The old man replied he could yet shoot a buck or knife a bear, but he could not write a book; "he had gone to school only a quarter," and that at least two generations before. He was at length persuaded in this way to write the book, which is a credit to a man of his limited education and advantages. It was written at the house of his son, Thomas Browning, of Muddy Creek, Allegany County, after the death of his second wife. The manuscript of the book was submitted to Mr. Stabler for revision, but the only liberty he took with it was to correct the grammar, spelling, and punctuation. The language and composition remain as they came from the vigorous mind of the author. The manuscript of the book is in possession of his grandson, R. L. Browning, at Sang Run, and the famous rifle that slaughtered so many deer, bears, panthers, and other game is on deposit at the Smithsonian Institute, Washington.

William Browning, the eldest son of Meshach, was a prominent and respectable citizen in his county. He held the offices of county commissioner and justice of the peace, and was once a candidate for the Legislature. He died a few years ago, aged seventy-five years. He left a large family of children, among them a number of sons, one of whom, Richard L., was recently a member of the Legislature from Garrett, and in 1879 a candidate for clerk of his county. He was a Union soldier in the late war, and was severely wounded at Lynchburg. He lived on the old Browning homestead, near Gough River. William inherited his father's hunting traits, and was very expert with the rifle.

John Lynn, the next oldest son, is a prosperous farmer on Deep Creek, the famous trout stream of olden times. He was county commissioner for Allegany County before it was divided. He, too, is something of a Nimrod. For long years he has been afflicted with a maimed hand from a terrible cut of a butcher-knife in a life and death struggle with a bear in the cliffs of Meadow Mountain. He was victorious in the fight, but came off with a crippled member for life. James is a well-to-do farmer in Preston County, W. Va., and Allen has for many years resided in the State of Missouri. The Brownings are locally famous for their skill in playing the violin. This trait extends to some of the females of the family. It is no uncommon thing to see a full string band at Oakland composed entirely of members of the family.

Thomas, the fifth son, lives on Muddy Creek, fifteen miles from Oakland, where a dam and house were built for the benefit of trout-fishers.

Jeremiah, the youngest, lives about twelve miles from Oakland.

The five daughters of Meshach Browning were all married, and all have had children. Three have died since the death of their father.

Holmes Wiley, who died recently, aged seventy-seven years, was the last of the three hunters of the olden times in Garrett. First, Christian Garlitz, father of B. T. Garlitz, of Cumberland, died many years ago, whom Meshach Browning, the Nimrod of the forest, and historian of his own achievements, followed some twenty years since, and recently the junior of the trio expired.

Wiley was a remarkable man in many respects; of a commanding presence, with a powerful constitution, capable in his better days of enduring almost any hardship, endowed with excellent judgment and strong common sense, and a memory that scarcely ever failed him. He was a farmer by vocation, but the rifle and the hunt were his enjoyments throughout a long life. None but himself could enumerate his many achievements in the mountains of what is now Garrett County. One of his exciting adventures he narrated somewhat as follows: While out hunting on a winter day he came upon the track of a powerful wolf. He pursued the animal to its den in a cavern in Negro Mountain. He at once saw that it was beyond his reach unless he could follow the beast to its lair. The entrance to the cave was only large enough to allow a man to approach in a crawling attitude. In this manner he felt his way in utter darkness for a long distance, with the reliable rifle at his side, until the glare of the eyes of the enraged animal disclosed its position. A crack from the gun, and in a moment the fierce growl ceased. The old huntsman was too well skilled in forest life to rush upon his game at once, but when he approached it was found to be dead. The leaden missive had struck a vital point, and to his surprise and satisfaction he found six live whelps with the dead mother, all of which were brought forth and scalped, for which trophies he secured one hundred and thirty dollars, under the law as it then stood in regard to the destruction of these animals. Wiley often said this was a pretty good return for an ounce of lead, half as much powder, and a little trembling in the boots. But he observed that there was a little more grumbling that fiscal year than usual among the tax-payers. He said this was his last encounter with the wolf tribe, as soon after, the Baltimore and Ohio Railroad Company extended its road through the bounds of the county, and drove them off entirely. Wiley was somewhat primitive in his habits, but a kind-hearted and generous man. He raised a large family of children, but none of his sons inherited his fondness for the "woods."

His second wife was the noted Nancy Hufford, who was tried and acquitted in 1856 of the charge of poisoning Mrs. Engle.

Holmes Wiley's father was Thomas Wiley, a native of England, one of the first settlers of Garrett County. He died about 1850. He took great pleasure in being able to vote without having been naturalized (though born in the old country), from the fact of his being older than the constitution of 1789. Joseph T. Wiley, the youngest son of Thomas, and a brother of Holmes Wiley, the hunter, fell dead Nov. 10, 1881, of heart disease, on the streets of Grantsville, in his sixty-second year. He was the last living child of Thomas, the pioneer.

Among the most distinguished men of Garrett County is the Hon. Patrick Hamill, now a resident of Oakland. He was born at the Green Glades, Garrett Co., Md., April 28, 1817. His father, Patrick Hamill, was born at Balymede, Ireland, April 15, 1781. He was a revolutionist under Emmet in 1798, and was forced to leave Ireland to save his life, and sought a home in America. He married, May 12, 1805, at Westernport, Allegany Co., Md., Mary Morrison, who was born in Baltimore, Oct. 27, 1786. They had five children, of whom Judge Hamill was the youngest. The elder Hamill was a successful farmer, and died at Green Glades, March 23, 1818. His wife survived him, and died Sept. 21, 1862.

Judge Patrick Hamill was educated at the common schools of his neighborhood until he was of age, after which he prosecuted his studies under a private teacher at his own expense. He also learned the carpenter's trade, at which he worked for one year, at the expiration of which he engaged in farming and stock-raising. In 1841 he was appointed tax-collector for Allegany County, which position he held for two years. In 1843 he was elected to the Legislature, and was re-elected in 1844. In 1845 he engaged in mercantile business, having stores at Westernport, Bloomington, and Shaw's Mills (now Moscow), and continued in the business for ten years. He was nominated to the Constitutional Convention which met in 1851, but declined, and held no public office until appointed judge of the Orphans' Court by Governor Ligon. He was elected to the same office for a second term. In 1866 he was elected to the Legislature, but declined to take his seat, because of the test-oath and for other reasons. In 1868 he was elected judge of the Orphans' Court for Allegany County, of which he was chief judge.

P Hamill

He was also president of the Allegany County convention for the nomination of delegates to the convention which framed the present constitution of Maryland, and was tendered the nomination of delegate, but declined. In 1868 he was nominated and elected to the Forty-first Congress, to succeed ex-Governor Francis Thomas, and served on the Committees on Public Expenditures and the Navy Department. Since his retirement from Congress he has held no office, except that of director of the Chesapeake and Ohio Canal. He was influential in the formation of Garrett County, with Oakland as the county-seat, in which place he now resides. He married Isabella, daughter of Enoch and Anna Kight. They have had eight children,—four sons and four daughters,—Mary Ann, born Dec. 14, 1844, wife of E. R. Browning; Rebecca Rawlings, born Nov. 14, 1846, died Sept. 15, 1860; Gilmor Semmes, born Dec. 11, 1848, who is among the most successful lawyers of Garrett County, and who is married and residing in Oakland; Sydney McNeal, born Feb. 5, 1851, wife of T. W. Casteel, a farmer of Garrett County; Henry P., born Feb. 28, 1853, a clergyman of the Methodist Church South, now stationed in Frederick City; Kansas, born Aug. 24, 1855, living at home; Patrick, Jr., born May 13, 1859, an engineer in the employ of the West Virginia Central Railroad; James D., born May 8, 1861; and Susan Offutt, born Feb. 8, 1863, the two latter living at home. Mr. Hamill is a thoroughly honest and conscientious gentleman, and has been closely and prominently identified with the important interests of Western Maryland. His record in Congress and in other public positions has been uniformly creditable, and there are few men in his section of the State who enjoy a more firmly rooted or a more extensive popularity.

First Court Proceedings.—The first Circuit Court held in Garrett County convened May 19, 1873, at which Associate Judges William Motter and George A. Pearre presided. The grand jury were Jonas Wass, D. A. Friend, Elisha Umbel, Henry Myers, Robert E. Lee, Isaac Spiker, S. J. Livengood, Adam Garringer, Christian J. Beachy, Frederick Englehardt, Silas Fitzwater, Charles Warwick, Charles Bill, Israel Garlitz, W. E. George, E. Falkenstine, J. F. Frantz, John Friend, of N., Josiah Bowcher, Patrick Hamill, John Frantz, of Joseph, Thomas Cuppett, John C. Dunham. The petit jury were James Poland, Normand Barnard, Wm. Sharpless, John G. Riley, George Ruckle, P. M. Stemple, J. F. Robinson, W. C. Broadwater, Samuel Beachy, John Edgar, Sr., John Tice, Nelson Irwin, Wm. B. Stanton, W. W. Ashby, Amos W. Friend, Clark Deberry, Stephen W. Friend, Emanuel Custer, Robert Green, Joseph Mart, A. C. Hamill, George Roth, Elijah Friend, of J. The court-crier was William Smoose; messenger, James Bell; bailiff to the grand jury, Wm. Waltz; and to the petit jury, Thomas Bosley. The first jury trial was the suit of William Lipscomb *vs.* Samuel Rodaharer, an appeal from Ezekiel Totten, justice of the peace, and the jury found for appellee in the sum of forty dollars, whereas before the magistrate a judgment had been rendered for plaintiff of forty-six dollars and fifty cents.

The court was in session three days, and thirty-three witnesses were examined before the grand jury. The first twelve original suits (out of twenty-five) brought for this (May) term were:

George A. Pearre *vs.* Wm. Harvey and Washington Mosley.

Elhart Weltz *vs.* H. F. Leininger.

Wilson Proctor *vs.* Baltimore and Ohio Railroad.

Wm. Price, assignee, *vs.* Joel Pennington and J. G. Barnard.

Harriet Punnell *vs.* E. W. Cecil.

State of Maryland for use of Louis Klegel *vs.* Baltimore and Ohio Railroad.

Samuel J. Edwards *vs.* John Friend, of N.

Joel Wyland *vs.* Conrad Myers (two cases).

George Smith *vs.* Margaret Kennedy.

Philson Black *vs.* Louis Leininger.

The second court was held in December, 1873, Judge George A. Pearre on the bench.

The grand jury were Samuel Harshberger, J. A. Dunham, John L. Browning, George Beall, George McKenzie, Middleton Biggs, Henry Fuller, Henry Yoder, Joshua Fazenbaker, Garrett V. Moon, Aaron Boyer, Theophilus Witt, Hiram Duckworth, Andrew Miller, Meshach Mattingly, Bowie Johnson, David Michael, John G. Barnard, J. W. Blocher, Charles O. Michaels, David Fike, Thomas Grimes, Israel Frankhouser. The petit jury were Louis Nydigger, George Stark, Thomas Ravenscraft, Michael Nathan, H. H. Miller, Moses Kemp, Henry Smouse, David Kent, John C. Chaney, Henry Muhlenburg, John Swalp, Andrew Pysell, G. W. Blocher, Joseph Spyker, A. J. Rhoades, N. M. Ambrose, W. H. Barnard, Samuel Specht, Edward Bishoff, Basil Anderson, Jarvis Custer, Jackson Umble, Daniel Carey.

Forty-one witnesses testified before the grand jury. The first case tried was that of M. J. Beachy *vs.* George L. Layman, in which the jury found for the plaintiff in a verdict of ninety-nine dollars. The first five original suits brought for this term of court were:

George A. Pearre *vs.* Washington Mosley.

Peter McCleary *vs.* Valentine Boeltner.

David McIntyre *vs.* Francis Thomas and William Witt.

Laughlin & Bushfield *vs.* A. C. Good.

Louisa Witt *vs.* John E. Barnard.

From the organization of the county until Aug. 1, 1873, the following marriage-licenses were issued by the clerk of the Circuit Court:

1873.

Feb.	2.	C. H. Liston and Lucretia A. Lowdermilk.
"	27.	George Sperline and Abigail Beechley.
March	30.	D. A. Friend and Phebe M. Rush.
"	"	Albion Coles and Antoinette Barnes.
"	25.	Simon Matthews and Elizabeth A. Totten.
"	27.	J. F. Trehern and Cyrene Edwards.
"	29.	W. H. Chidester and Francis Friend.
"	30.	James W. White and Flora May McCrum.
April	24.	John W. Harvey and Sarah E. Davis.
"	26.	J. C. Rodeheaver and Jennie Friend.
"	27.	J. E. Barnard and Ellen Sharpless.
May	4.	G. J. Ferguson and Mary Ann Friend.
"	"	John W. Harvey and Mary C. Thompson.
"	8.	Manarah Tannehill and Katie Clark.
June	10.	W. H. Frazee and Felicie Frantz.
"	5.	Isaac W. Abernethy and Sophia K. Savage.
"	4.	J. W. Kisner and Mary M. Wable.
"	20.	Henry Jordan and Justina Cope.
June	16.	Benj. Thrasher and Margaret J. Williams.
"	15.	Reuben Fulk and Mary Johnson.
July	1.	John Grimes and Emily Musser.
"	6.	F. P. Layton and Susan Gould.

The first mortgage recorded was on Feb. 12, 1873. It was from Harmon and Helen S. Hesser to Humbird & Long, for $230, on six and five-eighths acres of land, on the Youghiogheny, and dated Feb. 10, 1873.

The first deed recorded was March 4, 1873, and was from Ezekiel Totten to Adelia M. Merrill, for a lot in Oakland, dated Feb. 6, 1873, consideration $125. The second deed was recorded March 4, 1873, from Henry G. Davis *et al.* to James Cassey, for a lot in Deer Park, consideration $100, dated Oct. 1, 1872. The next deed recorded was on Feb. 20, 1873, from Emily F. Droege *et al.* to Robert J. Head, for a lot in Deer Park, dated Feb. 20, 1873, consideration $1400. The next deed was recorded March 4, 1873, from Edward and Mary N. Lloyd to R. T. Browning, for one hundred acres of "Small Meadows," dated May 31, 1872, consideration $800.

The second mortgage recorded was on Feb. 19, 1873, from James Q. Robinson to Elias Whitesel, for $161, on eighty-nine and three-fourths acres, part of "Lochiel," dated Feb. 1, 1873.

The fifth deed recorded was Feb. 21, 1873, from J. L. Campbell to J. F. Browning, for a lot in Pennington's Addition to Oakland, dated Aug. 12, 1872, consideration $1625.

The first Orphans' Court was held Feb. 11, 1873, by Judges D. Harrison Friend (chief justice), William Harvey, and Joseph DeWitt. The bond of W. L. Rawlings, register of wills, with W. A. Brydon and Elijah Kemp securities, was presented and approved. Letters of administration were granted to Charles C. Hauft on the estate of Conrad Hauft, and Samuel Beachey and John Abel were appointed appraisers of decedent's personalty.

February 25. Letters of administration were granted to Joseph Kemp on the personal estate of David E. Hauser, on which David Fike and Thomas Grimes were appointed appraisers.

March 11. Letters of administration were granted to G. W. Wilson on the personal estate of Henry Kemp, and W. H. Kitzmiller and James F. Liller were selected as appraisers. The wills of the following deceased parties were admitted to record:

1. Christian Fike, of John, dated Dec. 17, 1872, proven Feb. 21, 1873.
2. Joseph McKinney, dated Dec. 7, 1871, proven Dec. 31, 1872.
3. Hannah R. Turney, dated March 26, 1873, proven April 22, 1873.
4. Elisha McRobie, dated March 16, 1870, proven April 22, 1873.

5. Jacob Youtsey, dated July 7, 1866, proven May 20, 1873.
6. Joseph Beeghley, dated Feb. 14, 1852, and certified copy admitted to record in 1873.
7. William Fike, dated March 4, 1870, proven in Allegany County, June 28, 1870, and a certified copy admitted to record in Garrett County in 1873.
8. Walter Steele, dated Jan. 1, 1872, proven July 22, 1873.
9. Ulysses Ward, of Washington, D. C., dated Feb. 11, 1867, proven April 7, 1868, and a certified copy admitted to record in 1873.

The first nominating convention (composed of members of both political parties) for Garrett County met at the Glades Hotel, in Oakland, Dec. 14, 1872. William A. Brydon was chairman of the meeting, and Messrs. Ralph Thayer and Gilmore S. Hamill, secretaries.

A committee was appointed, composed of two delegates from each district (one of each political party), to present a ticket to the convention. The committee reported the following ticket:

Clerk, R. T. Browning, District No. 15, Dem.; Register of Wills, Ralph Thayer, Rep., District 15; Sheriff, Sol. Turner, Dem., District No. 1; State's Attorney, Gilmore S. Hamill, Dem., District No. 15; Judges of Orphans' Court, Joseph B. Davis, Rep., District No. 15; J. McMason, Dem., District No. 10; D. H. Friend, Rep., District No. 14; County Commissioners, D. E. Offutt, Dem., District No. 15; Jacob Boyer, Rep., District No. 11; W. H. Barnard, Dem., District No. 4; County Surveyor, A. M. Ambrose, Rep.

The ticket was nominated by the convention after some few objections, the delegates from Grantsville withdrawing from the hall and declining to take part in the further proceedings. Following are the votes at the different important elections:

Vote for Congressman in 1876.

Districts.	Wm. Walsh. (Democrat.)	L. E. McComas. (Republican.)
Altamont	124	119
Selbysport	74	123
Grantsville	203	214
Bloomington	86	96
Accident	119	96
Sang Run	32	98
Oakland	196	164
Ryan's Glades	55	92
Johnson's	61	18
Total	950	1020

Gubernatorial Election in 1879.

Districts.	W. T. Hamilton. (Democrat.)	J. A. Gary. (Republican.)
Altamont	125	141
Selbysport	96	125
Grantsville	204	226
Bloomington	99	93
Accident	107	108
Sang Run	42	105
Oakland	205	199
Ryan's Glades	69	104
Johnson's	54	23
Total	1001	1122

Presidential Vote in 1880.

	W. S. Hancock.	J. A. Garfield.
Altamont	155	162
Selbysport	96	132
Grantsville	230	224
Bloomington	125	110
Accident	130	124
Sang Run	45	101
Oakland	200	203
Ryan's Glades	74	122
Johnson's	69	32
Total	1124	1210

State and County Election, Tuesday, Nov. 8, 1881.

Comptroller.

Thomas Gorsuch, R.	1074
Thomas J. Keating, D.	1000
Frank T. Morling, G. L.	60

Senate.

Geo. W. Wilson, R.	985
William R. Getty, D.	1075
David B. White, G. L.	53

House of Delegates.

Samuel J. Beachey, R.	1053
Howard M. Kemp, R.	1027
Wm. D. Hoye, D.	1012
George T. Michaels, D.	1042
Patrick Carey, G. L.	55
A. F. George, G. L.	64

County Commissioners.

S. L. Townshend, R.	1043
Eli McMillen, R.	1061
Thomas B. Wiley, R.	993
James R. Bishop, D.	1016
Meshach Mattingly, D.	1056
Otho Speelman, D.	1004
John C. Beckman, G. L.	67
Ashford Warnick, G. L.	56
A. H. Griffin, G. L.	56

Sheriff.

W. S. Pew, R.	975
Edmund T. Jamison, D.	1096
George H. Allen, G. L.	54

Surveyor.

John Harned, R.	1055
J. T. Mitchell, D.	1038

Given below is a list of the officers of the county from its formation to the present time (1881).

CIRCUIT COURT JUDGES.

1873, Richard H. Alvey, chief justice; George A. Pearre, William Motter, associate judges.

CLERK OF CIRCUIT COURT.

1873, William H. Tower.

SHERIFFS.

1873, William Coddington; 1875, Edmund Jamison; 1877, John P. Dunham; 1879, George A. White; 1881, Edmund T. Jamison.

JUDGES OF ORPHANS' COURT.

1873, William Harvey, D. H. Friend, Joseph De Witt; 1875, A. J. Michaels, Joseph De Witt, William Harvey; 1879, Isaac H. Kooken (chief justice), Joseph De Witt, William Harvey.

REGISTERS OF WILLS.

1873, William L. Rawlings; 1879, William H. Hagans.

COUNTY COMMISSIONERS.

1873 (Jan. 30 to Dec. 4), William Casteel, H. M. Frazee, A. Boning; 1873–75, H. E. Friend, G. W. Blocher, Elisha Umbel; 1875–77, Isaiah Boucher, Henry Winterberg, John E. Knaggey; 1877–79, E. C. Fillson, Jeremiah Guard, John Riley, of George; 1879–81, D. H. Friend, John Wilhelm, W. W. Broadwater; 1881–83, Meshach Mattingly, S. L. Townshend, Eli McMillen.

CLERKS TO COUNTY COMMISSIONERS.

1873, Wm. H. Hagans; 1874, G. W. Merrill; 1878, W. H. Hagans; 1879, F. A. Thayer.

DEPUTY CLERKS OF CIRCUIT COURT.

1873, C. F. Newman; 1874, W. H. Hagans; 1876, W. P. Townshend; 1878, F. A. Thayer; 1879, E. Z. Tower.

School Commissioners.

1873, W. A. Brydon, G. W. Delander, Andrew Arendt; 1874, G. W. Delander, W. A. Brydon, T. W. Frost; 1875, W. G. Burns; 1879, S. D. Yutsy, Thomas H. Bittinger.

School Examiners, Secretaries, and Treasurers.

1873, A. Matthews; 1877, Dr. E. H. Bartlett.

Collectors.

1873, Charles Bell, J. C. Dunham, J. Z. Browning; 1874-75, Ira E. Friend; 1876-77, Abraham Miller; 1878, J. Z. Browning, Edward Margraff, Jasper Guard.

Attorneys-at-Law, with dates of admission to the Garret County Bar.

1873, J. H. Gordon, John M. Read, Joseph A. Cahill, R. Chew Jones, S. A. Cox, A. H. Blackistone, Thomas J. Peddicord, John B. Fay, Gilmor S. Hamill, John W. Veitch, W. W. McKaig, James M. Schley, J. J. McHenry, A. Hunter Boyd, M. A. Healey, A. Beall McCaig, F. Williams, Jacob Brown, W. M. Price, William Brace, Jr., G. W. Wolf, R. H. Gordon, William Devecmon; 1874, R. T. Semmes, Thomas J. McKaig, J. W. Mason, B. F. Martin, Lloyd Lowndes; 1875, J. S. Grove, J. F. Harrison, C. A. Snyder, G. T. Porter, John Ritchie, B. A. Richmond; 1876, W. J. Read, Philetus Lipscomb, James A. McHenry, H. W. Hoffman, R. T. Merrick, B. F. M. Hurley, William Walsh; 1877, D. W. Sloan, Andrew B. Gouder, Thomas McCleave; 1878, W. L. Boughner, D. J. Blackistone, L. H. Vandiver, Robert McDonald, H. Wheeler Combs; 1879, W. A. Daily, J. Frank Seiss, A. G. Sturgess; 1880, W. P. Townshend, A. A. Wilson; 1881, A. K. Syester, C. C. Willison, M. Bannon.

State's Attorneys.

1873, Gilmor S. Hamill, James M. Schley; 1874, John W. Wolf; 1876, John W. Veitch.

Notaries Public.

1874, Richard B. Jamison, J. C. Read; 1878, Andrew B. Gouder.

Justices of the Peace.

1874.—1st Dist., Wm. Sharpless, J. H. Wilson; 2d, Benjamin Griffith, Isaac Umbel; 3d, J. F. Patterson; 4th, A. J. Warnick; 5th, Sylvanus Butler, Wm. Hinebaugh; 6th, William Browning; 7th, E. G. Hall, A. C. Good.

1876.—1st Dist., J. H. Wilson, Henry Rasche; 2d, Isaac Umbel, Benj. Griffith; 3d, Sylvanus Butler, J. F. Patterson; 4th, A. J. Warnick; 5th, W. M. Miller; 6th, Wm. Browning, Francis Sebold; 7th, E. G. Hall, A. C. Good; 9th, Perry Wimer.

1878.—1st Dist., Henry Rasche, Wm. Sharpless; 2d, Isaac Umbel; 3d, Sylvanus Butler; 4th, A. J. Warnick; 5th, Wm. Hinebaugh, W. M. Miller; 6th, Wm. Browning, Francis Sebold; 7th, A. L. Osbourn, R. B. Jamison; 9th, Perry Wimer.

1880.—1st Dist., J. W. Davis, Wm. Sharpless; 2d, J. M. Kessler; 3d, Henry Winterberg, Sylvanus Butler; 4th, A. J. Warnick; 5th, William Hinebaugh; 6th, R. T. Browning, Francis Sebold; 7th, A. L. Osbourn, Richard B. Jamison, A. B. Gouder; 9th, Perry Wimer; District not known, Emil F. Davege.

County Surveyors.

1873, A. C. Mason; 1875, W. R. Hamill; 1877-81, John Harned.

Deputy County Surveyors.

1875-77, John B. Brant; 1878, A. C. Mason.

Constables.

1873.—Dist. No. 15, John B. Brant, L. Harvey.

1874.—Aaron Boyer, W. L. Barnthouse, B. F. Hoye, Geo. D. White, John B. Brant, F. McKizie, W. A. Willison, E. J. Fringer.

1875.—John Barnes, Jacob Flegel, Chauncey Kimmel, Charles Atkinson.

1876.—Dist. No. 1, J. Miller, Jr.; No. 2, W. R. Barnthouse; No. 3, F. McKizie; No. 5, Aaron Boyer; No. 6, E. A. Browning; No. 7, J. F. White, Jacob Flegel; No. 9, Isaac Larue.

1878.—Dist. No. 1, W. S. Pew, J. Miller, Jr.; No. 2, S. F. Cuppert, W. R. Barnthouse; No. 3, F. McKizie; No. 4, D. J. Reeves; No. 5, Aaron Boyer; No. 6, E. R. Browning; No. 7, G. D. White, J. S. Johnson; No. 8, Louis Nydigger; No. 9, Isaac Larue.

1880.—Dist. No. 1, John Miller, F. C. Browning; No. 2, J. W. Savage; No. 3, Joseph Blocher; No. 4, G. Hallen; No. 7, G. W. Paugh, W. S. Wolf, J. S. Johnson; No. 9, Isaac Larue; Districts not known, Frederick Kolb, David Hurst, Jacob Flegel.

Registers of Election.

1874.—Dist. No. 1, G. W. Kitzmiller; No. 2, J. H. Rush; No. 3, Isaiah Fuller; No. 4, W. H. Barnard; No. 5, Eli McMillen; No. 6, Thos. Browning; No. 7, W. H. Hall; No. 8, Isaac S. Thompson; No. 9, Geo. S. Layman.

1876.—Dist. No. 1, J. H. Beekman; No. 2, J. H. Rush; No. 3, Isaiah Fuller; No. 4, W. H. Barnard; No. 5, Daniel Hinebaugh; No. 6, Thos. Browning; No. 7, W. H. Hall; No. 8, Isaac S. Thompson; No. 9, J. Fazenbaker.

1878.—Dist. No. 1, H. O. Hamill; No. 2, J. H. Rush; No. 3, Isaiah Fuller; No. 4, W. H. Barnard; No. 5, Daniel Hinebaugh; No. 6, Thos. Browning; No. 7, R. T. Browning; No. 8, W. F. Deakins; No. 9, Joshua Fazenbaker.

1880.—Dist. No. 1, H. O. Hamill; No. 2, B. G. Green; No. 3, Isaiah Fuller; No. 4, W. H. Barnard; No. 5, Daniel Hinebaugh; No. 6, Thos. Browning; No. 7, W. H. Hall; No. 8, W. F. Deakins; No. 9, Daniel Carey.

Board of Control and Review.

1876.—Adam Garringer, William H. Barnard, Charles J. Pennington.

Assessors.

1874, R. T. Browning, Edward Saggart; 1876, Dist. No. 1, J. McClure Mason, Samuel C. Hoye, William Browning; No. 2, Eli Stanton, Christian Snyder, E. M. Friend.

Road Supervisors.

Dist. No. 1, S. W. Friend; No. 2, Isaac Myers; No. 3, P. J. Stephens; No. 4, David Evans; No. 5, William Englehart; No. 6, Elijah Hoye; No. 7, W. M. Coddington; No. 8, J. G. Knauer; No. 9, Andrew Blocher.

Miscellaneous Officials.

Court-crier, William Smouse; Auditor, W. P. Townshend; Standing Commissioners, A. B. Gouder, G. S. Hamill; Messenger, James M. Bell; Bailiffs, William Waitz, T. Bosley.

State Senators from Garrett County.

1874, William R. Getty; 1878, Balthasar Welfley; 1882, William R. Getty.

Members of the House of Delegates.

1874, Richard J. West, E. H. Glotfelty; 1876, William R. Barnard, Richard T. Browning; 1878, George W. Wilson, George W. Blocher; 1880, Austin Speicher, George W. Wilson; 1882, Samuel J. Beachey, George T. Michaels.

Garrett County Schools for year ending Sept. 30, 1880.

Number of school-houses (of which 77 were frame, 1 brick, 1 log)	83
Number male teachers (principals)	58
" female " "	25
" male " (assistants)	2
" female " "	5
" fenced lots	6
" schools having outbuildings	13
" " " sufficient blackboards	25
" " " good furniture	24
" terms schools were open	2
" male pupils	1810
" female "	1533
" pupils over 16 years of age	226
" official school visits paid by examiner	54
Average attendance in schools	2142
Number pupils in algebra	27
" " philosophy	2
" " geometry	13
" " physiology	4

RECEIPTS AND DISBURSEMENTS FOR PUBLIC SCHOOL PURPOSES FOR YEAR ENDING SEPT. 30, 1880.

Receipts.

Balance on hand Sept. 30, 1879	$1,252.67
State school tax	3,804.46
" free school fund	1,214.14
" donation	1,200.00
County school tax	4,516,93
Amount of levy, $10,000.	
Sales of books	367.51
State donation, due July, 1879, paid February, 1880.	1,200.00
April appropriations, State school tax for the years 1877, '78, '79, and '80	4,705.74
License for sale of liquors in Garrett County	255.00
Tax collected on levy of June, 1880, and not due until Oct. 15, 1880	1,309.04
Total	$19,826.14

Disbursements.

Teachers' salaries	$9,808.91
Fuel	575.50
Incidental expenses of schools	183.45
Rent	170.50
Books and stationery	1,388.18
Building school-houses	1,714.82
Repairing " "	213.60
Furniture, blackboards, and stoves	87.00
Interest	1,172.82
Salary of secretary, treasurer, and examiner	950.00
Per diem of school commissioners	265.00
Office expenses and account books	232.20
Printing and advertising	67.25
Attorney's fees	25.00
Balance on hand Sept. 30, 1880	2,971.91
Total	$19,826.14

Population and Financial Exhibit in 1881.—The national census report of 1880 gives the following population by districts and villages:

District No. 1	1,561	District No. 7	2,077
" " 2	1,250	" " 8	1,033
" " 3	2,152	" " 9	402
" " 4	1,357		
" " 5	1,369	Total	12,175
" " 6	794		

Included in the above are the following villages, whose population was:

Oakland	910	Grantsville	220
Bloomington	341	Deer Park	195
Franklin Hill	260	Accident	114

Of the total population, 6212 were males, 5963 females, 11,389 were born in the county, 786 were of foreign birth, 12,063 were white, and 112 colored.

The agricultural productions of Garrett, as given by the census of 1880, were for that year: barley, acreage, 1; number of bushels, 25; buckwheat, acreage, 4989; number of bushels, 72,333; Indian corn, acreage, 3714; bushels, 90,777; oats, acreage, 8657; bushels, 171,-723; rye, acreage, 2746; bushels, 21,552; wheat, acreage, 4122; bushels, 44,399; tobacco, acreage, 4; pounds, 1927. The average yield per acre of corn was 24½ bushels, and of wheat, 11 bushels.

Annual Levy List for Garrett County, Md., for the year 1881, levied by the County Commissioners at June Session, 1881.

RECAPITULATION.

Road levy	$3,775.17
Elections	267.12
Magistrates' fees	82.20
Constables' fees	40.95
Registrars	433.82
Taxes paid in error	95.47
Foxes and wild-cats	295.00
Bridges	206.13
Road appropriations	298.92
Road expenses	93.00
Pensions	325.00
Sheriff's fees	898.70
Clerk's office	4,370.13
Orphans' Court	400.71
Court-house fund	1,660.00
Hospitals	1,523.75
Attorney's fees	599.98
Coroner's inquests	25.00
County commissioners	1,135.50
Miscellaneous	2,604.76
Public schools	8,500.00
Contingent fund	1,318.19
Collector's commissions	1,910.23
Special road and bridge levy	870.00
Total	$31,792.56

Total assessment of Garrett County $3,636,626.00

The State tax is fixed by law at 18¾ cents on the $100 of assessable property, which added to 87¼ cents for county and other purposes, makes the sum of $1.06 on every $100 of assessable property of Garrett County for the year 1881.

Altamont District, No. 1, is bounded on the north by Grantsville and Sang Run Districts, east by Bloomington District and West Virginia, south by West Virginia and the district of Ryan's Glades and Oakland, and west by Oakland. The first settlers were the Friend family, followed by the Kitzmillers, Carmangs, Appels, Wilsons, Armiths, Wests, Staidings, McRobies, Millers, Rexrodes, Kimmels, Spikers, Rites, Roons, Saucers, Rowans, Kerns, Hills, Herveys, Baldwins, Beckmans, Brownings, Grims, Blackburns, Greens, Georges, Garretts, Wilsons, Camps, Carrolls, Edvans, Edmonds, Custers, Charitans, Clians, and Cassidys, Hamills, Sharplesses, Paughs, Rafters, Tuesings, Taskers.

Altamont Village is situated on the Baltimore and Ohio Railroad, nine miles east of Oakland and two hundred and twenty-three from Baltimore. The situation is upon the extreme summit of the Alleganies, 2620 feet above sea-level. Near here the interesting phenomenon is seen of two streams of water or rivers running in opposite directions,—the Potomac runs east, and the Youghiogheny, within a few yards of it, runs west. The Potomac courses to the Chesapeake Bay, and the Youghiogheny flows towards and discharges into the Ohio River. The head-waters of the Potomac have their source a short distance from Altamont, near Fairfax stone, a monument which indicates the boundary between West Virginia and Maryland. From Altamont westward, for a distance of nearly twenty miles, are beautiful meadows known as the "Glades," lying along the upper waters of the Youghiogheny and its numerous tributaries, divided by ridges of moderate elevation and gentle slopes, with fine ranges of mountains in the backgrounds. John Friend, of N., is postmaster of the town, and E. G. Blackburn and J. H. Wilson are the merchants. Altamont takes its name from its high location.

Kitzmillersville is eight miles from Wilson's Station, on the Baltimore and Ohio Railroad, and fourteen from Oakland, near the North Branch of the Potomac. Its name is derived from the pioneer family of Kitzmiller, which settled here over a century ago. The merchants are G. W. Kitzmiller, J. H. Rafter & Co., and G. W. Wilson. J. H. Rafter is postmaster, William H. Pool is a wool manufacturer, Ebenezer Kitzmiller, miller, and Andrew Barnhouse, Henry Brey, William Brey, and Charles Tuesing are coopers. The carpenters are Henry Hamill, John Rank, and John Sharpless; the blacksmiths, William Wilson and J. H. Tice; stone-mason, Alex. Reid; wheelwright, G. F. Richardson; chair-maker, Henry Sowers; and shoemakers, Henry Tuesing, W. S. Pew, and John J. McRobie.

Swanton is situated on the Baltimore and Ohio Railroad, thirteen miles east of Oakland, and two hundred and nineteen from Baltimore. C. T. West has a store and mill, A. Fairall is railroad agent and postmaster, Charles Murphy is a miller, William Sharpless, a sand-refiner, Theo. Beckman runs a saw-mill, and J. F. Friend and J. D. Ashenfelter are blacksmiths.

The school-teachers in the district for the year ending May 13, 1881, are as follows:

School No. 1.—T. A. Van Horn.
No. 2.—Lou E. Dewitt.
No. 3.—A. S. Spear.
No. 4.—W. W. Dewitt, T. D. Collins.
No. 5.—C. F. Glotfeltz.
No. 6.—A. J. Wilson.
No. 7.—Clenning Hepburn.
No. 8.—Nannie Hepburn.
No. 9.—H. O. Hamill.
No. 10.—L. C. Hamill.
No. 11.—R. L. Hamill.
No. 12.—A. T. Dewitt, A. C. Hamill.
No. 13.—W. H. Speicher.
No. 14.—Mollie Cunningham.

The school trustees for year ending May, 1882, are as follows:

School No. 1. Deer Park.—Henry Sisk, John Jankey, Benjamin Thrasher.
No. 2. Delawder School.—John Friend, of N., M. V. Grim, Herman Beckman.
No. 3. Little England.—Samuel Greene, William E. George, George Hill.
No. 4. Glendale.—George O'Brien, H. O. Hamill, James L. McCrobie.
No. 5. North Glade.—John L. Fitzwater, E. Howell, Theodore Beckman.
No. 6. Wilson School.—J. H. Wilson, W. H. Wright, Michael T. Brady.
No. 7. Swanton.—A. Fairall, C. Murphy, Joseph F. Friend,
No. 8. Frankville.
No. 9. Paugh.—Andrew F. McCrobie, John Paugh, Abraham Lee.
No. 10. Fairview.—Robert C. Wilson, John A. Junkins, John H. Rafter.
No. 11. Tichnell.—Joseph Paugh, William Tichnell.
No. 12. Mount Zion.—William Sharpless, Henry Lee, F. R. Sharpless.
No. 13. Armistead.—Joseph Speicher, William Nine, R. J. Head.
No. 14. Meadow Mountain.—Joseph Knox, Daniel O'Brien, Alexander Lohr.

Selbysport District, No. 2, is bounded on the north by Pennsylvania, east by Accident District, south by Sang Run District, and west by West Virginia. The first settlers were the Frazees, Welches, Fikes, Coddingtons, Frantzes, Friends, Rushes, Umbersons, Teates, Browns, Gearys, Tankasters, Groves, Spears, Hilemans, Rileys, Kesslers, Matthews, Lancascasters, Listers, Swalps, Speelmans, Polands, Guards, Griffiths, and Greens.

Selbysport Village is located twelve miles from Confluence, Pa. John H. Kessler is the postmaster, and Jeremiah Guard the merchant of the hamlet. H. Frazee is carpenter; H. M. Frazee and Otho Speelman, millers; Jasper Guard, shoemaker; and Alpheus Welsh, blacksmith.

Friendsville is eighteen miles from Oakland, near the Youghiogheny River and Bear Creek, and derives its name from the Friend family, one of the first to settle in the county. O. M. Hatfield is the merchant and postmaster. Scott Friend is the blacksmith; D. Kent and Hiram Frazier, millers; John Frantz, tanner; and Thomas Cuppett and John Curling, carpenters. The village is 1699 feet above tide-water.

Mineral Spring is nine miles from Confluence,

Pa., and near the Youghiogheny River. There are several veins of coal in this vicinity, two, three, and five feet thick. The merchants are P. T. Garthright (postmaster) and Jeremiah Guard. The woolen-mills are run by Alfred Daniels, and the saw-mill by John M. Miller. Lewis Neil is the tinner, and August Neil, J. L. Sellers, and Otho Speelman, millers.

The school-teachers for the year ending May 13, 1881, were as follows:

School No. 1.—Jennie A. Miller.
No. 2.—John Steele.
No. 3.—R. F. Liston.
No. 4.—G. M. Steele.
No. 5.—Samuel E. Friend, George Dunham.
No. 6.—W. N. Myers.
No. 7.—Taylor Friend.
No. 8.—E. J. Stuck.
No. 9.—Jefferson Guard.

School trustees for the year ending May, 1882:

School No. 1. Elder Hill.—Morgan Conneway, Matthew Frazee, Robert Sterling.

No. 2. Friendsville.—W. A. Coddington, E. M. Friend, Joshua M. Friend.

No. 3. Selbysport.—John Frantz, H. M. Frazee, John Riley.

No. 4. Frazee Ridge.—S P. Lowdermilk, Lucian Frazee, H. B. Demmitt.

No. 5. Mount Holly, or Rush.—James H. Rush, Elijah Myers, George D. Frantz.

No. 6. Sandy Spring.—Isaac Myers, J. W. Frantz.

No. 7. Ira Friend.—Ira E. Friend, William Umbel, John H. Friend.

No. 8. Ashe's Glade.—Isaac C. Frazee, Elijah Thomas, Elisha Umbel.

No. 9. Mill Run.—Benjamin H. Green, Jonas Wass, Newton Guard.

Joseph Frantz, of Joseph, died at his residence near Selbysport, Nov. 23, 1879, aged seventy-three. He was at one time a county commissioner, and in 1851 was elected to the Legislature. With the exception of the venerable George Matthews, he was the last of the old citizens of the district.

Grantsville District, No. 3, is bounded on the north by Pennsylvania, east by Johnson's and Bloomington Districts, south by Bloomington and Altamont Districts, and west by Accident. It is the largest and wealthiest district in the county, being underlaid with the best coal, and having large tracts of valuable pine and other woods for lumber.

Among the earliest settlers were Jesse Tomlinson, the Bruces, Gettys, Durts, Fullers, Browns, Laymans, Glotfeltys, Wileys, Shultzes, Woodins, Yutseys, Bakers, Yoders, Sloans, Beacheys, Shaws, Mancolms, Stantons, Wagoners, Bevans, Broadwaters, Blochers, Dorseys, Custers, Comptons, Ottoes, Millers, Lohrs, Gnageys, George Matthews, John Farrell, Engles, Freshes, Hanson Grant, McKenzies, Spikers, Ridgeleys, Weitzells, and Thistles.

"Grassy Cabin Survey" was the earliest entered near Grantsville, and was made in 1768. John Sloan was the first settler upon it, a part of which he purchased before the Revolutionary war. He was twice married. By his first wife he had one child only,—Mary,—and by his second, six children. To his son John Joseph he conveyed his lands of four hundred and seventy-three and a half acres, part of "Grassy Cabin Survey." John Sloan died about 1826, and John Joseph Sloan died in 1832. The heirs of John Joseph Sloan conveyed by deed this land to Jacob and Daniel Blougher, but after the death of Sloan, Henry Brewer obtained out of the Land Office of the Western Shore of Maryland a special warrant to escheat this land for an alleged want of legal heirs, and a patent was issued to said Brewer. The lessee of Brewer brought suit in the Allegany County Court against the Bloughers (Jacob and Daniel) to recover the land, setting forth that John Joseph Sloan had no title and could not convey, and claimed it under the State escheat law and patent. The suit finally reached the United States Supreme Court, which (Judge Taney delivering the opinion) at its January term, in 1840, held that the title of the Bloughers was good. John Wesley Blougher now resides on this tract, a mile and a half east of Grantsville, upon which he has a beautiful mansion overlooking the National road.

More than a century ago a young man named Jesse Tomlinson removed from Will's Creek to the Little Meadows (three miles east of Grantsville), where he worked a farm and carried on a tavern. He was prosperous, considering the times, but was a bachelor and needed a helpmate in his business. The tide of immigration, then as now, was westward. On a lucky day a genteel family from the East passed along "Braddock's road," bound for "old Kentuck," and halted at the modest inn for shelter. Mine host was at once captivated, and the young lady never got any farther west than Little Meadows. They lived a happy and prosperous pair, and both died the same year,—1840. He represented the county for many years in the Legislature, and in his day was the most important and influential man in the upper part of Allegany. He was foremost in every enterprise, and in the course of his long life held many public positions, and acquired much property. He owned many slaves, one of whom, Reeson Sweet, still survives. Jesse Tomlinson had five sons, to all of whom he gave a generous education, but none had the thrift of the father. Henry, the youngest and favorite son, graduated at Washington College, Pennsylvania, and in 1825 became a member of the

Cumberland bar. He married in Washington, Pa., but lived on his father's ample estate most of his married life, and died while on a visit to his old college home in 1838, aged thirty-eight years, the last of the five brothers. Nearly all of this prominent family have for many years rested at the foot of the slope of Meadow Mountain, at a spot indicated by a beautiful marble shaft, in full view of the "Stone House," and quite near the site of a small fort built by Washington in one of his campaigns to Fort Pitt. Washington arrived here May 9, 1754, with one hundred and fifty men. This fort has been completely effaced.

Tomlinson's first inn was on the old Braddock road, and was called the "Red House." Afterwards he erected the splendid "Stone House," on the National road, and just a little distance from the former. He was the first postmaster in the region, and kept the post-office and a little store in his tavern. "Tomlinson's Stand" is twenty-one miles west of Cumberland, eight west of Frostburg, three east of Grantsville, and one hundred and nine miles east of Wheeling. After Tomlinson retired, William Reed kept the tavern until May, 1832, when Christopher and Jonathan Hillerd took it, and carried on the business for many years. The "Stone House" is a massive structure, three and a half stories in the rear and two in front. It has on its rear end a three-story porch and a veranda one story high in front. The lands attached are the most fertile in the State, and lie beautifully at the foot of the mountain. The place is owned now by Hon. John S. Combs, of Lonaconing, and occupied by William Shaw. "Little Meadows" and the "Stone House" are the most attractive sites on the old National road, and threescore years ago they were centres of politics and society in northwestern Allegany County.

Little Crossings is a half-mile east of Grantsville, on the National road, and is memorable from its having been in the Braddock campaign of 1755 the camp of Col. Dunbar's brigade, made up mostly of sick and disabled soldiers, who tarried at this place to recruit their enfeebled bodies, and were so much benefited that in two weeks' time they were enabled to proceed on their way to Fort Du Quesne, but they did not get farther than the top of Laurel Hill, some thirty miles west, before they were met by Maj. Washington, with the scattered remnant of Braddock's proud army, retreating from the disastrous battle on the banks of the Monongahela. Little Crossings was a considerable place when the sites of old and new Grantsville were a wilderness. Here Jesse Tomlinson built a store, which was kept by George Matthews, who is still living at Accident at a very advanced age. This old log weather-boarded store still stands, as does also the two-story log weather-board tavern-house Mr. Tomlinson also built, and which was once a noted inn. The Tomlinson saw and grist-mill was rebuilt in 1856 by Perry Shultz, and is now the property of Eli Stanton. The fine culvert bridge over the "Little Crossings" (Castleman River) was built on the National road in 1817. Andrew Fox built a large planing-mill here in 1878, but just after its completion it was destroyed by fire. Eli Stanton owns fifty acres, embracing the old seat of Little Crossings, where he has erected a handsome residence. A little east of his house lives his brother, Uriah M., half an owner in Schramm & Co.'s distillery (registered No. 17), and located a mile farther east on the National road. It has a capacity for distilling thirty gallons of whisky per day, and is about to be enlarged.

The progenitor of the Stanton family settled just after the Revolution on "Stanton's Purchase," a survey where Schramm & Co.'s distillery is located. He went out hunting one day, and was never seen or heard of afterwards, and was supposed to have been carried off by wandering Indians or killed by wild beasts. His son, John Stanton, was the father of William Stanton, who was born on "Stanton's Purchase," Dec. 18, 1798, and married, in 1822, Magdalena Blocher, by whom he had the following children: James, born March 24, 1823; Maria, May 9, 1825; Andrew J., April 27, 1827; Thomas J., March 26, 1829; Benjamin F., May 6, 1831; William, Dec. 27, 1833; and Samuel, March 31, 1836.

He was married the second time on Aug. 22, 1837, to Mary Ann Ridgely, born Aug. 31, 1818. She was the daughter of Eli and Eleanor Ridgely, early settlers three miles south of Little Crossings, near the North Fork, where they located about 1815, having come from the Eastern Shore. Mr. Stanton's children by this marriage were Ellen R., born July 6, 1838; Eli, Jan. 28, 1841; Levi H., July 10, 1843; George A., Feb. 21, 1847; Josephus, Aug. 11, 1849; Ruth T., June 9, 1851; Mary E., Aug. 7, 1853; Francis H., Aug. 5, 1855; and Uriah M., Feb. 22, 1858. William Stanton died April 20, 1869.

Piney Grove is a region of country in the eastern portion of this district, where the lands were originally covered with magnificent white-pine lumber. John Getty emigrated from Ireland in 1790 and settled at Cresaptown, Allegany Co., and in 1817 removed to this section and opened a tavern on the National road, which had been recently built. His son James married Jane McKenzie, and from this union was born William R. Getty, for twelve years the principal merchant at Grantsville, his place of residence. He was six years magistrate, and has held nearly all the district offices, having at one time, as a candidate for justice of the peace, received all the votes cast but nine. He was unanimously elected, in 1873, the first State senator from Garrett County. In 1881 he was again elected senator, by ninety majority, over George W. Wilson, the Republican nominee, though on the State ticket the Republicans had seventy-four majority in the county. In 1870 he was appointed tax-collector of Allegany County, and served two years. The old Getty tavern is now owned by William Bepler, of Frostburg, and occupied by George Jenks, but is no longer used as a tavern. Joshua Johnson built a fine tavern-stand at Piney Grove for Mortimer D. Cade, who died in 1842, and was succeeded in the tavern by John Rench. William Frost, son of Meshach Frost, lives between Piney Grove and Little Meadows, where he has an elegant estate and mansion.

St. Anne's Catholic church is three miles from the National road and twelve from Frostburg. It was built by Father V. F. Schmidt, of St. Michael's Church, Frostburg, who attends it.

Its congregation is mostly composed of farmers, and numbers three hundred. The building is a frame edifice, and is located in the Piney Grove country, where recently silver-mines have been discovered.

The dedication of St. Anne's Catholic church took place on Aug. 29, 1874. A procession was formed at St. Michael's church, Frostburg, and moved down the National road, a distance of twelve miles. The ceremony of dedication was commenced by Father Brennan, of Cumberland. There were many present from Allegany and Garrett Counties, Md., and Somerset, Pa. At the conclusion mass was celebrated for the first time by Rev. Father Anselm, of Cumberland, assisted by Rev. C. Schmidt as deacon, Rev. M. Brennan as sub-deacon, and Rev. E. McKinsil as master of ceremonies.

St. Anne's church is a small but very pretty structure, twenty-five by forty feet in size. The cost was about two thousand five hundred dollars.

George Bruce resided for many years on the fine property now owned by Isaiah Boucher, but upon his second marriage, about 1846, he removed to Frostburg, where he died in 1853. He was a leading man in his day in the community. By his first wife he had five children,—William, Elizabeth, George R., Henry B., and John Jesse. George R. died in 1853. Elizabeth, formerly the wife of the late Normand Bruce, now of Mr. Dickinson, lives in Baltimore, and Henry Basil Bruce resides in Pittsburgh. John J., the youngest, is a prominent business man of Cumberland. He has served in the Legislature, and was for several years a contractor on the Gunpowder Water Extension in Baltimore The Bruce influence was once potent in Allegany County, but the family have all gone from their old seat, near the old log school, at the "Stone House," where forty years ago Charles Slemaker was the popular teacher.

No one now knows when Caspar Durst came to this part of the country. He was the progenitor of all the Durst name who so numerously populate Garrett and Allegany Counties, to say nothing of those now scattered over the neighboring States and the West. His son, Lightfoot John, was a famous hunter, and finding himself short of ammunition on one occasion, and there being none nearer than Cumberland, twenty-seven miles distant, he donned his blue hunting-shirt and deer-skin moccasins, and went a-foot to that town, and returned home before sundown with replenished horn and pouch, and a buck was made to feel the quality of the new powder and lead the same evening. His son Henry married Barbara Garlitz, and moved from near Saulsbury, just over the State line, in Pennsylvania, about 1808, to near the "Stone House," and afterwards to "Maynadier's Ridge," where he and his wife died. His son, Henry Durst, now living in Grantsville, was born March 16, 1802, and married, Jan. 1, 1824, Mahala Young, by whom he had eleven children, of whom five sons and two daughters yet live. He is hale, hearty, and capable of doing a good day's work. When a boy he hunted a great deal, and killed many bears, wolves, and wild-cats.

John Farrell lives only a few hundred yards west of Grantsville, on the National road. He was born near Aker, in County Tyrone, Ireland, in November, 1796, and came to Maryland in September, 1819. He located at Frostburg, and was one of the first to help mine out coal with Meshach Frost, then a laborer on the old National road. He dug coal three years for Mr. Frost and his brothers. The National road was at that time nearly finished to Uniontown, Pa. After leaving Frostburg, he drove a stage for fourteen winters for Stockton & Stokes' stages, working at other labor the balance of the year. He drove from Cumberland to Uniontown, and during the last year was the agent of the stage company, having charge of three sets of coaches. He then settled on his farm. In the spring of 1835 he married Miss Nancy Holderman, who died several years ago, long before which an only son lost his life by the accidental discharge of a gun. He has one child, a daughter, who is married. He was twice elected county commissioner, and made one of the best officials the county ever had. In 1820, when Cumberland was scourged by an epidemic, he went down from his mountain home to act as nurse. He, too, was seized, and laid up for many months, and returned penniless, though he had taken several hundred dollars with him when he went on his charitable mission. He is a faithful member of the Catholic Church and an attendant on its services in Cumberland. He was formerly an active Democratic politician, and was a candidate for the Legislature, but, with his whole ticket, was defeated by the "Know-Nothings." When he came to Garrett there was no village at Grantsville. The site was a wilderness, the only houses being the two of Jesse Tomlinson at "Little Crossings" and "Little Meadows."

Henry Fuller was born in 1800 in Frederick County, but was raised up to manhood in Martinsburg, Va. From there he removed to Somerset County, Pa., where he married Drusilla Shockey. He came to Grantsville in 1837, and died at his home at "Shade Run" (a few yards from the residence of John Farrell), March 23, 1881, and his wife survived him but four months. He was a stonemason by trade, and for some years a hotel-keeper, being the builder of the "Slicer House," the first tavern in New Grantsville, as it was then called. But he abandoned hotel-keeping, and returned to the trowel, square, and plummet for the remainder of his working days. One of the first settlers of Grantsville, he lived a busy life of forty-four years in its midst or vicinity.

Adam Spiker served in the war of 1812, in Capt. Blair's company. He died in 1836, aged forty-seven years, leaving eight sons and four daughters, all of whom live in the county. His widow died in 1877.

The Broadwater family. The Broadwaters settled originally in the northern part of Bloomington District, No. 4, on Little Savage River, and came from Loudon County, Va. Three brothers, Charles, William, and Guy, settled there about 1805, and a fourth brother, Samuel, located near Barton. Of these, Charles was in the war of 1812, and died in 1859, aged eighty-five years. He married Mary Magdalene, of German descent, by whom he had twelve children,—1, Amos; 2, Jefferson; 3, Catharine, married to George Michaels; 4, Mary, married to John Warnick; 5, William C., born Oct. 4, 1812, and who has lived ten years at Grantsville; 6, Charles; 7, Samuel (deceased); 8, Peter (deceased); 9, Rebecca (deceased), married to Mr. Ingland; 10, Mahala, married to William Durst; 11, Ephraim; and 12, Ashford. Charles' wife, Mary (Magdalene), lived to be ninety-three years old. The Broadwater family is one of the largest and best known in the county.

The Beachey family came from Pennsylvania in 1840. John Beachey was a very muscular man, of great strength and activity, and at a "raising" or "muster" could throw any man in the county. But withal, he was a most peaceable citizen, and held in great esteem. His son, Samuel J. Beachey, of Grantsville, was in 1881 elected to the House of Delegates.

Samuel Brown was born in 1770, in Cecil County, Md. In the latter part of the last century he, in company with a young man named Bateman, left their homes on horseback for a six weeks' visit to the Glades, as Somerset County, Pa., was then called. Neither of the two young men ever returned to their homes. They made the acquaintance of two sisters, Emma and Amy Penrod, and were both married at the same time, in 1800, near Somerset, Pa. Mr. Brown and his wife lived in several places on that beautiful stream, Castleman's River, at each removal getting nearer to his native State, Maryland. His last removal was made in 1810, just across the State line to the "Brown Farm," two miles north of the Tomlinson Stone House at "Little Meadows." Here he died in 1829, leaving a wife and ten living children (one dead). He was of a slight and delicate frame, and for many years in poor health. He was a carpenter by trade, but left a good farm for the occupation of his family. He was a very estimable citizen and a man of more than ordinary intelligence, and was greatly respected and deferred to by his neighbors. A lapse of over half a century has nearly obliterated the acquaintances of this pioneer, but here and there still remains an old settler who speaks in the kindest terms of "Sammy Brown," and there is yet to be seen some of his neat and durable work as a carpenter. At his death his widow took charge of the large family and raised them all. Some of the sons pursued their father's calling, but the youngest, Jacob, is now a prominent attorney of Cumberland.

Another son, Capt. Henry Brown, formerly a member of the Legislature from Allegany County, was accidentally killed, May 20, 1869, at the stave-factory of McKaig & Charles. Capt. Brown was engaged in feeding the "head cutter," when the forty-inch saw with which it was supplied burst into fragments, portions of which struck him, carrying off both legs below the knee. Mr. Charles and a young man in his employ were in the building at the time, but providentially escaped injury. Capt. Brown only lived between four and five hours. He was in his sixtieth year, and had three times represented his county in the Legislature, viz., 1847, 1863, and 1865. He was elected a county commissioner in 1836 and 1838. He was born on Castleman's River, in Pennsylvania, Dec. 3, 1809, and had been a resident of the district over half a century. His mother was a woman of extraordinary strength of mind and body. For many years before and after the death of her husband she assumed the direction of the family. Much of her time, especially in her later years, was spent in visiting and ministering to the sick, and it is believed she shortened her life by her exposure and exertions in this manner. She died March 30, 1858, aged seventy-five years. Another son of hers was Col. Hanson Brown, who was murdered in the summer of 1881. A daughter of her son, Capt. Brown, is the wife of George Charles, of Cumberland.

Another leading family was the Custers, of which the late Gen. George A. Custer was a member. John Custer and Emanuel Custer left their native county, Frederick, Va., and went westward, the former stopping at Cresaptown, and the latter going into Somerset County, Pa., and afterwards settling down on a beautiful tract of land called Mount Nebo, near Grantsville, where he died in 1829. John Custer was at one time a hotel-keeper and blacksmith at Cresaptown, and died in 1830, leaving, among other sons, Emanuel Custer, who learned the same trade from his father. About 1824, Emanuel, at the age of nineteen, left his smithy at Clarysville, in Allegany County, with his whole possessions bound up in a cheap handkerchief, for the West. His objective-point was Harrison County, Ohio, to which some relatives had preceded him. About eight years after he returned to his home on a short visit, and again in the winter of 1878, spending about a month in Cumberland. These were the only two visits he ever made to his old home. After remaining for a number of years in Harrison County, he removed to Wood County, in the same State, and thence to Monroe, in Michigan, where he now resides. He was the father of Gen. Custer, who with a number of brave officers and men was killed at the Little Big Horn, in 1876, by Sitting Bull and his savage warriors. In this great disaster Emanuel Custer lost two sons, a grandson, and son-in-law.

The father of Gen. Custer is a man of intelligence, character, and sound principles. He is very modest in his demeanor, and never mentions the name of his distinguished son except when questioned. Though a man of retired manners, he has much influence. The great War Secretary, Stanton, was a devoted friend. More than once during the late war, when a wayward soldier would get into trouble, Emanuel Custer would help him out by appealing to the Secretary of War, who would say, familiarly, "Well, 'Manuel, what must I do now?" All the Custers have long since disappeared from the Cresaptown region.

Emanuel Custer, uncle of the father of Gen. Custer, died fifty years ago, leaving eight sons, — Adam, Jacob, Daniel, John, David, Samuel, Peter, and Jeremiah, and Catherine, an only daughter, long since dead. None of this large number of sons survived except Samuel, now sixty-five years of age, living on the beautiful old homestead, leading a farmer's life, amiable and gentle in his disposition, a good citizen, well liked and respected by all who know him. One of the brothers (Daniel) when a young man had his brains dashed out by being thrown from a sleigh against a tree. Another brother dropped dead in a harvest-field in Washington County from a sunstroke. David, who died some six years ago, was perhaps the strongest and most energetic. All were married except three, some of them leaving very large families, so this branch of the Custer family will not soon fade away in Garrett County as the other has done in Allegany. Jeremiah, the youngest of the family, died a long while ago in the early years of his manhood.

In the past two years two commodious churches, fine frame structures, have been built in the district by the Omish congregations. One is a mile from Grantsville, and the other some three miles distant. These are said to be the first Omish meeting-houses in the country. Previous to their erection these congregations had always held religious worship at their private residences.

Little Crossings is 1998 feet above tide-water, and Negro Mountain 2824. The latter takes its name from the negro man who accompanied Col. Cresap on an expedition against the Indians, and who fell in an encounter between Cresap's force and the savages on the mountain, being the only one of the party slain, while the Indians lost two killed.

Modern Grantsville is situated nearly half a mile from old Grantsville, founded more than three-quarters of a century ago by Hanson Grant, who came from Baltimore. He built on his vast tract of land a large log, weather-boarded house, in which afterwards a Mr. Clarke kept a tavern. It stood on the elevation just back of the residence of William C. Broadwater, but has been torn down for many years. His little village, consisting of about five houses and a church, has entirely disappeared, and the plow and the scythe annually move over the spot. Immediately adjacent is the cemetery, where hundreds of the people of this community, old and young, are buried. The name of Grant has not existed in the county for a generation. Mr. Grant built a costly grist and saw-mill three miles south on the North Fork, near its junction with the South Fork. But the mills being in advance of the settlements, they rotted down unused. The first tavern in old Grantsville was kept by Ned Clark, a colored man, and Peter McCann had a little store. The present village of Grantsville was never regularly laid out as a town, but after its foundation lots were at different times laid out by Joel Miller, Adam and Perry Schultze. The new village was begun in 1832. John Baker built the first house, a tavern, which he kept where Slicer's tavern is, and in which he carried on a store. The tavern-keepers after him were David Mahoney, George Smouse, and Adam Schultze, who built for a tavern the brick house afterwards converted into a school building. Archie Starner built the present Mellinger House in 1842, and kept it until his death in the fall of 1863. George Shaw then took charge until Mrs. Starner's death, after which it was closed as a hotel. In November, 1811, John Mellinger, who for the four previous years had been at the National House, opened it, and has made it a popular summer resort.

The first blacksmith was Joseph Glotfelty, and the first physician Dr. Patterson. The Slicer House was built after 1837, on the site where Baker's tavern had been. John Layman was the first regular merchant after John Baker, who kept a store and tavern together.

The village is situated twenty-five miles west of Cumberland and fourteen from Frostburg. It is on the National road, twelve miles from Myersdale and Petersburg, Pa., the former on the Pittsburgh and Connellsville Railroad, and the latter on the National road. It lies midway between Negro Mountain and Little Crossings, two points replete with historical incidents and Indian legends. Old Grantsville was on Braddock's road, traces of which are still plainly visible. Little Crossings was the voting-place of the district until, by act of the Legislature of March 9, 1850, it was changed to Grantsville. On the vote, Nov. 5, 1872, to locate the county-seat, this village received 590 votes to Oakland's 653 and McHenry's Glades 456, thus lacking only sixty-three votes of becoming the shiretown of the new county of Garrett. In the palmy days of the old National road the village was one of special note to travelers and stage-drivers.

The village was incorporated by the Legislature of 1864–65, and was rechartered about 1878. An effort is now being made to give the charter effect by the election of proper municipal officers.

The cemetery is adjacent to and nearly on the site of old Grantsville. Among the interments here are those of

Hannah, wife of John Smith, died Sept. 30, 1874, aged 82.
Adam Shultze, died July 27, 1864, aged 75.
Andrew Arendt, died Sept. 22, 1873, aged 57.
Peter Yeast, died Jan. 16, 1851, aged 42.
Sarah, wife of Philip Durst, died June 7, 1870, aged 60.
David Compton, died Aug. 14, 1866, aged 52.
Elisha Durst, died April 6, 1867, aged 34.
John Yeast, born Nov. 7, 1797, died July 22, 1833.
Mrs. McGillis, born July 7, 1805, died April 4, 1831.
James Wright, died March 17, 1858, aged 71; and his wife, Elizabeth, March 14, 1854, aged 66.
Sarah A., wife of David Johnson, died Jan. 7, 1863, aged 48.
William Woodin, died Oct. 3, 1834, aged 56; and Sally, his wife, March 7, 1843, aged 60.
Peter Shultz, born July 19, 1812, died Nov. 6, 1857.
Barbara, wife of John Kemp, died July 27, 1853, aged 59.
George Brown, died June 10, 1854, aged 33.
John Slicer, died March 8, 1873; and Rachel, his wife, Nov. 17, 1869, aged 69.
Simon Matthews, died Jan. 4, 1878, aged 43.
Maria, wife of Henry Smouser, died Nov. 6, 1868, aged 36.
Chris. Winterberg, died May 20, 1872, aged 69; and his wife, Elizabeth, Oct. 1, 1871, aged 69.
Margaret Sheets, died Aug. 20, 1851, aged 83.
Amy, wife of Samuel Brown, died March 30, 1858, aged 75.
Jacob Blocher, died June 26, 1872, aged 74; and his wife, Elizabeth, Dec. 12, 1841, aged 40.
William B. Stanton, died April 21, 1880, aged 46.
Ann M., wife of Jacob Arendt, died Jan. 28, 1858, aged 48.
George Smouse, died Feb. 6, 1855, aged 41.
John Layman, died Sept. 23, 1845, aged 39.
Mortimer D. Cade, died Oct. 3, 1842, aged 40.
Joseph Glotfelty, died May 27, 1864, aged 64; and his wife, Sarah A., Dec. 30, 1868, aged 59.

The Methodist Episcopal church, a frame edifice, was erected in 1847 under the auspices of Rev. Robert Laughlin, the preacher in charge. Before that period there was preaching in the old log school-house. Since then the pastors have been, as far as the church records show:

1847, Robert Laughlin; 1849, Benjamin Ison; 1851, Joseph Dewitt; 1853, William Smith; 1855, G. Martin; 1857, Eli Engle; 1858, Franklin Ball; 1859, D. O. Stuart; 1862, J. W. Webb; 1863, G. W. Arnold, W. L. Hindman; 1864, W. L. Hindman; 1865, J. B. Feather; 1869, J. B. Blakeny; 1870, J. W. Webb; 1871, W. J. Sharp; 1874, C. J. Tribbet; 1875, Wesley Chidester; 1876, Joseph Lee; 1877, C. J. Harrison; 1878, E. J. Price; 1879, David Flannigan, the present incumbent, who was born in Fayette County, Pa.

His circuit embraces this church, Zion church, in Johnson's District, just west of Layman's Half-way House, and a church at New Germany, seven miles south.

The church trustees are Samuel J. Beachey, William Chapman, Samuel Broadwater, William Broadwater, and David Durst. The superintendent of the Sunday-school is Charles Snider.

The Lutheran church, a frame building, was erected in 1856. Its pastors have been:

1856, Rev. Mr. Phaler; 1869, Richard Lazarus; 1871, Peter Lane; 1873, J. G. Brenniger; 1877, J. J. Young, present incumbent, who resides at Accident.

Rev. Mr. Phaler had preached in this section long years before the church was built, for some time in the German Reformed church, and before its erection in the old log school-house.

Henry Winterberg is superintendent of the Sunday-school.

The council are Henry Winterberg, Charles Bill (elders), Adolph Hoenig, David Popp, H. Lowenstein (deceased).

The trustees are Henry Wagoner, Sr., August Bonig, Charles Bill, Henry Winterberg, Charles Lowenstein (deceased), H. Wagoner, Jr., Henry Diffenbach.

Before 1849, when the German Reformed church was erected, the congregation worshiped in the old log school-house. Its pastor for several years has been Rev. C. M. Heilman, who resides at Saulsbury, Pa.

The merchants of the town are J. S. Broadwater, H. C. Shaw, and Mr. Bowser. The resident physicians are Drs. O. C. Getty, H. J. Bevans, and Asa Spiker. Conrad Bodis operates the woolen-mills near the village, and Patrick Dorsey, Samuel S. Durst, and E. J. Miller & Bro. the saw-mills. H. Muhlenberg is postmaster, and Henry Winterberg magistrate, appointed in 1879 by Governor Hamilton.

Its population, by the census of 1880, was 220. Joseph Glotfelty is the operator for the Western Union Telegraph line. The village is destined soon, from its fine location, to become a favorite summer resort. About a mile distant is the artesian well, dug to the depth of seven hundred and eighty feet a few years ago for coal-oil, but without success. A white sulphur spring, however, was reached, whose waters are unsurpassed in the country.

About the year 1836, Adam Schultz removed from Somerset County, Pa., to Grantsville, with a large family of children. He embarked in the tanning business, or rather, he continued it during the remainder of his life. At one period, during the flush times of the old National road, he was engaged in the hotel business. Mr. Schultz, in the latter part of his life, was not engaged actively in business, but his sound advice and strong common sense were constantly infused into it. He died in 1864, at the age of seventy-five. A beautiful and costly monument marks his resting-place in the cemetery. He was the father (by two marriages) of eighteen children,—ten sons and eight daughters. Out of this large family, but one, the wife of John Royer, remains in the vicinity.

The name of Schultz, once so general and respectable in this region, does not exist in the county. The aged widow is still living, with her surviving children, at or near St. Louis. Perry, one of the sons, was elected sheriff of Allegany County in 1853, but died of the cholera in St. Louis some ten years ago, after being in business there some years. Chauncey Forward (named after a distinguished Pennsylvania lawyer) has been living in St. Louis for about twenty years, and is now, and has been for years, one of the foremost men of the city. As a business man he stands very high, and politically, though not much of a partisan, he has held some very important and honorable positions.

John A. J. Schultz, a younger brother, went to St. Louis in 1864, and is now largely interested in and is running the Pittsburgh Tannery, which is the largest establishment of the kind west of the Mississippi. He is a practical tanner, and has lately obtained a patent for making belting leather by a hitherto unknown process, by which he says he can make the strongest and most durable belting leather in the world.

Norman Brown, a grandson of old Mr. Schultz, and son of the late George Brown, left Grantsville just after the war, a poor tanner-boy, without a dollar. To-day he is one of the first business men of St. Louis in the hide and leather trade, with a business of over half a million a year in his five extensive houses.

All those who have lived beyond the period of middle age will remember the wonderful traffic that was carried on by means of the pike,—there were some fourteen coaches each way every day of the Old Line and Good Intent Companies,—what emulation and even envy there would be between the different drivers as to the merits of their respective lines in regard to speed and endurance of horses. Then there were Adams' express wagons, then the line wagons, carrying freight to all points along the road; besides innumerable private vehicles of all descriptions. Whenever a farmer did not have much to do he would rig up his team and go to hauling on the pike.

In addition to all these were the droves of all kinds,—horses, mules, cattle, sheep, and hogs.

Most of the great men of the United States have passed over this road, particularly those from the West and Southwest, such as Jackson, Clay, Benton, Randolph, Allan, Scott, Taylor, and hosts of others. Repair-hands were constantly at work, and even then they could hardly keep the road in order, the big wagons crushing everything under them like egg-shells. The old pike still winds its way over mountains and through valleys, but its greatness has long since departed. The grass grows in some places in its very centre, and the grand old thoroughfare has been deserted for a swifter mode of transit.

It has been appropriately compared with the Appian Way, and the magnificent stone bridge over the Youghiogheny, at Somerfield, has never been excelled. Unless an earthquake should destroy it, it will last a thousand years. The silence and loneliness along the road to-day is absolutely painful. In the twenty-six miles between Petersburg and Uniontown the traveler frequently does not meet a single individual.

Upon the road between Petersburg and Grantsville the change is more striking, because the soil is more sterile, and people who formerly lived near the pike depended chiefly on the travel for their support. There is not between the points named a single public-house, where thirty years ago there were twelve; and there is not a single individual living on the pike now who lived there then, with one possible exception; and between Somerfield and Petersburg only two of the old-time tavern-keepers are living in the same houses now,—Hon. William Endsley and John Mitchell,—and they can hardly be said to keep public-houses, as they only do so for accommodation. In Somerfield there are three other houses besides Mr. Endsley's that used to be taverns. All did well. One of them is the stage-office, now between Somerfield and Petersburg. In Petersburg there is only one house, Lot Watson's, where the public can be accommodated, instead of the three at this point years ago. In Petersburg and vicinity, however, there are more persons living who remember and were in part identified with the rise and fall of the pike than anywhere on its line. In addition to John Mitchell, just named, there are now living upon this portion of the road the following persons who were prominently connected with the pike during its "palmiest" days: Andrew Mitchell, William Roddy, Capt. Glisan, Henry McGee, Henry Risheberger, Peter Stark, Gen. Ross, Ephraim Stuck, Jerry Strahan, William Wass, George W. and Philip Turney, Wesley Jeffries, Allen Nicklow, and James McCartney, who used to work the Rich Hill quarry, getting out limestone for the pike.

The Legislature of Maryland, by a recent act, gave so much of the road as runs through Garrett County, and through Allegany County, to the charge of the county; consequently no toll is collected, and the road is kept in repair by the local supervisors. In some places the bottom has been reached and the bed-rock has to be driven over. This is partly owing to mismanagement while the road remained under the control of the State. This portion of the road (between Grantsville and Petersburg) abounds with magnificent landscape views.

Within two miles east of Petersburg there were formerly four hotels, one known latterly as the Miller farm, another the Wentling farm and hotel, and lastly the house so successfully kept by Daniel Augustine. After this was the famous hostlery on the top of Winding Ridge. At each of these houses there would be a blacksmith-shop and a "tenant" house or two, in which resided persons who would do the "chores" around the hotel.

Near by was a house kept by Mr. Althouse, and another where Henry Walter dispensed hospitalities to the traveling public. Next was the Claggett property, kept by Harvey Beam, and afterwards by David Johnson; following this was John Woods' tavern. Then came the Fairall house, known the length of the pike, not a vestige of which remains,—the building, the commodious stables, and the extensive garden having all disappeared.

The next place is the Sheets' stand, formerly the objective-point of all hog-drovers. Not far from here was the Holderman, or Smouse tavern, well patronized in its day, and afterwards presided over by Polly Recknor.

The next hotel was where Maj. D. W. DeHaven, a prominent citizen of Addison township, served the public for several years. In Grantsville, where there used to be many hotels, there is now but one.

Of all the drivers on the pike only a few remain. "Sandy Conner," who drove Henry Clay from Keyser's Ridge to Somerfield in forty-five minutes, and whose reminiscences of his old coaching days are always listened to with great pleasure, still lives not far from Grantsville. Thomas Wilhern, who has since become a mighty hunter in Garrett County, and Fielding Montague, who lives in Fayette County, Pa., are about the only survivors in this region.

The following is a list of school-teachers in the district for the year ending May 13, 1881:

School No. 1.—Ephraim Enlow.
No. 2.—M. C. McClintock.
No. 3.—George Royer.
No. 4.—Maria Lininger, George P. Thistle.
No. 5.—Mary Newman.
No. 6.—F. M. Conneway.
No. 7.—J. H. McKinly.
No. 8.—Emanuel Custer.
No. 9.—Rufus M. Enlow.
No. 10.—Anna Baker.
No. 11.—A. J. Bevans.
No. 12.—W. N. Werner.
No. 13.—Annie L. Enlow.
No. 14.—Frank Listun.
No. 15.—Mrs. T. Brown.
No. 16.—N. A. Munst.
No. 17.—Annie E. Munst.

School trustees for year ending May, 1882:

School No. 1. Grantsville.—Eli Stanton, Henry Winterberg, Joseph Glotfelty.

No. 2. Shade Run, or Beachy.—John Farrell, Aaron Beachy, Henry H. Miller.

No. 3. Keyser Ridge.—S. Butler, John Ople, Samuel Leochel.

No. 4. Lancaster, or Pea Ridge.—John F. Robeson, Andrew J. Lancaster, John Wilhelm.

No. 5. McKenzie—Leo McKenzie, Morgan Robeson, Christian Blocher.

No. 6. Back Woods.—Ashford Warnick, John Warnick, Jas. H. Bowers.

No. 7. New Germany.—Joel Wyland, Henry Broadwater, Archibald Warnick.

No. 8. Dorsey.—Jacob Fresh, Samuel S. Durst, Patrick Dorsey.

No. 9. Wiley.—Thomas J. Stanton, James P. Wiley, Henry Stark.

No. 10. Maynadier Ridge.—Michael Custer, Charles Warnick, Josephus Broadwater.

No. 11.—Levi Kinsinger, Moses Kamp, Christian Ginerich.

No. 12. Werner.—Amos Butler, John Yomer, Chas. Werner.

No. 13. Lohr.—P. P. Lohr, Elias Orndorf, Thos. B. Wiley.

No. 14. Engle's Mills.—Henry Yost, Jonas J. Beachy, Solomon Baker.

No. 15. Pope.—B. Anderson, Joshua Turner, Michael S. Durst.

No. 16. Compton.—Ross Compton, Edward Harshbarger, W. H. Swanger.

No. 17. Maust.—A. A. Maust, Henry Newman.

Bloomington District, No. 4, is bounded on the north by Grantsville and Johnson's Districts, east by Allegany County, south by Altamont District and West Virginia, and west by Altamont District.

Among the first to settle in this district were the Barnards, Michaelses, Twiggses, Wilsons, Abernathys, Adamses, Warnicks, Tichnells, Brants, Copelands, Simpsons, Sharplesses, Paughs, Nethkins, Millers, Knights, Loars, Hamiltons, Groves, Duckworths, and Dawsons.

Bloomington Village, located 1037 feet above tidewater, is a station on the Baltimore and Ohio Railroad, two hundred and eight miles from Baltimore, and twenty-four east of Oakland. It is at the junction of the Potomac and Savage Rivers. The only church is that of the Methodist Episcopal congregation. M. E. Moody is the postmaster. The physician is Dr. E. H. Parsons, and the merchants William Moody, W. L. Rawlings, and Andrew Mullen. W. A. Brydon is a large coal operator, and J. Somerville is superintendent of the Empire Coal Company. James Cummings and Collins Hepburn are engineers, and William Mullen railroad and express agent. A well-kept hotel is conducted by Thomas Garvey. A. J. Warnick is, and has been for many years, the magistrate. Mr. W. L. Rawlings was the Democratic candidate for register of wills on the county ticket in 1879. Dr. Parsons settled here two years ago, and originally came from Tucker County, W. Va.

The Lochiel Lumber Company, of which J. I. Livingston is superintendent, is the largest in Maryland, and is connected with the Pennsylvania Standard Oil Company. Its many large mills are near the town, to whose prosperity it has largely contributed since its organization and location here seven years ago. Before the building of the Baltimore and Ohio Railroad this now thriving village (the second in the county in population and business) was but a small hamlet. Among the largest farmers in its vicinity are W. H. Barnard, Joshua Tichnell, Henry Paugh, and Otho Barnard, whose ancestors were the first settlers in this region. According to the census of 1880, Bloomington has 341 inhabitants.

The West Virginia Central Railroad, of which Henry G. Davis, United States senator from West Virginia, Hon. James G. Blaine, Senator Windom, of Minnesota, Senator Bayard, Governor W. T. Hamilton, Gen. Grant, and Augustus Schell, of New York, are leading owners, is already built over fourteen miles from near Bloomington, extending to the rich coal-fields and lumber districts of West Virginia. This railroad taps the Baltimore and Ohio Railroad near Bloomington. The Piedmont Coal and Iron Company, of which John Somerville is superintendent, is now successfully working its mine near the town. The West Virginia Central Railroad is beautifully laid out, and follows the North Branch of the Potomac closely. Three miles from the point to which it is now completed are the noted coal-mines of Elk Garden. The West Virginia Central and Pittsburgh Company have around Elk Garden over twenty-five thousand acres of the finest coal lands in this the great Piedmont coal-basin. Their tract, only sixteen miles from Bloomington, is in a section very rich, but as yet undeveloped, and for the purpose of developing it the railroad was built and the improvements made. Their tract extends for nearly thirty miles along the North Branch, and one thousand acres of it around Elk Garden is what is known as "Big Vein" coal, which is fourteen feet thick, and will yield eighteen thousand tons to the acre. The completion of this road and the opening of the mines upon a larger scale will be the making of Bloomington, which bids fair to become a great railroad point and the seat of the coal and lumber trade of Garrett County. The company obtained its charter in 1866, but nothing was done until about 1879. The Piedmont region has three good workable veins, four, six, and fourteen feet in width, which are estimated to contain two billion four hundred million tons of bituminous coal. The portion of this great basin that lies north of the Baltimore and Ohio Railroad was actively opened in 1842, and is now occupied by fifteen different coal companies, with an aggregate capital of over thirty million dollars. The West Virginia Central Railroad will be extended south to other rich fields, up the North Branch, through Grant County; thence to the iron-ore lands farther south; thence running through Randolph, Pocahontas, and Tucker Counties to the Greenbrier River, and to the southeastern part of the State, connecting with the Richmond and Allegany road. Since 1842 an enormous supply of coal has been drawn from only one end of the Cumberland region, and there is still a vast tract of coal lands four times as large as the tract now being worked in Pennsylvania and Maryland untouched.

Below is given a list of school-teachers for the year ending May 13, 1881:

School No. 1.—Eva F. Riggs.
No. 2.—William McRobie.
No. 3.—T. Bridendolph.
No. 4.—P. A. Michael.
No. 5.—Ella J. Lininger.
No. 6.—Mary E. Dougherty.
No. 7.—Katie Kause.

School trustees for year ending May, 1882:

School No. 1. Bloomington.—E. Kemp, W. L. Rawlings, Robert Somerville.

No. 2. Chestnut Grove.—William H. Barnard, Joshua Tichnell. Henry Warnick.

No. 3. Aaron Run.—To be appointed.

No. 4. Firm Rock.—Marcus Fazenbaker, John L. Michael, Dennis Collins.

No. 5. Magruder.—Joseph Inskeep, James Magruder, Robert Russell.

No. 6. Weir.—Simeon W. Green, James Weir, Jacob Beeman.

No. 7. Gregg.—W. W. Broadwater, Elias Merrill.

No. 8. Wilt.—George O. Broadwater, Theop. Wilt, John W. Wilt.

Accident District, No. 5, is bounded on the north by Pennsylvania, east by Grantsville District, south by Sang Run District, and west by Selbysport District.

Among the first settlers were the Gurneys, Engleharts, Beeghleys, Boyers, Frotzs, Kamps, Hinebaughs, Kolbs, Frushes, Growers, Swangers, Swalps, Pysells, Orndorffs, Mossers, Gorricks, Dixons, Turneys, Lees, Spikers, Lohrs, Hostetters, Garricks, Diehls, Leningers, Sperlings, Margraffs, Mossers, Richters, Millers, Snyders, Shartzers, Rushes, Schlossnagles, Wellers, Beckerds, and Engles.

The village of Accident is twenty miles from Oakland, and has a Lutheran and Tunker church.

The merchants are J. W. Boyer & Son, John E. Gnagey, and Mrs. A. B. Ries. The physicians are Drs. E. H. Glotfelty and A. F. Speicher. Melcher Weller and M. J. Miller operate distilleries. Henry Casey and Samuel Engle are millers. George T. Englehart is the undertaker. John L. Richter and William Hinebaugh are tanners; Christian Snyder and Eli McMillen, harness-makers; Henry Zinken and John Eckart, wagon-makers; Adam Gohringer, Ferdinand Grouse, Frederick Grower, and George F. Menhorn, blacksmiths; Henry & Van Kahl, carpenters; Alexander Hauftling, Edward Richter, and George Vagdon, boot and shoemakers.

Engle's Mills lies sixteen miles from Confluence, Pa., near Bear Creek. Henry Kease is postmaster, Samuel Engle and Henry Kease, millers; Frederick Krause, blacksmith; Josiah and M. J. Beeghley, carpenters. The place was named in honor of Samuel Engle, the proprietor of the mills.

The following is a list of school-teachers in the district for year ending May 13, 1881:

School No. 1.—A. W. Dewitt.
No. 2.—T. K. Welch.
No. 3.—E. A. Browning.
No. 4.—J. J. Beeghley.
No. 5.—Emma F. De Witt.
No. 6.—Allie M. Swalp.
No. 7.—W. W. Griffith.
No. 8.—George Dunham.
No. 9.—Leslie E. Friend.

School trustees for year ending May, 1882:

School No. 1. Accident.—Daniel Hinebaugh, V. Kahle, Adam Garringer.

No. 2. Fairview.—Henry Gonig, George Spoerline, Joseph Hostetter.

No. 3. Flat Woods.—Benjamin Shepp, John Wilburn, James Skiles.

No. 4. Cove.—W. M. Lohr, George Richter, Eli Brown.

No. 5. Bear Creek.—Austin Speicher, Jacob Mosser, Daniel Hostetter.

No. 6. Miller.—S. H. Ryland, Daniel Beeghley, Jeremiah Strawn.

No. 7. Winding Ridge.—John W. Bowman, Hiram Bowser, George Sheerer.

No. 8. Oak Hill.—Abraham Turney, James W. Lee, Henry Schlossnagle.

No. 9. Schrock.—Nimrod Glotfelty, Moses Schrock, D. D. Brenneman.

Sang Run District, No. 6, is bounded on the north by Selbysport District and Grantsville District, east by Grantsville and Altamont Districts, south by Oakland District, and west by West Virginia. Among the early settlers were the Yeagers, Blackburns, Weimers, Bowsers, Bowmans, Smiths, Spechts, Brants, Casteels, Pysells, Slones, Pecks, Dranes, Eckards, Frakers, Fulmers, Meeses, Keefers, McRobies, and Glotfeltys.

McHenry is fourteen miles from Oakland. E. J. Blackburn is the merchant, and George H. Fulmer postmaster. The saw-mills are run by F. Keefer,

Jonas and Mahlon Glotfelty, and the blacksmith-shop by S. A. McRobie.

Johnstown is situated fourteen miles from Deer Park and sixteen from Oakland. Daniel Smith is postmaster and merchant; Franklin Seebold, carpenter; Adam Fox, blacksmith; and Meshach Mattingly a prominent farmer.

The school-teachers in the district for the year ending May 13, 1881, are:

School No. 1.—G. D. Browning.
No. 2.—M. M. Levis.
No. 3.—Horace R. Dewitt.
No. 4.—Annie E. Fazenbaker.
No. 5.—A. W. Frederick.
No. 6.—Henry E. Friend.

School trustees for the year ending May, 1882:

School No. 1. Muddy Creek.—Thomas Browning, Eug. Teets, Thomas C. Friend.
No. 2. McHenry.—Joseph Meese, J. Glotfelty, Douglas McLane.
No. 3. Johnstown.—M. Mattingley, A. C. Dewitt, Wm. Dewitt.
No. 4. Sang Run.—R. T. Browning, Amos Friend, D. H. Friend.
No. 5. Pine Swamp.—J. M. Frankhouser, John E. Otto, E. Allbright.
No. 5. Bishoff.—George E. Bishoff, J. M. Lowdermilk, Briscon Welsh.

Oakland District, No. 7, is bounded on the north by Sang Run District, east by Altamont and Ryan's Glades Districts, south by Ryan's Glades District, and west by West Virginia. Among its first settlers were the Casteels, Ashbys, Schaffers, Thompsons, Lowers, Ridders, Brownings, Brays, Brants, Bowers, Bishops, Bernards, Beckmans, Yutzys, Whites, Wootrings, Tottens, Spikers, Combses, Davises, Eulows, De Berrys, Goodwins, Fazenbakers, Haigs, Gortners, Slabachs, Schleys, Russells, Ridders, Reynoldses, Rasches, Halls, Hanns, Harts, Hugheses, Proctors, Porters, Perrys, Johnsons, Irvins, Kepners, Kings, Lees, Taskers, Willsons, Friends, Harshbergers, Stemples, Paughs, Hinebaughs, Hayeses, Draeges, and Schooleys.

A number of eminent clergymen and laymen, chiefly of the Methodist Episcopal Church, in 1881 formed an association which projected the summer resort called "Mountain Lake Park," on the summit of the Alleganies. These gentlemen reside in Cincinnati, Wheeling, Parkersburg, Philadelphia, Baltimore, and Oakland. The tract of land purchased is on the Baltimore and Ohio Railroad, two miles east of Oakland, and contains nearly eight hundred acres, heavily timbered with white-oak. It has a front of three-quarters of a mile on the north side of the railroad, and extends back over a glade and gently-rising hills for a mile. A branch of the Youghiogheny flows through it, which by a series of dams is to be converted into three lakes. The water is pure and plentiful. Rev. C. P. Masden, of Wheeling, is president of the association; Mr. List, of the same city, treasurer; Maj. Anderson, secretary. The board of directors are Revs. C. P. Masden, J. F. Goucher, J. B. Van Meter, Dr. Logan, and John Davis, representing Wheeling, Oakland, and Baltimore. The other stockholders are Revs. E. W. Ryan, T. B. Hughes, W. C. Snodgrass, George C. Wilding, all of the West Virginia Conference; Rev. John Thompson, of Philadelphia; and Mr. Conner, of Wheeling. The capital stock is fifteen thousand dollars. One hundred lots have been disposed of upon the condition that the purchasers erect by 1882 a cottage upon each worth not less than three hundred dollars. At least one hundred and fifteen cottages will be built by the summer of 1882. The place is to be made a first order railroad station, where all trains will stop except Sunday trains, and the excursion rates are to be the same as to Deer Park or Oakland. The aim is to create a summer resort combining the religious, educational, and recreation features of the best establishments of the kind now in existence.

Sunday-school assemblies, temperance conventions, and other bodies will be invited to make use of its facilities. Courses of lectures will be delivered, and a camp-meeting held. Twenty acres of the best timbered ground are set apart for the use of these assemblies. Revs. J. F. Goucher and J. B. Van Meter represent the association in Baltimore.

The growing town of Oakland, the county-seat of Garrett, is two hundred and thirty-two miles from Baltimore, on the Baltimore and Ohio Railroad. It is located on the summit of a plateau of the Allegany Mountains, two thousand three hundred and seventy-two feet above tide-water, and its atmosphere is noted for purity and healthfulness. The neighboring streams abound with trout, and the surrounding mountains with game of all descriptions. It derives its name from the heavy and splendid oak timber that originally covered its beautiful site and the neighboring region. It is one of the most popular and attractive summer resorts in America. When the Baltimore and Ohio Railroad surveyed through Oakland the location for its road in 1848, and began work in 1849, Isaac McCarty owned the land on which the town now stands. In the year 1849 he laid it out into lots. The first house erected was the railroad depot, where Chisholm's drug-store now is. The second building put up was a store-house and residence by Daniel R. Brant, on the lot now owned by the heirs of Ezekiel Totten. The third building erected was a store-house and residence by J. L. Townshend, on the corner of

Oak and Second Streets, and now the property of Henry Rasche. The first merchants were Daniel R. Brant and J. L. Townshend. J. L. Townshend and D. E. Offutt have been in the mercantile business since 1863. The former settled here in 1853, and served many years as magistrate under the old elective system.

The first physician was Dr. J. H. Conn, who located here in 1851, and died in the spring of 1854. He was succeeded by Dr. J. F. Dorsey, from Monongahela County, W. Va. Dr. Samuel Mead located in 1857, and after him came Dr. Ramsey and Dr. J. Lee McComas. Dr. E. H. Bartlett, born on the island of Cuba, and a graduate of the Medical Department of Yale College, settled here at the close of the late war, in which he participated in the Confederate service.

One of the prominent citizens of Oakland, and a physician in large practice, is Dr. Bayard T. Keller, who was born in Cumberland, Allegany Co., Md., Feb. 22, 1850, and is the eldest of the six children of Daniel T. and Mary J. (Thistle) Keller. The family are of German origin, and settled in Frankfort, Hampshire Co., Va. (now West Virginia), before the Revolution. Daniel Keller, his grandfather, was a farmer there, and married a Miss Taylor, who bore him two children,—John and Daniel T. Soon after the birth of the latter his wife died. Daniel Keller died at the residence of his son Daniel, at Barton, Allegany Co., November, 1870. His son, and the father of the doctor, Daniel T. Keller, was a merchant at first at Patterson Creek Depot, on the Baltimore and Ohio Railroad. Having been elected sheriff of Hampshire County he moved to Romney, the county-seat, where he remained from 1859 to 1865. At the commencement of the civil war he joined the Confederate army as lieutenant in the Thirteenth Virginia Regiment, Gen. "Stonewall" Jackson's brigade. He was taken prisoner and confined for several months at Camp Chase. After the close of the war he carried on the mercantile business at Patterson's Depot for two years, then moved to Barton, where he continued in trade up to the time of his death, which occurred Feb. 8, 1871. His wife was Mary J., daughter of George and Ann (Bayard) Thistle. Her father emigrated from Ireland in 1798 and settled in Cumberland. On her mother s side she was a granddaughter of John H. Bayard, a brother of the elder James A. Bayard, senator from Delaware. The children of this union were Bayard T., the subject of this sketch; Maggie A., wife of C. B. Ludwig, editor of the *Democrat* at Oakland; Alice R., wife of O. G. Getty, a physician living at Grantsville; Charles G., a dentist at the same place; Ida, not living; and Mary C., living with her mother at Oakland.

Dr. B. T. Keller received his primary education at the Romney Classical Institute, and afterwards studied at Allegany County Academy, Cumberland. He began the study of medicine in 1868 with Dr. B. A. Dougherty, with whom he remained one year. Subsequently he attended two courses of lectures at the University of Maryland, from which institution he received his medical diploma in 1871. During the last course of lectures he was clinical assistant at the Baltimore Infirmary. In March, 1871, he commenced the practice of his profession at Grantsville, and continued there for nearly ten years. In February, 1881, he removed to Oakland, where he is now pursuing his profession. He married, Nov. 10, 1875, Elizabeth J., daughter of William and Charlotte (Brant) Casteel. Their children are Mary A., Alice M., Daniel C., and an infant. In politics he is a Democrat, and both himself and wife are members of the German Reformed Church in Grantsville. Dr. Keller is also a member of the American Legion of Honor.

DR. BAYARD T. KELLER.

The first blacksmith was Conrad Whetzel. The first hotel was built by White & Burton, near the present "Glades Hotel," and was called the "Glades." It was subsequently purchased by Perry Lyles, who was succeeded in 1858 by John Daily. It burned down in 1877, and was rebuilt the same year by Mr. Daily. Since Mr. Daily's death, in September, 1881, it has been under the management of John B. Brant,

OAKLAND HOTEL, Oakland, Md.

a popular gentleman, associated with Mr. Daily from the time the latter opened the hotel in 1858. This house has a national reputation, is very commodious, and elegantly furnished.

Oakland Hotel, erected by the Baltimore and Ohio Railroad in 1878, is at this place. It is situated on a mountain slope in the town of Oakland, and is shaded by handsome forest-trees. It is a spacious structure, and very attractive in appearance, with handsome verandas and roomy halls and apartments. It is a favorite summer hotel, and in its immediate vicinity are numerous localities to which excursions are made by the guests. In every direction the scenery is of a grand and diversified character, and the picturesque walks and drives are almost innumerable. In 1880 the manager was J. P. Dukehart, the famous conductor of treasure between the Atlantic and Pacific coasts, and in 1881 the hotel was in charge of Mr. Wood, proprietor of the Eutaw House, Baltimore. Both Oakland and Deer Park Hotels are fitted up with handsome furniture, Brussels carpets, spring beds, dressing-closets, and mantel and grate in every room, so that during cool weather fires can be lit at any time without trouble. Handsome verandas extend along the fronts of both these hotels, and adjoining them are billiard-rooms, ten-pin alleys, accomodations for horses and carriages, etc. Both are surrounded by handsome grounds, laid out with great taste and tended with scrupulous care, and in convenience of arrangement and beauty of design they are not surpassed by any similar buildings in the country.

The surrounding region is one of remarkable beauty, and the locality is noted for purity of atmosphere, coolness, and salubrity. The invigorating mountain air is relished alike by the robust and the delicate, and one of the enjoyable sensations in summer is a sound night's sleep under blankets, when those who are compelled to remain in the cities are sweltering from the excessive heat. The Deer Park and Oakland Hotels are connected by telephone, and the guests of the two houses can thus converse together whenever they desire. There are frequent interchanges of visits between the guests of the two hotels, and the season at both is always bright and animated. S. Spencer has general charge of the Baltimore and Ohio Railroad hotels; J. P. Gordon is general superintendent, and Maj. N. S. Hill is the purchasing agent in Baltimore.

The "Coddington House" was built before the war by James Caton, and is now owned by Ezekiel Totten's heirs. Oakland was on the old road from Winchester, Va., to Kingwood. Among the oldest settlers in this region were Stephen Merrill, yet living, and over one hundred years old, and Isaac McCarty, John Steyer, George Loar, Henry Lower, and William White, all deceased.

Thomas J. Peddicord was born near Lisbon, Anne Arundel Co. (now Howard), Md., Nov. 9, 1839. Jasper Peddicord, his great-grandfather, was the son of the emigrant, who came from Ireland and settled in Anne Arundel County. Thomas Peddicord, his

T. J. Peddicord

grandfather, was born there, and married Mary Landon, a native of Baltimore. By this union there were nine children,—four sons and five daughters,—all of whom but one (who died before reaching his majority) married and settled in Howard County. Washington A. Peddicord, his father, the eldest of the family, married Rebecca, daughter of John Crawford, of Howard County. Their children were Thomas J., Sarah C., Rebecca J., Mary E., Leanna W., Jeremiah E., Laura L., James A., and Josephine M. Three daughters, viz., Rebecca J., Leanna W., and Josephine M., are dead. The three sons and three daughters living are married, and, with the exception of Thomas J., are residents of Howard County. Washington A. Peddicord and wife are living about four miles from the old Peddicord homestead, in Howard County. Thomas J. lived at home on the farm up to the time of his majority, and attended the common school of his native county until sixteen years of age. Subsequently for two years he was under the private instruction of William T. Crapster, a graduate of Harvard College. He then commenced the study of medicine under Dr. John H. Owings, of his native place. At the end of a year's study his preceptor, fancying his pupil was bestowing more than a proportionate share of his time upon the young ladies, gave him the plain alternative of dropping the girls or medicine. He dropped medicine and returned home. At the age of twenty-one he married Rebecca, daughter of James H. and Mary Clagett. Mrs. Peddicord was born near Gaithersburg, Montgomery Co., Md., March 5, 1843. For five years after his marriage he carried on a farm, given him by his father. At the end of the five years he sold his farm and became deputy sheriff under his father-in-law, and for two years,—1868 and 1869,—while acting as sheriff, he devoted his spare time to the study of law. He was admitted to the bar January, 1871, and opened an office at Rockville, where he continued in the practice of his profession until 1873. In June of that year he moved to Oakland, and was the third lawyer to open an office in the new county of Garrett. Mr. Peddicord is thoroughly wedded to his profession, and though often solicited to become a candidate for different offices has uniformly declined. In 1878 he formed a law partnership with H. Wheeler Combs, and the firm of Peddicord & Combs do a leading legal business in Western Maryland. Up to the fall of 1879 Mr. Peddicord was identified with the Democratic party, since which time he has acted with the Republican party. Both himself and Mrs. Peddicord are members of the Methodist Episcopal Church of Oakland. Mr. Peddicord is a Past Master of the Masonic order, a Past Grand of the Odd-Fellows, and is now a representative to the Grand Lodge Independent Order of Odd-Fellows of Maryland. He is also a member of the Knights of Honor and of the Legion of Honor. Mr. and Mrs. Peddicord have four children, viz.: Ella May, Maggie Washington, Mary Rebecca, and James Clagett.

The Methodist Episcopal church edifice was built in 1853, under the charge of Rev. M. M. Eaton, and rebuilt in 1874.

Its pastors have been:

1853–54, M. M. Eaton; 1855, William Smith; 1856, A. Bower; 1857–58, D. O. Stewart; 1859–60, A. Hall; 1861–62, J. Dolliver; 1863, Spencer King; 1864–65, M. V. B. White; 1866, Charles King; 1867–69, J. M. Powell: 1870–71, R. M. Wallace; 1872, J. L. Clarke; 1873–74, J. P. Thatcher; 1875–76, Dr. J. A. Fullerton: 1877–78, Benjamin Ison; 1879, H. C. Sanford; 1880–81, S. E. Jones.

The first parsonage was built in 1853, and the second in 1867. S. L. Townshend has been recording steward since 1856. The superintendent of the Sunday-school is John M. Davis, and the assistant, S. L. Townshend. The church trustees are G. L. Bosley, E. D. Kepner, A. C. Brooks, John M. Davis, S. L. Townshend, D. H. Loar, Nathan Casteel, William White.

The Presbyterian church edifice, built of stone, is the finest in the county, and cost over eleven thousand dollars. It was erected by John W. Garrett, president of the Baltimore and Ohio Railroad, in memory of his deceased brother, Henry S. Garrett, who had intended to construct it, but died before his intentions were carried out. It was built for the Presbyterian Church, but when not used by it can be occupied by any Protestant denomination. It was constructed in 1868 of stone brought from the Cheat River region. The congregation was organized in 1869, and has since had preaching by stated supply. Rev. John A. Scott preached until 1879, with occasional services by other clergymen. Since then Rev. John S. Lefevre has supplied the pulpit. He came from Martinsburg, W. Va. The Sunday-school was organized in 1872, and its superintendent is W. H. Tower. The elders are James R. Bishop, William P. Totten, John W. Veitch, David Little, and W. H. Tower; Deacon, John A. Grant. Before its organization as a congregation there were occasional Presbyterian services in the town.

The congregation of the Lutheran Church was organized in 1850. The first pastor was Rev. Mr. Wyncoff, of West Aurora, W. Va., charge, who continued until 1858. Under his auspices the frame church edifice was built in 1854. He was succeeded by Rev. J. H. Cupp, at first from Aurora charge, who, when this church was separated from the Aurora charge and connected with Piedmont, removed his residence to Oakland. He remained until after the war, during which time Rev. Dr. Dosh preached occasionally as a missionary. His successor was Rev. O. C. Miller, who continued until 1880, when he was followed by Rev. William Stoudenmire, the present pastor. He came from Orangeburg, S. C., and was educated at Newberry College in that State. He subsequently studied at the Salem, Va., Theological Seminary. Before his installation over this church he had for four years had charge of various churches of his denomination in Virginia and South Carolina. John Shatzer is superintendent of the Sunday-school. The council (trustees) are W. D. Hoye, C. H. Sincell, John Shatzer, George Loughridge, Moses R. Hamill, and John Pfeiffer.

St. Peter's Roman Catholic church was erected in 1852–53, and has since been handsomely remodeled. It is now a commodious building, tastefully designed and substantially built. The first pastor was Father Slattery, who attended from Frostburg, and who was succeeded by Father Riley, from the same place. His successors were Fathers Lewis and McDonald, who attended from Cumberland. The next pastors were Fathers DeWolf and Sullivan, who attended from Westernport. They were followed by Father Gallen, the first resident pastor, whose successor (in 1880) was Father C. Schmidt, and who is the present learned and popular pastor, under whose charge the congregation is constantly increasing.

In the cemetery of this church, on the hillside overlooking the town, are the following interments:

Michael, son of Thomas and Ann Byrne, born in County Carlow, Ireland, died March 6, 1878; and his mother, Ann, born in County Wicklow, Ireland, died Sept. 1858, aged 45.

James Keefe, died Feb. 1, 1856, aged 60.

Patrick Cullen, born in County Carlow, Ireland, died July 12, 1863, aged 64; and Catherine, his wife, born in County Wicklow, Ireland, died Nov. 4, 1876, aged 72.

Ellen, wife of H. A. Rasche, died Feb. 12, 1875, aged 38.

Redmon Donahoe, a native of Parish Kilamen, County Galway, Ireland, born 1838, died Oct. 22, 1876.

Thomas T. Webster, son of John Skinner and Elizabeth Thornbury Webster, born Dec. 8, 1812, died Dec. 7, 1866.

The Protestant Episcopal church edifice was erected in 1873, and is kept open during the summer months, when the town and its hotels and boarding-houses are filled with visitors. It is on the hill, and is a neat Gothic structure. In its yard are the following tombstones:

Gracia Marcia, wife of Andrew Turnbull, of Charleston, S. C., born Jan. 5, 1803, died in Oakland, Jan. 28, 1877.

Elinor Donnell, wife of Samuel W. Smith, born in Baltimore, Jan. 1, 1806, died in Oakland, July 1, 1870.

Shealtiel Lodge, No. 122, I. O. O. F., was instituted July 17, 1871. Among its charter members were G. W. Merrill, James S. Johnson, and George W. Legge. The officers for the second term of 1881 were:

P. G., H. Wheeler Combs; N. G., George A. Spedden; V. G., F. A. Thayer; Rec. Sec., Thomas J. Peddicord; Per. Sec., W. H. Tower; C., John W. Smith: W., David Little; Chaplain, E. D. Kepner; R. S. to N. G., J. S. Johnson; L. S. to N. G., M. R. Hamill; I. G , Robert Thompson; O. G., D. H. Loar.

Its membership is fifty, and its meetings are held on Monday evenings at Legge's Hall. The trustees are G. W. Legge, M. R. Hamill, E. D. Kepner, D. H. Loar. The finance committee are T. J Peddicord, David Little, and J. S. Johnson. Dr. J. Lee McComas is District Deputy, and Thomas J. Peddicord representative to the Grand Lodge. In the I. O. O. F. Cemetery, east of the court-house, are the following interments:

Charlotte, wife of Thomas Bosley, died Aug. 8, 1878, aged 71.

Joseph Martin, died April 30, 1871, aged 60.

James Caton, died Oct. 26, 1880, aged 78.

Caroline, wife of R. M. Porter, died Jan. 13, 1875, aged 40.

Mariah, wife of W. D. Smouse, died July 13, 1879, aged 64.

James W. Smouse, born May 19, 1837, died Sept. 14, 1869.

A. J. Stottlemeyer, died Feb. 16, 1881, aged 47.

Margaret, wife of Samuel Loar, born March 25, 1797, died Feb. 4, 1869; and her husband, Samuel Loar, born Oct. 11, 1791, died May 27, 1860.

Rev. John Legge, died May 16, 1860, aged 51.

Isabel, wife of John Armstrong, died Dec. 22, 1860, aged 73.

Ellen, wife of J. G. Rinehart, died Nov. 30, 1869, aged 59.

Richard Fairall, died Nov. 27, 1865, aged 55.

Oakland Lodge, No. 133, A. F. and A. M., first met under a dispensation, July 13, 1867. Its officers were: W. M., Patrick Hamill; S. W., Jacob Gibson; J. W., J. A. Spedden; Treas., C. E. S. McKee; Sec., W. B. Kelly; S. D., M. Fadden; Tyler, E. G. Hall, who were installed by Past Master Vaner. At this meeting John M. Jarboe received the Fellow Craft degree.

Its Worshipful Masters have been Patrick Hamill, Dr. E. H. Bartlett, George Spedden, and John M. Jarboe. Its present membership is twenty-two. Its meeting-nights are the first and third Thursdays of every month.

The officers for 1881 are:

W. M., John M. Jarboe; S. W., S. L. Townshend; J. W., Dr. J. Lee McComas; Sec., Gilmor S. Hamill; Treas., Alexander L. Osbourn; Tyler, George Spedden.

Alta Lodge, No. 574, Knights of Pythias, was instituted April 3, 1877, by Deputy Teeple, of Mansfield, Ohio. The charter members were W. H. Tower, Dr. J. Lee McComas, Dr. E. H. Bartlett, J. H. Brooks, E. G. Sturgis, John M. Davis, E. H. Thalaker, N. B. Wayman, John W. Veitch, Bowie Johnson, Samuel Lawton, M. L. Scott, John M. Read.

It meets at Legge's Hall on the second and fourth Thursday evenings of every month.

Cherry Grange, No. 144, P. of H., is located here, of which B. F. Shaffer is Master, and Fannie Best, Secretary.

Patmos Council of the American Legion of Honor was instituted Jan. 4, 1881, in Legge's Hall, by Deputy Supreme Commander William H. Tower. Its officers for 1881 were:

P. C., H. Wheeler Combs; C., T. J. Peddicord; V. C., Dr. G. H. Hocking; Sec., F. A. Thayer; Col., E. Z. Tower; Treas., John W. Veitch; Guide, Dr. B. T. Keller; W., G. W. Legge; Sent., Lloyd Chambers; Med. Exs., Drs. E. H. Bartlett and G. H. Hocking.

It meets on the second and fourth Fridays of each month. The trustees are John W. Veitch, G. W. Legge, J. W. Smith.

A branch of the Order of the Iron Hall was established in November, 1881. It is a beneficial institution, and pays benefits to sick members.

A post-office was established in this vicinity as early as 1812, under the name of "Yough Glades," Allegany Co. The postmasters were appointed as follows: William Armstrong, April 1, 1812; John Armstrong, Oct. 29, 1831; William Armstrong, Nov. 26, 1832; Isaac McCarty, Jan. 12, 1843; James Taggart, March 11, 1852; Charles W. White, Nov. 1, 1852. On the 31st of January, 1854, the name of the office was changed to Oakland, and Charles W. White was continued as postmaster. He was succeeded, May 2, 1854, by John Matthews, who was followed by Rowan White, May 28, 1863. On the 23d of April, 1875, Ralph Thayer, the present postmaster, was appointed.

The town of Oakland was incorporated in 1861. Its officers are a burgess, four commissioners, a bailiff, and clerk. Since the erection of Garrett County the officers have been:

Burgesses.—1873-74, John Daily; 1875, R. T. Browning; 1876, D. M. Mason; 1877, John M. Read, Alexander L. Osbourn (*pro tem.*); 1878, D. E. Offutt; 1879, G. W. Delawder; 1880, Alexander L. Osbourn; 1881, Andrew B. Gouder.

Commissioners.—1878, G. W. Merrill, John M. Davis, G. W. Legge, G. L. Bosley; 1879, David Little, John Helbig, Edmund Jamison, Thomas Carr; 1880, Thomas Carr, J. W. Smith, Dr. E. H. Bartlett, W. M. Coddington; 1881, W. M. Coddington, J. C. Durham, J. O. Michael, S. L. Townshend.

Clerks.—1878, A. C. Good; 1879-82, King Delawder.

Bailiffs.—1878, J. W. White; 1879, J. M. Crim.

Among the lawyers of Oakland H. Wheeler Combs occupies a conspicuous position. Mr. Combs was born in Westernport, Allegany County, Md., Feb. 20, 1849. His grandfather, John Combs, whose ancestors were of Welsh origin, was a native of Virginia, and moved early in life to Frostburg, Md., where he married and raised a family of three children,—two sons and one daughter. His occupation was that of farmer, and he died at Frostburg at the age of ninety-four. William Combs, second son of John, and father of H. Wheeler Combs, was born at Frostburg, Aug. 13, 1799, and was twice married. His first wife was Maria Arnold, by whom he had two children,—John S. Combs, a merchant and prominent citizen of Lonaconing, and Althea M., widow of Thomas Devecmon, who was one of the foremost lawyers of Maryland. His second wife was Sarah A. Wheeler, of Hampshire County, Va., by whom he had five children, only two of whom are living,—Charles A., a farmer, residing near Oakland, and H. Wheeler. William Combs was a successful merchant, carrying on stores at Mount Savage, Frostburg, Pekin Mines, Lonaconing, Bloomington, Westernport, and Franklin Mines. He was among the first who engaged in flat-boating coal down the Potomac River. He died Aug. 18, 1879. His wife is living with her son Charles A.

H. Wheeler Combs

H. Wheeler Combs was partially educated in the common schools of his county, and was employed up to the age of seventeen principally as clerk in his father's stores. He then entered St. John's College at Annapolis, where he remained two years, but was obliged to leave school on account of health, and for two years was book-keeper for his brother, John S., at Lonaconing and Barton. During this period he occupied his spare time in the study of law. The confinement of bookkeeping proving injurious to him, he obtained an engagement with Stoneburner & Richards, a grocery house of Baltimore, as traveling salesman, and then with H. E. Pickert & Co., importers of teas and coffees, New York City. In the fall of 1870 he started a wholesale tea and spice business in Baltimore, but after carrying it on a short time was obliged, on account of ill health, to discontinue it. On the 15th of June, 1871, he married Flora, daughter of Israel and Eleanora Totton, of Yellow Springs, Ohio.

In the fall of 1872 Mr. Combs purchased a cotton

DEER PARK HOTEL,

GARRETT CO., MD.

plantation near Natchez, Miss., which he managed for two years. Having recovered his health he returned to Maryland, and engaged in mercantile business at Moscow, Allegany Co. His store was burned in the fall of 1875. He then became manager of a mercantile business at Danville, Knox Co., Ohio, and his wife died there Sept. 9, 1876. He continued in business at Danville about one year and then resumed the study of law, attending two courses of lectures at the University of Virginia. In 1878 he moved to Oakland, where he was admitted to the bar and opened an office for the practice of his profession. Nov. 13, 1879, he married Lucille, daughter of Charles and Amanda Morris. By his former marriage there were two children,—Myrtle, born and died in Mississippi, and Leslie, born and died in Danville. J. Morris is the only child by the last marriage.

Mr. Combs is a Republican in politics, and a leader of his party in the section of the State in which he resides. He was one of the electors on the Garfield ticket, and is at present chairman of the State Central Committee of Garrett County, and member of the Republican Executive Committee of the State. Though not a member of any religious denomination, he is a contributor to the support of the several churches at the place of his residence. He is a Past Grand in the I. O. O. F., and also a member of the American Legion of Honor.

The first paper published in what is now Garrett County was the *Glades Star*, established in 1871, at Oakland, by Mr. Zevely. It only lived a few months, but its influence was largely instrumental in stirring up a sentiment in favor of a new county. The next venture was the *Garrett County Herald*, started in June, 1873, by Hiram Tasker and W. H. Hagans. It was an independent paper, well edited, and of commanding influence.

C. T. Abel and Thomas J. Peddicord, in June, 1873, established the *Garrett County Gazette*, a Democratic journal. It was published until March 1, 1877, when it was sold to James A. Hayden, who changed it to *The Republican*, and it has since been the Republican organ of the county. *The Republican Ensign*, the first Republican paper of the county, was published in the fall of 1874 by W. H. Hagans, but was short-lived. *The Republican* was issued April 1, 1877. Mr. Hayden still continues its publication, and makes it one of the best county and local journals in Maryland. *The Democrat* was established Feb. 2, 1878, by John J. Smith and M. R. Hamill, who sold out his interest, April 20, 1878, to Mr. Smith. Mr. Smith continued its publication until Sept. 5, 1881, the date of his death. He was born Sept. 27, 1839, and married, May 2, 1876, Miss M. E. Groshon, of Frederick County. He was an able writer and a genial gentleman. His widow continued the paper under her management until Oct. 22, 1881, when she sold it to C. B. Ludwig. Mr. Ludwig, the present editor, publisher, and proprietor, was born in Chambersburg, Pa., and was for several years an able Lutheran preacher.

John Daily, the proprietor of the Glades Hotel, died Sept. 14, 1881. He was born in 1813, near Romney, W. Va., and in 1850 removed to Baltimore, where he engaged in the clothing business. His large store was burned in 1850. Not long after the breaking out of the civil war he came to Cumberland and kept the "Revere House" for several years. It was from this hotel that the Confederate scouts took Gens. Kelly and Crook when that town was full of Federal soldiers. At the close of the war he opened the old "Glades Hotel," at Oakland, which was burned in 1874. He conducted the "Deer Park Hotel" for one season. In 1879 he erected the present Glades Hotel, which he conducted with great success for several seasons, enlarging it greatly in the winter of 1880 and 1881. His wife died in 1878. He had four children, two of whom only survive, the wife of Maj.-Gen. Crook and Mrs. John M. Read. Mr. Daily was one of the best-known hotel proprietors in the country, and had a national reputation for urbanity and a thorough knowledge of his business.

The population of Oakland, according to the census of 1880, was 910.

The *Maryland Journal* of Oct. 6, 1789, has the following advertisement:

"Notice is hereby given that the subscribers intend applying to the next General Assembly for to confirm unto them a tract of land, called Deer Park, lying in Washington County, according to the field-notes and actual survey of the same.

"DANIEL JENIFER.
"GEO. SCOTT.
"JOHN SWAN."

The village is two hundred and twenty-four miles from Baltimore and six from Oakland, and takes its name from the original survey of the same name, given to it before the French and Indian war on account of its attractive site being the resort of the wild deer, then so plentiful in the mountains. It is 2800 feet above sea-level.

Deer Park Hotel is situated on the line of the Baltimore and Ohio Railroad, two hundred and twenty-four miles from Baltimore, two hundred miles from Washington, and six miles east of Oakland. It is on the summit of the Allegany Mountains, 2800 feet above tide-water, and was erected by the Baltimore and Ohio Railroad Company as a summer resort. As such it has proved extremely popular, and is thronged with visitors every season. Located in the midst of beautiful and romantic mountain scenery, and possessing a pure atmosphere, delicious water, and charming surroundings, it presents peculiar attractions for those in search of a spot in which to recuperate in the hot season. During the warmest nights in summer, when it is impossible to sleep in the city with comfort, if sleep visits the tired eyelids at all, the thermometer at Deer Park seldom indicates a higher temperature than fifty-eight degrees. The hotel is situated on the slope of one of the prettiest valleys on the summit of the mountain, and faces to the southeast, having a background of heavy timber. The valley slopes down to a beautiful meadow, through which the railroad runs. The opposite slope has been cleared of all undergrowth, leaving only stately oaks scattered here and there to the distant summit, where earth and sky seem to meet, and about which the clouds often gather and expand themselves in those sudden summer storms—always grand and beautiful as seen from the hotel—which preserve the continual freshness and verdure of the hills and valleys. Nearly all the land in the neighborhood has been cleared of timber, but the woods in the rear of the hotel is carefully preserved by the railroad company, and is one of the special attractions of the spot. Between the hotel and the railway-track there is an extensive lawn sloping to the centre of the valley, laid off in tan-bark walks and drives, and studded with pavilions, pagodas, and rustic benches. At night when there is no moon it is brilliantly illuminated. The hotel is large and handsome in appearance, and is fitted up in elegant style. It is provided with all the latest improvements and conveniences, and the food and service are of the very best character. Express trains from Baltimore reach Deer Park in less than eight hours, and from Cincinnati in eleven hours. Placed thus nearly midway between the two cities, it provides a convenient mountain resort for the people of both, and is largely patronized by visitors from Ohio and other Western States, as well as from Baltimore, Washington, New York, and other points in the East. In the neighborhood of Deer Park Hotel United States senator H. G. Davis, of West Virginia, has a cottage and extensive business interests, including a store and lumber depot, at which a number of the residents of the village of Deer Park find employment. Senator Davis resides at Piedmont, W. Va., but spends his summers at Deer Park. He owns a large portion of the valley, and has set an example in agricultural enterprise which might be profitably followed by others. He has thinned out the wooded growth of the slope opposite Deer Park, and is now reaping large crops of timothy from the meadow and hillside, where it grows with clover in great luxuriance. He has also cleared to its summit a bold, rounded hill, southeast of the hotel, on which a lofty observatory has been placed. This hill is three hundred feet above the hotel and a little over three thousand feet above tide-water. Its summit is an easy walk or short drive from the hotel, and affords a magnificent view of a grand range of hills and valleys on all sides, while the valley of Deer Park, with its village, cottages, hotel, and its delightful pleasure-grounds, are immediately beneath the eye. Flocks of sheep and herds of cattle add pastoral beauty to the scene. The cottage of Senator Davis is embowered in trees, and surrounded by handsome grounds, walks, etc.

The school-teachers in this district for the year ending May 13, 1881, were:

School No. 1.—J. T. Mitchell.
No. 2.—Emma McMillen.
No. 3.—J. H. Enlow.
No. 4.—J. W. Beechly.
No. 5.—J. F. Ashby.
No. 6.—W. B. Hutson.
No. 7.—Joseph S. Enos.
No. 8.—W. H. White.
No. 9.—Kate O'Sullivan.
No. 10.—Virginia A. Ringer.

School trustees for the year ending May, 1882:

School No. 1. Oakland.—William M. Coddington, John W. Smith, A. B. Gouder.

No. 2. Brant.—Bowie Johnson, Clark Deberry, Thomas Casteel.

No. 3. Thayer, or Deep Creek.—Wright Thayer, Thomas Wilburn, Jonas Glotfelty.

No. 4. Bray.—Thomas Cross, Chauncey Kimmel, John Riley.

No. 5. Hutton's Switch.—John Connell, Martin Hughes, John Harned.

No. 6. South Point.—William White, John Thompson, S. E. Switzer.

No. 7. Glade Valley.—Benjamin White, George W. Fazenbaker.

No. 8. Lindale.—Henry Beckman, Christian Slabaugh, John Moon.

No. 9. Lloyd's.—A. Kimmel, S. E. Flowers.

No. 10. Harrington.—Simon Wolf, William Hall, Daniel McRobie.

Ryan's Glades, District No. 8, is bounded on the north by Oakland and Altamont Districts, and east, south, and west by West Virginia. Among the first settlers were the Chisholms, Awnhalts, Wilsons, Wildesens, Harveys, Hendricksons, Kidds, Lees, Moons, Stigers, Nydiggers, Whites, Wheelers, Thompsons, Bigges, Blampels, Willisons, Serpels, Nines, Movelanes, Brownings, Clarks, Crows, Knepps, Kitzmillers, Henlines, Hayeses, and Everetts.

Chisholm's Mills is a small village ten miles from Oakland. M. C. Chisholm is the postmistress; S. D. White, miller; Louis Poole, painter; John M. White, shoemaker; and Benjamin Moon and J. F. Sebold, carpenters.

Fort Pendleton, a camp of the Federal army in the war of 1861–65, is twelve miles from Oakland, near the head-waters of the Potomac River. It is on the backbone of the Alleganies, 3300 feet above tide. The climate is delightful, and is said to be very beneficial to persons suffering from throat and pulmonary diseases. The Potomac here abounds in fine trout. Magnificent outcropping veins of coal underlie the whole district, and in the vicinity there are vast forests of virgin timber, as yet untouched by the woodman's axe. L. M. Deakins is postmaster, and Mrs. W. F. Deakins keeps the hotel, one of the finest summer resorts in the country. Mrs. James Chisholm has a store and mill, John Blampel and George Wilson own saw-mills, and Alexander Chisholm a flouring-mill.

In 1880, James Harvey, son of Elisha Harvey, captured a magnificent golden eagle, about ten miles south of Oakland. Some voracious animal had been feasting upon the carcass of a sheep on Mr. Harvey's farm, and young Harvey procured a so-called "gopher trap" and placed it near the partially-devoured sheep. The next morning, to his great surprise, instead of some wild animal, his trap had an eagle between its jaws by one of its terrible claws. It was, however, in no wise disabled, and was caged, taken to Oakland, and exhibited at Daniel Chisholm's drug-store. The bird measured between the tips of its wings seven feet, and stood three feet in height. Several years prior to this, Jacob Brown, an attorney of Cumberland, was in the woods near Grantsville hunting for squirrels in a beech thicket. He was about to shoot at a squirrel when a fearful dash was made, and the little animal instantly disappeared, and was not seen afterwards. An immense eagle turned several somersaults to check its tremendous speed, and lit on the limb of a tree, but in an instant was on the ground lifeless from the full charge of Mr. Brown's gun at short range.

The school-teachers for the year ending May 13, 1881, were:

School No. 1.—George T. Porter.
No. 2.—James W. Mason.
No. 3.—Arthur Ashby.
No. 4.—John H. Myers.
No. 5.—B. B. Savage.
No. 6.—Lou A. Savage.
No. 7.—R. A. McClintock.
No. 8.—M. L. Selby.
No. 9.—C. L. Paugh.

School trustees for year ending May, 1882:

School No. 1. Sunnyside.—Francis Martin, Peter Gortner, Solomon Yutzy.
No. 2. McMason.—J. McMason, Benjamin F. Shaffer, Joseph Moon.
No. 3. Abernathy.—George W. Wilson, Daniel Conneway, James W. Abernathy.
No. 4. Fairfax.—George L. Mosser, Wm. Arnold, M. McKimmey.
No. 5. Gauer.—Joseph Kemp, John H. Roth, George H. Gauer.
No. 6. Shook Shop.—Henry Thompson, Ephraim Kelso, Nath. Harvey.
No. 7. Bear Range.—James W. White, John G. Steyer, John G. Riley.
No. 8. Oak Grove.—John M. White, W. C. Wildeson, Benj. Harvey.
No. 9. Bethlehem.—Joshua B. Lipscomb, Garrett V. Moon, James E. Paugh.
No. 11. Red Oak.—Jeremiah Harvey, Thomas J. Schaffer, John A. Arnold.

Johnson's District, No. 9, is bounded on the north by Pennsylvania, east by Allegany County, south by Bloomington District, and west by Grantsville District. It was one of the last settled regions of the county, is the smallest in territory, and very mountainous. It contains no villages, and its lands are heavily timbered.

The school-teachers of the district for the year ending May 13, 1881, were:

School No. 1.—Ephraim Lee.
No. 2.—Charles A. Murphy.

School trustees for year ending May, 1882:

School No. 1. Johnson.—Perry Weimer, George Crow, Jerry McKenzie.
No. 2. Wilhelm.—Aaron Wilhelm, Francis McKenzie.

The congregation of Emmanuel chapel, Methodist Episcopal Church South, first worshiped in an old stone building, and was formed only a short time before the year 1872. Under the supervision and charge of Rev. L. W. Haslup the present edifice was erected, and it was formally dedicated in February, 1872, by Rev. Dr. G. H. Zimmerman. The congregation was known as Johnson's until it was christened Emmanuel at the dedication. The ministers of the Frostburg charge have always supplied this pulpit, viz.: Rev. L. W. Haslup, 1871 to 1875; Rev. Charles Semmes, 1875 to 1876; Rev. Charles G. Nevitt, 1876 to 1877. Rev. J. R. Andrew, the present pastor, began his duties in March, 1878. The board of trustees for 1881 were John D. Bernard, Samuel Johnson, Joshua Facenbaker, Perry Wimer, George Crow, Wm. Burton, Joseph Warren. Stewards, George Crow, Perry Wimer. Membership, twenty-nine.

APPENDIX.

Executive Officers of the United States.

Date.	President.	Vice-President.	Secretary of State.
April 30, 1789, to March 4, 1793	George Washington, Va	John Adams, Mass	Thos. Jefferson, Va., 1789.
March 4, 1793, to March 4, 1797	George Washington, Va	John Adams, Mass	Thos. Jefferson, reappointed. Edm'd Randolph, Va., 1794. T. Pickering, Pa., 1795.
March 4, 1797, to March 4, 1801	John Adams, Mass	Thomas Jefferson, Va	T. Pickering, reappointed. John Marshall, Va., 1800.
March 4, 1801, to March 4, 1805	Thomas Jefferson, Va	Aaron Burr, N. Y	James Madison, Va., 1801.
March 4, 1805, to March 4, 1809	Thomas Jefferson, Va	George Clinton, N. Y	Jas. Madison, reappointed.
March 4, 1809, to March 4, 1813	James Madison, Va	*George Clinton, N. Y †Wm. H. Crawford, Ga	Robert Smith, Md., 1809. James Monroe, Va., 1811.
March 4, 1813, to March 4, 1817	James Madison, Va	*Elbridge Gerry, Mass †John Gaillord, S. C.	Jas. Monroe, reappointed.
March 4, 1817, to March 4, 1821	James Monroe, Va	Daniel D. Tompkins, N. Y	John Q. Adams, Mass., 1817.
March 5, 1821, to March 4, 1825	James Monroe, Va	Daniel D. Tompkins, N. Y	John Q. Adams, reappointed.
March 4, 1825, to March 4, 1829	John Q. Adams, Mass	John C. Calhoun, S. C	Henry Clay, Ky., 1825.
March 4, 1829, to March 4, 1833	Andrew Jackson, Tenn	John C. Calhoun, S. C	M. Van Buren, N. Y., 1829. E. Livingston, La., 1831.
March 4, 1833, to March 4, 1837	Andrew Jackson, Tenn	Martin Van Buren, N. Y	Louis McLane, Del., 1833. John Forsyth, Ga., 1834.
March 4, 1837, to March 4, 1841	Martin Van Buren, N. Y	Richard M. Johnson, Ky	John Forsyth, reappointed.
March 4, 1841, to April 4, 1841	Wm. H. Harrison, Ohio	John Tyler, Va	Dan'l Webster, Mass., 1841.
April 4, 1841, to March 4, 1845	John Tyler, Va.	†Samuel L. Southard, N. J. †Willie P. Mangum, N. C.	Hugh S. Legare, S. C., 1843. Abel B. Upshur, Va., 1843. J. Nelson, Md. (act.), 1844. John C. Calhoun, S. C., 1844.
March 4, 1845, to March 4, 1849	James K. Polk, Tenn	Geo. M. Dallas, Pa	Jas. Buchanan, Pa., 1845.
March 5, 1849, to July 9, 1850	Zachary Taylor, La	Millard Fillmore, N. Y	John M. Clayton, Del., 1849.
July 9, 1850, to March 4, 1853	Millard Fillmore, N. Y	†Wm. R. King, Ala	Dan'l Webster, Mass., 1850. Edw'd Everett, Mass., 1852.
March 4, 1853, to March 4, 1857	Franklin Pierce, N. H	*Wm. R. King, Ala †D. R. Atchison. †J. D. Bright.	Wm. L. Marcy, N. Y., 1853.
March 4, 1857, to March 4, 1861	James Buchanan, Pa	John C. Breckenridge, Ky.	Lewis Cass., Mich., 1857. Jere. S. Black, Pa., 1860.
March 4, 1861, to March 4, 1865	Abraham Lincoln, Ill	Hannibal Hamlin, Me	Wm. H. Seward, N. Y., 1861.
March 4, 1865, to April 15, 1865	Abraham Lincoln, Ill	Andrew Johnson, Tenn	W. H. Seward, reappointed.
April 15, 1865, to March 4, 1869	Andrew Johnson, Tenn	†Lafayette S. Foster, Conn. †Benjamin F. Wade, Ohio.	W. H. Seward, continued.
March 4, 1869, to March 4, 1873	Ulysses S. Grant, Ill	Schuyler Colfax, Ind	E. B. Washburn, Ill., 1869. Hamilton Fish, N. Y., 1869.
March 4, 1873, to March 4, 1877	Ulysses S. Grant, Ill	*Henry M. Wilson, Mass †Thos. W. Ferry, Mich.	Hamilton Fish, reappointed.
March 5, 1877, to March 4, 1881	Rutherford B. Hayes, Ohio.	Wm. A. Wheeler, N. Y	Wm. M. Evarts, N. Y., 1877.
March 4, 1881, to Sept. 19, 1881	James A. Garfield, Ohio	Chester A. Arthur, N. Y	James G. Blaine, Me., 1881.
Sept. 19, 1881	Chester A. Arthur, N. Y	†Thos. F. Bayard, Del †David Davis, Ill.	T. F. Frelinghuysen, N. J., 1881.

* Died. † President *pro tem.* of the Senate.

Barons of Baltimore and Lords Proprietary of Maryland.

George Calvert, First Lord Baltimore.

LORDS PROPRIETARY.

1632.—Cæcilius Calvert, Second Lord Baltimore.
1675.—Charles Calvert, Third Lord Baltimore.
1715.—Benedict Leonard Calvert, Fourth Lord Baltimore.
1715.—Charles Calvert, Fifth Lord Baltimore.
1751.—Frederick Calvert, Sixth and last Lord Baltimore.
1771-76.—Sir Henry Harford, last Proprietary.

GOVERNORS OF MARYLAND.

PROPRIETARY GOVERNORS.

1633.—Leonard Calvert.
1647.—Thomas Greene.
1649.—William Stone.
1654.—Bennett and Matthews, commissioners under Parliament.
1658.—Josiah Fendall.
1661.—Philip Calvert.
1662.—Charles Calvert.
1667.—Charles, Lord Baltimore.
1678.—Thomas Notley.
1681.—Charles, Lord Baltimore.
1685.—William Joseph, president of Deputies.
1689.—Convention of Protestant Associations.

ROYAL GOVERNORS.

1691.—Sir Lionel Copley.
1693.—Sir Edmond Andros.
1694.—Francis Nicholson.
1699.—Nathaniel Blackistone.
1703.—Thomas Tench, president of Deputies.
1704.—John Seymour.
1709.—Edward Lloyd, president.
1714.—John Hart.

PROPRIETARY GOVERNORS.

1715.—John Hart.
1726.—Charles Calvert.
1727.—Benedict Leonard Calvert.
1732.—Samuel Ogle.
1733.—Charles, Lord Baltimore.
1735.—Samuel Ogle.
1742.—Thomas Bladen.
1747.—Samuel Ogle.
1752.—Benj. Tasker, president of Deputies.
1753.—Horatio Sharpe.
1769–74.—Robert Eden.

THE REVOLUTION.

1774–76.—Convention and Council of Safety.

STATE GOVERNORS.

Elected Annually by the Legislature with an Executive Council.

1777.—Thomas Johnson.
1779.—Thomas Sim Lee.
1782.—William Paca.
1785.—William Smallwood.
1788.—John Eager Howard.
1791.—George Plater.
1792.—Thomas Sim Lee.
1794.—John H. Stone.
1797.—John Henry.
1798.—Benjamin Ogle.
1801.—John Francis Mercer.
1803.—Robert Bowie.
1806.—Robert Wright.
1809.—Edward Lloyd.
1811.—Robert Bowie.
1812.—Levin Winder.
1815.—Charles Ridgely, of Hampton.
1818.—Charles Goldsborough.
1819.—Samuel Sprigg.
1822.—Samuel Stevens, Jr.
1825.—Joseph Kent.
1828.—Daniel Martin.
1829.—Thomas King Carroll.
1830.—Daniel Martin.
1831.—George Howard (acting).
1832.—George Howard.
1833.—James Thomas.
1835.—Thomas W. Veazey.

Elected under the amended Constitution of 1838 *for three years.*

1838.—William Grason, Queen Anne's County.
1841.—Francis Thomas, Frederick County.
1844.—Thomas G. Pratt, Prince George's County.
1847.—Philip F. Thomas, Talbot County.
1850.—Enoch Louis Lowe, Frederick County.

Elected under the Constitution of 1851 *for four years.*

1853.—Thomas Watkins Ligon, Howard County.
1857.—Thomas Holliday Hicks, Dorchester County.
1861.—Augustus W. Bradford, Baltimore County.

Elected under the Constitution of 1864 *for four years.*

1865.—Thomas Swann, of Baltimore City, Governor.
1865.—Christopher C. Cox, of Baltimore City, Lieutenant-Governor.

Elected under the Constitution of 1867 *for four years.*

1867.—Oden Bowie, Prince George's County.
1872.—William Pinkney Whyte, Baltimore City. Mr. Whyte was elected United States senator from Maryland on the 20th of January, 1874, and on the 27th of that month resigned the office of Governor, to take effect on the 4th of March following.
1874.—James Black Groome, Cecil County. Mr. Groome resigned his seat as a member of the House of Delegates Feb. 4, 1874, and on the same day was elected Governor, to fill the unexpired term of Senator Whyte.
1875.—John Lee Carroll, Howard County.
1879.—William T. Hamilton, Washington County.

United States Senators from Maryland.[1]

SENATORS FROM THE WESTERN SHORE.

1789, March 4.—Charles Carroll of Carrollton.
1793, Jan. 10.—Richard Potts, Frederick County.
1796, Nov. 30.—John Eager Howard, Baltimore County.
1803, March 4.—Samuel Smith, " "
1816, Jan. 29.—Robert G. Harper, " "
1816, Dec. 20.—Alexander Contee Hanson, " "
1819, Dec. 21.—William Pinkney, Baltimore City.
1822, Dec. 15.—Samuel Smith, Baltimore County.
1833, March 4.—Joseph Kent, Prince George's County.
1838, Jan. 4.—William D. Merrick, Charles County.
1845, March 4.—Reverdy Johnson, Baltimore City.
1849, Dec. 8.—David Stewart,[2] " "
1850, Jan. 10.—Thomas G. Pratt,[3] Prince George's County.
1857, March 4.—Anthony Kennedy, Baltimore City.
1863, March 4.—Reverdy Johnson, " "
1868, July 14.—William Pinkney Whyte,[4] Baltimore City.
1868, Jan. 17.—William T. Hamilton, Washington County.
1874, Jan. 27.—William Pinkney Whyte, Baltimore City.
1881, March 4.—Arthur P. Gorman, Howard County.

SENATORS FROM THE EASTERN SHORE.

1789, March 4.—John Henry, Talbot County.
1797, Dec. 11.—James Lloyd, " "
1800, Dec. 12.—Wm. Hindman, " "
1801, Nov. 19.—Robert Wright, " "
1806, Nov. 25.—Philip Reed, Kent County.
1813, May 21.—Robert H. Goldsborough, Dorchester County.
1818, Dec. 21.—Edward Lloyd, Talbot County.
1826, Jan. 24.—Ezekiel F. Chambers, Kent County.
1835, Jan. 13.—Robert H. Goldsborough, Dorchester County.
1836, Dec. 31.—John S. Spence, Dorchester County.
1841, Jan. 5.—John Leeds Kerr, Talbot County.
1843, March 4.—James Alfred Pearce, Kent County.
1862, March 6.—Thomas Holliday Hicks, Dorchester County.
1865, March 9.—John A. J. Creswell,[5] Cecil County.
1867, Jan. 25.—Thomas Swann,[6] Baltimore City.
1867, March 12.—Philip F. Thomas,[7] Talbot County.
1868, March 6.—George Vickers, Kent County.
1872, March 3.—George R. Dennis, Somerset County.
1878, Jan. 18.—James Black Groome, Cecil County.

Members of the Constitutional Conventions of Maryland.

FIRST STATE CONSTITUTION OF 1776.

Matthew Tilghman, President; Gabriel Duval, Secretary.

St. Mary's County.—Richard Barnes, Ignatius Fenwick, George Plater, Jeremiah Jordan.

Charles County.—Robert T. Hove, John Dent, Thomas Semmes, John Parnham.

Calvert County.—Benjamin Mackall, Charles Graham, Wm. Fitzhugh, John Mackall.

[1] The terms of senators begin on the 4th of March, and where other dates are given they indicate that the senators were elected to fill unexpired terms.

[2] Mr. Stewart was appointed by the Governor until the meeting of the next Legislature, in place of Hon. Reverdy Johnson (who had resigned to become attorney-general of the United States).

[3] Governor Pratt was elected by the Legislature to fill the unexpired term of Mr. Johnson.

[4] Governor Whyte was appointed to fill the unexpired term of Mr. Johnson, who was appointed minister to Great Britain.

[5] Mr. Creswell was appointed to fill the unexpired term of Governor Hicks, deceased.

[6] Governor Swann declined to accept the senatorship, March 1, 1867.

[7] Governor Thomas was not admitted on account of alleged disloyalty.

Prince George's County.—Walter Bowie, Benjamin Hall, Osborn Sprigg, Luke Marbury.

Anne Arundel County.—John Hall, Brice T. B. Worthington, Rezin Hammond, Samuel Chase.

Frederick County, Middle District.—Adam Fischer, Upton Sheredine, Christopher Edelen, David Schriver.

Frederick County, Lower District, now Montgomery County.—Thomas Sprigg Wootton, Jonathan Wilson, William Bayley, Jr., Elisha Williams.

Washington, including what is now Allegany County, Upper District.—Samuel Beall, Samuel Hughes, John Stull, Henry Schnebly.

Baltimore County.—Charles Ridgely, Thomas Cockey Deye, John Stephenson, Peter Shepherd.

Harford County.—Jacob Bond, Henry Wilson, Jr., John Love, and John Archer.

Cecil County.—Joseph Gilpin, Patrick Ewing, David Smith, and Benjamin Brevard.

Talbot County.—Pollard Edmondson, John Gibson, Matthew Tilghman, James Lloyd Chamberlaine.

Caroline County.—Nathaniel Potter, William Richardson, Richard Mason, and Henry Dickinson.

Dorchester County.—Robert Goldsborough, James Murray, John Ennalls, and James Ennalls.

Somerset County.—Gustavus Scott, George Scott, William Horsey, Henry Lowes.

Worcester County.—Samuel Handy, Peter Chaille, Smith Bishop, Josiah Mitchell.

Kent County.—Thomas Ringgold, William Ringgold, Joseph Earle, Thomas Smyth.

Queen Anne County.—Turbut Wright, James Kent, William Bruff, and Solomon Wright.

Baltimore Town.—John Smith and Jeremiah T. Chase.

Annapolis.—William Paca, Charles Carroll of Carrollton.

Ratification of the United States Constitution—State Convention of 1788.

George Plater, President; William Harwood, Secretary.

Annapolis.—Nicholas Carroll, Alexander Contee Hanson.

Baltimore Town.—James McHenry, John Coulter.

Anne Arundel County.—Jeremiah T. Chase, Samuel Chase, John F. Mercer, Benjamin Harrison.

St. Mary's County.—George Plater, Richard Barnes, Charles Shelton, and Nicholas L. Sewell.

Kent County.—William Tilghman, Donaldson Yates, Isaac Perkins, and William Granger.

Calvert County.—Joseph Wilkinson, Charles Graham, Walter Smith, and John Chesley.

Charles County.—Zeph. Turner, Gustavus R. Brown, Michael J. Stone, and William Craik.

Somerset County.—George Gale, John Stewart, John Gale, Henry Waggaman.

Talbot County.—Robert Goldsborough, Edward Lloyd, John Stevens, and Jeremiah Banning.

Dorchester County.—Robert Goldsborough, Nicholas Hammond, James Shaw, and Daniel Sulivare.

Baltimore County.—Charles Ridgely, Charles Ridgely, of William, Edward Cockey, and Nathan Cromwell.

Cecil County.—Henry Hollingsworth, James G. Heron, Joseph Gilpin, and William Evans.

Prince George's County.—Fielder Bowie, George Digges, Osborne Sprigg, Benjamin Hall.

Queen Anne's County.—James Tilghman (3d), James Hollyday, William Hemsley, John Seney.

Worcester County.—John Done, Peter Chaille, William Morris, James Martin.

Frederick County.—Thomas Johnson, Thomas Sim Lee, Richard Potts, Abraham Faw.

Harford County.—Luther Martin, William Paca, William Pinkney, John Love.

Caroline County.—William Richardson, Joseph Richardson, Matt. Driver, Peter Edmondson.

Washington County.—John Stull, Moses Rawlings, Thomas Sprigg, and Henry Shryock.

Montgomery County.—Benjamin Edwards, Richard Thomas, Thomas Cramphin, William Deakins, Jr.

State Constitutional Convention of 1851.

John G. Chapman, President; George G. Brewer, Secretary.

St. Mary's County.—George C. Morgan, William J. Blackistone, J. F. Dent, and J. R. Hopewell.

Kent County.—James B. Ricaud, John Lee, Ezekiel F. Chambers, and Joseph T. Mitchell.

Anne Arundel County.—Thomas Donaldson, Thomas B. Dorsey, George Wells, Alexander Randall, James Kent, John S. Sellman.

Calvert County.—George W. Weems, J. J. Dalrymple, John Bond, A. R. Sollers.

Baltimore County.—Benjamin C. Howard, James M. Buchanan, Ephraim Bell, Thomas J. Welsh, H. J. Chandler, and James L. Ridgely.

Charles County.—George Brent, John G. Chapman, William D. Merrick, and Daniel Jenifer.

Talbot County.—Edward Lloyd, S. P. Dickinson, C. Sherwood, M. O. Colston.

Somerset County.—John Dennis, James U. Dennis, J. W. Crisfield, J. J. Dashiell, William Williams.

Dorchester County.—Thomas H. Hicks, John N. Hodson, William T. Goldsborough, J. R. Eccleston, and Francis P. Phelps.

Cecil County.—Albert Constable, B. B. Chambers, William McCullough, John M. Miller, Louis McLane.

Prince George's County.—Thomas F. Bowie, William H. Tuck, Samuel Sprigg, John M. S. McCubbin, and J. D. Bowling.

Frederick County.—Francis Thomas, Edward Shriver, William Cost Johnson, John D. Gaither, Daniel S. Biser, Robert Annan.

Washington County.—George Schley, Lewis P. Fiery, Alexander Neill, Jr., John Newcomer, Thomas Harbine, and Michael Newcomer.

Montgomery County.—J. M. Kilgour, Allen Bowie Davis, Washington Waters, John Brewer, and James W. Anderson.

Baltimore City.—Charles J. M. Gwinn, David Stewart, Robert J. Brent, George W. Sherwood, Benjamin C. Frestman, and Elias Ware, Jr.

Worcester County.—L. L. Dirickson, S. S. McMaster, E. Hearn, James M. Fooks, Curtis W. Jacobs.

Harford County.—John Sappington, W. B. Stephenson, R. McHenry, Samuel M. McGraw, James Nelson.

Allegany County.—William Webber, William M. Holliday, John Slicer, James Fitzpatrick, Samuel P. Smith.

Queen Anne's County.—William A. Spencer, William Grason, Enoch George, and H. E. Wright.

Carroll County.—Andrew G. Ege, M. G. Cockey, Joseph M. Parke, Jacob Shower, Elias Brown.

Caroline County.—R. C. Carter, John Thawley, Thomas R. Stewart, and Edward Hardcastle.

In addition to the president and secretary, whose names have been given, the following were officers of the convention: Assistant Secretary, Washington B. Chichester, of Montgomery County; Sergeant-at-Arms, Richard Booth, of Carroll County;

Door-keepers, Samuel J. Lambdin and S. C. Herbert; Committee Clerks, J. W. Rider, George S. King, J. Morritz, S. Peacock, and William Hall. The convention assembled at Annapolis, Nov. 4, 1850, and adjourned May 13, 1851. The constitution was ratified by the people on the first Wednesday of June, and went into operation July 4, 1851.

STATE CONSTITUTIONAL CONVENTION OF 1864.

H. H. Goldsborough, President; William R. Cole, Secretary.

St. Mary's County.—Chapman Billingsley, John F. Dent, George W. Morgan.

Kent County.—Ezekiel F. Chambers, David C. Blackistone, George S. Holliday.

Anne Arundel County.—William B. Bond, Eli J. Henkle, Oliver Miller, Sprigg Harwood.

Calvert County.—James T. Briscoe, John Turner, and Charles S. Parran.

Charles County.—John W. Mitchell, Richard H. Edelen, and Peregrine Davis.

Baltimore County.—John S. Berry, James L. Ridgely, William H. Hoffman, Edwin L. Parker, David King, William H. Mace, Silas Larsh.

Talbot County.—Henry H. Goldsborough, James Valliant, and John F. Mullikin.

Somerset County.—Isaac D. Jones, James M. Dennis, William H. Gale, Andrew J. Crawford, and John C. Horsey.

Dorchester County.—Thomas J. Hodson, Alward Johnson, Washington A. Smith, and Thomas J. Dail.

Cecil County.—Thomas P. Jones, George Earle, Joseph B. Pugh, and David Scott.

Prince George's County.—Daniel Clarke, Samuel H. Berry, Edward W. Belt, Fendall Marbury.

Queen Anne s County.—John Lee, Pere Wilmer, John Brown.

Worcester County.—William T. Purnell, Thomas B. Smith, William H. W. Farrow, Francis T. Murray.

Frederick County.—Samuel Keefer, Frederick A. Schley, David J. Markey, Andrew Annan, Henry Baker, B. A. Cunningham, and Peter G. Schlosser.

Harford County.—John A. Hooper, William Galloway, George M. McComas, Thomas Russell.

Caroline County.—Robert W. Todd, James D. Carter, and Twiford S. Noble.

Baltimore City.—Samuel T. Hatch, Joseph H. Audoun, Henry Stockbridge, William Brooks, John Barron, Joseph M. Cushing, John L. Thomas, Jr., Baltis H. Kennard, Edwin A. Abbott, Archibald Sterling, Jr., William Daniels.

Washington County.—Peter Negley, Henry W. Dellinger, James P. Mayhugh, John R. Sneary, Lewis B. Nyman, and Joseph F. Davis.

Montgomery County.—Edmund P. Duvall, Thomas Lansdale, and George Peter.

Allegany County.—Albert C. Greene, Hopewell Hebb, Jasper Robinette, George A. Thruston, and Jacob Wickard.

Carroll County.—John E. Smith, Jonas Ecker, John Swope, Wm. S. Woodin.

Howard County.—Joel Hopkins, George W. Sands, James Sykes.

STATE CONSTITUTIONAL CONVENTION OF 1867.

Richard B. Carmichael, President; Milton Y. Kidd, Secretary.

Allegany County.—Thomas Perry, Alfred Spates, William Walsh, J. Philip Roman, Jacob Hoblitzell, Thomas J. McKaig.

Anne Arundel County.—James R. Howison, Thomas I. Hall, E. G. Kilbourne, Luther Giddings.

Baltimore City, First Legislative District.—Lindsay H. Reynolds, Ezra Whiteman, John H. Barnes, Isaac S. George, Joshua Vansant, Edward F. Flaherty, James A. Henderson.

Baltimore City, Second Legislative District.—George M. Gill, Albert Ritchie, George William Brown, Bernard Carter, Henry F. Garey, George W. Dobbin, J. Hall Pleasants.

Baltimore City, Third Legislative District.—James R. Brewer, John Ferry, J. Montgomery Peters, John Franck, Joseph P. Merryman, I. M. Denson, Walter S. Wilkinson.

Baltimore County.—Charles A. Buchanan, John Wethered, Ephraim Bell, Anthony Kennedy, Samuel W. Starr, Charles H. Nicolai, Robert C. Barry.

Calvert County.—John Parran, Charles S. Parran, John F. Ireland.

Caroline County.—R. E. Hardcastle, Charles E. Tarr, Tilghman H. Hubbard, W. H. Watkins.

Carroll County.—John K. Longwell, George W. Manro, Stirling Galt, Benjamin W. Bennett, Thomas F. Cover, William N. Hayden.

Cecil County.—Benjamin B. Chambers, George R. Howard, James B. Groome, James O. McCormick, Eli Cosgrove.

Charles County.—Walter Mitchell, Vivian Brent, John T. Stoddert.

Dorchester County.—James Wallace, William T. Goldsborough, George E. Austin, Levin Hodson.

Frederick County.—William P. Maulsby, Frederick J. Nelson, Harry W. Dorsey, Outerbridge Horsey, William S. McPherson, John B. Thomas, Dewitt C. Johnson.

Harford County.—Henry D. Farnandis, Henry W. Archer, John Evans, Evan S. Rogers, Henry A. Silver.

Howard County.—William M. Merrick, James Maccubbin, Henry O. Devries, James Morris.

Kent County.—Joseph A. Wickes, Richard W. Ringgold, C. H. B. Massey, William Janvier.

Montgomery County.—Greenbury M. Watkins, Nicholas Brewer, Samuel Riggs, of R., Washington Duvall.

Prince George's County.—J. F. Lee, J. B. Brooke, Fendall Marbury, Elbert G. Emack.

Queen Anne's County.—Richard B. Carmichael, Thomas J. Keating, Washington Finley, Stephen J. Bradley.

St. Mary's County.—Robert Ford, John F. Dent, Baker A. Jamison.

Somerset County.—Purnell Toadvine, Thomas F. J. Rider, James L. Horsey, Isaac D. Jones, Henry Page.

Talbot County.—William Goldsborough, Richard C. Hollyday, Henry E. Bateman, and Ormond Hammond.

Washington County.—Andrew K. Syester, Richard H. Alvey, Joseph Murray, S. S. Cunningham, William Motter, George Pole.

Worcester County.—J. Hopkins Tarr, Littleton P. Franklin, Thomas P. Parker, Samuel S. McMaster, George W. Covington.

Presidential Electors of Maryland.

First Presidential Election.—George Washington, President, 1789.

John Rogers, Philip Thomas.

1, George Plater; 2, Robert Smith; 3, William Tilghman; 4, William Richardson; 5, Alexander C. Hanson; 6, William Matthews.

Second Presidential Election.—George Washington, President, 1793.

Alexander C. Hanson, Joshua Seney.

1, John E. Howard; 2, Levin Winder; 3, Thomas Sim Lee; 4, William Smith; 5, Richard Potts; 6, Samuel Hughes; 7, William Richardson; 8, Donaldson Yates.

Third Presidential Election.—John Adams, President, 1797.

John R. Plater, John Archer.

1, Francis Deakins; 2, John Gilpin; 3, George Murdock; 4, John Roberts; 5, John Lynn; 6, John Eccleston; 7, Gabriel Duvall; 8, John Done.

Fourth Presidential Election.—Thomas Jefferson, President, 1801.

Edmund Plowden, Francis Deakins.

1, George Murdoch; 2, John Gilpin; 3, Martin Kershner; 4, Perry Spencer; 5, Gabriel Duvall; 6, William M. Robertson; 7, Nicholas B. Moore; 8, Littleton Dennis.

Fifth Presidential Election.—Thomas Jefferson, President, 1805.

John Parnham, Tobias E. Stansbury.

1, Joseph Wilkinson; 2, John Gilpin; 3, John Johnson; 4, William Gleaves; 5, Edward Johnson; 6, Perry Spencer; 7, John Tyler; 8, Ephraim K. Wilson; 9, Frisby Tilghman.

Sixth Presidential Election.—James Madison, President, 1809.

John R. Plater, Tobias E. Stansbury.

1, Robert Bowie; 2, Thomas W. Veazey; 3, Edward Johnson; 4, Richard Tilghman; 5, John Johnson; 6, Earle Perry Spencer; 7, John Tyler; 8, Henry James Carrol; 9, Nathaniel Rochester.

Seventh Presidential Election.—James Madison, President, 1813.

Henry H. Chapman, Tobias E. Stansbury.

1, Edward H. Calvert; 2, Thomas W. Veazey; 3, Edward Johnson; 4, Thomas Worrell; 5, John Stephen; 6, Edward Lloyd; 7, Henry Williams; 8, Littleton Dennis; 9, Daniel Rentch.

Eighth Presidential Election.—James Monroe, President, 1817.

William D. Beall, George Warner.

1, Joseph Kent; 2, William C. Nuller; 3, Edward Johnson; 4, Benjamin Massey; 5, John Stephen; 6, Thomas Ennalls; 7, John Buchanan; 8, Littleton Dennis; 9, Lawrence Brengle.

Ninth Presidential Election.—James Monroe, President, 1821.

James Forrest, Elias Brown.

1, Robert W. Bowie; 2, John Foward; 3, John Stephen; 4, William R. Stuart; 5, A. McKim; 6, John Boon; 7, William Gaby; 8, Joshua Prideaux; 9, Michael C. Sprigg.

Tenth Presidential Election.—John Quincy Adams, President, 1825.

Henry Brawner, William Brown.

1, John C. Herbert; 2, Thomas Hope; 3, George Winchester; 4, Samuel G. Osborn; 5, Dennis Claude; 6, James Sangston; 7, William Tyler; 8, Littleton Dennis; 9, Thomas Post.

Eleventh Presidential Election.—Andrew Jackson, President, 1829.

William Fitzhugh, Jr., Benjamin F. Forrest.

1, William Tyler; 2, James Sewell; 3, John S. Sellman; 4, Thomas Emory; 5, Benjamin C. Howard; 6, T. R. Lockerman; 7, Elias Brown; 8, Littleton Dennis; 9, Henry Brawner.

Twelfth Presidential Election.—Andrew Jackson, President, 1833.

R. H. Goldsborough, William Price.

1, J. S. Smith; 2, William B. Tyler; 3, William Frick; 4, Albert Constable; 5, U. S. Heath; 6, John L. Steele.

Thirteenth Presidential Election.—Martin Van Buren, President, 1837.

Elias Brown, David Hoffman.

1, J. B. Ricaud; 2, George Howard; 3, William Price; 4, J. M. Coale; 5, Anthony Kimmel; 6, Robert W. Bowie; 7, T. Burcheval; 8, Thomas G. Pratt.

Fourteenth Presidential Election.—William H. Harrison, President, 1841.

David Hoffman, John P. Kennedy.

1, J. L. Kerr; 2, George Howard; 3, Theo. R. Lockerman; 4, Richard J. Bowie; 5, Jacob A. Preston; 6, James M. Coale; 7, W. T. Wootton; 8, Thomas A. Spence.

Fifteenth Presidential Election.—James K. Polk, President, 1845.

William M. Gaither, William Price.

1, James B. Ricaud; 2, C. K. Stewart; 3, Thomas S. Alexander; 4, A. W. Bradford; 5, H. E. Wright; 6, Samuel Hambleton.

Sixteenth Presidential Election.—Zachary Taylor, President, 1849.

William M. Gaither, A. C. Edge.

1, Joseph S. Cottman; 2, J. D. Roman; 3, J. M. S. Causin; 4, J. M. Starris; 5, B. C. Wickes; 6, J. D. Derickson.

Seventeenth Presidential Election.—Franklin Pierce, President, 1853.

R. M. McLane, C. Humphries.

1, J. Parran; 2, R. H. Alvey; 3, Carroll Spence; 4, C. J. M. Gwinn; 5, J. A. Wickes; 6, E. K. Wilson.

Eighteenth Presidential Election.—James Buchanan, President, 1857.

J. D. Roman, James Wallace.

1, R. Goldsborough; 2, E. H. Webster; 3, C. L. Leary; 4, Thomas Swann; 5, F. A. Schley; 6, A. R. Sollers.

Nineteenth Presidential Election.—Abraham Lincoln, President, 1861.

E. Louis Lowe, James L. Martin.

1, Elias Griswold; 2, John Brooke Boyle; 3, Joshua Vansant; 4, T. Parkin Scott; 5, John Ritchie; 6, James S. Franklin.

Twentieth Presidential Election.—Abraham Lincoln, President, 1865.

William J. Albert, H. H. Goldsborough.

1, W. H. W. Farrow; 2, Isaac Nesbit; 3, William Smith Reese; 4, George W. Sands; 5, R. Stockett Matthews.

Twenty-first Presidential Election.—U. S. Grant, President, 1869.

George M. Gill, J. Thomson Mason.

1, A. Constable; 2, W. T. Allender; 3, H. Clay Dallam; 4, Charles B. Roberts; 5, George Peter.

Twenty-second Presidential Election.—U. S. Grant, President, 1873.

Augustus W. Bradford, Frederick Racine.

1, Philip D. Laird; 2, James B. Groome; 3, John M. Carter; 4, James A. Buchanan; 5, William Walsh.

Twenty-third Presidential Election.—R. B. Hayes, President, 1877.

Richard B. Carmichael, Frederick Raine.

1, James M. Dennis; 2, Richard J. Gittings; 3, Wm. Sheppard Bryan; 4, Charles G. Kerr; 5, Fendall Marbury; 6, Frederick J. Nelson.

Population of Maryland.

Year.	Whites.	Negro Slaves.	Free Colored.	Total.
1634	The first colony.	Population about		200
1638	....	....	....	700
1660	....	....	....	12,000
1665	....	....	....	16,000
1671	....	....	....	20,000
1701	....	....	....	30,000
1712	37,743	8,330	....	46,073
1715	40,700	9,500	....	50,200
1748	94,000	36,000	....	130,000
1756	107,963	46,225	....	154,188
1775 about	....	....	....	200,000
1780	170,688	83,362	....	254,050
1790	208,649	103,036	8,043	319,728
1800	222,402	107,703	19,587	341,548
1810	235,575	111,502	33,927	380,546
1820	261,305	107,306	39,730	407,350
1830	291,224	102,878	52,938	447,040
1840	317,575	89,619	62,078	470,019
1850	417,943	90,368	74,723	583,034
1860	515,918	87,189	83,942	687,049
1870	605,497	....	175,391	780,894
1880	724,718	....	209,914	934,632

The colored population in 1880 included 5 Chinese, 1 Japanese, and 11 Indians. Of the population, according to the census of 1880, 462,004 were males, 472,628 females, 851,984 native, and 82,648 foreign.

Maryland Judiciary.

COURT OF APPEALS.

James L. Bartol, chief judge; Levin T. H. Irving, John M. Robinson, Richard Grason, Richard H. Alvey, Oliver Miller, John Ritchie, Frederick Stone; Spencer C. Jones, clerk. Terms, first Monday in April and October.

CIRCUIT COURTS.

First Judicial Circuit.—Levin T. H. Irving, chief judge; Ephraim K. Wilson and Charles F. Goldsborough, associate judges. Worcester, Somerset, Dorchester, and Wicomico Counties. *Worcester*—Snow Hill—third Mondays in January, May, and July, and fourth Monday in October. *Somerset*—Princess Anne—second Mondays in January, April, July, and October. *Dorchester*—Cambridge—fourth Mondays in January, April, and July, second Monday in November. *Wicomico*—Salisbury—first Mondays in January and July, fourth Mondays in March and September.

Second Judicial Circuit.—John M. Robinson, chief judge; Joseph A. Wickes and Frederick Stump, associate judges. Caroline, Talbot, Queen Anne's, Kent, and Cecil. *Caroline*—Denton—Jury Terms, first Mondays in April and October. Non-Jury Terms, second Monday in January, fourth Monday in June. *Talbot*—Easton—Jury Terms, third Mondays in May and November. Non-Jury Terms, first Monday in February and fourth Monday in July. *Queen Anne's*—Centreville—Jury Terms, first Mondays in May and November. *Kent*—Chestertown—Jury Terms, third Mondays in April and October. *Cecil*—Elkton—Jury Terms, third Mondays in March and September, second Monday in December. Non-Jury Term, third Monday in June.

Third Judicial Circuit.—Richard Grason, chief judge; George Yellott and James D. Watters, associate judges. Baltimore and Harford. *Baltimore*—Towsontown—Jury Terms, first Monday in March, third Monday in May, second Monday in September, first Monday in December. *Harford*—Belair—second Mondays in February, May, September, and November.

Fourth Judicial Circuit.—Richard H. Alvey, chief judge; William Motter and George A. Pearre, associate judges. Allegany, Washington, and Garrett. *Allegany*—Cumberland—Jury Terms, first Monday in January, second Mondays in April and October. Non-Jury Term, first Thursday in July. *Washington*—Hagerstown—Law Terms, second Monday in February, second Monday in May, third Monday in November. Chancery Terms, second Monday in February, first Monday in April, second Monday in May, fourth Monday in July, third Mondays in September and November. *Garrett*—Jury Terms, first Monday in May, second Monday in September. Non-Jury Terms, first Monday in July, third Monday in December.

Fifth Judicial Circuit.—Oliver Miller, chief judge; Edward Hammond and William N. Hayden, associate judges. Carroll, Howard, and Anne Arundel. *Carroll*—Westminster—Jury Terms, second Mondays in May and November. *Howard*—Ellicott City—Jury Terms, third Monday in March, first Monday in September. *Anne Arundel*—Annapolis—Jury Terms, third Mondays in April and October.

Sixth Judicial Circuit.—John Ritchie, chief judge; William Viers Bouic and John A. Lynch, associate judges. Montgomery and Frederick. *Montgomery*—Rockville—third Monday in January, third Monday in March, first Monday in June, and second Monday in November. *Frederick*—Frederick City—third Mondays in February and September, second Mondays in May and December.

Seventh Judicial Circuit.—Frederick Stone, chief judge; Robert Ford and John B. Brooke, associate judges. Prince George's, Charles, Calvert, and St. Mary's. *Prince George's*—Upper Marlborough—Regular Terms, first Mondays in April and October. Non-Jury Terms, third Mondays in January and June. *Charles*—Port Tobacco—Regular Terms, third Mondays in May and November. Non-Jury Terms, third Mondays in July and February. *Calvert*—Prince Frederick—Regular Terms, first Monday in May, and the Wednesday next after the first Monday in November. Non-Jury Terms, first Mondays in July and February. *St. Mary's*—Leonardtown—Regular Terms, third Mondays in March and September. Non-Jury Terms, first Mondays in June and December.

THE SUPREME BENCH OF BALTIMORE CITY

Comprises judges of the following courts, with George William Brown as chief judge:

THE SUPERIOR COURT OF BALTIMORE CITY.

Robert Gilmor, Jr., judge.

THE COURT OF COMMON PLEAS OF BALTIMORE CITY.

George William Brown, judge.

THE CITY COURT OF BALTIMORE CITY.

Henry F. Garey, judge.

THE CIRCUIT COURT OF BALTIMORE CITY.

George W. Dobbin, judge.

THE CRIMINAL COURT OF BALTIMORE CITY.

Campbell W. Pinkney, judge.

Terms of Baltimore Courts.—Second Mondays in January, May, and September.

UNITED STATES CIRCUIT COURT, FOURTH CIRCUIT.

Hugh Lennox Bond, judge, Maryland, Virginia, West Virginia, North Carolina, South Carolina. Terms, Alexandria, Va., first Monday in January and July; Danville, Va., Tuesday after fourth Monday in February and August; Lynchburg, Va., Tuesday after third Monday in March and September; Baltimore, Md., first Monday in April and November; Richmond, Va., and Greensborough, N. C., first Monday in April and October; Charleston, S. C., first Monday in April; Stateville, N. C., third Monday in April and October; Norfolk, Va., Asheville, N. C., first Monday in May and November; Harrisonburg, Va., Tuesday after first Monday in May, and Tuesday after second Monday in October; Abingdon, Va., Tuesday after fourth Monday of May and October; Raleigh, N. C., first Monday in June and last Monday of November; Parkersburg, W. Va., first Monday in August; Columbia, S. C., fourth Monday in November.

UNITED STATES DISTRICT COURT FOR MARYLAND.

Thomas J. Morris, judge. Terms, Baltimore, first Monday in March, June, September, and December, James W. Chew, clerk; Henry T. Meloney, deputy clerk and clerk in bankruptcy; John M. McClintock, marshal.

UNITED STATES COMMISSIONERS, BALTIMORE CITY.

R. Lyon Rogers, Isaac Brooks, Jr., and G. Morris Bond.

Population of Maryland by Counties.

White.

Counties.	1880.	1870.	1860.	1850.	1840.	1830.	1820.	1810.	1800.	1790.
Allegany	38,012	37,370	27,215	21,632	14,663	9,569	7,664	6,176	5,703	4,539
Anne Arundel	28,526	12,725	11,704	16,542	14,630	13,872	13,482	12,439	11,030	11,664
Baltimore[1]	83,334	282,818	231,242	174,853	105,331	92,329	72,635	57,233	45,050	30,878
Calvert	10,538	4,332	3,997	3,630	3,585	3,788	3,711	3,680	3,889	4,211
Caroline	13,767	8,343	7,604	6,096	5,334	6,241	7,144	6,932	6,759	7,028
Carroll	30,992	26,444	22,525	18,667	15,221	......	......	......	......	......
Cecil	27,108	21,860	19,994	15,472	13,329	11,478	11,923	9,652	6,542	10,055
Charles	18,548	6,418	5,796	5,665	6,022	6,789	6,514	7,398	9,043	10,124
Dorchester	23,110	11,902	11,654	10,747	10,629	10,685	10,095	10,415	9,415	10,010
Frederick	50,482	39,999	38,391	33,314	28,975	36,703	31,997	27,983	26,478	26,937
Garrett	12,175	......	......	......	......	......	......	......	......	......
Harford	28,042	17,750	17,971	14,413	12,041	11,314	11,217	14,606	12,018	10,784
Howard	16,141	10,676	9,081	......	......	......	......	......	......	......
Kent	17,605	9,370	7,347	5,616	5,616	5,044	5,315	5,222	5,511	6,748
Montgomery	24,759	13,128	11,349	9,435	8,766	12,103	9,082	9,731	8,508	11,679
Prince George's	26,263	11,358	9,650	8,901	7,823	7,687	7,935	6,471	8,346	10,004
Queen Anne's	19,257	9,579	8,415	6,936	6,132	6,659	7,226	7,529	7,315	8,171
St. Mary's	16,934	7,218	6,798	6,223	6,070	6,097	6,033	6,158	6,678	8,216
Somerset	21,668	10,916	15,332	13,385	11,485	11,371	10,384	9,162	9,340	8,272
Talbot	19,065	9,471	8,106	7,084	6,063	6,291	7,387	7,249	7,070	7,231
Washington	38,561	31,874	28,305	26,930	24,724	21,277	19,247	15,591	16,108	14,472
Wicomico	18,016	11,396	......	......	......	......	......	......	......	......
Worcester	19,539	10,650	13,442	12,401	11,765	11,811	11,232	11,490	11,523	7,626
Total	934,632	605,497	515,918	417,943	318,203	291,108	260,223	235,117	216,326	208,649

[1] The population of Baltimore City, independent of the county, was, according to the census of 1880, 332,190.

Free Colored.

Counties.	1880.	1870.	1860.	1850.	1840.	1830.	1820.	1810.	1800.	1790.
Allegany	1,531	1,166	467	412	215	222	195	113	101	12
Anne Arundel	13,879	11,732	4,864	4,602	5,083	4,076	3,382	2,536	1,833	804
Baltimore[1]	......	47,921	29,911	29,075	21,453	17,888	12,489	7,208	4,307	927
Calvert	5,696	5,533	1,841	1,530	1,474	1,213	694	388	307	136
Caroline	4,166	3,758	2,786	2,788	1,720	1,652	1,390	1,001	602	421
Carroll	2,284	2,175	1,225	974	898	......	......	......	......	......
Cecil	4,466	4,014	2,918	2,623	2,551	2,229	1,783	947	373	163
Charles	10,852	9,318	1,068	913	819	851	567	412	571	404
Dorchester	8,472	7,556	4,684	3,848	3,987	3,000	2,496	2,661	2,365	528
Frederick	7,508	7,572	4,957	3,760	2,985	2,716	1,777	783	473	213
Garrett	112	......	......	......	......	......	......	......	......	......
Harford	6,649	4,855	3,644	2,777	2,436	2,058	1,387	2,221	1,344	775
Howard	4,398	3,474	1,395	......	......	......	......	......	......	......
Kent	7,207	7,732	3,411	3,143	2,491	2,266	2,067	1,979	1,786	655
Montgomery	9,151	7,434	1,552	1,311	1,313	1,266	922	677	262	294
Prince George's	12,313	9,780	1,198	1,138	1,080	1,202	1,096	4,929	648	164
Queen Anne's	7,192	6,592	3,372	3,278	2,541	2,866	2,138	2,738	1,025	618
St. Mary's	8,689	7,726	1,866	1,633	1,393	1,179	894	636	622	343
Somerset	8,637	7,274	4,571	3,483	2,646	2,239	1,954	1,058	586	268
Talbot	7,327	6,666	2,964	2,593	2,340	2,483	2,234	2,103	1,591	1,076
Washington	3,064	2,838	1,677	1,828	1,580	1,082	627	483	342	64
Wicomico	5,073	4,406	......	......	......	......	......	......	......	......
Worcester	6,984	5,869	3,571	3,014	3,073	2,430	1,638	1,054	449	178
Total[2]	209,914	175,391	83,942	74,723	62,078	52,938	39,730	33,927	19,587	8,043

[1] The returns for the census of 1880 for Baltimore City and Baltimore County are given separately. In the preceding enumerations the two are combined as above. The colored population of Baltimore City in 1880 was 53,703, and of Baltimore County 10,561.

[2] The colored population included 5 Chinese, 1 Japanese, and 11 Indians.

Population of Maryland by Counties.—*Continued.*

Slave.

Counties.	1860.	1850.	1840.	1830.	1820.	1810.	1800.	1790.
Allegany	666	724	812	818	795	620	499	258
Anne Arundel	7,332	11,249	9,819	10,347	10,301	11,693	9,760	10,130
Baltimore	5,400	6,718	7,595	10,653	11,077	11,369	9,673	7,132
Calvert	4,609	4,486	4,170	3,899	3,668	3,937	4,101	4,305
Caroline	739	808	752	1,177	1,574	1,520	1,865	2,057
Carroll	783	975	1,122	....	....	....	....	....
Cecil	950	844	1,352	1,705	2,342	2,467	2,103	3,407
Charles	9,653	9,584	9,182	10,129	9,419	12,435	9,558	10,085
Dorchester	4,123	4,282	4,227	5,001	5,168	5,032	4,566	5,337
Frederick	3,243	3,913	4,445	6,370	6,685	5,671	4,572	3,641
Harford	1,800	2,166	2,643	2,947	3,320	4,431	4,264	3,417
Howard	2,862	....	....	....	....	....	....	....
Kent	2,509	2,627	2,735	3,191	4,071	4,249	4,474	5,433
Montgomery	5,421	5,114	5,377	6,447	6,396	7,572	6,288	6,030
Prince George's	12,479	11,510	10,636	11,585	11,185	9,189	12,191	11,176
Queen Anne's	4,174	4,279	3,960	4,872	5,588	6,381	6,517	6,674
St. Mary's	6,549	5,842	5,761	6,183	6,047	6,000	6,399	6,985
Somerset	5,089	5,588	5,377	6,556	7,241	6,975	7,432	7,070
Talbot	3,725	4,134	3,687	4,173	4,768	4,878	4,775	4,777
Washington	1,435	2,090	2,546	2,909	3,201	2,656	2,200	1,286
Worcester	3,648	3,444	3,539	4,032	4,551	4,427	4,398	3,836
Total	87,189	90,368	89,737	102,994	107,397	111,502	105,635	103,036

Aggregate.

Counties.	1880.	1870.	1860.	1850.	1840.	1830.	1820.	1810.	1800.	1790.
Allegany	3,802	38,536	28,348	22,769	15,690	10,609	8,654	6,909	6,303	4,809
Anne Arundel	28,526	24,457	23,900	32,393	29,532	28,295	27,165	26,668	22,623	22,598
Baltimore County and City[1]	415,524	330,741	266,553	210,646	134,379	120,870	96,201	75,810	59,030	38,937
Calvert	10,538	9,865	10,447	9,646	9,229	8,900	8,073	8,005	8,297	8,652
Caroline	13,767	12,101	11,129	9,692	7,806	9,070	10,108	9,453	9,226	9,506
Carroll	30,992	28,619	24,533	20,616	17,241	....	....	....	....	....
Cecil	27,108	25,874	23,862	18,939	17,232	15,432	16,048	13,066	9,018	13,625
Charles	18,548	15,738	16,517	16,162	16,023	17,769	16,500	20,245	19,172	20,613
Dorchester	23,110	19,458	20,461	18,877	18,843	18,686	17,759	18,108	16,346	15,875
Frederick	50,482	47,572	46,591	40,987	36,405	45,789	40,459	34,437	31,523	30,791
Garrett	12,175	....	....	....	....	....	....	....	....	....
Harford	28,042	22,605	23,415	19,356	17,120	16,319	15,924	21,258	17,626	14,976
Howard	16,141	14,150	13,338	....	....	....	....	....	....	....
Kent	17,605	17,102	13,267	11,386	10,842	10,501	11,453	11,450	11,771	12,836
Montgomery	24,759	20,563	18,322	15,860	15,456	19,816	16,400	17,980	15,058	18,003
Prince George's	26,263	21,138	23,327	21,549	19,539	20,474	20,216	20,589	21,185	21,344
Queen Anne's	19,257	16,171	15,961	14,484	12,633	14,397	14,952	16,648	14,857	15,463
St. Mary's	16,934	14,944	15,213	13,698	13,224	13,459	12,974	12,794	13,699	15,544
Somerset	21,668	18,190	24,992	22,456	19,508	20,166	19,579	17,195	17,358	15,610
Talbot	19,065	16,137	14,795	13,811	12,090	12,947	14,389	14,230	13,436	13,084
Washington	38,561	34,712	31,417	30,848	28,850	25,268	23,075	18,730	18,659	15,822
Wicomico	18,016	15,802	....	....	....	....	....	....	....	....
Worcester	19,539	16,419	20,661	18,859	18,377	18,273	17,421	16,971	16,370	11,640
Total	934,632	780,894	687,049	583,034	470,019	447,040	407,350	380,546	341,548	319,728

Of the total population of Maryland, 462,004 were males, 472,628 females, 851,984 natives, 82,648 foreign, 724,718 white, and 209,914 colored.

[1] Baltimore City and County are separated in the census returns. The population of Baltimore City in 1880 was 332,190, and of Baltimore County 83,334.

Population of Baltimore Town and City.

	1880.	1870.	1860.	1850.	1840.	1830.	1820.	1810.	1800.	1790.
Total	332,190	267,559	212,418	169,054	102,313	80,625	62,738	35,583	26,114	13,503

INDEX.

CPSIA information can be obtained
at www.ICGtesting.com
Printed in the USA
BVOW01s0215031116
466649BV00002B/3/P

9 780806 352053